FINANCE
LITERATURE
•INDEX•

FINANCE
LITERATURE
•INDEX•

THIRD EDITION

Edited By

JEAN LOUIS HECK
Villanova University

McGraw-Hill, Inc.

New York   St. Louis   San Francisco   Auckland   Bogotá   Caracas
Lisbon   London   Madrid   Mexico   Milan   Montreal   New Delhi
Paris   San Juan   Singapore   Sydney   Tokyo   Toronto

1 2 3 4 5 6 7 8 9 0 MALMAL 9 0 9 8 7 6 5 4 3 2 1

ISBN 0-07-027785-0 / 0-07-027787-7

The editors were Kenneth MacLeod and Peitr Bohen;
the production supervisor was Anthony DiBartolomeo.
The cover was designed by Circa 86, Inc.
Malloy Lithographing, Inc., was printer and binder.

FINANCE LITERATURE INDEX
Table of Contents

PREFACE

In this third edition, 16 additional journals have been added to the second edition's listing, bringing to 35 the total number of journals indexed. The new additions include the leading journals from the Insurance and Real Estate areas, plus 11 finance journals that are fairly new on the market. The index contains complete bibliographic references for articles published in these 35 leading journals from their inaugural issue through 1990 (or later). The 35 journals and the abreviations used to reference them throughout the index include the following:

Advances in Financial Planning and Forecasting (AFPAF)
Advances in Working Capital Management (AWCM)
Financial Analysts Journal (FAJ)
Financial Management (FM)
Financial Practice and Education (FPE)
Financial Review (FR)
Financial Services Review (RSR)
Global Finance Journal (GFJ)
International Journal of Finance (IJOF)
Journal of the Am. Real Estate & Urban Economics Assoc. (AREUEA)
Journal of Applied Corporate Finance (JACF)
Journal of Bank Research (JBR)
Journal of Banking and Finance (JBF)
Journal of Business (JOB)
Journal of Business Finance and Accounting (JBFA)
Journal of Finance (JOF)
Journal of Financial and Quantitative Analysis (JFQA)
Journal of Financial Economics (JFEC)
Journal of Financial Education (JFED)
Journal of Financial Intermediation (JFI)
Journal of Financial Research (JFR)
Journal of Financial Services Research (JFSR)
Journal of Futures Markets (JFM)
Journal of International Money and Finance (JIMF)
Journal of Money, Credit and Banking (JMCB)
Journal of Portfolio Management (JPM)
Journal of Real Estate Finance and Economics (JREFEC)
Journal of Real Estate Research (JRER)
Journal of Risk and Insurance (JRI)
Journal of Risk and Uncertainty (JRU)
Recent Developments in International Banking and Finance (RDIBF)
Research in Finance (RIF)
Review of Financial Studies (RFS)
Review of Futures Markets (RFM)
Review of Quantitative Finance and Accounting (RQFA)

This index is divided into two parts. **Part One** contains a chronological listing of all articles by journal from the first issue published through 1990. For consistency, all journal issues are numbered. For readers desiring exact citations, **Appendix A** on page 527 contains a cross reference for each journal that notes any monthly, quarterly or seasonal names corresponding to particular issues. **Part Two** contains all articles from the 35 journals listed in alphabetical order by author. For multiple author articles, the citation is repeated in its entirety for each co-author.

In preparing this index, article titles and authors' names were obtained directly from the journal tables of contents which occasionally contain errors. Also, considering there are more than 17,000 references in the first section alone (approximately one and one-half times that number in the author section), there are no doubt some missed citations and typographical errors. All such errors are, of course, my responsibility. Bringing them to my attention at Villanova University will assure a correction in future editions.

My greatful appreciation to McGraw-Hill for recognizing the need for this index and their willing support of its publication, along with the companion Accounting Literature Index. This index would not have been possible without the early efforts of editors Scott Stratford and Susanne BeDell. A special note of thanks is due Kenneth MacLeod, Sponsoring Editor for Finance and Accounting at McGraw-Hill, for his tremendous support in making this expanded third edition both possible and an enjoyable task.

I hope this index proves valuable to each of you in your research endeavors. May your research efforts yield abundant and rewarding results.

Jean Louis Heck
Villanova University

FINANCE
LITERATURE
•INDEX•

PART ONE

JOURNAL
INDEX

ADVANCES IN FINANCIAL PLANNING AND FORECASTING

1

ADVANCES IN WORKING CAPITAL MANAGEMENT

FINANCIAL ANALYSTS JOURNAL

Financial Analysts Journal
Volume 6, 1950

Issue No. 2 Contains Discussions From The NFFAS Conference

Financial Analysts Journal
Volume 7, 1951

Issue No. 2 Contains Discussions From The NFFAS Conference

Financial Analysts Journal
Volume 8, 1952

Issue No. 1 Contains Discussions From The NFFAS Conference

Issue No. 4 Contains Discussions From The NFFAS Conference

Financial Analysts Journal
Volume 11, 1955

Issue No. 3 Contains Discussions From The NFFAS Conference

Financial Analsts Journal
Volume 12, 1956

Financial Analysts Journal
Volume 17, 1961

Financial Analysts Journal
Volume 18, 1962

Hall, Edward B. "Sound Money And The Voter," (1), 65-67.
Gross, Courtlandt S. "Wanted: A New Name For Aircrafts," (2), 11-14.
Poole, Alan C. "Gold, Money And The Economy - 1962," (2), 17-19.
Dobbins, Cris. "The Cement Industry In Search Of Its Future," (2), 21-26.
Storer, Robert W. "Business Earnings, High Employment And Economic Growth," (2), 29-32.
Boyle, Alexander R. M. and Victor E. Samuelson. "Disclosure Of Long-Term Leases," (2), 35-40.
Hansen, John W. "Rails' Potential For Remote And Automatic Control," (2), 43-46.
Molodowsky, Nicholas. "The Many Aspects Of Yields," (2), 49-86.
Herman, Hamilton and Delbert F. Jurgensen. "Challenge Of The National Water Problem," (2), 65-74.
Garwood, John D. "Economic Growth For The Sixties," (3), 9-11.
Zises, Alvin. "Long Term Leases: Case Against Capitalization; For Full Disclosures," (3), 13-64.
George, J. H. B. "Saline Water Conversion," (3), 23-28.
Hartill, Creighton. "For Growth Alone?," (3), 31-33.
Kotler, Philip. "Elements In A Theory Of Growth Stock Valuation," (3), 35-44.
Santow, Leonard Jay. "Ultimate Demise Of Preferred Stock As A Source Of Corporate Capital," (3), 47-54.
Ross, Carl D. "The Mexican Stock Market," (3), 57-64.
Baughman, G. W. "Step By Step Approach To The Crewless Train," (3), 67-78.
Taylor, Reese H. "Efficiency" Watchword Of The Oil Industry," (3), 81-84.
Ely, Roland T. "Partners In Progress: The Latin American Economy," (4), 9-60.
Lefkoe, M. R. "Government Intervention - Freedom's Greatest Threat," (4), 21-30.
Neil, Herbert E., Jr. and William C. Norby. "Dynamic Factors In Corporate Profits," (4), 33-39.
Beckers, Carl L. A. "Economic Survey Of The Far East," (4), 41-43.
Hoxter, Curtis J. "Western Europe, As Of Today," (4), 45-53.
Griffith, B. Barret. "The Gold Flow," (4), 63-64.
Margoshes, Sanford L. "Debt Financing And Investment Value Of Common Stock," (4), 67-72.
Kolb, Burton A. "Research, Development And Common Stock Values," (5), 9-16.
Maguire, W. G. "Natural Gas: New Era For A Growth Industry," (5), 19-21.
Poole, Alan C. "Canadian Austerity Program And Its Effect On American Economy," (5), 23-24.
Teck, Alan. "Population Study And Age Group Evaluation For Industry Growth," (5), 25-27.
Lifton, Robert K. "An Understanding Of Public Realty Firms," (5), 29-38.
Crofton, Sir Malby. "Investment Opportunities In The British Market," (5), 41-46.
Bower, Casper M. "Clinical Analysis Of Young Companies," (5), 49-51.
Hayes, Douglas A. "Ethical Considerations In The Professional Stature Of Analysts," (5), 53-56.
Sjostrom, Robert A. "What Are Life Insurance Stocks Worth?," (5), 59-62.
Heath, Loyd C. "Calculation And Meaning Of Cash Flow In Security Analysis," (5), 65-67.
Mennis, Edmund A. "Different Measures Of Corporate Profits," (5), 69-78.
Feick, Harry W. "Digging Deeper Into Research And Development," (5), 79-81.
Roddewig, Clair M. "Showdown Looms In Rail Transportation," (5), 85-88.
Bretey, Pierre R. "Railroads' Problem: 'A Compound Of Several Brews'," (5), 89-98.
Shelton, John P. "Influence Of Six-Month Capital Gains Rule On Short-Term Transactions," (5), 99-101.
Graham, Benjamin. "Our Balance Of Payments - The Conspiracy Of Silence," (6), 9-14.
Ferretti, Andrew P. "Long-Term Perspective On Common Stock Prices," (6), 19-26.
Shapiro, David. "Recent Trends In The Independent Telephone Industry," (6), 29-31.
Jones, David L. "Stock Options - An Incentive In Reverse?," (6), 33-34.
Quinn, James J. "Aerospace 'Envelope' (A New Conception)," (6), 41-44.
Reilly, Frank K. "What Determines Ratio Of Exchange In Corporate Mergers?," (6), 47-50.
Packer, Stephen B. "Forecasting Consumer Spending For Durable Goods," (6), 53-60.
Lehman, E. R. "Outlook For Liquefied Petroleum Gas Industry," (6), 63-65.
Waill, Robert S. "Old Thoughts On New Growth Rates," (6), 67-70.
Axelrad, Leonard I. "Over-the-Counter Market: Organization And Problems," (6), 71-73.
Chambers, Frank G. "Small Business Investment Companies," (6), 75-78.
O'Brien, James J. "A Review Of The Vending Industry," (6), 81-87.
Poole, Alan C. "Senior Financial Analysts Look Into Future (Beloit Seminar)," (6), 89-92.
Griffith, B. Barret. "Stock Market Bellwether - General Motors," (6), 94-95.
Noon, Theodore W., Jr. "Oil Company Analysis: Estimating Buy And Sell Prices," (6), 96-97.
Cook, Elizabeth E. "Greece Unafraid As She Joins Common Market," (6), 99-103.
Guthmann, Harry G. "British Corporate Law Scrutinized For Reforms (Aid To Analysts)," (6), 104-107.

Hartill, Creighton. "Oil In A Changing Era," (1), 13-16.
Stone, Frances. "Investments: Research And Development," (1), 19-23.
Pease, Fred. "The Warrant - Its Powers And Its Hazards," (1), 25-32.
North, Joseph E. "The Cosmetics And Toiletries Industry," (1), 39-50.
Coughtry, Lloyd S. "Computers, A Tool In Security Analysis," (1), 53-60.
Badger, Ralph E. "Investment Growth, Is It Overvalued?," (1), 63-68.
Poole, Alan C. "United States And The Free World Economy," (2), 9-11.
Knowlton, Winthrop. "The Seven Percent Investment Credit," (2), 13-15.
Gaubis, Anthony. "The Timing Factor In Business And Stock Market Forecasting," (2), 19-23.
Dean, Joel. "Outside Directors Appraise Stock Options," (2), 25-31.
Ascher, Leonard W. "The Savings And Loan Colossus," (2), 33-38.
Ruff, Raymond T. "Effect Of A 'Stock Of The Month' Recommendation," (2), 41-43.
Boericke, William F. "South African Gold Mining Accounts," (2), 45-47.
Weidenbaum, Murray L. "The United States Aircraft Industry," (2), 49-53.
Callister, T. K. "Foreign Security Investing," (2), 55-56.
Seligman, Barnard. "Financial Indexing - The 'Variable Payments' Approach To Fixed Income Investment," (2), 59-64.
Bowlin, Oswald D. "The Current Ratio In Current Position Analysis," (2), 67-72.
Molodovsky, Nicholas. "It's Good To Own Growth Stocks!," (2), 75-86,93-99.
Donovan, James E. "Greater Economic Role Of Service Industries," (2), 89-91.
Holdren, George C. "Toward Greater Comparability Of Financial Statements," (2), 101-103.
Jones, Robert H. "Investment Climate Of The European Common Market," (3), 9-19.
Broy, Anthony. "The Automatic Controls Industry," (3), 21-27,80.
Conklin, G. Howard. "Cigarette Stocks - Current Confusion Hides Profit Potential," (3), 29-30.
Hubbard, Philip M., Jr. "The Many Aspects Of Dilution," (3), 33-40.
Santow, Leonard Jay. "Cost Of Long-Term Capital From A Corporate Point Of View," (3), 43-50.
Griffith, B. Barret. "The Gold Flow (Continued)," (3), 52.
Kisor, M. Jr. and V. S. Whitbeck. "A New Tool In Investment Decision-Making," (3), 55-62.
Graham, Benjamin. "The Future Of Financial Analysis," (3), 65-70.
McLean, James H. "Depreciation: Its Relationship To Funds," (3),73-82.
Griesedieck, Joseph. "Brewing Crosses The Threshold," (3), 85-88.
Einzig, Robert S. "Tomorrow's Markets - The Competitive 1960's," (3), 91-97.
Kessler, Daniel. "Discount Retailing And Leased Departments," (3), 99-102.
Whitney, Jack M., II. "The S.E.C. And The Financial Analyst," (4), 11-14.
O'Rourke, Dennis. "Sugar Situation - 1963," (4), 17-24.
Molodovsky, Nicholas. "Economic Insight: Historical Vignettes," (4), 27-31,74-82.
Boorstin, Robert L. "Rational Dividend Policy For Savings & Loan Companies," (4), 33-46.
Margoshes, S. L. "Cost Of Capital - Guide To Managerial Decision-Making," (4), 49-53.
Schwinn, Leslie B. "Growth Of Credit Unions," (4), 55-58.
Brody, Eugene D. "The Rails As An Indicator Of Professional Sentiment," (4), 61-62.
Neil, Herbert E., Jr. "Implications Of The Proposed Tax Cut," (4),65-72.
Greene, Norvin R. "An Old Counselor Philosophizes," (4), 87-89.
Smith, Edgar Lawrence. "Low Tide In Sunspots - 1964," (4), 91-92.
Tobey, Julian E. "Expanding Use Of Coal By Electric Utility Industry," (5), 19-23.
Riggs, Henry E. "The Economics Of Tax Switching," (5), 25-31.
Broy, Anthony. "Investing In Swedish Securities," (5), 33-42.
Peale, Mundy J. "Research & Development - The True Capital Of The Space Age," (5), 45-47.
Heller, Philip. "More Office Space For An Expanding Economy," (5), 49-50.
Fredman, Herbert. "Implications Of The Dow-Jones Industrials' Price Level," (5), 53-54.
Freeman, George K. "Depreciation: Too Big To Write Off," (5), 57-59.
Hirsch, Joel H. "Improved Yardstick Of Common Stock Value," (5), 60-69.
Lang, Arthur H. "The Investment Aspects Of Water Flooding," (5), 71-73.
Randell, Donald H. "A Report: Financial Analysts Seminar (Beloit) 1963," (5), 75-76.
Raynolds, David R. "The United States Balance Of Payments," (6), 11-16.
Bretey, Pierre R. "Green Light Ahead For The Rails," (6), 19-25,78-89.
Mennis, Edmund A. "A Fresh Reappraisal Of The Steel Industry," (6), 27-32.
Kourday, Michael. "Relative Values - A Method Of Outperforming The Market," (6), 35-44.
Harper, Allen D. "How A Professional Investor Seeks Investment Opportunities," (6), 47-52.
Dolley, James C. "Inflation, The Balance Of Payments, And The Gold Flow," (6), 55-59.
Feldman, William. "Economic Analysis For The Financial Analyst," (6), 61-67.
Van Arsdell, Paul M. "Considerations Underlying Cost Of Capital," (6), 69-76.
Griffith, B. Barret. "Turn-Around In Raw Material Prices?," (6), 77.
Kimpton, Lawrence A. "The Growth Outlook For Petroleum," (6), 91-96.

Financial Analysts Journal
Volume 19, 1963

Jones, Donald P. "Can We Make The Right Decisions On Tax Reforms?," (1), 9-11.

Financial Analysts Journal
Volume 20, 1964

Ahearn, Daniel S. "Investment Management And Economic Research," (1), 15-20.

Financial Analysts Journal
Volume 21, 1965

Ziebarth, Karl. "On The Estimation Of Railroad Earnings," (6), 54-55.
Goodfriend, Herbert E. "Life Insurance Company Earnings," (6), 57-63.
Shelton, John P. "New Research And The Investment Profession (Keynote Review)," (6), 65-67.
Murphy, Joseph E., Jr. "Relative Growth Of Earnings Per Share," (6), 73-75.
Good, Walter R. "How To Avoid Over-Priced Stocks," (6), 79-81.
Milne, Robert D. "The Dow-Jones Industrial Average Re-Examined," (6), 83-88.
Carter, E. Eugene and Kalman J. Cohen. "Bias In The DJIA Caused By Stock Splits," (6), 90-94.
Stevenson, Richard A. "The Variability Of Common Stock Quality Ratings," (6), 97-101.
Conklin, George T., Jr. "The Money And Capital Markets (Keynote Review)," (6), 103-105.
Packer, Stephen B. "Monetary Policy - A Current Perspective," (6), 107-114.
Gumperz, Julian. "From A Closed To An Open System (Keynote Review)," (6), 117-119.
Spigelman, Joseph H. "Technological Transformation Of The Drug Industry - Part II," (6), 121-133.
Busschau, W. J. "The 'Paper Gold' Planners (Keynote Review)," (6), 135-137.
Marshall, Earle. "North Sea Gas Discoveries," (6), 139-144.
Soros, George. "European Financial Analysts' Congress," (6), 147-148.

Financial Analysts Journal
Volume 23, 1967

Crawford, Peter H. "Money And Household Liquidity," (1), 13-15.
Bonham, Howard B., Jr. "Input-Output In Common Stock Analysis," (1), 19-28.
Rogers, Stephen. "Accounting Practices: A Critique," (1), 31-32.
Carey, John L. "CPA's Under Fire?," (1), 35-37.
Arnett, Farold E. "Capital Gains And Losses," (1), 39-48.
Morrison, James and Paul Morrison. "Accounting And Business Acquisitions," (1), 51-56.
Spencer, Roger W. "LIFO Inventory In Meatpacking Industry," (1), 59-63.
Cunniff, Richard T. "The Magnetic Tape Industry," (1), 65-73.
Biggs, Barton M. "New Print-Out Horizons," (1), 75-80.
Yakowicz, Joseph V. "The Glass Container Industry," (1), 82-86.
Renshaw, Edward F. "The Stock Market And Prosperity," (1), 88-89.
Hammel, J. E. and D. A. Hodes. "Factors Influencing P/E Multiples," (1), 90-92.
Bauman, W. Scott. "Investment Analysis: Science Or Fiction?," (1), 93-97.
Ritter, Lucy E. "A Sense Of Values," (1), 98-99.
Snyder, Gerard L. "A Look At Options," (1), 100-103.
Ricks, R. Bruce. "Tight Money And Investment Management," (1), 104-105.
Hayes, S. L. and R. A. Taussig. "Are Cash Take-Over Bids Unethical?," (1), 107-111.
Gumperz, Julian. "Machines That Analyze - Or Analysts?," (1), 113-115.
Heisterberg, Robert G. "A Utility Earnings Growth Model," (1), 116-119.
Bower, Richard S., Christopher E. Nugent, Barbara C. Myers and J. Peter Williamson. "A Language For Financial Analysts," (1), 121.
Balles, John J. "Tight Money And The New Economics," (2), 15-18.
Leontiades, Milton. "The Use Of Capital Markets," (2), 19-23.
Schoetz, Robert F. "Profit Margins In The U.S. And Europe," (2), 25-33.
Harper, Allen D. "Investing In The Water Utility Industry," (2), 35-38.
Brennan, Joseph F. "The Water Industry - Regulation," (2), 41-48.
Walsh, Philip F. "Engineering And Operation Problems," (2), 49-55.
Baum, Dwight C. "Buying Water Company Equities," (2), 57-63.
Hammarskjold, Knut. "Giant Jets And Supersonic Aircraft," (2), 67-70.
Kerley, James J. "Financial Problems Of The Airlines," (2), 73-82.
Steiner, J. E. "Aircraft Evolution And Airline Growth," (2), 85-92.
Strong, George H. "Management's Fourth Dimension," (2), 97-102.
Guthart, Leo A. "Why Companies Buy Their Own Stock," (2), 105-112.
Seligman, Barnard. "Tax Effects Of State Investment Policy," (2), 113-115.
Gaines, Tilford C. "A New Look At Certificates Of Deposit," (2), 117-119.
Trefftzs, Kenneth L. "Let's Avoid The Next Panic," (2), 121-122.
Jen, Frank C. and James E. Wert. "Sinking Funds And Bond Yields," (2), 125-131.
Johnson, Robert L. "The Value Of The Call Privilege," (2), 134-138.
Warner, Adolphe J. "Inside Europe's Future Capital Market," (2), 141-143.
Genillard, Robert L. "The Eurobond Market," (2), 144-151.
Cole, James F. "Investing In Canada," (2), 153-156.
Conatser, R. Gene. "Decision Making Under Full Employment," (3), 15-17.
Neil, Herbert E., Jr. "The Consumer's Tomorrow's Buying," (3), 18-24.
Karo, Margherita. "The Cosmetics/Toiletries Industry," (3), 27-32.
Knobler, William M. "Food Stocks," (3), 35-40.
Molodovsky, Nicholas. "Building A Stock Market Measure," (3), 43-46.
Miller, Norman and Stan West. "Why The NYSE Common Stock Indexes?," (3), 49-54.
Schoomer, B. Alva, Jr. "American Stock Exchange Index System," (3), 57-61.
Kekish, Bohdan J. "Moody's Averages," (3), 65-69.
Schellbach, Lewis C. "When Did The DJIA Top 1200?," (3), 71-73.
Carter, E. E. and K. J. Cohen. "Stock Averages, Stock Splits, And Bias," (3), 77-81.
Hoffland, David L. "The Folklore Of Wall Street," (3), 85-88.
Murphy, Joseph E., Jr. "Return, Payout, And Growth," (3), 91-93.
Bing, Ralph A. "Scientific Investment Analysis," (3), 97.
Molodovsky, Nicholas. "Recent Studies Of P/E Ratios," (3), 101-108.
Beach, T. E. and P. F. Miller, Jr. "Price-Earnings Ratios: A Reply," (3), 109-110.
Smith, Keith V. "Needed: A Dynamic Approach," (3), 115-117.
Hayes, Douglas A. "The Undervalued Issue Strategy," (3), 121-127.

Shelton, John P., Eugene F. Brigham and Alfred E. Hofflander, Jr. "Dual Funds: An Appraisal," (3), 131-139.
Shelton, John P. "Warrant, Stock-Price Relations - Part I," (3), 143-151.
Saulnier, Raymond J. "Three Federal Budget Concepts," (4), 19-24.
Manus, Peter C. "The Inventory Syndrome," (4), 27-28.
Kennedy, James R. "Challenges In Chemical Fibers," (4), 31-35.
Doan, Herbert D. "Challenges In Petrochemicals," (4), 35-37.
Conklin, G. Howard. "Evaluation Of Savings And Loans," (4), 39-42.
Weston, Frank T. "Reporting Earnings Per Share," (4), 45-53.
Schwartz, William. "Convertibles Get Realistic Image," (4), 55-57.
Klaman, Saul B. "The Plenitude Of Scarcity," (4), 59-61.
Fichthorn, William H. "Bank Capital Notes," (4), 63-70.
Woods, Donald H. "A New Perspective," (4), 73-75.
Moriarty, D. P. and J. Balog. "Use Of Scientific Knowledge," (4), 76-79.
Renshaw, Edward F. "Stock Market Instability," (4), 80-83.
Netter, Joseph, II. "Dual-Purpose Funds," (4), 85-87.
Shelton, John P. "Warrant, Stock-Price Relations - Part II," (4), 88-99.
Johnson, C. R. and R. M. Soldofsky. "Rights Timing," (4), 101-104.
Marks, John H. D. "Australian Investment Outlook," (4), 107-110.
Thomas, Douglas P. "Canada-U.S. Auto Trade Agreement," (4), 113-117.
Patton, Henry H. "Investing In Latin America," (4), 119-126.
Rowen, Henry S. "Problems Of American Society," (5), 13-16.
Freeman, Orville L., Patrick J. James, and Robert Price. "World Food Needs: A Discussion," (5), 19-25.
Heneman, Harlow J. "Financial Analysts And Management," (5), 27-30.
Gearhart, John A. "Corporate Management And Analysts," (5), 31-32.
Collier, James R. "Management Business Planning," (5), 33-38.
Kim, Andrew B. "Air Cargo," (5), 41-48.
Mason, William F. "Air Freight," (5), 49-56.
Butler, Hartman L., Jr. "Aerospace Industry Revisited," (5), 57-62.
Longley, F. A. and G. S. Sarlo. "Current Trends In Integrated Circuits," (5), 65-69.
Ross, Lawrence. "Paper Industry - Wood Costs," (5), 71-72.
Greeley, Robert E. "Mutual Fund Management Companies," (5), 75-82.
Sprinkel, Beryl W. "Measuring Impact Of Monetary Policy," (5), 85-87.
Brickman, Myrtle. "New Federal Reserve Series," (5), 88-92.
Reilly, James F. "The Outlook For Municipal Bonds," (5), 93-95.
Cullity, John P. "Stock Recoveries After Recessions," (5), 98-100.
Kewley, T. J. and R. A. Stevenson. "The Odd Lot Theory," (5), 103-106.
Drew, Garfield A. "A Clarification Of The Odd Lot Theory," (5), 107-108.
Benjes, W. D. and L. J. Seidler. "Interim Financial Statements," (5), 109-115.
Young, Allan. "Common Stocks After Repurchase," (5), 117-121.
Briggs, George C. "Performance And Portfolio Management," (5), 123-127.
Babson, David L. "Performance Or Speculation?," (5), 129-132.
Aranyi, Janos. "Portfolio Diversification," (5), 133-139.
Lambert, E. W. and A. E. Hofflander. "Liquidity In Investing," (5), 141-145.
Miles, Joseph E. "Insurance Portfolio Strategies," (5), 147-154.
Lempert, Leonard H. "Do The Leading Indicators Lead?," (6), 19-27.
Hayes, Douglas A. "Potential For Professional Status," (6), 29-31.
Ketchum, Marshall D. "Is Financial Analysis A Profession?," (6), 33-37.
Sheppard, C. Stewart. "Professionalization Of The Analyst," (6), 39-41.
Salvino, S. M. "Rate Of Return Dilemma Of Utilities," (6), 45-49.
Greer, Carl C. "Commercial Broadcasting Industry," (6), 51-60.
Bretey, Pierre R. "The Railroads - Amber To Green," (6), 61-66.
Levy, Robert A. "Random Walks: Reality Or Myth," (6), 69-77.
Jensen, Michael C. "Random Walks: A Comment," (6), 77-85.
Van Horne, James C. and G. G. C. Parker. "An Empirical Test," (6), 87-92.
Meiselman, David. "New Economics And Monetary Policy," (6), 95-100.
Hart, Orson H. "National Economic Policy," (6), 101-102.
Neil, Herbert E., Jr. "The Surtax," (6), 105-107.
Mayer, Robert W. "Price Earnings Ratios: A Prospect," (6), 109.
Murphy, J. E., Jr. and H. W. Stevenson. "P/E Ratios And Future Growth," (6), 111-114.
Graham, Benjamin. "Some Observations," (6), 114.
Myers, John H. "Depreciation For Fun And Profits," (6), 117-123.
West, David A. "Risk Analysis In The 1960's," (6), 124-126.
Smith, R. G. E. "The `Marginal Opinion' Theory," (6), 127.
Marks, Lawrence J. "In Defense Of Performance," (6), 135-137.
Hubbard, Charles L. "A Control Chart For Stock Prices," (6), 139-145.
McCandlish, Randolph W., Jr. "Portfolio Evaluation," (6), 147-150.
Hofflander, Alfred E., Jr. "Multiple Line Insurance Companies," (6), 151-153.
van Eck, John C. "The German Stock Market," (6), 155-158.
Dodd, David K. "An International Capital Market," (6), 159-161.

Financial Analysts Journal
Volume 24, 1968

Grove, David L. "International Monetary Liquidity," (1), 19-26.
Corcoran, Eileen T. "Reporting On Leases," (1), 29-35.
O'glove, Thornton L. "Finance Company Accounting," (1), 37-44.
Gunness, Robert C. "The Economics Of Energy," (1), 47-50.
Neidig, C. P. "World Chemical Companies," (1), 51-65.
Williams, William D. "Industrial Gases," (1), 66-69.
Scanlan, F. V. and C. S. Goodwin. "The Advertising Industry," (1), 71-76.
Weidenbaum, Murray L. "Government Spending," (1), 77-80.
Miller, Donald C. "Financial Markets Under Stress," (1), 83-81.
Packer, Stephen B. "Higher Interest Rates Forever?," (1), 84-90.
Wendt, Paul F. "Determination Of Investment Policy," (1), 91-96.
Murphy, Joseph E., Jr. "Earnings Growth And Price Change," (1), 97-99.
Barges, Alexander. "Growth Rates And Debt Capacity," (1), 100-104.
Nicholson, S. Francis. "Price Ratios," (1), 105-109.
Stern, Walter P. "Performance-Transitory Or Real?," (1), 110-113.
Callard, Charles G. "The Third Yield," (1), 114-120.
Kassouf, Sheen T. "Warrant Price Behavior, 1945-1964," (1), 123-126.
Levy, Robert A. "Random Walks: Reality Or Myth-Reply," (1), 129-132.
Blake, C. W. and D. W. Riegle. "Data Processing," (1), 134-146.

Stone, Donald E. "Computer-Aided Financial Analysis," (1), 149-153.
Feuerstein, A. E. and P. G. Maggi. "Computer Investment Research," (1), 154-158.
Kaufman, Henry. "The New Financial Setting," (2), 19-21.
Molodovsky, Nicholas. "Mergers And Antitrust Policy," (2), 23-33.
Olsen, J. A. and T. A. Blancy. "The Copper Industry Study," (2), 35-39.
Burkhead, J. Gary. "Investing In The Shoe Industry," (2), 41-48.
Karo, Margherita. "The Jewelry Business," (2), 49-56,88.
Johnson, Leonard W. "The Offshore Service Industry," (2), 58-60.
Bretey, Pierre R. "Coal Industry's Expansion," (2), 61-64.
Savoie, Leonard M. "Financial Reports," (2), 67-79.
Briloff, Abraham J. "Pooling Of Interests Accounting," (2), 71-81.
Harmon, David Perry, Jr. "Pooling Of Interests: Case Study," (2), 82-88.
Leisy, Herbert F. and Robert D. Milne. "What Are Bank Earnings?," (2), 89-94.
Margoshes, Sanford L. "Modified Present Value Profile," (2), 97-104.
Niederhoffer, Victor. "Some Properties Of Stock Prices," (2), 105-111.
Renshaw, Edward F. "Portfolio Theory," (2), 114-119.
Mennis, Edmund A. "Growing Pension Funds," (2), 122-131.
Dietz, Peter O. "Pension Funds Performance," (2), 133-137.
Lorie, James H. "NABAC Study On Pension Funds," (2), 139-143.
Kopp, Bennett S. "Conglomerates In Portfolio," (2), 145-148.
Gentry, James A. and John R. Pike. "Dual Funds Revisited," (2), 149-157.
Wallich, Henry C. "Random Walk And Security Analysts," (2), 159-162.
Rinfret, Pierre A. "Investment Managers Are Needed," (2), 163-170.
Kimber, John R. "Stock Market Maturity In Canada," (2), 173-174.
Rist, Marcel. "Letters From France," (2), 175-181.
O'Leary, James J. "Economic Outlook For 1968," (3), 17-21.
McLaughlin, Frank C. "International Monetary System," (3), 23-27.
Molodovsky, Nicholas. "The Business Corporation," (3), 29-39.
Mascia, Joseph S. "Personal Credit In New York State," (3), 42-51.
Goodman, Roy M. "Congressional Testimony," (3), 59-64.
Reilly, James F. "Comments On Testimony," (3), 65-66.
Harries, Brenton W. "Standard And Poor's New Policy," (3), 68-71.
Riehle, Robert C. "Moody's Municipal Ratings," (3), 71-73.
Barges, Alexander and Brian R. Hickey. "Drug Industry Profits," (3), 75-83.
Brandon, Dick H. "Computer Leasing Industry," (3), 85-90.
Yakowicz, Joseph V. "Glass And Metal Containers," (3), 92-95.
Ahern, David P. "Auto Industry," (3), 96-102.
Bonham, Howard B., Jr. "Projections Of The DJIA," (3), 104-110.
May, Marvin M. "The Earnings Per Share Trap," (3), 113-117.
Howard, Godfrey G. "Investment Research In 1970s," (3), 120-123.
Keller, Philip R. "Utility Stocks Vs. Bonds," (3), 127-132.
Smith, Keith V. "Option Writing," (3), 135-138.
Nicholson, G. A., Jr. and T. E. O'Hara. "Investment Clubs," (3), 141-146.
Cohen, Manuel F. "The SEC And The Press," (4), 21-24.
Machlup, Fritz. "International Monetary Arrangement," (4), 25-30.
Amos, William W. "Insurance Holding Company Concepts," (4), 35-38.
Hayes, Douglas A. "The Evaluation Of Management," (4), 39-42.
Fisch, Gerald G. "Management In Financial Analysis," (4), 43-49.
Latane, Henry A. and Donald L. Tuttle. "Probability In Industry Analysis," (4), 51-61.
Londoner, David J. "Steel Industry Profit Outlook," (4), 63-68.
Goldstein, Lawrence J. "Investment In Business Services," (4), 71-74.
Homer, Sidney. "Distortions Within Money Markets," (4), 77-79.
Harris, John T. "Discount And Current Coupon Bonds," (4), 81-85.
Johnson, Harry G. "Current Issues In Monetary Policy," (4), 87-91.
Packer, Stephen B. "Municipal Bond Ratings," (4), 93-97.
Matteson, Archibald C. "In Defense Of Municipal Ratings," (4), 99-103.
Eiteman, David K. "A Computer Program," (4), 107-111.
Keefe, William C., Jr. "Cost Of Capital - Rate Of Return," (4), 113-116.
Murphy, Joseph E., Jr. "Some Effects Of Leverage," (4), 121-124.
Breen, William. "Low Price-Earnings Ratios," (4), 125-127.
Van Horne, James C. and G. G. C. Parker. "Technical Trading Rules," (4), 128-132.
Mennis, Edmund A. "Trends In Institutional Investing," (4), 133-138.
Pakkala, A. L. "Trust Department Income," (4), 140-144.
Jenkins, Roy. "United Kingdom's Economic Situation," (4), 145-147.
Bell, Geoffrey L. "Economic Conditions In The U.K.," (4), 147-150.
Albertini, Isidoro. "Fiscal Reform In Italy," (4), 151-153.
McLaughlin, Frank C. and John L. Moore, Jr. "Planning To Meet Retirement Costs," (5), 13-23.
Koeneman, John K. "Outlook For The Aerospace Industry," (5), 25-33.
Karo, Margherita. "Cosmetics/Toiletries Industry," (5), 34-44.
Schwartz, William D. "The Domestic Toy Industry," (5), 45-48.
Mackin, John J. "Machine Tool Industry," (5), 53-57.
Weston, Frank T. and Sidney Davidson. "Accounting Changes And Earnings," (5), 59-66.
Leveson, Sidney M. "Have We Solved The Dilution Problem?," (5), 69-70.
Luther, Ernest W. "New International Monetary System," (5), 73-76.
Winger, Alan R. "Mortgage Demands And Supplies," (5), 77-84.
Johannesen, Richard L., Jr. "Coupon Bond Price Fluctuations," (5), 89-91.
Treynor, Jack L., William W. Priest, Jr., Lawrence Fisher and Catherine A. Higgins. "Risk Estimates," (5), 93-100.
Molodovsky, Nicholas. "Growth Stocks: A Note," (5), 103-106.
Jones, Charles H., Jr. "The Growth Rate Appraiser," (5), 109-111.
Richard, Donald L. "Fiscal Use And Financial Reporting," (5), 113-115.
Ellis, Charles D. "Performance Investing," (5), 117-119.
Fox, Edward A. "Measuring Performance Of Equities," (5), 121-129.
Soldofsky, Robert M. "Yield-Risk Performance Measurements," (5), 130-139.
Rotch, William. "Venture Capital Financing," (5), 141-147.
Bracken, Jerome. "Models For Call Option Decisions," (5), 149-151.
Baker, James C. "The German Stock Market," (5), 153-156.
Studness, Charles M. "New York Stock Exchange Trading," (6), 26-36.
McCosker, Joseph S. "Need For Backlog Information," (6), 37-43.
Monks, Joseph G. "Nuclear Fuel Industry Trends," (6), 45-53.
Kingsley, Jean Richards. "The Furniture Industry," (6), 55-65.
Lynch, Thomas Edward. "Diversified Reporting," (6), 67-73.
Johnson, Arnold W. "Financial Statements," (6), 75-83.
Snavely, Howard J. "Pooling Is Good Accounting," (6), 85-89.

Kaufman, George G. "A Proposed Experiment," (6), 90-93.
Baskin, Elba F. and Gary M. Grooch. "Return On Flat Bonds," (6), 95-97.
Thompson, Arthur A. "Tax-Exempt Development Bonds," (6), 99-103.
Crepas, K. J. and R. A. Stevenson. "Industrial Aid Bonds," (6), 105-109.
Gumperz, Julian. "Scientific Input And Economic Output," (6), 111-113.
Whittall, David. "A Simulation Model," (6), 115-118.
Buff, Jerome H., G. Gordon Biggar,Jr. and J. Gary Burkhead. "Decision Analysis Techniques," (6), 123-128.
Fluegel, Frederick K. "High And Low P/E Ratio Stocks," (6), 130-133.
Molodovsky, Nicholas. "Stock Values And Stock Prices," (6), 134-148..
Smith, Randall D. "Short Interest And Stock Prices," (6), 151-154.
Johnston, George S,M. Louise Curley and Robert A. McIndoe. "Dual-Purpose Funds Undervalued?," (6), 157-163.
Fredman, Albert J. and James E. Wert. "Secondary Distributions," (6), 165-168.
Kolb, Burton A. "Capital Budgeting," (6), 170-174.

Financial Analysts Journal
Volume 25, 1969

Mennis, Edmund A. "New Tools For Profits Analysis," (1), 25-33.
Ferretti, Andrew P. "The Economist's Role," (1), 35-37.
O'Leary, James J. "Outlook For Interest Rates," (1), 39-44.
Baker, C. Austin. "The U. S. Money Crisis," (1), 45-50.
Kaufman, Henry. "The Economist And The Money Market," (1), 59-61.
Ely, Owen. "Case History Of Electric Utilities," (1), 63-67.
Flanagan, John R. "Pacific Northwest Forest Products," (1), 69-71.
Granger, Alix. "Canadian Financial Intermediaries," (1), 72-77.
Comiskey, Eugene E. "Depreciation And Comparability," (1), 78-80.
Norgaard, Corine T. "Comprehensive Income Tax Allocation," (1), 81-85.
Wolf, Charles R. "Bank Portfolio Gains And Losses," (1), 86-90.
Leisy, Herbert F. and Robert D. Milne. "Bank Portfolio Gains And Losses: A Comment," (1), 91.
Kramer, Donald. "Current Accounting Practices," (1), 92-97.
Kewley, Thomas J. and R. A. Stevenson. "The Odd-Lot Theory: A Reply," (1), 99-104.
Winer, Loen. "Using The Nomograph," (1), 105-108.
Kisor, Manown, Jr. and Van A. Messner. "Filter Approach To Earnings," (1), 109-115.
Latane, Henry A., Donald L. Tuttle and C. P. Jones. "E/P Ratios V. Changes In Earnings," (1), 117-120.
Renshaw, Edward F. "Return On S&P Industrials," (1), 121-123.
Reilly, Frank K. "First Look At O-T-C Volume," (1), 124-128.
Legan, Robert W. "The DJIA @ 2100 In Ten Years," (1), 129-133.
Bromberg, Alan R. "The Law Of Corporate Information," (2), 26-31.
Natrella, Vito. "Tax Returns Vs. Company Books," (2), 37-43.
Greenwald, Douglas and Margaret K. Matulis. "McGraw-Hill Survey Of Profits," (2), 44-46.
Savoie, Leonard M. "Meeting Financial Consumer Needs," (2), 47-51.
Graber, Dean E. "Real And Illusory Earnings Growth," (2), 52-54.
Comiskey, Eugene E. and Claude S. Colantoni. "Finance Company Earnings," (2), 55-59.
Baldwin, Rosecrans. "Principal And Income Accounting," (2), 60-67.
Carlson, Keith M. "Impact Of Fiscal Action," (2), 69-71.
Horton, Joseph J., Jr. "Rating Index For Municipal Bonds," (2), 72-75.
Murphy, Joseph E., Jr. and J. Russell Nelson. "Stability Of P/E Ratios," (2), 77-80.
Bird, Monroe M., Jr. "Investment Tax Credit," (2), 81-82.
Smith, Keith V. "Evaluation Of Wednesday Closings," (2), 83-87.
Kaish, Stanley. "Differential Odd-Lot Trading," (2), 88-91.
Spigelman, Joseph H. "The Data Service Industry," (2), 92-102.
Dutter, Philip H. "Quality Of Management," (2), 105-108.
Stern, Walter P. "The Investment Scene," (2), 109-112.
Hartwell, John M. "Performance: Its Promise And Problems," (2), 115-117.
Zeikel, Arthur. "Coordinating Research Information," (2), 119-123.
Warner, Adolphe J. "Report On European Trip," (2), 125-127.
Lockhart, J. Anthony. "Secondary Euro-Dollar Bonds," (2), 128-132.
Leach, H. Derrick. "Canadian Chartered Banks," (2), 133-140.
Neil, Herbert E., Jr. "Moderating Inflation In 1969," (3), 21-28.
Hummer, William B. "The Money Market Outlook," (3), 30-32.
Richardson, Lemont K. "Commercial Airplane Programs," (3), 37-48.
Vernon, Thomas H. "Airlines And The B-E Point," (3), 51-58.
Pickett, Ralph R. "Textbook Publishing Companies," (3), 59-62.
Devereux, John H. "Electric Utility Stocks," (3), 65-70.
Briloff, Abraham J. "The `Funny-Money' Game," (3), 73-79.
Leontiades, Milton. "Conglomerates: Another Look," (3), 80-86.
Spigelman, Joseph H. "The Data Service Industry - Part II," (3), 88-99.
Elliott, David C. "A New Index Of Equity Values," (3), 101-104.
Schneider, Theodore H. "Measuring Performance," (3), 105-111.
Fountain, John. "Growth Rates The Simple Way," (3), 112-114.
Bonham, Howard B., Jr. "Equity Investment Return In 1970: Reply," (3), 115-116.
Pyun, C. S. "DJIA AT 2100 In Ten Years' Examined," (3), 118-121.
Block, Frank E. "Elements Of Portfolio Construction," (3), 123-129.
Brown, Homer A., Jr. and Donald R. Nichols. "A Deterrent To Investment Mobility," (3), 131-137.
Baum, Clifford B. "Equity Lease Financing," (3), 138-141.
Crum, M. Colyer. "Performance Investing," (3), 142-147.
Wallich, Henry C. "The Spotty Economy," (4), 21-24.
Fand, David I. "CROS Theory Of Inflation," (4), 26-32.
Williams, Edward E. "Accounting And Capital Allocation," (4), 37-40.
Holdren, George C. "What Does The Auditor Really Say?," (4), 43-50.
Spigelman, Joseph H. "The Data Service Industry - Part III," (4), 52-70.
Spencer, Roger W. and Michael J. Heppen. "Economic Conditions And Life Insurance," (4), 73-79.
McClow, Richard J. "Is There A Renaissance In Steel?," (4), 80-84.
Birnbaum, Jerry L. "Participating In The Merger Mania," (4), 87-94.
Stone, David. "Input-Output And The Multi-Product Firm," (4), 96-102.
Mascia, Joseph S. "Corporate Earnings Predictions," (4), 107-110.
Elsaid, Hussein H. "Preferred Stock In Corporate Plan," (4), 112-117.
Lerner, Eugene M. and Rolf Auster. "Market Discounts Potential Dilution?," (4), 118-121.

Financial Analysts Journal
Volume 26, 1970

Financial Analysts Journal
Volume 27, 1971

Smidt, Seymour. "The Road To An Efficient Stock Market," (5), 18-20,64-69.
Hugon, James H. "The Euro-Money Market, Explained," (5), 21-24.
Ellis, Charles D. "Portfolio Operations," (5), 36-46.
Fanning, James E. "A System For Forecasting The Market," (5), 49-56.
Latane, Henry A., Donald L. Tuttle and William E. Young. "How To Choose A Market Index," (5), 75-85.
Beidleman, Carl R. "Pitfalls Of The Price-Earnings Ratio," (5), 86-91.
Heyne, Paul T. "The Market System Is The Best Guide," (5), 26-27,72-73.
Gray, Daniel H. "Corporate Standards Are Changing," (5), 28-29,73-74.
Bradshaw, Thornton F. "The Corporation Executive's View," (5), 30-31,70-72.
Hall, J. Parker, III. "The Professional Investor's View," (5), 32-34.
Davant, James W. "An Answer To The Critics," (6), 14-18,88.
Baker, Guthrie. "Blueprint For Constructive Reform," (6), 20-22,62.
Black, Fischer. "A Fully Computerized Stock Exchange - II," (6), 24-28,86-87.
West, Richard R. "Conflicts Of Interest," (6), 31-39.
Maynard, John. "The Most Rapidly Changing Industry," (6), 41-47.
Wagner, W. H. and S. C. Lau. "The Effect Of Diversification On Risk," (5), 48-53.
Levy, Robert A. "Stationarity Of Beta Coefficients," (6), 55-62.
Moor, Roy E. "Economics And Investment Analysis," (6), 63-69.
Mills, Robert H. "Accounting For The Investment Credit," (6), 71-77.
Miller, Jerry D. "Longevity Of Stock Purchase Warrants," (6), 78-85.

Financial Analysts Journal
Volume 28, 1972

Wallich, Henry C. "Reconstructing Humpty Dumpty," (1), 18-22,66-67.
Stern, Walter P. and William C. Norby. "Research And Market Structure," (1), 24-28,85-87.
Mark, Morris, Marvin L. Baris, Ronald K. Lytle and Leonard Marx, Jr. "Pitfalls In Real Estate Accounting," (1), 29-36.
Gibson, Ray G., Jr. "Domestic Gasoline: Prices And Margins," (1), 38-42,88-90.
Packer, Stephen B. "New Game Plan In Perspective," (1), 44-48,91-94.
Burton, John C. "Ethics In Financial Reporting," (1), 49-53.
Diefenbach, Robert E. "How Good Is Institutional Research?," (1), 54-60.
Mayne, L. S. and G. E. Philips. "Investment Assets And Bank Earnings," (1), 61-65.
Thompson, Howard E. "Coverage Ratios In Public Utilities," (1), 69-73.
Sharpe, William F. "Diversification And Portfolio Risk," (1), 74-79.
Bagehot, Walter. "Risk In Corporate Pension Funds," (1), 80-84.
Rudolph, J. Allan. "Stock Prices And The Money Supply," (1), 19-25.
Straszheim, Donald H. "Profits Vs. Phase 2 Margin Guidelines," (2), 27-32,83-85.
Norby, William C. "Profile Of The Financial Analyst," (2), 35-37.
Brown, R. Gene. "Financial Forecasting By Corporations," (2), 38-45,86-87.
Sharpe, W. F. and G. M. Cooper. "NYSE Stocks Classified By Risk, 1931-1967," (2), 46-54,81.
Pye, Gordon. "Minimax Portfolio Policies," (2), 56-60.
Dascher, Paul E. "Penn Central Was Predictable," (2), 61-64.
Hoffland, David L. "Municipal Bond Ratings And Prices," (2), 65-70.
Curran, Ward S. "Preferred Stock For Public Utilities," (2), 71-76.
Levy, Haim and Marshall Sarnat. "The Case For Mutual Funds," (2), 77-81.
Loomis, Philip, George S. Bissell, John G. Gillis and Walter P. Stern. "Corporate Disclosure And Inside Information," (3), 20-21,24-25,82-84,86-88.
FAJ Editors. "Integrating Our Securities Exchanges," (3), 28-30,32,34,90-91.
Benham, Isabel H. "Railroad-Based Conglomerates," (3), 43-48,51-53.
Trestrail, Richard W. "Eurodollars And The Money Supply," (3), 55-63.
Niederhoffer, Victor and Patrick Regan. "Earnings Changes And Stock Prices," (3), 65-71.
Bissell, George S. "Responsibility In Financial Forecasting," (3), 73-78.
Whitmarsh, Theodore F. "When To Sell Short Against The Box," (3), 80-81,78.
Weidenbaum, Murray L. "Matching National Goals And Resources," (4), 17-19,74-75.
Spigelman, Joseph H. "The Knowledge Revolution - I," (4), 22-24,26-27,30-32.
Norby, William C. and Frances Stone. "Objectives Of Financial Reporting," (4), 39-45,76-81.
Barrett, M. Edgar. "APB Opinion Number 18," (4), 47-50, 52-55.
Feuerstein, Donald M. "The Third And Fourth Markets," (4), 57-59,82-86.
Voorheis, Frank L. "Bank Trustee And Pension Performance," (4), 60-64.
Singhvi, Surendra S. "How Willing Is Management To Disclose," (4), 66-73.
Kaufman, George G. "How Not To Control The Money Supply," (5), 20-23,26,57.
Block, Frank E. "Time Horizon," (5), 30-31,60-62.
Spigelman, Joseph H. "The Knowledge Revolution - II," (5), 33-40.
Treynor, Jack L. "The Trouble With Earnings," (5), 41-43.
Damant, David C. "Financial Forecasting In The UK," (5), 44-46,59.
Good, Walter R. "Valuing Quality Growth Stocks," (5), 47-54,56-59.
Harlow, C. V. and R. J. Teweles. "Commodities And Securities Compared," (5), 64-70.
Vasicek, O. A. and J. A. McQuown. "The Efficent Market Model," (5), 71-84.
Packer, Stephen B. "A Look At The Balance Of Payments," (6), 20-21,24-25,28-29,86.
Casson, John J. "Business Economists' Forecast For 1973," (6), 32-34,91.
Monroe, Wilbur F. "Exchange Controls In Japan: 1971-72," (6), 43-46,88,91.
Bernstein, Leopold A. "Extraordinary Gains And Losses," (6), 49-52,88-89.
Ambachtsheer, Keith. "Portfolio Theory And Security Analysis," (6), 53-57.

Hodges, Stewart D. and Richard A. Brealey. "Dynamic Portfolio Selection," (6), 58-69.
Levin, Jesse. "The Bigger They Come The Harder They Fall," (6), 71-77.
Williamson, Peter J. "Measuring Mutual Fund Performance," (6), 78-80,82-84.
Groth, Stephen C. "The Trouble With Convertibles," (6), 92-95.

Financial Analysts Journal
Volume 29, 1973

Owens, Hugh F. "Investment Adviser Regulation," (1), 12-14,18,86-87.
Nelson, Harry L., Jr. "Make Investment Advisers Accountable!," (1), 19-22.
Herman, E. S. and C. F. Safanda. "Allocating Investment Information," (1), 23-28,88-91.
Akins, James E. "New Directions In Energy Policy," (1), 29-32,61-63,92.
Bethke, William M. "The Flat Glass Industry," (1), 41-47,92.
Kaplan, R. and R. W. Roll. "Accounting Changes And Stock Prices," (1), 48-53.
Reilly, Frank K. "Misdirected Emphasis In Stock Valuation," (1), 54-56,59-60.
Levy, Robert A. "On The Safety Of Low P/E Stocks," (1), 57-59.
Gray, William S., III. "Corporate Forecasts: FAF Proposal," (1), 64-71,85.
Gillis, John G. "Corporate Forecasts: Legal Aspects," (1), 72-76.
Stewart, Samuel S., Jr. "Corporate Forecasts: Research Report," (1), 77-85.
Grove, David L. "Solving The Dollar Overhang," (2), 14-15,18-19,22-23,33.
Harris, Louis. "Confidence In Financial Institutions," (2), 24-26,84-85.
DeVore, Donald C. "Managing The Management," (2), 28-30.
Appleman, Mark J. "Are You Genuinely Professional?," (2), 32-33.
Briloff, Abraham J. "Quo Vadis?," (2), 34-36,38,40-42,46-48,67-72.
Hodges, S. D. and R. A. Brealey. "Dynamic Portfolio Selection," (2), 50-65.
Brinson, Gary P. "How You Lose To Taxes And Inflation," (2), 74-75.
Turow, Daniel. "Warrants Of Dividend-Paying Stocks," (2), 76-78.
Jones, C. P. "Earnings Trends And Stock Selection," (2), 79-83.
Cook, G. Bradford. "Chairman Cook On The Role Of Analysts," (3), 18-20,22,76.
Hedberg, Robert D. "Let's Regulate Investment Advice," (3), 24-26,102.
Henderson, Hazel. "The Limits Of Traditional Economics," (3), 28-30,32,79-80,83-84,86-87.
Henwood, Thomas D. "Publicly Owned Broker-Dealer Stocks," (3), 41-44,46,48,50,88,90-91.
Hunt, Lacy H., II. "Evaluating The Reserve Aggregates," (3), 52-54,57-60,62-63.
Jahnke, William W. "The Growth Stock Mania," (3), 65-68.
Robbins, Stuart M. "The Fabric Retailing Industry," (3), 70-74,92-101.
Weidenbaum, Murray L. "A Hard Look At The Federal Budget," (4), 18-20,88-92.
Engel, Philip L. "Life Insurance Company Accounting," (4), 22-26,70-72.
Snyder, Gerard L. "Tender Offering For Stock Options," (4), 30-32.
Sedgwick, R. Minturn. "Alternative To Conventional Investing?," (4), 41-44.
Lorie, J. H. and M. T. Hamilton. "New Focus For Investment Counselling," (4), 46-50.
Fisher, Arthur L. "Investment Opportunities In Retailing," (4), 52-54,61.
Kaplan, Robert S. and Roman L. Weil. "Risk And The Value Line Contest," (4), 56-61.
Baylis, R. M. and S. L. Bhirud. "Growth Stock Analysis: A New Approach," (4), 63-70.
Radcliffe, Robert C. "Liquidity Costs And Block Trading," (4), 73-80.
Crowell, Richard A. "Five Applications Of Beta," (4), 81-87.
Gillis, John G. "Accountant Under Siege," (5), 18-19,22,90-91.
Shohet, Ruben. "New Investment Environment For The U. S.," (5), 26-32.
Gilbert, R. Alton. "Effect Of Lagged Reserve Requirements," (5), 34-36,38-40,42-43.
Whitman, Martin J. "Let's Reform Exchange Prospectuses," (5), 44-46,85-89.
Appleman, Mark J. "The Three Minds Of The Money Manager," (5), 49-52.
Gaskins, J. Peter. "Taxation Of Foreign Source Income," (5), 55-58,60-64.
Olstein, R. A. and T. L. O'glove. "Devaluation And Multinational Reporting," (5), 65-69,80-84.
Walker, C. James, III. "The United States Wine Industry," (5), 70-79,32.
NYSSA Round Table. "The Outlook For Security Analysts," (6), 22-24,26,28.
Bostian, David B., Jr. "The Impact Of Institutions On The Market," (6), 30-32,35-36,86-93.
Smith, Chas. B. "Rule 144 And Technological Innovation," (6), 38-41,85.
Good, Walter R. and Jack R. Meyer. "Adjusting The Price-Earnings Ratio Gap," (6), 42,44,48-49,81-84.
Paternotte, William L. "Supplying The Food Service Industry," (6), 50,52,54,56-57,80.
Norr, David. "Some Elements Of Oil Profitability," (6), 58-66.
Cross, Frank. "Price Movements On Fridays And Mondays," (6), 67-79.
Post, Lawrence A. "Yield To Early Maturity In Usable Bonds," (6), 70-73,84.
Sharpe, William F. "Bonds Vs. Stocks: Capital Market Theory," (6), 74-80.

Financial Analysts Journal
Volume 30, 1974

FAF Inside Information Committee. "New Guidelines On Inside Information," (1), 20-25.
Boudreaux, Kenneth J. "The Pricing Of Mutual Fund Shares," (1), 26-32.
Barrett, M. Edgar, Lee N. Price and Judith Ann Gehrke. "What Investors Need To Know About Japan," (1), 33-44.
Cullity, John P. "Market Recoveries Following Recessions," (1), 45-48.

Financial Analysts Journal
Volume 33, 1977

Gray, William S. "The Major Shortfall Of ERISA," (1), 18-20.

Fisher, Arthur L. "Money Managers Don't Behave Like Capitalists," (1), 21-25.

Klesch, A. Gary. "Interpreting The Prudent Man Rule Of ERISA," (1), 26-32.

Brown, Marilyn V. "Prudence Under ERISA: What Regulators Say," (1), 33-39.

Fouse, William, L. "Risk And Liquidity Revisited," (1), 40-44.

Falkenstein, Angela and Roman L. Weil. "Using Replacement Costs To Measure Income - Part I," (1), 46-57.

Renshaw, Edward F. "Short Selling And Financial Arbitrage," (1), 58-65.

Reints, William and Pieter Vandenberg. "Investment Performance Of Levered Bank Stocks," (1), 66-70.

McConnell, Walter S. and Stephen D. Leit. "Inflation, Stock Prices And Job Creation," (2), 25-29.

Pozen, Robert C. "The Prudent Man Rule And ERISA," (2), 30-35.

Hoffland, David L. "New York City And The Municipal Bond Market," (2), 36-39.

Rodriguez, Rita M. "FASB No. 8: What Has It Done To Us?," (2), 40-47.

Falkenstein, Angela and Roman L. Weil. "Using Replacement Costs To Measure Income - Part II," (2), 48-57.

Wilson, Paul N. and Robert I. Cummin. "Saving Management And Transaction Costs," (2), 58-62.

Hagaman, T. Carter and Arnold E. Jensen. "Investment Value: A Reference Point For Analysts," (2), 63-70.

Cottle, Sidney. "The Future Of Pension Management," (3), 23-25.

Kahn, Irving. "Lemmings Always Lose," (3), 27-29.

Beebower, Gilbert L. and Gary L. Bergstrom. "Pension Performance 1966-1975," (3), 31-42.

Banks, Stephen J. "The Origins Of The Great Inflation," (3), 43-55.

Bell, Philip W. "Portfolio Reports For Client And Manager," (3), 56-61.

Dimson, Elroy. "Instant Option Valuation," (3), 62-69.

Gastineau, Gary L. "An Index Of Listed Option Premiums," (3), 70-75.

Korschot, Benjamin C. "Prudence Before And After ERISA," (4), 18-21.

Butler, H. L., Jr., G. J. Podrasky and J. D. Allen. "Aerospace Industry Re-Revisited," (4), 32-35.

Calderwood, Stanford. "The Truth About Index Funds," (4), 36-47.

Chambers, R. J. "The Delusions Of Replacement Cost Accounting," (4), 48-52.

Lindsley, David A. and Douglas V. Austin. "A Sensational New Investment," (4), 53-54.

Hartland-Thunberg, Penelope. "Oil, Petrodollars And The LDC's," (4), 55-58.

Schaefer, Stephen M. "The Problem With Redemption Yields," (4), 59-67.

Zeikel, Arthur. "Stock Market Outlook: No Metamorphosis," (5), 25-28.

Hall, J. Parker, III. "CELI - Another Government Time Bomb?," (5), 30-32.

Howard, Godfrey G. "A Second Look At Inflation," (5), 35-47.

Pakkala, A. L. "The Market For Amateur Photography," (5), 48-52.

Butler, Hartman L., Jr., George J. Podrasky and J. Devon Allen. "Aerospace II - Commercial Aircraft," (5), 53-66.

Gutmann, Peter M. "The Subterranean Economy," (6), 26-27.

Schaefer, Jeffrey M. and Adolphe J. Warner. "Concentration In The Securities Industry," (6), 29-34.

Baylis, Robert M. "The Greening Of U.S. Investment Business," (6), 36-37.

Ambachtsheer, Keith P. "Investment Scenarios For The 1980's," (6), 38-46.

Hawkins, David F. "Toward An Old Theory Of Equity Valuation," (6), 48-53.

Christopherson, Paul C. "Product Pricing In The Chemical Industry," (6), 54-62.

Cole, James F. "What About The Anatomy Of The Stock?," (6), 63-64.

Bradley, James W. and Donald H. Korn. "Acquisition And Merger Trends," (6), 65-70.

Dimson, Elroy. "Option Valuation Nomograms," (6), 71-74.

Financial Analysts Journal
Volume 34, 1978

Williams, Dave H. "Changing Shape Of Investment Research," (1), 18-21.

Geyer, Carter T. "The Abrogation Of Rule 390," (1), 22-30.

Jensen, M. C. and W. H. Meckling. "Can The Corporation Survive?," (1), 31-37.

Woodworth, Jay N. "What Kind Of Research Do We Really Need?," (1), 38-40.

Williams, William D. "CIC 1976 Awards For Excellence," (1), 42-45.

Benston, G. J. and R. L. Hagerman. "Risk, Volume And Spread," (1), 46-49.

Gargett, Dave R. "The Link Between Stock Prices And Liquidity," (1), 50-54.

Basu, S. and J. R. Hanna. "GPL-Adjusted Earnings For Utilities," (1), 55-67.

Helms, Gary B. "Toward Bridging The Gap," (1), 68-72.

Wallich, Henry C. "Investment Income During Inflation," (2), 34-37.

White, Reba. "Coping With The Financial Reporter," (2), 38-40.

Colhoun, Howard P. "The New FAF Investment Workshop," (2), 41-42.

Treynor, Jack L. "What Prof. Galbraith Failed To Say On TV," (2), 43-44.

Schnepper, Jeff A. "'Going Private' And Minority Shareholders," (2), 45-47.

Woo, J. C. H. and S. B. Seth. "Replacement Costs And Historical Performance," (2), 48-54.

Fuller, R. J. and R. W. Metcalf. "How Analysts Use Management Forecasts," (2), 55-57.

Marcus, Robert P. "Residual Value And The Cost Of Leasing," (2), 58-60.

Dyl, Edward A. "Short Selling And The Capital Gains Tax," (2), 61-64.

Largay, James A., III and J. Leslie Livingstone. "Current Value Accounting Neglects Liabilities," (2), 65-71.

Black, Fischer. "The Ins And Outs Of Foreign Investment," (3), 25-32.

Wagner, W. H. and C. A. Zipkin. "Better Performance Via Inventory Funds," (3), 34-36,68.

Ferguson, Robert. "Do Inventory Funds Make Sense?," (3), 38-44.

West, Richard R. and Seha Tinic. "Critique Of Schaefer And Warner," (3), 46,50-56.

Schaefer, Jeffrey M. and Adolphe J. Warner. "Rejoinder To West And Tinic," (3), 47-49.

Brown, Marilyn V. "Reducing Corporate And Shareholder Taxes," (3), 57-63.

Hoffland, David L. "A Model Bank Investment Policy," (3), 64-76.

Miller, Edward M. "Portfolio Selection In A Fluctuating Economy," (3), 77-83.

Treynor, Jack L., P. J. Regan and W. W. Priest. "Pension Claims And Corporate Assets," (3), 84-88.

Peake, Junius W. "The National Market System," (4), 25-33.

Forrestal, Daniel J., III. "The Changing Economics Of Money Management," (4), 35-38.

Korschot, Benjamin C. "Measuring Research Analysts' Performance," (4), 41-46.

Pozen, Robert C. "When To Purchase A Protective Put," (4), 47-60.

Kupferman, Martin and Maurice D. Levi. "Taxation And Interest Rate Parity," (4), 61-64.

Beaver, William and Dale Morse. "What Determines Price-Earnings Ratios?," (4), 65-76.

Eisemann, Peter C. and Edward A. Moses. "Stock Dividends: Management's View," (4), 77-83.

Gutmann, Peter M. "Are The Unemployed, Unemployed?," (5), 26-29.

Ranson, R. David and Charles E. Babin. "What's Holding Up Capital Investment?," (5), 30-41.

West, Stan and Thomas T. Murphy. "Caveats For Market Technicians," (5), 42-48.

Lasman, Daniel A. and Roman L. Weil. "Adjusting The Debt-Equity Ratio," (5), 49-58.

Hale, David. "Inflation Accounting In The 1970s," (5), 59-72.

Good, Walter R. "Short-Term Clients And Long-Term Performance," (6), 21-26.

Hale, David. "Adjusting Tax Policies For Inflation," (6), 28-40.

Reed, Joel L. "Evaluating Oil And Gas Reserves," (6), 42-47.

Collins, Daniel W., Warren T. Dent and Melvin C. O'Conner. "Has Full Cost Accounting Helped Share Prices?," (6), 48-57.

Meyer, Kenneth R. "Yield Spreads And Interest Rate Levels," (6), 58-63.

Garcia, Gillian. "The Currency Ratio And The Subterranean Economy," (6), 64-66.

Gutmann, Peter M. "Professor Gutmann Replies," (6), 67-69.

Arditti, Fred D. and W. Andrew McCollough. "Real Versus Randomly Generated Stock Prices," (6), 70-74.

Financial Analysts Journal
Volume 35, 1979

Brealey, Richard A. "Government Assets: Key To Inflation?," (1), 18-21.

Patterson, Solon P., Dennis R. Bouwer, Theodore R. Lilley and Benjamin C. Korschot. "Long-Range Planning In The FAF," (1), 23-26.

Ingberman, Monroe, Joshua Ronen and George H. Sorter. "Lease Capitalization And Financial Ratios," (1), 28-31.

Groth, John C., Wilbur G. Lewellen, Gary G. Schlarbaum and Ronald C. Lease. "How Good Are Broker's Recommendations?," (1), 32-40.

Shank, John K., Jessie F. Dillard and Joseph F. Bylinski. "What `Subject To' Opinions Tell Investors," (1), 41-45.

Pakkala, A. L. "Fixed Costs And Earnings Predictions," (1), 46-48.

Rosenberg, Barr. "How Active Should Your Portfolio Be?," (1), 49-62.

Radcliffe, Robert C. and William G. Gillespie. "The Price Impact Of Reverse Splits," (1), 63-67.

Tyndall, D. G. "The Value Of Participation In A Loan Contract," (1), 68-77.

Modigliani, Franco and Richard A. Cohn. "Inflation And The Stock Market," (2), 24-44.

Norr, David. "Management And The Investor," (2), 45-48.

Wojtyla, Henry L. "Cashing In On Our Investment In People," (2), 49-52.

Zacks, Leonard. "EPS Forecasts - Accuracy Is Not Enough," (2), 53-55.

Ferguson, Robert F. "Where Are The Customers' Yachts?," (2), 56-62.

Bernstein, Peter L. "The Wedge Theory: Pie In The Sky?," (2), 63-67.

Haugen, Robert A. "Common Stock Quality Ratings And Risk," (2), 68-71.

Graber, Dean E. and Bill D. Jarnagin. "The FASB - Eliminator Of `Managed Earnings'?," (2), 72-76.

Ellis, Charles D. "Pension Funds Need Management Management," (3), 25-28.

Ayres, Herbert F. and John Y. Barry. "Dynamics Of The Government Yield Curve," (3), 31-39.

Davidson, Sidney, Skelton and Roman L. Weil. "The FASB's Inflation Accounting Proposal," (3), 41-54.

Kaiser, Ronald W. "Kondratieff's Gloomy News For Investors," (3), 57-66.

Leibowitz, Martin L. "The Horizon Annuity," (3), 68-74.

Dyckman, Thomas R. "Full Cost Accounting: Another View," (3), 75-80.

Wubbels, Rolf E. "The French Economic Miracle," (4), 23-27.

Gray, William S., III. "Long-Term Outlook For The Stock Market," (4), 29-39.

Ibbotson, R. G. and R. A. Sinquefield. "Stocks, Bonds, Bills And Inflation: Updates," (4), 40-44.

Stickney, Clyde P. "Analyzing Effective Corporate Tax Rates," (4), 45-54.

Miller, Edward M. "A Counter Example To The Random Walk," (4), 55-56,67.

Price, Lee N. "Choosing Between Growth And Yield," (4), 57-67.

Gross, William H. "The Effect Of Coupon On Yield Spreads," (4), 68-71.

Bernstein, Leopold A. and Joel G. Siegel. "The Concept Of Earnings Quality," (4), 72-75.

Balog, James. "Pyramids, Mesas And Mid-Career Crises," (5), 25-29.
Mendelson, M. and J. W. Peake. "Which Way To A National Market System?," (5), 31-34,37-42.
Easman, W. S., Jr., A. Falkenstein, Roman L. Weil and D. J. Guy. "Sustainable Income And Stock Returns," (5), 44-48.
Page, John R. and Paul Hooper. "Financial Statements For Security Analysts," (5), 50-55.
Sprouse, Robert T. "Prospects For Progress In Financial Reporting," (5), 56-60.
Gastineau, G. L. and A. Madansky. "Simulation Is No Guide To Option Strategies," (5), 61-76.
Butler, H. L., Jr. and J. D. Allen. "Dow Jones Industrial Average Re-Examined," (6), 23-30.
Nicholson, S. F., M. Smith and R. B. Willis. "Investment Perspectives - 150 Years," (6), 23-37.
Ambachtsheer, K. P. and J. L. Farrell, Jr. "Can Active Management Add Value?," (6), 39-47.
Rodriguez, Rita M. "Measuring Multinationals' Exchange Risk," (6), 49-55.
Rudd, Andrew T. "The Revised Dow Jones Industrial Average," (6), 57-61,63.
Gutmann, Peter M. "Taxes And The Supply Of National Output," (6), 64-66.
Mortimer, Terry. "Reporting Earnings: A New Approach," (6), 67-71.
Grubel, Herbert G. "The Peter Principle And Efficient Markets," (6), 72-75.
Bolten, Steven E. and John H. Crockett, Jr. "Are Auditors Independent?," (6), 76-78.

Financial Analysts Journal
Volume 36, 1980

Wanniski, Jude T. "Economic Policy And The Rise And Fall Of Empires," (1), 20-27.
Hitschler, W. Anthony. "The Caribou Weren't In The Estimates," (1), 28-32.
Bogle, John C. and Jan M. Twardowski. "Institutional Investment Performance Compared," (1), 33-41.
Ederington, Louis H. "New Futures And Options Markets," (1), 42-48.
Niederhoffer, Victor and Richard Zeckhauser. "Market Index Futures Contracts," (1), 49-55.
Babcock, Guilford C. "The Roots Of Risk And Return," (1), 56-63.
Norby, William C. and John C. Burton. "Financial Reporting In The 1980s," (1), 64-68.
Grinnell, D. J. and C. T. Norgaard. "Reporting Rules For Marketable Equity Securities," (1), 69-74.
Kripke, Homer. "Inside Information And Efficient Markets," (2), 20-24.
Fruhan, William E., Jr. "Lessons From Levitz: Creating Share Value," (2), 25-32,34-40,42-45.
Smaistrla, Charles J. and Adrian W. Throop. "A New Inflation In The 1970s?," (2), 47-52,54-57.
Bierman, Harold, Jr. "Convertible Bonds As Investments," (2), 59-61.
Kennedy, Robert E. and Millie H. Wilson. "Investor Relations And Security Analysts," (2), 63-69.
Broome, O. Whitfield, Jr. "The C.F.A. Program's Body Of Knowledge," (2), 71-74.
Lovell, Robert M., Jr. "Alternative Investments," (3), 19-21.
Baylis, Robert M. "Business Strategy For The Securities Industry," (3), 23-25.
Bodie, Zvi and Victor I. Rosansky. "Risk And Return In Commodity Futures," (3), 27-31,33-39.
Jenkins, James W. "Taxes, Margining And Bond Selection," (3), 41-47.
Murphy, J. Michael. "Why No One Can Tell Who's Winning," (3), 49-57.
Ferguson, Robert. "Performance Measurement Doesn't Make Sense," (3), 59-69.
Welch, Jonathan B. "Explaining Disintermediation At Mutual Savings Banks," (3), 71-76.
Black, Fischer. "The Tax Consequences Of Long-Run Pension Policy," (4), 21-28.
Porter, Michael E. "Industry Structure And Competitive Strategy: Keys To Profitability," (4), 30-41.
Ezra, D. Don. "How Actuaries Determine The Unfunded Pension Liability," (4), 43-50.
Largay, James A., III and Clyde P. Stickney. "Cash Flows, Ratio Analysis And The W. T. Grant Company Bankruptcy," (4), 51-54.
Piccini, Raymond. "Stock Market Behavior Around Business Cycle Peaks," (4), 55-57.
Reilly, Frank K. and Rupinder S. Sidhu. "The Many Uses Of Bond Duration," (4), 58-72.
Williams, Dave H. "Organizing For Superior Investment Returns," (5), 21-23,27.
Baylis, Robert M. "The Salesman And The Institutional Investment Process," (5), 25-27.
Schotland, Roy A. "Divergent Investing For Pension Funds," (5), 29-39.
Parry, Robert W., Jr. and Stuart K. Webster. "City Leases: Up Front, Out Back, In The Closet," (5), 41-47.
Allvine, Fred C. and Daniel E. O'Neill. "Stock Market Returns And The Presidential Election Cycle," (5), 49-56.
McCauley, Peter B. "The Quick Asset Effect: Missing Key To The Relation Between Inflation And The Investment Value Of The Firm," (5), 57-66.
Slivka, Ronald T. "Risk And Return For Option Investment Strategies," (5), 67-73.
Black, Fischer. "The Magic In Earnings: Economic Earnings Versus Accounting Earnings," (6), 19-24.
Terborgh, George. "The Indexation Issue In Inflation Accounting," (6), 26-31.
Laiderman, Richard. "The Sinking Fund Bond Game," (6), 33-36.
Dawson, James P., Peter M. Neupert and Clyde P. Stickney. "Restating Financial Statements For Alternative GAAPs: Is It Worth The Effort?," (6), 38-46.
Ezra, D. Don. "Mortgage In Canadian Pension Funds," (6), 48-54.
Arnott, Robert D. "Cluster Analysis And Stock Price Movement," (6), 56-62.
Alboini, Victor P. "The New Ontario Securities Act," (6), 64-69.

Dale, Charles and Rosemarie Workman. "The Arc Sine Law And The Treasury Bill Futures Market," (6), 71-74.
Lindahl-Stevens, Mary. "Redefining Bull And Bear Markets," (6), 76-77.

Financial Analysts Journal
Volume 37, 1981

Meigs, A. James. "The Fed And Financial Markets: Is It Killing Them With Kindness?," (1), 18-27.
Leuthold, Steven C. "Interest Rates, Inflation And Deflation," (1),28-41.
Leibowitz, Martin L. "A Yield Basis For Financial Futures," (1), 42-51.
Surz, Ronald J. "Elaborations On The Tax Consequences Of Long-Run Pension Policy," (1), 52-54,60.
Treynor, Jack L. "What Does It Take To Win The Trading Game?," (1), 55-60.
Moriarty, Eugene, Susan Phillips and Paula Tosini. "A Comparison Of Options And Futures In The Management Of Portfolio Risk," (1), 61-67.
Randall, Maury R. "Investment Planning In An Inflationary Environment," (1), 68-70.
Clarke, F. L. "Replacement Costs And Inflation Accounting: A Demurrer," (1), 71-75.
Wildavsky, Aaron. "Richer Is Safer," (2), 19-22.
Diller, Stanley. "Analyzing The Yield Curve: A New Approach," (2), 23-41.
Reader, A. Constant. "The Care And Feeding Of Buy-Side Analysts," (2), 42-43,51.
Gushee, Charles H. "How To Immunize A Bond Investment," (2), 44-51.
Reinganum, Marc R. "Abnormal Returns In Small Firm Portfolios," (2), 52-56,71.
Brick, John R. and Howard E. Thompson. "Portfolio Policies Of Private Mortgage Insurers," (2), 58-66.
Treynor, Jack L. "The Financial Objective In The Widely Held Corporation," (2), 68-71.
Holt, Robert N. and Rebecca E. Fincher. "The Foreign Corrupt Practices Act," (2), 73-76.
Revsine, Lawrence. "Inflation Accounting For Debt," (3), 20-29.
Jauch, Heinz. "Four Keys To Savings And Loan Profitability," (3), 31-39,41-43.
Hall, J. Parker, III. "Shouldn't You Own Fewer Long-Term Bonds?," (3), 45-48.
Storey, Reed K. "Conditions Necessary For Developing A Conceptual Framework," (3), 51-54,56-58.
Ellis, Charles D. "Jack Has Never Been Easy," (4), 25.
Fand, David I. "The Reagan Economic Program," (4), 28-34.
Freund, William C. "Productivity And Inflation," (4), 36-39.
Wallich, Henry C. "Techniques Of Monetary Policy," (4), 41-46,56.
Ladd, Edward H. "Thoughts On The Long-Term Implications Of Inflation: A Look At American Inflation From A British Perspective," (4), 48-56.
Terborgh, George. "The Decline Of Fiscal Discipline," (4), 58-62.
Rubinstein, Mark and Hayne E. Leland. "Replicating Options With Positions In Stock And Cash," (4), 63-72.
Laffer, Arthur B. "Supply-Side Economics," (5), 29-43.
Beaver, William H. "Interpreting Disclosures Of The Effects Of Changing Prices," (5), 45-55.
Condon, Kathleen A. "Measuring Equity Transaction Costs," (5), 57-60.
Ranson, R. David and William G. Shipman. "Institutional Buying Power And The Stock Market," (5), 62-68.
Clancy, Donald K. and John A. Yeakel. "On Reporting Dilutionary Exchanges," (5), 70-73.
Leibowitz, Martin L. "Volatility In Tax-Exempt Bonds: A Theoretical Model," (6), 31-33,35-39,41-47,49-52.
Mallman, Thomas L. "Volatility In Municipal Bonds: Estimating And Using Volatility Factors," (6), 54-59.
Hale, David. "Thatcher And Reagan: Different Roads To Recession," (6), 61-68,70-71.
Black, Fischer. "The ABCs Of Business Cycles," (6), 75-80.

Financial Analysts Journal
Volume 38, 1982

Tepper, Irwin. "The Future Of Private Pension Funding," (1), 25-31.
Burns, Joseph M. "Electronic Trading In Futures Markets," (1), 33-41.
Rosenberg, Barr. "The Current State And Future Of Investment Research," (1), 43-50.
Figlewski, Stephen and Stanley J. Kon. "Portfolio Management With Stock Index Futures," (1), 52-60.
Camerer, Colin. "The Pricing And Social Value Of Commodity Options," (1), 62-65.
Nichols, Donald R. "Operating Income And Distributable Income Under Replacement Cost Accounting: The Long-Life Asset Replacement Problem," (1), 68-73.
Ferguson, Robert and Philip Popkin. "Pulling Rabbits Out Of Hats In The Oil Business - And Elsewhere," (2), 24-27.
Black, Fischer. "The Trouble With Econometric Models," (2), 29-37.
Grauer, Robert R. and Nils H. Hakansson. "Higher Return, Lower Risk: Historical Returns On Long-Run, Actively Managed Portfolios Of Stocks, Bonds, And Bills, 1936-1978," (2), 39-53.
Liss, Herman. "A Backward Glance O'er Travelled Roads," (2), 55-59.
Siegel, Joel G. "The `Quality Of Earnings' Concept - A Survey," (2), 60-68.
Morse, Dale. "Wall Street Journal Announcements And The Securities Markets," (2), 69-76.
DeGroff, Carol C. "The 1981 F.A.F. Investment Management Workshop - A Study In Controversy," (2), 77-78.
Treynor, Jack L. "On The Quality Of Municipal Bonds," (3), 25-30.
Copeland, Basil L., Jr. "Inflation, Interest Rates And Equity Risk Premia," (3), 32-43.
Morrison, Russell J. "Investment (Savings) Elaborated - With Special Reference To Japan," (3), 45-48.
Amihud, Yakov and Haim Mendelson. "Asset Price Behavior In A Dealership Market," (3), 50-59.

Dowen, Richard, J. and W. Scott Bauman. "A Fundamental Multifactor Asset Pricing Model," (4), 45-51.
Rappaport, Alfred. "The Affordable Dividend Approach To Equity Valuation," (4), 52-58.
Butler, Hartman L., Jr. and Richard F. DeMong. "The Changing Dow Jones Industrial Average," (4), 59-62.
Arditti, Fred D., Sirri Ayaydin, Ravi K. Mattu and Stephen Rigsbee. "A Passive Futures Strategy That Outperforms Active Management," (4), 63-67.
Madden, Gerald P., Kenneth P. Nunn, Jr. and Alan Wiemann. "Mutual Fund Performance And Market Capitalization," (4), 67-70.
Paul, Jack W. "Do Timely Interim Reviews Lessen Accounting Error?," (4), 70-73.
Howe, John S. "Evidence On Stock Market Overreaction," (4), 74-77.
Leibowitz, Martin L. "Total Portfolio Duration: A New Perspective On Asset Allocation," (5), 18-29,77.
Canto, Victor A., J. Kimball Dietrich, Adish Jain and Vishwa Mudaliar. "Protectionism And The Stock Market: The Determinants And Consequences Of Trade Restrictions," (5), 32-42.
Sorensen, Eric H. and Terry Burke. "Portfolio Returns From Active Industry Group Rotation," (5), 43-50.
Pettit, R. Richardson and Ronald F. Singer. "Instant Option Betas," (5), 51-62.
Townsend, Henry. "Another Look At The Modigliani And Cohn Equation," (5), 63-66.
McConnell, Dennis, John A. Haslem and Virginia R. Gibson. "The President's Letter To Stockholders: A New Look," (5), 66-70.
Varela, Oscar. "Using The COMPUSTAT Tapes In Studying The Dow Jones Portfolios," (5), 70-75.
Babcock, Guilford. "On The Linearity Of Duration," (5), 75-77.
Bailey, Jeffrey V. and Robert D. Arnott. "Cluster Analysis And Manager Selection," (6), 20-21,24-28.
Benesh, Gary A. and Pamela P. Peterson. "On The Relation Between Earnings, Changes, Analysts' Forecasts And Stock Price Fluctuations," (6), 29-39,55.
Oppenheimer, Henry R. "Ben Graham's Net Current Asset Values: A Performance Update," (6), 40-47.
Brill, Edward A. and Richard B. Harriff. "Pricing American Options: Managing Risk With Early Exercise," (6), 48-55.
Malley, Susan L. and Susan Jayson. "Why Do Financial Executives Manage Pensions Funds The Way They Do?," (6), 56-62.
Rogalski, Richard and Seha M. Tinic. "The January Size Effect: Anomaly Or Risk Mismeasurement?," (6), 63-70.
Reichenstein, William. "When Stock Is Less Risky Than Treasury Bills," (6), 71-75.
Brief, Richard P. and Raef A. Lawson. "Estimating Security Returns: A Further Note," (6), 75-77.

Financial Analysts Journal
Volume 43, 1987

Davanzo, Lawrence E. and Stephen L. Nesbitt. "Performance Fees For Investment Management," (1), 14-20.
Kritzman, Mark P. "Incentive Fees: Some Problems And Some Solutions," (1), 21-26.
Grinold, Richard and Andrew Rudd. "Incentive Fees: Who Wins? Who Loses?," (1), 27-38.
Record, Eugene E., Jr. and Mary Ann Tynan. "Incentive Fees: The Basic Issues," (1), 39-43.
Canto, Victor A. "The Fat CATS Strategy For Portfolio Selection," (1), 44-51.
Nixon, Clair J., Casper Wiggins and L. Richard Johnson. "Repeal Of The Investment Tax Credit And Financial Statement Analysis," (1), 52-55.
Cinar, E. Mine and Joseph Vu. "Evidence On The Effect Of Option Expirations On Stock Prices," (1), 55-57.
Jain, Prem C. "The Effect On Stock Price Of Inclusion In Or Exclusion From The S&P 500," (1), 58-65.
Morrissey, Thomas F. and Chor Huang. "A Nomogram For Estimating Duration," (1),
Stoll, Hans R. and Robert E. Whaley. "Program Trading And Expiration-Day Effects," (2), 16-28.
Leibowitz, Martin L. "Pension Asset Allocation Through Surplus Management," (2), 29-40.
Craig, Darryl, Glenn Johnson and Maurice Joy. "Accounting Methods And P/E Ratios," (2), 41-45.
Senchack, A. J., Jr. and John D. Martin. "The Relative Performance Of The PSR And PER Investment Strategies," (2), 46-56.
Finnerty, Joseph E. and Hun Y. Park. "Stock Index Futures: Does The Tail Wag The Dog?," (2), 57-61.
Garcia, C. B. and F. J. Gould. "A Note On The Measurement Of Risk In A Portfolio," (2), 61-69.
Hegde, Shantaram P. "Coupon And Maturity Characteristics Of The Cheapest-To-Deliver Bonds On The Treasury Bond Futures Contract," (2), 70-76.
O'Connell, James A. "The Policy Level Management Gap In Corporate Pension Administration (And How One Corporation Bridged It)," (2), 76-79.
Brooks, Robert, Haim Levy and Jim Yoder. "Using Stochastic Dominance To Evaluate The Performance Of Portfolios With Options," (2), 79-82.
Queen, Maggie and Richard Roll. "Firm Mortality: Using Market Indicators To Predict Survival," (3), 9-26.
Rendleman, Richard J., Jr. and Richard W. McEnally. "Assessing The Costs Of Portfolio Insurance," (3), 27-37.
DeAngelo, Harry and Linda DeAngelo. "Management Buyouts Of Publicly Traded Corporations," (3), 38-49.
Treynor, Jack L. "Market Efficiency And The Bean Jar Experiment," (3), 50-53.
Clayman, Michelle. "In Search Of Excellence: The Investor's Viewpoint," (3), 54-63.
Varaiya, Nikhil P. and Kenneth R. Ferris. "Overpaying In Corporate Takeovers: The Winner's Curse," (3), 64-71.
Bierman, Harold, Jr. "Deferred Taxes, Income And The 1986 Tax Reform Act," (3), 72-73.

Gibson, Charles. "How Chartered Financial Analysts View Financial Ratios," (3), 73-76.
Jones, Charles P. and Bruce Bublitz. "The CAPM And Equity Return Regularities: An Extension," (3), 77-79.
Altman, Edward I. "The Anatomy Of The High-Yield Bond Market," (4), 12-25.
Blume, Marshall E. and Donald B. Keim. "Lower-Grade Bonds: Their Risks And Returns," (4), 26-33.
Estep, Tony. "Security Analysis And Stock Selection: Turning Financial Information Into Return Forecasts," (4), 34-43.
Garcia, C. B. and F. J. Gould. "An Empirical Study Of Portfolio Insurance," (4), 44-54.
Ferguson, Robert. "A Comparison Of The Mean-Variance And Long-Term Return Characteristics Of 3 Investment Strategies," (4), 55-66.
Wilson, Jack W. and Charles P. Jones. "Common Stock Prices And Inflation: 1857-1985," (4), 67-72.
Taylor, Richard W. "Bond Duration Analysis: A Pedagogical Note," (4), 72-74.
Brown, Keith C. and John S. Howe. "On The Use Of Gold As a Fixed Income Security," (4), 74-76.
Vu, Joseph D. and Paul Caster. "Why All The Interest In Short Interest?," (4), 77-79.
Ambachtsheer, Keith P. "Pension Fund Asset Allocation: In Defense Of A 60/40 Equity/Debt Asset Mix," (5), 14-24.
Sharpe, William F. "Integrated Asset Allocation," (5), 25-32.
Kling, Arnold. "How The Stock Market Can Learn To Live With Index Futures And Options," (5), 33-39.
Cullity, John P. "Signals Of Cyclical Movements In Inflation And Interest Rates," (5), 40-49.
Chua, Jess H., Richard S. Woodward and Eric C. To. "Potential Gains From Stock Market Timing In Canada," (5), 50-56.
Sondhi, Ashwinpaul C., George H. Sorter and Gerald I. White. "Transactional Analysis," (5), 57-64.
Chalk, Andrew J. and John W. Peavy, III. "Initial Public Offerings: Daily Returns, Offering Types And The Price Effect ," (5), 65-69.
Lee, Cheng F. and Hun Y. Park. "Value Line Investment Survey Rank Changes And Beta Coefficients," (5), 70-72.
Young, S. David, Michael A. Berry, David W. Harvey and John R. Page. "Systematic Risk And Accounting Information Under The Arbitrage Pricing Theory," (5), 73-76.
Millar, James A., Thakol Nunthirapakorn and Steve Courtenay. "A Note On The Information Content Of Primary And Fully Diluted Earnings Per Share," (5), 77-79.
Ippolito, Richard A. and John A. Turner. "Turnover, Fees And Pension Plan Performance," (6), 6-26.
Treynor, Jack L. "The Economics Of The Dealer Function," (6), 27-34.
Clarke, Roger G. and Robert D. Arnott. "The Cost Of Portfolio Insurance: Tradeoffs And Choices," (6), 35-47.
Jog, Vijay M. and Allan L. Riding. "Underpricing In Canadian IPOs," (6), 48-55.
Canto, Victor A. "Fine-Tuning The CATS Meow," (6), 56-66.
DeBrillembourg, Hilda Ochoa. "From Blue Jeans To Buyouts--Shrewd Portfolio Mangers Or A Nation Of Spendthrifts?," (6), 67-71.
Gordon, J. Douglas, Eugene J. Moriarty and Paula A. Tosini. "Stock Index Futures: Does The Dog Wag The Tail?," (6), 72-73.
Herbst, Anthony F. and Edwin Maberly. "Shoes And Ships And Sealing Wax, Cabbages And Kings: Now Tail-Wagged Dogs And Stock Index Futures," (6), 73-75.

Financial Analysts Journal
Volume 44, 1988

Perold, Andre F. and William F. Sharpe. "Dynamic Strategies For Asset Allocation," (1), 16-27.
Tosini, Paula A. "Stock Index Futures And Stock Market Activity In October 1987," (1), 28-37.
Rubinstein, Mark. "Portfolio Insurance And The Market Crash," (1), 38-47.
Gould, F. J. "Stock Index Futures: The Arbitrage Cycle And Portfolio Insurance," (1), 48-62.
Edwards, Franklin R. "Does Futures Trading Increase Stock Market Volatility?," (1), 63-69.
Bookstaber, Richard and Jeremy Gold. "In Search Of The Liability Asset," (1), 70-80.
Reinganum, Marc R. "The Anatomy Of A Stock Market Winner," (2), 16-28.
Berry, Michael A., Edwin Burmeister and Marjorie B. McElroy. "Sorting Out Risks Using Known APT Factors," (2), 29-42.
Leibowitz, Martin L. and Roy D. Henriksson. "Portfolio Optimization Within A Surplus Framework," (2), 43-51.
Fuller, Russell J. and G. Wenchi Wong. "Traditional Versus Theoretical Risk Measures," (2), 52-57.
Ezra, D. Don. "Economic Values: A Pension Pentateuch," (2), 58-67.
Thomas, Lee R., III. "Currency Risks In International Equity Portfolios," (2), 68-71.
Swales, George S., Jr. "Another Look At The President's Letter To Stockholders," (2), 71-73.
Jacobs, Bruce I. and Kenneth N. Levy. "Disentangling Equity Return Regularities: New Insights And Investment Opportunities," (3), 18-44.
Perold, Andre F. and Evan C. Schulman. "The Free Lunch In Currency Hedging: Implications For Investment Policy And Peformance Standards," (3), 45-52.
Dunetz, Mark L. and James M. Mahoney. "Using Duration And Convexity In The Analysis Of Callable Bonds," (3), 53-73.
Briloff, Abraham J. "Cannibalizing The Transcendent Margin: Reflections On Conglomeration, LBOs, Recapitalizations And Other Manifestations Of Corporate Mania," (3), 74-80.
Dyl, Edward A. and Edwin D. Maberly. "A Possible Explanation Of The Weekend Effect," (3), 83-84.
Bierman, Harold, Jr. "Defining And Evaluating Portfolio Insurance Strategies," (3), 84-87.
Grossman, Sanford J. "Program Trading And Market Volatility: A Report On Interday Relationships," (4), 18-28.

Hill, Joanne M. and Frank J. Jones. "Equity Trading, Program Trading, Portfolio Insurance, Computer Trading And All That," (4), 29-38.
Bierwag, G. O. and George G. Kaufman. "Durations Of Non-Default-Free Securities," (4), 39-46.
Jacobs, Bruce I. and Kenneth N. Levy. "On The Value Of 'Value'," (4), 47-62.
Seidenverg, Edward. "A Case Of Confused Identity," (4), 63-67.
Ferguson, Robert and Roken Ahmed. "How To Get Rich Quick (Without Losing Sleep)," (4), 68-75.
Errunza, Vihang R. and Prasad Padmanabhan. "Further Evidence On The Benefits Of Portfolio Investments In Emerging Markets," (4), 76-78.
Bauman, W. Scott and Richard Dowen. "Growth Projections And Common Stock Returns," (4), 79-80.
Roll, Richard. "The International Crash Of October 1987," (5), 19-35.
Wasserfallen, Walter. "The Behavior Of Flexible Exchange Rates: Evidence And Implications," (5), 36-44.
Solt, Michael E. and Meir Statman. "How Useful Is The Sentiment Index?," (5), 45-55.
Levy, Haim and Zvi Lerman. "The Benefits Of International Diversification In Bonds," (5), 56-64.
Chua, Jess H. "A Generalized Formula For Calculating Bond Duration," (5), 65-67.
Rodriguez, Ricardo J. "Investment Horizon, Taxes And Maturity Choice For Discount Coupon Bonds," (5), 67-69.
Hagigi, Moshe. "Industry Versus Country Risk In International Investments Of U.S. Pension Funds," (5), 70-74.
Dambolena, Ismael G. and Joel M. Shulman. "A Primary Rule For Detecting Bankruptcy: Watch The Cash," (5), 74-78.
Taylor, Richard W. "A Three-Phase Quarterly Dividend Discount Model," (5), 79-80.
Brenner, Menachem and Marti G. Subrahmanyan. "A Simple Formula To Compute The Implied Standard Deviation," (5), 80-83.
Pakkala, A. L. "There Is A Free Lunch," (5), 83-87.
Ennis, Richard M. "Is A Statewide Pension Fund A Person Or A Cookie Jar? The Answer Has Implications For Investment Policy," (6), 21-27.
Jacobs, Bruce I. and Kenneth N. Levy. "Calendar Anomalies: Abnormal Returns At Calendar Turning Points," (6), 28-39.
Leibowitz, Martin L. and William S. Krasker. "The Persistence Of Risk: Stocks Versus Bonds Over The Long Term," (6), 40-47.
Valentine, Jerome L. "Applying Expert Systems To Investment," (6), 48-53.
Schroder, Mark. "Adapting The Binomial Model To Value Options On Assets With Fixed-Cash Payouts," (6), 54-62.
Barrett, W. Brian. "Term Structure Modeling For Pension Liability Discounting," (6), 63-67.
Gold, Jeremy and Michael W. Peskin. "Longing For Duration," (6), 68-71.
Treynor, Jack L. "Portfolio Insurance And Market Volatility," (6), 71-73.
Jacques, William E. "The S&P 500 Membership Anomaly, Or Would You Join This Club?," (6), 73-75.
Golec, Joseph H. "Do Mutual Fund Managers Who Use Incentive Compensation Outperform Those Who Don't?," (6), 75-79.
Grantier, Bruce J. "Convexity And Bond Performance: The Benter The Better," (6), 79-81.
Nawalkha, Sanjay K. and Nelson J. Lacey. "Closed-Form Solutions Of Higher-Order Duration Measures," (6), 82-84.

Financial Analyst Journal
Volume 45, 1989

Speidell, Lawrence S., Deborah H. Miller and James R. Ullman. "Portfolio Optimization: A Primer," (1), 22-30.
Michaud, Richard O. "The Markowitz Optimization Enigma: Is 'Optimized' Optimal?," (1), 31-42.
Selling, Thomas I. and Clyde P. Stickney. "The Effects Of Business Environment And Strategy On A Firm's Rate Of Return On Assets," (1), 43-52.
Bostock, Paul, Paul Woolley and Martin Duffy. "Duration-Based Asset Allocation," (1), 53-60.
Revsine, Lawrence. "Understanding Financial Accounting Standard 87," (1), 61-68.
Guerard, John B., Jr. "Combining Time-Series Model Forecasts And Analysts' Forecasts For Superior Forecasts Of Annual Earnings," (1), 69-71.
Renshaw, Edward. "A Consensus Approach To The Determination Of Not-So-Good Years To Own Common Stock," (1), 71-72.
Droms, William G. "Market Timing As An Investment Policy," (1), 73-77.
Taylor, Richard W. "Bond Duration With Geometric Mean Returns," (1), 77-80.
Arnott, Robert D. and Roy D. Henriksson. "A Disciplined Approach To Global Asset Allocation," (2), 17-28.
Fong, H. Gifford and Oldrich A. Vasicek. "Forecast-Free International Asset Allocation," (2), 29-33.
Leibowitz, Martin L. and Roy D. Henriksson. "Portfolio Optimization With Shortfall Constraints: A Confidence-Limit Approach To Managing Downside Risk," (2), 34-41.
Ferguson, Robert. "On Crashes," (2), 42-52.
Jaffe, Jeffrey F. "Gold And Gold Stocks As Investments For Institutional Portfolios," (2), 53-59.
Pari, Robert, Steven Carvell and Timothy Sullivan. "Analyst Forecasts And Price/Earnings Ratios," (2), 60-62.
Jog, Vijay M. and Allan L. Riding. "Lunar Cycles In Stock Prices," (2), 63-68.
Barrett, W. Brian and John W. Pfenenger, II. "Proper Cash-Flow Discounting For Pension Fund Liabilities," (2), 68-70.
Greenleaf, Robert W. "Synthetic Instruments," (2), 71-73.
Johnson, Lewis D. "Equity Duration: Another Look," (2), 73-75.
Canto, Victor A. and Arthur B. Laffer. "A Not-So-Odd Couple: Small-Cap Stocks And The State Competitive Environment," (2), 75-78.
LeBaron, Dean, Gail Farrelly and Susan Gula. "Facilitating A Dialogue On Risk: A Questionnaire Approach," (3), 19-24.

Thomas, Lee R. "The Performance Of Currency-Hedged Foreign Bonds," (3), 25-31.
Farrell, James L., Jr. "A Fundamental Forecast Approach To Superior Asset Allocation," (3), 32-37.
Jacobs, Bruce I. and Kenneth N. Levy. "Forecasting The Size Effect," (3), 38-54.
Boyle, Phelim P. "Valuing Canadian Mortgage-Backed Securities," (3), 55-60.
Martin, John D. and A. J. Senchack, Jr. "Program Trading And Systematic Stock Price Behavior," (3), 61-67.
Anderson, Seth C. "Evidence On The Reflecting Barriers Model: New Opportunities For Technical Analysis?," (3), 67-71.
Peavy, John W., III. "Closed-End Fund IPOs: Caveat Emptor," (3), 71-74.
Sterge, Andrew J. "On The Distribution Of Financial Futures Price Changes," (3), 74-78.
Black, Fischer. "Universal Hedging: Optimizing Currency Risk And Reward In International Equity Portfolios," (4), 16-22.
Altman, Edward I. "The Convertible Debt Market: Are Returns Worth The Risk?," (4), 23-31.
Peters, Edgar E. "Fractal Structure In The Capital Markets," (4), 32-37.
Hradsky, Gregory T. and Robert D. Long. "High-Yield Default Losses And The Return Performance Of Bankrupt Debt," (4), 38-49.
Garland, James P. "A Market-Yield Spending Rule For Endowments And Trusts," (4), 50-60.
Brenner, Menachem and Dan Galai. "New Financial Instruments To Hedge Changes In Volatility," (4), 61-65.
Alexander, John, Delbert Goff and Pamela P. Peterson. "Profitability Of A Trading Strategy Based On Unexpected Earnings," (4), 65-71.
Dowen, Richard J. "What Are Analysts' Forecasts Worth? One-Period Growth Expectations And Subsequent Stock Returns," (4), 71-74.
Liano, Kartono and Benton E. Gup. "The Day-Of-The-Week Effect In Stock Returns Over Business Cycles," (4), 74-77.
Landskroner, Yoram and David Ruthenberg. "How Variable Interest Rates Affect Bank Duration And Immunization," (4), 77-80.
Rubinstein, Mark. "Market Basket Alternatives," (5), 20-29.
Leibowitz, Martin L., Eric H. Sorensen, Robert D. Arnott and H. Nicholas Hanson. "A Total Differential Approach To Equity Duration," (5), 30-37.
Harvey, Campbell R. "Forecasts Of Economic Growth From The Bond And Stock Markets," (5), 38-45.
Conroy, Robert and Mike Miles. "Commercial Forestland In The Pension Portfolio: The Biological Beta," (5), 46-54.
Kawaller, Ira G. "Interest Rate Swaps Versus Eurodollar Strips," (5), 55-61.
Visser, John R. and Hsiu-Kwang Wu. "The Effects Of Deregulation On Bank Stock Price-Earnings Ratios," (5), 62-67.
Chamberlain, Trevor W., C. Sherman Cheung and Clarence C. Y. Kwan. "Expiration-Day Effects Of Index Futures And Options: Some Canadian Evidence," (5), 67-71.
Winkelmann, Kurt. "Uses And Abuses Of Duration And Convexity," (5), 72-75.
Rystrom, David S. and Earl D. Benson. "Investor Psychology And The Day-Of-The-Week Effect," (5), 75-78.
Taylor, Richard W. "A Three-Phase Quarterly Earnings Model," (5), 79.
Jones, Charles P. and Jack W. Wilson. "Is Stock Price Volatility Increasing?," (6), 20-26.
Clarke, Roger G., Michael T. FitzGerald, Phillip Berent and Meir Statman. "Market Timing With Imperfect Information," (6), 27-36.
Bookstaber, Richard M. and Steven Pomerantz. "An Information-Based Model Of Market Volatility," (6), 37-46.
Kritzman, Mark. "A Simple Solution For Optimal Currency Hedging," (6), 47-50.
Johnson, Brian D. and Kenneth R. Meyer. "Managing Yield Curve Risk In An Index Environment," (6), 51-59.
Bauman, W. Scott. "Investment Research Analysis In An Emerging Market: Singapore And Malaysia," (6), 60-67.
Selling, Thomas I., Ashwinpaul C. Sondhi and George H. Sorter. "Consolidating Captive Finance Subsidiaries: The Impact Of SFAS 94 On Financial Statements," (6), 72-75.
Maberly, Edwin D., David S. Allen and Roy F. Gilbert. "Stock Index Futures And Cash Market Volatility," (6), 75-77.
Brooks, Robert. "A Closed-Form Equation For Bond Convexity," (6), 78-79.

Financial Analyst Journal
Volume 46, 1990

Celebuski, Matthew J., Joanne M. Hill and John J. Kilgannon. "Managing Currency Exposures In International Portfolios," (1), 16-23.
Ippolito, Richard A. "The Role Of Risk In A Tax-Arbitrage Pension Portfolio," (1), 24-32.
Black, Fischer, Emanuel Derman and William Toy. "A One-Factor Model Of Interest Rates And Its Application To Treasury Bond Options," (1), 33-39.
Collins, Bruce M. and Frank J. Fabozzi. "Considerations In Selecting A Small-Capitalization Benchmark," (1), 40-46
Townsend, Henry. "Stockholder Earnings," (1), 47-57.
Samorajski, Gregory S. and Bruce D. Phelps. "Using Treasury Bond Futures To Enhance Total Return," (1), 58-65.
Wolf, Jesse. "Calendar Spreads For Enhanced Index Fund Returns," (1), 66-74.
Nawalkha, Sanjay K., Nelson J. Lacey and Thomas Schneeweis. "Closed-Form Solutions Of Convexity And M-Square," (1), 75-77.
Bierman, Harold, Jr. "Total Stock Market Value With Reciprocal Ownership: A Note On The Japanese Situation," (1), 77.
Schnabel, Jacques A. "Is Benter Better: A Cautionary Note On Maximizing Convexity," (1), 78-79.
Brenner, Menachem, Marti J. Subrahmanyam and Jun Uno. "Arbitrage Opportunities In The Japanese Stock And Futures Markets," (2), 14-24.
Jones, Robert C. "Designing Factor Models For Different Types Of Stock: What's Good For The Goose Ain't Always Good For The Gander," (2), 25-30.

Burik, Paul and Richard M. Ennis. "Foreign Bonds In Diversified Portfolios: A Limited Advantage," (2), 31-40.

Michel, Allen and Israel Shaked. "The LBO Nightmare: Fraudulent Conveyance Risk," (2), 41-50.

Freiman, Howard A. "Understanding The Economics Of Leveraged ESOPs," (2), 51-55.

Keim, Donald B. "A New Look At The Effects Of Firm Size And E/P Ratio On Stock Returns," (2), 56-67.

Bannister, Barry B. "In Search Of Excellence: A Portfolio Management Perspective," (2), 68-71.

Renshaw, Edward. "Some Evidence In Support Of Stock Market Bubbles," (2), 71-73.

Warren, William E., Robert E. Stevens and C. William McConkey. "Using Demographic And Lifestyle Analysis To Segment Individual Investors," (2), 74-77.

Schwert, G. William. "Stock Market Volatility," (3), 23-34.

Bodurtha, Stephen G. and Thomas E. Quinn. "Does Patient Program Trading Really Pay?," (3), 35-42.

Leibowitz, Martin L., Stanley Kogelman and Eric B. Lindenberg. "A Shortfall Approach To The Creditor's Decision: How Much Leverage Can A Firm Support?," (3), 43-52.

Barth, Mary E., William H. Beaver and Mark A. Wolfson. "Components Of Earnings And The Structure Of Bank Share Prices," (3), 53-60.

Rendleman, Richard J., Jr. and Thomas J. O'Brien. "The Effects Of Volatility Misestimation On Option-Replication Portfolio Insurance," (3), 61-70.

Mauldin, Patrick D., Brian F. Olasov and Craig K. Ruff. "The Use Of Mortgage-Derivative Products By Southeastern Thrifts," (3), 71-76.

Fortin, Richard D., R. Corwin Grube and O. Maurice Joy. "Bid-Ask Spreads For OTC NASDAQ Firms," (3), 76-79.

Elton, Edwin J., Martin J. Gruber and Joel Rentzler. "The Performance Of Publicly Offered Commodity Funds," (4), 23-30.

Bailey, Jeffery V. "Some Thoughts On Performance-Based Fees," (4), 31-40.

Gentry, James A., Paul Newbold and David T. Whitford. "Profiles Of Cash Flow Components," (4), 41-48.

Tierney, David E. and Kenneth Winston. "Defining And Using Dynamic Completeness Funds To Enhance Total Fund Efficiency," (4), 49-54.

Wainscott, Craig B. "The Stock-Bond Correlation And Its Implications For Asset Allocation," (4), 55-60.

Fridson, Martin S. and Michael A. Cherry. "Initial Pricing As A Predictor Of Subsequent Performance Of High-Yield Bonds," (4), 61-67.

Lewis, Alan L. "Semivariance And The Performance Of Portfolios With Options," (4), 67-76.

Chua, Jess H., Gordon Sick and Richard S. Woodward. "Diversifying With Gold Stocks," (4), 76-79.

Rennie, Edward P. and Thomas J. Cowhey. "The Successful Use Of Benchmark Portfolios: A Case Study," (5), 18-26.

Bodie, Zvi. "The ABO, The PBO And Pension Investment Policy," (5), 27-34.

Langetieg, Terence C., Martin L. Leibowitz and Stanley Kogelman. "Duration Targeting And The Management Of Multiperiod Returns," (5), 35-45.

Fabozzi, T. Dessa, Tom Tong and Yu Zhu. "Symmetric Cash Matching," (5), 46-52.

Wigmore, Barrie A. "The Decline In Credit Quality Of New-Issue Junk Bonds," (5), 53-62.

Kester, George W. "Market Timing With Small Versus Large-Firm Stocks: Potential Gains And Required Predictive Ability," (5), 63-69.

Johnson, Lewis D. "Convexity For Equity Securities: Does Curvature Matter?," (5), 70-73.

Ramaswami, Murali. "Multiple Versus Multivariate Valuation Models," (5), 73-77.

Raftopoulos, Dimitri. "Pinning Down The Small-Stock Universe," (5), 77-79.

Leibowitz, Martin L. and Stanley Kogelman. "Inside The P/E Ratio: The Franchise Factor," (6), 17-35.

Vaga, Tonis. "The Coherent Market Hypothesis," (6), 36-49.

Harlow, W. V. and Keith C. Brown. "Understanding And Assessing Financial Risk Tolerance: A Biological Perspective," (6), 50-62.

Hawley, Delvin D., John D. Johnson and Dijjotam Raina. "Artificial Neural Systems: A New Tool For Financial Decision-Making," (6), 63-72.

Arnott, Robert D. and Wayne H. Wagner. "The Measurement And Control Of Trading Costs," (6), 73-80.

FINANCIAL MANAGEMENT

Financial Management
Volume 5, 1976

Financial Management
Volume 6, 1977

Van Horne, James C. "An Application Of The CAPM To Divisional Required Returns," (1), 14-19.

Conine, Thomas E., Jr. "Debt Capacity And The Capital Budgeting Decision: Comment," (1), 20-22.

Martin, John D. and David F. Scott. "Debt Capacity And The Capital Budgeting Decision: A Revisitation," (1), 23-26.

Mukherjee, Tarun K. and Larry M. Austin. "An Empirical Investigation Of Small Bank Stock Valuation And Dividend Policy," (1), 27-31.

Richards, Verlyn D. and Eugene J. Laughlin. "A Cash Conversion Cycle Approach To Liquidity Analysis," (1), 32-38.

Alexander, Gordon J. and Roger D. Stover. "The Effect Of Forced Conversions On Common Stock Prices," (1), 39-45.

Gau, George W. and Daniel B. Kohlhepp. "The Financial Planning And Management Of Real Estate Developments," (1), 46-52.

Backer, Morton and Martin L. Gosman. "The Use Of Financial Ratios In Credit Downgrade Decisions," (1), 53-56.

Rudd, Andrew. "Optimal Selection Of Passive Portfolios," (1), 57-66.

Schreiner, John. "Portfolio Revision: A Turnover-Constrained Approach," (1), 67-75.

Athanasopoulos, Peter J. and Peter W. Bacon. "The Evaluation Of Leveraged Leases," (1), 76-80.

Jenkins, James W. "Incentive Compensation And REIT Financial Leverage And Asset Risk," (1), 81-87.

Rothmeier, Steven G. "The Effect Of Financial Leverage On Air Carrier Earnings: Comment," (1), 88-89.

Findlay, M. C. and E. E. Williams. "A Positivist Evaluation Of The New Finance," (2), 7-17.

Riener, Kenneth D. "Financial Structure Effects Of Bond Refunding," (2), 18-23.

Idol, Charles R. "A Note On Specifying Debt Displacement And Tax Shield Borrowing Opportunities In Financial Lease Valuation Models," (2), 24-29.

Ruland, William. "On The Choice Of Simple Extrapolative Model Forecasts Of Annual Earnings," (2), 30-37.

Jaggi, Bikki and Paul Grier. "A Comparative Analysis Of Forecast Disclosing And Non-Disclosing Firms," (2), 38-43.

Huntsman, Blaine and James P. Hoban, Jr. "Investment In New Enterprise: Some Empirical Observations On Risk, Return, And Market Structure," (2), 44-51.

Collins, Robert A. "An Empirical Comparison Of Bankruptcy Prediction Models," (2), 52-57.

Branch, Ben. "The Laws Of The Marketplace And ROI Dynamics," (2), 58-65.

Elgers, Pieter T. and John J. Clark. "Merger Types And Shareholder Returns: Additional Evidence," (2), 66-72.

Baker, H. Kent and Patricia L. Gallagher. "Management's View Of Stock Splits," (2), 73-77.

Joehnk, Michael D., Oswald D. Bowlin and J. William Petty. "Preferred Dividend Rolls: A Viable Strategy For Corporate Money Managers?," (2), 78-87.

Clark, John J. "The Mobil Corporation: Perspectives By William P. Tavoulareas," (3), 7-14.

Farrelly, Gail. "A Behavioral Science Approach To Financial Research," (3), 15-22.

Eaker, Mark R. "Denomination Decision For Multinational Transactions," (3), 23-29.

Cornell, Bradford. "Inflation, Relative Price Changes, And Exchange Risk," (3), 30-34.

Stone, Bernell K. and Ned C. Hill. "Cash Transfer Scheduling For Efficient Cash Concentration," (3), 35-43.

Belkaoui, Ahmed. "Industrial Bond Ratings: A New Look," (3), 44-51.

Ferri, Michael G. and James P. Gaines. "A Study Of Yield Spreads In The Money Market: 1971 To 1978," (3), 52-59.

Schallheim, James and Robin DeMagistris. "New Estimates Of The Market Parameters," (3), 60-68.

Chew, I. Keong. "Implications Of Discount Rates And Financing Assumptions For Bond Refunding Decisions: Comment," (3), 69-71.

Gritta, Richard D. "The Effects Of Financial Leverage On Air Carrier Earnings: Reply," (3), 72-73.

McCallum, John S. "On Portfolio Theory, Holding Period Assumptions, And Bond Maturity Diversification: Comment," (3), 74-76.

Osteryoung, Jerome S., Daniel E. McCarty and Karen Fortin. "Optimal Tax Lives Of Depreciable Assets: Comment," (3), 77-78.

Johnson, James M. "Optimal Tax Lives: Reply," (3), 79.

Harris, Robert S. "The Refunding Of Discounted Debt: An Adjusted Present Value Analysis," (4), 7-12.

Horvitz, Paul M. and Charles P. Harper. "Regulation Of The Money Order Industry," (4), 13-20.

Millar, James R. and James A. Gentry. "The Soviet Experiment With Domestic Lottery Bonds," (4), 21-29.

Block, Stanley and Majorie Stanley. "The Financial Characteristics And Price Movement Patterns Of Companies Approaching The Unseasoned Securities Market In The Late 1970s," (4), 30-36.

Oblak, David J. and Roy J. Helm, Jr. "Survey And Analysis Of Capital Budgeting Methods Used By Multinationals," (4), 37-41.

Hill, Joanne M. "Reducing Forecast Error In Portfolio Management: Sample Clustering And Alternative Risk Specifications," (4), 42-50.

Wachowicz, John M., Jr. and Ronald E. Shrieves. "An Argument For `Generalized' Mean-Coefficient Of Variation Analysis," (4), 51-58.

Weston, J. Fred and Pham D. Tuan. "Comment On Analysis Of Credit Policy Changes," (4), 59-63.

Eaker, Mark R. "Covering Foreign Exchange Risks: Comment," (4), 64-65.

Financial Management
Volume 10, 1981

Weston, J. Fred. "From Practice To Theory," (1), 7-8.

Maier, Steven F., David W. Robinson and James H. Vander Weide. "A Short-Term Disbursement Forecasting Model," (1), 9-20.

Emery, Gary W. "Some Empirical Evidence On The Properties Of Daily Cash Flow," (1), 21-28.

Palmon, Dan and Uzi Yaari. "Retention And Tax Avoidance: A Clarification," (1), 29-36.

Roberts, Gordon S. and Jerry A. Viscione. "Captive Finance Subsidiaries: The Manager's View," (1), 36-42.

Fabozzi, Frank J. "Does Listing On The AMEX Increase The Value Of Equity?," (1), 43-50.

Chen, Kung H. and Thomas A. Shimerda. "An Empirical Analysis Of Useful Financial Ratios," (1), 51-60.

Rendleman, Richard J., Jr. "Optimal Long-Run Option Investment Strategies," (1), 61-76.

Bernhard, Richard H. "Avoiding Irrationality In The Use Of Two-Parameter Risk-Benefit Models For Investment Under Uncertainty," (1), 77-81.

Weston, J. Fred. "Developments In Finance Theory," Tenth Anniversary Edition, 5-22.

Cooley, Philip L. and J. Louis Heck. "Significant Contributions To Finance Literature," Tenth Anniversary Edition, 23-33.

Norgaard, Richard L. "The Evolution Of Business Finance Textbooks," Tenth Anniversary Edition, 34-45.

Sweetser, Albert G. and Glenn H. Petry. "A History Of The Seven Academic Finance Associations And Their Contributions To Development Of The Discipline," Tenth Anniversary Edition, 46-70.

Sweetser, Albert G. "The Financing Of The Seven Academic Finance Associations And Their Journals," Tenth Anniversary Edition, 71-92.

Petry, Glenn H. "A History And Analysis Of Scholarly Papers Presented At The Seven Academic Finance Associations From 1939 Thorugh 1980," Tenth Anniversary Editon, 93-104.

Hoffmeister, J. Ronald and Edward A. Dyl. "Financial Management Association - The First Ten Years: An Assessment Of Meeting And Journal Participation," Tenth Anniversary Edition, 105-111.

Andrews, Victor L. "The Early History Of FINANCIAL MANAGEMENT," Tenth Anniversary Edition, 112-115.

Langer, Leonard C. R. "A Financial Practitioner's View Of Professional Finance Associations," Tenth Anniversary Edition, 116-122.

Kerr, Halbert S. "A Bibliography For FINANCIAL MANAGEMENT," Tenth Anniversary Edition, 123-134.

Barnea, Amir, Robert A. Haugen and Lemma W. Senbet. "Market Imperfections, Agency Problems, And Capital Structure: A Review," (2), 7-22.

Altman, Edward I. and Paul S. Tubiana. "The Multi-Firm Bond Issue: A Fund-Raising Financial Instrument," (2), 23-33.

Kalotay, Andrew J. "On The Management Of Sinking Funds," (2), 34-40.

Martin, John D. and R. Malcolm Richards. "The Seasoning Process For Corporate Bonds," (2), 41-48.

Smith, L. Douglas and Robert E. Markland. "Measurement Of Business Risk For Inter-Industry Comparisons," (2), 49-63.

Reilly, Frank K. and Eugene F. Drzycimski. "Short-Run Profits From Stock Splits," (2), 64-74.

Officer, Dennis T. and Gary L. Trennepohl. "Price Behavior Of Corporate Equities Near Option Expiration Dates," (2), 75-80.

Crawford, Peggy J., Charles P. Harper and John J. McConnell. "Further Evidence On The Terms Of Financial Leases," (3), 7-14.

Capettini, Robert and Howard Toole. "Designing Leveraged Leases: A Mixed Integer Linear Programming Approach," (3), 15-23.

Ferri, Michael G. and H. Dennis Oberhelman. "A Study Of The Management Of Money Market Mutual Funds, 1975-1980," (3), 24-29.

Johnson, Dana J. "The Behavior Of Financial Structure And Sustainable Growth In An Inflationary Environment," (3), 30-35.

Higgins, Robert C. "Sustainable Growth Under Inflation," (3), 36-40.

Gatti, James F., John R. Mills and Peter J. McTague. "The Feasibility Of Small Denomination Consumer Note Issues As A Source Of Funds For Non-Financial Borrowers," (3), 41-53.

Maldonado, Rita and Anthony Saunders. "International Portfolio Diversification And The Inter-Temporal Stability Of International Stock Market Relationships, 1957-1978," (3), 54-63.

Mueller, Paul A. "Covered Options: An Alternative Investment Strategy," (3), 64-71.

Kolb, Robert W. and Raymond Chiang. "Improving Hedging Performance Using Interest Rate Futures," (3), 72-79.

Caks, John. "Sense And Nonsense About Depreciation," (3), 80-86.

Carlson, Phillip G. "An Argument For `Generalized' Mean-Coefficient Of Variation Analysis: Comment," (3), 87-88.

Durand, David. "Comprehensiveness In Capital Budgeting," (4), 7-13.

Gehr, Adam K., Jr. "Risk-Adjusted Capital Budgeting Using Arbitrage," (4), 14-19.

Crum, Roy L., Dan J. Laughhunn and John W. Payne. "Risk-Seeking Behavior And Its Implications For Financial Models," (4), 20-27.

Shim, Jae K. "Estimating Cash Collection Rates From Credit Sales: A Lagged Regression Approach," (4), 28-30.

Halloran, John A. and Howard P. Lanser. "The Credit Policy Decision In An Inflationary Environment," (4), 31-38.

Batlin, C. A. and Susan Hinko. "Lockbox Management And Value Maximization," (4), 39-44.

Sachdeva, Kanwal S. and Lawrence J. Gitman. "Accounts Receivable Decisions In A Capital Budgeting Framework," (4), 45-49.

Hoffmeister, J. Ronald and Edward A. Dyl. "Predicting Outcomes Of Cash Tender Offers," (4), 50-58.

Finnerty, John D. "The Behavior Of Electric Utility Common Stock Prices Near The Ex-Dividend Date," (4), 59-69.

Ang, James S. and Jess H. Chua. "Corporate Bankruptcy And Job Losses Among Top Level Managers," (4), 70-74.

Cooley, Philip L. "A Review Of The Use Of Beta In Regulatory Proceedings," (4), 75-81.

Singhvi, Surendra S. "One Financial Executive's Response To Surveys," (4), 82-83.

Financial Management
Volume 11, 1982

Rappaport, Alfred and Robert A. Taggart, Jr. "Evaluation Of Capital Expenditure Proposals Under Inflation," (1), 5-13.

Emery, Gary W. "Some Guidelines For Evaluating Capital Investment Alternatives With Unequal Lives," (1), 14-19.

Ben-Horim, Moshe, Shalom Hochman and Oded Palmon. "The Impact Of The 1986 Tax Reform Act On Corporate Financial Policy," (3), 29-35.

Garlicki, T. Dessa, Frank J. Fabozzi and Robert Fonfeder. "The Impact Of Earnings Under FASB 52 On Equity Returns," (3), 36-44.

Comiskey, Eugene E., Ruth Ann McEwen and Charles W. Mulford. "A Test Of Pro Forma Consolidation Of Finance Subsidiaries," (3), 45-50.

Howe, John S. and Kathryn Kelm. "The Stock Price Impacts Of Overseas Listings," (3), 51-56.

Emery, Douglas R., J. Ronald Hoffmeister and Ronald W. Spahr. "The Case For Indexing A Bond's Call Price," (3), 57-64.

Linke, Charles M. and J. Kenton Zumwalt. "The Irrelevance Of Compounding Frequency In Determining A Utility's Cost Of Equity," (3), 65-69.

Statman, Meir and David Caldwell. "Applying Behavioral Finance To Capital Budgeting: Project Terminations," (4), 7-15.

Yagil, Joseph. "Divisional Beta Estimation Under The Old And New Tax Laws," (4), 16-21.

Miller, Edward M. "The Competitive Market Assumption And Capital Budgeting Criteria," (4), 22-28.

Lewellen, Wilbur G. and William A. Kracaw. "Inflation, Corporate Growth, And Corporate Leverage," (4), 29-36.

Allen, David S., Robert E. Lamy and G. Rodney Thompson. "Agency Costs And Alternative Call Provisions: An Empirical Investigation," (4), 37-44.

Stone, Bernell K. and Tom W. Miller. "Daily Cash Forecasting With Multiplicative Models Of Cash Flow Patterns," (4), 45-54.

Gombola, Michael J., Mark E. Haskins, J. Edward Ketz and David D. Williams. "Cash Flow In Bankruptcy Prediction," (4), 55-65.

Neely, Walter P. "Banking Acquisitions: Acquirer And Target Shareholder Returns," (4), 66-73.

Financial Management
Volume 17, 1988

Amihud, Yakov and Haim Mendelson. "Liquidity And Asset Prices: Financial Management Implications," (1), 5-15.

Thatcher, Janet S. and John G. Thatcher. "Timing Performance And The Flotation Of Shelf-Registered Bonds," (1), 16-26.

Chen, Andrew H. and John W. Kensinger. "Puttable Stock: A New Innovation In Equity Financing," (1), 27-37.

Born, Jeffrey A. "Insider Ownership And Signals--Evidence From Dividend Initiation Announcement Effects," (1), 38-45.

Hsueh, L. Paul and David S. Kidwell. "Bond Ratings: Are Two Better Than One?," (1), 46-53.

Kwan, Clarence C. Y. and Yufei Yuan. "Optimal Sequential Selection In Capital Budgeting: A Shortcut," (1), 54-59.

Crum, Roy L. and Keqian Bi. "An Observation Of Estimating The Systematic Risk Of An Industry Segment," (1), 60-62.

Black, Fischer. "A Simple Discounting Rule," (2), 7-11.

Arak, Marcelle, Arturo Estrella,Laurie Goodman and Andrew Silver. "Interest Rate Swaps: An Alternative Explanation," (2), 12-18.

Johnson, James M. and Robert E. Miller. "Investment Banker Prestige And The Underpricing Of Initial Public Offerings," (2), 19-29.

Emery, Douglas R. and Adam K. Gehr, Jr. "Tax Options, Capital Structure, And Miller Equilibrium: A Numerical Illustration," (2), 30-40.

Gentry, James A. "State Of The Art Of Short-Run Financial Management," (2), 41-57.

Cooper, Kerry and R. Malcolm Richards. "Investing The Alaskan Project Cash Flows: The Sohio Experience," (2), 58-70.

Pohlman, Randolph A., Emmanuel S. Santiago and F. Lynn Markel. "Cash Flow Estimation Practices Of Large Firms," (2), 71-79.

Choi, Frederick D. S. "International Data Sources For Empirical Research In Financial Management," (2), 80-98.

Holsapple, Clyde W., Kar Yan Tam and Andrew B. Whinston. "Adapting Expert System Technology To Financial Management," (3), 12-22.

Myers, Stewart C. "Notes On An Expert System For Capital Budgeting," (3), 23-31.

Srinivasan, Venkat and Yong H. Kim. "Designing Expert Financial Systems: A Case Study Of Corporate Credit Management," (3), 32-44.

Shaw, Michael J. and James A. Gentry. "Using An Expert System With Inductive Learning To Evaluate Business Loans," (3), 45-56.

Duchessi, Peter, Hany Shawky and John P. Seagle. "A Knowledge-Engineered System For Commercial Loan Decisions," (3), 57-65.

Elmer, Peter J. and David M. Borowski. "An Expert System Approach To Financial Analysis: The Case Of S&L Bankruptcy," (3), 66-76.

Coats, Pamela K. "Why Expert Systems Fail," (3), 77-86.

Ravid, S. Abraham. "On Interactions Of Production And Financial Decisions," (3), 87-99.

Heck, Jean Louis and Philip L. Cooley. "Most Frequent Contributors To The Finance Literature," (3), 100-108.

Financial Management
Volume 18, 1989

Baskin, Jonathan. "An Empirical Investigation Of The Pecking Order Hypothesis," (1), 26-35.

Barton, Sidney L., Ned C. Hill and Srinivasan Sundaram. "An Empirical Test Of Stakeholder Theory Predictions Of Capital Structure," (1), 36-44.

Lee, Winson B. and Elizabeth S. Cooperman. "Conglomerates Is The 1980s: A Performance Appraisal," (1), 45-54.

Aziz, Abdul and Gerald H. Lawson. "Cash Flow Reporting And Financial Distress Models: Testing Of Hypotheses," (1), 55-63.

Murphy, J. Austin. "Analyzing Sub-Classes Of General Motors Common Stock," (1), 64-71.

Durand, David. "Afterthoughts On A Controversy With MM, Plus Thoughts On Growth And The Cost Of Capital," (2), 12-18.

Gordon, M. J. "Corporate Finance Under The MM Theorems," (2), 19-28.

Weston, J. Fred. "What MM Have Wrought," (2), 29-38.

Thakor, Anjan V. "Strategic Issues In Financial Contracting: An Overview," (2), 39-58.

Wall, Larry D. and John J. Pringle. "Alternative Explanations Of Interest Rate Swaps: A Theoretical And Empirical Analysis," (2), 59-73.

Harris, Robert S., Thomas J. O'Brien and Doug Wakeman. "Divisional Cost-Of-Capital Estimation For Multi-Industry Firms," (2), 74-84.

Woods, John C. and Maury R. Randall. "The Net Present Value Of Future Investment Opportunities: Its Impact On Shareholder Wealth And Implications For Capital Budgeting Theory," (2),85-92.

Bertin, William J., Farrokh Ghazanfari and Khalil M. Torabzadeh. "Failed Bank Acquisitions And Successful Bidders' Returns," (2), 93-100.

Jarrell, Gregg A. and Annette B. Poulsen. "The Returns To Acquiring Firms In Tender Orders: Evidence From Three Decades,"(3),12-19.

Ryngaert, Michael D. "Firm Valuation, Takeover Defenses, And The Delaware Supreme Court," (3), 20-28.

Netter, Jeffry and Annette Poulsen. "State Corporation Laws And Shareholders: The Recent Experience," (3), 29-40.

Mitchell, Mark L. and J. Harold Mulherin. "The Stock Price Response To Pension Terminations And The Relation Of Terminations With Corporate Takeovers," (3), 41-56.

Weiss, Kathleen. "The Post-Offering Price Performance Of Closed-End Funds," (3), 57-67.

Furbush, Dean. "Program Trading And Price Movement: Evidence From The October 1987 Market Crash," (3), 68-83.

Netter, Jeffry M. and Mark L. Mitchell. "Stock-Repurchase Announcements And Insider Transactions After The October 1987 Stock Market Crash," (3), 84-96.

Wansley, James W., William R. Lane and Salil Sarkar. "Managements' View On Share Repurchase And Tender Offer Premiums," (3), 97-110.

Butler, J. S. and Barry Schachter. "The Investment Decision: Estimation Risk And Risk Adjusted Discount Rates," (4), 13-22.

Timme, Stephen G. and Peter C. Eisemann. "On The Use Of Consensus Forecasts Of Growth In The Constant Growth Model: The Case Of Electric Utilities," (4), 23-35.

Crutchley, Claire E. and Robert S. Hansen. "A Test Of The Agency Theory Of Managerial Ownership, Corporate Leverage, And Corporate Dividends," (4), 36-46.

Marr, M. Wayne, Robert W. Rogowski and John L. Trimble. "The Competitive Effects Of U.S. And Japanese Commercial Bank Participation In Eurobond Underwriting," (4), 47-54.

Gardner, Mona J. and Dixie L. Mills. "Evaluating The Likelihood Of Default On Deliquent Loans," (4), 55-63.

Bosch, Jean-Claude and Mark Hirschey. "The Valuation Effects Of Corporate Name Changes," (4), 64-73.

Statman, Meir and James F. Sepe. "Project Termination Announcements And The Market Value Of The Firm," (4), 74-81.

Pinegar, J. Michael and Lisa Wilbricht. "What Managers Think Of Capital Structure Theory: A Survey," (4), 82-91.

Financial Management
Volume 19, 1990

Scholes, Myron S. and Mark A. Wolfson. "Employee Stock Ownership Plans And Corporate Restructuring: Myths And Realities," (1), 12-28.

Chaplinsky, Susan and Greg Niehaus. "The Tax And Distributional Effects Of Leveraged ESOPs," (1), 29-38.

Rosen, Corey. "The Record Of Employee Ownership," (1), 39-47.

Chang, Saeyoung. "Employee Stock Ownership Plans And Shareholder Wealth: An Empirical Investigation," (1), 48-58.

Bruner, Robert F. and E. Richard Brownlee, II. "Leveraged ESOPs, Wealth Transfers, And 'Shareholder Neutrality:' The Case Of Polaroid," (1), 59-74.

Laber, Gene. "Bond Covenants And Managerial Flexibility: Two Cases Of Special Redemption Provisions," (1), 82-89.

Gentry, James A., R. Vaidyanathan and Hei Wai Lee. "A Weighted Cash Conversion Cycle," (1), 90-99.

Lease, Ronald C., John J. McConnell and James S. Schallheim. "Realized Returns And The Default And Prepayment Experience Of Financial Leasing Contracts," (2), 11-20.

Chang, Rosita P. and S. Ghon Rhee. "The Impact Of Personal Taxes On Corporate Dividend Policy And Capital Structure Decisions," (2), 21-31.

Talmor, Eli and Sheridan Titman. "Taxes And Dividend Policy," (2), 32-35.

Chen, K. C. and R. Stephen Sears. "Pricing The SPIN," (2), 36-47.

Bae, Sung C. and Haim Levy. "The Valuation Of Firm Commitment Underwriting Contracts For Seasoned New Equity Issues: Theory And Evidence," (2), 48-59.

Furtado, Eugene P. H. and Vijay Karan. "Causes, Consequences, And Shareholder Wealth Effects Of Management Turnover: A Review Of The Empirical Evidence," (2), 60-75.

Hickman, Kent and Glenn H. Petry. "A Comparison Of Stock Price Predictions Using Court Accepted Formulas, Dividend Discount, And P/E Models," (2), 76-87.

Bodie, Zvi. "Pension Funds And Financial Innovation," (3), 11-22.

Long, Michael S. and Stephan E. Sefcik. "Participation Financing: A Comparison Of The Characteristics Of Convertible Debt And Straight Bonds Issued In Conjunction With Warrants," (3), 23-34.

Ritchken, Peter, L. Sandarasubramanian and Anand M. Vijh. "Averaging Options For Capping Total Costs," (3), 35-41.

Houston, Arthur L., Jr. and Carol Olson Houston. "Financing With Preferred Stock," (3), 42-54.

Carter, Richard B. and Frederick H. Dark. "The Use Of The Over-Allotment Option In Initial Public Offerings Of Equity: Risks And Underwriter Prestige," (3), 55-64.

Bjerksund, Petter and Steinar Ekern. "Managing Investment Opportunities Under Price Uncertainty: From 'Last Chance' To 'Wait And See' Strategies," (3), 65-83.

Gombola, Michael J. and Douglas R. Kahl. "Time-Series Processes Of Utility Betas: Implications For Forecasting Systematic Risk," (3), 84-93.

Loderer, Claudio and Kenneth Martin. "Corporate Acquisitions By Listed Firms: The Experience Of A Comprehensive Sample," (4), 17-33.

Bowers, Helen M. and Robert E. Miller. "Choice Of Investment Banker And Shareholders' Wealth Of Firms Involved In Acquisitions," (4), 34-44.

Aggarwal, Reena and Pietra Rivoli. "Fads In The Initial Public Offering Market?," (4), 45-57.

Wingler, Tony R. and G. Donald Jud. "Premium Debt Tenders:

Analysis And Evidence," (4), 58-67.

Fraser, Donald R. and Srinivasan Kannan. "Deregulation And Risk: Evidence From Earnings Forecasts And Stock Prices," (4), 68-76.

Mahajan, Arvind. "Pricing Expropriation Risk," (4), 77-86.

Alderson, Michael J. "Corporate Pension Policy Under OBRA 1987," (4), 87-97.

Pilotte, Eugene. "The Economic Recovery Tax Act Of 1981 And Corporate Capital Structure," (4), 98-107.

FINANCIAL PRACTICE AND EDUCATION

Financial Practice and Education
Volume 1, 1991

Paul, Chris W. and Paul H. Rubin. "Teaching And Research: The Human Capital Paradigm," (1), 7-10.

Dyl, Edward A. "Comment: The Teaching Vs. Research Conundrum," (1), 11-12.

Logue, Dennis E. "Comment: Some Observations On The Significance Of The Research Requirements In Academia," (1), 13-16.

West, Richard W. "Comment: Teaching, Research And The Human Capital Paradigm," (1), 17-20.

Forbes, Shawn M. and Chris W. Paul. "Reply: Eduation, Publishing And Academic Markets," (1), 21-24.

Bertin, William J. and Terry L. Zivney. "The New Hire Market For Finance: Productivity, Salaries And Other Market Factors," (1), 25-34.

Block, Stanley B. and Dan W. French. "The Student-Managed Investment Fund: A Special Opportunity In Learning," (1), 35-40.

Heck, Jean Louis and David E. Stout. "Initial Empirical Evidence On

The Relationship Between Finance Test-Question Sequencing And Student Performance Scores," (1), 41-48.

Dyl, Edward A. "Wall Street: A Case In Ethics," (1), 49-52.

Pettijohn, James, Gerald Udell and Stephen Parker. "The Quest For AACSB Accreditation: Must Finance Faculty Really Publish Or Perish?," (1), 53-56.

Baker, H. Kent and Sue E. Meeks. "Research On Exchange Listings And Delistings: A Review And Synthesis," (1), 57-72.

Mohan, Nancy, M. Fall Ainina, Daniel Kaufman and Bernard J. Winger. "Acquisition/Divestiture Valuation Practices In Major U.S. Firms," (1), 73-82.

Fosberg, Richard H. "Insider Trading And Security Market Investors," (1), 83-86.

Bhandari, Shyam B. "Compounding/Discounting Of Intrayear Cash Flows: Principles, Pedogogy, And Practices," (1), 87-89.

Chen, Carl R. "A Note On The Tax Loss Carryback And Carryforward: A Common Negligence Found In Finance Textbooks," (1), 90.

Forbes, Shawn W. "A Note On Teaching The Time Value Of Money," (1), 91.

FINANCIAL REVIEW

Financial Review
Volume 1, 1966-70

Dunkman, William E. "College Courses In Banking And Finance," (1), 5-18.

Bonner, Gordon R. "Some Notes On The Rehabilitation Of Preferred Stock," (1), 32-37.

Fredrikson, E. Bruce. "Consumer-Credit Charges In Philadelphia And Pittsburgh," (2), 2-14.

Olsen, John A. "The Evolution Of The Investment Advisers Act," (2), 58-65.

Seltzer, John. "Pension-Fund Investing," (2), 15-25.

Fichthorn, William H. "Current Investment Policies Of Pension Funds," (2), 26-32.

Wiltman, William J. "Administration Of Union Pension Plans In Multi-Employer Industries," (2), 33-40.

Fenstermaker, J. Van. "Cash-Flow Management For Universities," (2), 41-54.

Philippi, Dieter R. "Maximum Return On University Funds," (2), 55-57.

Fergusson, Donald A. "Capital Budgeting Decision-Making And New Theory," (3), 140-154.

Smidt, Seymour. "Evaluating The Risk Of Investment Projects," (3), 155-165.

Beranek, William. "Some Problems In Valuation Theory," (3), 166-170.

Nash, Lee J. "The New Era Of Finance," (3), 171-180.

Nickson, Jack W., Jr. and R. Bryan Grinnan III. "Should Banks Enter The Leasing Field?," (3), 181-190.

Wacht, Richard F. "Diversification And Capital Budgeting For Commercial Banks," (4), 204-209.

Horvitz, Paul M. "Price Uniformity And Banking Markets," (4), 213-219.

Tuttle, Donald L. and William L. Wilbur. "Holding-Period Yields On Highest-Grade Corporate Bonds," (4), 227-241.

Gup, Benton E. "Trends In Savings Flows And Mortgage Lending," (4), 244-249.

Leveson, Sidney M. "The Dividend-Payout Paradox," (4), 253-254.

Rapp, Wilbur A. "Treasury-Stock Purchases: Their Effects Upon The Price-Earnings Ratio," (4), 255-263.

Fenstermaker, J. Van and A. D. Issa. "Price Uniformity And Banking Markets: Evidence From The St. Louis Area," (4), 224-226.

Hane, George. "Recovery And Relapse In The Mortgage Market: The 1968 And 1969 Experience," (5), 291-295.

Guenther, Harry P. "The District Of Columbia Case For Amending The Bank Holding Company Act," (5), 296-302.

Smith, David L. "Characteristics Of Merging Banks," (5), 303-319.

Walters, Joan G. "Is The One-Bank Holding Company Doomed?," (5), 320-330.

Cheney, Harlan L. "The Value Of Industry Forecasting As An Aid To Portfolio Management," (5), 331-339.

Works, John W. "Clustering Of Stock Prices: A New Model," (5), 340-347.

Cole, David W. and Wilbur A. Rapp. "University Courses In Commercial Banking And Other Financial Institutions," (5), 348-358.

Sloane, William R. "A Scholarly Approach To The Teaching Of Finance," (5), 358-359.

Financial Review
Volume 2, 1971-72

Williamson, J. Peter. "Mutual Funds And Portfolio Selection," (1), 1-14.

Soldofsky, R. M. "Institutional Ownership Of Common Stock To The Year 2000," (1), 15-26.

Banda, J. Frederic. "Mutual Fund Ownership Of Air Transport Stocks," (1), 27-33.

Guenther, Harry P. "Bank Regulation: A Plan For Flexibility," (1), 34-43.

Furst, Richard W. and Robert E. Markland. "Exploiting Imperfections In Markets: A Preliminary Test Of A Mechanical Trading Rule," (1), 44-78.

Carlson, Phillip G. and Arthur T. Dietz. "Optimal Capital Budgeting Policies," (2), 103-114.

Baker, James C. and L. J. Beardsley. "Capital Budgeting By U.S. Multinational Companies," (2), 115-121.

Billings, C. David and John B. Legler. "Financing Equal Educational Opportunity," (2), 122-133.

Furst, Richard W. and Alan D. Bauerschmidt. "Community Funding Of Depreciation To Finance Change In The Health Care System," (2), 134-140.

Arpan, Jeffrey S. "Transfer Pricing In Multinational Financial Mangement," (2), 141-155.

Dalrymple, Brent B. and Ben J. Tuchi. "Hospital Pricing Under Economic Controls," (2), 156-162.

Financial Review
Volume 8, 1973

Lee, Sang M. and A. Joseph Lerro. "A Cash Management Model For Health Care Clinics," (1), 1-10.

Young, Allan E. "The Effects Of Share Distribution On Price Action," (1), 11-16.

Reilly, Frank G. and Thomas J. Zeller. "An Analysis Of Relative Industry Price-Earnings Ratios," (1), 17-33.

Bird, Monroe M. and Otha L. Gray. "Small Manufacturers' Reactions To The 1969 Repeal Of The Investment Tax Credit," (1), 34-37.

Logue, Dennis E. and Donald L. Tuttle. "Brokerage House Investment Advice," (1), 38-54.

Financial Review
Volume 9, 1974

Findlay, M. Chapman, III. "Financial Lease Evaluation: Survey And Synthesis," (1), 1-15.

Viscione, Jerry and John Neuhauser. "Capital Expenditure Decisions In Moderately Sized Firms," (1), 16-23.

Garant, Jean-Pierre. "An Inquiry Into Bond Types Used By Canadian Firms," (1), 24-28.

Brandon, Charles and Jeffrey Jarrett. "Accuracy Of Forecasts In Annual Reports," (1), 29-45.

Gressis, Nicholas, Jack Hayya and George Philippatos. "Multiperiod Portfolio Efficiency Analysis Via The Geometric Mean," (1), 46-63.

Shannon, Donald S. "Some Evidence Of Imperfections In The Market For Municipal Bonds," (1), 64-78.

Gitman, Lawrence J. "Estimating Corporate Liquidity Requirements: A Simplified Approach," (1), 79-88.

Financial Review
Volume 10, 1975

Hoeke, Robert S. and Roger E. Potter. "Stock Investor Objectives Of Demographic Segments," (1), 1-11.

Grossman, Stephen D. "An Application Of Communication Theory To Financial Statement Analysis," (1), 12,20.

Ezzell, John R. and Carlos Rubiales. "An Empirical Analysis Of The Determinants Of Stock Splits," (1), 21-30.

Cooley, Philip L. and Rodney L. Roenfeldt. "A Comparative Multivariate Analysis Of Factors Affecting Stock Returns," (1), 31-41.

Osteryoung, Jerome S. "A Call For Common Notation In Financial Literature," (1), 42-44.

DeThomas, Arthur R. and Carroll D. Aby, Jr. "Stock Price Trends And Point And Figure Charting: An Empirical Evaluation," (1), 45-54.

Shannon, Donald S. and Keith H. Johnson. "Error Terms And Asset Allocation Schemes," (1), 55-63.

Lavely, Joe. "Warrant Beta's," (1), 64-69.

Financial Review
Volume 11, 1976

Joy, O. Maurice, Don B. Panton, Frank K. Reilly and Stanley A. Martin. "Comovements Of Major International Equity Markets," (1), 1-20.

Gooding, Arthur E. "Some Preliminary Findings Regarding The Nature Of Investment Risk," (1), 21-35.

Findlay, M. Chapman, III and William Smith. "Some Canadian Implications Of International Portfolio Diversification," (1), 36-48.

Monahan, James P. "Some Programming Models For Administering Discretionary Profit Sharing," (1), 49-58.

Baesel, Jerome B. and Nahum Biger. "Inflation And Pension Plan Linkage Of Benefits To The Cost Of Living Index," (1), 59-68.

Fraser, Donald R. "The Determinants Of Bank Profits: An Analysis Of Extremes," (1), 69-87.

Financial Review
Volume 12, 1977

Jaggi, Bikki and Richard Kolodny. Selection Of The LIFO Method Of Inventory Valuation: Mangement's Motives And Investor's Reaction," (1), 1-19.

Cooley, Philip L., Rodney L. Roenfeldt and It-Keong Chew. "Clarification Of Three Capital Budgeting Criteria," (1), 20-27.

Baesel, Jerome B. "Adjusting 'Duration' Estimates For Tax Payments," (1), 28-35.

Nielsen, James F. "Empirical Evidence Of Institutional Timing Ability," (1), 36-47.

Osteryoung, Jerome S., Rodney L. Roenfeldt and Donald A. Nast. Capital Asset Pricing Model And Traditional Risk For Capital Budgeting," (1), 48-58.

Booth, G. Geoffrey and Gordon H. Dash. "Bank Portfolio Management Using Non-Linear Goal Programming," (1), 59-69.

Nichols, Donald R. "A Study Of The Market Valuation Of Extraordinary Items Reported In Financial Statements," (2), 1-17.

Arndt, Terry L. and James A. Miller. "Some Empirical Results On Financial Characteristics And Unusual Stock Prices," (2), 18-32.

Tole, Thomas M. and Robert Ford. "Performance Evaluation Of Sources Of Investment Research," (2), 33-46.

Fielitz, Bruce D. and Donald J. Thompson, II. "Performance Indexes Derived From The Sharpe-Lintner And Two-Factor Asset Pricing Models: Some Comparative Tests," (2), 47-75.

Brooks, LeRoy D. "Additional Evidence On The Market Reaction To Accounting Numbers," (2), 76-90.

Financial Review
Volume 13, 1978

Capozza, Dennis R. and Michael Asay. "Option Prices And Diffusion Processes: Some Empirical Tests," (1), 1-21.

Ruland, William. "Stock Prices And Management Forecasts Of Future Earnings," (1), 22-35.

Lee, Cheng F. and Kirnio Morimune. "Time Aggregation, Coefficient Of Determination And Systematic Risk Of The Market Model," (1), 36-47.

Mendelson, Morris. "Closed-End Fund Discounts Revisited," (1), 48-72.

Denison, R. D. "Practical Applications Of Financial Research," (1), 73-76.

Lee, Cheng F., Paul Newbold, Joseph E. Finnerty and Chen-Chin Chu. "On Accounting-Based, Market-Based And Composite-Based Beta Predictions: Methods And Implications," (1), 51-68.

Chiang, Thomas C. "On The Predictors Of The Future Spot Rates - A Multi-Currency Analysis," (1), 69-83.

Dubofsky, David A. and John C. Groth. "Relative Information Accessibility For OTC Stocks And Security Returns," (1), 85-102.

Gressis, Nicholas, George C. Phillippatos and George Vlahos. "Net Selectivity As A Component Measure Of Investment Performance," (1), 103-110.

Tiwari, Kashi Nath. "The Money Supply Process Under Deregulation," (1), 111-123.

Chang, Rosita P. and S. Ghon Rhee. "Does The Stock Market React To Announcements Of The Producer Price Index?," (1), 125-134.

Prakash, Arun J. and Robert M. Bear. "A Simplifying Performance Measure Recognizing Skewness," (1), 135-144.

Bolten, Steven E. and Susan W. Long. "A Note On Cyclical And Dynamic Aspects Of Stock Market Price Cycles," (1), 145-150.

Meyer, Richard L. and Murad J. Antia. "A Note On The Calculation Of Probabilistic Betas," (1), 151-156.

Akgiray, Vedat and Geoffrey Booth. "Stock Price Processes With Discontinuous Time Paths: An Empirical Examination," (2), 163-184.

Chua, Jess H. and Jacques A. Schnabel. "Nonpecuniary Benefits And Asset Market Equilibrium," (2), 185-190.

Chiang, Raymond and Robert W. Kolb. "An Analytical Model Of The Relationship Between Maturity And Bonds Risk Differentials," (2), 191-209.

Milonas, Nikolaos T. "Liquidity And Price Variability In Futures Markets," (2), 211-237.

Hancock, Diana. "Testing Price Taking In Loan And Deposit Markets By Financial Firms," (2), 239-257.

Fooladi, Iraj, Gordon Roberts and Jerry Viscione. "Captive Finance Subsidiaries: Overview And Synthesis," (2), 259-275.

Downs, Thomas W. "The User Cost And Capital Budgeting," (2), 277-287.

Dubofsky, David A. and John C. Groth. "An Examination Of Asked-Bid Spreads For Two Over-The-Counter Market Segments," (2), 289-298.

Sweeney, Richard J. and Arthur D. Warga. "The Possibility Of Estimating Risk Premia In Asset Pricing Models," (2), 299-308.

Lanser, Howard P. and John A. Halloran. "Evaluating Cash Flow Systems Under Growth," (2), 309-318.

Kryzanowski, Lawrence and Abolhassan Jalilvand. "Statistical Tests Of The Accuracy Of Alternative Forecasts: Some Results For U.S. Utility Betas," (2), 319-336.

Garven, James R. "A Pedagogic Note On The Derivation Of The Black-Scholes Option Pricing Formula," (2), 337-344.

Tehranian, Hassan and James F. Waegelein. "Short-Term Bonus Plan Adoption And Stock Market Performance - Proxy And Industry Effects: A Note," (2), 345-353.

Issue No. 3 Contains Preceedings Abstracts

Ronn, Ehud I. "On The Rationality Of Common Stock Return Volatility," (4), 355-381.

Elmer, Peter J. "Preferred Stock Arbitrage Of Municipal Bond Market Segmentation," (4), 383-398.

O'Brien, Thomas J. and Michael J. P. Selby. "Option Pricing Theory And Asset Expectations: A Review And Discussion In Tribute To James Boness," (4), 399-418.

Eddy, Albert and Bruce Seifert. "Dividend Changes Of Financially Weak Firms," (4), 419-431.

Johnson, Larry J. "Foreign-Currency Options, Ex Ante Exchange-Rate Volatility, And Market Efficiency: An Empirical Test," (4), 433-450.

Stock, Duane. "The Analytics Of Tax Effects In Discount Bond Valuation," (4), 451-462.

Raghid, Muhammad and Devinder K. Gandhi. "Tax And Savings Implications Of The Canadian Registered Retirement Savings Plans," (4), 463-471.

Skomp, Stephen E., Timothy P. Cronan and William L. Seaver. "On Application Of The Rank Transformation Discrimination Method To Financial Problems," (4), 473-483.

Grammatikos, Theoharry and George J. Papaioannou. "The Informational Value Of Listing On The New York Stock Exchange," (4), 485-499.

Trzcinka, Charles. "Risk, Segmentation, And The Municipal Term Structure," (4), 501-526.

McDaniel, William R. "The Economic Ordering Quantity Problem And Wealth Maximization," (4), 527-536.

Michas, Nicholas A. "The Performance Measurement And Evaluation Of A Corporate Retirement Plan: A Case Study," (4), 537-549.

French, Dan W. and Donald R. Fraser. "A Note On Interest Rates And The Risk Of Bank And Savings And Loan Stock," (4), 551-558.

Financial Review
Volume 22, 1987

Scherr, Frederick C. "A Multiperiod Mean-Variance Model Of Optimal Capital Structure," (1), 1-32.

Lindley, James T., Billy P. Helms and Mahmoud Haddad. "A Measurement Of The Errors In Intra-Period Compounding And Bond Valuation," (1), 33-52.

Lamoureux, Christopher G. and James W. Wansley. "Market Effects Of Changes In The Standard & Poor's 500 Index," (1), 53-70.

Liu, Pu and William T. Moore. "The Impact Of Split Bond Ratings On Risk Premia," (1), 71-86.

Pieptea, Dan R. "Leveraged Bond Portfolio Optimization Under Uncertainty," (1), 87-110.

Neely, Walter P. and David P. Rochester. "Operating Performance And Merger Benefits: The Savings And Loan Experience," (1), 111-130.

Rendleman, Richard J., Jr., Charles P. Jones and Henry A. Latane. "Further Insight Into The Standardized Unexpected Earnings Anomaly: Size And Serial Correlation Effects," (1), 131-144.

Benesh, Gary A. and Robert A. Pari. "Performance Of Stocks

Recommended On The Basis Of Insider Trading Activity," (1), 145-158.

Michel, Allen and Israel Shaked. "Airline Deregulation And The Probability Of Air Carrier Insolvency," (1), 159-174.

Goldenberg, David H. "Market Power And The Required Return To Electric Utilities," (1), 175-194.

Yagil, Joseph. "An Exchange Ratio Determination Model For Mergers: A Note," (1), 195-202.

Bierwag, G. O., George G. Kaufman and Cynthia M. Latta. "Bond Portfolio Immunization: Tests Of Maturity, One- And Two-Factor Duration Matching Strategies," (2), 203-220.

Peterson, Pamela P., David R. Peterson and Norman H. Moore. "The Adoption Of New-Issue Dividend Reinvestment Plans And Shareholder Wealth," (2), 221-232.

Davidson, Wallace N., III, Sharon Hatten Garrison and Glenn V. Henderson, Jr. "Examining Merger Synergy With The Capital Asset Pricing Model," (2), 233-248.

Cotner, John S. and Neil E. Seitz. "A Simplified Approach To Short-Term International Diversification," (2), 249-266.

Ramaswami, Murali. "Stock Market Perception Of Industrial Firm Bankruptcy," (2), 267-280.

Ferris, Stephen P. and Don M. Chance. "Trading Time Effects In Financial And Commodity Futures Markets," (2), 281-294.

Michel, Allen and Israel Shaked. "Trucking Deregulation And Motor-Carrier Performance: The Shareholders' Perspective," (2), 295-312.

Bagamery, Bruce D. "On The Correspondence Between The Baumol-Tobin And Miller-Orr Optimal Cash Balance Models," (2), 313-320.

Barges, Alexander. "The Marginal-Efficiency-Of-Capital Function Of The Firm," (2), 321-338.

Stewart, Scott D. "Biases In Performance Measurement During Contributions: A Note," (2), 339-343.

Issue No. 3 Contains Proceedings Abstracts

Barrett, W. Brian, Andrea J. Heuson, Robert W. Kolb and Gabriele H. Schropp. "The Adjustment Of Stock Prices To Completely Unanticipated Events," (4), 345-354.

Warschauer, Thomas and Antony Cherin. "Optimal Liquidity In Personal Financial Planning," (4), 355-368.

Gooptu, Sudarshan and Raymond Lombra. "Aggregation Across Heterogeneous Depository Institutions," (4), 369-378.

Jahera, John S., Jr., William P. Lloyd and Daniel E. Page. "The Relationship Between Financial Performance And Stock Market Based Measures Of Corporate Diversification," (4), 379-390.

Lasser, Dennis J. "Influence Of Treasury Bill Futures Trading On The Primary Sale Of The Deliverable Treasury Bill," (4), 391-402.

Wansley, James W., William R. Lane and Ho C. Yang. "Gains To Bidder Firms In Cash And Securities Transactions," (4), 403-414.

Calvet, A. L. and J. Lefoll. "Information Asymmetry And Wealth Effect Of Canadian Corporate Acquisitions," (4), 415-432.

Hoffer, George E., Stephen W. Pruitt and Robert J. Reilly. "Automotive Recalls And Informational Efficiency," (4), 433-442.

Financial Review
Volume 23, 1988

Johnson, W. Bruce. "Debt Refunding And Shareholder Wealth: The Price Effects Of Debt-For-Debt Exchange Offer Announcements," (1), 1-24.

Sears, R. Stephen and K. C. John Wei. "The Structure Of Skewness Preferences In Asset Pricing Models With Higher Moments: An Empirical Test," (1), 25-38.

Ma, Christopher K. and Ramesh P. Rao. "Information Asymmetry And Options Trading," (1), 39-52.

Kim, Wi Saeng, Jae Won Lee and Jack Clark Francis. "Investment Performance Of Common Stocks In Relation To Insider Ownership," (1), 53-64.

Rogers, Ronald C. "The Relationship Between Earnings Yield And Market Value: Evidence From The American Stock Exchange," (1), 65-80.

Swanson, Peggy E. "Interrelationships Among Domestic And Eurocurrency Deposit Yields: A Focus On The U.S. Dollar," (1), 81-94.

Kutner, George W. "Black-Scholes Revisited: Some Important Details," (1), 95-104.

Scott, William L., Mona J. Gardner and Dixie L. Mills. "Expense Preference And Minority Banking: A Note," (1), 105-116.

Cudd, Mike and Joe Morris. "Bias In Journal Ratings," (1), 117-125.

Douglas, Norman S. "Insider Trading: The Case Against The 'Victimless Crime' Hypothesis," (2), 127-142.

Beranek, William and James A. Miles. "The Excess Return Argument And Double Leverage," (2), 143-150.

Peterson, Pamela. "Reincorporation: Motives And Shareholder Wealth," (2), 151-160.

Jen, Frank C. "Financial Planning And Control For Commercial And Industrial Enterprises In China," (2), 161-174.

Ouyang, Ling-Nan. "Joint Ventures In China: Problems And Solutions," (2), 175-182.

Kim, Moon K. and Chunchi Wu. "Effects Of Inflation On Capital Structure," (2), 183-200.

Bera, Anil, Edward Bubnys and Hun Park. "Conditional Heteroscedasticity In The Market Model And Efficient Estimates Of Betas," (2), 201-214.

Vu, Joseph D. "An Empirical Analysis Of Ben Graham's Net Current Asset Value Rule," (2), 215-226.

Rodriguez, Ricardo J. "The Wealth Maximizing Ordering Quantity: An Extension," (2), 227-232.

Pari, Robert and John Caks. "A Note On Bond Defeasance," (2), 233-236.

Conine, Thomas E., Jr. and Maurry Tamarkin. "Textbook Inconsistencies In Graphing Valuation Equations: A Further Note," (2), 237-241.

Pettway, Richard H., T. Craig Tapley and Takeshi Yamada. "The Impacts Of Financial Deregulation Upon Trading Efficiency And The Levels Of Risk And Return Of Japanese Banks," (3), 243-268.

Gentry, James A., David T. Whitford and Paul Newbold. "Predicting Industrial Bond Ratings With A Probit Model And Funds Flow Components," (3), 269-286.

Born, Jeffrey A. and James T. Moser. "An Investigation Into The Role Of The Market Portfolio In The Arbitrage Pricing Theory," (3), 287-300.

Horvath, Philip A. "Disintermediation Revisited," (3), 301-312.

Bey, Roger P. and J. Markham Collins. "The Relationship Between Before- And After-Tax Yields On Financial Assets," (3), 313-332.

Tseng, Kuo C. "Low Price, Price-Earnings Ratio, Market Value, And Abnormal Stock Returns," (3), 333-344.

Ang, James S. and Tsong-Yue Lai. "Functional Forms Of The Capital Asset Pricing Model Under Different Market Risk Regimes," (3), 345-350.

Karafiath, Imre. "Using Dummy Variables In The Event Methodology," (3), 351-358.

Horvath, Philip A. "A Measurement Of The Errors In Intra-Period Compounding And Bond Valuation: A Short Extension," (3), 359-364.

Taylor, Richard W. "The Valuation Of Semiannual Bonds Between Interest Payment Dates," (3), 365-368.

McDaniel, William R., Daniel E. McCarty and Kenneth A. Jessell. "Discounted Cash Flow With Explicit Reinvestment Rates: Tutorial And Extension," (3), 369-385.

Eun, Cheol S. and Bruce G. Resnick. "Estimating The Dependence Structure Of Share Prices: A Comparative Study Of The United States And Japan," (4), 387-402.

Finucane, Thomas J. "Options On U.S. Treasury Coupon Issues," (4), 403-426.

Fabozzi, Frank J. and Christopher K. Ma. "The Over-The-Counter Market And New York Stock Exchange Trading Halts," (4),427-438.

Shome, Dilip K. and Stephen D. Smith. "An Econometric Analysis Of Equity Costs And Risk Premiums In The Electric Utility Industry: 1971-1985," (4), 439-452.

Gupta, Atul and Lalatendu Misra. "Illegal Insider Trading: Is It Rampant Before Corporate Takeovers?," (4), 453-464.

Kaufman, Daniel J., Jr. "Factors Affecting The Magnitude Of Premiums Paid To Target-Firm Shareholders In Corporate Acquisitions," (4), 465-482.

Zaima, Janis K. and Joseph McCarthy. "The Impact Of Bond Rating Changes On Common Stocks And Bonds: Tests Of The Wealth Redistribution Hypothesis," (4), 483-498.

Cebenoyan, A. Sinan. "Multiproduct Cost Functions And Scale Economies In Banking," (4), 499-512.

Muscarella, Chris J. "Price Performance Of Initial Public Offerings Of Master Limited Partnership Units," (4), 513-521.

Financial Review
Volume 24, 1989

Murphy, J. Austin and Jimmy E. Hilliard. "An Investigation Into The Equilibrium Structure Of The Commodity Futures Market Anomaly," (1), 1-18.

Bansal, Vipul K., Stephen W. Pruitt and K. C. John Wei. "An Empirical Reexamination Of The Impact. Of CBOE Option Initiation On Volatility And Trading Volume Of The Underlying Equities: 1973-1986," (1), 19-30.

Arshadi, Nasser. "Capital Structure, Agency Problems, And Deposit Insurance In Banking Firms," (1), 31-52.

Kelly, William A., Jr. and James A. Miles. "Capital Structure Theory And The Fisher Effect," (1), 53-74.

Chiang, Raymond and Dennis J. Lasser. "Tax Timing Options On Futures Contracts And The 1981 Economic Recovery Act," (1), 75-92.

Davidson, Wallace N., III and Sharon H. Garrison. "The Stock Market Reaction To Significant Tender Offer Repurchases Of Stock: Size And Purpose Perspective," (1), 93-108.

Dugan, Michael T. and Keith A. Shriver. "The Effects Of Estimation Period, Industry, And Proxy On The Calculation Of The Degree Of Operating Leverage," (1), 109-122.

Karafiath, Imre and John Glascock. "Intra-Industry Effects Of A Regulatory Shift: Capital Market Evidence From Penn Square," (1), 123-134.

Ferri, Michael G., Scott B. Moore and David C. Schirm. "The Listing, Size, And Value Of Equity Warrants," (1), 135-146.

Heuson, Andrea J. "Offering Rates On Fixed- And Adjustable-Rate Mortgage Loans," (1), 147-156.

Callahan, Carolyn M. and Rosanne M. Mohr. "The Determinants Of Systematic Risk: A Synthesis," (2), 157-182.

Lamoureux, Christopher G. and James W. Wansley. "The Pricing Of When-Issued Securities," (2), 183-198.

Callaway, Richard E. "Evidence Of The Nonstationarity Of The Variance Rate Of Return Of New York Stock Exchange Listed Common Stock," (2), 199-214.

Lau, Hon-Shiang and John R. Wingender. "The Analytics Of The Intervaling Effect On Skewness And Kurtosis Of Stock Returns," (2), 215-234.

Lee, Moon H. and Halim Bishara. "Recent Canadian Experience On The Profitability Of Insider Trades," (2), 235-250.

Rose, Peter S. "Diversification Of The Banking Firm," (2), 251-280.

Foote, William G. "The Rationality And Efficiency Of Stock Price Relative To Money Announcement Information," (2), 281-298.

D'Souza, Rudolph E., LeRoy D. Brooks and H. Dennis Oberhelman. "A General Stationary Stochastic Regression Model For Estimating And Predicting Beta," (2), 299-318.

Kolb, Robert W. and Ricardo J. Rodriguez. "The Regression Tendencies Of Betas: A Reappraisal," (2), 319-334.

Chang, S. J. and Son-Nan Chen. "A Study Of Call Price Behavior Under A Stationary Return Generating Process," (3), 335-354.

Sugrue, Timothy F. and Frederick C. Scherr. "An Empirical Test Of Ross's Cash Flow Beta Theory Of Capital Structure," (3), 355-370.

Kon, Stanley J. and John G. Thatcher. "The Effect Of Bankruptcy Laws On The Valuation Of Risky Consumer Debt," (3), 371-396.

Dwyer, Hubert J. and Richard Lynn. "Small Capitalization Companies: What Does Financial Analysis Tell Us About Them?," (3), 397-416.

Bundt, Thomas P. and Robert Schweitzer. "Deregulation, Deposit Markets, And Banks' Cost Of Funds," (3), 417-430.

Mitchell, Karlyn. "Interest Rate Risk At Commercial Banks: An Empirical Investigation," (3), 431-456.

Chen, Carl R. and Anthony Chan. "Interest Rate Sensitivity, Asymmetry, And The Stock Returns Of Financial Institutions," (3), 457-474.

Zivney, Terry L. and Richard D. Marcus. "The Day The United States Defaulted On Treasury Bills," (3), 475-490.

Gandhi, Devinder K., Muhammad Rashid and Kenneth D. Riener. "Intertemporal Resolution Of Uncertainty And Portfolio Behavior," (3), 491-498.

Johnson, R. Stafford, Lyle C. Fiore and Richard Zuber. "The Investment Performance Of Common Stocks In Relation To Their Price-Earnings Ratios: An Update Of The Basu Study," (3), 499-506.

Choi, Daniel F. S. and Charles W. R. Ward. "The Reconciliation Of The Smith's And Jarrow And Rudd's Option Sensitivity Formulae: A Teaching Note," (3), 507-510.

Brooks, Robert. "Investment Decision Making With Derivative Securities," (4), 511-528.

Dickinson, Amy and David R. Peterson. "Seasonality In The Option Market," (4), 529-540.

Aggarwal, Reena and Pietra Rivoli. "Seasonal And Day-Of-The-Week Effects In Four Emerging Stock Markets," (4), 541-550.

Murphy, Austin and Kevin Nathan. "An Analysis Of Merger Financing," (4), 551-566.

Syed, Azmat A., Pu Liu and Stanley D. Smith. "The Exploitation Of Inside Information At The Wall Street Journal: A Test Of Strong Form Efficiency," (4), 567-580.

Zivney, Terry L. and Donald J. Thompson, II. "The Specification And Power Of The Sign Test In Measuring Security Price Performance: Comments And Analysis," (4), 581-588.

Bey, Roger P. and Larry J. Johnson. "The Impact Of Taxes On Discount Bond Valuation And Risk," (4), 589-598.

Fry, Clifford L. and Insup Lee. "OSHA Sanctions And The Value Of The Firm," (4), 599-610.

Moser, James T. and James T. Lindley. "A Simple Formula For Duration: An Extension," (4), 611-615.

Financial Review
Volume 25, 1990

Bubnys, Edward L. "Simulating And Forecasting Utility Stock Returns: Arbitrage Pricing Theory Vs. Capital Asset Pricing Model," (1), 1-24.

Loviscek, Anthony L. and Frederick D. Crowley. "What Is In A Municipal Bond Rating?," (1), 25-54.

Wilson, Jack W. and Charles P. Jones. "Is There A January Effect In Corporate Bond And Paper Returns?," (1), 55-80.

Chu, Chen-Chin and Edward L. Bubnys. "A Likelihood Ratio Test Of Price Volatilities: Comparing Stock Index Spot And Futures," (1), 81-94.

Kao, Chihwa and Chunchi Wu. "Sinking Funds And The Agency Costs Of Corporate Debt," (1), 95-114.

Cebenoyan, A. Sinan. "Scope Economies In Banking: The Hybrid Box-Cox Function," (1), 115-126.

Pugh, William and John S. Jahera, Jr. "Stock Repurchases And Excess Returns: An Empirical Examination," (1), 127-142.

Followill, Richard A., Michael Schellenger and Patrick H. Marchand. "Economic Order Quantities, Volume Discounts, And Wealth Maximization," (1), 143-152.

Skantz, Terrance R., Dale O. Cloninger and Thomas H. Strickland. "Price-Fixing And Shareholder Returns: An Empirical Study," (1), 153-164.

Lawrence, Edward C. "Learning Portfolio Management By Experience: University Student Investment Funds," (1), 165-173.

Megginson, William L. "Restricted Voting Stock, Acquisition Premiums, And The Market Value Of Corporate Control," (2), 175-198.

Senteney, David L. "Dealers' Adverse Selection Costs And The Evaluation Of Alternative Measures Of The Earnings Release Signal," (2), 199-210.

Aggarwal, Raj and Ramesh P. Rao. "Institutional Ownership And Distribution Of Equity Returns," (2), 211-230.

Edelman, Richard B. and H. Kent Baker. "Liquidity And Stock Exchange Listing," (2), 231-250.

McCarthy, Joseph, Mohammad Najand and Bruce Seifert. "Empirical Tests Of The Proxy Hypothesis," (2), 251-264.

Wansley, James W., Fayez A. Elayan and Brian A. Maris. "Preferred Stock Returns, CreditWatch, And Preferred Stock Rating Changes," (2), 265-286.

Skinner, David L. and John E. Gilster, Jr. "Dividend Clienteles, The Tax-Clientele Hypothesis, And Utilities," (2), 287-296.

Burnie, David A. "An Empirical Evaluation Of The Friedman Hypothesis Of Inflation On Capital Asset Pricing," (2), 297-320.

Mansur, Iqbal, Steven J. Cochran and David K. Seagers. "The Relationship Between The Argentinean Debt Rescheduling Announcement And Bank Equity Returns," (2), 321-334.

Howe, Keith M. and Paul L. Gronewoller. "Issue Costs In Fisher's Two-Period Model," (2), 335-343.

Ho, Thomas S. Y. and Sang Bin Lee. "Interest Rate Futures Options And Interest Rate Options," (3), 345-370.

Fischer, K. P. and A. P. Palasvirta. "High Road To A Global Marketplace: The International Transmission Of Stock Market Fluctuations," (3), 371-394.

DeFusco, Richard A., George C. Philippatos and Dosoung Choi. "Differences In Factor Structures Between U.S. Multinational And Domestic Corporations: Evidence From Bilinear Paradigm Tests," (3), 395-404.

Sullivan, Michael J., Pamela P. Peterson and David R. Peterson. "Two-Stage Acquisitions, Free-Riding, And Corporate Control," (3), 405-420.

Chatfield, Robert E., Scott E. Hein and R. Charles Moyer. "Long-Term Earnings Forecasts In The Electric Utility Industry: Accuracy And Valuation Implications," (3), 421-440.

Sterk, William E. and Pieter A. Vandenberg. "The Market Valuation Of Cash Dividends And The Tax Differential Theory Of Dividend Policy: A Case Revisited," (3), 441-456.

Thompson, G. Rodney and Peter Vaz. "Dual Bond Ratings: A Test Of The Certification Function Of Rating Agencies," (3), 457-472.

Hsueh, L. Paul and Y. Angela Liu. "An Examination Of The Biases In Estimating The Benefit Of Debt Insurance," (3), 473-486.

Berry, S. Keith. "Flotation Cost Allowance Methodologies: A Synthesis Using Present Value Analysis," (3), 487-500.

Rodriguez, Ricardo J. "A Generalization Of The Tree Harvesting Paradigm," (3), 501-515.

Brewer, Elijah, III. "The Risk Of Banks Expanding Their Permissible Nonbanking Activities," (4), 517-538.

Wetmore, Jill L. T. and John R. Brick. "Interest Rate Risk And The Optimal Gap For Commercial Banks: An Empirical Study," (4), 539-558.

Gentry, James A. and Jesus M. De La Garza. "Monitoring Accounts Payables," (4), 559-576.

Odgen, Joseph P., Alan L. Tucker and Timothy W. Vines. "Arbitraging American Gold Spot And Futures Options," (4), 577-592.

Lukac, Louis P. and B. Wade Brorsen. "A Comprehensive Test Of Futures Market Disequilibrium," (4), 593-622.

Chung, Kee H. "Inventory Decision Under Demand Uncertainty: A Contingent Claims Approach," (4), 623-640.

Lee, Insup and Steve B. Wyatt. "The Effects Of International Joint Ventures On Shareholder Wealth," (4), 641-650.

Brooks, Robert and Billy Helms. "An N-Stage, Fractional Period, Quarterly Dividend Discount Model," (4), 651-658.

Tse, K. S. Maurice and Mark A. White. "The Valuation Of Semiannual Bonds Between Interest Payment Dates:A Correction," (4),659-662.

Financial Review
Volume 26, 1991

Kazemi, Hossein B. "Dispersion Of Beliefs, Asset Prices, And Noisy Aggregation Of Information," (1), 1-14.

Barry, Christopher B., Dan W. French and Ramesh K. S. Rao. "Estimation Risk And Adaptive Behavior In The Pricing Of Options," (1), 15-30.

Tew, Bernard V., Donald W. Reid and Craig A. Witt. "The Opportunity Cost Of A Mean-Variance Efficient Choice," (1), 31-44.

Reiter, Sara A. and David A. Ziebart. "Bond Yields, Ratings, And Financial Information: Evidence From Public Utility Issues," (1), 44-74.

Meric, Gulser, Serpil S. Leveen and Ilhan Meric. "The Financial Characteristics Of Commercial Banks Involved In Interstate Acquisitions," (1), 75-90.

Horvitz, Paul M., Insup Lee and Kerry L. Robertson. "Valuation Effects Of New Securities Issuance By Bank Holding Companies: New Evidence," (1), 91-104.

Gallagher, Timothy J. and J. Kenton Zumwalt. "Risk-Adjusted Discount Rates Revisited," (1), 105-114.

Kolb, Robert W. and Ricardo J. Rodriguez. "Markov Chains And Regression Toward The Mean," (1), 115-125.

Gregory-Allen, Russell B. and Glenn V. Henderson, Jr. "A Brief Review Of Catastrophe Theory And A Test In A Corporate Failure Context," (2), 127-156.

Chen, Son-Nan. "Optimal Asset Abandonment And Replacement: Tax And Inflation Considerations," (2), 157-178.

Castelino, Mark G., Jack C. Francis and Avner Wolf. "Cross-Hedging: Basis Risk And Choice Of The Optimal Hedging Vehicle," (2), 179-210.

Anderson, Seth C., Jeffery A. Born and T. Randolph Beard. "An Analysis Of Bond Investment Company Initial Public Offerings: Past And Present," (2), 211-222.

Guffey, Daryl M. and William T. Moore. "Direct Bankruptcy Costs: Evidence From The Trucking Industry," (2), 223-236.

Lasser, Dennis J. and W. Brian Barrett. "New Issue Yield Spreads In The 30-Year Treasury Bond Market," (2), 237-248.

Branch, Ben and David P. Echevarria. "The Impact Of Bid-Ask Prices On Market Anomalies," (2), 249-268.

Bolten, Steven E. and Scott Besley. "Long-Term Asset Allocation Under Dynamic Interaction Of Earnings And Interest Rates," (2), 269-274.

FINANCIAL SERVICES REVIEW

Financial Services Review
Volume 1, 1991

Markowitz, Harry M. "Individual Versus Institutional Investing," (1), 1-9.

Potts, Tom L. and William Reichenstein. "The Optimal Allocation Of Pension Fund Assets: An Individual's Perspective," (1), 11-26.

Kleiman, Robert T. and Anandi P. Sahu. "Life Insurance Companies As Investment Managers: New Implications For Consumers," (1), 27-40.

Murphy, Neil B. "Determinants Of Household Check Writing: The Impacts Of The Use Of Electronic Banking Services And Alternative Pricing Of Services," (1), 51-51.

Chinloy, Peter. "Real Estate Income And Relocation," (1), 53-65.

Cox, Larry A. "Review: Diability Income Insurance And The Individual," (1), 67-76.

GLOBAL FINANCE JOURNAL

Global Finance Journal
Volume 1, 1989/90

Chuppe, Terry M., Hugh R. Haworth and Marvin G. Watkins. "Global Finance: Causes, Consequences And Prospects For The Future," (1), 1-20.

Bodurtha, James N., Jr., D. Chinhyung Cho and Lemma W. Senbet. "Economic Forces In The Stock Market: An International Perspective," (1), 21-46.

Finnerty, John D. and Victor M. Borun. "An Analysis Of Unbundled Stock Units," (1), 47-70.

Ang, James S. and Tsong-Yue Lai. "A Simple Rule For Multinational Capital Budgeting," (1), 71-76.

Apsel, David, Jack Cogen and Michael Rabin. "Hedging Long Term Commodity Swaps With Futures," (1), 77-93.

Kwok, Chuck C. Y. "The Numeraire Problem, Forward Hedges And International Portfolio Selection," (2), 95-120.

Tiwari, Kashi Nath. "The Circular Flow Of Dollars In The World Financial Markets," (2), 121-138.

Rao, Spuma and Theodor Kohers. "The Effect Of Selected U.S. Market Conditions And Exchange Rate Variability On Merger And Acquisition Activities Of Foreign Companies In The United States," (2), 139-152.

Strickland, Thomas H. and Ghassem Homaifar. "Foreign Direct Investment: Evidence From Capital Market Data," (2), 153-162.

Haar, Jerry, Krishnan Dandapani and Stanley P. Haar. "The American Depositary Receipt (ADR): A Creative Financial Tool For Multinational Companies," (2), 163-171.

INTERNATIONAL JOURNAL OF FINANCE

International Journal of Finance
Volume 1, 1988/89

Marcus, Matityahu and Uzi Yaari. "How A Closed-End Fund Can Out-Perform Its Own Stock Portfolio, " (1), 1-14.

Baum, Donald N. and Dilip K. Ghosh. "Interest Rate, Wealth And The Consumption-Savings Decision: The Relationship Revisited," (1), 15-34.

Choi, Jongmoo Jay. "Pricing Exchange Risk And Location Costs: An Empirical Investigation Of The World Capital Markets," (1), 35-45.

Malindretos, John. "The Keynesian And The Monetary Approaches To International Finance: A Reexamination," (1), 46-89.

Ghosh, Dilip K. "Selection And Revision Theoretic Exercises In Portfolio Analysis," (1), 90-95.

Fooladi, Iraj and Gordon S. Roberts. "Dividend Changes And Preferred Stock Returns," (1), 96-112.

Lee, Cheng F., Frank C. Jen and K. C. John Wei. "The Real And Nominal Parameters In The CAPM: A Responsive Coefficient Approach," (1), 113-130.

Ndubizu, Gordian, Augustine C. Arize and P. R. Chandy. "The Market Model Specification And The Structural Stability Of The Beta," (2), 1-14.

Shalit, Haim and Shlomo Yitzhaki. "Evaluating The Mean-Gini Approach To Portfolio Selection," (2), 15-31.

Fatemi, Khosrow. "U.S. Trade Imbalance And The Dollar: Is There A Correlation?," (2), 32-51.

Kasibhatla, Krishnamoorti. "A Monetary Model Of The Brazilian Balance Of Payments," (2), 52-59.

Meric, Gulser and Ilhan Meric. "Industry Effect Of Financial Structure In Multinational Corporations," (2), 60-63.

Chatterjee, Sris. "Agency Cost Of Asset Substitution: Some Additional Results," (2), 64-71.

Hsu, Chih-Chang and Thomas Liaw. "Partial Equity Interests And Mangerial Incentives," (2), 72-81.

International Journal of Finance
Volume 2, 1989/90

Ho, Thomas S. Y. and Sang Bin Lee. "Pricing Of The Call And Sinking Fund Provisions On Corporate Bonds Under Interest Rate Risk: Empirical Evidence," (1), 1-17.

Chiang, Raymond C. and John M. Finkelstein. "The Multiplicity Of Financial Intermediary Types: The Rationale Re-Examined," (1), 18-29.

Rabinovitch, Ramon. "The Valuation Of Options Embedded In Government Agricultural Loans," (1), 30-49.

Rhee, Thomas A. and Fuad A. Abdullah. "The Intermarket Pricing Relations In The Foreign Currency Option Market," (1), 50-57.

Dhatt, Yashwant S. "Capital Regulation And Bank Portfolio Risk," (1), 58-66.

Varela, Oscar and P. R. Chandy. "Market Reaction To Listings And Delistings In The Dow Jones Portfolios," (1), 67-78.

Stone, Charles A. and Anne-Marie Zissu. "Does The Quality Of Investment Banks Foretell The Outcome Of Hostile Tender Offers?," (2), 1-11.

Bonitsis, Theologos Homer and Raj Aggarwal. "U.S. Direct Foreign Investment And Economic Growth In Brazil: An Econometric Causal Analysis," (2), 12-19.

Finkelstein, John M. "Bank Capital Ratios And Macroeconomic Stability," (2), 20-30.

Ziorklui, Sam Q. "Devaluation And Inflationary Pressures In The Less Developed Countries: A Test Of The Granger Causality," (2), 31-45.

Liaw, K. Thomas. "Systematic Risk, Monopoly Power, And Factor Prices," (2), 46-51.

Trippi, Robert R. and Rebecca Jacob Abraham. "Interest Rates Implied In The Prices Of S&P 100 Options: Evidence And Implications Of An Inverted Ultra-Short Term Structure," (2), 52-66.

Lee, Insup, R. Richardson Pettit and Ronald F. Singer. "Offer Premiums In Stock Exchange Mergers And The Distribution Of Stockholder's Wealth," (2), 67-87.

Arize, Augustine and Gordian Ndubizu. "Modelling Money Demand Functions With Exchange Rates: Regression Estimates And Diagnostic Tests," (2), 88-104.

International Journal of Finance
Volume 3, 1990/91

DeMaskey, Andrea L. and James C. Baker. "The Efficiency Of Option Markets In Foreign Currencies: An Empirical Analysis," (1), 1-38.

Brocato, Joe. "Evidence On The Comovement And Linkages Between National Equity Markets: 1980-1987," (1), 39-64.

Muoghalu, Michael I. "Valuation Of Toxic Waste Mismanagement Lawsuits: A Capital Market Approach," (1), 65-85.

Ariff, Mohamed and Matthew Varghese. "Risk Reduction From Currency Portfolio Diversification And Revision Gains," (1), 86-100.

Madura, Jeff and Wm. R. McDaniel. "The Reaction Of Bank Holding Company Share Prices To Citicorp's $1 Billion Stock Issue," (1), 101-120.

Hegde, Krishna and P. V. Viswanath. "Structure Stability With Ex-Ante Factor Spectification In APT," (1), 121-157.

Ghosh, Dilip K. "Capital Assets And Activity Analysis Of Firms In A General Equilibrium Model," (1), 158-169.

Langdana, Farrokh K. "Central Bank Intervention And Domestic Fiscal Policy," (1), 170-184.

JOURNAL OF THE AMERICAN REAL ESTATE AND URBAN ECONOMICS ASSOCIATION

Erber, Ernest. "Impact Of New Housing Construction On Racial Patterns," (3), 313-336.

Kidd, Phillip E. "Housing Statistics: Some Sources And Some Limitations," (3), 337-398.

Curcio, Richard J. and James P. Gaines. "Real Estate Portfolio Revision," (4), 399-410.

Field, Al and Henry J. Cassidy. "Simulation Analysis Of Alternative Mortgage Instruments," (4), 411-433.

Kamer, Pearl. "The Changing Spatial Relationship Between Residences And Worksites In The New York Metropolitan Region: Implications For Public Policy," (4), 434-454.

Ferri, Michael J. "An Application Of Hedonic Indexing Methods To Monthly Changes In Housing Prices: 1965-1975," (4), 455-462.

Hutchinson, Peter M., James R. Ostas and J. David Reed. "A Survey And Comparison Of Redlining Influences In Urban Mortgage Lending Markets," (4), 463-472.

Ahlbrandt, Roger S., Jr. "Exploratory Research On The Redlining Phenomenon," (4), 473-481.

Jaffe, Austin J. "Is There A 'New' Internal Rate Of Return Literature?," (4), 482-502.

Journal of the American Real Estate
and Urban Economics Association
Volume 6, 1978

Hempel, Donald J. and Subhash C. Jain. "House Buying Behavior: An Empirical Study In Cross-Cultural Buyer Behavior," (1), 1-21.

Wofford, Larry E. and R. Keith Preddy. "Real Estate Investment Perception: A Multidimensional Analysis," (1), 22-36.

Lusht, Kenneth M. "Inflation And Real Estate Investment Value," (1), 37-49.

Gau, George W. and Daniel B. Kohlhepp. "Multicollinearity And Reduced-Form Price Equations For Residential Markets," (1), 50-69.

Epley, Donald R. and William Burns. "The Correct Use Of Confidence Intervals And Regression Analysis In Determining The Value Of Residential Homes," (1), 70-85.

Teplin, Albert M. "Uses And Abuses Of Residential Building Permits In Forecasting Private Housing Starts," (1), 86-104.

Buckley, Robert M. "On Estimating The Tax Loss Of The Homeownership Incentive Plan," (1), 105-127.

Vandell, Kerry D. "Distributional Consequences Of Alternative Mortgage Instruments," (2), 129-152.

Schenk, Robert E. "A Theory Of Vacant Urban Land," (2), 153-163.

Miller, Norman G. "Time On The Market And Selling Price," (2), 164-174.

Goetze, Rolf. "Avoiding Both Disinvestment And Speculation In Private Multifamily Housing," (2), 175-185.

Haney, Richard L., Jr., Melvin R. Crask and Hans P. Isakson. "The Gatekeeper Appraiser's Role In An Era Of Higher Energy Prices," (2), 186-203.

Manski, Charles F. and Kenneth T. Rosen. "The Implications Of Demand Instability For The Behavior Of Firms: The Case Of Residential Construction," (2), 204-226.

Grigsby, William G. "AREUEA Presidential Address," (3), 241-246.

Goldberg, Michael A. and Blake Allan. "Urban Growth: A View From The Supply Side," (3), 247-270.

Stroud, Hubert B. "The Land Development Corporation: A System Of Selling Rural Real Estate," (3), 271-286.

Isakson, Hans R. and Richard L. Haney, Jr. "The Impact Of Market Experience Upon Appraisers' Energy Awareness," (3), 287-304.

Kain, John F. and Gary R. Fauth. "The Impact Of Urban Development On Auto Ownership And Transit Use," (3), 305-326.

Nourse, Hugh O. "A Cynic's View Of Zoning Reform," (3), 327-334.

Mandelker, Daniel R. "Zoning Reform: Comment," (3), 335-336.

Gruen, Claude. "A Cynic's View Of Zoning Reform: Comment," (3), 337-340.

Nourse, Hugh O. "A Cynic's View Of Zoning Reform: Response," (3), 341-342.

Thygerson, Kenneth J. "Hedging Forward Mortgage Loan Commitments: The Option Of Futures And A Future For Options," (4), 357-369.

Wofford, Larry E. "A Simulation Approach To The Appraisal Of Income Producing Real Estate," (4), 370-394.

Weicher, John C. "New Home Affordability, Equity, And Housing Market Behavior," (4), 395-416.

Rubin, Marilyn, Ilene Wagner and Pearl Kamer. "Industrial Migration: A Case Study Of Destination By City-Suburban Origin Within The New York Metropolitan Area," (4), 417-437.

Diamond, Douglas B., Jr. "A Note On Inflation And Relative Tenure Prices," (4), 438-450.

Fullerton, David J. and C. Duncan MacRae. "FHA, Racial Discrimination And Urban Mortgages," (4), 451-470.

Journal of the American Real Estate
and Urban Economics Association
Volume 7, 1979

Sternlieb, George and Robert W. Burchell. "Multifamily Housing Demand: 1980-2000," (1), 1-38.

Case, Fred E. "The Attraction Of Home Ownership," (1), 39-44.

Kawaller, Ira G. "Macroeconomic Determinants Of Multifamily Housing Starts: A Descriptive Analysis," (1), 45-62.

Rosen, Kenneth T. "A Regional Model Of Multifamily Housing Starts," (1), 63-76.

Stegman, Michael A. "Multifamily Distress: A Case For National Action," (1), 77-94.

Fredland, J. Eric and C. Duncan MacRae. "FHA Multifamily Financial Failure: A Review Of Empirical Studies," (1), 95-122.

Reid, Gary and Robert Schafer. "Multifamily Housing Demand: Comment," (1), 123-129.

Case, Fred E. "Multifamily Housing Demand: Comment," (1), 130.

Gloudemans, Robert J. "Confidence Intervals And The Evaluation Of Regression Based Appraisal Models," (1), 131-135.

Epley, Donald and William Burns. "The Correct Use Of Confidence Intervals And Regression Analysis In Determining The Value Of Residential Houses: A Reply," (1), 136-140.

Epstein, Ira. "A Property Tax Base Model," (2), 147-162.

Guntermann, Karl L. "FHA Mortgage Discount Points, House Prices And Consumer Behavior," (2), 163-176.

Hendershott, Patric H. "The Likely Impact Of Increases In Deposit Rate Ceilings On Thrift Earnings And Housing Construction," (2), 177-189.

Pearson, Thomas D. "Assessment Ratios And Property Tax Burdens In Norfolk, Virginia, 1974-1975," (2), 190-203.

Vernor, James D. "Simulations Of Savings Associations Using Alternative Mortgage Instruments," (2), 204-226.

Goering, John M. "What A National Commission On Neighborhoods Could Do: Comment," (2), 227-229.

Dahmann, Donald C. "North-South Differences In Housing And The Housing And Community Development Act Of 1977," (2), 230-242.

Lusht, Kenneth M. and Bruce E. Leidenberger. "A Research Note On Factors Associated With Troubled Residential Construction Loans," (2), 243-252.

Albaum, Gerald and George G. Kaufman. "The Mortgage Acquisition Process: A Comparison Of VRM And FRM Borrowers," (2), 253-264.

Case, Fred E. "The Value Of A Thing Is The Price It Will Bring," (2), 265-268.

Barnett, C. Lance. "Expected And Actual Effects Of Housing Allowances On Housing Prices," (3), 277-297.

Findlay, M. Chapman, III, Carl W. Hamilton, Stephen D. Messner and Jonathan S. Yormark. "Optimal Real Estate Portfolios," (3), 298-317.

Kohlhepp, Daniel B. and Charles A. Ingene. "The Effect Of Municipal Services And Local Taxes On Housing Values," (3), 318-343.

Lewis, W. Cris and Paul J. McNutt. "The Incidence Of Property Taxes On Single-Family Housing," (3), 344-361.

Mason, John M. "The Supply Curve For Housing," (3), 362-377.

Miller, Norman G. and Patrick G. McKeown. "Optimizing The Distributions Of Limited Partnership Returns," (3), 378-392.

Richardson, David H. and Richard Thalheimer. "Alternative Methods Of Variable Selection: An Application To Real Estate Assessment," (3), 393-409.

Wurtzebach, Charles H. and Kee S. Kim. "An Investment Analysis And Decision Making Framework For Real Estate Development," (3), 410-426.

Vandell, Kerry D. "Alternative Estimation Methods For Reduced Form Price Equations Under Conditions Of Multicollinearity: A Comment," (3), 427-436.

Gau, George W. and Daniel B. Kohlhepp. "Alternative Estimation Methods For Reduced Form Price Equations Under Conditions Of Multicollinearity: Reply," (3), 437-441.

Lang, James R. and Wesley H. Jones. "Hedonic Property Valuation Models: Are Subjective Measures Of Neighborhood Amenities Needed?," (4), 451-465.

Follain, James R., Jr. "How Well Do Section 8 FMRs (Fair Market Rent) Match The Cost Of Rental Housing? Data From Thirty-Nine Large Cities," (4), 466-481.

Altmann, James L. and Joseph S. DeSalvo. "Extension And Application Of The Mills-Muth Urban Residential Land Use Simulation Model: Milwaukee, 1977-2020," (4), 482-504.

Kain, John F. and William C. Apgar, Jr. "Simulation Of Housing Market Dynamics," (4), 505-538.

Grebler, Leo. "The Growth Of Residential Capital Since World War II," (4), 539-580.

Colton, Kent W., Donald R. Lessard and Arthur P. Solomon. "Borrower Attitudes Toward Alternative Mortgage Instruments," (4), 581-609.

Rabianski, Joseph and Jackson Harris. "A Descriptive Analysis Of The AREUEA Members: 1978," (4), 610-620.

Journal of the American Real Estate
and Urban Economics Association
Volume 8, 1980

Seiders, David F. "Major Developments In Residential Mortgage And Housing Markets Since The Hunt Commission," (1), 4-32.

Jaffee, Dwight and Kenneth Rosen. "The Changing Liability Structure Of Savings And Loan Associations," (1), 33-49.

Hendershott, Patric H. and Kevin E. Villani. "Secondary Mortgage Markets And The Cost Of Mortgage Funds," (1), 50-76.

King, A. Thomas. "Mortgage Lending, Social Responsibility, And Public Policy: Some Perspectives On HMDA And CRA," (1), 77-90.

Colton, Kent W. "Financial Reform: A Review Of The Past And Prospects For The Future," (1), 91-117.

Lindsay, Robert. "Housing Finance In The 1980's," (1), 118-147.

Marcis, Richard G. "Implications Of Financial Innovation And Reform For The Savings And Loan Industry," (1), 148-155.

Kaufman, George G. and George E. Morgan. "Standardizing Yields On Mortgages And Other Securities," (2), 163-179.

Ihlanfeldt, Keith Ray. "An Intertemporal Empirical Analysis Of The Renter's Decision To Purchase A Home," (2), 180-197.

Bible, Douglas S. and Stephen E. Celec. "Real Estate Investment Analysis: New Developments In Traditional Leverage Concepts," (2), 198-206.

Brewster, J. Alan, Irving Crespi, Richard Kaluzny, James Ohls and Cynthia Thomas. "Homeowner Warranties: A Study Of The Need And Demand For Protection Against Unanticipated Repair Expenses," (2), 207-217.

Sirmans, C. F. and James R. Webb. "Expected Equity Returns On Real Estate Financed With Life Insurance Company Loans: 1967-1977," (2), 218-228.

Clapp, John M. "A Model Of Localized Mortgage Lending Behavior," (2), 229-246.

Sirmans, C. F. "Minimum Tax, Recapture And Choice Of Depreciation Methods," (3), 255-267.

Gamble, Hays B., Roger H. Downing and Owen H. Sauerlender. "Community Growth Around Nuclear Power Plants," (3), 268-280.

Diamond, Douglas B., Jr. "Taxes, Inflation, Speculation And The Cost Of Homeownership," (3), 281-298.
Boehm, Thomas P. and Jonathan Mark. "A Principal Component Logistic Analysis Of The Mobility Decision In Transitional Neighborhoods," (3), 299-319.
Dunn, Kenneth B. and John J. McConnell. "Rates Of Return On GNMA Securities: The Cost Of Mortgage Funds," (3), 320-336.
Quinn, Michael A., Donald S. Elliott, Jr., Robert E. Mendelson and Jeffrey A. Thoman. "Maintenance Effort And The Professional Landlord: An Empirical Critique Of Neighborhood Decline," (4), 345-369.
Epstein, Ira and Brian Dittenhafer. "A Preliminary Investigation Into The Effects Of The Federal Override Of State Usury Ceilings On The Supply Of Mortgage Funds By FSLIC-Insured S&Ls In New York And New Jersey," (4), 370-386.
Gleeson, Michael E. "Housing Costs And The Elderly," (4), 387-394.
Rystrom, David. "Inflation And Real Estate Investment Value: A Comment," (4), 395-401.
Lusht, Kenneth M. "Inflation And Real Estate Investment Value: A Reply," (4), 402-403.
Dasso, Jerome and Lynn Woodward. "Real Estate Education: Past, Present And Future - The Search For A Discipline," (4), 404-416.
Wofford, Larry E. and R. Keith Preddy. "Assessing Student Perception Of Real Estate Careers," (4), 417-427.

Journal of the American Real Estate and Urban Economics Association
Volume 9, 1981

Johnson, Michael S. "A Cash Flow Model Of Rational Housing Tenure Choice," (1), 1-17.
Weinrobe, Maurice. "Savings And Loan Demand For Liquid Assets: Theory, Evidence And Implications For Policy," (1), 18-37.
Shulman, David. "Real Estate Valuation Under Rent Control: The Case Of Santa Monica," (1), 38-53.
O'Hare, Michael. "Improvement Of Owner-Occupied Rental Housing: A Game-Theoretic Study Of The Decision To Invest," (1), 54-66.
Beranek, William and Edward B. Selby, Jr. "Accelerated Depreciation And Income Growth," (1), 67-73.
Evans, Richard D. "Residential Construction Volatility: A Seasonal And Cyclical Inventory Adjustment Analysis," (1), 74-82.
Smith, Lawrence B. and Peter Tomlinson. "Rent Controls In Ontario: Roofs Or Ceilings?," (2), 93-114.
Elliott, Michael. "The Impact Of Growth Control Regulations On Housing Prices In California," (2), 115-133.
Hite, Gailen L. and Anthony B. Sanders. "Excess Depreciation And The Maximum Tax," (2), 134-147.
Brueggeman, William B., Jeffrey D. Fisher and Jerrold J. Stern. "Federal Income Taxes, Inflation And Holding Periods For Income-Producing Property," (2), 148-164.
Church, Albert M. "The Effects Of Local Government Expenditure And Property Taxes On Investment," (2), 165-180.
Skaburskis, A. "Determinants Of Canadian Housing Stock Losses," (2), 181-184.
Spellman, Lewis J. "Inflation And Housing Prices," (3), 205-222.
Whitaker, David. "Bidding For Land Development," (3), 223-233.
Black, Harold A. and Robert L. Schweitzer. "An Analysis Of Market Segmentation In Mortgage Lending Between A Commercial Bank And A Mutual Savings Bank," (3), 234-240.
Sandelin, Bo. "Price Behavior And Capital Gains On Residential Real Estate: The Case Of Sweden," (3), 241-264.
Tansey, Michael M. and Patricia Hoon Tansey. "An Analysis Of The Impact Of Usury Ceilings On Conventional Mortgage Loans," (3), 265-282.
Archer, Wayne R. "Determinants Of Location For General Purpose Office Firms Within Medium Size Cities," (3), 283-298.
Rosen, Kenneth T. and Lawrence F. Katz. "Growth Management And Land Use Controls: The San Francisco Bay Area Experience," (3), 321-344.
Case, Fred E. and Jeffrey Gale. "The Impact On Housing Costs Of The California Coastal Zone Conservation Act," (4), 345-366.
Belloit, Jerry D. and Halbert C. Smith. "The Coastal Construction Control Line: A Cost-Benefit Analysis," (4), 367-383.
Nicholas, James C. "Housing Costs And Prices Under Regional Regulation," (4), 384-396.
Peiser, Richard B. "Land Development Regulation: A Case Study Of Dallas And Houston, Texas," (4), 397-417.
Mark, Jonathan H. and Michael A. Goldberg. "Land Use Controls: The Case Of Zoning In Vancouver," (4), 418-435.
Clapp, John M. "The Impact Of Inclusionary Zoning On The Location And Type Of Construction Activity," (4), 436-456.
Shedd, Peter. "Land Use Controls: Can Landowners Force Government Bodies To Pay?," (4), 457-473.

Journal of the American Real Estate and Urban Economics Association
Volume 10, 1982

Greenless, John S. "An Empirical Evaluation Of The CPI Home Purchase Index, 1973-1978," (1), 1-24.
Boehm, Thomas P. and Joseph A. McKenzie. "Inflation, Taxes, And The Demand For Housing," (1), 25-38.
Galster, George C. "Black And White Preferences For Neighborhood Racial Composition," (1), 39-66.
Dowall, David E. and John D. Landis. "Land-Use Controls And Housing Costs: An Examination Of San Francisco Bay Area Communities," (1), 67-93.
Rudolph, Patricia M., Leonard V. Zumpano and Marvin J. Karson. "Mortgage Markets And Inter-Regional Differences In Convention Mortgage Terms," (1), 94-110.
Grebler, Leo and Leland S. Burns. "Construction Cycles In The United States Since World War II," (2), 123-151.
Draper, Dennis W. and M. Chapman Findlay. "Capital Asset Pricing And Real Estate Valuation," (2), 152-183.

Miles, Mike and Tom McCue. "Historic Returns And Institutional Real Estate Portfolios," (2), 184-199.
Hite, Gailen L. and Raymond J. Krasniewski. "The 1981 Tax Act: Cost Recovery Choices For Real Property," (2), 200-208.
Crockett, John H. "Competition And Efficiency In Transacting: The Case Of Residential Real Estate Brokerage," (2), 209-227.
Villani, Kevin E. and John Simonson. "Real Estate Settlement Pricing: A Theoretical Framework," (3), 249-275.
Swan, Craig. "Pricing Private Mortgage Insurance," (3), 276-296.
Ford, Deborah Ann. "Title Assurance And Settlement Charges," (3), 297-312.
Smith, Clifford W., Jr. "Pricing Mortgage Originations," (3), 313-330.
Carney, Michael. "Costs And Pricing Of Home Brokerage Services," (3), 331-354.
Hendershott, Patric H. and Joel Slemrod. "Taxes And The User Cost Of Capital For Owner-Occupied Housing," (4), 375-393.
Noan, Eli M. "The Interaction Of Building Codes And Housing Prices," (4), 394-404.
Shear, William B. and Anthony M. J. Yezer. "An Indirect Test For Differential Treatment Of Borrowers In Mortgage Markets," (4), 405-420.
Buckley, Robert M. and Robert A. Van Order. "Housing And The Economy: Popular Myths," (4), 421-441.
Clemmer, Richard B. and John C. Simonson. "Trends In Substandard Housing 1940-1980," (4), 442-464.
Meador, Mark. "The Effects On Mortgage Repayment Of Restrictions On The Enforcement Of Due-On-Sale Clauses: The California Experience," (4), 465-474.

Journal of the American Real Estate and Urban Economics Association
Volume 11, 1983

Weicher, John C. "Re-Evaluating Housing Policy Alternatives: What Do We Really Know?," (1), 1-10.
Colwell, Peter F., Roger E. Cannaday and Chunchi Wu. "The Analytical Foundations Of Adjustment Grid Methods," (1), 11-29.
Fallis, George. "Housing Tenure In A Model Of Consumer Choice: A Simple Diagrammatic Analysis," (1), 30-44.
Wieand, Kenneth F. "The Performance Of Annual Housing Survey Quality Measures In Explaining Dwelling Rentals In 20 Metropolitan Areas," (1), 45-68.
Jud, G. Donald. "Real Estate Brokers And The Market For Residential Housing," (1), 69-82.
Weinrobe, Maurice D. "Home Equity Conversion Instruments With Fixed Term To Maturity: Alternatives To End Of Term Pay-Off," (1), 83-96.
Bloom David E., Beth Preiss and James Trussell. "Mortgage Lending Discrimination And The Decision To Apply: A Methodological Note," (1), 97-103.
Weicher, John C. "The Report Of The President's Commission On Housing: Policy Proposals For Subsidized Housing," (2), 117-132.
Colton, Kent W. "The Report Of The President's Commission On Housing: The Nation's System Of Housing Finance," (2), 133-165.
Grebler, Leo. "The Commission's Recommendations On Housing Finance," (2), 166-181.
Downs, Anthony. "The President's Housing Commission And Two Tests Of Realistic Recommendations," (2), 182-191.
Wallace, James E. "Direct Household Assistance And Block Grants," (2), 192-202.
Chisholm, Nancy S. "A Future For Public Housing," (2), 203-220.
Clemmer, Richard B. and John C. Weicher. "The Individual Housing Account," (2), 221-236.
Seiders, David S. "Managing Mortgage Interest-Rate Risks In Forward, Futures, And Options Markets," (2), 237-263.
Seiders, David S. "Mortgage Pass-Through Securities: Progress And Prospects," (2), 264-287.
Tuccillo, John A. "The Tax Treatment Of Mortgage Investment," (2), 288-299.
Goldman, Ellis G. and Charles G. Field. "Summary Of An Article On Reforming Land-Use Regulations," (2), 300-318.
Mann, Bruce D. and Michael Veseth. "Moderate Rent Controls: A Microeconomic And Public Choice Analysis," (3), 333-343.
Elliott, Donald S., Jr. and Michael A. Quinn. "Concentrated Housing Code Enforcement In St. Louis," (3), 344-370.
Buser, Stephen A. and Anthony B. Sanders. "Tenure Decisions Under A Progressive Tax Structure," (3), 371-381.
Dale-Johnson, David. "Clientele Effects On The Demand For Housing Price Appreciation," (3), 382-396.
Mark, Jonathan H. "An Empirical Examination Of The Stability Of Housing Price Equations Over Time," (3), 397-415.
Bajic, Vladimir. "Urban Housing Markets Modelling: Short-Run Equilibrium Implications," (3), 416-438.
Gau, George W. and Michael A. Goldberg. "Interest Rate Risk, Residential Mortgages And Financial Futures Markets," (4), 445-461.
Johnson, Linda L. "The Impact Of Real Estate Political Action Committees On Congressional Voting And Elections," (4), 462-475.
Hendershott, Patric H., James D. Shilling and Kevin E. Villani. "Measurement Of The Spreads Between Yields On Various Mortgage Contracts And Treasury Securities," (4), 476-490.
Agarwal, Vinod B. and Richard A. Phillips. "The Effect Of Mortgage Rate Buydowns On Housing Prices: Recent Evidence From FHA-VA Transactions," (4), 491-503.
Hohm, Charles F. "The Reaction Of Landlords To Rent Control," (4), 504-520.
Clauretie, Terrence M. "A Note On The Bias In House Price Capitalization Models," (4), 521-524.
Shear, William B. "A Note On Occupancy Turnover In Rental Housing Units," (4), 525-538.

Journal of the American Real Estate and Urban Economics Association
Volume 12, 1984

Lusht, Kenneth M. and Jeffrey D. Fisher. "Anticipated Growth And The Specification Of Debt In Real Estate Value Models," (1), 1-11.

Peiser, Richard B. "Risk Analysis In Land Development," (1), 12-29.
Mark, Jonathan H. and Michael A. Goldberg. "Alternative Housing Price Indices: An Evaluation," (1), 30-49.
Moore, James S., Alan K. Riechert and Chien-Ching Cho. "Analyzing The Temporal Stability Of Appraisal Model Coefficients: An Application Of Ridge Regression Techniques," (1), 50-71.
Edmonds, Radcliffe G., Jr. "A Theoretical Basis For Hedonic Regression: A Research Primer," (1), 72-85.
Reid, Clifford E. "The Reliability Of Fair Housing Audits To Detect Racial Discrimination In Rental Housing Markets," (1), 86-96.
Vandell, Kerry D. and Robert H. Zerbst. "Estimates Of The Effect Of School Desegregation Plans On Housing Values Over Time," (2), 109-135.
Brueckner, Jan K. "The Flexible Mortgage Optimal Financing Of A Consumer Durable," (2), 136-152.
Smith, Stanley D. and G. Stacy Sirmans. "The Shifting Of FHA Discount Points: Actual Vs. Expectations," (2), 153-161.
Dale-Johnson, David and G. Michael Phillips. "Housing Attributes Associated With Capital Gain," (2), 162-175.
Corgel, John B. and Gerald D. Gay. "The Impact Of GNMA Futures Trading On Cash Market Volatility," (2), 176-190.
Diskin, Barry A. and Armen Tashchian. "Application Of Logit Analysis To The Determination Of Tenant Absorption In Condominium Conversion," (2), 191-205.
Ibbotson, Roger G. and Laurence B. Siegel. "Real Estate Returns: A Comparison With Other Investments," (3), 219-242.
Brennan, Thomas P., Roger E. Cannady and Peter F. Colwell. "Office Rent In The Chicago CBD," (3), 243-260.
Rosen, Kenneth T. "Toward A Model Of The Office Building Sector," (3), 261-269.
Vandell, Kerry D. "On The Assessment Of Default Risk In Commercial Mortgage Lending," (3), 270-296.
Hendershott, Patric H. and David C. Ling. "Prospective Changes In The Tax Law And The Value Of Depreciable Real Estate," (3), 297-317.
Hite, Gailen L., James E. Owers and Ronald C. Rogers. "The Separation Of Real Estate Operations By Spin-Off," (3), 318-331.
Brueckner, Jan K. "Creative Financing And House Prices: A Theoretical Inquiry Into The Capitalization Issue," (4), 417-426.
Sa-Aadu, J. "Another Look At The Economics Of Demand-Side Versus Supply-Side Strategies In Low-Income Housing," (4), 427-460.
Whinihan, Michael J. "Condominium Conversion And The Tax Reform Acts Of 1969 And 1976," (4), 461-472.
Ozanne, Larry. "The Financial Stakes In Due-On-Sale: The Case Of California's State-Chartered Savings And Loans," (4), 473-494.
Webb, James R. "Real Estate Investment Acquisition Rules For Life Insurance Companies And Pension Funds: A Survey," (4), 495-520.
Srivastava, R. K., H. R. Isakson, L. Price and T. H. McInish. "Analysis Of The Characteristics Of Individual Investors In Real Estate Securities And Income-Producing Property," (4), 521-541.

**Journal of the American Real Estate
and Urban Economics Association
Volume 13, 1985**

Goldberg, Michael A. "American Real Estate And Urban Economics: A Canadian Perspective," (1), 1-14.
Gau, George W. "Public Information And Abnormal Returns In Real Estate Investment," (1), 15-31.
Hekman, John S. "Rental Price Adjustment And Investment In The Office Market," (1), 32-47.
Agarwal, Vinod B. and Richard A. Philips. "The Effects Of Assumption Financing Across Housing Price Categories," (1), 48-57.
Bajic, Vladimir. "Housing-Market Segmentation And Demand For Housing Attributes: Some Empirical Findings," (1), 58-75.
Ostas, James R. "Reduced Form Coefficients, Structural Coefficients, And Mortgage Redlining," (1), 76-92.
Berry, Thomas D. and Adam K. Gehr, Jr. "FNMA Mortgage Purchase Commitments As Put Options: An Empirical Examination," (1), 93-105.
Kau, James B., Donald C. Keenan, Walter J. Muller, III and James F. Epperson. "Rational Pricing Of Adjustable Rate Mortgages," (2), 117-128.
Brueckner, Jan K. "A Simple Model Of Mortgage Insurance," (2), 129-142.
Benjamin, John D., James D. Shilling and C. F. Sirmans. "Contracts As Options: Some Evidence From Condominium Developments," (2), 143-152.
Rogers, Ronald C. and James E. Owers. "The Investment Of Performance Of Public Real Estate Limited Partnerships," (2), 153-166.
Lee, Cheng F. and Morgan J. Lynge, Jr. "Return, Risk And Cost Of Equity For Stock S&L Firms: Theory And Empirical Results," (2), 167-180.
Ling, David C. and Michael J. Whinihan. "Valuing Depreciable Real Estate: A New Methodology," (2), 181-194.
Harris, John M., Jr. and Daniel E. Page. "Rate Level Index Mortgage: An Evaluation," (2), 195-207.
Brennan, Michael J. and Eduardo S. Schwartz. "Determinants Of GNMA Mortgage Prices," (3), 209-228.
Hall, Arden R. "Valuing The Mortgage Borrower's Prepayment Option," (3), 229-247.
Buser, Stephen A., Patric H. Hendershott and Anthony B. Sanders. "Pricing Life Of Loan Rate Caps On Default-Free Adjustable-Rate Mortgages," (3), 248-260.
Epperson, James F., James B. Kau, Donald C. Keenan and Walter J. Muller, III. "Pricing Default Risk In Mortgages," (3), 261-272.
Foster, Chester and Robert Van Order. "FHA Terminations: A Prelude To Rational Mortgage Pricing," (3), 273-291.
Vandell, Kerry D. and Thomas Thibodeau. "Estimation Of Mortgage Defaults Using Disaggregate Loan History Data," (3), 292-316.
Hendershott, Patric H. and James D. Shilling. "Valuing ARM Rate Caps: Implications of 1970-84 Interest Rate Behavior," (3), 317-332.
Peiser, Richard B. and Lawrence B. Smith. "Homeownership Returns, Tenure Choice And Inflation," (4), 343-360.

Asabere, Paul K. and Barrie Harvey. "Factors Influencing The Value Of Urban Land: Evidence From Halifax-Dartmouth, Canada," (4), 361-377.
Guy, Donald C., John L. Hysom and Stephen R. Ruth. "The Effect Of Subsidized Housing On Values Of Adjacent Housing," (4), 378-387.
Dale-Johnson, David, M. Chapman Findlay, Arthur L. Schwartz, Jr. and Stephen D. Kapplin. "Valuation And Efficiency In The Market For Creatively Financed Houses," (4), 388-403.
Solt, Michael E. and Norman G. Miller. "Managerial Incentives: Implications For The Financial Performance Of Real Estate Investment Trusts," (4), 404-423.
Elliott, Donald S., Jr., Michael A. Quinn and Robert E. Mendelson. "Maintenance Behavior Of Large-Scale Landlords And Theories Of Neighborhood Succession," (4), 424-445.
Epley, Donald R., Timothy P. Cronan and Larry Perry. "A Research Note On Discrimination In Mortgage Lending," (4), 446-451.
Jud, G. Donald. "A Further Note On Schools And Housing Values," (4), 452-462.

**Journal of the American Real Estate
and Urban Economics Association
Volume 14, 1986**

Wu, Chunchi and Peter F. Colwell. "Equilibrium Of Housing And Real Estate Brokerage Markets Under Uncertainty," (1), 1-23.
Zorn, Thomas S. and James E. Larsen. "The Incentive Effects Of Flat-Fee And Percentage Commissions For Real Estate Brokers," (1), 24-47.
Boehm, Thomas P. and Keith R. Ihlanfeldt. "The Improvement Expenditures Of Urban Homeowners: An Empirical Analysis," (1), 48-60.
Vitaliano, Donald F. "Measuring The Efficiency Cost Of Rent Control," (1), 61-72.
Jackson, John D., Charlotte A. Jones and Philip W. Balsmeir. "An Empirical Analysis Of Tenant Selection Under Federal Rent Supplement Programs: A First Step," (1), 72-90.
Zumpano, Leonard V., Patricia M. Rudolph and David C. Cheng. "The Demand And Supply Of Mortgage Funds And Mortgage Loan Terms," (1), 91-109.
Anderson, Dan and Maurice Weinrobe. "Mortgage Default Risks And The 1971 San Fernando Earthquake," (1), 110-135.
Reichert, Alan K. and James S. Moore. "Using Latent Root Regression To Identify Nonpredictive Collinearity In Statistical Appraisal Models," (1), 136-152.
Dale-Johnson, David and M. Chapman Findlay. "Creative Financing And Housing Prices: A Comment On A Theoretical Inquiry Into The Capitalization Issue," (1), 153-157.
Brueckner, Jan K. "Creative Financing And Housing Prices: Reply," (1), 158-162.
Nourse, Hugh O. "Comment On Rental Price Adjustment And Investment In The Office Market," (1), 163-164.
Lusht, Kenneth M. "Real Estate Valuation And Appraisal," (2), 175-178.
Blackley, Dixie M., James R. Follain and Haeduck Lee. "An Evaluation Of Hedonic Price Indexes For 34 Large SMSAs," (2), 179-205.
Beaton, William and C. F. Sirmans. "Do Syndications Pay More For Real Estate?," (2), 206-215.
Chiang, Raymond, Tsong-Yue Lai and David C. Ling. "Retail Leasehold Interests: A Contingent Claim Analysis," (2), 216-229.
Hartzell, David, John Hekman and Mike Miles. "Diversification Categories In Investment Real Estate," (2), 230-254.
Cannaday, Roger E. and Mark A. Sunderman. "Estimation Of Depreciation For Single-Family Appraisals," (2), 255-273.
Isakson, Hans R. "The Nearest Neighbors Appraisal Technique: An Alternative To The Adjustment Grid Methods," (2), 274-286.
Fisher, Jeffrey D. and George H. Lentz. "Tax Reform And The Value Of Real Estate Income Property," (2), 287-315.
Cannaday, Roger E. and Peter F. Colwell. "Real Estate Valuation Models: Lender And Equity Investor Criteria," (2), 316-337.
Clauretie, Terrence M. and Melvin W. Harju. "The Expanding Concept Of Just Compensation And The Role Of The Appraiser," (2), 338-360.
Kowalski, Joseph G. and Peter F. Colwell. "Market Versus Assessed Values Of Industrial Land," (2), 361-373.
Frew, James R. and G. Donald Jud. "The Value Of A Real Estate Franchise," (2), 374-383.
Bosch, Jean-Claude, James R. Morris and Steve B. Wyatt. "The Investment In Housing As A Forward Market Transaction: Implications For Tenure Choice And Portfolio Selection," (3), 385-405.
Barney, L. Dwayne and Harry White. "The Optimal Mortgage Payment Path Under Price Uncertainty," (3), 406-413.
Titman, Sheridan and Arthur Warga. "Risk And The Performance Of Real Estate Investment Trusts: A Multiple Index Approach," (3), 414-431.
Lea, Michael J. and Peter M. Zorn. "Adjustable-Rate Mortgages, Economic Fluctuations, And Lender Portfolio Change," (3), 432-447.
Schnitzel, Paul. "Do Deposit Rates Cause Mortgage Loan Rates?: The Evidence From Causality Tests," (3), 448-464.
Webb, James R. and Jack H. Rubens. "Portfolio Considerations In The Valuation Of Real Estate," (3), 465-495.
Hendershott, Patric H. "Mortgage Pricing: What Have We Learned So Far?," (4), 497-509.
Rosen, Kenneth T. and Lawrence B. Smith. "The Resale Housing Market," (4), 510-524.
Fortura, Peter and Joseph Kushner. "Canadian Inter-City House Price Differentials," (4), 525-536.
Leppel, Karen. "A Trinomial Logit Analysis Of Household Composition," (4), 537-556.
Goodman, John L., Jr. "Reducing The Error In Monthly Housing Starts Estimates," (4), 557-566.
Johnson, Linda L. and Christine Loucks. "The Effect Of State Licensing Regulations On The Real Estate Brokerage Industry," (4), 567-582.
Colwell, Peter F. and David W. Marshall. "Market Share In The Real Estate Brokerage Industry," (4), 583-599.

Journal of the American Real Estate and Urban Economics Association
Volume 15, 1987

Mills, Edwin S. "Has The United States Overinvested In Housing?," (1), 601-616.

Hartzell, David, John S. Hekman and Mike E. Miles. "Real Estate Returns And Inflation," (1), 617-637.

Goodman, John L., Jr. "Housing And The Weather," (1), 638-663.

Melchert, David and Joel L. Naroff. "Central City Revitalization: A Predictive Model," (1), 664-683.

Moore, James S. "An Investigation Of The Major Influences Of Residential Liquidity: A Multivariate Approach," (1), 684-703.

Newman, Sandra and James Reschovsky. "An Evaluation Of The One-Time Capital Gains Exclusion For Older Homeowners," (1), 704-724.

Buckley, Robert M. and John Simonson. "Effective Property Tax Rates And Capital Formation Issues: Manvel, Acton And Darby," (1), 725-738.

Johnson, Larry J. and Larry E. Wofford. "On Contracts As Options: Some Evidence From Condominium Developments," (1), 739-741.

Shilling, James D., C. F. Sirmans and John D. Benjamin. "On Option-Pricing Models In Real Estate: A Critique," (1), 742-752.

Gau, George W. "Efficient Real Estate Markets: Paradox Or Paradigm?," (2), 1-12.

Walden, Michael L. "Effects Of Housing Codes On Local Housing Markets," (2), 13-31.

Tanzer, Ellen P. "Housing Quality And The Structure Tax: Evidence From Microdata," (2), 32-45.

Pantalone, Colleen C. and Marjorie B. Platt. "Predicting Failure Of Savings And Loan Associations," (2), 46-64.

Weinrobe, Maurice. "An Analysis Of Home Equity Conversion In The RAM Program," (2), 65-78.

Park, Hun Y. and Anil K. Bera. "Interest-Rate Volatility, Basis Risk And Heteroscedasticity In Hedging Mortgages," (2), 79-97.

Guntermann, Karl L. and Richard L. Smith. "Derivation Of Cost Of Capital And Equity Rates From Market Data," (2), 98-109.

Smith, Donald J. "The Borrower's Choice Between Fixed And Adjustable Rate Loan Contracts," (2), 110-115.

Kim, Taewon. "A Contingent Claims Analysis Of Price Level-Adjusted Mortgages," (2), 117-131.

Sa-Aadu, J. "Consumer Welfare Under The Adjustable Rate Mortgage: Some Empirical Evidence," (3), 132-151.

Clauretie, Terrence M. "The Impact Of Interstate Foreclosure Cost Differences And The Value Of Mortgages On Default Rates," (3), 152-167.

Kau, James B. and Donald Keenan. "Taxes, Points And Rationality In The Mortgage Market," (3), 168-184.

Archer, Wayne R. and David J. Nye. "An Insurance Apporach To Risk Analysis Of Debt Home Equity Conversion Programs," (3), 185-198.

Grissom, Terry V., David Hartzell and Crocker H. Liu. "An Approach To Industrial Real Estate Market Segmentation And Valuation Using The Arbitrage Pricing Paradigm," (3), 199-219.

Rayburn, William, Michael Devaney and Richard Evans. "A Test Of Weak-Form Efficiency In Residential Real Estate Returns," (3), 220-233.

Kling, John L. and Thomas E. McCue. "Office Building Investment And The Macroeconomy: Empirical Evidence, 1973-1985," (3), 234-255.

Corgel, John B. and Gerald D. Gay. "Local Economic Base, Geographic Diversification, And Risk Management Of Mortgage Portfolios," (3), 256-267.

Gabriel, Stuart A. "Economic Effects Of Racial Integration: An Analysis Of Hedonic Housing Prices And The Willingness To Pay," (3), 268-279.

Wheaton, Willam C. "The Cyclic Behavior Of The National Office Market," (4), 281-299.

Kent, Richard J. "Dynamic Credit Rationing In The Home Mortgage Market," (4), 300-320.

Guntermann, Karl L. and Stefan Norrbin. "Explaining The Variability Of Apartment Rents," (4), 321-340.

Huffman, Forrest E. and Arthur E. Warner. "Toward The Development Of An Urban Growth Model That Recognizes The Importance Of The Basic Nature Of Services," (4), 341-358.

Harris, Curtis C., Jr. and Virginia D. McConnell. "Surpluses In Disequilibrium Urban Land Markets," (4), 359-373.

Sklarz, Michael A., Norman G. Miller and Will Gersch. "Forecasting Using Long-Order Autoregressive Processes: An Example Using Housing Starts," (4), 374-388.

Lerman, Donald L. and William J. Reeder. "The Affordability Of Adequate Housing," (4), 389-404.

Journal of the American Real Estate and Urban Economics Association
Volume 16, 1988

Zumpano, Leonard V. and Donald L. Hooks. "The Real Estate Brokerage Market: A Critical Reevaluation," (1), 1-16.

Rudolph, Patricia M. and Bassum Hamden. "An Analysis Of Post-Deregulation Savings-And-Loan Failures," (1), 17-33.

Houston, Arthur L., Jr. "A Comparison Of The Reinvestment Risk Of The Price Level Adjusted Mortgage And The Standard Fixed Payment Mortgage," (1), 34-49.

Edmister, Robert O. and Harry E. Merriken. "Pricing Efficiency In The Mortgage Market," (1), 50-62.

Kapplin, Steven D. and Arthur L. Schwartz, Jr. "Public Real Estate Limited Partnership Returns: A Preliminary Comparison With Other Investments," (1), 63-68.

Ault, Richard W. and Robert B. Ekelund, Jr. "Rent Seeking In A Static Model Of Zoning," (1), 69-76.

Giliberto, S. Michael. "A Note On The Use Of Appraisal Data In Indexes Of Performance Measurement," (1), 77-83.

Ford, Deborah Ann and Michele Gilligan. "The Effect Of Lead Point Abatement Laws On Rental Property Values," (1), 84-94.

Lusht, Kenneth M. "The Real Estate Pricing Puzzle," (2), 95-104.

Ravichandran, R. and J. Sa-Aadu. "Resource Combination And Security Price Reactions: The Case Of Real Estate Joint Ventures," (2), 105-122.

Webb, James R. and Jack H. Rubens. "The Effect Of Alternative Return Measures On Restricted Mixed-Asset Portfolios," (2), 123-137.

Nelson, Theron R. and Joseph Rabianski. "Consumer Preferences In Housing Market Analysis: An Application Of Multidimensional Scaling Techniques," (2), 138-159.

Heuson, Andrea J. "Managing The Short-Term Interest Rate Exposure Inherent In Adjustable Rate Mortgage Loans," (2), 160-172.

Miceli, Thomas J. "Information Costs And The Organization Of The Real Estate Brokerage Industry In The U.S. And Great Britain," (2), 173-188.

Kinnard, William N., Herman G. Berkman, Hugh O. Nourse and John C. Weicher. "The First Twenty Years Of AREUEA," (2), 189-205.

Follain, James R. and David C. Ling. "Another Look At Tenure Choice, Inflation, And Taxes," (3), 207-229.

Jaffe, Austin J. "Toward An Evolutionary Theory Of Trade Associations: The Case Of Real Estate Appraisers," (3), 230-256.

Sa-Aadu, J. and James D. Shilling. "Ranking Of Contributing Authors To The AREUEA Journal By Doctoral Origin And Employer," (3), 257-270.

Hendershott, Patric H. and Donald R. Haurin. "Adjustments In The Real Estate Market," (4), 343-353.

Read, Colin. "Advertising And Natural Vacancies In Rental Housing Markets," (4), 354-363.

Hendershott, Patric H. and Marc T. Smith. "Housing Inventory Change And The Role Of Existing Structures, 1961-1985," (4), 364-378.

Read, Colin. "Price Strategies For Idiosyncratic Goods - The Case Of Housing," (4), 379-395.

Haurin, Donald. "The Duration Of Marketing Time Of Residential Housing," (4), 396-410.

Reece, B. F. "The Price-Adjustment Process For Rental Housing: Some Further Evidence," (4), 411-418.

Gabriel, Stuart A. and Frank E. Nothaft. "Rental Housing Markets And The Natural Vacancy Rate," (4), 419-429.

Wheaton, William C. and Raymond G. Torto. "Vacancy Rates And The Future Of Office Rents," (4), 430-436.

Voith, Richard and Theodore Crone. "National Vacancy Rates And The Persistence Of Shocks In U.S. Office Markets," (4), 437-458.

Harmon, Oskar R. and Michael J. Potepan. "Housing Adjustment Costs: Their Impact On Mobility And Housing Demand Elasticities," (4), 459-478.

Ziegert, A. L. "The Demand For Housing Additions: An Empirical Analysis," (4), 479-492.

Journal of the American Real Estate and Urban Economics Association
Volume 17, 1989

Zorn, Peter M. "Mobility-Tenure Decisions And Financial Credit: Do Mortgage Qualification Requirements Constrain Home Ownership?," (1), 1-16.

Jones, Lawrence D. "Current Wealth And Tenure Choice," (1), 17-40.

Delaney, Charles J. and Marc T. Smith. "The Price Effect Of Impact Fees And The Price On New Housing: An Empirical Study," (1), 41-54.

Giliberto, S. Michael and Arthur L. Houston, Jr. "Relocation Opportunities And Mortgage Default," (1), 55-69.

Guilkey, David, Mike Miles and Rebel Cole. "The Motivation For Institutional Real Estate Sales And Implications For Asset Class Returns," (1), 70-86.

Francois, Joseph F. "Estimating Homeownership Costs: Owners' Estimates Of Implicit Rents And The Relative Importance Of Rental Equivalence In The Consumer Price Index," (1), 87-99.

Thibodeau, Thomas G. "Housng Price Indexes From The 1974-83 SMSA Annual Housing Surveys," (1), 100-117.

Zorn, Peter M. and Michael J. Lea. "Mortgage Borrower Repayment Behavior: A Microeconomic Analysis With Canadian Adjustable Rate Mortgage Data," (1), 118-136.

Geltner, David. "On The Use Of The Financial Option Price Model To Value And Explain Vacant Urban Land," (2), 142-158.

Capozza, Dennis R. and Gregory M. Schwann. "The Asset Approach To Pricing Urban Land: Empirical Evidence," (2), 161-174.

Smith, Bruce D. and Michael J. Stutzer. "Credit Rationing And Government Loan Programs: A Welfare Analysis," (2), 177-193.

Mills, Edwin S. "Social Returns To Housing And Other Fixed Capital," (2), 197-211.

Quan, Daniel C. and John M. Quigley. "Inferring An Investment Return Series For Real Estate From Observations On Sales," (2), 218-230.

Vandell, Kerry D. and Jonathan S. Lane. "The Economics Of Architecture And Urban Design: Some Preliminary Findings," (2), 235-260.

Miceli, Thomas J. "The Optimal Duration Of Real Estate Listing Contracts," (3), 267-277.

Chen, Andrew and David Ling. "Optimal Mortgage Refinancing With Stochastic Interest Rates," (3), 278-299.

Cammarota, Mark. "The Impact Of Unseasonable Weather On Housing Starts," (3), 300-313.

Lentz, George H. and Jeffrey D. Fisher. "Tax Reform And Organizational Forms For Holding Investment Real Estate: Corporation Vs. Partnership," (3), 314-337.

Geltner, David. "Bias In Appraisal-Based Returns," (3), 338-352.

Ford, Deborah Ann. "The Effect Of Historic District Designation On Single-Family Home Prices," (3), 353-362.

Mays, Elizabeth and Edward J. DeMarco. "The Demand For Federal Home Loan Bank Advances By Thrift Institutions: Some Recent Evidence," (3), 363-379.

Linneman, Peter and Susan Wachter. "The Impacts Of Borrowing Constraints On Homeownership," (4), 389-402.

Miceli, Thomas J. "Housing Rental Contracts And Adverse Selection With An Application To The Rent-Own Decision," (4), 403-421.

Larsen, James E. and Won J. Park. "Non-Uniform Percentage Brokerage Commissions And Real Estate Market Performance," (4), 422-438.

Wheaton, William C. and Raymond G. Torto. "Income And Appraised Values: A Reexamination Of The FRC Returns Data," (4), 439-449.

Rudolph, Patricia M. "The Insolvent Thrifts Of 1982: Where Are They Now?," (4), 450-462.

Geltner, David. "Estimating Real Estate's Systematic Risk From Aggregate Level Appraisal-Based Returns," (4), 463-481.

Journal of the American Real Estate and Urban Economics Association
Volume 18, 1990

Goodman, Allen C. "Modeling And Computing Transactions Costs For Purchasers Of Housing Services," (1), 1-21.

Maris, Brian A. and Fayez A. Elayan. "Capital Structure And The Cost Of Capital For Untaxed Firms: The Case Of REITS," (1), 22-39.

Gau, George W. and Ko Wang. "A Further Examination Of Appraisal Data And The Potential Bias In Real Estate Return Indexes," (1), 40-48.

Liu, Crocker H., David J. Hartzell, Terry V. Grissom and Wylie Grieg. "The Composition Of The Market Portfolio And Real Estate Investment Performance," (1), 49-75.

Crockett, John H. "Workouts, Deep Pockets, And Fire Sales: An Analysis Of Distressed Real Estate," (1), 76-90.

Leung, Wai K. and C. F. Sirmans. "A Lattice Approach To Fixed-Rate Mortgage Pricing With Default And Prepayment Options," (1), 91-104.

Glascock, John L., Shirin Jahanian and C. F. Sirmans. "An Analysis Of Office Market Rents: Some Empirical Evidence," (1), 105-120.

Follain, James R. "Mortgage Choice," (2), 125-144.

Kluger, Brian D. and Norman G. Miller. "Measuring Residential Real Estate Liquidity," (2), 145-159.

Reschovsky, James D. "Residential Immobility Of The Elderly: An Empirical Investigation," (2), 160-183.

Rosenberg, Sidney B. and John B. Corgel. "Agency Costs In Property Management Contracts," (2), 184-201.

Clauretie, Terrence M. "A Note On Mortgage Risk: Default Vs. Loss Rates," (2), 202-206.

Ma, Christopher K. "Mean Reversions In GNMA Returns," (2), 207-226.

Quigley, John M. and Robert Van Order. "Efficiency In The Mortgage Market: The Borrower's Perspective," (3), 237-252.

Case, Karl E. and Robert J. Shiller. "Forecasting Prices And Excess Returns In The Housing Market," (3), 253-273.

Clapp, John M. "A Methodology For Constructing Vacant Land Price Indices," (3), 274-293.

Jud, G. Donald and James Frew. "Atypicality And The Natural Vacancy Rate Hypothesis," (3), 294-301.

Benjamin, John D., Glenn W. Boyle and C. F. Sirmans. "Retail Leasing: The Determinants Of Shopping Center Rents," (3), 302-312.

O'Keef, Michael and Robert Van Order. "Mortgage Pricing: Some Provisional Empirical Results," (3), 313-322.

Hendershott, Patric H. and Thomas G. Thibodeau. "The Relationship Between Median And Constant Quality House Prices: Implications For Setting FHA Loan Limits," (3), 323-334.

White, Michelle J. "Commuting And Congestion: A Simulation Model Of A Decentralized Metropolitan Area," (3), 335-368.

Hendershott, Patric H. and Donald R. Haurin. "Research On Real Estate Investment," (4), 369-376.

Geltner, David. "Return Risk And Cash Flow Risk With Long-Term Riskless Leases In Commercial Real Estate," AREUEA, 1990, v18(4), 377-402.

Miles, Mike, Rebel Cole and David Guikey. "A Different Look At Commercial Real Estate Returns," (4), 403-430.

Chan, K. C., Patric H. Hendershott and Anthony B. Sanders. "Risk And Return On Real Estate: Evidence From Equity REITs," (4), 431-452.

Liu, Crocker H., Terry V. Grissom and David J. Hartzell. "The Impact Of Market Imperfections On Real Estate Returns And Optimal Investment Portfolios," (4), 453-478.

Howe, James S. and James D. Shilling. "REIT Advisor Performance," (4), 479-500.

Gau, George W. and Ko Wang. "Capital Structure Decisions In Real Estate Investment," (4), 501-521.

Rutherford, Ronald C. "Empirical Evidence On Shareholder Value And The Sale-Leaseback Of Corporate Real Estate," (4), 522-529.

Wheaton, William C. and Raymond G. Torto. "An Investment Model Of The Demand And Supply For Industrial Real Estate," (4), 530-547.

JOURNAL OF APPLIED CORPORATE FINANCE

Shapiro, Alan C. "The Economic Import Of Europe 1992," (4), 25-36.

Bland, Christopher, Manfred Klein, Henri Blanchet and Christian Moretti. "Perspectives On Restructuring In Europe: Interviews With Four European Executives," (4), 37-45.

Wright, Mike, Ken Robbie and Steve Thompson. "Corporate Restructuring, Buy-Outs, And Managerial Equity: The European Dimension," (4), 46-58.

Lessard, Donald R. "Global Competition And Corporate Finance In The 1900s," (4), 59-72.

Pringle, John J. "Managing Foreign Exchange Exposure," (4), 73-82.

Millman, Gregory J. "Financing The Uncreditworthy: New Financial Structures For LDCs," (4), 83-89.

Kester, W. Carl. "The Hidden Costs Of Japanese Success," (4), 90-97.

Ohmae, Kenichi. "'Lies, Damned Lies, And Statistics': Why The Trade Deficit Doesn't Matter In A Borderless World," (4), 98-106.

JOURNAL OF BANK RESEARCH

Journal of Bank Research
Volume 1, 1970/71

McQuown, J. A. "Research: Building An Effective Trilogy," (1), 7-12.

Cohen, Kalman J. "Improving The Capital Adequacy Formula," (1), 13-16.

Pogue, Gerald A. "An Inter-Temporal Model For Investment Management," (1), 17-34.

Gray, Kenneth B., Jr. "Managing The Balance Sheet: A Mathematical Approach To Decision Making," (1), 35-42.

Cohen, Kalman J. and Sten Thore. "Programming Bank Portfolios Under Uncertainty," (1), 43-61.

Eisenbeis, R. A. "A Study Of Geographic Banking Markets For Business Loans," (1), 62-63.

Vandeven, William J. "Bank Communication Standards Research," (1), 63-64.

Boughton, James M. "Econometric Models: A Decision Making Tool For Bank Management," (2), 9-19.

Strawser, Robert H. "Trends In The Financial Reporting Practices Of Commercial Banks," (2), 20-29.

Kramer, Robert L. "Arbitrage In U.S. Government Bonds: A Management Science Approach," (2), 30-44.

Cohen, Bruce C. "Economies Of Scale And Cash Balances," (2), 45-48.

Crane, Dwight B. "Marketing Strategy And Bank Service Interaction," (2), 49-56.

Murphy, Neil B. "Banking Research: Objectives Goals And Priorities," (2), 57-59.

Miller, F. Byers. "Research In The 1970's," (2), 59-60.

Waterman, Robert H., Jr. and William D. Clendenin. "Problem Solving For Commercial Banks," (2), 60-62.

Fenner, Linda M. "Payment Services In Transition," (2), 62-63.

Black, Fischer. "Banking And Interest Rates In A World Without Money: The Effects Of Uncontrolled Banking," (3), 8-20.

Poor, Riva. "4-Days, 40-Hours: Reporting A Revolution In Work And Leisure," (3), 21-28.

Horton, Joseph J., Jr. "Statistical Classification Of Municipal Bonds," (3), 29-40.

Slocum, John W., Jr. and Robert H. Strawser. "The Impact Of Job Level, Geographical Location And Organizational Size On The Managerial Satisfaction Of Bankers," (3), 41-49.

Kraus, Alan, Christian Janssen and Alan McAdams. "The Lock-Box Location Problem," (3), 50-58.

Reich, Kenneth E., Kenneth B. Gray, Jr. and Wolfgang P. Hochenwarter. "Balance Sheet Management: A Simulation Approach," (3), 59-62.

Towey, Richard E. "The Prohibition Of Interest On Demand Deposits," (4), 8-16.

Kramer, Robert L. "Forecasting Branch Bank Growth Patterns," (4), 17-24.

Weinberg, Eli. "Solving The Paper Crisis In The Security Industry," (4), 25-40.

Cohen, Kalman J. and David P. Rutenberg. "Toward A Comprehensive Framework For Bank Financial Planning," (4), 41-57.

Budzeika, George. "A Model Of Business Loan Behavior Of Large New York City Banks," (4), 58-72.

Journal of Bank Research
Volume 2, 1971/72

Van Fenstermaker, J. and Donald Perry. "An Examination Of A Charge Card System Operating In A Smaller Community Through Correspondent Banks," (1), 9-13.

Jacobs, Donald P., Eugene M. Lerner and Joseph S. Moag. "Guidelines For Designing Bank Planning Models And Information Systems," (1), 14-24.

Williams, George P., Jr. "An Incentive Plan For Bank Managed Pension Funds," (1), 25-30.

Orgler, Yair E. "Evaluation Of Bank Consumer Loans With Credit Scoring Models," (1), 31-37.

Komar, Robert L. "Developing A Liquidity Management Model," (1), 38-53.

Kramer, Robert L. "The Lock Box Problem: Comment," (1), 54-55.

Fenner, Linda M. "The Status Of Payment Services Today," (1), 60-68.

Lastavica, John. "Asset Management And Other Financial Simulation Models," (1), 69-70.

Gilbert, Gary G. and Neil B. Murphy. "Competition Between Thrift Institutions And Commercial Banks: An Examination Of The Evidence," (2), 8-18.

Neave, Edwin H. and David C. Nachman. "A Framework For Evaluating Securities Performance Forecasts," (2), 19-29.

Eisenbeis, Robert A. "Local Banking Markets For Business Loans," (2), 30-39.

Walsh, Cornelius F. and Gail Simonton. "The Confidence Index As A Stock Market Indicator," (2), 40-44.

Ramsey, David D. and Paul E. Smith. "Relative Lags In The Effect Of Monetary And Fiscal Policy," (2), 45-55.

Hochenwarter, Wolfgang P. "Guidelines For The Development Of Problem Oriented Software Systems," (2), 56-59.

Bower, Richard S. and David H. Downes. "The Time-Sharing Decision In Banking," (3), 9-21.

Chandross, Robert H. "The Impact Of New Bank Entry On Unit Banks In One Bank Towns," (3), 22-30.

Mathieson, Robert F. "Input-Output: A Tool For Investment Research," (3), 31-38.

Hooper, Carolyn N. "SBA's Business Loan Program: Retrospect And Prospect," (3), 39-49.

White, George C., Jr. "Reducing The Flow Of Stock Certificates By Use Of A Depository: Comment," (3), 50-54.

Stansell, Stanley R. "Some Further Comments On The Confidence Index," (3), 55-57.

Gray, Kenneth B., Jr. "Measuring Investment Performance: The Time-Weighted Rate - Appropriate Measure Of Manager Performance," (3), 58-60.

Murphy, Neil B. "A Statistical Approach To Determining The Weights To Be Assigned Activity Items In The Demand Deposit Function," (3), 61-63.

Cohen, Kalman J. "Dynamic Balance Sheet Management: A Management Science Approach," (4), 9-19.

Mathews, H. Lee and John W. Slocum, Jr. "Correlatives Of Commercial Bank Credit Card Use," (4), 20-27.

Booth, G. Geoffrey. "Programming Bank Portfolios Under Uncertainty: An Extension," (4), 28-40.

Eisenbeis, Robert A. "Nonlocal Banking Markets For Business Loans," (4), 41-47.

Strawser, Robert H. "A Comparative Study Of Perceived Adequacy Of Financial Reporting Practices Of Commercial Banks," (4), 48-58.

Benston, George J. "Banking And A World Without Money: Comment," (4), 59-61.

Shanker, Roy J. and Andris A. Zoltners. "An Extension Of The Lock-Box Location Problem: Comment," (4), 62.

Journal of Bank Research
Volume 3, 1972/73

Benston, George J. "Overdraft Banking: Its Implications For Monetary Policy, The Commercial Banking Industry & Individual Banks," (1), 7-25.

Kaufman, George G. "The Thrift Institution Problem Reconsidered," (1), 26-33.

Watson, Ronald D. "Tests Of Maturity Structures Of Commercial Bank Government Securities Portfolios: A Simulation Approach," (1), 34-46.

Shanker, Roy J. and Andris A. Zoltners. "The Corporate Payment Problem," (1), 47-53.

Dince, Robert R. and James C. Fortson. "The Use Of Discriminant Analysis To Predict The Capital Adequacy Of Commercial Banks," (1), 54-62.

Rao, M. R. and H. Martin. "A Note On Optimal Municipal Bond Coupon Schedules: Maximum Difference Between The Highest And Lowest Coupon," (1), 63-64.

Meltzer, Allan H. "Aggregative Consequences Of Removing Restrictions," (2), 72-83.

Derwa, Leon. "Computer Models: Aids To Management At Societe Generale De Banque," (2), 84-94.

Herbst, Anthony F. "Truth In Lending, Regulaton Z: Comments On Closed-End Contract Interest Rate Disclosure Requirements," (2), 95-101.

Wagner, W. H. and S. R. Quay. "New Concepts In Portfolio Management," (2), 102-110.

Williamson, J. Peter. "Mortgage Loan Extensions After An Interest Rate Change: A Problem In Blended Interest Rates," (2), 111-117.

Sullivan, John L., Jr. "Current Trends In The Reduction Of Stock Certificates," (2), 118-122.

Brenner, Vincent C. and Paul E. Dascher. "Bankers' Views Of Reporting Current Cost Information," (2), 123-126.

Hosemann, Michael J. "Measuring The Impact Of Electronic Funds Transfer Systems On Float," (3), 136-154.

Boorman, John T. and Manferd Peterson. "The Hunt Commission & The Mortgage Market: An Appraisal," (3), 155-165.

Smith, Keith V. and Maurice B. Goudzwaard. "The Profitability Of Bank Trust Management," (3), 166-177.

Hagerman, Robert L. "The Value Of Regulation F: An Empirical Test," (3), 178-185.

Watson, Hugh J. and H. William Vronen. "A Heuristic Model For Processing Overdrafts," (3), 186-188.

Mason, Joseph Barry and Morris L. Mayer. "Consumer Perceptions Of Affiliated Banking," (3), 189-191.

Durand, David. "Indices Of Profitability As Aids To Judgment In Capital Budgeting," (4), 200-219.

Benston, George J. "The Optimal Banking Structure: Theory And Evidence," (4), 220-237.

McWilliams, James D. "A Closer Look At Incentive Fees For Bank Managed Pension Funds," (4), 238-246.

Murray, Roger F. "Pension Funds: Newest Among Major Financial Institutions," (4), 247-260.

Richardson, Dennis W. "The Emerging Era Of Electronic Money: Some Implications For Monetary Policy," (4), 261-264.

White, Douglas and Arch G. Woodside. "Marketing In Banking: Philosophies And Actions," (4), 265-268.

Journal of Bank Research
Volume 4, 1973/74

McQuown, J. A. "Technical And Fundamental Analysis And Capital Market Theory," (1), 8-17.

Bradley, Stephen P. and Dwight B. Crane. "Management Of Commercial Bank Government Security Portfolios: An Optimization Approach Under Uncertainty," (1), 18-30.

Nicholson, Edward A. and Robert L. Litschert. "Long-Range Planning In Banking: Ten Cases In The U.S. And Britain," (1), 31-40.

Mayne, Lucille S. "The Deposit Reserve Requirement Recommendations Of The Commission On Financial Structure & Regulation: An Analysis And Critique," (1), 41-51.

Snider, Thomas E. "The Effect Of Merger On The Lending Behavior Of Rural Unit Banks In Virginia," (1), 52-57.

Johnson, Rodney D. and David R. Meinster. "The Analysis Of Bank Holding Company Acquisitions: Some Methodological Issues," (1), 58-61.

Zwick, Charles J. "Strategic Planning And Its Role In The Banking Environment Of The Seventies," (2), 74-78.

Johnson, Herbert E. "Strategic Planning For Banks," (2), 79-83.

Moag, Joseph S. "Strategic Planning In Banks - A Behavioral Science Perspective," (2), 84-92.

Long, Robert H. "Planning For Tomorrow's Customer," (2), 93-99.

Levy, Sidney J. "Consumer Views Of Bank Services," (2), 100-104.

Falkenberg, John F. "The Sources Of Bank Profitability," (2), 105-110.

Boyd, John H. "Bank Strategies In The Retail Demand Deposit Markets," (2), 111-121.

Cramer, Robert H. and Robert B. Miller. "Development Of A Deposit Forcasting Procedure For Use In Bank Financial Management," (2), 122-138.

Longbrake, William A. "Murphy's Method For Determining The Weights Assigned To Demand Deposit Items: A Clarification And Extension," (2), 139-144.

Gilbert, Gary G. and William A. Longbrake. "The Effects Of Branching By Financial Institutions On Competition, Productive Efficiency, And Stability: An Examination Of The Evidence," (3), 154-167.

Verbrugge, James A. "The Effects Of Pledging Regulations On Bank Asset Composition," (3), 168-176.

Kurtz, Robert D. and Joseph F. Sinkey, Jr. "Bank Disclosure Policy And Procedures, Adverse Publicity And Bank Deposit Flows," (3), 177-184.

Shank, John K. "Long Range Planning Systems: Achieveing Both `Realism' And `Reach'," (3), 185-193.

Longbrake, William A. "Computers And The Cost Of Producing Banking Services: Planning And Control Considerations," (3), 194-202.

Murphy, Neil B. "The Implications Of Econometric Analysis Of Bank Cost Functions For Bank Planning," (3), 203-206.

Yeo, Edwin H., III. "A Management View Of Financial Planning, Or The Best Laid Schemes," (3), 207-211.

Robinson, Randall S. "Bank Mod: An Interactive Simulation Aid For Bank Financial Planning," (3), 212-224.

Thomson, Michael R. "Forecasting For Financial Planning," (3), 225-231.

Snider, William D. "Building An On-Line Financial Planning Model," (3), 232-238.

Lifson, K. A. and Brian R. Blackmarr. "Simulation And Optimization Models For Asset Deployment And Funds Sources Balancing Profit, Liquidity And Growth," (3), 239-255.

Boorman, John T. "The Prospects For Minority-Owned Commercial Banks: A Comparative Performance Analysis," (4), 263-279.

Garand, John J. "Fixed Income Portfolio Performance: A Discussion Of The Issues," (4), 280-297.

Gilbert, Gary G. and William A. Longbrake. "The Effects Of Branching By Financial Institutions On Competition, Productive Efficiency And Stability: An Examination Of The Evidence," (4), 298-307.

Pattison, John C. "Bank Deposit Variability: Some Further Evidence," (4), 308-310.

Oliver, Bruce L. "Selected Insights On Bankers' Loan Decisions," (4), 311-313.

Fulmer, John. "The Effect Of Federal Reserve System Membership On The Earnings Of Commercial Banks In South Carolina," (4), 314-315.

Journal of Bank Research
Volume 5, 1974/75

Peterson, Manferd O. and Hugh S. McLaughlin. "Conflict Of Interest And The Financing Of Commercial Bank Stock Ownership," (1), 7-12.

Pool, Albert A. "Application Of Discriminant Analysis In Formulation Of Promotional Strategy For Cash Dispensing Machines," (1),13-19.

Durand, David. "Payout Period, Time Spread And Duration: Aids To Judgment In Capital Budgeting," (1), 20-34.

Reback, Robert. "The Single Index Model For Portfolio Selection With Unstable Parameters," (1), 35-37.

Gilbert, Gary G. and Manfred O. Peterson. "Uniform Reserve Requirements On Demand Deposits: Some Policy Issues: Comment," (1), 38-44.

Walker, Michael C. "The Thrift Institution Problem Further Reconsidered: Comment," (1), 45-51.

Kaufman, George G. "The Thrift Institution Problem Further Reconsidered: Reply," (1), 52-54.

Jessup, Paul F. "Analyzing Acquisitions By Bank Holding Companies," (1), 55-63.

Longbrake, William A. and Sandra B. Cohan. "The Now Account Experiment," (2), 71-85.

Morris, Russell D. "The FED's RCPC Performance: What Does It Imply For Electronic Funds Transfer?," (2), 86-91.

Maier, Steven F. and James H. Vander Weide. "The Lock-Box Location Problem: A Practical Reformulation," (2), 92-95.

White, Daniel L. "The Present Value Approach to Selecting Bank Customers," (2), 96-101.

Lane, Morton. "Short-Term Money Management For Bank Portfolios," (2), 102-119.

Becker, Wolf-Dieter. "The Crisis Of German Financial Institutions In 1973," (2), 120-124.

Horton, William L. and Howard S. Gross. "Opportunities For Commercial Banks In The Business Lease/Instalment Loan Market," (2), 125-128.

Moore, W. Robert. "The Impact Of Technological Change On Internal Bank Operations," (3), 136-140.

Long, Robert H. "The Impact Of Technological Change On Bank Products And Customers," (3), 141-144.

Jacobs, Donald P. and H. Prescott Beighley. "The Changing Structure Of Banking And Its Future Impact On Banks," (3), 145-155.

Marcus, Warren R. "Financing Tomorrow's Bank Growth," (3), 156-160.

Melvin, Donald J. "Future Direction Of Bank Regulation And Legislation," (3), 161-164.

Carroll, John P. "Organizational Structure: How Change Will Impact The Organization," (3), 165-169.

Hoskins, Charles R. "Impact Of Change On Bank Personnel And The Management Process," (3), 170-173.

Hammer, Frederick S. "Banking's Present And Future Competitors: Finance And Insurance Companies," (3), 174-181.

Benson, Donald. "Banking's Present And Future Competitors: Thrift Institutions," (3), 182-184.

White, George C., Jr. "Bank Cooperation And Competition: Where To Draw The Line," (3), 185-189.

Gaines, Tilford C. "Banking And The Energy Crisis," (3), 190-192.

White, Hubert D. and David A. Torgerson. "The Fed's Performance: What Does It Imply For EFTS?: Comment," (3), 193-196.

Szatrowski, Z. Ted. "A Conceptual Overview Of The Electronic Funds Transfer System," (3), 197-199.

Sinkey, Joseph F., Jr. and David A. Walker. "Problem Banks: Indentification & Characteristics," (4), 208-217.

Solnik, Bruno H. and Jean Grall. "Eurobonds: Determining The Demand For Capital And The International Interest Rate Structure," (4), 218-230.

Moag, Joseph S. and Donald P. Jacobs. "The Effects Of Direct Payroll Deposits On The Use Of Bank Services," (4), 231-236.

Royer, Marc H. "Simulation At Banque De Bruxelles," (4), 237-245.

Aghili, Parvis, Robert H. Cramer and Howard E. Thompson. "Small Bank Balance Sheet Management: Applying Two-Stage Programming Models," (4), 246-256.

Morris, Russell D. "The Fed's RCPC Performance: What Does It Imply For EFTS?: Reply," (4), 257-259.

Haslem, John A. "A Note On The Profitability Of Commercial Bank Trust Departments," (4), 260-263.

Echols, M. E. and J. W. Elliott. "Measuring The Shoulder Of The Yield Curve," (4), 264-268.

Journal of Bank Research
Volume 6, 1975/76

Sinkey, Joseph F., Jr. "The Failure Of United States National Bank Of San Diego: A Portfolio & Performance Analysis," (1), 8-24.

Meinster, David R. and Rajesh K. Mohindru. "Determinants Of The Demand For Correspondent Balances By Small & Medium Sized Banks," (1), 25-34.

Rhoades, Stephen A. "A Clarification Of The Potential Competition Doctrine In Bank Merger Analysis," (1), 35-42.

Eisenbeis, Robert A. "The Allocative Effects Of Branch Banking Restrictions On Business Loan Markets," (1), 43-47.

Stone, Bernell K. and Robert Reback. "Constructing A Model For Managing Portfolio Revisions," (1), 48-60.

Greer, Douglas F. and Stephen A. Rhoades. "Evaluation Of A Study On Competition In Financial Services: Comment," (1), 61-66.

Christophe, Cleveland A. "Evaluation Of `Competition In Financial Services': Reply," (1), 66-69.

Viswanathan, P. and Cesar Mayo. "The Feds RCPC Performance: Comment," (1), 70-72.

Morris, Russell D. "The Feds RCPC Performance: Reply," (1), 72-73.

Carleton, Willard T. "TUCKBANK: A New Bank Management Game," (1), 74-76.

Johnson, Rodney D. and Robert V. Swanick. "New Insights Into Forecasting And Long Range Planning," (1), 77-79.

Kane, Edward J. "Costs And Benefits Of The Proposed Tax Credit On Residential Mortgage Income," (2), 88-99.

Biederman, Kenneth R., John A. Tuccillo and George J. Viksnins. "An Analysis Of The Mortgage Tax Credit Provision Of The Financial Institutions Act," (2), 100-108.

Sinkey, Joseph F., Jr. "Adverse Publicity And Bank Deposit Flows: The Cases Of Franklin National Bank Of New York And United States National Bank Of San Diego," (2), 109-112.

Havrilesky, Thomas and Robert Schweitzer. "Non-Price Competition Among Banking Firms," (2), 113-121.

Bradley, Stephen P. and Dwight B. Crane. "Simulation Of Bond Portfolio Strategies: Laddered Vs. Barbell Maturity Structure," (2), 122-134.

Jessup, Paul F. and Richard W. Stolz. "Customer Alternatives Among Rural Banks," (2), 135-139.

Shick, Richard A. and James A. Verbrugge. "An Analysis Of Bank Price-Earnings Ratios," (2), 140-149.

Boczar, Gregory E. "The Evidence On Competition Between Commercial Banks And Finance Companies," (2), 150-156.

Bellenger, Danny N. and Jac L. Goldstucker. "Discrimination Against Women: An Opportunity For Bank Marketing," (2), 155-159.

Carey, Gerard V. "Reassessing The Role Of Bank Capital," (3), 165-169.

Watson, Justin T. "A Regulatory View Of Capital Adequacy," (3), 170-172.

Gallant, Richard A. "Approaches To Capital Planning," (3), 173-176.

Langley, William C., Jr. "Strategies In Today's Capital Environment," (3), 177-178.

Chaps, Ben. "Capital Alternatives For Smaller Banks," (3), 179-182.

Hagaman, T. Carter and Herbert J. Marks. "Earnings Stability: Key To The Equity Market," (3), 183-185.

Clinch, J. Houstoun M., Jr. "Liquidity Imbalances: Profits & Penalties," (3), 186-189.

Beighley, H. Prescott, John H. Boyd and Donald P. Jacobs. "Bank Equities And Investor Risk Perceptions: Some Entailments For Capital Adequacy Regulation," (3), 190-201.

Silverberg, Stanley C. "Bank Holding Companies And Capital Adequacy," (3), 202-207.

Friedman, Benjamin M. and Peter Formuzis. "Bank Capital: The Deposit-Protection Incentive," (3), 208-218.

Jessup, Paul F. "Testing Hypotheses Involving Nonaffiliate Banks," (3), 219-221.

Neveu, Raymond P. "A Note On Environmental Planning For Banks," (3), 222-223.

Ang, James S. and Dembel Balcha. "Bond Swap Profitability," (3), 224-227.

Balzano, Raymond V. "A Model To Forecast A Banks Daily Net Clearing House Liability," (3), 228-231.

Gambs, Carl M. "The Cost Of The U.S. Payment System," (4), 240-244.
Powers, R. William. "A Survey Of Bank Check Volume," (4), 245-256.
Hochenwarter, Wolfgang P. "Method For Evaluaton Of The Economic Characteristics Of Loan Portfolios," (4), 257-267.
Mayne, Lucille S. "Deposit Reserve Requirements: Time For Change," (4), 268-274.
Milutinovich, Jugoslav S. and Stephen C. Stremmel. "Reduction Of Terminal Response Time In An Expanding Real Time Banking System," (4), 275-282.
Echols, Michael E. and J. Walter Elliott. "Forecasting Vs. Allocation Efficiency In Bank Asset Planning," (4), 283-295.
Edelstein, Robert and Jack Guttentag. "On The Alleged Profitability Of Borrowing At 8% to Lend At 6%," (4), 296-298.
Moondra, Shyam L. "An L.P. Model For Workforce Scheduling For Banks," (4), 299-301.

Journal of Bank Research
Volume 7, 1976/77

Longbrake, William A. "Commercial Bank Capacity To Pay Interest On Demand Deposits," (1), 8-21.
McWilliams, James D. "The Benefits And Costs Of Timing Equity Investments," (1), 22-29.
Dingle, James F. "The Public Policy Implications Of EFTS," (1), 30-36.
Mayne, Lucille S. "Management Policies Of Bank Holding Companies And Bank Performance," (1), 37-48.
Simkin, Mark G. and Ralph H. Sprague, Jr. "Staffing For Bank Telephone Inquiry Systems: A Decision Analysis," (1), 49-55.
Boehlje, Michael and Glen Fisher. "A Competitive Management Game For Non-Metropolitan Commercial Banks," (1), 56-67.
Eisemann, Peter C. "Diversification And The Congeneric Bank Holding Company," (1), 68-77.
McCallum, John S. "The Canadian Chartered Banks & The Government Of Canada Bond Market: Ex Post Efficient Portfolios And Actual Holding," (1), 78-87.
Pool, A. A. "Attitudes Toward Consumer Banking Packages: An Empirical Analysis," (1), 88-92.
Serfaty, Abraham. "The Kinked Supply Function For Savings Banks Deposits," (1), 93-96.
Gonyer, George H. and Steven J. Weiss. "The Competitive Effects Of Demand Deposit Powers For Thrift Institutions In Connecticut," (2), 104-112.
Sinkey, Joseph F., Jr. "The Collapse Of Franklin National Bank Of New York," (2), 113-122.
Coats, Warren L., Jr. "What Do Reserve Carry-Overs Mean For Bank Management And For Free Reserves," (2), 123-133.
Longbrake, William A. "Commercial Bank Capacity To Pay Interest On Demand Deposits. Part Two: Earnings And Cost Analysis," (2), 134-149.
Barnea, Amir and Dennis E. Logue. "Stock Trading And Portfolio Performance," (2), 150-157.
Berman, Peter I. "Differentials In Discount Facility Administration: Some Empirical Evidence," (2), 158-165.
Maier, Steven F. and James H. Vander Weide. "A Unified Location Model For Cash Disbursements And Lock-Box Collections," (2), 166-172.
Fabozzi, Frank J. and Sal Trovato. "The Use Of Quantitative Techniques In Commercial Banks," (2), 173-178.
Kaufman, George G. "The Thrift Institution Problem Reconsidered: A Historical Oversight Corrected," (2), 179-180.
Brown, Brendan D. "Money In A Competive Banking Industry," (2), 181-183.
Humphrey, David B. "100% Deposit Insurance: What Would It Cost?," (3), 192-198.
Fitzpatrick, Dennis B. "An Analysis Of Bank Credit Card Profits," (3), 199-205.
Long, Michael S. "Effect Of Lending Rate Ceilings And Money Costs On Extensions Of Consumer Credit," (3), 206-212.
Crane, Dwight B. "A Study Of Interest Rate Spreads In The 1974 CD Market," (3), 213-224.
Taylor, Bernard W., III and Laurence J. Moore. "A Simulation Approach To Planning Bank Projects," (3), 225-228.
Cramer, Robert H. and James A. Seifert. "Measuring The Impact Of Maturity On Expected Return And Risk," (3), 229-235.
Rose, Peter S. "The Pattern Of Bank Holding Company Acquisitions," (3), 236-240.
DePamphilis, Donald M. "Establishing Confidence Levels For Economic Indicators Used In Forecasting Bank Related Variables," (3), 241-246.
Murphy, Neil B. "Removing Deposit Interest Ceilings: An Analysis Of Deposit Flows, Portfolio Response And Income Effects In Boston Co-Operative Banks," (4), 256-265.
Walker, David A. "An Analysis Of Cash Dispenser And Automated Teller Activity Levels And Costs," (4), 266-275.
Robertson, Dan H. and Danny N. Bellenger. "Identifying Bank Market Segments," (4), 276-283.
Rose, John T. "The Attractiveness Of Banking Markets For De Novo Entry," (4), 284-293.
McConnell, John J. "Mortgage Company Bids On the GNMA Auction," (4), 294-302.
Spong, Kenneth and Thomas Hoenig. "An Examination Of Individual Bank Growth," (4), 303-310.
Fortson, James C. and Robert R. Dince. "An Application Of Goal Programming To Management Of A Country Bank," (4), 311-319.
Allison, William H. "Check Volumes And Costs: Comment," (4), 320-321.

Journal of Bank Research
Volume 8, 1977/78

Rhoades, Stephen A. "Sharing Arrangements In An Electronic Funds Transfer System," (1), 8-15.
Dyl, Edward A. and Michael D. Joehnk. "Prepayment Penalties Inherent In The Rule Of 78s," (1), 16-21.

Gaines, James P. and Kathleen M. Kaiser. "An Analysis Of RESPA 1974 And the RESPA Amendments Of 1975," (1), 22-30.
Goldberg, Lawrence G. and John T. Rose. "Do State Reserve Requirements Matter?," (1), 31-39.
Brzozowski, Leonard J., Lee D. Turner and Eric E. Olsen. "Project Financing Evaluation: A Simulation Approach," (1), 40-49.
Pulliam, Kenneth P. "A Liquidity Portfolio Management Strategy Approach," (1), 50-58.
Hathaway, Donald D. "Managing Balances In Lock Box Accounts," (1), 59-62.
Mandell, Lewis and Lorman L. Lundsten. "Diversion Of Credit Life Insurance Commissions By Bankers," (2), 72-76.
Rose, Peter S. "Banker Attitudes Toward The Federal Reserve System: Survey Results," (2), 77-84.
Beighley, H. Prescott. "The Risk Perceptions Of Bank Holding Company Debtholders," (2), 85-93.
Brown, Stephen W., Richard L. Smith, II and George J. Zurowski. "The Appropriateness And Applicability Of Image Research To Banking," (2), 94-100.
Boyd, Kevin and Vincent A. Mabert. "A Two Stage Forecasting Approach At Chemical Bank Of New York For Check Processing," (2), 101-107.
Durkin, Thomas A. "Consumer Loan Costs And The Regulatory Basis Of Loan Sharking," (2), 108-117.
Lavin, David and Robert Libby. "The Effect Of The Perceived Independence Of The Auditor On The Loan Decision," (2), 118-121.
McKinney, George. "A Perspective On The Use Of Models In The Management Of Bank Funds," (2), 122-127.
Watson, Ronald D. "The Marginal Cost Of Funds Concept In Banking," (3), 136-147.
Haas, Gary and Andris A. Zoltners. "A Computerized Bank Check Collection Vehicle Routing System," (3), 148-158.
Walker, David A. "Contrasts Among Banks With Retail Electronic Banking Machines And All Insured Banks: 1974 Versus 1976," (3), 159-170.
Spellman, Lewis J. "Nonrate Competition For Savings Deposits," (3), 171-178.
Johnson, James M. and Paul G. Weber. "The Impact Of The Problem Bank Disclosure On Bank Share Prices," (3), 179-182.
Harrison, William B. "Observed Characteristics Of Fifth District Member Banks' Deposit Distributions," (3), 183-185.
Johnsen, Thore and Charles Wolf. "The Strategic Profitability Of Borrowing At 8% To Lend At 6%: A Comment," (3), 186-187.
Kaufman, George. "Sharing Arrangements In An Electronic Transfer System: A Comment," (3), 188.
Fraser, Donald R. "Further Evidence On Bank Equities And Investor Risk Perceptions," (3), 189-191.
Lewin, Wayne B. "NCEFT Recommendations: An Overview," (4), 200-204.
White, George C., Jr. "Evaluation Of The Final Report Of The National Commission Of Electronic Fund Transfers," (4), 205-208.
Bernard, Jules E., Gary G. Gilbert and Robert P. Rogers. "Final Report Of The National Commission On Electronic Fund Transfers: Implications For Federal Regulation Of Depository Institutions," (4), 209-217.
Stover, Roger D. and Gordon J. Alexander. "Bank Managed Equity Common Trust Funds: A Performance Analysis," (4), 218-223.
Etzel, Michael J. and Wesley H. Jones. "A Method For Developing Promotional Themes Based On Attitudes And Usage Patterns Of Bank Credit Card Holders," (4), 224-232.
Fraser, Donald R. and Peter S. Rose. "Commercial Bank Adjustments To Monetary Policy: The Peed Of Response," (4), 233-241.
Black, Harold. "The Dichotomization Of Bank Markets Over Time: The Case Of Washington D.C.," (4), 242-248.
Schwarzbach, Henry. "The Role Of Independent Audit Reports In Commercial Bank Business Loan Decision Making: A Study Of Rhode Island Banks," (4), 249-250.
Heggestad, Arnold A. and John J. Mingo. "On The Usefulness Of Functional Cost Analysis Data," (4), 251-256.

Journal of Bank Research
Volume 9, 1978/79

Martell, Terrence F. and Robert L. Fitts. "Determinants Of Bank Trust Department Usage," (1), 8-14.
Wolkowitz, Benjamin. "The Case For The Federal Reserve Actively Participating In Electronic Funds Transfer," (1), 15-25.
Lane, Morton. "Applying Risk/Return Analysis To Short-Term Fixed-Income Portfolios," (1), 26-37.
Lewis, John H. and Dillard B. Tinsley. "Personnnel Administration In Bank Holding Companies," (1), 38-42.
Burke, Jim. "Bank Holding Company Behavior And Structural Change," (1), 43-51.
Choudhury, Pravat K. "Marketing Bank Services To Blacks," (1), 52-58.
Johnson, James M. "Efficiency Of The Federal Reserves's Instalment Loan Break-Even Formula," (1), 59-60.
Trolle-Schultz, Erik. "International Money Transfer Developments," (2), 72-77.
Lewin, Wayne B. "The Check Collection System: Present And Future Status," (2), 78-81.
Kaufman, George G. "Measuring Risk And Return For Bonds: A New Approach," (2), 82-90.
Benbow, Robert F. "A New Approach For Analysis And Control Of The Yield From Commercial Customer," (2), 91-103.
Roering, Kenneth J. and Paul E. Smith. "A Distributed Lag Forecasting Model For Bank Loans And The Money Supply," (2), 104-111.
Mears, Peter, Daniel E. McCarty and Robert Osborn. "An Empirical Investigation Of Banking Customers' Perception Of Bank Machines," (2), 112-115.
Hobson, Hugh A., John T. Masten and Jacobus T. Severiens. "Holding Company Acquisitions And Bank Performance: A Comparative Study," (2), 116-120.
Ricketts, Donald and Roger Stover. "An Examination Of Commercial Bank Financial Ratios," (2), 121-124.

Winningham, Scott. "More On The Alleged Profitability Of Borrowing At 8% To Lend At 6%: Comment," (2), 125-127.

Morris, Russell D. "An Empirical Analysis Of Costs And Revenue Requirements For Point-Of-Sale EFTS," (3), 136-145.

Arditti, Fred D. "Interest Rate Futures: An Intermediate Stage Toward Efficient Risk Reallocation," (3), 146-150.

Dufey, Gunter and Ian H. Giddy. "Measuring The Eurocurrency Market," (3), 151-160.

Smith, Terrence R. and Daniel Martin. "The Determinants Of Manpower Costs In The Examination Of Banks In The Second Federal Reserve District," (3), 161-167.

Durand, Richard M., Donald W. Eckrich and C. Ronald Sprecher. "Bank Image: An Adequacy-Importance Approach," (3), 168-172.

Gardener, E. P. M. "Capital Adequacy And Bank Prudential Regulation," (3), 173-180.

Reynolds, Fred D. and William D. Wells. "Life Style Analysis: A Dimension For Future-Oriented Bank Research," (3), 181-185.

Lackman, Conway L. and Warren N. Minami. "Market Profiles By Lending Institutions," (3), 186-190.

Dyl, Edward A. "The Marginal Cost Of Funds Controversy: Comment," (3), 191-192.

Murphy, Neil B. and Lewis Mandell. "Reforming The Structure And Regulation Of Financial Institutions: The Evidence From The State Of Maine," (4), 200-212.

McAlister, M. Khris and George A. Overstreet. "Comparative Job Satisfaction Levels Among Bank Managers," (4), 213-217.

Schweitzer, Paul and Joshua Greene. "Determinants And Consequences Of Market Entry: A Case Study Of Two Wisconsin Banking Markets," (4), 218-226.

Eatman, John L. and C. W. Sealey, Jr. "A Multiobjective Linear Programming Model For Commercial Bank Balance Sheet Management," (4), 227-236.

Firth, Michael. "Qualified Audit Reports And Bank Lending Decisions," (4), 237-241.

Evans, Richard H. "Bank Selection: It All Depends On The Situation," (4), 242-245.

Miller, Randall J. "A Note On The Cost Analysis Of A Commercial Bank Regulatory Agency As A Multiproduct Firm: Implications For Regulatory Reorganization," (4), 246-250.

Blazek, Lubomir J. and David L. Wark. "Profits Hidden In The Balance Sheet," (4), 251-255.

Journal of Bank Research
Volume 10, 1979/80

Rose, John T. "Federal Reserve System Attrition Since 1960," (1), 8-27.

Karna, Adi S. "Bank Holding Company Profitability: Nonbanking Subsidiaries And Financial Leverage," (1), 28-35.

Anderson, Carl R. "Bank Forecasting: A Developmental Group Approach," (1), 36-44.

Guttentag, Jack M. and Kenneth H. Thomas. "Branch Banking And Bank Structure: Some Evidence From Alabama," (1), 45-53.

Bellenger, Danny N., Dan H. Robertson and Barnett A. Greenberg. "Female Attitudes Toward The Use Of Credit Vs. Cash," (1), 54-57.

Clayman, Charles F. and Alan K. Severn. "The Effect Of Random Disturbances In Float On The Federal Funds Rate," (1), 58-60.

Benston, George J. and Dan Horsky. "Redlining And The Demand For Mortgages In The Central City And Suburbs," (2), 72-87.

Murphy, Neil B. "Disclosure Of The Problem Bank Lists: A Test Of The Impact," (2), 88-96.

Melnik, Arie. "Demand Deposit Variability In Banks: A Time Series Analysis," (2), 97-101.

Olson, Lola M. and J. Dennis Lord. "Market Area Characteristics And Branch Bank Performance," (2), 102-110.

Courtney, James F., Jr. "Differentiating Capital Appreciation And Income In Portfolio Selection/Revision," (2), 111-118.

Evans, Richard H. "The Validity Of Service And Situational Perceptions: A Caution," (2), 119-123.

Shin, Tai S. and Morgan J. Lynge, Jr. "Rural Banking Markets In Illinois: An Empirical Test," (2), 124-127.

Guenther, Harry and Joseph White. "EFT System Privacy Safeguards: A Preliminary Inquiry Into The Privacy-Leisure Time Trade-Off," (3), 136-144.

Pany, Kurt and Lawrence F. Sherman. "Information Analysis Of Several Large Failed Banks," (3), 145-151.

Cohen, Kalman J. and Chun H. Lam. "A Linear Programming Planning Model For Bank Holding Companies," (3), 152-164.

Watne, Donald A. "Cross-Selling The Bank Customer," (3), 165-172.

Mabert, Vincent A., Randy Fairhurst and Michael A. Kilpatrick. "Chemical Bank's Encoder Daily Shift Scheduling System," (3), 173-180.

Myers, Forest E. and Thomas Hoenig. "Relative Operating Performance Of Withdrawing 10th Federal Reserve District Member Banks," (3), 181-183.

Cowen, Scott S. and Albert L. Page. "Factors Affecting The Performance Of Loans To Minority Small Businessmen: A Case Study," (3), 184-188.

Allardice, David R. "The Johnson Wax Effect: Setting The Record Straight," (3), 189-192.

Nathan, Harold C. "Economic Analysis Of Usury Laws," (4), 200-211.

Rogowski, Robert J. "Underwriting Competition And Issuer Borrowing Costs In The Municipal Revenue Bond Market," (4), 212-220.

Heard, Edwin L. and Jerry E. Wheat. "Management Engineering In Large U.S. Banks," (4), 221-227.

Swinyard, William R. "Strategy Development With Importance Analysis," (4), 228-234.

Buser, Stephen A. "Efficient Risk/Return Management In Commercial Banking," (4), 235-247.

Murphy, Neil B. "Economies Of Scale In The Cost Of Compliance With Consumer Credit Protection Laws: The Case Of The Implementation Of The Equal Credit Opportunity Act Of 1974," (4), 248-250.

Stone, Bernell K. "Lock-Box Selection And Collection-System Design: Objective Function Validity," (4), 251-254.

Veit, E. Theodore, Mary Lee Avey, Jerry L. Corley and Timothy

Summers. "The Role Of Stock Options In Bank Trust Departments: Fifth Federal Reserve District Banks," (4), 255-256.

Journal of Bank Research
Volume 11, 1980/81

Humphrey, David Burras. "Are There Economies Of Scale In Check Processing At The Federal Reserve?," (1), 8-19.

Mayne, Lucille S. "Funds Transfer Between Bank Holding Companies And Their Affiliates," (1), 20-27.

Miller, Randall J. "Examination Man-Hour Cost For Independent, Joint And Divided Examination Programs," (1), 28-35.

Euske, Kenneth J., Donald W. Jackson, Jr. and William E. Reif. "Performance And Satisfaction Of Bank Managers," (1), 36-42.

Stover, Roger D. "The Single-Subsidiary Bank Holding Company," (1), 43-50.

Giroux, Gary A. "A Survey Of Forecasting Techniques Used By Commercial Banks," (1), 51-53.

McCallum, John S. "The Canadian Conversion Loan: A Remembrance," (1), 54-56.

Benston, George J. "Federal Reserve Membership: Consequences, Costs, Benefits And Alternatives," (1), 57-60.

Ogilvie, Nigel R. "Foreign Banks In The U.S. And Geographic Restrictions On Banking," (2), 72-79.

Nathan, Harold C. "Nonbank Organizations And The McFadden Act," (2), 80-86.

McCall, Alan S. and John T. Lane. "Multi-Office Banking And The Safety And Soundness Of Commercial Banks," (2), 87-94.

McCall, Alan S. "Economies Of Scale, Operating Efficiencies And The Organizational Structure Of Commercial Banks," (2), 95-100.

McCall, Alan S. "The Impact Of Bank Structure On Bank Service To Local Communities," (2), 101-110.

Savage, Donald T. and Elinor H. Solomon. "Branch Banking: The Competitive Issues," (2), 110-121.

McCall, Alan S. and Donald T. Savage. "Branching Policy: The Options," (2), 122-126.

Shick, Richard A. and Lawrence F. Sherman. "Bank Stock Prices As An Early Warning System For Changes In Condition," (3), 136-146.

Boczar, Gregory E. "The External Growth Of Multibank Holding Companies," (3), 147-158.

Fellows, James A. and Thomas R. Beard. "Some Welfare Implications Of Legal Restrictions On Commercial Bank Entry," (3), 159-168.

Jahankhani, Ali and Morgan J. Lynge, Jr. "Commercial Bank Financial Policies And Their Impact On Market-Determined Measures Of Risk," (3), 169-178.

LaForge, R. Lawrence and D. Robley Wood, Jr. "The Use Of Operations Research In The Planning Activities Of Large U.S. Banks," (3), 179-183.

Black, Harold and Robert L. Schweitzer. "Discrimination In The Lending Decision: Home Improvement Loans," (3), 184-186.

Simonson, Donald G. and Peter C. Marks. "Breakeven Balances On NOW Accounts: Perils In Pricing," (3), 187-191.

Schweitzer, Paul R. and Joshua E. Greene. "The Johnson Wax Effect: Reply," (3), 192.

Kearney, Kevin J. "The New Payment Technology," (4), 197-199.

White, George C., Jr. "Developments In United States Payment Systems," (4), 200-205.

Marbacher, Josef. "Characteristics And Problems Of Modern Payment Systems," (4), 206-213.

Soleil, M. "A New Payment Technique: The Memory Card," (4), 214-218.

Hogg, Gordon H. J. "Payment Systems Developments In New Zealand," (4), 219-222.

Starke, Wolfgang. "Payment Methods Of The Future," (4), 223-226.

Williamson, J. M. "Pricing Money Transfer Services," (4), 227-232.

Engler, Rolf. "Automation Of Payments In The Federal Republic Of Germany: Status And Future Prospects," (4), 233-241.

No Author. "Payment Systems In Norway," (4), 242-244.

McCallum, John S. "The Empirical Impact Of Changes In Government On Bond Yields: The Canadian Provencial Experience," (4), 245-247.

Journal of Bank Research
Volume 12, 1981/82

Benston, George J. "Mortgage Redlining Research: A Review And Critical Analysis," (1), 8-23.

Kaufman, George G. "Municipal Bond Underwriting: Market Structure," (1), 24-31.

Spellman, Lewis J. "Commercial Banks And The Profits Of Savings And Loan Markets," (1), 32-36.

Kwast, Myron L. "New Minority-Owned Commercial Banks: A Statistical Analysis," (1), 37-45.

Peterson, Richard L. and Michael D. Ginsberg. "Determinants Of Commercial Bank Auto Loan Rates," (1), 46-55.

Hartman, Bart P. and Johng Y. Lee. "Influence Of Company Debt Burden On Reported Replacement Cost Values," (1), 56-59.

Selby, Edward B., Jr. "The Role Of Director Deposits In New Bank Growth," (1), 60-61.

Humphrey, David Burras. "Scale Economies At Automated Clearinghouses," (2), 71-81.

Curry, Timothy J. "The Pre-Acquisition Characteristics Of Banks Acquired By Multibank Holding Companies," (2), 82-89.

Doyle, P., I. Fenwick and G. P. Savage. "A Model For Evaluating Branch Location And Performance," (2), 90-95.

Mandell, Lewis, Ran Lachman and Yair Orgler. "Interpreting The Image Of Banking," (2), 96-104.

Klein, Hans E. "The Impact Of Planning On Growth And Profit," (2), 105-109.

Lakonishok, Josef. "Performance Of Mutual Funds Versus Their Expenses," (2), 110-113.

McCabe, George M. and James M. Blackwell. "The Hedging Strategy: A New Approach To Spread Management Banking And Commercial Lending," (2), 114-118.

Scheiner, James H. "Income Smoothing: An Analysis In The Banking Industry," (2), 119-123.

Priewasser, Erich. "Implementation Of OR/MS Models In German Banks," (2), 124-127.

Koch, Timothy W. "Commercial Bank Size, Relative Profitability And The Demand For Tax-Exempt Securities," (3), 136-144.

Kaufman, Herbert M. "FNMA And Its Relationship To The Mortgage Market," (3), 145-152.

Stock, Duane and Terry Robertson. "Improved Techniques For Predicting Municipal Bond Ratings," (3), 153-160.

Gouldey, Bruce K. and Gary J. Gray. "Implementing Mean-Variance Theory In The Selection Of U.S. Government Bond Portfolios," (3), 161-173.

Nauss, Robert M. and Bradford R. Keeler. "Optimizing Municipal Bond Bids," (3), 174-181.

Rudd, Andrew. "Using Options To Increase Reward And Decrease Risk," (3), 182-191.

Pol, Louis and Rebecca F. Guy. "Discrimination In Home Improvement Loans: A Rejoinder," (3), 192.

Savage, Donald T. "Branch Banking Laws, Deposits, Market Share And Profitability Of New Banks," (4), 200-206.

Cramer, Robert H. and William E. Sterk. "The Present Value Approach To Commercial Loan Pricing," (4), 207-217.

Holmberg, Stevan R. and H. Kent Baker. "The CEO's Role In Strategic Planning," (4), 218-227.

Gheva, David and Meir Sokoler. "An Alternative Approach To The Problem Of Classification - The Case Of Bank Failures In Israel," (4), 228-238.

Fry, Clifford L.,Charles P. Harper and Stanley R. Stansell. "An Analysis Of Credit Union Costs: A New Approach To Analyzing Cost Of Financial Institutions," (4), 239-249.

Altman, Edward I. "Computerized Bond Rating Replication: Worthwhile Or Futile?," (4), 250-253.

Rhoades, Stephen A. "Bank Expansion And Merger Activity By State, 1960-1975," (4), 254-256.

Journal of Bank Research
Volume 13, 1982/83

Stone, Bernell K. and Ned C. Hill. "Alternative Cash Transfer Mechanisms And Methods: Evaluation Frameworks," (1), 7-16.

Fielitz, Bruce D. and Daniel L. White. "An Evaluation And Linking Of Alternative Solution Procedures For The Lock Box Location Problem," (1), 17-27.

Bradford, William D. "The Deposit Demand Of Minority Savings And Loan Associations," (1), 28-35.

Hughes, John S. and James Vander Weide. "Incentive Considerations In The Reporting Of Leveraged Leases," (1), 36-41.

Karna, Adi S. and Duane B. Graddy. "Bank Holding Company Leverage And The Return On Stockholders' Equity," (1), 42-48.

Nielsen, James F. "Trading Small Bank Stocks: An Oregon Case Study," (1), 49-52.

Olson, Ronald L. and Donald G. Simonson. "Gap Management And Market Rate Sensitivity In Banks," (1), 53-58.

McCallum, John S. "Return And Risk In The Canadian Federal Bond Market," (1), 59-61.

King, B. Frank. "Future Holding Company Lead Banks: Federal Reserve Standards And Record," (2), 72-79.

Frieder, Larry A. and Vincent P. Apilado. "Bank Holding Company Research: Classification, Synthesis And New Directions," (2), 80-95.

Rose, John T. and Donald T. Savage. "Bank Holding Company De Novo Entry And Banking Market Deconcentration," (2), 96-100.

Stover, Roger D. "A Re-Examination Of Bank Holding Company Acquisitions," (2), 101-108.

Simonson, Donald G. and George H. Hempel. "Improving Gap Management for Controlling Interest Rate Risk," (2), 109-115.

Warner, Arthur E. and F. Jerry Ingram. "A Test For Discrimination In A Mortgage Market," (2), 116-124.

Gardener, E. P. M. "Capital Adequacy And Banking Supervision - Towards A Practical System," (2), 125-136.

Goldberg, Ellen S. "Comparative Cost Analysis Of Foreign Owned U.S. Banks," (3), 144-159.

Basch, Donald L. "Circumventive Innovation: The Case Of NOW Accounts In Massachusetts, 1972-1977," (3), 160-167.

Morgan, George Emir and Susan M. Becker. "Environmental Factors In Pricing NOW Accounts In 1981," (3), 168-178.

Edmister, Robert O. "Margin Analysis For Consumer Deposit Interest Rate Policy," (3), 179-184.

Davis, Samuel G., Nicholas Ceto, Jr. and J. Mac. Rabb. "A Comprehensive Check Processing Simulation Model," (3), 185-194.

Mabert, Vincent A. and Robert Stocco. "Managing And Monitoring A Forecasting System: The Chemical Bank Experience," (3), 195-201.

Langrehr, Frederick W. "Money Market Mutual Fund Investors' Savings Account Holdings And Demographic Profile," (3), 202-206.

Benston, George J. "Discrimination In Home Improvement Loans: A Comment On A Rejoinder," (3), 207-208.

Benston, George J. "Federal Regulation Of Banking Analysis And Policy Recommendations," (4), 216-244.

Horvitz, Paul M. "Reorganization Of The Financial Regulatory Agencies," (4), 245-263.

Basch, Donald L. "Regulatory Transition And Depositor Inertia: The Response Of Massachusetts Commercial Banks To NOW Accounts," (4), 264-273.

Keen, Howard, Jr. "The Impact Of A Dividend Cut Announcement On Bank Share Prices," (4), 274-281.

Bierwag, G. O., George G. Kaufman and Aldan Toevs. "Bond Portfolio Immunization And Stochastic Process Risk," (4), 282-291.

Kennedy, William F. and David F. Scott, Jr. "Some Observations On The Dividend Policies Of Large Commercial Banks," (4), 292-296.

Marks, Barry R. "Calculating The Rate Of Return On A Leveraged Lease - A Constant Leverage Approach," (4), 297-299.

James, Christopher. "Pricing Alternatives For Loan Commitments: A Note," (4), 300-303.

Hisrich, Robert D.,Michael P. Peters and John Krasnakevich. "Effectively Managing Consumer Credit Through Computer Graphics," (4), 304-308.

Martell, Terrence F. "The Accuracy Of Deposit Forecasts Generated By The Bank Chartering Process," (4), 309-311.

Flannery, Mark J. "Can State Bank Examination Data Replace FDIC Visits?," (4), 312-316.

Booth, James R. "NOW Accounts: The Competitive Battle In The Western States," (4), 317-320.

Journal of Bank Research
Volume 14, 1983/84

Cohen, Kalman J. "The Reform Of Banking Regulation: An Overview," (1), 3-7.

Kaufman, George, Larry Mote and Harvey Rosenblum. "Implications Of Deregulation For Product Lines And Geographical Markets Of Finanical Institutions," (1), 8-20.

Elliott, James V. "What Is The Role Of Government In A Major Restructuring Of Financial Institutions In The 1980s?," (1), 25-32.

Crane, Dwight B. and Samuel L. Hayes, III. "The Evolution Of International Banking Competition And Its Implications For Regulation," (1), 39-52.

Greenbaum, Stuart I. "Legal Reserve Requirements: A Case Study In Bank Regulation," (1), 59-68.

White, George C., Jr. "The Conflicting Roles Of The Fed As A Regulator And A Competitor," (1), 75-89.

Hester, Donald D. "Deregulation And Locational Rents In Banking," (1), 96-106.

Sinkey, Joseph F., Jr. "The Performance Of First Pennsylvania Bank Prior To Its Bail Out," (2), 119-133.

Zoltners, Andris A. "A Manpower Sizing And Resource Allocation Model For Commercial Lending," (2), 134-143.

Houpt, James A. "Foreign Ownership Of U.S. Banks: Trends And Effects," (2), 144-156.

Hannan, Timothy. "Bank Profitability And The Threat Of Entry," (2), 157-163.

Giroux, Gary, Winston Shearon and Steven Grossman. "How Does Inflation Affect A BHC's Rate Of Return?," (2), 164-169.

Rose, John T. "Branch Banking And The State/National Charter Decision," (2), 170-172.

Bierman, Harold, Jr. "A Comment On Optimizing Municipal Bond Bids," (2), 173-174.

McCallum, John S. "A Comment On Implementing Mean-Variance Theory In Selection Of U.S. Government Bond Portfolios," (2), 175-176.

Dalton, Dan R., David M. Krackhardt and Lyman W. Porter. "The Impact Of Teller Turnover In Banking: First Appearances Are Deceiving," (3), 184-192.

Jacobs, Rodney L. "Fixed-Rate Lending And Interest Rate Futures Hedging," (3), 193-202.

Davis, Samuel G., Gary A. Kochenberger and Edward T. Reutzel. "Expressend: A Check Clearing Decision Support System For Endpoint Selection," (3), 203-211.

Curry, Timothy J. and John T. Rose. "Multibank Holding Companies: Recent Evidence On Competition And Performance In Banking Markets," (3), 212-220.

Hicks, Sydney Smith. "Aggregate Bank Portfolio Statistics: Do They Tell Us Anything?," (3), 221-226.

Marlow, Michael L. "Entry And Performance In Financial Markets," (3), 227-230.

Murphy, Neil B. "Determinants Of ATM Activity: The Impact Of Card Base, Location, Time In Place And System," (3), 231-233.

Reeve, James M. "Loan Evaluations Under Accounting Disclosure Alternatives," (3), 234-236.

Gouldey, Bruce K. and Gary J. Gray. "Implementing Mean-Variance Theory In The Selection Of U.S. Government Bond Portfolios: Reply To A Comment," (3), 237-238.

Nauss, Robert M. and Bradford R. Keeler. "Optimizing Municipal Bond Bids: Reply To A Comment," (3), 239-240.

Dunkelberg, William C., Jonathan A. Scott and Edwin L. Cox. "Small Business And The Value Of Bank-Customer Relationships," (4), 248-258.

Curry, Timothy J. and John T. Rose. "Bank Holding Company Presence And Banking Market Performance," (4), 259-265.

Osteryoung, Jerome S., Daniel E. McCarty and Gordon S. Roberts. "Riding A Hedged Yield Curve With Treasury Bill Futures," (4), 266-273.

Lobue, Marie. "Categorical Bank Acquisitions," (4), 274-282.

Graddy, Duane B. and Adi S. Karna. "Net Interest Margin Sensitivity Among Banks Of Different Sizes," (4), 283-290.

Reichert, Alan, William Strauss, David Northcutt and Warren Spector. "The Impact Of Economic Conditions And Electronic Payments Technology On Federal Reserve Check Volume," (4), 291-296.

Reese, Richard M. and Wilbur W. Stanton. "Further Segmenting A Minority Bank's Customer Set," (4), 297-301.

Woodard, George D. and James E. Goldsberry. "Economic Research As An Aid To Regional Bank Holding Company Expansion," (4), 302-304.

Journal of Bank Finance
Volume 15, 1984/85

Hannan, Timothy H. "Competition Between Commercial Banks And Thrift Institutions: An Empirical Examination," (1), 8-14.

Booth, James R., Richard L. Smith and Richard W. Stolz. "Use Of Interest Rate Futures By Financial Institutions," (1), 15-20.

Murphy, Neil B. and Ronald C. Rogers. "The Line Of Commerce In Retail Financial Institution Mergers: Some Evidence From Consumer Data In New England," (1), 21-25.

Gardner, Mona J. "Minority Owned Banks: A Managerial And Performance Analysis," (1), 26-34.

Weber, Edward A. "Instalment Credit For Autos: A Literature Survey Of Sources, Terms And Demand Effects," (1), 35-43.

Hadaway, Beverly L. and Samuel C. Hadaway. "Implications Of Savings And Loan Conversions In A Deregulated World," (1), 44-55.

Schuster, Leo. "Profitability And Market Share Of Banks," (1), 56-61.

Rogowski, Robert J. "Pricing The Money Market Deposit And Super-NOW Accounts In 1983," (2), 72-81.

Brodt, Abraham I. "International Bank Asset And Liability Management," (2), 82-94.

Rose, John T. and Donald T. Savage. "De Novo Entry And Performance: Bank Holding Companies Versus Independent Banks," (2), 95-107.

Jacobs, Rodney L. "The Rate Maturity Of Prime And Other Indexed Assets Or Liabilities," (2), 108-114.

Graddy, Duane B., Ghassem Homaifar and Adi S. Karna. "Double Leverage As A Source Of Systematic Risk In Bank Holding Company Stocks," (2), 115-122.

Booth, James R. and Richard L. Smith, II. "The Impact Of The Community Reinvestment Act On Branching Activity Of Financial Institutions," (2), 123-128.

Giroux, Gary A. and Peter S. Rose. "An Update Of Bank Planning Systems: Results Of A Nationwide Survey Of Large U.S. Banks," (3), 136-147.

Huertas, Thomas F. "An Economic Brief Against Glass-Steagall," (3), 148-159.

Ladenson, Mark L. "Money Stock Control: The Effects Of A Reduction In The Number Of Depository Institutions," (3), 160-166.

Scott, Jonathan A. and William C. Dunkelberg. "Rural Versus Urban Bank Performance: An Analysis Of Market Competition For Small Business Loans," (3), 167-178.

Giroux, Gary A. and Casper E. Wiggins. "An Events Approach To Corporate Bankruptcy," (3), 179-187.

Vogt, Michael G. and R. S. Hanna. "Variations Of The Federal Funds Rate And Bank Reserve Management," (3), 188-192.

Revell, Jack. "Payment Systems Over The Next Decade," (4), 200-210.

De Mattia, Renato. "The Forces At Work In The Evolution Of Payment Systems In The 1980's," (4), 211-221.

Reichert, Alan K., William Strauss and Randall C. Merris. "An Economic Analysis Of Short-Run Fluctuations In Federal Reserve Wire Transfer Volume," (4), 222-228.

Myers, Forest E. and Joe Van Walleghem. "Management Transferability In Rural Banks," (4), 229-233.

Dyl, Edward A. and J. Ronald Hoffmeister. "Efficiency And Volatility In The Federal Funds Market," (4), 234-239.

Wall, Larry. "Why Are Some Banks More Profitable Than Others?," (4), 240-256.

Journal of Bank Research
Volume 16, 1985/86

Beatty, Randolph P., John F. Reim and Robert F. Schapperle. "The Effect Of Barriers To Entry On Bank Shareholder Wealth: Implications For Interstate Banking," (1), 8-15.

Duncan, F. H. "Intermarket Bank Expansions: Implications For Interstate Banking," (1), 16-21.

Cornell, Bradford and Ole Christian Sand. "The Value Of Base Rate Options In The Eurocredit Market," (1), 22-27.

Goldberg, Michael A. and Peter R. Lloyd-Davies. "Standby Letters Of Credit: Are Banks Overextending Themselves?," (1), 28-39.

Thottathil, Pelis. "A Note On Eurodollar Borrowing By U.S. Banks: Derivation Of Reg D Equation," (1), 40-44.

Humphrey, David Burras. "Resource Use In Federal Reserve Check And ACH Operations After Pricing," (1), 45-53.

Churchill, Neil C. and Virginia L. Lewis. "Profitability Of Small-Business Lending," (2), 63-71.

Rose, Peter S., James W. Kolari and Kenneth D. Riener. "A National Survey Study Of Bank Services And Prices Arrayed By Size And Structure," (2), 72-85.

Dermine, Jean. "The Measurement Of Interest-Rate Risk By Financial Intermediaries," (2), 86-90.

van Leeuwen, Peter H. "The Prediction Of Business Failure At Rabobank," (2), 91-98.

Teas, R. Kenneth and W. L. Dellva. "Conjoint Measurement Of Consumers' Preferences For Multiattribute Financial Services," (2), 99-112.

Glascock, John L. and Wallace N. Davidson, III. "The Effect Of Bond Deratings On Bank Stock Returns," (3), 120-127.

Billingsley, Randall S. and G. Rodney Thompson. "Determinants Of Stock Repurchases By Bank Holding Companies," (3), 128-135.

Fraser, Donald R. and John C. Groth. "Listing And The Liquidity Of Bank Stocks," (3), 136-144.

Rogers, Ronald C., Neil B. Murphy and James E. Owers. "Financial Innovation, Balance Sheet Cosmetics And Market Response: The Case Of Equity-For-Debt Exchanges In Banking," (3), 145-149.

Kolari, James and John DiClemente. "A Case Study Of Geographic Deregulation: The New Illinois Bank Holding Company Act," (3), 150-157.

Welch, Patrick J. and Jude L. Naes, Jr. "The Merger Guidelines, Concentration And Excess Capacity In Local Commercial Banking Markets," (3), 158-160.

Owens, Robert W. and G. Lee Willinger. "Investment Potential Of An Individual Retirement Account," (3), 161-168.

Morelli, G. "Payment Systems In Eleven Developed Countries," (4), 173-174.

Mitchell, George W. "Similarities And Contrasts In Payment Systems," (4), 175-177.

Sullivan, Barry F. "Meeting The Challenge Of Controlling Banking Costs And Developing Pricing Strategies," (4), 178-181.

Evans, John J. "Commercial Banks And The Consumer Services Revolution," (4), 182-185.

Witt, Horst J. "The Cost Of Developing And Implementing Electronic Payment Systems," (4), 186-189.

Meyer, Hans. "The Role Of The Swiss National Bank In The Payment System," (4), 190-193.

Dingle, James F. "The Role Of The Bank Of Canada In The Canadian Payment System," (4), 194-197.

Child, Denis M. "Payment Issues In The United Kingdom," (4), 198-201.

Hopper, Max. "Strategies For The Development Of Electronic Systems," (4), 202-205.

Douglas, William E. "Evolution Of Electronic Payments And Collections In The U.S. Government," (4), 206-208.

Heldring, Frederick. "Payment Systems Risk In The United States," (4), 209-213.

Hartmann, Wendelin. "Deutsche Bundesbank And Payment System Risk In The Federal Republic Of Germany," (4), 214-217.

Aoki, Tatsuo. "ATMs, POS And Home Banking Developments In Japan," (4), 218-220.

Moniez, Jean-Claude. "The Smart Card In France," (4), 221-222.

Starke, Wolfgang. "Efficiencies In Credit-Based Transfer Systems," (4), 223-226.

Hager, Karl Erik. "The Swedish Postal Giro And Its Progress," (4), 227-231.

Moore, W. Robert. "Large Value Payment Systems," (4), 232-234.

Barbe, Henri-Jean. "Cheque Truncation In Belgium," (4), 235-240.

Urkowitz, Michael. "Paper-Based Payments - A System In Transition," (4), 241-243.

St. Germain, Fernand J. "Consumer Banking Issues," (4), 244-247.

Brobeck, Stephen. "Consumer Perspective On Payments Systems," (4), 248-251.

Appleman, Norman. "Payment System Needs Of Corporations," (4), 252-253.

Level, Leon J. "Meeting The Needs Of Multinational Corporations," (4), 254-257.

Mitchell, George W. "It's The Old Time Religion, But Is It Good Enough Today?," (4), 258-260.

Journal of Bank Research
Volume 17, 1986/87

Murphy, Neil B. and Ronald C. Rogers. "Life Cycle And The Adoption Of Consumer Financial Innovation: An Empirical Study Of The Adoption Process," (1), 3-8.

Anderson, Richard G., E. Jayne McCarthy and Leslie A. Patern. "Valuing The Core Deposits Of Financial Institutions: A Statistical Analysis," (1), 9-17.

Reidenbach, R. Eric, Donald L. Moak and Robert E. Pitts. "The Impact Of Marketing Operating On Bank Performance: A Structural Investigation," (1), 18-27.

Cesarini, Francesco. "Equity Financing By Banks In The Italian Market: The 1980-1984 Experience And The New Trends," (1), 28-39.

Gualandri, Elisabetta. "Italian Banks And Interest Rate Risk," (1), 40-44.

Rose, John T. and Donald T. Savage. "Bank Holding Company De Novo Entry And Banking Market Performance," (1), 45-50.

Schuster, Leo. "Concentration And Competition In Banking," (1), 51-53.

Journal of Bank Research Discountinued
Publication after Volume 17, Issue 1

JOURNAL OF BANKING AND FINANCE

**Journal of Banking and Finance
Volume 1, 1977**

Merton, Robert C. "An Analytic Derivation Of The Cost Of Deposit Insurance And Loan Guarantees: An Application Of Modern Option Pricing Theory," (1), 3-11.

Levasseur, Michel G. "An Option Model Approach To Firm Liquidity Management," (1), 13-28.

Altman, Edward I., Robert G. Haldeman and P. Narayanan. "ZETA Analysis: A New Model To Identify Bankruptcy Risk Of Corporations," (1), 29-54.

Stapleton, Richard C. and Christopher M. Burke. "European Tax Systems And The Neutrality Of Corporate Financing Policy," (1), 55-70.

Guy, James R. F. "The Behavior Of Equity Securities On The German Stock Exchange," (1), 71-93.

Aharony, Joseph and Martin Loeb. "Mean-Variance Vs. Stochastic Dominance: Some Empirical Findings On Efficient Sets," (1), 95-102.

Friend, Irwin. "Recent Developments In Finance," (2), 103-117.

Zu Selhausen, Hermann Meyer. "Commercial Bank Balance Sheet Optimization," (2), 119-142.

Gavish, Bezalel. "A Relaxation Algorithm For Building Undominated Portfolios," (2), 143-150.

Garbade, Kenneth and Zvi Lieber. "On The Independence Of Transactions On The N.Y. Stock Exchange," (2), 151-172.

Hendershott, Patric H. "Model Simulations Of The Impact Of Selective Credit Policies And Financial Reforms," (2), 173-184.

Santomero, Anthony M. and Joseph D. Vinso. "Estimating The Probability Of Failure For Commercial Banks And The Banking System," (2), 185-205.

Kahane, Yehuda. "Capital Adequacy And The Regulation Of Financial Intermediaries," (2), 207-218.

Cohen, Kalman J., Steven F. Maier, Walter L. Ness, Jr., Hitoshi Okuda, Robert A. Schwartz and David K. Whitcomb. "The Impact Of Designated Market Makers On Security Prices," (3), 219-247.

Martin, Daniel. "Early Warning Of Bank Failure: A Logit Regression Approach," (3), 249-276.

Ben-Horim, Moshe and William L. Silber. "Financial Innovation: A Linear Programming Approach," (3), 277-296.

Mazzoleni, P. "The Influence Of Reserve Regulation And Capital On Optimal Bank Asset Management," (3), 297-309.

Mueller, Dennis C. "The Effects Of Conglomerate Mergers: A Survey Of The Empirical Evidence," (4), 315-347.

Aftalion, Florin and Lawrence J. White. "A Study Of A Monetary System With A Pegged Discount Rate Under Different Market Structures," (4), 349-371.

Galai, Dan. "Characterization Of Options," (4), 373-386.

**Journal of Banking and Finance
Volume 2, 1978**

Aftalion, Florin and Lawrence J. White. "On The Choice Of Immediate Monetary Targets," (1), 1-13.

Levy-Garboua, V. and G. Maarek. "Bank Behavior And Monetary Policy," (1), 15-46.

Brenner, Menachem and Dan Galai. "The Determinants Of The Return On Index Bonds," (1), 47-64.

Walker, David A. "Economies Of Scale In Electronic Funds Transfer Systems," (1), 65-78.

Nielsen, Niels Christian. "On The Financing And Investment Decisions Of The Firm," (1), 79-102.

Ophir, Tsvi. "The Geometric-Mean Principle Revisited," (1), 103-107.

Stein, Jerome L. "Inflation And Stagflation," (2), 109-131.

Beveridge, Stephen and Rolf Mirus. "An Empirical Evaluation Of The Rationality Of Eurocurrency Market Expectations," (2), 133-141.

Tuttle, Donald L., Wayne Y. Lee and Terry S. Maness. "Stochastic Cash Flow Constraints And The Term Structure Of Interest," (2), 143-162.

Paroush, Jacob and Yoram C. Peles. "Search For Information And Portfolio Selection," (2), 163-177.

Borch, Karl. "Portfolio Theory Is For Risk Lovers," (2), 179-182.

Fabry, Jaak and Willy Van Grembergen. "Further Evidence On The Stationarity Of Betas And Errors In Their Estimates," (3), 189-204.

Eisenbeis, Robert A. "Problems In Applying Discriminant Analysis In Credit Scoring Models," (3), 205-220.

Brodt, Abraham I. "A Dynamic Balance Sheet Management Model For A Canadian Chartered Bank," (3), 221-241.

Kinberg, Yoram and Ephraim F. Sudit. "Successive Retention Of Funds, Loan Profitability And Marketing Implications In Banking," (3), 243-255.

Eilon, Samuel. "Earning Per Share And Takeovers," (3), 257-268.

Agmon, Tamir and Ruth Arad. "Exchange Risk And Unanticipated Changes In Exchange Rates," (3), 269-280.

Solnik, B. "International Parity Conditions And Exchange Risk: A Review," (3), 281-293.

Landskroner, Yoram. "Effects Of Interest Rate Policy On External Balances," (3), 295-301.

Jacquillat, Bertrand C., John G. McDonald and Jacques Rolfo. "French Auctions Of Common Stock: New Issues, 1966-1974," (4), 305-322.

Eisenbeis, Robert A. and Alan S. McCall. "The Impact Of Legislation Prohibiting Director-Interlocks Among Depository Financial Institutions," (4), 323-337.

Vuchelen, J. "A Study Of A Monetary System With A Pegged Discount Rate Under Different Market Structures: Comments On The Article By F. Aftalion And L. White," (4), 339-350.

Aftalion, Florin and Lawrence J. White. "A Study Of A Monetary System With Pegged Discount Rate Under Different Market

Structures: A Reply To J. Vuchelen," (4), 351-354.

Melnik, Arie and Aharon R. Ofer. "Determinants Of Commission Rates For Bank Trust Stock Transactions," (4), 355-366.

Mingo, John J. "The Effect Of Deposit Rate Ceilings On Bank Risk," (4), 367-378.

Franks, Julian R. "Insider Information And The Efficiency Of The Acquisitions' Market," (4), 379-393.

Latane, Henry A. "The Geometric-Mean Principle Revisited: A Reply," (4), 395-398.

Szego, G. P. "A Note On Co-Variance Properties Of Efficient Portfolios," (4), 399-401.

**Journal of Banking and Finance
Volume 3, 1979**

Mehta, Dileep R., Peter C. Eisemann, Edward A. Moses and Benoit Deschamps. "Capital Structure And Capital Adequacy Of Bank Holding Companies: A Market Test," (1), 5-22.

Bierwag, G. O. "Dynamic Portfolio Immunization Policies," (1), 23-41.

Humphrey, David Burras. "Large Bank Intra-Deposit Maturity Composition: CDs And Small Time Deposits 1970-77," (1), 43-66.

Booth, G. Geoffrey and Gordon H. Dash, Jr. "Alternate Programming Structures For Bank Portfolios," (1), 67-82.

Van Nieuwkerk, Marius. "Domestic And Foreign Trade Credit In The Netherlands: An Econometric Analysis," (1), 83-105.

Dyl, Edward A. "A Note On The Optimal Bad Debt Expense In Installment Lending," (1), 107-109.

Hendershott, Patric H. and James P. Winder. "Commercial Bank Asset Portfolio Behavior In The United States: Evidence Of A Change In Structure," (2), 113-131.

Brennan, Michael J. and Eduardo S. Schwartz. "A Continuous Time Approach To The Pricing Of Bonds," (2), 133-156.

Baron, David P. "The Incentive Problem And The Design Of Investment Banking Contracts," (2), 157-175.

Kanniainen, Vesa. "The Redistribution Of Wealth In Inflation," (2), 177-185.

Halloran, John A. and Jess B. Yawitz. "The Effect Of Mortgage Form On Borrower Interest Rate Risk: A Portfolio Theory Approach," (2), 187-200.

Bertoneche, Marc L. "Spectral Analysis Of Stock Market Prices," (2), 201-208.

Short, Brock K. "The Relation Between Commercial Bank Profit Rates And Banking Concentration In Canada, Western Europe, And Japan," (3), 209-219.

Hannan, Timothy H. "The Theory Of Limit Pricing: Some Applications To The Banking Industry," (3), 221-234.

Brito, Ney O. "The Efficiency Of Inflation Expectations In Treasury Bill Markets: The Brazilian Evidence," (3), 235-251.

Jonkhart, Marius J. L. "On The Term Structure Of Interest Rates And The Risk Of Default: An Analytical Approach," (3), 253-261.

Cornell, Bradford. "Relative Price Changes And Deviations From Purchasing Power Parity," (3), 263-280.

Fung, W. K. H. "On The Process Of Risk Reduction Through Diversification," (3), 281-299.

Ophir, Tsvi. "The Geometric Mean Principle Revisited: A Reply To A 'Reply'," (4), 301-304.

Samuelson, Paul A. "Why We Should Not Make Mean Log Of Wealth Big Though Years To Act Are Long," (4), 305-308.

Latane, Henry A. "The Geometric Mean Criterion Continued," (4), 309-311.

Gordon, Myron J. and Clarence C. Y. Kwan. "Debt Maturity, Default Risk, And Capital Structure," (4), 313-329.

Rose, John T. and Peter S. Rose. "The Burden Of Federal Reserve System Membership: A Review Of The Evidence," (4), 331-346.

Mason, J. M. "Modeling Mutual Funds And Commercial Banks: A Comparative Analysis," (4), 347-353.

Errunza, Vihang E. "Efficiency And The Programs To Develop Capital Markets: The Brazilian Experience," (4), 355-382.

Smith, Paul F. "Changing Patterns In The Cycles In Short-Term Interest Rates," (4), 383-396.

Bertoneche, Marc L. "An Empirical Analysis Of The Interrelationships Among Equity Markets Under Changing Exchange Rate Systems," (4), 397-405.

**Journal of Banking and Finance
Volume 4, 1980**

Mayer, Thomas. "Competitive Equality As A Criterion For Financial Reform," (1), 7-15.

Rose, Harold B. "The Competition For Deposits And The Impact Of Monetary Policy," (1), 17-32.

Krummel, Hans-Jacob. "German Universal Banking Scrutinized: Some Remarks Concerning The Gessler Report," (1), 33-55.

Lamy, Pascal and Jean-Francois Vincensini. "The Decentralization Of Credit: A Selected Summary Of The Mayoux Report," (1), 57-63.

Dothan, Uri and Joseph Williams. "Banks, Bankruptcy, And Regulation," (1), 65-87.

Jones, E. Philip and Scott P. Mason. "Valuation Of Loan Guarantees," (1), 89-107.

Meeker, Larry G. and Forest E. Myers. "Financing Bank Stock Ownership: A Question Of Conflict Of Interest," (1), 109-124.

Hicks, Sydney Smith. "Commercial Banks And Business Loan Behavior," (2), 125-142.

Rhoades, Stephen A. "Entry And Competition In Banking," (2), 143-150.

Chateau, Jean-Pierre D. "The Demand For And Supply Of Deposits By Credit Unions: The Caisses Populaires' Case," (2), 151-173.

Elton, Edwin, Martin Gruber and Joel Rentzler. "A Simple Examination Of The Empirical Relationship Between Dividend Yields And Deviations From The CAPM," (1), 135-146.

Peavy, John W., III and S. Michael Edgar. "A Multiple Discriminant Analysis Of BHC Commercial Paper Ratings," (2), 161-174.

Meeker, Larry G., O. Maurice Joy and Kenneth O. Cogger. "Valuation Of Controlling Shares In Closely Held Banks," (2), 175-188.

Amihud, Yakov, Jacob Y. Kamin and Joshua Ronen. "'Management', 'Ownerism', And Risk," (2), 189-196.

Huffman, Lucy. "Operating Leverage, Financial Leverage, And Equity Risk," (2), 197-212.

Swary, Itzhak. "Bank Acquisition Of Non-Bank Firms: An Empirical Analysis Of Administrative Decisions," (2), 213-230.

Poncet, Patrice. "Optimum Consumption And Portfolio Rules With Money As An Asset," (2), 231-252.

Browne, F. X. "Departures From Interest Rates Parity: Further Evidence," (2), 253-272.

Hansen, Robert S. and John G. Thatcher. "On The Nature Of Credit Demand And Credit Rationing In Competitive Credit Markets," (2), 273-284.

Smith, Donald J. "The Demand For And Supply Of Deposits By Credit Unions: The Caisses Populaires' Case-Correction And Comment," (2), 285-287.

Chateau, John-Peter D. "The Demand For And Supply Of Deposits By Credit Unions: The Caisses Populaires' Case-Reply And Comments," (2), 289-293.

Jarrow, Robert and Andrew Rudd. "A Comparison Of The APT And CAPM: A Note," (2), 295-303.

Lam, Chun H. and Kenneth J. Boudreaux. "Compensating Balances, Deficiency Fees, And Lines Of Credit," (3), 307-322.

Galai, Dan. "Pricing Of Optional Bonds," (3), 323-338.

Bashir, B. A. "Portfolio Management Of Islamic Banks: 'Certainty Model'," (3), 339-354.

Galitz, Lawrence C. "InterBank: A Bank Management Simulation Exercise," (3), 355-382.

VanHoose, David D. "Monetary Policy Under Alternative Bank Market Structures," (3), 383-404.

Koskela, Erkki. "Credit Rationing And Non-Price Loan Terms: A Reexamination," (3), 405-416.

Woodward, R. S. "The Performance Of U. K. Investment Trusts As Internationally Diversified Portfolios Over The Period 1968 To 1977," (3), 417-426.

Rhoades, Stephen A. "Concentration Of World Banking And The Role Of U. S. Banks Among The 100 Largest, 1956-1980," (3), 427-437.

Teeters, Nancy. "The Role Of Banks In The International Financial System," (4), 447-451.

McKenzie, George and Stephen Thomas. "Liquidity, Credit Creation And International Banking: An Econometric Investigation," (4), 467-480.

Agmon, Tamir and J. Kimball Dietrich. "International Lending And Income Redistribution: An Alternative View Of Country Risk," (4), 483-495.

Szego, Giorgio P. "The Role Of International Banking In The `Oil Surplus' Adjustment Process," (4), 497-518.

Lessard, Donald. "North-South: The Implications For Multinational Banking," (4), 521-536.

Niehans, Jurg. "Financial Innovation, Multinational Banking, And Monetary Policy," (4), 537-551.

Greene, James. "Bank Lending To Third World Countries In The 1980's," (4), 553-558.

Torell, John R., III. "U. S. Financial Deregulation: Upheaval And Promise," (4), 561-566.

Walker, David A. "U. S. Banking Regulations And Foreign Banks' Entry Into The United States," (4), 569-580.

Kindleberger, Charles P. "International Banks As Leaders Or Followers Of International Business: An Historical Perspective," (4), 583-595.

Walter, Ingo and H. Peter Gray. "Protectionism And International Banking: Sectoral Efficiency, Competitive Structure And National Policy," (4), 597-610.

Heimann, John G. "The Effects Of Political, Economic And Institutional Development On International Banks," (4), 615-622.

Zecher, J. Richard. "The Effects Of The Current Turbulent Times On American Multinational Banking: An Overview," (4), 625-637.

Journal of Banking and Finance
Volume 8, 1984

Spindt, Paul A. and Vefa Tarhan. "Bank Reserve Adjustment Process And The Use Of Reserve Carryover As A Reserve Management Tool: A Microeconometric Approach," (1), 5-20.

Billingsley, Randall S. and Robert E. Lamy. "Market Reaction To The Formation Of One-Bank Holding Companies And The 1970 Bank Holding Company Act Amendment," (1), 21-33.

Bierwag, G. O., George G. Kaufman and Paul H. Leonard. "Interest Rate Effects Of Commercial Bank Underwriting Of Municipal Revenue Bonds: Additional Evidence," (1), 35-50.

Thore, Sten. "Spatial Models Of The Eurodollar Market," (1), 51-65.

Gilligan, Thomas W. and Michael L. Smirlock. "An Empirical Study Of Joint Production And Scale Economies In Commercial Banking," (1), 67-78.

Molho, Lazaros E. "Loan Rates As A Selective Credit Control," (1), 79-98.

Slovin, Myron B. and Marie Elizabeth Sushka. "A Note On The Evidence On Alternative Models Of The Banking Firm: A Cross Section Study Of Commercial Loan Rates," (1), 99-108.

Jahera, John S., Jr. and Joseph F. Sinkey, Jr. "A Note On The Intracyclical Balance-Sheet Behavior Of Large Commercial Banks: 1972-1978," (1), 109-118.

Rhoades, Stephen A. and Alice P. White. "Output In Relation To Labor Input In The Banking And Savings And Loan Industries: 1927-1979," (1), 119-130.

Bennett, Paul. "Applying Portfolio Theory To Global Bank Lending," (2), 153-170.

Altman, Edward I. "The Success Of Business Failure Prediction Models: An International Survey," (2), 171-198.

Taffler, Richard J. "Empirical Models For The Monitoring Of UK Corporations," (2), 199-228.

Takahashi, Kichinosuke, Yukiharu Kurokawa and Kazunori Watase. "Corporate Bankruptcy Prediction In Japan," (2), 229-247.

von Stein, Johann Heinrich and Werner Ziegler. "The Prognosis And Surveillance Of Risks From Commercial Credit Borrowers," (2), 249-268.

Appetiti, Sandro. "Identifying Unsound Firms In Italy: An Attempt To Use Trend Variables," (2), 269-280.

Micha, Bernard. "Analysis Of Business Failures In France," (2), 281-292.

Tamari, Meir. "The Use Of A Bankruptcy Forecasting Model To Analyze Corporate Behavior In Israel," (2), 293-302.

Izan, H. Y. "Corporate Distress In Australia," (2), 303-320.

Lincoln, Mervyn. "An Empirical Study Of The Usefulness Of Accounting Ratios To Describe Levels Of Insolvency Risk," (2), 321-340.

Saini, Krishan G. and Philip S. Bates. "A Survey Of The Quantitative Approaches To Country Risk Analysis," (2), 341-356.

Schmidt, Reinhart. "Early Warning Of Debt Rescheduling," (2), 357-370.

Ahking, Francis W. "The Predictive Performance Of The Time-Series Model And The Regression Model Of The Income Velocity Of Money: Evidence From Five EEC Countries," (3), 389-415.

Srivastava, Rajendra K., Thomas H. McInish and Linda L. Price. "Information Costs And Portfolio Selection," (3), 417-429.

Borch, Karl. "Premiums In A Competitive Insurance Market," (3), 431-441.

Calderon-Rossell, Jorge R. "Optimal Financial Structure Of Finance Companies In A Regulated Environment Of A Developing Country," (3), 443-457.

Beckers, Stan. "On The Efficiency Of The Gold Options Market," (3), 459-470.

Ball, Ray. "The Natural Taxation Of Capital Gains And Losses When Income Is Taxed," (3), 471-481.

Lahiri, Kajal and Mark Zaporowski. "A Note On The Variability Of Real Interest Rates, Business Cycles, And The Livingston Data," (3), 483-490.

Jaffe, Jeffrey F. and Randolph Westerfield. "Leverage And The Value Of A Firm Under A Progressive Income Tax: A Correction And Extension," (3), 491-494.

Gordon, Myron J. "Leverage And The Value Of A Firm Under A Progressive Personal Income Tax: Reply," (3), 495-498.

Kroll, Yoram. "The Analysis Of Risky Investment: A State-Contingent Approach," (4), 509-524.

Dotan, Amihud and Aharon Ofer. "Variable Versus Stationary Beta In The Market Model: A Comparative Analysis," (4), 525-534.

Micossi, S. and S. Rebecchini. "A Case Study On The Effectiveness Of Foreign Exchange Market Intervention: The Italian Lira (September 1975-March 1977)," (4), 535-555.

Marcus, Alan J. "Deregulation And Bank Financial Policy," (4), 557-565.

Dufey, Gunter and Ian H. Giddy. "Eurocurrency Deposit Risk," (4), 567-589.

Journal of Banking and Finance
Volume 9, 1985

Taub, Bart. "Equilibrium Traits Of Durable Commodity Money," (1), 5-34.

Alexander, Gordon J. and Bruce G. Resnick. "Using Linear And Goal Programming To Immunize Bond Portfolios," (1), 35-54.

Wasserfallen, Walter and Heinz Zimmermann. "The Behavior Of Intra-Daily Exchange Rates," (1), 55-72.

Dhrymes, Phoebus J., Irwin Friend, N. Bulent Gultekin and Mustafa N. Gultekin. "An Empirical Examination Of The Implications Of Arbitrage Pricing Theory," (1), 73-99.

Ball, Clifford A., Walter N. Torous and Adrian E. Tschoegl. "An Empirical Investigation Of The EOE Gold Options Market," (1), 101-113.

McShane, R. W. and I. G. Sharpe. "A Time Service/Cross Section Analysis Of The Determinants Of Australian Trading Bank Loan/Deposit Interest Margins: 1962-1981," (1), 115-136.

McCulloch, J. Huston. "Interest-Risk Sensitive Deposit Insurance Premia: Stable ACH Estimates," (1), 137-156.

Gehrlein, William V. and Thomas H. McInish. "Cyclical Variability Of Bond Risk Premia: A Note," (1), 157-166.

Nelson, Richard W. "Branching, Scale Economies, And Banking Costs," (2), 177-192.

Sealey, C. W., Jr. and Robert Heinkel. "Asymmetric Information And A Theory Of Compensating Balances," (2), 193-205.

Geske, Robert and Kuldeep Shastri. "The Early Exercise Of American Puts," (2), 207-219.

Eaker, Mark R. and Dwight Grant. "Optimal Hedging Of Uncertain And Long-Term Foreign Exchange Exposure," (2), 221-231.

Scott, Jonathan A., George H. Hempel and John W. Peavy, III. "The Effect Of Stock-For-Debt Swaps On Bank Holding Companies," (2), 233-251.

West, Robert Craig. "A Factor-Analytic Approach To Bank Condition," (2), 253-266.

Korobow, Leon and David Stuhr. "Performance Measurement Of Early Warning Models: Comments On West And Other Weakness/Failure Prediction Models," (2), 267-273.

Granziol, Markus J. "Direct Price Controls As A Source Of Instability In The Interest Rate/Inflation Rate Relationship," (2), 275-288.

Bryant, John. "A Clower Constraint Model Of Unbacked Money," (2), 289-295.

Sherman, H. David and Franklin Gold. "Bank Branch Operating Efficiency: Evaluation With Data Envelopment Analysis," (2), 297-316.

Raveh, Adi. "A Note On Factor Analysis And Arbitrage Pricing Theory," (2), 317-322.

Koppenhaver, G. D. "A Note On Managing Deposit Flows With Cash And Futures Market Decisions," (2), 323-332.

Hasbrouck, Joel. "The Characteristics Of Takeover Targets," (3), 351-362.

Torous, Walter N. "Differential Taxation And The Equilibrium Structure Of Interest Rates," (3), 363-385.

Journal of Banking and Finance

Ohlson, James A. "Ex Post Stockholder Unanimity," (3), 387-399.
Plaut, Steven E. "The Theory Of Collateral," (3), 401-419.
Kling, John L. "The Dynamic Behavior Of Business Loans And The Prime Rate," (3), 421-442.
Fung, William K. H., Robert A. Schwartz and David K. Whitcomb. "Adjusting For The Intervalling Effect Bias In Beta," (3), 443-460.
Sealey, C. W., Jr. "Portfolio Separation For Stockholder Owned Depository Financial Intermediaries," (4), 477-490.
Day, Theodore E. "Expected Inflation And The Real Rate Of Interest: A Note," (4), 491-498.
Sprenkle, Case M. "On The Precautionary Demand For Assets," (4), 499-515.
Gandhi, Devinder K., Robert Hausmann, Jr. and Anthony Saunders. "On Syndicate Sharing Rules For Unanimous Project Rankings," (4), 517-534.
Langohr, Herwig and Anthony M. Santomero. "Commercial Bank Refinancing And Economic Stability: An Analysis Of European Features," (4), 535-552.
Hawawini, Gabriel A., Pierre A. Michel and Albert Corhay. "New Evidence On Beta Stationarity And Forecast For Belgian Common Stocks," (4), 553-560.
Errunza, Vihang R. and Etienne Losq. "The Behavior Of Stock Prices On LDC Markets," (4), 561-575.
Angeloni, Ignazio. "The Dynamic Behavior Of Business Loans And The Prime Rate: A Comment," (4), 577-580.
Kling, John L. "The Dynamic Behavior Of Business Loans And The Prime Rate: Reply," (4), 581-584.
Fraser, Donald R., R. Malcolm Richards and Richard H. Fosberg. "A Note On Deposit Rate Deregulation, Super NOWS, And Bank Security Returns," (4), 585-596.

Journal of Banking and Finance
Volume 10, 1986

Mahajan, Arvind and Dileep Mehta. "Swaps, Expectations, And Exchange Rates," (1), 7-20.
Conroy, Robert M. and Robert L. Winkler. "Market Structure: The Specialist As Dealer And Broker," (1), 21-36.
Hancock, Diana. "A Model Of The Financial Firm With Imperfect Asset And Deposit Elasticities," (1), 37-54.
Cornell, Bradford and Alan C. Shapiro. "The Reaction Of Bank Stock Prices To The International Debt Crisis," (1), 55-73.
Guttentag, Jack and Richard Herring. "Disclosure Policy And International Banking," (1), 75-97.
Dermine, J. "Deposit Rates, Credit Rates And Bank Capital: The Klein-Monti Model Revisited," (1), 99-114.
Lakonishok, Josef and Alan C. Shapiro. "Systematic Risk, Total Risk And Size As Determinants Of Stock Market Returns," (1), 115-132.
Dymits, Lee and Michael L. Murray. "Another Look At Implied Tax Rates," (1), 133-142.
Murphy, James M. and Allen Rappaport. "A Multiple Discriminant Analysis Of BHC Commercial Paper Ratings: A Comment," (1), 143-144.
Peavy, John W., III and S. Michael Edgar. "A Multiple Discriminant Analysis Of BHC Commercial Paper Ratings: A Reply," (1), 145-146.
Van Hoose, David D. "A Note On Interest On Required Reserves As An Instrument Of Monetary Control," (1), 147-156.
Kane, Edward J. "Appearance And Reality In Deposit Insurance: The Case For Reform," (2), 175-188.
Pyle, David H. "Capital Regulation And Deposit Insurance," (2), 189-201.
Goodman, Laurie S. and Anthony M. Santomero. "Variable-Rate Deposit Insurance: A Re-Examination," (2), 203-218.
Allen, Linda and Anthony Saunders. "The Large-Small Bank Dichotomy In The Federal Funds Market," (2), 219-230.
Crouhy, Michel and Dan Galai. "An Economic Assessment Of Capital Requirements In The Banking Industry," (2), 231-241.
Chan, Yuk-Shee, Stuart I. Greenbaum and Anjan V. Thakor. "Information Reusability, Competition And Bank Asset Quality," (2), 243-253.
Lieber, Zvi and Yair E. Orgler. "Optimal Borrowing And Bank Lending Policies: An Interactive Approach," (2), 255-266.
Melnik, Arie and Steven E. Plaut. "The Economics Of Loan Commitment Contracts: Credit Pricing And Utilization," (2), 267-280.
Eaton, Jonathan. "Lending With Costly Enforcement Of Repayment And Potential Fraud," (2), 281-293.
Szego, Giorgio P. "Bank Asset Management And Financial Insurance," (2), 295-308.
Jaffee, Dwight M. "Term Structure Intermediation By Depository Institutions," (2), 309-326.
Zechner, Josef and Peter Swoboda. "The Critical Implicit Tax Rate And Capital Structure," (3), 327-341.
Penati, Alessandro. "The Sources Of The Movements In Interest Rates: An Empirical Investigation," (3), 343-360.
Matolcsy, Z. P. "The Distributive Nominal And Real Micro Effects Of Inflation On Security Returns: Some Australian Evidence," (3), 361-376.
Wahlroos, Bjorn and Tom Berglund. "Stock Returns, Inflationary Expectations And Real Activity: New Evidence," (3), 377-389.
Green, Richard C. and Eli Talmor. "Asset Substitution And The Agency Costs Of Debt Financing," (3), 391-400.
Amihud, Yakov, Peter Dodd and Mark Weinstein. "Conglomerate Mergers, Managerial Motives And Stockholder Wealth," (3), 401-410.
Clark, Jeffrey A. and Paul J. Speaker. "Compensating Balance Requirements And The Firm's Demand For Transactions Balances," (3), 411-429.
Laurence, Martin M. "Weak-Form Efficiency In The Kuala Lumpur And Singapore Stock Markets," (3), 431-446.
Morgan, George Emir, III and Stephen D. Smith. Basis Risk, Partial Takedown And Hedging By Financial Intermediaries," (4), 467-490.
Prisman, Eliezer Z. Immunization As A Maxmin Strategy: A New Look," (4), 491-510.

Lane, William R., Stephen W. Looney and James W. Wansley. "An Application Of The Cos Proportional Hazards Model To Bank Failure," (4), 511-532.
Liang, Ming-Yih. "Bank Float, Mail Float And The Definition Of Money," (4), 533-548.
Jehle, Geoffrey A. "Regulation And The Public Interest In Banking," (4), 549-574.
Canarella, Giorgio and Stephen K. Pollard. "The `Efficiency' Of The London Metal Exchange: A Test With Overlapping And Non-Overlapping Data," (4), 575-594.
Hansen, Robert S., John M. Pinkerton and Tai Ma. "On The Rightholders' Subscription To The Underwritten Rights Offering," (4), 595-604.
Perry, Larry G. and Timothy P. Cronan. "A Note On Rank Transformation Discriminant Analysis: An Alternative Procedure For Classifying Bank Holding Company Commercial Paper Ratings," (4), 605-610.
Havrilesky, Thomas. "A Comment On Niehans' Innovation In Monetary Policy," (4), 611-614.
Niehans, Jurg. "Further Comment," (4), 615-616.

Journal of Banking and Finance
Volume 11, 1987

Grube, R. Corwin, O. Maurice Joy and John S. Howe. "Some Empirical Evidence On Stock Returns And Security Credit Regulation In The OTC Equity Market," (1), 17-32.
Arshadi, Nasser and Edward C. Lawrence. "An Empirical Investigation Of New Bank Performance," (1), 33-48.
Aggarwal, Raj and P. S. Sundararaghavan. "Efficiency Of The Silver Futures Market: An Empirical Study Using Daily Data," (1), 49-64.
Fung, W. K. H. and M. F. Theobald. "Taxes, Unequal Access, Public Debt And Corporate Financial Policy In The United Kingdom," (1), 65-78.
Barnea, Amir, Eli Talmor and Robert A. Haugen. "Debt And Taxes: A Multiperiod Investigation," (1), 79-98.
Tarhan, Vefa. "Unanticipated Interest Rates, Bank Stock Returns And The Nominal Contracting Hypothesis," (1), 99-116.
Kryzanowski, Lawrence and Minh Chau To. "The E-V Stationarity Of Security Returns: Some Empirical Evidence," (1), 117-136.
Melnik, Arie and Steven E. Plaut. "Interest Rate Indexation And The Pricing Of Loan Commitment Contracts," (1), 137-146.
Sprenkle, Case M. "Liability And Asset Uncertainty For Banks," (1), 147-160.
Meeker, Larry G. and Laura Gray. "A Note On Non-Performing Loans As An Indicator Of Asset Quality," (1), 161-168.
Burdett, Kenneth and Maureen O'Hara. "Building Blocks: An Introduction To Block Trading," (2), 193-212.
Martin, John D. and Arthur J. Keown. "One-Bank Holding Company Formation And The 1970 Bank Holding Company Act Amendment: An Empirical Examination Allowing For Industry Group Effects," (2), 213-222.
Vanthienen, Lambert and Theo Vermaelen. "The Effect Of Personal Taxes On Common Stock Prices: The Case Of A Belgian Tax Reform," (2), 223-244.
Shastri, Kuldeep and Kishore Tandon. "Valuation Of American Options On Foreign Currency," (2), 245-270.
Thakor, Anjan V. and Gregory F. Udell. "An Economic Rationale For The Pricing Structure Of Bank Loan Commitments," (2), 271-290.
Pennacchi, George G. "Alternative Forms Of Deposit Insurance: Pricing And Bank Incentive Issues," (2), 291-312.
Friend, Irwin and Ichiro Tokutsu. "The Cost Of Capital To Corporations In Japan And The U.S.A.," (2), 313-328.
Nauss, Robert M. "Generating Optimal True Interest Cost Bids For New Municipal Bond Competitive Issues," (2), 329-344.
Karceken, John H. "The Emergence And Regulation Of Contingent Commitment Banking," (3), 359-378.
Greenbaum, Stuart I. and Anjan V. Thakor. "Bank Funding Modes: Securitization Versus Deposits," (3), 379-402.
Benveniste, Lawrence M. and Allen N. Berger. "Securitization With Recourse: An Instrument That Offers Uninsured Bank Depositors Sequential Claims," (3), 403-424.
Kanatas, George. "Commercial Paper, Bank Reserve Requirements, And The Informational Role Of Loan Commitments," (3), 425-448.
Boot, Arnoud, Anjan V. Thakor and Gregory F. Udell. "Competition, Risk Neutrality And Loan Commitments," (3), 449-472.
Lucas, Deborah and Robert L. McDonald. "Bank Portfolio Choice With Private Information About Loan Quality: Theory And Implications For Regulation," (3), 473-498.
Ronn, Ehud I. and Avinash K. Verma. "A Multi-Attribute Comparative Evaluation Of Relative Risk For A Sample Of Banks," (3), 499-524.
Kau, James B., Donald C. Keenan, Walter J. Muller, III and James F. Epperson. "The Valuation And Securitization Of Commercial And Multifamily Mortgages," (3), 525-546.
Adams, Paul D. and Steve B. Wyatt. "Biases In Option Prices: Evidence From The Foreign Currency Option Market," (4), 549-562.
VanHoose, David D. "A Note On Discount Rate Policy And The Variability Of Discount Window Borrowing," (4), 563-570.
Carrington, Samantha and Robert Crouch. "Interest Rate Differentials On Short-Term Securities And Rational Expectations Of Inflation," (4), 571-580.
Wall, Larry D. and David R. Peterson. "The Effect Of Capital Adequacy Guidelines On Large Bank Holding Companies," (4), 581-600.

Journal of Banking and Finance
Volume 12, 1988

Friend, Irwin and Larry H. P. Lang. "The Size Effect On Stock Returns: Is It Simply A Risk Effect Not Adequately Reflected By The Usual Measures?," (1), 13-30.
Smirlock, Michael and Laura Starks. "An Empirical Analysis Of The Stock Price-Volume Relationship," (1), 31-42.
Lessard, Donald R. and Adrian E. Tschoegl. "Panama's International Banking Center: The Direct Employment Effects," (1), 43-50.

Journal of Banking and Finance
Volume 13, 1989

Zilberfarb, Ben Zion. "Overdraft Banking: An Empirical Analysis," (6), 869-882.
Furlong, Frederick T. and Michael C. Keeley. "Capital Regulation And Bank Risk-Taking: A Note," (6), 883-892.

Journal of Banking and Finance
Volume 14, 1990

O'Hara, M. "Financial Contracts And International Lending," (1), 11-32.
Prisman, E. Z. "Bond Pricing In Markets With Taxes: The Tax-Clientele Model Vs. The Non-Clientele Model," (1), 33-40.
Choi, J. J. and S. Hauser. "The Effects Of Domestic And Foreign Yield Curves On The Value Of Currency American Call Options," (1), 41-54.
Niehaus, Gregory R. "The PBGC's Flat Fee Schedule, Moral Hazard, And Promised Pension Benefits," (1), 55-68.
Keeley, M. C. and F. T. Furlong. "A Reexamination Of Mean-Variance Analysis Of Bank Capital Regulation," (1), 69-84.
Hirschey, M., M. B. Slovin and J. K. Zaima. "Bank Debt, Insider Trading, And The Return To Corporate Selloffs," (1), 85-98.
McInish, T. H. and R. A. Wood. "A Transactions Data Analysis Of The Variability Of Common Stock Returns During 1980-1984," (1), 99-112.
Kemna, A. G. Z. and A. C. F. Vorst. "A Pricing Method For Options Based On Average Asset Values," (1), 113-130.
Evanoff, D. D. "An Empirical Examination Of Bank Reserve Management Behavior," (1), 131-144.
Papadia, F. and S. Rossi. "More On Monetarist Arithmetic," (1), 145-154.
Sprenkle, C. M., S. J. Turnovsky and R. A. Fujihara. "Assets, Aggregates And Optimal Monetary Control," (1), 155-178.
Eyssell, T. and N. Arshadi. "The Wealth Effects Of The Risk-Based Capital Requirement In Banking: The Evidence From The Capital Market," (1), 179-198.
Corradi, V., M. Galeotti and R. Rovelli. "A Cointegration Analysis Of The Relationship Between Bank Reserves, Deposits And Loans: The Case Of Italy, 1965-1987," (1), 199-214.
Brooks, R. and M. Livingston. "A Note On The Variance Of Spot Interest Rates," (1), 215-226.
Bergstrom, C. and K. Rydqvist. "The Determinants Of Corporate Ownership: An Empirical Study Of Swedish Data," (2/3), 237-254.
Bergstrom, C. and K. Rydqvist. "Ownership Of Equity In Dual-Class Firms," (2/3), 255-270.
Limmack, R. J. and C. W. R. Ward. "The October 1987 Stock Market Crash: An Exploratory Analysis Of Share Price Models," (2/3), 273-290.
Saunders, A. and J. Lim. "Underpricing And The New Issue Process In Singapore," (2/3), 291-310.
Ann, Wong Kie and Lye Meng Siong. "Market Values, Earnings' Yields And Stock Returns: Evidence From Singapore," (2/3), 311-326.
Hietala, P. T. "Equity Markets And Personal Taxation: The Ex-Dividend Day Behaviour Of Finnish Stock Prices," (2/3), 327-350.
Alonso, A., G. Rubio and F. Tusell. "Asset Pricing And Risk Aversion In The Spanish Stock Market," (2/3), 351-370.
Kawaller, I. G., P. D. Koch and T. W. Koch. "Intraday Relationships Between Volatility In S&P 500 Futures Prices And Volatility In The S&P 500 Index," (2/3), 373-398.
Dimson, E. and P. Marsh. "Volatility Forecasting Without Data-Snooping," (2/3), 399-422.
Amihud, Y., H. Mendelson and M. Murgia. "Stock Market, Microstructure And Return Volatility: Evidence From Italy," (2/3), 423-440.
McInish, T. H. and R. A. Wood. "An Analysis Of Transactions Data For The Toronto Stock Exchange: Return Patterns And End-Of-The-Day Effect," (2/3), 441-458.
Solnik, B. and L. Bousquet. "Day-Of-The-Week Effect On The Paris Bourse," (2/3), 461-468.
Alonso, A. and G. Rubio. "Overreaction In The Spanish Equity Market," (2/3), 469-482.
Barone, E. "The Italian Stock Market: Efficiency And Calendar Anomalies," (2/3), 483-510.
Grauer, R. R., N. H. Hakansson and F. C. Shen. "Industry Rotation In The U.S. Stock Market: 1934-1986 Returns On Passive, Semi-Passive, And Active Strategies," (2/3), 513-538.
Dumas, B. and B. Jacquillat. "Performance Of Currency Portfolios Chosen By A Bayesian Technique: 1967-1985," (2/3), 539-558.
Wijmenga, R. T. "The Performance Of Published Dutch Stock Recommendations," (2/3), 559-582.
Heffernan, S. A. "A Characteristics Definition Of Financial Markets," (2/3), 583-610.
Dumas, B. and B. Jacquillat. "The Money And Bond Markets In France: Segmentation Vs. Integration," (2/3), 613-636.
Tessaromatis, N. "Money Supply Announcements And Real Interest Rates: Evidence From The U.K. Index-Linked Bond Market, " (2/3), 637-648.
Gibson-Asner, R. "Valuing Swiss Default-Free Callable Bonds: Theory And Empirical Evidence," (2/3), 649-672.
Sofianos, G., P. Wachtel and A. Melnik. "Loan Commitments And Monetary Policy," (4), 677-690.
Kraizberg, E. "The Market Making Of Forward Contracts With Premature Delivery Provision," (4), 691-716.
Chateau, J. P. D. "Valuation Of 'Capped' Variable Rate Loan Commitments," (4), 717-728.
Slovin, M. B. and J. E. Young. "Bank Lending And Initial Public Offering," (4), 729-740.

Hegde, S. P. "An Ex Post Valuation Of The Quality Option Implicit In The Treasury Bond Futures Contract," (4), 741-760.
Kyle, S. C. and R. G. Wirick. "The Impact Of Sovereign Risk On The Market Valuation Of U.S. Bank Equities," (4), 761-780.
Detemple, J. and Ph. Jorion. "Option Listing And Stock Returns: An Empirical Analysis," (4), 781-802.
Yourougou, P. "Interest-Rate Risk And The Pricing Of Depository Financial Intermediary Common Stock: Empirical Evidence," (4), 803-820.
Stein, J. L. "Introduction To Special Issue On 'Real And Nominal Exchange Rates'," (5), 839-844.
Allen, P. R. "The Private ECU Markets: What They Are, Why They Exist, And Where They May Go," (5), 845-876.
Van Marrewijk, C. and C. G. De Vries. "The Customs Union Argument For A Monetary Union," (5), 877-888.
De Boissieu, Ch. "The Dynamics Of The EMS In The Light Of European Financial Integration: Some Reflections From A French Perspective," (5), 889-908.
Allen, P. R. and J. L. Stein. "Capital Market Integration," (5), 909-928.
Argy, V. E. "The Transmission Of Foreign Disturbances Under Different Exchange Rate Regimes," (5), 929-946.
Boughton, J. M. "External Adjustment In Large Countries: Is The Exchange Rate Irrelevant?," (5), 947-964.
Gandolfo, G., P. C. Padoan and G. Paladino. "Exchange Rate Determination: Single-Equation Or Economy-Wide Models? A Test Against The Random Walk," (5), 965-992.
Rich, G. "Exchange-Rate Management Under Floating Exchange Rates: A Skeptical Swiss View," (5), 993-1022.
Marston, R. C. "Systematic Movements In Real Exchange Rates In The G-5: Evidence On The Integration Of Internal And External Markets," (5), 1023-1044.
Stein, J. L. "The Real Exchange Rate," (5), 1045-1078.
Ueda, K. "Japanese Capital Outflows," (5), 1079-1102.
Kim, M. and V. Maksimovic. "Technology, Debt And The Exploitation Of Growth Options," (6), 1113-1132.
Howe, J. S. and J. Madura. "The Impact Of International Listings On Risk: Implications For Capital Market Integration," (6), 1133-1142.
Nawalkha, S. K. and N. J. Lacey. "Generalized Solutions Of Higher-Order Duration Measures," (6), 1143-1150.
Buono, M. J. and B. K. Eakin. "Branching Restrictions And Banking Costs," (6), 1151-1162.
Moazzami, B. "Interest Rates And Inflationary Expectations: Long-Run Equilibrium And Short-Run Adjustment," (6), 1163-1170.
Grammatikos, T. and P. Yourougou. "Market Expectations Of The Effects Of The Tax Reform Act Of 1986 On Banking Organizations," (6), 1171-1188.
Muller, U. A., M. M. Dacorogna, R. B. Olsen, O. V. Pictet, M. Schwarz and C. Morgenegg. "Statistical Study Of Foreign Exchange Rates, Empirical Evidence Of A Price Change Scaling Law, And Intraday Analysis," (6), 1189-1208.
Dahl, D. and R. E. Shrieves. "The Impact Of Regulation On Bank Equity Infusions," (6), 1209-1228.
Baradwaj, B. G., D. R. Fraser and E. P. H. Furtado. "Hostile Bank Takeover Offers: Analysis And Implications," (6), 1229-1242.
Lockwood, L. J. and T. H. McInish. "Tests Of Stability For Variances And Means Of Overnight/Intraday Returns During Bull And Bear Markets," (6), 1243-1254.

Journal of Banking and Finance
Volume 15, 1991

Lee, Suk Hun. "Ability And Willingness To Service Debt As Explanation For Commercial And Official Rescheduling Cases," (1), 5-27.
Blake, David and Mahmood Pradhan. "Debt-Equity Swaps As Bond Conversions: Implications For Pricing," (1), 29-41.
Kaufold, Howard and Michael Smirlock. "The Impact Of Credit Risk On The Pricing And Duration Of Floating-Rate Notes," (1), 43-52.
Espahbodi, Pouran. "Identification Of Problem Banks And Binary Choice Models," (1), 53-71.
Crouhy, Michel and Dan Galai. "A Contingent Claim Analysis Of A Regulated Depository Institution," (1), 73-90.
Goldberg, Lawrence G., Gerald A. Hanweck, Michael Keenan and Allan Young. "Economies Of Scale And Scope In The Securities Industry," (1), 91-107.
Gupta, Kanhaya L. "Interest Rates, Inflation Expectations And The Inverted Fisher Hypothesis," (1), 109-116.
Elton, Edwin J. and Martin J. Gruber. "Differential Information And Timing Ability," (1), 117-131.
Hannan, Timothy H. "Bank Commercial Loan Markets And The Role Of Market Structure: Evidence From Surveys Of Commercial Lending," (1), 133-149.
Madura, Jeff, Ann Marie White and Wm. R. McDaniel. "Reaction Of British Bank Share Prices To Citicorp's Announced $3 Billion Increase In Loan-Loss Reserves," (1), 151-163.
Shilling, James D. "On The Gains To Acquiring Capital-Stock Savings And Loan Associations In Merger Conversions: A Re-Examination Of The Regulatory-Approval Hypothesis," (1), 165-172.
Avery, Robert B. and Allen N. Berger. "Loan Commitments And Bank Risk Exposure," (1), 173-192.
McInish, Thomas H. and Robert A. Wood. "Autocorrelation Of Daily Index Returns: Intraday-to-Intraday Versus Close-To-Close Intervals," (1), 193-206.
Goldberg, Lawrence G. and Gerald A. Hanweck. "The Growth Of The World's 300 Largest Banking Organizations By Country," (1), 207-223.

Howard, John A. "Collusive Behavior," (3), 196-204.
Leavitt, Harold J. "A Note On Some Experimental Findings About The Meanings Of Price," (3), 205-210.
Loescher, Samuel M. "Geographical Pricing Policies And The Law," (3), 211-224.
McGee, John S. "The Decline And Fall Of Quantity Discounts: The Quantity Limit Rule In Rubber Tires And Tubes," (3), 225-234.
Riefler, Winfield W. "Monetary Policy," (3), 235-242.
Due, John F. "Canada's Experience With The Manufacturers' Sales Tax," (3), 243-253.
Burns, Robert K. "The Comparative Economic Position Of Manual And White-Collar Employees," (3), 257-267.
Solomon, Benjamin. "The Growth Of The White-Collar Work Force," (4), 268-275.
Goldstein, Bernard. "Unions And The Professional Employee," (4), 276-284.
Waters, Elinor. "Unionization Of Office Employees," (4), 285-292.
Scigliano, Robert G. "Trade-Unionism And The Industrial Foreman," (4), 293-300.
Zundel, Raulston G. "Conflict And Co-Operation Among Retail Unions," (4), 301-311.
Smyth, Henry D. "Industrial Application Of Atomic Energy," (4), 312-320.

Journal of Business
Volume 28, 1955

Argyris, Chris. "Organizational Leadership And Participative Management," (1), 1-7.
Leavitt, Harold J. "Small Groups In Large Organizations," (1), 8-17.
Albrecht, Paul A. "Projective Methods In Industry," (1), 18-28.
Whisler, Thomas L. "A Realistic Role For Merit Rating," (1), 29-36.
Krulee, Gilbert K. "Company-Wide Incentive Systems," (1), 37-47.
Stolz, Robert K. "Is Executive Development Coming Of Age?," (1), 48-57.
Moore, David G. and Richard Renck. "The Professional Employee In Industry," (1), 58-66.
Caldwell, J. E. and Charlotte Panimon. "Projective Testing In An Industrial Research Organization: One Experience," (1), 67-71.
Wallace, Thomas H. "Pre-Employment Tests And Post-Employment Performance," (1), 72-75.
Worthy, James C. "Education For Business Leadership," (1), 76-82.
Cook, Paul W., Jr. "Decentralization And The Transfer-Price Problem," (2), 87-94.
Solomon, Ezra. "The Current Recovery: An Analysis," (2), 95-99.
Krulee, Gilbert K. "The Scanlon Plan: Co-Operation Through Participation," (2), 100-113.
Kecker, Fred M. "Admissibility In Courts Of Law Of Economic Data Based On Samples," (2), 114-127.
Tull, Donald S. "A Re-Examination Of The Causes Of The Decline In Sales Of Sapolio," (2), 128-137.
Walter, James E. "The Use Of Borrowed Funds," (2), 138-147.
Chapin, Ned. "The Development Of The Break-Even Chart: A Bibliographical Note," (2), 148-149.
Drucker, Peter F. "The Management Horizon," (3), 155-164.
Keezer, Dexter Merriam. "The Short-Run Outlook For Busness Investment In New Plant And Equipment," (3), 165-168.
Chernick, Jack and Monroe Berkowitz. "The Guaranteed Wage - The Economics Of Opulence In Collective Bargaining," (3), 169-181.
Frankel, Marvin. "The Effects Of Fair Trade: Fact And Fiction In The Statistical Finds," (3), 182-194.
Henderson, John P. "A Deviation In The Pattern Of Relative Earnings For Production Workers And Office Personnel," (3), 195-205.
Carpenter, Walter H. and Charles L. Webster. "Communicating Business Ideas To Europe: A Case Study," (3), 206-212.
Solomon, Ezra. "Economic Growth And Common Stock Values," (3), 213-221.
Lorie, James H. and Leonard J. Savage. "Three Problems In Rationing Capital," (4), 229-239.
Solomon, Ezra. "Measuring A Company's Cost Of Capital," (4), 240-252.
Gordon, Myron J. "The Payoff Period And The Rate Of Profit," (4), 253-260.
Dean, Joel and Winfield Smith. "Has MAPI A Place In A Comprehensive System Of Capital Controls?," (4), 261-274.
Shillinglaw, Gordon. "Residual Values In Investment Analysis," (4), 275-284.
Hill, Horance G., Jr. "Capital Expenditure Management," (4), 285-290.
Norton, Frank E. "Administrative Organization In Capital Budgeting," (4), 291-295.
Villers, Raymond. "The Origin Of The Break-Even Chart," (4), 296-297.

Journal of Business
Volume 29, 1956

Roos, Charles F. "Problems Of Business Forecasting And The Outlook For Business," (1), 1-13.
Meier, R. L. "Automatism In The American Economy," (1), 14-27.
Clark, Clifford D. "Economic Appraisal Of Depreciation Policy," (1), 28-40.
McCarthy, E. J. "Wage Guarantees And Annual Earnings: A Case Study Of George A. Hormell And Company," (1), 41-51.
Shepard, Herbert A. "Patterns Of Organization For Applied Research And Development," (1), 52-58.
Dean, Joel. "Four Ways To Write Off Capital Investment: Management Should Have A Wider Tax Choice," (2), 79-89.
Schweiger, Irving. "Forecasting Short-Term Consumer Demand From Consumer Anticipations," (2), 90-100.
Martin, Norman H. and Anselm L. Strauss. "Patterns Of Mobility Within Industrial Organizations," (2), 101-110.
Crutchfield, James A. and Earl C. Hald. "Economic Expansion And The American Banking System," (2), 111-123.
Solomon, Ezra. "The Arithmetic Of Capital Budgeting-Decisions," (2), 124-129.
Danhof, Clarence. "Business Leadership In The South," (2), 130-137.

Terborgh, George. "Some Comments On The Dean-Smith Article On The MAPI Formula," (2), 138-140.
Cooper, Lyle. "Wage Guaranties At Hormel: A Comment," (2), 141-145.
Edwards, Corwin D. "Twenty Years Of The Robinson-Patman Act," (3), 149-159.
Caswell, W. Cameron. "Taking Stock Of Divisionalization," (3), 160-171.
Hirshleifer, Jack. "On The Economics Of Transfer Pricing," (3), 172-184.
Ulin, Robert P. "Financing Business Expansion-The Next Five Years," (3), 185-190.
Anderson, Clay J. "Consumer Instalment And Home-Mortgage Debt," (3), 191-200.
Segall, Joel. "The Effect Of Maturity On Price Fluctuations," (3), 202-206.
Carter, John P. "The New Maritime Nations," (3), 207-215.
McCarthy, E. J. "Wage Guaranties At Hormel: A Reply," (3), 216-217.
Riesman, David and Mark Benney. "Asking And Answering," (4), 225-236.
Cyert, Richard M., Herbert A. Simon, and Donald B. Trow. "Observation Of A Business Decision," (4), 237-248.
Martin, Norman H. "Differential Decisions In The Management Of An Industrial Plant," (4), 249-260.
Shepard, Herbert A. "Superiors And Subordinates In Research," (4), 261-267.
Morris, James R. "Job Rotation," (4), 268-273.
Whisler, Thomas L. "The Assistant To The Man In Motley," (4), 274-279.

Journal of Business
Volume 30, 1957

Craig, Paul G. and W. E. Schlender. "Some Relationships Between GAW And Seniority," (1), 1-11.
Roberts, Harry V. "Current Problems In The Economics Of Capital Budgeting," (1), 12-16.
Shillinglaw, Gordon. "Profit Analysis For Abandonment Decisions," (1), 17-29.
Walter, James E. "Determination Of Technical Solvency," (1), 30-43.
Maher, John E. "The Interpretation Of Wage Data," (1), 44-49.
Owen, C. F. "Cost Factors In The Integration Of Company Unemployment Benefits And Unemployment Insurance," (1), 50-59.
Stocking, George W. and Willard F. Mueller. "Business Reciprocity And The Size Of Firms," (2), 73-95.
Hirshleifer, Jack. "Economics Of The Divisionalized Firm," (2), 96-108.
Oakes, Ralph H. "Resale Price Maintenance In Chicago, 1953-55 (A Study Of Three Products)," (2), 109-130.
Bornemann, Alfred. "The Development Of Economics And Administration In The School Of Business," (2), 131-140.
Evans, Franklin B. "Motivation Research And Advertising Readership," (2), 141-146.
Leavitt, Harold J. "On The Export Of American Management Education," (3), 153-161.
Hoag, Malcolm W. "Operations Research - A New Science?," (3), 162-171.
Lorie, James H. "Two Important Problems In Sales Forecasting," (3), 172-179.
Cerf, Alan Robert. "Diverse Accounting Procedures, Price-Level Changes, And Financial Statement Ratios," (3), 180-192.
Renshaw, Ed. "A Note On The Arithmetic Of Capital Budgeting Decisions," (3), 193-201.
Strauss, George. "The Changing Role Of The Working Supervisor," (3), 202-211.
Shiskin, Julius. "Electronic Computers And Business Indicators," (4), 219-267.
Emmer, Robert E. "Compensating Balances And The Cost Of Loanable Funds," (4), 268-275.
Bierman, Harold and Seymour Smidt. "Capital Budgeting And The Problem Of Reinvesting Cash Proceeds," (4), 276-279.

Journal of Business
Volume 31, 1958

Mason, Edward S. "The Apologetics Of 'Managerialism'," (1), 1-11.
Fand, David I. and Ira O. Scott, Jr. "The Federal Reserve System's 'Bills Only' Policy: A Suggested Interpretation," (1), 12-18.
Whisler, Thomas L. "Performance Appraisal And The Organization Man," (1), 19-27.
Eilbirt, Henry. "A Study Of Current Counseling Practices In Industry," (1), 28-37.
Scherer, Joseph. "Labor Force: Concepts, Measurement, And Use Of Data," (1), 38-62.
Drucker, Peter F. "Business Objectives And Survival Needs: Notes On A Discipline Of Business Enterprise," (2), 81-90.
Yntema, Theodore. "Transferable Skills And Abilities," (2), 91-94.
Brozen, Yale. "Time, Demand, And Market Position," (2), 95-106.
Derber, Milton, W. Ellison Chalmers, and Ross Stagner. "Collective Bargaining And Management Functions: An Empirical Study," (2), 107-120.
Coughlan, John W. "Tax Reductions And Tax Deferrals," (2), 121-131.
Smith, Lincoln. "Businessmen As Regulatory Commissioners," (2), 132-144.
Burns, Arthur F. "The Current Business Recession," (2), 145-153.
Stigler, George. "The Goals Of Economic Policy," (3), 169-176.
Maffei, Richard B. "Simulation, Sensitivity, And Management Decision Rules," (3), 177-186.
Margolis, Julius. "The Analysis Of The Firm: Rationalism, Conventionalism, And Behaviorism," (3), 187-199.
Lamberton, D. McL. "Economic Growth And Stock Prices: The Australian Experience," (3), 200-212.
Fagg, Donald R., Carl Kaysen and Roland N. McKean. "What The Factory Worker Knows About His Factory," (3), 213-234.
Banks, Seymour and Albert Madansky. "Estimation Of Multimagazine Readership," (3), 235-242.

Turner, Robert C. "The Apologetics Of 'Managerialism'": Comment," (3), 243-248.

Clark, Colin. "International Comparisons Of Productivity Trends," (4), 267-279.

Enke, Stephen. "On The Economic Management Of Large Organizations: A Laboratory Study," (4), 280-292.

Worthy, James C. "Religion And Its Role In The World Of Business," (4), 293-303.

Strotz, Robert H. "On Being Fooled By Figures: The Case Of Trading Stamps," (4), 304-310.

Jung, Allen F. "Price Variations On Automatic Washing Machines In Chicago, Illinois, Among Different Types Of Retail Outlets," (4), 311-317.

Montgomery, Royal E., Irwin M. Stelzer, and Rosalind Roth. "Collective Bargaining Over Profit Sharing: The Automobile Union's Effort To Extend Its Frontier Of Control," (4), 318-334.

Renshaw, Ed. "Utility Regulation: A Re-Examination," (4), 335-343.

Mayer, Raymond R. "A Case Study Of Effective Communication In Industry," (4), 344-350.

Journal of Business
Volume 32, 1959

Stark, Stanley. "Research Criteria Of Executive Success," (1), 1-14.

Wright, David McCord. "Community,' Mobility, Security: A Footnote On Economic Growth," (1), 15-19.

Charnes, A., W. W. Cooper, and M. H. Miller. "Application Of Linear Programming To Financial Budgeting And The Costing Of Funds," (1), 20-46.

Sorter, George H. "Reported Income And Inventory Change," (1),47-51.

Grunfeld, Yehuda. "The Effect Of The Per Diem Rate On The Efficiency And Size Of The American Railroad Freight-Car Fleet," (1), 52-73.

Solomon, Ezra. "The Economic Outlook-1959," (1), 74-78.

Nelson, Richard R. "The Economics Of Invention: A Survey Of The Literature," (2), 101-127.

McCarthy, E. J. "Organization For New Product Development?," (2), 128-132.

Jung, Allen F. "Price Variations On Automatic Washing Machines In Chicago, Illinois, Among Different Types Of Retail Outlets-1955 Versus 1958," (2), 133-140.

Davis, Otto A. "The Economics Of Trading Stamps," (2), 141-150.

Weber, C. Edward. "Change In Managerial Manpower With Mechanization Of Data-Processing," (2), 151-163.

Bodenhorn, Diran. "A Note On The Theory Of The Firm," (2), 164-174.

Jehring, J. J. "Profit-Sharing And Collective Bargaining," (2), 175-177.

Margolis, Julius. "Traditional And Revisionist Theories Of The Firm: A Comment," (2), 178-182.

Arthur, H. B. "'Religion And Its Role In The World Of Business': A Comment," (2), 183-184.

Okun, Arthur M. "A Review Of Some Economic Forecasts For 1955-57," (3), 199-211.

George, Edwin B. and Robert J. Landry. "The Federal Reserve Board Report On Small-Business Financing," (3), 212-228.

Richards, Kenneth E. "A New Concept Of Performance Appraisal," (3), 229-243.

Wellisz, Stanislaw. "The European Common Market And American Foreign Trade And Investment," (3), 244-257.

Daly, Donald J. "Seasonal Variations And Business Expectations," (3), 258-270.

Nerlove, Marc. "On The Efficiency Of The Coal Industry," (3), 271-278.

Beem, Eugene R. "On Being Fooled By Statisticians: The Case Of Professor Strotz," (3), 279-282.

Strotz, Robert H. "Trading Comments On Trading Stamps: A Rejoinder," (3), 283-286.

Jung, Allen F. "Price Variations Among Automobile Dealers In Chicago, Illinois," (4), 315-325.

Fouraker, L. E. "Trouble In The Technique Industry," (4), 327-339.

Evans, Franklin B. "Psychological And Objective Factors In The Prediction Of Brand Choice: Ford Versus Chevrolet," (4), 340-369.

Van Lierde, Paul A. "Price-Level Changes And Capital Consumption Allowances," (4), 370-382.

Weisbrod, Burton A. "The Per Diem Freight-Car Rate And Railroad Efficiency-The Short-Run Problem," (4), 383-385.

Journal of Business
Volume 33, 1960

Myers, Charles A. "Lessons From Abroad For American Management," (1), 1-9.

Kilbridge, Maurice D. "The Effort Bargain In Industrial Society," (1), 10-20.

Roberts, Harry V. "The New Business Statistics," (1), 21-30.

Jung, Allen F. "Price Variations Among Automobile Dealers In Metropolitan Chicago," (1), 31-42.

Landon, Charles E. "Technological Progress In Transportation On The Mississippi River System," (1), 43-62.

Paarlberg, Don. "The Economic Challenge Of The Soviet Union," (2), 93-100.

Okun, Arthur M. "On The Appraisal Of Cyclical Turning-Point Predictors," (2), 101-120.

Jung, Allen F. "Prices Of Falcon And Corvair Cars In Chicago And Selected Cities," (2), 121-126.

Mayer, Thomas. "Plant And Equipment Lead Times," (2), 127-132.

Marschak, Thomas. "Capital Budgeting And Pricing In The French Nationalized Industries," (2), 133-156.

Boiteux, M. "Peak-Load Pricing," (2), 157-179.

Bain, Joe S. "Price Leaders, Barometers, And Kinks," (3), 193-203.

Brozen, Yale. "Trends In Industrial Research And Development," (3), 204-217.

Green, David, Jr. "A Moral To The Direct-Costing Controversy?," (3), 218-226.

Nicols, Alfred. "Economic Issues In THe DuPont-General Motors Case," (3), 227-251.

Jung, Allen F. "Compact-Car Prices In Major Cities," (3), 252-257.

Kruskal, William H. and Lester G. Telser. "Food Prices And The Bureau Of Labor Statistics," (3), 258-279.

Clague, Ewan. "Comment: Food Prices And The Bureau Of Labor Statistics," (3), 280-284.

Kruskal, William H. and Lester G. Telser. "Rejoinder: Food Prices And The Bureau Of Labor Statistics," (3), 285.

Cohen, K. J., R. M. Cyert, W. R. Dill, A. A. Kuehn, M. H. Miller, T. A. VanWormer, and P. R. Winters. "The Carnegie Tech Management Game," (4), 303-321.

Brozen, Yale. "The New Competition-International Markets: How Should We Adapt?," (4), 322-326.

Dryden, Myles M. "The MAPI Urgency Rating As An Investment-Ranking Criterion," (4), 327-341.

Jung, Allen F. "Price Policy And Discounts In The Medium- And High-Priced Car Market," (4), 342-347.

Weissman, Jacob. "The Role Of Law In Education For Business," (4), 348-356.

Kilbridge, Maurice D. "Reduced Costs Through Job Enlargement: A Case," (4), 357-362.

Donhowe, G. M. "Economic Analysis In Norwegian Collective Bargaining," (4), 363-372.

Pessemier, Edgar A. "An Experimental Method For Estimating Demand," (4), 373-383.

Journal of Business
Volume 34, 1961

Calkins, Robert D. "The Problems Of Business Education," (1), 1-9.

Sobotka, Stephen P. and Constance Schnabel. "Linear Programming As A Device For Depicting Market Value: Prices Of Used Commercial Aircraft, 1959-65," (1), 10-30.

Stark, Stanley. "Executive Foresight: Definitions, Illustrations, Importance," (1), 31-44.

Istvan, Donald F. "The Economic Evaluation Of Capital Expenditures," (1), 45-51.

Jung, Allen F. "Price Variations Among Home-Remodeling Contractors," (1), 52-56.

Steiner, Gary A. "Notes On Franklin B. Evans' 'Psychological And Objective Factors In The Prediction Of Brand Choice'," (1), 57-60.

Winick, Charles. "The Relationship Among Personality Needs, Objective Factors, And Brand Choice: A Re-Examination," (1), 61-66.

Evans, Franklin B. "Reply: 'You Still Can't Tell A Ford Owner From A Chevrolet Owner'," (1), 67-73.

Shubik, Martin. "Approaches To The Study Of Decision-Making Relevant To The Firm," (2), 101-118.

Sobotka, Stephen P. "Michigan's Employment Problem: The Substitution Against Labor," (2), 119-128.

Weston, J. Fred. "The Management Of Corporate Capital: A Review Article," (2), 129-139.

Pauling, N. G. "Experience With An Industrial Research Program In The Social Sciences," (2), 140-152.

Solo, Robert A. "Intra-Enterprise Conspiracy And The Theory Of The Firm," (2), 153-166.

Jung, Allen F. "Impact Of The Compact Cars On New-Car Prices," (2), 167-182.

Schweiger, Irving and John S. McGee. "Chicago Banking," (3), 203-366.

Rees, Albert. "The Waste-Makers And The String-Savers," (3), 367-373.

Foss, Murray. "How Rigid Are Construction Costs During Recessions?," (3), 374-383.

Rottenberg, Simon. "The Irrelevance Of Union Apprentice/Journeyman Ratios," (3), 384-386.

Ferber, Robert, Nai-Ruenn Chen and Fadil Zuwaylif. "Employers' Forecasts Of Manpower: An Interview Study," (3), 387-395.

Miller, Merton H. and Franco Modigliani. "Dividend Policy, Growth, And The Valuation Of Shares," (4), 411-433.

Brozen, Yale. "The Future Of Industrial Research," (4), 434-441.

Davidson, Sidney and David F. Drake. "Capital Budgeting And The 'Best' Tax Depreciation Method," (4), 442-452.

Herrnstadt, Irwin L. and Benson Soffer. "Recent Labor Disputes Over 'Restrictive' Practices And 'Inflationary' Wage Increases," (4), 453-470.

Hirshleifer, Jack. "The Bayesian Approach To Statistical Decision: An Exposition," (4), 471-489.

Jung, Allen F. "Indexes Of Retail Prices Of New Cars-Consumer Price Index," (4), 490-494.

DeJanosi, Peter E. "A Note On Provisional Estimates Of The Gross National Product And Its Major Components," (4), 495-499.

Journal of Business
Volume 35, 1962

Stigler, George J. "Administered Prices And Oligopolistic Inflation," (1), 1-13.

Blank, David M. "Cyclical Behavior Of National Advertising," (1), 14-27.

Solomons, David. "The Determination Of Asset Values," (1), 28-42.

Frank, Ronald E. "Brand Choice As A Probability Process," (1), 43-56.

Uhl, Kenneth P. "Shareowner Brand Preferences," (1), 57-69.

Jung, Allen F. "Impact Of The Compact Cars On New-Car Prices - A Reappraisal," (1), 70-76.

Denison, Edward F. "United States Economic Growth," (2), 109-121.

Sprinkel, Beryl W. and B. Kenneth West. "Effects Of Capital Gains Taxes On Investment Decisions," (2), 122-134.

McKersie, Robert B. and William W. Shropshire, Jr. "Avoiding Written Grievances: A Successful Program," (2), 135-152.

Bailey, Martin J. "Steel And The Postwar Rise In The Wholesale Price Index," (2), 153-157.

Douglas, Edna. "Size Of Firm And The Structure Of Costs In Retailing," (2), 158-190.

Northrup, Herbert R. "Engineers, Unions, And Management Organization: A Review Article," (2), 191-195.

Stekler, H. O. "A Simulation Of The Forecasting Performance Of The Diffusion Index," (2), 196-200.

Hirshleifer, Jack. "The Firm's Cost Function: A Successful Reconstruction?," (3), 235-255.
Hicks, John R. "Economic Theory And The Evaluation Of Consumers' Wants," (3), 256-263.
Adams, Walter. "Consumer Needs And Consumer Sovereignty In The American Economy," (3), 264-277.
McKenney, James L. "An Evaluation Of A Business Game In An MBA Curriculum," (3), 278-286.
Thorelli, Hans B., Robert L. Graves and Lloyd T. Howells. "The International Operations Simulation At The University Of Chicago," (3), 287-297.
Wolfe, Harry Deane and Gerald Albaum. "Inequality In Products, Orders, Customers, Salesmen, And Sales Territories," (3), 298-301.
Barron, J. P. "Mandatory Functional Discounts: An Appraisal," (3), 302-316.
Levy, Seymour and Gordon Donhowe. "Exploration Of A Biological Model Of Industrial Organization," (4), 335-342.
Lewis, John P. "Short-Term General Business Conditions Forecasting: Some Comments On Method," (4), 343-356.
Baumol, William J. and Associates. "The Role Of Cost In The Minimum Pricing Of Railroad Services," (4), 357-366.
Osborn, Richards C. "Postwar Control Of Restrictive Trade Practices In Great Britain," (4), 367-385.
Jung, Allen F. "Charges For Appliance And Automobile Installment Credit In Major Cities," (4), 386-391.
Becker, Selwyn and David Green, Jr. "Budgeting And Employee Behavior," (4), 392-402.
Nicosia, F. M. "Marketing And Alderson's Functionalism," (4), 403-413.

Journal of Business
Volume 36, 1963

Shultz, George P. "A Note On Forecasting," (1), 1.
Fackler, Walter D. "Business Spending And Government Fiscal Policy," (1), 2-5.
Sprinkel, Beryl W. "Monetary Policy, Balance Of Payments, And Financial Markets," (1), 6-9.
Schweiger, Irving. "Gross National Product, Consumer Spending, Saving, And Housing," (1), 10-13.
Cloos, George W. "How Good Are The National Bureau's Reference Dates?," (1), 14-32.
Blank, David M. "A Note On The Golden Age Of Advertising," (1), 33-38.
Kaufman, Gordon M. "Sequential Investment Analysis Under Uncertainty," (1), 39-64.
Porter, Albert. "Intelligence-Test Score As A Predictor Of Executive Success," (1), 65-68.
Orr, Daniel. "Two Books On Simulation In Economics And Business," (1), 69-76.
Bass, Frank M. "Marketing Research Expenditures: A Decision Model," (1), 77-90.
Sprowls, R. Clay. "Computer Education In The Business Curriculum," (1), 91-96.
Guthrie, Harold W. "Intergeneration Transfers Of Wealth And The Theory Of Saving," (1), 97-108.
Solomon, Benjamin and Robert K. Burns. "Unionization Of White-Collar Employees: Extent, Potential, And Implications,"(2),141-165.
Solo, Robert A. "Automation: Technique, Mystique, Critique," (2), 166-178.
Zarnowitz, Victor. "On The Dating Of Business Cycles," (2), 179-199.
Regan, William J. "Economic Growth And Services," (2), 200-209.
Northrup, Herbert R. and Richard L. Rowan. "State Seizure In Public Interest Disputes," (2), 210-227.
Weigand, Robert E. "The Marketing Organization, Channels, And Firm Size," (2), 228-236.
Kuehn, Alfred A. "Demonstration Of A Relationship Between Psychological Factors And Brand Choice," (2), 237-241.
Evans, Franklin B. and Harry V. Roberts. "Fords, Chevrolets, And The Problem Of Discrimination," (2), 242-249.
Johnson, Harry G. "An Overview Of Price Levels, Employment, And The Balance Of Payments," (3), 279-289.
Vatter, William J. "Operating Confusion In Accounting-Two Reports Or One?," (3), 290-301.
Weber, Arnold R. and David P. Taylor. "Procedures For Employee Displacement: Advance Notice Of Plant Shutdown," (3), 302-315.
Cohan, Avery B. "The Theory Of The Firm: A View On Methodology," (3), 316-324.
Miner, John B. "Evidence Regarding The Value Of A Management Course Based On Behavioral Science Subject Matter," (3), 325-335.
Rose, Joseph R. "The Role Of Cost In The Minimum Pricing Of Railroad Services: A Comment," (3), 336-337.
Hershey, J. W. "The Rest Of The Story On The Role Of Cost In The Minimum Pricing Of Railroad Services"," (3), 338-340.
Robinson, Romney. "Cost In The Minimum Pricing Of Railroad Services: A Comment," (3), 341-347.
Baumol, William J. and Associates. "Statement Of Clarification," (3), 348-351.
Cloos, George W. "More On Reference Dates And Leading Indicators," (3), 352-364.
Lentz, Arthur and Harvey Tschirgi. "The Ethical Content Of Annual Reports," (4), 387-393.
Mandelbrot, Benoit. "The Variation Of Certain Speculative Prices," (4), 394-419.
Fama, Eugene F. "Mandelbrot And The Stable Paretian Hypothesis," (4), 420-429.
Jung, Allen F. "Dealer Pricing Practices And Finance Charges For New Mobile Homes," (4), 430-439.
Ito, Rikuma. "An Analysis Of Response Errors: A Case Study," (4), 440-447.
Bodenhorn, Diran. "Depreciation, Price Level Changes, And Investment Decisions," (4), 448-457.
Dryden, Myles M. "A Note On An Approximation To The Post-Tax Rate Of Return," (4), 458-460.
Zarnowitz, Victor. "Cloos On Reference Dates And Leading Indicators: A Comment," (4), 461-463.

Journal of Business
Volume 37, 1964

Fisher, L. and J. H. Lorie. "Rates Of Return On Investments In Common Stocks," (1), 1-21.
Fackler, Walter D. "Business Spending And Government Fiscal Policies," (1), 22-24.
Sprinkel, Beryl W. "Monetary Policy, Balance Of Payments, And Financial Markets," (1), 25-27.
Schweiger, Irving. "Gross National Product, Consumer Spending, Saving, And Housing," (1), 28-31.
Johnson, Leland L. "Joint Cost And Price Discrimination: The Case Of Communications Satellites," (1), 32-46.
Fischer, Gerald C. "Bank Holding-Company Affiliates: Branches Or Unit Banks?," (1), 47-48.
O'Donnell, John L. "Operating Confusion In Accounting-Two Reports Or One?," (1), 49-50.
Orr, Daniel. "Costs And Outputs: An Appraisal Of Dynamic Aspects," (1), 51-60.
Gould, J. R. "Internal Pricing In Firms When There Are Costs Of Using An Outside Market," (1), 61-67.
Blair, John M. "Administered Prices And Oligopolistic Inflation: A Reply," (1), 68-81.
Stigler, George J. "Comment: Administered Prices And Oligopolistic Inflation," (1), 82-83.
McAllister, Harry E. "Comments On 'Administered Prices And Oligopolistic Inflation: A Reply'," (1), 84-86.
Stigler, George J. "Public Regulation Of The Securities Markets," (2), 117-142.
Adelman, M. A. "Oil Prices In The Long Run (1963-75)," (2), 143-161.
DeAlessi, Louis. "Do Business Firms Gain From Inflation?," (2), 162-166.
Nelson, Robert A. "Interest Conflicts In Transportation," (2), 167-178.
Wright, F. K. "Project Evaluation And The Managerial Limit," (2), 179-185.
Tull, D. S., R. A. Boring and M. H. Gonsior. "A Note On The Relationship Of Price And Imputed Quality," (2), 186-191.
Brooks, Robert C., Jr. "A Neglected Approach To Ethical Business Behavior," (2), 192-194.
Stedry, Andrew C. "Budgeting And Employee Behavior: A Reply," (2), 195-202.
Becker, Selwyn W. and David Green, Jr. "Budgeting And Employee Behavior: A Rejoinder To A 'Reply'," (2), 203-205.
Cyert, Richard M. and William R. Dill. "The Future Of Business Education," (3), 221-237.
Seidman, Joel and Glen G. Cain. "Unionized Engineers And Chemists: A Case Study Of A Professional Union," (3), 238-257.
Davidson, Sidney and David F. Drake. "The 'Best' Tax Depreciation Method-1964," (3), 258-260.
Pauling, Norman G. "Some Neglected Areas Of Research On The Effects Of Automation And Other Technological Change On Workers," (3), 261-273.
Jung, Allen F. "Mortgage Availability And Terms In Florida," (3), 274-279.
Page, Alfred N. "The Variation Of Mortgage Interest Rates," (3), 280-294.
Dilbeck, Harold R. "The Responses Of Local Residential Construction To Changes In National Credit Conditions, 1953-59," (3), 295-308.
Kolb, Burton A. "The Rise And Fall Of Public Utilities: An Appraisal Of Risk," (3), 329-345.
Baumol, William J., Richard E. Quandt and Harold T. Shapiro. "Oligopoly Theory And Retail Food Pricing," (4), 346-363.
Holland, Thomas E. "Cyclical Movements Of Interest Rates, 1948-61," (4), 364-369.
Farley, John U. "Brand Loyalty' And The Economics Of Information," (4), 370-381.
Friend, Irwin and Edward S. Herman. "The S.E.C. Through A Glass Darkly," (4), 382-405.
Robbins, Sidney and Walter Werner. "Professor Stigler Revisited," (4), 406-413.
Stigler, George J. "Comment: Professor Stigler Revisited," (4), 414-422.

Journal of Business
Volume 38, 1965

Fackler, Walter D. "Private Investment And Fiscal Policy," (1), 1-4.
Sprinkel, Beryl W. "1965 Economic And Financial Prospects," (1), 5-8.
Schweiger, Irving. "1965 Forecast Of Gross National Product, Consumer Spending, Saving, And Housing," (1), 9-11.
Scheinfeld, Aaron. "A Proposal To Accelerate The Flow Of Private Capital Into Under-Developed Nations," (1), 12-17.
Weisbrod, Burton A. "Some Problems Of Pricing And Resource Allocation In A Non-Profit Industry-The Hospitals," (1), 18-28.
Schwartz, Eli. "Note On A Theory Of Firm Growth," (1), 29-33.
Fama, Eugene F. "The Behavior Of Stock Market Prices," (1), 34-105.
Friend, Irwin and Edward S. Herman. "Professor Stigler On Securities Regulation: A Further Comment," (1), 106-110.
West, Richard. "New Issue Concessions On Municipal Bonds: A Case Of Monopsony Pricing," (2), 135-148.
Fisher, Lawrence. "Outcomes For 'Random' Investments In Common Stocks Listed On The New York Stock Exchange," (2), 149-161.
Palda, Kristian S. "The Measurement Of Cumulative Advertising Effects," (2), 162-179.
Jung, Allen F. "A Different Retail Price Pattern: The Case Of Carpeting," (2), 180-185.
Frank, Ronald E. and William F. Massy. "Market Segmentation And The Effectiveness Of A Brand's Price And Dealing Policies," (2), 186-200.
Hardin, Einar. "Michigan's Employment Problem And The Elasticity Of Substitution," (2), 201-206.
Lindholm, Richard W. "Comment: Michigan's Employment Problem And The Elasticity Of Substitution," (2), 207-209.
Reimer, Richard D. "A Comment On Oligopoly Pricing Practices And Economic Theory," (2), 210-211.
Heller, Walter W. "The Future Of Our Fiscal System," (3), 235-244.

Journal of Business
Volume 42, 1969

Journal of Business
Volume 43, 1970

Coates, Robert and David E. Updegraff. "The Relationship Between Organizational Size And The Administrative Component Of Banks," (4), 576-588.

Weil, Roman L. "Macaulay's Duration: An Appreciation," (4), 589-592.

Hughes, G. David, Joseph B. Juhasz and Bruno Contini. "The Influence Of Personality On The Bargaining Process," (4), 593-604.

Rubinstein, Mark E. "A Comparative Statics Analysis Of Risk Premiums," (4), 605-615.

Walsh, Cornelius F. "Does Listing Increase The Market Price Of Common Stocks?--Comment," (4), 616-620.

Journal of Business
Volume 47, 1974

Sprinkel, Beryl W. "Slow Growth And High Inflation For 1974," (1), 1-4.

Schweiger, Irving. "1974 Forecast Of Gross National Product, Consumer Spending, Saving, And Housing," (1), 5-10.

Daub, Mervin. "On The Cost To The Firm Of Aggregate Prediction Errors," (1), 11-22.

Frech, H. E., III and Paul B. Ginsburg. "Optimal Scale In Medical Practice: A Survivor Analysis," (1), 23-36.

McDonald, John G. and Bertrand C. Jacquillat. "Pricing Of Initial Equity Issues: The French Sealed-Bid Auction," (1), 37-47.

Branch, Ben. "Common Stock Performance And Inflation: An International Comparison," (1), 48-52.

Sharir, Shmuel. "'Brand Loyalty' And The Household's Cost Of Time," (1), 53-55.

Henry, William R. and E. Earl Burch. "Institutional Contributions To Scholarly Journals Of Business," (1), 56-66.

Weil, Roman L. and Lawrence Fisher. "TIAA/CREF: Who Gets What? An Analysis Of Wealth Transfers In A Variable Annuity," (1), 67-87.

Daub, Mervin. "A Comparison Of The Accuracy Of American And Canadian Short-Term Predictions Of Gross National Product," (2), 173-185.

Farrell, James L., Jr. "Analyzing Covariation Of Returns To Determine Homogeneous Stock Groupings," (2), 186-207.

Fishelson, Gideon. "Help-Wanted Advertisements: A Case Study, Israel 1965-71.," (2), 208-217.

Wise, Gordon L. "Differential Pricing And Treatment By New-Car Salesmen: The Effect Of The Propsect's Race, Sex, And Dress," (2), 218-230.

Elton, Edwin J. and Martin J. Gruber. "On The Optimality Of Some Multiperiod Portfolio Selection Criteria," (2), 231-243.

Blattberg, Robert C. and Nicholas J. Gonedes. "A Comparison Of The Stable And Student Distributions As Statistical Models For Stock Prices," (2), 244-280.

Eilbott, Peter. "Trends In The Value Of Individual Stockholdings," (3), 339-348.

Cocks, Douglas L. and John R. Virts. "Pricing Behavior Of The Ethical Pharmaceutical Industry," (3), 349-362.

Longbrake, William A. "Computers And The Cost Of Producing Various Types Of Banking Services," (3), 363-381.

McGugan, Vincent J. and Richard E. Caves. "Integration And Competition In The Equipment Leasing Industry," (3), 382-396.

Gould, John P. and Roman L. Weil. "The Rule Of 69," (3), 397-398.

Cunningham, William H., W. Thomas Anderson, Jr. and John H. Murphy. "Are Students Real People?," (3), 399-409.

Jaffe, Jeffrey F. "Special Information And Insider Trading," (3), 410-428.

Krainer, Robert E. "A Reexamination Of The Theory Of Monopsonistic Discrimination In The Capital Market," (3), 429-439.

Gustafson, David P. and Charles R. Kuehl. "Citation Age Distributions For Three Areas Of Business," (3), 440-447.

Steinwald, Bruce and Frank A. Sloan. "Determinants Of Physicians' Fees," (4), 493-511.

Berger, Paul D. and James P. Monahan. "A Planning Model To Cope With Absenteeism," (4), 512-517.

Boness, A. James, Andrew H. Chen and Som Jatusipitak. "Investigations Of Nonstationarity In Prices," (4), 518-537.

Sexton, Donald E., Jr. "Food Sales Mix And Profitability: Ghetto Supermarkets Revisited," (4), 538-542.

Crandall, Robert W. "The Profitability Of Cable Television: An Examination Of Acquisition Prices," (4), 543-563.

Reback, Robert. "Nonrandom Price Changes In Association With Trading In Large Blocks: A Comment," (4), 564-565.

Grier, Paul. "Reply To Robert Reback's Comment: Nonrandom Price Changes In Association With Trading In Large Blocks," (4), 566-567.

Zaltman, Gerald. "Comments On 'Institutional Contributions To Scholarly Journals Of Business'," (4), 568-570.

Johnson, Thomas E. "Institutional Contributions To Scholarly Journals Of Business: Comment," (4), 571-573.

Journal of Business
Volume 48, 1975

Sprinkel, Beryl W. "1975: A Year Of Recession, Recovery, And Decelerating Inflation," (1), 1-4.

Schweiger, Irving. "1975 Forecast Of Gross National Product, Consumer Spending, Saving, And Housing," (1), 5-10.

Mancke, Richard B. "The Future Of OPEC," (1), 11-19.

Pesando, James E. "On The Accuracy And Formation Of Life Insurance Company Cash Flow Forecasts," (1), 20-26.

Sandor, Richard L. and Howard B. Sosin. "The Determinants Of Mortgage Risk Premiums: A Case Study Of The Portfolio Of A Savings And Loan Association," (1), 27-38.

Mazzolini, Renato. "Creating Europe's Multinationals: The International Merger Route," (1), 39-51.

Malone, Erwin L. "The Non-Linear Systems Experiment In Participative Management," (1), 52-64.

Bomball, Mark R., Walter J. Primeaux and Donald E. Pursell. "Forecasting Stage 2 Of The Family Life Cycle," (1), 65-73.

Tanner, J. Ernest. "The Determinants Of Interest Cost On New Municipal Bonds: A Reevaluation," (1), 74-80.

Martin, John D. and Robert C. Klemkosky. "Evidence Of Heteroscedasticity In The Market Model," (1), 81-86.

Stickney, Clyde P. "Window Dressing The Interim-Earnings Report: An Empirical Assessment For Firms Initially Going Public," (1), 87-97.

Sullivan, James A. and Richard G. Marcis. "Forecasting Consumer Installment Credit: An Application Of Parametric Time Series Modeling," (1), 98-107.

Hewett, Wendell C. "The Significance Of Human Curiosity In An Outdoor Advertising Experiment," (1), 108-110.

Mansfield, Edwin and Samuel Wagner. "Organizational And Strategic Factors Associated With Probabilities Of Success In Industrial R & D," (2), 179-198.

Yeats, Alexander J., Edward D. Irons and Stephen A. Rhoades. "An Analysis Of New Bank Growth," (2), 199-203.

Johnson, Rodney D. and David R. Meinster. "The Performance Of Bank Holding Company Acquisitions: A Multivariate Analysis," (2), 204-212.

Nelson, Phillip. "The Economic Consequences Of Advertising," (2), 213-241.

Kamerschen, David R. "The Return Of Target Pricing?," (2), 242-252.

Durkin, Thomas A. "Consumer Awareness Of Credit Terms: Review And New Evidence," (2), 253-362.

De Alessi, Louis. "Do Business Firms Gain From Inflation? Reprise," (2), 264-266.

Honeycutt, T. Crawford. "The Microeconomic Consequences Of Corporate Mergers: A Comment," (2), 267-274.

Reid, Samuel Richardson. "The Microeconomic Consequences Of Corporate Mergers: Comment," (2), 275-280.

Lev, Baruch and Gerhon Mandelker. "Rejoinder To Reid And Honeycutt: The Microeconomic Consequences Of Corporate Mergers," (2), 281-303.

Nelson, Charles R. "Rational Expectations And The Predictive Efficiency Of Economic Models," (3), 331-343.

Rhoades, Stephen A. "The Effect Of Bank-Holding-Company Acquisitions Of Mortgage Bankers On Mortgage Lending Activity," (3), 344-348.

Wolfe, Joseph and Gary R. Guth. "The Case Approach Versus Gaming In The Teaching Of Business Policy: An Experimental Evaluation," (3), 349-364.

Barksdale, Hiram C. and Jimmy E. Hilliard. "A Cross-Spectral Analysis Of Retail Inventories And Sales," (3), 365-382.

Shuptrine, F. Kelly. "On The Validity Of Using Students As Subjects In Consumer Behavior Investigations," (3), 383-390.

Vanlommel, E. and B. De Brabander. "The Organization Of Electronic Data Processing (EDP) Activities And Computer Use," (3), 391-410.

Ling, Robert F. and Harry V. Roberts. "IDA: An Approach To Interactive Data Analysis In Teaching And Research," (3), 411-451.

Link, Charles R. "Graduate Education, School Quality, Experience, Student Ability, And Earnings," (4), 477-491.

Primeaux, Walter J., Jr. "The Newspaper Rate Differential: Another Element In The Explanation," (4), 492-499.

Heggestad, Arnold A. and John J. Mingo. "Capital Management By Holding Company Banks," (4), 500-505.

Bildersee, John S. "Some New Bond Indexes," (4), 506-525.

Weinstein, David and John U. Farley. "Market Segmentation And Parameter Inequalities In A Buyer Behavior Model," (4), 526-540.

Bates, Timothy. "Government As Financial Intermediary For Minority Entrepreneurs: An Evaluation," (4), 541-557.

Zufryden, Fred S. "On The Dual Optimization Of Media Reach And Frequency," (4), 558-570.

Mitchell, Daniel J. B. and Ross E. Azevedo. "Price Controls And Shortages: A Note," (4), 571-574.

Journal of Business
Volume 49, 1976

Sprinkel, Beryl W. "1976: A Year Of Moderate Expansion And Contained Inflation," (1), 1-4.

Schweiger, Irving. "1976 Forecast Of Gross National Product, Consumer Spending, Saving, And Housing," (1), 5-10.

Ibbotson, Roger G. and Rex A. Sinquefield. "Stocks, Bonds, Bills, And Inflation: Year-By-Year Historical Returns (1926-1974)," (1), 11-47.

Klemkosky, Robert C. "Additional Evidence On The Risk Level Discriminatory Powers Of The Wiesenberger Classifications," (1), 48-50.

Woodside, Arch G. and J. William Davenport, Jr. "Effects Of Price And Salesman Expertise On Customer Purchasing Behavior," (1), 51-59.

Auerbach, Robert. "The Measurement Of Economies Of Scale: A Comment," (1), 60-61.

Murphy, Neil B. "The Relationship Between Organizational Size And The Administrative Component Of Banks: A Comment," (1), 62-65.

Coates, Robert and David E. Updegraff. "The Relationship Between Organizational Size And The Administrative Component Of Banks: A Reply," (1), 66-67.

Schnabel, Morton. "A Challenge To A Vote For Tonypandy," (1), 68-69.

Riesz, Peter C. "The Great Tonypandy Debate Continued," (1), 70-72.

Laub, P. Michael. "On The Informational Content Of Dividends," (1), 73-80.

Watts, Ross. "Comments On 'On The Informational Content Of Dividends'," (1), 81-85.

Pettit, R. Richardson. "The Impact Of Dividend And Earnings Announcements: A Reconciliation," (1), 86-96.

Watts, Ross. "Comments On 'The Impact Of Dividend And Earnings Announcements: A Reconciliation'," (1), 97-106.

Thompson, Donald J., II. "Sources Of Systematic Risk In Common Stocks," (2), 173-188.

Stekler, H. O. "The Savings Rate As A Tool Of Economic Analysis," (2), 189-193.

Ratchford, Brian T. and Gary T. Ford. "A Study Of Prices And Market Shares In The Computer Mainframe Industry," (2), 194-218.

Mason, Joseph Barry and J. B. Wilkinson. "Mispricing And Unavailability Of Advertised Food Products In Retail Food Outlets," (2), 219-225.

Grier, Paul and Steven Katz. "The Differential Effects Of Bond Rating

Gau, George W. "A Taxonomic Model For The Risk-Rating Of Residential Mortgages," (4), 687-706.

Journal of Business
Volume 52, 1979

Zarnowitz, Victor. "An Analysis Of Annual And Multiperiod Quarterly Forecasts Of Aggregate Income, Output, And The Price Level," (1), 1-34.

Wecker, William E. "Predicting The Turning Points Of A Time Series," (1), 35-50.

Cox, John C., Jonathan E. Ingersoll, Jr., and Stephen A. Ross. "Duration And The Measurement Of Basis Risk," (1), 51-62.

Brennan, Michael J. and Eduardo S. Schwartz. "Alternative Investment Strategies For The Issuers Of Equity Linked Life Insurance Policies With An Asset Value Guarantee," (1), 63-94.

Ambrose, David M. "Retail Grocery Pricing: Inner City, Suburban, And Rural Comparisons," (1), 95-102.

Anderson, Evan E. "An Analysis Of Retail Display Space: Theory And Methods," (1), 103-118.

Brock, Gerald W. "A Study Of Prices And Market Shares In The Computer Mainframe Industry: Comment," (1), 119-124.

Ratchford, Brian T. and Gary T. Ford. "A Study Of Prices And Market Shares In The Computer Mainframe Industry: Reply," (1), 125-33.

Fama, Eugene F. and G. William Schwert. "Inflation, Interest, And Relative Prices," (2), 183-210.

Telser, L. G. "A Theory Of Monopoly Of Complementary Goods," (2), 211-230.

Kaplan, Robert S. and Gabriel Urwitz. "Statistical Models Of Bond Ratings: A Methodological Inquiry," (2), 231-262.

Kon, Stanley J. and Frank C. Jen. "The Investment Performance Of Mutual Funds: An Empirical Investigation Of Timing, Selectivity, And Market Efficiency," (2), 263-290.

Lustgarten, Steven and Allan I. Mendelowitz. "The Covariability Of Industrial Concentration And Employment Fluctuations," (2), 291-304.

Qualls, P. David. "Market Structure And The Cyclical Flexibility Of Price-Cost Margins," (2), 305-325.

Demsetz, Harold. "Accounting For Advertising As A Barrier To Entry," (3), 345-360.

Courville, Leon and Warren H. Hausman. "Warranty Scope And Reliabiltiy Under Imperfect Information And Alternative Market Structures," (3), 361-378.

Zak, Thomas A., Cliff J. Huang and John J. Siegfried. "Production Efficiency: The Case Of Professional Basketball," (3), 379-392.

Venezia, Itzhak and Menachem Brenner. "The Optimal Duration Of Growth Investments And Search," (3), 393-408.

McRae, James J. and Francis Tapon. "A New Test Of The Administered Pricing Hypothesis With Canadian Data," (3), 409-428.

Morgan, Fred W., Jr. "Are Early Triers Heavy Users?," (3), 429-434.

Spiro, Rosann L. and William D. Perreault, Jr. "Influence Use By Industrial Salesmen: Influence-Strategy Mixes And Situational Determinants," (3), 435-455.

Jensen, Michael C. and William H. Meckling. "Rights And Production Functions: An Application To Labor-managed Firms And Codetermination," (4), 469-506.

Haring, John R., Jr. "Accountign Rules And 'The Accounting Establishment'," (4), 507-520.

Williams, Joseph T. "Uncertainty And The Accumulation Of Human Capital Over The Life Cycle," (4), 521-548.

Peterman, John L. "Differences Between The Levels Of Spot And Network Television Advertising Rates," (4), 549-562.

Winer, Russell S. "An Analysis Of The Time-Varying Effects Of Advertising: The Case Of Lydia Pinkham," (4), 563-576.

Hawkins, Del I. "The Impact Of Sponsor Identification And Direct Disclosure Of Respondent Rights On The Quantity And Quality Of Mail Survey Data," (4), 577-590.

Journal of Business
Volume 53, 1980

Irvine, F. Owen., Jr. "Econometric Tests Of The Hypothesis That Market-Maker Firms Follow A 'Short-Run Inventory-Based Pricing Policy'," (1), 1-26.

Telser, L. G. "A Theory Of Self-Enforcing Agreements," (1), 27-44.

DeVany, Arthur and Thomas R. Saving. "Competition And Highway Pricing For Stochastic Traffic," (1), 45-60.

Parkinson, Michael. "The Extreme Value Method For Estimating The Variance Of The Rate Of Return," (1), 61-66.

Garman, Mark B. and Michael J. Klass. "On The Estimation Of Security Price Volatilities From Historical Data," (1), 67-78.

Elnicki, Richard A. and Warren R. Hughes. "An Empirical Analysis Of Demands For Priority Computing Goods By Externally And Internally Funded Researchers," (1), 79-96.

Koenigsberg, Ernest. "Uncertainty, Capacity, And Market Share In Oligopoly: A Stochastic Theory Of Product Quality," (2), 151-164.

Liberman, Joseph. "Human Capital And The Financial Capital Market," (2), 165-192.

Carlson, Rodney L. and M. Michael Umble. "Statistical Demand Functions For Automobiles And Their Use For Forecasting In An Energy Crisis," (2), 193-204.

Lewis, Alan L., Sheen T. Kassouf, R. Dennis Brehm and Jack Johnston. "The Ibbotson-Sinquefield Simulation Made Easy," (2), 205-214.

Williams, Arlington W. "Computerized Double-Auction Markets: Some Initial Experimental Results," (3), Part 1, 235-258.

Dodd, Peter and Richard Leftwich. "The Market For Corporate Charters: 'Unhealthy Competition' Versus Federal Regulation," (3), Part 1, 259-284.

Lippman, Steven A., John M. McCall and Wayne L. Winston. "Constant Absolute Risk Aversion, Bankruptcy, And Wealth-Dependent Decisions," (3), Part 1, 285-296.

Mecker, Larry G. and O. Maurice Joy. "Price Premiums For Controlling Shares Of Closely Held Bank Stock," (3), Part 1, 297-314.

Bagozzi, Echard P. "The Nature And Causes Of Self-Esteem, Peformance, And Satisfaction In The Sales Force: A Structural Equation Approach," (3), Part 1, 315-331.

Horsky, Dan and Subrata K. Sen. "Interfaces Between Marketing And Economics: An Overview," (3) ,Part 2, S5-S12.

McFadden, Daniel. "Econometric Models For Probabilistic Choice Among Products," (3), Part 2, S13-S30.

Madansky, Albert. "On Conjoint Analysis And Quantal Choice Models," (3), Part 2, S37-S44.

Bass, Frank M. "The Relationship Between Diffusion Rates, Experience Curves, And Demand Elasticities For Consumer Durable Technological Innovations," (3), Part 2, S51-S68.

Lancaster, Kelvin. "Competition And Product Variety," (3), Part 2, S79-S104.

Verma, Vinod K. "A Price Theoretic Approach To The Specification And Estimation Of The Sales-Advertising Function," (3), Part 2, S115-S138.

Wilde, Louis L. "The Economics Of Consumer Information Acquisition," (3), Part 2, S143-S158.

Gould, John P. "The Economics Of Markets: A Simple Model Of The Market-Making Process," (3), Part 2, S167-S188.

Little, John D. C. and Jeremy F. Shapiro. "A Theory For Pricing Nonfeatured Products In Supermarkets," (3), Part 2, S199-S210.

Bradley, Michael. "Interfirm Tender Offers And The Market For Corporate Control," (4), 345-376.

Izan, Haji Y. "Mandatory Audit Regulation For Banks: An Empirical Evaluation Of Its Effects," (4), 377-396.

Gerner, Jennifer L. and W. Keith Bryant. "The Demand For Repair Service During Warranty," (4), 397-414.

Windal, Pierre M. and Doyle L. Weiss. "An Iterative GLS Procedure For Estimating The Parameters Of Models With Autocorrelated Errors Using Data Aggregted Over Time," (4), 415-424.

Journal of Business
Volume 54, 1981

Lindenberg, Eric B. and Stephen A. Ross. "Tobin's q Ratio And Industrial Organization," (1), 1-32.

McConnell, John J. and Gary G. Schlarbaum. "Returns, Risks, And Pricing Of Income Bonds, 1956-76 (Does Money Have An Odor?)," (1), 33-64.

McConnell, John J. and Gary G. Schlarbaum. "Evidence On The Impact Of Exchange Offers On Security Prices: The Case Of Income Bonds," (1), 65-86.

Smith, Rodney T. "In Search Of The 'Just' U.S. Oil Policy: A Review Of Arrow And Kalt And More," (1), 87-116.

Dothan, Uri and Joseph Williams. "Education As An Option," (1), 117-140.

Bookstaber, Richard M. "Observed Option Mispricing And The Nonsimultaneity Of Stock And Option Quotations," (1), 141-155.

Joines, Douglas H. "Estimates Of Effective Marginal Tax Rates On Factor Incomes," (2), 191-226.

Gonedes, Nicholas J. "Evidence On The 'Tax Effects' Of Inflation Under Historical Cost Accounting Methods," (2), 227-270.

Lynk, William J. "Information, Advertising, And The Structure Of The Market," (2), 271-304.

Schipper, Katherine and Rex Thompson. "Common Stocks As Hedges Against Shifts In The Consumption Or Investment Opportunity Set," (2), 305-328.

Hirschey, Mark. "The Effect Of Advertising On Industrial Mobility, 1947-72," (2), 329-340.

Merton, Robert C. "On Market Timing And Investment Performance. I. An Equilibrium Theory Of Value For Market Forecasts," (3), 363-406.

Mayers, David and Clifford W. Smith, Jr. "Contractual Provisions, Organizational Structure, And Conflict Control In Insurance Markets," (3), 407-434.

Bilson, John F. O. "The 'Speculative Efficiency' Hypothesis," (3), 435-452.

Solt, Michael E. and Paul J. Swanson. "On The Efficiency Of The Markets For Gold And Silver," (3), 453-478.

Freedman, David. "Some Pitfalls In Large Econometric Models: A Case Study," (3), 479-500.

Henriksson, Roy D. and Robert C. Merton. "On Market Timing And Investment Performance. II. Statistical Procedures For Evaluating Forecasting Skills," (4), 513-534.

LeRoy, Stephen F. and C. J. LaCivita. "Risk Aversion And The Dispersion Of Asset Prices," (4), 535-548.

Kiefer, Donald W. "The Effects Of Alternative Regulatory Treatments Of The Investment Tax Credit In The Public Utility Industry," (4), 549-578.

Gibbons, Michael R. and Patrick Hess. "Day Of The Week Effects And Asset Returns," (4), 579-596.

Farley, John U., Donald R. Lehmann and Michael J. Ryan. "Generalizing From 'Imperfect' Replication," (4), 597-610.

Crafton, Steven M. and George E. Hoffer. "Estimating A Transaction Price For New Automobiles," (4), 611-621.

Journal of Business
Volume 55, 1982

Merton, Robert C., Myron S. Scholes and Mathew L. Gladstein. "The Returns And Risks Of Alternative Put-Option Portfolio Investment Strategies," (1), 1-56.

Zarnowitz, Victor and Geoffrey H. Moore. "Sequential Signals Of Recession And Recovery," (1), 57-86.

Zarnowitz, Victor. "On Functions, Quality, And Timeliness Of Economic Information," (1), 87-120.

Ohlson, James and Barr Rosenberg. "Systematic Risk Of The CRSP Equal-Weighted Common Stock Index: A History Estimated By Stochastic-Parameter Regression," (1), 121-146.

Brenner, Gabrielle A. and Reuven Brenner. "Memory And Markets, Or Why Are You Paying $2.99 For A Widget?," (1), 147-158.

Fama, Eugene F. "Inflation, Output, And Money," (2), 201-232.

Dybvig, Philip H. and Jonathan E. Ingersoll, Jr. "Mean-Variance Theory In Complete Markets," (2), 233-252.

Constantinides, George M. "Intertemporal Asset Pricing With Heterogeneous Consumers And Without Demand Aggregation," (2), 253-268.

Gronberg, Timothy J. and Jack Meyer. "Spatial Pricing And Its Effect On Product Transportability," (2), 269-280.

Mayers, David and Clifford W. Smith, Jr. "On The Corporate Demand For Insurance," (2), 281-296.

Gay, Gerald D. and Steven Manaster. "Hedging Against Commodity Price Inflation: Stocks And Bills As Substitutes For Futures Contracts," (2), 317-344.

Bryant, W. Keith and Jennifer L. Gerner. "The Demand For Service Contracts," (3), 345-366.

Batlin, Carl Alan and Susan Hinko. "A Game Theoretic Approach To Cash Management," (3), 367-382.

Jondrow, James M., David E. Chase and Christopher L. Gamble. "The Price Differential Between Domestic And Imported Steel," (3), 383-400.

Jagpal, Harsharanjeet S., Ephraim F. Sudit and Hrishikesh D. Vinod. "Measuring Dynamic Marketing Mix Interactions Using Translog Functions," (3), 401-415.

Smith, Rodney T. "An Economic Analysis Of Income Growth By U.S. Oil Firms: The Roles Of U.S. Oil Regulation And OPEC," (4), 427-478.

Penman, Stephen H. "Insider Trading And The Dissemination Of Firms' Forecast Information," (4), 479-504.

Etgar, Michael and Pinhas Zusman. "The Marketing Intermediary As An Information Seller: A New Approach," (4), 505-516.

Clarke, Frank H., Masako N. Darrough and John Heincke. "Optimal Pricing Policy In The Presence Of Experience Effects," (4), 517-530.

Hirschman, Elizabeth C. "Consumer Payment Systems: The Relationship Of Attribute Structure To Preference And Usage," (4), 531-545.

Journal of Business
Volume 56, 1983

Cornell, Bradford. "Money Supply Announcements And Interest Rates: Another View," (1), 1-24.

Kellner, S. and Frank Mathewson. "Entry, Size Distribution, Scale, And Scope Economies In The Life Insurance Industry," (1), 25-44.

Galai, Dan. "The Components Of The Return From Hedging Options Against Stocks," (1), 45-54.

Evans, Kaye D., John J. Siegfried and George H. Sweeney. "The Economic Cost Of Suboptimal Manufacturing Capacity," (1), 55-76.

Asquith, Paul and David W. Mullins, Jr. "The Impact Of Initiating Dividend Payments On Shareholders' Wealth," (1), 77-96.

Beckers, Stan. "Variances Of Security Price Returns Based On High, Low, And Closing Prices," (1), 97-112.

Protopapadakis, Aris. "Some Indirect Evidence On Effective Capital Gains Tax Rates," (2), 127-138.

Maloney, Michael T. and Robert E. McCormick. "A Theory Of Cost And Intermittent Production," (2), 139-154.

Baldwin, Carliss. "Productivity And Labor Unions: An Application Of The Theory Of Self-Enforcing Contracts," (2), 155-186.

Tschoegl, Adrian E. "Size, Growth, And Transnationality Among The World's Largest Banks," (2), 187-202.

Spatt, Chester S. "Imperfect Price Discrimination And Variety," (2), 203-216.

Turnbull, S. M. "Additional Aspects Of Rational Insurance Purchasing," (2), 217-229.

Garbade, Kenneth D. and William L. Silber. "Futures Contracts On Commodities With Multiple Varieties: An Analysis Of Premiums And Discounts," (3), 249-272.

Clements, Kenneth W. and Lester W. Johnson. "The Demand For Beer, Wine, And Spirits: A Systemwide Analysis," (3), 273-304.

Aharony, Joseph and Itzhak Swary. "Contagion Effects Of Bank Failures: Evidence From Capital Markets," (3), 305-322.

Kon, Stanley J. "The Market-Timing Performance Of Mutual Fund Managers," (3), 323-348.

Ayanian, Robert. "The Advertising Capital Controversy," (3), 349-364.

Wildt, Albert R. and Russell S. Winer. "Modeling And Estimation In Changing Market Environments," (3), 365-388.

Doyle, Peter and Marcel Corstjens. "Optimal Growth Strategies For Service Organizations," (3), 389-405.

Barro, Robert J. and Chaipat Sahasakul. "Measuring The Average Marginal Tax Rate From The Individual Income Tax," (4), 419-452.

Schmalensee, Richard, Alvin J. Silk and Robert Bojanek. "The Impact Of Scale And Media Mix On Advertising Agency Costs," (4), 453-476.

Bittlingmayer, George. "A Model Of Vertical Restriction And Equilibrium In Retailing," (4), 477-496.

Mathewson, G. F. and R. A. Winter. "Vertical Integration By Contractual Restraints In Spatial Markets," (4), 497-518.

Alt, Christopher B., Michael G. Baumann and Martin B. Zimmerman. "The Economics Of Western Coal Severance Taxes," (4), 519-536.

Hess, Patrick J. "Tests For Tax Effects In The Pricing Of Financial Assets," (4), 537-554.

Doherty, Neil A. and Harris Schlesinger. "The Optimal Deductible For An Insurance Policy When Initial Wealth Is Random," (4), 555-565.

Journal of Business
Volume 57, 1984

Williams, Arlington W. and Vernon L. Smith. "Cyclical Double-Auction Markets With And Without Speculators," (1), Part 1, 1-34.

Bos, T. and P. Newbold. "An Empirical Investigation Of The Possibility Of Stochastic Systematic Risk In The Market Model," (1), Part 1, 35-42.

Lynk, William J. "Interpreting Rising Concentration: The Case Of Beer," (1), Part 1, 43-56.

Chang, Eric C. and Wilbur G. Lewellen. "Market Timing And Mutual Fund Investment Performance," (1), Part 1, 57-72.

Henriksson, Roy D. "Market Timing And Mutual Fund Performance: An Empirical Investigation," (1), Part 1, 73-96.

Ball, Clifford A. and Walter N. Torous. "The Maximum Likelihood Estimation Of Security Price Volatility: Theory, Evidence, And Application To Option Pricing," (1), Part 1, 97-112.

Kalay, Avner and Marti G. Subrahmanyam. "The Ex-Dividend Day Behavior Of Option Prices," (1), Part 1, 113-128.

Nagle, Thomas. "Economic Foundations For Pricing," (1), Part 2, S3-S26.

Rao, Vithala R. "Pricing Research In Marketing: The State Of The Art," (1), Part 2, S39-S60.

Oren, Shmuel, Stephen Smith and Robert Wilson. "Producing A Product Line," (1), Part 2, S73-S100.

Goldberg, Stephen M., Paul E. Green and Yoram Wind. "Conjoint Analysis Of Price Premiums For Hotel Amenities," (1), Part 2, S111-S132.

Katz, Michael L. "Firm-Specific Differentiation And Competition Among Multiproduct Firms," (1), Part 2, S149-S166.

Clarke, Darral G. and Robert J. Dolan. "A Simulation Of Alternative Pricing Strategies For Dynamic Environments," (1), Part 2, S179-S200.

Schmalensee, Richard. "Gaussian Demand And Commodity Bundling," (1), Part 2, S211-S230.

Asch, Peter, Burton G. Malkiel and Richard E. Quandt. "Market Efficiency In Racetrack Betting," (2), 165-176.

LeRoy, Stephen F. "Nominal Prices And Interest Rates In General Equilibrium: Money Shocks," (2), 177-196.

Ritter, Jay R. "The 'Hot Issue' Market Of 1980," (2), 215-240.

Gultekin, N. Bulent and Richard J. Rogalski. "Alternative Duration Specifications And The Measurement Of Basis Risk: Empirical Tests," (2), 241-264.

Hensher, David A. "Achieving Representativeness Of The Observable Component Of The Indirect Utility Function In Logit Choice Models: An Empirical Revelation," (2), 265-280.

Dye, Ronald A. "Insider Trading And Incentives," (3), 295-314.

Ho, Thomas and Donald F. Singer. "The Value Of Corporate Debt With A Sinking-Fund Provision," (3), 315-336.

Jarrow, Robert A. and Eric R. Rosenfeld. "Jump Risks And The Intertemporal Capital Asset Pricing Model," (3), 337-352.

Harrison, J. Michael, Richard Pitbladdo and Stephen M. Schaefer. "Continuous Price Processes In Frictionless Markets Have Infinite Variation," (3), 353-366.

MacCrimmon, Kenneth R. and Donald A. Wehrung. "The Risk In-Basket," (3), 367-388.

Gibbons, Joel C. "The Optimal Durability Of Fixed Capital When Demand Is Uncertain," (3), 389-403.

French, Kenneth R. and Robert E. McCormick. "Sealed Bids, Sunk Costs, And The Process Of Competition," (4), 417-442.

Lease, Ronald C., John J. McConnell and Wayne H. Mikkelson. "The Market Value Of Differential Voting Rights In Closely Held Corporations," (4), 443-468.

Bookstaber, Richard and Roger Clarke. "Option Portfolio Strategies: Measurement And Evaluation," (4), 469-492.

Sundaresan, Suresh M. "Equilibrium Valuation Of Natural Resources," (4), 493-518.

Eppen, Gary D. and Yehoshua Liebermann. "Why Do Retailers Deal? An Inventory Explanation," (4), 519-530.

Journal of Business
Volume 58, 1985

Admati, Anat R. and Stephen A. Ross. "Measuring Investment Performance In A Rational Expectations Equilibrium Model," (1), 1-26.

Bronars, Stephen G. "Fair Pricing Of Unemployment Insurance Premiums," (1), 27-48.

Pearce, Douglas K. and V. Vance Roley. "Stock Prices And Economic News," (1), 49-68.

Givoly, Dan and Dan Palmon. "Insider Trading And The Exploitation Of Inside Information: Some Empirical Evidence," (1), 69-88.

Hirschey, Mark. "Market Structure And Market Value," (1), 89-98.

Brennan, M. J. and E. S. Schwartz. "Evaluating Natural Resource Investments," (2), 135-158.

Wolfson, Mark. "Tax, Incentive, And Risk-Sharing Issues In The Allocation Of Property Rights: The Generalized Lease-Or-Buy Problem," (2), 159-172.

Mueller, Curt D. "Waiting For Physicians' Services: Model And Evidence," (2), 173-190.

Talmor, Eli, Robert Haugen and Amir Barnea. "The Value Of The Tax Subsidy On Risky Debt," (2), 191-202.

Park, Sang Yong and Joseph Williams. "Taxes, Capital Structure, And Bondholder Clienteles," (2), 203-224.

Feinberg, Robert M. "'Sales-At-Risk': A Test Of The Mutual Forbearance Theory Of Conglomerate Behavior," (2), 225-241.

Jorion, Philippe. "International Portfolio Diversification With Estimation Risk," (3), 259-278.

Sappington, David E. M. and Birger Wernerfelt. "To Brand Or Not To Brand? A Theoretical And Empirical Question," (3), 279-294.

Jeuland, Abel P. and Chakravarthi Narasimhan. "Dealing--Temporary Price Cuts--By Seller As A Buyer Discrimination Mechanism," (3), 295-308.

Narayanan, M. P. "Observability And The Payback Criterion," (3), 309-324.

Eckbo, B. Espen. "Mergers And The Market Concentration Doctrine: Evidence From The Capital Market," (3), 325-349.

Lawrence, Colin and Aloysius Siow. "Interest Rates And Investment Spending: Some Empirical Evidence For Postwar U.S. Producer Equipment, 1947-1980," (4), 359-376.

Hafer, R. W. and Scott E. Hein. "On The Accuracy Of Time-Series, Interest Rate, And Survey Forecasts Of Inflation," (4), 377-398.

Kaserman, David L. and John W. Mayo. "Advertising And The Residential Demand For Electricity," (4), 399-408.

Blair, Roger D., David L. Kaserman and Patricia L. Pacey. "A Note On Purchased Power Adjustment Clauses," (4), 409-418.

Tremblay, Victor J. "A Reappraisal Of Interpreting Rising Concentration: The Case Of Beer," (4), 419-432.

Lynk, William J. "The Price And Output Of Beer Revisited," (4), 433-437.

Journal of Business
Volume 59, 1986

Reder, M. W. "Introduction To The Symposium On Bank Regulation," (1), 1-2.

Kareken, John H. "Federal Bank Regulatory Policy: A Description And Some Observations," (1), 3-48.

Cagan, Phillip. "Financial Regulation: Comment On Kareken," (1), 49-54.

Diamond, Douglas W. and Philip H. Dybvig. "Banking Theory, Deposit Insurance, And Bank Regulation," (1), 55-68.

Kaufman, George G. "Federal Bank Regulatory Policy: Comment On Kareken," (1), 69-78.

McCulloch, J. Huston. "Bank Regulation And Deposit Insurance," (1), 79-86.

Mayer, Thomas. "Regulating Banks: Comment On Kareken," (1), 87-96.

Mussa, Michael. "Safety And Soundness As An Objective Of Regulation Of Depository Institutions: Comment On Kareken," (1), 97-118.

Perrakis, Stylianos. "Option Bounds In Discrete Time: Extensions And The Pricing Of The American Put," (1), 119-142.

Ross, Thomas W. "The Costs Of Regulating Price Differences," (1), 143-156.

Asch, Peter, Burton G. Malkiel and Richard E. Quandt. "Market Efficiency In Racetrack Betting: Further Evidence And A Correction," (1), 157-160.

Roll, Richard. "The Hubris Hypothesis Of Corporate Takeovers," (2), Part 1, 197-216.

Jagannathan, Ravi and Robert A. Korajczyk. "Assessing The Market Timing Performance Of Managed Portfolios," (2), Part 1, 217-236.

Kleidon, Allan W. "Bias In Small Sample Tests Of Stock Price Rationality," (2), Part 1, 237-262.

Lupoletti, William M. and Roy H. Webb. "Defining And Improving The Accuracy Of Macroeconomic Forecasts: Contributions From A VAR Model," (2), Part 1, 263-286.

Grauer, Robert R. and Nils H. Hakansson. "A Half Century Of Returns On Levered And Unlevered Portfolios Of Stocks, Bonds, And Bills, With And Without Small Stocks," (2), Part 1, 287-318.

Grammatikos, Theoharry and Anthony Saunders. "Futures Price Variability: A Test Of Maturity And Volume Effects," (2), Part 1, 319-330.

Dye, Ronald A. "Proprietary And Nonproprietary Disclosures," (2), Part 1, 331-366.

Admati, Anat R. and Stephen A. Ross. "Corrigendum," (2), Part 1, 367.

Coleman, Thomas C. and Roger D. Rutz. "Self-Regulation And Government Regulation Of Futures And Options Markets: Introduction," (2), Part 2, S1-S4.

Telser, Lester G. "Futures And Actual Markets: How They Are Related," (2), Part 2, S5-S20.

Barro, Robert J. "Futures Markets And The Fluctuations In Inflation, Monetary Growth, And Asset Returns," (2), Part 2, S21-S38.

French, Kenneth R. "Detecting Spot Price Forecasts In Futures Prices," (2), Part 2, S39-S54.

Pashigian, B. Peter. "The Political Economy Of Futures Market Regulation," (2), Part 2, S55-S84.

Fischel, Daniel R. "Regulatory Conflict And Entry Regulation Of New Futures Contracts," (2), Part 2, S85-S102.

Easterbrook, Frank H. "Monopoly, Manipulation, And The Regulation Of Futures Markets," (2), Part 2, S103-S128.

Grossman, Sanford J. "An Analysis Of The Role Of 'Insider Trading' On Futures Markets," (2), Part 2, S129-S146.

Hartzmark, Michael L. "The Effects Of Changing Margin Levels On Futures Market Activity, The Composition Of Traders In The Market, And Price Performance," (2), Part 2, S147-S180.

Chen, Nai-Fu, Richard Roll and Stephen A. Ross. "Economic Forces And The Stock Market," (3), 383-404.

Lazear, Edward P. "Salaries And Piece Rates," (3), 405-432.

Springer, Robert F. and H. E. Frech III. "Deterring Fraud: The Role Of Resale Price Maintenance," (3), 433-450.

Swary, Itzhak. "Stock Market Reaction To Regulatory Action In The Continental Illinois Crisis," (3), 451-474.

Levy, Robert A. and James M. Jondrow. "The Adjustment Of Employment To Technical Change In The Steel And Auto Industries," (3), 475-492.

Brenner, Menachem and Dan Galai. "Implied Interest Rates," (3), 493-508.

Boyer, Kenneth D. and Kent M. Lancaster. "Are There Scale Economies In Advertising?," (3), 509-526.

Hayes, Beth and Daniel Siegel. "Rate Of Return Regulation With Price Flexibility," (4), Part 1, 537-554.

Barro, Robert J. and Chaipat Sahasakul. "Average Marginal Tax Rates From Social Security And The Individual Income Tax," (4), Part 1, 555-566.

Hess, Alan C. and Sanjai Bhagat. "Size Effects Of Seasoned Stock Issues: Empirical Evidence," (4), Part 1, 567-584.

Breen, William, Ravi Jagannathan and Aharon R. Ofer. "Correcting For Heteroscedasticity In Tests For Market Timing Ability," (4), Part 1, 585-598.

Goldstein, Jonathan. "Markup Variability And Flexibility: Theory And Empirical Evidence," (4), Part 1, 599-622.

Srivastava, Rajendra K. and Robert T. Green. "Determinants Of Bilateral Trade Flows," (4), Part 1, 623-640.

Simon, Herbert A. "Rationality In Psychology And Economics," (4), Part 2, S209-S224.

Einhorn, Hillel J. and Robin M. Hogarth. "Decision Making Under Ambiguity," (4), Part 2, S225-S250.

Tversky, Amos and Daniel Kahneman. "Rational Choice And The Framing Of Decisions," (4), Part 2, S251-S278.

Kahneman, Daniel, Jack L. Knetsch and Richard H. Thaler. "Fairness And The Assumptions Of Economics," (4), Part 2, S285-S300.

Plott, Charles R. "Rational Choice In Experimental Markets," (4), Part 2, S301-S328.

Campbell, Donald T. "Rationality And Utility From The Standpoint Of Evolutionary Biology," (4), Part 2, S355-S364.

Coleman, James S. "Psychological Structure And Social Structure In Economic Models," (4), Part 2, S365-S370.

Gould, John P. "Is The Rational Expectations Hypothesis Enough?," (4), Part 2, S371-S378.

Lynn, Laurence E., Jr. "The Behavioral Foundations Of Public Policy-Making," (4), Part 2, S379-S384.

Arrow, Kenneth J. "Rationality Of Self And Others In An Economic System," (4), Part 2, S385-S400.

Lucas, Robert E., Jr. "Adaptive Behavior And Economic Theory," (2), Part 2, S401-S426.

Miller, Merton H. "Behavioral Rationality In Finance: The Case Of Dividends," (4), Part 2, S451-S468.

Kleidon, Allan W. "Anomalies In Financial Economics: Blueprint For Change?," (4), Part 2, S469-S500.

Journal of Business
Volume 60, 1987

Marsh, Terry A. and Robert C. Merton. "Dividend Behavior For The Aggregate Stock Market," (1), 1-40.

Hayes, Beth. "Competition And Two-Part Tariffs," (1), 41-54.

Fama, Eugene F. and Kenneth R. French. "Commodity Futures Prices: Some Evidence On Forecast Power, Premiums, And The Theory Of Storage," (1), 55-74.

Hansen, Robert G. "A Theory For The Choice Of Exchange Medium In Mergers And Acquisitions," (1), 75-96.

Grinblatt, Mark and Sheridan Titman. "The Relation Between Mean-Variance Efficiency And Arbitrage Pricing," (1), 97-112.

LaCivita, Charles J. "Currency, Trade, And Capital Flows In General Equilibrium," (1), 113-136.

Elton, Edwin J., Martin J. Gruber and Joel C. Rentzler. "Professionally Managed, Publicly Traded Commodity Funds," (2), 175-200.

Kling, John L. "Predicting The Turning Points Of Business And Economic Time Series," (2), 201-238.

Wilson, Jack W. and Charles P. Jones. "A Comparison Of Annual Common Stock Returns: 1871-1925 With 1926-85," (2), 239-258.

Nguyen, Dung. "Advertising, Random Sales Response, And Brand Competition: Some Theoretical And Econometric Implications," (2), 259-280.

Reinganum, Marc R. and Alan C. Shapiro. "Taxes And Stock Return Seasonality: Evidence From The London Stock Exchange," (2), 281-296.

Clark, Don P. "Regulation Of International Trade In The United States: The Tokyo Round," (2), 297-306.

Kormendi, Roger and Robert Lipe. "Earnings Innovations, Earnings Persistence, And Stock Returns," (3), 323-346.

Smirlock, Michael and Howard Kaufold. "Bank Foreign Lending, Mandatory Disclosure Rules, And The Reaction Of Bank Stock Prices To The Mexican Debt Crisis," (3), 347-364.

Png, I. P. L. and D. Hirshleifer. "Price Discrimination Through Offers To Match Price," (3), 365-384.

McFarland, Henry. "Did Railroad Deregulation Lead To Monopoly Pricing? An Application Of q," (3), 385-400.

Bookstaber, Richard M. and James B. McDonald. "A General Distribution For Describing Security Price Returns," (3), 401-424.

Collins, Daniel W., Johannes Ledolter and Judy Rayburn. "Some Further Evidence On The Stochastic Properties Of Systematic Risk," (3), 425-448.

Benvignati, Anita M. "Domestic Profit Advantages Of Multinational Firms," (3), 449-462.

Nelson, Charles R. and Andrew F. Siegel. "Parsimonious Modeling Of Yield Curves," (4), 473-490.

Gerstner, Eitan and James D Hess. "Why Do Hot Dogs Come In Packs Of 10 And Buns In 8s Or 12s? A Demand-Side Investigation," (4), 491-518.

Lustgarten, Steven and Stavros Thomadakis. "Mobility Barriers And Tobin's q," (4), 519-538.

Eckard, E. Woodrow, Jr. "Advertising, Competition, And Market Share Instability," (4), 539-552.

Benelli, Giuseppe, Claudio Loderer and Thomas Lys. "Labor Participation In Corporate Policy-Making Decisions: West Germany's Experience With Codetermination," (4), 553-576.

Huberman, Gur and Shmuel Kandel. "Value Line Rank And Firm Size," (4), 577-590.

Journal of Business
Volume 61, 1988

Seyhun, H. Nejat. "The Information Content Of Aggregate Insider Trading," (1), 1-24.

Rozeff, Michael S. and Mir A. Zaman. "Market Efficiency And Insider Trading: New Evidence," (1), 25-44.

Freeman, Scott. "Banking As The Provision Of Liquidity," (1), 45-64.

Navarro, Peter. "Why Do Corporations Give To Charity?," (1), 65-94.

Heath, David C. and Robert A. Jarrow. "Ex-Dividend Stock Price Behavior And Arbitrage Opportunities," (1), 95-108.

Chan, K. C. "On The Contrarian Investment Strategy," (2), 147-164.

Furubotn, Eirik G. "Codetermination And The Modern Theory Of The Firm: A Property-Rights Analysis," (2), 165-182.

Brown, David T. "The Construction Of Tender Offers: Capital Gains Taxes And The Free Rider Problem," (2), 183-196.

Norton, Seth W. "An Empirical Look At Franchising As An Organizational Form," (2), 197-218.

Jain, Prem C. "Response Of Hourly Stock Prices And Trading Volume To Economic News," (2), 219-232.

Benninga, Simon and Eli Talmor. "The Interaction Of Corporate And Government Financing In General Equilibrium," (2), 233-258.

Grossman, Sanford J. "An Analysis Of The Implications For Stock And Futures Price Volatility Of Program Trading And Dynamic Hedging Strategies," (3), 275-298.

Castanias, Rick, Ki-Young Chung and Herb Johnson. "Dividend Spreads," (3), 299-320.

Mayo, John W. and Joseph E. Flynn. "The Effects Of Regulation On Research And Development: Theory And Evidence," (3), 321-336.
Busche, Kelly and Christopher D. Hall. "An Exception To The Risk Preference Anomaly," (3), 337-346.
Davidson, Carl. "Equilibrium In Servicing Industries: An Economic Application Of Queuing Theory," (3), 347-368.
Dybvig, Philip H. "Distributional Analysis Of Portfolio Choice," (3), 369-394.
Conrad, Jennifer and Gautam Kaul. "Time-Variation In Expected Returns," (4), 409-426.
Narasimhan, Chakravarthi. "Competitive Promotional Strategies," (4), 427-450.
Badrinath, S. G. and Sangit Chatterjee. "On Measuring Skewness And Elongation In Common Stock Return Distributions: The Case Of The Market Index," (4), 451-472.
Holland, A. Steven. "Indexation And The Effect Of Inflation Uncertainty On Real GNP," (4), 473-484.
Carroll, Carolyn and K. C. John Wei. "Risk, Return, And Equilibrium: An Extension," (4), 485-500.

Journal of Business
Volume 62, 1989

Elton, Edwin J., Martin J. Gruber and Joel Rentzler. "New Public Offerings, Information, And Investor Rationality: The Case Of Publicly Offered Commodity Funds," (1), 1-16.
Clarke, Richard N. "SICs As Delineators Of Economic Markets," (1), 17-32.
Prager, Robin A. "The Effects Of Regulatory Policies On The Cost Of Debt For Electric Utilities: An Empirical Investigation," (1),33-54.
Akgiray, Vedat. "Conditional Heteroscedasticity In Time Series Of Stock Returns: Evidence And Forecasts," (1), 55-80.
Smith, Michael L. "Investment Returns And Yields To Holders Of Insurance," (1), 81-98.
Stensland, Gunnar and Dag Tjostheim. "Optimal Investments Using Empirical Dynamic Programming With Application To Natural Resources," (1), 99-120.
Grammatikos, Theoharry. "Dividend Stripping, Risk Exposure, And The Effect Of The 1984 Tax Reform Act On The Ex-Dividend Day Behavior," (2), 157-174.
Venkatesh, P. C. "The Impact Of Dividend Initiation On The Information Content Of Earnings Announcements And Returns Volatility," (2), 175-198.
Margolis, Stephen E. "Monopolistic Competition And Multiproduct Brand Names," (2), 199-210.
Glosten, Lawrence R. "Insider Trading, Liquidity, And The Role Of The Monopolist Specialist," (2), 211-236.
Darrough, Masako N. and Neal M. Stoughton. "A Bargaining Approach To Profit Sharing In Joint Ventures," (2), 237-270.
Kadapakkam, Palani-Rajan and Stanley J. Kon. "The Value Of Shelf Registration For New Debt Issues," (2), 271-292.
Scheinkman, Jose A. and Blake LeBaron. "Nonlinear Dynamics And Stock Returns," (3), 311-338.
Hsieh, David A. "Testing For Nonlinear Dependence In Daily Foreign Exchange Rates," (3), 339-368.
Diebold, Francis X. and Glenn D. Rudebusch. "Scoring The Leading Indicators," (3), 369-392.
Grinblatt, Mark and Sheridan Titman. "Mutual Fund Performance: An Analysis Of Quarterly Portfolio Holdings," (3), 393-416.
Shinnar, Reuel, Ofer Dressler, C. A. Feng and Alan I. Avidan. "Estimation Of The Economic Rate Of Return For Industrial Companies," (3), 417-446.
Brennan, Michael J. and Eduardo S. Schwartz. "Portfolio Insurance And Financial Market Equilibrium," (4), 455-472.
Grossman, Sanford J. and Jean-Luc Vila. "Portfolio Insurance In Complete Markets: A Note," (4), 473-476.
Kling, John L. and David A. Bessler. "Calibration-Based Predictive Distributions: An Application Of Prequential Analysis To Interest Rates, Money, Prices, And Output," (4), 477-500.
Allen, Linda, Stavros Peristiani and Anthony Saunders. "Bank Size, Collateral, And Net Purchase Behavior In The Federal Funds Market: Empirical Evidence," (4), 501-516.
Wedig, Gerard J., Mahmud Hassan and Frank A. Sloan. "Hospital Investment Decisions And The Cost Of Capital," (4), 517-538.
Maloney, Kevin J. and Richard J. Rogalski. "Call-Option Pricing And The Turn Of The Year," (4), 539-552.

Journal of Business
Volume 63, 1990

Hafer, R. W. and Scott E. Hein. "Forecasting Inflation Using Interest-Rate And Time-Series Models: Some International Evidence," (1), Part 1, 1-18.
Mayers, David and Clifford W. Smith, Jr. "On The Corporate Demand For Insurance: Evidence From The Reinsurance Market," (1), Part 1, 19-40.
Ippolito, Pauline M. "Bonding And Nonbonding Signals Of Product Quality," (1), Part 1, 41-60.
Hausch, Donald B. and William T. Ziemba. "Arbitrage Strategies For Cross-Track Betting On Major Horse Races," (1), Part 1, 61-78.
Feinberg, Robert M. and Donald J. Rousslang. "The Economic Effects Of Intellectual Property Right Infringements," (1), Part 1, 79-90.

Wernerfelt, Birger. "Advertising Content When Brand Choice Is A Signal," (1), Part 1, 91-98.
Schnader, M. H. and H. O. Stekler. "Evaluating Predictions Of Change," (1), Part 1, 99-108.
Brennan, Michael J. and Eduardo S. Schwartz. "Arbitrage In Stock Index Futures," (1), Part 2, S7-S32.
Buser, Stephen A., Patric H. Hendershott and Anthony B. Saunders. "Determinants Of The Value Of Call Options On Default-Free Bonds," (1), Part 2, S33-S50.
Chen, Nai-Fu, Bruce Grundy and Robert F. Stambaugh. "Changing Risk, Changing Risk Premiums, And Dividend Yield Effects," (1), Part 2, S51-S70.
Fama, Eugene F. "Contract Costs And Financing Decisions," (1), Part 2, S71-S92.
Huberman, Gur. "Dividend Neutrality With Transaction Costs," (1), Part 2, S93-S106.
Jaffee, Dwight and Andrei Shleifer. "Costs Of Financial Distress, Delayed Calls Of Convertible Bonds, And The Role Of Investment Banks," (1), Part 2, S107-S124.
Nelson, Charles R. and Richard Startz. "The Distribution Of The Instrumental Variables Estimator And Its t-Ratio When The Instrument Is A Poor One," (1), Part 2, S125-S140.
Scholes, Myron S. and Mark A. Wolfson. "The Effects Of Changes In Tax Laws On Corporate Reorganization Activity," (1), Part 2, S141-S164.
Stoll, Hans R. and Robert E. Whaley. "Program Trading And Individual Stock Returns: Ingredients Of The Triple-Witching Brew," (1), Part 2, S165-S192.
D'Arcy, Stephen P. and Neil A. Doherty. "Adverse Selection, Private Information, And Lowballing In Insurance Markets," (2), 145-164.
Golec, Joseph. "The Financial Effects Of Fuel Adjustment Clauses On Electric Utilities," (2), 165-186.
Huberman, Gur and Shmuel Kandel. "Market Efficiency And Value Line's Record," (2), 187-216.
Woglom, Geoffrey. "Systematic Risk And The Theory Of Wage Indexation," (2), 217-238.
Chaplinsky, Susan and H. Nejat Seyhun. "Dividends And Taxes: Evidence On Tax-Reduction Strategies," (2), 239-260.
Lee, Cheng-Few and Shafiqur Rahman. "Market Timing, Selectivity, And Mutual Fund Performance: An Empirical Investigation," (2), 261-278.
Pound, John and Richard Zeckhauser. "Clearly Heard On The Street: The Effect Of Takeover Rumors On Stock Prices," (3), 291-308.
Sullivan, Mary. "Measuring Image Spillovers In Umbrella-Branded Products," (3), 309-330.
Jorion, Philippe. "The Exchange-Rate Exposure Of U.S. Multinationals," (3), 331-346.
Hansen, Robert S. and Claire Crutchley. "Corporate Earnings And Financings: An Empirical Analysis," (3), 347-372.
Woodward, G. Thomas. "The Real Thing: A Dynamic Profile Of The Term Structure Of Real Interest Rates And Inflation Expectations In The United Kingdom, 1982-89," (3), 373-398.
Schwert, G. William. "Indexes Of U.S. Stock Prices From 1802 To 1987," (3), 399-426.
Seyhun, H. Nejat. "Do Bidder Managers Knowingly Pay Too Much For Target Firms?," (4), 439-464.
Zechner, Josef. "Tax Clienteles And Optimal Capital Structure Under Uncertainty," (4), 465-492.
Smith, Bruce D. and Michael J. Stutzer. "Adverse Selection, Aggregate Uncertainty, And The Role For Mutual Insurance Contracts," (4), 493-510.
Madan, Dilip B. and Eugene Seneta. "The Variance Gamma (V.G.) Model For Share Market Returns," (4), 511-524.
Mantell, Edmund H. "The Relationship Of Rent-Seeking Behavior To Impacted Information In Public Utility Regulation," (4), 525-536.

Journal of Business
Volume 64, 1991

De Long, J. Bradford, Andrei Shleifer, Lawrence H. Summers and Robert J. Waldmann. "The Survival Of Noise Traders In Financial Markets," (1), 1-20.
Hall, Christopher D. "Renting Ideas," (1), 21-48.
Hartzmark, Michael L. "Luck Versus Forecast Ability: Determinants Of Trader Performance In Futures Markets," (1), 49-74.
Dhillon, Upinder and Herb Johnson. "Changes In The Standard And Poor's 500 List," (1), 75-86.
Hamao, Yasushi. "A Standard Data Base For The Analysis Of Japanese Security Markets," (1), 87-102.
Jennings, Robert H. and Michael A. Mazzeo. "Stock Price Movements Around Acquisition Announcements And Management's Response," (2), 139-164.
Morck, Randall and Bernard Yeung. "Why Investors Value Multinationality," (2), 165-188.
Denis, David J. "Shelf Registration And The Market For Seasoned Equity Offerings," (2), 189-212.
Mann, Steven V. and Neil W. Sicherman. "The Agency Costs Of Free Cash Flow: Acquisition Activity And Equity Issues," (2), 213-228.
Erzan, Refik and Alexander J. Yeats. "Implications Of Current Factor Proportions Indices For The Competitive Position Of The U.S. Manufacturing And Service Industries In The Year 2000," (2), 229-254.
Kaserman, David L. and John W. Mayo. "Regulation, Advertising, And Economic Welfare," (2), 255-268.

JOURNAL OF BUSINESS FINANCE AND ACCOUNTING

Yoshida, Hiroshi. "Some Comments On CPP Accounting," (3), 113-116.
Nguyen, D. T. "Inflation, Inflation Accounting, And The Corporate Viability Condition," (3), 117-122.
Kennedy, Charles. "Holding Gains, Debt-Financing, Working Capital And Current Cost Accounting: Comment," (3), 123-128.
Lawson, G. H. "Holding Gains, Debt-Financing, Working Capital And Current Cost Accounting: A Reply," (3), 129-136.
Peasnell, K. V. and L. C. L. Skerratt. "Long-Term Debt And Shareholder Wealth: A Comment," (3), 137-142.
Briscoe, G. "Long-Term Debt And Shareholder Wealth: A Reply," (3), 143-146.
Climo, Tom. "Bourn On Borrowing Gains: A Short Comment On Losses To Lenders," (3), 147-148.
Bourn, Michael, P. J. M. Stoney and R. F. Wynn. "Price Indices For Current Cost Accounting," (3), 149-172.
Flamholtz, Eric. "Toward A Formal Model Of Group Dynamics In Task Performance Relevant To Accounting," (4), 3-26.
Davis, E. W. and K. A. Yeomans. "Market Discount On New Issues Of Equity: The Influence Of Firm Size, Method Of Issue And Market Volatility," (4), 27-42.
Emmanuel, C. R. and D. T. Otley. "The Usefulness Of Residual Income," (4), 43-51.
Keane, S. M. "The Tax-Deductibility Of Interest Payments And The Weighted Average Cost Of Capital," (4), 53-61.
Ashton, Raymond. "Cash Flow Accounting: A Review And Critique," (4), 63-81.
Ward, C. W. R. and A. Saunders. "U.K. Unit Trust Performance 1964-74," (4), 83-100.
Grinyer, John R. "The Cost Of Equity, The C.A.P.M. And Management Objectives Under Uncertainty," (4), 101-121.
Gee, Kenneth P. "Holding Gains, Inventory Decisions And The Measurement Of Purchasing Performance," (4), 123-142.
Groves, R. E. V. and J. M. Samuels. "A Note On The Cost Of Retained Earnings And Deferred Taxes In The U.K.," (4), 143-149.
Archer, Simon. "Holding Gains, Deferred Taxation And Capital Structure," (4), 151-167.
Redhead, Keith J. "Stock Appreciation And The Definition Of Profit - A Macroeconomic Perspective," (4), 169-178.

Journal of Business Finance and Accounting
Volume 4, 1977

Falk, Haim and James A. Heintz. "The Predictability Of Relative Risk Over Time," (1), 5-28.
Bird, R. G. and A. J. McHugh. "Financial Ratios - An Empirical Study," (1), 29-46.
Firth, Michael. "An Empirical Investigation Of The Impact Of The Announcement Of Capitalisation Issues On Share Prices," (1), 47-60.
Franklin, Peter J. "The Normal Cost Theory Of Price And The Internal Rate Of Return Method Of Investment Appraisal: An Integration," (1), 61-82.
Martin, Donald Dewayne. "Justification For Probability Depreciation," (1), 83-98.
Purdy, Derek E. "Accounting For Convertible Debt," (1), 99-114.
Laughlin, Richard C. "Accounting Objectives And The Corporate Report," (1), 115-130.
Newbould, G. D. and K. W. Wilson. "Alternative Measures Of Company Size - A Note For Researchers," (1), 131-132.
Gordon, Lawrence A. "Further Thoughts On The Accounting Rate Of Return Vs. The Economic Rate Of Return," (1), 133-134.
Buckley, Adrian. "Cash Flow Statements For Investors - A Comment," (1), 135-138.
Peasnell, K. V. and L. C. L. Skerratt. "Price Indices For Current Cost Accounting - A Reply And Some Further Evidence," (1), 139-144.
Bourn, Michael, P. J. M. Stoney and R. F. Wynn. "Price Indices For Current Cost Accounting: A Rejoinder," (1), 145-150.
Peasnell, K. V. "The Present Value Concept In Financial Reporting," (2), 153-168.
Ezejelue, A. C. "Financial Accounting And Optimality Criteria," (2), 169-176.
Dickinson, J. P. and K. Kyuno. "Corporate Valuation: A Reconciliation Of The Miller-Modigliani And Traditionalist Views," (2), 177-186.
Wilkes, F. M. "Dividend Policy And Investment Appraisal In Imperfect Capital Markets," (2), 187-200.
Keane, Simon M. "The Irrelevance Of The Firm's Cost Of Capital As An Investment Decision Tool," (2), 201-216.
Findlay, M. Chapman, III. "The Weighted Average Cost Of Capital And Finite Flows," (2), 217-227.
Hoskins, Colin G. "Benefit-Cost Ratio Ranking For Size Disparity Problems," (2), 229-232.
Bello, Olaseni A. "The Firm, Investment, Rate Of Return And The Monopolies Commission," (2), 233-246.
Jensen, Daniel L. and James C. McKeown. "Multiple-Step Investigations Of Standard Cost Variances," (2), 247-256.
Forrester, D. A. R. "German Principles Of Accounting: A Review Note," (2), 257-262.
Lowe, E. A. and A. M. Tinker. "Siting The Accounting Problematic: Towards An Intellectual Emancipation Of Accounting," (3), 263-276.
Zanker, F. W. A. "The Cost Of Capital For Debt-Financed Investments," (3), 277-284.
Tweedie, D. P. "ED18 And User Comprehension - The Need For An Explanatory Statement," (3), 285-298.
Saunders, Anthony and Richard S. Woodward. "Gains From International Portfolio Diversification: UK Evidence 1971-75," (3), 299-309.
Patz, Dennis H. "The State Of The Art In Translation Theory," (3), 311-325.
Turnbull, S. M. "Market Imperfections And The Capital Asset Pricing Model," (3), 327-337.
Fadel, Hisham. "The Predictive Power Of Financial Ratios In The British Construction Industry," (3), 339-352.
Stewart, J. C. "Multinational Companies And Transfer Pricing," (3), 353-372.

Cuthbert, N. H. and A. Whitaker. "Disclosure Of Information And Collective Bargaining: A Re-Examination," (3), 373-378.
King, Paul. "A Short Note On `Is The Emphasis Of Capital Budgeting Theory Misplaced?'," (3), 379-382.
Arnold, John. "An Approach To Pricing And Output Decisions When Prices Are Changing," (4), 383-406.
Emmanuel, C. R. and S. J. Gray. "Corporate Diversification And Segmental Disclosure Requirements In The USA," (4), 407-418.
Longbottom, D. A. and L. Wiper. "Capital Appraisal And The Case For Average Rate Of Return," (4), 419-426.
Nurnberg, Hugo. "An Unrecognized Ambiguity Of The High-Low Method," (4), 427-442.
Gordon, L. A. "Imperfect Markets And The Nature Of Goodwill," (4), 443-462.
Fox, A. F. "The Cost Of Retained Earnings - A Comment," (4), 463-468.
Briston, Richard J. and Richard Dobbins. "Institutional Shareholders And Equity Stability: A Corroboratory Note," (4), 469-476.
Glautier, M. W. E. and P. J. Taylor. "A Comment On The Application Of Group Dynamics In Task Performance Relevant To Accounting," (4), 477-480.
Flamholtz, Eric G. "Group Dynamics In Task Performance And Human Resource Accounting: A Reply," (4), 481-484.

Journal of Business Finance and Accounting
Volume 5, 1978

Lister, Roger J. "Business Finance - An Evolving Field Of Study," (1), 1-26.
Artto, Eero. "Money Flow Analyses," (1), 27-38.
Jarrett, Jeffrey E. "Estimating The Cost Of Capital For A Division Of A Firm, And The Allocation Problem In Accounting," (1), 39-48.
Amihud, Yakov. "Uncertainty In Future Interest Rates And The Term Structure," (1), 49-56.
Roenfeldt, Rodney L. and Philip L. Cooley. "Predicting Corporate Profitability For Investment Selection," (1), 57-65.
Spicer, Barry H. "Market Risk, Accounting Data And Companies' Pollution Control Records," (1), 67-83.
Weston, C. R. "The Information Content Of Rights Trading," (1), 85-92.
Belkaoui, Ahmed. "Financial Ratios As Predictors Of Canadian Takeovers," (1), 93-108.
Hull, J. C. "The Interpretation Of The Output From A Sensitivity Analysis In Investment Appraisal," (1), 109-122.
Theobald, Michael. "Intertemporal Dividend Models - An Empirical Analysis Using Recent UK Data," (1), 123-136.
Oliver, Jan and Eric Flamholtz. "Human Resource Replacement Cost Numbers, Cognitive Information Processing, And Personnel Decisions: A Laboratory Experiment," (2), 137-158.
Bhaskar, Krish. "Linear Programming And Capital Budgeting: The Financing Problem," (2), 159-194.
Watson, J. "A Study Of Possible Gains From International Investment," (2), 195-206.
Johnson, W. Bruce. "The Cross-Sectional Stability Of Financial Patterns," (2), 207-214.
Appleyard, A. R. "The Shape Of The Preference Function Under Uncertainty: A Note," (2), 215-221.
Roux, F. J. P. and B. P. Gilbertson. "The Behaviour Of Share Prices On The Johannesburg Stock Exchange," (2), 223-232.
Ashton, D. J. "The Reasons For Leasing - A Mathematical Programming Framework," (2), 233-251.
Bailey, R. A. and W. K. H. Fung. "A Note On Extreme Leverage, MM And Ezra Solomon," (2), 253-259.
Peasnell, K. V. and L. C. L. Skerratt. "Performance Of A Relative Decline Model: An Efficient Markets Interpretation Of Some Results Of Jones, Tweedie And Whittington," (2), 261-267.
Whittington, Geoffrey. "A Comment On The Efficient Markets Interpretation Of A Relative Decline Model," (2), 269-273.
Amigoni, Franco. "Planning Management Control Systems," (3), 279-292.
Mumford, M. J. "Monetary Assets And Capital Gearing," (3), 293-308.
Saunders, Anthony. "Expected Inflation, Unexpected Inflation And The Return On U.K. Shares, 1961-1973," (3), 309-320.
Meade, Nigel. "The Random Walk And A Thin Market," (3), 321-328.
Mao, James C. T. and Carl E. Sarndal. "Cash Management: Theory And Practice," (3), 329-338.
Keane, Simon M. "The Cost Of Capital As A Financial Decision Tool," (3), 339-354.
Sealey, C. W., Jr. "Utility Maximization And Programming Models For Capital Budgeting," (3), 355-366.
Blois, K. J. "The Pricing Of Supplies By Large Customers," (3), 367-380.
Keane, Simon M. "The Present Value Concept In Financial Reporting: A Comment," (3), 381-393.
Peasnell, K. V. "The Present Value Concept In Financial Reporting: A Reply," (3), 395.
Schwab, Bernhard. "Conceptual Problems In The Use Of Risk-Adjusted Discount Rates With Disaggregated Cash Flows," (4), 281-293.
Longbottom, David A. and Linda Wiper. "Necessary Conditions For The Existence Of Multiple Rates In The Use Of Internal Rate Of Return," (4), 295-304.
Dhingra, Harbans L. "Portfolio Volatility Adjustment By Canadian Mutual Funds," (4), 305-333.
Capettini, Robert and Dennis Collins. "The Investigation Of Deviations From Standard Costs In The Presence Of Unequal State Variances," (4), 335-352.
Leech, Stewart A., Denis J. Pratt and W. G. W. Magill. "Company Asset Revaluations And Inflation In Australia, 1950 To 1975," (4), 353-362.
Emery, Douglas R., Philip C. Parr, Per B. Mokkelbost, David Gandhi and Anthony Saunders. "An Investigation Of Real Investment Decision Making With The Options Pricing Model," (4), 363-369.
Courtis, John K. "Modelling A Financial Ratios Categoric Framework," (4), 371-386.
Grant, R. M. "The Monopolies Commission And The Rate Of Return On Capital: A Comment," (4), 387-391.
Kennedy, Charles. "Fixed Assets And The Hyde Gearing Adjustment," (4), 393-406.

Gandhi, Devinder K. and Anthony Saunders. "The Superiority Of Stochastic Dominance Over Mean-Variance Efficiency Criteria: Some Clarifications," (1), 51-59.

White, J. R. "Unit Trusts, Homogenous Beliefs And The Separation Property," (1), 61-78.

Buckland, R., P. J. Herbert and K. A. Yeomans. "Price Discount On New Equity Issues In The UK And Their Relationship To Investor Subscription In The Period 1965-75," (1), 79-95.

Partington, Graham H. "Financial Decisions, The Cost(s) Of Capital And The Capital Asset Pricing Model," (1), 97-112.

Oakford, R. V. and Arturo Salazar. "The Long Term Effectiveness Of 'Exact' And Approximate Capital Rationing Procedures Under Uncertainty And Incomplete Information," (1), 113-137.

Pope, P. F. and D. A. Peel. "Information Disclosure To Employees And Rational Expectations," (1), 139-146.

Lister, Roger. "The Cost Of Retained Earnings: A Comment On Some Recent Work," (2), 155-160.

Findlay, M. Chapman, III and Edward E. Williams. "The Problem Of 'Unequal Lives' Reconsidered," (2), 161-164.

Vickers, Douglas. "The Marginal Efficiency Of (Money) Capital," (2), 165-176.

Aivazian, Varouj A. and Jeffrey L. Callen. "The 'Unanimity' Literature And The Security Market Line Criterion: The Additive Risk Case," (2), 177-184.

Trennepohl, Gary L. and William P. Dukes. "An Empirical Test Of Option Writing And Buying Strategies Utilizing In-The-Money And Out-Of-The-Money Contracts," (2), 185-202.

Morris, R.C. and P.F. Pope. "The Jensen Measure Of Portfolio Performance In An Arbitrage Pricing Theory Context," (2), 203-220.

Barlev, Benzion and Haim Levy. "The Information Content Of Accounting Data And The Management Of Security Portfolios," (2), 221-248.

Raine, P. S., R. B. Flavell and G. R. Salkin. "A Likelihood Control System For Use With Formal Planning Models," (2), 249-266.

Fowler, David J., C. Harvey Rorke and Vijay M. Jog. "A Note On Beta Stability And Thin Trading On The Toronto Stock Exchange," (2), 267-278.

Calvet, A. L. and J. Lefoll. "Performance And Systematic Risk Stability Of Canadian Mutual Funds Under Inflation," (2), 279-289.

Benjamin, Wahjudi P. and John E. McEnroe. "The FASB's Policy Intervention And The Behavior Of Security Returns: An Empirical Investigation Of The Oil And Gas Industry Employing A Combination Of The ITS And The SUR Models," (3), 303-327.

Laughlin, Richard C. "On The Nature Of Accounting Methodology," (3), 329-351.

Pound, G. D. and J. R. Francis. "The Accounting Services Market: Theory And Evidence," (3), 353-371.

Ruland, William. "The Behavior Of Changes In Accounting Risk Measures," (3), 373-387.

Scapens, Robert W. and J. Timothy Sale. "Performance Measurement And Formal Capital Expenditure Controls In Divisionalised Companies," (3), 389-419.

Rao, Ramesh K. S. and John D. Martin. "Another Look At The Use Of Options Pricing Theory To Evaluate Real Asset Investment Opportunities," (3), 421-429.

Hasseldine, C. R. "The Information Content Of Rights Trading: A Comment," (3), 431-439.

Weston, C. R. "The Information Content Of Rights Trading: A Reply," (3), 441-443.

Castagna, A. D. and Z. P. Matolcsy. "The Market Characteristics Of Failed Companies: Extensions And Further Evidence," (4), 467-484.

Hong, Han Kang. "Finance Mix And Capital Structure," (4), 485-491.

Khumawala, Saleha B., Neil W. Polhemus and Woody M. Liao. "The Predictability Of Quarterly Cash Flows," (1), 493-510.

Pohlman, Randolph A. and Robert D. Hollinger. "Information Redundancy In Sets Of Financial Ratios," (4), 511-528.

Lapsley, Irvine. "Income Measurement At A State Railway Corporation: The 'Social Profit' Illusion?," (4), 529-548.

Thomas, Andrew P. "Towards A Value-Neutral Positive Science Of Accounting," (4), 549-572.

Ansari, Shahid L. and Masao Tsuji. "A Behavioral Extension To The Cost Variances Investigation Decision," (4), 573-591.

Findlay, M. Chapman, III and Edward E. Williams. "Discounting Deferred Tax Liabilities: A Reply," (4), 593-597.

Journal of Business Finance and Accounting
Volume 9, 1982

Baxter, W. T. "Lessors' Depreciation And Profit - An Approach Via Deprival Value," (1), 1-18.

Atkinson, Anthony A. and William R. Scott. "Current Cost Depreciation: A Programming Perspective," (1), 19-42.

Pointon, John. "Taxation And Mathematical Programming," (1), 43-50.

Barnes, Paul. "Methodological Implications Of Non-Normally Distributed Financial Ratios," (1), 51-62.

Salmi, Timo. "Estimating The Internal Rate Of Return From Published Financial Statements," (1), 63-74.

Singh, Saraswati P. and Prem P. Talwar. "Monetary And Fiscal Policies And Stock Prices," (1), 75-91.

Ward, C. W. R. "Arbitrage And Investment In Commercial Property," (1), 93-108.

Yallup, Peter J. "A Study Of Possible Gains From International Investment And The Stationarity Of Inter-Country Correlation Coefficients: A Comment," (1), 109-116.

Watson, J. "A Study Of Possible Gains From International Investment And The Stationarity Of Inter-Country Correlation Coefficients: A Reply," (1), 117-118

Zafiris, Nicos. "Interest On Equity Capital As An Ex Post Cost: A Comment," (1), 119-125.

Amey, Lloyd R. "Interest On Equity Capital As An Ex Post Cost: A Reply," (1), 127-132.

Zafiris, Nicos. "Interest On Equity Capital As An Ex Post Cost: A Rejoinder," (1), 133-134.

Hoshino, Yasuo. "The Performance Of Corporate Mergers In Japan,"

(2), 153-165.

McInish, Thomas H. and Donald J. Puglisi. "The Efficiency Of The International Money Markets," (2), 167-177.

Tang, Roger Y. W. "Environmental Variables Of Multinational Transfer Pricing: A UK Perspective," (2), 179-189.

Chua, J. and R. S. Woodward. "Gold As An Inflation Hedge: A Comparative Study Of Six Major Industrial Countries," (2), 191-197.

Conine, Thomas E., Jr. "On The Theoretical Relationship Between Business Risk And Systematic Risk," (2), 199-206.

Kolari, James W. and Vincent P. Apilado. "Bond Risk Premiums, Financial Data, And The Effect Of Market Segmentation," (2), 207-218.

Lohmann, Jack R. and R. V. Oakford. "The Effects Of Borrowing On The Rate Of Growth Of Capital And The Risk Of Ruin Of A Firm," (2), 219-238.

Bartley, Jon W. "Accounting For The Cost Of Capital: An Empirical Examination," (2), 239-254.

Dhaliwal, Dan S. "Some Economic Determinants Of Management Lobbying For Alternative Methods Of Accounting: Evidence From The Accounting For Interest Costs Issue," (2), 255-265.

Davies, J. R. and W. M. McInnes. "The Valuation Of Fixed Assets In The Financial Accounts Of UK Nationalised Industries And The Implications For Monitoring Performance: A Comment," (2), 267-272.

MacArthur, J. B. "The Valuation Of Fixed Assets In The Financial Accounts Of UK Nationalised Industries And The Implications For Monitoring Performance: A Reply," (2), 273-276.

Appleyard, A. R., N. Strong and M. Walker. "Mutual Fund Performance In The Context Of Models Of Equilibrium Capital Asset Pricing," (3), 289-296.

Cheung, Joseph K. "The Association Between Lease Disclosure And The Lessee's Systematic Risk," (3), 297-306.

Beedles, William L. and O. Maurice Joy. "Compounding Risk Over Time: A Note," (3), 307-311.

Kross, William. "Profitability, Earnings Announcement Time Lags, And Stock Prices," (3), 313-328.

Punter, Alan. "Optimal Cash Management Under Conditions Of Uncertainty," (3), 329-340.

Lee, T. A. "Cash Flow Accounting And The Allocation Problem," (3), 341-352.

Firth, Michael. "Some Time Series Properties Of Corporate Earnings In New Zealand: A Note," (3), 353-360.

Peasnell, K. V. "Some Formal Connections Between Economic Values And Yields And Accounting Numbers," (3), 361-381.

Morris, Michael H. and Bill McDonald. "Asset Pricing And Financial Reporting With Changing Prices," (3), 383-395.

Ro, Byung, T. "An Analytical Approach To Accounting Materiality," (3), 397-412.

Barlev, Benzion, Joshua Livnat and Aharon Yoran. "Advance Payments During Inflationary Periods," (3), 413-426.

Ryan, Robert J. "Capital Market Theory - A Case Study In Methodological Conflict," (4), 443-458.

Kanniainen, Vesa. "Unanticipated Inflation, Taxation, And Common Stocks," (4), 459-470.

Ashton, David J. "Stochastic Dominance And Mean Variance Rules In The Selection Of Risky Investments," (4), 471-482.

Yagil, Joseph. "Margin Trading: A Risk-Return Analysis," (4), 483-487.

Belkaoui, Ahmed. "Judgement Related Issues In Performance Evaluation," (4), 489-500.

Woodward, R. S. and J. Matatko. "Factors Affecting The Behaviour Of UK Closed End Fund Discounts 1968 to 1977," (4), 501-509.

Boardman, Calvin M., Walter J. Reinhart and Stephen E. Celec. "The Role Of The Payback Period In The Theory And Application Of Duration To Capital Budgeting," (4), 511-522.

Lawrence, S. R. "The Application Of Analysis Of Variance To Interfirm Comparison Ratios," (4), 523-530.

Hope, Tony and Rob Gray. "Power And Policy Making: The Development Of An R & D Standard," (4), 531-558.

Schnabel, Jacques A. "Variable Transactions Costs, The Capital Asset Pricing Model And The Corporate Dividend Decision: A Comment," (4), 559-562.

Theobald, Michael. "Variable Transactions Costs, The Capital Asset Pricing Model And The Corporate Dividend Decision: A Reply," (4), 563-564.

Ryan, Robert J. "Towards A Value-Neutral Positive Science Of Accounting: A Comment," (4), 565-566.

Laughlin, Richard C., E. Anthony Lowe and Anthony G. Puxty. "Towards A Value-Neutral Positive Science Of Accounting: A Comment," (4), 567-572.

Thomas, Andrew P. "Towards A Value-Neutral Positive Science Of Accounting: A Reply," (4), 573-578.

Draper, Dennis W. and M. Chapman Findlay, III. "A Note On Vickers' Marginal Cost Of Debt Capital," (4), 579-582.

Journal of Business Finance and Accounting
Volume 10, 1983

Nobes, C. W. "A Judgemental International Classification Of Financial Reporting Practices," (1), 1-19.

Chow, Chee W. "On The Measurement Of Auditing Standards," (1), 21-35.

Barnes, Paul and Colin Dodds. "The Structure And Performance Of The UK Building Society Industry 1970-78," (1), 37-56.

Foster, Taylor W., III, D. Randall Jenkins and Don W. Vickrey. "Additional Evidence On The Incremental Information Content Of The 10-K," (1), 57-66.

Booth, Peter J. "Decomposition Measures And The Prediction Of Financial Failure," (1), 67-82.

Grimlund, Richard A. and Robert Capettini. "Sign Tests For Actual Investments With Latter Period Net Cash Outflows," (1), 83-103.

Wilkes, F. M. "Dominance Criteria For The Ranking Of Projects With An Imperfect Capital Market," (1), 105-126.

Fabozzi, Frank J., Robert Fonfeder and Patrick Casabona. "An Empirical Examination Of The Impact Of Limited Review On

Equity Prices," (1), 127-138.

Bohren, Oyvind. "Bounding Certainty Equivalent Factors And Risk Adjusted Discount Rates," (1), 139-146.

Booth, Laurence D. "On The Negative Risk Premium For Risk Adjusted Discount Rates: A Comment And Extension," (1), 147-155.

Dyson, R. G. and R. H. Berry. "On The Negative Risk Premium For Risk Adjusted Discount Rates: A Reply," (1), 157-159.

Conine, Thomas E., Jr. "On The Theoretical Relationship Between Systematic Risk And Price Elasticity Of Demand," (2), 173-182.

Nawrocki, David. "A Comparison Of Risk Measures When Used In A Simple Portfolio Selection Heuristic," (2), 183-194.

Richardson, Frederick M. and Lewis F. Davidson. "An Exploration Into Bankruptcy Discriminant Model Sensitivity," (2), 195-207.

El Hennawy, R. H. A. and R. C. Morris. "The Significance Of Base Year In Developing Failure Prediction Models," (2), 209-223.

Castagna, A. D. and Z. P. Matolcsy. "The Evaluation Of Traded Options Pricing Models In Australia," (2), 225-233.

Benjamin, Wahjudi P. and John E. McEnroe. "The SEC Overruling Of SFAS 19 And The Behavior Of Security Returns," (2), 235-249.

Ashton, R. K. "An Economic Analysis Of Value To The Owner," (2), 251-256.

Oxelheim, Lars. "Proposals For New Accounting Standards For Foreign Monetary Items," (2), 257-288.

Jarrett, Jeffrey. "The Rate Of Return From Interim Financial Reports And The Allocation Problem In Financial Accounting," (2),289-298.

Belkaoui, Ahmed. "Accrual Accounting And Cash Accounting: Relative Merits Of Derived Accounting Indicator Numbers," (2), 299-312.

Rutherford, B. A. "Cash Flow Reporting And Distributional Allocations: A Note," (2), 313-316.

Williams, David J. and Keith D. Turpie. "The Accounting Services Market: Theory And Evidence: A Comment," (2), 317-321.

Francis, J. R. and G. Pound. "The Accounting Services Market: Theory And Evidence: A Reply," (2), 323-324.

Hawawini, Gabriel A., Pierre A. Michel and Claude J. Viallet. "As Assessment Of Risk And Return Of French Common Stocks," (3), 333-350.

Witt, Stephen F. and Richard Dobbins. "A Note On The Effect Of Institutional Trading Activities On The Real Value Of The Financial Times All-Share Index," (3), 351-358.

El Hennawy, R. H. A. and R. C. Morris. "Market Anticipation Of Corporate Failure In The UK," (3), 359-372.

Brandon, Charles, Jeffrey Jarrett and Saleha Khumuwala. "On The Predictability Of Growth In Earnings Per Share," (3), 373-387.

Lister, Roger. "The Cost Of Retained Earnings: A Further Note, An Illustration And A Computer Program," (3), 389-393.

French, Dan W. "Black-Scholes Vs. Kassouf Option Pricing: An Empirical Comparison," (3), 395-408.

Scapens, Robert W. "A Neoclassical Measure Of Profit: An Extension For Uncertainty," (3), 409-418.

Woodward, R. S. "The Performance Of UK Closed-End Funds: A Comparison Of The Various Ranking Criteria," (3), 419-428.

Edmonds, Thomas P. "The Effect Of Auditor Involvement On The Predictive Capacity Of Interim Financial Information," (3), 429-441.

Filios, Vassilios P. "The Cameralistic Method Of Accounting: A Historical Note," (3), 443-450.

Laughlin, Richard C. and Anthony G. Puxty. "Accounting Regulation: An Alternative Perspective," (3), 451-479.

Williams, David J. and Chanoch Shreiber. "Cost-Volume-Profit Complications Using A Simplified Form," (3), 481-488.

Walker, M. "Financial Accounting Reports: A Market Model Of Disclosure: A Comment," (3), 489-493.

Bird, Ron and Stuart Locke. "Financial Accounting Reports: A Market Model Of Disclosure: A Reply," (3), 495-497.

Scapens, Robert W. "The Gearing Adjustment: An Economic Profit Perspective," (4), 503-520.

Barnes, Paul. "The Consequences Of Growth Maximisation And Expense Preference Policies Of Managers: Evidence From UK Building Societies. A Study Of The Causes Of Profit Insufficiency During A Period Of Increased Competition Using Discriminant Analysis," (4), 521-530.

Purdy, Derek E. "The Enterprise Theory: An Extension," (4), 531-541.

Puxty, Anthony G. and Richard Laughlin. "A Rational Reconstruction Of The Decision-Usefulness Criterion," (4), 543-559.

Bowman, Robert G. "Understanding And Conducting Event Studies," (4), 561-584.

Pendlebury, Maurice and Rowan Jones. "Budget Auditing In Governmental Organisations Financed By Taxation," (4), 585-594.

Bhaskar, Krish and Patrick McNamee. "Multiple Objectives In Accounting And Finance," (4), 595-621.

Moore, J. S. and A. K. Reichert. "An Analysis Of The Financial Management Techniques Currently Employed By Large U.S. Corporations," (4), 623-645.

Wansley, James W., William R. Lane and Ho C. Yang. "Shareholder Returns To USA Acquired Firms In Foreign And Domestic Acquisitions," (4), 647-656.

Ang, James S., Jess H. Chua and Richard S. Woodward. "A Note On Investment Decision Rules Based On Utility Functions," (4), 657-661.

Pike, Richard H. "The Capital Budgeting Behaviour And Corporate Characteristics Of Capital Constrained Firms," (4), 663-671.

Vickers, Douglas. "A Note On The Marginal Cost Of Debt Capital," (4), 673-676.

Booth, L. D. "On The `Unanimity' Literature And The Security Market Line Criterion: A Note," (4), 677-681.

Horrigan, James O. "Methodological Implications Of Non-Normally Distributed Financial Ratios: A Comment," (4), 683-689.

Barnes, Paul. "Methodological Implications Of Non-Normally Distributed Financial Ratios: A Reply," (4), 691-693

Journal of Business Finance and Accounting
Volume 11, 1984

Lee, T. A. and A. W. Stark. "A Cash Flow Disclosure Of Government-Supported Enterprises' Results," (1), 1-11.

Bar-Yosef, Sasson and Yoram Landskroner. "The Impact Of The Government Sector On Financial Equilibrium And Corporate Financial Decisions," (1), 13-27.

Mahapatra, Sitikantha. "Investor Reaction To Corporate Social Accounting," (1), 29-40.

Pope, Peter F. "Information Asymmetries In Participative Budgeting: A Bargaining Approach," (1), 41-59.

Statman, Meir and James F. Sepe. "Managerial Incentive Plans And The Use Of The Payback Method," (1), 61-65.

Kudla, Ronald J. "A Note On Resolving Agency Problems Through Warrants," (1), 67-72.

Livnat, Joshua. "Disclosure Of Pension Liabilities: The Information Content Of Unfunded Vested Benefits And Unfunded Past Service Cost," (1), 73-88.

McDonald, Bill and Michael H. Morris. "The Statistical Validity Of The Ratio Method In Financial Analysis: An Empirical Examination," (1), 89-97.

Bayldon, R., A. Woods and N. Zafiris. "A Note On The `Pyramid' Technique Of Financial Ratio Analysis Of Firms' Performance," (1), 99-106.

Beckers, Stan and Luc Soenen. "Gold: More Attractive To Non-U.S. Than To U.S. Investors?," (1), 107-112.

McDaniel, Wm. R. "Operating Leverage And Operating Risk," (1), 113-125.

Henin, Claude and William F. Rentz. "Call Purchases, Stock Purchases, And Subjective Stochastic Dominance," (1), 127-138.

Kanniainen, Vesa and Vesa Kurikka. "On The Effects Of Inflation In The Stock Market: Empirical Evidence With Finnish Data 1968-1981," (2), 139-150.

Dawson, Steven M. "The Trend Toward Efficiency For Less Developed Stock Exchanges: Hong Kong," (2), 151-161.

Riding, Allan L. "The Information Content Of Dividends: An Other Test," (2), 163-176.

Peel, D. A. and P. F. Pope. "Corporate Accounting Data, Capital Market Information And Wage Increases Of The Firm," (2), 177-188.

Young, Colin M. "The Competitiveness Of Lease Markets: An Empirical Investigation Of The UK Local Authority Lease Market," (2), 189-198.

Bohren, Oyvind. "The Validity Of Conventional Valuation Models Under Multiperiod Uncertainty," (2), 199-211.

Luckett, Peter F. "ARR Vs. IRR: A Review And An Analysis," (2), 213-232.

Cheng, Peter, Fredric Jacobs and Ronald Marshall. "Cost Variance Investigation In A Linear Programming Framework," (2), 233-244.

Beedles, William L. "Some Notes On The Cost Of New Equity," (2), 245-251.

Wolk, Harry I., Lynn K. Saubert and Frank M. Tiernan. "A Further Note On Discounting Deferred Taxes," (2), 253-255.

Grinyer, John R. "On The Negative Risk Premium For Risk Adjusted Discount Rates: A Further Comment," (2), 257-262.

Berry, R. H. and R. G. Dyson. "On The Negative Risk Premium For Risk Adjusted Discount Rates: A Reply And Extension," (2), 263-268.

Brief, Richard P. "The Relationship Between Duration And Economic Depreciation: A Note," (3), 281-286.

Ashton, R. K. "A Microeconomic Analysis Of The Amey/Solomons Debate," (3), 287-294.

Amey, Lloyd R. "Joint Product Decisions, The Fixed Proportions Case: A Note," (3), 295-300.

Rege, Udayan P. "Accounting Ratios To Locate Take-Over Targets," (3), 301-311.

Elgers, Pieter T. and Dennis Murray. "LIFO-FIFO, Accounting Ratios And Market Risk: A Re-Assessment," (3), 313-325.

Bell, Jan. "The Effect Of Presentation Form On Judgment Confidence In Performance Evaluation," (3), 327-346.

Haley, Charles W. "Valuation And Risk-Adjusted Discount Rates," (3), 347-353.

Russell, Allen M. and John A. Rickard. "An Algorithm For Determining Unique Nonnegative Internal Rates Of Return," (3), 355-366.

Zeghal, Daniel. "Timeliness Of Accounting Reports And Their Informational Content On The Capital Market," (3), 367-380.

Kodde, David A. and Hein Schreuder. "Forecasting Corporate Revenue And Profit: Time-Series Models Versus Management And Analysts," (3), 381-395.

Peavy, John W. and S. Michael Edgar. "An Expanded Commercial Paper Rating Scale: Classification Of Industrial Issuers," (3), 397-407.

Copley, Ronald E.,Philip L. Cooley and Rodney L. Roenfeldt. "Autocorrelation In Market Model Residuals," (3), 409-417.

Wright, F. K. "An Economic Analysis Of Value To The Owner: A Comment," (3), 419-423.

Ashton, R. K. "An Economic Analysis Of Value To The Owner: A Reply," (3), 425-429.

Maupin, Rabekah J.,Clinton M. Bidwell and Alan K. Ortegren. "An Empirical Investigation Of The Characteristics Of Publicly-Quoted Corporations Which Change To Closely-Held Ownership Through Management Buyouts," (4), 435-450.

McKinnon, S. M. "A Cost-Benefit Study Of Disclosure Requirements For Multinational Corporations," (4), 451-468.

Chow, Chee W. "Financial Disclosure Regulation And Indirect Economic Consequences: An Analysis Of The Sales Disclosure Requirement Of The 1934 Securities And Exchange Act," (4), 469-483.

Draper, Paul. "Unit Trusts, Homogeneous Beliefs And The Separation Property: A Note," (4), 485-492.

Bodenhorn, Diran. "Balance Sheet Items As The Present Value Of Future Cash Flows," (4), 493-510.

Richardson, Frederick M. and Lewis F. Davidson. "On Linear Discrimination With Accounting Ratios," (4), 511-525.

Belkaoui, Ahmed and Ronald D. Picur. "The Smoothing Of Income Numbers: Some Empirical Evidence On Systematic Differences Between Core And Periphery Industrial Sectors," (4), 527-546.

Morris, Michael H., William D. Nichols and James W. Pattillo. "Capitalization Of Interest, Materiality Judgement Divergence And Users' Information Needs," (4), 547-555.

Trends In The Riskiness Of Electric Utility Shares," (3), 453-459.

Taylor, Peter and Stuart Turley. "Applying Economic Consequences Analysis In Accounting Standard Setting: A Tax Incidence Approach," (4), 467-488.

Diacogiannis, George P. "Arbitrage Pricing Model: A Critical Examination Of Its Empirical Applicability For The London Stock Exchange," (4), 489-504.

Miles, James A. and Raj Varma. "Using Financial Market Data To Make Trade Credit Decisions," (4), 505-518.

Burnie, David A. "Capital Asset Prices And The Friedman Hypothesis Of Inflation," (4), 519-534.

Gemmill, Gordon. "The Forecasting Performance Of Stock Options On The London Traded Options Market," (4), 535-546.

Lefebvre, Olivier. "Risk Sharing In The Bank Deposit Con tract," (4), 547-559.

Penno, Mark and Daniel T. Simon. "Accounting Choices: Public Versus Private Firms," (4), 561-569.

Lawrence, Edward C. and Robert M. Bear. "Corporate Bankruptcy Prediction And The Impact Of Leases," (4), 571-585.

Lackman, C. L. "The Impact Of Capital Adequacy Constraints On Bank Portfolios," (4), 587-596.

Lobo, Gerald J., R. D. Nair and In Man Song. "Additional Evidence On The Information Content Of Dividends," (4), 597-608.

Barnes, Paul. "Thin Trading And Stock Market Efficiency: The Case Of The Kuala Lumpur Stock Exchange," (4), 609-617.

Ashton, R. K. "Personal Leverage V. Corporate Leverage: An Extension To The Debate," (4), 619-626.

Barnes, Paul. "The Statistical Validity Of The Ratio Method In Financial Analysis: An Empirical Examination: A Comment," (4), 627-632.

McDonald, Bill and Michael H. Morris. "The Statistical Validity Of The Ratio Method In Financial Analysis: An Empirical Examination: A Reply," (4), 633-635.

Journal of Business Finance and Accounting
Volume 14, 1987

Nunthirapakorn, Thakol and James A. Millar. "Changing Prices, Accounting Earnings And Systematic Risk," (1), 1-26.

Wood, Douglas and Jenifer Piesse. "The Information Value Of MDA Based Financial Indicators," (1), 27-38.

Johnson, Raymond N. "Auditor Detected Errors And Related Client Traits--A Study Of Inherent And Control Risks In A Sample Of U.K. Audits," (1), 39-64.

Dawson, Steven M. "Secondary Stock Market Performance Of Initial Public Offers, Hong Kong, Singapore And Malaysia: 1978-1984," (1), 65-76.

Copeland, Ronald M. and Sharon McKinnon. "'Financial Distortion' And Consolidation Of Captive Finance Subsidiaries In The General Merchandising Industry," (1), 77-98.

Stark, Andrew W. "On The Observability Of The Cash Recovery Rate," (1), 99-108.

Ward, C.W.R. "Returns From The Indexed Mortgage: An Option Pricing Model Approach," (1), 109-120.

Brown, Sudro and Jeffrey Lippitt. "Are Deferred Taxes Discountable?," (1), 121-130.

Lee, C. Jevons. "Fundamental Analysis And The Stock Market," (1), 131-142.

Egginton, D. A. and I. R. Davidson. "A Test Of Income Dichotomization," (1), 143-153.

Condoyanni, L., J. O'Hanlon and C.W.R. Ward. "Day Of The Week Effects On Stock Returns: International Evidence," (1), 159-174.

Belkaoui, Ahmed and Ronald D. Picur. "Sources Of Feedback In A CPA Firm," (2), 175-186.

Keown, Arthur J., John M. Pinkerton and Son Nan Chen. "Portfolio Selection Based Upon P/E Ratios: Diversification, Risk Decomposition And Implications," (2), 187-198.

Hudson, John. "The Age, Regional, And Industrial Structure Of Company Liquidations," (2), 199-214.

Trivoli, George W. and William R. McDaniel. "Uncertainty, Capital Immobility And Capital Rationing In The Investment Decision," (2), 215-228.

Comiskey, Eugene E., Ralph A. Walkling and Michael A. Weeks. "Dispersion Of Expectations And Trading Volume," (2), 229-240.

Hagigi, Moshe and Brian Kluger. "Assessing Risk And Return Of Pension Funds' Portfolios By The Telser Safety-First Approach," (2), 241-254.

Etebari, Ahmad, James O. Horrigan and Jan L. Landwehr. "To Be Or Not To Be--Reaction Of Stock Returns To Sudden Deaths Of Corporate Chief Executive Officers," (2), 255-278.

Carvell, Steven A. and Paul J. Strebel. "Is There A Neglected Firm Effect?," (2), 279-290.

Hegde, Shantaram P. "The Forecast Performance Of Treasury Bond Futures Contracts," (2), 291-304.

Gietzmann, M. B. "Incentives To Introduce A Cost Reducing Technology In A Decentralized Organisation," (3), 313-322.

Betts, J. and D. Belhoul. "The Effectiveness Of Incorporating Stability Measures In Company Failure Models," (3), 323-334.

Keasey, K. and R. Watson. "Non-Financial Symptoms And The Prediction Of Small Company A Test Of Argenti's Hypotheses," (3), 335-354.

Ushman, Neal L. "A Comparison Of Cross-Sectional And Time-Series Beta Adjustment Techniques," (3), 355-376.

Abeysekera, Sarath P. and Arvind Mahajan. "A Test Of The APT In Pricing UK Stocks," (3), 377-392.

Wirth, A. and F. K. Wright. "New-Issue Costs And Project Evaluation: Ezzell And Porter Revisited," (3), 393-408.

Feroz, Ehsan H. "Corporate Demands And Changes In GPLA," (3), 409-424.

Wansley, James W. and William R. Lane. "A Financial Profile Of The Dividend Initiating Firm," (3), 425-436.

Conine, Thomas E., Jr. "A Pedagogical Note On Cash Break-Even Analysis," (3), 437-441.

Barnes, Paul. "The Analysis And Use of Financial Ratios: A Review Article," (4), 449-462.

Ezzamel, Mahmoud, Cecilio Mar-Molinero and Alistair Beecher. "On The Distributional Properties Of Financial Ratios," (4), 463-482.

So, Jacky C. "Some Empirical Evidence On The Outliers And The Non-Normal Distribution Of Financial Ratios," (4), 483-496.

Fieldsend, Susan, Nicholas Longford and Stuart McLeay. "Industry Effects And The Proportionality Assumption In Ratio Analysis: A Variance Component Analysis," (4), 497-518.

Ezzamel, Mahmoud, Judith Brodie and Cecilio Mar-Molinero. "Financial Patterns Of UK Manufacturing Companies," (4), 519-536.

Houghton, Keith A. and David R. Woodliff. "Financial Ratios: The Prediction Of Corporte 'Success' And Failure," (4), 537-554.

Thomas, Joseph, III and R. V. Evanson. "An Empirical Investigation Of Association Between Financial Ratio Use And Small Business Success," (4), 555-572.

Karels, Gordon V. and Arun J. Prakash. "Multivariate Normality And Forecasting Of Business Bankruptcy," (4), 573-594.

Gentry, James A., Paul Newbold and David T. Whitford. "Funds Flow Components, Financial Ratios, And Bankruptcy," (4), 595-606.

Journal of Business Finance and Accounting
Volume 15, 1988

Ashton, D. J. "On The Evaluation Of Bought-In Goods And Services," (1), 1-8.

Hutchinson, P., I. Meric and G. Meric. "The Financial Characteristics Of Small Firms Which Achieve Quotation On The UK Unlisted Securities Market," (1), 9-20.

Conine, Thomas E., Jr., Oscar W. Jensen and Maurry Tamarkin. "On Optimal Output In An Option Pricing Framework," (1), 21-26.

Zavgren, Christine V., Michael T. Dugan and James M. Reeve. "The Association Between Probabilities Of Bankruptcy And Market Responses--A Test Of Market Anticipation," (1), 27-46.

Cheung, Joseph K. "The PIP Grant Accounting Controversy In Canada: A Study Of The Economic Consequences Of Accounting Standards," (1), 47-66.

Bradley, D. P. and M. Walsh. "Portfolio Insurance And The UK Stock Market," (1), 67-76.

Thompson, Joel E. "More Methods That Make Little Difference In Event Studies," (1), 77-86.

Balachandran, K. R. and B. N. Srinidhi. "A Stable Cost Application Scheme For Service Center Usage," (1), 87-100.

Blann, Jack and B. V. Balachandran. "An Empirical Test Of The Statistical Association Of Market Risk And Financial Accounting Allocation," (1), 101-114.

Stewart, I. C. "The Explication Of The True And Fair View Doctrine: A Comment," (1), 115-124.

Rutherford, B. A. "The Explication Of The True And Fair View Doctrine: A Reply," (1), 125-127.

Garrod, N. W. and C. R. Emmanuel. "The Impact Of Company Profile On The Predictive Ability Of Disaggregated Data," (2), 135-154.

Lee, C. Jevons. "Capital Budgeting Under Uncertainty: The Issue Of Optimal Timing," (2), 155-168.

Knight, Rory F. and John F. Affleck-Graves. "Further Evidence On The Market Response To LIFO Adoptions," (2), 169-184.

Foster, Taylor W., III, Don R. Hansen and Don W. Vickrey. "Additional Evidence On The Abatement Of Errors In Predicting Beta Through Increases In Portfolio Size And On The Regression Tendency," (2), 185-198.

Board, J. L. G. and C. M. S. Sutcliffe. "The Weekend Effect In UK Stock Market Returns," (2), 199-214.

Dharan, Bala G. "The Association Between Corporate Dividends And Current Cost Disclosures," (2), 215-230.

Perry, Larry G., Pu Liu and Dorla A. Evans. "Modified Bond Ratings: Further Evidence On The Effect Of Split Ratings On Corporate Bond Yields," (2), 231-242.

Williams, David D. "The Potential Determinants Of Auditor Change," (2), 243-262.

Michel, Allen and Israel Shaked. "Corporate Takeovers: Excess Returns And The Multiple Bidding Phenomena," (2), 263-274.

Aharony, Joseph and Itzhak Swary. "A Note On Corporate Bankruptcy And The Market Model Risk Measures," (2), 275-282.

Garven, James R. "CML To SML: An Alternative Approach," (2), 283-288.

Dhaliwal, Dan S. "The Effect Of The Firm's Business Risk On The Choice Of Accounting Methods," (2), 289-302.

Arnold, A. J. and R. T. Wearing. "Cash Flows, Exit Prices And British Airways," (3), 311-334.

Linsmeier, Thomas J., R. D. Nair and Jerry J. Weygandt. "UK Tax Legislation And The Switch To The Liability Method For Income Taxes," (3), 335-352.

Kroll, Yoram. "Analytical Examination Of A Business Tax Reform Under Rapid Inflation: The Israeli Case," (3), 353-372.

Brown, Robert M. "A Comparison Of Market Efficiency Among Stock Exchanges," (3), 373-384.

Frankfurter, George M. and Christopher G. Lamoureux. "Stock Selection And Timing--A New Look At Market Efficiency," (3), 385-400.

Aharony, Joseph, Haim Falk and Itzhak Swary. "Information Content Of Dividend Increases: The Case Of Regulated Utilities," (3), 401-414.

Meyer, Richard L., Scott Besley and James R. Longstreet. "An Examination Of Capital Budgeting Decision Alternatives For Mutually Exclusive Investments With Unequal Lives," (3), 415-426.

Kudla, Ronald J. and Manjeet S. Dhatt. "An Empirical Test Of Operating Synergism," (3), 427-436.

Barr, Graham D. and Rory F. Knight. "Some Geometrical Characteristics Of The Risk-Return Plane," (3), 437-446.

Prakash, Arun J., Krishnan Dandapani and Gordon V. Karels. "Simple Resource Allocation Rules," (3), 447-452.

Peel, D. A. and P. F. Pope. "Stock Returns And Expected Inflation In The UK: Some New Evidence," (4), 459-468.

Reichert, Alan K., James S. Moore and Ezra Byler. "Financial Analysis Among Large US Corporations: Recent Trends And The Impact Of The Personal Computer," (4), 469-486.

Ma, Christopher K. "Loan Loss Reserves And Income Smoothing: The Experience In The US Banking Industry," (4), 487-498.

Lackman, Conway. "Forecasting Commercial Paper Rates," (4), 499-524.

Oppenheimer, Henry R. and Terry E. Dielman. "Firm Dividend Policy And Insider Activity: Some Empirical Results," (4), 525-542.

Roy, Asim. "Optimal Acquisition Fraction And A Theory For Partial Acquisitions," (4), 543-556.

Kim, Sang-Hoon and Hussein H. Elsaid. "Estimation Of Periodic Standard Deviations Under The PERT And Derivation Of Probabilistic Information," (4), 557-572.

Jean, William H. and Billy P. Helms. "Moment Orderings And Stochastic Dominance Tests," (4), 573-584.

Lister, Roger J. "Interest, Morality, Orthodoxy, Gambling And Karim," (4), 585-596.

Journal of Business Finance and Accounting
Volume 16, 1989

Thomson, Lydia and Robert Watson. "Historic Cost Earnings, Current Cost Earnings And The Dividend Decision," (1), 1-24.

Moon, Philip and Stewart Hodges. "Implications Of The Recent Tax Changes For Corporate Capital Investment," (1), 25-40.

Moizer, Peter and Stuart Turley. "Changes In The UK Market For Audit Services: 1972-1982," (1), 41-54.

Kross, William and Douglas A. Schroeder. "Firm Prominence And The Differential Information Content Of Quarterly Earnings Announcements," (1), 55-74.

Ashton, D. J. "The Cost Of Capital And The Imputation Tax System," (1), 75-88.

Choy, A. Y. F. and J. O'Hanlon. "Day Of The Week Effects In The UK Equity Market: A Cross Sectional Analysis," (1), 89-104.

Callen, Jeffrey L., M. W. Luke Chan and Clarence C. Y. Kwan. "Spot And Forward Exchange Rates: A Causality Analysis," (1), 105-118.

Cheshire, J. D. and E. H. Feroz. "Allison's Models And The FASB Statements No's 2, 5, 13 And 19," (1), 119-130.

Silhan, Peter A. "Using Quarterly Sales And Margins To Predict Corporate Earnings: A Time-Series Perspective," (1), 131-141.

Lui, Y. H. and K. V. Peasnell. "Time Series Behaviour, Predictability And Speculation In The Hong Kong Foreign Exchange Market," (2), 145-164.

Partington, Graham H. "Variables Influencing Dividend Policy In Australia: Survey Results," (2), 165-182.

Kamarotou, H. and J. O'Hanlon. "Informational Efficiency In The UK, US, Canadian And Japanese Equity Markets: A Note," (2), 183-192.

Karim, Rifaat Ahmed Abdel and Amal El-Tigani Ali. "Determinants Of The Financial Strategy Of Islamic Banks," (2), 193-212.

Emanuel, D. M. "Asset Revaluations And Share Price Revisions," (2), 213-228.

Craig, Russell and Paul Walsh. "Adjustments For 'Extraordinary Items' In Smoothing Reported Profits Of Listed Australian Companies: Some Empirical Evidence," (2), 229-246.

Brown, Robert L. "Adjusting Option Contracts To Reflect Capitalisation Changes," (2), 247-254.

Stanton, Harry G. and John A. Rickard. "The 'Rule Of 78' Cost Penalty: An Alternative Perspective," (2), 255-266.

Booth, Peter and Patrick Hutchinson. "Distinguishing Between Failing And Growing Firms: A Note On The Use Of Decomposition Measure Analysis," (2), 267-272.

Mak, Yuen Teen. "Contingency Fit, Internal Consistency And Financial Performance," (2), 273-300.

Grinyer, John R. and Robert A. Lyon. "The Need For Ex Post EEI," (3), 303-316.

Castagna, A. D. and Z. P. Matolcsy. "The Marginal Information Content Of Selected Items In Financial Statements," (3), 317-334.

Prakash, Arun J., A. M. Parhizgari and Gerald W. Perritt. "The Effect Of Listing On The Parameters Of Characteristic Lines Models," (3), 335-342.

Chung, Kee H. "The Impact Of The Demand Volatility And Leverages On The Systematic Risk Of Common Stocks," (3), 343-360.

BarNiv, Ran and Adi Raveh. "Identifying Financial Distress: A New Nonparametric Approach," (3), 361-384.

Murali, Ramaswami and Jonathan B. Welch. "Agents, Owners, Control And Performance," (3), 385-398.

Brick, Ivan E., Meir Statman and Daniel G. Weaver. "Event Studies And Model Misspecification: Another Look At The Benefits Of Outsiders From Public Information About Insider Trading," (3), 399-424.

Gordon, L. A. and A. W. Stark. "Accounting And Economic Rates Of Return: A Note On Depreciation And Other Accrurals," (3), 425-432.

Greenberg, Ralph H., Robert F. Sharp and Eric E. Spires. "A Practical Method Of Measuring Current Costs Of Technologically Inferior Assets," (3), 433-442.

Moon, Philip. "Paradoxes In The Cost Allocation For Joint Products," (3), 443-448.

Raymond, Arthur J. and Gordon Weil. "Diversification Benefits And Exchange-Rate Changes," (4), 455-466.

Prodhan, Bimal K. and Malcolm C. Harris. "Systematic Risk And The Discretionary Disclosure Of Geographical Segments: An Empirical Investigation Of US Multinationals," (4), 467-492.

De Villiers, J. U. "Inflation, Asset Structure And The Discrepancy Between Accounting And True Return," (4), 493-506.

Thompson, Joel E. "An Alternative Control Model For Event Studies," (4), 507-514.

Lee, Chi-Wen Jevons. "The Tax Effect Hypothesis And Inventory Accounting," (4), 515-530.

Chandy, P. R. and Imre Karafiath. "The Effect Of The WPPSS Crisis On Utility Common Stock Returns," (4), 531-542.

Steele, A. and N. Tessaromatis. "A Note On Dividend Policy And Beta: A Comment," (4), 543-548.

Shoenthal, Edward R. "Classification Of Accounting Systems Using Competencies As A Discriminating Variable: A Great Britain - United States Study," (4), 549-564.

Chen, Carl R. "The Impact Of Maturity And Yield Effects On The Systematic Risk Of Bonds," (4), 565-574.

Ashton, R. K. "Stockholding Costs And Stockholding Policies: A Field Test," (4), 575-586.

Maris, Brian A. "Analysis Of Bond Refunding With Overlapping Interest," (4), 587-591.

Soenen, Luc A. and Raj Aggarwal. "Cash And Foreign Exchange Management: Theory And Corporate Practice In Three Countries," (5), 599-620.

Brayshaw, R. E. and Ahmed E. K. Eldin. "The Smoothing Hypothesis And The Role Of Exchange Differences," (5), 621-634.

Mahapatra, S., M. Chase and W. Rogers. "Information Interaction Effects Of Inflation Adjusted Accounting Data On Individual Decision-Maker's Sophistication And Risk Preference," (5), 635-650.

Jose, Manuel L. and Jerry L. Stevens. "Capital Market Valuation Of Dividend Policy," (5), 651-662.

Karels, Gordon V., Arun J. Prakash and Emmanuel Roussakis. "The Relationship Between Bank Capital Adequacy And Market Measures Of Risk," (5), 663-674.

Jahera, John S., Jr. and William P. Lloyd. "Exchange Listing And Size: Effects On Excess Returns," (5), 675-680.

Liljeblom, Eva. "The Informational Impact Of Announcements Of Stock Dividends And Stock Splits," (5), 681-698.

Bao, Ben-Hsien and Da-Hsien Bao. "An Empirical Investigation Of The Association Between Productivity And Firm Value," (5), 699-718.

Chung, Kee H. "Debt And Risk: A Technical Note," (5), 719-728.

Rubio, Gonzalo. "An Empirical Evaluation Of The Intertemporal Capital Asset Pricing Model: The Stock Market In Spain," (5), 729-744.

Giaccotto, Carmelo. "Compounding And Discounting With Stochastic Interest Rates," (5), 745-769.

Journal of Business Finance and Accounting
Volume 17, 1990

Ezzamel, Mahmoud and Cocillo Mar-Molinero. "The Distributional Properties Of Financial Ratios In UK Manufacturing Companies," (1), 1-30.

Platt, Harlan D. and Marjorie B. Platt. "Development Of A Class Of Stable Predictive Variables: The Case Of Bankruptcy Prediction," (1), 31-52.

Bartley, Jon W. and Calvin M. Boardman. "The Relevance Of Inflation Adjusted Accounting Data To The Prediction Of Corporate Takeovers," (1), 53-72.

Barnes, Paul. "The Prediction Of Takeover Targets In The UK By Means Of Multiple Discriminant Analysis," (1), 73-84.

Amit, Raphael and Joshua Livnat. "Grouping Of Conglomerates By Their Segments' Economic Attributes: Towards A More Meaningful Ratio Analysis," (1), 85-100.

Moses, O. Douglas. "On Analysts' Earnings Forecasts For Failing Firms," (1), 101-118.

Keasey, Kevin and Paul McGuinness. "The Failure Of UK Industrial Firms For The Period 1976-1984, Logistic Analysis And Entropy Measures," (1), 119-136.

Skogsvik, Kenth. "Current Cost Accounting Ratios As Predictors Of Business Failures: The Swedish Case," (1), 137-160.

Gilbert, Lisa R., Krishnagopal Menon and Kenneth B. Schwartz. "Predicting Bankruptcy For Firms In Financial Distress," (1), 161-171.

Koh, Hian C. and Larry N. Killough. "The Use Of Multiple Discriminant Analysis In The Assessment Of Going-Concern Status Of An Audit Client," (2), 179-192.

Bhoocha-Oom, Areepong and Stanley R. Stansell. "A Study Of International Financial Market Integration: An Examination Of The US, Hong Kong And Singapore Markets," (2), 193-212.

Aitken, Michael. "The Australian Securities Industry Under Negotiated Brokerage Commissions: Evidence Of The Effects Of Change On The Structure Of The Industry," (2), 213-246.

Okunev, John. "An Alternative Measure Of Mutual Fund Performance," (2), 247-264.

Lee, Insup, R. Richardson Pettit and Mark V. Swankoski. "Daily Return Relationships Among Asian Stock Markets," (2), 265-284.

Low, Lay-Chin, Pearl Hock-Neo Tan and Hian-Chye Koh. "The Determination Of Audit Fees: An Analysis In The Singapore Context," (2), 285-296.

Loudon, G. F. "American Put Pricing: Australian Evidence," (2), 297-322.

Shastri, Kuldeep and Kulpatra Wethyavivorn. "Pricing Of Foreign Currency Options For Arbitrary Stochastic Processes," (2), 323-334.

Ashton, D. J. "A Problem In The Detection Of Superior Investment Performance," (3), 337-350.

Madden, Gerald P., Lynn W. Marples and Lal C. Chugh. "A Stock Market Evaluation Of Management Buyouts," (3), 351-358.

Pope, P. F., R. C. Morris and D. A. Peel. "Insider Trading: Some Evidence On Market Efficiency And Directors' Share Dealings In Great Britain," (3), 359-380.

Kim, Yong H. and Kee H. Chung. "An Integrated Evaluation Of Investment In Inventory And Credit: A Cash Flow Approach," (3), 381-390.

Tennyson, B. Mack, Robert W. Ingram and Michael T. Dugan. "Assessing The Information Content Of Narrative Disclosures In Explaining Bankruptcy," (3), 391-410.

Barnes, Tom and David Burnie. "Corporate Bonds, Term Structure Expectations And Optimal Portfolios: The Canadian Experience," (3), 411-420.

Lahey, Karen E. and Robert L. Conn. "Sensitivity Of Acquiring Firms' Returns To Alternative Model Specifications And Disaggregation," (3), 421-440.

Ma, Christopher K. and G. Wenchi Kao. "On Exchange Rate Changes And Stock Price Reactions," (3), 441-450.

Gray, J. Brian and Dan W. French. "Empirical Comparisons Of Distributional Models For Stock Index Returns," (3), 451-460.

Jog, Vijay M. and Allan L. Riding. "A Note On Insider Trading And Issuances Of Restricted-Voting Common Shares," (3), 461-470.

Murphy, J. Austin. "Using Bayesian Betas To Estimate Risk-Return Parameters: An Empirical Investigation," (3), 471-477.

Kellow, Ahmed. "Decomposition Of Stock Returns," (4), 481-496.

Gilbert, Erika W. and Esmeralda O. Lyn. "The Impact Of Target Managerial Resistence On The Shareholders Of Bidding Firms," (4), 497-510.

Booth, Peter and Neil Cocks. "Critical Research Issues In Accounting Standard-Setting," (4), 511-528.

Barnes, Paul, S. P. Chakravarty and J. Haslam. "Bargaining Power, Dissimulation And Takeovers In A Rational Market With Asymmetric Information," (4), 529-540.

Krueger, Thomas M. "Seasonal Aspects Of Anomaly Explanatory Power," (4), 541-556.

Haw, In-Mu and Byung T. Ro. "Firm Size, Reporting Lags And Market Reactions To Earnings Releases," (4), 557-574.

Conine, Thomas E., Jr. "A Note On The Theoretical Irrelevance Of FASB 94 On Equity Systematic Risk," (4), 575-578.

Balachandran, Kashi R. and B. N. Srinidhi. "A Note On Cost Allocation, Opportunity Costs And Optimal Utilization," (4), 579-584.

Jenkins, Elizabeth and Robert E. Seiler. "The Impact Of Executive Compensation Schemes Upon The Level Of Discretionary Expenditures And Growth In Stockholder Wealth," (4), 585-592.

Gupta, Yash P., Ramesh P. Rao and Prabir K. Bagchi. "Linear Goal Programming As An Alternative To Multivariate Discriminant Analysis: A Note," (4), 593-598.

Aczel, Michael, Jack Broyles and Bronek Masojada. "Participation In The Lloyd's Insurance Market As A Portfolio Investment," (5), 609-634.

Rezaee, Zabihollah. "Capital Market Reactions To Accounting Policy Deliberations: An Empirical Study Of Accounting For Foreign Currency Translation 1974-1982," (5), 635-648.

Kross, William and Douglas Schroeder. "An Investigation Of Seasonality In Stock Price Responses To Quarterly Earnings Announcements," (5), 649-676.

Homaifar, Ghassem and Duane B. Graddy. "Variance And Lower Partial Moment Betas As Alternative Risk Measures In Cost Of Capital Estimation: A Defense Of The CAPM Beta," (5), 677-688.

Conn, R. L. and F. Connell. "International Mergers: Returns To US And British Firms," (5), 689-712.

Albrecht, W. David and Frederick M. Richardson. "Income Smoothing By Economy Sector," (5), 713-730.

Denning, Karen Craft and Kuldeep Shastri. "Single Sale Divestments: The Impact On Stockholders And Bondholders," (5), 731-744.

Schnabel, Jacques A. "Optimal Output In An Option Pricing Framework: An Agency-Theoretic Perspective," (5), 745-750.

Jennergren, L. Peter. "Valuation By Linear Programming - A Pedagogical Note," (5), 751-756.

Collins, Brett, John Rickard and Michael Selby. "Discounting Of Deferred Tax Liabilities," (5), 757-758.

Anderson, Gary A. and Arun J. Prakash. "A Note On Simple Resource Allocation Rules: The Case Of Arithmetic Growth," (5), 759-762.

Journal of Business Finance and Accounting
Volume 18, 1991

Theobald, Michael. "Testing The Relationship Between Forward And Spot Rates In Foreign Exchange Markets," (1), 1-12.

Brief, Richard P. and Raef A. Lawson. "Approximate Error In Using Accounting Rates Of Return To Estimate Economic Returns," (1), 13-20.

Bartley, Jon W. and Alex B. Cameron. "Long-Run Earnings Forecasts By Managers And Financial Analysts," (1), 21-42.

Ehrhardt, Michael C. "Diversification And Interest Rate Risk," (1), 43-60.

Kim, Jeong-Bon and Roland Lipka. "Effects Of Accounting Choice On The Explanation Of The Market Risk In The Oil And Gas Industry," (1), 61-84.

Watson, Robert. "Modelling Directors' Remuneration Decisions In Small And Closely-Held UK Companies," (1), 85-98.

Fooladi, Iraj, Patricia McGraw and Gordon S. Roberts. "Preferred Stock And Taxes," (1), 99-108.

Millar, James A. and Ted Nunthirapakorn. "Earnings Per Share Reporting For Canadian Companies With Complex Capital Structures," (1), 109-116.

Leong, Kenneth K. and Janis K. Zaima. "Further Evidence Of The Small Firm Effect: A Comparison Of NYSE-AMEX And OTC Stocks," (1), 117-124.

O'Brien, Thomas J. "The Constant Growth Model And Personal Taxes," (1), 125-132.

Lam, Swee-Sum. "Venture Capital Financing: A Conceptual Framework," (2), 137-150.

Eddey, Peter H. "Corporate Raiders And Takeover Targets," (2), 151-172.

Walsh, Paul, Russell Craig and Frank Clarke. "'Big Bath Accounting' Using Extraordinary Items Adjustments: Australian Empirical Evidence," (2), 173-190.

Iselin, Errol R. "Individual Versus Group Decision-Making Performance: A Further Investigation Of Two Theories In A Bankruptcy Prediction Task," (2), 191-208.

Okunev, John. "The Generation Of Mean Gini Efficient Sets," (2), 209-218.

Ko, Kwang-Soo and Sang-Bin Lee. "A Comparative Analysis Of The Daily Behavior Of Stock Returns: Japan, The US And The Asian NICs," (2), 219-234.

Cheung, Yan-Leung and Yak-Ki Ho. "The Intertemporal Stability Of The Relationships Between Asian Emerging Equity Markets And The Developed Equity Markets," (2), 235-254.

Easton, Stephen. "Earnings And Dividends: Is There An Interaction Effect?," (2), 255-266.

Hodgson, Allan and Des Nicholls. "The Impact Of Index Futures Markets On Australian Sharemarket Volatility," (2), 267-280.

Hsia, Chi-Cheng. "Estimating A Firm's Cost Of Capital: An Option Pricing Approach," (2), 281-287.

Thorne, Daniel. "The Information Content Of The Trend Between Historical Cost Earnings And Current Cost Earnings (United States Of America)," (3), 289-304.

O'Hanlon, John. "The Relationship In Time Between Annual Accounting Returns And Annual Stock Market Returns In The UK," (3), 305-314.

Ghosh, Chinmoy and J. Randall Woolridge. "Dividend Omissions And Stock Market Rationality," (3), 315-330.

Bayless, Mark E. and J. David Diltz. "The Relevance Of Asymmetric Information To Financing Decisions," (3), 331-344.

Davidson, Ian R. "Ex-Effects: Taxes, Transactions Costs And The Short-Term Trading Hypothesis," (3), 345-358.

Nobes, C. W. and R. H. Parker. "'True And Fair': A Survey Of UK Financial Directors," (3), 359-376.

Chang, S. J. "A Study Of Empirical Return Generating Models: A Market Model, A Multifactor Model, And A Unified Model," (3), 377-392.

Ainina, M. Fall and Nancy K. Mohan. "When LBOs Go IPO," (3), 393-404.

Leong, Kenneth K., Janis K. Zaima and Thomas Buchman. "The Effect Of Ownership Control Status On Stock Price Reaction To The Adoption Of LIFO Inventory," (3), 405-420.

McGuire, Dan C. and Ronald J. Kudla. "Option Prices As An Indicator Of Stock Return Expectations," (3), 421-430.

Shaked, Israel, Allen Michel and David McClain. "The Foreign Acquirer Bonanza: Myth Or Reality?," (3), 431-448.

Berg, Menachem and Giora Moore. "Foreign Exchange Strategies: Spot, Forward And Options," (3), 449-457.

JOURNAL OF FINANCE

Journal of Finance
Volume 7, 1952

Journal of Finance
Volume 8, 1953

Journal of Finance
Volume 9, 1954

Dauten, Carl A. "A Fresh Approach To The Place Of Consumer Credit In Economic And Financial Thinking," (2), 111-123.
Weston, J. Fred. "Norms For Debt Levels," (2), 124-135.
Scott, Eldred H. "Probable Impact Of Atomic Energy On Electric Public Utility Securities," (2), 136-147.
Sutton, Ben B. "Recent Developments In Pension Planning - A Challenge To The Insurance Industry," (2), 148-159.
O'Leary, James J. "Valuation Of Life Insurance Company Holding Of Corporate Bonds And Stocks - Some Recent Developments," (2), 160-177.
Lent, George E. "Major Trends In The Market For Tax-Exempt Securities," (2), 178-187.
Soloway, Arnold M. "Economic Aspects Of The British Purchase Tax," (2), 188-208.
Maxwell, James A. "The Equalizing Effects Of Federal Grants," (2), 209-215.
Grebler, Leo. "Real Estate Investment Experience In New York City," (2), 216-218.
Levitt, Theodore. "Investment, Depression, And The Assurance Of Prosperity," (3), 235-251.
Latane, Henry Allan. "Price Changes In Equity Securities," (3), 252-264.
Weston, J. Fred. "The Finance Function," (3), 265-282.
Torgerson, Harold W. "Developments In Savings And Loan Associations, 1945-53," (3), 283-297.
Cooke, H. J. and M. Katzen. "The Public Debt Limit," (3), 298-303.
Grebler, Leo. "The Flow Of Funds Into New Residential Construction 1911-52," (4), 339-350.
Harriss, C. Lowell. "Government Expenditure: Significant Issues Of Definition," (4), 351-364.
Clendenin, John C. and Maurice Van Cleave. "Growth And Common Stock Values," (4), 365-376.
Williams, C. Arthur, Jr. "An Analysis Of Current Experience And Retrospective Rating Plans," (4), 377-411.

Journal of Finance
Volume 10, 1955

Johnson, Robert W. "Subordinated Debentures: Debt That Serves As Equity," (1), 1-16.
Dernberg, H. J. "The Blocked Mark Problem (1931-54)," (1), 17-40.
Case, Fred E. "The Use Of Junior Mortgages In Real Estate Financing," (1), 41-54.
Evans, George Heberton, Jr. "The Theoretical Value Of A Stock Right," (1), 55-61.
Dingle, Mona E. "Toward A More Meaningful Statistical Concept Of The Money Supply: A Comment," (1), 62-66.
Pritchard, Leland J. "Toward A More Meaningful Statistical Concept of The Money Supply: A Reply," (1), 66-68.
Dingle, Mona E. "Toward A More Meaningful Statistical Concept Of The Money Supply: A Rejoinder," (1), 69.
Buchanan, James M. "Professor Maxwell And Fiscal Equity: A Comment," (1), 70-71.
Maxwell, James A. "Professor Maxwell And Fiscal Equity: A Reply," (1), 71-72.
Dauten, Carl A. "The Necessary Ingredients Of A Theory Of Business Finance," (2), 107-120.
Sagan, John. "Toward A Theory Of Working Capital Management," (2), 121-129.
Weston, J. Fred. "Toward Theories Of Financial Policy," (2), 130-143.
Willis, George H. "Convertibility - The Current Approach," (2), 152-169.
Heatherington, Donald F. "Convertibility And The Business Community," (2), 170-179.
Ellis, Howard S. "Changing Concepts Of Convertibility And The Future Of Currencies," (2), 180-194.
Wood, David M. "Legal Aspects Of Revenue Bond Financing," (2), 201-208.
Kushell, C. J., Jr. "Operating Aspects Of Revenue Bond Financing," (2), 209-222.
Mitchell, George W. "Economic Aspects Of Revenue Bond Financing," (2), 223-229.
Tostlebe, Alvin S. "Trends In Capital Formation And Financing In Agriculture," (2), 234-249.
Dobrovolsky, S. "Capital Formation And Financing Trends In Manufacturing And Mining, 1900-1953," (2), 250-265.
Ulmer, Melville J. "Long-Term Trends In The Financing Of Regulated Industries, 1870-1950," (2), 266-276.
Koch, Albert R. "Money Market Developments - From The 'Accord' To Mid-1952," (2), 286-292.
Woodworth, G. Walter. "Money Market Developments, Mid-Year 1952 To Mid-Year 1953," (2), 292-295.
McWhinney, Madeline. "Money Markets Developments June, 1953 To December, 1954," (2), 296-301.
Reierson, Roy L. "Factors And Prospects In The Money Market," (2), 302-314.
Wood, Elmer. "Recent Monetary Policies," (3), 315-325.
Hellmuth, William F., Jr. "Depreciation And The 1954 Internal Revenue Code," (3), 326-349.
Kilpatrick, Wylie. "Florida City Debt - A Case Study," (3), 350-362.
Gillies, James and Clayton Curtis. "The Structure Of Local Mortgage Markets And Government Housing Finance Programs," (3), 363-375.
Gustus, Warren J. "Professor Levitt On 'Investment, Depression, And The Assurance Of Prosperity': A Comment," (3), 376-378.
Levitt, Theodore. "Professor Levitt On 'Investment, Depression, And The Assurance Of Prosperity': A Reply," (3), 378-380.
Campbell, James A. and William Beranek. "Stock Price Behavior On Ex-Dividend Dates," (4), 425-429.
Katz, Samuel I. "The Future Of Sterling," (4), 430-441.
Darling, Paul G. "A Surrogative Measure Of Business Confidence And Its Relation To Stock Prices," (4), 442-458.
Ratchford, B. U. "Some Constitutional Aspects Of Federal Expenditures," (4), 459-482.
Financial Research Program. "Research In The Capital And Securities Markets," (4), 483-503.

Journal of Finance
Volume 11, 1956

Sproul, Allan. "Reflections Of A Central Banker," (1), 1-14.
Goodman, Bernard. "The Price Of Gold And International Liquidity," (1), 15-28.
Walter, James E. "Dividend Policies And Common Stock Prices," (1), 29-41.
Kinnard, William N., Jr. "Junior Mortgages In Real Estate Finance: A Case Study," (1), 42-57.
Howard, William M. "Life Reinsurance Pools," (1), 58-67.
Allen, William R. "Interbank Deposits And Excess Reserves," (1), 68-73.
Linton, M. Albert. "The Variable Annuity: Problems And Prospects," (2), 121-141.
McCracken, Paul W. "Are Variable Annuities The Answer To Inflation," (2), 142-150.
Wood, Ramsey. "Government Mortgage Credit Commitments And Economic Stability," (2), 151-165.
Winnick, Louis. "The Burden Of The Residential Mortgage Debt," (2), 166-179.
Blough, Roy. "United States Taxation And Foreign Investment," (2), 180-194.
Keith, E. Gordon. "The Future Of The Corporation Income Tax," (2), 195-204.
Due, John F. "The Role Of Sales And Excise Taxation In The Over-All Tax Structure," (2), 205-220.
Nadler, Marcus. "The Outlook For Money Rates," (2), 221-222.
O'Leary, James J. "Outlook For The Long-Term Capital Market," (2), 223-228.
Shay, Robert. "Postwar Developments In The Market For Consumer Instalment Credit," (2), 229-248.
Lewis, Robert E. "Some Factors In The Growth Of Consumer Credit," (2), 249-256.
Gurley, John G. and Edward S. Shaw. "Financial Intermediaries And The Saving-Investment Process," (2), 257-276.
Saunders, R. Duane. "The Development Of The Flow Of Institutional Savings In The Analysis Of Treasury Borrowing Problems," (2), 277-287.
Moore, Geoffrey H. "The Quality Of Credit In Booms And Depressions," (2), 288-300.
Thompson, Donald S. "Changes In Quality Of Bank Credit," (2), 301-311.
McDonald, Stephen L. "Some Factors Affecting The Increased Relative Use Of Currency Since 1939," (3), 313-327.
Collery, Arnold P. "A Graphic Analysis Of The Theory Of The Determination Of The Money Supply," (3), 328-331.
Emmer, Robert E. "The Credit Expansion Equations Of An Individual Bank," (3), 322-346.
Croteau, John T. "The Large Credit Union," (3), 347-362.
Archer, Stephen H. "The Theoretical Value Of A Stock Right: A Comment," (3), 363-366.
Beranek, William. "The Theoretical Value Of A Stock Right: A Comment," (3), 367-370.
Simmons, Edward C. "A Note On The Revival Of Federal Reserve Discount Policy," (4), 413-421.
Keiser, Norman F. "The Development Of The Concept Of 'Automatic Stabilizers'," (4), 422-441.
Loewy, Harris. "Net Cash Moneyflows Through Life Insurance Companies," (4), 442-462.
McEvoy, Raymond H. "Variation In Bank Asset Portfolios," (4), 463-473.
Ronk, Sally S. "The Acceleration Of Corporate Income Tax Payments," (4), 474-481.

Journal of Finance
Volume 12, 1957

Worcester, Dean A., Jr. "Monetary Versus Fiscal Policy At Full Employment," (1), 1-15.
Bowyer, John W., Jr. "The Use Of Small Area Income Estimates In Municipal Credit Analysis," (1), 16-23.
Alhadeff, David A. and Charlotte P. Alhadeff. "An Integrated Model For Commercial Banks," (1), 24-43.
Clark, Clifford D. "A Note On Investment Activities And The Graduated Corporate Tax," (1), 44-50.
Carson, Deane. "Federal Reserve Support Of Treasury Refunding Operations," (1), 51-63.
Goldsmith, Raymond W. "The National Bureau's Postwar Capital Markets Study," (2), 121-125.
Robinson, Roland I. "Factors Accounting For The Sharply Increased Cost Of State And Local Government Borrowing," (2), 126-135.
Shapiro, Eli. "The Market For Corporate Securities: A Progress Report," (2), 136-147.
Klaman, Saul B. "Mortgage Companies In The Postwar Mortgage Market," (2), 148-158.
Mendelson, Morris. "The Flow Of Funds Through The Capital Market, 1953-55: A Progress Report," (2), 159-166.
Bernstein, E. M. "General Problems Of Financing Development Programs," (2), 167-177.
Patterson, Gardner. "Impact Of Deficit Financing In Underdeveloped Countries: Sometimes Neglected Aspects," (2), 178-189.
Bloomfield, Arthur I. "Some Problems Of Central Banking In Underdeveloped Countries," (2), 190-204.
Scott, Ira. "The Changing Significance Of Treasury Obligations In Commercial Bank Portfolios," (2), 213-222.
Walker, Charls E. "Discount Policy In The Light Of Recent Experience," (2), 223-237.
Horwich, George. "Elements Of Timing And Response In The Balance Sheet Of Banking, 1953-55," (2), 238-255.
Johnson, Norris O. "Financing Industrial Growth," (2), 264-271.
Scanlon, J. J. "Long-Range Outlook For Financing," (2), 272-278.
McKinley, Gordon W. "The Federal Home Loan Bank System And The Control Of Credit," (3), 319-332.
Jones, Dallas. "The European Monetary Agreement, The European Payments Union, And Convertibility," (3), 333-347.

Journal of Finance
Volume 16, 1961

Journal of Finance
Volume 17, 1962

Journal of Finance
Volume 18, 1963

Journal of Finance
Volume 19, 1964

Journal of Finance
Volume 20, 1965

Convertible Preferred Stocks," (5), 1187-1201.

Elton, Edwin J. and Martin J. Gruber. "Estimating The Dependence Structure Of Share Prices - Implications For Portfolio Selection," (5), 1203-1232.

Vasicek, Oldrich A. "A Note On Using Cross-Sectional Information In Bayesian Estimation Of Security Betas," (5), 1233-1239.

Davis, E. G., D. M. Dunn and W. H. Williams. "Ambiguities In The Cross-Section Analysis Of Per Share Financial Data," (5), 1241-1248.

Aigner, D. J. and C. M. Sprenkle. "On Optimal Financing Of Cyclical Cash Needs," (5), 1249-1254.

Joy, O. Maurice and Jerry O. Bradley. "A Note On Sensitivity Analysis Of Rates Of Return," (5), 1255-1261.

Melnik, A. and M. A. Pollatschek. "Debt Capacity, Diversification And Conglomeratge Mergers," (5), 1263-1273.

Wiar, Robert C. "Economic Implications Of Multiple Rates Of Return In The Leveraged Lease Context," (5), 1275-1286.

Kalish, Lionel, III and R. Alton Gilbert. "The Influence Of Bank Regulation On The Operating Efficiency Of Commercial Banks," (5), 1287-1301.

Harris, Duane G. "Some Evidence On Differential Lending Practices At Commercial Banks," (5), 1303-1311.

Clauretie, Terrence M. "Interest Rates, The Business Demand For Funds, And The Residential Mortgage Market: A Sectoral Econometric Study," (5), 1313-1326.

Nagata, Ernest A. "The Cost Structure Of Consumer Finance Small-Loan Operations," (5), 1327-1337.

Hempel, George H. "An Evaluation Of Municipal 'Bankruptcy' Laws And Procedures," (5), 1339-1351.

Weber, Harry. "God As Portfolio Manager," (5), 1353-1355.

Kamoike, Osamu. "Portfolio Selection When Future Prices Of Consumption Goods May Change: Comment," (5), 1357-1360.

Heckerman, Donald G. "Portfolio Selection When Future Prices Of Consumption Goods May Change: Reply," (5), 1361.

Puckett, Richard H. "Monetary Policy Effectiveness: The Case Of A Positively Sloped I-S Curve: Comment," (5), 1362-1364.

Silber, William L. "Monetary Policy Effectiveness: The Case Of A Positively Sloped I-S Curve: Reply," (5), 1365.

Hemmings, Dan B. "Leverage, Dividend Policy And The Cost Of Capital: Comment," (5), 1366-1370.

Rosenzweig, Adelle R. "The Random Walk Hypothesis, Domestic Borrowing, And Others: A Glossary Of Contempary Financial Terms," (5), 1371-1372.

Journal of Finance
Volume 29, 1974

Myers, Stewart C. "Interactions Of Corporate Financing And Investment Decisions - Implications For Capital Budgeting," (1), 1-25.

Samuelson, Paul A. and Robert C. Merton. "Generalized Mean-Variance Tradeoffs For Best Perturbation Correction To Approximate Portfolio Decisions," (1), 27-40.

Hinderliter, Roger H. "Market Access, Uncertainty, And Reserve-Position Adjustments Of Large Commercial Banks In The 1960's," (1), 41-56.

Towey, Richard E. "Money Creation And The Theory Of The Banking Firm," (1), 57-72.

Peterson, Richard E. "A Cross Section Study Of The Demand For Money: The United States, 1960-62," (1), 73-88.

Santomero, Anthony M. "A Model Of The Demand For Money By Households," (1), 89-102.

Levin, Jay H. "A Financial Sector Analysis Of The Eurodollar Market," (1), 103-117.

Adler, Michael. "The Cost Of Capital And Valuation Of A Two-Country Firm," (1), 119-132.

Schiff, Michael and Zvi Lieber. "A Model For The Integration Of Credit And Inventory Management," (1), 133-140.

Melicher, Ronald W. and David F. Rush. "Evidence On The Acquisition-Related Performance Of Conglomerate Firms," (1), 141-149.

Gilbert, Gary G. "Predicting De Novo Expansion In Bank Merger Cases," (1), 151-162.

Piper, Thomas R. and Steven J. Weiss. "The Profitability Of Multibank Holding Company Acquisitions," (1), 163-174.

Chen, Andrew H. Y., Frank C. Jen and Stanley Zionts. "The Joint Determination Of Portfolio And Transaction Demands For Money," (1), 175-186.

Bell, Frederick W. "The Relation Of The Structure Of Common Stock Prices To Historical, Expectational And Industrial Variables," (1), 187-197.

McEnally, Richard W. "A Note On The Return Behavior Of High Risk Common Stocks," (1), 199-202.

Logue, Dennis E. and John R. Lindvall. "The Behavior Of Investment Bankers: An Econometric Investigation," (1), 203-215.

Parker, George G. C. and Robert P. Shay. "Some Factors Affecting Awareness Of Annual Percentage Rates In Consumer Installment Credit Transactions," (1), 217-225.

Robins, Philip K. "The Effects Of State Usury Ceilings On Single Family Homebuilding," (1), 227-235.

Weston, J. Fred. "New Themes In Finance," (1), 237-243.

Gordon, Myron J. "A General Solution To The Buy Or Lease Decision: A Pedagogical Note," (1), 245-250.

Edwards, Charles E. and Stanley R. Stansell. " An Inter-Temporal Approach To The Optimization Of Dividend Policy with Predetermined Investments: Comment," (1), 251-253.

Higgins, Robert C. "An Inter-Temporal Approach To The Optimization Of Dividend Policy with Predetermined Investments: Comment," (1), 254-257.

Brennan, M. J. "An Inter-Temporal Approach To The Optimization Of Dividend Policy with Predetermined Investments: Comment," (1), 258-259.

Franke, Gunter. "Optimization Of Dividend Policy And Capital Structure with Predetermined Investments: Comment," (1), 260-263.

Wallingford, Buckner A., II. "An Inter-Temporal Approach To The Optimization Of Dividend Policy with Pre-determined Investments: Reply," (1), 264-266.

Horvitz, Paul M. "The Hunt Commission Report: A Further Comment," (1), 267-269.

Maisel, Sherman J. "The Economic And Finance Literature And Decision Making," (2), 313-322.

Shultz, Hon. George P. "Joint Session AFA-AEA Address Reflections On Political Economy," (2), 323-330.

Duesenberry, James S. and Barry Bosworth. "Policy Implications Of A Flow-Of-Funds Model," (2), 331-347.

Pierce, James L. and Thomas D. Thomson. "Short-Term Financial Models At The Federal Reserve Board," (2), 349-357.

Solnik, B. H. "The International Pricing Of Risk: An Empirical Investigation Of The World Capital Market Structure," (2), 365-378.

Lessard, Donald R. "World, National, And Industry Factors In Equity Returns," (2), 379-391.

Black, Fischer and Myron Scholes. "From Theory To A New Financial Product," (2), 399-412.

Lease, Ronald C.,Wilbur G. Lewellen and Gary G. Schlarbaum. "The Individual Investor: Attributes And Attitudes," (2), 413-433.

Robichek, Alexander A. and Richard A. Cohn. "The Economic Determinants Of Systematic Risk," (2), 439-447.

Merton, Robert C. "On The Pricing Of Corporate Debt: The Risk Structure Of Interest Rates," (2), 449-470.

Edelstein, Robert H. "The Value Of Information And The Optimal Governmental Guarantee On Its Agencies' Issues," (2), 471-484.

Martell, Terrence F. and George C. Philippatos. "Adaptation, Information, And Dependence In Commodity Markets," (2), 493-498.

Long, Michael S. and George A. Racette. "Stochastic Demand, Output And The Cost Of Capital," (2), 499-506.

Lau, Sheila C., Stuart R. Quay and Carl M. Ramsey. "The Tokyo Stock Exchange And The Capital Asset Pricing Model," (2), 507-514.

Barry, Christopher B. "Portfolio Analysis Under Uncertain Means, Variances, And Covariances," (2), 515-522.

Greenbaum, Stuart I. and Mukhtar M. Ali. "Entry, Control And The Market For Bank Charters," (2), 527-535.

Melicher, Ronald W. and David F. Rush. "Systematic Risk, Financial Data, And Bond Rating Relationships In A Regulated Industry Environment," (2), 537-544.

Severn, Alan K. "Investor Evaluation Of Foreign And Domestic Risk," (2), 545-550.

Katz, Steven. "The Price Adjustment Process Of Bonds To Rating Reclassifications: A Test Of Bond Market Efficiency," (2), 551-559.

White, William L. "Debt Management And The Form Of Business Financing," (2), 565-577.

Myers, Stewart C. and Gerald A. Pogue. "A Programming Approach To Corporate Financial Management," (2), 579-596.

Bogue, Marcus C. and Richard Roll. "Capital Budgeting Of Risky Projects With 'Imperfect' Markets For Physical Capital," (2), 601-613.

Johnson, Keith and Lawrence R. Klein. "Link Model Simulations Of International Trade: An Evaluation Of The Effects Of Currency Realignment," (2), 617-630.

Kenen, Peter B. "The Balance Of Payments And Policy Mix: Simulations Based On A U.S. Model," (2), 631-654.

Adler, Michael and Guy V. G. Stevens. "The Trade Effects Of Direct Investment," (2), 655-676.

Kain, John F. "What Should Housing Policies Be?," (2), 683-698.

De Leeuw, Frank. "What Should U.S. Housing Policies Be?," (2), 699-721.

Tinic, Seha M. and Richard R. West. "Marketability Of Common Stocks In Canada And The U.S.A.: A Comparison Of Agent Versus Dealer Dominated Markets," (3), 729-746.

Bates, Timothy. "Financing Black Enterprise," (3), 747-761.

Meltzer, Allan H. "Credit Availability And Economic Decisions: Some Evidence From The Mortgage And Housing Markets," (3), 763-777.

Pringle, John J. "The Capital Decision In Commercial Banks," (3), 779-795.

Shashua, L. and Y. Goldschmidt. "An Index For Evaluating Financial Performance," (3), 797-814.

Carleton, Willard T., Glen Kendall And Sanjiv Tandon. "Application Of The Decomposition Principle To The Capital Budgeting Problem In A Decentralized Firm," (3), 815-827.

Spies, Richard R. "The Dynamics Of Corporate Capital Budgeting," (3), 829-845.

Jacob, Nancy L. "A Limited-Diversification Portfolio Selection Model For The Small Investor," (3), 847-856.

Fama, Eugene F. and James D. MacBeth. "Long-Term Growth In A Short-Term Market," (3), 857-885.

Cooper, Richard V. L. "Efficient Capital Markets And The Quantity Theory Of Money," (3), 887-908.

Pesando, James E. "The Supply Of Money And Common Stock Prices: Further Observations On The Econometric Evidence," (3), 909-921.

Feige, Edgar L. "Temporal Cross-Section Specifications Of The Demand For Demand Deposits," (3), 923-940.

Hunt, Lacy H., II. "Bank Credit And The Money Stock: Their Roles In The Determination Of Income In The Post Accord Period," (3), 941-954.

Burrows, Paul. "The Upward Sloping IS Curve And The Control Of Income And The Balance Of Payments," (3), 955-961.

Greenbaum, Stuart I. and Mukhtar M. Ali. "Need Interest Rates On Bank Loans And Deposits Move Sympathetically?," (3), 963-971.

Awh, R. Y. and D. Waters. "A Discriminant Analysis Of Economic, Demographic, And Attitudinal Characteristics Of Bank Charge-Card Holders: A Case Study," (3), 973-980.

Monahan, James P. and Kenneth B. Monahan. "Company Contributions To Discretionary Profit-Sharing Plans: A Quantitative Approach," (3), 981-994.

Arditti, Fred D. "A Note On Discounting The Components Of An Income Stream," (3), 995-999.

Kwack, Sung Y. "A Note On The Balance Of Payments Effects Of The U. S. Capital Controls Programs: Simulation Estimates," (3), 1001-1005.

Warren, James M. "A Note On The Algebraic Equivalence Of The Holt And Malkiel Models Of Share Valuation," (3), 1007-1010.

Weston, J. Fred and Surendra K. Mansinghka. "Conglomerate Performance Measurement: Comment," (3), 1011-1012.

Reid, Samuel R. "Conglomerate Performance Measurement: Reply," (3), 1013-1015.

Slovin, Myron B. "Financial Disintermediation In A Macroeconomic Framework: Comment," (3), 1016-1019.

Seelig, Steven A. "Rising Interest Rates And Cost Push Inflation," (4), 1049-1061.

Holmes, David N., Jr. "Excess Demand, Undercapitalization, And The True Interest Rate For Credit Union Loans In Unorganized Money Markets," (4), 1063-1076.

Mason, John M. "A Structural Study Of The Income Velocity Of Circulation," (4), 1077-1086.

Herbst, Anthony F. "A Factor Analysis Approach To Determining The Relative Endogeneity Of Trade Credit," (4), 1087-1103.

Pesando, James E. "The Interest Sensitivity Of The Flow Of Funds Through Life Insurance Companies: An Econometric Analysis," (4), 1105-1121.

Boorman, John T. and Myron L. Kwast. "The Start-Up Experience Of Minority-Owned Commercial Banks: A Comparative Analysis," (4), 1123-1141.

Steindl, Frank G. "Money And Income: The View From The Government Budget Restraint," (4), 1143-1148.

Lewis, Kenneth A. "A Note On The Interest Elasticity Of Transaction Demand For Cash," (4), 1149-1152.

Gordon, Myron J. and Paul J. Halpern. "Cost Of Capital For A Division Of A Firm," (4), 1153-1163.

Burton, R. M. and W. W. Damon. "On The Existence Of A Cost Of Capital Under Pure Capital Rationing," (4), 1165-1173.

Kumar, Prem. "Market Equilibrium And Corporation Finance: Some Issues," (4), 1175-1188.

Higgins, Robert C. "Growth, Dividend Policy And Capital Costs In The Electric Utility Industry," (4), 1189-1201.

Schall, Lawrence D. "The Lease-Or-Buy And Asset Acquisition Decisions," (4), 1203-1214.

Brown, Keith C. "A Note On The Apparent Bias Of Net Revenue Estimates For Capital Investment Projects," (4), 1215-1216.

Albin, Peter S. "Information Exchange In Security Markets And The Assumption Of 'Homogeneous Beliefs'," (4), 1217-1227.

Haugen, Robert A. and Dean W. Wichern. "The Elasticity Of Financial Assets," (4), 1229-1240.

Sarnat, Marshall. "Capital Market Imperfections And The Composition Of Optimal Portfolios," (4), 1241-1253.

Baker, H. Kent and John A. Haslem. "Toward The Development Of Client-Specified Valuation Models," (4), 1255-1263.

Elton, Edwin J. and Martin J. Gruber. "Portfolio Theory When Investment Relatives Are Lognormally Distributed," (4), 1265-1273.

Norgaard, Richard L. "An Examination Of The Yields Of Corporate Bonds And Stocks," (4), 1275-1286.

Carr, J. L., P. J. Halpern and J. S. McCallum. "Correcting The Yield Curve: A Re-Interpretation Of The Duration Problem," (4), 1287-1294.

Hamelman, Paul W. and Edward M. Mazze. "Citation Patterns In Finance Journals," (4), 1295-1301.

Rosenberg, Barr and Michel Houglet. "Error Rates In CRSP And COMPUSTAT Data Bases And Their Implications," (4), 1303-1310.

Adler, Michael and Reuven Horesh. "The Relationship Among Equity Markets: Comment," (4), 1311-1317.

Agmon, Tamir. "The Relationship Among Equity Markets: Reply," (4), 1318-1319.

Pippenger, John E. "A Time Series Analysis Of Post-Accord Interest Rates: Comment," (4), 1320-1325.

Smith, V. Kerry and Richard G. Marcis. "Post Accord Interest Rates: A Reply," (4), 1326-1327.

Greer, Douglas F. "Rate Ceilings, Market Structure, And The Supply Of Finance Company Personal Loans," (5), 1363-1382.

Avio, Kenneth L. "On The Effects Of Statutory Interest Rate Ceilings," (5), 1383-1395.

Rhoades, S. A. and A. J. Yeats. "Growth, Consolidation And Mergers In Banking," (5), 1397-1405.

Sullivan, Timothy G. "Market Power, Profitability And Financial Leverage," (5), 1407-1414.

Marcis, Richard G. and V. Kerry Smith. "Efficient Estimation Of Multivariate Financial Relationships," (5), 1415-1423.

Zwick, Burton. "The Interest-Induced Wealth Effect And The Behavior Of Real And Nominal Interest Rates," (5), 1425-1435.

Jaffe, Jeffrey F. and Larry J. Merville. "Stock Price Dependencies And The Valuation Of Risky Assets with Discountinuous Temporal Returns," (5), 1437-1448.

Rush, David F. and Ronald W. Melicher. "An Empirical Examination Of Factors Which Influence Warrant Prices," (5), 1449-1466.

Kolodny, Richard. "The Refunding Decision In Near Perfect Markets," (5), 1467-1477.

Porter, R. Burr and Roger P. Bey. "An Evaluation Of The Empirical Significance Of Optimal Seeking Algorithms In Portfolio Selection," (5), 1479-1490.

Baesel, Jerome B. "On The Assessment Of Risk: Some Further Considerations," (5), 1491-1494.

Altman, Edward I., Bertrand Jacquillat And Michel Levasseur. "Comparative Analysis Of Risk Measures: France And The United States," (5), 1495-1511.

Mirus, Rolf. "The Impact Of Bank Portfolio Decisions On The Balance Of Payments: The German Experience," (5), 1513-1522.

Zecher, Richard. "Monetary Equilibrium And International Reserve Flows In Australia," (5), 1523-1530.

Ederington, Louis H. "The Yield Spread On New Issues Of Corporate Bonds," (5), 1531-1543.

Von Furstenberg, George M. and R. Jeffery Green. "Home Mortgage Delinquencies: A Cohort Analysis," (5), 1545-1548.

Tepper, Irwin and A. R. P. Affleck. "Pension Plan Liabilities And Corporate Financial Strategies," (5), 1549-1564.

Orr, Daniel. "A Note On The Uselessness Of Transaction Demand Models," (5), 1565-1572.

Taylor, Walton. "A Note On Mao's Growth Stock-Investment Opportunities Approach," (5), 1573-1576.

Sprenkle, Case M. "An Overdue Note On Some 'Ancient But Popular' Literature," (5), 1577-1580.

Keehn, Richard H. "A Note On The Cost Of Trade Credit And The Discriminatory Effects Of Monetary Policy," (5), 1581-1582.

Stapleton, Richard C. "Capital Budgeting Under Uncertainty: A Reformation: Comment," (5), 1583-1584.

Bierman, Harold, Jr. and Jerome E. Hass. "Capital Budgeting Under Uncertainty: A Reformation: Reply," (5), 1585.

Journal of Finance
Volume 30, 1975

Adler, Michael and Bernard Dumas. "Optimal International Acquisitions," (1), 1-19.

Sinkey, Joseph F., Jr. "A Multivariate Statistical Analysis Of The Characteristics Of Problem Banks," (1), 21-36.

Edelstein, Robert H. "Improving The Selection Of Credit Risks: An Analysis Of A Commercial Bank Minority Lending Program," (1), 37-55.

Becker, William E., Jr. "Determinants Of The United States Currency-Demand Deposit Ratio," (1), 57-74.

Lev, Baruch and Dov Pekelman. "A Multiperiod Adjustment Model For The Firm's Capital Structure," (1), 75-91.

Higgins, Robert C. and Lawrence D. Schall. "Corporate Bankruptcy And Conglomerate Merger," (1), 93-113.

Logue, Dennis E. "Market-Making And The Assessment Of Market Efficiency," (1), 115-123.

Brealey, R. A. and S. D. Hodges. "Playing With Portfolios," (1), 125-134.

Granger, Clive W. J. "Some Consequences Of The Valuation Model When Expectations Are Taken To Be Optimum Forecasts," (1), 135-145.

Klemkosky, Robert C. and John D. Martin. "The Effect Of Market Risk On Portfolio Diversification," (1), 147-154.

Roberts, Gordon S. "Endogenous Endowments And Capital Asset Prices," (1), 155-162.

Leabo, Dick A. and Richard J. Rogalski. "Warrant Price Movements And The Efficient Market Model," (1), 163-177.

Winkler, Robert L. and Christopher B. Barry. "A Bayesian Model For Portfolio Selection And Revision," (1), 179-192.

Schwendiman, Carl J. and George E. Pinches. "An Analysis Of Alternative Measures Of Investment Risk," (1), 193-200.

Pinches, George E. and Kent A. Mingo. "The Role Of Subordination And Industrial Bond Ratings," (1), 201-206.

Frankle, A. W. and C. A. Hawkins. "Beta Coefficients For Convertible Bonds," (1), 207-210.

Paul, Ronda S. "Valuation, Leverage And The Cost Of Capital In The Case Of Depreciable Assets: Comment," (1), 211-213.

Bradford, William D. "Valuation, Leverage And The Cost Of Capital In The Case Of Depreciable Assets: Comment," (1), 214-220.

Levy, Haim and Fred D. Arditti. "Valuation, Leverage And The Cost Of Capital In The Case Of Depreciable Assets: A Reply," (1), 221-223.

Jean, William H. "A General Class Of Three-Parameter Risk Measures: Comment," (1), 224-225.

Lintner, John. "Inflation And Security Returns," (2), 259-280.

Chase, Samuel B., Jr. and John J. Mingo. "The Regulation Of Bank Holding Companies," (2), 281-292.

Storrs, Thomas L. "Freedom For Banks," (2), 293-302.

McCallum, John S. "The Expected Holding Period Return, Uncertainty And The Term Structure Of Interest Rates," (2), 307-323.

Yawitz, Jess B., George H. Hempel and William J. Marshall. "The Use Of Average Maturity As A Risk Proxy In Investment Portfolios," (2), 325-333.

Brimmer, Andrew F. and Frederick R. Dahl. "Growth Of American International Banking: Implications For Public Policy," (2), 341-363.

Aliber, Robert Z. "Monetary Interdependence Under Floating Exchange Rates," (2), 365-376.

Hewson, John and Eisuke Sakakibara. "A Qualitative Analysis Of Euro-Currency Controls," (2), 377-400.

Elton, Edwin J., Martin J. Gruber and Zvi Lieber. "Valuation, Optimum Investment And Financing For The Firm Subject To Regulation," (2), 401-425.

Quirin, G. David And William R. Waters. "Market Efficiency And The Cost Of Capital: The Strange Case Of Fire And Casualty Insurance Companies," (2), 427-445.

Biger, Nahum. "The Assessment Of Inflation And Portfolio Selection," (2), 451-467.

Chen, Andrew H. and A. James Boness. "Effects Of Uncertain Inflation On The Investment And Financing Decisions Of A Firm," (2), 469-483.

Shapiro, Alan C. "Exchange Rate Changes, Inflation, And The Value Of The Multinational Corporation," (2), 485-502.

Ofer, Aharon R. "Investors' Expectations Of Earnings Growth, Their Accuracy And Effects On The Structure Of Realized Rates Of Returns," (2), 509-523.

Fewings, David R. "The Impact Of Corporate Growth On The Risk Of Common Stocks," (2), 525-531.

Kumar, Prem. "Growth Stocks And Corporate Capital Structure Theory," (2), 533-547.

Nathan, Richard P. "The Uses Of Shared Revenue," (2), 557-565.

Okner, Benjamin A. "The Social Security Payroll Tax: Some Alternatives For Reform," (2), 567-578.

Blume, Marshall E. and Irwin Friend. "The Asset Structure Of Individual Portfolios And Some Implications For Utility Functions," (2), 585-603.

Cohn, Richard A., Wilbur G. Lewellen, Ronald C. Lease and Gary G. Schlarbaum. "Individual Investor Risk Aversion And Investment Portfolio Composition," (2), 605-620.

Ang, James S. and Kiritkumar A. Patel. "Bond Rating Methods: Comparison And Validation," (2), 631-640.

Fraser, Donald R., Peter S. Rose and Gary L. Schugart. "Federal Reserve Membership And Bank Performance: The Evidence From Texas," (2), 641-658.

Hasty, John M., Jr. and Bruce D. Fielitz. "Systematic Risk For Heterogeneous Time Horizons," (2), 659-673.

Poole, William. "The Relationship Of Monetary Decelerations To Business Cycle Peaks: Another Look At The Evidence,"(3),697-719.

Gilbert, Gary G. and Manferd O. Peterson. "The Impact Of Changes In Federal Reserve Membership On Commercial Bank Performance," (3), 713-720.

Slovin, Myron B. and Marie Elizabeth Sushka. "The Structural Shift In The Demand For Money," (3), 721-731.

Hendershott, Patric H. and Richard C. Lemmon. "The Financial Behavior Of Households: Some Empirical Estimates," (3), 733-759.

Cargill, Thomas F. "The Term Structure Of Interest Rates: A Test Of The Expectations Hypothesis," (3), 761-771.

Santomero, Anthony M. "The Error-Learning Hypothesis And The Term Structure Of Interest Rates In Eurodollars," (3), 773-783.

Blume, Marshall E. "Betas And Their Regression Tendencies," (3), 785-795.

Arditti, Fred D. and Haim Levy. "Portfolio Efficiency Analysis In Three Moments: The Multiperiod Case," (3), 797-809.

McCulloch, J. Huston. "The Tax-Adjusted Yield Curve," (3), 811-830.

Jaffe, Jeffrey F. "On The Use Of Public Information In Financial Markets," (3), 831-839.

Gonedes, Nicholas J. "Information-Production And Capital Market Equilibrium," (3), 841-864.

Ripley, Duncan M. "Capital Control Policies And Foreign Share Prices," (3), 865-868.

Ang, James S. "The Two Faces Of Bond Refunding," (3), 869-874.

Pazner, Elisha A. and Assaf Razin. "On Expected Value Vs. Expected Future Value," (3), 875-877.

Findlay, M. Chapman, III. "The Weighted Average Cost Of Capital: Some Questions On Its Definition, Interpretation, And Use: Comment," (3), 879-880.

Pettit, R. Richardson. "The Weighted Average Cost Of Capital: Some Questions On Its Definition, Interpretation, And Use: Comment," (3), 881-882.

McConnell, John J. and Carl M. Sandberg. "The Weighted Average Cost Of Capital: Some Questions On Its Definition, Interpretation, And Use: Comment," (3), 883-886.

Bloomfield, Ted and Ronald Ma. "The Weighted Average Cost Of Capital: Some Questions On Its Definition, Interpretation, And Use: Comment," (3), 887-888.

Arditti, Fred D. "The Weighted Average Cost Of Capital: Some Questions On Its Definition, Interpretation, And Use: Reply," (3), 889-892.

Boatler, Robert W. "Treasury Bill Auction Procedures: An Empirical Investigation: Comment," (3), 893-894.

Goldstein, Henry N. and George G. Kaufman. "Treasury Bill Auction Procedures: An Empirical Investigation: Comment," (3), 895-899.

Bolten, Steven. "Treasury Bill Auction Procedures: An Empirical Investigation: Reply," (3), 900-901.

Jones-Lee, M. W. "Optimal Life Insurance: Comment," (3), 902-903.

Klein, Michael A. "Optimal Life Insurance: Comment," (3), 904-908.

Fortune, Peter. "Optimal Life Insurance: Reply," (3), 909-910.

Starleaf, Dennis R. "Nonmember Banks And Monetary Control," (4), 955-975.

Sundem, Gary L. "Evaluating Capital Budgeting Models In Simulated Environments," (4), 977-991.

Litzenberger, Robert H. and O. Maurice Joy. "Decentralized Capital Budgeting Decisions And Shareholder Wealth Maximization," (4), 993-1002.

Haugen, Robert A. and Terence C. Langetieg. "An Empirical Test For Synergism In Merger," (4), 1003-1014.

Ben-Zion, Uri and Sol S. Shalit. "Size, Leverage, And Dividend Record As Determinants Of Equity Risk," (4), 1015-1026.

Ibbotson, Roger G. and Jeffrey F. Jaffe. "'Hot Issue' Markets," (4), 1027-1042.

Cargill, Thomas F. and Gordon C. Rausser. "Temporal Price Behavior In Commodity Futures Markets," (4), 1043-1053.

Mangoletsis, I. D. "The Microeconomics Of Indirect Finance," (4), 1055-1063.

Lewis, Kenneth A. and Francis F. Breen. "Empirical Issues In The Demand For Currency: A Multinational Study," (4), 1065-1079.

Koot, Ronald S. "A Factor Analytic Approach To An Empirical Definition Of Money," (4), 1081-1089.

Wilbratte, Barry J. "Some Essential Differences In The Demand For Money By Households And By Firms," (4), 1091-1099.

Hewson, John and Eisuke Sakakibara. "The Effect Of U. S. Controls On The U. S. Commercial Bank Borrowing In The Euro-Dollar Market," (4), 1101-1110.

Mingo, John J. "Regulatory Influence On Bank Capital Investment," (4), 1111-1121.

Klemkosky, Robert C. and John D. Martin. "The Adjustment Of Beta Forecasts," (4), 1123-1128.

Johnson, Keith B., T. Gregory Morton And M. Chapman Findlay, III. "An Empirical Analysis Of The Flotation Cost Of Corporate Securities, 1971-1972," (4), 1129-1133.

Grace, H. Stephen, Jr. "On Optimal Financing Of Cyclical Cash Needs: Comment," (4), 1135-1136.

Khang, Chulsoon. "Expectations, Prices, Coupons And Yields: Comment," (4), 1137-1140.

Buse, A. "Expectations, Prices, Coupons And Yields: Reply," (4), 1141-1142.

Storoy, Sverre, Sten Thore and Marcel Boyer. "Equilibrium In Linear Capital Market Networks," (5), 1197-1211.

Kraus, Alan and Robert H. Litzenberger. "Market Equilibrium In A Multiperiod State Preference Model With Logarithmic Utility," (5), 1213-1227.

Arzac, Enrique R. "Structural Planning Under Controllable Business Risk," (5), 1229-1237.

Appleyard, A. R. and G. K. Yarrow. "The Relationship Between Take-Over Activity And Share Valuation," (5), 1239-1249.

Baron, David P. "Firm Valuation, Corporate Taxes, And Default Risk," (5), 1251-1264.

Firth, Michael. "The Information Content Of Large Investment Holdings," (5), 1265-1281.

Haugen, Robert A. and Dean W. Wichern. "The Intricate Relationship Between Financial Leverage And The Stability Of Stock Prices," (5), 1283-1292.

Schneller, Meir I. "Mean-Variance Portfolio Composition When Investors' Revision Horizon Is Very Long," (5), 1293-1300.

Gooding, Arthur E. "Quantification Of Investors' Perceptions Of Common Stocks: Risk And Return Dimensions," (5), 1301-1316.

Pesando, James E. "Determinants Of Term Premiums In The Market For United States Treasury Bills," (5), 1317-1327.

Shoup, Carl S. "Surrey's Pathways To Tax Reform - A Review Article," (5), 1329-1341.

Nantell, Timothy J. and C. Robert Carlson. "The Cost Of Capital As A Weighted Average," (5), 1343-1355.

Wrightsman, Dwayne and James O. Horrigan. "Retention, Risk Of Success, And The Price Of Stock: A Note," (5), 1357-1359.

Boquist, John A., George A. Racette and Gary G. Schlarbaum. "Duration And Risk Assessment For Bonds And Common Stocks: A Note," (5), 1360-1365.

Orgler, Yair E. "Capital Adequacy And Recoveries From Failed Banks: A Note," (5), 1366-1375.

Greer, Douglas F. "Rate Ceilings And Loan Turndowns: A Note," (5), 1376-1383.

Robichek, Alexander A. "Interpreting The Results Of Risk Analysis: A Note," (5), 1384-1388.

Journal of Finance
Volume 31, 1976

Gonedes, Nicholas J. "Capital Market Equilibrium For A Class Of Heterogeneous Expectations In A Two-Parameter World," (1), 1-15.

Ederington, Louis H. "Negotiated Versus Competitive Underwritings Of Corporate Bonds," (1), 17-28.

Morris, James R. "On Corporate Debt Maturity Strategies," (1), 29-37.

Mason, R. Hal and Maurice B. Goudzwaard. "Performance Of Conglomerate Firms: A Portfolio Approach," (1), 39-48.

Jaffe, Jeffrey F. and Robert L. Winkler. "Optimal Speculation Against An Efficient Market," (1), 49-61.

Whisler, William D. "Sensitivity Analysis Of Rates Of Return," (1), 63-69.

Practz, Peter D. "Rates Of Return On Filter Tests," (1), 71-75.

Barro, Robert J. "Integral Constraints And Aggregation In An Inventory Model Of Money Demand," (1), 77-88.

Greenbaum, Stuart I., Mukhtar M. Ali and Randall C. Merris. "Monetary Policy And Banking Profits," (1), 89-101.

Yeager, Leland. "Bootstrap Inflation," (1), 103-112.

Eastwood, David B. and Robert Anderson. "Consumer Credit And Consumer Demand For Automobiles," (1), 113-124.

Thompson, Howard E. "Mathematical Programming, The Capital Asset Pricing Model And Capital Budgeting Of Interrelated Projects," (1), 125-131.

Razin, Assaf. "Rational Insurance Purchasing," (1), 133-137.

LeRoy, Stephen F. "Efficient Capital Markets: Comment," (1), 139-141.

Fama, Eugene F. "Efficient Capital Markets: Reply," (1), 143-145.

Henderson, Glenn V., Jr. "A General Solution To The Buy Or Lease Decision: A Pedagogical Note: Comment," (1), 147-151.

Goldman, M. Barry. "Portfolio Returns And The Random Walk Theory: Comment," (1), 153-156.

Cheng, Pao L. and M. King Deets. "Portfolio Returns And The Random Walk Theory: Reply," (1), 157-161.

Gray, H. Peter. "Determinants Of The Aggregate Profit Margin: Comment," (1), 163-165.

Finkel, Sidney R. and Donald L. Tuttle. "Determinants Of The Aggregate Profit Margin: Reply," (1), 167-168.

Gordon, Myron J. "A Portfolio Theory Of The Social Discount Rate And The Public Debt," (2), 199-214.

Benston, George J. and Clifford W. Smith, Jr. "A Transactions Cost Approach To The Theory Of Financial Intermediation," (2), 215-231.

Mullins, David Wiley, Jr. "Restrictions On The Rate Of Interest On Demand Deposits And A Theory Of Compensating Balances," (2), 233-252.

Andersen, Leonall C. "Is There A Capital Shortage: Theory And Recent Empirical Evidence," (2), 257-268.

Wachtel, Paul, Arnold Sametz and Harry Shuford. "Capital Shortages: Myth Or Reality?," (2), 269-286.

Brimmer, Andrew F. and Allen Sinai. "The Effects Of Tax Policy On Capital Formation, Corporate Liquidity And The Availability Of Investible Funds: A Simulation Study," (2), 287-308.

Scholes, Myron. "Taxes And The Pricing Of Options," (2), 319-332.

Merton, Robert C. "The Impact On Option Pricing Of Specification Error In The Underlying Stock Price Returns," (2), 333-350.

Black, Fischer and John C. Cox. "Valuing Corporate Securities: Some Effects Of Bond Indenture Provisions," (2), 351-367.

Latane, Henry A. and Richard J. Rendleman, Jr. "Standard Deviations Of Stock Price Ratios Implied In Option Prices," (2), 369-381.

Cox, John C. and Stephen A. Ross. "A Survey Of Some New Results In Financial Option Pricing Theory," (2), 383-402.

Cohn, Richard A. and Donald R. Lessard. "Recent Research On Indexation And The Housing Market," (2), 403-413.

Stansell, Stanley R. and James A. Millar. "An Empirical Study Of Mortgage Payment To Income Ratios In A Variable Rate Mortgage Program," (2), 415-425.

Tucker, Donald P. "Financial Innovation And The Mortgage Market: The Possibilities For Liability Management By Thrifts," (2), 427-437.

Jaffe, Jeffrey F. and Gershon Mandelker. "The 'Fisher Effect' For Risky Assets: An Empirical Investigation," (2), 447-458.

Bodie, Zvi. "Common Stocks As A Hedge Against Inflation," (2), 459-470.

Nelson, Charles R. "Inflation And Rates Of Return On Common Stock," (2), 471-483.

Mehta, Dileep R. "The Impact Of Outstanding Convertible Bonds On Corporate Dividend Policy," (2), 489-506.

Glenn, David W. "Super Premium Security Prices And Optimal Corporate Financing Decisions," (2), 507-524.

Elton, Edwin J. and Martin J. Gruber. "Valuation And Asset Selection Under Alternative Investment Opportunities," (2), 525-539.

Journal of Finance
Volume 32, 1977

Franks, J. R., J. E. Broyles and M. J. Hecht. "An Industry Study Of The Profitability Of Mergers In The United Kingdom," (5), 1513-1525.
Lee, Li Way. "Co-Insurance And Conglomerate Merger," (5), 1527-1537.
O'Brien, James M. "On The Incidence Of Selective Credit And Related Policies In A Multi-Asset Framework," (5), 1539-1556.
Hamburger, Michael J. and Burton Zwick. "Installment Credit Controls, Consumer Expenditures And The Allocation Of Real Resources," (5), 1557-1569.
Kearl, J. R. and Frederic S. Mishkin. "Illiquidity, The Demand For Residential Housing, And Monetary Policy," (5), 1571-1586.
McCall, Alan S. and Manferd O. Peterson. "The Impact Of DE NOVO Commercial Bank Entry," (5), 1587-1604.
Mingo, John and Benjamin Wolkowitz. "The Effects Of Regulation On Bank Balance Sheet Decisions," (5), 1605-1616.
Weinrobe, Maurice. "An Analysis Of The Effectiveness Of FHLBB Liquidity Policy, 1971-1975," (5), 1617-1637.
Pfaff, Philip. "Evaluation Of Some Money Stock Forecasting Models," (5), 1639-1646.
Hopewell, Michael H. and George G. Kaufman. "Commercial Bank Bidding On Municipal Revenue Bonds: New Evidence," (5), 1647-1656.
Kohlhagen, Steven W. "The Stability Of Exchange Rate Expectations And Canadian Capital Flows," (5), 1657-1669.
Landskroner, Yoram. "Intertemporal Determination Of The Market Price Of Risk," (5), 1671-1681.
Baron, David P. "On The Utility Theoretic Foundations Of Mean-Variance Analysis," (5), 1683-1697.
Brennan, M. J. and E. S. Schwartz. "Convertible Bonds: Valuation And Optimal Strategies For Call And Conversion," (5), 1699-1715.
Ng, David S. "Pareto-Optimality Of Authentic Information," (5), 1717-1728.
Bar-Yosef, Sasson and Roger Mesnick. "On Some Definitional Problems With The Method Of Certainty Equivalents," (5), 1729-1737.
Yawitz, Jess B. and James A. Anderson. "The Effect Of Bond Refunding On Shareholder Wealth," (5), 1738-1746.
Livingston, Miles. "A Theory Of Humpbacked Bond Yield Curves," (5), 1747-1751.
Sutherland, Ronald J. "Income Velocity And Commercial Bank Portfolios," (5), 1752-1758.
Morgan, I. G. "Grouping Procedures For Portfolio Formation," (5), 1759-1765.
Zerbst, Robert H. and William B. Brueggeman. "FHA And VA Mortgage Discount Points And Housing Prices," (5), 1766-1773.
Ostas, James R. "Regional Differences In Mortgage Financing Costs: A Reexamination," (5), 1774-1778.
Weston, J. Fred and Wayne Y. Lee. "Cost Of Capital For A Division Of A Firm: Comment," (5), 1779-1780.
Gordon, Myron J. and Paul J. Halpern. "Cost Of Capital For A Division Of A Firm: Reply," (5), 1781-1782.
Bates, Timothy M. and Donald D. Hester. "Analysis Of A Commercial Bank Minority Lending Program: Comment," (5), 1783-1789.
Edelstein, Robert H. "Improving The Selection Of Credit Risks - An Analysis Of A Commercial Bank Minority Lending Program: Reply," (5), 1790-1794.
Salomon, Gerald L. and E. Dan Smith. "Additional Evidence On The Time Series Properties Of Reported Earnings Per Share: Comment," (5), 1795-1801.
Ball, Ray and Ross Watts. "Additional Evidence On The Time Series Properties Of Reported Earnings Per Share: Reply," (5), 1802-1808.
Peterson, Richard L. "On The Effects Of Statutory Interest Rate Ceilings: Comment," (5), 1809-1810.
Avio, Kenneth L. "On The Effects Of Statutory Interest Rate Ceilings: Reply," (5), 1811-1813.
Auerbach, Robert D. and Jack L. Rutner. "A Negative View Of The Negative Money Multiplier: Comment," (5), 1814-1817.
Steindl, Frank G. "The Negative View Of The Negative Money Multiplier: Reply," (5), 1818-1821.

Journal of Finance
Volume 33, 1978

Brown, Lawrence D. and Michael S. Rozeff. "The Superiority Of Analyst Forecasts As Measures Of Expectations: Evidence From Earnings," (1), 1-16.
Brown, Stewart L. "Earnings Changes, Stock Prices, And Market Efficiency," (1), 17-28.
Pinches, George E. and J. Clay Singleton. "The Adjustment Of Stock Prices To Bond Rating Changes," (1), 29-44.
Kim, E. Han. "A Mean-Variance Theory Of Optimal Capital Structure And Corporate Debt Capacity," (1), 45-63.
Arditti, Fred D. and John M. Pinkerton. "The Valuation And The Cost Of Capital Of The Levered Firm With Growth Opportunities," (1), 65-73.
Dobson, Steven W. "Estimating Term Structure Equations With Individual Bond Data," (1), 75-92.
Brick, John R. and Howard E. Thompson. "Time Series Analysis Of Interest Rates: Some Additional Evidence," (1), 93-103.
Garbade, Kenneth D. and Joseph F. Hunt. "Risk Premiums On Federal Agency Debt," (1), 105-116.
Cornell, Bradford. "Monetary Policy, Inflation Forecasting And The Term Structure Of Interest Rates," (1), 117-127.
Schmalensee, Richard and Robert R. Trippi. "Common Stock Volatility Expectations Implied By Option Premia," (1), 129-147.
Cohen, Kalman J., Steven F. Maier, Robert A. Schwartz and David K. Whitcomb. "The Returns Generating Process, Returns Variance, And The Effect Of Thinness In Securities Markets," (1), 149-167.
Fischer, Stanley. "Call Option Pricing When The Exercise Price Is Uncertain, And The Valuation Of Index Bonds," (1), 169-176.
Margrabe, William. "The Value Of An Option To Exchange One Asset For Another," (1), 177-186.
Harper, Charles P. and Clifford L. Fry. "Consistent Empirical Results With Almon's Method: Implications For The Monetary Versus Fiscal Policy Debate," (1), 187-198.
Clotfelter, Charles and Charles Lieberman. "On The Distributional Impact Of Federal Interest Rate Restrictions," (1), 199-213.
Lapp, John S. "The Determination Of Savings And Loan Association Deposit Rates In The Absence Of Rate Ceilings: A Cross-Section Approach," (1), 215-230.
Campbell, Tim S. "A Model Of The Market For Lines Of Credit," (1), 231-244.
Boczar, Gregory E. "Competition Between Banks And Finance Companies: A Cross Section Study Of Personal Loan Debtors," (1), 245-258.
Mullineaux, Donald J. "Economies Of Scale, And Organizational Efficiency In Banking: A Profit-Function Approach," (1), 259-280.
Schall, Lawrence D., Gary L. Sundem and William R. Geijsbeek. "Survey And Analysis Of Capital Budgeting Methods," (1), 281-287.
Beedles, William L. and Michael A. Simkowitz. "A Note On Skewness And Data Errors," (1), 288-292.
Livingston, Miles. "Duration And Risk Assessment For Bonds And Common Stocks: A Note," (1), 293-295.
Elton, Edwin J., Martin J. Gruber and Manfred W. Padberg. "Simple Criteria For Optimal Portfolio Selection: Tracing Out The Efficient Frontier," (1), 296-302.
Kumar, P. C., George C. Philippatos and John R. Ezzell. "Goal Programming And The Selection Of Portfolios By Dual-Purpose Funds," (1), 303-310.
Kopecky, Kenneth J. "Nonmember Banks And Empirical Measures Of The Variability Of Reserves And Money: A Theoretical Appraisal," (1), 311-318.
Wilford, Walton T. and D. Sykes Wilford. "On The Monetary Approach To The Balance Of Payments: The Small, Open Economy," (1), 319-323.
Eisenbeis, Robert A. "A Multivariate Analysis Of Industrial Bond Ratings' And The Role Of Subordination: A Comment," (1), 325-335.
Pinches, George E. "'A Multivariate Analysis Of Industrial Bond Ratings' And The Role Of Subordination: Reply," (1), 336-344.
Granito, Michael and Patrick Walsh. "Portfolio Efficiency Analysis In Three Moments-The Multiperiod Case: Comment," (1), 345-348.
Mayor, Thomas H. and Kenneth G. McCoin. "Bond Refunding: One Or Two Faces?," (1), 349-353.
Ang, James S. "The Two Faces Of Bond Refunding: Reply," (1), 354-356.
Haugen, Robert A. and Lemma W. Senbet. "The Insignificance Of Bankruptcy Costs To The Theory Of Optimal Capital Structure," (2), 383-393.
Senbet, Lemma W. and Howard E. Thompson. "The Equivalence Of Alternative Mean-Variance Capital Budgeting Models," (2), 395-401.
Kim, Yong H. and Joseph C. Atkins. "Evaluating Investments In Accounts Receivable: A Wealth Maximizing Framework," (2), 403-412.
Dole, Walter. "Capital Markets And The Short Run Behavior Of Life Cycle Savers," (2), 413-428.
Schlarbaum, Gary G.,Wilbur G. Lewellen and Ronald C. Lease. "The Common Stock-Portfolio Performance Record Of Individual Investors: 1954-70," (2), 429-441.
Guy, James R. F. "The Performance Of The British Investment Trust Industry," (2), 443-455.
Kon, Stanley J. and Frank C. Jen. "Estimation Of Time-Varying Systematic Risk And Performance For Mutual Fund Portfolios: An Application Of Switching Regression," (2), 457-475.
Edmister, Robert O. "Commission Cost Structure: Shifts And Scale Economies," (2), 477-486.
Hamilton, James L. "Marketplace Organization And Marketability: NASDAQ, The Stock Exchange, And The National Market System," (2), 487-503.
Kummer, Donald R. and J. Ronald Hoffmeister. "Valuation Consequences Of Cash Tender Offers," (2), 505-516.
Makin, John H. "Portfolio Theory And The Problem Of Foreign Exchange Risk," (2), 517-534.
Yardini, Edward E. "A Portfolio - Balance Model Of Corporate Working Capital," (2), 535-552.
Levy, Haim and Yoram Kroll. "Ordering Uncertain Options With Borrowing And Lending," (2), 553-574.
Rabinovitch, Ramon and Joel Owen. "Nonhomogeneous Expectations And Information In The Capital Asset Market," (2), 575-587.
Brito, Ney O. "Portfolio Selection In An Economy With Marketability And Short Sales Restrictions," (2), 589-601.
Constantinides, George M. "Market Risk Adjustment In Project Valuation," (2), 603-616.
Geske, Robert. "The Pricing Of Options With Stochastic Dividend Yield," (2), 617-625.
Eddy, Albert R. "Interest Rate Risk And Systematic Risk: An Interpretation," (2), 626-630.
Klemkosky, Robert C. and Terry S. Maness. "The Predictability Of Real Portfolio Risk Levels," (2), 631-639.
Lee, Cheng-Few and William P. Lloyd. "Block Recursive Systems In Asset Pricing Models: An Extension," (2), 640-644.
Hsaio, Frank S. T. and James W. Smith. "An Analytical Approach To Sensitivity Analysis Of The Internal Rate Of Return Model," (2), 645-649.
Wrightsman, Dwayne. "Tax Shield Valuation And The Capital Structure Decision," (2), 650-656.
Franks, Julian R. and Stewart D. Hodges. "Valuation Of Financial Lease Contracts: A Note," (2), 657-669.
Firth, Michael. "Synergism In Mergers: Some British Results," (2), 670-672.
Robichek, Alexander A. "Regulation And Modern Finance Theory," (3), 693-705.
Haugen, Robert A., Alvin L. Stroyny and Dean W. Wichern. "Rate Regulation, Capital Structure, And The Sharing Of Interest Rate Risk In The Electric Utility Industry," (3), 707-721.
Cohen, Kalman J., Steven F. Maier, Robert A. Schwartz and David K. Whitcomb. "Limit Orders, Market Structure, And The Returns Generation Process," (3), 723-736.
Litzenberger, Robert H. and James C. Van Horne. "Elimination Of The Double Taxation Of Dividends And Corporate Financial Policy," (3), 737-750.

Hakansson, Nils H. "Welfare Aspects Of Options And Supershares," (3), 759-776.

Ross, Stephen. "Some Notes On Financial Incentive-Signalling Models, Activity Choice And Risk Preferences," (3), 777-794.

Kafka, Alexandre. "The New Exchange Rate Regime And The Developing Countries," (3), 795-802.

Junz, Helen B. "The Balance Of Payments Adjustment Process Revisited," (3), 803-813.

Garbade, Kenneth D. and William L. Silber. "Technology, Communication And The Performance Of Financial Markets: 1840-1975," (3), 819-832.

Friedman, Benjamin M. "Who Puts The Inflation Premium Into Nominal Interest Rates?," (3), 833-845.

Gordon, Myron J. and Lawrence I. Gould. "The Cost Of Equity Capital: A Reconsideration," (3), 849-861.

Chen, Andrew. "Recent Developments In The Cost Of Debt Capital," (3), 863-877.

Ross, Stephen. "The Current Status Of The Capital Asset Pricing Model," (3), 885-901.

Friend, Irwin, Randolph Westerfield and Michael Granito. "New Evidence On The Capital Asset Pricing Model," (3), 903-917.

Kane, Edward J. "Getting Along Without Regulation Q: Testing The Standard View Of Deposit-Rate Competition During The 'Wild-Card Experience'," (3), 921-932.

Jaffee, Dwight M. and Kenneth T. Rosen. "Estimates Of The Effectiveness Of Stabilization Policies For The Mortgage And Housing Markets," (3), 933-946.

Litzenberger, Robert H. and Howard Sosin. "Taxation And The Incidence Of Home Ownership Across Income Groups," (3), 947-961.

Clark, Peter K. "Capital Formation And The Recent Productivity Slowdown," (3), 965-975.

McCarthy, Michael D. "Current Prospects For Productivity Growth," (3), 977-988.

Von Furstenberg, George M. "The Long-Term Effects Of Government Deficits On The U. S. Output Potential," (3), 989-1007.

Robichek, Alexander A. and Mark R. Eaker. "Foreign Exchange Hedging And The Capital Asset Pricing Model," (3), 1011-1018.

Dumas, Bernard. "The Theory Of The Trading Firm Revisited," (3), 1019-1030.

Roll, Richard. "Ambiguity When Performance Is Measured By The Securities Line," (4), 1051-1069.

Kalay, Avner and Ramon Rabinovitch. "On Individual Loans Pricing Credit Rationing And Interest Rate Regulation," (4), 1071-1085.

Koot, Ronald S. "On Economies Of Scale In Credit Unions," (4), 1087-1094.

Bart, John T. "The Nature Of The Conflict Between Transactors' Expectations Of Capital Gains," (4), 1095-1107.

Snyder, Wayne W. "Horse Racing: Testing The Efficient Markets Model," (4), 1109-1118.

Grant, Dwight. "Market Timing And Portfolio Mangement," (4), 1119-1131.

Stoll, Hans R. "The Supply Of Dealer Services In Securities Markets," (4), 1133-1151.

Stoll, Hans R. "The Pricing Of Security Dealer Services: An Empirical Study Of NASDAQ Stocks," (4), 1153-1172.

Cook, Timothy Q. and Patric H. Hendershott. "The Impact Of Taxes, Risk And Relative Security Supplies On Interest Rate Differentials," (4), 1173-1186.

Bodie, Zvi and Robert A. Taggart. "Future Investment Opportunities And The Value Of The Call Provision On A Bond," (4), 1187-1200.

Gordon, M. J. and L. I. Gould. "The Cost Of Equity Capital With Personal Income Taxes And Flotation Costs," (4), 1201-1212.

Hagerman, Robert L. "More Evidence On The Distribution Of Security Returns," (4), 1213-1221.

Schwartz, Eli and James A. Greenleaf. "A Comment On Investment Decisions, Repetitive Games And The Unequal Distribution Of Wealth," (4), 1222-1227.

Sosin, Howard B. "Neutral Recapitalizations: Predictions And Tests Concerning Valuation And Welfare," (4), 1228-1234.

Jarrow, Robert A. "The Relationship Between Yield, Risk, And Return Of Corporate Bonds," (4), 1235-1240.

Carr, J. L., P. J. Halpern and J. S. McCallum. "Comments On Single-Valued Duration Measures," (4), 1241-1243.

Robison, Lindon and Peter J. Barry. "Risk Efficiency Using Stochastic Dominance And Expected Gain-Confidence Limits," (4), 1244-1249.

Brown, Keith C. "The Rate Of Return Of Selected Investment Projects," (4), 1250-1253.

Vandell, Kerry D. "Default Risk Under Alternative Mortgage Instruments," (5), 1279-1296.

Caks, John. "Corporate Debt Decisions: A New Analytical Framework," (5), 1297-1315.

Bhattacharya, Sudipto. "Project Valuation With Mean-Reverting Cash Flow Streams," (5), 1317-1331.

Galai, Dan and Meir I. Schneller. "Pricing Of Warrants And The Value Of The Firm," (5), 1333-1342.

Weinstein, Mark I. "The Seasoning Process Of New Corporate Bond Issues," (5), 1343-1354.

Hopewell, Michael H. and Arthur L. Schwartz. "Temporary Trading Suspensions In Individual NYSE Securities," (5), 1355-1373.

Elton, Edwin J., Martin J. Gruber and Thomas J. Urich. "Are Betas Best?," (5), 1375-1384.

Lewellen, Wilbur G., Kenneth L. Stanley, Ronald C. Lease and Gary G. Schlarbaum. "Some Direct Evidence On The Dividend Clientele Phenomenon," (5), 1385-1399.

Gooding, Arthur E. "Perceived Risk And Capital Asset Pricing," (5), 1401-1424.

Guy, James R. F. "An Examination Of The Effects Of International Diversification From The British Viewpoint On Both Hypothetical And Real Portfolios," (5), 1425-1438.

Jaffe, Jeffrey F. "A Note On Taxation And Investment," (5), 1439-1445.

Ashton, D. J. and D. R. Atkins. "Interactions In Corporate Financing And Investment Decisions - Implications For Capital Budgeting: A Further Comment," (5), 1447-1454.

Epps, Thomas W. "Financial Risk And The St. Petersburg Paradox: Comment," (5), 1455-1456.

Smith, W. James. "Sensitivity Analysis Of Rates Of Return: Comment," (5), 1457-1460.

Joy, O. Maurice and Jerry O. Bradley. "Sensitivity Analysis Of Rates Of Return: Reply," (5), 1461.

Journal of Finance
Volume 34, 1979

Graddy, Duane B. and Reuben Kyle, III. "The Simultaneity Of Bank Decision-Making, Market Structure, And Bank Performance," (1), 1-18.

Kane, Edward J. and Stephen A. Buser. "Portfolio Diversification At Commercial Banks," (1), 19-34.

Levi, Maurice D. and John H. Makin. "Fisher, Phillips, Friedman And The Measured Impact Of Inflation On Interest," (1), 35-52.

Brennan, M. J. "The Pricing Of Contingent Claims In Discrete Time Models," (1), 53-68.

Grauer, Frederick L. A. and Robert H. Litzenberger. "The Pricing Of Commodity Futures Contracts, Nominal Bonds And Other Risky Assets Under Commodity Price Uncertainty," (1), 69-83.

Aivazian, Varouj A. and Jeffrey L. Callen. "Investment, Market Structure, And The Cost Of Capital," (1), 85-92.

Manaster, Steven. "Real And Nominal Efficient Sets," (1), 93-102.

Hilliard, Jimmy E. "The Relationship Between Equity Indices On World Exchanges," (1), 103-114.

Copeland, Thomas E. "Liquidity Changes Following Stock Splits," (1), 115-141.

Alexander, Gordon J., Roger D. Stover and David B. Kuhnau. "Market Timing Strategies In Convertible Debt Financing," (1), 143-155.

Ederington, Louis H. "The Hedging Performance Of The New Futures Markets," (1), 157-170.

Hamilton, James L. "Marketplace Fragmentation, Competition, And The Efficiency Of The Stock Exchange," (1), 171-187.

Livingston, Miles. "Bond Taxation And The Shape Of The Yield-To-Maturity Curve," (1), 189-196.

Ball, Ray and Ross Watts. "Some Additional Evidence On Survival Biases," (1), 197-206.

Baron, David P. "Investment Policy, Optimality, And The Mean-Variance Model," (1), 207-232.

Berger, Paul D. and Zvi Bodie. "Portfolio Selection In A 'Winner-Take-All' Environment," (1), 233-236.

Selby, Edward B., Jr. "The Recognition Lag Of The Federal Advisory Council," (1), 237-240.

Livingston, Miles. "A Note On The Issue Of Long-Term Pure Discount Bonds," (1), 241-246.

Smith, Clifford W., Jr. and Jerold B. Warner. "Bankruptcy, Secured Debt, And Optimal Capital Structure: Comment," (1), 247-251.

Scott, James H., Jr. "Bankruptcy, Secured Debt, And Optimal Capital Structure: Reply," (1), 253-260.

Elgers, Pieter T., James R. Haltiner and William H. Hawthorne. "Beta Regression Tendencies: Statistical And Real Causes," (1), 261-263.

Blume, Marshall E. "Betas And Their Regression Tendencies: Some Further Evidence," (1), 265-267.

Malkiel, Burton G. "The Capital Formation Problem In The United States," (2), 291-306.

Scott, James H., Jr. "The Tax Effects Of Investment In Marketable Securities On Firm Valuation," (2), 307-324.

Benninga, Simon. "General Equilibrium With Financial Markets: Existence, Uniqueness, And Implications For Corporate Finance," (2), 325-342.

Hamada, Robert S. "Financial Theory And Taxation In An Inflationary World: Some Public Policy Issues," (2), 347-369.

Chen, Andrew H. and E. Han Kim. "Theories Of Corporate Debt Policy: A Synthesis," (2), 371-384.

Bierwag, G. O. and Chulsoon Khang. "An Immunization Strategy Is A Minimax Strategy," (2), 389-399.

Goldman, M. Barry, Howard B. Sosin and Lawrence A. Shepp. "On Contingent Claims That Insure Ex-post Optimal Stock Market Timing," (2), 401-414.

Goodman, Stephen H. "Foreign Exchange Rate Forecasting Techniques: Implications For Business And Policy," (2), 415-427.

Fisk, Charles and Frank Rimlinger. "Nonparametric Estimates Of LDC Repayment Prospects," (2), 429-436.

Castanias, Richard P., II. "Macroinformation And The Variability Of Stock Market Prices," (2), 439-450.

Kon, Stanley J. and W. Patrick Lau. "Specification Tests For Portfolio Regression Parameter Stationarity And The Implications For Empirical Research," (2), 451-465.

Poole, William. "Burnsian Monetary Policy: Eight Years Of Progress?," (2), 473-484.

Pierce, James L. "The Political Economy Of Arthur Burns," (2), 485-496.

Goldman, M. Barry. "Anti-Diversification Or Optimal Programmes For Infrequently Revised Portfolios," (2), 505-516.

Cooper, Ian A. and Willard T. Carleton. "Dynamics Of Borrower-Lender Interaction: Partitioning Final Payoff In Venture Capital Finance," (2), 517-529.

Ciccolo, John and Gary Fromm. "'q' And The Theory Of Investment," (2), 535-547.

Malkiel, Burton G., George M. Von Furstenberg and Harry S. Watson. "Expectations, Tobin's q, And Industry Investment," (2), 549-561.

Garbade, Kenneth D. and William L. Silber. "Structural Organization Of Secondary Markets: Clearing Frequency, Dealer Activity And Liquidity Risk," (2), 577-593.

Goldman, M. Barry and Avraham Beja. "Market Prices Vs. Equilibrium Prices: Returns' Variance, Serial Correlation, And The Role Of The Specialist," (3), 595-607.

Singer, Ronald F. "Endogenous Marginal Income Tax Rates, Investor Behavior And The Capital Asset Pricing Model," (3), 609-616.

Bowman, Robert G. "The Theoretical Relationship Between Systematic Risk And Financial (Accounting) Variables," (3), 617-630.

Ferri, Michael G. and Wesley H. Jones. "Determinants Of Financial Structure: A New Methodological Approach," (3), 631-644.

Practz, Peter D. "Testing For A Flat Spectrum On Efficient Market Price Data," (3), 645-658.

Journal of Finance
Volume 35, 1980

DeAngelo, Harry and Ronald W. Masulis. "Leverage And Dividend Irrelevancy Under Corporate And Personal Taxation," (2), 453-464.

Litzenberger, Robert H. and Krishna Ramaswamy. "Dividends, Short Selling Restrictions, Tax-Induced Investor Clienteles And Market Equilibrium," (2), 469-482.

Anderson, Ronald W. and Jean-Pierre Danthine. "Hedging And Joint Production: Theory And Illustrations," (2), 487-498.

Breeden, Douglas T. "Consumption Risk In Futures Markets," (2), 503-520.

Foster, George. "Externalities And Financial Reporting," (2), 521-533.

Ohlson, James A. and A. Gregory Buckman. "Toward A Theory Of Financial Accounting," (2), 537-547.

Sunder, Shyam. "Corporate Capital Investment, Accounting Methods And Earnings: A Test Of The Control Hypothesis," (2), 553-565.

Hoag, James W. "Towards Indices Of Real Estate Value And Return," (2), 569-580.

Leland, Hayne E. "Who Should Buy Portfolio Insurance?," (2), 581-594.

Rudd, Andrew and Barr Rosenberg. "The 'Market Model' In Investment Management," (2), 597-607.

Epstein, Larry G. and Stuart M. Turnbull. "Capital Asset Prices And The Temporal Resolution Of Uncertainty," (3), 627-643.

Taggart, Robert A., Jr. "Taxes And Corporate Capital Structure In An Incomplete Market," (3), 645-659.

Beckers, Stan. "The Constant Elasticity Of Variance Model And Its Implications For Option Pricing," (3), 661-673.

Ohlson, James A. and Mark B. Garman. "A Dynamic Equilibrium For The Ross Arbitrage Model," (3), 675-684.

Amihud, Yakov. "General Risk Aversion And Attitude Towards Risk," (3), 685-691.

Marsh, Paul. "Valuation Of Underwriting Agreements For UK Rights Issues," (3), 693-716.

Hendershott, Patric H. and Timothy W. Koch. "The Demand For Tax-Exempt Securities By Financial Institutions," (3), 717-727.

Oldfield, George S., Jr. and Richard J. Rogalski. "A Theory Of Common Stock Returns Over Trading And Non-Trading Periods," (3), 729-751.

Bates, Timothy and William Bradford. "An Analysis Of The Portfolio Behavior Of Black-Owned Commercial Banks," (3), 753-768.

Wolken, John D. and Frank J. Navratil. "Economies Of Scale In Credit Unions: Further Evidence," (3), 769-777.

Ungar, Meyer and Benzion Zilberfarb. "The Demand For Money By Firms: The Stability And Other Issues Reexamined," (3), 779-785.

Akhtar, M. A. and Bluford H. Putnam. "Money Demand And Foreign Exchange Risk: The German Case, 1972-1976," (3), 787-794.

Booth, Laurence D. "Stochastic Demand, Output And The Cost Of Capital: A Clarification," (3), 795-798.

Hodges, S. D. and R. A. Brealey. "The Rate Of Return On New Investment In The UK," (3), 799-800.

Starleaf, Dennis R. "A Comment On 'Nonmember Banks And Empirical Measures Of The Variability Of Reserves And Money: A Theoretical Appraisal'," (3), 801-805.

Kopecky, Kenneth J. "Nonmember Banks And Monetary Control: Reply," (3), 807.

Campbell, Tim S. and William A. Kracaw. "Information Production, Market Signalling, And The Theory Of Financial Intermediation," (4), 863-882.

Sunder, Shyam. "Stationarity Of Market Risk: Random Coefficient Tests For Individual Stocks," (4), 883-896.

Friend, Irwin and Randolph Westerfield. "Co-Skewness And Capital Assets Pricing," (4), 897-913.

Scott, Robert C. and Philip A. Horvath. "On The Direction Of Preference For Moments Of Higher Order Than The Variance," (4), 915-919.

Lakonishok, Josef. "Stock Market Return Expectations: Some General Properties," (4), 921-932.

Deschamps, Benoit and Dileep R. Mehta. "Predictive Ability And Descriptive Validity Of Earnings Forecasting Models," (4), 933-949.

Graddy, Duane B. and Reuben Kyle, III. "Affiliated Bank Performance And The Simultaneity Of Financial Decision-Making," (4), 952-957.

Rosen, Kenneth T. and David E. Bloom. "A Microeconomic Model Of Federal Home Loan Mortgage Corporate Activity," (4), 959-971.

Stowe, John D., Collin J. Watson and Terry D. Robertson. "Relationships Between The Two Sides Of The Balance Sheet: A Canonical Correlation Analysis," (4), 973-980.

Elliott, J. Walter. "The Cost Of Capital And US Capital Investment: A Test Of Alternative Concepts," (4), 981-999.

Aharony, Joseph, Charles P. Jones and Itzhak Swary. "An Analysis Of Risk And Return Characteristics Of Corporate Bankruptcy Using Capital Market Data," (4), 1001-1016.

Dambolena, Ismael G. and Sarkis J. Khoury. "Ratio Stability And Corporate Failure," (4), 1017-1026.

Bryant, John. "Nontransferable Interest-Bearing National Debt," (4), 1027-1031.

Conine, Thomas E., Jr. "Corporate Debt And Corporate Taxes: An Extension," (4), 1033-1037.

Losey, Robert L. and John C. Talbott, Jr. "Back On The Track With The Efficient Markets Hypothesis," (4), 1039-1043.

Pesando, James E. "On Forecasting Long-Term Interest Rates: Is The Success Of The No-Change Prediction Surprising: Comment," (4), 1045-1047.

Elliott, J. Walter and J. R. Baier. "Econometric Models And Current Interest Rates: How Well Do They Predict Future Rates: A Reply," (4), 1049-1050.

Aivazian, Varouj A. and Jeffrey L. Callen. "Future Investment Opportunities And The Value Of The Call Provision On A Bond: Comment," (4), 1051-1054.

Bodie, Zvi and Robert A. Taggart, Jr. "Future Investment Opportunities And The Value Of The Call Provision On A Bond: Reply," (4), 1055-1056.

Roll, Richard and Stephen A. Ross. "An Empirical Investigation Of The Arbitrage Pricing Theory," (5), 1073-1103.

Jarrow, Robert. "Heterogeneous Expectations, Restrictions On Short Sales, And Equilibrium Asset Prices," (5), 1105-1113.

Baron, David P. and Bengt Holmstrom. "The Investment Banking Contract For New Issues Under Asymmetric Information: Delegation And The Incentive Problem," (5), 1115-1138.

Sealey, C. W., Jr. "Deposit Rate-Setting, Risk Aversion And The Theory Of Depository Financial Intermediaries," (5), 1139-1154.

Campbell, Ritchie A. "The Demand For Life Insurance: An Application Of The Economics Of Uncertainty," (5), 1155-1172.

Ferber, Robert and Luch Chao Lee. "Asset Accumulation In Early Married Life," (5), 1173-1188.

Ho, Thomas and Anthony Saunders. "A Catastrophe Model Of Bank Failure," (5), 1189-1207.

Sosin, Howard B. "On The Valuation Of Federal Loan Guarantees To Corporations," (5), 1209-1221.

Barnea, Amir, Robert A. Haugen and Lemma W. Senbet. "A Rationale For Debt Maturity Structure And Call Provisions In The Agency Theoretic Framework," (5), 1223-1234.

Koehn, Michael and Anthony M. Santomero. "Regulation Of Bank Capital And Portfolio Risk," (5), 1235-1244.

Brealey, R. A. and C. M. Young. "Debt, Taxes And Leasing - A Note," (5), 1245-1250.

Peterson, David and Michael L. Rice. "A Note On Ambiguity In Portfolio Performance Measures," (5), 1251-1256.

Gup, Benton E. "The Financial Consequences Of Corporate Growth," (5), 1257-1265.

Bennin, Robert. "Error Rates In CRSP And COMPUSTAT: A Second Look," (5), 1267-1271.

Franckle, Charles T. "The Hedging Performance Of The New Futures Markets: Comment," (5), 1272-1279.

Journal of Finance
Volume 36, 1981

Tepper, Irwin. "Taxation And Corporate Pension Policy," (1), 1-13.

Schwert, G. William. "The Adjustment Of Stock Prices To Information About Inflation," (1), 15-29.

Huang, Roger D. "The Monetary Approach To Exchange Rate In An Efficient Foreign Exchange Market: Tests Based On Volatility," (1), 31-41.

Longworth, David. "Testing The Efficiency Of The Canadian-U.S. Exchange Market Under The Assumption Of No Risk Premium," (1), 43-49.

Buser, Stephen A., Andrew H. Chen And Edward J. Kane. "Federal Deposit Insurance, Regulatory Policy, And Optimal Bank Capital," (1), 51-60.

Kent, Richard J. "An Analysis Of Countercyclical Policies Of The FHLBB," (1), 61-79.

Winter, Ralph A. "On The Rate Structure Of The American Life Insurance Market," (1), 81-96.

Lewellen, Wilbur G. and Douglas R. Emery. "On The Matter Of Parity Among Financial Obligations," (1), 97-111.

Agmon, T., A. R. Ofer and A. Tamir. "Variable Rate Debt Instruments And Corporate Debt Policy," (1), 113-125.

Grauer, Robert R. "Investment Policy Implications Of The Capital Asset Pricing Model," (1), 127-141.

Jennings, Robert H., Laura T. Starks and John C. Fellingham. "An Equilibrium Model Of Asset Trading With Sequential Information Arrival," (1), 143-161.

Bhattacharya, Sudipto. "Notes On Multiperiod Valuation And The Pricing Of Options," (1), 163-180.

Osborne, D. K. and Jeanne Wendel. "A Note On Concentration And Checking Account Prices," (1), 181-186.

Adler, Michael. "Investor Recognition Of Corporation International Diversification: Comment," (1), 187-190.

Agmon, Tamir and Donald Lessard. "Investor Recognition Of Corporate International Diversification: A Note," (1), 191-192.

Nicol, David J. "A Note On Capital Budgeting Techniques And The Reinvestment Rate: Comment," (1), 193-195.

Turnbull, Stuart M. "Debt Capacity: Erratum," (1), 197.

Sharpe, William F. "Decentralized Investment Management," (2), 217-234.

Stiglitz, Joseph E. "Pareto Optimality And Competition," (2), 235-251.

Grossman, Sanford J. and Oliver D. Hart. "The Allocation Role Of Takeover Bids In Situations Of Asymmetric Information," (2), 253-270.

Allen, Franklin. "The Prevention Of Default," (2), 271-276.

Cohn, Richard A. and Donald R. Lessard. "The Effect Of Inflation On Stock Prices: International Evidence," (2), 277-289.

Shiller, Robert J. "The Use Of Volatility Measures In Assessing Market Efficiency," (2), 291-304.

Reinganum, Marc R. "The Arbitrage Pricing Theory: Some Empirical Results," (2), 313-321.

Fogler, H. Russell, Kose John and James Tipton. "Three Factors, Interest Rate Differentials And Stock Groups," (2), 323-335.

Oldfield, George S., Jr. and Richard J. Rogalski. "Treasury Bill Factors And Common Stock Returns," (2), 337-354.

Kane, Edward J. "Accelerating Inflation, Technological Innovation, And The Decreasing Effectiveness Of Banking Regulation," (2), 355-367.

Farrar, Donald E. and Lance Girton. "Institutional Investors And Concentration Of Financial Power: Berle And Means Revisited," (2), 369-381.

Taggart, Robert A., Jr. "Rate-of-Return Regulation And Utility Capital Structure Decisions," (2), 383-393.

Errunza, Vihang R. and Lemma W. Senbet. "The Effects Of International Operations On The Market Value Of The Firm: Theory And Evidence," (2), 401-417.

Eaker, Mark R. "The Numeraire Problem And Foreign Exchange Risk," (2), 419-426.

Rodriguez, Rita M. "Corporate Exchange Risk Management: Theme And Aberrations," (2), 427-438.

Figlewski, Stephen. "Futures Trading And Volatility In The GNMA Market," (2), 445-456.

Black, Deborah G., Kenneth D. Garbade and William L. Silber. "The Impact Of The GNMA Pass-through Program On FHA Mortgage Costs," (2), 457-469.

Dunn, Kenneth B. and John J. McConnell. "A Comparison Of Alternative Models For Pricing GNMA Mortgage-Backed Securities," (2), 471-484.

Tinsley, P., G. Fries, B. Garrett, A. Norman, P.A.V.B. Swamy and P.

Journal of Finance
Volume 38, 1983

Investing Decisions When The Firm has Unused Tax Credits," (2), 571-583.

Gordon, Roger H. and Joel Slemrod. "A General Equilibrium Simulation Study Of Subsidies To Municipal Expenditures," (2), 585-594.

Fabozzi, Frank J. and Uzi Yaari. "Valuation Of Safe Harbor Tax Benefit Transfer Leases," (2), 595-606.

Dunn, Kenneth B. and Kenneth J. Singleton. "An Empirical Analysis Of The Pricing Of Mortgage-Backed Securities," (2), 613-623.

Skelton, Jeffrey L. "Relative Risk In Municipal And Corporate Debt," (2), 625-634.

Marsh, Terry A. and Eric R. Rosenfeld. "Stochastic Processes For Interest Rates And Equilibrium Bond Prices," (2), 635-646.

Gultekin, N. Bulent. "Stock-Market Returns And Inflations Forecasts," (3), 663-673.

Cornell, Bradford and Kenneth R. French. "Taxes And The Pricing Of Stock Index Futures," (3), 675-694.

Figlewski, Stephen and Thomas Urich. "Optimal Aggregation Of Money Supply Forecasts: Accuracy, Profitability And Market Efficiency," (3), 695-710.

Brown, Stephen J. and Mark I. Weinstein. "A New Approach To Testing Asset Pricing Models: The Bilinear Paradigm," (3), 711-743.

Owen, Joel and Ramon Rabinovitch. "On The Class Of Elliptical Distributions And Their Application To The Theory Of Portfolio Choice," (3), 745-752.

Dimson, E. and P. R. Marsh. "The Stability Of UK Risk Measures And The Problem Of Thin Trading," (3), 753-783.

Hochman, Shalom and Oded Palmon. "The Irrelevance Of Capital Structure For The Impact Of Inflation On Investment," (3), 785-794.

Hendershott, Patric H. and Sheng Cheng Hu. "The Allocation Of Capital Between Residential And Nonresidential Uses: Taxes, Inflation And Capital Market Constraints," (3), 795-812.

Carleton, Willard T., David K. Guilkey, Robert S. Harris and John F. Stewart. "An Empirical Analysis Of The Role Of The Medium Of Exchange In Mergers," (3), 813-826.

Santomero, Anthony M. "Controlling Monetary Aggregates: The Discount Window," (3), 827-843.

Friedman, Richard M. and William W. Roberts. "The Carry-Forward Provision And Management Of Bank Reserves," (3), 845-855.

Sealey, C. W., Jr. "Valuation, Capital Structure, And Shareholder Unanimity For Depository Financial Intermediaries," (3), 857-875.

Deshmukh, Sudhakar D., Stuart I. Greenbaum and George Kanatas. "Lending Policies Of Financial Intermediaries Facing Credit And Funding Risk," (3), 873-886.

Murray, John D. And Robert W. White. "Economies Of Scale And Economies Of Scope In Multiproduct Financial Institutions: A Study Of British Columbia Credit Unions," (3), 887-902.

Easley, David and Robert A. Jarrow. "Consensus Beliefs Equilibrium And Market Efficiency," (3), 903-911.

Trueman, Brett. "Optimality Of The Disclosure Of Private Information In A Production-Exchange Economy," (3), 913-924.

Adler, Michael and Bernard Dumas. "International Portfolio Choice And Corporation Finance: A Synthesis," (3), 925-984.

Chen, Nai-Fu and Jonathan E. Ingersoll, Jr. "Exact Pricing In Linear Factor Models With Finitely Many Assets: A Note," (3), 985-988.

Baesel, Jerome B., George Shows and Edward Thorp. "The Cost Of Liquidity Services In Listed Options: A Note," (3), 989-995.

Ingram, Robert W., LeRoy D. Brooks and Ronald M. Copeland. "The Information Content Of Municipal Bond Rating Changes: A Note," (3), 997-1003.

McDonald, Bill. "Beta Nonstationarity And The Use Of The Chen And Lee Estimator: A Note," (3), 1005-1009.

Rosen, Kenneth T. and Larry Katz. "Money Market Mutual Funds: An Experiment In Ad Hoc Deregulation: A Note," (3), 1011-1017.

Rosenfeld, James. "The Effect Of Common-Stock Dividend Reductions On The Returns Of Nonconvertible Preferred Stocks: A Note," (3), 1019-1024.

Struck, Peter L. and Lewis Mandell. "The Effect Of Bank Deregulation On Small Business: A Note," (3), 1025-1031.

Kroll, Yoram. "Stochastic Choice In Insurance And Risk Sharing: A Comment," (3), 1033-1035.

Doherty, Neil A. "Stochastic Choice In Insurance And Risk Sharing: A Reply," (3), 1037-1038.

Brief, Richard P. "Yield Approximations: A Historical Perspective: A Correction," (3), 1039-1039.

Modigliani, Franco. "Debt, Dividend Policy, Taxes, Inflation, And Market Valuation: Erratum," (3), 1041-1042.

Ho, Thomas S. Y. and Hans R. Stoll. "The Dynamics Of Dealer Markets Under Competition," (4), 1053-1074.

James, Christopher and Robert O. Edmister. "The Relation Between Common Stock Returns, Trading Activity And Market Value," (4), 1075-1086.

Chen, Son-Nan and Stephen J. Brown. "Estimation Risk And Simple Rules For Optimal Portfolio Selection," (4), 1087-1094.

Taylor, William M. "The Estimation Of Quality-Adjusted Rates Of Return In Stamp Auctions," (4), 1095-1109.

Peek, Joe and James A. Wilcox. "The Postwar Stability Of The Fisher Effect," (4), 1111-1124.

Harris, John M., Jr., Rodney L. Roenfeldt and Philip L. Cooley. "Evidence Of Financial Leverage Clienteles," (4), 1125-1132.

Emanuel, David. "A Theoretical Model For Valuing Preferred Stock," (4), 1133-1155.

Lakonishok, Josef and Theo Vermaelen. "Tax Reform And Ex-Dividend Day Behavior," (4), 1157-1179.

Penman, Stephen H. "The Predictive Content Of Earnings Forecasts And Dividends," (4), 1181-1199.

Morin, Roger A. and A. Fernandez Suarez. "Risk Aversion Revisited," (4), 1201-1216.

Marcus, Alan J. "The Bank Capital Decision: A Time Series-Cross Section Analysis," (4), 1217-1232.

Barth, James R., Padma Gotur, Neela Manage and Anthony M. J. Yezer. "The Effect Of Government Regulations On Personal Loan Markets: A Tobit Estimation Of A Microeconomic Model," (4), 1233-1251.

Trueman, Brett. "Motivating Mangement To Reveal Inside Information," (4), 1253-1269.

Geske, Robert, Richard Roll and Kuldeep Shastri. "Over-the-Counter Option Market Dividend Protection And 'Biases' In The Black-Scholes Model: A Note," (4), 1271-1277.

Maloney, Kevin J., William J. Marshall and Jess B. Yawitz. "The Effect Of Risk On The Firm's Optimal Capital Stock: A Note," (4), 1279-1284.

Hill, Joanne and Thomas Schneeweis. "The Effect Of Three Mile Island On Electric Utility Stock Prices: A Note," (4), 1285-1292.

Choi, Dosoung and Robert A. Strong. "The Pricing Of When-Issued Common Stock: A Note," (4), 1293-1298.

Peterson, Richard L. "Usury Laws And Consumer Credit: A Note," (4), 1299-1304.

Hubbard, Carl M. "Money Market Funds, Money Supply, And Monetary Control: A Note," (4), 1305-1310.

Pitts, C. G. C. and M. J. P. Selby. "The Pricing Of Corporate Debt: A Further Note," (4), 1311-1313.

I'Costa, Joan E. Richart and Stuart I. Greenbaum. Bank Forward Lending: A Note," (4), 1315-1322.

Pearce, Douglas K. and V. Vance Roley. "The Reaction Of Stock Prices To Unanticipated Changes In Money: A Note," (4), 1323-1333.

Patterson, Cleveland S. "Flotation Cost Allowance In Rate Of Return Regulation: Comment," (4), 1335-1338.

Arzac, Enrique R. and Matityahu Marcus. "Flotation Cost Allowance In Rate Of Return Regulation: A Reply," (4), 1339-1341.

Santomero, Anthony M. "Fixed Versus Varible Rate Loans," (5), 1363-1380.

Kraus, Alan and Robert Litzenberger. "On The Distributional Conditions For A Consumption-Oriented Three Moment CAPM," (5), 1381-1391.

Chen, Nai-Fu. "Some Empirical Tests Of The Theory Of Arbitrage Pricing," (5), 1393-1414.

Weinstein, Mark I. "Bond Systematic Risk And The Option Pricing Model," (5), 1415-1429.

Protopapadakis, Aris and Hans R. Stoll. "Spot And Futures Prices And The Law Of One Price," (5), 1431-1455.

Copeland, Thomas E. and Dan Galai. "Information Effects Of The Bid-Ask Spread," (5), 1457-1469.

Adler, Michael and Bruce Lehmann. "Deviations From Purchasing Power Parity In The Long Run," (5), 1471-1487.

Eaton, Jonathan and Harvey S. Rosen. "Agency, Delayed Compensation, And The Structure Of Executive Remuneration," (5), 1489-1505.

Lee, Wayne L., Anjan V. Thakor and Gautam Vora. "Screening, Market Signalling, And Capital Structure Theory," (5), 1507-1518.

Brenner, Menachem and Itzhak Venezia. "The Effects Of Inflation And Taxes On Growth Investments And Replacement Policies," (5), 1519-1528.

Walsh, Carl E. "Taxation Of Interest Income, Deregulation And The Banking Industry," (5), 1529-1542.

Chan, Yuk-Shee. "On The Positive Role Of Financial Intermediation In Allocation Of Venture Capital In A Market With Imperfect Information," (5), 1543-1568.

Campbell, Tim S. and J. Kimball Dietrich. "The Determinants Of Default On Insured Conventional Residential Mortgage Loans," (5), 1569-1581.

Slovin, Myron B. and Marie Elizabeth Sushka. "A Model Of The Commercial Loan Rate," (5), 1583-1596.

Miles, James A. and James D. Rosenfeld. "The Effect Of Voluntary Spin-off Announcements On Shareholder Wealth," (5), 1597-1606.

Woolridge, J. Randall. "Dividend Changes And Security Prices," (5), 1607-1615.

Castanias, Richard. "Bankruptcy Risk And Optimal Capital Structure," (5), 1617-1635.

Stapleton, R. C. and M. G. Subrahmanyam. "The Market Model And Capital Asset Pricing Theory: A Note," (5), 1637-1642.

Van Horne, James C. and Hal B. Heaton. "Government Security Dealers' Positions, Information And Interest-Rate Expectations: A Note," (5), 1643-1649.

Dietrich, J. Kimball and Christopher James. "Regulation And The Determination Of Bank Capital Changes: A Note," (5), 1651-1658.

Smirlock, Michael and William Marshall. "An Examination Of The Empirical Relationship Between The Dividend And Investment Decisions: A Note," (5), 1659-1667.

Amoako-Adu, Ben. "The Canadian Tax Reform And Its Effect On Stock Prices: A Note," (5), 1669-1675.

Journal of Finance
Volume 39, 1984

Litzenberger, Robert H. and Jacques Rolfo. "An International Study Of Tax Effects On Government Bonds," (1), 1-22.

Ho, Thomas S. Y. and Richard G. Macris. "Dealer Bid-Ask Quotes And Transaction Prices: An Empirical Study Of Some AMEX Options," (1), 23-45.

Kroll, Yoram, Haim Levy and Harry M. Markowitz. "Mean-Variance Versus Direct Utility Maximization," (1), 47-62.

Kandel, Shmuel. "On The Exclusion Of Assets From Tests Of The Mean Variance Efficiency Of The Market Portfolio," (1), 63-75.

Sundaresan, M. "Consumption And Equilibrium Interest Rates In Stochastic Production Economies," (1), 77-92.

Senbet, Lemma W. and Robert A. Taggart, Jr. "Capital Structure Equilibrium Under Market Imperfections And Incompleteness," (1), 93-103.

Schall, Lawrence D. "Taxes, Inflation And Corporate Financial Policy," (1), 105-126.

Jalilvand, Abolhassan and Robert S. Harris. "Corporate Behavior In Adjusting To Capital Structure And Dividend Targets: An Econometric Study," (1), 127-145.

Kon, Stanley J. "Models Of Stock Returns - A Comparison," (1), 147-165.

Ashton, D. J. and D. R. Atkins. "A Partial Theory Of Takeover Bids," (1), 167-183.

Berges, Angel, John J. McConnell and Gary G. Schlarbaum. "The Turn-of-the-Year In Canada," (1), 185-192.

Fong, H. Gifford and Oldrich A. Vasicek. "A Risk Minimizing Strategy For Portfolio Immunization," (5), 1541-1546.
Hilliard, Jimmy E. "Hedging Interest Rate Risk With Futures Portfolios Under Term Structure Effects," (5), 1547-1569.
Grinols, Earl L. "Production And Risk Leveling In The Intertemporal Capital Asset Pricing Model," (5), 1571-1595.
Roberts, Gordon S. and Jerry A. Viscione. "The Impact Of Seniority And Security Covenants On Bond Yields: A Note," (5), 1597-1602.
Rogalski, Richard J. "New Findings Regarding Day-Of-The-Week Returns Over Trading And Non-Trading Periods: A Note," (5), 1603-1614.
Smith, Richard L. and Manjeet Dhatt. "Direct Equity Financing; A Resolution Of A Paradox: A Comment," (5), 1615-1618.
Hansen, Robert S. and John M. Pinkerton. "Direct Equity Financing; A Resolution Of A Paradox: A Reply," (5), 1619-1624.

Journal of Finance
Volume 40, 1985

Hakansson, Nils H., Avraham Beja and Jivendra Kale. "On The Feasibility Of Automated Market Making By A Programmed Specialist," (1), 1-20.
Ho, Thomas S. Y., Robert A. Schwartz and David K. Whitcomb. "The Trading Decision And Market Clearing Under Transaction Price Uncertainty," (1), 21-42.
Gultekin, N. Bulent and Richard J. Rogalski. "Government Bond Returns, Measurement Of Interest Rate Risk, And The Arbitrage Pricing Theory," (1), 43-61.
Walsh, Carl E. "A Rational Expectations Model Of Term Premia With Some Implications For Empirical Asset Demand Equations," (1), 63-83.
Best, Michael J. and Robert R. Grauer. "Capital Asset Pricing Compatible With Observed Market Value Weights," (1), 85-103.
Errunza, Vihang and Etienne Losq. "International Asset Pricing Under Mild Segmentation: Theory And Test," (1), 105-124.
Alexander, Gordon J. and Bruce G. Resnick. "More On Estimation Risk And Simple Rules For Optimal Portfolio Selection," (1), 125-133.
Gottlieb, Gary and Avner Kalay. "Implications Of The Discreteness Of Observed Stock Prices," (1), 135-153.
Ball, Clifford A. and Walter N. Torous. "On Jumps In Common Stock Prices And Their Impact On Call Pricing," (1), 155-173.
Jagannathan, Ravi. "An Investigation Of Commodity Futures Prices Using The Consumption-Based Intertemporal Capital Asset Pricing Model," (1), 175-191.
Chang, Eric C. "Returns To Speculators And The Theory Of Normal Backwardation," (1), 193-208.
Jain, Prem C. "The Effect Of Voluntary Sell-Off Announcements On Shareholder Wealth," (1), 209-224.
Babbel, David F. "The Price Elasticity Of Demand For Whole Life Insurance," (1), 225-239.
Koppenhaver, G. D. "Bank Funding Risks, Risk Aversion, And The Choice Of Futures Hedging Instrument," (1), 241-255.
Green, Richard C. and Sanjay Srivastava. "Risk Aversion And Arbitrage," (1), 257-268.
Frydman, Halina, Edward I. Altman and Duen-Li Kao. "Introducing Recursive Partitioning For Financial Classification: The Case Of Financial Distress," (1), 269-291.
Dunn, Kenneth B. and Chester S. Spatt. "An Analysis Of Mortgage Contracting: Prepayment Penalties And The Due-on-Sale Clause," (1), 293-308.
Varian, Hal R. "Divergence Of Opinion In Complete Markets: A Note," (1), 309-317.
Shea, Gary S. "Interest Rate Term Structure Estimation With Exponential Splines: A Note," (1), 319-325.
Ang, James, David Peterson and Pamela Peterson. "Marginal Tax Rates: Evidence From Nontaxable Corporate Bonds: A Note," (1), 327-332.
Schultz, Paul. "Personal Income Taxes And The January Effect: Small Firm Stock Returns Before The War Revenue Act Of 1917: A Note," (1), 333-343.
Dybvig, Philip H. "Acknowledgment: Kinks On The Mean-Variance Frontier," (1), 345.
Dyl, Edward A. and Stanley A. Martin, Jr. "Weekend Effects On Stock Returns: A Comment," (1), 347-350.
Lakonishok, Josef and Maurice Levi. "Weekend Effects On Stock Returns: A Reply," (1), 351-352.
Brown, David P. and Michael R. Gibbons. "A Simple Econometric Approach For Utility-Based Asset Pricing Models," (2), 359-382.
Dybvig, Philip H. and Stephen A. Ross. "Performance Measurement Using Differential Information And A Security Market Line," (2), 383-399.
Dybvig, Philip H. and Stephen A. Ross. "The Analytics Of Performance Measurement Using A Security Market Line," (2), 401-416.
Bawa, Vijay S., James N. Bodurtha, Jr., M. R. Rao and Hira L. Suri. "On Determination Of Stochastic Dominance Optimal Sets," (2), 417-431.
Jaffe, Jeffrey and Randolph Westerfield. "The Week-End Effect In Common Stock Returns: The International Evidence," (2), 433-454.
Rubinstein, Mark. "Nonparametric Tests Of Alternative Option Pricing Models Using All Reported Trades And Quotes On The 30 Most Active CBOE Option Classes From August 23, 1976 Through August 31, 1978," (2), 455-480.
Halpern, Paul J. and Stuart M. Turnbull. "Empirical Tests Of Boundary Conditions For Toronto Stock Exchange Options," (2), 481-500.
Dotan, Amihud and S. Abraham Ravid. "On The Interaction Of Real And Financial Decisions Of The Firm Under Uncertainty," (2), 501-517.
McConnell, John J. and Timothy J. Nantell. "Corporate Combinations And Common Stock Returns: The Case Of Joint Ventures," (2), 519-536.
Ang, James S. and David R. Peterson. "Return, Risk, And Yield: Evidence From Ex Ante Data," (2), 537-548.
Thatcher, Janet S. "The Choice Of Call Provision Terms: Evidence Of The Existence Of Agency Costs Of Debt," (2), 549-561.
Lam, Chun H. and Andrew H. Chen. "Joint Effects Of Interest Rate Deregulation And Capital Requirements On Optimal Bank Portfolio Adjustments," (2), 563-575.
Briys, Eric P. and Henri Louberge. "On The Theory Of Rational Insurance Purchasing: A Note," (2), 577-581.
Cornell, Bradford. "The Weekly Pattern In Stock Returns: Cash Versus Futures: A Note," (2), 583-588.
Jordan, Bradford D. and Richard H. Pettway. "The Pricing Of Short-Term Debt And The Miller Hypothesis: A Note," (2), 589-594.
Mitchell, Douglas W. "Expected Inflation And Interest Rates In A Multi-Asset Model," (2), 595-599.
Pulley, Lawrence B. "Comment On 'Mean-Variance Versus Direct Utility Maximization'," (2), 601-602.
Lehmann, Bruce and Arthur Warga. "Optimal Distribution-Free Tests And Further Evidence Of Heteroscedasticity In The Market Model: A Comment," (2), 603-605.
Giaccotto, Carmelo and Mukhtar M. Ali. "Optimal Distribution-Free Tests And Further Evidence Of Heteroscedasticity In The Market Model: A Reply," (2), 607.
Van Horne, James C. "The Presidential Address: Of Financial Innovations And Excesses," (3), 621-631.
Summers, Lawrence H. "On Economics And Finance," (3), 633-636.
Ross, Stephen A. "Debt And Taxes And Uncertainty," (3), 637-657.
Dhrymes, Phoebus J., Irwin Friend, Mustafa N. Gultekin and N. Bulent Gultekin. "New Tests Of The APT And Their Implications," (3), 659-674.
Mankiw, N. Gregory, David Romer and Matthew D. Shapiro. "An Unbiased Reexamination Of Stock Market Volatility," (3), 677-687.
Huffman, Gregory W. "Adjustment Costs And Capital Asset Pricing," (3), 691-705.
Fogler, H. Russell, Michael R. Granito and Laurence R. Smith. "A Theoretical Analysis Of Real Estate Returns," (3), 711-719.
Wood, Robert A., Thomas H. McInish and J. Keith Ord. "An Investigation Of Transactions Data For NYSE Stocks," (3), 723-739.
Evnine, Jeremy and Andrew Rudd. "Index Options: The Early Evidence," (3), 743-758.
Treynor, Jack L. and Robert Ferguson. "In Defense Of Technical Analysis," (3), 757-773.
Shefrin Hersh and Meir Statman. "The Disposition To Sell Winners Too Early And Ride Losers Too Long: Theory And Evidence," (3), 777-782.
DeBondt, Werner F. M. and Richard Thaler. "Does The Stock Market Overreact?," (3), 793-805.
DeJong, Douglas V., Robert Forsythe and Russell J. Lundholm. "Ripoffs, Lemons, And Reputation Formation In Agency Relationships: A Laboratory Market Study," (3), 809-820.
Ang, James S. and Thomas Schwarz. "Risk Aversion And Information Structure: An Experimental Study Of Price Variability In The Securities Markets," (3), 825-844.
Garman, Mark B. "Towards A Semigroup Pricing Theory," (3), 847-861.
John, Kose and David C. Nachman. "Risky Debt, Investment Incentives, And Reputation In A Sequential Equilibrium," (3), 863-878.
Shapiro, Alan C. "Currency Risk And Country Risk In International Banking," (3), 881-891.
Smith, Clifford W., Jr. and L. MacDonald Wakeman. "Determinants Of Corporate Leasing Policy," (3), 895-908.
Marcus, Alan J. "Spinoff/Terminations And The Value Of Pension Insurance," (3), 911-924.
Pesando, James E. "The Usefulness Of The Wind-Up Measure Of Pension Liabilities: A Labor Market Perspective," (3), 927-940.
Bicksler, James L. and Andrew H. Chen. "The Integration Of Insurance And Taxes In Corporate Pension Strategy," (3), 943-955.
Chan, Yuk-Shee and King-Tim Mak. "Depositors' Welfare, Deposit Insurance, And Deregulation," (3), 959-974.
Ho, Thomas S. Y. and Anthony Saunders. "A Micro Model Of The Federal Funds Market," (3), 977-988.
Loderer, Claudio. "A Test Of The OPEC Cartel Hypothesis: 1974-1983," (3), 991-1006.
Miller, Merton H. and Charles W. Upton. "The Pricing Of Oil And Gas: Some Further Results," (3), 1009-1018.
Miller, Merton H. and Kevin Rock. "Dividend Policy Under Asymmetric Information," (4), 1031-1051.
John, Kose and Joseph Williams. "Dividends, Dilution, And Taxes: A Signalling Equilibrium," (4), 1053-1070.
Diamond, Douglas W. "Optimal Release Of Information By Firms," (4), 1071-1094.
Green, Richard C. and Eli Talmor. "The Structure And Incentive Effects Of Corporate Tax Liabilities," (4), 1095-1114.
Hochman, Shalom and Oded Palmon. "The Impact Of Inflation On The Aggregate Debt-Asset Ratio," (4), 1115-1125.
Yawitz, Jess B., Kevin J. Maloney and Louis H. Ederington. "Taxes, Default Risk, And Yield Spreads," (4), 1127-1140.
Smirlock, Michael and Jess Yawitz. "Asset Returns, Discount Rate Changes, And Market Efficiency," (4), 1141-1158.
Landskroner, Yoram and David Ruthenberg. "Optimal Bank Behavior Under Uncertain Inflation," (4), 1159-1171.
Dybvig, Philip H. and Stephen A. Ross. "Yes, The APT Is Testable," (4), 1173-1188.
Shanken, Jay. "Multi-Beta CAPM Or Equilibrium APT?: A Reply," (4), 1189-1196.
Levy, Haim. "Upper And Lower Bounds Of Put And Call Option Value: Stochastic Dominance Approach," (4), 1197-1217.
Ritchken, Peter H. "On Option Pricing Bounds," (4), 1219-1233.
Amershi, Amin H. "A Complete Analysis Of Full Pareto Efficiency In Financial Markets For Arbitrary Preferences," (4), 1235-1243.
Makowski, Louis and Lynne Pepall. "Easy Proofs Of Unanimity And Optimality Without Spanning: A Pedagogical Note," (4), 1245-1250.
Sears, Stephen and K. C. John Wei. "Asset Pricing, Higher Moments, And The Market Risk Premium: A Note," (4), 1251-1253.
Harris, Milton and Artur Raviv. "A Sequential Signalling Model Of Convertible Debt Call Policy," (5), 1263-1281.
Leland, Hayne E. "Option Pricing And Replication With Transactions Costs," (5), 1283-1301.
Brenner, Menachem, Georges Courtadon And Marti Subrahmanyam. "Options On The Spot And Options On Futures," (5), 1303-1317.

110

Zardkoohi, Asghar, Nanda Rangan and James Kolari. "Homogeneity Restrictions On The Translog Cost Model: A Note," (5), 1153-1156.
Farmer, Roger E. A. and Ralph A. Winter. "The Role Of Options In The Resolution Of Agency Problems: A Comment," (5), 1157-1170.
Haugen, Robert A. and Lemma W. Senbet. "The Role Of Options In The Resolution Of Agency Problems: A Reply," (5), 1171-1174.
Cadsby, Charles Bram. "Performance Hypothesis Testing With The Sharpe And Treynor Measures: A Comment," (5), 1175-1176.
Tew, Bernard V. and Donald W. Reid. "Mean-Variance Versus Direct Utility Maximization: A Comment," (5), 1177-1180.
Levy, Haim. "Upper And Lower Bonds Of Put And Call Option Value: Stochastic Dominance Approach-Erratum," (5), 1181-1182.

Journal of Finance
Volume 42, 1987

Huberman, Gur, Shmuel Kandel and Robert F. Stambaugh. "Mimicking Portfolios And Exact Arbitrage Pricing," (1), 1-9.
Bar-Yosef, Sasson, Jeffrey L. Callen and Joshua Livnat. "Autoregressive Modeling Of Earnings--Investment Causality," (1), 11-28.
Williams, Joseph. "Perquisites, Risk, And Capital Structure," (1), 29-48.
Corhay, Albert, Gabriel Hawawini and Pierre Michel. "Seasonality In The Risk-Return Relationship: Some International Evidence," (1), 49-68.
Huang, Roger D. "Expectations Of Exchange Rates And Differential Inflation Rates: Further Evidence On Purchasing Power Parity In Efficient Markets," (1), 69-79.
Fons, Jerome S. "The Default Premium And Corporate Bond Experience," (1), 81-97.
Ogden, Joseph P. "An Analysis Of Yield Curve Notes," (1), 99-110.
Atchison, Michael D., Kirt C. Butler and Richard R. Simonds. "Nonsynchronous Security Trading And Market Index Autocorrelation," (1), 111-118.
McConnell, John J. and Gary C. Sanger. "The Puzzle In Post-Listing Common Stock Returns," (1), 119-140.
Solnik, Bruno. "Using Financial Prices To Test Exchange Rate Models: A Note," (1), 141-149.
Alexander, Gordon J., Cheol S. Eun and S. Janakiramanan. "Asset Pricing And Dual Listing On Foreign Capital Markets: A Note," (1), 151-158.
Dawson, Steven M. "Initial Public Offer Underpricing: The Issuer's View--A Note," (1), 159-162.
Dravid, Ajay R. "A Note On The Behavior Of Stock Returns Around Ex-Dates Of Stock Distributions," (1), 163-168.
Aivazian, Varouj A. and Jeffrey L. Callen. "Miller's Irrelevance Mechanism: A Note," (1), 169-180.
So, Jacky C. "The Distribtuion Of Foreign Exchange Price Changes: Trading Day Effects And Risk Measurement--A Comment," (1), 181-188.
McFarland, James W., R. Richardson Pettit and Sam K. Sung. "The Distribution Of Foreign Exchange Price Changes: Trading Day Effects And Risk Measurement--A Reply," (1), 189-194.
Ferson, Wayne E., Shmuel Kandel and Robert F. Stambaugh. "Tests Of Asset Pricing With Time-Varying Expected Risk Premiums And Market Betas," (2), 201-220.
Shanken, Jay. "Nonsynchronous Data And The Covariance-Factor Structure Of Returns," (2), 221-231.
Lehmann, Bruce N. and David M. Modest. "Mutual Fund Performance Evaluation: A Comparison Of Benchmarks And Benchmark Comparisons," (2), 233-265.
Johnson, Herb and Rene Stulz. "The Pricing Of Options With Default Risk," (2), 267-280.
Hull, John and Alan White. "The Pricing Of Options On Assets With Stochastic Volatilities," (2), 281-300.
Barone-Adesi, Giovanni and Robert E. Whaley. "Efficient Analytic Approximation Of American Option Values," (2), 301-320.
Ambarish, Ramasastry, Kose John and Joseph Williams. "Efficient Signalling With Dividends And Investments," (2), 321-343.
Chan, Yuk-Shee and Anjan V. Thakor. "Collateral And Competitive Equilibria With Moral Hazard And Private Information," (2), 345-363.
Ofer, Aharon R. and Anjan V. Thakor. "A Theory Of Stock Price Responses To Alternative Corporate Cash Disbursement Methods: Stock Repurchases And Dividends," (2), 365-394.
Wolff, Christian C. P. "Forward Foreign Exchange Rates, Expected Spot Rates, And Premia: A Signal-Extraction Approach," (2), 395-406.
Hardouvelis, Gikas A. "Reserves Announcements And Interest Rates: Does Monetary Policy Matter?," (2), 407-422.
Mester, Loretta J. "A Multiproduct Cost Study Of Savings And Loans," (2), 423-445.
Piros, Christopher D. "Taxable Vs. Tax-Exempt Bonds: A Note On The Effect Of Uncertain Taxable Income," (2), 447-451.
Jones, Charles P., Douglas K. Pearce and Jack W. Wilson. "Can Tax-Loss Selling Explain The January Effect? A Note," (2), 453-461.
Omberg, Edward. "A Note On The Convergence Of Binomial-Pricing And Compound-Option Models," (2), 463-469.
Nielsen, Lars Tyge. "Positively Weighted Frontier Portfolios: A Note," (2), 471.
Gilles, Christian and Stephen F. LeRoy. "A Note On The Local Expectations Hypothesis: A Discrete-Time Exposition-Erratum," (2), 473-474.
Merton, Robert C. "Presidential Address: A Simple Model Of Capital Market Equilibrium With Incomplete Information," (3), 483-510.
Neal, Robert. "Potential Competition And Actual Competition In Equity Options," (3), 511-531.
Amihud, Yakov and Haim Mendelson. "Trading Mechanisms And Stock Returns: An Empirical Investigation," (3), 533-553.
DeBondt, Werner F. M. and Richard H. Thaler. "Further Evidence On Investor Overreaction And Stock Market Seasonality," (3), 557-581.
Herring, Richard J. and Prashant Vankudre. "Growth Opportunities And Risk-Taking By Financial Intermediaries," (3), 583-600.
Lehmann, Bruce N. "Orthogonal Frontiers And Alternative Mean-Variance Efficiency Tests," (3), 601-619.
John, Kose. "Risk-Shifting Incentives And Signalling Through

Corporate Capital Structure," (3), 632-641.
Strong, John S. and John R. Meyer. "Asset Writedowns: Managerial Incentives And Security Returns," (3), 643-661.
Srinivasan, Venkat and Yong H. Kim. "Credit Granting: A Comparative Analysis Of Classification Procedures," (3), 665-681.
Mayers, David and Clifford W. Smith, Jr. "Death And Taxes: The Market For Flower Bonds," (3), 685-698.
Smith, Richard L. "The Choice Of Issuance Procedure And The Cost Of Competitive And Negotiated Underwriting: An Examination Of The Impact Of Rule 50," (3), 703-720.
Grauer, Robert R. and Nils H. Hakansson. "Gains From International Diversification: 1968-85 Returns On Portfolios Of Stocks And Bonds," (3), 721-739.
Balcer, Yves and Kenneth L. Judd. "Effects Of Capital Gains Taxation On Life-Cycle Investment And Portfolio Management," (3), 743-758.
Copeland, Thomas E. and Daniel Friedman. "The Effect Of Sequential Information Arrival On Asset Prices: An Experimental Study," (3), 763-797.
Franke, Gunter. "Costless Signalling In Financial Markets," (4), 809-822.
Agrawal, Anup and Gershon N. Mandelker. "Managerial Incentives And Corporate Investment And Financing Decisions," (4), 823-838.
Blazenko, George W. "Managerial Preference, Asymmetric Information, And Financial Structure," (4), 839-862.
Smith, Janet Kiholm. "Trade Credit And Informational Asymmetry," (4), 863-872.
Huberman, Gur and Shmuel Kandel. "Mean-Variance Spanning," (4), 873-888.
Ofer, Aharon R. and Daniel R. Siegel. "Corporate Financial Policy, Information, And Market Expectations: An Empirical Investigation Of Dividends," (4), 889-911.
Lakonishok, Josef and Baruch Lev. "Stock Splits And Stock Dividends: Why, Who, And When," (4), 913-932.
Tehranian, Hassan, Nickolaos G. Travlos and James F. Waegelein. "The Effect Of Long-Term Performance Plans On Corporate Sell-Off-Induced Abnormal Returns," (4), 933-942.
Travlos, Nickolaos G. "Corporate Takeover Bids, Methods Of Payment, And Bidding Firms' Stock Returns," (4), 943-963.
Bhagat, Sanjai, James A. Brickley and Uri Loewenstein. "The Pricing Effects Of Interfirm Cash Tender Offers," (4), 965-986.
Franks, Julian R. and Stewart D. Hodges. "Lease Valuation When Taxable Earnings Are A Scarce Resource," (4), 987-1005.
Kamara, Avraham and Andrew F. Siegel. "Optimal Hedging In Futures Markets With Multiple Delivery Specifications," (4), 1007-1021.
Morgan, George Emir and Stephen D. Smith. "Maturity Intermediation And Intertemporal Lending Policies Of Financial Intermediaries," (4), 1023-1034.
Hasbrouck, Joel and Thomas S. Y. Ho. "Order Arrival, Quote Behavior, And The Return-Generating Process," (4), 1035-1048.
Bosshardt, Donald I. "A Model Of Intertemporal Discount Rates In The Presence Of Real And Inflationary Autocorrelations," (4), 1049-1070.
Carr, Peter. "A Note On The Pricing Of Commodity-Linked Bonds," (4), 1071-1076.
Ferris, Stephen P. and Don M. Chance. "The Effect Of 12b-1 Plans On Mutual Fund Expense Ratios: A Note," (4), 1077-1082.
Narayanan, M. P. "On The Resolution Of Agency Problems By Complex Financial Instruments: A Comment," (4), 1083-1090.
Haugen, Robert A. and Lemma W. Senbet. "On The Resolution Of Agency Problems By Complex Financial Instruments: A Reply," (4), 1091-1095.
Darrough, Masako N. "Managerial Incentives For Short-Term Results: A Comment," (4), 1097-1102.
Narayanan, M. P. "Managerial Incentives For Short-Term Results: A Reply," (4), 1103-1104.
Schaefer, Stephen M. and Eduardo S. Schwartz. "Time-Dependent Variance And The Pricing Of Bond Options," (5), 1113-1128.
Heath, David C. and Robert A. Jarrow. "Arbitrage, Continuous Trading, And Margin Requirements," (5), 1129-1142.
Dammon, Robert M. and Richard C. Green. "Tax Arbitrage And The Existence Of Equilibrium Prices For Financial Assets," (5), 1143-1166.
MacMinn, Richard D. "Forward Markets, Stock Markets, And The Theory Of The Firm," (5), 1167-1185.
Bailey, Warren. "An Empirical Investigation Of The Market For COMEX Gold Futures Options," (5), 1187-1194.
Cho, D. Chinhyung and William M. Taylor. "The Seasonal Stability Of The Factor Structure Of Stock Returns," (5), 1195-1211.
Gultekin, Mustafa N. and N. Bulent Gultekin. "Stock Return Anomalies And The Tests Of The APT," (5), 1213-1224.
Brennan, Michael and Alan Kraus. "Efficient Financing Under Asymmetric Information," (5), 1225-1243.
Bradford, William D. "The Issue Decision Of Manager-Owners Under Information Asymmetry," (5), 1245-1260.
Sicherman, Neil W. and Richard H. Pettway. "Acquisition Of Divested Assets And Shareholders' Wealth," (5), 1261-1273.
Mauer, David C. and Wilbur G. Lewellen. "Debt Management Under Corporate And Personal Taxation," (5), 1275-1291.
Glosten, Lawrence R. "Components Of The Bid-Ask Spread And The Statistical Properties Of Transactions Prices," (5), 1293-1307.
Kawaller, Ira G., Paul D. Koch and Timothy W. Koch. "The Temporal Price Relationship Between S&P 500 Futures And The S&P 500 Index," (5), 1309-1329.
Hamilton, James L. "Off-Board Trading Of NYSE-Listed Stocks: The Effects Of Deregulation And The National Market System," (5), 1331-1345.
Lamoureux, Christopher G. and Percy Poon. "The Market Reaction To Stock Splits," (5), 1347-1370.
Nielsen, Lars Tyge. "Portfolio Selection In The Mean-Variance Model: A Note," (5), 1371-1376.
Smith, Stephen D., Deborah Wright Gregory and Kathleen A. Weiss. "A Note On Quantity Versus Price Risk And The Theory Of Financial Intermediation," (5), 1377-1383.
Kolb, Robert W. and Ricardo J. Rodriguez. "Friday The Thirteenth: 'Part VII'--A Note," (5), 1385-1387.
Niemi, Albert W., Jr. "Institutional Contributions To The Leading Finance Journals, 1975 Through 1986: A Note," (5), 1389-1397.

Latham, Mark. "The Arbitrage Pricing Theory And Supershares," (2), 263-282.

Froot, Kenneth A. "New Hope For The Expectations Hypothesis Of The Term Structure Of Interest Rates," (2), 283-306.

Giovannini, Alberto and Philippe Jorion. "The Time Variation Of Risk And Return In The Foreign Exchange And Stock Markets," (2), 307-326.

Bolster, Paul J., Lawrence B. Lindsey and Andrew Mitrusi. "Tax-Induced Trading: The Effect Of The 1986 Tax Reform Act On Stock Market Activity," (2), 327-344.

Titman, Sheridan and Walter Torous. "Valuing Commercial Mortgages: An Empirical Investigation Of The Contingent-Claims Approach To Pricing Risky Debt," (2), 345-374.

Schwartz, Eduardo S. and Walter N. Torous. "Prepayment And The Valuation Of Mortgage-Backed Securities," (2), 375-392.

Grinblatt, Mark and Chuan Yang Hwang. "Signalling And The Pricing Of New Issues," (2), 393-420.

Welch, Ivo. "Seasoned Offerings, Imitation Costs, And The Underpricing Of Initial Public Offerings," (2), 421-450.

Cornett, Marcia Million and Nickolaos G. Travlos. "Information Effects Associated With Debt-For-Equity And Equity-For-Debt Exchange Offers," (2), 451-468.

Gale, Ian and Joseph E. Stiglitz. "The Information Content Of Initial Public Offerings," (2), 469-478.

Amihud, Yakov and Haim Mendelson. "The Effects Of Beta, Bid-Ask Spread, Residual Risk, And Size On Stock Returns," (2), 479-486.

Conrad, Jennifer. "The Price Effect Of Option Introduction," (2), 487-498.

Chari, V. V. and Ravi Jagannathan. "Adverse Selection In A Model Of Real Estate Lending," (2), 499-508.

Pruitt, Stephen W. and K. C. John Wei. "Institutional Ownership And Changes In The S&P 500," (2), 509-514.

Omberg, Edward. "The Expected Utility Of The Doubling Strategy," (2), 515-524.

Maksimovic, Vojislav, Gordon Sick and Josef Zechner. "Forward Markets, Stock Markets, And The Theory Of The Firm: Comment," (2), 525-528.

Ross, Stephen A. "Presidential Address: Institutional Markets, Financial Marketing, And Financial Innovation," (3), 541-556.

Kraus, Alan and Maxwell Smith. "Market Created Risk," (3), 557-570.

Kishimoto, Naoki. "Pricing Contingent Claims Under Interest Rate And Asset Price Risk," (3), 571-590.

Bliss, Robert R., Jr. and Ehud I. Ronn. "Arbitrage-Based Estimation Of Nonstationary Shifts In The Term Structure Of Interest Rates," (3), 591-610.

Kaplan, Steven. "Management Buyouts: Evidence On Taxes As A Source Of Value," (3), 611-632.

Fishman, Michael J. and Kathleen M. Hagerty. "Disclosure Decisions By Firms And The Competition For Price Efficiency," (3), 633-646.

Bower, Nancy L. "Firm Value And The Choice Of Offering Method In Initial Public Offerings," (3), 647-662.

Errunza, Vihang R. and Arthur F. Moreau. "Debt-For-Equity Swaps Under A Rational Expectations Equilibrium," (3), 663-680.

DeLong, J. Bradford, Andrei Shleifer, Lawrence H. Summers and Robert J. Waldmann. "The Size And Incidence Of The Losses From Noise Trading," (3), 681-696.

Hietala, Pekka T. "Asset Pricing In Partially Segmented Markets: Evidence From The Finnish Market," (3), 697-718.

Shiller, Robert J. "Comovements In Stock Prices And Comovements In Dividends," (3), 719-730.

Lang, William W. and Leonard I. Nakamura. "Information Losses In A Dynamic Model Of Credit," (3), 731-746.

Franks, Julian R. and Walter N. Torous. "An Empirical Investigation Of U.S. Firms In Reorganization," (3), 747-770.

Lehn, Kenneth and Annette Poulsen. "Free Cash Flow And Stockholder Gains In Going Private Transactions," (3), 771-788.

Feldman, David. "The Term Structure Of Interest Rates In A Partially Observable Economy," (3), 789-812.

Blume, Marshall E., A. Craig MacKinlay and Bruce Terker. "Order Imbalances And Stock Price Movements On October 19 And 20, 1987," (4), 827-848.

Gultekin, Mustafa N., N. Bulent Gultekin and Alessandro Penati. "Capital Controls And International Capital Market Segmentation: The Evidence From The Japanese And American Stock Markets," (4), 849-870.

Longstaff, Francis A. "Temporal Aggregation And The Continuous-Time Capital Asset Pricing Model," (4), 871-888.

Affleck-Graves, John and Bill McDonald. "Nonnormalities And Tests Of Asset Pricing Theories," (4), 889-908.

Altman, Edward I. "Measuring Corporate Bond Mortality And Performance," (4), 909-922.

Asquith, Paul, David W. Mullins, Jr. and Eric D. Wolff. "Original Issue High Yield Bonds: Aging Analyses Of Defaults, Exchanges, And Calls," (4), 923-952.

Hite, Gailen L. and Michael R. Vetsuypens. "Management Buyouts Of Divisions And Shareholder Wealth," (4), 953-970.

Hirschey, Mark and Janis K. Zaima. "Insider Trading, Ownership Structure, And The Market Assessment Of Corporate Sell-Offs," (4), 971-980.

Parsons, John E. "Estimating The Strategic Value Of Long-Term Forward Purchase Contracts Using Auction Models," (4), 981-1010.

Stein, Jeremy. "Overreactions In The Options Market," (4), 1011-1024.

Errunza, Vihang and Etienne Losq. "Capital Flow Controls, International Asset Pricing, And Investors' Welfare: A Multi-Country Framework," (4), 1025-1038.

Malitz, Ileen B. "A Re-Examination Of The Wealth Expropriation Hypothesis: The Case Of Captive Finance Subsidiaries," (4), 1039-1048.

Johnson, James M., Robert A. Pari and Leonard Rosenthal. "The Impact Of In-Substance Defeasance On Bondholder And Shareholder Wealth," (4), 1049-1058.

Loderer, Claudio P. and Dennis P. Sheehan. "Corporate Bankruptcy And Managers' Self-Serving Behavior," (4), 1059-1076;.

Davidson, Wallace N., III, Dipa Dutia and Louis Cheng. "A Re-Examination Of The Market Reaction To Failed Mergers," (4), 1077-1084.

Ma, Christopher K., Ramesh P. Rao and Richard L. Peterson. "The Resiliency Of The High-Yield Bond Market: The LTV Default," (4), 1085-1098.

Barry, Christopher B. "Initial Public Offering Underpricing: The Issuer's View: Comment," (4), 1099-1104.

Schwert, G. William. "Why Does Stock Market Volatility Change Over Time?," (5), 1115-1154.

Harris, Lawrence. "S&P 500 Cash Stock Price Volatilities," (5), 1155-1176.

Breen, William, Lawrence R. Glosten and Ravi Jagannathan. "Economic Significance Of Predictable Variations In Stock Index Returns," (5), 1177-1190.

Ferson, Wayne E. "Changes In Expected Security Returns, Risk, And The Level Of Interest Rates," (5), 1191-1218.

Lamoureux, Christopher G. and Gary C. Sanger. "Firm Size And Turn-Of-The-Year Effects In The OTC/NASDAQ Market," (5), 1219-1246.

Brown, Stephen J. "The Number Of Factors In Security Returns," (5), 1247-1262.

Jarrow, Robert A. and Maureen O'Hara. "Primes And Scores: An Essay On Market Imperfections," (5), 1263-1288.

Figlewski, Stephen. "Options Arbitrage In Imperfect Markets," (5), 1289-1312.

Acharya, Sankarshan and Jean-Francois Dreyfus. "Optimal Bank Reorganization Policies And The Pricing Of Federal Deposit Insurance," (5), 1313-1334.

Froot, Kenneth A., David S. Scharfstein and Jeremy C. Stein. "LDC Debt: Forgiveness, Indexation, And Investment Incentives," (5), 1335-1350.

Sarig, Oded and Arthur Warga. "Some Empirical Estimates Of The Risk Structure Of Interest Rates," (5), 1351-1360.

Sheikh, Aamir M. "Stock Splits, Volatility Increases, And Implied Volatilities," (5), 1361-1372.

Shimko, David C. "The Equilibrium Valuation Of Risky Discrete Cash Flows In Continuous Time," (5), 1373-1384.

Zarowin, Paul. "Does The Stock Market Overreact To Corporate Earnings Information?," (5), 1385-1400.

Mais, Eric L., William T. Moore and Ronald C. Rogers. "A Re-Examination Of Shareholder Wealth Effects Of Calls Of Convertible Preferred Stock," (5), 1401-1410.

Ahn, Chang Mo. "The Effect Of Temporal Risk Aversion On Optimal Consumption, The Equity Premium, And The Equilibrium Interest Rate," (5), 1411-1420.

Korkie, Bob. "Corrections For Trading Frictions In Multivariate Returns," (5), 1421-1434.

Aneja, Yash P., Ramesh Chandra and Erdal Gunay. "A Portfolio Approach To Estimating The Average Correlation Coefficient For The Constant Correlation Model," (5), 1435-1438.

Journal of Finance
Volume 45, 1990

Hsieh, David A. and Merton H. Miller. "Margin Regulation And Stock Market Volatility," (1), 3-30.

Morck, Randall, Andrei Shleifer and Robert W. Vishny. "Do Managerial Objectives Drive Bad Acquisitions?," (1), 31-48.

Gorton, Gary and George Pennacchi. "Financial Intermediaries And Liquidity Creation," (1), 49-72.

Seppi, Duane J. "Equilibrium Block Trading And Asymmetric Information," (1), 73-94.

Cornett, Marcia Million and Hassan Tehranian. "An Examination Of The Impact Of The Garn-St. Germain Depository Institutions Act Of 1982 On Commercial Banks And Savings And Loans," (1), 95-112.

Kane, Edward J. and Haluk Unal. "Modeling Structural And Temporal Variation In The Market's Valuation Of Banking Firms," (1), 113-136.

Berkovitch, Elazar and Naveen Khanna. "How Target Shareholders Benefit From Value-Reducing Defensive Strategies In Takeovers," (1), 137-156.

Abuaf, Niso and Philippe Jorion. "Purchasing Power Parity In The Long Run," (1), 157-174.

Kocherlakota, Narayana R. "Disentangling The Coefficient Of Relative Risk Aversion From The Elasticity Of Intertemporal Substitution: An Irrelevance Result," (1), 175-190.

Stephan, Jens A. and Robert E. Whaley. "Intraday Price Changes And Trading Volume Relations In The Stock And Stock Option Markets," (1), 191-220.

Lamoureux, Christopher G. and William D. Lastrapes. "Heteroskedasticity In Stock Return Data: Volume Versus GARCH Effects," (1), 221-230.

Lakonishok, Josef and Edwin Maberly. "The Weekend Effect: Trading Patterns Of Individual And Institutional Investors," (1), 231-244.

Mishkin, Frederic S. "Can Futures Market Data Be Used To Understand The Behavior Of Real Interest Rates?," (1), 245-258.

Ritchken, Peter and Kickie Boenawan. "On Arbitrage-Free Pricing Of Interest Rate Contingent Claims," (1), 259-264.

Chance, Don M. "Default Risk And The Duration Of Zero Coupon Bonds," (1), 265-274.

Allen, David S., Robert E. Lamy and G. Rodney Thompson. "The Shelf Registration Of Debt And Self Selection Bias," (1), 275-288.

Slovin, Myron B., Marie E. Sushka and John A. Polonchek. "Corporate Sale-And-Leasebacks And Shareholder Wealth," (1), 289-300.

Chung, Kee H. and Raymond A. K. Cox. "Patterns Of Productivity In The Finance Literature: A Study Of The Bibliometric Distributions," (1), 301-310.

Harris, Milton and Artur Raviv. "Capital Structure And The Informational Role Of Debt," (2), 321-350.

Seward, James K. "Corporate Financial Policy And The Theory Of Financial Intermediation," (2), 351-378.

De Long, J. Bradford, Andrei Shleifer, Lawrence H. Summers and Robert J. Waldmann. "Positive Feedback Investment Strategies And Destabilizing Rational Speculation," (2), 379-396.

Ferson, Wayne E. "Are The Latent Variables In Time-Varying Expected Returns Compensation For Consumption Risk?," (2), 397-430.

Clarkson, Peter M. and Rex Thompson. "Empirical Estimates Of Beta When Investors Face Estimation Risk," (2), 431-454.

Lakonishok, Josef and Theo Vermaelen. "Anomalous Price Behavior Around Repurchase Tender Offers," (2), 455-478.

Kaul, Gautam and H. Nejat Seyhun. "Relative Price Variability, Real Shocks, And The Stock Market," (2), 479-496.

Cumby, Robert E. and Jack D. Glen. "Evaluating The Performance Of International Mutual Funds," (2), 497-522.

Bonser-Neal, Catherine, Greggory Brauer, Robert Neal and Simon Wheatley. "International Investment Restrictions And Closed-End Country Fund Prices," (2), 523-548.

Triantis, Alexander J. and James E. Hodder. "Valuing Flexibility As A Complex Option," (2), 549-566.

Simon, David P. "Expectations And The Treasury Bill-Federal Funds Rate Spread Over Recent Monetary Policy Regimes," (2), 567-578.

Harris, Lawrence. "Statistical Properties Of The Roll Serial Covariance Bid/Ask Spread Estimator," (2), 579-590.

Lockwood, Larry J. and Scott C. Linn. "An Examination Of Stock Market Return Volatility During Overnight And Intraday Periods, 1964-1989," (2), 591-602.

Amihud, Yakov, Baruch Lev and Nickolaos G. Travlos. "Corporate Control And The Choice Of Investment Financing: The Case Of Corporate Acquisitions," (2), 603-616.

DeFusco, Richard A., Robert R. Johnson. "The Effect Of Executive Stock Option Plans On Stockholders And Bondholders," (2), 617-628.

Elton, Edwin J., Martin J. Gruber and Roni Michaely. "The Structure Of Spot Rates And Immunization," (2), 629-642.

Saunders, Anthony, Elizabeth Strock and Nickolaos G. Travlos. "Ownership Structure, Deregulation, And Bank Risk Taking," (2), 643-654.

Boyle, Glenn W. "International Interest Rates, Exchange Rates, And The Stochastic Structure Of Supply," (2), 655-672.

Bick, Avi. "On Viable Diffusion Price Processes Of The Market Portfolio," (2), 673-690.

Krueger, Thomas M. and William F. Kennedy. "An Examination Of The Super Bowl Stock Market Predictor," (2), 691-698.

Brennan, Michael J. "Presidential Address: Latent Assets," (3), 709-730.

Barth, James R., Philip F. Bartholomew and Michael G. Bradley. "Determinants Of Thrift Institution Resolution Costs," (3), 731-754.

Kane, Edward J. "Principal-Agent Problems In S&L Salvage," (3), 755-764.

Berkovitch, Elazar and E. Han Kim. "Financial Contracting And Leverage Induced Over- And Under-Investment Incentives," (3), 765-794.

Kim, Moshe and Vojislav Maksimovic. "Debt And Input Misallocation," (3), 795-816.

Stulz, Rene M., Ralph A. Walkling and Moon H. Song. "The Distribution Of Target Ownership And The Division Of Gains In Successful Takeovers," (3), 817-834.

John, Kose and BaniKanta Mishra. "Information Content Of Insider Trading Around Corporate Announcements: The Case Of Capital Expenditures," (3), 835-856.

McNichols, Maureen and Ajay David. "Stock Dividends, Stock Splits and Signaling," (3), 857-880.

Jegadeesh, Narasimhan. "Evidence Of Predictable Behavior Of Security Returns," (3), 881-898.

Black, Fischer. "Equilibrium Exchange Rate Hedging," (3), 899-908.

Jordan, James V. and George Emir Morgan. "Default Risk In Futures Markets: The Customer-Broker Relationship," (3), 909-934.

Longstaff, Francis A. "Pricing Options With Extendible Maturities: Analysis And Applications," (3), 935-958.

Gibson, Rajna and Eduardo S. Schwartz. "Stochastic Convenience Yield And The Pricing Of Oil Contingent Claims," (3), 959-976.

Brennan, Michael J. and Anjan V. Thakor. "Shareholder Preferences And Dividend Policy," (4), 993-1019.

Lucas, Deborah J. and Robert J. McDonald. "Equity Issues And Stock Price Dynamics," (4), 1020-1043.

Carter, Richard and Steven Manaster. "Initial Public Offerings And Underwriter Reputation," (4), 1045-1067.

Sharpe, Steven A. "Asymmetric Information, Bank Lending, And Implicit Contracts: A Stylized Model Of Customer Relationships," (4), 1069-1087.

Fama, Eugene F. "Stock Returns, Expected Returns, And Real Activity," (4), 1089-1108.

Balvers, Ronald J., Thomas F. Cosimano and Bill McDonald. "Predicting Stock Returns In An Efficient Market," (4), 1109-1128.

Schwert, G. William and Paul J. Seguin. "Heteroskedasticity In Stock Returns," (4), 1129-1155.

Vijh, Anand M. "Liquidity Of The CBOE Equity Options," (4), 1157-1179.

Lauterbach, Beni and Paul Schultz. "Pricing Warrants: An Empirical Study Of The Black-Scholes Model And Its Alternatives," (4), 1181-1209.

Lewis, Karen K. "The Behavior Of Eurocurrency Returns Across Different Holding Periods And Monetary Regimes," (4), 1211-1236.

Schwert, G. William. "Stock Returns And Real Activity: A Century Of Evidence," (4), 1237-1257.

Ogden, Joseph P. "Turn-Of-Month Evaluations Of Liquid Profits And Stock Returns: A Common Explanation For The Monthly And January Effects," (4), 1259-1272.

Lin, Ji-Chai and John S. Howe. "Insider Trading In The OTC Market," (4), 1273-1284.

Conroy, Robert M., Robert S. Harris and Bruce A. Benet. "The Effects Of Stock Splits On Bid-Ask Spreads," (4), 1285-1295.

Becker, Kent G., Joseph E. Finnerty and Manoj Gupta. "The Intertemporal Relation Between The U.S. And Japanese Stock Markets," (4), 1297-1306.

Longstaff, Francis A. "Time Varying Term Premia And Traditional Hypotheses About The Term Structure," (4), 1307-1314.

Briys, Eric, Michel Crouhy and Harris Schlesinger. "Optimal Hedging Under Intertemporally Dependent Preferences," (4), 1315-1324.

Agrawal, Anup and Nandu J. Nagarajan. "Corporate Capital Structure, Agency Costs, And Ownership Control: The Case Of All-Equity Firms," (4), 1325-1331.

Chang, Carolyn W. and Jack S. K. Chang. "Forward And Futures Prices: Evidence From The Foreign Exchange Markets," (4), 1333-1336.

Le Compte, Richard L. B. and Stephen D. Smith. "Changes In The Cost Of Intermediation: The Case Of Savings And Loans," (4),1337-1346.

Seyhun, H. Nejat. "Overreaction Or Fundamentals: Some Lessons From Insiders' Response To The Market Crash Of 1987," (5), 1363-1388.

Muscarella, Chris J. and Michael R. Vetsuypens. "Efficiency And Organizational Structure: A Study Of Reverse LBOs," (5), 1389-1414.

DeAngelo, Harry and Linda DeAngelo. "Dividend Policy And Financial Distress: An Empirical Investigation Of Troubled NYSE Firms," (5), 1415-1432.

Denis, David J. "Defensive Changes In Corporate Payout Policy: Share Repurchases And Special Dividends," (5), 1433-1456.

Eberhart, Allan C., William T. Moore and Rodney L. Roenfeldt. "Security Pricing And Deviations From The Absolute Priority Rule In Bankruptcy Proceedings," (5), 1457-1470.

MacKie-Mason, Jeffrey K. "Do Taxes Affect Corporate Financing Decisions?," (5), 1471-1494.

Hodder, James E. and Lemma W. Senbet. "International Capital Structure Equilibrium," (5), 1495-1516.

Boehmer, Ekkehart and William L. Megginson. "Determinants Of Secondary Market Prices For Developing Country Syndicated Loans," (5), 1517-1540.

Shukla, Ravi and Charles Trzcinka. "Sequential Tests Of The Arbitrage Pricing Theory: A Comparison Of Principal Components And Maximum Likelihood Factors," (5), 1541-1564.

Hemler, Michael L. "The Quality Delivery Option In Treasury Bond Futures Contracts," (5), 1565-1586.

O'Hara, Maureen and Wayne Shaw. "Deposit Insurance And Wealth Effects: The Value Of Being Too Big To Fail," (5), 1587-1600.

Solnik, Bruno. "The Distribution Of Daily Stock Returns And Settlement Procedures: The Paris Bourse," (5), 1601-1610.

Ariel, Robert. "High Cost Returns Before Holidays: Existence And Evidence On Possible Causes," (5), 1611-1626.

McWilliams, Victoria B. "Managerial Share Ownership And The Stock Price Effects Of Antitakeover Amendment Proposals," (5), 1627-1640.

Maksimovic, Vojislav. "Product Market Imperfections And Loan Commitments," (5), 1641-1654.

Gendron, Michel and Christian Genest. "Performance Measurement Under Asymmetric Information And Investment Constraints," (5), 1655-1662.

Black, Harold A., M. Andrew Fields and Robert L. Schweitzer. "Changes In Interstate Banking Laws: The Impact On Shareholder Wealth," (5), 1663-1672.

Campbell, Tim S. and William A. Kracaw. "Corporate Risk Management And The Incentive Effects Of Debt," (5), 1673-1686.

Cunnngham, Donald F. and Charles A. Capone, Jr. "The Relative Termination Experience Of Adjustable To Fixed-Rate Mortgages," (5), 1687-1704.

Campbell, Tim S. and William A. Kracaw. "Bank Funding Risks, Risk Aversion, And The Choice Of Futures Hedging Instrument: Comment," (5), 1705-1708.

Moore, Norman H. and Stephen W. Pruitt. "Excess Asset Reversions And Shareholder Wealth: Comment," (5), 1709-1714.

Journal of Finance
Volume 46, 1991

Ritter, Jay R. "The Long Run Performance Of Initial Public Offerings," (1), 3-28.

Cornell, Bradford and Kevin Green. "The Investment Performance Of Low-Grade Bond Funds," (1), 29-48.

Blume, Marshall E., Donald B. Keim and Sandeep A. Patel. "Returns And Volatility Of Low-Grade Bonds, 1977-1989," (1), 49-74.

Lee, Charles, Andrei Shleifer and Richard Thaler. "Investor Sentiment And The Closed-End Fund Puzzle," (1), 75-110.

Harvey, Campbell R. "The World Price Of Covariance Risk," (1), 111-158.

Neumark, David, P. A. Tinsley and Suzanne Tosini. "After-Hours Stock Prices And Post-Crash Hangovers," (1), 159-178.

Hasbrouck, Joel. "Measuring The Information Content Of Stock Trades," (1), 179-208.

Cochrane, John H. "Production-Based Asset Pricing And The Link Between Stock Returns And Economic Fluctuations," (1), 209-238.

McQueen, Grant and Steven Thorley. "Are Stock Returns Predictable? A Test Using Markov Chains," (1), 239-264.

Copeland, Thomas E. and Daniel Friedman. "Partial Revelation Of Information In Experimental Asset Markets," (1), 265-296.

Harris, Milton and Artur Raviv. "The Theory Of Capital Structure," (1), 297-356.

DeAngelo, Harry. "Payout Policy And Tax Deferral," (1), 357-368.

Badrinath, S. G. and Wilbur G. Lewellen. "Evidence On Tax-Motivated Securities Trading Behavior," (1), 369-382.

Ang, James S., David W. Blackwell and William L. Megginson. "The Effect Of Taxes On The Relative Valuation Of Dividends And Capital Gains: Evidence From Dual-Class British Investment Trusts," (1), 383-399.

Jaffe, Jeffrey F. "Taxes And The Capital Structure Of Partnerships, REIT's, And Related Entities," (1), 401-408.

Servaes, Henri. "Tobin's Q And The Gains From Takeovers," (1), 409-420.

Dubofsky, David A. "Volatility Increases Subsequent To NYSE And AMEX Stock Splits," (1), 421-432.

Jang, Hasung and P. C. Venkatesh. "Consistency Between Predicted And Actual Bid-Ask Quote Revisions," (1), 433-446.

Ikeda, Shinsuke. "Arbitrage Asset Pricing Under Exchange Risk," (1), 447-456.

JOURNAL OF FINANCIAL AND QUANTITATIVE ANALYSIS

Journal of Financial and Quantitative Analysis
Volume 1, 1966

Archer, Stephen H. "A Model For The Determination Of Firm Cash Balances," (1), 1-10.
Woods, Donald H. and Eugene F. Brigham. "Stockholder Distribution Decisions: Share Repurchases Or Dividends," (1), 15-25.
Michaelsen, Jacob B. "The Determinants Of Corporate Dividend Policies," (1), 29-29a.
Martin, Preston. "Affluence And High Household Liquidity: Problems And Opportunities," (1), 30-52.
Mitchell, Howard R. "Implications Of Balance Of Payments Deficits For Bank Liquidity," (1), 56-75.
Widicus, Wilbur W., Jr. "A Quantitative Analysis Of The Small Business Investment Company Program," (1), 81-110.
Robichek, Alexander A. and Stewart C. Myers. "Problems In The Theory Of Optimal Capital Structure," (2), 1-35.
Schink, William A. and John S. Y. Chiu. "A Simulation Study Of Effects Of Multicollinearity And Autocorrelation On Estimates Of Parameters," (2), 36-67.
Van Horne, James. "A Linear-Programming Approach To Evaluating Restrictions Under A Bond Indenture Or Loan Agreement," (2), 68-83.
Scott, Robert Haney. "A Conditional Theory Of Banking Enterprise," (2), 84-98.
Haydon, Randall B. and John H. Wicks. "A Model Of Commercial Banking Earning Assets Selection," (2), 99-114.
Weingartner, H. Martin. "The Generalized Rate Of Return," (3), 1-29.
Cohen, Jacob. "Federal Reserve Margin Requirements And The Stock Market," (3), 30-54.
Mullick, Satinder K. "Optimal Design Of A Stochastic System With Dominating Fixed Costs," (3), 55-74.
Kaufman, George G. and Cynthia M. Latta. "The Demand For Money: Preliminary Evidence From Industrial Countries," (3), 75-89.
Dince, Robert R. "Portfolio Income: A Test Of A Formula Plan," (3), 90-107.
Benavie, A. "Monetary-Fiscal Policy And The Debt Burden," (3), 108-123.
Bierman, Harold. "The Bond Issue Size Decision," (4), 1-14.
Cohen, Kalman J. and Samuel Richardson Reid. "The Benefits And Costs Of Bank Mergers," (4), 15-57.
Jolivet, Vincent M. "The Control Of Savings And Loan Associations," (4), 58-71.
Haley, Charles W. "A Note On The Cost Of Debt," (4), 72-93.

Journal of Financial and Quantitative Analysis
Volume 2, 1967

Samuelson, Paul A. "General Proof That Diversification Pays," (1),1-13.
Diamond, James J. "Earnings Distribution And The Evaluation Of Shares: Some Recent Evidence," (1), 14-29.
Meier, Robert C. "The Application Of Optimum-Seeking Techniques To Simulation Studies: A Preliminary Evaluation," (1), 30-51.
Murphy, Neil B. "A Test Of The Deposit Relationship Hypothesis," (1), 51-59.
Nimrod, Vance L. and Richard S. Bower. "Commodities And Computers," (1), 58-73.
Sharpe, William F. "Portfolio Analysis," (2), 76-84.
Wallingford, Buckner A. "A Survey And Comparison Of Portfolio Selection Models," (2), 85-106.
Samuelson, Paul A. "Efficient Portfolio Selection For Pareto-Levy Investments," (2), 107-122.
Renshaw, Edward F. "Portfolio Balance Models In Perspective: Some Generalizations That Can Be Derived From The Two-Asset Case," (2), 123-149.
Hofflander, Alfred E., Jr. and Richard M. Duvall. "The Ruin Problem In Multiple Line Insurance: A Simplified Model," (2), 150-165.
Michaelsen, Jacob B. and Robert C. Goshay. "Portfolio Selection Financial Intermediaries: A New Approach," (2), 166-199.
Mumey, Glen A. "An Amendment To The Note On The Cost Of Debt," (2), 200-201.
Carleton, Willard T. and Eugene M. Lerner. "Measuring Corporate Profit Opportunities," (3), 225-240.
West, Richard R. "Determinants Of Underwriters' Spreads On Tax Exempt Bond Issues," (3), 241-263.
Teichroew, Daniel, William Lesso, Kevin Rice and Gordon Wright. "Optimizing Models Of After-Tax Earnings Incorporating Depletion Allowance," (3), 265-297.
Scott, Robert Haney. "Some Additional Estimates Of The Liquidity Preference Function For The United States," (3), 299-312.
Chen, Houng-Yhi. "Valuation Under Uncertainty," (3), 313-325.
Bierman, Harold, Jr. "The Valuation Of Stock Options," (3), 327-334.
Byrne, R., A. Charnes, W. W. Cooper and K. Kortanek. "A Chance-Constrained Approach To Capital Budgeting With Portfolio Type Payback And Liquidity Constraints And Horizon Posture Controls," (4), 339-364.
Allerdice, F. B. and D. E. Farrar. "Factors That Affect Mutual Fund Growth," (4), 365-382.
Arzac, E. R. "The Dynamic Characteristics Of Chow's Model: A Simulation Study," (4), 383-397.
Greer, Carl C. "The Optimal Credit Acceptance Policy," (4), 399-415.
West, Richard R. "Homemade' Diversification Vs. Corporate Diversification," (4), 417-420.

Journal of Financial and Quantitative Analysis
Volume 3, 1968

Myers, Stewart C. "A Time-State-Preference Model Of Security Valuation," (1), 1-33.

Levy, Robert A. "Measurement Of Investment Performance," (1), 35-57.
Soldofsky, Robert M. and Roger Biderman. "Yield-Risk Measurements Of The Performance Of Common Stocks," (1), 59-74.
Baxter, Nevins D. "Marketability, Default Risk, And Yields On Money Market Instruments," (1), 75-85.
Murphy, Neil B. "A Cross-Section Analysis Of Demand Deposit Variability," (1), 87-95.
Wacht, Richard F. "Branch Banking And Risk," (1), 97-108.
Beckwith, R. E. "Continuous Financial Processes," (2), 113-133.
Mao, James C. T. and Roger L. Wright. "A Chance-Constrained Approach To Urban Renewal Decisions," (2), 135-150.
Bierman, Harold, Jr. "Using Investment Portfolios To Change Risk," (2), 151-156.
Jen, Frank C. and James E. Wert. "The Deferred Call Provision And Corporate Bond Yields," (2), 157-170.
Sloane, William R. and Arnold Reisman. "Stock Evaluation Theory: Classification, Reconciliation, And General Model," (2), 171-204.
Conley, Ronald W. "A Note On The Liquidity And Stabilization Effects Of Savings Deposits," (2), 205-213.
Mendelson, Morris. "Determinants Of Underwriters' Spreads On Tax-Exempt Bond Issues: Comment," (2), 215-224.
Boness, A. James. "The Valuation Of Stock Options: Comment," (2), 225-226.
Bierman, Harold, Jr. "The Valuation Of Stock Options: Reply," (2), 227-228.
Smidt, Seymour. "A New Look At The Random Walk Hypothesis," (3), 235-261.
Seelenfreund, Alan, George G. C. Parker and James C. Van Horne. "Stock Price Behavior And Trading," (3), 263-281.
Mayor, Thomas H. "Short Trading Activities And The Price Of Equities: Some Simulation And Regression Results," (3), 283-298.
Zakon, Alan J. and James C. Pennypacker. "An Analysis Of The Advance-Decline Line As A Stock Market Indicator," (3), 299-314.
James, F. E., Jr. "Monthly Moving Averages--An Effective Investment Tool?," (3), 315-326.
Evans, John L. "The Random Walk Hypothesis, Portfolio Analysis And The Buy-And-Hold Criterion," (3), 327-342.
Hausman, W. H. and W. L. White. "Theory Of Option Strategy Under Risk Aversion," (3), 343-358.
Smith, Keith V. "Alternative Procedures For Revising Investment Portfolios," (4), 371-403.
Breen, William. "Homogeneous Risk Measures And The Construction Of Composite Assets," (4), 405-413.
Bierman, Harold, Jr. "Risk And The Addition Of Debt To The Capital Structure," (4), 415-426.
Lusztig, Peter and Bernhard Schwab. "A Note On The Application Of Linear Programming To Capital Budgeting," (4), 427-431.
Levy, Haim. "A Note On The Payback Method," (4), 433-443.
Vaughn, Donald E. and Hite Bennett. "Adjusting For Risk In The Capital Budget Of A Growth-Oriented Company," (4), 445-461.
Marshall, Wayne S. and Alan E. Young. "A Mathematical Model For Re-Acquisition Of Small Shareholdings," (4), 463-469.
Diwan, Romesh K. "Bias In The Measurement Of Technical Change," (4), 471-477.
Robichek, Alexander A. and Stewart C. Myers. "Valuation Under Uncertainty: Comment," (4), 479-483.

Journal of Financial and Quantitative Analysis
Volume 4, 1969

Borch, Karl. "Equilibrium, Optimum And Prejudices In Capital Markets," (1), 1-14.
McKean, John R. "A Note On Administered Prices With Fluctuating Demand," (1), 15-23.
Saunders, Robert J. "On The Interpretation Of Models Explaining Cross Section Differences Among Commercial Banks," (1), 25-35.
Mauer, Laurence Jay. "Commercial Bank Maturity Demand For United States Government Securities And The Determinants Of The Term Structure Of Interest Rates," (1), 37-52.
von Lanzenauer, Christoph Haehling. "A Model For Determining Optimal Profit Sharing Plans," (1), 53-63.
Hakansson, Nils H. "On The Dividend Capitalization Model Under Uncertainty," (1), 65-87.
Krainer, Robert E. "Liquidity Preference And Stock Market Speculation," (1), 89-97.
Bernhard, Richard H. "Mathematical Programming Models For Capital Budgeting -- A Survey, Generalization, And Critique," (2), 111-158.
Gonedes, Nicholas J. "A Test Of The Equivalent-Risk Class Hypothesis," (2), 159-177.
Young, William E. and Robert H. Trent. "Geometric Mean Approximations Of Individual Security And Portfolio Performance," (2), 179-199.
Pogue, Thomas F. and Robert M. Soldofsky. "What's In A Bond Rating?," (2), 201-228.
Breen, William. "An Exploratory Econometric Model Of Financial Markets," (3), 233-269.
Roll, Richard. "Bias In Fitting The Sharpe Model To Time Series Data," (3), 271-289.
Melnik, Arie and Alan Kraus. "Short-Run Interest Rate Cycles In The U. S.: 1954-1967," (3), 291-299.
Litzenberger, Robert H. and Charles P. Jones. "Adjusting For Risk In The Capital Budget Of A Growth-Oriented Company: Comment," (3), 301-304.
Ziemba, William T. "A Myopic Capital Budgeting Model," (3), 305-327.
Daellenbach, Hans G. and Stephen H. Archer. "The Optimal Bank Liquidity: A Multi-Period Stochastic Model," (3), 329-343.
Lintner, John. "The Aggregation Of Investor's Diverse Judgments And Preferences In Purely Competitive Security Markets," (4), 347-400.

Hakansson, Nils H. "Risk Disposition And The Separation Property In Portfolio Selection," (4), 401-416.
Bower, Richard S. and Ronald F. Wippern. "Risk-Return Measurement In Portfolio Selection And Performance Appraisal Models: Progress Report," (4), 417-447.
Smith, Keith V. and Dennis A. Tito. "Risk-Return Measures Of Ex Post Portfolio Performance," (4), 449-471.
Machol, Robert E. and Eugene M. Lerner. "Risk, Ruin And Investment Analysis," (4), 473-492.
Adler, Michael. "On The Risk-Return Trade-Off In The Valuation Of Assets," (4), 493-512.
Robichek, Alexander A. "Risk And The Value Of Securities," (4), 513-538.

Journal of Financial and Quantitative Analysis
Volume 5, 1970

Carlson, Robert S. "Aggregate Performance Of Mutual Funds, 1948-1967," (1), 1-32.
Tinsley, P. A. "Capital Structure, Precautionary Balances, And Valuation Of The Firm: The Problem Of Financial Risk," (1),33-62.
Levy, Haim and Giora Hanoch. "Relative Effectiveness Of Efficiency Criteria For Portfolio Selection," (1), 63-76.
Krouse, Clement G. "Portfolio Balancing Corporate Assets And Liabilities With Special Application To Insurance Management," (1), 77-104.
Whitmore, G. A. "Market Demand Curve For Common Stock And The Maximization Of Market Value," (1), 105-114.
West, Richard R. "Simulating Securities Markets Operations: Some Examples, Observations, And Comments," (1), 115-137.
Brown, Keith C. "Estimating Frequency Functions From Limited Data," (1), 139-148.
Hakansson, Nils H. "An Induced Theory Of The Firm Under Risk: The Pure Mutual Fund," (2), 155-178.
Gentry, James and John Pike. "An Empirical Study Of The Risk-Return Hypothesis Using Common Stock Portfolios Of Life Insurance Companies," (2), 179-185.
Edwards, Charles E. and James G. Hilton. "Some Comments On Short-Run Earnings Fluctuation Bias," (2), 187-201.
Fried, Joel. "Bank Portfolio Selection," (2), 203-227.
von Furstenberg, George M. "Interstate Differences In Mortgage Lending Risks: An Analysis Of The Causes," (2), 229-242.
Lockett, A. Geoffrey and Cyril Tomkins. "The Discount Rate Problem In Capital Rationing Situations: Comment," (2), 245-260.
Lusztig, Peter and Bernhard Schwab. "The Discount Rate Problem In Capital Rationing Situations: Reply," (2), 261-261.
Whitmore, G. A. "Diversification And The Reduction Of Dispersion: A Note," (2), 263-264.
Colin, J. W. and Richard J. Bayer. "Calculation Of Tax Effective Yields For Discount Instruments," (2), 265-273.
Boness, A. James and Frank C. Jen. "A Model Of Information Diffusion, Stock Market Behavior, And Equilibrium Price," (3), 279-296.
Haugen, Robert A. "Expected Growth, Required Return, And The Variability Of Stock Prices," (3), 297-307.
Stoll, Hans R. and Anthony J. Curley. "Small Business And The New Issues Market For Equities," (3), 309-322.
Lauch, Louis H. and Neil B. Murphy. "A Test Of The Impact Of Branching On Deposit Variability," (3), 323-327.
Theilman, Ward. "Commercial Bank Liability Management And Monetary Control," (3), 329-339.
Cohen, Bruce and Damodar Gujarati. "The Student's t Test In Multiple Regression Under Simple Collinearity," (3), 341-351.
Sharpe, William F. "Computer-Assisted Economics," (3), 353-366.
Smith, V. Kerry and Joseph J. Seneca. "A Further Note On The Cost Implications Of Fluctuating Demand," (3), 369-376.
Schwab, Bernard and Peter Lusztig. "A Note On Abandonment Value And Capital Budgeting," (3), 377-379.
Sethi, Suresh P. and Gerald L. Thompson. "Applications Of Mathematical Control Theory To Finance: Modeling Simple Dynamic Cash Balance Problems," (4), 381-394.
Litzenberger, Robert H. and Alan P. Budd. "Corporate Investment Criteria And The Valuation Of Risk Assets," (4), 395-419.
Mehta, Dileep. "Optimal Credit Policy Selection: A Dynamic Approach," (4), 421-444.
Chervany, Norman L. "A Simulation Analysis Of Causal Relationships Within The Cash Flow Process," (4), 445-467.
Bower, Richard S. and John M. Scheidell. "Operationalism In Finance And Economics," (4), 469-495.
Burns, Joseph M. "An Examination Of The Operating Efficiency Of Three Financial Intermediaries," (5), 541-558.
Murphy, Neil B. and Harry Weintrob. "Evaluating Liquidity Under Conditions Of Uncertainty In Mutual Savings Banks," (5), 559-568.
Van den Dool, Peter. "Some Observations On The Operations Of Foreign Banks In California," (5), 569-580.
Elton, Edwin J. and Martin J. Gruber. "Homogeneous Groups And The Testing Of Economic Hypotheses," (5), 581-602.
Altman, Edward I. and Robert A. Schwartz. "Common Stock Price Volatility Measures And Patterns," (5), 603-626.
Woods, Donald H. and Thomas A. Caverly. "Development Of A Linear Programming Model For The Analysis Of Merger/ Acquisition Situations," (5), 627-642.
Shapiro, David L. "Conglomerate Mergers And Optimal Investment Policy," (5), 643-656.
Mao, James C. T. "Models Of Capital Budgeting, E-V Vs. E-S," (5), 657-676.
Upson, Roger B. and Paul F. Jessup. "Risk-Return Relationships In Regional Securities," (5), 677-696.
Stitzel, Thomas E. "Investing In Intrastate Issues Of Common Stock," (5), 697-706.

Journal of Financial and Quantitative Analysis
Volume 6, 1971

Jean, William H. "The Extension Of Portfolio Analysis To Three Or More Parameters," (1), 505-515.

Hakansson, Nils H. "Capital Growth And The Mean-Variance Approach To Portfolio Selection," (1), 517-557.
Kalymon, Basil A. "Estimation Risk In The Portfolio Selection Model," (1), 559-582.
Handa, Jagdish. "An Empirical Study Of Financial Intermediation In Canada," (1), 583-600.
Fraser, Donald R. and Peter S. Rose. "More On Banking Structure And Performance: The Evidence From Texas," (1), 601-611.
Vernon, Jack R. "Separation Of Ownership And Control And Profit Rates, The Evidence from Banking: Comment," (1), 615-625.
Breen, William and Richard Jackson. "An Efficient Algorithm For Solving Large-Scale Portfolio Problems," (1), 627-637.
Levy, Haim and Marshall Sarnat. "A Note On Portfolio Selection And Investors' Wealth," (1), 639-642.
Peles, Yoram. "A Note On Risk And The Theory Of Asset Value," (1), 643-647.
Jean, William H. "Terminal Value Or Present Value In Capital Budgeting Programs," (1), 649-651.
Van Horne, James C. "A Note On Biases In Capital Budgeting Introduced By Inflation," (1), 653-658.
Sethi, Suresh P. "A Note On A Planning Horizon Model Of Cash Management," (1), 659-664.
Strangways, Raymond and Bruce Yandle, Jr. "Effect Of State Usury Laws On Housing Starts In 1966," (1), 665-669.
Litzenberger, R. H. and O. M. Joy. "Target Rates Of Return And Corporate Asset And Liability Structure Under Uncertainty," (2), 675-686.
McEnally, Richard W. "An Investigation Of The Extrapolative Determinants Of Short-Run Earnings Expectations," (2), 687-706.
Tuttle, Donald L. and William L. Wilbur. "A Multivariate Time-Series Investigation Of Annual Returns On Highest Grade Corporate Bonds," (2), 707-721.
Magen, S. D. "Cost Of Capital And Dividend Policies In Commercial Banks," (2), 733-746.
Klein, Michael A. and Neil B. Murphy. "The Pricing Of Bank Deposits: A Theoretical And Empirical Analysis," (2), 747-761.
Emery, John T. "Risk, Return, And The Morphology Of Commercial Banking," (2), 763-776.
Mokkelbost, Per B. "Unsystematic Risk Over Time," (2), 785-796.
Jennings, Edward H. "An Empirical Analysis Of Some Aspects Of Common Stock Diversification," (2), 797-813.
Jacob, Nancy L. "The Measurement Of Systematic Risk For Securities And Portfolios: Some Empirical Results," (2), 815-833.
Tysseland, Milford S. "Further Tests Of The Validity Of The Industry Approach To Investment Analysis," (2), 835-847.
Friedman, Harris C. "Real Estate Investment And Portfolio Theory," (2), 861-874.
Murphy, Joseph E., Jr. and J. Russell Nelson. "Random And Nonrandom Relationships Among Financial Variables: A Financial Model," (2), 875-885.
Arditti, Fred D. "Another Look At Mutual Fund Performance," (3), 909-912.
Wippern, Ronald F. "Utility Implications Of Portfolio Selection And Performance Appraisal Models," (3), 913-924.
Schall, Lawrence D. "Firm Financial Structure And Investment," (3), 925-942.
Haugen, Robert A. and James L. Pappas. "Equilibrium In The Pricing Of Capital Assets, Risk-Bearing Debt Instruments, And The Question Of Optimal Capital Structure," (3), 943-953.
Crane, Dwight B. "A Stochastic Programming Model For Commercial Bank Bond Portfolio Management," (3), 955-976.
Cheng, Pao L. and M. King Deets. "Statistical Biases And Security Rates Of Return," (3), 977-994.
Brown, George F., Jr. and Richmond M. Lloyd. "Static Models Of Bank Credit Expansion," (3), 995-1014.
Johnson, Glenn L., Frank K. Reilly and Ralph E. Smith. "Individual Common Stocks As Inflation Hedges," (3), 1015-1024.
Fielitz, Bruce D. "Stationarity Of Random Data: Some Implications For The Distribution Of Stock Price Changes," (3), 1025-1034.
Heinze, David Charles. "Decision Models For University Budget Requests," (3), 1035-1040.
Percival, John. "A Comment: "Short-Run Interest Rate Cycles In The U. S.: 1954-1967"," (3), 1043-1045.
Melnik, Arie and Alan Kraus. "More On The Short Cycles Of Interest Rates," (3), 1047-1052.
Smith, V. Kerry. "A Note On Student's t Test In Multiple Regression," (3), 1053-1056.
Litzenberger, Robert H., O. Maurice Joy and Charles P. Jones. "Ordinal Predictions And The Selection Of Common Stocks," (3), 1059-1068.
Norgaard, Richard L. "Evaluating Intercorporate Risk, Returns, And Trends," (4), 1069-1082.
Rosenberg, Barr. "Statistical Analysis Of Price Series Obscured By Averaging Measures," (4), 1083-1094.
Williams, W. H. and M. L. Goodman. "A Statistical Grouping Of Corporations By Their Financial Characteristics," (4), 1095-1104.
Mao, James C. T. "Security Pricing In An Imperfect Capital Market," (4), 1105-1116.
Spitz, A. Edward and Andre DeKorvin. "A New Theoretical Model For Depicting Profit Optimality," (4), 1117-1121.
Mumey, G. A. and R. M. Korkie. "Balance Sheet Additivity Of Risk Measures," (4), 1123-1133.
Bierman, Harold, Jr. and Jerome Hass. "Normative Stock Price Models," (4), 1135-1144.
Krainer, Robert E. "A Pedagogic Note On Dividend Policy," (4), 1147-1154.
Cohen, Bruce C. "Money Market Development And The Demand For Money," (4), 1155-1157.
Mendleson, Morris. "A Comment On Payback," (4), 1159-1160.
Levy, Haim. "A Comment On Payback: A Reply," (4), 1161-1161.
Colin, J. W. and Edward A. Dyl. "Calculation Of Tax Effective Yields: A Correction," (4), 1163-1164.
McCall, Alan S. and Neil B. Murphy. "A Note On Evaluating Liquidity Under Conditions Of Uncertainty In Mutual Savings Banks," (4), 1165-1169.
Lintner, John. "The Effect Of Short Selling And Margin Requirements In Perfect Capital Markets," (5), 1173-1195.

Brennan, M. J. "Capital Market Equilibrium With Divergent Borrowing And Lending Rates," (5), 1197-1205.

Cheng, Pao L. "Efficient Portfolio Selections Beyond The Markowitz Frontier," (5), 1207-1233.

Stevens, Guy G. V. "Two Problems In Portfolio Analysis: Conditional And Multiplicative Random Variables," (5), 1235-1250.

Frankfurter, George M., Herbert E. Phillips and John P. Seagle. "Portfolio Selection: The Effects Of Uncertain Means, Variances, And Covariances," (5), 1251-1262.

Sharpe, William F. "A Linear Programming Approximation For The General Portfolio Analysis Problem," (5), 1263-1275.

Litzenberger, Robert H. and A. P. Budd. "A Note On Geometric Mean Portfolio Selection And The Market Prices Of Equities," (5), 1277-1282.

Haugen, Robert A. and Charles O. Kroncke. "Rate Regulation And The Cost Of Capital In The Insurance Industry," (5), 1283-1305.

Journal of Financial and Quantitative Analysis
Volume 7, 1972

Elliott, J. W. "Control, Size, Growth, And Financial Performance In The Firm," (1), 1309-1320.

Wu, Hsiu-Kwang. "Odd-Lot Trading In The Stock Market And Its Market Impact," (1), 1321-1341.

Litzenberger, Robert H. and David P. Rutenberg. "Size And Timing Of Corporate Bond Flotations," (1), 1343-1359.

Bierman, Harold, Jr. and L. Joseph Thomas. "Ruin Considerations And Debt Issuance," (1), 1361-1378.

Lane, Sylvia. "Submarginal Credit Risk Classification," (1), 1379-1385.

Haugen, Robert A. and Jon G. Udell. "Rates Of Return To Stockholders Of Acquired Companies," (1), 1387-1398.

Johnson, Craig G. "Dimensional Analysis And The Interpretation Of Regression Coefficients," (1), 1399-1406.

Jennergren, Peter. "Decentralization On The Basis Of Price Schedules In Linear Decomposable Resource-Allocation Problems," (1), 1407-1417.

Carol, Arthur. "An Investment Paradox," (1), 1421-1422.

Frankfurter, George M., Herbert E. Phillips and John P. Seagle. "Estimation Risk In The Portfolio Selection Model: A Comment," (1), 1423-1424.

Robertson, Matthew. "A Note On The Flow Of Capital In Outstanding Common And Preferred Shares Between Canada And The United States," (1), 1425-1427.

Arditti, Fred D. and Haim Levy. "Distribution Moments And Equilibrium: A Comment," (1), 1429-1433.

Jean, William H. "Distribution Moments And Equilibrium: Reply," (1), 1435-1437.

Litzenberger, Robert H. and Cherukuri U. Rao. "Portfolio Theory And Industry Cost-Of-Capital Estimates," (2), 1443-1462.

Edmister, Robert O. "An Empirical Test Of Financial Ratio Analysis For Small Business Failure Prediction," (2), 1477-1493.

Elliott, J. Walter. "Forecasting And Analysis Of Corporate Financial Performance With An Econometric Model Of The Firm," (2), 1499-1526.

Higgins, Robert C. "The Corporate Dividend-Saving Decision," (2), 1527-1541.

Johnson, Harry G. "The Monetary Approach To Balance-Of-Payments Theory," (2), 1555-1572.

Gibson, William E. "Deposit Insurance In The United States: Evaluation And Reform," (2), 1575-1594.

Monroe, Robert J. and James Trieschmann. "Portfolio Performance Of Property-Liability Insurance Companies," (2), 1595-1611.

Kaufman, George G. "The Strange Journey Of Monetary Indicators," (2), 1625-1639.

Pesek, B. P. "Four Ways Of Aggregating Monies," (2), 1641.

Pettit, R. Richardson and Randolph Westerfield. "A Model Of Capital Asset Risk," (2), 1649-1668.

Freund, William C. "Issues Confronting The Stock Markets In A Period Of Rising Institutionalization," (2), Supp, 1687-1690.

Friend, Irwin. "Institutionalization Of Savings And The Long-Term Outlook For The Securities Industry," (2), Supp, 1691-1695.

Weeden, Donald E. "Competition: Key To Market Structure," (2), Supp, 1696-1701.

Tinic, Seha M. and Richard R. West. "Competition And The Pricing Of Dealer Service In The Over-The-Counter Stock Market," (3), 1707-1727.

Hastie, K. Larry. "Determinants Of Municipal Bond Yields," (3), 1729-1748.

Taylor, Ryland A. "The Demand For Credit Union Shares: A Cross-Sectional Analysis," (3), 1749-1756.

Higgins, Robert C. "Dividend Policy And Increasing Discount Rates: A Clarification," (3), 1757-1762.

Rao, N. Krishna. "Equivalent-Risk Class Hypothesis: An Empirical Study," (3), 1763-1771.

Pinches, George E. and Gary Simon. "An Analysis Of Portfolio Accumulation Strategies Employing Low-Priced Common Stocks," (3), 1773-1796.

Bierman, Harold, Jr., David H. Downes and Jerome E. Hass. "Closed-Form Stock Price Models," (3), 1797-1808.

Ziemba, William T. "Solving Nonlinear Programming Problems With Stochastic Objective Functions," (3), 1809-1827.

Levy, Haim and Marshall Sarnat. "Safety First - An Expected Utility Principle," (3), 1829-1834.

Norstrom, Carl J. "A Sufficient Condition For A Unique Nonnegative Internal Rate Of Return," (3), 1835-1839.

Barnea, Amir. "A Note On The Cash-Flow Approach To Valuation And Depreciation Of Productive Assets," (3), 1841-1846.

Richards, Larry E. and William H. Parks. "A Note On Model Specification," (3), 1847-1850.

Merton, Robert C. "An Analytic Derivation Of The Efficient Portfolio Frontier," (4), 1851-1872.

Hakansson, Nils H. "Mean-Variance Analysis In A Finite World," (4), 1873-1880.

Hogan, William W. and James M. Warren. "Computation Of The Efficient Boundary In The E-S Portfolio Selection Model," (4), 1881-1896.

Upson, Roger B. "Random Walk And Forward Exchange Rates: A Spectral Analysis," (4), 1897-1905.

Bear, Robert M. "Margin Levels And The Behavior Of Futures Prices," (4), 1907-1930.

Sartoris, William L. "The Effect Of Regulation, Population Characteristics, And Competition On The Market For Personal Cash Loans," (4), 1931-1956.

Boot, John C. G. and George M. Frankfurter. "The Dynamics Of Corporate Debt Management, Decision Rules, And Some Empirical Evidence," (4), 1957-1965.

Boness, A. James, Andrew H. Chen and Som Jatusipitak. "On Relations Among Stock Price Behavior And Changes In The Capital Structure Of The Firm," (4), 1967-1982.

Rothstein, Marvin. "On Geometric And Arithmetic Portfolio Performance Indexes," (4), 1983-1992.

Ziemba, William T. "Note On 'Optimal Growth Portfolios When Yields Are Serially Correlated'," (4), 1995-2000.

Imai, Yutaka and Mark Rubinstein. "Equilibrium In The Pricing Of Capital Assets, Risk-Bearing Debt Instruments, And The Question Of Optimal Capital Structure: A Comment," (4), 2001-2003.

Haugen, Robert A. and James L. Pappas. "Equilibruim In Pricing Of Capital Assets, Risk-Bearing Debt Instruments, And The Question Of Optimal Capital Structure: A Reply," (4), 2005-2008.

Pyle, David H. "Descriptive Theories Of Financial Institutions Under Uncertainty," (5), 2009-2029.

Brown, George F., Jr. "Optimal Management Of Bank Reserves," (5), 2031-2054.

Walker, David A. "A Recursive Programming Approach To Bank Asset Management," (5), 2055-2075.

Stone, Bernell K. "The Cost Of Bank Loans," (5), 2077-2086.

Kaufman, George G. "Deposit Variability And Bank Size," (5), 2087-2096.

Murphy, Neil B. "A Reestimation Of The Benston-Bell-Murphy Cost Functions For A Larger Sample With Greater Size And Geographic Dispersion," (5), 2097-2105.

Kraus, Alan and Hans R. Stoll. "Parallel Trading By Institutional Investors," (5), 2107-2138.

Bryan, William R. "Treasury Advanced Refundings: An Empirical Investigation," (5), 2139-2150.

Lippman, Steven A. "Optimal Reinsurance," (5), 2151-2155.

Journal of Financial and Quantitative Analysis
Volume 8, 1973

McGuigan, James R. and William R. King. "Security Option Strategy Under Risk Aversion: An Analysis," (1), 1-15.

Ryan, Terence M. "Security Prices As Markov Processes," (1), 17-36.

Shapiro, Alan. "Optimal Inventory And Credit-Granting Strategies Under Inflation And Devaluation," (1), 37-46.

Merville, L. J. and L. A. Tavis. "Optimal Working Capital Policies: A Chance-Constrained Programming Approach," (1), 47-59.

Rubinstein, Mark E. "The Fundamental Theorem Of Parameter-Preference Security Valuation," (1), 61-69.

Porter, R. Burr, James R. Wart and Donald L. Ferguson. "Efficient Algorithms For Conducting Stochastic Dominance Tests On Large Numbers Of Portfolios," (1), 71-81.

Reilly, Frank K. "Further Evidence On Short-Run Results For New Issues Investors," (1), 83-90.

Logue, Dennis E. "On The Pricing Of Unseasoned Equity Issues: 1965-1969," (1), 91-103.

Folks, William R., Jr. "The Optimal Level Of Forward Exchange Transactions," (1), 105-110.

Brumelle, Shelby L. and Bernhard Schwab. "Capital Budgeting With Uncertain Future Opportunities: A Markovian Approach," (1), 111-122.

Reilly, Raymond R. and William E. Wecker. "On The Weighted Average Cost Of Capital," (1), 123-126.

Whitmore, G. A. and Lloyd R. Amey. "Capital Budgeting Under Rationing: Comments On The Lusztig And Schwab Procedure," (1), 127-135.

Nielsen, James F. and Ronald W. Melicher. "A Financial Analysis Of Acquisition And Merger Premiums," (2), 139-148.

Stevens, Donald L. "Financial Characteristics Of Merged Firms: A Multivariate Analysis," (2), 149-158.

Reilly, Frank K. and William C. Slaughter. "The Effect Of Dual Markets On Common Stock Market Making," (2), 167-182.

Emery, John T. "The Information Content Of Daily Market Indicators," (2), 183-190.

Lewellen, Wilbur G. and Robert O. Edmister. "A General Model For Accounts-Receivable Analysis And Control," (2), 195-206.

Marcis, Richard G. and V. Kerry Smith. "The Demand For Liquid Asset Balances By U. S. Manufacturing Corporations: 1959-1970," (2), 207-218.

Alberts, W. W. and S. H. Archer. "Some Evidence On The Effect Of Company Size On The Cost Of Equity Capital," (2), 229-242.

Oudet, Bruno A. "The Variation Of The Return On Stocks In Periods Of Inflation," (2), 247-258.

Simkowitz, Michael A. and Dennis E. Logue. "The Interdependent Structure Of Security Returns," (2), 259-272.

Bicksler, James L. and Edward O. Thorp. "The Capital Growth Model: An Empirical Investigation," (2), 273-287.

Cheng, Pao L. and M. King Deets. "Systematic Risk And The Horizon Problem," (2), 299-316.

Rosenberg, Barr and Walt McKibben. "The Prediction Of Systematic And Specific Risk In Common Stocks," (2), 317-333.

Huntsman, Blaine. "Natural Behavior Toward Risk And The Question Of Value Determination," (2), 335-350.

Bauman, W. Scott. "Presidential Address," (2), 369-380.

Winkler, Robert L. "Bayesian Models For Forecasting Future Security Prices," (3), 387-405.

Gonedes, Nicholas J. "Evidence On The Information Content Of Accounting Numbers: Accounting-Based And Market-Based Estimates Of Systematic Risk," (3), 407-443.

Philippatos, George C. and David N. Nawrocki. "The Information Inaccuracy Of Stock Market Forecasts: Some New Evidence Of Dependence On The New York Stock Exchange," (3), 445-458.

Elton, Edwin J. and Martin J. Gruber. "Asset Selection With Changing Capital Structure," (3), 459-474.

Jean, William H. "More On Multidimensional Portfolio Analysis," (3), 475-490.

Berger, Paul D. and William K. Harper. "Determination Of An Optimal Revolving Credit Agreement," (3), 491-497.

Bierman, Harold, Jr. "The Cost Of Warrants," (3), 499-503.

Klemkosky, Robert C. "The Bias In Composite Performance Measures," (3), 505-514.

Neave, Edwin H. and C. Harvey Rorke. "Risk, Ruin, And Investment Analysis: A Comment," (3), 517-526.

Stevenson, Richard A. "Odd-Lot Trading In The Stock Market And Its Market Impact: Comment," (3), 527-533.

Wu, Hsiu-Kwang. "Odd-Lot Trading In The Stock Market And Its Market Impact: A Reply," (3), 535.

Krouse, Clement G. and Wayne Y. Lee. "Optimal Equity Financing Of The Corporation," (4), 539-563.

McEnally, Richard W. "Some Portfolio-Relevant Risk Characteristics Of Long-Term Marketable Securities," (4), 565-585.

Porter, R. Burr. "An Empirical Comparison Of Stochastic Dominance And Mean-Variance Portfolio Choice Criteria," (4), 587-608.

Jordan, Ronald J. "An Empirical Investigation Of The Adjustment Of Stock Prices To New Quarterly Earnings Information," (4), 609-620.

Stone, Bernell K. "A Linear Programming Formulation Of The General Portfolio Selection Problem," (4), 621-636.

McCall, Alan S. and David A. Walker. "The Effects Of Control Status On Commercial Bank Profitability," (4), 637-645.

Moyer, R. Charles and Edward Sussna. "Registered Bank Holding Company Acquisitions: A Cross-Section Analysis," (4), 647-661.

Pettway, Richard H. "Integer Programming In Capital Budgeting: A Note On Computational Experience," (4), 665-672.

Gup, Benton E. "A Note On Stock Market Indicators And Stock Prices," (4), 673-682.

de Faro, Clovis. "A Sufficient Condition For A Unique Nonnegative Internal Rate Of Return: A Comment," (4), 683-684.

Sethi, Suresh P. "A Note On Modeling Simple Dynamic Cash Balance Problems," (4), 685-687.

Carleton, Willard T., Charles L. Dick, Jr. and David H. Downes. "Financial Policy Models: Theory And Practice," (5), 691-709.

Stone, Bernell K. "Cash Planning And Credit-Line Determination With A Financial Statement Simulator: A Cash Report On Short-Term Financial Planning," (5), 711-729.

Gupta, Manak C. "Optimal Financing Policy For A Firm With Uncertain Fund Requirements," (5), 731-747.

Rubinstein, Mark E. "Corporate Financial Policy In Segmented Securities Markets," (5), 749-761.

Inselbag, Isik. "Financing Decisions And The Theory Of The Firm," (5), 763-776.

Lewellen, Wilbur G. and George A. Racette. "Convertible Debt Financing," (5), 777-792.

Kraus, Alan. "The Bond Refunding Decision In An Efficient Market," (5), 793-806.

von Furstenberg, George M. "The Equilibrium Spread Between Variable Rates And Fixed Rates On Long-Term Financing Instruments," (5), 807-819.

Van Horne, James C. "Implied Fixed Costs Of Long-Term Debt Issues," (5), 821-833.

Wakoff, Gary I. "On Shareholders' Indifference To The Proceeds Price In Preemptive Rights Offerings," (5), 835-836.

Journal of Financial and Quantitative Analysis
Volume 9, 1974

Hogan, William W. and James M. Warren. "Toward The Development Of An Equilibrium Capital-Market Model Based On Semivariance," (1), 1-11.

Santomero, Anthony M. "The Economic Effects Of NASDAQ: Some Preliminary Results," (1), 13-24.

Joy, O. Maurice and R. Burr Porter. "Stochastic Dominance And Mutual Fund Performance," (1), 25-31.

Jennings, Edward H. "An Estimate Of Convertible Bond Premiums," (1), 33-56.

Gupta, Manak C. "Money Supply And Stock Prices: A Probabilistic Approach," (1), 57-68.

Pringle, John J. "The Imperfect-Markets Model Of Commercial Bank Financial Management," (1), 69-87.

Schlarbaum, Gary G. "The Investment Performance Of The Common Stock Portfolios Of Property-Liability Insurance Companies," (1), 89-106.

Merville, L. J. and L. A. Tavis. "A Total Real Asset Planning System," (1), 107-115.

Aldrich, Carole A. "A Model For Funding Interrelated Research And Development Projects Under Uncertainty," (1), 117-129.

Pye, Gordon. "A Note On Diversification," (1), 131-136.

Emery, John T. "Efficient Capital Markets And The Information Content Of Accounting Numbers," (2), 139-149.

Hopewell, Michael H. and George G. Kaufman. "The Cost Of Inefficient Coupons On Municipal Bonds," (2), 155-164.

Neuberger, Brian M. and Carl T. Hammond. "A Study Of Underwriters' Experience With Unseasoned New Issues," (2), 165-177.

Severn, Alan K. and Martin M. Laurence. "Direct Investment, Research Intensity, And Profitability," (2), 181-190.

Altman, Edward I., Michel Margaine, Michel Schlosser and Pierre Vernimmen. "Financial And Statistical Analysis For Commercial Loan Evaluation: A French Experience," (2), 195-211.

Joehnk, Michael D. and James F. Nielsen. "The Effects Of Conglomerate Merger Activity On Systematic Risk," (2), 215-225.

Melicher, Ronald W. "Financial Factors Which Influence Beta Variations Within An Homogeneous Industry Environment," (2), 231-241.

Heathcotte, Bryan and Vincent P. Apilado. "The Predictive Content Of Some Leading Economic Indicators For Future Stock Prices," (2), 247-258.

Rosenberg, Barr. "Extra-Market Components Of Covariance In Security Returns," (2), 263-273.

Apilado, Vincent P., Don C. Warner and Joel J. Dauten. "Evaluative Techniques In Consumer Finance--Experimental Results And Policy Implications For Financial Institutions," (2), 275-283.

Fraser, Donald R., Wallace Phillips, Jr. and Peter S. Rose. "A Canonical Analysis Of Bank Performance," (2), 287-295.

McDonald, John G. "Objectives And Performance Of Mutual Funds, 1960-1969," (3), 311-333.

Edmister, Robert O. and Gary G. Schlarbaum. "Credit Policy In Lending Institutions," (3), 335-356.

Tepper, Irwin. "Optimal Financial Strategies For Trusteed Pension Plans," (3), 357-376.

Herbst, Anthony F. "Some Empirical Evidence On The Determinants Of Trade Credit At The Industry Level Of Aggregation," (3), 377-394.

Warren, James M. "An Operational Model For Security Analysis And Valuation," (3), 395-422.

Reilly, Frank K. and Eugene F. Drzycimski. "Alternative Industry Performance And Risk," (3), 423-446.

Dickinson, J. P. "The Reliability Of Estimation Procedures In Portfolio Analysis," (3), 447-463.

Sharpe, William F. "Imputing Expected Security Returns From Portfolio Composition," (3), 462-472.

Brumelle, Shelby L. "When Does Diversification Between Two Investments Pay?," (3), 473-483.

Fogler, H. Russell and Robert C. Radcliffe. "A Note On Measurement Of Skewness," (3), 485-489.

Lee, Feng-Yao. "On The Dummy Variable Technique And Covariance Analysis In Testing Equality Among Sets Of Coefficients In Linear Regressions: An Expository Note," (3), 491-495.

Hodges, Stewart and Stephen Schaefer. "The Interpretation Of The Geometric Mean: A Note," (3), 497-504.

Rothstein, Marvin. "The Geometric Index Revisited: A Rejoinder," (3), 505-506.

Barnea, Amir. "Performance Evaluation Of New York Stock Exchange Specialists," (4), 511-535.

Solnik, Bruno H. "An International Market Model Of Security Price Behavior," (4), 537-554.

Baron, David P. "Information, Investment Behavior, And Efficient Portfolios," (4), 555-566.

McGuigan, James and William R. King. "Evaluating Alternative Stock Option Timing Strategies," (4), 567-578.

Pettit, R. Richardson and Randolph Westerfield. "Using The Capital Asset Pricing Model And The Market Model To Predict Security Returns," (4), 579-605.

Daellenbach, Hans G. "Are Cash Management Optimization Models Worthwhile?," (4), 607-626.

Lev, Baruch. "On The Association Between Operating Leverage And Risk," (4), 627-641.

Schwartz, Robert A. "An Economic Model Of Trade Credit," (4), 643-657.

Reinmuth, James E. and Dick R. Wittink. "Recursive Models For Forecasting Seasonal Processes," (4), 659-684.

Sarnat, Marshall. "A Note On The Implications Of Quadratic Utility For Portfolio Theory," (4), 687-689.

Jaffe, Jeffrey F. and Larry J. Merville. "The Value Of Risk-Reducing Information," (5), 697-707.

Stone, Bernell K. "Systematic Interest-Rate Risk In A Two-Index Model Of Returns," (5), 709-721.

Davis, Richard G. "Monetary And Credit Restraint In 1973 And Early 1974," (5), 733-741.

Kane, Edward J. "The Re-Politicization Of The Fed," (5), 743-752.

Eiteman, David K. and Keith V. Smith. "A Portfolio Analysis Of The Teaching Of Investments," (5), 771-780.

Christy, George A. "Teaching Of Investments: A 'Utilitarian' View," (5), 781-787.

West, Richard R. "The Teaching Of Investments - Is 'Witchcraft' Still Appropriate?," (5), 789-793.

Phillips, Almarin. "Regulatory Reform For The Deposit Financial Institutions--Retrospect And Prospects," (5), 795-802.

Gibson, William E. "Reform Of Financial Institutions," (5), 803-814.

Farrar, Donald E. "Toward A Central Market System: Wall Street's Slow Retreat Into The Future," (5), 815-827.

Rodriguez, Rita M. "Management Of Foreign Exchange Risk In The U. S. Multinationals," (5), 849-857.

Naumann-Etienne, Ruediger. "A Framework For Financial Decisions In Multinational Corporations--Summary Of Recent Research," (5), 859-874.

Toy, Norman, Arthur Stonehill, Lee Remmers, Richard Wright and Theo Beekhuisen. "A Comparative International Study Of Growth, Profitability, And Risk As Determinants Of Corporate Debt Ratios In The Manufacturing Sector," (5), 875-886.

Olsen, Robert A. "The Effect Of Interest-Rate Risk On Liquidity Premiums: An Empirical Investigation," (5), 901-909.

Pogue, Gerald A. and Bruno H. Solnik. "The Market Model Applied To European Common Stocks: Some Empirical Results," (6), 917-944.

Brenner, Menachem. "On The Stability Of The Distribution Of The Market Component In Stock Price Changes," (6), 945-961.

Bonin, Joseph M. and Edward A. Moses. "Seasonal Variations In Prices Of Individual Dow Jones Industrial Stocks," (6), 963-991.

Arzac, Enrique R. "Utility Analysis Of Chance-Constrained Portfolio Selection," (6), 993-1007.

Chung, Peter S. "An Investigation Of The Firm Effects Influence In The Analysis Of Earnings To Price Ratios Of Industrial Common Stocks," (6), 1009-1029.

Haugen, Robert A. and Prem Kumar. "The Traditional Approach To Valuing Levered-Growth Stocks: A Clarification," (6), 1031-1044.

Chiattello, Marion L. "Comment: On The Use Of Principal Components Analysis To Interpret Cross-Sectional Differences Among Commercial Banks," (6), 1047-1051.

Saunders, Robert J. "Further Comment: Cross-Sectional Differences Among Commercial Banks," (6), 1053-1055.

Gressis, Nicholas and William A. Remaley. "Comment: Safety First - An Expected Utility Principle," (6), 1057-1061.

Levy, Haim and Marshall Sarnat. "Reply: Safety First - An Expected Utility Principle," (6), 1063-1064.

Thakkar, Rashmi B. "Comment: The Dynamics Of Corporate Debt

Journal of Financial and Quantitative Analysis
Volume 12, 1977

Journal of Financial and Quantitative Analysis
Volume 13, 1978

Journal of Financial and Quantitative Analysis
Volume 14, 1979

McEnally, Richard W. and David E. Upton. "A Reexamination Of The Ex Post Risk-Return Tradeoff On Common Stocks," (2), 395-419.

Bachrach, Benjamin and Dan Galai. "The Risk-Return Relationship And Stock Prices," (2), 421-441.

Constantinides, George M. "A Note On The Suboptimality Of Dollar-Cost Averaging As An Investment Policy," (2), 443-450.

Senbet, Lemma W. "International Capital Market Equilibrium And The Multinational Firm Financing And Investment Policies," (3), 455-480.

Christofides, N., R. D. Hewins and G. R. Salkin. "Graph Theoretic Approaches To Foreign Exchange Operations," (3), 481-500.

Shrieves, Ronald E. and Donald L. Stevens. "Bankruptcy Avoidance As A Motive For Merger," (3), 501-515.

Livingston, Miles. "The Pricing Of Premium Bonds," (3), 517-527.

Dyl, Edward A. "A State Preference Model Of Capital Gains Taxation," (3), 529-535.

Trauring, Mitchell. "A Capital Asset Pricing Model With Investors' Taxes And Three Categories Of Investment Income," (3), 537-545.

Kearns, Richard B. and Richard C. Burgess. "An Effective Algorithm For Estimating Stochastic Dominance Efficient Sets," (3), 547-552.

Baesel, Jerome B. and Garry R. Stein. "The Value Of Information: Inferences From The Profitability Of Insider Trading," (3), 553-571.

Groth, John C. "Security-Relative Information Market Efficiency: Some Empirical Evidence," (3), 573-593.

Umstead, David A. and Gary L. Bergstrom. "Dynamic Estimation Of Portfolio Betas," (3), 595-614.

Saniga, Erwin, Nicholas Gressis and Jack Hayya. "The Effects Of Sample Size And Correlation On The Accuracy Of The EV Efficient Criterion," (3), 615-628.

Gultekin, N. Bulent and Richard J. Rogalski. "Comment: A Test Of Stone's Two-Index Model Of Returns," (3), 629-639.

Chance, Don M. "Comment: A Test Of Stone's Two-Index Model Of Returns," (3), 641-644.

Miller, Edward M. "Comment: The Optimal Price To Trade," (3), 645-647.

Branch, Ben. "Reply: The Optimal Price To Trade," (3), 649-651.

Beedles, William L. "On The Assymmetry Of Market Returns," (3), 653-660.

Haugen, Robert A. and Lemma W. Senbet. "New Perspectives On Informational Asymmetry And Agency Relationships," (4), 671-694.

Kraus, Alan and Gordon A. Sick. "Communication Of Aggregate Preferences Through Market Prices," (4), 695-703.

Hakansson, Nils H. "The Fantastic World Of Finance: Progress And The Free Lunch," (4), 717-734.

Brueggeman, William B. and Richard B. Peiser. "Housing Choice And Relative Tenure Prices," (4), 735-751.

Edelstein, Robert. "The Residential Property Tax Progresses," (4), 753-768.

Follain, James R., Jr. "A Study Of The Demand For Housing By Low Versus High Income Households," (4), 769-782.

Noland, Charles W. "Assessing Hedonic Indexes For Housing," (4), 783-800.

Cohen, Kalman J., Stephen F. Maier, Robert A. Schwartz and David K. Whitcomb. "Market Makers And The Market Spread: A Review Of Recent Literature," (4), 813-835.

Smidt, Seymour. "Continuous Versus Intermittent Trading On Auction Markets," (4), 837-867.

Stoll, Hans R. "Commodity Futures And Spot Price Determination And Hedging In Capital Market Equilibrium," (4), 873-894.

Murray, Roger F. "A New Role For Options," (4), 895-899.

Campbell, Tim S. "Optimal Investment Financing Decisions And The Value Of Confidentiality," (5), 913-925.

Frankfurter, George M. and Thomas J. Frecka. "Efficient Portfolios And Superfluous Diversification," (5), 925-938.

Schneeweis, Thomas and J. Randall Woolridge. "Capital Market Seasonality: The Case Of Bond Returns," (5), 939-958.

Jaffe, Jeffrey F. and Gershon Mandelker. "Inflation And The Holding Period Returns On Bonds," (5), 959-979.

Francis, Jack Clark. "Statistical Analysis Of Risk Surrogates For NYSE Stocks," (5), 981-997.

Gahlon, James M. and Roger D. Stover. "Diversification, Financial Leverage, And Conglomerate Systematic Risk," (5), 999-1013.

Kim, Moon K. and J. Kenton Zumwalt. "An Analysis Of Risk In Bull And Bear Markets," (5), 1015-1025.

Brown, Stewart L. "Autocorrelation, Market Imperfections, And The CAPM," (5), 1027-1034.

Johnson, W. Bruce. "The Cross-Sectional Stability Of Financial Ratio Patterns," (5), 1035-1048.

Ederington, Louis H. and William R. Henry. "On Costs Of Capital In Programming Approaches To Capital Budgeting," (5), 1049-1058.

Bey, Roger P. "Estimating The Optimal Stochastic Dominance Efficient Set With A Mean-Semivariance Algorithm," (5), 1059-1070.

Stone, Bernell K. and Ned C. Hill. "Portfolio Management And The Shrinking Knapsack Algorithm," (5), 1071-1083.

Khang, Chulsoon. "Bond Immunization When Short-Term Interest Rates Fluctuate More Than Long-Term Rates," (5), 1085-1090.

Capettini, Robert, Richard A. Grimlund and Howard R. Toole. "Comment: The Unique, Real Internal Rate Of Return," (5), 1091-1094.

Miles, James and Dosoung Choi. "Comment: Evaluating Negative Benefits," (5), 1095-1099.

Journal of Financial and Quantitative Analysis
Volume 15, 1980

Arditti, Fred D. and Kose John. "Spanning The State Space With Options," (1), 1-9.

Rendleman, Richard J., Jr. and Brit J. Bartter. "The Pricing Of Options On Debt Securities," (1), 11-24.

White, R. W. and P. A. Lusztig. "The Price Effects Of Rights Offerings," (1), 25-40.

Haugen, Robert A. and Dean W. Wichern. "The Term Of A Risk-Free Security," (1), 41-52.

Lee, Wayne Y., Terry S. Maness and Donald L. Tuttle. "Nonspeculative Behavior And The Term Structure," (1), 53-83.

Higgins, W. W. and B. J. Moore. "Market Structure Versus Information Costs As Determinants Of Underwriters' Spreads On Municipal Bonds," (1), 85-97.

Harris, Richard G. "A General Equilibrium Analysis Of The Capital Asset Pricing Model," (1), 99-122.

Alexander, Gordon J. and Norman L. Chervany. "On The Estimation And Stability Of Beta," (1), 123-137.

Hawawini, Gabriel A. "Intertemporal Cross-Dependence In Securities Daily Returns And The Short-Run Intervaling Effect On Systematic Risk," (1), 139-149.

Chen, Son-Nan. "Time Aggregation, Autocorrelation, And Systematic Risk Estimates--Additive Versus Multiplicative Assumptions," (1), 151-174.

Dielman, Terry, Timothy J. Nantell and Roger L. Wright. "Price Effects Of Stock Repurchasing: A Random Coefficient Regression Approach," (1), 175-189.

Feder, Gershon. "A Note On Debt, Assets And Lending Under Default Risk," (1), 191-200.

Bernhard, Richard H. "A Simplification And An Extension Of The Bernhard-deFaro Sufficient Condition For A Unique Non-Negative Internal Rate Of Return," (1), 201-209.

Karson, Marvin J. and Terrence F. Martell. "On The Interpretation Of Individual Variables In Multiple Discriminant Analysis," (1), 211-217.

Pettway, Richard H. "Potential Insolvency, Market Efficiency And Bank Regulation Of Large Commercial Banks," (1), 219-236.

Milne, Frank and Clifford Smith, Jr. "Capital Asset Pricing With Proportional Transaction Costs," (2), 253-266.

Larcker, David F., Lawrence A. Gordon and George E. Pinches. "Testing For Market Efficiency: A Comparison Of The Cumulative Average Residual Methodology And Intervention Analysis," (2), 267-287.

Ben-Horim, Moshe and Haim Levy. "Total Risk, Diversifiable Risk And Non-Diversifiable Risk: A Pedagogic Note," (2), 289-298.

Bey, Roger P. and George E. Pinches. "Additional Evidence Of Heteroschedasticity In The Market Model," (2), 299-322.

Saunders, Anthony, Charles Ward and Richard Woodward. "Stochastic Dominance And The Performance Of U.K. Unit Trusts," (2), 323-330.

Hawawini, Gabriel A. and Ashok Vora. "Evidence Of Intertemporal Systematic Risks In The Daily Price Movements Of NYSE And AMEX Common Stocks," (2), 331-339.

Van Landingham, M. H. "The Day Trader: Some Additional Evidence," (2), 341-355.

Frankfurter, George M. and Herbert E. Phillips. "Portfolio Selection: An Analytic Approach For Selecting Securities From A Large Universe," (2), 357-377.

Lee, Wayne Y. and Andrew J. Senchak, Jr. "On The Social Optimality Of The Value Maximization Criterion," (2), 379-389.

Beranek, William. "The AB Procedure And Capital Budgeting," (2), 391-406.

Gaumnitz, Jack E. and Douglas R. Emery. "Asset Growth, Abandonment Value And The Replacement Decision Of Like-For-Like Capital Assets," (2), 407-419.

Bernhard, Richard H. and Carl J. Norstrom. "A Further Note On Unrecovered Investment, Uniqueness Of The Internal Rate, And The Question Of Project Acceptability," (2), 421-423.

Pyun, C. S. "A Note On Capital Asset Pricing Model Under Uncertain Inflation," (2), 425-434.

Sorensen, Eric H. "An Analysis Of The Relationship Between Underwriter Spread And The Pricing Of Municipal Bonds," (2), 435-447.

Fogler, H. Russell and S. Ganapathy. "Comment On: `A Quantitative Yield Curve Model For Estimating The Term Structure Of Interest Rates'," (2), 449-456.

Baesel, Jerome B. and Nahum Biger. "The Allocation Of Risk: Some Implications Of Fixed Versus Index-Linked Mortgages," (2), 457-468.

Mayne, Lucille S. "Bank Dividend Policy And Holding Company Affiliation," (2), 469-480.

Owen, Joel and Ramon Rabinovitch. "The Cost Of Information And Equilibrium In The Capital Asset Market," (3), 497-508.

Cheng, Pao L. "Divergent Rates, Financial Restrictions And Relative Prices In Capital Market Equilibrium," (3), 509-540.

Riley, William B. and William A. Luksetich. "The Market Prefers Republicans: Myth Or Reality," (3), 541-560.

Levy, Haim. "The Capital Asset Pricing Model, Inflation, And The Investment Horizon: The Israeli Experience," (3), 561-593.

Hill, Ned C. and Bernell K. Stone. "Accounting Betas, Systematic Operating Risk, And Financial Leverage: A Risk-Composition Approach To The Determinants Of Systematic Risk," (3), 595-637.

Miller, Tom W. and Nicholas Gressis. "Nonstationarity And Evaluation Of Mutual Fund Performance," (3), 639-654.

Kroll, Yoram and Haim Levy. "Sampling Errors And Portfolio Efficient Analysis," (3), 655-688.

Langetieg, Terence C., Robert A. Haugen and Dean W. Wichern. "Merger And Stockholder Risk," (3), 689-711.

Miles, James A. and John R. Ezzell. "The Weighted Average Cost Of Capital, Perfect Capital Markets, And Project Life: A Clarification," (3), 719-730.

Lynge, Morgan J., Jr. and J. Kenton Zumwalt. "An Empirical Study Of The Interest Rate Sensitivity Of Commercial Bank Returns: A Multi-Index Approach," (3), 731-742.

Finnerty, Joseph E., Thomas Schneeweis and Shantaram P. Hegde. "Interest Rates In The $Eurobond Market," (3), 743-755.

Wiginton, John C. "A Note On The Comparison Of Logit And Discriminant Models Of Consumer Credit Behavior," (3), 757-771.

Arrow, Kenneth J. "Real And Nominal Magnitude In Economics," (4), 773-783.

Talmor, Eli. "A Normative Approach To Bank Capital Adequacy," (4), 785-811.

Altman, Edward I. "Commercial Bank Lending: Process, Credit Scoring, And Costs Of Errors In Lending," (4), 813-832.

Kau, James B. and Donald Keenan. "The Theory Of Housing And Interest Rates," (4), 833-847.

Kalay, Avner. "Signaling, Information Content, And The Reluctance To

Journal of Financial and Quantitative Analysis
Volume 18, 1983

Journal of Financial and Quantitative Analysis
Volume 19, 1984

Howe, Keith M. and Harvey Lapan. "Inflation And Asset Life: The Darby Versus The Fisher Effect," (2), 249-258.

Bick, Avi. "On The Consistency Of The Black-Scholes Model With A General Equilibrium Framework," (3), 259-276.

Johnson, Herb. "Options On The Maximum Or The Minimum Of Several Assets," (3), 277-284.

Levy, Haim and Azriel Levy. "Equilibrium Under Uncertain Inflation: A Discrete Time Approach," (3), 285-298.

Kidwell, David S., Eric H. Sorensen and John M. Wachowicz, Jr. "Estimating The Signaling Benefits Of Debt Insurance: The Case Of Municipal Bonds," (3), 299-314.

Campbell, Tim S. and William A. Kracaw. "Optimal Managerial Incentive Contracts And The Value Of Corporate Insurance," (3), 315-328.

Ogden, Joseph P. "The End Of The Month As A Preferred Habitat: A Test Of Operational Efficiency In The Money Market," (3), 329-344.

Klein, April and James Rosenfeld. "The Influence Of Market Conditions On Event-Study Residuals," (3), 345-352.

Statman, Meir. "How Many Stocks Make A Diversified Portfolio?," (3), 353-364.

Heaton, Hal. "On The Bias Of The Corporate Tax Against High-Risk Projects," (3), 365-372.

Chang, Jack S. K. and Latha Shanker. "A Risk-Return Measure Of Hedging Effectiveness: A Comment," (3), 373-376.

Howard, Charles T. and Louis J. D'Antonio. "A Risk-Return Measure Of Hedging Effectiveness: A Reply," (3), 377-381.

Brick, Ivan E. and Lawrence Fisher. "Effects Of Classifying Equity Or Debt On The Value Of The Firm Under Uncertainty," (3), 383-400.

Chen, Nai-Fu, Thomas E. Copeland and David Mayers. "A Comparison Of Single And Multifactor Portfolio Performance Methodologies," (4), 401-418.

Scott, Louis O. "Option Pricing When The Variance Changes Randomly: Theory, Estimation, And An Application," (4), 419-438.

Ronn, Ehud I. "A New Linear Programming Approach To Bond Portfolio Management," (4), 439-466.

Saunders, Anthony and Michael Smirlock. "Intra- And Interindustry Effects Of Bank Securities Market Activities: The Case Of Discount Brokerage," (4), 467-482.

Peterson, David R. "Security Price Reactions To Initial Reviews Of Common Stock By The Value Line Investment Survey," (4), 483-494.

McDonald, Bill. "Event Studies And Systems Methods: Some Additional Evidence," (4), 495-504.

Frankfurter, George M. and Christopher G. Lamoureux. "The Relevance Of The Distributional Form Of Common Stock Returns To The Construction Of Optimal Portfolios," (4), 505-511.

Journal of Financial and Quantitative Analysis
Volume 23, 1988

Boyle, Phelim P. "A Lattice Framework For Option Pricing With Two State Variables," (1), 1-12.

Blomeyer, Edward C. and Herb Johnson. "An Empirical Examination Of The Pricing Of American Put Options," (1), 13-22.

Grinblatt, Mark and Herb Johnson. "A Put Option Paradox," (1), 23-26.

Haugen, Robert A. and Lemma W. Senbet. "Bankruptcy And Agency Costs: Their Significance To The Theory Of Optimal Capital Structure," (1), 27-38.

Narayanan, M. P. "Debt Versus Equity Under Asymmetric Information," (1), 39-52.

Ho, Thomas S. Y. and Roni Michaely. "Information Quality And Market Efficiency," (1), 53-70.

Heinkel, Robert and Alan Kraus. "Measuring Event Impacts In Thinly Traded Stocks," (1), 71-88.

Chambers, Donald R., Willard T. Carleton and Richard W. McEnally. "Immunizing Default-Free Bond Portfolios With A Duration Vector," (1), 89-104.

Siegel, Andrew F. and Charles R. Nelson. "Long-Term Behavior Of Yield Curves," (1), 105-110.

Rodriguez, Ricardo J. "Default Risk, Yield Spreads, And Time To Maturity," (1), 111-117.

Mikkelson, Wayne H. and M. Megan Partch. "Withdrawn Security Offerings," (2), 119-134.

Alexander, Gordon J., Cheol S. Eun and S. Janakiramanan. "International Listings And Stock Returns: Some Empirical Evidence," (2), 135-152.

Bick, Avi. "Producing Derivative Assets With Forward Contracts," (2), 153-160.

Omberg, Edward. "Efficient Discrete Time Jump Process Models In Option Pricing," (2), 161-174.

Stoughton, Neal M. "The Information Content Of Corporate Merger And Acquisition Offers," (2), 175-198.

Bruner, Robert F. "The Use Of Excess Cash And Debt Capacity As A Motive For Merger," (2), 199-218.

Choi, J. Y., Dan Salandro and Kuldeep Shastri. "On The Estimation Of Bid-Ask Spreads: Theory And Evidence," (2), 219-230.

Allen, Linda. "The Determinants Of Bank Interest Margins: A Note," (2), 231-235.

Hull, John and Alan White. "The Use Of The Control Variate Technique In Option Pricing," (3), 237-252.

Joerding, Wayne. "Excess Stock Price Volatility As A Misspecified Euler Equation," (3), 253-268.

Jain, Prem C. and Gun-Ho Joh. "The Dependence Between Hourly Prices And Trading Volume," (3), 269-284.

Sweeney, Richard J. "Some New Filter Rule Tests: Methods And Results," (3), 285-300.

Jayaraman, Narayanan and Kuldeep Shastri. "The Valuation Impacts Of Specially Designated Dividends," (3), 301-312.

Stock, Duane and Donald G. Simonson. "Tax-Adjusted Duration For Amortizing Debt Instruments," (3), 313-328.

Nielsen, Lars Tyge. "Uniqueness Of Equilibrium In The Classical Capital Asset Pricing Model," (3), 329-336.

Kane, Alex and Alan J. Marcus. "The Delivery Option On Forward Contracts: A Note," (3), 337-342.

Barnhill, Theodore M. "The Delivery Option On Forward Contracts: A Comment," (3), 343-348.

Ogden, Joseph P. and Alan L. Tucker. "The Relative Valuation Of American Currency Spot And Futures Options: Theory And Empirical Tests," (4), 351-368.

Masulis, Ronald W. and Brett Trueman. "Corporate Investment And Dividend Decisions Under Differential Personal Taxation," (4), 369-386.

Lewellen, Wilbur G. and David C. Mauer. "Tax Options And Corporate Capital Structures," (4), 387-400.

Spindt, Paul A. and J. Ronald Hoffmeister. "The Micromechanics Of The Federal Funds Market: Implications For Day-Of-The-Week Effects In Funds Rate Variability," (4), 401-416.

Sanders, Anthony B. and Haluk Unal. "On The Intertemporal Behavior Of The Short-Term Rate Of Interest," (4), 417-424.

Kane, Alex and Stephen Gary Marks. "Performance Evaluation Of Market Timers: Theory And Evidence," (4), 425-436.

Overdahl, James A. "The Early Exercise Of Options On Treasury Bond Futures," (4), 437-450.

Merrick, John J., Jr. "Hedging With Mispriced Futures," (4), 451-464.

Goldenberg, David H. "Trading Frictions And Futures Price Movements," (4), 465-480.

Journal of Financial and Quantitative Analysis
Volume 24, 1989

Bailey, Warren and Rene M. Stulz. "The Pricing Of Stock Index Options In A General Equilibrium Model," (1), 1-12.

McCardle, Kevin F. and Robert L. Winkler. "All Roads Lead To Risk Preference: A Turnpike Theorem For Conditionally Independent Returns," (1), 13-28.

Harris, Lawrence. "A Day-End Transaction Price Anomaly," (1), 29-46.

Titman, Sheridan and Arthur Warga. "Stock Returns As Predictors Of Interest Rates And Inflation," (1), 47-58.

Chang, Eric C. and J. Michael Pinegar. "Seasonal Fluctuations In Industrial Production And Stock Market Seasonals," (1), 59-74.

Hegde, Shantaram P. and Robert E. Miller. "Market-Making In Initial Public Offerings Of Common Stocks: An Empirical Analysis," (1), 75-90.

Narayanan, M. P. and Suk-Pil Lim. "On The Call Provision In Corporate Zero-Coupon Bonds," (1), 91-104.

Hall, Joyce A., B. Wade Brorsen and Scott H. Irwin. "The Distribution Of Futures Prices: A Test Of The Stable Paretian And Mixture Of Normals Hypotheses," (1), 105-116.

Lai, Tsong-Yue. "An Equilibrium Model Of Asset Pricing With Progressive Personal Taxes," (1), 117-128.

Panton, Don B. "The Relevance Of The Distributional Form Of Common Stock Returns To The Construction Of Optimal Portfolios: Comment," (1), 129-131.

Frankfurter, G. M. and C. G. Lamoureux. "The Relevance Of The Distributional Form Of Common Stock Returns To The Construction Of Optimal Portfolios: Reply," (1), 131.

Connolly, Robert A. "An Examination Of The Robustness Of The Weekend Effect," (2), 133-170.

Bebchuk, Lucian Arye. "Takeover Bids Below The Expected Value Of Minority Shares," (2), 171-184.

Jobson, J. D. and Bob Korkie. "A Performance Interpretation Of Multivariate Tests Of Asset Set Intersection, Spanning, And Mean-Variance Efficiency," (2), 185-204.

Lim, Kian-Guan. "A New Test Of The Three-Moment Capital Asset Pricing Model," (2), 205-216.

Hilliard, Jimmy E. and Susan D. Jordan. "Hedging Interest Rate Risk With Futures Portfolios Under Full-Rank Assumptions," (2), 217-240.

Eun, Cheol S. and Sangdal Shim. "International Transmission Of Stock Market Movements," (2), 241-256.

Krinsky, I. and W. Rotenberg. "Signalling And The Valuation Of Unseasoned New Issues Revisited," (2), 257-265.

Chesney, Marc and Louis Scott. "Pricing European Currency Options: A Comparison Of The Modified Black-Scholes Model And A Random Variance Model," (3), 267-284.

Harlow, W. V. and Ramesh K. S. Rao. "Asset Pricing In A Generalized Mean-Lower Partial Moment Framework: Theory And Evidence," (3), 285-312.

Hirshleifer, David. "Determinants Of Hedging And Risk Premia In Commodity Futures Markets," (3), 313-332.

Froot, Kenneth A. "Consistent Covariance Matrix Estimation With Cross-Sectional Dependence And Heteroskedasticity In Financial Data," (3), 333-356.

Simon, David P. "Expectations And Risk In The Treasury Bill Market: An Instrumental Variables Approach," (3), 357-366.

Sarig, Oded and Arthur Warga. "Bond Price Data And Bond Market Liquidity," (3), 367-378.

Leeth, John D. and Jonathan A. Scott. "The Incidence Of Secured Debt: Evidence From The Small Business Community," (3), 379-394.

Fortin, Richard D., R. Corwin Grube and O. Maurice Joy. "Seasonality In NASDAQ Dealer Spreads," (3), 395-407.

Lambert, Richard A., William N. Lanen and David F. Larcker. "Executive Stock Option Plans And Corporate Dividend Policy," (4), 409-426.

Fischer, Edwin O., Robert Heinkel and Josef Zechner. "Dynamic Recapitalization Policies And The Role Of Call Premia And Issue Discounts," (4), 427-446.

Rabinovitch, Ramon. "Pricing Stock And Bond Options When The Default-Free Rate Is Stochastic," (4), 447-458.

Lewellen, Wilbur, Claudio Loderer and Ahron Rosenfeld. "Mergers, Executive Risk Reduction, And Stockholder Wealth," (4), 459-472.

Morck, Randall, Eduardo Schwartz and David Stangeland. "The Valuation Of Foresty Resources Under Stochastic Prices And Inventories," (4), 473-488.

Hull, John. "Assessing Credit Risk In A Financial Institution's Off-Balance Sheet Commitments," (4), 489-502.

Moyer, R. Charles, Robert E. Chatfield and Phillip M. Sisneros. "Security Analyst Monitoring Activity: Agency Costs And

Information Demands," (4), 503-512.

Thomson, James B. "Errors In Recorded Security Prices And The Turn-Of-The-Year Effect," (4), 513-526.

Finucane, Thomas J. "Black-Scholes Approximations Of Call Option Prices With Stochastic Volatilities: A Note," (4), 527-532.

Ehrhardt, Michael C. "A New Linear Programming Approach To Bond Portfolio Management: A Comment," (4), 533-537.

Journal of Financial and Quantitative Analysis
Volume 25, 1990

Heinkel, Robert and Josef Zechner. "The Role Of Debt And Preferred Stock As A Solution To Adverse Investment Incentives," (1), 1-24.

Lewis, Craig M. "A Multiperiod Theory Of Corporate Financial Policy Under Taxation," (1), 25-44.

Kamara, Avraham. "Delivery Uncertainty And The Efficiency Of Futures Markets," (1), 45-64.

Barnhill, Theodore M. "Quality Option Profits, Switching Option Profits, And Variation Margin Costs: An Evaluation Of Their Size And Impact On Treasury Bond Futures Prices," (1), 65-86.

Hull, John and Alan White. "Valuing Derivative Securities Using The Explicit Finite Difference Method," (1), 87-100.

Dezhbakhsh, Hashem and Asli Demirguc-Kunt. "On The Presence Of Speculative Bubbles In Stock Prices," (1), 101-112.

Zarowin, Paul. "Size, Seasonality, And Stock Market Overreaction," (1), 113-126.

Prisman, Eliezer Z. "A Unified Approach To Term Structure Estimation: A Methodology For Estimating The Term Structure In A Market With Frictions," (1), 127-141.

Agrawal, Anup and Gershon N. Mandelker. "Large Shareholders And The Monitoring Of Managers: The Case Of Antitakeover Charter Amendments," (2), 143-162.

Affleck-Graves, John and Bill McDonald. "Multivariate Tests Of Asset Pricing: The Comparative Power Of Alternative Statistics," (2), 163-186.

Peterson, David R. "Stock Return Seasonalities And Earnings Information," (2), 187-202.

Baillie, Richard T. and Ramon P. DeGennaro. "Stock Returns And Volatility," (2), 203-214.

Boyle, Phelim P. and Y. K. Tse. "An Algorithm For Computing Values Of Options On The Maximum Or Minimum Of Several Assets," (2), 215-228.

Kim, Yong O. "Informative Conversion Ratios: A Signalling Approach," (2), 229-244.

Blackwell, David W., M. Wayne Marr and Michael F. Spivey. "Shelf Registration And The Reduced Due Diligence Argument: Implications Of The Underwriter Certification And The Implicit Insurance Hypotheses," (2), 245-260.

Sanger, Gary C. and James D. Peterson. "An Empirical Analysis Of Common Stock Delistings," (2), 261-272.

Brent, Averil, Dale Morse and E. Kay Stice. "Short Interest: Explanations And Tests," (2), 273-289.

Harris, Lawrence. "Estimation Of Stock Price Variances And Serial Covariances From Discrete Observations," (3), 291-306.

Kaul, Gautam. "Monetary Regimes And The Relation Between Stock Returns And Inflationary Expectations," (3), 307-322.

Chang, Eric C. and Roger D. Huang. "Time-Varying Return And Risk In The Corporate Bond Market," (3), 323-340.

Mauer, David C. and Wilbur G. Lewellen. "Securityholder Taxes And Corporate Restructurings," (3), 341-360.

Lee, Cheng F., Chunchi Wu and K. C. John Wei. "The Heterogeneous Investment Horizon And The Capital Asset Pricing Model: Theory And Implications," (3), 361-376.

Wiggins, James B. "The Relation Between Risk And Optimal Debt Maturity," (3), 377-386.

Darrat, Ali F. "Stock Returns, Money, And Fiscal Deficits," (3), 387-398.

Liu, Pu, Stanley D. Smith and Azmat A. Syed. "Stock Price Reactions To The Wall Street Journal's Securities Recommendations," (3), 399-410.

Corrado, Charles J. and John Schatzberg. "A Nonparametric Distribution-Free Test For Serial Independence In Stock Returns: A Correction," (3), 411-416.

Ashley, Richard and Douglas Patterson. "A Nonparametric Distribution-Free Test For Serial Independence In Stock Returns: A Comment," (3), 417-418.

Heath, David, Robert Jarrow and Andrew Morton. "Bond Pricing And The Term Structure Of Interest Rates: A Discrete Time Approximation," (4), 419-440.

Stoll, Hans R. and Robert E. Whaley. "The Dynamics Of Stock Index And Stock Index Futures Returns," (4), 441-468.

Igawa, Kazuhiro and George Kanatas. "Asymmetric Information, Collateral, And Moral Hazard," (4), 469-490.

Eckbo, B. Espen. "Valuation Effects Of Greenmail Prohibition," (4), 491-506.

Gilster, John E., Jr. "The Systematic Risk Of Discretely Rebalanced Option Hedges," (4), 507-516.

Chang, Eric C. and J. Michael Pinegar. "Stock Market Seasonals And Prespecified Multifactor Pricing Relations," (4), 517-534.

Atkins, Allen B. and Edward A. Dyl. "Price Reversals, Bid-Ask Spreads, And Market Efficiency," (4), 535-548.

Cowan, Arnold R., Nandkumar Nayar and Ajai K. Singh. "Stock Returns Before And After Calls Of Convertible Bonds," (4), 549-554.

Journal of Financial and Quantitative Analysis
Volume 26, 1991

John, Kose and Haim Reisman. "Fundamentals, Factor Structure, And Multibeta Models In Large Asset Markets," (1), 1-10.

Handa, Puneet and Scott C. Linn. "Equilibrium Factor Pricing With Heterogeneous Beliefs," (1), 11-22.

Johnston, Elizabeth Tashijan, William A. Kracaw and John J. McConnell. "Day-Of-The-Week Effects In Financial Futures: An Analysis Of GNMA, T-Bond, T-Note, And T-Bill Contracts," (1), 23-44.

Stickel, Scott E. "The Ex-Dividend Behavior Of Nonconvertible Preferred Stock Returns And Trading Volume," (1), 45-62.

Brick, Ivan E. and S. Abraham Ravid. "Interest Rate Uncertainty And The Optimal Debt Maturity Structure," (1), 63-82.

Berkovitch, Elazar and Stuart I. Greenbaum. "The Loan Commitment As An Optimal Financing Contract," (1), 83-96.

Simon, David P. "Segmentation In The Treasury Bill Market: Evidence From Cash Management Bills," (1), 97-108.

Booth, Laurence. "The Influence Of Production Technology On Risk And The Cost Of Capital," (1), 109-128.

Zivney, Terry L. "The Value Of Early Exercise In Option Prices: An Empirical Investigation," (1), 129-138.

Dodd, Peter and Richard Ruback. "Tender Offers And Stockholder Returns: An Empirical Analysis," (3), 351-373.

Boyle, P. P. and A. L. Ananthanarayanan. "The Impact Of Variance Estimation In Option Valuation Models," (3), 375-387.

Oldfield, George S., Jr., R. J. Rogalski and Robert A. Jarrow. "An Autoregressive Jump Process For Common Stock Returns," (3), 389-418.

Pettit, R. Richardson. "Taxes, Transaction Costs And The Clientele Effect Of Dividends," (3), 419-436.

Journal of Financial Economics
Volume 6, 1978

Garman, Mark B. "The Pricing Of Supershares," (1), 3-10.

Grauer, Robert R. "Generalized Two Parameter Asset Pricing Models: Some Empirical Evidence," (1), 11-32.

Richard, Scott F. "An Arbitrage Model Of The Term Structure Of Interest Rates," (1), 33-57.

Dothan, L. Uri. "On The Term Structure Of Interest Rates," (1), 59-69.

Gleit, Alan. "Valuation Of General Contingent Claims: Existence, Uniqueness, And Comparisons Of Solutions," (1), 71-87.

Jensen, Michael C. "Some Anomalous Evidence Regarding Market Efficiency," (2/3), 95-101.

Ball, Ray. "Anomalies In Relationships Between Securities' Yields And Yield-Surrogates," (2/3), 103-126.

Watts, Ross L. "Systematic `Abnormal' Returns After Quarterly Earnings Announcements," (2/3), 127-150.

Thompson, Rex. "The Information Content Of Discounts And Premiums On Closed-End Fund Shares," (2/3), 151-186.

Galai, Dan. "Empirical Tests Of Boundary Conditions For CBOE Options," (2/3), 187-211.

Chiras, Donald P. and Steven Manaster. "The Information Content Of Option Prices And A Test Of Market Efficiency," (2/3), 213-234.

Long, John B., Jr. "The Market Valuation Of Cash Dividends: A Case To Consider," (2/3), 235-264.

Charest, Guy. "Split Information, Stock Returns And Market Efficiency - I," (2/3), 265-296.

Charest, Guy. "Dividend Information, Stock Returns And Market Efficiency - II," (2/3), 297-330.

Miller, Merton H. and Myron S. Scholes. "Dividends And Taxes," (4), 333-364.

Langetieg, Terence C. "An Application Of A Three-Factor Performance Index To Measure Stockholder Gains From Merger," (4), 365-384.

Morgan, I. G. "Market Proxies And The Conditional Prediction Of Returns," (4), 385-398.

Elton, Edwin J. and Martin J. Gruber. "Taxes And Portfolio Composition," (4), 399-410.

Journal of Financial Economics
Volume 7, 1979

Mayers, David and Edward M. Rice. "Measuring Portfolio Performance And The Empirical Content Of Asset Pricing Models," (1), 3-28.

Goldman, M. Barry and Howard B. Sosin. "Information Dissemination, Market Efficiency And The Frequency Of Transactions," (1), 29-61.

Geske, Robert. "The Valuation Of Compound Options," (1), 63-82.

Kim, E. Han, Wilbur G. Lewellen and John J. McConnell. "Financial Leverage Clienteles: Theory And Evidence," (1), 83-109.

Smith, Clifford W., Jr. and Jerold B. Warner. "On Financial Contracting: An Analysis Of Bond Covenants," (2), 117-162.

Litzenberger, Robert H. and Krishna Ramaswamy. "The Effect Of Personal Taxes And Dividends On Capital Asset Prices: Theory And Empirical Evidence," (2), 163-196.

Dimson, Elroy. "Risk Measurement When Shares Are Subject To Infrequent Trading," (2), 197-226.

Cox, John C., Stephen A. Ross and Mark Rubinstein. "Option Pricing: A Simplified Approach," (3), 229-264.

Breeden, Douglas T. "An Intertemporal Asset Pricing Model With Stochastic Consumption And Investment Opportunities," (3), 265-296.

Shiller, Robert J. and Franco Modigliani. "Coupon And Tax Effects On New And Seasoned Bond Yields And The Measurement Of The Cost Of Debt Capital," (3), 297-318.

Hillmer, S. C. and P. L. Yu. "The Market Speed Of Adjustment To New Information," (4), 321-346.

Baldwin, Carliss Y. and Richard F. Meyer. "Liquidity Preference Under Uncertainty: A Model Of Dynamic Investment In Illiquid Opportunities," (4), 347-374.

Geske, Robert. "A Note On An Analytical Valuation Formula For Unprotected American Call Options On Stocks With Known Dividends," (4), 375-380.

Cornell, Bradford. "Asymmetric Information And Portfolio Performance Measurement," (4), 381-390.

Roll, Richard. "Measuring Portfolio Performance And The Empirical Content Of Asset Pricing Models: A Reply," (3), 391-400.

Journal of Financial Economics
Volume 8, 1980

DeAngelo, Harry and Ronald W. Masulis. "Optimal Capital Structure Under Corporate And Personal Taxation," (1), 3-27.

Amihud, Yakov and Haim Mendelson. "Dealership Market: Market-Making With Inventory," (1), 31-53.

French, Kenneth R. "Stock Returns And The Weekend Effect," (1), 55-69.

Constantinides, George M. "Admissible Uncertainty In The Intertemporal Asset Pricing Model," (1), 71-86.

Verrecchia, Robert E. "The Mayers-Rice Conjecture: A Counterexample," (1), 87-100.

Dodd, Peter. "Merger Proposals, Management Discretion And Stockholder Wealth," (2), 105-138.

Masulis, Ronald W. "The Effects Of Capital Structure Change On Security Prices: A Study Of Exchange Offers," (2), 139-177.

Phillips, Susan M. and Clifford W. Smith, Jr. "Trading Costs For Listed Options: The Implications For Market Efficiency," (2), 179-201.

Brown, Stephen J. and Jerold B. Warner. "Measuring Security Price Information," (3), 205-258.

Boyle, Phelim P. and David Emanuel. "Discretely Adjusted Option Hedges," (3), 259-282.

Gatto, Mary Ann, Robert Geske, Robert Litzenberger and Howard Sosin. "Mutual Fund Insurance," (3), 283-317.

Merton, Robert C. "On Estimating The Expected Return On The Market: An Exploratory Investigation," (4), 323-361.

Klemkosky, Robert C. and Bruce G. Resnick. "An Ex Ante Analysis Of Put Call Parity," (4), 363-378.

Aivazian, Varouj A. and Jeffrey L. Callen. "Corporate Leverage And Growth: The Game-Theoretic Issues," (4), 379-399.

Journal of Financial Economics
Volume 9, 1981

Banz, Rolf W. "The Relationship Between Return And Market Value Of Common Stocks," (1), 3-18.

Reinganum, Marc R. "Misspecification Of Capital Asset Pricing: Empirical Anomalies Based On Earnings' Yields And Market Values," (1), 19-46.

Ho, Thomas and Hans R. Stoll. "Optimal Dealer Pricing Under Transactions And Return Uncertainty," (1), 47-73.

Lee, Wayne Y., Ramesh K. S. Rao and J. F. G. Auchmuty. "Option Pricing In A Lognormal Securities Market, With Discrete Trading," (1), 75-102.

Cornell, Bradford. "The Consumption Based Asset Pricing Model: A Note On Potential Tests And Application," (1), 103-108.

Dann, Larry Y. "Common Stock Repurchases: An Analysis Of Returns To Bondholders And Stockholders," (2), 113-138.

Vermaelen, Theo. "Common Stock Repurchases And Market Signalling: An Empirical Study," (2), 138-183.

Schmalensee, Richard. "Risk And Return On Long-Lived Tangible Assets," (2), 185-205.

Whaley, Robert E. "On The Valuation Of American Call Options On Stocks With Known Dividends," (2), 207-211.

Geske, Robert. "On The Valuation Of American Call Options On Stocks With Known Dividends: A Comment," (2), 213-215.

Diamond, Douglas W. and Robert E. Verrecchia. "Information Aggregation In A Noisy Rational Expectations Economy," (3), 221-236.

Mikkelson, Wayne H. "Convertible Calls And Security Returns," (3), 237-264.

Feenberg, Daniel. "Does The Investment Interest Limitation Explain The Existence Of Dividends?," (3), 265-270.

Garman, Mark B. and James A. Ohlson. "Valuation Of Risky Assets In Arbitrage-Free Economies With Transactions Costs," (3), 271-280.

Mason, Scott P. and Sudipto Bhattacharya. "Risky Debt, Jump Processes, And Safety Covenants," (3), 281-307.

Nichols, William D. and Stewart L. Brown. "Assimilating Earnings And Split Information: Is The Capital Market Becoming More Efficient?," (3), 309-315.

Cox, John C., Jonathan E. Ingersoll, Jr. and Stephen A. Ross. "The Relation Between Forward Prices And Futures Prices," (4), 321-346.

Richard, Scott F. and M. Sundaresan. "A Continuous Time Equilibrium Model Of Forward Prices And Future Prices In A Multigood Economy," (4), 347-371.

Jarrow, Robert A. and George S. Oldfield. "Forward Contracts And Futures Contracts," (4), 373-382.

Stulz, Rene M. "A Model Of International Asset Pricing," (4), 383-406.

Journal of Financial Economics
Volume 10, 1982

Gibbons, Michael R. "Multivariate Tests Of Financial Models: A New Approach," (1), 3-27.

Whaley, Robert E. "Valuation Of American Call Options On Dividend-Paying Stocks: Empirical Tests," (1), 29-58.

Hawkins, Gregory D. "An Analysis Of Revolving Credit Agreements," (1), 59-81.

Ruback, Richard S. "The Effect Of Discretionary Price Control Decisions On Equity Values," (1), 83-105.

Park, Soo-Bin. "Spot And Forward Rates In The Canadian Treasury Bill Market," (1), 107-114.

Gupta, Keshav. "Determinants Of Corporate Borrowing: A Note," (1), 115-116.

Schaefer, Stephen M. "Tax-Induced Clientele Effects In The Market For British Government Securities: Placing Bounds On Security Values In An Incomplete Market," (2), 121-159.

Stulz, Rene M. "Options On The Minimum Or The Maximum Of Two Risky Assets: Analysis And Applications," (2), 161-185.

Asch, Peter, Burton G. Malkiel and Richard E. Quandt. "Racetrack Betting And Informed Behavior," (2), 187-194.

Grossman, Sanford J. and Robert J. Shiller. "Consumption Correlatedness And Risk Measurement In Economies With Non-Traded Assets And Heterogeneous Information," (2), 195-210.

Kalay, Avner. "Stockholder-Bondholder Conflict And Dividend Constraints," (2), 211-233.

Stambaugh, Robert F. "On The Exclusion Of Assets From Tests Of The Two-Parameter Model: A Sensitivity Analysis," (3), 237-268.

Rendleman, Richard J., Jr., Charles P. Jones and Henry A. Latane. "Empirical Anomalies Based On Unexpected Earnings And The Importance Of Risk Adjustment," (3), 269-287.

Copeland, Thomas E. and David Mayers. "The Value Line Enigma (1965-1978): A Case Study Of Performance Evaluation Issues," (3), 289-322.

Startz, Richard. "Do Forecast Errors Or Term Premia Really Make The Difference Between Long And Short Rates?," (3), 323-329.

Bick, Avi. "Comments On The Valuation Of Derivative Assets," (3), 331-345.

Jarrow, Robert and Andrew Rudd. "Approximate Option Valuation For

Journal of Financial Economics

Garman, Mark B. "The Duration Of Option Portfolios," (2), 309-316.
Chen, Nai-Fu and Herb Johnson. "Hedging Options," (2), 317-321.
Shanken, Jay. "Multivariate Tests Of The Zero-Beta CAPM," (3), 327-348.
Roll, Richard. "A Note On The Geometry Of Shanken's CSR T-Squared Test For Mean/Variance Efficiency," (3), 349-358.
Amsler, Christine E. and Peter Schmidt. "A Monte Carlo Investigation Of The Accuracy Of Multivariate CAPM Tests," (3), 359-376.
Parsons John E. and Arthur Raviv. "Underpricing Of Seasoned Issues," (3), 377-397.
McConnell, John J. and Chris J. Muscarella. "Corporate Capital Expenditure Decisions And The Market Value Of The Firm," (3), 399-422.
Kalay, Avner and Uri Loewenstein. "Predictable Events And Excess Returns: The Case Of Dividend Announcements," (3), 423-449.
Chan, K. C.,Nai-Fu Chen and David A. Hsieh. "An Exploratory Investigation Of The Firm Size Effect," (3), 451-471.
Keim, Donald B. "Dividend Yields And Stock Returns: Implications Of Abnormal January Returns," (3), 473-489.
Brown, Stephen J. and Mark I. Weinstein. "Derived Factors In Event Studies," (3), 491-495.
Stulz, Rene M. and Herb Johnson. "An Analysis Of Secured Debt," (4), 501-522.
Mikkelson, Wayne H. and Richard S. Ruback. "An Empirical Analysis Of The Interfirm Equity Investment Process," (4), 523-553.
Holderness, Clifford G. and Dennis P. Sheehan. "Raiders Or Saviors? The Evidence On Six Controversial Investors," (4), 555-579.
Eades, Kenneth M., Patrick J. Hess and E. Han Kim. "Market Rationality And Dividend Annoucements," (4), 581-604.

Journal of Financial Economics
Volume 15, 1986

Smith, Clifford W., Jr. "Investment Banking And The Capital Acquisition Process," (1/2), 3-29.
Mikkelson, Wayne H. and M. Megan Partch. "Valuation Effects Of Security Offerings And The Issuance Process," (1/2), 31-60.
Asquith, Paul and David W. Mullins, Jr. "Equity Issues And Offering Dilution," (1/2), 61-89.
Masulis, Ronald W. and Ashok N. Korwar. "Seasoned Equity Offerings: An Empirical Investigation," (1/2), 91-118.
Eckbo, B. Espen. "Valuation Effects Of Corporate Debt Offerings," (1/2), 119-152.
Schipper, Katherine and Abbie Smith. "A Comparison Of Equity Carve-Outs And Seasoned Equity Offerings: Share Price Effects And Corporate Restructuring," (1/2), 153-186.
Rock, Kevin. "Why New Issues Are Underpriced," (1/2), 187-212.
Beatty, Randolph P. and Jay R. Ritter. "Investment Banking, Reputation, And The Underpricing Of Initial Public Offerings," (1/2), 213-232.
Bhagat, Sanjai and Peter A. Frost. "Issuing Costs To Existing Shareholders In Competitive And Negotiated Underwritten Public Utility Equity Offerings," (1/2), 233-260.
Booth, James R. and Richard L. Smith, II. "Capital Raising, Underwriting And The Certification Hypothesis," (1/2), 261-281.
Bernard, Victor L. "Unanticipated Inflation And The Value Of The Firm," (3), 285-322.
Ruback, Richard S. "Calculating The Market Value Of Riskless Cash Flows," (3), 323-340.
Butler, J. S. and Barry Schachter. "Unbiased Estimation Of The Black/Scholes Formula," (3), 341-357.
Marsh, Terry A. and Eric R. Rosenfeld. "Non-Trading Market Making, And Estimates Of Stock Price Volatility," (3), 359-372.
Connor, Gregory and Robert A. Korajczyk. "Performance Measurement With The Arbitrage Pricing Theory: A New Framework For Analysis," (3), 373-394.
Poterba, James M. "The Market Valuation Of Cash Dividends: The Citizens Utilities Cash Reconsidered," (3), 395-406.

Journal of Financial Economics
Volume 16, 1986

Breeden, Douglas T. "Consumption, Production, Inflation And Interest Rates: A Synthesis," (1), 3-40.
Gay, Gerald D. and Steven Manaster. "Implicit Delivery Options And Optimal Delivery Strategies For Financial Futures Contracts," (1), 41-72.
Mayers, David and Clifford W. Smith, Jr. "Ownership Structure And Control: The Mutualization Of Stock Life Insurance Companies," (1), 73-98.
Harris, Lawrence. "A Transaction Data Study Of Weekly And Intradaily Patterns In Stock Returns," (1), 99-118.
Scott, Jonathan A. and Terrence C. Smith. "The Effect Of The Bankruptcy Reform Act Of 1978 On Small Business Loan Pricing," (1), 119-140.
Dennis, Debra K. and John J. McConnell. "Corporate Mergers And Security Returns," (2), 143-187.
Seyhun, H. Nejat. "Insiders' Profits, Cost Of Trading, And Market Efficiency," (2), 189-212.
Brennan, Michael J. "A Theory Of Price Limits In Futures Markets," (2), 213-233.
Vu, Joseph D. "An Empirical Investigation Of Calls Of Non-Convertible Bonds," (2), 235-265.
Park, Sang Yong and Marc R. Reinganum. "The Puzzling Price Behavior Of Treasury Bills That Mature At The Turn Of Calendar Months," (2), 267-283.
Lakonishok, Josef and Theo Vermaelen. "Tax-Induced Trading Around Ex-Dividend Days," (3), 287-319.
Dietrich-Campbell, Bruce and Eduardo Schwartz. "Valuing Debt Options: Empirical Evidence," (3), 321-343.
Brickley, James A. and Christopher M. James. "Access To Deposit Insurance, Insolvency Rules And The Stock Returns Of Financial Institutions," (3), 345-372.
Kalay, Avner and Uri Loewenstein. "The Informational Content Of The Timing Of Dividend Announcements," (3), 373-388.
Benninga, Simon and Aris Protopapadakis. "General Equilibrium Properties Of The Term Structure Of Interest Rates," (3), 389-410.

Journal of Financial Economics
Volume 17, 1986

French, Kenneth R. and Richard Roll. "Stock Return Variances: The Arrival Of Information And The Reaction Of Traders," (1), 5-26.
Dunn, Kenneth B. and Kenneth J. Singleton. "Modeling The Term Structure Of Interest Rates Under Non-Separable Utility And Durability Of Goods," (1), 27-56.
Holthausen, Robert W. and Richard W. Leftwich. "The Effect Of Bond Rating Changes On Common Stock Prices," (1), 57-90.
Barone-Adesi, Giovanni and Robert E. Whaley. "The Valuation Of American Call Options And The Expected Ex-Dividend Stock Price Decline," (1), 91-111.
Dimson, Elroy and Paul Marsh. "Event Study Methodologies And The Size Effect: The Case Of UK Press Recommendations," (1), 113-142.
Lo, Andrew W. "Statistical Tests Of Contingent-Claims Asset-Pricing Models: A New Methodology," (1), 143-174.
Fama, Eugene F. "Term Premiums And Default Premiums In Money Markets," (1), 175-196.
Smirlock, Michael and Laura Starks. "Day-Of-The-Week And Intraday Effects In Stock Returns," (1), 197-210.
Mankiw, N. Gregory. "The Equity Premium And The Concentration Of Aggregate Shocks," (1), 211-219.
Amihud, Yakov and Haim Mendelson. "Asset Pricing And The Bid-Asked Spread," (2), 223-249.
Ramaswamy, Krishna and Suresh M. Sundaresan. "The Valuation Of Floating-Rate Instruments: Theory And Evidence," (2), 251-272.
Langohr, Herwig M. and Claude J. Viallet. "Compensation And Wealth Transfers In The French Nationalizations: 1981-1982," (2), 273-312.
Richardson, Gordon, Stephen E. Sefcik and Rex Thompson. "A Test Of Dividend Irrelevance Using Volume Reactions To A Change In Dividend Policy," (2), 313-333.
Buser, Stephen A. and Patrick J. Hess. "Empirical Determinants Of The Relative Yields On Taxable And Tax-Exempt Securities," (2), 335-355.
Keim, Donald B. and Robert F. Stambaugh. "Predicting Returns In The Stock And Bond Markets," (2), 357-390.
Chang, Eric C. and J. Michael Pinegar. "Return Seasonality And Tax-Loss Selling In The Market For Long-Term Government And Corporate Bonds," (2), 391-416.

Journal of Financial Economics
Volume 18, 1987

Majd, Saman and Robert S. Pindyck. "Time To Build, Option Value, And Investment Decisions," (1), 7-28.
Masulis, Ronald W. "Changes In Ownership Structure: Conversions Of Mutual Savings And Loans To Stock Charter," (1), 29-60.
Kandel, Shmuel and Robert F. Stambaugh. "On Correlations And Inferences About Mean--Variance Efficiency," (1), 61-90.
Shanken, Jay. "Multivariate Proxies And Asset Pricing Relations: Living With The Roll Critique," (1), 91-110.
Larcker, David F. and Thomas Lys. "An Empirical Analysis Of The Incentives To Engage In Costly Information Acquisition: The Case Of Risk Arbitrage," (1), 111-126.
Ferson, Wayne E. and John J. Merrick, Jr. "Non-Stationarity And Stage-Of-The-Business-Cycle Effects In Consumption-Based Asset Pricing Relations," (1), 127-146.
Furtado, Eugene P. H. and Michael S. Rozeff. "The Wealth Effects Of Company Initiated Management Changes," (1), 147-160.
Ariel, Robert A. "A Monthly Effect In Stock Returns," (1), 161-174.
Allen, Paul R. and C. F. Sirmans. "An Analysis Of Gains To Acquiring Firm's Shareholders: The Special Case Of REITs," (1), 175-184.
McCulloch, J. Huston. "The Monotonicity Of The Term Premium: A Closer Look," (1), 185-192.
Penman, Stephen H. "The Distribution Of Earnings News Over Time And Seasonalities In Aggregate Stock Returns," (2), 199-228.
Hite, Gailen L., James E. Owers and Ronald C. Rogers. "The Market For Interfirm Asset Sales: Partial Sell-Offs And Total Liquidations," (2), 229-252.
Kaul, Gautam. "Stock Returns And Inflation: The Role Of The Monetary Sector," (2), 253-276.
Diamond, Douglas W. and Robert E. Verrecchia. "Constraints On Short-Selling And Asset Price Adjustment To Private Information," (2), 277-312.
Partch, M. Megan. "The Creation Of A Class Of Limited Voting Common Stock And Shareholder Wealth," (2), 313-340.
MacKinlay, A. Craig. "On Multivariate Tests Of The CAPM," (2), 341-372.
Campbell, John Y. "Stock Returns And The Term Structure," (2), 373-400.
Brickley, James A. and Frederick H. Dark. "The Choice Of Organizational Form: The Case Of Franchising," (2), 401-420.

Journal of Financial Economics
Volume 19, 1987

French, Kenneth R., G. William Schwert and Robert F. Stambaugh. "Expected Stock Returns And Volatility," (1), 3-30.
Barclay, Michael J. "Dividends, Taxes, And Common Stock Prices: The Ex-Dividend Day Behavior Of Common Stock Prices Before The Income Tax," (1), 31-44.
Schallheim, James S., Ramon E. Johnson, Ronald C. Lease and John J. McConnell. "The Determinants Of Yields On Financial Leasing Contracts," (1), 45-68.
Easley, David and Maureen O'Hara. "Price, Trade Size, And Information In Securities Markets," (1), 69-90.

Ofer, Aharon R. and Ashok Natarajan. "Convertible Call Policies: An Empirical Analysis Of An Information-Signaling Hypothesis," (1), 91-108.

Kalay, Avner and Adam Shimrat. "Firm Value And Seasoned Equity Issues: Price Pressure, Wealth Redistribution, Or Negative Information," (1), 109-126.

Jarrell, Gregg A. and Annette B. Poulsen. "Shark Repellents And Stock Prices: The Effects Of Antitakeover Amendments Since 1980," (1), 127-168.

Cumby, Robert E. and David M. Modest. "Testing For Market Timing Ability: A Framework For Forecast Evaluation," (1), 169-190.

Shanken, Jay. "A Bayesian Approach To Testing Portfolio Efficiency," (2), 195-216.

James, Christopher. "Some Evidence On The Uniqueness Of Bank Loans," (2), 217-236.

Holthausen, Robert W., Richard W. Leftwich and David Mayers. "The Effect Of Large Block Transactions On Security Prices: A Cross-Sectional Analysis," (2), 237-268.

Ritter, Jay R. "The Costs Of Going Public," (2), 269-282.

Comment, Robert and Gregg A. Jarrell. "Two-Tier And Negotiated Tender Offers: The Imprisonment Of The Free-Riding Shareholder," (2), 283-310.

Kim, E. Han and John D. Schatzberg. "Voluntary Corporate Liquidations," (2), 311-328.

Huang, Yen-Sheng and Ralph A. Walkling. "Target Abnormal Returns Associated With Acquisition Announcements: Payment, Acquisition Form, And Managerial Resistance," (2), 329-350.

Wiggins, James B. "Option Values Under Stochastic Volatility: Theory And Empirical Estimates," (2), 351-372.

Lo, Andrew W. "Semi-Parametric Upper Bounds For Option Prices And Expected Payoffs," (2), 373-388.

Gibbons, Michael R. and Jay Shanken. "Subperiod Aggression And The Power Of Multivariate Tests Of Portfolio Efficiency," (2), 389-394.

Journal of Financial Economics
Volume 20, 1988

Jensen, Michael C. and Jerold B. Warner. "The Distribution Of Power Among Corporate Managers, Shareholders, And Directors," (1/2), 3-24.

Stulz, Rene M. "Managerial Control Of Voting Rights: Financing Policies And The Market For Corporate Control," (1/2), 25-54.

Harris, Milton and Artur Raviv. "Corporate Control Contests And Capital Structure," (1/2), 55-86.

Dann, Larry Y. and Harry DeAngelo. "Corporate Financial Policy And Corporate Control: A Study Of Defensive Adjustments In Asset And Ownership Structure," (1/2), 87-128.

Jarrell, Gregg A. and Annette B. Poulsen. "Dual-Class Recapitalizations As Antitakeover Mechanisms: The Recent Evidence," (1/2), 129-152.

Ruback, Richard S. "Coercive Dual-Class Exchange Offers," (1/2), 153-174.

Grossman, Sanford J. and Oliver D. Hart. "One Share--One Vote And The Market For Corporate Control," (1/2), 175-202.

Harris, Milton and Artur Raviv. "Corporate Governance: Voting Rights And Majority Rules," (1/2), 203-236.

Pound, John. "Proxy Contests And The Efficiency Of Shareholder Oversight," (1/2), 237-266.

Brickley, James A., Ronald C. Lease and Clifford W. Smith, Jr. "Ownership Structure And Voting On Antitakeover Amendments," (1/2), 267-292.

Morck, Randall, Andrei Shleifer and Robert W. Vishny. "Management Ownership And Market Valuation: An Empirical Analysis," (1/2), 293-316.

Holderness, Clifford G. and Dennis P. Sheehan. "The Role Of Majority Shareholders In Publicly Held Corporations: An Exploratory Analysis," (1/2), 317-346.

Malatesta, Paul H. and Ralph A. Walkling. "Poison Pill Securities: Stockholder Wealth, Profitability, And Ownership Structure," (1/2), 347-376.

Ryngaert, Michael. "The Effect Of Poison Pill Securities On Shareholder Wealth," (1/2), 377-418.

Kamma, Sreenivas, Joseph Weintrop and Peggy Wier. "Investors' Perceptions Of The Delaware Supreme Court Decision In Unocal V. Mesa," (1/2), 419-430.

Weisbach, Michael S. "Outside Directors And CEO Turnover," (1/2), 431-460.

Warner, Jerold B., Ross L. Watts and Karen H. Wruck. "Stock Prices And Top Management Changes," (1), 461-492.

Klein, April and James Rosenfeld. "Targeted Share Repurchases And Top Management Changes," (1), 493-506.

Journal of Financial Economics
Volume 21, 1988

Bradley, Michael, Anand Desai and E. Han Kim. "Synergistic Gains From Corporate Acquisitions And Their Division Between The Stockholders Of Target And Acquiring Firms," (1), 3-40.

Stambaugh, Robert F. "The Information In Forward Rates: Implications For Models Of The Term Structure," (1), 41-70.

Barclay, Michael J. and Robert H. Litzenberger. "Announcement Effects Of New Equity Issues And The Use Of Intraday Price Data," (1), 71-100.

Chari, V. V., Ravi Jagannathan and Aharon R. Ofer. "Seasonalities In Security Returns: The Case Of Earnings Announcements," (1), 101-122.

Glosten, Lawrence R. and Lawrence E. Harris. "Estimating The Components Of The Bid/Ask Spread," (1), 123-142.

Healy, Paul M. and Krishna G. Palepu. "Earnings Information Conveyed By Dividend Initiations And Omissions," (2), 149-176.

Wheatley, Simon. "Some Tests Of International Equity Integration," (2), 177-212.

Lehmann, Bruce N. and David M. Modest. "The Empirical Foundations Of The Arbitrage Pricing Theory," (2), 213-254.

Connor, Gregory and Robert A. Korajczyk. "Risk And Return In An Equilibrium APT: Application Of A New Test Methodology," (2), 255-290.

Karpoff, Jonathan M. and Ralph A. Walkling. "Short-Term Trading Around Ex-Dividend Days: Additional Evidence," (2), 291-298.

Journal of Financial Economics
Volume 22, 1988

Fama, Eugene F. and Kenneth R. French. "Dividend Yields And Expected Stock Returns," (1), 3-26.

Poterba, James M. and Lawrence H. Summers. "Mean Reversion In Stock Prices: Evidence And Implications," (1), 27-60.

Barclay, Michael J. and Clifford W. Smith, Jr. "Corporate Payout Policy: Cash Dividends Versus Open-Market Repurchases," (1), 61-82.

Brennan, Michael J. and Thomas E. Copeland. "Stock Splits, Stock Prices, And Transaction Costs," (1), 83-102.

Day, Theodore E. and Craig M. Lewis. "The Behavior Of The Volatility Implicit In The Prices Of Stock Index Options," (1), 103-122.

Ball, Clifford A. and Walter N. Torous. "Investigating Security-Price Performance In The Presence Of Event-Date Uncertainty," (1), 123-154.

Linn, Scott C. and J. Michael Pinegar. "The Effect Of Issuing Preferred Stock On Common And Preferred Stockholder Wealth," (1), 155-184.

Kim, Yong Cheol and Rene M. Stulz. "The Eurobond Market And Corporate Financial Policy: A Test Of The Clientele Hypothesis," (2), 189-206.

Pound, John. The Information Effects Of Takeover Bids And Resistance," (2), 207-228.

Hasbrouck, Joel. Trades, Quotes, Inventories, And Information," (2), 229-252.

Blackwell, David W. and David S. Kidwell. "An Investigation Of Cost Differences Between Public Sales And Private Placements Of Debt," (2), 253-278.

Coles, Jeffrey L. and Uri Loewenstein. "Equilibrium Pricing And Portfolio Composition In The Presence Of Uncertain Parameters," (2), 279-304.

Harvey, Campbell R. "The Real Term Structure And Consumption Growth," (2), 305-334.

Mark, Nelson C. "Time-Varying Betas And Risk Premia In The Pricing Of Forward Foreign Exchange Contracts," (2), 335-354.

Brown, Keith C., W. V. Harlow and Seha M. Tinic. "Risk Aversion, Uncertain Information, And Market Efficiency," (2), 355-386.

Journal of Financial Economics
Volume 23, 1989

Wruck, Karen Hopper. "Equity Ownership Concentration And Firm Value: Evidence From Private Equity Financings," (1), 3-28.

DeAngelo, Harry and Linda DeAngelo. "Proxy Contests And The Governance Of Publicly Held Corporations," (1), 29-60.

Skinner, Douglas J. "Options Markets And Stock Return Volatility," (1), 61-78.

Handa, Puneet, S. P. Kothari and Charles Wasley. "The Relation Between The Return Interval And Betas: Implications For The Size Effect," (1), 79-100.

Nathan, Kevin S. and Terrence B. O'Keefe. "The Rise In Takeover Premiums: An Exploratory Study," (1), 101-120.

Hayn, Carla. "Tax Attributes As Determinants Of Shareholder Gains In Corporate Acquisitions," (1), 121-154.

Marais, Laurentius, Katherine Schipper and Abbie Smith. "Wealth Effects Of Going Private For Senior Securities," (1), 155-191.

Longstaff, Francis A. "A Nonlinear General Equilibrium Model Of The Term Structure Of Interest Rates," (2), 195-224.

Franks, Julian R. and Robert S. Harris. "Shareholder Wealth Effects Of Corporate Takeovers: The U.K. Experience 1955-1985," (2),225-250.

Koh, Francis and Terry Walter. "A Direct Test Of Rock's Model Of The Pricing Of Unseasoned Issues," (2), 251-272.

Dunn, Kenneth B. and Kenneth M. Eades. "Voluntary Conversion Of Convertible Securities And The Optimal Call Strategy," (2), 273-302.

Allen, Franklin and Gerald R. Faulhaber. "Signaling By Underpricing In The IPO Market," (2), 303-324.

Wheatley, Simon M. "A Critique Of Latent Variable Tests Of Asset Pricing Models," (2), 325-338.

Gay, Gerald D., Robert W. Kolb and Kenneth Yung. "Trader Rationality In The Exercise Of Futures Options," (2), 339-362.

Brenner, Menachem, Marti G. Subrahmanyam and Jun Uno. "The Behavior Of Prices In The Nikkei Spot And Futures Market," (2), 363-384.

Corrado, Charles J. "A Nonparametric Test For Abnormal Security-Price Performance In Event Studies," (2), 385-396.

Journal of Financial Economics
Volume 24, 1989

Scholes, Myron S. and Mark A. Wolfson. "Decentralized Investment Banking: The Case Of Discount Dividend-Reinvestment And Stock-Purchase Plans," (1), 7-36.

Mitchell, Mark L. and Jeffry M. Netter. "Triggering The 1987 Stock Market Crash: Antitakeover Provisions In The Proposed House Ways And Means Tax Bill," (1), 37-68.

Karpoff, Jonathan M. and Edward M. Rice. "Organizational Form, Share Transferability, And Firm Performance: Evidence From The ANCSA Corporations," (1), 69-106.

Moore, William T., Donald G. Christensen and Rodney L. Roenfeldt. "Equity Valuation Effects Of Forming Master Limited Partnerships," (1), 107-124.

Muscarella, Chris J. and Michael R. Vetsuypens. "A Simple Test Of Baron's Model Of IPO Underpricing," (1), 125-136.

Lang, Larry H. P., Rene M. Stulz and Ralph A. Walkling. "Managerial Performance, Tobin's Q, And The Gains From Successful Tender Offers," (1), 137-154.

Lauterbach, Beni. "Consumption Volatility, Production Volatility, Spot-Rate Volatility, And The Returns On Treasury Bills And Bonds," (1), 155-180.

Lang, Larry H. P. and Robert H. Litzenberger. "Dividend Announcements: Cash Flow Signalling Vs. Free Cash Flow Hypothesis?," (1), 181-192.

Merville, Larry J. and Dan R. Pieptea. "Stock-Price Volatility, Mean-Reverting Diffusion, And Noise," (1), 193-214.

Kaplan, Steven. "The Effects Of Management Buyouts On Operating Performance And Value," (2), 217-254.

Harris, Milton and Artur Raviv. "The Design Of Securities," (2), 255-288.

Harvey, Campbell R. "Time-Varying Conditional Covariances In Tests Of Asset Pricing Models," (2), 289-318.

Young, Leslie and Glenn W. Boyle. "Forward And Futures Prices In A General Equilibrium Monetary Model," (2), 319-342.

Benveniste, Lawrence M. and Paul A. Spindt. "How Investment Bankers Determine The Offer Price And Allocation Of New Issues," (2), 343-362.

Eckbo, B. Espen and Herwig Langohr. "Information Disclosure, Method Of Payment, And Takeover Premiums: Public And Private Tender Offers In France," (2), 363-404.

Journal of Financial Economics
Volume 25, 1989

Turner, Christopher M., Richard Startz and Charles R. Nelson. "A Markov Model Of Heteroskedasticity, Risk, And Learning In The Stock Market," (1), 3-20.

Fama, Eugene F. and Kenneth R. French. "Business Conditions And Expected Returns On Stocks And Bonds," (1), 23-50.

Ball, Ray and S. P. Kothari. "Nonstationary Expected Returns: Implications For Tests Of Market Efficiency And Serial Correlations In Returns," (1), 51-74.

Keim, Donald B. "Trading Patterns, Bid-Ask Spreads, And Estimated Security Returns: The Case Of Common Stocks At Calendar Turning Points," (1), 75-98.

Lummer, Scott L. and John J. McConnell. "Further Evidence On The Bank Lending Process And The Capital-Market Response To Bank Loan Agreements," (1), 99-122.

Shleifer, Andrei and Robert W. Vishny. "Management Entrenchment: The Case Of Manager-Specific Investments," (1), 123-140.

Kale, Jayant R., Thomas H. Noe and Gerald D. Gay. "Share Repurchase Through Transferable Put Rights: Theory And Case Study," (1), 141-160.

Baker, George P. and Karen H. Wruck. "Organizational Changes And Value Creation In Leveraged Buyouts: The Case Of The O.M. Scott & Sons Company," (2), 163-190.

Kaplan, Steven N. "Campeau's Acquisition Of Federated: Value Destroyed Or Value Added," (2), 191-212.

Tufano, Peter. "Financial Innovation And First-Mover Advantages," (2), 213-240.

Gilson, Stuart C. "Management Turnover And Financial Distress," (2), 241-262.

Mikkelson, Wayne H. and M. Megan Partch. "Managers' Voting Rights And Corporate Control," (2), 263-290.

Karpoff, Jonathan M. and Paul H. Malatesta. "The Wealth Effects Of Second-Generation State Takeover Legislation," (2), 291-322.

Richardson, Matthew and James H. Stock. "Drawing Inferences From Statistics Based On Multiyear Asset Returns," (2), 323-348.

Israel, Ronen, Aharon R. Ofer and Daniel R. Siegel. "The Information Content Of Equity-For-Debt Swaps: An Investigation Of Analyst Forecasts Of Firm Cash Flows," (2), 349-370.

Barclay, Michael J. and Clifford G. Holderness. "Private Benefits From Control Of Public Corporations," (2), 371-396.

Journal of Financial Economics
Volume 26, 1990

Stulz, Rene M. "Managerial Discretion And Optimal Financing Policies," (1), 3-28.

Long, John B., Jr. "The Numeraire Portfolio," (1), 29-70.

Holthausen, Robert W., Richard W. Leftwich and David Mayers. "Large-Block Transactions, The Speed Of Response, And Temporary And Permanent Stock-Price Effects," (1), 71-96.

Longstaff, Francis A. "The Valuation Of Options On Yields,"(1),97-122.

Rosenthal, Leonard and Colin Young. "The Seemingly Anomalous Price Behavior Of Royal Dutch/Shell And Unilever N.V./PLC," (1), 123-142.

Kaen, Fred R. and Hassan Tehranian. "Information Effects In Financial Distress: The Case Of Seabrook Station," (1), 143-171.

Rosenstein, Stuart and Jeffrey G. Wyatt. "Outside Directors, Board Independence, And Shareholder Wealth," (2), 175-192.

Bajaj, Mukesh. and Anand M. Vijh. "Dividend Clienteles And The Information Content Of Dividend Changes," (2), 193-220.

Harvey, Campbell R. and Guofu Zhou. "Bayesian Inference In Asset Pricing Tests," (2), 221-254.

Chan, Su Han, John D. Martin and John W. Kensinger. "Corporate Research And Development Expenditures And Share Value," (2), 255-276.

Blackwell, David W., M. Wayne Marr and Michael F. Spivey. "Plant-Closing Decisions And The Market Value Of The Firm," (2), 277-288.

Varma, Raj and Donald R. Chambers. "The Role Of Financial Innovation In Raising Capital: Evidence From Deep Discount Debt Offers," (2), 289-298.

Journal of Financial Economics
Volume 27, 1990

Roe, Mark J. "Political And Legal Restraints On Ownership And Control Of Public Companies," (1), 7-42.

Prowse, Stephen D. "Institutional Investment Patterns And Corporate Financial Behavior In The United States And Japan," (1), 43-66.

Hoshi, Takeo, Anil Kashyap and David Scharfstein. "The Role Of Banks In Reducing The Costs Of Financial Distress In Japan," (1), 67-88.

Grundfest, Joseph A. "Subordination Of American Capital," (1), 89-114.

Donaldson, Gordon. "Voluntary Restructuring: The Case Of General Mills," (1), 117-142.

Smith, Abbie J. "Corporate Ownership Structure And Performance: The Case Of Management Buyouts," (1), 143-164.

Lichtenberg, Frank R. and Donald Siegel. "The Effects Of Leveraged Buyouts On Productivity And Related Aspects Of Firm Behavior," (1), 165-194.

Asquith, Paul and Thierry A. Wizman. "Event Risk, Covenants, And Bondholder Returns In Leveraged Buyouts," (1), 195-214.

Kaplan, Steven N. and Jeremy C. Stein. "How Risky Is The Debt Of Highly Leveraged Transactions?," (1), 215-246.

Palepu, Krishna G. "Consequences Of Leveraged Buyouts," (1), 247-262.

Rosett, Joshua G. "Do Union Wealth Concessions Explain Takeover Premiums? The Evidence On Contract Wages," (1), 263-282.

Weiss, Lawrence A. "Bankruptcy Resolution: Direct Costs And Violaton Of Priority Of Claims," (2), 285-314.

Gilson, Stuart C., Kose John and Larry H. P. Lang. "Troubled Debt Restructurings: An Empirical Study Of Private Reorganiztion Of Firms In Default," (2), 315-354.

Gilson, Stuart C. "Bankruptcy, Boards, Banks, And Blockholders: Evidence On Changes In Corporate Ownership And Control When Firms Default," (2), 355-388.

Kaplan, Steven N. and David Reishus. "Outside Directorships And Corporate Performance," (2), 389-410.

Easterbrook, Frank H. "Is Corporate Bankruptcy Efficient?," (2), 411-418.

Wruck, Karen Hopper. "Financial Distress, Reorganiztion, And Organizational Efficiency," (2), 419-444.

Barry, Christopher B., Chris J. Muscarella, John W. Peavy, III and Michael R. Vetsuypens. "The Role Of Venture Capital In The Creation Of Public Companies: Evidence From The Going-Public Process," (2), 447-472.

Sahlman, William A. "The Structure And Governance Of Venture-Capital Organizations," (2), 473-524.

Gordon, Lilli A. and John Pound. "ESOPs And Corporate Control," (2), 525-556.

Lehn, Kenneth, Jeffry Netter and Annette Poulsen. "Consolidating Corporate Control: Dual-Class Recapitalizations Versus Leveraged Buyouts," (2) 557-580.

Herzel, Leo. "Corporate Governance Through Statistical Eyes," (2), 581-594.

McConnell, John J. and Henri Servaes. "Additional Evidence On Equity Ownership And Corporate Value," (2), 595-612.

D'Ambrosio, Charles A. "A Multi-Optioned Computer Program To Illustrate Investment Concepts," 73-76.
Osteryoung, Jerome S. "The Use Of Computers In Teaching Capital Budgeting," 77-79.
Glimpse, Warren G. "The Compustat Analysis System: An Integrated Software Package For Financial Analysis And Modeling," 80-87.
Eckardt, Walter L., Jr. "PORTU: A Computer Program To Construct Portfolio Returns," 88-90.
Abranovic, Wynn A. "An Interactive Computer Program For Financial Break-Even Analysis," 91-93.
Hoffmeister, J. Ronald. "Student Evaluation Of Financial Simulation Games As A Learning Experience," 94-96.

Journal of Financial Education
Volume 6, 1977

Cooley, Philip L. and J. Louis Heck. "A Survey Of The Introductory Business Finance Course: The Professor's Viewpoint," 3-8.
Granger, Fred W., Jr. and Carroll D. Aby, Jr. "A Survey Of The Introductory Investment Course Design," 9-13.
Valachi, Donald J. "An Investment Framework For The Real Estate Course," 14-16.
Findlay, M. Chapman, III and R. A. Tarantello. "An M.B.A. Program In Real Estate With A Financial Emphasis," 17-18.
Finnerty, Joseph E. "The Impact Of The New Copyright Revision Bill On Finance Teachers," 19.
Walker, Michael C. "A Course In The Financial Management Of Not-For-Profit Organizations," 20-23.
Springate, David J. "Designing A Course In Non-Profit Financial Management," 24-26.
Einhorn, Raymond and H. Kent Baker. "The Institute For Applied Public Financial Management: An Innovative Approach," 27-32.
Bidwell, Clinton M. "Oral Classroom Examinations," 33-35.
Lewis, John H. and Dillard B. Tinsley. "Curriculum Development For Commercial Bank Management," 36-39.
McCarty, Daniel E. and Philip M. Scherer. "The Demand For Finance Majors By Financial Institutions In The Southwest," 40-44.
Branch, Ben. "Guidelines For Students Studying Finance," 45-50.
Sanderson, George Robert. "The Classroom Professor As A Manager," 51-53.
Sussman, Jeffrey. "Individualized Student Learning Contracts In Finance," 54-56.
Hirt, Geoffrey A. "Real Dollar Portfolios Managed By Students - An Evaluation," 57-61.
Petry, Glenn H. "Economic Feasibility Studies As Assigned In The Graduate Finance Course," 62-65.
Baker, H. Kent. "Understanding International Finance Through A Study Tour Program," 66-69.
Singhvi, Surendra S. and Harsha B. Desai. "An Overview Of The Case Method Of Instruction," 70-74.
Schaffer, Burton F. and D. Ordell Calkins. "Compustat: Bringing The Real World Into The Classroom," 75-78.
Grambo, Ralph W. and Alan R. Peslak. "MAXFINANCE: A Package Of Programs For Comprehensive Capital Budgeting Cases," 79-80.
Eckardt, Walter L., Jr. "An Academic Resources Management Information System (ARMIS)," 81-83.
Edelman, Richard B. "A Filter Rule Program Used In Teaching Investments," 84-86.
Trykowski, Ben L. "Integrating A Computerized Examination Generating System Into The Basic Business Finance Course," 87-89.
Bednar, Dick. "Residual Analysis Using Compustat Data," 90-92.
Bavishi, Vinod B., Michael R. Czinkota, Harry A. Shawky and David A. Ricks. "International Financial Management -- A Survey Of Research Trends And An Annotated Bibliography, 1973-1976," 93-95.
Aggarwal, Raj. "International Business Finance: A Selected Bibliography," 96.
Senchack, Andrew J., Jr. "Modern Capital Market Theory: A Bibliography Of Its Influence In The Finance, Economics, And Accounting Literature," 97-98.

Journal of Financial Education
Volume 7, 1978

Brigham, Eugene F. "Alternative Approaches To Teaching The Basic Finance Course," 3-6.
Stonehill, Arthur. "Internationalizing The Business Core: The Finance Component," 7-12.
Goulet, Peter G. "Introductory Investments: A Survey Of Practice And A Note On Direction," 13-17.
Crane, Donald B. "Personal Finance: A Team-Teaching Approach," 18-20.
Sanderson, George Robert. "A Bank Management Simulation Game As A Learning Device," 21-24.
Claiborn, Stephen A. and J. Markham Collins. "The Entering Job Market For Careers In Finance," 25-29.
Perlick, Walter W. "Bank Hiring Practices And Training Programs," 30-33.
Branch, Ben. "Guiding Students In Conducting Original Research," 34-36.
Render, Barry, William Wagoner, James R. Bobo and Stephen Corliss. "Finance Doctorates In The South: A 1977-1981 Supply And Demand Analysis," 37-41.
Mayo, Herbert. "Advising College Students," 42-43.
Blevins, Dallas R. "The Need For Education In Municipal Finance," 44-46.
Finnerty, Joseph E. "The Master Of Science In Finance As An Alternative To The M.B.A.," 47-48.
Viscione, Jerry A. and George Aragon. "The Case Method In Undergraduate Finance," 49-52.
Johnson, Keith B. "Long-Term Financial Planning Using A Live Case," 53-55.
Vandenberg, Pieter A. "Individualized Case Studies For Students," 56-58.

Young, Charles W. "Computer-Assisted Analysis As The Focus For A Course In Financial Management," 59-62.
Brooks, LeRoy D. "An Evaluation Of Financial Management Learning Simulations," 63-68.
Zock, Richard. "Injecting Realism Into Computer Games: A Negotiation With The Investment Banker," 69-71.
Eckhardt, Walter L., Jr. "PERS: The Evolution Of A Computer-Based Portfolio Game," 72-75.
Runyon, L. Richard. "The Use Of A Computer Simulation Game In The Investments Course," 76-79.
Simonds, Richard R. "Case Management Simulation," 80-82.
Ellis, John W. and David J. O'Farrell. "Utilizing Mixed Integer Programming In The Construction Of Income-Oriented Portfolios," 83-85.
Cretien, Paul D., Jr. "A Computer Program To Derive Option Price Curves," 86-87.
Chesser, Delton L. and Pamela K. Coats. "A Computer-Based Instructional Tool For Capital Budgeting," 88-89.
Kudla, Ronald J. "A Computer Program For Solving The Capital Rationing Problem," 90-91.
Alexander, Gordon J. "PORTFO: A Computer Program Involving The Application Of Portfolio Theory," 92-94.
Senchack, Andrew J., Jr. "A Bibliography Of Corporate Financial Theory And Empirics," 95-96.

Journal of Financial Education
Volume 8, 1979

Hill, Ned C. "A Course In Short-Term Financial Management For The M.B.A.," 3-10.
Becker, Charles M. "Integration Of The Security Analysis Course With The C.F.A. Program," 11-18.
Crane, Donald B. "Portfolio Management As A Second Course In Investments," 19-22.
Daigler, Robert T. "Personal Financial Planning As A New Major Within Finance," 23-29.
Warschauer, Thomas. "The Use Of Project/Contract Method In The Investments Course," 30-32.
Racette, George A. "The Role Of Financial Theory In Educating The Financial Manager," 33-39.
Hogan, Stephen D. and Donald A. Boyd. "PSI: A Favorable Experience," 40-44.
DeMong, Richard F., Laurence C. Pettit and B. J. Campsey. "Finance Curriculum For The Future: Perceptions Of Practitioners Versus Academicians," 45-48.
Abdelsamad, M. H. and J. E. Thornton. "An Evaluation Of Business Masters Programs By Graduates," 49-52.
Petry, Glenn H. and Russell J. Fuller. "A Comparison Of Institutions Publishing In Finance Journals With Those Presenting Papers At Finance Association Meetings," 53-57.
Simpson, W. Gary and Brenda P. Sumrall. "The Determinants Of Objective Test Scores By Finance Students," 58-62.
Simon, Simon M. "The Case Method Approach To Teaching Decision Making And Analysis," 63-70.
Fischer, Donald E. and Gerald P. Madden. "Improving The Investments Course With A Securities Trading Game," 71-76.
Pettit, Laurence C., Jr. "A Course In Small Business Finance," 77-79.
Sachlis, J. Minor. "A Business Finance Simulation," 80-85.
Daniel, Donnie L. and William A. Sirmon. "Computerized Bank Financial Statements: Classroom Applications," 86-89.
Maness, Terry S. "A Financial Planning Model: A Teaching Tool," 90-93.
Clouse, Maclyn L. "A Simulation Model To Link The Economic Environment With Corporate Financial Decisions," 94-96.
Hand, Herbert H. and W. Palmer. "A Bibliography Of Operating Expense Information Sources For Small Businesses," 97-98.

Journal of Financial Education
Volume 9, 1980

Carter, E. Eugene and Rita M. Rodriquez. "Internationalizing The Corporate Finance Course According To AACSB Guidelines," 3-7.
O'Conner, Dennis J. and Alberto T. Bueso. "The New Managerial Finance: The Key Course In The Business Administration Curriculum," 8-11.
Sanderson, G. Robert. "Intuitive Versus Analytical Thinking In Investment Decision-Making," 12-16.
D'Ambrosio, Charles A. "Financial Theory In Personal Finance Courses," 17-18.
Kerr, Halbert S. "The Evaluation Of Acquisition Candidates As A Comprehensive Financial Management Project," 19-23.
Crabbs, Roger A. "Teaching Small Business Management -- A Living Experience," 24-26.
Hirt, Geoffrey A. and Charles M. Becker. "Merits And Guidelines For Industry-Security Analysis Term Papers," 27-32.
Grablowsky, Bernie J. and Dexter R. Rowell. "The Market For Finance Majors: The Myths And Realities Reconsidered," 33-41.
Peters, Robert M. and William Poppei. "An Accelerated Program For Bankers In Accounting/Finance," 42-45.
Wurtzebach, Charles H. "Integrating A Real Estate Sequence Into The Finance Curriculum," 46-50.
Schaffer, Burton F. and D. Ordell Calkins. "An Appraisal Of Prerequisites To Business Finance," 51-55.
Sherman, Lawrence F. "A Proposed Method For Financial Case Analysis," 57-65.
Blevins, Dallas R. "A Student's Guide To The Case Method," 66-73.
McInish, Thomas H. "Teaching The Art Of Market Making With A Game Simulation," 74-76.
Dothan, Uri and Joseph Williams. "Financial Game: Capital Market Equilibrium," 77-78.
O'Connell, John J. and Dwight Anderson. "Risk And Insurance As Part Of Teaching Financial Analysis," 79-82.
Klein, Richard. "Teaching Computer-Based Financial Modeling," 83-88.
Riley, William B. and Austin H. Montgomery, Jr. "The Use Of

Overstreet, George A., Lawrence C. Pettit and Robert S. Kemp. "A Professional Approach To Building An Undergraduate Finance Program: The McIntire Experience," 42-52.

Avard, Stephen L. and Jane H. White. "Readability Study Of Principles Of Financial Management Textbooks," 53-62.

Strong, Robert A. "Using Gunning's Fog Index With Term Papers And Outside Reading Lists," 63-67.

Milano, Duane R., Stephen L. Avard and John Russell Arens. "Microcomputer Applications For Preparing Tests In Entry Level Financial Management Courses," 68-78.

Singleton, J. Clay. "A Stock Options Game," 79-88.

Journal of Financial Education
Volume 16, 1987

Malitz, Ileen and Richard Cohn. "The Nonequivalence Of Subordinated Debt And Equity From The Senior Creditor's Standpoint: A Pedagogical Note," 1-5.

Murphy, J. Austin. "The Effect Of Portfolio Insurance On The Probability Distribution Of Return," 6-11.

Jessell, Kenneth A. and Daniel E. McCarty. "A Note On Marginal Analysis, NPV Criterion And Wealth Maximization," 12-15.

Rose, John T. "The Weighted Average Cost Of Capital And The Marginal Cost Of Capital: A Pedagogical Note," 16-18.

Kester, George W. "An Overview Of Dow Jones News/Retrieval For Teaching Investments," 19-25.

Johnson, Robert R. and Jerome F. Sherman. "The Financial World: A Campus And Travel Course," 26-31.

Hamilton, Arthur J. and S. Brooks Marshall. "The Chartered Financial Analyst Certification: Implications For The Finance Curriculum," 32-39.

Tatar, Daniel D. "Teaching Securities Analysis With Real Funds," 40-45.

Pope, Ralph A. "An Analysis Of The Need To Develop A Tax Course," 46-55.

Gitman, Lawrence J., William F. Lewis and Rebecca M. J. Yates. "An Approach For Assessing, Selecting And Using Finance Cases," 56-64.

Berry, Thomas D. and Edward J. Farragher. "A Survey Of Introductory Financial Management Courses," 65-72.

Taylor, Richard W. "Option Valuation For Alternative Instruments With The Black-Scholes Model: A Pedagogical Note," 73-77.

Liao, Shu S. "A Spreadsheet Approach To Receivable Payments Pattern Analysis," 78-85.

Journal of Financial Education
Volume 17, 1988

Boyd, G. Michael. "A Pedagogical Note On Pro Forma Feedback Effects," 1-5.

Harris, John M., Jr. and Richard H. Klein. "Analysis Of Leveraged Buyouts: Application Of A Simple Option Pricing Model," 6-14.

Fairchild, Keith William. "Inflation And Discounted Cash Flows," 15-18.

Rodriguez, Ricardo J. "The Quadratic Approximation To The Yield To Maturity," 19-25.

Smith, Donald J. "The Duration Of A Bond As A Price Elasticity And A Fulcrum," 26-38.

Blevins, Dallas R. "CMA: A Professional Designation For Professors And Students Of Managerial Finance," 39-43.

Planisek, Sandra L. and James P. Sanford. "Video Case Materials For Enhanced Classroom Learning: Observations And Student Reactions," 44-54.

Grablowsky, Bernie J. "The Market For MBAs: The Myths And Realities," 55-63.

Shin, Tai S. and Elbert T. Hubbard. "Current Status Of Doctoral Programs In Finance," 64-79.

Scott, David F., Jr. and Brian Rungeling. "Business Doctoral Programs: What Are The Incremental Costs Of Starting New Ones?," 80-88.

Carr, Peter. "A Calculator Program For Option Values And Implied Standard Deviations," 89-93.

Kutner, George W. "A Computerized Black-Scholes Option Valuation Model With Applications," 94-103.

Journal of Financial Education
Volume 18, 1989

Hilliard, Jimmy and Joseph F. Sinkey, Jr. "Duration Analysis As A Tool For Predicting Interest-Sensitive Cash Flows," 1-7.

Liesz, Thomas J. and Mario G. C. Reyes. "The Use Of Piagetian Concepts To Enhance Student Performance In The Introductory Finance Course," 8-14.

Followill, Richard. "Present Value And Future Value Of An Annuity Growing By A Constant Amount," 15-18.

Daskin, Allan J. "A Pedagogic Approach To Real And Nominal Interest Rates," 19-24.

Newman, Joseph A. and John M. Wachowicz, Jr. "Memorandums In The Classroom," 25-28.

Boyd, G. Michael. "Some Suggestions For A 'New And Improved' DuPont Model," 29-32.

Tessema, Asrat. "A Stock Market Game In Teaching Investments," 33-37.

Kester, George W. "A Group Project Approach To Teaching Finance Cases," 38-42.

DeFusco, Richard A., Gordon V. Karels and Thomas S. Zorn. "Agency Theory: An Application To Grading Group Projects," 43-44.

Planisek, Sandra L. "International Topics In Corporate Finance: What To Teach?," 45-53.

Taube, Paul M. and Don N. MacDonald. "The Job Market For Finance Ph.D's," 54-59.

Cudd, Mike, John R. Tanner and Michael C. Budden. "The Issue Of Student Preparedness: Perceptions Of Finance Professors," 60-64.

Madden, Gerald P. "Using Value/Screen Plus For A Portfolio Management Project," 65-70.

Ma, James C. "A Survey Of Finance Department Computer Usage In The California State University And Colleges," 71-74.

Journal of Financial Education
Volume 19, 1990

Gardner, Mona J. and Dixie L. Mills. "Financial Institutions Management Courses: A Survey Of Current Content And The Outlook For The 1990s," 1-4.

Fehrs, Donald H. "Management Decisions, Market Events, And Stock Price Changes: A Student Project For Finance Courses," 5-9.

Millar, James A. "Primary And Fully Diluted Earnings Per Share: Some Clarifying Comments," 10-14.

Saunders, Edward M., Jr. "Developing A Real-Time Microcomputerized Investment Arbitrage Course," 15-18.

Stine, Bert and Dwayne Key. "Reconciling Degrees Of Freedom When Partitioning Risk: A Teaching Note," 19-22.

Singer, Daniel and Walter Holman. "The Effective Use Of Writing In Financial Case Analysis," 23-26.

Eades, Kenneth M. and Diana Harrington. "Using A Moot Court To Teach The Dividend-Relevance Controversy," 27-32.

White, Charles S., Marilyn M. Helms and Barbara Parker. "Simulations Versus Cases: Impact On The Analysis And Interpretation Of Financial Statements," 33-36.

Brown, Kate M. "The Use Of Role Play In Teaching Corporate Finance," 37-43.

PonArul, Richard. "Treatment Of Flotation Cost Of Equity In Capital Budgeting," 44-45.

Kester, George W. "An Integrative Model For Presenting Common Stock Valuation," 46-48.

Liao, Shu S. "Spreadsheet-Based Simulation Modeling For Risk Analysis," 49-58.

Ely, David P. and Linda Hittle. "The Impact Of Math Background On Performance In Managerial Economics And Basic Finance Courses," 59-61.

Winkler, Daniel T., George B. Flanigan and Joseph E. Johnson. "Solving For The Number Of Cash Flows And Periods In Financial Problems," 62-65.

JOURNAL OF FINANCIAL INTERMEDIATION

Journal of Financial Intermediation
Volume 1, 1990

Allen, Franklin. "The Market For Information And The Origin Of Financial Intermediation," (1), 3-30.

Lacker, Jeffrey M., Robert J. Levy and John A. Weinberg. "Incentive-Compatible Financial Contracts, Asset Prices, And The Value Of Control," (1), 31-56.

Kihlstrom, Richard E. and Steven A. Matthews. "Managerial Incentives In An Entrepreneurial Stock Market Model," (1), 57-79.

Peck, James. "Liquidity Without Money: A General Equilibrium Model Of Market Microstructure," (1), 80-103.

Roell, Ailsa. "Dual-Capacity Trading And The Quality Of The Market," (2), 105-124.

Smith, Bruce D. and Michael J. Stutzer. "Adverse Selection And Mutuality: The Case Of The Farm Credit System," (2), 125-149.

Kane, Alex and Stephen G. Marks. "The Delivery Of Market Timing Services: Newsletters Versus Market Timing Funds," (2), 150-166.

Domowitz, Ian. "The Mechanics Of Automated Trade Execution Systems," (2), 167-194.

JOURNAL OF FINANCIAL RESEARCH

Journal of Financial Research
Volume 1, 1978

Ferri, Michael G. "Systematic Return Risk And The Call Risk Of Corporate Debt Instruments," (1), 1-13.

Beedles, William L. "On The Use Of Certainty Equivalent Factors As Risk Proxies," (1), 15-21.

Howe, Keith M. "Capital Budgeting And Search: An Overview," (1), 23-33.

Gombola, Michael J., Rodney L. Roenfeldt and Philip L. Cooley. "Spreading Strategies In CBOE Options: Evidence On Market Performance," (1), 35-44.

Jacob, Nancy and Rich Pettit. "Research Output And Capital Market Efficiency Under Alternative Commission Rate Structures," (1), 45-60.

Fraser, Donald R. "Does Branching Matter?," (1), 61-69.

Storey, Ronald G. and Cecil R. Dipchand. "Factors Related To The Conversion Record Of Convertible Securities: The Canadian Experience 1946-1975," (1), 71-83.

Journal of Financial Research
Volume 2, 1979

Smith, Keith V. "Constituencies, Attributes, And Goals In Financial Research," (1), 1-12.

Bey, Roger P. "Mean-Variance, Mean-Semivariance, And DCF Estimates Of A Public Utility's Cost Of Equity," (1), 13-26.

McEnally, Richard W. and Calvin M. Boardman. "Aspects Of Corporate Bond Portfolio Diversification," (1), 27-36.

Trennepohl, Gary L. and William P. Dukes. "Return And Risk From Listed Option Investments," (1), 37-49.

Joy, O. Maurice and Charles P. Jones. "Earnings Reports And Market Efficiencies: An Analysis Of The Contrary Evidence," (1), 51-63.

Johnson, Dana J., Richard E. Bennett and Richard J. Curcio. "A Note On The Deceptive Nature Of Bayesian Forecasted Betas,"(1),65-69.

Beedles, William L. "Return, Dispersion, And Skewness: Synthesis And Investment Strategy," (1), 71-80.

Cooley, Philip L. "On The Nature Of Risk: A Comment," (1), 81-85.

Ang, James S., Jess H. Chua and Anand S. Desai. "Evidence That The Common Stock Market Adjusts Fully For Expected Inflation," (2), 97-109.

Chen, Son-Nan. "Re-Examining The Market Model Given Evidence Of Heteroskedasticity," (2), 111-118.

Senchack, Andrew J., Jr. and William L. Beedles. "Price Behavior In A Regional Over-The-Counter Securities Market," (2), 119-131.

Johnson, Keith B., Gregory Morton and M. Chapman Findlay, III. "An Analysis Of The Flotation Cost Of Utility Bonds, 1971-76," (2), 133-142.

Hays, Patrick A., Michael D. Joehnk and Ronald W. Melicher. "Differential Determinants Of Risk Premiums In The Public And Private Corporate Bond Markets," (2), 143-152.

Marks, Barry R. "A Reevaluation Of The Arditti And Levy Capital Budgeting Procedure," (2), 153-159.

Gitman, Lawrence J. and Mark D. Goodwin. "An Assessment Of Marketable Securities Management Practices," (2), 161-169.

Brown, Stewart L. "Earnings Announcement And Autocorrelation: An Empirical Test," (2), 171-183.

Journal of Financial Research
Volume 3, 1980

Kaufman, George G. "Duration, Planning Period And Tests Of The Capital Asset Pricing Model," (1), 1-9.

Bookstabler, Richard. "The Efficiency Of The Exchange Market And The Biasness Of The Forward Rate: A Joint Test," (1), 11-21.

Schweser, Carl and Thomas Schneesweis. "Risk Return And The Multi-Dimensional Security Pricing Market," (1), 23-31.

Marquette, R. Penny and Dana Johnson. "Ridge Regression And The Multicollinearity Problem In Financial Research: A Case Study," (1), 33-47.

Chance Don M. and William R. Lane. "A Re-Examination Of Interest Rate Sensitivity In The Common Stocks Of Financial Institutions," (1), 49-55.

Dipchand, Cecil R., Arthur C. Gudikunst and Gordon S. Roberts. "An Empirical Analysis Of Canadian Railroad Leases," (1), 57-68.

Stone, John D. and Michael C. Walker. "The Effect Of Executive Stock Options On Corporate Financial Decisions," (1), 69-83.

Barry, Christopher B. "Bayesian Betas And Deception: A Comment," (1), 85-89.

Lewellen, Wilbur G., John J. McConnell and Jonathan A. Scott. "Capital Market Influences On Trade Credit Policies," (2), 105-113.

Moosa, Suleman A. "Inflation And Common Stock Prices," (2), 115-128.

McInish, Thomas H. "The Determinants Of Municipal Bond Risk Premiums By Maturity," (2), 129-138.

Bey, Roger P. "Calculating Means And Variances Of NPVs When The Life Of The Project Is Uncertain," (2), 139-152.

Hawawini, Gabriel A. "The Intertemporal Cross Price Behavior Of Common Stocks: Evidence And Implications," (2), 153-167.

Vignola, Anthony J. and Charles Dale. "The Efficiency Of The Treasury Bill Futures Market: An Analysis Of Alternative Specifications," (2), 169-188.

Hendershott, Patric H. and Chang-tseh Hsieh. "Inflation And The Growth In Home Mortgage Debt, 1964-78," (2), 189-202.

Marshall, William and Jess B. Yawitz. "Optimal Terms Of The Call Provision On A Corporate Bond," (2), 203-211.

Wacht, Richard F. "The Southern Finance Association: The First Twenty Years," (3), 221-228.

Rozelle, James P. and Bruce D. Fielitz. "Stationarity Of Common Stock Returns," (3), 229-242.

Gouldey, Bruce K. "Evidence Of Nonmarket Risk Premiums In Common Stock Returns," (3), 243-260.

Schnabel, J. A. "A Note On Inflation, The Capital Asset Pricing Model, And Beta Estimation With Nominal Data," (3), 261-267.

Chen, Son-Non and John D. Martin. "Beta Nonstationarity And Pure Extra-Market Covariance Effects On Portfolio Risk," (3), 269-282.

Harris, Robert S. "The Impact Of Corporate Mergers On Acquiring Firms," (3), 283-295.

Peterson, Pamela Parrish. "A Re-Examination Of Seemingly Unrelated Regressions Methodology Applied To Estimation Of Financial Relationships," (3), 297-308.

Ang, James S., Jess H. Chua and Anand S. Desai. "Efficient Portfolios Versus Efficient Market," (3), 309-319.

Journal of Financial Research
Volume 4, 1981

Stanley, Kenneth L., Wilbur G. Lewellen and Gary G. Schlarbaum. "Further Evidence On The Value Of Professional Investment Research," (1), 1-9.

Trennepohl, Gary. "A Comparison Of Listed Option Premiums And Black And Scholes Model Prices: 1973-1979," (1), 11-20.

French, Dan W. and Glenn V. Henderson, Jr. "Substitute Hedged Option Portfolios: Theory And Evidence," (1), 21-31.

Rao, Ramesh K. S. "Modern Option Pricing Models: A Dichotomous Classification," (1), 33-44.

Verbrugge, James A. and Steven J. Goldstein. "Risk Return And Managerial Objectives: Some Evidence From The Savings And Loan Industry," (1), 45-58.

Zumpano, Leonard V. and Patricia M. Rudolph. "Another Look At Residential Mortgage Lending By Savings And Loans," (1), 59-67.

Palmon, Dan and Uzi Yaari. "Stock Repurchase As A Tax-Saving Distribution," (1), 69-79.

Sartoris, William L. and Ned C. Hill. "Evaluating Credit Policy Alternatives: A Present Value Framework," (1), 81-89.

Yawitz, Jess B. and William J. Marshall. "The Shortcomings Of Duration As A Risk Measure For Bonds," (1), 91-101.

Wilson, Jack W. and Charles P. Jones. "The Relationship Between Performance And Risk: Whence The Bias?," (2), 103-108.

Leonard, David C. and Nicholas R. Noble. "Estimation Of Time-Varying Systematic Risk And Investment Performance: Closed-End Investment Companies," (2), 109-120.

Buell, Stephen G., Carl Beidleman and R. Charles Moyer. "On The Linkage Between Corporate Savings And Earnings Growth," (2), 121-128.

Saniga, Erwin M., Thomas H. McInish and Bruce K. Gouldey. "The Effect Of Differencing Interval Length On Beta," (2), 129-135.

Steinberg, Joan S. and Larry R. Arnold. "An Interactive Approach For Optimizing Debt Repayment Schedules," (2), 137-146.

Dran, John J., Jr. and Brian E. Campbell. "Hospital Investment And Medicare Reimbursement," (2), 147-160.

Miller, Edward M. "Time Preference And Interest Rates In An Uncertain Multiperiod World," (2), 161-168.

Daigler, Robert T. and Bruce D. Fielitz. "A Multiple Discriminant Analysis Of Technical Indicators On The New York Stock Exchange," (3), 169-182.

Lloyd, William P., John H. Hand and Naval K. Modani. "The Effect Of Portfolio Construction Rules On The Relationship Between Portfolio Size And Effective Diversification," (3), 183-193.

Hadaway, Beverly L. and Samuel C. Hadaway. "An Analysis Of The Performance Characteristics Of Converted Savings And Loan Associations," (3), 195-206.

Nunn, Kenneth P., Jr. "The Strategic Determinants Of Working Capital: A Product-Line Perspective," (3), 207-219.

Hsia, Chi-Cheng. "Optimal Debt Of A Firm: An Option Pricing Approach," (3), 221-231.

Baker, H. Kent, Patricia L. Gallagher and Karen E. Morgan. "Management's View Of Stock Repurchase Programs," (3), 233-247.

Duvall, Richard M. and Judith L. Quinn. "Skewness Preference In Stable Markets," (3), 249-263.

Brick, Ivan E. and Meir Statman. "A Note On Beta And The Probability Of Default," (3), 265-269.

Journal of Financial Research
Volume 5, 1982

Hawawini, Gabriel A. and Ashok Vora. "Investment Horizon, Diversification, And The Efficiency Of Alternative Beta Forecasts," (1), 1-15.

Tezel, Ahmet. "The Effect Of Inflation On Common Stock Values," (1), 17-25.

Lloyd, William P. and Steven J. Goldstein. "Simulation Of Portfolio Returns: Varying Numbers Of Securities And Holding Periods," (1), 27-38.

Burgess, Richard C. and Maurry J. Tamarkin. "Regulatory Influences On Portfolio Performance: Short Selling And Regulation T," (1), 39-54.

Upton, David E. "Single-Period Mean-Variance In A Multiperiod Context," (1), 55-68.

Celec, Stephen E. "Incorrect Preference Orderings With The Coefficient Of Variation," (1), 69-73.

Johnson, Ramon E., Richard T. Pratt and Samuel S. Stewart, Jr. "The Economic Consequences Of ESOPs," (1), 75-82.

Booth, G. Geoffrey, Fred R. Kaen and Peter E. Koveos. "Persistent Dependence In Gold Prices," (1), 85-93.

Hill, Joanne and Thomas Schneeweis. "The Hedging Effectiveness Of Foreign Currency Futures," (1), 95-104.

Lewellen, Wilbur G. and James S. Ang. "Inflation, Security Values, And Risk Premia," (2), 105-123.

Peterson, Pamela Parrish and David R. Peterson. "Divergence Of Opinion And Return," (2), 125-134.

Kolluri, Bharat R. "Anticipated Price Changes, Inflation Uncertainty, And Capital Stock Returns," (2), 135-149.

Jahankhani, Ali and George E. Pinches. "Duration And The Nonstationarity Of Systematic Risk For Bonds," (2), 151-160.

Kolb, Robert W. and Raymond Chiang. "Duration, Immunization, And Hedging With Interest Rate Futures," (2), 161-170.

Stock, Duane. "Empirical Analysis Of Municipal Bond Portfolio Structure And Performance," (2), 171-180.

Murphy, Neil B. and Yair E. Orgler. "Cost Analysis For Branching Systems: Methodology, Test Results, And Implications For Management," (2), 181-188.

Dipchand, Cecil R.,Gordon S. Roberts and Jerry A. Viscione. "Agency Costs And Captive Finance Subsidiaries In Canada," (2), 189-199.

Kaufman, George G. "Search Theory And The Prohibition Against Commercial Bank Underwriting Of Municipal Revenue Bonds," (3), 201-205.

Benson, Earl D. "The Dispersion Of Bids On Individual New Municipal Issues," (3), 207-219.

Wingler, Tony R. and James M. Watts. "Electric Utility Bond Rating Changes: Methodological Issues And Evidence," (3), 221-235.

Woolridge, J. Randall. "The Information Content Of Dividend Changes," (3), 237-247.

Rozeff, Michael S. "Growth, Beta And Agency Costs As Determinants Of Dividend Payout Ratios," (3), 249-259.

Chu, Chen-Chin and David T. Whitford. "Stock Market Returns And Inflationary Expectations: Additional Evidence For 1975-1979," (3), 261-271.

Emery, Gary W. "Optimal Liquidity Policy: A Stochastic Process Approach," (3), 273-283.

Morris, James R. "Taxes, Bankruptcy Costs And The Existence Of An Optimal Capital Structure," (3), 285-299.

Journal of Financial Research
Volume 6, 1983

Woolridge, J. Randall. "Stock Dividends As Signals," (1), 1-12.

Harris, Robert S. and John J. Pringle. "Implications Of Miller's Argument For Capital Budgeting," (1), 13-23.

Ezzell, John R. and James A. Miles. "Capital Project Analysis And The Debt Transaction Plan," (1), 25-31.

Modani, Naval K., Philip L. Cooley and Rodney L. Roenfeldt. "Stability Of Market Risk Surrogates," (1), 33-40.

Hsia, Chi-Cheng. "On Binomial Option Pricing," (1), 41-46.

Swidler, Steve and Paul Vanderheiden. "Another Opinion Regarding Divergence Of Opinion And Return," (1), 47-50.

McDaniel, William R. "Convertible Bonds In Perfect And Imperfect Markets," (1), 51-65.

Frieder, Larry A. and Vincent P. Apilado. "Bank Holding Company Expansion: A Refocus On Its Financial Rationale," (1), 67-81.

Puglisi, Donald J. and Anthony J. Vignola, Jr. "An Examination Of Federal Agency Debt Pricing Practices," (2), 83-92.

Van Horne, James C. and Hal B. Heaton. "Securities Inventories And Excess Returns," (2), 93-102.

Bosch, Jean-Claude. "Speculation And The Market For Recommendations," (2), 103-113.

McDonald, Bill and Michael H. Morris. "The Existence Of Heteroscedasticity And Its Effect On Estimates Of The Market Model Parameters," (2), 115-126.

Smith, David B. "A Framework For Analyzing Nonconvertible Preferred Stock Risk," (2), 127-139.

Shawky, Hany, Ronald Forbes and Alan Frankle. "Liquidity Services And Capital Market Equilibrium: The Case For Money Market Mutual Funds," (2), 141-152.

Harris, John M., Jr. "Alternative Mortgage Instruments: Comparisons And A Proposal," (2), 153-162.

Grier, Paul and Paul Strebel. "An Implicit Clientele Test Of The Relationship Between Taxation And Capital Structure," (2), 163-174.

Bey, Roger P. "Capital Budgeting Decisions When Cash Flows And Project Lives Are Stochastic And Dependent," (3), 175-185.

Gay, Gerald D., Robert W. Kolb and Raymond Chiang. "Interest Rate Hedging: An Empirical Test Of Alternative Strategies," (3), 187-197.

Sears, R. Stephen and Gary L. Trennepohl. "Diversification And Skewness In Option Portfolios," (3), 199-212.

Hessel, Christopher A. and Lucy T. Huffman. "Incorporation Of Tax Considerations Into The Computation Of Duration," (3), 213-215.

Spiceland, J. David and Jerry E. Trapnell. "The Effect Of Market Conditions And Risk Classifications On Market Model Parameters," (3), 217-222.

Carpenter, Michael D. and I. Keong Chew. "The Effects Of Default Risk On The Market Model," (3), 223-229.

Eckardt, Walter L., Jr. and Bruce D. Bagamery. "Short Selling: The Mutual Fund Alternative," (3), 231-238.

Choi, Dosoung and George C. Philippatos. "An Examination Of Merger Synergism," (3), 239-256.

Swanson, Peggy J. "Compensating Balances And Foreigners' Dollar Deposits In United States Banks," (3), 257-263.

Dyl, Edward A. and Ronald W. Spahr. "Taxes And The Refunding Of Discount Bonds," (4), 265-273.

Bey, Roger P. "The Market Model As An Appropriate Description Of The Stochastic Process Generating Security Returns," (4), 275-288.

Pettway, Richard H. and Bradford D. Jordan. "Diversification, Double Leverage, And The Cost Of Capital," (4), 289-300.

Bernard, Victor L. and Thomas J. Frecka. "Evidence On The Existence Of Common Stock Inflation Hedges," (4), 301-312.

Whiteside, Mary M., William P. Dukes and Patrick M. Dunne. "Short Term Impact Of Option Trading On Underlying Securities," (4), 313-321.

Stover, Roger D. "The Interaction Between Pricing And Underwriting Spread In The New Issue Convertible Debt Market," (4), 323-332.

Hill, Joanne and Thomas Schneeweis. "International Diversification Of Equities And Fixed-Income Securities," (4), 333-343.

Coe, Robert K. and Irwin Weinstock. "Evaluating The Finance Journals: The Department Chairman's Perspective," (4), 345-349.

Journal of Financial Research
Volume 7, 1984

Peterson, David R. and Donald M. Waldman. "A Model Of Heterogeneous Expectations As A Determinant Of Short Sales," (1), 1-16.

Muller, Frederick L., Bruce D. Fielitz and Myron T. Greene. "Portfolio Performance In Relation To Quality, Earnings, Dividends, Firm Size, Leverage, And Return On Equity," (1), 17-26.

Perry, Larry G., Glenn V. Henderson, Jr. and Timothy P. Cronan. "Multivariate Analysis Of Corporate Bond Ratings And Industry Classifications," (1), 27-36.

Wacht, Richard F. "A Financial Management Theory Of The Nonprofit Organization," (1), 37-45.

Eisemann, Peter C. and Stephen G. Timme. "Intraweek Seasonality In The Federal Funds Market," (1), 47-56.

Miles, Mike and Tom McCue. "Diversification In The Real Estate Portfolio," (1), 57-68.

Gehr, Adam K., Jr. "Financial Structure And Financial Strategy," (1), 69-80.

Davidson, Wallace N., III. "The Effect Of Rate Cases On Public Utility Stock Returns," (1), 81-93.

Brauer, Greggory A. "The Value Impacts Of Capital Adequacy Regulation And Stochastic Deposits," (2), 95-104.

Koppenhaver, G. D. "Selective Hedging Of Bank Assets With Treasury Bill Futures Contracts," (2), 105-119.

Pari, Robert A. and Son-Nan Chen. "An Empirical Test Of The Arbitrage Pricing Theory," (2), 121-130.

Benesh, Gary A., Arthur J. Keown and John M. Pinkerton. "An Examination Of Market Reaction To Substantial Shifts In Dividend Policy," (2), 131-140.

Ferri, Michael G., H. Dennis Oberhelman and Rodney L. Roenfeldt. "Market Timing And Mutual Fund Portfolio Composition," (2), 143-150.

Beedles, William L. "The Anomalous And Asymmetric Nature Of Equity Returns: An Empirical Synthesis," (2), 151-160.

Trent, Robert H. and Robert S. Kemp. "The Writings Of Henry A. Latane: A Compilation And Analysis," (2), 161-174.

McKenzie, Joseph A. "Who Holds Alternative Market-Yield Accounts?," (2), 175-183.

Bey, Roger P., Richard C. Burgess and Richard B. Kearns. "Moving Stochastic Dominance: An Alternative Method For Testing Market Efficiency," (3), 185-196.

Mahajan, Arvind and Dileep Mehta. "Strong Form Efficiency Of The Foreign Exchange Market And Bank Positions," (3), 197-207.

Rose, John T. and Samuel H. Talley. "Financial Transactions Within Bank Holding Companies," (3), 209-217.

Ang, James S. and David R. Peterson. "An Empirical Study Of The Diffusion Process Of Securities And Portfolios," (3), 219-229.

Cook, Thomas J. and Michael S. Rozeff. "Coskewness, Dividend Yield And Capital Asset Pricing," (3), 231-241.

Duvall, Richard M. and John M. Cheney. "Bond Beta And Default Risk," (3), 243-254.

Rosenfeld, James D. "Returns On High-Quality And Low-Quality Preferred Stocks In Periods Of Common-Stock Dividend Reductions," (3), 255-258.

Antia, Murad J. and Richard L. Meyer. "The Growth Optimal Capital Structure: Manager Versus Shareholder Objectives," (3), 259-267.

Goldberg, Michael A. "The Sensitivity Of The Prime Rate To Money Market Conditions," (4), 269-280.

Kaen, Fred R., Evangelos O. Simos and George A. Hachey. "The Response Of Forward Exchange Rates To Interest Rate Forecasting Errors," (4), 281-290.

Dubofsky, David A. and John C. Groth. "Exchange Listing And Stock Liquidity," (4), 291-302.

Glick, Reuven. "The Geometry Of Asset Adjustment With Adjustment Costs," (4), 303-314.

McDonald, Bill and William D. Nichols. "Nonstationarity Of Beta And Tests Of Market Efficiency," (4), 315-322.

Marr, M. Wayne and G. Rodney Thompson. "The Influence Of Offering Yield On Underwriting Spread," (4), 323-328.

Settle, John W., Glenn H. Petry and Chi-Cheng Hsia. "Synergy, Diversification, And Incentive Effects Of Corporate Merger On Bondholder Wealth: Some Evidence," (4), 329-339.

Chen, K. C. and R. Stephen Sears. "How Many Small Firms Are Enough?," (4), 341-349.

Journal of Financial Research
Volume 8, 1985

Stock, Duane. "Price Volatility Of Municipal Discount Bonds," (1),1-13.

Chang, Eric C. and Wilbur G. Lewellen. "An Arbitrage Pricing Approach To Evaluating Mutual Fund Performance," (1), 15-30.

Wansley, James W. and Terrence M. Clauretie. "The Impact Of CreditWatch Placement On Equity Returns And Bond Prices," (1), 31-42.

Dhaliwal, Dan S. "The Agency Cost Rationale For Refunding Discounted Bonds," (1), 43-50.

Booth, James R. and Dennis T. Officer. "Expectations, Interest Rates, And Commercial Bank Stocks," (1), 51-58.

Murray, Dennis. "Further Evidence On The Liquidity Effects Of Stock Splits And Stock Dividends," (1), 59-67.

McInish, Thomas H. and Robert A. Wood. "A New Approach To Controlling For Thin Trading," (1), 69-75.

Bedingfield, James P., Philip M. J. Reckers and A. J. Stagliano. "Distributions Of Financial Ratios In The Commercial Banking Industry," (1), 77-81.

Smith, Richard L. and James R. Booth. "The Risk Structure Of Interest Rates And Interdependent Borrowing Costs: The Impact Of Major Defaults," (2), 83-94.

Kim, Moon and Geoffrey Booth. "Yield Structure Of Taxable Vs. Nontaxable Bonds," (2), 95-105.

Navratil, Frank J. "The Estimation Of Mortgage Prepayment Rates," (2), 107-117.

McInish, Thomas H. and Robert A. Wood. "Intraday And Overnight Returns And Day-Of-The-Week Effects," (2), 119-126.

Kolodny, Richard and Diane Rizzuto Suhler. "Changes In Capital Structure, New Equity Issues, And Scale Effects," (2), 127-136.

Schultz, Joseph J., Jr., Sandra G. Gustavson and Frank K. Reilly. "Factors Influencing The New York Stock Exchange Specialists' Price-Setting Behavior: An Experiment," (2), 137-144.

Desai, Anand S. and Roger D. Stover. "Bank Holding Company Acquisitions, Stockholder Returns, And Regulatory Uncertainty," (2), 145-156.

Kolb, Robert W. and Gerald D. Gay. "A Pricing Anomaly In Treasury Bill Futures," (2), 157-167.

Kross, William. "The Size Effect Is Primarily A Price Effect," (3), 169-179.

Barnes, Tom. "Markowitz Allocation - Fixed Income Securities," (3), 181-191.

Black, Harold A. and Robert L. Schweitzer. "Black-Controlled Credit Unions: A Comparative Analysis," (3), 193-202.

Yaari, Uzi and Frank J. Fabozzi. "Why IRA And Keogh Plans Should Avoid Growth Stocks," (3), 203-216.

Smirlock, Michael and Laura Starks. "A Further Examination Of Stock Price Changes And Transaction Volume," (3), 217-236.

Zaima, Janis K. and Douglas Hearth. "The Wealth Effects Of Voluntary Selloffs: Implications For Divesting And Acquiring Firms," (3), 217-226.

Harris, Robert S. and John J. Pringle. "Risk-Adjusted Discount Rates - Extensions From The Average-Risk Case," (3), 237-244.

Caks, John, William R. Lane, Robert W. Greenleaf and Reginald G. Joules. "A Simple Formula For Duration," (3), 245-249.

Greenbaum, Stuart I. and Itzhak Venezia. "Partial Exercise Of Loan Commitments Under Adaptive Pricing," (4), 251-263.

Park, Hun Y. and R. Stephen Sears. "Changing Volatility And The Pricing Of Options On Stock Index Futures," (4), 265-274.

Tucker, Alan L. "Empirical Tests Of The Efficiency Of The Currency Option Market," (4), 275-285.

Mabry, Rodney H. and Arthur D. Sharplin. "The Relative Importance Of Journals Used In Finance Research," (4), 287-296.

Thies, Clifford F. "New Estimates Of The Term Structure Of Interest Rates: 1920-1939," (4), 297-306.

Perry, Larry G. "The Effect Of Bond Rating Agencies On Bond Rating Models," (4), 307-315.

Davidson, Wallace N., III and John L. Glascock. "The Announcement Effects Of Preferred Stock Re-Ratings," (4), 317-325.

Beranek, William and Ronnie Clayton. "Risk Differences And Financial Reporting," (4), 327-334.

Journal of Financial Research
Volume 9, 1986

Little, Patricia Knain. "Financial Futures And Immunization," (1), 1-12.

Woolridge, J. Randall and Chinmoy Ghosh. "Institutional Trading And Security Prices: The Case Of Changes In The Composition Of The S&P 500 Index," (1), 13-24.

Howard, Charles T. and Louis J. D'Antonio. "Treasury Bill Futures As A Hedging Tool: A Risk-Return Approach," (1), 25-39.

Bellante, Don and Richard P. Saba. "Human Capital And Life-Cycle Effects On Risk Aversion," (1), 41-51.

King, Raymond. "Convertible Bond Valuation: An Empircial Test," (1), 53-69.

Peterson, Richard L. "Creditors' Use Of Collection Remedies," (1), 71-86.

Chen, Carl R. and Steve Stockum. "Selectivity, Market Timing, And Random Beta Behavior Of Mutual Funds: A Generalized Model," (1), 87-96.

Wong, Shee Q. "The Contribution Of Inflation Uncertainty To The Variable Impacts Of Money On Stock Prices," (1), 97-101.

Lamy, Robert E. and G. Rodney Thompson. "Penn Square, Problem Loans, And Insolvency Risk," (2), 103-111.

Pruitt, Stephen W. and David R. Peterson. "Security Price Reactions Around Product Recall Announcements," (2), 113-122.

Hsia, Chi-Cheng. "Comparative Efficiency Of Market Indices: An Empirical Study," (2), 123-136.

Luft, Carl F. and Bruce D. Fielitz. "An Empirical Test Of The Commodity Option Pricing Model Using Ginnie Mae Call Options," (2), 137-151.

Chiang, Thomas C. "Empirical Analysis On The Predictors Of Future Spot Rates," (2), 153-162.

Roden, Peyton Foster and Robert L. Bland. "Issuer Sophistication And Underpricing In The Negotiated Municipal Bond Market," (2), 163-170.

Lloyd, William P., John S. Jahera, Jr. and Steven J. Goldstein. "The Relation Between Returns, Ownership Structure, And Market Value," (2), 171-177.

Wansley, James W. and Elayan Fayez. "Stock Repurchases And Securityholder Returns: A Case Study Of Teledyne," (2), 179-191.

Cornell, Bradford. "Inflation Measurement, Inflation Risk, And The Pricing Of Treasury Bills," (3), 193-202.

Peterson, David R. "An Empirical Test Of An Ex-Ante Model Of The Determination Of Stock Return Volatility," (3), 203-214.

Grammatikos, Theoharry and George Papaioannou. "Market Reaction to NYSE Listings: Tests Of The Marketability Gains Hypothesis," (3), 215-228.

Officer, Dennis T. and Richard L. Smith, II. "Announcement Effects Of Withdrawn Security Offerings: Evidence On The Wealth Redistribution Hypothesis," (3), 229-238.

Bosch, J. C. "Portfolio Choices, Consumption, And Prices In A Market With Durable Assets," (3), 239-250.

Billingsley, Randall S., Robert E. Lamy and G. Rodney Thompson. "Valuation Of Primary Issue Convertible Bonds," (3), 251-260.

Born, Jeffery A. and Seth C. Anderson. "A Comparison Of Intervention And Residual Analysis," (3), 261-270.

Booth, G. Geoffrey and Peter E. Koveos. "A Programming Model For Bank Hedging Decisions," (3), 271-279.

Leonard, David C. and Michael E. Solt. "Recent Evidence On The Accuracy And Rationality Of Popular Inflation Forecasts,"(4),281-290.

Blum, Gerald A., William A. Kracaw and Wilbur G. Lewellen. "Determinants Of The Execution Costs Of Common Stock Trades By Individual Investors," (4), 291-301.

Barrett, W. Brian, Andrea J. Heuson and Robert W. Kolb. "The Differential Effects Of Sinking Funds On Bond Risk Premia," (4), 303-312.

Ferris, Stephen P., Dana J. Johnson and Dilip K. Shome. "Regulatory Environment And Market Response To Public Utility Rate Decisions," (4), 313-318.

Fooladi, Iraj and Gordon S. Roberts. "On Preferred Stock," (4),319-324.

Scott, William L. and Richard L. Peterson. "Interest Rate Risk And Equity Values Of Hedged And Unhedged Financial Intermediaries," (4), 325-329.

Shome, Dilip K., Stephen D. Smith and Arnold A. Heggestad. "Capital Adequacy And The Valuation Of Large Commercial Banking Organizations," (4), 331-341.

Atchison, Michael D. "Non-Representative Trading Frequencies And The Detection Of Abnormal Performance," (4), 343-348.

Journal of Financial Research
Volume 10, 1987

Chang, Jack S. K. and Latha Shanker. "Option Pricing And The Arbitrage Pricing Theory," (1), 1-16.

Livingston, Miles. "Flattening Of Bond Yield Curves," (1), 17-24.

Shilling, James D. and C. F. Sirmans. "Pricing Fast-Pay Mortgages: Some Simulation Results," (1), 25-32.

Morgan, George Emir and Stephen D. Smith. "The Role Of Capital Adequacy Regulation In The Hedging Decisions Of Financial Intermediaries," (1), 33-46.

Belongia, Michael T. and G. J. Santoni. "Interest Rate Risk, Market Value, And Hedging Financial Portfolios," (1), 47-57.

Leonard, David C. and Michael E. Solt. "Stock Market Signals Of Changes In Expected Inflation," (1), 57-64.

Skantz, Terrance R. and Roberto Marchesini. "The Effect Of Voluntary Corporate Liquidation On Shareholder Wealth," (1), 65-76.

Booth, James R. and Richard L. Smith. "An Examination Of The Small-Firm Effect On The Basis Of Skewness Preference," (1), 77-88.

Kim, Moon K. and Chunchi Wu. "Macro-Economic Factors And Stock Returns," (2), 87-98.

Zivney, Terry L. and Donald J. Thompson, II. "Relative Stock Prices And The Firm Size Effect," (2), 99-110.

Ehrhardt, Michael C. "Arbitrage Pricing Models: The Sufficient Number Of Factors And Equilibrium Conditions," (2), 111-120.

Barnhill, Theodore M., James V. Jordan and William E. Seale. "Maturity And Refunding Effects On Treasury-Bond Futures Price Variance," (2), 121-132.

Anderson, Gary and Raymond Chiang. "Interest Rate Risk Hedging For Due-On-Sale Mortgages With Early Termination," (2), 133-142.

Rahman, Abdul, Lawrence Kryzanowski and Ah Boon Sim. "Systematic Risk In A Purely Random Market Model: Some Empirical Evidence For Individual Public Utilities," (2), 143-152.

Moore, Norman H. and Stephen W. Pruitt. "The Market Pricing Of Net Operating Loss Carryforwards: Implications Of The Tax Motivations Of Mergers," (2), 153-160.

Jose, Manuel L. and Jerry L. Stevens. "Product Market Structure, Capital Intensity, And Systematic Risk: Empirical Results From The Theory Of The Firm," (2), 161-175.

Taggart, Robert A., Jr. "Allocating Capital Among A Firm's Divisions: Hurdle Rates Vs. Budgets," (3), 177-190.

Bierwag, Gerald O. "Bond Returns, Discrete Stochastic Processes, And Duration," (3), 191-210.

Ederington, Louis J., Jess B. Yawitz and Brian E. Roberts. "The Informational Content Of Bond Ratings," (3), 211-226.

Pettway, Richard H. and Bradford D. Jordan. "APT Vs. CAPM Estimates Of The Return-Generating Function Parameters For Regulated Public Utilities," (3), 227-238.

Peavy, John W., III and George H. Hempel. "The Effect Of The WPPSS Crisis On The Tax-Exempt Bond Market," (3), 239-248.

Tew, Bernard V. and Donald W. Reid. "More Evidence On Expected Value-Variance Analysis Versus Direct Utility Maximization," (3), 249-258.

Stein, William E., Roger C. Pfaffenberger and Dan W. French. "Sampling Error In First Order Stochastic Dominance," (3), 259-268.

Akgiray, Vedat and G. Geoffrey Booth. "Compound Distribution Models Of Stock Returns," (3), 269-280.

Shastri, Kuldeep and Kulpatra Wethyavivorn. "The Valuation Of Currency Options For Alternate Stochastic Processes," (3), 283-294.

Kolari, James W. "An Analytical Model Of Risky Yield Curves," (3), 295-304.

Trifts, Jack W. and Kevin P. Scanlon. "Interstate Bank Mergers: The Early Evidence," (4), 305-312.

Torabzadeh, Khalil M. and William J. Bertin. "Leveraged Buyouts And Shareholder Returns," (4), 313-320.

Davidson, Wallace N., III and James L. McDonald. "Evidence Of The Effect On Shareholder Wealth Of Corporate Spinoffs: The Creation Of Royalty Trusts," (4), 321-328.

Ogden, Joseph P. "Determinants Of The Ratings And Yields On Corporate Bonds: Tests Of The Contingent Claims Model," (4), 329-340.

Rashid, Muhammad and Ben Amoako-Adu. "Personal Taxes, Inflation, And Market Valuation," (4), 341-352.

Larson, John C. and Joel N. Morse. "Intervalling Effects In Hong Kong Stocks," (4), 353-362.

Journal of Financial Research
Volume 11, 1988

Trennepohl, Gary L., James R. Booth and Hassan Tehranian. "An Empirical Analysis Of Insured Portfolio Strategies Using Listed Options," (1), 1-12.

Heuson, Andrea J. "The Term Premia Relationship Implicit In The Term Structure Of Treasury Bills," (1), 13-20.

Chance, Don M. "Boundary Condition Tests Of Bid And Ask Prices Of Index Call Options," (1), 21-32.

Gombola, Michael J., Douglas R. Kahl and Kenneth P. Nunn, Jr. "Valuation Of The Preferred Stock Sinking Fund Feature: A Time-Series Approach," (1), 33-42.

Billingsley, Randall S., Robert E. Lamy and G. Rodney Thompson.

"The Choice Among Debt, Equity, And Convertible Bonds," (1), 43-56.

Pettengill, Glenn N. and Bradford D. Jordan. "A Comprehensive Examination Of Volume Effects And Seasonality In Daily Security Returns," (1), 57-70.

Klein, Linda S. and David R. Peterson. "Investor Expectations Of Volatility Increases Around Large Stock Splits As Implied In Call Option Premia," (1), 71-80.

Haw, In-Mu, William Ruland and Ahmed Hamdallah. "Investor Evauation Of Overfunded Pension Plan Terminations," (1), 81-88.

Klein, April and James Rosenfeld. "The Impact Of Targeted Share Repurchases On The Wealth Of Non-Participating Shareholders," (2), 89-98.

Emery, Douglas R., Wilbur G. Lewellen and David C. Mauer. "Tax-Timing Options, Leverage, And The Choice Of Corporate Form," (2), 99-110.

Fehrs, Donald H., Gary A. Benesh and David R. Peterson. "Evidence Of A Relation Between Stock Price Reactions Around Cash Dividend Changes And Yields," (2), 111-124.

Jordan, Bradford D., James A. Verbrugge and Richard M. Burns. "Returns To Initial Shareholders In Savings Institution Covnersions: Evidence And Regulatory Implications," (2), 125-136.

Grube, R. Corwin and O. Maurice Joy. "Some Evidence On The Efficacy Of Security Credit Regulation In The OTC Equity Market," (2), 137-142.

Heuson, Andrea J. "Mortgage Terminations And Pool Characteristics: Some Additional Evidence," (2), 143-152.

Burgess, Richard C. and Roger P. Bey. "Optimal Portfolios: Markowitz Full Covariance Versus Simple Selection Rules," (2), 153-164.

Loo, Jean C. H. "Common Stock Returns, Expected Inflation, And The Rational Expectations Hypothesis," (2), 165-170.

Karpoff, Jonathan M. "Costly Short Sales And The Correlation Of Returns With Volume," (3), 173-188.

Gilmer, R. H., Jr. and Duane R. Stock. "Yield Volatility Of Discount Coupon Bonds," (3), 189-200.

Tucker, Alan L., David R. Peterson and Elton Scott. "Tests Of The Black-Scholes And Constant Elasticity Of Variance Currency Call Option Valuation Models," (3), 201-214.

Tezel, Ahmet. "The Value Line Stock Rankings And The Option Model Implied Standard Deviations," (3), 215-226.

Hall, Thomas W. and Jeffrey J. Tsay. "An Evaluation Of The Performance Of Portfolios Selected From Value Line Rank One Stocks: 1976-1982," (3), 227-240.

Levy, Haim and Zvi Lerman. "Testing The Predicitve Power Of Ex-Post Efficient Portfolios," (3), 241-254.

Chang, Philip. "Economies Of Scope, Synergy, And The CAPM," (3), 255-263.

Ang, James S. and Alan L. Tucker. "The Shareholder Wealth Effects Of Corporate Greenmail," (4), 265-280.

Ghosh, Chinmoy and J. Randall Woolridge. "An Analysis Of Share-holder Reaction To Dividend Cuts And Omissions," (4), 281-294.

Eddy, Albert and Bruce Seifert. "Firm Size And Dividend Announcements," (4), 295-302.

Hassell, John M., Robert H. Jennings and Dennis J. Lasser. "Management Earnings Forecasts: Their Usefulness As A Source Of Firm-Specific Information To Security Analysts," (4), 303-320.

Finucane, Thomas J. "Some Empirical Evidence On The Use Of Financial Leases," (4), 321-334.

Ma, Christopher K., Ramesh P. Rao and Herbert J. Weinraub. "The Seasonality In Convertible Bond Markets: A Stock Effect Or Bond Effect?," (4), 335-348.

Journal of Financial Research
Volume 12, 1989

Kidwell, David S., M. Wayne Marr and Joseph P. Ogden. "The Effect Of A Sinking Fund On The Reoffering Yields Of New Public Utility Bonds," (1), 1-14.

Brooks, Robert, Haim Levy and Miles Livingston. "The Coupon Effect On Term Premiums," (1), 15-22.

Fowler, David J., C. Harvey Rorke and Vijay M. Jog. "A Bias-Correcting Procedure For Beta Estimation In The Presence Of Thin Trading," (1), 23-32.

Johnson, Dana J. "The Risk Behavior Of Equity Of Firms Approaching Bankruptcy," (1), 33-50.

Wingender, John and James E. Groff. "On Stochastic Dominance Analysis Of Day-Of-The-Week Return Patterns," (1), 51-56.

Pettengill, Glenn N. "Holiday Closings And Security Returns," (1), 57-68.

Walz, Daniel T. and Roger W. Spencer. "The Informational Content Of Forward Rates: Further Evidence," (1), 69-82.

Sa-Aadu, J., C. F. Sirmans and John D. Benjamin. "Financing And House Prices," (1), 83-91.

Bhandari, Arvind, Theoharry Grammatikos, Anil K. Makhija and George Papaioannou. "Risk And Return On Newly Listed Stocks: The Post-Listing Experience," (2), 93-102.

Scanlon, Kevin P., Jack W. Trifts and Richard H. Pettway. "Impacts Of Relative Size And Industrial Relatedness On Returns To Shareholders Of Acquiring Firms," (2), 103-112.

Chaney, Paul K. "Moral Hazard And Capital Budgeting," (2), 113-128.

Choi, Jongmoo Jay, Frank J. Fabozzi and Uzi Yaari. "Optimum Corporate Leverage With Risky Debt: A Demand Approach," (2), 129-142.

Ben-Horim, Moshe and Jeffrey L. Callen. "The Cost Of Capital, Macaulay's Duration, And Tobin's q," (2), 143-156.

Castelino, Mark G. "Basis Volatility: Implications For Hedging," (2), 157-172.

Frankfurter, George M. and Christopher G. Lamoureux. "Estimation And Selection Bias In Mean-Variance Portfolio Selection," (2), 173-181.

Muscarella, Chris J. and Michael R. Vetsuypens. "The Underpricing Of 'Second' Initial Public Offerings," (2), 183-192.

Affleck-Graves, John and Robert E. Miller. "Regulatory And Procedural Effects On The Underpricing Of Initial Public Offerings," (3), 193-202.

Spivey, Michael F. "The Cost Of Including A Call Provision In Municipal Debt Contracts," (3), 203-216.

Wansley, James W. and Upinder S. Dhillon. "Determinants Of Valuation Effects For Security Offerings Of Commercial Bank Holding Companies," (3), 217-234.

Hsueh, L. Paul and P. R. Chandy. "An Examination Of The Yield Spread Between Insured And Uninsured Debt," (3), 235-244.

Davidson, Wallace N., III and Dipa Dutia. "A Note On The Behavior Of Security Returns: A Test Of Stock Market Overreaction And Efficiency," (3), 245-252.

Aggarwal, Raj, Ramesh P. Rao and Takato Hiraki. "Skewness And Kurtosis In Japanese Equity Returns: Empirical Evidence," (3), 253-260.

Fraser, Donald R. and Srinivasan Kannan. "The Risk Implications Of Forecast Errors Of Bank Earnings, 1976-1986," (3), 261-268.

Guth, Michael A. S. "Intrinsic Uncertainty And Common-Knowledge Priors In Financial Economics," (4), 269-284.

Lusht, Kenneth M. and Edward M. Saunders. "Direct Tests Of The Divergence Of Opinion Hypothesis In The Market For Racetrack Betting," (4), 285-292.

Zivney, Terry L. and Donald J. Thompson, II. "The Effect Of Market Proxy Rebalancing Policies On Detecting Abnormal Performance," (4), 293-300.

Ang, James S. and William L. Megginson. "Restricted Voting Shares, Ownership Structure, And The Market Value Of Dual-Class Firms," (4), 301-318.

Klein, Linda S. and David R. Peterson. "Earnings Forecast Revisions Associated With Stock Split Announcements," (4), 319-328.

Buono, Mark J. "The Relationship Between The Variability Of Inflation And Stock Returns: An Empirical Investigation," (4), 329-340.

Jones, Charles P. and Jack W. Wilson. "An Analysis Of The January Effect In Stocks And Interest Rates Under Varying Monetary Regimes," (4), 341-354.

Journal of Financial Research
Volume 13, 1990

Cornell, Bradford. "Volume And R-Square: A First Look," (1), 1-6.

Ehrhardt, Michael C. and Alan L. Tucker. "Pricing CRB Futures Contracts," (1), 7-14.

Chatterjee, Sangit and Robert A. Pari. "Bootstrapping The Number Of Factors In The Arbitrage Pricing Theory," (1), 15-22.

Bierwag, G. O. and Gordon S. Roberts. "Single-Factor Duration Models: Canadian Tests," (1), 23-38.

Rosenstein, Stuart and David F. Rush. "The Stock Return Performance Of Corporations That Are Partially Owned By Other Corporations," (1), 39-52.

Janjigian, Vahan and Paul J. Bolster. "The Elimination Of Director Liability And Stockholder Returns: An Empirical Investigation," (1), 53-60.

Madura, Jeff and Richard H. Fosberg. "The Impact Of Financing Sources On Multinational Projects," (1), 61-70.

Bae, Sung C. "Interest Rate Changes And Common Stock Returns Of Financial Institutions: Revisited," (1), 71-79.

Leonard, David C. and Michael E. Solt. "On Using The Black-Scholes Model Of Value Warrants," (2), 81-92.

Heuson, Andrea J. and Dennis J. Lasser. "Tax-Timing Options And The Pricing Of Government Bonds," (2), 93-104.

Ben-Horim, Moshe. "Stochastic Dominance And Truncated Sample Data," (2), 105-116.

Peterson, David R. "A Transaction Data Study Of Day-Of-The-Week And Intraday Patterns In Option Returns," (2), 117-132.

DeGennaro, Ramon P. "The Effect Of Payment Delays On Stock Prices," (2), 133-146.

Akella, Srinivas R. and Su-Jane Chen. "Interest Rate Sensitivity Of Bank Stock Returns: Specification Effects And Structural Changes," (2), 147-154.

Kale, Jayant R. and Thomas H. Noe. "Risky Debt Maturity Choice In A Sequential Game Equilibrium," (2), 155-166.

Trifts, Jack W., Neil W. Sicherman, Rodney L. Roenfeldt and Francisco De Cossio. "Divestiture To Unit Managers And Shareholder Wealth," (2), 167-172.

Ancel, Esther Weinstein and Ramesh K. S. Rao. "Stock Returns And Option Prices: An Exploratory Study," (3), 173-186.

Billingsley, Randall S., Robert E. Lamy and David M. Smith. "Units Of Debt With Warrants: Evidence Of The 'Penalty-Free' Issuance Of An Equity-Like Security," (3), 187-200.

Manakyan, Herman and Carolyn Carroll. "An Empirical Examination Of The Existence Of A Signaling Value Function For Dividends," (3), 201-210.

Jameson, Mel, James D. Shilling and C. F. Sirmans. "Regional Variation Of Mortgage Yields And Simultaneity Bias," (3), 211-220.

Pugh, William N. and John S. Jahera, Jr. "State Antitakeover Legislation And Shareholder Wealth," (3), 221-232.

Murphy, J. Austin. "Using The CAPM As A General Framework For Asset Pricing Analysis," (3), 233-242.

Fortin, Rich. "Transaction Costs And Day-Of-The-Week Effects In The OTC/NASDAQ Equity Market," (3), 243-248.

Aggarwal, Raj, Ramesh P. Rao and Takato Hiraki. "Regularities In Tokyo Stock Exchange Security Returns: P/E, Size, And Seasonal Influences," (3), 249-263.

Kale, Jayant R. and Thomas H. Noe. "Dividends, Uncertainty, And Underwriting Costs Under Asymmetric Information," (4), 265-278.

Kolb, Robert W. and Ricardo J. Rodriguez. "Is The Distribution Of Betas Stationary?," (4), 279-284.

Ritchey, Robert J. "Call Option Valuation For Discrete Normal Mixtures," (4), 285-296.

Chang, Jack S. K., Jean C. H. Loo and Carolyn C. Wu Chang. "The Pricing Of Futures Contracts And The Arbitrage Pricing Theory," (4), 297-306.

Hammer, Jerry A. "Hedging Performance And Hedging Objectives: Tests Of New Performance Measures In The Foreign Currency Market," (4), 307-324.

Baker, H. Kent and Richard B. Edelman. "OTC Market Switching And Stock Returns: Some Empirical Evidence," (4), 325-338.

Fraser, Donald R. and James W. Kolari. "The 1982 Depository Institutions Act And Security Returns In The Savings And Loan Industry," (4), 339-348.

Kamara, Avraham. "Issues In Futures Markets: A Survey," (3), 261-294.
Howard, Charles T. "Are T-Bill Futures Good Forecasters Of Interest Rates?," (4), 305-315.
Kroch, Eugene. "Do Futures Markets Help Intertemporal Allocation Of Resources?," (4), 317-332.
Miller, Stephen E. "Forward Pricing Feeder Pigs," (4), 333-340.
Hegde, Shantaram P. "The Impact Of Interest Rate Level And Volatility On The Performance Of Interest Rate Hedges," (4), 341-356.
Simpson, W. Gary and Timothy C. Ireland. "The Effect Of Futures Trading On The Price Volatility Of GNMA Securities," (4), 357-366.
Weaver, Robert D. and Aniruddha Banerjee. "Cash Price Variation In The Live Beef Cattle Market: The Causal Role Of Futures Trade," (4), 367-389.
Wolf, Avner. "Fundamentals Of Commodity Options On Futures," (4), 391-408.
Laborde, P. "A Note On Net And Double Gains, Or Losses, In Spreading Operations," (4), 409-414.
von Furstenberg, George M. "Comment On `Future Markets And The Supply Of Storage With Rational Expectations'," (4), 415-417.

Journal of Futures Markets
Volume 3, 1983

Cornell, Bradford and Kenneth R. French. "The Pricing Of Stock Index Futures," (1), 1-14.
Modest, David M. and Mahadevan Sundaresan. "The Relationship Between Spot And Futures Prices In Stock Index Futures Markets: Some Preliminary Evidence," (1), 15-41.
McDonald, Robert and Daniel Siegel. "A Note On The Design Of Commodity Options Contracts: A Comment," (1), 43-46.
Scherr, Bruce A. and Howard C. Madsen. "Observations On The Relationship Between Agricultural Commodity Prices And Real Interest Rates," (1), 47-54.
Kolb, Robert W. and Gerald D. Gay. "The Performance Of Live Cattle Futures As Predictors Of Subsequent Spot Prices," (1), 55-63.
Arak, Marcelle. "The Effect Of The Tax Treatment Of Treasury-Bill Futures On Their Rates," (1), 65-73.
Hirschfeld, David J. "A Fundamental Overview Of The Energy Futures Market," (1), 75-100.
Leuthold, Raymond M. "Commercial Use And Speculative Measures Of The Livestock Commodity Futures Markets," (2), 113-135.
Guttentag, Jack M. "A Note On Hedging And Solvency: The Case Of A Phoenix," (2), 137-141.
Giddy, Ian H. "Foreign Exchange Options," (2), 143-166.
Spilka, Walter, Jr. "An Overview Of The USDA Crop And Livestock Information System," (2), 167-176.
Batlin, Carl Alan. "Interest Rate Risk, Prepayment Risk, And The Futures Market Hedging Strategies Of Financial Intermediaries," (2), 177-184.
Speakes, Jeffrey K. "The Phased-In Money Market Certificate Hedge," (2), 185-190.
Edwards, Franklin R. "Futures Markets In Transition: The Uneasy Balance Between Government And Self-Regulation," (2), 191-206.
Ward, Ronald W. and Robert M. Behr. "Futures Trading Liquidity: An Application Of A Futures Trading Model," (2), 207-224.
Goldenberg, David H. "Comment On `Usefulness Of Treasury Bill Futures As Hedging Instruments'," (2), 225-226.
Rosen, Jeffrey S. "The Impact Of The Futures Trading Act of 1982 Upon Commodity Regulaton," (3), 235-258.
Strahm, Norman D. "Preference Space Evaluation Of Trading System Performance," (3), 259-281.
Veit, E. Theodore and Wallace W. Reiff. "Commercial Banks And Interest Rate Futures: A Hedging Survey," (3), 283-293.
Grammatikos, Theoharry and Anthony Saunders. "Stability And The Hedging Performance Of Foreign Currency Futures," (3), 295-305.
Koppenhaver, G. D. "The Forward Pricing Efficiency Of The Live Cattle Futures Market," (3), 307-319.
Bigman, David, David Goldfarb and Edna Schechtman. "Futures Market Efficiency And The Time Content Of The Information Sets," (3), 321-334.
Asay, Michael R. "A Note On The Design Commodity Option Contracts: A Reply," (3), 335-338.
Kuberek, Robert C. and Norman G. Pefley. "Hedging Corporate Debt With U.S. Treasury Bond Futures," (4), 345-353.
Adler, Michael. "Designing Spreads In Forward Exchange Contracts And Foreign Exchange Futures," (4), 355-368.
Edwards, Franklin R. "The Clearing Association In Futures Markets: Guarantor And Regulator," (4), 369-392.
Ward, Ronald W. and Robert M. Behr. "Allocating Nonreported Futures Commitments," (4), 393-401.
Hill, Joanne, Joseph Liro and Thomas Schneeweis. "Hedging Performance Of GNMA Futures Under Rising And Falling Interest Rates," (4), 403-413.
Goodman, Laurie S. and Martha J. Langer. "Accounting For Interest Rate Futures In Bank Asset-Liability Management," (4), 415-428.
Senchack, Andrew J., Jr. and John C. Easterwood. "Cross Hedging CDs With Treasury Bill Futures," (4), 429-438.
Conroy, Robert M. and Richard J. Rendleman, Jr. "Pricing Commodities When Both Price And Output Are Uncertain," (4), 439-450.
Garbade, Kenneth D. and William L. Silber. "Cash Settlement Of Futures Contracts: An Economic Analysis," (4), 451-472.

Journal of Futures Markets
Volume 4, 1984

Pitts, Mark and Robert W. Kopprasch. "Reducing Inter-Temporal Risk In Financial Futures Hedging," (1), 1-14.
Tomek, William G. and Scott F. Querin. "Random Processes In Prices And Technical Analysis," (1), 15-23.
Bortz, Gary A. "Does The Treasury Bond Futures Market Destabilize The Treasury Bond Cash Market?," (1), 25-38.

Castelino, Mark G. and Ashok Vora. "Spread Volatility In Commodity Futures: The Length Effect," (1), 39-46.
Kolb, Robert W., Stephen G. Timme and Gerald D. Gay. "Macro Versus Micro Futures Hedges At Commercial Banks," (1), 47-54.
Kane, Alex and Alan J. Marcus. "Conversion Factor Risk And Hedging In The Treasury-Bond Futures Market," (1), 55-64.
Gehm, Fred. "Techniques For Making Decisions Under Uncertainty," (1), 65-74.
Eckardt, Walter L., Jr. "Equivalent Delivery Procedures For GNMA Futures Contracts And Options," (1), 75-85.
Herbst, Anthony F. and Nicholas O. Ordway. "Stock Index Futures Contracts And Separability Of Returns," (1), 87-102.
Kawaller, Ira G. and Timothy W. Koch. "Cash-And-Carry Trading And The Pricing Of Treasury Bill Futures," (2), 115-124.
Draper, Dennis W. "The Behavior Of Event-Related Returns On Oil Futures Contracts," (2), 125-132.
Eldridge, Robert M. "Intertemporal Price Volatility Of Foreign Currency Futures Contracts," (2), 133-140.
Hayenga, Marvin L., Dennis D. Dipietre, J. Marvin Skadberg and Ted C. Schroeder. "Profitable Hedging Opportunities And Risk Premiums For Producers In Live Cattle And Live Hog Futures Markets," (2), 141-154.
Benninga, Simon, Rafael Eldor and Itzhak Zilcha. "The Optimal Hedge Ratio In Unbiased Futures Markets," (2), 155-159.
Livingston, Miles. "The Cheapest Deliverable Bond For The CBT Treasury Bond Futures Contract," (2), 161-172.
Chambers, Donald R. "An Immunization Strategy For Futures Contracts On Government Securities," (2), 173-188.
Raynauld, Jacques and Jacques Tessier. "Risk Premiums In Futures Markets: An Empirical Investigation," (2), 189-211.
Finnerty, Joseph E. "The Mexican Peso And The Chicago International Money Market: A Case Study In Foreign Currency Futures," (2), 213-224.
Gay, Gerald D. and Robert W. Kolb. "Removing Bias In Duration Based Hedging Models: A Note," (2), 225-228.
Carlton, Dennis W. "Futures Markets: Their Purpose, Their History, Their Growth, Their Successes And Failures," (3), 237-272.
Fischel, Daniel R. and Sanford J. Grossman. "Customer Protection In Futures And Securities Markets," (3), 273-296.
Anderson, Ronald W. "The Regulation Of Futures Contract Innovations In The United States," (3), 297-332.
Edwards, Linda N. and Franklin R. Edwards. "A Legal And Economic Analysis Of Manipulation In Futures Markets," (3), 333-366.
Kane, Edward J. "Regulatory Structure In Futures Markets: Jurisdictional Competition Between The SEC, The CFTC, And Other Agencies," (3), 367-384.
Figlewski, Stephen. "Margins And Market Integrity: Margin Setting For Stock Index Futures And Options," (3), 385-416.
Jaffee, Dwight M. "The Impact Of Financial Futures And Options On Capital Formation," (3), 417-447.
Gordon, Kathryn M. and Gordon C. Rausser. "Country Hedging For Real Income Stabilization: A Case Study Of South Korea And Egypt," (4), 449-464.
Neftci, Salih N. and Andrew J. Policano. "Can Chartists Outperform The Market? Market Efficiency Tests For `Technical Analysis'," (4), 465-478.
Oldfield, George S. and Carlos E. Rovira. "Futures Contract Options," (4), 479-490.
Wolf, Anver. "Options Of Futures: Pricing And The Effect Of An Anticipated Price Change," (4), 491-512.
Martin, Larry J. and David Hope. "Risk And Returns From Alternative Marketing Strategies For Corn Producers," (4), 513-530.
Cornew, Ronald W., Donald E. Town and Lawrence D. Crowson. "Stable Distributions, Futures Prices, And The Measurement Of Trading Performance," (4), 531-558.
Helms, Billy P., Fred R. Kaen and Robert E. Rosenman. "Memory In Commodity Futures Contracts," (4), 559-567.
Meisner, James F. and John W. Labuszewski. "Treasury Bond Futures Delivery Bias," (4), 569-577.
Feuerstein, Jay R. "Trading Bond Spreads In The Delivery Month," (4), 579-583.

Journal of Futures Markets
Volume 5, 1985

Bigman, David and David Goldfarb. "Efficiency And Efficient Trading Rules For Food And Feed Grains In The World Commodity Markets: The Israeli Experience," (1), 1-10.
Pluhar, Darwin M., Carl E. Shafer and Thomas L. Sporleder. "The Systematic Downward Bias In Live Cattle Futures: A Further Evaluation," (1), 11-20.
Miller, Stephen E. "Simple And Multiple Cross-Hedging Of Millfeeds," (1), 21-28.
Ball, Clifford A., Walter N. Torous and Adrian E. Tschoegl. "The Degree Of Price Resolution: The Case Of The Gold Market," (1), 29-43.
Nelson, Ray D. and Robert A. Collins. "A Measure Of Hedging's Performance," (1), 45-55.
Canarella, Giorgio and Stephen K. Pollard. "Efficiency Of Commodity Futures: A Vector Autoregression Analysis," (1), 57-76.
Park, Hun Y. and Andrew H. Chen. "Differences Between Futures And Forward Prices: A Further Investigation Of The Marking-to-Market Effect," (1), 77-88.
Cornell, Bradford. "Taxes And The Pricing Of Stock Index Futures: Empirical Results," (1), 89-101.
Kahl, Kandace H., Roger D. Rutz and Jeanne C. Sinquefield. "The Economics Of Performance Margins In Futures Markets," (1), 103-112.
Milonas, Nicholaos T., Peter E. Koveos and G. Geoffrey Booth. "Memory In Commodity Futures Contracts: A Comment," (1), 113-114.
Jones, Robert A. "Conversion Factor Risk In Treasury Bond Futures: Comment," (1), 115-120.
Baxter, Jennefer, Thomas E. Conine, Jr. and Maurry Tamarkin. "On Commodity Market Risk Premiums: Additional Evidence," (1), 121-

Abken, Peter A. "An Analysis Of Intra-Market Spreads In Heating Oil Futures," (1), 77-87.

Braga, Francesco S., Larry J. Martin and Karl D. Meilke. "Cross Hedging The Italian Lira/US Dollar Exchange Rate With Deutsch Mark Futures," (2), 87-100.

Merrick, John J., Jr. "Early Unwindings And Rollovers Of Stock Index Futures Arbitrage Programs: Analysis And Implications For Predicting Expiration Day Effects," (2), 101-112.

Oellermann, Charles M., B. Wade Brorsen and Paul L. Farris. "Price Discovery For Feeder Cattle," (2), 113-122.

Poitras, Geoff. "Optimal Futures Spread Positions," (2), 123-134.

Eldor, Rafael, David Pines and Abba Schwartz. "Determinants Of An Individual's Demand For Hedging Instruments," (2), 135-142.

Brooks, Robert. "Investment Decision Making With Index Futures And Index Futures Options," (2), 143-162.

Lien, Da-Hsiang Donald. "Optimal Hedging And Spreading On Wheat Futures Markets," (2), 163-170.

Levy, Azriel. "A Note On The Relationship Between Forward And Futures Contracts," (2), 171-174.

Ma, Christopher K., G. Wenchi Wong and Edwin D. Maberly. "The Daily Effect In The Gold Market: A Reply," (2), 175-178.

Herbst, A. F., D. D. Kare and S. C. Caples. "Hedging Effectiveness And Minimum Risk Hedge Ratios In The Presence Of Autocorrelation: Foreign Currency Futures," (3), 185-198.

Goldenberg, David H. "Memory And Equilibrium Futures Prices," (3), 199-214.

Shalen, C. T. "The Optimal Maturity Of Hedges And Participation Of Hedgers In Futures And Forward Markets," (3), 215-224.

Brorsen, B. Wade. "Liquidity Costs And Scalping Returns In The Corn Futures Market," (3), 225-236.

Kahl, Kandice H., Michael A. Hudson and Clement E. Ward. "Cash Settlement Issues For Live Cattle Futures Contracts," (3), 237-248.

MacDonald, S. Scott and Scott E. Hein. "Future Rates And Forward Rates As Predictors Of Near-Term Treasury Bill Rates," (3), 249-262.

Lien, Da-Hsiang Donald. "Cash Settlement Provisions On Futures Contracts," (3), 263-270.

Maberly, Edwin D. "The Relationship Between Stock Indices And Stock Index Futures From 3:00-3:15: A Note," (3), 271-273.

Brorsen, B. Wade, Charles M. Oellermann and Paul L. Farris. "The Live Cattle Futures Market And Daily Cash Price," (4), 273-282.

Bailey, Warren. "The Market For Japanese Index Futures: Some Preliminary Evidence," (4), 283-296.

Lauterbach, Beni and Margaret Monroe. "Evidence On The Effect Of Information And Noise Trading On Intraday Gold Futures Returns," (4), 297-306.

Miller, Stephen E. and Kandice H. Kahl. "Performance Of Estimated Hedging Ratios Under Yield Uncertainty," (4), 307-320.

Ma, Christopher K., Ramesh P. Rao and R. Stephen Sears. "Limit Moves And Price Resolution: The Case Of The Treasury Bond Futures Market," (4), 321-336.

Dalal, Ardeshir J. and Bala G. Arshanapalli. "Effects Of Expected Cash And Futures Prices On Hedging And Production: Comments And Extensions," (4), 337-346.

Carter, Colin A. "Arbitrage Opportunities Between Thin And Liquid Futures Markets," (4), 347-354.

Lien, Da-Hsiang Donald. "Optical Settlement Specification On Futures Contracts," (4), 355-358.

Jorion, Philippe and Neal M. Stoughton. "An Empirical Investigation Of The Early Exercise Premium Of Foreign Currency Options," (5), 365-376.

Wilson, William W. "Price Discovery And Hedging In The Sunflower Market," (5), 377-392.

Ma, Cindy W. "Forecasting Efficiency Of Energy Futures Prices," (5), 393-420.

Hegde, Shantaram P. "On The Value Of The Implicit Delivery Options," (5), 421-438.

Yano, Adrian S. "Configurations For Arbitrage Using Financial Futures Contracts," (5), 439-448.

Cotner, John S. and James F. Horrell. "An Analysis Of Index Option Pricing," (5), 449-460.

Moylan, James J., Laren A. Ukman and Peter S. Lake. "Exchange Memberships: An Overview Of The Issues Pertaining To The Property Rights Of A Bankrupt Member And His Creditors," (5), 461-468.

Lindahl, Mary. "Measuring Hedging Effectiveness With R-Square: A Note," (5), 469-475.

Leistikow, Dean. "Announcements And Futures Price Variability," (6), 477-486.

Babbel, David F. "Insuring Banks Against Systematic Credit Risk," (6), 487-506.

Savit, Robert. "Nonlinearities And Chaotic Effects In Options Prices," (6), 507-518.

Wood, Wendell C., Carl E. Shafer and Carl G. Anderson. "Frequency And Duration Of Profitable Hedging Margins For Texas Cotton Producers, 1980-1986," (6), 519-528.

McCabe, George M. and Donald P. Solberg. "Hedging In The Treasury Bill Futures Market When The Hedged Instrument And The Deliverable Instrument Are Not Matched," (6), 529-538.

Kawaller, Ira G. and Timothy W. Koch. "Yield Opportunities And Hedge Ratio Considerations With Fixed Income Cash-And-Carry Trades," (6), 539-546.

Paroush, Jacob and Avner Wolf. "Production And Hedging Decisions In The Presence Of Basis Risk," (6), 547-564.

Shyy, Gang. "Gambler's Ruin And Optimal Stop Loss Strategy," (6), 565-572.

Khoury, Nabil T. and Jean-Marc Martel. "A Supply Of Storage Theory With Asymmetric Information," (6), 573-582.

Lien, Da-Hsiang Donald. "Sampled Data As A Basis Of Cash Settlement Price," (6), 583-588.

Journal of Futures Markets
Volume 10, 1990

Koppenhaver, G. D. "An Empirical Analysis Of Bank Hedging In Futures Markets," (1), 1-12.

Wilson, William W. and Hung-Gay Fung. "Information Content Of Volatilities Implied By Option Premiums In Grain Futures Markets," (1), 13-28.

Chang, Eric C., Chao Chen and Son-Nan Chen. "Risk And Return In Copper, Platinum, And Silver Futures," (1), 29-40.

Weaver, Robert D. and Aniruddha Banerjee. "Does Futures Trading Destabilize Cash Prices? Evidence For U.S. Live Beef Cattle," (1), 41-60.

Cheung, C. Sherman, Clarence C. Y. Kwan and Patrick C. Y. Yip. "The Hedging Effectiveness Of Options And Futures: A Mean-Gini Approach," (1), 61-74.

Murphy, Austin and Doug Gordon. "An Empirical Note On Hedging Mortgages With Puts," (1), 75-78.

Chambers, Scott and Colin Carter. "U.S. Futures Exchanges As Nonprofit Entities," (1), 79-88.

Lien, Da-Hsiang Donald. "Entry-Deterring Contract Specification On Futures Markets," (1), 89-96.

Melvin, Michael and Jahangir Sultan. "South African Political Unrest, Oil Prices, And The Time Varying Risk Premium In The Gold Futures Market," (2), 103-112.

Ouattara, Korotoumou, Ted C. Schroeder and L. Orlo Sorenson. "Potential Use Of Futures Markets For International Marketing Of Cote D'Ivoire Coffee," (2), 113-122.

Koontz, Stephen R., Philip Garcia and Michael A. Hudson. "Dominant-Satellite Relationships Between Live Cattle Cash And Futures Markets," (2), 123-136.

Ma, Christopher K., William H. Dare and Darla R. Donaldson. "Testing Rationality In Futures Markets," (2), 137-152.

Thompson, Sarahelen, Thomas J. McNeill and James S. Eales. "Expiration And Delivery On The World Sugar Futures Contract," (2), 153-168.

Blank, Steven C. "Determining Futures 'Hedging Reserve' Capital Requirements," (2), 169-178.

Harris, Lawrence. "The Economics Of Cash Index Alternatives," (2), 179-194.

Shen, Chung-Hua and Lee-Rong Wang. "Examining The Validity Of A Test Of Futures Market Efficiency: A Comment," (2), 195-196.

Deaves, Richard. "Hedging Canadian Corporate Debt: A Comment And Extensions," (2), 197-200.

Lien, Da-Hsiang Donald. "A Note On Hedging Performance And Portfolio Effects," (2), 201-204.

Eales, James and Robert J. Hauser. "Analyzing Biases In Valuation Models Of Options On Futures," (3), 211-228.

Braga, Francesco S. and Larry J. Martin. "Out Of Sample Effectiveness Of A Joint Commodity And Currency Hedge: The Case Of Soybean Meal In Italy," (3), 229-246.

Brorsen, B. Wade and Louis P. Lukac. "Optimal Portfolios For Commodity Futures Funds," (3), 247-258.

Park, Timothy and Frances Antonovitz. "Basis Risk And Optimal Decision Making For California Feedlots," (3), 259-272.

Han, Li-Ming and Lalatendu Misra. "The Relationship Between The Volatilities Of The S&P Index And Futures Contracts Implicit In Their Call Option Prices," (3), 273-286.

Benet, Bruce A. "Commodity Futures Cross Hedging Of Foreign Exchange Exposure," (3), 287-306.

Chang, Jack S. K. and Hsing Fang. "An Intertemporal Measure Of Hedging Effectiveness," (3), 307-322.

Herbst, Anthony F. and Edwin D. Maberly. "Stock Index Futures, Expiration Day Volatility, And The 'Special' Friday Opening: A Note," (3), 323-325.

Lieu, Derming. "Option Pricing With Futures-Style Margining," (4), 327-338.

Followill, Richard A. and Billy P. Helms. "Put-Call-Futures Parity And Arbitrage Opportunity In The Market For Options On Gold Futures Contracts," (4), 339-352.

Turvey, Calum G. "Alternative Estimates Of Weighted Implied Volatilities From Soybean And Live Cattle Options," (4), 353-366.

Bhatt, Swati and Nusret Cakici. "Premiums On Stock Index Futures - Some Evidence," (4), 367-376.

Leistikow, Dean. "The Relative Responsiveness To Information And Variability Of Storable Commodity Spot And Futures Prices," (4), 377-396.

Kamara, Avraham. "Forecasting Accuracy And Development Of A Financial Market: The Treasury Bill Futures Market," (4), 397-406.

Hill, Joanne, Thomas Schneeweis and Jot Yau. "International Trading/Non Trading Time Effects On Risk Estimation In Futures Markets," (4), 407-424.

O'Neill, William D. "Estimation And Revision Of A Sequential Auction Model For The Soybean Futures Current Contract," (4), 425-441.

Ritchken, Peter and L. Sankarasubramanian. "On Valuing Complex Interest Rate Claims," (5), 443-456.

Moser, James T. and Billy Helms. "An Examination Of Basis Risk Due To Estimation," (5), 457-468.

Harpaz, Giorra, Steven Krull and Joseph Yagil. "The Efficiency Of The US Dollar Index Futures Market," (5), 469-480.

Gosnell, Thomas F. and Andrea J. Heuson. "A Discretionary Approach To Hedging A Lender's Exposure In Adjustable Rate Mortgages," (5), 481-496.

Tzang, Dah-Nein and Raymond M. Leuthold. "Hedge Ratios Under Inherent Risk Reduction In A Commodity Complex," (5), 497-504.

Morard, Bernard and Ahmed Naciri. "Options And Investment Strategies," (5), 505-518.

Heinkel, Robert, Maureen E. Howe and John S. Hughes. "Commodity Convenience Yields As On Option Profit," (5), 519-534.

Eytan, T. Hanan. "Corporate Taxes And Hedging With Futures," (5), 535-540.

Fishe, Raymond P. H., Lawrence G. Goldberg, Thomas F. Gosnell and Sujata Sinha. "Margin Requirements In Futures Markets: Their Relationship To Price Volatility," (5), 541-554.

Hein, Scott E., Christopher K. Ma and S. Scott MacDonald. "Testing Unbiasedness In Futures Markets: A Clarification," (5), 555-562.

Moser, James T. "Public Policy Intervention Through Futures Market Operations," (6), 567-572.

Yadav, Pradeep K. and Peter F. Pope. "Stock Index Futures Arbitrage: International Evidence," (6), 573-604.

Blenman, Lloyd P. "Price Forecasts And Interest Rate Forecasts: An

Extension Of Levy's Hypothesis," (6), 605-610.

Cho, Dong W. and Gerald S. McDougall. "The Supply Of Storage In Energy Futures Markets," (6), 611-622.

Fujihara, Roger and Keehwan Park. "The Probability Distribution Of Futures Prices In The Foreign Exchange Market: A Comparison Of Candidate Processes," (6), 623-642.

Poitras, Geoffrey. "The Distribution Of Gold Futures Spreads," (6), 643-660.

Martell, Terrence F. and Ruben C. Trevino. "The Intraday Behavior Of Commodity Futures Prices," (6), 661-672.

Kuserk, Gregory J. "Limit Moves And Price Resolution: The Case Of The Treasury Bond Futures Market: A Comment," (6), 673-674.

Journal of Futures Markets
Volume 11, 1991

Cotner, John S. "Index Option Pricing: Do Investors Pay For Skewness?," (1), 1-8.

Junkus, Joan C. "Systematic Skewness In Futures Contracts," (1), 9-24.

Johnson, Robert L., Carl R. Zulauf, Scott H. Irwin and Mary E. Gerlow.

"The Soybean Complex Spread: An Examination Of Market Efficiency From The Viewpoint Of A Production Process," (1), 25-38.

Myers, Robert J. "Estimating Time-Varying Optimal Hedge Ratios On Futures Markets," (1), 39-54.

Malliaris, A. G. and Jorge Urrutia. "Tests Of Random Walk Of Hedge Ratios And Measures Of Hedging Effectiveness For Stock Indexes And Foreign Currencies," (1), 55-68.

Khoury, Nabil T. and Pierre Yourougou. "The Informational Content Of The Basis: Evidence From Canadian Barley, Oats, And Canola Futures Markets," (1), 69-80.

Stevens, Stanley C. "Evidence For A Weather Persistence Effect On The Corn, Wheat, And Soybean Growing Season Price Dynamics," (1), 81-88.

Rumsey, John. "Pricing Cross-Currency Options," (1), 89-94.

Martin, John D. and A. J. Senchack, Jr. "Index Futures, Program Trading, And The Covariability Of The Major Market Index Stocks," (1), 95-112.

Flesaker, Bjorn. "The Relationship Between Forward And Futures Contracts: A Comment," (1), 113-116.

Polakoff, Michael A. "A Note On The Role Of Futures Indivisibility: Reconciling The Theoretical Literature," (1), 117-120.

Journal of International Money and Finance
Volume 1, 1982

Friedman, Milton and Anna J. Schwartz. "Interrelations Between The United States And The United Kingdom, 1873-1975," (1), 3-19.

Eaton, Jonathan and Stephen J. Turnovsky. "Effects Of Monetary Disturbances On Exchange Rates With Risk Averse Speculation," (1), 21-37.

Hooper, Peter and John Morton. "Fluctuations In The Dollar: A Model Of Nominal And Real Exchange Rate Determination," (1), 39-56.

Laskar, Daniel M. "Short-Run Independence Of Monetary Policy Under A Pegged-Exchange-Rates System: An Econometric Approach," (1), 57-80.

von Furstenberg, George M. "New Estimates Of The Demand For Non-Gold Reserves Under Floating Exchange Rates," (1), 81-96.

Kane, Alex and Leonard Rosenthal. "International Interest Rates And Inflationary Expectations," (1), 97-110.

Pippenger, John. "Some Evidence On The Relationship Between Spot And Forward Exchange Rates," (1), 111-113.

Murray, John D. "The Tax Sensitivity Of US Direct Investment In Canadian Manufacturing," (2), 117-140.

Laney, Leroy O. and Thomas D. Willett. "The International Liquidity Explosion And Worldwide Inflation: The Evidence From Sterilization Coefficient Estimates," (2), 141-152.

Connolly, Michael. "The Choice Of An Optimum Currency Peg For A Small, Open Country," (2), 153-164.

Branson, William H. and Jorge Braga De Macedo. "The Optimal Weighting Of Indicators For A Crawling Peg," (2), 165-178.

Djajic, Slobodan. "Balance-Of-Payments Dynamics And Exchange-Rate Management," (2), 179-191.

Meyer, Stephen A. and Richard Startz. "Real Versus Nominal Forecast Errors In The Prediction Of Foreign Exchange Rates," (2), 193-200.

Cornell, Bradford. "Money Supply Announcements, Interest Rates, And Foreign Exchange," (2), 201-208.

Edwards, Sebastian. "Exchange Rate And `News': A Multi-Currency Approach," (3), 211-224.

De Grauwe, Paul. "The Exchange Rate In A Portfolio Balance Model With A Banking Sector," (3), 225-240.

Harris, Richard G. and Douglas D. Purvis. "Incomplete Information And Equilibrium Determination Of The Forward Exchange Rate," (3), 241-254.

Frankel, Jeffrey A. "In Search Of The Exchange Risk Premium: A Six-Currency Test Assuming Mean-Variance Optimization," (3), 255-274.

Bhandari, Jagdeep S. "Staggered Wage Setting And Exchange Rate Policy In An Economy With Capital Assets," (3), 275-292.

Laidler, David. "Friedman And Schwartz On Monetary Trends: A Review Article," (3), 293-305.

Fratianni, Michele and Lee MacDonald Wakeman. "The Law Of One Price In The Eurocurrency Market," (3), 307-324.

Driskill, Robert and Stephen McCafferty. "Equilibrium Price-Output Dynamics And The (Non) Insulating Properties Of Fixed Exchange Rates," (3), 325-332.

Solnik, Bruno H. "An Empirical Investigation Of The Determinants Of National Interest Rate Differences," (3), 333-339.

Journal of International Money and Finance
Volume 2, 1983

Eichengreen, Barry J. "Effective Protection And Exchange-Rate Determination," (1), 1-16.

Kim, Inchul. "A Partial Adjustment Theory Of The Balance Of Payments," (1), 17-26.

Kimbrough, Kent P. "The Information Content Of The Exchange Rate And The Stability Of Real Output Under Alternative Exchange-Rate Regimes," (1), 27-38.

Frankel, Jeffrey A. "The Effect Of Excessively Elastic Expectations On Exchange-Rate Volatility In The Dornbusch Overshooting Model," (1), 39-46.

Protopapadakis, Aris. "Expectations, Exchange Rates, And Monetary Theory: The Case Of The German Hyperinflation," (1), 47-65.

Clifton, Eric V. "The Effects Of Increased Interest-Rate Volatility On LDCs," (1), 67-74.

Benavie, Arthur. "Achieving External And Internal Targets With Exchange-Rate And Interest-Rate Intervention," (1), 75-85.

Horne, Jocelyn. "The Asset Market Model Of The Balance Of Payments And The Exchange Rate: A Survey Of Empirical Evidence," (2), 89-109.

Cuddington, John T. "Currency Substitution, Capital Mobility, And Money Demand," (2), 111-133.

Obstfeld, Maurice. "Intertemporal Price Speculation And The Optimal Current-Account Deficit," (2), 135-145.

Stockman, Alan C. "Real Exchange Rates Under Alternative Nominal Exchange-Rate Systems," (2), 147-166.

Choudhri, Ehsan U. "The Transmission Of Inflation In A Small Economy: An Empirical Analysis Of The Influence Of US Monetary Disturbances On Canadian Inflation, 1962-80," (2), 167-178.

Djajic, Slobodan. "Intermediate Inputs and International Trade: An Analysis Of The Real And Monetary Aspects Of A Change In The Price Of Oil," (2), 179-195.

McDermott, John. "Exchange-Rate Indexation In A Monetary Model: Theory And Evidence," (2), 197-213.

Razin, Assaf and Lars E. O. Svensson. "The Current Account And The Optimal Government Debt," (2), 215-224.

Garman, Mark B. and Steven W. Kohlhagen. "Foreign Currency Option Values," (3), 231-237.

Grabbe, J. Orlin. "The Pricing Of Call And Put Options On Foreign Exchange," (3), 239-253.

Vander Kraats, R. H. and L. D. Booth. "Empirical Tests Of The Monetary Approach To Exchange-Rate Determination," (3), 255-278.

Flood, Robert P. and Nancy P. Marion. "Exchange-Rate Regimes In Transition: Italy 1974," (3), 279-294.

Shapiro, Alan C. "What Does Purchasing Power Parity Mean?," (3), 295-318.

Beenstock, Michael. "Rational Expectations And The Effect Of Exchange-Rate Intervention On The Exchange Rate," (3), 319-331.

Kimbrough, Kent P. "Exchange-Rate Policy And Monetary Information," (3), 333-346.

Gardner, Grant W. "The Choice Of Monetary Policy Instruments In An Open Economy," (3), 347-354.

Minford, Patrick. "Equilibrium Price-Output Dynamics And The (Non)Insulating Properties Of Fixed Exchange Rates: A Comment," (3), 355-356.

Journal of International Money and Finance
Volume 3, 1984

Hodrick, Robert J. and Sanjay Srivastava. "An Investigation Of Risk And Return In Forward Foreign Exchange," (1), 5-29.

Rush, Mark. "A Classical Model Of A Small Fixed Exchange Rate Economy," (1), 31-49.

Bigman, David. "Semi-Rational Expectations And Exchange-Rate Dynamics," (1), 51-66.

BenZion, Uri and J. Weinblatt. "Purchasing Power, Interest Rate Parities And The Modified Fisher Effect In Presence Of Tax Agreements," (1), 67-73.

Brissimis, Sophocles N. and John A. Leventakis. "An Empirical Inquiry Into The Short-Run Dynamics Of Output, Prices, And Exchange Market Pressure," (1), 75-89.

Hartman, David G. "The International Financial Market And US Interest Rates," (1), 91-104.

Levi, Maurice. "Spot Versus Forward Speculation And Hedging: A Diagrammatic Exposition," (1), 105-109.

Swanson, Peggy E. "External Currency Market Data: An Application From BIS Series," (1), 111-117.

Longworth, David. "Exchange Rates And `News': A Comment," (1), 119-122.

Edwards, Sebastian. "Exchange Rates And `News': Reply," (1), 123-126.

Meese, Richard A. "Is The Sticky Price Assumption Reasonable For Exchange Rate Models?," (1), 131-139.

Hsieh, David A. "International Risk Sharing And The Choice Of Exchange-Rate Regime," (2), 141-151.

Huang, Roger D. "Some Alternative Tests Of Forward Exchange Rates As Predictors Of Future Spot Rates," (2), 153-168.

Park, Keehwan. "Tests Of The Hypothesis Of The Existence Of Risk Premium In The Foreign Exchange Market," (2), 169-178.

Papell, David H. "Anticipated And Unanticipated Disturbances: The Dynamics Of The Exchange Rate And The Current Account," (2), 179-193.

Cumby, Robert E. "Monetary Policy Under Dual Exchange Rates," (2), 195-208.

Booth, Laurence D. "Bid-Ask Spreads In The Market For Forward Exchange," (2), 209-222.

Neumann, Manfred J. M. "Intervention In The Mark/Dollar Market: The Authorities' Reaction Function," (2), 223-240.

Wallace, Myles S. "World Money Or Domestic Money: Which Predicts US Inflation Best?," (2), 241-244.

Loopesko, Bonnie E. "Relationships Among Exchange Rates, Intervention, And Interest Rates: An Empirical Investigation," (3), 257-277.

Batten, Dallas S. and Daniel L. Thornton. "Discount Rate Changes And The Foreign Exchange Market," (3), 279-292.

Papell, David H. "Activist Monetary Policy And Exchange-Rate Overshooting: The Deutsche Mark/Dollar Rate," (3), 293-310.

Sheffrin, Steven M. and Thomas Russell. "Sterling And Oil Discoveries: The Mystery Of Nonappreciation," (3), 311-326.

Murphy, Robert G. "Capital Mobility And The Relationship Between Saving And Investment Rates In OECD Countries," (3), 327-342.

Lee, Moon H. and Josef Zechner. "Debt, Taxes, And International Equilibrium," (3), 343-355.

Gregory, Allan W. and Thomas H. McCurdy. "Testing The Unbiasedness Hypothesis In the Forward Foreign Exchange Market: A Specification Analysis," (3), 357-368.

Melvin, Michael and David Bernstein. "Trade Concentration, Openness, And Deviations From Purchasing Power Parity," (3), 369-376.

Journal of International Money and Finance
Volume 4, 1985

Aizenman, Joshua. "Openness, Relative Prices, And Macro-Policies," (1), 5-18.

Bhandari, Jagdeep S. "The Flexible Exchange Basket: A Macroeconomic Analysis," (1), 19-41.

Calvo, Guillermo A. "Reserves And The Managed Float: A Search For The Essentials," (1), 43-60.

Chand, Sheetal K. and Yusuke Onitsuka. "Stocks, Flows, And Some Exchange-Rate Dynamics For The Currency Substitution Model," (1), 61-82.

Eaton, Jonathan. "Optimal And Time Consistent Exchange-Rate Management In An Overlapping-Generations Model," (1), 83-100.

Harkness, Jon. "Optimal Exchange Intervention For A Small Open Economy," (1), 101-112.

Kimbrough, Kent P. "An Examination Of The Effects Of Government Purchases In An Open Economy," (1), 113-134.

Currency In Intra-Firm Trade Transactions," (4), 449-464.

Tucker, Alan L. and Elton Scott. "A Study Of Diffusion Processes For Foreign Exchange Rates," (4), 465-478.

Glassman, Debra. "Exchange Rate Risk And Transactions Costs: Evidence From Bid-Ask Spreads," (4), 479-490.

Chadha, Binky. "Contract Length, Monetary Policy And Exchange Rate Variability," (4), 491-504.

Fratianni, Michele, Hyung-Doh Hur and Heejoon Kang. "Random Walk And Monetary Causality In Five Exchange Markets," (4), 505-514.

Journal of International Money and Finance
Volume 8, 1988

Lewis, Karen K. "The Persistence Of The 'Peso Problem' When Policy Is Noisy," (1), 5-22.

Hardouvelis, Gikas A. "Economic News, Exchange Rates And Interest Rates," (1), 23-36.

Akgiray, Vedat, G. Geoffrey Booth and Bruce Seifert. "Distribution Properties Of Latin American Black Market Exchange Rates," (1), 37-48.

Wolff, Christian C. P. "Exchange Rates, Innovations And Forecasting," (1), 49-62.

Kaplanis, Evi C. "Stability And Forecasting Of The Comovement Measures Of International Stock Market Returns," (1), 63-76.

Johnson, David. "The Currency Denomination Of Long-Term Debt In The Canadian Corporate Sector: An Empirical Analysis," (1), 77-90.

Lyons, Richard K. "Tests Of The Foreign Exchange Risk Premium Using The Expected Second Moments Implied By Option Pricing," (1), 91-108.

Pagan, Adrian. "A Note On The Magnitude Of Risk Premia," (1), 109-110.

Giovannini, Alberto and Philippe Jorion. "Foreign Exchange Risk Premia Volatility Once Again," (1), 111-114.

Frankel, Jeffrey A. "Recent Estimates Of Time-Variation In The Conditional Variance And In The Exchange Risk Premium," (1), 115-125.

Benninga, Simon and Aris Protopapadakis. "The Equilibrium Pricing Of Exchange Rates And Assets When Trade Takes Time," (2), 129-150.

Rasmussen, Bo Sandemann. "Stabilization Policies In Open Economies With Imperfect Current Information," (2), 151-166.

Stulz, Rene M. "Capital Mobility And The Current Account," (2), 167-180.

Koch, Paul D., Jeffrey A. Rosenweig and Joseph A. Whitt, Jr. "The Dynamic Relationship Between The Dollar And US Prices: An Intensive Empirical Investigation," (2), 181-204.

Bomhoff, Eduard J. and Kees G. Koedijk. "Bilateral Exchange Rates And Risk Premia," (2), 205-220.

Chen, Chau-nan, Ching-chong Lai and Tien-wang Tsaur. "The Loanable Funds Theory And The Dynamics Of Exchange Rates: The Mundell Model Revisited," (2), 221-230.

Barnhart, Scott W. and Ali F. Darrat. "Budget Deficits, Money Growth And Causality: Further OECD Evidence," (2), 231-242.

Tabellini, Guido. "Learning And The Volatility Of Exchange Rates," (2), 243-250.

Marini, Giancarlo. "Flexible Exchange Rates And Stabilizing Speculation," (2), 251-257.

Hutchison, Michael M. "Monetary Control With An Exchange Rate Objective: The Bank Of Japan, 1973-86," (3), 261-272.

Lewis, Karen K. "Inflation Risk And Asset Market Disturbances: The Mean-Variance Model Revisited," (3), 273-288.

Slovin, Myron B., Marie E. Sushka and Carl D. Hudson. "Corporate Commercial Paper, Note Issuance Facilities, And Shareholder Wealth," (3), 289-302.

Phylaktis, Kate. "Capital Controls: The Case Of Argentina," (3), 303-320.

Chrystal, K. Alec and Daniel L. Thornton. "On The Informational Content Of Spot And Forward Exchange Rates," (3), 321-330.

Canarella, Giorgio and Stephen K. Pollard. "Efficiency In Foreign Exchange Markets: A Vector Autoregression Approach," (3), 331-346.

McClure, J. Harold. "PPP, Interest Rate Parities, And The Modified Fisher Effect In The Presence Of Tax Agreements: A Comment," (3), 347-350.

Scarth, William. "Deficits And Debt In An Open Economy," (3), 351-358.

Cushman, David O. "The Impact Of Third-Country Exchange Risk: A Correction," (3), 359.

Claessen, Stijn. "Balance-Of-Payments Crises In A Perfect Foresight Optimizing Model," (4), 363-372.

Blackburn, Keith. "Collapsing Exchange Rate Regimes And Exchange Rate Dynamics: Some Further Examples," (4), 373-386.

McKibbin, Warwick J. and Jeffrey D. Sachs. "Comparing The Global Performance Of Alternative Exchange Arrangements," (4), 387-410.

Leiderman, Leonardo and Assaf Razin. "Foreign Trade Shocks And The Dynamics Of High Inflation: Israel, 1978-85," (4), 411-424.

O'Connell, Joan. "Sterilization And Interest Rates," (4), 425-428.

Poitras, Geoffrey. "Arbitrage Boundaries, Treasury Bills, And Covered Interest Parity," (4), 429-446.

Morande, Felipe G. "Domestic Currency Appreciation And Foreign Capital Inflows: What Comes First? (Chile, 1977-82)," (4), 447-466.

Journal of International Money and Finance
Volume 8, 1989

Aizenman, Joshua. "Monopolistic Competition, Relative Prices, And Output Adjustment In The Open Economy," (1), 5-28.

Guidotti, Pablo E. "Exchange Rate Determination, Interest Rates, And An Integrative Approach To The Demand For Money," (1), 29-46.

Engel, Charles. "The Trade Balance And Real Exchange Rate Under Currency Substitution," (1), 47-58.

Enders, Walter. "Unit Roots And The Real Exchange Rate Before World War I: The Case Of Britain And The USA," (1), 59-74.

Hakkio, Craig S. and Mark Rush. "Market Efficiency And Cointegration: An Application To The Sterling And Deutschemark Exchange Markets," (1), 75-88.

Reagan, Patricia B. and Rene M. Stulz. "Contracts, Delivery Lags, And Currency Risk," (1), 89-104.

Caskey, John P. "The IMF And Concerted Lending In Latin American Debt Restructurings: A Formal Analysis," (1), 105-120.

Diwan, Ishac. "Foreign Debt, Crowding Out And Capital Flight," (1), 121-136.

Belongia, Michael T. and Mack Ott. "The US Monetary Policy Regime, Interest Differentials, And Dollar Exchange Rate Risk Premia," (1), 137-146.

Cornell, Bradford. "The Impact Of Data Errors On Measurement Of The Foreign Exchange Risk Premium," (1), 147-157.

Levine, Ross. "The Pricing Of Forward Exchange Rates," (2), 163-180.

Gavin, Michael. "The Stock Market And Exchange Rate Dynamics," (2), 181-200.

Boschen, John F. and John L. Newman. "Monetary Effects On The Real Interest Rate In An Open Economy: Evidence From The Argentine Indexed Bond Market," (2), 201-218.

Ambler, Steve. "The International Transmission Of Policy Announcement Effects," (2), 219-232.

Ceglowski, Janet. "Dollar Depreciation And US Industry Performance," (2), 233-252.

Sheen, Jeffrey. "Modelling The Floating Australian Dollar," (2), 253-276.

Isaac, Alan G. "Exchange Rate Volatility And Currency Substitution," (2), 277-284.

Golub, Stephen S. "Foreign-Currency Government Debt, Asset Markets, And The Balance Of Payments," (2), 285-294.

Buttler, Hans-Jurg. "An Expository Note On The Valuation Of Foreign Exchange Options," (2), 295-304.

Adams, Paul D. and Steve B. Wyatt. "On The Pricing Of European And American Foreign Currency Options: A Clarification," (2), 305-311.

Fry, Maxwell J. "Foreign Debt Instability: An Analysis Of National Saving And Domestic Investment Responses To Foreign Debt Accumulation In 28 Developing Countries," (3), 315-344.

Murphy, Robert G. "Import Pricing And The Trade Balance In A Popular Model Of Exchange Rate Determination," (3), 345-358.

Brennan, M. J. and B. Solnik. "International Risk Sharing And Capital Mobility," (3), 359-374.

Schinasi, Garry J. and P. A. V. B. Swamy. "The Out-Of-Sample Forecasting Performance Of Exchange Rate Models When Coefficients Are Allowed To Change," (3), 375-390.

Ayanian, Robert. "Geopolitics And The Dollar," (3), 391-400.

Burdekin, Richard C. K. "International Transmission Of US Macroeconomic Policy And The Inflation Record Of Western Europe," (3), 401-424.

Moffett, Michael H. "The J-Curve Revisited: An Empirical Examination For The United States," (3), 425-444.

Sephton, Peter S. "On Exchange Intervention, Sterlization, And Bank Reserve Accounting," (3), 445-450.

Sundaram, Anant K. "Syndications In Sovereign Lending," (3), 451-464.

Finn, Mary. "An Econometric Analysis Of The Intertemporal General-Equilibrium Approach To Exchange Rate And Current Account Determination," (4), 467-486.

Froot, Kenneth A. and Takatoshi Ito. "On The Consistency Of Short-Run And Long-Run Exchange Rate Expectations," (4), 487-510.

Pesaran, M. Hashem. "Consistency Of Short-Term And Long-Term Expectations," (4), 511-516.

Koedijk, Kees and Peter Schotman. "Dominant Real Exchange Rate Movements," (4), 517-532.

McNown, Robert and Myles S. Wallace. "National Price Levels, Purchasing Power Parity, And Cointegration: A Test Of Four High Inflation Economies," (4), 533-546.

Moore, Michael J. "Dual Exchange Rates, Capital Controls, And Sticky Prices," (4), 547-558.

Djajic, Slobodan. "Dynamics Of The Exchange Rate In Anticipation Of Pegging," (4), 559-572.

Thornton, Daniel L. "The Effect Of Unanticipated Money On The Money And Foreign Exchange Markets," (4), 573-588.

Journal of International Money and Finance
Volume 9, 1990

Bui, Nhuong and John Pippenger. "Commodity Prices, Exchange Rates And Their Relative Volatility," (1), 3-20.

Goodwin, Barry K., Thomas Grennes and Michael K. Wohlgenant. "Testing The Law Of One Price When Trade Takes Time," (1), 21-40.

Browne, Francis X. and Paul D. McNelis. "Exchange Controls And Interest Rate Determination With Traded And Nontraded Assets: The Irish-United Kingdom Experience," (1), 41-59.

Wong, David Y. "What Do Saving-Investment Relationships Tell Us About Capital Mobility?," (1), 60-74.

Manzur, Meher. "An International Comparison Of Prices And Exchange Rates: A New Test Of Purchasing Power Parity," (1), 75-91.

Wasserfallen, Walter. "Expected And Unexpected Changes In Nominal And Real Variables - Evidence From The Capital Markets," (1), 92-107.

Von Hagen, Juergen. "Policy Effectiveness In An Open Multi-Market Economy With Risk Neutral Exchange Rate Speculation," (2), 110-122.

Goldberg, Lawrence G. and Denise Johnson. "The Determinants Of US Banking Activity Abroad," (2), 123-137.

Aizenman, Joshua. "External Debt, Planning Horizon, And Distorted Credit Markets," (2), 138-158.

Grilli, Enzo R. and Maw Cheng Yang. "Internationally Traded Good Prices, World Money, And Economic Activity: 1900-83," (2), 159-181.

Cumby, Robert E. "Consumption Risk And International Equity Returns: Some Empirical Evidence," (2), 182-192.

Schroeder, Juergen. "International Risk And Exchange Rate Overshooting," (2), 193-205.

Edwards, Sebastian and Jonathan D. Ostry. "Anticipated Protectionist Policies, Real Exchange Rates, And The Current Account: The Case Of Rigid Wages," (2), 206-219.

Sheffrin, Steven M. and Wing Thye Woo. "Testing An Optimizing Model Of The Current Account Via The Consumption Function," (2), 220-233.

Kugler, Peter. "The Term Structure Of Euro Interest Rates And Rational Expectations," (2), 234-244.

Bacchetta, Philippe. "Temporary Capital Controls In A Balance-Of-Payments Crisis," (3), 246-257.

Grilli, Vittorio. "Managing Exchange Rate Crises: Evidence From The 1890s," (3), 258-275.

Barone-Adesi, Giovanni and Bernard Yeung. "Price Flexibility And Output Volatility: The Case For Flexible Exchange Rates," (3), 276-298.

Klein, Michael W. "Sectoral Effects Of Exchange Rate Volatility On United States Exports," (3), 299-308.

Baillie, Richard T. and Tim Bollerslev. "A Multivariate Generalized ARCH Approach To Modeling Risk Premia In Forward Foreign Exchange Rate Markets," (3), 309-324.

Bergstrand, Jeffrey H. and Thomas P. Bundt. "Currency Substitution And Monetary Autonomy: The Foreign Demand For US Demand Deposits," (3), 325-334.

Hertzel, Michael G., Coleman S. Kendall and Peter E. Kretzmer. "The Volatility Of Asset Returns During Trading And Nontrading Hours: Some Evidence From The Foreign Exchange Markets," (3), 335-343.

Bailey, Warren. "US Money Supply Announcements And Pacific Rim Stock Markets: Evidence And Implications," (3), 344-356.

Von Hagen, Jurgen and Michele Fratianni. "German Dominance In The EMS: Evidence From Interest Rates," (4), 358-375.

Klein, Michael W. "Macroeconomic Aspects Of Exchange Rate Pass-Through," (4), 376-387.

Adler, Oliver. "Some Macroeconomic Effects Of Nationalizing Private Sector Foreign Debt," (4), 388-401.

Lastrapes, William D. and Faik Koray. "International Transmission Of Aggregate Shocks Under Fixed And Flexible Exchange Rate Regimes: United Kingdom, France, And Germany, 1959 To 1985," (4), 402-423.

Golub, Stephen S. "International Capital Mobility: Net Versus Gross Stocks And Flows," (4), 424-439.

Savvides, Andreas. "Real Exchange Rate Variability And The Choice Of Exchange Rate Regime By Developing Countries," (4), 440-454.

De Haan, Jakob and Dick Zelhorst. "The Impact Of Government Deficits On Money Growth In Developing Countries," (4), 455-469.

Journal of International Money and Finance
Volume 10, 1991

Mishkin, Frederic S. "A Multi-Country Study Of The Information In The Shorter Maturity Term Structure About Future Inflation," (1), 2-22.

Goodhart, C. A. E. and L. Figliuoli. "Every Minute Counts In Financial Markets," (1), 23-52.

Edison, Hali J. and Eric O'N. Fisher. "A Long-View Of The European Monetary System," (1), 53-70.

Baxter, Marianne. "Business Cycles, Stylized Facts, And The Exchange Rate Regime: Evidence From The United States," (1), 71-88.

Osler, Carol L. "Explaining The Absence Of International Factor-Price Convergence," (1), 89-107.

Zilcha, Itzhak and Rafael Eldor. "Exporting Firm And Forward Markets: The Multiperiod Case," (1), 108-117.

Ceglowski, Janet. "Intertemporal Substitution In Import Demand," (1), 118-130.

Kroner, Kenneth F. and Stijn Claessens. "Optimal Dynamic Hedging Portfolios And The Currency Composition Of External Debt," (1), 131-148.

Papadia, Francesco and Salvatore Rossi. "Are Asymmetric Exchange Controls Effective?," (1), 149-160.

Dooley, Michael P. and Peter Isard. "A Note On Fiscal Policy, Investment Location Decisions, And Exchange Rates," (1), 161-167.

Lothian, James R. "Political Factors In International Economics: An Overview," (Supp), S4-S15.

Edwards, Sebastian and Guido Tabellini. "Explaining Fiscal Policies And Inflation In Developing Countries," (Supp) S16-S48.

Roubini, Nouriel. "Economic And Political Determinants Of Budget Deficits In Developing Countries," (Supp), S49-S72.

Ito, Takatoshi. "International Impacts On Domestic Political Economy: A Case Of Japanese General Elections," (Supp) S73-S89.

Hogan, Ked, Michael Melvin and Dan J. Roberts. "Trade Balance News And Exchange Rates: Is There A Policy Signal?," (Supp), S90-S99.

Stone, Mark R. "Are Sovereign Debt Secondary Market Returns Sensitive To Macroeconomic Fundamentals?," (Supp) S100-S122.

Journal of Money, Credit and Banking
Volume 4, 1972

Benston, George J. "Discussion Of The Hunt Commission Report," (4), 985-989.
Jaffee, Dwight M. "Discussion Of The Hunt Commission Report," (4), 990-1000.
Peltzman, Samuel. "The Costs Of Competition: An Appraisal Of The Hunt Commission Report," (4), 1001-1004.
Meltzer, Allan H. "What The Commission Didn't Recommend," (4), 1005-1009.
Pankratz, Alan. "On Modernized Liquidity Preference Theory: A Comment," (4), 1010-1015.
Villanueva, Delano P. "Public Debt, 'Efficient' Labor, And Growth: A Comment," (4), 1016-1018.

Journal of Money, Credit and Banking
Volume 5, 1973

Rasche, Robert H. "Simulations Of Stabilization Policies For 1966-1970," (1), 1-25.
Andersen, Leonall C. "A Comparison Of Stabilization Policies: 1966-67 And 1969-70," (1), 26-38.
Kane, Edward J. "A Comparison Of Stabilization Policies: 1966-67 And 1969-70" Comment," (1), 39-42.
Meiselman, David. "A Comparison Of Stabilization Policies: 1966-67 And 1969-70: Comment," (1), 43-46.
Burns, Joseph M. "Academic Views On Improving The Federal Reserve Discount Mechanism: A Review Essay," (1), 47-60.
Griffiths, Brian. "Resource Efficiency, Monetary Policy And The Reform Of The U.K. Banking System," (1), 61-77.
Arcelus, Francisco and Allan H. Meltzer. "The Markets For Housing And Housing Services," (1), 78-99.
Cohan, Sandra B. "The Determinants Of Supply And Demand For Certificates Of Deposit," (1), 100-112.
Silveira, Antonio M. "The Demand For Money: The Evidence From The Brazilian Economy," (1), 113-140.
Dornbusch, Rudiger and Jacob A. Frenkel. "Inflation And Growth: Alternative Approaches," (1), 141-156.
Laidler, David. "Expectations, Adjustment, And The Dynamic Response Of Income To Policy Changes," (1), 157-172.
Alchian Armen A. and Benjamin Klein. "On A Correct Measure Of Inflation," (1), 173-191.
Sinkey, Joseph F., Jr. "The Term Structure Of Interest Rates: A Time-Series Test Of The Kane Expected-Change Model Of Interest-Rate Forecasting," (1), 192-200.
Mullineaux, Donald J. "Deposit-Rate Ceilings And Noncompetitive Bidding For U.S. Treasury Bills," (1), 201-212.
Niehans, Jurg. "Veendorp On Optimal Payment Arrangements: A Reply," (1), 213-214.
Kliman, M. L. and E. H. Oksanen. "The Keynesian Demand-For-Money Function: A Comment," (1), 215-220.
Silverman, Lester P. "Credit Standards And Tight Money: A Comment," (1), 221-223.
Schwartz, Anna J. "Secular Price Change In Historical Perspective," (1), Part II, 243-269.
Christ, Carl F. "Monetary And Fiscal Influences On U.S. Money Income, 1891-1970," (1), Part II, 279-300.
Bruner, Karl, Michele Fratianni, Jerry L. Jordan, Allan H. Meltzer and Manfred J. Neumann. "Fiscal And Monetary Policies In Moderate Inflation," (1), Part II, 313-354.
Brechling, Frank. "Wage Inflation And The Structure Of Regional Unemployment," (1), Part II, 355-379.
Sargent, Thomas J. "Interest Rates And Prices In The Long Run," (1), Part II, 385-449.
Nordhaus, William D. "The Effects Of Inflation On The Distribution Of Economic Welfare," (1), Part II, 465-504.
Johnson, Harry G. "Secular Inflation And The International Monetary System," (1), Part II, 509-519.
Stein, Jerome L. and Ettore F. Infante. "Optimal Stabilization Paths," (1), Part II, 525-562.
Perry, George L. "The Success Of Anti-Inflation Policies In The United States," (1), Part II, 569-593.
Park, Yung Chul. "The Transmission Process And The Relative Effectiveness Of Monetary And Fiscal Policy In A Two-Sector Neoclassical Model," (2), 595-622.
Yeats, Alexander. "An Analysis Of The Effect Of Mergers On The Banking Market Structure," (2), 623-636.
Acheson, Keith and John F. Chant. "Bureaucratic Theory And The Choice Of Central Bank Goals: The Case Of The Bank Of Canada," (2), 637-655.
Klein, Benjamin. "Income Velocity, Interest Rates, And The Money Supply Multiplier: A Reinterpretation Of The Long-Term Evidence," (2), 656-668.
Melitz, Jacques and Morris Pardue. "The Demand And Supply Of Commercial Bank Loans," (2), 669-692.
Niskanen, William and Robert Berry. "The 1973 Economic Report Of The President," (2), 693-703.
Fischer, Stanley. "A Neoclassical Monetary Growth Model: A Comment," (2), 704-706.
Villanueva, Delano P. "A Neoclassical Monetary Growth Model: A Reply," (2), 707.
Klein, Michael. "Credit Standards And Tight Money: A Comment," (2), 708-712.
Pippenger, John E. "The Determination Of The Stock Of Reserves And The Balance Of Payments In A Neo-Keynesian Model: A Comment," (2), 713-719.
Hamburger, Michael. "The Demand For Money In 1971: Was There A Shift?: A Comment," (2), 720-725.
Boyd, John H. "Some Recent Developments In The Savings And Loan Deposit Markets," (3), 733-750.
Greisel, Martin S. "Bayesian Comparisons Of Simple Macroeconomic Models," (3), 751-772.
Clark, Carolyn. "The Demand For Money And The Choice Of A Permanent Income Estimate: Some Canadian Evidence, 1962-65," (3), 773-793.
Silveira, Antonio M. "Interest Rate And Rapid Inflation: The Evidence From The Brazilian Economy," (3), 794-805.

Formuzis, Peter. "The Demand For Eurodollars And The Optimum Stock Of Bank Liabilities," (3), 806-818.
Aliber, Robert Z. "Gold, SDR's, And Central Bank Swaps," (3), 819-825.
Tullock, Gordon. "Inflation And Unemployment: The Discussion Continued: A Comment," (3), 826-835.
Sarnat, Marshall. "Purchasing Power Risk, Portfolio Analysis, And The Case For Index-Linked Bonds: A Comment," (3), 836-845.
Hagerman, Robert L. "The Efficiency Of The Market For Bank Stocks: An Empirical Test: A Comment," (3), 846-855.
Shiller, Robert J. "Rational Expectations And The Term Structure Of Interest Rates: A Comment," (3), 856-860.
Feldstein, Martin and Gary Chamberlain. "Multimarket Expectations And The Rate Of Interest," (4), 873-902.
Roll, Richard. "Assets, Money, And Commodity Price Inflation Under Uncertainty: Demand Theory," (4), 903-923.
Levin, Fred J. "Examination Of The Money-Stock Control Approach Of Burger, Kalishn, And Babb," (4), 924-938.
Steindl, Frank G. "Price Expectations And Interest Rates," (4), 939-949.
Neumann, Manfred J. M. "The 1972 Report Of The German Council Of Economic Experts: Inflation And Stabilization," (4), 950-959.
Swan, Craig. "The Markets For Housing And Housing Services: A Comment," (4), 960-972.
Arcelus, Francisco and Allan H. Meltzer. "A Reply To Craig Swan," (4), 973-978.
Kane, Edward J. "The Central Bank As Big Brother: A Comment," (4), 979-981.
Tobin, James. "More On Inflation: A Reply," (4), 982-984.
Chen, Chau-nan. "A Graphical Note On The Aggregative Effect Of Payments Of Interest On Deposits: A Comment," (4), 985-987.
Johnson, Elizabeth S. and Harry G. Johnson. "Keynes, The Wider Bank, And The Crawling Peg: A Comment," (4), 988-989.
Pringle, John J. "A Theory Of The Banking Firm," (4), 990-996.
Van Belle, John J. "Spot Rates, Forward Rates, And The Interest-Rate Differentials: A Comment," (4), 997-999.
Shetler, Douglas. "Monetary Aggregates Prior To The Civil War: A Closer Look: A Comment," (4), 1000-1006.

Journal of Money, Credit and Banking
Volume 6, 1974

Cooper, J. Phillip and Stanley Fischer. "Monetary And Fiscal Policy In The Fully Stochastic St. Louis Econometric Model," (1), 1-22.
Benston, George J. and John Tepper Marlin. "Bank Examiners' Evaluation Of Credit: An Analysis Of The Usefulness Of Substandard Loan Data," (1), 23-44.
Karni, Edi. "The Value Of Time And The Demand For Money," (1), 45-64.
Hynes, J. Allan. "On The Theory Of Real Balance Effects," (1), 65-83.
Johnson, Omotunde E. G. "Credit Controls As Instruments Of Development Policy In The Light Of Economic Theory," (1), 85-99.
Griffiths, Brian. "Two Monetary Inquiries In Great Britain: Comments On The Macmillan Report Of 1931 And The Radcliffe Committee Of 1959: A Comment," (1), 101-114.
Fratianni, Michele. "The Problem Of Coexistence Of SDRs And A Reserve Currency: A Comment," (1), 115-118.
Warner, P. D., III and Stephen M. Miller. "The Deficient Treatment Of Money In Basic Undergraduate Texts: An Opposing View: A Reply," (1), 119-121.
Saving, T. R. "The Value Of Time And Economies Of Scale In The Demand For Cash Balances: A Comment," (1), 122-124.
Rockoff, Hugh. "The Free Banking Era: A Reexamination," (2), 141-167.
Cathcart, Charles D. "Monetary Dynamics, Growth, And The Efficiency Of Inflationary Finance," (2), 169-190.
Officer, Lawrence H. "Reserve-Asset Preferences In The Crisis Zone, 1958-67," (2), 191-212.
Laurent, Robert D. "Currency In Circulation And The Real Value Of Notes," (2), 213-226.
Harris, Duane G. "Credit Rationing At Commercial Banks: Some Empirical Evidence," (2), 227-240.
Feige, Edgar L. and P. A. V. B. Swamy. "A Random Coefficient Model Of The Demand For Liquid Assets," (2), 241-252.
Koot, Ronald S. and David A. Walker. "Rules Versus Discretion: An Analysis Of Income Stability And The Money Supply: A Comment," (2), 253-261.
Ben-Zion, Uri. "The Cost Of Capital And The Demand For Money By Firms: A Comment," (2), 263-296.
Allais, Maurice. "The Psychological Rate Of Interest," (3), 285-331.
Mussa, Michael. "A Monetary Approach To Balance-Of-Payments Analysis," (3), 333-351.
Slovin, Myron B. "On The Relationships Among Monetary Aggregates," (3), 353-366.
Wagner, Richard E. "Politics, Bureaucracy, And Budgetary Choice: The Brookings Budget For 1974," (3), 367-383.
Kochin, Levis A. "Are Future Taxes Anticipated By Consumers?: A Comment," (3), 385-394.
Yeats, A. J. "A Framework For Evaluating Potential Competition As A Factor In Bank Mergers And Acquisitions: A Comment," (3), 395-402.
Fry, Clifford L. "An Explanation Of Short-Run Fluctuations In The Ratio Of Currency to Demand Deposits: A Comment," (3),403-412.
Klein, Benjamin. "The Competitive Supply Of Money," (4), 423-453.
Caligiuri, Gian Franco, Antonio Fazio and Tommaso Padoa-Schioppa. "Demand And Supply Of Bank Credit In Italy," (4), 455-479.
Meyer, Laurence H. "Wealth Effects And The Effectiveness Of Monetary And Fiscal Policies," (4), 481-502.
Cargill, Thomas F. and Robert A. Meyer. "Estimating Term Structure Phenomena From Data Aggregated Over Time," (4), 503-515.
Stillson, Richard T. "An Analysis Of Information And Transaction Services In Financial Institutions," (4), 517-535.
Jaffee, Dwight M. "What To Do About Savings And Loan Associations?," (4), 537-549.
Hambor, John C. and Robert E. Weintraub. "The Term Structure: Another Look: A Comment," (4), 551-557.

Journal of Money, Credit and Banking
Volume 12, 1980

Barro, Robert J. "Federal Deficit Policy And The Effects Of Public Debt Shocks," (4), Part 2, 747-762.

Fellner, William. "The Valid Core Of Rationality Hypotheses In The Theory Of Expectations," (4), Part 2, 763-787.

Tobin, James. "Are New Classical Models Plausible Enough To Guide Policy?," (4), Part 2, 788-799.

Burmeister, Edwin. "On Some Conceptual Issues In Rational Expectations Modeling," (4), Part 2, 800-816.

Okun, Arthur M. "Rational-Expectations-With-Misperceptions As A Theory Of The Business Cycle," (4), Part 2, 817-825.

Cagan, Phillip. "Reflections On Rational Expectations," (4), Part 2, 826-832.

Haberler, Gottfried. "Critical Notes On Rational Expectations," (4), Part 2, 833-836.

Journal of Money, Credit and Banking
Volume 13, 1981

Nelson, Charles R. "Adjustment Lags Versus Information Lags: A Test Of Alternative Explanations Of The Phillips Curve Phenomenon," (1), 1-11.

Girton, Lance and Don Roper. "Theory And Implications Of Currency Substitution," (1), 12-30.

Hetzel, Robert L. "The Federal Reserve System And Control Of The Money Supply In The 1970s," (1), 31-43.

Beenstock, Michael and J. Andrew Longbottom. "The Term Structure Of Interest Rates In A Small Open Economy," (1), 44-59.

Yawitz, Jess B. and William J. Marshall. "Measuring The Effect Of Callability On Bond Yields," (1), 60-71.

Arzac, Enrique R., Robert A. Schwartz and David K. Whitcomb. "The Leverage Structure Of Interest Rates," (1), 72-88.

Cargill, Thomas F. "A Tribute To Clark Warburton, 1896-1979," (1), 89-93.

Frydman, Roman. "Sluggish Price Adjustments And The Effectiveness Of Monetary Policy Under Rational Expectations: A Comment," (1), 94-102.

McCallum, Bennett T. "Sluggish Price Adjustments And The Effectiveness Of Monetary Policy Under Rational Expectations: A Reply," (1), 103-104.

Ballendux, Frans J. and Marius J. L. Jonkhart. "A Possible Error In The Expectations Theory: A Comment," (1), 105-106.

Amihud, Yakov. "A Possible Error In The Expectations Theory: A Rejoinder," (1), 107-108.

Stauffer, Robert F. "The Bank Failures Of 1930-31: A Comment," (1), 109-113.

Brittain, Bruce. "International Currency Substitution And The Apparent Instability Of Velocity In Some Western European Economies And In The United States," (2), 135-155.

Turnovsky, Stephen J. "Monetary Policy And Foreign Disturbances Under Flexible Exchange Rates: Stochastic Approach," (2), 156-176.

Turnbull, Stuart M. "Measurement Of The Real Rate Of Interest And Related Problems In A World Of Uncertainty," (2), 177-191.

Dwyer, Gerald P., Jr. "The Effects Of The Banking Acts Of 1933 And 1935 On Capital Investment In Commercial Banking," (2), 192-204.

Landskroner, Yoram and Nissan Liviatan. "Risk Premia And The Sources Of Inflation," (2), 205-214.

Woglom, Geoffrey. "A Reexamination Of The Role Of Stocks In The Consumption Function And The Transmission Mechanism," (2), 215-220.

McMillin, W. Douglas. "A Dynamic Analysis Of The Impact Of Fiscal Policy On The Money Supply," (2), 221-226.

Barrett, Richard N. "Purchasing Power Parity And The Equilibrium Exchange Rate," (2), 227-233.

Modeste, Nelson C. "Exchange Market Pressure During The 1970s In Argentina: An Application Of The Girton Roper Monetary Model," (2), 234-240.

Beedles, William L. and Nancy K. Buschmann. "Describing Bank Equity Returns: The Year-By-Year Record," (2), 241-247.

Gale, William A. "Temporal Variability Of United States Consumer Price Index," (3), 273-297.

Johannes, James M. and Robert H. Rasche. "Can The Reserves Approach To Monetary Control Really Work?," (3), 298-313.

Laurent, Robert D. "Reserve Requirements, Deposit Insurance, And Monetary Control," (3), 314-324.

Levy, Haim. "Optimal Portfolio Of Foreign Currencies With Borrowing And Lending," (3), 325-341.

Cuddington, John T. "Money, Income, And Causality In The United Kingdom: An Empirical Reexamination," (3), 342-351.

Kaufman, Herbert M. and Don E. Schlagenhauf. "FNMA Auction Results As A Forecaster Of Residential Mortgage Yields," (3), 352-364.

Goldberg, Lawrence G. and Anthony Saunders. "The Growth Of Organizational Forms Of Foreign Banks In The U.S.," (3), 365-374.

Rose, John T. and Roger D. Rutz. "Organization Form And Risk In Bank-Affiliated Mortgage Companies," (3), 375-380.

Corbo, Vittorio. "Inflation Expectations And The Specification Of Demand For Money Equations," (3), 381-387.

Maris, Brian A. "Indirect Evidence On The Efficacy Of Selective Credit Controls: The Case Of Consumer Credit," (3), 388-390.

Chappell, David. "On The Revenue Maximizing Rate Of Inflation: A Comment," (3), 391-392.

Grossman, Jacob. "The 'Rationality' Of Money Supply Expectations And The Short-Run Response Of Interest Rates To Monetary Surprises," (4), 409-424.

Blinder, Alan S. "Monetary Accomodation Of Supply Shocks Under Rational Expectations," (4), 425-438.

Fethke, Gary C. and Andrew J. Policano. "Long-Term Contracts And The Effectiveness Of Demand And Supply Policies," (4), 439-453.

Bryant, John. "Bank Collapse And Depression," (4), 454-464.

Verbrugge, James A. and John S. Jahera, Jr. "Expense-Preference Behavior In The Savings And Loan Industry," (4), 465-476.

Phaup, E. Dwight. "A Reinterpretation Of The Modern Theory Of Forward Exchange Rates," (4), 477-484.

Barnett, William A. "The New Monetary Aggregates: A Comment," (4), 485-489.

Frenkel, Jacob A. "Adjustment Lags Versus Information Lags: A Test Of Alternative Explanations Of The Phillips Curve Phenomenon: A Comment," (4), 490-493.

Nelson, Charles R. "Adjustment Lags Versus Information Lags: A Test Of Alternative Explanations Of The Phillips Curve Phenomenon: A Comment," (4), 494-496.

Logue, Dennis E. and Richard James Sweeney. "Inflation And Real Growth: Some Empirical Results," (4), 497-501.

Journal of Money, Credit and Banking
Volume 14, 1982

Fischer, Stanley and John Huizinga. "Inflation, Unemployment, And Public Opinion Polls," (1), 1-19.

Saurman, David S. "Transactions Costs, Foreign Exchange Demands, And The Expected Rates Of Change Of Exchange Rates," (1), 20-32.

Ebrill, Liam P. and Uri M. Possen. "Inflation And The Taxation Of Equity In Corporations And Owner-Occupied Housing," (1), 33-47.

Bordo, Michael D. and Ehsan U. Choudhri. "Currency Substitution And The Demand For Money: Some Evidence For Canada," (1), 48-57.

Wihlborg, Clas. "Interest Rates, Exchange Rate Adjustments And Currency Risks: An Empirical Study, 1967-75," (1), 58-75.

Seater, John J. "On The Estimation Of Permanent Income," (1), 76-83.

Goodman, Laurie S. "Bank Foreign Exchange Operations: A Portfolio Approach," (1), 84-91.

Richardson, David H. and Mickey T. C. Wu. "Tests Of The Goods Market Integration Hypothesis," (1), 92-97.

Friedman, Milton. "Monetary Policy: Theory And Practice," (1), 98-118.

Meltzer, Allan H. and Robert H. Rasche. "Is The Federal Reserve's Monetary Control Policy Misdirected? Resolved: That The Federal Reserve's Current Operating Procedures For Controlling Money Should Be Replaced: Affirmative," (1), 119-147.

Axilrod, Stephen H. and Peter D. Sternlight. "Is The Federal Reserve's Monetary Control Policy Misdirected? Resolved: That The Federal Reserve's Current Operating Procedures For Controlling Money Should Be Replaced: Negative," (1), 119-147.

Tobin, James. "Money And Finance In The Macroeconomic Process," (2), 171-204.

Baltensperger, Ernst. "Reserve Requirements And Economic Stability," (2), 205-215.

Gertler, Mark L. and Earl L. Grinols. "Unemployment, Inflation, And Common Stock Returns," (2), 216-233.

Hetzel, Robert L. "The October 1979 Regime Of Monetary Control And The Behavior Of The Money Supply In 1980," (2), 234-251.

Klovland, Jan Tore. "The Stability Of The Demand For Money In The Interwar Years: The Case Of Norway, 1925-39," (2), 252-264.

Mills, Terence C. and Geoffrey E. Wood. "Econometric Evaluation Of Alternative Money Stock Series, 1880-1913," (2), 265-277.

Smith, Gary. "Monetarism, Bondism, And Inflation," (2), 278-286.

Turnovsky, Stephen J. and Jagdeep S. Bhandari. "The Degree Of Capital Mobility And The Stability Of An Open Economy Under Rational Expectations," (3), 303-326.

Saidi, Nasser H. "Expectations, International Business Cycles, And The Balance Of Payments," (3), 327-346.

Khan, Mohsin S. and Malcolm D. Knight. "Unanticipated Monetary Growth And Inflationary Finance," (3), 347-364.

Mitchell, Douglas W. "Kalman Filters And The Target Values Of Monetary Aggregates," (3), 365-375.

Seater, John J. "Are Future Taxes Discounted?," (3), 376-389.

Amihud, Yakov and Haim Mendelson. "Relative Price Dispersion And Economic Shocks: An Inventory-Adjustment Approach," (3), 390-398.

Levin, Fred J. and Ann-Marie Meulendyke. "Monetary Policy: Theory And Practice: A Comment," (3), 399-403.

Friedman, Milton. "Monetary Policy: Theory And Practice: Reply," (3), 404-406.

Friedman, Benjamin M. "Interest Rate Implications For Fiscal And Monetary Policies: A Postscript On The Government Budget Constraint," (3), 407-412.

Benston, George J., Gerald A. Hanweck and David B. Humphrey. "Scale Economies In Banking: A Restructuring And Reassessment," (4), Part 1, 435-456.

Bhandari, Jagdeep S. "Informational Efficiency And The Open Economy," (4), Part 1, 457-478.

Osborne, Dale K. "The Cost Of Servicing Demand Deposits," (4), Part 1, 479-493.

Hagemann, Robert P. "The Variability Of Inflation Rates Across Household Types," (4), Part 1, 494-510.

Umbeck, John and Robert E. Chatfield. "The Structure Of Contracts And Transaction Costs," (4), Part 1, 511-516.

Batavia, Bala and Nicholas A. Lash. "The Impact Of Bank Portfolio Composition On GNP," (4), Part 1, 517-524.

Allen, Stuart D. "Klein's Price Variability Terms In The U.S. Demand For Money," (4), Part 1, 525-530.

Madura, Jeff and E. Joe Nosari. "Optimal Portfolio Of Foreign Currencies With Borrowing And Lending: A Comment," (4), Part 1, 531.

Noble, Nicholas R. "Granger Causality And Expectational Rationality," (4), Part 1, 532-537.

Schwartz, Anna J. "Reflections On The Gold Commission Report," (4), Part 1, 538-551.

Poole, William. "Federal Reserve Operating Procedures: A Survey And Evaluation Of The Historical Record Since October 1979," (4), Part 2, 575-596.

Bryant, Ralph C. "Federal Reserve Control Of The Money Stock," (4), Part 2, 597-625.

Fellner, William. "Criteria For Useful Targeting: Money Versus The Base And Other Variables," (4), Part 2, 641-660.

Cagan, Phillip. "The Choice Among Monetary Aggregates As Targets And Guides For Monetary Policy," (4), Part 2, 661-686.

Barnett, William A. "The Optimal Level Of Monetary Aggregation," (4), Part 2, 687-710.

Friedman, Benjamin M. "Federal Reserve Policy, Interest Rate Volatility, And The U.S. Capital Raising Mechanism," (4), Part 2, 721-745.

Black, Stanley W. "The Effects Of Alternative Monetary Control Procedures On Exchange Rates And Output," (4), Part 2, 746-760.

Pierce, James L. "How Regulations Affect Monetary Control," (4), Part 2, 775-787.

Anderson, Richard G. and Robert H. Rasche. "What Do Money Market Models Tell Us About How To Implement Monetary Policy?," (4), Part 2, 796-828.

Tinsley, Peter A., Helen T. Farr, Gerhard Fries, Bonnie Garrett and Peter von zur Muehlen. "Policy Robustness: Specification And Simulation Of A Monthly Money Market Model," (4), Part 2, 829-856.

Journal of Money, Credit and Banking
Volume 15, 1983

Peek, Joe. "Capital Gains And Personal Saving Behavior," (1), 1-23.

Capie, Forrest and Alan Webber. "Total Coin And Coin In Circulation In The United Kingdom, 1868-1914," (1), 24-39.

Kidwell, David S. and Timothy W. Koch. "Market Segmentation And The Term Structure Of Municipal Yields," (1), 40-55.

Connolly, Michael B. "Optimum Currency Pegs For Latin America," (1), 56-72.

Edwards, Sebastian. "Floating Exchange Rates In Less-Developed Countries: A Monetary Analysis Of The Peruvian Experience, 1950-54," (1), 73-81.

Bull, Clive and Roman Frydman. "The Derivation And Interpretation Of The Lucas Supply Function," (1), 82-95.

McCallum, Bennett T. and James G. Hoehn. "Instrument Choice For Money Stock Control With Contemporaneous And Lagged Reserve Requirements," (1), 96-101.

Braswell, Ronald C., E. Joe Nosari and DeWitt L. Sumners. "A Comparison Of The True Interest Costs Of Competitive And Negotiated Underwritings In The Municipal Bond Market," (1), 102-106.

Mayer, Thomas and Harold Nathan. "Mortgage Rates And Regulation Q," (1), 107-115.

Gehr, Adam K., Jr. and Thomas Berry. "FNMA Auction Results As A Forecaster Of Residential Mortgage Yields: A Comment," (1), 116-119.

Molho, Lazaros E. "On Testing The Efficacy Of Selective Credits Controls: A Comment," (1), 120-122.

Hercowitz, Zvi. "Anticipated Inflation, The Frequency Of Transactions, And The Slope Of The Phillips Curve," (2), 139-154.

Gramlich, Edward M. "Models Of Inflation Expectations Formation: A Comparison Of Household And Economist Forecasts," (2), 155-173.

Ortiz, Guillermo. "Currency Substitution In Mexico: The Dollarization Problem," (2), 174-185.

Benavie, Arthur and Richard T. Froyen. "Combination Monetary Policies To Stablize Price And Output Under Rational Expectations," (2), 186-198.

Canarella, Giorgio and Neil Garston. "Monetary And Public Debt Shocks: Tests And Efficient Estimates," (2), 199-211.

Orgler, Yair E. and Robert A. Taggart, Jr. "Implications Of Corporate Capital Structure Theory For Banking Institutions," (2), 212-221.

Merrick, John J., Jr. "Financial Market Efficiency, The Decomposition Of 'Anticipated' Verus 'Unanticipated' Monetary Growth, And Further Tests Of The Relation Between Money And Real Output," (2), 222-232.

Cothren, Richard. "On The Trigger Mechanism For Indexing Wages," (2), 233-236.

Klein, Lawrence R., Edward Friedman and Stephen Able. "Money In The Wharton Quarterly Model," (2), 237-259.

Kaufman, Roger T. and Geoffrey Woglom. "Estimating Models With Rational Expectations," (3), 275-285.

Engle, Robert F. "Estimates Of The Variance Of U.S. Inflation Based Upon The ARCH Model," (3), 286-301.

Greenfield, Robert L. and Leland B. Yeager. "A Laissez-Faire Approach To Monetary Stability," (3), 302-315.

Grieves, Robin. "The Demand For Consumer Durables," (3), 316-326.

Kaen, Fred R. and George A. Hachey. "Eurocurrency And National Money Market Interest Rates: An Empirical Investigation Of Causality," (3), 327-338.

Friedman, Milton. "Monetary Variability: United States And Japan," (3), 339-343.

Roley, V. Vance. "The Response Of Short-Term Interest Rates To Weekly Money Announcements," (3), 344-354.

Flannery, Mark J. "Interest Rates And Bank Profitability: Additional Evidence," (3), 355-362.

Siegel, Jeremy J. "Technological Change And The Superneutrality Of Money," (3), 363-367.

Auernheimer, Leonardo. "The Revenue-Maximizing Inflation Rate And The Treatment Of The Transition To Equilibrium," (3), 368-376.

Gendreau, Brian C. "The Implicit Return On Bankers' Balances," (4), 411-424.

O'Hara, Maureen. "Tax-Exempt Financing: Some Lessons From History," (4), 425-441.

Attfield, Clifford L. F. and Nigel W. Duck. "The Influence Of Unanticipated Money Growth On Real Output: Some Cross-Country Estimates," (4), 442-454.

Howard, David H. and Karen H. Johnson. "The Behavior Of Monetary Aggregates In Major Industrialized Countries," (4), 455-468.

Blejer, Mario I. "On The Anatomy Of Inflation: The Variability Of Relative Commodity Prices In Argentina," (4), 469-482.

Gilbert, R. Alton. "Economics Of Scale In Correspondent Banking," (4), 483-488.

Rotemberg, Julio J. "Supply Shocks, Sticky Prices, And Monetary Policy," (4), 489-498.

Ochs, Jack and Mark Rush. "The Persistence Of Interest-Rate Effects On The Demand For Currency," (4), 499-505.

Tobin, James. "Monetary Policy: Rules, Targets, And Shocks," (4), 506-518.

Journal of Money, Credit and Banking
Volume 16, 1984

Timberlake, Richard H., Jr. "The Central Banking Role Of Clearinghouse Associations," (1), 1-15.

Turnovsky, Stephen J. and Marcus H. Miller. "The Effects Of Government Expenditure On The Term Structure Of Interest Rates," (1), 16-33.

Ewis, Nabil A. and Douglas Fisher. "The Translog Utility Function And The Demand For Money In The United States," (1), 34-52.

Clark, Jeffrey A. "Estimation Of Economies Of Scale In Banking Using A Generalized Functional Form," (1), 53-68.

Weintraub, Robert E. "Money In The Wharton Quarterly Model: A Comment," (1), 69-75.

Klein, Lawrence R. "Money In The Wharton Quarterly Model: A Reply," (1), 76-78.

Weintraub, Robert E. "Money In The Wharton Quarterly Model: A Rejoinder," (1), 79-80.

Kopecky, Kenneth J. "Monetary Control Under Reverse Lag And Contemporaneous Reserve Accounting: A Comparison: A Comment," (1), 81-88.

Laurent, Robert D. "Monetary Control Under Reverse Lag And Contemporaneous Reserve Accounting: A Comparison: A Reply," (1), 89-92.

Forbes, Ronald W. and Paul A. Leonard. "The Effects Of Statutory Portfolio Constraints On Tax-Exempt Interest Rates," (1), 93-99.

Shaffer, Sherrill. "Cross-Subsidization In Checking Accounts," (1), 100-109.

Balbes, John J. "The Federal Reserve: The Role Of Reserve Banks," (1), 110-117.

Walsh, Carl E. "Interest Rate Volatility And Monetary Policy," (2), 133-150.

O'Brien, James M. "The Information Value Of The FOMC Policy Directive Under The New Operating Procedures," (2), 151-164.

Ladenson, Mark L. and Kenneth J. Bombara. "Entry In Commercial Banking: 1962-78," (2), 165-174.

Mayor, Thomas H. and Lawrence R. Pearl. "Life-Cycle Effects, Structural Change, And Long-Run Movements In The Velocity Of Money," (2), 175-184.

Hetzel, Robert L. "Estimating Money Demand Functions," (2), 185-193.

Connolly, Michael B. and Dean Taylor. "The Exact Timing Of The Collapse Of An Exchange Rate Regime And Its Impact On The Relative Price Of Traded Goods," (2), 194-207.

Obstfeld, Maurice. "Balance-Of-Payments Crises And Devaluation," (2), 208-217.

Maccini, Louis J. and Robert J. Rossana. "Joint Production, Quasi-Fixed Factors Of Production, And Investment In Finished Goods Inventory," (2), 218-236.

Sheehey, Edmund J. "The Neutrality Of Money In The Short Run: Some Tests," (2), 237-241.

Miller, Edward M. "Bank Deposits In The Monetary Theory Of Keynes," (2), 242-245.

Hafer, R. W. and Scott E. Hein. "Financial Innovations And The Interest Elasticity Of Money Demand: Some Historical Evidence," (2), 247-252.

Cukierman, Alex and Leonardo Leiderman. "Price Controls And The Variability Of Relative Prices," (3), 271-284.

Marston, Richard C. "Real Wages And The Terms Of Trade: Alternative Indexation Rules For An Open Economy," (3), 285-301.

Stulz, Rene M. "Currency Preferences, Purchasing Power Risks, And The Determination Of Exchange Rates," (3), 302-316.

Pearce, Douglas K. "An Empirical Analysis Of Expected Stock Price Movements," (3), 317-327.

King, A. Thomas. "Thrift Institution Deposits: The Influence Of MMCs And MMMFs," (3), 328-334.

Papadia, Francesco. "Estimates Of Ex Ante Real Rates Of Interest In The EEC Countries And In The United States, 1973-82," (3), 335-344.

Liu, Pu and Anjan V. Thakor. "Interest Yields, Credit Ratings, And Economic Characteristics Of State Bonds: An Empirical Analysis," (3), 344-351.

Kaufman, George G. "The Academic Preparation Of Economists Employed By Commercial And Investment Banks," (3), 351-359.

Choi, Sang-Rim and Adrian E. Tschoegl. "Bank Employment In The World's Largest Banks: An Update," (3), 359-362.

Trescott, Paul B. "The Behavior Of The Currency-Deposit Ratio During The Great Depression: A Comment," (3), 362-365.

Boughton, James M. and Elmus R. Wicker. "The Behavior Of The Currency-Deposit Ratio During The Great Depression: A Reply," (3), 366-367.

Kimbrough, Kent P. "The Derivation And Interpretation Of The Lucas Supply Function: A Comment," (3), 367-377.

Bull, Clive and Roman Frydman. "The Derivation And Interpretation Of The Lucas Supply Function: A Reply," (3), 377-379.

Gordon, Robert J. "The Short-Run Demand For Money: A Reconsideration," (4), Part 1, 403-434.

Flannery, Mark J. and Christopher M. James. "Market Evidence Of The Effective Maturity Of Bank Assets And Liabilities," (4), Part 1, 435-445.

Marcus, Alan J. and Israel Shaked. "The Valuation Of FDIC Deposit Insurance Using Option-Pricing Estimates," (4), Part 1, 446-460.

Shah, Anup. "Crowding Out, Capital Accumulation, The Stock Market, And Money-Financed Fiscal Policy," (4), Part 1, 461-473.

Tybout, James R. "Interest Controls And Credit Allocation In Developing Countries," (4), Part 1, 474-487.

Williams, Jeffrey C. "Fractional Reserve Banking In Grain," (4), Part 1, 488-496.

Benavie, Arthur and Richard T. Froyen. "Optimal Combination Monetary Policies: A Two-Stage Process," (4), Part 1, 497-505.

Montgomery, Edward. "Aggregate Dynamics And Staggered Contracts: A Test Of The Importance Of Spillover Effects," (4), Part 1, 505-514.

Ahmed, Ehsan and James M. Johannes. "St. Louis Equation Restrictions And Criticisms Revisited," (4), Part 1, 514-520.

Fishe, Raymond P. H. "On Testing Hypotheses Using The Livingston Price Expectations Data," (4), Part 1, 520-527.

Peterson, Richard L. and Dan A. Black. "Consumer Credit Search," (4), Part 1, 527-536.

Santomero, Anthony M. "Modeling The Banking Firm: A Survey," (4), Part 2, 576-602.

Gilbert, R. Alton. "Bank Market Structure And Competition: A Survey," (4), Part 2, 617-645.

Saurman, David S. "Currency Substitution, The Exchange Rate, And The Real Interest Rate (Non)Differential: Shipping The Bad Money In," (4), 512-518.

Kilbride, Bernard J., Bill McDonald and Robert E. Miller. "A Reexamination Of Economies Of Scale In Banking Using A Generalized Functional Form," (4), 519-526.

Barth, James R., Frank S. Russek and George H. K. Wang. "The Measurement And Significance Of The Cyclically Adjusted Federal Budget And Debt: A Comment," (4), 527-538.

Bryan, Michael F. and William T. Gavin. "Models Of Inflation Expectations Formation: A Comparison Of Household And Economist Forecasts: A Comment," (4), 539-544.

Journal of Money, Credit and Banking
Volume 19, 1987

Williams, Arlington W. "The Formation Of Price Forecasts In Experimental Markets," (1), 1-18.

Calvo, Guillermo A. "Balance Of Payments Crises In A Cash-In-Advance Economy," (1), 19-32.

Niehans, Jurg. "Monetary Policy And Investment Dynamics In Interdependent Economics," (1), 33-45.

Bruner, Robert F. and John M. Simms, Jr. "The International Debt Crisis And Bank Security Returns In 1982," (1), 46-55.

Campbell, John Y. "Money Announcements, The Demand For Bank Reserves And The Behavior Of The Federal Funds Rate Within The Statement Week," (1), 56-67.

Cothren, Richard. "Asymmetric Information And Optimal Bank Reserves," (1), 68-77.

Jain, Arvind K. and Satyadev Gupta. "Some Evidence On 'Herding' Behavior By U.S. Banks," (1), 78-89.

Hochman, Shalom and Oded Palmon. "Expected Inflation And The Real Rates Of Interest On Taxable And Tax-Exempt Bonds," (1), 90-103.

Diba, Behzad T. "A Critique Of Variance Bounds Tests Of Monetary Exchange Rate Models," (1), 104-111.

Hall, Thomas E. and Nicholas R. Noble. "Velocity And The Variability Of Money Growth: Evidence From Granger-Causality Tests," (1), 112-116.

Duca, John V. "The Spillover Effects Of Nominal Wage Rigidity In A Multisector Economy," (1), 117-121.

Feltenstein, Andrew and Ziba Farhadian. "Fiscal Policy, Monetary Targets, And The Price Level In A Centrally Planned Economy: An Application To The Case Of China," (2), 137-156.

Turnovsky, Stephen J. "Optimal Monetary Policy And Wage Indexation Under Alternative Disturbances And Information Structures," (2), 157-180.

Bordo, Michael D., Ehsan U. Choudhri and Anna J. Schwartz. "The Behavior Of Money Stock Under Interest Rate Control: Some Evidence For Canada," (2), 181-198.

Cosimano, Thomas F. "Reserve Accounting And Variability In The Federal Funds Market," (2), 199-209.

Darity, William A., Jr. and Allin F. Cottrell. "Meade's General Theory Model: A Geometric Reprise," (2), 210-221.

Sweeney, Richard J. "Some Macro Implications Of Risk," (2), 222-234.

Gapinski, James H. "Capital Lessons In Leaning Against The Wind," (2), 235-245.

Kitchen, John and Mark Denbaly. "Commodity Prices, Money Surprises, And Fed Credibility: Comment," (2), 246-251.

Van der Ploeg, Frederick. "Benefits Of Contingent Rules For Optimal Taxation Of A Monetary Economy," (2), 252-259.

Dhillon, Upinder S., James D. Shilling and C. F. Sirmans. "Choosing Between Fixed And Adjustable Rate Mortgages," (2), 260-267.

Peek, Joe and James A. Wilcox. "Monetary Policy Regimes And The Reduced Form For Interest Rates," (3), 273-291.

Roley, V. Vance. "The Effects Of Money Announcements Under Alternative Monetary Control Procedures," (3), 292-307.

Havrilesky, Thomas M. "A Partisanship Theory Of Fiscal And Monetary Regimes," (3), 308-325.

Cosimano, Thomas F. "The Federal Funds Market Under Bank Deregulation," (3), 326-339.

Pennacchi, George G. "A Reexamination Of The Over-(Or Under-) Pricing Of Deposit Insurance," (3), 340-360.

Koray, Faik. "Government Debt, Economic Activity, And Transmission Of Economic Disturbances," (3), 361-375.

Edison, Hali J. "Purchasing Power Parity In The Long Run: A Test Of The Dollar/Pound Exchange Rate (1890-1978)," (3), 376-387.

Pearce, Douglas K. "Short-Term Inflation Expectations: Evidence From A Monthly Survey," (3), 388-395.

Guth, Michael A. S. "Functional Form In Finished Goods Inventory Investment," (3), 396-407.

Niehans, Jurg. "Classical Monetary Theory, New And Old," (4), 409-424.

Tabellini, Guido. "Secrecy Of Monetary Policy And The Variability Of Interest Rates," (4), 425-436.

Timberlake, Richard H. "Private Production Of Scrip-Money In The Isolated Community," (4), 437-447.

White, Lawrence H. "Accounting For Non-Interest-Bearing Currency: A Critique Of The Legal Restrictions Theory Of Money," (4), 448-456.

Gorton, Gary and Donald J. Mullineaux. "The Joint Production Of Confidence: Endogenous Regulation And Nineteenth Century Commercial-Bank Clearinghouses," (4), 457-468.

Maling, Charles. "On The Consumers' Surplus Of Money Holders And The Measuring Of Money's Services," (4), 469-483.

Williamson, Stephen. "Transactions Costs, Inflation, And The Variety Of Intermediation Services," (4), 484-498.

Woo, Wing Thye. "Some Evidence Of Speculative Bubbles In The Foreign Exchange Market," (4), 499-514.

Takagi, Shinji. "Transactions Costs And The Term Structure Of Interest Rates In The OTC Bond Market In Japan," (4), 515-527.

Thomson, James B. "The Use Of Market Information In Pricing Deposit Insurance," (4), 528-537.

Mester, Loretta J. "Multiple Market Contact Between Savings And Loans," (4), 538-549.

Journal of Money, Credit and Banking
Volume 20, 1988

Leiderman, Leonardo and Assaf Razin. "Testing Ricardian Neutrality With An Intertemporal Stochastic Model," (1), 1-21.

Dotsey, Michael. "The Demand For Currency In The United States," (1), 22-40.

Aschauer, David Alan. "The Equilibrium Approach To Fiscal Policy," (1), 41-62.

Alesina, Alberto and Jeffrey Sachs. "Political Parties And The Business Cycle In The United States, 1948-1984," (1), 63-82.

Havrilesky, Thomas. "Monetary Policy Signaling From The Administration To The Federal Reserve," (1), 83-101.

Tabellini, Guido. "Centralized Wage Setting And Monetary Policy In A Reputational Equilibrium," (1), 102-118.

Smith, Donald J. "Credit Union Rate And Earnings Retention Decisions Under Uncertainty And Taxation," (1), 119-131.

Sommariva, Andrea and Giuseppe Tullio. "International Gold Flows In Gold Standard Germany: A Test Of The Monetary Approach To The Balance Of Payments, 1880-1911," (1), 132-140.

Marty, Alvin L. and Frank J. Chaloupka. "Optimal Inflation Rates: A Generalization," (1), 141-144.

McCallum, John. "Is Increased Credibility Stabilizing?," (2), 155-166.

Cook, Timothy and Thomas Hahn. "The Information Content Of Discount Rate Announcements And Their Effect On Market Interest Rates," (2), 167-180.

Boyes, William J., William Stewart Mounts and Clifford Sowell. "The Federal Reserve As A Bureaucracy: An Examination Of Expense-Preference Behavior," (2), 181-190.

Evanoff, Douglas D. "Branch Banking And Service Accessibility," (2), 191-202.

Hannan, Timothy H. and Gerald A. Hanweck. "Bank Insolvency Risk And The Market For Large Certificates Of Deposit," (2), 203-211.

Chiang, Thomas C. "The Forward Rate As A Predictor Of The Future Spot Rate--A Stochastic Coefficient Approach," (2), 212-232.

Lahiri, Kajal, Christie Teigland and Mark Zaporowski. "Interest Rates And The Subjective Probability Distribution Of Inflation Forecasts," (2), 233-248.

Economopoulos, Andrew J. "Illinois Free Banking Experience," (2), 249-264.

Kelly, Gary Wayne. "Some Regulatory Determinants Of Bank Risk Behavior: Comment," (2), 265-269.

Mitchell, Douglas W. "Explicit Interest And Demand Deposit Service Charges: Comment," (2), 270-274.

Beckman, Steven R. and Joshua N. Foreman. "An Experimental Test Of The Baumol-Tobin Transactions Demand For Money," (3), Part 1, 291-305.

Wasserfallen, Walter. "Trends, Random Walks, And The Expectations-Augmented Phillips Curve -Evidence From Six Countries," (3), Part 1, 306-318.

McMillin, W. Douglas. "Money Growth Volatility And The Macroeconomy," (3), Part 1, 319-335.

Long, C. Richard and Mark L. Gardner. "Alternative U.S. Monetary And Deficit Reduction Policies For The 1980s," (3), Part 1, 336-352.

Darrat, Ali F. "On Fiscal Policy And The Stock Market," (3), Part 1, 353-363.

Allen, Paul R. and William J. Wilhelm. "The Impact Of The 1980 Depository Institutions Deregulation And Monetary Control Act On Market Value And Risk: Evidence From The Capital Markets," (3), Part 1, 364-380.

Devereux, Michael. "The Optimal Mix Of Wage Indexation And Foreign Exchange Market Intervention," (3), Part 1, 381-392.

Walsh, Carl E. "Testing For Real Effects Of Monetary Policy Regime Shifts," (3), Part 1, 393-401.

Karamouzis, Nicholas and Raymond E. Lombra. "Forecasts And U.S. Monetary Policy, 1974-78: The Role Of Openness," (3), Part 1, 402-408.

Cosimano, Thomas F. and Dennis W. Jansen. "Estimates Of The Variance Of U.S. Inflation Based Upon The ARCH Model: Comment," (3), Part 1, 409-421.

Engle, Robert F. "Estimates Of The Variance Of U.S. Inflation Based Upon The ARCH Model: Reply," (3), Part 1, 422-423.

Mankiw, N. Gregory. "Recent Developments In Macroeconomics: A Very Quick Refresher Course," (3), Part 2, 436-449.

McCallum, Bennet T. "Postwar Developments In Business Cycle Theory: A Moderately Classical Perspective," (3), Part 2, 459-471.

Kotlikoff, Laurence J. "What Microeconomics Teaches Us About The Dynamic Macro Effects Of Fiscal Policy," (3), Part 2, 479-495.

Katz, Lawrence F. "Some Recent Developments In Labor Economics And Their Implications For Macroeconomics," (3), Part 2, 507-522.

Stockman, Alan C. "On The Roles Of International Financial Markets And Their Relevance For Economic Policy," (3), Part 2, 531-549.

Gertler, Mark. "Financial Structure And Aggregate Economic Activity: An Overview," (3), Part 2, 559-588.

Avery, Robert B., Terrence M. Belton and Michael A. Goldberg. "Market Discipline In Regulating Bank Risk: New Evidence From The Capital Markets," (3), 597-610.

Bailey, Warren. "Money Supply Announcements And The Ex Ante Volatility Of Asset Prices," (4), 611-620.

Gerlach, Stefan. "World Business Cycles Under Fixed And Flexible Exchange Rates," (4), 621-632.

Boyer, Russell S. and F. Charles Adams. "Forward Premia And Risk Premia In A Simple Model Of Exchange Rate Determination," (4), 633-644.

Woodward, R. S. "Some New Evidence On The Profitability Of One-Way Versus Round-Trip Arbitrage," (4), 645-652.

Anderson, Robert B., William A. Bomberger, and Gail E. Makinen. "The Demand For Money, The 'Reform Effect,' And The Money Supply Process In Hyperinflation: The Evidence From Greece And Hungary II Reexamined," (4), 653-672.

Kaufman, Herbert M. "FNMA's Role In Deregulated Markets: Implications From Past Behavior," (4), 673-683.

DeGennaro, Ramon P. "Payment Delays: Bias In The Yield Curve," (4), 684-690.

Cranford, Brian K. and Roger D. Stover. "Interest Yields, Credit Ratings, And Economic Characteristics Of State Bonds: Comment,"

(4), 691-695.

Liu, Pu and Anjan V. Thakor. "Interest Yields, Credit Ratings, And Economic Characteristics Of State Bonds: Reply," (4), 696-697.

Cohen, Darrel. "Money Demand And The Effects Of Fiscal Policies: Comment," (4), 698-705.

McGibany, James M. and Farrokh Nourzad. "Money Demand And The Effects Of Fiscal Policies: Comment," (4), 706-714.

Mankiw, N. Gregory and Lawrence H. Summers. "Money Demand And The Effects Of Fiscal Policies: Reply," (4), 715-717.

Journal of Money, Credit and Banking
Volume 21, 1989

Herring, Richard J. "The Economics Of Workout Lending," (1), 1-15.

Manchester, Joyce. "How Money Affects Real Output," (1), 16-32.

Koray, Faik. "Money And Functional Distribution Of Income,"(1),33-48.

Sibert, Anne. "The Risk Premium In The Foreign Exchange Market," (1), 49-65.

Lastrapes, William D. "Exchange Rate Volatility And U.S. Monetary Policy: An ARCH Application," (1), 66-77.

Calomiris, Charles W. and Ian Domowitz. "Asset Substitutions, Money Demand, And The Inflation Process In Brazil," (1), 78-89.

Makinen, Gail E. and G. Thomas Woodward. "The Taiwanese Hyperinflation And Stabilization Of 1945-1952," (1), 90-105.

Brock, Philip L. "Reserve Requirements And The Inflation Tax," (1), 106-121.

Siklos, Pierre L. "The End Of The Hungarian Hyperinflation Of 1945-1946," (2), 135-147.

Kiguel, Miguel A. "Budget Deficits, Stability, And The Dynamics Of Hyperinflation," (2), 148-157.

Allen, Stuart D. and Robert A. Connolly. "Financial Market Effects On Aggregate Money Demand: A Bayesian Analysis," (2), 158-175.

Daniel, Betty C. "One-Sided Uncertainty About Future Fiscal Policy," (2), 176-189.

Viswanath, P. V. "Taxes And The Futures-Forward Price Difference In The 91-Day T-Bill Market," (2), 190-205.

Unal, Haluk. "Impact Of Deposit-Rate Ceiling Changes On Bank Stock Returns," (2), 206-220.

Cowen, Tyler and Randall Kroszner. "Scottish Banking Before 1845: A Model For Laissez-Faire?," (2), 221-231.

VanHoose, David D. "Monetary Targeting And Price Level Non-Trend-Stationarity," (2), 232-239.

Bryant, John. "Interest-Bearing Currency, Legal Restrictions, And The Rate Of Return Dominance Of Money," (2), 240-245.

Whitesell, William C. "The Demand For Currency Versus Debitable Accounts," (2), 246-251.

Batchelor, Roy A. and Pami Dua. "Household Versus Economist Forecasts Of Inflation: A Reassessment," (2), 252-257.

Brocato, Joe and Kenneth L. Smith. "Velocity And The Variability Of Money Growth: Evidence From Granger-Causality Tests: Comment," (2), 258-261.

Mehra, Yash P. "Velocity And The Variability Of Money Growth: Evidence From Granger-Causality Tests: Comment," (2), 262-271.

Dotsey, Michael. "Monetary Control Under Alternative Operating Procedures," (3), 273-290.

Wilcox, David W. "The Sustainability Of Government Deficits: Implications Of The Present-Value Borrowing Constraint," (3), 291-306.

Strong, John S. "The Market Valuation Of Credit Market Debt," (3), 307-320.

Turnovsky, Stephen J. "The Term Structure Of Interest Rates And The Effects Of Macroeconomic Policy," (3), 321-347.

Lee, Bong-Soo. "A Nonlinear Expectations Model Of The Term Structure Of Interest Rates With Time-Varying Risk Premia," (3), 348-367.

Lawrence, Colin. "Banking Costs, Generalized Functional Forms, And Estimation Of Economies Of Scale And Scope," (3), 368-379.

Hayford, Marc. "Liquidity Constraints And The Ricardian Equivalence Theorem," (3), 380-387.

Simon, David P. "The Rationality Of Federal Funds Rate Expectations: Evidence From A Survey," (3), 388-393.

Schirm, David C., Richard G. Sheehan and Michael G. Ferri. "Financial Market Responses To Treasury Debt Announcements," (3), 394-400.

Falk, Barry and Peter F. Orazem. "The Role Of Systematic Fed Errors In Explaining The Money Supply Announcements Puzzle," (3), 401-406.

Grubaugh, Stephen and Scott Sumner. "Commodity Prices, Money Surprises, And Fed Credibility: Comment," (3), 407-408.

Garman, David M. and Daniel J. Richards. "Policy Rules, Inflationary Bias, And Cyclical Stability," (4), 409-421.

Waller, Christopher J. "Monetary Policy Games And Central Bank Politics," (4), 422-431.

Belden, Susan. "Policy Preferences Of FOMC Members As Revealed By Dissenting Votes," (4), 432-441.

Spencer, David E. "Does Money Matter? The Robustness Of Evidence From Vector Autoregressions," (4), 442-454.

Hetzel, Robert L. and Yash P. Mehra. "The Behavior Of Money Demand In The 1980s," (4), 455-463.

Beenstock, Michael. "The Determinants Of The Money Multiplier In The United Kingdom," (4), 464-480.

Chadha, Binky. "Is Increased Price Inflexibility Stabilizing?," (4), 481-497.

Evans, George W. "The Conduct Of Monetary Policy And The Natural Rate Of Unemployment," (4), 498-507.

Garner, C. Alan. "Commodity Prices: Policy Target Or Information Variable?," (4), 508-514.

Haslag, Joseph H. and Scott E. Hein. "Federal Reserve System Reserve Requirements, 1959-1988," (4), 515-523.

Cheng, David C., Benton E. Gup and Larry D. Wall. "Financial Determinants Of Bank Takeovers," (4), 524-536.

Journal of Money, Credit and Banking
Volume 22, 1990

Poterba, James M. and Julio J. Rotemberg. "Inflation And Taxation With Optimizing Governments," (1), 1-18.

Basu, Susanto, Miles S. Kimball, N. Gregory Mankiw and David N. Weil. "Optimal Advice For Monetary Policy," (1), 19-36.

Havrilesky, Thomas. "The Influence Of The Federal Advisory Council On Monetary Policy," (1), 37-50.

Dowd, Kevin. "The Value Of Time And The Transactions Demand For Money," (1), 51-64.

Swidler, Steve and David Ketcher. "Economic Forecasts, Rationality, And The Processing Of New Information Over Time," (1), 65-76.

Kormendi, Roger C. and Philip Meguire. "A Multicountry Characterization Of The Nonstationarity Of Aggregate Output," (1), 77-93.

Noulas, Athanasios G., Subhash C. Ray and Stephen M. Miller. "Returns To Scale And Input Substitution For Large U.S. Banks," (1), 94-108.

Sumner, Scott. "The Forerunners Of 'New Monetary Economics' Proposals To Stabilize The Unit Of Account," (1), 109-118.

Gorton, Gary and Anthony M. Santomero. "Market Discipline And Bank Subordinated Debt," (1), 119-128.

Strongin, Steven and Vefa Tarhan. "Money Supply Announcements And The Market's Perception Of Federal Reserve Policy," (2), 135-153.

Deaves, Richard. "Money Supply Announcements And Market Reactions In An Open Economy," (2), 154-164.

Grossman, Herschel I. "Inflation And Reputation With Generic Policy Preferences," (2), 165-177.

Duca, John V. and David VanHoose. "Loan Commitments And Optimal Monetary Policy," (2), 178-194.

Rogers, John H. "Foreign Inflation Transmission Under Flexible Exchange Rates And Currency Substitution," (2), 195-208.

Musumeci, James J. and Joseph F. Sinkey, Jr. "The International Debt Crisis, Investor Contagion, And Bank Security Returns In 1987: The Brazilian Experience," (2), 209-220.

Clauretie, Terrence M. and Thomas Herzog. "The Effect Of State Foreclosure Laws On Loan Losses: Evidence From The Mortgage Insurance Industry," (2), 221-233.

Feltenstein, Andrew, David Lebow and S. Van Wijnbergen. "Savings, Commodity Market Rationing, And The Real Rate Of Interest In China," (2), 234-252.

Fissel, Gary S. and Tullio Jappelli. "Do Liquidity Constraints Vary Over Time? Evidence From Survey And Panel Data," (2), 253-262.

Rassekh, Farhad and Barry Wilbratte. "The Effect Of Import Price Changes On Domestic Inflation: An Empirical Test Of The Ratchet Effect," (2), 263-267.

Canzoneri, Matthew B. and Anne C. Sibert. "The Macroeconomic Implications Of Contract Models With Asymmetric Information," (3), 273-287.

Glick, Reuven and Michael Hutchison. "New Results In Support Of The Fiscal Policy Ineffectiveness Proposition," (3), 288-304.

Haug, Alfred A. "Ricardian Equivalence, Rational Expectations, And The Permanent Income Hypothesis," (3), 305-326.

Hakes, David R. "The Objectives And Priorities Of Monetary Policy Under Different Federal Reserve Chairmen," (3), 327-337.

Huang, Roger D. "Risk And Parity In Purchasing Power," (3), 338-356.

Brewer, Thomas L. and Pietra Rivoli. "Politics And Perceived Country Creditworthiness In International Banking," (3), 357-369.

Musumeci, James J. and Joseph F. Sinkey, Jr. "The International Debt Crisis And Bank Loan-Loss-Reserve Decisions: The Signaling Content Of Partially Anticipated Events," (3), 370-387.

Karfakis, Costas J. and Demetrios M. Moschos. "Interest Rate Linkages Within The European Monetary System: A Time Series Analysis," (3), 388-394.

Thornton, John and Sri Ram Poudyal. "Money And Capital In Economic Development: A Test Of The McKinnon Hypothesis For Nepal," (3), 395-399.

Barney, L. Dwayne, Jr., Alan Frankle and Harry White. "Reserve Requirements And The Inflation Tax," (3), 400-401.

Wheelock, David C. "Member Bank Borrowing And The Fed's Contractionary Monetary Policy During The Great Depression," (4), 409-426.

Reinhart, Vincent. "Targeting Nominal Income In A Dynamic Model," (4), 427-443.

Fackler, James S. "Federal Credit, Private Credit, And Economic Activity," (4), 444-464.

Baum, Christopher F. and Marilena Furno. "Analyzing The Stability Of Demand-For-Money Equations Via Bounded-Influence Estimation Techniques," (4), 465-477.

Salyer, Kevin D. "The Term Structure And Time Series Properties Of Nominal Interest Rates: Implications From Theory," (4), 478-490.

Kim, Yoonbai. "Purchasing Power Parity In The Long Run: A Cointegration Approach," (4), 491-503.

Hunter, William C., Stephen G. Timme and Won Keun Yang. "An Examination Of Cost Subadditivity And Multiproduct Production In Large U.S. Banks," (4), 504-525.

White, Lawrence H. "Scottish Banking And The Legal Restrictions Theory: A Closer Look," (4), 526-536.

JOURNAL OF PORTFOLIO MANAGEMENT

Goodman, Laurie S. and Robert A. Schwartz. "Coffee Pots And Limit Orders," (3), 5-6.
Lloyd, William P. and Naval K. Modani. "Stocks, Bonds, Bills, And Time Diversification," (3), 7-11.
Bodie, Zvi. "Commodity Futures As A Hedge Against Inflation," (3), 12-17.
Nunn, Kenneth P., Jr., Gerald P. Madden and Michael J. Gombola. "Are Some Insiders More 'Inside' Than Others?," (3), 18-22.
Bethke, William M. and Susan E. Boyd. "Should Dividend Discount Models Be Yield-Tilted?," (3), 23-27.
Glickstein, David A. and Rolf E. Wubbels. "Dow Theory Is Alive And Well!," (3), 28-32.
Korkie, Bob. "External Vs. Internal Performance Evaluation," (3), 36-42.
Unger, Raymond F. "Using Outside Research," (3), 43-45.
Fong, Gifford, Charles Pearson and Oldrich Vasicek. "Bond Performance: Analyzing Sources Of Return," (3), 46-50.
Cheney, John M. "Rating Classification And Bond Yield Volatility," (3), 51-57.
Fielitz, Bruce D. "Calculating The Bond Equivalent Yield For T-Bills," (3), 58-60.
Ritchken, Peter H. and Harvey M. Salkin. "Safety First Selection Techniques For Option Spreads," (3), 61-67.
Sherman, Eugene J. "A Gold Pricing Model," (3), 68-70.
Estep, Tony, Nick Hanson and Cal Johnson. "Sources Of Value And Risk In Common Stocks," (4), 5-13.
Edmister, Robert O. and Christopher James. "Is Illiquidity A Bar To Buying Small Cap Stocks?," (4), 14-19.
Brush, John S. and Keith E. Boles. "The Predictive Power In Relative Strength And CAPM," (4), 20-23.
Hetherington, Norriss S. "Taking The Risk Out Of Risk Arbitrage," (4), 24-25.
Lerner, Eugene M. and Pochara Theerathorn. "The Returns Of Different Investment Strategies," (4), 26-28.
Sorensen, Roy A. "An 'Essential Reservation' About The EMH," (4), 29-30.
Ferguson, Robert. "An Efficient Stock Market? Ridiculous!," (4), 31-38.
Muller, Frederick L., Bruce D. Fielitz and Myron T. Greene. "S&P Quality Group Rankings: Risk And Return," (4), 39-42.
Madura, Jeff. "Empirical Measurement Of Exchange Rate Betas," (4), 43-46.
Dunn, Patricia C. and Rolf D. Theisen. "How Consistently Do Active Managers Win?," (4), 47-50.
Kritzman, Mark. "Can Bond Managers Perform Consistently?," (4), 54-56.
Miller, Paul F., Jr. "Managing Investment Portfolios: A Review Article," (4), 57-58.
Saulnier, Raymond J. "The President's Economic Report: A Critique," (4), 58-59.
Sorensen, Eric. "Who Puts The Slope In The Municipal Yield Curve?," (4), 61-65.
Christofi, Andreas. "How To Maximize Stationarity Of Beta: Comment," (4), 67-68.
Tole, Thomas M. "How To Maximize Stationarity Of Beta: Reply," (4), 67-68.

Journal of Portfolio Management
Volume 10, 1983/84

Arnott, Robert D. "What Hath MPT Wrought: Which Risks Reap Rewards?," (1), 5-11.
French, Dan W., John C. Groth and James W. Kolari. "Current Investor Expectations And Better Betas," (1), 12-17.
Olsen, Robert. "Sample Size And Markowitz Diversification," (1), 18-22.
Hawawini, Gabriel A. and Ashok Vora. "Is Adjusting Beta Estimates An Illusion?," (1), 23-26.
Merrett, A. J. and Gerald D. Newbould. "Integrating Financial Performance And Stock Valuation," (1), 27-35.
Reilly, Frank K., Frank T. Griggs and Wenchi Wong. "Determinants Of The Aggregate Stock Market Earnings Multiple," (1), 36-45.
Edelman, Richard B. "Telecommunications Betas: Are They Stable And Unique?," (1), 46-52.
Renshaw, Edward F. "The Anatomy Of Stock Market Cycles," (1), 53-57.
Strong, Robert A. "Do Share Price And Stock Splits Matter?," (1),58-64.
Gay, Gerald D. and Robert W. Kolb. "Interest Rate Futures As A Tool For Immunization," (1), 65-70.
Dyl, Edward A. and Stanley A. Martin. "Rules Of Thumb For The Analysis Of Tax Swaps," (1), 71-74.
Fogler, H. Russell. "20% In Real Estate: Can Theory Justify It?," (2), 6-13.
Howe, John S. and William L. Beedles. "Defensive Investing Using Fundamental Data," (2), 14-17.
Jones, Charles P., Richard J. Rendleman, Jr. and Henry Latane. "Stock Returns And SUEs During The 1970s," (2), 18-22.
Evnine, Jeremy and Andrew Rudd. "Option Portfolio Risk Analysis," (2), 23-27.
Shiller, Robert J. "Theories Of Aggregate Stock Price Movements," (2), 28-37.
Mantell, Edmund H. "How To Measure Expected Returns On Foreign Investments," (2), 38-43.
Kane, Alex. "Coins: Anatomy Of A Fad Asset," (2), 44-51.
Casabona, Patrick A., Frank J. Fabozzi and Jack C. Francis. "How To Apply Duration To Equity Analysis," (2), 52-58.
Barnes, Tom, Keith Johnson and Don Shannon. "A Test Of Fixed-Income Strategies," (2), 60-65.
Speakes, Jeffrey K. "Risk Measurement And Risk Management," (2), 66-70.
Cabanilla, Nathaniel B. "Directly-Placed Bonds: A Test Of Market Efficiency," (2), 72-74.
Goldie, Raymond. "Are Some Insiders More 'Inside' Than Others?: Comment," (2), 75.
Brooks, LeRoy D.,Charles E. Edwards and Eurico J. Ferreira. "Risk-Return Characteristics Of Convertible Preferred Stock: Comment," (2), 76-78.

Soldofsky, Robert M. "Risk-Return Characteristics Of Convertible Preferred Stock: Reply," (2), 79.
Bernstein, Peter L. "How To Take Reinvestment Risk Without Really Trying," (3), 4.
Zerbst, Robert H. and Barbara R. Cambon. "Real Estate: Historical Returns And Risks," (3), 5-20.
Kopcke, Richard W. and Peter C. Aldrich. "A Real Estate Crisis: Averted Or Just Postponed?," (3), 21-29.
Trainer, Francis H., Jr., David A. Levine and Jonathan A. Reiss. "A Systematic Approach To Bond Management In Pension Funds," (3), 30-35.
Johnson, James M. "When Are Zero Coupon Bonds The Better Buy?," (3), 36-71.
Galai, Dan and Robert Geske. "Option Performance Measurement," (3), 42-46.
Gressis, N., G. Vlahos and G. C. Philippatos. "A CAPM-Based Analysis Of Stock Index Futures," (3), 47-52.
Nordhauser, Fred. "Using Stock Index Futures To Reduce Market Risk," (3), 56-62.
Singleton, J. Clay and Robin Grieves. "Synthetic Puts And Portfolio Insurance Strategies," (3), 63-69.
Statman, Meir. "Growth Opportunities Vs. Growth Stocks," (3), 70-74.
McWilliams, James D. "Watchman, Tell Us Of The Night!," (3), 75-80.
Khoury, Sarkis J. "Dow Theory Is Alive And Well: Comment," (3), 81-83.
Johnson, Lewis D. "Sources Of Risk And Value In Common Stocks: Comment," (3), 84.
Farrelly, Gail E. and William R. Reichenstein. "Risk Perceptions Of Institutional Investors," (4), 5-12.
Klemkosky, Robert C. and William P. Miller. "When Forecasting Earnings, It Pays To Be Right!," (4), 13-18.
Kerrigan, Thomas J. "When Forecasting Earnings, It Pays To Watch Forecasts," (4), 19-26.
Taylor, Richard W. "Portfolio Management With A Hand-Held Calculator," (4), 27-31.
Dhrymes, Phoebus. "Arbitrage Pricing Theory," (4), 35-44.
Cole, John A. "Are Dividend Surprises Independently Important?," (4), 45-50.
Modest, David M. "On The Pricing Of Stock Index Futures," (4), 51-57.
Babcock, Guilford C. "Duration As A Link Between Yield And Value," (4), 58-65.
Fuller, Russell J. and John W. Settle. "Determinants Of Duration And Bond Volatility," (4), 66-72.
Gray, William S. "The Stock Market And The Economy In 1988," (4), 73-80.
Saulnier, Raymond J. "The President's Economic Report: A Critique," (4), 81-83.
French, Dan W. and Debra K. Dennis. "CEPS: The Illusion Of Corporate Growth: Comment," (4), 83-85.
Michaud, Richard O. "Should Dividend Discount Models Be Yield-Tilted?: Comment," (4), 85.

Journal of Portfolio Management
Volume 11, 1984/85

Kaplan, Gilbert E. "A Tenth Anniversary," (1), 3.
Bernstein, Peter L. "Surprising The Smoothies," (1), 7-11.
Markowitz, Harry M. "The 'Two Beta' Trap," (1), 12-20.
Sharpe, William F. "Factor Models, CAPMs, And The ABT," (1), 21-25.
Tobin, James. "A Mean-Variance Approach To Fundamental Valuations," (1), 26-32.
Jeffrey, Robert H. "A New Paradigm For Portfolio Risk," (1), 33-40.
Kosmicke, Ralph. "The Contradiction Between Keynes And The EMH," (1), 41-43.
Rosenberg, Barr. "Prediction Of Common Stock Investment Risk," (1), 44-53.
Ross, Stephen A. "A Reply to Dhrymes: APT Is Empirically Relevant," (1), 54-56.
Soldofsky, Robert M. "Risk And Return For Long-Term Securities: 1971-1982," (1), 57-67.
Rozeff, Michael S. "Dividend Yields Are Equity Risk Premiums," (1), 68-75.
Kirby, Robert G. "The Coffee Can Portfolio," (1), 76-80.
Carvell, Steven and Paul Strebel. "A New Beta Incorporating Anaysts' Forecasts," (1), 81-85.
Blume, Marshall E. "The Use Of 'Alphas' To Improve Performance," (1), 86-92.
Leibowitz, Martin L., Thomas E. Klaffky, Steven Mandel and Alfred Weinberger. "Horizon Matching: A New Approach To Dedicated Portfolios," (1), 93-96.
Babcock, Guilford C. "Duration As A Link Between Yield And Value: Erratum," (1), 97-98.
Rosenberg, Barr. "Prediction Of Common Stock Betas," (2), 5-14.
French, Dan W. and Glenn V. Henderson, Jr. "How Well Does Performance Evaluation Perform?," (2), 15-18.
McDonald, Bill. "Making Sense Out Of Unstable Alphas And Betas," (2), 19-22.
Whitford, David T. and Frank K. Reilly. "What Makes Stock Prices Move?," (2), 23-30.
Levy, Haim and Zvi Lerman. "Testing P/E Ratio Filters With Stochastic Dominance," (2), 31-40.
Pitts, Mark. "The Pricing Of Options On Debt Securities," (2), 41-50.
Yawitz, Jess B. and William J. Marshall. "The Use Of Futures In Immunized Portfolios," (2), 51-58.
Goodman, Laurie S. "Put-Call Parity With Coupon Instruments," (2), 59-60.
Anthony, Robert N. "How To Measure Fixed-Income Performance Correctly," (2), 61-65.
Murphy, J. E. and M. F. M. Osborne. "Predicting The Volatility Of Interest Rates," (2), 66-69.
Kalotay, Andrew J. "The After-Tax Duration Of Original Issue Discount Bonds," (2), 70-72.
Kaplan, Howard M. "Farmland As A Portfolio Investment," (2), 73-78.
Shaked, Saul. "International Equity Markets And The Investment Horizon," (2), 80-84.

Journal of Portfolio Management
Volume 14, 1987/88

Journal of Portfolio Management
Volume 15, 1988/89

Haugen, Robert A. and Nardin L. Baker. "The Efficient Market Inefficiency Of Capitalization-Weighted Stock Portfolios,"(3),35-40.

Butler, Kirt C. and Dale L. Domian. "Risk, Diversification, And The Investment Horizon," (3), 41-48.

Peters, Donald J. "Valuing A Growth Stock," (3), 49-51.

Litterman, Robert and Thomas Iben. "Corporate Bond Valuation And The Term Structure Of Credit Spreads," (3), 52-64.

Finnerty, John D. and Michael Rose. "Arbitrage-Free Spread: A Consistent Measure Of Relative Value," (3), 65-81.

Reitano, Robert R. "Non-Parallel Yield Curve Shifts And Spread Leverage," (3), 82-87.

Eun, Cheol S., Richard Kolodny and Bruce G. Resnick. "U.S.-Based International Mutual Funds: A Performance Evaluation," (3), 88-94.

JOURNAL OF REAL ESTATE FINANCE AND ECONOMICS

Journal of Real Estate Research
Volume 1, 1986

Smith, Halbert C. "Inconsistencies In Appraisal Theory And Practice," (1), 1-17.

Cronan, Timothy P., Donald R. Epley and Larry G. Perry. "The Use Of Rank Transformation And Multiple Regression Analysis In Estimating Residential Property Values With A Small Sample," (1), 19-31.

Kapplin, Steven D. and Arthur L. Schwartz, Jr. "An Anlaysis Of Recent Rates Of Return And Of The Secondary Market For Public Real Estate Limited Partnerships," (1), 33-44.

Manning, Christopher A. "Intercity Differences In Home Price Appreciation," (1), 45-66.

Kuhle, James L., Carl H. Walther and Charles H. Wurtzebach. "The Financial Performance Of Real Estate Investment Trusts," (1), 67-75.

Webb, James R. and Willard McIntosh. "Real Estate Investment Acquisition Rules For REITs: A Survey," (1), 77-98.

Miller, Norman G. and Michael A. Sklarz. "A Note On Leading Indicators Of Housing Market Price Trends," (1), 99-109.

Journal of Real Estate Research
Volume 2, 1987

Kang, Han Bin and Alan K. Reichert. "An Evaluation Of Alternative Estimation Techniques And Functional Forms In Developing Statistical Appraisal Models," (1), 1-29.

Miller, Norman G. and Michael A. Sklarz. "Pricing Strategies And Residential Property Selling Prices," (1), 31-40.

Johnson, Larry J., James L. Kuhle and Carl H. Walther. "An Elasticity Approach To Equity Risk Evaluation," (1), 41-49.

Nourse, Hugh O. and Dorothy Kingery. "Survey Of Approaches To Disposing Of Suplus Corporate Real Estate," (1), 51-59.

Perry, Larry G., Timothy P. Cronan and Donald R. Epley. "A Procedure For Unconvering Acceptable And Nonacceptable Mortgage Applications Through Discriminant Analysis Using Ranked Data," (1), 61-72.

Follain, James R., Terry Lutes and David A. Meier. "Why Do Some Real Estate Salespeople Earn More Than Others?," (1), 73-81.

Christiansen, William A. and Clarence C. Elebash. "A Note On The Attitude Of Pension Fund Investment Managers Toward Mortgage-Backed Securities," (1), 83-92.

Ball, Jay N. "A Note On The Importance Of Real Estate Course Titles," (1), 93-97.

Isakson, Hans R. and Nicholas Ordway. "Real Estate Programs: A Note On Publication Performance," (1), 99-111.

Kuhle, James L. "Portfolio Diversification And Return Benefits - Common Stock Vs. Real Estate Investment Trusts (REITs)," (2), 1-9.

Webb, James R. and Jack H. Rubens. "Tax Rates And Implicit Rates Of Return On Owner-Occupied Single-Family Housing," (2), 11-28.

Ferreira, Eurico J. and G. Stacy Sirmans. "Interest-Rate Changes, Transaction Costs, And Assumable Loan Value," (2), 29-40.

Richins, Marsha L., William C. Black and C. F. Sirmans. "Strategic Orientation And Marketing Strategy: An Analysis Of Residential Real Estate Brokerage Firms," (2), 41-54.

Bible, Douglas S. "Rehabilitation Tax Credits And Rate Of Return On Real Estate Under Recent Tax Reform Measures," (2), 55-61.

Gardner, Mona J., Han Bin Kang and Dixie L. Mills. "Consumer Profiles And Acceptance Of ARM Features: An Application Of Logit Regression," (2), 63-74.

Skantz, Terrance R. and Thomas H. Strickland. "House Prices And A Flood Event: An Empirical Investigation Of Market Efficiency," (2), 75-83.

Hartzell, David J., David G. Shulman and Charles H. Wurtzebach. "Refining The Analysis Of Regional Diversification For Income-Producing Real Estate," (2), 85-95.

Harris, John M., Jr. and G. Stacy Sirmans. "Discount Points, Effective Yields And Mortgage Prepayments," (2), 97-104.

Smith, Charles A. and George D. Greenwade. "The Rankings Of Real Estate Publications And Tenure Requirements At AACSB Versus Non-AACSB Schools," (2), 105-112.

Journal of Real Estate Research
Volume 3, 1988

Frew, James and G. Donald Jud. "Vacancy Rates In Rent Levels In The Commercial Office Market," (1), 1-8.

Merriken, Harry. "Mortgage Loan Market Segmentation And Lender Pricing Behavior," (1), 9-18.

Ferguson, Jerry T. "After-Sale Evaluations: Appraisals Or Justifications?," (1), 19-26.

Kroll, Mark J. and Charles Smith. "Buyer's Response Technique - A Framework For Improving Comparable Selection And Adjustment In Single-Family Appraising," (1), 27-35.

Boyd, James W. "Asset Status Proxies And Consumer Preference For ARMs: An Empirical Investigation Using Probit Analysis," (1), 37-49.

Goolsby, William C. and Lehahan O'Connell. "Overbuilt Housing: Criteria For Success," (1), 51-59.

Haney, Richard L., Jr. "Sticky Mortgage Rates: Some Empirical Evidence," (1), 61-73.

Devaney, Michael and William Rayburn. "When A House Is More Than A Home: Performance Of The Household Portfolio," (1), 75-85.

Clauretie, Terrance M. "Regional Economic Diversification And Residential Mortgage Default Risk," (1), 87-97.

Shilling, James D. and C. F. Sirmans. "The Effects Of Occupational Licensing On Complaints Against Real Estate Agents," (2), 1-9.

Guntermann, Karl L. and Richard L. Smith. "Licensing Requirements, Enforcement Effort And Complaints Against Real Estate Agents," (2), 11-20.

Johnson, Linda L., Michael J. Dotson and B. J. Dunlap. "Service Quality Determinants And Effectiveness In The Real Estate Brokerage Industry," (2), 21-36.

Chinloy, Peter. "The Real Estate Brokerage: Commissioned Sales And Market Values," (2), 37-51.

Glower, Michel and Patric H. Hendershott. "The Determinants Of REALTOR Income," (2), 53-68.

Crellin, Glenn E., James R. Frew and G. Donald Jud. "The Earnings Of REALTORS: Some Empirical Evidence," (2), 69-78.

Goolsby, William C. and Barbara J. Childs. "Brokerage Firm Competition In Real Estate Commission Rates," (2), 79-85.

Nelson, Theron R. and Susan Logan Nelson. "Franchise Affiliation And Brokerage Firm Selection: A Perceptual Investigation," (2), 87-107.

Johnson, Joyce M., Hugh O. Nourse and Ellen Day. "Factors Related To The Selection Of A Real Estate Agency," (2), 109-118.

Ball, Jay N. and Hugh O. Nourse. "Testing The Conventional Representation Model For Residential Real Estate Brokerage," (2), 119-131.

Levi, Donald R. and Curtis D. Terflinger. "A Legal-Economic Analysis Of Changing Liability Rules Affecting Real Estate Brokers And Appraisers," (2), 133-149.

Marsh, Gene A. and Leonard V. Zumpano. "Agency Theory And The Changing Role Of The Real Estate Broker: Conflicts And Possible Solutions," (2), 151-164.

Webb, James R. "The Assimilation Of New Services Into The Real Estate Brokerage Firm," (2), 165-175.

Dotzour, Mark G. "Quantifying Estimation Bias In Residential Appraisal," (3), 1-11.

Chen, K. C. and Daniel T. Tzang. "Interest-Rate Sensitivity Of Real Estate Investment Trusts," (3), 13-22.

G.-Yohannes, Arefaine. "Evaluating Alternative Fast-Pay Mortgages," (3), 23-29.

Hartzell, David J. and James R. Webb. "Real Estate Risk And Return Expectations: Recent Survey Results," (3), 31-37.

Miller, Norman G., Michael A. Sklarz and Nicholas Ordway. "Japanese Purchases, Exchange Rates And Speculation In Residential Real Estate Markets," (3), 39-49.

Born, Waldo L. "A Real Estate Market Research Method To Screen Areas For New Construction Potential," (3), 51-62.

Green, G. Hayden. "Strategic Management Practices Of Real Estate Developers In A Volatile Economic Climate," (3), 63-72.

Rutherford, Ronald C. and Hugh O. Nourse. "The Impact Of Corporate Real Estate Unit Formation On The Parent Firm's Value," (3), 73-84.

Wright, Arthur L. "The Impact Of Residential Rent Controls On Lender Policies And Activities," (3), 85-90.

Journal of Real Estate Research
Volume 4, 1989

Shilton, Leon G. and James R. Webb. "Commercial Loan Underwriting And Option Valuation," (1), 1-12.

Larsen, James E. "Money Illusion And Residential Real Estate Transfers," (1), 13-19.

Kang, Han Bin and Mona J. Gardner. "Selling Price And Marketing Time In The Residential Real Estae Market," (1), 21-35.

Epley, Donald R. and Alireza Tahai. "Consumer-Revealed Preferences For A Margin And Other Associated Adjustable-Rate Mortgage Features," (1), 37-51.

Leung Wai K. "Option Theory And Defaultable Mortgage Pricing," (1), 53-59.

Smith, Charles A. and Mark J. Kroll. "Utility Theory And Rent Optimization: Utilizing Cluster Analysis To Segment Rental Markets," (1), 61-71.

Taube, Paul M. and Don N. MacDonald. "A Note On Residential Mortgage Selection: Borrower Decisions And Inflation Expectations," (1), 73-79.

Miller, Norman G. and Michael A. Sklarz. "Tax Rates And Implicit Rates Of Return On Owner-Occupied Single-Family Housing: A Comment," (1), 81-84.

Webb, James R. and Jack H. Rubens. "Tax Rates And Implicit Rates Of Return On Owner-Occupied Single-Family Housing: A Reply," (1), 85-86.

Donnelly, William A. "The Methodology Of Housing Value Assessment: An Analysis," (2), 1-12.

Kutner, George W. and James A. Seifert. "The Valuation Of Mortgage Loan Commitments Using Option Pricing Estimates," (2), 13-20.

Lacey, Nelson J. and Nikolaos T. Milonas. "The Determinants Of GNMA Prepayments: A Pool-By-Pool Analysis," (2), 21-32.

Sirmans, G. Stacy, C. F. Sirmans and John D. Benjamin. "Determining Apartment Rent: The Value Of Amenities, Services And External Factors," (2), 33-43.

Rubens, Jack H., Michael T. Bond and James R. Webb. "The Inflation-Hedging Effectiveness Of Real Estate," (2), 45-55.

Goebel, Paul R. and Kee S. Kim. "Performance Evaluation Of Finite-Life Real Estate Investment Trusts," (2), 57-69.

Elebash, Clarence C. and William A. Christiansen. "State Pension Funds: What Is Their Future In Real Estate?," (2), 71-79.

Tucker, Michael. "Adjustable-Rate And Fixed-Rate Mortgage Choice: A Logit Analysis," (2), 81-91.

Veale, Peter R. "Managing Corporate Real Estate Assets: Current Executive Attitudes And Prospects For An Emergent Discipline," (3), 1-22.

Journal of Real Estate Research
Volume 5, 1990

JOURNAL OF RISK AND INSURANCE

Journal of Risk and Insurance
Volume 1, 1934

Nerlove, S. H. "Some Problems Related To Life Insurance Receiverships," 3-9.
Mowbray, Albert H. "How Far Should Further Increase In Insurance Facilities Be Permitted?," 1-12.
Kulp, C. A. "Investment Of Unemployment Insurance Funds," 1-12.
Linton, M. Albert. "The Effect Of Inflation Upon Life Insurance," 1-8.
Riegel, Robert. "Life Insurance And The Moratorium," 1-7.
Dickinson, Frank G. "Would Federal Control Of Life Insurance Mean Improvement?," 1-3.
Loman, H. J. "Is A Change In Investment Policy Of Life Insurance Companies Towards Greater Liquidity Desirable?," 1-4.
Laird, J. M. "Should Surrender And Loan Values Be Restricted," 1-7.
Bowers, Edison L. "The Attitude Of Companies In Accepting Large Amounts Of Single Premium And Annuity Contracts," 1-4.

Journal of Risk and Insurance
Volume 2, 1935

Blanchard, Ralph H. "University Instruction In Insurance Curricula And Teaching Methods," 2-8.
McCahan, David. "University Instruction For Insurance Leadership," 9-21.
Goble, George W. "Regulation Of Insurance Companies In A Period Of Emergency," 29-36.
Douglas, Paul H. "Is A General Problem Of Social Insurance Desirable?," 37-47.
Lippincott, Lincoln H. "A General System Of Social Insurance Is Not A Practicable Ideal," 48-55.
Dingman, H. W. "Experience In Disability Income Insurance," 56-64.
Leslie, William. "The Condition Of The Workmen's Compensation Business," 65-71.

Journal of Risk and Insurance
Volume 3, 1936

Loman, H. J. "A Course Of Study For Students Specializing In Insurance," 1-9.
Mowbray, A. H. "Content, Arrangement And Method Of A General Course For Students Not Specializing In Insurance," 10-22.
Riegel, Robert. "Content, Arrangement And Method Of A General Course For Students Not Specializing In Insurance," 23-30.
Pink, Louis H. "The Problems Of A Superintendent Of Insurance," 43-54.
Taylor, C. G. "How Can The Universities And University Teachers Best Serve In Their Fields?," 55-60.
Falls, L. E. "How Can The Universities And University Teachers Best Serve In Their Fields?,"61-67.
Michelbacher, G. F. "How Can The Universities And University Teachers Best Serve In Their Fields?,"68-79.

Journal of Risk and Insurance
Volume 4, 1937

Loman, H. J., E. L. Bowers and J. E. Partington. "Report Of The Committee On Standards And Topics For Courses In Insurance," 5-9.
Parry, C. L., G. L. Amrhein and C. D. Spangler. "Interim Report Of The Committee On Insurance Bibliography," 25-27.
Manes, Alfred. "Relationship Between Insurance Practice And Theory," 32-36.
Goble, George W. "Proposed Revision Of The Standard Fire Insurance Policy With Special Reference To Moral Hazard Clauses," 37-53.
Sawyer, E. W. "Liability At Law And Insurance Against It," 72-78.

Journal of Risk and Insurance
Volume 5, 1938

Wood, J. Harry. "Training Courses Conducted By Life Insurance Companies," 5-12.
Herd, J. Victor. "Training Courses Conducted By Fire And Marine Insurance Companies," 17-22.
Leslie, William. "Training Courses Conducted By Casualty Insurance Companies," 26-36.
Magrath, Joseph J. "The Proposed Revision Of The New York Insurance Law," 40-46.
Robbins, Rainard B. "The Effect Of Social Security Legislation On Private Pension Plans," 47-55.
Thurman, Oliver. "The Future Of Disability Income Insurance," 59-65.

Journal of Risk and Insurance
Volume 6, 1939

Linton, M. Albert. "Permanent Insurance Vs. Term And Separate Investment," 5-19.
Jackson, Henry H. "Individual Reserves And Kindred Delusions," 24-35.
Morrison, Laurence S. "Selling Method In Life Insurance," 40-51.
Travers, Frank J. "Some Life Insurance Investment Problems," 56-61.
Bowers, Edison L. "Social Insurance In The University Curriculum," 62-69.

Journal of Risk and Insurance
Volume 7, 1940

Reed, Henry H. "War Problems In Marine Insurance," 5-10.
Dickinson, Frank. "Insurance Developments After 1940," 11-26.
Heymann, Hans. "Property Life Insurance," 31-43.
Miller, A. Van Court. "The Buyer's Viewpoint On Insurance," 53-58.
Taylor, Paul. "Savings Bank Life Insurance," 61-69.
Shepherd, Pearce. "War Clauses In Life Insurance," 75-82.

Journal of Risk and Insurance
Volume 8, 1941

Berolzheimer, Howard, Edwin A. Gaumnitz, C. M. Kahler and Joseph Pillion. "Round Table Discussion: The Objectives And Content Of The Survey Course In Insurance," 5-38.
Havighurst, Harold C. "State Vs. Federal Regulation Of Insurance," 57-67.

Journal of Risk and Insurance
Volume 9, 1942

Huebner, S. S. "Report Of Committee On Professional Standards In Property And Casualty Insurance," 5-16.
Loman, Harry J. "Report Of Committee On Collegiate Preparation For Insurance Careers," 17-19.
Hedges, J. Edward. "Report Of Publications Committee," 20-21.
Harvey, Julien H. "The Place Of Manpower In Our Victory Program," 22-28.
Bielaski, A. Bruce. "The Risk Of Arson," 29-38.
Winter, William D. "Marine Insurance In A World At War," 39-44.
Hill, Reese F. "The Role Of Insurance In The Defense Program," 45-52.
Parry, Corliss L. "The Insurance Industry In Defense And War Finance," 53-62.
Field, Kenneth. "The Impact Of Federal Policies On Equity Capital," 63-72.

Journal of Risk and Insurance
Volume 10, 1943

Huebner, S. S. "The College Of Property And Casualty Underwriters: A Report Of Progress," 5-18.
Breen, John M. "The Outlook For Automobile Insurance, " 19-25.
Reede, Arthur H. "The Impact Of The War Upon Workmen's Compensation Underwriting And Loss Prevention," 26-40.
O'Connor, James C. "Fire Insurance In Wartime," 41-45.
Magee, John H. "The Position Of The Government As An Insurer Of Ocean Marine War Risks," 46-58.
Sommer, Armand. "The War And Accident And Health Insurance," 59-68.
Goldin, A. J. "War Damage Insurance," 69-75.
Beck, Lester F. "Insurance Coverage For War Projects," 76-87.

Journal of Risk and Insurance
Volume 11, 1944

Jackson, Henry H. "Annuity Problems Today," 5-21.
Dickinson, Frank G. "Annuities For An Aging Population," 22-45.
Guertin, Alfred N. "The Standard Non-Forfeiture And Valuation Laws," 46-60.
Mitchell, Robert B. "Review Of Life Insurance In 1943," 61-71.

Journal of Risk and Insurance
Volume 12, 1945

Fisher, Paul S. "Group Accident And Health Insurance," 5-10.
Falk, I. S. "Long-Term Disability Insurance," 11-21.
Klem, Margaret C. "Prepayment Medical Care Organizations," 22-31.
Van Steenwyk, E. A. "Non-Profit Health Service Plans," 32-38.
Goldstein, Meyer M. "Employee Pension And Profit Sharing Plans," 39-53.

Journal of Risk and Insurance
Volume 13, 1946

Guertin, Alfred N. "Developments In Standard Non-Forfeiture And Valuation Legislation," 5-15.
Cover, Clyde J. "Developments In State Life Insurance Legislation Resulting From Public Law 15," 25-44.
Diemand, John A. "Developments In Comprehensive Property-Casualty Insurance (Multiple Line Underwriting)," 50-62.
Stone, Edward C. "Developments In Property-Casualty Insurance Legislation Resulting From Public Law 15," 63-70.
Dressel, Walter. "Some Post-War Insurance Problems," 74-79.

Journal of Risk and Insurance
Volume 14, 1947

McCahan, David and Harry J. Loman. "College Education For Insurance: A Minimum Program," 5-24.
Gravengaard, H. P. "Life Insurance Company Sales Training Programs," 25-35.

Bodine, William W. "Private Lending," 41-47.
Maine, Robert F. "Common Stocks As Life Insurance Investments," 48-54.
Sawyer, Elmer Warren. "Meeting The Problems Of Insurance As Interstate Commerce," 57-67.

Journal of Risk and Insurance
Volume 15, 1948

Gardiner, Harold. "A Life Company Training Program," 5-15.
Abbott, H. Paul. "A Property-Casualty Educational Program," 16-25.
Dickinson, Frank G. "Cost, Supply And Demand Problems Of Medical Care," 38-46.
Pike, Albert. "Commercial Group Medical-Hospitalization Covers," 47-51.
Ketchum, J. C. "Medical Society And Hospital-Sponsored Plans," 52-56.
Williamson, W. R. "Non-Governmental Medical Care Programs," 57-62.

Journal of Risk and Insurance
Volume 16, 1949

Kellogg, Chester M. "The Capacity Problem," 5-13.
Danforth, Warner C. "A Property Insurance Executive Views Education For Insurance On The University Level," 14-17.
Kenagy, H. G. "A Life Insurance Executive Looks At The Academic Program Of Education In Insurance," 18-20.
McCahan, David. "Report On Survey Of College And University Courses In Insurance And Related Subjects," 21-26.
Mehr, Robert I. "A University Professor's Viewpoint," 27-34.
Fraine, Harold G. "Direct Sale Of Security Issues," 40-56.
Vance, Eric C. "Direct Sales Of Large Industrial And Miscellaneous Bond Issues," 71-73.

Journal of Risk and Insurance
Volume 17, 1950

Carlson, Thomas O. "Statistical And Actuarial Procedures In Liability Insurance," 5-12.
Kormes, Mark. "Statistical Problems And Methods Of Pre-Paid Blue Cross And Blue Shield Hospital And Medical Plans," 13-23.
Irwin, Hampton H. "The University Teacher Looks At Company Educational Programs - Life Insurance," 56-64.
Kahler, Clyde M. "The University Teacher Looks At Company Educational Programs - Property and Casualty Insurance," 65-73.
Ringer, L. Ray. "My Reaction To Property And Casualty Insurance Education On The University Level," 74-78.
Metzger, C. B. "The Company Executive Looks At Life Insurance Instruction At The University Level," 79-85.
Randall, Jesse W. "Insurance - The American Way," 90-96.

Journal of Risk and Insurance
Volume 18, 1951

Kelsey, R. Wilfred. "Visual Aids In Life Insurance Teaching," 5-13.
Abbott, H. Paul. "Visual Aids In Property-Casualty Insurance Teaching," 14-27.
Jackson, Henry H. "The Half-Century In Personal Insurance," 35-45.
Mays, Milton W. "The Half-Century In Property-Casualty Insurance," 46-53.
McCahan, David. "The Half-Century In Insurance Education," 54-72.
Harris, Seymour E. "The British Experiment," 73-87.
Kulp, Clarence A. "Alternate Solutions: Voluntary And Compulsory Medical Care Insurance," 88-95.
Rothenberg, Jerome. "Welfare Implications Of Alternative Methods Of Financing," 96-106.

Journal of Risk and Insurance
Volume 19, 1952

Irwin, Hampton H. "Introducing And Developing Insurance In A Curriculum," 5-14.
Johnson, H. Clay. "The Impact Of Multiple Line Powers On The Insurance Industry," 21-28.
Miller, John H. "The Impact Of New Disability Coverages On The Life Insurance Companies," 29-39.
Anthony, Julian D. "Running A Life Insurance Company Is Fun," 40-47.

Journal of Risk and Insurance
Volume 20, 1953

Ivry, David A. "The Basic Survey Course In Insurance," 5-6.
Wherry, Ralph H. "The Basic Survey Course In Insurance," 7-8.
Beadles, William T. "The Basic Survey Course In Insurance," 9-11.
Lyons, Daniel J. "The Revision Of Section 213 - A Major Life Insurance Problem," 12-17.
McCarty, Spencer L. "The Revision Of Section 213 - A Major Life Insurance Problem," 18-23.
Leslie, William. "Automobile Insurance - A Major Property Insurance Problem," 24-28.
Breen, John M. "Automobile Insurance - A Major Property Insurance Problem," 29-34.
Bronson, Dorrance C. "The Concept Of Actuarial Soundness," 36-47.
Peterson, Ray M. "Actuarial Soundness In Pension Plans With Insurance Companies," 48-53.
Buck, George B. "Actuarial Soundness In Trusteed And Governmental Retirement Plans," 54-58.
Cohen, Edwin S. "Legal Implications Of Actuarial Soundness," 59-62.
Barkin, Solomon. "Labor's View Of Actuarial Requirements For Pension Plans," 63-69.
Williams, C. Arthur, Jr. "The Deductible In Medical Expense Insurance," 107-116.

Journal of Risk and Insurance
Volume 21, 1954

McGill, Dan. "The Basic Life Insurance Course In The Curriculum," 5-9.
Trosper, Joseph F. "The Basic Life Insurance Course In The Curriculum," 10-12.
Hedges, J. Edward. "The Basic Life Insurance Course In The Curriculum," 13-17.
Fischer, Carl H. "The Basic Life Insurance Course In The Curriculum," 18-21.
Wallace, S. Rains, Jr. "Research In Insurance," 22-26.
Lang, Frank. "Research In Insurance," 27-36.
Bickley, John S. "Research In Insurance," 37-42.
Lew, Edward A. "Insurance Mortality Investigations Of Physical Impairments," 43-55.
Myers, Robert J. "Factors In Interpreting Mortality After Retirement," 56-63.
Bohlinger, Alfred J. "1954 - The Year For Action," 64-70.
Greene, Mark R. "Life Insurance Buying In Inflation," 99-113.
Bickley, John S. "The Nature And Methodology Of The Insurance Survey Course," 114-117.

Journal of Risk and Insurance
Volume 22, 1955

Loman, Harry J. "College Education For Insurance: A Minimum Program," 5-18.
Hedges, J. Edward. "Teaching Insurance At An Advanced Level On The 'Line' Basis," 19-22.
Kulp, C. A. "Tomorrow In The Automobile Liability Business," 23-27.
Thore, Eugene M. "The Ingratiating Intervention," 40-51.

Journal of Risk and Insurance
Volume 23, 1956

Bowers, Edison L. "Teaching Social Insurance As A Course In The Insurance Curriculum," 5-16.
Zimmerman, Charles J. "The Place Of The College Graduate In Life Insurance Sales," 20-26.
Johnson, Holgar J. "The Place Of The College Graduate In Life Insurance Home Offices," 27-33.
Warfield, Guy T. "The Place Of The College Graduate In Property And Casualty Sales," 34-41.
Mays, Milton W. "The Place Of The College Graduate In Fire And Casualty Insurance Company Home Offices," 42-46.
Johnson, George E. "Some Answers To The Variable Annuity Puzzle," 47-54.
Dowell, Dudley. "Life Insurance In Its New Competitive Frame," 55-60.
Sellers, Richard M. "Life Insurance In Its New Competitive Frame," 61-68.
Herrick, Kenneth W. "Teaching The Basic Property And Casualty Course," 69-76.
Pfeffer, Irving. "A Survey Of Current Faculty Retirement Programs In American Universities And Colleges," 82-93.
Greenough, William C. "College Retirement Systems: Social Security And Variable Annuities," 94-105.
Farley, Jarvis. "Recent Developments In Sickness And Accident Insurance," 112-119.
Serbein, Oscar N. "Paying For Medical Care In The United States," 120-122.
Botts, Ralph R. "Federal Crop Insurance," 123-128.
Howard, William M. "Fire Insurance Written Under Perpetual Contracts," 129-134.
Adams, John F. "Research Dealing With The Financial Consequences Of Automobile Accidents," 135-141.
Hedges, Robert A. "Experiment In Financial Analysis Of Property Insurers," 142-146.
Wandel, William H. "Insurance Consumption Patterns," 147-151.
Long, John D. "Research On Property Agency Continuation," 152-156.

Journal of Risk and Insurance
Volume 24, 1957

Faulkner, E. J. "Meeting Health Care Costs Through Insurance," (1), 9-22.
Klarman, Herbert E. "Medical Care Costs And Voluntary Health Insurance," (1), 23-41.
Davidson, George F. "Canadian Programs For Meeting The Sickness Risks," (1), 42-60.
Newman, Monroe. "Issues In Temporary Disability Insurance," (1), 61-72.
Heins, Richard M. "Compensating The Automobile Accident Victim," (1), 73-100.
Wise, Paul S. "The Problem Of The Financially Irresponsible Motorist And The Uncompensated Accident Victim," (1), 101-113.
Lusby, R. Newell. "The Uninsured Motorist - Several Points Of View," (1), 114-122.
Mertz, Arthur C. "The Uninsured Motorist," (1), 123-132.
Rodda, William H. "Multiple Line Underwriting: Rating Methods," (1), 133-144.
McPherson, James Roland. "Multiple-Multiple Lines," (1), 145-150.
Tomlinson, C. E. "Business Contracts: Developments And Trends In Multiple Line Underwriting," (1), 151-157.
Bagby, Wesley S. "Automation In Insurance," (1), 158-167.
Austin, C. Henry. "The Integrated Insurance Department," (1), 168-173.
Roos, Nestor R. "Recent Federal Activity In Insurance Regulation," (1), 174-180.
Williams, C. Arthur, Jr. "Some Economic And Legal Aspects Of Insurance Rate Discrimination," (2), 9-23.

Solberg, Harry J. "The Profit Factor In Fire Insurance Rates," (2), 24-33.

Kedzie, Daniel P. "Marketing Consumer Credit Insurance," (2), 34-42.

McPherson, James Roland. "The Trillion Dollar Question," (2), 43-55.

Valenti, Raymond F. "Theoretical Approaches To Taxing Life Insurance Companies For Federal Income Tax Purposes," (2), 56-70.

Berridge, William A. "Economic Facts Bearing On Some 'Variable Annuity' Arguments: With Special Reference To Cyclical Price Fluctuations In Common-Stock And Consumer-Goods Markets," (2), 71-87.

Howard, William M. "A Note On Mortality Tables And Interest Rates," (2), 88-92.

Bakerman, Theodore. "Is The Insurance Industry Attracting Younger Men?," (2), 93-95.

Huebner, S. S. "Future Patterns Of Life Insurance Distribution - An Educator's View," (3), 9-20.

Zimmerman, Charles J. "Future Patterns Of Life Insurance Distribution - A Company View," (3), 21-31.

Rennie, Robert A. "Management's Approach To Alternative Methods Of Insurance Distribution," (3), 32-41.

Greene, Mark R. "Marketing Research As An Aid To Insurance Management," (3), 42-55.

Berridge, William A. "Economic Research As An Aid To Management Planning: A Case Study Of One Life Insurance Company," (3), 56-69.

Mehr, Robert I. "A Blueprint For Long-Range Planning By Insurance Companies," (3), 70-77.

Cockerell, H. A. L. "Insurance Education In Great Britain," (3), 78-85.

McGuinness, John S. "The Job Of Insurance Company Top Management," (4), 9-21.

Launstein, Howard C. "Managerial Accounting Tools For Casualty Insurance Companies," (4), 22-35.

Bakerman, Theodore. "How Old Is Top Management In Insurance Companies? The Data And Some Implications," (4), 36-44.

Athearn, James L. "Uncertainty And The OASI Program," (4), 45-63.

Fischer, Carl H. "Social Security In The Philippines," (4), 64-75.

Kline, Chester A. "A Visual Aids Program For The College Teacher Of Insurance," (4), 76-88.

Journal of Risk and Insurance
Volume 25, 1958

Guertin, Alfred N. "Price Competition In The Life Insurance Business," (1), 1-10.

McCullough, Roy C. "Philosophy And Background Of Multiple-Line Underwriting," (1), 11-14.

Perlet, Harry F. "Impact Of Multiple Line Underwriting On Coverages, Contracts, And Operating Results," (1), 15-22.

Mehr, Robert I. "A Philosophy Of Learning - A Summary View," (1), 23-25.

Ratcliffe, David T. "The Case Method Of Instruction In Insurance," (1), 26-31.

Daniels, Arthur C., Albert I. Hermalin, Alfred Cranwill and James R. Williams. "The Research Facilities Of The Institute Of Life Insurance," (1), 32-41.

Kenney, Roger. "Critique Of American Agency System," (1), 42-49.

Schwentker, Frank J. "The Life Insurance Agency System," (1), 50-60.

Davis, Shelby Cullom. "Impact Of Multiple Line Underwriting On The Capital Structure Of Insurance Companies," (1), 61-64.

Navarre, Joseph A. "Perfecting The System Of State Regulation Of The Business Of Insurance," (1), 65-68.

Hooley, Richard W. "Life Insurance Investments In Natural Gas Pipelines," (2), 1-9.

Houston, David B. "Deficiency Reserves And The X17 Mortality Table," (2), 10-21.

Mayerson, Allen L. "Is A New Mortality Table Needed?," (2), 22-36.

Eggertsen, Paul. "Some Aspects Of Denmark's Insurance Industry," (2), 37-46.

Hardin, Rector R. "Contributions Of Life Insurance To Capital Formation In The South," (2), 47-52.

Center, Charles C. "A Philosophical Approach To Student Insurance Societies," (2), 53-57.

Strain, Robert W. "The Insurance Society As An Integral Part Of An Insurance Program," (2), 58-63.

Larson, Robert E. "Note On The Education Of Actuarial Students," (2), 64-66.

Davis, Ralph C. "A Philosophy Of Management," (3), 1-7.

McWhorter, Suzanne S. "Advertising And Public Relations Activities Of Insurance Companies: With Special Emphasis On Health Insurers," (3), 8-20.

Allan, W. Scott. "Rehabilitation As A Practical Insurance Program," (3), 21-28.

Valenti, Raymond F. "Taxation Of Life Insurance Companies: The Treasury Proposal," (3), 29-38.

McAuliff, Joseph L. "The Impact Of Selected Socio-Economic Factors On Life Insurance: A Case Study Of Arkansas," (3), 39-42.

Shelton, David H. "Private Insurance In Latin America: Prospects And Problems," (3), 43-56.

Mittelman, Jonas E. "Liability Insurance For Private And Public Schools," (3), 57-61.

Gregg, Davis W. "A Note On Insurance Terminology," (3), 62-64.

Hedges, Bob A. "Evaluation Of Property Insurance Companies' Expense Ratios," (4), 1-16.

Johnson, George E. "The Market For Equity Annuities," (4), 17-21.

Greene, Mark R. "Federal Income Taxes And The Variable Annuitant," (4), 22-27.

Strain, Robert W. "The Impact Of Increased Life Insurance Purchases On The Consumption Function," (4), 28-31.

Bickley, John H. "The Nature Of Business Risk," (4), 32-42.

Newman, Monroe. "Joint Administration Of Social Insurance Programs," (4), 43-50.

Quantius, Frances. "Federal Loan Insurance: Its Relation To Federal Reserve Policy," (4), 51-54.

Krogh, Harold C. "Faculty Retirement And Insurance Programs In Midwestern Universities," (4), 55-60.

Muller-Lutz, Heinz L. "Property-Liability Insurance Distribution In Germany," (4), 61-69.

Toelle, R. Maynard. "A Commentary On Foreign Insurance Practices," (4), 70-75.

Gregg, Davis W. "A Note On The Desirability Of Organizing An International Society Of Insurance," (4), 76-78.

Leganger, Gunnar. "A Note On The Norwegian School Of Insurance," (4), 79-81.

Journal of Risk and Insurance
Volume 26, 1959

Loman, Harry J. "The Insurance Curriculum," (1), 1-7.

Blanchard, Ralph H. "Risk As A Special Subject Of Study," (1), 8-11.

Trosper, Joseph F. "A Challenge To AAUTI Members," (1), 12-15.

Cowee, John W. "Insurance Company Taxation - A General Review," (1), 16-19.

Hogg, Robert L. "Taxation Of Life Insurance Companies," (1), 20-30.

Haskell, George D. "Taxation Of Property And Casualty Insurance Companies," (1), 31-39.

Hansen, Victor R. "Insurance And The Antitrust Laws," (1), 40-48.

Gerber, Joseph F. "A Regulator Faces The Facts," (1), 49-56.

O'Connor, James C. "All-Line Insurance," (1), 57-60.

Dickinson, Frank D. "Health Insurance For Retired Persons," (1),61-64.

Dickerson, O. D. "The Problem Of Overutilization In Health Insurance," (1), 65-72.

Elkin, Philip. "A Report On A Study To Estimate The Financial Loss Proximatley Caused By Automobile Operations In New Jersey," (1), 73-75.

Krogh, Harold C., W. O. Bryson, Jr., William M. Howard and Robert M. Stevenson. "The Insurance Curriculum In Collegiate Business Education," (1), 76-81.

Graebner, Herbert C. "Some Thoughts On A Life Insurance Internship Program," (2), 1-6.

Weimer, Arthur M. "Suggestions Regarding Education For Business," (2), 7-12.

Williams, C. Arthur, Jr. "Workmen's Compensation And The Handicapped," (2), 13-28.

Gerdes, Victor. "International Compulsory Automobile Insurance," (2), 29-34.

Bickley, John H. "Public Utility Stability And Risk," (2), 35-58.

McDiarmid, F. J. "Inflation And Life Insurance," (2), 59-62.

Bakerman, Theodore. "Selected Unemployment Compensation Benefit Problems: Disregarded Earnings And The Determination Of Labor Force Status," (2), 63-68.

Beadles, William T. "Control Of Abuses Under Credit Life And Health Insurance," (3), 1-12.

Houston, David B. "A Comparison Of Mortality Rates Of Insured Lives With Those Of The General Population," (3), 13-24.

Adams, John F. "Some Observations On Experience Rating In Unemployment Insurance," (3), 25-32.

Schultz, Raymond G. "Investment Income And Casualty Insurance Profits," (3), 33-40.

Roos, Nestor R. "Life Insurance In Mexico," (3), 41-56.

Prochazka, Jaroslav. "Insurance In Czechoslovakia," (3), 57-60.

Launstein, Howard C. "The Agent's Responsibility For Developing Sound Insurance Programs," (3), 61-68.

Bryson, W. O., Jr. "The Negro Insurance Market In Baltimore, 1957," (3), 69-74.

Quantius, Frances. "Duplication Of Government Insurance In Commercial Banks," (3), 75-78.

Dickerson, O. D. "The Insurance Curriculum: Retrospect And Prospect," (4), 1-10.

Houston, David B. "Elizur Wright: The Man And His Work," (4), 11-36.

Dover, Victor. "Forty Years In Insurance Education," (4), 37-50.

Soldofsky, Robert M. "Private Placement Loans For Small Business," (4), 51-58.

Byrne, Mother Martin. "The Role Of Life Insurance Companies In Financing Religious Institution Expansion," (4), 59-64.

Sevier, John C. "Life Insurance Reserves And Aggregate Savings," (4), 65-68.

Myers, John H. "Federal Taxation Of Fire And Casualty Insurance Companies," (4), 69-71.

Journal of Risk and Insurance
Volume 27, 1960

Neal, Robert R. "Current Developments And Problems In Health Insurance," (1), 1-10.

Myers, Robert J. "Current Developments And Problems In Social Insurance," (1), 11-22.

Kelly, Ambrose B. "Current Developments And Problems In Property Insurance," (1), 23-28.

Thore, Eugene M. "Current Developments And Problems In Life Insurance," (1), 29-36.

Flemming, Arthur S. "Social Insurance: A Prospective View," (1), 37-42.

Buchan, Leslie J. "The Place Of Insurance In The Collegiate Curriculum Orientation Address," (1), 43-52.

Solomon, Robert J. "Testing Techniques In Insurance," (1), 53-64.

Herrick, Kenneth W. "Credit Life And Health Insurance In Texas," (1), 65-76.

Houston, David B. "Risk Theory," (1), 77-82.

Bakerman, Theodore. "OASI Statistics - A Program For Insurance Industry Employment Research," (1), 83-90.

Greenough, William C. "Variable Annuities Through CREF," (1), 91-104.

Cleveland, Harold Van B. "The Status Of Self Insured Employee-Benefit Plans Under The Insurance Laws," (2), 1-16.

Wagner, Ludwig A. and Theodore Bakerman. "Wage Earner's Opinions Of Insurance Fringe Benefits," (2), 17-28.

Athearn, James L. "The Structure Of The Life Insurance Industry," (2), 29-36.

Wermel, Michael T. "The Role Of Management In Retirement Preparation Programs," (2), 37-44.

Follmann, J. F., Jr. "Some Medico-Economic Trends," (2), 45-58.
Alrich, William. "Substantive Report Of The AAUTI Census Committee," (2), 59-64.
Wandel, William H. "Rising Medical Care Costs With Special Reference To Hospital Expenses," (2), 65-68.
Schwentker, Frank J. "The Structure Of Life Insurance Agents' Compensation," (2), 69-72.
Carton, John H. "The Assigned Risk As A Separate Classification," (2), 73-80.
Trosper, Joseph F. "Appraising The Life Value For Key Man Life Insurance," (2), 81-92.
MacDonald, D. L. "Life Insurance: A Study In Location Of Industry," (2), 93-100.
Williams, Walter. "A Comment On Insurance And The Consumption Function," (2), 109-112.
Roberts, Mark O. "Mandatory Pretrial Disclosure Of Automobile Liability Insurance Limits," (3), 1-6.
Provost, Theodore E. "Payment Of Claims Under The Uniform Simultaneous Death Acts," (3), 7-18.
Nilsen, James B. "The Use Of Formula Timing Plans For Investment By Property And Casualty Insurance Companies," (3), 19-28.
Valenti, Raymond F. "The 1959 Insurance Company Tax Law - Attitudes And Insights," (3), 29-36.
Snider, H. Wayne. "Population, Prejudice And Pensions," (3), 37-42.
Williams, Walter. "Insurance As A Segment Of The Liberal Business Education," (3), 43-48.
Bakerman, Theodore. "OASI Statistics - A Program For Insurance Industry Employment Research," (3), 49-54.
Jung, Allen F. "Charges For Credit Life Insurance In Major Cities," (3), 55-60.
Mittelman, Jonas E. "Automobile Insurance Commission Litigation," (3), 61-66.
Arbuckle, Ernest C., Richard L. Kozelka and Arthur M. Weimer. "Dean's Forum: The Place Of Insurance In The Collegiate Curriculum," (3), 67-70.
Dickinson, Frank G. "The Social Security Principle," (4), 1-14.
Cohen, Wilbur J. "The Challenge Of Aging To Insurance," (4), 15-18.
Marples, William F. "Pensions And The Cost Of Living," (4), 19-32.
Even, John T. "Notes From A Graduate Course In Insurance Administration," (4), 33-46.
Williams, C. Arthur, Jr. "Game-Theory And Insurance Consumption," (4), 47-56.
Schultz, Robert E. and Raymond G. Schultz. "The Regulation Of Life Insurance Company Investments," (4), 57-62.
Lent, George E. "A More Permanent Formula For The Taxation Of Life Insurance," (4), 63-74.
Otjen, Theo P. and Arthur J. Pabst. "Updating Life Insurance Settlement Options," (4), 75-84.
Bagby, Wesley S. "Insurance, Automation, And The Individual Employee," (4), 85-90.
Chastain, James J. "The A, B, Cs Of Life Insurance Rate And Reserve Computation," (4), 91-98.
Farmer, Lee R. "Exploration Of A New Era Of Insurance: Dental Insurance," (4), 99-102.
Grimley, Cecil A. "Supervision Of Insurance In Australia," (4), 103-108.
Conley, Howard H. "Factors Influencing The Training Of Life Insurance Salesmen," (4), 109-112.
Gaumnitz, Erwin A., George E. Manners, James R. Surface, Maurice W. Lee and Paul Garner. "Dean's Forum: The Place Of Insurance In The Collegiate Curriculum," (4), 113-120.
Gregg, Davis W. and Mechthild K. Longo. "Insurance Education Abroad," (4), 121-125.

Journal of Risk and Insurance
Volume 28, 1961

Hedges, J. Edward. "Presidential Address," (1), 1-6.
Dickerson, O. D. "Potential Innovations In Health Insurance," (1), 7-20.
Faulkner, E. J. "Potential Innovations In Health Insurance," (1), 21-26.
Gerdes, Victor. "Application Of The Theory Of Marketing Tangible Goods To The Marketing Of Insurance," (1), 27-28.
Cordell, Warren N. "Application Of The Theory Of Marketing Tangible Goods To The Marketing Of Insurance," (1), 29-34.
Miner, Robert B. "Application Of The Theory Of Marketing Tangible Goods To The Marketing Of Insurance," (1), 35-40.
Johnson, Raymond C. "Application Of The Theory Of Marketing Tangible Goods To The Marketing Of Insurance," (1), 41-44.
Pierce, Frederic M. "The Responsibility Of The Insurance Industry," (1), 45-52.
Otto, Ingolf H. E. "Capacity," (1), 53-70.
Williams, C. Arthur, Jr. "Analyzing The Expenses Incurred By Private Workmen's Compensation Insurers," (1), 71-82.
Rennie, Robert A. "The Measurement Of Risk," (1), 83-92.
Greene, Mark R. "Application Of Mathematics To Insurance And Risk Management," (1), 93-104.
Otto, Ingolf H. E. "The British Insurance Scene," (1), 105-111.
Baker, Richard. "Emotional Factors In Marketing Insurance," (2), 1-10.
Hansen, Knud. "The Reinsurance Game - A Tool For Education And Research," (2), 11-18.
Hoffman, William H., Jr. "Tax Planning And The Deferred Pay Contract," (2), 19-28.
Chastain, James J. "Teaching Techniques: Property Insurance Contract Analysis," (2), 29-34.
Osborn, Grant. "Teaching The Analysis Of Financial Statements," (2), 35-40.
Snider, H. Wayne. "Teaching Risk Management," (2), 41-44.
Nichols, Archie. "The Liquidation Of Insurance Carriers In The Commonwealth Of Pennsylvania," (2), 45-50.
Schwarzchild, Stuart. "Rights Of Creditors In Life Insurance Policies," (2), 51-58.
Mehr, Robert I. and George R. Jordan. "A Life Adjustment Policy," (2), 59-70.
Hedges, Bob. "Proper Limits In Liability Insurance," (2), 71-76.
Williams, Walter. "Measuring The Macroeconomic Effects Of Life And Health Insurance," (2), 77-82.

Houston, David B. "The Effectiveness Of Rating Classifications," (2), 83-86.
Bakerman, Theodore. "OASI Statistics: A Program For Insurance Industry Employment Research, Part III," (2), 87-92.
Athearn, James L. "Self Insuring The Workmen's Compensation Risk: A Case Study," (2), 93-96.
Abel, Burl M. "Tools For Recruiting College Men For Life Insurance," (2), 97-98.
Krogh, Harold C. "Accident Proneness And The Uninsured Motorist," (2), 99-102.
Malisih, Harry. "The Insurance Principle And Unemployment Insurance," (2), 103-106.
Alrich, William. "Problems In Defining 'All Lines' Insurance," (2), 107-110.
Williamson, W. Rulon. "The Social Security Principle: Comment," (2), 111-114.
Peterson, Ray M. "The Social Security Principle: Comment," (2), 115-119.
Myers, Robert J. "The Social Security Principle: Comment," (2), 120-122.
Dickinson, Frank G. "The Social Security Principle: Reply," (2), 123-127.
Blaisdell, Paul H. "20,000 Aids To Students Of Insurance," (2), 128.
Gould, Jay M. "The Sanborn Buying Power Maps," (2), 129-130.
Lampman, Robert J. and S. F. Miyamoto. "Effects Of Coverage Of Home And Office Calls In A Physician-Sponsored Health Insurance Plan," (3), 1-16.
Feight, James S. "Blue Cross And The Community Health Problem," (3), 17-24.
Applebaum, Leon. "The Development Of Voluntary Health Insurance In The United States," (3), 25-34.
Borch, Karl. "Some Elements Of A Theory Of Reinsurance," (3), 35-44.
Dickerson, O. D., Shriniwas K. Katti and Alfred E. Hofflander. "Loss Distributions In Non-Life Insurance," (3), 45-54.
Long, John D. "Proposal For A New Course: Risk In The Enterprise System," (3), 55-64.
Ivry, David A. "Historical Development Of Some Basic Life Insurance Terminology," (3), 65-70.
Felton, Robert S. "Retaliatory Insurance Company Taxation: An Evaluation," (3), 71-80.
Fonseca, John R. "The Impact Of Automation On Insurance Education And Management," (3), 81-88.
Schmidt, Richard F. "Does A Deductible Curb Moral Hazard?," (3), 89-92.
Peterson, Ray M. "The Challenge Of Aging To Insurance: Comment," (3), 93-97.
Cohen, Wilbur J. "The Challenge Of Aging To Insurance: Reply," (3), 98-101.
Dickerson, O. D. "Monetary Values For The C.S.A. Table: Comment," (3), 102-104.
Chastain, James J. "Monetary Values For The C.S.A. Table: Reply," (3), 105-106.
Magarick, Patrick. "Training Problems Involved In The Handling Of Foreign Claims," (3), 107-109.
Ulfers, D. D. "Insuring The Senior Citizen - A Case Study," (4), 1-12.
Bombaugh, Robert L. "The Economic Significance Of Loss Shifting In The United States," (4), 13-22.
Belth, Joseph M. "The Cost Of Life Insurance To The Policyowner - A Single Year Attained Age System," (4), 23-32.
Lassiter, Roy L., Jr. "The Wife's Contribution To Family Income," (4), 33-40.
Lay, Paul E. "Common Stock Investments Of Mutual Fire And Casualty Insurance Companies," (4), 41-48.
Schultz, Raymond G. and Robert E. Schultz. "The Regulation Of Multiple-Line Insurance Company Investments," (4), 49-56.
Hall, Charles P., Jr. "Compensation Of Executives In The Insurance Industry," (4), 57-64.
Stalnaker, Armand C. "A Look At The Future Life Agency Force," (4), 65-72.
Johnson, Alton C. and Roger T. Reinemann. "Recruiting Practices And Attitudes In Selected Insurance Companies," (4), 73-78.
Sarason, Harry M. "Association Insurance," (4), 79-84.
Diaz, Manuel Orlando. "The Spanish Average System Of Insurance And Loss Prevention," (4), 85-92.
Smith, R. Lee. "Life Insurance Language - Past And Present," (4), 93-98.
Dickerson, O. D. "The Reinsurance Game - A Tool For Education And Research: Comment," (4), 99.
Hansen, Knud. "The Reinsurance Game - A Tool For Education And Research: Reply," (4), 100-104.
Dickerson, O. D. "The S.O.B.'s," (4), 105-116.
Otto, Ingolf H. E. "The Hierarchic Hubris Of Abstractions," (4), 117-123.

Journal of Risk and Insurance
Volume 29, 1962

Gregg, Davis W. "And The Truth Shall Make Us Free," (1), 1-6.
Cohen, Wilbur J. "Health Insurance And The Government," (1), 7-18.
Kimball, Spencer J. "The Goals Of Insurance Law: Means Versus Ends," (1), 19-30.
Mehr, Robert I., R. W. Osler and Meyer Melnikoff. "Has The Life Insurance Company Product Become Obsolete?," (1), 31-48.
Belth, Joseph M. "The Question Of Life Company Ownership Of A Property-Liability Subsidiary," (1), 49-56.
Bakerman, Theodore. "Development Of Statistics Of The Insurance Industry By Government," (1), 57-68.
Kellogg, Chester M. "Joint ARIA-IASA Program," (1), 69-74.
Earnest, Robert C. and John J. Andrews. "A Comparison Of The Federal Deposit Insurance Corporation And The Federal Savings And Loan Insurance Corporation," (1), 75-86.
Denenberg, Herbert S. "The Right To Income: Social Insurance Versus Public Assistance," (1), 87-98.
Jung, Allen F. "Credit Life Insurance Charges In Selected Areas," (1), 99-106.
Levine, Louis. "University Consultation On Employment Security - A Cooperative Venture," (1), 107-114.

Rokes, Willis P. "The Role Of The Sales Finance Company Insurance Affiliate In Writing Automobile Insurance," (1), 115-122.

Chapman, F. P. "A Life Adjustment Policy: Comment," (1), 123-124.

Knepper, William E. "Law, Insurance And The Automobile Accident Victim," (2), 159-168.

Fougner, Arne. "Rehabilitation For Automobile Accident Victims," (2), 169-176.

Rennie, Robert A. "An Experiment In Limited Absolute Liability," (2), 177-184.

McCrae, William. "Legal Aspects Of Automobile Compensation," (2), 185-198.

Malisoff, Harry. "Duration Issues In Unemployment Insurance," (2), 199-204.

Mittelman, Jonas E. "The Electronics Age In Life Insurance," (2), 205-220.

Foody, Walter M. and Eldon J. Klaassen. "Financing Medical Care For The Aged," (2), 221-228.

Belth, Joseph M. "Participating Life Insurance - The Stock Company Version," (2), 229-238.

Johnson, Alton C. and Roger T. Reinemann. "Reactions Of Students And Agents To Recruiting Practices," (2), 239-244.

McClelland, Harold F. "Do Variable Annuities Have A Tax Advantage?," (2), 245-255.

Cocheu, Lincoln C., Jr. "Association Insurance: Comment," (2), 265-268.

Overman, Edwin S. "Evolution Of A Science - An Introduction," (3), 305-320.

Childress, Donald R. "Contributions To Risk And Insurance Theory From The Field Of Philosophy," (3), 321-328.

Athearn, James L. "Contributions To Risk And Insurance Theory From The Field Of Economics," (3), 329-342.

Howard, William M. "Mathematical Contributions To Risk And Insurance Theory," (3), 343-350.

Lynn, Arthur D., Jr. "Contributions To Risk And Insurance Theory From The Field Of Law," (3), 351-354.

Williams, Walter. "The Life Insurance-Consumer Saving Relationship," (3), 355-372.

Rokes, Willis P. "The Saskatchewan Plan," (3), 373-384.

Eilers, Robert D. "The Fundamental Nature Of Blue Cross And Blue Shield," (3), 385-402.

Follmann, J. F., Jr. "Experience Rating Vs. Community Rating," (3), 403-416.

Floyd, Joe S., Jr. "Rate Of Return And Allocation Of Life Insurance Company Investments," (3), 417-423.

Moorhead, E. J. and Herbert S. Bright. "Cost Of Life Insurance To The Policyholder: Comment," (3), 424-426.

Belth, Joseph M. "Cost Of Life Insurance To The Policyholder: Reply," (3), 427-429.

Greene, Mark R. "Marketing Efficiency And Workmen's Compensation - A Case Study," (4), 467-502.

Hammond, J. D. "Pension Financing In Corporate Consolidations," (4), 503-516.

Ramey, W. J. "Anti-Selection Of Agents Through Selection Of Field Management," (4), 517-522.

Adams, John F. "Law, Insurance, And The Automobile Accident Victim - Social And Economic Aspects," (4), 523-532.

Rejda, George E. "The Role Of Dollar Averaging In The Common Stock Investment Operations Of Life Insurance Companies," (4), 533-546.

Athearn, James L. "Economic Significance Of Insurance Activity In The United States," (4), 547-551.

Myers, Robert J. "Insuring The Senior Citizen - A Case Study: Comment," (4), 556.

Overman, Edwin S. "The Most Appropriate Generic Term To Identify The Property-Casualty Field Of Insurance," (4), 558-566.

Cristy, James. "A Risk Manager Looks At Curricular Concepts In Risk And Insurance," (4), 567-568.

Leslie, William, Jr. "Comments Concerning Curricular Concepts," (4), 569-570.

Journal of Risk and Insurance
Volume 30, 1963

McGrath, Earl J. "College Schools Of Business: A Further Appraisal," (1), 1-10.

Thore, Eugene M. "The Washington Scene," (1), 11-16.

Carlson, T. O. "Trends In Casualty Insurance Rate Making," (1), 17-22.

Longley-Cook, L. H. "Trends In Property Insurance Rate Making," (1), 23-28.

Williams, C. Arthur, Jr. "Trends In Property And Liability Insurance Rate Making: An Academic Viewpoint," (1), 29-34.

Fraine, Harold G. "Criticism Of Requirements For Valuation Of Life Insurance Company Security Holdings," (1), 35-46.

Cristy, James. "Organizational Problems In Control Of The Risk Of Accidental Loss And Management Of Employee Benefit Plans," (1), 47-52.

Moeller, Charles. "New Areas For Research - Some Practical Aspects," (1), 53-60.

Snider, H. Wayne. "Inland Marine Rating And Rate Regulation," (1), 61-80.

Belth, Joseph M. "The Replacement Problem In Life Insurance - With Special Emphasis On Comparative Costs," (1), 81-96.

Applebaum, Leon. "Collectively Bargained Health Insurance Plans In Milwaukee County," (1), 97-100.

Crum, Lawrence L. and James L. Athearn. "An Experiment In Central Banking For Life Insurance Companies," (1), 101-108.

Roos, Nestor R. "The Fundamental Nature Of Blue Cross And Blue Shield: Comment," (1), 109-111.

Williams, C. Arthur, Jr. "Social Insurance - Proper Terminology?," (1), 112-128.

Greene, Mark R., John W. McPherrin and Herbert W. Florer. "Curricular Concepts In Risk And Insurance," (1), 129-132.

Greene, Mark R. "Attitudes Toward Risk And A Theory Of Insurance Consumption," (2), 165-182.

Murray, Merrill G. "Social Insurance Perspectives: Background Philosophy And Early Program Developments," (2), 183-196.

Faulkner, E. J. "Social Security And Insurance - Some Relationships In Perspective," (2), 197-218.

Blyth, John W. "Programmed Learning," (2), 219-228.

Wickman, James A. "The Case Method," (2), 229-236.

Tootle, Columbus E. "Doctoral Dissertations In Insurance And Closely Related Fields, 1940-1962," (2), 237-244.

Spaid, Oricon M. "The Calculated Risk In Business," (2), 245-256.

Brainard, Calvin H. "A Comparison And Integration Of Economic And Actuarial Explanations Of Life Insurance Premium Computations," (2), 257-268.

Ratcliffe, Davis T. "Risk," (2), 269-272.

Rogers, Paul P. "A Survey Of Insurance In The USSR," (2), 273-280.

Snider, H. Wayne. "Educational Requirements For Agents' Licensing," (2), 281-285.

Kelly, Ambrose B. "Confusion Thrice Confounded," (2), 286-288.

Long, John D. "Curricular Concepts In Risk And Insurance," (2), 289-294.

Denenberg, Herbert S. "The Legal Definition Of Insurance," (3), 319-344.

Williams, C. Arthur, Jr. "Competitive Bidding And Municipal Property And Liability Insurance," (3), 345-362.

Harms, Louis T. "Philosophical Preconceptions And The Social Security System," (3), 363-376.

Bakerman, Theodore. "Unable To Work: A Study Of Socio-Economic Influence On The Census Statistic In A Selected Area," (3),377-384.

Elkin, Philip. "The Future Family Economic Unit: Economic And Social Security Perspectives," (3), 385-392.

Solomon, E. Ray. "Inheritance Taxation Of Life Insurance," (3), 393-402.

Abelle, Barnie E., Jr. "An Evaluation Of The Life Insurance Company Income Tax Act Of 1959," (3), 403-422.

Crane, Frederick G. "Public Control Of Automobile Insurance Rate Adequacy And Excessiveness," (3), 423-432.

Alrich, William M. and William B. Buckman. "Debit Insurance," (3), 433-446.

Rogers, George E. "The Risk Manager And Insurance Legislation," (3), 447-450.

Gregg, Davis W. "A Progress Report," (3), 451-453.

Gregg, Davis W. "A Terminology Note," (3), 454-455.

Melone, Joseph J. "Actuarial Cost Methods - New Pension Terminology," (3), 456-464.

Long, John D. "Curricular Concepts In Risk And Insurance," (3), 465-472.

Eilers, Robert E. "Inter-Insurer Arrangements To Provide Over-65 Medical Care Coverage," (4), 483-504.

Melone, Joseph J. "Are Non-Insured Pension Plans Engaged In The Business Of Insurance?," (4), 505-516.

Felton, Robert S. "An Analysis Of The Adjustments To The Tax Base In State Taxation Of Fire And Casualty Insurance Companies," (4), 517-524.

Rejda, George E. "The Impact Of The Business Cycle On New Life Insurance Purchases," (4), 525-534.

Dover, Victor. "Vocational Education In Insurance," (4), 535-546.

Gerdes, Victor. "Insuring The Flood Peril," (4), 547-554.

Salzman, Gary. "Murder, Wagering, And Insurable Interest In Life Insurance," (4), 555-562.

Snider, H. Wayne. "Problems Of Professionalism," (4), 563-572.

Jung, Allen F. "Rate Variations Among Suppliers Of Automobile Insurance," (4), 573-576.

Thomas, Roy E. "The Mexican Automobile Insurance Problem For Tourists," (4), 577-581.

Anderson, Ronald T. "Educational Requirements For Agent's Licensing: Comment," (4), 582-583.

Myers, Robert J. "Some Factual Points On Papers Dealing With Social Insurance And Social Security Perspective," (4), 584-586.

McIntosh, Kenneth L. "Risk: Comment," (4), 587-589.

Carlson, Thomas O. "Risk: Comment," (4), 590-592.

Tootle, Columbus E. "Supplement To Doctoral Dissertations In Insurance And Closely Related Fields, 1940-1962," (4), 593-594.

Aponte, Juan B. and Herbert S. Denenberg. "Life Insurance And The Investment Texts," (4), 595-605.

Journal of Risk and Insurance
Volume 31, 1964

Nelli, Humbert O. "Insurance Transactions And The U.S. Balance Of Payments," (1), 1-12.

Bickelhaupt, David L. "Insurance And The European Common Market: Faction, Fiction Or Fancy?," (1), 13-26.

Greene, Mark R. "Insurance Mindedness' - Implications For Insurance Theory," (1), 27-38.

Walker, R. W. "Writing A Life Insurance Policy," (1), 39-50.

Norgaard, Richard L. "What Is A Reciprocal?," (1), 51-62.

Hall, Charles P. "Special Risks Health Insurance: Partial Solution To Growing Bodily Injury Awards?," (1), 63-72.

Wenck, Thomas L. "Standard Hospitalization Insurance Contracts," (1), 73-82.

Wood, Oliver G. "Evolution Of The Concept Of Risk," (1), 83-92.

Hashmi, Sajjad A. "Unsatisfied Judgment Funds," (1), 93-110.

Seligman, Barnard. "A Note On Cost Of Living Adjustment In Annuities," (1), 111-112.

Denenberg, Herbert S. "Science, Government And Information," (1), 113-116.

Hogan, John D. "Western European Capital Markets And The Role Of Life Insurance Companies," (2), 157-168.

Gerdes, Victor. "The Insurance Worker In The Labor Movement," (2), 169-178.

Crowe, Robert M. "Rate Making For Automobile Physical Damage Insurance," (2), 179-192.

Schultz, Raymond G. "Trends In Life Insurance Company Competition For Pension Funds," (2), 193-206.

Griffith, Reynolds. "A Note On Life Insurance Accounting," (2), 207-216.

Curry, Harold E. "Refinement Of Automobile Rate And Underwriting Classes," (2), 217-224.

Journal of Risk and Insurance
Volume 32, 1965

Journal of Risk and Insurance
Volume 33, 1966

Hekimian, James S. "A Profit Calculation For Agency Management," (1), 73-84.

Tracy, Myles A. "Insurance And Theology: The Background And The Issues," (1), 85-94.

Sichel, Werner. "Fire Insurance: Imperfectly Regulated Collusion," (1), 95-114.

Nye, William A. "The Case For Social Insurance In The Undergraduate Curriculum," (1), 115-124.

Josephson, Halsey D., Glenn L. Wood and C. Arthur Williams, Jr. "High Cash Value Life Insurance Policies And Unfair Discrimination: Comment," (1), 125-134.

Myers, Robert J. "An Actuarial Appraisal Of Congressional Proposals For Hospital Insurance For The Aged: Comment," (1), 135-138.

Keir, Jack C. "Cash Flow And Solvency Of Life Insurance Companies: Comment," (1), 139-144.

Bragg, John M. "Prices And Commissions Based On The Theory Of Games," (2), 169-194.

Rejda, George E. "Unemployment Insurance As An Automatic Stabilizer," (2), 195-208.

Lambert, Eugene W., Jr. and Alfred E. Hofflander. "Impact Of New Multiple Line Underwriting On Investment Portfolios Of Property-Liability Insurers," (2), 209-223.

Gerdes, Victor. "Social Security And Family Income Requirements," (2), 225-236.

Countryman, Gary L. "A Study Of Fire And Casualty Stock Price Determination With Some Price Movement Implications," (2), 237-252.

Hall, Charles P., Jr. "Deductibles In Health Insurance: An Evaluation," (2), 253-264.

Molnar, Daniel E. and T. H. Rockwell. "Analysis Of Policy Movement In A Merit-Rating Program: An Application Of Markov-Processes," (2), 265-276.

Frahm, Donald R. "The Domestic Excess And Surplus Market," (2), 277-284.

Friedman, Lloyd K., Harold A. Jensen, Jr., Spencer L. Kimball and Jon S. Hanson. "The Regulation Of Specialty Policies In Life Insurance: Comment," (2), 305-316.

Rejda, George E., Joseph M. Belth and Glenn L. Wood. "Life Insurance Policy Loans: The Emergency Fund Concept: Comment," (2), 317-328.

Leavitt, Gordon and Calvin H. Brainard. "Reviews Of 'Savings Bank Life Insurance': Comment," (2), 329-332.

Myers, Robert J. "A Method Of Automatically Adjusting The Maximum Earnings Base Under OASDI: Author's Comment," (2), 333-335.

Wickman, James A. "Teachers, Computers, And Teaching," (2), 336-342.

Belth, Joseph M. "Price Competition In Life Insurance," (3), 365-379.

Hofflander, Alfred E. "The Human Life Value: An Historical Perspective," (3), 381-391.

Johnson, Harry Mack. "The Nature Of Title Insurance," (3), 393-410.

Williams, C. Arthur, Jr. and O. D. Dickerson. "Game-Theory And Insurance Consumption: The Worry Factor Revisited," (3), 411-426.

Schkade, Lawrence L. and George H. Menefee. "A Normative Model For Deductible Collision Insurance Selection," (3), 427-436.

Hickman, James C. and Douglas A. Zahn. "Some Mathematical Views Of Risk," (3), 437-446.

Strain, Robert W. "Insurance Pricing And Its Role In Relation To Economic Theory And Marketing Management," (3), 447-458.

Norgaard, Richard L. "A Monte Carlo Simulation In Insurance Company Portfolio Management," (3), 459-468.

Tootle, Columbus E. "Second Supplement To: Doctoral Dissertations In Insurance And Closely Related Fields, 1940-1962," (3), 469-470.

Horn, Ronald C. "Report Of The Committee On Curricular Concepts In Risk And Insurance," (3), 471-474.

Larson, Robert E. "The Actuarial Curriculum: Comment," (3), 475-477.

Fischer, Carl H. "The Actuarial Curriculum: Comment," (3), 477-478.

Hickman, James C. "The Actuarial Curriculum: Comment," (3), 478-480.

Crofts, Geoffrey. "The Actuarial Curriculum: Comment," (3), 480-482.

Black, Kenneth, Jr. and Eli A. Zubay. "The Actuarial Curriculum: Reply," (3), 482-483.

Townsend, Frederick S. "Insurance Stocks - Measuring Values And Earnings: Comment," (3), 485-488.

Graaskamp, James A. "Implications Of Vested Benefits In Private Pension Plans: Comment," (3), 489-494.

Malisoff, Harry. "Welfare And Social Insurance In A Great Society," (4), 513-527.

Hofflander, Alfred E. "The Human Life Value: A Theoretical Model," (4), 529-536.

Eilers, Robert D. "Blue Shield: Current Issues And Future Direction," (4), 537-552.

Osler, Robert W. and Harry M. Johnson. "Major Policy Provisions In Guaranteed Renewable Major Medical Expense Insurance," (4), 553-561.

Goshay, Robert C. "Net Income Taxation Of The Life Insurance Industry At The State Level," (4), 563-575.

Williams, C. Arthur, Jr. "Attitudes Toward Speculative Risks As An Indicator Of Attitudes Toward Pure Risks," (4), 577-586.

Carlson, Valdemar. "Institutional Change In A Welfare State: Sweden," (4), 587-596.

Pfeffer, Irving and Seev Neumann. "The Survival Probability Of A New Life Insurance Company," (4), 597-602.

Peterson, Ray M. "The Future Of Private Pension Plans," (4), 603-620.

Farmer, Richard N. "The Long Term Crisis In Life Insurance," (4), 621-630.

Keir, Jack C. "A Second Look At Programmed Learning In The C.L.U. Diploma Program," (4), 631-638.

Wickman, James A. "Salary Scales: An Aggregate Approach: Comment," (4), 639-640.

Hofflander, Alfred E., Jr. "Salary Scales: An Aggregate Approach: Reply," (4), 641-642.

Borg, Robert W. "An Employee Benefits Reporting Service," (4), 643-645.

Denenberg, Herbert S. and J. Robert Ferrari. "New Perspectives On Risk Management: The Search For Principles," (4), 647-660.

Adams, John F. "Some Observations On The Insurance Educator's Quest For Security," (1), 1-8.

Pfeffer, Irving and Seev Neumann. "The Survival Probability Of A New Life Insurance Company," (1), 9-13.

Bernstein, Merton C. "The Future Of Private Pension Plans," (1), 15-26.

Murray, Rogert F. "The Future Of Private Pensions: Some Economic Aspects," (1), 27-32.

Young, Howard. "Discussion Of Papers On The Future Of Private Pensions," (1), 33-37.

Harding, Forrest E. "The Standard Automobile Insurance Policy: A Study Of Its Readability," (1), 39-46.

Graaskamp, James. "Development And Structure Of Mortgage Loan Guaranty Insurance In The United States," (1), 47-68.

Reinmuth, Dennis F. "Managerial Control Of The Reciprocal: A Regulatory Void," (1), 69-80.

Fletcher, Linda Pickthorne. "Prepaid Drug Plans Sponsored By Pharmacists," (1), 81-94.

Mayerson, Allen L. "How To Rewrite An Insurance Code," (1), 95-120.

Gahin, Fikry S. "A Theory Of Pure Risk Management In The Business Firm," (1), 121-129.

Collier, James A. "Structuring The Beginning Insurance Course," (1), 131-134.

Myers, Robert J. "What Would `Medicare' Cost?: Comment," (1), 141-147.

Sanders, Barkev S. "What Would `Medicare' Cost?: Reply," (1), 148-166.

Bickley, John S. "An Overview Of Insurance Marketing," (2), 175-183.

Evans, Campbell K. "Financial Proportionality In Insurance Agencies," (2), 187-204.

Head, George L. "An Alternative To Defining Risk As Uncertainty," (2), 205-214.

Whitman, Andrew F. and Howard E. Thompson. "The Impact Of The 1959 Income Tax Act On Stock And Mutual Companies: A Simulation Study," (2), 215-230.

Stone, Gary K. "A Trend In Complaints Processed By State Insurance Departments," (2), 231-236.

Pursell, Garry L. "Rate Control And Government Competition In Australian Non-Life Insurance," (2), 237-254.

Beightler, Charles S. and Robert L. Street. "Profit Planning In Non-Life Insurance Companies Through The Use Of A Probability Model," (2), 255-268.

Soldofsky, Robert M. "College Retirement Benefit Planning: A Snare Of Uncertainty For All Concerned," (2), 269-288.

Bobbitt, H. Randolph, Jr. "The University Professor Of Insurance As Viewed By The Insurance Professor," (2), 289-300.

Luck, Thomas J. "The Insurance Industry And The Insurance Professor," (2), 301-304.

Gaumnitz, E. A. "Graduate Curriculum Planning In Risk," (2), 305-310.

Malisoff, Harry. "Social Insurance In The Liberal Arts Curriculum," (2), 311-314.

Welty, Dan M. "A Need For Federal Insurance Regulation," (2), 329-332.

Peet, William. "Should Consultants In Different Disciplines Merge?," (2), 333-334.

Projector, Murray. "A Profit Calculation For Agency Management: Comment," (2), 335-336.

Leverett, E. J., Jr. "A Profit Calculation For Agency Management: Comment," (2), 336-339.

Moorhead, E. J. "A Profit Calculation For Agency Management: Comment," (2), 339-341.

Hekimian, James. "A Profit Calculation For Agency Management: Reply," (2), 341-344.

Hofflander, Alfred E., and Richard Duvall. "Inflation And Sales Of Life Insurance," (3), 355-362.

Hashmi, Sajjad A. "The Problem Of The Uninsured Motorist: A Proposed Solution," (3), 363-370.

Denenberg, Herbert S. "Is `A-Plus' Really A Passing Grade? Insurer Risk Capacity And Financial Ratings," (3), 371-384.

Belth, Joseph M. "Calculation Of Life Insurance Gross Premiums," (3), 385-396.

Hammond, J. D., David B. Houston and Eugene R. Melander. "Determinants Of Household Life Insurance Premium Expenditures," (3), 397-408.

Braverman, Jerome D. "A Critique Of Credibility Tables," (3), 409-416.

O'Donnell, William. "Is Social Insurance A Profession?," (3), 417-422.

Schultz, Raymond C. "Administrative Issues In Workmen's Compensation," (3), 423-434.

Schwarzschild, Stuart. "A Model For Determining The Rate Of Return On Investment In Life Insurance Policies," (3), 435-444.

Best, Paul J. "Some Notes On The Soviet Foreign Insurance System," (3), 445-450.

Clickner, Edwin K. "Risk Management Principles Applied To Mortgage Lending," (3), 451-458.

Crowe, Robert M. and Ronald C. Horn. "The Meaning Of Risk," (3), 459-474.

Gupta, Om S. "A Note On Life Insurance Cash Values," (3), 475-476.

Mehr, Robert I. "New Settings For Old Stones," (3), 477-480.

Proschansky, Harris. "Anti-Insurance Activities," (3), 481-482.

Myers, Robert J. "Social Security And Family Income Requirements: Comment," (3), 483-484.

Belth, Joseph M. "A Note On The Consumers Union Life Insurance Series," (3), 485-490.

Long, John D. "The Future And Insurance - Presidential Address," (4), 515-523.

Pfeffer, Irving. "The Social Responsibility Of Insurance: A Case Study At Watts," (4), 525-537.

Belth, Joseph M. "Observations On Solvency In The Context Of Life Insurance Regulation," (4), 539-560.

Denenberg, Herbert S. "How To Rewrite An Insurance Code: Comment," (4), 561-574.

McHugh, Donald P. "Towards A Rational Regulatory System - Discussion," (4), 575-580.

Borch, Karl. "The Theory Of Control Processes Applied To Insurance Companies," (4), 581-592.

Journal of Risk and Insurance
Volume 39, 1972

Forbes, Stephen W. "Loss Reserve Valuations And Financial Results In Nonlife Insurance," (3), 369-382.
Gentry, James A. "Simulation Of The Financial Planning Process Of P-L Insurers," (3), 383-396.
Apilado, Vincent P. "Pension Funds, Personal Savings, And Economic Growth," (3), 397-404.
Johnson, Harry M. "The History Of British And American Fire Marks," (3), 405-418.
Howard, William M. "Florida Relative Values For Surgical And Medical Procedures," (3), 419-430.
Krogh, Harold C. "Insurer Post-Insolvency Guaranty Funds," (3), 431-450.
Stone, Gary K. "Insurance In The Undergraduate Curriculum," (3), 451-456.
Ratcliffe, Davis T. "The Omnibus Clause," (3), 457-458
Gahin, Fikry S. "Review Of The Literature On Risk Management," (3), 463-470.
Myers, Robert J. "The Family Assistance Plan As A Solution To The Welfare Crisis: Comment," (3), 471-472.
Kamerschen, David R. "A Note On Economies Of Scale In Life Insurance," (3), 473-474.
Sugars, Edmund G. "A Risk Theoretic Prescription For Regulated Ratemaking," (3), 475-478.
Markle, John L. "Profitability In The Property And Liability Insurance Industry: Comment," (3), 479-483.
Norgaard, Richard and George Schick. "Profitability In The Property And Liability Insurance Industry: Reply," (3), 483-485.
Cummins, J. David and David J. Nye. "The Cost Of Capital Of Insurance Companies: Comment," (3), 487-491.
Forbes, Stephen W. "The Cost Of Capital Of Insurance Companies: Comment," (3), 491-492.
Launie, J. J. "The Cost Of Capital Of Insurance Companies: Reply," (3), 492-495.
Rodha, Rodney R. "Variable Life Insurance Product Design: Comment," (3), 497-499.
Miller, Walter N. "Variable Life Insurance Product Design: Reply," (3), 499.
Belth, Joseph M. "A Note On The Price Of Split Life Insurance," (3), 501-505.
Crane, Frederick G. "Insurance Rate Regulation: The Reasons Why," (4), 511-534.
Jonish, James E. and Reginald G. Worthley. "Unemployment Insurance Fund Adequacy: An Alternative Measure," (4), 535-544.
Trieschmann, James S. and Robert J. Monroe. "Investment Performance Of Property-Liability Insurers' Common Stock Portfolios," (4), 545-554.
Long, John D. "Is The U.S. Insurance Poor?," (4), 555-571.
Zelten, Robert A. "Solvency Surveillance: The Problem And A Solution," (4), 573-588.
Klock, David R. "Competitive Rating Laws And Insurer Conduct," (4), 589-601.
Gagnon, Jean P. and Christopher A. Rodowskas, Jr. "Two Controversial Problems In Third-Party Outpatient Prescription Plans," (4), 603-611.
Dorfman, Mark S. "Workable Product Competition In The Life Insurance Market," (4), 613-626.
Johnson, Richard E. "A Test Of The Effectiveness Of An Innovative Teaching Technique," (4), 627-630.
Belth, Joseph M. "The Second Edition Of Cost Facts On Life Insurance: A Review Article," (4), 631-644.
Wood, Glenn L. and William Rudelius. "The Product Performance Of The Life Insurance Industry: Revisited: Comment," (4), 651-652.
Dorfman, Mark S. "The Product Performance Of The Life Insurance Industry: Revisited: Reply," (4), 652-654.
Schott, Francis H. "Investment Implications Of The Actuarial Design Of Life Insurance Products: Comment," (4), 655-658.
Cummins, J. David. "Property-Liability Company Exits: Comment," (4), 659-664.
Brightman, Harvey J. and Mark S. Dorfman. "Acceptability Of Three Normative Methods In Insurance Decision Making: Comment 465-466.
Neter, John and C. Arthur Williams, Jr. "Acceptability Of Three Normative Methods In Insurance Decision Making: Reply," (4), 466-467.

Journal of Risk and Insurance
Volume 40, 1973

Hedges, Bob A. "On The Skinning Of Cats," (1), 1-6.
Posnak, Robert L. "Perspectives On Life Insurance Financial Reporting," (1), 7-30.
Keeton, Robert E. "Beyond Current Reforms In Automobile Reparations," (1), 31-37.
Bleakney, Thomas P. "Problems And Issues In Public Employee Retirement Systems," (1), 39-54.
Herrick, Kenneth W. "Auto Accidents And Alcohol In Great Britain - An Analysis," (1), 55-74.
Witt, Robert Charles. "Pricing Problems In Automobile Insurance: An Economic Analysis," (1), 75-93.
Brainard, Clavin H. "Massachusetts Loss Experience Under No-Fault In 1971: Analysis And Implications," (1), 95-101.
Williams, Harold M. "The Future Of ARIA," (1), 103-114.
Belth, Joseph M. "Credit Life Insurance Prices," (1), 115-128.
MacPhee, Craig R. "Insurance And Reciprocity: Comment," (1),139-141.
Denenberg, Herbert S. and J. David Cummins. "Insurance And Reciprocity: Reply," (1), 141-142.
Braverman, Jerome D. and Gerald R. Hartman. "The Process Of Classifying Drivers: A Suggestion For Insurance Ratemaking: Comment," (1), 142-146.
Kroncke, Charles O. "The Process Of Classifying Drivers: A Suggestion For Insurance Ratemaking: Reply," (1), 147-148.
Pritchett, S. Travis. "Operating Expenses Of Life Insurers, 1961-70: Implication For Economies Of Size," (2), 157-165.
Stone, Gary K. "Life Insurance Sales Practices On The College Campus," (2), 167-179.

Allen, Tom C. and Richard M. Duvall. "Determinants Of Property Loss Ratios In The Retail Industry," (2), 181-190.
Ingraham, Harold G., Jr. "Problems In Agents' Compensation," (2), 191-208.
Kensicki, Peter R. and David Richmond. "Consumerism And Automobile Insurance," (2), 209-220.
Duker, Jacob M. and Charles E. Hughes. "The Black-Owned Life Insurance Company: Issues And Recommendations," (2), 221-230.
Stone, James M. "A Theory Of Capacity And The Insurance Of Catastrophe Risks (Part I)," (2), 231-243.
Scheel, William C. "A Critique Of The Interest-Adjusted Net Cost Index," (2), 245-262.
Tuan, Kailin. "A Preliminary Note On The Study Of Hazards," (2), 279-286.
Malisoff, Harry. "Beyond The Limits Of State Workmen's Compensation: Comment," (2), 287-290.
McLure, Charles E., Jr. "Investment Life Insurance Versus Term Insurance And Separate Investment: A Determination Of Expected-Return Equivalents: Comment," (2), 291-293.
Schonberger, Richard J. "Management Information Systems In Insurance: Comment," (2), 294-296.
Anderson, Dan R. "Risk Management, Insurance, And Actuarial Science In The Changing Curriculum," (2), 297-303.
Rejda, George E. and Richard J. Shepler. "The Impact Of Zero Population Growth On The OASDHI Program," (3), 313-325.
Trieschmann, James S. and George E. Pinches. "A Multivariate Model For Predicting Financially Distressed P-L Insurers," (3), 327-338.
Stone, James M. "A Theory Of Capacity And The Insurance Of Catastrophe Risks (Part II)," (3), 339-355.
Ziock, Richard W. "A Realistic Profit Model For Individual Non-Participating Life Insurance," (3), 357-374.
Prohaska, Charles R. and Walton Taylor. "Minimizing Losses In A Hostile Environment: The Costs Of Defending One's Castle,"(3),375-388.
Mehr, Robert I. and Stephen W. Forbes. "The Risk Management Decision In The Total Business Setting," (3), 389-402.
Winklevoss, Howard E. and Robert A. Zelten. "An Empirical Analysis Of Mutual Life Insurance Company Surplus," (3), 403-426.
Kamien, Morton I. and Nancy L. Schwartz. "Payment Plans And The Efficient Delivery Of Health Care Services," (3), 427-436.
Winklevoss, Howard E. "An Explantory Analysis Of The Insurable Value Concept," (3), 437-442.
McEnally, Richard W. and Lee A. Tavis. "Further Studies Of Property-Liability Return Adequacy: Comment," (3), 443-459.
Forbes, Stephen W. "Further Studies Of Property-Liability Return Adequacy: Reply," (3), 460-462.
Trieschmann, James S. "Further Studies Of Property-Liability Return Adequacy: Further Reply," (3), 463-464.
Weil, Roman L. "Annuitants Can Afford CREF's Projecting Earnings At A Rate Larger Than 4 Percent," (3), 465-472.
Greene, Mark R. "A Note On Loading Charges For Variable Annuities," (3), 473-478.
Williams, C. Arthur, Jr. and Andrew F. Whitman. "Open Competition Rating Laws And Price Competition," (4), 483-496.
Duvall, Richard M. and Tom C. Allen. "Least Cost Deductible Decisions," (4), 497-507.
Witt, Robert Charles. "Pricing And Underwriting Risk In Automobile Insurance: A Probabilistic View," (4), 509-531.
Cummins, J. David. "An Econometric Model Of The Life Insurance Sector Of The U.S. Economy," (4), 533-554.
Levine, Kenneth C. "Corporate Modeling Of A Life Insurance Company: A Developmental Game Plan," (4), 555-564.
Tyler, George R. and George E. Hoffer. "Reform Of The Non-Commercial Vehicle Liability Insurance Market," (4), 565-574.
Fitzgerald, John F., Jr. "Demutalization Of Mutual Property And Liability Insurers," (4), 575-584.
Greene, Mark R. "Should Variable Policy Loan Interest Rates Be Adopted?," (4), 585-597.
Meyer, Richard L. and Fred B. Power. "Total Insurance Costs And The Frequency Of Premium Payments," (4), 599-606.
Abelle, Barnie E. "The Teaching-Learning Implications Of Educational Technology," (4), 607-616.
Epley, D. R. "A Price Index For Life Insurance: Comment," (4), 629.
Lin, Cheyeh. "A Price Index For Life Insurance: Reply," (4), 630.
Neamann, Secv. "Ownership And Performance: Stock And Mutual Life Insurance Companies: Comment," (4), 631-635.
Spiller, Richard. "Ownership And Performance: Stock And Mutual Life Insurance Companies: Reply," (4), 635-638.
Cockerell, Hugh. "The History Of British And American Fire Marks: Comment," (4), 639-641.
Johnson, Harry M. "The History Of British And American Fire Marks: Reply," (4), 641-642.
Brightman, Harvey J. and Mark S. Dorfman. "Birth Order, Anxiety, Affiliation And The Purchase Of Life Insurance: Comment," (4), 643-646.
Berekson, Leonard L. "Birth Order, Anxiety, Affiliation And The Purchase Of Life Insurance: Reply," (4), 646-648.

Journal of Risk and Insurance
Volume 41, 1974

Bickelhaupt, David L. "Rx For Rational Responsibility," (1), 1-8.
Belth, Joseph M. "Money, Communications, And The Integrity Of ARIA," (1), 11-23.
Brainard, Calvin H. and John F. Fitzgerald. "First-Year Cost Results Under No-Fault Automobile Insurance: A Comparison Of The Florida And Massachusetts Experience," (1), 25-39.
Pfeffer, Irving. "Residual Risks In Europe," (1), 41-56.
Winklevoss, Howard E. "Cost Sensitivity Analysis Of Mandatory Funding And Vesting Standards In Pension Plans," (1), 57-73.
Clark, Russell D., III. "Risk Taking In Groups: A Social Psychological Analysis," (1), 75-92.
Pritchett, S. Travis and James S. Trieschmann. "Faculty Benefits At Fifty Major Universities," (1), 93-108.
Witt, Robert Charles. "Pricing, Investment Income, And Underwriting Risk In Auto Insurance: A Stochastic View," (1), 109-134.

Journal of Risk and Insurance
Volume 42, 1975

Pupp, Roger L. "Community Rating And Cross Subsidies In Health Insurance," (4), 610-627.

Bellhouse, David R. and Harry H. Panjer. "Stochastic Modelling Of Interest Rates With Applications To Life Contingencies - Part II," (4), 628-637.

Roussel, H. Lee and Moses K. Rosenberg. "The High Price Of 'Reform': Title Insurance Rates And The Benefits Of Rating Bureaus," (4), 638-648.

Hedges, Bob A. "On Positive Correlation Between Means And Standard Deviations Of Claims Ratios: Comment," (4), 649-652.

Witt, Robert C. "Underwriting Risk And Return: Some Additional Comments: Reply," (4), 653-661.

Todd, Jerry D. and David N. Goldstein. "A Computerized Simulation Model For Analyzing Profit Sharing Plans," (4), 662-673.

Smith, Michael L. "The Effects Of Risk Reduction Inherent In Universal Life Insurance: Comment," (4), 674-681.

Rose, Terry L. and John H. Hand. "The Effects Of Risk Reduction Inherent In Universal Life Insurance: Comment," (4), 682-689.

Scheel, William C. "The Effects Of Risk Reduction Inherent In Universal Life Insurance: Reply," (4), 690-693.

Smith, Stanley D. and Kenneth L. Stanley. "Social Security Retirement Age: Alternatives And Cost Comparisons," (4), 694-699.

Journal of Risk and Insurance
Volume 49, 1982

Rosenbloom, Jerry S. "1981 Presidential Address - Is ARIA Facing A Mid-Life Crisis?," (1), 8-18.

Clark, Robert L. and Ann Archibald McDermed. "Inflation, Pension Benefits, And Retirement," (1), 19-38.

Greenspan, Nancy T. and Ronald J. Vogel. "An Econometric Analysis Of The Effects Of Regulation In The Private Health Insurance Market," (1), 39-58.

Keyfitz, Nathan and Andrei Rogers. "Simplified Multiple Contingency Calculations," (1), 59-72.

Adelman, Saul W. and Mark S. Dorfman. "A Comparison Of TDA And Non-TDA Investment Returns," (1), 73-90.

Spahr, Ronald W. and Edmond L. Escolas. "1979 Automobile Accident Reports: Do Driver Characteristics Support Rate Discrimination?," (1), 91-103.

Greenough, William C. "Pensions. What Now?," (1), 104-113.

D'Arcy, Stephen P. "Regulated Firms Under Uncertain Price Change: The Case Of Property And Liability Insurance Companies: Comment," (1), 114-119.

Walter, James E. "Regulated Firms Under Uncertain Price Change: The Case Of Property And Liability Insurance Companies: Reply," (1), 120.

Balcer, Yves and Izzet Sahin. "Modeling The Impact Of Pension Reform - A Case Study," (2), 158-192.

McKenna, Fred W. "Pension Plan Cost Risk," (2), 193-217.

Skogh, Goran. "Returns To Scale In The Swedish Property-Liability Insurance Industry," (2), 218-228.

Harrington, Scott E. "Operating Expenses For Agency And Nonagency Life Insurers: Further Evidence," (2), 229-255.

Huszagh, Sandra M. and Mark R. Greene. "FCIA: Help Or Hindrance To Exports?," (2), 256-268.

Lee, Cheng F. and Stephen W. Forbes. "Income Measures, Ownership, Capacity Ratios And The Dividend Decision Of The Non-Life Insurance Industry: Some Empirical Evidence," (2), 269-289.

Gustavson, Sandra G. "Flexible Income Programming: Comment," (2), 290-296.

Rose, Terry and Robert I. Mehr. "Flexible Income Programming: Reply," (2), 297-299.

Hosek, William R. "Problems In The Use Of Historical Data In Estimating Economic Loss In Wrongful Death And Injury Cases," (2), 300-308.

Sioshansi, F. Perry. "Insurance For Irreplaceable Commodities," (2), 309-320.

Worrall, John D. and David Appel. "The Wage Replacement Rate And Benefit Utilization In Workers' Compensation Insurance," (3), 361-371.

Kihlstrom, Richard E. and Alvin E. Roth. "Risk Aversion And The Negotiation Of Insurance Contracts," (3), 372-387.

Meidan, Arthur. "Marketing Strategies, Organisation And Performance Control In Insurance," (3), 388-404.

Dionne, Georges. "Moral Hazard And State-Dependent Utility Function," (3), 405-422.

Van Matre, Joseph G. and George A. Overstreet, Jr. "Motor Vehicle Inspection And Accident Mortality: A Reexamination," (3), 423-435.

Hershbarger, Robert A. and Ronald K. Miller. "The Investment Performance Of Minority Controlled Life Insurance Companies," (3), 436-442.

Dowd, Bryan E. "The Logic Of Moral Hazard: A Game Theoretic Illustration," (3), 443-447.

Williams, Stephen J., Paula Diehr, William L. Drucker and William C. Richardson. "Limitations And Exclusions In Two Provider Systems With Comprehensive Care," (3), 448-462.

Myers, Robert J. "The Case For Extending Social Security To Government Employees: Comment," (3), 463.

Morgan, Norma. "The Case For Extending Social Security To Government Employees: Comment," (3), 464-467.

Levy, Mickey D. "The Case For Extending Social Security To Government Employees: Reply," (3), 468-471.

Outreville, J. Francois. "Report On Canadian And United States Risk And Insurance Curricula," (3), 472-476.

Winter, Ralph A. "On The Choice Of An Index For Disclosure In The Life Insurance Market: An Axiomatic Approach," (4), 513-538.

Weisberg, Herbert I. and Thomas J. Tomberlin. "A Statistical Perspective On Actuarial Methods For Estimating Pure Premiums From Cross-Classified Data," (4), 539-563.

Harrington, Scott E. "New York Regulation Of General Agency Expense Allowances," (4), 564-582.

Smith, Michael L. "The Life Insurance Policy As An Options Package," (4), 583-601.

Feldman, Roger. "Equilibrium In Monopolistic Insurance Markets: An Extension To The Sales-Maximizing Monopolist," (4), 602-612.

Belth, Joseph M. "A Note On Disclosure Of Realized Rates Of Return For Retirement Accumulations, Savings Accounts, And The Savings Component Of Universal Life Insurance Policies," (4), 613-617.

Venezian, Emilio C. "Comments On The Exchange Between Hedges And Witt," (4), 618-620.

Brockett, Patrick L. and Robert C. Witt. "The Underwriting Risk And Return Paradox Revisited," (4), 621-627.

Michel, Allen and James Norris. "On The Determination Of Appropriate Profit Margins In Insurance Industry Regulation," (4), 628-633.

Headen, Alvin E., Jr. "The Relationship Between The Blue Cross Market Share And The Blue Cross 'Discount' On Hospital Charges: Comment," (4), 634.

Journal of Risk and Insurance
Volume 50, 1983

Trieschmann, James S. "1982 Presidential Address - The American Risk And Insurance Association Today And Tomorrow," (1), 8-18.

Venezian, Emilio C. "Insurer Capital Needs Under Parameter Uncertainty," (1), 19-32.

Goldsmith, Art. "Household Life Cycle Protection: Human Capital Versus Life Insurance," (1), 33-43.

Louberge, Henri. "A Portfolio Model Of International Reinsurance Operations," (1), 44-60.

Schlesinger, Harris. "Nonlinear Pricing Strategies For Competitive And Monopolistic Insurance Markets," (1), 61-83.

Gahin, Fikry S. "The Financial Feasibility Of Tax-Sheltered Individual Retirement Plans," (1), 84-106.

Sprecher, C. Ronald and Mars A. Pertl. "Large Losses, Risk Management And Stock Prices," (1), 107-117.

Hogan, Andrew J. "Crop Credit Insurance And Technical Change In Agricultural Development: A Theoretical Analysis," (1), 118-130.

Roach, William L. "Pay-At-The-Pump Automobile Liability Insurance," (1), 131-139.

Main, Brian G. "Risk Management And The Theory Of The Firm: Comment," (1), 140-144.

Cummins, J. David. "Risk Management And The Theory Of The Firm: Reply," (1), 145-150.

Meyer, Richard L. and Fred B. Power. "The Investment Value Of Corporate Insurance," (1), 151-156.

Smith, Barry D. "A Note On The Application Of The Normal Power Method When Estimating Maximum Probable Yearly Aggregate Loss," (1), 157-160.

Mumy, Gene E. and William D. Manson. "Payroll Taxes, Social Security, And The Unique Tax Advantage Of Company Pensions," (1), 161-165.

Main, Brian G. M. "Corporate Insurance Purchases And Taxes," (2), 197-223.

Doherty, Neil A. "The Measurement Of Firm And Market Capacity," (2), 224-234.

Dillingham, Alan E. "The Effect Of Labor Force Age Distribution On Workers' Compensation Costs," (2), 235-248.

Samson, Danny and Howard Thomas. "Reinsurance Decision Making And Expected Utility," (2), 249-264.

Harris, William G. "Inflation Risk As A Determinant Of The Discount Rate In Tort Settlements," (2), 265-280.

Cho, Dongsae. "Integrated Risk Management Decision-Making: A Workers' Compensation Loss Exposure Case Study," (2), 281-300.

Achampong, Francis. "The Means And Ends Of Insurance Regulation - Basic Ideas," (2), 301-306.

Gustavson, Sandra G. and Joseph J. Schultz, Jr. "Property-Liability Loss Reserve Certification: Independent Or In-House?," (2), 307-314.

Long, Blair M. "University Insurance Instruction: It Is Time To Teach Problem Solving," (2), 315-322.

Weese, Samuel H. "Another Look At Nuclear Liability After Three Mile Island," (2), 323-327.

Wood, William C. "Nuclear Liability After Three Mile Island: Reply," (2), 328-329.

Jung, Alan F. "Automobile Insurance Rates In Chicago Illinois: A Correction," (2), 330-331.

Cummins, J. David and Laurel J. Wiltbank. "Estimating The Total Claims Distribution Using Multivariate Frequency And Severity Distributions," (3), 377-403.

Cozzolino, John M. "The Evaluation Of Loss Control Options," (3), 404-416.

Cross, Mark L. and John H. Thornton. "The Probable Effect Of An Extreme Hurrican On Texas Catastrophe Plan Insurers," (3), 417-444.

Williams, C. Arthur, Jr. "Regulatory Property And Liability Insurance Rates Through Excess Profits Statutes," (3), 445-472.

Goldsmith, Art. "Household Life Cycle Protection: Human Capital Versus Life Insurance," (3), 473-486.

Miller, Elbert G. and George E. Hoffer. "Pay-At-The-Pump Automobile Liability Insurance: Reply," (3), 487-492.

Rosen, Corey M. "The Effect Of Employee Stock Ownership Plans On Corporate Profits: Comment," (3), 493-494.

Granados, Luis L. "The Effect Of Employee Stock Ownership Plans On Corporate Profits - Additional Comment," (3), 495-497.

Livingston, D. T. and James B. Henry. "The Effect Of Employee Stock Ownership Plans On Corporate Profits: Reply," (3), 498-499.

Barth, James R. and Anthony M. J. Yezer. "Default Risk On Home Mortgages: A Further Test Of Competing Hypotheses," (3), 500-505.

Kott, Phillip S. "Returns To Scale In The U.S. Life Insurance Industry: Comment," (3), 506-507.

Praetz, Peter. "Returns To Scale In The U.S. Life Insurance Industry: Reply," (3), 508-509.

Burnett, John J. and Bruce A. Palmer. "Reliance On Life Insurance Agents: A Demographic And Psychographic Analysis Of Consumers," (3), 510-520.

Smith, Barry D. "A Model For Workers' Compensation Group Self Insurance: The Delaware Valley School Districts Plan," (3), 521-

532.

Myers, Phyllis Schiller and S. Travis Pritchett. "Rate Of Return On Differential Premiums For Selected Participating Life Insurance Contracts," (4), 569-586.

Harrington, Scott E. "The Relationship Between Risk And Return: Evidence For Life Insurance Stock," (4), 587-610.

Oppenheimer, Henry R. and Ben Graham. "Investment Policies Of Property - Liability Insurers And pension Plans: A Lesson From Ben Graham," (4), 611-630.

Witt, Robert C. and Jorge Urrutia. "A Comparative Economic Analysis Of Tort Liability And No-Fault Compensation Systems In Automobile Insurance," (4), 631-669.

Cristiansen, Hanne D. "Equality And Equilibrium: Weaknesses Of The Overlap Argument For Unisex Pension Plans," (4), 670-680.

Hickman, James C. "Pensions And Sex," (4), 681-687.

Babbel, David F. and Kim B. Staking. "An Engel Curve Analysis Of Gambling And Insurance In Brazil," (4), 688-696.

Reilly, Robert J. "Some Evidence On The Reliability Of Variance As A Proxy For Risk," (4), 697-702.

Freifelder, Leonard R. "Collegiate Sports Risk Management," (4), 703-718.

Boyle, Phelim P. and Jennifer Mao. "An Exact Solution For The Optimal Stop Loss Limit," (4), 719-726.

Brockett, Patrick L. "On The Misuse Of The Central Limit Theorem In Some Risk Calculation," (4), 727-730.

Journal of Risk and Insurance
Volume 51, 1984

Lau, Hon-Shiang. "An Effective Approach For Estimating The Aggregate Loss Of An Insurance Portfolio," (1), 20-30.

Friedman, Bernard, Caroline Ross and Glen Misek. "On The Surprisingly Low Cost Of State Catastrophic Health Insurance Programs," (1), 31-48.

Sherden, William A. "An Analysis Of The Determinants Of The Demand For Automobile Insurance," (1), 49-62.

Venezia, Itzhak. "Aspects Of Optimal Automobile Insurance," (1), 63-79.

Cho, Dongsae. "Rehabilitation For Worker's Compensation Loss Exposures," (1), 80-98.

Morgan, N. C. "An Analysis Of Selected Hospice Programs," (1), 99-114.

Peterson, Timothy M. "Loss Reserving - Property/Casualty Insurance: A Summary Of The Book," (1), 115-121.

Harris, William G. "Problems In The Use Of Historical Data In Estimating Economic Loss In Wrongful Death And Injury Cases: Comment," (1), 122-125.

Hosek, William R. "Problems In The Use Of Historical Data In Estimating Economic Loss In Wrongful Death And Injury Cases: Reply," (1), 126-130.

Schlesinger, Harris. "Optimal Insurance For Irreplaceable Commodities," (1), 131-137.

Brady, Dennis P., Michael L. Brookshire and William E. Cobb. "The Development And Solution Of A Tax-Adjusted Model For Personal Injury Awards," (1), 138-142.

Sahin, Izzet. "Bruce's Spider And The Employee's Risk Under A Pension System," (1), 143-149.

Venezian, Emilio C. "Are Insurers Under-Earning?," (1), 150-156.

Venezian, Emilio C. "Efficiency And Equity In Insurance," (2), 190-204.

Doherty, Neil A. "Portfolio Efficient Insurance Buying Strategies," (2), 205-224.

Ledolter, Johannes and Mark L. Power. "A Study Of ERISA's Impact On Private Retirement Plan Growth," (2), 225-243.

Fogler, H. Russell. "Bond Portfolio Immunization, Inflation, And The Fisher Equation," (2), 244-264.

Todd, Jerry D. "A Retirement Plan Decision Model For Small Business," (2), 265-285.

Beliveau, Barbara C. "Theoretical And Empirical Aspects Of Implicit Information In The Market For Life Insurance," (2), 286-307.

White, Lawrence J. "The Title Insurance Industry, Reverse Competition, And Controlled Business - A Different View," (2), 308-319.

Outreville, Jean-Francois. "The Impact Of The Government No-Fault Plan For Automobile Insurance In The Province Of Quebec," (2), 320-335.

Weissbrod, Doron. "Index-Linked Life Insurance In Israel And The Sharir Committee," (2), 336-341.

Hogan, Andrew J. and Robert T. Aubey. "Compulsory Insurance And Allocative Efficiency In Agriculture," (2), 342-348.

Nielson, Norma. "Capacity Of The Property-Casualty Insurance Industry," (3), 393-411.

Klugman, Stuart A. and Michael L. Murray. "Bodily Injury Claim Payments As A Function Of Automobile Liability Insurance Limits," (3), 412-432.

Venezian, Emilio C. "Cost-Based Pricing And Price-Based Costing In Private Passenger Automobile Insurance," (3), 433-452.

Burnett, John J. and Bruce A. Palmer. "Examining Life Insurance Ownership Through Demographic And Psychographic Characteristics," (3), 453-467.

Borch, Karl. "Equilibrium Premiums In An Insurance Market," (3), 468-476.

Baltz, Richard B. "An Incentive Early Retirement Model For College And University Faculty," (3), 477-497.

Watson, Harry. "The Effects Of Compensation For Uninsured But Insurable Losses," (3), 498-512.

Skinner, Steven J. and Alan J. Dubinsky. "Purchasing Insurance: Predictors Of Family Decision-Making Responsibility," (3),513-523.

Halperin, Sanford B. and Rodney H. Mabry. "Property And Casualty Insurance Lines Comparisons: A Shift-Share Analysis," (3), 524-535.

Hamwi, Iskandar S. and Edward Nissan. "Determination Of Net Rate In Property And Liability Insurance: An Alternative Approach," (3), 536-548.

Harrington, Scott. "The Impact Of Rate Regulation On Prices And Underwriting Results In The Property-Liability Insurance Industry: A Survey," (4), 577-623.

King, Francis P. "An Increasing Annuity Based On Nominal Interest Rates And Debt Instruments," (4), 624-639.

Rejda, George E. and James R. Schmidt. "The Impact Of Social Security And ERISA On Insured Private Pension Contributions," (4), 640-651.

Baker, Yves and Izzet Sahin. "Dynamics Of Pension Reform: The Case Of Ontario," (4), 652-686.

Marlin, Paul. "Fitting The Log-Normal Distribution To Loss Data Subject To Multiple Deductibles," (4), 687-701.

Hofflander, Alfred E. and Blaine F. Nye. "Self-Insurance, Captives And Income Taxation," (4), 702-709.

Kahane, Yehuda and M. Moshe Porat. "Financial Analysis Of Underwriting Results - A Corrected Approach To Loss Ratio Analysis, With Special Reference To Inflation," (4), 710-719.

Brockett, Patrick L., Samuel H. Cox, Jr. and Robert C. Witt. "Self-Insurance And The Probability Of Financial Regret," (4), 720-729.

Journal of Risk and Insurance
Volume 52, 1985

Cummins, J. David and Scott Harrington. "Property-Liability Insurance Rate Regulation: Estimation Of Underwriting Betas Using Quarterly Profit Data," (1), 16-43.

Walden, Michael L. "The Whole Life Insurance Policy As An Options Package: An Empirical Investigation," (1), 44-58.

Shaked, Israel. "Measuring Prospective Probabilities Of Insolvency: An Application To The Life Insurance Industry," (1), 59-80.

Shapiro, Arnold F. "Contributions To The Evolution Of Pension Cost Analysis," (1), 81-99.

Schilling, Don. "Estimating The Present Value Of Future Income Losses: An Historical Simulation 1900-1982," (1), 100-116.

Huszagh, Sandra M. and Mark R. Greene. "How Exporters View Credit Risk And FCIA Insurance - The Georgia Experience," (1), 117-132.

Jorgensen, Jerry L. and Ronald M. Mano. "Financial Statement Disclosure Of Uninsured Risks," (1), 133-143.

Jones, David D. "Inflation Rates Implicit In Discounting Personal Injury Economic Losses," (1), 144-150.

Gogol, Daniel. "The Much Greater Profitability Of New York Workers' Compensation Risks With Higher Modifications," (1), 151-156.

Panara, Philip, Jr. and Warren Greenberg. "The Impact Of Competition And Regulation On Blue Cross Enrollment Of Non-Group Individuals," (2), 185-198.

Weiss, Mary. "A Multivariate Analysis Of Loss Reserving Estimates In Property-Liability Insurers," (2), 199-221.

Stowe, John D. and Collin J. Watson. "A Multivariate Analysis Of The Composition Of Life Insurer Balance Sheets," (2), 222-240.

Krinsky, Itzhak. "Mean-Variance Utility Functions, Flexible Functional Forms, And The Investment Behaviour Of Canadian Life Insurers," (2), 241-268.

Kochanowski, Paul S. and Madelyn V. Young. "Deterrent Aspects Of No-Fault Automobile Insurance: Some Empirical Findings," (2), 269-288.

Myers, Robert J. "Income Of Social Security Beneficiaries As Affected By Earnings Test And Income Taxes On Benefits," (2), 289-300.

Gustavson, Sandra G. "Moving Insurance Education Into The Computer Age," (2), 301-310.

Mack, Thomas and Matthias Kulessa. "Reinsurance Decision Making And Expected Utility: Comment," (2), 311.

Samson, Danny and Howard Thomas. "Reinsurance Decision Making And Expected Utility: Reply," (2), 312-314.

Praetz, Peter. "A Note On Economies Of Scale In The United Kingdom Property-Liability Insurance Industry," (2), 315-320.

Cather, David A., Sandra G. Gustavson and James S. Trieschmann. "A Profitability Analysis Of Property-Liability Insurers Using Alternative Distribution Systems," (2), 321-332.

Smith, Michael L. and Robert C. Witt. "An Economic Analysis Of Retroactive Liability Insurance," (3), 379-401.

Schlesinger, Harris and Neil A. Doherty. "Incomplete Markets For Insurance: An Overview," (3), 402-423.

Appel, David, John D. Worrall and Richard J. Butler. "Survivorship And The Size Distribution Of The Property-Liability Insurance Industry," (3), 424-440.

Smith, Barry D. "The Effect Of Life Insurance Underwriting Practices On Mortality Results," (3), 441-463.

Lambrinos, James. "On The Use Of Historical Data In The Estimation Of Economic Losses," (3), 464-476.

Venezian, Emilio C. "Ratemaking Methods And Profit Cycles In Property And Liability Insurance," (3), 477-500.

Dubinsky, Alan J. and Francis J. Yammarino. "Job-Related Responses Of Insurance Agents: A Multi-Firm Investigation," (3), 501-517.

Johnson, Larry J. and John R. Phelps. "The Development And Solution Of A Tax-Adjusted Model Of Personal Injury Awards: A Clarification," (3), 518-519.

Brady, Dennis, Michael Brookshire and William Cobb. "The Development And Solution Of A Tax-Adjusted Model Of Personal Injury Awards: A Response," (3), 520-521.

Schlesinger, Harris. "Choosing A Deductible For Insurance Contracts: Best Or Worst Insurance Policy?," (3), 522-527.

Vernon, Jack. "Inflation Risk As Determinant Of The Discount Rate In Tort Settlements: Comment," (3), 528-532.

Harris, William G. "Inflation Risk As Determinant Of The Discount Rate In Tort Settlements: Reply," (3), 533-536.

Venezian, Emilio C. "Interactions In Insurance Classifications," (4), 571-584.

Warshawsky, Mark. "Life Insurance Savings And The After-Tax Life Insurance Rate Of Return," (4), 585-606.

Freifelder, Leonard R. "Measuring The Impact Of Merit Rating On Ratemaking Efficiency," (4), 607-626.

Chang, Rosita P., Blair M. Lord and S. Ghon Rhee. "Inflation-Caused Wealth-Transfer: A Case Of The Insurance Industry," (4), 627-643.

Lee, Yoong-Sin. "A Graphical Treatment Of The Coinsurance Clause," (4), 644-661.

Kimball, Spencer L. "The Context Of `No-Fault'," (4), 662-666.

Rolph, John E., James K. Hammitt and Robert L. Houchens. "Automobile Accident Compensation: Who Pays How Much How Soon?," (4), 667-685.

Lane, Julia and Dennis Glennon. "The Estimation Of Age/Earnings Profiles In Wrongful Death And Injury Cases," (4), 686-695.

Vernon, Jack. "Discounting After-Tax Earnings With After-Tax Yields In Torts Settlements," (4), 696-703.

Szpiro, George G. "Optimal Insurance Coverage," (4), 704-710.

Manning, Richard L., Matilde K. Stephenson and Jerry D. Todd. "Information Technology In The Insurance Industry: A Forecast Of Utilization And Impact," (4), 711-722.

Outreville, J. Francois and Jean-Louis Malouin. "What Are The Major Journals That Members Of ARIA Read?," (4), 723-733.

Venezian, Emilio C. "Coding Errors And Classification Refinement," (4), 734-742.

Journal of Risk and Insurance
Volume 53, 1986

McKenna, Fred W. and Yong H. Kim. "Managerial Risk Preferences, Real Pension Costs, And Long-Run Corporate Pension Fund Investment Policy," (1), 29-48.

Weiss, Mary A. "Analysis Of Productivity At The Firm Level: An Application To Life Insurers," (1), 49-84.

Smith, Barry D. "Analyzing The Tax Deductibility Of Premiums Paid To Captive Insurers," (1), 85-103.

Carpenter, Michael D., David R. Lange, Donald S. Shannon and William Thomas Stevens. "Methodologies Of Valuing Lost Earnings: A Review, A Criticism, And A Recommendation," (1), 104-118.

Bar-Niv, Ran and David L. Bickelhaupt. "Research In International Risk And Insurance: Summary, Synthesis, And Prospects," (1), 119-134.

Freifelder, Leonard R. "Estimation Of Classification Factor Relativities: A Modelling Approach," (1), 135-143.

Nye, David J. and Robert W. Kolb. "Inflation, Interest Rates And Property-Liability Insurer Risk," (1), 144-154.

Simmons, LeRoy F. and Mark L. Cross. "The Underwriting Cycle And The Risk Manager," (1), 155-163.

Williams, C. Arthur, Jr. "Higher Interest Rates, Longer Lifetimes, And The Demand For Life Annuities," (1), 164-171.

Chen, K. C. and Stephen P. D'Arcy. "Market Sensitivity To Interest Rate Assumptions In Corporate Pension Plans," (2), 209-225.

Zador, Paul and Adrian Lund. "Re-Analyses Of The Effects Of No-Fault Auto Insurance On Fatal Crashes," (2), 226-241.

Brockett, Patrick L., Samuel H. Cox, Jr. and Robert C. Witt. "Insurance Versus Self-Insurance: A Risk Management Perspective," (2), 242-257.

Blazenko, George. "The Economics Of Reinsurance," (2), 258-277.

Globerman, Steven. "Firm Size And Dynamic Efficiency In The Life Insurance Industry," (2), 278-293.

Ramsay, Colin M. "An Optimum And Equitable Net Risk Premium Payment Plan," (2), 294-300.

Sinha, Tapen. "The Effects Of Survival Probabilities, Transactions Costs And The Attitude Towards Risk On The Demand For Annuities," (2), 301-307.

Spahr, Ronald W. and Edmond L. Escolas. "Mortgage Guaranty Insurance: A Unique Style Of Insurance," (2), 308-319.

Schmit, Joan T. "A New View Of The Requisites Of Insurability," (2), 320-329.

Venezian, Emilio C. "Use Of Risk Loads And Distributional Fitting In Ratemaking: Comment," (2), 330-333.

Krogh, Harold C. and Murray S. Levin. "Recent Trends: State Insurance Guaranty Funds And Insurance Company Insurance Assessment Operations," (2), 335-342.

Venezian, Emilio C. "Risk Management And Financial Regret," (3), 395-408.

Carlson, Severin and Blair Lord. "Unisex Retirement Benefits And The Market For Annuity 'Lemons'," (3), 409-418.

Broverman, Samuel. "The Rate Of Return On Life Insurance And Annuities," (3), 419-434.

Giaccotto, Carmelo. "Stochastic Modelling Of Interest Rates: Actuarial Vs. Equilibrium Approach," (3), 435-453.

Scott, Cuthbert L., III. "Effects Of Differing Unemployment Insurance Taxable Wage Bases On System Capacity," (3), 454-470.

Cross, Mark L., Wallace N. Davidson, III and John H. Thornton. "The Impact Of Captive Insurer Formation On The Parent Firm's Value," (3), 471-483.

McGuire, Thomas G. "Financing Psychotherapy," (3), 484-491.

Brown, Ralph J. "Implicit Inflation And Interest Rates In Discounting Personal Injury Economic Losses: Comment," (3), 492-495.

Schilling, Don. "Implicit Inflation And Interest Rates In Discounting Personal Injury Economic Losses: Reply," (3), 496-497.

Jones, David D. "Rejoinder To Brown's Comment On A Reaction To Schilling's Paper," (3), 498-500.

Anderson, Dan R. and Maurice Weinrobe. "Insurance Issues Related To Mortgage Default Risks Associated With Natural Disasters," (3), 501-513.

Smith, Dean G. and Lawrence C. Rose. "The Effects Of Insurance Policy Limits On Product Choice," (3), 514-520.

Panjer, Harry H. "Direct Calculation Of Ruin Probabilities," (3), 521-529.

Horvitz, Sigmund A. "Implications Of Projecting Future Losses Of Earning Capacity With Deterministic Models," (3), 530-537.

D'Arcy, Stephen P. "Legislative Reform Of The Medical Malpractice Tort System In Illinois," (3), 538-550.

Harrington, Scott E. and Jack M. Nelson. "A Regression-Based Methodology For Solvency Surveillance In The Property-Liability Insurance Industry," (4), 583-605.

Karni, Edi and Itzhak Zilcha. "Risk Aversion In The Theory Of Life Insurance: The Fisherian Model," (4), 606-620.

Meador, Joseph W., Gerald P. Madden and David J. Johnston. "On The Probability Of Acquisition Of Non-Life Insurers," (4), 621-643.

De Wit, G. W. "The Politics Of Rate Discrimination: An International Perspective," (4), 644-661.

Welland, Deborah A. "Workers' Compensation Liability Changes And The Distribution Of Injury Claims," (4), 662-678.

Funatsu, Hideki. "Export Credit Insurance," (4), 679-692.

Smith, Clifford W., Jr. "On The Convergence Of Insurance And Finance Research," (4), 693-717.

Briys, Eric. "Insurance And Consumption: The Continuous Time Case," (4), 718-733.

Glennon, Dennis and Julia Lane. "Imputing A Housewife's Earnings In A Wrongful Death And Injury Case," (4), 734-743.

Murray, Michael L. "An Alternative To Workers' Compensation - 24 Hour Benefits," (4), 744-754.

Outreville, J. Francois and Carole Helie. "More Evidence On The Systematic Underwriting Risk In Automobile Insurance," (4), 755-766.

Journal of Risk and Insurance
Volume 54, 1987

Worrall, John D., David Appel and Richard J. Butler. "Sex, Marital Status, And Medical Utilization By Injured Workers," (1), 27-44.

Mayers, David and Clifford W. Smith, Jr. "Corporate Insurance And The Underinvestment Problem," (1), 45-54.

Skipper, Harold D., Jr. "Protectionism In The Provision Of International Insurance Services," (1), 55-85.

Fitzgerald, John. "The Effects Of Social Security On Life Insurance Demand By Married Couples," (1), 86-99.

Aiuppa, Thomas A. and James S. Trieschmann. "An Empirical Analysis Of The Magnitude And Accuracy Of Incurred-But-Not-Reported Reserves," (1), 100-118.

Curatola, Anthony P., Thomas L. Dickens and Kent T. Fields. "Increased Salary As An Alternative To Group Term Life Insurance," (1), 119-130.

VanDerhei, Jack L. "The Effect Of Voluntary Termination Of Overfunded Pension Plans On Shareholder Wealth," (1), 131-156.

Gebotys, Robert J., Alan Auerbach and Adriana Petrucci. "The Insurance Branch Manager: Correlates Of Success," (1), 157-161.

Davidson, Wallace N., III, P. R. Chandy and Mark Cross. "Large Losses, Risk Management And Stock Returns In The Airline Industry," (1), 162-172.

Fields, Joseph A. and Emilio C. Venezian. "Investment Income - Is There A Company Effect?," (1), 173-178.

Schlesinger, Harris. "Monopoly Profits For Contingent-Claims Contracts When Preferences Are State Dependent," (1), 179-184.

Smith, Michael L. and Stephen A. Buser. "Risk Aversion, Insurance Costs And Optimal Property-Liability Coverages," (2), 225-245.

Cummins, J. David and J. Francois Outreville. "An International Analysis Of Underwriting Cycles In Property-Liability Insurance," (2), 246-262.

Danzon, Patricia M. "Compensation For Occupational Disease: Evaluating The Options," (2), 263-282.

Antler, Jacob and Yehuda Kahane. "The Gross And Net Replacement Ratios In Designing Pension Schemes And In Financial Planning: The Israeli Experience," (2), 283-297.

Feldman, Roger. "Health Insurance In The United States: Is Market Failure Avoidable?," (2), 298-313.

Gollier, Christian. "The Design Of Optimal Insurance Contracts Without The Nonnegativity Constraint On Claims," (2), 314-324.

Dahlby, B. G. "Monopoly Versus Competition In An Insurance Market With Adverse Selection," (2), 325-331.

Schmit, Joan T. "Lump-Sum Awards In Workers' Compensation," (2), 332-340.

Chung, Yosup and Harold D. Skipper, Jr. "The Effect Of Interest Rates On Surrender Values Of Universal Life Policies," (2), 341-347.

Cabanilla, Nathaniel B. "Life Insurers In The Public And Private Security Markets," (2), 348-356.

Trieschmann, James S. and E. J. Leverett, Jr. "A Sensitivity Analysis Of Selected Variables In Agency Valuation," (2), 357-363.

Becker, William E. and George C. Alter. "The Probabilities Of Life And Work Force Status In The Calculation Of Expected Earnings," (2), 364-375.

Anderson, Dan R. "Financing Asbestos Claims: Coverage Issues, Manville's Bankruptcy And The Claims Facility," (2), 429-451.

D'Arcy, Stephen P. and Keun Chang Lee. "Universal Variable Life Insurance Versus Similar Unbundled Investment Strategies," (3), 452-477.

Rokes, Willis Park. "Remedies Afforded Private Parties Against Insurers For Unfair Claims Practices," (3), 478-501.

Nye, Blaine F. and Alfred E. Hofflander. "Economics Of Oligopoly: Medical Malpractice Insurance As A Classic Illustration," (3), 502-519.

Cresta, Jean-Paul and Jean-Jacques Laffont. "Incentive Compatibility Of Insurance Contracts And The Value Of Information," (3), 520-540.

Cameron, Norman E. "Inflation And Nominal Policy Yields On Participating Life Insurance," (3), 541-556.

Outreville, J. Francois. "The Transactions Demand For Cash Balances By Property And Liability Insurance Companies," (3), 557-568.

Tryfos, Peter. "The Equity Of Classification Systems In Automobile Insurance," (3), 569-581.

Weiss, Mary A. "Macroeconomic Insurance Output Estimation," (3), 582-593.

Tapiero, Charles S. and Laurent Jacque. "The Expected Cost Of Ruin And Insurance Premiums In Mutual Insurance," (3), 594-602.

Forbes, Stephen W. "Life Insurance Financial Management Issues," (3), 603-613.

MacMinn, Richard D. "Insurance And Corporate Risk Management," (4), 658-677.

Tolley, H. Dennis, Kenneth G. Manton and James Vertrees. "An Evaluation Of Three Payment Strategies For Capitation For Medicare," (4), 678-690.

Cherin, Antony C. and Robert C. Hutchins. "The Rate Of Return On Universal Life Insurance," (4), 691-711.

Rejda, George E., James R. Schmidt and Michael J. McNamara. "The Impact Of Social Security Tax Contributions On Group Life Insurance Premiums," (4), 712-720.

Bhagat, Sanjai, James A. Brickley and Jeffrey L. Coles. "Managerial Indemnification And Liability Insurance: The Effect On Sharholder Wealth," (4), 721-736.

Lipka, Roland. "Effects Of Taxation Of Social Security Benefits On Portfolio Revisions," (4), 737-751.

Myers, Daniel A., Richard V. Burkhauser and Karen C. Holden. "The Transition From Wife To Widow: The Importance Of Survivor Benefits To Widows," (4), 752-759.

Hofflander, Alfred E. and Blaine F. Nye. "An Analysis Of Premium Tax Revenue And Rate In California: The Case Of Structured Settlement Annuities," (4), 760-766.

Ang, James S. and Tsong-Yue Lai. "Insurance Premium Pricing And Ratemaking In Competitive Insurance And Capital Asset Markets," (4), 767-779.

Venezian, Emilio C. and Joseph A. Fields. "Informational Asymmetries In Retroactive Insurance," (4), 780-789.

Rhine, Sherrie L. W. "The Determinants Of Fringe Benefits: Additional Evidence," (4), 790-799.

Outreville, J. Francois and Michel Zins. "Job-Related Responses Of Insurance Agents: More Evidence," (4), 800-803.

Yammarino, Francis J. and Alan J. Dubinsky. "On Job Satisfaction: It's The Relationships That Count!," (4), 804-809.

Schlesinger, Harris. "Optimal Insurance Coverage: Comment," (4), 810-812.

Szpiro, George G. "Optimal Insurance Coverage: Reply," (4), 813-815.

Journal of Risk and Insurance
Volume 55, 1988

Cummins, J. David and Scott E. Harrington. "The Relationship Between Risk And Return: Evidence For Property-Liability Insurance Stocks," (1), 15-31.

Holland, Rodger G. and Nancy A. Sutton. "The Liability Nature Of Unfunded Pension Obligations Since ERISA," (1), 32-58.

VanDerhei, Jack L. and Francois P. Joanette. "Economic Determinants For The Choice Of Actuarial Cost Methods," (1), 59-74.

Katzman, Martin T. "Pollution Liability Insurance And Catastrophic Environmental Risk," (1), 75-100.

Wu, Chunchi and Peter F. Colwell. "Moral Hazard And Moral Imperative," (1), 101-117.

Cho, Dongsae. "The Impact Of Risk Management Decisions On Firm Value: Gordon's Growth Model Approach," (1), 118-131.

Dubinsky, Alan J., Terry L. Childers, Steven J. Skinner and Esra Gencturk. "Impact Of Sales Supervisor Leadership Behavior On Insurance Agent Attitudes And Performance," (1), 132-144.

Lee, Hyong J. and George E. Pinches. "On Optimal Insurance Purchasing," (1), 145-149.

Nye, Blaine F. and Aflred E. Hofflander. "Experience Rating In Medical Professional Liability Insurance," (1), 150-157.

Vaughn, Therese M. "The Financial Feasibility Of Tax-Sheltered Individual Retirement Plans: Comment," (1), 158-163.

Gahin, Fikry S. "The Financial Feasibility Of Tax-Sheltered Individual Retirement Plans: Reply," (1), 164-167.

Bryan, William R. and Charles M. Linke. "The Estimation Of The Age/Earnings Profiles In Wrongful Death And Injury Cases: Comment," (1), 168-173.

Lane, Julia and Dennis Glennon. "The Estimation Of Age/Earnings Profiles In Wrongful Death And Injury Cases: Reply," (1), 174-179.

Eeckhoudt, L., J. F. Outreville, M. Lauwers and F. Calcoen. "The Impact Of A Probationary Period On The Demand For Insurance," (2), 217-228.

Ambrose, Jan Mills and J. Allen Seward. "Best's Ratings, Financial Ratios And Prior Probabilities In Insolvency Prediction," (2), 229-244.

Director, Steven M. and Frederick J. Englander. "Requiring Unemployment Insurance Recipients To Register With The Public Employment Service," (2), 245-258.

Beenstock, Michael, Gerry Dickinson and Sajay Khajuria. "The Relationship Between Property-Liability Insurance Premiums And Income: An International Analysis," (2), 259-272.

Bryan, William R. and Charles M. Linke. "Estimating Present Value Of Future Earnings: Experience With Dedicated Portfolios," (2), 273-286.

Segal, Uzi. "Probabilistic Insurance And Anticipated Utility," (2), 287-297.

Berger, Lawrence A. "A Model Of The Underwriting Cycle In The Property/Liability Insurance Industry," (2), 298-306.

Venezia, Itzhak. "On The Economic Advantages Of The Coinsurance Clause," (2), 307-314.

Chelius, James R. and Karen Kavanaugh. "Workers' Compensation And The Level Of Occupational Injuries," (2), 315-323.

Cho, Dongsae. "Some Evidence Of Scale Economies In Worker's Compensation Insurance," (2), 324-330.

Cross, Mark L., Wallace N. Davidson, III and John H. Thornton. "Taxes, Stock Returns And Captive Insurance Subsidiaries," (2), 331-338.

Abel, Andrew B. "The Implications Of Insurance For The Efficacy Of Fiscal Policy," (2), 339-378.

Aiuppa, Thomas A. "Evaluation Of Pearson Curves As An Approximation Of The Maximum Probable Annual Aggregate Loss," (3), 425-441.

Cox, Larry A. and Gary L. Griepentrog. "The Pure-Play Cost Of Equity For Insurance Divisions," (3), 442-452.

Schmit, Joan T., S. Travis Pritchett and Paige Fields. "Punitive Damages: Punishment Or Further Compensation?," (3), 453-466.

Thies, Clifford F. and Thomas Sturrock. "The Pension-Augmented Balance Sheet," (3), 467-480.

D'Arcy, Stephen P. "Use Of The CAPM To Discount Property-Liability Loss Reserves," (3), 481-491.

Nicswiadomy, Michael and Eugene Silberberg. "Calculating Changes In Worklife Expectancies And Lost Earnings In Personal Injury Cases," (3), 492-498.

Lacey, Nelson J. "Recent Evidence On The Liability Crisis," (3), 499-508.

Sobti, Rajiv. "Increasing Social Variability And Insurance Equilibrium," (3), 509-517.

Warshawsky, Mark. "Private Annuity Markets In The United States: 1919-1984," (3), 518-528.

Gustavson, Sandra G. and James S. Trieschmann. "Universal Life Insurance As An Alternative To The Joint And Survivor Annuity," (3), 529-538.

Nicswiadomy, Michael L. and D. J. Slottje. "Estimating Lost Future Earnings Using The New Worklife Tables: Comment," (3), 539-544.

Becker, William E. and George C. Alter. "Estimating Lost Future Earnings Using The New Worklife Tables: Reply," (3), 545-547.

Smith, Michael L. and Robert C. Witt. "Informational Asymmetries In Retroactive Insurance: A Response," (3), 548-554.

Fields, Joseph A. and Emilio C. Venezian. "Informational Asymmetries In Retroactive Insurance: Reply," (3), 555-558.

Jablonowski, Mark. "The Underwriting Cycle And The Risk Manager: Comment," (3), 559-560.

Cross, Mark L. and LeRoy F. Simmons. "The Underwriting Cycle And The Risk Manager: Reply," (3), 561-562.

Cox, Larry A. and Gary L. Griepentrog. "Systematic Risk, Unsystematic Risk, And Property-Liability Rate Regulation," (4), 606-627.

Troutt, Marvin D. "A Purchase Timing Model For Life Insurance Decision Support Systems," (4), 628-643.

Weinrobe, Maurice. "An Insurance Plan To Guarantee Reverse Mortgages," (4), 644-659.

Lemaire, Jean. "A Comparative Analysis Of Most European And Japanese Bonus-Malus Systems," (4), 660-681.

Chan, M. W. Luke and Itzhak Krinsky. "Expectations Formation And Portfolio Models For Life Insurers," (4), 682-700.

Babbel, David F. and David R. Klock. "Insurance Pedagogy: Executive Opinions And Priorities," (4), 701-712.

Briys, Eric, Yehuda Kahane and Yoram Kroll. "Voluntary Insurance Coverage, Compulsory Insurance, And Risky-Riskless Portfolio Opportunities," (4), 713-722.

Cornett, Marcia Millon. "Undetected Theft As A Social Hazard: The Role Of Financial Institutions In The Choice Of Protection Mechanisms," (4), 723-733.

Shows, E. Warren, Fred B. Power and Dale A. Johnson. "Lump-Sum Awards In Workers' Compensation: Comment," (4), 734-739.

Schmit, Joan T. "Lump-Sum Awards In Workers' Compensation: Reply," (4), 740-741.

Eeckhoudt, Louis and Henri Louberge. "Export Credit Insurance: Comment," (4), 742-747.

Funatsu, Hideki. "Export Credit Insurance: Reply," (4), 748-750.

Brotman, Billie Ann and Pauline Fox. "The Impact Of Economic Conditions On The Incidence Of Arson: Comment," (4), 751-754.

Hershbarger, Robert A. and Ronald K. Miller. "The Impact Of Economic Conditions On The Incidence Of Arson: Reply," (4), 755-757.

Journal of Risk and Insurance
Volume 56, 1989

Berger, Lawrence A., Paul R. Kleindorfer and Howard Kunreuther. "A Dynamic Model Of The Transmission Of Price Information In Auto Insurance Markets," (1), 17-33.

Sharp, Keith P. "Mortgage Rate Insurance Pricing Under An Interest Rate Diffusion With Drift," (1), 34-49.

Anderson, Gary A. and David L. Robert. "Stability In The Present Value Assessment Of Lost Earnings," (1), 50-66.

Homan, Rick K., Gerald L. Glandon and Michael A. Counte. "Perceived Risk: The Link To Plan Selection And Future Utilization," (1), 67-82.

Schleef, Harold J. "Whole Life Cost Comparisons Based Upon The Year Of Required Protection," (1), 83-103.

Willinger, Marc. "Risk Aversion And The Value Of Information," (1), 104-112.

Johnson, Steven B. and Jack VanDerhei. "Fiduciary Decision Making And The Nature Of Private Pension Fund Investment Behavior," (1), 113-121.

Jennings, William P. and G. Michael Phillips. "Risk As A Discount Rate Determinant In Wrongful Death And Injury Cases," (1), 122-127.

Cross, Mark L., Wallace N. Davidson and John H. Thornton. "The Impact Of Directors And Officers' Liability Suits On Firm Value," (1), 128-136.

Moore, William T. and Joan T. Schmit. "The Risk Retention Act Of 1986: Effects On Insurance Firm Shareholders' Wealth," (1), 137-145.

Bacon, Peter W., Lawrence J. Gitman, Khurshid Ahmad and M. Fall Ainina. "Long-Term Catastrophic Care: A Financial Planning Perspective," (1), 146-154.

Schnabel, Jacques A. and Ebrahim Roumi. "Corporate Insurance And The Underinvestment Problem: An Extension," (1), 155-159.

Lee, Keun Chang and Stephen P. D'Arcy. "The Optimal Investment Strategy Through Variable Universal Life Insurance," (2), 201-217.

Anderson, Gary A. and David L. Roberts. "A Historical Perspective On The Present Value Assessment Of Medical Care," (2), 218-232.

Diallo, Alahassane and Sangphill Kim. "Asymmetric Information, Captive Insurer's Formation, And Manager's Welfare Gain," (2), 233-251.

Hansen, Ronald W., Paul W. MacAvoy and Clifford W. Smith, Jr. "Compensation Alternatives For Occupational Disease And Disability," (2), 252-274.

Grabowski, Henry, W. Kip Viscusi and William N. Evans. "Price And Availability Tradeoffs Of Automobile Insurance Regulation," (2), 275-299.

Hiebert, L. Dean. "Optimal Loss Reduction And Increases In Risk Aversion," (2), 300-305.

Chen, Charng Y. and Richard PonArul. "On The Tax Incentive For Corporate Insurance Purchase," (2), 306-311.

Fields, Joseph A. and Emilio C. Venezian. "Interest Rates And Profit Cycles: A Disaggregated Approach," (2), 312-319.

Willinger, Marc. "Risk Aversion And The Value Of Information," (2), 320-328.

Klugman, Stuart. "Experience Rating In Medical Professional Liability Insurance: Comment," (2), 329-332.

Nye, Blaine F. and Alfred E. Hofflander. "Experience Rating In Medical Professional Liability Insurance: Reply," (2), 333-335.

JOURNAL OF RISK AND UNCERTAINTY

RECENT DEVELOPMENTS IN
INTERNATIONAL BANKING AND FINANCE

RESEARCH IN FINANCE

Cho, D. Chinhyung and Edward W. Frees. "Estimating The Volatility Of Discrete Stock Prices," 23-58.

De Jong, Piet and Rex Thompson. "Testing Linear Hypothesis In The Sur Framework With Identical Explanatory Variables," 59-76.

Kalay, Avner and Adam Shimrat. "The Maintained Flexibility Of Divided Constraints: A Cross-Sectional And Time Series Analysis," 77-96.

Ang, James S. and William L. Megginson. "A Test Of The Before-Tax Versus After-Tax Equilibrium Models Of Corporate Debt," 97-118.

Kensinger, John W. and John D. Martin. "Project Financing For Research And Development," 119-148.

Guerard, John B., Jr. and George M. McCabe. "A Further Look At The Interdependencies Of Corporate Expenditures And Implications For Strategic-Planning Models," 149-178.

Shastri, Kuldeep. "The Differential Effects Of Mergers On Corporate Security Values," 179-202.

Chalk, Andrew J. and John W. Peavy, III. "Understanding The Pricing Of Initial Public Offerings," 203-240.

Vu, Joseph D. "An Anomalous Evidence Regarding Market Efficiency: The Net Current Asset Value Rule," 241-254.

Osterberg, William P. and James B. Thomson. "Deposit Insurance And The Cost Of Capital," 255-270.

REVIEW OF FINANCIAL STUDIES

Review of Financial Studies
Volume 1, 1988

Williams, Joseph. "A Message From The President Of The Society For Financial Studies," (1), 1-2.

Admati, Anat R. and Paul Pfleiderer. "A Theory Of Intraday Patterns: Volume And Price Variability," (1), 3-40.

Lo, Andrew W. and A. Craig MacKinlay. "Stock Market Prices Do Not Follow Random Walks: Evidence From A Simple Specification Test," (1), 41-66.

Dybvig, Philip H. "Inefficient Dynamic Portfolio Strategies Or How To Throw Away A Million Dollars In The Stock Market," (1), 67-88.

Bagnoli, Mark and Barton L. Lipman. "Successful Takeovers Without Exclusion," (1), 89-110.

Kumar, Praveen. "Shareholder-Manager Conflict And The Information Content Of Dividends," (2), 111-136.

MacKinlay, A. Craig and Krishna Ramaswamy. "Index-Futures Arbitrage And The Behavior Of Stock Index Futures Prices," (2), 137-158.

Jarrow, Robert A. "Preferences, Continuity, And The Arbitrage Pricing Theory," (2), 159-172.

Hirshleifer, David. "Residual Risk, Trading Costs, And Commodity Futures Risk Premia," (2), 173-193.

Campbell, John Y. and Robert J. Shiller. "The Dividend-Price Ratio And Expectations Of Future Dividends And Discount Factors," (3), 195-228.

Allen, Franklin and Douglas Gale. "Optimal Security Design," (3), 229-263.

Giammarino, Ronald and Tracy Lewis. "A Theory Of Negotiated Equity Financing," (3), 265-288.

Hansen, Robert S. "The Demise Of The Rights Issue," (3), 289-309.

Nachman, David C. "Spanning And Completeness With Options," (3), 311-328.

Noe, Thomas H. "Capital Structure And Signaling Game Equilibria," (4), 331-355.

Kamara, Avraham. "Market Trading Structures And Asset Pricing: Evidence From The Treasury-Bill Markets," (4), 357-375.

Dybvig, Philip H. and Chi-fu Huang. "Nonnegative Wealth, Absence Of Arbitrage, And Feasible Consumption Plans," (4), 377-401.

Lakonishok, Josef and Seymour Smidt. "Are Seasonal Anomalies Real? A Ninety-Year Perspective," (4), 403-425.

Jorion, Philippe. "On Jump Processes In The Foreign Exchange And Stock Markets," (4), 427-445.

Review of Financial Studies
Volume 2, 1989

Johnston, Elizabeth Tashjian and John J. McConnell. "Requiem For A Market: An Analysis Of The Rise And Fall Of A Financial Futures Contract," (1), 1-24.

Giammarino, Ronald M. "The Resolution Of Financial Distress," (1), 25-48.

Thakor, Anjan V. "Competitive Equilibrium With Type Convergence In An Asymmetrically Informed Market," (1), 49-72.

Sundaresan, Suresh M. "Intertemporally Dependent Preferences And The Volatility Of Consumption And Wealth," (1), 73-90.

Ronn, Aimee Gerbarg and Ehud I. Ronn. "The Box Spread Arbitrage Conditions: Theory, Tests, And Investment Strategies," (1), 91-108.

Brown, David T. "Claimholder Incentive Conflicts In Reorganization: The Role Of Bankruptcy Law," (1), 109-123.

Kandel, Shmuel and Robert F. Stambaugh. "A Mean-Variance Framework For Tests Of Asset Pricing Models," (2), 125-156.

Dumas, Bernard. "Two-Person Dynamic Equilibrium In The Capital Market," (2), 157-188.

Admati, Anat R. and Paul Pfleiderer. "Divide And Conquer: A Theory Of Intraday And Day-Of-The-Week Mean Effects," (2), 189-224.

Conrad, Jennifer and Gautam Kaul. "Mean Reversion In Short-Horizon Expected Returns," (2), 225-240.

Boyle, Phelim P., Jeremy Evnine and Stephen Gibbs. "Numerical Evaluation Of Multivariate Contingent Claims," (2), 241-250.

Madan, Dilip B., Frank Milne and Hersh Shefrin. "The Multinomial Option Pricing Model And Its Brownian And Poisson Limits," (2), 251-266.

Duffie, Darrell and Matthew O. Jackson. "Optimal Innovation Of Futures Contracts," (3), 275-296.

Cornell, Bradford and Alan C. Shapiro. "The Mispricing Of U.S. Treasury Bonds: A Case Study," (3), 297-310.

Bikhchandani, Sushil and Chi-Fu Huang. "Auctions With Resale Markets: An Exploratory Model Of Treasury Bill Markets," (3), 311-340.

Dammon, Robert M., Kenneth B. Dunn and Chester S. Spatt. "A Reexamination Of The Value Of Tax Options," (3), 341-372.

Connor, Gregory and Robert A. Korajczyk. "An Intertemporal Equilibrium Beta Pricing Model," (3), 373-392.

Grinblatt, Mark and Sheridan Titman. "Portfolio Performance Evaluation: Old Issues And New Insights," (3), 393-422.

Bagnoli, Mark, Roger Gordon and Barton L. Lipman. "Stock Repurchase As A Takeover Defense," (3), 423-443.

Constantinides, George M. and Bruce D. Grundy. "Optimal Investment With Stock Repurchase And Financing As Signals," (4), 445-466.

Bossaerts, Peter and Richard C. Green. "A General Equilibrium Model Of Changing Risk Premia: Theory And Tests," (4), 467-494.

Grundy, Bruce D. and Maureen McNichols. "Trade And Revelation Of Information Through Prices And Direct Disclosure," (4), 495-526.

Brown, David P. and Robert H. Jennings. "On Technical Analysis," (4), 527-552.

Korajczyk, Robert A. and Claude J. Viallet. "An Empirical Investigation Of International Asset Pricing," (4), 553-586.

Hirshleifer, David and I. P. L. Png. "Facilitation Of Competing Bids And The Price Of A Takeover Target," (4), 587-606.

Damodaran, Aswath. "The Weekend Effect In Information Releases: A Study Of Earnings And Dividend Announcements," (4), 607-623.

Review of Financial Studies
Volume 3, 1990

King, Mervyn A. and Sushil Wadhwani. "Transmission Of Volatility Between Stock Markets," (1), 5-33.

Stoll, Hans R. and Robert E. Whaley. "Stock Market Structure And Volatility," (1), 37-71.

Schwert, G. William. "Stock Volatility And The Crash Of '87," (1), 77-102.

Black, Fischer. "Mean Reversion And Consumption Smoothing," (1), 107-114.

Barro, Robert J. "The Stock Market And Investment," (1), 115-132.

Bernanke, Ben S. "Clearing And Settlement During The Crash," (1), 133-151.

Berkovitch, Elazar and M. P. Narayanan. "Competition And The Medium Of Exchange In Takeovers," (2), 153-174.

Lo, Andrew W. and A. Craig MacKinlay. "When Are Contrarian Profits Due To Stock Market Overreaction?," (2), 175-206.

Kandel, Shmuel and Robert F. Stambaugh. "Expectations And Volatility Of Consumption And Asset Returns," (2), 207-232.

Barclay, Michael J., Robert H. Litzenberger and Jerold B. Warner. "Private Information, Trading Volume, And Stock-Return Variances," (2), 233-254.

Brauer, Greggory A. and Eric C. Chang. "Return Seasonality In Stocks And Their Underlying Assets: Tax Loss Selling Versus Information Explanations," (2), 255-280.

Hamao, Yasushi, Ronald W. Masulis and Victor Ng. "Correlations In Price Changes And Volatility Across International Stock Markets," (2), 281-308.

Cadsby, Charles Bram, Murray Frank and Vojislav Maksimovic. "Pooling, Separating, And Semiseparating Equilibria In Financial Markets: Some Experimental Evidence," (3), 315-342.

Eckbo, B. Espen, Vojislav Maksimovic and Joseph Williams. "Consistent Estimation Of Cross-Sectional Models In Event Studies," (3), 343-366.

Rotemberg, Julio J. and David S. Scharfstein. "Shareholder-Value Maximization And Product-Market Competition," (3), 367-392.

Nelson, Daniel B. and Krishna Ramaswamy. "Simple Binomial Processes As Diffusion Approximations In Financial Models," (3), 393-430.

Lo, Andrew W. and A. Craig MacKinlay. "Data-Snooping Biases In Tests Of Financial Asset Pricing Models," (3), 431-468.

Carr, Peter P. and Robert A. Jarrow. "The Stop-Loss Start-Gain Paradox And Option Valuation: A New Decomposition Into Intrinsic And Time Value," (3), 469-492.

Naik, Vasanttilak and Moon Lee. "General Equilibrium Pricing Of Options On The Market Portfolio With Discontinuous Returns," (4), 493-522.

He, Hua. "Convergence From Discrete- To Continuous-Time Contingent Claims Prices," (4), 523-546.

Kim, In Joon. "The Analytic Valuation Of American Options," (4), 547-572.

Hull, John and Alan White. "Pricing Interest-Rate-Derivative Securities," (4), 573-592.

Foster, F. Douglas and S. Viswanathan. "A Theory Of The Interday Variations In Volume, Variance, And Trading Costs In Securities Markets," (4), 593-624.

Scholes, Myron S., G. Peter Wilson and Mark A. Wolfson. "Tax Planning, Regulatory Capital Planning, And Financial Reporting Strategy For Commercial Banks," (4), 625-650.

Eckbo, B. Espen, Ronald M. Giammarino and Robert L. Heinkel. "Asymmetric Information And The Medium Of Exchange In Takeovers: Theory And Tests," (4), 651-676.

Stapleton, R. C. and M. G. Subrahmanyam. "Risk Aversion And The Intertemporal Behavior Of Asset Prices," (4), 677-694.

Peavy, John W., III. "Returns On Initial Public Offerings Of Closed-End Funds," (4), 695-709.

REVIEW OF FUTURES MARKETS

Review of Futures Markets
Volume 1, 1982

Wardrep, Bruce N. and James F. Buck. "Characteristics Of The Speculator's Position In Financial Futures," (1), 1-14.

Bookstaber, Richard. "Interest Rate Hedging For The Mortgage Banker: The Effect Of Interest Rate Futures And Loan Commitments On Portfolio Return Distributions," (1), 22-51.

Firch, Robert S. "Futures Markets As Inverse Forecasters Of Post-harvest Prices For Storable Agricultural Commodities," (1), 62-73.

Figlewski, Stephen and M. Desmond Fitzgerald. "The Price Behaviour Of London Commodity Options," (1), 90-104.

Issue No. 2 contains panel discussions

Thiessen, G. Willard. "Spread Trading In The Grains," (3), 188-194.

Hill, Mark. "How A Commercial Bank Trader Uses The Treasury Bond Market For Various Hedging Applications," (3), 204-209.

Owens, Patricia A. "How A Pension Fund Manager Uses Financial Futures To Hedge A Portfolio," (3), 218-226.

Johnson, James J. "How A Pharmaceutical Company Uses The Futures Markets For Cross-Hedging," (3), 238-246.

Review of Futures Markets
Volume 2, 1983

Conklin, Neilson C. "Grain Exports, Futures Markets, And Pricing Efficiency," (1), 1-25.

Marsh, Terry A. and Robert I. Webb. "Information Dissemination Uncertainty, The Continuity Of Trading, And The Structure Of International Futures Markets," (1), 36-71.

Draper, Dennis W. and James W. Hoag. "Portfolio Strategies Using Treasury Bond Options And Futures," (1), 82-98.

Kolb, Robert W., James V. Jordan and Gerald D. Gay. "Futures Prices And Expected Future Spot Prices," (1), 110-123.

Hill, Joanne, Thomas Schneeweis and Robert Mayerson. "An Analysis Of The Impact Of Marking-To-Market In Hedging With Treasury Bond Futures," (1), 136-159.

Gregory, Owen K. "Banking And Commodity Market Structure: The Early Chicago Board Of Trade," (2), 168-189.

Rothstein, Morton. "The Rejection And Acceptance Of A Marketing Innovation: Hedging In The Late 19th Century," (2), 200-214.

Hieronymus, Thomas A. "Survival And Change: Post-World War II At The Chicago Board Of Trade," (2), 222-238.

Howard, James A. "Grain Trading In The 1970s," (2), 252-261.

Resnick, Bruce G. and Elizabeth Hennigar. "The Relationship Between Futures And Cash Prices For U.S. Treasury Bonds," (3), 282-299.

Martin, Stanley A. and Ronald W. Spahr. "Futures Market Efficiency As A Function Of Market Speculation," (3), 314-328.

Schneeweis, Thomas R., Joanne M. Hill and Michael G. Philipp. "Hedge Ratio Determination Based On Bond Yield Forecasts," (3),338-349.

Chiang, Raymond C. and T. Craig Tapley. "Day-Of-The-Week Effects And The Futures Market," (3), 356-410.

Review of Futures Markets
Volume 3, 1984

Dahlgran, Roger A. and Dale W. Jergensen. "The Feasibility Of Hedging Working Capital Costs In Financial Futures Markets By Small Agribusiness Firms," (1), 1-12.

Khoury, Sarkis J. and Gerald L. Jones. "Daily Price Limits On Futures Contracts: Nature, Impact, And Justification," (1), 22-36.

Heymann, Hans G. and Richard E. Cohan. "The Effect Of Financial Futures Trading On The Bid-Ask Spread Of Cash Market T-Bonds," (1), 48-57.

Wilson, William W. "Hedging Effectiveness Of U.S. Wheat Futures Markets," (1), 64-79.

Resnick, Bruce G. "The Relationship Between Futures Prices For U.S. Treasury Bonds," (1), 88-104.

Wilson, Stephen D. "Hedging A Mortgage Pipeline," (2), 116-121.

Gunnin, Robert G. "Petroleum Futures Trading: Practical Applications By The Trade," (2), 128-140.

Phillips, Susan M. "Regulation Of Futures Markets: Theory And Practice," (2), 150-158.

Sheldon, Randall E. "Options Contracts," (2), 166-170.

Brophy, Daniel F. "Commercial Use Of Options," (2), 174-178.

Behr, Robert M. and Ronald W. Ward. "A Simultaneous Equation Model Of Futures Market Trading Activity," (3), 194-212.

Leuck, Richard C. and Raymond M. Leuthold. "Agribusiness Firms As Users Of Financial Futures: The Case Of Grain Elevators," (3), 222-234.

Pan, Fung-Shine and James W. Hoag. "The Pricing Of GNMA Futures Using Dealer Quotations And Spot Transactions," (3), 244-255.

Irwin, Scott H. and J. William Uhrig. "Do Technical Analysts Have Holes In Their Shoes?," (3), 264-277.

Rzepczynski, Mark S. "The Behavior Of Primary Government Security Dealers And Their Use Of Financial Futures," (3), 282-317.

Review of Futures Markets
Volume 4, 1985

Kolb, Robert W., Gerald D. Gay and William C. Hunter. "Liquidity And Capital Requirements For Futures Market Hedges," (1), 1-25.

Sholund, J. Douglas. "The Impact Of Financial Futures On The Firm's Cost Of Capital And Investment Decisions," (1), 36-49.

Bookstaber, Richard M. and James B. McDonald. "A Generalized Option Valuation Model For The Pricing Of Bond Options," (1),60-73.

Brorsen, B. Wade and Scott H. Irwin. "Examination Of Commodity Fund Performance," (1), 84-94.

Barnhill, Theodore M., William W. Hardgrave and Rehman P. Kassam. "An Empirical Study Of T-Bond Futures Contract Price Change Patterns Around U.S. Treasury Quarterly Refundings," (1),106-131.

Chance, Don M. "The Reaction Of The Chicago Board Of Trade GNMA Futures Contract To The Announcement Of Inflation Rates: A Study Of Market Efficiency," (1), 132-154.

Maxwell, Chris D. "Commercial Banks And Financial Futures: Current Practice," (2), 170-177.

Lodge, Howard R. "Variations In The Use Of Futures By Commercial Banks," (2), 178-184.

Pomeranz, Robert J. "Thrift Industry Usage Of Financial Futures: A Regulator's Perspective," (2), 190-195.

Beighley, Scott. "Financial Futures Applications By The Thrift Industry," (2), 196-206.

Matteson, David M. "The Insurance Industry And Futures Markets: Regulatory Problems," (2), 212-217.

O'Connor, Kevin J. "The Insurance Industry And Futures Markets: Current Practice," (2), 218-223.

DeRonne, William A. "Pension Funds And Futures Markets: Option Hedging Of Fixed-Rate Assets," (2), 232-241.

Rutz, Roger D. "Key Features Of The Municipal Bond Futures Contract," (2), 252-259.

Hegel, Peter W. "Potential Uses Of The Municipal Bond Futures Contract By A Unit Investment Trust," (2), 260-267.

Trader, William A. "Dealer Uses Of The Municipal Bond Futures Contract," (2), 268-272.

Barnhill, Theodore M. and William C. Handorf. "An Application Of Monte Carlo Simulation Modeling To Commercial Bank Interest Rate Management," (3), 282-305.

Milonas, Nikolaos T. and Ashok Vora. "Sources Of Nonstationarity In Cash And Futures Prices," (3), 314-326.

Lacey, Nelson J. and Donald R. Chambers. "The Investigation Of A Systematic Prepayment Option In GNMA Futures," (3), 338-353.

Epps, T. W. and Michael J. Kukanza. "Predictions Of Returns To Commodities Speculation Based On Current Information: Some Evidence Of Informational Inefficiency In Futures Markets," (3), 366-382.

Craine, Roger. "Maturity Intermediation And Interest Rate Risks: Hedging Strategies For S&Ls," (3), 390-403.

Review of Futures Markets
Volume 5, 1986

Morowitz, Jacob J. "Speculation In The Metals Markets," (1), 1-14.

Tesar, Robert. "Agricultural Options: Practical Usage By A Commercial Firm," (1), 24-34.

Kelly, Thomas M., Jr. "Arbitrage In Government Security Markets," (1), 44-52.

Selmer, Brian. "Stock Index Futures Trading," (1), 60-69.

Koop, Dwight. "Pricing Options: Variations On The Black-Scholes Model," (1), 80-89.

Bookstaber, Richard M. "Contract And Market Hedging: A Comparison Of Futures Contracts And Adjustable Rate Mortgages In Hedging Interest Rate Risk," (1), 100-123.

Chance, Don M. "Futures Contracts And Immunization," (2), 124-141.

Maness, Terry S. and A. J. Senchack. "Futures Hedging And The Reported Financial Position Of Thrift Institutions," (2), 142-159.

Hunter, William C. "Rational Margins On Futures Contracts: Initial Margins," (2), 160-173.

Rendleman, Richard J., Jr. "Commentary On The Effects Of Stock Index Futures Trading On The Market For Underlying Stocks," (3), 174-187.

Randolph, William Lewis. "The Relative Pricing Of Options On Futures And Options On The Spot," (3), 198-215.

Kahl, Kandice H. and Charles E. Curtis, Jr. "A Comparative Analysis Of The Corn Basis In Feed Grain Deficit And Surplus Areas," (3), 220-232.

Hartzmark, Michael L. "Regulating Futures Margin Requirements," (3), 242-260.

Heuson, Andrea J. "Market Maturation Effects In Options On Treasury Bond Futures," (3), 274-283.

Whaley, Robert E. "Expiration-Day Effects Of Index Futures And Options--Empirical Results," (3), 292-308.

Stoll, Hans R. "Expiration-Day Effects Of Index Futures And Options--Alternative Proposals," (3), 309-312.

Review of Futures Markets
Volume 6, 1987

Chiang, Raymond C., Gerald D. Gay and Robert W. Kolb. "Commodity Exchange Seat Prices," (1), 1-10.

Miller, Stephen E. and Kandice H. Kahl. "Forward Pricing When Yields Are Uncertain," (1), 20-39.

Swidler, Steven and Terry L. Zivney. "An Empirical Analysis Of The Early Exercise Premium," (1), 46-56.

Geske, Robert L. and Dan R. Pieptea. Controlling Interest Rate Risk And Return With Futures," (1), 64-86.

Goodman, Laurie S. and N. R. Vijayaraghavan. "Generalized Duration Hedging With Futures Contracts," (1), 94-108.

Brorsen, B. Wade and Scott H. Irwin. "Futures Funds And Price Volatility," (1), 118-135.

Koppenhaver, Gary D. "Regulating Financial Intermediary Use Of Futures And Options," (2), 144-164.

Curtis, Charles E., Jr., Kandice H. Kahl and Cathy S. McKinnell. "Risk-Efficient Soybean Marketing: The Contribution Of Commodity Options To The Producing Firm," (2), 176-190.

Whittaker, Gregg, Linda E. Bowyer and Daniel P. Klein. "The Effect Of Futures Trading On The Municipal Bond Market," (2), 196-204.

Monke, Eric A. and Alessandro Sorrentino. "Exchange Rate Changes

REVIEW OF QUANTITATIVE FINANCE AND ACCOUNTING

PART TWO

AUTHOR
INDEX

Abbott, Charles C. "Notes On Federal Reserve Policy, August 1945-June, 1948," JOF, 1949, v4(2), 101-110.

Abbott, H. Paul. "A Property-Casualty Educational Program," JRI, 1948, v15, 16-25.

Abbott, H. Paul. "Visual Aids In Property-Casualty Insurance Teaching," JRI, 1951, v18, 14-27.

Abbott, Jarold G. and Neil E. Seitz. "An Evaluation Of An Innovative Approach To Graduate Business Education," JFED, 1974, v3,28-38.

Abdelsamad, M. H. and J. E. Thornton. "An Evaluation Of Business Masters Programs By Graduates," JFED, 1979, v8, 49-52.

Abdullah, Fuad A. (Rhee, Thomas A. and Fuad Abdullah. "The Intermarket Pricing Relations In The Foreign Currency Option Market," IJOF, 1989, v2(1), 50-57.)

Abel, Andrew B. "The Implications Of Insurance For The Efficacy Of Fiscal Policy," JRI, 1988, v55(2), 339-378.

Abel, Burl M. "Tools For Recruiting College Men For Life Insurance," JRI, 1961, v28(2), 97-98.

Abelle, Barnie E. "The Teaching-Learning Implications Of Educational Technology," JRI, 1973, v40(4), 607-616.

Abelle, Barnie E., Jr. "An Evaluation Of The Life Insurance Company Income Tax Act Of 1959," JRI, 1963, v30(3), 403-422.

Abelle, Barnie E., Jr. "An Evaluation Of The Life Insurance Company Income Tax Act Of 1959: Comment," JRI, 1964, v31(2), 298-300.

Abelson, Michael A., K. Michele Kacmar and Ellen F. Jackofsky. "Factors Influencing Real Estate Brokerage Sales Staff Performance," JRER, 1990, v5(2), 265-275.

Aber, John W. "Industry Effects And Multivariate Stock Price Behavior," JFQA, 1976, v11(4), 617-624.

Abeysekera, Sarath P. and Arvind Mahajan. "A Test Of The APT In Pricing UK Stocks," JBFA, 1987, v14(3), 377-392.

Abitala, Pekka. "The Effects Of Foreign Disturbances Under Flexible Exchange Rates," JIMF, 1987, v6(4), 387-400.

Abken, Peter A. "An Analysis Of Intra-Market Spreads In Heating Oil Futures," JFM, 1989, v9(1), 77-87.

Able, Stephen. (Klein, Lawrence R., Edward Friedman and Stephen Able. "Money In The Wharton Quarterly Model," JMCB, 1983, v15(2), 237-259.)

Abraham, Rebecca Jacob. (Trippi, Robert R. and Rebecca Jacob Abraham. "Interest Rates Implied In The Prices Of S&P 100 Options: Evidence And Implications Of An Inverted Ultra-Short Term Structure," IJOF, 1990, v2(2), 52-66.)

Abrahamson, Allen A. and John T. Emery. "An Alternative Approach To Asset Selection Under Uncertainty," AREUEA, 1974, v2(1), 75-88.

Abrams, Richard K., Richard Froyen and Roger N. Waud. "Monetary Policy Reaction Functions, Consistent Expectations, And The Burns Era," JMCB, 1980, v12(1), 30-42.

Abranovic, Wynn A. "An Interactive Computer Program For Financial Break-Even Analysis," JFED, 1976, v5, 91-93.

Abuaf, Niso and Philippe Jorion. "Purchasing Power Parity In The Long Run," JOF, 1990, v45(1), 157-174.

Aby, Carroll D., Jr. (DeThomas, Arthur R. and Carroll D. Aby, Jr. "Stock Price Trends And Point And Figure Charting: An Empirical Evaluation," FR, 1975, v10(1), 45-54.)

Aby, Carroll D., Jr. (Granger, Fred W., Jr. and Carroll D. Aby, Jr. "A Survey Of The Introductory Investment Course Design," JFED, 1977, v6, 9-13.)

Achampong, Francis. "The Means And Ends Of Insurance Regulation - Basic Ideas," JRI, 1983, v50(2), 301-306.

Acharya, Sankarshan and Jean-Francois Dreyfus. "Optimal Bank Reorganization Policies And The Pricing Of Federal Deposit Insurance," JOF, 1989, v44(5), 1313-1334.

Acharya, Sankarshan. "A Generalized Econometric Model And Tests Of A Signalling Hypothesis With Two Discrete Signals," JOF, 1988, v43(2), 413-429.

Acheson, Keith and John F. Chant. "Bureaucratic Theory And The Choice Of Central Bank Goals: The Case Of The Bank Of Canada," JMCB, 1973, v5(2), 637-655.

Acheson, Keith. "The Allocation Of Government Deposits Among Private Banks: The Canadian Case," JMCB, 1977, v9(3), 447-459.

Acheson, Marcus W., IV and David W. Halstead. "Trends In Securitization - Private And Public," JACF, 1988, v1(3), 52-60.

Ackerman, George F. "Japanese Silk Industry," FAJ, 1961, v17(5), 81-83.

Ackley, Gardner. "The Contribution Of Economists To Policy Formation," JOF, 1966, v21(2), 169-177.

Aczel, Michael, Jack Broyles and Bronek Masojada. "Participation In The Lloyd's Insurance Market As A Portfolio Investment," JBFA, 1990, v17(5), 609-634.

Adamche, Killard W. (Rossiter, Lewis F., Killard W. Adamche and Tamara Faulknier. "A Blended Sector Rate Adjustment For The Medicare AAPCC When Risk-Based Market Penetration Is High," JRI, 1990, v57(2), 220-239.)

Adams, Charles and Russell S. Boyer. "Efficiency And A Simple Model Of Exchange-Rate Determination," JIMF, 1986, v5(3), 285-302.

Adams, F. Charles. (Boyer, Russell S. and F. Charles Adams. "Forward Premia And Risk Premia In A Simple Model Of Exchange Rate Determination," JMCB, 1988, v20(4), 633-644.)

Adams, F. Gerard and Helen B. Junz. "The Effect Of The Business Cycle On Trade Flows Of Industrial Countries," JOF, 1971, v26(2), 251-268.

Adams, John F. "Consumer Attitudes, Judical Decision, Government Regulation, And The Insurance Market," JRI, 1976, v43(3), 501-512.

Adams, John F. "Law, Insurance, And The Automobile Accident Victim - Social And Economic Aspects," JRI, 1962, v29(4), 523-532.

Adams, John F. "Research Dealing With The Financial Consequences Of Automobile Accidents," JRI, 1956, v23, 135-141.

Adams, John F. "Some Observations On Experience Rating In Unemployment Insurance," JRI, 1959, v26(3), 25-32.

Adams, John F. "Some Observations On The Insurance Educator's Quest For Security," JRI, 1967, v34(1), 1-8.

Adams, Paul D. and Steve B. Wyatt. "On The Pricing Of European And American Foreign Currency Call Options," JIMF, 1987, v6(3), 315-338.

Adams, Paul D. and Steve B. Wyatt. "Biases In Option Prices: Evidence From The Foreign Currency Option Market," JBF, 1987, v11(4), 549-562.

Adams, Paul D. and Steve B. Wyatt. "On The Pricing Of European And American Foreign Currency Options: A Clarification," JIMF, 1989, v8(2), 305-311.

Adams, Richard A. (Hawkins, Clark A. and Richard A. Adams. "A Goal Programming Model For Capital Budgeting," FM, 1974, v3(1), 52-57.)

Adams, Rodney H. "Endowment Funds Are A Distinct Case," JPM, 1977, v3(2), 37-45.

Adams, Walter. "Consumer Needs And Consumer Sovereignty In The American Economy," JOB, 1962, v35(3), 264-277.

Adams, William C. "Trading: The Fixable Leak: Comment," JPM, 1982, v8(4), 76.

Adar, Zvi and Seev Neumann. "On Optimal Property Insurance Policies," JRI, 1978, v45(1), 95-108.

Adar, Zvi, Tamir Agmon and Yair E. Orgler. "Output Mix And Jointness In Production In The Banking Firm," JMCB, 1975, v7(2), 235-243.

Adderley, Terence E. and Douglas A. Hayes. "The Investment Performance Of Selected Growth Stock Portfolios: 1939-55," FAJ, 1957, v13(2), 65-78.

Adelberger, Otto L. "SIMULFIN: A General Financial Simulation Model Of The Firm For Teaching And Research Purposes," JFED, 1974, v3, 96-104.

Adelman, M. A. "Business Size And Public Policy," JOB, 1951, v24(4), 269-279.

Adelman, M. A. "Oil Prices In The Long Run (1963-75)," JOB, 1964, v37(2), 143-161.

Adelman, Maurice A. and Barry C. Good. "The 7 Sisters: Comment," JPM, 1976, v3(1), 72.

Adelman, Saul W. and Mark S. Dorfman. "A Comparison Of TDA And Non-TDA Investment Returns," JRI, 1982, v49(1), 73-90.

Adkisson, J. Amanda and Donald R. Fraser. "The Effect Of Geographical Deregulation On Bank Acquisition Premiums," JFSR, 1990, v4(2), 145-156.

Adler, Michael and Bernard Dumas. "The Exposure Of Long-Term Foreign Currency Bonds," JFQA, 1980, v15(4), 973-994.

Adler, Michael and Bernard Dumas. "Optimal International Acquisitions," JOF, 1975, v30(1), 1-19.

Adler, Michael and Bernard Dumas. "International Portfolio Choice And Corporation Finance: A Synthesis," JOF, 1983, v38(3), 925-984.

Adler, Michael and Bernard Dumas. "Exposure To Currency Risk: Definition And Measurement," FM, 1984, v13(2), 41-50.

Adler, Michael and Bruce Lehmann. "Deviations From Purchasing Power Parity In The Long Run," JOF, 1983, v38(5), 1471-1487.

Adler, Michael and David Simon. "Exchange Risk Surprises In International Portfolios," JPM, 1986, v12(2), 44-53.

Adler, Michael and Guy V. G. Stevens. "The Trade Effects Of Direct Investment," JOF, 1974, v29(2),655-676.

Adler, Michael and Reuven Horesh. "The Relationship Among Equity Markets: Comment," JOF, 1974, v29(4), 1311-1317.

Adler, Michael and G. C. Hufbauer. "On Balance-Of-Payments Payback Periods," JOB, 1972, v45(3),416-421.

Adler, Michael and Jerome B. Detemple. "On The Optimal Hedge Of A Nontraded Cash Position," JOF, 1988, v43(1), 143-153.

Adler, Michael and Jerome Detemple. "Hedging With Futures In An Intertemporal Portfolio Context," JFM, 1988, v8(3), 249-270.

Adler, Michael and Michael Granito. "Should International Portfolios Be Permanently Hedged?," RDIBF, 1991, v4/5, 271-309.

Adler, Michael. "Designing Spreads In Forward Exchange Contracts And Foreign Exchange Futures," JFM, 1983, v3(4), 355-368.

Adler, Michael. "Global Fixed-Income Portfolio Management," FAJ, 1983, v39(5), 41-48.

Adler, Michael. "Investor Recognition Of Corporation International Diversification: Comment," JOF, 1981, v36(1), 187-190.

Adler, Michael. "On Risk-Adjusted Capitalization Rates And Valuation By Individuals," JOF, 1970, v25(4), 819-835.

Adler, Michael. "On The Risk-Return Trade-Off In The Valuation Of Assets," JFQA, 1969, v4(4), 493-512.

Adler, Michael. "The Cost Of Capital And Valuation Of A Two-Country Firm," JOF, 1974, v29(1),119-132.

Adler, Michael. "The Cost Of Capital And Valuation Of A Two-Country Firm: Reply," JOF, 1977, v32(4), 1354-1357.

Adler, Oliver. "Some Macroeconomic Effects Of Nationalizing Private Sector Foreign Debt," JIMF, 1990, v9(4), 388-401.

Admati, Anat R. and Paul Pfleiderer. "A Theory Of Intraday Patterns: Volume And Price Variability," RFS, 1988-89, v1(1), 3-40.

Admati, Anat R. and Paul Pfleiderer. "Divide And Conquer: A Theory Of Intraday And Day-Of-The-Week Mean Effects," RFS, 1989, v2(2), 189-224.

Admati, Anat R. and Stephen A. Ross. "Measuring Investment Performance In A Rational Expectations Equilibrium Model," JOB, 1985, v58(1), 1-26.

Admati, Anat R. and Stephen A. Ross. "Corrigendum," JOB, 1986, v59(2), Part 1, 367.

Admati, Anat R., Sudipto Bhattacharya, Paul Pfleiderer and Stephen A. Ross. "On Timing And Selectivity," JOF, 1986, v41(3), 715-729.

Affleck, A. R. P. (Tepper, Irwin and A. R. P. Affleck. "Pension Plan Liabilities And Corporate Financial Strategies," JOF, 1974, v29(5), 1549-1564.)

Affleck-Graves, J. F. (Knight, R. F. and J. F. Affleck-Graves," The Impact Of Disclosure Requirements On The Systematic Risk Of South African Companies," **JBFA**, 1986, v13(1), 87-94.)

Affleck-Graves, John F. (Carter, Kevin J., John F. Affleck-Graves and Arthur H. Money. "Are Gold Shares Better Than Gold For Diversification?," **JPM**, 1982, v9(1), 52-55.)

Affleck-Graves, John F. (Knight, Rory F. and John F. Affleck-Graves. "Further Evidence On The Market Response To LIFO Adoptions," **JBFA**, 1988, v15(2), 169-184.)

Affleck-Graves, John and Bill McDonald. "Nonnormalities And Tests Of Asset Pricing Theories," **JOF**, 1989, v44(4), 889-908.

Affleck-Graves, John and Bill McDonald. "Multivariate Tests Of Asset Pricing: The Comparative Power Of Alternative Statistics," **JFQA**, 1990, v25(2), 163-186.

Affleck-Graves, John and Robert E. Miller. "Regulatory And Procedural Effects On The Underpricing Of Initial Public Offerings," **JFR**, 1989, v12(3), 193-202.

Aftalion, Florin and Lawrence J. White. "On The Choice Of Immediate Monetary Targets," **JBF**, 1978, v2(1), 1-13.

Aftalion, Florin and Lawrence J. White. "A Study Of A Monetary System With A Pegged Discount Rate Under Different Market Structures," **JBF**, 1977, v1(4), 349-371.

Aftalion, Florin and Lawrence J. White. "A Study Of A Monetary System With Pegged Discount Rate Under Different Market Structures: A Reply To J. Vuchelen," **JBF**, 1978, v2(4), 351-354.

Agarwal, Vinod B. and Richard A. Phillips. "The Effect Of Mortgage Rate Buydowns On Housing Prices: Recent Evidence From FHA-VA Transactions," **AREUEA**, 1983, v11(4), 491-503.

Agarwal, Vinod B. and Richard A. Philips. "The Effects Of Assumption Financing Across Housing Price Categories," **AREUEA**, 1985, v13(1), 48-57.

Aggarwal, Raj and Luc A. Soenen. "The Nature And Efficiency Of The Gold Market," **JPM**, 1988, v14(3), 18-21.

Aggarwal, Raj and P. S. Sundararaghavan. "Efficiency Of The Silver Futures Market: An Empirical Study Using Daily Data," **JBF**, 1987, v11(1), 49-64.

Aggarwal, Raj and Ramesh P. Rao. "Institutional Ownership And Distribution Of Equity Returns," **FR**, 1990, v25(2), 211-230.

Aggarwal, Raj, Ramesh P. Rao and Takato Hiraki. "Skewness And Kurtosis In Japanese Equity Returns: Empirical Evidence," **JFR**, 1989, v12(3), 253-260.

Aggarwal, Raj, Ramesh P. Rao and Takato Hiraki. "Regularities In Tokyo Stock Exchange Security Returns: P/E, Size, And Seasonal Influences," **JFR**, 1990, v13(3), 249-263.

Aggarwal, Raj. "International Business Finance: A Selected Bibliography," **JFED**, 1977, v6, 96.

Aggarwal, Raj. "The Distribution Of Exchange Rates And Forward Risk Premia," **AFPAF**, 1989, v4(Supp), 43-54.

Aggarwal, Raj. (Baliga, Gurudutt and Raj Aggarwal. "Domestic Versus Transnational Mergers: Differences In Participating Firms," **AFPAF**, 1990, v5(1), 315-335.)

Aggarwal, Raj. (Bonitsis, Theologos Homer and Raj Aggarwal. "U.S. Direct Foreign Investment And Economic Growth In Brazil: An Econometric Causal Analysis," **IJOF**, 1990, v2(2), 12-19.)

Aggarwal, Raj. (Soenen, Luc A. and Raj Aggarwal. "Cash And Foreign Exchange Management: Theory And Corporate Practice In Three Countries," **JBFA**, 1989, v16(5), 599-620.)

Aggarwal, Reena and Pietra Rivoli. "Fads In The Initial Public Offering Market?," **FM**, 1990, v19(4), 45-57.

Aggarwal, Reena and Pietra Rivoli. "Seasonal And Day-Of-The-Week Effects In Four Emerging Stock Markets," **FR**, 1989, v24(4), 541-550.

Aggarwal, Reena. "Stock Index Futures And Cash Market Volatility," **RFM**, 1988, v7(2), 290-299.

Aggarwal, Reena. (Chen, Son-Nan and Reena Aggarwal. "Optimal Portfolio Selection And Uncertain Inflation," **JPM**, 1986, v13(1), 44-49.)

Aghili, Parvis, Robert H. Cramer and Howard E. Thompson. "Small Bank Balance Sheet Management: Applying Two-Stage Programming Models," **JBR**, 1974-75, v5(4), 246-256.

Agmon, T., A. R. Ofer and A. Tamir. "Variable Rate Debt Instruments And Corporate Debt Policy," **JOF**, 1981, v36(1), 113-125.

Agmon, Tamir and Donald Lessard. "Investor Recognition Of Corporate International Diversification: A Note," **JOF**, 1981, v36(1), 191-192.

Agmon, Tamir and Donald R. Lessard. "Investor Recognition Of Corporate International Diversification," **JOF**, 1977, v32(4), 1049-1055.

Agmon, Tamir and J. Kimball Dietrich. "International Lending And Income Redistribution: An Alternative View Of Country Risk," **JBF**, 1983, v7(4), 483-495.

Agmon, Tamir and M. Chapman Findlay. "Domestic Political Risk And Stock Valuation," **FAJ**, 1982, v38(6), 74-77.

Agmon, Tamir and Ruth Arad. "Exchange Risk And Unanticipated Changes In Exchange Rates," **JBF**, 1978, v2(3), 269-280.

Agmon, Tamir and Saul Bronfield. "The International Mobility Of Short-Term Covered Arbitrage Capital," **JBFA**, 1975, v2(2), 269-278.

Agmon, Tamir and Yakov Amihud. "The Forward Exchange Rate And The Prediction Of The Future Spot Rate: Empirical Evidence," **JBF**, 1981, v5(3), 425-437.

Agmon, Tamir. "The Relations Among Equity Markets: A Study Of Share Price Co-Movements In The United States, United Kingdom, Germany And Japan," **JOF**, 1972, v27(4), 839-855.

Agmon, Tamir. "Capital Budgeting And Unanticipated Changes In The Exchange Rate," **AFPAF**, 1990, v5(1), 295-314.

Agmon, Tamir. "Country Risk: The Significance Of The Country Factor For Share-price Movements In The United Kingdom, Germany, And Japan," **JOB**, 1973, v46(1), 24-32.

Agmon, Tamir. "The Relationship Among Equity Markets: Reply," **JOF**, 1974, v29(4), 1318-1319.

Agmon, Tamir. (Adar, Zvi, Tamir Agmon and Yair E. Orgler. "Output Mix And Jointness In Production In The Banking Firm," **JMCB**, 1975, v7(2), 235-243.)

Agnello, W., W. Brueggeman, G. Decker, R. Griffith, R. Leftwich, R. Moore, J. Neal, B. Sternlicht, B. Wallach, W. Wardrop and C. Zinngrabe. "Panel: Corporate Real Estate Roundtable," **JACF**, 1990, v3(1), 6-38.

Agrawal, Anup and Gershon N. Mandelker. "Managerial Incentives And Corporate Investment And Financing Decisions," **JOF**, 1987, v42(4), 823-838.

Agrawal, Anup and Gershon N. Mandelker. "Large Shareholders And The Monitoring Of Managers: The Case Of Antitakeover Charter Amendments," **JFQA**, 1990, v25(2), 143-162.

Agrawal, Anup and Nandu J. Nagarajan. "Corporate Capital Structure, Agency Costs, And Ownership Control: The Case Of All-Equity Firms," **JOF**, 1990, v45(4), 1325-1331.

Aharony, Joseph and Itzhak Swary. "Quarterly Dividend And Earnings Announcements And Stockholders' Returns: An Empirical Analysis," **JOF**, 1980, v35(1), 1-12.

Aharony, Joseph and Itzhak Swary. "Effects Of The 1970 Bank Holding Company Act: Evidence From Capital Markets," **JOF**, 1981, v36(4), 841-853.

Aharony, Joseph and Martin Loeb. "Mean-Variance Vs. Stochastic Dominance: Some Empirical Findings On Efficient Sets," **JBF**, 1977, v1(1), 95-102.

Aharony, Joseph and Itzhak Swary. "Contagion Effects Of Bank Failures: Evidence From Capital Markets," **JOB**, 1983, v56(3), 305-322.

Aharony, Joseph and Itzhak Swary. "A Note On Corporate Bankruptcy And The Market Model Risk Measures," **JBFA**, 1988, v15(2), 275-282.

Aharony, Joseph, Anthony Saunders and Itzhak Swary. "The Effects Of The International Banking Act On Domestic Bank Profitability And Risk," **JMCB**, 1985, v17(4), Part 1, 493-506.

Aharony, Joseph, Charles P. Jones and Itzhak Swary. "An Analysis Of Risk And Return Characteristics Of Corporate Bankruptcy Using Capital Market Data," **JOF**, 1980, v35(4), 1001-1016.

Aharony, Joseph, Anthony Saunders and Itzhak Swary. "The Effects Of DIDMCA On Bank Stockholders' Returns And Risk," **JBF**, 1988, v11(3), 317-332.

Aharony, Joseph, Haim Falk and Itzhak Swary. "Information Content Of Dividend Increases: The Case Of Regulated Utilities," **JBFA**, 1988, v15(3), 401-414.

Ahearn, Daniel S. "Investment Management And Economic Research," **FAJ**, 1964, v20(1), 15-20.

Ahearn, Daniel S. "The Strategic Role Of Fixed Income Securities," **JPM**, 1975, v1(3), 12-16.

Ahern, David P. "Auto Industry," **FAJ**, 1968, v24(3), 96-102.

Ahking, Francis W. "The Predictive Performance Of The Time-Series Model And The Regression Model Of The Income Velocity Of Money: Evidence From Five EEC Countries," **JBF**, 1984, v8(3), 389-415.

Ahlbrandt, Roger S., Jr. "Public Policies For The Preservation Of Capital In Older Areas," **AREUEA**, 1977, v5(1), 68-84.

Ahlbrnadt, Roger S., Jr. "Exploratory Research On The Redlining Phenomenon," **AREUEA**, 1977, v5(4), 473-481.

Ahmad, Khurshid. (Bacon, Peter W., Lawrence J. Gitman, Khurshid Ahmad and M. Fall Ainina. "Long-Term Catastrophic Care: A Financial Planning Perspective," **JRI**, 1989, v56(1), 146-154.)

Ahmad, Syed. "The `Paradox Of Bliss' And Money As Net Wealth: A Comment," **JMCB**, 1975, v7(3), 385-390.

Ahmed, Ehsan and James M. Johannes. "St. Louis Equation Restrictions And Criticisms Revisited," **JMCB**, 1984, v16(4), Part 1, 514-520.

Ahmed, Roken. (Ferguson, Robert and Roken Ahmed. "How To Get Rich Quick (Without Losing Sleep)," **FAJ**, 1988, v44(4), 68-75.)

Ahn, Chang Mo and Howard E. Thompson. "Jump-Diffusion Processes And Term Structure Of Interest Rates," **JOF**, 1988, v43(1), 155-174.

Ahn, Chang Mo. "The Effect Of Temporal Risk Aversion On Optimal Consumption, The Equity Premium, And The Equilibrium Interest Rate," **JOF**, 1989, v44(5), 1411-1420.

Ahn, Chul Won and W. Jung. "The Choice Of A Monetary Instrument In A Small Open Economy: The Case Of Korea," **JIMF**, 1985, v4(4), 469-484.

Ahsan, Syed M. "Relative Risk-Aversion And The Demand For Cash Balances," **JOF**, 1977, v32(3), 769-774.

Aigner, D. J. and C. M. Sprenkle. "On Optimal Financing Of Cyclical Cash Needs," **JOF**, 1973, v28(5), 1249-1254.

Aigner, D. J. and C. M. Sprenkle. "A Simple Model Of Information And Lending Behavior," **JOF**, 1968, v23(1), 151-166.

Aigner, Dennis J. and William R. Bryan. "The Determinants Of Member Bank Borrowing: A Critique," **JOF**, 1968, v23(5), 832-837.

Ainina, M. Fall (Mohan, Nancy, M. Fall Ainina, Daniel Kaufman and Bernard J. Winger. "Acquisition/Divestiture Valuation Practices In Major U.S. Firms," **FPE**, 1991, v1(1), 73-82.)

Ainina, M. Fall and Nancy K. Mohan. "When LBOs Go IPO," **JBFA**, 1991, v18(3), 393-404.

Ainina, M. Fall. (Bacon, Peter W., Lawrence J. Gitman, Khurshid Ahmad and M. Fall Ainina. "Long-Term Catastrophic Care: A Financial Planning Perspective," **JRI**, 1989, v56(1), 146-154.)

Aitken, Michael. "The Australian Securities Industry Under Negotiated Brokerage Commissions: Evidence Of The Effects Of Change On The Structure Of The Industry," **JBFA**, 1990, v17(2), 213-246.

Aiuppa, Thomas A. "Evaluation Of Pearson Curves As An Approximation Of The Maximum Probable Annual Aggregate Loss," **JRI**, 1988, v55(3), 425-441.

Aiuppa, Thomas A. and James S. Trieschmann. "An Empirical Analysis Of The Magnitude And Accuracy Of Incurred-But-Not-Reported Reserves," **JRI**, 1987, v54(1), 100-118.

Aivazian, Varouj A. and Jeffrey L. Callen. "Investment, Market Structure, And The Cost Of Capital," **JOF**, 1979, v34(1), 85-92.

Aivazian, Varouj A. and Jeffrey L. Callen. "The `Unanimity' Literature And The Security Market Line Criterion: The Additive Risk Case," **JBFA**, 1981, v8(2),177-184.

Aivazian, Varouj A. and Jeffrey L. Callen. "Reorganization In Bankruptcy And The Issue Of Strategic Risk," **JBF**, 1983, v7(1), 119-134.

Aivazian, Varouj A. and Jeffrey L. Callen. "Future Investment Opportunities And The Value Of The Call Provision On A Bond: Comment," **JOF**, 1980, v35(4), 1051-1054.

Aivazian, Varouj A. and Jeffrey L. Callen. "Corporate Leverage And Growth: The Game-Theoretic Issues," **JFEC**, 1980, v8(4), 379-399.

Aivazian, Varouj A. and Jeffrey L. Callen. "On Unanimity And Monopoly Power," JBFA, 1985, v12(1), 145-149.

Aivazian, Varouj A. and Jeffrey L. Callen. "Miller's Irrelevance Mechanism: A Note," JOF, 1987, v42(1), 169-180.

Aivazian, Varouj A., J. L. Callen, I. Krinsky and Clarence C. Y. Kwan. "Mean-Variance Utility Functions And The Demand For Risky Assets: An Empirical Analysis Using Flexible Functional Forms," JFQA, 1983, v18(4), 411-424.

Aivazian, Varouj A., Jeffrey L. Callen, Itzhak Krinsky and Clarence C. Y. Kwan. "International Exchange Risk And Asset Substitutability," JIMF, 1986, v5(4), 449-466.

Aivazian, Varouj. "The Demand For Assets Under Conditions Of Risk: Comment," JOF, 1977, v32(3),927-929.

Aizenman, Joshua and Jacob A. Frenkel. "Supply Shocks, Wage Indexation, And Monetary Accommodation," JMCB, 1986,v18(3),304-322.

Aizenman, Joshua. "External Debt, Planning Horizon, And Distorted Credit Markets," JIMF, 1990, v9(2), 138-158.

Aizenman, Joshua. "Monopolistic Competition, Relative Prices, And Output Adjustment In The Open Economy," JIMF, 1989,v8(1),5-28.

Aizenman, Joshua. "Openness, Relative Prices, And Macro-Policies," JIMF, 1985, v4(1), 5-18.

Aizenman, Joshua. "Testing Deviations From Purchasing Power Parity," JIMF, 1986, v5(1), 25-35.

Ajinkya, Bipin B. and Michael J. Gift. "Dispersion Of Financial Analysts' Earnings Forecasts And The (Option Model) Implied Standard Deviations Of Stock Returns," JOF, 1985, v40(5), 1353-1365.

Akella, Srinivas R. and Stuart I. Greenbaum. "Savings And Loan Ownership Structure And Expense-Preference," JBF, 1988, v11(3), 419-428.

Akella, Srinivas R. and Su-Jane Chen. "Interest Rate Sensitivity Of Bank Stock Returns: Specification Effects And Structural Changes," JFR, 1990, v13(2), 147-154.

Akemann, Charles A. and Werner E. Keller. "Relative Strength Does Persist!," JPM, 1977, v4(1), 38-45.

Akemann, Charles A. "Predicting Changes In T-Bond Futures Spreads Using Implied Yields From T-Bill Futures," JFM, 1986, v6(2), 223-230.

Akgiray, Vedat and Geoffrey Booth. "Stock Price Processes With Discontinuous Time Paths: An Empirical Examination," FR, 1986, v21(2), 163-184.

Akgiray, Vedat and G. Geoffrey Booth. "Compound Distribution Models Of Stock Returns," JFR, 1987, v10(3), 269-280.

Akgiray, Vedat, G. Geoffrey Booth and Bruce Seifert. "Distribution Properties Of Latin American Black Market Exchange Rates," JIMF, 1988, v7(1), 37-48.

Akgiray, Vedat. "Conditional Heteroscedasticity In Time Series Of Stock Returns: Evidence And Forecasts," JOB, 1989, v62(1), 55-80.

Akhoury, Ravi. (Seix, Christina and Ravi Akhoury. "Bond Indexation: The Optimal Quantitative Approach," JPM, 1986, v12(3), 50-53.)

Akhtar, M. A. and Bluford H. Putnam. "Money Demand And Foreign Exchange Risk: The German Case, 1972-1976," JOF, 1980, v35(3), 787-794.

Akhtar, M. A., Bluford H. Putnam and D. Sykes Wilford. "Fiscal Constraints, Domestic Credit, And International Reserves Flows In The United Kingdom, 1952-71," JMCB, 1979, v11(2), 202-208.

Akins, James E. "New Directions In Energy Policy," FAJ, 1973, v29(1), 29-32,61-63,92.

Albach, Horst. "The Development Of The Capital Structure Of German Companies," JBFA, 1975, v2(3),281-294.

Albaum, Gerald and George G. Kaufman. "The Mortgage Acquisition Process: A Comparison Of VRM And FRM Borrowers," AREUEA, 1979, v7(2), 253-264.

Albaum, Gerald. (Hawkins, Del I., Gerald Albaum and Roger Best. "An Investigation Of Two Issues In The Use Of Students As Surrogates For Housewives In Consumer Behavior Studies," JOB, 1977, v50(2), 216-221.)

Albaum, Gerald. (Wolfe, Harry Deane and Gerald Albaum. "Inequality In Products, Orders, Customers, Salesmen, And Sales Territories," JOB, 1962, v35(3), 298-301.)

Albert, Joseph D. and Willard McIntosh. "Identifying Risk-Adjusted Indifference Rents For Alternative Operating Leases," JRER, 1989, v4(3), 81-93.

Albertini, Isidoro. "Fiscal Reform In Italy," FAJ, 1968, v24(4), 151-153.

Alberts, W. W. and S. H. Archer. "Some Evidence On The Effect Of Company Size On The Cost Of Equity Capital," JFQA, 1973, v8(2), 229-242.

Alberts, William W. and Gailen L. Hite. "The Modigliani-Miller Leverage Equation Considered In A Product Market Context," JFQA, 1983, v18(4), 425-437.

Alberts, William W. "Capital Investment By The Firm In Plant And Equipment," JOF, 1966, v21(2), 178-201.

Albin, Peter S. "Information Exchange In Security Markets And The Assumption Of `Homogeneous Beliefs'," JOF, 1974, v29(4), 1217-1227.

Albin, Peter S. (Grier, Paul C. and Peter S. Albin. "Nonrandom Price Changes In Association With Trading In Large Blocks," JOB, 1973, v46(3), 425-433.)

Alboini, Victor P. "The New Ontario Securities Act," FAJ, 1980, v36(6), 64-69.

Albon, Robert P. and Thomas J. Valentine. "Price Expectations, Partial Adjustment, And The Sectoral Demand For Money In Australia," JMCB, 1978, v10(3), 290-307.

Albrecht, Paul A. "Projective Methods In Industry," JOB, 1955, v28(1), 18-28.

Albrecht, W. David and Frederick M. Richardson. "Income Smoothing By Economy Sector," JBFA, 1990, v17(5), 713-730.

Alcaly, Roger E. and Alvin K. Klevorick. "Food Prices In Relation To Income Levels In New York City," JOB, 1971, v44(4), 380-397.

Alchian Armen A. and Benjamin Klein. "On A Correct Measure Of Inflation," JMCB, 1973, v5(1), 173-191.

Alchian, Armen A. "Why Money?," JMCB, 1977, v9(1), Part 2, 133-140.

Alchian, Armen. "Review Of The Council Of Economic Advisers' 1972 Report: A Comment," JMCB, 1972, v4(3), 704-712.

Alder, Robert J. "Are Indexed Funds Un-American?," JPM, 1990, v17(1), 94-95.

Alderfer, Clayton P. and Harold Bierman, Jr. "Choices With Risk: Beyond The Mean And Variance," JOB, 1970, v43(3), 341-353.

Alderson, Michael J. and K. C. Chen. "Excess Asset Reversions And Shareholder Wealth," JOF, 1986, v41(1), 225-242.

Alderson, Michael J. "Corporate Pension Policy Under OBRA 1987," FM, 1990, v19(4), 87-97.

Alderson, Michael J. "On Research In Corporate Pension Policy," AFPAF, 1989, v3(1), 263-280.

Alderson, Michael J. (Zivney, Terry L. and Michael J. Alderson. "Hedged Dividend Capture With Stock Index Options," FM, 1986, v15(2), 5-12.)

Alderson, Michael J. and Terry L. Zivney. "Optimal Cross-Hedge Portfolios For Hedging Stock Index Options," JFM, 1989, v9(1), 67-76.

Alderson, Michael J., Keith C. Brown and Scott L. Lummer. "Dutch Auction Rate Preferred Stock," FM, 1987, v16(2), 68-73.

Aldrich, Carole A. "A Model For Funding Interrelated Research And Development Projects Under Uncertainty," JFQA, 1974, v9(1), 117-129.

Aldrich, Peter C. "Active Versus Passive: A New Look," JPM, 1987, v14(1), 9-11.

Aldrich, Peter C. (Kopcke, Richard W. and Peter C. Aldrich. "A Real Estate Crisis: Averted Or Just Postponed?," JPM, 1984, v10(3), 21-29.)

Aldrich, Winthrop W. "The Management Of The Public Debt," JOF, 1949, v4(1), 1-12.

Alemann, Roberto T. "The Discipline Of The Balance Of Payments: Monetary Stabilization in Latin America," JOF,1961,v16(2),167-175.

Alesina, Alberto and Jeffrey Sachs. "Political Parties And The Business Cycle In The United States, 1948-1984," JMCB, 1988, v20(1), 63-82.

Alexander, Gordon J. and Bruce G. Resnick. "More On Estimation Risk And Simple Rules For Optimal Portfolio Selection," JOF, 1985, v40(1), 125-133.

Alexander, Gordon J. and Bruce G. Resnick. "Using Linear And Goal Programming To Immunize Bond Portfolios," JBF, 1985, v9(1), 35-54.

Alexander, Gordon J. and Norman L. Chervany. "On The Estimation And Stability Of Beta," JFQA, 1980, v15(1), 123-137.

Alexander, Gordon J. and P. George Benson. "More On Beta As A Random Coefficient," JFQA, 1982, v17(1), 27-36.

Alexander, Gordon J. and Roger D. Stover. "Pricing In The New Issue Convertible Debt Market," FM, 1977, v6(3), 35-39.

Alexander, Gordon J. and Roger D. Stover. "The Effect Of Forced Conversions On Common Stock Prices," FM, 1980, v9(1), 39-45.

Alexander, Gordon J. "A Reevaluation Of Alternative Portfolio Selection Models Applied To Common Stocks," JFQA, 1978, v13(1), 71-78.

Alexander, Gordon J. "An Algorithmic Approach To Deriving The Minimum-Variance Zero-Beta Portfolio," JFEC, 1977, v4(2), 231-236.

Alexander, Gordon J. "Applying The Market Model To Long-Term Corporate Bonds," JFQA, 1980, v15(5), 1063-1080.

Alexander, Gordon J. "Mixed Security Testing Of Alternative Portfolio Selection Models," JFQA, 1977, v12(5), 817-832.

Alexander, Gordon J. "PORTFO: A Computer Program Involving The Application Of Portfolio Theory," JFED, 1978, v7, 92-94.

Alexander, Gordon J. "PORTID: A Computer Program Involving The Interaction Of Utility Theory And Portfolio Theory," JFED, 1981, v10, 88-90.

Alexander, Gordon J. "The Derivation Of Efficient Sets," JFQA, 1976, v11(5), 817-830.

Alexander, Gordon J. (Garbisch, Michael W. and Gordon J. Alexander. "Is Standard And Poor's Master List Worthless?," JPM, 1977, v4(1), 34-37.)

Alexander, Gordon J. (Stover, Roger D. and Gordon J. Alexander. "Bank Managed Equity Common Trust Funds: A Performance Analysis," JBR, 1977-78, v8(4), 218-223.)

Alexander, Gordon J., P. George Benson and Joan M. Kampmeyer. "Investigating The Valuation Effects Of Announcements Of Voluntary Corporate Selloffs," JOF, 1984, v39(2), 503-517.

Alexander, Gordon J., P. George Benson and Carol E. Eger. "Timing Decisions And The Behavior Of Mutual Fund Systematic Risk," JFQA, 1982, v17(4), 579-602.

Alexander, Gordon J., P. George Benson and Elizabeth W. Gunderson. "Asset Redeployment: Trans World Corporation's Spinoff Of TWA," FM, 1986, v15(2), 50-58.

Alexander, Gordon J., Roger D. Stover and David B. Kuhnau. "Market Timing Strategies In Convertible Debt Financing," JOF, 1979, v34(1), 143-155.

Alexander, Gordon J., Cheol S. Eun and S. Janakiramanan. "Asset Pricing And Dual Listing On Foreign Capital Markets: A Note," JOF, 1987, v42(1),151-158.

Alexander, Gordon J., Cheol S. Eun and S. Janakiramanan. "International Listings And Stock Returns: Some Empirical Evidence," JFQA, 1988, v23(2), 135-152.

Alexander, Gordon, Thomas R. Hoffman and Bruce Resnick. "Immunization: A Computer Program Involving The Implementation Of A Bond Portfolio Immunization Strategy," JFED, 1985, v14, 60-69.

Alexander, John, Delbert Goff and Pamela P. Peterson. "Profitability Of A Trading Strategy Based On Unexpected Earnings," FAJ, 1989, v45(4), 65-71.

Alexander, William E. (Haas, Richard D. and William E. Alexander. "A Model Of Exchange Rates And Capital Flows: The Canadian Floating Rate Experience," JMCB, 1979, v11(4), 467-482.)

Alhadeff, Charlotte P. (Alhadeff, David A. and Charlotte P. Alhadeff. "An Integrated Model For Commercial Banks," JOF, 1957, v12(1), 24-43.)

Alhadeff, Charlotte P. (Alhadeff, David A. and Charlotte P. Alhadeff. "Growth And Survival Patterns Of New Banks, 1948-70," JMCB, 1976, v8(2), 199-208.)

Alhadeff, Charlotte P. (Alhadeff, David A. and Charlotte P. Alhadeff. "A Note On Bank Earnings And Savings Deposit Rate Policy," JOF, 1959, v14(3), 410-413.)

Alhadeff, David A. and Charlotte P. Alhadeff. "An Integrated Model For Commercial Banks," JOF, 1957, v12(1), 24-43.

Alhadeff, David A. and Charlotte P. Alhadeff. "Growth And Survival Patterns Of New Banks, 1948-70," **JMCB,** 1976, v8(2), 199-208.

Alhadeff, David A. and Charlotte P. Alhadeff. "A Note On Bank Earnings And Savings Deposit Rate Policy," **JOF,** 1959, v14(3), 403-410.

Alhadeff, David A., P.L. Bernstein, C.D. Campbell, L.V. Chandler, E.C. Ettin, V.R. Farhi, J.M. Guttentag, H.A. Latane and K.E. Poole. "The Commission On Money And Credit's Research Studies," **JOF,** 1964, v19(3), 497-533.

Ali, Amal El-Tigani. (Karim, Rifaat Ahmed Abdel and Amal El-Tigani Ali. "Determinants Of The Financial Strategy Of Islamic Banks," **JBFA,** 1989, v16(2), 193-212.)

Ali, M. M. "Stochastic Dominance And Portfolio Analysis," **JFEC,** 1975, v2(2), 205-229.

Ali, Mukhtar M. and Stuart I. Greenbaum. "A Spatial Model Of The Banking Industry," **JOF,** 1977, v32(4), 1283-1303.

Ali, Mukhtar M. (Giaccotto, Carmelo and Mukhtar M. Ali. "Optimum Distribution-Free Tests And Further Evidence Of Heteroscedasticity In The Market Model," **JOF,** 1982, v37(5), 1247-1258.)

Ali, Mukhtar M. (Giaccotto, Carmelo and Mukhtar M. Ali. "Optimal Distribution-Free Tests And Further Evidence Of Heteroscedasticity In The Market Model: A Reply," **JOF,** 1985, v40(2), 607.)

Ali, Mukhtar M. (Greenbaum, Stuart I., Mukhtar M. Ali and Randall C. Merris. "Monetary Policy And Banking Profits," **JOF,** 1976, v31(1), 89-101.)

Ali, Mukhtar M. (Greenbaum, Stuart I. and Mukhtar M. Ali. "Need Interest Rates On Bank Loans And Deposits Move Sympathetically?," **JOF,** 1974, v29(3),963-971.)

Ali, Mukhtar M. (Greenbaum, Stuart I. and Mukhtar M. Ali. "Entry, Control And The Market For Bank Charters," **JOF,** 1974, v29(2), 527-535.)

Aliber, Robert Z. "Exchange Risk, Political Risk, And Investor Demand For External Currency Deposits," **JMCB,** 1975, v7(2), 161-179.

Aliber, Robert Z. "Exchange Risk, Yield Curves, And The Pattern Of Capital Flows," **JOF,** 1969, v24(2), 361-370.

Aliber, Robert Z. "Gold, SDR's, And Central Bank Swaps," **JMCB,** 1973, v5(3), 819-825.

Aliber, Robert Z. "International Banking: A Survey," **JMCB,** 1984, v16(4), Part 2, 661-678.

Aliber, Robert Z. "Monetary Independence Under Floating Exchange Rates," **JOF,** 1975, v30(2), 365-376.

Aliber, Robert Z. "The Commission On Money And Credit: Ten Years Later," **JMCB,** 1972, v4(4), 915-929.

Allais, Maurice. "Forgetfulness And Interest," **JMCB,** 1972, v4(1), 40-73.

Allais, Maurice. "Growth And Inflation," **JMCB,** 1969, v1(3), 355-426.

Allais, Maurice. "The Psychological Rate Of Interest," **JMCB,** 1974, v6(3), 285-331.

Allan, Blake. (Goldberg, Michael A. and Blake Allan. "Urban Growth: A View From The Supply Side," **AREUEA,** 1978, v6(3), 247-270.)

Allan, W. Scott. "Rehabilitation As A Practical Insurance Program," **JRI,** 1958, v25(3), 21-28.

Allardice, David R. "The Johnson Wax Effect: Setting The Record Straight," **JBR,** 1979-80, v10(3),189-192.

Allen, David S. (Maberly, Edwin D., David S. Allen and Roy F. Gilbert. "Stock Index Futures And Cash Market Volatility," **FAJ,** 1989, v45(6), 75-77.)

Allen, David S., Robert E. Lamy and G. Rodney Thompson. "Agency Costs And Alternative Call Provisions: An Empirical Investigation," **FM,** 1987, v16(4),37-44.

Allen, David S., Robert E. Lamy and G. Rodney Thompson. "The Shelf Registration Of Debt And Self Selection Bias," **JOF,** 1990, v45(1), 275-288.

Allen, Everett T., Jr. "Survivor's Income Benefits," **JRI,** 1970, v37(3), 397-406.

Allen, Ferry B. "Does Going Into Debt Lower The Cost Of Capital?," **FAJ,** 1954, v10(4), 57-62.

Allen, Ferry B. "Measurement Of Public Utility Risk," **FAJ,** 1960, v16(2), 63-70.

Allen, Franklin and Andrew Postelwaite. "Rational Expectations And The Measurement Of A Stock's Elasticity Of Demand," **JOF,** 1984, v39(4), 1119-1125.

Allen, Franklin and Douglas Gale. "Optimal Security Design," **RFS,** 1988-89, v1(3), 229-263.

Allen, Franklin and Gerald R. Faulhaber. "Signaling By Underpricing In The IPO Market," **JFEC,** 1989, v23(2), 303-324.

Allen, Franklin. "The Market For Information And The Origin Of Financial Intermediation," **JFI,** 1990, v1(1), 3-30.

Allen, Franklin. "The Prevention Of Default," **JOF,** 1981, v36(2), 271-276.

Allen, Helen and Mark P. Taylor. "Chart Analysis And The Foreign Exchange Market," **RFM,** 1989, v8(2), 288-319.

Allen, J. D. (Butler, H. L., Jr.; G. J. Podrasky and J. D. Allen. "Aerospace Industry Re-Revisited," **FAJ,** 1977, v33(4), 32-35.)

Allen, J. D. (Butler, H. L., Jr. and J. D. Allen. "Dow Jones Industrial Average Re-Examined," **FAJ,** 1979, v35(6), 23-30.)

Allen, J. Devon. (Butler, Hartman L., Jr., George J. Podrasky and J. Devon Allen. "Aerospace II - Commercial Aircraft," **FAJ,** 1977, v33(5), 53-66.)

Allen, Linda and Anthony Saunders. "The Large-Small Bank Dichotomy In The Federal Funds Market," **JBF,** 1986, v10(2), 219-230.

Allen, Linda and Thom Thurston. "Cash-Futures Arbitrage And Forward-Futures Spreads In The Treasury Bill Market," **JFM,** 1988, v8(5), 563-574.

Allen, Linda, Stavros Peristiani and Anthony Saunders. "Bank Size, Collateral, And Net Purchase Behavior In The Federal Funds Market: Empirical Evidence," **JOB,** 1989, v62(4), 501-516.

Allen, Linda. "The Determinants Of Bank Interest Margins: A Note," **JFQA,** 1988, v23(2), 231-235.

Allen, P. R. "The Private ECU Markets: What They Are, Why They Exist, And Where They May Go," **JBF,** 1990, v14(5), 845-876.

Allen, P. R. and J. L. Stein. "Capital Market Integration," **JBF,** 1990, v14(5), 909-928.

Allen, Paul R. and C. F. Sirmans. "An Analysis Of Gains To Acquiring Firm's Shareholders: The Special Case Of REITs," **JFEC,** 1987, v18(1), 175-184.

Allen, Paul R. and William J. Wilhelm. "The Impact Of The 1980 Depository Institutions Deregulation And Monetary Control Act On Market Value And Risk: Evidence From The Capital Markets," **JMCB,** 1988, v20(3), Part 1, 364-380.

Allen, Robert F. "The Supply Function Of Urban Property Insurance: Comment," **JRI,** 1970, v37(3), 459-462.

Allen, Stuart D. "Klein's Price Variability Terms In The U.S. Demand For Money," **JMCB,** 1982, v14(4), Part 1, 525-530.

Allen, Stuart D. "The Federal Reserve And The Electoral Cycle," **JMCB,** 1986, v18(1), 88-94.

Allen, Stuart D. and Robert A. Connolly. "Financial Market Effects On Aggregate Money Demand: A Bayesian Analysis," **JMCB,** 1989, v21(2), 158-175.

Allen, Tom C. (Duvall, Richard M. and Tom C. Allen. "Least Cost Deductible Decisions," **JRI,** 1973, v40(4), 497-507.)

Allen, Tom C. and Richard M. Duvall. "Determinants Of Property Loss Ratios In The Retail Industry," **JRI,** 1973, v40(2), 181-190.

Allen, William R. "Interbank Deposits And Excess Reserves," **JOF,** 1956, v11(1), 68-73.

Allerdice, F. B. and D. E. Farrar. "Factors That Affect Mutual Fund Growth," **JFQA,** 1967, v2(4),365-382.

Allison, Robert. "Atomic Energy And Electric Power," **FAJ,** 1956, v12(1), 59-60.

Allison, Stephen L. (Heins, A. James and Stephen L. Allison. "Some Factors Affectidng Stock Price Variability," **JOB,** 1966, v39(1), Part I, 19-23.)

Allison, William H. "Check Volumes And Costs: Comment," **JBR,** 1976-77, v7(4), 320-321.

Allvine, Fred C. and Daniel E. O'Neill. "Stock Market Returns And The Presidential Election Cycle," **FAJ,** 1980, v36(5), 49-56.

Alm, James and James R. Follain, Jr. "Alternative Mortgage Instruments, The Tilt Problem, And Consumer Welfare," **JFQA,** 1984, v19(1), 113-126.

Alonso, A. and G. Rubio. "Overreaction In The Spanish Equity Market," **JBF,** 1990, v14(2/3), 469-482.

Alonso, A., G. Rubio and F. Tusell. "Asset Pricing And Risk Aversion In The Spanish Stock Market," **JBF,** 1990, v14(2/3), 351-370.

Alpert, Bernard. "Non-Businessmen As Surrogates For Businessmen In Behavioral Experiments," **JOB,** 1967, v40(2), 203-207.

Alrich, William M. and William B. Buckman. "Debit Insurance," **JRI,** 1963, v30(3), 433-446.

Alrich, William. "Problems In Defining 'All Lines' Insurance," **JRI,** 1961, v28(2), 107-110.

Alrich, William. "Substantive Report Of The AAUTI Census Committee," **JRI,** 1960, v27(2), 59-64.

Alt, Christopher B., Michael G. Baumann and Martin B. Zimmerman. "The Economics Of Western Coal Severance Taxes," **JOB,** 1983, v56(4), 519-536.

Alten, K. W. "A New Tool For Security Analysis," **FAJ,** 1956, v12(4), 78-84.

Alter, George C. (Becker, William E. and George C. Alter. "Estimating Lost Future Earnings Using The New Worklife Tables: Reply," **JRI,** 1988, v55(3), 545-547.)

Altman, Edward I. and Joseph Spivack. "Predicting Bankruptcy: The Value Line Relative Financial Strength System Vs. The Zeta Bankruptcy Classification Approach," **FAJ,** 1983, v39(6), 60-67.

Altman, Edward I. and Menachem Brenner. "Information Effects And Stock Market Response To Signs Of Firm Deterioration," **JFQA,** 1981, v16(1), 35-51.

Altman, Edward I. and Paul S. Tubiana. "The Multi-Firm Bond Issue: A Fund-Raising Financial Instrument," **FM,** 1981, v10(3), 23-33.

Altman, Edward I. and Robert A. Schwartz. "Common Stock Price Volatility Measures And Patterns," **JFQA,** 1970, v5(5), 603-626.

Altman, Edward I. and Robert A. Eisenbeis. "Financial Applications Of Discriminant Analysis: A Clarification," **JFQA,** 1978, v13(1), 185-195.

Altman, Edward I. and Scott A. Nammacher. "The Default Rate Experience On High-Yield Corporate Debt," **FAJ,** 1985, v41(4), 25-41.

Altman, Edward I. "A Financial Early Warning System For Over-The-Counter Broker-Dealers," **JOF,** 1976, v31(4), 1201-1224.

Altman, Edward I. "A Further Empirical Investigation Of The Bankruptcy Cost Question," **JOF,** 1984, v39(4), 1067-1089.

Altman, Edward I. "Bankruptcy Identification: Virtue Or Necessity?," **JPM,** 1977, v3(3), 63-67.

Altman, Edward I. "Commercial Bank Lending: Process, Credit Scoring, And Costs Of Errors In Lending," **JFQA,** 1980, v15(4), 813-832.

Altman, Edward I. "Computerized Bond Rating Replication: Worthwhile Or Futile?," **JBR,** 1981-82, v12(4), 250-253.

Altman, Edward I. "Corporate Bankruptcy Potential, Stockholder Returns And Share Valuation: Reply," **JOF,** 1972, v27(3), 718-721.

Altman, Edward I. "Corporate Bankruptcy Potential, Stockholder Returns And Share Valuation," **JOF,** 1969, v24(5), 887-900.

Altman, Edward I. "Equity Securities Of Bankrupt Firms," **FAJ,** 1969, v25(4), 129-133.

Altman, Edward I. "Examining Moyer's Re-Examination Of Forecasting Financial Failure," **FM,** 1978, v7(4), 76-79.

Altman, Edward I. "Financial Ratios, Discriminant Analysis And The Prediction Of Corporate Bankruptcy," **JOF,** 1968, v23(4), 589-609.

Altman, Edward I. "Measuring Corporate Bond Mortality And Performance," **JOF,** 1989, v44(4), 909-922.

Altman, Edward I. "Railroad Bankruptcy Propensity," **JOF,** 1971, v26(2), 333-345.

Altman, Edward I. "Ratio Analysis And The Prediction Of Firm Failure: Reply," **JOF,** 1970, v25(5), 1169-1172.

Altman, Edward I. "Setting The Record Straight On Junk Bonds: A Review Of The Research On Default Rates And Returns," **JACF,** 1990, v3(2), 82-95.

Altman, Edward I. "The Anatomy Of The High-Yield Bond Market," **FAJ,** 1987, v43(4), 12-25.

Altman, Edward I. "The Convertible Debt Market: Are Returns Worth The Risk?," **FAJ,** 1989, v45(4), 23-31.

Altman, Edward I. "The Success Of Business Failure Prediction Models: An International Survey," **JBF,** 1984, v8(2), 171-198.

Altman, Edward I. (Frydman, Halina, Edward I. Altman and Duen-Li Kao. "Introducing Recursive Partitioning For Financial Classification: The Case Of Financial Distress," **JOF**, 1985, v40(1), 269-291.)

Altman, Edward I. (Schwartz, Robert A. and Edward I. Altman. "Volatility Behavior Of Industrial Stock Price Indices," **JOF**, 1973, v28(4), 957-971.)

Altman, Edward I., Michel Margaine, Michel Schlosser and Pierre Vernimmen. "Financial And Statistical Analysis For Commercial Loan Evaluation: A French Experience," **JFQA**, 1974, v9(2), 195-211.

Altman, Edward I., Robert G. Haldeman and P. Narayanan. "ZETA Analysis: A New Model To Identify Bankruptcy Risk Of Corporations," **JBF**, 1977, v1(1), 29-54.

Altman, Edward I., Bertrand Jacquillat and Michel Levasseur. "Comparative Analysis Of Risk Measures: France And The United States," **JOF**, 1974, v29(5), 1495-1511.

Altman, M. (Vickson, R. G. and M. Altman. "On The Relative Effectiveness Of Stochastic Dominance Rules: Extension To Decreasingly Risk-Averse Utility Functions," **JFQA**, 1977, v12(1), 73-84.)

Altman, Oscar L. "The Integration Of European Capital Markets," **JOF**, 1965, v20(2), 209-221.

Altmann, James L. and Joseph S. DeSalvo. "Extension And Application Of The Mills-Muth Urban Residential Land Use Simulation Model: Milwaukee, 1977-2020," **AREUEA**, 1979, v7(4), 482-504.

Altschul, Selig. "Significant Air Line Trends," **FAJ**, 1946, v2(3), 3-11.

Altschul, Selig. "The Airline Challenge - Pitfall Or Opportunity," **FAJ**, 1957, v13(5), 91-97.

Alvayay, Jaime and John S. Baen. "The Implications Of Federal Wetland Protection Programs For The Real Estate Appraisal Industry," **JRER**, 1990, v5(1), 153-165.

Ambachtsheer, K. P. and J. L. Farrell, Jr. "Can Active Man-agement Add Value?," **FAJ**, 1979, v35(6),39-47.

Ambachtsheer, Keith P. "Can Selectivity Pay In An Efficient Market?," **JPM**, 1976, v2(4), 19-22.

Ambachtsheer, Keith P. "International Investing: Structuring The Process," **JPM**, 1981, v8(1),23-27.

Ambachtsheer, Keith P. "Investment Scenarios For The 1980's," **FAJ**, 1977, v33(6), 38-46.

Ambachtsheer, Keith P. "Pension Fund Asset Allocation: In Defense Of A 60/40 Equity/Debt Asset Mix," **FAJ**, 1987, v43(5), 14-24.

Ambachtsheer, Keith P. "Pensions In The American Economy: A Review Article," **JPM**, 1985, v11(3), 77-78.

Ambachtsheer, Keith P. "The Persistence Of Investment Risk," **JPM**, 1989, v16(1), 69-71.

Ambachtsheer, Keith P. "Where Are The Customers' Alphas?," **JPM**, 1977, v4(1), 52-56.

Ambachtsheer, Keith P. (Ezra, D. Don and Keith P. Ambachtsheer. "Pension Funds: Rich Or Poor?," **FAJ**, 1985, v41(2), 43-56.)

Ambachtsheer, Keith. "Portfolio Theory And Security Analysis," **FAJ**, 1972, v28(6), 53-57.

Ambachtsheer, Keith. "Profit Potential In An `Almost Efficient' Market," **JPM**, 1974, v1(1), 84-87.

Ambachtsheer, Keith. (Goldie, Raymond and Keith Ambachtsheer. "The Battle Of Insider Trading: Comment," **JPM**, 1981, v7(2), 88.)

Ambarish, Ramasastry, Kose John and Joseph Williams. "Efficient Signalling With Dividends And Investments," **JOF**, 1987, v42(2), 321-343.

Ambler, Steve. "The International Transmission Of Policy Announcement Effects," **JIMF**, 1989, v8(2), 219-232.

Ambrose, Brent W. "An Analysis Of The Factors Affecting Light Industrial Property Valuation," **JRER**, 1990, v5(3), 355-370.

Ambrose, Brent William. "Corporate Real Estate's Impact On The Takeover Market," **JREFEC**, 1990, v3(4), 307-322.

Ambrose, David M. "Retail Grocery Pricing: Inner City, Suburban, And Rural Comparisons," **JOB**, 1979, v52(1), 95-102.

Ambrose, Jan Mills and J. Allen Seward. "Best's Ratings, Financial Ratios And Prior Probabilities In Insolvency Prediction," **JRI**, 1988, v55(2), 229-244.

Amernic, J. H. "Accounting: A Source Of Market Imperfection: A Comment," **JBFA**, 1975, v2(3),373-382.

Amershi, Amin H. "A Complete Analysis Of Full Parerto Efficiency In Financial Markets For Arbitrary Preferences," **JOF**, 1985, v40(4), 1235-1243.

Amey, Lloyd R. "Interest On Equity Capital As An Ex Post Cost," **JBFA**, 1980, v7(3), 347-364.

Amey, Lloyd R. "Interest On Equity Capital As An Ex Post Cost: A Reply," **JBFA**, 1982, v8(1), 127-132.

Amey, Lloyd R. "Joint Product Decisions, The Fixed Proportions Case: A Note," **JBFA**, 1984, v11(3), 295-300.

Amey, Lloyd R. (Whitmore, G. A. and Lloyd R. Amey. "Capital Budgeting Under Rationing: Comments On The Lusztig And Schwab Procedure," **JFQA**, 1973, v8(1)127-135.)

Amey, Lloyd. "Tomkins On `Residual Income'," **JBFA**,1975,v2(1),55-68.

Amigoni, Franco. "Planning Management Control Systems," **JBFA**, 1978, v5(3), 279-292.

Amihud, Y. and A. Barnea. "A Note On Fisher Hypothesis And Price Level Uncertainty," **JFQA**, 1977, v12(3), 525-530.

Amihud, Y., C. Brunie, C. Ferenbach, R. Fredericks, J. Grundfest, J. Lafferty, B. Lev, B. Shorts, J. Stern, B. Stewart and R. Zeckhauser. "Panel: 'Lead Steer' Roundtable," **JACF**, 1989, v2(3), 24-44.

Amihud, Y., H. Mendelson and M. Murgia. "Stock Market, Microstructure And Return Volatility: Evidence From Italy," **JBF**, 1990, v14(2/3), 423-440.

Amihud, Yakov and Haim Mendelson. "Dealership Market: Market-Making With Inventory," **JFEC**, 1980, v8(1), 31-53.

Amihud, Yakov and Haim Mendelson. "Asset Pricing And The Bid-Asked Spread," **JFEC**, 1986, v17(2),223-249.

Amihud, Yakov and Haim Mendelson. "Relative Price Dispersion And Economic Shocks: An Inventory-Adjustment Approach," **JMCB**, 1982, v14(3), 390-398.

Amihud, Yakov and Haim Mendelson. "Liquidity And Stock Returns," **FAJ**, 1986, v42(3), 43-48.

Amihud, Yakov and Haim Mendelson. "Asset Price Behavior In A Dealership Market," **FAJ**, 1982, v38(3),50-59.

Amihud, Yakov and Haim Mendelson. "Trading Mechanisms And Stock Returns: An Empirical Investigation," **JOF**, 1987, v42(3), 533-553.

Amihud, Yakov and Haim Mendelson. "Liquidity And Asset Prices: Financial Management Implications," **FM**, 1988, v17(1), 5-15.

Amihud, Yakov and Haim Mendelson. "Are Trading Rule Profits Feasible?," **JPM**, 1987, v14(1), 77-78.

Amihud, Yakov and Haim Mendelson. "Liquidity And Cost Of Capital: Implications For Corporate Management," **JACF**, 1989, v2(3),65-73.

Amihud, Yakov and Haim Mendelson. "The Effects Of Beta, Bid-Ask Spread, Residual Risk, And Size On Stock Returns," **JOF**, 1989, v44(2), 479-486.

Amihud, Yakov and Haim Mendelson. "Explaining Intra-Day And Overnight Price Behavior: Comment," **JPM**, 1990, v16(2), 85-86.

Amihud, Yakov, Jacob Y. Kamin and Joshua Ronen. "`Management', `Ownerism', And Risk," **JBF**, 1983, v7(2), 189-196.

Amihud, Yakov, Peter Dodd and Mark Weinstein. "Conglomerate Mergers, Managerial Motives And Stockholder Wealth," **JBF**, 1986, v10(3), 401-410.

Amihud, Yakov, Baruch Lev and Nickolaos G. Travlos. "Corporate Control And The Choice Of Investment Financing: The Case Of Corporate Acquisitions," **JOF**, 1990, v45(2), 603-616.

Amihud, Yakov, Haim Mendelson and Robert A. Wood. "Liquidity And The 1987 Stock Market Crash," **JPM**, 1990, v16(3), 65-69.

Amihud, Yakov. "A Note On Risk Aversion And Indifference Curves," **JFQA**, 1977, v12(3), 509-513.

Amihud, Yakov. "A Possible Error In The Expectations Theory: A Rejoinder," **JMCB**, 1981, v13(1), 107-108.

Amihud, Yakov. "A Possible Error In The Expectations Theory," **JMCB**, 1979, v11(2), 243-245.

Amihud, Yakov. "General Risk Aversion And Attitude Towards Risk," **JOF**, 1980, v35(3), 685-691.

Amihud, Yakov. "Uncertainty In Future Interest Rates And The Term Structure," **JBFA**, 1978, v5(1),49-56.

Amihud, Yakov. (Agmon, Tamir and Yakov Amihud. "The Forward Exchange Rate And The Prediction Of The Future Spot Rate: Empirical Evidence," **JBF**, 1981, v5(3), 425-437.)

Amit, Raphael and Joshua Livnat. "Grouping Of Conglomerates By Their Segments' Economic Attributes: Towards A More Meaningful Ratio Analysis," **JBFA**, 1990, v17(1), 85-100.

Amling, Frederick. "Suggested: An Improved Statistical Unit For Comparison In Investment Analysis," **FAJ**, 1958, v14(4), 39-40.

Amoako-Adu, Ben. "Corporate Valuation And Personal Taxes: Extension And Application To Canada," **FR**, 1983, v18(4), 281-291.

Amoako-Adu, Ben. "The Canadian Tax Reform And Its Effect On Stock Prices: A Note," **JOF**, 1983, v38(5), 1669-1675.

Amoako-Adu, Ben. (Rashid, Muhammad and Ben Amoako-Adu. "Personal Taxes, Inflation, And Market Valuation," **JFR**, 1987, v10(4), 341-352.)

Amos, William W. "Insurance Holding Company Concepts," **FAJ**, 1968, v24(4), 35-38.

Amos, William W. "New Accounting Rules For Fire And Casualty Companies," **FAJ**, 1966, v22(5),35-38.

Amos, William W. "New Holding Company Moves By Insurance Companies," **FAJ**, 1966, v22(2), 133-135.

Amrhein, G. L. (Parry, C. L., G. L. Amrhein and C. D. Spangler. "Interim Report Of The Committee On Insurance Bibliography," **JRI**, 1937, v4, 25-27.)

Amsler, Christine E. and Peter Schmidt. "A Monte Carlo Investigation Of The Accuracy Of Multivariate CAPM Tests," **JFEC**, 1985, v14(3), 359-376.

Ananthanarayanan, A. L. and Eduardo S. Schwartz. "Retractable And Extendible Bonds: The Canadian Experience," **JOF**, 1980, v35(1), 31-47.

Ananthanarayanan, A. L. (Boyle, P. P. and A. L. Ananthanarayanan. "The Impact Of Variance Estimation In Option Valuation Models," **JFEC**, 1977, v5(3),375-387.)

Ancel, Esther Weinstock and Ramesh K. S. Rao. "Stock Returns And Option Prices: An Exploratory Study," **JFR**, 1990, v13(3), 173-186.

Andersen, Hans Christian. "The Emperor's New Clothes," **JPM**, 1977, v3(2), 78-79.

Andersen, Leonall C. and Albert E. Burger. "Asset Management And Commercial Bank Portfolio Behavior: Theory And Practice," **JOF**, 1969, v24(2), 207-222.

Andersen, Leonall C. "A Comparison Of Stabilization Policies: 1966-67 And 1969-70," **JMCB**, 1973, v5(1), 26-38.

Andersen, Leonall C. "Dilemmas In The Trends Of Capital And Productivity," **JPM**, 1976, v2(4), 59-64.

Andersen, Leonall C. "Is There A Capital Shortage: Theory And Recent Empirical Evidence," **JOF**, 1976, v31(2), 257-268.

Andersen, Leonall C. "Will Banking Boom In The `70s," **FAJ**, 1971, v27(4), 45-48,87.

Andersen, Leonall C. (Carleton, Willard T. and Leonall C. Andersen. "A Principal Components Test Of Bank Debits As A Local Economic Indicator," **JOB**, 1965, v38(4), 409-415.)

Andersen, Theodore A. "Trends In Profit Sensitivity," **JOF**, 1963, v18(4), 637-646.

Anderson, Burt T. "Railway Signaling," **FAJ**, 1948, v4(2), 3-12.

Anderson, Carl G. (Wood, Wendell C., Carl E. Shafer and Carl G. Anderson. "Frequency And Duration Of Profitable Hedging Margins For Texas Cotton Producers, 1980-1986," **JFM**, 1989, v9(6), 519-528.)

Anderson, Carl R. "Bank Forecasting: A Developmental Group Approach," **JBR**, 1979-80, v10(1), 36-44.

Anderson, Clay J. "Consumer Instalment And Home-Mortgage Debt," **JOB**, 1956, v29(3), 191-200.

Anderson, Dan R. "All Risks Rating Within A Catastrophe Insurance System," **JRI**, 1976, v43(4), 629-652.

Anderson, Dan R. "Financing Asbestos Claims: Coverage Issues, Manville's Bankruptcy And The Claims Facility," **JRI**, 1987, v54(3), 429-451.

Anderson, Dan R. "Limits On Liability: The Price-Anderson Act Versus Other Laws," **JRI**, 1978, v45(4), 651-674.

Anderson, Dan R. "Risk Management, Insurance, And Actuarial Science In The Changing Curriculum," **JRI**, 1973, v40(2), 297-303.

Anderson, Dan R. "The National Flood Insurance Problems - Programs And Potential," **JRI**, 1974, v41(4), 579-599.

Books," **FR**, 1983, v18(2), 196-205.

Ang, James S., Jess H. Chua and Richard S. Woodward. "A Note On Investment Decision Rules Based On Utility Functions," **JBFA**, 1983, v10(4), 657-661.

Ang, James S., Jess H. Chua and Anand S. Desai. "Evidence That The Common Stock Market Adjusts Fully For Expected Inflation," **JFR**, 1979, v2(2), 97-109.

Ang, James S., David W. Blackwell and William L. Megginson. "The Effect Of Taxes On The Relative Valuation Of Dividends And Capital Gains: Evidence From Dual-Class British Investment Trusts," **JOF**, 1991, v46(1), 383-400.

Ang, James, David Peterson and Pamela Peterson. "Marginal Tax Rates: Evidence From Nontaxable Corporate Bonds: A Note," **JOF**, 1985, v40(1), 327-332.

Ang, James. (Peterson, Pamela, David Peterson and James Ang. "The Extinguishment Of Debt Through In-Substance Defeasance," **FM**, 1985, v14(1), 59-67.)

Angell, Frank J. "Some Effects Of The Truth-In-Lending Legislation," **JOB**, 1971, v44(2), 78-85.

Angell, Robert J. and Jerry G. Hunt. "Is The Denver Market Efficient?," **JPM**, 1982, v8(3), 10-16.

Angell, Robert J. and Tony R. Wingler. "A Note On Expensing Versus Depreciating Under The Accelerated Cost Recovery System," **FM**, 1982, v11(4), 34-35.

Angell, Robert J. "Depreciable Basis/ITC Decisions When The ITC Is Deferred," **FM**, 1985, v14(2), 43-47.

Angell, Robert J. "The Effect Of The Tax Reform Act On Capital Investment Decisions," **FM**, 1988, v17(4), 82-86.

Angeloni, Ignazio. "The Dynamic Behavior Of Business Loans And The Prime Rate: A Comment," **JBF**, 1985, v9(4), 577-580.

Ann, Wong Kie and Lye Meng Siong. "Market Values, Earnings' Yields And Stock Returns: Evidence From Singapore," **JBF**, 1990, v14(2/3), 311-326.

Annett, Douglas R. "Canada's Economy: Coyne-Fleming Controversy," **FAJ**, 1961, v17(4), 75-78.

Anonymous. "Comparison Of British And U.S. Steel," **FAJ**, 1959, v15(2), 19-26.

Ansari, Shahid L. and Masao Tsuji. "A Behavioral Extension To The Cost Variances Investigation Decision," **JBFA**, 1981, v8(4), 573-591.

Anshen, Melvin and William D. Guth. "Strategies For Research In Policy Formulation," **JOB**, 1973, v46(4), 499-511.

Anstaett, Kurt W., Dennis P. McCrary and Stephen T. Monahan, Jr. "Practical Debt Policy Considerations For Growth Companies: A Case Study Approach," **JACF**, 1988, v1(2), 71-78.

Anthony, Joseph H. "The Interrelation Of Stock And Options Market Trading-Volume Data," **JOF**, 1988, v43(4), 949-964.

Anthony, Julian D. "Running A Life Insurance Company Is Fun," **JRI**, 1952, v19, 40-47.

Anthony, Philip K. "If You Are So Smart, Why Are You Not Rich?," **FAJ**, 1955, v11(1), 69-70.

Anthony, Philip K. "New Enterprise, The Investor, And The Investment Banker," **FAJ**, 1953, v9(1), 31-34.

Anthony, Robert N. "How To Measure Fixed-Income Performance Correctly," **JPM**, 1985, v11(2), 61-65.

Antia, Murad J. and Richard L. Meyer. "The Growth Optimal Capital Structure: Manager Versus Shareholder Objectives," **JFR**, 1984, v7(3), 259-267.

Antia, Murad J. (Meyer, Richard L. and Murad J. Anitia. "A Note On The Calculation Of Probabilistic Betas," **FR**, 1986, v21(1), 151-156.)

Antler, Jacob and Yehuda Kahane. "The Gross And Net Replacement Ratios In Designing Pension Schemes And In Financial Planning: The Israeli Experience," **JRI**, 1987, v54(2), 283-297.

Antliff, John C. and William C. Freund. "Some Basic Research Into Historical Results Under Pension Plans With Benefits Based On Common Stock Performance," **JOF**, 1967, v22(2), 169-191.

Anton, Mark. "Liquefied Petroleum Gas: The Industry Today," **FAJ**, 1959, v15(2), 59-66.

Antoncic, Madelyn. "High And Volatile Real Interest Rates: Where Does The Fed Fit In?," **JMCB**, 1986, v18(1), 18-27.

Antonovitz, Frances and Terry Roe. "Effects Of Expected Cash And Futures Prices On Hedging And Production," **JFM**, 1986, v6(2), 187-206.

Antonovitz, Frances. (Park, Timothy and Frances Antonovitz. "Basis Risk And Optimal Decision Making For California Feedlots," **JFM**, 1990, v10(3), 259-272.)

Anvari, M. "Efficient Scheduling Of Cross-Border Cash Transfers," **FM**, 1986, v15(2), 40-49.

Anvari, Mohsen. "Corporate Cash Management In Canada: A Comparison With The United States," **AWCM**, 1990, v1(1), 79-98.

Aoki, Masanao. "Misadjustment To Anticipated Shocks: An Example Of Exchange-Rate Responses," **JIMF**, 1985, v4(3), 415-420.

Aoki, Tatsuo. "ATMs, POS And Home Banking Developments In Japan," **JBR**, 1985-86, v16(4), 218-220.

Apgar, William C., Jr. (Kain, John F. and William C. Apgar, Jr. "Simulation Of Housing Market Dynamics," **AREUEA**, 1979, v7(4), 505-538.)

Apilado, Vincent P. "Pension Funds, Personal Savings, And Economic Growth," **JRI**, 1972, v39(3), 397-404.

Apilado, Vincent P. (Frieder, Larry A. and Vincent P. Apilado. "Bank Holding Company Expansion: A Refocus On Its Financial Rationale," **JFR**, 1983, v6(1), 67-81.)

Apilado, Vincent P. (Frieder, Larry A. and Vincent P. Apilado. "Bank Holding Company Research: Classification, Synthesis And New Directions," **JBR**, 1982-83, v13(2), 80-95.)

Apilado, Vincent P. (Heathcotte, Bryan and Vincent P. Apilado. "The Predictive Content Of Some Leading Economic Indicators For Future Stock Prices," **JFQA**, 1974, v9(2), 247-258.)

Apilado, Vincent P. (Kolari, James W. and Vincent P. Apilado. "Bond Risk Premiums, Financial Data, And The Effect Of Market Segmentation," **JBR**, 1982, v8(2), 207-218.)

Apilado, Vincent P., Don C. Warner and Joel J. Dauten. "Evaluative Techniques In Consumer Finance--Experimental Results And Policy Implications For Financial Institutions," **JFQA**, 1974, v9(2), 275-283.

Aponte, Juan B. and Herbert S. Denenberg. "Life Insurance And The Investment Texts," **JRI**, 1963, v30(4), 595-605.

Aponte, Juan B. and Herbert S. Denenberg. "The Automobile Problem In Puerto Rico: Dimensions And Proposed Solution," **JRI**, 1968, v35(2), 227-236.

Aponte, Juan B. and Herbert S. Denenberg. "A New Concept Of The Economics Of Life Value And The Human Life Value: A Rationale For Term Insurance As The Cornerstone Of Insurance Marketing," **JRI**, 1968, v35(3), 337-356.

Aponte, Juan B. and Herbert S. Denenberg. "The Automobile Problem In Puerto Rico: Comment," **JRI**, 1968, v35(4), 637.

Appel, David, John D. Worrall and Richard J. Butler. "Survivorship And The Size Distribution Of The Property-Liability Insurance Industry," **JRI**, 1985, v52(3), 424-440.

Appel, David. (Worrall, John D. and David Appel. "The Wage Replacement Rate And Benefit Utilization In Workers' Compensation Insurance," **JRI**, 1982, v49(3), 361-371.)

Appel, David. (Worrall, John D., David Appel and Richard J. Butler. "Sex, Marital Status, And Medical Utilization By Injured Workers," **JRI**, 1987, v54(1), 27-44.)

Appelbaum, E., J. Burns, R. Evans, J. Gould, T. Hamachek, R. Kidder, M. Jensen, J. Johnstone, M. Murray, R. Sim, J. Stern, B. Stewart and C. Zaner. "Panel: CEO Roundtable On Corporate Structure And Management Incentives," **JACF**, 1990, v3(3), 6-35.

Appetiti, Sandro. "Identifying Unsound Firms In Italy: An Attempt To Use Trend Variables," **JBF**, 1984, v8(2), 269-280.

Applebaum, Leon. "Collectively Bargained Health Insurance Plans In Milwaukee County," **JRI**, 1963, v30(1), 97-100.

Applebaum, Leon. "The Development Of Voluntary Health Insurance In The United States," **JRI**, 1961, v28(3), 25-34.

Appleman, Mark J. "Are You Genuinely Professional?," **FAJ**, 1973, v29(2), 32-33.

Appleman, Mark J. "The Three Minds Of The Money Manager," **FAJ**, 1973, v29(5), 49-52.

Appleman, Norman. "Payment System Needs Of Corporations," **JBR**, 1985-86, v16(4), 252-253.

Appleyard, A. R. and G. K. Yarrow. "The Relationship Between Take-Over Activity And Share Valuation," **JOF**, 1975, v30(5), 1239-1249.

Appleyard, A. R. and N.C. Strong. "Textbook Inconsistencies In Graphing Valuation Equations: A Note," **FR**, 1985, v20(4), 361-367.

Appleyard, A. R. "Takeovers: Accounting Policy, Financial Policy And The Case Against Accounting Measures Of Performance," **JBFA**, 1980, v7(4), 541-554.

Appleyard, A. R. "The Shape Of The Preference Function Under Uncertainty: A Note," **JBFA**, 1978, v5(2), 215-221.

Appleyard, A. R., N. Strong and M. Walker. "Mutual Fund Performance In The Context Of Models Of Equilibrium Capital Asset Pricing," **JBFA**, 1982, v8(3), 289-296.

Apsel, David, Jack Cogen and Michael Rabin. "Hedging Long Term Commodity Swaps With Futures," **GFJ**, 1989, v1(1), 77-93.

Arad, Ruth. (Agmon, Tamir and Ruth Arad. "Exchange Risk And Unanticipated Changes In Exchange Rates," **JBF**, 1978, v2(3), 269-280.)

Aragon, George. (Viscione, Jerry A. and George Aragon. "The Case Method In Undergraduate Finance," **JFED**, 1978, v7, 49-52.)

Arak, Marcelle and Andrew Silver. "The Value Of The Tax Treatment Of Original-Issue Deep-Discount Bonds: A Note," **JOF**, 1984, v39(1), 253-259.

Arak, Marcelle and Laurie S. Goodman. "Treasury Bond Futures: Valuing The Delivery Options," **JFM**, 1987, v7(3), 269-286.

Arak, Marcelle, Laurie S. Goodman and Joseph Snailer. "Duration Equivalent Bond Swaps: A New Tool," **JPM**, 1986, v12(4), 26-32.

Arak, Marcelle, Arturo Estrella, Laurie Goodman and Andrew Silver. "Interest Rate Swaps: An Alternative Explanation," **FM**, 1988, v17(2), 12-18.

Arak, Marcelle, Philip Fischer, Laurie Goodman and Raj Daryanani. "The Municipal-Treasury Futures Spread," **JFM**, 1987, v7(4), 355-372.

Arak, Marcelle. "Profit Opportunities With Old OIDs," **JPM**, 1985, v11(3), 63-66.

Arak, Marcelle. "The Effect Of The Tax Treatment Of Treasury-Bill Futures On Their Rates," **JFM**, 1983, v3(1), 65-73.

Aranyi, Janos. "Portfolio Diversification," **FAJ**, 1967, v23(5), 133-139.

Arbel, Avner and Bikki Jaggi. "Market Information Assimilation Related To Extreme Daily Price Jumps," **FAJ**, 1982, v38(6), 60-66.

Arbel, Avner and Paul Strebel. "The Neglected And Small Firm Effects," **FR**, 1982, v17(4), 201-218.

Arbel, Avner, Richard Kolodny and Josef Lakonishok. "The Relationship Between Risk Of Default And Return On Equity: An Empirical Investigation," **JFQA**, 1977, v12(4), 615-625.

Arbel, Avner, Steven Carvell and Paul Strebel. "Giraffes, Institutions And Neglected Firms," **FAJ**, 1983, v39(3), 57-63.

Arbel, Avner. "Generic Stocks: The Key To Market Anomalies," **JPM**, 1985, v11(4), 4-13.

Arbel, Avner. (Strebel, Paul J. and Avner Arbel. "Pay Attention To Neglected Firms!," **JPM**, 1983, v9(2), 37-42.)

Arbit, Hal L. (Boldt, Bob L. and Hal L. Arbit. "Efficient Markets And The Professional Investor," **FAJ**, 1984, v40(4), 22-34.)

Arbit, Hal. "The Nature Of The Game," **JPM**, 1981, v8(1), 5-9.

Arbit, Harold L. and James E. Rhodes. "Performance Goals In A Generally Efficient Market," **JPM**, 1976, v3(1), 57-61.

Arbuckle, Ernest C., Richard L. Kozelka and Arthur M. Weimer. "Dean's Forum: The Place Of Insurance In The Collegiate Curriculum," **JRI**, 1960, v27(3), 67-70.

Arcelus, Francisco and Allan H. Meltzer. "A Reply To Craig Swan," **JMCB**, 1973, v5(4), 973-978.

Arcelus, Francisco and Allan H. Meltzer. "The Markets For Housing And Housing Services," **JMCB**, 1973, v5(1), 78-99.

Archer, Edouard. (Scott, David F., Jr., Laurence J. Moore, Andre Saint-Denis, Edouard Archer and Bernard W. Taylor, III. "Implementation Of A Cash Budget Simulator At Air Canada," **FM**, 1979, v8(2), 46-52.)

Archer, S. H. (Alberts, W. W. and S. H. Archer. "Some Evidence On The Effect Of Company Size On The Cost Of Equity Capital," **JFQA**, 1973, v8(2), 229-242.)

Archer, Simon. "Holding Gains, Deferred Taxation And Capital Structure," **JBFA**, 1974, v3(4),151-167.

Archer, Stephen H. and LeRoy G. Faerber. "Firm Size And The Cost Of Externally Secured Equity Capital," **JOF**, 1966, v21(1), 69-83.

Archer, Stephen H. "A Model For The Determination Of Firm Cash Balances," JFQA, 1966, v1(1), 1-10.

Archer, Stephen H. "Common Stock As An Inflation Hedge," FAJ, 1960, v16(5), 41-45.

Archer, Stephen H. "The Theoretical Value Of A Stock Right: A Comment," JOF, 1956, v11(3), 363-366.

Archer, Stephen H. (Choate, G. Marc and Stephen H. Archer. "Irving Fisher, Inflation And The Nominal Rate Of Interest," JFQA, 1975, v10(4), 675-685.)

Archer, Stephen H. (Daellenbach, Hans G. and Stephen H. Archer. "The Optimal Bank Liquidity: A Multi-Period Stochastic Model," JFQA, 1969, v4(3), 329-343.)

Archer, Stephen H. (Evans, John L. and Stephen H. Archer. "Diversification And The Reduction Of Dispersion: An Empirical Analysis," JOF, 1968, v23(5), 761-767.)

Archer, Wayne R. "Determinants Of Location For General Purpose Office Firms Within Medium Size Cities," AREUEA, 1981, v9(3), 283-298.

Archer, Wayne R. "Toward A Model Of Real Estate Project Demand Under Uncertainty: An Exploratory Example Of Market Simulation," AREUEA, 1976, v4(3), 19-48.

Archer, Wayne R. and David J. Nye. "An Insurance Apporach To Risk Analysis Of Debt Home Equity Conversion Programs," AREUEA, 1987, v15(3), 185-198.

Archibald, T. Ross. "The Motives Behind Depreciation Switchbacks," FAJ, 1976, v32(5), 67-73.

Arditti, Fred D. and Haim Levy. "Distribution Moments And Equilibrium: A Comment," JFQA, 1972, v7(1), 1429-1433.

Arditti, Fred D. and Haim Levy. "The Weighted Average Cost Of Capital As A Cutoff Rate: A Critical Analysis Of The Classical Textbook Weighted Average," FM, 1977, v6(3), 24-34.

Arditti, Fred D. and Haim Levy. "Portfolio Efficiency Analysis In Three Moments: The Multiperiod Case," JOF, 1975, v30(3), 797-809.

Arditti, Fred D. and John M. Pinkerton. "The Valuation And Cost Of Capital Of The Levered Firm With Growth Opportunities," JOF, 1978, v33(1), 65-73.

Arditti, Fred D. and Kose John. "Spanning The State Space With Options," JFQA, 1980, v15(1), 1-9.

Arditti, Fred D. and Miles Livingston. "The Relative Price Volatility Of Taxable And Non-Taxable Bonds: A Note," JOF, 1982, v37(3), 877-881.

Arditti, Fred D. and Milford S. Tysseland. "Three Ways To Present The Marginal Cost Of Capital," FM, 1973, v2(2), 63-67.

Arditti, Fred D. and W. Andrew McCollough. "Real Versus Randomly Generated Stock Prices," FAJ, 1978, v34(6), 70-74.

Arditti, Fred D. and Yoram C. Peles. "The Regulatory Process And The Firm's Capital Structure," FR, 1980, v15(1), 1-8.

Arditti, Fred D. "A Note On Discounting The Components Of An Income Stream," JOF, 1974, v29(3),995-999.

Arditti, Fred D. "A Survey Of Valuation And The Cost Of Capital," RIF, 1980, v2, 1-56.

Arditti, Fred D. "A Utility Function Depending On The First Three Moments: Reply," JOF, 1969, v24(4), 720-720.

Arditti, Fred D. "Another Look At Mutual Fund Performance," JFQA, 1971, v6(3), 909-912.

Arditti, Fred D. "Discounting The Components Of An Income Stream: Reply," JOF, 1977, v32(1), 224-226.

Arditti, Fred D. "Interest Rate Futures: An Intermediate Stage Toward Efficient Risk Reallocation," JBR, 1978-79, v9(3), 146-150.

Arditti, Fred D. "On The Separation Of Production From The Developer," JOB, 1968, v41(3), 317-328.

Arditti, Fred D. "Risk And The Required Return On Equity," JOF, 1967, v22(1), 19-36.

Arditti, Fred D. "Skewness And Investors' Decisions: A Reply," JFQA, 1975, v10(1), 173-176.

Arditti, Fred D. "The Weighted Average Cost Of Capital: Some Questions On Its Definition, Interpretation, And Use: Reply," JOF, 1975, v30(3),889-892.

Arditti, Fred D. "The Weighted Average Cost Of Capital: Some Questions On Its Definition, Interpretation, And Use," JOF, 1973, v28(4), 1001-1007.

Arditti, Fred D. (Levy, Haim and Fred D. Arditti. "Valuation, Leverage And The Cost Of Capital In The Case Of Depreciable Assets: A Reply," JOF, 1975, v30(1), 221-223.)

Arditti, Fred D. (Levy, Haim and Fred D. Arditti. "Valuation, Leverage, And The Cost Of Capital In The Case Of Depreciable Assets," JOF, 1973, v28(3), 687-695.)

Arditti, Fred D., Haim Levy and Marshall Sarnat. "Taxes, Uncertainty And Optimal Dividend Policy," FM, 1976, v5(1), 46-52.

Arditti, Fred D., Sirri Ayaydin, Ravi K. Mattu and Stephen Rigsbee. "A Passive Futures Strategy That Outperforms Active Management," FAJ, 1986, v42(4),63-67.

Arenberg, J. T., Jr. "Life Insurance Accounting And Reporting And The Independent Public Accountant," JRI, 1970, v37(2), 253-261.

Arens, John Russell. (Milano, Duane R., Stephen L. Avard and John Russell Arens. "Microcomputer Applications For Preparing Tests In Entry Level Financial Management Courses," JFED, 1986, v15, 68-78.)

Argy, V. E. and G. L. Murray. "Effects Of Sterilising A Balance Of Payments Surplus On Domestic Yields - A Formal Analysis," JIMF, 1985, v4(2),223-236.

Argy, V. E. "The Transmission Of Foreign Disturbances Under Different Exchange Rate Regimes," JBF, 1990, v14(5), 929-946.

Argy, Victor. "Rules, Discretion In Monetary Management, And Short-Term Stability," JMCB, 1971, v3(1), 102-122.

Argyris, Chris. "Organizational Leadership And Participative Management," JOB, 1955, v28(1), 1-7.

Ariel, Robert A. "A Monthly Effect In Stock Returns," JFEC, 1987, v18(1), 161-174.

Ariel, Robert. "High Cost Returns Before Holidays: Existence And Evidence On Possible Causes," JOF, 1990, v45(5), 1611-1626.

Ariff, Mohamed and Matthew Varghese. "Risk Reduction From Currency Portfolio Diversification And Revision Gains," IJOF, 1990, v3(1), 86-100.

Arize, Augustine C. (Ndubizu, Gordian, Augustine C. Arize and P. R. Chandy. "The Market Model Specification And The Structural Stability Of The Beta," IJOF, 1989, v1(2), 1-14.)

Arize, Augustine and Gordian Ndubizu. "Modelling Money Demand Functions With Exchange Rates: Regression Estimates And Diagnostic Tests," IJOF, 1990, v2(2), 88-104.

Arjona, Enrique. (Haugen, Robert A., Edgar Ortiz and Enrique Arjona. "Market Efficiency: Mexico Versus The U.S.," JPM, 1985, v12(1), 28-32.)

Armstrong, Clive A. (Buiter, Willem H. and Clive A. Armstrong. "A Didactic Note On The Transactions Demand For Money And Behavior Towards Risk," JMCB, 1978, v10(4), 529-538.)

Armstrong, Dale. "The Flow Of Funds Statement - An Effective Tool," JRI, 1969, v36(1), 151-158.

Armstrong, David. "Were Mutual Funds Worth The Candle?," JPM, 1976, v2(4), 46-51.

Armstrong, J. Scott. "Econometric Forecasting And The Science Court," JOB, 1978, v51(4), 595-600.

Armstrong, J. Scott. "Forecasting With Econometric Methods: Folklore Versus Fact," JOB, 1978, v51(4), 549-564.

Armstrong, John B. "The Case For Mutual Fund Management," FAJ, 1960, v16(3), 33-38.

Armstrong, R. Wright. "The Railroads: A Year Of Decision," FAJ, 1959, v15(5), 39-44.

Armstrong, Thomas H. "Stock Option Warrants," FAJ, 1954, v10(2), 89-91.

Arnault, E. Jane. "Optimal Maintenance Under Rent Control With Quality Constraints," AREUEA, 1975, v3(2), 67-82.

Arndt, Terry L. and James A. Millar. "Some Empirical Results On Financial Characteristics And Unusual Stock Prices," FR, 1977, v12(2), 18-32.

Arnett, Farold E. "Capital Gains And Losses," FAJ, 1967, v23(1), 39-48.

Arnold, A. J. and R. T. Wearing. "Cash Flows, Exit Prices And British Airways," JBFA, 1988, v15(3), 311-334.

Arnold, John. "An Approach To Pricing And Output Decisions When Prices Are Changing," JBFA, 1977, v4(4), 383-406.

Arnold, Larry R. (Steinberg, Joan S. and Larry R. Arnold. "An Interactive Approach For Optimizing Debt Repayment Schedules," JFR, 1981, v4(2), 137-146.)

Arnott, Richard. "Housing Vacancies, Thin Markets, And Idiosyncratic Tastes," JREFEC, 1989, v2(1), 5-30.

Arnott, Richard. "Rent Control: The International Experience," JREFEC, 1988, v1(3), 203-216.

Arnott, Robert D. and James N. von Germeten. "Systematic Asset Allocation," FAJ, 1983, v39(6), 31-38.

Arnott, Robert D. and Stephen J. Vincent. "S&P Additions And Deletions: A Market Anomaly," JPM, 1986, v13(1), 29-33.

Arnott, Robert D. and William A. Copeland. "The Business Cycle And Security Selection," FAJ, 1985, v41(2), 26-32.

Arnott, Robert D. "Cluster Analysis And Stock Price Movement," FAJ, 1980, v36(6), 56-62.

Arnott, Robert D. "Modeling Portfolios With Options: Risks And Returns," JPM, 1980, v7(1), 66-73.

Arnott, Robert D. "Relative Strength Revisited," JPM, 1979, v5(3), 19-23.

Arnott, Robert D. "The Future For Quantitative Investment Products," JPM, 1988, v14(2), 52-56.

Arnott, Robert D. "The Pension Sponsor's View Of Asset Allocation," FAJ, 1985, v41(5), 17-19,22-23.

Arnott, Robert D. "The Use And Misuse Of Consensus Earnings," JPM, 1985, v11(3), 18-27.

Arnott, Robert D. "What Hath MPT Wrought: Which Risks Reap Rewards?," JPM, 1983, v10(1), 5-11.

Arnott, Robert D. (Bailey, Jeffrey V. and Robert D. Arnott. "Cluster Analysis And Manager Selection," FAJ, 1986, v42(6), 20-21,24-28.)

Arnott, Robert D. (Clarke, Roger G. and Robert D. Arnott. "The Cost Of portfolio Insurance: Tradeoffs And Choices," FAJ, 1987, v43(6), 35-47.)

Arnott, Robert D. (Leibowitz, Martin L., Eric H. Sorensen, Robert D. Arnott and H. Nicholas Hanson. "A Total Differential Approach To Equity Duration," FAJ, 1989, v45(5), 30-37.)

Arnott, Robert D. (Sorensen, Eric H. and Robert D. Arnott. "The Risk Premium And Stock Market Performance," JPM, 1988, v14(4), 50-55.)

Arnott, Robert D. and Roy D. Henriksson. "A Disciplined Approach To Global Asset Allocation," FAJ, 1989, v45(2), 17-28.

Arnott, Robert D. and Wayne H. Wagner. "The Measurement And Control Of Trading Costs," FAJ, 1990, v46(6), 73-80.

Arnott, Robert D., Charles M. Kelso, Jr., Stephan Kiscadden and Rosemary Macedo. "Forecasting Factor Returns: An Intriguing Possibility," JPM, 1989, v16(1), 28-35.

Arnstein, Melville G. "A Yardstick For Determining Rate Of Return," FAJ, 1954, v10(2), 41-46.

Aronson, J. Richard. "The Idle Cash Balances Of State And Local Governments: An Economic Problem Of National Concern," JOF, 1968, v23(3), 499-508.

Aronson, J. Richard. (Schwartz, Eli and J. Richard Aronson. "Some Surrogate Evidence In Support Of The Concept Of Optimal Financial Structure," JOF, 1967, v22(1), 10-18.)

Aronson, J. Richard. (Schwartz, Eli and J. Richard Aronson. "How To Integrate Corporate And Personal Income Taxation," JOF, 1972, v27(5), 1073-1080.)

Arpan, Jeffrey S. "Transfer Pricing In Multinational Financial Mangement," FR, 1972, v2(2),141-155.

Arrow, Kenneth J. "Futures Markets: Some Theoretical Perspectives," JFM, v1(2), 107-116.

Arrow, Kenneth J. "Rationality Of Self And Others In An Economic System," JOB, 1986, v59(4), Part 2, S385-S400.

Arrow, Kenneth J. "Real And Nominal Magnitude In Economics," JFQA, 1980, v15(4), 773-783.

Arshadi, N. (Eyssell, T. and N. Arshadi. "The Wealth Effects Of The Risk-Based Capital Requirement In Banking: The Evidence From The Capital Market," JBF, 1990, v14(1), 179-198.)

Arshadi, Nasser and Edward C. Lawrence. "An Empirical Investigation Of New Bank Performance," JBF, 1987, v11(1), 33-48.

Arshadi, Nasser. "Capital Structure, Agency Problems, And Deposit Insurance In Banking Firms," FR, 1989, v24(1), 31-52.

Arshadi, Nasser. (Lawrence, Edward C. and Nasser Arshadi. "The

Distributional Impact Of Foreign Deposits On Federal Deposit Insurance Premia," JBF, 1988, v12(1), 105-116.)

Arshadik, Nasser. (Kummer, Donald R., Nasser Arshadi and Edward C. Lawrence. "Incentive Problems In Bank Insider Borrowing," JFSR, 1989, v3(1), 17-32.)

Arshanapalli, Bala G. (Dalal, Ardeshir J. and Bala G. Arshanapalli. "Effects Of Expected Cash And Futures Prices On Hedging And Production: Comments And Extensions," JFM, 1989, v9(4), 337-346.)

Arthur, H. B. "`Religion And Its Role In The World Of Business': A Comment," JOB, 1959, v32(2), 183-184.

Artto, Eero. "Money Flow Analyses," JBFA, 1978, v5(1), 27-38.

Arzac, E. R. and M. Marcus. "Flotation Cost Allowance For The Regulated Firm: A Reply," JOF, 1984, v39(1), 293-294.

Arzac, E. R. "The Dynamic Characteristics Of Chow's Model: A Simulation Study," JFQA, 1967, v2(4), 383-397.

Arzac, E. R. "Utility Analysis Of Chance-Constrained Portfolio Selection: A Correction," JFQA, 1977, v12(2), 321-323.

Arzac, Enrique R. and Matityahu Marcus. "Flotation Cost Allowance In Rate Of Return Regulation: A Reply," JOF, 1983, v38(4),1339-1341.

Arzac, Enrique R. and Matityahu Marcus. "Flotation Cost Allowance In Rate Of Return Regulation: A Note," JOF, 1981, v36(5), 1199-1202.

Arzac, Enrique R. and Matityahu Marcus. "Flotation Cost Adjustment In Rate Of Return Regulation: A Reply," JOF, 1984, v39(2), 563.

Arzac, Enrique R. and Vijay S. Bawa. "Portfolio Choice And Equilibrium In Capital Markets With Safety-First Investors," JFEC, 1977, v4(3), 277-288.

Arzac, Enrique R. "A Mechanism For The Allocation Of Corporate Investment," JFQA, 1983, v18(2), 175-188.

Arzac, Enrique R. "Structural Planning Under Controllable Business Risk," JOF, 1975, v30(5), 1229-1237.

Arzac, Enrique R. "Utility Analysis Of Chance-Constrained Portfolio Selection," JFQA, 1974, v9(6), 993-1007.

Arzac, Enrique R., Robert A. Schwartz and David K. Whitcomb. "The Leverage Structure Of Interest Rates," JMCB, 1981, v13(1), 72-88.

Asabere, Paul K. "The Value Of A Neighborhood Street With Reference To The Cul-De-Sac," JREFEC, 1990, v3(2), 185-194.

Asabere, Paul K. and Barrie Harvey. "Factors Influencing The Value Of Urban Land: Evidence From Halifax-Dartmouth, Canada," AREUEA, 1985, v13(4), 361-377.

Asabere, Paul K., George Hachey and Steven Grubaugh. "Architecture, Historic Zoning, And The Value Of Homes," JREFEC, 1989, v2(3), 181-196.

Asay, Michael and Charles Edelsburg. "Can A Dynamic Strategy Replicate The Returns Of An Option?," JFM, 1986, v6(1), 63-70.

Asay, Michael R. "A Note On The Design Of Commodity Option Contracts," JFM, 1982, v2(1), 1-8.

Asay, Michael R. "A Note On The Design Commodity Option Contracts: A Reply," JFM, 1983, v3(3),335-338.

Asay, Michael R. "Implied Margin Requirements On Options And Stocks," JPM, 1981, v7(3), 55-59.

Asay, Michael R., Gisela A. Gonzalez and Benjamin Wolkowitz. "Financial Futures, Bank Portfolio Risk, And Accounting," JFM, v1(4), 607-618.

Asay, Michael. (Capozza, Dennis R. and Michael Asay. "Option Prices And Diffusion Processes: Some Empirical Tests," FR, 1978, v13(1), 1-21.)

Asch, Peter, Burton G. Malkiel and Richard E. Quandt. "Racetrack Betting And Informed Behavior," JFEC, 1982, v10(2), 187-194.

Asch, Peter, Burton G. Malkiel and Richard E. Quandt. "Market Efficiency In Racetrack Betting: Further Evidence And A Correction," JOB, 1986, v59(1), 157-160.

Asch, Peter, Burton G. Malkiel and Richard E. Quandt. "Market Efficiency In Racetrack Betting," JOB, 1984, v57(2), 165-176.

Aschauer, David Alan. "The Equilibrium Approach To Fiscal Policy," JMCB, 1988, v20(1), 41-62.

Ascher, Leonard W. "Dollar Averaging In Theory And In Practice," FAJ, 1960, v16(5), 51-53.

Ascher, Leonard W. "Eurodollars To The Rescue," FAJ, 1969, v25(4), 167-169.

Ascher, Leonard W. "Five Years Of Easy Money," FAJ, 1965, v21(4), 40-44.

Ascher, Leonard W. "Practical Limits To Bank Expansion," FAJ, 1961, v17(3), 23-27.

Ascher, Leonard W. "Selecting Bonds For Capital Gains," FAJ, 1971, v27(2), 74-79.

Ascher, Leonard W. "The Coming Chaos In Our Coinage," FAJ, 1964, v20(3), 99-102.

Ascher, Leonard W. "The Savings And Loan Colossus," FAJ, 1963, v19(2), 33-38.

Aschheim, Joseph. "Security-Reserve Requirements In The United States And The United Kingdom: Reply," JOF, 1959, v14(4), 545-547.

Aschheim, Joseph. "Supplementary Security-Reserve Requirements Reconsidered," JOF, 1958, v13(4), 473-487.

Ashley, Richard A. and Douglas M. Patterson. "A Nonparametric, Distribution-Free Test For Serial Independence In Stock Returns," JFQA, 1986, v21(2), 221-227.

Ashley, Richard and Douglas Patterson. "A Nonparametric Distribution-Free Test For Serial Independence In Stock Returns: A Comment," JFQA, 1990, v25(3), 417-418.

Ashton, D. J. and D. R. Atkins. "Interactions In Corporate Financing And Investment Decisions - Implications For Capital Budgeting: A Further Comment," JOF, 1978, v33(5), 1447-1454.

Ashton, D. J. and D. R. Atkins. "A Partial Theory Of Takeover Bids," JOF, 1984, v39(1), 167-183.

Ashton, D. J. "A Problem In The Detection Of Superior Investment Performance," JBFA, 1990, v17(3), 337-350.

Ashton, D. J. "Disagreements On Conditions For Unanimity," JBFA, 1985, v12(4), 507-513.

Ashton, D. J. "On The Evaluation Of Bought-In Goods And Services," JBFA, 1988, v15(1), 1-8.

Ashton, D. J. "The Cost Of Capital And The Imputation Tax System," JBFA, 1989, v16(1), 75-88.

Ashton, D. J. "The Reasons For Leasing - A Mathematical Programming Framework," JBFA, 1978, v5(2), 233-251.

Ashton, David J. "Stochastic Dominance And Mean Variance Rules In The Selection Of Risky Investments," JBFA, 1982, v8(4), 471-482.

Ashton, R. K. "A Microeconomic Analysis Of The Amey/Solomons Debate," JBFA, 1984, v11(3), 287-294.

Ashton, R. K. "An Economic Analysis Of Value To The Owner: A Reply," JBFA, 1984, v11(3), 425-427.

Ashton, R. K. "An Economic Analysis Of Value To The Owner," JBFA, 1983, v10(2), 251-256.

Ashton, R. K. "Personal Leverage V. Corporate Leverage: An Extension To The Debate," JBFA, 1986, v13(4), 619-626.

Ashton, R. K. "Stockholding Costs And Stockholding Policies: A Field Test," JBFA, 1989, v16(4), 575-586.

Ashton, Raymond. "Cash Flow Accounting: A Review And Critique," JBFA, 1976, v3(4), 63-81.

Askin, Sherry S. (Miller, Norman C. and Sherry S. Askin. "Monetary Policy And The Balance Of Payments In Brazil And Chile," JMCB, 1976, v8(2), 227-238.)

Aspinwall, Richard C. (Walker, David A., Richard C. Aspinwall, Stuart I. Greenbaum, Edward J. Kane and Perry D. Quick. "Panel Discussion On Federal Reserve Membership Issues," FR, 1979, v14(2), 58-74.)

Asplund, Nathan M., D. Lynn Forster and Thomas T. Stout. "Farmers' Use Of Forward Contracting And Hedging," RFM, 1989, v8(1), 24-37.

Asprem, Mads. "Stock Prices, Asset Portfolios And Macroeconomic Variables In Ten European Countries," JBF, 1989, v13(4/5), 589-612.

Asquith, Paul and David W. Mullins, Jr. "Equity Issues And Offering Dilution," JFEC, 1986, v15(1/2), 61-89.

Asquith, Paul and David W. Mullins, Jr. "Signalling With Dividends, Stock Repurchases, And Equity Issues," FM, 1986, v15(3), 27-44.

Asquith, Paul and E. Han Kim. "The Impact Of Merger Bids On The Participating Firms' Security Holders," JOF, 1982, v37(5), 1209-1228.

Asquith, Paul and David W. Mullins, Jr. "The Impact Of Initiating Dividend Payments On Shareholders' Wealth," JOB, 1983, v56(1), 77-96.

Asquith, Paul and Thierry A. Wizman. "Event Risk, Covenants, And Bondholder Returns In Leveraged Buyouts," JFEC, 1990, v27(1), 195-214.

Asquith, Paul, Robert F. Bruner and David W. Mullins, Jr. "The Gains To Bidding Firms From Merger," JFEC, 1983, v11(1), 121-139.

Asquith, Paul, David W. Mullins, Jr. and Eric D. Wolff. "Original Issue High Yield Bonds: Aging Analyses Of Defaults, Exchanges, And Calls," JOF, 1989, v44(4), 923-952.

Asquith, Paul. "Merger Bids, Uncertainty, And Stockholder Returns," JFEC, 1983, v11(1), 51-83.

Atchison, Michael D. "A Tool For Teaching The Weak Form Of Efficient Market Hypothesis," JFED, 1985, v14, 70-74.

Atchison, Michael D. "Non-Representative Trading Frequencies And The Detection Of Abnormal Performance," JFR, 1986, v9(4), 343-348.

Atchison, Michael D., Kirt C. Butler and Richard R. Simonds. "Nonsynchronous Security Trading And Market Index Autocorrelation," JOF, 1987, v42(1), 111-118.

Athanasopoulos, Peter J. and Peter W. Bacon. "The Evaluation Of Leveraged Leases," FM, 1980, v9(1), 76-80.

Athearn, James L. "1978 Presidential Address - The Riskless Society," JRI, 1978, v45(4), 565-573.

Athearn, James L. "Contributions To Risk And Insurance Theory From The Field Of Economics," JRI, 1962, v29(3), 329-342.

Athearn, James L. "Economic Significance Of Insurance Activity In The United States," JRI, 1962, v29(4), 547-551.

Athearn, James L. "Self Insuring The Workmen's Compensation Risk: A Case Study," JRI, 1961, v28(2), 93-96.

Athearn, James L. "The Structure Of The Life Insurance Industry," JRI, 1960, v27(2), 29-36.

Athearn, James L. "Uncertainty And The OASI Program," JRI, 1957, v24(4), 45-63.

Athearn, James L. "What Is Risk?," JRI, 1971, v38(4), 639-646.

Athearn, James L. (Crum, Lawrence L. and James L. Athearn. "An Experiment In Central Banking For Life Insurance Companies," JRI, 1963, v30(1), 101-108.)

Athearn, James L. and Harold E. Curry. "A Key To The Apartment," JRI, 1974, v41(1), 135-146.

Atkins, Allen B. and Edward A. Dyl. "Price Reversals, Bid-Ask Spreads, And Market Efficiency," JFQA, 1990, v25(4), 535-548.

Atkins, D. R. (Ashton, D. J. and D. R. Atkins. "A Partial Theory Of Takeover Bids," JOF, 1984, v39(1), 167-183.)

Atkins, D. R. (Ashton, D. J. and D. R. Atkins. "Interactions In Corporate Financing And Investment Decisions - Implications For Capital Budgeting: A Further Comment," JOF, 1978, v33(5), 1447-1454.)

Atkins, Joseph C. and Yong H. Kim. "Comment And Correction: Opportunty Cost In The Evaluation Of Investment In Accounts Receivable," FM, 1977, v6(4),71-74.

Atkins, Joseph C. (Kim, Yong H. and Joseph C. Atkins. "Evaluating Investments In Accounts Receivable: A Wealth Maximizing Framework," JOF, 1978, v33(2), 403-412.)

Atkinson, A. Sheridan. "The Management Factor In Security Analysis," FAJ, 1952, v8(5), 93-98.

Atkinson, Anthony A. and William R. Scott. "Current Cost Depreciation: A Programming Perspective," JBFA, 1982, v8(1), 19-42.

Atkinson, Stanley M. and R. Phil Malone. "The Use Of Low-Cost Microcomputers In Teaching Investments And Corporate Finance," JFED, 1983, v12, 78-81.

Atkinson, Sue N. "Financial Flows In Recent Business Cycles," JOF, 1965, v20(1), 14-35.

Atkinson, Thomas R. "Outlook For State And Local Government Securities," JOF, 1962, v17(2), 240-244.

Atkinson, Thomas R. "The Discount Proposal From The Standpoint Of Commercial Banks," JMCB, 1970, v2(2), 147-150.

Atkinson, Thomas R. "What Do Commercial Banks Want From The Presidential Commission?," JMCB, 1971, v3(1), 31-34.

Atkinson, Thomas R. (Ritter, Lawrence S. and Thomas R. Atkinson. "Monetary Theory And Policy In the Payments System Of The Future," **JMCB**, 1970, v2(4), 493-503.)

Atler, George C. (Becker, William E. and George C. Alter. "The Probabilities Of Life And Work Force Status In The Calculation Of Expected Earnings," **JRI**, 1987, v54(2), 364-375.)

Atrill, Verne Henry. (Healy, C. Ross and Verne Henry Atrill. "Objective Economics: Will The Real Laffer Curve Please Stand Up?," **FAJ**, 1983, v39(2), 15-24.)

Attfield, Clifford L. F. and Nigel W. Duck. "The Influence Of Unanticipated Money Growth On Real Output: Some Cross-Country Estimates," **JMCB**, 1983, v15(4), 442-454.

Atwater, Hubert F. "The Hobbs Bill (Railroad Reorganizations): The Bill Fosters False Hopes," **FAJ**, 1945, v1(2), 21-24.

Aubey, Robert T. (Hogan, Andrew J. and Robert T. Aubey. "Compulsory Insurance And Allocative Efficiency In Agriculture," **JRI**, 1984, v51(2), 342-348.)

Aucamp, Donald C. and Walter L. Eckardt, Jr. "An Intuitive Look at Ito's Lemma: A Pedagogical Note," **FR**, 1981, v16(2), 41-50.

Aucamp, Donald C. and Walter L. Eckardt, Jr. "A Sufficient Condition For A Unique Nonnegative Internal Rate Of Return--Comment," **JFQA**, 1976, v11(2), 329-332.

Auchmuty, J. F. G. (Lee, Wayne Y., Ramesh K. S. Rao and J. F. G. Auchmuty. "Option Pricing In A Lognormal Securities Market, With Discrete Trading," **JFEC**, 1981, v9(1), 75-102.)

Auerbach, Alan J. "Selections From The Senate And House Hearings On LBOs And Corporate Debt," **JACF**, 1989, v2(1), 52-57.

Auerbach, Alan. (Gebotys, Robert J., Alan Auerbach and Adriana Petrucci. "The Insurance Branch Manager: Correlates Of Success," **JRI**, 1987, v54(1), 157-161.)

Auerbach, Irving. "Should Federal Reserve Float Be Abolished And Its Check Activities Curtailed?: Comment," **JOF**, 1965, v20(3), 490-499.

Auerbach, Robert D. and Jack L. Rutner. "A Negative View Of The Negative Money Multiplier: Comment," **JOF**, 1977, v32(5), 1814-1817.

Auerbach, Robert. "The Measurement Of Economies Of Scale: A Comment," **JOB**, 1976, v49(1), 60-61.

Auerbach, Sylvia. "Investment: One Year's Study - Return: Profitable," **FAJ**, 1960, v16(4), 77-78.

Auernheimer, Leonardo. "The Revenue-Maximizing Inflation Rate And The Treatment Of The Transition To Equilibrium," **JMCB**, 1983, v15(3), 368-376.

Ault, Richard W. and Robert B. Ekelund, Jr. "Rent Seeking In A Static Model Of Zoning," **AREUEA**, 1988, v16(1), 69-76.

Ault, Richard and Richard Saba. "The Economic Effects Of Long-Term Rent Control: The Case Of New York City," **JREFEC**, 1990, v3(1), 25-42.

Ausman, Evan L., David M. Scott and Raymond T. Smith. "Life Insurance Stocks," **FAJ**, 1956, v12(4), 87-93.

Auster, Richard. (Silver, Morris and Richard Auster. "Entre-pre-neurship, Profit, And Limits On Firm Size," **JOB**, 1969, v42(3), 277-281.)

Auster, Rolf. (Lerner, Eugene M. and Rolf Auster. "Market Discounts Potential Dilution?," **FAJ**, 1969, v25(4), 118-121.)

Austin, C. Henry. "The Integrated Insurance Department," **JRI**, 1957, v24(1), 168-173.

Austin, Douglas V. and John M. Fall. "Capital Asset Financing Of Retirement Centers," **FM**, 1976, v5(1), 39-45.

Austin, Douglas V. "The Financial Management Of Tender Offer Takeovers," **FM**, 1974, v3(1), 37-43.

Austin, Douglas V. (Duvall, Richard M. and Douglas V. Austin. "Predicting The Results Of Proxy Contests," **JOF**, 1965, v20(3), 464-471.)

Austin, Douglas V. (Lindsley, David A. and Douglas V. Austin. "A Sensational New Investment," **FAJ**, 1977, v33(4), 53-54.)

Austin, Douglas V. and David A. Lindsley. "Ohio Usury Ceiling And Residential Real Estate Development," **AREUEA**, 1976, v4(1), 83-96.

Austin, Larry M. (Mukherjee, Tarun K. and Larry M. Austin. "An Empirical Investigation Of Small Bank Stock Valuation And Dividend Policy," **FM**, 1980, v9(1), 27-31.)

Auten, John H. "Forward Exchange Rates And Interest-Rate Differentials," **JOF**, 1963, v18(1), 11-19.

Auten, John H. "Monetary Policy And The Forward Exchange Market," **JOF**, 1961, v16(4), 546-558.

Auxier, Albert L. "A Test Of The Usefulness Of Policy Information In Ranking Life Insurance Alternatives," **JRI**, 1976, v43(1), 87-98.

Avard, Stephen L. and Jane H. White. "Readability Study Of Principles Of Financial Management Textbooks," **JFED**, 1986, v15, 53-62.

Avard, Stephen L. (Milano, Duane R., Stephen L. Avard and John Russell Arens. "Microcomputer Applications For Preparing Tests In Entry Level Financial Management Courses," **JFED**, 1986, v15, 68-78.)

Avery, Robert B. and Allen N. Berger. "Loan Commitments And Bank Risk Exposure," **JBF**, 1991, v15(1), 173-192.

Avery, Robert B., Terrence M. Belton and Michael A. Goldberg. "Market Discipline In Regulating Bank Risk: New Evidence From The Capital Markets," **JMCB**, 1988, v20(4), 597-610.

Avey, Mary Lee. (Veit, E. Theodore, Mary Lee Avey, Jerry L. Corley and Timothy Summers. "The Role Of Stock Options In Bank Trust Departments: Fifth Federal Reserve District Banks," **JBR**, 1979-80, v10(4),255-256.)

Avidan, Alan I. (Shinnar, Reuel, Ofer Dressler, C. A. Feng and Alan I. Avidan. "Estimation Of The Economic Rate Of Return For Industrial Companies," **JOB**, 1989, v62(3), 417-446.)

Avio, Kenneth L. "On The Effects Of Satutory Interest Rate Ceilings," **JOF**, 1974, v29(5), 1383-1395.

Avio, Kenneth L. "On The Effects Of Statutory Interest Rate Ceilings: Reply," **JOF**, 1977, v32(5),1811-1813.

Awh, R. Y. and D. Waters. "A Discriminant Analysis Of Economic, Demographic, And Attitudinal Characteristics Of Bank Charge-Card Holders: A Case Study," **JOF**, 1974, v29(3), 973-980.

Axelrad, Leonard I. "Over-the-Counter Market: Organization And Problems," **FAJ**, 1962, v18(6), 71-73.

Axelson, Kenneth S. "Accounting For Deferred Taxes," **FAJ**, 1966, v22(5), 23-26.

Ayanian, Robert. "Geopolitics And The Dollar," **JIMF**, 1989, v8(3), 391-400.

Ayanian, Robert. "The Advertising Capital Controversy," **JOB**, 1983, v56(3), 349-364.

Ayaydin, Sirri. (Arditti, Fred D., Sirri Ayaydin, Ravi K. Mattu and Stephen Rigsbee. "A Passive Futures Strategy That Outperforms Active Management," **FAJ**, 1986, v42(4), 63-67.)

Ayres, Herbert F. and John Y. Barry. "Prologue To A Unified Portfolio Theory," **JOF**, 1982, v37(2),625-635.

Ayres, Herbert F. and John Y. Barry. "Dynamics Of The Government Yield Curve," **FAJ**, 1979, v35(3), 31-39.

Azevedo, Ross E. (Mitchell, Daniel J. B. and Ross E. Azevedo. "Price Controls And Shortages: A Note," **JOB**, 1975, v48(4), 571-574.)

Aziz, Abdul and Gerald H. Lawson. "Cash Flow Reporting And Financial Distress Models: Testing Of Hypotheses," **FM**, 1989, v18(1), 55-63.

BBB

Babb, E. M., M. A. Leslie and M. D. Van Slyke. "The Potential Of Business-Gaming Methods In Research," **JOB**, 1966, v39(4), 465-472.

Babbel, David F. and Kim B. Staking. "A Capital Budgeting Analysis Of Life Insurance Costs In The United States: 1950-1979," **JOF**, 1983, v38(1), 149-170.

Babbel, David F. "A Mathematical Note On Inflation, Regulation, And The Cost Of Life Insurance," **JRI**, 1980, v47(1), 152-156.

Babbel, David F. "Consumer Valuation Of Life Insurance: Comment," **JRI**, 1978, v45(3), 516-521.

Babbel, David F. "Inflation's Impact On Life Insurance Costs: Brazilian Indexed And Nonindexed Policies," **JRI**, 1979, v46(4), 652-671.

Babbel, David F. "Inflation, Indexation, And Life Insurance Sales In Brazil," **JRI**, 1981, v48(1), 111-135.

Babbel, David F. "Insuring Banks Against Systematic Credit Risk," **JFM**, 1989, v9(6), 487-506.

Babbel, David F. "Interest Rate Dynamics And The Term Structure: A Note," **JBF**, 1988, v11(3),401-418.

Babbel, David F. "Measuring Inflation Impact On Life Insurance Costs," **JRI**, 1979, v46(3), 425-440.

Babbel, David F. "Real Immunization With Indexed Bonds," **FAJ**, 1984, v40(6), 49-54.

Babbel, David F. "The Price Elasticity Of Demand For Whole Life Insurance," **JOF**, 1985, v40(1), 225-239.

Babbel, David F. and David R. Klock. "Insurance Pedagogy: Executive Opinions And Priorities," **JRI**, 1988, v55(4), 701-712.

Babbel, David F. and Eisaku Ohrsuka. "Aspects Of Optimal Multiperiod Life Insurance," **JRI**, 1989, v56(3), 460-481.

Babbel, David F. and Kim B. Staking. "An Engel Curve Analysis Of Gambling And Insurance In Brazil," **JRI**, 1983, v50(4), 688-696.

Babcock, Guilford C. "A Note On Justifying Beta As A Measure Of Risk," **JOF**, 1972, v27(3),699-702.

Babcock, Guilford C. "Duration As A Link Between Yield And Value," **JPM**, 1984, v10(2), 58-65.

Babcock, Guilford C. "Duration As A Weighted Average Of Two Factors," **FAJ**, 1985, v41(2), 75-76.

Babcock, Guilford C. "Duration As A Link Between Yield And Value: Erratum," **JPM**, 1984, v11(1), 97-98.

Babcock, Guilford C. "The Roots Of Risk And Return," **FAJ**, 1980, v36(1), 56-63.

Babcock, Guilford C. "When Is Growth Sustainable?," **FAJ**, 1970, v26(3), 108-114.

Babcock, Guilford C., M. Chapman Findlay, III and Stephen D. Messner. "FMRR and Duration: Implications For Real Estate Investment Analysis," **AREUEA**, 1976, v4(3), 49-68.

Babcock, Guilford. "On The Linearity Of Duration," **FAJ**, 1986, v42(5), 75-77.

Babin, Charles E. (Ranson, R. David and Charles E. Babin. "What's Holding Up Capital Investment?," **FAJ**, 1978, v34(5), 30-41.)

Babson, David L. "Index Funds: Why Throw In The Towel?," **JPM**, 1976, v2(3), 53-55.

Babson, David L. "Investment Information Explosion," **FAJ**, 1964, v20(4), 33-34.

Babson, David L. "Performance Or Speculation?," **FAJ**, 1967, v23(5), 129-132.

Babson, David L. "Yesterday's Crash And Today's Inflation," **JPM**, 1979, v6(1), 49-51.

Bacchetta, Philippe. "Temporary Capital Controls In A Balance-Of-Payments Crisis," **JIMF**, 1990, v9(3), 246-257.

Bach, G. L. "A Further Note On Bank Supervision And Monetary Policy," **JOF**, 1950, v5(4), 421-424.

Bach, G. L. "Bank Supervision, Monetary Policy, And Governmental Reorganization," **JOF**, 1949, v4(4), 269-285.

Bach, G. L. "The Machinery And Politics Of Monetary Policy-Making," **JOF**, 1953, v8(2), 169-176.

Bachrach, Benjamin and Dan Galai. "The Risk-Return Relationship And Stock Prices," **JFQA**, 1979, v14(2), 421-441.

Backer, Morton and Martin L. Gosman. "Management's Perspective On Bond Downgrades," **FAJ**, 1985, v41(4), 77-79.

Backer, Morton and Martin L. Gosman. "The Use Of Financial Ratios In Credit Downgrade Decisions," **FM**, 1980, v9(1), 53-56.

Backer, Morton. "Innovation In Financial Reporting," **FAJ**, 1971, v27(2), 67-72,79.

Backman, Jules. "Merger Accounting: An Economist's View," **FAJ**, 1970, v26(4), 39-48.

Backus, David and Douglas Purvis. "An Integrated Model Of Household Flow-Of-Funds Allocations," **JMCB**, 1980, v12(2), Part 2, 400-421.

Backus, David, William C. Brainard, Gary Smith and James Tobin. "A Model Of U.S. Financial And Nonfinancial Economic Behavior," **JMCB**, 1980, v12(2), Part 1, 259-293.

Bacon, Peter and Richard Williams. "Interest Rate Futures Trading: New Tool For The Financial Manager," **FM**, 1976, v5(1), 32-38.

Bacon, Peter W. and Edward L. Winn, Jr. "The Impact Of Forced Conversion On Stock Prices," **JOF**, 1969, v24(5), 871-874.

Bacon, Peter W. "The Evaluation Of Mutually Exclusive Investments," FM, 1977, v6(2), 55-58.

Bacon, Peter W. "The Subscription Price In Rights Offerings," FM, 1972, v1(2), 59-64.

Bacon, Peter W. (Athanasopoulos, Peter J. and Peter W. Bacon. "The Evaluation Of Leveraged Leases," FM, 1980, v9(1), 76-80.)

Bacon, Peter W. (Logue, Dennis E. and Richard J. Rogalski. "Offshore Alphas: Should Diversification Begin At Home?," JPM, 1979, v5(2), 5-10.)

Bacon, Peter W., Lawrence J. Gitman, Khurshid Ahmad and M. Fall Ainina. "Long-Term Catastrophic Care: A Financial Planning Perspective," JRI, 1989, v56(1), 146-154.

Bacon, Peter. (Gitman, Lawrence and Peter Bacon. "Comprehensive Personal Financial Planning: An Emerging Opportunity," JFED, 1985, v14, 36-46.)

Badger, Ralph E. "Investment Growth, Is It Overvalued?," FAJ, 1963, v19(1), 63-68.

Badger, Sherwin C. "Unusual Features Of Life Insurance Investing," JOF, 1951, v6(2), 77-84.

Badrinath, S. G. and Sangit Chatterjee. "On Measuring Skewness And Elongation In Common Stock Return Distributions: The Case Of The Market Index," JOB, 1988, v61(4), 451-472.

Badrinath, S. G. and Wilbur G. Lewellen. "Evidence On Tax-Motivated Securities Trading Behavior," JOF, 1991, v46(1), 369-382.

Badrinath, S. G., Gerald D. Gay and Jayant R. Kale. "Patterns Of Institutional Investment, Prudence, And The Managerial 'Safety-Net' Hypothesis," JRI, 1989, v56(4), 605-629.

Bae, Sung C. "Interest Rate Changes And Common Stock Returns Of Financial Institutions: Revisited," JFR, 1990, v13(1), 71-79.

Bae, Sung C. and Haim Levy. "The Valuation Of Firm Commitment Underwriting Contracts For Seasoned New Equity Issues: Theory And Evidence," FM, 1990, v19(2), 48-59.

Baen, John S. (Alvayay, Jaime and John S. Baen. "The Implications Of Federal Wetland Protection Programs For The Real Estate Appraisal Industry," JRER, 1990, v5(1), 153-165.)

Baer, Herbert L., Jr. "Panel: Who Should Set Futures Margins?," RFM, 1988, v7(3), 410-412.

Baesel, Jerome and Dwight Grant. "Optimal Sequential Futures Trading," JPQA, 1982, v17(5),683-695.

Baesel, Jerome B. and Garry R. Stein. "The Value Of Information: Inferences From The Profitability Of Insider Trading," JFQA, 1979, v14(3), 553-571.

Baesel, Jerome B. and Nahum Biger. "The Allocation Of Risk: Some Implications Of Fixed Versus Index-Linked Mortgages," JFQA, 1980, v15(2), 457-468.

Baesel, Jerome B. and Nahum Biger. "Inflation And Pension Plan Linkage Of Benefits To The Cost Of Living Index," FR, 1976, v11(1), 59-68.

Baesel, Jerome B. "Adjusting `Duration' Estimates For Tax Payments," FR, v12(1), 28-35.

Baesel, Jerome B. "On The Assessment Of Risk: Some Further Considerations," JOF, 1974, v29(5), 1491-1494.

Baesel, Jerome B. (Johnson, James M. and Jerome B. Baesel. "The Nature And Significance Of Trend Betas," JPM, 1978, v4(3), 36-40.)

Baesel, Jerome B., David T. Methe and David Shulman. "Teaching Managerial Finance To Public Sector Students," JFED, 1981, v10, 23-32.

Baesel, Jerome B., George Shows and Edward Thorp. "The Cost Of Liquidity Services In Listed Options: A Note," JOF, 1983, v38(3), 989-995.

Baesel, Jerome, George Shows and Edward Thorp. "Can Joe Granville Time The Market?," JPM, 1982, v8(3), 5-9.

Bagamery, Bruce D. "On The Correspondence Between The Baumol-Tobin And Miller-Orr Optimal Cash Balance Models," FR, 1987, v22(2), 313-320.

Bagamery, Bruce D. (Eckardt, Walter L., Jr. and Bruce D. Bagamery. "Short Selling: The Mutual Fund Alternative," JFR, 1983, v6(3), 231-238.)

Bagby, Wesley S. "Automation In Insurance," JRI, 1957, v24(1), 158-167.

Bagby, Wesley S. "Insurance, Automation, And The Individual Employee," JRI, 1960, v27(4), 85-90.

Bagchi, Prabir K. (Gupta, Yash P., Ramesh P. Rao and Prabir K. Bagchi. "Linear Goal Programming As An Alternative To Multivariate Discriminant Analysis: A Note," JBFA, 1990, v17(4), 593-598.)

Bagehot, Walter. "Money Will Not Manage Itself," JPM, 1975, v1(3), 78-81.

Bagehot, Walter. "Risk In Corporate Pension Funds," FAJ, 1972, v28(1), 80-84.

Bagehot, Walter. "The Only Game In Town," FAJ, 1971, v27(2), 12-14,22.

Bagnoli, Mark and Barton L. Lipman. "Successful Takeovers Without Exclusion," RFS, 1988-89, v1(1), 89-110.

Bagnoli, Mark, Roger Gordon and Barton L. Lipman. "Stock Repurchase As A Takeover Defense," RFS, 1989, v2(3), 423-443.

Bagozzi, Echard P. "The Nature And Causes Of Self-Esteem, Peformance, And Satisfaction In The Sales Force: A Structural Equation Approach," JOB, 1980, v53(3), Part 1, 315-331.

Bagwell, J. (Franks, J. R., R. Miles and J. Bagwell. "A Review Of Acquisition Valuation Models," JBFA, 1974, v1(1), 35-53.)

Bahl, Roy W. and Robert J. Saunders. "Factors Associated With Variation In State And Local Government Spending," JOF, 1966, v21(3), 523-534.

Bahr, Michael D. (Tolley, H. Dennis, Michael D. Bahr and Peter K. Dotson. "A Statistical Method For Monitoring Social Insurance Claims," JRI, 1989, v56(4), 670-685.)

Baier, J. R. (Elliott, J. Walter and J. R. Baier. "Econometric Models And Current Interest Rates: How Well Do They Predict Future Rates: A Reply," JOF, 1980, v35(4), 1049-1050.)

Baier, Jerome R. (Elliott, J. Walter and Jerome R. Baier. "Econometric Models And Current Interest Rates: How Well Do They Predict Future Rates?," JOF, 1979, v34(4), 975-986.)

Bailey, Andrew D., Jr. and Daniel L. Jensen. "General Price Level Adjustments In The Capital Budgeting Decision," FM, 1977, v6(1), 26-32.

Bailey, E. Norman. "Real Estate Investment Trusts: An Appraisal," FAJ, 1966, v22(3), 107-114.

Bailey, E. Norman. "The Erroneous MEC Function: Reply," JOF, 1972, v27(1), 138-138.

Bailey, E. Norman. "The Erroneous MEC Function," JOF, 1970, v25(5), 1123-1124.

Bailey, F. A. and W. K. H. Fung. "A Note On Extreme Leverage, MM And Ezra Solomon," JBFA, 1978, v5(2), 253-259.

Bailey, George D. "Corporate Financial Reports And Accounting," FAJ, 1946, v2(2), 39-46.

Bailey, J. K. "The Responsibility For The Organizational Planning Function," JRI, 1965, v32(1), 91-104.

Bailey, Jeffry V. "Some Thoughts On Performance-Based Fees," FAJ, 1990, v46(4), 31-40.

Bailey, Jeffrey V. and Robert D. Arnott. "Cluster Analysis And Manager Selection," FAJ, 1986, v42(6), 20-21,24-28.

Bailey, Martin J. "Steel And The Postwar Rise In The Wholesale Price Index," JOB, 1962, v35(2),153-157.

Bailey, Warren and Rene M. Stulz. "The Pricing Of Stock Index Options In A General Equilibrium Model," JFQA, 1989, v24(1), 1-12.

Bailey, Warren and Rene M. Stulz. "Benefits Of International Diversification: The Case Of Pacific Basin Stock Markets," JPM, 1990, v16(4), 57-61.

Bailey, Warren. "An Empirical Investigation Of The Market For COMEX Gold Futures Options," JOF, 1987, v42(5), 1187-1194.

Bailey, Warren. "Canada's Dual Class Shares: Further Evidence On The Market Value Of Cash Dividends," JOF, 1988, v43(5), 1143-1160.

Bailey, Warren. "Money Supply Announcements And The Ex Ante Volatility Of Asset Prices," JMCB, 1988, v20(4), 611-620.

Bailey, Warren. "The Market For Japanese Index Futures: Some Preliminary Evidence," JFM, 1989, v9(4), 283-296.

Bailey, Warren. "US Money Supply Announcements And Pacific Rim Stock Markets: Evidence And Implications," JIMF, 1990, v9(3), 344-356.

Baillie, Richard T. and Ramon P. DeGennaro. "Stock Returns And Volatility," JFQA, 1990, v25(2), 203-214.

Baillie, Richard T. and Ramon P. DeGennaro. "The Impact Of Delivery Terms On Stock Return Volatility," JFSR, 1989, v3(1), 55-76.

Baillie, Richard T. and Tim Bollerslev. "Common Stochastic Trends In A System Of Exchange Rates," JOF, 1989, v44(1), 167-182.

Baillie, Richard T. and Tim Bollerslev. "A Multivariate Generalized ARCH Approach To Modeling Risk Premia In Forward Foreign Exchange Rate Markets," JIMF, 1990, v9(3), 309-324.

Bain, Joe S. "Price Leaders, Barometers, And Kinks," JOB, 1960, v33(3), 193-203.

Bajaj, Mukesh. and Anand M. Vijh. "Dividend Clienteles And The Information Content Of Dividend Changes," JFEC, 1990, v26(2), 193-220.

Bajic, Vladimir. "Housing-Market Segmentation And Demand For Housing Attributes: Some Empirical Findings," AREUEA, 1985, v13(1), 58-75.

Bajic, Vladimir. "Urban Housing Markets Modelling: Short-Run Equilibrium Implications," AREUEA, 1983, v11(3), 416-438.

Bakay, Archie J. (Guthmann, Harry G. and Archie J. Bakay. "The Market Impact Of The Sale Of Large Blocks Of Stock," JOF, 1965, v20(4), 617-631.)

Baker, C. Austin. "The U. S. Money Crisis," FAJ, 1969, v25(1), 45-50.

Baker, David A. "Investment Performance And The Range Of Choice," JPM, 1979, v5(3), 13-18.

Baker, George P. "Pay-For-Performance For Middle Managers: Causes And Consequences," JACF, 1990, v3(3), 50-61.

Baker, George P. and Karen H. Wruck. "Organizational Changes And Value Creation In Leveraged Buyouts: The Case Of The O.M. Scott & Sons Company," JFEC, 1989, v25(2), 163-190.

Baker, George P., Michael C. Jensen and Kevin J. Murphy. "Compensation And Incentives: Practice Vs. Theory," JOF, 1988, v43(3), 593-616.

Baker, Guthrie. "Blueprint For Constructive Reform," FAJ, 1971, v27(6), 20-22,62.

Baker, H. Kent and James Spitzfaden. "The Impact Of Exchange Listing On The Cost Of Equity Capital," FR, 1982, v17(3), 128-141.

Baker, H. Kent and John A. Haslem. "Toward The Development Of Client-Specified Valuation Models," JOF, 1974, v29(4), 1255-1263.

Baker, H. Kent and Patricia L. Gallagher. "Management's View Of Stock Splits," FM, 1980, v9(2), 73-77.

Baker, H. Kent and Richard B. Edelman. "OTC Market Switching And Stock Returns: Some Empirical Evidence," JFR, 1990, v13(4), 325-338.

Baker, H. Kent and Sue E. Meeks. "Research On Exchange Listings And Delistings: A Review And Synthesis," FPE, 1991, v1(1), 57-72.

Baker, H. Kent, Gail E. Farrelly and Richard B. Edelman. "A Survey Of Management Views On Dividend Policy," FM, 1985, v14(3), 78-84.

Baker, H. Kent, Michael B. Hargrove and John A. Haslem. "An Empirical Analysis Of The Risk-Return Preferences Of Individual Investors," JFQA, 1977, v12(3), 377-389.

Baker, H. Kent, Patricia L. Gallagher and Karen E. Morgan. "Management's View Of Stock Repurchase Programs," JFR, 1981, v4(3), 233-247.

Baker, H. Kent. "PSI: An Innovative Approach To Teaching Finance," JFED, 1974, v3, 16-20.

Baker, H. Kent. "Personal Finance As A Service Course," JFED, 1976, v5, 21-25.

Baker, H. Kent. "Understanding International Finance Through A Study Tour Program," JFED, 1977, v6, 66-69.

Baker, H. Kent. (Edelman, Richard B. and H. Kent Baker. "The Dynamics Of Neglect And Return," JPM, 1987, v14(1), 52-55.)

Baker, H. Kent. (Edelman, Richard B. and H. Kent Baker. "Liquidity And Stock Exchange Listing," FR, 1990, v25(2), 231-250.)

Baker, H. Kent. (Einhorn, Raymond and H. Kent Baker. "The Institute For Applied Public Financial Management: An Innovative Approach," JFED, 1977, v6, 27-32.)

Baker, H. Kent. (Holmberg, Stevan R. and H. Kent Baker. "The CEO's Role In Strategic Planning," JBR, 1981-82, v12(4), 218-227.)

Baker, James C. and L. J. Beardsley. "Capital Budgeting By U.S. Multinational Companies," FR, 1972, v2(2), 115-121.

Baker, James C. "The German Stock Market," FAJ, 1968, v24(5), 153-156.

Baker, James C. (DeMaskey, Andrea L. and James C. Baker. "The Efficiency Of Option Markets In Foreign Currencies: An Empirical Analysis," IJOF, 1990, v3(1), 1-38.)

Baker, Nardin L. (Haugen, Robert A. and Nardin L. Baker. "Dedicated Stock Portfolios," JPM, 1990, v16(4), 17-22.)

Baker, Nardin L. (Haugen, Robert A. and Nardin L. Baker. "The Efficient Market Inefficiency Of Capitalization-Weighted Stock Portfolios," JPM, 1991, v17(3), 35-40.)

Baker, Richard. "Emotional Factors In Marketing Insurance," JRI, 1961, v28(2), 1-10.

Bakerman, Theodore and George T. Doran. "Unemployment And Out-Of-The-Labor-Force Relationships: Static And Dynamic Analyses," JRI, 1964, v31(4), 573-587.

Bakerman, Theodore. "Development Of Statistics Of The Insurance Industry By Government," JRI, 1962, v29(1), 57-68.

Bakerman, Theodore. "How Old Is Top Management In Insurance Companies? The Data And Some Implications," JRI, 1957, v24(4), 36-44.

Bakerman, Theodore. "Is The Insurance Industry Attracting Younger Men?," JRI, 1957, v24(2), 93-95.

Bakerman, Theodore. "OASI Statistics - A Program For Insurance Industry Employment Research," JRI, 1960, v27(1), 83-90.

Bakerman, Theodore. "OASI Statistics: A Program For Insurance Industry Employment Research," JRI, 1960, v27(3), 49-54.

Bakerman, Theodore. "OASI Statistics: A Program For Insurance Industry Employment Research, Part III," JRI, 1961, v28(2), 87-92.

Bakerman, Theodore. "Selected Unemployment Compensation Benefit Problems: Disregarded Earnings And The Determination Of Labor Force Status," JRI, 1959, v26(2), 63-68.

Bakerman, Theodore. "Unable To Work: A Study Of Socio-Economic Influence On The Census Statistic In A Selected Area," JRI, 1963, v30(3), 377-384.

Bakerman, Theodore. (Wagner, Ludwig A. and Theodore Bakerman. "Wage Earner's Opinions Of Insurance Fringe Benefits," JRI, 1960, v27(2), 17-28.)

Balachandran, B. V. (Blann, Jack and B. V. Balachandran. "An Empirical Test Of The Statistical Association Of Market Risk And Financial Accounting Allocation," JBFA, 1988, v15(1), 101-114.)

Balachandran, Bala V., Nandu J. Nagarajan and Alfred Rappaport. "Threshold Margins For Creating Economic Value," FM, 1986, v15(1), 68-77.

Balachandran, K. R. and B. N. Srinidhi. "A Stable Cost Application Scheme For Service Center Usage," JBFA, 1988, v15(1), 87-100.

Balachandran, Kashi R. and B. N. Srinidhi. "A Note On Cost Allocation, Opportunity Costs And Optimal Utilization," JBFA, 1990, v17(4), 579-584.

Balbach, Anatol. "Karl Brunner: Early Years, UCLA," JMCB, 1977, v9(1), Part 2, 247-249.

Balbirer, Sheldon D. (Flanigan, George B. and Sheldon D. Balbirer. "Some Findings On The Costs And Benefits Of Mutual Fund Insurance," JRI, 1978, v45(4), 675-682.)

Balcer, Y. and P. Diamond. "Social Security Benefits With A Lengthening Average Period," JRI, 1977, v44(2), 259-265.

Balcer, Yves and Izzet Sahin. "Probabilistic Models For Pension Benefits," JRI, 1979, v46(1), 99-124.

Balcer, Yves and Izzet Sahin. "Modeling The Impact Of Pension Reform - A Case Study," JRI, 1982, v49(2), 158-192.

Balcer, Yves and Izzet Sahin. "Dynamics Of Pension Reform: The Case Of Ontario," JRI, 1984, v51(4), 652-686.

Balcer, Yves and Kenneth L. Judd. "Effects Of Capital Gains Taxation On Life-Cycle Investment And Portfolio Management," JOF, 1987, v42(3), 743-758.

Balcer, Yves. (Sahin, Izzet and Yves Balcer. "Qualifying Service Under ERISA Vesting Standards: A Comparative Analysis," JRI, 1979, v46(3), 483-496.)

Balcha, Dembel. (Ang, James S. and Dembel Balcha. "Bond Swap Profitability," JBR, 1975-76, v6(3), 224-227.)

Balding, Bruce E. "Public Offerings And Pre-Filing Publicity," FAJ, 1961, v17(2), 77-81.

Baldwin, Carliss Y. and Richard S. Ruback. "Inflation, Uncertainty And Investment," JOF, 1986, v41(3), 657-667.

Baldwin, Carliss Y. and Scott P. Mason. "The Resolution Of Claims In Financial Distress: The Case Of Massey Ferguson," JOF, 1983, v38(2), 505-516.

Baldwin, Carliss Y. "Optimal Sequential Investment When Capital Is Not Readily Reversible," JOF, 1982, v37(3), 763-782.

Baldwin, Carliss. "Productivity And Labor Unions: An Application Of The Theory Of Self-Enforcing Contracts," JOB, 1983, v56(2), 155-186.

Baldwin, Roger R. "An Approximate Formula For The Yield On Bonds Selling Close To Par," FAJ, 1958, v14(4), 77-78.

Baldwin, Rosecrans. "Principal And Income Accounting," FAJ, 1969, v25(2), 60-67.

Baliga, Gurudutt and Raj Aggarwal. "Domestic Versus Transnational Mergers: Differences In Participating Firms," AFPAF, 1990, v5(1), 315-335.

Ball, Clifford A. and Adrian E. Tschoegl. "The Decision To Establish A Foreign Bank Branch Or Subsidiary: An Application Of Binary Classification Procedures," JFQA, 1982, v17(3), 411-424.

Ball, Clifford A. and Walter N. Torous. "Futures Options And The Volatility Of Futures Prices," JOF, 1986, v41(4), 857-870.

Ball, Clifford A. and Walter N. Torous. "A Simplified Jump Process For Common Stock Returns," JFQA, 1983, v18(1), 53-65.

Ball, Clifford A. and Walter N. Torous. "Bond Price Dynamics And Options," JFQA, 1983, v18(4), 517-531.

Ball, Clifford A. and Walter N. Torous. "On Jumps In Common Stock Prices And Their Impact On Call Pricing," JOF, 1985, v40(1), 155-173.

Ball, Clifford A. "Estimation Bias Induced By Discrete Security Prices," JOF, 1988, v43(4), 841-865.

Ball, Clifford A. and Walter N. Torous. "Investigating Security-Price Performance In The Presence Of Event-Date Uncertainty," JFEC, 1988, v22(1), 123-154.

Ball, Clifford A. and Walter N. Torous. "The Maximum Likelihood Estimation Of Security Price Volatility: Theory, Evidence, And Application To Option Pricing," JOB, 1984, v57(1), Part 1, 97-112.

Ball, Clifford A., Walter N. Torous and Adrian E. Tschoegl. "An Empirical Investigation Of The EOE Gold Options Market," JBF, 1985, v9(1), 101-113.

Ball, Clifford A., Walter N. Torous and Adrian E. Tschoegl. "Gold And The `Weekend Effect'," JFM, 1982, v2(2), 175-182.

Ball, Clifford A., Walter N. Torous and Adrian E. Tschoegl. "The Degree Of Price Resolution: The Case Of The Gold Market," JFM, 1985, v5(1), 29-43.

Ball, Jay N. "A Note On The Importance Of Real Estate Course Titles," JRER, 1987, v2(1), 93-97.

Ball, Jay N. and Hugh O. Nourse. "Testing The Conventional Representation Model For Residential Real Estate Brokerage," JRER, 1988, v3(2), 119-131.

Ball, Michael. "Investment Company Performance (Another View)," FAJ, 1961, v17(5), 51-58.

Ball, Ray and Ross Watts. "Additional Evidence On The Time Series Properties Of Reported Earnings Per Share: Reply," JOF, 1977, v32(5), 1802-1808.

Ball, Ray and Ross Watts. "Some Additional Evidence On Survival Biases," JOF, 1979, v34(1),197-206.

Ball, Ray and Ross Watts. "Some Time Series Properties Of Accounting Income," JOF, 1972, v27(3),663-681.

Ball, Ray and Frank J. Finn. "The Effect Of Block Transactions On Share Prices: Australian Evidence," JBF, 1989, v13(3), 397-420.

Ball, Ray and S. P. Kothari. "Nonstationary Expected Returns: Implications For Tests Of Market Efficiency And Serial Correlations In Returns," JFEC, 1989, v25(1), 51-74.

Ball, Ray. "Anomalies In Relationships Between Securities' Yields And Yield-Surrogates," JFEC, 1978, v6(2/3), 103-126.

Ball, Ray. "Risk, Return And Disequilibrium: An Application To Changes In Accounting Techniques," JOF, 1972, v27(2), 343-353.

Ball, Ray. "The Natural Taxation Of Capital Gains And Losses When Income Is Taxed," JBF, 1984, v8(3), 471-481.

Ballam, S. H., Jr. "Preferred Stocks - They Can Be Attractive Investments," FAJ, 1955, v11(5), 53-58.

Ballen, Samuel. "Petroleum Reserves And The Security Analyst," FAJ, 1955, v11(2), 91-94.

Ballendux, Frans J. and Marius J. L. Jonkhart. "A Possible Error In The Expectations Theory: A Comment," JMCB, 1981, v13(1), 105-106.

Balles, John J. "The Federal Reserve: The Role Of Reserve Banks," JMCB, 1984, v16(1), 110-117.

Balles, John J. "The Outlook For Fiscal Monetary And Debt Management Policies," JOF, 1964, v19(2), Part 1, 403-410.

Balles, John J. "Tight Money And The New Economics," FAJ, 1967, v23(2), 15-18.

Ballman, R. J., Jr. "The Relative Stability Of Potato Velocity And The Exercise Multiplier In The United States," JOF, 1972, v27(4), 919-920.

Baloff, N. and R. McKersie. "Motivating Startups," JOB, 1966, v39(4), 473-484.

Balog, J. (Moriarty, D. P. and J. Balog. "Use Of Scientific Knowledge," FAJ, 1967, v23(4), 76- 79.)

Balog, James. "Forecasting Drug Earnings (A Review)," FAJ, 1966, v22(4), 39-40.

Balog, James. "Market Reaction To Merger Announcements," FAJ, 1975, v31(1), 24-26.

Balog, James. "Market Reaction To Merger Announcements," FAJ, 1975, v31(2), 84-88.

Balog, James. "Pyramids, Mesas And Mid-Career Crises," FAJ, 1979, v35(5), 25-29.

Balsmeir, Philip W. (Jackson, John D., Charlotte A. Jones and Philip W. Balsmeir. "An Empirical Analysis Of Tenant Selection Under Federal Rent Supplement Programs: A First Step," AREUEA, 1986, v14(1), 72-90.)

Baltensperger, Ernst and Hellmuth Milde. "Reserve Demand, Information Costs, And Bank Portfolio Behavior," JOF, 1976, v31(3), 835-843.

Baltensperger, Ernst. "Cost of Banking Activities: Interactions Between Risk And Operating Costs," JMCB, 1972, v4(3),595-611.

Baltensperger, Ernst. "Credit Rationing: Issues And Questions," JMCB, 1978, v10(2), 170-183.

Baltensperger, Ernst. "Economies Of Scale, Firm Size, And Concentration In Banking," JMCB, 1972, v4(3), 467-488.

Baltensperger, Ernst. "Reserve Requirements And Economic Stability," JMCB, 1982, v14(2), 205-215.

Baltz, Richard B. "An Incentive Early Retirement Model For College And University Faculty," JRI, 1984, v51(3), 477-497.

Balvers, Ronald J., Thomas F. Cosimano and Bill McDonald. "Predicting Stock Returns In An Efficient Market," JOF, 1990, v45(4), 1109-1128.

Balzano, Raymond V. "A Model To Forecast A Banks Daily Net Clearing House Liability," JBR, 1975-76, v6(3), 228-231.

Banda, J. Frederic. "Mutual Fund Ownership Of Air Transport Stocks," FR, 1971, v2(1), 27-33.

Bandari, Shyam B. "Discounted Payback Period," JFED, 1985, v14, 1-16.

Banerjee, Aniruddha. (Weaver, Robert D. and Aniruddha Banerjee. "Cash Price Variation In The Live Beef Cattle Market: The Causal Role Of Futures Trade," JFM, 1982, v2(4), 367-389.)

Banerjee, Aniruddha. (Weaver, Robert D. and Aniruddha Banerjee. "Does Futures Trading Destabilize Cash Prices? Evidence For U.S. Live Beef Cattle," JFM, 1990, v10(1), 41-60.)

Banks, Doyle W. "Information Uncertainty And Trading Volume," FR, 1985, v20(1), 83-94.

Banks, F. E. "A Note On A `Keynesian' Model Of Aggregate Demand," JOF, 1969, v24(1), 101-103.

Banks, J. Eugene. "Some Guides For Appraising The Bond Market," FAJ, 1958, v14(2), 57-62.

Banks, Seymour and Albert Madansky. "Estimation Of Multimagazine Readership," JOB, 1958, v31(3), 235-242.

Banks, Seymour. "The Measurement Of The Effect Of A New Packaging Material Upon Preference And Sales," JOB, 1950, v23(2), 71-80.

Banks, Seymour. "The Prediction Of Dress Purchases For A Mail-Order House," JOB, 1950, v23(1), 48-57.

Banks, Stephen J. "The Origins Of The Great Inflation," FAJ, 1977, v33(3), 43-55.

Bannister, Barry B. "In Search Of Excellence: A Portfolio Management Perspective," FAJ, 1990, v46(2), 68-71.

Bansal, Vipul K., Stephen W. Pruitt and K. C. John Wei. "An Empirical Reexamination Of The Impact Of CBOE Option Initiation On Volatility And Trading Volume Of The Underlying Equities: 1973-1986," FR, 1989, v24(1), 19-30.

Banz, Rolf W. and William J. Breen. "Sample Dependent Results Using Accounting And Market Data: Some Evidence," JOF, 1986, v41(4), 779-794.

Banz, Rolf W. "The Relationship Between Return And Market Value Of Common Stocks," JFEC, 1981, v9(1), 3-18.

Banz, Rolf W. and Merton H. Miller. "Prices For State-Contingent Claims: Some Estimates And Applications," JOB, 1978, v51(4), 653-672.

Bao, Ben-Hsien and Da-Hsien Bao. "An Empirical Investigation Of The Association Between Productivity And Firm Value," JBFA, 1989, v16(5), 699-718.

Bao, Da-Hsien. (Bao, Ben-Hsien and Da-Hsien Bao. "An Empirical Investigation Of The Association Between Productivity And Firm Value," JBFA, 1989, v16(5), 699-718.)

Bar-Lev, Dan and Steven Katz. "Fuel Procurement In The Electric Utility Industry," JOF, 1976, v31(3), 933-947.

Bar-Niv, Ran and David L. Bickelhaupt. "Research In International Risk And Insurance: Summary, Synthesis, And Prospects," JRI, 1986, v53(1), 119-134.

Bar-Yosef, Sasson and Baruch Lev. "Historical Cost Earnings Versus Inflation-Adjusted Earnings In The Dividend Decision," FAJ, 1983, v39(2), 41-50.

Bar-Yosef, Sasson and Lawrence D. Brown. "A Reexamination Of Stock Splits Using Moving Betas," JOF, 1977, v32(4), 1069-1080.

Bar-Yosef, Sasson and Lawrence D. Brown. "Share Price Levels And Beta," FM, 1979, v8(1), 60-63.

Bar-Yosef, Sasson and Lucy Huffman. "The Information Content Of Dividends: A Signalling Approach," JFQA, 1986, v21(1), 47-58.

Bar-Yosef, Sasson and Roger Mesznick. "On Some Definitional Problems With The Method Of Certainty Equivalents," JOF, 1977, v32(5), 1729-1737.

Bar-Yosef, Sasson and Yoram Landskroner. "The Impact Of The Government Sector On Financial Equilibrium And Corporate Financial Decisions," JBFA, 1984, v11(1),13-27.

Bar-Yosef, Sasson, Jeffrey L. Callen and Joshua Livnat. "Autoregressive Modeling Of Earnings--Investment Causality," JOF, 1987, v42(1), 11-28.

Bar-Yosef, Sasson. "Interactions Of Corporate Financing And Investment Decisions - Implications For Capital Budgeting: Comment," JOF, 1977, v32(1), 211-217.

BarNiv, Ran and Adi Raveh. "Identifying Financial Distress: A New Nonparametric Approach," JBFA, 1989, v16(3), 361-384.

BarNiv, Ran and Robert A. Hershbarger. "Classifying Financial Distress In The Life Insurance Industry," JRI, 1990, v57(1), 110-136.

Baradwaj, B. G., D. R. Fraser and E. P. H. Furtado. "Hostile Bank Takeover Offers: Analysis And Implications," JBF, 1990, v14(6), 1229-1242.

Baran, Arie, Josef Lakonishok and Aharon R. Ofer. "The Value Of General Price Level Adjusted Data To Bond Rating," JBFA, 1980, v7(1), 135-149.

Barban, Arnold M. "The Dilemma Of `Integrated' Advertising," JOB, 1969, v42(4), 477-496.

Barbe, Henri-Jean. "Cheque Truncation In Belgium," JBR, 1985-86, v16(4), 235-240.

Barber, James S. (Blau, Leslie A. and James S. Barber. "Proposed Amendment Of Section 4d(2) Of The Commodity Exchange Act: Concerning Investment Of Customer Funds," JFM, v1(4), 657-658.)

Barbour, Justin F. "Cowles Studies On The Dow Theory," FAJ, 1948, v4(4), 11-20.

Barclay, Michael J. "Dividends, Taxes, And Common Stock Prices: The Ex-Dividend Day Behavior Of Common Stock Prices Before The Income Tax," JFEC, 1987, v19(1), 31-44.

Barclay, Michael J. and Clifford W. Smith, Jr., "Corporate Payout Policy: Cash Dividends Versus Open-Market Repurchases," JFEC, 1988, v22(1), 61-82.

Barclay, Michael J. and Clifford G. Holderness. "Private Benefits From Control Of Public Corporations," JFEC, 1989, v25(2), 371-396.

Barclay, Michael J. and Robert H. Litzenberger. "Announcement Effects Of New Equity Issues And The Use Of Intraday Price Data," JFEC, 1988, v21(1), 71-100.

Barclay, Michael J., Robert H. Litzenberger and Jerold B. Warner. "Private Information, Trading Volume, And Stock-Return Variances," RFS, 1990, v3(2), 233-254.

Barefield, Russell M. and Eugene E. Comiskey. "The Differential Association Of Forecast Error And Earnings Variability With Systematic Risk," JBFA, 1979, v6(1), 1-8.

Barefield, Russell M. and Eugene E. Comiskey. "The Association Of Forecast Error With Other Risk Measures," JBFA, 1975, v2(3), 315-326.

Barger, Harold. "The Prospects For Federal Reserve Policy," JOF, 1960, v15(2), 278-280.

Barges, Alexander and Brian R. Hickey. "Drug Industry Profits," FAJ, 1968, v24(3), 75-83.

Barges, Alexander. "Growth Rates And Debt Capacity," FAJ, 1968, v24(1), 100-104.

Barges, Alexander. "The Marginal-Efficiency-Of-Capital Function Of The Firm," FR, 1987, v22(2), 321-338.

Baris, Marvin L. (Mark, Morris, Marvin L. Baris, Ronald K. Lytle and Leonard Marx, Jr. "Pitfalls In Real Estate Accounting," FAJ, 1972, v28(1), 29-36.

Barker, C. Austin. "Are Accounting Requirements For Stock Dividends Obsolete?," FAJ, 1958, v14(5),69-73.

Barker, C. Austin. "Price Changes Of Stock-Dividend Shares At Ex-Dividend Dates," JOF, 1959, v14(3), 373-378.

Barker, C. Austin. "Securities Market Levels Today And The Outlook For 1957," FAJ, 1957, v13(1), 45-50.

Barker, C. Austin. "The U.S. Balance Of Payments - Problems And Remedies," FAJ, 1965, v21(5), 118-132.

Barker, Robert R. "U.S. International Balance Of Payments," FAJ, 1960, v16(3), 49-54.

Barkin, Solomon. "Labor's View Of Actuarial Requirements For Pension Plans," JRI, 1953, v20, 63-69.

Barkin, Solomon. "New Industrial Giants In The Textile Industry," FAJ, 1956, v12(1), 41-46.

Barksdale, Hiram C. and Jimmy E. Hilliard. "A Cross-Spectral Analysis Of Retail Inventories And Sales," JOB, 1975, v48(3), 365-382.

Barlev, Benzion and Haim Levy. "The Information Content Of Accounting Data And The Management Of Security Portfolios," JBFA, 1981, v8(2), 221-248.

Barlev, Benzion and Joshua Livnat. "The Statement Of Changes In Financial Position: It Relationship With Security Prices," JBFA, 1986, v13(2),223-238.

Barlev, Benzion, Joshua Livnat and Aharon Yoran. "Advance Payments During Inflationary Periods," JBFA, 1982, v8(3), 413-426.

Barlev, Benzion, Wanda Denny and Haim Levy. "Using Accounting Data For Portfolio Management," JPM, 1988, v14(3), 70-77.

Barnea, A. and D. E. Logue. "Risk And The Market Maker's Spread," FAJ, 1975, v31(6), 45-49.

Barnea, A. and M. Brenner. "World Events And Stock Market Volume," FAJ, 1974, v30(4), 64-66.

Barnea, A. (Amihud, Y. and A. Barnea. "A Note On Fisher Hypothesis And Price Level Uncertainty," JFQA, 1977, v12(3), 525-530.)

Barnea, Amir and Dennis E. Logue. "Stock Trading And Portfolio Performance," JBR, 1976-77, v7(2), 150-157.

Barnea, Amir and Dennis E. Logue. "Evaluating The Forecasts Of A Security Analyst," FM, 1973, v2(2),38-45.

Barnea, Amir, Robert A. Haugen and Lemma W. Senbet. "An Equilibrium Analysis Of Debt Financing Under Costly Tax Arbitrage And Agency Problems," JOF, 1981, v36(3), 569-581.

Barnea, Amir, Robert A. Haugen and Lemma W. Senbet. "A Rationale For Debt Maturity Structure And Call Provisions In The Agency Theoretic Framework," JOF, 1980, v35(5), 1223-1234.

Barnea, Amir, Robert A. Haugen and Lemma W. Senbet. "Market Imperfections, Agency Problems, And Capital Structure: A Review," FM, 1981, v10(3), 7-22.

Barnea, Amir, Eli Talmor and Robert A. Haugen. "Debt And Taxes: A Multiperiod Investigation," JBF, 1987, v11(1), 79-98.

Barnea, Amir, Robert A. Haugen and Lemma W. Senbet. "Management Of Corporate Risk," AFPAF, 1985, v1(1), 1-28.

Barnea, Amir. "A Note On The Cash-Flow Approach To Valuation And Depreciation Of Productive Assets," JFQA, 1972, v7(3), 1841-1846.

Barnea, Amir. "Performance Evaluation Of New York Stock Exchange Specialists," JFQA, 1974, v9(4), 511-535.

Barnea, Amir. "Reply: Specialists' Performance And Serial Dependence Of Stock Price Change," JFQA, 1976, v11(5), 909-911.

Barnea, Amir. (Bierman, Harold, Jr. and Amir Barnea. "Expected Short-Term Interest Rates In Bond Refunding," FM, 1974, v3(1), 75-79.)

Barnea, Amir. (Talmor, Eli, Robert Haugen and Amir Barnea. "The Value Of The Tax Subsidy On Risky Debt," JOB, 1985, v58(2), 191-202.)

Barnea, Amir. (Yawitz, Jess B., Amir Barnea and Dennis E. Logue. "Evaluating The Forecasts Of A Security Analyst: Yawitz Vs. Barnea And Logue," FM, 1973, v2(4), 47-49.)

Barneby, T. Kirkham. (Good, Walter R., Roy W. Hermansen and T. Kirkham Barneby. "Opportunity: Actively Managed In-vestment Universes," FAJ, 1986, v42(1),49-57.)

Barnes, Leo. "Tax Relativity: The Missing `X' Factor In Stock And Portfolio Evaluation," FAJ, 1965, v21(1), 70-74.

Barnes, Paul and Colin Dodds. "The Structure And Performance Of The UK Building Society Industry 1970-78," JBFA, 1983, v10(1), 37-56.

Barnes, Paul, S. P. Chakravarty and J. Haslam. "Bargaining Power, Dissimulation And Takeovers In A Rational Market With Asymmetric Information," JBFA, 1990, v17(4), 529-540.

Barnes, Paul. "Methodological Implications Of Non-Normally Distributed Financial Ratios," JBFA, 1982, v8(1), 51-62.

Barnes, Paul. "Methodological Implications Of Non-Normally Distributed Financial Ratios: A Reply," JBFA, 1983, v10(4), 691-693.

Barnes, Paul. "The Analysis And Use of Financial Ratios: A Review Article," JBFA, 1987, v14(4), 449-462.

Barnes, Paul. "The Consequences Of Growth Maximisation And Expense Preference Policies of Managers," JBFA, 1983, v10(4), 521-530.

Barnes, Paul. "The Prediction Of Takeover Targets In The UK By Means Of Multiple Discriminant Analysis," JBFA, 1990, v17(1), 73-84.

Barnes, Paul. "The Statistical Validity Of The Ratio Method In Financial Analysis: A Comment," JBFA, 1986, v13(4), 627-632.

Barnes, Paul. "Thin Trading And Stock Market Efficiency: The Case Of The Kuala Lumpur Stock Exchange," JBFA, 1986, v13(4), 609-617.

Barnes, Paul. "UK Building Societies - A Study Of The Gains From Merger," JBFA, 1985, v12(1), 75-91.

Barnes, Tom and David Burnie. "Corporate Bonds, Term Structure Expectations And Optimal Portfolios: The Canadian Experience," JBFA, 1990, v17(3), 411-420.

Barnes, Tom, Keith Johnson and Don Shannon. "A Test Of Fixed-Income Strategies," JPM, 1984, v10(2), 60-65.

Barnes, Tom. "Markowitz Allocation - Fixed Income Securities," JFR, 1985, v8(3), 181-191.

Barnes, William R. "The Uses Of Urban Research: A Perspective On The Urban Observatory Experience," AREUEA, 1974, v2(2), 47-58.

Barnet, Herbert L. "Outlook For The Soft Drink Industry," FAJ, 1960, v16(5), 23-28.

Barnett, C. Lance. "Expected And Actual Effects Of Housing Allowances On Housing Prices," AREUEA, 1979, v7(3), 277-297.

Barnett, Stephen H. "Monetary Indicators At Turning Points," FAJ, 1970, v26(5), 29-32.

Barnett, William A. "The New Monetary Aggregates: A Comment," JMCB, 1981, v13(4), 485-489.

Barnett, William A. "The Optimal Level Of Monetary Aggregation," JMCB, 1982, v14(4), Part 2, 687-710.

Barnett, William, Edward Offenbacher and Paul Spindt. "New Concepts Of Aggregated Money," JOF, 1981, v36(2), 497-505.

Barney, L. Dwayne and Harry White. "The Optimal Mortgage Payment Path Under Price Uncertainty," AREUEA, 1986, v14(3), 406-413.

Barney, L. Dwayne, Jr., Alan Frankle and Harry White. "Reserve Requirements And The Inflation Tax," JMCB, 1990, v22(3), 400-401.

Barney, L. Dwayne. "Moral Hazard And Moral Imperative: Comment," JRI, 1990, v57(2), 329-331.

Barngrover, Charles. "A Survey Of M.B.A. Programs In Finance," JFED, 1976, v5, 29-34.

Barnhart, Scott W. "Commodity Futures Prices And Economic News: An Examination Under Alternative Monetary Regimes," JFM, 1988, v8(4), 483-510.

Barnhart, Scott W. and Ali F. Darrat. "Budget Deficits, Money Growth And Causality: Further OECD Evidence," JIMF, 1988, v7(2), 231-242.

Barnhart, Scott W. and Ali F. Darrat. "Federal Deficits And Money Growth In The United States: A Vector Autoregressive Analysis," JBF, 1989, v13(1), 137-150.

Barnhill, Theodore M. and James Powell. "Silver Price Volatility: A Perspective On the July 1979-April 1980 Period," JFM, v1(4), 619-647.

Barnhill, Theodore M. and William C. Handorf. "An Application Of Monte Carlo Simulation Modeling To Commercial Bank Interest Rate Management," RFM, 1985, v4(3), 282-305.

Barnhill, Theodore M. "Quality Option Profits, Switching Option Profits, And Variation Margin Costs: An Evaluation Of Their Size And Impact On Treasury Bond Futures Prices," JFQA, 1990, v25(1), 65-86.

Barnhill, Theodore M. "The Delivery Option On Forward Contracts: A Comment," JFQA, 1988, v23(3), 343-348.

Barnhill, Theodore M. and William E. Seale. "Optimal Exercise Of The Switching Option In Treasury Bond Arbitrages," JFM, 1988, v8(5), 517-532.

Barnhill, Theodore M., William W. Hardgrave and Rehman P. Kassam. "An Empirical Study Of T-Bond Futures Contract Price Change Patterns Around U.S. Treasury Quarterly Refundings," RFM, 1985, v4(1), 106-131.

Barnhill, Theodore M., James V. Jordan and William E. Seale. "Maturity And Refunding Effects On Treasury-Bond Futures Price Variance," JFR, 1987, v10(2), 121-132.

Baron, David P. and Bengt Holmstrom. "The Investment Banking Contract For New Issues Under Asymmetric Information: Delegation And The Incentive Problem," JOF, 1980, v35(5), 1115-1138.

Baron, David P. "A Model Of The Demand For Investment Banking Advising And Distribution Services For New Issues," JOF, 1982, v37(4), 955-976.

Baron, David P. "Firm Valuation, Corporate Taxes, And Default Risk," JOF, 1975, v30(5), 1251-1264.

Baron, David P. "Information, Investment Behavior, And Efficient Portfolios," JFQA, 1974, v9(4), 555-566.

Baron, David P. "Investment Policy, Optimality, And The Mean-Variance Model," JOF, 1979, v34(1), 207-232.

Baron, David P. "On The Utility Theoretic Foundations Of Mean-Variance Analysis," JOF, 1977, v32(5), 1683-1697.

Baron, David P. "Tender Offers And Management Resistance," JOF, 1983, v38(2), 331-343.

Baron, David P. "The Incentive Problem And The Design Of Investment Banking Contracts," JFBF, 1979, v3(2), 157-175.

Baron, Donald C. (McDonald, John G. and Donald C. Baron. "Risk And Return On Short Positions In Common Stocks," JOF, 1973, v28(1), 97-107.)

Barone, E. "The Italian Stock Market: Efficiency And Calendar Anomalies," JBF, 1990, v14(2/3), 483-510.

Barone, E. and D. Cuoco. "The Italian Market For 'Premium' Contracts: An Application Of Option Pricing Theory," JBF, 1989, v13(4/5), 709-746.

Barone, Robert N. "Risk And International Diversification: Another Look," FR, 1983, v18(2), 184-195.

Barone-Adesi, Giovanni and Robert E. Whaley. "The Valuation Of American Call Options And The Expected Ex-Dividend Stock Price Decline," JFEC, 1986, v17(1), 91-111.

Barone-Adesi, Giovanni and Bernard Yeung. "Price Flexibility And Output Volatility: The Case For Flexible Exchange Rates," JIMF, 1990, v9(3), 276-298.

Barone-Adesi, Giovanni and Robert E. Whaley. "Efficient Analytic Approximation Of American Option Values," JOF, 1987, v42(2), 301-320.

Barone-Adesi, Giovanni and Robert J. Elliott. "Pricing The Treasury Bond Futures Contract As The Minimum Value Of Deliverable Bond Prices," RFM, 1989, v8(3), 438-445.

Barone-Adesi, Giovanni. (Tinic, Seha M., Giovanni Barone-Adesi and Richard R. West. "Seasonality In Canadian Stock Prices: A Test Of The 'Tax-Loss-Selling' Hypothesis," JFQA, 1987, v22(1), 51-64.)

Barr, Graham D. and Rory F. Knight. "Some Geometrical Characteristics Of The Risk-Return Plane," JBFA, 1988, v15(3), 437-446.

Barr, James L. and Timothy L. Shaftel. "Solution Properties Of Deterministic Auctions," JFQA, 1976, v11(2), 287-311.

Barrett, Bob. (Lavely, Joe, Gordon Wakefield and Bob Barrett. "Toward Enhancing Beta Estimates," JPM, 1980, v6(4), 43-46.)

Barrett, M. E. and J. Roy. "Financial Reporting In France," FAJ, 1976, v32(1), 39-49.

Barrett, M. E. and L. L. Spero. "Foreign Exchange Gains And Losses," FAJ, 1975, v31(2), 26-30.

Barrett, M. Edgar, Lee N. Price and Judith Ann Gehrke. "What Investors Need To Know About Japan," FAJ, 1974, v30(2), 60-67,59.

Barrett, M. Edgar, Lee N. Price and Judith Ann Gehrke. "What Investors Need To Know About Japan," FAJ, 1974, v30(1), 33-44.

Barrett, M. Edgar. "APB Opinion Number 18," FAJ, 1972, v28(4), 47-50, 52-55.

Barrett, Michael J. (Ricketts, Donald E. and Michael J. Barrett. "Corporate Operating Income Forecasting Ability," FM, 1973, v2(2), 53-62.)

Barrett, Richard N. "Purchasing Power Parity And The Equilibrium Exchange Rate," JMCB, 1981, v13(2), 227-233.

Barrett, W. Brian and John W. Pfenenger, II. "Proper Cash-Flow Discounting For Pension Fund Liabilities," FAJ, 1989, v45(2), 68-70.

Barrett, W. Brian, Andrea J. Heuson and Robert W. Kolb. "The Differential Effects Of Sinking Funds On Bond Risk Premia," JFR, 1986, v9(4), 303-312.

Barrett, W. Brian, Andrea J. Heuson and Robert W. Kolb. "The Effect Of Three Mile Island On Utility Bond Risk Premia: A Note," JOF, 1986, v41(1), 255-262.

Barrett, W. Brian, Andrea J. Heuson, Robert W. Kolb and Gabriele H. Schropp. "The Adjustment Of Stock Prices To Completely Unanticipated Events," FR, 1987, v22(4), 345-354.

Barrett, W. Brian, Myron B. Slovin and Marie E. Sushka. "Reserve Regulation And Recourse As A Source Of Risk Premia In The Federal Funds Market," JBF, 1988, v11(4), 575-584.

Barrett, W. Brian. "Term Structure Modeling For Pension Liability Discounting," FAJ, 1988, v44(6), 63-67.

Barrett, W. Brian. (Lasser, Dennis J. and W. Brian Barrett. "New Issue Yield Spreads In The 30-Year Treasury Bond Market," FR, 1991, v26(2), 237-248.)

Barro, Robert J. and Anthony J. Santomero. "Household Money Holdings And The Demand Deposit Rate," JMCB, 1972, v4(2), 397-413.

Barro, Robert J. and Herschel I. Grossman. "Open-Market Operations And The Medium Of Exchange: A Comment," JMCB, 1971, v3(2), Part 1, 304-311.

Barro, Robert J. "Federal Deficit Policy And The Effects Of Public Debt Shocks," JMCB, 1980, v12(4), Part 2, 747-762.

Barro, Robert J. "Futures Markets And The Fluctuations In Inflation, Monetary Growth, And Asset Returns," JOB, 1986, v59(2), Part 2, S21-S38.

Barro, Robert J. "Integral Constraints And Aggregation In An Inventory Model Of Money Demand," JOF, 1976, v31(1), 77-88.

Barro, Robert J. "The Loan Market, Collateral, And Rates Of Interest," JMCB, 1976, v8(4), 439-456.

Barro, Robert J. "The Stock Market And Investment," RFS, 1990, v3(1), 115-132.

Barro, Robert J. and Chaipat Sahasakul. "Measuring The Average Marginal Tax Rate From The Individual Income Tax," JOB, 1983, v56(4), 419-452.

Barro, Robert J. and Chaipat Sahasakul. "Average Marginal Tax Rates From Social Security And The Individual Income Tax," JOB, 1986, v59(4), Part 1, 555-566.

Barron, J. F. "Mandatory Functional Discounts: An Appraisal," JOB, 1962, v35(3), 302-316.

Barry, Christopher B. and Laura T. Starks. "Investment Management And Risk Sharing With Multiple Managers," JOF, 1984, v39(2), 477-491.

Barry, Christopher B. and Robert L. Winkler. "Nonstationarity And Portfolio Choice," JFQA, 1976, v11(2), 217-235.

Barry, Christopher B. and Stephen J. Brown. "Limited Information As A Source Of Risk," JPM, 1986, v12(2), 66-73.

Barry, Christopher B. and Stephen J. Brown. "Differential Information And The Small Firm Effect," JFEC, 1984, v13(2), 283-294.

Barry, Christopher B. and Stephen J. Brown. "Differential Information And Security Market Equilibrium," JFQA, 1985, v20(4), 407-422.

Barry, Christopher B. "Bayesian Betas And Deception: A Comment," JFR, 1980, v3(1), 85-89.

Barry, Christopher B. "Effects Of Uncertain And Nonstationary Parameters Upon Capital Market Equilibrium Conditions," JFQA, 1978, v13(3), 419-433.

Barry, Christopher B. "Information Use And Expectations Formation In Security Markets," FR, 1979, v14(2), 45-57.

Barry, Christopher B. "Initial Public Offering Underpricing: The Issuer's View: Comment," JOF, 1989, v44(4), 1099-1104.

Barry, Christopher B. "Portfolio Analysis Under Uncertain Means, Variances, And Covariances," JOF, 1974, v29(2), 515-522.

Barry, Christopher B. (Brown, Stephen J. and Christopher B. Barry. "Anomalies In Security Returns And The Speculation Of The Market Model," JOF, 1984, v39(3), 807-815.)

Barry, Christopher B. (Jennings, Robert H. and Christopher B. Barry. "On Information Dissemination And Equilibrium Asset Prices: A Note," JFQA, 1984, v19(4), 395-402.)

Barry, Christopher B. (Jennings, Robert H. and Christopher B. Barry. "Information Dissemination And Portfolio Choice," JFQA, 1983, v18(1), 1-19.)

Barry, Christopher B. (Winkler, Robert L. and Christopher B. Barry. "A Bayesian Model For Portfolio Selection And Revision," JOF, 1975, v30(1), 179-192.)

Barry, Christopher B. and John W. Peavy, III. "Risk Characteristics Of Closed-End Stock Fund IPOs," JFSR, 1990, v4(1), 65-76.

Barry, Christopher B., Chris J. Muscarella, John W. Peavy, III and Michael R. Vetsuypens. "The Role Of Venture Capital In The Creation Of Public Companies: Evidence From The Going-Public Process," JFEC, 1990, v27(2), 447-472.

Barry, Christopher B., Dan W. French and Ramesh K. S. Rao. "Estimation Risk And Adaptive Behavior In The Pricing Of Options," FR, 1991, v26(1), 15-30.

Barry, John Y. (Ayres, Herbert F. and John Y. Barry. "Prologue To A Unified Portfolio Theory," JOF, 1982, v37(2), 625-635.)

Barry, John Y. (Ayres, Herbert F. and John Y. Barry. "Dynamics Of The Government Yield Curve," FAJ, 1979, v35(3), 31-39.)

Barry, Peter J. (Robison, Lindon and Peter J. Barry. "Risk Efficiency Using Stochastic Dominance And Expected Gain-Confidence Limits," JOF, 1978, v33(4), 1244-1249.)

Bart, John and Isidore J. Masse. "Divergence Of Opinion And Risk," JFQA, 1981, v16(1), 23-34.

Bart, John T. "The Nature Of The Conflict Between Transactors' Expectations Of Capital Gains," JFM, 1984, v33(4), 1095-1107.

Bartel, Henry, Michael Daly and Peter Wrage. "Reverse Mortgages: Supplementary Retirement Income From Homeownership," JRI, 1980, v47(3), 477-490.

Bartels, Robert. "Justification For Direct Regulation Of Consumer Credit Reappraised," JOF, 1953, v8(2), 261-271.

Barth, James R. and James T. Bennett. "Cost-Push Versus Demand-Pull Inflation: Some Empirical Evidence: A Comment," JMCB, 1975, v7(3), 391-397.

Barth, James R. and James T. Bennett. "Is The `Neutralized Money Stock' Unbiased: Comment," JOF, 1976, v31(5), 1509-1513.

Barth, James R. and Anthony M. J. Yezer. "Default Risk On Home Mortgages: A Further Test Of Competing Hypotheses," JRI, 1983, v50(3), 500-505.

Barth, James R. and Michael D. Bradley. "On Interest Rates, Inflationary Expectations And Tax Rates," JBF, 1988, v12(2), 215-220.

Barth, James R. and Michael G. Bradley. "Thrift Deregulation And Federal Deposit Insurance," JFSR, 1989, v2(3), 231-260.

Barth, James R., Frank S. Russek and George H. K. Wang. "The Measurement And Significance Of The Cyclically Adjusted Federal Budget And Debt: A Comment," JMCB, 1986, v18(4), 527-538.

Barth, James R., Padma Gotur, Neela Manage and Anthony M. J. Yezer. "The Effect Of Government Regulations On Personal Loan Markets: A Tobit Estimation Of A Microeconomic Model," JOF, 1983, v38(4),1233-1251.

Barth, James R., Philip F. Bartholomew and Michael G. Bradley. "Determinants Of Thrift Institution Resolution Costs," JOF, 1990, v45(3), 731-754.

Barth, James, Arthur Kraft and Philip Wiest. "A Utility Maximization Approach To Individual Bank Asset Selection," JMCB, 1977, v9(2), 316-327.

Barth, Mary E., William H. Beaver and Mark A. Wolfson. "Components Of Earnings And The Structure Of Bank Share Prices," FAJ, 1990, v46(3), 53-60.

Bartholmew, Philip F. (Barth, James R., Philip F. Bartholomew and Michael G. Bradley. "Determinants Of Thrift Institution Resolution Costs," JOF, 1990, v45(3), 731-754.)

Bartlett, Bruce. "The Case For Ending The Capital Gains Tax," FAJ, 1985, v41(3), 23-30.

Bartley, Jon W. "Accounting For The Cost Of Capital: An Empirical Examination," JBFA, 1982, v8(2), 239-254.

Bartley, Jon W. and Alex B. Cameron. "Long-Run Earnings Forecasts By Managers And Financial Analysts," JBFA, 1991, v18(1), 21-42.

Bartley, Jon W. and Calvin M. Boardman. "The Relevance Of Inflation Adjusted Accounting Data To The Prediction Of Corporate Takeovers," JBFA, 1990, v17(1), 53-72.

Barton, Sidney L., Ned C. Hill and Srinivasan Sundaram. "An Empirical Test Of Stakeholder Theory Predictions Of Capital Structure," FM, 1989, v18(1), 36-44.

Bartter, Brit J. and Richard J. Rendleman, Jr. "Fee-Based Pricing Of Fixed Rate Bank Loan Commitments," FM, 1979, v8(1), 13-20.

Bartter, Brit J. (Rendleman, Richard J., Jr. and Brit J. Bartter. "The Pricing Of Options On Debt Securities," JFQA, 1980, v15(1), 11-24.)

Bartter, Brit J. (Rendleman, Richard J., Jr. and Brit J. Bartter. "Two-State Option Pricing," JOF, 1979, v34(5), 1093-1110.)

Basch, Donald L. "Circumventive Innovation: The Case Of NOW Accounts In Massachusetts, 1972-1977," JBR, 1982-83, v13(3), 160-167.

Basch, Donald L. "Regulatory Transition And Depositor Inertia: The Response Of Massachusetts Commercial Banks To NOW Accounts," JBR, 1982-83, v13(4), 264-273.

Bashir, B. A. "Portfolio Management Of Islamic Banks: `Certainty Model'," JBF, 1983, v7(3),339-354.

Baskin, Elba F. and Gary M. Grooch. "Return On Flat Bonds," FAJ, 1968, v24(6), 95-97.

Baskin, Jonathan. "An Empirical Investigation Of The Pecking Order Hypothesis," FM, 1989, v18(1), 26-35.

Baskin, Jonathan. "Dividend Policy And The Volatility Of Common Stocks," JPM, 1989, v15(3), 19-25.

Bass, F. M. (Starbuck, W. H. and F. M. Bass. "An Experimental Study Of Risk-Taking And The Value Of Information In A New Product Context," JOB, 1967, v40(2), 155-165.)

Bass, F. M., E. A. Pessemier and D. J. Tigert. "A Taxonomy Of Magazine Readership Applied To Problems In Marketing Starategy And Media Selection," JOB, 1969, v42(3), 337-363.

Bass, Frank M. "Marketing Research Expenditures: A Decision Model," JOB, 1963, v36(1), 77-90.

Bass, Frank M. "The Relationship Between Diffusion Rates, Experience Curves, And Demand Elasticities For Consumer Durable Technological Innovations," JOB, 1980, v53(3), Part 2, S51-S68.

Bassett, Gilbert W., Jr. (France, Virginia G., Gilbert W. Bassett, Jr. and Stanley R. Pliska. "The MMI Cash-Futures Spread On October 19, 1987," RFM, 1989, v8(1), 118-138.)

Bassett, Gilbert W., Jr., Virginia G. France and Stanely R. Pliska. "Kalman Filter Estimation For Calculating Nontrading Securities, With Applications To The MMI Cash-Futures Spread On October 19 And 20, 1987," RQFA, 1991, v1(2), 135-152.

Basu, S. and J. R. Hanna. "GPL-Adjusted Earnings For Utilities," FAJ, 1978, v34(1), 55-67.

Basu, S. "The Investment Performance Of Common Stocks In Relation To Their Price-Earnings Ratios: A Test Of The Efficient Market Hypothesis," JOF, 1977, v32(3), 663-682.

Basu, Sanjoy. "The Information Content Of Price Earnings Ratios," FM, 1974, v4(2), 53-64.

Basu, Sanjoy. "The Relationship Between Earnings' Yield, Market Value And Return For NYSE Common Stocks: Further Evidence," JFEC, 1983, v12(1), 129-156.

Basu, Susanto, Miles S. Kimball, N. Gregory Mankiw and David N. Weil. "Optimal Advice For Monetary Policy," JMCB, 1990, v22(1), 19-36.

Batavia, Bala and Nicholas A. Lash. "The Impact Of Bank Portfolio Composition On GNP," JMCB, 1982, v14(4), Part 1, 517-524.

Batchelor, Roy A. and Pami Dua. "Household Versus Economist Forecasts Of Inflation: A Reassessment," JMCB, 1989, v21(2), 252-257.

Bateman, J. Carroll. "Five Bridges To Cross," JRI, 1970, v37(2), 225-232.

Bates, Philip S. (Saini, Krishan G. and Philip S. Bates. "A Survey Of The Quantitative Approaches To Country Risk Analysis," JBF, 1984, v8(2), 341-356.)

Bates, Thomas. (Stonehill, Arthur, Theo Beekhuisen, Richard Wright, Lee Remmers, Norman Toy, Antonio Pares, Alan Shapiro, Douglas Egan and Thomas Bates. "Financial Goals And Debt Ratio Determinants," FM, 1974, v4(3), 27-41.)

Bates, Timothy and William Bradford. "An Analysis Of The Portfolio Behavior Of Black-Owned Commercial Banks," JOF, 1980, v35(3), 753-768.

Bates, Timothy M. and Donald D. Hester. "Analysis Of A Commercial Bank Minority Lending Program: Comment," JOF, 1977, v32(5), 1783-1789.

Bates, Timothy. "Financing Black Enterprise," JOF,1974,v29(3),747-761.

Bates, Timothy. "Government As Financial Intermediary For Minority Entrepreneurs: An Evaluation," JOB, 1975, v48(4), 541-557.

Batkin, Carl A. "Hedging Mortgage-Backed Securities With Treasury Bond Futures," JFM, 1987, v7(6), 675-694.

Batlin, C. A. and Susan Hinko. "Lockbox Management And Value Maximization," FM, 1981, v10(5),39-44.

Batlin, Carl Alan and Susan Hinko. "A Game Theoretic Approach To Cash Management," JOB, 1982, v55(3), 367-382.

Batlin, Carl Alan. "Interest Rate Risk, Prepayment Risk, And The Futures Market Hedging Strategies Of Financial Intermediaries," JFM, 1983, v3(2), 177-184.

Batra, Harish. "Dynamic Interdependence In Demand For Savings Deposits," JOF, 1973, v28(2),507-514.

Batra, Raveendra N. and Nadeem Naqvi. "International Debt, Factor Accmulation, And The Balance Of Payments," RIF, 1986, v6, 261-277.

Battalio, Raymond C., John H. Kagel and Romain Jiranyakul. "Testing Between Alternative Models Of Choice Under Uncertainty: Some Intitial Results," JRU, 1990, v3(1), 25-50.

Battelle, Nicholas. "Notes From The Business Services Sector," FAJ, 1984, v40(6), 75-76.

Batten, Dallas S. and Daniel L. Thornton. "Discount Rate Changes And The Foreign Exchange Market," JIMF, 1984, v3(3), 279-292.

Batten, Dallas S. and Mack Ott. "The Interrelationship Of Monetary Policies Under Floating Exchange Rates," JMCB, 1985, v17(1), 103-110.

Batten, Dallas S. (Thornton, Daniel L. and Dallas S. Batten. "Lag-Length Selection And Tests Of Granger Causality Between Money And Income," JMCB, 1985, v17(2), 164-178.)

Bauder, Kenneth C. "Analysis Of Turnpike Revenue Bonds," FAJ, 1955, v11(2), 87-90.

Bauerschmidt, Alan D. "Payment Plans And The Efficient Delivery Of Health Care Services: Comment," JRI, 1975, v42(4), 673-674.

Bauerschmidt, Alan D. (Furst, Richard W. and Alan D. Bauerschmidt. "Community Funding Of Depreciation To Finance Change In The Health Care System," FR, 1972, v2(2), 134-140.)

Bauerschmidt, Alan D. (Furst, Richard W. and Alan D. Bauerschmidt. "Review Article: The Financial Management Of Hospitals (2nd Edition)," FM, 1974, v4(1), 25-31.)

Baughman, G. W. "Step By Step Approach To The Crewless Train," FAJ, 1962, v18(3), 67-78.

Baum, Bernard H. (Whisler, Thomas L., Harald Meyer, Bernard H. Baum and Peter F. Sorensen, Jr. "Centralization Of Organizational Control: An Empirical Study Of IT's Meaning And Measurement," JOB, 1967, v40(1), 10-26.)

Baum, Bernard H. and Peter F. Sorensen, Jr. "Influence Relationships As Administrative Organizational Data," JRI, 1966, v33(1), 63-71.

Baum, Christopher F. and Marilena Furno. "Analyzing The Stability Of Demand-For-Money Equations Via Bounded-Influence Estimation Techniques," JMCB, 1990, v22(4), 465-477.

Baum, Clifford B. "Equity Lease Financing," FAJ, 1969, v25(3), 138-141.

Baum, Donald N. and Dilip K. Ghosh. "Interest Rate, Wealth And The Consumption-Savings Decision: The Relationship Revisited," IJOF, 1988, v1(1), 15-34.

Baum, Dwight C. "Buying Water Company Equities," FAJ, 1967, v23(2), 57-63.

Baum, Sanford, Robert C. Carlson and James V. Jucker. "Some Problems In Applying The Continuous Portfolio Selection Model To The Discrete Capital Budgeting Problem," JFQA, 1978, v13(2), 333-344.

Bauman, W. Scott and Constance H. McClaren. "An Asset Allocation Model For Active Portfolios," JPM, 1982, v8(2), 76-86.

Bauman, W. Scott and James R. Haltiner. "Portfolio Capital Gains Disbursement Strategies," FR, 1982, v17(1), 26-49.

Bauman, W. Scott and Richard Dowen. "Growth Projections And Common Stock Returns," FAJ, 1988, v44(4), 79-80.

Bauman, W. Scott. "Education In Investment Analysis And The Institute Of Chartered Financial Analysts," JFED, 1975, v4, 46-53.

Bauman, W. Scott. "Evaluation Of Prospective Investment Performance," JOF, 1968, v23(2), 276-295.

Bauman, W. Scott. "Investment Value Of Common Stock Earnings And Dividends," FAJ, 1965, v21(6), 98-104.

Bauman, W. Scott. "Investment Experience With Less Popular Common Stocks," FAJ, 1964, v20(2), 79-88.

Bauman, W. Scott. "Investment Analysis: Science Or Fiction?," FAJ, 1967, v23(1), 93-97.

Bauman, W. Scott. "Investment Returns And Present Values," FAJ, 1969, v25(6), 107-120.

Bauman, W. Scott. "Investment Research Analysis In An Emerging Market: Singapore And Malaysia," FAJ, 1989, v45(6), 60-67.

Bauman, W. Scott. "Presidential Address," JFQA, 1973, v8(2), 369-380.

Bauman, W. Scott. "The 1976 C.F.A. Examinations," FAJ, 1976, v32(5), 60-69.

Bauman, W. Scott. "The C.F.A. Candidate Program," FAJ, 1974, v30(6), 68-84.

Bauman, W. Scott. "The Less Popular Stocks Vs. The Most Popular Stocks," FAJ, 1965, v21(1), 61-69.

Bauman, W. Scott. (Dowen, Richard J. and W. Scott Bauman. "The Relative Importance Of Size, P/E, And Neglect," JPM, 1986, v12(3), 30-35.)

Bauman, W. Scott. (Dowen, Richard, J. and W. Scott Bauman. "A Fundamental Multifactor Asset Pricing Model," FAJ, 1986, v42(4), 45-51.)

Bauman, W. Scott. (Slovic, Paul, Dan Fleissner and W. Scott Bauman. "Analyzing The Use Of Information In Investment Decision Making: A Methodological Proposal," JOB, 1972, v45(2), 283-301.)

Baumann, Michael G. (Alt, Christopher B., Michael G. Baumann and Martin B. Zimmerman. "The Economics Of Western Coal Severance Taxes," JOB, 1983, v56(4), 519-536.)

Baumol, Daniel. "A Modest (Pension Investment) Proposal," JPM, 1990, v17(1), 27-29.

Baumol, William J. "Mathematical Analysis Of Portfolio Selection," FAJ, 1966, v22(5), 95-99.

Baumol, William J. and Associates. "Statement Of Clarification," JOB, 1963, v36(3), 348-351.

Baumol, William J., Richard E. Quandt and Harold T. Shapiro. "Oligopoly Theory And Retail Food Pricing," JOB, 1964, v37(4), 346-363.

Bautista, Alberto J. (Myers, Stewart C., David A. Dill and Alberto J. Bautista. "Valuation Of Financial Lease Contracts," JOF, 1976, v31(3), 799-819.)

Bavishi, Vinod B., Michael R. Czinkota, Harry A. Shawky and David A. Ricks. "International Financial Management -- A Survey Of Research Trends And An Annotated Bibliography, 1977-1976," JFED, 1977, v6, 93-95.

Bawa, Vijay S. and E. B. Lindenberg. "Capital Market Equilibrium In A Mean-Lower Partial Moment Framework," JFEC, 1977, v5(2), 189-200.

Bawa, Vijay S. "Admissable Portfolios For All Individuals," JOF, 1976, v31(4), 1169-1183.

Bawa, Vijay S. "On Stochastic Dominance And Estimation Risk," RIF, 1980, v2, 57-68.

Bawa, Vijay S. "Optimal Rules For Ordering Uncertain Prospects," JFEC, 1975, v2(1), 95-121.

Bawa, Vijay S. "Safety-First, Stochastic Dominance, And Optimal Portfolio Choice," JFQA, 1978, v13(2), 255-271.

Bawa, Vijay S. (Arzac, Enrique R. and Vijay S. Bawa. "Portfolio Choice And Equilibrium In Capital Markets With Safety-First Investors," JFEC, 1977, v4(3), 277-288.)

Bawa, Vijay S. (Klein, Roger W. and Vijay S. Bawa. "The Effect Of Estimation Risk On Optimal Portfolio Choice," JFEC, 1976, v3(3), 215-231.)

Bawa, Vijay S. (Klein, Roger W. and Vijay S. Bawa. "The Effect Of Limited Information And Estimation Risk On Optimal Portfolio Diversification," JFEC, 1977, v5(1), 89-111.)

Bawa, Vijay S., Edwin J. Elton and Martin J. Gruber. "Simple Rules For Optimal Portfolio Selection In Stable Paretian Markets," JOF, 1979, v34(4),1041-1047.

Bawa, Vijay S., James N. Odurtha, Jr., M. R. Rao and Hira L. Suri. "On Determination Of Stochastic Dominance Optimal Sets," JOF, 1985, v40(2), 417-431.

Baxter, Jennefer, Thomas E. Conine, Jr. and Maurry Tamarkin. "On Commodity Market Risk Premiums: Additional Evidence," JFM, 1985, v5(1), 121-125.

Baxter, Marianne. "Business Cycles, Stylized Facts, And The Exchange Rate Regime: Evidence From The United States," JIMF, 1991, v10(1), 71-88.

Baxter, Nevins D. and Harold T. Shapiro. "Compensating-Balance Requirements: The Results Of A Survey," JOF, 1964, v19(3), 483-496.

Baxter, Nevins D. "Leverage, Risk Of Ruin And The Cost Of Capital," JOF, 1967, v22(3), 395-403.

Baxter, Nevins D. "Marketability, Default Risk, And Yields On Money Market Instruments," JFQA, 1968, v3(1), 75-85.

Baxter, W. T. "Lessors' Depreciation And Profit - An Approach Via Deprival Value," JBFA, 1982, v8(1), 1-18.

Baxter, W. T. "The Sandilands Report," JBFA, 1976, v3(1), 115-123.

Bayer, Alan E. (Holtmann, A. G. and Alan E. Bayer. "Determinants Of Professional Income Among Recent Recipients Of Natural Science Doctorates," JOB, 1970, v43(4), 410-418.)

Bayer, Richard J. (Colin, J. W. and Richard J. Bayer. "Calculation Of Tax Effective Yields For Discount Instruments," JFQA, 1970, v5(2), 265-273.)

Bayldon, R., A. Woods and N. Zafiris. "A Note On The `Pyramid' Technique Of Financial Ratio Analysis Of Firms' Performance," JBFA, 1984, v11(1), 99-106.

Bayless, Mark E. and J. David Diltz. "An Empirical Study Of The Debt Displacement Effects Of Leasing," FM, 1986, v15(4), 53-60.

Bayless, Mark E. and J. David Diltz. "The Relevance Of Asymmetric Information To Financing Decisions," JBFA, 1991, v18(3), 331-344.

Baylis, R. M. and S. L. Bhirud. "Growth Stock Analysis: A New Approach," FAJ, 1973, v29(4), 63-70.

Baylis, Robert M. "Business Strategy For The Securities Industry," FAJ, 1980, v36(3), 23-25.

Baylis, Robert M. "The Greening Of U.S. Investment Business," FAJ, 1977, v33(6), 36-37.

Baylis, Robert M. "The New Performance," FAJ, 1974, v30(4), 55-60,75.

Baylis, Robert M. "The Salesman And The Institutional Investment Process," FAJ, 1980, v36(5),25-27.

Beach, T. E. and P. F. Miller, Jr. "Price-Earnings Ratios: A Reply," FAJ, 1967, v23(3), 109-110.

Beadles, William T. "Control Of Abuses Under Credit Life And Health Insurance," JRI, 1959, v26(3), 1-12.

Beadles, William T. "The Basic Survey Course In Insurance," JRI, 1953, v20, 9-11.

Bear, Robert M. and Anthony J. Curley. "Unseasoned Equity Financing," JFQA, 1975, v10(2), 311-325.

Bear, Robert M. and Richard A. Stevenson. "On The Methodology Of Testing For Independence In Futures Prices: Reply," JOF, 1976, v31(3), 980-983.

Bear, Robert M. "Margin Levels And The Behavior Of Futures Prices," JFQA, 1972, v7(4), 1907-1930.

Bear, Robert M. (Lawrence, Edward C. and Robert M. Bear. "Corporate Bankruptcy Prediction And The Impact Of Leases," JBFA, 1986, v13(4), 571-585.)

Bear, Robert M. (Prakash, Arun J. and Robert M. Bear. "A Simplifying Performance Measure Recognizing Skewness," FR, 1986, v21(1), 135-144.)

Bear, Robert M. (Stevenson, Richard A. and Robert M. Bear. "Commodity Futures: Trends Or Random Walks?," JOF, 1970, v25(1), 65-81.)

Bear, Thomas. (Boyd, G. Michael and Thomas Bear. "An Applied Course In Investment Analysis And Portfolio Management," JFED, 1984, v13, 68-71.)

Beard, T. Randolph. (Anderson, Seth C., Jeffrey A. Born and T.

Randolph Beard. "An Analysis Of Bond Investment Company Initial Public Offerings: Past And Present," FR, 1991, v26(2), 211-222.)

Beard, Thomas R. (Fellows, James A. and Thomas R. Beard. "Some Welfare Implications Of Legal Restrictions On Commercial Bank Entry," JBR, 1980-81, v11(3), 159-168.)

Beard, Winston C. "An Epitaph For The Robertson Law," JRI, 1965, v32(4), 595-608.

Beardsley, George and Edwin Mansfield. "A Note On The Accuracy Of Industrial Forecasts Of The Profitability Of New Products And Processes," JOB, 1978, v51(1), 127-136.

Beardsley, L. J. (Baker, James C. and L. J. Beardsley. "Capital Budgeting By U.S. Multinational Companies," FR, 1972, v2(2), 115-121.)

Bearman, Arlene Erlich and Betsey Epstein Kuhn. "Test Of Efficiency: Cash Versus Future Markets," JPM, 1981, v8(1), 44-47.

Beaton, William and C. F. Sirmans. "Do Syndications Pay More For Real Estate?," AREUEA, 1986, v14(2), 206-215.

Beatty, Randolph P. and Jay R. Ritter. "Investment Banking, Reputation, And The Underpricing Of Initial Public Offerings," JFEC, 1986, v15(1/2), 213-232.

Beatty, Randolph P. "Estimation Of Convertible Security Systematic Risk: The Marginal Effect Of Time, Price, Premium Over Bond Value, And Conversion Value/Call Price," AFPAF, 1987, v2(1), 135-154.

Beatty, Randolph P., John F. Reim and Robert F. Schapperle. "The Effect Of Barriers To Entry On Bank Shareholder Wealth: Implications For Interstate Banking," JBR, 1985-86, v16(1), 8-15.

Beaver, William and Dale Morse. "What Determines Price-Earnings Ratios?," FAJ, 1978, v34(4), 65-76.

Beaver, William and James Manegold. "The Association Between Market-Determined And Accounting-Determined Measures Of Systematic Risk: Some Further Evidence," JFQA, 1975, v10(2), 231-284.

Beaver, William and Mark Wolfson. "Foreign Currency Translation Gains And Losses: What Effect Do They Have And What Do They Mean?," FAJ, 1984, v40(2), 28-29,32-36.

Beaver, William H. and Stephen G. Ryan. "How Well Do Statement No. 33 Earnings Explain Stock Returns?," FAJ, 1985, v41(5), 66-71.

Beaver, William H. "Interpreting Disclosures Of The Effects Of Changing Prices," FAJ, 1981, v37(5), 45-55.

Beaver, William H. (Barth, Mary E., William H. Beaver and Mark A. Wolfson. "Components Of Earnings And The Structure Of Bank Share Prices," FAJ, 1990, v46(3), 53-60.)

Beaver, William H., Paul A. Griffin and Wayne R. Landsman. "How Well Does Replacement Cost Income Explain Stock Return?," FAJ, 1983, v39(2), 26-30,39.

Beazer, William F. "Tax Law, Lock-Ins, And Bank Portfolio Choice," JOF, 1965, v20(4), 665-677.

Bebchuk, Lucian Arye. "Takeover Bids Below The Expected Value Of Minority Shares," JFQA, 1989, v24(2), 171-184.

Beck, Lester F. "Insurance Coverage For War Projects," JRI, 1943, v10, 76-87.

Beck, Paul J. and Thomas S. Zorn. "Managerial Incentives In A Stock Market Economy," JOF, 1982, v37(5), 1151-1168.

Beck, R. G. and J. M. Horne. "Economic Class And Risk Avoidance: Experience Under Public Medical Care Insurance," JRI, 1976, v43(1), 73-86.

Becker, Charles M. and Marjorie Stanley. "Equations As A Conceptual Basis For The Money And Banking Course," JFED, 1982, v11, 13-16.

Becker, Charles M. "Integration Of The Security Analysis Course With The C.F.A. Program," JFED, 1979, v8, 11-18.

Becker, Charles M. (Hirt, Geoffrey A. and Charles M. Becker. "Merits And Guidelines For Industry-Security Analysis Term Papers," JFED, 1980, v9, 27-32.)

Becker, Jack. "General Proof Of Modigliani-Miller Propositions I And II Using Parameter-Preference Theory," JFQA, 1978, v13(1), 65-69.

Becker, Joao L. and Rakesh K. Sarin. "Decision Analysis Using Lottery-Dependent Utility," JRU, 1989, v2(1), 105-118.

Becker, Kent G., Joseph E. Finnerty and Manoj Gupta. "The Intertemporal Relation Between The U.S. And Japanese Stock Markets," JOF, 1990, v45(4), 1297-1306.

Becker, Selwyn W. and David Green, Jr. "Budgeting And Employee Behavior: A Rejoinder To A `Reply'," JOB, 1964, v37(2), 203-205.

Becker, Selwyn W. and Frank Stafford. "Some Determinants Of Organizational Success," JOB, 1967, v40(4), 511-518.

Becker, Selwyn W. and Thomas L. Whisler. "The Innovative Organization: A Selective View Of Current Theory And Research," JOB, 1967, v40(4), 462-469.

Becker, Selwyn and David Green, Jr. "Budgeting And Employee Behavior," JOB, 1962, v35(4), 392-402.

Becker, Susan M. (Morgan, George Emir and Susan M. Becker. "Environmental Factors In Pricing NOW Accounts In 1981," JBR, 1982-83, v13(3), 168-178.)

Becker, Theodore M. and Robert N. Stern. "Professionalism, Professionalization, And Bias In The Commercial Human Relations Consulting Operation: A Survey Analysis," JOB, 1973, v46(2), 230-257.

Becker, William E. and George C. Alter. "The Probabilities Of Life And Work Force Status In The Calculation Of Expected Earnings," JRI, 1987, v54(2), 364-375.

Becker, William E. and George C. Alter. "Estimating Lost Future Earnings Using The New Worklife Tables: Reply," JRI, 1988, v55(3), 545-547.

Becker, William E., Jr. "Determinants Of The United States Currency-Demand Deposit Ratio," JOF, 1975, v30(1), 57-74.

Becker, Wolf-Dieter. "The Crisis Of German Financial Institutions In 1973," JBR, 1974-75, v5(2),120-124.

Beckers, Carl L. A. "Economic Survey Of The Far East," FAJ, 1962, v18(4), 41-43.

Beckers, Carl L. A. "Japan - A Reach For Self-Sufficiency," FAJ, 1960, v16(2), 9-16.

Beckers, Carl L. A. "Money Markets In Asia And The Middle East," FAJ, 1960, v16(6), 79-88.

Beckers, Stan and Luc Soenen. "Gold: More Attractive To Non-U.S.

Than To U.S. Investors?," JBFA, 1984, v11(1), 107-112.

Beckers, Stan and Piet Sercu. "Foreign Exchange Pricing Under Free Floating Versus Admissible Band Regimes," JIMF, 1985, v4(3), 317-329.

Beckers, Stan. "A Note On Estimating The Parameters Of The Diffusion-Jump Model Of Stock Returns," JFQA, 1981, v16(1), 127-140.

Beckers, Stan. "On The Efficiency Of The Gold Options Market," JBF, 1984, v8(3), 459-470.

Beckers, Stan. "Standard Deviations Implied In Option Prices As Predictors Of Future Stock Price Variability," JBF, 1981, v5(3), 363-381.

Beckers, Stan. "The Constant Elasticity Of Variance Model And Its Implications For Option Pricing," JOF, 1980, v35(3), 661-673.

Beckers, Stan. "Variances Of Security Price Returns Based On High, Low, And Closing Prices," JOB, 1983, v56(1), 97-112.

Beckman, Steven R. and Joshua N. Foreman. "An Experimental Test Of The Baumol-Tobin Transactions Demand For Money," JMCB, 1988, v20(3), Part 1, 291-305.

Beckwith, R. E. "Continuous Financial Processes," JFQA, 1968, v3(2), 113-133.

Bedford, G. Leighton. "Estimating Price-Earning Ratios," FAJ, 1947, v3(3), 14-19.

Bedford, George L. "Investment Opportunities In Revenue Bonds," FAJ, 1956, v12(1), 73-74.

Bedingfield, James P., Philip M. J. Reckers and A. J. Stagliano. "Distributions Of Financial Ratios In The Commercial Banking Industry," JBFA, 1985, v8(1), 77-81.

Bednar, Dick. "Residual Analysis Using Compustat Data," JFED, 1977, v6, 90-92.

Beebower, Gilbert L. and Gary L. Bergstrom. "Pension Performance 1966-1975," FAJ, 1977, v33(3), 31-42.

Beebower, Gilbert L. and William W. Priest, Jr. "The Tricks Of The Trade," JPM, 1980, v6(2), 36-42.

Beebower, Gilbert L. (Brinson, Gary P., L. Randolph Hood and Gilbert L. Beebower. "Determinants Of Portfolio Performance," FAJ, 1986, v42(4), 39-44.)

Beecher, Alistair. (Ezzamel, Mahmoud, Cecilio Mar-Molinero and Alistair Beecher. "On The Distributional Properties Of Financial Ratios," JBFA, 1987, v14(4), 463-482.)

Beedles, William L. and Donald L. Tuttle. "Portfolio Construction And Clientele Objective," JPM, 1978, v5(1), 25-28.

Beedles, William L. and Michael A. Simkowitz. "A Note On Skewness And Data Errors," JOF, 1978, v33(1), 288-292.

Beedles, William L. and Nancy K. Buschmann. "Describing Bank Equity Returns: The Year-By-Year Record," JMCB, 1981, v13(2), 241-247.

Beedles, William L. and O. Maurice Joy. "Compounding Risk Over Time: A Note," JBFA, 1982, v8(3),307-311.

Beedles, William L. "A Comparison Of Compustat And Value Line Financial Data Bases," JFED, 1983, v12, 100-102.

Beedles, William L. "A Micro-Econometric Investigation Of Multi-Objective Firms," JOF, 1977, v32(4), 1217-1233.

Beedles, William L. "Evaluating Negative Benefits," JFQA, 1978, v13(1), 173-176.

Beedles, William L. "On The Use Of Certainty Equivalent Factors As Risk Proxies," JFR, 1978, v1(1), 15-21.

Beedles, William L. "On The Assymmetry Of Market Returns," JFQA, 1979, v14(3), 653-660.

Beedles, William L. "Return, Dispersion, And Skewness: Synthesis And Investment Strategy," JFR, 1979, v2(1), 71-80.

Beedles, William L. "Some Notes On The Cost Of New Equity," JBFA, 1984, v11(2), 245-251.

Beedles, William L. "Some Notes On The Cost Of New Equity: A Reply," JBFA, 1986, v13(1), 153-154.

Beedles, William L. "The Anomalous And Asymmetric Nature Of Equity Returns: An Empirical Synthesis," JFR, 1984, v7(2), 151-160.

Beedles, William L. (Howe, John S. and William L. Beedles. "Defensive Investing Using Fundamental Data," JPM, 1984, v10(2), 14-17.)

Beedles, William L. (Senchack, Andrew J., Jr. and William L. Beedles. "Price Behavior In A Regional Over-The-Counter Securities Market," JFR, 1979, v2(2), 119-131.)

Beedles, William L. (Senchack, Andrew J., Jr. and William L. Beedles. "Is Indirect International Diversification Desirable?," JPM, 1980, v6(2), 49-57.)

Beedles, William L. (Simkowitz, Michael A. and William L. Beedles. "Diversification In A Three-Moment World," JFQA, 1978, v13(5), 927-941.)

Beedles, William L. (Strachan, James L., David B. Smith and William L. Beedles. "The Price Reaction To (Alleged) Corporate Crime," FR, 1983, v18(2),121-132.)

Beedles, William L., O. Maurice Joy and William Ruland. "Conglomeration And Diversification," FR, 1981, v16(1), 1-13.

Beekhuisen, Theo. (Remmers, Lee, Arthur Stonehill, Richard Wright and Theo Beekhuisen. "Industry And Size As Debt Ratio Determinants In Manufacturing Internationally," FM, 1974, v3(2), 24-32.)

Beekhuisen, Theo. (Stonehill, A., T. Beekhuisen, R. Wright, L. Remmers, N. Toy, A. Pares, A. Shapiro, D. Egan and T. Bates. "Financial Goals And Debt Ratio Determinants," FM, 1974, v4(3), 27-41.)

Beekhuisen, Theo. (Toy,N., A. Stonehill,L. Remmers,R. Wright and T. Beekhuisen. "A Comparative International Study Of Growth, Profitability, And Risk As Determinant Of Corporate Debt Ratios," JFQA, 1974, Vol.9(5), 875-886.)

Beem, E. and L. Isaacson. "Schizophrenia In Trading Stamp Analysis," JOB, 1968, v41(3), 340-344.

Beem, Eugene R. "On Being Fooled By Statisticians: The Case Of Professor Strotz," JOB, 1959, v32(3), 279-282.

Beenstock, Michael and J. Andrew Longbottom. "The Term Structure Of Interest Rates In A Small Open Economy," JMCB, 1981, v13(1), 44-59.

Beenstock, Michael, Gerry Dickinson and Sajay Khajuria. "The Relationship Between Property-Liability Insurance Premiums And Income: An International Analysis," JRI, 1988, v55(2), 259-272.

Beenstock, Michael. "Rational Expectations And The Effect Of Exchange-Rate Intervention On The Exchange Rate," JIMF, 1983, v2(3), 319-331.

Beenstock, Michael. "The Determinants Of The Money Multiplier In The United Kingdom," JMCB, 1989, v21(4), 464-480.

Behr, Robert M. and Ronald W. Ward. "A Simultaneous Equation Model Of Futures Market Trading Activity," RFM, 1984, v3(3), 194-212.

Behr, Robert M. (Ward, Ronald W. and Robert M. Behr. "Allocating Nonreported Futures Commitments," JFM, 1983, v3(4), 393-401.)

Behr, Robert M. (Ward, Ronald W. and Robert M. Behr. "Futures Trading Liquidity: An Application Of A Futures Trading Model," JFM, 1983, v3(2), 207-224.)

Behrman, Jack N. "Foreign Private Investment And The Government's Efforts To Reduce The Payments Deficit," JOF, 1966, v21(2), 283-296.

Beidleman, Carl R. "Pitfalls Of The Price-Earnings Ratio," FAJ, 1971, v27(5), 86-91.

Beidleman, Carl. (Buell, Stephen G., Carl Beidleman and R. Charles Moyer. "On The Linkage Between Corporate Savings And Earnings Growth," JFR, 1981, v4(2), 121-128.)

Beighley, H. Prescott and Alan S. McCall. "Market Power And Structure And Commercial Bank Installment Lending," JMCB, 1975, v7(4), 449-467.

Beighley, H. Prescott, John H. Boyd and Donald P. Jacobs. "Bank Equities And Investor Risk Perceptions: Some Entailments For Capital Adequacy Regulation," JBR, 1975-76, v6(3), 190-201.

Beighley, H. Prescott. "The Risk Perceptions Of Bank Holding Company Debtholders," JBR, 1977-78, v8(2), 85-93.

Beighley, H. Prescott. (Jacobs, Donald P. and H. Prescott Beighley. "The Changing Structure Of Banking And Its Future Impact On Banks," JBR, 1974-75, v5(3), 145-155.)

Beighley, Scott. "Financial Futures Applications By The Thrift Industry," RFM, 1985, v4(2), 196-206.

Beightler, Charles S. and Robert L. Street. "Profit Planning In Non-Life Insurance Companies Through The Use Of A Probability Model," JRI, 1967, v34(2), 255-268.

Beja, Avraham and M. Barry Goldman. "On The Dynamic Behavior Of Prices In Disequilibrium," JOF, 1980, v35(2), 235-248.

Beja, Avraham and Nils H. Hakansson. "Dynamic Market Processes And The Rewards To Up-to-date Information," JOF, 1977, v32(2), 291-304.

Beja, Avraham. "On Systematic And Unsystematic Components Of Financial Risk," JOF, 1972, v27(1), 37-45.

Beja, Avraham. (Goldman, M. Barry and Avraham Beja. "Market Prices Vs. Equilibrium Prices: Returns' Variance, Serial Correlation, And The Role Of The Specialist," JOF, 1979, v34(3), 595-607.)

Beja, Avraham. (Hakannsson, Nils H., Avraham Beja and Jivendra Kale. "On The Feasibility Of Automated Market Making By A Programmed Specialist," JOF, 1985, v40(1), 1-20.)

Belden, Susan. "Policy Preferences Of FOMC Members As Revealed By Dissenting Votes," JMCB, 1989, v21(4), 432-441.

Belfer, Nathan. "Construction Of Private Investors' Portfolios," FAJ, 1965, v21(3), 101-104.

Belhoul, D. (Betts, J. and D. Belhoul. "The Effectiveness Of Incorporating Stability Measures In Company Failure Models," JBFA, 1987, v14(3), 323-334.)

Belhouse, David R. (Panjer, Harry H. and David R. Bellhouse. "Stochastic Modelling Of Interest Rates With Applications To Life Contingencies," JRI, 1980, v47(1), 91-110.)

Beliveau, Barbara C. "Theoretical And Empirical Aspects Of Implicit Information In The Market For Life Insurance," JRI, 1984, v51(2), 286-307.

Belkaoui, Ahmed and Ronald D. Picur. "The Smoothing Of Income Numbers: Some Empirical Evidence On Systematic Differences Between Core And Periphery Industrial Sectors," JBFA, 1984, v11(4), 527-546.

Belkaoui, Ahmed and Alain Cousineau. "Accounting Information, Nonaccounting Information, And Common Stock Perception," JOB, 1977, v50(3), 334-342.

Belkaoui, Ahmed and Ronald D. Picur. "Sources Of Feedback In A CPA Firm," JBFA, 1987, v14(2), 175-186.

Belkaoui, Ahmed. "A Canadian Survey Of Financial Structure," FM, 1974, v4(1), 74-79.

Belkaoui, Ahmed. "Accrual Accounting And Cash Accounting: Relative Merits Of Derived Accounting Indicator Numbers," JBFA, 1983, v10(2), 299-312.

Belkaoui, Ahmed. "Canadian Evidence Of Heteroscedasticity In The Market Model," JOF, 1977, v32(4), 1320-1324.

Belkaoui, Ahmed. "Financial Ratios As Predictors Of Canadian Takeovers," JBFA, 1978, v5(1),93-108.

Belkaoui, Ahmed. "Industrial Bond Ratings: A New Look," FM, 1980, v9(3), 44-51.

Belkaoui, Ahmed. "Judgement Related Issues In Performance Evaluation," JBFA, 1982, v8(4), 489-500.

Belkaoui, Ahmed. "The Entropy Law, Information Decomposition Measures And Corporate Takeover," JBFA, 1976, v3(3), 41-52.

Belkaoui, Ahmed. "The Impact Of The Disclosure Of The Environmental Effects Of Organizational Behavior On The Market," FM, 1976, v5(4), 26-31.

Belkin, Jacob, Donald J. Hempel and Dennis W. McLeavey. "An Empirical Study Of Time On Market Using Multidimensional Segmentation Of Housing Markets," AREUEA, 1976, v4(2), 57-76.

Bell, Carolyn Shaw. "Reply: Schizophrenia In Trading Stamp Analysis," JOB, 1968, v41(3), 345-346.

Bell, Carolyn Shaw. "'Liberty And Property, And No Stamps'," JOB, 1967, v40(2), 194-202.

Bell, David E. and William S. Krasker. "Estimating Hedge Ratios," FM, 1986, v15(2), 34-39.

Bell, Edward B. and Allan J. Taub. "Selecting Income Growth And Discount Rates In Wrongful Death And Injury Cases: Comment," JRI, 1977, v44(1), 122-129.

Bell, Frederick W. "The Relation Of The Structure Of Common Stock Prices To Historical, Expectational And Industrial Variables," JOF, 1974, v29(1), 187-197.

Bell, Geoffrey L. "Economic Conditions In The U.K.," FAJ, 1968, v24(4), 147-150.

Bell, Geoffrey. "Monetary Policy Issues - U. S. And U. K.," FAJ, 1970, v26(2), 24-29.

Reexamination Of The Empirical Relationship Between Investment And Financing Decisions," **JFQA**, 1983, v18(4), 439-453.)

Benesh, Gary A. and Robert A. Pari. "Performance Of Stocks Recommended On The Basis Of Insider Trading Activity," **FR**, 1987, v22(1), 145-158.

Benesh, Gary A., Arthur J. Keown and John M. Pinkerton. "An Examination Of Market Reaction To Substantial Shifts In Dividend Policy," **JFR**, 1984, v7(2), 131-140.

Benet, Bruce A. "Commodity Futures Cross Hedging Of Foreign Exchange Exposure," **JFM**, 1990, v10(3), 287-306.

Benet, Bruce A. (Conroy, Robert M., Robert S. Harris and Bruce A. Benet. "The Effects Of Stock Splits On Bid-Ask Spreads," **JOF**, 1990, v45(4), 1285-1295.)

Benham, Isabel H. "Railroad-Based Conglomerates," **FAJ**, 1972, v28(3), 43-48,51-53.

Benham, Isabel H. "Railroad-Equipment Debt," **FAJ**, 1953, v9(5), 51-56.

Benishay, H. "On Benishay's Evaluation Of Policy: A Reply," **JMCB**, 1975, v7(3), 381-384.

Benishay, Haskel. "A Framework For The Evaluation Of Short-Term Fiscal And Monetary Policy," **JMCB**, 1972, v4(4), 779-810.

Benishay, Haskel. "On The Limitations Of Research In Finance," **FR**, 1978, v13(1), 85-88.

Benjamin, Anne F. (Girmes, D. H. and Anne E. Benjamin. "Random Walk Hypothesis For 543 Stocks And Shares Registered On The London Stock Exchange," **JBFA**, 1975, v2(1), 135-145.)

Benjamin, James J. (Richards, R. Malcolm, James J. Benjamin and Robert H. Strawser. "An Examination Of The Accuracy Of Earnings Forecasts," **FM**, 1977, v6(3),78-86.)

Benjamin, John D. (Sa-Aadu, J., C. F. Sirmans and John D. Benjamin. "Financing And House Prices," **JFR**, 1989, v12(1), 83-91.)

Benjamin, John D. (Shilling, James D., C. F. Sirmans and John D. Benjamin. "On Option-Pricing Models In Real Estate: A Critique," **AREUEA**, 1987, v15(1), 742-752.)

Benjamin, John D. (Shilling, James D., John D. Benjamin and C. F. Sirmans. "Estimating Net Realizable Value For Distressed Real Estate," **JRER**, 1990, v5(1), 129-140.)

Benjamin, John D. (Sirmans, C. F. and John D. Benjamin. "Pricing Fixed Rate Mortgages: Some Empirical Evidence," **JFSR**, 1990, v4(3), 191-202.)

Benjamin, John D. (Sirmans, G. Stacy, C. F. Sirmans and John D. Benjamin. "Determining Apartment Rent: The Value Of Amenities, Services And External Factors," **JRER**, 1989, v4(2), 33-43.)

Benjamin, John D. (Sirmans, G. Stacy, C. F. Sirmans and John D. Benjamin. "Rental Concessions And Property Values," **JRER**, 1990, v5(1), 141-151.)

Benjamin, John D., Glenn W. Boyle and C. F. Sirmans. "Retail Leasing: The Determinants Of Shopping Center Rents," **AREUEA**, 1990, v18(3), 302-312.

Benjamin, John D., James D. Shilling and C. F. Sirmans. "Contracts As Options: Some Evidence From Condominium Developments," **AREUEA**, 1985, v13(2), 143-152.

Benjamin, Wahjudi P. and John E. McEnroe. "The SEC Overruling Of SFAS 19 And The Behavior Of Security Returns," **JBFA**, 1983, v10(2), 235-249.

Benjamin, Wahjudi P. and John E. McEnroe. "The FASB's Policy Intervention And The Behavior Of Security Returns," **JBFA**, 1981, v8(3), 303-327.

Benjes, W. D. and L. J. Seidler. "Interim Financial Statements," **FAJ**, 1967, v23(5), 109-115.

Benktander, G. and B. Berliner. "Risk And Return In Insurance And Reinsurance," **JRI**, 1977, v44(2), 299-304.

Bennett, Alden S. "Determining Combined Fixed Charge And Preferred Dividend Coverage," **FAJ**, 1973, v3(4), 63-66.

Bennett, Hite. (Vaughn, Donald E. and Hite Bennett. "Adjusting For Risk In The Capital Budget Of A Growth-Oriented Company," **JFQA**, 1968, v3(4),445-461.)

Bennett, Jack F. "Europe's Money Game," **JOF**, 1952, v7(3), 434-446.

Bennett, James T. (Barth, James R. and James T. Bennett. "Is The 'Neutralized Money Stock' Unbiased: Comment," **JOF**, 1976, v31(5), 1509-1513.)

Bennett, James T. (Barth, James R. and James T. Bennett. "Cost-Push Versus Demand-Pull Inflation: Some Empirical Evidence: A Comment," **JMCB**, 1975, v7(3), 391-397.)

Bennett, Paul. "Applying Portfolio Theory To Global Bank Lending," **JBF**, 1984, v8(2), 153-170.

Bennett, Richard E. (Johnson, Dana J., Richard E. Bennett and Richard J. Curcio. "A Note On The Deceptive Nature Of Bayesian Forecasted Betas," **JFR**, 1979, v2(1), 65-69.)

Bennett, Richard E. (Swinnerton, Eugene A., Richard J. Curcio and Richard E. Bennett. "Index Arbitrage Program Trading And The Prediction Of Intraday Stock Price Changes," **RFM**, 1988, v7(2), 300-323.)

Bennett, Robert L. "Financial Innovation And Structural Change In The Early Stages Of Industrialization: Mexico, 1945-59," **JOF**, 1963, v18(4), 666-683.

Bennett, William M. "Accelerated Amortization And The Aluminum Companies," **FAJ**, 1954, v10(4),63-66.

Bennett, William M. "Accounting For Uranium And Plutonium," **FAJ**, 1953, v9(5), 81-84.

Bennett, William M. "Aluminum As An Earnings Stabilizer," **FAJ**, 1953, v9(2), 107-110.

Bennett, William M. "Capital Turnover Versus Profit Margins," **FAJ**, 1966, v22(2), 88-95.

Bennett, William M. "History Of San Francisco Security Analysts," **FAJ**, 1960, v16(1), 69-71.

Benney, Mark. (Riesman, David and Mark Benney. "Asking And Answering," **JOB**, 1956, v29(4), 225-236.)

Bennin, Robert. "Error Rates In CRSP And COMPUSTAT: A Second Look," **JOF**, 1980, v35(5), 1267-1271.

Benninga, Simon and Aris Protopapadakis. "General Equilibrium Properties Of The Term Structure Of Interest Rates," **JFEC**, 1986, v16(3), 389-410.

Benninga, Simon and Marshall Blume. "On The Optimality Of Portfolio Insurance," **JOF**, 1985, v40(5), 1341-1352.

Benninga, Simon and Michael Smirlock. "An Empirical Analysis Of The Delivery Option, Marking To Market, And The Pricing Of Treasury Bond Futures," **JFM**, 1985, v5(3), 361-374.

Benninga, Simon and Aris Protopapadakis. "The Equilibrium Pricing Of Exchange Rates And Assets When Trade Takes Time," **JIMF**, 1988, v7(2), 129-150.

Benninga, Simon and Eli Talmor. "The Interaction Of Corporate And Government Financing In General Equilibrium," **JOB**, 1988, v61(2), 233-258.

Benninga, Simon, Rafael Eldor and Itzhak Zilcha. "Optimal International Hedging In Commodity And Currency Forward Markets," **JIMF**, 1985, v4(4), 537-552.

Benninga, Simon, Rafael Eldor and Itzhak Zilcha. "The Optimal Hedge Ratio In Unbiased Futures Markets," **JFM**, 1984, v4(2), 155-159.

Benninga, Simon. "General Equilibrium With Financial Markets: Existence, Uniqueness, And Implications For Corporate Finance," **JOF**, 1979, v34(2),325-342.

Benninga, Simon. "Nonlinear Pricing Systems In Finance," **RIF**, 1983, v4, 21-42.

Bennington, George A. (Jensen, Michael C. and George A. Bennington. "Random Walks And Technical Theories: Some Additional Evidence," **JOF**, 1970, v25(2), 469-482.)

Benoit, Emile. "The Role Of Monetary And Fiscal Policies In Disarmament Adjustments," **JOF**, 1963, v18(2), 113-129.

Bensinger, B. E. "Bowling: A Billion Dollar Industry," **FAJ**, 1960, v16(1), 27-29.

Benson, Donald. "Banking's Present And Future Competitors: Thrift Institutions," **JBR**, 1974-75, v5(3), 182-184.

Benson, Earl D. and Robert J. Rogowski. "The Cyclical Behavior Of Risk Spreads On New Municipal Issues," **JMCB**, 1978, v10(3), 348-362.

Benson, Earl D. "The Dispersion Of Bids On Individual New Municipal Issues," **JFR**, 1982, v5(3),207-219.

Benson, Earl D. "The Search For Information By Underwriters And Its Impact On Municipal Interest Cost," **JOF**, 1979, v34(4), 871-885.

Benson, Earl D. (Rystrom, David S. and Earl D. Benson. "Investor Psychology And The Day-Of-The-Week Effect," **FAJ**, 1989, v45(5), 75-78.)

Benson, Earl D., David S. Kidwell, Timothy W. Koch and Robert J. Rogowski. "Systematic Variation In Yield Spreads For Tax-Exempt General Obligation Bonds," **JFQA**, 1981, v16(5), 685-702.

Benson, P. George. (Alexander, Gordon J., P. George Benson and Joan M. Kampmeyer. "Investigating The Valuation Effects Of Announcements Of Voluntary Corporate Selloffs," **JOF**, 1984, v39(2), 503-517.)

Benson, P. George. (Alexander, Gordon J., P. George Benson and Elizabeth W. Gunderson. "Asset Redeployment: Trans World Corporation's Spinoff Of TWA," **FM**, 1986, v15(2), 50-58.)

Benson, P. George. (Alexander, Gordon J. and P. George Benson. "More On Beta As A Random Coefficient," **JFQA**, 1982, v17(1), 27-36.)

Benson, P. George. (Alexander, Gordon J., P. George Benson and Carol E. Eger. "Timing Decisions And The Behavior Of Mutual Fund Systematic Risk," **JFQA**, 1982, v17(4), 579-602.)

Benston, G. J. and R. L. Hagerman. "Risk, Volume And Spread," **FAJ**, 1978, v34(1), 46-49.

Benston, George J. and Clifford W. Smith, Jr. "A Transactions Cost Approach To The Theory Of Financial Intermediation," **JOF**, 1976, v31(2), 215-231.

Benston, George J. and Dan Horsky. "Redlining And The Demand For Mortgages In The Central City And Suburbs," **JBR**, 1979-80, v10(2), 72-87.

Benston, George J. and John Tepper Marlin. "Bank Examiners' Evaluation Of Credit: An Analysis Of The Usefulness Of Substandard Loan Data," **JMCB**, 1974, v6(1), 23-44.

Benston, George J. and Robert L. Hagerman. "Determinants Of Bid-Asked Spreads In The Over-The-Counter Market," **JFEC**, 1974, v1(4), 353-364.

Benston, George J. "A Microeconomic Approach To Banking Competition: Comment," **JOF**, 1972, v27(3), 722-723.

Benston, George J. "An Analysis And Evaluation Of Alternative Reserve Requirement Plans," **JOF**, 1969, v24(5), 849-870.

Benston, George J. "Banking And A World Without Money: Comment," **JBR**, 1971-72, v2(4), 59-61.

Benston, George J. "Branch Banking And Economies Of Scale," **JOF**, 1965, v20(2), 312-331.

Benston, George J. "Commercial Bank Price Discrimination Against Small Loans: An Empirical Study," **JOF**, 1964, v19(4), 631-643.

Benston, George J. "Discrimination In Home Improvement Loans: A Comment On A Rejoinder," **JBR**, 1982-83, v13(3), 207-208.

Benston, George J. "Discussion Of The Hunt Commission Report," **JMCB**, 1972, v4(4), 985-989.

Benston, George J. "Economies Of Scale Of Financial Institutions," **JMCB**, 1972, v4(2), 312-341.

Benston, George J. "Federal Reserve Membership: Consequences, Costs, Benefits And Alternatives," **JBR**, 1980-81, v11(1), 57-60.

Benston, George J. "Federal Regulation Of Banking Analysis And Policy Recommendations," **JBR**, 1982-83, v13(4), 216-244.

Benston, George J. "Graduated Interest Rate Ceilings And Operating Costs By Size Of Small Consumer Cash Loans," **JOF**, 1977, v32(3), 695-707.

Benston, George J. "Mortgage Redlining Research: A Review And Critical Analysis," **JBR**, 1981-82, v12(1), 8-23.

Benston, George J. "Overdraft Banking: Its Implications For Monetary Policy, The Commercial Banking Industry & Individual Banks," **JBR**, 1972-73, v3(1),7-25.

Benston, George J. "Rate Ceiling Implications Of The Cost Structure Of Consumer Finance Companies," **JOF**, 1977, v32(4), 1169-1194.

Benston, George J. "Risk On Consumer Finance Company Personal Loans," **JOF**, 1977, v32(2),593-607.

Benston, George J. "Savings Banks And The Public Interest," **JMCB**, 1972, v4(1), Part II, 133-224.

Benston, George J. "The Federal 'Safety Net' And The Repeal Of The Glass-Steagall Act's Separation Of Commercial And Investment Banking," **JFSR**, 1989, v2(4), 287-306.

Benston, George J. "The Impact Of Maturity Regulation On High Interest Rate Lenders And Borrowers," JFEC, 1977, v4(1), 23-49.

Benston, George J. "The Optimal Banking Structure: Theory And Evidence," JBR, 1972-73, v3(4), 220-237.

Benston, George J., Gerald A. Hanweck and David B. Humphrey. "Scale Economies In Banking: A Restructuring And Reassessment," JMCB, 1982, v14(4), Part 1, 435-456.

Bentert, Joseph R. "Synthetic Fibers," FAJ, 1952, v8(3), 55-58.

Benveniste, Lawrence M. and Allen N. Berger. "Securitization With Recourse: An Instrument That Offers Uninsured Bank Depositors Sequential Claims," JBF, 1987, v11(3), 403-424.

Benveniste, Lawrence M. and Paul A. Spindt. "How Investment Bankers Determine The Offer Price And Allocation Of New Issues," JFEC, 1989, v24(2), 343-362.

Benvignati, Anita M. "Domestic Profit Advantages Of Multinational Firms," JOB, 1987, v60(3), 449-462.

Bera, Anil K. (Park, Hun Y. and Anil K. Bera. "Interest-Rate Volatility, Basis Risk And Heteroscedasticity In Hedging Mortgages," AREUEA, 1987, v15(2), 79-97.)

Bera, Anil, Edward Bubnys and Hun Park. "Conditional Heteroscedasticity In The Market Model And Efficient Estimates Of Betas," FR, 1988, v23(2),201-214.

Beranek, William and Gadis J. Dillon. "Pitfalls In Assessing Financial Risk From Consolidated Financial Statements," JFED, 1982, v11, 32-39.

Beranek, William and J. Fred Weston. "Programming Investment Portfolio Construction," FAJ, 1955, v11(2), 51-56.

Beranek, William and Ronnie Clayton. "Risk Differences And Financial Reporting," JFR, 1985, v8(4),327-334.

Beranek, William and Edward B. Selby, Jr. "Accelerated Depreciation And Income Growth," AREUEA, 1981, v9(1), 67-73.

Beranek, William and James A. Miles. "The Excess Return Argument And Double Leverage," FR, 1988, v23(2), 143-150.

Beranek, William, Thomas M. Humphrey and Richard H. Timberlake, Jr. "Fisher, Thornton, And The Analysis Of The Inflation Premium," JMCB, 1985, v17(3),371-377.

Beranek, William. "A Historical Perspective Of Research And Practice In Working Capital Management," AWCM, 1990, v1(1), 3-16.

Beranek, William. "A Little More On The Weighted Average Cost Of Capital," JFQA, 1975, v10(5),892-896.

Beranek, William. "Some New Capital Budgeting Theorems," JFQA, 1978, v13(5), 809-823.

Beranek, William. "Some Problems In Valuation Theory," FR, 1968, v1(3), 166-170.

Beranek, William. "The AB Procedure And Capital Budgeting," JFQA, 1980, v15(2), 391-406.

Beranek, William. "The Cost Of Capital, Capital Budgeting, And The Maximization Of Shareholder Wealth," JFQA, 1975, v10(1), 1-20.

Beranek, William. "The Theoretical Value Of A Stock Right: A Comment," JOF, 1956, v11(3), 367-370.

Beranek, William. "The Weighted Average Cost Of Capital And Shareholder Wealth Maximization," JFQA, 1977, v12(1), 17-31.

Beranek, William. (Campbell, James A. and William Beranek. "Stock Price Behavior On Ex-Dividend Dates," JOF, 1955, v10(4),, 425-429.)

Beranek, William. (Clayton, Ronnie J. and William Beranek. "Disassociations And Legal Combinations," FM, 1985, v14(2), 24-28.)

Beranek, William. (Mehta, Cyrus R. and William Beranek. "Tracking Asset Volatility By Means Of A Bayesian Switching Regression," JFQA, 1982, v17(2), 241-263.)

Beranek, William. (Williams, Alex O., William Beranek and James Kenkel. "Default Risk In Urban Mortgages: A Pittsburgh Prototype Analysis," AREUEA, 1974, v2(2), 101-116.)

Berck, Peter and Thomas Bible. "Wood Products Futures Markets And The Reservation Price Of Timber," JFM, 1985, v5(3), 311-316.

Bereksor, Leonard L. "Birth Order, Anxiety, Affiliation And The Purchase Of Life Insurance," JRI, 1972, v39(1), 93-108.

Bereksor, Leonard L. "Birth Order, Anxiety, Affiliation And The Purchase Of Life Insurance: Reply," JRI, 1973, v40(4), 646-648.

Bereksor, Leonard L. and Roger E. Severns. "Insurance Executives' Perceptions Of Insurance Instruction At The College And University Level," JRI, 1981, v48(2), 322-333.

Berent, Philip. (Clarke, Roger G., Michael T. Fitzgerald, Philip Berent and Meir Statman. "Diversifying Among Asset Allocators," JPM, 1990, v16(3), 9-14.)

Berent, Philip. (Clarke, Roger G., Michael T. Fitzgerald, Philip Berent and Meir Statman. "Required Accuracy For Successful Asset Allocation," JPM, 1990, v17(1), 12-19.)

Berent, Phillip. (Clarke, Roger G., Michael T. FitzGerald, Phillip Berent and Meir Statman. "Market Timing With Imperfect Information," FAJ, 1989, v45(6), 27-36.)

Berg, Gordon H. and John M. Tucker. "Techniques For Arranging Hospital Financing," FM, 1972, v1, FM, 1972, v1(1), 48-57.

Berg, Gordon H. "Hospitals As Long-Term Borrowers," FAJ, 1971, v27(2), 23-32.

Berg, Menachem and Giora Moore. "Foreign Exchange Strategies: Spot, Forward And Options," JBFA, 1991, v18(3), 449-457.

Berger, Allen N. (Avery, Robert B. and Allen N. Berger. "Loan Commitments And Bank Risk Exposure," JBF, 1991, v15(1), 173-192.)

Berger, Allen N. (Benveniste, Lawrence M. and Allen N. Berger. "Securitization With Recourse: An Instrument That Offers Uninsured Bank Depositors Sequential Claims," JBF, 1987, v11(3), 403-424.)

Berger, Allen N. and David B. Humphrey. "Interstate Banking And The Payments System," JFSR, 1988, v1(2), 131-146.

Berger, Lawrence A. "A Model Of The Underwriting Cycle In The Property/Liability Insurance Industry," JRI, 1988, v55(2), 298-306.

Berger, Lawrence A., Paul R. Kleindorfer and Howard Kunreuther. "A Dynamic Model Of The Transmission Of Price Information In Auto Insurance Markets," JRI, 1989, v56(1), 17-33.

Berger, Paul D. and William K. Harper. "Determination Of An Optimal Revolving Credit Agreement," JFQA, 1973, v8(3), 491-497.

Berger, Paul D. and Zvi Bodie. "Portfolio Selection In A 'Winner-Take-All' Environment," JOF, 1979, v34(1), 233-236.

Berger, Paul D. and James P. Monahan. "A Planning Model To Cope With Absenteeism," JOB, 1974, v47(4), 512-517.

Berges, Angel, John J. McConnell and Gary G. Schlarbaum. "The Turn-of-the-Year In Canada," JOF, 1984, v39(1), 185-192.

Bergh-Jacobsen, Stein. (Varvin, Kaare and Stein Bergh-Jacobsen. "As Two Norwegians Saw The Train Trip," FAJ, 1958, v14(4), 85.)

Berglund, Tom and Bjorn Wahlroos. "The Efficiency Of The Finnish Market For Rights Issues: An Application Of The Black-Scholes Model," JBFA, 1985, v12(1), 151-164.

Berglund, Tom and Eva Liljeblom. "Market Serial Correlation On A Small Security Market: A Note," JOF, 1988, v43(5), 1265-1274.

Berglund, Tom, Eva Liljeblom and Anders Loflund. "Estimating Betas On Daily Data For A Small Stock Market," JBF, 1989, v13(1), 42-64.

Berglund, Tom. (Wahlroos, Bjorn and Tom Berglund. "Stock Returns, Inflationary Expectations And Real Activity: New Evidence," JBF, 1986, v10(3), 377-389.)

Bergman, Yaacov Z. "Pricing Path Contingent Claims," RIF, 1985, v5, 229-242.

Bergman, Yaacov Z. "Time Preference And Capital Asset Pricing Models," JFEC, 1985, v14(1),145-159.

Bergstrand, Jeffrey H. and Thomas P. Bundt. "Currency Substitution And Monetary Autonomy: The Foreign Demand For US Demand Deposits," JIMF, 1990, v9(3), 325-334.

Bergstrom, C. and K. Rydqvist. "The Determinants Of Corporate Ownership: An Empirical Study Of Swedish Data," JBF, 1990, v14(2/3), 237-254.

Bergstrom, C. and K. Rydqvist. "Ownership Of Equity In Dual-Class Firms," JBF, 1990, v14(2/3), 255-270.

Bergstrom, Gary L. "A New Route To Higher Returns And Lower Risks," JPM, 1975, v2(1), 30-38.

Bergstrom, Gary L. (Beebower, Gilbert L. and Gary L. Bergstrom. "Pension Performance 1966-1975," FAJ, 1977, v33(3), 31-42.)

Bergstrom, Gary L. (Umstead, David A. and Gary L. Bergstrom. "Dynamic Estimation Of Portfolio Betas," JFQA, 1979, v14(3), 595-614.)

Berk, Jonathan and Richard Roll. "Adjustable Rate Mortgages: Valuation," JREFEC, 1988, v1(2), 163-184.

Berkman, Herman G. (Kinnard, William N., Herman G. Berkman, Hugh O. Nourse and John C. Weicher. "The First Twenty Years Of AREUEA," AREUEA, 1988, v16(2), 189-205.)

Berkman, Neil G. "The New Monetary Aggregates: A Critical Appraisal," JMCB, 1980, v12(2), Part 1, 135-154.

Berkovec, James. "A General Equilibrium Model Of Housing Consumption And Investment," JREFEC, 1989, v2(3), 157-172.

Berkovitch, Elazar and E. Han Kim. "Financial Contracting And Leverage Induced Over- And Under-Investment Incentives," JOF, 1990, v45(3), 765-794.

Berkovitch, Elazar and M. P. Narayanan. "Competition And The Medium Of Exchange In Takeovers," RFS, 1990, v3(2), 153-174.

Berkovitch, Elazar and Naveen Khanna. "How Target Shareholders Benefit From Value-Reducing Defensive Strategies In Takeovers," JOF, 1990, v45(1), 137-156.

Berkovitch, Elazar and Stuart I. Greenbaum. "The Loan Commitment As An Optimal Financing Contract," JFQA, 1991, v26(1), 83-96.

Berkowitz, Monroe. (Burton, John F., Jr. and Monroe Berkowitz. "Objectives Other Than Income Maintenance For Workmen's Compensation," JRI, 1971, v38(3), 343-355.)

Berkowitz, Monroe. (Chernick, Jack and Monroe Berkowitz. "The Guaranteed Wage - The Economics Of Opulence In Collective Bargaining," JOB, 1955, v28(3), 169-181.)

Berkowitz, Stephen A. and Dennis E. Logue. "The Portfolio Turnover Explosion Explored," JPM, 1987, v13(3), 38-45.

Berkowitz, Stephen A., Dennis E. Logue and Eugene A. Noser, Jr. "The Total Cost Of Transactions On The NYSE," JOF, 1988, v43(1), 97-112.

Berlin, Mitchell and Jan Loeys. "Bond Covenants And Delegated Monitoring," JOF, 1988, v43(2), 397-412.

Berliner, B. (Benktander, G. and B. Berliner. "Risk And Return In Insurance And Reinsurance," JRI, 1977, v44(2), 299-304.)

Berliner, Robert W. "Do Analysts Use Inflation-Adjusted Information? Results Of A Survey," FAJ, 1983, v39(2), 65-72.

Berman, Alfred. "Regulation Of Unlisted Securities," FAJ, 1961, v17(4), 45-52.

Berman, Daniel S. "Using Tax Laws To Help Finance Corporate Acquisitions," FAJ, 1956, v12(2), 119-123.

Berman, Howard. "A Method Of Increasing The Security Of Pension Benefits," JRI, 1968, v35(1), 155-158.

Berman, Peter I. "Differentials In Discount Facility Administration: Some Empirical Evidence," JBR, 1976-77, v7(2), 158-165.

Berman, Peter. (Weiner, Michael D. and Peter Berman. "Section 17: Registered Futures Associations," JFM, v1(Supp), 497-500.)

Bernanke, Ben S. "Clearing And Settlement During The Crash," RFS, 1990, v3(1), 133-151.

Bernard, Jules E., Gary G. Gilbert and Robert P. Rogers. "Final Report Of The National Commission On Electronic Fund Transfers: Implications For Federal Regulation Of Depository Institutions," JBR, 1977-78, v8(4), 209-217.

Bernard, Victor L. and Thomas J. Frecka. "Evidence On The Existence Of Common Stock Inflation Hedges," JFR, 1983, v6(4), 301-312.

Bernard, Victor L. "Unanticipated Inflation And The Value Of The Firm," JFEC, 1986, v15(3), 285-322.

Bernard, Victor L. (Kormendi, Roger C., Victor L. Bernard, S. Craig Pirrong and Edward A. Snyder. "The Origins And Resolution Of The Thrift Crisis," JACF, 1989, v2(3), 85-99.)

Bernard, Victor L. and Thomas J. Frecka. "Commodity Contracts And Common Stocks As Hedges Against Relative Consumer Price Risk," JFQA, 1987, v22(2), 169-188.

Bernardo, John J. and Howard P. Lanser. "A Capital Budgeting Decision Model With Subjective Criteria," JFQA, 1977, v12(2), 261-275.

Berndt, Ernst R., Karen Chant Sharp and G. Campbell Watkins. "Utility Bond Rates And Tax Normalization," JOF, 1979, v34(5), 1211-1220.

Bernenko, Herbert. "Public Utility Common Stocks," FAJ, 1949, v5(4), 47-51.

Berney, Robert E. "The Auction Of Long-Term Government Securities," JOF, 1964, v19(3), 470-482.

Bernhard, Arnold. "No Crash, But A Bull Market," JPM, 1979, v6(1), 77-81.

Bernhard, Arnold. "The Valuation Of Listed Stocks," FAJ, 1949, v5(2), 20-24.

Bernhard, Richard H. and Carl J. Norstrom. "A Further Note On Unrecovered Investment, Uniqueness Of The Internal Rate, And The Question Of Project Acceptability," JFQA, 1980, v15(2), 421-423.

Bernhard, Richard H. "A More General Sufficient Condition For A Unique Nonnegative Internal Rate Of Return," JFQA, 1979, v14(2), 337-341.

Bernhard, Richard H. "A Simplification And An Extension Of The Bernhard-deFaro Sufficient Condition For A Unique Non-Negative Internal Rate Of Return," JFQA, 1980, v15(1), 201-209.

Bernhard, Richard H. "Avoiding Irrationality In The Use Of Two-Parameter Risk-Benefit Models For Investment Under Uncertainty," FM, 1981, v10(1), 77-81.

Bernhard, Richard H. "Bhaskar's Mathematical Programming Models For Borrowing And Lending In Capital Budgeting: A Comment," JBFA, 1980, v7(3), 489-500.

Bernhard, Richard H. "Mathematical Programming Models For Capital Budgeting -- A Survey, Generalization, And Critique," JFQA, 1969, v4(2), 111-158.

Bernhard, Richard H. "Risk-Adjusted Values, Timing Of Uncertainty Resolution, And The Measurement Of Project Worth," JFQA, 1984, v19(1), 83-99.

Bernhard, Richard H. "Some New Capital Budgeting Theorems: Comment," JFQA, 1978, v13(5), 825-829.

Bernhard, Richard H. "Unrecovered Investment, Uniqueness Of The Internal Rate, And The Question Of Project Acceptability," JFQA, 1977, v12(1), 33-38.

Bernstein, David. (Melvin, Michael and David Bernstein. "Trade Concentration, Openness, And Deviations From Purchasing Power Parity," JIMF, 1984, v3(3), 369-376.)

Bernstein, E. M. "General Problems Of Financing Development Programs," JOF, 1957, v12(2), 167-177.

Bernstein, Edward. "Domestic And International Objectives Of United States Monetary Policy," JOF, 1963, v18(2), 161-173.

Bernstein, George K. "Critical Evaluation Of FAIR Plans," JRI, 1971, v38(2), 269-276.

Bernstein, Leonard. "Commodities: High Finance In Eggs," FAJ, 1960, v16(2), 93-96.

Bernstein, Leopold A. and Joel G. Siegel. "The Concept Of Earnings Quality," FAJ, 1979, v35(4), 72-75.

Bernstein, Leopold A. and Mostafa M. Maksy. "Again Now: How Do We Measure Cash Flow From Operations?," FAJ, 1985, v41(4), 74-77.

Bernstein, Leopold A. "Extraordinary Gains And Losses," FAJ, 1972, v28(6), 49-52,88-89.

Bernstein, Leopold A. "In Defense Of Fundamental Analysis," FAJ, 1975, v31(1), 56-61.

Bernstein, Leopold A. "Reserves For Future Costs And Losses," FAJ, 1970, v26(1), 45-48.

Bernstein, Merton C. "The Future Of Private Pension Plans," JRI, 1967, v34(1), 15-26.

Bernstein, Peter L. "Efficiency And Opportunity," JPM, 1977, v4(1), 4.

Bernstein, Peter L. "How I Came To Be The Oldest Man Around," JPM, 1979, v6(1), 47-48.

Bernstein, Peter L. "How To Take Reinvestment Risk Without Really Trying," JPM, 1984, v10(3), 4.

Bernstein, Peter L. "Liquidity, Stock Markets, And Market Makers," FM, 1987, v16(2), 54-62.

Bernstein, Peter L. "Markowitz Marked To Market," FAJ, 1983, v39(1), 18-22.

Bernstein, Peter L. "Reply: The Gibson Paradox Revisited," FR, 1983, v18(2), 218-219.

Bernstein, Peter L. "Surprising The Smoothies," JPM, 1984, v11(1), 7-11.

Bernstein, Peter L. "The Coming Labor Glut," FAJ, 1970, v26(6), 12-18.

Bernstein, Peter L. "The Gibson Paradox Revisited," FR, 1982, v17(3), 153-164.

Bernstein, Peter L. "The Wedge Theory: Pie In The Sky?," FAJ, 1979, v35(2), 63-67.

Bernstein, Peter L. "What Rate Of Return Can You 'Reasonably' Expect," JOF, 1973, v28(2), 273-282.

Bernstein, Peter L. (Alhadeff, D., P. Bernstein, C. Campbell, L. Chandler, E. Ettin, V. Farhi, J. Guttentag, H. Latane and K. Poole. "The Commission On Money And Credit's Research Studies," JOF, 1964, v19(3), 497-533.)

Berolzheimer, Howard, Edwin A. Gaumnitz, C. M. Kahler and Joseph Pillion. "Round Table Discussion: The Objectives And Content Of The Survey Course In Insurance," JRI, 1941, v8, 5-38.

Berridge, William A. "Economic Facts Bearing On Some 'Variable Annuity' Arguments: With Special Reference To Cyclical Price Fluctuations In Common-Stock And Consumer-Goods Markets," JRI, 1957, v24(2), 71-87.

Berridge, William A. "Economic Research As An Aid To Management Planning: A Case Study Of One Life Insurance Company," JRI, 1957, v24(3), 56-69.

Berry, Michael A. (Young, S. David, Michael A. Berry, David W. Harvey and John R. Page. "Systematic Risk And Accounting Information Under The Arbitrage Pricing Theory," FAJ, 1987, v43(5), 73-76.)

Berry, Michael A., Edwin Burmeister and Marjorie B. McElroy. "Sorting Out Risks Using Known APT Factors," FAJ, 1988, v44(2), 29-42.

Berry, R. H. and R. G. Dyson. "On The Negative Risk Premium For Risk Adjusted Discount Rates: A Reply And Extension," JBFA, 1984, v11(2), 263-268.

Berry, R. H. and R. G. Dyson. "A Mathematical Programming Approach To Taxation Induced Interdependencies In Investment Appraisal," JBFA, 1979, v6(4), 425-442.

Berry, R. H. and R. G. Dyson. "On The Negative Risk Premium For Risk Adjusted Discount Rates," JBFA, 1980, v7(3), 427-436.

Berry, R. H. (Dyson, R. G. and R. H. Berry. "On The Negative Risk Premium For Risk Adjusted Discount Rates: A Reply," JBFA, 1983, v10(1), 157-159.)

Berry, Robert. (Niskanen, William and Robert Berry. "The 1973 Economic Report Of The President," JMCB, 1973, v5(2), 693-703.)

Berry, S. Keith. "Flotation Cost Allowance Methodologies: A Synthesis Using Present Value Analysis," FR, 1990, v25(3), 487-500.

Berry, Thomas D. and William M. Poppei. "An Alternative Methodology For Developing Certainty Equivalents," JFED, 1983, v12, 51-53.

Berry, Thomas D. and Adam K. Gehr, Jr. "FNMA Mortgage Purchase Commitments As Put Options: An Empirical Examination," AREUEA, 1985, v13(1), 93-105.

Berry, Thomas D. and Edward J. Farragher. "A Survey Of Introductory Financial Management Courses," JFED, 1987, v16, 65-72.

Berry, Thomas. (Gehr, Adam K., Jr. and Thomas Berry. "FNMA Auction Results As A Forecaster Of Residential Mortgage Yields: A Comment," JMCB, 1983, v15(1), 116-119.)

Bertin, William J. "Money, Mobility, And Motivation In The Academic Finance Labor Market," FR, 1983, v18(4), 336-341.

Bertin, William J. (Torabzadeh, Khalil M. and William J. Bertin. "Leveraged Buyouts And Shareholder Returns," JFR, 1987, v10(4), 313-320.)

Bertin, William J. and Terry L. Zivney. "The New Hire Market For Finance: Productivity, Salaries And Other Market Factors," FPE, 1991, v1(1), 25-34.

Bertin, William J., Farrokh Ghazanfari and Khalil M. Torabzadeh. "Failed Bank Acquisitions And Successful Bidders' Returns," FM, 1989, v18(2), 93-100.

Bertoneche, Marc L. "An Empirical Analysis Of The Interrelationships Among Equity Markets Under Changing Exchange Rate Systems," JBF, 1979, v3(4), 397-405.

Bertoneche, Marc L. "Spectral Analysis Of Stock Market Prices," JBF, 1979, v3(2), 201-208.

Bertrand, Robert J. "Insurer Views On Property And Liability Insurance Rate Regulation: Comment," JRI, 1969, v36(2), 237-238.

Besley, Scott and Jerome S. Osteryoung. "Survey Of Current Practices In Establishing Trade-Credit Limits," FR, 1985, v20(1), 71-82.

Besley, Scott. (Bolten, Steven E. and Scott Besley. "Long-Term Asset Allocation Under Dynamic Interaction Of Earnings And Interest Rates," FR, 1991, v26(2), 269-274.)

Besley, Scott. (Meyer, Richard L., Scott Besley and James R. Longstreet. "An Examination Of Capital Budgeting Decision Alternatives For Mutually Exclusive Investments With Unequal Lives," JBFA, 1988, v15(3), 415-426.)

Bessler, David A. (Kling, John L. and David A. Bessler. "Calibration-Based Predictive Distributions: An Application Of Prequential Analysis To Interest Rates, Money, Prices, And Output," JOB, 1989, v62(4), 477-500.)

Best, Michael J. and Robert R. Grauer. "Capital Asset Pricing Compatible With Observed Market Value Weights," JOF, 1985, v40(1), 85-103.

Best, Paul J. "Some Notes On The Soviet Foreign Insurance System," JRI, 1967, v34(3), 445-450.

Best, Roger. (Hawkins, Del I., Gerald Albaum and Roger Best. "An Investigation Of Two Issues In The Use Of Students As Surrogates For Housewives In Consumer Behavior Studies," JOB, 1977, v50(2),216-221.)

Bethke, William M. and Susan E. Boyd. "Should Dividend Discount Models Be Yield-Tilted?," JPM, 1983, v9(3), 23-27.

Bethke, William M. "The Flat Glass Industry," FAJ, 1973, v29(1), 41-47,92.

Bettman, James R. and J. Morgan Jones. "Formal Models Of Consumer Behavior: A Conceptual Overview," JOB, 1972, v45(4), 544-562.

Betts, J. and D. Belhoul. "The Effectiveness Of Incorporating Stability Measures In Company Failure Models," JBFA, 1987, v14(3), 323-334.

Beveridge, Stephen and Rolf Mirus. "An Empirical Evaluation Of The Rationality Of Eurocurrency Market Expectations," JBF, 1978, v2(2), 133-141.

Bey, Roger P. and George E. Pinches. "Additional Evidence Of Heteroscedasticity In The Market Model," JFQA, 1980, v15(2), 299-322.

Bey, Roger P. and Keith M. Howe. "Gini's Mean Difference And Portfolio Selection: An Empirical Evaluation," JFQA, 1984, v19(3), 329-338.

Bey, Roger P. "Calculating Means And Variances Of NPVs When The Life Of The Project Is Uncertain," JFR, 1980, v3(2), 139-152.

Bey, Roger P. "Capital Budgeting Decisions When Cash Flows And Project Lives Are Stochastic And Dependent," JFR, 1983, v6(3), 175-185.

Bey, Roger P. "Estimating The Optimal Stochastic Dominance Efficient Set With A Mean-Semivariance Algorithm," JFQA, 1979, v14(5), 1059-1070.

Bey, Roger P. "Market Model Stationarity Of Individual Public Utilities," JFQA, 1983, v18(1),67-85.

Bey, Roger P. "Mean-Variance, Mean-Semivariance, And DCF Estimates Of A Public Utility's Cost Of Equity," JFR, 1979, v2(1), 13-26.

Bey, Roger P. "The Market Model As An Appropriate Description Of The Stochastic Process Generating Security Returns," JFR, 1983, v6(4), 275-288.

Bey, Roger P. (Burgess, Richard C. and Roger P. Bey. "Optimal Portfolios: Markowitz Full Covariance Versus Simple Selection Rules," JFR, 1988, v11(2), 153-164.)

Bey, Roger P. (Collins, J. Markham and Roger P. Bey. "The Master Limited Partnership: An Alternative To The Corporation," FM, 1986, v15(4), 5-14.)

Bey, Roger P. (Porter, R. Burr, Roger P. Bey and David C. Lewis. "The Development Of A Mean-Semivariance Approach To Capital Budgeting," JFQA, 1975, v10(4), 639-649.)

Bey, Roger P. (Porter, R. Burr and Roger P. Bey. "An Evaluation Of The Empirical Significance Of Optimal Seeking Algorithms In Portfolio Selection," JOF, 1974, v29(5), 1479-1490.)

Bey, Roger P. and J. Markham Collins. "The Relationship Between Before- And After-Tax Yields On Financial Assets," FR, 1988, v23(3), 313-332.

Bey, Roger P. and Larry J. Johnson. "The Impact Of Taxes On Discount Bond Valuation And Risk," FR, 1989, v24(4), 589-598.

Bey, Roger P., Richard C. Burgess and Richard B. Kearns. "Moving Stochastic Dominance: An Alternative Method For Testing Market Efficiency," JFR, 1984, v7(3), 185-196.

Beyer, Gerald D. and Gary J. Greenspan. "The AuCoin Amendment: Is It Sensible? Should It Be Repealed?," JFM, v1(Supp), 479-481.

Bhagat, Sanjai and Peter A. Frost. "Issuing Costs To Existing Shareholders In Competitive And Negotiated Underwritten Public Utility Equity Offerings," JFEC, 1986, v15(1/2), 233-260.

Bhagat, Sanjai, James A. Brickley and Ronald C. Lease. "The Authorization Of Additional Common Stock: An Empirical Investigation," FM, 1986, v15(3), 45-53.

Bhagat, Sanjai, James A. Brickley and Ronald C. Lease. "Incentive Effects Of Stock Purchase Plans," JFEC, 1985, v14(2), 195-216.

Bhagat, Sanjai, M. Wayne Marr and G. Rodney Thompson. "The Rule 415 Experiment: Equity Markets," JOF, 1985, v40(5), 1385-1401.

Bhagat, Sanjai, James A. Brickley and Uri Loewenstein. "The Pricing Effects Of Interfirm Cash Tender Offers," JOF, 1987, v42(4), 965-986.

Bhagat, Sanjai, James A. Brickley and Jeffrey L. Coles. "Managerial Indemnification And Liability Insurance: The Effect On Sharholder Wealth," JRI, 1987, v54(4), 721-736.

Bhagat, Sanjai. "The Effect Of Management's Choice Between Negotiated And Competitive Equity Offerings On Shareholder Wealth," JFQA, 1986, v21(2), 181-196.

Bhagat, Sanjai. "The Effect Of Pre-Emptive Right Amendments On Shareholder Wealth," JFEC, 1983, v12(3), 289-310.

Bhagat, Sanjai. (Hess, Alan C. and Sanjai Bhagat. "Size Effects Of Seasoned Stock Issues: Empirical Evidence," JOB, 1986, v59(4), Part 1, 567-584.)

Bhandari, Arvind, Theoharry Grammatikos, Anil K. Makhija and George Papaioannou. "Risk And Return On Newly Listed Stocks: The Post-Listing Experience," JFR, 1989, v12(2), 93-102.

Bhandari, Jagdeep S. "Informational Efficiency And The Open Economy," JMCB, 1982, v14(4), Part 1, 457-478.

Bhandari, Jagdeep S. "Staggered Wage Setting And Exchange Rate Policy In An Economy With Capital Assets," JIMF, 1982, v1(3), 275-292.

Bhandari, Jagdeep S. "The Flexible Exchange Basket: A Macroeconomic Analysis," JIMF, 1985, v4(1), 19-41.

Bhandari, Jagdeep S. "World Trade Patterns, Economic Disturbances, And Exchange-Rate Management," JIMF, 1985, v4(3), 331-360.

Bhandari, Jagdeep S. (Turnovsky, Stephen J. and Jagdeep S. Bhandari. "The Degree Of Capital Mobility And The Stability Of An Open Economy Under Rational Expectations," JMCB, 1982, v14(3), 303-326.)

Bhandari, Laxmi Chand. "Debt/Equity Ratio And Expected Common Stock Returns: Empirical Evidence," JOF, 1988, v43(2), 507-528.

Bhandari, Shyam B. "Compounding/Discounting Of Intrayear Cash Flows: Principles, Pedogogy, And Practices," FPE, 1991, v1(1), 87-89.

Bhandari, Shyam B., Robert M. Soldofsky and Warren J. Boe. "Bond Quality Rating Changes For Electric Utilities: A Multivariate Analysis," FM, 1979, v8(1),74-81.

Bhaskar, K. N. "Borrowing And Lending In A Mathematical Programming Model Of Capital Budgeting," JBFA, 1974, v1(2), 267-291.

Bhaskar, K. N. "Linear Programming And Capital Budgeting: A Reappraisal," JBFA, 1976, v3(3), 29-40.

Bhaskar, Krish and Patrick McNamee. "Multiple Objectives In Accounting And Finance," JBFA, 1983, v10(4), 595-621.

Bhaskar, Krish N. "Bhaskar's Mathematical Programming Models For Borrowing And Lending In Capital Budgeting: A Reply," JBFA, 1980, v7(3), 501-512.

Bhaskar, Krish. "Linear Programming And Capital Budgeting: The Financing Problem," JBFA, 1978, v5(2), 159-194.

Bhatt, Swati and Nusret Cakici. "Premiums On Stock Index Futures - Some Evidence," JFM, 1990, v10(4), 367-376.

Bhattacharya, Anand K. "Option Expirations And Treasury Bond Futures Prices," JFM, 1987, v7(1),49-64.

Bhattacharya, Anand K. "Synthetic Asset Swaps," JPM, 1990, v17(1), 56-65.

Bhattacharya, Anand K. "The Joint Effect Of Housing Start And Inflation Announcements On GNMA Futures Prices," JFM, 1986, v6(4), 645-658.

Bhattacharya, Anand K., Anju Ramjee and Balasubramani Ramjee. "The Causal Relationship Between Futures Price Volatility And The Cash Price Volatility Of GNMA Securities," JFM, 1986, v6(1), 29-40.

Bhattacharya, Mihir. "Empirical Properties Of The Black-Scholes Formula Under Ideal Conditions," JFQA, 1980, v15(5), 1081-1105.

Bhattacharya, Mihir. "Price Changes Of Related Securities: The Case Of Call Options And Stocks," JFQA, 1987, v22(1), 1-16.

Bhattacharya, Mihir. "Transactions Data Tests Of Efficiency Of The Chicago Board Options Exchange," JFEC, 1983, v12(2), 161-186.

Bhattacharya, Sudipto. "Aspects Of Monetary And Banking Theory And Moral Hazard," JOF, 1982, v37(2), 371-384.

Bhattacharya, Sudipto. "Notes On Multiperiod Valuation And The Pricing Of Options," JOF, 1981, v36(1), 163-180.

Bhattacharya, Sudipto. "Notes On Multiperiod Valuation And The Pricing Of Options: A Reply," JOF, 1984, v39(1), 309-312.

Bhattacharya, Sudipto. "Project Valuation With Mean-Reverting Cash Flow Streams," JOF, 1978, v33(5), 1317-1331.

Bhattacharya, Sudipto. "Welfare And Savings Effects Of Indexation," JMCB, 1979, v11(2), 192-201.

Bhattacharya, Sudipto. (Admati, Anat R., Sudipto Bhattacharya, Paul Pfleiderer and Stephen A. Ross. "On Timing And Selectivity," JOF, 1986, v41(3), 715-729.)

Bhattacharya, Sudipto. (Mason, Scott P. and Sudipto Bhattacharya. "Risky Debt, Jump Processes, And Safety Covenants," JFEC, 1981, v9(3), 281-307.)

Bhide, Amar. "Reversing Corporate Diversification," JACF, 1990, v3(2), 70-81.

Bhide, Amar. "The Causes And Consequences Of Hostile Takeovers," JACF, 1989, v2(2), 36-59.

Bhirud, S. L. (Baylis, R. M. and S. L. Bhirud. "Growth Stock Analysis: A New Approach," FAJ, 1973, v29(4), 63-70.)

Bhirud, Suresh L. "Market Valuation And Investment Strategy," JPM, 1975, v2(1), 22-29.

Bhoocha-Oom, Areepong and Stanley R. Stansell. "A Study Of International Financial Market Integration: An Examination Of The US, Hong Kong And Singapore Markets," JBFA, 1990, v17(2), 193-212.

Bi, Keqian. (Crum, Roy L. and Keqian Bi. "An Observation Of Estimating The Systematic Risk Of An Industry Segment," FM, 1988, v17(1), 60-62.)

Bible, Douglas S. "Rehabilitation Tax Credits And Rate Of Return On Real Estate Under Recent Tax Reform Measures," JRER, 1987, v2(2), 55-61.

Bible, Douglas S. and Stephen E. Celec. "Real Estate Investment Analysis: New Developments In Traditional Leverage Concepts," AREUEA, 1980, v8(2), 198-206.

Bible, Thomas. (Berck, Peter and Thomas Bible. "Wood Products Futures Markets And The Reservation Price Of Timber," JFM, 1985, v5(3), 311-316.)

Bick, Avi. "Comments On The Valuation Of Derivative Assets," JFEC, 1982, v10(3), 331-345.

Bick, Avi. "On The Consistency Of The Black-Scholes Model With A General Equilibrium Framework," JFQA, 1987, v22(3), 259-276.

Bick, Avi. "On Viable Diffusion Price Processes Of The Market Portfolio," JOF, 1990, v45(2), 673-690.

Bick, Avi. "Producing Derivative Assets With Forward Contracts," JFQA, 1988, v23(2), 153-160.

Bickelhaupt, David L. "Insurance And The European Common Market: Faction, Fiction Or Fancy?," JRI, 1964, v31(1), 13-26.

Bickelhaupt, David L. "Rx For Rational Responsibility," JRI, 1974, v41(1), 1-8.

Bickelhaupt, David L. (Bar-Niv, Ran and David L. Bickelhaupt. "Research In International Risk And Insurance: Summary, Synthesis, And Prospects," JRI, 1986, v53(1), 119-134.)

Bickelhaupt, David L. (Smith, Michael L. and David L. Bickelhaupt. "Is Coinsurance Becoming Obsolete?," JRI, 1981, v48(1), 95-110.)

Bickley, John H. "Public Utility Stability And Risk," JRI, 1959, v26(2), 35-58.

Bickley, John H. "The Nature Of Business Risk," JRI, 1958, v25(4), 32-42.

Bickley, John S. "An Overview Of Insurance Marketing," JRI, 1967, v34(2), 175-183.

Bickley, John S. "Research In Insurance," JRI, 1954, v21, 37-42.

Bickley, John S. "The Nature And Methodology Of The Insurance Survey Course," JRI, 1954, v21, 114-117.

Bicksler, J. L. "The State Of The Finance Field: A Further Comment," JOF, 1972, v27(4), 917-918.

Bicksler, J. L. (Hess, P. J. and J. L. Bicksler. "Capital Asset Prices Versus Time Series Models As Predictors Of Inflation: The Expected Real Rate Of Interest And Market Efficiency," JFEC, 1975, v2(4), 341-360.)

Bicksler, James and Andrew H. Chen. "An Economic Analysis Of Interest Rate Swaps," JOF, 1986, v41(3), 645-656.

Bicksler, James L. and Andrew H. Chen. "The Integration Of Insurance And Taxes In Corporate Pension Strategy," JOF, 1985, v40(3), 943-955.

Bicksler, James L. and Edward O. Thorp. "The Capital Growth Model: An Empirical Investigation," JFQA, 1973, v8(2), 273-287.

Bicksler, James L. and Pat J. Hess. "More On Purchasing Power Risk, Portfolio Analysis, And The Case For Index-Linked Bonds: A Comment," JMCB, 1976, v8(2), 265-266.

Bicksler, James and Patrick J. Hess. "A Note On The Profits And Riskiness Of Defense Contractors," JOB, 1976, v49(4), 555-557.

Biderman, Roger. (Soldofsky, Robert M. and Roger Biderman. "Yield-Risk Measurements Of The Performance Of Common Stocks," JFQA, 1968, v3(1), 59-74.)

Bidwell, Clinton M. "Oral Classroom Examinations," JFED, 1977, v6, 33-35.

Bidwell, Clinton M. (Maupin,R.,C. Bidwell and A. Ortegren. "An Empirical Investigation Of The Characteristics Of Publicly-Quoted Corporations Which Change To Closely-Held Ownership," JBFA, 1984, v11(4), 435-450.)

Bidwell, Clinton M., III and Robert W. Kolb. "The Impact And Value Of Broker's Sell Recommendations," FR, 1980, v15(3), 58-68.

Bidwell, Clinton M., III. "A Test Of Market Efficiency: SUE/PE," JPM, 1979, v5(4), 53-58.

Bidwell, Clinton M., III. "How Good Is Institutional Brokerage Research?," JPM, 1977, v3(2), 26-31.

Bidwell, Clinton M., III. "SUE/PE Revista," JPM, 1981, v7(2), 85-88.

Bidwell, Peter T. (Liebling, Herman, Peter T. Bidwell and Karen E. Hall. "The Recent Performance Of Anticipation Surveys And Econometric Model Projections Of Investment Spending In The United States," JOB, 1976, v49(4),451-477.)

Biederman, Kenneth R., John A. Tuccillo and George J. Viksnins. "An Analysis Of The Mortgage Tax Credit Provision Of The Financial Institutions Act," JBR, 1975-76, v6(2), 100-108.

Bielaski, A. Bruce. "The Risk Of Arson," JRI, 1942, v9, 29-38.

Bieri, H. G. "Karl Brunner As Seen By One Of His Friends From The Old Days," JMCB, 1977, v9(1), Part 2, 243-245.

Bierman, H., K. Chopra and J. Thomas. "Ruin Considerations: Optimal Working Capital And Capital Structure," JFQA, 1975, v10(1), 119-128.

Bierman, Harold and Seymour Smidt. "Capital Budgeting And The Problem Of Reinvesting Cash Proceeds," JOB, 1957, v30(4), 276-279.

Bierman, Harold, Jr. and Amir Barnea. "Expected Short-Term Interest Rates In Bond Refunding," FM, 1974, v3(1), 75-79.

Bierman, Harold, Jr. and George S. Oldfield, Jr. Corporate Debt And Corporate Taxes," JOF, 1979, v34(4), 951-956.

Bierman, Harold, Jr. and Jerome E. Hass. "An Analytical Model Of Bond Risk Differentials: A Reply," JFQA, 1978, v13(2), 379-381.

Bierman, Harold, Jr. and Jerome E. Hass. "Capital Budgeting Under Uncertainty: A Reformation: Reply," JOF, 1974, v29(5), 1585.

Bierman, Harold, Jr. and Jerome Hass. "Normative Stock Price Models," JFQA, 1971, v6(4), 1135-1144.

Bierman, Harold, Jr. and Jerome E. Hass. "Capital Budgeting Under Uncertainty: A Reformulation," JOF, 1973, v28(1), 119-129.

Bierman, Harold, Jr. and Jerome E. Hass. "An Analytical Model Of Bond Risk Differentials," JFQA, 1975, v10(5), 757-773.

Bierman, Harold, Jr. and Jerome E. Hass. "Investment Cut-Off Rates And Dividend Policy," FM, 1983, v12(4), 19-24.

Bierman, Harold, Jr. and L. Joseph Thomas. "Ruin Considerations And Debt Issuance," JFQA, 1972, v7(1), 1361-1378.

Bierman, Harold, Jr. and Richard West. "The Effect Of Share Repurchase On The Value Of The Firm: Some Further Comments," JOF, 1968, v23(5), 865-869.

Bierman, Harold, Jr. and Richard West. "The Acquisition Of Common Stock By The Corporate Issuer," JOF, 1966, v21(4), 687-696.

Bierman, Harold, Jr. and Seymour Smidt. "Application Of The Capital Asset Pricing Model To Multi-Period Investments," JBFA, 1975, v2(3), 327-340.

Bierman, Harold, Jr. and Vithala R. Rao. "Investment Decisions With Sampling," FM, 1978, v7(3), 19-24.

Bierman, Harold, Jr. "A Comment On Optimizing Municipal Bond Bids," JBR, 1983-84, v14(2), 173-174.

Bierman, Harold, Jr. "A Neglected Tax Incentive For Mergers," FM, 1985, v14(2), 29-32.

Bierman, Harold, Jr. "A Reconciliation Of Present Value Capital Budgeting And Accounting," FM, 1977, v6(2), 52-54.

Bierman, Harold, Jr. "Alternative Debt Bids By State And Local Governments," FM, 1972, v1(3), 51-54.

Bierman, Harold, Jr. "Analysis Of The Lease-Or-Buy Decision: Comment," JOF, 1973, v28(4), 1019-1021.

Bierman, Harold, Jr. "Buy Versus Leave With An Alternative Minimum Tax," FM, 1988, v17(4), 87-91.

Bierman, Harold, Jr. "Convertible Bonds As Investments," FAJ, 1980, v36(2), 59-61.

Bierman, Harold, Jr. "Deferred Taxes, Income And The 1986 Tax Reform Act," FAJ, 1987, v43(3), 72-73.

Bierman, Harold, Jr. "Defining And Evaluating Portfolio Insurance Strategies," FAJ, 1988, v44(3), 84-87.

Bierman, Harold, Jr. "Diversification: Is There Safety In Numbers?," JPM, 1978, v5(1), 29-32.

Bierman, Harold, Jr. "How Much Diversification Is Desirable?," JPM, 1980, v7(1), 42-44.

Bierman, Harold, Jr. "Inflation, Exchange Rates, And Investment In Common Stock," JPM, 1990, v17(1), 74-77.

Bierman, Harold, Jr. "Investing In Junk Bonds," JPM, 1990, v16(2), 60-62.

Bierman, Harold, Jr. "Risk And The Addition Of Debt To The Capital Structure," JFQA, 1968, v3(4),415-426.

Bierman, Harold, Jr. "The Cost Of Warrants," JFQA, 1973, v8(3), 499-503.

Bierman, Harold, Jr. "The Dow Jones Industrials: Do You Get What You See?," JPM, 1988, v15(1), 58-63.

Bierman, Harold, Jr. "The Valuation Of Stock Options: Reply," JFQA, 1968, v3(2), 227-228.

Bierman, Harold, Jr. "The Valuation Of Stock Options," JFQA, 1967, v2(3), 327-334.

Bierman, Harold, Jr. "Total Stock Market Value With Reciprocal Ownership: A Note On The Japanese Situation," FAJ, 1990, v46(1), 77.

Bierman, Harold, Jr. "Toward A Constant Price-Earnings Ratio," FAJ, 1982, v38(5), 62-65.

Bierman, Harold, Jr. "Using Investment Portfolios To Change Risk," JFQA, 1968, v3(2), 151-156.

Bierman, Harold, Jr. (Alderfer, Clayton P. and Harold Bierman, Jr. "Choices With Risk: Beyond The Mean And Variance," JOB, 1970, v43(3), 341-353.)

Bierman, Harold, Jr. (West, Richard R. and Harold Bierman, Jr. "Corporate Dividend Policy And Preemptive Security Issues," JOB, 1968, v41(1), 71-75.)

Bierman, Harold, Jr., David H. Downes and Jerome E. Hass. "Closed-Form Stock Price Models," JFQA, 1972, v7(3), 1797-1808.

Bierman, Harold. "The Bond Issue Size Decision," JFQA, 1966, v1(4), 1-14.

Bierman, Harold. "The Bond Refunding Decision," FM, 1972, v1(2), 27-29.

Bierwag, G. O. and Chulsoon Khang. "An Immunization Strategy Is A Minimax Strategy," JOF, 1979, v34(2), 389-399.

Bierwag, G. O. and George G. Kaufman. "Duration Gap For Financial Institutions," FAJ, 1985, v41(2), 68-71.

Bierwag, G. O. and George Kaufman. "Bond Portfolio Strategy Simulations: A Critique," JFQA, 1978, v13(3), 519-525.

Bierwag, G. O. and M. A. Grove. "On Capital Asset Prices: Comment," JOF, 1965, v20(1), 89-93.

Bierwag, G. O. and M. A. Grove. "A Model Of The Structure Of Prices Of Marketable U.S. Treasury Securities," JMCB, 1971, v3(3), 605-629.

Bierwag, G. O. "Dynamic Portfolio Immunization Policies," JBF, 1979, v3(1), 23-41.

Bierwag, G. O. "Immunization, Duration, And The Term Structure Of Interest Rates," JFQA, 1977, v12(5), 725-741.

Bierwag, G. O. and George G. Kaufman. "Coping With The Risk Of Interest-Rate Fluctuations: A Note," JOB, 1977, v50(3), 364-370.

Bierwag, G. O. and George G. Kaufman. "Durations Of Non-Default-Free Securities," FAJ, 1988, v44(4), 39-46.

Bierwag, G. O. and Gordon S. Roberts. "Single-Factor Duration Models: Canadian Tests," JFR, 1990, v13(1), 23-38.

Bierwag, G. O., G. G. Kaufman, R. Schweitzer and A. Toevs. "The Art Of Risk Management In Bond Portfolios," JPM, 1981, v7(3), 27-36.

Bierwag, G. O., George G. Kaufman and Alden Toevs. "Immunization Strategies For Funding Multiple Liabilities," JFQA, 1983, v18(1), 113-123.

Bierwag, G. O., George G. Kaufman and Paul H. Leonard. "Interest Rate Effects Of Commercial Bank Underwriting Of Municipal Revenue Bonds: Additional Evidence," JBF, 1984, v8(1), 35-50.

Bierwag, G. O., George G. Kaufman and Chulsoon Khang. "Duration And Bond Portfolio Analysis: An Overview," JFQA, 1978, v13(4), 671-681.

Bierwag, G. O., George G. Kaufman and Aldan Toevs. "Bond Portfolio Immunization And Stochastic Process Risk," JBR, 1982-83, v13(4), 282-291.

Bierwag, G. O., George G. Kaufman and Alden Toevs. "Duration: Its Development And Uses In Bond Portfolio Management," FAJ, 1983, v39(4), 15-35.

Bierwag, G. O., George G. Kaufman and Cynthia M. Latta. "Duration Models: A Taxonomy," JPM, 1988, v15(1), 50-54.

Bierwag, G. O., George G. Kaufman, Cynthia M. Latta and Gordon S. Roberts. "The Usefulness Of Duration: Response To Critics" JPM, 1987, v13(2), 48-52.

Bierwag, G. O., George G. Kaufman and Cynthia M. Latta. "Bond Portfolio Immunization: Tests Of Maturity, One- And Two-Factor Duration Matching Strategies," FR, 1987, v22(2), 203-220.

Bierwag, Gerald O. "Bond Returns, Discrete Stochastic Processes, And Duration," JFR, 1987, v10(3), 191-210.

Bierwag, Gerald O., Charles J. Corrado and George C. Kaufman. "Computing Durations For Bond Portfolios," JPM, 1990, v17(1), 51-55.

Bierwag, G. O., George G. Kaufman and Alden L. Toevs. "Single Factor Duration Models In A Discrete General Equilibrium Framework," JOF, 1982, v37(2), 325-338.

Biger, Nahum and John Hull. "The Valuation of Currency Options," FM, 1983, v12(1), 24-28.

Biger, Nahum and Ronen Israel. "A Note On The Pricing Of Double Choice Bonds," JBF, 1989, v13(2), 181-190.

Biger, Nahum and Yehuda Kahane. "Purchasing Power Risk And The Performance Of Non Life Insurance Companies," JRI, 1976, v43(2), 243-256.

Biger, Nahum. "Portfolio Selection And Purchasing Power Risk--Recent Canadian Experience," JFQA, 1976, v11(2), 251-267.

Biger, Nahum. "The Assessment Of Inflation And Portfolio Selection," JOF, 1975, v30(2), 451-467.

Biger, Nahum. (Baesel, Jerome B. and Nahum Biger. "Inflation And Pension Plan Linkage Of Benefits To The Cost Of Living Index," FR, 1976, v11(1),59-68.)

Biger, Nahum. (Baesel, Jerome B. and Nahum Biger. "The Allocation Of Risk: Some Implications Of Fixed Versus Index-Linked Mortgages," JPM, 1980, v15(2), 457-468.)

Biggar, G. Gordon, Jr. (Buff, Jerome H., G. Gordon Biggar, Jr. and J. Gary Burkhead. "Decision Analysis Techniques," FAJ, 1968, v24(6), 123-128.)

Biggs, Barton M. "Christmas Is Coming," FAJ, 1965, v21(6), 82-84.

Biggs, Barton M. "New Print-Out Horizons," FAJ, 1967, v23(1), 75-80.

Biggs, Barton M. "The Outlook For Sulphur," FAJ, 1964, v20(6), 49-52.

Biggs, Barton M. "The Outlook For The Cigarette Industry," FAJ, 1965, v21(3), 73-78.

Biggs, Barton M. "The Short Interest - A False Proverb," FAJ, 1966, v22(4), 111-116.

Biggs, Robert M. "Income At Product And Factor Prices," JOF, 1953, v8(1), 47-54.

Bigman, David and David Goldfarb. "Efficiency And Efficient Trading Rules For Food And Feed Grains In The World Commodity Markets: The Israeli Experience," JPM, 1985, v5(1), 1-10.

Bigman, David, David Goldfarb and Edna Schechtman. "Futures Market Efficiency And The Time Content Of The Information Sets," JFM, 1983, v3(3), 321-334.

Bigman, David. "Semi-Rational Expectations And Exchange-Rate Dynamics," JIMF, 1984, v3(1), 51-66.

Bigus, A. W. "Foreign Investment Potential - Mexico," FAJ, 1964, v20(6), 99-104.

Bigus, Anatol W. "Managing Portfolios With Graham & Dodd," JPM, 1977, v3(3), 58-62.

Bikhchandani, Sushil and Chi-Fu Huang. "Auctions With Resale Markets: An Exploratory Model Of Treasury Bill Markets," RFS, 1989, v2(3), 311-340.

Bildersee, John S. and Gordon S. Roberts. "Beta Instability When Interest Rate Levels Change," JPM, 1981, v16(3), 375-380.

Bildersee, John S. "Bid-Ask Price Spreads In The Agency Bond Market," JMCB, 1979, v11(2), 209-213.

Bildersee, John S. "Price Spreads, Performance, And The Seasoning Of New Treasury And Agency Bond Issues," JFQA, 1977, v12(3), 433-455.

Bildersee, John S. "Some Aspects Of The Performance Of Non-Convertible Preferred Stocks," JOF, 1973, v28(5), 1187-1201.

Bildersee, John S. "Some New Bond Indexes," JOB, 1975, v48(4), 506-525.

Bildersee, John S. "U.S. Government And Agency Securities: An Analysis Of Yield Spreads And Performance," JOB, 1978, v51(3), 499-520.

Billingham, Carol J. "Strategies For Enhancing Bond Portfolio Returns," FAJ, 1983, v39(3),50-56.

Billings, C. David and John B. Legler. "Financing Equal Educational Opportunity," FR, 1972, v2(2), 122-133.

Billingsley, Randall S. and Don M. Chance. "Options Market Efficiency And The Box Spread Strategy," FR, 1985, v20(4), 287-301.

Billingsley, Randall S. and Robert E. Lamy. "Market Reaction To The Formation Of One-Bank Holding Companies And The 1970 Bank Holding Company Act Amendment," JBF, 1984, v8(1), 21-33.

Billingsley, Randall S. and G. Rodney Thompson. "Determinants Of Stock Repurchases By Bank Holding Companies," JBR, 1985-86, v16(3), 128-135.

Billingsley, Randall S. and Donald R. Fraser. "Determinants Of Bank Holding Company Debt Ratings," FR, 1984, v19(1), 55-66.

Billingsley, Randall S. and Robert E. Lamy. "The Regulation Of International Lending: IMF Support, The Debt Crisis, And Bank Stockholder Wealth," JBF, 1988, v12(2), 255-274.

Billingsley, Randall S. and Don M. Chance. "The Pricing And Performance Of Stock Index Futures Spreads," JFM, 1988, v8(3), 303-318.

Billingsley, Randall S. and Don M. Chance. "Put-Call Ratios And Market Timing Effectiveness," JPM, 1988, v15(1), 25-28.

Billingsley, Randall S., Robert E. Lamy and G. Rodney Thompson. "Valuation Of Primary Issue Convertible Bonds," JFR, 1986, v9(3), 251-260.

Billingsley, Randall S., Robert E. Lamy, M. Wayne Marr and G. Rodney Thompson. "Split Ratings And Bond Reoffering Yields," *FM*, 1985, v14(2), 59-65.

Billingsley, Randall S., Robert E. Lamy and G. Rodney Thompson. "The Choice Among Debt, Equity, And Convertible Bonds," *JFR*, 1988, v11(1), 43-56.

Billingsley, Randall S., Robert E. Lamy and David M. Smith. "Units Of Debt With Warrants: Evidence Of The 'Penalty-Free' Issuance Of An Equity-Like Security," *JFR*, 1990, v13(3), 187-200.

Bilson, John F. O. "Purchasing Power Parity As A Trading Strategy," *JOF*, 1984, v39(3), 715-723.

Bilson, John F. O. "The `Speculative Efficiency' Hypothesis," *JOB*, 1981, v54(3), 435-452.

Bing, Ralph A. "Appraising Our Methods Of Stock Appraisal," *FAJ*, 1964, v20(3), 118-124.

Bing, Ralph A. "For The Record - A Rejoinder," *FAJ*, 1964, v20(4), 109-111.

Bing, Ralph A. "Scientific Investment Analysis," *FAJ*, 1967, v23(3), 97.

Bing, Ralph A. "Stock Valuation: Theory Vs. Practice," *FAJ*, 1971, v27(3), 55-60.

Bing, Ralph A. "The Appraisal Of Stocks," *FAJ*, 1958, v14(2), 41-48.

Bing, Ralph A. "The Fetish Of Youth In Management," *FAJ*, 1957, v13(4), 67-72.

Bing, Ralph A. "The Home State And Equity Financing Of Operating Utility Companies," *FAJ*, 1954, v10(4), 69-76.

Bingham, Albert Young. "Relative Performance - Nonsense," *FAJ*, 1966, v22(4), 101-104.

Birch, John W. (Sunderman, Mark A., John W. Birch, Roger E. Cannaday and Thomas W. Hamilton. "Testing For Vertical Inequity In Property Tax Systems," *JRER*, 1990, v5(3), 319-334.)

Bird, A. P. "Some Hypotheses On The Valuation Of Stock Warrants: A Comment," *JBFA*, 1975, v2(2), 219-232.

Bird, A. P. "The Valuation Of Stock Warrants: A Reply," *JBFA*, 1975, v2(3), 395-397.

Bird, Monroe M. and Otha L. Gray. "Small Manufacturers' Reactions To The 1969 Repeal Of The Investment Tax Credit," *FR*, 1973, v8(1), 34-37.

Bird, Monroe M., Jr. "Investment Tax Credit," *FAJ*, 1969, v25(2), 81-82.

Bird, Peter J. W. N. "Dependency And Efficiency In The London Terminal Markets," *JFM*, 1985, v5(3), 433-446.

Bird, R. G. and A. J. McHugh. "Financial Ratios - An Empirical Study," *JBFA*, 1977, v4(1), 29-46.

Bird, Ron and Stuart Locke. "Financial Accounting Reports: A Market Model Of Disclosure: A Reply," *JBFA*, 1983, v10(3), 495-497.

Bird, Ron, David Dennis and Mark Tippett. "A Stop Loss Approach To Portfolio Insurance," *JPM*, 1988, v15(1), 35-40.

Bird, Ronald G. and Stuart M. Locke. "Financial Accounting Reports: A Market Model Of Disclosure," *JBFA*, 1981, v8(1), 27-44.

Birdwell, Al E. "A Study Of The Influence Of Image Congruence On Consumer Choice," *JOB*, 1968, v41(1), 76-88.

Birdwell, Al E. "Automobiles And Self-Imagery: Reply," *JOB*, 1968, v41(4), 486-487.

Birkett, W. P. and R. G. Walker. "Accounting: A Source Of Market Imperfection," *JBFA*, 1974, v1(2), 171-193.

Birkinsha, Jack E. "Investment Income: The Legal Part," *JRI*, 1969, v36(3), 463-464.

Birmingham, John M., Jr. "The Quest For Performance (Keynote Review)," *FAJ*, 1966, v22(5), 93-94.

Birmingham, John M., Jr. (Mennis, Edmund A. and John M. Birmingham, Jr. "Diffusion Analysis As An Investment Guide," *FAJ*, 1957, v13(2), 47-58.)

Birnbaum, Jerry L. "Participating In The Merger Mania," *FAJ*, 1969, v25(4), 87-94.

Birren, James E. "Age Changes In Mental Abilities," *JOB*, 1954, v27(2), 156-163.

Bishara, Halim. (Lee, Moon H. and Halim Bishara. "Recent Canadian Experience On The Profitability Of Insider Trades," *FR*, 1989, v24(2), 235-250.)

Bishop, E. L., III and J. R. Rollins. "Lowry's Reports: A Denial Of Market Efficiency," *JPM*, 1977, v4(1), 21-27.

Bishop, George W., Jr. "Charles H. Dow And The Theory Of The Multiplier," *FAJ*, 1965, v21(1), 39-41.

Bishop, George W., Jr. "Evolution Of The Dow Theory," *FAJ*, 1961, v17(5), 23-26.

Bishop, George W., Jr. "Who Was The First American Financial Analyst?," *FAJ*, 1964, v20(2),26-28.

Bissell, George S. "Responsibility In Financial Forecasting," *FAJ*, 1972, v28(3), 73-78.

Bissell, George S. (Loomis, Philip, George S. Bissell, John G. Gillis and Walter P. Stern. "Corporate Disclosure And Inside Information," *FAJ*, 1972, v28(3), 20-21,24-25,82-84,86-88.)

Bittlingmayer, George. "A Model Of Vertical Restriction And Equilibrium In Retailing," *JOB*, 1983, v56(4), 477-496.

Bjerksund, Petter and Steinar Ekern. "Managing Investment Opportunities Under Price Uncertainty: From 'Last Chance' To 'Wait And See' Strategies," *FM*, 1990, v19(3), 65-83.

Bjerring, James H., Josef Lakonishok and Theo Vermaelen. "Stock Prices And Financial Analysts' Recommendations," *JOF*, 1983, v38(1), 187-204.

Black, Bernard S. and Joseph A. Grundfest. "Shareholder Gains From Takeovers And Restructurings Between 1981 And 1986," *JACF*, 1988, v1(1), 6-15.

Black, Dan A. (Peterson, Richard L. and Dan A. Black. "Consumer Credit Search," *JMCB*, 1984, v16(4), Part 1, 527-536.)

Black, Deborah G., Kenneth D. Garbade and William L. Silber. "The Impact Of The GNMA Pass-through Program On FHA Mortgage Costs," *JOF*, 1981, v36(2),457-469.

Black, Fischer and John C. Cox. "Valuing Corporate Securities: Some Effects Of Bond Indenture Provisions," *JOF*, 1976, v31(2), 351-367.

Black, Fischer and Moray P. Dewhurst. "A New Investment Strategy For Pension Funds," *JPM*, 1981, v7(4), 26-34.

Black, Fischer and Myron Scholes. "The Effects Of Dividend Yield And Dividend Policy On Common Stock Prices And Returns," *JFEC*, 1974, v1(1), 1-22.

Black, Fischer and Myron Scholes. "From Theory To A New Financial Product," *JOF*, 1974, v29(2),399-412.

Black, Fischer and Myron Scholes. "The Valuation Of Option Contracts And A Test Of Market Efficiency," *JOF*, 1972, v27(2), 399-417.

Black, Fischer and Robert Jones. "Simplifying Portfolio Insurance," *JPM*, 1987, v14(1), 48-51.

Black, Fischer and Robert Jones. "Simplifying Portfolio Insurance For Corporate Pension Plans," *JPM*, 1988, v14(4), 33-37.

Black, Fischer, Yale Hirsch and John Westergaard. "Nuggets," *JPM*, 1977, v3(2), 71-77.

Black, Fischer, Emanuel Derman and William Toy. "A One-Factor Model Of Interest Rates And Its Application To Treasury Bond Options," *FAJ*, 1990, v46(1), 33-39.

Black, Fischer, Merton H. Miller and Richard A. Posner. " An Approach To The Regulation Of Bank Holding Companies," *JOB*, 1978, v51(3), 379-412.

Black, Fischer. "A Fully Computerized Stock Exchange - II," *FAJ*, 1971, v27(6), 24-28,86-87.

Black, Fischer. "A New Investment Strategy For Pension Funds: Reply," *JPM*, 1982, v8(4), 74-76.

Black, Fischer. "A Simple Discounting Rule," *FM*, 1988, v17(2), 7-11.

Black, Fischer. "Active And Passive Monetary Policy In A Neoclassical Model," *JOF*, 1972, v27(4),801-814.

Black, Fischer. "Bank Funds Management In An Efficient Market," *JFEC*, 1975, v2(4), 323-340.

Black, Fischer. "Banking And Interest Rates In A World Without Money: The Effects Of Uncontrolled Banking," *JBR*, 1970-71, v1(3), 8-20.

Black, Fischer. "Can Portfolio Managers Outrun The Random Walkers?," *JPM*, 1974, v1(1), 32-36.

Black, Fischer. "Equilibrium Exchange Rate Hedging," *JOF*, 1990, v45(3),899-908.

Black, Fischer. "Fact And Fantasy In The Use Of Options," *FAJ*, 1975, v31(4), 36-41,61-72.

Black, Fischer. "How To Use The Holes In Black-Scholes," *JACF*, 1989, v1(4), 67-73.

Black, Fischer. "How We Came Up With The Option Formula," *JPM*, 1989, v15(2), 4-8.

Black, Fischer. "International Capital Market Equilibrium With Investment Barriers," *JFEC*, 1974, v1(4), 337-352.

Black, Fischer. "Mean Reversion And Consumption Smoothing," *RFS*, 1990, v3(1), 107-114.

Black, Fischer. "Presidential Address: Noise," *JOF*, 1986, v41(3), 529-544.

Black, Fischer. "Random Walk And Portfolio Management," *FAJ*, 1971, v27(2), 16-22.

Black, Fischer. "The ABCs Of Business Cycles," *FAJ*, 1981, v37(6), 75-80.

Black, Fischer. "The Dividend Puzzle," *JPM*, 1976, v2(2), 5-8.

Black, Fischer. "The Ins And Outs Of Foreign Investment," *FAJ*, 1978, v34(3), 25-32.

Black, Fischer. "The Investment Policy Spectrum," *FAJ*, 1976, v32(1), 23-31.

Black, Fischer. "The Magic In Earnings: Economic Earnings Versus Accounting Earnings," *FAJ*, 1980, v36(6), 19-24.

Black, Fischer. "The Pricing Of Commodity Contracts," *JFEC*, 1976, v3(1/2), 167-179.

Black, Fischer. "The Tax Consequences Of Long-Run Pension Policy," *FAJ*, 1980, v36(4), 21-28.

Black, Fischer. "The Trouble With Econometric Models," *FAJ*, 1982, v38(2), 29-37.

Black, Fischer. "Toward A Fully Automated Exchange," *FAJ*, 1971, v27(4), 28-35,44.

Black, Fischer. "Universal Hedging: Optimizing Currency Risk And Reward In International Equity Portfolios," *FAJ*, 1989, v45(4), 16-22.

Black, Fischer. (Treynor, Jack L. and Fischer Black. "How To Use Security Analysis To Improve Portfolio Selection," *JOB*, 1973, v46(1), 66-86.)

Black, Guy. (Evan, William M. and Guy Black. "Innovation In Business Organizations: Some Factors Associated With Success Or Failure Of Staff Proposals," *JOB*, 1967, v40(4), 519-530.)

Black, Harold and Robert H. Dugger. "Credit Union Structure, Growth And Regulatory Problems," *JOF*, 1981, v36(2), 529-538.

Black, Harold and Robert L. Schweitzer. "Discrimination In The Lending Decision: Home Improvement Loans," *JBR*, 1980-81, v11(3), 184-186.

Black, Harold A. and Robert L. Schweitzer. "Black-Controlled Credit Unions: A Comparative Analysis," *JFR*, 1985, v8(3), 193-202.

Black, Harold A. and Robert L. Schweitzer. "An Analysis Of Market Segmentation In Mortgage Lending Between A Commercial Bank And A Mutual Savings Bank," *AREUEA*, 1981, v9(3), 234-240.

Black, Harold A., M. Andrew Fields and Robert L. Schweitzer. "Changes In Interstate Banking Laws: The Impact On Shareholder Wealth," *JOF*, 1990, v45(5), 1663-1672.

Black, Harold. "Inflation And The Issue Of Unidirectional Causality," *JMCB*, 1978, v10(1), 99-101.

Black, Harold. "The Dichotomization Of Bank Markets Over Time: The Case Of Washington D.C.," *JBR*, 1977-78, v8(4), 242-248.

Black, Homer A. "Interperiod Allocation Of Corporate Income Taxes," *FAJ*, 1966, v22(5), 41-47.

Black, Kenneth, Jr. "A Dean's Perception Of Insurance Education," *JRI*, 1972, v39(2), 280-285.

Black, Kenneth, Jr. and Eli Zubay. "The Actuarial Curriculum," *JRI*, 1965, v32(2), 308-311.

Black, Kenneth, Jr. and Eli A. Zubay. "The Actuarial Curriculum: Reply," *JRI*, 1966, v33(3), 482-483.

Black, Stanley W. "An Econometric Study Of Euro-Dollar Borrowing By New York Banks And The Rate Of Interest On Euro-Dollars," *JOF*, 1971, v26(1), 83-88.

Black, Stanley W. "An Econometric Study Of Eurodollar Borrowing By New York Banks And The Rate Of Interest On Eurodollars: Reply," *JOF*, 1972, v27(4), 931-932.

Black, Stanley W. "Eurodollar Borrowing By New York Banks And The Rate Of Interest On Eurodollars: Reply," *JOF*, 1972, v27(1), 134-135.

Black, Stanley W. "The Effects Of Alternative Monetary Control Procedures On Exchange Rates And Output," *JMCB*, 1982, v14(4),

Part 2, 746-760.

Black, William C. (Richins, Marsha L., William C. Black and C. F. Sirmans. "Strategic Orientation And Marketing Strategy: An Analysis Of Residential Real Estate Brokerage Firms," JRER, 1987, v2(2), 41-54.)

Blackburn, Keith. "Collapsing Exchange Rate Regimes And Exchange Rate Dynamics: Some Further Examples," JIMF, 1988, v7(4), 373-386.

Blackett, George H. "Estimates Of Cigarette Consumption," FAJ, 1948, v4(3), 26-32.

Blackley, Dixie M., James R. Follain and Haeduck Lee. "An Evaluation Of Hedonic Price Indexes For 34 Large SMSAs," AREUEA, 1986, v14(2), 179-205.

Blackmarr, Brian R. (Lifson, K. A. and Brian R. Blackmarr. "Simulation And Optimization Models For Asset Deployment And Funds Sources Balancing Profit, Liquidity And Growth," JBR, 1973-74, v4(3), 239-255.)

Blackstock, Henry T. "New Era For Softgoods Suppliers," FAJ, 1974, v30(3), 62-64,66-68.

Blackwell, David W. (Ang, James S., David W. Blackwell and William L. Megginson. "The Effect Of Taxes On The Relative Valuation Of Dividends And Capital Gains: Evidence From Dual-Class British Investment Trusts," JOF, 1991, v46(1), 383-400.)

Blackwell, David W. and David S. Kidwell. "An Investigation Of Cost Differences Between Public Sales And Private Placements Of Debt," JFEC, 1988, v22(2),253-278.

Blackwell, David W., M. Wayne Marr and Michael F. Spivey. "Shelf Registration And The Reduced Due Diligence Argument: Implications Of The Underwriter Certification And The Implicit Insurance Hypotheses," JFQA, 1990, v25(2), 245-260.

Blackwell, David W., M. Wayne Marr and Michael F. Spivey. "Plant-Closing Decisions And The Market Value Of The Firm," JFEC, 1990, v26(2), 277-288.

Blackwell, J. Lloyd, III. "Branch Banking: A Note On A Theory Dilemma," JOB, 1977, v50(4), 520-525.

Blackwell, James M. (McCabe, George M. and James M. Blackwell. "The Hedging Strategy: A New Approach To Spread Management Banking And Commercial Lending," JBR, 1981-82, v12(2), 114-118.)

Blair, John M. "Administered Prices And Oligopolistic Inflation: A Reply," JOB, 1964, v37(1),68-81.

Blair, John P. "Local Mechanisms For Locational Efficiency," AREUEA, 1976, v4(3), 85-92.

Blair, Roger D. and Arnold A. Heggestad. "Bank Portfolio Regulation And The Probability Of Bank Failure," JMCB, 1978, v10(1), 88-93.

Blair, Roger D. and David L. Kaserman. "Tying Arrangements And Uncertainty," RIF, 1983, v4, (Supp), 1-14.

Blair, Roger D. and Ronald J. Vogel. "A Survivor Analysis Of Commerical Health Insurers," JOB, 1978, v51(3), 521-530.

Blair, Roger D., David L. Kaserman and Patricia L. Pacey. "A Note On Purchased Power Adjustment Clauses," JOB, 1985, v58(4), 409-418.

Blaisdell, Paul H. "20,000 Aids To Students Of Insurance," JRI, 1961, v28(2), 128.

Blake, C. W. and D. W. Riegle. "Data Processing," FAJ, 1968, v24(1), 134-146.

Blake, David and Mahmood Pradhan. "Debt-Equity Swaps As Bond Conversions: Implications For Pricing," JBF, 1991, v15(1), 29-41.

Blake, John C. "Consumer Credit And Its Effect On The Business Cycle," FAJ, 1957, v13(2), 103-108.

Blake, John C. "Looking At Business And The Stock Market," FAJ, 1958, v14(5), 15-16.

Blakeslee, Arthur L., III. "Is Variable Life Insurance A Competitor For Mutual Funds? A Position Paper," JRI, 1975, v42(3), 513-517.

Blakeslee, Arthur L., III. "Some Observations On Variable Life Insurance Product Design," JRI, 1975, v42(3), 518-521.

Blalack, Richard O., Herbert J. Davis and Harvey W. Rubin. "Sources Of Job Stress For The FLMI: A Comparative Analysis," JRI, 1979, v46(2), 123-138.

Blanchard, Ralph H. "Risk As A Special Subject Of Study," JRI, 1959, v26(1), 8-11.

Blanchard, Ralph H. "University Instruction In Insurance Curricula And Teaching Methods," JRI, 1935, v2, 2-8.

Blanchet, Henri. (Bland, Christopher, Manfred Klein, Henri Blanchet and Christian Moretti. "Perspectives On Restructuring In Europe: Interviews With Four European Executives," JACF, 1991, v3(4), 37-45.)

Bland, Christopher, Manfred Klein, Henri Blanchet and Christian Moretti. "Perspectives On Restructuring In Europe: Interviews With Four European Executives," JACF, 1991, v3(4), 37-45.

Bland, Robert L. (Roden, Peyton Foster and Robert L. Bland. "Issuer Sophistication And Underpricing In The Negotiated Municipal Bond Market," JFR, 1986, v9(2), 163-170.)

Blandon, Peter R. and C. W. R. Ward. "Investors' Perception Of Risk: A Re-Assessment," JBFA, 1979, v6(4), 443-454.

Blaney, T. A. (Olsen, J. A. and T. A. Blaney. "The Copper Industry Study," FAJ, 1968, v24(2), 35-39.)

Blank, David M. "A Note On The Golden Age Of Advertising," JOB, 1963, v36(1), 33-38.

Blank, David M. "Cyclical Behavior Of National Advertising," JOB, 1962, v35(1), 14-27.

Blank, David M. "Television Advertising: The Great Discount Illusion, Or Tony-Pandy Revisited," JOB, 1968, v41(1), 10-38.

Blank, David M. "Tonypandy Once Again," JOB, 1969, v42(1), 104-112.

Blank, Seymour. "Small Business And Tight Money," JOF, 1961, v16(1), 73-79.

Blank, Steven C. "Determining Futures 'Hedging Reserve' Capital Requirements," JFM, 1990, v10(2), 169-178.

Blann, Jack and B. V. Balachandran. "An Empirical Test Of The Statistical Association Of Market Risk And Financial Accounting Allocation," JBFA, 1988, v15(1), 101-114.

Blatt, Charles. "Factors In Analyzing Liquor Stocks," FAJ, 1947, v3(4), 67-74.

Blatt, John M. "Investment Evaluation Under Uncertainty," FM, 1979, v8(2), 66-81.

Blattberg, Robert C. and Nicholas J. Gonedes. "A Comparison Of The Stable And Student Distributions As Statistical Models For Stock Prices," JOB, 1974, v47(2), 244-280.

Blattberg, Robert C. and Nicholas J. Gonedes. "A Comparison Of The Stable And Student Distributions As Statistical Models For Stock Prices: Reply," JOB, 1977, v50(1), 78-79.

Blau, Leslie A. and James S. Barber. "Proposed Amendment Of Section 4d(2) Of The Commodity Exchange Act: Concerning Investment Of Customer Funds," JFM, 1994, v1(4), 657-658.

Blazek, Lubomir J. and David L. Wark. "Profits Hidden In The Balance Sheet," JBR, 1978-79, v9(4), 251-255.

Blazenko, George W. "Managerial Preference, Asymmetric Information, And Financial Structure," JOF, 1987, v42(4), 839-862.

Blazenko, George. "The Economics Of Reinsurance," JRI, 1986, v53(2), 258-277.

Bleakney, Thomas P. "Problems And Issues In Public Employee Retirement Systems," JRI, 1973, v40(1), 39-54.

Bleakney, Thomas P. "Problems And Issues In Public Employee Retirement Systems: Reply," JRI, 1974, v41(3), 533-536.

Bleiberg, Steven. "How Little We Know," JPM, 1989, v15(4), 26-31.

Bleibtreu, Jacob. "Japanese Impressions, 1953," FAJ, 1953, v9(4), 55-58.

Blejer, Mario I. "On The Anatomy Of Inflation: The Variability Of Relative Commodity Prices In Argentina," JMCB, 1983, v15(4), 469-482.

Blenman, Lloyd P. "Price Forecasts And Interest Rate Forecasts: An Extension Of Levy's Hypothesis," JFM, 1990, v10(6), 605-610.

Blevins, Dallas R. "A Student's Guide To The Case Method," JFED, 1980, v9, 66-73.

Blevins, Dallas R. "CMA: A Professional Designation For Professors And Students Of Managerial Finance," JFED, 1988, v17, 39-43.

Blevins, Dallas R. "The Need For Education In Municipal Finance," JFED, 1978, v7, 44-46.

Blevins, Dallas R. (Osteryoung, Jerome S., Ronald C. Braswell and Dallas R. Blevins. "PIC: An Alternative Approach To Accepting Bids On Local And State Government Bonds," FM, 1979, v8(2), 36-41.)

Blevins, Dallas R. (Osteryoung, Jerome S. and Dallas R. Blevins. "A New Approach To Ratings On State GO's," JPM, 1979,v5(3),69-74.)

Blinder, Alan S. "Monetary Accommodation Of Supply Shocks Under Rational Expectations," JMCB, 1981, v13(4), 425-438.

Blinder, Alan S. "More On The Speed Of Adjustment In Inventory Models," JMCB, 1986, v18(3), 355-365.

Blinder, Edward. (Gagnon, Louis, Samuel Mensah and Edward Blinder. "Hedging Canadian Corporate Debt: A Comparative Study Of The Hedging Effectiveness Of Canadian And U.S. Bond Futures," JFM, 1989, v9(1), 29-40.)

Bliss, John Alden. "The Picture Is Different With A Two-Dimensional Price," FAJ, 1954, v10(4),89-96.

Bliss, Robert R., Jr. and Ehud I. Ronn. "Arbitrage-Based Estimation Of Nonstationary Shifts In The Term Structure Of Interest Rates," JOF, 1989, v44(3), 591-610.

Bloch, Alan J. "An Option For The Age Of Stability," JPM, 1978, v4(2), 27-30.

Bloch, Ernest and Robert A. Schwartz. "The Great Debate Over NYSE Rule 390," JPM, 1978, v5(1), 5-10.

Bloch, Ernest. "Two Decades Of Evolution Of Financial Institutions And Public Policy," JMCB, 1971, v3(2), Part 2, 555-570.

Bloch, Howard and Roger Pupp. "The January Barometer Revisited And Rejected," JPM, 1983, v9(2), 48-50.

Bloch, Howard R. and Thomas J. Lareau. "Should We Invest In `Socially Irresponsible' Firms?," JPM, 1985, v11(4), 27-31.

Bloch, Ivan. "Alaska's Economic Outlook," FAJ, 1960, v16(1), 31-42.

Bloch, Ivan. "Growth Of Commerce On The Columbia River," FAJ, 1960, v16(4), 7-14.

Block, Frank E. "A Study Of The Price To Book Relationship," FAJ, 1964, v20(5), 108-117.

Block, Frank E. "Elements Of Portfolio Construction," FAJ, 1969, v25(3), 123-129.

Block, Frank E. "Per Share Adjustments For Rights," FAJ, 1965, v21(3), 58-60.

Block, Frank E. "Risk And Performance," FAJ, 1966, v22(2), 65-74.

Block, Frank E. "The Place Of Book Value In Common Stock Evaluation," FAJ, 1964, v20(2), 29-33.

Block, Frank E. "Time Horizon," FAJ, 1972, v28(5), 30-31,60-62.

Block, Frank E. "Understanding Commodity Shortages," FAJ, 1974, v30(6), 20-29,67.

Block, Stanley and Majorie Stanley. "The Financial Characteristics And Price Movement Patterns Of Companies Approaching The Unseasoned Securities Market In The Late 1970s," FM, 1980, v9(4), 30-36.

Block, Stanley B. and Timothy J. Gallagher. "The Use Of Interest Rate Futures And Options By Corporate Financial Managers," FM, 1986, v15(3), 73-78.

Block, Stanley B. "Teaching Investments In The Context Of The Efficient Market Hypothesis: Some Strategies To Consider," JFED, 1983, v12, 54-58.

Block, Stanley B. (Stanley, Majorie T. and Stanley B. Block. "A Survey Of Multinational Capital Budgeting," FR, 1984, v19(1), 36-54.)

Block, Stanley B. and Dan W. French. "The Student-Managed Investment Fund: A Special Opportunity In Learning," FPE, 1991, v1(1), 35-40.

Block, Stanley B. and Timothy J. Gallagher. "How Much Do Bank Trust Departments Use Derivatives?," JPM, 1988, v15(1), 12-15.

Block, Stanley. "Use Of Merger Analysis Project As An Instructive Tool In Managerial Finance," JFED, 1973, v2, 39-41.

Blois, K. J. "The Pricing Of Supplies By Large Customers," JBFA, 1978, v5(3), 367-380.

Blomeyer, Edward C. "An Analytic Approximation For The American Put Price For Options On Stocks With Dividends," JFQA, 1986, v21(2), 229-233.)

Blomeyer, Edward C. and Herb Johnson. "An Empirical Examination Of The Pricing Of American Put Options," JFQA, 1988, v23(1), 13-22.

Blomeyer, Edward C. and James C. Boyd. "Empirical Tests Of Boundary Conditions For Options On Treasury Bond Futures Contracts," JFM, 1988, v8(2), 185-198.

Bloom David E., Beth Preiss and James Trussell. "Mortgage Lending Discrimination And The Decision To Apply: A Methodological Note," AREUEA, 1983, v11(1), 97-103.

Bloom, David E. (Rosen, Kenneth T. and David E. Bloom. "A Microeconomic Model Of Federal Home Loan Mortgage Corporate Activity," **JOF**, 1980, v35(4), 959-971.)

Bloom, Robert, Pieter T. Elgers, James R. Haltiner and William H. Hawthorne. "Inflation Gains And Losses On Monetary Items: An Empirical Test," **JBFA**, 1980, v7(4), 603-618.

Bloom, Robert. "An Adaption Of Dicksee's Ship Model," **JBFA**, 1979, v6(2), 223-227.

Bloomfield, Arthur I. "Some Problems Of Central Banking In Underdeveloped Countries," **JOF**, 1957, v12(2), 190-204.

Bloomfield, T. R., Richard Leftwich and J. B. Long, Jr. "Portfolio Strategies And Performance," **JFEC**, 1977, v5(2), 210-218.

Bloomfield, Ted and Ronald Ma. "The Weighted Average Cost Of Capital: Some Questions On Its Definition, Interpretation, And Use: Comment," **JOF**, 1975, v30(3), 887-888.

Blough, Carman G. "LIFO Inventory Accounting In Period Of Declining Prices," **FAJ**, 1949, v5(2), 12-16.

Blough, Roy. "The Adjustment Process And The International Role Of The Dollar," **JOF**, 1969, v24(2), 345-359.

Blough, Roy. "United States Taxation And Foreign Investment," **JOF**, 1956, v11(2), 180-194.

Blucher, Lillian H. (Bellemore, Douglas H. and Lillian H. Blucher. "Stock Splits," **FAJ**, 1959, v15(5), 19-28.)

Blum, Gerald A. and Wilbur G. Lewellen. "Negotiated Brokerage Commissions And The Individual Investor," **JFQA**, 1983, v18(3), 331-343.

Blum, Gerald A., William A. Kracaw and Wilbur G. Lewellen. "Determinants Of The Execution Costs Of Common Stock Trades By Individual Investors," **JFR**, 1986, v9(4), 291-301.

Blume, Marshall E. and Frank Husic. "Price, Beta, And Exchange Listing," **JOF**, 1973, v28(2),283-299.

Blume, Marshall E. and Irwin Friend. "A New Look At The Capital Asset Pricing Model," **JOF**, 1973, v28(1), 19-33.

Blume, Marshall E. and Irwin Friend. "The Asset Structure Of Individual Portfolios And Some Implications For Utility Functions," **JOF**, 1975, v30(2), 585-603.

Blume, Marshall E. and Robert F. Stambaugh. "Biases In Computed Returns: An Application To The Size Effect," **JFEC**, 1983, v12(3), 387-404.

Blume, Marshall E. "Betas And Their Regression Tendencies: Some Further Evidence," **JOF**, 1979, v34(1), 265-267.

Blume, Marshall E. "Betas And Their Regression Tendencies," **JOF**, 1975, v30(3), 785-795.

Blume, Marshall E. "On The Assessment Of Risk," **JOF**, 1971, v26(1), 1-10.

Blume, Marshall E. "Portfolio Theory: A Step Toward Its Practical Application," **JOB**, 1970, v43(2), 152-173.

Blume, Marshall E. "The Pricing Of Capital Assets In A Multiperiod World," **JBF**, 1983, v7(1), 31-44.

Blume, Marshall E. "The Relative Efficiency Of Various Portfolios: Some Further Evidence," **JOF**, 1980, v35(2), 269-281.

Blume, Marshall E. "The Use Of `Alphas' To Improve Performance," **JPM**, 1984, v11(1), 86-92.

Blume, Marshall E. "Two Tiers - But How Many Decisions?," **JPM**, 1976, v3(3), 5-12.

Blume, Marshall E. (Fama, Eugene F. and Marshall E. Blume. "Filter Rules And Stock Market Trading," **JOB**, 1966, v39(1), Part II, 226-241.)

Blume, Marshall E. (Friend, Irwin and Marshall E. Blume. "Competitive Commissions On The New York Stock Exchange," **JOF**, 1973, v28(4), 795-819.)

Blume, Marshall E. and Donald B. Keim. "Lower-Grade Bonds: Their Risks And Returns," **FAJ**, 1987, v43(4), 26-33.

Blume, Marshall E., A. Craig MacKinlay and Bruce Terker. "Order Imbalances And Stock Price Movements On October 19 And 20, 1987," **JOF**, 1989, v44(4), 827-848.

Blume, Marshall E., Donald B. Keim and Sandeep A. Patel. "Returns And Volatility Of Low-Grade Bonds, 1977-1989," **JOF**, 1991, v46(1), 49-74.

Blume, Marshall. (Benninga, Simon and Marshall Blume. "On The Optimality Of Portfolio Insurance," **JOF**, 1985, v40(5), 1341-1352.)

Blutter, Arthur. "Dividend Policy And Valuation," **JFED**, 1972, v1, 111-115.

Blyth, John W. "Programmed Learning," **JRI**, 1963, v30(2), 219-228.

Board, J. L. G. and C. M. S. Sutcliffe. "Optimal Portfolio Diversification And The Effects Of Differing Intra Sample Measures Of Return," **JBFA**, 1985, v12(4), 561-574.

Board, J. L. G. and C. M. S. Sutcliffe. "The Weekend Effect In UK Stock Market Returns," **JBFA**, 1988, v15(2), 199-214.

Boardman, Calvin M. and Richard W. McEnally. "Factors Affecting Seasoned Corporate Bond Prices," **JFQA**, 1981, v16(2), 207-226.

Boardman, Calvin M. "The Role Of The Payback Period In The Theory And Application Of Duration To Capital Budgeting: A Reply," **JBFA**, 1985, v12(1), 169-171.

Boardman, Calvin M. (Bartley, Jon W. and Calvin M. Boardman. "The Relevance Of Inflation Adjusted Accounting Data To The Prediction Of Corporate Takeovers," **JBFA**, 1990, v17(1), 53-72.)

Boardman, Calvin M. (McEnally, Richard W. and Calvin M. Boardman. "Aspects Of Corporate Bond Portfolio Diversification," **JFR**, 1979, v2(1), 27-36.)

Boardman, Calvin M., Frederick H. Dark and Ronald C. Lease. "On The Listing Of Corporate Debt: A Note," **JFQA**, 1986, v21(1), 107-114.

Boardman, Calvin M., Walter J. Reinhart and Stephen E. Celec. "The Role Of The Payback Period In The Theory And Application Of Duration To Capital Budgeting," **JBFA**, 1982, v8(4), 511-522.

Boatler, Robert W. "Treasury Bill Auction Procedures: An Empirical Investigation: Comment," **JOF**, 1975, v30(3), 893-894.

Bobbitt, H. Randolph, Jr. "The University Professor Of Insurance As Viewed By The Insurance Professor," **JRI**, 1967, v34(2), 289-300.

Bober, William C. "The Construction Industry," **FAJ**, 1953, v9(2), 13-18.

Bobo, James R. (Render, Barry, William Wagoner, James R. Bobo and Stephen Corliss. "Finance Doctorates In The South: A 1977-1981 Supply And Demand Analysis," **JFED**, 1978, v7, 37-41.)

Bochnak, Mary. (Jessup, Paul F. and Mary Bochnak. "Why Not Deregulate Bank Debt Capital," **FM**, 1976, v5(4), 65-67.)

Boczar, Gregory E. "Competition Between Banks And Finance Companies: A Cross Section Study Of Personal Loan Debtors," **JOF**, 1978, v33(1), 245-258.

Boczar, Gregory E. "Market Characteristics And Multibank Holding Company Acquisitions," **JOF**, 1977, v32(1), 131-146.

Boczar, Gregory E. "Predicting DE NOVO Expansion In Bank Merger Cases: Comment," **JOF**, 1976, v31(4), 1239-1242.

Boczar, Gregory E. "The Evidence On Competition Between Commercial Banks And Finance Companies," **JBR**, 1975-76, v6(2), 150-156.

Boczar, Gregory E. "The External Growth Of Multibank Holding Companies," **JBR**, 1980-81, v11(3), 147-158.

Bodenhorn, Diran. "A Cash-Flow Concept Of Profit," **JOF**, 1964, v19(1), 16-31.

Bodenhorn, Diran. "A Note On The Theory Of The Firm," **JOB**, 1959, v32(2), 164-174.

Bodenhorn, Diran. "Balance Sheet Items As The Present Value Of Future Cash Flows," **JBFA**, 1984, v11(4), 493-510.

Bodenhorn, Diran. "Depreciation, Price Level Changes, And Investment Decisions," **JOB**, 1963, v36(4), 448-457.

Bodenhorn, Diran. "On The Problem Of Capital Budgeting," **JOF**, 1959, v14(4), 473-492.

Bodie, Zvi and Robert A. Taggart. "Future Investment Opportunities And The Value Of The Call Provision On A Bond," **JOF**, 1978, v33(4), 1187-1200.

Bodie, Zvi and Robert A. Taggart, Jr. "Future Investment Opportunities And The Value Of The Call Provision On A Bond: Reply," **JOF**, 1980, v35(4), 1055-1056.

Bodie, Zvi and Victor I. Rosansky. "Risk And Return In Commodity Futures," **FAJ**, 1980, v36(3), 27-31,33-39.

Bodie, Zvi, Alex Kane and Robert McDonald. "Why Haven't Nominal Rates Declined?," **FAJ**, 1984, v40(2), 16-19,22-27.

Bodie, Zvi, Jay O. Light, Randall Morck and Robert A. Taggart, Jr. "Corporate Pension Policy: An Empirical Investigation," **FAJ**, 1985, v41(5), 10-16.

Bodie, Zvi. "An Innovation For Stable Real Retirement Income," **JPM**, 1980, v7(1), 5-13.

Bodie, Zvi. "Commodity Futures As A Hedge Against Inflation," **JPM**, 1983, v9(3), 12-17.

Bodie, Zvi. "Common Stocks As A Hedge Against Inflation," **JOF**, 1976, v31(2), 459-470.

Bodie, Zvi. "Inflation Insurance," **JRI**, 1990, v57(4), 634-645.

Bodie, Zvi. "Inflation Risk And Capital Market Equilibrium," **FR**, 1982, v17(1), 1-25.

Bodie, Zvi. "Inflation, Index-Linked Bonds, And Asset Allocation," **JPM**, 1990, v16(2), 48-53.

Bodie, Zvi. "Pension Funds And Financial Innovation," **FM**, 1990, v19(3), 11-22.

Bodie, Zvi. "The ABO, The PBO And Pension Investment Policy," **FAJ**, 1990, v46(5), 27-34.

Bodie, Zvi. (Berger, Paul D. and Zvi Bodie. "Portfolio Selection In A `Winner-Take-All' Environment," **JOF**, 1979, v34(1), 233-236.)

Bodily, Jerry J. "The Effects Of Retaliation On The State Taxation Of Life Insurers," **JRI**, 1977, v44(1), 21-36.

Bodily, Samuel E. and Chelsea C. White. "Optimal Consumption And Portfolio Strategies In A Discrete-Time Model With Summary-Dependent Preferences," **JFQA**, 1982, v17(1), 1-14.

Bodine, William W. "Private Lending," **JRI**, 1947, v14, 41-47.

Bodurtha, James N., Jr. and Georges R. Courtadon. "Efficiency Tests Of The Foreign Currency Options Market," **JOF**, 1986, v41(1), 151-162.

Bodurtha, James N., Jr. and Georges R. Courtadon. "Tests Of An American Option Pricing Model On The Foreign Currency Options Market," **JFQA**, 1987, v22(2),153-168.

Bodurtha, James N., Jr. and Frederique Valnet. "Innovation In The International Money And Bond Markets: A Source Of Lower Borrowing Costs?," **RDIBF**, 1988, v2, 45-86.

Bodurtha, James N., Jr., D. Chinhyung Cho and Lemma W. Senbet. "Economic Forces In The Stock Market: An International Perspective," **GFJ**, 1989, v1(1), 21-46.

Bodurtha, Stephen G. and Thomas E. Quinn. "Does Patient Program Trading Really Pay?," **FAJ**, 1990, v46(3), 35-42.

Boe, Warren J. (Bhandari, Shyam B., Robert M. Soldofsky and Warren J. Boe. "Bond Quality Rating Changes For Electric Utilities: A Multivariate Analysis," **FM**, 1979, v8(1), 74-81.)

Boehlje, Michael and Glen Fisher. "A Competitive Management Game For Non-Metropolitan Commercial Banks," **JBR**, 1976-77, v7(1), 56-67.

Boehm, Thomas P. and Jonathan Mark. "A Principal Component Logistic Analysis Of The Mobility Decision In Transitional Neighborhoods," **AREUEA**, 1980, v8(3), 299-319.

Boehm, Thomas P. and Joseph A. McKenzie. "Inflation, Taxes, And The Demand For Housing," **AREUEA**, 1982, v10(1), 25-38.

Boehm, Thomas P. and Keith R. Ihlanfeldt. "The Improvement Expenditures Of Urban Homeowners: An Empirical Analysis," **AREUEA**, 1986, v14(1), 48-60.

Boehmer, Ekkehart and William L. Megginson. "Determinants Of Secondary Market Prices For Developing Country Syndicated Loans," **JOF**, 1990, v45(5), 1517-1540.

Boenawan, Kickie. (Ritchken, Peter and Kiekie Boenawan. "On Arbitrage-Free Pricing Of Interest Rate Contingent Claims," **JOF**, 1990, v45(1), 259-264.)

Boericke, William F. "Nonferrous Metals," **FAJ**, 1949, v5(4), 28-30.

Boericke, William F. "Outlook For Copper, Lead, And Zinc In 1953," **FAJ**, 1953, v9(1), 21-24.

Boericke, William F. "South African Gold Mining Accounts," **FAJ**, 1963, v19(2), 45-47.

Boericke, William F. "South African Gold," **FAJ**, 1959, v15(5), 55-60.

Bogan, Elizabeth C. and Thomas R. Bogan. "Individual Retirement Accounts And Preretirement Savings Goals," **FAJ**, 1982, v38(6), 45-47.

Bogan, Thomas R. (Bogan, Elizabeth C. and Thomas R. Bogan. "Individual Retirement Accounts And Preretirement Savings Goals," **FAJ**, 1982, v38(6), 45-47.)

Bogart, Leo. "Comment On Walter J. Primeaux, Jr., `The Newspaper Rate Differential: Another Element In The Explanation'," **JOB**,

1977, v50(1), 84-85.

Bogen, Jules I. "The Importance Of Equity Financing In The American Economy," JOF, 1950, v5(2),170-178.

Bogen, Mason. "Adjusting Railroad Operating Costs To The Revenue Trend," FAJ, 1946, v2(4), 26-30.

Bogle, John C. and Jan M. Twardowski. "Institutional Investment Performance Compared," FAJ, 1980, v36(1), 33-41.

Bogle, John C. "Investing In The 1990s: Remembrance Of Things Past, And Things Yet To Come," JPM, 1991, v17(3), 5-14.

Bogle, John C. "Mutual Fund Performance Evaluation," FAJ, 1970, v26(6), 25-33.

Bogle, John C. "Of Glory, Jest And Riddle: Professors, Professionals And Modern Portfolio Theory," FR, 1978, v13(2), 67-71.

Bogue, Marcus C. and Richard Roll. "Capital Budgeting Of Risky Projects With `Imperfect' Markets For Physical Capital," JOF, 1974, v29(2), 601-613.

Bogue, Marcus C. (Robichek, Alexander A. and Marcus C. Bogue. "A Note On The Behavior Of Expected Price/Earnings Ratios Over Time," JOF, 1971, v26(3), 731-735.)

Bohan, James. "Relative Strength: Further Positive Evidence," JPM, 1981, v8(1), 36-39.

Bohi, Douglas R. and Michael A. Toman. "Futures Trading And Oil Market Conditions," JFM, 1987, v7(2), 203-222.

Bohlinger, Alfred J. "1954 - The Year For Action," JRI, 1954, v21, 64-70.

Bohmfalk, John F., Jr. and Robert L. Newton. "A Look Ahead For Chemical Industry," FAJ, 1957, v13(2), 33-38.

Bohmfalk, John F., Jr. "Philosophy Of Growth Stocks," FAJ, 1960, v16(6), 113-123.

Bohren, Oyvind. "Bounding Certainty Equivalent Factors And Risk Adjusted Discount Rates," JBFA, 1983, v10(1), 139-146.

Bohren, Oyvind. "The Validity Of Conventional Valuation Models Under Multiperiod Uncertainty," JBFA, 1984, v11(2), 199-211.

Boies, D., D. Carroll, A. Fleischer, J. Grundfest, J. Ira Harris, M. Lipton, R. Monks, A. Oliver, L. Sachnoff and J. Wilcox. "Panel: Corporate Governance: The Role Of Boards Of Directors In Takeover Bids And Defenses," JACF, 1989, v2(2), 6-35.

Boiteux, M. "Peak-Load Pricing," JOB, 1960, v33(2), 157-179.

Bojanek, Robert. (Schmalensee, Richard, Alvin J. Silk and Robert Bojanek. "The Impact Of Scale And Media Mix On Advertising Agency Costs," JOB, 1983, v56(4), 453-476.)

Boland, Lawrence F. "Beryllium - Present And Potential Uses," FAJ, 1958, v14(5), 27-32.

Boldin, Robert. (Ziskind, Ross and Robert Boldin. "A Computer Simulation Model For Investment Portfolio Management," FM, 1973, v2(3), 23-33.)

Boldt, Bob L. and Hal L. Arbit. "Efficient Markets And The Professional Investor," FAJ, 1984, v40(4), 22-34.

Boles, Keith E. "A Generalized Approach To Managerial Finance," JFED, 1981, v10, 69-70.

Boles, Keith E. "An Integrative Approach To Risk Evaluation," JFED, 1983, v12, 47-50.

Boles, Keith E. (Brush, John S. and Keith E. Boles. "The Predictive Power In Relative Strength And CAPM," JPM, 1983, v9(4), 20-23.)

Bollerslev, Tim. (Baillie, Richard T. and Tim Bollerslev. "Common Stochastic Trends In A System Of Exchange Rates," JOF, 1989, v44(1), 167-182.)

Bollerslev, Tim. (Baillie, Richard T. and Tim Bollerslev. "A Multivariate Generalized ARCH Approach To Modeling Risk Premia In Forward Foreign Exchange Rate Markets," JIMF, 1990, v9(3), 309-324.)

Bolster, P. J. (Srinivasan, V., Y. H. Kim and P. J. Bolster. "A Framework For Integrating The Leasing Alternative With The Capital Budgeting Decision," AFPAF, 1989, v3(1), 75-94.)

Bolster, Paul J. (Janjigian, Vahan and Paul J. Bolster. "The Elimination Of Director Liability And Stockholder Returns: An Empirical Investigation," JFR, 1990, v13(1), 53-60.)

Bolster, Paul J., Lawrence B. Lindsey and Andrew Mitrusi. "Tax-Induced Trading: The Effect Of The 1986 Tax Reform Act On Stock Market Activity," JOF, 1989, v44(2), 327-344.

Bolten, Steven E. and John H. Crockett, Jr. "Are Auditors Independent?," FAJ, 1979, v35(6), 76-78.

Bolten, Steven E. and Susan W. Long. "A Note On Cyclical And Dynamic Aspects Of Stock Market Price Cycles," FR, 1986, v21(1), 145-150.

Bolten, Steven E. "Finance Frontiers Vs. Finance Education," JFED, 1981, v10, 63-65.

Bolten, Steven E. and Scott Besley. "Long-Term Asset Allocation Under Dynamic Interaction Of Earnings And Interest Rates," FR, 1991, v26(2), 269-274.

Bolten, Steven. "Treasury Bill Auction Procedures: An Empirical Investigation," JOF, 1973, v28(3), 577-585.

Bolten, Steven. "Treasury Bill Auction Procedures: An Empirical Investigation: Reply," JOF, 1975, v30(3), 900-903.

Bolten, Steven. (Claiborn, Stephen and Steven Bolten. "An Experiment In Competency-Based Financial Education," JFED, 1975, v4, 9-15.)

Bolten, Steven. (Mastrapasqua, Frank and Steven Bolten. "A Note On Financial Analyst Evaluation," JOF, 1973, v28(3), 707-712.)

Bolton, A. Hamilton. "General Characteristics Of Inflation," FAJ, 1961, v17(6), 71-79.

Bolton, A. Hamilton. "Newsprint Statistics In Business And Investment Analysis," FAJ, 1954, v10(2), 31-38.

Bolton, A. Hamilton. "Price & Monetary Inflation, And Stock Prices," FAJ, 1962, v18(1), 55-62.

Bolton, A. Hamilton. "Price-Earnings Ratios May Be Too Low!," FAJ, 1958, v14(5), 37-40.

Bolton, A. Hamilton. "The Money Equation And Common Stock Investments," FAJ, 1957, v13(4), 15-24.

Bolton, Hamilton. "Economy Of The Stock Market, 1929 And Now," FAJ, 1960, v16(1), 57-62.

Bolton, Hamilton. "The 1959 National Convention In Retrospect," FAJ, 1959, v15(3), 53-56.

Bomball, Mark R., Walter J. Primeaux and Donald E. Pursell. "Forecasting Stage 2 Of The Family Life Cycle," JOB, 1975, v48(1), 65-73.

Bombara, Kenneth J. (Ladenson, Mark L. and Kenneth J. Bombara. "Entry In Commercial Banking: 1962-78," JMCB, 1984, v16(2), 165-174.)

Bombara, Kenneth J. (Ladenson, Mark L. and Kenneth J. Bombara. "Entry In Commercial Banking: A Reply," JMCB, 1986, v18(3), 390-391.)

Bombaugh, Robert L. "The Economic Significance Of Loss Shifting In The United States," JRI, 1961, v28(4), 13-22.

Bomberger, W. A. and G. E. Makinen. "The Fischer Effect: Graphical Treatment And Some Econometric Implications," JOF, 1977, v32(3), 719-733.

Bomberger, William A. and William J. Frazer, Jr. "Interest Rates, Uncertainty And The Livingston Data," JOF, 1981, v36(3), 661-675.

Bomberger, William. (Anderson, Robert, William Bomberger, and Gail Makinen. "The Demand For Money, The `Reform Effect,' And The Money Supply Process In Hyperinflation: Evidence From Greece And Hungary," JMCB, 1988, v20(4), 653-672.)

Bomhoff, Eduard J. and Kees G. Koedijk. "Bilateral Exchange Rates And Risk Premia," JIMF, 1988, v7(2), 205-220.

Bond, F. M. "Yields On Convertible Securities: 1969-1974," JBFA, 1976, v3(2), 93-114.

Bond, Gary E. and Stanley R. Thompson. "Optimal Commodity Hedging Within The Capital Asset Pricing Model," JFM, 1986, v6(3), 421-432.

Bond, Gary E., Stanley R. Thompson and Benny M. S. Lee. "Application Of A Simplified Hedging Rule," JFM, 1987, v7(1), 65-72.

Bond, Michael T. (Rubens, Jack H., Michael T. Bond and James R. Webb. "The Inflation-Hedging Effectiveness Of Real Estate," JRER, 1989, v4(2), 45-55.)

Bond, Richard E. "Deposit Composition And Commercial Bank Earnings," JOF, 1971, v26(1), 39-50.

Boness, A. J. (Chen, A. H. and A. J. Boness. "Effects Of Uncertain Inflation On The Investment And Financing Decisions Of A Firm," JOF, 1975, v30(2), 469-483.)

Boness, A. James and Frank C. Jen. "A Model Of Information Diffusion, Stock Market Behavior, And Equilibrium Price," JFQA, 1970, v5(3), 279-296.

Boness, A. James and George M. Frankfurter. "Evidence Of Non-Homogeneity Of Capital Costs Within `Risk-Classes'," JOF, 1977, v32(3), 775-787.

Boness, A. James, Andrew H. Chen and Som Jatusipitak. "On Relations Among Stock Price Behavior And Changes In The Capital Structure Of The Firm," JFQA, 1972, v7(4), 1967-1982.

Boness, A. James, Andrew H. Chen and Som Jatusipitak. "Investigations Of Nonstationarity In Prices," JOB, 1974, v47(4), 518-537.

Boness, A. James. "A Pedagogic Note On The Cost Of Capital," JOF, 1964, v19(1), 99-106.

Boness, A. James. "The Valuation Of Stock Options: Comment," JFQA, 1968, v3(2), 225-226.

Boness, A. James. (Lai, Tsong-Yue and A. James Boness. "Investment In The Long Run," FR, 1984, v19(4), 285-300.)

Bonham, Howard B., Jr. "Creditor's Right To Inside Information," FAJ, 1970, v26(1), 115-118.

Bonham, Howard B., Jr. "Projections Of The DJIA," FAJ, 1968, v24(3), 104-110.

Bonham, T. W. (Klock, David R. and T. W. Bonham. "Life Insurance Agents And Executives: A Test Of Incongruent Perceptions," JRI, 1974, v41(2), 249-258.)

Boni, Alfred C. "Influence Of `Extras' & `Specials' On Yields," FAJ, 1959, v15(4), 51-54.

Bonin, Joseph M. and Edward A. Moses. "Seasonal Variations In Prices Of Individual Dow Jones Industrial Stocks," JFQA, 1974, v9(6), 963-991.

Bonini, Charles P. "Capital Investment Under Uncertainty With Abandonment Options," JFQA, 1977, v12(1), 39-54.

Bonitsis, Theologos Homer and Raj Aggarwal. "U.S. Direct Foreign Investment And Economic Growth In Brazil: An Econometric Causal Analysis," IJOF, 1990, v2(2), 12-19.

Bonker, Dick. "The `Rule Of 78'," JOF, 1976, v31(3), 877-888.

Bonner, Gordon R. "Some Notes On The Rehabilitation Of Preferred Stock," FR, 1966, v1(1), 32-37.

Bonomo, Vittorio and Charles Schotta. "Federal Open Market Operations And Variations In The Reserve Base," JOF, 1970, v25(3), 659-667.

Bonomo, Vittorio and Charles Schotta. "Federal Open Market Operations And Variations In The Reserve Base: Reply," JOF, 1972, v27(3), 730-732.

Bonser-Neal, Catherine, Greggory Brauer, Robert Neal and Simon Wheatley. "International Investment Restrictions And Closed-End Country Fund Prices," JOF, 1990, v45(2), 523-548.

Booher, Edward E. "Book Publishing 25 Years From Now," FAJ, 1961, v17(4), 13-17.

Bookstaber, Richard and David P. Jacob. "The Composite Hedge: Controlling The Credit Risk Of High-Yield Bonds," FAJ, 1986, v42(2), 25-36.

Bookstaber, Richard and Roger Clarke. "Problems In Evaluating The Performance Of Portfolios With Options," FAJ, 1985, v41(1), 48-62.

Bookstaber, Richard and Roger Clarke. "Options Can Alter Portfolio Return Distributions," JPM, 1981, v7(3), 63-70.

Bookstaber, Richard M. and James B. McDonald. "A Generalized Option Valuation Model For The Pricing Of Bond Options," RFM, 1985, v4(1), 60-73.

Bookstaber, Richard M. "Contract And Market Hedging: A Comparison Of Futures Contracts And Adjustable Rate Mortgages In Hedging Interest Rate Risk," RFM, 1986, v5(2), 100-123.

Bookstaber, Richard M. "Futures Market Participation With Differential Information," RIF, 1983, v4, 165-182.)

Bookstaber, Richard M. "Observed Option Mispricing And The Nonsimultaneity Of Stock And Option Quotations," JOB, 1981, v54(1), 141-155.

Bookstaber, Richard M. and James B. McDonald. "A General Distribution For Describing Security Price Returns," JOB, 1987, v60(3), 401-424.

Bookstaber, Richard M. and Steven Pomerantz. "An Information-Based Model Of Market Volatility," FAJ, 1989, v45(6), 37-46.

Bookstaber, Richard and Jeremy Gold. "In Search Of The Liability Asset," FAJ, 1988, v44(1), 70-80.

Bookstaber, Richard and Joseph A. Langsam. "Portfolio Insurance Trading Rules," **JFM**, 1988, v8(1), 15-32.

Bookstaber, Richard and Roger Clarke. "Option Portfolio Strategies: Measurement And Evaluation," **JOB**, 1984, v57(4), 469-492.

Bookstaber, Richard. "Interest Rate Hedging For The Mortgage Banker: The Effect Of Interest Rate Futures And Loan Commitments On Portfolio Return Distributions," **RFM**, 1982, v1(1), 22-51.

Bookstaber, Richard. "The Efficiency Of The Exchange Market And The Biasness Of The Forward Rate: A Joint Test," **JFR**, 1980, v3(1), 11-21.

Bookstaber, Richard. "The Use Of Options In Performance Structuring," **JPM**, 1985, v11(4), 36-50.

Boone, Louis E. "The Search For The Consumer Innovator," **JOB**, 1970, v43(2), 135-140.

Boorman, John T. "The Prospects For Minority-Owned Commercial Banks: A Comparative Performance Analysis," **JBR**, 1973-74, v4(4), 263-279.

Boorman, John T. "The Start-Up Experience Of Minority-Owned Commercial Banks: A Comparative Analysis," **JOF**, 1974, v29(4), 1123-1141.

Boorman, John T. and Manferd Peterson. "The Hunt Commission & The Mortgage Market: An Appraisal," **JBR**, 1972-73, v3(3), 155-165.

Boose, Mary Ann. "Agency Theory And Alternative Predictions For Life Insurers: An Empirical Test," **JRI**, 1990, v57(3), 499-518.

Boot, Arnoud, Anjan V. Thakor and Gregory F. Udell. "Competition, Risk Neutrality And Loan Commitments," **JBF**, 1987, v11(3), 449-472.

Boot, John C. G. and George M. Frankfurter. "The Dynamics Of Corporate Debt Management, Decision Rules, And Some Empirical Evidence," **JFQA**, 1972, v7(4), 1957-1965.

Boot, John C. G. and George M. Frankfurter. "Reply: The Dynamics Of Corporate Debt Management, Decision Rules And Some Empirical Evidence," **JFQA**, 1974, v9(6), 1067-1068.

Booth, G. Geoffrey and Fred R. Kaen. "Gold And Silver Spot Prices And Market Information Efficiency," **FR**, 1979, v14(2), 21-26.

Booth, G. Geoffrey and Gordon H. Dash, Jr. "Alternate Programming Structures For Bank Portfolios," **JBF**, 1979, v3(1), 67-82.

Booth, G. Geoffrey and Peter E. Koveos. "A Programming Model For Bank Hedging Decisions," **JFR**, 1986, v9(3), 271-279.

Booth, G. Geoffrey and Gordon H. Dash. "Bank Portfolio Management Using Non-Linear Goal Programming," **FR**, 1977, v12(1), 59-69.

Booth, G. Geoffrey and Peter E. Koveos. "Purchasing Power Parity: A Reexamination Of Prediction Errors," **AFPAF**, 1989, v3(1), 143-162.

Booth, G. Geoffrey, Fred R. Kaen and Peter E. Koveos. "Persistent Dependence In Gold Prices," **JFR**, 1982, v5(1), 85-93.

Booth, G. Geoffrey, Fred R. Kaen and Peter E. Koveos. "Currency Interdependence In Foreign Exchange Markets," **FR**, 1980, v15(3), 36-44.

Booth, G. Geoffrey, James E. Duggan and Peter E. Koveos. "Deviations From Purchasing Power Parity, Relative Inflation, And Exchange Rates: The Recent Experience," **FR**, 1985, v20(2), 195-218.

Booth, G. Geoffrey. "Programming Bank Portfolios Under Uncertainty: An Extension," **JBR**, 1971-72, v2(4), 28-40.

Booth, G. Geoffrey. (Akgiray, Vedat and G. Geoffrey Booth. "Compound Distribution Models Of Stock Returns," **JFR**, 1987, v10(3), 269-280.)

Booth, G. Geoffrey. (Akgiray, Vedat, G. Geoffrey Booth and Bruce Seifert. "Distribution Properties Of Latin American Black Market Exchange Rates," **JIMF**, 1988, v7(1), 37-48.)

Booth, G. Geoffrey. (Burt, John, Fred R. Kaen and G. Geoffrey Booth. "Foreign Exchange Market Efficiency Under Flexible Exchange Rates," **JOF**, 1977, v32(4), 1325-1330.)

Booth, G. Geoffrey. (Burt, John, Fred R. Kaen and G. Geoffrey Booth. "Foreign Exchange Market Efficiency Under Flexible Exchange Rates: Reply," **JOF**, 1979, v34(3), 791-793.)

Booth, G. Geoffrey. (Milonas, Nicholaos T., Peter E. Koveos and G. Geoffrey Booth. "Memory In Commodity Futures Contracts: A Comment," **JFM**, 1985, v5(1), 113-114.)

Booth, Geoffrey. (Akgiray, Vedat and Geoffrey Booth. "Stock Price Processes With Discontinuous Time Paths: An Empirical Examination," **FR**, 1986, v21(2), 163-184.)

Booth, Geoffrey. (Kim, Moon and Geoffrey Booth. "Yield Structure Of Taxable Vs. Nontaxable Bonds," **JFR**, 1985, v8(2), 95-105.)

Booth, James R. and Dennis T. Officer. "Expectations, Interest Rates, And Commercial Bank Stocks," **JFR**, 1985, v8(1), 51-58.

Booth, James R. and Richard L. Smith, II. "The Application Of Errors-In-Variables Methodology To Capital Market Research: Evidence On The Small Firm Effect," **JFQA**, 1985, v20(4), 501-516.

Booth, James R. and Richard L. Smith, II. "Capital Raising, Underwriting And The Certification Hypothesis," **JFEC**, 1986, v15(1/2), 261-281.

Booth, James R. and Richard L. Smith, II. "The Impact Of The Community Reinvestment Act On Branching Activity Of Financial Institutions," **JBR**, 1984-85, v15(2), 123-128.

Booth, James R. "NOW Accounts: The Competitive Battle In The Western States," **JBR**, 1982-83, v13(4), 317-320.

Booth, James R. (Smith, Richard L. and James R. Booth. "The Risk Structure Of Interest Rates And Interdependent Borrowing Costs: The Impact Of Major Defaults," **JFR**, 1985, v8(2), 83-94.)

Booth, James R. (Trennepohl, Gary L., James R. Booth and Hassan Tehranian. "An Empirical Analysis Of Insured Portfolio Strategies Using Listed Options," **JFR**, 1988, v11(1), 1-12.)

Booth, James R. and Richard L. Smith. "An Examination Of The Small-Firm Effect On The Basis Of Skewness Preference," **JFR**, 1987, v10(1), 77-88.

Booth, James R., Hassan Tehranian and Gary L. Trennepohl. "Efficiency Analysis And Option Portfolio Selection," **JFQA**, 1985, v20(4), 435-450.

Booth, James R., Richard L. Smith and Richard W. Stolz. "Use Of Interest Rate Futures By Financial Institutions," **JBR**, 1984-85, v15(1), 15-20.

Booth, L. D. and D. J. Johnston. "The Ex-Dividend Day Behavior Of Canadian Stock Prices: Tax Changes And Clientele Effects," **JOF**, 1984, v39(2), 457-476.

Booth, L. D. "On The `Unanimity' Literature And The Security Market Line Criterion: A Note," **JBFA**, 1983, v10(4), 677-681.

Booth, L. D. (Vander Kraats, R. H. and L. D. Booth. "Empirical Tests Of The Monetary Approach To Exchange-Rate Determination," **JIMF**, 1983, v2(3), 255-278.)

Booth, Laurence D. "Bid-Ask Spreads In The Market For Forward Exchange," **JIMF**, 1984, v3(2), 209-222.

Booth, Laurence D. "Correct Procedures For The Evaluation Of Risky Cash Outflows," **JFQA**, 1982, v17(2), 287-300.

Booth, Laurence D. "Market Structure Uncertainty And The Cost Of Equity Capital," **JBF**, 1981, v5(4), 467-482.

Booth, Laurence D. "On The Negative Risk Premium For Risk Adjusted Discount Rates: A Comment And Extension," **JBFA**, 1983, v10(1), 147-155.

Booth, Laurence D. "On The Relationship Between Time State Preference And Capital Asset Pricing Models," **FR**, 1984, v19(2), 251-265.

Booth, Laurence D. "Stochastic Demand, Output And The Cost Of Capital: A Clarification," **JOF**, 1980, v35(3), 795-798.

Booth, Laurence David. "Taxes, Funds Positioning, And The Cost Of Capital For Multinationals," **AFPAF**, 1990, v5(1), 245-270.

Booth, Laurence. "The Influence Of Production Technology On Risk And The Cost Of Capital," **JFQA**, 1991, v26(1), 109-128.

Booth, Peter J. "Decomposition Measures And The Prediction Of Financial Failure," **JBFA**, 1983, v10(1), 67-82.

Booth, Peter and Neil Cocks. "Critical Research Issues In Accounting Standard-Setting," **JBFA**, 1990, v17(4), 511-528.

Booth, Peter and Patrick Hutchinson. "Distinguishing Between Failing And Growing Firms: A Note On The Use Of Decomposition Measure Analysis," **JBFA**, 1989, v16(2), 267-272.

Boothe, Paul and David Longworth. "Foreign Exchange Market Efficiency Tests: Implications Of Recent Empirical Findings," **JIMF**, 1986, v5(2), 135-152.

Bopp, Anthony E. and Scott Sitzer. "Are Petroleum Prices Good Predictors Of Cash Value?," **JFM**, 1987, v7(6), 705-720.

Bopp, Karl R. "Central Banking Objectives, Guides, And Measures," **JOF**, 1954, v9(1), 12-22.

Boquist, John A. and William T. Moore. "Estimating The Systematic Risk Of An Industry Segment: A Mathematical Programming Approach," **FM**, 1983, v12(4), 11-18.

Boquist, John A. and William T. Moore. "Inter-Industry Leverage Differences And The DeAngelo-Masulis Tax Shield Hypothesis," **FM**, 1984, v13(1), 5-9.

Boquist, John A., George A. Racette and Gary G. Schlarbaum. "Duration And Risk Assessment For Bonds And Common Stocks: A Note," **JOF**, 1975, v30(5), 1360-1365.

Borch, Karl. "A Note On Option Prices," **FR**, 1984, v19(1), 124-127.

Borch, Karl. "A Shortcut To CAPM," **FR**, 1982, v17(3), 174-176.

Borch, Karl. "Additive Insurance Premiums: A Note," **JOF**, 1982, v37(5), 1295-1298.

Borch, Karl. "CAPM As A Special Case," **FR**, 1982, v17(4), 295-298.

Borch, Karl. "Capital Markets And The Supervision Of Insurance Companies," **JRI**, 1974, v41(3), 397-405.

Borch, Karl. "Equilibrium Premiums In An Insurance Market," **JRI**, 1984, v51(3), 468-476.

Borch, Karl. "Equilibrium, Optimum And Prejudices In Capital Markets," **JFQA**, 1969, v4(1), 1-14.

Borch, Karl. "Portfolio Theory Is For Risk Lovers," **JBF**, 1978, v2(2), 179-182.

Borch, Karl. "Premiums In A Competitive Insurance Market," **JBF**, 1984, v8(3), 431-441.

Borch, Karl. "Some Elements Of A Theory Of Reinsurance," **JRI**, 1961, v28(3), 35-44.

Borch, Karl. "The Monster In Loch Ness," **JRI**, 1976, v43(3), 521-525.

Borch, Karl. "The Theory Of Control Processes Applied To Insurance Companies," **JRI**, 1967, v34(4), 581-592.

Bordo, Michael D. and Ehsan U. Choudhri. "Currency Substitution And The Demand For Money: Some Evidence For Canada," **JMCB**, 1982, v14(1), 48-57.

Bordo, Michael D., Ehsan U. Choudhri and Anna J. Schwartz. "The Behavior Of Money Stock Under Interest Rate Control: Some Evidence For Canada," **JMCB**, 1987, v19(2), 181-198.

Borg, Robert W. "An Employee Benefits Reporting Service," **JRI**, 1966, v33(4), 643-645.

Boring, R. A. (Tull, D. S., R. A. Boring and M. H. Gonsior. "A Note On The Relationship Of Price And Imputed Quality," **JOB**, 1964, v37(2), 186-191.)

Borman, Clyde E. "Co-op Banks And Big Credit," **FAJ**, 1961, v17(2), 45-51.

Borman, Clyde E. "What About Agency Issues?," **FAJ**, 1959, v15(1), 61-66.

Born, Jeffery A. and Seth C. Anderson. "A Comparison Of Intervention And Residual Analysis," **JFR**, 1986, v9(3), 261-270.

Born, Jeffery A. (Anderson, Seth C. and Jeffery A. Born. "The Selling And Seasoning Of Investment Company Offerings," **JFSR**, 1989, v2(2), 115-132.)

Born, Jeffery A. "Insider Ownership And Signals--Evidence From Dividend Initiation Announcement Effects," **FM**, 1988, v17(1), 38-45.

Born, Jeffrey A. (Anderson, Seth C., Jeffrey A. Born and T. Randolph Beard. "An Analysis Of Bond Investment Company Initial Public Offerings: Past And Present," **FR**, 1991, v26(2), 211-222.)

Born, Jeffrey A. (McIntosh, Willard, Dennis T. Officer and Jeffrey A. Born. "The Wealth Effects Of Merger Activities: Further Evidence From Real Estate Investment Trusts," **JRER**, 1989, v4(3), 141-155.)

Born, Jeffrey A. and James T. Moser. "An Investigation Into The Role Of The Market Portfolio In The Arbitrage Pricing Theory," **FR**, 1988, v23(3), 287-300.

Born, Jeffrey A. and James T. Moser. "Bank-Equity Returns And Changes In The Discount Rate," **JFSR**, 1990, v4(3), 223-242.

Born, Jeffrey A., James T. Moser and Dennis T. Officer. "Changes In Dividend Policy And Subsequent Earnings," **JPM**, 1988, v14(4), 56-62.

Born, Jeffrey A., Robert A. Eisenbeis and Robert Harris. "The Benefits Of Geographical And Product Expansion In The Financial Services Industry," **JFSR**, 1988, v1(2), 161-182.

Born, Waldo L. "A Real Estate Market Research Method To Screen Areas For New Construction Potential," **JRER**, 1988, v3(3), 51-62.

Born, Waldo L. (Pyhrr, Stephen A., Waldo L. Born and James R. Webb. "Development Of A Dynamic Investment Strategy Under Alternative Inflation Cycle Scenarios," JRER, 1990, v5(2), 177-193.)

Born, Waldo and B. Earl Williams. "Electronic Data Transmission Pathways: Implications For Site Selection," JRER, 1989, v4(3), 95-105.

Bornemann, Alfred H. "The Emergence Of Incomes Policies," FAJ, 1966, v22(2), 19-26.

Bornemann, Alfred. "The Development Of Economics And Administration In The School Of Business," JOB, 1957, v30(2), 131-140.

Borowski, David M. (Elmer, Peter J. and David M. Borowski. "An Expert System Approach To Financial Analysis: The Case Of S&L Bankruptcy," FM, 1988, v17(3), 66-76.)

Borts, G. H. "The Benston Paper: Some Comments," JMCB, 1972, v4(2), 419-421.

Borts, George H. "Agenda For A Commission To Study Financial Markets, Their Structure, And Regulation," JMCB, 1971, v3(1), 2-6.

Bortz, Gary A. "Does The Treasury Bond Futures Market Destabilize The Treasury Bond Cash Market?," JFM, 1984, v4(1), 25-38.

Borun, Victor M. (Finnerty, John D. and Victor M. Borun. "An Analysis Of Unbundled Stock Units," GFJ, 1989, v1(1), 47-70.)

Bos, T. and P. Newbold. "An Empirical Investigation Of The Possibility Of Stochastic Systematic Risk In The Market Model," JOB, 1984, v57(1), Part 1, 35-42.

Bosch, J. C. "Portfolio Choices, Consumption, And Prices In A Market With Durable Assets," JFR, 1986, v9(3), 239-250.

Bosch, Jean-Claude and Mark Hirschey. "The Valuation Effects Of Corporate Name Changes," FM, 1989, v18(4), 64-73.

Bosch, Jean-Claude, James R. Morris and Steve B. Wyatt. "The Investment In Housing As A Forward Market Transaction: Implications For Tenure Choice And Portfolio Selection," AREUEA, 1986, v14(3), 385-405.

Bosch, Jean-Claude. "Speculation And The Market For Recommendations," JFR, 1983, v6(2), 103-113.

Boschen, John F. "Employment And Output Effects Of Observed And Unobserved Monetary Growth," JMCB, 1985, v17(2), 153-163.

Boschen, John F. "The Information Content Of Indexed Bonds," JMCB, 1986, v18(1), 76-87.

Boschen, John F. and John L. Newman. "Monetary Effects On The Real Interest Rate In An Open Economy: Evidence From The Argentine Indexed Bond Market," JIMF, 1989, v8(2), 201-218.

Bosland, Chelcie C. "Materials And Methods Of Teaching Business Finance (IV)," JOF, 1950, v5(3), 285-288.

Bosland, Chelcie C. "The Valuation Of Public Utility Enterprises By The Securities And Exchange Commission," JOF, 1961, v16(1), 52-64.

Bossaerts, Peter and Richard C. Green. "A General Equilibrium Model Of Changing Risk Premia: Theory And Tests," RFS, 1989, v2(4), 467-494.

Bosshardt, Donald I. "A Model Of Intertemporal Discount Rates In The Presence Of Real And Inflationary Autocorrelations," JOF, 1987, v42(4), 1049-1070.

Bosshardt, Donald I. "Equity Clienteles, Short-Sale Restrictions, And The Miller Equilibrium," FR, 1984, v19(2), 240-250.

Bostian, David B., Jr. "Market Analysis And Portfolio Strategy," JPM, 1975, v1(4), 44-53.

Bostian, David B., Jr. "The Impact Of Institutions On The Market," FAJ, 1973, v29(6), 30-32,35-36,86-93.

Bostock, Paul, Paul Woolley and Martin Duffy. "Duration-Based Asset Allocation," FAJ, 1989, v45(1), 53-60.

Bosworth, Barry P. "Nonmonetary Aspects Of Inflation," JMCB, 1980, v12(3), 527-539.

Bosworth, Barry. (Duesenberry, James and Barry Bosworth. "Policy Implications Of A Flow-Of-Funds Model," JOF, 1974, v29(2), 331-347.)

Bottlieb, Manuel. "The Capital Levy And Deadweight Debt In England - 1815-40," JOF, 1953, v8(1), 34-46.

Botts, Ralph R. "Federal Crop Insurance," JRI, 1956, v23, 123-128.

Boudreaux, Kenneth J. and Hugh W. Long. "Incorporating The Capital Asset Pricing Model Into The Basic Finance Course," JFED, 1976, v5, 15-20.

Boudreaux, Kenneth J. and Hugh W. Long. "The Weighted Average Cost Of Capital As A Cutoff Rate: A Further Analysis," FM, 1979, v8(2), 7-14.

Boudreaux, Kenneth J. "Competitive Rates And Market Efficiency," FAJ, 1975, v31(2),18-19,22-24,92.

Boudreaux, Kenneth J. "Discounts And Premiums On Closed-End Mutual Funds: A Study In Valuation," JOF, 1973, v28(2), 515-522.

Boudreaux, Kenneth J. "Divestiture And Share Price," JFQA, 1975, v10(4), 619-626.

Boudreaux, Kenneth J. "The Pricing Of Mutual Fund Shares," FAJ, 1974, v30(1), 26-32.

Boudreaux, Kenneth J. (Lam, Chun H. and Kenneth J. Boudreaux. "Compensating Balance, Rationality, And Optimality," JBF, 1981, v5(4), 451-466.)

Boudreaux, Kenneth J. (Lam, Chun H. and Kenneth J. Boudreaux. "Compensating Balances, Deficiency Fees, And Lines Of Credit," JBF, 1983, v7(3),307-322.)

Boudreaux, Kenneth J. (Lam, Chun H. and Kenneth J. Boudreaux. "Conglomerate Merger, Wealth Redistribution And Debt: A Note," JOF, 1984, v39(1), 275-281.)

Bougen, P. D. and J. C. Drury. "U.K. Statistical Distributions Of Financial Ratios, 1975," JBFA, 1980, v7(1), 39-47.

Boughton, J. M. "External Adjustment In Large Countries: Is The Exchange Rate Irrelevant?," JBF, 1990, v14(5), 947-964.

Boughton, James M. and Elmus R. Wicker. "The Behavior Of The Currency-Deposit Ratio During The Great Depression: A Reply," JMCB, 1984, v16(3), 366-367.

Boughton, James M. and Elmus R. Wicker. "The Behavior Of The Currency-Deposit Ratio During The Great Depression," JMCB, 1979, v11(4), 405-418.

Boughton, James M. "Econometric Models: A Decision Making Tool For Bank Management," JBR, 1970-71, v1(2), 9-19.

Boulton, Schroeder. "Federal Income Taxes, Business Enterprise And A Depreciating Dollar," FAJ, 1957, v13(2), 23-28.

Boulton, Schroeder. "Growth Of The Airline Industry," FAJ, 1955, v11(4), 29-34.

Boulton, Schroeder. "How Unpopular Should Steel Stocks Be?," FAJ, 1953, v9(5), 23-26.

Boulton, Schroeder. "Strength Of Textile Industry," FAJ, 1948, v4(2), 13-19.

Boulton, Schroeder. "The Bugaboo Of Labor Costs," FAJ, 1945, v1(2), 55-59.

Bourke, Philip. "Concentration And Other Determinants Of Bank Profitability In Europe, North America And Australia," JBF, 1989, v13(1), 65-80.

Bourke, Philip. "Some International Aspects Of Bank Stability, Deposit Insurance And Regulation," RDIBF, 1989, v3, 25-44.

Bourn, Michael, P. J. M. Stoney and R. F. Wynn. "Price Indices For Current Cost Accounting: A Rejoinder," JBFA, 1977, v4(1), 145-150.

Bourn, Michael, P. J. M. Stoney and R. F. Wynn. "Price Indices For Current Cost Accounting," JBFA, 1976, v3(3), 149-172.

Bourn, Michael. "The `Gain' On Borrowing," JBFA, 1976,v3(1),167-182.

Bousquet, L. (Solnik, B. and L. Bousquet. "Day-Of-The-Week Effect On The Paris Bourse," JBF, 1990, v14(2/3), 461-468.)

Bouwer, Dennis R. (Patterson, Solon P., Dennis R. Bouwer, Theodore R. Lilley and Benjamin C. Korschot. "Long-Range Planning In The FAF," FAJ, 1979, v35(1), 23-26.)

Bowen, Howard R. "The Teaching Of Money And Banking," JOF, 1949, v4(3), 231-237.

Bowen, Robert M., Lane A. Daley and Charles C. Huber, Jr. "Leverage Measures And Industrial Classification: Review And Additional Evidence," FM, 1982, v11(4), 10-20.

Bowen, Robert M., Richard P. Castanias and Lane A. Daley. "Intra-Industry Effects Of The Accident At Three Mile Island," JFQA, 1983, v18(1), 87-111.

Bower, Casper M. "Barometer Needed For Defense Costs," FAJ, 1959, v15(5), 33-38.

Bower, Casper M. "Clinical Analysis Of Young Companies," FAJ, 1962, v18(5), 49-51.

Bower, Casper M. "Freight In Flight," FAJ, 1958, v14(2), 93-97.

Bower, Dorothy H. and Richard S. Bower. "Test Of A Stock Valuation Model," JOF, 1970, v25(2),483-492.

Bower, Dorothy H. (Bower, Richard S. and Dorothy H. Bower. "The Salomon Brothers Electric Utility Model: Another Challenge To Market Efficiency," FAJ, 1984, v40(5), 57-67.)

Bower, Dorothy H., Richard S. Bower and Dennis E. Logue. "Arbitrage Pricing Theory And Utility Stock Returns," JOF, 1984, v39(4), 1041-1054.

Bower, Dorothy H., Richard S. Bower and Dennis E. Logue. "Equity Screening Rates Using Arbitrage Pricing Theory," AFPAF, 1985, v1(1), 29-48.

Bower, Nancy L. "Firm Value And The Choice Of Offering Method In Initial Public Offerings," JOF, 1989, v44(3), 647-662.

Bower, R. S. (Williamson, J. P. and R. S. Bower. "Measuring Pension Fund Performance: Another Comment," FAJ, 1966, v22(3), 143-149.)

Bower, Richard S. and David H. Downes. "The Time-Sharing Decision In Banking," JBR, 1971-72, v2(3), 9-21.)

Bower, Richard S. and Donald R. Lessard. "An Operational Approach To Risk-Screening," JOF, 1973, v28(2), 321-337.

Bower, Richard S. and Dorothy H. Bower. "The Salomon Brothers Electric Utility Model: Another Challenge To Market Efficiency," FAJ, 1984, v40(5),57-67.

Bower, Richard S. and Jeffrey M. Jenks. "Divisional Screening Rates," FM, 1974, v4(3), 42-49.

Bower, Richard S. and John M. Scheidell. "Operationalism In Finance And Economics," JFQA, 1970, v5(4), 469-495.

Bower, Richard S. and Kenneth J. McPartlin. "Oh, To Be In Equities, Now That Winter's Here," JPM, 1975, v2(1), 39-45

Bower, Richard S. and Ronald F. Wippern. "Risk-Return Measurement In Portfolio Selection And Performance Appraisal Models: Progress Report," JFQA, 1969, v4(4), 417-447.

Bower, Richard S. "Issues In Lease Financing," FM, 1973, v2(4), 25-34.

Bower, Richard S. "Time-Sharing At Tuck," JFED, 1972, v1, 92-94.

Bower, Richard S. (Bower, Dorothy H. and Richard S. Bower. "Test Of A Stock Valuation Model," JOF, 1970, v25(2), 483-492.)

Bower, Richard S. (Bower, Dorothy H., Richard S. Bower and Dennis E. Logue. "Arbitrage Pricing Theory And Utility Stock Returns," JOF, 1984, v39(4), 1041-1054.)

Bower, Richard S. (Bower, Dorothy H., Richard S. Bower and Dennis E. Logue. "Equity Screening Rates Using Arbitrage Pricing Theory," AFPAF, 1985, v1(1), 29-48.).

Bower, Richard S. (Nimrod, Vance L. and Richard S. Bower. "Commodities And Computers," JFQA, 1967, v2(1), 58-73.)

Bower, Richard S., Christopher E. Nugent, Barbara C. Myers and J. Peter Williamson. "A Language For Financial Analysts," FAJ, 1967, v23(1), 121.

Bowers, David A. and Lorraine E. Duro. "An Alternative Estimation Of The `Neutralized Money Stock'," JOF, 1972, v27(1), 61-64.

Bowers, David A. "A Warning Note On Empirical Research Using Foreign Exchange Rates," JFQA, 1977, v12(2), 315-319.

Bowers, E. L. (Loman, H. J., E. L. Bowers and J. E. Partington. "Report Of The Committee On Standards And Topics For Courses In Insurance," JRI, 1937, v4, 5-9.)

Bowers, Edison L. "Social Insurance In The University Curriculum," JRI, 1939, v6, 62-69.

Bowers, Edison L. "Teaching Social Insurance As A Course In The Insurance Curriculum," JRI, 1956, v23, 5-16.

Bowers, Edison L. "The Attitude Of Companies In Accepting Large Amounts Of Single Premium And Annuity Contracts," JRI, 1934, v1, 1-4.

Bowers, Helen M. and Robert E. Miller. "Choice Of Investment Banker And Shareholders' Wealth Of Firms Involved In Acquisitions," FM, 1990, v19(4), 34-44.

Bowes, Arthur S., Jr. and Wayne P. Hochmuth. "Investment Companies: Performances Vs. Charges (Part II)," FAJ, 1961, v17(2), 83-88.

Bowes, Arthur S., Jr. (Hochmuth, Wayne P. and Arthur S. Bowes, Jr. "Investment Companies: Performance Vs. Charges (Part I)," FAJ, 1961, v17(1), 43-49.

Bowlin, Lyle and Michael S. Rozeff. "Do Specialists' Short Sales Predict Returns?," JPM, 1987, v13(3), 59-63.

Bowlin, Oswald D. and William P. Dukes. "The Dual Nature Of Beta Responsiveness," JPM, 1983, v9(2), 51-56.

Bowlin, Oswald D. "The Current Ratio In Current Position Analysis," FAJ, 1963, v19(2), 67-72.

Bowlin, Oswald D. "The Refunding Decision: Another Special Case In Capital Budgeting," JOF, 1966, v21(1), 55-68.

Bowlin, Oswald D. (Joehnk, Michael D., Oswald D. Bowlin and J. William Petty. "Preferred Dividend Rolls: A Viable Strategy For Corporate Money Managers?," FM, 1980, v9(2), 78-87.)

Bowlin, Oswald D. (Petty, J. William and Oswald D. Bowlin. "The Financial Manager And Quantitative Decision Models," FM, 1976, v5(4), 32-41.)

Bowling, Clinton H. (Ang, James S., Jess H. Chua and Clinton H. Bowling. "The Profiles Of Late-Paying Consumer Loan Borrowers: An Exploratory Study: A Comment," JMCB, 1979, v11(2), 222-226.)

Bowman, Robert G. "The Role Of Utility In The State-Preference Framework," JFQA, 1975, v10(2), 341-352.

Bowman, Robert G. "The Theoretical Relationship Between Systematic Risk And Financial (Accounting) Variables," JOF, 1979, v34(3), 617-630.

Bowman, Robert G. "The Theoretical Relationship Between Systematic Risk And Financial (Accounting) Variables: Reply," JOF, 1981, v36(3), 749-750.

Bowman, Robert G. "Understanding And Conducting Event Studies," JBFA, 1983, v10(4), 561-584.

Bowman, Ward S., Jr. "Resale Price Maintenance--A Monopoly Problem," JOB, 1952, v25(3), 141-155.

Bowsher, Norman N., J. Dewey Daane and Robert Einzig. "The Flows Of Funds Between Regions Of The United States," JOF, 1958, v13(1), 1-20.

Bowyer, John W., Jr. "The Use Of Small Area Income Estimates In Municipal Credit Analysis," JOF, 1957, v12(1), 16-23.

Bowyer, Linda E. (Whittaker, Gregg, Linda E. Bowyer and Daniel P. Klein. "The Effect Of Futures Trading On The Municipal Bond Market," RFM, 1987, v6(2), 196-204.)

Boy, Alan D. "An Input-Output Planning Model That Takes Into Account Price-Level Changes," JBFA, v3(1), 15-31.

Boyce, W. M. and A. J. Kalotay. "Tax Differentials And Callable Bonds," JOF, 1979, v34(4), 825-838.

Boyd, Donald A. (Hogan, Stephen D. and Donald A. Boyd. "PSI: A Favorable Experience," JFED, 1979, v8, 40-44.)

Boyd, Fulton. "Investment Opportunities In Latin America," FAJ, 1960, v16(5), 7-20.

Boyd, G. Michael and Thomas Bear. "An Applied Course In Investment Analysis And Portfolio Management," JFED, 1984, v13, 68-71.

Boyd, G. Michael. "A Pedagogical Note On Pro Forma Feedback Effects," JFED, 1988, v17, 1-5.

Boyd, G. Michael. "Some Suggestions For A 'New And Improved' DuPont Model," JFED, 1989, v18, 29-32.

Boyd, James C. (Blomeyer, Edward C. and James C. Boyd. "Empirical Tests Of Boundary Conditions For Options On Treasury Bond Futures Contracts," JPM, 1988, v2(2), 185-198.)

Boyd, James W. "Asset Status Proxies And Consumer Preference For ARMs: An Empirical Investigation Using Probit Analysis," JRER, 1988, v3(1), 37-49.

Boyd, John A., Jr. "1961: An Industrial And Stock Market Forecast," FAJ, 1961, v17(1), 7-10.

Boyd, John H. and Eugene P. Schonfeld. "The Effect Of Financial Press Advertising On Stock Prices," FM, 1977, v6(2), 42-51.

Boyd, John H. "Bank Strategies In The Retail Demand Deposit Markets," JBR, 1973-74, v4(2), 111-121.

Boyd, John H. "Deposit Rate Setting By Savings And Loan Associations: Comment," JOF, 1971, v26(5), 1155-1157.

Boyd, John H. "Some Recent Developments In The Savings And Loan Deposit Markets," JMCB, 1973, v5(3), 733-750.

Boyd, John H. (Beighley, H. Prescott, John H. Boyd and Donald P. Jacobs. "Bank Equities And Investor Risk Perceptions: Some Entailments For Capital Adequacy Regulation," JBR, 1975-76, v6(3), 190-201.)

Boyd, John. (Breen, William and John Boyd. "Classroom Simulation As A Pedagogical Device In Teaching Money And Banking," JFQA, 1976, v11(4), 595-606.)

Boyd, Kevin and Vincent A. Mabert. "A Two Stage Forecasting Approach At Chemical Bank Of New York For Check Processing," JBR, 1977-78, v8(2), 101-107.

Boyd, Susan E. (Bethke, William M. and Susan E. Boyd. "Should Dividend Discount Models Be Yield-Tilted?," JPM, 1983, v9(3), 23-27.)

Boyd, William L. "Street-Name Stock Certificates," FAJ, 1970, v26(6), 52-54.

Boyer, Kenneth D. and Kent M. Lancaster. "Are There Scale Economies In Advertising?," JOB, 1986, v59(3), 509-526.

Boyer, Marcel. (Storoy, Sverre, Sten Thore and Marcel Boyer. "Equilibrium In Linear Capital Market Networks," JOF, 1975, v30(5), 1197-1211.)

Boyer, Russell S. (Adams, Charles and Russell S. Boyer. "Efficiency And A Simple Model Of Exchange-Rate Determination," JIMF, 1986, v5(3), 285-302.)

Boyer, Russell S. and F. Charles Adams. "Forward Premia And Risk Premia In A Simple Model Of Exchange Rate Determination," JMCB, 1988, v20(4), 633-644.

Boyer, Russell S. and Geoffrey H. Kingston. "Currency Substitution Under Finance Constraints," JIMF, 1987, v6(3), 235-250.

Boyes, W. J., Dennis Hoffman and Stuart Low. "Lender Reactions To Information Restrictions: The Case Of Banks And The ECOA," JMCB, 1986, v18(2), 211-219.

Boyes, William J. (Officer, Dennis T. and William J. Boyes. "The Behavior Of Brokerage Firm Shares," FAJ, 1984, v40(3), 41-46.)

Boyes, William J., William Stewart Mounts and Clifford Sowell. "The Federal Reserve As A Bureaucracy: An Examination Of Expense-Preference Behavior," JMCB, 1988, v20(2), 181-190.

Boyle, Alexander R. M. and Victor E. Samuelson. "Disclosure Of Long-Term Leases," FAJ, 1962, v18(2), 35-40.

Boyle, Glenn W. "International Interest Rates, Exchange Rates, And The Stochastic Structure Of Supply," JOF, 1990, v45(2), 655-672.

Boyle, Glenn W., John D., Glenn W. Boyle and C. F. Sirmans. "Retail Leasing: The Determinants Of Shopping Center Rents," AREUEA, 1990, v18(3), 302-312.)

Boyle, Glenn W. (Young, Leslie and Glenn W. Boyle. "Forward And Futures Prices In A General Equilibrium Monetary Model," JFEC, 1989, v24(2), 319-342.)

Boyle, P. P. and A. L. Ananthanarayanan. "The Impact Of Variance Estimation In Option Valuation Models," JFEC, 1977, v5(3), 375-387.

Boyle, Phelim P. and David Emanuel. "Discretely Adjusted Option Hedges," JFEC, 1980, v8(3), 259-282.

Boyle, Phelim P. "A Critique Of The Interest-Adjusted Net Cost Index: Comment," JRI, 1975, v42(3), 545-552.

Boyle, Phelim P. "A Lattice Framework For Option Pricing With Two State Variables," JFQA, 1988, v23(1), 1-12.

Boyle, Phelim P. "Financial Instruments For Retired Homeowners," JRI, 1977, v44(3), 513-520.

Boyle, Phelim P. "Karl Borch's Research Contributions To Insurance," JRI, 1990, v57(2), 307-320.

Boyle, Phelim P. "Options: A Monte Carlo Approach," JFEC, 1977, v4(3), 323-338.

Boyle, Phelim P. "Rates Of Return As Random Variables," JRI, 1976, v43(4), 693-714.

Boyle, Phelim P. "Review Of Economics And Insurance: Comment," JRI, 1975, v42(1), 163.

Boyle, Phelim P. "The Quality Option And Timing Option In Futures Contracts," JOF, 1989, v44(1), 101-114.

Boyle, Phelim P. "Valuing Canadian Mortgage-Backed Securities," FAJ, 1989, v45(3), 55-60.

Boyle, Phelim P. and Eduardo S. Schwartz. "Equilibrium Prices Of Guarantees Under Equity-Linked Contracts," JRI, 1977, v44(4), 639-660.

Boyle, Phelim P. and Jennifer Mao. "An Exact Solution For The Optimal Stop Loss Limit," JRI, 1983, v50(4), 719-726.

Boyle, Phelim P. and Stuart M. Turnbull. "Pricing And Hedging Capped Options," JPM, 1989, v9(1), 41-54.

Boyle, Phelim P. and Y. K. Tse. "An Algorithm For Computing Values Of Options On The Maximum Or Minimum Of Several Assets," JFQA, 1990, v25(2), 215-228.

Boyle, Phelim P., Jeremy Evnine and Stephen Gibbs. "Numerical Evaluation Of Multivariate Contingent Claims," RFS, 1989, v2(2), 241-250.

Boynton, Frank D. "Financing The Expanding Mobile Home Industry," FAJ, 1960, v16(2), 87-90.

Braas, Alberic and Charles N. Bralver. "An Analysis Of Trading Profits: How Trading Rooms Really Make Their Money," JACF, 1990, v2(4), 85-90.

Bracken, Jerome. "Models For Call Option Decisions," FAJ, 1968, v24(5), 149-151.

Bradburn, Norman M. (Sudman, Seymour, Norman M. Bradburn and Galen Gockel. "The Extent And Characteristics Of Racially Integrated Housing In The United States," JOB, 1969, v42(1), 50-92.)

Braden, Samuel E. "Income From Gold Output In The Sterling Area," FAJ, 1953, v9(4), 19-22.

Bradfield, James. "A Formal Dynamic Model Of Market Making," JFQA, 1979, v14(2), 275-291.

Bradford, William D. "Minority Savings And Loan Associations: Hypotheses And Tests," JFQA, 1978, v13(3), 533-547.

Bradford, William D. "The Deposit Demand Of Minority Savings And Loan Associations," JBR, 1982-83, v13(1), 28-35.

Bradford, William D. "The Issue Decision Of Manager-Owners Under Information Asymmetry," JOF, 1987, v42(5), 1245-1260.

Bradford, William D. "The Performance Of Merging Savings And Loan Associations," JOB, 1978, v51(1), 115-126.

Bradford, William D. "Valuation, Leverage And The Cost Of Capital In The Case Of Depreciable Assets: Comment," JOF, 1975, v30(1), 214-220.

Bradford, William D. (Spellman, Lewis J., Alfred E. Osborne, Jr. and William D. Bradford. "The Comparative Operating Efficiency Of Black Savings And Loan Associations," JOF, 1977, v32(2), 565-574.)

Bradford, William D., Alfred E. Osborne, Jr. and Lewis J. Spellman. "The Efficiency And Profitability Of Minority Controlled Savings And Loan Associations," JMCB, 1978, v10(1), 65-74.

Bradford, William. (Bates, Timothy and William Bradford. "An Analysis Of The Portfolio Behavior Of Black-Owned Commercial Banks," JOF, 1980, v35(3), 753-768.)

Bradley, Charles E. (Joehnk, Michael D., H. Russell Fogler and Charles E. Bradley. "The Price Elasticity Of Discounted Bonds: Some Empirical Evidence," JFQA, 1978, v13(3), 559-566.)

Bradley, D. P. and M. Walsh. "Portfolio Insurance And The UK Stock Market," JBFA, 1988, v15(1), 67-76.

Bradley, Finbarr. "Neglected Factors In The Market Pricing Of Eurodollar Bonds," JPM, 1991, v17(2), 62-73.

Bradley, James W. and Donald H. Korn. "Acquisition And Merger Trends," FAJ, 1977, v33(6), 65-70.

Bradley, Jerry O. (Joy, O. Maurice and Jerry O. Bradley. "A Note On Sensitivity Analysis Of Rates Of Return," JOF, 1973, v28(5), 1255-1261.)

Bradley, Jerry O. (Joy, O. Maurice and Jerry O. Bradley. "Sensitivity Analysis Of Rates Of Return: Reply," JOF, 1978, v33(5), 1461.)

Bradley, Joseph F. "Voting Rights Of Preferred Stockholders In Industrials," JOF, 1948, v3(3), 78-88.

Bradley, Michael and L. Macdonald Wakeman. "The Wealth Effects Of Targeted Share Repurchases," JFEC, 1983, v11(1), 301-328.

Bradley, Michael D. and Dennis W. Jansen. "Federal Reserve Operating Procedure In The Eighties: A Dynamic Analysis," JMCB, 1986, v18(3), 323-335.

Bradley, Michael D. (Barth, James R. and Michael D. Bradley. "On Interest Rates, Inflationary Expectations And Tax Rates," JBF, 1988, v12(2), 215-220.)

Bradley, Michael G. (Barth, James R., Philip F. Bartholomew and Michael G. Bradley. "Determinants Of Thrift Institution Resolution Costs," JOF, 1990, v45(3), 731-754.)

Bradley, Michael G. (Barth, James R. and Michael G. Bradley. "Thrift

Deregulation And Federal Deposit Insurance," **JFSR**, 1989, v2(3), 231-260.)

Bradley, Michael, Anand Desai and E. Han Kim. "The Rationale Behind Interfirm Tender Offers," **JFEC**, 1983, v11(1), 183-206.

Bradley, Michael, Gregg A. Jarrell and E. Han Kim. "On The Existence Of An Optimal Capital Structure: Theory And Evidence," **JOF**, 1984, v39(3), 857-878.

Bradley, Michael, Anand Desai and E. Han Kim. "Synergistic Gains From Corporate Acquisitions And Their Division Between The Stockholders Of Target And Acquiring Firms," **JFEC**, 1988, v21(1), 3-40.

Bradley, Michael. "Interfirm Tender Offers And The Market For Corporate Control," **JOB**, 1980, v53(4), 345-376.

Bradley, Philip D. "International Business Investment: Governmental And Private," **JOF**, 1952, v7(2), 359-371.

Bradley, Stephen P. and Dwight B. Crane. "Management Of Commercial Bank Government Security Portfolios: An Optimization Approach Under Uncertainty," **JBR**, 1973-74, v4(1), 18-30.

Bradley, Stephen P. and Dwight B. Crane. "Simulation Of Bond Portfolio Strategies: Laddered Vs. Barbell Maturity Structure," **JBR**, 1975-76, v6(2), 122-134.

Bradley, Stephen P. and Sherwood C. Frey, Jr. "Equivalent Mathematical Programming Models Of Pure Capital Rationing," **JFQA**, 1978, v13(2), 345-361.

Bradshaw, Thornton F. "The Corporation Executive's View," **FAJ**, 1971, v27(5), 30-31,70-72.

Brady, Dennis P., Michael L. Brookshire and William E. Cobb. "The Development And Solution Of A Tax-Adjusted Model For Personal Injury Awards," **JRI**, 1984, v51(1), 138-142.

Brady, Dennis, Michael Brookshire and William Cobb. "The Development And Solution Of A Tax-Adjusted Model Of Personal Injury Awards: A Response," **JRI**, 1985, v52(3), 520-521.

Bracutigam, Ronald R. "The Role Of Technological And Market Structure In Regulatory Reform," **JFSR**, 1989, v2(3), 189-204.

Braga, Francesco S. and Larry J. Martin. "Hedging The Corn And Wheat Variable Import Levy Of The European Community," **RFM**, 1987, v6(3), 390-408.

Braga, Francesco S. and Larry J. Martin. "Out Of Sample Effectiveness Of A Joint Commodity And Currency Hedge: The Case Of Soybean Meal In Italy," **JFM**, 1990, v10(3), 229-246.

Braga, Francesco S., Larry J. Martin and Karl D. Meilke. "Cross Hedging The Italian Lira/US Dollar Exchange Rate With Deutsch Mark Futures," **JFM**, 1989, v9(2), 87-100.

Bragg, John M. "Prices And Commissions Based On The Theory Of Games," **JRI**, 1966, v33(2), 169-194.

Brainard, Calvin H. "A Comparison And Integration Of Economic And Actuarial Explanations Of Life Insurance Premium Computations," **JRI**, 1963, v30(2), 257-268.

Brainard, Calvin H. "Rate Making For Automobile Physical Damage Insurance: Comment," **JRI**, 1965, v32(1), 121-128.

Brainard, Calvin H. (Leavitt, Gordon and Calvin H. Brainard. "Reviews Of 'Savings Bank Life Insurance': Comment," **JRI**, 1966, v33(2), 329-332.)

Brainard, Calvin H. and John F. Fitzgerald. "First-Year Cost Results Under No-Fault Automobile Insurance: A Comparison Of The Florida And Massachusetts Experience," **JRI**, 1974, v41(1), 25-39.

Brainard, Clavin H. "Massachusetts Loss Experience Under No-Fault In 1971: Analysis And Implications," **JRI**, 1973, v40(1), 95-101.

Brainard, William C. (Backus, David, William C. Brainard, Gary Smith and James Tobin. "A Model Of U.S. Financial And Nonfinancial Economic Behavior," **JMCB**, 1980, v12(2), Part 1, 259-293.)

Brainard, William. (Smith, Gary and William Brainard. "The Value Of A Priori Information In Estimating A Financial Model," **JOF**, 1976, v31(5), 1299-1322.)

Brainard, William. (Smith, Gary and William Brainard. "A Disequilibrium Model Of Savings And Loan Associations," **JOF**, 1982, v37(5), 1277-1294.)

Bralver, Charles N. (Braas, Alberic and Charles N. Bralver. "An Analysis Of Trading Profits: How Trading Rooms Really Make Their Money," **JACF**, 1990, v2(4), 85-90.)

Branch, Ben and Cornelius Ryan. "Tax Loss Trading: An Inefficiency Too Large To Ignore," **FR**, 1980, v15(1), 20-29.

Branch, Ben and Joseph E. Finnerty. "The Impact Of Option Listing On The Price And Volume Of The Underlying Stock," **FR**, 1981, v16(2), 1-15.

Branch, Ben and Kyungchun Chang. "Tax-Loss Trading - Is The Game Over Or Have The Rules Changed?," **FR**, 1985, v20(1), 55-70.

Branch, Ben and Ruth Newman. "Term Papers In Investments: Alternatives And Style," **JFED**, 1985, v14, 47-59.

Branch, Ben and Walter Freed. "Bid-Asked Spreads On The AMEX And The Big Board," **JOF**, 1977, v32(1), 159-163.

Branch, Ben and David P. Echevarria. "The Impact Of Bid-Ask Prices On Market Anomalies," **FR**, 1991, v26(2), 249-268.

Branch, Ben. "A Tax Loss Trading Rule," **JOB**, 1977, v50(2), 198-207.

Branch, Ben. "Common Stock Performance And Inflation: An International Comparison," **JOB**, 1974, v47(1), 48-52.

Branch, Ben. "Corporate Objectives And Market Performance," **FM**, 1973, v2(2), 24-29.

Branch, Ben. "Guidelines For Students Studying Finance," **JFED**, 1977, v6, 45-50.

Branch, Ben. "Guiding Students In Conducting Original Research," **JFED**, 1978, v3, 34-36.

Branch, Ben. "Reply: The Optimal Price To Trade," **JFQA**, 1979, v14(3), 649-651.

Branch, Ben. "Special Offerings And Market Efficiency," **FR**, 1984, v19(1), 26-35.

Branch, Ben. "Term Papers In The Investments Course," **JFED**, 1976, v5, 26-28.

Branch, Ben. "Testing The Unbiased Expectations Theory Of Interest Rates," **FR**, 1978, v13(2), 51-66.

Branch, Ben. "The Impact Of Operating Decisions On ROI Dynamics," **FM**, 1978, v7(4), 54-60.

Branch, Ben. "The Laws Of The Marketplace And ROI Dynamics," **FM**, 1980, v9(2), 58-65.

Branch, Ben. "The Optimal Price To Trade," **JFQA**, 1975, v10(3), 497-514.

Branch, Ben. "The Predictive Power Of Stock Market Indicators," **JFQA**, 1976, v11(2), 269-286.

Branch, Ben. "Use Of A Stock Market Game In Teaching Investments," **JFED**, 1975, v4, 72-76.

Branch, Ben. (Gleit, Alan and Ben Branch. "The Black-Scholes Model And Stock Price Forecasting," **FR**, 1980, v15(2), 13-22.)

Branch, Ben. (Hegde, Shantaram P. and Ben Branch. "An Empirical Analysis Of Arbitrage Opportunities In The Treasury Bill Futures Market," **JFM**, 1985, v5(3), 407-424.)

Brandenburg, Richard. (Mansfield, Edwin and Richard Brandenburg. "The Allocation, Characteristics, And Outcome Of The Firm's Research And Development Portfolio," **JOB**, 1966, v39(4), 447-464.)

Brandenburg, Richard. (Mansfield, Edwin and Richard Brandenburg. "Reply: The Allocation, Characteristics, And Outcome Of The Firm's Research And Development Portfolio," **JOB**, 1968, v41(1), 91-93.)

Brandon, Charles and Jeffrey Jarrett. "Accuracy Of Forecasts In Annual Reports," **FR**, 1974, v9(1), 29-45.

Brandon, Charles H. and Jeffrey E. Jarrett. "Evaluating Accounting Forecast," **JBFA**, 1976, v3(3), 67-78.

Brandon, Charles, Jeffrey Jarrett and Saleha Khumuwala. "On The Predictability Of Growth In Earnings Per Share," **JBFA**, 1983, v10(3), 373-387.

Brandon, Dick H. "Computer Leasing Industry," **FAJ**, 1968, v24(3), 85-90.

Brandt, Henry. "The Canadian Life Insurance Industry," **FAJ**, 1956, v12(5), 85-88.

Brandt, Jon A. (Holt, Matthew T. and Jon A. Brandt. "Combining Price Forecasting With Hedging Of Hogs: An Evaluation Using Alternative Measures Of Risk," **JFM**, 1985, v5(3), 297-309.)

Brannon, Gerard M. "Tax Policy And Depreciation: The Case For ADR," **JOF**, 1972, v27(2), 525-533.

Branson, William H. and Jorge Braga De Macedo. "The Optimal Weighting Of Indicators For A Crawling Peg," **JIMF**, 1982, v1(2), 165-178.

Branson, William H. and Raymond D. Hill, Jr. "Capital Movements Among Major OECD Countries: Some Preliminary Results," **JOF**, 1971, v26(2), 269-286.

Branson, William H. and Ronald L. Teigen. "Flow And Stock Equilibrium In A Dynamic Metzler Model," **JOF**, 1976, v31(5), 1323-1339.

Brassman, Mark D. "The Effect Of A Suburban Driving Population On Urban Auto Insurance Premiums," **JRI**, 1980, v47(4), 636-659.

Braswell, Ronald C. (Osteryoung, Jerome S., Ronald C. Braswell and Dallas R. Blevins. "PIC: An Alternative Approach To Accepting Bids On Local And State Government Bonds," **FM**, 1979, v8(2), 36-41.)

Braswell, Ronald C., E. Joe Nosari and Mark A. Browning. "The Effect Of Private Municipal Bond Insurance On The Cost To The Issuer," **FR**, 1982, v17(4), 240-251.

Braswell, Ronald C., E. Joe Nosari and DeWitt L. Summers. "A Comparison Of The True Interest Costs Of Competitive And Negotiated Underwritings In The Municipal Bond Market," **JMCB**, 1983, v15(1), 102-106.

Braswell, Ronald C., Walter J. Reinhart and James R. Hasselback. "The Tax Treatment Of Municipal Discount Bonds: Correction Of A Fallacy," **FM**, 1982, v11(1), 77-81.

Braswell, Ronald C., Barry R. Marks, Walter J. Reinhart and DeWitt L. Sumners. "The Effect Of Term Structure And Taxes On The Issuance Of Discount Bonds," **FM**, 1988, v17(4), 92-103.

Bratt, Elmer C. "Consumer Expenditures On Nondurables And Services In 1954," **JOB**, 1954, v27(1), 77-86.

Bratt, Elmer C. "Short- And Long-Term Capital Requirements," **JOF**, 1952, v7(2), 128-137.

Bratt, Elmer C. "The Future Character Of The Business Cycle," **FAJ**, 1953, v9(2), 19-22.

Bratt, Elmer Clark. "A Reconsideration Of The Postwar Forecasts," **JOB**, 1953, v26(2), 71-83.

Bratt, Elmer Clark. "Market Situation As A Basis For Forecasting," **FAJ**, 1974, v10(1), 27-34.

Brauer, Greggory A. and R. Ravichandran. "How Sweet Is Silver?," **JPM**, 1986, v12(4), 33-42.

Brauer, Greggory A. "Closed-End Fund Shares' Abnormal Returns And The Information Content Of Discounts And Premiums," **JOF**, 1988, v43(1), 113-127.

Brauer, Greggory A. "Evidence Of The Market Value Of Me-First Rules," **FM**, 1983, v12(1), 11-18.

Brauer, Greggory A. "The Value Impacts Of Capital Adequacy Regulation And Stochastic Deposits," **JFR**, 1984, v7(2), 95-104.

Brauer, Greggory A. "Using Jump-Diffusion Return Models To Measure Differential Information By Firm Size," **JFQA**, 1986, v21(4), 447-458.

Brauer, Greggory A. " `Open-Ending' Closed-End Funds," **JFEC**, 1984, v13(4), 491-507.

Brauer, Greggory A. and Eric C. Chang. "Return Seasonality In Stocks And Their Underlying Assets: Tax Loss Selling Versus Information Explanations," **RFS**, 1990, v3(2), 255-280.

Brauer, Greggory. (Bonser-Neal, Catherine, Greggory Brauer, Robert Neal and Simon Wheatley. "International Investment Restrictions And Closed-End Country Fund Prices," **JOF**, 1990, v45(2),523-548.)

Braverman, J. D. "Credibility Theory: A Probabilistic Development," **JRI**, 1968, v35(3), 411-423.

Braverman, Jerome D. "A Critique Of Credibility Tables," **JRI**, 1967, v34(3), 409-416.

Braverman, Jerome D. and Gerald R. Hartman. "The Process Of Classifying Drivers: A Suggestion For Insurance Ratemaking: Comment," **JRI**, 1973, v40(1), 142-146.

Brayshaw, R. E. and A. R. O. Miro. "The Information Content Of Inflation-Adjusted Financial Statements," **JBFA**, v20, 1985(2), 249-262.

Brayshaw, R. E. and Ahmed E. K. Eldin. "The Smoothing Hypothesis And The Role Of Exchange Differences," **JBFA**, 1989, v16(5), 621-634.

Brazer, Harvey E. "The Report Of The Royal Commission On Taxation: A Review Article," **JOF**, 1967, v22(4), 671-683.

Brazil, Alan Jay. "Citicorp's Mortgage Valuation Model: Option-Adjusted Spreads And Option-Based Durations," **JREFEC**, 1988, v1(2), 151-162.

Break, George F. "Fiscal Policy In A Fully Employed Economy," **JOF**, 1967, v22(2), 247-260.

Break, George F. "On The Deductibility Of Capital Losses Under The Income Tax," **JOF**, 1952, v7(2), 214-229.

Break, George F. "Revenue Sharing: Priorities And Policy Instruments," **JOF**, 1968, v23(2), 251-263.

Brealey, R. A. and C. M. Young. "Debt, Taxes And Leasing - A Note," **JOF**, 1980, v35(5), 1245-1250.

Brealey, R. A. and S. D. Hodges. "Playing With Portfolios," **JOF**, 1975, v30(1), 125-134.

Brealey, R. A. (Hodges, S. D. and R. A. Brealey. "The Rate Of Return On New Investment In The UK," **JOF**, 1980, v35(3), 799-800.)

Brealey, R. A. (Hodges, S. D. and R. A. Brealey. "Dynamic Portfolio Selection," **FAJ**, 1973, v29(2), 50-65.)

Brealey, Richard and Stephen Schaefer. "Term Structure And Uncertain Inflation," **JOF**, 1977, v32(2), 277-289.

Brealey, Richard A. "Government Assets: Key To Inflation?," **FAJ**, 1979, v35(1), 18-21.

Brealey, Richard A. "How To Combine Active Management With Index Funds," **JPM**, 1986, v12(2), 4-10.

Brealey, Richard A. "Portfolio Theory Versus Portfolio Practice," **JPM**, 1990, v16(4), 6-10.

Brealey, Richard A. (Hodges, Stewart D. and Richard A. Brealey. "Dynamic Portfolio Selection," **FAJ**, 1972, v28(6), 58-69.)

Brechling, Frank. "Wage Inflation And The Structure Of Regional Unemployment," **JMCB**, 1973, v5(1), Part II, 355-379.

Brecht, W. A. and Charles Kerr, Jr. "Electric Locomotives With Identical Basic Components," **FAJ**, 1948, v4(3), 33-44.

Breeden, Douglas T. "An Intertemporal Asset Pricing Model With Stochastic Consumption And Investment Opportunities," **JFEC**, 1979, v7(3), 265-296.

Breeden, Douglas T. "Consumption Risk In Futures Markets," **JOF**, 1980, v35(2), 503-520.

Breeden, Douglas T. "Consumption, Production, Inflation And Interest Rates: A Synthesis," **JFEC**, 1986, v16(1), 3-40.

Breeden, Douglas T. and Robert H. Litzenberger. "Prices Of State-Contingent Claims Implicit In Option Prices," **JOB**, 1978, v51(4), 621-652.

Breeden, Douglas T., Michael R. Gibbons and Robert H. Litzenberger. "Empirical Tests Of The Consumption-Oriented CAPM," **JOF**, 1989, v44(2), 231-262.

Breen, Francis F. (Lewis, Kenneth A. and Francis F. Breen. "Empirical Issues In The Demand For Currency: A Multinational Study," **JOF**, 1975, v30(4), 1065-1079.)

Breen, John M. "Automobile Insurance - A Major Property Insurance Problem," **JRI**, 1953, v20, 29-34.

Breen, John M. "The Outlook For Automobile Insurance," **JRI**, 1943, v10, 19-25.

Breen, William and James Savage. "Portfolio Distribution And Tests Of Security Selection Models," **JOF**, 1968, v23(5), 805-819.

Breen, William and John Boyd. "Classroom Simulation As A Pedagogical Device In Teaching Money And Banking," **JFQA**, 1976, v11(4), 595-606.

Breen, William and Richard Jackson. "An Efficient Algorithm For Solving Large-Scale Portfolio Problems," **JFQA**, 1971, v6(1), 627-637.

Breen, William J. and Eugene M. Lerner. "Corporate Financial Strategies And Market Measures Of Risk And Return," **JOF**, 1973, v28(2), 339-351.

Breen, William J. (Banz, Rolf W. and William J. Breen. "Sample Dependent Results Using Accounting And Market Data: Some Evidence," **JOF**, 1986, v41(4), 779-794.)

Breen, William, Lawrence R. Glosten and Ravi Jagannathan. "Economic Significance Of Predictable Variations In Stock Index Returns," **JOF**, 1989, v44(5), 1177-1190.

Breen, William, Ravi Jagannathan and Aharon R. Ofer. "Correcting For Heteroscedasticity In Tests For Market Timing Ability," **JOB**, 1986, v59(4), Part 1, 585-598.

Breen, William. "An Exploratory Econometric Model Of Financial Markets," **JFQA**, 1969, v4(3), 233-269.

Breen, William. "Homogeneous Risk Measures And The Construction Of Composite Assets," **JFQA**, 1968, v3(4), 405-413.

Breen, William. "Low Price-Earnings Ratios," **FAJ**, 1968, v24(4), 125-127.

Brehm, R. Dennis. (Lewis, Alan L., Sheen T. Kassouf, R. Dennis Brehm and Jack Johnston. "The Ibbotson-Sinquefield Simulation Made Easy," **JOB**, 1980, v53(2), 205-214.)

Brendsel, Leland. (Campbell, Tim and Leland Brendsel. "The Impact Of Compensating Balance Requirements On The Cash Balances Of Manufacturing Corporations: An Empirical Study," **JOF**, 1977, v32(1), 31-40.)

Brennan, Joseph F. "The Water Industry - Regulation," **FAJ**, 1967, v23(2), 41-48.

Brennan, M. J. and A. Kraus. "The Geometry Of Separation And Myopia," **JFQA**, 1976, v11(2), 171-194.

Brennan, M. J. and Alan Kraus. "Necessary Conditions For Aggregation In Securities Markets," **JFQA**, 1978, v13(3), 407-418.

Brennan, M. J. and E. S. Schwartz. "Convertible Bonds: Valuation And Optimal Strategies For Call And Conversion," **JOF**, 1977, v32(5), 1699-1715.

Brennan, M. J. and R. Solanki. "Optimal Portfolio Insurance," **JFQA**, 1981, v16(3), 279-300.

Brennan, M. J. "An Approach To The Valuation Of Uncertain Income Streams," **JOF**, 1973, v28(3), 661-674.

Brennan, M. J. "An Inter-Temporal Approach To The Optimization Of Dividend Policy With Predetermined Investments: Comment," **JOF**, 1974, v29(1), 258-259.

Brennan, M. J. "Capital Market Equilibrium With Divergent Borrowing And Lending Rates," **JFQA**, 1971, v6(5), 1197-1205.

Brennan, M. J. "The Optimal Number Of Securities In A Risky Asset Portfolio When There Are Fixed Costs Of Transacting: Theory And Some Empirical Results," **JFQA**, 1975, v10(3), 483-496.

Brennan, M. J. "The Pricing Of Contingent Claims In Discrete Time Models," **JOF**, 1979, v34(1), 53-68.

Brennan, M. J. and B. Solnik. "International Risk Sharing And Capital Mobility," **JIMF**, 1989, v8(3), 359-374.

Brennan, M. J. and E. S. Schwartz. "Evaluating Natural Resource Investments," **JOB**, 1985, v58(2), 135-158.

Brennan, M. J. and E. S. Schwartz. "Corporate Income Taxes, Valuation, And The Problem Of Optimal Capital Structure," **JOB**, 1978, v51(1), 103-114.

Brennan, M. J. and T. E. Copeland. "Beta Changes Around Stock Splits: A Note," **JOF**, 1988, v43(4), 1009-1014.

Brennan, Michael J. and Eduardo S. Schwartz. "Regulation And Corporate Investment Policy," **JOF**, 1982, v37(2), 289-300.

Brennan, Michael J. and Eduardo S. Schwartz. "The Valuation Of American Put Options," **JOF**, 1977, v32(2), 449-462.

Brennan, Michael J. and Eduardo S. Schwartz. "On The Geometric Mean Index: A Note," **JFQA**, 1985, v20(1), 119-122.

Brennan, Michael J. and Eduardo S. Schwartz. "An Equilibrium Model Of Bond Pricing And A Test Of Market Efficiency," **JFQA**, 1982, v17(3), 301-329.

Brennan, Michael J. and Eduardo S. Schwartz. "Finite Difference Methods And Jump Processes Arising In The Pricing Of Contingent Claims: A Synthesis," **JFQA**, 1978, v13(3), 461-474.

Brennan, Michael J. and Eduardo S. Schwartz. "The Pricing Of Equity-Linked Life Insurance Policies With An Asset Value Guarantee," **JFEC**, 1976, v3(3), 195-213.

Brennan, Michael J. and Eduardo S. Schwartz. "Savings Bonds, Retractable Bonds And Callable Bonds," **JFEC**, 1977, v5(1), 67-88.

Brennan, Michael J. and Eduardo S. Schwartz. "Conditional Predictions Of Bond Prices And Returns," **JOF**, 1980, v35(2), 405-417.

Brennan, Michael J. and Eduardo S. Schwartz. "Analyzing Convertible Bonds," **JFQA**, 1980, v15(4), 907-929.

Brennan, Michael J. and Eduardo S. Schwartz. "A Continuous Time Approach To The Pricing Of Bonds," **JBF**, 1979, v3(2), 133-156.

Brennan, Michael J. and Eduardo S. Schwartz. "Optimal Financial Policy And Firm Valuation," **JOF**, 1984, v39(3), 593-607.

Brennan, Michael J. and Eduardo S. Schwartz. "Bond Pricing And Market Efficiency," **FAJ**, 1982, v38(5), 49-56.

Brennan, Michael J. "A Theory Of Price Limits In Futures Markets," **JFEC**, 1986, v16(2), 213-233.

Brennan, Michael J. "Presidential Address: Latent Assets," **JOF**, 1990, v45(3), 709-730.

Brennan, Michael J. "Valuation And The Cost Of Capital For Regulated Industries: A Comment," **JOF**, 1972, v27(5), 1147-1149.

Brennan, Michael J. and Anjan V. Thakor. "Shareholder Preferences And Dividend Policy," **JOF**, 1990, v45(4), 993-1019.

Brennan, Michael J. and Eduardo S. Schwartz. "Time-Invariant Portfolio Insurance Strategies," **JOF**, 1988, v43(2), 283-299.

Brennan, Michael J. and Eduardo S. Schwartz. "Alternative Investment Strategies For The Issuers Of Equity Linked Life Insurance Policies With An Asset Value Guarantee," **JOB**, 1979, v52(1), 63-94.

Brennan, Michael J. and Eduardo S. Schwartz. "The Case For Convertibles," **JACF**, 1988, v1(2), 55-64.

Brennan, Michael J. and Eduardo S. Schwartz. "Determinants Of GNMA Mortgage Prices," **AREUEA**, 1985, v13(3), 209-228.

Brennan, Michael J. and Eduardo S. Schwartz. "Portfolio Insurance And Financial Market Equilibrium," **JOB**, 1989, v62(4), 455-472.

Brennan, Michael J. and Eduardo S. Schwartz. "Arbitrage In Stock Index Futures," **JOB**, 1990, v63(1), Part 2, S7-S32.

Brennan, Michael J. and Thomas E. Copeland. "Stock Splits, Stock Prices, And Transaction Costs," **JFEC**, 1988, v22(1), 83-102.

Brennan, Michael J., Vojislav Maksimovic and Josef Zechner. "Vendor Financing," **JOF**, 1988, v43(5), 1127-1141.

Brennan, Michael and Alan Kraus. "Efficient Financing Under Asymmetric Information," **JOF**, 1987, v42(5), 1225-1243.

Brennan, Michael. "A Note On Dividend Irrelevance And The Gordon Valuation Model," **JOF**, 1971, v26(5), 1115-1121.

Brennan, Thomas P., Roger E. Cannady and Peter F. Colwell. "Office Rent In The Chicago CBD," **AREUEA**, 1984, v12(3), 243-260.

Brenner, Gabrielle A. and Reuven Brenner. "Memory And Markets, Or Why Are You Paying $2.99 For A Widget?," **JOB**, 1982, v55(1), 147-158.

Brenner, M. (Barnea, A. and M. Brenner. "World Events And Stock Market Volume," **FAJ**, 1974, v30(4), 64-66.)

Brenner, Menachem and Dan Galai. "The Determinants Of The Return On Index Bonds," **JBF**, 1978, v2(1), 47-64.

Brenner, Menachem and Dan Galai. "On Measuring The Risk Of Common Stocks Implied By Options Prices: A Note," **JFQA**, 1984, v19(4), 403-412.

Brenner, Menachem and Itzhak Venezia. "The Effects Of Inflation And Taxes On Growth Investments And Replacement Policies," **JOF**, 1983, v38(5), 1519-1528.

Brenner, Menachem and Marti G. Subrahmanyam. "Intra-Equilibrium And Inter-Equilibrium Analysis In Capital Market Theory: A Clarification," **JOF**, 1977, v32(4), 1313-1319.

Brenner, Menachem and Seymour Smidt. "A Simple Model Of Non-Stationarity Of Systematic Risk," **JOF**, 1977, v32(4), 1081-1092.

Brenner, Menachem and Seymour Smidt. "Asset Characteristics And Systematic Risk," **FM**, 1978, v7(4), 33-39.

Brenner, Menachem and Dan Galai. "Implied Interest Rates," **JOB**, 1986, v59(5), 493-508.

Brenner, Menachem and Dan Galai. "New Financial Instruments To Hedge Changes In Volatility," **FAJ**, 1989, v45(4), 61-65.

Brenner, Menachem and Marti G. Subrahmanyam. "A Simple Formula To Compute The Implied Standard Deviation," **FAJ**, 1988, v44(5), 80-83.

Brenner, Menachem, Georges Courtadon And Marti Subrahmanyam. "Options On The Spot And Options On Futures," **JOF**, 1985, v40(5), 1303-1317.

Brenner, Menachem, Georges Courtadon and Marti Subrahmanyam. "Options On Stock Indices And Options On Futures," **JBF**, 1989, v13(4/5), 773-782.

Brenner, Menachem, Marti G. Subrahmanyam and Jun Uno. "Arbitrage Opportunities In The Japanese Stock And Futures Markets," **FAJ**, 1990, v46(2), 14-24.

Brenner, Menachem, Marti G. Subrahmanyam and Jun Uno. "The Behavior Of Prices In The Nikkei Spot And Futures Market," **JFEC**, 1989, v23(2), 363-384.

Brenner, Menachem. "On The Stability Of The Distribution Of The Market Component In Stock Price Changes," JFQA, 1974, v9(6), 945-961.

Brenner, Menachem. "The Effect Of Model Misspecification On Tests Of The Efficient Market Hypothesis," JOF, 1977, v32(1), 57-66.

Brenner, Menachem. "The Sensitivity Of The Efficient Market Hypothesis To Alternative Specifications Of The Market Model," JOF, 1979, v34(4), 915-929.

Brenner, Menachem. (Altman, Edward I. and Menachem Brenner. "Information Effects And Stock Market Response To Signs Of Firm Deterioration," JFQA, 1981, v16(1), 35-51.)

Brenner, Menachem. (Venezia, Itzhak and Menachem Brenner. "The Optimal Duration Of Growth Investments And Search," JOB, 1979, v52(3), 393-408.)

Brenner, Reuven. (Brenner, Gabrielle A. and Reuven Brenner. "Memory And Markets, Or Why Are You Paying $2.99 For A Widget?," JOB, 1982, v55(1), 147-158.)

Brenner, T. Webster. "Margin Authority: No Reason For A Change," JFM, v1(Supp), 487-490.

Brenner, Vincent C. and Paul E. Dascher. "Bankers' Views Of Reporting Current Cost Information," JBR, 1972-73, v3(2), 123-126.

Brent, Averil, Dale Morse and E. Kay Stice. "Short Interest: Explanations And Tests," JFQA, 1990, v25(2), 273-289.

Bretey, Pierre R. and Warren Burns. "First Convention Outside U. S.," FAJ, 1959, v15(3), 57-64.

Bretey, Pierre R. "AAR Convention," FAJ, 1947, v3(3),27-32.

Bretey, Pierre R. "Coal Industry's Expansion," FAJ, 1968, v24(2), 61-64.

Bretey, Pierre R. "Coal: The Giant Revived," FAJ, 1971, v27(1), 54-58,91.

Bretey, Pierre R. "Financial Benefits In Railroad Mergers," FAJ, 1961, v17(2), 103-106.

Bretey, Pierre R. "Green Light Ahead For The Rails," FAJ, 1963, v19(6), 19-25,78-89.

Bretey, Pierre R. "Impact Of Taxes On Class I Railroads," FAJ, 1951, v7(1), 31-33.

Bretey, Pierre R. "Importance Of Railroad Accounting Officer," FAJ, 1952, v8(5), 20-24.

Bretey, Pierre R. "Longer Term Prospects For The Coal Industry," FAJ, 1964, v20(4), 49-51.

Bretey, Pierre R. "Merger Progress Slow But Sure," FAJ, 1965, v21(2), 65-67.

Bretey, Pierre R. "Methods Of Gauging Rail Credit," FAJ, 1945, v1(1), 63-68.

Bretey, Pierre R. "Modern Technology And Operating Costs Of Railroads," FAJ, 1952, v8(2), 11-18.

Bretey, Pierre R. "Rail Diversification, An Income Producer," FAJ, 1960, v16(5), 71-78.

Bretey, Pierre R. "Railroad Mergers - Their Impact On Investors," FAJ, 1964, v20(3),25-31.

Bretey, Pierre R. "Railroads May Regain Investment Status," FAJ, 1961, v17(4), 55-73.

Bretey, Pierre R. "Railroads' Problem: `A Compound Of Several Brews'," FAJ, 1962, v18(5), 89-98.

Bretey, Pierre R. "The Railroad Renaissance - Cyclical Or Fundamental?," FAJ, 1966, v22(3), 35-38.

Bretey, Pierre R. "The Railroads - Amber To Green," FAJ, 1967, v23(6), 61-66.

Bretey, Pierre R. "Value Of Railroad Securities," FAJ, 1949, v5(4), 34-39.

Brewer, Betty L. (Grablowsky, Bernie J. and Betty L. Brewer. "The Market For Finance Majors: Some Myths And Some Realities," JFED, 1975, v4, 33-36.)

Brewer, Elijah, III and Gillian G. Garcia. "A Discriminant Analysis Of Savings And Loan Accounting Profits, 1976-1981," AFPAF, 1987, v2(1), 205-244.

Brewer, Elijah, III, Gillian G. Garcia and Alan K. Reichert. "A Statistical Analysis Of S&L Accounting Profits," AFPAF, 1989, v3(1), 163-194.

Brewer, Elijah, III. "The Risk Of Banks Expanding Their Permissible Nonbanking Activities," FR, 1990, v25(4), 517-538.

Brewer, H. L. "Investor Benefits From Corporate International Diversification," JFQA, 1981, v16(1), 113-126.

Brewer, H. L. "Risk Reduction For Mortgage Portfolios: The Role Of Portfolio Theory," AFPAF, 1989, v3(1), 245-262.

Brewer, Thomas L. and Pietra Rivoli. "Politics And Perceived Country Creditworthiness In International Banking," JMCB, 1990, v22(3), 357-369.

Brewster, Benjamin Y., Jr. (Pritchett, S. Travis and Benjamin Y. Brewster, Jr. "Comparison Of Ordinary Life Operating Expense Ratios For Agency And Nonagency Insurers," JRI, 1979, v46(1), 61-74.)

Brewster, J. Alan, Irving Crespi, Richard Kaluzny, James Ohls and Cynthia Thomas. "Homeowner Warranties: A Study Of The Need And Demand For Protection Against Unanticipated Repair Expenses," AREUEA, 1980, v8(2), 207-217.

Brick, Ivan E. and Buckner A. Wallingford. "The Relative Tax Benefits Of Alternative Call Features In Corporate Debt," JFQA, 1985, v20(1), 95-106.

Brick, Ivan E. and Daniel G. Weaver. "A Comparison Of Capital Budgeting Techniques In Identifying Profitable Investments," FM, 1984, v13(4), 29-39.

Brick, Ivan E. and Meir Statman. "A Note On Beta And The Probability Of Default," JFR, 1981, v4(3), 265-269.

Brick, Ivan E. and S. Abraham Ravid. "On The Relevance Of Debt Maturity Structure," JOF, 1985, v40(5), 1423-1437.

Brick, Ivan E. and William K. H. Fung. "Taxes And The Theory Of Trade Debt," JOF, 1984, v39(4), 1169-1176.

Brick, Ivan E. and William K. H. Fung. "The Effect Of Taxes On The Trade Credit Decision," FM, 1984, v13(2), 24-30.

Brick, Ivan E. (Fisher, Lawrence, Ivan E. Brick and Francis K. W. Ng. "Tax Incentives And Financial Innovation: The Case Of Zero-Coupon And Other Deep-Discount Corporate Bonds," FR, 1983, v18(4), 292-305.)

Brick, Ivan E. and Lawrence Fisher. "Effects Of Classifying Equity Or Debt On The Value Of The Firm Under Uncertainty," JFQA, 1987, v22(4), 383-400.

Brick, Ivan E. and S. Abraham Ravid. "Interest Rate Uncertainty And The Optimal Debt Maturity Structure," JFQA, 1991, v26(1), 63-82.

Brick, Ivan E., W. G. Mellon, Julius Surkis and Murray Mohl. "Optimal Capital Structure: A Multi-Period Programming Model For Use In Financial Planning," JBF, 1983, v7(1), 45-68.

Brick, Ivan E., Meir Statman and Daniel G. Weaver. "Event Studies And Model Misspecification: Another Look At The Benefits Of Outsiders From Public Information About Insider Trading," JBFA, 1989, v16(3), 399-424.

Brick, Ivan E., William Fung and Marti Subrahmanyam. "Leasing And Financial Intermediation: Comparative Tax Advantages," FM, 1987, v16(1), 55-59.

Brick, John R. and Howard E. Thompson. "Portfolio Policies Of Private Mortgage Insurers," FAJ, 1981, v37(2), 58-66.

Brick, John R. and Howard E. Thompson. "Time Series Analysis Of Interest Rates: Some Additional Evidence," JOF, 1978, v33(1), 93-103.

Brick, John R. and Howard E. Thompson. "The Economic Life Of An Investment And The Appropriate Discount Rate," JFQA, 1978, v13(5), 831-846.

Brick, John R. (Price, Kelly and John R. Brick. "Daily Interest Rate Relationships," JMCB, 1980, v12(2), Part 1, 215-220.)

Brick, John R. (Wetmore, Jill L. T. and John R. Brick. "Interest Rate Risk And The Optimal Gap For Commercial Banks: An Empirical Study," FR, 1990, v25(4), 539-558.)

Brick, John R. and Howard E. Thompson. "Investment Portfolios And Regulation Of Private Mortgage Insurance," JRI, 1978, v45(2), 261-273.

Brickley, James A. and Christopher M. James. "Access To Deposit Insurance, Insolvency Rules And The Stock Returns Of Financial Institutions," JFEC, 1986, v16(3), 345-372.

Brickley, James A. and James S. Schallheim. "Lifting The Lid On Closed-End Investment Companies: A Case Of Abnormal Returns," JFQA, 1985, v20(1), 107-118.

Brickley, James A. "Interpreting Common Stock Returns Around Proxy Statement Disclosures And Annual Shareholder Meetings," JFQA, 1986, v21(3),343-349.

Brickley, James A. "Shareholder Wealth Information Signaling And The Specially Designated Dividend: An Empirical Study," JFEC, 1983, v12(2),187-210.

Brickley, James A. (Bhagat, Sanjai, James A. Brickley and Uri Loewenstein. "The Pricing Effects Of Interfirm Cash Tender Offers," JOF, 1987, v42(4), 965-986.)

Brickley, James A. (Bhagat, Sanjai, James A. Brickley and Ronald C. Lease. "The Authorization Of Additional Common Stock: An Empirical Investigation," FM, 1986, v15(3), 45-53.)

Brickley, James A. (Bhagat, Sanjai, James A. Brickley and Ronald C. Lease. "Incentive Effects Of Stock Purchase Plans," JFEC, 1985, v14(2), 195-216.)

Brickley, James A. (Bhagat, Sanjai, James A. Brickley and Jeffrey L. Coles. "Managerial Indemnification And Liability Insurance: The Effect On Sharholder Wealth," JRI, 1987, v54(4), 721-736.)

Brickley, James A. and Frederick H. Dark. "The Choice Of Organizational Form: The Case Of Franchising," JFEC, 1987, v18(2), 401-420.

Brickley, James A., Ronald C. Lease and Clifford W. Smith, Jr. "Ownership Structure And Voting On Antitakeover Amendments," JFEC, 1988, v20(1/2), 267-292.

Brickman, Myrtle. "A Note: Has Federal Reserve Policy Changed?," FAJ, 1966, v22(5), 105-107.

Brickman, Myrtle. "New Federal Reserve Series," FAJ, 1967, v23(5), 88-92.

Bridges, Edson L. "A Year-End Review Of The 1961 Economy," FAJ, 1961, v17(6), 9-14.

Brief, R. P. and Joel Owen. "Accounting And Investment Analysis," FAJ, 1975, v31(1), 52-56.

Brief, R. P. "Limitations Of Using The Cash Recovery Rate To Estimate The IRR: A Note," JBFA, 1985, v12(3), 473-475.

Brief, Richard P. and Joel Owen. "A Note On Earnings Risk And The Coefficient Of Variation," JOF, 1969, v24(5), 901-904.

Brief, Richard P. and Joel Owen. "A Note On The Inclusion Of Earnings Risk In Measures Of Return: A Reply," JOF,1977,v32(4), 1367.

Brief, Richard P. and Raef A. Lawson. "Estimating Security Returns: A Further Note," FAJ, 1986, v42(6), 75-77.

Brief, Richard P. "The Relationship Between Duration And Economic Depreciation: A Note," JBFA, 1984, v11(3), 281-286.

Brief, Richard P. "Yield Approximations: A Historical Perspective: A Correction," JOF, 1983, v38(3), 1039-1039.

Brief, Richard P. and Raef A. Lawson. "Approximate Error In Using Accounting Rates Of Return To Estimate Economic Returns," JBFA, 1991, v18(1), 13-20.

Briggs, George C. "Performance And Portfolio Management," FAJ, 1967, v23(5), 123-127.

Brigham, E. F. (Pappas, J. L. and E. F. Brigham. "Growth Rate Changes And Common Stock Prices," FAJ, 1966, v22(3), 157-162.)

Brigham, E. F., D. E. Fischer, K. B. Johnson and R. J. Jordan. "What Makes Short Cases Work In The Basic Finance Course?," JFED, 1972, v1, 65-68.

Brigham, Eugene F. and Myron J. Gordon. "Leverage, Dividend Policy, And The Cost Of Capital," JOF, 1968, v23(1), 85-103.

Brigham, Eugene F. and Myron J. Gordon. "Leverage, Dividend Policy And The Cost Of Capital: Reply," JOF, 1970, v25(4), 904-908.

Brigham, Eugene F. and Richard H. Pettway. "Capital Budgeting By Utilities," FM, 1973, v2(3), 11-22.

Brigham, Eugene F. and Roy L. Crum. "On The Use Of The CAPM In Public Utility Rate Cases," FM, 1977, v6(2), 7-15.

Brigham, Eugene F. and Roy L. Crum. "Reply To Comments On `Use Of The CAPM In Public Utility Rate Cases'," FM, 1978, v7(3), 72-76.

Brigham, Eugene F. and T. Craig Tapley. "Financial Leverage And Use Of The Net Present Value Investment Criterion: A Reexamination," FM, 1985, v14(2), 48-52.

Brigham, Eugene F. "Alternative Approaches To Teaching The Basic Finance Course," JFED, 1978, v7, 3-6.

Brigham, Eugene F. "An Analysis Of Convertible Debentures: Theory And Some Empirical Evidence," JOF, 1966, v21(1), 35-54.

Brigham, Eugene F. "Florida's Public Utility Research Center: Improving College/Business Relationships," JFED, 1973, v2, 33-34.

Brigham, Eugene F. "Future Direction Of The Basic Finance Course," JFED, 1973, v2, 13-19.

Brigham, Eugene F. "Hurdle Rates For Screening Capital Expenditure Proposals," FM, 1974, v4(3), 17-26.

Brigham, Eugene F. "Programs Designed To Increase Interaction Between The Academic And Business Communities," JFED, 1975, v4, 54-56.

Brigham, Eugene F. (Reilly, Raymond R., Eugene F. Brigham, Charles M. Linke, Moon H. Kim and James S. Ang. "Weighted Average Vs. True Cost Of Capital: Reilly, Brigham, Linke and Kim Versus Ang," FM, 1974, v3(1), 80-85.)

Brigham, Eugene F. (Shelton, John P., Eugene F. Brigham and Alfred E. Hofflander, Jr. "Dual Funds: An Appraisal," FAJ, 1967, v23(3), 131-139.)

Brigham, Eugene F. (Woods, Donald H. and Eugene F. Brigham. "Stockholder Distribution Decisions: Share Repurchases Or Dividends," JFQA, 1966, v1(1), 15-25.)

Brigham, Eugene F. and James L. Pappas. "Rates Of Return On Common Stock," JOB, 1969, v42(3), 302-316.

Brigham, Eugene F., Dilip K. Shome and Steve R. Vinson. "The Risk Premium Approach To Measuring A Utility's Cost Of Equity," FM, 1985, v14(1), 33-45.

Bright, Herbert S. (Moorhead, E. J. and Herbert S. Bright. "Cost Of Life Insurance To The Policyholder: Comment," JRI, 1962, v29(3), 424-426.)

Brightman, Harvey J. and Mark S. Dorfman. "Acceptability Of Three Normative Methods In Insurance Decision Making: Comment 465-466.

Brightman, Harvey J. and Mark S. Dorfman. "Birth Order, Anxiety, Affiliation And The Purchase Of Life Insurance: Comment," JRI, 1973, v40(4), 643-646.

Brightman, Jon S. and Barbara L. Haslanger. "Past Investment Performance: Seductive But Deceptive," JPM, 1980, v6(2), 43-45.

Brill, Edward A. and Richard B. Harriff. "Pricing American Options: Managing Risk With Early Exercise," FAJ, 1986, v42(6), 48-55.

Brillembourg, Arturo and Mohsin S. Khan. "The Relationship Between Money, Income, And Prices: Has Money Mattered Historically?," JMCB, 1979, v11(3), 358-365.

Briloff, Abraham J. "At The Hump Of The Decades," FAJ, 1970, v26(3), 60-67.

Briloff, Abraham J. "Cannibalizing The Transcendent Margin: Reflections On Conglomeration, LBOs, Recapitalizations And Other Manifestations Of Corporate Mania," FAJ, 1988, v44(3), 74-80.

Briloff, Abraham J. "GAAP And The Life Insurance Companies," FAJ, 1974, v30(2), 30-36,81-85.

Briloff, Abraham J. "Pooling Of Interests Accounting," FAJ, 1968, v24(2), 71-81.

Briloff, Abraham J. "Quo Vadis?," FAJ, 1973, v29(2), 34-36,38,40-42,46-48,67-72.

Briloff, Abraham J. "The CPA And Fair Corporate Accountability," FAJ, 1966, v22(3), 51-55.

Briloff, Abraham J. "The `Funny-Money' Game," FAJ, 1969, v25(3), 73-79.

Brimmer, Andrew and Allen Sinai. "The Effects Of Tax Policy On Capital Formation, Corporate Liquidity And The Availability Of Investible Funds: A Simulation Study," JOF, 1976, v31(2), 287-308.

Brimmer, Andrew F. and Frederick R. Dahl. "Growth Of American International Banking: Implications For Public Policy," JOF, 1975, v30(2), 341-363.

Brimmer, Andrew F. "Central Banking And Economic Development: The Record Of Innovation," JMCB, 1971, v3(4), 780-792.

Brimmer, Andrew F. "Credit Conditions And Price Determination In The Corporate Bond Market," JOF, 1960, v15(3), 353-370.

Brimmer, Andrew F. "Direct Investment And Corporate Adjustment Techniques Under The Voluntary U. S. Balance Of Payments Program," JOF, 1966, v21(2),266-282.

Brimmer, Andrew F. "Multi-National Banks And The Management Of Monetary Policy In The United States," JOF, 1973, v28(2), 439-454.

Brimmer, Andrew F. "On The Financing Of Black Economic Development: Reply," JOF, 1972, v27(5), 1139-1140.

Brimmer, Andrew F. "The Black Banks: An Assessment Of Performance And Prospects," JOF, 1971, v26(2), 379-405.

Brinson, Gary P. and Nimrod Fachler. "Measuring Non-U.S. Equity Portfolio Performance," JPM, 1985, v11(3), 73-76.

Brinson, Gary P. "How You Lose To Taxes And Inflation," FAJ, 1973, v29(2), 74-75.

Brinson, Gary P., Jeffrey J. Diermeier and Gary G. Schlarbaum. "A Composite Portfolio Benchmark For Pension Plans," FAJ, 1986, v42(2), 15-24.

Brinson, Gary P., L. Randolph Hood and Gilbert L. Beebower. "Determinants Of Portfolio Performance," FAJ, 1986, v42(4), 39-44.

Brioschi, Francesco, Luigi Buzzacchi and Massimo G. Colombo. "Risk Capital Financing And The Separation Of Ownership And Control In Business Groups," JBF, 1989, v13(4/5), 747-772.

Brisco, John P. and Robert M. Jennings. "Present And Future Value Approximations," JFED, 1984, v13, 1-4.

Briscoe, G. and G. Hawke. "Long-Term Debt And Realisable Gains In Shareholder Wealth: An Empirical Study," JBFA, 1976, v3(1), 125-136.

Briscoe, G. "Long-Term Debt And Shareholder Wealth: A Reply," JBFA, 1976, v3(3), 143-146.

Briscoe, G., J. M. Samuels and D. J. Smyth. "The Treatment Of Risk In The Stock Market," JOF, 1969, v24(4), 707-713.

Brissimis, Sophocles N. and John A. Leventakis. "An Empirical Inquiry Into The Short-Run Dynamics Of Output, Prices, And Exchange Market Pressure," JIMF, 1984, v3(1), 75-89.

Briston, Richard J. and Richard Dobbins. "Institutional Shareholders And Equity Stability: A Corroboratory Note," JBFA, 1977, v4(4), 469-476.

Brito, Ney O. "Marketability Restrictions And The Valuation Of Capital Assets Under Certainty," JOF, 1977, v32(4), 1109-1123.

Brito, Ney O. "Portfolio Selection In An Economy With Marketability And Short Sales Restrictions," JOF, 1978, v33(2), 589-601.

Brito, Ney O. "The Efficiency Of Inflation Expectations In Treasury Bill Markets: The Brazilian Evidence," JBF, 1979, v3(3), 235-251.

Brittain, Bruce. "International Currency Substitution And The Apparent Instability Of Velocity In Some Western European Economies And In The United States," JMCB, 1981, v13(2), 135-155.

Brittain, Bruce. "Tests Of Theories Of Exchange Rate Determination," JOF, 1977, v32(2), 519-529.

Britto, Ronald. "Futures Markets And The Supply Of Storage With Rational Expectations," JFM, 1982, v2(3), 255-260.

Briys, Eric P. and Henri Louberge. "On The Theory Of Rational Insurance Purchasing: A Note," JOF, 1985, v40(2), 577-581.

Briys, Eric and Michel Crouhy. "Creating And Pricing Hybrid Foreign Currency Options," FM, 1988, v17(4), 59-65.

Briys, Eric, Georges Dionne and Louis Eeckhoudt. "More On Insurance As A Giffin Good," JRU, 1989, v2(4), 415-420.

Briys, Eric, Michel Crouhy and Harris Schlesinger. "Optimal Hedging Under Intertemporally Dependent Preferences," JOF, 1990, v45(4), 1315-1324.

Briys, Eric, Michel Crouhy and Harris Schlesinger. "An Intertemporal Model Of Consumption And Hedging," RFM, 1988, v7(Supp), 456-466.

Briys, Eric, Michel Crouhy and Daniel R. Pieptea. "Hedging Versus Speculating With Interest Rate Futures," RFM, 1988, v7(Supp), 620-635.

Briys, Eric, Yehuda Kahane and Yoram Kroll. "Voluntary Insurance Coverage, Compulsory Insurance, And Risky-Riskless Portfolio Opportunities," JRI, 1988, v55(4), 713-722.

Briys, Eric. "Insurance And Consumption: The Continuous Time Case," JRI, 1986, v53(4), 718-733.

Brobeck, Stephen. "Consumer Perspective On Payments Systems," JBR, 1985-86, v16(4), 248-251.

Brocato, Joe and Kenneth E. Smith. "Velocity And The Variability Of Money Growth: Evidence From Granger-Causality Tests: Comment," JMCB, 1989, v21(2), 258-261.

Brocato, Joe. Evidence On The Comovement And Linkages Between National Equity Markets: 1980-1987," IJOF, 1990, v3(1), 39-64.

Brock, Gerald W. "A Study Of Prices And Market Shares In The Computer Mainframe Industry: Comment," JOB, 1979, v52(1), 119-124.

Brock, Philip L. "Reserve Requirements And The Inflation Tax," JMCB, 1989, v21(1), 106-121.

Brockett, Patrick L. "On The Misuse Of The Central Limit Theorem In Some Risk Calculation," JRI, 1983, v50(4), 727-730.

Brockett, Patrick L. and Robert C. Witt. "The Underwriting Risk And Return Paradox Revisited," JRI, 1982, v49(4), 621-627.

Brockett, Patrick L., Samuel H. Cox, Jr. and Robert C. Witt. "Self-Insurance And The Probability Of Financial Regret," JRI, 1984, v51(4), 720-729.

Brockett, Patrick L., Samuel H. Cox, Jr. and Robert C. Witt. "Insurance Versus Self-Insurance: A Risk Management Perspective," JRI, 1986, v53(2), 242-257.

Brockhaus, William L. "Prospects For Malpractice Suits In The Business Consulting Profession," JOB, 1977, v50(1), 70-75.

Broder, Ivy E. "The Cost Of Accidental Death: A Capital Market Approach," JRU, 1990, v3(1), 51-64.

Broderick, John P. "A New Look At Puerto Rico And Puerto Rican Bonds," FAJ, 1955, v11(2), 107-110.

Brodie, Judith. (Ezzamel, Mahmoud, Judith Brodie and Cecilio Mar-Molinero. "Financial Patterns Of UK Manufacturing Companies," JBFA, 1987, v14(4), 519-536.)

Brodt, Abraham I. "A Dynamic Balance Sheet Management Model For A Canadian Chartered Bank," JBF, 1978, v2(3), 221-241.

Brodt, Abraham I. "International Bank Asset And Liability Management," JBR, 1984-85, v15(2), 82-94.

Brodt, Abraham I. "Optimal Bank Asset And Liability Management With Financial Futures," JFM, 1988, v8(4), 457-482.

Brody, Eugene D. "Options And The Mathematics Of Defense," JPM, 1975, v1(2), 35-29.

Brody, Eugene D. "The Rails As An Indicator Of Professional Sentiment," FAJ, 1963, v19(4), 61-62.

Bromberg, Alan R. "The Law Of Corporate Information," FAJ, 1969, v25(2), 26-31.

Bronars, Stephen G. "Fair Pricing Of Unemployment Insurance Premiums," JOB, 1985, v58(1), 27-48.

Bronfenbrenner, M. "Imperfect Competition On A Long-Run Basis," JOB, 1950, v23(2), 81-93.

Bronfield, Saul. (Agmon, Tamir and Saul Bronfield. "The International Mobility Of Short-Term Covered Arbitrage Capital," JBFA, 1975, v2(2), 269-278.)

Bronson, Dorrance C. "The Concept Of Actuarial Soundness," JRI, 1953, v20, 36-47.

Bronson, Howard C. (Brown, Jonathan A. and Howard C. Bronson. "New York Stock Exchange Research Program On Share Ownership," JOF, 1953, v8(2),129-136.)

Brooker, George and Phillip Shinoda. "Peer Ratings Of Graduate Programs For Business," JOB, 1976, v49(2), 240-251.

Brooks, LeRoy and Dale Buckmaster. "First Difference Signals And Accounting Income Time Series Properties," JBFA, 1980, v7(3), 437-454.

Brooks, LeRoy and Dale Buckmaster. "The Impact Of Price Changes On Accounting Income: Holding Gains And Losses On Monetary Assets And Liabilities," FM, 1977, v6(3), 60-65.

Brooks, LeRoy D. and Dale A. Buckmaster. "Further Evidence Of The Time Series Properties Of Accounting Income," JOF, 1976, v31(5), 1359-1373.

Brooks, LeRoy D. and Dale Buckmaster. "The Impact Of Price Changes On Accounting Income," FM, 1974, v4(1), 32-43.

Brooks, LeRoy D. "Additional Evidence On The Market Reaction To Accounting Numbers," FR, 1977, v12(1), 76-90.

Brooks, LeRoy D. "An Evaluation Of Financial Management Learning Simulations," JFED, 1978, v7, 63-68.

Brooks, LeRoy D. "Stock-Bond Swaps In Regulated Utilities," FM, 1984, v13(3), 5-10.

Brooks, LeRoy D. (D'Souza, Rudolph E., LeRoy D. Brooks and H. Dennis Oberhelman. "A General Stationary Stochastic Regression

Model For Estimating And Predicting Beta," **FR**, 1989, v24(2), 299-318.)

Brooks, LeRoy D. (Ingram, Robert W., LeRoy D. Brooks and Ronald M. Copeland. "The Information Content Of Municipal Bond Rating Changes: A Note," **JOF**, 1983, v38(3), 997-1003.)

Brooks, LeRoy D.,Charles E. Edwards and Eurico J. Ferreira. "Risk-Return Characteristics Of Convertible Preferred Stock: Comment," **JPM**, 1984, v10(2),76-78.

Brooks, Leroy D. "Financial Management Simulation Games And Decision-Making Skills," **JFED**, 1975, v4, 85-90.

Brooks, R. and M. Livingston. "A Note On The Variance Of Spot Interest Rates," **JBF**, 1990, v14(1), 215-226.

Brooks, Robert C., Jr. "A Neglected Approach To Ethical Business Behavior," **JOB**, 1964, v37(2), 192-194.

Brooks, Robert and Billy Helms. "An N-Stage, Fractional Period, Quarterly Dividend Discount Model," **FR**, 1990, v25(4), 651-658.

Brooks, Robert and John Hand. "Evaluating The Performance Of Stock Portfolios With Index Futures Contracts," **JFM**, 1988, v8(1), 33-46.

Brooks, Robert, Haim Levy and Jim Yoder. "Using Stochastic Dominance To Evaluate The Performance Of Portfolios With Options," **FAJ**, 1987, v43(2), 79-82.

Brooks, Robert, Haim Levy and Miles Livingston. "The Coupon Effect On Term Premiums," **JFI**, 1989, v12(1), 15-22.

Brooks, Robert. "A Closed-Form Equation For Bond Convexity," **FAJ**, 1989, v45(6), 78-79.

Brooks, Robert. "Investment Decision Making With Derivative Securities," **FR**, 1989, v24(4), 511-528.

Brooks, Robert. "Investment Decision Making With Index Futures And Index Futures Options," **JFM**, 1989, v9(2), 143-162.

Brooks, Robert. (Levy, Haim and Robert Brooks. "Financial Break-Even Analysis And The Value Of The Firm," **FM**, 1986, v15(3), 22-26.)

Brooks, Robert. (Levy, Haim and Robert Brooks. "An Empirical Analysis Of Term Premiums Using Stochastic Dominance," **JBF**, 1989, v13(2), 245-260.)

Brookshire, Michael L. (Brady, Dennis P., Michael L. Brookshire and William E. Cobb. "The Development And Solution Of A Tax-Adjusted Model For Personal Injury Awards," **JRI**, 1984, v51(1), 138-142.)

Brookshire, Michael. (Brady, Dennis, Michael Brookshire and William Cobb. "The Development And Solution Of A Tax-Adjusted Model Of Personal Injury Awards: A Response," **JRI**, 1985, v52(3), 520-521.)

Broom, Edward. (Crerend, William J. and Edward Broom. "A Taxonomy Of Money Management," **FAJ**, 1974, v30(3), 24-27,30,23.)

Broome, O. Whitfield, Jr. "The C.F.A. Program's Body Of Knowledge," **FAJ**, 1980, v36(2), 71-78.

Brophy, Daniel F. "Commercial Use Of Options," **RFM**, 1984, v3(2), 174-178.

Brophy, David J. (Chow, Brian G. and David J. Brophy. "The U.S. Treasury Bill Market And Hypotheses Regarding The Term Structure Of Interest Rates," **FR**, 1978, v13(2), 36-50.)

Brophy, David J. (Chow, Brian G. and David J. Brophy. "Treasury-Bill Futures Market: A Formulation And Interpretation," **JFM**, 1982, v2(1), 25-49.)

Brorsen, B. Wade and Scott H. Irwin. "Examination Of Commodity Fund Performance," **RFM**, 1985, v4(1), 84-94.

Brorsen, B. Wade and Scott H. Irwin. "Futures Funds And Price Volatility," **RFM**, 1987, v6(2), 118-135.

Brorsen, B. Wade and Louis P. Lukac. "Optimal Portfolios For Commodity Futures Funds," **JFM**, 1990, v10(3), 247-258.

Brorsen, B. Wade, Charles M. Oellermann and Paul L. Farris. "The Live Cattle Futures Market And Daily Cash Price," **JFM**, 1989, v9(4), 273-282.

Brorsen, B. Wade. "Liquidity Costs And Scalping Returns In The Corn Futures Markets," **JFM**, 1989, v9(3), 225-236.

Brorsen, B. Wade. (Irwin, Scott H. and B. Wade Brorsen. "Public Futures Funds," **JFM**, 1985, v5(2), 149-172.)

Brorsen, B. Wade. (Irwin, Scott H. and B. Wade Brorsen. "A Note On The Factors Affecting Technical Trading System Returns," **JFM**, 1987, v7(5), 591-596.)

Brorsen, B. Wade. (Irwin, Scott H. and B. Wade Brorsen. "Erratum To Public Futures Funds," **JFM**, 1985, v5(3), 461.)

Brorsen, B. Wade. (Lukac, Louis P., B. Wade Brorsen and Scott H. Irwin. "Similarity Of Computer Guided Technical Trading Systems," **JFM**, 1988, v8(1), 1-14.)

Brorsen, B. Wade. (Lukac, Louis P. and B. Wade Brorsen. "A Comprehensive Test Of Futures Market Disequilibrium," **FR**, 1990, v25(4), 593-622.)

Brorsen, B. Wade. (Lukac, Louis P. and B. Wade Brorsen. "The Usefulness Of Historical Data In Selecting Parameters For Technical Trading Systems," **JFM**, 1989, v9(1), 55-66.)

Brorsen, B. Wade. (Oellermann, Charles M., B. Wade Brorsen and Paul L. Farris. "Price Discovery For Feeder Cattle," **JFM**, 1989, v9(2), 113-122.)

Brorsen, B. Wage. (Hall, Joyce A., B. Wade Brorsen and Scott H. Irwin. "The Distribution Of Futures Prices: A Test Of The Stable Paretian And Mixture Of Normals Hypotheses," **JFQA**, 1989, v24(1), 105-116.)

Broske, Mary S. "The Measurement Of Bond Default Risk," **RIF**, 1985, v5, 107-144.

Brotman, Billie Ann and Pauline Fox. "The Impact Of Economic Conditions On The Incidence Of Arson: Comment," **JRI**, 1988, v55(4), 751-754.

Broughton, John B. (Chance, Don M. and John B. Broughton. "Market Index Depository Liabilities: Analysis, Interpretation, And Performance," **JFSR**, 1988, v1(4), 335-352.)

Broverman, Samuel. "The Rate Of Return On Life Insurance And Annuities," **JRI**, 1986, v53(3), 419-434.

Brown, Brendan D. "Money In A Competive Banking Industry," **JBR**, 1976-77, v7(2), 181-183.

Brown, David and Chi-Fu Huang. "Option Pricing In A Lognormal Securities Market With Discrete Trading: A Comment," **JFEC**, 1983, v12(2), 285-286.

Brown, David P. and Michael R. Gibbons. "A Simple Econometric Approach For Utility-Based Asset Pricing Models," **JOF**, 1985, v40(2), 359-382.

Brown, David P. "The Implications Of Nonmarketable Income For Consumption-Based Models Of Asset Pricing," **JOF**, 1988, v43(4), 867-880.

Brown, David P. and Robert H. Jennings. "On Technical Analysis," **RFS**, 1989, v2(4), 527-552.

Brown, David T. "Claimholder Incentive Conflicts In Reorganization: The Role Of Bankruptcy Law," **RFS**, 1989, v2(1), 109-123.

Brown, David T. "The Construction OF Tender Offers: Capital Gains Taxes And The Free Rider Problem," **JOB**, 1988, v61(2), 183-196.

Brown, E. Cary. "The Policy Acceptance In The United States Of Reliance On Automatic Fiscal Stablizers," **JOF**, 1959, v14(1), 40-51.

Brown, F. E. and Douglas Vickers. "Mutual Fund Portfolio Activity, Performance, And Market Impact," **JOF**, 1963, v18(2), 377-391.

Brown, George F., Jr. and Robert M. Bronson. "Static Models Of Bank Credit Expansion," **JFQA**, 1971, v6(3), 995-1014.

Brown, George F., Jr. "Optimal Management Of Bank Reserves," **JFQA**, 1972, v7(5), 2031-2054.

Brown, Gregory D. (Brown, Keith C. and Gregory D. Brown. "Does The Market Portfolio's Composition Matter?," **JPM**, 1987, v13(2), 26-32.)

Brown, H. A., Jr. and R. W. Estes. "Comparability Vs. Flexibility: A Practical Solution," **FAJ**, 1966, v22(3), 65-68.

Brown, Homer A., Jr. and Donald R. Nichols. "A Deterrent To Investment Mobility," **FAJ**, 1969, v25(3), 131-137.

Brown, J. Michael. "Post-Offering Experience Of Companies Going Public," **JOB**, 1970, v43(1), 10-18.

Brown, Jonathan A. and Howard C. Bronson. "New York Stock Exchange Research Program On Share Ownership," **JOF**, 1953, v8(2), 129-136.

Brown, Kate M. "The Use Of Role Play In Teaching Corporate Finance," **JFED**, 1990, v19, 37-43.

Brown, Keith C. and Michael V. Raymond. "Risk Arbitrage And The Prediction Of Successful Corporate Takeovers," **FM**, 1986, v15(3), 54-63.

Brown, Keith C. and Scott L. Lummer. "A Reexamination Of The Covered Call Option Strategy For Corporate Cash Management," **FM**, 1986, v15(2), 13-17.

Brown, Keith C. and Scott L. Lummer. "The Cash Management Implications Of A Hedged Dividend Capture Strategy," **FM**, 1984, v13(4), 7-17.

Brown, Keith C. "A Note On The Apparent Bias Of Net Revenue Estimates For Capital Investment Projects," **JOF**, 1974, v29(4), 1215-1216.

Brown, Keith C. "Estimating Frequency Functions From Limited Data," **JFQA**, 1970, v5(1), 139-148.

Brown, Keith C. "The Rate Of Return Of Selected Investment Projects," **JOF**, 1978, v33(4), 1250-1253.

Brown, Keith C. "The Significance Of Dummy Variables In Multiple Regressions Involving Financial And Economic Data: Comment," **JOF**, 1968, v23(3), 515-517.

Brown, Keith C. (Alderson, Michael J., Keith C. Brown and Scott L. Lummer. "Dutch Auction Rate Preferred Stock," **FM**, 1987, v16(2), 68-73.)

Brown, Keith C. (Harlow, W. V. and Keith C. Brown. "Understanding And Assessing Financial Risk Tolerance: A Biological Perspective," **FAJ**, 1990, v46(6), 50-62.)

Brown, Keith C. and Donald J. Smith. "Recent Innovations In Interest Rate Risk Management And The Reintermediation Of Commercial Banking," **FM**, 1988, v17(4), 45-58.

Brown, Keith C. and Gregory D. Brown. "Does The Market Portfolio's Composition Matter?," **JPM**, 1987, v13(2), 26-32.

Brown, Keith C. and John S. Howe. "On The Use Of Gold As a Fixed Income Security," **FAJ**, 1987, v43(4), 74-76.

Brown, Keith C. and W. V. Harlow. "Market Overreaction: Magnitude And Intensity," **JPM**, 1988, v14(2), 6-13.

Brown, Keith C., Larry J. Lockwood and Scott L. Lummer. "An Examination Of Event Dependency And Structural Change In Security Pricing Models," **JFQA**, 1985, v20(3), 315-334.

Brown, Keith C., W. V. Harlow and Seha M. Tinic. "Risk Aversion, Uncertain Information, And Market Efficiency," **JFEC**, 1988, v22(2), 355-386.

Brown, Keith C., W. V. Harlow and Seha M. Tinic. "How Rational Investors Deal With Uncertainty (Or, Reports Of The Death Of Efficient Market Theory Are Greatly Exaggerated)," **JACF**, 1989, v2(3), 45-58.

Brown, Keith and Donald J. Smith. "Forward Swaps, Swap Options, And The Management Of Callable Debt," **JACF**, 1990, v2(4), 59-71.

Brown, Lawrence D. and Michael S. Rozeff. "The Superiority Of Analyst Forecasts As Measures Of Expectations: Evidence From Earnings," **JOF**, 1978, v33(1), 1-16.

Brown, Lawrence D. and Michael S. Rozeff. "Analysts Can Forecast Accurately!," **JPM**, 1980, v6(3), 31-34.

Brown, Lawrence D. (Bar-Yosef, Sasson and Lawrence D. Brown. "A Reexamination Of Stock Splits Using Moving Betas," **JOF**, 1977, v32(4), 1069-1080.)

Brown, Lawrence D. (Bar-Yosef, Sasson and Lawrence D. Brown. "Share Price Levels And Beta," **FM**, 1979, v8(1), 60-63.)

Brown, Marilyn V. "Prudence Under ERISA: What Regulators Say," **FAJ**, 1977, v33(1), 33-39.

Brown, Marilyn V. "Reducing Corporate And Shareholder Taxes," **FAJ**, 1978, v34(3), 57-63.

Brown, Marilyn V. "The Prospects For Banking Reform," **FAJ**, 1976, v32(2), 14-24.

Brown, Philip and John W. Kennelly. "The Informational Content Of Quarterly Earnings: An Extension And Some Further Evidence," **JOB**, 1972, v45(3),403-415.

Brown, Philip, Allan W. Kleidon and Terry A. Marsh. "New Evidence On The Nature Of Size-Related Anomalies In Stock Prices," **JFEC**, 1983, v12(1), 33-56.

Brown, Philip, Donald B. Keim, Allan W. Kleidon and Terry A. Marsh. "Stock Return Seasonalities And The Tax-Loss Selling Hypothesis: Analysis Of The Arguments And Australian Evidence," **JFEC**, 1983, v12(1), 105-127.

Brown, Philip and Victor Niederhoffer. "The Predictive Content Of Quarterly Earnings," JOB, 1968, v41(4), 488-497.

Brown, R. Gene. "Financial Forecasting By Corporations," FAJ, 1972, v28(2), 38-45,86-87.

Brown, Ralph J. "Implicit Inflation And Interest Rates In Discounting Personal Injury Economic Losses: Comment," JRI, 1986, v53(3), 492-495.

Brown, Robert L. "Adjusting Option Contracts To Reflect Capitalization Changes," JBFA, 1989, v16(2), 247-254.

Brown, Robert M. "A Comparison Of Market Efficiency Among Stock Exchanges," JBFA, 1988, v15(3),373-384.

Brown, Robert M. "On Carrying Costs And The EOQ Model: A Pedagogical Note," FR, 1985, v20(4),357-360.

Brown, S. "The Effect Of Estimation Risk On Capital Market Equilibrium," JFQA, 1979, v14(2), 215-220.

Brown, Stephen and Philip H. Dybvig. "The Empirical Implications Of The Cox, Ingersoll, Ross Theory Of The Term Structure Of Interest Rates," JOF, 1986, v41(3), 616-628.

Brown, Stephen J. and Christopher B. Barry. "Anomalies In Security Returns And The Speculation Of The Market Model," JOF, 1984, v39(3), 807-815.

Brown, Stephen J. and Jerold B. Warner. "Using Daily Stock Returns: The Case Of Event Studies," JFEC, 1985, v14(1), 3-31.

Brown, Stephen J. and Jerold B. Warner. "Measuring Security Price Information," JFEC, 1980, v8(3), 205-258.

Brown, Stephen J. and Mark I. Weinstein. "A New Approach To Testing Asset Pricing Models: The Bilinear Paradigm," JOF, 1983, v38(3), 711-743.

Brown, Stephen J. and Mark I. Weinstein. "Derived Factors In Event Studies," JFEC, 1985, v14(3), 491-495.

Brown, Stephen J. "Heteroscedasticity In The Market Model: A Comment," JOB, 1977, v50(1), 80-83.

Brown, Stephen J. "The Number Of Factors In Security Returns," JOF, 1989, v44(5), 1247-1262.

Brown, Stephen J. (Barry, Christopher B. and Stephen J. Brown. "Limited Information As A Source Of Risk," JPM, 1986, v12(2), 66-73.)

Brown, Stephen J. (Barry, Christopher B. and Stephen J. Brown. "Differential Information And The Small Firm Effect," JFEC, 1984, v13(2), 283-294.)

Brown, Stephen J. (Barry, Christopher B. and Stephen J. Brown. "Differential Information And Security Market Equilibrium," JFQA, 1985, v20(4), 407-422.)

Brown, Stephen J. (Chen, Son-Nan and Stephen J. Brown. "Estimation Risk And Simple Rules For Optimal Portfolio Selection," JOF, 1983, v38(4), 1087-1094.)

Brown, Stephen W., Richard L. Smith, II and George J. Zurowski. "The Appropriateness And Applicability Of Image Research To Banking," JBR, 1977-78, v8(2), 94-100.

Brown, Stewart L. "Autocorrelation, Market Imperfections, And The CAPM," JFQA, 1979, v14(5),1027-1034.

Brown, Stewart L. "Earnings Announcement And Autocorrelation: An Empirical Test," JFR, 1979, v2(2), 171-183.

Brown, Stewart L. "Earnings Changes, Stock Prices, And Market Efficiency," JOF, 1978, v33(1),17-28.

Brown, Stewart L. (Nichols, William D. and Stewart L. Brown. "Assimilating Earnings And Split Information: Is The Capital Market Becoming More Efficient?," JFEC, 1981, v9(3), 309-315.)

Brown, Stewart. (Scott, Elton and Stewart Brown. "Biased Estimators And Unstable Betas," JOF, 1980, v35(1), 49-55.)

Brown, Sudro and Jeffrey Lippitt. "Are Deferred Taxes Discountable?," JBFA, 1987, v14(1), 121-130.

Brown, Theodore H. "Marketing Business Statistics," FAJ, 1954, v10(2), 11-14.

Brown, Theodore H. "Price-Earnings Discount Chart For Growth Stocks," FAJ, 1964, v20(5), 98-103.

Brown, Theodore H. "Security Prices And The Wage Earner," FAJ, 1951, v7(1), 21-24.

Browne, F. X. "Departures From Interest Rates Parity: Further Evidence," JBF, 1983, v7(2),253-272.

Browne, Francis X. and Paul D. McNelis. "Exchange Controls And Interest Rate Determination With Traded And Nontraded Assets: The Irish-United Kingdom Experience," JIMF, 1990, v9(1), 41-59.

Browning, Mark A. (Braswell, Ronald C., E. Joe Nosari and Mark A. Browning. "The Effect Of Private Municipal Bond Insurance On The Cost To The Issuer," FR, 1982, v17(4), 240-251.)

Brownlee, E. Richard, II. (Bruner, Robert F. and E. Richard Brownlee, II. "Leveraged ESOPs, Wealth Transfers, And 'Shareholder Neutrality:' The Case Of Polaroid," FM, 1990, v19(1), 59-74.)

Brownlee, Oswald. "The Economic Report Of The President, 1971: A Comment," JMCB, 1971, v3(4),833-839.

Brox, James A. "Money And Money Substitutes: A Comment," JMCB, 1978, v10(1), 112-114.

Broy, Anthony. "Investing In Swedish Securities," FAJ, 1963, v19(5), 33-42.

Broy, Anthony. "The Automatic Controls Industry," FAJ, 1963, v19(3), 21-27,80.

Broyles, J. E. (Franks, J. R., J. E. Broyles and M. J. Hecht. "An Industry Study Of The Profitability Of Mergers In The United Kingdom," JOF, 1977, v32(5), 1513-1525.)

Broyles, Jack. (Aczel, Michael, Jack Broyles and Bronek Masojada. "Participation In The Lloyd's Insurance Market As A Portfolio Investment," JBFA, 1990, v17(5), 609-634.)

Brozen, Yale. "Adapting To Technological Change," JOB, 1951, v24(2), 114-126.

Brozen, Yale. "The Future Of Industrial Research," JOB, 1961, v34(4), 434-441.

Brozen, Yale. "The New Competition-International Markets: How Should We Adapt?," JOB, 1960, v33(4), 322-326.

Brozen, Yale. "Time, Demand, And Market Position," JOB, 1958, v31(2), 95-106.

Brozen, Yale. "Trends In Industrial Research And Development," JOB, 1960, v33(3), 204-217.

Bruck, Nicholas K. and Francis A. Lees. "Foreign Content Of U.S. Corporate Activities," FAJ, 1966, v22(5), 127-132.

Brucker, Eric. "A Microeconomic Approach To Banking Competition,"

JOF, 1970, v25(5), 1133-1141.

Brucker, Eric. "A Microeconomic Approach To Banking Competition: Reply," JOF, 1972, v27(3), 724-726.

Brucker, Eric. "Usury Legislation And Market Structure: An Alternative Approach," JOF, 1977, v32(4), 1339-1344.

Brudno, Walter W. "The Effects Of Taxes On Business Policies And Practices In Great Britain," JOF, 1958, v13(2), 211-237.

Brueckner, Jan K. "A Simple Model Of Mortgage Insurance," AREUEA, 1985, v13(2), 129-142.

Brueckner, Jan K. "Creative Financing And House Prices: A Theoretical Inquiry Into The Capitalization Issue," AREUEA, 1984, v12(4), 417-426.

Brueckner, Jan K. "Creative Financing And Housing Prices: Reply," AREUEA, 1986, v14(1), 158-162.

Brueckner, Jan K. "The Flexible Mortgage Optimal Financing Of A Consumer Durable," AREUEA, 1984, v12(2), 136-152.

Brueggeman, W. (Agnello, W., W. Brueggeman, G. Decker, R. Griffith, R. Leftwich, R. Moore, J. Neal, B. Sternlicht, B. Wallach, W. Wardrop and C. Zinngrabe. "Panel: Corporate Real Estate Roundtable," JACF, 1990, v3(1), 6-38.)

Brueggeman, William B. and Richard B. Peiser. "Housing Choice And Relative Tenure Prices," JFQA, 1979, v14(4), 735-751.

Brueggeman, William B. and Robert H. Zerbst. "Discount Points And Housing Prices: Reply," JOF, 1979, v34(4), 1055-1060.

Brueggeman, William B. (Zerbst, Robert H. and William B. Brueggeman. "FHA And VA Mortgage Discount Points And Housing Prices," JOF, 1977, v32(5), 1766-1773.)

Brueggeman, William B., Jeffrey D. Fisher and Jerrold J. Stern. "Federal Income Taxes, Inflation And Holding Periods For Income-Producing Property," AREUEA, 1981, v9(2), 148-164.

Brueggeman, William B., Jeffrey D. Fisher and David M. Porter. "Rethinking Corporate Real Estate," JACF, 1990, v3(1), 39-50.

Brumelle, Shelby L. and Bernhard Schwab. "Capital Budgeting With Uncertain Future Opportunities: A Markovian Approach," JFQA, 1973, v8(1), 111-122.

Brumelle, Shelby L. "When Does Diversification Between Two Investments Pay?," JFQA, 1974, v9(3),473-483.

Bruner, Robert F. "Leveraged ESOPS And Corporate Restructuring," JACF, 1988, v1(1), 54-66.

Bruner, Robert F. "The Use Of Excess Cash And Debt Capacity As A Motive For Merger," JFQA, 1988, v23(2), 199-218.

Bruner, Robert F. and E. Richard Brownlee, II. "Leveraged ESOPs, Wealth Transfers, And 'Shareholder Neutrality:' The Case Of Polaroid," FM, 1990, v19(1), 59-74.

Bruner, Robert F. and John M. Simms, Jr. "The International Debt Crisis And Bank Security Returns In 1982," JMCB, 1987, v19(1), 46-55.

Brunie, C. (Amihud, Y., C. Brunie, C. Ferenbach, J. Fredericks, J. Grundfest, J. Lafferty, B. Lev, B. Shorts, J. Stern, B. Stewart and R. Zeckhauser. "Panel: 'Lead Steer' Roundtable," JACF, 1989, v2(3), 24-44.)

Brunner, Karl and Allan H. Meltzer. "Predicting Velocity: Implications For Theory And Policy," JOF, 1963, v18(2), 319-354.

Brunner, Karl and Allan H. Meltzer. "Some Further Investigations Of Demand And Supply Functions For Money," JOF, 1964, v19(2), Part 1, 240-283.

Brunner, Karl and Allan H. Meltzer. "Auerbach's Defense Of Defensive Operations: Comment," JOF, 1965, v20(3), 500-502.

Brunner, Karl and William H. Meckling. "The Perception Of Man And The Conception Of Government," JMCB, 1977, v9(1), 70-85.

Brunner, Karl, Michele Fratianni, Jerry L. Jordan, Allan H. Meltzer and Manferd J. Neumann. "Fiscal And Monetary Policies In Moderate Inflation," JMCB, 1973, v5(1), Part II, 313-354.

Brunner, Karl. "The Ambiguous Rationality Of Economic Policy," JMCB, 1972, v4(1), 3-12.

Brunner, Karl. "'Yale' And Money: A Review Article," JOF, 1971, v26(1), 165-174.

Brunner, Robert F. (Asquith, Paul, Robert F. Bruner and David W. Mullins, Jr. "The Gains To Bidding Firms From Merger," JFEC, 1983, v11(1), 121-139.)

Brush, John S. and Keith E. Boles. "The Predictive Power In Relative Strength And CAPM," JPM, 1983, v9(4), 20-23.

Brush, John S. "Eight Relative Strength Models Compared," JPM, 1986, v13(1), 21-28.

Brush, John S. and Anthony Spare. "Change In Dividend Yield And Portfolio Volatility," JPM, 1990, v16(3), 27-32.

Bryan, Lowell J. "Structured Securitized Credit," JACF, 1988, v1(3), 6-19.

Bryan, Michael F. and William T. Gavin. "Models Of Inflation Expectations Formation: A Comparison Of Household And Economist Forecasts: A Comment," JMCB, 1986, v18(4), 539-544.

Bryan, Robert F. "A Sound Structure For The Corporate Profits Tax," FAJ, 1945, v1(2), 44-54.

Bryan, William R. and A. James Heins. "Defensive Open-Market Operations, Proximate Objectives, And Monetary Instability: A Comment," JMCB, 1972, v4(1), 98-108.

Bryan, William R. and Timothy J. Gallagher. "The Role Of The Federal Funds Market," JMCB, 1978, v10(1), 102-104.

Bryan, William R. "Bank Responses To Reserve Changes: Comment," JOF, 1966, v21(3), 539-541.

Bryan, William R. "Treasury Advanced Refundings: An Empirical Investigation," JFQA, 1972, v7(5), 2139-2150.

Bryan, William R. (Aigner, Dennis J. and William R. Bryan. "The Determinants Of Member Bank Borrowing: A Critique," JOF, 1968, v23(5), 832-837.)

Bryan, William R. and Charles M. Linke. "The Estimation Of The Age/Earnings Profiles In Wrongful Death And Injury Cases: Comment," JRI, 1988, v55(1), 168-173.

Bryan, William R. and Charles M. Linke. "Estimating Present Value Of Future Earnings: Experience With Dedicated Portfolios," JRI, 1988, v55(2), 273-286.

Bryan, William R. and Charles M. Linke. "Estimating The Present Value Of Future Income Losses: An Historical Simulation 1900-1982: Comment," JRI, 1989, v56(3), 555-559.

Bryan, William R., Thomas Gruca and Charles M. Linke. "The Present Value Of Future Earnings: Contemporary Differentials And

Burgess, Richard C. and Bruce T. O'Dell. "An Empirical Examination Of Index Efficiency: Implications For Index Funds," JFQA, 1978, v13(1), 93-100.

Burgess, Richard C. and Keith H. Johnson. "The Effects Of Sampling Fluctuations On The Required Inputs Of Security Analysis," JFQA, 1976, v11(5), 847-855.

Burgess, Richard C. and Maurry J. Tamarkin. "Regulatory Influences On Portfolio Performance: Short Selling And Regulation T," JFR, 1982, v5(1), 39-54.

Burgess, Richard C. (Bey, Roger P., Richard C. Burgess and Richard B. Kearns. "Moving Stochastic Dominance: An Alternative Method For Testing Market Efficiency," JFR, 1984, v7(3), 185-196.)

Burgess, Richard C. (Johnson, Keith R. and Richard C. Burgess. "The Effects Of Sample Sizes On The Accuracy Of EV And SSD Efficiency Criteria," JFQA, 1975, v10(5), 813-820.)

Burgess, Richard C. (Kearns, Richard B. and Richard C. Burgess. "An Effective Algorithm For Estimating Stochastic Dominance Efficient Sets," JFQA, 1979, v14(3), 547-552.)

Burgess, Richard C. and Roger P. Bey. "Optimal Portfolios: Markowitz Full Covariance Versus Simple Selection Rules," JFR, 1988, v11(2), 153-164.

Burgess, W. Randolph. "Federal Reserve And Treasury Relations," JOF, 1954, v9(1), 1-11.

Burghardt, Galen and Morton Lane. "How To Tell If Options Are Cheap," JPM, 1990, v16(2), 72-78.

Burghardt, Galen, Jr. and Donald L. Kohn. "Comments On `Margins And Futures Contracts'," JFM, v1(2), 255-257.

Burik, Paul and Richard M. Ennis. "Foreign Bonds In Diversified Portfolios: A Limited Advantage," FAJ, 1990, v46(2), 31-40.

Burke, Alfred L. "The Investor Looks At Accounting Problems In The Utility Industry," FAJ, 1965, v21(5), 27-30.

Burke, Christopher M. (Stapleton, Richard C. and Christopher M. Burke. "European Tax Systems And The Neutrality Of Corporate Financing Policy," JBF, 1977, v1(1), 55-70.)

Burke, J. L. "Pipelines: Oil's Steel Arteries," FAJ, 1960, v16(3), 135-136.

Burke, Jim. "Bank Holding Company Behavior And Structural Change," JBR, 1978-79, v9(1), 43-51.

Burke, Terry. (Sorensen, Eric H. and Terry Burke. "Portfolio Returns From Active Industry Group Rotation," FAJ, 1986, v42(5), 43-50.)

Burkhauser, Richard V. (Myers, Daniel A., Richard V. Burkhauser and Karen C. Holden. "The Transition From Wife To Widow: The Importance Of Survivor Benefits To Widows," JRI, 1987, v54(4), 752-759.)

Burkhead, J. Gary. "Investing In The Shoe Industry," FAJ, 1968, v24(2), 41-48.

Burkhead, J. Gary. (Buff, Jerome H., G. Gordon Biggar, Jr. and J. Gary Burkhead. "Decision Analysis Techniques," FAJ, 1968, v24(6), 123-128.)

Burkhead, Jesse and Donald C. Steele. "The Effect Of State Taxation On The Migration Of Industry," JOB, 1950, v23(3), 167-172.

Burmeister, Edwin and Kent D. Wall. "The Arbitrage Pricing Theory And Macroeconomic Factor Measures," FR, 1986, v21(1), 1-20.

Burmeister, Edwin and Marjorie B. McElroy. "Joint Estimation Of Factor Sensitivities And Risk Premia For The Arbitrage Pricing Theory," JOF, 1988, v43(3), 721-733.

Burmeister, Edwin and Marjorie B. McElroy. "The Residual Market Factor, The APT, And Mean-Variance Efficiency," RQFA, 1991, v1(1), 27-50.

Burmeister, Edwin. "On Some Conceptual Issues In Rational Expectations Modeling," JMCB, 1980, v12(4), Part 2, 800-816.

Burmeister, Edwin. (Berry, Michael A., Edwin Burmeister and Marjorie B. McElroy. "Sorting OUt Risks Using Known APT Factors," FAJ, 1988, v44(2), 29-42.)

Burmesiter, Edwin and Edmund Phelps. "Money, Public Debt, Inflation, And Real Interest," JMCB, 1971, v3(2), Part 1, 153-182.

Burnett, John J. and Bruce A. Palmer. "Reliance On Life Insurance Agents: A Demographic And Psychographic Analysis Of Consumers," JRI, 1983, v50(3), 510-520.

Burnett, John J. and Bruce A. Palmer. "Examining Life Insurance Ownership Through Demographic And Psychographic Characteristics," JRI, 1984, v51(3), 453-467.

Burnham, James B. "Current Structure And Recent Developments In Foreign Exchange Markets," RDIBF, 1991, v4/5, 115-146.

Burnie, David A. "An Empirical Evaluation Of The Friedman Hypothesis Of Inflation On Capital Asset Pricing," FR, 1990, v25(2), 297-320.

Burnie, David A. "Capital Asset Prices And The Friedman Hypothesis Of Inflation," JBFA, 1986, v13(4), 519-534.

Burnie, David. (Barnes, Tom and David Burnie. "Corporate Bonds, Term Structure Expectations And Optimal Portfolios: The Canadian Experience," JBFA, 1990, v17(3), 411-420.)

Burns, Arthur F. "The Current Business Recession," JOB, 1958, v31(2), 145-153.

Burns, Arthur F. "Wages And Prices By Formula," JPM, 1978, v4(4), 58-65.

Burns, J. (Appelbaum, E., J. Burns, R. Evans, J. Gould, T. Hamachek, R. Kidder, M. Jensen, J. Johnstone, M. Murray, R. Sim, J. Stern, B. Stewart and C. Zaner. "Panel: CEO Roundtable On Corporate Structure And Management Incentives," JACF, 1990, v3(3), 6-35.)

Burns, Joseph M. "Academic Views On Improving The Federal Reserve Discount Mechanism: A Review Essay," JMCB, 1973, v5(1), 47-60.

Burns, Joseph M. "An Examination Of The Operating Efficiency Of Three Financial Intermediaries," JFQA, 1970, v5(5), 541-558.

Burns, Joseph M. "Electronic Trading In Futures Markets," FAJ, 1982, v38(1), 33-41.

Burns, Leland S. (Grebler, Leo and Leland S. Burns. "Construction Cycles In The United States Since World War II," AREUEA, 1982, v10(2), 123-151.)

Burns, Malcolm R. "New Evidence On The Value Additivity Principle," JFQA, 1987, v22(1), 65-78.

Burns, Michele A. "A Framework For Utilizing Interest Rate Data In Teaching Finance," JFED, 1984, v13, 47-54.

Burns, Michele. (Burns, William and Michele Burns. "The Use Of A Portfolio Management Simulation As A Learning Device," JFED, 1982, v11, 79-82.)

Burns, Richard M. (Jordan, Bradford D., James A. Verbrugge and

Richard M. Burns. "Returns To Initial Shareholders In Savings Institution Covnersions: Evidence And Regulatory Implications," JFR, 1988, v11(2), 125-136.)

Burns, Robert K. "Some Unsettled Issues Of Retirement Policy," JOB, 1954, v27(2), 137-145.

Burns, Robert K. "The Comparative Economic Position Of Manual And White-Collar Employees," JOB, 1954, v27(4), 257-267.

Burns, Robert K. (Solomon, Benjamin and Robert K. Burns. "Unionization Of White-Collar Employees: Extent, Potential, And Implications," JOB, 1963, v36(2), 141-165.)

Burns, Warren. "Analysts Bid Farewell To Europe," FAJ, 1961, v17(3), 75-78.

Burns, Warren. "Natural Gas Seminar - On Location: Louisiana," FAJ, 1960, v16(4), 67-74.

Burns, Warren. (Bretey, Pierre R. and Warren Burns. "First Convention Outside U. S.," FAJ, 1959, v15(3), 57-64.)

Burns, William and Michele Burns. "The Use Of A Portfolio Management Simulation As A Learning Device," JFED, 1982, v11, 79-82.

Burns, William L. and Donald R. Epley. "The Performance Of Portfolios Of REITs + Stocks," JPM, 1982, v8(3), 37-42.

Burns, William. (Epley, Donald R. and William Burns. "The Correct Use Of Confidence Intervals And Regression Analysis In Determining The Value Of Residential Homes," AREUEA, 1978, v6(1), 70-85.)

Burns, William. (Epley, Donald and William Burns. "The Correct Use Of Confidence Intervals And Regression Analysis In Determining The Value Of Residential Houses: A Reply," AREUEA, 1979, v7(1), 136-140.)

Burr, L. Clinton. "Reparations," JFM, 1981, v1(Supp), 505-514.

Burr, Ted. (Mano, Ronald M. and Ted Burr. "IRAs Versus Nonsheltered Alternatives For Retirement Savings Goals," FAJ, 1984, v40(3), 67-75.)

Burrell, O. K. "A Mathematical Approach To Growth Stock Valuation," FAJ, 1960, v16(3), 69-76.

Burrell, O. K. "Possibility Of An Experimental Approach To Investment Studies," JOF, 1951, v6(2), 211-219.

Burrell, O. K. "Savings Bonds In Personal Investment Programs," JOF, 1953, v8(2), 212-223.

Burrell, O. K. "The Growth Factor In Railroad Stock Analysis," FAJ, 1955, v11(4), 35-40.

Burroughs, Eugene B. "The Asset Manager As Stargazer," JPM, 1976, v2(3), 27-29.

Burrows, Paul. "The Upward Sloping IS Curve And The Control Of Income And The Balance Of Payments," JOF, 1974, v29(3), 955-961.

Burstein, Nancy R. "Effects On The Credit Markets Of The Abolition Of Holder-In-Due-Course," FR, 1979, v8(4), 19-27.

Burt, John, Fred R. Kaen and G. Geoffrey Booth. "Foreign Exchange Market Efficiency Under Flexible Exchange Rates," JOF, 1977, v32(4), 1325-1330.

Burt, John, Fred R. Kaen and G. Geoffrey Booth. "Foreign Exchange Market Efficiency Under Flexible Exchange Rates: Reply," JOF, 1979, v34(3), 791-793.

Burton, J. S. and J. R. Toth. "Forecasting Long-Term Interest Rates," FAJ, 1974, v30(5), 73-87.

Burton, John C. "Ethics In Financial Reporting," FAJ, 1972, v28(1), 49-53.

Burton, John C. (Norby, William C. and John C. Burton. "Financial Reporting In The 1980s," FAJ, 1980, v36(1), 64-68.)

Burton, John F., Jr. and Monroe Berkowitz. "Objectives Other Than Income Maintenance For Workmen's Compensation," JRI, 1971, v38(3), 343-355.

Burton, R. M. and W. W. Damon. "On The Existence Of A Cost Of Capital Under Pure Capital Rationing," JOF, 1974, v29(4), 1165-1173.

Busche, Kelly and Christopher D. Hall. "An Exception To The Risk Preference Anomaly," JOB, 1988, v61(3), 337-346.

Buschmann, Nancy K. (Beedles, William L. and Nancy K. Buschmann. "Describing Bank Equity Returns: The Year-By-Year Record," JMCB, 1981, v13(2),241-247.)

Buse, A. "Expectations, Prices, Coupons And Yields: Reply," JOF, 1975, v30(4), 1141-1142.

Buse, A. "Expectations, Prices, Coupons And Yields," JOF, 1970, v25(4), 809-818.

Buser, Stephen A. and Patrick J. Hess. "Empirical Determinants Of The Relative Yields On Taxable And Tax-Exempt Securities," JFEC, 1986, v17(2), 335-355.

Buser, Stephen A. "Efficient Risk/Return Management In Commercial Banking," JBR, 1979-80, v10(4), 235-247.

Buser, Stephen A. "Laplace Transforms As Present Value Rules: A Note," JOF, 1986, v41(1), 243-246.

Buser, Stephen A. "Mean-Variance Portfolio Selection With Either A Singular Or Nonsingular Variance-Covariance Matrix," JFQA, 1977, v12(3), 347-361.

Buser, Stephen A. (Kane, Edward J. and Stephen A. Buser. "Portfolio Diversification At Commercial Banks," JOF, 1979, v34(1), 19-34.)

Buser, Stephen A. (Smith, Michael L. and Stephen A. Buser. "Risk Aversion, Insurance Costs And Optimal Property-Liability Coverages," JRI, 1987, v54(2), 225-245.)

Buser, Stephen A. and Anthony B. Sanders. "Tenure Decisions Under A Progressive Tax Structure," AREUEA, 1983, v11(3), 371-381.

Buser, Stephen A., Andrew H. Chen And Edward J. Kane. "Federal Deposit Insurance, Regulatory Policy, And Optimal Bank Capital," JOF, 1981, v36(1), 51-60.

Buser, Stephen A., Patric H. Hendershott and Anthony B. Sanders. "Pricing Life Of Loan Rate Caps On Default-Free Adjustable-Rate Mortgages," AREUEA, 1985, v13(3), 248-260.

Buser, Stephen A., Patric H. Hendershott and Anthony B. Saunders. "Determinants Of The Value Of Call Options On Default-Free Bonds," JOB, 1990, v63(1), Part 2, S33-S50.

Bush, Ronald F. (Hair, Joseph F., Jr., Paul J. Solomon and Ronald F. Bush. "A Factor Analytic Study Of Black Models In Television Commercials," JOB, 1977, v50(2), 208-215.)

Bush, Ronald F. (Stern, Bruce L., Ronald F. Bush and Joseph F. Hair, Jr. "The Self-Image/Store Image Matching Process: An Empirical Test," JOB, 1977, v50(1), 63-69.)

Busschau, W. J. "The 'Paper Gold' Planners (Keynote Review)," FAJ, 1966, v22(6), 135-137.

Butler, Arthur D. and Stanton A. Warren. "An Optimal Temporary Loan Model For State Borrowers," JOF, 1977, v32(4), 1305-1312.

Butler, H. L., Jr. and J. D. Allen. "Dow Jones Industrial Average Re-Examined," FAJ, 1979, v35(6),23-30.

Butler, H. L., Jr., G. J. Podrasky and J. D. Allen. "Aerospace Industry Re-Revisited," FAJ, 1977, v33(4), 32-35.

Butler, Hartman L. "Aerospace Fundamentals And Industry Analysis - Part Two," FAJ, 1966, v22(2),41-48.

Butler, Hartman L., Jr. and Richard F. DeMong. "The Changing Dow Jones Industrial Average," FAJ, 1986, v42(4), 59-62.

Butler, Hartman L., Jr. and Martin G. Decker. "Security Check On Dow Jones Industrial Average," FAJ, 1953, v9(1), 37-46.

Butler, Hartman L., Jr. "Aerospace Industry Revisited," FAJ, 1967, v23(5), 57-62.

Butler, Hartman L., Jr. "Aerospace Fundamentals And Industry Analysis," FAJ, 1966, v22(1),55-60.

Butler, Hartman L., Jr., George J. Podrasky and J. Devon Allen. "Aerospace II - Commercial Aircraft," FAJ, 1977, v33(5), 53-66.

Butler, J. S. and Barry Schachter. "Unbiased Estimation Of The Black/Scholes Formula," JFEC, 1986, v15(3), 341-357.

Butler, J. S. and Barry Schachter. "The Investment Decision: Estimation Risk And Risk Adjusted Discount Rates," FM, 1989, v18(4), 13-22.

Butler, Kirt C. (Atchison, Michael D., Kirt C. Butler and Richard R. Simonds. "Nonsynchronous Security Trading And Market Index Autocorrelation," JOF, 1987, v42(1), 111-118.)

Butler, Kirt C. and Dale L. Domian. "Risk, Diversification, And The Investment Horizon," JPM, 1991, v17(3), 41-48.

Butler, Richard J. (Appel, David, John D. Worrall and Richard J. Butler. "Survivorship And The Size Distribution Of The Property-Liability Insurance Industry," JRI, 1985, v52(3), 424-440.)

Butler, Richard J. (Worrall, John D., David Appel and Richard J. Butler. "Sex, Marital Status, And Medical Utilization By Injured Workers," JRI, 1987, v54(1), 27-44.)

Butters, J. Keith and John Lintner. "Tax And Non-Tax Motivations For Mergers," JOF, 1951, v6(4), 361-382.

Butters, J. Keith. "Federal Income Taxation And External vs. Internal Financing," JOF, 1949, v4(3), 197-205.

Butters, J. Keith. (Thompson, Lawrence E. and J. Keith Butters. "Effects Of Taxation On The Investment Policies And Capacity Of Individuals," JOF, 1953, v8(2), 137-151.)

Buttler, Hans-Jurg. "An Expository Note On The Valuation Of Foreign Exchange Options," JIMF, 1989, v8(2), 295-304.

Buzby, Stephen L. (Falk, Haim and Stephen L. Buzby. "Borrowing Rates, Alternative Investment Sets, And The Life Insurance Purchase Decision," JRI, 1976, v43(2), 291-304.)

Buzzacchi, Luigi. (Brioschi, Francesco, Luigi Buzzacchi and Massimo G. Colombo. "Risk Capital Financing And The Separation Of Ownership And Control In Business Groups," JBF, 1989, v13(4/5), 747-772.)

Byfield, Robert S. "A Security Analyst Appraises The Impact Of Soviet Technique," FAJ, 1955, v11(5),43-48.

Byler, Ezra. (Reichert, Alan K., James S. Moore and Ezra Byler. "Financial Analysis Among Large US Corporations: Recent Trends And The Impact Of The Personal Computer," JBFA, 1988, v15(4), 469-486.)

Bylinski, Joseph F. (Shank, John K., Jessie F. Dillard and Joseph F. Bylinski. "What 'Subject To' Opinions Tell Investors," FAJ, 1979, v35(1), 41-45.)

Byrne, Mark J. (Maloney, Kevin J. and Mark J. Byrne. "An Equilibrium Debt Option Pricing Model In Discrete Time," JBF, 1989, v13(3), 421-442.)

Byrne, Mother Martin. "The Role Of Life Insurance Companies In Financing Religious Institution Expansion," JRI, 1959, v26(4), 59-64.

Byrne, R., A. Charnes, W. W. Cooper and K. Kortanek. "A Chance-Constrained Approach To Capital Budgeting With Portfolio Type Payback And Liquidity Constraints And Horizon Posture Controls," JFQA, 1967, v2(4), 339-364.

Byrne, Sister Martin. "Class Presentation Of Cases," JFED, 1972, v1, 75.

CCC

Cabanilla, Nathaniel B. "Directly-Placed Bonds: A Test Of Market Efficiency," JPM, 1984, v10(2), 72-74.

Cabanilla, Nathaniel B. "Life Insurers In The Public And Private Security Markets," JRI, 1987, v54(2), 348-356.

Cabral, Jose Sarsfield and Rui Campos Guimaraes. "Are Commodity Futures Markets Really Efficient? A Purchasing-Oriented Study Of The Chicago Corn Futures Market," RFM, 1988, v7(Supp), 598-617.

Cadsby, Charles Bram, Murray Frank and Vojislav Maksimovic. "Pooling, Separating, And Semiseparating Equilibria In Financial Markets: Some Experimental Evidence," RFS, 1990, v3(3), 315-342.

Cadsby, Charles Bram. "Performance Hypothesis Testing With The Sharpe And Treynor Measures: A Comment," JOF, 1986, v41(5), 1175-1176.

Caffrey, Edward R. "Polyester Fiber And Film," FAJ, 1953, v9(1), 69-70.

Cagan, Phillip and Anna J. Schwartz. "Has The Growth Of Money Substitutes Hindered Monetary Policy?," JMCB, 1975, v7(2), 137-159.

Cagan, Phillip. "Financial Futures Markets: Is More Regulation Needed?," JFM, v1(2), 169-189.

Cagan, Phillip. "Financial Regulation: Comment On Kareken," JOB, 1986, v59(1), 49-54.

Cagan, Phillip. "Imported Inflation 1973-74 And The Accommodation Issue," JMCB, 1980, v12(1), 1-16.

Cagan, Phillip. "Reflections On Rational Expectations," JMCB, 1980, v12(4), Part 2, 826-832.

Cagan, Phillip. "The Choice Among Monetary Aggregates As Targets And Guides For Monetary Policy," JMCB, 1982, v14(4), Part 2, 661-686.

Cagan, Phillip. "The Hodgman And Mayer Papers: Some Comments," JMCB, 1972, v4(2), 422-425.

Cagan, Phillip. "The Non-Neutrality Of Money In The Long Run: A Discussion Of The Critical Assumptions And Some Evidence," JMCB, 1969, v1(2), 207-227.

Cain, Glen G. (Seidman, Joel and Glen G. Cain. "Unionized Engineers And Chemists: A Case Study Of A Professional Union," JOB, 1964, v37(3), 238-257.)

Cakici, Nusret, T. Hanan Eytan and Giora Harpaz. "American Vs. European Options On The Value Line Index," JFM, 1988, v8(3), 373-388.

Cakici, Nusret. (Bhatt, Swati and Nusret Cakici. "Premiums On Stock Index Futures - Some Evidence," JFM, 1990, v10(4), 367-376.)

Caks, John, William R. Lane, Robert W. Greenleaf and Reginald G. Joules. "A Simple Formula For Duration," JFR, 1985, v8(3),245-249.

Caks, John. "Corporate Debt Decisions: A New Analytical Framework," JOF, 1978, v33(5), 1297-1315.

Caks, John. "Sense And Nonsense About Depreciation," FM, 1981, v10(4), 80-86.

Caks, John. "The Coupon Effect On Yield To Maturity," JOF, 1977, v32(1), 103-115.

Caks, John. "The Pricing Of Premium Bonds: Comment," JFQA, 1981, v16(3), 397-401.

Caks, John. (Livingston, Miles and John Caks. "A 'Duration' Fallacy," JOF, 1977, v32(1), 185-187.)

Caks, John. (Pari, Robert and John Caks. "A Note On Bond Defeasance," FR, 1988, v23(2), 233-236.)

Calcoen, F. (Eeckhoudt, L., J. F. Outreville, M. Lauwers and F. Calcoen. "The Impact Of A Probationary Period On The Demand For Insurance," JRI, 1988, v55(2), 217-228.)

Calderon-Rossell, Jorge R. "Optimal Financial Structure Of Finance Companies In A Regulated Environment Of A Developing Country," JBF, 1984, v8(3), 443-457.

Calderon-Rossell, Jorge R. "Covering Foreign Exchange Risks Of Single Transactions: A Framework For Analysis," FM, 1979, v8(3), 78-85.

Calderwood, Stanford. "The Truth About Index Funds," FAJ, 1977, v33(4), 36-47.

Caldwell, David. (Statman, Meir and David Caldwell. "Applying Behavioral Finance To Capital Budgeting: Project Terminations," FM, 1987, v16(4), 7-15.)

Caldwell, J. E. and Charlotte Panimon. "Projective Testing In An Industrial Research Organization: One Experience," JOB, 1955, v28(1), 67-71.

Caligiuri, Gian Franco, Antonio Fazio and Tommaso Padoa-Schioppa. "Demand And Supply Of Bank Credit In Italy," JMCB, 1974, v6(4), 455-479.

Calkins, D. Ordell. (Schaffer, Burton F. and D. Ordell Calkins. "An Appraisal Of Prerequisites To Business Finance," JFED, 1980, v9, 51-55.)

Calkins, D. Ordell. (Schaffer, Burton F. and D. Ordell Calkins. "Compustat: Bringing The Real World Into The Classroom," JFED, 1977, v6, 75-78.)

Calkins, Francis J. "Corporate Reorganization Under Chapter X - A Post-Mortem," JOF, 1948, v3(2), 19-28.

Calkins, Francis J. "Courts And Chapter X Reorganization," FAJ, 1948, v4(1), 42-48.

Calkins, Francis J. "Materials And Methods Of Teaching Business Finance (II)," JOF, 1950, v5(3), 275-279.

Calkins, Francis J. "University Courses In Finance," JOF, 1949, v4(3), 244-265.

Calkins, Robert D. "The Problems Of Business Education," JOB, 1961, v34(1), 1-9.

Call, Ivan T., Terry N. Lee and Gary F. McKinnon. "Teaching Financial Management As Part Of An Integrated Management Core," JFED, 1975, v4, 19-27.

Callahan, Carolyn M. and Rosanne M. Mohr. "The Determinants Of Systematic Risk: A Synthesis," FR, 1989, v24(2), 157-182.

Callahan, John L. "Evaluation Of Metropolitan Conflict And Cooperation," AREUEA, 1973, v1(2), 141-151.

Callahan, John and William H. Wilken. "School Finance Reform And Property Tax Relief Programs: Their Effect On Urban Fiscal Disparities," AREUEA, 1974, v2(1), 39-56.

Callard, Charles G. and David C. Kleinman. "Inflation-Adjusted Accounting: Does It Matter?," FAJ, 1985, v41(3), 51-59.

Callard, Charles G. "The Third Yield," FAJ, 1968, v24(1), 114-120.

Callaway, Richard E. "Evidence Of The Nonstationarity Of The Variance Rate Of Return Of New York Stock Exchange Listed Common Stock," FR, 1989, v24(2), 199-214.

Callaway, Richard. (Thakor, Anjan V. and Richard Callaway. "Costly Information Production Equilibria In The Bank Credit Market With Applications To Credit Rationing," JFQA, 1983, v18(2), 229-256.)

Callen, Jeffrey L. (Aivazian, Varouj A. and Jeffrey L. Callen. "The 'Unanimity' Literature And The Security Market Line Criterion: The Additive Risk Case," JBFA, 1981, v8(2), 177-184.)

Callen, Jeffrey L. (Aivazian, Varouj A., Jeffrey L. Callen, Itzhak Krinsky and Clarence C. Y. Kwan. "International Exchange Risk And Asset Substitutability," JIMF, 1986, v5(4), 449-466.)

Callen, Jeffrey L. (Aivazian, Varouj A. and Jeffrey L. Callen. "Corporate Leverage And Growth: The Game-Theoretic Issues," JFEC, 1980, v8(4), 379-399.)

Callen, Jeffrey L. (Aivazian, Varouj A. and Jeffrey L. Callen. "Future Investment Opportunities And The Value Of The Call Provision On A Bond: Comment," JOF, 1980, v35(4), 1051-1054.)

Callen, Jeffrey L. (Aivazian, Varouj A. and Jeffrey L. Callen. "On Unanimity And Monopoly Power," JBFA, 1985, v12(1), 145-149.)

Callen, Jeffrey L. (Aivazian, Varouj A. and Jeffrey L. Callen. "Reorganization In Bankruptcy And The Issue Of Strategic Risk," JBF, 1983, v7(1),119-134.)

Callen, Jeffrey L. (Aivazian, Varouj A. and Jeffrey L. Callen. "Investment, Market Structure, And The Cost Of Capital," JOF, 1979, v34(1), 85-92.)

Callen, Jeffrey L. (Aivazian, Varouj A. and Jeffrey L. Callen. "Miller's Irrelevance Mechanism: A Note," JOF, 1987, v42(1), 169-180.)

Callen, Jeffrey L. (Bar-Yosef, Sasson, Jeffrey L. Callen and Joshua Livnat. "Autoregressive Modeling Of Earnings--Investment Causality," JOF, 1987, v42(1), 11-28.)

Callen, Jeffrey L. (Ben-Horim, Moshe and Jeffrey L. Callen. "The Cost Of Capital, Macaulay's Duration, And Tobin's q," *JFR*, 1989, v12(2), 143-156.)

Callen, Jeffrey L., M. W. Luke Chan and Clarence C. Y. Kwan. "Spot And Forward Exchange Rates: A Causality Analysis," *JBFA*, 1989, v16(1), 105-118.

Calley, Nicholas O., Donald R. Chambers and J. Randall Woolridge. "A Note On Standardized Unexpected Earnings: The Case Of The Electric Utility Industry," *FR*, 1985, v20(1), 102-110.

Callier, Philippe. "One Way Arbitrage Foreign Exchange And Securities Markets: A Note," *JOF*, 1981, v36(5), 1177-1186.

Callier, Philippe. "Speculation And The Forward Foreign Exchange Rate: A Note," *JOF*, 1980, v35(1), 173-176.

Callister, T. K. "Central Value And P/E Estimation By Formula Approach," *FAJ*, 1961, v17(6), 57-59.

Callister, T. K. "Foreign Security Investing," *FAJ*, 1963, v19(2), 55-56.

Calomiris, Charles W. "Commercial Paper, Bank Reserve Requirements, And The Informational Role Of Loan Commitments: A Comment," *JBF*, 1989, v13(2), 271-278.

Calomiris, Charles W. and Ian Domowitz. "Asset Substitutions, Money Demand, And The Inflation Process In Brazil," *JMCB*, 1989, v21(1), 78-89.

Calvet, A. L. and J. Lefoll. "Performance And Systematic Risk Stability Of Canadian Mutual Funds Under Inflation," *JBFA*, 1981, v8(2), 279-289.

Calvet, A. L. and J. Lefoll. "Information Asymmetry And Wealth Effect Of Canadian Corporate Acquisitions," *FR*, 1987, v22(4), 415-432.

Calvo, Guillermo A. "Balance Of Payments Crises In A Cash-In-Advance Economy," *JMCB*, 1987, v19(1),19-32.

Calvo, Guillermo A. "Currency Substitution And The Real Exchange Rate: The Utility Maximization Approach," *JIMF*, 1985, v4(2), 175-188.

Calvo, Guillermo A. "Reserves And The Managed Float: A Search For The Essentials," *JIMF*, 1985, v4(1), 43-60.

Cambon, Barbara R. (Zerbst, Robert H. and Barbara R. Cambon. "Real Estate: Historical Returns And Risks," *JPM*, 1984, v10(3), 5-20.)

Camerer, Colin F. "An Experimental Test Of Several Generalized Utility Theories," *JRU*, 1989, v2(1), 61-104.

Camerer, Colin and Howard Kunreuther. "Experimental Markets For Insurance," *JRU*, 1989, v2(3), 265-300.

Camerer, Colin. "The Pricing And Social Value Of Commodity Options," *FAJ*, 1982, v38(1), 62-65.

Cameron, Alex B. (Bartley, Jon W. and Alex B. Cameron. "Long-Run Earnings Forecasts By Managers And Financial Analysts," *JBFA*, 1991, v18(1), 21-42.)

Cameron, Norman E. "Capital Gains, Losses, And Financial Results In The Non-Life Insurance Industry: Comment," *JRI*, 1976, v43(4), 720.

Cameron, Norman E. "Inflation And Nominal Policy Yields On Participating Life Insurance," *JRI*, 1987, v54(3), 541-556.

Cameron, Norman. "The Accuracy Of Hill's Linear Method Of Rate Of Return Calculation," *JRI*, 1976, v43(1), 164-167.

Cameron, Stephen, Kevin Holme and Alice Rapoport. "Managing Interest Rate Risk," *JACF*, 1990, v3(1), 56-64.

Cammarota, Mark. "The Impact Of Unseasonable Weather On Housing Starts," *AREUEA*, 1989, v17(3), 300-313.

Camp, Kathryn Page. "The Public Interest Test: An Anticompetitive Anomaly," *JPM*, 1981, v1(Spec), 475-478.

Camp, Robert C. and Arthur A. Eubank, Jr. "The Beta Quotient: A New Measure Of Portfolio Risk," *JPM*, 1981, v7(4), 53-57.

Campbell, Brian E. (Dran, John J., Jr. and Brian E. Campbell. "Hospital Investment And Medicare Reimbursement," *JFR*, 1981, v4(2), 147-160.)

Campbell, Colin D. (Alhadeff, D., P. Bernstein, C. Campbell, L. Chandler, E. Ettin, V. Farhi, J. Guttentag, H. Latane and K. Poole. "The Commission On Money And Credit's Research Studies," *JOF*, 1964, v19(3), 497-533.)

Campbell, Donald T. "Rationality And Utility From The Standpoint Of Evolutionary Biology," *JOB*, 1986, v59(4), Part 2, S355-S364.

Campbell, James A. and William Beranek. "Stock Price Behavior On Ex-Dividend Dates," *JOF*, 1955, v10(4),, 425-429.

Campbell, John Y. "A Defense Of Traditional Hypotheses About The Term Structure Of Interest Rates," *JOF*, 1986, v41(1), 183-194.

Campbell, John Y. "Money Announcements, The Demand For Bank Reserves And The Behavior Of The Federal Funds Rate Within The Statement Week," *JMCB*, 1987, v19(1), 56-67.

Campbell, John Y. "Stock Returns And The Term Structure," *JFEC*, 1987, v18(2), 373-400.

Campbell, John Y. and Robert J. Shiller. "The Dividend-Price Ratio And Expectations Of Future Dividends And Discount Factors," *RFS*, 1988-89, v1(3), 195-228.

Campbell, Kenneth R. "Problems And Issues In Public Employee Retirement Systems: Comment," *JRI*, 1974, v41(3), 527-529.

Campbell, Ritchie A. "The Demand For Life Insurance: An Application Of The Economics Of Uncertainty," *JOF*, 1980, v35(5), 1155-1172.

Campbell, Robert J. "An Evaluation Of The Need For New Information Technology To Support Branch Operations," *JRI*, 1978, v45(3), 401-412.

Campbell, Tim and Leland Brendsel. "The Impact Of Compensating Balance Requirements On The Cash Balances Of Manufacturing Corporations: An Empirical Study," *JOF*, 1977, v32(1), 31-40.

Campbell, Tim S. and David Glenn. "Deposit Insurance In A Deregulated Environment," *JOF*, 1984, v39(3), 775-785.

Campbell, Tim S. and J. Kimball Dietrich. "The Determinants Of Default On Insured Conventional Residential Mortgage Loans," *JOF*, 1983, v38(5), 1568-1581.

Campbell, Tim S. and William A. Kracaw. "Information Production, Market Signalling, And The Theory Of Financial Intermediation," *JOF*, 1980, v35(4), 863-882.

Campbell, Tim S. and William A. Kracaw. "The Market For Managerial Services And Capital Market Equilibrium," *JFQA*, 1985, v20(3), 277-298.

Campbell, Tim S. and William A. Kracaw. "Sorting Equilibria In Financial Markets: The Incentive Problem," *JFQA*, 1981, v16(4), 477-492.

Campbell, Tim S. and William A. Kracaw. "Information Production, Market Signalling, And The Theory Of Financial Intermediation: A Reply," *JOF*, 1982, v37(4), 1097-1099.

Campbell, Tim S. "A Model Of The Market For Lines Of Credit," *JOF*, 1978, v33(1), 231-244.

Campbell, Tim S. "Monetary Policy And Bank Portfolio Composition: An Analysis Of Their Impact On GNP," *JMCB*, 1978, v10(2), 239-251.

Campbell, Tim S. "On The Extent Of Segmentation In The Municipal Securities Market," *JMCB*, 1980, v12(1), 71-83.

Campbell, Tim S. "On The Optimal Regulation Of Financial Guarantees," *JREFEC*, 1988, v1(1), 61-74.

Campbell, Tim S. "Optimal Investment Financing Decisions And The Value Of Confidentiality," *JFQA*, 1979, v14(5), 913-925.

Campbell, Tim S. and William A. Kracaw. "Optimal Managerial Incentive Contracts And The Value Of Corporate Insurance," *JFQA*, 1987, v22(3), 315-328.

Campbell, Tim S. and William A. Kracaw. "Corporate Risk Management And The Incentive Effects Of Debt," *JOF*, 1990, v45(5), 1673-1686.

Campbell, Tim S. and William A. Kracaw. "Bank Funding Risks, Risk Aversion, And The Choice Of Futures Hedging Instrument: Comment," *JOF*, 1990, v45(5), 1705-1708.

Campsey, B. J. (DeMong, Richard F., Laurence C. Pettit and B. J. Campsey. "Finance Curriculum For The Future: Perceptions Of Practitioners Versus Academicians," *JFED*, 1979, v8, 45-48.)

Canarella, Giorgio and Neil Garston. "Monetary And Public Debt Shocks: Tests And Efficient Estimates," *JMCB*, 1983, v15(2), 199-211.

Canarella, Giorgio and Stephen K. Pollard. "Efficiency Of Commodity Futures: A Vector Autoregression Analysis," *JFM*, 1985, v5(1), 57-76.

Canarella, Giorgio and Stephen K. Pollard. "The Efficiency Of The London Metal Exchange: A Test With Overlapping And Non-Overlapping Data," *JBF*, 1986, v10(4), 575-594.

Canarella, Giorgio and Stephen K. Pollard. "Efficiency In Foreign Exchange Markets: A Vector Autoregression Approach," *JIMF*, 1988, v7(3), 331-346.

Canes, Michael. (Lloyd-Davies, Peter and Michael Canes. "Stock Prices And The Publication Of Second-Hand Information," *JOB*, 1978, v51(1), 43-56.)

Cannaday, Roger E. (Brennan, Thomas P., Roger E. Cannady and Peter F. Colwell. "Office Rent In The Chicago CBD," *AREUEA*, 1984, v12(3), 243-260.)

Cannaday, Roger E. (Colwell, Peter F., Roger E. Cannaday and Chunchi Wu. "The Analytical Foundations Of Adjustment Grid Methods," *AREUEA*, 1983, v11(1), 11-29.)

Cannaday, Roger E. (Sunderman, Mark A., Roger E. Cannaday and Peter F. Colwell. "The Value Of Mortgage Assumptions: An Empirical Test," *JRER*, 1990, v5(2), 247-257.)

Cannaday, Roger E. (Sunderman, Mark A., John W. Birch, Roger E. Cannaday and Thomas W. Hamilton. "Testing For Vertical Inequity In Property Tax Systems," *JRER*, 1990, v5(3), 319-334.)

Cannaday, Roger E. and Mark A. Sunderman. "Estimation Of Depreciation For Single-Family Appraisals," *AREUEA*, 1986, v14(2), 255-273.

Cannaday, Roger E. and Peter F. Colwell. "Real Estate Valuation Models: Lender And Equity Investor Criteria," *AREUEA*, 1986, v14(2), 316-337.

Cannaday, Roger E. and Peter F. Colwell. "Optimization Of Subdivision Development," *JREFEC*, 1990, v3(2), 195-206.

Cannell, Peter B. "New Profits From Chemical Research," *FAJ*, 1960, v16(3), 41-43.

Cannell, Peter B. "Our Terrible Thirst," *FAJ*, 1966, v22(4), 49-53.

Cannon, Susanne. (Wang, Ko, James R. Webb and Susanne Cannon. "Estimating Project-Specific Absorption," *JRER*, 1990, v5(1), 107-116.)

Canto, Victor A. "Fine-Tuning The CATS Meow," *FAJ*, 1987, v43(6), 56-66.

Canto, Victor A. "Monetary Policy, 'Dollarization,' And Parallel Market Exchange Rates: The Case Of The Dominican Republic," *JIMF*, 1985, v4(4), 507-521.

Canto, Victor A. "The CATS Meow: A Portfolio Strategy For Modified Flat Tax," *FAJ*, 1986, v42(1),35-48.

Canto, Victor A. "The Fat CATS Strategy For Portfolio Selection," *FAJ*, 1987, v43(1), 44-51.

Canto, Victor A. and Arthur B. Laffer. "A Not-So-Odd Couple: Small-Cap Stocks And The State Competitive Environment," *FAJ*, 1989, v45(2), 75-78.

Canto, Victor A., Arthur B. Laffer and James C. Turney. "Trade Policy And The U.S. Economy," *FAJ*, 1982, v38(5), 27-46.

Canto, Victor A., J. Kimball Dietrich, Adish Jain and Vishwa Mudaliar. "Protectionism And The Stock Market: The Determinants And Consequences Of Trade Restrictions," *FAJ*, 1986, v42(5), 32-42.

Canto, Victor A., M. C. Findlay and Marc R. Reinganum. "Inflation, Money, And Stock Prices: An Alternative Interpretation," *FR*, 1985, v20(1), 95-101.

Cantor, Richard and Nelson C. Mark. "International Debt And World Business Fluctuations," *JIMF*, 1987, v6(2), 153-166.

Canvin, Jack H. "Introduction To Investments: TV Educational," *FAJ*, 1959, v15(4), 81.

Canzoneri, Matthew B. "The Intermediate Control Problem," *JMCB*, 1977, v9(2), 368-371.

Canzoneri, Matthew B. and Anne C. Sibert. "The Macroeconomic Implications Of Contract Models With Asymmetric Information," *JMCB*, 1990, v22(3), 273-287.

Capen, Gary T. "Oil And Gas In The North Sea," *FAJ*, 1964, v20(1), 111-114.

Caperaa, P. and L. Eeckhoudt. "Delayed Risk And Risk Premiums," *JFEC*, 1975, v2(3), 309-319.

Caperaa, Philippe and Jean Lefoll. "Changes In The Riskless Rate Of Interest And Financial Markets' Equilibrium," *FR*, 1982, v17(4), 252-258.

Capettini, Robert and Dennis Collins. "The Investigation Of Deviations From Standard Costs In The Presence Of Unequal State Variances," *JBFA*, 1978, v5(4), 335-352.

Capettini, Robert and Howard Toole. "Designing Leveraged Leases: A Mixed Integer Linear Programming Approach," **FM**, 1981, v10(4), 15-23.

Capettini, Robert, Richard A. Grimlund and Howard R. Toole. "Comment: The Unique, Real Internal Rate Of Return," **JFQA**, 1979, v14(5), 1091-1094.

Capettini, Robert. (Grimlund, Richard A. and Robert Capettini. "Sign Tests For Actual Investments With Latter Period Net Cash Outflows," **JBFA**, 1983, v10(1), 83-103.)

Capettini, Robert. (Grimlund, Richard A. and Robert Capettini. "A Note On The Evaluation On Leveraged Leases And Other Investments," **FM**, 1982, v11(2), 68-72.)

Capie, Forrest and Alan Webber. "Total Coin And Coin In Circulation In The United Kingdom, 1868-1914," **JMCB**, 1983, v15(1), 24-39.

Caples, S. C. (Herbst, A. F., D. D. Kare and S. C. Caples. "Hedging Effectiveness And Minimum Risk Hedge Ratios In The Presence Of Autocorrelation: Foreign Currency Futures," **JFM**, 1989, v9(3), 185-198.)

Capone, Charles A., Jr. (Cunnngham, Donald F. and Charles A. Capone, Jr. "The Relative Termination Experience Of Adjustable To Fixed-Rate Mortgages," **JOF**, 1990, v45(5), 1687-1704.)

Capozza, Dennis R. and Bradford Cornell. "A Variance Forecasting Test Of The Option Pricing Model," **FR**, 1979, v14(3), 52-60.

Capozza, Dennis R. and Michael Asay. "Option Prices And Diffusion Processes: Some Empirical Tests," **FR**, 1978, v13(1), 1-21.

Capozza, Dennis R. "Forecasting Long-Run Land Use Patterns With An Aggressive Model Of Urban Housing And Transportation: The Case Of Los Angeles," **AREUEA**, 1976, v4(1), 23-40.

Capozza, Dennis R. (Findlay, M. Chapman, III and Dennis R. Capozza. "The Variable-Rate Mortgage And Risk In The Mortgage Market: An Option Theory Perspective," **JMCB**, 1977, v9(2), 356-364.)

Capozza, Dennis R. and Gregory M. Schwann. "The Asset Approach To Pricing Urban Land: Empirical Evidence," **AREUEA**, 1989, v17(2), 161-174.

Capozza, Dennis R. and Gregory M. Schwann. "The Value Of Risk In Real Estate Markets," **JREFEC**, 1990, v3(2), 117-140.

Carabini, Christopher E. (Rendleman, Richard J., Jr. and Christopher E. Carabini. "The Efficiency Of The Treasury Bill Futures Market," **JOF**, 1979, v34(4), 895-914.)

Carasik, Karen S. "Exchange-Traded Clearinghouse (Offset) Options," **JFM**, 1981, v1(Supp), 539-542.

Carey, Gerard V. "Reassessing The Role Of Bank Capital," **JBR**, 1975-76, v6(3), 165-169.

Carey, John L. "CPA's Under Fire?," **FAJ**, 1967, v23(1), 35-37.

Carey, Kenneth J. "Nonrandom Price Changes In Association With Trading In Large Blocks: Evidence Of Market Efficiency In Behavior Of Investor Returns," **JOB**, 1977, v50(4), 407-414.

Carey, Kenneth J. "Persistence Of Profitability," **FM**, 1974, v3(2), 43-48.

Cargill, Thomas F. and Gordon C. Rausser. "Temporal Price Behavior In Commodity Futures Markets," **JOF**, 1975, v30(4), 1043-1053.

Cargill, Thomas F. and Robert A. Meyer. "Estimating Term Structure Phenomena From Data Aggregated Over Time," **JMCB**, 1974, v6(4), 503-515.

Cargill, Thomas F. and Robert A. Meyer. "The Term Structure Of Inflationary Expectations And Market Efficiency," **JOF**, 1980, v35(1), 57-70.

Cargill, Thomas F. and Robert A. Meyer. "Intertemporal Stability Of The Relationship Between Interest Rates And Price Changes," **JOF**, 1977, v32(4),1001-1015.

Cargill, Thomas F. and Robert A. Meyer. "Municipal Interest Rates And The Term Structure Of Inflationary Expectations," **FR**, 1984, v19(2), 135-152.

Cargill, Thomas F. "A Tribute To Clark Warburton, 1896-1979," **JMCB**, 1981, v13(1), 89-93.

Cargill, Thomas F. "CAMEL Ratings And The CD Market," **JFSR**, 1989, v3(4), 347-358.

Cargill, Thomas F. "The Term Structure Of Interest Rates: A Test Of The Expectations Hypothesis," **JOF**, 1975, v30(3), 761-771.

Cargill, Thomas F. (Smith, Donald J., Thomas F. Cargill and Robert A. Meyer. "An Economic Theory Of A Credit Union," **JOF**, 1981, v36(2), 519-528.)

Cargill, Thomas F. and Robert A. Meyer. "Multiperiod Portfolio Optimization And The Value Of Risk Information," **AFPAF**, 1987, v2(1), 245-268.

Cargill, Thomas F. and Robert A. Meyer. "Estimating The Value Of Risk Information," **RIF**, 1983, v4, 43-62.

Cargill, Thomas F. and Terrie E. Troxel. "Modeling Life Insurance Savings: Some Methodological Issues," **JRI**, 1979, v46(3), 391-410.

Carleton, Willard T. and Eugene M. Lerner. "Measuring Corporate Profit Opportunities," **JFQA**, 1967, v2(3), 225-240.

Carleton, Willard T. and Eugene M. Lerner. "Statistical Credit Scoring Of Municipal Bonds," **JMCB**, 1969, v1(4), 750-764.

Carleton, Willard T. and Ian A. Cooper. "Estimation And Uses Of The Term Structure Of Interest Rates," **JOF**, 1976, v31(4), 1067-1083.

Carleton, Willard T. and Irwin H. Silberman. "Joint Determination Of Rate Of Return And Capital Structure: An Econometric Analysis," **JOF**, 1977, v32(3), 811-821.

Carleton, Willard T. and Josef Lakonishok. "Risk And Return On Equity: The Use And Misuse Of Historical Estimates," **FAJ**, 1985, v41(1), 38-47,62.

Carleton, Willard T. and Josef Lakonishok. "The Size Anomaly: Does Industry Group Matter?," **JPM**, 1986, v12(3), 36-40.

Carleton, Willard T. "A Highly Personal Comment On 'On The Use Of The CAPM In Public Utility Rate Cases'," **FM**, 1978, v7(3) 57-59.

Carleton, Willard T. "An Agenda For More Effective Research In Corporate Finance," **FM**, 1978, v7(4), 7-9.

Carleton, Willard T. "An Analytical Model For Long-Range Financial Planning," **JOF**, 1970, v25(2),291-315.

Carleton, Willard T. "Linear Programming And Capital Budgeting Models: A New Interpretation," **JOF**, 1969, v24(5), 825-833.

Carleton, Willard T. "TUCKBANK: A New Bank Management Game," **JBR**, 1975-76, v6(1), 74-76.

Carleton, Willard T. (Chambers, Donald R., Willard T. Carleton and Donald W. Waldman. "A New Approach To Estimation Of The Term Structure Of Interest Rates," **JFQA**, 1984, v19(3), 233-252.)

Carleton, Willard T. (Chambers, Donald R., Willard T. Carleton and Richard W. McEnally. "Immunizing Default-Free Bond Portfolios With A Duration Vector," **JFQA**, 1988, v23(1), 89-104.)

Carleton, Willard T. (Chambers, Donald R. and Willard T. Carleton. "A Generalized Approach To Duration," **RIF**, 1988, v7, 163-182.)

Carleton, Willard T. (Cooper, Ian A. and Willard T. Carleton. "Dynamics Of Borrower-Lender Interaction: Partitioning Final Payoff In Venture Capital Finance," **JOF**, 1979, v34(2), 517-529.)

Carleton, Willard T. (Lerner, Eugene M. and Willard T. Carleton. "Financing Decisions Of The Firm," **JOF**, 1966, v21(2), 202-214.)

Carleton, Willard T. (Lerner, Eugene M. and Willard T. Carleton. "A Note On The Lerner-Carleton Analysis: Reply," **JOF**, 1968, v23(5), 862-864.)

Carleton, Willard T. (Machado, Ezequiel L. and Willard T. Carleton. "Financial Planning In A Regulated Environment," **JFQA**, 1978, v13(4), 759-777.)

Carleton, Willard T. (Moag, Joseph S., Willard T. Carleton and Eugene M. Lerner. "Defining The Finance Function: A Model-Systems Approach," **JOF**, 1967, v22(4), 543-555.)

Carleton, Willard T. (Vander Weide, James H. Vander and Willard T. Carleton. "Investor Growth Expectations: Analysts Vs. History," **JPM**, 1988, v14(3), 78-83.)

Carleton, Willard T. and Leonall C. Andersen. "A Principal Components Test Of Bank Debits As A Local Economic Indicator," **JOB**, 1965, v38(4), 409-415.

Carleton, Willard T., Charles L. Dick, Jr. and David H. Downes. "Financial Policy Models: Theory And Practice," **JFQA**, 1973, v8(5), 691-709.

Carleton, Willard T., David K. Guilkey, Robert S. Harris and John F. Stewart. "An Empirical Analysis Of The Role Of The Medium Of Exchange In Mergers," **JOF**, 1983, v38(3), 813-826.

Carleton, Willard T., Donald R. Chambers and Josef Lakonishok. "Inflation Risk And Regulatory Lag," **JOF**, 1983, v38(2), 419-431.

Carleton, Willard T., Glen Kendall And Sanjiv Tandon. "Application Of The Decomposition Principle To The Capital Budgeting Problem In A Decentralized Firm," **JOF**, 1974, v29(3), 815-827.

Carlisle, Charles T., Jr. "Handouts," **JFED**, 1972, v1, 108.

Carlson, C. Robert. (Nantell, Timothy J. and C. Robert Carlson. "The Cost Of Capital As A Weighted Average," **JOF**, 1975, v30(5), 1343-1355.)

Carlson, Keith M. "Impact Of Fiscal Action," **FAJ**, 1969, v25(2), 69-71.

Carlson, Phillip G. and Arthur T. Dietz. "Optimal Capital Budgeting Policies," **FR**, 1972, v2(2),103-114.

Carlson, Phillip G. "An Argument For 'Generalized' Mean-Coefficient Of Variation Analysis: Comment," **FM**, 1981, v10(3), 87-88.

Carlson, Phillip G. "Planning, Growth And The Efficient Use Of Capital," **FM**, 1974, v4(2), 27-38.

Carlson, Robert C. (Baum, Sanford, Robert C. Carlson and James V. Jucker. "Some Problems In Applying The Continuous Portfolio Selection Model To The Discrete Capital Budgeting Problem," **JFQA**, 1978, v13(2), 333-344.)

Carlson, Robert S. "Aggregate Performance Of Mutual Funds, 1948-1967," **JFQA**, 1970, v5(1), 1-32.

Carlson, Rodney L. "Seemingly Unrelated Regression And The Demand For Automobiles Of Different Sizes, 1965-75: A Disaggregate Approach," **JOB**, 1978, v51(2), 243-262.

Carlson, Rodney L. and M. Michael Umble. "Statistical Demand Functions For Automobiles And Their Use For Forecasting In An Energy Crisis," **JOB**, 1980, v53(2), 193-204.

Carlson, Russell C. "What Price Maturity?," **FAJ**, 1961, v17(1), 51-53.

Carlson, Ruth I. "Adequacy Of Corporate Reporting," **FAJ**, 1946, v2(2), 3-10.

Carlson, Severin and Blair Lord. "Unisex Retirement Benefits And The Market For Annuity 'Lemons'," **JRI**, 1986, v53(3), 409-418.

Carlson, T. O. "Trends In Casualty Insurance Rate Making," **JRI**, 1963, v30(1), 17-22.

Carlson, Thomas O. "Risk: Comment," **JRI**, 1963, v30(4), 590-592.

Carlson, Thomas O. "Statistical And Actuarial Procedures In Liability Insurance," **JRI**, 1950, v17, 5-12.

Carlson, Valdemar. "Democratizing Money," **JOF**, 1947, v2(2), 68-71.

Carlson, Valdemar. "Institutional Change In A Welfare State: Sweden," **JRI**, 1966, v33(4), 587-596.

Carlton, Dennis W. "Futures Markets: Their Purpose, Their History, Their Growth, Their Successes And Failures," **JFM**, 1984, v4(3), 237-272.

Carman, Peter. "The Trouble With Asset Allocation," **JPM**, 1981, v8(1), 17-22.

Carmichael, Jeffrey. "The Effects Of Mission-Oriented Public R & D Spending On Private Industry," **JOF**, 1981, v36(3), 617-627.

Carnes, W. Stansbury, Gerald D. Gay and Paul A. McCulley. "Fed-Watching, Monetary Policy Regimes, And The Response Of Financial Futures To Money Announcements," **RFM**, 1989, v8(3), 384-401.

Carney, Michael. "Costs And Pricing Of Home Brokerage Services," **AREUEA**, 1982, v10(3), 331-354.

Carney, Michael. (Peterman, John L. and Michael Carney. "A Comment On Television Network Price Discrimination," **JOB**, 1989, v51(2), 343-352.)

Carney, Owen. "Comments On 'The Regulation Of Futures And Forward Trading By Depository Institutions: A Legal And Economic Analysis'," **JFM**, v1(2), 219-223.

Carol, Arthur. "An Investment Paradox," **JFQA**, 1972, v7(1), 1421-1422.

Carpenter, Anna E. "College And University Endowment Funds," **FAJ**, 1956, v12(2), 63-66.

Carpenter, Leroy. (Ricks, David A. and Leroy Carpenter. "An Annotated Bibliography For International Finance," **JFED**, 1973, v2, 92-108.)

Carpenter, Michael D. and David E. Upton. "Trading Volume And Beta Stability," **JPM**, 1981, v7(2), 60-64.

Carpenter, Michael D. and I. Keong Chew. "The Effects Of Default Risk On The Market Model," **JFR**, 1983, v6(3), 223-229.

Carpenter, Michael D. and Jack E. Miller. "A Reliable Framework For Monitoring Accounts Receivable," **FM**, 1979, v8(4), 37-40.

Carpenter, Michael D., David R. Lange, Donald S. Shannon and William Thomas Stevens. "Methodologies Of Valuing Lost Earnings: A Review, A Criticism, And A Recommendation," **JRI**,

1986, v53(1), 104-118.

Carpenter, Orville S. "Pipeline Transportation Of Energy," **FAJ**, 1960, v16(3), 127-132.

Carpenter, Walter H. and Charles L. Webster. "Communicating Business Ideas To Europe: A Case Study," **JOB**, 1955, v28(3), 206-212.

Carr, Hobart C. "A Note On Regional Differences In Discount Rates," **JOF**, 1960, v15(1), 62-68.

Carr, Hobart C. "Why And How To Read The Federal Reserve Statement," **JOF**, 1959, v14(4), 504-519.

Carr, J. L., P. J. Halpern and J. S. McCallum. "Correcting The Yield Curve: A Re-Interpretation Of The Duration Problem," **JOF**, 1974, v29(4), 1287-1294.

Carr, J. L., P. J. Halpern and J. S. McCallum. "Comments On Single-Valued Duration Measures," **JOF**, 1978, v33(4), 1241-1243.

Carr, Jack and Lawrence B. Smith. "Money Supply, Interest Rates, And The Yield Curve," **JMCB**, 1972, v4(3), 582-594.

Carr, Peter P. and Robert A. Jarrow. "The Stop-Loss Start-Gain Paradox And Option Valuation: A New Decomposition Into Intrinsic And Time Value," **RFS**, 1990, v3(3), 469-492.

Carr, Peter. "A Calculator Program For Option Values And Implied Standard Deviations," **JFED**, 1988, v17, 89-93.

Carr, Peter. "A Note On The Pricing Of Commodity-Linked Bonds," **JOF**, 1987, v42(4), 1071-1076.

Carr, Peter. "The Valuation Of Sequential Exchange Opportunities," **JOF**, 1988, v43(5), 1235-1256.

Carr, Richard C. (Ibbotson, Roger G., Richard C. Carr and Anthony W. Robinson. "International Equity And Bond Returns," **FAJ**, 1982, v38(4), 61-83.)

Carret, Philip L. "Useless Paper Work," **FAJ**, 1970, v26(5), 48-50.

Carrington, Samantha and Robert Crouch. "Interest Rate Differentials On Short-Term Securities And Rational Expectations Of Inflation," **JBF**, 1987, v11(4), 571-580.

Carroll, Carolyn and K. C. John Wei. "Risk, Return, And Equilibrium: An Extension," **JOB**, 1988, v61(4), 485-500.

Carroll, Carolyn. (Manakyan, Herman and Carolyn Carroll. "An Empirical Examination Of The Existence Of A Signaling Value Function For Dividends," **JFR**, 1990, v13(2), 201-210.)

Carroll, D. (Boies, D., D. Carroll, A. Fleischer, J. Grundfest, J. Ira Harris, M. Lipton, R. Monks, A. Oliver, L. Sachnoff and J. Wilcox. "Panel: Corporate Governance: The Role Of Boards Of Directors In Takeover Bids And Defenses," **JACF**, 1989, v2(2), 6-35.)

Carroll, Jean. "A Note On Departmental Autonomy And Innovation In Medical Schools," **JOB**, 1967, v40(4), 531-534.

Carroll, John P. "Organizational Structure: How Change Will Impact The Organization," **JBR**, 1974-75, v5(3), 165-169.

Carroll, Stephen J., Jr. and Henry L. Tosi. "The Relationship Of Characteristics Of The Review Process To The Success Of The 'Management By Objectives' Approach," **JOB**, 1971, v44(3), 299-305.

Carroll, Wayne. "Fixed-Percentage Commissions And Moral Hazard In Residential Real Estate Brokerage," **JREFEC**, 1989, v2(4), 349-365.

Carron, Andrew S. and Marjorie Hogan. "The Option Valuation Approach To Mortgage Pricing," **JREFEC**, 1988, v1(2), 131-150.

Carson, Deane. "Changes In The Discount Mechanism: The Joint Economic Committee Hearings And Report," **JMCB**, 1970, v2(2), 158-165.

Carson, Deane. "Federal Reserve Support Of Treasury Refunding Operations," **JOF**, 1957, v12(1), 51-63.

Carson, Deane. "Is The Federal Reserve System Really Necessary,?," **JOF**, 1964, v19(4), 652-661.

Carson, Deane. "Is The Federal Reserve System Really Necessary?': Reply," **JOF**, 1965, v20(3), 486-489.

Carson, Deane. "Should Federal Reserve Float Be Abolished And Its Check Activities Curtailed?': Reply," **JOF**, 1965, v20(3), 503-503.

Carson, Richard T. (Horowitz, John K. and Richard T. Carson. "Discounting Statistical Lives," **JRU**, 1990, v3(4), 403-413.)

Carson, Richard T. (Kiel, Katherine A. and Richard T. Carson. "An Examination Of Systematic Differences In The Appreciation Of Individual Housing Units," **JRER**, 1990, v5(3), 301-318.)

Carswell, Howard J. "Petrochemicals - A Dynamic Trend," **FAJ**, 1952, v8(2), 57-60.

Carter, Arthur L. "Marginal Opportunities In U. S. Government Securities," **FAJ**, 1960, v16(2), 43-45.

Carter, Colin A. "Arbitrage Opportunities Between Thin And Liquid Futures Markets," **JFM**, 1989, v9(4), 347-354.

Carter, Colin. (Chambers, Scott and Colin Carter. "U.S. Futures Exchanges As Nonprofit Entities," **JFM**, 1990, v10(1), 79-88.)

Carter, E. E. and K. J. Cohen. "Stock Averages, Stock Splits, And Bias," **FAJ**, 1967, v23(3), 77-81.

Carter, E. Eugene and Kalman J. Cohen. "Bias In The DJIA Caused By Stock Splits," **FAJ**, 1966, v22(6), 90-94.

Carter, E. Eugene and Rita M. Rodriquez. "Internationalizing The Corporate Finance Course According To AACSB Guidelines," **JFED**, 1980, v9, 3-7.

Carter, E. Eugene. "A Simultaneous Equation Approach To Financial Planning: Comment," **JOF**, 1973, v28(4), 1035-1038.

Carter, E. Eugene. "Using Interactive Computer Programs In A Basic Finance Course," **JFED**, 1975, v4, 99-102.

Carter, John P. "The New Maritime Nations," **JOB**, 1956, v29(3), 207-215.

Carter, Kevin J., John F. Affleck-Graves and Arthur H. Money. "Are Gold Shares Better Than Gold For Diversification?," **JPM**, 1982, v9(1), 52-55.

Carter, R. L. and N. A. Doherty. "Tariff Control And The Public Interest: Report On British Fire Insurance," **JRI**, 1974, v41(3), 483-496.

Carter, Richard B. and Frederick H. Dark. "The Use Of The Over-Allotment Option In Initial Public Offerings Of Equity: Risks And Underwriter Prestige," **FM**, 1990, v19(3), 55-64.

Carter, Richard B. and Howard E. Van Auken. "Security Analysis And Portfolio Management: A Survey And Analysis," **JPM**, 1990, v16(3), 81-85.

Carter, Richard B. and Roger D. Stover. "The Effects Of Mutual To Stock Conversion Of Thrift Institutions On Managerial Behavior," **JFSR**, 1990, v4(2), 127-144.

Carter, Richard and Steven Manaster. "Initial Public Offerings And Underwriter Reputation," **JOF**, 1990, v45(4), 1045-1067.

Carter, William A. "World Gold Production And The Money Supply," **JOF**, 1963, v18(3), 494-510.

Carter, William D. "Quality Of Mutual Fund Portfolio Supervision," **FAJ**, 1950, v6(4), 32-36.

Carton, John H. "The Assigned Risk As A Separate Classification," **JRI**, 1960, v27(2), 73-80.

Caruthers, J. Kent. (Pinches, George E., Kent A. Mingo and J. Kent Caruthers. "The Stability Of Financial Patterns In Industrial Organizations," **JOF**, 1973, v28(2), 389-396.)

Carvell, Steven and Paul Strebel. "A New Beta Incorporating Anaysts' Forecasts," **JPM**, 1984, v11(1), 81-85.

Carvell, Steven A. and Paul J. Strebel. "Is There A Neglected Firm Effect?," **JBFA**, 1987, v14(2), 279-290.

Carvell, Steven. (Arbel, Avner, Steven Carvell and Paul Strebel. "Giraffes, Institutions And Neglected Firms," **FAJ**, 1983, v39(3), 57-63.)

Carvell, Steven. (Pari, Robert, Steven Carvell and Timothy Sullivan. "Analyst Forecasts And Price/Earnings Ratios," **FAJ**, 1989, v45(2), 60-62.)

Casabona, Patrick A. and Ashok Vora. "The Bias Of Conventional Risk Premiums In Empirical Tests Of The Capital Asset Pricing Model," **FM**, 1982, v11(2),90-96.

Casabona, Patrick A., Frank J. Fabozzi and Jack C. Francis. "How To Apply Duration To Equity Analysis," **JPM**, 1984, v10(2), 52-58.

Casabona, Patrick. (Fabozzi, Frank J., Robert Fonfeder and Patrick Casabona. "An Empirical Examination Of The Impact Of Limited Review On Equity Prices," **JBFA**, 1983, v10(1), 127-138.)

Casazza, Charles T. (O'Hay, Charles F. and Charles T. Casazza. "A New Screen For Superior Stock Selection," **JPM**, 1976, v2(3), 45-52.)

Case, Fred E. "Housing The Underhoused In The Inner City," **JOF**, 1971, v26(2), 427-444.

Case, Fred E. "Multifamily Housing Demand: Comment," **AREUEA**, 1979, v7(1), 130.

Case, Fred E. "The Attraction Of Home Ownership," **AREUEA**, 1979, v7(1), 39-44.

Case, Fred E. "The Budget As A Measure Of The Federal Urban Housing Programs," **JOF**, 1951, v6(4),429-439.

Case, Fred E. "The Use Of Junior Mortgages In Real Estate Financing," **JOF**, 1955, v10(1), 41-54.

Case, Fred E. "The Value Of A Thing Is The Price It Will Bring," **AREUEA**, 1979, v7(2), 265-268.

Case, Fred E. and Jeffrey Gale. "The Impact On Housing Costs Of The California Coastal Zone Conservation Act," **AREUEA**, 1981, v9(4), 345-366.

Case, Fred. (Gale, Jeffrey and Fred Case. "A Study Of Corporate Real Estate Resource Management," **JRER**, 1989, v4(3), 23-34.)

Case, Karl E. and Robert J. Shiller. "Forecasting Prices And Excess Returns In The Housing Market," **AREUEA**, 1990, v18(3), 253-273.

Casey, Walter J. (Lund, Harry A., Walter J. Casey and Philip K. Chamberlain. "A Financial Analysis Of The ESOT," **FAJ**, 1976, v32(1), 55-61.)

Cashdan, Daniel M., Jr. (Graff, Richard A. and Daniel M. Cashdan, Jr. "Some New Ideas In Real Estate Finance," **JACF**, 1990, v3(1), 77-89.)

Caskey, John P. "The IMF And Concerted Lending In Latin American Debt Restructurings: A Formal Analysis," **JIMF**, 1989, v8(1), 105-120.

Cason, Roger L. "Leasing, Asset Lives And Uncertainty: A Practitioner's Comments," **FM**, 1987, v16(2), 13-16.

Cass, Roger H. "A Global Approach To Portfolio Management," **JPM**, 1975, v1(2), 40-51.

Cassel, Norman S. and Herbert B. Woodman. "Looking Behind Research Costs," **FAJ**, 1957, v13(4), 11-14.

Cassidy, Henry J. and Josephine McElhone. "The Pricing Of Variable Rate Mortgages," **FM**, 1974, v4(4), 37-45.

Cassidy, Henry J. "Estimates Of The Aggregate Impact Of Expected Windfalls For A Portion Of The S&L Industry," **JMCB**, 1976, v8(4), 477-485.

Cassidy, Henry J. (Field, Al and Henry J. Cassidy. "Simulation Analysis Of Alternative Mortgage Instruments," **AREUEA**, 1977, v5(4), 411-433.)

Cassidy, Steven N., Richard L. Constand and Richard B. Corbett. "The Market Value Of The Corporate Risk Management Function," **JRI**, 1990, v57(4), 664-670.

Casson, John J. "Business Economists' Forecast For 1973," **FAJ**, 1972, v28(6), 32-34,91.

Castagna, A. D. and Z. P. Matolcsy. "The Market Characteristics Of Failed Companies: Extensions And Further Evidence," **JBFA**, 1981, v8(4), 467-484.

Castagna, A. D. and Z. P. Matolcsy. "The Evaluation Of Traded Options Pricing Models In Australia," **JBFA**, 1983, v10(2), 225-233.

Castagna, A. D. and Z. P. Matolcsy. "A Two Stage Experimental Design To Test The Efficiency Of The Market For Traded Stock Options And The Australian Evidence," **JBF**, 1982, v6(4), 521-532.

Castagna, A. D. and Z. P. Matolcsy. "The Marginal Information Content Of Selected Items In Financial Statements," **JBFA**, 1989, v16(3), 317-334.

Castanias, Richard P. (Bowen, Robert M., Richard P. Castanias and Lane A. Daley. "Intra-Industry Effects Of The Accident At Three Mile Island," **JFQA**, 1983, v18(1), 87-111.)

Castanias, Richard P., II. "Macroinformation And The Variability Of Stock Market Prices," **JOF**, 1979, v34(2), 439-450.

Castanias, Richard. "Bankruptcy Risk And Optimal Capital Structure," **JOF**, 1983, v38(5), 1617-1635.

Castanias, Rick, Ki-Young Chung and Herb Johnson. "Dividend Spreads," **JOB**, 1988, v61(3), 299-320.

Castelino, Mark G. and Jack Clark Francis. "Basis Speculation In Commodity Futures: The Maturity Effect," **JFM**, 1982, v2(2), 195-206.

Castelino, Mark G. "Basis Volatility: Implications For Hedging," **JFR**, 1989, v12(2), 157-172.

Castelino, Mark G. "Minimum-Variance Hedging With Futures Revisited," **JPM**, 1990, v16(3), 74-80.

Castelino, Mark G., Jack C. Francis and Avner Wolf. "Cross-Hedging:

Basis Risk And Choice Of The Optimal Hedging Vehicle," **FR**, 1991, v26(2), 179-210.

Castelino, Mark. (Wolf, Avner, Mark Castelino and Jack Francis. "Hedging Mispriced Options," **JFM**, 1987, v7(2), 147-156.)

Castellano, Vincent S. "Replacement Cost Data: What Can We Do With It?," **JPM**, 1978, v5(1), 57-65.

Caster, Paul. (Vu, Joseph D. and Paul Caster. "Why All The Interest In Short Interest?," **FAJ**, 1987, v43(4), 77-79.)

Caswell, Jerry W. "Economic Efficiency In Pension Plan Administration: A Study Of The Construction Industry," **JRI**, 1976, v43(2), 257-274.

Caswell, Jerry W. and Steve C. Goodfellow. "Effect Of Including Investment Income In Ratemaking Upon Profitability Of Non-Life Insurers," **JRI**, 1976, v43(2), 305-316.

Caswell, W. Cameron. "Taking Stock Of Divisionalization," **JOB**, 1956, v29(3), 160-171.

Cataldo, J. T. "Semiconductors: Young Giant Of Electronics," **FAJ**, 1959, v15(4), 71-72.

Cathcart, Charles D. "Monetary Dynamics, Growth, And The Efficiency Of Inflationary Finance," **JMCB**, 1974, v6(2), 169-190.

Cather, David A. and Vince Howe. "Conflict And Channel Management In Property-Liability Distribution Systems," **JRI**, 1989, v56(3), 535-543.

Cather, David A., Sandra G. Gustavson and James S. Trieschmann. "A Profitability Analysis Of Property-Liability Insurers Using Alternative Distribution Systems," **JRI**, 1985, v52(2), 321-332.

Cathles, Lawrence M., Jr. "Minimum Premium Health Plans: Insured Non-Insurance: Comment," **JRI**, 1970, v37(3), 477-480.

Cavanaugh, Kenneth L. "Price Dynamics In Foreign Currency Futures Markets," **JIMF**, 1987, v6(3),295-314.

Caverly, Thomas A. (Woods, Donald H. and Thomas A. Caverly. "Development Of A Linear Programming Model For The Analysis Of Merger/Acquisition Situations," **JFQA**, 1970, v5(5), 627-642.)

Caves, Richard E. (McGugan, Vincent J. and Richard E. Caves. "Integration And Competition In The Equipment Leasing Industry," **JOB**, 1974, v47(3), 382-396.)

Cebenoyan, A. Sinan. "Multiproduct Cost Functions And Scale Economies In Banking," **FR**, 1988, v23(4), 499-512.

Cebenoyan, A. Sinan. "Scope Economies In Banking: The Hybrid Box-Cox Function," **FR**, 1990, v25(1), 115-126.

Ceglowski, Janet. "Dollar Depreciation And US Industry Performance," **JIMF**, 1989, v8(2), 233-252.

Ceglowski, Janet. "Intertemporal Substitution In Import Demand," **JIMF**, 1991, v10(1), 118-130.

Celebuski, Matthew J., Joanne M. Hill and John J. Kilgannon. "Managing Currency Exposures In International Portfolios," **FAJ**, 1990, v46(1), 16-23.

Celec, Stephen E. and Joe D. Icerman. "A Comprehensive Approach To Accounts Receivable Management," **FR**, 1980, v15(2), 23-34.

Celec, Stephen E. and Richard H. Pettway. "Some Observations On Risk-Adjusted Discount Rates: A Comment," **JOF**, 1979, v34(4), 1061-1063.

Celec, Stephen E. "Incorrect Preference Orderings With The Coefficient Of Variation," **JFR**, 1982, v5(1), 69-73.

Celec, Stephen E. (Benesh, Gary A. and Stephen E. Celec. "A Simplified Approach For Calculating Bond Duration," **FR**, 1984, v19(4), 394-396.)

Celec, Stephen E. (Bible, Douglas S. and Stephen E. Celec. "Real Estate Investment Analysis: New Developments In Traditional Leverage Concepts," **AREUEA**, 1980, v8(2), 198-206.)

Celec, Stephen E. (Boardman, Calvin M., Walter J. Reinhart and Stephen E. Celec. "The Role Of The Payback Period In The Theory And Application Of Duration To Capital Budgeting," **JBFA**, 1982, v8(4), 511-522.)

Center, Charles C. "A Philosophical Approach To Student Insurance Societies," **JRI**, 1958, v25(2), 53-57.

Cerf, Alan Robert. "Diverse Accounting Procedures, Price-Level Changes, And Financial Statement Ratios," **JOB**, 1957, v30(3), 180-192.

Cesarini, Francesco. "Equity Financing By Banks In The Italian Market: The 1980-1984 Experience And The New Trends," **JBR**, 1986-87, v17(1), 28-39.

Ceto, Nicholas, Jr. (Davis, Samuel G., Nicholas Ceto, Jr. and J. Mac. Rabb. "A Comprehensive Check Processing Simulation Model," **JBR**, 1982-83, v13(3), 185-194.)

Chadha, Binky. "Contract Length, Monetary Policy And Exchange Rate Variability," **JIMF**, 1987, v6(4), 491-504.

Chadha, Binky. "Is Increased Price Inflexibility Stabilizing?," **JMCB**, 1989, v21(4), 481-497.

Chakravarty, S. P. (Barnes, Paul, S. P. Chakravarty and J. Haslam. "Bargaining Power, Dissimulation And Takeovers In A Rational Market With Asymmetric Information," **JBFA**, 1990, v17(4), 529-540.)

Chalk, Andrew J. and John W. Peavy, III. "Initial Public Offerings: Daily Returns, Offering Types And The Price Effect ," **FAJ**, 1987, v43(5), 65-69.

Chalk, Andrew J. and John W. Peavy, III. "Understanding The Pricing Of Initial Public Offerings," **RIF**, 1990, v8, 203-240.

Chalmers, E. L., Jr. "The Reconstruction Of Higher Education," **JRI**, 1971, v38(4), 505-513.

Chalmers, W. Ellison. (Derber, Milton, W. Ellison Chalmers, and Ross Stagner. "Collective Bargaining And Management Functions: An Empirical Study," **JOB**, 1958, v31(2), 107-120.)

Chaloupka, Frank J. (Marty, Alvin L. and Frank J. Chaloupka. "Optimal Inflation Rates: A Generalization," **JMCB**, 1988, v20(1), 141-144.)

Chamberlain, Gary. (Feldstein, Martin and Gary Chamberlain. "Multimarket Expectations And The Rate Of Interest," **JMCB**, 1973, v5(4), 873-902.)

Chamberlain, Philip K. (Lund, Harry A., Walter J. Casey and Philip K. Chamberlain. "A Financial Analysis Of The ESOT," **FAJ**, 1976, v32(1), 55-61.)

Chamberlain, Trevor W., C. Sherman Cheung and Clarence C. Y. Kwan. "Expiration-Day Effects Of Index Futures And Options: Some Canadian Evidence," **FAJ**, 1989, v45(5), 67-71.

Chamberlin, Stanley C. (Hawkins, Eugene H., Stanley C. Chamberlin and Wayne E. Daniel. "Earnings Expectations And Security Prices," **FAJ**, 1984, v40(5), 24-27,30-38,74.)

Chambers, Donald R. (Lacey, Nelson J. and Donald R. Chambers. "The Investigation Of A Systematic Prepayment Option In GNMA Futures," **RFM**, 1985, v4(3), 338-353.)

Chambers, Donald R. "An Immunization Strategy For Futures Contracts On Government Securities," **JFM**, 1984, v4(2), 173-188.

Chambers, Donald R. (Calley, Nicholas O., Donald R. Chambers and J. Randall Woolridge. "A Note On Standardized Unexpected Earnings: The Case Of The Electric Utility Industry," **FR**, 1985, v20(1),102-110.)

Chambers, Donald R. (Carleton, Willard T., Donald R. Chambers and Josef Lakonishok. "Inflation Risk And Regulatory Lag," **JOF**, 1983, v38(2),419-431.)

Chambers, Donald R. (Kelly, William A., Jr. and Donald R. Chambers. "Inflation, Taxes, And Savings 'Incentives'," **FR**, 1984, v19(2), 222-231.)

Chambers, Donald R. (Varma, Raj and Donald R. Chambers. "The Role Of Financial Innovation In Raising Capital: Evidence From Deep Discount Debt Offers," **JFEC**, 1990, v26(2), 289-298.)

Chambers, Donald R. (Woolridge, J. Randall and Donald R. Chambers. "Reverse Splits And Shareholder Wealth," **FM**, 1983, v12(3), 5-15.)

Chambers, Donald R. and Willard T. Carleton. "A Generalized Approach To Duration," **RIF**, 1988, v7, 163-182.

Chambers, Donald R., Robert S. Harris and John J. Pringle. "Treatment Of Financing Mix In Analyzing Investment Opportunities," **FM**, 1982, v11(2), 24-41.

Chambers, Donald R., Willard T. Carleton and Donald W. Waldman. "A New Approach To Estimation Of The Term Structure Of Interest Rates," **JFQA**, 1984, v19(3), 233-252.

Chambers, Donald R., Willard T. Carleton and Richard W. McEnally. "Immunizing Default-Free Bond Portfolios With A Duration Vector," **JFQA**, 1988, v23(1),89-104.

Chambers, R. J. "The Delusions Of Replacement Cost Accounting," **FAJ**, 1977, v33(4), 48-52.

Chambers, Scott and Colin Carter. "U.S. Futures Exchanges As Nonprofit Entities," **JFM**, 1990, v10(1), 79-88.

Chan, Anthony. (Chen, Carl R. and Anthony Chan. "Interest Rate Sensitivity, Asymmetry, And The Stock Returns Of Financial Institutions," **FR**, 1989, v24(3), 457-474.)

Chan, K. C. "On The Contrarian Investment Strategy," **JOB**, 1988, v61(2), 147-164.

Chan, K. C. and Nai-Fu Chen. "An Unconditional Asset-Pricing Test And The Role Of Firm Size As An Instrumental Variable For Risk," **JOF**, 1988, v43(2), 309-325.

Chan, K. C., Nai-Fu Chen and David A. Hsieh. "An Exploratory Investigation Of The Firm Size Effect," **JFEC**, 1985, v14(3), 451-471.

Chan, K. C., Patric H. Hendershott and Anthony B. Sanders. "Risk And Return On Real Estate: Evidence From Equity REITs," **AREUEA**, 1990, v18(4), 431-452.

Chan, K. Hung and Kwok Ho. "Forecasting Of Seasonal And Cyclical Financial Variables: The Wiener-Kolmogorov Method Vs. The Box-Jenkins Method," **AFPAF**, 1987, v2(1), 103-118.

Chan, M. W. Luke and Itzhak Krinsky. "Expectations Formation And Portfolio Models For Life Insurers," **JRI**, 1988, v55(4), 682-700.

Chan, M. W. Luke, Itzhak Krinsky and Dean C. Mountain. "Analysis Of Productivity At The Firm Level: An Application To Life Insurers: Comment," **JRI**, 1989, v56(2), 336-340.

Chan, M. W. Luke. (Callen, Jeffrey L., M. W. Luke Chan and Clarence C. Y. Kwan. "Spot And Forward Exchange Rates: A Causality Analysis," **JBFA**, 1989, v16(1), 105-118.)

Chan, Patrick S. T. (Pattison, John C. and Patrick S. T. Chan. "Cash Management Of Foreign Note Holdings By Banks," **JBF**, 1981, v5(4), 511-522.)

Chan, Su Han, John D. Martin and John W. Kensinger. "Corporate Research And Development Expenditures And Share Value," **JFEC**, 1990, v26(2), 255-276.

Chan, Su Hun. (Wang, Ko, Terry V. Grissom and Su Hun Chan. "The Functional Relationships And Use Of Going-In And Going-Out Capitalization Rates," **JRER**, 1990, v5(2), 231-245.)

Chan, Yuk-Shee and George Kanatas. "Asymmetric Valuations And The Role Of Collateral In Loan Agreements," **JMCB**, 1985, v17(1), pp 84-95.

Chan, Yuk-Shee and King-Tim Mak. "Depositors' Welfare, Deposit Insurance, And Deregulation," **JOF**, 1985, v40(3), 959-974.

Chan, Yuk-Shee and Anjan V. Thakor. "Collateral And Competitive Equilibria With Moral Hazard And Private Information," **JOF**, 1987, v42(2), 345-363.

Chan, Yuk-Shee, Stuart I. Greenbaum and Anjan V. Thakor. "Information Reusability, Competition And Bank Asset Quality," **JBF**, 1986, v10(2), 243-253.

Chan, Yuk-Shee. "Information Production, Market Signalling, And The Theory Of Financial Intermediation: A Comment," **JOF**, 1982, v37(4), 1095-1096.

Chan, Yuk-Shee. "On The Positive Role Of Financial Intermediation In Allocation Of Venture Capital In A Market With Imperfect Information," **JOF**, 1983, v38(5), 1543-1568.

Chance, Don M. "Futures Contracts And Immunization," **RFM**, 1986, v5(2), 124-141.

Chance, Don M. and Stephen P. Ferris. "The CBOE Call Option Index: A Historical Record," **JPM**, 1985, v12(1), 75-83.

Chance, Don M. and Stephen P. Ferris. "Summer Rallies," **FAJ**, 1986, v42(1), 6-9.

Chance, Don M. and William R. Lane. "A Re-Examination Of Interest Rate Sensitivity In The Common Stocks Of Financial Institutions," **JFR**, 1980, v3(1), 49-55.

Chance, Don M. "A Semi-Strong Form Test Of The Efficiency Of The Treasury Bond Futures Market," **JFM**, 1985, v5(3), 385-405.

Chance, Don M. "An Immunized-Hedge Procedure For Bond Futures," **JFM**, 1982, v2(3), 231-242.

Chance, Don M. "Boundary Condition Tests Of Bid And Ask Prices Of Index Call Options," **JFR**, 1988, v11(1), 21-32.

Chance, Don M. "Comment: A Test Of Stone's Two-Index Model Of Returns," **JFQA**, 1979, v14(3), 641-644.

Chance, Don M. "Default Risk And The Duration Of Zero Coupon Bonds," **JOF**, 1990, v45(1), 265-274.

Chance, Don M. "Empirical Estimates Of Equivalent Risk Classes And The Effect Of Financial Leverage On Systematic Risk," FR, 1981, v16(3), 12-29.

Chance, Don M. "Evidence On A Simplified Model Of Systematic Risk," FM, 1982, v11(3), 53-63.

Chance, Don M. "Floating Rate Notes And Immunization," JFQA, 1983, v18(3), 365-380.

Chance, Don M. "Interest Sensitivity And Dividend Yields," JPM, 1982, v8(2), 69-75.

Chance, Don M. "Option Volume And Stock Market Performance," JPM, 1990, v16(4), 42-51.

Chance, Don M. "The Reaction Of The Chicago Board Of Trade GNMA Futures Contract To The Announcement Of Inflation Rates: A Study Of Market Efficiency," RFM, 1985, v4(1), 132-154.

Chance, Don M. (Billingsley, Randall S. and Don M. Chance. "Options Market Efficiency And The Box Spread Strategy," FR, 1985, v20(4), 287-301.)

Chance, Don M. (Billingsley, Randall S. and Don M. Chance. "Put-Call Ratios And Market Timing Effectiveness," JPM, 1988, v15(1), 25-28.)

Chance, Don M. (Billingsley, Randall S. and Don M. Chance. "The Pricing And Performance Of Stock Index Futures Spreads," JFM, 1988, v8(3), 303-318.)

Chance, Don M. (Ferris, Stephen P. and Don M. Chance. "Trading Time Effects In Financial And Commodity Futures Markets," FR, 1987, v22(2), 281-294.)

Chance, Don M. (Ferris, Stephen P. and Don M. Chance. "The Effect Of 12b-1 Plans On Mutual Fund Expense Ratios: A Note," JOF, 1987, v42(4), 1077-1082.)

Chance, Don M. and John B. Broughton. "Market Index Depository Liabilities: Analysis, Interpretation, And Performance," JFSR, 1988, v1(4), 335-352.

Chance, Don M., M. Wayne Marr and G. Rodney Thompson. "Hedging Shelf Registrations," JFM, 1986, v6(1), 11-28.

Chand, Sheetal K. and Yusuke Onitsuka. "Stocks, Flows, And Some Exchange-Rate Dynamics For The Currency Substitution Model," JIMF, 1985, v4(1), 61-82.

Chandler, Lester V. and Dwight M. Jaffee. "Regulating The Regualtors: A Review Of The FINE Regulatory Reforms," JMCB, 1977, v9(4), 619-635.

Chandler, Lester V. "From Wampum To Money-Supply Rules: The Documentary History Of Banking In The United States: A Review Article," JOF, 1970, v25(1),158-160.

Chandler, Lester V. "The Impact Of Low Interest Rates On The Economy," JOF, v6(2), 252-263.

Chandler, Lester V. (Alhadeff, D., P. Bernstein, C. Campbell, L. Chandler, E. Ettin, V. Farhi, J. Guttentag, H. Latane and K. Poole. "The Commission On Money And Credit's Research Studies," JOF, 1964, v19(3), 497-533.)

Chandohl, Marie A. (Pinkus, Scott M. and Marie A. Chandohl. "The Relative Price Volatility Of Mortgage Securities," JPM, 1986, v12(4), 9-22.)

Chandra, Ramesh. (Aneja, Yash P., Ramesh Chandra and Erdal Gunay. "A Portfolio Approach To Estimating The Average Correlation Coefficient For The Constant Correlation Model," JOF, 1989, v44(5), 1435-1438.)

Chandross, Robert H. "The Impact Of New Bank Entry On Unit Banks In One Bank Towns," JBR, 1971-72, v2(3), 22-30.

Chandy, P. R. (Davidson, Wallace N., III and P. R. Chandy. "The Regulatory Environment For Public Utilities: Indications Of The Importance Of Political Process," FAJ, 1983, v39(6), 50-53.)

Chandy, P. R. (Davidson, Wallace N., III, P. R. Chandy and Mark Cross. "Large Losses, Risk Management And Stock Returns In The Airline Industry," JRI, 1987, v54(1), 162-172.)

Chandy, P. R. (Hsueh, L. Paul and P. R. Chandy. "An Examination Of The Yield Spread Between Insured And Uninsured Debt," JFR, 1989, v12(3), 235-244.)

Chandy, P. R. (Ndubizu, Gordian, Augustine C. Arize and P. R. Chandy. "The Market Model Specification And The Structural Stability Of The Beta," IJOF, 1989, v1(2), 1-14.)

Chandy, P. R. (Varela, Oscar and P. R. Chandy. "Market Reaction To Listings And Delistings In The Dow Jones Portfolios," IJOF, 1989, v2(1), 67-78.)

Chandy, P. R. and Imre Karafiath. "The Effect Of The WPPSS Crisis On Utility Common Stock Returns," JBFA, 1989, v16(4), 531-542.

Chandy, P. R., Wallace N. Davidson and Sharon Garrison. "Bad News = Good News! Who Can Tell?," JPM, 1985, v12(1), 24-27.

Chaney, John and Jack McDonnell. "An Experiment In A Completely Self-Paced Home Study Finance Course," JFED, 1976, v5, 40-42.

Chaney, John S. "Utilization Of Desktop Computers In Financial Education," JFED, 1982, v11, 101-104.

Chaney, Paul K. "Moral Hazard And Capital Budgeting," JFR, 1989, v12(2), 113-128.

Chang, Carolyn C. Wu. (Chang, Jack S. K., Jean C. H. Loo and Carolyn C. Wu Chang. "The Pricing Of Futures Contracts And The Arbitrage Pricing Theory," JFR, 1990, v13(4), 297-306.)

Chang, Carolyn W. and Jack S. K. Chang. "Forward And Futures Prices: Evidence From The Foreign Exchange Markets," JOF, 1990, v45(4), 1333-1336.)

Chang, Davis L. S. and Shu S. Liao. "Forecasting And Control Of Accounts Receivable Characterized By Unstable Payment Patterns: A Field Test," AFPAF, 1985, v1(1), 241-264.

Chang, Eric C. and J. Michael Pinegar. "Return Seasonality And Tax-Loss Selling In The Market For Long-Term Government And Corporate Bonds," JFEC, 1986, v17(2), 391-416.

Chang, Eric C. and Richard A. Stevenson. "The Timing Performance Of Small Traders," JFM, 1985, v5(4), 517-527.

Chang, Eric C. and Wilbur G. Lewellen. "An Arbitrage Pricing Approach To Evaluating Mutual Fund Performance," JFR, 1985, v8(1), 15-30.

Chang, Eric C. "A Monthly Effect In Commodity Price Changes: An Note," JFM, 1988, v8(6),717-722.

Chang, Eric C. "Returns To Speculators And The Theory Of Normal Backwardation," JOF, 1985, v40(1), 193-208.

Chang, Eric C. (Brauer, Greggory A. and Eric C. Chang. "Return Seasonality In Stocks And Their Underlying Assets: Tax Loss Selling Versus Information Explanations," RFS, 1990, v3(2), 255-280.)

Chang, Eric C. and Chan-Wung Kim. "Day Of The Week Effects And Commodity Price Changes," JFM, 1988, v8(2), 229-242.

Chang, Eric C. and J. Michael Pinegar. "Does The Market Reward Risk In Non-January Months?," JPM, 1988, v15(1), 55-57.

Chang, Eric C. and J. Michael Pinegar. "A Fundamental Study Of The Seasonal Risk-Return Relationship: A Note," JOF, 1988, v43(4), 1035-1039.

Chang, Eric C. and J. Michael Pinegar. "Risk And Inflation," JFQA, 1987, v22(1), 89-100.

Chang, Eric C. and J. Michael Pinegar. "Seasonal Fluctuations In Industrial Production And Stock Market Seasonals," JFQA, 1989, v24(1), 59-74.

Chang, Eric C. and J. Michael Pinegar. "Stock Market Seasonals And Prespecified Multifactor Pricing Relations," JFQA, 1990, v25(4), 517-534.

Chang, Eric C. and J. Michael Pinegar. "Another Look At Risk And Reward In January And Non-January Months: Reply," JPM, 1990, v16(4), 82-83.

Chang, Eric C. and Roger D. Huang. "Time-Varying Return And Risk In The Corporate Bond Market," JFQA, 1990, v25(3), 323-340.

Chang, Eric C. and Wilbur G. Lewellen. "Market Timing And Mutual Fund Investment Performance," JOB, 1984, v57(1), Part 1, 57-72.

Chang, Eric C., Chao Chen and Son-Nan Chen. "Risk And Return In Copper, Platinum, And Silver Futures," JFM, 1990, v10(1), 29-40.

Chang, Hui-shyong and Cheng F. Lee. "Using Pooled Time-Series And Cross-Section Data To Test The Firm And Time Effects In Financial Analyses," JFQA, 1977, v12(3), 457-471.

Chang, Jack S. K. and Latha Shanker. "Hedging Effectiveness Of Currency Options And Currency Futures," JFM, 1986, v6(2), 289-306.

Chang, Jack S. K. (Chang, Carolyn W. and Jack S. K. Chang. "Forward And Futures Prices: Evidence From The Foreign Exchange Markets," JOF, 1990, v45(4), 1333-1336.)

Chang, Jack S. K. and Hsing Fang. "An Intertemporal Measure Of Hedging Effectiveness," JFM, 1990, v10(3), 307-322.

Chang, Jack S. K. and Jean C. H. Loo. "Marking-To-Market, Stochastic Interest Rates And Discounts On Stock Index Futures," JFM, 1987, v7(1), 15-20.

Chang, Jack S. K. and Latha Shanker. "A Risk-Return Measure Of Hedging Effectiveness: A Comment," JFQA, 1987, v22(3), 373-376.

Chang, Jack S. K. and Latha Shanker. "Option Pricing And The Arbitrage Pricing Theory," JFR, 1987, v10(1), 1-16.

Chang, Jack S. K., Jean C. H. Loo and Carolyn C. Wu Chang. "The Pricing Of Futures Contracts And The Arbitrage Pricing Theory," JFR, 1990, v13(4), 297-306.

Chang, Kyungchun. (Branch, Ben and Kyungchun Chang. "Tax-Loss Trading - Is The Game Over Or Have The Rules Changed?," FR, 1985, v20(1), 55-70.)

Chang, Lena and William B. Fairley. "Pricing Automobile Insurance Under Multivariate Classification Of Risks: Additive Versus Multiplicative," JRI, 1979, v46(1), 75-98.

Chang, Philip. "Economies Of Scope, Synergy, And The CAPM," JFR, 1988, v11(3), 255-263.

Chang, Rosita P. and S. Ghon Rhee. "Does The Stock Market React To Announcements Of The Producer Price Index?," FR, 1986, v21(1), 125-134.

Chang, Rosita P. and S. Ghon Rhee. "The Impact Of Personal Taxes On Corporate Dividend Policy And Capital Structure Decisions," FM, 1990, v19(2), 21-31.

Chang, Rosita P., Blair M. Lord and S. Ghon Rhee. "Inflation-Caused Wealth-Transfer: A Case Of The Insurance Industry," JRI, 1985, v52(4), 627-643.

Chang, Rosita P., Peter E. Koveos and S. Ghon Rhee. "Financial Planning For International Long-Term Debt Financing," AFPAF, 1990, v5(1), 33-58.

Chang, S. J. "A Study Of Empirical Return Generating Models: A Market Model, A Multifactor Model, And A Unified Model," JBFA, 1991, v18(3), 377-392.

Chang, S. J. and Son-Nan Chen. "A Study Of Call Price Behavior Under A Stationary Return Generating Process," FR, 1989, v24(3), 335-354.

Chang, Saeyoung. "Employee Stock Ownership Plans And Shareholder Wealth: An Empirical Investigation," FM, 1990, v19(1), 48-58.

Chang, T. L. (Yen, Gili, T. L. Chang and Eva C. Yen. "On The Measurement Of State-Owned Enterprises In Taiwan: An Application Of Financial Ratio Analysis," AFPAF, 1985, v1(Supp), 243-260.)

Chant, John F. (Acheson, Keith and John F. Chant. "Bureaucratic Theory And The Choice Of Central Bank Goals: The Case Of The Bank Of Canada," JMCB, 1973, v5(2), 637-655.)

Chant, Peter D. "On The Predictability Of Corporate Earnings Per Share Behavior," JOF, 1980, v35(1), 13-21.

Chapin, Ned. "A Look At The Computer Industry," FAJ, 1958, v14(4), 79-84.

Chapin, Ned. "The Development Of The Break-Even Chart: A Bibliographical Note," JOB, 1955, v28(2), 148-149.

Chaplinksy, Susan and Greg Niehaus. "The Tax And Distributional Effects Of Leveraged ESOPs," FM, 1990, v19(1), 29-38.

Chaplinsky, Susan and H. Nejat Seyhun. "Dividends And Taxes: Evidence On Tax-Reduction Strategies," JOB, 1990, v63(2), 239-260.

Chapman, F. P. "A Life Adjustment Policy: Comment," JRI, 1962, v29(1), 123-124.

Chapman, Frederic P. and Joseph M. Belth. "The Replacement Problem In Life Insurance - With Special Emphasis On Comparative Costs: Comment," JRI, 1964, v31(3), 479-484.

Chapman, Ronald W. "Performance Based Mortgage-Backed Securities Indexing," JREFEC, 1988, v1(2), 185-193.

Chappell, David. "On The Revenue Maximizing Rate Of Inflation: A Comment," JMCB, 1981, v13(3),391-392.

Chappell, Henry W., Jr. and David C. Cheng. "Expectations, Tobin's q, And Investment: A Note," JOF, 1982, v37(1), 231-236.

Chaps, Ben. "Capital Alternatives For Smaller Banks," JBR, 1975-76, v6(3), 179-182.

Charest, Guy. "Dividend Information, Stock Returns And Market Efficiency - II," JFEC, 1978, v6(2/3), 297-330.

Charest, Guy. "Split Information, Stock Returns And Market Efficiency - I," JFEC, 1978, v6(2/3), 265-296.

Chari, V. V. and Ravi Jagannathan. "Banking Panics, Information, And Rational Expectations Equilibrium," JOF, 1988, v43(3), 749-761.

Chari, V. V. and Ravi Jagannathan. "Adverse Selection In A Model Of Real Estate Lending," JOF, 1989, v44(2), 499-508.

Chari, V. V., Ravi Jagannathan and Aharon R. Ofer. "Seasonalities In Security Returns: The Case Of Earnings Announcements," JFEC, 1988, v21(1), 101-122.

Charnes, A. and Sten Thore. "Planning For Liquidity In Financial Institutions: The Chance-Constrained Method," JOF, 1966, v21(4), 649-674.

Charnes, A. (Byrne, R., A. Charnes, W.W. Cooper and K. Kortanek. "A Chance-Constrained Approach To Capital Budgeting With Portfolio Type Payback And Liquidity Constraints And Horizon Posture Controls," JFQA, 1967, v2(4),339-364.)

Charnes, A., W. W. Cooper, and M. H. Miller. "Application Of Linear Programming To Financial Budgeting And The Costing Of Funds," JOB, 1959, v32(1), 20-46.

Chase, David E. (Jondrow, James M., David E. Chase and Christopher L. Gamble. "The Price Differential Between Domestic And Imported Steel," JOB, 1982, v55(3), 383-400.)

Chase, John P. "Selecting Securities In A One-World Economy," FAJ, 1960, v16(1), 67-69.

Chase, M. (Mahapatra, S., M. Chase and W. Rogers. "Information Interaction Effects Of Inflation Adjusted Accounting Data On Individual Decision-Maker's Sophistication And Risk Preference," JBFA, 1989, v16(5), 635-650.)

Chase, Samuel B., Jr. and John J. Mingo. "The Regulation Of Bank Holding Companies," JOF, 1975, v30(2), 281-292.

Chase, Samuel B., Jr. "Financial Structure And Regulation: Some Knotty Problems," JOF, 1971, v26(2), 585-597.

Chase, Samuel B., Jr. "Household Demand For Savings Deposits, 1921-1965," JOF, 1969, v24(4), 643-658.

Chase, Samuel B., Jr. "Introduction To Symposium On Bank Regulation," JOB, 1978, v51(3), 375-378.

Chastain, James J. "Monetary Values For The C.S.A. Table: Reply," JRI, 1961, v28(3), 105-106.

Chastain, James J. "Teaching Techniques: Property Insurance Contract Analysis," JRI, 1961, v28(2), 29-34.

Chastain, James J. "The A, B, Cs Of Life Insurance Rate And Reserve Computation," JRI, 1960, v27(4), 91-98.

Chateau, J. P. D. "Valuation Of 'Capped' Variable Rate Loan Commitments," JBF, 1990, v14(4), 717-728.

Chateau, Jean-Pierre D. "Dividend Policy Revisited Within - And Out-Of-Sample Tests," JBFA, 1979, v6(3), 355-372.

Chateau, Jean-Pierre D. "The Demand For And Supply Of Deposits By Credit Unions: The Caisses Populaires' Case," JBF, 1980, v4(2), 151-173.

Chateau, Jean-Pierre D. "The Capital Budgeting Problem Under Conflicting Financial Policies," JBFA, 1975, v2(1), 83-103.

Chateau, John Peter D. (Losq, Etienne and John Peter D. Chateau. "A Generalization Of The CAPM Based On A Property Of The Covariance Operator," JFQA, 1982, v17(5), 783-797.)

Chateau, John-Peter D. "On DFI's Liability Management: Deposit Capacity, Multideposit Supply, And Risk-Efficient Rate Setting," JBF, 1982, v6(4), 533-548.

Chateau, John-Peter D. "The Demand For And Supply Of Deposits By Credit Unions: The Caisses Populaires' Case-Reply And Comments," JBF, 1983, v7(2), 289-293.

Chatfield, Robert E. and R. Charles Moyer. "'Putting' Away Bond Risk: An Empirical Examination Of The Value Of The Put Option On Bonds," FM, 1986, v15(2),26-33.

Chatfield, Robert E. (Moyer, R. Charles, Robert E. Chatfield and Phillip M. Sisneros. "Security Analyst Monitoring Activity: Agency Costs And Information Demands," JFQA, 1989, v24(4), 503-512.)

Chatfield, Robert E. (Umbeck, John and Robert E. Chatfield. "The Structure Of Contracts And Transaction Costs," JMCB, 1982, v14(4), Part 1, 511-516.)

Chatfield, Robert E., Scott E. Hein and R. Charles Moyer. "Long-Term Earnings Forecasts In The Electric Utility Industry: Accuracy And Valuation Implications," FR, 1990, v25(3), 421-440.

Chatterjee, Sangit and Robert A. Pari. "Bootstrapping The Number Of Factors In The Arbitrage Pricing Theory," JFR, 1990, v13(1), 15-22.

Chatterjee, Sangit. (Badrinath, S. G. and Sangit Chatterjee. "On Measuring Skewness And Elongation In Common Stock Return Distributions: The Case Of The Market Index," JOB, 1988, v61(4), 451-472.)

Chatterjee, Sangit. (Tomczyk, Stephen and Sangit Chatterjee. "Estimating The Market Model Robustly," JBFA, 1984, v11(4), 563-573.)

Chatterjee, Sris and James H. Scott, Jr. "Explaining Differences In Corporate Capital Structure: Theory And New Evidence," JBF, 1989, v13(2), 283-310.

Chatterjee, Sris. Agency Cost Of Asset Substitution: Some Additional Results," IJOF, 1989, v1(2), 64-71.

Chau, To Minh. (Kryzanowski, Lawrence and To Minh Chau. "Asset Pricing Models When The Number Of Securities Held Is Constrained: A Comparison And Reconciliation Of The Mao And Levy Models," JFQA, 1982, v17(1), 63-73.)

Che, Wen-Kuei. (Ritchken, Peter H. and Wen-Kuei Chen. "Downside Risk Option Pricing Models," RDIBF, 1988, v2, 205-226.)

Chelius, James R. and Karen Kavanaugh. "Workers' Compensation And The Level Of Occupational Injuries," JRI, 1988, v55(2), 315-323.

Chen, A. H. and A. J. Boness. "Effects Of Uncertain Inflation On The Investment And Financing Decisions Of A Firm," JOF, 1975, v30(2), 469-483.

Chen, A. H., E. Han Kim and S. J. Kon. "Cash Demand, Liquidation Costs And Capital Market Equilibrium Under Uncertainty," JFEC, 1975, v2(3), 293-308.

Chen, Andrew H. and E. Han Kim. "Theories Of Corporate Debt Policy: A Synthesis," JOF, 1979, v34(2), 371-384.

Chen, Andrew H. and Gary C. Sanger. "An Analysis Of The Impact Of Regulatory Change: The Case Of Natural Gas Deregulation," FR, 1985, v20(1), 36-54.

Chen, Andrew H. and John W. Kensinger. "Innovations In Corporate Financing: Tax-Deductible Equity," FM, 1985, v14(4), 44-51.

Chen, Andrew H. and Larry J. Merville. "An Analysis Of Divestiture Effects Resulting From Deregulation," JOF, 1986, v41(5), 997-1010.

Chen, Andrew H. Y. "A Model Of Warrant Pricing In A Dynamic Market," JOF, 1970, v25(5), 1041-1059.

Chen, Andrew H. Y., Frank C. Jen and Stanley Zionts. "The Joint Determination Of Portfolio And Transaction Demands For Money," JOF, 1974, v29(1), 175-186.

Chen, Andrew H. Y., Frank C. Jen and Stanley Zionts. "Optimal Portolio Revision Policy," JOB, 1971, v44(1), 51-61.

Chen, Andrew H. "Effects Of Purchasing Power Risk On Portfolio Demand For Money," JFQA, 1979, v14(2), 243-254.

Chen, Andrew H. "Portfolio Selection With Stochastic Cash Demand," JFQA, 1977, v12(2), 197-312.

Chen, Andrew H. (Bicksler, James and Andrew H. Chen. "An Economic Analysis Of Interest Rate Swaps," JOF, 1986, v41(3), 645-656.)

Chen, Andrew H. (Bicksler, James L. and Andrew H. Chen. "The Integration Of Insurance And Taxes In Corporate Pension Strategy," JOF, 1985, v40(3), 943-955.)

Chen, Andrew H. (Boness, A. James, Andrew H. Chen and Som Jatusipitak. "Investigations Of Nonstationarity In Prices," JOB, 1974, v47(4), 518-537.)

Chen, Andrew H. (Boness, A. James, Andrew H. Chen and Som Jatusipitak. "On Relations Among Stock Price Behavior And Changes In The Capital Structure Of The Firm," JFQA, 1972, v7(4), 1967-1982.)

Chen, Andrew H. (Buser, Stephen A., Andrew H. Chen And Edward J. Kane. "Federal Deposit Insurance, Regulatory Policy, And Optimal Bank Capital," JOF, 1981, v36(1), 51-60.)

Chen, Andrew H. (Lam, Chun H. and Andrew H. Chen. "Joint Effects Of Interest Rate Deregulation And Capital Requirements On Optimal Bank Portfolio Adjustments," JOF, 1985, v40(2), 563-575.)

Chen, Andrew H. (Lam, Chun H. and Andrew H. Chen. "A Note On Optimal Credit And Pricing Policy Under Uncertainty: A Contingent-Claims Approach," JOF, 1986, v41(5), 1141-1148.)

Chen, Andrew H. (Park, Hun Y. and Andrew H. Chen. "Differences Between Futures And Forward Prices: A Further Investigation Of The Marking-to-Market Effect," JFM, 1985, v5(1), 77-88.)

Chen, Andrew H. (Wei, K. C. John, Cheng-few Lee and Andrew H. Chen. "Multivariate Regression Tests Of The Arbitrage Pricing Theory: The Instrumental-Variables Approach," RQFA, 1991, v1(2), 191-208.)

Chen, Andrew H. and John W. Kensinger. "Puttable Stock: A New Innovation In Equity Financing," FM, 1988, v17(1), 27-37.

Chen, Andrew H. and John W. Kensinger. "Beyond The Tax Benefits Of ESOP Financing," JACF, 1988, v1(1), 67-75.

Chen, Andrew H. and John W. Kensinger. "An Analysis Of Market-Index Certificates Of Deposit," JFSR, 1990, v4(2), 93-110.

Chen, Andrew H. and Marcia H. Millon. "The Secondary Market And Dynamic Swap Management," RDIBF, 1989, v3, 131-148.

Chen, Andrew H., E. Han Kim and Stanley J. Kon. "Cash Demand, Liquidation Costs, And Capital Market Equilibrium Under Uncertainty: Reply," JFEC, 1976, v3(3), 297-298.

Chen, Andrew H., K. C. Chen and R. Stephen Sears. "The Value Of Loan Guarantees: The Case Of Chrysler Corporation," RIF, 1986, v6, 101-118.

Chen, Andrew H., Neil A. Doherty and Hun Y. Park. "The Optimal Capital Structure Decision Of Depository Financial Intermediaries: A Contingent-Claim Analysis," RIF, 1988, v7, 91-112.

Chen, Andrew and David Ling. "Optimal Mortgage Refinancing With Stochastic Interest Rates," AREUEA, 1989, v17(3), 278-299.

Chen, Andrew. "Recent Developments In The Cost Of Debt Capital," JOF, 1978, v33(3), 863-877.

Chen, Carl R. and Steve Stockum. "Selectivity, Market Timing, And Random Beta Behavior Of Mutual Funds: A Generalized Model," JFR, 1986, v9(1), 87-96.

Chen, Carl R. "A Note On The Tax Loss Carryback And Carryforward: A Common Negligence Found In Finance Textbooks," FPE, 1991, v1(1), 90.

Chen, Carl R. "The Impact Of Maturity And Yield Effects On The Systematic Risk Of Bonds," JBFA, 1989, v16(4), 565-574.

Chen, Carl R. "Time-Series Analysis Of Beta Stationarity And Its Determinants: A Case Of Public Utilities," FM, 1982, v11(3), 64-70.

Chen, Carl R. (Mohan, Nancy and Carl R. Chen. "A Review Of The RJR-Nabisco Buyout," JACF, 1990, v3(2), 102-108.)

Chen, Carl R. (Winger, Bernard J., Carl R. Chen, John D. Martin, J. William Petty and Steven C. Hayden. "Adjustable Rate Preferred Stock," FM, 1986, v15(1), 48-57.)

Chen, Carl R. and Anthony Chan. "Interest Rate Sensitivity, Asymmetry, And The Stock Returns Of Financial Institutions," FR, 1989, v24(3), 457-474.

Chen, Chao. (Chang, Eric C., Chao Chen and Son-Nan Chen. "Risk And Return In Copper, Platinum, And Silver Futures," JFM, 1990, v10(1), 29-40.)

Chen, Charng Y. and Richard PonArul. "On The Tax Incentive For Corporate Insurance Purchase," JRI, 1989, v56(2), 306-311.

Chen, Charng Yi. "Risk-Preferences And Tax-Induced Dividend Clienteles: Evidences From The Insurance Industry," JRI, 1990, v57(2), 199-219.

Chen, Chau-nan, Ching-chong Lai and Tien-wang Tsaur. "The Loanable Funds Theory And The Dynamics Of Exchange Rates: The Mundell Model Revisited," JIMF, 1988, v7(2), 221-230.

Chen, Chau-nan. "A Graphical Note On The Aggregative Effect Of Payments Of Interest On Deposits: A Comment," JMCB, 1973, v5(4), 985-987.

Chen, Chau-nan. "Flexible Bimetallic Exchange Rates In China, 1650-1850: A Historical Example Of Optimum Currency Areas," JMCB, 1975, v7(3), 359-376.

Chen, Houng-Yhi. "Valuation Under Uncertainty," JFQA, 1967, v2(3), 313-325.

Chen, K. C. and R. Stephen Sears. "How Many Small Firms Are Enough?," JFR, 1984, v7(4), 341-349.

Chen, K. C. (Alderson, Michael J. and K. C. Chen. "Excess Asset Reversions And Shareholder Wealth," JOF, 1986, v41(1), 225-242.)

Chen, K. C. (Chen, Andrew H., K. C. Chen and R. Stephen Sears. "The

Value Of Loan Guarantees: The Case Of Chrysler Corporation," RIF, 1986, v6, 101-118.)

Chen, K. C. and Daniel T. Tzang. "Interest-Rate Sensitivity Of Real Estate Investment Trusts," JRER, 1988, v3(3), 13-22.

Chen, K. C. and R. Stephen Sears. "Pricing The SPIN," FM, 1990, v19(2), 36-47.

Chen, K. C. and Stephen P. D'Arcy. "Market Sensitivity To Interest Rate Assumptions In Corporate Pension Plans," JRI, 1986, v53(2), 209-225.

Chen, K. C., R. Stephen Sears and Dah-Nein Tzang. "Oil Prices And Energy Futures," JFM, 1987, v7(5), 501-518.

Chen, Kung H. and Thomas A. Shimerda. "An Empirical Analysis Of Useful Financial Ratios," FM, 1981, v10(1), 51-60.

Chen, Nai-Fu and Herb Johnson. "Hedging Options," JFEC, 1985, v14(2), 317-321.

Chen, Nai-Fu and Jonathan E. Ingersoll, Jr. "Exact Pricing In Linear Factor Models With Finitely Many Assets: A Note," JOF, 1983, v38(3), 985-988.

Chen, Nai-Fu, Bruce Grundy and Robert F. Stambaugh. "Changing Risk, Changing Risk Premiums, And Dividend Yield Effects," JOB, 1990, v63(1), Part 2, S51-S70.

Chen, Nai-Fu, Richard Roll and Stephen A. Ross. "Economic Forces And The Stock Market," JOB, 1986, v59(3), 383-404.

Chen, Nai-Fu, Thomas E. Copeland and David Mayers. "A Comparison Of Single And Multifactor Portfolio Performance Methodologies," JFQA, 1987, v22(4), 401-418.

Chen, Nai-Fu. "Some Empirical Tests Of The Theory Of Arbitrage Pricing," JOF, 1983, v38(5), 1393-1414.

Chen, Nai-Fu. (Chan, K. C. and Nai-Fu Chen. "An Unconditional Asset-Pricing Test And The Role Of Firm Size As An Instrumental Variable For Risk," JOF, 1988, v43(2), 309-325.)

Chen, Nai-Fu. (Chan, K. C., Nai-Fu Chen and David A. Hsieh. "An Exploratory Investigation Of The Firm Size Effect," JFEC, 1985, v14(3), 451-471.)

Chen, Nai-Fu. (Weston, J. Fred and Nai-Fu Chen. "A Note On Capital Budgeting And The Three Rs," FM, 1980, v9(1), 12-13.)

Chen, Son Nan. (Keown, Arthur J., John M. Pinkerton and Son Nan Chen. "Portfolio Selection Based Upon P/E Ratios: Diversification, Risk Decomposition And Implications," JBFA, 1987, v14(2), 187-198.)

Chen, Son-Nan and Arthur J. Keown. "Risk Composition And Portfolio Diversification When Beta Is Nonstationary: A Note," JOF, 1981, v36(4), 941-947.

Chen, Son-Nan and Arthur J. Keown. "Group Effects And Beta Nonstationarity," JBFA, 1985, v12(4),595-608.

Chen, Son-Nan and Arthur J. Keown. "An Examination Of The Relationship Between Pure Residual And Market Risk: A Note," JOF, 1981, v36(5), 1202-1209.

Chen, Son-Nan and Reena Aggarwal. "Optimal Portfolio Selection And Uncertain Inflation," JPM, 1986, v13(1), 44-49.

Chen, Son-Nan and Stephen J. Brown. "Estimation Risk And Simple Rules For Optimal Portfolio Selection," JOF, 1983, v38(4), 1087-1094.

Chen, Son-Nan and William T. Moore. "Multi-Period Asset Pricing: The Effects Of Uncertain Inflation," FR, 1984, v19(2), 208-221.

Chen, Son-Nan and William T. Moore. "Investment Decisions Under Uncertainty: Application Of Estimation Risk In The Hillier Approach," JFQA, 1982, v17(3), 425-440.

Chen, Son-Nan and William T. Moore. "Project Abandonment Under Uncertainty: A Bayesian Approach," FR, 1983, v18(4), 306-313.

Chen, Son-Nan and William T. Moore. "Uncertain Inflation And Optimal Portfolio Approach: A Simplified Approach," FR, 1985, v20(4), 343-356.

Chen, Son-Nan and William T. Moore. "The Expected Net Present Value Rule Under Informative And Noninformative Prior Distributions," AFPAF, 1985, v1(1), 209-224.

Chen, Son-Nan. "An Examination Of Risk-Return Relationship In Bull And Bear Markets Using Time-Varying Betas," JFQA, 1982, v17(2), 265-286.

Chen, Son-Nan. "Beta Nonstationarity, Portfolio Residual Risk And Diversification," JFQA, 1981, v16(1), 95-111.

Chen, Son-Nan. "Optimal Asset Abandoment And Replacement: Tax And Inflation Considerations," FR, 1991, v26(2), 157-178.

Chen, Son-Nan. "Re-Examining The Market Model Given Evidence Of Heteroskedasticity," JFR, 1979, v2(2), 111-118.

Chen, Son-Nan. "Simple Optimal Asset Allocation Under Uncertainty," JPM, 1987, v13(4), 69-76.

Chen, Son-Nan. "Time Aggregation, Autocorrelation, And Systematic Risk Estimates--Additive Versus Multiplicative Assumptions," JFQA, 1980, v15(1),151-174.

Chen, Son-Nan. (Chang, Eric C., Chao Chen and Son-Nan Chen. "Risk And Return In Copper, Platinum, And Silver Futures," JFM, 1990, v10(1), 29-40.)

Chen, Son-Nan. (Chang, S. J. and Son-Nan Chen. "A Study Of Call Price Behavior Under A Stationary Return Generating Process," FR, 1989, v24(3), 335-354.)

Chen, Son-Nan. (Moore, William T. and Son-Nan Chen. "Implementing the IRR Criterion When Cash Flow Parameters Are Unknown," FR, 1984, v19(4), 351-358.)

Chen, Son-Nan. (Pari, Robert A. and Son-Nan Chen. "Estimation Risk And Optimal Portfolios," JPM, 1985, v12(1), 40-43.)

Chen, Son-Nan. (Pari, Robert A. and Son-Nan Chen. "An Empirical Test Of The Arbitrage Pricing Theory," JFR, 1984, v7(2), 121-130.)

Chen, Son-Non and John D. Martin. "Beta Nonstationarity And Pure Extra-Market Covariance Effects On Portfolio Risk," JFR, 1980, v3(3), 269-282.

Chen, Su-Janc. (Akella, Srinivas R. and Su-Jane Chen. "Interest Rate Sensitivity Of Bank Stock Returns: Specification Effects And Structural Changes," JFR, 1990, v13(2), 147-154.)

Chen, T. J. and K. C. John Wei. "Risk Premiums In Foreign Exchange Markets: Theory And Evidence," AFPAF, 1989, v4(Supp), 23-42.

Chen, Thomas P. "The Internationalization Of The Taiwanese Economy," AFPAF, 1985, v1(Supp), 201-212.

Chen, Yung-Ping and Kwang-Wen Chu. "Tax-Benefit Ratios And Rates Of Return Under OASI: 1974 Retirees And Entrants," JRI, 1974, v41(2), 189-206.

Chen, Yung-Ping and Kwang-Wen Chu. "Tax-Benefit Ratios And Rates Of Return Under OASI: 1974 Retirees And Entrants: Reply," JRI, 1976, v43(1), 145-151.

Cheney, Harlan L. "The Value Of Industry Forecasting As An Aid To Portfolio Management," FR, 1970, v1(5), 331-339.

Cheney, John M. and E. Theodore Veit. "Evidence Of Shifts In Portfolio Asset Composition As A Market Timing Tool," FR, 1983, v18(1), 56-78.

Cheney, John M. "Rating Classification And Bond Yield Volatility," JPM, 1983, v9(3), 51-57.

Cheney, John M. (Duvall, Richard M. and John M. Cheney. "Bond Beta And Default Risk," JFR, 1984, v7(3), 243-254.)

Cheney, John M. (Veit, E. Theodore and John M. Cheney. "Are Mutual Funds Market Timers?," JPM, 1982, v8(2), 35-42.)

Cheney, John M. (Veit, E. Theodore and John M. Cheney. "Managing Investment Portfolios: A Survey Of Mutual Funds," FR, 1984, v19(4), 321-338.)

Cheng, David C. (Chappell, Henry W., Jr. and David C. Cheng. "Expectations, Tobin's q, And Investment: A Note," JOF, 1982, v37(1), 231-236.)

Cheng, David C. (Zumpano, Leonard V., Patricia M. Rudolph and David C. Cheng. "The Demand And Supply Of Mortgage Funds And Mortgage Loan Terms," AREUEA, 1986, v14(1), 91-109.)

Cheng, David C., Benton E. Gup and Larry D. Wall. "Financial Determinants Of Bank Takeovers," JMCB, 1989, v21(4), 524-536.

Cheng, Louis. (Davidson, Wallace N., III, Dipa Dutia and Louis Cheng. "A Re-Examination Of The Market Reaction To Failed Mergers," JOF, 1989, v44(4), 1077-1084.)

Cheng, Pao L. and John P. Shelton. "A Contribution To The Theory Of Capital Budgeting - The Multi-Investment Case: Reply," JOF, 1964, v19(4), 671-672.

Cheng, Pao L. and John P. Shelton. "A Contribution To The Theory Of Capital Budgeting - The Multi-Investment Case," JOF, 1963, v18(4), 622-636.

Cheng, Pao L. and M. King Deets. "Statistical Biases And Security Rates Of Return," JFQA, 1971, v6(3), 977-994.

Cheng, Pao L. and M. King Deets. "Portfolio Returns And The Random Walk Theory: Reply," JOF, 1973, v28(3), 742-745.

Cheng, Pao L. and M. King Deets. "Systematic Risk And The Horizon Problem," JFQA, 1973, v8(2), 299-316.

Cheng, Pao L. and M. King Deets. "Portfolio Returns And The Random Walk Theory," JOF, 1971, v26(1), 11-30.

Cheng, Pao L. and M. King Deets. "Test Of Portfolio Building Rules: Comment," JOF, 1971, v26(4), 965-972.

Cheng, Pao L. and M. King Deets. "Portfolio Returns And The Random Walk Theory: Reply," JOF, 1976, v31(1), 157-161.

Cheng, Pao L. "Divergent Rates, Financial Restrictions And Relative Prices In Capital Market Equilibrium," JFQA, 1980, v15(3), 509-540.

Cheng, Pao L. "Efficient Portfolio Selections Beyond The Markowitz Frontier," JFQA, 1971, v6(5), 1207-1233.

Cheng, Pao L. "Unbiased Estimators Of Long-Run Expected Returns Revisited," JFQA, 1984, v19(4),375-393.

Cheng, Pao L. (Heaney, W. John and Pao L. Cheng. "Continuous Maturity Diversification Of Default-Free Bond Portfolios And A Generalization Of Efficient Diversification," JOF, 1984, v39(4), 1101-1117.)

Cheng, Pao Lun. "A Note On The Progressive Consumption Tax," JOF, 1953, v8(3), 333-342.

Cheng, Peter, Fredric Jacobs and Ronald Marshall. "Cost Variance Investigation In A Linear Programming Framework," JBFA, 1984, v11(2), 233-244.

Cherin, Antony C. and Robert C. Hutchins. "The Rate Of Return On Universal Life Insurance," JRI, 1987, v54(4), 691-711.

Cherin, Antony. (Warschauer, Thomas and Antony Cherin. "Optimal Liquidity In Personal Financial Planning," FR, 1987, v22(4), 355-368.)

Cherry, Michael A. (Fridson, Martin S. and Michael A. Cherry. "Initial Pricing As A Predictor Of Subsequent Performance Of High-Yield Bonds," FAJ, 1990, v46(4), 61-67.)

Cherry, R. and E. J. Ford, Jr. "Concentration Of Rental Housing Property And Rental Housing Markets In Urban Areas," AREUEA, 1975, v3(1), 7-16.

Chervany, Norman L. "A Simulation Analysis Of Causal Relationships Within The Cash Flow Process," JFQA, 1970, v5(4), 445-467.

Chervany, Norman L. (Alexander, Gordon J. and Norman L. Chervany. "On The Estimation And Stability Of Beta," JFQA, 1980, v15(1), 123-137.)

Cheshire, J. D. and E. H. Feroz. "Allison's Models And The FASB Statements No's 2, 5, 13 And 19," JBFA, 1989, v16(1), 119-130.

Chesney, Marc and Louis Scott. "Pricing European Currency Options: A Comparison Of The Modified Black-Scholes Model And A Random Variance Model," JFQA, 1989, v24(3), 267-284.

Chesser, Delton L. and Pamela K. Coats. "A Computer-Based Instructional Tool For Capital Budgeting," JFED, 1978, v7, 88-89.

Chesser, Delton L. (Lee, Sang M. and Delton L. Chesser. "Goal Programming For Portfolio Selection," JPM, 1980, v6(3), 22-26.)

Cheung, C. Sherman and Clarence C. Y. Kwan. "A Note On Simple Criteria For Optimal Portfolio Selection," JOF, 1988, v43(1), 241-245.

Cheung, C. Sherman, Clarence C. Y. Kwan and Patrick C. Y. Yip. "The Hedging Effectiveness Of Options And Futures: A Mean-Gini Approach," JFM, 1990, v10(1), 61-74.

Cheung, C. Sherman. (Chamberlain, Trevor W., C. Sherman Cheung and Clarence C. Y. Kwan. "Expiration-Day Effects Of Index Futures And Options: Some Canadian Evidence," FAJ, 1989, v45(5), 67-71.)

Cheung, Joseph K. "The Association Between Lease Disclosure And The Lessee's Systematic Risk," JBFA, 1982, v8(3), 297-306.

Cheung, Joseph K. "The PIP Grant Accounting Controversy In Canada: A Study Of The Economic Consequences Of Accounting Standards," JBFA, 1988, v15(1), 47-66.

Cheung, Yan-Leung and Yak-Ki Ho. "The Intertemporal Stability Of The Relationships Between Asian Emerging Equity Markets And The Developed Equity Markets," JBFA, 1991, v18(2), 235-254.

Chew, I. Keong and Ronnie J. Clayton. "Bond Valuation: A Clarification," FR, 1983, v18(2), 234-236.

Chew, I. Keong. "Implications Of Discount Rates And Financing Assumptions For Bond Refunding Decisions: Comment," FM, 1980, v9(3), 69-71.

Chew, I. Keong. (Carpenter, Michael D. and I. Keong Chew. "The Effects Of Default Risk On The Market Model," JFR, 1983, v6(3), 223-229.)

Chew, It-Keong. (Cooley, Philip L., Rodney L. Roenfeldt and It-Keong Chew. "Capital Budgeting Procedures Under Inflation," FM, 1974, v4(4), 18-27.)

Chew, It-Keong. (Cooley, Philip L., Rodney L. Roenfeldt and It-Keong Chew. "Clarification Of Three Capital Budgeting Criteria," FR, v12(1), 20-27.)

Chew, It-Keong. (Ferri, Michael G., Steven J. Goldstein and It-Keong Chew. "Interest Rates And The Announcement Of Inflation," FM, 1983, v12(3), 52-61.)

Chew, It-Keong. (Findlay, M. Chapman, III, Arthur E. Gooding and Wallace Q. Weaver, Jr. "On The Relevant Risk For Determining Capital Expenditure Hurdle Rates," FM, 1976, v5(4), 9-17.)

Chew, It-Keong. (Park, Jeong Yun, Donald J. Mullineaux and It-Keong Chew. "Are REITs Inflation Hedges?," JREFEC, 1990, v3(1), 91-103.)

Chew, S. H. and Larry G. Epstein. "The Law Of Large Numbers And The Attractiveness Of Compound Gambles," JRU, 1988, v1(1), 125-132.

Cheyney, John M. (Moses, Edward A., John M. Cheyney and E. Theodore Veit. "A New And More Complete Performance Measure," JPM, 1987, v13(4), 24-33.)

Chiang, R. (Venkatesh, P. C. and R. Chiang. "Information Asymmetry And The Dealer's Bid-Ask Spread: A Case Study Of Earnings And Dividend Announcements," JOF, 1986, v41(5), 1089-1102.)

Chiang, Raymond and Robert W. Kolb. "An Analytical Model Of The Relationship Between Maturity And Bonds Risk Differentials," FR, 1986, v21(2), 191-209.

Chiang, Raymond C. and T. Craig Tapley. "Day-Of-The-Week Effects And The Futures Market," RFM, 1983, v2(3), 356-410.

Chiang, Raymond C. and John M. Finkelstein. "The Multiplicity Of Financial Intermediary Types: The Rationale Re-Examined," IJOF, 1989, v2(1), 18-29.

Chiang, Raymond C., Gerald D. Gay and Robert W. Kolb. "Commodity Exchange Seat Prices," RFM, 1987, v6(1), 1-10.

Chiang, Raymond and Dennis J. Lasser. "Tax Timing Options On Futures Contracts And The 1981 Economic Recovery Act," FR, 1989, v24(1), 75-92.

Chiang, Raymond and P. C. Venkatesh. "Insider Holdings And Perceptions Of Information Asymmetry: A Note," JOF, 1988, v43(4), 1041-1048.

Chiang, Raymond, Tsong-Yue Lai and David C. Ling. "Retail Leasehold Interests: A Contingent Claim Analysis," AREUEA, 1986, v14(2), 216-229.

Chiang, Raymond. (Anderson, Gary and Raymond Chiang. "Interest Rate Risk Hedging For Due-On-Sale Mortgages With Early Termination," JFR, 1987, v10(2), 133-142.)

Chiang, Raymond. (Gay, Gerald D., Robert W. Kolb and Raymond Chiang. "Interest Rate Hedging: An Empirical Test Of Alternative Strategies," JFR, 1983, v6(3), 187-197.)

Chiang, Raymond. (Kolb, Robert W. and Raymond Chiang. "Duration, Immunization, And Hedging With Interest Rate Futures," JFR, 1982, v5(2), 161-170.)

Chiang, Raymond. (Kolb, Robert A. and Raymond Chiang. "Improving Hedging Performance Using Interest Rate Futures," FM, 1981, v10(4), 72-79.)

Chiang, Thomas C. "Empirical Analysis On The Predictors Of Future Spot Rates," JFR, 1986, v9(2),153-162.

Chiang, Thomas C. "On The Predictors Of The Future Spot Rates - A Multi-Currency Analysis," FR, 1986, v21(1), 69-83.

Chiang, Thomas C. "The Forward Rate As A Predictor Of The Future Spot Rate--A Stochastic Coefficient Approach," JMCB, 1988, v20(2), 212-232.

Chiattello, Marion L. "Comment: On The Use Of Principal Components Analysis To Interpret Cross-Sectional Differences Among Commercial Banks," JFQA, 1974, v9(6), 1047-1051.

Child, Denis M. "Payment Issues In The United Kingdom," JBR, 1985-86, v16(4), 198-201.

Childers, Terry L. (Dubinsky, Alan J., Terry L. Childers, Steven J. Skinner and Esra Gencturk. "Impact Of Sales Supervisor Leadership Behavior On Insurance Agent Attitudes And Performance," JRI, 1988, v55(1), 132-144.)

Childers, Terry L. and O. C. Ferrell. "Husband-Wife Decision Making In Purchasing And Renewing Auto Insurance," JRI, 1981, v48(3), 482-493.

Childress, Donald R. "Contributions To Risk And Insurance Theory From The Field Of Philosophy," JRI, 1962, v29(3), 321-328.

Childs, Barbara J. (Goolsby, William C. and Barbara J. Childs. "Brokerage Firm Competition In Real Estate Commission Rates," JRER, 1988, v3(2), 79-85.)

Chinloy, Peter. "Real Estate Income And Relocation," FSR, 1991, v1(1), 53-65.

Chinloy, Peter. "The Probability Of Prepayment," JREFEC, 1989, v2(4), 267-284.

Chinloy, Peter. "The Real Estate Brokerage: Commissioned Sales And Market Values," JRER, 1988, v3(1), 1-21.

Chiplin, Brian and Mike Wright. "Inter-Industry Differences In The Response Of Trade Credit To Changes In Monetary Policy," JBFA, 1985, v12(2), 221-248.

Chiras, Donald P. and Steven Manaster. "The Information Content Of Option Prices And A Test Of Market Efficiency," JFEC, 1978, v6(2/3), 213-234.

Chisholm, Nancy S. "A Future For Public Housing," AREUEA, 1983, v11(2), 203-220.

Chittenden, George H. "The Changing Role Of U. S. Banks In International Financing," JOF, 1965, v20(2), 172-181.

Chiu, John S. Y. (Schink, William A. and John S. Y. Chiu. "A Simulation Study Of Effects Of Multicollinearity And Autocorrelation On Estimates Of Parameters," JFQA, 1966, v1(2), 36-67.)

Cho, Chien-Ching. (Moore, James S., Alan K. Riechert and Chien-Ching Cho. "Analyzing The Temporal Stability Of Appraisal Model Coefficients: An Application Of Ridge Regression Techniques," AREUEA, 1984, v12(1), 50-71.)

Cho, D. Chinhyung and Edward W. Frees. "Estimating The Volatility Of Discrete Stock Prices," JOF, 1988, v43(2), 451-466.

Cho, D. Chinhyung and Edward W. Frees. "Estimating The Volatility Of Discrete Stock Prices," RIF, 1990, v8, 23-58.

Cho, D. Chinhyung and William M. Taylor. "The Seasonal Stability Of The Factor Structure Of Stock Returns," JOF, 1987, v42(5), 1195-1211.

Cho, D. Chinhyung, Cheol S. Eun and Lemma W. Senbet. "International Arbitrage Pricing Theory: An Empirical Investigation," JOF, 1986, v41(2), 313-330.

Cho, D. Chinhyung, Edwin J. Elton and Martin J. Gruber. "On The Robustness Of The Roll And Ross Arbitrage Pricing Theory," JFQA, 1984, v19(1), 1-10.

Cho, D. Chinhyung. "On Testing The Arbitrage Pricing Theory: Inter-Battery Factor Analysis," JOF, 1984, v39(5), 1485-1502.

Cho, D. Chinhyung. (Bodurtha, James N., Jr., D. Chinhyung Cho and Lemma W. Senbet. "Economic Forces In The Stock Market: An International Perspective," GFJ, 1989, v1(1), 21-46.)

Cho, Dong W. "IRA Investments: Liquidity Considerations," FAJ, 1986, v42(2), 71-74.

Cho, Dong W. and Gerald S. McDougall. "The Supply Of Storage In ?8 Energy Futures Markets," JFM, 1990, v10(6), 611-622. 3X

Cho, Dongsae. "Integrated Risk Management Decision-Making: A Workers' Compensation Loss Exposure Case Study," JRI, 1983, v50(2), 281-300.

Cho, Dongsae. "Rehabilitation For Worker's Compensation Loss Exposures," JRI, 1984, v51(1), 80-98.

Cho, Dongsae. "Some Evidence Of Scale Economies In Worker's Compensation Insurance," JRI, 1988, v55(2), 324-330.

Cho, Dongsae. "The Impact Of Risk Management Decisions On Firm Value: Gordon's Growth Model Approach," JRI, 1988, v55(1), 118-131.

Cho, Yoon Je. "Inefficiencies From Financial Liberalization In The Absence Of Well-Functioning Equity Markets," JMCB, 1986, v18(2), 191-199.

Choate, Algie. "Security Purchases Of Small Business Investment Companies," JOF, 1961, v16(2), 304-308.

Choate, G. Marc and Stephen H. Archer. "Irving Fisher, Inflation And The Nominal Rate Of Interest," JFQA, 1975, v10(4), 675-685.

Choi, Daniel F. S. and Charles W. R. Ward. "The Reconciliation Of The Smith's And Jarrow And Rudd's Option Sensitivity Formulae: A Teaching Note," FR, 1989, v24(3), 507-510.

Choi, Dosoung and George C. Philippatos. "Post-Merger Performance Among Homogeneous Firm Samples," FR, 1984, v19(2), 173-194.

Choi, Dosoung and George C. Philippatos. "An Examination Of Merger Synergism," JFR, 1983, v6(3),239-256.

Choi, Dosoung and Robert A. Strong. "The Pricing Of When-Issued Common Stock: A Note," JOF, 1983, v38(4), 1293-1298.

Choi, Dosoung and Frank C. Jen. "The Relation Between Stock Returns And Short-Term Interest Rates," RQFA, 1991, v1(1),75-90.

Choi, Dosoung. (DeFusco, Richard A., George C. Philippatos and Dosoung Choi. "Differences In Factor Structures Between U.S. Multinational And Domestic Corporations: Evidence From Bilinear Paradigm Tests," FR, 1990, v25(3), 395-404.)

Choi, Dosoung. (Miles, James and Dosoung Choi. "Comment: Evaluating Negative Benefits," JFQA, 1979, v14(5), 1095-1099.)

Choi, Frederick D. S. "International Data Sources For Empirical Research In Financial Management," FM, 1988, v17(2), 80-98.

Choi, Frederick D. S. "Teaching International Finance--An Accountant's Perspective," JFQA, 1977, v12(4), 609-614.

Choi, Frederick D. S. and Sungbin Chun Hong. "The Feasibility And Decision Utility Of Restating Accounting Information Sets: Korea," AFPAF, 1990, v5(1), 123-144.

Choi, J. J. and S. Hauser. "The Effects Of Domestic And Foreign Yield Curves On The Value Of Currency American Call Options," JBF, 1990, v14(1), 41-54.

Choi, J. Y. and Kuldeep Shastri. "Bid-Ask Spreads And Volatility Estimates: The Implications For Option Pricing," JBF, 1989, v13(2), 207-220.

Choi, J. Y., Dan Salandro and Kuldeep Shastri. "On The Estimation Of Bid-Ask Spreads: Theory And Evidence," JFQA, 1988, v23(2), 219-230.

Choi, Jin W. and Francis A. Longstaff. "Pricing Options On Agricultural Futures: An Application Of The Constant Elasticity Of Variance Option Pricing Model," JFM, 1985, v5(2), 247-258.

Choi, Jongmoo Jay and Shmuel Hauser. "The Value Of Foreign Currency Options And The Term Structure Of Interest Rates," RDIBF, 1989, v3, 149-158.

Choi, Jongmoo Jay, Frank J. Fabozzi and Uzi Yaari. "Optimum Corporate Leverage With Risky Debt: A Demand Approach," JFR, 1989, v12(2), 129-142.

Choi, Jongmoo Jay. "Consumption Basket, Exchange Risk, And Asset Demand," JFQA, 1984, v19(3), 287-298.

Choi, Jongmoo Jay. Pricing Exchange Risk And Location Costs: An Empirical Investigation Of The World Capital Markets," IJOF, 1988, v1(1), 35-45.

Choi, Sang-Rim and Adrian E. Tschoegl. "Bank Employment In The World's Largest Banks: An Update," JMCB, 1984, v16(3), 359-362.

Choie, Kenneth S. "A Simplified Approach To Bond Portfolio Management: DDS," JPM, 1990, v16(3), 40-45.

Choie, Kenneth S. and Eric J. Seff. "TIPP: Insurance Without Complexity: Comment," JPM, 1989, v16(1), 107-108.

Choie, Kenneth S. and Frederick Novomestky. "Replication Of Long-Term With Short-Term Options," JPM, 1989, v15(2), 17-19.

Cholerton, Kenneth, Pierre Pieraerts and Bruno Solnik. "Why Invest In Foreign Currency Bonds?," JPM, 1986, v12(4), 4-8.

Chopra, K. (Bierman, H., K. Chopra and J. Thomas. "Ruin Considerations: Optimal Working Capital And Capital Structure," JFQA, 1975, v10(1), 119-128.)

Chopra, Navin. (Ritter, Jay R. and Navin Chopra. "Portfolio Rebalancing And The Turn-Of-The-Year Effect," JOF, 1989, v44(1), 149-166.)

Chottiner, Sherman, Catherine May, and Nicholas Molodovsky. "Common Stock Valuation: Theory And Tables," **FAJ,** 1965, v21(2), 104-123.

Chottiner, Sherman. "Optimum Investor - Stock Market Efficiency Standard," **FAJ,** 1964, v20(1), 57-62.

Choudhri, Ehsan U. and Levis A. Kochin. "The Exchange Rate And The International Transmission Of Business Cycle Disturbances: Some Evidence From The Great Depression," **JMCB,** 1980, v12(4), Part 1, 565-574.

Choudhri, Ehsan U. "The Transmission Of Inflation In A Small Economy: An Empirical Analysis Of The Influence Of US Monetary Disturbances On Canadian Inflation, 1962-80," **JIMF,** 1983, v2(2), 167-178.

Choudhri, Ehsan U. (Bordo, Michael D., Ehsan U. Choudhri and Anna J. Schwartz. "The Behavior Of Money Stock Under Interest Rate Control: Some Evidence For Canada," **JMCB,** 1987, v19(2), 181-198.)

Choudhri, Ehsan U. (Bordo, Michael D. and Ehsan U. Choudhri. "Currency Substitution And The Demand For Money: Some Evidence For Canada," **JMCB,** 1982, v14(1), 48-57.)

Choudhury, Pravat K. "Marketing Bank Services To Blacks," **JBR,** 1978-79, v9(1), 52-58.

Chow, Brian G. and David J. Brophy. "The U.S. Treasury Bill Market And Hypotheses Regarding The Term Structure Of Interest Rates," **FR,** 1978, v13(2), 36-50.

Chow, Brian G. and David J. Brophy. "Treasury-Bill Futures Market: A Formulation And Interpretation," **JFM,** 1982, v2(1), 25-49.

Chow, Chee W. "Financial Disclosure Regulation And Indirect Economic Consequences: An Analysis Of The Sales Disclosure Requirement Of The 1934 Securities And Exchange Act," **JBFA,** 1984, v11(4), 469-483.

Chow, Chee W. "On The Measurement Of Auditing Standards," **JBFA,** 1983, v10(1), 21-35.

Chow, Gregory C. "Are Econometric Methods Useful For Forecasting?," **JOB,** 1978, v51(4), 565-568.

Chow, Gregory C. "Friedman On Money: A Review Article," **JOF,** 1970, v25(3), 687-689.

Chow, Gregory C. "Optimal Stochastic Control Of Linear Economic Systems," **JMCB,** 1970, v2(3),291-302.

Choy, A. Y. F. and J. O'Hanlon. "Day Of The Week Effects In The UK Equity Market: A Cross Sectional Analysis," **JBFA,** 1989, v16(1), 89-104.

Christ, Carl F. "A Model Of Monetary And Fiscal Policy Effects On The Money Stock, Price Level, And Real Output," **JMCB,** 1969, v1(4), 683-705.

Christ, Carl F. "Econometric Models Of The Financial Sector," **JMCB,** 1971, v3(2), Part 2, 419-449.

Christ, Carl F. "Karl Brunner At The Cowles Commission: A Reminiscence," **JMCB,** 1977, v9(1), Part 2, 245-246.

Christ, Carl F. "Monetary And Fiscal Influences On U.S. Money Income, 1891-1970," **JMCB,** 1973, v5(1), Part II, 279-300.

Christensen, Donald G. (Moore, William T., Donald G. Christensen and Rodney L. Roenfeldt. "Equity Valuation Effects Of Forming Master Limited Partnerships," **JFEC,** 1989, v24(1), 107-124.)

Christian, James W. "A Further Analysis Of The Objectives Of American Monetary Policy," **JOF,** 1968, v23(3), 465-477.

Christiansen, William A. (Elebash, Clarence C. and William A. Christiansen. "State Pension Funds: What Is Their Future In Real Estate?," **JRER,** 1989, v4(2), 71-79.)

Christiansen, William A. and Clarence C. Elebash. "A Note On The Attitude Of Pension Fund Investment Managers Toward Mortgage-Backed Securities," **JRER,** 1987, v2(1), 83-92.

Christie, Andrew A. "The Stochastic Behavior Of Common Stock Variances: Value, Leverage And Interest Rate Effects," **JFEC,** 1982, v10(4), 407-432.

Christner, Ronald C. and Roger D. Stover. "Institutional Research And Regulation Are On The Wrong Track," **JPM,** 1975, v1(2), 12-20.

Christofi, A. (Philippatos, G. C., A. Christofi and P. Christofi. "The Inter-Temporal Stability Of International Stock Market Relationships: Another View," **FM,** 1983, v12(4), 63-69.)

Christofi, Andreas. "How To Maximize Stationarity Of Beta: Comment," **JPM,** 1983, v9(4), 67-68.

Christofi, P. (Philippatos, G. C., A. Christofi and P. Christofi. "The Inter-Temporal Stability Of International Stock Market Relationships: Another View," **FM,** 1983, v12(4), 63-69.)

Christofides, N., R. D. Hewins and G. R. Salkin. "Graph Theoretic Approaches To Foreign Exchange Operations," **JFQA,** 1979, v14(3), 481-500.

Christophe, Cleveland A. "Evaluation Of 'Competition In Financial Services': Reply," **JBR,** 1975-76, v6(1), 66-69.

Christopherson, Paul C. "Product Pricing In The Chemical Industry," **FAJ,** 1977, v33(6), 54-62.

Christy, George A. "Teaching Of Investments: A 'Utilitarian' View," **JFQA,** 1974, v9(5), 781-787.

Chrystal, K. Alec and Daniel L. Thornton. "On The Informational Content Of Spot And Forward Exchange Rates," **JIMF,** 1988, v7(3), 321-330.

Chu, Chen-Chin and David T. Whitford. "Stock Market Returns And Inflationary Expectations: Additional Evidence For 1975-1979," **JFR,** 1982, v5(3), 261-271.

Chu, Chen-Chin and Edward L. Bubnys. "A Likelihood Ratio Test Of Price Volatilities: Comparing Stock Index Spot And Futures," **FR,** 1990, v25(1), 81-94.

Chu, Chen-Chin. "A Risk Premium Under Uncertain Inflation: The Inflation Futures Evidence," **JFM,** 1988, v8(3), 353-364.

Chu, Chen-Chin. (Lee, Cheng F., Paul Newbold, Joseph E. Finnerty and Chen-Chin Chu. "On Accounting-Based, Market-Based And Composite-Based Beta Predictions: Methods And Implications," **FR,** 1986, v21(1), 51-68.)

Chu, Kwang-Wen. (Chen, Yung-Ping and Kwang-Wen Chu. "Tax-Benefit Ratios And Rates Of Return Under OASI: 1974 Retirees And Entrants: Reply," **JRI,** 1978, v43(1), 145-151.)

Chu, Seok C. (Lee, Jae K., Robert R. Trippi, Seok C. Chu and Hyun Kim. "K-FOLIO: Integrating The Markowitz Model With A Knowledge-Based System," **JPM,** 1990, v17(1), 89-93.)

Chua, J. and R. S. Woodward. "Gold As An Inflation Hedge: A Comparative Study Of Six Major Industrial Countries," **JBFA,** 1982, v8(2), 191-197.

Chua, J. H. and R. S. Woodward. "The Investment Wizardry Of J. M. Keynes," **FAJ,** 1983, v39(3), 35-37.

Chua, Jess H. and Jacques A. Schnabel. "Nonpecuniary Benefits And Asset Market Equilibrium," **FR,** 1986, v21(2), 185-190.

Chua, Jess H. and Richard S. Woodward. "J. M. Keynes's Investment Performance: A Note," **JOF,** 1983, v38(1), 232-235.

Chua, Jess H. "A Closed-Form Formula For Calculating Bond Duration," **FAJ,** 1984, v40(3), 76-78.

Chua, Jess H. "A Generalized Formula For Calculating Bond Duration," **FAJ,** 1988, v44(5), 65-67.

Chua, Jess H. "Calculating Bond Duration: Further Simplification," **FAJ,** 1985, v41(5), 80-81.

Chua, Jess H. "Calculating Bond Duration: Further Simplification," **FAJ,** 1985, v41(6), 76.

Chua, Jess H. (Ang, James A., Jess H. Chua and Walter J. Reinhart. "Monetary Appreciation And Inflation-Hedging Characteristics Of Comic Books," **FR,** 1983, v18(2), 196-205.)

Chua, Jess H. (Ang, James S. and Jess H. Chua. "Corporate Bankruptcy And Job Losses Among Top Level Managers," **FM,** 1981, v10(5), 70-74.)

Chua, Jess H. (Ang, James S., Jess H. Chua and Clinton H. Bowling. "The Profiles Of Late-Paying Consumer Loan Borrowers: An Exploratory Study: A Comment," **JMCB,** 1979, v11(2), 222-226.)

Chua, Jess H. (Ang, James S., Jess H. Chua and Richard S. Woodward. "A Note On Investment Decision Rules Based On Utility Functions," **JBFA,** 1983, v10(4), 657-661.)

Chua, Jess H. (Ang, James S., Jess H. Chua and John J. McConnell. "The Administrative Costs Of Corporate Bankruptcy: A Note," **JOF,** 1982, v37(1),219-226.)

Chua, Jess H. (Ang, James S., Jess H. Chua and Ronald Sellers. "Generating Cash Flow Estimates: An Actual Study Using The Delphi Technique," **FM,** 1979, v8(1), 64-67.)

Chua, Jess H. (Ang, James S., Jess H. Chua and Anand S. Desai. "Evidence That The Common Stock Market Adjusts Fully For Expected Inflation," **JFR,** 1979, v2(2), 97-109.)

Chua, Jess H. (Ang, James S. and Jess H. Chua. "Composite Measures For The Evaluation Of Investment Performance," **JFQA,** 1979, v14(2), 361-384.)

Chua, Jess H. (Ang, James S., Jess H. Chua and Anand S. Desai. "Efficient Portfolios Versus Efficient Market," **JFR,** 1980, v3(3), 309-319.)

Chua, Jess H. (Ang, James S. and Jess H. Chua. "Mutual Funds: Different Strokes For Different Folks?," **JPM,** 1982, v8(2), 43-47.)

Chua, Jess H., Gordon Sick and Richard S. Woodward. "Diversifying With Gold Stocks," **FAJ,** 1990, v46(4), 76-79.

Chua, Jess H., Richard S. Woodward and Eric C. To. "Potential Gains From Stock Market Timing In Canada," **FAJ,** 1987, v43(5), 50-56.

Chue, Kwnag-Wen. (Chen, Yung-Ping and Kwang-Wen Chu. "Tax-Benefit Ratios And Rates Of Return Under OASI: 1974 Retirees And Entrants," **JRI,** 1974, v41(2), 189-206.)

Chugh, Lal C. and Joseph W. Meador. "The Stock Valuation Process: The Analysts' View," **FAJ,** 1984, v40(6), 41-43,46-48.

Chugh, Lal C. (Madden, Gerald P., Lynn W. Marples and Lal C. Chugh. "A Stock Market Evaluation Of Management Buyouts," **JBFA,** 1990, v17(3), 351-358.)

Chung, Chang Young. (Schollhammer, Hans and Chang Young Chung. "The Effect Of Exchange Rate Changes On The Interdependence Among National Equity Markets: An Empirical Investigation Of The United States, Japan, Britain And Germany," **RDIBF,** 1989, v3, 229-246.)

Chung, Kee H. "Debt And Risk: A Technical Note," **JBFA,** 1989, v16(5), 719-728.

Chung, Kee H. "Inventory Decision Under Demand Uncertainty: A Contingent Claims Approach," **FR,** 1990, v25(4), 623-640.

Chung, Kee H. "The Impact Of The Demand Volatility And Leverages On The Systematic Risk Of Common Stocks," **JBFA,** 1989, v16(3), 343-360.

Chung, Kee H. (Kim, Yong H. and Kee H. Chung. "An Integrated Evaluation Of Investment In Inventory And Credit: A Cash Flow Approach," **JBFA,** 1990, v17(3), 381-390.)

Chung, Kee H. and Raymond A. K. Cox. "Patterns Of Productivity In The Finance Literature: A Study Of The Bibliometric Distributions," **JOF,** 1990, v45(1), 301-310.

Chung, Ki-Young. (Castanias, Rick, Ki-Young Chung and Herb Johnson. "Dividend Spreads," **JOB,** 1988, v61(3), 299-320.)

Chung, Peter S. "An Investigation Of The Firm Effects Influence In The Analysis Of Earnings To Price Ratios Of Industrial Common Stocks," **JFQA,** 1974, v9(6), 1009-1029.

Chung, Yosup and Harold D. Skipper, Jr. "The Effect Of Interest Rates On Surrender Values Of Universal Life Policies," **JRI,** 1987, v54(2), 341-347.

Chuppe, Terry M., Hugh R. Haworth and Marvin G. Watkins. "Public Policy Toward The International Bond Markets In The 1980s," **AFPAF,** 1990, v5(1), 3-30.

Chuppe, Terry M., Hugh R. Haworth and Marvin G. Watkins. "Global Finance: Causes, Consequences And Prospects For The Future," **GFJ,** 1989, v1(1), 1-20.

Church, Albert M. "An Econometric Model For Appraising," **AREUEA,** 1975, v3(1), 17-32.

Church, Albert M. "The Effects Of Local Government Expenditure And Property Taxes On Investment," **AREUEA,** 1981, v9(2), 165-180.

Churchill, Neil C. and Virginia L. Lewis. "Profitability Of Small-Business Lending," **JBR,** 1985-86, v16(2), 63-71.

Cicchetti, Paul, Charles Dale and Anthony J. Vignola. "Usefulness Of Treasury Bill Futures As Hedging Instruments," **JFM,** v1(3), 379-387.

Ciccolo, John and Gary Fromm. "'q' And The Theory Of Investment," **JOF,** 1979, v34(2), 535-547.

Ciccolo, John and Gary Fromm. "'q,' Corporate Investment, And Balance Sheet Behavior," **JMCB,** 1980, v12(2), Part 1, 294-307.

Ciccolo, John H., Jr. "Money, Equity Values, And Income: Test For

Exogeneity," **JMCB**, 1978, v10(1), 46-64.
Cinar, E. Mine and Joseph Vu. "Evidence On The Effect Of Option Expirations On Stock Prices," **FAJ**, 1987, v43(1), 55-57.
Cisler, Walker L. "Nuclear Fuels And The Electric Power Industry," **FAJ**, 1964, v20(5), 144-147.
Claessens, Stijn. (Kroner, Kenneth F. and Stijn Claessens. "Optimal Dynamic Hedging Portfolios And The Currency Composition Of External Debt," **JIMF**, 1991, v10(1), 131-148.)
Clague, Ewan. "Comment: Food Prices And The Bureau Of Labor Statistics," **JOB**, 1960, v33(3), 280-284.
Claiborn, Stephen and Steven Bolten. "An Experiment In Competency-Based Financial Education," **JFED**, 1975, v4, 9-15.
Claiborn, Stephen A. and J. Markham Collins. "The Entering Job Market For Careers In Finance," **JFED**, 1978, v7, 25-29.
Clancy, Donald K. and John A. Yeakel. "On Reporting Dilutionary Exchanges," **FAJ**, 1981, v37(5),70-73.
Clapp, John M. "A Methodology For Constructing Vacant Land Price Indices," **AREUEA**, 1990, v18(3), 274-293.
Clapp, John M. "A Model Of Localized Mortgage Lending Behavior," **AREUEA**, 1980, v8(2), 229-246.
Clapp, John M. "A New Test For Equitable Real Estate Tax Assessment," **JREFEC**, 1990, v3(3), 233-250.
Clapp, John M. "The Impact Of Inclusionary Zoning On The Location And Type Of Construction Activity," **AREUEA**, 1981, v9(4), 436-456.
Clapp, John M., Joseph A. Fields and Chinmoy Ghosh. "An Examination Of Profitability In Spatial Markets: The Case Of Life Insurance Agency Locations," **JRI**, 1990, v57(3), 431-454.
Clapper, James M. (Willenborg, John F. and James M. Clapper. "Life Insurance Demand And Household Portfolio Behavior: Comment," **JRI**, 1976, v43(2), 325-331.)
Clarida, Richard H. and Benjamin M. Friedman. "The Behavior Of U.S. Short-Term Interest Rates Since October, 1979," **JOF**, 1984, v39(3), 671-682.
Clark, Carolyn. "The Demand For Money And The Choice Of A Permanent Income Estimate: Some Canadian Evidence, 1962-65," **JMCB**, 1973, v5(3), 773-793.
Clark, Clifford D. "A Note On Investment Activities And The Graduated Corporate Tax," **JOF**, 1957, v12(1), 44-50.
Clark, Clifford D. "Economic Appraisal Of Depreciation Policy," **JOB**, 1956, v29(1), 28-40.
Clark, Colin. "International Comparisons Of Productivity Trends," **JOB**, 1958, v31(4), 267-279.
Clark, David A. (Willis, John R. and David A. Clark. "An Introduction To Mezzanine Finance And Private Equity," **JACF**, 1989, v2(2), 77-86.)
Clark, Don P. "Regulation Of International Trade In The United States: The Tokyo Round," **JOB**, 1987, v60(2), 297-306.
Clark, Frederick W. and Joseph D. Davis. "Interest Rates Caught Between Inflationary And Monetary Forces," **FAJ**, 1964, v20(6), 77-83.
Clark, Jeffrey A. and Paul J. Speaker. "Compensating Balance Requirements And The Firm's Demand For Transactions Balances," **JBF**, 1986, v10(3), 411-429.
Clark, Jeffrey A. "Estimation Of Economies Of Scale In Banking Using A Generalized Functional Form," **JMCB**, 1984, v16(1), 53-68.
Clark, John D. "Can Government Influence Business Stability?," **JOF**, 1947, v2(1), 65-75.
Clark, John D. "Gaps In The Patman Committee Report," **JOF**, 1953, v8(2), 206-211.
Clark, John J. and Brenton W. Harries. "Some Recent Trends In Municipal And Corporate Securities Markets: An Interview With Brenton W. Harries, President Of Standard & Poor's Corporation," **FM**, 1976, v5(1),9-17.
Clark, John J. "The Mobil Corporation: Perspectives By William P. Tavoulareas," **FM**, 1980, v9(3), 7-14.
Clark, John J. (Elgers, Pieter T. and John J. Clark. "Merger Types And Shareholder Returns: Additional Evidence," **FM**, 1980, v9(2),66-72.)
Clark, John N., Jr. "Common Stock Price Fluctuations," **FAJ**, 1964, v20(3), 71-74.
Clark, John N., Jr. "The Adjustment Of Life Insurance Company Earnings," **FAJ**, 1966, v22(5), 71-73.
Clark, Peter K. "Capital Formation And The Recent Productivity Slowdown," **JOF**, 1978, v33(3),965-975.
Clark, Robert A., Joan M. Jantorni and Robert R. Gann. "Analysis Of The Lease-Or-Buy Decision: Comment," **JOF**, 1973, v28(4), 1015-1016.
Clark, Robert D. "Business Education: Agent For Social Change," **JRI**, 1970, v37(1), 1-8.
Clark, Robert L. "The Energy Industry In The World Of Tomorrow," **FAJ**, 1966, v22(5), 59-66.
Clark, Robert L. "The Impact Of Zero Population Growth On The OASDHI Program: Further Comment," **JRI**, 1976, v43(2), 322-324.
Clark, Robert L. and Ann Archibald McDermed. "Inflation, Pension Benefits, And Retirement," **JRI**, 1982, v49(1), 19-38.
Clark, Russell D., III. "Risk Taking In Groups: A Social Psychological Analysis," **JRI**, 1974, v41(1), 75-92.
Clark, Simon J. "The Effects Of Government Expenditure On The Term Structure Of Interest Rates: A Comment," **JMCB**, 1985, v17(3), 397-400.
Clark, Truman A. and Mark I. Weinstein. "The Behavior Of The Common Stock Of Bankrupt Firms," **JOF**, 1983, v38(2), 489-504.
Clarke, Darral G. "A Simulation Of Alternative Pricing Strategies For Dynamic Environments," **JOB**, 1984, v57(1), Part 2, S179-S200.
Clarke, F. L. "Replacement Costs And Inflation Accounting: A Demurrer," **FAJ**, 1981, v37(1), 71-75.
Clarke, Frank H., Masako N. Darrough and John Heineke. "Optimal Pricing Policy In The Presence Of Experience Effects," **JOB**, 1982, v55(4), 517-530.
Clarke, Frank. (Walsh, Paul, Russell Craig and Frank Clarke. "'Big Bath Accounting' Using Extraordinary Items Adjustments: Australian Empirical Evidence," **JBFA**, 1991, v18(2), 173-190.)
Clarke, Richard N. "SICs As Delineators Of Economic Markets," **JOB**, 1989, v62(1), 17-32.
Clarke, Robert L. "Selections From The Senate And House Hearings On LBOs And Corporate Debt," **JACF**, 1989, v2(1), 58-63.
Clarke, Roger G. "The Effect Of Fuel Adjustment Clauses On The Systematic Risk And Market Values Of Electric Utilities," **JOF**, 1980, v35(2), 347-358.
Clarke, Roger G. "The Impact Of A Fuel Adjustment Clause On The Regulated Firms's Value And Cost Of Capital," **JFQA**, 1978, v13(4), 745-757.
Clarke, Roger G. and Robert D. Arnott. "The Cost Of Portfolio Insurance: Tradeoffs And Choices," **FAJ**, 1987, v43(6), 35-47.
Clarke, Roger G., Michael T. FitzGerald, Phillip Berent and Meir Statman. "Market Timing With Imperfect Information," **FAJ**, 1989, v45(6), 27-36.
Clarke, Roger G., Michael T. Fitzgerald, Philip Berent and Meir Statman. "Diversifying Among Asset Allocators," **JPM**, 1990, v16(3), 9-14.
Clarke, Roger G., Michael T. Fitzgerald, Philip Berent and Meir Statman. "Required Accuracy For Successful Asset Allocation," **JPM**, 1990, v17(1), 12-19.
Clarke, Roger. (Bookstaber, Richard and Roger Clarke. "Options Can Alter Portfolio Return Distributions," **JPM**, 1981, v7(3), 63-70.)
Clarke, Roger. (Bookstaber, Richard and Roger Clarke. "Problems In Evaluating The Performance Of Portfolios With Options," **FAJ**, 1985, v41(1), 48-62.)
Clarke, Roger. (Bookstaber, Richard and Roger Clarke. "Option Portfolio Strategies: Measurement And Evaluation," **JOB**, 1984, v57(4), 469-492.)
Clarkson, Geoffrey P. and Allan H. Meltzer. "Portfolio Selection: A Heuristic Approach," **JOF**, 1960, v15(4), 465-480.
Clarkson, Peter M. and Rex Thompson. "Empirical Estimates Of Beta When Investors Face Estimation Risk," **JOF**, 1990, v45(2), 431-454.
Classens, Stijn. "Balance-Of-Payments Crises In A Perfect Foresight Optimizing Model," **JIMF**, 1988, v7(4), 363-372.
Clauretie, Terrance M. "Regional Economic Diversification And Residential Mortgage Default Risk," **JRER**, 1988, v3(1), 87-97.
Clauretie, Terrence M. "A Note On The Bias In House Price Capitalization Models," **AREUEA**, 1983, v11(4), 521-524.
Clauretie, Terrence M. "A Note On Mortgage Risk: Default Vs. Loss Rates," **AREUEA**, 1990, v18(2), 202-206.
Clauretie, Terrence M. "Interest Rates, The Business Demand For Funds, And The Residential Mortgage Market: A Sectoral Econometric Study," **JOF**, 1973, v28(5), 1313-1326.
Clauretie, Terrence M. "Resolution Of Incentive Conflicts In The Mortgage Industry: Comment," **JREFEC**, 1989, v2(1), 71-72.
Clauretie, Terrence M. "The Impact Of Interstate Foreclosure Cost Differences And The Value Of Mortgages On Default Rates," **AREUEA**, 1987, v15(3), 152-167.
Clauretie, Terrence M. "Why Do GNMAs Yield More Than Treasuries?," **JPM**, 1982, v8(3), 72-74.
Clauretie, Terrence M. (Wansley, James W. and Terrence M. Clauretie. "The Impact Of CreditWatch Placement On Equity Returns And Bond Prices," **JFR**, 1985, v8(1), 31-42.)
Clauretie, Terrence M. and Melvin W. Harju. "The Expanding Concept Of Just Compensation And The Role Of The Appraiser," **AREUEA**, 1986, v14(2), 338-360.
Clauretie, Terrence M. and Mel Jameson. "Interest Rates And The Foreclosure Process: An Agency Problem In FHA Mortgage Insurance," **JRI**, 1990, v57(4), 701-711.
Clauretie, Terrence M. and Thomas Herzog. "The Effect Of State Foreclosure Laws On Loan Losses: Evidence From The Mortgage Insurance Industry," **JMCB**, 1990, v22(2), 221-233.
Clauretie, Terrence M., Mel Jameson and Ronald C. Rogers. "A Note On Refinancing Costs, Prepayment Assumptions, And The Value Of Mortgage-Backed Securities," **JREFEC**, 1990, v3(3), 295-300.
Clauretie, Terrence. M. "State Foreclosure Laws, Risk Shifting, And The Private Mortgage Insurance Industry," **JRI**, 1989, v56(3), 544-554.
Clay, John. (Kenyon, David and John Clay. "Analysis Of Profit Margin Hedging Strategies For Hog Producers," **JFM**, 1987, v7(2), 183-202.)
Clayman, Charles F. and Alan K. Severn. "The Effect Of Random Disturbances In Float On The Federal Funds Rate," **JBR**, 1979-80, v10(1), 58-60.
Clayman, Michelle. "In Search Of Excellence: The Investor's Viewpoint," **FAJ**, 1987, v43(3), 54-63.
Clayton, Ronnie J. and Frank J. Navratil. "The Management Of Interest Rate Risk: Comment," **JPM**, 1985, v11(4), 64-66
Clayton, Ronnie J. and William Beranek. "Disassociations And Legal Combinations," **FM**, 1985, v14(2), 24-28.
Clayton, Ronnie J. (Chew, I. Keong and Ronnie J. Clayton. "Bond Valuation: A Clarification," **FR**, 1983, v18(2), 234-236.)
Clayton, Ronnie, John Delozier and Michael C. Ehrhardt. "A Note On January Returns In The U.S. Government Bond Market: The Term Effect," **JFSR**, 1989, v2(4), 307-318.
Clayton, Ronnie. (Beranek, William and Ronnie Clayton. "Risk Differences And Financial Reporting," **JFR**, 1985, v8(4), 327-334.)
Cleaver, James S. "Bank Bonanza In Dallas," **FAJ**, 1954, v10(5), 53-54.
Cleaver, James S. "Some Aspects Of The Oil Industry Today," **FAJ**, 1953, v9(4), 39-40.
Clements, Kenneth W. and Lester W. Johnson. "The Demand For Beer, Wine, And Spirits: A Systemwide Analysis," **JOB**, 1983, v56(3), 273-304.
Clemmer, Richard B. and John C. Simonson. "Trends In Substandard Housing 1940-1980," **AREUEA**, 1982, v10(4), 442-464.
Clemmer, Richard B. and John C. Weicher. "The Individual Housing Account," **AREUEA**, 1983, v11(2), 221-236.
Clendenin, John C. and Maurice Van Cleave. "Growth And Common Stock Values," **JOF**, 1954, v9(4), 365-376.
Clendenin, John C. "Price-Level Variations And The Tenets Of High-Grade Investment," **JOF**, 1959, v14(2), 245-262.
Clendenin, John C. "Quality Versus Price As Factors Influencing Common Stock Price Fluctuations," **JOF**, 1951, v6(4), 398-405.
Clendenin, William D. (Waterman, Robert H., Jr. and William D. Clendenin. "Problem Solving For Commercial Banks," **JBR**, 1970-71, v1(2), 60-62.)
Cleveland, Harold Van B. "The Status Of Self Insured Employee-Benefit Plans Under The Insurance Laws," **JRI**, 1960, v27(2), 1-16.
Cleveland, William P. (Pierce, David A., Darrel W. Parke, William P. Cleveland and Agustin Maravall. "Uncertainty In The Monetary

Aggregates: Sources, Measurement And Policy Effects," JOF, 1981, v36(2), 507-515.)

Cleverley, Graham. (Bello, Olaseni A. and Graham Cleverley. "Capital Growth-Sharing Schemes And The Value Of The Firm," JBFA, 1980, v7(1), 19-38.)

Clickner, Edwin K. "Risk Management Principles Applied To Mortgage Lending," JRI, 1967, v34(3), 451-458.

Clifton, Eric V. "The Currency Futures Market And Interbank Foreign Exchange Trading," JFM, 1985, v5(3), 375-384.

Clifton, Eric V. "The Effects Of Increased Interest-Rate Volatility On LDCs," JIMF, 1983, v2(1),67-74.

Climo, T. A. "Cash Flow Statements For Investors," JBFA, 1976, v3(3), 3-16.

Climo, Tom. "Bourn On Borrowing Gains: A Short Comment On Losses To Lenders," JBFA, 1976, v3(3), 147-148.

Clinch, J. Houstoun M., Jr. "Liquidity Imbalances: Profits & Penalties," JBR, 1975-76, v6(3), 186-189.

Cline, Robert S. "Should There Be An Undergraduate Insurance Program?," JRI, 1972, v39(2), 275-279.

Clinton, Kevin. "Interest Rate Expectations And The Demand For Money In Canada: Comment," JOF, 1973, v28(1), 207-212.

Cloninger, Dale O. "Arson And Abandonment: A Restatement," JRI, 1990, v57(3), 540-545.)

Cloninger, Dale O. "Risk, Arson And Abandonment," JRI, 1981, v48(3), 494-504.

Cloninger, Dale O. (Skantz, Terrance R., Dale O. Cloninger and Thomas H. Strickland. "Price-Fixing And Shareholder Returns: An Empirical Study," FR, 1990, v25(1), 153-164.)

Cloos, George W. "How Good Are The National Bureau's Reference Dates?," JOB, 1963, v36(1), 14-32.

Cloos, George W. "More On Reference Dates And Leading Indicators," JOB, 1963, v36(3), 352-364.

Cloos, George W. "Pre-War Monetary Conditions," FAJ, 1966, v22(1), 26-32.

Close, Darwin B. "An Organization Behavior Approach To Risk Management," JRI, 1974, v41(3), 435-460.

Close, Darwin B. "Contract Design And Marketing Philosophies," JRI, 1972, v39(1), 125-129.

Close, Darwin B. "Property-Liability Underwriting Under The Continental Codes," JRI, 1970, v37(4), 621-626.

Close, Darwin B. "Teaching Principles Of Insurance And Risk By The Contract Method," JRI, 1974, v41(4), 719-725.

Close, Frank Alexander. "Commodities: High Finance In Cocoa," FAJ, 1959, v15(2), 75-82.

Close, Nicholas. "Price Effects Of Large Transactions," FAJ, 1975, v31(6), 50-57.

Clotfelter, Charles and Charles Lieberman. "On The Distributional Impact Of Federal Interest Rate Restrictions," JOF, 1978, v33(1), 199-213.

Clouse, Maclyn L. "A Simulation Model To Link The Economic Environment With Corporate Financial Decisions," JFED, 1979, v8, 94-96.

Clower, Robert W. "Is There An Optimal Money Supply?," JOF, 1970, v25(2), 425-433.

Clubb, C. D. B. and M. Walker. "On The Association Between General And Relative Price Movements In The CCA Price Indices," JBFA, 1986, v13(2), 197-208.

Clune, Daniel A. (Salzman, Jerrold E. and Daniel A. Clune. "Judicial Review Of CFTCs Invocation Of Emergency Powers," JFM, 1981, v1(Supp), 465-467.)

Clurman, David. "An Inquiry Into Trading In Levitz," FAJ, 1974, v30(2), 23-28.

Coates, J. H. and P. K. Woolley. "Corporate Gearing In The EEC," JBFA, 1975, v2(1), 1-18.

Coates, Robert and David E. Updegraff. "The Relationship Between Organizational Size And The Administrative Component Of Banks," JOB, 1973, v46(4), 576-588.

Coats, Pamela K. "A Testing Innovation For Large Enrollment Finance Courses," JFED, 1981, v10, 14-19.

Coats, Pamela K. "Why Expert Systems Fail," FM, 1988, v17(3), 77-86.

Coats, Pamela K. (Chesser, Delton L. and Pamela K. Coats. "A Computer-Based Instructional Tool For Capital Budgeting," JFED, 1978, v7, 88-89.)

Coats, Warren L., Jr. "Lagged Reserve Accounting And The Money Supply Mechanism," JMCB, 1976, v8(2), 167-180.

Coats, Warren L., Jr. "Regulation D And The Vault Cash Game," JOF, 1973, v28(3), 601-607.

Coats, Warren L., Jr. "The Weekend Eurodollar Game," JOF, 1981, v36(3), 649-659.

Coats, Warren L., Jr. "What Do Reserve Carry-Overs Mean For Bank Management And For Free Reserves," JBR, 1976-77, v7(2), 123-133.

Cobb, William E. (Brady, Dennis P., Michael L. Brookshire and William E. Cobb. "The Development And Solution Of A Tax-Adjusted Model For Personal Injury Awards," JRI, 1984, v51(1), 138-142.)

Cobb, William. (Brady, Dennis, Michael Brookshire and William Cobb. "The Development And Solution Of A Tax-Adjusted Model Of Personal Injury Awards: A Response," JRI, 1985, v52(3), 520-521.)

Cocheu, Lincoln C., Jr. "Association Insurance: Comment," JRI, 1962, v29(2), 265-268.

Cochran, Steven J. (Mansur, Iqbal, Steven J. Cochran and David K. Seagers. "The Relationship Between The Argentinean Debt Rescheduling Announcement And Bank Equity Returns," FR, 1990, v25(2), 321-334.)

Cochrane, John H. "Production-Based Asset Pricing And The Link Between Stock Returns And Economic Fluctuations," JOF, 1991, v46(1), 209-238.

Cockerell, H. A. L. "Insurance Education In Great Britain," JRI, 1957, v24(3), 78-85.

Cockerell, Hugh. "The History Of British And American Fire Marks: Comment," JRI, 1973, v40(4), 639-641.

Cocks, Douglas L. and John R. Virts. "Pricing Behavior Of The Ethical Pharmaceutical Industry," JOB, 1974, v47(3), 349-362.

Cocks, Neil. (Booth, Peter and Neil Cocks. "Critical Research Issues In Accounting Standard-Setting," JBFA, 1990, v17(4), 511-528.)

Coe, Robert K. and Irwin Weinstock. "Evaluating The Finance Journals: The Department Chairman's Perspective," JFR, 1983, v6(4), 345-349.

Coenenberg, A. and K. Macharzina. "Accounting For Price Changes: An Analysis Of Current Developments In Germany," JBFA, 1976, v3(1), 53-68.

Coffin, Lamar. "The Salesmanship Economy," FAJ, 1957, v13(5), 79-82.

Coffman, Richard. "Is Profit Maximization Vs. Value Maximization: Also Economics Vs. Finance?," JFED, 1983, v12, 37-40.

Cogan, J. A. "The Technological Progress And Petroleum Securities," FAJ, 1952, v8(2), 83-84.

Cogen, Jack. (Apsel, David, Jack Cogen and Michael Rabin. "Hedging Long Term Commodity Swaps With Futures," GFJ, 1989, v1(1), 77-93.)

Cogger, Kenneth O. and Gary W. Emery. "A Determination Of The Risk Of Ruin: Comment," JFQA, 1981, v16(5), 759-764.

Cogger, Kenneth O. (Meeker, Larry G., O. Maurice Joy and Kenneth O. Cogger. "Valuation Of Controlling Shares In Closely Held Banks," JBF, 1983, v7(2), 175-188.)

Coggin, T. Daniel and John E. Hunter. "Measuring Stability And Growth In Annual EPS," JPM, 1983, v9(2), 75-78.

Coggin, T. Daniel and John E. Hunter. "Problems In Measuring The Quality Of Investment Information: The Perils Of The Information Coefficient," FAJ, 1983, v39(3), 25-33.

Coggin, T. Daniel and John E. Hunter. "Are High-Beta, Large-Capitalization Stocks Overpriced?," FAJ, 1985, v41(6), 70-71.

Coggin, T. Daniel and John E. Hunter. "A Meta-Analysis Of Spicing 'Risk' Factors In APT," JPM, 1987, v14(1), 35-38.

Coggin, T. Daniel. (Hunter, John E. and T. Daniel Coggin. "An Analysis Of The Diversification Benefit From International Equity Investment," JPM, 1990, v17(1), 33-36.)

Coghlan, Richard T. "Analysis Within The 'New View'," JMCB, 1977, v9(3), 410-427.

Cogitator. "Hippocratic Methods Of Security Analysis," FAJ, 1946, v2(2), 47-50.

Cogitator. "On Being Right In Security Analysis," FAJ, 1946, v2(1), 18-21.

Cogitator. "The S.E.C. Method Of Security Analysis," FAJ, 1946, v2(3), 32-35.

Cohan, Avery B. "An Analytical Model Of Bond Risk Differentials: A Comment," JFQA, 1978, v13(2), 371-377.

Cohan, Avery B. "The Theory Of The Firm: A View On Methodology," JOB, 1963, v36(3), 316-324.

Cohan, Avery B. "Yields On New Underwritten Corporate Bonds, 1935-58," JOF, 1962, v17(4), 585-606.

Cohan, Richard E. (Heymann, Hans G. and Richard E. Cohan. "The Effect Of Financial Futures Trading On The Bid-Ask Spread Of Cash Market T-Bonds," RFM, 1984, v3(1), 48-57.)

Cohan, Sandra B. "The Determinants Of Supply And Demand For Certificates Of Deposit," JMCB, 1973, v5(1), 100-112.

Cohan, Sandra B. (Longbrake, William A. and Sandra B. Cohan. "The Now Account Experiment," JBR, 1974-75, v5(2), 71-85.)

Cohen, Alan H. (Goodman, Laurie S. and Alan H. Cohen. "Pay-In-Kind Debentures: An Innovation," JPM, 1989, v15(2), 9-16.)

Cohen, Ayala, Judith M. Schilling and Irma Terpenning. "Dealer-Issued Commercial Paper: Analysis Of Data," RIF, 1985, v5, 71-106.

Cohen, Benjamin J. "The Euro-Dollar, The Common Market, And Currency Unification," JOF, 1963, v18(4), 605-621.

Cohen, Bruce and Damodar Gujarati. "The Student's t Test In Multiple Regression Under Simple Collinearity," JFQA, 1970, v5(3), 341-351.

Cohen, Bruce C. and George G. Kaufman. "Factors Determining Bank Deposit Growth By State: An Empirical Analysis," JOF, 1965, v20(1), 59-70.

Cohen, Bruce C. "Economies Of Scale And Cash Balances," JBR, 1970-71, v1(2), 45-48.

Cohen, Bruce C. "Money Market Development And The Demand For Money," JFQA, 1971, v6(4), 1155-1157.

Cohen, Darrel and J. Stuart McMenamin. "The Role Of Fiscal Policy In A Financially Disaggregated Macroeconomic Model," JMCB, 1978, v10(3), 322-336.

Cohen, Darrel. "Money Demand And The Effects Of Fiscal Policies: Comment," JMCB, 1988, v20(4), 698-705.

Cohen, Edwin S. "Legal Implications Of Actuarial Soundness," JRI, 1953, v20, 59-62.

Cohen, Jacob and Asatoshi Maeshiro. "The Significance Of Money On the State Level," JMCB, 1977, v9(4), 672-678.

Cohen, Jacob and James N. Morgan. "The Effect Of Cash Buying And Credit Buying On Consumer Liquid Savings," JOF, 1962, v17(1), 110-120.

Cohen, Jacob. "Distributional Effects Of The Federal Debt," JOF, 1951, v6(3), 267-275.

Cohen, Jacob. "Federal Reserve Margin Requirements And The Stock Market," JFQA, 1966, v1(3), 30-54.

Cohen, Jacob. "Integrating The Real And Financial Via The Linkage Of Financial Flow," JOF, 1968, v23(1), 1-27.

Cohen, Jacob. "The Treatment Of The Means Of Payment In Social Accounting," JOF, 1957, v12(4),423-437.

Cohen, Jerome. "Fiscal Policy In Japan," JOF, 1950, v5(1), 110-125.

Cohen, K. J. (Carter, E. E. and K. J. Cohen. "Stock Averages, Stock Splits, And Bias," FAJ, 1967, v23(3), 77-81.)

Cohen, K. J., R. M. Cyert, W. R. Dill, A. A. Kuehn, M. H. Miller, T. A. VanWormer, and P. R. Winters. "The Carnegie Tech Management Game," JOB, 1960, v33(4), 303-321.

Cohen, Kalman J. and Chun H. Lam. "A Linear Programming Planning Model For Bank Holding Companies," JBR, 1979-80, v10(3), 152-164.

Cohen, Kalman J. and David P. Rutenberg. "Toward A Comprehensive Framework For Bank Financial Planning," JBR, 1970-71, v1(4), 41-57.

Cohen, Kalman J. and Frederick S. Hammer. "Linear Programming And Optimal Bank Asset Management Decisions," JOF, 1967, v22(2), 147-165.

Cohen, Kalman J. and Samuel Richardson Reid. "The Benefits And Costs Of Bank Mergers," JFQA, 1966, v1(4), 15-57.

Cohen, Kalman J. and Sten Thore. "Programming Bank Portfolios Under Uncertainty," JBR, 1970-71, v1(1), 43-61.

Cohen, Kalman J. "Dynamic Balance Sheet Management: A Management Science Approach," JBR, 1971-72, v2(4), 9-19.

Cohen, Kalman J. "Improving The Capital Adequacy Formula," JBR, 1970-71, v1(1), 13-16.

Cohen, Kalman J. "The Reform Of Banking Regulation: An Overview," JBR, 1983-84, v14(1), 3-7.

Cohen, Kalman J. (Carter, E. Eugene and Kalman J. Cohen. "Bias In The DJIA Caused By Stock Splits," FAJ, 1966, v22(6), 90-94.)

Cohen, Kalman J. and Jerry A. Pogue. "An Empirical Evaluation Of Alternative Portfolio Selection Models," JOB, 1967, v40(2), 166-193.

Cohen, Kalman J. and Jerry A. Pogue. "Some Comments Concerning Mutual Fund Versus Random Portfolio Performance," JOB, 1968, v41(2), 180-190.

Cohen, Kalman J. and Richard M. Cyert. "Strategy: Formulation, Implementation, and Monitoring," JOB, 1973, v46(3), 349-367.

Cohen, Kalman J., Gabriel A. Hawawini, Steven F. Maier, Robert Schwartz and David K. Whitcomb. "Implications Of Microstructure Theory For Empirical Research On Stock Price Behavior," JOF, 1980, v35(2), 249-257.

Cohen, Kalman J., Gabriel A. Hawawini, Steven F. Maier, Robert A. Schwartz and David K. Whitcomb. "Friction In The Trading Process And The Estimation Of Systematic Risk," JFEC, 1983, v12(2), 263-278.

Cohen, Kalman J., Stephen F. Maier, Robert A. Schwartz and David K. Whitcomb. "Market Makers And The Market Spread: A Review Of Recent Literature," JFQA, 1979, v14(4), 813-835.

Cohen, Kalman J., Steven F. Maier, Robert A. Schwartz and David K. Whitcomb. "An Analysis Of The Economic Justification For Consolidation In A Secondary Security Market," JBF, 1982, v6(1), 117-136.

Cohen, Kalman J., Steven F. Maier, Walter L. Ness, Jr., Hitoshi Okuda, Robert A. Schwartz and David K. Whitcomb. "The Impact Of Designated Market Makers On Security Prices," JBF, 1977, v1(3), 219-247.

Cohen, Kalman J., Steven F. Maier, Robert A. Schwartz and David K. Whitcomb. "The Returns Generating Process, Returns Variance, And The Effect Of Thinness In Securities Markets," JOF, 1978, v33(1), 149-167.

Cohen, Kalman J., Steven F. Maier, Robert A. Schwartz and David K. Whitcomb. "Limit Orders, Market Structure, And The Returns Generation Process," JOF, 1978, v33(3), 723-736.

Cohen, Kalman J., Walter L. Ness, Jr., Hitoshi Okuda, Robert A. Schwartz and David K. Whitcomb. "The Determinants Of Common Stock Returns Volatility: An International Comparison," JOF, 1976, v31(2), 733-739.

Cohen, Manuel F. "The SEC And The Press," FAJ, 1968, v24(4), 21-24.

Cohen, Wilbur J. "Health Insurance And The Government," JRI, 1962, v29(1), 7-18.

Cohen, Wilbur J. "The Challenge Of Aging To Insurance," JRI, 1960, v27(4), 15-18.

Cohen, Wilbur J. "The Challenge Of Aging To Insurance: Reply," JRI, 1961, v28(3), 98-101.

Cohn, Richard A. and Donald R. Lessard. "The Effect Of Inflation On Stock Prices: International Evidence," JOF, 1981, v36(2), 277-289.

Cohn, Richard A. and Donald R. Lessard. "Recent Research On Indexation And The Housing Market," JOF, 1976, v31(2), 403-413.

Cohn, Richard A. and John J. Pringle. "Imperfections In International Financial Markets: Implications For Risk Premia And The Cost Of Capital To Firms," JOF, 1973, v28(1), 59-66.

Cohn, Richard A. "Capital Market Equilibrium With Restricted Borrowing," JOB, 1972, v45(3), 444-455.

Cohn, Richard A. "Mutual Life Insurer's Portfolio And Policyholder Utility Functions," JRI, 1974, v41(3), 407-414.

Cohn, Richard A. (Modigliani, Franco and Richard A. Cohn. "Inflation And The Stock Market," FAJ, 1979, v35(2), 24-44.)

Cohn, Richard A. (Monroe, Margaret A. and Richard A. Cohn. "The Relative Efficiency Of The Gold And Treasury Bill Futures Markets," JFM, 1986, v6(3),477-494.)

Cohn, Richard A. (Robichek, Alexander A., Richard A. Cohn and John J. Pringle. "Returns On Alternative Investment Media And Implications For Portfolio Construction," JOB, 1975, v45(3), 427-443.)

Cohn, Richard A. (Robichek, Alexander A. and Richard A. Cohn. "The Economic Determinants Of Systematic Risk," JOF, 1974, v29(2), 439-447.)

Cohn, Richard A., Wilbur G. Lewellen, Ronald C. Lease and Gary G. Schlarbaum. "Individual Investor Risk Aversion And Investment Portfolio Composition," JOF, 1975, v30(2), 605-620.

Cohn, Richard. (Malitz, Ileen and Richard Cohn. "The Nonequivalence Of Subordinated Debt And Equity From The Senior Creditor's Standpoint: A Pedagogical Note," JFED, 1987, v16, 1-5.)

Colantoni, Claude S. (Comiskey, Eugene E. and Claude S. Colantoni. "Finance Company Earnings," FAJ, 1969, v25(2), 55-59.)

Colberg, Marshall R. (Franklin, Charles B. and Marshall R. Colberg. "Puts And Calls: A Factual Survey," JOF, 1958, v13(1), 21-34.)

Colberg, Marshall R. (Franklin, Charles B. And Marshall R. Colberg. "Puts And Calls: A Factual Survey," JOF, 1959, v14(1), 71-74.)

Cole, Charles W. and James A. Millar. "The Impact Of Municipal Bond Banking On Municipal Interest Costs," FM, 1982, v11(1), 70-76.

Cole, Charles W. and Dennis T. Officer. "The Interest Cost Effect Of Private Municipal Bond Insurance," JRI, 1981, v48(3), 435-449.

Cole, David W. and Wilbur A. Rapp. "University Courses In Commercial Banking And Other Financial Institutions," FR, 1970, v1(5), 348-358.

Cole, James F. "Investing In Canada," FAJ, 1967, v23(2), 153-156.

Cole, James F. "What About The Anatomy Of The Stock?," FAJ, 1977, v33(6), 63-64.

Cole, John A. "Are Dividend Surprises Independently Important?," JPM, 1984, v10(4), 45-50.

Cole, Rebel. (Guilkey, David, Mike Miles and Rebel Cole. "The Motivation For Institutional Real Estate Sales And Implications For Asset Class Returns," AREUEA, 1989, v17(1), 70-86.)

Cole, Rebel. (Miles, Mike, Rebel Cole and David Guikey. "A Different Look At Commercial Real Estate Returns," AREUEA, 1990, v18(4), 403-430.)

Cole, W. D. "Federal Aid For Education And The Book Publishers," FAJ, 1966, v22(5), 53-56.

Colean, Miles L. "A Review Of Federal Mortgage Lending And Insuring Practices," JOF, 1953, v8(2),249-256.

Colean, Miles L. "Civic And Community Construction For The Next Ten Years," JOF, 1960, v15(2), 274-278.

Colean, Miles L. "Prospects For The Mortgage Market In 1962," JOF, 1962, v17(2), 237-239.

Coleman, David. "Rent Control: The British Experience And Policy Response," JREFEC, 1988, v1(3), 233-256.

Coleman, James S. "Psychological Structure And Social Structure In Economic Models," JOB, 1986, v59(4), Part 2, S365-S370.

Coleman, Thomas C. "Panel: Trading Halts And Price Limits," RFM, 1988, v7(3), 435-439.

Coleman, Thomas C. and Roger D. Rutz. "Self-Regulation And Government Regulation Of Futures And Options Markets: Introduction," JOB, 1986, v59(2), Part 2, S1-S4.

Colenutt, D. W. "Determinants Of Expense Ratios In United Kingdom Life Assurers," JRI, 1977, v44(1), 77-86.

Colenutt, Dennis. "The Regulation Of Insurance Intermediaries In The United Kingdom," JRI, 1979, v46(2), 77-86.

Coles, Jeffrey L. (Bhagat, Sanjai, James A. Brickley and Jeffrey L. Coles. "Managerial Indemnification And Liability Insurance: The Effect On Sharholder Wealth," JRI, 1987, v54(4), 721-736.)

Coles, Jeffrey L. and Uri Loewenstein. "Equilibrium Pricing And Portfolio Composition In The Presence Of Uncertain Parameters," JFEC, 1988, v22(2), 279-304.

Coley, Stephen C. (Honig, Lawrence E. and Stephen C. Coley. "An After-Tax Equivalent Payment Approach To Conventional Lease Analysis," FM, 1974, v4(4), 28-36.)

Colhoun, Howard P. "The New FAF Investment Workshop," FAJ, 1978, v34(2), 41-42.

Colin, J. W. and Edward A. Dyl. "Calculation Of Tax Effective Yields: A Correction," JFQA, 1971, v6(4), 1163-1164.

Colin, J. W. and Richard J. Bayer. "Calculation Of Tax Effective Yields For Discount Instruments," JFQA, 1970, v5(2), 265-273.

Collery, Arnold P. "A Graphic Analysis Of The Theory Of The Determination Of The Money Supply," JOF, 1956, v11(3), 328-331.

Collery, Arnold. "On Money, Wealth, And Economic Theory: A Review Article," JOF, 1967, v22(4), 684-692.

Collier, James A. "Mergers And The Special Dividend," JRI, 1965, v32(2), 255-266.

Collier, James A. "Structuring The Beginning Insurance Course," JRI, 1967, v34(1), 131-134.

Collier, James R. "Management Business Planning," FAJ, 1967, v23(5), 33-38.

Collins, Brett, John Rickard and Michael Selby. "Discounting Of Deferred Tax Liabilities," JBFA, 1990, v17(5), 757-758.

Collins, Bruce M. and Frank J. Fabozzi. "Considerations In Selecting A Small-Capitalization Benchmark," FAJ, 1990, v46(1), 40-46

Collins, Charles J. "An Inquiry Into The Effect Of Sunspot Activity On The Stock Market," FAJ, 1965, v21(6), 45-56.

Collins, Charles J. "No More Depressions," FAJ, 1954, v10(5), 37-42.

Collins, Charles J. "Stock Market Decline Ended?," FAJ, 1958, v14(1), 33-36.

Collins, Charles J. "The Dow-Jones Industrial Average," FAJ, 1961, v17(5), 7-10.

Collins, Charles J. "Why Be Optimistic?," FAJ, 1953, v9(4), 27-30.

Collins, D. W. "SEC Product-Line Reporting And Market Efficiency," JFEC, 1975, v2(2), 125-164.

Collins, Daniel W. (DeJong, Douglas V. and Daniel W. Collins. "Explanations For The Instability Of Equity Beta: Risk-Free Rate Changes and Leverage Effects," JFQA, v20(1), 73-94.)

Collins, Daniel W., Warren T. Dent and Melvin C. O'Conner. "Has Full Cost Accounting Helped Share Prices?," FAJ, 1978, v34(6), 48-57.

Collins, Daniel W., Johannes Ledolter and Judy Rayburn. "Some Further Evidence On The Stochastic Properties Of Systematic Risk," JOB, 1987, v60(3), 425-448.

Collins, Dennis. (Capettini, Robert and Dennis Collins. "The Investigation Of Deviations From Standard Costs In The Presence Of Unequal State Variances," JBFA, 1978, v5(4), 335-352.)

Collins, J. A. "British And American Prices During The Next 40 Years," FAJ, 1961, v17(1), 55-58.

Collins, J. Markham and Roger P. Bey. "The Master Limited Partnership: An Alternative To The Corporation," FM, 1986, v15(4), 5-14.

Collins, J. Markham and William S. Sekely. "The Relationship Of Headquarters Country And Industry Classification To Financial Structure," FM, 1983, v12(3), 45-51.

Collins, J. Markham. (Bey, Roger P. and J. Markham Collins. "The Relationship Between Before- And After-Tax Yields On Financial Assets," FR, 1988, v23(3), 313-332.)

Collins, J. Markham. (Claiborn, Stephen A. and J. Markham Collins. "The Entering Job Market For Careers In Finance," JFED, 1978, v7, 25-29.)

Collins, John. "How To Study The Behavior Of Bank Stocks," FAJ, 1957, v13(2), 109-114.

Collins, Robert A. "An Empirical Comparison Of Bankruptcy Prediction Models," FM, 1980, v9(2), 52-57.

Collins, Robert A. (Nelson, Ray D. and Robert A. Collins. "A Measure Of Hedging's Performance," JFM, 1985, v5(1), 45-55.)

Collyer, John. "Rubber Manufacturing - A Growth Industry," FAJ, 1953, v9(4), 23-26.

Colm, Gerhard. "National Goals And The American Economy," FAJ, 1964, v20(6), 25-30.

Colodney, Bernard. "Commodities: High Finance In Sugar," FAJ, 1959, v15(4), 59-66.

Colodney, Bernard. "Commodities: High Finance In Coffee," FAJ, 1959, v15(5), 69-80.

Colombo, Massimo G. (Brioschi, Francesco, Luigi Buzzacchi and Massimo G. Colombo. "Risk Capital Financing And The Separation Of Ownership And Control In Business Groups," JBF, 1989, v13(4/5), 747-772.)

Colton, Kent W. "Financial Reform: A Review Of The Past And Prospects For The Future," AREUEA, 1980, v8(1), 91-117.

Colton, Kent W. "The Report Of The President's Commission On Housing: The Nation's System Of Housing Finance," AREUEA, 1983, v11(2), 133-165.

Colton, Kent W., Donald R. Lessard and Arthur P. Solomon. "Borrower Attitudes Toward Alternative Mortgage Instruments," AREUEA, 1979, v7(4), 581-609.

Colwell, Peter F. "Power Lines And Land Value," JRER, 1990, v5(1), 117-127.

Colwell, Peter F. (Brennan, Thomas P., Roger E. Cannady and Peter F. Colwell. "Office Rent In The Chicago CBD," AREUEA, 1984, v12(3), 243-260.)

Colwell, Peter F. (Cannaday, Roger E. and Peter F. Colwell. "Real Estate Valuation Models: Lender And Equity Investor Criteria," AREUEA, 1986, v14(2), 316-337.)

Colwell, Peter F. (Cannaday, Roger E. and Peter F. Colwell. "Optimization Of Subdivision Development," JREFEC, 1990, v3(2), 195-206.)

Colwell, Peter F. (Kowalski, Joseph G. and Peter F. Colwell. "Market Versus Assessed Values Of Industrial Land," AREUEA, 1986, v14(2), 361-373.)

Colwell, Peter F. (Sunderman, Mark A., Roger E. Cannaday and Peter F. Colwell. "The Value Of Mortgage Assumptions: An Empirical Test," JRER, 1990, v5(2), 247-257.)

Colwell, Peter F. (Wu, Chunchi and Peter F. Colwell. "Equilibrium Of Housing And Real Estate Brokerage Markets Under Uncertainty," AREUEA, 1986, v14(1), 1-23.)

Colwell, Peter F. (Wu, Chunchi and Peter F. Colwell. "Moral Hazard And Moral Imperative," JRI, 1988, v55(1), 101-117.)

Colwell, Peter F. (Wu, Chunchi and Peter F. Colwell. "Moral Hazard And Moral Imperative: Reply," JRI, 1990, v57(2), 332-335.)

Colwell, Peter F. and David W. Marshall. "Market Share In The Real Estate Brokerage Industry," AREUEA, 1986, v14(4), 583-599.

Colwell, Peter F. and Hun Y. Park. "Seasonality And Size Effects: The Case Of Real-Estate-Related Investment," JREFEC, 1990, v3(3), 251-260.

Colwell, Peter F., Karl L. Guntermann and C. F. Sirmans. "Discount Points And Housing Prices: Comment," JOF, 1979, v34(4), 1049-1054.

Colwell, Peter F., Roger E. Cannaday and Chunchi Wu. "The Analytical Foundations Of Adjustment Grid Methods," AREUEA, 1983, v11(1), 11-29.

Comanor, William S. "The Drug Industry And Medical Research: The Economics Of The Kefauver Committee Investigations," JOB, 1966, v39(1) Part I, 12-18.

Combs, Barbara. (Slovic, Paul, Baruch Fischhoff, Sarah Lichtenstein, Bernard Corrigan and Barbara Combs. "Preference For Insuring Against Probable Small Losses: Insurance Implications," JRI, 1977, v44(2), 237-258.)

Comer, Harry D. "High Prices Hidden By Stock Splits," FAJ, 1958, v14(1), 79-80.

Comer, Harry D. "Is The 'Dow' Already Above 1200?," FAJ, 1964, v20(3), 69-70.

Comer, Harry D. "Low Priced Versus High Priced Stocks," FAJ, 1945, v1(2), 15-20.

Comeskey, James R. "Investing By Corporate Trustees," FAJ, 1966, v22(1), 77-79.

Comiskey, Eugene E. and Claude S. Colantoni. "Finance Company Earnings," FAJ, 1969, v25(2), 55-59.

Comiskey, Eugene E. and James R. Hasselback. "Analyzing The Profit-Tax Relationship," FM, 1973, v2(4), 57-62.

Comiskey, Eugene E. and Monojit Ghosal. "Tax Analysis Of The Operating Loss Company," FAJ, 1984, v40(6), 56-61.

Comiskey, Eugene E. "Depreciation And Comparability," FAJ, 1969, v25(1), 78-80.

Comiskey, Eugene E. (Barefield, Russell M. and Eugene E. Comiskey. "The Association Of Forecast Error With Other Risk Measures," JBFA, 1975, v2(3), 315-326.)

Comiskey, Eugene E. (Barefield, Russell M. and Eugene E. Comiskey. "The Differential Association Of Forecast Error And Earnings Variability With Systematic Risk," JBFA, 1979, v6(1), 1-8.)

Comiskey, Eugene E., Charles W. Mulford and Thomas L. Porter. "Forecast Error, Earnings Variability And Systematic Risk: Additional Evidence," JBFA, 1986, v13(2), 257-265.

Comiskey, Eugene E., Ralph A. Walkling and Michael A. Weeks. "Dispersion Of Expectations And Trading Volume," JBFA, 1987, v14(2), 229-240.

Comiskey, Eugene E., Ruth Ann McEwen and Charles W. Mulford. "A Test Of Pro Forma Consolidation Of Finance Subsidiaries," FM, 1987, v16(3), 45-50.

Comment, Robert and Gregg A. Jarrell. "Two-Tier And Negotiated Tender Offers: The Imprisonment Of The Free-Riding Shareholder," JFEC, 1987, v19(2), 283-310.

Comrie, Allan. "Property And Casualty Company Portfolios," FAJ, 1965, v21(4), 95-97.

Conant, Lawrence W. "Tomorrow's Investment Information Tonight," FAJ, 1961, v17(2), 31-35.

Conant, Michael. "Competition In The Farm-Machinery Industry," JOB, 1953, v26(1), 26-36.

Conatser, R. Gene. "Decision Making Under Full Employment," FAJ, 1967, v23(3), 15-17.

Condon, Kathleen A. "Measuring Equity Transaction Costs," FAJ, 1981, v37(5), 57-60.

Condoyanni, L., J. O'Hanlon and C.W.R. Ward. "Day Of The Week Effects On Stock Returns: International Evidence," JBFA, 1987, v14(1), 159-174.

Conine, Thomas E. and Maurry J. Tamarkin. "On Diversification Given Asymmetry In Returns," JOF, 1981, v36(5), 1143-1155.

Conine, Thomas E., Jr. and Maurry Tamarkin. "Divisional Cost Of Capital Estimation: Adjusting For Leverage," FM, 1985, v14(1), 54-58.

Conine, Thomas E., Jr. and Maurry Tamarkin. "A Pedagogic Note On The Derivation Of The Comparative Statics Of The Option Pricing Model," FR, 1984, v19(4), 397-400.

Conine, Thomas E., Jr. and Maurry Tamarkin. "Implications Of Skewness In Returns For Utilities' Cost Of Equity Capital," FM, 1985, v14(4), 66-71.

Conine, Thomas E., Jr. and Maurry Tamarkin. "On Diversification Given Asymmetry In Returns: Erratum," JOF, 1982, v37(4), 1101-1101.

Conine, Thomas E., Jr. "A Note On The Theoretical Irrelevance Of FASB 94 On Equity Systematic Risk," JBFA, 1990, v17(4), 575-578.

Conine, Thomas E., Jr. "A Pedagogical Note On Cash Break-Even Analysis," JBFA, 1987, v14(3), 437-441.

Conine, Thomas E., Jr. "Corporate Debt And Corporate Taxes: An Extension," JOF, 1980, v35(4), 1033-1037.

Conine, Thomas E., Jr. "Debt Capacity And The Capital Budgeting Decision: Comment," FM, 1980, v9(1), 20-22.

Conine, Thomas E., Jr. "On The Theoretical Relationship Between Business Risk And Systematic Risk," JBFA, 1982, v8(2), 199-206.

Conine, Thomas E., Jr. "On The Theoretical Relationship Between Systematic Risk And Price Elasticity Of Demand," JBFA, 1983, v10(2), 173-182.

Conine, Thomas E., Jr. (Baxter, Jennefer, Thomas E. Conine, Jr. and Maurry Tamarkin. "On Commodity Market Risk Premiums: Additional Evidence," JFM, 1985, v5(1), 121-125.)

Conine, Thomas E., Jr. and Maurry Tamarkin. "Textbook Inconsistencies In Graphing Valuation Equations: A Further Note," FR, 1988, v23(2), 237-241.

Conine, Thomas E., Jr., Oscar W. Jensen and Maurry Tamarkin. "On Optimal Output In An Option Pricing Framework," JBFA, 1988, v15(1), 21-26.

Conklin, G. Howard. "A Sleeping Giant Awakes," FAJ, 1965, v21(2), 59-64.

Conklin, G. Howard. "Airlines: A Bright Future," FAJ, 1962, v18(1), 9-14.

Conklin, G. Howard. "Cigarette Stocks - Current Confusion Hides Profit Potential," FAJ, 1963, v19(3), 29-30.

Conklin, G. Howard. "Evaluation Of Savings And Loans," FAJ, 1967, v23(4), 39-42.

Conklin, G. Howard. "Growth Stocks - A Critical View," FAJ, 1958, v14(1), 49-52.

Conklin, G. Howard. "Is Steel A Growth Industry?" FAJ, 1959, v15(2), 15-18.

Conklin, G. Howard. "Oil Well Drilling - A Security Analyst's Approach," FAJ, 1955, v11(5), 25-28.

Conklin, G. Howard. "Profit Potentials In Atomic Energy," FAJ, 1954, v10(4), 13-16.

Conklin, G. Howard. "Steel As A Growth Industry," FAJ, 1956, v12(4), 13-16.

Conklin, G. Howard. "The Airline Industry," FAJ, 1971, v27(1), 40-43.

Conklin, George T., Jr. "Corporate Bond Market," JOF, 1961, v16(2), 265-271.

Conklin, George T., Jr. "Direct Placements," JOF, 1951, v6(2), 85-118.

Conklin, George T., Jr. "The Money And Capital Markets (Keynote Review)," FAJ, 1966, v22(6), 103-105.

Conklin, George T., Jr. "The Bond Market, 1962 And 1963," JOF, 1963, v18(2), 417-422.

Conklin, George T., Jr. "The Outlook For The Corporate Bond Market," JOF, 1962, v17(2), 234-236.

Conklin, George T., Jr. "Treasury Financial Policy From The Institutional Point Of View," JOF, 1953, v8(2), 226-234.

Conklin, Neilson C. "Grain Exports, Futures Markets, And Pricing Efficiency," RFM, 1983, v2(1), 1-25.

Conley, Howard H. "Factors Influencing The Training Of Life Insurance Salesmen," JRI, 1960, v27(4), 109-112.

Conley, Ronald W. "A Note On The Liquidity And Stabilization Effects Of Savings Deposits," JFQA, 1968, v3(2), 205-213.

Conlon, Edwin J. and Marya L. Leatherwood. "Sunk Costs And Financial Decision Making: Integration And Implications," AFPAF, 1989, v3(1), 37-62.

Conn, Mabel V. and Robert W. Storer. "Stock Market Leading Indicators," FAJ, 1961, v17(5), 61-64.

Conn, R. L. and F. Connell. "International Mergers: Returns To US And British Firms," JBFA, 1990, v17(5), 689-712.

Conn, Robert L. and James F. Nielsen. "An Empirical Test Of The Larson-Gonedes Exchange Ratio Determination Model," JOF, 1977, v32(3), 749-759.

Conn, Robert L. "Performance Of Conglomerate Firms: Comment," JOF, 1973, v28(3), 754-758.

Conn, Robert L. (Lahey, Karen E. and Robert L. Conn. "Sensitivity Of Acquiring Firms' Returns To Alternative Model Specifications And Disaggregation," JBFA, 1990, v17(3), 421-440.)

Connell, F. (Conn, R. L. and F. Connell. "International Mergers: Returns To US And British Firms," JBFA, 1990, v17(5), 689-712.)

Conners, Donald. "Fresh Look At The Electric Utilities," FAJ, 1970, v26(6), 35-45.

Connolly, John D. "Corporate And Investor Returns: A Guide To Strategy," JPM, 1976, v2(3), 39-44.

Connolly, Michael B. and Dean Taylor. "The Exact Timing Of The Collapse Of An Exchange Rate Regime And Its Impact On The Relative Price Of Traded Goods," JMCB, 1984, v16(2), 194-207.

Connolly, Michael B. "Optimum Currency Pegs For Latin America," JMCB, 1983, v15(1), 56-72.

Connolly, Michael. "The Choice Of An Optimum Currency Peg For A Small, Open Country," JIMF, 1982, v1(2), 153-164.

Connolly, Michael. "The Speculative Attack On The Peso And The Real Exchange Rate: Argentina, 1979-81," JIMF, 1986, v5(Supp), S117-S130.

Connolly, Robert A. "An Examination Of The Robustness Of The Weekend Effect," JFQA, 1989, v24(2), 133-170.

Connolly, Robert A. (Allen, Stuart D. and Robert A. Connolly. "Financial Market Effects On Aggregate Money Demand: A Bayesian Analysis," JMCB, 1989, v21(2), 158-175.)

Connor, Gregory and Robert A. Korajczyk. "Performance Measurement With The Arbitrage Pricing Theory: A New Framework For Analysis," JFEC, 1986, v15(3), 373-394.

Connor, Gregory and Barry Dillon. "Organized Exchanges In Small Economies: The Case Of Irish Futures Trading," RFM, 1989, v8(2), 326-345.

Connor, Gregory and Robert A. Korajczyk. "Risk And Return In An Equilibrium APT: Application Of A New Test Methodology," JFEC, 1988, v21(2), 255-290.

Connor, Gregory and Robert A. Korajczyk. "An Intertemporal Equilibrium Beta Pricing Model," RFS, 1989, v2(3), 373-392.

Connor, Gregory and Robert A. Korajczyk. "The Attributes, Behavior

And Performance Of U.S. Mutual Funds," **RQFA**, 1991, v1(1), 5-26.

Conrad, B. Lynne. (Thistle, Paul D., Robert W. McLeod and B. Lynne Conrad. "Interest Rates And Bank Portfolio Adjustments," **JBF**, 1989, v13(1), 151-162.)

Conrad, Jennifer and Gautam Kaul. "Time-Variation In Expected Returns," **JOB**, 1988, v61(4),409-426.

Conrad, Jennifer and Gautam Kaul. "Mean Reversion In Short-Horizon Expected Returns," **RFS**, 1989, v2(2), 225-240.

Conrad, Jennifer. "The Price Effect Of Option Introduction," **JOF**, 1989, v44(2), 487-498.

Conroy, Robert M. and Richard J. Rendleman, Jr. "Pricing Commodities When Both Price And Output Are Uncertain," **JFM**, 1983, v3(4), 439-450.

Conroy, Robert M. and Robert L. Winkler. "Market Structure: The Specialist As Dealer And Broker," **JBF**, 1986, v10(1), 21-36.

Conroy, Robert M. and Robert L. Winkler. "Informational Difference Between Limit And Market Orders For A Market Maker," **JFQA**, 1981, v16(5), 703-724.

Conroy, Robert M. and Richard J. Rendleman, Jr. "A Test Of Market Efficiency In Government Bonds," **JPM**, 1987, v13(4), 57-64.

Conroy, Robert M., Robert S. Harris and Bruce A. Benet. "The Effects Of Stock Splits On Bid-Ask Spreads," **JOF**, 1990, v45(4), 1285-1295.

Conroy, Robert and Mike Miles. "Commercial Forestland In The Pension Portfolio: The Biological Beta," **FAJ**, 1989, v45(5), 46-54.

Constand, Richard L. (Cassidy, Steven N., Richard L. Constand and Richard B. Corbett. "The Market Value Of The Corporate Risk Management Function," **JRI**, 1990, v57(4), 664-670.)

Constantinides, George M. and Jonathan E. Ingersoll, Jr. "Optimal Bond Trading With Personal Taxes," **JFEC**, 1984, v13(3), 299-335.

Constantinides, George M. and Jonathan E. Ingersoll, Jr. "Optimal Bond Trading With Personal Tax: Implications For Bond Prices And Estimated Tax Brackets And Yield Curves," **JOF**, 1982, v37(2), 349-352.

Constantinides, George M. and Myron S. Scholes. "Optimal Liquidation Of Assets In The Presence Of Personal Taxes: Implications For Asset Pricing," **JOF**, 1980, v35(2), 439-449.

Constantinides, George M. "A Note On The Suboptimality Of Dollar-Cost Averaging As An Investment Policy," **JFQA**, 1979, v14(2), 443-450.

Constantinides, George M. "Admissible Uncertainty In The Intertemporal Asset Pricing Model," **JFEC**, 1980, v8(1), 71-86.

Constantinides, George M. "Cash Demand, Liquidation Costs, And Capital Market Equilibrium Under Uncertainty: Comment," **JFEC**, 1976, v3(3), 295-296.

Constantinides, George M. "Intertemporal Asset Pricing With Heterogeneous Consumers And Without Demand Aggregation," **JOB**, 1982, v55(2), 253-268.

Constantinides, George M. "Market Risk Adjustment In Project Valuation," **JOF**, 1978, v33(2),603-616.

Constantinides, George M. "Optimal Stock Trading With Personal Taxes: Implications For Prices And The Abnormal January Returns," **JFEC**, 1984, v13(1), 65-89.

Constantinides, George M. "Warrant Exercise And Bond Conversion In Competitive Markets," **JFEC**, 1984, v13(3), 371-397.

Constantinides, George M. and Bruce D. Grundy. "Optimal Investment With Stock Repurchase And Financing As Signals," **RFS**, 1989, v2(4), 445-466.

Contini, Bruno. (Hughes, G. David, Joseph B. Juhasz and Bruno Contini. "The Influence Of Personality On The Bargaining Process," **JOB**, 1973, v46(4), 593-604.)

Cook, Elizabeth F. "Greece Unafraid As She Joins Common Market," **FAJ**, 1962, v18(6), 99-103.

Cook, G. Bradford. "Chairman Cook On The Role Of Analysts," **FAJ**, 1973, v29(3), 18-20,22,76.

Cook, Thomas J. and Michael S. Rozeff. "Size And Earnings/ Price Ratio Anomalies: One Effect Or Two?," **JFQA**, 1984, v19(4), 449-466.

Cook, Thomas J. and Michael S. Rozeff. "Coskewness, Dividend Yield And Capital Asset Pricing," **JFR**, 1984, v7(3), 231-241.

Cook, Timothy Q. and Patric H. Hendershott. "The Impact Of Taxes, Risk And Relative Security Supplies On Interest Rate Differentials," **JOF**, 1978, v33(4), 1173-1186.

Cook, Timothy and Thomas Hahn. "The Information Content Of Discount Rate Announcements And Their Effect On Market Interest Rates," **JMCB**, 1988, v20(2),167-180.

Cook, Victor. (Polli, Rolando and Victor Cook. "Validity Of The Product Life Cycle," **JOB**, 1969, v42(4), 385-400.)

Cooke, H. J. and M. Katzen. "The Public Debt Limit," **JOF**, 1954, v9(3), 298-303.

Cooley, Philip L. and Charles E. Edwards. "Ownership Effects On Managerial Salaries In Small Business," **FM**, 1982, v11(4), 5-9.

Cooley, Philip L. and J. Louis Heck. "A Survey Of The Introductory Business Finance Course: The Professor's Viewpoint," **JFED**, 1977, v6, 3-8.

Cooley, Philip L. and J. Louis Heck. "Significant Contributions To Finance Literature," **FM**, 1981, v10(2), Tenth Anniversary Edition, 23-33.

Cooley, Philip L. and Rodney L. Roenfeldt. "A Comparative Multivariate Analysis Of Factors Affecting Stock Returns," **FR**, 1975, v10(1), 31-41.

Cooley, Philip L. "A Multidimensional Analysis Of Institutional Investor Perception Of Risk," **JOF**, 1977, v32(1), 67-78.

Cooley, Philip L. "A Review Of The Use Of Beta In Regulatory Proceedings," **FM**, 1981, v10(5), 75-81.

Cooley, Philip L. "Bayesian And Cost Considerations For Optimal Classification With Discriminant Analysis," **JRI**, 1975, v42(2), 277-288.

Cooley, Philip L. "On The Nature Of Risk: A Comment," **JFR**, 1979, v2(1), 81-85.

Cooley, Philip L. (Copley, Ronald E., Philip L. Cooley and Rodney L. Roenfeldt. "Autocorrelation In Market Model Residuals," **JBFA**, 1984, v11(3), 409-417.)

Cooley, Philip L. (Findlay, M. C., III, A. W. Frankle, P. L. Cooley, R. L. Roenfeldt and It-Keong Chew. "Capital Budgeting Procedures Under Inflation: Cooley, Roenfeldt, And Chew Vs. Findlay And Frankle," **FM**, 1976, v5(3), 83-95.)

Cooley, Philip L. (Gombola, Michael J., Rodney L. Roenfeldt and Philip L. Cooley. "Some Additional Evidence On Pricing Efficiency Of CBOE Options," **FR**, 1980, v15(1), 9-19.)

Cooley, Philip L. (Gombola, Michael J., Rodney L. Roenfeldt and Philip L. Cooley. "Spreading Strategies In CBOE Options: Evidence On Market Performance," **JFR**, 1978, v1(1), 35-44.)

Cooley, Philip L. (Harris, John M., Jr., Rodney L. Roenfeldt and Philip L. Cooley. "Evidence Of Financial Leverage Clienteles," **JOF**, 1983, v38(4), 1125-1132.)

Cooley, Philip L. (Heck, J. Louis, Philip L. Cooley and Carl M. Hubbard. "Contributing Authors And Institutions To The Journal Of Finance: 1946-1985," **JOF**, 1986, v41(5), 1129-1140.)

Cooley, Philip L. (Heck, Jean Louis and Philip L. Cooley. "Most Frequent Contributors To The Finance Literature," **FM**, 1988, v17(3), 100-108.)

Cooley, Philip L. (Modani, Naval K., Philip L. Cooley and Rodney L. Roenfeldt. "Covariation Of Risk Measures Under Inflation," **JBFA**, 1980, v7(3), 393-400.)

Cooley, Philip L. (Modani, Naval K., Philip L. Cooley and Rodney L. Roenfeldt. "Stability Of Market Risk Surrogates," **JFR**, 1983, v6(1), 33-40.)

Cooley, Philip L. (Roenfeldt, Rodney L. and Philip L. Cooley. "Predicting Corporate Profitability For Investment Selection," **JBFA**, 1978, v5(1), 57-65.)

Cooley, Philip L. (Wansley, James W., Rodney L. Roenfeldt and Philip L. Cooley. "Abnormal Returns From Merger Profiles," **JFQA**, 1983, v18(2), 149-162.)

Cooley, Philip L., Rodney L. Roenfeldt and It-Keong Chew. "Capital Budgeting Procedures Under Inflation," **FM**, 1974, v4(4), 18-27.

Cooley, Philip L., Rodney L. Roenfeldt and It-Keong Chew. "Clarification Of Three Capital Budgeting Criteria," **FR**, 1977, v12(1), 20-27.

Cooley, Philip L., Rodney L. Roenfeldt and Naval K. Modani. "Interdependence Of Market Risk Measures," **JOB**, 1977, v50(3), 356-363.

Cooley, Philip L. (Heck, Jean L. and Philip L. Cooley. "From Intellectual Wave To Nobel Laureate," **RQFA**, 1991, v1(2), 215-216.)

Coolidge, Francis P. "Are Farmers Getting More Than Their Share?," **FAJ**, 1955, v11(2), 71-74.

Cooper, G. M. (Sharpe, W. F. and G. M. Cooper. "NYSE Stocks Classified By Risk, 1931-1967," **FAJ**, 1972, v28(2), 46-54,81.)

Cooper, George. "Saving Estate Taxes For The duPonts," **JPM**, 1979, v5(4), 64-68.

Cooper, I. A. "Asset Changes, Interest-Rate Changes, And Duration," **JFQA**, 1977, v12(5), 701-723.

Cooper, Ian and Julian R. Franks. "The Interaction Of Financing And Investing Decisions When The Firm Has Un- used Tax Credits," **JOF**, 1983, v38(2), 571-583.

Cooper, Ian A. and Willard T. Carleton. "Dynamics Of Borrower-Lender Interaction: Partitioning Final Payoff In Venture Capital Finance," **JOF**, 1979, v34(2), 517-529.

Cooper, Ian A. (Carleton, Willard T. and Ian A. Cooper. "Estimation And Uses Of The Term Structure Of Interest Rates," **JOF**, 1976, v31(4), 1067-1083.)

Cooper, J. Phillip and Charles R. Nelson. "The Ex Ante Prediction Performance Of The St. Louis And FRB-MIT-PENN Econometric Models And Some Results On Composite Predictors," **JMCB**, 1975, v7(1), 1-32.

Cooper, J. Phillip and Stanley Fischer. "Monetary And Fiscal Policy In The Fully Stochastic St. Louis Econometric Model," **JMCB**, 1974, v6(1), 1-22.

Cooper, J. Phillip and Stanley Fischer. "Simulations Of Monetary Rules In The FRB-MIT-Penn Model," **JMCB**, 1972, v4(2), 384-396.

Cooper, J. Phillip and Stanley Fischer. "The Use Of The Secant Method In Econometric Models," **JOF**, 1973, v46(2), 274-277.

Cooper, J. Phillip. (Modigliani, Franco, Robert Rasche and J. Philip Cooper. "Central Bank Policy, The Money Supply, And The Short-Term Rate Of Interest," **JMCB**, 1970, v2(2), 166-218.)

Cooper, Jack L. "Continuous Borrowing From The Federal Reserve System: Some Empirical Evidence," **JOF**, 1969, v24(1), 33-48.

Cooper, James R. "Housing Needs Of The Urban Poor. The Problems And Alternatives," **AREUEA**, 1975, v3(1), 33-48.

Cooper, Kerry and Robert H. Strawser. "Evaluation Of Capital Investment Projects Involving Asset Leases," **FM**, 1974, v4(1), 44-49.

Cooper, Kerry and R. Malcolm Richards. "Investing The Alaskan Project Cash Flows: The Sohio Experience," **FM**, 1988, v17(2), 58-70.

Cooper, Lyle. "Wage Guaranties At Hormel: A Comment," **JOB**, 1956, v29(2), 141-145.

Cooper, Richard V. L. "Efficient Capital Markets And The Quantity Theory Of Money," **JOF**, 1974, v29(3), 887-908.

Cooper, W. W. (Byrne, R., A. Charnes, W.W. Cooper and K. Kortanek. "A Chance-Constrained Approach To Capital Budgeting With Portfolio Type Payback And Liquidity Constraints And Horizon Posture Controls," **JFQA**, 1967, v2(4),339-364.)

Cooper, W. W. (Charnes, A., W. W. Cooper, and M. H. Miller. "Application Of Linear Programming To Financial Budgeting And The Costing Of Funds," **JOB**, 1959, v32(1), 20-46.)

Cooperman, Daniel. (Parker, George G. C. and Daniel Cooperman. "Competitive Bidding In The Underwriting Of Public Utilities Securities," **JFQA**, 1978, v13(5), 885-902.)

Cooperman, Elizabeth S. (Lee, Winson B. and Elizabeth S. Cooperman. "Conglomerates Is The 1980s: A Performance Appraisal," **FM**, 1989, v18(1), 45-54.)

Cooperman, Elizabeth S., Winson B. Lee and James P. Lesage. "Commercial Bank And Thrift Interdependence And Local Market Competition For Retail Certificates Of Deposit," **JFSR**, 1990, v4(1), 37-52.

Cootner, Paul H. and David H. Pyle, Ed. "Capital Asset Pricing In A General Equilibrium Framework," **JFQA**, 1978, v13(4), 613-624.

Cootner, Paul H. "The Theorems Of Modern Finance In A General Equilibrium Setting: Paradoxes Resolved," **JFQA**, 1977, v12(4), 553-562.

Cope, A. C. "A Financial Survey Of British Housing Since 1919," **JOF**, 1951, v6(1), 32-45.

Copeland, Basil L., Jr. "Inflation, Interest Rates And Equity Risk Premia," **FAJ**, 1982, v38(3),32-43.
Copeland, Basil L., Jr. (Severn, Alan D., James C. Mills and Basil L. Copeland, Jr. "Capital Gains Taxes After Tax Reform," **JPM**, 1987, v13(3), 69-75.
Copeland, Ronald M. and Joseph F. Wojdak. "Goodwill In Merger-Minded Firms," **FAJ**, 1969, v25(5),57-62.
Copeland, Ronald M. (Ingram, Robert W., LeRoy D. Brooks and Ronald M. Copeland. "The Information Content Of Municipal Bond Rating Changes: A Note," **JOF**, 1983, v38(3), 997-1003.)
Copeland, Ronald M. and Hassan Espahbodi. "Accomodating Multicollinearity In Financial Forecasting And Business Research," **AFPAF**, 1989, v3(1), 311-322.
Copeland, Ronald M. and Robert J. Marioni. "Executives' Forecasts Of Earnings Per Share Versus Forecasts Of Naive Models," **JOB**, 1972, v45(4), 497-512.
Copeland, Ronald M. and Sharon McKinnon. "'Financial Distortion' And Consolidation Of Captive Finance Subsidiaries In The General Merchandising Industry," **JBFA**, 1987, v14(1), 77-98.
Copeland, T. E. (Brennan, M. J. and T. E. Copeland. "Beta Changes Around Stock Splits: A Note," **JOF**, 1988, v43(4), 1009-1014.)
Copeland, Thomas E. and Dan Galai. "Information Effects Of The Bid-Ask Spread," **JOF**, 1983, v38(5), 1457-1469.
Copeland, Thomas E. and David Mayers. "The Value Line Enigma (1965-1978): A Case Study Of Performance Evaluation Issues," **JFEC**, 1982, v10(3), 289-322.
Copeland, Thomas E. and J. Fred Weston. "A Note On The Evaluation Of Cancellable Operating Leases," **FM**, 1982, v11(2), 60-67.
Copeland, Thomas E. "A Model Of Asset Trading Under The Assumption Of Sequential Information Arrival," **JOF**, 1976, v31(4), 1149-1168.
Copeland, Thomas E. "A Probability Model Of Asset Trading," **JFQA**, 1977, v12(4), 563-578.
Copeland, Thomas E. "Liquidity Changes Following Stock Splits," **JOF**, 1979, v34(1), 115-141.
Copeland, Thomas E. (Brennan, Michael J. and Thomas E. Copeland. "Stock Splits, Stock Prices, And Transaction Costs," **JFEC**, 1988, v22(1), 83-102.)
Copeland, Thomas E. (Chen, Nai-Fu, Thomas E. Copeland and David Mayers. "A Comparison Of Single And Multifactor Portfolio Performance Methodologies," **JFQA**, 1987, v22(4), 401-418.)
Copeland, Thomas E. and Daniel Friedman. "The Effect Of Sequential Information Arrival On Asset Prices: An Experimental Study," **JOF**, 1987, v42(3), 763-797.
Copeland, Thomas E. and Daniel Friedman. "Partial Revelation Of Information In Experimental Asset Markets," **JOF**, 1991, v46(1), 265-296.
Copeland, William A. (Arnott, Robert D. and William A. Copeland. "The Business Cycle And Security Selection," **FAJ**, 1985, v41(2), 26-32.)
Copley, Ronald E.,Philip L. Cooley and Rodney L. Roenfeldt. "Autocorrelation In Market Model Residuals," **JBFA**, 1984, v11(3), 409-417.
Coppock, Joseph D. "Cushioning The Impact Of United States Economic Fluctuations On The Rest Of The World," **JOF**, 1959, v14(2), 302-311.
Corbeau, Andre B. (Meyer, Carl F. and Andre B. Corbeau. "The Application Of Spectral Analysis To Demonstrate The Stochastic Distortion In The Delta Midrange Of Price Series," **JFQA**, 1975, v10(2), 221-230.)
Corbett, Gary and Reynolds Griffith. "A Note On Life Insurance Accounting: Comment," **JRI**, 1965, v32(2), 277-282.
Corbett, Richard B. (Cassidy, Steven N., Richard L. Constand and Richard B. Corbett. "The Market Value Of The Corporate Risk Management Function," **JRI**, 1990, v57(4), 664-670.)
Corbin, Donald A. "Analysis Of Financial Statements During Inflation," **FAJ**, 1956, v12(5), 73-80.
Corbo, Vittorio. "Inflation Expectations And The Specification Of Demand For Money Equations," **JMCB**, 1981, v13(3), 381-387.
Corcoran, Eileen T. "Reporting On Leases," **FAJ**, 1968, v28(1), 29-35.
Corcoran, Patrick J. "Commercial Mortgages: Measuring Risk And Return," **JPM**, 1989, v15(2), 69-74.
Corcoran, Patrick J. "Explaining The Commerical Real Estate Market," **JPM**, 1987, v13(3), 15-21.
Cordell, Warren N. "Application Of The Theory Of Marketing Tangible Goods To The Marketing Of Insurance," **JRI**, 1961, v28(1), 29-34.
Cordes, Joseph J. and Steven M. Sheffrin. "Estimating The Tax Advantage Of Corporate Debt," **JOF**, 1983, v38(1), 95-105.
Cordier, Jean E. (Lee, Cheng F., Raymond M. Leuthold and Jean E. Cordier. "The Stock Market And The Commodity Futures Market: Diversification And Arbitrage Potential," **FAJ**, 1985, v41(4), 53-60.)
Corgel, Jack B. "Long-Term Effects Of Firm Size On Life Insurer Mortgage Investment," **JRI**, 1981, v48(2), 296-307.
Corgel, John B. (Rosenberg, Sidney B. and John B. Corgel. "Agency Costs In Property Management Contracts," **AREUEA**, 1990, v18(2), 184-201.)
Corgel, John B. and Gerald D. Gay. "The Impact Of GNMA Futures Trading On Cash Market Volatility," **AREUEA**, 1984, v12(2), 176-190.
Corgel, John B. and Gerald D. Gay. "Local Economic Base, Geographic Diversification, And Risk Management Of Mortgage Portfolios," **AREUEA**, 1987, v15(3), 256-267.
Corhay, Albert, Gabriel Hawawini and Pierre Michel. "Seasonality In The Risk-Return Relationship: Some International Evidence," **JOF**, 1987, v42(1), 49-68.
Corhay, Albert. (Hawawini, Gabriel A., Pierre A. Michel and Albert Corhay. "New Evidence On Beta Stationarity And Forecast For Belgian Common Stocks," **JBF**, 1985, v9(4), 553-560.)
Coriolanus. "The Glass Container Industry," **FAJ**, 1958, v14(4), 65-68.
Corley, Jerry L. (Veit, E. Theodore, Mary Lee Avey, Jerry L. Corley and Timothy Summers. "The Role Of Stock Options In Bank Trust Departments: Fifth Federal Reserve District Banks," **JBR**, 1979-80, v10(4), 255-256.)
Corliss, Stephen. (Render, Barry, William Wagoner, James R. Bobo and Stephen Corliss. "Finance Doctorates In The South: A 1977-1981 Supply And Demand Analysis," **JFED**, 1978, v7, 37-41.)
Cornell, Bradford and Alan C. Shapiro. "Interest Rates And Exchange Rates: Some New Empirical Results," **JIMF**, 1985, v4(4), 431-442.
Cornell, Bradford and Alan C. Shapiro. "The Reaction Of Bank Stock Prices To The International Debt Crisis," **JBF**, 1986, v10(1), 55-73.
Cornell, Bradford and Dhafrallah Hammani. "Option Pricing In Bear And Bull Markets," **JPM**, 1978, v4(4), 30-34.
Cornell, Bradford and J. Kimball Dietrich. "Mean-Absolute-Deviation Versus Least-Squares Regression Estimation Of Beta Coefficients," **JFQA**, 1978, v13(1),123-131.
Cornell, Bradford and Kenneth R. French. "Taxes And The Pricing Of Stock Index Futures," **JOF**, 1983, v38(3), 675-694.
Cornell, Bradford and Kenneth R. French. "The Pricing Of Stock Index Futures," **JFM**, 1983, v3(1),1-14.
Cornell, Bradford and Marc R. Reinganum. "Forward And Futures Prices: Evidence From The Foreign Exchange Markets," **JOF**, 1981, v36(5), 1035-1045.
Cornell, Bradford and Ole Christian Sand. "The Value Of Base Rate Options In The Eurocredit Market," **JBR**, 1985-86, v16(1), 22-27.
Cornell, Bradford and Alan C. Shapiro. "Corporate Stakeholders And Corporate Finance," **FM**, 1987, v16(1), 5-14.
Cornell, Bradford and Alan C. Shapiro. "Financing Corporate Growth," **JACF**, 1988, v1(2), 6-22.
Cornell, Bradford and Alan C. Shapiro. "The Mispricing Of U.S. Treasury Bonds: A Case Study," **RFS**, 1989, v2(3), 297-310.
Cornell, Bradford and Kevin Green. "The Investment Performance Of Low-Grade Bond Funds," **JOF**, 1991, v46(1), 29-48.
Cornell, Bradford. "A Note On Taxes And The Pricing Of Treasury Bill Futures Contracts," **JOF**, 1981, v36(5), 1169-1176.
Cornell, Bradford. "Asymmetric Information And Portfolio Performance Measurement," **JFEC**, 1979, v7(4), 381-390.
Cornell, Bradford. "Do Money Supply Announcements Affect Short-Term Interest Rates?," **JMCB**, 1979, v11(1), 80-86.
Cornell, Bradford. "Inflation Measurement, Inflation Risk, And The Pricing Of Treasury Bills," **JFR**, 1986, v9(3), 193-202.
Cornell, Bradford. "Inflation, Relative Price Changes, And Exchange Risk," **FM**, 1980, v9(3), 30-34.
Cornell, Bradford. "Monetary Policy, Inflation Forecasting And The Term Structure Of Interest Rates," **JOF**, 1978, v33(1), 117-127.
Cornell, Bradford. "Money Supply Announcements, Interest Rates, And Foreign Exchange," **JIMF**, 1982, v1(2), 201-208.
Cornell, Bradford. "Money Supply Announcements And Interest Rates: Another View," **JOB**, 1983, v56(1),1-24.
Cornell, Bradford. "Relative Price Changes And Deviations From Purchasing Power Parity," **JBF**, 1979, v3(3), 263-280.
Cornell, Bradford. "Spot Rates, Forward Rates And Exchange Market Efficiency," **JFEC**, 1977, v5(1),55-65.
Cornell, Bradford. "Taxes And The Pricing Of Stock Index Futures: Empirical Results," **JFM**, 1985, v5(1), 89-101.
Cornell, Bradford. "The Consumption Based Asset Pricing Model: A Note On Potential Tests And Application," **JFEC**, 1981, v9(1), 103-108.
Cornell, Bradford. "The Denomination Of Foreign Trade Contracts Once Again," **JFQA**, 1980, v15(4), 933-944.
Cornell, Bradford. "The Impact Of Data Errors On Measurement Of The Foreign Exchange Risk Premium," **JIMF**, 1989, v8(1), 147-157.
Cornell, Bradford. "The Relationship Between Volume And Price Variability In Futures Markets," **JFM**, v1(3), 303-316.
Cornell, Bradford. "The Weekly Pattern In Stock Returns: Cash Versus Futures: A Note," **JOF**, 1985, v40(2), 583-588.
Cornell, Bradford. "Using The Option Pricing Model To Measure The Uncertainty Producing Effect Of Major Announcements," **FM**, 1978, v7(1), 54-59.
Cornell, Bradford. "Volume And R-Square: A First Look," **JFR**, 1990, v13(1), 1-6.
Cornell, Bradford. (Capozza, Dennis R. and Bradford Cornell. "A Variance Forecasting Test Of The Option Pricing Model," **FR**, 1979, v14(3), 52-60.)
Cornell, Richard A. "You Can NOT Live With One Decision," **JPM**, 1974, v1(1), 50-73.
Cornell, Theodore E., III. "Employees Of CTAs: Are They CTAs? Should The Act Be Amended To Make Them APs?," **JFM**, 1981, v1(Supp), 531-534.
Cornell, W. Bradford. "Are Deep Discount Convertibles Underpriced?," **JPM**, 1977, v3(3), 55-57.
Cornett, Marcia Millon and Hassan Tehranian. "An Examination Of The Impact Of The Garn-St. Germain Depository Institutions Act Of 1982 On Commercial Banks And Savings And Loans," **JOF**, 1990, v45(1), 95-112.
Cornett, Marcia Millon and Nickolaos G. Travlos. "Information Effects Associated With Debt-For-Equity And Equity-For-Debt Exchange Offers," **JOF**, 1989, v44(2), 451-468.
Cornett, Marcia Millon and Ruben C. Trevino. "Monthly Return Patterns On Commodity Futures Contracts," **RFM**, 1989, v8(1), 86-104.
Cornett, Marcia Millon. "Undetected Theft As A Social Hazard: The Role Of Financial Institutions In The Choice Of Protection Mechanisms," **JRI**, 1988, v55(4), 723-733.
Cornew, Ronald W. "Commodity Pool Operators And Their Pools: Expenses And Profitability," **JFM**, 1988, v8(5), 617-637.
Cornew, Ronald W. "Note On Initial Margin To Net Asset Value: Average Values For The Commodity Pool Industry," **JFM**, 1986, v6(3), 495-502.
Cornew, Ronald W. "Response To A Comment On 'Stable Distributions, Futures Prices, And The Measurement Of Trading Performance," **JFM**, 1986, v6(4), 677-680.
Cornew, Ronald W., Donald E. Town and Lawrence D. Crowson. "Stable Distributions, Futures Prices, And The Measurement Of Trading Performance," **JFM**, 1984, v4(4), 531-558.
Corradi, V., M. Galeotti and R. Rovelli. "A Cointegration Analysis Of The Relationship Between Bank Reserves, Deposits And Loans: The Case Of Italy, 1965-1987," **JBF**, 1990, v14(1), 199-214.
Corrado, Charles J. and Dean Taylor. "The Cost Of A Central Bank Leaning Against A Random Walk," **JIMF**, 1986, v5(3), 303-314.
Corrado, Charles J. "A Nonparametric Test For Abnormal Security-Price Performance In Event Studies," **JFEC**, 1989, v23(2), 385-396.
Corrado, Charles J. (Bierwag, Gerald O., Charles J. Corrado and

George C. Kaufman. "Computing Durations For Bond Portfolios," **JPM**, 1990, v17(1), 51-55.)

Corrado, Charles J. and John Schatzberg. "A Nonparametric Distribution-Free Test For Serial Independence In Stock Returns: A Correction," **JFQA**, 1990, v25(3), 411-416.

Corrigan, Bernard. (Slovic, Paul, Baruch Fischhoff, Sarah Lichtenstein, Bernard Corrigan and Barbara Combs. "Preference For Insuring Against Probable Small Losses: Insurance Implications," **JRI**, 1977, v44(2), 237-258.)

Corson, John J. "Sources Of Income For The Aged," **JOF**, 1952, v7(2), 243-251.

Corstjens, Marcel. (Doyle, Peter and Marcel Corstjens. "Optimal Growth Strategies For Service Organizations," **JOB**, 1983, v56(3), 389-405.)

Cosandier, Pierre-Alexis and Bruno R. Lang. "Interest Rate Parity Tests: Switzerland And Some Major Western Countries," **JBF**, 1981, v5(2), 187-200.

Cosimano, Thomas F. "Reserve Accounting And Variability In The Federal Funds Market," **JMCB**, 1987, v19(2), 199-209.

Cosimano, Thomas F. "The Banking Industry Under Uncertain Monetary Policy," **JBF**, 1988, v12(1),117-140.

Cosimano, Thomas F. "The Federal Funds Market Under Bank Deregulation," **JMCB**, 1987, v19(3), 326-339.

Cosimano, Thomas F. (Balvers, Ronald J., Thomas F. Cosimano and Bill McDonald. "Predicting Stock Returns In An Efficient Market," **JOF**, 1990, v45(4), 1109-1128.)

Cosimano, Thomas F. and Dennis W. Jansen. "Estimates Of The Variance Of U.S. Inflation Based Upon The ARCH Model: Comment," **JMCB**, 1988, v20(3), Part 1,409-421.

Cossaboom, Roger A. "A Technique To Generalize Learning In Case Courses," **JFED**, 1976, v5, 65-68.

Cothren, Richard. "Asymmetric Information And Optimal Bank Reserves," **JMCB**, 1987, v19(1), 68-77.

Cothren, Richard. "On The Trigger Mechanism For Indexing Wages," **JMCB**, 1983, v15(2), 233-236.

Cotlar, Morton and Ralph Sprague. "Multi-Media Cases In Finance," **JFED**, 1974, v3, 69-72.

Cotlar, Morton. (Green, Thad B. and Morton Cotlar. "An Evaluation Of A Novel Business Simulation Technique For Management Devleopment," **JOB**, 1973, v46(2), 212-229.)

Cotner, John S. "Index Option Pricing: Do Investors Pay For Skewness?," **JFM**, 1991, v11(1), 1-8.

Cotner, John S. and James F. Horrell. "An Analysis Of Index Option Pricing," **JFM**, 1989, v9(5), 449-460.

Cotner, John S. and Neil E. Seitz. "A Simplified Approach To Short-Term International Diversification," **FR**, 1987, v22(2), 249-266.

Cotter, Kevin D. and Gail A. Jensen. "Choice Of Purchasing Arrangements In Insurance Markets," **JRU**, 1989, v2(4), 405-414.

Cottle, C. Sidney and W. Tate Whitman. "Testing Formula Plans," **JOF**, 1951, v6(2), 220-228.

Cottle, Edmund A. (Mennis, Sidney and Edmund A. Cottle. "Corporate Earnings - Short Term," **FAJ**, 1971, v27(4), 24-25,51,53,55,57,59,61.)

Cottle, Edmund A., Sidney Mennis and Robert A. Schuelke. "Corporate Earnings - Long Term," **FAJ**, 1971, v27(4), 22-23,50-52,54,56,58,60,62,64.

Cottle, Sidney. "Corporate Earnings: A Record Of Contrast And Change," **FAJ**, 1965, v21(6), 67-81.

Cottle, Sidney. "The Earnings Performance Of The Consumer Finance Industry," **JOF**, 1960, v15(3),387-406.

Cottle, Sidney. "The Future Of Pension Management," **FAJ**, 1977, v33(3), 23-25.

Cottrell, Allin F. (Darity, William A., Jr. and Allin F. Cottrell. "Meade's General Theory Model: A Geometric Reprise," **JMCB**, 1987, v19(2), 210-221.)

Coughlan, John W. "Tax Reductions And Tax Deferrals," **JOB**, 1958, v31(2), 121-131.

Coughtry, Lloyd S. "Computers, A Tool In Security Analysis," **FAJ**, 1963, v19(1), 53-60.

Counte, Michael A. (Homan, Rick K., Gerald L. Glandon and Michael A. Counte. "Perceived Risk: The Link To Plan Selection And Future Utilization," **JRI**, 1989, v56(1), 67-82.)

Countryman, Gary L. "A Study Of Fire And Casualty Stock Price Determination With Some Price Movement Implications," **JRI**, 1966, v33(2), 237-252.

Courchene, Thomas J. and Alex K. Kelly. "Money Supply And Money Demand: An Econoteric Analysis For Canada," **JMCB**, 1971, v3(2), Part 1, 219-244.

Courchene, Thomas J. "Recent Canadian Monetary Policy," **JMCB**, 1971, v3(1), 35-56.

Courtadon, Georges R. (Bodurtha, James N., Jr. and Georges R. Courtadon. "Tests Of An American Option Pricing Model On The Foreign Currency Options Market," **JFQA**, 1987, v22(2), 153-168.)

Courtadon, Georges R. (Bodurtha, James N., Jr. and Georges R. Courtadon. "Efficiency Tests Of The Foreign Currency Options Market," **JOF**, 1986, v41(1),151-162.)

Courtadon, Georges. "A More Accurate Finite Difference Approximation For The Valuation Of Options," **JFQA**, 1982, v17(5), 697-703.

Courtadon, Georges. "A Note On The Premium Market Of The Paris Stock Exchange," **JBF**, 1982, v6(4), 561-565.

Courtadon, Georges. "The Pricing Of Options On Default-Free Bonds," **JFQA**, 1982, v17(1), 75-100.

Courtadon, Georges. (Brenner, Menachem, Georges Courtadon and marti Subrahmanyam. "Options On The Spot And Options On Futures," **JOF**, 1985, v40(5), 1303-1317.)

Courtadon, Georges. (Brenner, Menachem, Georges Courtadon and Marti Subrahmanyam. "Options On Stock Indices And Options On Futures," **JBF**, 1989, v13(4/5), 773-782.)

Courtenay, Steve. (Millar, James A., Thakol Nunthirapakorn and Steve Courtenay. "A Note On The Information Content Of Primary And Fully Diluted Earnings Per Share," **FAJ**, 1987, v43(5), 77-79.)

Curtis, John K. "Modelling A Financial Ratios Categoric Frame work," **JBFA**, 1978, v5(4), 371-386.

Courtney, James F., Jr. "Differentiating Capital Appreciation And Income In Portfolio Selection/Revision," **JBR**, 1979-80, v10(2), 111-118.

Courville, Leon and Warren H. Hausman. "Warranty Scope And Reliability Under Imperfect Information And Alternative Market Structures," **JOB**, 1979, v52(3), 361-378.

Cousineau, Alain. (Belkaoui, Ahmed and Alain Cousineau. "Accounting Information, Nonaccounting Information, And Common Stock Perception," **JOB**, 1977, v50(3), 334-342.)

Cover, Clyde J. "Developments In State Life Insurance Legislation Resulting From Public Law 15," **JRI**, 1946, v13, 25-44.

Cowan, Arnold R., Nandkumar Nayar and Ajai K. Singh. "Stock Returns Before And After Calls Of Convertible Bonds," **JFQA**, 1990, v25(4), 549-554.

Cowan, David. "Could Natural Gas Reports Be More Informative?," **FAJ**, 1953, v9(5), 57-60.

Cowan, T. K. "The Maintenance Of Financial Viability Under Inflationary Conditions: A Planning Model," **JBFA**, 1975, v2(3), 361-371.

Cowee, John W. "Insurance Company Taxation - A General Review," **JRI**, 1959, v26(1), 16-19.

Cowen, Scott S. and Albert L. Page. "Factors Affecting The Performance Of Loans To Minority Small Businessmen: A Case Study," **JBR**, 1979-80, v10(3), 184-188.

Cowen, Tyler and Randall Kroszner. "Scottish Banking Before 1845: A Model For Laissez-Faire?," **JMCB**, 1989, v21(2), 221-231.

Cowhey, Thomas J. (Rennie, Edward P. and Thomas J. Cowhey. "The Successful Use Of Benchmark Portfolios: A Case Study," **FAJ**, 1990, v46(5), 18-26.)

Cowton, Christopher J. "The Earnings Effect Of Shareholder Concessions," **JBFA**, 1986, v13(3), 451-452.

Cox, Albert H., Jr. and Ralph F. Leach. "Open Market Operations And Reserve Settlement Periods: A Proposed Experiment," **JOF**, 1964, v19(3), 534-539.

Cox, Albert H., Jr. and Ralph F. Leach. "Defensive Open Market Operations And The Reserve Settlement Periods Of Member Banks," **JOF**, 1964, v19(1), 76-93.

Cox, Albert H., Jr. "Regulation Of Interest On Deposits: An Historical Review," **JOF**, 1967, v22(2), 274-296.

Cox, Edwin L. (Dunkelberg, William C., Jonathan A. Scott and Edwin L. Cox. "Small Business And The Value Of Bank-Customer Relationships," **JBR**, 1983-84, v14(4), 248-258.)

Cox, Eli P., III, Paul W. Hamelman and James B. Wilcox. "Relational Characteristics Of The Business Literature: An Interpretive Procedure," **JOB**, 1976, v49(2), 252-265.

Cox, Garfield, V. "Forecasting Expenditures For Plant And Equipment," **JOB**, 1954, v27(1), 22-31.

Cox, James C. (Walker, James M., Vernon L. Smith and James C. Cox. "Inducing Risk-Neutral Preferences: An Examination In A Controlled Market Environment," **JRU**, 1990, v3(1), 5-24.)

Cox, James C. and Ronald L. Oaxaca. "Laboratory Experiments With A Finite-Horizon Job-Search Model," **JRU**, 1989, v2(3), 301-329.

Cox, James C., Vernon L. Smith and James M. Walker. "Theory And Behavior Of Multiple Unit Discriminative Auctions," **JOF**, 1984, v39(4), 983-1010.

Cox, James C., Vernon L. Smith and James M. Walker. "Theory And Individual Behavior Of First-Price Auctions," **JRU**, 1988, v1(1), 61-100.

Cox, John C. and Stephen A. Ross. "A Survey Of Some New Results In Financial Option Pricing Theory," **JOF**, 1976, v31(2), 383-402.

Cox, John C. and Stephen A. Ross. "The Valuation Of Options For Alternative Stochastic Processes," **JFEC**, 1976, v3(1/2), 145-166.

Cox, John C. (Black, Fischer and John C. Cox. "Valuing Corporate Securities: Some Effects Of Bond Indenture Provisions," **JOF**, 1976, v31(2), 351-367.)

Cox, John C., Jonathan E. Ingersoll, Jr. and Stephen A. Ross. "The Relation Between Forward Prices And Futures Prices," **JFEC**, 1981, v9(4), 321-346.

Cox, John C., Jonathan E. Ingersoll, Jr. and Stephen A. Ross. "A Re-examination Of Traditional Hyptheses About The Term Structure Of Interest Rates," **JOF**, 1981, v36(4), 769-799.

Cox, John C., Jonathan E. Ingersoll, Jr. and Stephen A. Ross. "An Analysis Of Variable Rate Loan Contracts," **JOF**, 1980, v35(2), 389-403.

Cox, John C., Stephen A. Ross and Mark Rubinstein. "Option Pricing: A Simplified Approach," **JFEC**, 1979, v7(3), 229-264.

Cox, John C., Jonathan E. Ingersoll, Jr., and Stephen A. Ross. "Duration And The Measurement Of Basis Risk," **JOB**, 1979, v52(1), 51-62.

Cox, Larry A. "Review: Diability Income Insurance And The Individual," **FSR**, 1991, v1(1), 67-76.

Cox, Larry A. and Gary L. Griepentrog. "The Pure-Play Cost Of Equity For Insurance Divisions," **JRI**, 1988, v55(3), 442-452.

Cox, Larry A. and Gary L. Griepentrog. "Systematic Risk, Unsystematic Risk, And Property-Liability Rate Regulation," **JRI**, 1988, v55(4), 606-627.

Cox, Larry A. and Sandra G. Gustavson. "Leading Contributors To Insurance Research," **JRI**, 1990, v57(2), 260-281.

Cox, Raymond A. K. (Chung, Kee H. and Raymond A. K. Cox. "Patterns Of Productivity In The Finance Literature: A Study Of The Bibliometric Distributions," **JOF**, 1990, v45(1), 301-310.)

Cox, Samuel H., Jr. (Brockett, Patrick L., Samuel H. Cox, Jr. and Robert C. Witt. "Self-Insurance And The Probability Of Financial Regret," **JRI**, 1984, v51(4), 720-729.)

Cox, Samuel H., Jr. (Brockett, Patrick L., Samuel H. Cox, Jr. and Robert C. Witt. "Insurance Versus Self-Insurance: A Risk Management Perspective," **JRI**, 1986, v53(2), 242-257.)

Cox, William E., Jr. "Product Life Cycles As Marketing Models," **JOB**, 1967, v40(4), 375-384.

Coyne, Thomas J., Waldemar M. Goulet and Mario J. Picconi. "Residential Real Estate Versus Financial Assets," **JPM**, 1980, v7(1), 20-24.

Coyne, Thomas Joseph. "Commercial Bank Profitability By Function," **FM**, 1973, v2(1), 64-73.

Cozier, Barry V. "A Model Of Output Fluctuations In A Small, Specialized Economy," **JMCB**, 1986, v18(2), 179-190.

Cozzolino, John M. "A Method For The Evaluation Of Retained Risk," **JRI**, 1978, v45(3), 449-471.

Cozzolino, John M. "The Evaluation Of Loss Control Options," **JRI**, 1983, v50(3), 404-416.

Crabb, Ronald R. "A Computer Approach To Teaching The Fundamentals Of Life Insurance Mathematics," **JRI**, 1979, v46(4), 715-726.

Crabbs, Roger A. "Teaching Small Business Management -- A Living Experience," **JFED**, 1980, v9, 24-26.

Crafton, Steven M. and George E. Hoffer. "Estimating A Transaction Price For New Automobiles," **JOB**, 1981, v54(4), 611-621.

Cragg, John G. and Burton G. Malkiel. "The Consensus And Accuracy Of Some Predictions Of The Growth Of Corporate Earnings," **JOF**, 1968, v23(1), 67-84.

Craig, Darryl, Glenn Johnson and Maurice Joy. "Accounting Methods And P/E Ratios," **FAJ**, 1987, v43(2), 41-45.

Craig, Russell and Paul Walsh. "Adjustments For 'Extraordinary Items' In Smoothing Reported Profits Of Listed Australian Companies: Some Empirical Evidence," **JBFA**, 1989, v16(2), 229-246.

Craig, Russell. (Walsh, Paul, Russell Craig and Frank Clarke. "Big Bath Accounting' Using Extraordinary Items Adjustments: Australian Empirical Evidence," **JBFA**, 1991, v18(2), 173-190.)

Craine, Roger N. and James L. Pierce. "Interest Rate Risk," **JFQA**, 1978, v13(4), 719-734.

Craine, Roger. "Maturity Intermediation And Interest Rate Risks: Hedging Strategies For S&Ls," **RFM**, 1985, v4(3), 390-403.

Cramer, Edison H. "The Philosophy Of Bank Capitalization," **JOF**, 1951, v6(1), 62-66.

Cramer, Joe J., Jr. and William J. Schrader. "Elements Of 'Pension Costs'," **JRI**, 1968, v35(2), 237-245.

Cramer, Robert H. and James A. Seifert. "Measuring The Impact Of Maturity On Expected Return And Risk," **JBR**, 1976-77, v7(3), 229-235.

Cramer, Robert H. and Robert B. Miller. "Dynamic Modeling Of Multivariate Time Series For Use In Bank Analysis," **JMCB**, 1976, v8(1), 85-96.

Cramer, Robert H. and Robert B. Miller. "Multivariate Time Series Analysis Of Bank Financial Behavior," **JFQA**, 1978, v13(5), 1003-1017.

Cramer, Robert H. and Robert B. Miller. "Development Of A Deposit Forcasting Procedure For Use In Bank Financial Management," **JBR**, 1973-74, v4(2), 122-138.

Cramer, Robert H. and Stephen L. Hawk. "The Consideration Of Coupon Levels, Taxes, Reinvestment Rates, And Maturity In The Investment Management Of Financial Institutions," **JFQA**, 1975, v10(1), 67-84.

Cramer, Robert H. and William E. Sterk. "The Present Value Approach To Commercial Loan Pricing," **JBR**, 1981-82, v12(4), 207-217.

Cramer, Robert H. (Aghili, Parvis, Robert H. Cramer and Howard E. Thompson. "Small Bank Balance Sheet Management: Applying Two-Stage Programming Models," **JBR**, 1973-74, v5(4), 246-256.

Crandall, Robert W. "The Decline Of The Franchised Dealer In The Automobile Repair Market," **JOB**, 1970, v43(1), 19-30.

Crandall, Robert W. "The Profitability Of Cable Television: An Examination Of Acquisition Prices," **JOB**, 1974, v47(4), 543-563.

Crane, Donald B. "A Closer Look At The Effects Of Leverage," **JFED**, 1982, v11, 50-54.

Crane, Donald B. "Personal Finance: A Team-Teaching Approach," **JFED**, 1978, v7, 18-20.

Crane, Donald B. "Portfolio Management As A Second Course In Investments," **JFED**, 1979, v8, 19-22.

Crane, Dwight B. and Samuel L. Hayes, III. "The Evolution Of International Banking Competition And Its Implications For Regulation," **JBR**, 1983-84, v14(1), 39-52.

Crane, Dwight B. "A Stochastic Programming Model For Commercial Bank Bond Portfolio Management," **JFQA**, 1971, v6(3), 955-976.

Crane, Dwight B. "A Study Of Interest Rate Spreads In The 1974 CD Market," **JBR**, 1976-77, v7(3),213-224.

Crane, Dwight B. "Marketing Strategy And Bank Service Interaction," **JBR**, 1970-71, v1(2), 49-56.

Crane, Dwight B. (Bradley, Stephen P. and Dwight B. Crane. "Management Of Commercial Bank Government Security Portfolios: An Optimization Approach Under Uncertainty," **JBR**, 1973-74, v4(1), 18-30.)

Crane, Dwight B. (Bradley, Stephen P. and Dwight B. Crane. "Simulation Of Bond Portfolio Strategies: Laddered Vs. Barbell Maturity Structure," **JBR**, 1975-76, v6(2), 122-134.)

Crane, Frederick G. "Insurance Education For High School Teachers," **JRI**, 1970, v37(4), 627-629.

Crane, Frederick G. "Insurance Rate Regulation: The Reasons Why," **JRI**, 1972, v39(4), 511-534.

Crane, Frederick G. "Public Control Of Automobile Insurance Rate Adequacy And Excessiveness," **JRI**, 1963, v30(3), 423-432.

Crane, Frederick G. and Allen F. Jung. "Rate Variations Among Suppliers Of Automobile Insurance: Comment," **JRI**, 1964, v31(3), 469-474.

Crane, Nicholas E. "The Outlook For Uranium," **FAJ**, 1955, v11(5), 21-24.

Cranford, Brian K. and Roger D. Stover. "Interest Yields, Credit Ratings, And Economic Characteristics Of State Bonds: Comment," **JMCB**, 1988, v20(4),691-695.

Cranshaw, T. E. "The Evaluation Of Investment Performance," **JOB**, 1977, v50(4), 462-485.

Cranwill, Alfred. (Daniels, Arthur C., Albert I. Hermalin, Alfred Cranwill and James R. Williams. "The Research Facilities Of The Institute Of Life Insurance," **JRI**, 1958, v25(1), 32-41.)

Crary, D. T. (Norgaard, R. L. and D. T. Crary. "Insurance Industry Merger Targets," **FAJ**, 1970, v26(1), 91-94.)

Crary, David, Gary Fromm and Milton Kelenson. "Financial And Nonfinancial Data For Detailed U.S. Industries," **JMCB**, 1980, v12(2), Part 2, 308-316.

Crash, Melvin R. (Haney, Richard L., Jr., Melvin R. Crask and Hans P. Isakson. "The Gatekeeper Appraiser's Role In An Era Of Higher Energy Prices," **AREUEA**, 1978, v6(2), 186-203.)

Craswell, A. T. "Studies Of The Information Content Of Qualified Audit Reports," **JBFA**, 1985, v12(1), 93-115.

Crawford, Peggy J.,Charles P. Harper and John J. McConnell. "Further Evidence On The Terms Of Financial Leases," **FM**, 1981, v10(4), 7-14.

Crawford, Peter H. Money And Household Liquidity," **FAJ**, 1967, v23(1), 13-15.

Crellin, Glenn E., James R. Frew and G. Donald Jud. "The Earnings Of REALTORS: Some Empirical Evidence," **JRER**, 1988, v3(2), 69-78.

Crepas, K. J. and R. A. Stevenson. "Industrial Aid Bonds," **FAJ**, 1968, v24(6), 105-109.

Crerend, William J. and Edward Broom. "A Taxonomy Of Money Management," **FAJ**, 1974, v30(3), 24-27,30,23.

Crespi, Irving. (Brewster, J. Alan, Irving Crespi, Richard Kaluzny, James Ohls and Cynthia Thomas. "Homeowner Warranties: A Study Of The Need And Demand For Protection Against Unanticipated Repair Expenses," **AREUEA**, 1980, v8(2), 207-217.)

Cresson, George V. "Relationship Analysis Applied To Oils," **FAJ**, 1949, v5(3), 11-14.

Cresson, George Vaux. "Puts And Calls: The Writing Of Options," **FAJ**, 1959, v15(2), 43-50.

Cresta, Jean-Paul and Jean-Jacques Laffont. "Incentive Compatibility Of Insurance Contracts And The Value Of Information," **JRI**, 1987, v54(3), 520-540.

Cretien, Paul D., Jr. "A Computer Program To Derive Option Price Curves," **JFED**, 1978, v7, 86-87.

Cretien, Paul D., Jr. "Convertible Premiums Vs. Stock Prices," **FAJ**, 1969, v25(6), 90-95.

Cretien, Paul D., Jr. "Premiums On Convertible Bonds: Comment," **JOF**, 1970, v25(4), 917-922.

Cristiansen, Hanne D. "Equality And Equilibrium: Weaknesses Of The Overlap Argument For Unisex Pension Plans," **JRI**, 1983, v50(4), 670-680.

Cristy, James. "A Risk Manager Looks At Curricular Concepts In Risk And Insurance," **JRI**, 1962, v29(4), 567-568.

Cristy, James. "Organizational Problems In Control Of The Risk Of Accidental Loss And Management Of Employee Benefit Plans," **JRI**, 1963, v30(1), 47-52.

Crockett, Jean and Irwin Friend. "Consumption And Saving In Economic Development," **RIF**, 1979, v1, 1-52.

Crockett, John H. "Competition And Efficiency In Transacting: The Case Of Residential Real Estate Brokerage," **AREUEA**, 1982, v10(2), 209-227.

Crockett, John H. "Workouts, Deep Pockets, And Fire Sales: An Analysis Of Distressed Real Estate," **AREUEA**, 1990, v18(1), 76-90.

Crockett, John H., Jr. (Bolten, Steven E. and John H. Crockett, Jr. "Are Auditors Independent?," **FAJ**, 1979, v35(6), 76-78.)

Crofton, Sir Malby. "Investment Opportunities In The British Market," **FAJ**, 1962, v18(5), 41-46.

Crofts, Geoffrey. "The Actuarial Curriculum: Comment," **JRI**, 1966, v33(3), 480-482.

Cronan, Timothy P. (Epley, Donald R., Timothy P. Cronan and Larry Perry. "A Research Note On Discrimination In Mortgage Lending," **AREUEA**, 1985, v13(4), 446-451.)

Cronan, Timothy P. (Perry, Larry and Timothy P. Cronan. "A Note On Rank Transformation Discriminant Analysis: An Alternative Procedure For Classifying Bank Holding Company Commercial Paper Ratings," **JBF**, 1986, v10(4),605-610.)

Cronan, Timothy P. (Perry, Larry G., Glenn V. Henderson, Jr. and Timothy P. Cronan. "Multivariate Analysis Of Corporate Bond Ratings And Industry Classifications," **JFR**, 1984, v7(1), 27-36.)

Cronan, Timothy P. (Perry, Larry G., Timothy P. Cronan and Donald R. Epley. "A Procedure For Uncovering Acceptable And Nonacceptable Mortgage Applications Through Discriminant Analysis Using Ranked Data," **JRER**, 1987, v2(1), 61-72.)

Cronan, Timothy P. (Skomp, Stephen E., Timothy P. Cronan and William L. Seaver. "On Application Of The Rank Transformation Discrimination Method To Financial Problems," **FR**, 1986, v21(4), 473-483.)

Cronan, Timothy P. (Wilson, Joseph W. and Timothy P. Cronan. "Computer System Use In The Finance Major," **JFED**, 1982, v11, 97-100.)

Cronan, Timothy P., Donald R. Epley and Larry G. Perry. "The Use Of Rank Transformation And Multiple Regression Analysis In Estimating Residential Property Values With A Small Sample," **JRER**, 1986, v1(1), 19-31.

Crone, Theodore. (Voith, Richard and Theodore Crone. "National Vacancy Rates And The Persistence Of Shocks In U.S. Office Markets," **AREUEA**, 1988, v16(4), 437-458.)

Cropper, Maureen L. and Paul R. Portney. "Discounting And The Evaluation Of Lifesaving Programs," **JRU**, 1990, v3(4), 369-380.

Cross, Frank "Price Movements On Fridays And Mondays," **FAJ**, 1973, v29(6), 67-79.

Cross, Mark L. (Shelor, Roger M., Dwight C. Anderson and Mark L. Cross. "The Impact Of The California Earthquake On Real Estate Firms' Stock Value," **JRER**, 1990, v5(3), 335-340.)

Cross, Mark L. (Shelor, Roger M. and Mark L. Cross. "Insurance Firm Market Response To California Proposition 103 And The Effects Of Firm Size," **JRI**, 1990, v57(4), 682-690.)

Cross, Mark L. (Simmons, LeRoy F. and Mark L. Cross. "The Underwriting Cycle And The Risk Manager," **JRI**, 1986, v53(1), 155-163.)

Cross, Mark L. and John H. Thornton. "The Probable Effect Of An Extreme Hurrican On Texas Catastrophe Plan Insurers," **JRI**, 1983, v50(3), 417-444.

Cross, Mark L. and LeRoy F. Simmons. "The Underwriting Cycle And The Risk Manager: Reply," **JRI**, 1988, v55(3), 561-562.

Cross, Mark L. and Robert A. Hershbarger. "Price Discrimination In The Homeowners Program," **JRI**, 1979, v46(1), 147-157.

Cross, Mark L., Wallace N. Davidson, III and John H. Thornton. "The Impact Of Captive Insurer Formation On The Parent Firm's Value," **JRI**, 1986, v53(3), 471-483.

Cross, Mark L., Wallace N. Davidson, III and John H. Thornton. "Taxes, Stock Returns And Captive Insurance Subsidiaries," **JRI**, 1988, v55(2), 331-338.

Cross, Mark L., Wallace N. Davidson and John H. Thornton. "The Impact Of Directors And Officers' Liability Suits On Firm Value," **JRI**, 1989, v56(1), 128-136.

Cross, Mark. (Davidson, Wallace N., III, P. R. Chandy and Mark Cross. "Large Losses, Risk Management And Stock Returns In The Airline Industry," **JRI**, 1987, v54(1), 162-172.)

Cross, Stephen M. "A Note On Inflation, Taxation And Investment Returns," *JOF*, 1980, v35(1),177-180.

Crosse, Howard D. "Banking Structure And Competition," *JOF*, 1965, v20(2), 349-357.

Croteau, John T. "Federal Credit Union Liquidations, 1935-1951," *JOB*, 1952, v25(3), 187-203.

Croteau, John T. "Sources Of Consumer Credit: Instalment Debt Among Institutional Creditors," *JOF*, 1960, v15(4), 531-545.

Croteau, John T. "The Large Credit Union," *JOF*, 1956, v11(3), 347-362.

Crouch, Robert L. "Market Volume And Price Changes," *FAJ*, 1970, v26(4), 104-109.

Crouch, Robert. (Carrington, Samantha and Robert Crouch. "Interest Rate Differentials On Short-Term Securities And Rational Expectations Of Inflation," *JBF*, 1987, v11(4), 571-580.)

Croughy, Michel. (Briys, Eric, Michel Crouhy and Daniel R. Pieptea. "Hedging Versus Speculating With Interest Rate Futures," *RFM*, 1988, v7(Supp), 620-635.)

Crouhy, Michel and Dan Galai. "An Economic Assessment Of Capital Requirements In The Banking Industry," *JBF*, 1986, v10(2), 231-241.

Crouhy, Michel and Dan Galai. "A Contingent Claim Analysis Of A Regulated Depository Institution," *JBF*, 1991, v15(1), 73-90.

Crouhy, Michel. (Briys, Eric and Michel Crouhy. "Creating And Pricing Hybrid Foreign Currency Options," *FM*, 1988, v17(4), 59-65.)

Crouhy, Michel. (Briys, Eric, Michel Crouhy and Harris Schlesinger. "Optimal Hedging Under Intertemporally Dependent Preferences," *JOF*, 1990, v45(4), 1315-1324.)

Crouhy, Michel. (Briys, Eric, Michel Crouhy and Harris Schlesinger. "An Intertemporal Model Of Consumption And Hedging," *RFM*, 1988, v7(Supp), 456-466.)

Crowe, Robert M. "An Undergraduate Curriculum In Risk And Insurance For Non-Majors," *JRI*, 1965, v32(4), 645-648.

Crowe, Robert M. "Rate Making For Automobile Physical Damage Insurance," *JRI*, 1964, v31(2), 179-192.

Crowe, Robert M. and Ronald C. Horn. "The Meaning Of Risk," *JRI*, 1967, v34(3), 459-474.

Crowell, Richard A. "Five Applications Of Beta," *FAJ*, 1973, v29(4), 81-87.

Crowley, Frederick D. (Loviscek, Anthony L. and Frederick D. Crowley. "What Is In A Municipal Bond Rating?," *FR*, 1990, 25(1), 25-54.)

Crowson, Lawrence D. (Cornew, Ronald W., Donald E. Town and Lawrence D. Crowson. "Stable Distributions, Futures Prices, And The Measurement Of Trading Performance," *JFM*, 1984, v4(4), 531-558.)

Crum, Lawrence L. and James L. Athearn. "An Experiment In Central Banking For Life Insurance Companies," *JRI*, 1963, v30(1), 101-108.

Crum, M. Colyer. "Performance Investing," *FAJ*, 1969, v25(3), 142-147.

Crum, Roy L. (Brigham, Eugene F. and Roy L. Crum. "On The Use Of The CAPM In Public Utility Rate Cases," *FM*, 1977, v6(2), 7-15.)

Crum, Roy L. (Brigham, Eugene F. and Roy L. Crum. "Reply To Comments On 'Use Of The CAPM In Public Utility Rate Cases'," *FM*, 1978, v7(3), 72-76.)

Crum, Roy L. and Keqian Bi. "An Observation Of Estimating The Systematic Risk Of An Industry Segment," *FM*, 1988, v17(1), 60-62.

Crum, Roy L. and Lee A. Tavis. "Allocating Multinational Resources When Objectives Conflict: A Problem Of Overlapping Systems," *AFPAF*, 1990, v5(1), 271-294.

Crum, Roy L., Dan J. Laughhunn and John W. Payne. "Risk-Seeking Behavior And Its Implications For Financial Models," *FM*, 1981, v10(5), 20-27.

Crum, Roy L., Darwin D. Klingman and Lee A. Tavis. "Implementation Of Large-Scale Financial Planning Models: Solution Efficient Transformations," *JFQA*, 1979, v14(1), 137-152.

Crumbley, D. Larry. (Rivers, Richard and D. Larry Crumbley. "The Timing Problem For The Unified Estate And Gift Tax," *JRI*, 1979, v46(1), 125-138.)

Crutchfield, James A. and Earl C. Hald. "Economic Expansion And The American Banking System," *JOB*, 1956, v29(2), 111-123.

Crutchley, Claire E. and Robert S. Hansen. "A Test Of The Agency Theory Of Managerial Ownership, Corporate Leverage, And Corporate Dividends," *FM*, 1989, v18(4), 36-46.

Crutchley, Claire. (Hansen, Robert S. and Claire Crutchley. "Corporate Earnings And Financings: An Empirical Analysis," *JOB*, 1990, v63(3), 347-372.)

Crysler, Edwin W., Jr. "Growth Of The Mutual Fund Industry," *FAJ*, 1962, v18(1), 31-38.

Cudd, Mike and Joe Morris. "Bias In Journal Ratings," *FR*, 1988, v23(1), 117-125.

Cudd, Mike, John R. Tanner and Michael C. Budden. "The Issue Of Student Preparedness: Perceptions Of Finance Professors," *JFED*, 1989, v18, 60-64.

Cuddington, John T. "Currency Substitution, Capital Mobility, And Money Demand," *JIMF*, 1983, v2(2), 111-133.

Cuddington, John T. "Money, Income, And Causality In The United Kingdom: An Empirical Reexamination," *JMCB*, 1981, v13(3), 342-351.

Cuikey, David. (Miles, Mike, Rebel Cole and David Guikey. "A Different Look At Commercial Real Estate Returns," *AREUEA*, 1990, v18(4), 403-430.)

Cukierman, A. (Ben-Shahar, H. and A. Cukierman. "The Term-Structure Of Interest Rates And Expectations Of Price Increase And Devaluation," *JOF*, 1973, v28(3), 567-575.)

Cukierman, Alex and Leonardo Leiderman. "Price Controls And The Variability Of Relative Prices," *JMCB*, 1984, v16(3), 271-284.

Culbertson, John M. "Terms Of Reference For The President's Commission On Financial Structure And Regulation," *JMCB*, 1971, v3(1), 7-12.

Culbertson, John M. "Timing Changes In Monetary Policy," *JOF*, 1959, v14(2), 145-160.

Cullity, John P. "Market Recoveries Following Recessions," *FAJ*, 1974, v30(1), 45-48.

Cullity, John P. "Signals Of Cyclical Movements In Inflation And Interest Rates," *FAJ*, 1987, v43(5), 40-49.

Cullity, John P. "Stock Recoveries After Recessions," *FAJ*, 1967, v23(5), 98-100.

Cumby, Robert E. and Frederic S. Mishkin. "The International Linkage Of Real Interest Rates: The European-US Connection," *JIMF*, 1986, v5(1), 5-23.

Cumby, Robert E. and Maurice Obstfeld. "A Note On Exchange-Rate Expectations And Nominal Interest Differentials: A Test Of The Fisher Hypothesis," *JOF*, 1981, v36(3), 697-703.

Cumby, Robert E. "Consumption Risk And International Equity Returns: Some Empirical Evidence," *JIMF*, 1990, v9(2), 182-192.

Cumby, Robert E. "Monetary Policy Under Dual Exchange Rates," *JIMF*, 1984, v3(2), 195-208.

Cumby, Robert E. and David M. Modest. "Testing For Market Timing Ability: A Framework For Forecast Evaluation," *JFEC*, 1987, v19(1), 169-190.

Cumby, Robert E. and Jack D. Glen. "Evaluating The Performance Of International Mutual Funds," *JOF*, 1990, v45(2), 497-522.

Cummin, Robert I. "If You Are So Smart, Why Are You Not Rich?," *FAJ*, 1955, v11(5), 81-84.

Cummin, Robert I. "Knowledge And Insight (A Review)," *FAJ*, 1966, v22(4), 65-67.

Cummin, Robert I. "Lucky Strikes Again: L.S./M.G.W.H.," *FAJ*, 1983, v39(2), 56-57.

Cummin, Robert I. "The Mechanics Of Corporate Growth," *FAJ*, 1957, v13(4), 25-30.

Cummin, Robert I. "Unfriendly Corporate Takeovers - Old Style," *FAJ*, 1982, v38(4), 85,87.

Cummin, Robert I. "Upon What Meat Doth This Our Caesar Feed That He Is Grown So Great?," *FAJ*, 1982, v38(6), 68-69.

Cummin, Robert I. (Wilson, Paul N. and Robert I. Cummin. "Saving and Management Transaction Costs," *FAJ*, 1977, v22(2), 58.62.)

Cummins, J. David and David J. Nye. "Optimizing The Structure Of Capital Claims And Assets Of A Stock Insurance Company: Comment," *JRI*, 1972, v39(2), 310-313.

Cummins, J. David and David J. Nye. "The Cost Of Capital Of Insurance Companies: Comment," *JRI*, 1972, v39(3), 487-491.

Cummins, J. David and David J. Nye. "The Stochastic Characteristics Of Property-Liability Insurance Company Underwriting Profits," *JRI*, 1980, v47(1), 61-77.

Cummins, J. David and Douglas G. Olson. "An Analysis Of The Black Lung Compensation Program," *JRI*, 1974, v41(4), 633-654.

Cummins, J. David and J. Francois Outreville. "An International Analysis Of Underwriting Cycles In Property-Liability Insurance," *JRI*, 1987, v54(2), 246-262.

Cummins, J. David and Laurel J. Wiltbank. "Estimating The Total Claims Distribution Using Multivariate Frequency And Severity Distributions," *JRI*, 1983, v50(3), 377-403.

Cummins, J. David and Leonard R. Freifelder. "A Comparative Analysis Of Alternative Maximum Probable Yearly Aggregate Loss Estimators," *JRI*, 1978, v45(1), 27-52.

Cummins, J. David and Randolph Westerfield. "Patterns Of Concentration In Private Pension Plan Common Stock Portfolios Since ERISA," *JRI*, 1981, v48(2), 201-219.

Cummins, J. David and Scott Harrington. "Property-Liability Insurance Rate Regulation: Estimation Of Underwriting Betas Using Quarterly Profit Data," *JRI*, 1985, v52(1), 16-43.

Cummins, J. David and Scott E. Harrington. "The Relationship Between Risk And Return: Evidence For Property-Liability Insurance Stocks," *JRI*, 1988, v55(1), 15-31.

Cummins, J. David, Herbert S. Denenberg and William C. Scheel. "Concentration In The U.S. Life Insurance Industry," *JRI*, 1972, v39(2), 177-200.

Cummins, J. David, John R. Percival, Randolph Westerfield and J. G. Ramage. "Effects Of ERISA On The Investment Policies Of Private Pension Plans: Survey Evidence," *JRI*, 1980, v47(3), 447-476.

Cummins, J. David. "An Econometric Model Of The Life Insurance Sector Of The U.S. Economy," *JRI*, 1973, v40(4), 533-554.

Cummins, J. David. "Economies Of Scale In Independent Insurance Agencies," *JRI*, 1977, v44(4), 539-553.

Cummins, J. David. "Insurer's Risk: A Restatement," *JRI*, 1974, v41(1), 147-158.

Cummins, J. David. "Multi-Period Discounted Cash Flow Ratemaking Models In Property-Liability Insurance," *JRI*, 1990, v57(1), 79-109.

Cummins, J. David. "Property-Liability Company Exits: Comment," *JRI*, 1972, v39(4), 659-664.

Cummins, J. David. "Risk Management And The Theory Of The Firm," *JRI*, 1976, v43(4), 587-609.

Cummins, J. David. "Risk Management And The Theory Of The Firm: Reply," *JRI*, 1983, v50(1), 145-150.

Cummins, J. David. "Risk-Based Premiums For Insurance Guaranty Funds," *JOF*, 1988, v43(4), 823-839.

Cummins, J. David. (Denenberg, Herbert S. and J. David Cummins. "Insurance And Reciprocity," *JRI*, 1971, v38(3), 367-384.)

Cummins, J. David. (Denenberg, Herbert S. and J. David Cummins. "Insurance And Reciprocity: Reply," *JRI*, 1973, v40(1), 141-142.)

Cuneo, L. J. and W. H. Wagner. "Reducing The Cost Of Stock Trading," *FAJ*, 1975, v31(6), 35-44.

Cuneo, R. L. (Zenoff, D. B. and R. L. Cuneo. "Trading With Eastern Europe," *FAJ*, 1971, v27(4), 66-70,91-95.)

Cunningham, William H., W. Thomas Anderson, Jr. and John H. Murphy. "Are Students Real People?," *JOB*, 1974, v47(3), 399-409.

Cunngham, Donald F. and Charles A. Capone, Jr. "The Relative Termination Experience Of Adjustable To Fixed-Rate Mortgages," *JOF*, 1990, v45(5), 1687-1704.

Cuoco, D. (Barone, E. and D. Cuoco. "The Italian Market For 'Premium' Contracts: An Application Of Option Pricing Theory," *JBF*, 1989, v13(4/5), 709-746.)

Curatola, Anthony P., Kent T. Fields and William D. Samson. "The Benefits Of The Salary Reduction Plan," *FAJ*, 1984, v40(3), 53-58.

Curatola, Anthony P., Thomas L. Dickens and Kent T. Fields. "Increased Salary As An Alternative To Group Term Life Insurance," *JRI*, 1987, v54(1), 119-130.

Curcio, Richard J. (Johnson, Dana J., Richard E. Bennett and Richard J. Curcio. "A Note On The Deceptive Nature Of Bayesian Forecasted Betas," *JFR*, 1979, v2(1), 65-69.)

Curcio, Richard J. (Swinnerton, Eugene A., Richard J. Curcio and Richard E. Bennett. "Index Arbitrage Program Trading And The

Prediction Of Intraday Stock Price Changes," **RFM**, 1988, v7(2), 300-323.)

Curcio, Richard J. (Webb, James R. and Richard J. Curcio. "Interest Rate Illusions And Real Property Purchases," **JPM**, 1982, v8(4), 67-73.)

Curcio, Richard J. and James P. Gaines. "Real Estate Portfolio Revision," **AREUEA**, 1977, v5(4), 399-410.

Curley, Anthony J. and Jack M. Guttentag. "Value And Yield Risk On Outstanding Insured Residential Mortgages," **JOF**, 1977, v32(2), 403-412.

Curley, Anthony J. "Monte Carlo Evaluation Of Life Insurance Strategy," **JRI**, 1974, v41(4), 667-684.

Curley, Anthony J. "Reconciling Investment Planning And Accounting Control Mechanisms," **JBFA**, 1976, v3(3), 17-28.

Curley, Anthony J. (Bear, Robert M. and Anthony J. Curley. "Unseasoned Equity Financing," **JFQA**, 1975, v10(2), 311-325.)

Curley, Anthony J. (Stoll, Hans R. and Anthony J. Curley. "Small Business And The New Issues Market For Equities," **JFQA**, 1970, v5(3), 309-322.)

Curley, John F. "Negotiation Vs. Competitive Bidding In The Sale Of Securities By Public Utilities: Comment," **FM**, 1978, v7(4), 75.

Curley, M. Louise. (Johnston, George S., M. Louise Curley and Robert A. McIndoe. "Dual-Purpose Funds Undervalued?," **FAJ**, 1968, v24(6), 157-163.)

Curley, Michael D. (Mehta, Dileep R., Michael D. Curley and Hung-Gay Fung. "Inflation, Cost Of Capital, And Capital Budgeting Procedures," **FM**, 1984, v13(4), 48-54.)

Curran, Ward S. "Preferred Stock For Public Utilities," **FAJ**, 1972, v28(2), 71-76.

Curran, Ward S. "Teaching Finance As A Branch Of Economics," **JFED**, 1972, v1, 19-21.

Curry, H. E. "Investment Income In Fire And Casualty Rate Making," **JRI**, 1969, v36(3), 447-454.

Curry, Harold E. "Refinement Of Automobile Rate And Underwriting Classes," **JRI**, 1964, v31(2), 217-224.

Curry, Harold E. (Athearn, James L. and Harold E. Curry. "A Key To The Apartment," **JRI**, 1974, v41(1), 135-146.)

Curry, Timothy J. and John T. Rose. "Bank Holding Company Presence And Banking Market Performance," **JBR**, 1983-84, v14(4), 259-265.

Curry, Timothy J. and John T. Rose. "Multibank Holding Companies: Recent Evidence On Competition And Performance In Banking Markets," **JBR**, 1983-84, v14(3), 212-220.

Curry, Timothy J. "The Pre-Acquisition Characteristics Of Banks Acquired By Multibank Holding Companies," **JBR**, 1981-82, v12(2), 82-89.

Curtis, Charles E., Jr. (Kahl, Kandice H. and Charles E. Curtis, Jr. "A Comparative Analysis Of The Corn Basis In Feed Grain Deficit And Surplus Areas," **RFM**, 1986, v5(3), 220-232.)

Curtis, Charles E., Jr., Kandice H. Kahl and Cathy S. McKinnell. "Risk-Efficient Soybean Marketing: The Contribution Of Commodity Options To The Producing Firm," **RFM**, 1987, v6(2), 176-190.

Curtis, Clayton. (Gillies, James and Clayton Curtis. "A Note On The Small Mortgage Market," **JOF**, 1959, v14(3), 411-414.)

Curtis, Clayton. (Gillies, James and Clayton Curtis. "The Structure Of Local Mortgage Markets And Government Housing Finance Programs," **JOF**, 1955, v10(3), 363-375.)

Cushing, Barry E. "The Application Potential Of Integer Programming," **JOB**, 1970, v43(4), 456-467.

Cushman, David O. "Has Exchange Risk Depressed International Trade? The Impact Of Third Country Exchange Risk," **JIMF**, 1986, v5(3), 361-379.

Cushman, David O. "The Impact Of Third-Country Exchange Risk: A Correction," **JIMF**, 1988, v7(3), 359.

Cuthbert, N. H. and A. Whitaker. "Disclosure Of Information And Collective Bargaining: A Re-Examination," **JBFA**, 1977, v4(3), 373-378.

Cutler, David M., James M. Poterba and Lawrence H. Summers. "What Moves Stock Prices?," **JPM**, 1989, v15(3), 4-12.

Cyert, R. M. (Cohen, K. J., R. M. Cyert, W. R. Dill, A. A. Kuehn, M. H. Miller, T. A. VanWormer, and P. R. Winters. "The Carnegie Tech Management Game," **JOB**, 1960, v33(4), 303-321.)

Cyert, R. M. and G. L. Thompson. "Selecting A Portfolio Of Credit Risks By Markov Chains," **JOB**, 1968, v41(1), 39-46.

Cyert, Richard M. (Cohen, Kalman J. and Richard M. Cyert. "Strategy: Formulation, Implementation, And Monitoring," **JOB**, 1973, v46(3), 349-367.)

Cyert, Richard M. and William R. Dill. "The Future Of Business Education," **JOB**, 1964, v37(3), 21-237.

Cyert, Richard M., Herbert A. Simon, and Donald B. Trow. "Observation Of A Business Decision," **JOB**, 1956, v29(4), 237-248.

Czinkota, Michael R. (Bavishi, Vinod B., Michael R. Czinkota, Harry A. Shawky and David A. Ricks. "International Financial Management -- A Survey Of Research Trends And An Annotated Bibliography, 1977-1976," **JFED**, 1977, v6, 93-95.)

DDD

DaMotta, L. F. J. (Langetieg, T. C., M. C. Findlay and L. F. J. da Motta. "Multiperiod Pension Plans And ERISA," **JFQA**, 1982, v17(4), 603-631.)

Daane, J. Dewey. (Bowsher, Norman N., J. Dewey Daane and Robert Einzig. "The Flows Of Funds Between Regions Of The United States," **JOF**, 1958, v13(1),1-20.)

Dacorogna, M. M. (Muller, U. A., M. M. Dacorogna, R. B. Olsen, O. V. Pictet, M. Schwarz and C. Morgenegg. "Statistical Study Of Foreign Exchange Rates, Empirical Evidence Of A Price Change Scaling Law, And Intraday Analysis," **JBF**, 1990, v14(6), 1189-1208.)

Dadkhah, Kamran M. and Rajen Mookerjee. "Money And Corporate Profits In A Developing Country: Theory And Evidence," **JBF**, 1989, v13(2), 191-206.

Daellenbach, Hans G. and Stephen H. Archer. "The Optimal Bank Liquidity: A Multi-Period Stochastic Model," **JFQA**, 1969, v4(3), 329-343.

Daellenbach, Hans G. "Are Cash Management Optimization Models Worthwhile?," **JFQA**, 1974, v9(4),607-626.

Daenzer, Bernard John. "The Non-Admitted Market Abroad," **JRI**, 1966, v33(1), 33-42.

Dahl, D. and R. E. Shrieves. "The Impact Of Regulation On Bank Equity Infusions," **JBF**, 1990, v14(6), 1209-1228.

Dahl, Drew and Ronald E. Shrieves. "Evidence On The Role Of Holding Company Acquisitions In The Management Of Bank Capital," **JFSR**, 1989, v2(1), 21-38.

Dahl, Frederick R. (Brimmer, Andrew F. and Frederick R. Dahl. "Growth Of American International Banking: Implications For Public Policy," **JOF**, 1975, v30(2), 341-363.)

Dahlby, B. G. "Monopoly Versus Competition In An Insurance Market With Adverse Selection," **JRI**, 1987, v54(2), 325-331.

Dahlgran, Roger A. and Dale W. Jergenson. "The Feasibility Of Hedging Working Capital Costs In Financial Futures Markets By Small Agribusiness Firms," **RFM**, 1984, v3(1), 1-12.

Dahmann, Donald C. "North-South Differences In Housing And The Housing And Community Development Act Of 1977," **AREUEA**, 1979, v7(2), 230-242.

Daigler, Robert T. and Bruce D. Fielitz. "A Multiple Discriminant Analysis Of Technical Indicators On The New York Stock Exchange," **JFR**, 1981, v4(3), 169-182.

Daigler, Robert T. "Current And Future Developments In Finance," **JFED**, 1976, v5, 35-39.

Daigler, Robert T. "Developing A Futures Markets Course For A Finance Curriculum," **JFED**, 1981, v10, 42-50.

Daigler, Robert T. "Personal Financial Planning As A New Major Within Finance," **JFED**, 1979, v8, 23-29.

Daigler, Robert T. (Parker, Jack W. and Robert T. Daigler. "Hedging Money Market CDs With Treasury-Bill Futures," **JFM**, v1(4), 597-606.)

Daily, James M. (Lucas, Vane B. and James M. Daily. "An Adult Learning Research Center At Bryn Mawr," **JRI**, 1969, v36(1), 125-128.)

Daines, Robert. "An Analysis Of The Impact Of The Underwriting Function On Investment In Common Stocks For Multiple Line Insurers," **JRI**, 1968, v35(3), 357-370.

Dake, Leland E. "Are Analysts' Techniques Adequate For Growth Stocks?," **FAJ**, 1960, v16(6), 45-49.

Dalal, Ardeshir J. "On The Use Of A Covariance Function In A Portfolio Model," **JFQA**, 1983, v18(2),223-227.

Dalal, Ardeshir J. and Bala G. Arshanapalli. "Effects Of Expected Cash And Futures Prices On Hedging And Production: Comments And Extensions," **JFM**, 1989, v9(4), 337-346.

Dale, Charles and Rosemarie Workman. "The Arc Sine Law And The Treasury Bill Futures Market," **FAJ**, 1980, v36(6), 71-74.

Dale, Charles J. (Vignola, Anthony J. and Charles J. Dale. "Is The Futures Market For Treasury Bills Efficient?," **JPM**, 1979, v5(2), 78-81.)

Dale, Charles. "The Hedging Effectiveness Of Currency Futures Markets," **JFM**, v1(1), 77-88.

Dale, Charles. (Cicchetti, Paul, Charles Dale and Anthony J. Vignola. "Usefulness Of Treasury Bill Futures As Hedging Instruments," **JFM**, v1(3), 379-387.)

Dale, Charles. (Vignola, Anthony J. and Charles Dale. "The Efficiency Of The Treasury Bill Futures Market: An Analysis Of Alternative Specifications," **JFR**, 1980, v3(2), 169-188.)

Dale, Ernest. "New Perspectives In Managerial Decision Making," **JOB**, 1953, v26(1), 1-8.

Dale-Johnson, David and G. Michael Phillips. "Housing Attributes Associated With Capital Gain," **AREUEA**, 1984, v12(2), 162-175.

Dale-Johnson, David and Hyang K. Yim. "Coastal Development Moratoria And Housing Prices," **JREFEC**, 1990, v3(2), 173-184.

Dale-Johnson, David and M. Chapman Findlay. "Creative Financing And Housing Prices: A Comment On A Theoretical Inquiry Into The Capitalization Issue," **AREUEA**, 1986, v14(1), 153-157.

Dale-Johnson, David. "Clientele Effects On The Demand For Housing Price Appreciation," **AREUEA**, 1983, v11(3), 382-396.

Dale-Johnson, David, M. Chapman Findlay, Arthur L. Schwartz, Jr. and Stephen D. Kapplin. "Valuation And Efficiency In The Market For Creatively Financed Houses," **AREUEA**, 1985, v13(4), 388-403.

Daley, Lane A. (Bowen, Robert M., Richard P. Castanias and Lane A. Daley. "Intra-Industry Effects Of The Accident At Three Mile Island," **JFQA**, 1983, v18(1), 87-111.)

Daley, Lane A. (Bowen, Robert M., Lane A. Daley and Charles C. Huber, Jr. "Leverage Measures And Industrial Classification: Review And Additional Evidence," **FM**, 1982, v11(4), 10-20.)

Dalrymple, Brent B. and Ben J. Tuchi. "Hospital Pricing Under Economic Controls," **FR**, 1972, v2(2), 156-162.

Dalton, Dan R., David M. Krackhardt and Lyman W. Porter. "The Impact Of Teller Turnover In Banking: First Appearances Are Deceiving," **JBR**, 1983-84, v14(3), 184-192.

Daly, Donald J. "Seasonal Variations And Business Expectations," **JOB**, 1959, v32(3), 258-270.

Daly, George. "The Impact Of Monetary Policy And The Maturity Of Savings And Loan Association Assets: A Critique Of Reform Proposals: A Comment," **JMCB**, 1972, v4(2), 441-444.

Daly, Michael. (Bartel, Henry, Michael Daly and Peter Wrage. "Reverse Mortgages: Supplementary Retirement Income From Homeownership," **JRI**, 1980, v47(3), 477-490.)

Damant, David C. "Financial Forecasting In The UK," **FAJ**, 1972, v28(5), 44-46,59.

Dambolena, Ismael G. and Sarkis J. Khoury. "Ratio Stability And Corporate Failure," **JOF**, 1980, v35(4), 1017-1026.

Dambolena, Ismael G. and Joel M. Shulman. "A Primary Rule For Detecting Bankruptcy: Watch The Cash," **FAJ**, 1988, v44(5), 74-78.

D'Ambrosio, Charles A. "A Multi-Optioned Computer Program To Illustrate Investment Concepts," **JFED**, 1976, v5, 73-76.

D'Ambrosio, Charles A. "Financial Theory In Personal Finance Courses," **JFED**, 1980, v9, 17-18.

D'Ambrosio, Charles A. "Random Walk And The Stock Exchange Of Singapore," **FR**, 1980, v15(2), 1-12.

D'Ambrosio, Charles A. "Risks And Returns In Continuous Option Writing: A Comment," **JPM**, 1979, v5(4), 72-73.

Dammon, Robert M. "A Security Market And Capital Structure Equilibrium Under Uncertainty With Progressive Personal Taxes," **RIF**, 1988, v7, 53-74.

Dammon, Robert M. and Lemma W. Senbet. "The Effect Of Taxes And Depreciation On Corporate Investment And Financial Leverage," JOF, 1988, v43(2), 357-373.

Dammon, Robert M. and Richard C. Green. "Tax Arbitrage And The Existence Of Equilibrium Prices For Financial Assets," JOF, 1987, v42(5), 1143-1166.

Dammon, Robert M., Kenneth B. Dunn and Chester S. Spatt. "A Reexamination Of The Value Of Tax Options," RFS, 1989, v2(3), 341-372.

Damodaran, Aswath. "Economic Events, Information Structure, And The Return-Generating Process," JFQA, 1985, v20(4), 423-434.

Damodaran, Aswath. "Information Structure In International Markets: Measures And Implications," RDIBF, 1988, v2, 277-298.

Damodaran, Aswath. "Information And Price Adjustment Processes: A Comparison Of U.S. And Japanese Stocks," RDIBF, 1991, v4/5, 370-389.

Damodaran, Aswath. "The Weekend Effect In Information Releases: A Study Of Earnings And Dividend Announcements," RFS, 1989, v2(4), 607-623.

Damon, W. W. (Burton, R. M. and W. W. Damon. "On The Existence Of A Cost Of Capital Under Pure Capital Rationing," JOF, 1974, v29(4), 1165-1173.)

Damordaran, Aswath. "The Impact Of Information Structure On Stock Returns," JPM, 1987, v13(3), 53-58.

Dandapani, Krishnan. (Haar, Jerry, Krishnan Dandapani and Stanley P. Haar. "The American Depositary Receipt (ADR): A Creative Financial Tool For Multinational Companies," GFJ, 1990, v1(2), 163-171.)

Dandapani, Krishnan. (Prakash, Arun J., Krishnan Dandapani and Gordon V. Karels. "Simple Resource Allocation Rules," JBFA, 1988, v15(3), 447-452.)

Danforth, Warner C. "A Property Insurance Executive Views Education For Insurance On The University Level," JRI, 1949, v16, 14-17.

Danhof, Clarence. "Business Leadership In The South," JOB, 1956, v29(2), 130-137.

Daniel, Betty C. "One-Sided Uncertainty About Future Fiscal Policy," JMCB, 1989, v21(2), 176-189.

Daniel, Betty C. "Optimal Foreign Exchange Policy For A Small Open Economy," JIMF, 1985, v4(4), 523-536.

Daniel, Donnie L. and William A. Sirmon. "Computerized Bank Financial Statements: Classroom Applications," JFED, 1979, v8, 86-89.

Daniel, Donnie L., William A. Longbrake and Neil B. Murphy. "The Effect Of Technology On Bank Economies Of Scale For Demand Deposits," JOF, 1973, v28(1), 131-146.

Daniel, Eleanor Bagley. "Some Observations On Recent Studies Of Investment Risk," JOF, 1953, v8(2), 99-112.

Daniel, Wayne E. (Hawkins, Eugene H., Stanley C. Chamberlin and Wayne E. Daniel. "Earnings Expectations And Security Prices," FAJ, 1984, v40(5), 24-27, 30-38, 74.)

Danielian, N. R. "Financing The Seaway," FAJ, 1956, v12(2), 93-96.

Daniels, Arthur C., Albert I. Hermalin, Alfred Cranwill and James R. Williams. "The Research Facilities Of The Institute Of Life Insurance," JRI, 1958, v25(1), 32-41.

Daniels, Richard L. and L. Robin Keller. "An Experimental Evaluation Of The Descriptive Validity Of Lottery-Dependent Utility Theory," JRU, 1990, v3(2), 115-134.

Dann, Larry Y. and Christopher M. James. "An Analysis Of The Impact Of Deposit Rate Ceilings On The Market Values Of Thrift Institutions," JOF, 1982, v37(5), 1259-1275.

Dann, Larry Y. and Harry DeAngelo. "Standstill Agreements, Privately Negotiated Stock Repurchases, And The Market For Corporate Control," JFEC, 1983, v11(1), 275-300.

Dann, Larry Y. and Wayne H. Mikkelson. "Convertible Debt Issuance, Capital Structure Change And Financing-Related Information: Some New Evidence," JFEC, 1984, v13(2), 157-186.

Dann, Larry Y. "Common Stock Repurchases: An Analysis Of Returns To Bondholders And Stockholders," JFEC, 1981, v9(2), 113-138.

Dann, Larry Y. and Harry DeAngelo. "Corporate Financial Policy And Corporate Control: A Study Of Defensive Adjustments In Asset And Ownership Structure," JFEC, 1988, v20(1/2), 87-128.

Dann, Larry Y., David Mayers and Robert J. Raab, Jr. "Trading Rules, Large Blocks And The Speed Of Price Adjustment," JFEC, 1977, v4(1), 3-22.

Danthine, Jean-Pierre. (Anderson, Ronald W. and Jean-Pierre Danthine. "Hedging And Joint Production: Theory And Illustrations," JOF, 1980, v35(2), 487-498.)

D'Antonio, Louis J. and Ronald W. Melicher. "Changes In Federal Reserve Membership: A Risk-Return Profitability Analysis," JOF, 1979, v34(4), 987-997.

D'Antonio, Louis J. (Howard, Charles T. and Louis J. D'Antonio. "A Risk-Return Measure Of Hedging Effectiveness," JFQA, 1984, v19(1), 101-112.)

D'Antonio, Louis J. (Howard, Charles T. and Louis J. D'Antonio. "Treasury Bill Futures As A Hedging Tool: A Risk-Return Approach," JFR, 1986, v9(1), 25-39.)

D'Antonio, Louis J. (Howard, Charles T. and Louis J. D'Antonio. "A Risk-Return Measure Of Hedging Effectiveness: A Reply," JFQA, 1987, v22(3), 377-381.)

Danzon, Patricia M. "Compensation For Occupational Disease: Evaluating The Options," JRI, 1987, v54(2), 263-282.

Dar, A. and C. Dodds. "Interest Rates, The Emergency Fund Hypothesis And Saving Through Endowment Policies: Some Empirical Evidence For The U.K.," JRI, 1989, v56(3), 415-433.

Darby, Michael R. "Rational Expectations Under Conditions Of Costly Information," JOF, 1976, v31(3), 889-895.

Darby, Michael R. "The Internationalization Of American Banking And Finance: Structure, Risk, And World Interest Rates," JIMF, 1986, v5(4), 403-428.

D'Arcy, Stephen P. "Legislative Reform Of The Medical Malpractice Tort System In Illinois," JRI, 1986, v53(3), 538-550.

D'Arcy, Stephen P. "Regulated Firms Under Uncertain Price Change: The Case Of Property And Liability Insurance Companies: Comment," JRI, 1982, v49(1), 114-119.

D'Arcy, Stephen P. "Use Of The CAPM To Discount Property-Liability Loss Reserves," JRI, 1988, v55(3), 481-491.

D'Arcy, Stephen P. (Chen, K. C. and Stephen P. D'Arcy. "Market Sensitivity To Interest Rate Assumptions In Corporate Pension Plans," JRI, 1986, v53(2), 209-225.)

D'Arcy, Stephen P. (Lee, Keun Chang and Stephen P. D'Arcy. "The Optimal Investment Strategy Through Variable Universal Life Insurance," JRI, 1989, v56(2), 201-217.)

D'Arcy, Stephen P. and James R. Garven. "Property-Liability Insurance Pricing Models: An Empirical Evaluation," JRI, 1990, v57(3), 391-430.

D'Arcy, Stephen P. and Keun Chang Lee. "Universal Variable Life Insurance Versus Similar Unbundled Investment Strategies," JRI, 1987, v54(3), 452-477.

D'Arcy, Stephen P. and Neil A. Doherty. "Adverse Selection, Private Information, And Lowballing In Insurance Markets," JOB, 1990, v63(2), 145-164.

Dare, William H. (Ma, Christopher K., William H. Dare and Darla R. Donaldson. "Testing Rationality In Futures Markets," JFM, 1990, v10(2), 137-152.)

Darity, William A., Jr. and Allin F. Cottrell. "Meade's General Theory Model: A Geometric Reprise," JMCB, 1987, v19(2), 210-221.

Dark, Frederick H. (Boardman, Calvin M., Frederick H. Dark and Ronald C. Lease. "On The Listing Of Corporate Debt: A Note," JFQA, 1986, v21(1), 107-114.)

Dark, Frederick H. (Brickley, James A. and Frederick H. Dark. "The Choice Of Organizational Form: The Case Of Franchising," JFEC, 1987, v18(2), 401-420.)

Dark, Frederick H. (Carter, Richard B. and Frederick H. Dark. "The Use Of The Over-Allotment Option In Initial Public Offerings Of Equity: Risks And Underwriter Prestige," FM, 1990, v19(3), 55-64.)

Darling, John R. (Hackett, Donald W. and John R. Darling. "A Comparison Of Consumer And Realtor Attitudes Regarding Consumer Issues Affecting The Housing Industry," AREUEA, 1976, v4(2), 91-99.)

Darling, Paul G. "A Surrogative Measure Of Business Confidence And Its Relation To Stock Prices," JOF, 1955, v10(4), 442-458.

Darrat, Ali F. "On Fiscal Policy And The Stock Market," JMCB, 1988, v20(3), Part 1, 353-363.

Darrat, Ali F. "Stock Returns, Money, And Fiscal Deficits," JFQA, 1990, v25(3), 387-398.

Darrat, Ali F. (Barnhart, Scott W. and Ali F. Darrat. "Budget Deficits, Money Growth And Causality: Further OECD Evidence," JIMF, 1988, v7(2), 231-242.)

Darrat, Ali F. (Barnhart, Scott W. and Ali F. Darrat. "Federal Deficits And Money Growth In The United States: A Vector Autoregressive Analysis," JBF, 1989, v13(1), 137-150.)

Darrat, Ali F. and John L. Glascock. "Real Estate Returns, Money And Fiscal Deficits: Is The Real Estate Market Efficient?," JREFEC, 1989, v2(3), 197-208.

Darrough, Masako N. and Neal M. Stoughton. "Moral Hazard And Adverse Selection: The Question Of Financial Structure," JOF, 1986, v41(2), 501-514.

Darrough, Masako N. "Managerial Incentives For Short-Term Results: A Comment," JOF, 1987, v42(4), 1097-1102.

Darrough, Masako N. (Clarke, Frank H., Masako N. Darrough and John Heineke. "Optimal Pricing Policy In The Presence Of Experience Effects," JOB, 1982, v55(4), 517-530.)

Darrough, Masako N. and Neal M. Stoughton. "A Bargaining Approach To Profit Sharing In Joint Ventures," JOB, 1989, v62(2), 237-270.

Daryanani, Raj. (Arak, Marcelle, Philip Fischer, Laurie Goodman and Raj Daryanani. "The Municipal-Treasury Futures Spread," JFM, 1987, v7(4), 355-372.)

Daryanani, Raj. (Goodman, Laurie S., Raj Daryanani and Arthur Rones. "The Credit Exposure Of Cross-Currency And Nondollar Interest Rate Swaps," RDIBF, 1988, v2, 193-204.)

Dascher, Paul E. "Penn Central Was Predictable," FAJ, 1972, v28(2), 61-64.

Dascher, Paul E. (Brenner, Vincent C. and Paul E. Dascher. "Bankers' Views Of Reporting Current Cost Information," JBR, 1972-73, v3(2), 123-126.)

Dash, Gordon H. (Booth, G. Geoffrey and Gordon H. Dash. "Bank Portfolio Management Using Non-Linear Goal Programming," FR, v12(1), 59-69.)

Dash, Gordon H., Jr. (Booth, G. Geoffrey and Gordon H. Dash, Jr. "Alternate Programming Structures For Bank Portfolios," JBF, 1979, v3(1), 67-82.)

Dash, Gordon H., Jr. (Sanghvi, Arun P. and Gordon H. Dash, Jr. "Core Securities: Widening The Decision Dimensions," JPM, 1978, v4(3), 20-24.)

Daskin, Allan J. "A Pedagogic Approach To Real And Nominal Interest Rates," JFED, 1989, v18, 19-24.

Dasso, Jerome and Lynn Woodward. "Real Estate Education: Past, Present And Future - The Search For A Discipline," AREUEA, 1980, v8(4), 404-416.

Dasso, Jerome, William Kinnard and Joseph Rabianski. "Corporate Real Estate: A Course Outline And Rationale," JRER, 1989, v4(3), 35-46.

Dattatreya, Ravi E. and Frank J. Fabozzi. "A Simplified Model For Valuing Debt Options," JPM, 1989, v15(3), 64-73.

Daub, Mervin. "A Comparison Of The Accuracy Of American And Canadian Short-Term Predictions Of Gross National Product," JOB, 1974, v47(2), 173-185.

Daub, Mervin. "On The Cost To The Firm Of Aggregate Prediction Errors," JOB, 1974, v47(1), 11-22.

Dauer, Ernst A. "Increasing Public Understanding Of Consumer Credit," JOF, 1953, v8(2), 113-118.

Dauten, Carl A. and Merle T. Welshans. "Investment Development Companies," JOF, 1951, v6(3), 276-290.

Dauten, Carl A. "A Fresh Approach To The Place Of Consumer Credit In Economic And Financial Thinking," JOF, 1954, v9(2), 111-123.

Dauten, Carl A. "Recent Institutional Developments In The Field Of Consumer Credit," JOF, 1960, v15(2), 206-220.

Dauten, Carl A. "The Necessary Ingredients Of A Theory Of Business Finance," JOF, 1955, v10(2), 107-120.

Dauten, Joel J. (Apilado, Vincent P., Don C. Warner and Joel J. Dauten. "Evaluative Techniques In Consumer Finance -- Experimental Results And Policy Implications For Financial Institutions," JFQA, 1974, v9(2), 275-283.)

Davant, James W. "An Answer To The Critics," **FAJ**, 1971, v27(6), 14-18,88.

Davanzo, Lawrence E. and Stephen L. Nesbitt. "Performance Fees For Investment Management," **FAJ**, 1987, v43(1), 14-20.

Davenport, J. William, Jr. (Woodside, Arch G. and J. William Davenport, Jr. "Effects Of Price And Salesman Expertise On Customer Purchasing Behavior," **JOB**, 1976, v49(1), 51-59.)

Davenport, Martin W. "Appreciation With Safety In Convertibles," **FAJ**, 1954, v10(4), 37-40.

Davenport, Martin W. "Measuring Earnings Protection For Preferred Stocks," **FAJ**, 1956, v12(4), 31-34.

Davenport, Michael. "Leverage, Dividend Policy And The Cost Of Capital: A Comment," **JOF**, 1970, v25(4), 893-897.

David, Ajay. (McNichols, Maureen and Ajay David. "Stock Dividends, Stock Splits And Signaling," **JOF**, 1990, v45(3), 857-880.)

David, Martin. "Increased Taxation With Increased Acceptability - A Discussion Of Net Worth Taxation As A Federal Revenue Alternative," **JOF**, 1973, v28(2), 481-495.

Davidson, Andrew S., Michael D. Herskovitz and Leonard D. Van Drunen. "The Refinancing Threshold Pricing Model: An Economic Approach To Valuing MBS," **JREFEC**, 1988, v1(2), 117-130.

Davidson, Carl. "Equilibrium In Servicing Industries: An Economic Application Of Queuing Theory," **JOB**, 1988, v61(3), 347-368.

Davidson, George F. "Canadian Programs For Meeting The Sickness Risks," **JRI**, 1957, v24(1), 42-60.

Davidson, Harold A. "College Endowment Fund Management," **FAJ**, 1971, v27(1), 69-74.

Davidson, I. R. "Takeovers: Partitioning Of Gains And Pareto Improvement In A Rational Market With Asymmetric Information," **JBFA**, 1985, v12(3), 373-385.

Davidson, I. R. (Egginton, D. A. and I. R. Davidson. "A Test Of Income Dichotomization," **JBFA**, 1987, v14(1), 143-153.)

Davidson, Ian R. "Ex-Effects: Taxes, Transactions Costs And The Short-Term Trading Hypothesis," **JBFA**, 1991, v18(3), 345-358.

Davidson, Ian. "An Optimal Control Theory Framework For Dividend Determination And The Implications For Intertemporal Dividend Change," **JBFA**, 1980, v7(4), 527-540.

Davidson, Lewis F. (Richardson, Frederick M. and Lewis F. Davidson. "An Exploration Into Bankruptcy Discriminant Model Sensitivity," **JBFA**, 1983, v10(2), 195-207.)

Davidson, Lewis F. (Richardson, Frederick M. and Lewis F. Davidson. "On Linear Discrimination With Accounting Ratios," **JBFA**, 1984, v11(4), 511-525.)

Davidson, S. and R. L. Weil. "Predicting Inflation - Adjusted Results," **FAJ**, 1975, v31(1), 27-31.

Davidson, Sidney and Roman L. Weil. "Replacement Cost Disclosure," **FAJ**, 1976, v32(2), 57-66.

Davidson, Sidney and Roman L. Weil. "Inflation Accounting For Utilities," **FAJ**, 1975, v31(3), 30-34,62.

Davidson, Sidney and Roman L. Weil. "Inflation Accounting And 1974 Earnings," **FAJ**, 1975, v31(5), 42-54.

Davidson, Sidney and Roman L. Weil. "Inflation Accounting And Leases," **FAJ**, 1975, v31(6), 22-29,57.

Davidson, Sidney and David F. Drake. "Capital Budgeting And The 'Best' Tax Depreciation Method," **JOB**, 1961, v34(4), 442-452.

Davidson, Sidney and David F. Drake. "The 'Best' Tax Depreciation Method-1964," **JOB**, 1964, v37(3), 258-260.

Davidson, Sidney, George H. Sorter, and Hemu Kalle. "Measuring The Defensive Position Of A Firm," **FAJ**, 1964, v20(1), 23-29.

Davidson, Sidney, Lisa B. Skelton and Roman L. Weil. "The FASB's Inflation Accounting Proposal," **FAJ**, 1979, v35(3), 41-54.

Davidson, Sidney. "Government Intervention In Financial Reporting," **RIF**, 1983, v4, (Supp), 15-30.

Davidson, Sidney. (Weston, Frank T. and Sidney Davidson. "Accounting Changes And Earnings," **FAJ**, 1968, v24(5), 59-66.)

Davidson, Wallace N. (Chandy, P. R., Wallace N. Davidson and Sharon Garrison. "Bad News = Good News! Who Can Tell?," **JPM**, 1985, v12(1), 24-27.)

Davidson, Wallace N. (Cross, Mark L., Wallace N. Davidson and John H. Thornton. "The Impact Of Directors And Officers' Liability Suits On Firm Value," **JRI**, 1989, v56(1), 128-136.)

Davidson, Wallace N. (Glascock, John L., Wallace N. Davidson and C. F. Sirmans. "An Analysis Of The Acquisition And Dispositon Of Real Estate Assets," **JRER**, 1989, v4(3), 131-140.)

Davidson, Wallace N., III and P. R. Chandy. "The Regulatory Environment For Public Utilities: Indications Of The Importance Of Political Process," **FAJ**, 1983, v39(6), 50-53.

Davidson, Wallace N., III and James L. McDonald. "Evidence Of The Effect On Shareholder Wealth Of Corporate Spinoffs: The Creation Of Royalty Trusts," **JFR**, 1987, v10(4), 321-328.

Davidson, Wallace N., III and Sharon H. Garrison. "The Stock Market Reaction To Significant Tender Offer Repurchases Of Stock: Size And Purpose Perspective," **FR**, 1989, v24(1), 93-108.

Davidson, Wallace N., III and Dipa Dutia. "A Note On The Behavior Of Security Returns: A Test Of Stock Market Overreaction And Efficiency," **JFR**, 1989, v12(3), 245-252.

Davidson, Wallace N., III, and John L. Glascock. "The Announcement Effects Of Preferred Stock Re-Ratings," **JFR**, 1985, v8(4), 317-325.

Davidson, Wallace N., III, Dipa Dutia and Louis Cheng. "A Re-Examination Of The Market Reaction To Failed Mergers," **JOF**, 1989, v44(4), 1077-1084.

Davidson, Wallace N., III, P. R. Chandy and Mark Cross. "Large Losses, Risk Management And Stock Returns In The Airline Industry," **JRI**, 1987, v54(1), 162-172.

Davidson, Wallace N., III, Sharon Hatten Garrison and Glenn V. Henderson, Jr. "Examining Merger Synergy With The Capital Asset Pricing Model," **FR**, 1987, v22(2), 233-248.

Davidson, Wallace N., III. "The Effect Of Rate Cases On Public Utility Stock Returns," **JFR**, 1984, v7(1), 81-93.

Davidson, Wallace N., III. "An Examination Of The Finance Programs At Liberal Arts Colleges," **JFED**, 1984, v13, 40-46.

Davidson, Wallace N., III. (Glascock, John L. and Wallace N. Davidson, III. "The Effect Of Bond Deratings On Bank Stock Returns," **JBR**, 1985-86, v16(3), 120-127.)

Davidson, Wallace N., III. (Cross, Mark L., Wallace N. Davidson, III and John H. Thornton. "The Impact Of Captive Insurer Formation On The Parent Firm's Value," **JRI**, 1986, v53(3), 471-483.)

Davidson, Wallace N., III. (Cross, Mark L., Wallace N. Davidson, III and John H. Thornton. "Taxes, Stock Returns And Captive Insurance Subsidiaries," **JRI**, 1988, v55(2), 331-338.)

Davies, David G. "Commodity Taxation And Equity," **JOF**, 1961, v16(4), 581-590.

Davies, J. R. and W. M. McInnes. "The Valuation Of Fixed Assets In The Financial Accounts Of UK Nationalised Industries And The Implications For Monitoring Performance: A Comment," **JBFA**, 1982, v8(2),267-272.

Davies, Laurie and Gerd Ronning. "A Note On The Uniqueness Of Portfolio Choice," **JFQA**, 1976, v11(3), 481-484.

Davis, Alfred H. R. "Effective Tax Rates As Determinants Of Canadian Capital Structure," **FM**, 1987, v16(3), 22-28.

Davis, E. G., D. M. Dunn and W. H. Williams. "Ambiguities In The Cross-Section Analysis Of Per Share Financial Data," **JOF**, 1973, v28(5), 1241-1248.

Davis, E. G., D. M. Dunn and W. H. Williams. "Invariance And Scaling In The Per Share Analysis Of Financial Data: Reply," **JOF**, 1977, v32(3), 937-938.

Davis, E. W. and K. A. Yeomans. "Market Discount On New Issues Of Equity: The Influence Of Firm Size, Method Of Issue And Market Volatility," **JBFA**, 1976, v3(4), 27-42.

Davis, Harry L. (Peacock, Peter and Harry L. Davis. "The Alphabet As An Independent Variable: A Reply To J. Douglas McConnell," **JOB**, 1970, v43(2),205-209.)

Davis, Herbert J. (Blalack, Richard O., Herbert J. Davis and Harvey W. Rubin. "Sources Of Job Stress For The FLMI: A Comparative Analysis," **JRI**, 1979, v46(2), 123-138.)

Davis, Herbert J. and Harvey W. Rubin. "Perceived Benefits Of Professional Certification," **JRI**, 1976, v43(1), 152-155.

Davis, Joseph D. (Clark, Frederick W. and Joseph D. Davis. "Interest Rates Caught Between Inflationary And Monetary Forces," **FAJ**, 1964, v20(6), 77-83.)

Davis, Joseph S. "Population Centers As Investment Wells," **FAJ**, 1952, v8(2), 23-26.

Davis, K. Roscoe. (Trieschmann, James S., K. Roscoe Davis and E. J. Leverett, Jr. "A Probabilistic Valuation Model For A Property-Liability Insurance Agency," **JRI**, 1975, v42(2), 289-302.)

Davis, Otto A. "The Economics Of Trading Stamps," **JOB**, 1959, v32(2), 141-150.

Davis, Paul L. (Michaud, Richard O. and Paul L. Davis. "Valuation Model Bias And The Scale Structure Of Dividend Discount Returns," **JOF**, 1982, v37(1), 562-573.)

Davis, Ralph C. "A Philosophy Of Management," **JRI**, 1958, v25(3), 1-7.

Davis, Richard G. and Jack M. Guttentag. "Are Compensating Balance Requirements Irrational?," **JOF**, 1962, v17(1), 121-126.

Davis, Richard G. "Monetary And Credit Restraint In 1973 And Early 1974," **JFQA**, 1974, v9(5), 733-741.

Davis, Robert R. "Panel: Trading Halts And Price Limits," **RFM**, 1988, v7(3), 442-445.

Davis, Samuel G., Gary A. Kochenberger and Edward T. Reutzel. "Expressend: A Check Clearing Decision Support System For Endpoint Selection," **JBR**, 1983-84, v14(3), 203-211.

Davis, Samuel G., Nicholas Ceto, Jr. and J. Mac. Rabb. "A Comprehensive Check Processing Simulation Model," **JBR**, 1982-83, v13(3), 185-194.

Davis, Shelby Cullom. "How Fire And Casualty Companies Invest," **FAJ**, 1961, v17(6), 19-23.

Davis, Shelby Cullom. "Impact Of Multiple Line Underwriting On The Capital Structure Of Insurance Companies," **JRI**, 1958, v25(1), 61-64.

Davis, Shelby Cullom. "Insurance Companies And The Interest Rate," **FAJ**, 1953, v9(4), 15-18.

Davis, Shelby Cullom. "It's Only A Matter Of Money," **FAJ**, 1948, v4(4), 3-10.

Davis, Shelby Cullom. "Nothing But The Best," **FAJ**, 1954, v10(4), 9-12.

Davis, Shelby Cullom. "Only A Matter Of Money," **FAJ**, 1966, v22(5), 67-71.

Davis, Shelby Cullom. "Opportunities In Life Insurance Stocks," **FAJ**, 1957, v13(4), 97-101.

Davis, Shelby Cullom. "Our Mid-20th Century Capitalists," **FAJ**, 1950, v6(4), 15-20.

Davis, Shelby Cullom. "Pauper And Prince," **FAJ**, 1956, v12(5), 9-12.

Davis, Shelby Cullom. "There's Life In Them," **FAJ**, 1952, v8(5), 46-50.

Davis, Shelby Cullom. "Treatment Results Of Fire And Casualty Companies," **FAJ**, 1947, v3(2), 3-9.

Davis, Shelby Cullom. "Types Of Analysts Abroad," **FAJ**, 1955, v11(5), 9-12.

Davis, Shelby M.C. "Elements Of Perspective And Policy," **FAJ**, 1965, v21(3), 98-100.

Davis, Wayne J. and David T. Whitford. "Tests Of Competition Models For Resource Allocation: Good News And Bad News," **AFPAF**, 1989, v3(1), 375-393.

Davis, William A., Jr. and Edward B. Roberts. "The Management Of Department Of Defense Laser Research Contracts," **JOB**, 1970, v43(1), 44-55.

Dawson, Frederic C. "Risks And Returns In Continuous Option Writing: Reply," **JPM**, 1980, v6(2), 71-73.

Dawson, Frederic C. "Risks And Returns In Continuous Option Writing: A Reply," **JPM**, 1979, v5(4), 74.

Dawson, Frederic C. "Risks And Returns In Continuous Option Writing," **JPM**, 1979, v5(2), 58-63.

Dawson, James P., Peter M. Neupert and Clyde P. Stickney. "Restating Financial Statements For Alternative GAAPs: Is It Worth The Effort?," **FAJ**, 1980, v36(6), 38-46.

Dawson, Steve. "A Number Fifteenth Euroconvertible Bond Reunion," **JPM**, 1985, v11(2), 85-87.

Dawson, Steve. "Is The Hong Kong Market Efficient?," **JPM**, 1982, v8(3), 17-20.

Dawson, Steven M. "Initial Public Offer Underpricing: The Issuer's View—A Note," **JOF**, 1987, v42(1), 159-162.

Dawson, Steven M. "Local Adaptation Of Cases," **JFED**, 1973, v2, 62-63.

Dawson, Steven M. "Secondary Stock Market Performance Of Initial Public Offers, Hong Kong, Singapore And Malaysia: 1978-1984," **JBFA**, 1987, v14(1), 65-76.

Dawson, Steven M. "The Trend Toward Efficiency For Less Developed Stock Exchanges: Hong Kong," JBFA, 1984, v11(2), 151-161.

Dawson, Steven M. "Timing Interest Payments For Convertible Bonds," FM, 1974, v3(2), 14-16.

Day, A. Edward and Patric H. Hendershott. "Household Demand For Policy Loans," JRI, 1977, v44(3), 411-423.

Day, Ellen. (Johnson, Joyce M., Hugh O. Nourse and Ellen Day. "Factors Related To The Selection Of A Real Estate Agency," JRER, 1988, v3(2), 109-118.)

Day, Theodore E. "Expected Inflation And The Real Rate Of Interest: A Note," JBF, 1985, v9(4), 491-498.

Day, Theodore E. "Real Stock Returns And Inflation," JOF, 1984, v39(2), 493-502.

Day, Theodore E. and Craig M. Lewis. "The Behavior Of The Volatility Implicit In The Prices Of Stock Index Options," JFEC, 1988, v22(1), 103-122.

DeAlessi, Louis. "Do Business Firms Gain From Inflation? Reprise," JOB, 1975, v48(2), 264-266.

DeAlessi, Louis. "Do Business Firms Gain From Inflation?," JOB, 1964, v37(2), 162-166.

DeAlessi, Louis. "Private Property And Dispersion Of Ownership In Large Corporations," JOF, 1973, v28(4), 839-851.

Dean, James W. "The Rise And Fall Of Neomonetarism," FAJ, 1985, v41(5), 72-78.

Dean, Joel and Winfield Smith. "Has MAPI A Place In A Comprehensive System Of Capital Controls?," JOB, 1955, v28(4), 261-274.

Dean, Joel. "Better Management Of Capital Expenditures Through Research," JOF, 1953, v8(2), 119-128.

Dean, Joel. "Four Ways To Write Off Capital Investment: Management Should Have A Wider Tax Choice," JOB, 1956, v29(2), 79-89.

Dean, Joel. "Outside Directors Appraise Stock Options," FAJ, 1963, v19(2), 25-31.

Dean, Joel. "Product Line Policy," JOB, 1950, v23(4), 248-258.

DeAngelo, Harry and Edward M. Rice. "Antitakeover Charter Amendments And Stockholder Wealth," JFEC, 1983, v11(1), 329-360.

DeAngelo, Harry and Linda DeAngelo. "Managerial Ownership Of Voting Rights: A Study Of Public Corporation With Dual Classes Of Common Stock," JFEC, 1985, v14(1), 33-69.

DeAngelo, Harry and Ronald W. Masulis. "Optimal Capital Structure Under Corporate And Personal Taxation," JFEC, 1980, v8(1), 3-27.

DeAngelo, Harry and Ronald W. Masulis. "Leverage And Dividend Irrelevancy Under Corprate And Personal Taxation," JOF, 1980, v35(2), 453-464.

DeAngelo, Harry and Linda DeAngelo. "Management Buyouts Of Publicly Traded Corporations," FAJ, 1987, v43(3), 38-49.

DeAngelo, Harry and Linda DeAngelo. "Dividend Policy And Financial Distress: An Empirical Investigation Of Troubled NYSE Firms," JOF, 1990, v45(5), 1415-1432.

DeAngelo, Harry and Linda DeAngelo. "Proxy Contests And The Governance Of Publicly Held Corporations," JFEC, 1989, v23(1), 29-60.

DeAngelo, Harry. "Payout Policy And Tax Deferral," JOF, 1991, v46(1), 357-368.

DeAngelo, Harry. (Dann, Larry Y. and Harry DeAngelo. "Standstill Agreements, Privately Negotiated Stock Repurchases, And The Market For Corporate Control," JFEC, 1983, v11(1), 275-300.)

DeAngelo, Harry. (Dann, Larry Y. and Harry DeAngelo. "Corporate Financial Policy And Corporate Control: A Study Of Defensive Adjustments In Asset And Ownership Structure," JFEC, 1988, v20(1/2), 87-128.)

DeAngelo, Linda. (DeAngelo, Harry and Linda DeAngelo. "Management Buyouts Of Publicly Traded Corporations," FAJ, 1987, v43(3), 38-49.)

DeAngelo, Linda. (DeAngelo, Harry and Linda DeAngelo. "Managerial Ownership Of Voting Rights: A Study Of Public Corporation With Dual Classes Of Common Stock," JFEC, 1985, v14(1), 33-69.)

DeAngelo, Linda. (DeAngelo, Harry and Linda DeAngelo. "Dividend Policy And Financial Distress: An Empirical Investigation Of Troubled NYSE Firms," JOF, 1990, v45(5), 1415-1432.)

DeAngelo, Linda. (DeAngelo, Harry and Linda DeAngelo. "Proxy Contests And The Governance Of Publicly Held Corporations," JFEC, 1989, v23(1), 29-60.)

Deaton, Robert B. "Domestic Trunk Airlines," FAJ, 1966, v22(4), 61-63.

Deaves, Richard. "Hedging Canadian Corporate Debt: A Comment And Extensions," JFM, 1990, v10(2), 197-200.

Deaves, Richard. "Money Supply Announcements And Market Reactions In An Open Economy," JMCB, 1990, v22(2), 154-164.

Debe, A. Joseph. "Investment Aspects Of The Trucking Industry," FAJ, 1965, v21(4), 72-77.

DeBoissieu, Ch. "The Dynamics Of The EMS In The Light Of European Financial Integration: Some Reflections From A French Perspective," JBF, 1990, v14(5), 889-908.

DeBondt, Werner F. M. and Richard Thaler. "Does The Stock Market Overreact?," JOF, 1985, v40(3), 793-805.

DeBondt, Werner F. M. and Richard H. Thaler. "Further Evidence On Investor Overreaction And Stock Market Seasonality," JOF, 1987, v42(3), 557-581.

DeBondt, Werner F. M. "What Do Economists Know About The Stock Market?," JPM, 1991, v17(2), 84-91.

DeBrabander, B. (Vanlommel, E. and B. De Brabander. "The Organization Of Electronic Data Processing (EDP) Activities And Computer Use," JOB, 1975, v48(3), 391-410.)

DeBrabander, B., D. Deschoolmeester, R. Leyder and E. Vanlommel. "The Effect Of Task Volume And Complexity Upon Computer Use," JOB, 1972, v45(1),56-84.

DeBrillembourg, Hilda Ochoa. "From Blue Jeans To Buyouts—Shrewd Portfolio Mangers Or A Nation Of Spendthrifts?," FAJ, 1987, v43(6), 67-71.

DeCandia, Angelo. (Fridson, Martin S. and Angelo De Candia. "Trends: Follow, Buck, Or Ignore?," JPM, 1991, v17(2), 50-55.)

Decker, G. (Agnello, W., W. Brueggeman, G. Decker, R. Griffith, R. Leftwich, R. Moore, J. Neal, B. Sternlicht, B. Wallach, W. Wardrop and C. Zinngrabe. "Panel: Corporate Real Estate Roundtable," JACF, 1990, v3(1), 6-38.)

Decker, Martin G. (Butler, Hartman L., Jr. and Martin G. Decker. "Security Check On Dow Jones Industrial Average," FAJ, 1953, v9(1), 37-46.)

DeCossio, Francisco. (Trifts, Jack W., Neil W. Sicherman, Rodney L. Roenfeldt and Francisco De Cossio. "Divestiture To Unit Managers And Shareholder Wealth," JFR, 1990, v13(2), 167-172.)

DeCossio, Francisco. (Trifts, Jack W., Neil W. Sicherman, Rodney L. Roenfeldt and Francisco De Cossio. "Divestiture To Unit Managers And Shareholder Wealth," JFR, 1990, v13(2), 167-172.)

Dedalus, Adam I. "The Effect Of Inflation On The Stock Market," FAJ, 1958, v14(4), 73-76.

Dee, John J. (Hettenhouse, George W. and John J. Dee. "A Component Analysis Of Rates Of Return In Real Estate Investment," AREUEA, 1976, v4(1), 7-22.)

Deegan, James. (McMillan, T. E., Jr., Louis E. Buck, Jr. and James Deegan. "The 'Fisher Theorem' - An Illusion, But Whose?," FAJ, 1984, v40(6), 63-69.)

Deely, Cathy. (Morse, Dale and Cathy Deely. "Regional Differences In Municipal Bond Ratings," FAJ, 1983, v39(6), 54-59.)

Deets, M. King. (Cheng, Pao L. and M. King Deets. "Statistical Biases And Security Rates Of Return," JFQA, 1971, v6(3), 977-994.)

Deets, M. King. (Cheng, Pao L. and M. King Deets. "Systematic Risk And The Horizon Problem," JFQA, 1973, v8(2), 299-316.)

Deets, M. King. (Cheng, Pao L. and M. King Deets. "Portfolio Returns And The Random Walk Theory," JOF, 1971, v26(1), 11-30.)

Deets, M. King. (Cheng, Pao L. and M. King Deets. "Test Of Portfolio Building Rules: Comment," JOF, 1971, v26(4), 965-972.)

Deets, M. King. (Cheng, Pao L. and M. King Deets. "Portfolio Returns And The Random Walk Theory: Reply," JOF, 1976,v31(1),157-161.)

Deets, M. King. (Cheng, Pao L. and M. King Deets. "Portfolio Returns And The Random Walk Theory: Reply," JOF, 1973, v28(3), 742-745.)

deFaro, Clovis. "A Sufficient Condition For A Unique Nonnegative Internal Rate Of Return: Further Comments," JFQA, 1978, v13(3), 577-584.

deFaro, Clovis. "A Sufficient Condition For A Unique Nonnegative Internal Rate Of Return: A Comment," JFQA, 1973, v8(4), 683-684.

deFaro, Clovis. (Jucker, James V. and Clovis de Faro. "The Selection Of International Borrowing Sources," JFQA, 1975, v10(3), 381-407.)

deFaro, Clovis. (Jucker, James V. and Clovis de Faro. "A Simple Algorithm For Stone's Version Of The Portfolio Selection Problem," JFQA, 1975, v10(5), 859-870.)

DeFelice, Frank. "Security And Investment: More Evidence," JOF, 1970, v25(4), 803-807.

DeFreitas, Arlei. (Solnik, Bruno and Arlei De Freitas. "International Factors Of Stock Price Behavior," RDIBF, 1988, v2, 259-276.)

DeFusco, Richard A. and Robert R. Johnson. "The Effect Of Executive Stock Option Plans On Stockholders And Bondholders," JOF, 1990, v45(2), 617-628.

DeFusco, Richard A., George C. Philippatos and Dosoung Choi. "Differences In Factor Structures Between U.S. Multinational And Domestic Corporations: Evidence From Bilinear Paradigm Tests," FR, 1990, v25(3), 395-404.

DeFusco, Richard A., Gordon V. Karels and Thomas S. Zorn. "Agency Theory: An Application To Grading Group Projects," JFED, 1989, v18, 43-44.

Defusco, Richard. (Tsetsekos, George P. and Richard Defusco. "Portfolio Performance, Managerial Ownership, And The Size Effect," JPM, 1990, v16(3), 33-39.)

DeGennaro, Ramon P. and Sangphill Kim. "The CAPM And Beta In An Imperfect Market: Comment," JPM, 1986, v12(4), 78-80.

DeGennaro, Ramon P. "Payment Delays: Bias In The Yield Curve," JMCB, 1988, v20(4), 684-690.

DeGennaro, Ramon P. "The Effect Of Payment Delays On Stock Prices," JFR, 1990, v13(2), 133-146.

DeGennaro, Ramon P. (Baillie, Richard T. and Ramon P. DeGennaro. "Stock Returns And Volatility," JFQA, 1990, v25(2), 203-214.)

DeGennaro, Ramon P. (Baillie, Richard T. and Ramon P. DeGennaro. "The Impact Of Delivery Terms On Stock Return Volatility," JFSR, 1989, v3(1), 55-76.)

DeGennaro, Ramon P. and James T. Moser. "Delivery, Failed And Daily Treasury Bill Returns," JFSR, 1990, v4(3), 203-222.

deGoumois, Marc. "A 'Character Of The Market Method' Is Facing A Crucial Test," FAJ, 1957, v13(1), 55-60.

deGoumois, Marc. "Pre-Determined Resistance Levels For Dow-Jones," FAJ, 1960, v16(5), 59-60.

DeGrauwe, Paul. "The Exchange Rate In A Portfolio Balance Model With A Banking Sector," JIMF, 1982, v1(3), 225-240.

DeGroff, Carol C. "The 1981 F.A.F. Investment Management Workshop - A Study In Controversy," FAJ, 1982, v38(2), 77-78.

DeHaan, Jakob and Dick Zelhorst. "The Impact Of Government Deficits On Money Growth In Developing Countries," JIMF, 1990, v9(4), 455-469.

DeHaan, Menno. (Gerking, Shelby, Menno De Haan and William Schulze. "The Marginal Value Of Job Safety: A Contingent Valuation Study," JRU, 1988, v1(2), 185-200.)

DeJanosi, Peter E. "A Note On Provisional Estimates Of The Gross National Product And Its Major Components," JOB, 1961, v34(4), 495-499.

DeJong, Douglas V. and Daniel W. Collins. "Explanations For The Instability Of Equity Beta: Risk-Free Rate Changes And Leverage Effects," JFQA, 1985, v20(1), 73-94.

DeJong, Douglas V., Robert Forsythe and Russell J. Lundholm. "Ripoffs, Lemons, And Reputation Formation In Agency Relationships: A Laboratory Market Study," JOF, 1985, v40(3), 809-820.

DeJong, Piet and Rex Thompson. "Testing Linear Hypothesis In The Sur Framework With Identical Explanatory Variables," RIF, 1990, v8, 59-76.

DeKorvin, Andre. (Spitz, A. Edward and Andre DeKorvin. "A New Theoretical Model For Depicting Profit Optimality," JFQA, 1971, v6(4), 1117-1121.)

DeLaGarza, Jesus M. (Gentry, James A. and Jesus M. De La Garza. "A Generalized Model For Monitoring Accounts Receivable," FM, 1985, v14(4), 28-38.)

DeLaGarza, Jesus M. (Gentry, James A. and Jesus M. De La Garza. "Monitoring Accounts Payables," FR, 1990, v25(4), 559-576.)

delaMare, R. F. "An Investigation Into The Discounting Formula Used In Capital Budgeting Models," **JBFA**, 1975, v2(2), 203-218.

Delaney, Charles J. and Marc T. Smith. "The Price Effect Of Impact Fees And The Price On New Housing: An Empirical Study," **AREUEA**, 1989, v17(1), 41-54.

DeLeeuw, Frank and Edward M. Gramlich. "The Channels Of Monetary Policy: A Further Report On The Federal Reserve - M.I.T. Model," **JOF**, 1969, v24(2),265-290.

DeLeeuw, Frank and Thomas M. Holloway. "The Measurement And Significance Of The Cyclically Adjusted Federal Budget And Debt," **JMCB**, 1985, v17(2), 232-242.

DeLeeuw, Frank. "What Should U.S. Housing Policies Be?," **JOF**, 1974, v29(2), 699-721.

DeLeeuw, Frank. (Hendershott, Patric H. and Frank De Leeuw. "Free Reserves, Interest Rates, And Deposits: A Synthesis," **JOF**, 1970, v25(3), 599-613.)

Dellas, Harris. "A Real Model Of The World Business Cycle," **JIMF**, 1986, v5(3), 381-394.

Dellva, W. L. (Teas, R. Kenneth and W. L. Dellva. "Conjoint Measurement Of Consumers' Preferences For Multiattribute Financial Services," **JBR**, 1985-86, v16(2), 99-112.)

DeLong, J. Bradford, Andrei Shleifer, Lawrence H. Summers and Robert J. Waldmann. "The Survival Of Noise Traders In Financial Markets," **JOB**, 1991, v64(1), 1-20.

DeLong, J. Bradford, Andrei Shleifer, Lawrence H. Summers and Robert J. Waldmann. "Positive Feedback Investment Strategies And Destabilizing Rational Speculation," **JOF**, 1990, v45(2), 379-396.

DeLong, J. Bradford, Andrei Shleifer, Lawrence H. Summers and Robert J. Waldmann. "The Size And Incidence Of The Losses From Noise Trading," **JOF**, 1989, v44(3), 681-696.

Delozier, John. (Clayton, Ronnie, John Delozier and Michael C. Ehrhardt. "A Note On January Returns In The U.S. Government Bond Market: The Term Effect," **JFSR**, 1989, v2(4), 307-318.)

DeLung, John. "Playing FINANSIM - An Undergraduate's View," **JFED**, 1973, v2, 78-79.

DelVale, Marguerite. (Petruzzi, Chirstoher, Marguerite Del Valle and Stephen Judlowe. "Patent And Copyright Protection For Innovations In Finance," **FM**, 1988, v17(4), 66-71.)

DeMacedo, Jorge Braga. (Branson, William H. and Jorge Braga De Macedo. "The Optimal Weighting Of Indicators For A Crawling Peg," **JIMF**, 1982, v1(2), 165-178.)

DeMagistris, Robin. (Schallheim, James and Robin DeMagistris. "New Estimates Of The Market Parameters," **FM**, 1980, v9(3), 60-68.)

DeMarco, Edward J. (Mays, Elizabeth and Edward J. DeMarco. "The Demand For Federal Home Loan Bank Advances By Thrift Institutions: Some Recent Evidence," **AREUEA**, 1989, v17(3), 363-379.)

DeMaskey, Andrea L. and James C. Baker. "The Efficiency Of Option Markets In Foreign Currencies: An Empirical Analysis," **IJOF**, 1990, v3(1), 1-38.

DeMattia, Renato. "The Forces At Work In The Evolution Of Payment Systems In The 1980s," **JBR**, 1984-85, v15(4), 211-221.

Demers, Donald P. "The Offshore Drilling Industry," **FAJ**, 1970, v26(1), 32-44.

DeMong, Richard F. (Butler, Hartman L., Jr. and Richard F. DeMong. "The Changing Dow Jones Industrial Average," **FAJ**, 1986, v42(4), 59-62.)

DeMong, Richard F., Laurence C. Pettit and B. J. Campsey. "Finance Curriculum For The Future: Perceptions Of Practitioners Versus Academicians," **JFED**, 1979, v8, 45-48.

Dempsey, B. W. "There Is No Discount Rate," **FAJ**, 1955, v11(5), 79-80.

Demsetz, Harold. "Accounting For Advertising As A Barrier To Entry," **JOB**, 1979, v52(3), 345-360.

Denbaly, Mark. (Kitchen, John and Mark Denbaly. "Commodity Prices, Money Surprises, And Fed Credibility: Comment," **JMCB**, 1987, v19(2), 246-251.)

Denenberg, Herbert S. "A New Concept Of The Economics Of Life Value And The Human Life Value: Reply," **JRI**, 1970, v37(4), 648-654.

Denenberg, Herbert S. "How To Rewrite An Insurance Code: Comment," **JRI**, 1967, v34(4), 561-574.

Denenberg, Herbert S. "Is 'A-Plus' Really A Passing Grade? Insurer Risk Capacity And Financial Ratings," **JRI**, 1967, v34(3), 371-384.

Denenberg, Herbert S. "Review Article - A Basic Look At Operations Research," **JRI**, 1968, v35(1), 159-162.

Denenberg, Herbert S. "Science, Government And Information," **JRI**, 1964, v31(1), 113-116.

Denenberg, Herbert S. "The Insurance Professor: Captive Or Critic, Countervailence Or Capitulation," **JRI**, 1970, v37(4), 513-525.

Denenberg, Herbert S. "The Legal Definition Of Insurance," **JRI**, 1963, v30(3), 319-344.

Denenberg, Herbert S. "The Right To Income: Social Insurance Versus Public Assistance," **JRI**, 1962, v29(1), 87-98.

Denenberg, Herbert S. (Aponte, Juan B. and Herbert S. Denenberg. "Life Insurance And The Investment Texts," **JRI**, 1963, v30(4), 595-605.)

Denenberg, Herbert S. (Aponte, Juan B. and Herbert S. Denenberg. "The Automobile Problem In Puerto Rico: Dimensions And Proposed Solution," **JRI**, 1968, v35(2), 227-236.)

Denenberg, Herbert S. (Aponte, Juan B. and Herbert S. Denenberg. "A New Concept Of The Economics Of Life Value And The Human Life Value: A Rationale For Term Insurance As The Cornerstone Of Insurance Marketing," **JRI**, 1968, v35(3), 337-356.)

Denenberg, Herbert S. (Aponte, Juan B. and Herbert S. Denenberg. "The Automobile Problem In Puerto Rico: Comment," **JRI**, 1968, v35(4), 637.)

Denenberg, Herbert S. (Cummins, J. David, Herbert S. Denenberg and William C. Scheel. "Concentration In The U.S. Life Insurance Industry," **JRI**, 1972, v39(2), 177-200.)

Denenberg, Herbert S. and Gerald R. Hartman. "Insurance Rate Making In Louisiana," **JRI**, 1967, v34(4), 635-646.

Denenberg, Herbert S. and J. Robert Ferrari. "New Perspectives On Risk Management: The Search For Principles," **JRI**, 1966, v33(4), 647-660.

Denenberg, Herbert S. and J. Robert Ferrari. "New Perspectives On Risk Management: Reply," **JRI**, 1968, v35(4), 623-627.

Denenberg, Herbert S. and J. David Cummins. "Insurance And Reciprocity," **JRI**, 1971, v38(3), 367-384.

Denenberg, Herbert S. and J. David Cummins. "Insurance And Reciprocity: Reply," **JRI**, 1973, v40(1), 141-142.

DeNeufville, Richard. (Shpilberg, David and Richard De Neufville. "Use Of Decision Analysis For Optimizing Choice Of Fire Protection And Insurance: An Airport Study," **JRI**, 1975, v42(1), 133-150.)

Denis, David J. "Defensive Changes In Corporate Payout Policy: Share Repurchases And Special Dividends," **JOF**, 1990, v45(5), 1433-1456.

Denis, David J. "Shelf Registration And The Market For Seasoned Equity Offerings," **JOB**, 1991, v64(2), 189-212.

Denis, Jack, Jr. "How To Hedge Foreign Currency Risk," **FAJ**, 1976, v32(1), 50-54.

Denison, Edward F. "United States Economic Growth," **JOB**, 1962, v35(2), 109-121.

Denison, R. D. "Practical Applications Of Financial Research," **FR**, 1978, v13(1), 73-76.

Dennehy, Gerald. "Compounded Growth Rates (A Nomograph)," **FAJ**, 1965, v21(6), 97.

Denning, Karen Craft and Kuldeep Shastri. "Single Sale Divestments: The Impact On Stockholders And Bondholders," **JBFA**, 1990, v17(5), 731-744.

Dennis, Charles N. "An Investigation Into The Effects Of Independent Investor Relations Firms On Common Stock Prices," **JOF**, 1973, v28(2), 373-380.

Dennis, David. (Bird, Ron, David Dennis and Mark Tippett. "A Stop Loss Approach To Portfolio Insurance," **JPM**, 1988, v15(1), 35-40.)

Dennis, Debra K. and John J. McConnell. "Corporate Mergers And Security Returns," **JFEC**, 1986, v16(2), 143-187.

Dennis, Debra K. (French, Dan W. and Debra K. Dennis. "CEPS: The Illusion Of Corporate Growth: Comment," **JPM**, 1984,v10(4),83-85.)

Dennis, W. M. "Chemicals A Growth Industry," **FAJ**, 1952, v8(2), 61-65.

Denny, Wanda. (Barlev, Benzion, Wanda Denny and Haim Levy. "Using Accounting Data For Portfolio Management," **JPM**, 1988, v14(3), 70-77.)

Dent, Warren T. (Collins, Daniel W., Warren T. Dent and Melvin C. O'Conner. "Has Full Cost Accounting Helped Share Prices?," **FAJ**, 1978, v34(6), 48-57.)

Denyon, David E. (Jordan, James V., William E. Seale, Stephen J. Dinehart and David E. Kenyon. "The Intraday Variability Of Soybean Futures Prices: Information And Trading Effects," **RFM**, 1988, v7(1), 96-109.)

Deoul, Neal. "An Investment Approach To Microwave Securities," **FAJ**, 1961, v17(5), 67-72.

DePamphilis, Donald M. "Establishing Confidence Levels For Economic Indicators Used In Forecasting Bank Related Variables," **JBR**, 1976-77, v7(3), 241-246.

DePamphilis, Donald M. "Variation On Individual Life Insurance Premium Revenues: An Econometric Approach," **JRI**, 1977, v44(1), 67-76.

Deravi, M. Keivan and Massoud Metghalchi. "The European Monetary System: A Note," **JBF**, 1988, v11(3), 505-512.

Derber, Milton, W. Ellison Chalmers, and Ross Stagner. "Collective Bargaining And Management Functions: An Empirical Study," **JOB**, 1958, v31(2),107-120.

Derber, Milton. "A History Of American Labor And Organized Labor In American History: A Review Article," **JOB**, 1967, v40(1), 85-86.

Derman, Emanuel. (Black, Fischer, Emanuel Derman and William Toy. "A One-Factor Model Of Interest Rates And Its Application To Treasury Bond Options," **FAJ**, 1990, v46(1), 33-39.)

Dermine, J. "Deposit Rates, Credit Rates And Bank Capital: The Klein-Monti Model Revisited," **JBF**, 1986, v10(1), 99-114.

Dermine, Jean. "Inflation, Taxes And Banks' Market Values," **JBFA**, 1985, v12(1), 65-71.

Dermine, Jean. "The Measurement Of Interest-Rate Risk By Financial Intermediaries," **JBR**, 1985-86, v16(2), 86-90.

Dermody, Jaime Cuevas and Eliezer Zeev Prisman. "Term Structure Multiplicity And Clientele In Markets With Transactions Costs And Taxes," **JOF**, 1988, v43(4), 893-911.

Dernburg, H. J. "Foreign Dollar Bonds: Present Status And Possibilities Of Future Financing," **JOF**, 1950, v5(3), 217-240.

Dernburg, H. J. "Some Basic Aspects Of The German Debt Settlement," **JOF**, 1953, v8(3), 298-318.

Dernburg, H. J. "The Blocked Mark Problem (1931-54)," **JOF**, 1955, v10(1), 17-40.

DeRonne, William A. "Pension Funds And Futures Markets: Option Hedging Of Fixed-Rate Assets," **RFM**, 1985, v4(2), 232-241.

DeRosa, Paul. "Mortgage Rationing And Residential Investment: Some Results From A Brainard-Tobin Model," **JMCB**, 1978, v10(1), 75-87.

Derwa, Leon. "Computer Models: Aids To Management At Societe Generale De Banque," **JBR**, 1972-73, v3(2), 84-94.

Desai, Anand S. and Roger D. Stover. "Bank Holding Company Acquisitions, Stockholder Returns, And Regulatory Uncertainty," **JFR**, 1985, v8(2), 145-156.

Desai, Anand S. (Ang, James S., Jess H. Chua and Anand S. Desai. "Evidence That The Common Stock Market Adjusts Fully For Expected Inflation," **JFR**, 1979, v2(2), 97-109.)

Desai, Anand S. (Ang, James S., Jess H. Chua and Anand S. Desai. "Efficient Portfolios Versus Efficient Market," **JFR**, 1980, v3(3), 309-319.)

Desai, Anand. (Bradley, Michael, Anand Desai and E. Han Kim. "The Rationale Behind Interfirm Tender Offers," **JFEC**, 1983, v11(1), 183-206.)

Desai, Anand. (Bradley, Michael, Anand Desai and E. Han Kim. "Synergistic Gains From Corporate Acquisitions And Their Division Between The Stockholders Of Target And Acquiring Firms," **JFEC**, 1988, v21(1), 3-40.)

Desai, Harsha B. (Singhvi, Surendra S. and Harsha B. Desai. "An Overview Of The Case Method Of Instruction," **JFED**, 1977, v6, 70-74.)

DeSalvia, Donald N. "An Application Of Peak-Load Pricing," **JOB**, 1969, v42(4), 458-476.

Dipietre, Dennis D. (Hayenga, M. L., D. D. Dipietre, J. M. Skadberg and T. C. Schroeder. "Profitable Hedging Opportunities And Risk Premiums For Producers In Live Cattle And Live Hog Futures Markets," JFM, 1984, v4(2), 141-154.)

Director, Steven M. and Frederick J. Englander. "Requiring Unemployment Insurance Recipients To Register With The Public Employment Service," JRI, 1988, v55(2), 245-258.

Dirks, Frederick C. "Recent Investment Return On Industrial Stocks," JOF, 1958, v13(3), 370-385.

Diskin, Barry A. and Armen Tashchian. "Application Of Logit Analysis To The Determination Of Tenant Absorption In Condominium Conversion," AREUEA, 1984, v12(2), 191-205.

Dittenhafer, Brian. (Epstein, Ira and Brian Dittenhafer. "A Preliminary Investigation Into The Effects Of The Federal Override Of State Usury Ceilings On The Supply Of Mortgage Funds By FSLIC-Insured S&Ls In New York And New Jersey," AREUEA, 1980, v8(4), 370-386.)

Divecha, Arjun and Dale Morse. "Market Responses To Dividend Increases and Changes In Payout Ratios," JFQA, 1983, v18(2), 163-173.

Diwan, Ishac. "Foreign Debt, Crowding Out And Capital Flight," JIMF, 1989, v8(1), 121-136.

Diwan, Romesh K. "Bias In The Measurement Of Technical Change," JFQA, 1968, v3(4), 471-477.

Dixon, Bruce L. (Elam, Emmett and Bruce L. Dixon. "Examining The Validity Of A Test Of Futures Market Efficiency," JFM, 1988, v8(3), 365-372.)

Dixon, Richard L. (Wagner, Wayne H., Allen Emkin and Richard L. Dixon. "South African Divestment: The Investment Issues," FAJ, 1984, v40(6), 14-19,22.)

Djajic, Slobodan. "Balance-Of-Payments Dynamics And Exchange-Rate Management," JIMF, 1982, v1(2), 179-191.

Djajic, Slobodan. "Dynamics Of The Exchange Rate In Anticipation Of Pegging," JIMF, 1989, v8(4), 559-572.

Djajic, Slobodan. "Effects Of Budgetary Policies In Open Economies: The Role Of Intertemporal Consumption Substitution," JIMF, 1987, v6(3), 373-383.

Djajic, Slobodan. "Intermediate Inputs And International Trade: An Analysis Of The Real And Monetary Aspects Of A Change In The Price Of Oil," JIMF, 1983, v2(2), 179-195.

Doan, Herbert D. "Challenges In Petrochemicals," FAJ, 1967, v23(4), 35-37.

Dobbins, Cris. "The Cement Industry In Search Of Its Future," FAJ, 1962, v18(2), 21-26.

Dobbins, Richard and Michael J. Greenwood. "Institutional Shareholders And Equity Market Stability," JBFA, 1975, v2(2), 257-268.

Dobbins, Richard and Stephen F. Witt. "Stock Market Prices And Sector Activity," JBFA, 1980, v7(2), 261-276.

Dobbins, Richard. (Briston, Richard J. and Richard Dobbins. "Institutional Shareholders And Equity Stability: A Corroboratory Note," JBFA, 1977, v4(4), 469-476.)

Dobbins, Richard. (Witt, Stephen F. and Richard Dobbins. "A Note On The Effect Of Institutional Trading Activities On The Real Value Of The Financial Times All-Share Index," JBFA, 1983, v10(3), 351-358.)

Dobrovolsky, S. P. "Business Income Taxation And Asset Expansion," JOF, 1949, v4(3), 185-193.

Dobrovolsky, S. P. "Economics Of Corporate Internal And External Financing," JOF, 1958, v13(1), 35-47.

Dobrovolsky, S. "Capital Formation And Financing Trends In Manufacturing And Mining, 1900-1953," JOF, 1955, v10(2), 250-265.

Dobson, Steven W. "Estimating Term Structure Equations With Individual Bond Data," JOF, 1978, v33(1), 75-92.

Dobson, Steven W., Richard C. Sutch and David E. Vanderford. "An Evaluation Of Alternative Empirical Models Of The Firm Structure Of Interest Rates," JOF, 1976, v31(4), 1035-1065.

Dodd, David K. "An International Capital Market," FAJ, 1967, v23(6), 159-161.

Dodd, Peter and Jerold B. Warner. "On Corporate Governance," JFEC, 1983, v11(1), 401-438.

Dodd, Peter and Richard Ruback. "Tender Offers And Stockholder Returns: An Empirical Analysis," JFEC, 1977, v5(3), 351-373.

Dodd, Peter and Richard Leftwich. "The Market For Coprorate Charters: 'Unhealthy Competition' Versus Federal Regulation," JOB, 1980, v53(3), Part 1, 259-284.

Dodd, Peter. "Merger Proposals, Management Discretion And Stockholder Wealth," JFEC, 1980, v8(2),105-138.

Dodd, Peter. (Amihud, Yakov, Peter Dodd and Mark Weinstein. "Conglomerate Mergers, Managerial Motives And Stockholder Wealth," JBF, 1986, v10(3), 401-410.)

Dodds, C. (Dar, A. and C. Dodds. "Interest Rates, The Emergency Fund Hypothesis And Saving Through Endowment Policies: Some Empirical Evidence For The U.K.," JRI, 1989, v56(3), 415-433.)

Dodds, Colin. (Barnes, Paul and Colin Dodds. "The Structure And Performance Of The UK Building Society Industry 1970-78," JBFA, 1983, v10(1), 37-56.)

Dodds, J. C. and J. P. Quek. "Effect Of Mergers On Share Price Movement Of The Acquiring Firms: A UK Study," JBFA, 1985, v12(2), 285-296.

Dodin, Bajis. (Khoury, Sarkis J., Bajis Dodin and Hirokazu Takada. "Multiple Time Series Analysis Of National Stock Markets And Their Structure: Some Implications," RDIBF, 1987, v1, 169-186.)

Doenges, R. Conrad. "The 'Reinvestment Problem' In A Practical Perspective," FM, 1972, v1(1), 85-91.

Doerpinghaus, Helen I. "Effect Of Ambulatory Surgery Policy Provisions On Medical Expense Insurance Claims," JRI, 1990, v57(4), 608-622.

Doherty, N. A. and S. M. Tinic. "Reinsurance Under Conditions Of Capital Market Equilibrium: A Note," JOF, 1981, v36(4), 949-953.

Doherty, N. A. "Contingency Loans For Financing Corporate Loss," JRI, 1978, v45(3), 491-506.

Doherty, N. A. "Some Fundamental Theorems Of Risk Management," JRI, 1975, v42(3), 447-460.

Doherty, N. A. "Stochastic Choice In Insurance And Risk Sharing," JOF, 1977, v32(3), 921-926.

Doherty, N. A. (Carter, R. L. and N. A. Doherty. "Tariff Control And The Public Interest: Report On British Fire Insurance," JRI, 1974, v41(3), 483-496.)

Doherty, Neil A. and James R. Garven. "Price Regulation In Property-Liability Insurance: A Contingent-Claims Approach," JOF, 1986, v41(5), 1031-1050.

Doherty, Neil A. "A Portfolio Theory Of Insurance Capacity," JRI, 1980, v47(3), 405-420.

Doherty, Neil A. "Insurer And Provider As The Same Firm: HMO's And Moral Hazard: Comment," JRI, 1979, v46(3), 550-553.

Doherty, Neil A. "Is Rate Classification Profitable?," JRI, 1981, v48(2), 286-295.

Doherty, Neil A. "Moral Hazard And Pricing In The U.K. Fire Insurance Market," JRI, 1980, v47(2), 240-257.

Doherty, Neil A. "Portfolio Efficient Insurance Buying Strategies," JRI, 1984, v51(2), 205-224.

Doherty, Neil A. "Risk-Bearing Contracts For Space Enterprises," JRI, 1989, v56(3), 397-414.

Doherty, Neil A. "Stochastic Choice In Insurance And Risk Sharing: A Reply," JOF, 1983, v38(3), 1037-1038.

Doherty, Neil A. "The Measurement Of Output And Economies Of Scale In Property-Liability Insurance," JRI, 1981, v48(3), 390-402.

Doherty, Neil A. "The Measurement Of Firm And Market Capacity," JRI, 1983, v50(2), 224-234.

Doherty, Neil A. (Chen, Andrew H., Neil A. Doherty and Hun Y. Park. "The Optimal Capital Structure Decision Of Depository Financial Intermediaries: A Contingent-Claim Analysis," RIF, 1988, v7, 91-112.)

Doherty, Neil A. (D'Arcy, Stephen P. and Neil A. Doherty. "Adverse Selection, Private Information, And Lowballing In Insurance Markets," JOB, 1990, v63(2), 145-164.)

Doherty, Neil A. (Schlesinger, Harris and Neil A. Doherty. "Incomplete Markets For Insurance: An Overview," JRI, 1985, v52(3), 402-423.)

Doherty, Neil A. and Han Bin Kang. "Interest Rates And Insurance Price Cycles," JBF, 1988, v12(2), 199-214.

Doherty, Neil A. and Harris Schlesinger. "The Optimal Deductible For An Insurance Policy When Initial Wealth Is Random," JOB, 1983, v56(4), 555-565.

Doherty, Richard P. "Is The Television Industry Still In The Growth Stage?," FAJ, 1954, v10(5), 35-36.

Dokko, Yoon, Robert H. Edelstein and E. Scott Unlang. "Does Credit Rationing Affect Residential Investment? Deja Vu All Over Again," JREFEC, 1990, v3(4), 357-372.

Dolan, Robert J. (Clarke, Darral G. and Robert J. Dolan. "A Simulation Of Alternative Pricing Strategies For Dynamic Environments," JOB, 1984, v57(1), Part 2, S179-S200.

Dole, Walter. "Capital Markets And The Short Run Behavior Of Life Cycle Savers," JOF, 1978, v33(2), 413-428.

Dolley, James C. "Inflation, The Balance Of Payments, And The Gold Flow," FAJ, 1963, v19(6), 55-59.

Domian, Dale L. (Butler, Kirt C. and Dale L. Domian. "Risk, Diversification, And The Investment Horizon," JPM, 1991, v17(3), 41-48.)

Dominick, Everett. "Finance And Industry," FAJ, 1955, v11(2), 101-106.

Dominick, Everett. "Some Economics Of Forestry," FAJ, 1952, v8(3), 108-115.

Domowitz, Ian. "The Mechanics Of Automated Trade Execution Systems," JFI, 1990, v1(2), 167-194.

Domowitz, Ian. (Calomiris, Charles W. and Ian Domowitz. "Asset Substitutions, Money Demand, And The Inflation Process In Brazil," JMCB, 1989, v21(1), 78-89.)

Donaldson, Darla R. (Ma, Christopher K., William H. Dare and Darla R. Donaldson. "Testing Rationality In Futures Markets," JFM, 1990, v10(2), 137-152.)

Donaldson, Gordon. "Voluntary Restructuring: The Case Of General Mills," JFEC, 1990, v27(1), 117-142.

Donaldson, Gordon. "Making Intellectual Waves," FM, 1977, v6(4),7-10.

Donaldson, Loraine and Raymond S. Strangways. "Can Ghetto Groceries Price Competitively And Make A Profit?," JOB, 1973, v46(1), 61-65.

Donchian, Richard D. "Commodities: High Finance In Copper," FAJ, 1960, v16(6), 133-142.

Donhowe, G. M. "Economic Analysis In Norwegian Collective Bargaining," JOB, 1960, v33(4), 363-372.

Donhowe, Gordon. (Levy, Seymour and Gordon Donhowe. "Exploration Of A Biological Model Of Industrial Organization," JOB, 1962, v35(4), 335-342.)

Donnelly, William A. "The Methodology Of Housing Value Assessment: An Analysis," JRER, 1989, v4(2), 1-12.

Donoghue, William E. "Developing Seminars Oriented Toward The Financial Executive," JFED, 1975, v4, 28-32.

Donovan, James E. "Greater Economic Role Of Service Industries," FAJ, 1963, v19(2), 89-91.

Dooley, Michael P. and Peter Isard. "A Note On Fiscal Policy, Investment Location Decisions, And Exchange Rates," JIMF, 1991, v10(1), 161-167.

Doran, George T. (Bakerman, Theodore and George T. Doran. "Unemployment And Out-Of-The-Labor-Force Relationships: Static And Dynamic Analyses," JRI, 1964, v31(4), 573-587.)

Dorfman, Mark S. "Insurance In The Undergraduate Curriculum," JRI, 1990, v57(1), 47-65.

Dorfman, Mark S. "Life Insurance Product Innovations: Comment," JRI, 1972, v39(1), 140-141.

Dorfman, Mark S. "Reformation In Life Insurance Agents' Compensation," JRI, 1976, v43(3), 447-461.

Dorfman, Mark S. "The Product Performance Of The Life Insurance Industry: Revisited," JRI, 1971, v38(4), 613-626.

Dorfman, Mark S. "The Product Performance Of The Life Insurance Industry: Revisited: Reply," JRI, 1972, v39(4), 652-654.

Dorfman, Mark S. "The Theory And Practice Of Innovation In The Private Insurance Industry: Comment," JRI, 1978, v45(4), 689-691.

Dorfman, Mark S. "Workable Product Competition In The Life Insurance Market," JRI, 1972, v39(4), 613-626.

Dorfman, Mark S. (Adelman, Saul W. and Mark S. Dorfman. "A Comparison Of TDA And Non-TDA Investment Returns," JRI, 1982, v49(1), 73-90.)

Dorfman, Mark S. (Brightman, Harvey J. and Mark S. Dorfman. "Acceptability Of Three Normative Methods In Insurance Decision Making: Comment 465-466.)

Dorfman, Mark S. (Brightman, Harvey J. and Mark S. Dorfman. "Birth Order, Anxiety, Affiliation And The Purchase Of Life Insurance: Comment," JRI, 1973, v40(4), 643-646.)

Dorfman, Robert. "The Meaning Of Internal Rates Of Return," JOF, 1981, v36(5), 1011-1021.

Dornbusch, Rudiger and Clarice Pechman. "The Bid-Ask Spread In The Black Market For Dollars In Brazil," JMCB, 1985, v17(4), Part 1, 517-520.

Dornbusch, Rudiger and Jacob A. Frenkel. "Inflation And Growth: Alternative Approaches," JMCB, 1973, v5(1), 141-156.

Dornbusch, Rudiger. "Inflation, Capital, And Deficit In Finance," JMCB, 1977, v9(1), Part 2, 141-150.

Dorsey, Harold B. "An Analysis Of A Current Problem Of Analysts," FAJ, 1957, v13(2), 19-22.

Dorsey, Harold B. "Impact On Business Indicators," FAJ, 1951, v7(1), 39-42.

Dotan, Amihud and Aharon Ofer. "Variable Versus Stationary Beta In The Market Model: A Comparative Analysis," JBF, 1984, v8(4), 525-534.

Dotan, Amihud and S. Abraham Ravid. "On The Interaction Of Real And Financial Decisions Of The Firm Under Uncertainty," JOF, 1985, v40(2), 501-517.

Dothan, L. Uri. "On The Term Structure Of Interest Rates," JFEC, 1978, v6(1), 59-69.

Dothan, Uri and David Feldman. "Equilibrium Interest Rates And Multiperiod Bonds In A Partially Observable Economy," JOF, 1986, v41(2), 369-382.

Dothan, Uri and Joseph Williams. "Banks, Bankruptcy, And Regulation," JBF, 1980, v4(1), 65-87.

Dothan, Uri and Joseph Williams. "Term-Risk Structures And The Valuation Of Projects," JFQA, 1980, v15(4), 875-905.

Dothan, Uri and Joseph Williams. "Financial Game: Capital Market Equilibrium," JFED, 1980, v9, 77-78.

Dothan, Uri and Joseph Williams. "Education As An Option," JOB, 1981, v54(1), 117-140.

Dotsey, Michael. "Monetary Control Under Alternative Operating Procedures," JMCB, 1989, v21(3), 273-290.

Dotsey, Michael. "The Demand For Currency In The United States," JMCB, 1988, v20(1), 22-40.

Dotsey, Michael. "The Use Of Electronic Funds Transfers To Capture The Effects Of Cash Management Practices On The Demand For Demand Deposits: A Note," JOF, 1985, v40(5), 1493-1503.

Dotson, Michael J. (Johnson, Linda L., Michael J. Dotson and B. J. Dunlap. "Service Quality Determinants And Effectiveness In The Real Estate Brokerage Industry," JRER, 1988, v3(2), 21-36.)

Dotson, Peter K. (Tolley, H. Dennis, Michael D. Bahr and Peter K. Dotson. "A Statistical Method For Monitoring Social Insurance Claims," JRI, 1989, v56(4), 670-685.)

Dotterweich, W. W. "Businessmen-In-Residence," JRI, 1971, v38(4), 627-632.

Dotterweich, William and James S. Trieschmann. "Use Of Computers In Teaching Insurance, Revisited," JRI, 1974, v41(3), 553-560.

Dotzour, Mark G. "An Empirical Analysis Of The Realiability And Precision Of The Cost Approach In Residential Appraisal," JRER, 1990, v5(1), 67-74.

Dotzour, Mark G. "Quantifying Estimation Bias In Residential Appraisal," JRER, 1988, v3(3), 1-11.

Dotzour, Mark G. and Donald R. Levi. "Reducing The Cost Of Corporate Employee Relocation," JRER, 1989, v4(3), 157-168.

Dotzour, Mark G., Terry V. Grissom, Crocker H. Liu and Thomas Pearson. "Highest And Best Use: The Evolving Paradigm," JRER, 1990, v5(1), 17-32.

Doudna, Donald J. "Effect Of The Economy On Group Long Term Disability Claims," JRI, 1977, v44(2), 223-236.

Douds, H. James. "The (Non) Franchising Relationship Of The Life Insurance Agent," JRI, 1976, v43(3), 513-520.

Douglas, Edna. "Buying Practices Of Out-Of-Town Customers," JOB, 1950, v23(4), 259-272.

Douglas, Edna. "Size Of Firm And The Structure Of Costs In Retailing," JOB, 1962, v35(2), 158-190.

Douglas, Honorable Paul H. "The Federal Budget," JOF, 1950, v5(2), 129-147.

Douglas, James M. "Bigger Role For Generic Drugs?," FAJ, 1970, v26(5), 113-118.

Douglas, James M. "Prospects For Generic Drugs - II," FAJ, 1971, v27(1), 59-63.

Douglas, Norman S. "Insider Trading: The Case Against The 'Victimless Crime' Hypothesis," FR, 1988, v23(2), 127-142.

Douglas, Patricia P. "Professionalism: Its Presence And Absence In The Insurance Industry," JRI, 1971, v38(2), 215-224.

Douglas, Paul H. "Is A General Problem Of Social Insurance Desirable?," JRI, 1935, v2, 37-47.

Douglas, Susan P. (Frank, Ronald E., Susan P. Douglas and Rolando E. Polli. "Household Correlates Of 'Brand Loyalty' For Grocery Products," JOB, 1968, v41(2), 237-245.)

Douglas, William E. "Evolution Of Electronic Payments And Collections In The U.S. Government," JBR, 1985-86, v16(4), 206-208.

Doukas, John and Abdul Rahman. "Stable Distributions, Futures Prices, And The Measurement Of Trading Performance: A Comment," JFM, 1986, v6(3),505-506.

Doukas, John and Abdul Rahman. "Foreign Currency Futures And Monetary Policy Announcements: An Intervention Analysis," JFM, 1986, v6(3), 343-374.

Doukas, John and Abdul Rahman. "Unit Roots Tests: Evidence From The Foreign Exchange Futures Market," JFQA, 1987, v22(1), 101-108.

Doukas, John and Nickolaos G. Travlos. "The Effect Of Corporate Multinationalism On Shareholders' Wealth: Evidence From International Acquisitions," JOF, 1988, v43(5), 1161-1175.

Doukas, John. "The Rationality Of Money Supply Expectations And The Canadian-US Exchange Rate Response To Money Supply Announcements," FR, 1985, v20(2), 180-194.

Dover, Victor. "Forty Years In Insurance Education," JRI, 1959, v26(4), 37-50.

Dover, Victor. "Vocational Education In Insurance," JRI, 1963, v30(4), 535-546.

Dow, Votaw. (Hirsch, Werner Z. and Votaw Dow. "Giant Grocery Retailing And The Antitrust Laws," JOB, 1952, v25(1), 1-17.)

Dowall, David E. and John D. Landis. "Land-Use Controls And Housing Costs: An Examination Of San Francisco Bay Area Communities," AREUEA, 1982, v10(1), 67-93.

Dowd, Bryan E. "The Logic Of Moral Hazard: A Game Theoretic Illustration," JRI, 1982, v49(3), 443-447.

Dowd, James. "Collective Forecasting Of Business Activity," FAJ, 1957, v13(5), 45-50.

Dowd, Kevin. "Option Clauses And The Stability Of A Laisser Faire Monetary System," JFSR, 1988, v1(4), 319-334.

Dowd, Kevin. "The Value Of Time And The Transactions Demand For Money," JMCB, 1990, v22(1), 51-64.

Dowell, C. Dwayne and R. Corwin Grube. "Common Stock Return Distributions During Homogeneous Activity Periods," JFQA, 1978, v13(1), 79-92.

Dowell, Dudley. "Life Insurance In Its New Competitive Frame," JRI, 1956, v23, 55-60.

Dowen, Richard J. and W. Scott Bauman. "A Fundamental Multifactor Asset Pricing Model," FAJ, 1986, v42(4), 45-51.

Dowen, Richard J. and W. Scott Bauman. "The Relative Importance Of Size, P/E, And Neglect," JPM, 1986, v12(3), 30-35.

Dowen, Richard J. "A Note: Hedging Market Risk For Capital Investments Projects," JFM, 1985, v5(4), 621-624.

Dowen, Richard J. "What Are Analysts' Forecasts Worth? One-Period Growth Expectations And Subsequent Stock Returns," FAJ, 1989, v45(4), 71-74.

Dowen, Richard. (Bauman, W. Scott and Richard Dowen. "Growth Projections And Common Stock Returns," FAJ, 1988, v44(4), 79-80.)

Downes, David H. and Robert Heinkel. "Signaling And The Valuation Of Unseasoned New Issues," JOF, 1982, v37(1), 1-10.

Downes, David H. (Bierman, Harold, Jr., David H. Downes and Jerome E. Hass. "Closed-Form Stock Price Models," JFQA, 1972, v7(3), 1797-1808.)

Downes, David H. (Bower, Richard S. and David H. Downes. "The Time-Sharing Decision In Banking," JBR, 1971-72, v2(3), 9-21.)

Downes, David H. (Carelton, Willard T., Charles L. Dick, Jr. and David H. Downes. "Financial Policy Models: Theory And Practice," JFQA, 1973, v8(5), 691-709.)

Downing, Roger H. (Gamble, Hays B., Roger H. Downing and Owen H. Sauerlender. "Community Growth Around Nuclear Power Plants," AREUEA, 1980, v8(3), 268-280.)

Downs, Anthony. "The President's Housing Commission And Two Tests Of Realistic Recommendations," AREUEA, 1983, v11(2), 182-191.

Downs, Thomas W. "An Alternative Approach To Fundamental Analysis: The Asset Side Of The Equation," JPM, 1991, v17(2), 6-17.

Downs, Thomas W. "The User Cost And Capital Budgeting," FR, 1986, v21(2), 277-287.

Doyle, P., I. Fenwick and G. P. Savage. "A Model For Evaluating Branch Location And Performance," JBR, 1981-82, v12(2), 90-95.

Doyle, Peter and Marcel Corstjens. "Optimal Growth Strategies For Service Organizations," JOB, 1983, v56(3), 389-405.

Doyle, Robert J., Jr. "IRA's And The Capital-Gains Tax Effect," FAJ, 1984, v40(3), 60-65.

Drake, David F. (Davidson, Sidney and David F. Drake. "Capital Budgeting And The 'Best' Tax Depreciation Method," JOB, 1961, v34(4), 442-452.)

Drake, David F. (Davidson, Sidney and David F. Drake. The 'Best' Tax Depreciation Method-1964," JOB, 1964, v37(3), 258-260.)

Drake, Francis. "Decrease In Oil Field Discoveries," FAJ, 1948, v4(2), 31-34.

Dran, John J., Jr. and Brian E. Campbell. "Hospital Investment And Medicare Reimbursement," JFR, 1981, v4(2), 147-160.

Drandell, Milton. "A Resource Association Model For Insurance Management Utilizing Goal Programming," JRI, 1977, v44(2), 311-315.

Drandell, Milton. (Hofflander, A. E. and Milton Drandell. "A Linear Programming Model Of Profitability, Capacity And Regulation In Insurance Management," JRI, 1969, v36(1), 41-54.)

Draper, Dennis W. and James W. Hoag. "Portfolio Strategies Using Treasury Bond Options And Futures," RFM, 1983, v2(1), 82-98.

Draper, Dennis W. and James W. Hoag. "Financial Intermediation And The Theory of Agency," JFQA, 1978, v13(4), 595-611.

Draper, Dennis W. and M. Chapman Findlay, III. "A Note On Vickers' Marginal Cost Of Debt Capital," JBFA, 1982, v8(4), 579-582.

Draper, Dennis W. "The Behavior Of Event-Related Returns On Oil Futures Contracts," JFM, 1984, v4(2), 125-132.

Draper, Dennis W. and M. Chapman Findlay. "Capital Asset Pricing And Real Estate Valuation," AREUEA, 1982, v10(2), 152-183.

Draper, J. E. and C. A. Hawkins. "On The Transactions Demand For Cash: Comment," JOF, 1969, v24(5), 942-949.

Draper, P. R. "Industry Influences On Share Price Variability," JBFA, 1975, v2(2), 169-185.

Draper, Paul. "Unit Trusts, Homogeneous Beliefs And The Separation Property: A Note," JBFA, 1984, v11(4), 485-492.

Dravid, Ajay R. "A Note On The Behavior Of Stock Returns Around Ex-Dates Of Stock Distributions," JOF, 1987, v42(1), 163-168.

Dreese, G. Richard. (Dewald, William G. and G. Richard Dreese. "Bank Behavior With Respect To Deposit Variability," JOF, 1970, v25(4), 869-879.)

Dreher, William A. "Does Portfolio Insurance Ever Make Sense?," JPM, 1988, v14(4), 25-32.

Drennan, Matthew and Emanuel Tobier. "Taxation Of Residential Property In New York City: The Sources Of Differential Treatment," AREUEA, 1977, v5(1), 85-110.

Dressel, Walter. "Some Post-War Insurance Problems," JRI, 1946, v13, 74-79.

Dressler, Ofer. (Shinnar, Reuel, Ofer Dressler, C. A. Feng and Alan I. Avidan. "Estimation Of The Economic Rate Of Return For Industrial Companies," JOB, 1989, v62(3), 417-446.)

Drew, Garfield A. "A Clarification Of The Odd Lot Theory," FAJ, 1967, v23(5), 107-108.

Dreyfus, Jean-Francois. (Acharya, Sankarshan and Jean-Francois Dreyfus. "Optimal Bank Reorganization Policies And The Pricing Of Federal Deposit Insurance," JOF, 1989, v44(5), 1313-1334.)

Driskill, Robert and Stephen McCafferty. "Equilibrium Price-Output Dynamics And The (Non) Insulating Properties Of Fixed Exchange Rates," JIMF, 1982, v1(3), 325-332.

Droms, William G. "Market Timing As An Investment Policy," FAJ, 1989, v45(1), 73-77.

Drucker, Peter F. "Business Objectives And Survival Needs: Notes On A Discipline Of Business Enterprise," JOB, 1958, v31(2), 81-90.

Drucker, Peter F. "The Management Horizon," JOB, 1955, v28(3), 155-164.

Drucker, William L. (Williams, Stephen J., Paula Diehr, William L. Drucker and William C. Richardson. "Limitations And Exclusions In Two Provider Systems With Comprehensive Care," JRI, 1982, v49(3), 448-462.)

Drury, J. C. (Bougen, P. D. and J. C. Drury. "U.K. Statistical Distributions Of Financial Ratios, 1975," JBFA, 1980, v7(1), 39-47.)

Dryden, Myles M. "A Note On An Approximation To The Post-Tax Rate Of Return," JOB, 1963, v36(4), 458-460.

Dryden, Myles M. "A Source Of Bias In Filter Tests Of Share Prices," JOB, 1969, v42(3), 321-325.

Dryden, Myles M. "Share Price Movements: A Markovian Approach," JOF, 1969, v24(1), 49-60.

Dryden, Myles M. "The MAPI Urgency Rating As An Investment-Ranking Criterion," JOB, 1960, v33(4),327-341.

Drzycimski, Eugene F. (Reilly, Frank K. and Eugene F. Drzycimski. "An Analysis Of The Effects Of A Multi-Tier Market," JFQA, 1981, v16(4), 559-575.)

Drzycimski, Eugene F. (Reilly, Frank K. and Eugene F. Drzycimski. "Short-Run Profits From Stock Splits," FM, 1981, v10(3), 64-74.)

Drzycimski, Eugene F. (Reilly, Frank K. and Eugene F. Drzycimski. "Exchange Specialists And World Events," FAJ, 1975, v31(4),27-32.)

Drzycimski, Eugene F. (Reilly, Frank K. and Eugene F. Drzycimski. "Alternative Industry Performance And Risk," JFQA, 1974, v9(3), 423-446.)

Dua, Pami. (Batchelor, Roy A. and Pami Dua. "Household Versus Economist Forecasts Of Inflation: A Reassessment," JMCB, 1989, v21(2), 252-257.)

Dubinsky, Alan J. (Skinner, Steven J. and Alan J. Dubinsky. "Purchasing Insurance: Predictors Of Family Decision-Making Responsibility," JRI, 1984, v51(3), 513-523.)

Dubinsky, Alan J. and Francis J. Yammarino. "Job-Related Responses Of Insurance Agents: A Multi-Firm Investigation," JRI, 1985, v52(3), 501-517.

Dubinsky, Alan J., Terry L. Childers, Steven J. Skinner and Esra Gencturk. "Impact Of Sales Supervisor Leadership Behavior On Insurance Agent Attitudes And Performance," JRI, 1988, v55(1), 132-144.

Dubinsky, Alan. (Yammarino, Francis J. and Alan J. Dubinsky. "On Job Satisfaction: It's The Relationships That Count!," JRI, 1987, v54(4), 804-809.)

Dubofsky, David A. and John C. Groth. "Relative Information Accessibility For OTC Stocks And Security Returns," FR, 1986, v21(1), 85-102.

Dubofsky, David A. and John C. Groth. "Exchange Listing And Stock Liquidity," JFR, 1984, v7(4), 291-302.

Dubofsky, David A. and John C. Groth. "An Examination Of Asked-Bid Spreads For Two Over-The-Counter Market Segments," FR, 1986, v21(2), 289-298.

Dubofsky, David A. "Hedging Dividend Capture Strategies With Stock Index Futures," JFM, 1987, v7(5), 471-482.

Dubofsky, David A. "Volatility Increases Subsequent To NYSE And AMEX Stock Splits," JOF, 1991, v46(1), 421-432.

Dubofsky, David A. (French, Dan W. and David A. Dubofsky. "Stock Splits and Implied Stock Price Volatility," JPM, 1986, v12(4), 55-59.)

Dubofsky, David A. and Donald R. Fraser. "The Differential Impact Of Two Significant Court Decisions Concerning Banking Consolidation," JBF, 1989, v13(3), 339-354.

Duca, John V. "The Spillover Effects Of Nominal Wage Rigidity In A Multisector Economy," JMCB, 1987, v19(1), 117-121.

Duca, John V. and David VanHoose. "Loan Commitments And Optimal Monetary Policy," JMCB, 1990, v22(2), 178-194.

Duchessi, Peter, Hany Shawky and John P. Seagle. "A Knowledge-Engineered System For Commercial Loan Decisions," FM, 1988, v17(3), 57-65.

Duck, Nigel W. (Attfield, Clifford L. F. and Nigel W. Duck. "The Influence Of Unanticipated Money Growth On Real Output: Some Cross-Country Estimates," JMCB, 1983, v15(4), 442-454.)

Dudley, Carlton L., Jr. "A Note On Reinvestment Assumptions In Choosing Between Net Present Value And Internal Rate Of Return," JOF, 1972, v27(4), 907-915.

Dudley, D. A. and Charles S. Sherwood. "Which Computer Skills For Finance Graduates?," JFED, 1984, v13, 80-86.

Due, John F. "American And Canadian Experience With The Sales Tax," JOF, 1952, v7(3), 463-473.

Due, John F. "An Empirical Study Of Abandonment Decisions," JOF, 1959, v14(3), 361-372.

Due, John F. "Canada's Experience With The Manufacturers' Sales Tax," JOB, 1954, v27(3), 243-253.

Due, John F. "The Role Of Sales And Excise Taxation In The Over-All Tax Structure," JOF, 1956, v11(2), 205-220.

Duesenberg, Richard W. "Are Non-Insured Pension Plans Engaged In The Business Of Insurance?: Comment," JRI, 1964, v31(3), 475-478.

Duesenberry, James and Barry Bosworth. "Policy Implications Of A Flow-Of-Funds Model," JOF, 1974, v29(2), 331-347.

Duesenberry, James. "Domestic Policy Objectives And The Balance Of Payments," JOF, 1966, v21(2), 345-353.

Dufey, Gunter and Ian H. Giddy. "Measuring The Eurocurrency Market," JBR, 1978-79, v9(3), 151-160.

Dufey, Gunter and Ian H. Giddy. "Eurocurrency Deposit Risk," JBF, 1984, v8(4), 567-58).

Dufey, Gunter and S. L. Srinivasulu. "The Case For Corporate Management Of Foreign Exchange Risk," FM, 1983, v12(4), 54-62.

Dufey, Gunter. "Corporate Finance And Exchange Rate Variations," FM, 1972, v1(2), 51-57.

Duff, J. Kenneth. "A Critical Look At Risk And Insurance Education And Educators," JRI, 1971, v38(1), 107-112.

Duffie, Darrell and Matthew O. Jackson. "Optimal Innovation Of Futures Contracts," RFS, 1989, v2(3), 275-296.

Duffy, Martin. (Bostock, Paul, Paul Woolley and Martin Duffy. "Duration-Based Asset Allocation," FAJ, 1989, v45(1), 53-60.)

Dugan, Michael T. (Tennyson, B. Mack, Robert W. Ingram and Michael T. Dugan. "Assessing The Information Content Of Narrative Disclosures In Explaining Bankruptcy," JBFA, 1990, v17(3), 391-410.)

Dugan, Michael T. (Zavgren, Christine V., Michael T. Dugan and James M. Reeve. "The Association Between Probabilities Of Bankruptcy And Market Responses--A Test Of Market Anticipation," JBFA, 1988, v15(1), 27-46.)

Dugan, Michael T. and Keith A. Shriver. "The Effects Of Estimation Period, Industry, And Proxy On The Calculation Of The Degree Of Operating Leverage," FR, 1989, v24(1), 109-122.

Duggan, James E. (Booth, G. Geoffrey, James E. Duggan and Peter E. Koveos. "Deviations From Purchasing Power Parity, Relative Inflation, And Exchange Rates: The Recent Experience," FR, 1985, v20(2),195-218.)

Duggar, Jan Warren. "Federal Open Market Operations And Variations In The Reserve Base: Comment," JOF, 1972, v27(3), 727-729.

Duggar, Jan Warren. "The Federal Open Market Committee's Proviso Clause: Usage And Analysis," JOF, 1971, v26(4), 885-895.

Dugger, Robert H. (Black, Harold and Robert H. Dugger. "Credit Union Structure, Growth And Regulatory Problems," JOF, 1981, v36(2), 529-538.)

Duke, Henry K. (Hedges, Bob A., Walter Williams and Henry K. Duke. "What Is Wrong With Insurance Theory?," JRI, 1964, v31(2), 279-284.)

Duker, Jacob M. "Expenditures For Life Insurance Among Working-Wife Families," JRI, 1969, v36(4), 525-534.

Duker, Jacob M. (Morton, T. Gregory and Jacob M. Duker. "Black Financial Institutions: An Appraisal," FM, 1978, v7(2), 28-36.)

Duker, Jacob M. and Charles E. Hughes. "The Black-Owned Life Insurance Company: Issues And Recommendations," JRI, 1973, v40(2), 221-230.

Duker, Jacob M. and Charles E. Hughes. "The Black-Owned Life Insurance Company: Reply," JRI, 1975, v42(2), 355-358.

Dukes, William P. (Bowlin, Oswald D. and William P. Dukes. "The Dual Nature Of Beta Responsiveness," JPM, 1983, v9(2), 51-56.)

Dukes, William P. (Trennepohl, Gary L. and William P. Dukes. "An Empirical Test Of Option Writing And Buying Strategies Utilizing In-The-Money And Out-Of-The-Money Contracts," JBFA, 1981, v8(2), 185-202.)

Dukes, William P. (Trennepohl, Gary L. and William P. Dukes. "Return And Risk From Listed Option Investments," JFR, 1979, v2(1), 37-49.)

Dukes, William P. (Whiteside, Mary M., William P. Dukes and Patrick M. Dunne. "Short Term Impact Of Option Trading On Underlying Securities," JFR, 1983, v6(4), 313-321.)

Dukes, William P. and Claude C. Lilly. "Short Term Risk-Return Impact Of The Holding Company Movement," JRI, 1977, v44(2), 320-328.

Dulan, Harold A. "Diversification And Yields In Common Stock Portfolios," FAJ, 1965, v21(4), 98-108.

Dumas, B. and B. Jacquillat. "Performance Of Currency Portfolios Chosen By A Bayesian Technique: 1967-1985," JBF, 1990, v14(2/3), 539-558.

Dumas, B. and B. Jacquillat. "The Money And Bond Markets In France: Segmentation Vs. Integration," JBF, 1990, v14(2/3), 613-636.

Dumas, Bernard. "The Theory Of The Trading Firm Revisited," JOF, 1978, v33(3), 1019-1030.

Dumas, Bernard. "Two-Person Dynamic Equilibrium In The Capital Market," RFS, 1989, v2(2), 157-188.

Dumas, Bernard. (Adler, Michael and Bernard Dumas. "Optimal International Acquisitions," JOF, 1975, v30(1), 1-19.)

Dumas, Bernard. (Adler, Michael and Bernard Dumas. "International Portfolio Choice And Corporation Finance: A Synthesis," JOF, 1983, v38(3), 925-984.)

Dumas, Bernard. (Adler, Michael and Bernard Dumas. "Exposure To Currency Risk: Definition And Measurement," FM, 1984, v13(2), 41-50.)

Dumas, Bernard. (Adler, Michael and Bernard Dumas. "The Exposure Of Long-Term Foreign Currency Bonds," JFQA, 1980, v15(4), 973-994.)

Dumpty, Humpty S. "Is The Committee On General Insurance Terminology Really General?," JRI, 1964, v31(3), 485-486.

Dumpty, Humpty S. "Is The Committee On General Insurance Terminology Really General?: Reply," JRI, 1965, v32(1), 140.

Duncan, F. H. "Intermarket Bank Expansions: Implications For Interstate Banking," JBR, 1985-86, v16(1), 16-21.

Duncan, Gregory M. "The Effect Of Probabilistic Demands On The Structure Of Cost Functions," JRU, 1990, v3(3), 211-220.

Dunetz, Mark L. and James M. Mahoney. "Using Duration And Convexity In The Analysis Of Callable Bonds," FAJ, 1988, v44(3), 53-73.

Dunham, Allison. "Unconscionable Conduct And The Uniform Consumer Credit Code," JOF, 1968, v23(2), 312-319.

Dunkelberg, William C. and Robert H. Smiley. "Subsidies In The Use Of Revolving Credit," JMCB, 1975, v7(4), 469-490.

Dunkelberg, William C. (Scott, Jonathan A. and William C. Dunkelberg. "Rural Versus Urban Bank Performance: An Analysis Of Market Competition For Small Business Loans," JBR, 1984-85, v15(3), 167-178.)

Dunkelberg, William C., Jonathan A. Scott and Edwin L. Cox. "Small Business And The Value Of Bank-Customer Relationships," JBR, 1983-84, v14(4), 248-258.

Dunkman, William E. "College Courses In Banking And Finance," FR, 1966, v1(1), 5-18.

Dunkman, William E. "Postwar Commercial Bank Lending Policies," JOF, 1949, v4(2), 87-100.

Dunkman, William E. "The Teaching Of Money And Banking," JOF, 1949, v4(3), 237.

Dunlap, B. J. (Johnson, Linda L., Michael J. Dotson and B. J. Dunlap. "Service Quality Determinants And Effectiveness In The Real Estate Brokerage Industry," JRER, 1988, v3(2), 21-36.)

Dunn, D. M. (Davis, E. G., D. M. Dunn and W. H. Williams. "Invariance And Scaling In The Per Share Analysis Of Financial Data: Reply," JOF, 1977, v32(3), 937-938.)

Dunn, D. M. (Davis, E. G., D. M. Dunn and W. H. Williams. "Ambiguities In The Cross-Section Analysis Of Per Share Financial Data," JOF, 1973, v28(5),1241-1248.)

Dunn, Kenneth B. and Chester S. Spatt. "An Analysis Of Mortgage Contracting: Prepayment Penalties And The Due-on-Sale Clause," JOF, 1985, v40(1), 293-308.

Dunn, Kenneth B. and Chester S. Spatt. "A Strategic Analysis Of Sinking Fund Bonds," JFEC, 1984, v13(3), 399-424.

Dunn, Kenneth B. and John J. McConnell. "Valuation Of GNMA Mortgage-Backed Securities," JOF, 1981, v36(3), 599-616.

Dunn, Kenneth B. and John J. McConnell. "A Comparison Of Alternative Models For Pricing GNMA Mortgage-Backed Securities," JOF, 1981, v36(2), 471-484.

Dunn, Kenneth B. and John J. McConnell. "Rate Of Return Indexes For GNMA Securities," JPM, 1981, v7(2), 65-74.

Dunn, Kenneth B. and Kenneth J. Singleton. "Modeling The Term Structure Of Interest Rates Under Non-Separable Utility And Durability Of Goods," JFEC, 1986, v17(1), 27-56.

Dunn, Kenneth B. and Kenneth J. Singleton. "An Empirical Analysis Of The Pricing Of Mortgage-Backed Securities," JOF, 1983, v38(2), 613-623.

Dunn, Kenneth B. (Dammon, Robert M., Kenneth B. Dunn and Chester S. Spatt. "A Reexamination Of The Value Of Tax Options," RFS, 1989, v2(3), 341-372.)

Dunn, Kenneth B. and Chester S. Spatt. "Private Information And Incentives: Implications For Mortgage Contract Terms And Pricing," JREFEC, 1988, v1(1), 47-60.

Dunn, Kenneth B. and John J. McConnell. "Rates Of Return On GNMA Securities: The Cost Of Mortgage Funds," AREUEA, 1980, v8(3), 320-336.

Dunn, Kenneth B. and Kenneth M. Eades. "Voluntary Conversion Of Convertible Securities And The Optimal Call Strategy," JFEC, 1989, v23(2), 273-302.

Dunn, Marshall and Richard E. Weeks. "Railroad Pro Forma Tabulations," FAJ, 1947, v3(1), 43-51.

Dunn, Patricia C. and Rolf D. Theisen. "How Consistently Do Active Managers Win?," JPM, 1983, v9(4), 47-50.

Dunne, Patrick M. (Whiteside, Mary M., William P. Dukes and Patrick M. Dunne. "Short Term Impact Of Option Trading On Underlying Securities," JPM, 1983, v6(4), 313-321.)

Durand, David and Alan M. May. "The Ex-Dividend Behavior Of American Telephone And Telegraph Stock," JOF, 1960, v15(1), 19-31.

Durand, David. "A Quarterly Series Of Corporate Basic Yields, 1952-57, And Some Attendant Reservations," JOF, 1958, v13(3), 348-356.

Durand, David. "Afterthoughts On A Controversy With MM, Plus Thoughts On Growth And The Cost Of Capital," FM, 1989, v18(2), 12-18.

Durand, David. "Comprehensiveness In Capital Budgeting," FM, 1981, v10(5), 7-13.

Durand, David. "Growth Stocks And The Petersburg Paradox," JOF, 1957, v12(3), 348-363.

Durand, David. "Indices Of Profitability As Aids To Judgment In Capital Budgeting," JBR, 1972-73, v3(4), 200-219.

Durand, David. "Payout Period, Time Spread And Duration: Aids To Judgment In Capital Budgeting," JBR, 1974-75, v5(1), 20-34.

Durand, David. "State Of The Finance Field: Further Comment," JOF, 1968, v23(5), 848-852.

Durand, Richard M., Donald W. Eckrich and C. Ronald Sprecher. "Bank Image: An Adequacy-Importance Approach," JBR, 1978-79, v9(3), 168-172.

Durkin, Thomas A. "Consumer Loan Costs And The Regulatory Basis Of Loan Sharking," JBR, 1977-78, v8(2), 108-117.

Durkin, Thomas A. "Consumer Awareness Of Credit Terms: Review And New Evidence," JOB, 1975, v48(2), 253-362.

Durkin, Thomas A. (Elliehausen, Gregory E. and Thomas A. Durkin. "Theory And Evidence Of The Impact Of Equal Credit Opportunity: An Agnostic Review Of The Literature," JFSR, 1989, v2(2), 89-114.)

Duro, Lorraine E. (Bowers, David A. and Lorraine E. Duro. "An Alternative Estimation Of The 'Neutralized Money Stock'," JOF, 1972, v27(1), 61-64.)

Duston, Thomas E. "Insurer And Provider As The Same Firm: HMOs And Moral Hazard," JRI, 1978, v45(1), 141-147.

Duston, Thomas E. "Insurer And Provider As The Same Firm: HMO's And Moral Hazard: Reply," JRI, 1979, v46(3), 554-555.

Dutia, Dipa. (Davidson, Wallace N., III, Dipa Dutia and Louis Cheng. "A Re-Examination Of The Market Reaction To Failed Mergers," JOF, 1989, v44(4), 1077-1084.)

Dutia, Dipa. (Davidson, Wallace N., III and Dipa Dutia. "A Note On The Behavior Of Security Returns: A Test Of Stock Market Overreaction And Efficiency," JFR, 1989, v12(3), 245-252.)

Dutkowsky, Donald. "The Demand For Borrowed Reserves: A Switching Regression Model," JOF, 1984, v39(2), 407-424.

Dutter, Philip H. "Quality Of Management," FAJ, 1969, v25(2), 105-108.

Dutton, Dean S. "A Model Of Self-Generating Inflation: The Argentine Case," JMCB, 1971, v3(2), Part 1, 245-262.

Dutton, Dean S. "The Demand For Money And The Expected Rate Of Price Change: A Comment," JMCB, 1971, v3(4), 861-866.

Dutton, Richard E. "The Need For Variable Life Contracts," JRI, 1965, v32(3), 435-446.

Duvall, Richard M. and Douglas V. Austin. "Predicting The Results Of Proxy Contests," JOF, 1965, v20(3), 464-471.

Duvall, Richard M. and John M. Cheney. "Bond Beta And Default Risk," JFR, 1984, v7(3), 243-254.

Duvall, Richard M. and Judith L. Quinn. "Skewness Preference In Stable Markets," JFR, 1981, v4(3), 249-263.

Duvall, Richard M. (Allen, Tom C. and Richard M. Duvall. "Determinants Of Property Loss Ratios In The Retail Industry," JRI, 1973, v40(2), 181-190.)

Duvall, Richard M. (Hofflander, Alfred E., Jr. and Richard M. Duvall. "The Ruin Problem In Multiple Line Insurance: A Simplified Model," JFQA, 1967, v2(2), 150-165.)

Duvall, Richard M. (Hofflander, Alfred E., Jr. and Richard M. Duvall. "Inflation And Sales Of Life Insurance: Reply," JRI, 1968, v35(4), 632-636.)

Duvall, Richard M. and Tom C. Allen. "Least Cost Deductible Decisions," JRI, 1973, v40(4), 497-507.

Duvall, Richard M., Alfred E. Hofflander, Jr. and Eugene W. Lambert, Jr. "Optimum Liquidity Levels For Multiple Line Insurance Companies," JRI, 1968, v35(2), 199-205.

Duvall, Richard. (Hofflander, Alfred E., Jr. and Richard Duvall. "Inflation And Sales Of Life Insurance," JRI, 1967, v34(3), 355-362.)

Duvel, David Tell. "Premiums On Convertible Bonds: Comment," JOF, 1970, v25(4), 923-927.

Dworsky, Alan J. "The Case For Raising The Capital Gains Tax (Undoing The Damage From Venture Capital)," FAJ, 1986, v42(2), 69-71.

Dwyer, Gerald P., Jr. "Federal Deficits, Interest Rates, And Monetary Policy," JMCB, 1985, v17(4), Part 2, 655-681.

Dwyer, Gerald P., Jr. "The Effects Of The Banking Acts Of 1933 And 1935 On Capital Investment In Commercial Banking," JMCB, 1981, v13(2), 192-204.

Dwyer, Hubert J. and Richard Lynn. "Small Capitalization Companies: What Does Financial Analysis Tell Us About Them?," FR, 1989, v24(3), 397-416.

Dybvig, Philip H. and Stephen A. Ross. "The Analytics Of Performance Measurement Using A Security Market Line," JOF, 1985, v40(2), 401-416.

Dybvig, Philip H. and Stephen A. Ross. "Tax Clienteles And Asset Pricing," JOF, 1986, v41(3), 751-771.

Dybvig, Philip H. and Stephen A. Ross. "Yes, The APT Is Testable," JOF, 1985, v40(4), 1173-1188.

Dybvig, Philip H. and Stephen A. Ross. "Performance Measurement Using Differential Information And A Security Market Line," JOF, 1985, v40(2), 383-399.

Dybvig, Philip H. and Stephen A. Ross. "The Analytics Of Performance Measurement Using A Security Market Line," JOF, 1985, v40(2), 401-416.

Dybvig, Philip H. "Acknowledgment: Kinks On The Mean-Variance Frontier," JOF, 1985, v40(1), 345.

Dybvig, Philip H. "An Explicit Bound On Individual Assets Deviations From APT Pricing In A Finite Economy," JFEC, 1983, v12(4), 483-496.

Dybvig, Philip H. "Distributional Analysis Of Portfolio Choice," JOB, 1988, v61(3), 369-394.

Dybvig, Philip H. "Inefficient Dynamic Portfolio Strategies Or How To Throw Away A Million Dollars In The Stock Market," RFS, 1988-89, v1(1), 67-88.

Dybvig, Philip H. "Short Sales Restrictions And Kinks Of The Mean Variance Frontier," JOF, 1984, v39(1), 239-244.

Dybvig, Philip H. (Brown, Stephen and Philip H. Dybvig. "The Empirical Implications Of The Cox, Ingersoll, Ross Theory Of The Term Structure Of Interest Rates," JOF, 1986, v41(3), 616-628.)

Dybvig, Philip H. (Diamond, Douglas W. and Philip H. Dybvig. "Banking Theory, Deposit Insurance, And Bank Regulation," JOB, 1986, v59(1), 55-68.)

Dybvig, Philip H. and Chi-fu Huang. "Nonnegative Wealth, Absence Of Arbitrage, And Feasible Consumption Plans," RFS, 1988-89, v1(4), 377-401.

Dybvig, Philip H. and Jonathan E. Ingersoll, Jr. "Mean-Variance Theory In Complete Markets," JOB, 1982, v55(2), 233-252.

Dyckman, Thomas R. "An Aggregate Demand Model For Automobiles," JOB, 1965, v38(3), 252-266.

Dyckman, Thomas R. "Full Cost Accounting: Another View," FAJ, 1979, v35(3), 75-80.

Dye, Ronald A. "Insider Trading And Incentives," JOB, 1984, v57(3), 295-314.

Dye, Ronald A. "Proprietary And Nonproprietary Disclosures," JOB, 1986, v59(2), Part 1, 331-366.

Dyer, William W., Jr. "Life Insurance Accounting Under Fire," FAJ, 1974, v30(5), 42-44,46-50.

Dyl, Edward A. and Edwin D. Maberly. "The Daily Distribution Of Changes In The Price Of Stock Index Futures," JFM, 1986, v6(4), 513-522.

Dyl, Edward A. and Edwin D. Maberly. "The Weekly Pattern In Stock Index Futures: A Further Note," JOF, 1986, v41(5), 1149-1152.

Dyl, Edward A. and Hugh W. Long. "Abandonment Value And Capital Budgeting: Comment," JOF, 1969, v24(1), 88-95.

Dyl, Edward A. and J. Ronald Hoffmeister. "Efficiency And Volatility In The Federal Funds Market," JBR, 1984-85, v15(4), 234-239.

Dyl, Edward A. and J. Ronald Hoffmeister. "A Note On Dividend Policy And Beta," JBFA, 1986, v13(1), 107-115.

Dyl, Edward A. and Michael D. Joehnk. "Riding The Yield Curve: Does It Work?," JPM, 1981, v7(3), 13-17.

Dyl, Edward A. and Michael D. Joehnk. "Effect Of Latest IRS Regulations On Advance Refundings," FM, 1977, v6(2), 71-72.

Dyl, Edward A. and Michael D. Joehnk. "Prepayment Penalties Inherent In The Rule Of 78s," JBR, 1977-78, v8(1), 16-21.

Dyl, Edward A. and Michael D. Joehnk. "Sinking Funds And The Cost Of Corporate Debt," JOF, 1979, v34(4), 887-893.

Dyl, Edward A. and Michael D. Joehnk. "Refunding Tax Exempt Bonds," FM, 1976, v5(2), 59-66.

Dyl, Edward A. and Ronald A. Spahr. "Taxes And The Refunding Of Discount Bonds," JFR, 1983, v6(4), 265-273.

Dyl, Edward A. and Stanley A. Martin, Jr. "Setting Terms For Leveraged Leases," FM, 1977, v6(4),20-27.

Dyl, Edward A. and Stanley A. Martin, Jr. "Rules Of Thumb For The Analysis Of Tax Swaps," JPM, 1983, v10(1), 71-74.

Dyl, Edward A. and Stanley A. Martin, Jr. "Weekend Effects On Stock Returns: A Comment," JOF, 1985, v40(1), 347-350.

Dyl, Edward A. and Stanley A. Martin, Jr. "Another Look At Barbells Versus Ladders," JPM, 1986, v12(3), 54-59.

Eckardt, Walter L., Jr. (Aucamp, Donald C. and Walter L. Eckardt, Jr. "An Intuitive Look at Ito's Lemma: A Pedagogical Note," FR, 1981, v16(2), 41-50.)

Eckardt, Walter L., Jr. (Aucamp, Donald C. and Walter L. Eckardt, Jr. "A Sufficient Condition For A Unique Nonnegative Internal Rate Of Return--Comment," JFQA, 1976, v11(2), 329-332.)

Eckarkt, Walter L., Jr. and Donald L. Rogoff. "100% Margins Revisited," JOF, 1976, v31(3), 995-1001.

Eckbo, B. Espen and Herwig Langohr. "Information Disclosure, Method Of Payment, And Takeover Premiums: Public And Private Tender Offers In France," JFEC, 1989, v24(2), 363-404. 3 = '?8

Eckbo, B. Espen, Ronald M. Giammarino and Robert L. Heinkel. "Asymmetric Information And The Medium Of Exchange In Takeovers: Theory And Tests," RFS, 1990, v3(4), 651-676.

Eckbo, B. Espen, Vojislav Maksimovic and Joseph Williams. "Consistent Estimation Of Cross-Sectional Models In Event Studies," RFS, 1990, v3(3), 343-366.

Eckbo, B. Espen. "Horizontal Mergers, Collusion, And Stockholder Wealth," JFEC, 1983, v11(1), 241-273.

Eckbo, B. Espen. "Mergers And The Market Concentration Doctrine: Evidence From The Capital Market," JOB, 1985, v58(3), 325-349.

Eckbo, B. Espen. "Valuation Effects Of Corporate Debt Offerings," JFEC, 1986, v15(1/2), 119-152.

Eckbo, B. Espen. "Valuation Effects Of Greenmail Prohibition," JFQA, 1990, v25(4), 491-506.

Eckel, Jeffrey. (Fredrikson, E. Bruce and Jeffrey Eckel. "Electric Utilities: Assessing A Troubled Investment Environment," FAJ, 1983, v39(6), 40-45.)

Eckel, Norm. "An EPS Forecasting Model Utilizing Macroeconomic Performance Expectations," FAJ, 1982, v38(3), 68-77.

Eckrich, Donald W. (Durand, Richard M., Donald W. Eckrich and C. Ronald Sprecher. "Bank Image: An Adequacy-Importance Approach," JBR, 1978-79, v9(3), 168-172.)

Eckstein, Otto. "Federal Expenditure Policy For Economic Growth," JOF, 1962, v17(2), 280-288.

Economides, Nicholas. "The Demand For Life Insurance: An Application Of The Economics Of Uncertainty: A Comment," JOF, 1982, v37(5), 1305-1309.

Economopoulos, Andrew J. "Illinois Free Banking Experience," JMCB, 1988, v20(2), 249-264.

Eddey, Peter H. "Corporate Raiders And Takeover Targets," JBFA, 1991, v18(2), 151-172.

Eddy, Albert and Bruce Seifert. "Inflation, The Fisher Hypothesis, And Long-Term Bonds," FR, 1985, v20(1), 21-35.

Eddy, Albert and Bruce Seifert. "Dividend Changes Of Financially Weak Firms," FR, 1986, v21(4),419-431.

Eddy, Albert R. "Interest Rate Risk And Systematic Risk: An Interpretation," JOF, 1978, v33(2), 626-630.

Eddy, Albert and Bruce Seifert. "Firm Size And Dividend Announcements," JFR, 1988, v11(4), 295-302.

Edelman, Richard B. "A Filter Rule Program Used In Teaching Investments," JFED, 1977, v6, 84-86.

Edelman, Richard B. "A New Approach To Ratings On Utility Bonds: Reply," JPM, 1980, v6(4), 71-74.

Edelman, Richard B. "A New Approach To Ratings On Utility Bonds," JPM, 1979, v5(3), 63-68.

Edelman, Richard B. "Telecommunications Betas: Are They Stable And Unique?," JPM, 1983, v10(1), 46-52.

Edelman, Richard B. "The Impact On Electric Utility Bond Ratings Of Substituting Debt For Preferred Stock," FM, 1979, v8(1), 51-59.

Edelman, Richard B. (Baker, H. Kent, Gail E. Farrelly and Richard B. Edelman. "A Survey Of Management Views On Dividend Policy," FM, 1985, v14(3), 78-84.)

Edelman, Richard B. (Baker, H. Kent and Richard B. Edelman. "OTC Market Switching And Stock Returns: Some Empirical Evidence," JFR, 1990, v13(4), 325-338.)

Edelman, Richard B. and H. Kent Baker. "The Dynamics Of Neglect And Return," JPM, 1987, v14(1), 52-55.

Edelman, Richard B. and H. Kent Baker. "Liquidity And Stock Exchange Listing," FR, 1990, v25(2), 231-250.

Edelsburg, Charles. (Asay, Michael and Charles Edelsburg. "Can A Dynamic Strategy Replicate The Returns Of An Option?," JFM, 1986, v6(1), 63-70.)

Edelstein, Harold M. "Can Information Please?," JPM, 1976, v2(3), 30-33.

Edelstein, Robert and Jack Guttentag. "On The Alleged Profitability Of Borrowing At 8% to Lend At 6%," JBR, 1975-76, v6(4), 296-298.

Edelstein, Robert H. "Improving The Selection Of Credit Risks: An Analysis Of A Commercial Bank Minority Lending Program," JOF, 1975, v30(1), 37-55.

Edelstein, Robert H. "Improving The Selection Of Credit Risks - An Analysis Of A Commercial Bank Minority Lending Program: Reply," JOF, 1977, v32(5), 1790-1794.

Edelstein, Robert H. "The Value Of Information And The Optimal Governmental Guarantee On Its Agencies' Issues," JOF, 1974, v29(2), 471-484.

Edelstein, Robert H. (Dokko, Yoon, Robert H. Edelstein and E. Scott Unlang. "Does Credit Rationing Affect Residential Investment? Deja Vu All Over Again," JREFEC, 1990, v3(4), 357-372.)

Edelstein, Robert. "The Residential Property Tax Progresses," JFQA, 1979, v14(4), 753-768.

Ederington, L. H. "Uncertainty, Competition, And Costs In Corporate Bond Underwriting," JFEC, 1975, v2(1), 71-94.

Ederington, Louis H. and Samuel L. Skogstad. "Measurement Of Banking Competition And Geographic Markets: The Market For Checking Account Services," JMCB, 1977, v9(3), 469-482.

Ederington, Louis H. "Aspects Of The Production Of Significant Financial Research," JOF, 1979, v34(3), 777-786.

Ederington, Louis H. "Bidding For Securities: The Effect On The Issuer's Interest Costs," JOB, 1978, v51(4), 673-686.

Ederington, Louis H. "Classification Models And Bond Ratings," FR, 1985, v20(4), 237-262.

Ederington, Louis H. "Negotiated Versus Competitive Underwritings Of Corporate Bonds," JOF, 1976, v31(1), 17-28.

Ederington, Louis H. "New Futures And Options Markets," FAJ, 1980, v36(1), 42-48.

Ederington, Louis H. and William R. Henry. "On Costs Of Capital In Programming Approaches To Capital Budgeting," JFQA, 1979, v14(5), 1049-1058.

Ederington, Louis H. "The Hedging Performance Of The New Futures Markets," JOF, 1979, v34(1),157-170.

Ederington, Louis H. "The Yield Spread On New Issues Of Corporate Bonds," JOF, 1974, v29(5), 1531-1543.

Ederington, Louis H. "Why Split Ratings Occur," FM, 1986, v15(1), 37-47.

Ederington, Louis H. (Yawitz, Jess B., Kevin J. Maloney and Louis H. Ederington. "Taxes, Default Risk, And Yield Spreads," JOF, 1985, v40(4), 1127-1140.)

Ederington, Louis H., Jess B. Yawitz and Brian E. Roberts. "The Informational Content Of Bond Ratings," JFR, 1987, v10(3), 211-226.

Edesess, Michael and George A. Hambrecht. "Scenario Forecasting: Necessity, Not Choice," JPM, 1980, v6(3), 10-15.

Edgar, S. Michael. "Product Control Is A Problem At The FED," FAJ, 1974, v30(1), 82-91.

Edgar, S. Michael. (Peavy, John W., III and S. Michael Edgar. "A Multiple Discriminant Analysis Of BHC Commercial Paper Ratings," JBF, 1983, v7(2), 161-174.)

Edgar, S. Michael. (Peavy, John W. and S. Michael Edgar. "An Expanded Commercial Paper Rating Scale: Classification Of Industrial Issuers," JBF, 1984, v11(3), 397-407.)

Edgar, S. Michael. (Peavy, John W., III and S. Michael Edgar. "A Multiple Discriminant Analysis Of BHC Commercial Paper Ratings: A Reply," JBF, 1986, v10(1), 145-146.)

Edison, Hali J. and Eric O'N. Fisher. "A Long-View Of The European Monetary System," JIMF, 1991, v10(1), 53-70.

Edison, Hali J. "Purchasing Power Parity In The Long Run: A Test Of The Dollar/Pound Exchange Rate (1890-1978)," JMCB, 1987, v19(3), 376-387.

Edison, Hali J. "Purchasing Power Parity: A Quantitative Reassessment Of The 1920s Experience," JIMF, 1985, v4(3), 361-372.

Editor. "The Sensuous Investor," FAJ, 1971, v27(3), 42-43,93.

Edmister, Robert O. and Christopher James. "Is Illiquidity A Bar To Buying Small Cap Stocks?," JPM, 1983, v9(4), 14-19.

Edmister, Robert O. and Gary G. Schlarbaum. "Credit Policy In Lending Institutions," JFQA, 1974, v9(3), 335-356.

Edmister, Robert O. and James B. Greene. "Performance Of Super-Low-Price Stocks," JPM, 1980, v7(1), 36-41.

Edmister, Robert O. and N. Subramanian. "Determinants Of Brokerage Commission Rates For Institutional Investors: A Note," JOF, 1982, v37(4), 1087-1093.

Edmister, Robert O. and Ralph A. Walkling. "Trends In Institutional Commission Costs Following Deregulation: Evidence From The U.S.A.," JBFA, 1985, v12(4), 553-559.

Edmister, Robert O. "An Empirical Test Of Financial Ratio Analysis For Small Business Failure Prediction," JFQA, 1972, v7(2), 1477-1493.

Edmister, Robert O. "Commission Cost Structure: Shifts And Scale Economies," JOF, 1978, v33(2),477-486.

Edmister, Robert O. "Margin Analysis For Consumer Deposit Interest Rate Policy," JBR, 1982-83, v13(3), 179-184.

Edmister, Robert O. (James, Christopher and Robert O. Edmister. "The Relation Between Common Stock Returns, Trading Activity And Market Value," JOF, 1983, v38(4), 1075-1086.)

Edmister, Robert O. (Lewellen, Wilbur G. and Robert O. Edmister. "A General Model For Accounts-Receivable Analysis And Control," JFQA, 1973, v8(2), 195-206.)

Edmister, Robert O. (Walkling, Ralph A. and Robert O. Edmister. "Are There Commission Cost Side-Effects From Portfolio Management Decisions?," FAJ, 1983, v39(4), 52-59.)

Edmister, Robert O. (Walkling, Ralph A. and Robert O. Edmister. "Determinants Of Tender Offer Premiums," FAJ, 1985, v41(1), 27,30-37.)

Edmister, Robert O. and Harry E. Merriken. "Pricing Efficiency In The Mortgage Market," AREUEA, 1988, v16(1), 50-62.

Edmister, Robert O. and Harry E. Merriken. "Measuring Interest Rate Sensitivity Of Consumer Depositors," JFSR, 1989, v2(2), 133-145.

Edmonds, Radcliffe G., Jr. "A Theoretical Basis For Hedonic Regression: A Research Primer," AREUEA, 1984, v12(1), 72-85.

Edmonds, Thomas P. "The Effect Of Auditor Involvement On The Predictive Capacity Of Interim Financial Information," JBFA, 1983, v10(3), 429-441.

Edmunds, John. "A Comment On Greenstone's 'The Coffee Cartel: Manipulation In The Public Interest'," JFM, 1982, v2(1), 19-24.

Edwards, Charles E. and James G. Hilton. "A Note On The High-Low Price Average As An Estimator Of Annual Average Stock Prices," JOF, 1966, v21(1), 112-115.

Edwards, Charles E. and James G. Hilton. "Some Comments On Short-Run Earnings Fluctuation Bias," JFQA, 1970, v5(2), 187-201.

Edwards, Charles E. and Stanley R. Stansell. " An Inter-Temporal Approach To The Optimization Of Dividend Policy With Predetermined Investments: Comment," JOF, 1974, v29(1), 251-253.

Edwards, Charles E. (Brooks, LeRoy D., Charles E. Edwards and Eurico J. Ferreira. "Risk-Return Characteristics Of Convertible Preferred Stock: Comment," JPM, 1984, v10(2), 76-78.)

Edwards, Charles E. (Cooley, Philip L. and Charles E. Edwards. "Ownership Effects On Managerial Salaries In Small Business," FM, 1982, v11(4), 5-9.)

Edwards, Corwin D. "Public Policy And Business Size," JOB, 1951, v24(4), 280-292.

Edwards, Corwin D. "Twenty Years Of The Robinson-Patman Act," JOB, 1956, v29(3), 149-159.

Edwards, Edgar O. "Funds Statements Further Considered," JOB, 1953, v26(2), 133-140.

Edwards, Edgar O. "Funds Statements For Short-And Long-Run Analyses," JOB, 1952, v25(3), 156-174.

Edwards, Edward E. "Changing Character Of The Real Estate Mortgage Markets," JOF, 1964, v19(2), Part 1, 313-320.

Edwards, Franklin R. "Does Futures Trading Increase Stock Market Volatility?," FAJ, 1988, v44(1),63-69.

Edwards, Franklin R. "Futures Trading And Cash Market Volatility: Stock Index And Interest Rate Futures," JFM, 1988, v8(4), 421-440.

Edwards, Franklin R. "Futures Markets In Transition: The Uneasy Balance Between Government And Self-Regulation," JFM, 1983, v3(2), 191-206.

Edwards, Franklin R. "More On Substitutability Between Money And Near Monies," JMCB, 1972, v4(3), 551-571.

Edwards, Franklin R. "Studies Of The 1987 Stock Market Crash: Review And Appraisal," JFSR, 1988, v1(3), 231-252.

Edwards, Franklin R. "The Clearing Association In Futures Markets: Guarantor And Regulator," JFM, 1983, v3(4), 369-392.

Edwards, Franklin R. "The Regulation Of Futures And Forward Trading By Depository Institutions: A Legal And Economic Analysis," JFM, v1(2), 201-218.

Edwards, Franklin R. "The Regulation Of Futures Markets: A Conceptual Framework," JFM, 1981, v1(Supp), 417-439.

Edwards, Franklin R. (Edwards, Linda N. and Franklin R. Edwards. "A Legal And Economic Analysis Of Manipulation In Futures Markets," JFM, 1984, v4(3), 333-366.)

Edwards, Franklin R. and Cindy Ma. "Commodity Pool Performance: Is The Information Contained In Pool Prospectuses Useful?," JFM, 1988, v8(5), 589-616.

Edwards, Franklin R. and Salih N. Neftci. "Extreme Price Movements And Margin Levels In Futures Markets," JFM, 1988, v8(6), 639-656.

Edwards, Linda N. and Franklin R. Edwards. "A Legal And Economic Analysis Of Manipulation In Futures Markets," JFM, 1984, v4(3), 333-366.

Edwards, N. Fayne. "Selecting The Discount Rate In Personal Injury And Wrongful Death Cases," JRI, 1975, v42(2), 342-345.

Edwards, Nathan D. "Significance Of Price Fluctuations In Securities," FAJ, 1958, v14(2), 87-92.

Edwards, Sebastian and Guido Tabellini. "Explaining Fiscal Policies And Inflation In Developing Countries," JIMF, 1991, v10(Supp), S16-S48.

Edwards, Sebastian and Jonathan D. Ostry. "Anticipated Protectionist Policies, Real Exchange Rates, And The Current Account: The Case Of Rigid Wages," JIMF, 1990, v9(2), 206-219.

Edwards, Sebastian. "Country Risk, Foreign Borrowing, And The Social Discount Rate In An Open Developing Economy," JIMF, 1986, v5(Supp), S79-S96.

Edwards, Sebastian. "Exchange Rates And 'News': Reply," JIMF, 1984, v3(1), 123-126.

Edwards, Sebastian. "Exchange Rate And 'News': A Multi-Currency Approach," JIMF, 1982, v1(3),211-224.

Edwards, Sebastian. "Floating Exchange Rates In Less-Developed Countries: A Monetary Analysis Of The Peruvian Experience, 1950-54," JMCB, 1983, v15(1), 73-81.

Edwards, Sebastian. "Money, The Rate Of Devaluation, And Interest Rates In A Semiopen Economy: Columbia, 1968-82," JMCB, 1985, v17(1), 59-68.

Edwards, Sebastian. "On The Interest-Rate Elasticity Of The Demand For International Reserves: Some Evidence From Developing Countries," JIMF, 1985, v4(2), 287-295.

Edwards, Thomas C. "A Benefit Manager's Guide To Sex," JRI, 1975, v42(2), 189-200.

Edwards, William F. "Fundamentals Plus Statistics In Appraising The Business Outlook," FAJ, 1947, v3(4),3-11.

Edwards, William F. "Judgement Versus Mechanical Investment Plans," FAJ, 1946, v2(1), 3-8.

Eeckhoudt, L. (Caperaa, P. and L. Eeckhoudt. "Delayed Risk And Risk Premiums," JFEC, 1975, v2(3), 309-319.)

Eeckhoudt, L., J. F. Outreville, M. Lauwers and F. Calcoen. "The Impact Of A Probationary Period On The Demand For Insurance," JRI, 1988, v55(2), 217-228.

Eeckhoudt, Louis and Henri Louberge. "Export Credit Insurance: Comment," JRI, 1988, v55(4), 742-747.

Eeckhoudt, Louis. (Brys, Eric, Georges Dionne and Louis Eeckhoudt. "More On Insurance As A Giffin Good," JRU, 1989, v2(4), 415-420.)

Egan, Douglas. (Stonehill, Arthur, T. Beekhuisen, R. Wright, L. Remmers, N. Toy, A. Pares, A. Shapiro, D. Egan and T. Bates. "Financial Goals And Debt Ratio Determinants," FM, 1974, v4(3), 27-41.)

Eger, Carol E. (Alexander, Gordon J., P. George Benson and Carol E. Eger. "Timing Decisions And The Behavior Of Mutual Fund Systematic Risk," JFQA, 1982, v17(4), 579-602.)

Eger, Carol Ellen. "An Empirical Test Of The Redistribution Effect In Pure Exchange Mergers," JFQA, 1983, v18(4), 547-572.

Eggertsen, Paul. "Some Aspects Of Denmark's Insurance Industry," JRI, 1958, v25(2), 37-46.

Egginton, D. A. and I. R. Davidson. "A Test Of Income Dichotomization," JBFA, 1987, v14(1),143-153.

Ehrhardt, Michael C. "A Mean-Variance Derivation Of A Multi-Factor Equilibrium Model," JFQA, 1987, v22(2), 227-236.

Ehrhardt, Michael C. "A New Linear Programming Approach To Bond Portfolio Management: A Comment," JFQA, 1989, v24(4), 533-537.

Ehrhardt, Michael C. "Arbitrage Pricing Models: The Sufficient Number Of Factors And Equilibrium Conditions," JFR, 1987, v10(2), 111-120.

Ehrhardt, Michael C. "Diversification And Interest Rate Risk," JBFA, 1991, v18(1), 43-60.

Ehrhardt, Michael C. (Clayton, Ronnie, John Delozier and Michael C. Ehrhardt. "A Note On January Returns In The U.S. Government Bond Market: The Term Effect," JFSR, 1989, v2(4), 307-318.)

Ehrhardt, Michael C. and Alan L. Tucker. "Pricing CRB Futures Contracts," JFR, 1990, v13(1), 7-14.

Ehrhardt, Michael C., James V. Jordan and Ralph A. Walkling. "An Application Of Arbitrage Pricing Theory To Futures Markets: Tests Of Normal Backwardation," JFM, 1987, v7(1), 21-34.

Ehrlich, Harold. "Tight Money: Deflationary Or Inflationary?," FAJ, 1957, v13(4), 79-84.

Ehrman, Libert and Stuart A. Rice. "Effective Shareowner Relations Through Research," FAJ, 1956, v12(2), 11-16.

Eichengreen, Barry J. "Effective Protection And Exchange-Rate Determination," JIMF, 1983, v2(1),1-16.

Eichengreen, Barry. "Conducting The International Orchestra: Bank Of England Leadership Under The Classical Gold Standard," JIMF, 1987, v6(1), 5-30.

Eiger, Nahum and Yehuda Kahane. "Risk Considerations In Insurance Ratemaking," JRI, 1978, v45(1), 121-132.

Eilbirt, Henry. "A Study Of Current Counseling Practices In Industry," JOB, 1958, v31(1), 28-37.

Eilbott, Peter. "Trends In The Value Of Individual Stockholdings," JOB, 1974, v47(3), 339-348.

Eilers, Robert D. "Blue Shield: Current Issues And Future Direction," JRI, 1966, v33(4), 537-552.

Eilers, Robert D. "Minimum Premium Health Plans: Insured Non-Insurance," JRI, 1969, v36(1), 63-81.

Eilers, Robert D. "Post-Payment Health Coverage: Contributions And Limitations," JRI, 1970, v37(3), 381-396.

Eilers, Robert D. "The Fundamental Nature Of Blue Cross And Blue Shield," JRI, 1962, v29(3), 385-402.

Eilers, Robert E. "Inter-Insurer Arrangements To Provide Over-65 Medical Care Coverage," JRI, 1963, v30(4), 483-504.

Eilon, Samuel. "Earning Per Share And Takeovers," JBF, 1978, v2(3), 257-268.

Eilon, Samuel. "Earnings Per Share Can Be Misleading: A Note," JBFA, 1975, v2(2), 239-241.

Einhorn, Hillel J. (Gallagher, William E., Jr. and Hillel J. Einhorn. "Motivation Theory And Job Design," JOB, 1976, v49(3), 358-373.)

Einhorn, Hillel J. (Hogarth, Robin M. and Hillel J. Einhorn. "Optimal Strategies For Personnel Selection When Candidates Can Reject Offers," JOB, 1976, v49(4), 478-495.)

Einhorn, Hillel J. and Robin M. Hogarth. "Decision Making Under Ambiguity," JOB, 1986, v59(4), Part 2, S225-S250.

Einhorn, Madeline W. "Breaking Tradition In Bond Portfolio Investment," JPM, 1975, v1(3), 38-43.

Einhorn, Raymond and H. Kent Baker. "The Institute For Applied Public Financial Management: An Innovative Approach," JFED, 1977, v6, 27-32.

Einhorn, Steven G. and Patricia Shangquan. "Using The Dividend Discount Model For Asset Allocation," FAJ, 1984, v40(3), 30-32.

Einzig, Paul. "Some Recent Changes In The Euro-Dollar System," JOF, 1964, v19(3), 443-449.

Einzig, Robert S. "Tomorrow's Markets - The Competitive 1960's," FAJ, 1963, v19(3), 91-97.

Einzig, Robert and Bruce Lange. "Swaps At Transamerica: Applications And Analysis," JACF, 1990, v2(4), 48-58.

Einzig, Robert. (Bowsher, Norman N., J. Dewey Daane and Robert Einzig. "The Flows Of Funds Between Regions Of The United States," JOF, 1958, v13(1),1-20.)

Eisemann, Peter C. and Edward A. Moses. "Stock Dividends: Management's View," FAJ, 1978, v34(4),77-83.

Eisemann, Peter C. and Stephen G. Timme. "Intraweek Seasonality In The Federal Funds Market," JFR, 1984, v7(1), 47-56.

Eisemann, Peter C. "Diversification And The Congeneric Bank Holding Company," JBR, 1976-77, v7(1),68-77.

Eisenbeis, R. A. "A Study Of Geographic Banking Markets For Business Loans," JBR, 1970-71, v1(1), 62-63.

Eisenbeis, Robert A. and Alan S. McCall. "The Impact Of Legislation Prohibiting Director-Interlocks Among Depository Financial Institutions," JBF, 1978, v2(4), 323-337.

Eisenbeis, Robert A. and Alan S. McCall. "Some Effects Of Affiliations Among Mutual Savings And Commercial Banks," JOF, 1972, v27(4), 865-877.

Eisenbeis, Robert A. "Differences In Federal Regulatory Agencies' Bank Merger Policies," JMCB, 1975, v7(1), 93-104.

Eisenbeis, Robert A. "Local Banking Markets For Business Loans," JBR, 1971-72, v2(2), 30-39.

Eisenbeis, Robert A. "Nonlocal Banking Markets For Business Loans," JBR, 1971-72, v2(4), 41-47.

Eisenbeis, Robert A. "Pitfalls In The Application Of Discriminant Analysis In Business, Finance, And Economics," JOF, 1977, v32(3), 875-900.

Eisenbeis, Robert A. "Problems In Applying Discriminant Analysis In Credit Scoring Models," JBF, 1978, v2(3), 205-220.

Eisenbeis, Robert A. "The Allocative Effects Of Branch Banking Restrictions On Business Loan Markets," JBR, 1975-76, v6(1), 43-47.

Eisenbeis, Robert A. "A Multivariate Analysis Of Industrial Bond Ratings' And The Role Of Subordination: A Comment," JOF, 1978, v33(1), 325-335.

Eisenbeis, Robert A. (Altman, Edward I. and Robert A. Eisenbeis. "Financial Applications Of Discriminant Analysis: A Clarification," JFQA, 1978, v13(1), 185-195.)

Eisenbeis, Robert A. (Born, Jeffrey A., Robert A. Eisenbeis and Robert Harris. "The Benefits Of Geographical And Product Expansion In The Financial Services Industry," JFSR, 1988, v1(2), 161-182.)

Eisenbeis, Robert A.,Robert S. Harris and Josef Lakonishok. "Benefits Of Bank Diversification: The Evidence From Shareholder Returns," JOF, 1984, v39(3), 881-892.

Eisenmann, Peter C. (Mehta, Dileep R., Peter C. Eisemann, Edward A. Moses and Benoit Deschamps. "Capital Structure And Capital Adequacy Of Bank Holding Companies: A Market Test," JBF, 1979, v3(1), 5-22.)

Eisenmann, Peter C. (Timme, Stephen G. and Peter C. Eisemann. "On The Use Of Consensus Forecasts Of Growth In The Constant Growth Model: The Case Of Electric Utilities," FM, 1989, v18(4), 23-35.)

Eisenstadt, Samuel. "How Good Is Investment For Individuals?," JPM, 1979, v5(2), 76-77.

Eiteman, David K. and J. Fred Weston. "Economic Trends And Security Values - A Bleak Or Bountiful Future For Investors?," FAJ, 1965, v21(1), 21-32.

Eiteman, David K. and Keith V. Smith. "A Portfolio Analysis Of The Teaching Of Investments," JFQA, 1974, v9(5), 771-780.

Eiteman, David K. "A Computer Program," FAJ, 1968, v24(4), 107-111.

Eiteman, David K. "A Computer Program For Financial Statement Analysis," FAJ, 1964, v20(6), 61-68.

Eiteman, David K. "Interdependence Of Utility Rate-Base Type, Permitted Rate Of Return, And Utility Earnings," JOF, 1962, v17(1), 38-52.

Eiteman, David K. "The S. E. C. Special Study And The Exchange Markets," JOF, 1966, v21(2),311-323.

Eiteman, Wilford J. "Yield On Common Stock Investments," **FAJ**, 1957, v13(1), 13-18.

Eizman, Ethan S. "Rebalance Disciplines For Portfolio Insurance," **JPM**, 1986, v13(1), 59-62.

Ekelund, Robert B., Jr. (Ault, Richard W. and Robert B. Ekelund, Jr. "Rent Seeking In A Static Model Of Zoning," **AREUEA**, 1988, v16(1), 69-76.)

Ekern, Steinar. "On The Adequacy Of A Probabilistic Internal Rate Of Return," **JBFA**, 1979, v6(2), 229-238.

Ekern, Steinar. "Time Dominance Efficiency Analysis," **JOF**, 1981, v36(5), 1023-1034.

Ekern, Steinar. (Bjerksund, Petter and Steinar Ekern. "Managing Investment Opportunities Under Price Uncertainty: From 'Last Chance' to 'Wait And See' Strategies," **FM**, 1990, v19(3), 65-83.)

El Hennawy, R. H. A. and R. C. Morris. "Market Anticipation Of Corporate Failure In The UK," **JBFA**, 1983, v10(3), 359-372.

El Hennawy, R. H. A. and R. C. Morris. "The Significance Of Base Year In Developing Failure Prediction Models," **JBFA**, 1983, v10(2), 209-223.

Elam, Emmet W. and Daniel Vaught. "Risk And Return In Cattle And Hog Futures," **JFM**, 1988, v8(1), 79-88.

Elam, Emmett and Bruce L. Dixon. "Examining The Validity Of A Test Of Futures Market Efficiency," **JFM**, 1988, v8(3), 365-372.

Elayan, Fayez A. (Maris, Brian A. and Fayez A. Elayan. "Capital Structure And The Cost Of Capital For Untaxed Firms: The Case Of REITS," **AREUEA**, 1990, v18(1), 22-39.)

Elayan, Fayez A. (Wansley, James W., Fayez A. Elayan and Brian A. Maris. "Preferred Stock Returns, CreditWatch, And Preferred Stock Rating Changes," **FR**, 1990, v25(2), 265-286.)

Eldin, Ahmed E. K. (Brayshaw, R. E. and Ahmed E. K. Eldin. "The Smoothing Hypothesis And The Role Of Exchange Differences," **JBFA**, 1989, v16(5), 621-634.)

Eldor, Rafael, David Pines and Abba Schwartz. "Determinants Of An Individual's Demand For Hedging Instruments," **JFM**, 1989, v9(2), 135-142.

Eldor, Rafael, David Pines and Aba Schwartz. "The Demand For Domestic Assets And Consumption Risk," **RDIBF**, 1988, v2, 349-362.

Eldor, Rafael. (Benninga, Simon, Rafael Eldor and Itzhak Zilcha. "The Optimal Hedge Ratio In Unbiased Futures Markets," **JFM**, 1984, v4(2), 155-159.)

Eldor, Rafael. (Benninga, Simon, Rafael Eldor and Itzhak Zilcha. "Optimal International Hedging In Commodity And Currency Forward Markets," **JIMF**, 1985, v4(4), 537-552.)

Eldor, Rafael. (Zilcha, Itzhak and Rafael Eldor. "Exporting Firm And Forward Markets: The Multiperiod Case," **JIMF**, 1991, v10(1), 108-117.)

Eldred, Gary W. "Does The Public Support The Social Security Program?," **JRI**, 1977, v44(2), 179-191.

Eldred, Gary W. "Factors To Be Examined In Terminating A Social Security Coverage Agreement," **JRI**, 1975, v42(3), 433-446.

Eldred, Gary W. "Social Security: A Conceptual Alternative," **JRI**, 1981, v48(2), 220-234.

Eldred, Gary W. (Mehr, Robert I. and Gary W. Eldred. "Should The 'No-Fault' Concept Be Applied To Automobile Property Damage?," **JRI**, 1975, v42(1), 17-33.)

Eldred, Gary W. (Mehr, Robert I. and Gary W. Eldred. "Public Desires And Automobile Property Damage Insurance," **JRI**, 1975, v42(1), 151-155.))

Eldridge, Robert M. "Intertemporal Price Volatility Of Foreign Currency Futures Contracts," **JFM**, 1984, v4(2), 133-140.

Elebash, Clarence C. (Christiansen, William A. and Clarence C. Elebash. "A Note On The Attitude Of Pension Fund Investment Managers Toward Mortgage-Backed Securities," **JRER**, 1987, v2(1), 83-92.)

Elebash, Clarence C. and William A. Christiansen. "State Pension Funds: What Is Their Future In Real Estate?," **JRER**, 1989, v4(2), 71-79.

Elgers, Pieter T. and Dennis Murray. "LIFO-FIFO, Accounting Ratios And Market Risk: A Re-Assessment," **JBFA**, 1984, v11(3), 313-325.

Elgers, Pieter T. and Dennis Murray. "Financial Characteristics Related To Managements' Stock Split And Stock Dividend Decisions," **JBFA**, 1985, v12(4), 543-551.

Elgers, Pieter T. and John J. Clark. "Merger Types And Shareholder Returns: Additional Evidence," **FM**, 1980, v9(2), 66-72.

Elgers, Pieter T. (Bloom, Robert, Pieter T. Elgers, James R. Haltiner and William H. Hawthorne. "Inflation Gains And Losses On Monetary Items: An Empirical Test," **JBFA**, 1980, v7(4), 603-618.)

Elgers, Pieter T., James R. Haltiner and William H. Hawthorne. "Beta Regression Tendencies: Statistical And Real Causes," **JOF**, 1979, v34(1), 261-263.

Elgers, Pieter, Joanne Hill and Thomas Schneeweis. "Research Design For Systematic Risk Prediction," **JPM**, 1982, v8(3), 43-52.

Elkin, Philip. "A Report On A Study To Estimate The Financial Loss Proximately Caused By Automobile Operations In New Jersey," **JRI**, 1959, v26(1), 73-75.

Elkin, Philip. "The Future Family Economic Unit: Economic And Social Security Perspectives," **JRI**, 1963, v30(3), 385-392.

Ellebracht, Pat. "The Telelecturer — An Innovative Classroom Tool," **JFED**, 1975, v4, 82-83.

Ellert, James C. "Mergers, Antitrust Law Enforcement And Stockholder Returns," **JOF**, 1976, v31(2), 715-732.

Elliehausen, Gregory E. (Lawrence, Edward C. and Gregory E. Elliehausen. "The Impact Of Federal Interest Rate Regulations On The Small Saver: Further Evidence," **JOF**, 1981, v36(3), 677-684.)

Elliehausen, Gregory E. and Robert D. Kurtz. "Scale Economies And Compliance Costs For Federal Consumer Credit Regulations," **JFSR**, 1988, v1(2), 147-160.

Elliehausen, Gregory E. and Thomas A. Durkin. "Theory And Evidence Of The Impact Of Equal Credit Opportunity: An Agnostic Review Of The Literature," **JFSR**, 1989, v2(2), 89-114.

Elliehausen, Gregory E. and John D. Wolken. "Market Definition And Product Segmentation For Household Credit," **JFSR**, 1990, v4(1), 21-36.

Elliott, David C. "A New Index Of Equity Values," **FAJ**, 1969, v25(3), 101-104.

Elliott, Donald S., Jr. (Quinn, Michael A., Donald S. Elliott, Jr., Robert E. Mendelson and Jeffrey A. Thoman. "Maintenance Effort And The Professional Landlord: An Empirical Critique Of Neighborhood Decline," **AREUEA**, 1980, v8(4), 345-369.)

Elliott, Donald S., Jr. and Michael A. Quinn. "Concentrated Housing Code Enforcement In St. Louis," **AREUEA**, 1983, v11(3), 344-370.

Elliott, Donald S., Jr., Michael A. Quinn and Robert E. Mendelson. "Maintenance Behavior Of Large-Scale Landlords And Theories Of Neighborhood Succession," **AREUEA**, 1985, v13(4), 424-445.

Elliott, J. W. "A Direct Comparison Of Short-Run GNP Forecasting Models," **JOB**, 1973, v46(1), 33-60.

Elliott, J. W. "Control, Size, Growth, And Financial Performance In The Firm," **JFQA**, 1972, v7(1), 1309-1320.

Elliott, J. W. "The Expected Return To Equity And International Asset Prices," **JFQA**, 1978, v13(5), 987-1002.

Elliott, J. W. "The Influence Of Monetary And Fiscal Actions On Total Spending: The St. Louis Total Spending Equation Revisited," **JMCB**, 1975, v7(2), 181-192.

Elliott, J. W. (Echols, M. E. and J. W. Elliott. "Measuring The Shoulder Of The Yield Curve," **JBR**, 1974-75, v5(4), 264-268.)

Elliott, J. Walter and J. R. Baier. "Econometric Models And Current Interest Rates: How Well Do They Predict Future Rates: A Reply," **JOF**, 1980, v35(4), 1049-1050.

Elliott, J. Walter and Jerome R. Baier. "Econometric Models And Current Interest Rates: How Well Do They Predict Future Rates?," **JOF**, 1979, v34(4), 975-986.

Elliott, J. Walter and Michael E. Echols. "Expected Yield Curve Movements And Rational Term Structure Expectations: An Empirical Note," **JMCB**, 1977, v9(1), 90-96.

Elliott, J. Walter. "Forecasting And Analysis Of Corporate Financial Performance With An Econometric Model Of The Firm," **JFQA**, 1972, v7(2), 1499-1526.

Elliott, J. Walter. "The Cost Of Capital And US Capital Investment: A Test Of Alternative Concepts," **JOF**, 1980, v35(4), 981-999.

Elliott, J. Walter. (Echols, Michael E. and J. Walter Elliott. "Forecasting Vs. Allocation Efficiency In Bank Asset Planning," **JBR**, 1975-76, v6(4), 283-295.)

Elliott, James V. "What Is The Role Of Government In A Major Restructuring Of Financial Institutions In The 1980s?," **JBR**, 1983-84, v14(1), 25-32.

Elliott, Jan Walter. (Echols, Michael E. and Jan Walter Elliott. "A Quantitative Yield Curve Model For Estimating The Term Structure Of Interest Rates," **JFQA**, 1976, v11(1), 87-114.)

Elliott, Martin A. and Marvin Chandler. "The Bright Future For The Gas Industry," **FAJ**, 1958, v14(4), 47-52.

Elliott, Michael. "The Impact Of Growth Control Regulations On Housing Prices In California," **AREUEA**, 1981, v9(2), 115-133.

Elliott, Robert J. (Barone-Adesi, Giovanni and Robert J. Elliott. "Pricing The Treasury Bond Futures Contract As The Minimum Value Of Deliverable Bond Prices," **RFM**, 1989, v8(3), 438-445.)

Ellis, C. A. and J. S. Wadsworth, Jr. "U.S. Corporations And The International Capital Market Abroad," **FAJ**, 1966, v22(3), 169-175.

Ellis, Charles D. "Ben Graham: Ideas As Mementos," **FAJ**, 1982, v38(4), 41-42,44-48.

Ellis, Charles D. "Bonds For Long Term Investors," **FAJ**, 1970, v26(2), 81-85.

Ellis, Charles D. "How To Manage Investor Relations," **FAJ**, 1985, v41(2), 34-41.

Ellis, Charles D. "Jack Has Never Been Easy," **FAJ**, 1981, v37(4), 25.

Ellis, Charles D. "Pension Funds Need Management Management," **FAJ**, 1979, v35(3), 25-28.

Ellis, Charles D. "Performance Investing," **FAJ**, 1968, v24(5), 117-119.

Ellis, Charles D. "Portfolio Operations," **FAJ**, 1971, v27(5), 36-46.

Ellis, Charles D. "Tax Cut Implications For Financial Analysis," **FAJ**, 1964, v20(3), 53-55.

Ellis, Charles D. "The Brokerage Industry After May Day," **FAJ**, 1976, v32(5), 25-26.

Ellis, Charles D. "The Great 1970 Market Crash," **FAJ**, 1970, v26(5), 22-27.

Ellis, Charles D. "The Loser's Game," **FAJ**, 1975, v31(4), 19-20,22-24,26.

Ellis, Howard S. "Changing Concepts Of Convertibility And The Future Of Currencies," **JOF**, 1955, v10(2), 180-194.

Ellis, John W. and David J. O'Farrell. "Utilizing Mixed Integer Programming In The Construction Of Income-Oriented Portfolios," **JFED**, 1978, v7, 83-85.

Ellis, John W. "A Computerized Projection Model For Stock Market Evaluation," **JFED**, 1975, v4, 106-110.

Ellis, M. E. (Ma, Christopher K. and M. E. Ellis. "Selecting Industries As Inflation Hedges," **JPM**, 1989, v15(4), 45-48.)

Ellis, Peter M. "Characterization Of The Annual Pattern Of Life Insurance Sales," **JRI**, 1974, v41(4), 735-738.

Ellis, Peter M. "Motor Vehicle Mortality Reductions Since The Energy Crisis," **JRI**, 1977, v44(3), 373-381.

Ellis, Randall P., Cynthia L. Gallup and Thomas G. McGuire. "Should Medical Professional Liability Insurance Be Experience Rated?," **JRI**, 1990, v57(1), 66-78.

Ellsworth, D. Bruce. "Divergence In The Market Not New," **FAJ**, 1954, v10(2), 73-76.

Elmer, Peter J. "Preferred Stock Arbitrage Of Municipal Bond Market Segmentation," **FR**, 1986, v21(4), 383-398.

Elmer, Peter J. and David M. Borowski. "An Expert System Approach To Financial Analysis: The Case Of S&L Bankruptcy," **FM**, 1988, v17(3), 66-76.

Elnicki, Richard A. and Warren R. Hughes. "An Empirical Analysis Of Demands For Priority Computing Goods By Externally And Internally Funded Researchers," **JOB**, 1980, v53(1), 79-96.

Elsaid, Hussein H. "Non-Convertible Preferred Stock As A Financing Instrument 1950-1965: Comment," **JOF**, 1969, v24(5), 939-941.

Elsaid, Hussein H. "Preferred Stock In Corporate Plan," **FAJ**, 1969, v25(4), 112-117.

Elsaid, Hussein H. (Kim, Sang-Hoon and Hussein H. Elsaid. "Safety Margin Allocation And Risk Assessment Under The NPV Method," **JBFA**, 1985, v12(1), 133-144.)

Elsaid, Hussein H. (Kim, Sang-Hoon and Hussein H. Elsaid. "Estimation Of Periodic Standard Deviations Under The PERT And Derivation Of Probabilistic Information," **JBFA**, 1988, v15(4),

557-572.)

Elsom, Harold B. "Common Stocks And The Short-Term Interest Rate," **FAJ**, 1961, v17(2), 21-26.

Elsom, Harold B. "The Law Of Trust Investments," **FAJ**, 1960, v16(4), 27-33.

Elton, Edwin and Martin Gruber. "The Effect Of Share Repurchase On The Value Of The Firm: Reply," **JOF**, 1968, v23(5), 870-874.

Elton, Edwin and Martin Gruber. "The Effect Of Share Repurchases On The Value Of The Firm," **JOF**, 1968, v23(1), 135-149.

Elton, Edwin J. and Martin J. Gruber. "Valuation And The Cost Of Capital For Regulated Industries: Reply," **JOF**, 1972, v27(5), 1150-1155.

Elton, Edwin J. and Martin J. Gruber. "Asset Selection With Changing Capital Structure," **JFQA**, 1973, v8(3), 459-474.

Elton, Edwin J. and Martin J. Gruber. "Taxes And Portfolio Composition," **JFEC**, 1978, v6(4), 399-410.

Elton, Edwin J. and Martin J. Gruber. "Valuation And Asset Selection Under Alternative Investment Opportunities," **JOF**, 1976, v31(2), 525-539.

Elton, Edwin J. and Martin J. Gruber. "Estimating The Dependence Structure Of Share Prices - Implications For Portfolio Selection," **JOF**, 1973, v28(5), 1203-1232.

Elton, Edwin J. and Martin J. Gruber. "Homogeneous Groups And The Testing Of Economic Hypotheses," **JFQA**, 1970, v5(5), 581-602.

Elton, Edwin J. and Martin J. Gruber. "The Economic Value Of The Call Option," **JOF**, 1972, v27(4), 891-901.

Elton, Edwin J. and Martin J. Gruber. "Valuation And The Cost Of Capital For Regulated Industries," **JOF**, 1974, v26(3), 661-670.

Elton, Edwin J. and Martin J. Gruber. "Non-Standard C.A.P.M.'s And The Market Portfolio," **JOF**, 1984, v39(3), 911-924.

Elton, Edwin J. and Martin J. Gruber. "Portfolio Theory When Investment Relatives Are Lognormally Distributed," **JOF**, 1974, v29(4), 1265-1273.

Elton, Edwin J. and Martin J. Gruber. "Optimal Investment And Financing Patterns For A Firm Subject To Regulation With A Lag," **JOF**, 1977, v32(5), 1485-1500.

Elton, Edwin J. and Martin J. Gruber. "Dynamic Programming Applications In Finance," **JOF**, 1971, v26(2), 473-506.

Elton, Edwin J. "Capital Rationing And External Discount Rates," **JOF**, 1970, v25(3), 573-584.

Elton, Edwin J. (Bawa, Vijay S., Edwin J. Elton and Martin J. Gruber. "Simple Rules For Optimal Portfolio Selection In Stable Paretian Markets," **JOF**, 1979, v34(4), 1041-1047.)

Elton, Edwin J. (Cho, D. Chinhyung, Edwin J. Elton and Martin J. Gruber. "On The Robustness Of The Roll And Ross Arbitrage Pricing Theory," **JFQA**, 1984, v19(1), 1-10.)

Elton, Edwin J. and Martin J. Gruber. "On The Optimality Of Some Multiperiod Portfolio Selection Criteria," **JOB**, 1974, v47(2), 231-243.

Elton, Edwin J. and Martin J. Gruber. "Risk Reduction And Portfolio Size: An Analytical Solution," **JOB**, 1977, v50(4), 415-437.

Elton, Edwin J. and Martin J. Gruber. "Improved Forecasting Through The Design Of Homogeneous Groups," **JOB**, 1971, v44(4), 432-450.

Elton, Edwin J. and Martin J. Gruber. "Differential Information And Timing Ability," **JBF**, 1991, v15(1), 117-131.

Elton, Edwin J., Martin J. Gruber and Seth Grossman. "Discrete Expectational Data And Portfolio Performance," **JOF**, 1986, v41(3), 699-712.

Elton, Edwin J., Martin J. Gruber and Zvi Lieber. "Valuation, Optimum Investment And Financing For The Firm Subject To Regulation," **JOF**, 1975, v30(2), 401-425.

Elton, Edwin J., Martin J. Gruber and Manfred W. Padberg. "Simple Rules For Optimal Portfolio Selection: The Multi Group Case," **JFQA**, 1977, v12(3), 329-345.

Elton, Edwin J., Martin J. Gruber and Joel Rentzler. "The Ex-Dividend Day Behavior Of Stock Prices; A Reexamination Of The Clientele Effect: A Comment," **JOF**, 1984, v39(2), 551-556.

Elton, Edwin J., Martin J. Gruber and Thomas J. Urich. "Are Betas Best?," **JOF**, 1978, v33(5), 1375-1384.

Elton, Edwin J., Martin J. Gruber and Manfred W. Padberg. "Optimal Portfolios From Simple Ranking Devices," **JPM**, 1978, v4(3), 15-19.

Elton, Edwin J., Martin J. Gruber and Mustafa N. Gultekin. "Professional Expectations: Accuracy And Diagnosis Of Errors," **JFQA**, 1984, v19(4), 351-363.

Elton, Edwin J., Martin J. Gruber and Manfred W. Padberg. "Simple Criteria For Optimal Portfolio Selection," **JOF**, 1976, v31(5), 1341-1357.

Elton, Edwin J., Martin J. Gruber and Joel C. Rentzler. "Professionally Managed, Publicly Traded Commodity Funds," **JOB**, 1987, v60(2), 175-200.

Elton, Edwin J., Martin J. Gruber and Joel Rentzler. "The Performance Of Publicly Offered Commodity Funds," **JOF**, 1990, v46(4), 23-30.

Elton, Edwin J., Martin J. Gruber and Joel Rentzler. "New Public Offerings, Information, And Investor Rationality: The Case Of Publicly Offered Commodity Funds," **JOB**, 1989, v62(1), 1-16.

Elton, Edwin J., Martin J. Gruber and Roni Michaely. "The Structure Of Spot Rates And Immunization," **JOF**, 1990, v45(2), 629-642.

Elton, Edwin J., Martin J. Gruber and John B. Lightstone. "The Impact Of Bankruptcy On The Firm's Capital Structure, The Reasonableness Of Mergers, And The Risk Independence Of Projects," **RIF**, 1981, v3, 143-156.

Elton, Edwin J., Martin J. Gruber and Suk Mo Koo. "Effect Of Quarterly Earnings Announcements On Analysts' Forecasts," **RIF**, 1986, v6, 247-260.

Elton, Edwin, Martin Gruber and Joel Rentzler. "The Arbitrage Pricing Model And Returns On Assets Under Uncertain Inflation," **JOF**, 1983, v38(2), 525-537.

Elton, Edwin, Martin Gruber and Joel Rentzler. "A Simple Exam-ination Of The Empirical Relationship Between Dividend Yields And Deviations From The CAPM," **JBF**, 1983, v7(1), 135-146.

Elton, Edwin, Martin J. Gruber and Manfred W. Padberg. "Simple Criteria For Optimal Portfolio Selection: Tracing Out The Efficient Frontier," **JOF**, 1978, v33(1), 296-302.

Ely, David P. and Linda Hittle. "The Impact Of Math Background On Performance In Managerial Economics And Basic Finance Courses," **JFED**, 1990, v19, 59-61.

Ely, Owen. "Analyzing Electric Utility Stocks," **FAJ**, 1955, v11(1), 25-28.

Ely, Owen. "Case History Of Electric Utilities," **FAJ**, 1969, v25(1), 63-67.

Ely, Roland T. "Partners In Progress: The Latin American Economy," **FAJ**, 1962, v18(4), 9-60.

Elyasiani, Elyas and Seyed M. Mehdian. "A Nonparametric Approach To Measurement Of Efficiency And Technological Change: The Case Of Large U.S. Commercial Banks," **JFSR**, 1990, v4(2),157-168.

Elyasiani, Elyas. (Meinster, David R. and Elyas Elyasiani. "The Performance Of Foreign Owned, Minority Owned, And Holding COmpany Owned Banks In The U.S.," **JBF**, 1988, v12(2), 293-314.)

Emanuel, D. M. "Asset Revaluations And Share Price Revisions," **JBFA**, 1989, v16(2), 213-228.

Emanuel, David C. and James D. MacBeth. "Further Results On The Constant Elasticity Of Variance Call Option Pricing Model," **JFQA**, 1982, v17(4), 533-554.

Emanuel, David C. "Warrant Valuation And Exercise Strategy," **JFEC**, 1983, v12(2), 211-235.

Emanuel, David M. "The Market Model In New Zealand," **JBFA**, 1980, v7(4), 591-601.

Emanuel, David. "A Theoretical Model For Valuing Preferred Stock," **JOF**, 1983, v38(4), 1133-1155.

Emanuel, David. (Boyle, Phelim P. and David Emanuel. "Discretely Adjusted Option Hedges," **JFEC**, 1980, v8(3), 259-282.)

Emerson, Frank D. "Institutional And Individual Participation Under The SEC's Shareholder Proposal Rule," **FAJ**, 1955, v11(5), 59-66.

Emerson, Frank D. "The Shareholder Proposal Rule," **FAJ**, 1953, v9(5), 87-94.

Emery, Douglas R. and Wilbur G. Lewellen. "Refunding Noncallable Debt," **JFQA**, 1984, v19(1),73-82.

Emery, Douglas R. "Overlapping Interest Bond Refunding: A Reconsideration," **FM**, 1978, v7(2), 19-20.

Emery, Douglas R. (Gaumnitz, Jack E. and Douglas R. Emery. "Asset Growth, Abandonment Value And The Replacement Decision Of Like-For-Like Capital Assets," **JFQA**, 1980, v15(2), 407-419.)

Emery, Douglas R. (Lewellen, Wilbur G. and Douglas R. Emery. "Corporate Debt Management And The Value Of The Firm," **JFQA**, 1986, v21(4), 415-426.)

Emery, Douglas R. (Lewellen, Wilbur G. and Douglas R. Emery. "On The Matter Of Parity Among Financial Obligations," **JOF**, 1981, v36(1), 97-111.)

Emery, Douglas R. and Adam K. Gehr, Jr. "Tax Options, Capital Structure, And Miller Equilibrium: A Numerical Illustration," **FM**, 1988, v17(2), 30-40.

Emery, Douglas R., Philip C. Parr, Per B. Mokkelbost, David Gandhi and Anthony Saunders. "An Investigation Of Real Investment Decision Making With The Options Pricing Model," **JBFA**, 1978, v5(4), 363-369.

Emery, Douglas R., J. Ronald Hoffmeister and Ronald W. Spahr. "The Case For Indexing A Bond's Call Price," **FM**, 1987, v16(3), 57-64.

Emery, Douglas R., Wilbur G. Lewellen and David C. Mauer. "Tax-Timing Options, Leverage, And The Choice Of Corporate Form," **JFR**, 1988, v11(2), 99-110.

Emery, Gary W. "A Pure Financial Explanation For Trade Credit," **JFQA**, 1984, v19(3), 271-285.

Emery, Gary W. "An Optimal Financial Response To Variable Demand," **JFQA**, 1987, v22(2), 209-226.

Emery, Gary W. "Optimal Liquidity Policy: A Stochastic Process Approach," **JFR**, 1982, v5(3),273-283.

Emery, Gary W. "Positive Theories Of Trade Credit," **AWCM**, 1990, v1(1), 115-130.

Emery, Gary W. "Some Empirical Evidence On The Properties Of Daily Cash Flow," **FM**, 1981, v10(1),21-28.

Emery, Gary W. "Some Guidelines For Evaluating Capital Investment Alternatives With Unequal Lives," **FM**, 1982, v11(1), 14-19.

Emery, Gary W. (Cogger, Kenneth O. and Gary W. Emery. "A Determination Of The Risk Of Ruin: Comment," **JFQA**, 1981, v16(5), 759-764.)

Emery, John T. "Efficient Capital Markets And The Information Content Of Accounting Numbers," **JFQA**, 1974, v9(2), 139-149.

Emery, John T. "Risk, Return, And The Morphology Of Commercial Banking," **JFQA**, 1971, v6(2), 763-776.

Emery, John T. "The Information Content Of Daily Market Indicators," **JFQA**, 1973, v8(2), 183-190.

Emery, John T. (Abrahamson, Allen A. and John T. Emery. "An Alternative Approach To Asset Selection Under Uncertainty," **AREUEA**, 1974, v2(1), 75-88.)

Emkin, Allen. (Wagner, Wayne H., Allen Emkin and Richard L. Dixon. "South African Divestment: The Investment Issues," **FAJ**, 1984, v40(6), 14-19,22.)

Emmanuel, C. R. and D. T. Otley. "The Usefulness Of Residual Income," **JBFA**, 1976, v3(4), 43-51.

Emmanuel, C. R. and R. H. Pick. "The Predictive Ability Of UK Segment Reports," **JBFA**, 1980, v7(2), 201-218.

Emmanuel, C. R. and S. J. Gray. "Corporate Diversification And Segmental Disclosure Requirements In The USA," **JBFA**, 1977, v4(4), 407-418.

Emmanuel, C. R. (Garrod, N. W. and C. R. Emmanuel. "The Impact Of Company Profile On The Predictive Ability Of Disaggregated Data," **JBFA**, 1988, v15(2), 135-154.)

Emmer, Robert E. "Compensating Balances And The Cost Of Loanable Funds," **JOB**, 1957, v30(4), 268-275.

Emmer, Robert E. "The Credit Expansion Equations Of An Individual Bank," **JOF**, 1956, v11(3),322-346.

Enders, Walter. "Portfolio Balance And Exchange Rate Stability," **JMCB**, 1977, v9(3), 491-499.

Enders, Walter. "Unit Roots And The Real Exchange Rate Before World War I: The Case Of Britain And The USA," **JIMF**, 1989, v8(1), 59-74.

Engel, Charles M. and Robert P. Flood. "Exchange Rate Dynamics, Sticky Prices, And The Current Account," **JMCB**, 1985, v17(3), 312-327.

Engel, Charles M. "On The Correlation Of Exchange Rates And Interest Rates," **JIMF**, 1986, v5(1), 125-128.

Engel, Charles. "The Trade Balance And Real Exchange Rate Under Currency Substitution," **JIMF**, 1989, v8(1), 47-58.

Engel, Philip L. "Life Insurance Company Accounting," **FAJ**, 1973, v29(4), 22-26,70-72.

Engelbourg, Saul. "Some Consequences Of The Leasing Of Industrial Machinery," **JOB**, 1966, v39(1), Part I, 52-66.

Englander, Frederick J. (Director, Steven M. and Frederick J. Englander. "Requiring Unemployment Insurance Recipients To Register With The Public Employment Service," **JRI**, 1988, v55(2), 245-258.)

Engle, Robert F. "Estimates Of The Variance Of U.S. Inflation Based Upon The ARCH Model: Reply," **JMCB**, 1988, v20(3), Part 1, 422-423.

Engle, Robert F. "Estimates Of The Variance Of U.S. Inflation Based Upon The ARCH Model," **JMCB**, 1983, v15(3), 286-301.

Engler, George N. "The Use Of Flow Diagrams In Teaching The Basic Finance Course," **JFED**, 1976, v5, 8-14.

Engler, Rolf. "Automation Of Payments In The Federal Republic Of Germany: Status And Future Prospects," **JBR**, 1980-81, v11(4), 233-241.

Enke, Stephen. "On The Economic Management Of Large Organizations: A Laboratory Study," **JOB**, 1958, v31(4), 280-292.

Ennes, Howard. "A Note On The Urban Crisis, Health Care, And Health Insurance," **JRI**, 1970, v37(1), 148-150.

Ennis, Richard M. and Roberta L. Parkhill. "South African Divestment: Social Responsibility Or Fiduciary Folly?," **FAJ**, 1986, v42(4), 30-38.

Ennis, Richard M. "Is A Statewide Pension Fund A Person Or A Cookie Jar? The Answer Has Implications For Investment Policy," **FAJ**, 1988, v44(6), 21-27.

Ennis, Richard M. (Burik, Paul and Richard M. Ennis. "Foreign Bonds In Diversified Portfolios: A Limited Advantage," **FAJ**, 1990, v46(2), 31-40.)

Entine, Alan D. "Government Securities Holdings Of Selected Financial Intermediaries, 1954-1962," **JOF**, 1964, v19(4), 644-652.

Enzler, Jared J. and H. O. Stekler. "An Analysis Of The 1968-69 Economic Forecasts," **JOB**, 1971, v44(3), 271-281.

Epley, D. R. "A Price Index For Life Insurance: Comment," **JRI**, 1973, v40(4), 629.

Epley, D. R. "The Issue Of Fractional Assessment," **AREUEA**, 1974, v2(1), 57-74.

Epley, Donald R. "The Concept And Market Extraction Of Effective Age For Residential Properties," **JRER**, 1990, v5(1), 41-52.

Epley, Donald R. (Burns, William L. and Donald R. Epley. "The Performance Of Portfolios Of REITs + Stocks," **JPM**, 1982, v8(3), 37-42.)

Epley, Donald R. (Cronan, Timothy P., Donald R. Epley and Larry G. Perry. "The Use Of Rank Transformation And Multiple Regression Analysis In Estimating Residential Property Values With A Small Sample," **JRER**, 1986, v1(1), 19-31.)

Epley, Donald R. (Perry, Larry G., Timothy P. Cronan and Donald R. Epley. "A Procedure For Unconvering Acceptable And Nonacceptable Mortgage Applications Through Discriminant Analysis Using Ranked Data," **JRER**, 1987, v2(1), 61-72.)

Epley, Donald R. and Alireza Tahai. "Consumer-Revealed Preferences For A Margin And Other Associated Adjustable-Rate Mortgage Features," **JRER**, 1989, v4(1), 37-51.

Epley, Donald R. and William Burns. "The Correct Use Of Confidence Intervals And Regression Analysis In Determining The Value Of Residential Homes," **AREUEA**, 1978, v6(1), 70-85.

Epley, Donald R., Timothy P. Cronan and Larry Perry. "A Research Note On Discrimination In Mortgage Lending," **AREUEA**, 1985, v13(4), 446-451.

Epley, Donald and William Burns. "The Correct Use Of Confidence Intervals And Regression Analysis In Determining The Value Of Residential Houses: A Reply," **AREUEA**, 1979, v7(1), 136-140.

Epley, Donald. "A Re-Examination Of Federal Mortgage Rate Insurance," **JRI**, 1977, v44(1), 151-154.

Eppen, Gary D. and Eugene F. Fama. "Solutions For Cash-Balance And Simple Dynamic-Portfolio Problems," **JOB**, 1968, v41(1), 94-112.

Eppen, Gary D. and Yehoshua Liebermann. "Why Do Retailers Deal? An Inventory Explanation," **JOB**, 1984, v57(4), 519-530.

Epperson, James F. (Kau, James B., Donald C. Keenan, Walter J. Muller, III and James F. Epperson. "The Valuation And Securitization Of Commercial And Multifamily Mortgages," **JBF**, 1987, v11(3), 525-546.)

Epperson, James F. (Kau, James B., Donald C. Keenan, Walter J. Muller, III and James F. Epperson. "Pricing Commercial Mortgages And Their Mortgage-Backed Securities," **JREFEC**, 1990, v3(4), 333-356.)

Epperson, James F., James B. Kau, Donald C. Keenan and Walter J. Muller, III. "Pricing Default Risk In Mortgages," **AREUEA**, 1985, v13(3), 261-272.

Epperson, James P. (Kau, James B., Donald C. Keenan, Walter J. Muller, III and James P. Epperson. "Rational Pricing Of Adjustable Rate Mortgages," **AREUEA**, 1985, v13(2), 117-128.)

Epps, T. W. and Michael J. Kukanza. "Predictions Of Returns To Commodities Speculation Based On Current Information: Some Evidence Of Informational Inefficiency In Futures Markets," **RFM**, 1985, v4(3), 366-382.

Epps, Thomas W. "Financial Risk And The St. Petersburg Paradox: Comment," **JOF**, 1978, v33(5), 1455-1456.

Epps, Thomas W. "Necessary And Sufficient Conditions For The Mean-Variance Portfolio Model With Constant Risk Aversion," **JFQA**, 1981, v16(2), 169-176.

Epps, Thomas W. "Security Price Changes And Transaction Volumes: Some Additional Evidence," **JFQA**, 1977, v12(1), 141-146.

Epstein, Ira and Brian Dittenhafer. "A Preliminary Investigation Into The Effects Of The Federal Override Of State Usury Ceilings On The Supply Of Mortgage Funds By FSLIC-Insured S&Ls In New York And New Jersey," **AREUEA**, 1980, v8(4), 370-386.

Epstein, Ira. "A Property Tax Base Model," **AREUEA**, 1979, v7(2), 147-162.

Epstein, Larry G. and Stuart M. Turnbull. "Capital Asset Prices And The Temporal Resolution Of Uncertainty," **JOF**, 1980, v35(3), 627-643.

Epstein, Larry G. (Chew, S. H. and Larry G. Epstein. "The Law Of Large Numbers And The Attractiveness Of Compound Gambles," **JRU**, 1988, v1(1), 125-132.)

Erber, Ernest. "Impact Of New Housing Construction On Racial Patterns," **AREUEA**, 1977, v5(3), 313-336.

Erion, Gene L. "A Defense Of Orthodoxy In The Analysis Of War Finance," **FAJ**, 1955, v11(2), 111-116.

Errunza, Vihang and Etienne Losq. "International Asset Pricing Under Mild Segmentation: Theory And Test," **JOF**, 1985, v40(1), 105-124.

Errunza, Vihang R. and Barr Rosenberg. "Investment In Developed And Less Developed Countries," **JFQA**, 1982, v17(5), 741-762.

Errunza, Vihang R. and Etienne Losq. "The Behavior Of Stock Prices On LDC Markets," **JBF**, 1985, v9(4), 561-575.

Errunza, Vihang R. and Lemma W. Senbet. "International Corporate Diversification, Market Valuation, And Size-Adjusted Evidence," **JOF**, 1984, v39(3), 727-743.

Errunza, Vihang R. and Lemma W. Senbet. "The Effects Of International Operations On The Market Value Of The Firm: Theory And Evidence," **JOF**, 1981, v36(2), 401-417.

Errunza, Vihang R. "Determinants Of Financial Structure In The Central American Common Market," **FM**, 1979, v8(3), 72-77.

Errunza, Vihang R. "Efficiency And The Programs To Develop Capital Markets: The Brazilian Experience," **JBF**, 1979, v3(4), 355-382.

Errunza, Vihang R. "Emerging Markets: A New Opportunity For Improving Global Portfolio Performance," **FAJ**, 1983, v39(5), 51-58.

Errunza, Vihang R. "Pricing Of National Index Funds," **RQFA**, 1991, v1(1), 91-100.

Errunza, Vihang R. and Arthur F. Moreau. "Debt-For-Equity Swaps Under A Rational Expectations Equilibrium," **JOF**, 1989, v44(3), 663-680.

Errunza, Vihang R. and Prasad Padmanabhan. "Further Evidence On The Benefits Of Portfolio Investments In Emerging Markets," **FAJ**, 1988, v44(4), 76-78.

Errunza, Vihang and Etienne Losq. "How Risky Are Emerging Markets," **JPM**, 1987, v14(1), 62-67.

Errunza, Vihang and Etienne Losq. "Capital Flow Controls, International Asset Pricing, And Investors' Welfare: A Multi-Country Framework," **JOF**, 1989, v44(4), 1025-1038.,

Erzan, Refik and Alexander J. Yeats. "Implications Of Current Factor Proportions Indices For The Competitive Position Of The U.S. Manufacturing And Service Industries In The Year 2000," **JOB**, 1991, v64(2), 229-254.

Escolas, Edmond L. "Review Of The Hospital Insurance Puzzle: Comment," **JRI**, 1975, v42(1), 165-166.

Escolas, Edmond L. (Spahr, Ronald W. and Edmond L. Escolas. "1979 Automobile Accident Reports: Do Driver Characteristics Support Rate Discrimination?," **JRI**, 1982, v49(1), 91-103.)

Escolas, Edmond L. (Spahr, Ronald W. and Edmond L. Escolas. "Mortgage Guaranty Insurance: A Unique Style Of Insurance," **JRI**, 1986, v53(2), 308-319.)

Eskew, Robert K. and William F. Wright. "An Empirical Analysis Of Differential Capital Market Reactions To Extraordinary Accounting Items," **JOF**, 1976, v31(2), 651-674.

Espahbodi, Hassan. (Copeland, Ronald M. and Hassan Espahbodi. "Accomodating Multicollinearity In Financial Forecasting And Business Research," **AFPAF**, 1989, v3(1), 311-322.) 3\ 3

Espahbodi, Pouran. "Identification Of Problem Banks And Binary Choice Models," **JBF**, 1991, v15(1), 53-71.

Estep, Preston W. "A New Method For Valuing Common Stocks," **FAJ**, 1985, v41(6), 26-27,30-33.

Estep, Tony and Mark Kritzman. "TIPP: Time Invariant Portfolio Protection," **JPM**, 1988, v14(4),38-42.

Estep, Tony, Nick Hanson and Cal Johnson. "Sources Of Value And Risk In Common Stocks," **JPM**, 1983, v9(4), 5-13.

Estep, Tony. "Manager Style And The Sources Of Equity Returns," **JPM**, 1987, v13(2), 4-10.

Estep, Tony. "Security Analysis And Stock Selection: Turning Financial Information Into Return Forecasts," **FAJ**, 1987, v43(4), 34-43.

Estes, R. W. (Brown, H. A., Jr. and R. W. Estes. "Comparability Vs. Flexibility: A Practical Solution," **FAJ**, 1966, v22(3), 65-68.)

Estrella, Arturo. (Arak, Marcelle, Arturo Estrella, Laurie Goodman and Andrew Silver. "Interest Rate Swaps: An Alternative Explanation," **FM**, 1988, v17(2), 12-18.)

Esty, Arthur. (Miles, Mike and Arthur Esty. "How Well Do Commingled Real Estate Funds Perform?," **JPM**, 1982, v8(2), 62-68.)

Etebari, Ahmad and James O. Horrigan. "A Note On The Use Of Objective Exams In Basic Finance Courses," **JFED**, 1982, v11, 61-66.

Etebari, Ahmad, James O. Horrigan and Jan L. Landwehr. "To Be Or Not To Be--Reaction Of Stock Returns To Sudden Deaths Of Corporate Chief Executive Officers," **JBFA**, 1987, v14(2), 255-278.

Etgar, Michael and Pinhas Zusman. "The Marketing Intermediary As An Information Seller: A New Approach," **JOB**, 1982, v55(4), 505-516.

Etgar, Michael. "Cost Effectiveness In Insurance Distribution," **JRI**, 1977, v44(2), 211-222.

Etgar, Michael. "Service Performance Of Insurance Distributors," **JRI**, 1976, v43(3), 487-500.

Etgar, Michael. "Unfair Price Discrimination In P-L Insurance And The Reliance On Loss Ratios," **JRI**, 1975, v42(4), 615-524.

Etherington, Edwin D. "Wall Street: No Place To Go But Up," **JPM**, 1976, v3(1), 5-10.

Ethier, Wilfred. "Financial Assets And Economic Growth In A 'Keynesian' Economy," **JMCB**, 1975, v7(2), 215-233.

Ettin, Edward C. (Alhadeff, D., P. Bernstein, C. Campbell, L. Chandler, E. Ettin, V. Farhi, J. Guttentag, H. Latane and K. Poole. "The Commission On Money And Credit's Research Studies," **JOF**, 1964, v19(3),497-533.)

Ettredge, Michael and Russell J. Fuller. "The Negative Earnings Effect," **JPM**, 1991, v17(3), 27-34.

Etzel, Michael J. and Wesley H. Jones. "A Method For Developing Promotional Themes Based On Attitudes And Usage Patterns Of Bank Credit Card Holders," **JBR**, 1977-78, v8(4), 224-232.

Eubank, Arthur A. (Camp, Robert C. and Arthur A. Eubank, Jr. "The Beta Quotient: A New Measure Of Portfolio Risk," **JPM**, 1981, v7(4), 53-57.)

Eubank, Arthur A., Jr. and J. Kenton Zumwalt. "An Analysis Of The Forecast Error Impact Of Alternative Beta Adjustment Techniques And Risk Classes," **JOF**, 1979, v34(3), 761-776.

Eubank, Arthur A., Jr. and J. Kenton Zumwalt. "How To Determine The Stability Of Beta Values," *JPM*, 1979, v5(2), 22-26.

Eubank, Arthur A., Jr. (West, David A. and Arthur A. Eubank, Jr. "An Automatic Cost Of Capital Adjustment Model For Regulating Public Utilities," *FM*, 1976, v5(1), 23-31.)

Eubank, Arthur E., Jr. "Risk/Return Contrasts: NYSE, Amex, And OTC," *JPM*, 1977, v3(4), 25-30.

Eun, Cheol S. and Bruce G. Resnick. "Estimating The Correlation Structure Of International Share Prices," *JOF*, 1984, v39(5), 1311-1324.

Eun, Cheol S. and S. Janakiramanan. "A Model Of International Asset Pricing With A Constraint On The Foreign Equity Ownership," *JOF*, 1986, v41(4),897-914.

Eun, Cheol S. "Global Purchasing Power View Of Exchange Risk," *JFQA*, 1981, v16(5), 639-650.

Eun, Cheol S. (Alexander, Gordon J., Cheol S. Eun and S. Janakiramanan. "Asset Pricing And Dual Listing On Foreign Capital Markets: A Note," *JOF*, 1987, v42(1), 151-158.)

Eun, Cheol S. (Alexander, Gordon J., Cheol S. Eun and S. Janakiramanan. "International Listings And Stock Returns: Some Empirical Evidence," *JFQA*, 1988, v23(2), 135-152.)

Eun, Cheol S. (Cho, D. Chinhyung, Cheol S. Eun and Lemma W. Senbet. "International Arbitrage Pricing Theory: An Empirical Investigation," *JOF*, 1986, v41(2), 313-330.)

Eun, Cheol S. and Bruce G. Resnick. "Exchange Rate Uncertainty, Forward Contracts, And International Portfolio Selection," *JOF*, 1988, v43(1), 197-215.

Eun, Cheol S. and Bruce G. Resnick. "Estimating The Dependence Structure Of Share Prices: A Comparative Study Of The United States And Japan," *FR*, 1988, v23(4), 387-402.

Eun, Cheol S. and Bruce G. Resnick. "International Diversification Under Estimation Risk: Actual Versus Potential Gains," *RDIBF*, 1987, v1, 135-148.

Eun, Cheol S. and S. Janakiramanan. "Bilateral Cross-Listing And The Equilibrium Security Prices," *AFPAF*, 1990, v5(1), 59-74.

Eun, Cheol S. and Sangdal Shim. "International Transmission Of Stock Market Movements," *JFQA*, 1989, v24(2), 241-256.

Eun, Cheol S., Richard Kolodny and Bruce G. Resnick. "U.S.-Based International Mutual Funds: A Performance Evaluation," *JPM*, 1991, v17(3), 88-94.

Euske, Kenneth J., Donald W. Jackson, Jr. and William E. Reif. "Performance And Satisfaction Of Bank Managers," *JBR*, 1980-81, v11(1), 36-42.

Evan, William M. and Guy Black. "Innovation In Business Organizations: Some Factors Associated With Success Or Failure Of Staff Proposals," *JOB*, 1967, v40(4), 519-530.

Evanoff, D. D. "An Empirical Examination Of Bank Reserve Management Behavior," *JPM*, 1990, v14(1), 131-144.

Evanoff, Douglas D. "Branch Banking And Service Accessibility," *JMCB*, 1988, v20(2), 191-202.

Evanoff, Douglas D. and Diana L. Fortier. "Reevaluation Of The Structure-Conduct-Performance Paradigm In Banking," *JFSR*, 1988, v1(3), 277-294.

Evans, Bruce D. and Gary Richardson. "Stop Loss Reinsurance - A New Look," *JRI*, 1971, v38(2), 251-262.

Evans, Campbell K. "Basic Financial Differences Of Substandard Automobile Insurers," *JRI*, 1968, v35(4), 489-513.

Evans, Campbell K. "Financial Proportionality In Insurance Agencies," *JRI*, 1967, v34(2), 187-204.

Evans, Campbell K. "Model Of Certain Relationships Within The Structure Of Insurance Agencies," *JRI*, 1969, v36(4), 535-544.

Evans, Dorla A. (Perry, Larry G., Pu Liu and Dorla A. Evans. "Modified bond Ratings: Further Evidence On The Effect Of Split Ratings On Corporate Bond Yields," *JBFA*, 1988, v15(2), 231-242.)

Evans, Franklin B. "Automobiles And Self-Imagery: Comment," *JOB*, 1968, v41(4), 484-485.

Evans, Franklin B. "Ford Versus Chevrolet: Park Forest Revisited," *JOB*, 1968, v41(4), 445-459.

Evans, Franklin B. "Motivation Research And Advertising Readership," *JOB*, 1957, v30(2), 141-146.

Evans, Franklin B. "Psychological And Objective Factors In The Prediction Of Brand Choice: Ford Versus Chevrolet," *JOB*, 1959, v32(4), 340-369.

Evans, Franklin B. "Reply: 'You Still Can't Tell A Ford Owner From A Chevrolet Owner'," *JOB*, 1961, v34(1), 67-73.

Evans, Franklin B. and Harry V. Roberts. "Fords, Chevrolets, And The Problem Of Discrimination," *JOB*, 1963, v36(2), 242-249.

Evans, George Herbert, Jr. "The Theoretical Value Of A Stock Right," *JOF*, 1955, v10(1), 55-61.

Evans, George W. "The Conduct Of Monetary Policy And The Natural Rate Of Unemployment," *JMCB*, 1989, v21(4), 498-507.

Evans, John J. "Commercial Banks And The Consumer Services Revolution," *JBR*, 1985-86, v16(4), 182-185.

Evans, John L. and Stephen H. Archer. "Diversification And The Reduction Of Dispersion: An Empirical Analysis," *JOF*, 1968, v23(5), 761-767.

Evans, John L. "An Analysis Of Portfolio Maintenance Strategies," *JOF*, 1970, v25(3), 561-571.

Evans, John L. "An Examination Of The Principle Of Diversification," *JBFA*, 1975, v2(2), 243-255.

Evans, John L. "The Random Walk Hypothesis, Portfolio Analysis And The Buy-And-Hold Criterion," *JFQA*, 1968, v3(3), 327-342.

Evans, Jr. Robert. "'Render Unto Caesar': Federal District Courts And Unfair Labor-Practice Jurisdiction," *JOB*, 1966, v39(3), 400-412.

Evans, Kaye D., John J. Siegfried and George H. Sweeney. "The Economic Cost Of Suboptimal Manufacturing Capacity," *JOB*, 1983, v56(1), 55-76.

Evans, R. (Appelbaum, E., J. Burns, R. Evans, J. Gould, T. Hamachek, R. Kidder, M. Jensen, J. Johnstone, M. Murray, R. Sim, J. Stern, B. Stewart and C. Zaner. "Panel: CEO Roundtable On Corporate Structure And Management Incentives," *JACF*, 1990, v3(3), 6-35.)

Evans, Richard D. "A Transfer Function Analysis Of Real Estate Capitalization Rates," *JRER*, 1990, v5(3), 371-379.

Evans, Richard D. "Residential Construction Volatility: A Seasonal And Cyclical Inventory Adjustment Analysis," *AREUEA*, 1981, v9(1), 74-82.

Evans, Richard H. "Bank Selection: It All Depends On The Situation," *JBR*, 1978-79, v9(4), 242-245.

Evans, Richard H. "The Validity Of Service And Situational Perceptions: A Caution," *JBR*, 1979-80, v10(2), 119-123.

Evans, Richard. (Rayburn, William, Michael Devaney and Richard Evans. "A Test Of Weak-Form Efficiency In Residential Real Estate Returns," *AREUEA*, 1987, v15(3), 220-233.) 3! ?8

Evans, William N. (Grabowski, Henry, W. Kip Viscusi and William N. Evans. "Price And Availability Tradeoffs Of Automobile Insurance Regulation," *JRI*, 1989, v56(2), 275-299.)

Evans, William N. and John D. Graham. "Risk Reduction Or Risk Compensation? The Case Of Mandatory Safety-Belt Use Laws," *JRU*, 1991, v4(1), 61-74.

Evanson, R. V. (Thomas, Joseph, III and R. V. Evanson. "An Empirical Investigation Of Association Between Financial Ratio Use And Small Business Success," *JBFA*, 1987, v14(4), 555-572.)

Even, John T. "Notes From A Graduate Course In Insurance Administration," *JRI*, 1960, v27(4), 33-46.

Everett, E. J., Jr. (Umble, M. Michael, Paul F. York and E. J. Everett, Jr. "Agent Retention Rates In The Independent Agency System," *JRI*, 1977, v44(3), 481-486.)

Everett, J. E. and J. P. Dickinson. "Some Aspects Of Inflation, Tax, And The Investing Borrower," *JBFA*, 1979, v6(4), 527-538.

Everett, James E. and Bernhard Schwab. "On The Proper Adjustment For Risk Through Discount Rates In A Mean-Variance Framework," *FM*, 1979, v8(2),61-65.

Everett, John O. and Curtis L. Norton. "Evaluating The Effectiveness Of Code Section 1091 As A Deterrent To Wash Sales," *FR*, 1981, v16(3), 44-56.

Everitt, Walter A. "Investing In Foreign Securities," *FAJ*, 1956, v12(1), 75-78.

Evnine, Jeremy and Andrew Rudd. "Option Portfolio Risk Analysis," *JPM*, 1984, v10(2), 23-27.

Evnine, Jeremy and Andrew Rudd. "Index Options: The Early Evidence," *JOF*, 1985, v40(3), 743-758.

Evnine, Jeremy and Roy Henriksson. "Asset Allocation And Options," *JPM*, 1987, v14(1), 56-61.

Evnine, Jeremy. (Boyle, Phelim P., Jeremy Evnine and Stephen Gibbs. "Numerical Evaluation Of Multivariate Contingent Claims," *RFS*, 1989, v2(2), 241-250.)

Ewing, William F. C. "The Floor Coverings Industry," *FAJ*, 1952, v8(3), 79-84.

Ewis, Nabil A. and Douglas Fisher. "The Translog Utility Function And The Demand For Money In The United States," *JMCB*, 1984, v16(1), 34-52.

Eyssell, T. and N. Arshadi. "The Wealth Effects Of The Risk-Based Capital Requirement In Banking: The Evidence From The Capital Market," *JBF*, 1990, v14(1), 179-198.

Eyssell, Thomas H., Donald R. Fraser and Nanda K. Rangan. "Debt-Equity Swaps, Regulation K, And Bank Stock Returns," *JBF*, 1989, v13(6), 853-868.

Eytan, T. Hanan and Giora Harpaz. "The Pricing Of Futures And Options Contracts On The Value Line Index," *JOF*, 1986, v41(4), 843-856.

Eytan, T. Hanan, Giora Harpaz and Steven Krull. "The Pricing Of Dollar Index Futures Contracts," *JFM*, 1988, v8(2), 127-140.

Eytan, T. Hanan. "Corporate Taxes And Hedging With Futures," *JFM*, 1990, v10(5), 535-540.

Eytan, T. Hanan. (Cakici, Nusret, T. Hanan Eytan and Giora Harpaz. "American Vs. European Options On The Value Line Index," *JFM*, 1988, v8(3), 373-388.)

Ezejelue, A. C. "Financial Accounting And Optimality Criteria," *JBFA*, 1977, v4(2), 169-176.

Ezra, D. Don and Keith P. Ambachtsheer. "Pension Funds: Rich Or Poor?," *FAJ*, 1985, v41(2), 43-56.

Ezra, D. Don. "Economic Values: A Pension Pentateuch," *FAJ*, 1988, v44(2), 58-67.

Ezra, D. Don. "How Actuaries Determine The Unfunded Pension Liability," *FAJ*, 1980, v36(4), 43-50.

Ezra, D. Don. "Immunization: A New Look For Actuarial Liabilities," *JPM*, 1976, v2(2), 50-53.

Ezra, D. Don. "Mortgage In Canadian Pension Funds," *FAJ*, 1980, v36(4), 48-54.

Ezzamel, Mahmoud A. and Kenneth Hilton. "Can Divisional Discretion Be Measured?," *JBFA*, 1980, v7(2), 311-329.

Ezzamel, Mahmoud A. "Divisional Cost Of Capital And The Measurement Of Divisional Performance," *JBFA*, 1979, v6(3), 307-319.

Ezzamel, Mahmoud A. "Estimating The Cost Of Capital For A Division Of A Firm, And The Allocation Problem In Accounting: A Comment," *JBFA*, 1980, v7(1), 65-69.

Ezzamel, Mahmoud and Cocillo Mar-Molinero. "The Distributional Properties Of Financial Ratios In UK Manufacturing Companies," *JBFA*, 1990, v17(1), 1-30.

Ezzamel, Mahmoud, Cecilio Mar-Molinero and Alistair Beecher. "On The Distributional Properties Of Financial Ratios," *JBFA*, 1987, v14(4), 463-482.

Ezzamel, Mahmoud, Judith Brodie and Cecilio Mar-Molinero. "Financial Patterns Of UK Manufacturing Companies," *JBFA*, 1987, v14(4), 519-536.

Ezzell, John R. and Carlos Rubiales. "An Empirical Analysis Of The Determinants Of Stock Splits," *FR*, 1975, v10(1), 21-30.

Ezzell, John R. and James A. Miles. "Capital Project Analysis And The Debt Transaction Plan," *JFR*, 1983, v6(1), 25-31.

Ezzell, John R. and R. Burr Porter. "Correct Specification Of The Cost Of Capital And Net Present Value," *FM*, 1979, v8(2), 15-17.

Ezzell, John R. and R. Burr Porter. "Flotation Costs And The Weighted Average Cost Of Capital," *JFQA*, 1976, v11(3), 403-413.

Ezzell, John R. and William A. Kelly, Jr. "An APV Analysis Of Capital Budgeting Under Inflation," *FM*, 1984, v13(3), 49-54.

Ezzell, John R. (Kumar, P. C., George C. Philippatos and John R. Ezzell. "Goal Programming And The Selection Of Portfolios By Dual-Purpose Funds," *JOF*, 1978, v33(1), 303-310.)

Ezzell, John R. (Miles, James A. and John R. Ezzell. "Reformulating Tax Shield Valuation: A Note," *JOF*, 1985, v40(5), 1484-1492.)

Ezzell, John R. (Miles, James A. and John R. Ezzell. "The Weighted

Average Cost Of Capital, Perfect Capital Markets, And Project Life: A Clarification," JFQA, 1980, v15(3), 719-730.)

FFF

FAF Inside Information Committee. "New Guidelines On Inside Information," FAJ, 1974, v30(1), 20-25.

FAJ Editor. "A Conversation With Benjamin Graham," FAJ, 1976, v32(5), 20-23.

FAJ Editors. "Integrating Our Securities Exchanges," FAJ, 1972, v28(3), 28-30,32,34,90-91.

Fabozzi, Frank J. and Jack C. Francis. "Mutual Fund Systematic Risk For Bull And Bear Markets: An Empirical Examination," JOF, 1979, v34(5), 1243-1250.

Fabozzi, Frank J. and Jack Clark Francis. "Stability Tests For Alphas And Betas Over Bull And Bear Market Conditions," JOF, 1977, v32(4), 1093-1099.

Fabozzi, Frank J. and Jack Clark Francis. "Beta As A Random Coefficient," JFQA, 1978, v13(1), 101-116.

Fabozzi, Frank J. and Richard R. West. "Negotiated Versus Competitive Underwritings of Public Utility Bonds: Just One More Time," JFQA, 1981, v16(3), 323-339.

Fabozzi, Frank J. and Robert Fonfeder. "Have You Seen Any Good Quarterly Statements Lately?," JPM, 1983, v9(2), 71-74.

Fabozzi, Frank J. and Sal Trovato. "The Use Of Quantitative Techniques In Commercial Banks," JBR, 1976-77, v7(2), 173-178.

Fabozzi, Frank J. and Thom B. Thurston. "State Taxes And Reserve Requirements As Major Determinants Of Yield Spreads Among Money Market Instruments," JFQA, 1986, v21(4), 427-436.

Fabozzi, Frank J. and Uzi Yaari. "Valuation Of Safe Harbor Tax Benefit Transfer Leases," JOF, 1983, v38(2), 595-606.

Fabozzi, Frank J. "Does Listing On The AMEX Increase The Value Of Equity?," FM, 1981, v10(1), 43-50.

Fabozzi, Frank J. "Quality Of Earnings: A Test Of Market Efficiency," JPM, 1978, v5(1), 53-56.

Fabozzi, Frank J. (Casabona, Patrick A., Frank J. Fabozzi and Jack C. Francis. "How To Apply Duration To Equity Analysis," JPM, 1984, v10(2), 52-58.)

Fabozzi, Frank J. (Choi, Jongmoo Jay, Frank J. Fabozzi and Uzi Yaari. "Optimum Corporate Leverage With Risky Debt: A Demand Approach," JFR, 1989, v12(2), 129-142.)

Fabozzi, Frank J. (Collins, Bruce M. and Frank J. Fabozzi. "Considerations In Selecting A Small-Capitalization Benchmark," FAJ, 1990, v46(1), 40-46)

Fabozzi, Frank J. (Dattatreya, Ravi E. and Frank J. Fabozzi. "A Simplified Model For Valuing Debt Options," JPM, 1989, v15(3), 64-73.)

Fabozzi, Frank J. (Feldstein, Sylvan G. and Frank J. Fabozzi. "Analyzing The Credit Worthiness Of Short-Term Tax-Exempt Obligations," FAJ, 1985, v41(6), 71-76.)

Fabozzi, Frank J. (Fong, H. Gifford and Frank J. Fabozzi. "How To Enhance Bond Returns With Naive Strategies," JPM, 1985, v11(4), 57-60.)

Fabozzi, Frank J. (Francis, Jack Clark and Frank J. Fabozzi. "The Effects Of Changing Macroeconomic Conditions On The Parameters Of The Single Index Market Model," JFQA, 1979, v14(2), 351-360.)

Fabozzi, Frank J. (Francis, Jack Clark, Harold M. Hastings and Frank J. Fabozzi. "Bankruptcy As A Mathematical Catastrophe," RIF, 1983, v4, 63-90.)

Fabozzi, Frank J. (Garlicki, T. Dessa, Frank J. Fabozzi and Robert Fonfeder. "The Impact Of Earnings Under FASB 52 On Equity Returns," FM, 1987, v16(3),36-44.)

Fabozzi, Frank J. (Yaari, Uzi and Frank J. Fabozzi. "Why IRA And Keogh Plans Should Avoid Growth Stocks," JFR, 1985, v8(3), 203-216.)

Fabozzi, Frank J. and Christopher K. Ma. "The Over-The-Counter Market And New York Stock Exchange Trading Halts," FR, 1988, v23(4), 427-438.

Fabozzi, Frank J., Jack C. Francis and Cheng F. Lee. "Generalized Functional Form For Mutual Fund Returns," JFQA, 1980, v15(5), 1107-1120.

Fabozzi, Frank J., Robert Fonfeder and Patrick Casabona. "An Empirical Examination Of The Impact Of Limited Review On Equity Prices," JBFA, 1983, v10(1), 127-138.

Fabozzi, Frank J., Eileen Moran and Christopher K. Ma. "Market Uncertainty And The Least-Cost Offering Method Of Public Utility Debt: A Note," JOF, 1988, v43(4), 1025-1034.

Fabozzi, Frank J., Michael G. Ferri, T. Dessa Fabozzi and Julia Tucker. "A Note On Unsuccessful Tender Offers And Stockholder Returns," JOF, 1988, v43(5), 1275-1283.

Fabozzi, T. Dessa, Tom Tong and Yu Zhu. "Symmetric Cash Matching," FAJ, 1990, v46(5), 46-52.

Fabozzi, T. Dessa. (Fabozzi, Frank J., Michael G. Ferri, T. Dessa Fabozzi and Julia Tucker. "A Note On Unsuccessful Tender Offers And Stockholder Returns," JOF, 1988, v43(5), 1275-1283.)

Fabricant, Solomon. "Factors Affecting Foreign Investment," FAJ, 1952, v8(5), 25-28.

Fabry, Jaak and Willy Van Grembergen. "Further Evidence On The Stationarity Of Betas And Errors In Their Estimates," JBF, 1978, v2(3), 189-204.

Fachler, Nimrod. (Brinson, Gary P. and Nimrod Fachler. "Measuring Non-U.S. Equity Portfolio Performance," JPM, 1985, v11(3), 73-76.)

Fackler, James and Bryan Stanhouse. "Rationality Of The Michigan Price Expectations Data," JMCB, 1977, v9(4), 662-666.

Fackler, James S. "An Empirical Analysis Of The Markets For Goods, Money, And Credit," JMCB, 1985, v17(1), 28-42.

Fackler, James S. "Federal Credit, Private Credit, And Economic Activity," JMCB, 1990, v22(4), 444-464.

Fackler, Walter D. "Business Spending And Government Fiscal Policies," JOB, 1964, v37(1), 22-24.

Fackler, Walter D. "Business Spending And Government Fiscal Policy," JOB, 1963, v36(1), 2-5.

Fackler, Walter D. "Business Spending And Government Fiscal Policy," JOB, 1966, v39(1), Part I, 1-4.

Fackler, Walter D. "Private Investment And Fiscal Policy," JOB, 1965, v38(1), 1-4.

Fadel, Hisham. "The Predictive Power Of Financial Ratios In The British Construction Industry," JBFA, 1977, v4(3), 339-352.

Fadner, Kenneth. (Grubel, Hebert G. and Kenneth Fadner. "The Interdependence Of International Equity Markets," JOF, 1971, v26(1), 89-94.)

Faerber, LeRoy G. (Archer, Stephen H. and LeRoy G. Faerber. "Firm Size And The Cost Of Externally Secured Equity Capital," JOF, 1966, v21(1), 69-83.)

Fagg, Donald R., Carl Kaysen, and Roland N. McKean. "What The Factory Worker Knows About His Factory," JOB, 1958, v31(3), 213-234.

Fair, Ray and Burton Malkiel. "The Determination Of Yield Differentials Between Debt Instruments Of The Same Maturity," JMCB, 1971, v3(4), 733-749.

Fair, Ray C. "A Criticism Of One Class Of Macroeconomic Models With Rational Expectations," JMCB, 1978, v10(4), 411-417.

Fair, Ray C. "Disequilibrium In Housing Models," JOF, 1972, v27(2), 207-221.

Fairchild, Keith William. "Inflation And Discounted Cash Flows," JFED, 1988, v17, 15-18.

Fairhurst, Randy. (Mabert, Vincent A., Randy Fairhurst and Michael A. Kilpatrick. "Chemical Bank's Encoder Daily Shift Scheduling System," JBR, 1979-80, v10(3), 173-180.)

Fairley, William B. (Chang, Lena and William B. Fairley. "Pricing Automobile Insurance Under Multivariate Classification Of Risks: Additive Versus Multiplicative," JRI, 1979, v46(1), 75-98.)

Fairley, William B., Thomas J. Tomberlin and Herbert I. Weisberg. "Pricing Automobile Insurance Under A Cross-Classification Of Risks: Evidence From New Jersey," JRI, 1981, v48(3), 505-514.

Falk, Barry and Peter F. Orazem. "The Role Of Systematic Fed Errors In Explaining The Money Supply Announcements Puzzle," JMCB, 1989, v21(3), 401-406.

Falk, Haim and James A. Heintz. "The Predictability Of Relative Risk Over Time," JBFA, 1977, v4(1), 5-28.

Falk, Haim and Serge Matulich. "The Effect Of Personal Characteristics On Attitudes Toward Risk," JRI, 1976, v43(2), 215-241.

Falk, Haim and Stephen L. Buzby. "Borrowing Rates, Alternative Investment Sets, And The Life Insurance Purchase Decision," JRI, 1976, v43(2), 291-304.

Falk, Haim. "Accounting For Cash Value Policies," JRI, 1975, v42(3), 403-417.

Falk, Haim. (Aharony, Joseph, Haim Falk and Itzhak Swary. "Information Content Of Dividend Increases: The Case Of Regulated Utilities," JBFA, 1988, v15(3), 401-414.)

Falk, I. S. "Long-Term Disability Insurance," JRI, 1945, v12, 11-21.

Falkenberg, John F. "The Sources Of Bank Profitability," JBR, 1973-74, v4(2), 105-110.

Falkenstein, A. (Easman, W. S., Jr., A. Falkenstein, Roman L. Weil and D. J. Guy. "Sustainable Income And Stock Returns," FAJ, 1979, v35(5), 44-48.)

Falkenstein, Angela and Roman L. Weil. "Using Replacement Costs To Measure Income - Part II," FAJ, 1977, v33(2), 48-57.

Falkenstein, Angela and Roman L. Weil. "Using Replacement Costs To Measure Income - Part I," FAJ, 1977, v33(1), 46-57.

Fall, Carol L. (Ibbotson, Roger G. and Carol L. Fall. "The United States Market Wealth Portfolio," JPM, 1979, v6(1), 82-92.)

Fall, John M. (Austin, Douglas V. and John M. Fall. "Capital Asset Financing Of Retirement Centers," FM, 1976, v5(1), 39-45.)

Fallis, George. "Housing Tenure In A Model Of Consumer Choice: A Simple Diagrammatic Analysis," AREUEA, 1983, v11(1), 30-44.

Fallis, George. "Rent Control: The Citizen, The Market, And The State," JREFEC, 1988, v1(3), 309-320.

Falls, L. E. "How Can The Universities And University Teachers Best Serve In Their Fields?," JRI, 1936, v3, 61-67.

Fama, Eugene F. and G. William Schwert. "Asset Returns And Inflation," JFEC, 1977, v5(2), 115-146.

Fama, Eugene F. and G. William Schwert. "Human Capital And Capital Market Equilibrium," JFEC, 1977, v4(1), 95-125.

Fama, Eugene F. and J. D. MacBeth. "Tests Of The Multi-Period Two-Parameter Model," JFEC, 1974, v1(1), 43-66.

Fama, Eugene F. and James D. MacBeth. "Long-Term Growth In A Short-Term Market," JOF, 1974, v29(3), 857-885.

Fama, Eugene F. and Michael C. Jensen. "Organizational Forms And Investment Decisions," JFEC, 1985, v14(1), 101-118.

Fama, Eugene F. "A Note On The Market Model And The Two-Parameter Model," JOF, 1973, v28(5), 1181-1185.

Fama, Eugene F. "Components Of Investment Performance," JOF, 1972, v27(3), 551-567.

Fama, Eugene F. "Contract Costs And Financing Decisions," JOB, 1990, v63(1), Part 2, S71-S92. 3v~?8

Fama, Eugene F. "Efficient Capital Markets: A Review Of Theory And Empirical Work," JOF, 1970, v25(2), 383-417.

Fama, Eugene F. "Efficient Capital Markets: Reply," JOF, 1976, v31(1), 143-145.

Fama, Eugene F. "Financial Intermediation And Price Level Control," RIF, 1983, v4, (Supp), 279-301.

Fama, Eugene F. "Forward Rates As Predictors Of Future Spot Rates," JFEC, 1976, v3(4), 361-377.

Fama, Eugene F. "Inflation, Output, And Money," JOB, 1982, v55(2), 201-232.

Fama, Eugene F. "Mandelbrot And The Stable Paretian Hypothesis," JOB, 1963, v36(4), 420-429.

Fama, Eugene F. "Random Walks In Stock Market Prices," FAJ, 1965, v21(5), 55-59.

Fama, Eugene F. "Risk, Return And Equilibrium: Some Clarifying Comments," JOF, 1968, v23(1), 29-40.

Fama, Eugene F. "Risk-Adjusted Discount Rates And Capital Budgeting Under Uncertainty," JFEC, 1977, v5(1), 3-24.

Fama, Eugene F. "Stock Returns, Expected Returns, And Real Activity," JOF, 1990, v45(4), 1089-1108.

Fama, Eugene F. "Term Premiums And Default Premiums In Money Markets," JFEC, 1986, v17(1), 175-196.

Fama, Eugene F. "Term Premiums In Bond Returns," JFEC, 1984, v13(4), 529-546.

Fama, Eugene F. "The Behavior Of Stock Market Prices," JOB, 1965, v38(1), 34-105.

Fama, Eugene F. "The Information In The Term Structure," JFEC, 1984, v13(4), 509-528.

Fama, Eugene F. "Tomorrow On The New York Stock Exchange," JOB, 1965, v38(3), 285-299.

Fama, Eugene F. (Eppen, Gary D. and Eugene F. Fama. "Solutions For Cash-Balance And Simple Dynamic-Portfolio Problems," JOB, 1968, v41(1), 94-112.)

Fama, Eugene F. and Arthur B. Laffer. "Information And Capital Markets," JOB, 1971, v44(3),289-298.

Fama, Eugene F. and G. William Schwert. "Inflation, Interest, And Relative Prices," JOB, 1979, v52(2), 183-210.

Fama, Eugene F. and Kenneth R. French. "Commodity Futures Prices: Some Evidence On Forecast Power, Premiums, And The Theory Of Storage," JOB, 1987, v60(1), 55-74.

Fama, Eugene F. and Kenneth R. French. "Dividend Yields And Expected Stock Returns," JFEC, 1988, v22(1), 3-26.

Fama, Eugene F. and Kenneth R. French. "Business Cycles And The Behavior Of Metals Prices," JOF, 1988, v43(5), 1075-1093.

Fama, Eugene F. and Kenneth R. French. "Business Conditions And Expected Returns On Stocks And Bonds," JFEC, 1989,v25(1),23-50.

Fama, Eugene F. and Marshall E. Blume. "Filter Rules And Stock Market Trading," JOB, 1966, v39(1), Part II, 226-241.

Fan, Chuen-Mei and Liang-Shing Fan. "The Demand For International Reserve Of Asian Countries And The Irrational Case Of Taiwan," AFPAF, 1985, v1(Supp), 191-200.

Fan, Liang-Shing. (Fan, Chuen-Mei and Liang-Shing Fan. "The Demand For International Reserve Of Asian Countries And The Irrational Case Of Taiwan," AFPAF, 1985, v1(Supp), 191-200.)

Fanara, Philip, Jr. and Warren Greenberg. "The Impact Of Competition And Regulation On Blue Cross Enrollment Of Non-Group Individuals," JRI, 1985, v52(2), 185-198.

Fand, David I. "A Monetarist Model Of The Monetary Process," JOF, 1970, v25(2), 275-289.

Fand, David I. "CROS Theory Of Inflation," FAJ, 1969, v25(4), 26-32.

Fand, David I. "Interest Rate Behavior In '69-'70," FAJ, 1971, v27(1), 23-29,88-90.

Fand, David I. "Monetary Policy And Inflation," FAJ, 1970, v26(2), 17-22,29.

Fand, David I. "The Reagan Economic Program," FAJ, 1981, v37(4), 28-34.

Fand, David I. and Ira O. Scott, Jr. "The Federal Reserve System's 'Bills Only' Policy: A Suggested Interpretation," JOB, 1958, v31(1), 12-18.

Fand, David. "Keynesian Monetary Theories, Stabilization Policy, And The Recent Inflation," JMCB, 1969, v1(3), 556-587.

Fang, Hsing. (Chang, Jack S. K. and Hsing Fang. "An Intertemporal Measure Of Hedging Effectiveness," JFM, 1990, v10(3), 307-322.)

Fanning, James E. "A System For Forecasting The Market," FAJ, 1971, v27(5), 49-56.

Farhadian, Ziba. (Feltenstein, Andrew and Ziba Farhadian. "Fiscal Policy, Monetary Targets, And The Price Level In A Centrally Planned Economy: An Application To The Case Of China," JMCB, 1987, v19(2), 137-156.)

Farhi, Victor L. (Alhadeff, D.A., P.L. Bernstein, C.D. Campbell, L.V. Chandler, E.C. Ettin, V.R. Farhi, J.Guttentag, H.A. Latane and K.E. Poole. "The Commission On Money And Credit's Research Sudies," JOF, 1964, v19(3), 497-533.)

Faricy, William T. "Railroads Anticipate The Future," FAJ, 1956, v12(5), 45-50.

Faricy, William T. "What About The Next Ten Years?," FAJ, 1958, v14(1), 11-14.

Farkas, Karen L. and Robert E. Hoskin. "Testing A Valuation Model For American Puts," FM, 1979, v8(3), 51-56.

Farley, Dennis E. and Thomas D. Simpson. "Graduated Reserve Requirements And Monetary Control," JOF, 1979, v34(4), 999-1012.

Farley, Jarvis. "Recent Developments In Sickness And Accident Insurance," JRI, 1956, v23, 112-119.

Farley, John U. "'Brand Loyalty' And The Economics Of Information," JOB, 1964, v37(4), 370-381.

Farley, John U. (Weinstein, David and John U. Farley. "Market Segmentation And Parameter Inequalities In A Buyer Behavior Model," JOB, 1975, v48(4), 526-540.)

Farley, John U., Donald R. Lehmann and Michael J. Ryan. "Generalizing From 'Imperfect' Replication," JOB, 1981, v54(4), 597-610.

Farmer, Lee R. "Exploration Of A New Era Of Insurance: Dental Insurance," JRI, 1960, v27(4), 99-102.

Farmer, Richard N. "The Long Term Crisis In Life Insurance," JRI, 1966, v33(4), 621-630.

Farmer, Richard N. "The Long Term Crisis In Life Insurance: Reply," JRI, 1968, v35(2), 152-154.

Farmer, Richard N. (Mantis, George and Richard N. Farmer. "Demand For Life Insurance," JRI, 1968, v35(2), 247-256.)

Farmer, Richard N. (Mantis, George and Richard N. Farmer. "Demand For Life Insurance: Reply," JRI, 1970, v37(1), 156-159.)

Farmer, Roger E. A. and Ralph A. Winter. "The Role Of Options In The Resolution Of Agency Problems: A Comment," JOF, 1986, v41(5), 1157-1170.

Farr, F. W. E. and William B. Eagleson. "Quality Vs. 'Value' In Insurance Stock Selection," FAJ, 1957, v13(5), 17-20.

Farr, F. W. Elliott. "Effect Of Market Price On Economic Earnings," FAJ, 1958, v14(5), 67-68.

Farr, F. W. Elliott. "Future Level Of Industrial Stocks Prices," FAJ, 1949, v5(3), 26-27.

Farr, F. W. Elliott. "Pros And Cons Of Bank Stocks," FAJ, 1953, v9(1), 81-84.

Farr, Helen T. (Tinsley, Peter A., Helen T. Farr, Gerhard Fries, Bonnie Garrett and Peter von zur Muehlen. "Policy Robustness: Specification And Simulation Of A Monthly Money Market Model," JMCB, 1982, v14(4), Part 2, 829-856.)

Farragher, Edward J. (Berry, Thomas D. and Edward J. Farragher. "A Survey Of Introductory Financial Management Courses," JFED, 1987, v16, 65-72.)

Farrar, D. E. (Allerdice, F. B. and D. E. Farrar. "Factors That Affect Mutual Fund Growth," JFQA, 1967, v2(4), 365-382.)

Farrar, Donald E. and Lance Girton. "Institutional Investors And Concentration Of Financial Power: Berle And Means Revisited," JOF, 1981, v36(2), 369-381.

Farrar, Donald E. "Implications Of The Martin Report," FAJ, 1971, v27(5), 14-16,59-62.

Farrar, Donald E. "Toward A Central Market System: Wall Street's Slow Retreat Into The Future," JFQA, 1974, v9(5), 815-827.

Farrell, J. L., Jr. (Ambachtsheer, K. P. and J. L. Farrell, Jr. "Can Active Management Add Value?," FAJ, 1979, v35(6), 39-47.)

Farrell, James L., Jr. "A Fundamental Forecast Approach To Superior Asset Allocation," FAJ, 1989, v45(3), 32-37.

Farrell, James L., Jr. "Analyzing Covariation Of Returns To Determine Homogeneous Stock Groupings," JOB, 1974, v47(2), 186-207.

Farrell, James L., Jr. "Homogeneous Stock Groupings," FAJ, 1975, v31(3), 50-56,58-62.

Farrell, James L., Jr. "The Dividend Discount Model: A Primer," FAJ, 1985, v41(6), 16-19,22-25.

Farrell, James L., Jr. (Martin, John D., Arthur J. Keown, Jr. and James L. Farrell, Jr. "Do Fund Objectives Affect Diversification Policies?," JPM, 1982, v8(2), 19-28.)

Farrelly, Gail E. and William R. Reichenstein. "Risk Perceptions Of Institutional Investors," JPM, 1984, v10(4), 5-12.

Farrelly, Gail E. (Baker, H. Kent, Gail E. Farrelly and Richard B. Edelman. "A Survey Of Management Views On Dividend Policy," FM, 1985, v14(3), 78-84.)

Farrelly, Gail. "A Behavioral Science Approach To Financial Research," FM, 1980, v9(3), 15-22.

Farrelly, Gail. (LeBaron, Dean, Gail Farrelly and Susan Gula. "Facilitating A Dialogue On Risk: A Questionnaire Approach," FAJ, 1989, v45(3), 19-24.)

Farris, Paul L. (Brorsen, B. Wade, Charles M. Oellermann and Paul L. Farris. "The Live Cattle Futures Market And Daily Cash Price," JFM, 1989, v9(4), 273-282.)

Farris, Paul L. (Oellermann, Charles M. and Paul L. Farris. "Trader Concentration Effects In Live Cattle Futures," JFM, 1986, v6(4), 565-574.)

Farris, Paul L. (Oellermann, Charles M. and Paul L. Farris. "Futures Or Cash: Which Market Leads Live Beef Cattle Prices?," JFM, 1985, v5(4), 529-538.)

Farris, Paul L. (Oellermann, Charles M., B. Wade Brorsen and Paul L. Farris. "Price Discovery For Feeder Cattle," JFM, 1989, v9(2), 113-122.)

Farris, Paul L. (Vellermann, Charles M. and Paul L. Farris. "Note On Trader Concentration Effects In Feeder Cattle Futures And Comparison With Live Cattle," JFM, 1988, v8(1), 103-114.)

Fatemi, Ali M. "Shareholder Benefits From Corporate International Diversification," JOF, 1984, v39(5), 1325-1344.

Fatemi, Ali M. (Ang, James S. and Ali M. Fatemi. "Financial Planning And Performance: An Empirical Investigation," AFPAF, 1985, v1(1), 225-240.)

Fatemi, Ali M. (Ang, James S. and Ali M. Fatemi. "A Test Of The Rationality Of Forward Exchange Rate," AFPAF, 1989, v4(Supp), 3-22.)

Fatemi, Ali M. and Eugene P. H. Furtado. "An Empirical Investigation Of The Wealth Effects Of Foreign Acquisitions," RDIBF, 1988, v2, 363-380.

Fatemi, Ali. (Dilts, David A. and Ali Fatemi. "Student Evaluation Of Instructors: Investment Or Moral Hazard?," JFED, 1982, v11, 67-70.)

Fatemi, Khosrow. U.S. Trade Imbalance And The Dollar: Is There A Correlation?," IJOF, 1989, v1(2), 32-51.

Faulhaber, Gerald R. (Allen, Franklin and Gerald R. Faulhaber. "Signaling By Underpricing In The IPO Market," JFEC, 1989, v23(2), 303-324.)

Faulkner, E. J. "Meeting Health Care Costs Through Insurance," JRI, 1957, v24(1), 9-22.

Faulkner, E. J. "Potential Innovations In Health Insurance," JRI, 1961, v28(1), 21-26.

Faulkner, E. J. "Social Security And Insurance - Some Relationships In Perspective," JRI, 1963, v30(2), 197-218.

Faulknier, Tamara. (Rossiter, Lewis F., Killard W. Adamche and Tamara Faulknier. "A Blended Sector Rate Adjustment For The Medicare AAPCC When Risk-Based Market Penetration Is High," JRI, 1990, v57(2), 220-239.)

Fauth, Gary R. (Kain, John F. and Gary R. Fauth. "The Impact Of Urban Development On Auto Ownership And Transit Use," AREUEA, 1978, v6(3), 305-326.)

Fauver, Clarke L. and Ralph A. Young. "Measuring The Impact Of Consumer Credit Controls On Spending," JOF, 1952, v7(2),388-402.

Fawthrop, R. A. and Brian Terry. "The Evaluation Of An Integrated Investment And Lease-Financing Decision: A Reply," JBFA, 1979, v6(1), 89-93.

Fawthrop, R. A. and Brian Terry. "Debt Management And The Use Of Leasing Finance In UK Corporate Financing Strategies," JBFA, 1975, v2(3), 295-314.

Fawthrop, R. A. and Brian Terry. "The Evaluation Of An Integrated Investment And Lease-Financing Decision," JBFA, 1976, v3(3), 79-112.

Payez, Elayan. (Wansley, James W. and Elayan Fayez. "Stock Repurchases And Securityholder Returns: A Case Study of Teledyne," JFR, 1986, v9(2), 179-191.)

Fazio, Antonio. (Caligiuri, Gian Franco, Antonio Fazio and Tommaso Padoa-Schioppa. "Demand And Supply Of Bank Credit In Italy," JMCB, 1974, v6(4),455-479.)

Feay, Herbert L. and Irwin W. Kabak. "Frequency Formulas For Determining Stop-Loss Reinsurance Premiums," JRI, 1968, v35(3), 371-391.

Feder, Gershon and Knud Ross. "Risk Assessments And Risk Premiums In The Eurodollar Market," JOF, 1982, v37(3), 679-691.

Feder, Gershon, Richard Just and Knud Ross. "Projecting Debt Servicing Capacity Of Developing Countries," JFQA, 1981, v16(5), 651-669.

Feder, Gershon. "A Note On Debt, Assets and Lending Under Default Risk," JFQA, 1980, v15(1), 191-200.

Feenberg, Daniel. "Does The Investment Interest Limitation Explain The Existence Of Dividends?," **JFEC**, 1981, v9(3), 265-270.

Fefferman, Arthur S. "Private Pension Plans: A 1968 Prospectus," **JRI**, 1969, v36(3), 433-436.

Fehrs, Donald H. "Management Decisions, Market Events, And Stock Price Changes: A Student Project For Finance Courses," **JFED**, 1990, v19, 5-9.

Fehrs, Donald H., Gary A. Benesh and David R. Peterson. "Evidence Of A Relation Between Stock Price Reactions Around Cash Dividend Changes And Yields," **JFR**, 1988, v11(2), 111-124.

Feick, Harry W. "Digging Deeper Into Research And Development," **FAJ**, 1962, v18(5), 79-81.

Feige, Edgar L. and P. A. V. B. Swamy. "A Random Coefficient Model Of The Demand For Liquid Assets," **JMCB**, 1974, v6(2), 241-252.

Feige, Edgar L. and Robert McGee. "Money Supply Control And Lagged Reserve Accounting," **JMCB**, 1977, v9(4), 536-551.

Feige, Edgar L. and Robert McGee. "Has The Federal Reserve Shifted From A Policy Of Interest Rate Targets To A Policy Of Monetary Aggregate Targets?," **JMCB**, 1979, v11(4), 381-404.

Feige, Edgar L. and Robert T. McGee. "Federal Reserve Policy And Interest Rate Instability," **FR**, 1982, v17(1), 50-62.

Feige, Edgar L. "Temporal Cross-Section Specifications Of The Demand For Demand Deposits," **JOF**, 1974, v29(3), 923-940.

Feiger, George and Bertrand Jacquillat. "Currency Option Bonds, Puts And Calls On Spot Exchange And The Hedging Of Contingent Foreign Earnings," **JOF**, 1979, v34(5), 1129-1139.

Feight, James S. "Blue Cross And The Community Health Problem," **JRI**, 1961, v28(3), 17-24.

Feinberg, Robert M. "'Sales-At-Risk': A Test Of The Mutual Forbearance Theory Of Conglomerate Behavior," **JOB**, 1985, v58(2), 225-241.

Feinberg, Robert M. and Donald J. Rousslang. "The Economic Effects Of Intellectual Property Right Infringements," **JOB**, 1990, v63(1), Part 1, 79-90.

Feit, Evelyn B. (Feit, Theodore and Evelyn B. Feit. "The Day The Stock Market Stood Still," **FAJ**, 1982, v38(5), 57-58.)

Feit, Theodore and Evelyn B. Feit. "The Day The Stock Market Stood Still," **FAJ**, 1982, v38(5),57-58.

Feldman, David. "The Term Structure Of Interest Rates In A Partially Observable Economy," **JOF**, 1989, v44(3), 789-812.

Feldman, David. (Dothan, Uri and David Feldman. "Equilibrium Interest Rates And Multiperiod Bonds In A Partially Observable Economy," **JOF**, 1986, v41(2), 369-382.)

Feldman, Richard L. (Rippe, Richard D. and Richard L. Feldman. "The Impact Of Residential Construction On The Demand For Automobiles: An Omitted Variable," **JOB**, 1976, v49(3), 389-401.)

Feldman, Roger and Warren Greenberg. "The Relation Between The Blue Cross Market Share And The Blue Cross 'Discount' On Hospital Charges," **JRI**, 1981, v48(2), 235-246.

Feldman, Roger. "Equilibrium In Monopolistic Insurance Markets: An Extension To The Sales-Maximizing Monopolist," **JRI**, 1982, v49(4), 602-612.

Feldman, Roger. "Health Insurance In The United States: Is Market Failure Avoidable?," **JRI**, 1987, v54(2), 298-313.

Feldman, William. "Cyclical Effects Of Capital Gains Tax On The Market," **FAJ**, 1954, v10(4), 47-50.

Feldman, William. "Economic Analysis For The Financial Analyst," **FAJ**, 1963, v19(6), 61-67.

Feldstein, Martin and Gary Chamberlain. "Multimarket Expectations And The Rate Of Interest," **JMCB**, 1973, v5(4), 873-902.

Feldstein, Martin and Randall Morck. "Pension Funds And The Value Of Equities," **FAJ**, 1983, v39(5),29-39.

Feldstein, Martin and Stephanie Seligman. "Pension Funding, Share Prices, And National Savings," **JOF**, 1981, v36(4), 801-824.

Feldstein, Paul J. (Renshaw, Edward F. and Paul J. Feldstein. "The Case For An Unmanaged Investment Co.," **FAJ**, 1960, v16(1), 43-46.)

Feldstein, Sylvan G. and Frank J. Fabozzi. "Analyzing The Credit Worthiness Of Short-Term Tax-Exempt Obligations," **FAJ**, 1985, v41(6), 71-76.

Fellingham, John C. (Jennings, Robert H., Laura T. Starks and John C. Fellingham. "An Equilibrium Model Of Asset Trading With Sequential Information Arrival," **JOF**, 1981, v36(1), 143-161.)

Fellner, William. "Criteria For Useful Targeting: Money Versus The Base And Other Variables," **JMCB**, 1982, v14(4), Part 2, 641-660.

Fellner, William. "The Valid Core Of Rationality Hypotheses In The Theory Of Expectations," **JMCB**, 1980, v12(4), Part 2, 763-787.

Fellows, James A. and Thomas R. Beard. "Some Welfare Implications Of Legal Restrictions On Commercial Bank Entry," **JBR**, 1980-81, v11(3), 159-168.

Feltenstein, Andrew and Ziba Farhadian. "Fiscal Policy, Monetary Targets, And The Price Level In A Centrally Planned Economy: An Application To The Case Of China," **JMCB**, 1987, v19(2), 137-156.

Feltenstein, Andrew, David Lebow and S. Van Wijnbergen. "Savings, Commodity Market Rationing, And The Real Rate Of Interest In China," **JMCB**, 1990, v22(2), 234-252.

Felton, Robert S. "An Analysis Of The Adjustments To The Tax Base In State Taxation Of Fire And Casualty Insurance Companies," **JRI**, 1963, v30(4), 517-524.

Felton, Robert S. "Relationship Of The Insurance Curricula To The Subject Area Of Finance," **JRI**, 1965, v32(4), 617-620.

Felton, Robert S. "Retaliatory Insurance Company Taxation: An Evaluation," **JRI**, 1961, v28(3), 71-80.

Felton, Robert S. "The Market For Industrial Life Insurance In Developing Nations: Central America," **JRI**, 1968, v35(2), 273-282.

Felton, Robert S. (Fletcher, Linda Pickthorne and Robert S. Felton. "Toward The Development Of A 'Bibliography Of Teaching And Research Material'," **JRI**, 1969, v36(2), 299-304.)

Felton, Robert S., William K. Ghee and John E. Stinton. "A Mid-1970 Report On The National Flood Insurance Program," **JRI**, 1971, v38(1), 1-14.

Feng, C. A. (Shinnar, Reuel, Ofer Dressler, C. A. Feng and Alan I. Avidan. "Estimation Of The Economic Rate Of Return For Industrial Companies," **JOB**, 1989, v62(3), 417-446.)

Fenner, Linda M. "Payment Services In Transition," **JBR**, 1970-71, v1(2), 62-63.

Fenner, Linda M. "The Status Of Payment Services Today," **JBR**, 1971-72, v2(1), 60-68.

Fenstermaker, J. Van and A. D. Issa. "Price Uniformity And Banking Markets: Evidence From The St. Louis Area," **FR**, 1969, v1(4), 224-226.

Fenstermaker, J. Van. "Cash-Flow Management For Universities," **FR**, 1967, v1(2), 41-54.

Fenwick, I. (Doyle, P., I. Fenwick and G. P. Savage. "A Model For Evaluating Branch Location And Performance," **JBR**, 1981-82, v12(2), 90-95.)

Ferber, David. "Disclosure Of Corporate Information," **FAJ**, 1966, v22(4), 19-22.

Ferber, Robert and Luch Chao Lee. "Asset Accumulation In Early Married Life," **JOF**, 1980, v35(5), 1173-1188.

Ferber, Robert and Lucy Choa Lee. "Acquisition And Accumulation Of Life Insurance In Early Married Life," **JRI**, 1980, v47(4), 713-734.

Ferber, Robert, Nai-Ruenn Chen and Fadil Zuwaylif. "Employers' Forecasts Of Manpower: An Interview Study," **JOB**, 1961, v34(3), 387-395.

Ferber, Robert. "Short-Run Effects Of Stock Market Services On Stock Prices," **JOF**, 1958, v13(1), 80-95.

Ferenbach, C. (Amihud, Y., C. Brunie, C. Ferenbach, R. Fredericks, J. Grundfest, J. Lafferty, B. Lev, B. Shorts, J. Stern, B. Stewart and R. Zeckhauser. "Panel: 'Lead Steer' Roundtable," **JACF**, 1989, v2(3), 24-44.)

Ferguson, Daniel M. (Hill, Ned C. and Daniel M. Ferguson. "Negotiating Payment Terms In An Electronic Environment," **AWCM**, 1990, v1(1), 131-146.)

Ferguson, Donald A. "A Suggested Reorganization Of Monetary Policy Formation," **JOB**, 1951, v24(1), 25-42.

Ferguson, Donald A. "Public Service Industries And Capital Markets," **FAJ**, 1960, v16(2), 73-76.

Ferguson, Donald L. (Porter, R. Burr, James R. Wart and Donald L. Ferguson. "Efficient Algorithms For Conducting Stochastic Dominance Tests On Large Numbers Of Portfolios," **JFQA**, 1973, v8(1), 71-81.)

Ferguson, Donald. "Public Utilities, Growth Industry Of '50's," **FAJ**, 1959, v15(1), 81-100

Ferguson, James M. "Advertising And Liquor," **JOB**, 1967, v40(4), 414-434.

Ferguson, Jerry T. "After-Sale Evaluations: Appraisals Or Justifications?," **JRER**, 1988, v3(1), 19-26.

Ferguson, John, Jr. "Corporate Income Accounts," **FAJ**, 1948, v4(1), 10-22.

Ferguson, Robert and Philip Popkin. "Pulling Rabbits Out Of Hats In The Oil Business - And Elsewhere," **FAJ**, 1982, v38(2), 24-27.

Ferguson, Robert and Richard Lynn. "A Security Market Plane Approach To Stock Selection," **FAJ**, 1984, v40(5), 75-80.

Ferguson, Robert F. "Where Are The Customers' Yachts?," **FAJ**, 1979, v35(2), 56-62.

Ferguson, Robert and John O'Brien. "Stabilizing Forwards: For A More Stable Market," **JPM**, 1988, v14(4), 4.

Ferguson, Robert and Roken Ahmed. "How To Get Rich Quick (Without Losing Sleep)," **FAJ**, 1988, v44(4), 68-75.

Ferguson, Robert. "A Comparison Of The Mean-Variance And Long-Term Return Characteristics Of 3 Investment Strategies," **FAJ**, 1987, v43(4), 55-66.

Ferguson, Robert. "A Nomograph For Valuing Growth Stocks," **FAJ**, 1961, v17(3), 29-34.

Ferguson, Robert. "An Efficient Stock Market? Ridiculous!," **JPM**, 1983, v9(4), 31-38.

Ferguson, Robert. "Do Inventory Funds Make Sense?," **FAJ**, 1978, v34(3), 38-44.

Ferguson, Robert. "How To Beat The Index Funds," **FAJ**, 1975, v31(3), 63-72.

Ferguson, Robert. "How To Beat The S&P 500 (Without Losing Sleep)," **FAJ**, 1986, v42(2), 37-46.

Ferguson, Robert. "On Crashes," **FAJ**, 1989, v45(2), 42-52.

Ferguson, Robert. "Performance Measurement Doesn't Make Sense," **FAJ**, 1980, v36(3), 59-69.

Ferguson, Robert. "The Trouble With Performance Measurement," **JPM**, 1986, v12(3), 4-9.

Ferguson, Robert. "Unbundling: No More Analysts At A Discount," **JPM**, 1975, v1(3), 44-48.

Ferguson, Robert. "What To Do, Or Not Do, About The Markets," **JPM**, 1988, v14(4), 14-19.

Ferguson, Robert. (Good, Walter R., Robert Ferguson and Jack Treynor. "A Guide To The Index Fund Controversy," **FAJ**, 1976, v32(6), 27-38.)

Ferguson, Robert. (Treynor, Jack L. and Robert Ferguson. "In Defense Of Technical Analysis," **JOF**, 1985, v40(3), 757-773.)

Ferguson, William. (Flanigan, George B., Joseph E. Johnson, Daniel T. Winkler and William Ferguson. "Experience From Early Tort Reforms: Comparative Negligence Since 1974," **JRI**, 1989, v56(3), 525-534.)

Fergusson, Donald A. "Capital Budgeting Decision-Making And New Theory," **FR**, 1968, v1(3), 140-154.

Fergusson, Donald A. "Preferred Stock Valuation In Recapitalizations," **JOF**, 1958, v13(1), 48-69.

Fergusson, Donald A. "Price-Level Stabilization And Full Employment As Objectives Of Monetary Policy," **JOB**, 1951, v24(3), 220-231.

Fergusson, Donald A. "Recent Developments In Preferred Stock Financing," **JOF**, 1952, v7(3), 447-462.

Fernholz, Robert and Brian Shay. "Stochastic Portfolio Theory And Stock Market Equilibrium," **JOF**, 1982, v37(2), 615-624.

Fernow, Donald. "International Oils," **FAJ**, 1966, v22(1), 137-148.

Feroz, E. H. (Cheshire, J. D. and E. H. Feroz. "Allison's Models And The FASB Statements No's 2, 5, 13 And 19," **JBFA**, 1989, v16(1), 119-130.)

Feroz, Ehsan H. "Corporate Demands And Changes In GPLA," **JBFA**, 1987, v14(3), 409-424.

Ferrara, William L. and Joseph F. Wojdak. "Valuation Of Long-Term Leases," **FAJ**, 1969, v25(6), 29-32.

Ferrari, J. Robert. (Denenberg, Herbert S. and J. Robert Ferrari. "New Perspectives On Risk Management: The Search For Principles," **JRI**, 1966, v33(4), 647-660.)

Ferrari, J. Robert. "Implications Of Viewing Interest Foregone As An

Opportunity Cost Of Life Insurance," **JRI**, 1969, v36(2), 253-268.

Ferrari, J. Robert. "Implications Of Viewing Interest Foregone As An Opportunity Cost Of Life Insurance: Reply," **JRI**, 1970, v37(2), 322-325.

Ferrari, J. Robert. "Investment Life Insurance Versus Term Insurance And Separate Investment," **JRI**, 1968, v35(2), 181-198.

Ferrari, J. Robert. (Denenberg, Herbert S. and J. Robert Ferrari. "New Perspectives On Risk Management: Reply," **JRI**, 1968, v35(4), 623-627.)

Ferreira, Eurico J. (Brooks, LeRoy D., Charles E. Edwards and Eurico J. Ferreira. "Risk-Return Characteristics Of Convertible Preferred Stock: Comment," **JPM**, 1984, v10(2), 76-78.)

Ferreira, Eurico J. and G. Stacy Sirmans. "Selling Price, Financing Premiums, And Days On The Market," **JREFEC**, 1989, v2(3), 209-222.

Ferreira, Eurico J. and G. Stacy Sirmans. "Interest-Rate Changes, Transaction Costs, And Assumable Loan Value," **JRER**, 1987, v2(2), 29-40.

Ferrell, O. C. (Childers, Terry L. and O. C. Ferrell. "Husband-Wife Decision Making In Purchasing And Renewing Auto Insurance," **JRI**, 1981, v48(3), 482-493.)

Ferretti, Andrew P. "Long-Term Perspective On Common Stock Prices," **FAJ**, 1962, v18(6), 19-26.

Ferretti, Andrew P. "The Economist's Role," **FAJ**, 1969, v25(1), 35-37.

Ferri, Michael G. and Charles G. Martin. "The Cyclical Pattern In Corporate Bond Quality," **JPM**, 1980, v6(2), 26-29.

Ferri, Michael G. and H. Dennis Oberhelman. "How Well Do Money Market Funds Perform?," **JPM**, 1981, v7(3), 18-26.

Ferri, Michael G. and H. Dennis Oberhelman. "A Study Of The Management Of Money Market Mutual Funds, 1975-1980," **FM**, 1981, v10(4), 24-29.

Ferri, Michael G. and James P. Gaines. "A Study Of Yield Spreads In The Money Market: 1971 To 1978," **FM**, 1980, v9(3), 52-59.

Ferri, Michael G. and Wesley H. Jones. "Determinants Of Financial Structure: A New Methodological Approach," **JOF**, 1979, v34(3), 631-644.

Ferri, Michael G. "An Empirical Examination Of The Determinants Of Bond Yield Spreads," **FM**, 1978, v7(3), 40-46.

Ferri, Michael G. "How Do Call Provisions Influence Bond Yields?," **JPM**, 1979, v5(2), 55-57.

Ferri, Michael G. "How Do Call Provisions Influence Bond Yields?: A Reply," **JPM**, 1979, v5(4),71-72.

Ferri, Michael G. "Systematic Return Risk And The Call Risk Of Corporate Debt Instruments," **JFR**, 1978, v1(1), 1-13.

Ferri, Michael G. (Fabozzi, Frank J., Michael G. Ferri, T. Dessa Fabozzi and Julia Tucker. "A Note On Unsuccessful Tender Offers And Stockholder Returns," **JOF**, 1988, v43(5), 1275-1283.)

Ferri, Michael G. (Lewellen, Wilbur G. and Michael G. Ferri. "Strategies For The Merger Game: Management And The Market," **FM**, 1983, v12(4), 25-35.)

Ferri, Michael G. (Ritchken, Peter H. and Michael G. Ferri. "Recursion Models For Warrant Pricing," **RDIBF**, 1987, v1, 257-272.)

Ferri, Michael G. (Schirm, David C., Richard G. Sheehan and Michael G. Ferri. "Financial Market Responses To Treasury Debt Announcements," **JMCB**, 1989, v21(3), 394-400.)

Ferri, Michael G., H. Dennis Oberhelman and Steven J. Goldstein. "Yield Sensitivities Of Short-Term Securities," **JPM**, 1982, v8(3), 65-71.

Ferri, Michael G., H. Dennis Oberhelman and Rodney L. Roenfeldt. "Market Timing And Mutual Fund Portfolio Composition," **JFR**, 1984, v7(2), 143-150.

Ferri, Michael G., Steven J. Goldstein and It-Keong Chew. "Interest Rates And The Announcement Of Inflation," **FM**, 1983, v12(3), 52-61.

Ferri, Michael G., Steven J. Goldstein and H. Dennis Oberhelman. "The Performance Of The When-Issued Market For T-Bills," **JPM**, 1985, v11(3), 57-61.

Ferri, Michael G., Scott B. Moore and David C. Schirm. "Investor Expectations About Callable Warrants," **JPM**, 1988, v14(3), 84-86.

Ferri, Michael G., Scott B. Moore and David C. Schirm. "The Listing, Size, And Value Of Equity Warrants," **FR**, 1989, v24(1), 135-146.

Ferri, Michael J. "An Application Of Hedonic Indexing Methods To Monthly Changes In Housing Prices: 1965-1975," **AREUEA**, 1977, v5(4), 455-462.

Ferris, Kenneth R. "The Apparent Effects Of Profit Forecast Disclosure On Managerial Behaviour: An Empirical Examination," **JBFA**, 1976, v3(3), 53-66.

Ferris, Kenneth R. (Eaker, Mark R. and Kenneth R. Ferris. "Long-Term Supply Agreements: A New Albatross?," **FAJ**, 1982, v38(6), 70-73)

Ferris, Kenneth R. (Varaiya, Nikhil P. and Kenneth R. Ferris. "Overpaying In Corporate Takeovers: The Winner's Curse," **FAJ**, 1987, v43(3), 64-71.)

Ferris, Stephen P. (Chance, Don M. and Stephen P. Ferris. "Summer Rallies," **FAJ**, 1986, v42(1), 6-9.)

Ferris, Stephen P. (Chance, Don M. and Stephen P. Ferris. "The CBOE Call Option Index: A Historical Record," **JPM**, 1985, v12(1), 75-83.)

Ferris, Stephen P. and Don M. Chance. "The Effect Of 12b-1 Plans On Mutual Fund Expense Ratios: A Note," **JOF**, 1987, v42(4), 1077-1082.

Ferris, Stephen P. and Don M. Chance. "Trading Time Effects In Financial And Commodity Futures Markets," **FR**, 1987, v22(2), 281-294.

Ferris, Stephen P., Dana J. Johnson and Dilip K. Shome. "Regulatory Environment And Market Response To Public Utility Rate Decisions," **JFR**, 1986, v9(4), 313-318.

Ferris, Stephen P., Robert A. Haugen and Anil K. Makhija. "Predicting Contemporary Volume With Historic Volume At Differential Price Levels: Evidence Supporting The Disposition Effect," **JOF**, 1988, v43(3), 677-697.

Ferson, Wayne E. "Are The Latent Variables In Time-Varying Expected Returns Compensation For Consumption Risk?," **JOF**, 1990, v45(2), 397-430.)

Ferson, Wayne E. "Changes In Expected Security Returns, Risk, And The Level Of Interest Rates," **JOF**, 1989, v44(5), 1191-1218.

Ferson, Wayne E. "Expectations Of Real Interest Rates And Aggregate Consumption: Empirical Tests," **JFQA**, 1983, v18(4), 477-497.

Ferson, Wayne E. and John J. Merrick, Jr. "Non-Stationarity And Stage-Of-The-Business-Cycle Effects In Consumption-Based Asset Pricing Relations," **JFEC**, 1987, v18(1), 127-146.

Ferson, Wayne E., Shmuel Kandel and Robert F. Stambaugh. "Tests Of Asset Pricing With Time-Varying Expected Risk Premiums And Market Betas," **JOF**, 1987, v42(2), 201-220.

Ferson, Wayne. (Gibbons, Michael R. and Wayne Ferson. "Testing Asset Pricing Models With Changing Expectations And An Unobservable Market Portfolio," **JFEC**, 1985, v14(2), 217-236.)

Fertuck, Leonard. "A Test Of Industry Indices Based On SIC Codes," **JFQA**, 1975, v10(5), 837-848.

Fethke, Gary C. and Andrew J. Policano. "Long-Term Contracts And The Effectiveness Of Demand And Supply Policies," **JMCB**, 1981, v13(4), 439-453.

Fetters, Michael L. (Anderson, Dan R. and Michael L. Fetters. "An Empirical Analysis Of State Examiners' Reactions To Loss Reserving Patterns," **JRI**, 1975, v42(2), 243-262.)

Feuerstein, A. E. and P. G. Maggi. "Computer Investment Research," **FAJ**, 1968, v24(1), 154-158.

Feuerstein, Donald M. "The Third And Fourth Markets," **FAJ**, 1972, v28(4), 57-59,82-86.

Feuerstein, Jay R. "Trading Bond Spreads In The Delivery Month," **JFM**, 1984, v4(4), 579-583.

Fewings, David R. "The Impact Of Corporate Growth On The Risk Of Common Stocks," **JOF**, 1975, v30(2), 525-531.

Fey, John T. "Insurance In The Public Interest," **JRI**, 1971, v38(4), 521-526.

Fichthorn, William H. "Bank Capital Notes," **FAJ**, 1967, v23(4), 63-70.

Fichthorn, William H. "Current Investment Policies Of Pension Funds," **FR**, 1967, v1(2), 26-32.

Fiegenbaum, Avi and Walter J. Primeaux, Jr. "An Empirical Examination Of Strategic Groups In Three Manufacturing Industries," **AFPAF**, 1989, v3(1), 281-310.

Field, Al and Henry J. Cassidy. "Simulation Analysis Of Alternative Mortgage Instruments," **AREUEA**, 1977, v5(4), 411-433.

Field, Charles G. "Evaluating The Administrative Delivery Of Housing Goals," **AREUEA**, 1973, v1(2), 21-34.

Field, Charles G. (Goldman, Ellis G. and Charles G. Field. "Summary Of An Article On Reforming Land-Use Regulations," **AREUEA**, 1983, v11(2), 300-318.)

Field, Irving M. "Collective Merchandising Of Automobile Insurance And Auto Insurance As A Fringe Benefit: Comment," **JRI**, 1971, v38(1), 133-136.

Field, Irving M. "Group Property And Liability Insurance," **JRI**, 1968, v35(1), 35-48.

Field, Kenneth. "The Impact Of Federal Policies On Equity Capital," **JRI**, 1942, v9, 63-72.

Field, Robert E. "Accounting Problems In The Utility Industry," **FAJ**, 1966, v22(1), 42.

Fields, Joseph A. "Expense Preference Behavior In Mutual Life Insurers," **JFSR**, 1988, v1(2), 113-130.

Fields, Joseph A. (Clapp, John M., Joseph A. Fields and Chinmoy Ghosh. "An Examination Of Profitability In Spatial Markets: The Case Of Life Insurance Agency Locations," **JRI**, 1990, v57(3), 431-454.)

Fields, Joseph A. (Venezian, Emilio C. and Joseph A. Fields. "Informational Asymmetries In Retroactive Insurance," **JRI**, 1987, v54(4), 780-789.)

Fields, Joseph A. and Emilio C. Venezian. "Investment Income - Is There A Company Effect?," **JRI**, 1987, v54(1), 173-178.

Fields, Joseph A. and Emilio C. Venezian. "Informational Asymmetries In Retroactive Insurance: Reply," **JRI**, 1988, v55(3), 555-558.

Fields, Joseph A. and Emilio C. Venezian. "Interest Rates And Profit Cycles: A Disaggregated Approach," **JRI**, 1989, v56(2), 312-319.

Fields, Joseph A. and Neil B. Murphy. "An Analysis Of Efficiency In The Delivery Of Financial Services: The Case Of Life Insurance Agencies," **JFSR**, 1989, v2(4), 343-356.

Fields, Kent T. (Curatola, Anthony P., Kent T. Fields and William D. Samson. "The Benefits Of The Salary Reduction Plan," **FAJ**, 1984, v40(3), 53-58.)

Fields, Kent T. (Curatola, Anthony P., Thomas L. Dickens and Kent T. Fields. "Increased Salary As An Alternative To Group Term Life Insurance," **JRI**, 1987, v54(1), 119-130.)

Fields, M. Andrew. (Black, Harold A., M. Andrew Fields and Robert L. Schweitzer. "Changes In Interstate Banking Laws: The Impact On Shareholder Wealth," **JOF**, 1990, v45(5), 1663-1672.)

Fields, Paige. (Schmit, Joan T., S. Travis Pritchett and Paige Fields. "Punitive Damages: Punishment Or Further Compensation?," **JRI**, 1988, v55(3), 453-466.)

Fieldsend, Susan, Nicholas Longford and Stuart McLeay. "Industry Effects And The Proportionality Assumption In Ratio Analysis: A Variance Component Analysis," **JBFA**, 1987, v14(4), 497-518.

Fieleke, Norman S. "Exchange-Rate Flexibility And The Efficiency Of The Foreign-Exchange Markets," **JFQA**, 1975, v10(3), 409-428.

Fieleke, Norman S. "The Foreign Currency Futures Market: Some Reflections On Competitiveness And Growth," **JFM**, 1985, v5(4), 625-631.

Fielitz, Bruce D. and Daniel L. White. "An Evaluation And Linking Of Alternative Solution Procedures For The Lock Box Location Problem," **JBR**, 1982-83, v13(1), 17-27.

Fielitz, Bruce D. and Donald J. Thompson, II. "Performance Indexes Derived From The Sharpe-Lintner And Two-Factor Asset Pricing Models: Some Comparative Tests," **FR**, 1977, v12(2), 47-75.

Fielitz, Bruce D. and Frederick L. Muller. "The Asset Allocation Decision," **FAJ**, 1983, v39(4),44-50.

Fielitz, Bruce D. and Frederick L. Muller. "A Simplified Approach To Common Stock Valuation," **FAJ**, 1985, v41(6), 35-41.

Fielitz, Bruce D. and Gerald D. Gay. "Managing Cash Flow Risks In Stock Index Futures," **JPM**, 1986, v12(2), 74-78.

Fielitz, Bruce D. and Myron T. Greene. "Shortcomings In Performance Evaluation Via MPT," **JPM**, 1980, v6(4), 13-19.

Fielitz, Bruce D. and Myron T. Greene. "New Evidence Of Persistence In Stock Returns," **JPM**, 1979, v5(1), 38-42.

Fielitz, Bruce D. and Thomas A. Loeffler. "A Linear Programming Model For Commercial Bank Liquidity Management," **FM**, 1979, v8(3), 41-50.

Fielitz, Bruce D. "Calculating The Bond Equivalent Yield For T-Bills," JPM, 19883, v9(3), 58-60.

Fielitz, Bruce D. "Further Results On Asymmetric Stable Distributions Of Stock Price Changes," JPQA, 1976, v11(1), 39-55.

Fielitz, Bruce D. "Indirect Versus Direct Diversification," FM, 1974, v3(4), 54-62.

Fielitz, Bruce D. "On The Stationarity Of Transition Probability Matrices Of Common Stocks," JPQA, 1975, v10(2), 327-339.

Fielitz, Bruce D. "Stationarity Of Random Data: Some Implications For The Distribution Of Stock Price Changes," JPQA, 1971, v6(3), 1025-1034.

Fielitz, Bruce D. (Daigler, Robert T. and Bruce D. Fielitz. "A Multiple Discriminant Analysis Of Technical Indicators On The New York Stock Exchange," JFR, 1981, v4(3), 169-182.)

Fielitz, Bruce D. (Greene, Myron T. and Bruce D. Fielitz. "Long-Term Dependence In Common Stock Returns," JFEC, 1977, v4(3), 339-349.)

Fielitz, Bruce D. (Hasty, John M., Jr. and Bruce D. Fielitz. "Systematic Risk For Heterogeneous Time Horizons," JOF, 1975, v30(2), 659-673.)

Fielitz, Bruce D. (Luft, Carl F. and Bruce D. Fielitz. "An Empirical Test Of The Commodity Option Pricing Model Using Ginnie Mae Call Options," JFR, 1986, v9(2), 137-151.)

Fielitz, Bruce D. (Millar, James A. and Bruce D. Fielitz. "Stock-Split And Stock-Dividend Decisions," FM, 1973, v2(4), 35-45.)

Fielitz, Bruce D. (Muller, Frederick L., Bruce D. Fielitz and Myron T. Greene. "Portfolio Performance In Relation To Quality, Earnings, Dividends, Firm Size, Leverage, And Return On Equity," JFR, 1984, v7(1), 17-26.)

Fielitz, Bruce D. (Muller, Frederick L. and Bruce D. Fielitz. "Standard & Poor's Quality Rankings Revisited," JPM, 1987, v13(3), 64-68.)

Fielitz, Bruce D. (Muller, Frederick L., Bruce D. Fielitz and Myron T. Greene. "S&P Quality Group Rankings: Risk And Return," JPM, 1983, v9(4), 39-42.)

Fielitz, Bruce D. (Rozelle, James P. and Bruce D. Fielitz. "Stationarity Of Common Stock Returns," JFR, 1980, v3(3), 229-242.)

Fielitz, Bruce D. (Rozelle, James P. and Bruce D. Fielitz. "Skewness In Common Stock Returns," FR, 1980, v15(3), 1-23.)

Figlewski, Stephen and M. Desmond Fitzgerald. "The Price Behaviour Of London Commodity Options," RFM, 1982, v1(1), 90-104.

Figlewski, Stephen and Stanley J. Kon. "Portfolio Management With Stock Index Futures," FAJ, 1982, v38(1), 52-60.

Figlewski, Stephen and Thomas Urich. "Optimal Aggregation Of Money Supply Forecasts: Accuracy, Profitability And Market Efficiency," JOF, 1983, v38(3), 695-710.

Figlewski, Stephen. "Arbitrage-Based Pricing Of Stock Index Options," RFM, 1988, v7(2), 250-271.

Figlewski, Stephen. "Explaining The Early Discounts On Stock Index Futures: The Case For Disequilibrium," FAJ, 1984, v40(4), 43-47,67.

Figlewski, Stephen. "Futures Trading And Volatility In The GNMA Market," JOF, 1981, v36(2), 445-456.

Figlewski, Stephen. "Hedging With Stock Index Futures: Theory And Application In A New Market," JFM, 1985, v5(2), 183-199.

Figlewski, Stephen. "Hedging Performance And Basis Risk In Stock Index Futures," JOF, 1984, v39(2), 657-669.

Figlewski, Stephen. "Information Diversity And Market Behavior: A Reply," JOF, 1984, v39(1),299-302.

Figlewski, Stephen. "Information Diversity And Market Behavior," JOF, 1982, v37(1), 87-102.

Figlewski, Stephen. "Margins And Market Integrity: Margin Setting For Stock Index Futures And Options," JFM, 1984, v4(3), 385-416.

Figlewski, Stephen. "Options Arbitrage In Imperfect Markets," JOF, 1989, v44(5), 1289-1312.

Figlewski, Stephen. "The Informational Effects Of Restrictions On Short Sales: Some Empirical Evidence," JPQA, 1981, v16(4), 463-476.

Figliuoli, L. (Goodhart, C. A. E. and L. Figliuoli. "Every Minute Counts In Financial Markets," JIMF, 1991, v10(1), 23-52.)

Fildes, Robert A. and M. Desmond Fitzgerald. "Efficiency And Premiums In The Short-Term Money Market," JMCB, 1980, v12(4), Part 1, 615-629.

Filer, Herbert. "Investing In Options," FAJ, 1955, v11(1), 77-78.

Filer, John E. (Van Fenstermaker, J. and John E. Filer. "Impact Of The First And Second Banks Of The United States And The Suffolk System On New England Bank Money: 1791-1837," JMCB, 1986, v18(1), 28-40.)

Filios, Vassilios P. "The Cameralistic Method Of Accounting: A Historical Note," JBFA, 1983, v10(3), 443-450.

Filkins, James H. "The Finance Of Higher Education," JFED, 1972, v1, 23.

Filler, Ronald H. "Bring Us Forth From the Land Of Duplicative Regulation: An Appraisal Of State Jurisdiction Over Commodity Pools," JFM, 1981, v1(Supp), 449-452.

Filter, Eunice M. "How To Puff Up Computer Earnings," FAJ, 1971, v27(3), 44-52.

Fincher, Rebecca E. (Holt, Robert N. and Rebecca E. Fincher. "The Foreign Corrupt Practices Act," FAJ, 1981, v37(2), 73-76.)

Findlay, M. C. and E. E. Williams. "A Positivist Evaluation Of The New Finance," FM, 1980, v9(2), 7-17.

Findlay, M. C. (Canto, Victor A., M. C. Findlay and Marc R. Reinganum. "Inflation, Money, And Stock Prices: An Alternative Interpretation," FR, 1985, v20(1), 95-101.)

Findlay, M. C. (Langetieg, T. C., M. C. Findlay and L. F. J. da Motta. "Multiperiod Pension Plans And ERISA," JPQA, 1982, v17(4), 603-631.)

Findlay, M. C., III and E. E. Williams. "Better Debt Service Coverage Ratios," FAJ, 1975, v31(6), 58-61.

Findlay, M. Chapman, III and Elko J. Kleinschmidt. "Error-Learning In The Eurodollar Market," JPQA, 1975, v10(3), 429-446.

Findlay, M. Chapman, III and Edward E. Williams. "The Problem Of 'Unequal Lives' Reconsidered," JBFA, 1981, v8(2), 161-164.

Findlay, M. Chapman, III and Dennis R. Capozza. "The Variable-Rate Mortgage And Risk In The Mortgage Market: An Option Theory Perspective," JMCB, 1977, v9(2), 356-364.

Findlay, M. Chapman, III and Edward E. Williams. "Opportunity Cost, Discounting, And Deferred Tax Liabilities: A Final Note," JBFA, 1985, v12(2), 183-185.

Findlay, M. Chapman, III and Edward E. Williams. "Capital Allocation And The Nature Of Ownership Equities," FM, 1972, v1(2), 68-76.

Findlay, M. Chapman, III and Edward E. Williams. "Discounting Deferred Tax Liabilities: A Reply," JBFA, 1981, v8(4), 593-597.

Findlay, M. Chapman, III and R. A. Tarantello. "An M.B.A. Program In Real Estate With A Financial Emphasis," JFED, 1977, v6, 17-18.

Findlay, M. Chapman, III and Edward E. Williams. "Owners' Surplus, The Marginal Efficiency Of Capital And Market Equilibrium," JBFA, 1979, v6(1), 17-36.

Findlay, M. Chapman, III and G. A. Whitmore. "Beyond Shareholder Wealth Maximization," FM, 1974, v3(4), 25-35.

Findlay, M. Chapman, III and Edward E. Williams. "A Post Keynesian View Of Modern Financial Economics: In Search Of Alternative Paradigms," JBFA, 1985, v12(1), 1-18.

Findlay, M. Chapman, III and William Smith. "Some Canadian Implications Of International Portfolio Diversification," FR, 1976, v11(1), 36-48.

Findlay, M. Chapman, III and Edward E. Williams. "Better Betas Didn't Help The Boat People," JPM, 1986, v13(1), 4-9.

Findlay, M. Chapman, III and Hugh R. Howson. "Optimal Intertemporal Real Estate Ownership, Valuation And Use," AREUEA, 1975, v3(2), 51-66.

Findlay, M. Chapman, III, Alan W. Frankle, Philip L. Cooley, Rodney L. Roenfeldt and It-Keong Chew. "Capital Budgeting Procedures Under Inflation: Cooley, Roenfeldt, And Chew Vs. Findlay And Frankle," FM, 1976, v5(3), 83-95.

Findlay, M. Chapman, III, Arthur E. Gooding and Wallace Q. Weaver, Jr. "On The Relevant Risk For Determining Capital Expenditure Hurdle Rates," FM, 1976, v5(4), 9-17.

Findlay, M. Chapman, III, Edward E. Williams and Lawrence A. Gordon. "Toward More Adequate Measures Of Lender Protection," FM, 1974, v4(3), 54-61.

Findlay, M. Chapman, III, Carl W. Hamilton, Stephen D. Messner and Jonathan S. Yormark. "Optimal Real Estate Portfolios," AREUEA, 1979, v7(3), 298-317.

Findlay, M. Chapman, III. "Corporate Finance And Normalised Price," JBFA, 1976, v3(2), 115-130.

Findlay, M. Chapman, III. "Financial Lease Evaluation: Survey And Synthesis," FR, 1974, v9(1),1-15.

Findlay, M. Chapman, III. "Operating Decisions And The CAPM," JBFA, 1979, v6(2), 131-144.

Findlay, M. Chapman, III. "Stochastic Interest Rates And Investment Appraisal: A Comment," JBFA, 1980, v7(4), 639-641.

Findlay, M. Chapman, III. "The Weighted Average Cost Of Capital And Finite Flows," JBFA, 1977, v4(2), 217-227.

Findlay, M. Chapman, III. "The Weighted Average Cost Of Capital: Some Questions On Its Definition, Interpretation, And Use: Comment," JOF, 1975, v30(3), 879-880.

Findlay, M. Chapman, III. (Babcock, Guilford C., M. Chapman Findlay, III and Stephen D. Messner. "FMRR And Duration: Implications For Real Estate Investment Analysis," AREUEA, 1976, v4(3), 49-68.)

Findlay, M. Chapman, III. (Draper, Dennis W. and M. Chapman Findlay, III. "A Note On Vickers' Marginal Cost Of Debt Capital," JBFA, 1982, v8(4), 579-582.)

Findlay, M. Chapman, III. (Johnson, Keith B., Gregory Morton and M. Chapman Findlay, III. "An Analysis Of The Flotation Cost Of Utility Bonds, 1971-76," JFR, 1979, v2(2), 133-142.)

Findlay, M. Chapman, III. (Johnson, Keith B., T. Gregory Morton and M. Chapman Findlay, III. "An Analysis Of The Flotation Cost Of Corporate Quasi-Equity Securities, 1971-72," FM, 1974,v4(4),12-17.)

Findlay, M. Chapman, III. (Johnson, Keith B., T. Gregory Morton And M. Chapman Findlay, III. "An Empirical Analysis Of The Flotation Cost Of Corporate Securities, 1971-1972," JOF, 1975, v30(4), 1129-1133.)

Findlay, M. Chapman, III. (Williams, Edward E. and M. Chapman Findlay, III. "Discounting Deferred Tax Liabilities: Some Clarifying Comments," JBFA, 1975, v2(1), 121-133.)

Findlay, M. Chapman, III. (Williams, Edward E. and M. Chapman Findlay, III. "Capital Budgeting, Cost Of Capital And Ex Ante Static Equilibrium," JBFA, 1979, v6(4), 455-474.)

Findlay, M. Chapman. (Agmon, Tamir and M. Chapman Findlay. "Domestic Political Risk And Stock Valuation," FAJ, 1982, v38(6), 74-77.)

Findlay, M. Chapman. (Dale-Johnson, David, M. Chapman Findlay, Arthur L. Schwartz, Jr. and Stephen D. Kapplin. "Valuation And Efficiency In The Market For Creatively Financed Houses," AREUEA, 1985, v13(4), 388-403.)

Findlay, M. Chapman. (Dale-Johnson, David and M. Chapman Findlay. "Creative Financing And Housing Prices: A Comment On A Theoretical Inquiry Into The Capitalization Issue," AREUEA, 1986, v14(1), 153-157.)

Findlay, M. Chapman. (Draper, Dennis W. and M. Chapman Findlay. "Capital Asset Pricing And Real Estate Valuation," AREUEA, 1982, v10(2), 152-183.)

Finkel, Sidney R. and Donald L. Tuttle. "Determinants Of The Aggregate Profits Margin," JOF, 1971, v26(5), 1067-1075.

Finkel, Sidney R. "Comment: The Gibson Paradox Revisited," FR, 1983, v18(2), 214-217.

Finkelstein, John M. and Subbarao Uppaluri. "A Method For Optimal Deposit Liability Assignment," JBF, 1980, v4(3), 249-256.

Finkelstein, John M. "A Note On The Aggregate Effect Of Deposit Rate Ceilings," FR, 1981, v16(3), 67-75.

Finkelstein, John M. "A Note On An Interest Rate Strategies Framework For Teaching The Money And Capital Markets Course," JFED, 1981, v10, 6-9.

Finkelstein, John M. "The Macroeconomic Impact Of A Loan Reserve Requirement," FR, 1980, v15(3),24-35.

Finkelstein, John M. (Chiang, Raymond C. and John M. Finkelstein. "The Multiplicity Of Financial Intermediary Types: The Rationale Re-Examined," IJOF, 1989, v2(1), 18-29.)

Finkelstein, John M. Bank Capital Ratios And Macroeconomic Stability," IJOF, 1990, v2(2), 20-30.

Finkler, Steven A. "What Is Money? The Goldsmith Myth Revisited," JMCB, 1979, v11(4), 483-485.

Finn, Frank J. "Stock Splits: Prior And Subsequent Price Relationships," JBFA, 1974, v1(1), 93-108.

Finn, Frank J. (Ball, Ray and Frank J. Finn. "The Effect Of Block Transactions On Share Prices: Australian Evidence," JBF, 1989, v13(3), 397-420.)

Finn, Frank J. and Ron Higham. "The Performance Of Unseasoned New Equity Issues-Cum-Stock Exchange Listings In Australia," JBF, 1988, v11(3), 333-352.

Finn, Mark T. (Vandell, Robert F. and Mark T. Finn. "Portfolio Objective: Win Big, Lose Little!," JPM, 1982, v8(4), 37-45.)

Finn, Mary G. "Forecasting The Exchange Rate: A Monetary Or Random Walk Phenomenon?," JIMF, 1986, v5(2), 181-193.

Finn, Mary. "An Econometric Analysis Of The Intertemporal General-Equilibrium Approach To Exchange Rate And Current Account Determination," JIMF, 1989, v8(4), 467-486.

Finnerty, John D. "Bank Discount, Coupon Equivalent, And Compound Yields: Comment," FM, 1983, v12(2), 40-44.

Finnerty, John D. "Evaluating The Economics Of Refunding High-Coupon Sinking-Fund Debt," FM, 1983, v12(1), 5-10.

Finnerty, John D. "Measuring The Duration Of A Floating-Rate Bond," JPM, 1989, v15(4), 67-72.

Finnerty, John D. "Preferred Stock Refunding Analysis: Synthesis And Extension," FM, 1984, v13(3), 22-28.

Finnerty, John D. "Real Money Balances And The Firm's Production Function," JMCB, 1980, v12(4), Part 1, 666-671.

Finnerty, John D. "Refunding Discounted Debt: A Clarifying Analysis," JFQA, 1986, v21(1), 95-106.

Finnerty, John D. "Stock-For-Debt Swaps And Shareholder Returns," FM, 1985, v14(3), 5-17.

Finnerty, John D. "The Behavior Of Electric Utility Common Stock Prices Near The Ex-Dividend Date," FM, 1981, v10(5), 59-69.

Finnerty, John D. "The Stock Market's Reaction To The Switch From Flow-Through To Normalization," FM, 1982, v11(4), 36-47.

Finnerty, John D. "Zero Coupon Bond Arbitrage: An Illustration Of The Regulatory Dialectic At Work," FM, 1985, v14(4), 13-17.

Finnerty, John D. Financial Engineering In Corporate Finance: An Overview,"FM, 1988, v17(4),14-33.

Finnerty, John D. and Michael Rose. "Arbitrage-Free Spread: A Consistent Measure Of Relative Value," JPM, 1991, v17(3), 65-81.

Finnerty, John D. and Victor M. Borun. "An Analysis Of Unbundled Stock Units," GFJ, 1989, v1(1), 47-70.

Finnerty, Joseph E. and Kenneth P. Nunn, Jr. "Comparative Yield Spreads On U.S. Corporate Bonds And $Eurobonds," FAJ, 1985, v41(4), 68-73.

Finnerty, Joseph E. and Rick N. Fitzsimmons. "Bank Directors, Interlocking Directorships And Inside Information," FR, 1979, v14(3), 61-67.

Finnerty, Joseph E. "Corporate Stock Issue And Repurchase," FM, 1974, v4(3), 62-66.

Finnerty, Joseph E. "Insiders' Activity And Inside Information: A Multivariate Analysis," JFQA, 1976, v11(2), 205-215.

Finnerty, Joseph E. "Insiders And Market Efficiency," JOF, 1976, v31(4), 1141-1148.

Finnerty, Joseph E. "The Chicago Board Options Exchange And Market Efficiency," JFQA, 1978, v13(1),29-38.

Finnerty, Joseph E. "The Impact Of The New Copyright Revision Bill On Finance Teachers," JFED, 1977, v6, 19.

Finnerty, Joseph E. "The Master Of Science In Finance As An Alternative To The M.B.A.," JFED, 1978, v7, 47-48.

Finnerty, Joseph E. "The Mexican Peso And The Chicago International Money Market: A Case Study In Foreign Currency Futures," JFM, 1984, v4(2),213-224.

Finnerty, Joseph E. (Becker, Kent G., Joseph E. Finnerty and Manoj Gupta. "The Intertemporal Relation Between The U.S. And Japanese Stock Markets," JOF, 1990, v45(4), 1297-1306.)

Finnerty, Joseph E. (Branch, Ben and Joseph E. Finnerty. "The Impact Of Option Listing On The Price And Volume Of The Underlying Stock," FR, 1981, v16(2), 1-15.)

Finnerty, Joseph E. (Lee, Cheng F., Paul Newbold, Joseph E. Finnerty and Chen-Chin Chu. "On Accounting-Based, Market-Based And Composite-Based Beta Predictions: Methods And Implications," FR, 1986, v21(1), 51-68.)

Finnerty, Joseph E. and Hun Y. Park. "Stock Index Futures: Does The Tail Wag The Dog?," FAJ, 1987, v43(2), 56-61.

Finnerty, Joseph E. and Kenneth P. Nunn, Jr. "Valuation And The Impact Of Corporate Firm, Taxes, And Leverage On Multinational Net Income Under FASB #8 And FASB #52," AFPAF, 1987, v2(1), 87-102.

Finnerty, Joseph E. and Thomas W. Oliver. "The Impact Of Qualified Audit Opinions On Systematic Risk," AFPAF, 1985, v1(1), 293-306.

Finnerty, Joseph E., Thomas Schneeweis and Shantaram P. Hegde. "Interest Rates In The $Eurobond Market," JFQA, 1980, v15(3), 743-755.

Finnerty, Joseph E. and Hun Y. Park. "How To Profit From Program Trading," JPM, 1988, v14(2),40-46.

Finucane, Thomas J. "A Simple Linear Weighting Scheme For Black-Scholes Implied Volatilities - A Note," JBF, 1989, v13(2), 321-326.

Finucane, Thomas J. "Black-Scholes Approximations Of Call Option Prices With Stochastic Volatilities: A Note," JFQA, 1989, v24(4), 527-532.

Finucane, Thomas J. "Options On U.S. Treasury Coupon Issues," FR, 1988, v23(4), 403-426.

Finucane, Thomas J. "Some Empirical Evidence On The Use Of Financial Leases," JFR, 1988, v11(4),321-334.

Fiore, Lyle C. (Johnson, R. Stafford, Lyle C. Fiore and Richard Zuber. "The Investment Performance Of Common Stocks In Relation To Their Price-Earnings Ratios: An Update Of The Basu Study," FR, 1989, v24(3), 499-506.)

Firch, Robert S. "Futures Markets As Inverse Forecasters Of Postharvest Prices For Storable Agricultural Commodities," RFM, 1982, v1(1), 62-73.

Firstenberg, Paul B. (Malkiel, Burton G. and Paul B. Firstenberg. "A Winning Strategy For An Efficient Market," JPM, 1978, v4(4), 20-25.)

Firstenberg, Paul M., Stephen A. Ross and Randall C. Zisler. "Real Estate: The Whole Story," JPM, 1988, v14(3), 22-34.

Firth, Michael A. "The Investment Performance Of Unit Trusts In The Period 1965-75," JMCB, 1977, v9(4), 597-604.

Firth, Michael. "A Note On The Impact Of Audit Qualifications On Lending And Credit Decisions," JBF, 1980, v4(3), 257-267.

Firth, Michael. "An Empirical Investigation Of The Impact Of The Announcement Of Capitalisation Issues On Share Prices," JBFA, 1977, v4(1), 47-60.

Firth, Michael. "Qualified Audit Reports And Bank Lending Decisions," JBR, 1978-79, v9(4), 237-241.

Firth, Michael. "Synergism In Mergers: Some British Results," JOF, 1978, v33(2), 670-672.

Firth, Michael. "The Information Content Of Large Investment Holdings," JOF, 1975, v30(5),1265-1281.

Firth, Michael. "The Relationship Between Stock Market Returns And Rates Of Inflation," JOF, 1979, v34(3), 743-749.

Fisch, Gerald G. "Management In Financial Analysis," FAJ, 1968, v24(4), 43-49.

Fischel, Daniel R. and Sanford J. Grossman. "Customer Protection In Futures And Securities Markets," JFM, 1984, v4(3), 273-296.

Fischel, Daniel R. "Regulatory Conflict And Entry Regulation Of New Futures Contracts," JOB, 1986, v59(2), Part 2, S85-S102.

Fischer, Carl H. "Social Security In The Philippines," JRI, 1957, v24(4), 64-75.

Fischer, Carl H. "The Actuarial Curriculum: Comment," JRI, 1966, v33(3), 477-478.

Fischer, Carl H. "The Basic Life Insurance Course In The Curriculum," JRI, 1954, v21, 18-21.

Fischer, D. E. (Brigham, E. F., D. E. Fischer, K. B. Johnson and R. J. Jordan. "What Makes Short Cases Work In The Basic Finance Course?," JFED, 1972, v1, 65-68.)

Fischer, Donald E. and Gerald P. Madden. "Improving The Investments Course With A Securities Trading Game," JFED, 1979, v8, 71-76.

Fischer, Donald E. and Glenn A. Wilt, Jr. "Non-Convertible Preferred Stock As A Financing Instrument, 1950-1965," JOF, 1968, v23(4), 611-624.

Fischer, Donald E. "A Simplification Of FINANSIM," JFED, 1974, v3, 85-89.

Fischer, Edwin O., Robert Heinkel and Josef Zechner. "Dynamic Capital Structure Choice: Theory And Tests," JOF, 1989, v44(1), 19-40.

Fischer, Edwin O., Robert Heinkel and Josef Zechner. "Dynamic Recapitalization Policies And The Role Of Call Premia And Issue Discounts," JFQA, 1989, v24(4), 427-446.

Fischer, Gerald C. and Lawrence J. Minet. "No-Load Mutual Funds," FAJ, 1964, v20(1), 64-68.

Fischer, Gerald C. "Bank Holding-Company Affiliates: Branches Or Unit Banks?," JOB, 1964, v37(1), 47-48.

Fischer, K. P. and A. P. Palasvirta. "High Road To A Global Marketplace: The International Transmission Of Stock Market Fluctuations," FR, 1990, v25(3), 371-394.

Fischer, Philip J. (Shawky, Hany A. and Philip J. Fischer. "Imperfect Contracts, Me-First Rules, And Firm Value," FR, 1983, v18(1), 79-93.)

Fischer, Philip. (Arak, Marcelle, Philip Fischer, Laurie Goodman and Raj Daryanani. "The Municipal-Treasury Futures Spread," JFM, 1987, v7(4), 355-372.)

Fischer, R. M. "Intangibles In Market Value Of Successful Companies," FAJ, 1951, v7(4), 91.

Fischer, R. M. "Measuring Stability," FAJ, 1948, v4(3), 19-25.

Fischer, R. M. "The Accuracy Of Forecasts," FAJ, 1954, v10(1), 73-80.

Fischer, Stanley and John Huizinga. "Inflation, Unemployment, And Public Opinion Polls," JMCB, 1982, v14(1), 1-19.

Fischer, Stanley. "A Neoclassical Monetary Growth Model: A Comment," JMCB, 1973, v5(2), 704-706.

Fischer, Stanley. "Call Option Pricing When The Exercise Price Is Uncertain, And The Valuation Of Index Bonds," JOF, 1978, v33(1), 169-176.

Fischer, Stanley. "Supply Shocks, Wage Stickiness, And Accommodation," JMCB, 1985, v17(1), 1-15.

Fischer, Stanley. (Cooper, J. Phillip and Stanley Fischer. "Monetary And Fiscal Policy In The Fully Stochastic St. Louis Econometric Model," JMCB, 1974, v6(1), 1-22.)

Fischer, Stanley. (Cooper, J. Phillip and Stanley Fischer. "The Use Of The Secant Method In Econometric Models," JOB, 1973, v46(2), 274-277.)

Fischer, Stanley. (Cooper, J. Phillip and Stanley Fischer. "Simulations Of Monetary Rules In The FRB-MIT-Penn Model," JMCB, 1972, v4(2), 384-396.)

Fischhoff, Baruch and Lita Furby. "Measuring Values: A Conceptual Framework For Interpreting Transactions With Special Reference To Contingent Valuation Of Visibility," JRU, 1988, v1(2), 147-184.

Fischhoff, Baruch. "Understanding Long-Term Environmental Risks," JRU, 1990, v3(4), 315-330.

Fischhoff, Baruch. (Slovic, Paul, Baruch Fischhoff, Sarah Lichtenstein, Bernard Corrigan and Barbara Combs. "Preference For Insuring Against Probable Small Losses: Insurance Implications," JRI, 1977, v44(2), 237-258.)

Fishbein, Richard. "Closed-End Investment Companies," FAJ, 1970, v26(2), 67-73.

Fishburn, Peter C. "Expected Utility: An Anniversary And A New Era," JRU, 1988, v1(3), 267-284.

Fishburn, Peter C. "Stochastic Dominance And The Foundations Of Mean-Variance Analyses," RIF, 1980, v2, 69-98.

Fishburn, Peter C. (Luce, R. Duncan and Peter C. Fishburn. "Rank-And Sign-Dependent Linear Utility Models For Finite First-Order Gambles," JRU, 1991, v4(1), 29-60.)

Fishburn, Peter. "Retrospective On The Utility Theory Of Von Neumann And Morgenstern," JRU, 1989, v2(2), 127-158.

Fishe, Raymond P. H. and Lawrence G. Goldberg. "The Effects Of Margins On Trading In Futures Markets," JFM, 1986, v6(2), 261-272.

Fishe, Raymond P. H. "On Testing Hypotheses Using The Livingston Price Expectations Data," JMCB, 1984, v16(4), Part 1, 520-527.

Fishelson, Gideon. "Now is the time for all good men to come to the Sujata Sinha. "Margin Requirements In Futures Markets: Their Relationship To Price Volatility," JFM, 1990, v10(5), 541-554.

Fishelson, Gideon. "Help-Wanted Advertisements: A Case Study, Israel 1965-71.," JOB, 1974, v47(2), 208-217.

Fisher, A. K. (McDonald, J. G. and A. K. Fisher. "New-Issue Stock Price Behavior," JOF, 1972, v27(1), 97-102.)

Fisher, Ann. (Fisher, Warren, Norman Starler and Ann Fisher. "A Method For Building A Property Values' Index For Use In Local Public Policy Decisions," AREUEA, 1976, v4(2), 77-90.)

Fisher, Ann. (Smith, V. Kerry, William H. Desvousges, Ann Fisher and F. Reed Johnson. "Learning About Radon's Risk," JRU, 1988, v1(2), 233-258.)

Fisher, Arthur L. "Investment Opportunities In Retailing," FAJ, 1973, v29(4), 52-54,61.

Fisher, Arthur L. "Money Managers Don't Behave Like Capitalists," FAJ, 1977, v33(1), 21-25.

Fisher, Douglas. "The Objectives Of British Monetary Policy, 1951-1964," JOF, 1968, v23(5), 821-831.

Fisher, Douglas. (Ewis, Nabil A. and Douglas Fisher. "The Translog Utility Function And The Demand For Money In The United States," JMCB, 1984, v16(1), 34-52.)

Fisher, Eric O'N. (Edison, Hali J. and Eric O'N. Fisher. "A Long-View Of The European Monetary System," JIMF, 1991, v10(1), 53-70.)

Fisher, Ernest M. "Overcrowded' Households In The United States," AREUEA, 1976, v4(3), 93-111.

Fisher, Ernest M. "Changing Institutional Patterns Of Mortgage Lending," JOF, 1950, v5(4),307-315.

Fisher, Ernest M. "Evaluation Of National Housing Goals," AREUEA, 1973, v1(2), 5-20.

Fisher, Ernest M. "Speculative Development Of Residential Land And Residential Structures During The 1920's And The 1960's And 1970's," AREUEA, 1973, v1(1), 123-139.

Fisher, G. H. "Input-Output Technique As An Aid In Security Analysis," FAJ, 1953, v9(1), 85-94.

Fisher, Glen. (Boehlje, Michael and Glen Fisher. "A Competitive Management Game For Non-Metropolitan Commercial Banks," JBR, 1976-77, v7(1), 56-67.)

Fisher, Jeffrey C. (Brueggeman, William B., Jeffrey D. Fisher and David M. Porter. "Rethinking Corporate Real Estate," JACF, 1990, v3(1), 39-50.)

Fisher, Jeffrey D. (Brueggeman, William B., Jeffrey D. Fisher and Jerrold J. Stern. "Federal Income Taxes, Inflation And Holding Periods For Income-Producing Property," AREUEA, 1981, v9(2), 148-164.)

Fisher, Jeffrey D. (Lentz, George H. and Jeffrey D. Fisher. "Tax Reform And Organizational Forms For Holding Investment Real Estate: Corporation Vs. Partnership," AREUEA, 1989, v17(3), 314-337.) 3 ?8

Fisher, Jeffrey D. (Lusht, Kenneth M. and Jeffrey D. Fisher. "Anticipated Growth And The Specification Of Debt In Real Estate Value Models," AREUEA, 1984, v12(1), 1-11.)

Fisher, Jeffrey D. and George H. Lentz. "Tax Reform And The Value Of Real Estate Income Property," AREUEA, 1986, v14(2), 287-315.

Fisher, Jeffrey D. and George H. Lentz. "Business Enterprise Value In Shopping Malls: An Empirical Test," JRER, 1990, v5(1), 167-175.

Fisher, L. and J. H. Lorie. "Rates Of Return On Investments In Common Stocks," JOB, 1964, v37(1), 1-21.

Fisher, Lawrence and James H. Lorie. "Knowledge Makes A Difference - A Reply To Dr. Leo Barnes," FAJ, 1965, v21(6), 118-120.

Fisher, Lawrence and Jules H. Kamin. "Forecasting Systematic Risk: Estimates Of 'Raw' Beta That Take Account Of The Tendency Of Beta To Change And The Heteroskedasticity Of Residual Returns," JFQA, 1985, v20(2), 127-150.

Fisher, Lawrence and Roman L. Weil. "Coping With The Risk Of Interest-Rate Fluctuations: Returns To Bondholders From Naive And Optimal Strategies," JOB, 1971, v44(4), 408-431.

Fisher, Lawrence and James H. Lorie. "Rates Of Return On Investments In Common Stock: The Year-By-Year Record, 1926-65," JOB, 1968, v41(3), 291-316.

Fisher, Lawrence and James H. Lorie. "Some Studies Of Variability Of Returns On Investments In Common Stocks," JOB, 1970, v43(2), 99-134.

Fisher, Lawrence, Ivan E. Brick and Francis K. W. Ng. "Tax Incentives And Financial Innovation: The Case Of Zero-Coupon And Other Deep-Discount Corporate Bonds," FR, 1983, v18(4), 292-305.

Fisher, Lawrence. "An Algorithm For Finding Exact Rates Of Return," JOB, 1966, v39(1), Part II, 111-118.

Fisher, Lawrence. "Analysts' Input And Portfolio Changes," FAJ, 1975, v31(3), 73-85.

Fisher, Lawrence. "Outcomes For 'Random' Investments In Common Stocks Listed On The New York Stock Exchange," JOB, 1965, v38(2), 149-161.

Fisher, Lawrence. "Some New Stock Market Indexes," JOB, 1966, v39(1), Part II, 191-225.

Fisher, Lawrence. (Brick, Ivan E. and Lawrence Fisher. "Effects Of Classifying Equity Or Debt On The Value Of The Firm Under Uncertainty," JFQA, 1987, v22(4), 383-400.)

Fisher, Lawrence. (Treynor, Jack L., William W. Priest, Jr., Lawrence Fisher and Catherine A. Higgins. "Risk Estimates," FAJ, 1968, v24(5), 93-100.)

Fisher, Lawrence. (Weil, Roman L. and Lawrence Fisher. "TIAA/CREF: Who Gets What? An Analysis Of Wealth Transfers In A Variable Annuity," JOB, 1974, v47(1), 67-87.)

Fisher, Lawrence. "Some Reflections On The Context Of The Discoveries of Markowitz, Miller, And Sharpe And Their Significance Immediately After They Were Made," RQFA, 1991, v1(2), 210-213.

Fisher, Lee. (Steves, Buddy, Archer McWhorter, Jr. and Lee Fisher. "An Empirical Analysis Of The Capacity Crisis In Medical Malpractice Insurance," JRI, 1979, v46(1), 139-146.)

Fisher, Paul S. "Group Accident And Health Insurance," JRI, 1945, v12, 5-10.

Fisher, Philip A. "Why Do Not Financial Analysts Make More Money?," FAJ, 1954, v10(2), 65-68.

Fisher, Robert Moore and Charles J. Siegman. "Patterns Of Housing Experience During Periods Of Credit Restraint In Industrialized Countries," JOF, 1972, v27(2), 193-205.

Fisher, Robert Moore. "Housing Production, Consumption, Statistics, And Policy," AREUEA, 1976, v4(3), 7-18.

Fisher, Robert Moore. "Outlook For Mortgage Markets," JOF, 1960, v15(2), 280-284.

Fisher, Robert Moore. "Public Costs Of Urban Renewal," JOF, 1962, v17(2), 379-386.

Fisher, Warren, Norman Starler and Ann Fisher. "A Method For Building A Property Values' Index For Use In Local Public Policy Decisions," AREUEA, 1976, v4(2), 77-90.

Fishman, Gerald L. "Dealer Options," JPM, 1981, v1(Supp), 535-538.

Fishman, Leo. "Limitations Of The Business Executive As Government Administrator," JOB, 1952, v25(2), 89-94.

Fishman, Michael J. "Preemptive Bidding And The Role Of The Medium Of Exchange In Acquisitions," JOF, 1989, v44(1), 41-58.

Fishman, Michael J. and Kathleen M. Hagerty. "Disclosure Decisions By Firms And The Competition For Price Efficiency," JOF, 1989, v44(3), 633-646.

Fisk, Charles and Frank Rimlinger. "Nonparametric Estimates Of LDC Repayment Prospects," JOF, 1979, v34(2), 429-436.

Fissel, Gary S. and Tullio Jappelli. "Do Liquidity Constraints Vary Over Time? Evidence From Survey And Panel Data," JMCB, 1990, v22(2), 253-262.

Fitts, Robert L. (Martell, Terrence F. and Robert L. Fitts. "Determinants Of Bank Trust Department Usage," JBR, 1978-79, v9(1), 8-14.)

FitzGerald, Michael T. (Clarke, Roger G., Michael T. FitzGerald, Phillip Berent and Meir Statman. "Market Timing With Imperfect Information," FAJ, 1989, v45(6), 27-36.)

Fitzgerald, John F. (Brainard, Calvin H. and John F. Fitzgerald. "First-Year Cost Results Under No-Fault Automobile Insurance: A Comparison Of The Florida And Massachusetts Experience," JRI, 1974, v41(1), 25-39.)

Fitzgerald, John F., Jr. "Demutalization Of Mutual Property And Liability Insurers," JRI, 1973, v40(4), 575-584.

Fitzgerald, John. "The Effects Of Social Security On Life Insurance Demand By Married Couples," JRI, 1987, v54(1), 86-99.

Fitzgerald, M. Desmond. (Figlewski, Stephen and M. Desmond Fitzgerald. "The Price Behaviour Of London Commodity Options," RFM, 1982, v1(1), 90-104.)

Fitzgerald, M. Desmond. (Fildes, Robert A. and M. Desmond Fitzgerald. "Efficiency And Premiums In The Short-Term Money Market," JMCB, 1980, v12(4), Part 1, 615-629.)

Fitzgerald, Michael T. (Clarke, Roger G., Michael T. Fitzgerald, Philip Berent and Meir Statman. "Diversifying Among Asset Allocators," JPM, 1990, v16(3), 9-14.)

Fitzgerald, Michael T. (Clarke, Roger G., Michael T. Fitzgerald, Philip Berent and Meir Statman. "Required Accuracy For Successful Asset Allocation," JPM, 1990, v17(1), 12-19.)

Fitzpatrick, Dennis B. "An Analysis Of Bank Credit Card Profits," JBR, 1976-77, v7(3), 199-205.

Fitzpatrick, John D. and Jacobus T. Severiens. "Hickman Revisited: The Case For Junk Bonds," JPM, 1978, v4(4), 53-57.

Fitzsimmons, Rick N. (Finnerty, Joseph E. and Rick N. Fitzsimmons. "Bank Directors, Interlocking Directorships And Inside Information," FR, 1979, v14(3), 61-67.)

Fix, Robert F. and Charles M. Sivesind. "An Assessment Of The Income Stabilization Impact Of Monetary Policy In Twelve Industrialized Countries," JMCB, 1978, v10(4), 476-490.

Flaherty, Ross A. "Realistic Analysis Projects For The Fundamental Business Finance Course," JFED, 1974, v3, 79-81.

Flamholtz, Eric G. "Group Dynamics In Task Performance And Human Resource Accounting: A Reply," JBFA, 1977, v4(4), 481-484.

Flamholtz, Eric. "Toward A Formal Model Of Group Dynamics In Task Performance Relevant To Accounting," JBFA, 1976, v3(4), 3-26.

Flamholtz, Eric. (Oliver, Jan and Eric Flamholtz. "Human Resource Replacement Cost Numbers, Cognitive Information Processing, And Personnel Decisions: A Laboratory Experiment," JBFA, 1978, v5(2), 137-158.)

Flanagan, John R. "Pacific Northwest Forest Products," FAJ, 1969, v25(1), 69-71.

Flanigan, George B. "Investment Income In Rate-Making And Managerial Investment Attitudes," JRI, 1974, v41(2), 229-237.

Flanigan, George B. (Johnson, Joseph E. and George B. Flanigan. "Exceptions To Current Risk Dichotomies," JRI, 1977, v44(2), 329-334.)

Flanigan, George B. (Johnson, Joseph E., George B. Flanigan and Steven N. Weisbart. "Returns To Scale In The Property And Liability Insurance Industry," JRI, 1981, v48(1), 18-45.)

Flanigan, George B. (Winkler, Daniel T., George B. Flanigan and Joseph E. Johnson. "Solving For The Number Of Cash Flows And Periods In Financial Problems," JFED, 1990, v19(1), 62-65.)

Flanigan, George B. and Sheldon D. Balbirer. "Some Findings On The Costs And Benefits Of Mutual Fund Insurance," JRI, 1978, v45(4), 675-682.

Flanigan, George B., Joseph E. Johnson, Daniel T. Winkler and William Ferguson. "Experience From Early Tort Reforms: Comparative Negligence Since 1974," JRI, 1989, v56(3), 525-534.

Flannery, Mark J. and Christopher M. James. "Market Evidence Of The Effective Maturity Of Bank Assets And Liabilities," JMCB, 1984, v16(4), Part 1, 435-445.

Flannery, Mark J. and Christopher M. James. "The Effect Of Interest Rate Changes On The Common Stock Returns Of Financial Institutions," JOF, 1984, v39(4), 1141-1153.

Flannery, Mark J. "Asymmetric Information And Risky Debt Maturity Choice," JOF, 1986, v41(1), 19-38.

Flannery, Mark J. "Can State Bank Examination Data Replace FDIC Visits?," JBR, 1982-83, v13(4),312-316.

Flannery, Mark J. "Correspondent Services And Cost Economies In Commercial Banking," JBF, 1983, v7(1), 83-99.

Flannery, Mark J. "Interest Rates And Bank Profitability: Additional Evidence," JMCB, 1983, v15(3), 355-362.

Flannery, Mark J. "Market Interest Rates And Commercial Bank Profitability: An Empirical Investigation," JOF, 1981, v36(5), 1085-1101.

Flannery, Mark J. and Aris A. Protopapadakis. "From T-Bills To Common Stocks: Investigating The Generality Of Intra-Week Return Seasonality," JOF, 1988, v43(2), 431-450.

Flath, David and Charles R. Knoeber. "Taxes, Failure Costs, And

Optimal Industry Capital Structure: An Empirical Test," JOF, 1980, v35(1), 99-117.

Flavell, R. B. and G. R. Salkin. "A Sequential Analysis Of Large-Scale Investment Projects," JBFA, 1974, v1(1), 75-91.

Flavell, R. B. (Raine, P. S., R. B. Flavell and G. R. Salkin. "A Likelihood Control System For Use With Formal Planning Models," JBFA, 1981, v8(2),249-266.)

Flechsig, Theodore G. "The Effect Of Concentration On Bank Loan Rates," JOF, 1965, v20(2), 298-311.

Fleischer, A. (Boies, D., D. Carroll, A. Fleischer, J. Grundfest, J. Ira Harris, M. Lipton, R. Monks, A. Oliver, L. Sachnoff and J. Wilcox. "Panel: Corporate Governance: The Role Of Boards Of Directors In Takeover Bids And Defenses," JACF, 1989, v2(2), 6-35.)

Fleischman, Edward H., William E. Seale, Karsten Mahlmann and Hans R. Stoll. "Panel Discussion On Regulatory Issues Facing The Futures Industry," RFM, 1981, v7(1), 200-216.

Fleissner, Dan. (Slovic, Paul, Dan Fleissner and W. Scott Bauman. "Analyzing The Use Of Information In Investment Decision Making: A Methodological Proposal," JOB, 1972, v45(2), 283-301.)

Fleming, Robert M. "How Risky Is The Market?," JOB, 1973, v46(3), 404-424.

Flemming, Arthur S. "Social Insurance: A Prospective View," JRI, 1960, v27(1), 37-42.

Flesaker, Bjorn and Ehud I. Ronn. "Inflation Futures And A Riskless Real Interest Rate," RFM, 1988, v7(1), 36-67.

Flesaker, Bjorn and Ehud I. Ronn. "Inflation Futures And A Riskless Real Interest Rate," RFM, 1988, v7(1), 36-67.

Flesaker, Bjorn. "The Relationship Between Forward And Futures Contracts: A Comment," JFM, 1991, v11(1), 113-116.

Fletcher, Harold D. (Holman, Walter R. and Harold D. Fletcher. "Flow Through Versus Normalization Accounting For Electric Utilities - The Phantom Tax Issue," FR, 1981, v16(2), 30-40.)

Fletcher, Leslie. (Scapens, Robert W., Robert J. Ryan and Leslie Fletcher. "Explaining Corporate Failure: A Catastrophe Theory Approach," JBFA, 1981, v8(1), 1-26.)

Fletcher, Linda Pickthorne and Robert S. Felton. "Toward The Development Of A 'Bibliography Of Teaching And Research Material'," JRI, 1969, v36(2), 299-304.

Fletcher, Linda Pickthorne and Susan Phillips. "The Cost Of Funding Benefits Under The ERISA: A Statistical Survey: Reply," JRI, 1979, v46(3), 547-549.

Fletcher, Linda Pickthorne. "Motivations Underlying The Mutualization Of Stock Life Insurance Companies," JRI, 1966, v33(1), 19-32.

Fletcher, Linda Pickthorne. "Prepaid Drug Plans Sponsored By Pharmacists," JRI, 1967, v34(1), 81-94.

Fletcher, Linda Pickthorne. "Two Controversial Problems In Third-Party Outpatient Prescription Plans: Comment," JRI, 1974, v41(4), 739-741.

Fletcher, Linda Pickthorne. (Phillips, Susan and Linda Pickthorne Fletcher. "The Cost Of Funding Benefits Under ERISA: A Statistical Survey," JRI, 1976, v43(4), 569-585.)

Fletcher, Linda Pickthorne. (Phillips, Susan Meridith and Linda Pickthorne Fletcher. "The Cost Of Funding Benefits Under The ERISA: A Statistical Survey: Reply," JRI, 1978, v45(1), 137-140.)

Fletcher, Linda Pickthrone. "The Black-Owned Life Insurance Company: Comment," JRI, 1975, v42(2), 351-354.

Flood, Eugene, Jr. and Donald R. Lessard. "On The Measurement Of Operating Exposure To Exchange Rates: A Conceptual Approach," FM, 1986, v15(1),25-36.

Flood, Robert P. and Nancy P. Marion. "Exchange-Rate Regimes In Transition: Italy 1974," JIMF, 1983, v2(3), 279-294.

Flood, Robert P. and Robert J. Hodrick. "Asset Price Volatility, Bubbles, And Process Switching," JOF, 1986, v41(4), 831-842.

Flood, Robert P. (Engel, Charles M. and Robert P. Flood. "Exchange Rate Dynamics, Sticky Prices, And The Current Account," JMCB, 1985, v17(3), 312-327.)

Florer, Herbert W. (Greene, Mark R., John W. McPherrin and Herbert W. Florer. "Curricular Concepts In Risk And Insurance," JRI, 1963, v30(1), 129-132.)

Flowers, Edward B. "Taiwan's Potential For Foreign Direct Investment In The United States," AFPAF, 1985, v1(Supp), 91-118.

Floyd, Joe S., Jr. "Rate Of Return And Allocation Of Life Insurance Company Investments," JRI, 1962, v29(3), 417-423.

Floyd, John E. and J. Allan Hynes. "The Structure Of Production, The Composition Of Financial Demand, And The Determination Of Price Level And Employment," JMCB, 1978, v10(2), 222-238.

Floyd, John E. and J. Allan Hynes. "The Contribution Of Real Money Balances To The Level Of Wealth," JMCB, 1972, v4(2), 260-271.

Floyd, Richard. (Starleaf, Dennis R. and Richard Floyd. "Some Evidence With Respect To The Efficacy Of Friedman's Monetary Policy Proposals: A Comment," JMCB, 1972, v4(3), 713-722.)

Fluegel, Frederick K. "High And Low P/E Ratio Stocks," FAJ, 1968, v24(6), 130-133.

Flynn, Joseph E. (Mayo, John W. and Joseph E. Flynn. "The Effects Of Regulation On Research And Development: Theory And Evidence," JOB, 1988, v61(3), 321-336.)

Fogler, H. Russell and Michael Joehnk. "Deep Discount Bonds: How Well Do They Perform?," JPM, 1979, v5(3), 59-62.

Fogler, H. Russell and Robert C. Radcliffe. "A Note On Measurement Of Skewness," JFQA, 1974, v9(3), 485-489.

Fogler, H. Russell and S. Ganapathy. "Comment On: 'A Quantitative Yield Curve Model For Estimating The Term Structure Of Interest Rates'," JFQA, 1980, v15(2), 449-456.

Fogler, H. Russell and William A. Groves. "How Much Can Active Bond Management Raise Returns?," JPM, 1976, v3(1), 35-40.

Fogler, H. Russell, Kose John and James Tipton. "Three Factors, Interest Rate Differentials And Stock Groups," JOF, 1981, v36(2), 323-335.

Fogler, H. Russell, William A. Groves and James G. Richardson. "Bond Management: Are 'Dumbbells', Smart?," JPM, 1976, v2(2), 54-60.

Fogler, H. Russell, William A. Groves and James G. Richardson. "Bond Portfolio Strategies, Returns, And Skewness: A Note," JFQA, 1977, v12(1), 127-140.

Fogler, H. Russell, Michael R. Granito and Laurence Smith. "A Theoretical Analysis Of Real Estate Returns," JOF, 1985, v40(3), 711-719.

Fogler, H. Russell. "20% In Real Estate: Can Theory Justify It?," JPM, 1984, v10(2), 6-13.

Fogler, H. Russell. "Bond Portfolio Immunization, Inflation, And The Fisher Equation," JRI, 1984, v51(2), 244-264.

Fogler, H. Russell. "Common Sense On CAPM, APT, And Correlated Residuals," JPM, 1982, v8(4),20-28.

Fogler, H. Russell. "Common Stock Management In The 1990s," JPM, 1990, v16(2), 26-35.

Fogler, H. Russell. "Overkill In Capital Budgeting Techniques?," FM, 1972, v1(1), 92-96.

Fogler, H. Russell. (Dietz, Peter O., H. Russell Fogler and Donald J. Hardy. "The Challenge Of Analyzing Bond Portfolio Returns," JPM, 1980, v6(3), 53-58.)

Fogler, H. Russell. (Dietz, Peter O., H. Russell Fogler and Anthony U. Rivers. "Duration, Nonlinearity, And Bond Portfolio Performance," JPM, 1981, v7(3), 37-41.)

Fogler, H. Russell. (Dietz, Peter O. and H. Russell Fogler. "Pension Portfolio Objective: Connecting The Loop," FM, 1978, v7(2), 56-62.)

Fogler, H. Russell. (Joehnk, Michael D., H. Russell Fogler and Charles E. Bradley. "The Price Elasticity Of Discounted Bonds: Some Empirical Evidence," JFQA, 1978, v13(3), 559-566.)

Foley, B. J. (Maunders, K. T. and B. J. Foley. "Accounting Information, Employees And Collective Bargaining," JBFA, 1974, v1(1),109-127.)

Folks, William R., Jr. "Decision Analysis For Exchange Risk Management," FM, 1972, v1(3), 101-112.

Folks, William R., Jr. "International Finance In The Master Of International Business Studies Program," JFED, 1974, v3, 45-50.

Folks, William R., Jr. "Integrating International Finance Into A Unified Business Program," JFQA, 1977, v12(4), 599-600.

Folks, William R., Jr. "Optimal Foreign Borrowing Strategies With Operations In Forward Exchange Markets," JFQA, 1978, v13(2), 245-254.

Folks, William R., Jr. "The Optimal Level Of Forward Exchange Transactions," JFQA, 1973, v8(1), 105-110.

Folks, William R., Jr. "The Analysis Of Short-Term Cross-Border Financing Decisions," FM, 1976, v5(3), 19-27.

Folks, William R., Jr. and Chuck C. Y. Kwok. "A New Way To Cover Foreign Currency Bonds," RDIBF, 1987, v1, 103-116.

Follain, James R. "Mortgage Choice," AREUEA, 1990, v18(2), 125-144.

Follain, James R. (Blackley, Dixie M., James R. Follain and Haeduck Lee. "An Evaluation Of Hedonic Price Indexes For 34 Large SMSAs," AREUEA, 1986, v14(2), 179-205.)

Follain, James R. and David C. Ling. "Another Look At Tenure Choice, Inflation, And Taxes," AREUEA, 1988, v16(3), 207-229.

Follain, James R. and Hun Y. Park. "Hedging The Interest Rate Risk Of Mortgages With Prepayment Options," RFM, 1989, v8(1), 62-78.

Follain, James R., Jr. "A Study Of The Demand For Housing By Low Versus High Income Households," JFQA, 1979, v14(4), 769-782.

Follain, James R., Jr. "How Well Do Section 8 FMRs (Fair Market Rent) Match The Cost Of Rental Housing? Data From Thirty-Nine Large Cities," AREUEA, 1979, v7(4), 466-481.

Follain, James R., Jr. (Alm, James and James R. Follain, Jr. "Alternative Mortgage Instruments, The Tilt Problem, And Consumer Welfare," JFQA, 1984, v19(1), 113-126.)

Follain, James R., Terry Lutes and David A. Meier. "Why Do Some Real Estate Salespeople Earn More Than Others?," JRER, 1987, v2(1), 73-81.

Follain, James and Raymond Struyk. "Homeownership Effects Of Alternative Mortgage Instruments," AREUEA, 1977, v5(1), 1-43.

Follmann, J. F., Jr. "Experience Rating Vs. Community Rating," JRI, 1962, v29(3), 403-416.

Follmann, J. F., Jr. "Some Medico-Economic Trends," JRI, 1960, v27(2), 45-58.

Follmann, J. F., Jr. "The Growth Of Group Health Insurance," JRI, 1965, v32(1), 105-112.

Followill, Richard A. "Relative Call Futures Option Pricing: An Examination Of Market Efficiency," RFM, 1987, v6(3), 354-381.

Followill, Richard A. and Billy P. Helms. "Put-Call-Futures Parity And Arbitrage Opportunity In The Market For Options On Gold Futures Contracts," JPM, 1990, v10(4), 339-352.

Followill, Richard A., Michael Schellenger and Patrick H. Marchand. "Economic Order Quantities, Volume Discounts, And Wealth Maximization," FR, 1990, v25(1), 143-152.

Followill, Richard. "Present Value And Future Value Of An Annuity Growing By A Constant Amount," JFED, 1989, v18, 15-18.

Fonfeder, Robert. (Fabozzi, Frank J., Robert Fonfeder and Patrick Casabona. "An Empirical Examination Of The Impact Of Limited Review On Equity Prices," JBFA, 1983, v10(1), 127-138.)

Fonfeder, Robert. (Fabozzi, Frank J. and Robert Fonfeder. "Have You Seen Any Good Quarterly Statements Lately?," JPM, 1983, v9(2), 71-74.)

Fonfeder, Robert. (Garlicki, T. Dessa, Frank J. Fabozzi and Robert Fonfeder. "The Impact Of Earnings Under FASB 52 On Equity Returns," FM, 1987, v16(3),36-44.)

Fong, Gifford, Charles Pearson and Oldrich Vasicek. "Bond Performance: Analyzing Sources Of Return," JPM, 1983, v9(3), 46-50.

Fong, H. Gifford and Frank J. Fabozzi. "How To Enhance Bond Returns With Naive Strategies," JPM, 1985, v11(4), 57-60.

Fong, H. Gifford and Oldrich A. Vasicek. "A Risk Minimizing Strategy For Portfolio Immunization," JOF, 1984, v39(5), 1541-1546.

Fong, H. Gifford and Oldrich Vasicek. "The Tradeoff Between Return And Risk In Immunized Portfolios," FAJ, 1983, v39(5), 73-78.

Fong, H. Gifford and Eric M. P. Tang. "Immunized Bond Portfolios In Portfolio Protection," JPM, 1988, v14(2), 63-68.

Fong, H. Gifford and Oldrich A. Vasicek. "Forecast-Free International Asset Allocation," FAJ, 1989, v45(2), 29-33.

Fong, H. Gifford. "An Alternative To Indexing," JPM, 1978, v5(1), 33-37.

Fong, H. Gifford. "An Asset Allocation Framework," JPM, 1980, v6(2), 58-66.

Fong, H. Gifford. (Vasicek, Oldrich A. and H. Gifford Fong. "Term Structure Modeling Using Exponential Splines," JOF, 1982, v37(2), 339-348.)

Fons, Jerome S. "The Default Premium And Corporate Bond Experience," JOF, 1987, v42(1), 81-97.

Fonseca, John R. "The Impact Of Automation On Insurance Education And Management," JRI, 1961, v28(3), 81-88.

Foody, Walter M. and Eldon J. Klaassen. "Financing Medical Care For The Aged," JRI, 1962, v29(2), 221-228.

Fooladi, Iraj and Gordon S. Roberts. "On Preferred Stock," JFR, 1986, v9(4), 319-324.

Fooladi, Iraj and Gordon S. Roberts. "Dividend Changes And Preferred Stock Returns," IJOF, 1988, v1(1), 96-112.

Fooladi, Iraj, Gordon Roberts and Jerry Viscione. "Captive Finance Subsidiaries: Overview And Synthesis," FR, 1986, v21(2), 259-275.

Fooladi, Iraj, Patricia McGraw and Gordon S. Roberts. "Preferred Stock And Taxes," JBFA, 1991, v18(1), 99-108.

Foote, William G. "The Rationality And Efficiency Of Stock Price Relative To Money Announcement Information," FR, 1989, v24(2), 281-298.

Forbes, Ronald W. and Paul A. Leonard. "The Effects Of Statutory Portfolio Constraints On Tax-Exempt Interest Rates," JMCB, 1984, v16(1), 93-99.

Forbes, Ronald. (Shawky, Hany, Ronald Forbes and Alan Frankle. "Liquidity Services And Capital Market Equilibrium: The Case For Money Market Mutual Funds," JFR, 1983, v6(2), 141-152.)

Forbes, Shawn M. and Chris W. Paul. "Reply: Eduation, Publishing And Academic Markets," FPE, 1991, v1(1), 21-24.

Forbes, Shawn M. and Lucille S. Mayne. "A Friction Model Of The Prime," JBF, 1989, v13(1), 127-136.

Forbes, Shawn W. "A Note On Teaching The Time Value Of Money," FPE, 1991, v1(1), 91.

Forbes, Stephen W. "Automobile Bodily Injury Liability Loss Reserving Techniques And Simulation," JRI, 1969, v36(4), 597-614.

Forbes, Stephen W. "Capital Gains, Losses, And Financial Results In The Non-Life Insurance Industry," JRI, 1975, v42(4), 625-638.

Forbes, Stephen W. "Capital Gains, Losses, And Financial Results In The Nonlife Insurance Industry: Reply," JRI, 1977, v44(4), 707-708.

Forbes, Stephen W. "Further Studies Of Property-Liability Return Adequacy: Reply," JRI, 1973, v40(3), 460-462.

Forbes, Stephen W. "Growth Performances Of Nonlife Insurance Companies: 1955-1966," JRI, 1970, v37(3), 341-360.

Forbes, Stephen W. "Life Insurance Financial Management Issues," JRI, 1987, v54(3), 603-613.

Forbes, Stephen W. "Loss Reserving Performance Within The Regulatory Framework," JRI, 1970, v37(4), 527-538.

Forbes, Stephen W. "Loss Reserve Valuations And Financial Results In Nonlife Insurance," JRI, 1972, v39(3), 369-382.

Forbes, Stephen W. "Rates Of Return In The Nonlife Insurance Industry," JRI, 1971, v38(3), 409-422.

Forbes, Stephen W. "The Cost Of Capital Of Insurance Companies: Comment," JRI, 1972, v39(3), 491-492.

Forbes, Stephen W. (Lee, Cheng F. and Stephen W. Forbes. "Dividend Policy, Equity Value, And Cost Of Capital Estimates For The Property And Liability Insurance Industry," JRI, 1980, v47(2), 205-222.)

Forbes, Stephen W. (Lee, Cheng F. and Stephen W. Forbes. "Income Measures, Ownership, Capacity Ratios And The Dividend Decision Of The Non-Life Insurance Industry: Some Empirical Evidence," JRI, 1982, v49(2), 269-289.)

Forbes, Stephen W. (Mehr, Robert I. and Stephen W. Forbes. "The Risk Management Decision In The Total Business Setting," JRI, 1973, v40(3), 389-402.)

Ford, Allen. (Gaumnitz, Jack E. and Allen Ford. "The Lease Or Sell Decision," FM, 1978, v7(4), 69-74.)

Ford, Deborah Ann and Michele Gilligan. "The Effect Of Lead Point Abatement Laws On Rental Property Values," AREUEA, 1988, v16(1), 84-94.

Ford, Deborah Ann. "The Effect Of Historic District Designation On Single-Family Home Prices," AREUEA, 1989, v17(3), 353-362.

Ford, Deborah Ann. "Title Assurance And Settlement Charges," AREUEA, 1982, v10(3), 297-312.

Ford, E. J., Jr. (Cherry, R. and E. J. Ford, Jr. "Concentration Of Rental Housing Property And Rental Housing Markets In Urban Areas," AREUEA, 1975, v3(1), 7-16.)

Ford, Gary T. (Ratchford, Brian T. and Gary T. Ford. "A Study Of Prices And Market Shares In The Computer Mainframe Industry: Reply," JOB, 1979, v52(1), 125-129.)

Ford, Gary T. (Ratchford, Brian T. and Gary T. Ford. "A Study Of Prices And Market Shares In The Computer Mainframe Industry," JOB, 1976, v49(2),194-218.)

Ford, Robert. (Tole, Thomas M. and Robert Ford. "Performance Evaluation Of Sources Of Investment Research," FR, 1977, v12(2), 33-46.)

Foreman, Joshua N. (Beckman, Steven R. and Joshua N. Foreman. "An Experimental Test Of The Baumol-Tobin Transactions Demand For Money," JMCB, 1988, v20(3), Part 1, 291-305.)

Forgash, Morris. "Freight Forwarders: Coordinators Of Transportation," FAJ, 1960, v16(3), 123-125.

Formisano, Roger A. "The NAIC Model Life Insurance Solicitation Regulation: Measuring The Consumer Impact In New Jersey," JRI, 1981, v48(1), 59-79.

Formuzis, Peter. "The Demand For Eurodollars And The Optimum Stock Of Bank Liabilities," JMCB, 1973, v5(3), 806-818.

Formuzis, Peter. (Friedman, Benjamin M. and Peter Formuzis. "Bank Capital: The Deposit-Protection Incentive," JBR, 1975-76, v6(3), 208-218.)

Fornell, Claes and David F. Larcker. "The Use Of Canonical Correlation Analysis In Accounting Research," JBFA, 1980, v7(3), 455-474.

Forrestal, Daniel J., III. "The Changing Economics Of Money Management," FAJ, 1978, v34(4), 35-38.

Forrester, D. A. R. "German Principles Of Accounting: A Review Note," JBFA, 1977, v4(2), 257-262.

Forrester, D. Keith. (Gitman, Lawrence J., D. Keith Forrester and John R. Forrester, Jr. "Maximizing Cash Disbursement Float," FM, 1976, v5(2),15-24.)

Forrester, Jay W. "A New View Of Business Cycle Dynamics," JPM, 1976, v3(1), 22-34.

Forrester, John R., Jr. (Gitman, Lawrence J. and John R. Forrester, Jr. "A Survey Of Capital Budgeting Techniques Used By Major U.S.

Firms," FM, 1977, v6(3), 66-71.)

Forster, D. Lynn. (Asplund, Nathan M., D. Lynn Forster and Thomas T. Stout. "Farmers' Use Of Forward Contracting And Hedging," RFM, 1989, v8(1), 24-37.)

Forster, Edgar and Heinz Steinmuller. "An Alternative View On Moral Hazard," JRI, 1978, v45(3), 531-534.

Forsyth, J. D. and D. J. Laughhunn. "Rationing Capital In A Telephone Company," FM, 1974, v3(3), 36-43.

Forsythe, Joseph R. "Coal's Comeback! An Evaluation," FAJ, 1958, v14(5), 33-36.

Forsythe, Robert and Gerry L. Suchanek. "The Impossibility Of Efficient Decision Rules For Firms In Competitive Stock Market Economies," JFQA, 1982, v17(4), 555-574.

Forsythe, Robert, Thomas R. Palfrey and Charles R. Plott. "Futures Markets And Information Efficiency: A Laboratory Examination," JOF, 1984, v39(4),955-981.

Forsythe, Robert. (DeJong, Douglas V., Robert Forsythe and Russell J. Lundholm. "Ripoffs, Lemons, And Reputation Formation In Agency Relationships: A Laboratory Market Study," JOF, 1985, v40(3),809-820.)

Fortier, Diana L. (Evanoff, Douglas D. and Diana L. Fortier. "Reevaluation Of The Structure-Conduct-Performance Paradigm In Banking," JFSR, 1988, v1(3), 277-294.)

Fortin, Karen. (Osteryoung, Jerome S., Daniel E. McCarty and Karen Fortin. "Optimal Tax Lives Of Depreciable Assets: Comment," FM, 1980, v9(3), 77-78.)

Fortin, Michel and Nabil T. Khoury. "Effectiveness Of Hedging Interest Rate Risks And Stock Market Risks With Financial Futures," JFM, 1988, v8(3),319-334.

Fortin, Rich. "Transaction Costs And Day-Of-The-Week Effects In The OTC/NASDAQ Equity Market," JFR, 1990, v13(3), 243-248.

Fortin, Richard D., R. Corwin Grube and O. Maurice Joy. "Bid-Ask Spreads For OTC NASDAQ Firms," FAJ, 1990, v46(3), 76-79.

Fortin, Richard D., R. Corwin Grube and O. Maurice Joy. "Seasonality In NASDAQ Dealer Spreads," JFQA, 1989, v24(3), 395-407.

Fortson, James C. and Robert R. Dince. "An Application Of Goal Programming To Management Of A Country Bank," JBR, 1976-77, v7(4), 311-319.

Fortson, James C. "Asset Replacement," JFED, 1972, v1, 104.

Fortson, James C. (Dince, Robert R. and James C. Fortson. "The Use Of Discriminant Analysis To Predict The Capital Adequacy Of Commercial Banks," JBR, 1972-73, v3(1), 54-62.)

Fortune, Peter. "A Theory Of Optimal Life Insurance: Development And Tests," JOF, 1973, v28(3), 587-600.

Fortune, Peter. "Inflation And Saving Through Life Insurance: Comment," JRI, 1972, v39(2), 317-326.

Fortune, Peter. "Optimal Life Insurance: Reply," JOF, 1975, v30(3), 909-910.

Fortune, Peter. "The Effect Of FHLB Bond Operations On Savings Inflows At Savings And Loan Associations: Comment," JOF, 1976, v31(3), 963-972.

Fortune, Peter. "The Effectiveness Of Recent Policies To Maintain Thrift-Deposit Flows," JMCB, 1975, v7(3), 297-315.

Fortura, Peter and Joseph Kushner. "Canadian Inter-City House Price Differentials," AREUEA, 1986, v14(4), 525-536.

Fosberg, Richard H. "Insider Trading And Security Market Investors," FPE, 1991, v1(1), 83-86.

Fosberg, Richard H. (Fraser, Donald R., R. Malcolm Richards and Richard H. Fosberg. "A Note On Deposit Rate Deregulation, Super Nows, And Bank Security Returns," JBF, 1985, v9(4), 585-596.)

Fosberg, Richard H. (Madura, Jeff and Richard H. Fosberg. "The Impact Of Financing Sources On Multinational Projects," JFR, 1990, v13(1), 61-70.)

Foss, Murray. "How Rigid Are Construction Costs During Recessions?," JOB, 1961, v34(3), 374-383.

Foster, Chester and Robert Van Order. "FHA Terminations: A Prelude To Rational Mortgage Pricing," AREUEA, 1985, v13(3), 273-291.

Foster, Earl M. "Growth And P/E Ratios: A Revision," FAJ, 1970, v26(4), 115-118.

Foster, Earl M. "The Price Earnings Ratio And Growth," FAJ, 1970, v26(1), 96-103.

Foster, Edward, Jr. (Robbins, Sidney and Edward Foster, Jr. "Profit-Planning And The Finance Function," JOF, 1957, v12(4), 451-467.)

Foster, F. Douglas and S. Viswanathan. "A Theory Of The Interday Variations In Volume, Variance, And Trading Costs In Securities Markets," RFS, 1990, v3(4), 593-624.

Foster, F. Douglas. "Syndicate Size, Spreads, And Market Power During The Introduction Of Shelf Registration," JOF, 1989, v44(1), 195-204.

Foster, George. "Asset Pricing Models: Further Tests," JFQA, 1978, v13(1), 39-53.

Foster, George. "Externalities And Financial Reporting," JOF, 1980, v35(2), 521-533.

Foster, George. "Valuation Parameters Of Property-Liability Companies," JOF, 1977, v32(3), 823-835.

Foster, Taylor W., III, D. Randall Jenkins and Don W. Vickrey. "Additional Evidence On The Incremental Information Content Of The 10-K," JBFA, 1983, v10(1), 57-66.

Foster, Taylor W., III, Don R. Hansen and Don W. Vickrey. "Additional Evidence On The Abatement Of Errors In Predicting Beta Through Increases In Portfolio Size And On The Regression Tendency," JBFA, 1988, v15(2), 185-198.

Fougner, Arne. "Rehabilitation For Automobile Accident Victims," JRI, 1962, v29(2), 169-176.

Fountain, John. "A Study Of Today's Foriegn Currencies," FAJ, 1961, v17(1), 37-41.

Fountain, John. "Growth Rates The Simple Way," FAJ, 1969, v25(3), 112.

Fountain, John. "Premium Dollars," FAJ, 1975, v31(2), 70-76.

Fouraker, L. E. "Trouble In The Technique Industry," JOB, 1959, v32(4), 327-339.

Fouse, William L. "Risk And Liquidity Revisited," FAJ, 1977, v33(1), 40-44.

Fouse, William L. "Risk, Liquidity, And Common Stock Prices," FAJ, 1976, v32(3), 35-45.

Fouse, William L., William W. Jahnke and Barr Rosenberg. "Is Beta Phlogiston?," *FAJ*, 1974, v30(1), 70-80.

Fousek, Peter G. "Prerequisites For The Growth Of Consumer Instalment Credit," *JOF*, 1958, v13(2),163-175.

Fowler, David J. (Gordon, Myron J. and David J. Fowler. "Price And Expenditure Performance Of The Multinational Drug Industry In A Home And A Host Company," *RIF*, 1983, v4, (Supp), 59-84.)

Fowler, David J., C. Harvey Rorke and Vijay M. Jog. "Heteroscedasticity, R-Squared And Thin Trading On The Toronto Stock Exchange," *JOF*, 1979, v34(5),1201-1210.

Fowler, David J., C. Harvey Rorke and Vijay M. Jog. "A Note On Beta Stability And Thin Trading On The Toronto Stock Exchange," *JBFA*, 1981, v8(2), 267-278.

Fowler, David J., and C. Harvey Rorke. "Risk Measurement When Shares Are Subject To Infrequent Trading: Comment," *JFEC*, 1983, v12(2), 279-283.

Fowler, David J., C. Harvey Rorke and Vijay M. Jog. "A Bias-Correcting Procedure For Beta Estimation In The Presence Of Thin Trading," *JFI*, 1989, v12(1), 23-32.

Fowler, Isabelle I. (Halpern, Philip and Isabelle I. Fowler. "Investment Management Fees And Determinants Of Pricing Structure In The Industry," *JPM*, 1991, v17(2), 74-79.)

Fowler, J. and C. Harvey Rorke. "Capital Budgeting, Capital Asset Pricing And Externalities," *JBFA*, 1979, v6(2), 145-156.

Fox, A. F. "The Cost Of Retained Earnings - A Comment," *JBFA*, 1977, v4(4), 463-468.

Fox, Edward A. "Measuring Performance Of Equities," *FAJ*, 1968, v24(5), 121-129.

Fox, Harold W. and Robert L. Thistlethwaite. "Variable Annuities At State Universities: The Illinois Case," *JRI*, 1970, v37(3), 465-473.

Fox, Mortimer J., Jr. "At The Threshold Of New Horizons," *FAJ*, 1959, v15(2), 27-32.

Fox, Pauline. (Brotman, Billie Ann and Pauline Fox. "The Impact Of Economic Conditions On The Incidence Of Arson: Comment," *JRI*, 1988, v55(4), 751-754.)

Frahm, Donald R. "The Domestic Excess And Surplus Market," *JRI*, 1966, v33(2), 277-284.

Fraine, H. G. "The Valuation Of Security Holdings Of Life Insurance Companies," *JOF*, 1951, v6(2), 124-138.

Fraine, Harold G. and Robert H. Mills. "Effect Of Defaults And Credit Deterioration On Yields Of Corporate Bonds," *JOF*, 1961, v16(3), 423-434.

Fraine, Harold G. "Criticism Of Requirements For Valuation Of Life Insurance Company Security Holdings," *JRI*, 1963, v30(1), 35-46.

Fraine, Harold G. "Direct Sale Of Security Issues," *JRI*, 1949, v16, 40-56.

France, Virginia G. (Bassett, Gilbert W., Jr., Virginia G. France and Stanely R. Pliska. "Kalman Filter Estimation For Valuing Nontrading Securities, With Applications To The MMI Cash-Futures Spread On October 19 And 20, 1987," *RQFA*, 1991, v1(2), 135-152.)

France, Virginia G., Gilbert W. Bassett, Jr. and Stanley R. Pliska. "The MMI Cash-Futures Spread On October 19, 1987," *RFM*, 1989, v8(1), 118-138.

Francis, J. R. and G. Pound. "The Accounting Services Market: Theory And Evidence: A Reply," *JBFA*, 1983, v10(2), 323-324

Francis, J. R. (Pound, G. D. and J. R. Francis. "The Accounting Services Market: Theory And Evidence," *JBFA*, 1981, v8(3), 353-371.)

Francis, Jack C. (Casabona, Patrick A., Frank J. Fabozzi and Jack C. Francis. "How To Apply Duration To Equity Analysis," *JPM*, 1984, v10(2), 52-58.)

Francis, Jack C. (Castelino, Mark G., Jack C. Francis and Avner Wolf. "Cross-Hedging: Basis Risk And Choice Of The Optimal Hedging Vehicle," *FR*, 1991, v26(2), 179-210.)

Francis, Jack C. (Fabozzi, Frank J., Jack C. Francis and Cheng F. Lee. "Generalized Functional Form For Mutual Fund Returns," *JFQA*, 1980, v15(5), 1107-1120.)

Francis, Jack C. (Fabozzi, Frank J. and Jack C. Francis. "Mutual Fund Systematic Risk For Bull And Bear Markets: An Empirical Examination," *JOF*, 1979, v34(5), 1243-1250.)

Francis, Jack Clark and Dexter R. Rowell. "A Simultaneous Equation Model Of The Firm For Financial Anlaysis And Planning," *FM*, 1978, v7(1), 29-44.

Francis, Jack Clark and Frank J. Fabozzi. "The Effects Of Changing Macroeconomic Conditions On The Parameters Of The Single Index Market Model," *JFQA*, 1979, v14(2), 351-360.

Francis, Jack Clark and Cheng Few Lee. "Investment Horizon, Risk Proxies, Skewness, And Mutual Fund Performance: A Theoretical Analysis And Empirical Investigation," *RIF*, 1983, v4, 1-20.

Francis, Jack Clark, Harold M. Hastings and Frank J. Fabozzi. "Bankruptcy As A Mathematical Catastrophe," *RIF*, 1983, v4, 63-90.

Francis, Jack Clark. "Intertemporal Differences In Systematic Stock Price Movements," *JFQA*, 1975, v10(2), 205-219.

Francis, Jack Clark. "Skewness And Investors' Decisions," *JFQA*, 1975, v10(1), 163-172.

Francis, Jack Clark. "Statistical Analysis Of Risk Surrogates For NYSE Stocks," *JFQA*, 1979, v14(5), 981-997.

Francis, Jack Clark. (Castelino, Mark G. and Jack Clark Francis. "Basis Speculation In Commodity Futures: The Maturity Effect," *JFM*, 1982, v2(2),195-206.)

Francis, Jack Clark. (Fabozzi, Frank J. and Jack Clark Francis. "Beta As A Random Coefficient," *JFQA*, 1978, v13(1), 101-116.)

Francis, Jack Clark. (Fabozzi, Frank J. and Jack Clark Francis. "Stability Tests For Alphas And Betas Over Bull And Bear Market Conditions," *JOF*, 1977, v32(4), 1093-1099.)

Francis, Jack Clark. (Kim, Wi Saeng, Jae Won Lee and Jack Clark Francis. "Investment Performance Of Common Stocks In Relation To Insider Ownership," *FR*, 1988, v23(1), 53-64.)

Francis, Jack Clark. "Some Thoughts About Harry M. Markowitz," *RQFA*, 1991, v1(2), 214-215.

Francis, Jack. (Wolf, Avner, Mark Castelino and Jack Francis. "Hedging Mispriced Options," *JFM*, 1987, v7(2), 147-156.)

Francis, Jere R. "Debt Reporting By Parent Companies: Parent-Only Versus Consolidated Statements," *JBFA*, 1986, v13(3), 393-403.

Franck, Peter and Allan Young. "Stock Price Reaction Of Multinational Firms To Exchange Realignments," *FM*, 1972, v1(3), 66-73.

Franckle, Charles T. and Andrew J. Senchack, Jr. "Economic Considerations In The Use Of Interest Rate Futures," *JFM*, 1982, v2(1), 107-116.

Franckle, Charles T. "The Hedging Performance Of The New Futures Markets: Comment," *JOF*, 1980, v35(5), 1272-1279.

Franckle, Charles T. (McCabe, George M. and Charles T. Franckle. "The Effectiveness Of Rolling The Hedge Forward In The Treasury Bill Futures Market," *FM*, 1983, v12(2), 21-29.)

Francois, Joseph F. "Estimating Homeownership Costs: Owners' Estimates Of Implicit Rents And The Relative Importance Of Rental Equivalence In The Consumer Price Index," *AREUEA*, 1989, v17(1), 87-99.

Frank, Henry J. "Federal Revenues From Taxing Municipals," *JOF*, 1961, v16(3), 387-408.

Frank, Murray. (Cadsby, Charles Bram, Murray Frank and Vojislav Maksimovic. "Pooling, Separating, And Semiseparating Equilibria In Financial Markets: Some Experimental Evidence," *RFS*, 1990, v3(3), 315-342.)

Frank, Ronald E. "Brand Choice As A Probability Process," *JOB*, 1962, v35(1), 43-56.

Frank, Ronald E. and William F. Massy. "Market Segmentation And The Effectiveness Of A Brand's Price And Dealing Policies," *JOB*, 1965, v38(2), 186-200.

Frank, Ronald E., Susan P. Douglas and Rolando E. Polli. "Household Correlates Of 'Brand Loyalty' For Grocery Products," *JOB*, 1968, v41(2), 237-245.

Frank, Werner G. and Charles O. Kroncke. "Classifying Conversions Of Convertible Debentures Over Four Years," *FM*, 1974, v3(2), 33-39.

Franke, Gunter. "An Inter-Temporal Approach To The Optimization Of Dividend Policy With Predetermined Investment: Reply," *JOF*, 1977, v32(4), 1362.

Franke, Gunter. "Conditions For Myopic Valuation And Serial Independence Of The Market Excess Return In Discrete Time Models," *JOF*, 1984, v39(2), 425-442.

Franke, Gunter. "Costless Signalling In Financial Markets," *JOF*, 1987, v42(4), 809-822.

Franke, Gunter. "Optimization Of Dividend Policy And Capital Structure With Predetermined Investments: Comment," *JOF*, 1974, v29(1), 260-263.

Frankel, Jeffrey A. and Gikas A. Hardouvelis. "Commodity Prices, Money Surprises, And Fed Credibility," *JMCB*, 1985, v17(4), Part 1, 425-438.

Frankel, Jeffrey A. "In Search Of The Exchange Risk Premium: A Six-Currency Test Assuming Mean-Variance Optimization," *JIMF*, 1982, v1(3), 255-274.

Frankel, Jeffrey A. "Portfolio Shares As 'Beta Breakers'," *JPM*, 1985, v11(4), 18-23.

Frankel, Jeffrey A. "Recent Estimates Of Time-Variation In The Conditional Variance And In The Exchange Risk Premium," *JIMF*, 1988, v7(1), 115-125.

Frankel, Jeffrey A. "The Effect Of Excessively Elastic Expectations On Exchange-Rate Volatility In The Dornbusch Overshooting Model," *JIMF*, 1983, v2(1), 39-46.

Frankel, Jeffrey A. "The Implications Of Mean-Variance Optimization For Four Questions In International Macroeconomics," *JIMF*, 1986, v5(Supp), S53-S75.

Frankel, Jeffrey A. and James H. Stock. "Regression Vs. Volatility Tests Of Efficiency Of Foreign Exchange Markets," *JIMF*, 1987, v6(1), 49-56.

Frankel, Jeffrey. "Flexible Exchange Rates: Experience Versus Theory," *JPM*, 1989, v15(2), 45-54.

Frankel, Marvin. "The Effects Of Fair Trade: Fact And Fiction In The Statistical Finds," *JOB*, 1955, v28(3), 182-194.

Frankel, Paul H. and Walter L. Newton. "Profitability Of International Oil Companies," *FAJ*, 1959, v15(5), 81-86.

Frankfurter, G. M. and C. G. Lamoureux. "The Relevance Of The Distributional Form Of Common Stock Returns To The Construction Of Optimal Portfolios: Reply," *JFQA*, 1989, v24(1), 131.

Frankfurter, George E. and Herbert M. Phillips. "Catch 500: The Irony Of Indexing: Comment," *JPM*, 1980, v7(1), 80-81.

Frankfurter, George M. and Herbert E. Phillips. "Efficient Algorithms For Conducting Stochastic Dominance Tests On Large Numbers Of Portfolios: A Comment," *JFQA*, 1975, v10(1), 177-179.

Frankfurter, George M. and Herbert E. Phillips. "Alpha-Beta Theory: A Word Of Caution," *JPM*, 1977, v3(4), 35-42.

Frankfurter, George M. and Herbert E. Phillips. "MPT Plus Security Analysis For Better Performance," *JPM*, 1982, v8(4), 29-36.

Frankfurter, George M. and Herbert E. Phillips. "Portfolio Selection: An Analytic Approach For Selecting Securities From A Large Universe," *JFQA*, 1980, v15(2), 357-377.

Frankfurter, George M. and Joanne M. Hill. "A Normative Approach To Pension Fund Management," *JPM*, 1981, v16(4), 533-555.

Frankfurter, George M. and Thomas J. Frecka. "Efficient Portfolios And Superfluous Diversification," *JFQA*, 1979, v14(5), 925-938.

Frankfurter, George M. "Ex-Post Performance Of The Sharpe Portfolio Selection Model," *JOF*, 1976, v31(3), 949-955.

Frankfurter, George M. "The Price We Pay For The Games We Play," *FR*, 1982, v17(3), 177-183.

Frankfurter, George M. (Boness, A. James and George M. Frankfurter. "Evidence Of Non-Homogeneity Of Capital Costs Within 'Risk-Classes'," *JOF*, 1977, v32(3), 775-787.)

Frankfurter, George M. (Boot, John C. G. and George M. Frankfurter. "Reply: The Dynamics Of Corporate Debt Management, Decision Rules And Some Empirical Evidence," *JFQA*, 1974, v9(6), 1067-1068.)

Frankfurter, George M. (Boot, John C. G. and George M. Frankfurter. "The Dynamics Of Corporate Debt Management, Decision Rules, And Some Empirical Evidence," *JFQA*, 1972, v7(4), 1957-1965.)

Frankfurter, George M. and Christopher G. Lamoureux. "The Relevance Of The Distributional Form Of Common Stock Returns To The Construction Of Optimal Portfolios," *JFQA*, 1987, v22(4), 505-511.

Frankfurter, George M. and Christopher G. Lamoureux. "Stock Selection And Timing--A New Look At Market Efficiency," *JBFA*, 1988, v15(3), 385-400.

Frankfurter, George M. and Christopher G. Lamoureux. "Estimation And Selection Bias In Mean-Variance Portfolio Selection," *JFR*, 1989, v12(2), 173-181.

Frankfurter, George M., Herbert E. Phillips and John P. Seagle. "Portfolio Selection: The Effects Of Uncertain Means, Variances, And Covariances," *JFQA*, 1971, v6(5), 1251-1262.

Frankfurter, George M., Herbert E. Phillips and John P. Seagle. "Estimation Risk In The Portfolio Selection Model: A Comment," *JFQA*, 1972, v7(1), 1423-1424.

Frankfurter, George M., Herbert E. Phillips and John P. Seagle. "Performance Of The Sharpe Portfolio Selection Model: A Comparison," *JFQA*, 1976, v11(2), 195-204.

Frankfurter, George M., Herbert E. Phillips and John P. Seagle. "A Proposed Normative Procedure For Portfolio Selection Under Conditions Of Uncertainty," *FM*, 1977, v6(4), 43-50.

Frankfurter, George M., Richard Stevenson and Allan Young. "Option Spreading: Theory And An Illustration," *JPM*, 1979, v5(4), 59-63.

Frankfurter, George and Allan Young. "Option Spreading: Reply," *JPM*, 1981, v7(2), 89-93.

Frankfurter, George. "Efficient Portfolios And Non-Systematic Risk," *FR*, 1981, v16(2), 1-11.

Frankle, A. W. and C. A. Hawkins. "Beta Coefficients For Convertible Bonds," *JOF*, 1975, v30(1), 207-210.

Frankle, Alan W. "An Estimate Of Convertible Bond Premiums: Comment," *JFQA*, 1975, v10(2), 369-373.

Frankle, Alan W. "The Impact Of The Disclosure Of The Environmental Effects Of Organizational Behavior On The Market: Comment," *FM*, 1978, v7(2), 76-78.

Frankle, Alan W. (Findlay, M. C., III, A. W. Frankle, P. L. Cooley, R. L. Roenfeldt and It-Keong Chew. "Capital Budgeting Procedures Under Inflation: Cooley, Roenfeldt, And Chew Vs. Findlay And Frankle," *FM*, 1990, v5(3),83-95.

Frankle, Alan. (Barney, L. Dwayne, Jr., Alan Frankle and Harry White. "Reserve Requirements And The Inflation Tax," *JMCB*, 1990, v22(3), 400-401.)

Frankle, Alan. (Shawky, Hany, Ronald Forbes and Alan Frankle. "Liquidity Services And Capital Market Equilibrium: The Case For Money Market Mutual Funds," *JFR*, 1983, v6(2), 141-152.)

Franklin, Charles B. and Marshall R. Colberg. "Puts And Calls: A Factual Survey," *JOF*, 1959, v14(1), 71-74.

Franklin, Charles B. and Marshall R. Colberg. "Puts And Calls: A Factual Survey," *JOF*, 1958, v13(1), 21-34.

Franklin, Peter J. "Acquisitions And Mergers By UK Insurance Institutions 1966-1975," *JRI*, 1978, v45(3), 413-429.

Franklin, Peter J. "The Normal Cost Theory Of Price And The Internal Rate Of Return Method Of Investment Appraisal: An Integration," *JBFA*, 1977, v4(1), 61-82.

Franklin, Robert. "Tight Money - A Complete Look," *FAJ*, 1958, v14(2), 67-72.

Franks, Edward C. "A Simple Portfolio Revision Strategy For Achieving Prespecified Target Returns," *JPM*, 1990, v16(3), 15-20.

Franks, J. R. and J. J. Pringle. "Debt Financing, Corporate Financial Intermediaries And Firm Valuation," *JOF*, 1982, v37(3), 751-761.

Franks, J. R., J. E. Broyles and M. J. Hecht. "An Industry Study Of The Profitability Of Mergers In The United Kingdom," *JOF*, 1977, v32(5), 1513-1525.

Franks, J. R., R. Miles and J. Bagwell. "A Review Of Acquisition Valuation Models," *JBFA*, 1974, v1(1), 35-53.

Franks, Julian R. and Stewart D. Hodges. "Valuation Of Financial Lease Contracts: A Note," *JOF*, 1978, v33(2), 657-669.

Franks, Julian R. "Insider Information And The Efficiency Of The Acquisitions' Market," *JBF*, 1978, v2(4), 379-393.

Franks, Julian R. (Cooper, Ian and Julian R. Franks. "The Interaction Of Financing And Investing Decisions When The Firm has Unused Tax Credits," *JOF*, 1983, v38(2), 571-583.)

Franks, Julian R. and Robert S. Harris. "Shareholder Wealth Effects Of Corporate Takeovers: The U.K. Experience 1955-1985," *JFEC*, 1989, v23(2), 225-250.

Franks, Julian R. and Stewart D. Hodges. "Lease Valuation When Taxable Earnings Are A Scarce Resource," *JOF*, 1987, v42(4), 987-1005.

Franks, Julian R. and Walter N. Torous. "An Empirical Investigation Of U.S. Firms In Reorganization," *JOF*, 1989, v44(3), 747-770.

Franz, Wolfgang W. "A Solution To Problems Arising From Inflation When Determining Damages," *JRI*, 1978, v45(2), 323-333.

Fraser, D. R. (Baradwaj, B. G., D. R. Fraser and E. P. H. Furtado. "Hostile Bank Takeover Offers: Analysis And Implications," *JBF*, 1990, v14(6), 1229-1242.)

Fraser, Don R. (Richards, R. Malcolm, Don R. Fraser and John C. Groth. "Winning Strategies For Closed-End Funds," *JPM*, 1980, v7(1), 50-55.)

Fraser, Donald R. and J. Patrick McCormack. "Large Bank Failures And Investor Risk Perceptions: Evidence From The Debt Market," *JFQA*, 1978, v13(3),527-532.

Fraser, Donald R. and John C. Groth. "Listing And The Liquidity Of Bank Stocks," *JBR*, 1985-86, v16(3), 136-144.

Fraser, Donald R. and Peter S. Rose. "More On Banking Structure And Performance: The Evidence From Texas," *JFQA*, 1971, v6(1), 601-611.

Fraser, Donald R. and Peter S. Rose. "Bank Entry And Bank Performance," *JOF*, 1972, v27(1), 65-78.

Fraser, Donald R. and Peter S. Rose. "Commercial Bank Adjustments To Monetary Policy: The Peed Of Response," *JBR*, 1977-78, v8(4), 233-241.

Fraser, Donald R. and Peter S. Rose. "Short-Run Bank Portfolio Behavior: An Examination Of Selected Liquid Assets," *JOF*, 1973, v28(2), 531-537.

Fraser, Donald R. and R. Malcolm Richards. "The Penn Square Failure And The Inefficient Market," *JPM*, 1985, v11(3), 34-36.

Fraser, Donald R. "A Note On Bank Response To Reserve Changes: A Note," *JOF*, 1967, v22(1), 86-87.

Fraser, Donald R. "Does Branching Matter?," *JFR*, 1978, v1(1), 61-69.

Fraser, Donald R. "Further Evidence On Bank Equities And Investor Risk Perceptions," *JBR*, 1977-78, v8(3), 189-191.

Fraser, Donald R. "The Determinants Of Bank Profits: An Analysis Of Extremes," *FR*, 1976, v11(1), 69-87.

Fraser, Donald R. (Adkisson, J. Amanda and Donald R. Fraser. "The Effect Of Geographical Deregulation On Bank Acquisition Premiums," *JFSR*, 1990, v4(2), 145-156.)

Fraser, Donald R. (Billingsley, Randall S. and Donald R. Fraser. "Determinants Of Bank Holding Company Debt Ratings," *FR*, 1984, v19(1), 55-66.)

Fraser, Donald R. (Dubofsky, David A. and Donald R. Fraser. "The Differential Impact Of Two Significant Court Decisions Concerning Banking Consolidation," *JBF*, 1989, v13(3), 339-354.)

Fraser, Donald R. (Eyssell, Thomas H., Donald R. Fraser and Nanda K. Rangan. "Debt-Equity Swaps, Regulation K, And Bank Stock Returns," *JBF*, 1989, v13(6), 853-868.)

Fraser, Donald R. (French, Dan W. and Donald R. Fraser. "A Note On Interest Rates And The Risk Of Bank And Savings And Loan Stock," *FR*, 1986, v21(4), 551-558.)

Fraser, Donald R. (Richards, R. Malcolm, Donald R. Fraser and John C. Groth. "The Attractions Of Closed-End Bond Funds," *JPM*, 1982, v8(2), 56-61.)

Fraser, Donald R. (Richards, R. Malcolm, Donald R. Fraser and John C. Groth. "Premiums, Discounts, And The Volatility Of Closed-End Mutual Funds," *FR*, 1979, v14(3), 25-33.)

Fraser, Donald R. (Seaver, William L. and Donald R. Fraser. "Branch Banking And The Availability Of Banking Services In Metropolitan Areas," *JFQA*, 1979, v14(1), 153-160.)

Fraser, Donald R. (Uselton, Gene C., James W. Kolari and Donald R. Fraser. "Long-Term Trends In The Riskiness Of Electric Utility Shares," *JBFA*, 1986, v13(3), 453-459.)

Fraser, Donald R. and James W. Kolari. "The 1982 Depository Institutions Act And Security Returns In The Savings And Loan Industry," *JFR*, 1990, v13(4), 339-348.

Fraser, Donald R. and Srinivasan Kannan. "Deregulation And Risk: Evidence From Earnings Forecasts And Stock Prices," *FM*, 1990, v19(4), 68-76.

Fraser, Donald R. and Srinivasan Kannan. "The Risk Implications Of Forecast Errors Of Bank Earnings, 1976-1986," *JFR*, 1989, v12(3), 261-268.

Fraser, Donald R., Peter S. Rose and Gary L. Schugart. "Federal Reserve Membership And Bank Performance: The Evidence From Texas," *JOF*, 1975, v30(2), 641-658.

Fraser, Donald R., R. Malcolm Richards and Richard H. Fosberg. "A Note On Deposit Rate Deregulation, Super NOWS, And Bank Security Returns," *JBF*, 1985, v9(4), 585-596.

Fraser, Donald R., Wallace Phillips, Jr. and Peter S. Rose. "A Canonical Analysis Of Bank Performance," *JFQA*, 1974, v9(2), 287-295.

Fratianni, Michele and Lee MacDonald Wakeman. "The Law Of One Price In The Eurocurrency Market," *JIMF*, 1982, v1(3), 307-324.

Fratianni, Michele, Hyung-Doh Hur and Heejoon Kang. "Random Walk And Monetary Causality In Five Exchange Markets," *JIMF*, 1987, v6(4), 505-514.

Fratianni, Michele. "Price And Output Adjustments In A Closed Economy," *JMCB*, 1979, v9(1), Part 2, 151-164.

Fratianni, Michele. "The Problem Of Coexistence Of SDRs And A Reserve Currency: A Comment," *JMCB*, 1974, v6(1), 115-118.

Fratianni, Michele. (Bruner, Karl, Michele Fratianni, Jerry L. Jordan, Allan H. Meltzer and Manfred J. Neumann. "Fiscal And Monetary Policies In Moderate Inflation," *JMCB*, 1973, v5(1), Part II, 313-354.)

Fratianni, Michele. (Von Hagen, Jurgen and Michele Fratianni. "German Dominance In The EMS: Evidence From Interest Rates," *JIMF*, 1990, v9(4), 358-375.)

Frazer, William J., Jr. "Large Manufacturing Corporations As Suppliers Of Funds To The United States Government Securities Market," *JOF*, 1958, v13(4), 499-509.

Frazer, William J., Jr. (Bomberger, William A. and William J. Frazer, Jr. "Interest Rates, Uncertainty And The Livingston Data," *JOF*, 1981, v36(3),661-675.)

Frazer, William J., Jr. (Terrell, William T. and William J. Frazer, Jr. "Interest Rates, Portfolio Behavior And Marketable Government Securities," *JOF*, 1972, v27(1), 1-35.)

Frazier, Emma L. (Ingram, F. Jerry and Emma L. Frazier. "Alternative Multivariate Tests In Limited Dependent Variable Models: An Empirical Assessment," *JFQA*, 1982, v17(2), 227-240.)

Frech, H. E., III and Paul B. Ginsburg. "Optimal Scale In Medical Practice: A Survivor Analysis," *JOB*, 1974, v47(1), 23-36.

Frech, H. E., III. (Springer, Robert F. and H. E. Frech, III. "Deterring Fraud: The Role Of Resale Price Maintenance," *JOB*, 1986, v59(3), 433-450.)

Frecka, Thomas J. "The Effects Of Complex Capital Structure On The Market Values Of Firms," *FR*, 1982, v17(3), 86-111.

Frecka, Thomas J. (Bernard, Victor L. and Thomas J. Frecka. "Evidence On The Existence Of Common Stock Inflation Hedges," *JFR*, 1983, v6(4), 301-312.)

Frecka, Thomas J. (Bernard, Victor L. and Thomas J. Frecka. "Commodity Contracts And Common Stocks As Hedges Against Relative Consumer Price Risk," *JFQA*, 1987, v22(2), 169-188.)

Frecka, Thomas J. (Frankfurter, George M. and Thomas J. Frecka. "Efficient Portfolios And Superfluous Diversification," *JFQA*, 1979, v14(5), 925-938.)

Frecka, Thomas J. (Silhan, Peter A. and Thomas J. Frecka. "On The Sales Forecasting Benefits Of Form 10-K Backlog Information," *JBFA*, 1986, v13(3), 425-431.)

Fredericks, R. (Amihud, Y., C. Brunie, C. Ferenbach, R. Fredericks, J. Grundfest, J. Lafferty, B. Lev, B. Shorts, J. Stern, B. Stewart and R. Zeckhauser. "Panel: 'Lead Steer' Roundtable," *JACF*, 1989, v2(3), 24-44.)

Fredland, J. Eric and C. Duncan MacRae. "FHA Multifamily Financial Failure: A Review Of Empirical Studies," *AREUEA*, 1979, v7(1), 95-122.

Fredman, Albert J. and James E. Wert. "Secondary Distributions," *FAJ*, 1968, v24(6), 165-168.

Fredman, Herbert. "Implications Of The Dow-Jones Industrials' Price Level," *FAJ*, 1963, v19(5), 53-54.

Fredrikson, E. Bruce and Jeffrey Eckel. "Electric Utilities: Assessing A Troubled Investment Environment," *FAJ*, 1983, v39(6), 40-45.

Fredrikson, E. Bruce. "Consumer-Credit Charges In Philadelphia And Pittsburgh," *FR*, 1967, v1(2), 2-14.

Friedman, Benjamin M. (Clarida, Richard H. and Benjamin M. Friedman. "The Behavior Of U.S. Short-Term Interest Rates Since October, 1979," **JOF**, 1984, v39(3), 671-682.)

Friedman, Bernard, Caroline Ross and Glen Misek. "On The Surprisingly Low Cost Of State Catastrophic Health Insurance Programs," **JRI**, 1984, v51(1), 31-48.

Friedman, Daniel. "Makin's MARP: A Comment," **JOF**, 1981, v36(3), 739-741.

Friedman, Daniel. (Copeland, Thomas E. and Daniel Friedman. "The Effect Of Sequential Information Arrival On Asset Prices: An Experimental Study," **JOF**, 1987, v42(3), 763-797.)

Friedman, Daniel. (Copeland, Thomas E. and Daniel Friedman. "Partial Revelation Of Information In Experimental Asset Markets," **JOF**, 1991, v46(1), 265-296.)

Friedman, Edward. (Klein, Lawrence R., Edward Friedman and Stephen Able. "Money In The Wharton Quarterly Model," **JMCB**, 1983, v15(2), 237-259.)

Friedman, Elisha M. "The Hobbs Bill (Railroad Reorganizations): The Bill Should Be Enacted," **FAJ**, 1945, v1(2),25-28.

Friedman, Harris C. "Real Estate Investment And Portfolio Theory," **JFQA**, 1971, v6(2), 861-874.

Friedman, Lloyd K., Harold A. Jensen, Jr., Spencer L. Kimball and Jon S. Hanson. "The Regulation Of Specialty Policies In Life Insurance: Comment," **JRI**, 1966, v33(2), 305-316.

Friedman, Milton and Anna J. Schwartz. "Interrelations Between The United States And The United Kingdom, 1873-1975," **JIMF**, 1982, v1(1), 3-19.

Friedman, Milton and Anna L. Schwartz. "The Definition Of Money: Net Wealth And Neutrality As Criteria," **JMCB**, 1969, v1(1), 1-14.

Friedman, Milton and Robert V. Roosa. "Free Versus Fixed Exchange Rates: A Debate," **JPM**, 1977, v3(3), 68-73.

Friedman, Milton and Rose D. Friedman. "The Anatomy Of Crisis," **JPM**, 1979, v6(1), 15-21.

Friedman, Milton. "Controls On Interest Rates Paid By Banks," **JMCB**, 1970, v2(1), 15-32.

Friedman, Milton. "Monetary Variability: United States And Japan," **JMCB**, 1983, v15(3), 339-343.

Friedman, Milton. "Monetary Policy: Theory And Practice," **JMCB**, 1982, v14(1), 98-118.

Friedman, Milton. "Monetary Policy: Theory And Practice: Reply," **JMCB**, 1982, v14(3), 404-406.

Friedman, Milton. "Using The Free Market To Resolve The Balance Of Payments Problem," **FAJ**, 1964, v20(2), 21-25.

Friedman, Richard M. and William W. Roberts. "The Carry-Forward Provision And Management Of Bank Reserves," **JOF**, 1983, v38(3), 845-855.

Friedman, Rose D. (Friedman, Milton and Rose D. Friedman. "The Anatomy Of Crisis," **JPM**, 1979, v6(1), 15-21.)

Friedrich, Klaus. "The Euro-Dollar System And International Liquidity," **JMCB**, 1970, v2(3), 337-347.

Friend, Irwin and Douglas Vickers. "Portfolio Selection And Investment Performance," **JOF**, 1965, v20(3), 391-415.

Friend, Irwin and Marshall E. Blume. "Competitive Commissions On The New York Stock Exchange," **JOF**, 1973, v28(4), 795-819.

Friend, Irwin and Randolph Westerfield. "Co-Skewness And Capital Assets Pricing," **JOF**, 1980, v35(4), 897-913.

Friend, Irwin and Randolph Westerfield. "Risk And Capital Asset Prices," **JBF**, 1981, v5(3), 291-315.

Friend, Irwin and Douglas Vickers. "Re-Evaluation Of Alternative Portfolio-Selection Models," **JOB**, 1968, v41(2), 174-179.

Friend, Irwin and Edward S. Herman. "The S.E.C. Through A Glass Darkly," **JOB**, 1964, v37(4), 382-405.

Friend, Irwin and Edward S. Herman. "Professor Stigler On Securities Regulation: A Further Comment," **JOB**, 1965, v38(1), 106-110.

Friend, Irwin and Ichiro Tokutsu. "The Cost Of Capital To Corporations In Japan And The U.S.A.," **JBF**, 1987, v11(2), 313-328.

Friend, Irwin and Joel Hasbrouck. "Determinants Of Capital Structure," **RIF**, 1988, v7, 1-20.

Friend, Irwin and Larry H. P. Lang. "The Size Effect On Stock Returns: Is It Simply A Risk Effect Not Adequately Reflected By The Usual Measures?," **JBF**, 1988, v12(1), 13-30.

Friend, Irwin and Larry H. P. Lang. "An Empirical Test Of The Impact Of Managerial Self-Interest On Coprorate Capital Structure," **JOF**, 1988, v43(2), 271-281.

Friend, Irwin, Randolph Westerfield and Michael Granito. "New Evidence On The Capital Asset Pricing Model," **JOF**, 1978, v33(3), 903-917.

Friend, Irwin, Yoram Landskroner and Etienne Losq. "The Demand For Risky Assets Under Uncertain Inflation," **JOF**, 1976, v31(5), 1287-1297.

Friend, Irwin. "Broad Implications Of The S. E. C. Special Study," **JOF**, 1966, v21(2), 324-332.

Friend, Irwin. "Economic And Equity Aspects Of Securities Regulation," **RIF**, 1983, v4, (Supp), 31-58.

Friend, Irwin. "Institutionalization Of Savings And The Long-Term Outlook For The Securities Industry," **JFQA**, 1972, v7(2), Supp, 1691-1695.

Friend, Irwin. "Mythodology In Finance," **JOF**, 1973, v28(2), 257-272.

Friend, Irwin. "Recent Developments In Finance," **JBF**, 1977, v1(2), 103-117.

Friend, Irwin. (Blume, Marshall E. and Irwin Friend. "A New Look At The Capital Asset Pricing Model," **JOF**, 1973, v28(1), 19-33.)

Friend, Irwin. (Blume, Marshall E. and Irwin Friend. "The Asset Structure Of Individual Portfolios And Some Implications For Utility Functions," **JOF**, 1975, v30(2), 585-603.)

Friend, Irwin. (Crockett, Jean and Irwin Friend. "Consumption And Saving In Economic Development," **RIF**, 1979, v1, 1-52.)

Friend, Irwin. (Dhrymes, Phoebus J., Irwin Friend, Mustafa N. Gultekin and N. Bulent Gultekin. "New Tests Of The APT And Their Implications," **JOF**, 1985, v40(3), 659-674.)

Friend, Irwin. (Dhrymes, Phoebus J., Irwin Friend, N. Bulent Gultekin and Mustafa N. Gultekin. "An Empirical Examination Of The Implications Of Arbitrage Pricing Theory," **JBF**, 1985, v9(1), 73-99.)

Friend, Irwin. (Dhrymes, Phoebus J., Irwin Friend and N. Bulent

Gultekin. "A Critical Reexamination Of The Empirical Evidence On The Arbitrage Pricing Theory," **JOF**, 1984, v39(2), 323-346.)

Friend, Irwin. (Zhu, Yu and Irwin Friend. "The Effects Of Different Taxes On Risky And Risk-Free Investment And On The Cost Of Capital," **JOF**, 1986, v41(1), 53-66.)

Fries, G. (Tinsley, P., G. Fries, B. Garrett, A. Norman, P.A.V.B. Swamy and P. Von Zur Muehlen. "The Impact Of Uncertainty On The Feasibility Of Humphrey-Hawkins Objectives," **JOF**, 1981, v36(2), 489-496.)

Fries, Gerhard. (Tinsley, Peter A., Helen T. Farr, Gerhard Fries, Bonnie Garrett and Peter von zur Muehlen. "Policy Robustness: Specification And Simulation Of A Monthly Money Market Model," **JMCB**, 1982, v14(4), Part 2, 829-856.)

Frodin, Joanna H. and Richard Startz. "The NOW Account Experiment And The Demand For Money," **JBF**, 1982, v6(2), 179-193.

Froewiss, Kenneth C. "Comments On 'Financial Futures Markets: Is More Regulation Needed?'," **JFM**, v1(2), 191-192.

Froland, Charles, Robert Gorlow and Richard Sampson. "The Market Risk Of Real Estate," **JPM**, 1986, v12(3), 12-19.

Froland, Charles. "What Determines Cap Rates On Real Estate?," **JPM**, 1987, v13(4), 77-82.

Froman, Lewis A. "Can Individual Investors Be Induced To Furnish More Equity Capital?," **JOF**, 1950, v5(2), 192-200.

Froman, Lewis A. "The Adequacy Of Bank Equities," **JOF**, 1947, v2(2), 22-30.

Fromm, Gary. (Ciccolo, John and Gary Fromm. "'q' And The Theory Of Investment," **JOF**, 1979, v34(2), 535-547.)

Fromm, Gary. (Ciccolo, John and Gary Fromm. "'q', Corporate Investment, And Balance Sheet Behavior," **JMCB**, 1980, v12(2), Part 1, 294-307.)

Fromm, Gary. (Crary David, Gary Fromm and Milton Kelenson. "Financial And Nonfinancial Data For Detailed U.S. Industries," **JMCB**, 1980, v12(2), Part 2, 308-316.)

Froomkin, Joseph N. (Shapiro, Eli and Joseph N. Froomkin. "Devaluation Procedures And The Role Of The International Monetary Fund," **JOB**, 1950, v23(2), 103-109.)

Froot, Kenneth A. "Consistent Covariance Matrix Estimation With Cross-Sectional Dependence And Heteroskedasticity In Financial Data," **JFQA**, 1989, v24(3), 333-356.

Froot, Kenneth A. "New Hope For The Expectations Hypothesis Of The Term Structure Of Interest Rates," **JOF**, 1989, v44(2), 283-306.

Froot, Kenneth A. and Takatoshi Ito. "On The Consistency Of Short-Run And Long-Run Exchange Rate Expectations," **JIMF**, 1989, v8(4), 487-510.

Froot, Kenneth A., David S. Scharfstein and Jeremy C. Stein. "LDC Debt: Forgiveness, Indexation, And Investment Incentives," **JOF**, 1989, v44(5), 1335-1350.

Frost, Peter A. and James E. Savarino. "Portfolio Size And Estimation Risk," **JPM**, 1986, v12(4), 60-64.

Frost, Peter A. and James E. Savarino. "An Empirical Bayes Approach To Efficient Portfolio Selection," **JFQA**, 1986, v21(3), 293-305.

Frost, Peter A. and Thomas J. Sargent. "Money-Market Rates, The Discount Rate, And Borrowing From The Federal Reserve," **JMCB**, 1970, v2(1), 56-82.

Frost, Peter A. "Banking Services, Minimum Cash Balances, And The Firm's Demand For Money," **JOF**, 1970, v25(5), 1029-1039.

Frost, Peter A. "Comments On The Session On The Evolution Of Financial Institutions," **JMCB**, 1971, v3(2), Part 2, 593-598.

Frost, Peter A. "Short-Run Fluctuations In The Money Multiplier And Monetary Control," **JMCB**, 1977, v9(1), Part 2, 165-181.

Frost, Peter A. (Bhagat, Sanjai and Peter A. Frost. "Issuing Costs To Existing Shareholders In Competitive And Negotiated Underwritten Public Utility Equity Offerings," **JFEC**, 1986, v15(1/2), 233-260.)

Frost, Peter A. (Hess, Alan C. and Peter A. Frost. "Tests For Price Effects Of New Issues Of Seasoned Securities," **JOF**, 1982, v37(1), 11-25.)

Frost, Peter A. and James E. Savarino. "For Better Performance: Constrain Portfolio Weights," **JPM**, 1988, v15(1), 29-34.

Froyen, Richard T. and Kenneth J. Kopecky. "A Note On Reserve Requirements And Monetary Control With A Flexible Deposit Rate," **JBF**, 1983, v7(1),101-110.

Froyen, Richard T. (Benavie, Arthur and Richard T. Froyen. "Optimal Combination Monetary Policies: A Two-Stage Process," **JMCB**, 1984, v16(4), Part 1, 497-505.)

Froyen, Richard T. (Benavie, Arthur and Richard T. Froyen. "Combination Monetary Policies To Stabilize Price And Output Under Rational Expectations," **JMCB**, 1983, v15(2), 186-198.)

Froyen, Richard. (Abrams, Richard K., Richard Froyen and Roger N. Waud. "Monetary Policy Reaction Functions, Consistent Expectations, And The Burns Era," **JMCB**, 1980, v12(1), 30-42.)

Fruhan, William E., Jr. "Lessons From Levitz: Creating Share Value," **FAJ**, 1980, v36(2), 25-32,34-40,42-45.

Fry, Clifford L. "An Explanation Of Short-Run Fluctuations In The Ratio Of Currency to Demand Deposits: A Comment," **JMCB**, 1974, v6(3), 403-412.

Fry, Clifford L. (Harper, Charles P. and Clifford L. Fry. "Consistent Empirical Results With Almon's Method: Implications For The Monetary Versus Fiscal Policy Debate," **JOF**, 1978, v33(1), 187-198.)

Fry, Clifford L. and Insup Lee. "OSHA Sanctions And The Value Of The Firm," **FR**, 1989, v24(4), 599-610.

Fry, Clifford L., Charles P. Harper and Stanley R. Stansell. "An Analysis Of Credit Union Costs: A New Approach To Analyzing Cost Of Financial Institutions," **JBR**, 1981-82, v12(4), 239-249.

Fry, Joseph N., David C. Shaw, C. Haehling Von Lanzenauer and Cecil R. Dipchand. "Customer Loyalty To Banks: A Longitudinal Study," **JOB**, 1973, v46(4), 517-525.

Fry, Maxwell J. "A Monetary Approach to Afghanistan's Flexible Exchange Rate," **JMCB**, 1976, v8(2), 219-225.

Fry, Maxwell J. "Foreign Debt Instability: An Analysis Of National Saving And Domestic Investment Responses To Foreign Debt Accumulation In 28 Developing Countries," **JIMF**, 1989, v8(3), 315-344.

Fry, Maxwell J. "Money And Capital Or Financial Deepening In Economic Development?," **JMCB**, 1978, v10(4), 464-475.

Fry, Maxwell J. "Terms-Of-Trade Dynamics In Asia: An Analysis Of National Saving And Domestic Investment Responses To Terms-Of-Trade Changes In 14 Asian LDCs," **JIMF**, 1986, v5(1), 57-73.

Frydman, Halina, Edward I. Altman and Duen-Li Kao. "Introducing Recursive Partitioning For Financial Classification: The Case Of Financial Distress," **JOF**, 1985, v40(1), 269-291.

Frydman, Roman. "Sluggish Price Adjustments And The Effectiveness Of Monetary Policy Under Rational Expectations: A Comment," **JMCB**, 1981, v13(1), 94-102.

Frydman, Roman. (Bull, Clive and Roman Frydman. "The Derivation And Interpretation Of The Lucas Supply Function," **JMCB**, 1983, v15(1), 82-95.)

Frydman, Roman. (Bull, Clive and Roman Frydman. "The Derivation And Interpretation Of The Lucas Supply Function: A Reply," **JMCB**, 1984, v16(3), 377-379.)

Fuchs, Victor R. "The Growing Importance Of The Service Industries," **JOB**, 1965, v38(4), 344-373.

Fujihara, R. A. (Sprenkle, C. M., S. J. Turnovsky and R. A. Fujihara. "Assets, Aggregates And Optimal Monetary Control," **JBF**, 1990, v14(1), 155-178.)

Fujihara, Roger and Keehwan Park. "The Probability Distribution Of Futures Prices In The Foreign Exchange Market: A Comparison Of Candidate Processes," **JFM**, 1990, v10(6), 623-642.

Fuller, Beverly R. (Hansen, Robert S., Beverly R. Fuller and Vahan Janjigian. "The Over-Allotment Option And Equity Financing Flotation Costs: An Empirical Investigation," **FM**, 1987, v16(2), 24-32.)

Fuller, R. J. and R. W. Metcalf. "How Analysts Use Management Forecasts," **FAJ**, 1978, v34(2), 55-57.

Fuller, Russell J. and Chi-Cheng Hsia. "A Simplified Common Stock Valuation Model," **FAJ**, 1984, v40(5), 49-56.

Fuller, Russell J. and Glenn H. Petry. "Inflation, Return On Equity, And Stock Prices," **JPM**, 1981, v7(4), 19-25.

Fuller, Russell J. and Halbert S. Kerr. "Estimating The Divisional Cost Of Capital: An Analysis Of The Pure-Play Technique," **JOF**, 1981, v36(5),997-1008.

Fuller, Russell J. and John W. Settle. "Determinants Of Duration And Bond Volatility," **JPM**, 1984, v10(4), 66-72.

Fuller, Russell J. and Sang-Hoon Kim. "Inter-Temporal Correlation Of Cash Flows And The Risk Of Multi-Period Investment Projects," **JFQA**, 1980, v15(5), 1149-1162.

Fuller, Russell J. "Programming The Three-Phase Dividend Discount Model," **JPM**, 1979, v5(4), 28-32.

Fuller, Russell J. "Teaching Portfolio Theory To Undergraduates Using Proofs By Example," **JFED**, 1983, v12, 64-68.

Fuller, Russell J. "The January Barometer: What's Its Batting Average?," **JPM**, 1978, v4(2), 5-7.

Fuller, Russell J. "Timing Versus Selection: Which Holds The Key?," **JPM**, 1977, v3(2), 53-59.

Fuller, Russell J. (Ettredge, Michael and Russell J. Fuller. "The Negative Earnings Effect," **JPM**, 1991, v17(3), 27-34.)

Fuller, Russell J. (Petry, Glenn H. and Russell J. Fuller. "A Comparison Of Institutions Publishing In Finance Journals With Those Presenting Papers At Finance Association Meetings," **JFED**, 1979, v8, 53-57.)

Fuller, Russell J. (Petry, Glenn H. and Russell J. Fuller. "The Geographic Distribution Of Papers At The Seven Finance Associations In The United States," **JFQA**, 1978, v13(4), 785-794.)

Fuller, Russell J. and G. Wenchi Wong. "Traditional Versus Theoretical Risk Measures," **FAJ**, 1988, v44(2), 52-57.

Fuller, Russell J. and John L. Kling. "Is The Stock Market Predictable?," **JPM**, 1990, v16(4), 28-36.

Fullerton, David J. and C. Duncan MacRae. "FHA, Racial Discrimination And Urban Mortgages," **AREUEA**, 1978, v6(4), 451-470.

Fulmer, John. "The Effect Of Federal Reserve System Membership On The Earnings Of Commercial Banks In South Carolina," **JBR**, 1973-74, v4(4), 314-315.

Funatsu, Hideki. "Export Credit Insurance," **JRI**, 1986, v53(4), 679-692.

Funatsu, Hideki. "Export Credit Insurance: Reply," **JRI**, 1988, v55(4), 748-750.

Fung, Hung-Gay. (Mehta, Dileep R., Michael D. Curley and Hung-Gay Fung. "Inflation, Cost Of Capital, And Capital Budgeting Procedures," **FM**, 1984, v13(4), 48-54.)

Fung, Hung-Gay. (Wilson, William W., Hung-Gay Fung and Michael Ricks. "Option Price Behavior In Grain Futures Markets," **JFM**, 1988, v8(1), 47-66.)

Fung, Hung-Gay. (Wilson, William W. and Hung-Gay Fung. "Information Content Of Volatilities Implied By Option Premiums In Grain Futures Markets," **JFM**, 1990, v10(1), 13-28.)

Fung, W. K. H. and Andrew Rudd. "Pricing New Corporate Bond Issues: An Analysis Of Issue Cost And Seasoning Effects," **JOF**, 1986, v41(3), 633-642.

Fung, W. K. H. "Gains From International Portfolio Diversification: A Comment," **JBFA**, 1979, v6(1), 45-50.

Fung, W. K. H. "On The Process Of Risk Reduction Through Diversification," **JBF**, 1979, v3(3), 281-299.

Fung, W. K. H. "Taxes, Clientele Effect Of Dividend And Risk, Return Linearity," **JBF**, 1981, v5(3), 405-424.

Fung, W. K. H. (Bailey, F. A. and W. K. H. Fung. "A Note On Extreme Leverage, MM And Ezra Solomon," **JBFA**, 1978, v5(2), 253-259.)

Fung, W. K. H. and M. F. Theobald. "Taxes, Unequal Access, Public Debt And Corporate Financial Policy In The United Kingdom," **JBF**, 1987, v11(1), 65-78.

Fung, William K. H., Robert A. Schwartz and David K. Whitcomb. "Adjusting For The Intervalling Effect Bias In Beta," **JBF**, 1985, v9(3), 443-460.

Fung, William K. H. and Michael F. Theobald. "Dividends And Debt Under Alternative Tax Systems," **JFQA**, 1984, v19(1), 59-72.

Fung, William K. H. (Brick, Ivan E. and William K. H. Fung. "The Effect Of Taxes On The Trade Credit Decision," **FM**, 1984, v13(2), 24-30.)

Fung, William K. H. (Brick, Ivan E. and William K. H. Fung. "Taxes And The Theory Of Trade Debt," **JOF**, 1984, v39(4), 1169-1176.)

Fung, William. (Brick, Ivan E., William Fung and Marti Subrahmanyam. "Leasing And Financial Intermediation: Comparative Tax Advantages," **FM**, 1987, v16(1), 55-59.)

Furbush, Dean. "Program Trading And Price Movement: Evidence From The October 1987 Market Crash," **FM**, 1989, v18(3), 68-83.

Furby, Lita. (Fischhoff, Baruch and Lita Furby. "Measuring Values: A Conceptual Framework For Interpreting Transactions With Special Reference To Contingent Valuation Of Visibility," **JRU**, 1988, v1(2), 147-184.)

Furlong, F. T. (Keeley, M. C. and F. T. Furlong. "A Reexamination Of Mean-Variance Analysis Of Bank Capital Regulation," **JBF**, 1990, v14(1), 69-84.)

Furlong, Frederick T. and Michael C. Keeley. "Capital Regulation And Bank Risk-Taking: A Note," **JBF**, 1989, v13(6), 883-892.

Furno, Marilena. (Baum, Christopher F. and Marilena Furno. "Analyzing The Stability Of Demand-For-Money Equations Via Bounded-Influence Estimation Techniques," **JMCB**, 1990, v22(4), 465-477.)

Furst, Richard W. and Alan D. Bauerschmidt. "Community Funding Of Depreciation To Finance Change In The Health Care System," **FR**, 1972, v2(2), 134-140.

Furst, Richard W. and Alan D. Bauerschmidt. "Review Article: The Financial Management Of Hospitals (2nd Edition), **FM**, 1974, v4(1), 25-31.

Furst, Richard W. and Robert E. Markland. "Exploiting Imperfections In Markets: A Preliminary Test Of A Mechanical Trading Rule," **FR**, 1971, v2(1), 44-78.

Furst, Richard W. "Does Listing Increase The Market Price Of Common Stocks?," **JOB**, 1970, v43(2),174-180.

Furtado, E. P. H. (Baradwaj, B. G., D. R. Fraser and E. P. H. Furtado. "Hostile Bank Takeover Offers: Analysis And Implications," **JBF**, 1990, v14(6), 1229-1242.) 3¨?8

Furtado, Eugene P. H. (Fatemi, Ali M. and Eugene P. H. Furtado. "An Empirical Investigation Of The Wealth Effects Of Foreign Acquisitions," **RDIBF**, 1988, v2, 363-380.)

Furtado, Eugene P. H. and Michael S. Rozeff. "The Wealth Effects Of Company Initiated Management Changes," **JFEC**, 1987, v18(1), 147-160.

Furtado, Eugene P. H. and Vijay Karan. "Causes, Consequences, And Shareholder Wealth Effects Of Management Turnover: A Review Of The Empirical Evidence," **FM**, 1990, v19(2), 60-75.

Furubotn, Eirik G. "Codetermination And The Modern Theory Of The Firm: A Property-Rights Analysis," **JOB**, 1988, v61(2), 165-182.

Fuss, Daniel J. "Investing For Small Life Insurance Companies," **FAJ**, 1966, v22(2), 115-119.

GGG

G.-Yohannes, Arefaine. "Evaluating Alternative Fast-Pay Mortgages," **JRER**, 1988, v3(3), 23-29.

Gabriel, Stuart A. "Economic Effects Of Racial Integration: An Analysis Of Hedonic Housing Prices And The Willingness To Pay," **AREUEA**, 1987, v15(3), 268-279.

Gabriel, Stuart A. (Rothberg, James P., Frank E. Nothaft and Stuart A. Gabriel. "On The Determinants Of Yield Spreads Between Mortgage Pass-Through And Treasury Securities," **JREFEC**, 1989, v2(4), 301-316)

Gabriel, Stuart A. and Frank E. Nothaft. "Rental Housing Markets And The Natural Vacancy Rate," **AREUEA**, 1988, v16(4), 419-429.

Gage, Alan K. "Radio And Its Booming Next 10 Years With Financial Commentary On Its Resurgence," **FAJ**, 1960, v16(2), 40-41.

Gagnon, Jean P. and Christopher A. Rodowskas, Jr. "Two Controversial Problems In Third-Party Outpatient Prescription Plans," **JRI**, 1972, v39(4), 603-611.

Gagnon, Jean P. and Christopher A. Rodowskas, Jr. "Two Controversial Problems In Third-Party Outpatient Prescription Plans: Reply," **JRI**, 1974, v41(4), 742-747.

Gagnon, Louis, Samuel Mensah and Edward Blinder. "Hedging Canadian Corporate Debt: A Comparative Study Of The Hedging Effectiveness Of Canadian And U.S. Bond Futures," **JFM**, 1989, v9(1), 29-40.

Gahin, Fikry S. "A Theory Of Pure Risk Management In The Business Firm," **JRI**, 1967, v34(1), 121-129.

Gahin, Fikry S. "Review Article - Review Of The Literature On Risk Management," **JRI**, 1971, v38(2), 309-313.

Gahin, Fikry S. "Review Of The Literature On Risk Management," **JRI**, 1972, v39(3), 463-470.

Gahin, Fikry S. "The Financial Feasibility Of Tax-Sheltered Individual Retirement Plans," **JRI**, 1983, v50(1), 84-106.

Gahin, Fikry S. "The Financial Feasibility Of Tax-Sheltered Individual Retirement Plans: Reply," **JRI**, 1988, v55(1), 164-167.

Gahlon, James M. and James A. Gentry. "On the Relationship Between Systematic Risk And The Degrees Of Operating And Financial Leverage," **FM**, 1982, v11(2), 15-23.

Gahlon, James M. and Roger D. Stover. "Debt Capacity And The Capital Budgeting Decisions: A Caveat," **FM**, 1979, v8(4), 55-59.

Gahlon, James M. and Roger D. Stover. "Diversification, Financial Leverage, And Conglomerate Systematic Risk," **JFQA**, 1979, v14(5), 999-1013.

Gailliot, Henry J. "Purchasing Power Parity As An Explanation Of Long-Term Changes In Exchange Rates," **JMCB**, 1970, v2(3), 348-357.

Gaines, James P. and Kathleen M. Kaiser. "An Analysis Of RESPA 1974 And the RESPA Amendments Of 1975," **JBR**, 1977-78, v8(1), 22-30.

Gaines, James P. (Curcio, Richard J. and James P. Gaines. "Real Estate Portfolio Revision," **AREUEA**, 1977, v5(4), 399-410.) 3A?8

Gaines, James P. (Ferri, Michael G. and James P. Gaines. "A Study Of Yield Spreads In The Money Market: 1971 To 1978," **FM**, 1980, v9(3), 52-59.)

Gaines, Tilford C. "A Modest Proposal," **FAJ**, 1970, v26(3), 14-17.

Gaines, Tilford C. "A New Look At Certificates Of Deposit," **FAJ**, 1967, v23(2), 117-119.

Gaines, Tilford C. "Banking And The Energy Crisis," **JBR**, 1974-75, v5(3), 190-192.

Gainsbrugh, Martin R. "What Price Economic Expansion," FAJ, 1950, v6(3), 7-12.

Gal, Joseph J. "Man-Machine Interactive Systems And Financial Analysis," FAJ, 1966, v22(3), 126-136.

Galai, Dan and Mier I. Schneller. "Pricing Of Warrants And The Value Of The Firm," JOF, 1978, v33(5), 1333-1342.

Galai, Dan and Robert Geske. "Option Performance Measurement," JPM, 1983-84, v10(3), 42-46.

Galai, Dan and Ronald W. Masulis. "The Option Pricing Model And The Risk Factor Of Stock," JFEC, 1976, v3(1/2), 53-81.

Galai, Dan. "A Proposal For Indexes For Traded Call Options," JOF, 1979, v34(5), 1157-1172.

Galai, Dan. "Characterization of Options," JBF, 1977, v1(4), 373-386.

Galai, Dan. "Corporate Income Taxes And The Valuation Of The Claims On The Corporation," RIF, 1988, v7, 75-90.

Galai, Dan. "Empirical Tests Of Boundary Conditions For CBOE Options," JFEC, 1978, v6(2/3), 187-211.

Galai, Dan. "On The Boness And Black-Scholes Models For Valuation Of Call Options," JFQA, 1978, v13(1), 15-27.

Galai, Dan. "Pricing Of Optional Bonds," JBF, 1983, v7(3), 323-338.

Galai, Dan. "Tests Of Market Efficiency Of The Chicago Board Options Exchange," JOB, 1977, v50(2), 167-197.

Galai, Dan. "The Components Of The Return From Hedging Options Against Stocks," JOB, 1983, v56(1), 45-54.

Galai, Dan. (Bachrach, Benjamin and Dan Galai. "The Risk-Return Relationship And Stock Prices," JFQA, 1979, v14(2), 421-441.)

Galai, Dan. (Brenner, Menachem and Dan Galai. "On Measuring The Risk Of Common Stocks Implied By Options Prices: A Note," JFQA, 1984, v19(4), 403-412.)

Galai, Dan. (Brenner, Menachem and Dan Galai. "Implied Interest Rates," JOB, 1986, v59(3),493-508.)

Galai, Dan. (Brenner, Menachem and Dan Galai. "The Determinants Of The Return On Index Bonds," JBF, 1978, v2(1), 47-64.)

Galai, Dan. (Brenner, Menachem and Dan Galai. "New Financial Instruments To Hedge Changes In Volatility," FAJ, 1989, v45(4), 61-65.)

Galai, Dan. (Copeland, Thomas E. and Dan Galai. "Information Effects Of The Bid-Ask Spread," JOF, 1983, v38(5), 1457-1469.)

Galai, Dan. (Crouhy, Michel and Dan Galai. "An Economic Assessment Of Capital Requirements In The Banking Industry," JBF, 1986, v10(2), 231-241.)

Galai, Dan. (Crouhy, Michel and Dan Galai. "A Contingent Claim Analysis Of A Regulated Depository Institution," JBF, 1991, v15(1), 73-90.)

Galai, Dan. (Gould, J. P. and Dan Galai. "Transactions Costs And The Relationship Between Put And Call Prices," JFEC, 1974, v1(2), 105-129.)

Galanis, Joseph M. "A Primer For Field Contact Work," FAJ, 1956, v12(4), 17-22.

Galanis, Joseph M. "Household Equipment," FAJ, 1949, v5(4), 24-27.

Galanis, Joseph M. "Shortcomings Of Financial Statements," FAJ, 1947, v3(4), 35-50.

Galanis, Joseph. "Retail Trade Outlook," FAJ, 1956, v12(1), 85-92.

Galbraith, John Kenneth. "The Great Crash: What Was It Really Like?," JPM, 1974-75, v1(2), 74-80.

Galbraith, John Kenneth. "The Great Crash," JPM, 1979-80, v6(1), 60-62.

Gale, Douglas. (Allen, Franklin and Douglas Gale. "Optimal Security Design," RFS, 1988-89, v1(3), 229-263.)

Gale, Ian and Joseph E. Stiglitz. "The Information Content Of Initial Public Offerings," JOF, 1989, v44(2), 469-478.

Gale, Jeffrey and Fred Case. "A Study Of Corporate Real Estate Resource Management," JRER, 1989, v4(3), 23-34.

Gale, Jeffrey. (Case, Fred E. and Jeffrey Gale. "The Impact On Housing Costs Of The California Coastal Zone Conservation Act," AREUEA, 1981, v9(4), 345-366.)

Gale, William A. "Temporal Variability Of United States Consumer Price Index," JMCB, 1981, v13(3), 273-297.

Galeotti, M. (Corradi, V., M. Galeotti and R. Rovelli. "A Cointegration Analysis Of The Relationship Between Bank Reserves, Deposits And Loans: The Case Of Italy, 1965-1987," JBF, 1990, v14(1), 199-214.)

Galitz, Lawrence C. "InterBank: A Bank Management Simulation Exercise," JBF, 1983, v7(3), 355-382.

Gallagher, J. P. "Oil And Gas Potential In The Arctic," FAJ, 1969, v25(6), 44-56.

Gallagher, Patricia L. (Baker, H. Kent and Patricia L. Gallagher. "Management's View Of Stock Splits," FM, 1980, v9(2), 73-77.)

Gallagher, Patricia L. (Baker, H. Kent, Patricia L. Gallagher and Karen E. Morgan. "Management's View Of Stock Repurchase Programs," JFR, 1981, v4(3), 233-247.)

Gallagher, Timothy J. "A Pedagogical Note On Risk Aversion," JFED, 1982, v11, 40-46.

Gallagher, Timothy J. "Correction On Gallagher Article," JFED, 1983, v12, 107.

Gallagher, Timothy J. (Block, Stanley B. and Timothy J. Gallagher. "How Much Do Bank Trust Departments Use Derivatives?," JPM, 1988-89, v15(1), 12-15.)

Gallagher, Timothy J. (Block, Stanley B. and Timothy J. Gallagher. "The Use Of Interest Rate Futures And Options By Corporate Financial Managers," FM, 1986, v15(3), 73-78.)

Gallagher, Timothy J. (Bryan, William R. and Timothy J. Gallagher. "The Role Of The Federal Funds Market," JMCB, 1978, v10(1), 102-104.)

Gallagher, Timothy J. and J. Kenton Zumwalt. "Risk-Adjusted Discount Rates Revisited," FR, 1991, v26(1), 105-114.

Gallagher, William E., Jr. and Hillel J. Einhorn. "Motivation Theory And Job Design," JOB, 1976, v49(3), 358-373.

Gallant, Richard A. "Approaches To Capital Planning," JBR, 1975-76, v6(3), 173-176.

Gallaway, Lowell E. "The Negro And Poverty," JOB, 1967, v40(1), 27-35.

Gallaway, Lowell E. "Unemployment Levels Among Nonwhite Teen-Agers," JOB, 1969, v42(3), 265-276.

Gallaway, Lowell E. (Scully, Gerald W. and Lowell E. Gallaway. "A Spectral Analysis Of The Demographic Structure Of American Unemployment," JOB, 1973, v46(1), 87-102.)

Gallinger, George W. and A. James Ifflander. "Monitoring Accounts Receivable Using Variance Analysis," FM, 1986, v15(4), 69-76.

Gallinger, George W. "A New Approach To Ratings On Utility Bonds: Comment," JPM, 1979-80, v6(4), 71-74.

Gallinger, George W. and Glenn V. Henderson, Jr. "Hurdle Rates For Strategic Investments," AFPAF, 1985, v1(1), 125-144.

Gallup, Cynthia L. (Ellis, Randall P., Cynthia L. Gallup and Thomas G. McGuire. "Should Medical Professional Liability Insurance Be Experience Rated?," JRI, 1990, v57(1), 66-78.)

Galper, Harvey. "The Impacts Of The Vietnam War On Defense Spending: A Simulation Approach," JOB, 1969, v42(4), 401-415.

Galster, George C. "Black And White Preferences For Neighborhood Racial Composition," AREUEA, 1982, v10(1), 39-66.

Gamble, Christopher L. (Jondrow, James M., David E. Chase and Christopher L. Gamble. "The Price Differential Between Domestic And Imported Steel," JOB, 1982, v55(3), 383-400.)

Gamble, Hays B., Roger H. Downing and Owen H. Sauerlender. "Community Growth Around Nuclear Power Plants," AREUEA, 1980, v8(3), 268-280.

Gambling, T. E. and R. A. A. Karim. "Islam And 'Social Accounting'," JBFA, 1986, v13(1), 39-50.

Gambs, Carl M. "State Reserve Requirements And Bank Cash Assets," JMCB, 1980, v12(3), 462-470.

Gambs, Carl M. "The Cost Of The U.S. Payment System," JBR, 1975-76, v6(4), 240-244.

Gambs, Carl M. "Variable Rate Mortgages - Their Potential In The United States: A Comment," JMCB, 1975, v7(2), 245-251.

Gammill, James F., Jr. and James M. Stone. "Options, Futures, And Business Risk," JFM, 1982, v2(2), 141-149.

Gammill, James F., Jr. "Panel: Who Should Set Futures Margins?," RFM, 1988, v7(3), 413-420.

Gammill, James F., Jr. and Andre F. Perold. "The Changing Character Of Stock Market Liquidity," JPM, 1989, v15(3), 13-18.

Ganapathy, S. (Fogler, H. Russell and S. Ganapathy. "Comment On: 'A Quantitative Yield Curve Model For Estimating The Term Structure Of Interest Rates'," JFQA, 1980, v15(2), 449-456.)

Gandar, John, Richard Zuber, Thomas O'Brien and Ben Russo. "Testing Rationality In The Point Spread Betting Market," JOF, 1988, v43(4), 995-1008.

Gandhi, David. (Emery, Douglas R., Philip C. Parr, Per B. Mokkelbost, David Gandhi and Anthony Saunders. "An Investigation Of Real Investment Decision Making With The Options Pricing Model," JBFA, 1978, v5(4), 363-369.)

Gandhi, Devinder K. and Anthony Saunders. "The Superiority Of Stochastic Dominance Over Mean-Variance Efficiency Criteria: Some Clarifications," JBFA, 1981, v8(1), 51-59.

Gandhi, Devinder K. (Raghid, Muhammad and Devinder K. Gandhi. "Tax And Savings Implications Of The Canadian Registered Retirement Savings Plans," FR, 1986, v21(4), 463-471.)

Gandhi, Devinder K., Anthony Saunders, Richard Woodward and Charles Ward. "The British Investor's Gains From International Portfolio Investment," JBF, 1981, v5(2), 155-165.

Gandhi, Devinder K., Robert Hausmann, Jr. and Anthony Saunders. "On Syndicate Sharing Rules For Unanimous Project Rankings," JBF, 1985, v9(4),517-534.

Gandhi, Devinder K., Muhammad Rashid and Kenneth D. Riener. "Intertemporal Resolution Of Uncertainty And Portfolio Behavior," FR, 1989, v24(3), 491-498.

Gandolfi, Arthur E. "Inflation, Taxation, And Interest Rates," JOF, 1982, v37(3), 797-807.

Gandolfi, Arthur E. "Taxation And The 'Fischer Effect'," JOF, 1976, v31(5), 1375-1386.

Gandolfo, G., P. C. Padoan and G. Paladino. "Exchange Rate Determination: Single-Equation Or Economy-Wide Models? A Test Against The Random Walk," JBF, 1990, v14(5), 965-992.

Gangopadhyay, Partha. (Reinganum, Marc R. and Partha Gangopadhyay. "On Information Release And The January Effect: Accounting-Information Hypothesis," RQFA, 1991, v1(2), 169-176.)

Gann, Robert R. (Clark, Robert A., Joan M. Jantorni and Robert R. Gann. "Analysis Of The Lease-Or-Buy Decision: Comment," JOF, 1973, v28(4), 1015-1016.)

Gapenski, Louis C. and W. Andrew McCullough. "A Televised Replay Approach To Teaching The Basic Finance Course," JFED, 1982, v11, 1-4.

Gapinski, James H. "Capital Lessons In Leaning Against The Wind," JMCB, 1987, v19(2), 235-245.

Garand, John J. "Fixed Income Portfolio Performance: A Discussion Of The Issues," JBR, 1973-74, v4(4), 280-297.

Garant, Jean-Pierre. "An Inquiry Into Bond Types Used By Canadian Firms," FR, 1974, v9(1), 24-28.

Garbade, Kenneth and Zvi Lieber. "On The Independence Of Transactions On The N.Y. Stock Exchange," JBF, 1977, v1(2), 151-172.

Garbade, Kenneth D. and Chandra P. Sekaran. "Opening Prices On The New York Stock Exchange," JBF, 1981, v5(3), 345-355.

Garbade, Kenneth D. and Joseph F. Hunt. "Risk Premiums On Federal Agency Debt," JOF, 1978, v33(1), 105-116.

Garbade, Kenneth D. and William L. Silber. "Technology, Communication And The Performance Of Financial Markets: 1840-1975," JOF, 1978, v33(3), 819-832.

Garbade, Kenneth D. and William L. Silber. "Cash Settlement Of Futures Contracts: An Economic Analysis," JFM, 1983, v3(4), 451-472.

Garbade, Kenneth D. and William L. Silber. "Best Execution In Securities Markets: An Application Of Signaling And Agency Theory," JOF, 1982, v37(2), 493-504.

Garbade, Kenneth D. and William L. Silber. "Structural Organization Of Secondary Markets: Clearing Frequency, Dealer Activity And Liquidity Risk," JOF, 1979, v34(3), 577-593.

Garbade, Kenneth D. "The Effect Of Interdealer Brokerage On The Transactional Characteristics Of Dealer Markets," JOB, 1978, v51(3), 477-498.

Garbade, Kenneth D. (Black, Deborah G., Kenneth D. Garbade and William L. Silber. "The Impact Of The GNMA Pass-through Program On FHA Mortgage Costs," JOF, 1981, v36(2), 457-469.)

Garbade, Kenneth D. and William L. Silber. "Futures Contracts On Commodities With Multiple Varieties: An Analysis Of Premiums And Discounts," **JOB**, 1983, v56(3), 249-272.

Garber, Peter M. "Interwar Movements Of Dollars To Europe And The US Currency Supply," **JIMF**, 1986, Supp, S135-S156.

Garber, Peter M. "Who Put The Mania In Tulipmania?," **JPM**, 1989, v16(1), 53-60.

Garbisch, Michael W. and Gordon J. Alexander. "Is Standard And Poor's Master List Worthless?," **JPM**, 1977-78, v4(1), 34-37.

Garcia, C. B. and F. J. Gould. "A Note On The Measurement Of Risk In A Portfolio," **FAJ**, 1987, v43(2), 61-69.

Garcia, C. B. and F. J. Gould. "An Empirical Study Of Portfolio Insurance," **FAJ**, 1987, v43(4), 44-54.

Garcia, Gillian and Simon Pak. "The Rate Of Currency To Demand Deposits In The United States," **JOF**, 1979, v34(3), 703-715.

Garcia, Gillian G. (Brewer, Elijah, III and Gillian G. Garcia. "A Discriminant Analysis Of Savings And Loan Accounting Profits, 1976-1981," **AFPAF**, 1987, v2(1), 205-244.)

Garcia, Gillian G. (Brewer, Elijah, III, Gillian G. Garcia and Alan K. Reichert. "A Statistical Analysis Of S&L Accounting Profits," **AFPAF**, 1989, v3(1), 163-194.)

Garcia, Gillian. "The Currency Ratio And The Subterranean Economy," **FAJ**, 1978, v34(6), 64-66.

Garcia, Philip, Raymond M. Leuthold and Hector Zapata. "Lead-Lag Relationships Between Trading Volume And Price Variability: New Evidence," **JFM**, 1986, v6(1), 1-10.

Garcia, Philip. (Koontz, Stephen R., Philip Garcia and Michael A. Hudson. "Dominant-Satellite Relationships Between Live Cattle Cash And Futures Markets," **JFM**, 1990, v10(2), 123-136.)

Gardener, E. P. M. "Capital Adequacy And Banking Supervision - Towards A Practical System," **JBR**, 1982-83, v13(2), 125-136.

Gardener, E. P. M. "Capital Adequacy And Bank Prudential Regulation," **JBR**, 1978-79, v9(3), 173-180.

Gardiner, Harold. "A Life Company Training Program," **JRI**, 1948, v15, 5-15.

Gardner, Grant W. "The Choice Of Monetary Policy Instruments In An Open Economy," **JIMF**, 1983, v2(3), 347-354.

Gardner, Mark L. (Long, C. Richard and Mark L. Gardner. "Alternative U.S. Monetary And Deficit Reduction Policies For The 1980s," **JMCB**, 1988, v20(3), Part 1, 336-352.)

Gardner, Mona J. "Minority Owned Banks: A Managerial And Performance Analysis," **JBR**, 1984-85, v15(1), 26-34.

Gardner, Mona J. "The Integration Of Hedging Strategies In The Finance Curriculum," **JFED**, 1982, v11, 21-24.

Gardner, Mona J. (Kang, Han Bin and Mona J. Gardner. "Selling Price And Marketing Time In The Residential Real Estae Market," **JRER**, 1989, v4(1), 21-35.)

Gardner, Mona J. (Scott, William L., Mona J. Gardner and Dixie L. Mills. "Expense Preference And Minority Banking: A Note," **FR**, 1988, v23(1),105-116.)

Gardner, Mona J. and Dixie L. Mills. "Evaluating The Likelihood Of Default On Deliquent Loans," **FM**, 1989, v18(4), 55-63.

Gardner, Mona J. and Dixie L. Mills. "Financial Institutions Management Courses: A Survey Of Current Content And The Outlook For The 1990s," **JFED**, 1990, v19, 1-4.

Gardner, Mona J., Han Bin Kang and Dixie L. Mills. "Consumer Profiles And Acceptance Of ARM Features: An Application Of Logit Regression," **JRER**, 1987, v2(2), 63-74.

Gargett, Dave R. "The Link Between Stock Prices And Liquidity," **FAJ**, 1978, v34(1), 50-54.

Garland, James P. "A Market-Yield Spending Rule For Endowments And Trusts," **FAJ**, 1989, v45(4), 50-60.

Garland, James P. "Taxable Portfolios: Value And Performance," **JPM**, 1986-87, v13(2), 19-25.

Garlicki, T. Dessa, Frank J. Fabozzi and Robert Fonfeder. "The Impact Of Earnings Under FASB 52 On Equity Returns," **FM**, 1987, v16(3), 36-44.

Garman, David M. and Daniel J. Richards. "Policy Rules, Inflationary Bias, And Cyclical Stability," **JMCB**, 1989, v21(4), 409-421.

Garman, Mark B. and James A. Ohlson. "Valuation Of Risky Assets In Arbitrage-Free Economies With Transactions Costs," **JFEC**, 1981, v9(3), 271-280.

Garman, Mark B. and Steven W. Kohlhagen. "Foreign Currency Option Values," **JIMF**, 1983, v2(3), 231-237.

Garman, Mark B. and Steven W. Kohlhagen. "Inflation And Foreign Exchange Rates Under Production And Monetary Uncertainty," **JFQA**, 1980, v15(4), 949-967.

Garman, Mark B. "An Algebra For Evaluating Hedge Portfolios," **JFEC**, 1976, v4(4), 403-427.

Garman, Mark B. "Market Microstructure," **JFEC**, 1976, v3(3), 257-275.

Garman, Mark B. "The Duration Of Option Portfolios," **JFEC**, 1985, v14(2), 309-316.

Garman, Mark B. "The Pricing Of Supershares," **JFEC**, 1978, v6(1), 3-10.

Garman, Mark B. "Towards A Semigroup Pricing Theory," **JOF**, 1985, v40(3), 847-861.

Garman, Mark B. (Ohlson, James A. and Mark B. Garman. "A Dynamic Equilibrium For The Ross Arbitrage Model," **JOF**, 1980, v35(3), 675-684.)

Garman, Mark B. and Michael J. Klass. "On The Estimation Of Security Price Volatilities From Historical Data," **JOB**, 1980, v53(1), 67-78.

Garner, C. Alan. "Commodity Prices: Policy Target Or Information Variable?," **JMCB**, 1989, v21(4), 508-514.

Garner, Paul. (Gaumnitz, Erwin A., George E. Manners, James R. Surface, Maurice W. Lee and Paul Garner. "Dean's Forum: The Place Of Insurance In The Collegiate Curriculum," **JRI**, 1960, v27(4), 113-120.)

Garrett, B. (Tinsley, P., G. Fries, B. Garrett, A. Norman, P.A.V.B. Swamy and P. Von Zur Muehlen. "The Impact Of Uncertainty On The Feasibility Of Humphrey-Hawkins Objectives," **JOF**, 1981, v36(2), 489-496.)

Garrett, Bonnie. (Tinsley, P. A., H. T. Farr, G. Fries, B. Garrett and Peter von zur Muehlen. "Policy Robustness: Specification And Simulation Of A Monthly Money Market Model," **JMCB**, 1982, v14(4), Part 2, 829-856.)

Garrison, Sharon H. (Davidson, Wallace N., III and Sharon H. Garrison. "The Stock Market Reaction To Significant Tender Offer Repurchases Of Stock: Size And Purpose Perspective," **FR**, 1989, v24(1), 93-108.)

Garrison, Sharon Hatten. (Davidson, Wallace N., III, Sharon Hatten Garrison and Glenn V. Henderson, Jr. "Examining Merger Synergy With The Capital Asset Pricing Model," **FR**, 1987, v22(2), 233-248.)

Garrison, Sharon. (Chandy, P. R., Wallace N. Davidson and Sharon Garrison. "Bad News = Good News! Who Can Tell?," **JPM**, 1985-86, v12(1), 24-27.)

Garrod, N. W. and C. R. Emmanuel. "The Impact Of Company Profile On The Predictive Ability Of Disaggregated Data," **JBFA**, 1988, v15(2), 135-154.

Garrone, Francois and Bruno Solnik. "A Global Approach To Money Management," **JPM**, 1975-76, v2(4), 5-14.

Garry, Mark. (Goetzmann, William N. and Mark Garry. "Does Delisting From The S&P 500 Affect Stock Price?," **FAJ**, 1986, v42(2), 64-69.)

Garsombke, H. Perrin. "The Relationship Between Corporate Disclosure And Firm Risk," **JBFA**, 1979, v6(1), 53-70.

Garston, Neil. (Canarella, Giorgio and Neil Garston. "Monetary And Public Debt Shocks: Tests And Efficient Estimates," **JMCB**, 1983, v15(2), 199-211.)

Garven, J. R. "On The Application Of Finance Theory To The Insurance Firm," **JFSR**, 1987, v1(1), 57-76.

Garven, James A. "CML To SML: An Alternative Approach," **JBFA**, 1988, v15(2), 283-288.

Garven, James R. "A Pedagogic Note On The Derivation Of The Black-Scholes Option Pricing Formula," **FR**, 1986, v21(2), 337-344.

Garven, James R. (D'Arcy, Stephen P. and James R. Garven. "Property-Liability Insurance Pricing Models: An Empirical Evaluation," **JRI**, 1990, v57(3), 391-430.)

Garven, James R. (Doherty, Neil A. and James R. Garven. "Price Regulation In Property-Liability Insurance: A Contingent-Claims Approach," **JOF**, 1986, v41(5), 1031-1050.)

Garven, James R. (Gentry, James A. and James R. Garven. "Video Graphics And The Teaching Of Financial Management Concepts," **JFED**, 1983, v12, 17-26.)

Garvin, W. J. "The Small Business Capital Gap: The Special Case Of Minority Enterprise," **JOF**, 1971, v26(2), 445-457.

Garvy, George. "Changing Patterns Of Income Distribution," **FAJ**, 1954, v10(5), 21-28.

Garvy, George. "What Do Personal Savings Figures Tell Us?," **FAJ**, 1951, v7(4), 27-28.

Garwood, John D. "A Commonsense Explanation Of War Finance," **FAJ**, 1954, v10(4), 83-88.

Garwood, John D. "Economic Growth For The Sixties," **FAJ**, 1962, v18(3), 9-11.

Garwood, John D. "Industrial Location And Migrant Firm," **FAJ**, 1952, v8(5), 102-103.

Garwood, John D. "Western Development Via The Potomac," **FAJ**, 1953, v9(4), 73-76.

Gaskins, J. Peter. "Taxation Of Foreign Source Income," **FAJ**, 1973, v29(5), 55-58,60-64.

Gasper, L. C. (Yohe, W. P. and L. C. Gasper. "'Even Keel' Decisions Of The FOMC," **FAJ**, 1970, v26(6), 105-115.)

Gastineau, G. L. and A. Madansky. "Simulation Is No Guide To Option Strategies," **FAJ**, 1979, v35(5), 61-76.

Gastineau, Gary and Albert Madansky. "S&P 500 Stock Index Futures Evaluation Tables," **FAJ**, 1983, v39(6), 68-76.

Gastineau, Gary L. and Albert Madansky. "Some Comments On The CBOE Call Option Index," **FAJ**, 1984, v40(4), 58-67.

Gastineau, Gary L. "An Index Of Listed Option Premiums," **FAJ**, 1977, v33(3), 70-75.

Gatti, James F., John R. Mills and Peter J. McTague. "The Feasibility Of Small Denomination Consumer Note Issues As A Source Of Funds For Non-Financial Borrowers," **FM**, 1981, v10(4), 41-53.

Gatto, Mary Ann, Robert Geske, Robert Litzenberger and Howard Sosin. "Mutual Fund Insurance," **JFEC**, 1980, v8(3), 283-317.

Gatto, Mary Ann. (Goldman, M. Barry, Howard B. Sosin and Mary Ann Gatto. "Path Dependent Options: 'Buy At The Low, Sell At The High'," **JOF**, 1979, v34(5), 1111-1127.)

Gau, George W. and Daniel B. Kohlhepp. "The Financial Planning And Management Of Real Estate Developments," **FM**, 1980, v9(1), 46-52.

Gau, George W. "A Taxonomic Model For The Risk-Rating Of Residential Mortgages," **JOB**, 1978, v51(4), 687-706.

Gau, George W. "Efficient Real Estate Markets: Paradox Or Paradigm?," **AREUEA**, 1987, v15(2), 1-12.

Gau, George W. "Public Information And Abnormal Returns In Real Estate Investment," **AREUEA**, 1985, v13(1), 15-31.

Gau, George W. "Weak Form Tests Of The Efficiency Of Real Estate Investment Markets," **FR**, 1984, v19(4), 301-320.

Gau, George W. and Daniel B. Kohlhepp. "Reinvestment Rates And The Sensitivity Of Rates Of Return In Real Estate Investment," **AREUEA**, 1976, v4(3), 69-84.

Gau, George W. and Daniel B. Kohlhepp. "Multicollinearity And Reduced-Form Price Equations For Residential Markets," **AREUEA**, 1978, v6(1), 50-69.

Gau, George W. and Daniel B. Kohlhepp. "Alternative Estimation Methods For Reduced Form Price Equations Under Conditions Of Multicollinearity: Reply," **AREUEA**, 1979, v7(3), 437-441.

Gau, George W. and Ko Wang. "A Further Examination Of Appraisal Data And The Potential Bias In Real Estate Return Indexes," **AREUEA**, 1990, v18(1), 40-48.

Gau, George W. and Michael A. Goldberg. "Interest Rate Risk, Residential Mortgages And Financial Futures Markets," **AREUEA**, 1983, v11(4), 445-461.

Gau, George W. and Ko Wang. "Capital Structure Decisions In Real Estate Investment," **AREUEA**, 1990, v18(4), 501-521.

Gaubis, Anthony. "The Best Stock Average From A Practical Viewpoint," **FAJ**, 1952, v8(5), 70-74.

Gaubis, Anthony. "The Timing Factor In Business And Stock Market Forecasting," **FAJ**, 1963, v19(2),19-23.

Gaumnitz, E. A. "Graduate Curriculum Planning In Risk," **JRI**, 1967, v34(2), 305-310.

Gaumnitz, Edwin A. (Berolzheimer, Howard, Edwin A. Gaumnitz, C. M. Kahler and Joseph Pillion. "Round Table Discussion: The Objectives And Content Of The Survey Course In Insurance," JRI, 1941, v8, 5-38.)

Gaumnitz, Erwin A., George E. Manners, James R. Surface, Maurice W. Lee and Paul Garner. "Dean's Forum: The Place Of Insurance In The Collegiate Curriculum," JRI, 1960, v27(4), 113-120.

Gaumnitz, Jack E. and Allen Ford. "The Lease Or Sell Decision," FM, 1978, v7(4), 69-74.

Gaumnitz, Jack E. and Douglas R. Emery. "Asset Growth, Abandonment Value And The Replacement Decision Of Like-For-Like Capital Assets," JFQA, 1980, v15(2), 407-419.

Gaumnitz, Jack E. "Appraising Performance Of Investment Portfolios," JOF, 1970, v25(3), 555-560.

Gaver, Kenneth M. and Jerold L. Zimmerman. "An Analysis Of Competitive Bidding On BART Contracts," JOB, 1977, v50(3), 279-295.

Gavin, Michael. "The Stock Market And Exchange Rate Dynamics," JIMF, 1989, v8(2), 181-200.

Gavin, William T. (Bryan, Michael F. and William T. Gavin. "Models Of Inflation Expectations Formation: A Comparison Of Household And Economist Forecasts: A Comment," JMCB, 1986, v18(4), 539-544.)

Gavish, Bezalel and Avner Kalay. "On The Asset Substitution Problem," JFQA, 1983, v18(1), 21-30.

Gavish, Bezalel. "A Relaxation Algorithm For Building Undominated Portfolios," JBF, 1977, v1(2), 143-150.

Gay, Gerald D. (Chiang, Raymond C., Gerald D. Gay and Robert W. Kolb. "Commodity Exchange Seat Prices," RFM, 1987, v6(1), 1-10.)

Gay, Gerald D. (Kolb, Robert W., Gerald D. Gay and William C. Hunter. "Liquidity And Capital Requirements For Futures Market Hedges," RFM, 1985, v4(1),1-25.)

Gay, Gerald D. (Kolb, Robert W., James V. Jordan and Gerald D. Gay. "Futures Prices And Expected Future Spot Prices," RFM, 1983, v2(1), 110-123.)

Gay, Gerald D. and Robert W. Kolb. "Interest Rate Futures As A Tool For Immunization," JPM, 1983-84, v10(1), 65-70.

Gay, Gerald D. and Robert W. Kolb. "Removing Bias In Duration Based Hedging Models: A Note," JFM, 1984, v4(2), 225-228.

Gay, Gerald D. and Robert W. Kolb. "The Management Of Interest Rate Risk," JPM, 1982-83, v9(2), 65-70.

Gay, Gerald D. and Steven Manaster. "Implicit Delivery Options And Optimal Delivery Strategies For Financial Futures Contracts," JFEC, 1986, v16(1),41-72.

Gay, Gerald D. and Steven Manaster. "The Quality Option Implicit In Futures Contracts," JFEC, 1984, v13(3), 353-370.

Gay, Gerald D. (Badrinath, S. G., Gerald D. Gay and Jayant R. Kale. "Patterns Of Institutional Investment, Prudence, And The Managerial 'Safety-Net' Hypothesis," JRI, 1989, v56(4), 605-629.)

Gay, Gerald D. (Carnes, W. Stansbury, Gerald D. Gay and Paul A. McCulley. "Fed-Watching, Monetary Policy Regimes, And The Response Of Financial Futures To Money Announcements," RFM, 1989, v8(3), 384-401.)

Gay, Gerald D. (Corgel, John B. and Gerald D. Gay. "The Impact Of GNMA Futures Trading On Cash Market Volatility," AREUEA, 1984, v12(2), 176-190.)

Gay, Gerald D. (Corgel, John B. and Gerald D. Gay. "Local Economic Base, Geographic Diversification, And Risk Management Of Mortgage Portfolios," AREUEA, 1987, v15(3), 256-267.)

Gay, Gerald D. (Fielitz, Bruce D. and Gerald D. Gay. "Managing Cash Flow Risks In Stock Index Futures," JPM, 1985-86, v12(2), 74-78.)

Gay, Gerald D. (Kale, Jayant R., Thomas H. Noe and Gerald D. Gay. "Share Repurchase Through Transferable Put Rights: Theory And Case Study," JFEC, 1989, v25(1), 141-160.)

Gay, Gerald D. (Kolb, Robert W. and Gerald D. Gay. "Immunizing Bond Portfolios With Interest Rate Futures," FM, 1982, v11(2), 81-89.)

Gay, Gerald D. (Kolb, Robert W. and Gerald D. Gay. "The Performance Of Live Cattle Futures As Predictors Of Subsequent Spot Prices," JFM, 1983, v3(1), 55-63.)

Gay, Gerald D. (Kolb, Robert W., Roger A. Morin and Gerald D. Gay. "Regulation, Regulatory Lag, And The Use Of Fu- tures Markets," JOF, 1983, v38(2), 405-418.)

Gay, Gerald D. (Kolb, Robert W., Gerald D. Gay and William C. Hunter. "Liquidity Requirements For Financial Futures Investments," FAJ, 1985, v41(3), 60-68.)

Gay, Gerald D. (Kolb, Robert W., Gerald D. Gay and James V. Jordan. "Managing Foreign Interest Rate Risk," JPM, 1982, v2(2), 151-158.)

Gay, Gerald D. (Kolb, Robert W., Stephen G. Timme and Gerald D. Gay. "Macro Versus Micro Futures Hedges At Commercial Banks," JFM, 1984, v4(1), 47-54.)

Gay, Gerald D. (Kolb, Robert W. and Gerald D. Gay. "A Pricing Anomaly In Treasury Bill Futures," JFR, 1985, v8(2), 157-167.)

Gay, Gerald D. (Kolb, Robert W., Gerald D. Gay and James V. Jordan. "Markets Are There Arbitrage Opportunities In The Treasury-Bond Futures Markets," JFM, 1982, v2(3), 217-230.)

Gay, Gerald D. and Steven Manaster. "Hedging Against Commodity Price Inflation: Stocks And Bills As Substitutes For Futures Contracts," JOB, 1982, v55(2), 317-344.

Gay, Gerald D. and Tae-Hyuk Kim. "An Investigation Into Seasonality In The Futures Market," JFM, 1987, v7(2), 169-182.

Gay, Gerald D., Robert W. Kolb and Raymond Chiang. "Interest Rate Hedging: An Empirical Test Of Alternative Strategies," JFR, 1983, v6(3),187-197.

Gay, Gerald D., William C. Hunter and Robert W. Kolb. "A Comparative Analysis Of Futures Contract Margins," JFM, 1986, v6(2), 307-324.

Gay, Gerald D., Robert W. Kolb and Kenneth Yung. "Trader Rationality In The Exercise Of Futures Options," JFEC, 1989, v23(2), 339-362.

Gaynor, Joseph F. N. "Great Northern Railway Electrification," FAJ, 1948, v4(2), 20-30.

Gear, Anthony E. (Lockett, A. Geoffrey and Anthony E. Gear. "Multistage Capital Budgeting Under Uncertainty," JFQA, 1975, v10(1), 21-36.)

Gearhart, John A. "Corporate Management And Analysts," FAJ, 1967, v23(5), 31-32.

Gebotys, Robert J., Alan Auerbach and Adriana Petrucci. "The Insurance Branch Manager: Correlates Of Success," JRI, 1987, v54(1), 157-161.

Gee, Arthur. "Ranking Company Management," FAJ, 1954, v10(2), 83-88.

Gee, Kenneth P. "A Note On Cost Escalation Clauses," JBFA, 1979, v6(3), 339-346.

Gee, Kenneth P. "A Note On The Estimation Of Replacement Cost For A Job," JBFA, 1979, v6(1), 37-44.

Gee, Kenneth P. "Holding Gains, Inventory Decisions And The Measurement Of Purchasing Performance," JBFA, 1976, v3(4), 123-142.

Gehm, Fred. "Techniques For Making Decisions Under Uncertainty," JFM, 1984, v4(1), 65-74.

Gehm, Fred. "Who Is R. N. Elliott And Why Is He Making Waves?," FAJ, 1983, v39(1), 51-58.

Gehr, Adam K. (Miller, Robert E. and Adam K. Gehr. "Sample Size Bias And Sharpe's Performance Measure: A Note," JFQA, 1978, v13(5), 943-946.)

Gehr, Adam K., Jr. and Thomas Berry. "FNMA Auction Results As A Forecaster Of Residential Mortgage Yields: A Comment," JMCB, 1983, v15(1), 116-119.

Gehr, Adam K., Jr. "Financial Structure And Financial Strategy," JFR, 1984, v7(1), 69-80.

Gehr, Adam K., Jr. "Risk And Return," JOF, 1979, v34(4), 1027-1030.

Gehr, Adam K., Jr. "Risk-Adjusted Capital Budgeting Using Arbitrage," FM, 1981, v10(4), 14-19.

Gehr, Adam K., Jr. "Undated Futures Markets," JFM, 1988, v8(1), 89-98.

Gehr, Adam K., Jr. (Berry, Thomas D. and Adam K. Gehr, Jr. "FNMA Mortgage Purchase Commitments As Put Options: An Empirical Examination," AREUEA, 1985, v13(1), 93-105.)

Gehr, Adam K., Jr. (Emery, Douglas R. and Adam K. Gehr, Jr. "Tax Options, Capital Structure, And Miller Equilibrium: A Numerical Illustration," FM, 1988, v17(2), 30-40.)

Gehrels, Franz. "Monetary Systems For The Common Market," JOF, 1959, v14(2), 312-321.

Gehrke, Judith Ann. (Barrett, M. Edgar, Lee N. Price and Judith Ann Gehrke. "What Investors Need To Know About Japan," FAJ, 1974, v30(2), 60-67.)

Gehrke, Judith Ann. (Barrett, M. Edgar, Lee N. Price and Judith Ann Gehrke. "What Investors Need To Know About Japan," FAJ, 1974, v30(1), 33-44.)

Gehrlein, William V. and Thomas H. McInish. "Cyclical Variability Of Bond Risk Premia: A Note," JBF, 1985, v9(1), 157-166.

Geier, Frederick V. "The Machine Tool Industry," FAJ, 1950, v6(3), 27-30.

Geijsbeek, William R., Jr. (Schall, Lawrence D., Gary L. Sundem and William R. Geijsbeek, Jr. "Survey And Analysis Of Capital Budgeting Methods," JOF, 1978, v33(1), 281-287.)

Geltner, David. "Bias In Appraisal-Based Returns," AREUEA, 1989, v17(3), 338-352.

Geltner, David. "Estimating Real Estate's Systematic Risk From Aggregate Level Appraisal-Based Returns," AREUEA, 1989, v17(4), 463-481.

Geltner, David. "On The Use Of The Financial Option Price Model To Value And Explain Vacant Urban Land," AREUEA, 1989, v17(2), 142-158.

Geltner, David. "Return Risk And Cash Flow Risk With Long-Term Riskless Leases In Commercial Real Estate," AREUEA, 1990, v18(4), 377-402.

Gemmill, Gordon. "Hedging Crude Oil: How Many Markets Are Needed In The World?," RFM, 1988, v7(Supp), 556-571.

Gemmill, Gordon. "The Forecasting Performance Of Stock Options On The London Traded Options Market," JBFA, 1986, v13(4), 535-546.

Gemmill, R. F. "Notes On The Measurement Of International Liquidity," JOF, 1960, v15(1), 53-61.

Gemmill, Robert F. "Interest Rates And Foreign Dollar Balances," JOF, 1961, v16(3), 363-376.

Gencturk, Esra. (Dubinsky, Alan J., Terry L. Childers, Steven J. Skinner and Esra Gencturk. "Impact Of Sales Supervisor Leadership Behavior On Insurance Agent Attitudes And Performance," JRI, 1988, v55(1), 132-144.)

Gendreau, Brian C. "Bankers' Balances, Demand Deposit Interest, And Agricultural Credit Before The Banking Act Of 1933," JMCB, 1979, v11(4), 506-514.

Gendreau, Brian C. "Carrying Costs And Treasury Bill Futures," JPM, 1985-86, v12(1), 58-64.

Gendreau, Brian C. "The Implicit Return On Bankers' Balances," JMCB, 1983, v15(4), 411-424.

Gendron, Michel and Christian Genest. "Performance Measurement Under Asymmetric Information And Investment Constraints," JOF, 1990, v45(5), 1655-1662.

Genest, Christian. (Gendron, Michel and Christian Genest. "Performance Measurement Under Asymmetric Information And Investment Constraints," JOF, 1990, v45(5), 1655-1662.)

Gennotte, Gerard. "Optimal Portfolio Choice Under Incomplete Information," JOF, 1986, v41(3), 733-746.

Gentry, James and John Pike. "An Empirical Study Of The Risk-Return Hypothesis Using Common Stock Portfolios Of Life Insurance Companies," JFQA, 1970, v5(2), 179-185.

Gentry, James A. and Darrel Greifzu. "Short-Run Financial Management Model On Lotus 1-2-3," JFED, 1985, v14, 75-85.

Gentry, James A. and James R. Garven. "Video Graphics And The Teaching Of Financial Management Concepts," JFED, 1983, v12, 17-26.

Gentry, James A. and Jesus M. De La Garza. "A Generalized Model For Monitoring Accounts Receivable," FM, 1985, v14(4), 28-38.

Gentry, James A. and John R. Pike. "Dual Funds Revisited," FAJ, 1968, v24(2), 149-157.

Gentry, James A. and Stephen A. Pyhrr. "Simulating An EPS Growth Model," FM, 1973, v2(2), 68-75.

Gentry, James A. "Management Of Information, Competitive Advantages And Short-Run Financial Management Systems," AWCM, 1990, v1(1), 177-186.

Gentry, James A. "Rates Of Return On Common Stock Portfolios Of Life Insurance Companies: Addendum," JRI, 1971, v38(2), 285-292.

Gentry, James A. "Simulating Financial Decision Making," JFED, 1972, v1, 106.

Gentry, James A. "Simulation Of The Financial Planning Process Of P-L Insurers," JRI, 1972, v39(3), 383-396.

Gentry, James A. "State Of The Art Of Short-Run Financial Management," FM, 1988, v17(2), 41-57.

Gentry, James A. (Gahlon, James M. and James A. Gentry. "On the Relationship Between Systematic Risk And The Degrees Of Operating And Financial Leverage," FM, 1982, v11(2), 15-23.)

Gentry, James A. (Linke, Charles M. and James A. Gentry. "Life Insurers, Variable Annuities And Mutual Funds: A Critical Study: Comment," JRI, 1971, v38(3), 477-483.)

Gentry, James A. (Millar, James R. and James A. Gentry. "The Soviet Experiment With Domestic Lottery Bonds," FM, 1980, v9(4), 21-29.)

Gentry, James A. (Shaw, Michael J. and James A. Gentry. "Using An Expert System With Inductive Learning To Eval- uate Business Loans," FM, 1988, v17(3), 45-56.)

Gentry, James A. and Charles M. Linke. "Characteristics Of Life Insurers Entering The Mutual Fund Industry," JRI, 1971, v38(2), 237-250.

Gentry, James A. and Cheng F. Lee. "Financial Forecasting And The X-11 Model: Preliminary Evidence," AFPAF, 1987, v2(1), 27-50.

Gentry, James A. and Jesus M. De La Garza. "Monitoring Accounts Payables," FR, 1990, v25(4), 559-576.

Gentry, James A. and John R. Pike. "Rates Of Return On Common Stock Portfolios Of Life Insurance Companies," JRI, 1969, v36(4), 545-552.

Gentry, James A., Paul Newbold and David T. Whitford. "Predicting Bankruptcy: If Cash Flow's Not The Bottom Line, What Is?," FAJ, 1985, v41(5), 47-56.

Gentry, James A., David T. Whitford and Paul Newbold. "Predicting Industrial Bond Ratings With A Probit Model And Funds Flow Components," FR, 1988, v23(3), 269-286.

Gentry, James A., Paul Newbold and David T. Whitford. "Funds Flow Components, Financial Ratios, And Bankruptcy," JBFA, 1987, v14(4), 595-606.

Gentry, James A., Paul Newbold and David T. Whitford. "Profiles Of Cash Flow Components," FAJ, 1990, v46(4), 41-48.

Gentry, James A., R. Vaidyanathan and Hei Wai Lee. "A Weighted Cash Conversion Cycle," FM, 1990, v19(1), 90-99.

George, Edwin B. "The Rate Of Military Deliveries," FAJ, 1952, v8(5), 37-38.

George, Edwin B. and Robert J. Landry. "The Federal Reserve Board Report On Small-Business Financing," JOB, 1959, v32(3), 212-228.

George, Henry. "The Lazzaroni And The Leperos," JPM, 1975-76, v2(1), 72-74.

George, J. H. B. "Saline Water Conversion," FAJ, 1962, v18(3), 23-28.

Gerber, Joseph F. "A Regulator Faces The Facts," JRI, 1959, v26(1), 49-56.

Gerdes, Victor. "Application Of The Theory Of Marketing Tangible Goods To The Marketing Of Insurance," JRI, 1961, v28(1), 27-28.

Gerdes, Victor. "Insuring The Flood Peril," JRI, 1963, v30(4), 547-554.

Gerdes, Victor. "International Compulsory Automobile Insurance," JRI, 1959, v26(2), 29-34.

Gerdes, Victor. "Social Security In Developing African Nations," JRI, 1965, v32(3), 455-464.

Gerdes, Victor. "Social Security And Family Income Requirements," JRI, 1966, v33(2), 225-236.

Gerdes, Victor. "The Insurance Worker In The Labor Movement," JRI, 1964, v31(2), 169-178.

Gerking, Shelby, Menno De Haan and William Schulze. "The Marginal Value Of Job Safety: A Contingent Valuation Study," JRU, 1988, v1(2), 185-200.

Gerlach, Stefan. "World Business Cycles Under Fixed And Flexible Exchange Rates," JMCB, 1988, v20(4), 621-632.

Gerlow, Mary E. (Johnson, Robert L., Carl R. Zulauf, Scott H. Irwin and Mary E. Gerlow. "The Soybean Complex Spread: An Examination Of Market Efficiency From The Viewpoint Of A Production Process," JFM, 1991, v11(1), 25-38.)

Gerner, Jennifer L. (Bryant, W. Keith and Jennifer L. Gerner. "The Demand For Service Contracts," JOB, 1982, v55(3), 345-366.)

Gerner, Jennifer L. and W. Keith Bryant. "The Demand For Repair Service During Warranty," JOB, 1980, v53(4), 397-414.

Gersch, Will. (Sklarz, Michael A., Norman G. Miller and Will Gersch. "Forecasting Using Long-Order Autoregressive Processes: An Example Using Housing Starts," AREUEA, 1987, v15(4), 374-388.)

Gerstenfeld, Arthur. "Technological Forecasting," JOB, 1971, v44(1), 10-18.

Gerstner, Eitan and James D. Hess. "Why Do Hot Dogs Come In Packs Of 10 And Buns In 8s Or 12s? A Demand-Side Investigation," JOB, 1987, v60(4), 491-518.

Gertler, Mark L. and Earl L. Grinols. "Unemployment, Inflation, And Common Stock Returns," JMCB, 1982, v14(2), 216-233.

Gertler, Mark. "Financial Structure And Aggregate Economic Activity: An Overview," JMCB, 1988, v20(3), Part 2, 559-588.

Geske, Robert and H. E. Johnson. "The American Put Option Valued Analytically," JOF, 1984, v39(5), 1511-1524.

Geske, Robert and H. E. Johnson. "The Valuation Of Corporate Liabilities As Compound Options: A Correction," JFQA, 1984, v19(2), 231-232.

Geske, Robert and Kuldeep Shastri. "The Early Exercise Of American Puts," JBF, 1985, v9(2), 207-219.

Geske, Robert and Kuldeep Shastri. "Valuation By Approximation: A Comparison Of Alternative Option Valuation Techniques," JFQA, 1985, v20(1), 45-72.

Geske, Robert and Richard Roll. "The Fiscal And Monetary Linkage Between Stock Returns And Inflation," JOF, 1983, v38(1), 1-33.

Geske, Robert and Richard Roll. "On Valuing American Call Options With The Black-Scholes European Formula," JOF, 1984, v39(2), 443-455.

Geske, Robert, Richard Roll and Kuldeep Shastri. "Over-the-Counter Option Market Dividend Protection And 'Biases' In The Black-Scholes Model: A Note," JOF, 1983, v38(4), 1271-1277.

Geske, Robert L. and Dan R. Pieptea. Controlling Interest Rate Risk And Return With Futures," RFM, 1987, v6(1), 64-86.

Geske, Robert. "A Note On An Analytical Valuation Formula For Unprotected American Call Options On Stocks With Known Dividends," JFEC, 1979, v7(4), 375-380.

Geske, Robert. "On The Valuation Of American Call Options On Stocks With Known Dividends: A Comment," JFEC, 1981, v9(2), 213-215.

Geske, Robert. "The Pricing Of Options With Stochastic Dividend Yield," JOF, 1978, v33(2), 617-625.

Geske, Robert. "The Valuation Of Corporate Liabilities As Compound Options," JFQA, 1977, v12(4), 541-552.

Geske, Robert. "The Valuation Of Compound Options," JFEC, 1979, v7(1), 63-82.

Geske, Robert. (Galai, Dan and Robert Geske. "Option Performance Measurement," JPM, 1983-84, v10(3), 42-46.)

Geske, Robert. (Gatto, Mary Ann, Robert Geske, Robert Litzenberger and Howard Sosin. "Mutual Fund Insurance," JFEC, 1980, v8(3), 283-317.)

Geyer, Carter T. "The Abrogation Of Rule 390," FAJ, 1978, v34(1), 22-30.

Ghandhi, J. K. S. "On The Measurement Of Leverage," JOF, 1966, v21(4), 715-726.

Ghazanfari, Farrokh. (Bertin, William J., Farrokh Ghazanfari and Khalil M. Torabzadeh. "Failed Bank Acquisitions And Successful Bidders' Returns," FM, 1989, v18(2), 93-100.)

Ghee, William K. (Felton, Robert S., William K. Ghee and John E. Stinton. "A Mid-1970 Report On The National Flood Insurance Program," JRI, 1971, v38(1), 1-14.)

Gheva, David and Meir Sokoler. "An Alternative Approach To The Problem Of Classification - The Case Of Bank Failures In Israel," JBR, 1981-82, v12(4), 228-238.

Ghidini, Giulio. "Comment: An Investment Paradox," JFQA, 1977, v12(5), 891-894.

Ghosal, Monojit. (Comiskey, Eugene E. and Monojit Ghosal. "Tax Analysis Of The Operating Loss Company," FAJ, 1984, v40(6), 56-61.)

Ghosh, Arabinda. (Kolodny, Richard, Martin Laurence and Arabinda Ghosh. "In Search Of Excellence ... For Whom?," JPM, 1989, v15(3), 56-60.)

Ghosh, Chinmoy and J. Randall Woolridge. "An Analysis Of Shareholder Reaction To Dividend Cuts And Omissions," JFR, 1988, v11(4), 281-294.

Ghosh, Chinmoy and J. Randall Woolridge. "Dividend Omissions And Stock Market Rationality," JBFA, 1991, v18(3), 315-330.

Ghosh, Chinmoy. (Clapp, John M., Joseph A. Fields and Chinmoy Ghosh. "An Examination Of Profitability In Spatial Markets: The Case Of Life Insurance Agency Locations," JRI, 1990, v57(3), 431-454.)

Ghosh, Chinmoy. (Woolridge, J. Randall and Chinmoy Ghosh. "Institutional Trading And Security Prices: The Case Of Changes In The Composition Of The S&P 500 Index," JFR, 1986, v9(1), 13-24.)

Ghosh, Dilip K. "Capital Assets And Activity Analysis Of Firms In A General Equilibrium Model," IJOF, 1990, v3(1), 158-169.

Ghosh, Dilip K. (Baum, Donald N. and Dilip K. Ghosh. "Interest Rate, Wealth And The Consumption-Savings Decision: The Relationship Revisited," IJOF, 1988, v1(1), 15-34.)

Ghosh, Dilip K. Selection And Revision Theoretic Exercises In Portfolio Analysis," IJOF, 1988, v1(1), 90-95.

Giaccotto, Carmelo and Mukhtar M. Ali. "Optimal Distribution-Free Tests And Further Evidence Of Heteroscedasticity In The Market Model: A Reply," JOF, 1985, v40(2), 607.

Giaccotto, Carmelo and Mukhtar M. Ali. "Optimum Distribution-Free Tests And Further Evidence Of Heteroscedasticity In The Market Model," JOF, 1982, v37(5), 1247-1258.

Giaccotto, Carmelo. "A Note On Tests Of The Capital Asset Pricing Model," FR, 1984, v19(1), 97-102.

Giaccotto, Carmelo. "Compounding And Discounting With Stochastic Interest Rates," JBFA, 1989, v16(5), 745-769.

Giaccotto, Carmelo. "Stochastic Modelling Of Interest Rates: Actuarial Vs. Equilibrium Approach," JRI, 1986, v53(3), 435-453.

Giammarino, Ronald M. and Robert L. Heinkel. "A Model Of Dynamic Takeover Behavior," JOF, 1986, v41(2), 465-480.

Giammarino, Ronald M. (Eckbo, B. Espen, Ronald M. Giammarino and Robert L. Heinkel. "Asymmetric Information And The Medium Of Exchange In Takeovers: Theory And Tests," RFS, 1990, v3(4), 651-676.)

Giammarino, Ronald M. and Ed Nosal. "Debt Overhang And The Efficiency Of International Rescheduling," RDIBF, 1991, v4/5, 474-504.

Giammarino, Ronald and Tracy Lewis. "A Theory Of Negotiated Equity Financing," RFS, 1988-89, v1(3), 265-288.

Gibb, William T. "Critical Evaluation Of Pension Plans," JOF, 1968, v23(2), 337-343.

Gibbons, Joel C. "The Optimal Durability Of Fixed Capital When Demand Is Uncertain," JOB, 1984, v57(3), 389-403.

Gibbons, Michael R. and Wayne Ferson. "Testing Asset Pricing Models With Changing Expectations And An Unobservable Market Portfolio," JFEC, 1985, v14(2), 217-236.

Gibbons, Michael R. "Multivariate Tests Of Financial Models: A New Approach," JFEC, 1982, v10(1), 3-27.

Gibbons, Michael R. (Breeden, Douglas T., Michael R. Gibbons and Robert H. Litzenberger. "Empirical Tests Of The Consumption-Oriented CAPM," JOF, 1989, v44(2), 231-262.)

Gibbons, Michael R. and Jay Shanken. "Subperiod Aggression And The Power Of Multivariate Tests Of Portfolio Efficiency," JFEC, 1987, v19(2), 389-394.

Gibbons, Michael R. and Patrick Hess. "Day Of The Week Effects And Asset Returns," JOB, 1981, v54(4), 579-596.

Gibbs, Stephen. (Boyle, Phelim P., Jeremy Evnine and Stephen Gibbs. "Numerical Evaluation Of Multivariate Contingent Claims," RFS, 1989, v2(2), 241-250.)

Gibson, Charles. "How Chartered Financial Analysts View Financial Ratios," FAJ, 1987, v43(3), 73-76.

Gibson, J. Douglas. "Canada's Economic Development And Problems, FAJ, 1953, v9(2), 111-116.

Premia Volatility Once Again," **JIMF**, 1988, v7(1), 111-114.

Giovannini, Alberto and Philippe Jorion. "The Time Variation Of Risk And Return In The Foreign Exchange And Stock Markets," **JOF**, 1989, v44(2), 307-326.

Giovannini, Alberto. "'Rules Of The Game' During The International Gold Standard: England And Germany," **JIMF**, 1986, v5(4), 467-483.

Gipson, James H. "Investing In A Zero Sum Economy," **JPM**, 1980-81, v7(4), 15-16.

Gipson, James. "Growth On The Demand Curve: The New Kind Of Growth," **JPM**, 1979-80, v6(2), 46-48.

Girmes, D. H. and Anne E. Benjamin. "Random Walk Hypothesis For 543 Stocks And Shares Registered On The London Stock Exchange," **JBFA**, 1975, v2(1), 135-145.

Giroux, Gary A. and Casper E. Wiggins. "An Events Approach To Corporate Bankruptcy," **JBR**, 1984-85, v15(3), 179-187.

Giroux, Gary A. and Peter S. Rose. "An Update Of Bank Planning Systems: Results Of A Nationwide Survey Of Large U.S. Banks," **JBR**, 1984-85, v15(3), 136-147.

Giroux, Gary A. "A Survey Of Forecasting Techniques Used By Commercial Banks," **JBR**, 1980-81, v11(1),51-53.

Giroux, Gary, Winston Shearon and Steven Grossman. "How Does Inflation Affect A BHC's Rate Of Return?," **JBR**, 1983-84, v14(2), 164-169.

Girton, Lance and Dayle Nattress. "Monetary Innovations And Interest Rates," **JMCB**, 1985, v17(3),289-297.

Girton, Lance and Don Roper. "Theory And Implications Of Currency Substitution," **JMCB**, 1981, v13(1), 12-30.

Girton, Lance. (Farrar, Donald E. and Lance Girton. "Institutional Investors And Concentration Of Financial Power: Berle And Means Revisited," **JOF**, 1981, v36(2), 369-381.)

Gisser, Micha and Thomas H. Goodwin. "Crude Oil And The Macroeconomy: Tests Of Some Popular Notions," **JMCB**, 1986, v18(1), 95-103.

Gitman, Lawrence and Peter Bacon. "Comprehensive Personal Financial Planning: An Emerging Opportunity," **JFED**, 1985, v14, 36-46.

Gitman, Lawrence J. and Charles E. Maxwell. "Financial Activities Of Major U.S. Firms: Survey And Analysis Of Fortune's 1000," **FM**, 1985, v14(4), 57-65.

Gitman, Lawrence J. and John R. Forrester, Jr. "A Survey Of Capital Budgeting Techniques Used By Major U.S. Firms," **FM**, 1977, v6(3), 66-71.

Gitman, Lawrence J. and Mark D. Goodwin. "An Assessment Of Marketable Securities Management Practices," **JFR**, 1979, v2(2), 161-169.

Gitman, Lawrence J. and Vincent A. Mercurio. "Cost Of Capital Techniques Used By Major U.S. Firms: Survey And Analysis Of Fortune's 1000," **FM**, 1982, v11(4), 21-29.

Gitman, Lawrence J. "Estimating Corporate Liquidity Requirements: A Simplified Approach," **FR**, 1974, v9(1), 79-88.

Gitman, Lawrence J. (Bacon, Peter W., Lawrence J. Gitman, Khurshid Ahmad and M. Fall Ainina. "Long-Term Catastrophic Care: A Financial Planning Perspective," **JRI**, 1989, v56(1), 146-154.)

Gitman, Lawrence J. (Pruitt, Stephen W. and Lawrence J. Gitman. "Capital Budgeting Forecast Biases: Evidence From The Fortune 500," **FM**, 1987, v16(1), 46-51.)

Gitman, Lawrence J. (Sachdeva, Kanwal S. and Lawrence J. Gitman. "Accounts Receivable Decisions In A Capital Bud- geting Framework," **FM**, 1981, v10(5), 45-49.)

Gitman, Lawrence J., D. Keith Forrester and John R. Forrester, Jr. "Maximizing Cash Disbursement Float," **FM**, 1976, v5(2), 15-24.

Gitman, Lawrence J., Edward A. Moses and I. Thomas White. "An Assessment Of Corporate Cash Management Practices," **FM**, 1979, v8(1), 32-41.

Gitman, Lawrence J., William F. Lewis and Rebecca M. J. Yates. "An Approach For Assessing, Selecting And Using Finance Cases," **JFED**, 1987, v16, 56-64.

Givoly, Dan and Arie Ovadia. "Year-End Tax-Induced Sales And Stock Market Seasonality," **JOF**, 1983, v38(1), 171-185.

Givoly, Dan and Josef Lakonishok. "The Quality Of Analysts' Forecasts Of Earnings," **FAJ**, 1984, v40(5), 40-47.

Givoly, Dan and Josef Lakonishok. "Financial Analysts' Forecasts Of Earnings: Their Value To Investors," **JBF**, 1980, v4(3), 221-234.

Givoly, Dan and Dan Palmon. "Insider Trading And The Exploitation Of Inside Information: Some Empirical Evidence," **JOB**, 1985, v58(1), 69-88.

Givoly, Dan, Dan Palmon and Mier Schneller. "Perception Of Stock Similarity By Financial Analysts," **FR**, 1981, v16(3), 30-43.

Gjerde, Oystein. "A Simple Risk-Reducing Cross-Hedging Strategy: Using Soybean Oil Futures With Fish Oil Sales," **RFM**, 1989, v8(2), 180-195.

Gjerde, Oystein. "Measuring Hedging Effectiveness In A Traditional One-Periodic Portfolio Framework," **JFM**, 1987, v7(6), 663-674.

Gladstein, Mathew L. (Merton, Robert C., Myron S. Scholes and Mathew L. Gladstein. "The Returns And Risk Of Alternative Call Option Portoflio Investment Strategies," **JOB**, 1978, v51(2), 183-242.)

Gladstein, Mathew L. (Merton, Robert C., Myron S. Scholes and Mathew L. Gladstein. "The Returns And Risks Of Alternative Put-Option Portfolio Investment Strategies," **JOB**, 1982, v55(1), 1-56.)

Glahe, Fred R. "The Behavior Of Professional Risk-Bearers: A Better Test Of A Theory," **JMCB**, 1975, v7(4), 533-534.

Glandon, Gerald L. (Homan, Rick K., Gerald L. Glandon and Michael A. Counte. "Perceived Risk: The Link To Plan Selection And Future Utilization," **JRI**, 1989, v56(1), 67-82.)

Glascock, John L. and Wallace N. Davidson, III. "The Effect Of Bond Deratings On Bank Stock Returns," **JBR**, 1985-86, v16(3), 120-127.

Glascock, John L. (Darrat, Ali F. and John L. Glascock. "Real Estate Returns, Money And Fiscal Deficits: Is The Real Estate Market Efficient?," **JREFEC**, 1989, v2(3), 197-208.)

Glascock, John L. (Davidson, Wallace N., III. and John L. Glascock. "The Announcement Effects Of Preferred Stock Re-Ratings," **JFR**, 1985, v8(1), 317-325.)

Glascock, John L., Glenn V. Henderson, Jr. and Linda J. Martin. "When E. F. Hutton Talks," **FAJ**, 1986, v42(3), 69-72.

Glascock, John L., Shirin Jahanian and C. F. Sirmans. "An Analysis Of Office Market Rents: Some Empirical Evidence," **AREUEA**, 1990, v18(1), 105-120.

Glascock, John L., Wallace N. Davidson and C. F. Sirmans. "An Analysis Of The Acquisition And Dispositon Of Real Estate Assets," **JRER**, 1989, v4(3), 131-140.

Glascock, John. (Karafiath, Imre and John Glascock. "Intra-Industry Effects Of A Regulatory Shift: Capital Market Evidence From Penn Square," **FR**, 1989, v24(1), 123-134.)

Glasgo, Philip W., William J. Landes and A. Frank Thompson. "Bank Discount, Coupon Equivalent, And Compound Yields," **FM**, 1982, v11(3), 80-84.

Glasser, Peter. "A New Investment Strategy For Pension Funds: Comment," **JPM**, 1981-82, v8(4),74-76.

Glassman, David M. "Spin-Offs And Spin-Outs: Using 'Securitization' To Beat The Bureaucracy," **JACF**, 1988, v1(3), 82-89.

Glassman, David. (Stewart, G. Bennett and David Glassman. "The Motives And Methods Of Corporate Restructuring," **JACF**, 1988, v1(1), 85-99.)

Glassman, David. (Stewart, G. Bennett and David Glassman. "The Motives And Methods Of Corporate Restructuring: Part II," **JACF**, 1988, v1(2), 79-88.)

Glassman, Debra. "Exchange Rate Risk And Transactions Costs: Evidence From Bid-Ask Spreads," **JIMF**, 1987, v6(4), 479-490.

Glassman, Debra. "The Efficiency Of Foreign Exchange Futures Markets In Turbulent And Non-Turbulent Periods," **JFM**, 1987, v7(3), 245-268.

Glassmire, William F., Jr. (Van Horne, James C. and William F. Glassmire, Jr. "The Impact Of Unanticipated Changes In Inflation On The Value Of Common Stock," **JOF**, 1972, v27(5), 1081-1092.)

Glautier, M. W. E. and P. J. Taylor. "A Comment On The Application Of Group Dynamics In Task Performance Relevant To Accounting," **JBFA**, 1977, v4(4), 477-480.

Glautier, M. W. E. "Human Resource Accounting: A Critique Of Research Objectives For The Development Of Human Resource Accounting Models," **JBFA**, 1976, v3(2), 3-22.

Gleason, John M. (Lilly, Claude C. and John M. Gleason. "A Dynamic Programming Approach To Equipment Loss Analysis," **JRI**, 1977, v44(2), 305-310.)

Gleeson, Michael E. "Housing Costs And The Elderly," **AREUEA**, 1980, v8(4), 387-394.

Gleit, Alan and Ben Branch. "The Black-Scholes Model And Stock Price Forecasting," **FR**, 1980, v15(2), 13-22.

Gleit, Alan. "Valuation Of General Contingent Claims: Existence, Uniqueness, And Comparisons Of Solutions," **JFEC**, 1978, v6(1), 71-87.

Glen, Jack D. (Cumby, Robert E. and Jack D. Glen. "Evaluating The Performance Of International Mutual Funds," **JOF**, 1990, v45(2), 497-522.)

Glenn, David W. "Super Premium Security Prices And Optimal Corporate Financing Decisions," **JOF**, 1976, v31(2), 507-524.

Glenn, David W. and Robert H. Litzenberger. "An Interindustry Approach To Econometric Cost Of Capital Estimation," **RIF**, 1979, v1, 53-76.

Glenn, David. (Campbell, Tim S. and David Glenn. "Deposit Insurance In A Deregulated Environment," **JOF**, 1984, v39(3), 775-785.)

Glennon, Dennis and Julia Lane. "Imputing A Housewife's Earnings In A Wrongful Death And Injury Case," **JRI**, 1986, v53(4), 734-743.

Glennon, Dennis. (Lane, Julia and Dennis Glennon. "The Estimation Of Age/Earnings Profiles In Wrongful Death And Injury Cases," **JRI**, 1985, v52(4), 686-695.)

Glennon, Dennis. (Lane, Julia and Dennis Glennon. "The Estimation Of Age/Earnings Profiles In Wrongful Death And Injury Cases: Reply," **JRI**, 1988, v55(1), 174-179.)

Glick, Reuven and Clas Wihlborg. "The Role Of Information Acquisition And Financial Markets In International Macroeconomic Adjustment," **JIMF**, 1986, v5(3), 257-283.

Glick, Reuven and Michael Hutchison. "New Results In Support Of The Fiscal Policy Ineffectiveness Proposition," **JMCB**, 1990, v22(3), 288-304.

Glick, Reuven. "Market Neutrality Conditions And Valuation Of A Foreign Affiliate," **JBFA**, 1986, v13(2), 239-249.

Glick, Reuven. "The Geometry Of Asset Adjustment With Adjustment Costs," **JFR**, 1984, v7(4),303-314.

Glickstein, David A. and Rolf E. Wubbels. "Dow Theory Is Alive And Well!," **JPM**, 1982-83, v9(3),28-32.

Glimpse, Warren G. "The Compustat Analysis System: An Integrated Software Package For Financial Analysis And Modeling," **JFED**, 1976, v5, 80-87.

Globerman, Steven. "Firm Size And Dynamic Efficiency In The Life Insurance Industry," **JRI**, 1986, v53(2), 278-293.

Glosten, Lawrence R. and Paul R. Milgrom. "Bid, Ask And Transaction Prices In A Specialist Market With Heterogeneously Informed Traders," **JFEC**, 1985, v14(1), 71-100.

Glosten, Lawrence R. "Components Of The Bid-Ask Spread And The Statistical Properties Of Transactions Prices," **JOF**, 1987, v42(5), 1293-1307.

Glosten, Lawrence R. "Insider Trading, Liquidity, And The Role Of The Monopolist Specialist," **JOB**, 1989, v62(2), 211-236.

Glosten, Lawrence R. (Breen, William, Lawrence R. Glosten and Ravi Jagannathan. "Economic Significance Of Predictable Variations In Stock Index Returns," **JOF**, 1989, v44(5), 1177-1190.)

Glosten, Lawrence and Lawrence E. Harris. "Estimating The Components Of The Bid/Ask Spread," **JFEC**, 1988, v21(1), 123-142.

Gloudemans, Robert J. "Confidence Intervals And The Evaluation Of Regression Based Appraisal Models," **AREUEA**, 1979, v7(1), 131-135.

Glower, Michel and Patric H. Hendershott. "The Determinants Of REALTOR Income," **JRER**, 1988, v3(2), 53-68.

Glutekin, N. Bulent. (Gultekin, Mustafa N., N. Bulent Gultekin and Alessandro Penati. "Capital Controls And International Capital Market Segmentation: The Evidence From The Japanese And American Stock Markets," **JOF**, 1989, v44(4), 849-870.)

Goble, George W. "Proposed Revision Of The Standard Fire Insurance Policy With Special Reference To Moral Hazard Clauses," **JRI**, 1937, v4, 37-53.

Goble, George W. "Regulation Of Insurance Companies In A Period Of Emergency," **JRI**, 1935, v2, 29-36.

Gochoco, Maria S. "Tests Of The Money Neutrality And Rationality Hypotheses: The Case Of Japan 1973-1985," **JMCB**, 1986, v18(4), 458-466.

Gockel, Galen. (Sudman, Seymour, Norman M. Bradburn and Galen Gockel. "The Extent And Characteristics Of Racially Integrated Housing In The United States," **JOB**, 1969, v42(1), 50-92.)

Godfrey, Jaso P. "What Is An Analyst?," **FAJ**, 1953, v9(5), 103-105.

Goebel, Paul R. and Kee S. Kim. "Performance Evaluation Of Finite-Life Real Estate Investment Trusts," **JRER**, 1989, v4(2), 57-69.

Goering, John M. "What A National Commission On Neighborhoods Could Do: Comment," **AREUEA**, 1979, v7(2), 227-229.

Goetz, Raymond. "The Case Against State Regulation Of Uninsured Employee Welfare Plans," **JRI**, 1968, v35(2), 311-316.

Goetze, Rolf. "Avoiding Both Disinvestment And Speculation In Private Multifamily Housing," **AREUEA**, 1978, v6(2), 175-185.

Goetzmann, William N. and Mark Garry. "Does Delisting From The S&P 500 Affect Stock Price?," **FAJ**, 1986, v42(2), 64-69.

Goetzmann, William N. and Roger G. Ibbotson. "The Performance Of Real Estate As An Asset Class," **JACF**, 1990, v3(1), 65-76.

Goff, Delbert. (Alexander, John, Delbert Goff and Pamela P. Peterson. "Profitability Of A Trading Strategy Based On Unexpected Earnings," **FAJ**, 1989, v45(4), 65-71.)

Gogol, Daniel. "The Much Greater Profitability Of New York Workers' Compensation Risks With Higher Modifications," **JRI**, 1985, v52(1), 151-156.

Golbe, Devra L. and Barry Schachter. "The Net Present Value Rule And An Algorithm For Maintaining A Constant Debt-Equity Ratio," **FM**, 1985, v14(2), 53-58.

Gold, Franklin. (Sherman, H. David and Franklin Gold. "Bank Branch Operating Efficiency: Evaluation With Data Envelopment Analysis," **JBF**, 1985, v9(2), 297-316.)

Gold, Jeremy and Michael W. Peskin. "Longing For Duration," **FAJ**, 1988, v44(6), 68-71.

Gold, Jeremy. (Bookstaber, Richard and Jeremy Gold. "In Search Of The Liability Asset," **FAJ**, 1988, v44(1), 70-80.)

Goldberg, Craig J. and Karen Rogers. "An Introduction To Asset Backed Securities," **JACF**, 1988, v1(3), 20-31.

Goldberg, Ellen S. "Comparative Cost Analysis Of Foreign Owned U.S. Banks," **JBR**, 1982-83, v13(3), 144-159.

Goldberg, Harold H. "Asset Securitization And Corporate Financial Health," **JACF**, 1988, v1(3), 45-51.

Goldberg, Lawrence G. and Anthony Saunders. "The Causes Of U.S. Bank Expansion Overseas: The Case Of Great Britain," **JMCB**, 1980, v12(4), Part 1, 630-634.

Goldberg, Lawrence G. and Anthony Saunders. "The Growth Of Organizational Forms Of Foreign Banks In The U.S.," **JMCB**, 1981, v13(3),365-374.

Goldberg, Lawrence G. and Anthony Saunders. "The Determinants Of Foreign Banking Activity In The United States," **JBF**, 1981, v5(1), 17-32.

Goldberg, Lawrence G. and John T. Rose. "Do State Reserve Requirements Matter?," **JBR**, 1977-78, v8(1), 31-39.

Goldberg, Lawrence G. and John T. Rose. "Mutual Savings Bank Membership In The FHLBS: Motivations Behind Recent Membership Growth," **JBF**, 1981, v5(2),241-260.

Goldberg, Lawrence G. and John T. Rose. "The Effect On Nonmember Banks Of The Imposition Of Member Bank Reserve Requirements - With And Without Federal Reserve Services," **JOF**, 1976, v31(5), 1457-1469.

Goldberg, Lawrence G. "Bank Holding Company Acquisitions And Their Impact On Market Shares: A Comment," **JMCB**, 1976, v8(1), 127-130.

Goldberg, Lawrence G. "The Effect Of State Banking Regulations On Bank Credit Card Use: A Comment," **JMCB**, 1975, v7(1), 105-112.

Goldberg, Lawrence G. (Fishe, Raymond P. H. and Lawrence G. Goldberg. "The Effects Of Margins On Trading In Futures Markets," **JFM**, 1986, v6(2), 261-272.)

Goldberg, Lawrence G. (Fishe, Raymond P. H., Lawrence G. Goldberg, Thomas F. Gosnell and Sujata Sinha. "Margin Requirements In Futures Markets: Their Relationship To Price Volatility," **JFM**, 1990, v10(5), 541-554.)

Goldberg, Lawrence G. and Denise Johnson. "The Determinants Of US Banking Activity Abroad," **JIMF**, 1990, v9(2), 123-137.

Goldberg, Lawrence G. and Gerald A. Hanweck. "What We Can Expect From Interstate Banking," **JBF**, 1988, v12(1), 51-68.

Goldberg, Lawrence G. and Gerald A. Hanweck. "The Growth Of The World's 300 Largest Banking Organizations By Country," **JBF**, 1991, v15(1), 207-223.

Goldberg, Lawrence G., Gerald A. Hanweck, Michael Keenan and Allan Young. "Economies Of Scale And Scope In The Securities Industry," **JBF**, 1991, v15(1), 91-107.

Goldberg, Michael A. and Ashok Vora. "Dividend Yield, Regulation, And The Return On U.S. Public Utility Stocks," **JBFA**, 1985, v12(1), 47-70.

Goldberg, Michael A. and Ashok Vora. "Bivariate Spectral Analysis Of The Capital Asset Pricing Model," **JFQA**, 1978, v13(3), 435-459.

Goldberg, Michael A. and Peter R. Lloyd-Davies. "Standby Letters Of Credit: Are Banks Overextending Themselves?," **JBR**, 1985-86, v16(1), 28-39.

Goldberg, Michael A. and Wayne Y. Lee. "The Cost Of Capital And Valuation Of A Two-Country Firm: Comment," **JOF**, 1977, v32(4), 1348-1353.

Goldberg, Michael A. "American Real Estate And Urban Economics: A Canadian Perspective," **AREUEA**, 1985, v13(1), 1-14.

Goldberg, Michael A. "The Impact Of Regulatory And Monetary Factors On Bank Loan Charges," **JFQA**, 1981, v16(2), 227-246.

Goldberg, Michael A. "The Pricing Of The Prime Rate," **JBF**, 1982, v6(2), 277-296.

Goldberg, Michael A. "The Relevance Of Margin Regulations," **JMCB**, 1985, v17(4), Part 1, 521-527.

Goldberg, Michael A. "The Sensitivity Of The Prime Rate To Money Market Conditions," **JFR**, 1984, v7(4), 269-280.

Goldberg, Michael A. (Avery, Robert B., Terrence M. Belton and Michael A. Goldberg. "Market Discipline In Regulating Bank Risk:

New Evidence From The Capital Markets," **JMCB**, 1988, v20(4), 597-610.)

Goldberg, Michael A. (Gau, George W. and Michael A. Goldberg. "Interest Rate Risk, Residential Mortgages And Financial Futures Markets," **AREUEA**, 1983, v11(4), 445-461.)

Goldberg, Michael A. (Mark, Jonathan H. and Michael A. Goldberg. "Land Use Controls: The Case Of Zoning In Vancouver," **AREUEA**, 1981, v9(4), 418-435.)

Goldberg, Michael A. (Mark, Jonathan H. and Michael A. Goldberg. "Alternative Housing Price Indices: An Evaluation," **AREUEA**, 1984, v12(1), 30-49.)

Goldberg, Michael A. and Blake Allan. "Urban Growth: A View From The Supply Side," **AREUEA**, 1978, v6(3), 247-270.

Goldberg, Murray A. "Current Events As Cases," **JFED**, 1972, v1, 73.

Goldberg, Stephen M., Paul E. Green and Yoram Wind. "Conjoint Analysis Of Price Premiums For Hotel Amenities," **JOB**, 1984, v57(1), Part 2, S111-S132.

Goldenberg, David H. "Comment On 'Usefulness Of Treasury Bill Futures As Hedging Instruments'," **JFM**, 1983, v3(2), 225-226.

Goldenberg, David H. "Market Power And The Required Return To Electric Utilities," **FR**, 1987, v22(1), 175-194.

Goldenberg, David H. "Memory And Equilibrium Futures Prices," **JFM**, 1989, v9(3), 199-214.

Goldenberg, David H. "Sample Path Properties Of Futures Prices," **JFM**, 1986, v6(1), 127-140.

Goldenberg, David H. "Trading Frictions And Futures Price Movements," **JFQA**, 1988, v23(4), 465-480.

Goldenweiser, E. A. "Gold," **FAJ**, 1951, v7(4), 17-20.

Goldenweiser, E. A. "The Teaching Of Money And Banking," **JOF**, 1949, v4(3), 230-231.

Goldfarb, David R. "Hedging Interest Rate Risk In Banking," **JFM**, 1987, v7(1), 35-48.

Goldfarb, David. (Bigman, David and David Goldfarb. "Efficiency And Efficient Trading Rules For Food And Feed Grains In The World Commodity Markets: The Israeli Experience," **JFM**, 1985, v5(1), 1-10.)

Goldfarb, David. (Bigman, David, David Goldfarb and Edna Schechtman. "Futures Market Efficiency And The Time Content Of The Information Sets," **JFM**, 1983, v3(3), 321-334.)

Goldfeld, Stephen M. and Dwight M. Jaffee. "Deposit Rate Setting By Savings And Loan Associations: Reply," **JOF**, 1971, v26(5), 1158-1160.

Goldfeld, Stephen M. and Dwight M. Jaffee. "The Determinants Of Deposit-Rate Setting By Savings And Loan Associations," **JOF**, 1970, v25(3), 615-632.

Goldfeld, Stephen M. and Edward J. Kane. "The Determinants Of Member Bank Borrowing: A Reply," **JOF**, 1968, v23(5), 838-847.

Goldfeld, Stephen M. and Edward J. Kane. "The Determinants Of Member-Bank Borrowing: An Econometric Study," **JOF**, 1966, v21(3), 499-514.

Goldie, Raymond and Keith Ambachtsheer. "The Battle Of Insider Trading: Comment," **JPM**, 1980-81, v7(2), 88.

Goldie, Raymond. "Are Some Insiders More 'Inside' Than Others?: Comment," **JPM**, 1983-84, v10(2), 75.

Goldin, A. J. "War Damage Insurance," **JRI**, 1943, v10, 69-75.

Goldman, Ellis G. and Charles G. Field. "Summary Of An Article On Reforming Land-Use Regulations," **AREUEA**, 1983, v11(2), 300-318.

Goldman, M. Barry and Avraham Beja. "Market Prices Vs. Equilibrium Prices: Returns' Variance, Serial Correlation, And The Role Of The Specialist," **JOF**, 1979, v34(3), 595-607.

Goldman, M. Barry and Howard B. Sosin. "Information Dissemination, Market Efficiency And The Frequency Of Transactions," **JFEC**, 1979, v7(1), 29-61.

Goldman, M. Barry, Howard B. Sosin and Lawrence A. Shepp. "On Contingent Claims That Insure Ex-post Optimal Stock Market Timing," **JOF**, 1979, v34(2), 401-414.

Goldman, M. Barry, Howard B. Sosin and Mary Ann Gatto. "Path Dependent Options: 'Buy At The Low, Sell At The High'," **JOF**, 1979, v34(5), 1111-1127.

Goldman, M. Barry. "A Negative Report On The 'Near Optimality' Of The Max-Expected-Log Policy As Applied To Bounded Utilities For Long Lived Programs," **JFEC**, 1974, v1(1), 97-103.

Goldman, M. Barry. "Anti-Diversification Or Optimal Programmes For Infrequently Revised Portfolios," **JOF**, 1979, v34(2), 505-516.

Goldman, M. Barry. "Portfolio Returns And The Random Walk Theory: Comment," **JOF**, 1976, v31(1),153-156.

Goldman, M. Barry. (Beja, Avraham and M. Barry Goldman. "On The Dynamic Behavior Of Prices In Disequilibrium," **JOF**, 1980, v35(2), 235-248.)

Goldsberry, James E. (Woodard, George D. and James E. Goldsberry. "Economic Research As An Aid To Regional Bank Holding Company Expansion," **JBR**, 1983-84, v14(4), 302-304.)

Goldschmidt, Amnon. "On The Definition And Measurement Of Bank Output," **JBF**, 1981, v5(4), 575-585.

Goldschmidt, Y. (Shashua, L. and Y. Goldschmidt. "An Index For Evaluating Financial Performance," **JOF**, 1974, v29(3), 797-814.)

Goldschmidt. Y. "A Tool For Inflation Adjustment Of Financial Statements," **JBFA**, 1976, v3(1), 33-42.

Goldsmith, Art. "Household Life Cycle Protection: Human Capital Versus Life Insurance," **JRI**, 1983, v50(1), 33-43.

Goldsmith, Art. "Household Life Cycle Protection: Human Capital Versus Life Insurance," **JRI**, 1983, v50(3), 473-486.

Goldsmith, David. "Transactions Costs And The Theory Of Portfolio Selection," **JOF**, 1976, v31(4), 1127-1139.

Goldsmith, Raymond W. and Eli Shapiro. "An Estimate Of Bank-Administered Personal Trust Funds," **JOF**, 1959, v14(1), 11-17.

Goldsmith, Raymond W. "The National Balance Sheet - Another Tool In The Economist's Kit," **FAJ**, 1956, v12(1), 9-16.

Goldsmith, Raymond W. "The National Bureau's Postwar Capital Markets Study," **JOF**, 1957, v12(2), 121-125.

Goldstein, Alice B. and Barbara G. Markowitz. "SOFASIM: A Dynamic Insurance Model With Investment Structure, Policy Benefits And Taxes," **JOF**, 1982, v37(2), 595-604.

Goldstein, Bernard. "Unions And The Professional Employee," **JOB**, 1954, v27(4), 276-284.

Goldstein, David N. (Todd, Jerry D. and David N. Goldstein. "A Computerized Simulation Model For Analyzing Profit Sharing Plans," JRI, 1981, v48(4), 662-673.)

Goldstein, Henry N. and George G. Kaufman. "Treasury Bill Auction Procedures: An Empirical Investigation: Comment," JOF, 1975, v30(3), 895-899.

Goldstein, Henry N. "Can SDRs And A Reserve Currency Coexist?: A Comment," JMCB, 1974, v6(4), 567-570.

Goldstein, Henry N. "Should The Treasury Auction Long-Term Securities?," JOF, 1962, v17(3), 444-464.

Goldstein, Henry N. "The Implications Of Triangular Arbitrage For Forward Exchange Policy," JOF, 1964, v19(3), 544-551.

Goldstein, Jonathan. "Markup Variability And Flexibility: Theory And Empirical Evidence," JOB, 1986, v59(4), Part 1, 599-622.

Goldstein, Lawrence J. "Investment In Business Services," FAJ, 1968, v24(4), 71-74.

Goldstein, Meyer M. "Employee Pension And Profit Sharing Plans," JRI, 1945, v12, 39-53.

Goldstein, Steven J. (Ferri, Michael G., Steven J. Goldstein and It-Keong Chew. "Interest Rates And The Announcement Of Inflation," FM, 1983, v12(3), 52-61.)

Goldstein, Steven J. (Ferri, Michael G., Steven J. Goldstein and H. Dennis Oberhelman. "The Performance Of The When-Issued Market For T-Bills," JPM, 1984-85, v11(3), 57-61.)

Goldstein, Steven J. (Ferri, Michael G., H. Dennis Oberhelman and Steven J. Goldstein. "Yield Sensitivities Of Short-Term Securities," JPM, 1981-82, v8(3), 65-71.)

Goldstein, Steven J. (Lloyd, William P. and Steven J. Goldstein. "Simulation Of Portfolio Returns: Varying Numbers Of Securities And Holding Periods," JFR, 1982, v5(1), 27-38.)

Goldstein, Steven J. (Lloyd, William P., John S. Jahera, Jr. and Steven J. Goldstein. "The Relation Between Returns, Ownership Structure, And Market Value," JFR, 1986, v9(2), 171-177.)

Goldstein, Steven J. (Lloyd, William P. and Steven J. Goldstein. "Called Bonds: How Does The Investor Fare?," JPM, 1981-82, v8(1), 62-63.)

Goldstein, Steven J. (Lloyd, William P., Steven J. Goldstein and Robert B. Rogow. "International Portfolio Diversification Of Real Assets: An Update," JBFA, 1981, v8(1), 45-50.)

Goldstein, Steven J. (Roenfeldt, Rodney L, Robert J. Sweeney, Steven J. Goldstein and Helen M. Kleschick. "Commentary On 1982 FMA Program," FM, 1982, v11(4), 52-54.)

Goldstein, Steven J. (Verbrugge, James A. and Steven J. Goldstein. "Risk Return And Managerial Objectives: Some New Evidence From The Savings And Loan Industry," JFR, 1981, v4(1), 45-58.)

Goldstine, Abner D. (Netzer, Dick and Abner D. Goldstine. "Types Of Money Use In The 1950's," JOF, 1962, v17(4), 606-621.)

Goldstucker, Jac L. (Bellenger, Danny N. and Jac L. Goldstucker. "Discrimination Against Women: An Opportunity For Bank Marketing," JBR, 1975-76, v6(2), 155-159.)

Golec, Joseph H. "Do Mutual Fund Managers Who Use Incentive Compensation Outperform Those Who Don't?," FAJ, 1988, v44(6), 75-79.

Golec, Joseph. "The Financial Effects Of Fuel Adjustment Clauses On Electric Utilities," JOB, 1990, v63(2), 165-186.

Golembe, Carter H. "Long-Term Trends In Bank Regulation," JFSR, 1989, v2(3), 171-184.

Golembo, Leslie. (Simon, Julian L. and Leslie Golembo. "The Spread Of A Cost-Free Business Innovation," JOB, 1967, v40(4), 385-388.)

Golembre, Carter H. "The Future Shape Of Banking Regulation," JOF, 1971, v26(2), 599-604.

Golen, Steven and Robert Kozub. "Systems Flowchart: A Key To Understanding The Concepts Of Present And Future Value," JFED, 1981, v10, 74-77.

Gollier, Christian. "The Design Of Optimal Insurance Contracts Without The Nonnegativity Constraint On Claims," JRI, 1987, v54(2), 314-324.

Golub, Stephen S. "Foreign-Currency Government Debt, Asset Markets, And The Balance Of Payments," JIMF, 1989, v8(2), 285-294.

Golub, Stephen S. "International Capital Mobility: Net Versus Gross Stocks And Flows," JIMF, 1990, v9(4), 424-439.

Gombola, Michael J. and J. Edward Ketz. "A Caveat On Measuring Cash Flow And Solvency," FAJ, 1983, v39(5), 66-72.

Gombola, Michael J. and J. Edward Ketz. "Financial Ratio Patterns In Retail And Manufacturing Organizations," FM, 1983, v12(2), 45-56.

Gombola, Michael J. (Nunn, Kenneth P., Jr., Gerald P. Madden and Michael J. Gombola. "Are Some Insiders More 'Inside' Than Others?," JPM, 1982-83, v9(3), 18-22.)

Gombola, Michael J. and Douglas R. Kahl. "Time-Series Processes Of Utility Betas: Implications For Forecasting Systematic Risk," FM, 1990, v19(3), 84-93.

Gombola, Michael J. and Kenneth P. Nunn, Jr. "Valuation Of The Preferred Stock Sinking Fund Feature: A Time-Series Approach," JFR, 1988, v11(1), 33-42.

Gombola, Michael J., Rodney L. Roenfeldt and Philip L. Cooley. "Some Additional Evidence On Pricing Efficiency Of CBOE Options," FR, 1980, v15(1), 9-19.

Gombola, Michael J., Rodney L. Roenfeldt and Philip L. Cooley. "Spreading Strategies In CBOE Options: Evidence On Market Performance," JFR, 1978, v1(1), 35-44.

Gombola, Michael J., Mark E. Haskins, J. Edward Ketz and David D. Williams. "Cash Flow In Bankruptcy Prediction," FM, 1987, v16(4), 55-65.

Gonedes, Nicholas J. "A Note On Accounting-Based And Market-Based Estimates Of Systematic Risk," JFQA, 1975, v10(2), 355-365.

Gonedes, Nicholas J. "A Test Of The Equivalent-Risk Class Hypothesis," JFQA, 1969, v4(2), 159-177.

Gonedes, Nicholas J. "Capital Market Equilibrium For A Class Of Heterogeneous Expectations In A Two-Parameter World," JOF, 1976, v31(1), 1 -15.

Gonedes, Nicholas J. "Evidence On The 'Tax Effects' Of Inflation Under Historical Cost Accounting Methods," JOB, 1981, v54(2), 227-270.

Gonedes, Nicholas J. "Evidence On The Information Content Of Accounting Numbers: Accounting-Based And Market-Based Estimates Of Systematic Risk," JFQA, 1973, v8(3), 407-443.

Gonedes, Nicholas J. "Income-Smoothing Behavior Under Selected Stochastic Processes," JOB, 1972, v45(4), 570-584.

Gonedes, Nicholas J. "Information-Production And Capital Market Equilibrium," JOF, 1975, v30(3), 841-864.

Gonedes, Nicholas J. "The Capital Market, The Market For Information, And External Accounting," JOF, 1976, v31(2), 611-630.

Gonedes, Nicholas J. (Blattberg, Robert C. and Nicholas J. Gonedes. "A Comparison Of The Stable And Student Distributions As Statistical Models For Stock Prices: Reply," JOB, 1977, v50(1), 78-79.)

Gonedes, Nicholas J. (Blattberg, Robert C. and Nicholas J. Gonedes. "A Comparison Of The Stable And Student Distributions As Statistical Models For Stock Prices," JOB, 1974, v47(2), 244-280.)

Gonyer, George H. and Steven J. Weiss. "The Competitive Effects Of Demand Deposit Powers For Thrift Institutions In Connecticut," JBR, 1976-77, v7(2),104-112.

Gonzales, Nestor, Robert Litzenberger and Jacques Rolfo. "On Mean Variance Models Of Capital Structure And The Absurdity Of Their Predictions," JFQA, 1977, v12(2), 165-179.

Gonzalez, Gisela A. (Asay, Michael R., Gisela A. Gonzalez and Benjamin Wolkowitz. "Financial Futures, Bank Portfolio Risk, And Accounting," JFM, v1(4), 607-618.)

Good, Barry C. (Adelman, Maurice A. and Barry C. Good. "The 7 Sisters: Comment," JPM, 1976-77, v3(1), 72.)

Good, Walter R. and Jack R. Meyer. "Adjusting The Price-Earnings Ratio Gap," FAJ, 1973, v29(6), 42,44,48-49,81-84.

Good, Walter R. "Accountability For Pension Fund Performance," FAJ, 1984, v40(1), 39-42.

Good, Walter R. "How To Avoid Over-Priced Stocks," FAJ, 1966, v22(6), 79-81.

Good, Walter R. "Interpreting Analysts' Recommendations," FAJ, 1975, v31(3), 42-46,48,62.

Good, Walter R. "Measuring Performance," FAJ, 1983, v39(3), 19-23.

Good, Walter R. "Short-Term Clients And Long-Term Performance," FAJ, 1978, v34(6), 21-26.

Good, Walter R. "Valuing Quality Growth Stocks," FAJ, 1972, v28(5), 47-54,56-59.

Good, Walter R., Robert Ferguson and Jack Treynor. "A Guide To The Index Fund Controversy," FAJ, 1976, v32(6), 27-38.

Good, Walter R., Roy W. Hermansen and T. Kirkham Barneby. "Opportunity: Actively Managed Investment Universes," FAJ, 1986, v42(1), 49-57.

Goode, Richard. "Imputed Rent Of Owner-Occupied Dwellings Under The Income Tax," JOF, 1960, v15(4), 504-530.

Goodfellow, Steve C. (Caswell, Jerry W. and Steve C. Goodfellow. "Effect Of Including Investment Income In Ratemaking Upon Profitability Of Non-Life Insurers," JRI, 1976, v43(2), 305-316.)

Goodfriend, Herbert E. and Frank T. Pratt. "Community Antenna Television," FAJ, 1970, v26(2),48-57.

Goodfriend, Herbert E. "Adjusting Insurance Earnings," FAJ, 1970, v26(3), 51-58.

Goodfriend, Herbert E. "Life Insurance Company Earnings," FAJ, 1966, v22(6), 57-63.

Goodhart, C. A. E. and L. Figliuoli. "Every Minute Counts In Financial Markets," JIMF, 1991, v10(1), 23-52.

Goodhart, Charles A. E. and Richard G. Smith. "The Impact Of News On Financial Markets In The United Kingdom," JMCB, 1985, v17(4), Part 1, 507-511.

Gooding, Arthur E. and Terence P. O'Malley. "Market Phase And The Stationarity Of Beta," JFQA, 1977, v12(5), 833-857.

Gooding, Arthur E. "Perceived Risk And Capital Asset Pricing," JOF, 1978, v33(5), 1401-1424.

Gooding, Arthur E. "Quantification Of Investors' Perceptions Of Common Stocks: Risk And Return Dimensions," JOF, 1975, v30(5), 1301-1316.

Gooding, Arthur E. "Some Preliminary Findings Regarding The Nature Of Investment Risk," FR, 1976, v11(1), 21-35.

Gooding, Arthur E. (Findlay, M. Chapman, III, Arthur E. Gooding and Wallace Q. Weaver, Jr. "On The Relevant Risk For Determining Capital Expenditure Hurdle Rates," FM, 1976, v5(4), 9-17.)

Goodman, Allen C. "Modeling And Computing Transactions Costs For Purchasers Of Housing Services," AREUEA, 1990, v18(1), 1-21.

Goodman, Bernard. "The Price Of Gold And International Liquidity," JOF, 1956, v11(1), 15-28.

Goodman, David A. and John W. Peavy, III. "Industry Relative Price-Earnings Ratios As Indicators Of Investment Returns," FAJ, 1983, v39(4), 60-66.

Goodman, David A. and John W. Peavy, III. "The Risk Universal Nature Of The P/E Effect," JPM, 1984-85, v11(4), 14-16.

Goodman, David A. and John W. Peavy, III. "The Interaction Of Firm Size And Price-Earnings Ratio On Portfolio Performance," FAJ, 1986, v42(1), 9-12.

Goodman, David A. (Peavy, John W., III and David A. Goodman. "The Significance Of P/Es For Portfolio Returns," JPM, 1982-83, v9(2), 43-47.)

Goodman, David A. (Peavy, John W., III and David A. Goodman. "How Inflation, Risk And Corporate Profitability Affect Common Stock Returns," FAJ, 1985, v41(5), 59-65.)

Goodman, John L., Jr. "Housing And The Weather," AREUEA, 1987, v15(1), 638-663.

Goodman, John L., Jr. "Reducing The Error In Monthly Housing Starts Estimates," AREUEA, 1986, v14(4), 557-566.

Goodman, Laurie S. and Anthony M. Santomero. "Variable-Rate Deposit Insurance: A Re-Examination," JBF, 1986, v10(2), 203-218.

Goodman, Laurie S. and Martha J. Langer. "Accounting For Interest Rate Futures In Bank Asset-Liability Management," JFM, 1983, v3(4), 415-428.

Goodman, Laurie S. and N. R. Vijayaraghavan. "Generalized Duration Hedging With Futures Contracts," RFM, 1987, v6(1), 94-108.

Goodman, Laurie S. and Robert A. Schwartz. "Coffee Pots And Limit Orders," JPM, 1982-83, v9(3), 5-6.

Goodman, Laurie S. "A Note On The Effects Of Euromarket Regulation On Bank Balance Sheet Decisions," JBF, 1982, v6(4), 587-596.

Goodman, Laurie S. "Bank Foreign Exchange Operations: A Portfolio Approach," JMCB, 1982, v14(1), 84-91.

Goodman, Laurie S. "High-Yield Default Rates: Is There Cause For Concern?," JPM, 1990, v16(2), 54-59.

Goodman, Laurie S. "Put-Call Parity With Coupon Instruments," JPM, 1984-85, v11(2), 59-60.

Goodman, Laurie S. "The Uses Of Interest Rate Swaps In Managing Corporate Liabilities," JACF, 1990, v2(4), 35-47.

Goodman, Laurie S. (Arak, Marcelle, Laurie S. Goodman and Joseph Snailer. "Duration Equivalent Bond Swaps: A New Tool," JPM, 1985-86, v12(4), 26-32.)

Goodman, Laurie S. (Arak, Marcelle and Laurie S. Goodman. "Treasury Bond Futures: Valuing The Delivery Options," JFM, 1987, v7(3), 269-286.)

Goodman, Laurie S. and Alan H. Cohen. "Pay-In-Kind Debentures: An Innovation," JPM, 1989, v15(2), 9-16.

Goodman, Laurie S., Susan Ross and Frederick Schmidt. "Are Foreign Currency Options Overvalued? The Early Experience Of The Philadelphia Stock Exchange," JPM, 1985, v5(3), 349-359.

Goodman, Laurie S., Raj Daryanani and Arthur Rones. "The Credit Exposure Of Cross-Currency And Nondollar Interest Rate Swaps," RDIBF, 1988, v2, 193-204.

Goodman, Laurie. (Arak, Marcelle, Philip Fischer, Laurie Goodman and Raj Daryanani. "The Municipal-Treasury Futures Spread," JFM, 1987, v7(4), 355-372.)

Goodman, Laurie. (Arak, Marcelle, Arturo Estrella, Laurie Goodman and Andrew Silver. "Interest Rate Swaps: An Alternative Explanation," FM, 1988, v17(2), 12-18.)

Goodman, M. L. (Williams, W. H. and M. L. Goodman. "A Statistical Grouping Of Corporations By Their Financial Characteristics," JFQA, 1971, v6(4), 1095-1104.)

Goodman, Oscar R. "A Statement Before The NAIC On Protection Of The Public Interest And The Misstatement Of Age Clause In Life Insurance Contracts," JRI, 1971, v38(1), 147-152.

Goodman, Oscar R. "Antitrust And Competitive Issues In United States Banking Structure," JOF, 1971, v26(2), 615-646.

Goodman, Oscar R. "Insurance Agents And The Insolvency Loss Exposure," JRI, 1971, v38(4), 647-648.

Goodman, Oscar R. "Public Policy And The Age And Incontestable Clauses In Life Insurance Contracts," JRI, 1968, v35(4), 515-536.

Goodman, Roy M. "Congressional Testimony," FAJ, 1968, v24(3), 59-64.

Goodman, Stephen H. "Foreign Exchange Rate Forecasting Techniques: Implications For Business And Policy," JOF, 1979, v34(2), 415-427.

Goodspeed, Bennett W. "The World's Smartest Man Syndrome," JPM, 1977-78, v4(4), 41-44.

Goodwin, Barry K., Thomas Grennes and Michael K. Wohlgenant. "Testing The Law Of One Price When Trade Takes Time," JIMF, 1990, v9(1), 21-40.

Goodwin, C. S. (Scanlan, F. V. and C. S. Goodwin. "The Advertising Industry," FAJ, 1968, v24(1), 71-76.)

Goodwin, Daniel R. "If You Are So Smart, Why Are You Not Rich?," FAJ, 1955, v11(4), 75-76.

Goodwin, Mark D. (Gitman, Lawrence J. and Mark D. Goodwin. "An Assessment Of Marketable Securities Management Practices," JFR, 1979, v2(2), 161-169.)

Goodwin, Thomas H. (Gisser, Micha and Thomas H. Goodwin. "Crude Oil And The Macroeconomy: Tests Of Some Popular Notions," JMCB, 1986, v18(1), 95-103.)

Goolsby, William C. and Barbara J. Childs. "Brokerage Firm Competition In Real Estate Commission Rates," JRER, 1988, v3(2), 79-85.

Goolsby, William C. and Lehahan O'Connell. "Overbuilt Housing: Criteria For Success," JRER, 1988, v3(1), 51-59.

Gooptu, Sudarshan and Raymond Lombra. "Aggregation Across Heterogeneous Depository Institutions," FR, 1987, v22(4), 369-378.

Gordon, David A., Myron J. Gordon and Lawrence I. Gould. "Choice Among Methods Of Estimating Share Yield," JPM, 1989, v15(3), 50-55.

Gordon, Doug. (Murphy, Austin and Doug Gordon. "An Empirical Note On Hedging Mortgages With Puts," JPM, 1990, v10(1), 75-78.)

Gordon, J. Douglas, Eugene J. Moriarty and Paula A. Tosini. "Stock Index Futures: Does The Dog Wag The Tail?," FAJ, 1987, v43(6), 72-73.

Gordon, Joseph. "Techniques For Appraising The Petroleum Industry," FAJ, 1945, v1(1), 30-36.

Gordon, Kathryn M. and Gordon C. Rausser. "Country Hedging For Real Income Stabilization: A Case Study Of South Korea And Egypt," JPM, 1984, v4(4), 449-464.

Gordon, Kenneth R. and Michael Palmer. "A Comparison Of The Financial Institutions' View And The Market's View Of Country Creditworthiness," JIFSR, 1989, v2(2), 78-88.

Gordon, L. A. "Imperfect Markets And The Nature Of Goodwill," JBFA, 1977, v4(4), 443-462.

Gordon, L. A. and A. W. Stark. "Accounting And Economic Rates Of Return: A Note On Depreciation And Other Accruals," JBFA, 1989, v16(3), 425-432.

Gordon, Lawrence A. "Accounting Rate Of Return Vs. Economic Rate Of Return," JBFA, 1974, v1(3),343-356.

Gordon, Lawrence A. "Further Thoughts On The Accounting Rate Of Return Vs. The Economic Rate Of Return," JBFA, 1977, v4(1), 133-134.

Gordon, Lawrence A. (Findlay, M. Chapman, III, Edward E. Williams and Lawrence A. Gordon. "Toward More Adequate Measures Of Lender Protection," FM, 1974, v4(2), 54-61.)

Gordon, Lawrence A. (Larcker, D. F., L. A. Gordon and G. E. Pinches. "Testing For Market Efficiency: A Comparison Of The Cumulative Average Residual Methodology And Intervention Analysis," JFQA, 1980, v15(2), 267-287.)

Gordon, Lilli A. and John Pound. "ESOPs And Corporate Control," JFEC, 1990, v27(2), 525-556.

Gordon, M. J. and L. I. Gould. "Comparison Of The DCF And HPR Measures Of The Yield On Common Shares," FM, 1984, v13(4), 40-47.

Gordon, M. J. and L. I. Gould. "The Cost Of Equity Capital With Personal Income Taxes And Flotation Costs," JOF, 1978, v33(4), 1201-1212.

Gordon, M. J. "Corporate Finance Under The MM Theorems," FM,

Gordon, M. J. "Leverage And The Value Of A Firm Under A Progressive Personal Income Tax," JBF, 1982, v6(4), 483-493.

Gordon, M. J. "Optimal Investment And Financing Policy," JOF, 1963, v18(2), 264-272.

Gordon, M. J. "Towards A Theory Of Financial Distress," JOF, 1971, v26(2), 347-356.

Gordon, Monte J. "European Businessmen See Free Enterprise Secure," FAJ, 1961, v17(3), 79-86.

Gordon, Monte J. "European Stock Exchanges," FAJ, 1959, v15(3), 31-36.

Gordon, Myron J. and Clarence C. Y. Kwan. "Debt Maturity, Default Risk, And Capital Structure," JBF, 1979, v3(4), 313-329.

Gordon, Myron J. and John S. McCallum. "Valuation And The Cost Of Capital For Regulated Utilities: Comment," JOF, 1972, v27(5), 1141-1146.

Gordon, Myron J. and Lawrence I. Gould. "The Cost Of Equity Capital: A Reconsideration," JOF, 1978, v33(3), 849-861.

Gordon, Myron J. and Paul J. Halpern. "Cost Of Capital For A Division Of A Firm: Reply," JOF, 1977, v32(5), 1781-1782.

Gordon, Myron J. and Paul J. Halpern. "Cost Of Capital For A Division Of A Firm," JOF, 1974, v29(4), 1153-1163.

Gordon, Myron J. "A General Solution To The Buy Or Lease Decision: A Pedagogical Note," JOF, 1974, v29(1), 245-250.

Gordon, Myron J. "A Portfolio Theory Of The Social Discount Rate And The Public Debt," JOF, 1976, v31(2), 199-214.

Gordon, Myron J. "Comparison Of Historical Cost And General Price Level Adjusted Cost Rate Base Regulation," JOF, 1977, v32(5), 1501-1512.

Gordon, Myron J. "Leverage And The Value Of A Firm Under A Progressive Personal Income Tax: Reply," JBF, 1984, v8(3), 495-498.

Gordon, Myron J. "Security And Investment: Theory And Evidence," JOF, 1964, v19(4), 607-618.

Gordon, Myron J. "The Impact Of Real Factors And Inflation On The Performance Of The U. S. Stock Market From 1960 To 1980," JOF, 1983, v38(2), 553-563.

Gordon, Myron J. "The Payoff Period And The Rate Of Profit," JOB, 1955, v28(4), 253-260.

Gordon, Myron J. (Brigham, Eugene F. and Myron J. Gordon. "Leverage, Dividend Policy And The Cost Of Capital: Reply," JOF, 1970, v25(4), 904-908.)

Gordon, Myron J. (Brigham, Eugene F. and Myron J. Gordon. "Leverage, Dividend Policy, And The Cost Of Capital," JOF, 1968, v23(1), 85-103.)

Gordon, Myron J. (Gordon, David A., Myron J. Gordon and Lawrence I. Gould. "Choice Among Methods Of Estimating Share Yield," JPM, 1989, v15(3), 50-55.)

Gordon, Myron J. and Charles Ying. "The Assignment Of Costs To Joint Products In A Decentralized Firm," JOB, 1968, v41(3), 363-374.

Gordon, Myron J. and David J. Fowler. "Price And Expenditure Performance Of The Multinational Drug Industry In A Home And A Host Company," RIF, 1983, v4, (Supp), 59-84.

Gordon, Myron J. and Joseph Yagil. "Financial Gain From Conglomerate Mergers," RIF, 1981, v3, 103-142.

Gordon, R. A. "Wesley Mitchell And The Study Of Business Cycles," JOB, 1952, v25(2), 101-107.

Gordon, Robert J. "Notes On Money, Income, And Gramlich: A Comment," JMCB, 1971, v3(2), Part 2, 533-545.

Gordon, Robert J. "The Short-Run Demand For Money: A Reconsideration," JMCB, 1984, v16(4), Part 1, 403-434.

Gordon, Roger H. and Joel Slemrod. "A General Equilibrium Simulation Study Of Subsidies To Municipal Expenditures," JOF, 1983, v38(2), 585-594.

Gordon, Roger. (Bagnoli, Mark, Roger Gordon and Barton L. Lipman. "Stock Repurchase As A Takeover Defense," RFS, 1989, v2(3), 423-443.)

Gordon, Scott. "Two Monetary Inquiries In Great Britain," JMCB, 1972, v4(4), 957-977.

Gorham, Michael. "The Effects Of Inflation On the Rules Of Futures Exchanges: A Case Study Of The Chicago Mercantile Exchange," JFM, v1(3), 337-345.

Gorlow, Robert. (Froland, Charles, Robert Gorlow and Richard Sampson. "The Market Risk Of Real Estate," JPM, 1985-86, v12(3), 12-19.)

Gornick, Alan L. "An Excess Profits Tax? If So, What Kind?," FAJ, 1951, v7(1), 55-56.

Gorski, Roman S. "Investment Security In An Uncertain World," FAJ, 1954, v10(4), 33-36.

Gort, Michael. "The Planning Of Investment: A Study Of Capital Budgeting In The Electric-Power Industry. II," JOB, 1951, v24(3), 181-202.

Gort, Michael. "The Planning Of Investment: A Study Of Capital Budgeting In The Electric-Power Industry. I," JOB, 1951, v24(2), 79-95.

Gorton, Gary and Anthony M. Santomero. "Market Discipline And Bank Subordinated Debt," JMCB, 1990, v22(1), 119-128.

Gorton, Gary and Donald J. Mullineaux. "The Joint Production Of Confidence: Endogenous Regulation And Nineteenth Century Commercial-Bank Clearinghouses," JMCB, 1987, v19(4), 457-468.

Gorton, Gary and George Pennacchi. "Financial Intermediaries And Liquidity Creation," JOF, 1990, v45(1), 49-72.

Goshay, Robert C. "Economic Impact Of Self-Insurance Reserve Trusteed Funds: Product And General Liability Exposures," JRI, 1977, v44(3), 521-526.

Goshay, Robert C. "Net Income Taxation Of The Life Insurance Industry At The State Level," JRI, 1966, v33(4), 563-575.

Goshay, Robert C. "Net Income As A Base For Life Insurance Company Taxation In California: Implications," JRI, 1976, v43(1), 17-41.

Goshay, Robert C. "Pay Benefits During Retraining Under Unemployment Insurance?," JRI, 1970, v37(1), 49-62.

Goshay, Robert C. (Michaelsen, Jacob B. and Robert C. Goshay. "Portfolio Selection Financial Intermediaries: A New Approach," JFQA, 1967, v2(2),166-199.)

Gosman, Martin L. (Backer, Morton and Martin L. Gosman. "The Use

Of Financial Ratios In Credit Downgrade Decisions," **FM**, 1980, v9(1), 53-56.)

Gosman, Martin L. (Backer, Morton and Martin L. Gosman. "Management's Perspective On Bond Downgrades," **FAJ**, 1985, v41(4), 77-79.)

Gosnell, Thomas F. (Fishe, Raymond P. H., Lawrence G. Goldberg, Thomas F. Gosnell and Sujata Sinha. "Margin Requirements In Futures Markets: Their Relationship To Price Volatility," **JFM**, 1990, v10(5), 541-554.)

Gosnell, Thomas F. and Andrea J. Heuson. "A Discretionary Approach To Hedging A Lender's Exposure In Adjustable Rate Mortgages," **JFM**, 1990, v10(5), 481-496.

Gostomski, Adam and Bohdan J. Kekish. "A Criterion Of Business Activity," **FAJ**, 1965, v21(2),37-41.

Gostomski, Adam and Bohdan J. Kekish. "Composite Indicators: A Rejoinder," **FAJ**, 1965, v21(6), 60.

Gottfries, Nils. "Multiple Perfect Foresight Equilibriums And Convergence Of Learning Processes," **JMCB**, 1985, v17(1), 111-117.

Gottlieb, Gary and Avner Kalay. "Implications Of The Discreteness Of Observed Stock Prices," **JOF**, 1985, v40(1), 135-153.

Gotur, Padma. (Barth, James R., Padma Gotur, Neela Manage and Anthony M. J. Yezer. "The Effect Of Government Regulations On Personal Loan Markets: A Tobit Estimation Of A Microeconomic Model," **JOF**, 1983, v38(4), 1233-1251.)

Goudzwaard, Maurice B. "Price Ceilings And Credit Rationing," **JOF**, 1968, v23(1), 177-185.

Goudzwaard, Maurice B. "The Economic Impact Of Credit Insurance Charges," **JRI**, 1969, v36(4), 515-524.

Goudzwaard, Maurice B. (Mason, R. Hal and Maurice B. Goudzwaard. "Performance Of Conglomerate Firms: A Portfolio Approach," **JOF**, 1976, v31(1), 39-48.)

Goudzwaard, Maurice B. (Smith, Keith V. and Maurice B. Goudzwaard. "Survey Of Investment Management: Teaching Versus Practice," **JOF**, 1970, v25(2), 329-347.)

Goudzwaard, Maurice B. (Smith, Keith V. and Maurice B. Goudzwaard. "The Porfitability Of Bank Trust Management," **JBR**, 1972-73, v3(3), 166-177.)

Gould, Alex and Maurice Buchsbaum. "A Filter Approach To Stock Selection," **FAJ**, 1969, v25(6),61,65-67.

Gould, F. J. "Stock Index Futures: The Arbitrage Cycle And Portfolio Insurance," **FAJ**, 1988, v44(1), 48-62.

Gould, F. J. (Garcia, C. B. and F. J. Gould. "A Note On The Measurement Of Risk In A Portfolio," **FAJ**, 1987, v43(2), 61-69.)

Gould, F. J. (Garcia, C. B. and F. J. Gould. "An Empirical Study Of Portfolio Insurance," **FAJ**, 1987, v43(4), 44-54.)

Gould, J. B. and Eric H. Sorensen. "Duration: A Factor In Equity Pricing," **JPM**, 1986-87, v13(1),38-43.

Gould, J. P. and Dan Galai. "Transactions Costs And The Relationship Between Put And Call Prices," **JFEC**, 1974, v1(2), 105-129.

Gould, J. R. "Internal Pricing In Firms When There Are Costs Of Using An Outside Market," **JOB**, 1964, v37(1), 61-67.

Gould, J. (Appelbaum, E., J. Burns, R. Evans, J. Gould, T. Hamacek, R. Kidder, M. Jensen, J. Johnstone, M. Murray, R. Sim, J. Stern, B. Stewart and C. Zaner. "Panel: CEO Roundtable On Corporate Structure And Management Incentives," **JACF**, 1990, v3(3), 6-35.)

Gould, Jay M. "The Sanborn Buying Power Maps," **JRI**, 1961, v28(2), 129-130.

Gould, John P. "Inventories And Stochastic Demand: Equilibrium Models Of The Firm And Industry," **JOB**, 1978, v51(1), 1-42.

Gould, John P. "Is The Rational Expectations Hypothesis Enough?," **JOB**, 1986, v59(4), Part 2, S371-S378.

Gould, John P. "The Economics Of Markets: A Simple Model Of The Market-Making Process," **JOB**, 1980, v53(3), Part 2, S167-S188.

Gould, John P. "The Expected Utility Hypothesis And The Selection Of Optimal Deductibles For A Given Insurance Policy," **JOB**, 1969, v42(2), 143-151.

Gould, John P. and Roman L. Weil. "The Rule Of 69," **JOB**, 1974, v47(3), 397-398.

Gould, L. I. (Gordon, M. J. and L. I. Gould. "The Cost Of Equity Capital With Personal Income Taxes And Flotation Costs," **JOF**, 1978, v33(4), 1201-1212.)

Gould, L. I. (Gordon, M. J. and L. I. Gould. "Comparison Of The DCF And HPR Measures Of The Yield On Common Shares," **FM**, 1984, v13(4), 40-47.)

Gould, Lawrence I. (Gordon, Myron J. and Lawrence I. Gould. "The Cost Of Equity Capital: A Reconsideration," **JOF**, 1978, v33(3), 849-861.)

Gould, Lawrence I. (Gordon, David A., Myron J. Gordon and Lawrence I. Gould. "Choice Among Methods Of Estimating Share Yield," **JPM**, 1989, v15(3), 50-55.)

Gould, Leon B. "Banks And The Commercial Paper Market," **FAJ**, 1969, v25(6), 25-28.

Gouldey, Bruce K. and Gary J. Gray. "Implementing Mean-Variance Theory In The Selection Of U.S. Government Bond Portfolios," **JBR**, 1981-82, v12(3), 161-173.

Gouldey, Bruce K. and Gary J. Gray. "Implementing Mean-Variance Theory In The Selection Of U.S. Government Bond Portfolios: Reply To A Comment," **JBR**, 1983-84, v14(3), 237-238.

Gouldey, Bruce K. "Evidence Of Nonmarket Risk Premiums In Common Stock Returns," **JFR**, 1980, v3(3), 243-260.

Gouldey, Bruce K. (Saniga, Erwin M., Thomas H. McInish and Bruce K. Gouldey. "The Effect Of Differencing Interval Length On Beta," **JFR**, 1981, v4(2), 129-135.)

Goulet, Peter G. "How Sophisticated Are Bond Portfolio Managers?," **JPM**, 1977-78, v4(2), 23-26.

Goulet, Peter G. "Introductory Investments: A Survey Of Practice And A Note On Direction," **JFED**, 1978, v7, 13-17.

Goulet, Waldemar M. "Price Changes, Managerial Actions And Insider Trading At The Time Of Listing," **FM**, 1974, v3(1), 30-36.

Goulet, Waldemar M. (Coyne, Thomas J., Waldemar M. Goulet and Mario J. Picconi. "Residential Real Estate Versus Financial Assets," **JPM**, 1980-81, v7(1),20-24.)

Graaskamp, James A. "Implications Of Vested Benefits In Private Pension Plans: Comment," **JRI**, 1966, v33(3), 489-494.

Graaskamp, James. "Development And Structure Of Mortgage Loan Guaranty Insurance In The United States," **JRI**, 1967, v34(1), 47-68.

Grabbe, J. Orlin. "Foreign Currency Options: A Survey," **RDIBF**, 1987, v1, 203-230.

Grabbe, J. Orlin. "The Pricing Of Call And Put Options On Foreign Exchange," **JIMF**, 1983, v2(3), 239-253.

Graber, Dean E. and Bill D. Jarnagin. "The FASB - Eliminator Of 'Managed Earnings'?," **FAJ**, 1979, v35(2), 72-76.

Graber, Dean E. "Real And Illusory Earnings Growth," **FAJ**, 1969, v25(2), 52-54.

Grablowsky, Bernie J. and Betty L. Brewer. "The Market For Finance Majors: Some Myths And Some Realities," **JFED**, 1975, v4, 33-36.

Grablowsky, Bernie J. and Dexter R. Rowell. "The Market For Finance Majors: The Myths And Realities Reconsidered," **JFED**, 1980, v9, 33-41.

Grablowsky, Bernie J. "The Market For MBAs: The Myths And Realities," **JFED**, 1988, v17, 55-63.

Grabowski, Henry, W. Kip Viscusi and William N. Evans. "Price And Availability Tradeoffs Of Automobile Insurance Regulation," **JRI**, 1989, v56(2), 275-299.

Grace, Elizabeth V. "Property-Liability Insurer Reserve Errors: A Theoretical And Empirical Analysis," **JRI**, 1990, v57(1), 28-46.

Grace, H. Stephen, Jr. "On Optimal Financing Of Cyclical Cash Needs: Comment," **JOF**, 1975, v30(4), 1135-1136.

Graddy, Duane B. and Adi S. Karna. "Net Interest Margin Sensitivity Among Banks Of Different Sizes," **JBR**, 1983-84, v14(4), 283-290.

Graddy, Duane B. and Reuben Kyle, III. "The Simultaneity Of Bank Decision-Making, Market Structure, And Bank Performance," **JOF**, 1979, v34(1), 1-18.

Graddy, Duane B. and Reuben Kyle, III. "Affiliated Bank Performance And The Simultaneity Of Financial Decision-Making," **JOF**, 1980, v35(4), 952-957.

Graddy, Duane B. (Homaifar, Ghassem and Duane B. Graddy. "Variance And Lower Partial Moment Betas As Alternative Risk Measures In Cost Of Capital Estimation: A Defense Of The CAPM Beta," **JBFA**, 1990, v17(5), 677-688.)

Graddy, Duane B. (Karna, Adi S. and Duane B. Graddy. "Bank Holding Company Leverage And The Return On Stockholders' Equity," **JBR**, 1982-83, v13(1), 42-48.)

Graddy, Duane B., Ghassem Homaifar and Adi S. Karna. "Double Leverage As A Source Of Systematic Risk In Bank Holding Company Stocks," **JBR**, 1984-85, v15(2), 115-122.

Graebner, Herbert C. "Some Thoughts On A Life Insurance Internship Program," **JRI**, 1959, v26(2), 1-6.

Graff, Richard A. and Daniel M. Cashdan, Jr. "Some New Ideas In Real Estate Finance," **JACF**, 1990, v3(1), 77-89.

Graham, Ben. (Oppenheimer, Henry R. and Ben Graham. "Investment Policies Of Property - Liability Insurers And pension Plans: A Lesson From Ben Graham," **JRI**, 1983, v50(4), 611-630.)

Graham, Benjamin. "Our Balance Of Payments - The Conspiracy Of Silence'," **FAJ**, 1962, v18(6), 9-14.

Graham, Benjamin. "Questionnaire On Stockholder-Management Relationship," **FAJ**, 1947, v3(4), 57-62.

Graham, Benjamin. "Relief From Double Tax On Corporate Profits," **FAJ**, 1954, v10(1), 15-18.

Graham, Benjamin. "Should Security Analysts Have A Professional Rating?: The Affirmative Case," **FAJ**, 1945, v1(1), 37-40.

Graham, Benjamin. "Some Investment Aspects Of Accumulation Through Equities," **JOF**, 1962, v17(2),203-214.

Graham, Benjamin. "Some Observations," **FAJ**, 1967, v23(6), 114.

Graham, Benjamin. "Special Situations," **FAJ**, 1946, v2(4), 31-38.

Graham, Benjamin. "Structural Relationships Bearing On Full Employment," **FAJ**, 1955, v11(2), 13-18.

Graham, Benjamin. "The Future Of Common Stocks," **FAJ**, 1974, v30(5), 20-23,26-27,30.

Graham, Benjamin. "The Future Of Financial Analysis," **FAJ**, 1963, v19(3), 65-70.

Graham, Benjamin. "The War Economy And Stock Values," **FAJ**, 1951, v7(1), 34-38.

Graham, Benjamin. "Two Illustrative Approaches To Formula Valuations Of Common Stocks," **FAJ**, 1957, v13(5), 11-16.

Graham, David R. and David Burras Humphrey. "Bank Examination Data As Predictors Of Bank Net Loan Losses," **JMCB**, 1978, v10(4), 491-504.

Graham, David and Robert Jennings. "Systematic Risk, Dividend Yield And The Hedging Performance Of Stock Index Futures," **JFM**, 1987, v7(1), 1-14.

Graham, Donald M. "A Trust Investor Looks At Public Utility Equities," **FAJ**, 1965, v21(5), 37-39.

Graham, Frank D. "Exchange Rates: Bound Or Free?," **JOF**, 1949, v4(1), 13-27.

Graham, James. (Palme, Lennart A., Jr. and James Graham. "The Systematic Downward Bias In Live Cattle Futures: An Evaluation," **JFM**, v1(3), 359-366.)

Graham, John D. (Evans, William N. and John D. Graham. "Risk Reduction Or Risk Compensation? The Case Of Mandatory Safety-Belt Use Laws," **JRU**, 1991, v4(1), 61-74.)

Graham, Malise L. "Economic Significance Of Europe's 'Outer Seven'," **FAJ**, 1960, v16(3), 95-102.

Graham, Robert E. and Lester W. Johnson. "A Unified Bayesian Approach To Optimal Classification With Discriminant Analysis," **JRI**, 1977, v44(2), 316-319.

Grall, Jean. (Solnik, Bruno H. and Jean Grall. "Eurobonds: Determining The Demand For Capital And The International Interest Rate Structure," **JBR**, 1974-75, v5(4), 218-230.)

Grambo, Ralph W. and Alan R. Peslak. "MAXFINANCE: A Package Of Programs For Comprehensive Capital Budgeting Cases," **JFED**, 1977, v6, 79-80.

Gramlich, Edward M. "Models Of Inflation Expectations Formation: A Comparison Of Household And Economist Forecasts," **JMCB**, 1983, v15(2), 155-173.

Gramlich, Edward M. "The Usefulness Of Monetary And Fiscal Policy As Discretionary Stabilization Tools," **JMCB**, 1971, v3(2), Part 2, 506-532.

Gramlich, Edward M. (De Leeuw, Frank and Edward M. Gramlich. "The Channels Of Monetary Policy: A Further Report On The Federal Reserve - M.I.T. Model," **JOF**, 1969, v24(2), 265-290.)

Gramm, William P. and Robert T. Nash. "The Impact Of Changes In

Risk Assessment," JRU, 1990, v3(3), 283-305.)

Gray, William S. "Discount Rates And Return Forecasts," FAJ, 1974, v30(3), 53-61.

Gray, William S. "Measuring The Analyst's Performance," FAJ, 1966, v22(2), 56-63.

Gray, William S. "The Anatomy Of A Stock Market Forecast," JPM, 1989, v16(1), 36-44.

Gray, William S. "The Major Shortfall Of ERISA," FAJ, 1977, v33(1), 18-20.

Gray, William S. "The Stock Market And The Economy In 1988," JPM, 1983-84, v10(4), 73-80.

Gray, William S., III. "Corporate Forecasts: FAF Proposal," FAJ, 1973, v29(1), 64-71,85.

Gray, William S., III. "Long-Term Outlook For The Stock Market," FAJ, 1979, v35(4), 29-39.

Grebler, Leo and Leland S. Burns. "Construction Cycles In The United States Since World War II," AREUEA, 1982, v10(2), 123-151.

Grebler, Leo. "Growing Scale Of Real Estate Firms And Projects," AREUEA, 1973, v1(1), 107-122.

Grebler, Leo. "Real Estate Investment Experience In New York City," JOF, 1954, v9(2), 216-218.

Grebler, Leo. "The Commission's Recommendations On Housing Finance," AREUEA, 1983, v11(2), 166-181.

Grebler, Leo. "The Effect Of FHLB Bond Operations On Savings Inflows At Savings And Loan Associations: Comment," JOF, 1973, v28(1), 198-202.

Grebler, Leo. "The Flow Of Funds Into New Residential Construction 1911-52," JOF, 1954, v9(4), 339-350.

Grebler, Leo. "The Growth Of Residential Capital Since World War II," AREUEA, 1979, v7(4), 539-580.

Grede, Wm. J. "Changing Farm Scene And Agricultural Equipment," FAJ, 1960, v16(6), 23-29.

Greeley, Harold Dudley. "Practical Objections To Excess Profit Taxation," FAJ, 1951, v7(1), 57-58.

Greeley, Robert E. "Forecasting: 'Growth Stocks For Income'," FAJ, 1959, v15(1), 109.

Greeley, Robert E. "Mutual Fund Management Companies," FAJ, 1967, v23(5), 75-82.

Greeley, Robert E. "What Are The Investment Objectives Of Private Pension Plans," FAJ, 1957, v13(5), 75-78.

Green, D. E. W. "The Evaluation Of An Integrated Investment And Lease-Financing Decision: A Comment," JBFA, 1979, v6(1), 71-88.

Green, David O. (Weil, Roman L, Joel E. Segall and David O. Green. "Premium On Convertible Bonds: Reply," JOF, 1972, v27(5), 1163-1170.)

Green, David, Jr. "Taxable Stock Dividends," JOB, 1953, v26(4), 224-230.

Green, David, Jr. (Becker, Selwyn and David Green, Jr. "Budgeting And Employee Behavior," JOB, 1962, v35(4), 392-402.)

Green, David, Jr. (Becker, Selwyn W. and David Green, Jr. "Budgeting And Employee Behavior: A Rejoinder To A 'Reply'," JOB, 1964, v37(2), 203-205.)

Green, David, Jr. (Weil, Roman L., Joel E. Segall and David Green, Jr. "Premiums On Convertible Bonds: Reply," JOF, 1970, v25(4), 931-933.)

Green, David, Jr. (Weil, Roman L., Jr., Joel E. Segall and David Green, Jr. "Premiums On Convertible Bonds," JOF, 1968, v23(3), 445-463.)

Green, David, Jr. and Joel Segall. "The Predictive Power Of First-Quarter Earnings Reports," JOB, 1967, v40(1), 44-55.

Green, David, Jr. and Joel Segall. "Return Of Strawman," JOB, 1970, v43(1), 63-65.

Green, David, Jr. and Joel Segall. "Brickbats And Straw Men: A Reply To Brown And Niederhoffer," JOB, 1968, v41(4), 498-502.

Green, G. Hayden. "Strategic Management Practices Of Real Estate Developers In A Volatile Economic Climate," JRER, 1988, v3(3), 63-72.

Green, Jerry and John B. Shoven. "The Effects Of Interest Rates On Mortgage Prepayments," JMCB, 1986, v18(1), 41-59.

Green, Jerry R. and Bruno Jullien. "Ordinal Independence In Nonlinear Utility Theory," JRU, 1988, v1(4), 355-388.

Green, Jerry R. and Bruno Julien. "Erratum: Ordinal Independence In Nonlinear Utility Theory," JRU, 1989, v2(1), 119.

Green, Jr. David. "A Moral To The Direct-Costing Controversy?," JOB, 1960, v33(3), 218-226.

Green, Kevin. (Cornell, Bradford and Kevin Green. "The Investment Performance Of Low-Grade Bond Funds," JOF, 1991, v46(1), 29-48.)

Green, Lillian B. "Facts And Fiction Behind Price-Earnings Ratios Of The Steel Stocks," FAJ, 1957, v13(4), 35-44.

Green, Paul E. (Goldberg, Stephen M., Paul E. Green and Yoram Wind. "Conjoint Analysis Of Price Premiums For Hotel Amenities," JOB, 1984, v57(1), Part 2, S111-S132.

Green, Paul E. and Arun Maheshwari. "Common Stock Perception And Preference: An Application Of Multidimensional Scaling.," JOB, 1969, v42(4), 439-457.

Green, R. Jeffery. (Von Furstenberg, George M. and R. Jeffery Green. "Home Mortgage Delinquencies: A Cohort Analysis," JOF, 1974, v29(5), 1545-1548.)

Green, R. Jeffrey. (Von Furstenberg, George M. and R. Jeffrey Green. "Estimation Of Delinquency Risk For Home Mortgage Portfolios," AREUEA, 1974, v2(1), 5-20.) 3a?8

Green, Richard C. and Eli Talmor. "Asset Substitution And The Agency Costs Of Debt Financing," JBF, 1985, v10(2), 391-400.

Green, Richard C. and Eli Talmor. "The Structure And Incentive Effects Of Corporate Tax Liabilities," JOF, 1985, v40(5), 1095-1114.

Green, Richard C. and Sanjay Srivastava. "Risk Aversion And Arbitrage," JOF, 1985, v40(1), 257-268.

Green, Richard C. "Benchmark Portfolio Inefficiency And Deviations From The Security Market Line," JOF, 1986, v41(2), 295-312.

Green, Richard C. "Investment Incentives, Debt, And Warrants," JFEC, 1984, v13(1), 115-136.

Green, Richard C. "Positively Weighted Portfolios On The Minimum-Variance Frontier," JOF, 1986, v41(5), 1051-1068.

Green, Richard C. (Bossaerts, Peter and Richard C. Green. "A General Equilibrium Model Of Changing Risk Premia: Theory And Tests," RFS, 1989, v2(4), 467-494.)

Green, Richard C. (Dammon, Robert M. and Richard C. Green. "Tax Arbitrage And The Existence Of Equilibrium Prices For Financial Assets," JOF, 1987, v42(5), 1143-1166.)

Green, Robert T. (Srivastava, Rajendra K. and Robert T. Green. "Determinants Of Bilateral Trade Flows," JOB, 1986, v59(4), Part 1, 623-640.)

Green, Thad B. and Morton Cotlar. "An Evaluation Of A Novel Business Simulation Technique For Management Development," JOB, 1973, v46(2), 212-229.

Greenawalt, Mary Brady and Joseph F. Sinkey, Jr. "Bank Loan-Loss Provisions And The Income-Smoothing Hypothesis: An Empirical Analysis, 1976-1984," JFSR, 1988, v1(4), 301-318.

Greenbaum, S. I. and C. F. Haywood. "Secular Change In The Financial Services Industry," JMCB, 1971, v3(2), Part 2, 571-589.

Greenbaum, Stuart I. and Itzhak Venezia. "Partial Exercise Of Loan Commitments Under Adaptive Pricing," JFR, 1985, v8(4), 251-263.

Greenbaum, Stuart I. and Mukhtar M. Ali. "Entry, Control And The Market For Bank Charters," JOF, 1974, v29(2), 527-535.

Greenbaum, Stuart I. and Mukhtar M. Ali. "Need Interest Rates On Bank Loans And Deposits Move Sympathetically?," JOF, 1974, v29(3), 963-971.

Greenbaum, Stuart I. "Legal Reserve Requirements: A Case Study In Bank Regulation," JBR, 1983-84, v14(1), 59-68.

Greenbaum, Stuart I. (Akella, Srinivas R. and Stuart I. Greenbaum. "Savings And Loan Ownership Structure And Expense-Preference," JBF, 1988, v11(3), 419-428.)

Greenbaum, Stuart I. (Ali, Mukhtar M. and Stuart I. Greenbaum. "A Spatial Model Of The Banking Industry," JOF, 1977, v32(4), 1283-1303.)

Greenbaum, Stuart I. (Berkovitch, Elazar and Stuart I. Greenbaum. "The Loan Commitment As An Optimal Financing Contract," JFQA, 1991, v26(1), 83-96.)

Greenbaum, Stuart I. (Chan, Yuk-Shee, Stuart I. Greenbaum and Anjan V. Thakor. "Information Reusability, Competition And Bank Asset Quality," JBF, 1986, v10(2), 243-253.)

Greenbaum, Stuart I. (Deshmukh, Sudhakar D., Stuart I. Greenbaum and George Kanatas. "Bank Forward Lending In Alternative Funding Environments," JOF, 1982, v37(4), 925-940.)

Greenbaum, Stuart I. (Deshmukh, Sudhakar D., Stuart I. Greenbaum and Anjan V. Thakor. "Capital Accumulation And Deposit Pricing In Mutual Financial Institutions," JFQA, 1982, v17(5), 705-725.)

Greenbaum, Stuart I. (Deshmukh, Sudhakar D., Stuart I. Greenbaum and George Kanatas. "Lending Policies Of Financial Intermediaries Facing Credit And Funding Risk," JOF, 1983, v38(3), 873-886.)

Greenbaum, Stuart I. (Deshmukh, Sudhakar D., Stuart I. Greenbaum and George Kanatas. "Interest Rate Uncertainty And The Financial Intermediary's Choice Of Exposure," JOF, 1983, v38(1), 141-147.)

Greenbaum, Stuart I. (I'Costa, Joan E. Richart and Stuart I. Greenbaum. Bank Forward Lending: A Note," JOF, 1983, v38(4), 1315-1322.)

Greenbaum, Stuart I. (Kanatas, George and Stuart I. Greenbaum. "Bank Reserve Requirements And Monetary Aggregates," JBF, 1982, v6(4), 507-520.)

Greenbaum, Stuart I. (Taggart, Robert A., Jr. and Stuart I. Greenbaum. "Bank Capital And Public Regulation," JMCB, 1978, v10(2), 158-169.)

Greenbaum, Stuart I. (Thakor, Anjan, Hai Hong and Stuart I. Greenbaum. "Bank Loan Commitments And Interest Rate Volatility," JBF, 1981, v5(4), 497-510.)

Greenbaum, Stuart I. (Walker, David A., Richard C. Aspinwall, Stuart I. Greenbaum, Edward J. Kane and Perry D. Quick. "Panel Discussion On Federal Reserve Membership Issues," FR, 1979, v14(2), 58-74.)

Greenbaum, Stuart I. and Anjan V. Thakor. "Bank Funding Modes: Securitization Versus Deposits," JBF, 1987, v11(3), 379-402.

Greenbaum, Stuart I., Mukhtar M. Ali and Randall C. Merris. "Monetary Policy And Banking Profits," JOF, 1976, v31(1), 89-101.

Greenbaum, Stuart I., George Kanatas and Itzhak Venezia. "Equilibrium Loan Pricing Under The Bank-Client Relationship," JBF, 1989, v13(2), 221-236.

Greenberg, Barnett A. (Bellenger, Danny N., Dan H. Robertson and Barnett A. Greenberg. "Female Attitudes Toward The Use Of Credit Vs. Cash," JBR, 1979-80, v10(1), 54-57.)

Greenberg, Edward. (Marshall, William J., Jess B. Yawitz and Edward Greenberg. "Optimal Regulation Under Uncertainty," JOF, 1981, v36(4), 909-921.)

Greenberg, Penelope Sue. "Modeling Time-Dependent Processes For Cost Variance Analysis," JBFA, 1986, v13(3), 311-336.

Greenberg, Ralph H., Robert F. Sharp and Eric E. Spires. "A Practical Method Of Measuring Current Costs Of Technologically Inferior Assets," JBFA, 1989, v16(3), 433-442.

Greenberg, Warren. (Fanara, Philip, Jr. and Warren Greenberg. "The Impact Of Competition And Regulation On Blue Cross Enrollment Of Non-Group Individuals," JRI, 1985, v52(2), 185-198.)

Greenberg, Warren. (Feldman, Roger and Warren Greenberg. "The Relation Between The Blue Cross Market Share And The Blue Cross 'Discount' On Hospital Charges," JRI, 1981, v48(2), 235-246.)

Greenblatt, Joel M., Richard Pzena and Bruce L. Newberg. "How The Small Investor Can Beat The Market," JPM, 1980-81, v7(4), 48-52.

Greene, James B. (Edmister, Robert O. and James B. Greene. "Performance Of Super-Low-Price Stocks," JPM, 1980-81, v7(1), 36-41.)

Greene, James. "Bank Lending To Third World Countries In The 1980's," JBF, 1983, v7(4), 553-558.

Greene, Joshua E. (Schweitzer, Paul R. and Joshua E. Greene. "The Johnson Wax Effect: Reply," JBR, 1980-81, v11(3), 192.)

Greene, Joshua. (Schweitzer, Paul and Joshua Greene. "Determinants And Consequences Of Market Entry: A Case Study Of Two Wisconsin Banking Markets," JBR, 1978-79, v9(4), 218-226.)

Greene, Lancaster M. "Financing Of Signal Equipment And Cost To Railroads," FAJ, 1952, v8(3), 29-30.

Greene, Lawrence M. "The Investment Company - Useful Medium For American Private Investment Abroad," JOF, 1959, v14(4), 493-503.

Greene, Mark R. "Insurance Mindedness' - Implications For Insurance Theory," JRI, 1964, v31(1), 27-38.

Greene, Mark R. "A Note On Loading Charges For Variable Annuities," JRI, 1973, v40(3), 473-478.

Greene, Mark R. "A Note On Loading Charges For Variable Annuities: Reply," JRI, 1974, v41(3), 525-526.

Greene, Mark R. "Application Of Mathematics To Insurance And Risk Management," JRI, 1961, v28(1), 93-104.

Greene, Mark R. "Attitudes Toward Risk And A Theory Of Insurance Consumption," JRI, 1963, v30(2), 165-182.

Greene, Mark R. "Doctoral Education For Risk And Insurance In Leading U.S. Universities," JRI, 1969, v36(4), 505-514.

Greene, Mark R. "Export Credit Insurance - Its Role In Expanding World Trade," JRI, 1965, v32(2), 177-194.

Greene, Mark R. "Federal Income Taxes And The Variable Annuitant," JRI, 1958, v25(4), 22-27.

Greene, Mark R. "International Levels Of Employee Benefits - An Exploratory Study," JRI, 1968, v35(1), 1-16.

Greene, Mark R. "International Levels Of Employee Benefits - An Exploratory Study: Reply," JRI, 1971, v38(1), 144-145.

Greene, Mark R. "Life Care Centers - A New Concept In Insurance," JRI, 1981, v48(3), 403-421.

Greene, Mark R. "Life Insurance Buying In Inflation," JRI, 1954, v21, 99-113.

Greene, Mark R. "Marketing Efficiency And Workmen's Compensation - A Case Study," JRI, 1962, v29(4), 467-502.

Greene, Mark R. "Marketing Research As An Aid To Insurance Management," JRI, 1957, v24(3), 42-55.

Greene, Mark R. "Should Variable Policy Loan Interest Rates Be Adopted?," JRI, 1973, v40(4), 585-597.

Greene, Mark R. "The Effect Of Insurance Settlements In A Disaster," JRI, 1964, v31(3), 381-392.

Greene, Mark R. "The Government As An Insurer," JRI, 1976, v43(3), 393-407.

Greene, Mark R. "The Spanish Insurance Industry - An Analysis," JRI, 1972, v39(2), 221-244.

Greene, Mark R. (Huszagh, Sandra M. and Mark R. Greene. "FCIA: Help Or Hindrance To Exports?," JRI, 1982, v49(2), 256-268.)

Greene, Mark R. (Huszagh, Sandra M. and Mark R. Greene. "How Exporters View Credit Risk And FCIA Insurance - The Georgia Experience," JRI, 1985, v52(1), 117-132.)

Greene, Mark R. (Severiens, Jacobus T. and Mark R. Greene. "Variable Life Insurance In The Netherlands - A Case Study," JRI, 1974, v41(3), 511-522.)

Greene, Mark R. and Michael L. Murray. "Self-Insurance Of State-Owned Property," JRI, 1978, v45(1), 109-120.

Greene, Mark R. and Richard E. Johnson. "Stocks Vs. Mutuals: Who Controls?," JRI, 1980, v47(1), 165-174.

Greene, Mark R., John Neter and Lester I. Tenney. "Annuity Rents And Rates - Guaranteed Vs. Current," JRI, 1977, v44(3), 383-401.

Greene, Mark R., John W. McPherrin and Herbert W. Florer. "Curricular Concepts In Risk And Insurance," JRI, 1963, v30(1), 129-132.

Greene, Myron T. and Bruce D. Fielitz. "Long-Term Dependence In Common Stock Returns," JFEC, 1977, v4(3), 339-349.

Greene, Myron T. (Fielitz, Bruce D. and Myron T. Greene. "New Evidence Of Persistence In Stock Returns," JPM, 1978-79, v5(1), 38-42.)

Greene, Myron T. (Fielitz, Bruce D. and Myron T. Greene. "Shortcomings In Performance Evaluation Via MPT," JPM, 1979-80, v6(4), 13-19.)

Greene, Myron T. (Muller, Frederick L., Bruce D. Fielitz and Myron T. Greene. "S&P Quality Group Rankings: Risk And Return," JPM, 1982-83, v9(4), 39-42.)

Greene, Myron T. (Muller, Frederick L., Bruce D. Fielitz and Myron T. Greene. "Portfolio Performance In Relation To Quality, Earnings, Dividends, Firm Size,Leverage, And Return On Equity," JFR, 1984, v7(1), 17-26.)

Greene, Norvin R. "An Investment Adviser's Letters To Clients," FAJ, 1954, v10(2), 55-60.

Greene, Norvin R. "An Old Counselor Philosophizes," FAJ, 1963, v19(4), 87-89.

Greene, Norvin R. "Are Stock Rights Obsolete?," FAJ, 1957, v13(5), 41-44.

Greene, Norvin R. "Discard Conventional Investment Advice," FAJ, 1956, v12(4), 41-42.

Greene, Norvin R. "Responsibility Of Management For Price Level Of Stock," FAJ, 1952, v8(5), 42-43.

Greene, Norvin R. "Successful Investing," FAJ, 1955, v11(5), 89-91.

Greene, Norvin R. "United States Depreciation Tax Policies," FAJ, 1961, v17(1), 79-81.

Greene, Norvin. "American Telephone - A Growth Stock?," FAJ, 1960, v16(5), 55-56.

Greenfield, Harry. "A Decade Of Electronics Activity," FAJ, 1960, v16(5), 31-33.

Greenfield, Robert L. and Leland B. Yeager. "A Laissez-Faire Approach To Monetary Stability," JMCB, 1983, v15(3), 302-315.

Greenfield, Robert L., Maury R. Randall and John C. Woods. "Financial Leverage And Use Of The Net Present Value Investment Criterion," FM, 1983, v12(3), 40-44.

Greenleaf, James A. (Schwartz, Eli and James A. Greenleaf. "A Comment On Investment Decisions, Repetitive Games And The Unequal Distribution Of Wealth," JOF, 1978, v33(4), 1222-1227.)

Greenleaf, Robert W. "Synthetic Instruments," FAJ, 1989, v45(2), 71-73.

Greenleaf, Robert W. (Caks, John, William R. Lane, Robert W. Greenleaf and Reginald G. Joules. "A Simple Formula For Duration," JFR, 1985, v8(3), 245-249.)

Greenless, John S. "An Empirical Evaluation Of The CPI Home Purchase Index, 1973-1978," AREUEA, 1982, v10(1), 1-24.

Greenough, William C. "A New Approach To Retirement Income," JOF, 1952, v7(2), 285-295.

Greenough, William C. "College Retirement Systems: Social Security And Variable Annuities," JRI, 1956, v23, 94-105.

Greenough, William C. "Pensions. What Now?," JRI, 1982, v49(1), 104-113.)

Greenough, William C. "Variable Annuities Through CREF," JRI, 1960, v27(1), 91-104.

Greenspan, Alan. "Liquidity As A Determinant Of Industrial Prices And Interest Rates," JOF, 1964, v19(2), Part 1, 159-169.

Greenspan, Alan. "Selections From The Senate And House Hearings On LBOs And Corporate Debt," JACF, 1989, v2(1), 31-34.

Greenspan, Gary J. (Beyer, Gerald D. and Gary J. Greenspan. "The AuCoin Amendment: Is It Sensible? Should It Be Repealed?," JFM, 1981, v1(Supp), 479-481.)

Greenspan, Nancy T. and Ronald J. Vogel. "An Econometric Analysis Of The Effects Of Regulation In The Private Health Insurance Market," JRI, 1982, v49(1), 39-58.

Greenstone, Wayne D. "The Coffee Cartel: Manipulation In The Public Interest," JFM, v1(1), 3-16.

Greenwade, George D. (Smith, Charles A. and George D. Greenwade. "The Rankings Of Real Estate Publications And Tenure Requirements At AACSB Versus Non-AACSB Schools," JRER, 1987, v2(2), 105-112.)

Greenwald, Bruce C. "Admissible Rate Bases, Fair Rates Of Return And The Structure Of Regulation," JOF, 1980, v35(2), 359-368.

Greenwald, Douglas and Margaret K. Matulis. "McGraw-Hill Survey Of Profits," FAJ, 1969, v25(2), 44-46.

Greenwald, Douglas. "Sizing Up Research," FAJ, 1956, v12(5), 37-42.

Greenwald, William I. "The Control Of Foreign Trade: A Half-Century Of Film Trade With Great Britain," JOB, 1952, v25(1), 39-49.

Greenwood, Michael J. Greenwood. "Institutional Shareholders And Equity Market Stability," JBFA, 1975, v2(2), 257-268.)

Greenwood, Paul R. (Kim, E. Han, John J. McConnell and Paul R. Greenwood. "Capital Structure Rearrangements And Me-First Rules In An Efficient Capital Market," JOF, 1977, v32(3), 789-810.)

Greer, Carl C. "Commercial Broadcasting Industry," FAJ, 1967, v23(6), 51-60.

Greer, Carl C. "The Optimal Credit Acceptance Policy," JFQA, 1967, v2(4), 399-415.

Greer, Douglas F. and Stephen A. Rhoades. "Evaluation Of A Study On Competition In Financial Services: Comment," JBR, 1975-76, v6(1), 61-66

Greer, Douglas F. "Rate Ceilings And Loan Turndowns: A Note," JOF, 1975, v30(5), 1376-1383.

Greer, Douglas F. "Rate Ceilings, Market Structure, And The Supply Of Finance Company Personal Loans," JOF, 1974, v29(5), 1363-1382.

Greer, Douglas F. "Usury Legislation And Market Structure: Reply," JOF, 1977, v32(4), 1345-1347.

Greer, Robert J. "Conservative Commodities: A Key Inflation Hedge," JPM, 1977-78, v4(4), 26-29.

Greer, Willis R., Jr. and James A. Largay, III. "Decision Model Diagnostics: A Key To Information System Design," FR, 1979, v14(2), 36-44.

Greer, Willis R., Jr. and James A. Largay, III. "Interim Inventory Estimation Error And The Volatility Of Stock Prices," JBFA, 1980, v7(3), 401-414.

Gregg, Davis W. "A Note On Insurance Terminology," JRI, 1958, v25(3), 62-64.

Gregg, Davis W. "A Note On The Desirability Of Organizing An International Society Of Insurance," JRI, 1958, v25(4), 76-78.

Gregg, Davis W. "A Progress Report," JRI, 1963, v30(3), 451-453.

Gregg, Davis W. "A Terminology Note," JRI, 1963, v30(3), 454-455.

Gregg, Davis W. "And The Truth Shall Make Us Free," JRI, 1962, v29(1), 1-6.

Gregg, Davis W. and Mechthild K. Longo. "Insurance Education Abroad," JRI, 1960, v27(4), 121-125.

Gregory, Allan W. and Jacques Raynauld. "An Econometric Model Of Canadian Monetary Policy Over The 1970s," JMCB, 1985, v17(1), 43-58.

Gregory, Allan W. and Thomas H. McCurdy. "Testing The Unbiasedness Hypothesis In the Forward Foreign Exchange Market: A Specification Analysis," JIMF, 1984, v3(3), 357-368.

Gregory, Douglas D. "Multiplicative Risk Premiums," JFQA, 1978, v13(5), 947-963.

Gregory, Douglas D. "Risk Analysis Of An Employee Health Benefit Decision Under Hospital Reimbursement," JRI, 1981, v48(4), 577-595.

Gregory, N. A. "Testing An Aggressive Investment Strategy Using Value Line Ranks: A Comment," JOF, 1983, v38(1), 257-258.

Gregory, Owen K. "Banking And Commodity Market Structure: The Early Chicago Board Of Trade," RFM, 1983, v2(2), 168-189.

Gregory-Allen, Russell B. and Glenn V. Henderson, Jr. "A Brief Review Of Catastrophe Theory And A Test In A Corporate Failure Context," FR, 1991, v26(2), 127-156.

Greifzu, Darrel. (Gentry, James A. and Darrel Greifzu. "Short-Run Financial Management Model On Lotus 1-2-3," JFED, 1985, v14, 75-85.)

Greig, Wylie. (Liu, Crocker H., David J. Hartzell, Wylie Greig and Terry V. Grissom. "The Integration Of The Real Estate Market And The Stock Market: Some Preliminary Evidence," JREFEC, 1990, v3(3), 261-282.)

Greisel, Martin S. "Bayesian Comparisons Of Simple Macroeconomic Models," JMCB, 1973, v5(3), 751-772.

Grembergen, Willy Van. (Fabry, Jaak and Willy Van Grembergen. "Further Evidence On The Stationarity Of Betas And Errors In Their Estimates," JBF, 1978, v2(3), 189-204.)

Grennes, Thomas and John S. Lapp. "Neutrality Of Inflation In The Agricultural Sector," JIMF, 1986, v5(2), 231-243.

Grennes, Thomas. (Goodwin, Barry K., Thomas Grennes and Michael K. Wohlgenant. "Testing The Law Of One Price When Trade Takes Time," JIMF, 1990, v9(1), 21-40.)

Gressis, N. "A CAPM-Based Analysis Of Stock Index Futures," JPM, 1983-84, v10(3), 47-52.

Gressis, N., G. C. Philippatos and J. Hayya. "Multiperiod Portfolio Analysis And The Inefficiency Of The Market Portfolio," JOF, 1976, v31(4), 1115-1126.

Gressis, Nicholas and William A. Remaley. "Comment: Safety First - An Expected Utility Principle," JFQA, 1974, v9(6), 1057-1061.

Gressis, Nicholas, George C. Philippatos and George Vlahos. "Net Selectivity As A Component Measure Of Investment Performance," FR, 1986, v21(1), 103-110.

Gressis, Nicholas, Jack Hayya and George Philippatos. "Multiperiod Portfolio Efficiency Analysis Via The Geometric Mean," FR, 1974, v9(1), 46-63.

Gressis, Nicholas. (Miller, Tom W. and Nicholas Gressis. "Nonstationarity And Evaluation Of Mutual Fund Performance," *JFQA*, 1980, v15(3), 639-654.)

Gressis, Nicholas. (Saniga, Erwin, Nicholas Gressis and Jack Hayya. "The Effects Of Sample Size And Correlation On The Accuracy Of The EV Efficient Criterion," *JFQA*, 1979, v14(3), 615-628.)

Grether, Ewald T. "The Cigarette Industry's Price Policies," *JOB*, 1952, v25(4), 264-267.

Grieg, Wylie. (Liu, Crocker H., David J. Hartzell, Terry V. Grissom and Wylie Grieg. "The Composition Of The Market Portfolio And Real Estate Investment Performance," *AREUEA*, 1990, v18(1), 49-75.)

Griepentrog, Gary L. (Cox, Larry A. and Gary L. Griepentrog. "The Pure-Play Cost Of Equity For Insurance Divisions," *JRI*, 1988, v55(3), 442-452.)

Griepentrog, Gary L. (Cox, Larry A. and Gary L. Griepentrog. "Systematic Risk, Unsystematic Risk, And Property-Liability Rate Regulation," *JRI*, 1988, v55(4), 606-627.)

Griepentrog, Gary L. (Roenfeldt, Rodney L., Gary L. Griepentrog and Christopher C. Pflaum. "Further Evidence On The Stationarity Of Beta Coefficients," *JFQA*, 1978, v13(1), 117-121.)

Grier, Kevin B. "A Note On Unanticipated Money Growth And Interest Rate Surprises: Mishkin And Makin Revisited," *JOF*, 1986, v41(4), 981-986.

Grier, Paul and Paul Strebel. "An Implicit Clientele Test Of The Relationship Between Taxation And Capital Structure," *JFR*, 1983, v6(2), 163-174.

Grier, Paul and Paul Strebel. "The Empirical Relationship Between Taxation And Capital Structure," *FR*, 1980, v15(3), 45-57.

Grier, Paul C. and Peter S. Albin. "Nonrandom Price Changes In Association With Trading In Large Blocks," *JOB*, 1973, v46(3), 425-433.

Grier, Paul and Steven Katz. "The Differential Effects Of Bond Rating Changes Among Industrial And Public Utility Bonds By Maturity," *JOB*, 1976, v49(2), 226-239.

Grier, Paul. "Reply To Robert Reback's Comment: Nonrandom Price Changes In Association With Trading In Large Blocks," *JOB*, 1974, v47(4), 566-567.

Grier, Paul. (Jaggi, Bikki and Paul Grier. "A Comparative Analysis Of Forecast Disclosing And Non-Disclosing Firms," *FM*, 1980, v9(2), 38-43.)

Griesedieck, Joseph. "Brewing Crosses The Threshold," *FAJ*, 1963, v19(3), 85-88.

Grieves, Robin and J. Clay Singleton. "Analytical Methods Of The All-America Research Team," *JPM*, 1987-88, v14(1), 4-8.

Grieves, Robin. "Hedging Corporate Bond Portfolios," *JPM*, 1985-86, v12(4), 23-25.

Grieves, Robin. "The Demand For Consumer Durables," *JMCB*, 1983, v15(3), 316-326.

Grieves, Robin. (Khaksari, Shahriar, Ravindra Kamath and Robin Grieves. "A New Approach To Determining Optimum Portfolio Mix," *JPM*, 1989, v15(3), 43-49.)

Grieves, Robin. (Singleton, J. Clay and Robin Grieves. "Synthetic Puts And Portfolio Insurance Strategies," *JPM*, 1983-84, v10(3), 63-69.)

Griffin, Paul A. and Antonio Z. Sanvicente. "Common Stock Returns And Rating Changes: A Methodological Comparison," *JOF*, 1982, v37(1), 103-119.

Griffin, Paul A. "Competitive Information In The Stock Market: An Empirical Study Of Earnings, Dividends And Analysts' Forecasts," *JOF*, 1976, v31(2), 631-650.

Griffin, Paul A. (Beaver, William H., Paul A. Griffin and Wayne R. Landsman. "How Well Does Replacement Cost Income Explain Stock Return?," *FAJ*, 1983, v39(2), 26-30,39.)

Griffith, B. Barret. "Deflation - What Is It?," *FAJ*, 1958, v14(5), 74-78.

Griffith, B. Barret. "Gold," *FAJ*, 1957, v13(4), 65-66.

Griffith, B. Barret. "Gold," *FAJ*, 1953, v9(4), 71-72.

Griffith, B. Barret. "Stock Market Bellwether - General Motors," *FAJ*, 1962, v18(6), 94-95.

Griffith, B. Barret. "The Gold Glow," *FAJ*, 1961, v17(5), 85-86.

Griffith, B. Barret. "The Gold Flow," *FAJ*, 1959, v15(5), 51-54.

Griffith, B. Barret. "The Gold Flow," *FAJ*, 1962, v18(4), 63-64.

Griffith, B. Barret. "The Gold Flow (Continued)," *FAJ*, 1963, v19(3), 52.

Griffith, B. Barret. "The Gold Flow," *FAJ*, 1964, v20(3), 97-98.

Griffith, B. Barret. "The Gold Flow (An Economic Barometer)," *FAJ*, 1960, v16(6), 67-68.

Griffith, B. Barret. "Turn-Around In Raw Material Prices?," *FAJ*, 1963, v19(6), 77.

Griffith, B. Barret. "Unsophisticated Investments Against Inflation," *FAJ*, 1952, v8(3), 25-28.

Griffith, R. (Agnello, W., W. Brueggeman, G. Decker, R. Griffith, R. Leftwich, R. Moore, J. Neal, B. Sternlicht, B. Wallach, W. Wardrop and C. Zinngrabe. "Panel: Corporate Real Estate Roundtable," *JACF*, 1990, v3(1), 6-38.)

Griffith, Reynolds and J. Michael Murphy. "'Why You Can't Win'," *JPM*, 1977-78, v4(2), 76-78.

Griffith, Reynolds. "A Note On Life Insurance Accounting," *JRI*, 1964, v31(2), 207-216.

Griffith, Reynolds. "Valuation Of Life Insurance Stocks," *JRI*, 1965, v32(1), 77-84.

Griffith, Reynolds. (Corbett, Gary and Reynolds Griffith. "A Note On Life Insurance Accounting: Comment," *JRI*, 1965, v32(2), 277-282.)

Griffith, Sanford. "The Saar Steps Into Large Production," *FAJ*, 1955, v11(4), 25-28.

Griffiths, Brian. "Resource Efficiency, Monetary Policy And The Reform Of The U.K. Banking System," *JMCB*, 1973, v5(1), 61-77.

Griffiths, Brian. "The Welfare Cost Of The U.K. Clearing Banks' Cartel," *JMCB*, 1972, v4(2), 227-244.

Griffiths, Brian. "Two Monetary Inquiries In Great Britain: Comments On The Macmillan Report Of 1931 And The Radcliffe Committee Of 1959: A Comment," *JMCB*, 1974, v6(1), 101-114.

Griggs, Frank T. (Reilly, Frank K., Frank T. Griggs and Wenchi Wong. "Determinants Of The Aggregate Stock Market Earnings Multiple," *JPM*, 1983-84, v10(1), 36-45.)

Grigsby, William G. "AREUEA Presidential Address," *AREUEA*, 1978, v6(3), 241-246.

Grigsby, William G. "Real Estate And Urban Land Economics: Illusions Of Progress?," *AREUEA*, 1973, v1(1), 4-7.

Grilli, Enzo R. and Maw Cheng Yang. "Internationally Traded Good Prices, World Money, And Economic Activity: 1900-83," *JIMF*, 1990, v9(2), 159-181.

Grilli, Vittorio. "Managing Exchange Rate Crises: Evidence From The 1890s," *JIMF*, 1990, v9(3), 258-275.

Grimley, Cecil A. "Supervision Of Insurance In Australia," *JRI*, 1960, v27(4), 103-108.

Grimlund, Richard A. and Robert Capettini. "Sign Tests For Actual Investments With Latter Period Net Cash Outflows," *JBFA*, 1983, v10(1), 83-103.

Grimlund, Richard A. and Robert Capettini. "A Note On The Evaluation On Leveraged Leases And Other Investments," *FM*, 1982, v11(2), 68-72.

Grimlund, Richard A. (Capettini, Robert, Richard A. Grimlund and Howard R. Toole. "Comment: The Unique, Real Internal Rate Of Return," *JFQA*, 1979, v14(5), 1091-1094.)

Grimm, Eldon A. "One Must Be In Style," *FAJ*, 1956, v12(1), 25-28.

Grimm, Richard W. "A Case For Municipal Bond Funds," *FAJ*, 1958, v14(5), 79-84.

Grinblatt, Mark and Sheridan Titman. "Approximate Factor Structures: Interpretations And Implications For Empirical Tests," *JOF*, 1985, v40(5), 1367-1373.

Grinblatt, Mark and Sheridan Titman. "Factor Pricing In A Finite Economy," *JFEC*, 1983, v12(4), 497-508.

Grinblatt, Mark S., Ronald W. Masulis and Sheridan Titman. "The Valuation Effects Of Stock Splits And Stock Dividends," *JFEC*, 1984, v13(4), 461-490.

Grinblatt, Mark and Chuan Yang Hwang. "Signalling And The Pricing Of New Issues," *JOF*, 1989, v44(2), 393-420.

Grinblatt, Mark and Herb Johnson. "A Put Option Paradox," *JFQA*, 1988, v23(1), 23-26.

Grinblatt, Mark and Sheridan Titman. "How Clients Can Win The Gaming Game," *JPM*, 1986-87, v13(4),14-20.

Grinblatt, Mark and Sheridan Titman. "The Relation Between Mean-Variance Efficiency And Arbitrage Pricing," *JOB*, 1987, v60(1), 97-112.

Grinblatt, Mark and Sheridan Titman. "Mutual Fund Performance: An Analysis Of Quarterly Portfolio Holdings," *JOB*, 1989, v62(3), 393-416.

Grinblatt, Mark and Sheridan Titman. "Portfolio Performance Evaluation: Old Issues And New Insights," *RFS*, 1989, v2(3), 393-422.

Grinnan, R. Bryan, III. (Nickson, Jack W., Jr. and R. Bryan Grinnan III. "Should Banks Enter The Leasing Field?," *FR*, 1968, v1(3), 181-190.)

Grinnell, D. J. and C. T. Norgaard. "Reporting Rules For Marketable Equity Securities," *FAJ*, 1980, v36(1), 69-74.

Grinold, Richard C. "The Fundamental Law Of Active Management," *JPM*, 1989, v15(3), 30-37.

Grinold, Richard and Andrew Rudd. "Incentive Fees: Who Wins? Who Loses?," *FAJ*, 1987, v43(1), 27-38.

Grinold, Richard, Andrew Rudd and Dan Stefek. "Global Factors: Fact Or Fiction?," *JPM*, 1989, v16(1), 79-89.

Grinols, Earl L. "Production And Risk Leveling In The Intertemporal Capital Asset Pricing Model," *JOF*, 1984, v39(5), 1571-1595.

Grinols, Earl L. (Gertler, Mark L. and Earl L. Grinols. "Unemployment, Inflation, And Common Stock Returns," *JMCB*, 1982, v14(2), 216-233.)

Grinyer, John R. "Relevant Criterion Rates In Capital Budgeting," *JBFA*, 1974, v1(3), 357-374.

Grinyer, John R. "Inflation And Capital Budgeting Decisions: A Comment," *JBFA*, 1974, v1(1), 149-155.

Grinyer, John R. "On The Negative Risk Premium For Risk Adjusted Discount Rates: A Further Comment," *JBFA*, 1984, v11(2), 257-262.

Grinyer, John R. "The Cost Of Equity Capital - A Reply," *JBFA*, 1975, v2(3), 383-388.

Grinyer, John R. "The Cost Of Equity, The C.A.P.M. And Management Objectives Under Uncertainty," *JBFA*, 1979, v3(4), 101-121.

Grinyer, John R. "The Term Structure And The Irrelevance Of The Firm's Cost Of Capital: A Comment," *JBFA*, 1980, v7(2), 305-310.

Grinyer, John R. and Robert A. Lyon. "The Need For Ex Post EEI," *JBFA*, 1989, v16(3), 303-316.

Grissom, Terry V. (Dotzour, Mark G., Terry V. Grissom, Crocker H. Liu and Thomas Pearson. "Highest And Best Use: The Evolving Paradigm," *JRER*, 1990, v5(1), 17-32.)

Grissom, Terry V. (Liu, Crocker H., David J. Hartzell, Terry V. Grissom and Wylie Grieg. "The Composition Of The Market Portfolio And Real Estate Investment Performance," *AREUEA*, 1990, v18(1), 49-75.)

Grissom, Terry V. (Liu, Crocker H., Terry V. Grissom and David J. Hartzell. "The Impact Of Market Imperfections On Real Estate Returns And Optimal Investment Portfolios," *AREUEA*, 1990, v18(4), 453-478.)

Grissom, Terry V. (Liu, Crocker H., David J. Hartzell, Wylie Greig and Terry V. Grissom. "The Integration Of The Real Estate Market And The Stock Market: Some Preliminary Evidence," *JREFEC*, 1990, v3(3), 261-282.)

Grissom, Terry V. (Wang, Ko, Terry V. Grissom and Su Hun Chan. "The Functional Relationships And Use Of Going-In And Going-Out Capitalization Rates," *JRER*, 1990, v5(2), 231-245.)

Grissom, Terry V., David Hartzell and Crocker H. Liu. "An Approach To Industrial Real Estate Market Segmentation And Valuation Using The Arbitrage Pricing Paradigm," *AREUEA*, 1987, v15(3), 199-219.

Grissom, Terry V., James L. Kuhle and Carl H. Walther. "Diversification Works In Real Estate, Too," *JPM*, 1986-87, v13(2), 66-71.

Gritta, Richard D. "The Effects Of Financial Leverage On Air Carrier Earnings: Reply," *FM*, 1980, v9(3), 72-73.

Gritta, Richard D. "The Effect Of Financial Leverage On Air Carrier Earnings: A Break-Even Analysis," *FM*, 1979, v8(2), 53-60.

Gritta, Richard D. "The Impact Of Lease Capitalization," *FAJ*, 1974, v30(2), 47-52.

Groff, James E. (Wingender, John and James E. Groff. "On Stochastic Dominance Analysis Of Day-Of-The-Week Return Patterns," *JFR*, 1989, v12(1), 51-56.)

Gronberg, Timothy J. and Jack Meyer. "Spatial Pricing And Its Effect On Product Transportability," JOB, 1982, v55(2), 269-280.

Gronewoller, Paul L. (Howe, Keith M. and Paul L. Gronewoller. "Issue Costs In Fisher's Two-Period Model," FR, 1990, v25(2), 335-343.)

Grooch, Gary M. (Baskin, Elba F. and Gary M. Grooch. "Return On Flat Bonds," FAJ, 1968, v24(6), 95-97.)

Groomer, S. Michael. "A Software System For Financial Analysis And Modeling," JFED, 1980, v9, 98-101.

Gross, Courtlandt S. "Wanted: A New Name For Aircrafts," FAJ, 1962, v18(2), 11-14.

Gross, David J. (Buckley, Robert M. and David J. Gross. "Selective Credit Policies And The Mortgage Market: Cross-Sectional Evidence," JMCB, 1985, v17(3), 358-370.)

Gross, Howard S. (Horton, William L. and Howard S. Gross. "Opportunities For Commercial Banks In The Business Lease/Instalment Loan Market," JBR, 1974-75, v5(2), 125-128.)

Gross, Martin. "A Semi-Strong Test Of The Efficiency Of The Aluminum And Copper Markets At The LME," JFM, 1988, v8(1), 67-78.

Gross, William H. "Selling The Noise," JPM, 1989, v15(3), 61-63.

Gross, William H. "The Effect Of Coupon On Yield Spreads," FAJ, 1979, v35(4), 68-71.

Grossman, Blake R. and William F. Sharpe. "Financial Implications Of South African Divestment," FAJ, 1986, v42(4), 15-29.

Grossman, Herschel I. "Expectations, Transactions Costs, And Asset Demands," JOF, 1969, v24(3), 491-506.

Grossman, Herschel I. "Inflation And Reputation With Generic Policy Preferences," JMCB, 1990, v22(2), 165-177.

Grossman, Herschel I. "Risk Aversion, Financial Intermediation, And The Term Structure Of Interest Rates," JOF, 1967, v22(4), 611-622.

Grossman, Herschel I. (Barro, Robert J. and Herschel I. Grossman. "Open-Market Operations And The Medium Of Exchange: A Comment," JMCB, 1971, v3(2), Part 1, 304-311.)

Grossman, Jacob. "The 'Rationality' Of Money Supply Expectations And The Short-Run Response Of Interest Rates To Monetary Surprises," JMCB, 1981, v13(4), 409-424.

Grossman, S. J. and J. E. Stiglitz. "On Value Maximization And Alternative Objectives Of The Firm," JOF, 1977, v32(2), 389-402.

Grossman, S. J. and O. D. Hart. "Disclosure Laws And Takeover Bids," JOF, 1980, v35(2), 323-333.

Grossman, Sanford J. and Merton H. Miller. "Economic Costs And Benefits Of The Proposed One-Minute Time Bracketing Regulation," JFM, 1986, v6(1), 141-166.

Grossman, Sanford J. and Oliver D. Hart. "The Allocation Role Of Takeover Bids In Situations Of Asymmetric Information," JOF, 1981, v36(2), 253-270.

Grossman, Sanford J. and Robert J. Shiller. "Consumption Correlatedness And Risk Measurement In Economies With Non-Traded Assets And Heterogeneous Information," JFEC, 1982, v10(2), 195-210.

Grossman, Sanford J. "An Analysis Of The Role Of 'Insider Trading' On Futures Markets," JOB, 1986, v59(2), Part 2, S129-S146.

Grossman, Sanford J. "An Analysis Of The Implications For Stock And Futures Price Volatility Of Program Trading And Dynamic Hedging Strategies," JOB, 1988, v61(3), 275-298.

Grossman, Sanford J. "Insurance Seen And Unseen: The Impact On Markets," JPM, 1987-88, v14(4), 5-8.

Grossman, Sanford J. "Program Trading And Market Volatility: A Report On Interday Relationships," FAJ, 1988, v44(4), 18-28.

Grossman, Sanford J. "Program Trading And Stock And Futures Price Volatility," JFM, 1988, v8(4),413-420.

Grossman, Sanford J. (Fischel, Daniel R. and Sanford J. Grossman. "Customer Protection In Futures And Securities Markets," JFM, 1984, v4(3), 273-296.)

Grossman, Sanford J. and Jean-Luc Vila. "Portfolio Insurance In Complete Markets: A Note," JOB, 1989, v62(4), 473-476.

Grossman, Sanford J. and Merton H. Miller. "Liquidity And Market Structure," JOF, 1988, v43(3),617-633.

Grossman, Sanford J. and Oliver D. Hart. "One Share—One Vote And The Market For Corporate Control," JFEC, 1988, v20(1/2), 175-202.

Grossman, Sanford. "On The Efficiency Of Competitive Stock Markets Where Trades Have Diverse Information," JOF, 1976, v31(2), 573-585.

Grossman, Seth. (Elton, Edwin J., Martin J. Gruber and Seth Grossman. "Discrete Expectational Data And Portfolio Performance," JOF, 1986, v41(3), 699-712.)

Grossman, Stephen D. "An Application Of Communication Theory To Financial Statement Analysis," FR, 1975, v10(1), 12-20.

Grossman. Steven D., Gary L. Schugart and Robert H. Strawser. "An Intra And Inter-Industry Comparison Of Performance Measures Based On Alternative Income Concepts," FR, 1979, v14(3), 13-24.

Grossman, Steven. (Giroux, Gary, Winston Shearon and Steven Grossman. "How Does Inflation Affect A BHCs Rate Of Return?," JBR, 1983-84, v14(2), 164-169.)

Groth, John C. "Security-Relative Information Market Efficiency: Some Empirical Evidence," JFQA, 1979, v14(3), 573-593.

Groth, John C. (Dubofsky, David A. and John C. Groth. "Relative Information Accessibility For OTC Stocks And Security Returns," FR, 1986, v21(1),85-102.)

Groth, John C. (Dubofsky, David A. and John C. Groth. "Exchange Listing And Stock Liquidity," FR, 1987, v7(4), 291-302.)

Groth, John C. (Dubofsky, David A. and John C. Groth. "An Examination Of Asked-Bid Spreads For Two Over-The-Counter Market Segments," FR, 1986, v21(2), 289-298.)

Groth, John C. (Fraser, Donald R. and John C. Groth. "Listing And The Liquidity Of Bank Stocks," JBR, 1985-86, v16(3), 136-144.)

Groth, John C. (French, Dan W., John C. Groth and James W. Kolari. "Current Investor Expectations And Better Betas," JPM, 1983-84, v10(1), 12-17.)

Groth, John C. (Phillips, Paul D., John C. Groth and R. Malcolm Richards. "Financing The Alaskan Project: The Experience Of Sohio," FM, 1979, v8(3),7-16.)

Groth, John C. (Richards, R. Malcolm, Donald R. Fraser and John C. Groth. "The Attractions Of Closed-End Bond Funds," JPM, 1981-82, v8(2), 56-61.)

Groth, John C. (Richards, R. Malcolm, Donald R. Fraser and John C. Groth. "Premiums, Discounts, And The Volatility Of Closed-End Mutual Funds," FR, 1979, v14(3), 25-33.)

Groth, John C. (Richards, R. Malcolm, Don R. Fraser and John C. Groth. "Winning Strategies For Closed-End Funds," JPM, 1980-81, v7(1), 50-55.)

Groth, John C., Wilbur G. Lewellen, Gary G. Schlarbaum and Ronald C. Lease. "Security Analysts: Some Are More Equal," JPM, 1977-78, v4(3), 43-48.

Groth, John C., Wilbur G. Lewellen, Gary G. Schlarbaum and Ronald C. Lease. "How Good Are Broker's Recommendations?," FAJ, 1979, v35(1), 32-40.

Groth, Stephen C. "The Trouble With Convertibles," FAJ, 1972, v28(6), 92-95.

Grotz, W. Arthur. "Does Depreciation Make Sense," FAJ, 1956, v12(4), 23-26.

Grove, David L. "International Liquidity - Needs And Problems," FAJ, 1966, v22(1), 13-19.

Grove, David L. "International Monetary Liquidity," FAJ, 1968, v24(1), 19-26.

Grove, David L. "Monetary Policy And The Balance Of Payments," FAJ, 1965, v21(3), 39-44.

Grove, David L. "Solving The Dollar Overhang," FAJ, 1973, v29(2), 14-15,18-19,22-23,33.

Grove, Hugh. (Rizzuto, Ronald and Hugh Grove. "How To Lie With Accounting: A Unique Extension Of Security Analysis," JFED, 1981, v10, 33-37.)

Grove, M. A. (Bierwag, G. O. and M. A. Grove. "A Model Of The Structure Of Prices Of Marketable U.S. Treasury Securities," JMCB, 1971, v3(3), 605-629.)

Grove, M. A. (Bierwag, G. O. and M. A. Grove. "On Capital Asset Prices: Comment," JOF, 1965, v20(1), 89-93.)

Groves, Harold M. "Personal Versus Corporate Income Taxes," JOF, 1946, v1(1), 52-60.

Groves, R. E. V. and J. M. Samuels. "A Note On The Cost Of Retained Earnings And Deferred Taxes In The U.K.," JBFA, 1976, v3(4), 143-149.

Groves, R. E. V. (Rickwood, C. P. and Groves, R. E. V. "Tax And The Integration Of Finance And Investment," JBFA, 1979, v6(2), 157-172.)

Groves, William A. (Fogler, H. Russell and William A. Groves. "How Much Can Active Bond Management Raise Returns?," JPM, 1976-77, v3(1), 35-40.)

Groves, William A. (Fogler, H. Russell, William A. Groves and James G. Richardson. "Bond Management: Are 'Dumbbells' Smart?," JPM, 1975-76, v2(2), 54-60.)

Groves, William A. (Fogler, H. Russell, William A. Groves and James G. Richardson. "Bond Portfolio Strategies, Returns, And Skewness: A Note," JFQA, 1977, v12(1), 127-140.)

Grubaugh, Stephen and Scott Sumner. "Commodity Prices, Money Surprises, And Fed Credibility: Comment," JMCB, 1989, v21(3), 407-408.

Grubaugh, Steven. (Asabere, Paul K., George Hachey and Steven Grubaugh. "Architecture, Historic Zoning, And The Value Of Homes," JREFEC, 1989, v2(3), 181-196.)

Grubbs, Donald S., Jr. (Johnson, George E. and Donald S. Grubbs, Jr. "Media For Funding Variable Annuities," JRI, 1968, v35(2), 257-272.)

Grube, R. Corwin and Don B. Panton. "How Well Do Filter-Rule Strategies Work For Options?," JPM, 1977-78, v4(2), 52-57.

Grube, R. Corwin and O. Maurice Joy. "Some Evidence On The Efficacy Of Security Credit Regulation In The OTC Equity Market," JFR, 1988, v11(2), 137-142.

Grube, R. Corwin, Don B. Panton and J. Michael Terrell. "Risks And Rewards In Covered Call Positions," JPM, 1978-79, v5(2), 64-68.

Grube, R. Corwin, O. Maurice Joy and Don B. Panton. "Market Responses To Federal Reserve Changes In The Initial Margin Requirement," JOF, 1979, v34(3), 659-674.

Grube, R. Corwin, O. Maurice Joy and John S. Howe. "Some Empirical Evidence On Stock Returns And Security Credit Regulation In The OTC Equity Market," JBF, 1987, v11(1), 17-32.

Grube, R. Corwin. (Fortin, Richard D., R. Corwin Grube and O. Maurice Joy. "Bid-Ask Spreads For OTC NASDAQ Firms," FAJ, 1990, v46(3), 76-79.)

Grube, R. Corwin. (Fortin, Richard D., R. Corwin Grube and O. Maurice Joy. "Seasonality In NASDAQ Dealer Spreads," JFQA, 1989, v24(3), 395-407.)

Grubel, Hebert G. and Kenneth Fadner. "The Interdependence Of International Equity Markets," JOF, 1971, v26(1), 89-94.

Grubel, Herbert G. "A Neglected Aspect Of Forward Exchange Theory And Policy," JOF, 1963, v18(3), 537-548.

Grubel, Herbert G. "Basic Methods For Distributing Special Drawing Rights And The Problem Of International Aid," JOF, 1972, v27(5), 1009-1022.

Grubel, Herbert G. "Risk, Uncertainty And Moral Hazard," JRI, 1971, v38(1), 99-106.

Grubel, Herbert G. "The M.B.A. Education Myth," JOB, 1969, v42(1), 42-49.

Grubel, Herbert G. "The Peter Principle And Efficient Markets," FAJ, 1979, v35(6), 72-75.

Grubel, Herbert G. "Triangular Arbitrage For Forward Exchange Policy: Reply," JOF, 1964, v19(3), 552-554.

Gruber, Martin J. (Bawa, Vijay S., Edwin J. Elton and Martin J. Gruber. "Simple Rules For Optimal Portfolio Selection In Stable Paretian Markets," JOF, 1979, v34(4), 1041-1047.)

Gruber, Martin J. (Cho, D. Chinhyung, Edwin J. Elton and Martin J. Gruber. "On The Robustness Of The Roll And Ross Arbitrage Pricing Theory," JFQA, 1984, v19(1), 1-10.)

Gruber, Martin J. (Elton, Edwin J. and Martin J. Gruber. "Improved Forecasting Through The Design Of Homogeneous Groups," JOB, 1971, v44(4), 432-450.)

Gruber, Martin J. (Elton, Edwin J. and Martin J. Gruber. "Valuation And The Cost Of Capital For Regulated Industries," JOF, 1971, v26(3), 661-670.)

Gruber, Martin J. (Elton, Edwin J. and Martin J. Gruber. "The Economic Value Of The Call Option," JOF, 1972, v27(4), 891-901.)

Gruber, Martin J. (Elton, Edwin J. and Martin J. Gruber. "Valuation And Asset Selection Under Alternative Investment Opportunities," JOF, 1976, v31(2), 525-539.)

Gruber, Martin J. (Elton, Edwin J., Martin J. Gruber and Manfred W. Padberg. "Simple Rules For Optimal Portfolio Selection: The Multi Group Case," JFQA, 1977, v12(3), 329-345.)

Gruber, Martin J. (Elton, Edwin J., Martin J. Gruber and Manfred W. Padberg. "Simple Criteria For Optimal Portfolio Selection," JOF, 1976, v31(5), 1341-1357.)

Gruber, Martin J. (Elton, Edwin J., Martin J. Gruber and Seth Grossman. "Discrete Expectational Data And Portfolio Performance," JOF, 1986, v41(3), 699-712.)

Gruber, Martin J. (Elton, Edwin J., Martin J. Gruber and Joel Rentzler. "The Ex-Dividend Day Behavior Of Stock Prices; A Reexamination Of The Clientele Effect: A Comment," JOF, 1984, v39(2), 551-556.)

Gruber, Martin J. (Elton, Edwin J., Martin J. Gruber and Manfred W. Padberg. "Simple Criteria For Optimal Portfolio Selection: Tracing Out The Efficient Frontier," JOF, 1978, v33(1), 296-302.)

Gruber, Martin J. (Elton, Edwin J. and Martin J. Gruber. "Estimating The Dependence Structure Of Share Prices - Implications For Portfolio Selection," JOF, 1973, v28(5), 1203-1232.)

Gruber, Martin J. (Elton, Edwin J. and Martin J. Gruber. "Risk Reduction And Portfolio Size: An Analytical Solution," JOB, 1977, v50(4), 415-437.)

Gruber, Martin J. (Elton, Edwin J. and Martin J. Gruber. "Portfolio Theory When Investment Relatives Are Lognormally Distributed," JOF, 1974, v29(4), 1265-1273.)

Gruber, Martin J. (Elton, Edwin J. and Martin J. Gruber. "Dynamic Programming Applications In Finance," JOF, 1971, v26(2), 473-506.)

Gruber, Martin J. (Elton, Edwin J. and Martin J. Gruber. "Non-Standard C.A.P.M.'s And The Market Portfolio," JOF, 1984, v39(3), 911-924.)

Gruber, Martin J. (Elton, Edwin J., Martin J. Gruber and Zvi Lieber. "Valuation, Optimum Investment And Financing For The Firm Subject To Regulation," JOF, 1975, v30(2), 401-425.)

Gruber, Martin J. (Elton, Edwin J. and Martin J. Gruber. "Optimal Investment And Financing Patterns For A Firm Subject To Regulation With A Lag," JOF, 1977, v32(5), 1485-1500.)

Gruber, Martin J. (Elton, Edwin J. and Martin J. Gruber. "Asset Selection With Changing Capital Structure," JFQA, 1973, v8(3), 459-474.)

Gruber, Martin J. (Elton, Edwin J., Martin J. Gruber and Mustafa N. Gultekin. "Professional Expectations: Accuracy And Diagnosis Of Errors," JFQA, 1984, v19(4), 351-363.)

Gruber, Martin J. (Elton, Edwin J. and Martin J. Gruber. "On The Optimality Of Some Multiperiod Portfolio Selection Criteria," JOB, 1974, v47(2), 231-243.)

Gruber, Martin J. (Elton, Edwin J. and Martin J. Gruber. "Valuation And The Cost Of Capital For Regulated Industries: Reply," JOF, 1972, v27(5), 1150-1155.)

Gruber, Martin J. (Elton, Edwin J. and Martin J. Gruber. "Homogeneous Groups And The Testing Of Economic Hypotheses," JFQA, 1970, v5(5), 581-602.)

Gruber, Martin J. (Elton, Edwin J., Martin J. Gruber and Thomas J. Urich. "Are Betas Best?," JOF, 1978, v33(5), 1375-1384.)

Gruber, Martin J. (Elton, Edwin J. and Martin J. Gruber. "Taxes And Portfolio Composition," JFEC, 1978, v6(4), 399-410.)

Gruber, Martin J. (Elton, Edwin J., Martin J. Gruber and Joel C. Rentzler. "Professionally Managed, Publicly Traded Commodity Funds," JOB, 1987, v60(2), 175-200.)

Gruber, Martin J. (Elton, Edwin J. and Martin J. Gruber and Manfred W. Padberg. "Optimal Portfolios From Simple Ranking Devices," JPM, 1977-78, v4(3),15-19.)

Gruber, Martin J. (Elton, Edwin J., Martin J. Gruber and Joel Rentzler. "The Performance Of Publicly Offered Commodity Funds," FAJ, 1990, v46(4), 23-30.)

Gruber, Martin J. (Elton, Edwin J. and Martin J. Gruber. "Differential Information And Timing Ability," JBF, 1991, v15(1), 117-131.)

Gruber, Martin J. (Elton, Edwin J., Martin J. Gruber and Joel Rentzler. "New Public Offerings, Information, And Investor Rationality: The Case Of Publicly Offered Commodity Funds," JOB, 1989, v62(1), 1-16.)

Gruber, Martin J. (Elton, Edwin J., Martin J. Gruber and Roni Michaely. "The Structure Of Spot Rates And Immunization," JOF, 1990, v45(2), 629-642.)

Gruber, Martin J. (Elton, Edwin J., Martin J. Gruber and John B. Lightstone. "The Impact Of Bankruptcy On The Firm's Capital Structure, The Reasonableness Of Mergers, And The Risk Independence Of Projects," RIF, 1981, v3, 143-156.)

Gruber, Martin J. (Elton, Edwin J., Martin J. Gruber and Suk Mo Koo. "Effect Of Quarterly Earnings Announcements On Analysts' Forecasts," RIF, 1986, v6, 247-260.)

Gruber, Martin. (Elton, Edwin, Martin Gruber and Joel Rentzler. "A Simple Examination Of The Empirical Relationship Between Dividend Yields And Deviations From The CAPM," JBF, 1983, v7(1), 135-146.)

Gruber, Martin J. (Elton, Edwin J., Martin Gruber and Joel Rentzler. "The Arbitrage Pricing Model And Returns On Assets Under Uncertain Inflation," JOF, 1983, v38(2), 525-537.)

Gruber, Martin. (Elton, Edwin and Martin Gruber. "The Effect Of Share Repurchases On The Value Of The Firm," JOF, 1968, v23(1), 135-149.)

Gruber, Martin. (Elton, Edwin and Martin Gruber. "The Effect Of Share Repurchase On The Value Of The Firm: Reply," JOF, 1968, v23(5), 870-874.)

Gruca, Thomas. (Bryan, William R., Thomas Gruca and Charles M. Linke. "The Present Value Of Future Earnings: Contemporary Differentials And The Performance Of Dedicated Portfolios," JRI, 1990, v57(3), 530-539.)

Gruen, Claude. "A Cynic's View Of Zoning Reform: Comment," AREUEA, 1978, v6(3), 337-340.

Gruge, R. Corwin. (Dowell, C. Dwayne and R. Corwin Grube. "Common Stock Return Distributions During Homogeneous Activity Periods," JFQA, 1978, v13(1),79-92.)

Grundfest, J. (Amihud, Y., C. Brunie, C. Ferenbach, R. Fredericks, J. Grundfest, J. Lafferty, B. Lev, B. Shorts, J. Stern, B. Stewart and R. Zeckhauser. "Panel: 'Lead Steer' Roundtable," JACF, 1989, v2(3), 24-44.)

Grundfest, J. (Boies, D., D. Carroll, A. Fleischer, J. Grundfest, J. Ira Harris, M. Lipton, R. Monks, A. Oliver, L. Sachnoff and J. Wilcox. "Panel: Corporate Governance: The Role Of Boards Of Directors In Takeover Bids And Defenses," JACF, 1989, v2(2), 6-35.)

Grundfest, Joseph A. "Subordination Of American Capital," JFEC, 1990, v27(1), 89-114.

Grundfest, Joseph A. (Black, Bernard S. and Joseph A. Grundfest. "Shareholder Gains From Takeovers And Restructurings Between 1981 And 1986," JACF, 1988, v1(1), 6-15.)

Grundy, Bruce D. (Constantinides, George M. and Bruce D. Grundy. "Optimal Investment With Stock Repurchase And Financing As Signals," RFS, 1989, v2(4), 445-466.)

Grundy, Bruce D. and Maureen McNichols. "Trade And Revelation Of Information Through Prices And Direct Disclosure," RFS, 1989, v2(4), 495-526.

Grundy, Bruce. (Chen, Nai-Fu, Bruce Grundy and Robert F. Stambaugh. "Changing Risk, Changing Risk Premiums, And Dividend Yield Effects," JOB, 1990, v63(1), Part 2, S51-S70.)

Grunewald, Adolph E. "Stock Is Worth What You Can Get Out Of It," FAJ, 1957, v13(5), 61-64.

Grunewald, Adolph E. "West German Stock Investments," FAJ, 1960, v16(5), 35-38.

Gualandri, Elisabetta. "Italian Banks And Interest Rate Risk," JBR, 1986-87, v17(1), 41-44.

Gudikunst, Arthur C. (Dipchand, Cecil R., Arthur C. Gudikunst and Gordon S. Roberts. "An Empirical Analysis Of Canadian Railroad Leases," JFR, 1980, v3(1), 57-68.)

Gudikunst, Arthur C. (Roberts, Gordon S. and Arthur C. Gudikunst. "Equipment Financial Leasing Practices And Costs: Comment," FM, 1978, v7(2), 79-81.)

Guenther, Harry and Joseph White. "EFT System Privacy Safeguards: A Preliminary Inquiry Into The Privacy-Leisure Time Trade-Off," JBR, 1979-80, v10(3), 136-144.

Guenther, Harry P. "Bank Regulation: A Plan For Flexibility," FR, 1971, v2(1), 34-43.

Guenther, Harry P. "The District Of Columbia Case For Amending The Bank Holding Company Act," FR, 1970, v1(5), 296-302.

Guerard, John B., Jr. "Combining Time-Series Model Forecasts And Analysts' Forecasts For Superior Forecasts Of Annual Earnings," FAJ, 1989, v45(1), 69-71.

Guerard, John B., Jr. and George M. McCabe. "A Further Look At The Interdependencies Of Corporate Expenditures And Implications For Strategic-Planning Models," RIF, 1990, v8, 149-178.

Guertin, Alfred N. "Developments In Standard Non-Forfeiture And Valuation Legislation," JRI, 1946, v13, 5-15.

Guertin, Alfred N. "Life Insurance Premiums," JRI, 1965, v32(1), 23-50.

Guertin, Alfred N. "Price Competition In The Life Insurance Business," JRI, 1958, v25(1), 1-10.

Guertin, Alfred N. "The Standard Non-Forfeiture And Valuation Laws," JRI, 1944, v11, 46-60.

Guffey, Daryl M. and William T. Moore. "Direct Bankruptcy Costs: Evidence From The Trucking Industry," FR, 1991, v26(2), 223-236.

Guidotti, Pablo E. "Exchange Rate Determination, Interest Rates, And An Integrative Approach To The Demand For Money," JIMF, 1989, v8(1), 29-46.

Guild, S. E. "Foresight, Hindsight, And Foresight," FAJ, 1956, v12(4), 55-60.

Guild, S. Eliot. "The Case For Stock Value Tables," FAJ, 1964, v20(5), 80-97.

Guilkey, David K. (Carleton, Willard T., David K. Guilkey, Robert S. Harris and John F. Stewart. "An Empirical Analysis Of The Role Of The Medium Of Exchange In Mergers," JOF, 1983, v38(5), 813-826.)

Guilkey, David, Mike Miles and Rebel Cole. "The Motivation For Institutional Real Estate Sales And Implications For Asset Class Returns," AREUEA, 1989, v17(1), 70-86.

Guimaraes, Rui Campos. (Cabral, Jose Sarsfield and Rui Campos Guimaraes. "Are Commodity Futures Markets Really Efficient? A Purchasing-Oriented Study Of The Chicago Corn Futures Market," RFM, 1988, v7(Supp), 598-617.)

Guithues, Henry J. (Kim, Suk H. and Henry J. Guithues. "A Survey Of Graduate Finance Case Courses," JFED, 1982, v11, 83-86.)

Gujarati, D. N. "The Economics Of The Davis-Bacon Act," JOB, 1967, v40(3), 303-316.

Gujarati, Damodar. (Cohen, Bruce and Damodar Gujarati. "The Student's t Test In Multiple Regression Under Simple Collinearity," JFQA, 1970, v5(3),341-351.)

Gula, Susan. (LeBaron, Dean, Gail Farrelly and Susan Gula. "Facilitating A Dialogue On Risk: A Questionnaire Approach," FAJ, 1989, v45(3), 19-24.)

Gultekin, Bulent and Anthony M. Santomero. "Indexation, Expectations, And Stability," JMCB, 1979, v11(1), 1-21.

Gultekin, Mustafa N. and N. Bulent Gultekin. "Stock Market Seasonality: International Evidence," JFEC, 1983, v12(4), 469-481.

Gultekin, Mustafa N. (Dhrymes, Phoebus J., Irwin Friend, Mustafa N. Gultekin and N. Bulent Gultekin. "New Tests Of The APT And Their Implications," JOF, 1985, v40(3), 659-674.)

Gultekin, Mustafa N. (Dhrymes, Phoebus J., Irwin Friend, N. Bulent Gultekin and Mustafa N. Gultekin. "An Empirical Examination Of The Implications Of Arbitrage Pricing Theory," JBF, 1985, v9(1), 73-99.)

Gultekin, Mustafa N. and N. Bulent Gultekin. "Stock Return Anomalies And The Tests Of The APT," JOF, 1987, v42(5), 1213-1224.

Gultekin, Mustafa N., N. Bulent Gultekin and Alessandro Penati. "Capital Controls And International Capital Market Segmentation: The Evidence From The Japanese And American Stock Markets," JOF, 1989, v44(4), 849-870. 3k ?8

Gultekin, Mustafa N. (Elton, Edwin J., Martin J. Gruber and Mustafa N. Gultekin. "Professional Expectations: Accuracy And Diagnosis Of Errors," JFQA, 1984, v19(4), 351-363.)

Gultekin, N. Bulent. "Stock Market Returns And Inflation: Evidence From Other Countries," JOF, 1983, v38(1), 49-65.

Gultekin, N. Bulent and Richard J. Rogalski. "Government Bond Returns, Measurement Of Interest Rate Risk, And The Arbitrage Pricing Theory," JOF, 1985, v40(1), 43-61.

Gultekin, N. Bulent and Richard J. Rogalski. "Comment: A Test Of Stone's Two-Index Model Of Returns," JFQA, 1979, v14(3), 629-639.

Gultekin, N. Bulent and Richard J. Rogalski. "Alternative Duration Specifications And The Measurement Of Basis Risk: Empirical Tests," JOB, 1984, v57(2), 241-264.

Gultekin, N. Bulent, Richard Rogalski and Seha M. Tinic. "Option Pricing Model Estimates: Some Empirical Results," FM, 1982, v11(1), 58-69.

Gultekin, N. Bulent. "Stock-Market Returns And Inflations Forecasts," JOF, 1983, v38(3), 663-673.

Gultekin, N. Bulent. (Dhrymes, Phoebus J., Irwin Friend and N. Bulent Gultekin. "A Critical Reexamination Of The Empirical Evidence On The Arbitrage Pricing Theory," JOF, 1984, v39(2), 323-346.)

Gultekin, N. Bulent. (Dhrymes, Phoebus J., Irwin Friend, N. Bulent Gultekin and Mustafa N. Gultekin. "An Empirical Examination Of The Implications Of Arbitrage Pricing Theory," JBF, 1985, v9(1), 73-99.)

Gultekin, N. Bulent. (Dhrymes, Phoebus J., Irwin Friend, Mustafa N. Gultekin and N. Bulent Gultekin. "New Tests Of The APT And Their Implications," JOF, 1985, v40(3), 659-674.)

Gultekin, N. Bulent. (Gultekin, Mustafa N. and N. Bulent Gultekin. "Stock Market Seasonality: International Evidence," JFEC, 1983, v12(4), 469-481.)

Gultekin, N. Bulent. (Gultekin, Mustafa N. and N. Bulent Gultekin. "Stock Return Anomalies And The Tests Of The APT," JOF, 1987, v42(5), 1213-1224.)

Gumperz, Julian and E. W. Page, Jr. "Pension Fund Performance," FAJ, 1970, v26(3), 30-32,72-77.

Gumperz, Julian and J. H. Spigelman. "Prospects For Nuclear Energy," FAJ, 1964, v20(1), 95-101.

Gumperz, Julian. "Discontinuities In Pension Planning," FAJ, 1970, v26(6), 20-24.

Gumperz, Julian. "From A Closed To An Open System (Keynote Review)," FAJ, 1966, v22(6), 117-119.

Gumperz, Julian. "Machines That Analyze - Or Analysts?," FAJ, 1967, v23(1), 113-115.

Gumperz, Julian. "Scientific Input And Economic Output," FAJ, 1968, v24(6), 111-113.

Gumperz, Julian. "The Therapeutic Factory (Keynote Review)," FAJ, 1966, v22(5), 109-111.

Gun-Ho, Joh. (Jain, Prem C. and Gun-Ho Joh. "The Dependence Between Hourly Prices And Trading Volume," JFQA, 1988, v23(3), 269-284.)

Gunay, Erdal. (Aneja, Yash P., Ramesh Chandra and Erdal Gunay. "A Portfolio Approach To Estimating The Average Correlation Coefficient For The Constant Correlation Model," JOF, 1989, v44(5), 1435-1438.)

Gunderson, Elizabeth W. (Alexander, Gordon J., P. George Benson and Elizabeth W. Gunderson. "Asset Redeployment: Trans World Corporation's Spinoff Of TWA," FM, 1986, v15(2), 50-58.)

Gunness, Robert C. "The Economics Of Energy," FAJ, 1968, v24(1), 47-50.

Gunnin, Robert G. "Petroleum Futures Trading: Practical Applications By The Trade," RFM, 1984, v3(2), 128-140.

Guntermann, Karl L. "FHA Mortgage Discount Points, House Prices And Consumer Behavior," AREUEA, 1979, v7(2), 163-176.

Guntermann, Karl L. (Colwell, Peter F., Karl L. Guntermann and C. F. Sirmans. "Discount Points And Housing Prices: Comment," JOF, 1979, v34(4), 1049-1054.)

Guntermann, Karl L. and Richard L. Smith. "Derivation Of Cost Of Capital And Equity Rates From Market Data," AREUEA, 1987, v15(2), 98-109.

Guntermann, Karl L. and Richard L. Smith. "Licensing Requirements, Enforcement Effort And Complaints Against Real Estate Agents," JRER, 1988, v3(2), 11-20.

Guntermann, Karl L. and Stefan Norrbin. "Explaining The Variability Of Apartment Rents," AREUEA, 1987, v15(4), 321-340.

Gup, Benton E. and Samuel W. Norwood, III. "Divisional Cost Of Capital: A Practical Approach," FM, 1982, v11(1), 20-24.

Gup, Benton E. "A Note On Stock Market Indicators And Stock Prices," JFQA, 1973, v8(4), 673-682.

Gup, Benton E. "The Financial Consequences Of Corporate Growth," JOF, 1980, v35(5), 1257-1265.

Gup, Benton E. "Trends In Savings Flows And Mortgage Lending," FR, 1969, v1(4), 244-249.

Gup, Benton E. (Cheng, David C., Benton E. Gup and Larry D. Wall. "Financial Determinants Of Bank Takeovers," JMCB, 1989, v21(4), 524-536.)

Gup, Benton E. (Liano, Kartono and Benton E. Gup. "The Day-Of-The-Week Effect In Stock Returns Over Business Cycles," FAJ, 1989, v45(4), 74-77.)

Gupta, Atul and Lalatendu Misra. "Illegal Insider Trading: Is It Rampant Before Corporate Takeovers?," FR, 1989, v23(4), 453-464.

Gupta, Kanhaya L. "Interest Rates, Inflation Expectations And The Inverted Fisher Hypothesis," JBF, 1991, v10(3), 109-116.

Gupta, Kanhaya L. "Some Controversial Aspects Of The Demand For Money," JMCB, 1980, v12(4), Part 1, 660-665.

Gupta, Keshav. "Determinants Of Corporate Borrowing: A Note," JFEC, 1982, v10(1), 115-116.

Gupta, Manak C. and David A. Walker. "Dividend Disbursal Practices In Commercial Banking," JFQA, 1975, v10(3), 515-529.

Gupta, Manak C. "Differential Effects Of Tight Money: An Economic Rationale," JOF, 1972, v27(4), 825-838.

Gupta, Manak C. "Money Supply And Stock Prices: A Probabilistic Approach," JFQA, 1974, v9(1), 57-68.

Gupta, Manak C. "Optimal Financing Policy For A Firm With Uncertain Fund Requirements," JFQA, 1973, v8(5), 731-747.

Gupta, Manak C. "The Effect Of Size, Growth, And Industry On The Financial Structure Of Manufacturing Companies," JOF, 1969, v24(3), 517-529.

Gupta, Manak C. (Lee, Cheng F. and Manak C. Gupta. "An Inter-Temporal Approach To The Optimization Of Dividend Policy With Predetermined Investment: A Further Comment," JOF, 1977, v32(4), 1358-1361.)

Gupta, Manoj. (Becker, Kent G., Joseph E. Finnerty and Manoj Gupta. "The Intertemporal Relation Between The U.S. And Japanese Stock Markets," JOF, 1990, v45(4), 1297-1306.)

Gupta, Om S. "A Note On Life Insurance Cash Values," JRI, 1967, v34(3), 475-476.

Gupta, Sanjeev. "A Note On The Efficiency Of Black Markets In Foreign Currencies," JOF, 1981, v36(3), 705-710.

Gupta, Satyadev. (Jain, Arvind K. and Satyadev Gupta. "Some Evidence On 'Herding' Behavior By U.S. Banks," JMCB, 1987, v19(1), 78-89.)

Gupta, Yash P., Ramesh P. Rao and Prabir K. Bagchi. "Linear Goal Programming As An Alternative To Multivariate Discriminant Analysis: A Note," JBFA, 1990, v17(4), 593-598.

Gurel, Eitan and David Pyle. "Bank Income Taxes And Interest Rate Risk Management: A Note," JOF, 1984, v39(4), 1199-1206.

Gurel, Eitan. (Harris, Lawrence and Eitan Gurel. "Price And Volume Effects Associated With Changes In The S&P 500: New Evidence For The Existence Of Price Pressures," JOF, 1986, v41(4), 815-830.)

Gurley, John G. and Edward S. Shaw. "Financial Intermediaries And The Saving-Investment Process," JOF, 1956, v11(2), 257-276.

Gushee, Charles H. "How To Immunize A Bond Investment," FAJ, 1981, v37(2), 44-51.

Gustafson, Dale R. "A New Concept Of The Economics Of Life Value And The Human Life Value: Comment," JRI, 1970, v37(4), 645-648.

Gustafson, Dale R. "Solving A Risk Theory Problem Under Time Pressure (Life Insurance Adjusted Earnings)," JRI, 1974, v41(2), 259-266.

Gustafson, David P. and Charles R. Kuehl. "Citation Age Distributions For Three Areas Of Business," JOB, 1974, v47(3), 440-447.

Gustavson, Sandra G. "Flexible Income Programming: Comment," JRI, 1982, v49(2), 290-296.

Gustavson, Sandra G. "Moving Insurance Education Into The Computer Age," JRI, 1985, v52(2), 301-310.

Gustavson, Sandra G. "Pension Plans And The Writing Of Fully-Covered Exchange Traded Call Options," JRI, 1980, v47(3), 421-446.

Gustavson, Sandra G. (Cather, David A., Sandra G. Gustavson and James S. Trieschmann. "A Profitability Analysis Of Property-Liability Insurers Using Alternative Distribution Systems," JRI, 1985, v52(2), 321-332.)

Gustavson, Sandra G. (Cox, Larry A. and Sandra G. Gustavson. "Leading Contributors To Insurance Research," JRI, 1990, v57(2), 260-281.)

Gustavson, Sandra G. (Reilly, Frank K. and Sandra G. Gustavson. "Investing In Options On Stocks Announcing Splits," FR, 1985, v20(2), 121-142.)

Gustavson, Sandra G. (Schultz, Joseph J., Jr., Sandra G. Gustavson and Frank K. Reilly. "Factors Influencing The New York Stock Exchange Specialists' Price-Setting Behavior: An Experiment," JFR, 1985, v8(2), 137-144.)

Gustavson, Sandra G. and James S. Trieschmann. "Universal Life Insurance As An Alternative To The Joint And Survivor Annuity," JRI, 1988, v55(3), 529-538.

Gustavson, Sandra G. and Joseph J. Schultz, Jr. "Property-Liability Loss Reserve Certification: Independent Or In-House?," JRI, 1983, v50(2), 307-314.

Gustus, Warren J. "Professor Levitt On 'Investment, Depression, And The Assurance Of Prosperity': Comment," JOF, 1955, v10(3), 376-378.

Guth, Gary R. (Wolfe, Joseph and Gary R. Guth. "The Case Approach Versus Gaming In The Teaching Of Business Policy: An Experimental Evaluation," JOB, 1975, v48(3), 349-364.)

Guth, Michael A. S. "Functional Form In Finished Goods Inventory Investment," JMCB, 1987, v19(3), 396-407.

Guth, Michael A. S. "Intrinsic Uncertainty And Common-Knowledge Priors In Financial Economics," JFR, 1989, v12(4), 269-284.

Guth, William D. "Toward A Social System Theory Of Corporate Strategy," JOB, 1976, v49(3), 374-388.

Guth, William D. (Anshen, Melvin and William D. Guth. "Strategies For Research In Policy Formulation," JOB, 1973, v46(4), 499-511.)

Guthart, Leo A. "Why Companies Buy Their Own Stock," FAJ, 1967, v23(2), 105-112.

Guthmann, Harry G. and Archie J. Bakay. "The Market Impact Of The Sale Of Large Blocks Of Stock," JOF, 1965, v20(4), 617-631.

Guthmann, Harry G. "British Corporate Law Scrutinized For Reforms (Aid To Analysts)," FAJ, 1962, v18(6), 104-107.

Guthmann, Harry G. "Competition From Tax-Exempt Business," JOF, 1951, v6(2), 161-177.

Guthmann, Harry G. "Effect On The Economy Of Channeling Savings Through Pension Funds," JOF, 1952, v7(2), 260-277.

Guthmann, Harry G. "The Movement Of Debt To Institutions And Its Implications For The Interest Rate," JOF, 1950, v5(1), 70-87.

Guthrie, Harold W. "Intergeneration Transfers Of Wealth And The Theory Of Saving," JOB, 1963, v36(1), 97-108.

Gutman, Walter K. "Book Value - Market Value Patterns," FAJ, 1946, v2(3), 36-43.

Gutman, Walter K. "Economic Consequences Of The Rise Of Russia," FAJ, 1955, v11(5), 49-52.

Gutman, Walter K. "Legal Status For Our Profession," FAJ, 1950, v6(1), 13-16.

Gutman, Walter K. "Report Of Committee On Legal Status," FAJ, 1950, v6(3), 45.

Gutman, Walter Knowlton. "Growth Companies Have Grown Surprisingly Powerful," FAJ, 1950, v6(4), 40-42.

Gutman, Walter Knowlton. "Nuclear Reactions And Security Analysis," FAJ, 1953, v9(1), 63-68.

Gutman, Walter. "Bull And Bear Market Psychology," FAJ, 1948, v4(3), 15-18.

Gutmann, Peter M. "Are The Unemployed, Unemployed?," FAJ, 1978, v34(5), 26-29.

Gutmann, Peter M. "Professor Gutmann Replies," FAJ, 1978, v34(6), 67-69.

Gutmann, Peter M. "Taxes And The Supply Of National Output," FAJ, 1979, v35(6), 64-66.

Gutmann, Peter M. "The Subterranean Economy," FAJ, 1977, v33(6), 26-27.

Guttentag, Jack and Richard Herring. "Credit Rationing And Financial Disorder," JOF, 1984, v39(5), 1359-1382.

Guttentag, Jack and Richard Herring. "Disclosure Policy And International Banking," JBF, 1986, v10(1), 75-97.

Guttentag, Jack M. and Edward S. Herman. "Do Large Banks Neglect Small Business?," JOF, 1966, v21(3), 535-538.

Guttentag, Jack M. and Kenneth H. Thomas. "Branch Banking And Bank Structure: Some Evidence From Alabama," JBR, 1979-80, v10(1), 45-53.

Guttentag, Jack M. "A Note On Hedging And Solvency: The Case Of A Phoenix," JFM, 1983, v3(2), 137-141.

Guttentag, Jack M. "Defensive And Dynamic Open Market Operations, Discounting, And The Federal Reserve System's Crisis-Prevention Responsibilities," JOF, 1969, v24(2), 249-263.

Guttentag, Jack M. (Alhadeff, D., P. Bernstein, C. Campbell, L. Chandler, E. Ettin, V. Farhi, J. Guttentag, H. Latane and K. Poole. "The Commission On Money And Credit's Research Studies," JOF, 1964, v19(3), 497-533.)

Guttentag, Jack M. (Curley, Anthony J. and Jack M. Guttentag. "Value And Yield Risk On Outstanding Insured Residential Mortgages," JOF, 1977, v32(2), 403-412.)

Guttentag, Jack M. (Davis, Richard G. and Jack M. Guttentag. "Are Compensating Balance Requirements Irrational?," JOF, 1962, v17(1), 121-126.)

Guttentag, Jack and Richard Herring. "Strategic Planning To Cope With Uncertainty," RDIBF, 1987, v1, 61-86.

Guttentag, Jack. "Mortgage Warehousing," JOF, 1957, v12(4), 438-450.

Guttentag, Jack. (Edelstein, Robert and Jack Guttentag. "On The Alleged Profitability Of Borrowing At 8% to Lend At 6%," JBR, 1975-76, v6(4), 296-298.)

Guy, D. J. (Easman, W. S., Jr., A. Falkenstein, Roman L. Weil and D. J. Guy. "Sustainable Income And Stock Returns," FAJ, 1979, v35(5), 44-48.)

Guy, Donald C., John L. Hysom and Stephen R. Ruth. "The Effect Of Subsidized Housing On Values Of Adjacent Housing," AREUEA, 1985, v13(4), 378-387.

Guy, James R. F. "An Examination Of The Effects Of International Diversification From The British Viewpoint On Both Hypothetical And Real Portfolios," JOF, 1978, v33(5), 1425-1438.

Guy, James R. F. "The Behavior Of Equity Securities On The German Stock Exchange," JBF, 1977, v1(1), 71-93.

Guy, James R. F. "The Performance Of The British Investment Trust Industry," JOF, 1978, v33(2), 443-455.

Guy, James. (Rosenberg, Barr and James Guy. "Beta And Investment Fundamentals - II," FAJ, 1976, v32(4), 62-70.)

Guy, James. (Rosenberg, Barr and James Guy. "Beta And Investment Fundamentals," FAJ, 1976, v32(3), 60-72.)

Guy, Rebecca F. (Pol, Louis and Rebecca F. Guy. "Discrimination In Home Improvement Loans: A Rejoinder," JBR, 1981-82, v12(3), 192.)

Gyourko, Joseph and Peter Linneman. "Owner-Occupied Homes, Income-Producing Properties, And REITs As Inflation Hedges: Empirical Findings," JREFEC, 1988, v1(4), 347-372.

HHH

Haack, Robert W. "The S. E. C. Special Study And The Over-The-Counter Markets," JOF, 1966, v21(2), 333-338.

Haar, Jerry, Krishnan Dandapani and Stanley P. Haar. "The American Depositary Receipt (ADR): A Creative Financial Tool For Multinational Companies," GFJ, 1990, v1(2), 163-171.

Haar, Stanley P. (Haar, Jerry, Krishnan Dandapani and Stanley P. Haar. "The American Depositary Receipt (ADR): A Creative Financial Tool For Multinational Companies," GFJ, 1990, v1(2), 163-171.)

Haas, G. M. and J. J. Quinn. "American Corporation Earnings," FAJ, 1950, v6(4), 25-28.

Haas, Gary and Andris A. Zoltners. "A Computerized Bank Check Collection Vehicle Routing System," JBR, 1977-78, v8(3), 148-158.

Haas, Richard D. and **William E. Alexander.** "A Model Of Exchange Rates And Capital Flows: The Canadian Floating Rate Experience," JMCB, 1979, v11(4), 467-482.

Haberler, Gottfried. "Critical Notes On Rational Expectations," JMCB, 1980, v12(4), Part 2, 833-836.

Hachey, George A. (Kaen, Fred R. and George A. Hachey. "Eurocurrency And National Money Market Interest Rates: An Empirical Investigation Of Causality," JMCB, 1983, v15(3), 327-338.)

Hachey, George A. (Kaen, Fred R., Evangelos O. Simos and George A. Hachey. "The Response Of Forward Exchange Rates To Interest Rate Forecasting Errors," JFR, 1984, v7(4), 281-290.)

Hachey, George. (Asabere, Paul K., George Hachey and Steven Grubaugh. "Architecture, Historic Zoning, And The Value Of Homes," JREFEC, 1989, v2(3), 181-196.)

Hackett, Donald W. and John R. Darling. "A Comparison Of Consumer And Realtor Attitudes Regarding Consumer Issues Affecting The Housing Industry," AREUEA, 1976, v4(2), 91-99.

Hadar, Josef and Tae Kun Seo. "Ross' Measure Of Risk Aversion And Portfolio Selection," JRU, 1990, v3(1), 93-99.

Hadar, Josef and Tae Kun Seo. "Stochastic Dominance And The Case For Specialization," RIF, 1980, v2, 99-110.

Hadaway, Beverly L. and **Samuel C. Hadaway.** "An Analysis Of The Performance Characteristics Of Converted Savings And Loan Associations," JFR, 1981, v4(3),195-206.

Hadaway, Beverly L. and Samuel C. Hadaway. "Implications Of Savings And Loan Conversions In A Deregulated World," JBR, 1984-85, v15(1), 44-55.

Hadaway, Beverly L. and Samuel C. Hadaway. "Do Institutional Constraints Hobble Performance?," JPM, 1989, v15(2), 33-37.

Hadaway, Samuel C. (Hadaway, Beverly L. and Samuel C. Hadaway. "Implications Of Savings And Loan Conversions In A Deregulated World," JBR, 1984-85, v15(1), 44-55.)

Hadaway, Samuel C. (Hadaway, Beverly L. and Samuel C. Hadaway. "An Analysis Of The Performance Characteristics Of Converted Savings And Loan Associations," JFR, 1981, v4(3), 195-206.)

Hadaway, Samuel C. (Hadaway, Beverly L. and Samuel C. Hadaway. "Do Institutional Constraints Hobble Performance?," JPM, 1989, v15(2), 33-37.)

Hadaway, Samuel C., Jr. (Rochester, David P. and Samuel C. Hadaway, Jr. "Further Evidence Of Seasonal Adjustment Of Time Series Data," JFQA, 1978, v13(1), 133-141.)

Haddad, Kamal M. "Incorporating Actual Financial Management Practices Into Finance Courses: A Tool To Increase Student Motivation And Understanding," JFED, 1986, v15, 22-41.

Haddad, Mahmoud. (Lindley, James T., Billy P. Helms and Mahmoud Haddad. "A Measurement Of The Errors In Intra-Period Compounding And Bond Valuation," FR, 1987, v22(1), 33-52.)

Hadley, Galen D. "Aversion To Loss In Sale Of Bonds In The Life Insurance Industry," JRI, 1977, v44(4), 661-668.

Haegert, Lutz. "An Analysis Of The Kuhn-Tucker Conditions Of Stochastic Programming With Reference To The Estimate Of Discount Rates And Risk Premia," JBFA, 1974, v1(3), 319-334.

Haessler, Robert W. and Donald H. Peters. "More On The Coupon Rate Of Return: Haesser Versus Peters," FM, 1973, v2(3), 45-49.

Hafer, R. W. "Money Demand Predictability: Erratum," JMCB, 1986, v18(3), 391.

Hafer, R. W. and Scott E. Hein. "Financial Innovations And The Interest Elasticity Of Money Demand: Some Historical Evidence," JMCB, 1984, v16(2), 247-252.

Hafer, R. W. and Scott E. Hein. "On The Accuracy Of Time-Series, Interest Rate, And Survey Forecasts Of Inflation," JOB, 1985, v58(4), 377-398.

Hafer, R. W. and Scott E. Hein. "Forecasting Inflation Using Interest-Rate And Time-Series Models: Some International Evidence," JOB, 1990, v63(1), Part 1, 1-18.

Hagaman, T. Carter and Arnold E. Jensen. "Investment Value: A Reference Point For Analysts," FAJ, 1977, v33(2), 63-70.

Hagaman, T. Carter and Herbert J. Marks. "Earnings Stability: Key To The Equity Market," JBR, 1975-76, v6(3), 183-185.

Hagemann, Robert P. "The Variability Of Inflation Rates Across Household Types," JMCB, 1982, v14(4), Part 1, 494-510.

Hagen, Everett E. "Direct vs. Fiscal-Monetary Controls: A Critique," JOF, 1950, v5(1), 49-62.

Hager, Karl Erik. "The Swedish Postal Giro And Its Progress," JBR, 1985-86, v16(4), 227-231.

Hagerman, R. L. (Benston, G. J. and R. L. Hagerman. "Risk, Volume And Spread," FAJ, 1978, v34(1),46-49.)

Hagerman, Robert L. "Finance Theory In Rate Hearings," FM, 1976, v5(1), 18-22.

Hagerman, Robert L. "More Evidence On The Distribution Of Security Returns," JOF, 1978, v33(4), 1213-1221.

Hagerman, Robert L. "The Efficiency Of The Market For Bank Stocks: An Empirical Test: A Comment," JMCB, 1973, v5(3), 846-855.

Hagerman, Robert L. "The Value Of Regulation F: An Empirical Test," JBR, 1972-73, v3(3), 178-185.

Hagerman, Robert L. (Benston, George J. and Robert L. Hagerman. "Determinants Of Bid-Asked Spreads In The Over-The-Counter Market," JFEC, 1974, v1(4), 353-364.)

Hagerman, Robert L. and E. Han Kim. "Capital Asset Pricing With Price Level Changes," JFQA, 1976, v11(3), 381-391.

Hagerman, Robert L. and Lemma W. Senbet. "A Test Of Accounting Bias And Market Structure," JOB, 1976, v49(4), 509-514.

Hagerman, Robert L. and Richard D. Richmond. "Random Walks, Martingales And The OTC," JOF, 1973, v28(4), 897-909.

Hagerty, Kathleen M. (Fishman, Michael J. and Kathleen M. Hagerty. "Disclosure Decisions By Firms And The Competition For Price Efficiency," JOF, 1989, v44(3), 633-646.)

Hagigi, Moshe and Brian Kluger. "Safety-First: An Alternative Performance Measure," JPM, 1986-87, v13(4), 34-40.

Hagigi, Moshe and Brian Kluger. "Assessing Risk And Return Of Pension Funds' Portfolios By The Telser Safety-First Approach," JBFA, 1987, v14(2), 241-254.

Hagigi, Moshe. "Industry Versus Country Risk In International Investments Of U.S. Pension Funds," FAJ, 1988, v44(5), 70-74.

Hahn, Frank. "On Money And Growth," JMCB, 1969, v1(2), 172-189.

Hahn, Robert W. and Roger G. Noll. "Environmental Markets In The Year 2000," JRU, 1990, v3(4), 351-368.

Hahn, Thomas. (Cook, Timothy and Thomas Hahn. "The Information Content Of Discount Rate Announcements And Their Effect On Market Interest Rates," JMCB, 1988, v20(2), 167-180.)

Hahn, Walter F. "The Railroad Security Outlook," FAJ, 1947, v3(4), 26-34.

Haidt, Frances. "Analysts Explore European Investments," FAJ, 1959, v15(3), 13-22.

Haidt, Frances. "Denmark And Sweden (Successful Scandinavia)," FAJ, 1961, v17(3), 95-100.

Haim, Levy and Yoram Kroll. "Stochastic Dominance With Riskless Assets," JFQA, 1976, v11(5),743-778.

Hair, Joseph F., Jr. (Stern, Bruce L., Ronald F. Bush and Joseph F. Hair, Jr. "The Self-Image/Store Image Matching Process: An Empirical Test," JOB, 1977, v50(1), 63-69.)

Hair, Joseph F., Jr., Paul J. Solomon and Ronald F. Bush. "A Factor Analytic Study Of Black Models In Television Commercials," JOB, 1977, v50(2), 208-215.

Hakala, Donald R. "Certification Programs: A Means For Enriching Business Finance Program Objectives," JFED, 1983, v12, 41-46.

Hakala, Donald R. and Kenneth M. Huggins. "Has ERISA Had An Impact On Pension Investing?," JPM, 1978-79, v5(2), 44-47.

Hakanoglu, Erol, Robert Kopprasch and Emmanuel Roman. "Constant Proportion Portfolio Insurance For Fixed-Income Investment," JPM, 1989, v15(4), 58-66.

Hakansson, N. H. (Grauer, R. R., N. H. Hakansson and P. C. Shen. "Industry Rotation In The U.S. Stock Market: 1934-1986 Returns On Passive, Semi-Passive, And Active Strategies," JBF, 1990, v14(2/3), 513-538.)

Hakansson, Nils H. "Changes In The Financial Market: Welfare And Price Effects And The Basic Theorems Of Value Conservation," JOF, 1982, v37(4), 977-1004.

Hakansson, Nils H. "An Induced Theory Of The Firm Under Risk: The Pure Mutual Fund," JFQA, 1970, v5(2), 155-178.

Hakansson, Nils H. "Capital Growth And The Mean-Variance Approach To Portfolio Selection," JFQA, 1971, v6(1), 517-557.

Hakansson, Nils H. "Convergence To Isoelastic Utility And Policy In Multiperiod Portfolio Choice," JFEC, 1974, v1(3), 201-224.

Hakansson, Nils H. "Fallacy Of The Log-Normal Approximation To Optimal Portfolio Decision-Making Over Many Periods: Comment," JFEC, 1974, v1(1), 95-96.

Hakansson, Nils H. "Mean-Variance Analysis In A Finite World," JFQA, 1972, v7(4), 1873-1880.

Hakansson, Nils H. "Multi-Period Mean-Variance Analysis: Toward A General Theory Of Portfolio Choice," JOF, 1971, v26(4), 857-884.

Hakansson, Nils H. "On Optimal Myopic Portfolio Policies, With And Without Serial Correlation Of Yields," JOB, 1971, v44(3), 324-334.

Hakansson, Nils H. "On The Dividend Capitalization Model Under Uncertainty," JFQA, 1969, v4(1),65-87.

Hakansson, Nils H. "Purchasing Power Funds," FAJ, 1976, v32(6), 49-59.

Hakansson, Nils H. "Risk Disposition And The Separation Property In Portfolio Selection," JFQA, 1969, v4(4), 401-416.

Hakansson, Nils H. "The Fantastic World Of Finance: Progress And The Free Lunch," JFQA, 1979, v14(4), 717-734.

Hakansson, Nils H. "To Pay Or Not To Pay Dividends," JOF, 1982, v37(2), 415-428.

Hakansson, Nils H. "Welfare Aspects Of Options And Supershares," JOF, 1978, v33(3), 759-776.

Hakansson, Nils H. (Beja, Avraham and Nils H. Hakansson. "Dynamic Market Processes And The Rewards To Up-to-date Information," JOF, 1977, v32(2), 291-304.)

Hakansson, Nils H. (Grauer, Robert R. and Nils H. Hakansson. "A Half Century Of Returns On Levered And Unlevered Portfolios Of Stocks, Bonds, And Bills, With And Without Small Stocks," JOB, 1986, v59(2), Part 1, 287-318.)

Hakansson, Nils H. (Grauer, Robert R. and Nils H. Hakansson. "Returns On Levered, Actively Managed Long-Run Portfolios Of Stocks, Bonds, And Bills, 1934-1983," FAJ, 1985, v41(5), 24-27,30-43.)

Hakansson, Nils H. (Grauer, Robert R. and Nils H. Hakansson. "Gains From International Diversification: 1968-85 Returns On Portfolios Of Stocks And Bonds," JOF, 1987, v42(3), 721-739.)

Hakansson, Nils H. (Grauer, Robert R. and Nils H. Hakansson. "Higher Return, Lower Risk: Historical Returns On Long-Run, Actively Managed Portfolios Of Stocks, Bonds, And Bills, 1936-1978," FAJ, 1982, v38(2), 39-53.)

Hakansson, Nils H., Avraham Beja and Jivendra Kale. "On The Feasibility Of Automated Market Making By A Programmed Specialist," JOF, 1985, v40(1), 1-20.

Hakansson, Nils H., J. Gregory Kunkel and James A. Ohlson. "Sufficient And Necessary Conditions For Information To Have Social Value In Pure Exchange, JOF, 1982, v37(5), 1169-1181.

Hakes, David R. "The Objectives And Priorities Of Monetary Policy Under Different Federal Reserve Chairmen," JMCB, 1990, v22(3), 327-337.

Hakkio, Craig S. "Does The Exchange Rate Follow A Random Walk? A Monte Carlo Study Of Four Tests For A Random Walk," JIMF, 1986, v5(2), 221-229.

Hakkio, Craig S. and Mark Rush. "Market Efficiency And Cointegration: An Application To The Sterling And Deutschemark Exchange Markets," JIMF, 1989, v8(1), 75-88.

Hald, Earl C. (Crutchfield, James A. and Earl C. Hald. "Economic Expansion And The American Banking System," JOB, 1956, v29(2), 111-123.)

Haldeman, Robert G. (Altman, Edward I., Robert G. Haldeman and P. Narayanan. "ZETA Analysis: A New Model To Identify Bankruptcy Risk Of Corporations," JBF, 1977, v1(1), 29-54.)

Hale, David. "Adjusting Tax Policies For Inflation," FAJ, 1978, v34(6), 28-40.

Hale, David. "Inflation Accounting In The 1970s," FAJ, 1978, v34(5), 59-72.

Hale, David. "Thatcher And Reagan: Different Roads To Recession," FAJ, 1981, v37(6), 61-68,70-71.

Hale, Irving. "The Stock Selection 'Game Theory'," FAJ, 1960, v16(2), 53-56.

Haley, Charles W. and Lawrence D. Schall. "Problems With The Concept Of The Cost Of Capital," JFQA, 1978, v13(5), 847-870.

Haley, Charles W. and Lawrence D. Schall. "A Note On Investment Policy With Imperfect Capital Martkets," JOF, 1972, v27(1), 93-96.

Haley, Charles W. "A Note On The Cost Of Debt," JFQA, 1966, v1(4), 72-93.

Haley, Charles W. "A Theoretical Foundation For The Basic Finance Course," JFQA, 1975, v10(4),691-694.

Haley, Charles W. "Taxes, The Cost Of Capital, And The Firm's Investment Decisions," JOF, 1971, v26(4), 901-917.

Haley, Charles W. "Valuation And Risk-Adjusted Discount Rates," JBFA, 1984, v11(3), 347-353.

Halford, Frank A. "Income Bonds - The Sleeping Giant," FAJ, 1964, v20(1), 73-79.

Hall, Arden R. "Valuing The Mortgage Borrower's Prepayment Option," AREUEA, 1985, v13(3), 229-247.

Hall, Charles P. "Special Risks Health Insurance: Partial Solution To Growing Bodily Injury Awards?," JRI, 1964, v31(1), 63-72.

Hall, Charles P., Jr. "1979 Presidential Address - ARIA: Yesterday, Today And Tomorrow - Who, What And Why Are We?," JRI, 1979, v46(4), 589-602.

Hall, Charles P., Jr. "Compensation Of Executives In The Insurance Industry," JRI, 1961, v28(4), 57-64.

Hall, Charles P., Jr. "Deductibles In Health Insurance: An Evaluation," JRI, 1966, v33(2), 253-264.

Hall, Charles P., Jr. "The Basic Function Of Undergraduate Risk And Insurance Instruction," JRI, 1972, v39(1), 109-118.

Hall, Charles P., Jr. "The Maligned Business School: What Is A Liberal Education?," JRI, 1968, v35(4), 597-601.

Hall, Charles P., Jr., Stanley M. Henemier and Arnold H. Raphaelson. "Some Issues In Limiting Hospital Cost Reimbursement: A Maryland Experience," JRI, 1977, v44(2), 267-288.

Hall, Christopher D. "Renting Ideas," JOB, 1991, v64(1), 21-48.

Hall, Christopher D. (Busche, Kelly and Christopher D. Hall. "An Exception To The Risk Preference Anomaly," JOB, 1988, v61(3), 337-346.)

Hall, Edward B. "Sound Money And The Voter," FAJ, 1962, v18(1), 65-67.

Hall, J. Parker, III. "CELI - Another Government Time Bomb?," FAJ, 1977, v33(5), 30-32.

Hall, J. Parker, III. "Shouldn't You Own Fewer Long-Term Bonds?," FAJ, 1981, v37(3), 45-48.

Hall, J. Parker, III. "The Professional Investor's View," FAJ, 1971, v27(5), 32-34.

Hall, J. Parker, III. "Toward Effective Portfolio Management," FAJ, 1966, v22(1), 91-95.

Hall, J. Parker, III. "Two Gift Horses, Or Some Contrary Ideas On Asset Allocation And Manager Selection," FAJ, 1982, v38(6), 49-52.

Hall, J. Parker. "Current Tendencies In College Investments," JOF, 1949, v4(2), 129-139.

Hall, Joyce A., B. Wade Brorsen and Scott H. Irwin. "The Distribution Of Futures Prices: A Test Of The Stable Paretian And Mixture Of Normals Hypotheses," JFQA, 1989, v24(1), 105-116.

Hall, Karen E. (Liebling, Herman, Peter T. Bidwell and Karen E. Hall. "The Recent Performance Of Anticipation Surveys And Econometric Model Projections Of Investment Spending In The United States," JOB, 1976, v49(4), 451-477.)

Hall, Lincoln W. "Security Analysis From A Trust Company Viewpoint," FAJ, 1953, v9(2), 123-126.

Hall, Sherman M. "Effects Of A Depression On A Utility," FAJ, 1954, v10(1), 55-56.

Hall, Sherman M. "The Corporations Can Help Too," FAJ, 1951, v7(4), 29-30.

Hall, Stephen G. and Mark P. Taylor. "Modeling Risk Premia In Commodity Forward Prices: Some Evidence Form The London Metal Exchange," RFM, 1989, v8(2), 200-217.

Hall, Thomas E. and Nicholas R. Noble. "Velocity And The Variability Of Money Growth: Evidence From Granger-Causality Tests," JMCB, 1987, v19(1),112-116.

Hall, Thomas W. and Jeffrey J. Tsay. "An Evaluation Of The Performance Of Portfolios Selected From Value Line Rank One Stocks: 1976-1982," JFR, 1988, v11(3), 227-240.

Hall, William D. "Accounting For Installment Sales," FAJ, 1966, v22(5), 27-31.

Hall, William P. "Management Appraisal," FAJ, 1966, v22(5), 85-88.

Haller, Andreas and Hans R. Stoll. "Market Structure And Transaction Costs: Implied Spreads In The German Stock Market," JBF, 1989, v13(4/5), 697-708.

Halley, Donald M. "Materials And Methods Of Teaching Business Finance (I)," JOF, 1950, v5(3),270-274.

Hallingby, Paul Jr. "Speculative Opportunities In Stock Purchase Warrants," FAJ, 1947, v3(3), 41-49.

Hallman, G. Victor, III. "True Catastrophe Medical Expense Insurance," JRI, 1972, v39(1), 1-16.

Halloran, John A. and Howard P. Lanser. "Inflation-Induced Biases In The Evaluation And Selection Of Capital Investments," FR, 1983, v18(4), 314-325.

Halloran, John A. and Howard P. Lanser. "The Credit Policy Decision In An Inflationary Environment," FM, 1981, v10(5), 31-38.

Halloran, John A. and Jess B. Yawitz. "The Effect Of Mortgage Form On Borrower Interest Rate Risk: A Portfolio Theory Approach," JBF, 1979, v3(2), 187-200.

Halloran, John A. "A Note On The Impact Of FHLB Advances On The Cost And Availability Of Funds At S&Ls," JOF, 1979, v34(5), 1255-1261.

Halloran, John A. (Lanser, Howard P. and John A. Halloran. "Evaluating Cash Flow Systems Under Growth," FR, 1986, v21(2), 309-318.)

Halperin, Sanford B. "Change In Student Attitudes Toward Life Insurance Salesmen After An Insurance Course," JRI, 1974, v41(2), 327-338.

Halperin, Sanford B. and Rodney H. Mabry. "Property And Casualty Insurance Lines Comparison: A Shift-Share Analysis," JRI, 1984, v51(3), 524-535.

Halpern, P. J. (Carr, J. L., P. J. Halpern and J. S. McCallum. "Correcting The Yield Curve: A Re-Interpretation Of The Duration Problem," JOF, 1974, v29(4), 1287-1294.)

Halpern, P. J. (Carr, J. L., P. J. Halpern and J. S. McCallum. "Comments On Single-Valued Duration Measures," JOF, 1978, v33(4), 1241-1243.)

Halpern, Paul and Yehuda Kahane. "A Pedagogical Note On Baumol's Gain-Confidence Limit Criterion For Portfolio Selection And The Probability Of Ruin," JBF, 1980, v4(2), 189-195.

Halpern, Paul J. and Stuart M. Turnbull. "Empirical Tests Of Boundary Conditions For Toronto Stock Exchange Options," JOF, 1985, v40(2), 481-500.

Halpern, Paul J. "Empirical Estimates Of The Amount And Distribution Of Gains To Companies In Mergers," JOB, 1973, v46(4), 554-575.

Halpern, Paul J. (Gordon, Myron J. and Paul J. Halpern. "Cost Of Capital For A Division Of A Firm: Reply," JOF, 1977, v32(5), 1781-1782.)

Halpern, Paul J. (Gordon, Myron J. and Paul J. Halpern. "Cost Of Capital For A Division Of A Firm," JOF, 1974, v29(4), 1153-1163.)

Halpern, Paul. "Corporate Acquisitions: A Theory Of Special Cases? A Review Of Event Studies Applied To Acquisitions," JOF, 1983, v38(2), 297-317.

Halpern, Philip and Isabelle I. Fowler. "Investment Management Fees And Determinants Of Pricing Structure In The Industry," JPM, 1991, v17(2), 74-79.

Halstead, David W. (Acheson, Marcus W., IV and David W. Halstead. "Trends In Securitization - Private And Public," JACF, 1988, v1(3), 52-60.)

Haltiner, James R. (Bauman, W. Scott and James R. Haltiner. "Portfolio Capital Gains Disbursement Strategies," FR, 1982, v17(1), 26-49.)

Haltiner, James R. (Bloom, Robert, Pieter T. Elgers, James R. Haltiner and William H. Hawthorne. "Inflation Gains And Losses On Monetary Items: An Empirical Test," JBFA, 1980, v7(4), 603-618.)

Haltiner, James R. (Elgers, Pieter T., James R. Haltiner and William H. Hawthorne. "Beta Regression Tendencies: Statistical And Real Causes," JOF, 1979, v34(1), 261-263.)

Hamachek, T. (Appelbaum, E., J. Burns, R. Evans, J. Gould, T. Hamachek, R. Kidder, M. Jensen, J. Johnstone, M. Murray, R. Sim, J. Stern, B. Stewart and C. Zaner. "Panel: CEO Roundtable On Corporate Structure And Management Incentives," JACF, 1990, v3(3), 6-35.)

Hamada, Robert S. "Differential Taxes And The Structure Of Equilibrium Rates Of Return: Managerial Implications And Remaining Conundrums," AFPAF, 1987, v2(1), 1-26.

Hamada, Robert S. "Financial Theory And Taxation In An Inflationary World: Some Public Policy Issues," JOF, 1979, v34(2), 347-369.

Hamada, Robert S. "The Effect Of The Firm's Capital Structure On The Systematic Risk Of Common Stocks," JOF,1972,v27(2),435-452.

Hamada, Robert. "Portfolio Analysis, Market Equilibrium And Corporation Finance," JOF, 1969, v24(1), 13-31.

Hamao, Yasushi, Ronald W. Masulis and Victor Ng. "Correlations In Price Changes And Volatility Across International Stock Markets," RFS, 1990, v3(2), 281-308.

Hamao, Yasushi. "A Standard Data Base For The Analysis Of Japanese Security Markets," JOB, 1991, v64(1), 87-102.

Hamao, Yasushi. "Japanese Stocks, Bonds, Bills, And Inflation, 1973-1987," JPM, 1989, v15(2), 20-26.

Hambor, John C. and Robert E. Weintraub. "The Term Structure: Another Look: A Comment," JMCB, 1974, v6(4), 551-557.

Hambrecht, George A. (Edesess, Michael and George A. Hambrecht. "Scenario Forecasting: Necessity, Not Choice," JPM, 1979-80, v6(3), 10-15.)

Hamburger, Michael J. and Burton Zwick. "Installment Credit Controls, Consumer Expenditures And The Allocation Of Real Resources," JOF, 1977, v32(5), 1557-1569.

Hamburger, Michael J. and Burton Zwick. "The Efficacy Of Selective Credit Policies: An Alternative Test," JMCB, 1979, v11(1), 106-110.

Hamburger, Michael J. and Cynthia M. Latta. "The Term Structure Of Interest Rates: Some Additional Evidence," JMCB, 1969, v1(1), 71-83.

Hamburger, Michael J. and Levis A. Kochin. "Money And Stock Prices: The Channels Of Influence," JOF, 1972, v27(2), 231-249.

Hamburger, Michael. "The Demand For Money In 1971: Was There A Shift?: A Comment," JMCB, 1973, v5(2), 720-725.

Hamdallah, Ahmed. (Haw, In-Mu, William Ruland and Ahmed Hamdallah. "Investor Evaluation Of Overfunded Pension Plan Terminations," JFR, 1988, v11(1),81-88.)

Hamden, Bassum. (Rudolph, Patricia M. and Bassum Hamden. "An Analysis Of Post-Deregulation Savings-And-Loan Failures," AREUEA, 1988, v16(1), 17-33.)

Hamelman, Paul W. and Edward M. Mazze. "Citation Patterns In Finance Journals," JOF, 1974, v29(4), 1295-1301.

Hamelman, Paul W. (Cox, Eli P., III, Paul W. Hamelman and James B. Wilcox. "Relational Characteristics Of The Business Literature: An Interpretive Procedure," JOB, 1976, v49(2), 252-265.)

Hamilton, Arthur J. and S. Brooks Marshall. "The Chartered Financial Analyst Certification: Implications For The Finance Curriculum," JFED, 1987, v16, 32-39.

Hamilton, Carl W. (Findlay, M. Chapman, III, Carl W. Hamilton, Stephen D. Messner and Jonathan S. Yormark. "Optimal Real Estate Portfolios," AREUEA, 1979, (3), 298-317.)

Hamilton, James L. "Competition, Scale Economies, And Transaction Cost In The Stock Market," JFQA, 1976, v11(5), 779-802.

Hamilton, James L. "Marketplace Organization And Marketability: NASDAQ, The Stock Exchange, And The National Market System," JOF, 1978, v33(2), 487-503.

Hamilton, James L. "Marketplace Fragmentation, Competition, And The Efficiency Of The Stock Exchange," JOF, 1979, v34(1), 171-187.

Hamilton, James L. "Off-Board Trading Of NYSE-Listed Stocks: The Effects Of Deregulation And The National Market System," JOF, 1987, v42(5),1331-1345.

Hamilton, M. T. (Lorie, J. H. and M. T. Hamilton. "New Focus For Investment Counselling," FAJ, 1973, v29(4), 46-50.)

Hamilton, Thomas W. (Sunderman, Mark A., John W. Birch, Roger E. Cannaday and Thomas W. Hamilton. "Testing For Vertical Inequity In Property Tax Systems," JRER, 1990, v5(3), 319-334.)

Hamlen, Susan S. (Jen, Frank C. and Susan S. Hamlen. "Net Present Value Method And Agency Theory In Financial Planning," AFPAF, 1985, v1(1), 49-76.)

Hammani, Dhafrallah. (Cornell, Bradford and Dhafrallah Hammani. "Option Pricing In Bear And Bull Markets," JPM, 1977-78, v4(4), 30-34.)

Hammarskjold, Knut. "Giant Jets And Supersonic Aircraft," FAJ, 1967, v23(2), 67-70.

Hammel, J. E. and D. A. Hodes. "Factors Influencing P/E Multiples," FAJ, 1967, v23(1), 90-92.

Hammer, Frederick S. "Banking's Present And Future Competitors: Finance And Insurance Companies," JBR, 1974-75, v5(3), 174-181.

Hammer, Frederick S. (Cohen, Kalman J. and Frederick S. Hammer. "Linear Programming And Optimal Bank Asset Management Decisions," JOF, 1967, v22(2), 147-165.)

Hammer, Harold Harlan. "ABCs Of Oil Payments," FAJ, 1954, v10(4), 41-46.

Hammer, Jerry A. "Hedging And Risk Aversion In The Foreign Currency Market," JFM, 1988, v8(6), 657-686.

Hammer, Jerry A. "Hedging Performance And Hedging Objectives: Tests Of New Performance Measures In The Foreign Currency Market," JFR, 1990, v13(4), 307-324.

Hammet, Richard. (London, Jack, Bernard Karsh, Joel Seidman and Richard Hammet. "Management Views The Local Union," JOB, 1953, v26(2), 91-102.)

Hammitt, James K. (Rolph, John E., James K. Hammitt and Robert L. Houchens. "Automobile Accident Compensation: Who Pays How Much How Soon?," JRI, 1985, v52(4), 667-685.)

Hammond, Carl T. (Neuberger, Brian M. and Carl T. Hammond. "A Study Of Underwriters' Experience With Unseasoned New Issues," JFQA, 1974, v9(2), 165-177.)

Hammond, J. D. "Interlocks In Corporate Management," JRI, 1965, v32(4), 649-651.

Hammond, J. D. "Pension Financing In Corporate Consolidations," JRI, 1962, v29(4), 503-516.

Hammond, J. D. "Research And Development Activities Of Life Insurance Companies," JRI, 1966, v33(1), 43-56.

Hammond, J. D. and N. Shilling. "Review Article - The Little Report On Prices And Profits In The Property And Liability Insurance Industry," JRI, 1969, v36(1), 129-144.

Hammond, J. D. and N. Shilling. "Some Relationships Of Portfolio Theory To The Regulation Of Insurer Solidity," JRI, 1978, v45(3), 377-400.

Hammond, J. D. and Ned Shilling. "Review Article: Some Empirical Implications Of The Return On Investible Funds Measure Of Profitability," JRI, 1970, v37(4), 659-663.

Hammond, J. D., E. R. Melander and N. Shilling. "Risk, Return, And The Capital Market: The Insurer Case," JFQA, 1976, v11(1), 115-131.

Hammond, J. D., David B. Houston and Eugene R. Melander. "Determinants Of Household Life Insurance Premium Expenditures," JRI, 1967, v34(3), 397-408.

Hammond, J. D., E. R. Melander and N. Shilling. "Economies Of Scale In The Property And Liability Insurance Industry," JRI, 1971, v38(2), 181-191.

Hammond, J. D., and E. R. Melander. "The Long Term Crisis In Life Insurance: Comment," JRI, 1968, v35(1), 147-148.

Hammond, John S., III. (Pratt, John W. and John S. Hammond, III. "Evaluating And Comparing Projects: Simple Detection Of False Alarms," JOF, 1979, v34(5), 1231-1242.)

Hamwi, Iskandar S. "A Note On The Influence Of Withdrawal Rates On Natural Reserves," JRI, 1978, v45(2), 340-343.

Hamwi, Iskandar S. "Cash Value: An Examination Of Company Practices," JRI, 1975, v42(1), 35-50.

Hamwi, Iskandar S. and Edward Nissan. "Determination Of Net Rate In Property And Liability Insurance: An Alternative Approach," JRI, 1984, v51(3), 536-548.

Han, Doug. (Lee, Cheng F., Donald H. Wort and Doug Han. "The Relationship Between Dividend Yield And Earnings Yield And Its Implication For Forecasting," AFPAF, 1987, v2(1), 155-178.)

Han, Li-Ming and Lalatendu Misra. "The Relationship Between The Volatilities Of The S&P Index And Futures Contracts Implicit In Their Call Option Prices," JFM, 1990, v10(3), 273-286.

Han, Li-Ming. (MacMinn, Richard D. and Li-Ming Han. "Limited Liability, Corporate Value, And The Demand For Liability Insurance," JRI, 1990, v57(4), 581-607.)

Hanchett, Paul E. and George R. McCoy. "An Actuarial Appraisal Of Congressional Proposals For Hospital Insurance For The Aged," JRI, 1964, v31(4), 597-602.

Hancock, Diana. "A Model Of The Financial Firm With Imperfect Asset And Deposit Elasticities," JBF, 1986, v10(1), 37-54.

Hancock, Diana. "Bank Profitability, Interest Rates, And Monetary Policy," JMCB, 1985, v17(2),189-202.

Hancock, Diana. "Testing Price Taking In Loan And Deposit Markets By Financial Firms," FR, 1986, v21(2), 239-257.

Hancort, Joseph S. "Relative Values In Growth Stocks," FAJ, 1956, v12(1), 67-72.

Hand, Herbert H. and W. Palmer. "A Bibliography Of Operating Expense Information Sources For Small Businesses," JFED, 1979, v8, 97-98.

Hand, John H. (Lloyd, William P., John H. Hand and Naval K. Modani. "The Effect Of Portfolio Construction Rules On The Relationship Between Portfolio Size And Effective Diversification," JFR, 1981, v4(3),183-193.)

Hand, John H. (Rose, Terry L. and John H. Hand. "The Effects Of Risk Reduction Inherent In Universal Life Insurance: Comment," JRI, 1981, v48(4), 682-689.)

Hand, John H., William P. Lloyd and Robert B. Rogow. "Agency Relationships In The Close Corporation," FM, 1982, v11(1), 25-30.

Hand, John R. M. and Patricia Hughes. "The Motives And Consequences Of Debt-Equity Swaps And Defeasances: More Evidence That It Does Not Pay To Manipulate Earnings," JACF, 1990, v3(3), 77-81.

Hand, John. (Brooks, Robert and John Hand. "Evaluating The Performance Of Stock Portfolios With Index Futures Contracts," JFM, 1988, v8(1), 33-46.)

Handa, Jagdish. "An Empirical Study Of Financial Intermediation In Canada," JFQA, 1971, v6(1),583-600.

Handa, Puneet, S. P. Kothari and Charles Wasley. "The Relation Between The Return Interval And Betas: Implications For The Size Effect," JFEC, 1989, v23(1), 79-100.

Handa, Puneet. "An Economic Analysis Of Leasebacks," RQFA, 1991, v1(2), 177-190.

Handa, Puneet and Scott C. Linn. "Equilibrium Factor Pricing With Heterogeneous Beliefs," JFQA, 1991, v26(1), 11-22.

Handjinicolaou, George and Avner Kalay. "Wealth Redistributions Or Changes In Firm Value: An Analysis Of Returns To Bondholders And The Stockholders Around Dividend Announcements," JFEC, 1984, v13(1), 35-63.

Handmaker, David. "Low-Frequency Filters In Seasonal Analysis," JFM, v1(3), 367-378.

Handorf, William C. (Barnhill, Theodore M. and William C. Handorf. "An Application Of Monte Carlo Simulation Modeling To Commercial Bank Interest Rate Management," RFM, 1985, v4(3), 282-305.)

Handorf, William C. and William Margrabe. "The Dow-Jones Futures Market: A Role-Playing Case," JFED, 1982, v11, 87-93.

Handorf, William C. "Flexible Debt Financing," FM, 1974, v3(2), 17-23.

Handorf, William C. "The Underemphasis Of Bond Analysis In The Financial Investments Course," JFED, 1974, v3, 53-55.

Handorf, William C. and J. Minor Sachlis. "A Note On The Accounting Model For Problem Real Estate Loans," JRER, 1990, v5(3), 381-391.

Hane, George. "Recovery And Relapse In The Mortgage Market: The 1968 And 1969 Experience," FR, 1970, v1(5), 291-295.

Haner, Charles F. "Prediction Of Automobile Claims By Psychological Methods," JRI, 1968, v35(1), 49-60.

Haney, Lewis H. "Income From Short Loans, Bonds, And Stocks," FAJ, 1954, v10(1), 9-14.

Haney, Richard L. (Lloyd, William P. and Richard L. Haney, Jr. "Time Diversification: Surest Route To Lower Risk," **JPM**, 1979-80, v6(3), 5-9.)

Haney, Richard L., Jr. "An Analysis Of Yield Spreads Between Ginnie Mae Pass-Through And Aaa Corporate Bonds," **FM**, 1978, v7(1), 17-28.

Haney, Richard L., Jr. "Sticky Mortgage Rates: Some Empirical Evidence," **JRER**, 1988, v3(1), 61-73.

Haney, Richard L., Jr. (Isakson, Hans R. and Richard L. Haney, Jr. "The Impact Of Market Experience Upon Appraisers' Energy Awareness," **AREUEA**, 1978, v6(3), 287-304.)

Haney, Richard L., Jr. (Wendt, Paul F. and Richard L. Haney, Jr. "Secondary Mortgage Market Performance Under Pressure," **AREUEA**, 1975, v3(2), 31-42.)

Haney, Richard L., Jr., Melvin R. Crask and Hans P. Isakson. "The Gatekeeper Appraiser's Role In An Era Of Higher Energy Prices," **AREUEA**, 1978, v6(2), 186-203.

Hankla, William B., Jr. "Automotive Production Declines 15%," **FAJ**, 1952, v8(2), 69-72.

Hanna, J. R. (Basu, S. and J. R. Hanna. "GPL-Adjusted Earnings For Utilities," **FAJ**, 1978, v34(1), 55-67.)

Hanna, Mark. "A Stock Price Predictive Model Based On Changes In Ratios Of Short Interest To Trading Volume," **JFQA**, 1976, v11(5), 857-872.

Hanna, Mark. "An Investor Expectations Stock Price Predictive Model Using Closed-End Fund Premiums: Comment," **JOF**, 1977, v32(4), 1368-1371.

Hanna, Mark. "Corporate Bankruptcy Potential, Stockholder Returns And Share Valuation: Comment," **JOF**, 1972, v27(3), 711-717.

Hanna, Mark. "Short Interest: Bullish Or Bearish?: Comment," **JOF**, 1968, v23(3), 520-523.

Hanna, Mark. "Testing An Aggressive Investment Strategy Using Value Line Ranks: A Comment," **JOF**, 1983, v38(1), 259-262.

Hanna, R. S. (Vogt, Michael G. and R. S. Hanna. "Variations Of The Federal Funds Rate And Bank Reserve Management," **JBR**, 1984-85, v15(3), 188-192.)

Hannan, Timothy H. "Bank Commercial Loan Markets And The Role Of Market Structure: Evidence From Surveys Of Commercial Lending," **JBF**, 1991, v15(1), 133-149.

Hannan, Timothy H. "Competition Between Commercial Banks And Thrift Institutions: An Empirical Examination," **JBR**, 1984-85, v15(1), 8-14.

Hannan, Timothy H. "The Theory Of Limit Pricing: Some Applications To The Banking Industry," **JBF**, 1979, v3(3), 221-234.

Hannan, Timothy H. and Gerald A. Hanweck. "Bank Insolvency Risk And The Market For Large Certificates Of Deposit," **JMCB**, 1988, v20(2), 203-211.

Hannan, Timothy H. and John D. Wolken. "Returns To Bidders And Targets In The Acquisition Process: Evidence From The Banking Industry," **JFSR**, 1989, v3(1), 5-16.

Hannan, Timothy. "Bank Profitability And The Threat Of Entry," **JBR**, 1983-84, v14(2), 157-163.

Hannan, Timothy. "Limit Pricing And The Banking Industry," **JMCB**, 1979, v11(4), 438-446.

Hanoch, Giora and Haim Levy. "Efficient Portfolio Selection With Quadratic And Cubic Utility," **JOB**, 1970, v43(2), 181-189.

Hanoch, Giora. (Levy, Haim and Giora Hanoch. "Relative Effectiveness Of Efficiency Criteria For Portfolio Selection," **JFQA**, 1970, v5(1), 63-76.)

Hanraahn, L Michael. "International Levels Of Employee Benefits - An Exploratory Study: Comment," **JRI**, 1971, v38(1), 143-144.

Hanrahan, J. Robert. (Dipchand, Cecil R. and J. Robert Hanrahan. "Exit And Exchange Option Values On Government Of Canada 'Retractable Bonds," **FM**, 1979, v8(3), 62-71.)

Hansen, Don R. (Foster, Taylor W., Don Hansen and Don Vickrey. "Additional Evidence On The Abatement Of Errors In Predicting Beta Through Increases In Portfolio Size And On The Regression Tendency," **JBFA**, 1988, v15(2), 185-198.)

Hansen, Knud. "The Reinsurance Game - A Tool For Education And Research," **JRI**, 1961, v28(2), 11-18.

Hansen, Knud. "The Reinsurance Game - A Tool For Education And Research: Reply," **JRI**, 1961, v28(4), 100-104.

Hansen, Robert G. "A Theory For The Choice Of Exchange Medium In Mergers And Acquisitions," **JOB**, 1987, v60(1), 75-96.

Hansen, Robert S. and John G. Thatcher. "On The Nature Of Credit Demand And Credit Rationing In Competitive Credit Markets," **JBF**, 1993, v7(2), 273-284.

Hansen, Robert S. and John M. Pinkerton. "Direct Equity Finacing; A Resolution Of A Paradox: A Reply," **JOF**, 1984, v39(5), 1619-1624.

Hansen, Robert S. and John M. Pinkerton. "Direct Equity Financing: A Resolution Of A Paradox," **JOF**, 1982, v37(3), 651-665.

Hansen, Robert S. "The Demise Of The Rights Issue," **RFS**, 1988-89, v1(3), 289-309.

Hansen, Robert S. (Crutchley, Claire E. and Robert S. Hansen. "A Test Of The Agency Theory Of Managerial Ownership, Corporate Leverage, And Corporate Dividends," **FM**, 1989, v18(4), 36-46.)

Hansen, Robert S. and Claire Crutchley. "Corporate Earnings And Financings: An Empirical Analysis," **JOB**, 1990, v63(3), 347-372.

Hansen, Robert S., John M. Pinkerton and Tai Ma. "On The Rightholders' Subscription To The Underwritten Rights Offering," **JBF**, 1986, v10(4), 595-604.

Hansen, Robert S., Beverly R. Fuller and Vahan Janjigian. "The Over-Allotment Option And Equity Financing Flotation Costs: An Empirical Investigation," **FM**, 1987, v16(2), 24-32.

Hansen, Robert S., John M. Pinkerton and Tai Ma. "The Allocation Ratio Decision In The Underwritten Rights Offering," **RIF**, 1988, v7, 201-226.

Hansen, Ronald W., Paul W. MacAvoy and Clifford W. Smith, Jr. "Compensation Alternatives For Occupational Disease And Disability," **JRI**, 1989, v56(2), 252-274.

Hansen, Victor R. "Insurance And The Antitrust Laws," **JRI**, 1959, v26(1), 40-48.

Hanson, H. Nicholas. (Leibowitz, Martin L., Eric H. Sorensen, Robert D. Arnott and H. Nicholas Hanson. "A Total Differential Approach To Equity Duration," **FAJ**, 1989, v45(5), 30-37.)

Hanson, Jon S. (Friedman, Lloyd K., Harold A. Jensen, Jr., Spencer L.

Kimball and Jon S. Hanson. "The Regulation Of Specialty Policies In Life Insurance: Comment," **JRI**, 1966, v33(2), 305-316.)

Hanson, Nick. (Estep, Tony, Nick Hanson and Cal Johnson. "Sources Of Value And Risk In Common Stocks," **JPM**, 1982-83, v9(4), 5-13.)

Hanweck, Gerald A. (Benston, George J., Gerald A. Hanweck and David B. Humphrey. "Scale Economies In Banking: A Restructuring And Reassessment," **JMCB**, 1982, v14(4), Part 1, 435-456.)

Hanweck, Gerald A. (Goldberg, Lawrence G. and Gerald A. Hanweck. "What We Can Expect From Interstate Banking," **JBF**, 1988, v12(1), 51-68.)

Hanweck, Gerald A. (Goldberg, Lawrence G., Gerald A. Hanweck, Michael Keenan and Allan Young. "Economies Of Scale And Scope In The Securities Industry," **JBF**, 1991, v15(1), 91-107.)

Hanweck, Gerald A. (Goldberg, Lawrence G. and Gerald A. Hanweck. "The Growth Of The World's 300 Largest Banking Organizations By Country," **JBF**, 1991, v15(1), 207-223.)

Hanweck, Gerald A. (Hannan, Timothy H. and Gerald A. Hanweck. "Bank Insolvency Risk And The Market For Large Certificates Of Deposit," **JMCB**, 1988, v20(2), 203-211.)

Harben, George A. (Moskowitz, Arnold X. and George A. Harben. "Keep Profits: The True Discount Factor," **JPM**, 1977-78, v4(4), 5-15.)

Harberger, Arnold C. "A Primer On Inflation," **JMCB**, 1978, v10(4), 505-521.

Hardgrave, William W. (Barnhill, Theodore M., William W. Hardgrave and Rehman P. Kassam. "An Empirical Study Of T-Bond Futures Contract Price Change Patterns Around U.S. Treasury Quarterly Refundings," **RFM**, 1985, v4(1), 106-131.)

Hardin, Einar. "Michigan's Employment Problem And The Elasticity Of Substitution," **JOB**, 1965, v38(2), 201-206.

Hardin, Rector R. "Contributions Of Life Insurance To Capital Formation In The South," **JRI**, 1958, v25(2), 47-52.

Harding, Forrest E. "The Standard Automobile Insurance Policy: A Study Of Its Readability," **JRI**, 1967, v34(1), 39-46.

Hardouvelis, Gikas A. "Economic News, Exchange Rates And Interest Rates," **JIMF**, 1988, v7(1), 23-36.

Hardouvelis, Gikas A. "Exchange Rates, Interest Rates, And Money-Stock Announcements: A Theoretical Exposition," **JIMF**, 1985, v4(4), 443-454.

Hardouvelis, Gikas A. "Optimal Wage Indexation And Monetary Policy In An Economy With Imported Raw Materials," **JIMF**, 1987, v6(4), 419-432.

Hardouvelis, Gikas A. "Reserves Announcements And Interest Rates: Does Monetary Policy Matter?," **JOF**, 1987, v42(2), 407-422.

Hardouvelis, Gikas A. "The Predictive Power Of The Term Structure During Recent Monetary Regimes," **JOF**, 1988, v43(2), 339-356.

Hardouvelis, Gikas A. (Frankel, Jeffrey A. and Gikas A. Hardouvelis. "Commodity Prices, Money Surprises, And Fed Credibility," **JMCB**, 1985, v17(4), Part 1, 425-438.)

Hardy, Daniel. "Market Timing And International Diversification," **JPM**, 1990, v16(4), 23-27.

Hardy, Donald J. (Dietz, Peter O., H. Russell Fogler and Donald J. Hardy. "The Challenge Of Analyzing Bond Portfolio Returns," **JPM**, 1979-80, v6(3), 53-58.)

Hargrove, Michael B. (Baker, H. Kent, Michael B. Hargrove and John A. Haslem. "An Empirical Analysis Of The Risk-Return Preferences Of Individual Investors," **JFQA**, 1977, v12(3), 377-389.)

Hariff, Richard B. (Brill, Edward A. and Richard B. Harriff. "Pricing American Options: Managing Risk With Early Exercise," **FAJ**, 1986, v42(6), 48-55.)

Haring, John R., Jr. "Accounting Rules And 'The Accounting Establishment'," **JOB**, 1979, v52(4), 507-520.

Harju, Melvin W. (Clauretie, Terrence M. and Melvin W. Harju. "The Expanding Concept Of Just Compensation And The Role Of The Appraiser," **AREUEA**, 1986, v14(2), 338-360.)

Harkavy, Oscar. "The Relation Between Retained Earnings And Common Stock Prices For Large, Listed Corporations," **JOF**, 1953, v8(3), 283-297.

Harkness, Jon. "Optimal Exchange Intervention For A Small Open Economy," **JIMF**, 1985, v4(1), 101-112.

Harlow, C. V. and R. J. Teweles. "Commodities And Securities Compared," **FAJ**, 1972, v28(5), 64-70.

Harlow, W. V. (Brown, Keith C., W. V. Harlow and Seha M. Tinic. "Risk Aversion, Uncertain Information, And Market Efficiency," **JFEC**, 1988, v22(2), 355-386.)

Harlow, W. V. (Brown, Keith C. and W. V. Harlow. "Market Overreaction: Magnitude And Intensity," **JPM**, 1987-88, v14(2), 6-13.)

Harlow, W. V. (Brown, Keith C., W. V. Harlow and Seha M. Tinic. "How Rational Investors Deal With Uncertainty (Or, Reports Of The Death Of Efficient Market Theory Are Greatly Exaggerated)," **JACF**, 1989, v2(3), 45-58.)

Harlow, W. V. and Keith C. Brown. "Understanding And Assessing Financial Risk Tolerance: A Biological Perspective," **FAJ**, 1990, v46(6), 50-62.

Harlow, W. V. and Ramesh K. S. Rao. "Asset Pricing In A Generalized Mean-Lower Partial Moment Framework: Theory And Evidence," **JFQA**, 1989, v24(3), 285-312.

Harm, Christian. "A Contingent Claims Analysis Of Sovereign Debt," **RDIBF**, 1989, v3, 69-108.

Harmelink, Philip J. "Prediction Of Best's General Policyholders' Ratings," **JRI**, 1974, v41(4), 621-632.

Harmon, David Perry, Jr. "Pooling Of Interests: Case Study," **FAJ**, 1968, v24(2), 82-88.

Harmon, Oskar R. and Michael J. Potepan. "Housing Adjustment Costs: Their Impact On Mobility And Housing Demand Elasticities," **AREUEA**, 1988, v16(4), 459-478.

Harmon, Oskar R. (Lambinos, James and Oskar R. Harmon. "An Empirical Evaluation Of Two Methods For Estimating Economic Damages," **JRI**, 1989, v56(4), 733-739.)

Harms, Louis T. "Philosophical Preconceptions And The Social Security System," **JRI**, 1963, v30(3), 363-376.

Harnett, Donald L., G. David Hughes and Larry L. Cummings. "Bilateral Monopolistic Bargaining Through An Intermediary," **JOB**, 1968, v41(2), 251-259.

Harp, Anne. "Guide To Games: Second Edition," JFED, 1972, v1, 91.

Harpaz, Giora and Stavros B. Thomadakis. "Systematic Risk And The Firm's Experimental Strategy," JFQA, 1982, v17(3), 363-389.

Harpaz, Giora and Stavros B. Thomadakis. "Capital Budgeting With Imperfect Information And Bayesian Learning," RIF, 1985, v5, 207-228.

Harpaz, Giora. "Firm Learning And Systematic Risk," RIF, 1985, v5, 57-76.

Harpaz, Giora. (Cakici, Nusret, T. Hanan Eytan and Giora Harpaz. "American Vs. European Options On The Value Line Index," JFM, 1988, v8(3), 373-388.)

Harpaz, Giora. (Eytan, T. Hanan and Giora Harpaz. "The Pricing Of Futures And Options Contracts On The Value Line Index," JOF, 1986, v41(4), 843-856.)

Harpaz, Giora. (Eytan, T. Hanan, Giora Harpaz and Steven Krull. "The Pricing Of Dollar Index Futures Contracts," JFM, 1988, v8(2), 127-140.)

Harpaz, Gioria, Steven Krull and Joseph Yagil. "The Efficiency Of The US Dollar Index Futures Market," JFM, 1990, v10(5), 469-480.

Harper, Allen D. "How A Professional Investor Seeks Investment Opportunities," FAJ, 1963, v19(6), 47-52.

Harper, Allen D. "Investing In The Water Utility Industry," FAJ, 1967, v23(2), 35-38.

Harper, Charles P. and Clifford L. Fry. "Consistent Empirical Results With Almon's Method: Implications For The Monetary Versus Fiscal Policy Debate," JOF, 1978, v33(1), 187-198.

Harper, Charles P. (Crawford, Peggy J., Charles P. Harper and John J. McConnell. "Further Evidence On The Terms Of Financial Leases," FM, 1981, v10(4), 7-14.)

Harper, Charles P. (Fry, Clifford L., Charles P. Harper and Stanley R. Stansell. "An Analysis Of Credit Union Costs: A New Approach To Analyzing Cost Of Financial Institutions," JBR, 1981-82, v12(4), 239-249.)

Harper, Charles P. (Horvitz, Paul M. and Charles P. Harper. "Regulation Of The Money Order Industry," FM, 1980, v9(4), 13-20.)

Harper, William K. (Berger, Paul D. and William K. Harper. "Determination Of An Optimal Revolving Credit Agreement," JFQA, 1973, v8(3), 491-497.)

Harries, Brenton W. "Standard And Poor's New Policy," FAJ, 1968, v24(3), 68-71.

Harries, Brenton W. (Clark, John and Brenton Harries. "Some Recent Trends In Municipal And Corporate Securities Markets: An Interview With Brenton W. Harries, President Of Standard & Poor's Corporation," FM, 1976, v5(1),9-17.)

Harrington, Diana R. "Whose Beta Is Best?," FAJ, 1983, v39(4), 67-73.

Harrington, Diana. (Eades, Kenneth M. and Diana Harrington. "Using A Moot Court To Teach The Dividend-Relevance Controversy," JFED, 1990, v19, 27-32.)

Harrington, John J., Jr. and Edward D. Zinbarg. "The Stock Market's 'Seasonal Pattern'," FAJ, 1964, v20(1), 53-55.

Harrington, Joseph E., Jr. "The Role Of Risk Preferences In Bargaining When Acceptance Of A Proposal Requires Less Than Unanimous Approval," JRU, 1990, v3(2), 135-154.

Harrington, Scott E. "New York Regulation Of General Agency Expense Allowances," JRI, 1982, v49(4), 564-582.

Harrington, Scott E. "Operating Expenses For Agency And Nonagency Life Insurers: Further Evidence," JRI, 1982, v49(2), 229-255.

Harrington, Scott E. "Stock Life Insurer Shareholder Dividend Policy And Holding Company Affiliation," JRI, 1981, v48(4), 550-576.

Harrington, Scott E. "The Relationship Between Risk And Return: Evidence For Life Insurance Stock," JRI, 1983, v50(4), 587-610.

Harrington, Scott E. "The Relationship Between Voluntary And Involuntary Market Rates And Rate Regulation In Automobile Insurance," JRI, 1990, v57(1), 9-27.

Harrington, Scott E. (Cummins, J. David and Scott E. Harrington. "The Relationship Between Risk And Return: Evidence For Property-Liability Insurance Stocks," JRI, 1988, v55(1), 15-31.)

Harrington, Scott E. and Jack M. Nelson. "A Regression-Based Methodology For Solvency Surveillance In The Property-Liability Insurance Industry," JRI, 1986, v53(4), 583-605.

Harrington, Scott. "The Impact Of Rate Regulation On Prices And Underwriting Results In The Property-Liability Insurance Industry: A Survey," JRI, 1984, v51(4), 577-623.

Harrington, Scott. (Cummins, J. David and Scott Harrington. "Property-Liability Insurance Rate Regulation: Estimation Of Underwriting Betas Using Quarterly Profit Data," JRI, 1985, v52(1), 16-43.)

Harris, Clyde E., Jr. (Perreault, William D., Jr., Warren A. French and Clyde E. Harris, Jr. "Use Of Multiple Discriminant Analysis To Improve The Salesman Selection Process," JOB, 1977, v50(1), 50-62.)

Harris, Curtis C., Jr. and Virginia D. McConnell. "Surpluses In Disequilibrium Urban Land Markets," AREUEA, 1987, v15(4), 359-373.

Harris, Duane G. "Credit Rationing At Commercial Banks: Some Empirical Evidence," JMCB, 1974, v6(2), 227-240.

Harris, Duane G. "Some Evidence On Differential Lending Practices At Commercial Banks," JOF, 1973, v28(5), 1303-1311.

Harris, I. (Gilmour, A., M. Jensen, R. Mercer, N. Minow, J. Morley, R. Siefert, B. Stewart, L. Summers and I. Harris. "Panel: The Economic Consequences Of High Leverage And Stock Market Pressures On Corporate Management: A Roundtable Discussion," JACF, 1990, v3(2), 6-37.)

Harris, J. Ira. (Boies, D., D. Carroll, A. Fleischer, J. Grundfest, J. Ira Harris, M. Lipton, R. Monks, A. Oliver, L. Sachnoff and J. Wilcox. "Panel: Corporate Governance: The Role Of Boards Of Directors In Takeover Bids And Defenses," JACF, 1989, v2(2), 6-35.)

Harris, Jack C. "The Effect Of Real Rates Of Interest On Housing Prices," JREFEC, 1989, v2(1), 47-60.

Harris, Jackson. (Rabianski, Joseph and Jackson Harris. "A Descriptive Analysis Of The AREUEA Members: 1978," AREUEA, 1979, v7(4), 610-620.)

Harris, John M., Jr. and Richard H. Klein. "Analysis Of Leveraged Buyouts: Application Of A Simple Option Pricing Model," JFED, 1988, v17, 6-14.

Harris, John M., Jr. "Alternative Mortgage Instruments: Comparisons And A Proposal," JFR, 1983, v6(2), 153-162.

Harris, John M., Jr. and Daniel E. Page. "Rate Level Index Mortgage: An Evaluation," AREUEA, 1985, v13(2), 195-207.

Harris, John M., Jr. and G. Stacy Sirmans. "Discount Points, Effective Yields And Mortgage Prepayments," JRER, 1987, v2(2), 97-104.

Harris, John M., Jr., Rodney L. Roenfeldt and Philip L. Cooley. "Evidence Of Financial Leverage Clienteles," JOF, 1983, v38(4), 1125-1132.

Harris, John T. "Discount And Current Coupon Bonds," FAJ, 1968, v24(4), 81-85.

Harris, Lawrence and Eitan Gurel. "Price And Volume Effects Associated With Changes In The S&P 500: New Evidence For The Existence Of Price Pressures," JOF, 1986, v41(4), 815-830.

Harris, Lawrence E. (Glosten, Lawrence R. and Lawrence E. Harris. "Estimating The Components Of The Bid/Ask Spread," JFEC, 1988, v21(1), 123-142.)

Harris, Lawrence. "A Day-End Transaction Price Anomaly," JFQA, 1989, v24(1), 29-46.

Harris, Lawrence. "A Transaction Data Study Of Weekly And Intradaily Patterns In Stock Returns," JFEC, 1986, v16(1), 99-118.

Harris, Lawrence. "Cross-Security Tests Of The Mixture Of Distributions Hypothesis," JFQA, 1986, v21(1), 39-46.

Harris, Lawrence. "Estimation Of Stock Price Variances And Serial Covariances From Discrete Observations," JFQA, 1990, v25(3), 291-306.

Harris, Lawrence. "How To Profit From Intradaily Stock Returns," JPM, 1985-86, v12(2), 61-65.

Harris, Lawrence. "S&P 500 Cash Stock Price Volatilities," JOF, 1989, v44(5), 1155-1176.

Harris, Lawrence. "Statistical Properties Of The Roll Serial Covariance Bid/Ask Spread Estimator," JOF, 1990, v45(2), 579-590.

Harris, Lawrence. "The Economics Of Cash Index Alternatives," JFM, 1990, v10(2), 179-194.

Harris, Lawrence. "The October 1987 S&P 500 Stock-Futures Basis," JOF, 1989, v44(1), 77-100.

Harris, Lawrence. "Transaction Data Tests Of The Mixture Of Distribution Distribution," JFQA, 1987, v22(2), 127-142.

Harris, Louis. "Confidence In Financial Institutions," FAJ, 1973, v29(2), 24-26,84-85.

Harris, Malcolm C. (Prodhan, Bimal K. and Malcolm C. Harris. "Systematic Risk And The Discretionary Disclosure Of Geographical Segments: An Empirical Investigation Of US Multinationals," JBFA, 1989, v16(4), 467-492.)

Harris, Milton and Artur Raviv. "A Sequential Signalling Model Of Convertible Debt Call Policy," JOF, 1985, v40(5), 1263-1281.

Harris, Milton and Artur Raviv. "Corporate Governance: Voting Rights And Majority Rules," JFEC, 1988, v20(1/2), 203-236.

Harris, Milton and Artur Raviv. "Corporate Control Contests And Capital Structure," JFEC, 1988, v20(1/2), 55-86.

Harris, Milton and Artur Raviv. "Capital Structure And The Informational Role Of Debt," JOF, 1990, v45(2), 321-350. 3K ?8

Harris, Milton and Artur Raviv. "The Theory Of Capital Structure," JOF, 1991, v46(1), 297-356.

Harris, Milton and Artur Raviv. "The Design Of Securities," JFEC, 1989, v24(2), 255-288.

Harris, Richard G. and Douglas D. Purvis. "Incomplete Information And Equilibrium Determination Of The Forward Exchange Rate," JIMF, 1982, v1(3), 241-254.

Harris, Richard G. "A General Equilibrium Analysis Of The Capital Asset Pricing Model," JFQA, 1980, v15(1), 99-122.

Harris, Robert S. and John J. Pringle. "Implications Of Miller's Argument For Capital Budgeting," JFR, 1983, v6(1), 13-23.

Harris, Robert S. and John J. Pringle. "Risk-Adjusted Discount Rates - Extensions From The Average-Risk Case," JFR, 1985, v8(3), 237-244.

Harris, Robert S. "The Impact Of Corporate Mergers On Acquiring Firms," JFR, 1980, v3(3), 283-295.

Harris, Robert S. "The Refunding Of Discounted Debt: An Adjusted Present Value Analysis," FM, 1980, v9(4), 7-12.

Harris, Robert S. "Using Analysts' Growth Forecasts To Estimate Shareholder Required Rates Of Return," FM, 1986, v15(1), 58-67.

Harris, Robert S. (Carleton, Willard T., David K. Guilkey, Robert S. Harris and John F. Stewart. "An Empirical Analysis Of The Role Of The Medium Of Exchange In Mergers," JOF, 1983, v38(3), 813-826.)

Harris, Robert S. (Chambers, Donald R., Robert S. Harris and John J. Pringle. "Treatment Of Financing Mix In Analyzing Investment Opportunities," FM, 1982, v11(2), 24-41.)

Harris, Robert S. (Conroy, Robert M., Robert S. Harris and Bruce A. Benet. "The Effects Of Stock Splits On Bid-Ask Spreads," JOF, 1990, v45(4), 1285-1295.)

Harris, Robert S. (Eisenbeis, Robert A., Robert S. Harris and Josef Lakonishok. "Benefits Of Bank Diversification: The Evidence From Shareholder Returns," JOF, 1984, v39(3), 881-892.)

Harris, Robert S. (Franks, Julian R. and Robert S. Harris. "Shareholder Wealth Effects Of Corporate Takeovers: The U.K. Experience 1955-1985," JFEC, 1989, v23(2), 225-250.)

Harris, Robert S. (Jalilvand, Abolhassan and Robert S. Harris. "Corporate Behavior In Adjusting To Capital Structure And Dividend Targets: An Econometric Study," JOF, 1984, v39(1), 127-145.)

Harris, Robert S., Thomas J. O'Brien and Doug Wakeman. "Divisional Cost-Of-Capital Estimation For Multi-Industry Firms," FM, 1989, v18(2), 74-84.

Harris, Robert. (Born, Jeffrey A., Robert A. Eisenbeis and Robert Harris. "The Benefits Of Geographical And Product Expansion In The Financial Services Industry," JFSR, 1988, v1(2), 161-182.)

Harris, Seymour E. "The British Experiment," JRI, 1951, v18, 73-87.

Harris, William G. "Inflation Risk As A Determinant Of The Discount Rate In Tort Settlements," JRI, 1983, v50(2), 265-280.

Harris, William G. "Inflation Risk As Determinant Of The Discount Rate In Tort Settlements: Reply," JRI, 1985, v52(3), 533-536.

Harris, William G. "Problems In The Use Of Historical Data In Estimating Economic Loss In Wrongful Death And Injury Cases: Comment," JRI, 1984, v51(1), 122-125.

Harris, William G. "Selecting Income Growth And Discount Rates In Wrongful Death And Injury Cases: Comment," *JRI*, 1977, v44(1), 117-122.

Harrison, J. Michael, Richard Pitbladdo and Stephen M. Schaefer. "Continuous Price Processes In Frictionless Markets Have Infinite Variation," *JOB*, 1984, v57(3), 353-366.

Harrison, R. (Wilkes, F. M. and R. Harrison. "Classified Pricing Rules, Cost-Plus Pricing And The Capacity Constrained Firm," *JBFA*, 1975, v2(1),19-38.)

Harrison, William B. "Observed Characteristics Of Fifth District Member Banks' Deposit Distributions," *JBR*, 1977-78, v8(3), 183-185.

Harriss, C. Lowell. "Government Expenditure: Significant Issues Of Definition," *JOF*, 1954, v9(4), 351-364.

Harriss, C. Lowell. "Stock Prices, Death Tax Revenues, And Tax Equity," *JOF*, 1950, v5(3), 257-269.

Hart, Ira Royal. (Howell, Paul L. and Ira Royal Hart. "The Promoting And Financing Of Transcontinental Gas Pipe Line Corporation," *JOF*, 1951, v6(3),311-324.)

Hart, James F. "The Riskless Option Hedge: An Incomplete Guide," *JPM*, 1977-78, v4(2), 58-63.

Hart, O. D. (Grossman, S. J. and O. D. Hart. "Disclosure Laws And Takeover Bids," *JOF*, 1980, v35(2), 323-333.)

Hart, Oliver D. (Grossman, Sanford J. and Oliver D. Hart. "The Allocation Role Of Takeover Bids In Situations Of Asymmetric Information," *JOF*, 1981, v36(2), 253-270.)

Hart, Oliver D. (Grossman, Sanford J. and Oliver D. Hart. "One Share—One Vote And The Market For Corporate Control," *JFEC*, 1988, v20(1/2), 175-202.)

Hart, Orson H. "Life Insurance Companies And The Equity Capital Markets," *JOF*, 1965, v20(2),358-367.

Hart, Orson H. "National Economic Policy," *FAJ*, 1967, v23(6), 101-102.

Hart, Orson H. "The Outlook For Long-Term Funds," *JOF*, 1958, v13(2), 305-310.

Hart, Orson. "Risk Factors In Public Utility Securities," *JOF*, 1948, v3(3), 52-64.

Hartill, Creighton. "For Growth Alone?," *FAJ*, 1962, v18(3), 31-33.

Hartill, Creighton. "Oil In A Changing Era," *FAJ*, 1963, v19(1), 13-16.

Hartill, Creighton. "Stock Rights Make Sense," *FAJ*, 1958, v14(2), 63-66.

Hartill, Creighton. "What Is Wrong With The Airlines?," *FAJ*, 1957, v13(4), 49-52.

Hartland-Thunberg, Penelope. "Oil, Petrodollars And The LDC's," *FAJ*, 1977, v33(4), 55-58.

Hartman, Bart P. and Johng Y. Lee. "Influence Of Company Debt Burden On Reported Replacement Cost Values," *JBR*, 1981-82, v12(1), 56-59.

Hartman, David G. "The International Financial Market And US Interest Rates," *JIMF*, 1984, v3(1),91-104.

Hartman, Gerald R. "Application Of A Mathematical Concept Of Risk To Property-Liability Insurance Ratemaking: Comment," *JRI*, 1971, v38(2), 293-298.

Hartman, Gerald R. "Insurance Experience And Rating Laws," *JRI*, 1970, v37(2), 203-224.

Hartman, Gerald R. "The Loss-Ratio Method Of Rating And The Feedback Control Loop Concept: Comment," *JRI*, 1971, v38(1), 129-132.

Hartman, Gerald R. (Braverman, Jerome D. and Gerald R. Hartman. "The Process Of Classifying Drivers: A Suggestion For Insurance Ratemaking: Comment," *JRI*, 1973, v40(1), 142-146.)

Hartman, Gerald R. (Denenberg, Herbert S. and Gerald R. Hartman. "Insurance Rate Making In Louisiana," *JRI*, 1967, v34(4), 635-646.)

Hartmann, Wendelin. "Deutsche Bundesbank And Payment System Risk In The Federal Republic Of Germany," *JBR*, 1985-86, v16(4), 214-217.

Hartnett, Harry D. "A Locational Analysis Of Manufacturing Plants Within The City Of Chicago: 1959-1968," *AREUEA*, 1973, v1(1), 31-47.

Hartwell, John M. "Performance: Its Promise And Problems," *FAJ*, 1969, v25(2), 115-117.

Hartzell, David J. (Liu, Crocker H., David J. Hartzell, Terry V. Grissom and Wylie Grieg. "The Composition Of The Market Portfolio And Real Estate Investment Performance," *AREUEA*, 1990, v18(1), 49-75.)

Hartzell, David J. (Liu, Crocker H., Terry V. Grissom and David J. Hartzell. "The Impact Of Market Imperfections On Real Estate Returns And Optimal Investment Portfolios," *AREUEA*, 1990, v18(4), 453-478.)

Hartzell, David J. (Liu, Crocker H., David J. Hartzell, Wylie Greig and Terry V. Grissom. "The Integration Of The Real Estate Market And The Stock Market: Some Preliminary Evidence," *JREFEC*, 1990, v3(3), 261-282.)

Hartzell, David J. and James R. Webb. "Real Estate Risk And Return Expectations: Recent Survey Results," *JRER*, 1988, v3(3), 31-37.

Hartzell, David J., David G. Shulman, Terrence C. Langetieg and Martin L. Leibowitz. "A Look At Real Estate Duration," *JPM*, 1988-89, v15(1), 16-24.

Hartzell, David J., David G. Shulman and Charles H. Wurtzebach. "Refining The Analysis Of Regional Diversification For Income-Producing Real Estate," *JRER*, 1987, v2(2), 85-95.

Hartzell, David, John Hekman and Mike Miles. "Diversification Categories In Investment Real Estate," *AREUEA*, 1986, v14(2), 230-254.

Hartzell, David, John S. Hekman and Mike E. Miles. "Real Estate Returns And Inflation," *AREUEA*, 1987, v15(1), 617-637.

Hartzell, David. (Grissom, Terry V., David Hartzell and Crocker H. Liu. "An Approach To Industrial Real Estate Market Segmentation And Valuation Using The Arbitrage Pricing Paradigm," *AREUEA*, 1987, v15(3), 199-219.)

Hartzmark, Michael L. "Regulating Futures Margin Requirements," *RFM*, 1986, v5(3), 242-260.

Hartzmark, Michael L. "Is Risk Aversion A Theoretical Diversion?," *RFM*, 1988, v7(1), 1-26.

Hartzmark, Michael L. "Is Risk Aversion A Theoretical Diversion?," *RFM*, 1988, v7(1), 1-26.

Hartzmark, Michael L. "Luck Versus Forecast Ability: Determinants Of Trader Performance In Futures Markets," *JOB*, 1991, v64(1), 49-74.

Hartzmark, Michael L. "The Effects Of Changing Margin Levels On Futures Market Activity, The Composition Of Traders In The Market, And Price Performance," *JOB*, 1986, v59(2), Part 2, S147-S180.

Hartzog, B. G., Jr. (Kaplan, Donald M. and B. G. Hartzog, Jr. "Residential Mortgage Markets: Current Developments And Future Prospects," *AREUEA*, 1977, v5(3), 302-312.)

Harvey, Barrie. (Asabere, Paul K. and Barrie Harvey. "Factors Influencing The Value Of Urban Land: Evidence From Halifax-Dartmouth, Canada," *AREUEA*, 1985, v13(4), 361-377.)

Harvey, Campbell R. "Forecasts Of Economic Growth From The Bond And Stock Markets," *FAJ*, 1989, v45(5), 38-45.

Harvey, Campbell R. "The Real Term Structure And Consumption Growth," *JFEC*, 1988, v22(2), 305-334.

Harvey, Campbell R. "The World Price Of Covariance Risk," *JOF*, 1991, v46(1), 111-158.

Harvey, Campbell R. "Time-Varying Conditional Covariances In Tests Of Asset Pricing Models," *JFEC*, 1989, v24(2), 289-318.

Harvey, Campbell R. and Guofu Zhou. "Bayesian Inference In Asset Pricing Tests," *JFEC*, 1990, v26(2), 221-254.

Harvey, David W. (Young, S. David, Michael A. Berry, David W. Harvey and John R. Page. "Systematic Risk And Accounting Information Under The Arbitrage Pricing Theory," *FAJ*, 1987, v43(5), 73-76.)

Harvey, Julien H. "The Place Of Manpower In Our Victory Program," *JRI*, 1942, v9, 22-28.

Harwayne, Frank. "Personal Premium Saving Under Basic Protection," *JRI*, 1969, v36(2), 239-252.

Hasbrouck, Joel and Robert A. Schwartz. "Liquidity And Execution Costs In Equity Markets," *JPM*, 1987-88, v14(3), 10-17.

Hasbrouck, Joel and Thomas S. Y. Ho. "Order Arrival, Quote Behavior, And The Return-Generating Process," *JOF*, 1987, v42(4), 1035-1048.

Hasbrouck, Joel. "Measuring The Information Content Of Stock Trades," *JOF*, 1991, v46(1), 179-208.

Hasbrouck, Joel. "On Estimates Of Long-Run Rates Of Return: A Note," *JFQA*, 1983, v18(4), 455-461.

Hasbrouck, Joel. "Stock Returns, Inflation, And Economic Activity: The Survey Evidence," *JOF*, 1984, v39(5), 1293-1310.

Hasbrouck, Joel. "The Characteristics Of Takeover Targets," *JBF*, 1985, v9(3), 351-362.

Hasbrouck, Joel. (Friend, Irwin and Joel Hasbrouck. "Determinants Of Capital Structure," *RIF*, 1988, v7, 1-20.)

Hasbrouck, Joel. Trades, Quotes, Inventories, And Information," *JFEC*, 1988, v22(2), 229-252.

Hashmi, Sajjad A. "The Problem Of The Uninsured Motorist: A Proposed Solution," *JRI*, 1967, v34(3), 363-370.

Hashmi, Sajjad A. "Unsatisfied Judgment Funds," *JRI*, 1964, v31(1), 93-110.

Haskell, George D. "Taxation Of Property And Casualty Insurance Companies," *JRI*, 1959, v26(1), 31-39.

Haskins, Mark E. (Gombola, Michael J., Mark E. Haskins, J. Edward Ketz and David D. Williams. "Cash Flow In Bankruptcy Prediction," *FM*, 1987, v16(4),55-65.)

Haslag, Joseph H. and Scott E. Hein. "Federal Reserve System Reserve Requirements, 1959-1988," *JMCB*, 1989, v21(4), 515-523.

Haslam, J. (Barnes, Paul, S. P. Chakravarty and J. Haslam. "Bargaining Power, Dissimulation And Takeovers In A Rational Market With Asymmetric Information," *JBFA*, 1990, v17(4), 529-540.)

Haslanger, Barbara L. (Brightman, Jon S. and Barbara L. Haslanger. "Past Investment Performance: Seductive But Deceptive," *JPM*, 1979-80, v6(2), 43-45.)

Haslem, John A. and William Longbrake. "A Credit-Scoring Model For Commercial Loans: A Comment," *JMCB*, 1972, v4(3), 733-734.

Haslem, John A. and William A. Longbrake. "A Note On Average Interest Charges On Bank Loans, The Loan Mix, And Measures Of Competition," *JOF*, 1971, v26(1), 159-164.

Haslem, John A. "A Note On The Profitability Of Commercial Bank Trust Departments," *JBR*, 1974-75, v5(4), 260-263.

Haslem, John A. "A Statistical Analysis Of The Relative Profitability Of Commercial Banks," *JOF*, 1968, v23(1), 167-176.

Haslem, John A. "A Statistical Estimation Of Commercial Bank Profitability," *JOB*, 1969, v42(1),22-35.

Haslem, John A. (Anderson, R. N., John A. Haslem and John B. Leonard. "An Empirical Analysis Of The Impact Of Branching On Demand Deposit Variability," *JFQA*, 1976, v11(3), 455-464.)

Haslem, John A. (Baker, H. Kent and John A. Haslem. "Toward The Development Of Client-Specified Valuation Models," *JOF*, 1974, v29(4), 1255-1263.)

Haslem, John A. (Baker, H. Kent, Michael B. Hargrove and John A. Haslem. "An Empirical Analysis Of The Risk-Return Preferences Of Individual Investors," *JFQA*, 1977, v12(3), 377-389.)

Haslem, John A. (Longbrake, W.A. and J.A. Haslem. "Productive Efficiency In Commercial Banking: The Effects Of Size And Legal Form Of Organization On The Cost Of Producing Demand Deposit Services," *JMCB*, 1975, v7(3),317-330.)

Haslem, John A. (McConnell, Dennis, John A. Haslem and Virginia R. Gibson. "The President's Letter To Stockholders: A New Look," *FAJ*, 1986, v42(5), 66-70.)

Haslem, John A. (Rice, John G. and John A. Haslem. "Use Of Computer-Based Simulation Cases For Educational Programs In Financial Institutions," *JFED*, 1981, v10, 91-108.)

Hass, Jerome E. "Prescription For An Ailing Con Ed," *FAJ*, 1974, v30(6), 30-37.

Hass, Jerome E. (Bierman, Harold, Jr. and Jerome E. Hass. "An Analytical Model Of Bond Risk Differentials," *JFQA*, 1975, v10(5), 757-773.)

Hass, Jerome E. (Bierman, Harold, Jr. and Jerome E. Hass. "Capital Budgeting Under Uncertainty: A Reformulation," *JOF*, 1973, v28(1), 119-129.)

Hass, Jerome E. (Bierman, Harold, Jr. and Jerome E. Hass. "An Analytical Model Of Bond Risk Differentials: A Reply," *JFQA*, 1978, v13(2), 379-381.)

Hass, Jerome E. (Bierman, Harold, Jr., David H. Downes and Jerome E. Hass. "Closed-Form Stock Price Models," *JFQA*, 1972, v7(3), 1797-1808.)

Hass, Jerome E. (Bierman, Harold, Jr. and Jerome E. Hass. "Investment Cut-Off Rates And Dividend Policy," **FM**, 1983, v12(4), 19-24.)

Hass, Jerome E. (Bierman, Harold, Jr. and Jerome E. Hass. "Capital Budgeting Under Uncertainty: A Reformation: Reply," **JOF**, 1974, v29(5), 1585.)

Hass, Jerome. (Bierman, Harold, Jr. and Jerome Hass. "Normative Stock Price Models," **JFQA**, 1971, v6(4), 1135-1144.)

Hassan, Mahmud. (Hoerger, Thomas J., Frank A. Sloan and Mahmud Hassan. "Loss Volatility, Bankruptcy, And The Demand For Reinsurance," **JRU**, 1990, v3(3), 221-246.)

Hassan, Mahmud. (Wedig, Gerard, Frank A. Sloan, Mahmud Hassan and Michael A. Morrisey. "Capital Structure, Ownership, And Capital Payment Policy: The Case Of Hospitals," **JOF**, 1988, v43(1), 21-40.)

Hassan, Mahmud. (Wedig, Gerard J., Mahmud Hassan and Frank A. Sloan. "Hospital Investment Decisions And The Cost Of Capital," **JOB**, 1989, v62(4), 517-538.)

Hasselback, James R. (Braswell, Ronald C., Walter J. Reinhart and James R. Hasselback. "The Tax Treatment Of Municipal Discount Bonds: Correction Of A Fallacy," **FM**, 1982, v11(1), 77-81.)

Hasselback, James R. (Comiskey, Eugene E. and James R. Hasselback. "Analyzing The Profit-Tax Relationship," **FM**, 1973, v2(4), 57-62.)

Hasseldine, C. R. "The Information Content Of Rights Trading: A Comment," **JBFA**, 1981, v8(3),431-439.

Hassell, John M., Robert H. Jennings and Dennis J. Lasser. "Management Earnings Forecasts: Their Usefulness As A Source Of Firm-Specific Information To Security Analysts," **JFR**, 1988, v11(4), 303-320.

Hastie, K. Larry. "A Perspective On Management Education," **FM**, 1982, v11(4), 55-62.

Hastie, K. Larry. "Determinants Of Municipal Bond Yields," **JFQA**, 1972, v7(3), 1729-1748.

Hastie, K. Larry. "One Businessman's View Of Capital Budgeting," **FM**, 1974, v3(4), 36-44.

Hastings, Alan W. "Depreciation And Utility Security Analysis," **FAJ**, 1945, v1(4), 3-12.

Hastings, Harold M. (Francis, Jack Clark, Harold M. Hastings and Frank J. Fabozzi. "Bankruptcy As A Mathematical Catastrophe," **RIF**, 1983, v4, 63-90.)

Hasty, John M., Jr. and Bruce D. Fielitz. "Systematic Risk For Heterogeneous Time Horizons," **JOF**, 1975, v30(2), 659-673.

Hatch, James E. and Robert W. White. "A Canadian Perspective On Canadian And United States Capital Market Returns: 1950-1983," **FAJ**, 1986, v42(3),60-68.

Hatfield, Kenneth. (Reilly, Frank K. and Kenneth Hatfield. "Experience With New Stock Issues," **FAJ**, 1969, v25(5), 73-78.)

Hathaway, Donald D. "Managing Balances In Lock Box Accounts," **JBR**, 1977-78, v8(1), 59-62.

Haubrich, Joseph G. "Financial Intermediation: Delegated Monitoring And Long-Term Relationships," **JBF**, 1989, v13(1), 9-20.

Haug, Alfred A. "Ricardian Equivalence, Rational Expectations, And The Permanent Income Hypothesis," **JMCB**, 1990, v22(3), 305-326.

Haugen, Robert A. and A. James Heins. "Risk And Rate Of Return On Financial Assets: Some Old Wine In New Bottles," **JFQA**, 1975, v10(5), 775-784.

Haugen, Robert A. and Charles O. Kroncke. "Rate Regulation And The Cost Of Capital In The Insurance Industry," **JFQA**, 1971, v6(5), 1283-1305.

Haugen, Robert A. and Dean W. Wichern. "The Intricate Relationship Between Financial Leverage And The Stability Of Stock Prices," **JOF**, 1975, v30(5), 1283-1292.

Haugen, Robert A. and Dean W. Wichern. "The Term Of A Risk-Free Security," **JFQA**, 1980, v15(1), 41-52.

Haugen, Robert A. and Dean W. Wichern. "The Elasticity Of Financial Assets," **JOF**, 1974, v29(4), 1229-1240.

Haugen, Robert A. and Dean W. Wichern. "The Diametric Effects Of The Capital Gains Tax On The Stability Of Stock Prices," **JOF**, 1973, v28(4), 987-996.

Haugen, Robert A. and James L. Pappas. "A Comment On The Capital Structure And The Cost Of Capital: A Suggested Exposition," **JOF**, 1970, v25(3), 674-677.

Haugen, Robert A. and James L. Pappas. "Equilibrium In The Pricing Of Capital Assets, Risk-Bearing Debt Instruments, And The Question Of Optimal Capital Structure," **JFQA**, 1971, v6(3), 943-953.

Haugen, Robert A. and James L. Pappas. "Equilibrium In Pricing Of Capital Assets, Risk-Bearing Debt Instruments, And The Question Of Optimal Capital Structure: A Reply," **JFQA**, 1972, v7(4), 2005-2008.

Haugen, Robert A. and Jon G. Udell. "Rates Of Return To Stockholders Of Acquired Company Rates," **JFQA**, 1972, v7(1), 1387-1398.

Haugen, Robert A. and Lemma W. Senbet. "Resolving The Agency Problems Of External Capital Through Options," **JOF**, 1981, v36(3), 629-647.

Haugen, Robert A. and Lemma W. Senbet. "The Role Of Options In The Resolution Of Agency Problems: A Reply," **JOF**, 1986, v41(5), 1171-1174.

Haugen, Robert A. and Lemma W. Senbet. "New Perspectives On Informational Asymmetry And Agency Relationships," **JFQA**, 1979, v14(4), 671-694.

Haugen, Robert A. and Lemma W. Senbet. "The Insignificance Of Bankruptcy Costs To The Theory Of Optimal Capital Structure," **JOF**, 1978, v33(2), 383-393.

Haugen, Robert A. and Lemma W. Senbet. "Corporate Finance And Taxes: A Review," **FM**, 1985, v15(3),5-21.

Haugen, Robert A. and Prem Kumar. "The Traditional Approach To Valuing Levered-Growth Stocks: A Clarification," **JFQA**, 1974, v9(6), 1031-1044.

Haugen, Robert A. and Terence C. Langetieg. "An Empirical Test For Synergism In Merger," **JOF**, 1975, v30(4), 1003-1014.

Haugen, Robert A. "Common Stock Quality Ratings And Risk," **FAJ**, 1979, v35(2), 68-71.

Haugen, Robert A. "Expected Growth, Required Return, And The Variability Of Stock Prices," **JFQA**, 1970, v5(3), 297-307.

Haugen, Robert A. "Insurer Risk Under Alternative Investment And Financing Strategies," **JRI**, 1971, v38(1), 71-80.

Haugen, Robert A. "Pension Management In The Context Of Corporate Risk Management," **JPM**, 1989, v16(1), 72-78.

Haugen, Robert A. (Barnea, Amir, Robert A. Haugen and Lemma W. Senbet. "A Rationale For Debt Maturity Structure And Call Provisions In The Agency Theoretic Framework," **JOF**, 1980, v35(5), 1223-1234.)

Haugen, Robert A. (Barnea, Amir, Robert A. Haugen and Lemma W. Senbet. "Market Imperfections, Agency Problems, And Capital Structure: A Review," **FM**, 1981, v10(3), 7-22.)

Haugen, Robert A. (Barnea, Amir, Eli Talmor and Robert A. Haugen. "Debt And Taxes: A Multiperiod Investigation," **JBF**, 1987, v11(1), 79-98.)

Haugen, Robert A. (Barnea, Amir, Robert A. Haugen and Lemma W. Senbet. "An Equilibrium Analysis Of Debt Financing Under Costly Tax Arbitrage And Agency Problems," **JOF**, 1981, v36(3), 569-581.)

Haugen, Robert A. (Barnea, Amir, Robert A. Haugen and Lemma W. Senbet. "Management Of Corporate Risk," **AFPAF**, 1985, v1(1), 1-28.)

Haugen, Robert A. (Ferris, Stephen, Robert Haugen and Anil K. Makhija. "Predicting Contemporary Volume With Historic Volume At Differential Price Levels: Evidence Supporting The Disposition Effect," **JOF**, 1988, v43(3), 677-697.)

Haugen, Robert A. (Langetieg, Terence C., Robert A. Haugen and Dean W. Wichern. "Merger And Stockholder Risk," **JFQA**, 1980, v15(3), 689-717.)

Haugen, Robert A. (Schlater, John E., Robert A. Haugen and Dean W. Wichern. "Trading Based On Forecasts Of Earnings Per Share: A Test Of The Efficient Market Hypothesis," **JBF**, 1980, v4(2), 197-211.)

Haugen, Robert A. and Charles O. Kroncke. "Optimizing The Structure Of Capital Claims And Assets Of A Stock Insurance Company," **JRI**, 1970, v37(1), 41-48.

Haugen, Robert A. and Charles O. Kroncke. "Optimizing The Structure Of Capital Claims And Assets Of A Stock Insurance Company: Reply," **JRI**, 1972, v39(2), 313-316.

Haugen, Robert A. and Lemma W. Senbet. "On The Resolution Of Agency Problems By Complex Financial Instruments: A Reply," **JOF**, 1987, v42(4), 1091-1095.

Haugen, Robert A. and Lemma W. Senbet. "Bankruptcy And Agency Costs: Their Significance To The Theory Of Optimal Capital Structure," **JFQA**, 1988, v23(1), 27-38.

Haugen, Robert A. and Nardin L. Baker. "Dedicated Stock Portfolios," **JPM**, 1990, v16(4), 17-22.

Haugen, Robert A. and Nardin L. Baker. "The Efficient Market Inefficiency Of Capitalization-Weighted Stock Portfolios," **JPM**, 1991, v17(3), 35-40.

Haugen, Robert A., Alvin L. Stroyny and Dean W. Wichern. "Rate Regulation, Capital Structure, And The Sharing Of Interest Rate Risk In The Electric Utility Industry," **JOF**, 1978, v33(2), 707-721.

Haugen, Robert A., Edgar Ortiz and Enrique Arjona. "Market Efficiency: Mexico Versus The U.S.," **JPM**, 1985-86, v12(1), 28-32.

Haugen, Robert A., Lemma W. Senbet and Eli Talmor. "Debt, Dividends, And Taxes: Equilibrium Conditions For Simultaneous Tax Neutrality Of Debt And Dividend Policies," **RIF**, 1986, v6, 1-28.

Haugen, Robert. (Talmor, Eli, Robert Haugen and Amir Barnea. "The Value Of The Tax Subsidy On Risky Debt," **JOB**, 1985, v58(2), 191-202.)

Haurin, Donald R. (Hendershott, Patric H. and Donald R. Haurin. "Adjustments In The Real Estate Market," **AREUEA**, 1988, v16(4), 343-353.)

Haurin, Donald R. (Hendershott, Patric H. and Donald R. Haurin. "Research On Real Estate Investment," **AREUEA**, 1990, v18(4), 369-376.)

Haurin, Donald. "The Duration Of Marketing Time Of Residential Housing," **AREUEA**, 1988, v16(4), 396-410.

Hausafus, Kurt F. "Financial Institutions And International Capital Movements: Portfolio Selection Or Trade Finance?," **JMCB**, 1976, v8(3), 359-371.

Hausch, Donald B. and William T. Ziemba. "Arbitrage Strategies For Cross-Track Betting On Major Horse Races," **JOB**, 1990, v63(1), Part 1, 61-78.

Hauser, R. J. and J. S. Eales. "On Marketing Strategies With Options: A Technique To Measure Risk And Return," **JFM**, 1986, v6(2), 273-288.

Hauser, Robert J. and David Neff. "Pricing Options On Agricultural Futures: Departures From Traditional Theory," **JFM**, 1985, v5(4), 539-577.

Hauser, Robert J. (Eales, James and Robert J. Hauser. "Analyzing Biases In Valuation Models Of Options On Futures," **JFM**, 1990, v10(3), 211-228.)

Hauser, Robert J. and Jordan Buck. "The Feasibility Of A Futures Market For Barge Grain Freight," **RFM**, 1989, v8(1), 1-15.

Hauser, S. (Choi, J. J. and S. Hauser. "The Effects Of Domestic And Foreign Yield Curves On The Value Of Currency American Call Options," **JBF**, 1990, v14(1), 41-54.)

Hauser, Shmuel. (Choi, Jongmoo Jay and Shmuel Hauser. "The Value Of Foreign Currency Options And The Term Structure Of Interest Rates," **RDIBF**, 1989, v3, 149-158.)

Hausman, W. H. and W. L. White. "Theory Of Option Strategy Under Risk Aversion," **JFQA**, 1968, v3(3), 343-358.

Hausman, W. H., R. R. West and J. A. Largay. "Stock Splits, Price Changes, And Trading Profits: A Synthesis," **JOB**, 1971, v44(1), 69-77.

Hausman, Warren H. "A Note On 'The Value Line Contest: A Test Of The Predictability Of Stock-Price Changes'," **JOB**, 1969, v42(3), 317-320.

Hausman, Warren H. (Courville, Leon and Warren H. Hausman. "Warranty Scope And Reliability Under Imperfect Information And Alternative Market Structures," **JOB**, 1979, v52(3), 361-378.)

Hausmann, Robert, Jr. (Gandhi, Devinder K., Robert Hausmann, Jr. and Anthony Saunders. "On Syndicate Sharing Rules For Unanimous Project Rankings," **JBF**, 1985, v9(4), 517-534.)

Havighurst, Harold C. "State Vs. Federal Regulation Of Insurance," **JRI**, 1941, v8, 57-67.

Havrikesky, Thomas. "A Comment On Niehans' Innovation In Monetary Policy," JBF, 1986, v10(4), 611-614.
Havrilesky, Thomas and Robert Schweitzer. "Non-Price Competition Among Banking Firms," JBR, 1975-76, v6(2), 113-121.
Havrilesky, Thomas M. "A Partisanship Theory Of Fiscal And Monetary Regimes," JMCB, 1987, v19(3), 308-325.
Havrilesky, Thomas. "A Practicable Program For Monetary Stability," FR, 1982, v17(1), 63-66.
Havrilesky, Thomas. "Finding The Optimal Monetary Strategy With Information Constraints," JOF, 1972, v27(5), 1045-1056.
Havrilesky, Thomas. "Informationally Optimal Monetary And Fiscal Policy," FR, 1982, v17(4), 259-270.
Havrilesky, Thomas. "Monetary Policy Signaling From The Administration To The Federal Reserve," JMCB, 1988, v20(1), 83-101.
Havrilesky, Thomas. "The Causes And Consequences Of Big Bank PAC Contributions," JFSR, 1990, v4(3), 243-249.
Havrilesky, Thomas. "The Influence Of The Federal Advisory Council On Monetary Policy," JMCB, 1990, v22(1), 37-50.
Havrilesky, Thomas. "The Optimal Proximity Of Monetary Policy Target Variable: A Comment," JMCB, 1972, v4(2), 456-464.
Haw, In-Mu and Byung T. Ro. "Firm Size, Reporting Lags And Market Reactions To Earnings Releases," JBFA, 1990, v17(4), 557-574.
Haw, In-Mu, William Ruland and Ahmed Hamdallah. "Investor Evaluation Of Overfunded Pension Plan Terminations," JFR, 1988, v11(1), 81-88.
Hawawini, Gabriel A. and Ashok Vora. "Is Adjusting Beta Estimates An Illusion?," JPM, 1983-84, v10(1), 23-26.
Hawawini, Gabriel A. and Ashok Vora. "The CAPM And The Investment Horizon: Comment," JPM, 1982-83, v9(1), 66-68.
Hawawini, Gabriel A. and Ashok Vora. "Investment Horizon, Diversification, And The Efficiency Of Alternative Beta Forecasts," JFR, 1982, v5(1), 1-15.
Hawawini, Gabriel A. and Ashok Vora. "Evidence Of Intertemporal Systematic Risks In The Daily Price Movements Of NYSE And AMEX Common Stocks," JFQA, 1980, v15(2), 331-339.
Hawawini, Gabriel A. and Ashok Vora. "Yield Approximations: A Historical Perspective," JOF, 1982, v37(1), 145-156.
Hawawini, Gabriel A. and Pierre A. Michel. "The Pricing Of Risky Assets On The Belgian Stock Market," JBF, 1982, v6(2), 161-178.
Hawawini, Gabriel A. "An Analytical Examination Of The Intervaling Effect Of Skewness And Other Moments," JFQA, 1980, v15(5), 1121-1127.
Hawawini, Gabriel A. "Intertemporal Cross-Dependence In Securities Daily Returns And The Short-Run Intervaling Effect On Systematic Risk," JFQA, 1980, v15(1), 139-149.
Hawawini, Gabriel A. "The Intertemporal Cross Price Behavior Of Common Stocks: Evidence And Implications," JFR, 1980, v3(2), 153-167.
Hawawini, Gabriel A. (Cohen, Kalman, Gabriel Hawawini, Steven Maier, Robert Schwartz And David Whitcomb. "Implications Of Microstructure Theory For Empirical Research On Stock Price Behavior," JOF, 1980, v35(2), 249-257.)
Hawawini, Gabriel A. (Cohen, Kalman J., Gabriel A. Hawawini, Steven F. Maier, Robert A. Schwartz and David K. Whitcomb. "Friction In The Trading Process And The Estimation Of Systematic Risk," JFEC, 1983, v12(2), 263-278.)
Hawawini, Gabriel A., Pierre A. Michel and Claude J. Viallet. "As Assessment Of Risk And Return Of French Common Stocks," JBFA, 1983, v10(3), 333-350.
Hawawini, Gabriel A., Pierre A. Michel and Albert Corhay. "New Evidence On Beta Stationarity And Forecast For Belgian Common Stocks," JBF, 1985, v9(4), 553-560.
Hawawini, Gabriel. "Why Beta Shifts As The Return Interval Changes," FAJ, 1983, v39(3), 73-77.
Hawawini, Gabriel. (Corhay, Albert, Gabriel Hawawini and Pierre Michel. "Seasonality In The Risk-Return Relationship: Some International Evidence," JOF, 1987, v42(1), 49-68.)
Hawawini, Garbriel and Ashok Vora. "Proportional Vs. Logarithmic Models Of Asset Pricing," RIF, 1985, v5, 1-24.
Hawk, Stephen L. (Cramer, Robert H. and Stephen L. Hawk. "The Consideration Of Coupon Levels, Taxes, Reinvestment Rates, And Maturity In The Investment Management Of Financial Institutions," JFQA, 1975, v10(1), 67-84.)
Hawke, G. (Briscoe, G. and G. Hawke. "Long-Term Debt And Realisable Gains In Shareholder Wealth: An Empirical Study," JBFA, 1976, v3(1), 125-136.)
Hawke, John D., Jr. (Miller, Merton H., Burton Malkiel, Myron Scholes and John D. Hawke, Jr. "Stock Index Futures And The Crash Of '87," JACF, 1989, v1(4), 6-17.)
Hawkins, C. A. (Draper, J. E. and C. A. Hawkins. "On The Transactions Demand For Cash: Comment," JOF, 1969, v24(5), 942-949.)
Hawkins, C. A. (Frankle, A. W. and C. A. Hawkins. "Beta Coefficients For Convertible Bonds," JOF, 1975, v30(1), 207-210.)
Hawkins, Clark A. and Richard A. Adams. "A Goal Programming Model For Capital Budgeting," FM, 1974, v3(1), 52-57.
Hawkins, Clark A. (Sorensen, Eric H. and Clark A. Hawkins. "The Demand For Preferred Stock With Sinking Funds And Without: A Note," JOF, 1982, v37(1),237-241.)
Hawkins, Clark A. (Sorensen, Eric H. and Clark A. Hawkins. "On The Pricing Of Preferred Stock," JFQA, 1981, v16(4), 515-528.)
Hawkins, David F. "Toward An Old Theory Of Equity Valuation," FAJ, 1977, v33(6), 48-53.
Hawkins, Del I. "The Impact Of Sponsor Identification And Direct Disclosure Of Respondent Rights On The Quantity And Quality Of Mail Survey Data," JOB, 1979, v52(4), 577-590.
Hawkins, Del I., Gerald Albaum and Roger Best. "An Investigation Of Two Issues In The Use Of Students As Surrogates For Housewives In Consumer Behavior Studies," JOB, 1977, v50(2), 216-221.
Hawkins, Eugene H., Stanley C. Chamberlin and Wayne E. Daniel. "Earnings Expectations And Security Prices," FAJ, 1984, v40(5), 24-27,30-38,74.
Hawkins, Gregory D. "An Analysis Of Revolving Credit Agreements," JFEC, 1982, v10(1), 59-81.
Hawkins, Robert G. and C. Rangarajan. "On The Distribution Of New International Reserves," JOF, 1970, v25(4), 881-891.
Hawkins, Robert G. and Donald Macaluso. "The Avoidance Of Restrictive Monetary Policies In Host Countries By Multinational Firms," JMCB, 1977, v9(4), 562-571.
Hawley, Delvin D., John D. Johnson and Dijjotam Raina. "Artificial Neural Systems: A New Tool For Financial Decision-Making," FAJ, 1990, v46(6), 63-72.
Haworth, Hugh R. (Chuppe, Terry M., Hugh R. Haworth and Marvin G. Watkins. "Public Policy Toward The International Bond Markets In The 1980s," AFPAF, 1990, v5(1), 3-30.)
Haworth, Hugh R. (Chuppe, Terry M., Hugh R. Haworth and Marvin G. Watkins. "Global Finance: Causes, Consequences And Prospects For The Future," GFJ, 1989, v1(1), 1-20.)
Hawthorne, William H. (Bloom, Robert, Pieter T. Elgers, James R. Haltiner and William H. Hawthorne. "Inflation Gains And Losses On Monetary Items: An Empirical Test," JBFA, 1980, v7(4), 603-618.)
Hawthorne, William H. (Elgers, Pieter T., James R. Haltiner and William H. Hawthorne. "Beta Regression Tendencies: Statistical And Real Causes," JOF, 1979, v34(1), 261-263.)
Hayden, Steven C. (Winger, Bernard J., Carl R. Chen, John D. Martin, J. William Petty and Steven C. Hayden. "Adjustable Rate Preferred Stock," FM, 1986, v15(1), 48-57.)
Haydon, Randall B. and John H. Wicks. "A Model Of Commercial Banking Earning Assets Selection," JFQA, 1966, v1(2), 99-114.
Hayenga, Marvin L. and Dennis D. Dipietre. "Hedging Wholesale Meat Prices: Analysis Of Basis Risk," JFM, 1982, v2(2), 131-140.
Hayenga, Marvin L. (Schroeder, Ted C. and Marvin L. Hayenga. "Comparison Of Selective Hedging And Options Strategies In Cattle Feedlot Risk Management," JFM, 1988, v8(2), 141-156.)
Hayenga, Marvin L. (Witt, Harvey J., Ted C. Schroeder and Marvin L. Hayenga. "Comparison Of Analytical Approaches For Estimating Hedge Ratios For Agricultural Commodities," JFM, 1987, v7(2), 135-146.)
Hayenga, Marvin L., Dennis D. Dipietre, J. Marvin Skadberg and Ted C. Schroeder. "Profitable Hedging Opportunities And Risk Premiums For Producers In Live Cattle And Live Hog Futures Markets," JFM, 1984, v4(2), 141-154.
Hayes, Beth and Daniel Siegel. "Rate Of Return Regulation With Price Flexibility," JOB, 1986, v59(4), Part 1, 537-554.
Hayes, Beth. "Competition And Two-Part Tariffs," JOB, 1987, v60(1), 41-54.
Hayes, Douglas A. "Common Stocks And 'Safety Of Principal'," JOF, 1950, v5(4), 387-399.
Hayes, Douglas A. "Depreciation Policies And Earning Power," FAJ, 1955, v11(2), 79-86.
Hayes, Douglas A. "Ethical Considerations In The Professional Stature Of Analysts," FAJ, 1962, v18(5), 53-56.
Hayes, Douglas A. "Evaluating The Investment Management Record Of Fire Insurance Companies," FAJ, 1958, v14(4), 57-60.
Hayes, Douglas A. "Potential For Professional Status," FAJ, 1967, v23(6), 29-31.
Hayes, Douglas A. "Public Utility Returns On Equity," FAJ, 1970, v26(5), 102-106.
Hayes, Douglas A. "Techniques For Appraising Growth Rates," FAJ, 1964, v20(4), 96-101.
Hayes, Douglas A. "The Dimensions Of Analysis (Keynote Review)," FAJ, 1966, v22(5), 81.
Hayes, Douglas A. "The Evaluation Of Management," FAJ, 1968, v24(4), 39-42.
Hayes, Douglas A. "The Multi-Dimensional Aspects Of Risk," JPM, 1975-76, v2(4), 23-28.
Hayes, Douglas A. "The Undervalued Issue Strategy," FAJ, 1967, v23(3), 121-127.
Hayes, Douglas A. (Adderley, Terence E. and Douglas A. Hayes. "The Investment Performance Of Selected Growth Stock Portfolios: 1939-55," FAJ, 1957, v13(2), 65-78.)
Hayes, S. L. and R. A. Taussig. "Are Cash Take-Over Bids Unethical?," FAJ, 1967, v23(1), 107-111.
Hayes, Samuel L., III and Michael E. Tennenbaum. "The Impact Of Listed Options On The Underlying Shares," FM, 1979, v8(4), 72-76.
Hayes, Samuel L., III. (Crane, Dwight B. and Samuel L. Hayes, III. "The Evolution Of International Banking Competition And Its Implications For Regulation," JBR, 1983-84, v14(1), 39-52.)
Hayes, William and T. Mills Shepard. "How Publishing People Follow Magazine Fortunes," FAJ, 1951, v7(4), 34-36.
Hayford, Marc. "Liquidity Constraints And The Ricardian Equivalence Theorem," JMCB, 1989, v21(3), 380-387.
Haymes, Harmon H. "'Is The Federal Reserve System Really Necessary?': Comment," JOF, 1965, v20(3), 480-482.
Hayn, Carla. "Tax Attributes As Determinants Of Shareholder Gains In Corporate Acquisitions," JFEC, 1989, v23(1), 121-154.
Hayre, Lakhbir S. "Understanding Option-Adjusted Spreads And Their Use," JPM, 1990, v16(4), 68-69.
Hays, Ellen M. (Meehan, John P. and Ellen M. Hays. "Hidden Dangers In Modern Portfolio Theory," JPM, 1978-79, v5(3), 48-51.)
Hays, Patrick A. and David E. Upton. "A Shifting Regimes Approach To The Stationarity Of The Market Model Parameters Of Individual Securities," JFQA, 1986, v21(3), 307-321.
Hays, Patrick A., David S. Kidwell and M. Wayne Marr. "The Effect Of Market Uncertainty On Negotiated And Competitively Underwritten Public Utility Bonds," FR, 1984, v19(4), 339-350.
Hays, Patrick A., Michael D. Joehnk and Ronald W. Melicher. "Differential Determinants Of Risk Premiums In The Public And Private Corporate Bond Markets," JFR, 1979, v2(2), 143-152.
Haywood, C. F. (Greenbaum, S. I. and C. F. Haywood. "Secular Change In The Financial Services Industry," JMCB, 1971, v3(2), Part 2, 571-589.)
Haywood, Charles F. "A Comment On 'The Federal Home Loan Bank System And The Control Of Credit'," JOF, 1958, v13(4), 542-544.
Haywood, Charles F. "The Adequacy Of Federal Reserve Powers To Discharge Responsibilities," JOF, 1959, v14(2), 135-144.
Hayya, J. (Gressis, N., G. C. Philippatos and J. Hayya. "Multiperiod Portfolio Analysis And The Inefficiency Of The Market Portfolio," JOF, 1976, v31(4), 1115-1126.)
Hayya, Jack C. (Saniga, Erwin M. and Jack C. Hayya. "Simple Goodness-Of-Fit Tests For Symmetric Stable Distributions," JFQA,

1977, v12(2), 276-289.)

Hayya, Jack. (Gressis, Nicholas, Jack Hayya and George Philippatos. "Multiperiod Portfolio Efficiency Analysis Via The Geometric Mean," FR, 1974, v9(1),46-63.)

Hayya, Jack. (Saniga, Erwin, Nicholas Gressis and Jack Hayya. "The Effects Of Sample Size And Correlation On The Accuracy Of The EV Efficient Criterion," JFQA, 1979, v14(3), 615-628.)

Hazuka, Thomas B. "Consumption Betas And Backwardation In Commodity Markets," JOF, 1984, v39(3),647-655.

He, Hua. "Convergence From Discrete- To Continuous-Time Contingent Claims Prices," RFS, 1990, v3(4), 523-546.

Head, George L. "An Alternative To Defining Risk As Uncertainty," JRI, 1967, v34(2), 205-214.

Head, George L. "Optimizing Property Insurance Deductibles, A Theoretical Model For The Corporate Buyer," JRI, 1965, v32(3), 337-348.

Head, George L. "Underwriting - In Five Easy Lessons?," JRI, 1968, v35(2), 307-310.

Head, George L. (Smith, Michael L. and George L. Head. "Guidelines For Insurers In Pricing Deductibles," JRI, 1978, v45(2), 217-238.)

Headen, Alvin E., Jr. "The Relationship Between The Blue Cross Market Share And The Blue Cross 'Discount' On Hospital Charges: Comment," JRI, 1982, v49(4), 634.

Headen, Robert S. and J. Finley Lee. "Life Insurance Demand And Household Portfolio Behavior," JRI, 1974, v41(4), 685-698.

Headen, Robert S. and J. Finley Lee. "Life Insurance Demand And Household Portfolio Behavior: Reply," JRI, 1976, v43(2), 331-334.

Healy, C. Ross and Verne Henry Atrill. "Objective Economics: Will The Real Laffer Curve Please Stand Up?," FAJ, 1983, v39(2), 15-24.

Healy, Paul M. and Krishna G. Palepu. "Earnings Information Conveyed By Dividend Initiations And Omissions," JFEC, 1988, v21(2), 149-176.

Healy, Paul M. and Krishna G. Palepu. "How Investors Interpret Changes In Corporate Financial Policy," JACF, 1989, v2(3), 59-64.

Heaney, W. John and Pao L. Cheng. "Continuous Maturity Diversification Of Default-Free Bond Portfolios And A Generalization Of Efficient Diversification," JOF, 1984, v39(4), 1101-1117.

Heard, Edwin L. and Jerry E. Wheat. "Management Engineering In Large U.S. Banks," JBR, 1979-80, v10(4), 221-227.

Heard, Jamie. "Investor Responsibility: An Idea Whose Time Has Come?," JPM, 1977-78, v4(3), 12-14.

Hearth, Douglas and Janis K. Zaima. "Voluntary Corporate Divestitures And Value," FM, 1984, v13(1), 10-16.

Hearth, Douglas and Janis K. Zaima. "Divestiture Uncertainty And Shareholder Wealth: Evidence From The U.S.A. (1975-1982)," JBFA, 1986, v13(1), 71-85.

Hearth, Douglas. (Zaima, Janis K. and Douglas Hearth. "The Wealth Effects Of Voluntary Selloffs: Implications For Divesting And Acquiring Firms," JFR, 1985, v8(3), 217-226.)

Heath, Chip and Amos Tversky. "Preference And Belief: Ambiguity And Competence In Choice Under Uncertainty," JRU, 1991, v4(1), 5-28.

Heath, David C. and Robert A. Jarrow. "Arbitrage, Continuous Trading, And Margin Requirements," JOF, 1987, v42(5), 1129-1142.

Heath, David C. and Robert A. Jarrow. "Ex-Dividend Stock Price Behavior And Arbitrage Opportunities," JOB, 1988, v61(1), 95-108.

Heath, David, Robert Jarrow and Andrew Morton. "Bond Pricing And The Term Structure Of Interest Rates: A Discrete Time Approximation," JFQA, 1990, v25(4), 419-440.

Heath, Loyd C. "Calculation And Meaning Of Cash Flow In Security Analysis," FAJ, 1962, v18(5), 65-67.

Heathcotte, Bryan and Vincent P. Apilado. "The Predictive Content Of Some Leading Economic Indicators For Future Stock Prices," JFQA, 1974, v9(2), 247-258.

Heaton, C. P. "NGSEDECMH And HSCRCNGSEDECMH For Wealth Maximizing," JPM, 1976-77, v3(3), 5-17.

Heaton, Hal B. (Van Horne, James C. and Hal B. Heaton. "Securities Inventories And Excess Returns," JFR, 1983, v6(2), 93-102.)

Heaton, Hal B. (Van Horne, James C. and Hal B. Heaton. "Government Security Dealers' Positions, Information And Interest-Rate Expectations: A Note," JOF, 1983, v38(5), 1643-1649.)

Heaton, Hal. "Corporate Taxation And Leasing," JFQA, 1986, v21(3), 351-359.

Heaton, Hal. "On The Bias Of The Corporate Tax Against High-Risk Projects," JFQA, 1987, v22(3), 365-372.

Heaton, Hal. "On The Possible Tax-Driven Arbitrage Opportunities In The New Municipal Bonds Futures Contract," JFM, 1988, v8(3), 291-302.

Heaton, Hal. "The Relative Yields On Taxable And Tax-Exempt Debt," JMCB, 1986, v18(4), 482-494.

Heaton, Hal. "Volatilities Implied By Options Premia: A Test Of Market Efficiency," FR, 1986, v21(1), 37-49.

Heberton, William B. "Electric Utility Regulation," FAJ, 1961, v17(1), 61-69.

Hecht, M. J. (Franks, J. R., J. E. Broyles and M. J. Hecht. "An Industry Study Of The Profitability Of Mergers In The United Kingdom," JOF, 1977, v32(5), 1513-1525.)

Heck, J. Louis, Philip L. Cooley and Carl M. Hubbard. "Contributing Authors And Institutions To The Journal Of Finance: 1946-1985," JOF, 1986, v41(5), 1129-1140.

Heck, J. Louis. "A Historical Bibliography Of Finance Pedagogy," JFED, 1984, v13, 94-95.

Heck, J. Louis. (Cooley, Philip L. and J. Louis Heck. "A Survey Of The Introductory Business Finance Course: The Professor's Viewpoint," JFED, 1977, v6, 3-8.)

Heck, J. Louis. (Cooley, Philip L. and J. Louis Heck. "Significant Contributions To Finance Literature," FM, 1981, v10(2), Tenth Anniversary Edition, 23-33.)

Heck, J. Louis. (Holland, Michael M. and J. Louis Heck. "Investment Yields And Magic Triangles: A Computer Solution Based On The Newton-Rapheson Convergence Technique," JFED, 1984, v13, 72-79.)

Heck, Jean Louis and David E. Stout. "Initial Empirical Evidence On The Relationship Between Finance Test-Question Sequencing And Student Performance Scores," FPE, 1991, v1(1), 41-48.

Heck, Jean Louis and Philip L. Cooley. "Most Frequent Contributors To The Finance Literature," FM, 1988, v17(3), 100-108.

Heck, Jean L. and Philip L. Cooley. "From Intellectual Wave To Nobel Laureate," RQFA, 1991, v1(2), 215-216.

Heckerman, D. G. "Motivating Managers To Make Investment Decisions," JFEC, 1975, v2(3), 273-292.

Heckerman, Donald G. "Portfolio Selection When Future Prices Of Consumption Goods May Change: Reply," JOF, 1973, v28(5), 1361.

Heckerman, Donald G. "Portfolio Selection And The Structure Of Capital Asset Prices When Relative Prices Of Consumption Goods May Change," JOF, 1972, v27(1), 47-60.

Heckerman, Donald G. "Inefficient' European Capital Markets As An Explanation Of International Capital Movements: A Comment," JMCB, 1969, v1(1), 121-123.

Heckerman, Donald. "The Exchange Risks Of Foreign Operations," JOB, 1972, v45(1), 42-48.

Hedberg, Robert D. "Let's Regulate Investment Advice," FAJ, 1973, v29(3), 24-26,102.

Hedberg, Robert D. "Will The Boom Resume?," FAJ, 1958, v14(4), 9-14.

Hedberg, Robert. "The Nuclear Industry," FAJ, 1957, v13(2), 29-32.

Hedges, Bob A. "A Methodology For A Course In Risk Management," JRI, 1965, v32(4), 609-616.

Hedges, Bob A. "Content Of Education And Training Needed For Risk Management," JRI, 1970, v37(2), 278-280.

Hedges, Bob A. "Criteria For The Total Curriculum Of A School Of Business," JRI, 1968, v35(4), 602-606.

Hedges, Bob A. "Evaluation Of Property Insurance Companies' Expense Ratios," JRI, 1958, v25(4), 1-16.

Hedges, Bob A. "Gender Discrimination In Pension Plans: Comment," JRI, 1977, v44(1), 141-144.

Hedges, Bob A. "Insurance Rates And Investment Earnings Considered Together," JRI, 1969, v36(3), 455-462.

Hedges, Bob A. "Myths In Risk And Insurance: Maximum Risk Is A 50% Change Of Loss," JRI, 1978, v45(4), 699-703.

Hedges, Bob A. "On Positive Correlation Between Means And Standard Deviations Of Claims Ratios: Comment," JRI, 1981, v48(4), 649-652.

Hedges, Bob A. "On The Skinning Of Cats," JRI, 1973, v40(1), 1-6.

Hedges, Bob A. "Pricing And Underwriting Risk In Automobile Insurance: A Probabilistic View: Comment," JRI, 1975, v42(4), 647-650.

Hedges, Bob A. "Risk: Further Comments," JRI, 1964, v31(2), 301-302.

Hedges, Bob A. "Substandard Automobile Insurers: Comment," JRI, 1969, v36(4), 640-642.

Hedges, Bob A. "The Survival Probability Of A New Life Insurance Company: Comment," JRI, 1968, v35(3), 471-472.

Hedges, Bob A. (Mehr, Robert I. and Bob A. Hedges. "New Perspectives On Risk Management: Comment," JRI, 1968, v35(4), 615-623.)

Hedges, Bob A., Walter Williams and Henry K. Duke. "What Is Wrong With Insurance Theory?," JRI, 1964, v31(2), 279-284.

Hedges, Bob A. "Modifying The Business Financial Plan To Reduce Static Risk Management Costs," JOF, 1964, v19(2), Part 1, 340-348.

Hedges, Bob. "Proper Limits In Liability Insurance," JRI, 1961, v28(2), 71-76.

Hedges, J. Edward. "Presidential Address," JRI, 1961, v28(1), 1-6.

Hedges, J. Edward. "Report Of Publications Committee," JRI, 1942, v9, 20-21.

Hedges, J. Edward. "Teaching Insurance At An Advanced Level On The 'Line' Basis," JRI, 1955, v22, 19-22.

Hedges, J. Edward. "The Basic Life Insurance Course In The Curriculum," JRI, 1954, v21, 13-17.

Hedges, Robert A. "Experiment In Financial Analysis Of Property Insurers," JRI, 1956, v23, 142-146.

Heep, Don M. (Senchack, Andrew J., Jr. and Don M. Heep. "Auction Profits In The Treasury Bill Market," FM, 1974, v4(2), 45-52.)

Heffernan, S. A. "A Characteristics Definition Of Financial Markets," JBF, 1990, v14(2/3), 583-610.

Heffernan, Shelagh A. "Country Risk Analysis: The Demand And Supply Of Sovereign Loans," JIMF, 1985, v4(3), 389-413.

Heffley, Dennis R. and Daniel P. Hewitt. "Land-Use Zoning In A Local Economy With Optimal Property Taxes And Public Expenditures," JREFEC, 1988, v1(4), 373-392.

Heflebower, Richard B. "Economics Of Size," JOB, 1951, v24(4), 253-268.

Heflebower, Richard B. "Some Observations On Industrial Prices," JOB, 1954, v27(3), 187-195.

Hegde, Krishna and P. V. Viswanath. "Structure Stability With Ex-Ante Factor Specification In APT," IJOF, 1990, v3(1), 121-157.

Hegde, S. P. "An Ex Post Valuation Of The Quality Option Implicit In The Treasury Bond Futures Contract," JBF, 1990, v14(4), 741-760.

Hegde, Shantaram P. and Ben Branch. "An Empirical Analysis Of Arbitrage Opportunities In The Treasury Bill Futures Market," JFM, 1985, v5(3), 407-424.

Hegde, Shantaram P. and Bill McDonald. "On The Informational Role Of Treasury Bill Futures," JFM, 1986, v6(4), 629-643.

Hegde, Shantaram P. and Kenneth P. Nunn, Jr. "Interest Rate Volatility, Trading Volume, And The Hedging Performance Of T-Bond And GNMA Futures - A Note," JFM, 1985, v5(2), 273-286.

Hegde, Shantaram P. and Kenneth P. Nunn, Jr. "A Multivariate Analysis Of The Cross-Hedging Performance Of T-Bond And GNMA Futures Markets," FR, 1985, v20(2), 143-163.

Hegde, Shantaram P. "An Empirical Analysis Of Implicit Delivery Options In The Treasury Bond Futures Contract," JBF, 1988, v11(3), 469-492.

Hegde, Shantaram P. "Coupon And Maturity Characteristics Of The Cheapest-To-Deliver Bonds On The Treasury Bond Futures Contract," FAJ, 1987, v43(2), 70-76.

Hegde, Shantaram P. "On The Value Of The Implicit Delivery Options," JFM, 1989, v9(5), 421-438.

Hegde, Shantaram P. "The Forecast Performance Of Treasury Bond Futures Contracts," JBFA, 1987, v14(2), 291-304.

Hegde, Shantaram P. "The Impact Of Interest Rate Level And Volatility On The Performance Of Interest Rate Hedges," JFM, 1982, v2(4), 341-356.

Hegde, Shantaram P. (Finnerty, Joseph E., Thomas Schneeweis and Shantaram P. Hegde. "Interest Rates In The $Eurobond Market," *JFQA*, 1980, v15(3), 743-755.)

Hegde, Shantaram P. and Kenneth P. Nunn, Jr. "Non-Infinitesimal Rate Changes And Macaulay Duration," *JPM*, 1987-88, v14(2), 69-78.

Hegde, Shantaram P. and Robert E. Miller. "Market-Making In Initial Public Offerings Of Common Stocks: An Empirical Analysis," *JFQA*, 1989, v24(1), 75-90.

Hegel, Peter W. "Potential Uses Of The Municipal Bond Futures Contract By A Unit Investment Trust," *RFM*, 1985, v4(2), 260-267.

Heggestad, Arnold A. and John J. Mingo. "The Competitive Condition Of U. S. Banking Markets And The Impact Of Structural Form," *JOF*, 1977, v32(3),649-661.

Heggestad, Arnold A. and John J. Mingo. "Prices, Nonprices, And Concentration In Commercial Banking," *JMCB*, 1976, v8(1), 107-117.

Heggestad, Arnold A. and John J. Mingo. "On The Usefulness Of Functional Cost Analysis Data," *JBR*, 1977-78, v8(4), 251-256.

Heggestad, Arnold A. "Market Structure, Risk And Profitability In Commercial Banking," *JOF*, 1977, v32(4), 1207-1216.

Heggestad, Arnold A. (Blair, Roger D. and Arnold A. Heggestad. "Bank Portfolio Regulation And The Probability Of Bank Failure," *JMCB*, 1978, v10(1), 88-93.)

Heggestad, Arnold A. (Shome, Dilip K., Stephen D. Smith and Arnold A. Heggestad. "Capital Adequacy And The Valuation Of Large Commercial Banking Organizations," *JFR*, 1986, v9(4), 331-341.)

Heggestad, Arnold A. and John J. Mingo. "Capital Management By Holding Company Banks," *JOB*, 1975, v48(4), 500-505.

Heilbroner, Robert L. "The Adam Smith Nobody Knows," *JPM*, 1975-76, v2(4), 65-66.

Heilbrunn, Robert. "A Practical Approach To Common Stock Valuation," *FAJ*, 1958, v14(2), 49-52.

Heimann, John G. "The Effects Of Political, Economic And Institutional Development On International Banks," *JBF*, 1983, v7(4), 615-622.

Heimann, John. "The Problem Of Confidence In Domestic And International Banking Systems," *JBF*, 1982, v6(3), 429-435.

Hein, John. "A Note On The Giro Transfer System," *JOF*, 1959, v14(4), 548-554.

Hein, John. "A Note On The Use Of Index Clauses Abroad," *JOF*, 1960, v15(4), 546-552.

Hein, Scott E. "The Response Of Short-Term Interest Rates To Weekly Money Announcements: A Comment," *JMCB*, 1985, v17(2), 264-270.

Hein, Scott E. (Chatfield, Robert E., Scott E. Hein and R. Charles Moyer. "Long-Term Earnings Forecasts In The Electric Utility Industry: Accuracy And Valuation Implications," *FR*, 1990, v25(3), 421-440.)

Hein, Scott E. (Hafer, R. W. and Scott E. Hein. "On The Accuracy Of Time-Series, Interest Rate, And Survey Forecasts Of Inflation," *JOB*, 1985, v58(4), 377-398.)

Hein, Scott E. (Hafer, R. W. and Scott E. Hein. "Financial Innovations And The Interest Elasticity Of Money Demand: Some Historical Evidence," *JMCB*, 1984, v16(2), 247-252.)

Hein, Scott E. (Hafer, R. W. and Scott E. Hein. "Forecasting Inflation Using Interest-Rate And Time-Series Models: Some International Evidence," *JOB*, 1990, v63(1), Part 1, 1-18.)

Hein, Scott E. (Haslag, Joseph H. and Scott E. Hein. "Federal Reserve System Reserve Requirements, 1959-1988," *JMCB*, 1989, v21(4), 515-523.)

Hein, Scott E. (MacDonald, S. Scott and Scott E. Hein. "Future Rates And Forward Rates As Predictors Of Near-Term Treasury Bill Rates," *JFM*, 1989, v9(3), 249-262.)

Hein, Scott E. and S. Scott MacDonald. "On The Difference Between Daily Treasury Bill Futures Contract Rates And Implied Forward Rates," *RFM*, 1989, v8(3), 446-470.

Hein, Scott E., Christopher K. Ma and S. Scott MacDonald. "Testing Unbiasedness In Futures Markets: A Clarification," *JFM*, 1990, v10(5), 555-562.

Heincke, John. (Clarke, Frank H., Masako N. Darrough and John Heincke. "Optimal Pricing Policy In The Presence Of Experience Effects," *JOB*, 1982, v55(4), 517-530.)

Heinevetter, Bernd. "Liquidity Creation In The Euromarkets: A Comment," *JMCB*, 1979, v11(2), 231-234.

Heinkel, Rober. (Fischer, Edwin O., Robert Heinkel and Josef Zechner. "Dynamic Capital Structure Choice: Theory And Tests," *JOF*, 1989, v44(1), 19-40.)

Heinkel, Robert and Eduardo S. Schwartz. "Rights Versus Underwritten Offerings: An Asymmetric Information Approach," *JOF*, 1986, v41(1), 1-18.

Heinkel, Robert L. (Eckbo, B. Espen, Ronald M. Giammarino and Robert L. Heinkel. "Asymmetric Information And The Medium Of Exchange In Takeovers: Theory And Tests," *RFS*, 1990, v3(4), 651-676.)

Heinkel, Robert L. (Giammarino, Ronald M. and Robert L. Heinkel. "A Model Of Dynamic Takeover Behavior," *JOF*, 1986, v41(2), 465-480.)

Heinkel, Robert and Alan Kraus. "Measuring Event Impacts In Thinly Traded Stocks," *JFQA*, 1988, v23(1), 71-88.

Heinkel, Robert and Josef Zechner. "The Role Of Debt And Preferred Stock As A Solution To Adverse Investment Incentives," *JFQA*, 1990, v25(1), 1-24.

Heinkel, Robert, Maureen E. Howe and John S. Hughes. "Commodity Convenience Yields As On Option Profit," *JFM*, 1990, v10(5), 519-534.

Heinkel, Robert. "A Theory Of Capital Structure Relevance Under Imperfect Information," *JOF*, 1982, v37(5), 1141-1150.

Heinkel, Robert. (Downes, David H. and Robert Heinkel. "Signaling And The Valuation Of Unseasoned New Issues," *JOF*, 1982, v37(1), 1-10.)

Heinkel, Robert. (Fischer, Edwin O., Robert Heinkel and Josef Zechner. "Dynamic Recapitalization Policies And The Role Of Call Premia And Issue Discounts," *JFQA*, 1989, v24(4), 427-446.)

Heinkel, Robert. (Sealey, C. W., Jr. and Robert Heinkel. "Asymmetric Information And A Theory Of Compensating Balances," *JBF*, 1985, v9(2), 193-205.)

Heins, A. James and Stephen L. Allison. "Some Factors Affecting Stock Price Variability," *JOB*, 1966, v39(1), Part I, 19-23.

Heins, A. James. (Bryan, William R. and A. James Heins. "Defensive Open-Market Operations, Proximate Objectives, And Monetary Instability: A Comment," *JMCB*, 1972, v4(1), 98-108.)

Heins, A. James. (Haugen, Robert A. and A. James Heins. "Risk And Rate Of Return On Financial Assets: Some Old Wine In New Bottles," *JFQA*, 1975, v10(5), 775-784.)

Heins, Richard M. "Compensating The Automobile Accident Victim," *JRI*, 1957, v24(1), 73-100.

Heintz, James A. (Falk, Haim and James A. Heintz. "The Predictability Of Relative Risk Over Time," *JBFA*, 1977, v4(1), 5-28.)

Heinze, David Charles. "Decision Models For University Budget Requests," *JFQA*, 1971, v6(3), 1035-1040.

Heisterberg, Robert G. "A Utility Earnings Growth Model," *FAJ*, 1967, v23(1), 116-119.

Hekimian, James S. "A Profit Calculation For Agency Management," *JRI*, 1966, v33(1), 73-84.

Hekimian, James. "A Profit Calculation For Agency Management: Reply," *JRI*, 1967, v34(2), 341-344.

Hekman, Christine R. "Measuring Foreign Exchange Exposure: A Practical Theory And Its Application," *FAJ*, 1983, v39(5), 59-65.

Hekman, John S. "Rental Price Adjustment And Investment In The Office Market," *AREUEA*, 1985, v13(1), 32-47.

Hekman, John S. (Hartzell, David, John S. Hekman and Mike E. Miles. "Real Estate Returns And Inflation," *AREUEA*, 1987, v15(1), 617-637.)

Hekman, John. (Hartzell, David, John Hekman and Mike Miles. "Diversification Categories In Investment Real Estate," *AREUEA*, 1986, v14(2), 230-254.)

Heldring, Frederick. "Payment Systems Risk In The United States," *JBR*, 1985-86, v16(4), 209-213.

Helie, Carole. (Outreville, J. Francois and Carole Helie. "More Evidence On The Systematic Underwriting Risk In Automobile Insurance," *JRI*, 1986, v53(4), 755-766.)

Heller, H. Robert. "Determinants Of Exchange Rate Practices," *JMCB*, 1978, v10(3), 308-321.

Heller, H. Robert. "More On Projecting, Forecasting, And Hindcasting: A Reply," *JMCB*, 1971, v3(2), Part I, 288-292.

Heller, H. Robert. "The United States Balance Of Payments In 1968: A Comment," *JMCB*, 1970, v2(3), 370-382.

Heller, Philip. "More Office Space For An Expanding Economy," *FAJ*, 1963, v19(5), 49-50.

Heller, Walter W. "Limitations Of The Federal Individual Income Tax," *JOF*, 1952, v7(2), 185-202.

Heller, Walter W. "The Future Of Our Fiscal System," *JOB*, 1965, v38(3), 235-244.

Heller, Walter W. "What's Right With Economics," *JPM*, 1974-75, v1(4), 7-14.

Helliwell, John F. (Mao, James C. T. and John F. Helliwell. "Investment Decisions Under Uncertainty: Theory And Practice," *JOF*, 1969, v24(2), 323-338.)

Hellmuth, William F., Jr. "Depreciation And The 1954 Internal Revenue Code," *JOF*, 1955, v10(3), 326-349.

Hellweg, Douglas. "A Note On Compensatory Balance Requirements," *JOF*, 1961, v16(1), 80-84.

Helm, Roy J., Jr. (Oblak, David J. and Roy J. Helm, Jr. "Survey And Analysis Of Capital Budgeting Methods Used By Multinationals," *FM*, 1980, v9(4), 37-41.)

Helmer, Borden. "Economic Perspective For Planning," *FAJ*, 1964, v20(4), 23-30.

Helmer, Borden. "Perspective On Timing Equity Investments," *FAJ*, 1965, v21(3), 21-25.

Helms, Billy P. and Terrence F. Martell. "An Examination Of The Distribution Of Futures Price Changes," *JFM*, 1985, v5(2), 259-272.

Helms, Billy P. (Followill, Richard A. and Billy P. Helms. "Put-Call-Futures Parity And Arbitrage Opportunity In The Market For Options On Gold Futures Contracts," *JFM*, 1990, v10(4), 339-352.)

Helms, Billy P. (Jean, William H. and Billy P. Helms. "Geometric Mean Approximations," *JFQA*, 1983, v18(3), 287-293.)

Helms, Billy P. (Jean, William H. and Billy P. Helms. "Moment Orderings And Stochastic Dominance Tests," *JBFA*, 1988, v15(4), 573-584.)

Helms, Billy P. (Jean, William H. and Billy P. Helms. "The Identification Of Stochastic Dominance Efficient Sets By Moment Combination Orderings," *JBF*, 1988, v12(2), 243-254.)

Helms, Billy P. (Lindley, James T., Billy P. Helms and Mahmoud Haddad. "A Measurement Of The Errors In Intra-Period Compounding And Bond Valuation," *FR*, 1987, v22(1), 33-52.)

Helms, Billy P. (Tehranian, Hassan and Billy P. Helms. "An Empirical Comparison Of Stochastic Dominance Among Lognormal Prospects," *JFQA*, 1982, v17(2), 217-226.)

Helms, Billy P. (Wu, Hsiu-Kwang and Billy P. Helms. "Confidential Bank Examination Data And The Efficiency Of Bank Share Prices," *FAJ*, 1984, v40(6), 31-33.)

Helms, Billy P., Fred R. Kaen and Robert E. Rosenman. "Memory In Commodity Futures Contracts," *JFM*, 1984, v4(4), 559-567.

Helms, Billy. (Brooks, Robert and Billy Helms. "An N-Stage, Fractional Period, Quarterly Dividend Discount Model," *FR*, 1990, v25(4), 651-658.)

Helms, Billy. (Moser, James T. and Billy Helms. "An Examination Of Basis Risk Due To Estimation," *JFM*, 1990, v10(5), 457-468.)

Helms, Gary B. "Toward Bridging The Gap," *FAJ*, 1978, v34(1), 68-72.

Helms, Marilyn M. (White, Charles S., Marilyn M. Helms and Barbara Parker. "Simulations Versus Cases: Impact On The Analysis And Interpretation Of Financial Statements," *JFED*, 1990, v19, 33-36.)

Helmsley, Harry B. "Real Estate Syndications," *FAJ*, 1958, v14(1), 30-32.

Helmuth, John W. "A Report On The Systematic Downward Bias In Live Cattle Future Prices," *JFM*, v1(3), 347-358.

Helton, Don. "Contingent Immunization With Zero Coupon Bonds," *FAJ*, 1985, v41(3), 76-77.

Hemler, Michael L. "The Quality Delivery Option In Treasury Bond Futures Contracts," *JOF*, 1990, v45(5), 1565-1586.

Hemmings, Dan B. "Leverage, Dividend Policy And The Cost Of Capital: Comment," *JOF*, 1973, v28(5), 1366-1370.

Hempel, Donald J. (Belkin, Jacob, Donald J. Hempel and Dennis W.

McLeavey. "An Empirical Study Of Time On Market Using Multidimensional Segmentation Of Housing Markets," **AREUEA,** 1976, v4(2), 57-76.)

Hempel, Donald J. and Subhash C. Jain. "House Buying Behavior: An Empirical Study In Cross-Cultural Buyer Behavior," **AREUEA,** 1978, v6(1), 1-21.

Hempel, G. H. (Yawitz, J. B., G. H. Hempel and W. J. Marshall. "Is Average Maturity A Proxy For Risk?," **JPM,** 1975-76, v2(3), 60-63.)

Hempel, George H. "An Evaluation Of Municipal 'Bankruptcy' Laws And Procedures," **JOF,** 1973, v28(5), 1339-1351.

Hempel, George H. "Quantitative Borrower Characteristics Associated With Defaults On Municipal General Obligations," **JOF,** 1973, v28(2), 523-530.

Hempel, George H. "Teaching And Research In Finance: Perceptions, Conflicts, And The Future," **FM,** 1983, v12(4), 5-10.

Hempel, George H. (Peavy, John W., III and George H. Hempel. "The Effect Of The WPPSS Crisis On The Tax-Exempt Bond Market," **JFR,** 1987, v10(3), 239-248.)

Hempel, George H. (Peavy, John W., III and George H. Hempel. "The Penn Square Bank Failure: Effect On Commercial Bank Security Returns--A Note," **JBF,** 1988, v12(1), 141-150.)

Hempel, George H. (Scott, Jonathan A., George H. Hempel and John W. Peavy, III. "The Effect Of Stock-For-Debt Swaps On Bank Holding Companies," **JBF,** 1985, v9(2), 233-251.)

Hempel, George H. (Simonson, Donald G. and George H. Hempel. "Improving Gap Management for Controlling Interest Rate Risk," **JBR,** 1982-83, v13(2), 109-115.)

Hempel, George H. (Yawitz, Jess B., George H. Hempel and William J. Marshall. "The Use Of Average Maturity As A Risk Proxy In Investment Portfolios," **JOF,** 1979, v30(2), 325-333.)

Hempel, George H. (Yawitz, Jess B., George H. Hempel and William J. Marshall. "A Risk-Return Approach To The Selection Of Optimal Government Bond Portfolios," **FM,** 1976, v5(3), 36-47.)

Hemsted, J. R. "The Cost Of Equity Capital - A Comment," **JBFA,** 1974, v1(3), 445-448.

Hendershott, P. and R. Van Order. "Pricing Mortgages: An Interpretation Of The Model And Results," **JFR,** 1987, v1(1), 19-56.

Hendershott, Patric H. and Chang-tseh Hsieh. "Inflation And The Growth In Home Mortgage Debt, 1964-78," **JFR,** 1980, v3(2), 189-202.

Hendershott, Patric H. and David S. Kidwell. "The Impact Of Relative Security Supplies: A Test With Data From A Regional Tax Exempt Bond Market," **JMCB,** 1978, v10(3), 337-347.

Hendershott, Patric H. and Frank De Leeuw. "Free Reserves, Interest Rates, And Deposits: A Synthesis," **JOF,** 1970, v25(3), 599-613.

Hendershott, Patric H. and James P. Winder. "Commercial Bank Asset Portfolio Behavior In The United States: Evidence Of A Change In Structure," **JBF,** 1979, v3(2), 113-131.

Hendershott, Patric H. and James C. Van Horne. "Expected Inflation Implied By Capital Market Rates," **JOF,** 1973, v28(2), 301-314.

Hendershott, Patric H. and Richard C. Lemmon. "The Financial Behavior Of Households: Some Empirical Estimates," **JOF,** 1975, v30(3), 733-759.

Hendershott, Patric H. and Sheng Cheng Hu. "The Allocation Of Capital Between Residential And Nonresidential Uses: Taxes, Inflation And Capital Market Constraints," **JOF,** 1983, v38(3), 795-812.

Hendershott, Patric H. and Timothy W. Koch. "The Demand For Tax-Exempt Securities By Financial Institutions," **JOF,** 1980, v35(3), 717-727.

Hendershott, Patric H. "A Flow-Of-Funds Model: Estimates For The Nonbank Finance Sector," **JMCB,** 1971, v3(4), 815-832.

Hendershott, Patric H. "A Tax Cut In A Multiple Security Model: Crowding Out, Pulling In And The Term Structure Of Interest Rates," **JOF,** 1976, v31(4), 1185-1199.

Hendershott, Patric H. "Analysis Of The Impact Of Capital-Specific Policies Or Legislation: Application To Reforms Of The Tax-Exempt Market," **JMCB,** 1980, v12(2), Part 2, 377-399.

Hendershott, Patric H. "Expectations, Surprises, And Treasury Bill Rates: 1960-1982," **JOF,** 1984, v39(3), 685-696.

Hendershott, Patric H. "Financial Disintermediation In A Macroeconomic Framework: Reply," **JOF,** 1973, v28(4), 1033-1034.

Hendershott, Patric H. "Financial Disintermediation In A Macroeconomic Framework," **JOF,** 1971, v26(4), 843-856.

Hendershott, Patric H. "Government Policy And The Allocation Of Capital Between Residential And Industrial Uses," **FAJ,** 1983, v39(4), 37-42.

Hendershott, Patric H. "Model Simulations Of The Impact Of Selective Credit Policies And Financial Reforms," **JBF,** 1977, v1(2), 173-184.

Hendershott, Patric H. "Mortgage Pricing: What Have We Learned So Far?," **AREUEA,** 1986, v14(4), 497-509.

Hendershott, Patric H. "Policy And Statistical Exogeneity: Reply," **JOF,** 1976, v31(5), 1514-1516.

Hendershott, Patric H. "Recent Development Of The Financial Sector Of Economic Models," **JOF,** 1968, v23(1), 41-84.

Hendershott, Patric H. "The Structure Of International Rates: The U. S. Treasury Bill Rate And The Eurodollar Deposit Rate," **JOF,** 1967, v22(3), 455-465.

Hendershott, Patric H. "The Likely Impact Of Increases In Deposit Rate Ceilings On Thrift Earnings And Housing Construction," **AREUEA,** 1979, v7(2), 177-189.

Hendershott, Patric H. (Buser, Stephen A., Patric H. Hendershott and Anthony B. Sanders. "Pricing Life Of Loan Rate Caps On Default-Free Adjustable-Rate Mortgages," **AREUEA,** 1985, v13(3), 248-260.)

Hendershott, Patric H. (Buser, Stephen A., Patric H. Hendershott and Anthony B. Saunders. "Determinants Of The Value Of Call Options On Default-Free Bonds," **JOB,** 1990, v63(1), Part 2, S33-S50.)

Hendershott, Patric H. (Chan, K. C., Patric H. Hendershott and Anthony B. Sanders. "Risk And Return On Real Estate: Evidence From Equity REITs," **AREUEA,** 1990, v18(4), 431-452.)

Hendershott, Patric H. (Cook, Timothy Q. and Patric H. Hendershott, "The Impact Of Taxes, Risk And Relative Security Supplies On Interest Rate Differentials," **JOF,** 1978, v33(4), 1173-1186.)

Hendershott, Patric H. "The Full-Employment Interest Rate And The Neutralized Money Stock: Comment," **JOF,** 1971, v26(1), 127-136.

Hendershott, Patric H. (Day, A. Edward and Patric H. Hendershott. "Household Demand For Policy Loans," **JRI,** 1977, v44(3), 411-423.)

Hendershott, Patric H. (Glower, Michel and Patric H. Hendershott. "The Determinants Of REALTOR Income," **JRER,** 1988, v3(2), 53-68.)

Hendershott, Patric H. and David C. Ling. "Prospective Changes In The Tax Law And The Value Of Depreciable Real Estate," **AREUEA,** 1984, v12(3), 297-317.

Hendershott, Patric H. and Donald R. Haurin. "Adjustments In The Real Estate Market," **AREUEA,** 1988, v16(4), 343-353.

Hendershott, Patric H. and Donald R. Haurin. "Research On Real Estate Investment," **AREUEA,** 1990, v18(4), 369-376.

Hendershott, Patric H. and Joel Slemrod. "Taxes And The User Cost Of Capital For Owner-Occupied Housing," **AREUEA,** 1982, v10(4), 375-393.

Hendershott, Patric H. and James D. Shilling. "Valuing ARM Rate Caps: Implications Of 1970-84 Interest Rate Behavior," **AREUEA,** 1985, v13(3), 317-332.

Hendershott, Patric H. and James D. Shilling. "Reforming Conforming Loan Limits: The Impact On Thrift Earnings And Taxpayer Outlays," **JFSR,** 1989, v3(4), 311-332.

Hendershott, Patric H. and James D. Shilling. "The Impact Of The Agencies On Conventional Fixed-Rate Mortgage Yields," **JREFEC,** 1989, v2(2), 101-116.

Hendershott, Patric H. and Kevin E. Villani. "Secondary Mortgage Markets And The Cost Of Mortgage Funds," **AREUEA,** 1980, v8(1), 50-76.

Hendershott, Patric H. and Marc T. Smith. "Housing Inventory Change And The Role Of Existing Structures, 1961-1985," **AREUEA,** 1988, v16(4), 364-378.

Hendershott, Patric H. and Thomas G. Thibodeau. "The Relationship Between Median And Constant Quality House Prices: Implications For Setting FHA Loan Limits," **AREUEA,** 1990, v18(3), 323-334.

Hendershott, Patric H., James D. Shilling and Kevin E. Villani. "Measurement Of The Spreads Between Yields On Various Mortgage Contracts And Treasury Securities," **AREUEA,** 1983, v11(4), 476-490.

Henderson, Glenn and Stephan E. Skomp. "Geometric Exposition Of CAPM-Based Capital Budgeting," **JFED,** 1983, v12, 1-16.

Henderson, Glenn V., Jr. and Stephen E. Skomp. "A Pedagogical Note On CAPM-Based Capital Budgeting," **FR,** 1981, v16(2), 51-58.

Henderson, Glenn V., Jr. "A General Solution To The Buy Or Lease Decision: A Pedagogical Note: Comment," **JOF,** 1976, v31(1), 147-151.

Henderson, Glenn V., Jr. "An Organizing Concept For The Financial Management Case Course," **JFED,** 1976, v5, 69-72.

Henderson, Glenn V., Jr. "In Defense Of The WACC," **FM,** 1979, v8(3), 57-61.

Henderson, Glenn V., Jr. "On Capitalization Rates For Riskless Streams," **JOF,** 1976, v31(5), 1491-1493.

Henderson, Glenn V., Jr. "Problems And Solutions In Conducting Event Studies," **JRI,** 1990, v57(2), 282-306.

Henderson, Glenn V., Jr. "Shareholder Taxation And The Required Rate Of Return On Internally Generated Funds," **FM,** 1976, v5(2), 25-31.

Henderson, Glenn V. (Davidson, Wallace N., III, Sharon Hatten Garrison and Glenn V. Henderson, Jr. "Examining Merger Synergy With The Capital Asset Pricing Model," **FR,** 1987, v22(2), 233-248.)

Henderson, Glenn V., Jr. (French, Dan W. and Glenn V. Henderson, Jr. "How Well Does Performance Evaluation Perform?," **JPM,** 1984-85, v11(2), 15-18.)

Henderson, Glenn V., Jr. (French, Dan W. and Glenn V. Henderson, Jr. "Substitute Hedged Option Portfolios: Theory And Evidence," **JFR,** 1981, v4(1), 21-31.)

Henderson, Glenn V., Jr. (Gallinger, George W. and Glenn V. Henderson, Jr. "Hurdle Rates For Strategic Investments," **AFPAF,** 1985, v1(1), 125-144.)

Henderson, Glenn V., Jr. (Glascock, John L., Glenn V. Henderson, Jr. and Linda J. Martin. "When E. F. Hutton Talks," **FAJ,** 1986, v42(3), 69-72.)

Henderson, Glenn V., Jr. (Gregory-Allen, Russell B. and Glenn V. Henderson, Jr. "A Brief Review Of Catastrophe Theory And A Test In A Corporate Failure Context," **FR,** 1991, v26(2), 127-156.)

Henderson, Glenn V., Jr. (Martin, Linda J. and Glenn V. Henderson, Jr. "On Bond Ratings And Pension Obligations: A Note," **JFQA,** 1983, v18(4), 463-470.)

Henderson, Glenn V., Jr. (Martin, Linda J. and Glen V. Henderson, Jr. "The Effect Of ERISA On Capital Structure Measures," **FR,** 1980, v15(2), 39-49.)

Henderson, Glenn V., Jr. (McIntosh, Willard and Glenn V. Henderson, Jr. "Efficiency Of The Office Properties Market," **JREFEC,** 1989, v2(1), 61-70.)

Henderson, Glenn V., Jr. (Perry, Larry G., Glenn V. Henderson, Jr. and Timothy P. Cronan. "Multivariate Analysis Of Corporate Bond Ratings And Industry Classifications," **JFR,** 1984, v7(1), 27-36.)

Henderson, Hazel. "The Limits Of Traditional Economics," **FAJ,** 1973, v29(3),28-30,32,79-80,83-84,86-87.

Henderson, James W. and Terry S. Maness. "Financial Analysis And Forecasting: A Cash Flow Approach," **JFED,** 1983, v12, 92-99.

Henderson, John P. "A Deviation In The Pattern Of Relative Earnings For Production Workers And Office Personnel," **JOB,** 1955, v28(3), 195-205.

Henderson, Ronald H. "Ruminations On Performance," **FAJ,** 1969, v25(6), 103-104,121-123.

Heneman, Harlow J. "Financial Analysts And Management," **FAJ,** 1967, v23(5), 27-30.

Henemier, Stanley M. (Hall, Charles P., Jr., Stanley M. Henemier and Arnold H. Raphaelson. "Some Issues In Limiting Hospital Cost Reimbursement: A Maryland Experience," **JRI,** 1977, v44(2), 267-288.)

Henin, Claude and William F. Rentz. "Call Purchases, Stock Purchases, And Subjective Stochastic Dominance," **JBFA,** 1984, v11(1), 127-138.

Hennigar, Elizabeth. (Resnick, Bruce G. and Elizabeth Hennigar. "The Relationship Between Futures And Cash Prices For U.S. Treasury Bonds," **RFM**, 1983, v2(3), 282-299.)

Henningsen, Victor E. "Policy Loan Interest Rates: A Critical Evaluation: Comment," **JRI**, 1972, v39(1), 156.

Henrici, Stanley. "The Perversity, Peril and Pathos Of ROI," **FAJ**, 1983, v39(5), 79-80.

Henriksson, Roy D. "Market Timing And Mutual Fund Performance: An Empirical Investigation," **JOB**, 1984, v57(1), Part 1, 73-96.

Henriksson, Roy D. (Arnott, Robert D. and Roy D. Henriksson. "A Disciplined Approach To Global Asset Allocation," **FAJ**, 1989, v45(2), 17-28.)

Henriksson, Roy D. (Leibowitz, Martin L. and Roy D. Henriksson. "Portfolio Optimization Within A Surplus Framework," **FAJ**, 1988, v44(2), 43-51.)

Henriksson, Roy D. (Leibowitz, Martin L. and Roy D. Henriksson. "Portfolio Optimization With Shortfall Constraints: A Confidence-Limit Approach To Managing Downside Risk," **FAJ**, 1989, v45(2), 34-41.)

Henriksson, Roy D. and Robert C. Merton. "On Market Timing And Investment Performance. II. Statistical Procedures For Evaluating Forecasting Skills," **JOB**, 1981, v54(4), 513-534.

Henriksson, Roy. (Evnine, Jeremy and Roy Henriksson. "Asset Allocation And Options," **JPM**, 1987-88, v14(1), 56-61.)

Henry, James B. (Livingston, D. T. and James B. Henry. "The Effect Of Employee Stock Ownership Plans On Corporate Profits," **JRI**, 1980, v47(3), 491-505.)

Henry, James B. (Livingston, D. T. and James B. Henry. "The Effect Of Employee Stock Ownership Plans On Corporate Profits: Reply," **JRI**, 1983, v50(3), 498-499.)

Henry, James B. (Roenfeldt, Rodney L. and James B. Henry. "Lease-Cost Measurement Of Hospital Equipment Under Cost-Based Reimbursement," **FM**, 1979, v8(2), 24-35.)

Henry, William R. (Ederington, Louis H. and William R. Henry. "On Costs Of Capital In Programming Approaches To Capital Budgeting," **JFQA**, 1979, v14(5), 1049-1058.)

Henry, William R. and E. Earl Burch. "Institutional Contributions To Scholarly Journals Of Business," **JOB**, 1974, v47(1), 56-66.

Hensher, David A. "Achieving Representativeness Of The Observable Component Of The Indirect Utility Function In Logit Choice Models: An Empirical Revelation," **JOB**, 1984, v57(2), 265-280.

Henwood, Thomas D. "Publicly Owned Broker-Dealer Stocks," **FAJ**, 1973, v29(3), 41-44,46,48,50,88,90-91.

Heppen, Michael J. (Spencer, Roger W. and Michael J. Heppen. "Economic Conditions And Life Insurance," **FAJ**, 1969, v25(4), 73-79.)

Herbert, P. J. (Buckland, R., P. J. Herbert and K. A. Yeomans. "Price Discount On New Equity Issues In The UK And Their Relationship To Investor Subscription In The Period 1965-75," **JBFA**, 1981, v8(1), 79-95.)

Herbst, A. F., D. D. Kare and S. C. Caples. "Hedging Effectiveness And Minimum Risk Hedge Ratios In The Presence Of Autocorrelation: Foreign Currency Futures," **JFM**, 1989, v9(3), 185-198.

Herbst, Anthony F. and Craig W. Slinkman. "Political-Economic Cycles In The U.S. Stock Market," **FAJ**, 1984, v40(2), 38-44.

Herbst, Anthony F. and Joseph P. McCormack. "An Examination Of The Risk/Return Characteristics Of Portfolios Combining Commodity Futures Contracts With Common Stocks," **RFM**, 1987, v6(3), 416-425.

Herbst, Anthony F. and Nicholas O. Ordway. "Stock Index Futures Contracts And Separability Of Returns," **JFM**, 1984, v4(1), 87-102.

Herbst, Anthony F. "A Factor Analysis Approach To Determining The Relative Endogeneity Of Trade Credit," **JOF**, 1974, v29(4), 1087-1103.

Herbst, Anthony F. "Gold Versus U.S. Common Stocks: Some Evidence On Inflation Hedge Performance And Cyclical Behavior," **FAJ**, 1983, v39(1), 66-74.

Herbst, Anthony F. "Hedging Against Price Index Inflation With Futures Contracts," **JFM**, 1985, v5(4), 489-504.

Herbst, Anthony F. "Some Empirical Evidence On The Determinants Of Trade Credit At The Industry Level Of Aggregation," **JFQA**, 1974, v9(3), 377-394.

Herbst, Anthony F. "Truth In Lending, Regulation Z: Comments On Closed-End Contract Interest Rate Disclosure Requirements," **JBR**, 1972-73, v3(2), 95-101.

Herbst, Anthony F. and Edwin Maberly. "Shoes And Ships And Sealing Wax, Cabbages And Kings: Now Tail-Wagged Dogs And Stock Index Futures," **FAJ**, 1987, v43(6), 73-75.

Herbst, Anthony F. and Edwin D. Maberly. "A Further Investigation Of The Day-Of-The-Week Effect In The Gold Market: A Comment," **JFM**, 1988, v8(3),389-390.

Herbst, Anthony F. and Edwin D. Maberly. "Stock Index Futures, Expiration Day Volatility, And The 'Special' Friday Opening: A Note," **JFM**, 1990, v10(3), 323-325.

Herbst, Anthony F., Edwin Maberly and Hans U. Sieber. "Sovereign Debt: Historical Perspective As Portent For Today," **RDIBF**, 1989, v3, 45-68.

Herbst, Anthony F., Joseph P. McCormack and Elizabeth N. West. "Investigation Of A Lead-Lag Relationship Between Spot Indices And Their Futures Contracts," **JFM**, 1987, v7(4), 373-382.

Herbst, Anthony. "The Unique Real Internal Rate Of Return: Caveat Emptor!," **JFQA**, 1978, v13(2),363-370.

Hercowitz, Zvi. "Anticipated Inflation, The Frequency Of Transactions, And The Slope Of The Phillips Curve," **JMCB**, 1983, v15(2), 139-154.

Hercowitz, Zvi. "On The Determination Of The External Debt: The Case Of Israel," **JIMF**, 1986, v5(3),315-334.

Herd, J. Victor. "Training Courses Conducted By Fire And Marine Insurance Companies," **JRI**, 1938, v5, 17-22.

Hermalin, Albert I. (Daniels, Arthur C., Albert I. Hermalin, Alfred Cranwill and James R. Williams. "The Research Facilities Of The Institute Of Life Insurance," **JRI**, 1958, v25(1), 32-41.)

Herman, E. S. and C. F. Safanda. "Allocating Investment Information," **FAJ**, 1973, v29(1),23-28,88-91.

Herman, Edward S. "Mutual Fund Management Fee Rates," **JOF**, 1963, v18(2), 360-376.

Herman, Edward S. (Friend, Irwin and Edward S. Herman. "Professor Stigler On Securities Regulation: A Further Comment," **JOB**, 1965, v38(1), 106-110.)

Herman, Edward S. (Friend, Irwin and Edward S. Herman. "The S.E.C. Through A Glass Darkly," **JOB**, 1964, v37(4), 382-405.)

Herman, Edward S. (Guttentag, Jack M. and Edward S. Herman. "Do Large Banks Neglect Small Business?," **JOF**, 1966, v21(3), 535-538.)

Herman, Hamilton and Delbert F. Jurgensen. "Challenge Of The National Water Problem," **FAJ**, 1962, v18(2), 65-74.

Hermann, Mildred M. "Looking Back - Looking Forward 35 Years For The FAF," **FAJ**, 1982, v38(4),15,17-21.

Hermansen, Roy W. (Good, Walter R., Roy W. Hermansen and T. Kirkham Barneby. "Opportunity: Actively Managed Investment Universes," **FAJ**, 1986, v42(1), 49-57.)

Herrick, Kenneth W. "Auto Accidents And Alcohol In Great Britain - An Analysis," **JRI**, 1973, v40(1), 55-74.

Herrick, Kenneth W. "Credit Life And Health Insurance In Texas," **JRI**, 1960, v27(1), 65-76.

Herrick, Kenneth W. "Teaching The Basic Property And Casualty Course," **JRI**, 1956, v23, 69-76.

Herring, Richard J. "The Economics Of Workout Lending," **JMCB**, 1989, v21(1), 1-15.

Herring, Richard J. and Prashant Vankudre. "Growth Opportunities And Risk-Taking By Financial Intermediaries," **JOF**, 1987, v42(3), 583-600.

Herring, Richard. (Guttentag, Jack and Richard Herring. "Disclosure Policy And International Banking," **JBF**, 1986, v10(1), 75-97.)

Herring, Richard. (Guttentag, Jack and Richard Herring. "Credit Rationing And Financial Disorder," **JOF**, 1984, v39(5), 1359-1382.)

Herring, Richard. (Guttentag, Jack and Richard Herring. "Strategic Planning To Cope With Uncertainty," **RDIBF**, 1987, v1, 61-86.)

Herrmann, Arthur L. "Business Failure: A Timely Special Topic In The Core Course," **JFED**, 1975, v4, 57-59.

Herrnstadt, Irwin L. and Benson Soffer. "Recent Labor Disputes Over 'Restrictive' Practices And 'Inflationary' Wage Increases," **JOB**, 1961, v34(4), 453-470.

Hershbarger, Robert A. "Are The Loss And Expense Ratios Of Insurance Companies Normally Distributed?," **JRI**, 1975, v42(3), 522-528.

Hershbarger, Robert A. "Insurance Underwriting Capacity: A Psychometric Approach," **JRI**, 1975, v42(1), 51-68.

Hershbarger, Robert A. "Life Insurance Sales Policies Of American Colleges And Universities," **JRI**, 1977, v44(1), 133-140.

Hershbarger, Robert A. (BarNiv, Ran and Robert A. Hershbarger. "Classifying Financial Distress In The Life Insurance Industry," **JRI**, 1990, v57(1), 110-136.)

Hershbarger, Robert A. (Cross, Mark L. and Robert A. Hershbarger. "Price Discrimination In The Homeowners Program," **JRI**, 1979, v46(1), 147-157.)

Hershbarger, Robert A. and Ronald K. Miller. "A Procedure For Calculating The Annual Change In Value For Investment," **JRI**, 1975, v42(4), 663-668.

Hershbarger, Robert A. and Ronald K. Miller. "The Impact Of Economic Conditions On The Incidence Of Arson," **JRI**, 1978, v45(2), 275-290.

Hershbarger, Robert A. and Ronald K. Miller. "The Investment Performance Of Minority Controlled Life Insurance Companies," **JRI**, 1982, v49(3), 436-442.

Hershbarger, Robert A. and Ronald K. Miller. "The Impact Of Economic Conditions On The Incidence Of Arson: Reply," **JRI**, 1988, v55(4), 755-757.

Hershey, J. W. "The Rest Of The Story On The Role Of Cost In The Minimum Pricing Of Railroad Services'," **JOB**, 1963, v36(3), 338-340.

Hershey, John C. and Paul J. H. Schoemaker. "Risk Taking And Problem Context In The Domain Of Losses: An Expected Utility Analysis," **JRI**, 1980, v47(1), 111-132.

Herskovitz, Michael D. (Davidson, Andrew S., Michael D. Herskovitz and Leonard D. Van Drunen. "The Refinancing Threshold Pricing Model: An Economic Approach To Valuing MBS," **JREFEC**, 1988, v1(2), 117-130.)

Herskovitz, D. S. "U. S. Economic Projection: 1969-71," **FAJ**, 1969, v25(6), 22-24.

Herskovitz, David S. "Fiscal Versus Monetary Policy," **FAJ**, 1970, v26(2), 35-42.

Hertzel, Michael G., Coleman S. Kendall and Peter E. Kretzmer. "The Volatility Of Asset Returns During Trading And Nontrading Hours: Some Evidence From The Foreign Exchange Markets," **JIMF**, 1990, v9(3), 335-343.

Herzel, Leo. "Corporate Governance Through Statistical Eyes," **JFEC**, 1990, v27(2), 581-594.

Herzog, John P. "Investor Experience In Corporate Securities: A New Technique For Measurement," **JOF**, 1964, v19(1), 46-62.

Herzog, Thomas. (Clauretie, Terrence M. and Thomas Herzog. "The Effect Of State Foreclosure Laws On Loan Losses: Evidence From The Mortgage Insurance Industry," **JMCB**, 1990, v22(2), 221-233.)

Hess, Alan C. and Peter A. Frost. "Tests For Price Effects Of New Issues Of Seasoned Securities," **JOF**, 1982, v37(1), 11-25.

Hess, Alan C. "An Explanation Of Short-Run Fluctuations In The Ratio Of Currency To Demand Deposits," **JMCB**, 1971, v3(3), 666-679.

Hess, Alan C. "Variable Rate Mortgages," **FAJ**, 1984, v40(1), 67-70.

Hess, Alan C. and Clifford W. Smith, Jr. "Elements Of Mortgage Securitization," **JREFEC**, 1988, v1(4), 331-346.

Hess, Alan C. and Sanjai Bhagat. "Size Effects Of Seasoned Stock Issues: Empirical Evidence," **JOB**, 1986, v59(4), Part 1, 567-584.

Hess, Arleigh, Jr. (Win, Willis F. and Arleigh Hess, Jr. "The Value Of The Call Privilege," **JOF**, 1959, v14(2), 182-195.)

Hess, Arthur E. "Medicare After One Year," **JRI**, 1968, v35(1), 119-132.

Hess, James D. (Gerstner, Eitan and James D. Hess. "Why Do Hot Dogs Come In Packs Of 10 And Buns In 8s Or 12s? A Demand-Side Investigation," **JOB**, 1987, v60(4), 491-518.)

Hess, P. J. and J. L. Bicksler. "Capital Asset Prices Versus Time Series Models As Predictors Of Inflation: The Expected Real Rate Of Interest And Market Efficiency," **JFEC**, 1975, v2(4), 341-360.

Hess, Pat J. (Bicksler, James L. and Pat J. Hess. "More On Purchasing Power Risk, Portfolio Analysis, And The Case For Index-Linked

Bonds: A Comment," **JMCB**, 1976, v8(2), 265-266.)
Hess, Patrick J. "Tests For Tax Effects In The Pricing Of Financial Assets," **JOB**, 1983, v56(4),537-554.
Hess, Patrick J. "The Ex-Dividend Day Behavior Of Stock Returns: Further Evidence On Tax Effects," **JOF**, 1982, v37(2), 445-456.
Hess, Patrick J. (Bicksler, James and Patrick J. Hess. "A Note On The Profits And Riskiness Of Defense Contractors," **JOB**, 1976, v49(4), 555-557.)
Hess, Patrick J. (Buser, Stephen A. and Patrick J. Hess. "Empirical Determinants Of The Relative Yields On Taxable And Tax-Exempt Securities," **JFEC**, 1986, v17(2), 335-355.)
Hess, Patrick J. (Eades, Kenneth M., Patrick J. Hess and E. Han Kim. "Market Rationality And Dividend Announcements," **JFEC**, 1985, v14(4), 581-604.)
Hess, Patrick J. (Eades, Kenneth M., Patrick J. Hess and E. Han Kim. "On Interpreting Security Returns During The Exdividend Period," **JFEC**, 1984, v13(1),3-34.)
Hess, Patrick. (Gibbons, Michael R. and Patrick Hess. "Day Of The Week Effects And Asset Returns," **JOB**, 1981, v54(4), 579-596.)
Hessel, Christopher A. and Lucy Huffman. The Effect Of Taxation On Immunization Rules And Duration Estimation," **JOF**, 1981, v36(5), 1127-1142.
Hessel, Christopher A. and Lucy T. Huffman. "Incorporation Of Tax Considerations Into The Computation Of Duration," **JFR**, 1983, v6(3), 213-215.
Hessel, Christopher A. "Extensions To Portfolio Theory To Reflect Vast Wealth Differences Among Investors," **JFQA**, 1981, v16(1), 53-70.
Hester, Donald D. "Customer Relationships And Terms Of Loans; Evidence From A Pilot Survey," **JMCB**, 1979, v11(3), 349-357.
Hester, Donald D. "Deregulation And Locational Rents In Banking," **JBR**, 1983-84, v14(1), 96-106.
Hester, Donald D. "Financial Disintermediation And Policy," **JMCB**, 1969, v1(3), 600-617.
Hester, Donald D. "Innovations And The Portfolios Of Weekly Reporting," **JBF**, 1982, v6(1), 89-112.
Hester, Donald D. "Monetary Policy In The 'Checkless' Economy," **JOF**, 1972, v27(2), 279-293.
Hester, Donald D. "Reflections On The Discount Window," **JMCB**, 1970, v2(2), 151-157.
Hester, Donald D. "Special Interests: The FINE Situation," **JMCB**, 1977, v9(4), 652-661.
Hester, Donald D. (Bates, Timothy M. and Donald D. Hester. "Analysis Of A Commercial Bank Minority Lending Program: Comment," **JOF**, 1977, v32(5), 1783-1789.)
Hetherington, Norriss S. "Taking The Risk Out Of Risk Arbitrage," **JPM**, 1982-83, v9(4), 24-25.
Hetherington, Norriss. "High Return And Low Risk In Called Preferreds," **JPM**, 1986-87, v13(3), 81-82.
Hettenhouse, G. W. and D. J. Puglisi. "Investor Experience With Options," **FAJ**, 1975, v31(4), 53-58.
Hettenhouse, George W. "A Rationale For Restructuring Stock Plans," **FM**, 1972, v1(2), 30-35.
Hettenhouse, George W. "Financial Theory And Financial Practice: Are They Really Incompatible?," **JFED**, 1981, v10, 59-62.
Hettenhouse, George W. and John J. Dee. "A Component Analysis Of Rates Of Return In Real Estate Investment," **AREUEA**, 1976, v4(1), 7-22.
Hetzel, Robert L. "Estimating Money Demand Functions," **JMCB**, 1984, v16(2), 185-193.
Hetzel, Robert L. "The Federal Reserve System And Control Of The Money Supply In The 1970s," **JMCB**, 1981, v13(1), 31-43.
Hetzel, Robert L. "The October 1979 Regime Of Monetary Control And The Behavior Of The Money Supply In 1980," **JMCB**, 1982, v14(2), 234-251.
Hetzel, Robert L. and Yash P. Mehra. "The Behavior Of Money Demand In The 1980s," **JMCB**, 1989, v21(4), 455-463.
Heumann, Leonard F. "Interracial Price Trends In A Neighborhood Seeking Stable Integration," **AREUEA**, 1975, v3(2), 7-30.
Heuson, Andrea J. "Market Maturation Effects In Options On Treasury Bond Futures," **RFM**, 1986, v5(3), 274-283.
Heuson, Andrea J. "Managing The Short-Term Interest Rate Exposure Inherent In Adjustable Rate Mortgage Loans," **AREUEA**, 1988, v16(2), 160-172.
Heuson, Andrea J. "Mortgage Terminations And Pool Characteristics: Some Additional Evidence," **JFR**, 1988, v11(2), 143-152.
Heuson, Andrea J. "Offering Rates On Fixed- And Adjustable-Rate Mortgage Loans," **FR**, 1989, v24(1), 147-156.
Heuson, Andrea J. "The Term Premia Relationship Implicit In The Term Structure Of Treasury Bills," **JFR**, 1988, v11(2), 1-20.
Heuson, Andrea J. (Barrett, W. Brian, Andrea J. Heuson and Robert W. Kolb. "The Differential Effects Of Sinking Funds On Bond Risk Premia," **JFR**, 1986, v9(4), 303-312.)
Heuson, Andrea J. (Barrett, W. Brian, Andrea J. Heuson and Robert W. Kolb. "The Effect Of Three Mile Island On Utility Bond Risk Premia: A Note," **JOF**, 1986, v41(1), 255-262.)
Heuson, Andrea J. (Barrett, W. Brian, Andrea J. Heuson, Robert W. Kolb and Gabriele R. Schropp. "The Adjustment Of Stock Prices To Completely Unanticipated Events," **FR**, 1987, v22(4), 345-354.)
Heuson, Andrea J. (Gosnell, Thomas F. and Andrea J. Heuson. "A Discretionary Approach To Hedging A Lender's Exposure In Adjustable Rate Mortgages," **JFM**, 1990, v10(5), 481-496.)
Heuson, Andrea J. and Dennis J. Lasser. "Tax-Timing Options And The Pricing Of Government Bonds," **JFR**, 1990, v13(2), 93-104.
Heuson, Andrea Jane. "Institutional Disparities In The Pricing Of Adjustable Rate Mortgage Loans," **JREFEC**, 1989, v2(1), 31-46.
Hewett, Wendell C. "The Significance Of Human Curiosity In An Outdoor Advertising Experiment," **JOB**, 1975, v48(1), 108-110.
Hewins, R. D. (Christofides, N., R. D. Hewins and G. R. Salkin. "Graph Theoretic Approaches To Foreign Exchange Operations," **JFQA**, 1979, v14(3), 481-500.)
Hewitt, Daniel P. (Heffley, Dennis R. and Daniel P. Hewitt. "Land-Use Zoning In A Local Economy With Optimal Property Taxes And Public Expenditures," **JREFEC**, 1988, v1(3), 373-392.)
Hewson, John and Eisuke Sakakibara. "A Qualitative Analysis Of Euro-Currency Controls," **JOF**, 1975, v30(2), 377-400.

Hewson, John and Eisuke Sakakibara. "The Effect Of U. S. Controls On The U. S. Commercial Bank Borrowing In The Euro-Dollar Market," **JOF**, 1975, v30(4), 1101-1110.
Hewson, John and Eisuke Sakakibara. "A General Equilibrium Approach To The Eurodollar Market," **JMCB**, 1976, v8(3), 297-323.
Hewson, John. (Niehans, Jurg and John Hewson. "The Eurodollar Market And Monetary Theory," **JMCB**, 1976, v8(1), 1-27.)
Hexter, J. Lawrence. "A Test Of Hammer's Demand For Physical Capital Model Using Firm Data," **JOF**, 1968, v23(1), 105-111.
Heymann, Hans G. and Richard E. Cohan. "The Effect Of Financial Futures Trading On The Bid-Ask Spread Of Cash Market T-Bonds," **RFM**, 1984, v3(1), 48-57.
Heymann, Hans. "Property Life Insurance," **JRI**, 1940, v7, 31-43.
Heyne, Paul T. "The Market System Is The Best Guide," **FAJ**, 1971, v27(5), 26-27,72-73.
Hiatt, John C. "Panel: Clearance, Payment, And Settlement Systems In The Futures, Options, And Stock Markets," **RFM**, 1988, v7(3), 387-391.
Hickey, Brian R. (Barges, Alexander and Brian R. Hickey. "Drug Industry Profits," **FAJ**, 1968, v24(3), 75-83.)
Hickman, Edgar P. "Selecting Income Growth And Discount Rates In Wrongful Death And Injury Cases: Comment," **JRI**, 1977, v44(1), 129-132.
Hickman, James C. "Investment Implications Of The Actuarial Design Of Life Insurance Products," **JRI**, 1971, v38(4), 571-583.
Hickman, James C. "New Perspectives On Risk Management: Comment," **JRI**, 1968, v35(4), 607-610.
Hickman, James C. "Pensions And Sex," **JRI**, 1983, v50(4), 681-687.
Hickman, James C. "Some Remarks About Mathematical Models In Insurance: Comment," **JRI**, 1965, v32(1), 129-132.
Hickman, James C. "The Actuarial Curriculum: Comment," **JRI**, 1966, v33(3), 478-480.
Hickman, James C. and Douglas A. Zahn. "Some Mathematical Views Of Risk," **JRI**, 1966, v33(3), 437-446.
Hickman, James C. and Robert B. Miller. "Insurance Premiums And Decision Analysis," **JRI**, 1970, v37(4), 567-578.
Hickman, Kent and Glenn H. Petry. "A Comparison Of Stock Price Predictions Using Court Accepted Formulas, Dividend Discount, And P/E Models," **FM**, 1990, v19(2), 76-87.
Hicks, John R. "Economic Theory And The Evaluation Of Consumers' Wants," **JOB**, 1962, v35(3),256-263.
Hicks, Sir John. "Automatists, Hawtreyans, And Keynesians," **JMCB**, 1969, v1(3), 307-318.
Hicks, Sydney Smith. "Aggregate Bank Portfolio Statistics: Do They Tell Us Anything?," **JBR**, 1983-84, v14(3), 221-226.
Hicks, Sydney Smith. "Commercial Banks And Business Loan Behavior," **JBF**, 1980, v4(2), 125-142.
Hiebert, L. Dean. "Deregulation And Gains To Search In The Property Liability Insurance Market," **JRI**, 1977, v44(4), 585-593.
Hiebert, L. Dean. "Optimal Loss Reduction And Increases In Risk Aversion," **JRI**, 1989, v56(2), 300-305.
Hiebert, L. Dean. "Regulation And Price Rigidity In The Property-Liability Insurance Industry," **JRI**, 1976, v43(1), 129-138.
Hieronymus, Thomas A. "Survival And Change: Post-World War II At The Chicago Board Of Trade," **RFM**, 1983, v2(2), 222-238.
Hietala, P. T. "Equity Markets And Personal Taxation: The Ex-Dividend Day Behaviour Of Finnish Stock Prices," **JBF**, 1990, v14(2/3), 327-350.
Hietala, Pekka T. "Asset Pricing In Partially Segmented Markets: Evidence From The Finnish Market," **JOF**, 1989, v44(3), 697-718.
Higgins, Catherine A. (Treynor, Jack L., William W. Priest, Jr., Lawrence Fisher and Catherine A. Higgins. "Risk Estimates," **FAJ**, 1968, v24(5), 93-100.)
Higgins, David P. "Integrating A Personal Financial Planning Major Into Existing Curricula," **JFED**, 1983, v12, 31-36.
Higgins, Robert C. and Lawrence D. Schall. "Corporate Bankruptcy And Conglomerate Merger," **JOF**, 1975, v30(1), 93-113.
Higgins, Robert C. "An Inter-Temporal Approach To The Optimization Of Dividend Policy With Predetermined Investments: Comment," **JOF**, 1974, v29(1), 254-257.
Higgins, Robert C. "Dividend Policy And Increasing Discount Rates: A Clarification," **JFQA**, 1972, v7(3), 1757-1762.
Higgins, Robert C. "Growth, Dividend Policy And Capital Costs In The Electric Utility Industry," **JOF**, 1974, v29(4), 1189-1201.
Higgins, Robert C. "How Much Growth Can A Firm Afford?," **FM**, 1977, v6(3), 7-16.
Higgins, Robert C. "Sustainable Growth Under Inflation," **FM**, 1981, v10(4), 36-40.
Higgins, Robert C. "The Corporate Dividend-Saving Decision," **JFQA**, 1972, v7(2), 1527-1541.
Higgins, Robert C. (Robichek, Alexander, Robert C. Higgins and Michael Kinsman. "The Effect Of Leverage On The Cost Of Equity Capital Of Electric Utility Firms," **JOF**, 1973, v28(2), 353-367.)
Higgins, W. W. and B. J. Moore. "Market Structure Versus Information Costs As Determinants Of Underwriters' Spreads On Municipal Bonds," **JFQA**, 1980, v15(1), 85-97.
Higham, Ron. (Finn, Frank J. and Ron Higham. "The Performance Of Unseasoned New Equity Issues-Cum-Stock Exchange Listings In Australia," **JBF**, 1988, v11(3), 333-352.)
Hill, David A. "Appraisal Of Railroad Securities," **FAJ**, 1946, v2(1), 37-47.
Hill, Horance G., Jr. "Capital Expenditure Management," **JOB**, 1955, v28(4), 285-290.
Hill, J. S. "An Evaluation Of The Life Insurance Company Income Tax Act Of 1959: Comment," **JRI**, 1964, v31(2), 294-297.
Hill, J. Stanley. "A Model For Determining The Rate Of Return On Investment In Life Insurance Policies: Comment," **JRI**, 1968, v35(3), 473-475.
Hill, Joanne and Joel L. Naroff. "The Effect Of Location On The Performance Of High Technology Firms," **FM**, 1984, v13(1), 27-36.
Hill, Joanne and Thomas Schneeweis. "International Diversification Of Equities And Fixed-Income Securities, **JFR**, 1983, v6(4), 333-343.
Hill, Joanne and Thomas Schneeweis. "A Note On The Hedging Effectiveness Of Foreign Currency Futures," **JFM**, v1(4), 659-664.
Hill, Joanne and Thomas Schneeweis. "The Hedging Effectiveness Of Foreign Currency Futures," **JFR**, 1982, v5(1), 95-104.

Hill, Joanne and Thomas Schneeweis. "The Effect Of Interval Selection On The Parameters Of The Market Model As Applied To Bond Returns," FR, 1979, v14(3),34-51.

Hill, Joanne and Thomas Schneeweis. "The Effect Of Three Mile Island On Electric Utility Stock Prices: A Note," JOF, 1983, v38(4), 1285-1292.

Hill, Joanne M. (Schneeweis, Thomas R., Joanne M. Hill and Michael G. Philipp. "Hedge Ratio Determination Based On Bond Yield Forecasts," RFM, 1983, v2(3), 338-349.)

Hill, Joanne M. and Joseph R. Liro. "Incorporating Expected Inflation Into Market Model Estimates," FR, 1982, v17(3), 112-127.

Hill, Joanne M. and Thomas Schneeweis. "Reducing Volatility With Financial Futures," FAJ, 1984, v40(6), 34-40.

Hill, Joanne M. "Is Optimal Portfolio Management Worth The Candle?," JPM, 1980-81, v7(4), 59-69.

Hill, Joanne M. "Reducing Forecast Error In Portfolio Management: Sample Clustering And Alternative Risk Specifications," FM, 1980, v9(4), 42-50.

Hill, Joanne M. (Celebuski, Matthew J., Joanne M. Hill and John J. Kilgannon. "Managing Currency Exposures In International Portfolios," FAJ, 1990, v46(1), 16-23.)

Hill, Joanne M. (Frankfurter, George M. and Joanne M. Hill. "A Normative Approach To Pension Fund Management," JFQA, 1981, v16(4), 533-555.)

Hill, Joanne M. and Frank J. Jones. "Equity Trading, Program Trading, Portfolio Insurance, Computer Trading And All That," FAJ, 1988, v44(4), 29-38.

Hill, Joanne M., Anshuman Jain and Robert A. Wood, Jr. "Insurance: Volatility Risk And Futures Mispricing," JPM, 1987-88, v14(2), 23-29.

Hill, Joanne and Thomas Schneeweis. "On The Estimation Of Hedge Ratios For Corporate Bond Positions," AFPAF, 1985, v1(1), 307-323.

Hill, Joanne, Joseph Liro and Thomas Schneeweis. "Hedging Performance Of GNMA Futures Under Rising And Falling Interest Rates," JFM, 1983, v3(4), 403-413.

Hill, Joanne, Thomas Schneeweis and Robert Mayerson. "An Analysis Of The Impact Of Marking-To-Market In Hedging With Treasury Bond Futures," RFM, 1983, v2(1), 136-159.

Hill, Joanne, Thomas Schneeweis and Jot Yau. "International Multi-Asset Diversification: A Further Analysis," AFPAF, 1989, v4(Supp), 197-214.

Hill, Joanne, Thomas Schneeweis and Jot Yau. "International Trading/Non Trading Time Effects On Risk Estimation In Futures Markets," JPM, 1990, v10(4), 407-424.

Hill, Joanne. (Elgers, Pieter, Joanne Hill and Thomas Schneeweis. "Research Design For Systematic Risk Prediction," JPM, 1981-82, v8(3), 43-52.)

Hill, Joanne. (Nunn, Kenneth P., Jr., Joanne Hill and Thomas Schneeweis. "Corporate Bond Price Data Sources And Return/Risk Measurement," JFQA, 1986, v21(2), 197-208.)

Hill, Joanne. (Schneeweis, Thomas and Joanne Hill. "A Note On The Comovement Of International Equity And Bond Markets," FR, 1980, v15(1), 30-37.)

Hill, Mark. "How A Commercial Bank Trader Uses The Treasury Bond Market For Various Hedging Applications," RFM, 1982, v1(3), 204-209.

Hill, Ned C. and Bernell K. Stone. "Accounting Betas, Systematic Operating Risk, And Financial Leverage: A Risk-Composition Approach To The Determinants Of Systematic Risk," JFQA, 1980, v15(3), 595-637.

Hill, Ned C. and Kenneth D. Riener. "Determining The Cash Discount In The Firm's Credit Policy," FM, 1979, v8(1), 68-73.

Hill, Ned C. "A Course In Short-Term Financial Management For The M.B.A.," JFED, 1979, v8, 3-10.

Hill, Ned C. (Barton, Sidney L., Ned C. Hill and Srinivasan Sundaram. "An Empirical Test Of Stakeholder Theory Predictions Of Capital Structure," FM, 1989, v18(1), 36-44.)

Hill, Ned C. (Sartoris, William L. and Ned C. Hill. "A Generalized Cash Flow Approach To Short-Term Financial Decisions," JOF, 1983, v38(2), 349-360.)

Hill, Ned C. (Sartoris, William L. and Ned C. Hill. "Evaluating Credit Policy Alternatives: A Present Value Framework," JFR, 1981, v4(1), 81-89.)

Hill, Ned C. (Sartoris, William L. and Ned C. Hill. "The Relationship Between Credit Policies And Firm Financial Characteristics," AWCM, 1990, v1(1), 99-114.)

Hill, Ned C. (Stone, Bernell K. and Ned C. Hill. "Cash Transfer Scheduling For Efficient Cash Concentration," FM, 1980, v9(3), 35-43.)

Hill, Ned C. (Stone, Bernell K. and Ned C. Hill. "Portfolio Management And The Shrinking Knapsack Algorithm," JFQA, 1979, v14(5), 1071-1083.)

Hill, Ned C. (Stone, Bernell K. and Ned C. Hill. "The Design Of A Cash Concentration System," JFQA, 1981, v16(3), 301-322.)

Hill, Ned C. (Stone, Bernell K. and Ned C. Hill. "Alternative Cash Transfer Mechanisms And Methods: Evaluation Frameworks," JBR, 1982-83, v13(1), 7-16.)

Hill, Ned C. and Daniel M. Ferguson. "Negotiating Payment Terms In An Electronic Environment," AWCM, 1990, v1(1), 131-146.

Hill, Raymond D., Jr. (Branson, William H. and Raymond D. Hill, Jr. "Capital Movements Among Major OECD Countries: Some Preliminary Results," JOF, 1971, v26(2), 269-286.)

Hill, Reese F. "The Role Of Insurance In The Defense Program," JRI, 1942, v9, 45-52.

Hill, Rowland R. "An Algorithm For Counting The Number Of Possible Portfolios Given Linear Restrictions On The Weights," JFQA, 1976, v11(3), 479-480.

Hiller, Randall S. and Christian Schaack. "A Classification Of Structured Bond Portfolio Modeling Techniques," JPM, 1990, v17(1), 37-50.

Hiller, Stanley, Jr. "The Helicopter Soars Into The Blue," FAJ, 1960, v16(6), 17-21.

Hilliard, Jimmy E. and Robert A. Leitch. "Analysis Of The Warrant Hedge In A Stable Paretian Market," JFQA, 1977, v12(1), 85-103.

Hilliard, Jimmy E. "Asset Pricing Under A Subset Of Linear Risk

Tolerance Functions And Log-Normal Market Returns," JFQA, 1980, v15(5), 1041-1061.

Hilliard, Jimmy E. "Hedging Interest Rate Risk With Futures Portfolios Under Term Structure Effects," JOF, 1984, v39(5), 1547-1569.

Hilliard, Jimmy E. "The Geometric Mean In Investment Application: Transient And Steady-State Parameters," FR, 1983, v18(4), 326-335.

Hilliard, Jimmy E. "The Relationship Between Equity Indices On World Exchanges," JOF, 1979, v34(1),103-114.

Hilliard, Jimmy E. (Barksdale, Hiram C. and Jimmy E. Hilliard. "A Cross-Spectral Analysis Of Retail Inventories And Sales," JOB, 1975, v48(3), 365-382.)

Hilliard, Jimmy E. (Murphy, J. Austin and Jimmy E. Hilliard. "An Investigation Into The Equilibrium Structure Of The Commodity Futures Market Anomaly," FR, 1989, v24(1), 1-18.)

Hilliard, Jimmy E. and Susan D. Jordan. "Hedging Interest Rate Risk With Futures Portfolios Under Full-Rank Assumptions," JFQA, 1989, v24(2), 217-240.

Hilliard, Jimmy E., Cheng F. Lee and Robert A. Leitch. "Stochastic Analysis Of Earnings And Leverage Measures," FR, 1983, v18(2), 220-233.

Hilliard, Jimmy and Joseph F. Sinkey, Jr. "Duration Analysis As A Tool For Predicting Interest-Sensitive Cash Flows," JFED, 1989, v18, 1-7.

Hillmer, S. C. and P. L. Yu. "The Market Speed Of Adjustment To New Information," JFEC, 1979, v7(4), 321-346.

Hills, Gerald E. "The Black-Owned Life Insurance Company: Comment," JRI, 1975, v42(2), 346-351.

Hilson, John Francis. (Mattar, Edward Paul, III and John Francis Hilson. "Exposure Of Corporate Directors: An Overview Of Indemnification And Liability Insurance," JRI, 1979, v46(3), 411-424.)

Hilton, James G. (Edwards, Charles E. and James G. Hilton. "Some Comments On Short-Run Earnings Fluctuation Bias," JFQA, 1970, v5(2), 187-201.)

Hilton, James G. (Edwards, Charles E. and James G. Hilton. "A Note On The High-Low Price Average As An Estimator Of Annual Average Stock Prices," JOF, 1966, v21(1), 112-115.)

Hilton, Kenneth. (Ezzamel, Mahmoud A. and Kenneth Hilton. "Can Divisional Discretion Be Measured?," JBFA, 1980, v7(2), 311-329.)

Hiltz, Starr Roxanne. "Why Black Families Own Less Life Insurance," JRI, 1971, v38(2), 225-236.

Himarios, Daniel. "The Effects Of Devaluation On The Trade Balance: A Critical View And Re-Examination Of Miles's 'New Results'," JIMF, 1985, v4(4), 553-563.

Hinderliter, Roger H. "Market Access, Uncertainty, And Reserve-Position Adjustments Of Large Commercial Banks In The 1960's," JOF, 1974, v29(1), 41-56.

Hinich, Melvin J. and Richard Roll. "Measuring Nonstationarity In The Parameters Of The Market Model," RIF, 1981, v3, 1-52.

Hinkle, John. "Financial Analysts Meet European Bankers," FAJ, 1961, v17(3), 91-94.

Hinko, Susan. (Batlin, C. A. and Susan Hinko. "Lockbox Management And Value Maximization," FM, 1981, v10(5), 39-44.)

Hinko, Susan. (Batlin, Carl Alan and Susan Hinko. "A Game Theoretic Approach To Cash Management," JOB, 1982, v55(3), 367-382.)

Hiraki, Takato. (Aggarwal, Raj, Ramesh P. Rao and Takato Hiraki. "Skewness And Kurtosis In Japanese Equity Returns: Empirical Evidence," JFR, 1989, v12(3), 253-260.)

Hiraki, Takato. (Aggarwal, Raj, Ramesh P. Rao and Takato Hiraki. "Regularities In Tokyo Stock Exchange Security Returns: P/E, Size, And Seasonal Influences," JFR, 1990, v13(3), 249-263.)

Hirsch, Joel H. "An Effective Yardstick Of Common Stock Value," FAJ, 1961, v17(3), 13-20.

Hirsch, Joel H. "Improved Yardstick Of Common Stock Value," FAJ, 1963, v19(5), 60-69.

Hirsch, Michael D. "Liquidity Filters: Tools For Better Performance," JPM, 1975-76, v2(1), 46-50.

Hirsch, Yale. (Black, Fischer, Yale Hirsch and John Westergaard. "Nuggets," JPM, 1976-77, v3(2), 71-77.)

Hirschey, M., M. B. Slovin and J. K. Zaima. "Bank Debt, Insider Trading, And The Return To Corporate Selloffs," JBF, 1990, v14(1), 85-98.

Hirschey, Mark and Janis K. Zaima. "Insider Trading, Ownership Structure, And The Market Assessment Of Corporate Sell-Offs," JOF, 1989, v44(4), 971-980.

Hirschey, Mark. "Market Structure And Market Value," JOB, 1985, v58(1), 89-98.

Hirschey, Mark. "The Effect Of Advertising On Industrial Mobility, 1947-72," JOB, 1981, v54(2),329-340.

Hirschey, Mark. (Bosch, Jean-Claude and Mark Hirschey. "The Valuation Effects Of Corporate Name Changes," FM, 1989, v18(4), 64-73.)

Hirschfeld, David J. "A Fundamental Overview Of The Energy Futures Market," JFM, 1983, v3(1), 75-100.

Hirschhorn, Eric and David Zervos. "Policies To Change The Priority Of Claimants: The Case Of Depositor Preference Laws," JFSR, 1990, v4(2), 111-126.

Hirschman, Elizabeth C. "Consumer Payment Systems: The Relationship Of Attribute Structure To Preference And Usage," JOB, 1982, v55(4), 531-545.

Hirshleifer, D. (Png, I. P. L. and D. Hirshleifer. "Price Discrimination Through Offers To Match Price," JOB, 1987, v60(3), 365-384.)

Hirshleifer, David and I. P. L. Png. "Facilitation Of Competing Bids And The Price Of A Takeover Target," RFS, 1989, v2(4), 587-606.

Hirshleifer, David. "Determinants Of Hedging And Risk Premia In Commodity Futures Markets," JFQA, 1989, v24(3), 313-332.

Hirshleifer, David. "Residual Risk, Trading Costs, And Commodity Futures Risk Premia," RFS, 1988-89, v1(2), 173-193.

Hirshleifer, J. "On Multiple Rates Of Return: Comment," JOF, 1969, v24(1), 98-99.

Hirshleifer, J. "The Theory Of Speculation Under Alternative Regimes Of Markets," JOF, 1977, v32(4), 975-999.

Hirshleifer, Jack. "Economics Of The Divisionalized Firm," JOB, 1957, v30(2), 96-108.

Hirshleifer, Jack. "On The Economics Of Transfer Pricing," JOB, 1956, v29(3), 172-184.

Hirshleifer, Jack. "The Bayesian Approach To Statistical Decision: An Exposition," JOB, 1961, v34(4), 471-489.

Hirshleifer, Jack. "The Firm's Cost Function: A Successful Reconstruction?," JOB, 1962, v35(3),235-255.

Hirt, Geoffrey A. and Charles M. Becker. "Merits And Guidelines For Industry-Security Analysis Term Papers," JFED, 1980, v9, 27-32.

Hirt, Geoffrey A. "Integrating Financial Theory And Practice With Institutional-Descriptive Finance," JFED, 1984, v13, 19-27.

Hirt, Geoffrey A. "Real Dollar Portfolios Managed By Students - An Evaluation," JFED, 1977, v6, 57-61.

Hisrich, Robert D., Michael P. Peters and John Krasnakevich. "Effectively Managing Consumer Credit Through Computer Graphics," JBR, 1982-83, v13(4), 304-308.

Hite, Gailen L. and James E. Owers. "Security Price Reactions Around Corporate Spin-Off Announcements," JFEC, 1983, v12(4), 409-436.

Hite, Gailen L. "Leverage, Output Effects, And The M-M Theorems," JFEC, 1977, v4(2), 177-202.

Hite, Gailen L. (Alberts, William W. and Gailen L. Hite. "The Modigliani-Miller Leverage Equation Considered In A Product Market Context," JFQA, 1983, v18(4), 425-437.)

Hite, Gailen L. and Anthony B. Sanders. "Excess Depreciation And The Maximum Tax," AREUEA, 1981, v9(2), 134-147.

Hite, Gailen L. and Michael R. Vetsuypens. "Management Buyouts Of Divisions And Shareholder Wealth," JOF, 1989, v44(4), 953-970.

Hite, Gailen L. and Raymond J. Krasniewski. "The 1981 Tax Act: Cost Recovery Choices For Real Property," AREUEA, 1982, v10(2), 200-208.

Hite, Gailen L., James E. Owers and Ronald C. Rogers. "The Market For Interfirm Asset Sales: Partial Sell-Offs And Total Liquidations," JFEC, 1987, v18(2), 229-252.

Hite, Gailen L., James E. Owers and Ronald C. Rogers. "The Separation Of Real Estate Operations By Spin-Off," AREUEA, 1984, v12(3), 318-331.

Hitschler, W. Anthony. "The Caribou Weren't In The Estimates," FAJ, 1980, v36(1), 28-32.

Hittle, Linda. (Ely, David P. and Linda Hittle. "The Impact Of Math Background On Performance In Managerial Economics And Basic Finance Courses," JFED, 1990, v19, 59-61.)

Ho, Kwok S. "An Empirical Analysis Of A Causality Relationship Between Corporate Investment And Financing Decisions," RIF, 1986, v6, 179-196.

Ho, Kwok. (Chan, K. Hung and Kwok Ho. "Forecasting Of Seasonal And Cyclical Financial Variables: The Wiener-Kolmogorov Method Vs. The Box-Jenkins Method," AFPAF, 1987, v2(1), 103-118.)

Ho, Peter C. (Paulson, Albert S. and Peter C. Ho. "Portfolio Selection Via Factor Analysis," JPM, 1979-80, v6(3), 27-30.)

Ho, Thomas and Anthony Saunders. "A Catastrophe Model Of Bank Failure," JOF, 1980, v35(5), 1189-1207.

Ho, Thomas and Hans R. Stoll. "On Dealer Markets Under Competition," JOF, 1980, v35(2), 259-267.

Ho, Thomas and Hans R. Stoll. "Optimal Dealer Pricing Under Transactions And Return Uncertainty," JFEC, 1981, v9(1), 47-73.

Ho, Thomas S. Y. and Anthony Saunders. "Fixed Rate Loan Commitments, Take-Down Risk, And The Dynamics Of Hedging With Futures," JFQA, 1983, v18(4), 499-516.

Ho, Thomas S. Y. and Anthony Saunders. "The Determinants Of Bank Interest Margins: Theory And Empirical Evidence," JFQA, 1981, v16(4), 581-600.

Ho, Thomas S. Y. and Anthony Saunders. "A Micro Model Of The Federal Funds Market," JOF, 1985, v40(3), 977-988.

Ho, Thomas S. Y. and Hans R. Stoll. "The Dynamics Of Dealer Markets Under Competition," JOF, 1983, v38(4), 1053-1074.

Ho, Thomas S. Y. and Richard G. Macris. "Dealer Bid-Ask Quotes And Transaction Prices: An Empirical Study Of Some AMEX Options," JOF, 1984, v39(1),23-45.

Ho, Thomas S. Y. and Ronald F. Singer. "Bond Indenture Provisions And The Risk Of Corporate Debt," JFEC, 1982, v10(4), 375-406.

Ho, Thomas S. Y. and Sang-Bin Lee. "Term Structure Movements And Pricing Interest Rate Contingent Claims," JOF, 1986, v41(5), 1011-1030.

Ho, Thomas S. Y. "Intertemporal Commodity Futures Hedging And The Production Decision," JOF, 1984, v39(2), 351-377.

Ho, Thomas S. Y. (Hasbrouck, Joel and Thomas S. Y. Ho. "Order Arrival, Quote Behavior, And The Return-Generating Process," JOF, 1987, v42(4), 1035-1048.)

Ho, Thomas S. Y. and Roni Michaely. "Information Quality And Market Efficiency," JFQA, 1988, v23(1), 53-70.

Ho, Thomas S. Y. and Sang Bin Lee. "Interest Rate Futures Options And Interest Rate Options," FR, 1990, v25(3), 345-370.

Ho, Thomas S. Y. and Sang Bin Lee. "Pricing Of The Call And Sinking Fund Provisions On Corporate Bonds Under Interest Rate Risk: Empirical Evidence," IJOF, 1989, v2(1), 1-17.

Ho, Thomas S. Y. and Sang Bin Lee. "The Pricing Of Corporate Bond Provisions Under Interest Rate Risks," RIF, 1988, v7, 139-162.

Ho, Thomas S. Y., Robert A. Schwartz and David K. Whitcomb. "The Trading Decision And Market Clearing Under Transaction Price Uncertainty," JOF, 1985, v40(1), 21-42.

Ho, Thomas and Donald F. Singer. "The Value Of Corporate Debt With A Sinking-Fund Provision," JOB, 1984, v57(3), 315-336.

Ho, Yak-Ki. (Cheung, Yan-Leung and Yak-Ki Ho. "The Intertemporal Stability Of The Relationships Between Asian Emerging Equity Markets And The Developed Equity Markets," JBFA, 1991, v18(2), 235-254.)

Hoadley, Walter E. "Facing The Problems Of 1958," FAJ, 1958, v14(2), 19-22.

Hoag, James W. (Draper, Dennis W. and James W. Hoag. "Portfolio Strategies Using Treasury Bond Options And Futures," RFM, 1983, v2(1), 82-98.)

Hoag, James W. (Pan, Fung-Shine and James W. Hoag. "The Pricing Of GNMA Futures Using Dealer Quotations And Spot Transactions," RFM, 1984, v3(3), 244-255.)

Hoag, James W. "Towards Indices Of Real Estate Value And Return," JOF, 1980, v35(2), 569-580.

Hoag, James W. (Draper, Dennis W. and James W. Hoag. "Financial Intermediation And The Theory Of Agency," JFQA, 1978, v13(4), 595-611.)

Hoban, James P., Jr. (Huntsman, Blaine and James P. Hoban, Jr. "Investment In New Enterprise: Some Empirical Observations On Risk, Return, And Market Structure," FM, 1980, v9(2), 44-51.)

Hobbs, C. D. "Instructional Objectives In Finance," JFED, 1972, v1, 12-18.

Hobbs, Gerald R. and William B. Riley. "Profiting From A Presidential Election," FAJ, 1984, v40(2), 46-52.

Hobman, Richard J. "Setting Investment Policy In An ERISA Environment," JPM, 1975-76, v2(1), 17-21.

Hobson, Hugh A., John T. Masten and Jacobus T. Severiens. "Holding Company Acquisitions And Bank Performance: A Comparative Study," JBR, 1978-79, v9(2), 116-120.

Hochheimer, Frank. (Vaughn, Richard, Frank Hochheimer and Marvin Kelly. "Identifying Seasonality In Futures Prices Using X-11," JFM, v1(1), 93-102.)

Hochman, Shalom and Oded Palmon. "The Irrelevance Of Capital Structure For The Impact Of Inflation On Investment," JOF, 1983, v38(3), 785-794.

Hochman, Shalom and Oded Palmon. "The Impact Of Inflation On The Aggregate Debt-Asset Ratio," JOF, 1985, v40(4), 1115-1125.

Hochman, Shalom and Ramon Rabinovitch. "Financial Leasing Under Inflation," FM, 1984, v13(1), 17-26.

Hochman, Shalom and Oded Palmon. "A Tax-Induced Clientele For Index-Linked Corporate Bonds," JOF, 1988, v43(5), 1257-1263.

Hochman, Shalom and Oded Palmon. "Expected Inflation And The Real Rates Of Interest On Taxable And Tax-Exempt Bonds," JMCB, 1987, v19(1), 90-103.

Hochman, Shalom. "The Beta Coefficient: An Instrumental Variables Approach," RIF, 1983, v4, 123-152.

Hochman, Shalom. (Ben-Horim, Moshe, Shalom Hochman and Oded Palmon. "The Impact Of The 1986 Tax Reform Act On Corporate Financial Policy," FM, 1987, v16(3), 29-35.)

Hochmuth, Wayne P. and Arthur S. Bowes, Jr. "Investment Companies: Performance Vs. Charges (Part I)," FAJ, 1961, v17(1), 43-49.

Hochmuth, Wayne P. (Bowes, Arthur S., Jr. and Wayne P. Hochmuth. "Investment Companies: Performances Vs. Charges (Part II)," FAJ, 1961, v17(2),83-88.)

Hockstader, Harry G., Jr. "Trends In Railroad Earnings," FAJ, 1948, v4(3), 3-14.

Hodder, James E. and Adrian E. Tschoegl. "Some Aspects Of Japanese Corporate Finance," JFQA, 1985, v20(2), 173-192.

Hodder, James E. "Evaluation Of Manufacturing Investments: A Comparison Of U.S. And Japanese Practices," FM, 1986, v15(1), 17-24.

Hodder, James E. (Triantis, Alexander J. and James E. Hodder. "Valuing Flexibility As A Complex Option," JOF, 1990, v45(2), 549-566.)

Hodder, James E. and Lemma W. Senbet. "International Capital Structure Equilibrium," JOF, 1990, v45(5), 1495-1516.

Hodes, D. A. (Hammel, J. E. and D. A. Hodes. "Factors Influencing P/E Multiples," FAJ, 1967, v23(1), 90-92.)

Hodes, Daniel A. "Modular Housing," FAJ, 1970, v26(3), 80-89.

Hodges, J. Frank, Jr. "Effect Of Fire Loss And Loss Adjustments On Consumer Attitudes Toward Insurance," JRI, 1974, v41(2), 267-285.

Hodges, S. D. and R. A. Brealey. "The Rate Of Return On New Investment In The UK," JOF, 1980, v35(3), 799-800.

Hodges, S. D. and R. A. Brealey. "Dynamic Portfolio Selection," FAJ, 1973, v29(2), 50-65.

Hodges, S. D. and S. M. Schaefer. "A Model For Bond Portfolio Improvement," JFQA, 1977, v12(2), 243-260.

Hodges, S. D. (Brealey, R. A. and S. D. Hodges. "Playing With Portfolios," JOF, 1975, v30(1),125-134.)

Hodges, Stewart and Stephen Schaefer. "The Interpretation Of The Geometric Mean: A Note," JFQA, 1974, v9(3), 497-504.

Hodges, Stewart D. and Richard A. Brealey. "Dynamic Portfolio Selection," FAJ, 1972, v28(6), 58-69.

Hodges, Stewart D. "The Valuation Of Variable Rate Leases," FM, 1985, v14(1), 68-74.

Hodges, Stewart D. (Franks, Julian R. and Stewart D. Hodges. "Lease Valuation When Taxable Earnings Are A Scarce Resource," JOF, 1987, v42(4), 987-1005.)

Hodges, Stewart D. (Franks, Julian R. and Stewart D. Hodges. "Valuation Of Financial Lease Contracts: A Note," JOF, 1978, v33(2), 657-669.)

Hodges, Stewart D. and Anthony Neuberger. "Optimal Replication Of Contingent Claims Under Transactions Costs," RFM, 1989, v8(2), 222-239.

Hodges, Stewart. (Moon, Philip and Stewart Hodges. "Implications Of The Recent Tax Changes For Corporate Capital Investment," JBFA, 1989, v16(1), 25-40.)

Hodgetts, Richard M. "Corporate Planning And The Holding Company: Comment," JRI, 1970, v37(1), 138-140.

Hodgman, Donald R. "British Techniques Of Monetary Policy: A Critical Review," JMCB, 1971, v3(4), 760-779.

Hodgman, Donald R. "Member-Bank Borrowing: A Comment," JOF, 1961, v16(1), 90-93.

Hodgman, Donald R. "Selective Credit Controls," JMCB, 1972, v4(2), 342-359.

Hodgman, Donald R. "Member-Bank Borrowing: An Additional Comment," JOF, 1961, v16(1), 98-98.

Hodgson, Allan and Des Nicholls. "The Impact Of Index Futures Markets On Australian Sharemarket Volatility," JBFA, 1991, v18(2), 267-280.

Hodnette, J. K. "Gas Turbine As Railroad Motive Power," FAJ, 1953, v9(1), 55-58.

Hodrick, Robert J. and Sanjay Srivastava. "The Covariation Of Risk Premiums And Expected Future Spot Exchange Rates," Supplement, JIMF, 1986, v5(Supp), S5-S21.

Hodrick, Robert J. and Sanjay Srivastava. "An Investigation Of Risk And Return In Forward Foreign Exchange," JIMF, 1984, v3(1), 5-29.

Hodrick, Robert J. (Flood, Robert P. and Robert J. Hodrick. "Asset Price Volatility, Bubbles, And Process Switching," JOF, 1986, v41(4), 831-842.)

Hoehenwarter, Wolfgang P. "Guidelines For The Development Of Problem Oriented Software Systems," JBR, 1971-72, v2(2), 56-59.

Hoisington, Frederick R. "Commodities: High Finance In Rubber," FAJ, 1960, v16(3), 105-116.

Holbrook, Robert S. "Optimal Policy Choice Under A Nonlinear Constraint: An Iterative Application Of Linear Techniques," JMCB, 1975, v7(1), 33-49.

Hold, William T. "Graduate Insurance Education For The Non-Insurance Major," JRI, 1968, v35(3), 467-470.

Holden, Karen C. (Myers, Daniel A., Richard V. Burkhauser and Karen C. Holden. "The Transition From Wife To Widow: The Importance Of Survivor Benefits To Widows," JRI, 1987, v54(4), 752-759.)

Holderness, Clifford G. and Dennis P. Sheehan. "Raiders Or Saviors? The Evidence On Six Controversial Investors," JFEC, 1985, v14(4), 555-579.

Holderness, Clifford G. (Barclay, Michael J. and Clifford G. Holderness. "Private Benefits From Control Of Public Corporations," JFEC, 1989, v25(2), 371-396.)

Holderness, Clifford G. and Dennis P. Sheehan. "The Role Of Majority Shareholders In Publicly Held Corporations: An Exploratory Analysis," JFEC, 1988, v20(1/2), 317-346.

Holdren, George C. "Toward Greater Comparability Of Financial Statements," FAJ, 1963, v19(2), 101-103.

Holdren, George C. "What Does The Auditor Really Say?," FAJ, 1969, v25(4), 43-50.

Holland, A. Steven. "Indexation And The Effect Of Inflation Uncertainty On Real GNP," JOB, 1988, v61(4), 473-484.

Holland, Cylde W. (Dyl, Edward A. and Clyde W. Holland. "Why A Weekend Effect? Comment," JPM, 1990, v16(2), 88-89.)

Holland, Daniel M. "Business Tax Provisions Of The 1962 And 1964 Acts," JOF, 1965, v20(2), 273-291.

Holland, Daniel M. "Dividend Underreporting On Tax Returns," JOF, 1958, v13(2), 238-260.

Holland, Michael M. and J. Louis Heck. "Investment Yields And Magic Triangles: A Computer Solution Based On The Newton-Rapheson Convergence Technique," JFED, 1984, v13, 72-79.

Holland, Robert C. "Bank Holding Companies And Financial Stability," JFQA, 1975, v10(4), 577-587.

Holland, Robert C. "The Federal Reserve Discount Mechanism As An Instrument For Dealing With Banking Market Imperfections," JMCB, 1970, v2(2), 138-146.

Holland, Rodger G. and Nancy A. Sutton. "The Liability Nature Of Unfunded Pension Obligations Since ERISA," JRI, 1988, v55(1), 32-58.

Holland, Thomas E. "Cyclical Movements Of Interest Rates, 1948-61," JOB, 1964, v37(4), 364-369.

Hollas, Daniel R. (Stansell, Stanley R. and Daniel R. Hollas. "An Examination Of The Relative Economic Efficiency Of Mutual Vs. Stock Savings Institutions," JREFEC, 1990, v3(1), 73-90.)

Hollinger, Robert D. (Pohlman, Randolph A., James S. Ang and Robert D. Hollinger. "Performance And Timing: A Test Of Hedge Funds," JPM, 1977-78, v4(3), 69-72.)

Hollinger, Robert D. (Pohlman, Randolph A. and Robert D. Hollinger. "Information Redundancy In Sets Of Financial Ratios," JBFA, 1981, v8(4), 511-528.)

Holloway, Clark. "A Note On Testing An Aggressive Investment Strategy Using Value Line Ranks," JOF, 1981, v36(3), 711-719.

Holloway, Clark. "Testing An Aggressive Investment Strategy Using Value Line Ranks: A Reply," JOF, 1983, v38(1), 263-270.

Holloway, Thomas M. (de Leeuw, Frank and Thomas M. Holloway. "The Measurement And Significance Of The Cyclically Adjusted Federal Budget And Debt," JMCB, 1985, v17(2), 232-242.)

Holman, Walter R. and Harold D. Fletcher. "Flow Through Versus Normalization Accounting For Electric Utilities - The Phantom Tax Issue," FR, 1981, v16(2), 30-40.

Holman, Walter. (Singer, Daniel and Walter Holman. "The Effective Use Of Writing In Financial Case Analysis," JFED, 1990,v19,23-26.)

Holmberg, Stevan R. and H. Kent Baker. "The CEO's Role In Strategic Planning," JBR, 1981-82, v12(4), 218-227.

Holme, Kevin. (Cameron, Stephen, Kevin Holme and Alice Rapoport. "Managing Interest Rate Risk," JACF, 1990, v3(1), 56-64.)

Holmes, Alexander B. and Myron L. Kwast. "Interest Rates And Inflationary Expectations: Tests For Structural Change 1952-1976," JOF, 1979, v34(3),733-741.

Holmes, David N., Jr. "Excess Demand, Undercapitalization, And The True Interest Rate For Credit Union Loans In Unorganized Money Markets," JOF, 1974, v29(4), 1063-1076.

Holmes, John Russell. "100 Years Of Common Stock Investing," FAJ, 1974, v30(6), 38-44,85.

Holmes, John Russell. "Growth, Risk, And Stock Valuation," FAJ, 1976, v32(3), 46-55.

Holmes, R. A. "British Columbia's Need For No Fault Automobile Insurance," JRI, 1970, v37(4), 609-619.)

Holmes, R. A. "Inequities In Canadian Automobile Insurance Rates For Risky Groups," JOB, 1971, v44(2), 180-183.

Holmstrom, Bengt. (Baron, David P. and Bengt Holmstrom. "The Investment Banking Contract For New Issues Under Asymmetric Information: Delegation And The Incentive Problem," JOF, 1980, v35(5), 1115-1138.)

Holsapple, Clyde W., Kar Yan Tam and Andrew B. Whinston. "Adapting Expert System Technology To Financial Management," FM, 1988, v17(3), 12-22.

Holt, Charles C. and John P. Shelton. "The Implications Of The Capital Gains Tax For Investment Decisions," JOF, 1961, v16(4), 559-580.

Holt, Charles C. "The Influence Of Growth Duration On Share Prices," JOF, 1962, v17(3), 465-475.

Holt, Matthew T. and Jon A. Brandt. "Combining Price Forecasting With Hedging Of Hogs: An Evaluation Using Alternative Measures Of Risk," JFM, 1985, v5(3), 297-309.

Holt, Robert N. and Rebecca E. Fincher. "The Foreign Corrupt Practices Act," FAJ, 1981, v37(2), 73-76.

Holthausen, Duncan M. and John S. Hughes. "Commodity Returns And Capital Asset Pricing," FM, 1978, v7(2), 37-44.

Holthausen, Duncan McC. "A Critical Evaluation Of Available Consumer Credit Statistics," JOF, 1952, v7(2), 372-387.

Holthausen, Robert W. and Richard W. Leftwich. "The Effect Of Bond Rating Changes On Common Stock Prices," JFEC, 1986, v17(1), 57-90.

Holthausen, Robert W., Richard W. Leftwich and David Mayers. "The Effect Of Large Block Transactions On Security Prices: A Cross-Sectional Analysis," JFEC, 1987, v19(2), 237-268.

Holthausen, Robert W., Richard W. Leftwich and David Mayers. "Large-Block Transactions, The Speed Of Response, And Temporary And Permanent Stock-Price Effects," JFEC, 1990, v26(1), 71-96.

Holtmann, A. G. and Alan E. Bayer. "Determinants Of Professional Income Among Recent Recipients Of Natural Science Doctorates," JOB, 1970, v43(4), 410-418.

Holton, Richard H. "The Record Of Corporate Profits," FAJ, 1964, v20(4), 45-48.

Holton, Thomas L. "The Growing Confusion In Profit Accounting," FAJ, 1964, v20(2), 52-56.

Holtrop, M. V. "On The Effectiveness Of Monetary Policy: The Experience Of The Netherlands In The Years 1954-1969," JMCB, 1972, v4(2), 283-311.

Homa, Kenneth E. and Dwight M. Jaffee. "The Supply Of Money And Common Stock Prices," JOF, 1971, v26(5), 1045-1066.

Homaifar, Ghassem and Duane B. Graddy. "Variance And Lower Partial Moment Betas As Alternative Risk Measures In Cost Of Capital Estimation: A Defense Of The CAPM Beta," JBFA, 1990, v17(5), 677-688.

Homaifar, Ghassem. (Graddy, Duane B., Ghassem Homaifar and Adi S. Karna. "Double Leverage As A Source Of Systematic Risk In Bank Holding Company Stocks," JBR, 1984-85, v15(2), 115-122.)

Homaifar, Ghassem. (Strickland, Thomas H. and Ghassem Homaifar. "Foreign Direct Investment: Evidence From Capital Market Data," GFJ, 1990, v1(2), 153-162.)

Homan, Rick K., Gerald L. Glandon and Michael A. Counte. "Perceived Risk: The Link To Plan Selection And Future Utilization," JRI, 1989, v56(1), 67-82.

Homer, Sidney. "Distortions Within Money Markets," FAJ, 1968, v24(4), 77-79.

Homer, Sidney. "Inflation And The Capital Markets," FAJ, 1969, v25(4), 143-145.

Homer, Sidney. "Spring Tide In The Money Market (Keynote Review)," FAJ, 1966, v22(5), 101-102.

Homer, Sidney. "The High-Grade Bond Market During The Great Crash," JPM, 1979-80, v6(1), 24-25.

Homer, Sidney. "The Historical Evolution Of Today's Bond Market," JPM, 1974-75, v1(3), 6-11.

Homer, Sidney. "The Outlook For Long-Term Interest Rates," JOF, 1959, v14(2), 271-278.

Honeycutt, T. Crawford. "The Microeconomic Consequences Of Corporate Mergers: A Comment," JOB, 1975, v48(2), 267-274.

Hong, Hai and Alfred Rappaport. "Debt Capacity, Optimal Capital Structure, And Capital Budgeting Analysis," FM, 1978, v7(3), 7-11.

Hong, Hai. "Inflation And The Market Value Of The Firm: Theory And Tests," JOF, 1977, v32(4), 1031-1048.

Hong, Hai. "Inflationary Tax Effects On The Assets Of Business Corporations," FM, 1977, v6(3),51-59.

Hong, Hai. (Thakor, Anjan, Hai Hong and Stuart I. Greenbaum. "Bank Loan Commitments And Interest Rate Volatility," JBF, 1981, v5(4), 497-510.)

Hong, Han Kang. "Finance Mix And Capital Structure," JBFA, 1981, v8(4), 485-491.

Hong, Sungbin Chun. (Choi, Frederick D. S. and Sungbin Chun Hong. "The Feasibility And Decision Utility Of Restating Accounting Information Sets: Korea," AFPAF, 1990, v5(1), 123-144.)

Honig, Lawrence E. and Stephen C. Coley. "An After-Tax Equivalent Payment Approach To Conventional Lease Analysis," FM, 1974, v4(2), 8-16.

Honohan, Patrick and R. P. Kinsella. "Comparing Bank Concentration Across Countries," JBF, 1982, v6(2), 255-262.

Hood, L. Randolph. (Brinson, Gary P., L. Randolph Hood and Gilbert L. Beebower. "Determinants Of Portfolio Performance," FAJ, 1986, v42(4), 39-44.)

Hood, Oakman. "The Science Of Volatility," FAJ, 1958, v14(4), 35-38.

Hooks, Donald L. (Zumpano, Leonard V. and Donald L. Hooks. "The Real Estate Brokerage Market: A Critical Reevaluation," AREUEA, 1988, v16(1), 1-16.)

Hooley, Richard W. "Life Insurance Investments In Natural Gas Pipelines," JRI, 1958, v25(2), 1-9.

Hooper, Carolyn N. "SBA's Business Loan Program: Retrospect And Prospect," JBR, 1971-72, v2(3), 39-49.

Hooper, Lucien O. "American Involvement In International Politics," FAJ, 1947, v3(2), 10-15.

Hooper, Lucien O. "Federation Plans First Annual Meeting," FAJ, 1947, v3(4), 54-56.

Hooper, Lucien O. "Should Security Analysts Have A Professional Rating?: The Negative Case," FAJ, 1945, v1(1), 41-44.

Hooper, Lucien O. "The Shrinking Volume Of Trading," FAJ, 1954, v10(5), 43-46.

Hooper, Lucien O. "The Theory Of Emergency Controls," FAJ, 1951, v7(1), 45-46.

Hooper, Paul. (Page, John R. and Paul Hooper. "Financial Statements For Security Analysts," FAJ, 1979, v35(5), 50-55.)

Hooper, Peter and John Morton. "Fluctuations In The Dollar: A Model Of Nominal And Real Exchange Rate Determination," JIMF, 1982, v1(1), 39-56.

Hoover, Calvin B. "What Can Europe Do For Itself?," JOF, 1948, v3(1), 16-31.

Hoover, Edgar M. "The Outlook For Capital Expenditures," FAJ, 1951, v7(4), 37-40.

Hope, David. (Martin, Larry J. and David Hope. "Risk And Returns From Alternative Marketing Strategies For Corn Producers," JFM, 1984, v4(4), 513-530.)

Hope, Tony and Rob Gray. "Power And Policy Making: The Development Of An R & D Standard," JBFA, 1982, v8(4), 531-558.

Hopelain, David G. and Donald W. Jones. "Managing Change In Investment Institutions," FAJ, 1976, v32(5), 27-34.

Hopewell, Michael H. and Arthur L. Schwartz. "Temporary Trading Suspensions In Individual NYSE Securities," JOF, 1978, v33(5), 1355-1373.

Hopewell, Michael H. and Arthur L. Schwartz, Jr. "Stock Price Movement Associated With Temporary Trading Suspensions: Bear Market Versus Bull Market," JFQA, 1976, v11(4), 577-590.

Hopewell, Michael H. and George G. Kaufman. "Commercial Bank Bidding On Municipal Revenue Bonds: New Evidence," JOF, 1977, v32(5), 1647-1656.

Hopewell, Michael H. and George G. Kaufman. "Comment On PIC: An Alternative Approach," FM, 1979, v8(2), 42-45.

Hopewell, Michael H. and George G. Kaufman. "The Cost Of Inefficient Coupons On Municipal Bonds," JFQA, 1974, v9(2), 155-164.

Hopkinson, Edward, Jr. "The Fruition Of Philadelphia's Ambition," FAJ, 1953, v9(1), 25-27.

Hopper, Max. "Strategies For The Development Of Electronic Systems," JBR, 1985-86, v16(4), 202-205.

Horesh, Reuven. (Adler, Michael and Reuven Horesh. "The Relationship Among Equity Markets: Comment," JOF, 1974, v29(4), 1311-1317.)

Horn, Ronald C. "Report Of The Committee On Curricular Concepts In Risk And Insurance," JRI, 1966, v33(3), 471-474.

Horn, Ronald C. (Crowe, Robert M. and Ronald C. Horn. "The Meaning Of Risk," JRI, 1967, v34(3), 459-474.)

Horne, J. M. (Beck, R. G. and J. M. Horne. "Economic Class And Risk Avoidance: Experience Under Public Medical Care Insurance," JRI, 1976, v43(1), 73-86.)

Horne, Jocelyn. "The Asset Market Model Of The Balance Of Payments And The Exchange Rate: A Survey Of Empirical Evidence," JIMF, 1983, v3(2), 89-109.

Horner, Melchior R. "The Value Of The Corporate Voting Right: Evidence From Switzerland," JBF, 1988, v12(1), 69-84.

Horngren, Charles T. "Depreciation, Flow Of Funds, And The Price Level," FAJ, 1957, v13(4), 45-48.

Horngren, Lars. "Regulatory Monetary Policy And Uncontrolled Financial Intermediaries," JMCB, 1985, v17(2), 203-219.

Horowitz, Ira. "The 'Reward-To-Variability' Ratio And Mutual Fund Performance," JOB, 1966, v39(4), 485-488.

Horowitz, John K. and Richard T. Carson. "Discounting Statistical Lives," JRU, 1990, v3(4), 403-413.

Horowitz, Robert. "Net Present Value IN BASIC," JFED, 1973, v2, 80-81.

Horowitz, Robert. "Price Level Adjustments In Capital Budgeting," JFED, 1972, v1, 100-103.

Horrell, James F. (Cotner, John S. and James F. Horrell. "An Analysis Of Index Option Pricing," JFM, 1989, v9(5), 449-460.)

Horrigan, James O. "Methodological Implications Of Non-Normally Distributed Financial Ratios: A Comment," JBFA, 1983, v10(4), 683-689.

Horrigan, James O. "Some Hypotheses On The Valuation Of Stock Warrants," JBFA, 1974, v1(2), 239-248.

Horrigan, James O. (Etebari, Ahmad, James O. Horrigan and Jan L. Landwehr. "To Be Or Not To Be--Reaction Of Stock Returns To Sudden Deaths Of Corporate Chief Executive Officers," JBFA, 1987, v14(2), 255-278.)

Horrigan, James O. (Etebari, Ahmad and James O. Horrigan. "A Note On The Use Of Objective Exams In Basic Finance Courses," JFED, 1982, v11, 61-66.)

Horrigan, James O. (Wrightsman, Dwayne and James O. Horrigan. "Retention, Risk Of Success, And The Price Of Stock: A Note," JOF, 1975, v30(5), 1357-1359.)

Horsky, Dan and Subrata K. Sen. "Interfaces Between Marketing And Economics: An Overview," JOB, 1980, v53(3), Part 2, S5-S12.

Horsky, Dan. (Benston, George J. and Dan Horsky. "Redlining And The Demand For Mortgages In The Central City And Suburbs," JBR, 1979-80, v10(2), 72-87.)

Horton, Joseph J., Jr. "Rating Index For Municipal Bonds," FAJ, 1969, v25(2), 72-75.

Horton, Joseph J., Jr. "Statistical Classification Of Municipal Bonds," JBR, 1970-71, v1(3), 29-40.

Horton, Joseph. "Personal Finance In The Finance Curriculum," JFED, 1972, v1, 22.

Horton, William L. and Howard S. Gross. "Opportunities For Commercial Banks In The Business Lease/Instalment Loan Market," JBR, 1974-75, v5(3), 125-128.

Horvath, Philip A. and Robert C. Scott. "An Expected Utility Explanation Of Plunging And Dumping Behavior," FR, 1985, v20(2), 219-228.

Horvath, Philip A. "A Measurement Of The Errors In Intra-Period Compounding And Bond Valuation: A Short Extension," FR, 1988, v23(3), 359-364.

Horvath, Philip A. "A Pedagogic Note on Intra-Period Compounding And Discounting," FR, 1985, v20(1), 116-118.

Horvath, Philip A. "Disintermediation Revisited," FR, 1988, v23(3), 301-312.

Horvath, Philip A. (Scott, Robert C. and Philip A. Horvath. "On The Direction Of Preference For Moments Of Higher Order Than The Variance," JOF, 1980, v35(4), 915-919.)

Horvitz, Paul M. and Charles P. Harper. "Regulation Of The Money Order Industry," FM, 1980, v9(4), 13-20.

Horvitz, Paul M. "A Reconsideration Of The Role Of Bank Examination," JMCB, 1980, v12(4), Part 1, 654-659.

Horvitz, Paul M. "Failures Of Large Banks: Implications For Banking Supervision And Deposit Insurance," JFQA, 1975, v10(4), 589-601.

Horvitz, Paul M. "Price Uniformity And Banking Markets," FR, 1969, v1(4), 213-219.

Horvitz, Paul M. "Reorganization Of The Financial Regulatory Agencies," JBR, 1982-83, v13(4), 245-263.

Horvitz, Paul M. "Stimulating Bank Competition Through Regulatory Action," JOF, 1965, v20(1), 1-13.

Horvitz, Paul M. "The Hunt Commission Report: A Further Comment," JOF, 1974, v29(1), 267-269.

Horvitz, Paul M., Insup Lee and Kerry L. Robertson. "Valuation Effects Of New Securities Issuance By Bank Holding Companies: New Evidence," FR, 1991, v26(1), 91-104.

Horvitz, Sigmund A. "Implications Of Projecting Future Losses Of Earning Capacity With Deterministic Models," JRI, 1986, v53(3), 530-537.

Horwich, George. "Elements Of Timing And Response In The Balance Sheet Of Banking, 1953-55," JOF, 1957, v12(2), 238-255.

Horwich, George. "Tight Money As A Cause Of Inflation: Reply," JOF, 1971, v26(1), 156-158.

Horwich, George. "Tight Money, Monetary Restraint, And The Price Level," JOF, 1966, v21(1), 15-33.

Horwitz, Bertrand N. "Profit Responsibility In Soviet Enterprise," JOB, 1968, v41(1), 47-55.

Hosek, William R. "Problems In The Use Of Historical Data In Estimating Economic Loss In Wrongful Death And Injury Cases," JRI, 1982, v49(2), 300-308.

Hosek, William R. "Problems In the Use Of Historical Data In Estimating Economic Loss In Wrongful Death And Injury Cases: Reply," JRI, 1984, v51(1), 126-130.

Hosek, William R. (Weintraub, Robert and William R. Hosek. "Further Reflections On And Investigations Of Money Demand," JOF, 1970, v25(1), 109-125.)

Hosemann, Michael J. "Measuring The Impact Of Electronic Funds Transfer Systems On Float," JBR, 1972-73, v3(3), 136-154.

Hoshik, Takeo, Anil Kashyap and David Scharfstein. "The Role Of Banks In Reducing The Costs Of Financial Distress In Japan," JFEC, 1990, v27(1), 67-88.

Hoshino, Yasuo. "The Performance Of Corporate Mergers In Japan," JBFA, 1982, v8(2), 153-165.

Hoshower, Leon B. "Dividends, Reinvestment, And Stock Price," JFED, 1983, v12, 59-63.

Hoskin, C. A. "What About Public Utility Capitalization Ratios?," FAJ, 1957, v13(2), 39-46.

Hoskin, Robert E. (Farkas, Karen L. and Robert E. Hoskin. "Testing A Valuation Model For American Puts," FM, 1979, v8(3), 51-56.)

Hoskins, C. G. "Benefit-Cost Ratios Versus Net Present Value: Revisited," JBFA, 1974, v1(2), 249-265.

Hoskins, C. G. "Capital Appraisal And The Case For Average Rate Of Return: A Comment," JBFA, 1979, v6(2), 239-241.

Hoskins, Charles R. "Impact Of Change On Bank Personnel And The Management Process," JBR, 1974-75, v5(3), 170-173.

Hoskins, Colin D. "Benefit-Cost Ratio Ranking For Size Disparity Problems," JBFA, 1977, v4(2), 229-232.

Host-Madsen, Poul. "The Changing Role Of International Capital Flows," JOF, 1963, v18(2), 187-210.

Hotson, John H. "Tight Money As A Cause Of Inflation: Comment," JOF, 1971, v26(1), 152-155.

Hou-Shun, Lieu. "The Concept Of Economic Homeostasis," FAJ, 1956, v12(4), 51-54.

Houchens, Robert L. (Rolph, John E., James K. Hammitt and Robert L. Houchens. "Automobile Accident Compensation: Who Pays How Much How Soon?," JRI, 1985, v52(4), 667-685.)

Houghton, Keith A. and David R. Woodliff. "Financial Ratios: The Prediction Of Corporte 'Success' And Failure," JBFA, 1987, v14(4), 537-554.

Houglet, Michel. (Rosenberg, Barr and Michel Houglet. "Error Rates In CRSP And COMPUSTAT Data Bases And Their Implications," JOF, 1974, v29(4), 1303-1310.)

Houpt, James A. "Foreign Ownership Of U.S. Banks: Trends And Effects," JBR, 1983-84, v14(2), 144-156.

Houston, Arthur L., Jr. "A Comparison Of The Reinvestment Risk Of The Price Level Adjusted Mortgage And The Standard Fixed Payment Mortgage," AREUEA, 1988, v16(1), 34-49.

Houston, Arthur L., Jr. (Giliberto, S. Michael and Arthur L. Houston, Jr. "Relocation Opportunities And Mortgage Default," AREUEA, 1989, v17(1), 55-69.)

Houston, Arthur L., Jr. and Carol Olson Houston. "Financing With Preferred Stock," FM, 1990, v19(3), 42-54.

Houston, Carol Olson. (Houston, Arthur L., Jr. and Carol Olson Houston. "Financing With Preferred Stock," FM, 1990, v19(3), 42-54.)

Houston, David B. "A Comparison Of Mortality Rates Of Insured Lives With Those Of The General Population," JRI, 1959, v26(3), 13-24.

Houston, David B. "Deficiency Reserves And The X17 Mortality Table," JRI, 1958, v25(2), 10-21.

Houston, David B. "Elizur Wright: The Man And His Work," JRI, 1959, v26(4), 11-36.

Houston, David B. "Risk Theory," JRI, 1960, v27(1), 77-82.

Houston, David B. "Risk, Insurance And Sampling," JRI, 1964, v31(4), 511-538.

Houston, David B. "The Effectiveness Of Rating Classifications," JRI, 1961, v28(2), 83-86.

Houston, David B. (Hammond, J. D., David B. Houston and Eugene R. Melander. "Determinants Of Household Life Insurance Premium Expenditures," JRI, 1967, v34(3), 397-408.)

Houston, Franklin S. (Weiss, Doyle L., Franklin S. Houston and Pierre Windal. "The Periodic Pain Of Lydia E. Pinkham," JOB, 1978, v51(1), 91-102.)

Houston, John L. (Markese, John D. and John L. Houston. "Bond Portfolio Management: Emphasis Missing - Treatment Required," JFED, 1981, v10, 3-5.)

Houthakker, Hendrik S. "The Regulation Of Financial And Other Futures Markets," JOF, 1982, v37(2), 481-492.

Houthakker, Hendrik S. "The Extension Of Futures Trading To The Financial Sector," JBF, 1982, v6(1), 37-48.

Howard, Charles T. and Louis J. D'Antonio. "A Risk-Return Measure Of Hedging Effectiveness," JFQA, 1984, v19(1), 101-112.

Howard, Charles T. and Louis J. D'Antonio. "Treasury Bill Futures As A Hedging Tool: A Risk-Return Approach," JFR, 1986, v9(1), 25-39.

Howard, Charles T. "Are T-Bill Futures Good Forecasters Of Interest Rates?," JFM, 1982, v2(4), 305-315.

Howard, Charles T. and Louis J. D'Antonio. "A Risk-Return Measure Of Hedging Effectiveness: A Reply," JFQA, 1987, v22(3), 377-381.

Howard, David H. and Karen H. Johnson. "The Behavior Of Monetary Aggregates In Major Industrialized Countries," JMCB, 1983, v15(4), 455-468.

Howard, Edward Douglas. "The Relative Vulnerability Of Growth And Income Stocks," FAJ, 1955, v11(4), 19-24.

Howard, Godfrey G. "A Second Look At Inflation," FAJ, 1977, v33(5), 35-47.

Howard, James A. "Grain Trading In The 1970s," **RFM**, 1983, v2(2), 252-261.

Howard, John A. "A Note On Corporate Forecasting Practices," **JOB**, 1954, v27(1), 101-105.

Howard, John A. "Collusive Behavior," **JOB**, 1954, v27(3), 196-204.

Howard, Robert. (Racster, Ronald L. and Robert Howard. "Evaluation Of Multiple Subsidy Programs In A Local Market," **AREUEA**, 1973, v1(2), 104-118.)

Howard, W. M. "Catastrophe Reinsurance Coverage Of American Fire Insurance Companies," **JOF**, 1953, v8(4), 388-406.

Howard, William M. and Harry J. Solberg. "Perpetual Fire Insurance," **JOF**, 1958, v13(1), 70-79.

Howard, William M. "A Note On Mortality Tables And Interest Rates," **JRI**, 1957, v24(2), 88-92.

Howard, William M. "Cost Sensitivity Analysis Of Mandatory Funding And Vesting Standards In Pension Plans: Comment," **JRI**, 1976, v43(4), 715-719.

Howard, William M. "Fire Insurance Written Under Perpetual Contracts," **JRI**, 1956, v23, 129-134.

Howard, William M. "Florida Relative Values For Surgical And Medical Procedures," **JRI**, 1972, v39(3), 419-430.

Howard, William M. "Life Reinsurance Pools," **JOF**, 1956, v11(1), 58-67.

Howard, William M. "Mathematical Contributions To Risk And Insurance Theory," **JRI**, 1962, v29(3), 343-350.

Howard, William M. "Problems And Issues In Public Employee Retirement Systems: Comment," **JRI**, 1974, v41(3), 529-532.

Howard, William M. "Professional Ethics For Professors Of Insurance," **JRI**, 1964, v31(3), 405-410.

Howard, William M. "Use Of Computers In Teaching University Courses In Risk And Insurance," **JRI**, 1969, v36(1), 119-124.

Howard, William M. (Krogh, Harold C., W. O. Bryson, Jr., William M. Howard and Robert M. Stevenson. "The Insurance Curriculum In Collegiate Business Education," **JRI**, 1959, v26(1), 76-81.)

Howe, J. S. and J. Madura. "The Impact Of International Listings On Risk: Implications For Capital Market Integration," **JBF**, 1990, v14(6), 1133-1142.

Howe, James S. and James D. Shilling. "REIT Advisor Performance," **AREUEA**, 1990, v18(4), 479-500.

Howe, John S. and Gary G. Schlarbaum. "SEC Trading Suspensions: Empirical Evidence," **JFQA**, 1986, v21(3), 323-333.

Howe, John S. and William L. Beedles. "Defensive Investing Using Fundamental Data," **JPM**, 1983-84, v10(2), 14-17.

Howe, John S. "A Rose By Any Other Name? A Note On Corporate Name Changes," **FR**, 1987, v17(4), 271-278.

Howe, John S. "Evidence On Stock Market Overreaction," **FAJ**, 1986, v42(4), 74-77.

Howe, John S. (Brown, Keith C. and John S. Howe. "On The Use Of Gold As a Fixed Income Security," **FAJ**, 1987, v43(4), 74-76.)

Howe, John S. (Lin, Ji-Chai and John S. Howe. "Insider Trading In The OTC Market," **JOF**, 1990, v45(4), 1273-1284.)

Howe, John S. and James D. Shilling. "Capital Structure Theory And REIT Security Offerings," **JOF**, 1988, v43(4), 983-993.

Howe, John S. and Kathryn Kelm. "The Stock Price Impacts Of Overseas Listings," **FM**, 1987, v16(3), 51-56.

Howe, Keith M. and George M. McCabe. "On Optimal Asset Abandonment And Replacement," **JFQA**, 1983, v18(3), 295-305.

Howe, Keith M. and James H. Patterson. "Capital Investment Decisions Under Economies Of Scale In Flotation Costs," **FM**, 1985, v14(3), 61-69.

Howe, Keith M. "A Note On Flotation Costs And Capital Budgeting," **FM**, 1982, v11(4), 30-33.

Howe, Keith M. "Capital Budgeting And Search: An Overview," **JFR**, 1978, v1(1), 23-33.

Howe, Keith M. "Does Inflationary Change Affect Capital Asset Life?," **FM**, 1987, v16(2), 63-67.

Howe, Keith M. "Flotation Cost Allowance For The Regulated Firm: A Comment," **JOF**, 1984, v39(1), 289-291.

Howe, Keith M. (Bey, Roger P. and Keith M. Howe. "Gini's Mean Difference And Portfolio Selection: An Empirical Evaluation," **JFQA**, 1984, v19(3), 329-338.)

Howe, Keith M. and Harvey Lapan. "Inflation And Asset Life: The Darby Versus The Fisher Effect," **JFQA**, 1987, v22(2), 249-258.

Howe, Keith M. and Paul L. Gronewoller. "Issue Costs In Fisher's Two-Period Model," **FR**, 1990, v25(2), 335-343.

Howe, Maureen E. (Heinkel, Robert, Maureen E. Howe and John S. Hughes. "Commodity Convenience Yields As On Option Profit," **JFM**, 1990, v10(5), 519-534.)

Howe, Thomas H. (Robbins, Sidney M., Robert B. Stobaugh, Francis L. Sterling and Thomas H. Howe. "The Impact Of Exchange-Traded Options On The Market For New Issues Of Common Stock Of Small Companies," **FR**, 1979, v14(1),1-22.)

Howe, Vince. (Cather, David A. and Vince Howe. "Conflict And Channel Management In Property-Liability Distribution Systems," **JRI**, 1989, v56(3), 535-543.)

Howell, Paul L. and Ira Royal Hart. "The Promoting And Financing Of Transcontinental Gas Pipe Line Corporation," **JOF**, 1951, v6(3), 311-324.

Howell, Paul L. "A Re-Examination Of Pension Fund Investment Policies," **JOF**, 1958, v13(2), 261-274.

Howell, Paul L. "Competition In Investment Banking," **JOF**, 1953, v8(2), 278-282.

Howell, Paul L. "The Effects Of Federal Income Taxation On The Form Of External Financing By Business," **JOF**, 1949, v4(3), 208-222.

Howells, Lloyd T. (Thorelli, Hans B., Robert L. Graves and Lloyd T. Howells. "The International Operations Simulation At The University Of Chicago," **JOB**, 1962, v35(3), 287-297.)

Howitt, Peter. (Fried, Joel and Peter Howitt. "Credit Rationing And Implicit Contract Theory," **JMCB**, 1980, v12(3), 471-487.)

Howson, Hugh R. (Findlay, M. Chapman, III and Hugh R. Howson. "Optimal Intertemporal Real Estate Ownership, Valuation And Use," **AREUEA**, 1975, v3(2), 51-66.)

Hoxter, Curtis J. "Western Europe, As Of Today," **FAJ**, 1962, v18(4), 45-53.

Hoyt, G. Calvin. "The Process And Problems Of Retirement," **JOB**, 1954, v27(2), 164-168.

Hoyt, Homer. "Financing The Future Commercial And Industrial Requirements In Metropolitan Growth Of The United States," **JOF**, 1960, v15(2), 263-273.

Hoyt, Homer. "The Effect Of Cyclical Fluctuations Upon Real Estate Finance," **JOF**, 1947, v2(1), 51-64.

Hoyt, Newton H., Jr. "The Management Of Currency Exchange Risk By The Singer Company," **FM**, 1972, v1(1), 13-20.

Hoyt, Robert E. "Use Of Financial Futures By Life Insurers," **JRI**, 1989, v56(4), 740-759.

Hradsky, Gregory T. and Robert D. Long. "High-Yield Default Losses And The Return Performance Of Bankrupt Debt," **FAJ**, 1989, v45(4), 38-49.

Hsaio, Frank S. T. and James W. Smith. "An Analytic Approach To Sensitivity Analysis Of The Internal Rate Of Return Model," **JOF**, 1978, v33(2), 645-649.

Hsia, Chi-Cheng and J. Fred Weston. "Price Behavior Of Deep Discount Bonds," **JBF**, 1981, v5(3), 357-361.

Hsia, Chi-Cheng. "Coherence Of The Modern Theories Of Finance," **FR**, 1981, v16(1), 27-42.

Hsia, Chi-Cheng. "Comparative Efficiency Of Market Indices: An Empirical Study," **JFR**, 1986, v9(2), 123-136.

Hsia, Chi-Cheng. "Estimating A Firm's Cost Of Capital: An Option Pricing Approach," **JBFA**, 1991, v18(2), 281-287.

Hsia, Chi-Cheng. "On Binomial Option Pricing," **JFR**, 1983, v6(1), 41-46.

Hsia, Chi-Cheng. "Optimal Debt Of A Firm: An Option Pricing Approach," **JFR**, 1981, v4(3),221-231.

Hsia, Chi-Cheng. (Fuller, Russell J. and Chi-Cheng Hsia. "A Simplified Common Stock Valuation Model," **FAJ**, 1984, v40(5), 49-56.)

Hsia, Chi-Cheng. (Settle, John W., Glenn H. Petry and Chi-Cheng Hsia. "Synergy, Diversification, And Incentive Effects Of Corporate Merger On Bondholder Wealth: Some Evidence," **JFR**, 1984, v7(4), 329-339.)

Hsiao, Frank S. T. and Mei-Chu W. Hsiao. "Japanese Experience Of Industralization And Economic Performance Of Korea And Taiwan - Tests Of Similarity," **AFPAF**, 1985, v1(Supp), 157-190.

Hsiao, Mei-Chu W. (Hsiao, Frank S. T. and Mei-Chu W. Hsiao. "Japanese Experience Of Industralization And Economic Performance Of Korea And Taiwan - Tests Of Similarity," **AFPAF**, 1985, v1(Supp), 157-190.)

Hsieh, Chang-Tseh and Mark Stephens. "A Simultaneous Equations Model For Examining Taiwan-U.S. Trade Relations," **AFPAF**, 1985, v1(Supp), 139-156.

Hsieh, Chang-tseh. (Hendershott, Patric H. and Chang-tseh Hsieh. "Inflation And The Growth In Home Mortgage Debt, 1964-78," **JFR**, 1980, v3(2), 189-202.)

Hsieh, David A. and Nalin Kulatilaka. "Rational Expectations And Risk Premia In Forward Markets: Primary Metals At The London Metals Exchange," **JOF**, 1982, v37(5), 1199-1208.

Hsieh, David A. "International Risk Sharing And The Choice Of Exchange-Rate Regime," **JIMF**, 1984, v3(2), 141-151.

Hsieh, David A. "Testing For Nonlinear Dependence In Daily Foreign Exchange Rates," **JOB**, 1989, v62(3), 339-368.

Hsieh, David A. (Chan, K. C., Nai-Fu Chen and David A. Hsieh. "An Exploratory Investigation Of The Firm Size Effect," **JFEC**, 1985, v14(3), 451-471.)

Hsieh, David A. and Merton H. Miller. "Margin Regulation And Stock Market Volatility," **JOF**, 1990, v45(1), 3-30.

Hsu, Chih-Chang and Thomas Liaw. "Partial Equity Interests And Mangerial Incentives," **IJOF**, 1989, v19(1), 72-81.

Hsu, D. A. "The Behavior Of Stock Returns: Is It Stationary Or Evolutionary," **JFQA**, 1984, v19(1), 11-28.

Hsueh, L. Paul and David S. Kidwell. "Bond Ratings: Are Two Better Than One?," **FM**, 1988, v17(1), 46-53.

Hsueh, L. Paul and P. R. Chandy. "An Examination Of The Yield Spread Between Insured And Uninsured Debt," **JFR**, 1989, v12(3), 235-244.

Hsueh, L. Paul and Y. Angela Liu. "An Examination Of The Biases In Estimating The Benefit Of Debt Insurance," **FR**, 1990, v25(3), 473-486.

Hsueh, L. Paul and Y. Angela Liu. "The Effectiveness Of Debt Insurance As A Valid Signal Of Bond Quality," **JRI**, 1990, v57(4), 691-700.

Hu, Joseph C. "Derivative Mortgage Securities: An Overview," **JREFEC**, 1988, v1(2), 95-116.

Huang, C. C., I. Vertinsky and W. T. Ziemba. "On Multiperiod Stochastic Dominance," **JFQA**, 1978, v13(1), 1-13.

Huang, Chi-Fu. (Bikhchandani, Sushil and Chi-Fu Huang. "Auctions With Resale Markets: An Exploratory Model Of Treasury Bill Markets," **RFS**, 1989, v2(3), 311-340.)

Huang, Chi-Fu. (Brown, David and Chi-Fu Huang. "Option Pricing In A Lognormal Securities Market With Discrete Trading: A Comment," **JFEC**, 1983, v12(2), 285-286.)

Huang, Chi-Fu. (Dybvig, Philip H. and Chi-fu Huang. "Nonnegative Wealth, Absence Of Arbitrage, And Feasible Consumption Plans," **RFS**, 1988-89, v1(4), 377-401.)

Huang, Chi-fu and Robert Litzenberger. "On The Necessary Condition For Linear Sharing And Separation: A Note," **JFQA**, 1985, v20(3), 381-384.

Huang, Chor. (Morrissey, Thomas F. and Chor Huang. "A Nomogram For Estimating Duration," **FAJ**, 1987, v43(1), 65-67.)

Huang, Cliff J. "An Unbiased Estimator Of The N-Period Relative," **JFQA**, 1977, v12(3), 505-507.

Huang, Cliff J. (Zak, Thomas A., Cliff J. Huang and John J. Siegfried. "Production Efficiency: The Case Of Professional Basketball," **JOB**, 1979, v52(3), 379-392.)

Huang, Roger D. and William A. Kracaw. "Stock Market Returns And Real Activity: A Note," **JOF**, 1984, v39(1), 267-273.

Huang, Roger D. "An Analysis Of Intertemporal Pricing For Forward Foreign Exchange Contracts," **JOF**, 1989, v44(1), 183-194.

Huang, Roger D. "Does Monetization Of Federal Debt Matter? Evidence From The Financial Markets," **JMCB**, 1986, v18(3), 275-289.

Huang, Roger D. "Expectations Of Exchange Rates And Differential Inflation Rates: Further Evidence On Purchasing Power Parity In Efficient Markets," **JOF**, 1987, v42(1), 69-79.

Huang, Roger D. "Common Stock Returns And Presidential Elections," FAJ, 1985, v41(2), 58-61.

Huang, Roger D. "Financial Asset Returns, Inflation, And Market Expectations," RIF, 1985, v5, 25-56.

Huang, Roger D. "Risk And Parity In Purchasing Power," JMCB, 1990, v22(3), 338-356.

Huang, Roger D. "Some Alternative Tests Of Forward Exchange Rates As Predictors Of Future Spot Rates," JIMF, 1984, v3(2), 153-168.

Huang, Roger D. "The Monetary Approach To Exchange Rate In An Efficient Foreign Exchange Market: Tests Based On Volatility," JOF, 1981, v36(1), 31-41.

Huang, Roger D. (Chang, Eric C. and Roger D. Huang. "Time-Varying Return And Risk In The Corporate Bond Market," JFQA, 1990, v25(3), 323-340.)

Huang, Roger D. and Hoje Jo. "Tests Of Market Models: Heteroskedasticity Or Misspecification?," JBF, 1988, v11(3), 439-456.

Huang, Roger D. and Tsong-Yue Lai. "Methodological And Empirical Comparisons Of Statistical Classifications Of Bond Ratings," AFPAF, 1985, v1(1), 145-166.

Huang, Roger D. and Tsong-Yue Lai. "Financial Asset Substitutability And International Asset Pricing," AFPAF, 1989, v4(Supp), 171-196.

Huang, Yen-Sheng and Ralph A. Walkling. "Target Abnormal Returns Associated With Acquisition Announcements: Payment, Acquisition Form, And Managerial Resistance," JFEC, 1987, v19(2), 329-350.

Hubbard, Carl M. "Financial Management In A Non-Traditional Graduate Program," JFED, 1982, v11, 9-12.

Hubbard, Carl M. "Flotation Costs In Capital Budgeting: A Note On The Tax Effect," FM, 1984, v13(2), 38-40.

Hubbard, Carl M. "Money Market Funds, Money Supply, And Monetary Control: A Note," JOF, 1983, v38(4), 1305-1310.

Hubbard, Carl M. (Heck, J. Louis, Philip L. Cooley and Carl M. Hubbard. "Contributing Authors And Institutions To The Journal Of Finance: 1946-1985," JOF, 1986, v41(5), 1129-1140.)

Hubbard, Charles L. and Terry Johnson. "Writing Calls With Convertible Bonds," FAJ, 1969, v25(6), 78-89.

Hubbard, Charles L. "A Control Chart For Stock Prices," FAJ, 1967, v23(6), 139-145.

Hubbard, Elbert T. (Shin, Tai S. and Elbert T. Hubbard. "Current Status Of Doctoral Programs In Finance," JFED, 1988, v17, 64-79.)

Hubbard, G. L. (Hull, J. C., and G. L. Hubbard. "Lease Evaluation In The UK: Current Theory And Practice," JBFA, 1980, v7(4), 619-638.)

Hubbard, Philip M., Jr. "The Many Aspects Of Dilution," FAJ, 1963, v19(3), 33-40.

Hubbard, R. Glenn. "Pension Wealth And Individual Saving: Some New Evidence," JMCB, 1986, v18(2), 167-178.

Huber, Charles C., Jr. (Bowen, Robert M., Lane A. Daley and Charles C. Huber, Jr. "Leverage Measures And Industrial Classification: Review And Additional Evidence," FM, 1982, v11(4), 10-20.)

Huber, George P. (Pappas, James L. and George P. Huber. "Probabilistic Short-Term Financial Planning," FM, 1973, v2(3), 36-44.)

Huber, Joel. (Magat, Wesley A., W. Kip Viscusi and Joel Huber. "Consumer Processing Of Hazard Warning Information," JRU, 1988, v1(2), 201-232.)

Huberman, Gur and Shmuel Kandel. "Mean-Variance Spanning," JOF, 1987, v42(4), 873-888.

Huberman, Gur and Shmuel Kandel. "Value Line Rank And Firm Size," JOB, 1987, v60(4), 577-590.

Huberman, Gur and Shmuel Kandel. "Market Efficiency And Value Line's Record," JOB, 1990, v63(2), 187-216.

Huberman, Gur, Shmuel Kandel and Robert F. Stambaugh. "Mimicking Portfolios And Exact Arbitrage Pricing," JOF, 1987, v42(1), 1-9.

Huberman, Gur. "Dividend Neutrality With Transaction Costs," JOB, 1990, v63(1), Part 2, S93-S106.

Huberman, Gur. "External Financing And Liquidity," JOF, 1984, v39(3), 895-908.

Hudson, Carl D. (Slovin, Myron B., Marie E. Sushka and Carl D. Hudson. "Corporate Commercial Paper, Note Issuance Facilities, And Shareholder Wealth," JIMF, 1988, v7(3), 289-302.)

Hudson, John. "The Age, Regional, And Industrial Structure Of Company Liquidations," JBFA, 1987, v14(2), 199-214.

Hudson, Michael A. (Kahl, Kandice H., Michael A. Hudson and Clement E. Ward. "Cash Settlement Issues For Live Cattle Futures Contracts," JFM, 1989, v9(3), 237-248.)

Hudson, Michael A. (Koontz, Stephen R., Philip Garcia and Michael A. Hudson. "Dominant-Satellite Relationships Between Live Cattle Cash And Futures Markets," JFM, 1990, v10(2), 123-136.)

Hudson, Michael A. (Purcell, Wayne D. and Michael A. Hudson. "The Certificate System For Delivery In Live Cattle: Conceptual Issues And Measures Of Performance," JFM, 1986, v6(3), 461-476.)

Hudson, Michael A., Raymond M. Leuthold and Gboroton F. Sarassoro. "Commodity Futures Price Changes: Recent Evidence For Wheat, Soybeans And Live Cattle," JFM, 1987, v7(3), 287-302.

Hudson, Michael. "Statistical Tests Of The Keynesian Demand Function For Money: Comment," JOF, 1968, v23(4), 672-673.

Huebner, S. S. "Future Patterns Of Life Insurance Distribution - An Educator's View," JRI, 1957, v24(3), 9-20.

Huebner, S. S. "Report Of Committee On Professional Standards In Property And Casualty Insurance," JRI, 1942, v9, 5-16.

Huebner, S. S. "The College Of Property And Casualty Underwriters: A Report Of Progress," JRI, 1943, v10, 5-18.

Huefner, Ronald J. "Alternative Approaches To Casualty Loss Recognition," FM, 1974, v4(1), 50-56.

Huelke, Donald F. "Automobile Accidents - What Needs To Be Done," JRI, 1968, v35(1), 61-66.

Huertas, Thomas F. "An Economic Brief Against Glass-Steagall," JBR, 1984-85, v15(3), 148-159.

Hufbauer, G. C. (Adler, Michael and G. C. Hufbauer. "On Balance-Of-Payments Payback Periods," JOB, 1972, v45(3), 416-421.)

Huff, Thomas. (Laibstain, S. and Thomas Huff. "Reporting Of Revised Loss Estimates," FAJ, 1971, v27(3), 62-69.)

Huffman, Forrest E. and Arthur E. Warner. "Toward The Development Of An Urban Growth Model That Recognizes The Importance Of The Basic Nature Of Services," AREUEA, 1987, v15(4), 341-358.

Huffman, Gregory W. "Adjustment Costs And Capital Asset Pricing," JOF, 1985, v40(3), 691-705.

Huffman, Lucy T. (Hessel, Christopher A. and Lucy T. Huffman. "Incorporation Of Tax Considerations Into The Computation Of Duration," JFR, 1983, v6(3), 213-215.)

Huffman, Lucy. "Operating Leverage, Financial Leverage, And Equity Risk," JBF, 1983, v7(2), 197-212.

Huffman, Lucy. (Bar-Yosef, Sasson and Lucy Huffman. "The Information Content Of Dividends: A Signalling Approach," JFQA, 1986, v21(1), 47-58.)

Huffman, Lucy. (Hessel, Christopher A. and Lucy Huffman. "The Effect Of Taxation On Immunization Rules And Duration Estimation," JOF, 1981, v36(5), 1127-1142.)

Huffman, Wallace E. and James R. Lothian. "Money In The United Kingdom, 1833-80," JMCB, 1980, v12(2), Part 1, 155-174.

Huggins, Kenneth M. (Hakala, Donald R. and Kenneth M. Huggins. "Has ERISA Had An Impact On Pension Investing?," JPM, 1978-79, v5(2), 44-47.)

Hughes, Charles E. (Duker, Jacob M. and Charles E. Hughes. "The Black-Owned Life Insurance Company: Issues And Recommendations," JRI, 1973, v40(2), 221-230.)

Hughes, Charles E. (Duker, Jacob M. and Charles E. Hughes. "The Black-Owned Life Insurance Company: Reply," JRI, 1975, v42(2), 355-358.)

Hughes, G. David and Philippe A. Naert. "A Computer-Controlled Experiment In Consumer Behavior," JOB, 1970, v43(3), 354-372.

Hughes, G. David, Joseph B. Juhasz and Bruno Contini. "The Influence Of Personality On The Bargaining Process," JOB, 1973, v46(4), 593-604.

Hughes, G. David. (Harnett, Donald L., G. David Hughes and Larry L. Cummings. "Bilateral Monopolistic Bargaining Through An Intermediary," JOB, 1968, v41(2), 251-259.)

Hughes, James F. "New Era Stock Markets," FAJ, 1955, v11(2), 25-30.

Hughes, James W. (Sternlieb, George and James W. Hughes. "Neighborhood Dynamics And Government Policy," AREUEA, 1974, v2(2), 7-24.)

Hughes, James W. (Sternlieb, George and James W. Hughes. "Condominium Conversion Profiles: Governmental Policy," AREUEA, 1975, v3(3), 61-80.)

Hughes, James W. (Sternlieb, George and James W. Hughes. "Regional Market Variations: The Northeast Versus The South," AREUEA, 1977, v5(1), 44-67.)

Hughes, John S. and James Vander Weide. "Incentive Considerations In The Reporting Of Leveraged Leases," JBR, 1982-83, v13(1), 36-41.

Hughes, John S. and Wilbur G. Lewellen. "Programming Solution To Capital Rationing Problems," JBFA, 1974, v1(1), 55-74.

Hughes, John S. "Agency Theory And Stochastic Dominance," JFQA, 1982, v17(3), 341-361.

Hughes, John S. (Heinkel, Robert, Maureen E. Howe and John S. Hughes. "Commodity Convenience Yields As On Option Profit," JFM, 1990, v10(5), 519-534.)

Hughes, John S. (Holthausen, Duncan M. and John S. Hughes. "Commodity Returns And Capital Asset Pricing," FM, 1978, v7(2), 37-44.)

Hughes, John S., Dennis E. Logue and Richard James Sweeney. "Corporate International Diversification And Market Assigned Measures Of Risk And Diversification," JFQA, 1975, v10(4), 627-637.

Hughes, Jonathan. "Variations On A Theme: Long-Term Growth Of Government," JFSR, 1989, v2(3), 153-166.

Hughes, Patricia. (Hand, John R. M. and Patricia Hughes. "The Motives And Consequences Of Debt-Equity Swaps And Defeasances: More Evidence That It Does Not Pay To Manipulate Earnings," JACF, 1990, v3(3), 77-81.)

Hughes, R. Eugene. "Self-Concept And Brand Preference: A Partial Replication," JOB, 1976, v49(4), 530-540.

Hughes, Warren R. (Elnicki, Richard A. and Warren R. Hughes. "An Empirical Analysis Of Demands For Priority Computing Goods By Externally And Internally Funded Researchers," JOB, 1980, v53(1), 79-96.)

Hugon, James H. "Management Versus The Stockholder," FAJ, 1966, v22(1), 20-21.

Hugon, James H. "The Euro-Money Market, Explained," FAJ, 1971, v27(5), 21-24.

Huizinga, John and Frederic S. Mishkin. "Inflation And Real Interest Rates On Assets With Different Risk Characteristics," JOF, 1984, v39(3), 699-712.

Huizinga, John. (Fischer, Stanley and John Huizinga. "Inflation, Unemployment, And Public Opinion Polls," JMCB, 1982, v14(1), 1-19.)

Hull, J. C. "The Interpretation Of The Output From A Sensitivity Analysis In Investment Appraisal," JBFA, 1978, v5(1), 109-122.

Hull, J. C., and G. L. Hubbard. "Lease Evaluation In The UK: Current Theory And Practice," JBFA, 1980, v7(4), 619-638.

Hull, John C. "A Note On The Risk-Adjusted Discount Rate Method," JBFA, 1986, v13(3), 445-450.

Hull, John C. "The Bargaining Positions Of The Parties To A Lease Agreement," FM, 1982, v11(3), 71-79.

Hull, John and Alan White. "Hedging The Risks From Writing Foreign Currency Options," JIMF, 1987, v6(2), 131-152.

Hull, John and Alan White. "The Pricing Of Options On Assets With Stochastic Volatilities," JOF, 1987, v42(2), 281-300.

Hull, John and Alan White. "The Use Of The Control Variate Technique In Option Pricing," JFQA, 1988, v23(3), 237-252.

Hull, John and Alan White. "Valuing Derivative Securities Using The Explicit Finite Difference Method," JFQA, 1990, v25(1), 87-100.

Hull, John and Alan White. "Pricing Interest-Rate-Derivative Securities," RFS, 1990, v3(4), 573-592.

Hull, John. "An Analysis Of The Credit Risks In Interest Rate Swaps And Currency Swaps," RDIBF, 1989, v3, 109-130.

Hull, John. "Assessing Credit Risk In A Financial Institution's Off-Balance Sheet Commitments," JFQA, 1989, v24(4), 489-502.

Hull, John. "The Valuation Of Currency Options: Reply," FM, 1984, v13(2), 53.

Hull, John. (Biger, Nahum and John Hull. "The Valuation of Currency Options," *FM*, 1983, v12(1),24-28.)

Hultman, Charles W. and L. Randolph McGee. "Factors Affecting The Foreign Banking Presence In The U.S.," *JBF*, 1989, v13(3), 383-396.

Hummel, Thomas J. "The Survival Of Cigarette Smokers," *JRI*, 1964, v31(4), 613-620.

Hummer, William B. "The Money Market Outlook," *FAJ*, 1969, v25, No, 3, 30-32.

Humphrey, David B. "100% Deposit Insurance: What Would It Cost?," *JBR*, 1976-77, v7(3), 192-198.

Humphrey, David B. (Benston, George J., Gerald A. Hanweck and David B. Humphrey. "Scale Economies In Banking: A Restructuring And Reassessment," *JMCB*, 1982, v14(4), Part I, 435-456.)

Humphrey, David B. (Berger, Allen N. and David B. Humphrey. "Interstate Banking And The Payments System," *JFSR*, 1988, v1(2), 131-146.)

Humphrey, David B. (Rosen, Richard J., Peter Lloyd-Davies and David B. Humphrey. "New Banking Powers: A Portfolio Analysis Of Bank Investment In Real Estate," *JBF*, 1989, v13(3), 355-366.)

Humphrey, David Burras. "Are There Economies Of Scale In Check Processing At The Federal Reserve?," *JBR*, 1980-81, v11(1), 8-19.

Humphrey, David Burras. "Intermediation And Cost Determinants Of Large Bank Liability Composition," *JBF*, 1981, v5(2), 167-185.

Humphrey, David Burras. "Large Bank Intra-Deposit Maturity Composition: CDs And Small Time Deposits 1970-77," *JBF*, 1979, v3(1), 43-66.

Humphrey, David Burras. "Resource Use In Federal Reserve Check And ACH Operations After Pricing," *JBR*, 1985-86, v16(1), 45-53.

Humphrey, David Burras. "Scale Economies At Automated Clearinghouses," *JBR*, 1981-82, v12(2),71-81.

Humphrey, David Burras. (Graham, David R. and David Burras Humphrey. "Bank Examination Data As Predictors Of Bank Net Loan Losses," *JMCB*, 1978, v10(4),491-504.)

Humphrey, David Burras. (Savage, Donald T. and David Burras Humphrey. "Branching Laws And Banking Offices," *JMCB*, 1979, v11(2), 227-230.)

Humphrey, Thomas M. (Beranek, William, Thomas M. Humphrey and Richard H. Timberlake, Jr. "Fisher, Thornton, And The Analysis Of The Inflation Premium," *JMCB*, 1985, v17(3), 371-377.)

Hunt, Janet C. and B. F. Kiker. "Valuation Of Household Services: Methodology And Estimation," *JRI*, 1979, v46(4), 697-706.

Hunt, Jerry G. (Angell, Robert J. and Jerry G. Hunt. "Is The Denver Market Efficient?," *JPM*, 1981-82, v8(3), 10-16.)

Hunt, Joseph F. (Garbade, Kenneth D. and Joseph F. Hunt. "Risk Premiums On Federal Agency Debt," *JOF*, 1978, v33(1), 105-116.)

Hunt, Lacy H., II. "Bank Credit And The Money Stock: Their Roles In The Determination Of Income In The Post Accord Period," *JOF*, 1974, v29(3), 941-954.

Hunt, Lacy H., II. "Determinants Of The Dividend Yield," *JPM*, 1976-77, v3(3), 43-48.

Hunt, Lacy H., II. "Evaluating The Reserve Aggregates," *FAJ*, 1973, v29(3), 52-54,57-60,62-63.

Hunt, Lacy H., II. (Rose, Peter S. and Lacy H. Hunt, II. "The Relative Importance Of Monetary And Fiscal Variables In Determining Price Level Movements: A Note," *JOF*, 1971, v26(1), 31-37.)

Hunt, Lacy H., II. (Rose, Peter S. and Lacy H. Hunt, II. "The Relative Importance Of Monetary And Fiscal Variables In Determining Price Level Movements: Reply," *JOF*, 1973, v28(1), 191-193.)

Hunt, Lacy H., II. (Valentini, John J. and Lacy H. Hunt, II. "Eurodollar Borrowing By New York Banks And The Rate Of Interest On Eurodollars: Comment," *JOF*, 1972, v27(1), 130-133.)

Hunt, Lawrence H., Jr. and William J. Nissen. "Section 4a(1) Should Be Revised," *JPM*, 1981, v1(Supp), 461-464.

Hunt, Pearson. "A Proposal For Precise Definitions Of 'Trading On The Equity' And 'Leverage'," *JOF*, 1961, v16(3), 377-386.

Hunt, Pearson. "A Proposal For Precise Definition Of 'Trading On The Equity' And 'Leverage': Reply," *JOF*, 1962, v17(1), 131-132.

Hunt, Pearson. "A System Developed In Countries With Persistent Inflation," *JBFA*, 1976, v3(1), 161-165.

Hunter, John E. (Coggin, T. Daniel and John E. Hunter. "A Meta-Analysis Of Spicing 'Risk' Factors In APT," *JPM*, 1987-88, v14(1), 35-38.)

Hunter, John E. and T. Daniel Coggin. "An Analysis Of The Diversification Benefit From International Equity Investment," *JPM*, 1990, v17(1), 33-36.

Hunter, William C. "Rational Margins On Futures Contracts: Initial Margins," *RFM*, 1986, v5(2), 160-173.

Hunter, William C. (Kolb, Robert W., Gerald D. Gay and William C. Hunter. "Liquidity And Capital Requirements For Futures Market Hedges," *RFM*, 1985, v4(1), 1-25.)

Hunter, William C. (Kolb, Robert W., Gerald D. Gay and William C. Hunter. "Liquidity Requirements For Financial Futures Investments," *FAJ*, 1985, v41(3), 60-68.)

Hunter, William C. and Stephen G. Timme. "Technical Change, Organizational Form, And The Structure Of Bank Production," *JMCB*, 1986, v18(2), 152-166.

Hunter, William C., Stephen G. Timme and Won Keun Yang. "An Examination Of Cost Subadditivity And Multiproduct Production In Large U.S. Banks," *JMCB*, 1990, v22(4), 504-525.

Hunter, William C. (Gay, Gerald D., William C. Hunter and Robert W. Kolb. "A Comparative Analysis Of Futures Contract Margins," *JFM*, 1986, v6(2), 307-324.)

Hur, Hyung-Doh. (Fratianni, Michele, Hyung-Doh Hur and Heejoon Kang. "Random Walk And Monetary Causality In Five Exchange Markets," *JIMF*, 1987, v6(4), 505-514.)

Hustedt, W. J. and Dick L. Rottman. "Insurance Professors' Relationships With Risk Managers," *JRI*, 1969, v36(4), 643-647.

Huszagh, Sandra M. and Mark R. Greene. "FCIA: Help Or Hindrance To Exports?," *JRI*, 1982, v49(2), 256-268.

Huszagh, Sandra M. and Mark R. Greene. "How Exporters View Credit Risk And FCIA Insurance - The Georgia Experience," *JRI*, 1985, v52(4), 659-672.

Hutchings, Murray R. and John S. McCallum. "Bond Price Volatility: A Numerical Analysis," *JRI*, 1975, v42(4), 669-672.

Hutchins, Robert C. and Charles E. Quenneville. "Rate Of Return Versus Interest-Adjusted Cost," *JRI*, 1975, v42(1), 69-80.

Hutchins, Robert C. (Cherin, Antony C. and Robert C. Hutchins. "The Rate Of Return On Universal Life Insurance," *JRI*, 1987, v54(4), 691-711.)

Hutchinson, P., I. Meric and G. Meric. "The Financial Characteristics Of Small Firms Which Achieve Quotation On The UK Unlisted Securities Market," *JBFA*, 1988, v15(1), 9-20.

Hutchinson, Patrick. (Booth, Peter and Patrick Hutchinson. "Distinguishing Between Failing And Growing Firms: A Note On The Use Of Decomposition Measure Analysis," *JBFA*, 1989, v16(2), 267-272.)

Hutchinson, Peter M., James R. Ostas and J. David Reed. "A Survey And Comparison Of Redlining Influences In Urban Mortgage Lending Markets," *AREUEA*, 1977, v5(4), 463-472.

Hutchison, Michael M. "Monetary Control With An Exchange Rate Objective: The Bank Of Japan, 1973-86," *JIMF*, 1988, v7(3), 261-272.

Hutchison, Michael. (Glick, Reuven and Michael Hutchison. "New Results In Support Of The Fiscal Policy Ineffectiveness Proposition," *JMCB*, 1990, v22(3), 288-304.)

Huth, William L. (MacDonald, Don N., Harry L. White, Paul M. Taube and William L. Huth. "Flood Hazard Pricing And Insurance Premium Differentials: Evidence From The Housing Market," *JRI*, 1990, v57(4), 654-663.)

Hwang, Chuan Yang. (Grinblatt, Mark and Chuan Yang Hwang. "Signalling And The Pricing Of New Issues," *JOF*, 1989, v44(2), 393-420.)

Hwang, Hong and Chao-Cheng Mai. "Sequential Entry And Plant Location In Oligopolistic Competition," *JREFEC*, 1990, v3(1), 43-54.

Hysom, John L. (Guy, Donald C., John L. Hysom and Stephen R. Ruth. "The Effect Of Subsidized Housing On Values Of Adjacent Housing," *AREUEA*, 1985, v13(4), 378-387.)

III

Ibbotson, R. G. and R. A. Sinquefield. "Stocks, Bonds, Bills And Inflation: Updates," *FAJ*, 1979, v35(4), 40-44.

Ibbotson, R. G. "Price Performance Of Common Stock New Issues," *JFEC*, 1975, v2(3), 235-272.

Ibbotson, Roger G. and Carol L. Fall. "The United States Market Wealth Portfolio," *JPM*, 1979-80, v6(1), 82-92.

Ibbotson, Roger G. and Jeffrey F. Jaffe. "'Hot Issue' Markets," *JOF*, 1975, v30(4), 1027-1042.

Ibbotson, Roger G. and Laurence B. Siegel. "The World Market Wealth Portfolio," *JPM*, 1982-83, v9(2), 5-17.

Ibbotson, Roger G. (Diermeier, Jeffrey J., Roger G. Ibbotson and Laurence B. Siegel. "The Supply Of Capital Market Returns," *FAJ*, 1984, v40(2), 74-80.)

Ibbotson, Roger G. (Goetzmann, William N. and Roger G. Ibbotson. "The Performance Of Real Estate As An Asset Class," *JACF*, 1990, v3(1), 65-76.)

Ibbotson, Roger G. and Laurence B. Siegel. "Real Estate Returns: A Comparison With Other Investments," *AREUEA*, 1984, v12(3), 219-242.

Ibbotson, Roger G. and Rex A. Sinquefield. "Stocks, Bonds, Bills, And Inflation: Year-By-Year Historical Returns (1926-1974)," *JOB*, 1976, v49(1), 11-47.

Ibbotson, Roger G. and Rex A. Sinquefield. "Stocks, Bonds, Bills, And Inflation: Simulations Of The Future (1976-2000)," *JOB*, 1976, v49(3), 313-338.

Ibbotson, Roger G., Jeffrey J. Diermeier and Laurence B. Siegel. "The Demand For Capital Market Returns: A New Equilibrium Theory," *FAJ*, 1984, v40(1),22-33.

Ibbotson, Roger G., Laurence B. Siegel and Kathryn S. Love. "World Wealth: Market Values And Returns," *JPM*, 1985-86, v12(1), 4-23.

Ibbotson, Roger G., Richard C. Carr and Anthony W. Robinson. "International Equity And Bond Returns," *FAJ*, 1982, v38(4), 61-83.

Ibbotson, Roger G., Jody L. Sindelar and Jay R. Ritter. "Initial Public Offerings," *JACF*, 1988, v1(2), 37-45.

Iben, Thomas. (Litterman, Robert and Thomas Iben. "Corporate Bond Valuation And The Term Structure Of Credit Spreads," *JPM*, 1991, v17(3), 52-64.)

Ibrahim, I. B. and Raburn M. Williams. "The Fisher Relationship Under Different Monetary Standards," *JMCB*, 1978, v10(3), 363-370.

Ibrahim, I. B. "Risk And The Macro Financial Investment Equations Of Pension Funds And Life Insurance Companies," *JRI*, 1974, v41(3), 451-461.

Icerman, Joe D. (Celec, Stephen E. and Joe D. Icerman. "A Comprehensive Approach To Accounts Receivable Management," *FR*, 1980, v15(2), 23-34.)

I'Costa, Joan E. Richart and Stuart I. Greenbaum. "Bank Forward Lending: A Note," *JOF*, 1983, v38(4), 1315-1322.

Idol, Charles R. "A Note On Specifying Debt Displacement And Tax Shield Borrowing Opportunities In Financial Lease Valuation Models," *FM*, 1980, v9(2), 24-29.

Ifflander, A. James. (Gallinger, George W. and A. James Ifflander. "Monitoring Accounts Receivable Using Variance Analysis," *FM*, 1986, v15(4), 69-76.)

Igawa, Kazuhiro and George Kanatas. "Asymmetric Information, Collateral, And Moral Hazard," *JFQA*, 1990, v25(4), 469-490.

Ihlanfeldt, Keith R. (Boehm, Thomas P. and Keith R. Ihlanfeldt. "The Improvement Expenditures Of Urban Homeowners: An Empirical Analysis," *AREUEA*, 1986, v14(1), 48-60.)

Ihlanfeldt, Keith Ray. "An Intertemporal Empirical Analysis Of The Renter's Decision To Purchase A Home," *AREUEA*, 1980, v8(2), 180-197.

Ihori, Toshihiro. "On The Welfare Cost Of Permanent Inflation," *JMCB*, 1985, v17(2), 220-231.

Ijiri, Yuji. "Approximations To Interest Formulas," *JOB*, 1972, v45(3), 398-402.

Ikeda, Shinsuke. "Arbitrage Asset Pricing Under Exchange Risk," *JOF*, 1991, v46(1), 447-456.

Jackson, Henry H. "Individual Reserves And Kindred Delusions," JRI, 1939, v6, 24-35.

Jackson, Henry H. "The Half-Century In Personal Insurance," JRI, 1951, v18, 35-45.

Jackson, J. T. Ross. "Market Psychology And Psi Theory," JPM, 1977-78, v4(4), 35-40.

Jackson, Jerry R. and David L. Kasserman. "Default Risk On Home Mortgage Loans: A Test Of Competing Hypotheses," JRI, 1980, v47(4), 678-690.

Jackson, John D., Charlotte A. Jones and Philip W. Balsmeir. "An Empirical Analysis Of Tenant Selection Under Federal Rent Supplement Programs: A First Step," AREUEA, 1986, v14(1), 72-90.

Jackson, Matthew O. (Duffie, Darrell and Matthew O. Jackson. "Optimal Innovation Of Futures Contracts," RFS, 1989, v2(3), 275-296.)

Jackson, Raymond. "The Consideration Of Eocnomies In Merger Cases," JOB, 1970, v43(4), 439-447.

Jackson, Richard. (Breen, William and Richard Jackson. "An Efficient Algorithm For Solving Large-Scale Portfolio Problems," JFQA, 1971, v6(1), 627-637.)

Jackson, Richard. "Forecasting Interest Rates In Stagflation, 1969-77," JPM, 1978-79, v5(1), 43-48.)

Jacob, David P. (Bookstaber, Richard and David P. Jacob. "The Composite Hedge: Controlling The Credit Risk Of High-Yield Bonds," FAJ, 1986, v42(2),25-36.)

Jacob, David P. (Toevs, Alden L. and David P. Jacob. "Futures And Alternative Hedge Ratio Methodologies," JPM, 1985-86, v12(3), 60-70.)

Jacob, David P., Graham Lord and James A. Tilley. "A Generalized Framework For Pricing Contingent Cash Flows," FM, 1987, v16(3), 5-14.

Jacob, Nancy and Rich Pettit. "Research Output And Capital Market Efficiency Under Alternative Commission Rate Structures," JFR, 1978, v1(1), 45-60.

Jacob, Nancy L. "A Limited-Diversification Portfolio Selection Model For The Small Investor," JOF, 1974, v29(3), 847-856.

Jacob, Nancy L. "The Future Of Research In Finance," FR, 1978, v13(1), 76-79.

Jacob, Nancy L. "The Measurement Of Systematic Risk For Securities And Portfolios: Some Empirical Results," JFQA, 1971, v6(2), 815-833.

Jacob, Nancy L. and Keith V. Smith. "The Value Of Perfect Market Forecasts In Portfolio Selection," JOF, 1972, v27(2), 355-369.

Jacob, Nancy. "The Measurement Of Market Similarity For Securities Under Uncertainty," JOB, 1970, v43(3), 328-340.

Jacobs, Bruce I. and Kenneth N. Levy. "Disentangling Equity Return Regularities: New Insights And Investment Opportunities," FAJ, 1988, v44(3), 18-44.

Jacobs, Bruce I. and Kenneth N. Levy. "Calendar Anomalies: Abnormal Returns At Calendar Turning Points," FAJ, 1988, v44(6), 28-39.

Jacobs, Bruce I. and Kenneth N. Levy. "On The Value Of 'Value'," FAJ, 1988, v44(4), 47-62.

Jacobs, Bruce I. and Kenneth N. Levy. "Forecasting The Size Effect," FAJ, 1989, v45(3), 38-54.

Jacobs, Bruce I. and Kenneth N. Levy. "The Complexity Of The Stock Market," JPM, 1989, v16(1), 19-27.

Jacobs, Donald P. and Almarin Phillips. "The Commission On Financial Structure And Regulation: Its Organization And Recommendations," JOF, 1972, v27(2), 319-328.

Jacobs, Donald P. and H. Prescott Beighley. "The Changing Structure Of Banking And Its Future Impact On Banks," JBR, 1974-75, v5(3), 145-155.

Jacobs, Donald P. "The Interaction Effects Of Restrictions On Branching And Other Bank Regulations," JOF, 1965, v20(2), 332-348.

Jacobs, Donald P. "The Marketable Security Portfolios Of Non-Financial Corporations, Investment Practices And Trends," JOF, 1960, v15(3), 341-352.

Jacobs, Donald P. (Beighley, H. Prescott, John H. Boyd and Donald P. Jacobs. "Bank Equities And Investor Risk Perceptions: Some Entailments For Capital Adequacy Regulation," JBR, 1975-76, v6(3), 190-201.)

Jacobs, Donald P. (Moag, Joseph S. and Donald P. Jacobs. "The Effects Of Direct Payroll Deposits On The Use Of Bank Services," JBR, 1974-75, v5(4),231-236.)

Jacobs, Donald P., Eugene M. Lerner and Joseph S. Moag. "Guidelines For Designing Bank Planning Models And Information Systems," JBR, 1971-72, v2(1),14-24.

Jacobs, Fredric. (Cheng, Peter, Fredric Jacobs and Ronald Marshall. "Cost Variance Investigation In A Linear Programming Framework," JBFA, 1984, v11(2), 233-244.)

Jacobs, Rodney L. "Fixed-Rate Lending And Interest Rate Futures Hedging," JBR, 1983-84, v14(3), 193-202.

Jacobs, Rodney L. "Hyperinflation And The Supply Of Money," JMCB, 1977, v9(2), 287-303.

Jacobs, Rodney L. "Restructuring The Maturity Of Regulated Deposits With Treasury-Bill Futures," JFM, 1982, v2(2), 183-194.

Jacobs, Rodney L. "The Effect Of Errors In Variables On Tests For A Risk Premium In Forward Exchange Rates," JOF, 1982, v37(3), 667-677.

Jacobs, Rodney L. "The Rate Maturity Of Prime And Other Indexed Assets Or Liabilities," JBR, 1984-85, v15(2), 108-114.

Jacobson, Robert. (Maisel, Sherman J. and Robert Jacobson. "Interest Rate Changes And Commercial Bank Revenues And Costs," JFQA, 1978, v13(4), 687-700.)

Jacobsson, Per. "The International Monetary Situation," JOF, 1958, v13(2), 295-304.

Jacoby, Neil H. "Demands For Funds By American Business Enterprises: Retrospect And Prospect. I," JOF, 1948, v3(2), 27-38.

Jacoby, Neil H. "The Conglomerate Corporation," FAJ, 1970, v26(3), 35-48.

Jacoby, Neil H. "The Demand For Funds By American Business Enterprises: Retrospect And Prospect. II," JOF, 1949, v4(1), 47-59.

Jacoby, Neil H. "The Fiscal Policy Of The Kennedy-Johnson Administration," JOF, 1964, v19(2), Part 1, 353-369.

Jacque, Laurent L., Pascal Lang and Charles S. Tapiero. "Towards An Expected Utility Paradigm For Foreign Exchange Risk Management: The Long And Short Of It'," RDIBF, 1989, v3, 191-228.

Jacque, Laurent. (Tapiero, Charles S. and Laurent Jacque. "The Expected Cost Of Ruin And Insurance Premiums In Mutual Insurance," JRI, 1987, v54(3), 594-602.)

Jacques, William E. "The S&P 500 Membership Anomaly, Or Would You Join This Club?," FAJ, 1988, v44(6), 73-75.

Jacquillat, B. (Dumas, B. and B. Jacquillat. "Performance Of Currency Portfolios Chosen By A Bayesian Technique: 1967-1985," JBF, 1990, v14(2/3), 539-558.)

Jacquillat, B. (Dumas, B. and B. Jacquillat. "The Money And Bond Markets In France: Segmentation Vs. Integration," JBF, 1990, v14(2/3), 613-636.)

Jacquillat, Bertrand and Richard Roll. "French Index-Linked Bonds For U.S. Investors," JPM, 1978-79, v5(3), 24-30.

Jacquillat, Bertrand C. (McDonald, John G. and Bertrand C. Jacquillat. "Pricing Of Initial Equity Issues: The French Sealed-Bid Auction," JOB, 1974, v47(1), 37-47.)

Jacquillat, Bertrand and Bruno Solnik. "Multinationals Are Poor Tools For Diversification," JPM, 1977-78, v4(2), 8-12.

Jacquillat, Bertrand. (Altman, Edward I., Bertrand Jacquillat And Michel Levasseur. "Comparative Analysis Of Risk Measures: France And The United States," JOF, 1974, v29(5), 1495-1511.)

Jacquillat, Bertrand. (Feiger, George and Bertrand Jacquillat. "Currency Option Bonds, Puts And Calls On Spot Exchange And The Hedging Of Contingent Foreign Earnings," JOF, 1979, v34(5), 1129-1139.)

Jacquillat, Bertrand. (McDonald, John G., Bertrand Jacquillat and Maurice Nussenbaum. "Dividend, Investment And Financing Decisions: Empirical Evidence On French Firms," JFQA, 1975, v10(5), 741-755.)

Jadlow, Janice Wickstead. "Market Assessment Of The Eurodollar Default Risk Premium," AFPAF, 1989, v4(Supp), 105-122.

Jadlow, Joseph M. "Adam Smith On Usury Laws," JOF, 1977, v32(4), 1195-1200.

Jaffe, Austin J. "Toward An Evolutionary Theory Of Trade Associations: The Case Of Real Estate Appraisers," AREUEA, 1988, v16(3), 230-256.

Jaffe, Austin J. "Is There A 'New' Internal Rate Of Return Literature?," AREUEA, 1977, v5(4), 482-502.

Jaffe, Jeffrey F. "Taxes And The Capital Structure Of Partnerships, REIT's, And Related Entities," JOF, 1991, v46(1), 401-408.

Jaffe, Jeffrey and Randolph Westerfield. "The Week-End Effect In Common Stock Returns: The International Evidence," JOF, 1985, v40(2), 433-454.

Jaffe, Jeffrey and Randolph Westerfield. "Patterns In Japanese Common Stock Returns: Day Of The Week And Turn Of The Year Effects," JFQA, 1985, v20(2), 261-272.

Jaffe, Jeffrey F. and Gershon Mandelker. "The 'Fisher Effect' For Risky Assets: An Empirical Investigation," JOF, 1976, v31(2), 447-458.

Jaffe, Jeffrey F. and Gershon Mandelker. "The Value Of The Firm Under Regulation," JOF, 1976, v31(2), 701-713.

Jaffe, Jeffrey F. and Gershon Mandelker. "Inflation And The Holding Period Returns On Bonds," JFQA, 1979, v14(5), 959-979.

Jaffe, Jeffrey F. and Larry J. Merville. "The Value Of Risk-Reducing Information," JFQA, 1974, v9(5), 697-707.

Jaffe, Jeffrey F. and Larry J. Merville. "Stock Price Dependencies And The Valuation Of Risky Assets with Discountinuous Temporal Returns," JOF, 1974, v29(5), 1437-1448.

Jaffe, Jeffrey F. and Robert L. Winkler. "Optimal Speculation Against An Efficient Market," JOF, 1976, v31(1), 49-61.

Jaffe, Jeffrey F. "A Note On Taxation And Investment," JOF, 1978, v33(5), 1439-1445.

Jaffe, Jeffrey F. "Corporate Taxes, Inflation, The Rate Of Interest, And The Return Of Equity," JFQA, 1978, v13(1), 55-64.

Jaffe, Jeffrey F. "Gold And Gold Stocks As Investments For Institutional Portfolios," FAJ, 1989, v45(2), 53-59. 31 3

Jaffe, Jeffrey F. "Inflation, The Interest Rate, And The Required Return On Equity," JFQA, 1985, v20(1), 29-44.

Jaffe, Jeffrey F. "On The Use Of Public Information In Financial Markets," JOF, 1975, v30(3),831-839.

Jaffe, Jeffrey F. "Special Information And Insider Trading," JOB, 1974, v47(3), 410-428.

Jaffe, Jeffrey F. "Speculating With A Specialist: Who Wins?," JPM, 1976-77, v3(3), 52-54.

Jaffe, Jeffrey F. (Ibbotson, Roger G. and Jeffrey F. Jaffe. "Hot Issue' Markets," JOF, 1975, v30(4), 1027-1042.)

Jaffe, Jeffrey F., Randolph Westerfield and Christopher Ma. "A Twist On The Monday Effect In Stock Prices: Evidence From The U.S. And Foreign Stock Markets," JBF, 1989, v13(4/5), 641-650.

Jaffe, Jeffrey and Randolph Westerfield. "Is There A Monthly Effect In Stock Market Returns?: Evidence From Foreign Countries," JBF, 1989, v13(2), 237-244.

Jaffe, Jeffrey, Donald B. Keim and Randolph Westerfield. "Earnings Yields, Market Values, And Stock Returns," JOF, 1989, v44(1), 135-148.

Jaffee, Dwight M. and Kenneth T. Rosen. "Estimates Of The Effectiveness Of Stabilization Policies For The Mortgage And Housing Markets," JOF, 1978, v33(3), 933-946.

Jaffee, Dwight M. "Discussion Of The Hunt Commission Report," JMCB, 1972, v4(4), 990-1000.

Jaffee, Dwight M. "The Impact Of Financial Futures And Options On Capital Formation," JFM, 1984, v4(3), 417-447.

Jaffee, Dwight M. "What To Do About Savings And Loan Associations?," JMCB, 1974, v6(4), 537-549.

Jaffee, Dwight M. (Chandler, Lester V. and Dwight M. Jaffee. "Regulating The Regualtors: A Review Of The FINE Regulatory Reforms," JMCB, 1977, v9(4), 619-635.)

Jaffee, Dwight M. (Goldfeld, Stephen M. and Dwight M. Jaffee. "The Determinants Of Deposit-Rate Setting By Savings And Loan Associations," JOF, 1970, v25(3), 615-632.)

Jaffee, Dwight M. (Goldfeld, Stephen M. and Dwight M. Jaffee. "Deposit Rate Setting By Savings And Loan Associations: Reply," JOF, 1971, v26(5), 1158-1160.)

Jaffee, Dwight M. (Homa, Kenneth E. and Dwight M. Jaffee. "The Supply Of Money And Common Stock Prices," JOF, 1971, v26(5), 1045-1066.)

Jaffee, Dwight and Andrei Shleifer. "Costs Of Financial Distress, Delayed Calls Of Convertible Bonds, And The Role Of Investment Banks," JOB, 1990, v63(1), Part 2, S107-S124.

Jaffee, Dwight and Kenneth Rosen. "The Changing Liability Structure Of Savings And Loan Associations," AREUEA, 1980, v8(1), 33-49.

Jagannathan, Ravi and Robert A. Korajczyk. "Assessing The Market Timing Performance Of Managed Portfolios," JOB, 1986, v59(2), Part 1, 217-236.

Jagannathan, Ravi. "An Investigation Of Commodity Futures Prices Using The Consumption-Based Intertemporal Capital Asset Pricing Model," JOF, 1985, v40(1), 175-191.

Jagannathan, Ravi. "Call Options And The Risk Of Underlying Securities," JFEC, 1984, v13(3), 425-434.

Jagannathan, Ravi. (Breen, William, Ravi Jagannathan and Aharon R. Ofer. "Correcting For Heteroscedasticity In Tests For Market Timing Ability," JOB, 1986, v59(4), Part 1, 585-598.)

Jagannathan, Ravi. (Breen, William, Lawrence R. Glosten and Ravi Jagannathan. "Economic Significance Of Predictable Variations In Stock Index Returns," JOF, 1989, v44(5), 1177-1190.)

Jagannathan, Ravi. (Chari, V. V., Ravi Jagannathan and Aharon R. Ofer. "Seasonalities In Security Returns: The Case Of Earnings Announcements," JFEC, 1988, v21(1), 101-122.)

Jagannathan, Ravi. (Chari, V. V. and Ravi Jagannathan. "Banking Panics, Information, And Rational Expectations Equilibrium," JOF, 1988, v43(3), 749-761.)

Jagannathan, Ravi. (Chari, V. V. and Ravi Jagannathan. "Adverse Selection In A Model Of Real Estate Lending," JOF, 1989, v44(2), 499-508.)

Jaggi, Bikki and Martin Freedman. "An Analysis Of The Informational Content Of Pollution Disclosures," FR, 1982, v17(3), 142-152.

Jaggi, Bikki and Paul Grier. "A Comparative Analysis Of Forecast Disclosing And Non-Disclosing Firms," FM, 1980, v9(2), 38-43.

Jaggi, Bikki and Richard Kolodny. Selection Of The LIFO Method Of Inventory Valuation: Mangement's Motives And Investor's Reaction," FR, v12(1), 1-19.

Jaggi, Bikki. "Comparative Accuracy Of Management's Annual Earnings Forecast," FM, 1978, v7(4), 24-32.

Jaggi, Bikki. (Arbel, Avner and Bikki Jaggi. "Market Information Assimilation Related To Extreme Daily Price Jumps," FAJ, 1982, v38(6), 60-66.)

Jagpal, Harsharanjeet S., Ephraim F. Sudit and Hrishikesh D. Vinod. "Measuring Dynamic Marketing Mix Interactions Using Translog Functions," JOB, 1982, v55(3), 401-415.

Jahanian, Shirin. (Glascock, John L., Shirin Jahanian and C. F. Sirmans. "An Analysis Of Office Market Rents: Some Empirical Evidence," AREUEA, 1990, v18(1), 105-120.)

Jahnkhani, Ali and George E. Pinches. "Duration And The Nonstationarity Of Systematic Risk For Bonds," JFR, 1982, v5(2), 151-160.

Jahankhani, Ali and Morgan J. Lynge, Jr. "Commercial Bank Financial Policies And Their Impact On Market-Determined Measures Of Risk," JBR, 1980-81, v11(3), 169-178.

Jahankhani, Ali. "E-V And E-S Capital Asset Pricing Models: Some Empirical Tests," JFQA, 1976, v11(4), 513-528.

Jahankhani, Ali. (Pinches, George E., J. Clay Singleton and Ali Jahankhani. "Fixed Coverage As A Determinant Of Electric Utility Bond Ratings," FM, 1978, v7(2), 45-55.)

Jahera, John S. (Lloyd, William P., John S. Jahera, Jr. and Steven J. Goldstein. "The Relation Between Returns, Ownership Structure, And Market Value," JFR, 1986, v9(2), 171-177.)

Jahera, John S., Jr. (Jahera, John S., Jr. and Joseph F. Sinkey, Jr. "A Note On The Intracyclical Balance-Sheet Behavior Of Large Commercial Banks: 1972-1978," JBF, 1984, v8(1), 109-118.)

Jahera, John S., Jr. (Pugh, William and John S. Jahera, Jr. "Stock Repurchases And Excess Returns: An Empirical Examination," FR, 1990, v25(1), 127-142.)

Jahera, John S., Jr. (Pugh, William N. and John S. Jahera, Jr. "State Antitakeover Legislation And Shareholder Wealth," JFR, 1990, v13(3), 221-232.)

Jahera, John S., Jr. (Verbrugge, James A. and John S. Jahera, Jr. "Expense-Preference Behavior In The Savings And Loan Industry," JMCB, 1981, v13(4), 465-476.)

Jahera, John S., Jr. and William P. Lloyd. "Exchange Listing And Size: Effects On Excess Returns," JBFA, 1989, v16(5), 675-680.

Jahera, John S., Jr., William P. Lloyd and Daniel E. Page. "The Relationship Between Financial Performance And Stock Market Based Measures Of Corporate Diversification," FR, 1987, v22(4), 379-390.

Jahnke, Gregg, Stephen Klaffke and Henry R. Oppenheimer. "Price Earnings Ratios And Security Performance," JPM, 1987-88, v14(1), 39-47.

Jahnke, William W. "The Growth Stock Mania Revisited," FAJ, 1975, v31(1), 42-44.

Jahnke, William W. "The Growth Stock Mania," FAJ, 1973, v29(3), 65-68.

Jahnke, William W. "What's Behind Stock Prices?," FAJ, 1975, v31(5), 69-76.

Jahnke, William W. (Fouse, William L., William W. Jahnke and Barr Rosenberg. "Is Beta Phlogiston?," FAJ, 1974, v30(1), 70-80.)

Jain, Adish. (Canto, Victor A., J. Kimball Dietrich, Adish Jain and Vishwa Mudaliar. "Protectionism And The Stock Market: The Determinants And Consequences Of Trade Restrictions," FAJ, 1986, v42(5), 32-42.)

Jain, Anshuman. (Hill, Joanne M., Anshuman Jain and Robert A. Wood, Jr. "Insurance: Volatility Risk And Futures Mispricing," JPM, 1987-88, v14(2), 23-29.)

Jain, Arvind K. and Satyadev Gupta. "Some Evidence On 'Herding' Behavior By U.S. Banks," JMCB, 1987, v19(1), 78-89.

Jain, Prem C. "Response Of Hourly Stock Prices And Trading Volume To Economic News," JOB, 1988, v61(2), 219-232.

Jain, Prem C. "The Effect Of Voluntary Sell-Off Announcements On Shareholder Wealth," JOF, 1985, v40(1), 209-224.

Jain, Prem C. "The Effect On Stock Price Of Inclusion In Or Exclusion From The S&P 500," FAJ, 1987, v43(1), 58-65.

Jain, Prem C. "The Time-Series Behavior Of Annual Accounting Earnings: A Comparison Of The Random Walk And The Constant-Percentage-Growth Models," AFPAF, 1987, v2(1), 179-204.

Jain, Prem C. and Gun-Ho Joh. "The Dependence Between Hourly Prices And Trading Volume," JFQA, 1988, v23(3), 269-284.

Jain, Subhash C. (Hempel, Donald J. and Subhash C. Jain. "House Buying Behavior: An Empirical Study In Cross-Cultural Buyer Behavior," AREUEA, 1978, v6(1), 1-21.)

Jain, Suresh. (Livingston, Miles and Suresh Jain. "Flattening Of Bond Yield Curves For Long Maturities," JOF, 1982, v37(1), 157-167.)

Jalilvand, Abolhassan and Robert S. Harris. "Corporate Behavior In Adjusting To Capital Structure And Dividend Targets: An Econometric Study," JOF, 1984, v39(1), 127-145.

Jalilvand, Abolhassan. (Kryzanowski, Lawrence and Abolhassan Jalilvand. "Statistical Tests Of The Accuracy Of Alternative Forecasts: Some Results For U.S. Utility Betas," FR, 1986, v21(2), 319-336.)

James, Christopher and Robert O. Edmister. "The Relation Between Common Stock Returns, Trading Activity And Market Value," JOF, 1983, v38(4), 1075-1086.

James, Christopher M. (Brickley, James A. and Christopher M. James. "Access To Deposit Insurance, Insolvency Rules And The Stock Returns Of Financial Institutions," JFEC, 1986, v16(3), 345-372.)

James, Christopher M. (Dann, Larry Y. and Christopher M. James. "An Analysis Of The Impact Of Deposit Rate Ceilings On The Market Values Of Thrift Institutions," JOF, 1982, v37(5), 1259-1275.)

James, Christopher M. (Flannery, Mark J. and Christopher M. James. "Market Evidence Of The Effective Maturity Of Bank Assets And Liabilities," JMCB, 1984, v16(4), Part 1, 435-445.)

James, Christopher M. (Flannery, Mark J. and Christopher M. James. "The Effect Of Interest Rate Changes On The Common Stock Returns Of Financial Institutions," JOF, 1984, v39(4), 1141-1153.)

James, Christopher and Peggy Wier. "Are Bank Loans Different?: Some Evidence From The Stock Market," JACF, 1988, v1(2), 46-54.

James, Christopher, Sergio Koreisha and Megan Partch. "A Varma Analysis Of The Causal Relations Among Stock Returns, Real Output, And Nominal Interest Rates," JOF, 1985, v40(5), 1375-1384.

James, Christopher. "An Analysis Of Bank Loan Rate Indexation," JOF, 1982, v37(3), 809-825.

James, Christopher. "Pricing Alternatives For Loan Commitments: A Note," JBR, 1982-83, v13(4), 300-303.

James, Christopher. "Self-Selection And The Pricing Of Bank Services: An Analysis Of The Market For Loan Commitments And The Role Of Compensating Balance Requirements," JFQA, 1981, v16(5), 725-746.

James, Christopher. "Some Evidence On The Uniqueness Of Bank Loans," JFEC, 1987, v19(2), 217-236.

James, Christopher. (Dietrich, J. Kimball and Christopher James. "Regulation And The Determination Of Bank Capital Changes: A Note," JOF, 1983, v38(5), 1651-1658.)

James, Christopher. (Edmister, Robert O. and Christopher James. "Is Illiquidity A Bar To Buying Small Cap Stocks?," JPM, 1982-83, v9(4), 14-19.)

James, F. E., Jr. "Monthly Moving Averages--An Effective Investment Tool?," JFQA, 1968, v3(3),315-326.

James, Franklin J. and Thomas Mueller. "Environmental Impact Evaluation, Land Use Planning, And The Housing Consumer," AREUEA, 1977, v5(3), 279-301.

James, John A. "Portfolio Selection With An Imperfectly Competitive Asset Market," JFQA, 1976, v11(5), 831-846.

Jameson, Mel, James D. Shilling and C. F. Sirmans. "Regional Variation Of Mortgage Yields And Simultaneity Bias," JFR, 1990, v13(3), 211-220.

Jameson, Mel. (Clauretie, Terrence M., Mel Jameson and Ronald C. Rogers. "A Note On Refinancing Costs, Prepayment Assumptions, And The Value Of Mortgage-Backed Securities," JREFEC, 1990, v3(3), 295-300.)

Jameson, Mel. (Clauretie, Terrence M. and Mel Jameson. "Interest Rates And The Foreclosure Process: An Agency Problem In FHA Mortgage Insurance," JRI, 1990, v57(4), 701-711.)

Jamshidian, Farshid. "An Exact Bond Option Formula," JOF, 1989, v44(1), 205-210.

Janakiramanan, S. (Alexander, Gordon J., Cheol S. Eun and S. Janakiramanan. "Asset Pricing And Dual Listing On Foreign Capital Markets: A Note," JOF, 1987, v42(1), 151-158.)

Janakiramanan, S. (Alexander, Gordon J., Cheol S. Eun and S. Janakiramanan. "International Listings And Stock Returns: Some Empirical Evidence," JFQA, 1988, v23(2), 135-152.)

Janakiramanan, S. (Eun, Cheol S. and S. Janakiramanan. "A Model Of International Asset Pricing With A Constraint On The Foreign Equity Ownership," JOF, 1986, v41(4), 897-914.)

Janakiramanan, S. (Eun, Cheol S. and S. Janakiramanan. "Bilateral Cross-Listing And The Equilibrium Security Prices," AFPAF, 1990, v5(1), 59-74.)

Jang, Hasung and P. C. Venkatesh. "Consistency Between Predicted And Actual Bid-Ask Quote Revisions," JOF, 1991, v46(1), 433-446.

Janjigian, Vahan and Paul J. Bolster. "The Elimination Of Director Liability And Stockholder Returns: An Empirical Investigation," JFR, 1990, v13(1), 53-60.

Janjigian, Vahan. "The Leverage Changing Consequences Of Convertible Debt Financing," FM, 1987, v16(3), 15-21.

Janjigian, Vahan. (Hansen, Robert S., Beverly R. Fuller and Vahan Janjigian. "The Over-Allotment Option And Equity Financing Flotation Costs: An Empirical Investigation," FM, 1987, v16(2), 24-32.)

Jankus, Jonathan C. "Is Beta A Useful Measure Of Security Risk: Comment," JPM, 1981-82, v8(1), 66.

Jansen, Dennis W. "Real Balances In An Ad Hoc Keynesian Model And Policy Ineffectiveness," JMCB, 1985, v17(3), 378-386.

Jansen, Dennis W. (Bradley, Michael D. and Dennis W. Jansen. "Federal Reserve Operating Procedure In The Eighties: A Dynamic Analysis," JMCB, 1986, v18(3), 323-335.)

Jansen, Dennis W. (Cosimano, Thomas F. and Dennis W. Jansen.

"Estimates Of The Variance Of U.S. Inflation Based Upon The ARCH Model: Comment," **JMCB**, 1988, v20(3), Part 1, 409-421.)

Janssen, Christian. (Kraus, Alan, Christian Janssen and Alan McAdams. "The Lock-Box Location Problem," **JBR**, 1970-71, v1(3), 50-58.)

Jantorni, Joan M. (Clark, Robert A., Joan M. Jantorni and Robert R. Gann. "Analysis Of The Lease-Or-Buy Decision: Comment," **JOF**, 1973, v28(4), 1015-1016.)

Jappelli, Tullio. (Fissel, Gary S. and Tullio Jappelli. "Do Liquidity Constraints Vary Over Time? Evidence From Survey And Panel Data," **JMCB**, 1990, v22(2), 253-262.)

Jarislowsky, Stephen A. "Investment In Canadian Development Stocks," **FAJ**, 1957, v13(5), 55-60.

Jarislowsky, Stephen A. (Brown, J. J. and Stephen A. Jarislowsky. "Statistical Approach To Security Analysis," **FAJ**, 1954, v10(5), 79-84.)

Jarnagin, Bill D. (Graber, Dean E. and Bill D. Jarnagin. "The FASB - Eliminator Of 'Managed Earnings'?," **FAJ**, 1979, v35(2), 72-76.)

Jarrell, Gregg A. (Bradley, Michael, Gregg A. Jarrell and E. Han Kim. "On The Existence Of An Optimal Capital Structure: Theory And Evidence," **JOF**, 1984, v39(3), 857-878.)

Jarrell, Gregg A. (Comment, Robert and Gregg A. Jarrell. "Two-Tier And Negotiated Tender Offers: The Imprisonment Of The Free-Riding Shareholder," **JFEC**, 1987, v19(2), 283-310.)

Jarrell, Gregg A. and Annette B. Poulsen. "Dual-Class Recapitalizations As Antitakeover Mechanisms: The Recent Evidence," **JFEC**, 1988, v20(1/2), 129-152.

Jarrell, Gregg A. and Annette B. Poulsen. "Shark Repellents And Stock Prices: The Effects Of Antitakeover Amendments Since 1980," **JFEC**, 1987, v19(1), 127-168.

Jarrell, Gregg A. and Annette B. Poulsen. "The Returns To Acquiring Firms In Tender Orders: Evidence From Three Decades," **FM**, 1989, v18(3), 12-19.

Jarrell, Gregg A. and Paul J. Seguin. "A Proposal To Stabilize Stock Prices: Comment," **JPM**, 1990, v16(2), 79-81.

Jarrett, Jeffrey E. "A Note On Earnings Risk And The Coefficient Of Variation: Comment," **JOF**, 1970, v25(5), 1159-1160.

Jarrett, Jeffrey E. "A Note On Investment Criteria And The Estimation Problem In Financial Accounting," **JBFA**, 1980, v7(2), 233-237.

Jarrett, Jeffrey E. "Estimating The Cost Of Capital For A Division Of A Firm, And The Allocation Problem In Accounting: A Reply," **JBFA**, 1980, v7(1), 71-73.

Jarrett, Jeffrey E. "Estimating The Cost Of Capital For A Division Of A Firm, And The Allocation Problem In Accounting," **JBFA**, 1978, v5(1), 39-48.

Jarrett, Jeffrey E. "Rising Hospital Costs And Service Intensity," **JRI**, 1981, v48(2), 261-271.

Jarrett, Jeffrey E. (Brandon, Charles H. and Jeffrey E. Jarrett. "Evaluating Accounting Forecast," **JBFA**, 1976, v3(3), 67-78.)

Jarrett, Jeffrey. "The Rate Of Return From Interim Financial Reports And The Allocation Problem In Financial Accounting," **JBFA**, 1983, v10(2), 289-298.

Jarrett, Jeffrey. (Brandon, Charles, Jeffrey Jarrett and Saleha Khumuwala. "On The Predictability Of Growth In Earnings Per Share," **JBFA**, 1983, v10(3), 373-387.)

Jarrett, Jeffrey. (Brandon, Charles and Jeffrey Jarrett. "Accuracy Of Forecasts In Annual Reports," **FR**, 1974, v9(1), 29-45.)

Jarrow, Robert and Andrew Rudd. "Approximate Option Valuation For Arbitrary Stochastic Processes," **JFEC**, 1982, v10(3), 347-369.

Jarrow, Robert A. and George S. Oldfield. "Forward Contracts And Futures Contracts," **JFEC**, 1981, v9(4), 373-382.

Jarrow, Robert A. "Preferences, Continuity, And The Arbitrage Pricing Theory," **RFS**, 1988-89, v1(2), 159-172.

Jarrow, Robert A. "The Relationship Between Yield, Risk, And Return Of Corporate Bonds," **JOF**, 1978, v33(4), 1235-1240.

Jarrow, Robert A. (Carr, Peter P. and Robert A. Jarrow. "The Stop-Loss Start-Gain Paradox And Option Valuation: A New Decomposition Into Intrinsic And Time Value," **RFS**, 1990, v3(3), 469-492.)

Jarrow, Robert A. (Easley, David and Robert A. Jarrow. "Consensus Beliefs Equilibrium And Market Efficiency," **JOF**, 1983, v38(3), 903-911.)

Jarrow, Robert A. (Heath, David C. and Robert A. Jarrow. "Ex-Dividend Stock Price Behavior And Arbitrage Opportunities," **JOB**, 1988, v61(1), 95-108.)

Jarrow, Robert A. (Heath, David C. and Robert A. Jarrow. "Arbitrage, Continuous Trading, And Margin Requirements," **JOF**, 1987, v42(5), 1129-1142.)

Jarrow, Robert A. (Logue, Dennis E. and Robert A. Jarrow. "Negotiated Vs. Competitive Bidding In The Sale Of Securities By Public Utilities," **FM**, 1978, v7(3), 31-39.)

Jarrow, Robert A. (Oldfield, George S., Jr., R. J. Rogalski and Robert A. Jarrow. "An Autoregressive Jump Process For Common Stock Returns," **JFEC**, 1977, v5(3), 389-418.)

Jarrow, Robert A. and Eric R. Rosenfeld. "Jump Risks And The Intertemporal Capital Asset Pricing Model," **JOB**, 1984, v57(3), 337-352.

Jarrow, Robert A. and Maureen O'Hara. "Primes And Scores: An Essay On Market Imperfections," **JOF**, 1989, v44(5), 1263-1288.

Jarrow, Robert. "Heterogeneous Expectations, Restrictions On Short Sales, And Equilibrium Asset Prices," **JOF**, 1980, v35(5), 1105-1113.

Jarrow, Robert. "The Relationship Between Arbitrage And First Order Stochastic Dominance," **JOF**, 1986, v41(4), 915-922.

Jarrow, Robert. (Heath, David, Robert Jarrow and Andrew Morton. "Bond Pricing And The Term Structure Of Interest Rates: A Discrete Time Approximation," **JFQA**, 1990, v25(4), 419-440.)

Jarvis, N. Leonard. "Selecting Investments For 1958," **FAJ**, 1958, v14(1), 53-56.

Jarvis, N. Leonard. "The Cement Industry," **FAJ**, 1949, v5(4), 10-12.

Jarvis, N. Leonard. "Yesterday, Today, And Tomorrow," **FAJ**, 1953, v9(1), 11-16.

Jastram, Roy W. "The Development Of Advertising Appropriation Policy," **JOB**, 1950, v23(3), 154-166.

Jatusipitak, Som. (Boness, A. James, Andrew H. Chen and Som Jatusipitak. "Investigations Of Nonstationarity In Prices," **JOB**, 1974, v47(4), 518-537.)

Jatusipitak, Som. (Boness, A. James, Andrew H. Chen and Som Jatusipitak. "On Relations Among Stock Price Behavior And Changes In The Capital Structure Of The Firm," **JFQA**, 1972, v7(4), 1967-1982.)

Jauch, Heinz. "Four Keys To Savings And Loan Profitability," **FAJ**, 1981, v37(3), 31-39,41-43.

Jayaraman, Narayanan and Kuldeep Shastri. "The Valuation Impacts Of Specially Designated Dividends," **JFQA**, 1988, v23(3), 301-312.

Jayson, Susan. (Malley, Susan L. and Susan Jayson. "Why Do Financial Executives Manage Pensions Funds The Way They Do?," **FAJ**, 1986, v42(6), 56-62.)

Jean, William H. and Billy P. Helms. "Geometric Mean Approximations," **JFQA**, 1983, v18(3), 287-293.

Jean, William H. "A General Class Of Three-Parameter Risk Measures: Comment," **JOF**,1975, v30(1), 224-225.

Jean, William H. "Comparison Of Moment And Stochastic Dominance Ranking Models," **JFQA**, 1975, v10(1), 151-161.

Jean, William H. "Distribution Moments And Equilibrium: Reply," **JFQA**, 1972, v7(1), 1435-1437.

Jean, William H. "More On Multidimensional Portfolio Analysis," **JFQA**, 1973, v8(3), 475-490.

Jean, William H. "On Multiple Rates Of Return: Reply," **JOF**, 1969, v24(1), 99-100.

Jean, William H. "On Multiple Rates Of Return," **JOF**, 1968, v23(1), 187-191.

Jean, William H. "Terminal Value Or Present Value In Capital Budgeting Programs," **JFQA**, 1971, v6(1), 649-651.

Jean, William H. "The Extension Of Portfolio Analysis To Three Or More Parameters," **JFQA**, 1971, v6(1), 505-515.

Jean, William H. "The Geometric Mean And Stochastic Dominance," **JOF**, 1980, v35(1), 151-158.

Jean, William H. "The Harmonic Means And Other Necessary Conditions For Stochastic Domonance," **JOF**, 1984, v39(2), 527-534.

Jean, William H. and Billy P. Helms. "The Identification Of Stochastic Dominance Efficient Sets By Moment Combination Orderings," **JBF**, 1988, v12(2), 243-254.

Jean, William H. and Billy P. Helms. "Moment Orderings And Stochastic Dominance Tests," **JBFA**, 1988, v15(4), 573-584.

Jee, Beomha. "A Comparative Analysis Of Alternative Pure Premium In The Automobile Risk Classification System," **JRI**, 1989, v56(3), 434-459.

Jeffers, James R. and Jene Kwon. "A Portfolio Approach To Corporate Demands For Government Securities," **JOF**, 1969, v24(5), 905-919.

Jeffrey, Robert H. "A New Paradigm For Portfolio Risk," **JPM**, 1984-85, v11(1), 33-40.

Jeffrey, Robert H. "Internal Portfolio Growth: The Better Measure," **JPM**, 1976-77, v3(4), 10-15.

Jeffries, William S. "A Claimsman's Rejoinder To Scheduled Compensation Proposals For Automobile Insurance Claims," **JRI**, 1970, v37(3), 474-476.

Jegadeesh, Narasimhan. "Evidence Of Predictable Behavior Of Security Returns," **JOF**, 1990, v45(3), 881-898.

Jegers, M. and W. Buijink. "Cross-Sectional Distributional Properties Of Financial Ratios In Belgian Manufacturing Industries: Aggregation Effects And Persistence Over Time," **JBFA**, 1986, v13(3), 337-363.

Jegers, M. "Estimating The Internal Rate Of Return From Published Financial Statements: A Comment," **JBFA**, 1985, v12(4), 609-610.

Jehle, Geoffrey A. "Regulatory And The Public Interest In Banking," **JBF**, 1986, v10(4), 549-574.

Jehring, J. J. "Profit-Sharing And Collective Bargaining," **JOB**, 1959, v32(2), 175-177.

Jen, Frank C. and James E. Wert. "Imputed Yields Of A Sinking Fund Bond And The Term Structure Of Interest Rates," **JOF**, 1966, v21(4), 697-713.

Jen, Frank C. and James E. Wert. "Sinking Funds And Bond Yields," **FAJ**, 1967, v23(2), 125-131.

Jen, Frank C. and James E. Wert. "The Effect Of Call Risk On Corporate Bond Yields," **JOF**, 1967, v22(4), 637-651.

Jen, Frank C. and James E. Wert. "The Deferred Call Provision And Corporate Bond Yields," **JFQA**, 1968, v3(2), 157-170.

Jen, Frank C. "Financial Planning And Control For Commercial And Industrial Enterprises In China," **FR**, 1988, v23(2), 161-174.

Jen, Frank C. (Boness, A. James and Frank C. Jen. "A Model Of Information Diffusion, Stock Market Behavior, And Equilibrium Price," **JFQA**, 1970, v5(3), 279-296.)

Jen, Frank C. (Chen, Andrew H. Y., Frank C. Jen and Stanley Zionts," **JOB**, 1971, v44(1), 51-61.)

Jen, Frank C. (Chen, Andrew H. Y., Frank C. Jen and Stanley Zionts. "The Joint Determination Of Portfolio And Transaction Demands For Money," **JOF**, 1974, v29(1), 175-186.)

Jen, Frank C. (Choi, Dosoung and Frank C. Jen. "The Relation Between Stock Returns And Short-Term Interest Rates," **RQFA**, 1991, v1(1), 75-90.)

Jen, Frank C. (Kon, Stanley J. and Frank C. Jen. "Estimation Of Time-Varying Systematic Risk And Performance For Mutual Fund Portfolios: An Application Of Switching Regression," **JOF**, 1978, v33(2), 457-475.)

Jen, Frank C. (Kon, Stanley J. and Frank C. Jen. "The Investment Performance Of Mutual Funds: An Empirical Investigation Of Timing, Selectivity, And Market Efficiency," **JOB**, 1979, v52(2), 263-290.)

Jen, Frank C. (Lee, Cheng F. and Frank C. Jen. "Effects Of Measurement Errors On Systematic Risk And Performance Measure Of A Portfolio," **JFQA**, 1978, v13(1), 299-312.)

Jen, Frank C. (Lee, Cheng F., Frank C. Jen and K. C. John Wei. "The Real And Nominal Parameters In The CAPM: A Responsive Coefficient Approach," **IJOF**, 1988, v1(1), 113-130.)

Jen, Frank C. (Lin, Winston T. and Frank C. Jen. "Consumption, Investment, Market Price Of Risk, And The Risk-Free Rate," **JFQA**, 1980, v15(5), 1025-1040.)

Jen, Frank C. (Shick, Richard A. and Frank C. Jen. "Merger Benefits To Shareholders Of Acquiring Firms," **FM**, 1974, v3(4), 45-53.)

Jen, Frank C. "Merton H. Miller, Co-Winner, 1990 Nobel Laureates In Economics," **RQFA**, 1991, v1(2), 216-217.

Jen, Frank C. and Susan S. Hamlen. "Net Present Value Method And Agency Theory In Financial Planning," AFPAF, 1985, v1(1), 49-76.

Jenkins, D. Randall. (Foster, Taylor W., III, D. Randall Jenkins and Don W. Vickrey. "Additional Evidence On The Incremental Information Content Of The 10-K," JBFA, 1983, v10(1), 57-66.)

Jenkins, Elizabeth and Robert E. Seiler. "The Impact Of Executive Compensation Schemes Upon The Level Of Discretionary Expenditures And Growth In Stockholder Wealth," JBFA, 1990, v17(4), 585-592.

Jenkins, James W. "Incentive Compensation And REIT Financial Leverage And Asset Risk," FM, 1980, v9(1), 81-87.

Jenkins, James W. "Taxes, Margining And Bond Selection," FAJ, 1980, v36(3), 41-47.

Jenkins, Roy. "United Kingdom's Economic Situation," FAJ, 1968, v24(4), 145-147.

Jenks, Jeffrey M. (Bower, Richard S. and Jeffrey M. Jenks. "Divisional Screening Rates," FM, 1974, v4(3), 42-49.)

Jenks, Jeremy C. "Financial Community's Role In Stockholder Relations," FAJ, 1948, v4(4), 34-42.

Jenks, Jeremy C. "Growth Industries," FAJ, 1957, v13(4), 91-96.

Jenks, Jeremy C. "History Of Money," FAJ, 1964, v20(2), 95-99.

Jenks, Jeremy C. "Investing In Industrial Research," FAJ, 1954, v10(1), 23-26.

Jenks, Jeremy C. "Investing In Growth Stock," FAJ, 1947, v3(2), 38-53.

Jenks, Jeremy C. "The History Of Money," FAJ, 1965, v21(5), 94-103.

Jenks, Jeremy C. "The Worth Of Chemical Securities," FAJ, 1949, v5(4), 13-16.

Jennergren, L. Peter. "Valuation By Linear Programming - A Pedagogical Note," JBFA, 1990, v17(5), 751-756.

Jennergren, Peter. "Decentralization On The Basis Of Price Schedules In Linear Decomposable Resource-Allocation Problems," JFQA, 1972, v7(1), 1407-1417.

Jennings, Edward H. "An Empirical Analysis Of Some Aspects Of Common Stock Diversification," JFQA, 1971, v6(2), 797-813.

Jennings, Edward H. "An Estimate Of Convertible Bond Premiums," JFQA, 1974, v9(1), 33-56.

Jennings, Edward H. "Reply: An Estimate Of Convertible Bond Premiums," JFQA, 1975, v10(2), 375-376.

Jennings, G. W. "Investment Opportunities In Fire Insurance Stocks," FAJ, 1948, v4(1), 33-41.

Jennings, Robert and Laura Starks. "Earnings Announcements, Stock Price Adjustment, And The Existence Of Option Markets," JOF, 1986, v41(1), 107-126.

Jennings, Robert H. and Christopher B. Barry. "On Information Dissemination And Equilibrium Asset Prices: A Note," JFQA, 1984, v19(4), 395-402.

Jennings, Robert H. and Christopher B. Barry. "Information Dissemination And Portfolio Choice," JFQA, 1983, v18(1), 1-19.

Jennings, Robert H. (Brown, David P. and Robert H. Jennings. "On Technical Analysis," RFS, 1989, v2(4), 527-552.)

Jennings, Robert H. (Hassell, John M., Robert H. Jennings and Dennis J. Lasser. "Management Earnings Forecasts: Their Usefulness As A Source Of Firm-Specific Information To Security Analysts," JFR, 1988, v11(4), 303-320.)

Jennings, Robert H. and Michael A. Mazzeo. "Stock Price Movements Around Acquisition Announcements And Management's Response," JOB, 1991, v64(2), 139-164.

Jennings, Robert H., Laura T. Starks and John C. Fellingham. "An Equilibrium Model Of Asset Trading With Sequential Information Arrival," JOF, 1981, v36(1), 143-161.

Jennings, Robert M. (Brisco, John P. and Robert M. Jennings. "Present And Future Value Approximations," JFED, 1984, v13, 1-4.)

Jennings, Robert. (Graham, David and Robert Jennings. "Systematic Risk, Dividend Yield And The Hedging Performance Of Stock Index Futures," JFM, 1987, v7(1), 1-14.)

Jennings, William P. and G. Michael Phillips. "Risk As A Discount Rate Determinant In Wrongful Death And Injury Cases," JRI, 1989, v56(1), 122-127.

Jensen, Arnold E. (Hagaman, T. Carter and Arnold E. Jensen. "Investment Value: A Reference Point For Analysts," FAJ, 1977, v33(2), 63-70.)

Jensen, Daniel L. and James C. McKeown. "Multiple-Step Investigations Of Standard Cost Variances," JBFA, 1977, v4(2), 247-256.

Jensen, Daniel L. (Bailey, Andrew D., Jr. and Daniel L. Jensen. "General Price Level Adjustments In The Capital Budgeting Decision," FM, 1977, v6(1),26-32.)

Jensen, Gail A. (Cotter, Kevin D. and Gail A. Jensen. "Choice Of Purchasing Arrangements In Insurance Markets," JRU, 1989, v2(4), 405-414.)

Jensen, Harold A., Jr. (Friedman, Lloyd K., Harold A. Jensen, Jr., Spencer L. Kimball and Jon S. Hanson. "The Regulation Of Specialty Policies In Life Insurance: Comment," JRI, 1966, v33(2), 305-316.)

Jensen, M. C. and W. H. Meckling. "Can The Corporation Survive?," FAJ, 1978, v34(1), 31-37.

Jensen, M. (Appelbaum, E., J. Burns, R. Evans, J. Gould, T. Hamachek, R. Kidder, M. Jensen, J. Johnstone, M. Murray, R. Sim, J. Stern, B. Stewart and C. Zaner. "Panel: CEO Roundtable On Corporate Structure And Management Incentives," JACF, 1990, v3(3), 6-35.)

Jensen, M. (Gilmour, A., M. Jensen, R. Mercer, N. Minow, J. Morley, R. Siefert, B. Stewart, L. Summers and I. Harris. "Panel: The Economic Consequences Of High Leverage And Stock Market Pressures On Corporate Management: A Roundtable Discussion," JACF, 1990, v3(2), 6-37.)

Jensen, Michael C. and George A. Bennington. "Random Walks And Technical Theories: Some Additional Evidence," JOF, 1970, v25(2), 469-482.

Jensen, Michael C. and Richard S. Ruback. "The Market For Corporate Control," JFEC, 1983, v11(1), 5-50.

Jensen, Michael C. and William H. Meckling. "Theory Of The Firm: Managerial Behavior, Agency Costs And Ownership Structure," JFEC, 1976, v3(4), 305-360.

Jensen, Michael C. (Baker, George P., Michael C. Jensen and Kevin J. Murphy. "Compensation And Incentives: Practice Vs. Theory," JOF, 1988, v43(3), 593-616.)

Jensen, Michael C. "Random Walks: A Comment," FAJ, 1967, v23(6), 77-85.

Jensen, Michael C. "Risk, The Pricing Of Capital Assets, And The Evaluation Of Investment Portfolios," JOB, 1969, v42(2), 167-247.

Jensen, Michael C. "Selections From The Senate And House Hearings On LBOs And Corporate Debt," JACF, 1989, v2(1), 35-44.

Jensen, Michael C. "Some Anomalous Evidence Regarding Market Efficiency," JFEC, 1978, v6(2/3), 95-101.

Jensen, Michael C. "The Performance Of Mutual Funds In The Period 1945-1964," JOF, 1968, v23(2),389-416.

Jensen, Michael C. (Fama, Eugene F. and Michael C. Jensen. "Organizational Forms And Investment Decisions," JFEC, 1985, v14(1), 101-118.)

Jensen, Michael C. and Jerold B. Warner. "The Distribution Of Power Among Corporate Managers, Shareholders, And Directors," JFEC, 1988, v20(1/2), 3-24.

Jensen, Michael C. and Kevin J. Murphy. "CEO Incentives - It's Not How Much You Pay, But How," JACF, 1990, v3(3), 36-49.

Jensen, Michael C. and William H. Meckling. "Rights And Production Functions: An Application To Labor-Managed Firms And Codetermination," JOB, 1979, v52(4), 469-506.

Jensen, Oscar W. (Conine, Thomas E., Jr., Oscar W. Jensen and Maurry Tamarkin. "On Optimal Output In An Option Pricing Framework," JBFA, 1988, v15(1), 21-26.)

Jensen, Robert E. "A Dynamic Analytic Hierarchy Process Analysis Of Capital Budgeting Under Stochastic Inflation Rates And Risk Premiums," AFPAF, 1987, v2(1), 269-302.

Jepson, James A. "Graduate Seminar In Financial Management," JFED, 1973, v2, 37-38.

Jergensen, Dale W. (Dahlgran, Roger A. and Dale W. Jergensen. "The Feasibility Of Hedging Working Capital Costs In Financial Futures Markets By Small Agribusiness Firms," RFM, 1984, v3(1), 1-12.)

Jessell, Kenneth A. (McDaniel, William R., Daniel E. McCarty and Kenneth A. Jessell. "Discounted Cash Flow With Explicit Reinvestment Rates: Tutorial And Extension," FR, 1988, v23(3), 369-385.)

Jessell, Kenneth A. and Daniel E. McCarty. "A Note On Marginal Analysis, NPV Criterion And Wealth Maximization," JFED, 1987, v16, 12-15.

Jessup, Paul F. and Mary Bochnak. "Why Not Deregulate Bank Debt Capital," FM, 1976, v5(4), 65-67.

Jessup, Paul F. and Richard W. Stolz. "Customer Alternatives Among Rural Banks," JBR, 1975-76, v6(2), 135-139.

Jessup, Paul F. and Roger B. Upson. "Opportunities In Regional Markets," FAJ, 1970, v26(2), 75-79.

Jessup, Paul F. "Analyzing Acquisitions By Bank Holding Companies," JBR, 1974-75, v5(1), 55-63.

Jessup, Paul F. "Testing Hypotheses Involving Nonaffiliate Banks," JBR, 1975-76, v6(3), 219-221.

Jessup, Paul F. (Upson, Roger B., Paul F. Jessup and Matsumoto. "Portfolio Diversification Strategies," FAJ, 1975, v31(3), 86-88.)

Jessup, Paul F. (Upson, Roger B. and Paul F. Jessup. "Risk-Return Relationships In Regional Securities," JFQA, 1970, v5(5), 677-696.)

Jeuland, Abel P. and Chakravarthi Narasimhan. "Dealing--Temporary Price Cuts--By Seller As A Buyer Discrimination Mechanism," JOB, 1985, v58(3), 295-308.

Jeynes, Paul H. "Evaluating Cost Of Capital," FAJ, 1964, v20(4), 102-108.

Jiranyakul, Romain. (Battalio, Raymond C., John H. Kagel and Romain Jiranyakul. "Testing Between Alternative Models Of Choice Under Uncertainty: Some Initial Results," JRU, 1990, v3(1), 25-50.)

Jo, Hoje. (Huang, Roger D. and Hoje Jo. "Tests Of Market Models: Heteroskedasticity Or Misspecification?," JBF, 1988, v11(3), 439-456.)

Joanette, Francois P. (VanDerhiei, Jack L. and Francois P. Joanette. "Economic Determinants For The Choice Of Actuarial Cost Methods," JRI, 1988, v55(1), 59-74.)

Jobson, J. D. and Bob Korkie. "Statistical Inference In Two-Parameter Portfolio Theory With Multiple Regression Software," JFQA, 1983, v18(2), 189-197.

Jobson, J. D. and Bob Korkie. "Putting Markowitz Theory To Work," JPM, 1980-81, v7(4), 70-74.

Jobson, J. D. and Bob Korkie. "Potential Performance And Tests Of Portfolio Efficiency," JFEC, 1982, v10(4), 433-466.

Jobson, J. D. and Bob Korkie. "On The Jensen Measure And Marginal Improvements In Portfolio Performance: A Note," JOF, 1984, v39(1), 245-251.

Jobson, J. D. and Bob M. Korkie. "Performance Hypothesis Testing With The Sharpe And Treynor Measures," JOF, 1981, v36(4), 889-908.

Jobson, J. D. "A Multivariate Linear Regression Test For The Arbitrage Pricing Theory," JOF, 1982, v37(4), 1037-1042.

Jobson, J. D. and Bob Korkie. "A Performance Interpretation Of Multivariate Tests Of Asset Set Intersection, Spanning, And Mean-Variance Efficiency," JFQA, 1989, v24(2), 185-204.

Joehnk, Michael D. and David S. Kidwell. "The Impact Of Market Uncertainty On Municipal Bond Underwriting Spread," FM, 1984, v13(1), 37-44.

Joehnk, Michael D. and David S. Kidwell. "Comparative Costs Of Competitive And Negotiated Underwritings In The State And Local Bond Market," JOF, 1979, v34(3), 725-731.

Joehnk, Michael D. and J. William Petty, III. "The Interest Sensitivity Of Common Stock Prices," JPM, 1979-80, v6(2), 19-25.

Joehnk, Michael D. and James F. Nielsen. "The Effects Of Conglomerate Merger Activity On Systematic Risk," JFQA, 1974, v9(2), 215-225.

Joehnk, Michael D. and Timothy P. Sullivan. "An Annotated Bibliography Of Bond Literature," JFED, 1974, v3, 106-113.

Joehnk, Michael D. (Dyl, Edward A. and Michael D. Joehnk. "Sinking Funds And The Cost Of Corporate Debt," JOF, 1979, v34(4), 887-893.)

Joehnk, Michael D. (Dyl, Edward A. and Michael D. Joehnk. "Prepayment Penalties Inherent In The Rule Of 78s," JBR, 1977-78, v8(1), 16-21.)

Joehnk, Michael D. (Dyl, Edward A. and Michael D. Joehnk. "Refunding Tax Exempt Bonds," FM, 1976, v5(2), 59-66.)

Joehnk, Michael D. (Dyl, Edward A. and Michael D. Joehnk. "Effect Of Latest IRS Regulations On Advance Refundings" FM, 1977, v6(2), 71-72.)

Joehnk, Michael D. (Dyl, Edward A. and Michael D. Joehnk. "Riding The Yield Curve: Does It Work?," JPM, 1980-81, v7(3), 13-17.)

Joehnk, Michael D. (Hays, Patrick A., Michael D. Joehnk and Ronald W. Melicher. "Differential Determinants Of Risk Premiums In The Public And Private Corporate Bond Markets," JFR, 1979, v2(2), 143-152.)

Joehnk, Michael D. (Reilly, Frank K. and Michael D. Joehnk. "The Association Between Market-Determined Risk Measures For Bonds And Bond Ratings," JOF, 1976, v31(5), 1387-1403.)

Joehnk, Michael D., H. Russell Fogler and Charles E. Bradley. "The Price Elasticity Of Discounted Bonds: Some Empirical Evidence," JFQA, 1978, v13(3), 559-566.

Joehnk, Michael D., Oswald D. Bowlin and J. William Petty. "Preferred Dividend Rolls: A Viable Strategy For Corporate Money Managers?," FM, 1980, v9(2), 78-87.

Joehnk, Michael. (Fogler, H. Russell and Michael Joehnk. "Deep Discount Bonds: How Well Do They Perform?," JPM, 1978-79, v5(3), 59-62.)

Joerding, Wayne. "Excess Stock Price Volatility As A Misspecified Euler Equation," JFQA, 1988, v23(3), 253-268.

Jog, V. M. and A. L. Riding. "Some Canadian Findings Regarding Infrequent Trading And Instability In The Single Factor Market Model," JBFA, 1986, v13(1), 125-135.

Jog, Vijay M. and Allan L. Riding. "Price Effects Of Dual-Class Shares," FAJ, 1986, v42(1), 58-67.

Jog, Vijay M. (Fowler, David J., C. Harvey Rorke and Vijay M. Jog. "A Note On Beta Stability And Thin Trading On The Toronto Stock Exchange," JBFA, 1981, v8(2), 267-278.)

Jog, Vijay M. (Fowler, David J., C. Harvey Rorke and Vijay M. Jog. "Heteroscedasticity, R-Squared And Thin Trading On The Toronto Stock Exchange," JOF, 1979, v34(5), 1201-1210.)

Jog, Vijay M. (Fowler, David J., C. Harvey Rorke and Vijay M. Jog. "A Bias-Correcting Procedure For Beta Estimation In The Presence Of Thin Trading," JFI, 1989, v12(1), 23-32.)

Jog, Vijay M. and Allan L. Riding. "Underpricing In Canadian IPOs," FAJ, 1987, v43(6), 48-55.

Jog, Vijay M. and Allan L. Riding. "Lunar Cycles In Stock Prices," FAJ, 1989, v45(2), 63-68.

Jog, Vijay M. and Allan L. Riding. "A Note On Insider Trading And Issuances Of Restricted-Voting Common Shares," JBFA, 1990, v17(3), 461-470.

Johannes, James M. and Robert H. Rasche. "Can The Reserves Approach To Monetary Control Really Work?," JMCB, 1981, v13(3), 298-313.

Johannes, James M. (Ahmed, Ehsan and James M. Johannes. "St. Louis Equation Restrictions And Criticisms Revisited," JMCB, 1984, v16(4), Part 1, 514-520.)

Johannesen, Richard I., Jr. "Coupon Bond Price Fluctuations," FAJ, 1968, v24(5), 89-91.

John, Kose and Anthony Saunders. "Asymmetry Of Information, Regulatory Lags And Optimal Incentive Contracts: Theory And Evidence," JOF, 1983, v38(2), 391-404.

John, Kose and Avner Kalay. "Costly Contracting And Optimal Payout Constraints," JOF, 1982, v37(2), 457-470.

John, Kose and David C. Nachman. "Risky Debt, Investment Incentives, And Reputation In A Sequential Equilibrium," JOF, 1985, v40(3), 863-878.

John, Kose and Joseph Williams. "Dividends, Dilution, And Taxes: A Signalling Equilibrium," JOF, 1985, v40(4), 1053-1070.

John, Kose and BaniKanta Mishra. "Information Content Of Insider Trading Around Corporate Announcements: The Case Of Capital Expenditures," JOF, 1990, v45(3), 835-856.

John, Kose and Haim Reisman. "Fundamentals, Factor Structure, And Multibeta Models In Large Asset Markets," JFQA, 1991, v26(1), 1-10.

John, Kose. "Efficient Funds In A Financial Market With Options: A New Irrelevance Proposition," JOF, 1981, v36(3), 685-695.

John, Kose. "Market Resolution And Valuation In Incomplete Markets," JFQA, 1984, v19(1), 29-44.

John, Kose. "Risk-Shifting Incentives And Signalling Through Corporate Capital Structure," JOF, 1987, v42(3), 632-641.

John, Kose. (Ambarish, Ramasastry, Kose John and Joseph Williams. "Efficient Signalling With Dividends And Investments," JOF, 1987, v42(2), 321-343.)

John, Kose. (Arditti, Fred D. and Kose John. "Spanning The State Space With Options," JFQA, 1980, v15(1), 1-9.)

John, Kose. (Fogler, H. Russell, Kose John and James Tipton. "Three Factors, Interest Rate Differentials And Stock Groups," JOF, 1981, v36(2), 323-335.)

John, Kose. (Gilson, Stuart C., Kose John and Larry H. P. Lang. "Troubled Debt Restructurings: An Empirical Study Of Private Reorganization Of Firms In Default," JFEC, 1990, v27(2), 315-354.)

John, Kose. (John, Teresa A. and Kose John. "Optimality Of Project Financing: Theory And Implications In Finance And Accounting," RQFA, 1991, v1(1), 51-74.)

John, Teresa A. "Mergers And Investment Incentives," JFQA, 1986, v21(4), 393-413.

John, Teresa A. and Kose John. "Optimality Of Project Financing: Theory And Implications In Finance And Accounting," RQFA, 1991, v1(1), 51-74.

Johnsen, Thore and Charles Wolf. "The Strategic Profitability Of Borrowing At 8% To Lend At 6%: A Comment," JBR, 1977-78, v8(3), 186-187.

Johnson, Alton C. and Roger T. Reinemann. "Recruiting Practices And Attitudes In Selected Insurance Companies," JRI, 1961, v28(4), 73-78.

Johnson, Alton C. and Roger T. Reinemann. "Reactions Of Students And Agents To Recruiting Practices," JRI, 1962, v29(2), 239-244.

Johnson, Arnold W. "Financial Statements," FAJ, 1968, v24(6), 75-83.

Johnson, Brian D. and Kenneth R. Meyer. "Managing Yield Curve Risk In An Index Environment," FAJ, 1989, v45(6), 51-59.

Johnson, C. R. and R. M. Soldofsky. "Rights Timing," FAJ, 1967, v23(4), 101-104.

Johnson, Cal. (Estep, Tony, Nick Hanson and Cal Johnson. "Sources Of Value And Risk In Common Stocks," JPM, 1982-83, v9(4), 5-13.)

Johnson, Craig G. "Dimensional Analysis And The Interpretation Of Regression Coefficients," JFQA, 1972, v7(1), 1399-1406.

Johnson, Craig G. "Ratio Analysis And The Prediction Of Firm Failure: Comment," JOF, 1970, v25(5), 1166-1168.

Johnson, Dale A. (Shows, E. Warren, Fred B. Power and Dale A. Johnson. "Lump-Sum Awards In Workers' Compensation: Comment," JRI, 1988, v55(4), 734-739.)

Johnson, Dana J. "The Behavior Of Financial Structure And Sustainable Growth In An Inflationary Environment," FM, 1981, v10(4), 30-35.

Johnson, Dana J. "The Risk Behavior Of Equity Of Firms Approaching Bankruptcy," JFR, 1989, v12(1), 33-50.

Johnson, Dana J. (Ferris, Stephen P., Dana J. Johnson and Dilip K. Shome. "Regulatory Environment And Market Response To Public Utility Rate Decisions," JFR, 1986, v9(4), 313-318.)

Johnson, Dana J. (Scott, David F., Jr. and Dana J. Johnson. "Financing Policies And Practices In Large Corporations," FM, 1982, v11(2), 51-59.)

Johnson, Dana J., Richard E. Bennett and Richard J. Curcio. "A Note On The Deceptive Nature Of Bayesian Forecasted Betas," JFR, 1979, v2(1), 65-69.

Johnson, Dana. (Marquette, R. Penny and Dana Johnson. "Ridge Regression And The Multicollinearity Problem In Financial Research: A Case Study," JFR, 1980, v3(1), 33-47.)

Johnson, David. "The Currency Denomination Of Long-Term Debt In The Canadian Corporate Sector: An Empirical Analysis," JIMF, 1988, v7(1), 77-90.

Johnson, Denise. (Goldberg, Lawrence G. and Denise Johnson. "The Determinants Of US Banking Activity Abroad," JIMF, 1990, v9(2), 123-137.)

Johnson, Dudley D. "Properties Of Alternative Seasonal Adjustment Techniques: A Comment On The OMB Model," JOB, 1973, v46(2), 284-303.

Johnson, Elizabeth S. and Harry G. Johnson. "Keynes, The Wider Bank, And The Crawling Peg: A Comment," JMCB, 1973, v5(4), 988-989.

Johnson, F. Reed. (Smith, V. Kerry, William H. Desvousges, Ann Fisher and F. Reed Johnson. "Learning About Radon's Risk," JRU, 1988, v1(2), 233-258.)

Johnson, G. L. (Reilly, F. K., G. L. Johnson and R. E. Smith. "Inflation Hedges And Common Stocks," FAJ, 1970, v26(1), 104-110.)

Johnson, George E. "Some Answers To The Variable Annuity Puzzle," JRI, 1956, v23, 47-54.

Johnson, George E. "The Market For Equity Annuities," JRI, 1958, v25(4), 17-21.

Johnson, George E. and Donald S. Grubbs, Jr. "Media For Funding Variable Annuities," JRI, 1968, v35(2), 257-272.

Johnson, Glenn L. (Reilly, Frank K., Ralph E. Smith and Glenn L. Johnson. "A Correction And Update Regarding Individual Common Stocks As Inflation Hedges," JFQA, 1975, v10(5), 871-880.)

Johnson, Glenn L., Frank K. Reilly and Ralph E. Smith. "Individual Common Stocks As Inflation Hedges," JFQA, 1971, v6(3), 1015-1024.

Johnson, Glenn. (Craig, Darryl, Glenn Johnson and Maurice Joy. "Accounting Methods And P/E Ratios," FAJ, 1987, v43(2), 41-45.)

Johnson, H. Clay. "The Impact Of Multiple Line Powers On The Insurance Industry," JRI, 1952, v19, 21-28.

Johnson, H. E. "An Analytic Approximation For The American Put Price," JFQA, 1983, v18(1), 141-148.

Johnson, H. E. (Geske, Robert and H. E. Johnson. "The Valuation Of Corporate Liabilities As Compound Options: A Correction," JFQA, 1984, v19(2), 231-232.)

Johnson, H. E. (Geske, Robert and H. E. Johnson. "The American Put Option Valued Analytically," JOF, 1984, v39(5), 1511-1524.)

Johnson, Harold L. "Socially Responsible Firms: An Empty Box Or A Universal Set?," JOB, 1966, v39(3), 394-399.

Johnson, Harry G. "A Note On The Theory Of Transactions Demand For Cash," JMCB, 1970, v2(3), 383-384.

Johnson, Harry G. "An Overview Of Price Levels, Employment, And The Balance Of Payments," JOB, 1963, v36(3), 279-289.

Johnson, Harry G. "Current International Economic Policy Issues," JOB, 1969, v42(1), 12-21.

Johnson, Harry G. "Current Issues In Monetary Policy," FAJ, 1968, v24(4), 87-91.

Johnson, Harry G. "Inside Money, Outside Money, Income, Wealth, And Welfare In Monetary Theory," JMCB, 1969, v1(1), 30-45.

Johnson, Harry G. "Is There An Optimal Money Supply?," JOF, 1970, v25(2), 435-442.

Johnson, Harry G. "Secular Inflation And The International Monetary System," JMCB, 1973, v5(1), Part II, 509-519.

Johnson, Harry G. "The Decade Ahead-In U.S. International Economic Relations," JOB, 1965, v38(3),245-251.

Johnson, Harry G. "The International Monetary Crisis Of 1971," JOB, 1973, v46(1), 11-23.

Johnson, Harry G. "The Monetary Approach To Balance-Of-Payments Theory," JFQA, 1972, v7(2),1555-1572.

Johnson, Harry G. "The Welfare Economics Of Monetary Transfers And Reversed Transfers," JMCB, 1977, v9(2), 259-275.

Johnson, Harry G. "United States Policy And The Problems Of Developing Countries," JOB, 1965, v38(4), 337-343.

Johnson, Harry G. (Johnson, Elizabeth S. and Harry G. Johnson. "Keynes, The Wider Bank, And The Crawling Peg: A Comment," JMCB, 1973, v5(4), 988-989.)

Johnson, Harry L. "Insurance Pricing And Its Role In Relation To Economic Theory And Market Management: Comment," JRI, 1968, v35(2), 317-319.

Johnson, Harry M. "Major Medical Expense Insurance," JRI, 1965, v32(2), 211-236.

Johnson, Harry M. "The History Of British And American Fire Marks," JRI, 1972, v39(3), 405-418.

Johnson, Harry M. "The History Of British And American Fire Marks: Reply," JRI, 1973, v40(4), 641-642.

Johnson, Harry Mack. "The Nature Of Title Insurance," JRI, 1966, v33(3), 393-410.

Johnson, Harry M. (Osler, Robert W. and Harry M. Johnson. "Major Policy Provisions In Guaranteed Renewable Major Medical Expense Insurance," JRI, 1966, v33(4), 553-561.)

Johnson, Herb and David Shanno. "Option Pricing When The Variance Is Changing," JFQA, 1987, v22(2), 143-152.

Johnson, Herb and Rene Stulz. "The Pricing Of Options With Default Risk," JOF, 1987, v42(2), 267-280.

Johnson, Herb. "Options On The Maximum Or The Minimum Of Several Assets," JFQA, 1987, v22(3),277-284.

Johnson, Herb. (Blomeyer, Edward C. and Herb Johnson. "An Empirical Examination Of The Pricing Of American Put Options," JFQA, 1988, v23(1), 13-22.)

Johnson, Herb. (Castanias, Rick, Ki-Young Chung and Herb Johnson. "Dividend Spreads," JOB, 1988, v61(3), 299-320.)

Johnson, Herb. (Chen, Nai-Fu and Herb Johnson. "Hedging Options," JFEC, 1985, v14(2), 317-321.)

Johnson, Herb. (Dhillon, Upinder and Herb Johnson. "Changes In The Standard And Poor's 500 List," JOB, 1991, v64(1), 75-86.)

Johnson, Herb. (Grinblatt, Mark and Herb Johnson. "A Put Option Paradox," JFQA, 1988, v23(1), 23-26.)

Johnson, Herb. (Stulz, Rene M. and Herb Johnson. "An Analysis Of Secured Debt," JFEC, 1985, v14(4), 501-522.)

Johnson, Herbert E. "Strategic Planning For Banks," JBR, 1973-74, v4(2), 79-83.

Johnson, Holgar J. "The Place Of The College Graduate In Life Insurance Home Offices," JRI, 1956, v23, 27-33.

Johnson, I. Richard. (Nixon, Clair J., Casper Wiggins and I. Richard Johnson. "Repeal Of The Investment Tax Credit And Financial Statement Analysis," FAJ, 1987, v43(1), 52-55.)

Johnson, James J. "How A Pharmaceutical Company Uses The Futures Markets For Cross-Hedging," RFM, 1982, v1(3), 238-246.

Johnson, James M. and Howard P. Lanser. "Dividend Risk Measurement And Tests Of The CAPM," JPM, 1980-81, v7(2), 50-54.

Johnson, James M. and Jerome B. Baesel. "The Nature And Significance Of Trend Betas," JPM, 1977-78, v4(3), 36-40.

Johnson, James M. and Paul G. Weber. "The Impact Of The Problem Bank Disclosure On Bank Share Prices," JBR, 1977-78, v8(3), 179-182.

Johnson, James M. "Efficiency Of The Federal Reserves's Instalment Loan Break-Even Formula," JBR, 1978-79, v9(1), 59-60.

Johnson, James M. "Optimal Tax Lives: Reply," FM, 1980, v9(3), 79.

Johnson, James M. "Optimal Tax Lives Of Depreciable Assets," FM, 1979, v8(3), 27-31.

Johnson, James M. "When Are Zero Coupon Bonds The Better Buy?," JPM, 1983-84, v10(3), 36-71.

Johnson, James M. and Robert E. Miller. "Investment Banker Prestige And The Underpricing Of Initial Public Offerings," FM, 1988, v17(2), 19-29.

Johnson, James M., Robert A. Pari and Leonard Rosenthal. "The Impact Of In-Substance Defeasance On Bondholder And Shareholder Wealth," JOF, 1989, v44(4), 1049-1058.

Johnson, Jerah. "The Money=Blood Metaphor, 1300-1800," JOF, 1966, v21(1), 119-122.

Johnson, John D. (Hawley, Delvin D., John D. Johnson and Dijjotam Raina. "Artificial Neural Systems: A New Tool For Financial Decision-Making," FAJ, 1990, v46(6), 63-72.)

Johnson, Joseph E. (Flanigan, George B., Joseph E. Johnson, Daniel T. Winkler and William Ferguson. "Experience From Early Tort Reforms: Comparative Negligence Since 1974," JRI, 1989, v56(3), 525-534.)

Johnson, Joseph E. (Winkler, Daniel T., George B. Flanigan and Joseph E. Johnson. "Solving For The Number Of Cash Flows And Periods In Financial Problems," JFED, 1990, v19, 62-65.)

Johnson, Joseph E. and George B. Flanigan. "Exceptions To Current Risk Dichotomies," JRI, 1977, v44(2), 329-334.

Johnson, Joseph E., George B. Flanigan and Steven N. Weisbart. "Returns To Scale In The Property And Liability Insurance Industry," JRI, 1981, v48(1), 18-45.

Johnson, Joyce M., Hugh O. Nourse and Ellen Day. "Factors Related To The Selection Of A Real Estate Agency," JRER, 1988, v3(2), 109-118.

Johnson, K. B. (Brigham, E. F., D. E. Fischer, K. B. Johnson and R. J. Jordan. "What Makes Short Cases Work In The Basic Finance Course?," JFED, 1972, v1, 65-68.)

Johnson, Karen H. (Howard, David H. and Karen H. Johnson. "The Behavior Of Monetary Aggregates In Major Industrialized Countries," JMCB, 1983, v15(4), 455-468.)

Johnson, Keith and Lawrence R. Klein. "Link Model Simulations Of International Trade: An Evaluation Of The Effects Of Currency Realignment," JOF, 1974, v29(2), 617-630.

Johnson, Keith B. "Investment Organization, Policy And Practice In Property-Liability Insurance," JRI, 1972, v39(1), 53-64.

Johnson, Keith B. "Living Cases: A Successful Experiment," JFED, 1973, v2, 45-48.

Johnson, Keith B. "Long-Term Financial Planning Using A Live Case," JFED, 1978, v7, 53-55.

Johnson, Keith B. "Stock Splits And Price Change," JOF, 1966, v21(4), 675-686.

Johnson, Keith B., Gregory Morton and M. Chapman Findlay, III. "An Analysis Of The Flotation Cost Of Utility Bonds, 1971-76," JFR, 1979, v2(2), 133-142.

Johnson, Keith B., T. Gregory Morton and M. Chapman Findlay, III. "An Analysis Of The Flotation Cost Of Corporate Quasi-Equity Securities, 1971-72," FM, 1974, v4(4), 12-17.

Johnson, Keith B., T. Gregory Morton and M. Chapman Findlay, III. "An Empirical Analysis Of The Flotation Cost Of Corporate Securities, 1971-1972," JPM, 1975, v30(4), 1129-1133.

Johnson, Keith H. and D. S. Shannon. "A Note Of Diversification And The Reduction Of Dispersion," JFEC, 1974, v1(4), 365-372.

Johnson, Keith H. (Burgess, Richard C. and Keith H. Johnson. "The Effects Of Sampling Fluctuations On The Required Inputs Of Security Analysis," JFQA, 1976, v11(5), 847-855.)

Johnson, Keith H. (Shannon, Donald S. and Keith H. Johnson. "Error Terms And Asset Allocation Schemes," FR, 1975, v10(1), 55-63.)

Johnson, Keith H. (Shannon, Donald S., Keith H. Johnson and Gregory

L. Neal. "How To Beat Those Index Funds," JPM, 1977-78, v4(1), 28-33.)

Johnson, Keith M. "Bank Management Simulation Update," JFED, 1981, v10, 109-110.

Johnson, Keith R. and Richard C. Burgess. "The Effects Of Sample Sizes On The Accuracy Of EV And SSD Efficiency Criteria," JFQA, 1975, v10(5), 813-820.

Johnson, Keith. (Barnes, Tom, Keith Johnson and Don Shannon. "A Test Of Fixed-Income Strategies," JPM, 1983-84, v10(2), 60-65.)

Johnson, Larry J. "Foreign-Currency Options, Ex Ante Exchange-Rate Volatility, And Market Efficiency: An Empirical Test," FR, 1986, v21(4), 433-450.

Johnson, Larry J. (Bey, Roger P. and Larry J. Johnson. "The Impact Of Taxes On Discount Bond Valuation And Risk," FR, 1989, v24(4), 589-598.)

Johnson, Larry J. and John R. Phelps. "The Development And Solution Of A Tax-Adjusted Model Of Personal Injury Awards: A Clarification," JRI, 1985, v52(3), 518-519.

Johnson, Larry J. and Larry E. Wofford. "On Contracts As Options: Some Evidence From Condominium Developments," AREUEA, 1987, v15(1), 739-741.

Johnson, Larry J., James L. Kuhle and Carl H. Walther. "An Elasticity Approach To Equity Risk Evaluation," JRER, 1987, v2(1), 41-49.

Johnson, Leland L. "Joint Cost And Price Discrimination: The Case Of Communications Satellites," JOB, 1964, v37(1), 32-46.

Johnson, Leonard W. "The Offshore Service Industry," FAJ, 1968, v24(2), 58-60.

Johnson, Lester W. (Clements, Kenneth W. and Lester W. Johnson. "The Demand For Beer, Wine, And Spirits: A Systemwide Analysis," JOB, 1983, v56(3), 273-304.)

Johnson, Lester W. (Graham, Robert E. and Lester W. Johnson. "A Unified Bayesian Approach To Optimal Classification With Discriminant Analysis," JRI, 1977, v44(2), 316-319.)

Johnson, Lewis D. "Convexity For Equity Securities: Does Curvature Matter?," FAJ, 1990, v46(5), 70-73.

Johnson, Lewis D. "Dividend Yields Are Equity Premiums: Comment," JPM, 1985-86, v12(2), 81-83.

Johnson, Lewis D. "Dividends And Share Value: Graham And Dodd Revisited, Again," FAJ, 1985, v41(5), 79-80.

Johnson, Lewis D. "Equity Duration: Another Look," FAJ, 1989, v45(2), 73-75.

Johnson, Lewis D. "Growth Prospects And Share Prices: A Systematic View," JPM, 1986-87, v13(2), 58-60.

Johnson, Lewis D. "Sources Of Risk And Value In Common Stocks: Comment," JPM, 1983-84, v10(3), 84.

Johnson, Lewis. "Keynesian Dynamics And Growth," JMCB, 1977, v9(2), 328-340.

Johnson, Linda L. "The Impact Of Real Estate Political Action Committees On Congressional Voting And Elections," AREUEA, 1983, v11(4), 462-475.

Johnson, Linda L. and Christine Loucks. "The Effect Of State Licensing Regulations On The Real Estate Brokerage Industry," AREUEA, 1986, v14(4), 567-582.

Johnson, Linda L., Michael J. Dotson and B. J. Dunlap. "Service Quality Determinants And Effectiveness In The Real Estate Brokerage Industry," JRER, 1988, v3(2), 21-36.

Johnson, Michael S. "A Cash Flow Model Of Rational Housing Tenure Choice," AREUEA, 1981, v9(1), 1-17.

Johnson, Norris O. "Financing Industrial Growth," JOF, 1957, v12(2), 264-271.

Johnson, Norris O. "Impact Of Recent Credit And Debt Management Policies Upon The Commercial Banks," JOF, 1952, v7(2), 296-306.

Johnson, Norris O. "Outlook For The Short-Term Money Market," JOF, 1960, v15(2), 285-288.

Johnson, Omotunde E. G. "Credit Controls As Instruments Of Development Policy In The Light Of Economic Theory," JMCB, 1974, v6(1), 85-99.

Johnson, Orace and Walter L. Johnson. "The Income Elasticity Of Corporate Philanthropy: Comment," JOF, 1970, v25(1), 149-152.

Johnson, Orace. "Corporate Philanthropy: An Analysis Of Corporate Contributions," JOB, 1966, v39(4), 489-504.

Johnson, Paul J. "Cutting The Ticker Tape Umbilical Cord," JPM, 1975-76, v2(2), 61-64.

Johnson, R. B. "What A Security Analyst Wants To Know," FAJ, 1960, v16(6), 71-77.

Johnson, R. Stafford, Lyle C. Fiore and Richard Zuber. "The Investment Performance Of Common Stocks In Relation To Their Price-Earnings Ratios: An Update Of The Basu Study," FR, 1989, v24(3), 499-506.

Johnson, Ramon E. "Term Structures Of Corporate Bond Yields As A Function Of Risk Of Default," JOF, 1967, v22(2), 313-345.

Johnson, Ramon E. (Schallheim, James S., Ramon E. Johnson, Ronald C. Lease and John J. McConnell. "The Determinants Of Yields On Financial Leasing Contracts," JFEC, 1987, v19(1), 45-68.)

Johnson, Ramon E. (Sorensen, Ivar W. and Ramon E. Johnson. "Equipment Financial Leasing Practices And Costs: An Empirical Study," FM, 1977, v6(1), 33-40.

Johnson, Ramon E., Richard T. Pratt and Samuel S. Stewart, Jr. "The Economic Consequences Of ESOPs," JFR, 1982, v5(1), 75-82.

Johnson, Raymond C. "Application Of The Theory Of Marketing Tangible Goods To The Marketing Of Insurance," JRI, 1961, v28(1), 41-44.

Johnson, Raymond N. "Auditor Detected Errors And Related Client Traits--A Study Of Inherent And Control Risks In A Sample Of U.K. Audits," JBFA, 1987, v14(1), 39-64.

Johnson, Richard E. "A Test Of The Effectiveness Of An Innovative Teaching Technique," JRI, 1972, v39(4), 627-630.

Johnson, Richard E. "Reinsurance: Theory, The New Applications, And The Future," JRI, 1977, v44(1), 55-66.

Johnson, Richard E. "The College Professor And The Adequacy Of His Insurance Coverages," JRI, 1970, v37(1), 105-114.

Johnson, Richard E. "The Mixed Class: Motivation And Measurement," JRI, 1971, v38(2), 277-280.

Johnson, Richard E. (Greene, Mark R. and Richard E. Johnson. "Stocks Vs. Mutuals: Who Controls?," JRI, 1980, v47(1), 165-174.)

Johnson, Richard. "A Retrospective Rating Of A Student Intern Program," JRI, 1977, v44(3), 508-512.

Johnson, Robert L. "The Value Of The Call Privilege," FAJ, 1967, v23(2), 134-138.

Johnson, Robert L., Carl R Zulauf, Scott H. Irwin and Mary E. Gerlow. "The Soybean Complex Spread: An Examination Of Market Efficiency From The Viewpoint Of A Production Process," JFM, 1991, v11(1), 25-38.

Johnson, Robert R. (DeFusco, Richard A. and Robert R. Johnson. "The Effect Of Executive Stock Option Plans On Stockholders And Bondholders," JOF, 1990, v45(2), 617-628.)

Johnson, Robert R. and Jerome F. Sherman. "The Financial World: A Campus And Travel Course," JFED, 1987, v16, 26-31.

Johnson, Robert W. and Wilbur G. Lewellen. "Analysis Of The Lease-Or-Buy Decision," JOF, 1972, v27(4), 815-823.

Johnson, Robert W. and Wilbur G. Lewellen. "Analysis Of The Lease-Or-Buy Decision: Reply," JOF, 1973, v28(4), 1024-1028.

Johnson, Robert W. "Economic Rationale Of The Uniform Consumer Credit Code," JOF, 1968, v23(2), 303-311.

Johnson, Robert W. "Subordinated Debentures: Debt That Serves As Equity," JOF, 1955, v10(1), 1-16.

Johnson, Robert W. (Gregory, Robert H. and Robert W. Johnson. "Income Determination By Sales Finance Companies," JOB, 1953, v26(2), 125-132.)

Johnson, Rodney and Richard Klein. "Corporate Motives In Repurchases Of Discounted Bonds," FM, 1974, v3(3), 44-49.

Johnson, Rodney D. and David R. Meinster. "The Analysis Of Bank Holding Company Acquisitions: Some Methodological Issues," JBR, 1973-74, v4(1), 58-61.

Johnson, Rodney D. and Robert V. Swanick. "New Insights Into Forecasting And Long Range Planning," JBR, 1975-76, v6(1), 77-79.

Johnson, Rodney D. and David R. Meinster. "The Performance Of Bank Holding Company Acquisitions: A Multivariate Analysis," JOB, 1975, v48(2), 204-212.

Johnson, Steven B. and Jack VanDerhei. "Fiduciary Decision Making And The Nature Of Private Pension Fund Investment Behavior," JRI, 1989, v56(1), 113-121.

Johnson, Terry. (Hubbard, Charles L. and Terry Johnson. "Writing Calls With Convertible Bonds," FAJ, 1969, v25(6), 78-89.)

Johnson, Thomas P. "Institutional Contributions To Scholarly Journals Of Business: Comment," JOB, 1974, v47(4), 571-573.

Johnson, Timothy E. and Thomas G. Schmitt. "Effectiveness Of Earnings Per Share Forecasts," FM, 1974, v3(2), 64-72.

Johnson, W. Bruce. "Debt Refunding And Shareholder Wealth: The Price Effects Of Debt-For-Debt Exchange Offer Announcements," FR, 1988, v23(1), 1-24.

Johnson, W. Bruce. "The Cross-Sectional Stability Of Financial Patterns," JBFA, 1978, v5(2), 207-214.

Johnson, W. Bruce. "The Cross-Sectional Stability Of Financial Ratio Patterns," JPQA, 1979, v14(5), 1035-1048.

Johnson, Walter L. (Johnson, Orace and Walter L. Johnson. "The Income Elasticity Of Corporate Philanthropy: Comment," JOF, 1970, v25(1), 149-152.)

Johnston, D. J. (Booth, L. D. and D. J. Johnston. "The Ex-Dividend Day Behavior Of Canadian Stock Prices: Tax Changes And Clientele Effects," JOF, 1984, v39(2), 457-476.)

Johnston, David J. (Meador, Joseph W., Gerald P. Madden and David J. Johnston. "On The Probability Of Acquisition Of Non-Life Insurers," JRI, 1986, v53(4), 621-643.)

Johnston, Elizabeth Tashijan, William A. Kracaw and John J. McConnell. "Day-Of-The-Week Effects In Financial Futures: An Analysis Of GNMA, T-Bond, T-Note, And T-Bill Contracts," JPQA, 1991, v26(1), 23-44.

Johnston, Elizabeth Tashijan and John J. McConnell. "Requiem For A Market: An Analysis Of The Rise And Fall Of A Financial Futures Contract," RFS, 1989, v2(1), 1-24.

Johnston, George S. "The Pursuit Of Value: 1929-1979," JPM, 1979-80, v6(1), 39-41.

Johnston, George S., M. Louise Curley and Robert A. McIndoe. "Dual-Purpose Funds Undervalued?," FAJ, 1968, v24(6), 157-163.

Johnston, Jack. (Lewis, Alan L., Sheen T. Kassouf, R. Dennis Brehm and Jack Johnston. "The Ibbotson-Sinquefield Simulation Made Easy," JOB, 1980, v53(2), 205-214.)

Johnston, Will. "The Other Eighteen Hundred," JRI, 1969, v36(3), 497-498.

Johnstone, Anne. (Rappaport, Allen and Anne Johnstone. "Toward Better Case Writing In Financial Management," JFED, 1984, v13, 55-64.)

Johnstone, J. (Appelbaum, E., J. Burns, R. Evans, J. Gould, T. Hamachek, R. Kidder, M. Jensen, J. Johnstone, M. Murray, R. Sim, J. Stern, B. Stewart and C. Zaner. "Panel: CEO Roundtable On Corporate Structure And Management Incentives," JACF, 1990, v3(3), 6-35.)

Joines, Douglas H. "Estimates Of Effective Marginal Tax Rates On Factor Incomes," JOB, 1981, v54(2), 191-226.

Joines, Douglas H. "International Currency Substitution And The Income Velocity Of Money," JIMF, 1985, v4(3), 303-316.

Jolivet, Vincent M. "The Control Of Savings And Loan Associations," JPQA, 1966, v1(4), 58-71.

Jollineau, R. W. and S. P. Singh. "Inflation And The Profitability Of Firms In Canada," JBFA, 1975, v2(1), 105-120.

Jonas, Stan. "Comment On Feuerstein's 'Trading Bond Spreads In The Delivery Month'," JFM, 1985, v5(3), 451-452.

Jondrow, James M. (Levy, Robert A. and James M. Jondrow. "The Adjustment Of Employment To Technical Change In The Steel And Auto Industries," JOB, 1986, v59(3), 475-492.)

Jondrow, James M., David E. Chase and Christopher L. Gamble. "The Price Differential Between Domestic And Imported Steel," JOB, 1982, v55(3), 383-400.

Jones, C. J., D. P. Tweedie and G. Whittington. "The Regression Portfolio: A Statistical Investigation Of A Relative Decline Model," JBFA, 1976, v3(2), 71-92.

Jones, C. P. "Earnings Trends And Stock Selection," FAJ, 1973, v29(2), 79-83.

Jones, C. P. (Latane, Henry A., Donald L. Tuttle and C. P. Jones. "E/P Ratios V. Changes In Earnings," FAJ, 1969, v25(1), 117-120.)

Jones, C. S. "Organisational Change And The Functioning Of Accounting," JBFA, 1986, v13(3), 283-310.

Jones, Charles H., Jr. "The Growth Rate Appraiser," FAJ, 1968, v24(5), 109-111.

Jones, Charles P. and Robert H. Litzenberger. "Earnings Seasonality And Stock Prices," FAJ, 1969, v25(6), 57-59.

Jones, Charles P. and Robert H. Litzenberger. "Quarterly Earnings Reports And Intermediate Stock Price Trends," JOF, 1970, v25(1), 143-148.

Jones, Charles P. (Aharony, Joseph, Charles P. Jones and Itzhak Swary. "An Analysis Of Risk And Return Characteristics Of Corporate Bankruptcy Using Capital Market Data," JOF, 1980, v35(4), 1001-1016.)

Jones, Charles P. (Joy, O. Maurice and Charles P. Jones. "Earnings Reports And Market Efficiencies: An Analysis Of The Contrary Evidence," JFR, 1979, v2(1), 51-63.)

Jones, Charles P. (Joy, O. Maurice and Charles P. Jones. "Should We Believe The Tests Of Market Efficiency?," JPM, 1985-86, v12(4), 49-54.)

Jones, Charles P. (Joy, O. Maurice and Charles P. Jones. "Predictive Value Of P/E Ratios," FAJ, 1970, v26(5), 61-64.)

Jones, Charles P. (Latane, Henry A. and Charles P. Jones. "Standardized Unexpected Earnings - A Progress Report," JOF, 1977, v32(5), 1457-1465.)

Jones, Charles P. (Latane, Henry A., O. Maurice Joy and Charles P. Jones. "Quarterly Data, Sort-Rank Routines, And Security Evaluation," JOB, 1970, v43(4), 427-438.)

Jones, Charles P. (Latane, Henry A. and Charles P. Jones. "Standardized Unexpected Earnings - 1971-77," JOF, 1979, v34(3), 717-724.)

Jones, Charles P. (Litzenberger, Robert H. and Charles P. Jones. "Adjusting For Risk In The Capital Budget Of A Growth-Oriented Company: Comment," JOF, 1969, v4(3), 301-304.)

Jones, Charles P. (Litzenberger, Robert H. and Charles P. Jones. "The Capital Structure And The Cost Of Capital: Comment," JOF, 1970, v25(3), 669-673.)

Jones, Charles P. (Litzenberger, Robert H., O. Maurice Joy and Charles P. Jones. "Ordinal Predictions And The Selection Of Common Stocks," JPQA, 1971, v6(4), 1059-1068.)

Jones, Charles P. (Rendleman, Richard J., Jr., Charles P. Jones and Henry A. Latane. "Empirical Anomalies Based On Unexpected Earnings And The Importance Of Risk Adjustment," JFEC, 1982, v10(3), 269-287.)

Jones, Charles P. (Rendleman, Richard J., Jr., Charles P. Jones and Henry A. Latane. "Further Insight Into The Standardized Unexpected Earnings Anomaly: Size And Serial Correlation Effects," FR, 1987, v22(1), 131-144.)

Jones, Charles P. (Simkowitz, Michael A. and Charles P. Jones. "A Note On The Simultaneous Nature Of Finance Methodology," JOF, 1972, v27(1), 103-108.)

Jones, Charles P. (Wilson, Jack W. and Charles P. Jones. "The Relationship Between Performance And Risk: Whence The Bias?," JFR, 1981, v4(2), 103-108.)

Jones, Charles P. (Wilson, Jack W. and Charles P. Jones. "Common Stock Prices And Inflation: 1857-1985," FAJ, 1987, v43(4), 67-72.)

Jones, Charles P. (Wilson, Jack W. and Charles P. Jones. "A Comparison Of Annual Common Stock Returns: 1871-1925 With 1926-85," JOB, 1987, v60(2), 239-258.)

Jones, Charles P. (Wilson, Jack W. and Charles P. Jones. "Is There A January Effect In Corporate Bond And Paper Returns?," FR, 1990, v25(1), 55-80.)

Jones, Charles P. and Bruce Bublitz. "The CAPM And Equity Return Regularities: An Extension," FAJ, 1987, v43(3), 77-79.

Jones, Charles P. and Jack W. Wilson. "Stocks, Bonds, Paper, And Inflation: 1870-1985," JPM, 1987-88, v14(1), 20-24.

Jones, Charles P. and Jack W. Wilson. "Is Stock Price Volatility Increasing?," FAJ, 1989, v45(6), 20-26.

Jones, Charles P. and Jack W. Wilson. "An Analysis Of The January Effect In Stocks And Interest Rates Under Varying Monetary Regimes," JFR, 1989, v12(4), 341-354.

Jones, Charles P., Richard J. Rendleman, Jr. and Henry Latane. "Stock Returns And SUEs During The 1970s," JPM, 1983-84, v10(2), 18-22.

Jones, Charles P., Richard J. Rendleman, Jr. and Henry A. Latane. "Earnings Announcements: Pre-And-Post Responses," JPM, 1984-85, v11(3), 28-33.

Jones, Charles P., Douglas K. Pearce and Jack W. Wilson. "Can Tax-Loss Selling Explain The January Effect? A Note," JOF, 1987, v42(2), 453-461.

Jones, Charlotte A. (Jackson, John D., Charlotte A. Jones and Philip W. Balsmeir. "An Empirical Analysis Of Tenant Selection Under Federal Rent Supplement Programs: A First Step," AREUEA, 1986, v14(1), 72-90.)

Jones, Colin J. "Financial Planning And Control Practices In UK Companies: A Longitudinal Study," JBFA, 1986, v13(2), 161-185.

Jones, David D. "Choosing A Discount Rate For Future Losses In Wrongful Death And Injury Cases," JRI, 1990, v57(1), 137-140.

Jones, David D. "Inflation Rates Implicit In Discounting Personal Injury Economic Losses," JRI, 1985, v52(1), 144-150.)

Jones, David D. "Rejoinder To Brown's Comment On A Reaction To Schilling's Paper," JRI, 1986, v53(3), 498-500.

Jones, David L. "Stock Options - An Incentive In Reverse?," FAJ, 1962, v18(6), 33-34.

Jones, Donald P. "Can We Make The Right Decisions On Tax Reforms?," FAJ, 1963, v19(1), 9-11.

Jones, Donald W. (Hopelain, David G. and Donald W. Jones. "Managing Change In Investment Institutions," FAJ, 1976, v32(5), 27-34.)

Jones, E. Philip, Scott P. Mason and Eric Rosenfeld. "Contingent Claims Analysis Of Corporate Capital Structures: An Empirical Investigation," JOF, 1984, v39(3), 611-625.

Jones, E. Philip. "Option Arbitrage And Strategy With Large Price Changes," JFEC, 1984, v13(1), 91-113.

Jones, Frank J. "A New Approach To Teaching Financial Institutions Using Flow Of Funds Data," JFED, 1974, v3, 51-52.

Jones, Frank J. "Spreads: Tails, Turtles, And All That," JFM, v1(4), 565-596.

Jones, Frank J. "The Economics Of Futures And Options Contracts Based On Cash Settlement," **JFM**, 1982, v2(1), 63-82.

Jones, Frank J. "The Integration Of Cash And Future Markets For Treasury Securities," **JFM**, v1(1), 33-57.

Jones, Frank J. (Hill, Joanne M. and Frank J. Jones. "Equity Trading, Program trading, Portfolio Insurance, Computer Trading And All That," **FAJ**, 1988, v44(4), 29-38.)

Jones, Gerald L. (Khoury, Sarkis J. and Gerald L. Jones. "Daily Price Limits On Futures Contracts: Nature, Impact, And Justification," **RFM**, 1984, v3(1), 22-36.)

Jones, Homer. "Investment In Equities By Life Insurance Companies," **JOF**, 1950, v5(2), 179-191.

Jones, Homer. "Investment Prospects," **JOF**, 1947, v2(1), 15-33.

Jones, Homer. "Some Aspects Of Demand For Consumer Durable Goods," **JOF**, 1954, v9(2), 93-110.

Jones, Homer. "The Flow Of Savings. II," **JOF**, 1949, v4(1), 28-46.

Jones, Homer. "The Flow Of Savings. I," **JOF**, 1948, v3(3), 4-26.

Jones, Howard L. "Chinese Mutual Savings And Loan Clubs," **JOB**, 1967, v40(3), 336-338.

Jones, Irwin E. "Test Of Portfolio Building Rules: Comment," **JOF**, 1971, v26(4), 973-975.

Jones, Lawrence D. "Current Wealth And Tenure Choice," **AREUEA**, 1989, v17(1), 17-40.

Jones, Lawrence D. "Some Contributions Of The Institutional Investor Study," **JOF**, 1972, v27(2), 305-317.

Jones, Oliver H. "The Mortgage Market," **JOF**, 1964, v19(2), Part 1, 411-416.

Jones, Oliver. "Private Secondary Market Facilities," **JOF**, 1968, v23(2), 359-366.

Jones, Oliver. "The Development Of An Effective Secondary Mortgage Market," **JOF**, 1962, v17(2),358-370.

Jones, Robert A. "Conversion Factor Risk In Treasury Bond Futures: Comment," **JFM**, 1985, v5(1),115-120.

Jones, Robert C. "Designing Factor Models For Different Types Of Stock: What's Good For The Goose Ain't Always Good For The Gander," **FAJ**, 1990, v46(2), 25-30.

Jones, Robert C. "Group Rotation From The Bottom Up," **JPM**, 1989, v15(4), 32-38.

Jones, Robert. (Black, Fischer and Robert Jones. "Simplifying Portfolio Insurance," **JPM**, 1987-88, v14(1), 48-51.)

Jones, Robert. (Black, Fischer and Robert Jones. "Simplifying Portfolio Insurance For Corporate Pension Plans," **JPM**, 1987-88, v14(4), 33-37.)

Jones, Rowan. (Pendlebury, Maurice and Rowan Jones. "Budget Auditing In Governmental Organisations Financed By Taxation," **JBFA**, 1983, v10(4), 585-594.)

Jones, Sidney L. "The Challenge Of Economic Leadership," **JFQA**, 1976, v11(4), 529-539.

Jones, Wesley H. (Etzel, Michael J. and Wesley H. Jones. "A Method For Developing Promotional Themes Based On Attitudes And Usage Patterns Of Bank Credit Card Holders," **JBR**, 1977-78, v8(4), 224-232.)

Jones, Wesley H. (Ferri, Michael G. and Wesley H. Jones. "Determinants Of Financial Structure: A New Methodological Approach," **JOF**, 1979, v34(3), 631-644.)

Jones, Wesley H. (Lang, James R. and Wesley H. Jones. "Hedonic Property Valuation Models: Are Subjective Measures Of Neighborhood Amenities Needed?," **AREUEA**, 1979, v7(4), 451-465.)

Jones-Lee, M. W. and D. S. Poskitt. "An Existence Proof For Equilibrium In A Capital Asset Market," **JBFA**, 1975, v2(3), 349-360.

Jones-Lee, M. W. "A Note On A Property Of The Inverse Of A Bordered Matrix And Its Implication For The Theory Of Portfolio Selection," **JFQA**, 1974, v9(6), 1081-1087.

Jones-Lee, M. W. "Some Portfolio Adjustment Theorems For The Case Of Non-Negativity Constraints On Security Holdings," **JOF**, 1971, v26(3), 763-775.

Jonish, James E. and Reginald G. Worthley. "Unemployment Insurance Fund Adequacy: An Alternative Measure," **JRI**, 1972, v39(4), 535-544.

Jonkhart, Marius J. L. (Ballendux, Frans J. and Marius J. L. Jonkhart. "A Possible Error In The Expectations Theory: A Comment," **JMCB**, 1981, v13(1), 105-106.)

Jonung, Lars. "Knut Wicksell And Gustav Cassel On Secular Movements In Prices," **JMCB**, 1979, v11(2), 165-181.

Jordan, Bradford D. and Richard H. Pettway. "The Pricing Of Short-Term Debt And The Miller Hypothesis: A Note," **JOF**, 1985, v40(2), 589-594.

Jordan, Bradford D. (Pettengill, Glenn N. and Bradford D. Jordan. "A Comprehensive Examination Of Volume Effects And Seasonality In Daily Security Returns," **JFR**, 1988, v11(1), 57-70.)

Jordan, Bradford D. (Pettengill, Glenn N. and Bradford D. Jordan. "The Overreaction Hypothesis, Firm Size, And Stock Market Seasonality," **JPM**, 1990, v16(3), 60-64.)

Jordan, Bradford D. (Pettway, Richard H. and Bradford D. Jordan. "Diversification, Double Leverage, And The Cost Of Capital," **JFR**, 1983, v6(4), 289-300.)

Jordan, Bradford D. (Pettway, Richard H. and Bradford D. Jordan. "APT Vs. CAPM Estimates Of The Return-Generating Function Parameters For Regulated Public Utilities," **JFR**, 1987, v10(3), 227-238.)

Jordan, Bradford D., James A. Verbrugge and Richard M. Burns. "Returns To Initial Shareholders In Savings Institution Conversions: Evidence And Regulatory Implications," **JFR**, 1988, v11(2), 125-136.

Jordan, George R. (Mehr, Robert I. and George R. Jordan. "A Life Adjustment Policy," **JRI**, 1961, v28(2), 59-70.)

Jordan, James V. (Kolb, Robert W., James V. Jordan and Gerald D. Gay. "Futures Prices And Expected Future Spot Prices," **RFM**, 1983, v2(1), 110-123.)

Jordan, James V. "Tax Effects In Term Structure Estimation," **JOF**, 1984, v39(2), 393-406.

Jordan, James V. (Barnhill, Theodore M., James V. Jordan and William E. Seale. "Maturity And Refunding Effects On Treasury-Bond Futures Price Variance," **JFR**, 1987, v10(2), 121-132.)

Jordan, James V. (Ehrhardt, Michael C., James V. Jordan and Ralph A. Walkling. "An Application Of Arbitrage Pricing Theory To Futures Markets: Tests Of Normal Backwardation," **JFM**, 1987, v7(1), 21-34.)

Jordan, James V. (Kolb, Robert W., Gerald D. Gay and James V. Jordan. "Managing Foreign Interest Rate Risk," **JFM**, 1982, v2(2), 151-158.)

Jordan, James V. (Kolb, Robert W., Gerald D. Gay and James V. Jordan. "Markets Are There Arbitrage Opportunities In The Treasury-Bond Futures Markets," **JFM**, 1982, v2(3), 217-230.)

Jordan, James V. and George Emir Morgan. "Default Risk In Futures Markets: The Customer-Broker Relationship," **JOF**, 1990, v45(3), 909-934.

Jordan, James V., William E. Seale, Stephen J. Dinehart and David E. Kenyon. "The Intraday Variability Of Soybean Futures Prices: Information And Trading Effects," **RFM**, 1988, v7(1), 96-109.

Jordan, James V., Robert S. Mackay and Eugene Moriarty. "The New Regulation Of Hybrid Debt Instruments," **JACF**, 1990, v2(4), 72-84.

Jordan, James V., William E. Seale, Nancy C. McCabe and David E. Kenyon. "Transaction Data Tests Of The Black Model For Soybean Futures Options," **JFM**, 1987, v7(5), 535-554.

Jordan, James V., William E. Seale, Stephen J. Dinehart and David E. Kenyon. "The Intraday Variability Of Soybean Futures Prices: Information And Trading Effects," **RFM**, 1988, v7(1), 96-109.

Jordan, Jerry L. (Bruner, Karl, Michele Fratianni, Jerry L. Jordan, Allan H. Meltzer and Manfred J. Neumann. "Fiscal And Monetary Policies In Moderate Inflation," **JMCB**, 1973, v5(1), Part II, 313-354.)

Jordan, Jim. (Kenyon, David, Kenneth Kling, Jim Jordan, William Seale and Nancy McCabe. "Factors Affecting Agricultural Futures Price Variance," **JFM**, 1987, v7(1), 73-92.)

Jordan, R. J. (Brigham, E. F., D. E. Fischer, K. B. Johnson and R. J. Jordan. "What Makes Short Cases Work In The Basic Finance Course?," **JFED**, 1972, v1, 65-68.)

Jordan, Ronald J. "An Empirical Investigation Of The Adjustment Of Stock Prices To New Quarterly Earnings Information," **JFQA**, 1973, v8(4), 609-620.

Jordan, Susan D. (Hilliard, Jimmy E. and Susan D. Jordan. "Hedging Interest Rate Risk With Futures Portfolios Under Full-Rank Assumptions," **JFQA**, 1989, v24(2), 217-240.)

Jorgensen, Jerry L. and Ronald M. Mano. "FASB Statement No. 5: Throwing Out The Baby (Disclosure) With The Bathwater (Accrual)," **FAJ**, 1982, v38(3), 64-66.

Jorgensen, Jerry L. "Executive Manpower Problems In The Life Insurance Industry," **JRI**, 1972, v39(1), 43-54.

Jorgensen, Jerry L. and Ronald M. Mano. "Financial Statement Disclosure Of Uninsured Risks," **JRI**, 1985, v52(1), 133-143.

Jorion, Ph. (Detemple, J. and Ph. Jorion. "Option Listing And Stock Returns: An Empirical Analysis," **JBF**, 1990, v14(4), 781-802.)

Jorion, Philippe and Eduardo Schwartz. "Integration Vs. Segmentation In The Canadian Stock Market," **JOF**, 1986, v41(3), 603-613.

Jorion, Philippe and Neal M. Stoughton. "An Empirical Investigation Of The Early Exercise Premium Of Foreign Currency Options," **JFM**, 1989, v9(5), 365-376.

Jorion, Philippe and Neal M. Stoughton. "The Valuation Of The Early Exercise Premium In The Foreign Currency Options Market," **RDIBF**, 1989, v3, 159-190.

Jorion, Philippe. "Asset Allocation With Hedged And Unhedged Foreign Stocks," **JPM**, 1989, v15(4), 49-54.

Jorion, Philippe. "Bayes-Stein Estimation For Portfolio Analysis," **JFQA**, 1986, v21(3), 279-292.

Jorion, Philippe. "International Portfolio Diversification With Estimation Risk," **JOB**, 1985, v58(3), 259-278.

Jorion, Philippe. "On Jump Processes In The Foreign Exchange And Stock Markets," **RFS**, 1988-89, v1(4), 427-445.

Jorion, Philippe. "The Exchange-Rate Exposure Of U.S. Multinationals," **JOB**, 1990, v63(3), 331-346.

Jorion, Philippe. (Abuaf, Niso and Philippe Jorion. "Purchasing Power Parity In The Long Run," **JOF**, 1990, v45(1), 157-174.)

Jorion, Philippe. (Giovannini, Alberto and Philippe Jorion. "Interest Rates And Risk Premia In The Stock Market And In The Foreign Exchange Market," **JIMF**, 1987, v6(1), 107-124.)

Jorion, Philippe. (Giovannini, Alberto and Philippe Jorion. "Foreign Exchange Risk Premia Volatility Once Again," **JIMF**, 1988, v7(1), 111-114.)

Jorion, Philippe. (Giovannini, Alberto and Philippe Jorion. "The Time Variation Of Risk And Return In The Foreign Exchange And Stock Markets," **JOF**, 1989, v44(2), 307-326.)

Jose, Manuel L. and Jerry L. Stevens. "Product Market Structure, Capital Intensity, And Systematic Risk: Empirical Results From The Theory Of The Firm," **JFR**, 1987, v10(2), 161-175.

Jose, Manuel L. and Jerry L. Stevens. "Capital Market Valuation Of Dividend Policy," **JBFA**, 1989, v16(5), 651-662.

Jose, Manuel L., Len M. Nichols and Jerry L. Stevens. "Contributions Of Diversification, Promotion, And R&D To The Value Of Multiproduct Firms: A Tobin's q Approach," **FM**, 1986, v15(4), 33-42.

Joseph, Hyman. "The Measurement Of Moral Hazard," **JRI**, 1972, v39(2), 257-262.

Joseph, Stephen L. "Investing For Automation," **FAJ**, 1956, v12(5), 33-36.

Joseph, Stephen L. "The New Capitalism," **FAJ**, 1955, v11(1), 71-76.

Josephson, Halsey D. "A New Concept Of The Economics Of Life Value And The Human Life Value: Comment," **JRI**, 1970, v37(4), 641-643.

Josephson, Halsey D. "Policy Loan Interest Rates: A Critical Evaluation: Comment," **JRI**, 1972, v39(1), 156-160.

Josephson, Halsey D., Glenn L. Wood and C. Arthur Williams, Jr. "High Cash Value Life Insurance Policies And Unfair Discrimination: Comment," **JRI**, 1966, v33(1), 125-134.

Joules, Reginald G. (Caks, John, William R. Lane, Robert W. Greenleaf and Reginald G. Joules. "A Simple Formula For Duration," **JFR**, 1985, v8(3), 245-249.)

Joy, Maurice. (Craig, Darryl, Glenn Johnson and Maurice Joy. "Accounting Methods And P/E Ratios," **FAJ**, 1987, v43(2), 41-45.)

Joy, O. M. (Litzenberger, R. H. and O. M. Joy. "Target Rates Of Return And Corporate Asset And Liability Structure Under Uncertainty," JFQA, 1971, v6(2), 675-686.)

Joy, O. Maurice and Charles P. Jones. "Earnings Reports And Market Efficiencies: An Analysis Of The Contrary Evidence," JFR, 1979, v2(1), 51-63.

Joy, O. Maurice and Charles P. Jones. "Should We Believe The Tests Of Market Efficiency?," JPM, 1985-86, v12(4), 49-54.

Joy, O. Maurice and Charles P. Jones. "Predictive Value Of P/E Ratios," FAJ, 1970, v26(5), 61-64.

Joy, O. Maurice and Jerry O. Bradley. "A Note On Sensitivity Analysis Of Rates Of Return," JOF, 1973, v28(5), 1255-1261.

Joy, O. Maurice and Jerry O. Bradley. "Sensitivity Analysis Of Rates Of Return: Reply," JOF, 1978, v33(5), 1461.

Joy, O. Maurice and John D. Tollefson. "Some Clarifying Comments On Discriminant Analysis," JFQA, 1978, v13(1), 197-200.

Joy, O. Maurice and John O. Tollefson. "On The Financial Applications Of Discriminant Analysis," JFQA, 1975, v10(5), 723-739.

Joy, O. Maurice and R. Burr Porter. "Stochastic Dominance And Mutual Fund Performance," JFQA, 1974, v9(1), 25-31.

Joy, O. Maurice, Don B. Panton, Frank K. Reilly and Stanley A. Martin. "Comovements Of Major International Equity Markets," FR, 1976, v11(1), 1-20.

Joy, O. Maurice. "Abandonment Values And Abandonment Decisions: A Clarification," JOF, 1976, v31(4), 1225-1228.

Joy, O. Maurice. (Beedles, William L., O. Maurice Joy and William Ruland. "Conglomeration And Diversification," FR, 1981, v16(1), 1-13.)

Joy, O. Maurice. (Beedles, William L. and O. Maurice Joy. "Compounding Risk Over Time: A Note," JBFA, 1982, v8(3), 307-311.)

Joy, O. Maurice. (Fortin, Richard D., R. Corwin Grube and O. Maurice Joy. "Bid-Ask Spreads For OTC NASDAQ Firms," FAJ, 1990, v46(3), 76-79.)

Joy, O. Maurice. (Fortin, Richard D., R. Corwin Grube and O. Maurice Joy. "Seasonality In NASDAQ Dealer Spreads," JFQA, 1989, v24(3), 395-407.)

Joy, O. Maurice. (Grube, R. Corwin and O. Maurice Joy. "Some Evidence On The Efficacy Of Security Credit Regulation In The OTC Equity Market," JFR, 1988, v11(2), 137-142.)

Joy, O. Maurice. (Grube, R. Corwin, Maurice Joy and John S. Howe. "Some Empirical Evidence On Stock Returns And Security Credit Regulation In The OTC Equity Market," JBF, 1987, v11(1), 17-32.)

Joy, O. Maurice. (Grube, R. Corwin, O. Maurice Joy and Don B. Panton. "Market Responses To Federal Reserve Changes In The Initial Margin Requirement," JOF, 1979, v34(3), 659-674.)

Joy, O. Maurice. (Latane, Henry A., O. Maurice Joy and Charles P. Jones. "Quarterly Data, Sort-Rank Routines, And Security Evaluation," JOB, 1970, v43(4), 427-438.)

Joy, O. Maurice. (Litzenberger, Robert H., O. Maurice Joy and Charles P. Jones. "Ordinal Predictions And The Selection Of Common Stocks," JFQA, 1971, v6(4), 1059-1068.)

Joy, O. Maurice. (Litzenberger, Robert H. and O. Maurice Joy. "Decentralized Capital Budgeting Decisions And Shareholder Wealth Maximization," JOF, 1975, v30(4), 993-1002.)

Joy, O. Maurice. (Meekder, Larry G. and O. Maurice Joy. "Price Premiums For Controlling Shares Of Closely Held Bank Stock," JOB, 1980, v53(3), Part 1, 297-314.)

Joy, O. Maurice. (Pan, Judy, Donald R. Nichols and O. Maurice Joy. "Sales Forecasting Practices Of Large U.S. Industrial Firms," FM, 1977, v6(3), 72-77.)

Joy, O. Maurice. (Panton, Don B., V. Parker Lessiq and O. Maurice Joy. "Comovement Of International Equity Markets: A Taxonomic Approach," JFQA, 1976, v11(3), 415-432.)

Joyce, Jon M. and Robert C. Vogel. "The Uncertainty In Risk: Is Variance Unambiguous?," JOF, 1970, v25(1), 127-134.

Jucker, James V. and Clovis de Faro. "A Simple Algorithm For Stone's Version Of The Portfolio Selection Problem," JFQA, 1975, v10(5), 859-870.

Jucker, James V. (Baum, Sanford, Robert C. Carlson and James V. Jucker. "Some Problems In Applying The Continuous Portfolio Selection Model To The Discrete Capital Budgeting Problem," JFQA, 1978, v13(2), 333-344.)

Jucker, James V. and Clovis de Faro. "The Selection Of International Borrowing Sources," JFQA, 1975, v10(3), 381-407.

Jud, G. Donald and James Frew. "Atypicality And The Natural Vacancy Rate Hypothesis," AREUEA, 1990, v18(3), 294-301.

Jud, G. Donald. "A Further Note On Schools And Housing Values," AREUEA, 1985, v13(4), 452-462.

Jud, G. Donald. "Real Estate Brokers And The Market For Residential Housing," AREUEA, 1983, v11(1), 69-82.

Jud, G. Donald. (Crellin, Glenn E., James R. Frew and G. Donald Jud. "The Earnings Of REALTORS: Some Empirical Evidence," JRER, 1988, v3(2), 69-78.)

Jud, G. Donald. (Frew, James R. and G. Donald Jud. "The Value Of A Real Estate Franchise," AREUEA, 1986, v14(2), 374-383.)

Jud, G. Donald. (Frew, James R., G. Donald Jud and Tony R. Wingler. "The Effects Of Zoning On Population And Employment Density," JREFEC, 1990, v3(2), 155-172.)

Jud, G. Donald. (Frew, James and G. Donald Jud. "Vacancy Rates In Rent Levels In The Commercial Office Market," JRER, 1988, v3(1), 1-8.)

Jud, G. Donald. (Frew, James R., G. Donald Jud and Daniel T. Winkler. "Atypicalities And Apartment Rent Concessions," JRER, 1990, v5(2), 195-201.)

Jud, G. Donald. (Wingler, Tony R. and G. Donald Jud. "Premium Debt Tenders: Analysis And Evidence," FM, 1990, v19(4), 58-67.)

Judd, John P. "Dynamic Implications Of Poole's Proposed Reserve Requirement Rule," JMCB, 1977, v9(4), 667-671.

Judd, Kenneth L. (Balcer, Yves and Kenneth L. Judd. "Effects Of Capital Gains Taxation On Life-Cycle Investment And Portfolio Management," JOF, 1987, v42(3), 743-758.)

Judlowe, Stephen. (Petruzzi, Chirstoher, Marguerite Del Valle and Stephen Judlowe. "Patent And Copyright Protection For Innovations In Finance," FM, 1988, v17(4), 66-71.)

Juhasz, Joseph B. (Hughes, G. David, Joseph B. Juhasz and Bruno Contini. "The Influence Of Personality On The Bargaining Process," JOB, 1973, v46(4), 593-604.)

Julien, Bruno. (Green, Jerry R. and Bruno Julien. "Erratum: Ordinal Independence In Nonlinear Utility Theory," JRU, 1989, v2(1), 119.)

Jullien, Bruno. (Green, Jerry R. and Bruno Jullien. "Ordinal Independence In Nonlinear Utility Theory," JRU, 1988, v1(4), 355-388.)

Jun, Kwang W. (Klemkosky, Robert C. and Kwang W. Jun. "The Monetary Impact On Return Variability And Market Risk Premia," JFQA, 1982, v17(5), 663-681.)

Juncker, George R. and George S. Oldfield. "Projecting Market Structure By Monte Carlo Simulation: A Study Of Bank Expansion In New Jersey," JOF, 1972, v27(5), 1101-1126.

Jung, Alan F. "Automobile Insurance Rates In Chicago, Illinois," JRI, 1978, v45(3), 507-515.

Jung, Alan F. "Automobile Insurance Rates In Chicago Illinois: A Correction," JRI, 1983, v50(2), 330-331.

Jung, Allen F. "A Different Retail Price Pattern: The Case Of Carpeting," JOB, 1965, v38(2), 180-185.

Jung, Allen F. "Charges For Appliance And Automobile Installment Credit In Major Cities," JOB, 1962, v35(4), 386-391.

Jung, Allen F. "Charges For Credit Life Insurance In Major Cities," JRI, 1960, v27(3), 55-60.

Jung, Allen F. "Compact-Car Prices In Major Cities," JOB, 1960, v33(3), 252-257.

Jung, Allen F. "Credit Life Insurance Charges In Selected Areas," JRI, 1962, v29(1), 99-106.

Jung, Allen F. "Dealer Pricing Practices And Finance Charges For New Mobile Homes," JOB, 1963, v36(4), 430-439.

Jung, Allen F. "Impact Of The Compact Cars On New-Car Prices-A Reappraisal," JOB, 1962, v35(1), 70-76.

Jung, Allen F. "Impact Of The Compact Cars On New-Car Prices," JOB, 1961, v34(2), 167-182.

Jung, Allen F. "Indexes Of Retail Prices Of New Cars-Consumer Price Index," JOB, 1961, v34(4), 490-494.

Jung, Allen F. "Major Appliance Prices In The Chicago Area," JOB, 1977, v50(2), 231-235.

Jung, Allen F. "Mortgage Availability And Terms In Florida," JOB, 1964, v37(3), 274-279.

Jung, Allen F. "Price Policy And Discounts In The Medium- And High-Priced Car Market," JOB, 1960, v33(4), 342-347.

Jung, Allen F. "Price Variations On Automatic Washing Machines In Chicago, Illinois, Among Different Types Of Retail Outlets," JOB, 1958, v31(4), 311-317.

Jung, Allen F. "Price Variations Among Home-Remodeling Contractors," JOB, 1961, v34(1), 52-56.

Jung, Allen F. "Price Variations Among Automobile Dealers In Metropolitan Chicago," JOB, 1960, v33(1), 31-42.

Jung, Allen F. "Price Variations On Automatic Washing Machines In Chicago, Illinois, Among Different Types Of Retail Outlets-1955 Versus 1958," JOB, 1959, v32(2), 133-140.

Jung, Allen F. "Price Variations Among Automobile Dealers In Chicago, Illinois," JOB, 1959, v32(4), 315-325.

Jung, Allen F. "Prices Of Falcon And Corvair Cars In Chicago And Selected Cities," JOB, 1960, v33(2), 121-126.

Jung, Allen F. "Rate Variations Among Suppliers Of Automobile Insurance," JRI, 1963, v30(4), 573-576.

Jung, Allen F. "Terms On Conventional Mortgage Loans On Existing Houses," JOF, 1962, v17(3),432-443.

Jung, Allen F. (Crane, Frederick G. and Allen F. Jung. "Rate Variations Among Suppliers Of Automobile Insurance: Comment," JRI, 1964, v31(3), 469-474.)

Jung, W. (Ahn, Chul Won and W. Jung. "The Choice Of A Monetary Instrument In A Small Open Economy: The Case Of Korea," JIMF, 1985, v4(4), 469-484.)

Jung, Woo S. and Peyton J. Marshall. "Inflation And Economic Growth: Some International Evidence On Structuralist And Distortionist Positions," JMCB, 1986, v18(2), 227-232.

Junkus, Joan C. and Cheng F. Lee. "Use Of Three Stock Index Futures In Hedging Decisions," JFM, 1985, v5(2), 201-222.

Junkus, Joan C. "Systematic Skewness In Futures Contracts," JFM, 1991, v11(1), 9-24.

Junkus, Joan C. "Weekend And Day Of The Week Effects In Returns On Stock Index Futures," JFM, 1986, v6(3), 397-408.

Junz, Helen B. "The Balance Of Payments Adjustment Process Revisited," JOF, 1978, v33(3), 803-813.

Junz, Helen B. (Adams, F. Gerard and Helen B. Junz. "The Effect Of The Business Cycle On Trade Flows Of Industrial Countries," JOF, 1971, v26(2), 251-268.)

Jurgensen, Delbert F. (Herman, Hamilton and Delbert F. Jurgensen. "Challenge Of The National Water Problem," FAJ, 1962, v18(2), 65-74.)

Just, Richard. (Feder, Gershon, Richard Just and Knud Ross. "Projecting Debt Servicing Capacity Of Developing Countries," JFQA, 1981, v16(5), 651-669.)

Juster, F. Thomas. "Consumer Sensitivity To The Price Of Credit," JOF, 1964, v19(2), Part 1, 222-233.

KKK

Kabak, Irwin W. (Feay, Herbert L. and Irwin W. Kabak. "Frequency Formulas For Determining Stop-Loss Reinsurance Premiums," JRI, 1968, v35(3), 371-391.)

Kacmar, K. Michele. (Abelson, Michael A., K. Michele Kacmar and Ellen F. Jackofsky. "Factors Influencing Real Estate Brokerage Sales Staff Performance," JRER, 1990, v5(2), 265-275.)

Kadapakkam, Palani-Rajan and Stanley J. Kon. "The Value Of Shelf Registration For New Debt Issues," JOB, 1989, v62(2), 271-292.

Kadish, Lloyd and Michael A. Weinberg. "If The Supreme Court Does Not Imply A Private Judicial Cause Of Action Under The Commodity Exchange Act," JFM, 1981, v1(Supp), 519-521.

Kadiyala, K. Rao. (Lockwood, Larry J. and K. Rao Kadiyala. "Measuring Investment Performance With A Stochastic Parameter Regression Model," JBF, 1988, v11(3), 457-468.)

Kaen, Fred R. and George A. Hachey. "Eurocurrency And National Money Market Interest Rates: An Empirical Investigation Of Causality," **JMCB**, 1983, v15(3), 327-338.

Kaen, Fred R. (Booth, G. Geoffrey, Fred R. Kaen and Peter E. Koveos. "Currency Interependence In Foreign Exchange Markets," **FR**, 1980, v15(3), 36-44.)

Kaen, Fred R. (Booth, G. Geoffrey and Fred R. Kaen. "Gold And Silver Spot Prices And Market Information Efficiency," **FR**, 1979, v14(2), 21-26.)

Kaen, Fred R. (Booth, G. Geoffrey, Fred R. Kaen and Peter E. Koveos. "Persistent Dependence In Gold Prices," **JFR**, 1982, v5(1), 85-93.

Kaen, Fred R. (Burt, John, Fred R. Kaen and G. Geoffrey Booth. "Foreign Exchange Market Efficiency Under Flexible Exchange Rates: Reply," **JOF**, 1979, v34(3), 791-793.)

Kaen, Fred R. (Burt, John, Fred R. Kaen and G. Geoffrey Booth. "Foreign Exchange Market Efficiency Under Flexible Exchange Rates," **JOF**, 1977, v32(4), 1325-1330.)

Kaen, Fred R. (Helms, Billy P., Fred R. Kaen and Robert E. Rosenman. "Memory In Commodity Futures Contracts," **JFM**, 1984, v4(4), 559-567.)

Kaen, Fred R. and Hassan Tehranian. "Information Effects In Financial Distress: The Case Of Seabrook Station," **JFEC**, 1990, v26(1), 143-171.

Kaen, Fred R., Evangelos O. Simos and George A. Hachey. "The Response Of Forward Exchange Rates To Interest Rate Forecasting Errors," **JFR**, 1984, v7(4), 281-290.

Kafer, R. W. "Comparing Time-Series And Survey Forecasts Of Weekly Changes In Money: A Methodological Note," **JOF**, 1984, v39(4), 1207-1213.

Kafka, Alexandre. "The New Exchange Rate Regime And The Developing Countries," **JOF**, 1978, v33(3), 795-802.

Kagel, John H. (Battalio, Raymond C., John H. Kagel and Romain Jiranyakul. "Testing Between Alternative Models Of Choice Under Uncertainty: Some Intitial Results," **JRU**, 1990, v3(1), 25-50.)

Kahane, Jehuda. (Levy, Haim and Jehuda Kahane. "Profitability Of Saving Through Insurance Companies," **JRI**, 1970, v37(2), 233-240.)

Kahane, Yehuda and David Nye. "A Portfolio Approach To The Property-Liability Insurance Industry," **JRI**, 1975, v42(4), 579-598.

Kahane, Yehuda and Haim Levy. "Regulation In The Insurance Industry: Determination Of Premiums In Automobile Insurance," **JRI**, 1975, v42(1), 117-132.

Kahane, Yehuda and M. Moshe Porat. "Financial Analysis Of Underwriting Results - A Corrected Approach To Loss Ratio Analysis, With Special Reference To Inflation," **JRI**, 1984, v51(4), 710-719.

Kahane, Yehuda. "Generation Of Investable Funds And The Portfolio Behavior Of Non-Life Insurers," **JRI**, 1978, v45(1), 65-78.

Kahane, Yehuda. (Antler, Jacob and Yehuda Kahane. "The Gross And Net Replacement Ratios In Designing Pension Schemes And In Financial Planning: The Israeli Experience," **JRI**, 1987, v54(2), 283-297.)

Kahane, Yehuda. (Briys, Eric, Yehuda Kahane and Yoram Kroll. "Voluntary Insurance Coverage, Compulsory Insurance, And Risky-Riskless Portfolio Opportunities," **JRI**, 1988, v55(4), 713-722.)

Kahane, Yehuda. (Eiger, Nahum and Yehuda Kahane. "Risk Considerations In Insurance Ratemaking," **JRI**, 1978, v45(1), 121-132.)

Kahl, Dandice H. (Curtis, Charles E., Jr., Kandice H. Kahl and Cathy S. McKinnell. "Risk-Efficient Soybean Marketing: The Contribution Of Commodity Options To The Producing Firm," **RFM**, 1987, v6(2), 176-190.)

Kahl, Douglas R. (Gombola, Michael J. and Douglas R. Kahl. "Time-Series Processes Of Utility Betas: Implications For Forecasting Systematic Risk," **FM**, 1990, v19(3), 84-93.)

Kahl, Kandace H., Roger D. Rutz and Jeanne C. Sinquefield. "The Economics Of Performance Margins In Futures Markets," **JFM**, 1985, v5(1), 103-112.

Kahl, Kandice H. (Miller, Stephen E. and Kandice H. Kahl. "Forward Pricing When Yields Are Uncertain," **RFM**, 1987, v6(1), 20-39.)

Kahl, Kandice H. and Charles E. Curtis, Jr. "A Comparative Analysis Of The Corn Basis In Feed Grain Deficit And Surplus Areas," **RFM**, 1986, v5(3), 220-232.

Kahl, Kandice H. and William G. Tomek. "Effectiveness Of Hedging In Potato Futures," **JFM**, 1982, v2(1), 9-18.

Kahl, Kandice H. "Effects Of Economic Recovery Tax Act Of 1981 On Futures Market Volume," **JFM**, 1985, v5(2), 239-246.

Kahl, Kandice H. (Miller, Stephen E. and Kandice H. Kahl. "Performance Of Estimated Hedging Ratios Under Yield Uncertainty," **JFM**, 1989, v9(4), 307-320.)

Kahl, Kandice H., Michael A. Hudson and Clement E. Ward. "Cash Settlement Issues For Live Cattle Futures Contracts," **JFM**, 1989, v9(3), 237-248.

Kahler, C. M. (Berolzheimer, Howard, Edwin A. Gaumnitz, C. M. Kahler and Joseph Pillion. "Round Table Discussion: The Objectives And Content Of The Survey Course In Insurance," **JRI**, 1941, v8, 5-38.)

Kahler, Clyde M. "The University Teacher Looks At Company Educational Programs - Property and Casualty Insurance," **JRI**, 1950, v17, 65-73.

Kahn, Irving. "Lemmings Always Lose," **FAJ**, 1977, v33(3), 27-29.

Kahn, Irving. "TV - The Second Decade," **FAJ**, 1958, v14(1), 67-72.

Kahn, Lawrence R. "Changing Status Of The Variety Chains," **FAJ**, 1955, v11(2), 31-34.

Kahn, Lawrence R. "Tailor Made Metals," **FAJ**, 1956, v12(5), 19-22.

Kahn, Lawrence R. "The Business Boom Of 1960," **FAJ**, 1960, v16(1), 7-9.

Kahn, Lawrence R. "The Corporate Annual Report," **FAJ**, 1961, v17(6), 25-27.

Kahn, Paul Markham. "Some Remarks About Mathematical Models In Insurance," **JRI**, 1964, v31(2), 253-258.

Kahn, Ronald N. and Roland Lochoff. "Convexity And Exceptional Return," **JPM**, 1990, v16(2), 43-47.

Kahne, Yehuda. (Biger, Nahum and Yehuda Kahane. "Purchasing Power Risk And The Performance Of Non Life Insurance Companies," **JRI**, 1976, v43(2), 243-256.)

Kahneman, Daniel, Jack L. Knetsch and Richard H. Thaler. "Fairness And The Assumptions Of Economics," **JOB**, 1986, v59(4), Part 2, S285-S300.

Kahneman, Daniel. (Tversky, Amos and Daniel Kahneman. "Rational Choice And The Framing Of Decisions," **JOB**, 1986, v59(4), Part 2, S251-S278.)

Kaimakliotis, Michael and Edward Renshaw. "Some Self-Perpetuating Patterns In The Stock Market?," **JPM**, 1991, v17(2), 41-43.

Kain, John F. "What Should Housing Policies Be?," **JOF**, 1974, v29(2), 683-698.

Kain, John F. (Ingram, Gregory K. and John F. Kain. "A Simple Model Of Housing Production And The Abandonment Problem," **AREUEA**, 1973, v1(1), 79-106.)

Kain, John F. and Gary R. Fauth. "The Impact Of Urban Development On Auto Ownership And Transit Use," **AREUEA**, 1978, v6(3), 305-326.

Kain, John F. and William C. Apgar, Jr. "Simulation Of Housing Market Dynamics," **AREUEA**, 1979, v7(4), 505-538.

Kaiser, Kathleen M. (Gaines, James P. and Kathleen M. Kaiser. "An Analysis Of RESPA 1974 And the RESPA Amendments Of 1975," **JBR**, 1977-78, v8(1), 22-30.)

Kaiser, Ronald W. "Kondratieff's Gloomy News For Investors," **FAJ**, 1979, v35(3), 57-66.

Kaish, Stanley. "Differential Odd-Lot Trading," **FAJ**, 1969, v25(2), 88-91.

Kaish, Stanley. "Odd Lot Profit And Loss Performance," **FAJ**, 1969, v25(5), 83-89.

Kalaba, Robert E., Terence C. Langetieg, Nima Rasakhoo and Mark I. Weinstein. "Estimation Of Implicit Bankruptcy Costs," **JOF**, 1984, v39(3), 629-642.

Kalay, Avner and Ramon Rabinovitch. "On Individual Loans Pricing Credit Rationing And Interest Rate Regulation," **JOF**, 1978, v33(4), 1071-1085.

Kalay, Avner and Uri Loewenstein. "The Informational Content Of The Timing Of Dividend Announcements," **JFEC**, 1986, v16(3), 373-388.

Kalay, Avner and Uri Loewenstein. "Predictable Events And Excess Returns: The Case Of Dividend Announcements," **JFEC**, 1985, v14(3), 423-449.

Kalay, Avner and Adam Shimrat. "Firm Value And Seasoned Equity Issues: Price Pressure, Wealth Redistribution, Or Negative Information," **JFEC**, 1987, v19(1), 109-126.

Kalay, Avner and Adam Shimrat. "The Maintained Flexibility Of Divided Constraints: A Cross-Sectional And Time Series Analysis," **RIF**, 1990, v8, 77-96.

Kalay, Avner and Marti G. Subrahmanyam. "The Ex-Dividend Day Behavior Of Option Prices," **JOB**, 1984, v57(1), Part 1, 113-128.

Kalay, Avner. "Signaling, Information Content, And The Reluctance To Cut Dividends," **JFQA**, 1980, v15(4), 855-869.

Kalay, Avner. "Stockholder-Bondholder Conflict And Dividend Constraints," **JFEC**, 1982, v10(2), 211-233.

Kalay, Avner. "The Ex-Dividend Day Behavior Of Stock Prices: A Re-Examination Of The Clientele Effect," **JOF**, 1982, v37(4), 1059-1070.

Kalay, Avner. "The Ex-Dividend Day Behavior Of Stock Prices; A Reexamination Of The Clientele Effect: A Reply," **JOF**, 1984, v39(2), 557-561.

Kalay, Avner. (Gavish, Bezalel and Avner Kalay. "On The Asset Substitution Problem," **JFQA**, 1983, v18(1), 21-30.)

Kalay, Avner. (Gottlieb, Gary and Avner Kalay. "Implications Of The Discreteness Of Observed Stock Prices," **JOF**, 1985, v40(1), 135-153.)

Kalay, Avner. (Handjinicolaou, George and Avner Kalay. "Wealth Redistributions Or Changes In Firm Value: An Analysis Of Returns To Bondholders And The Stockholders Around Dividend Announcements," **JFEC**, 1984, v13(1), 35-63.)

Kalay, Avner. (John, Kose and Avner Kalay. "Costly Contracting And Optimal Payout Constraints," **JOF**, 1982, v37(2), 457-470.)

Kale, Jayant R. (Badrinath, S. G., Gerald D. Gay and Jayant R. Kale. "Patterns Of Institutional Investment, Prudence, And The Managerial 'Safety-Net' Hypothesis," **JRI**, 1989, v56(4), 605-629.)

Kale, Jayant R. and Thomas H. Noe. "Risky Debt Maturity Choice In A Sequential Game Equilibrium," **JFR**, 1990, v13(2), 155-166.

Kale, Jayant R. and Thomas H. Noe. "Dividends, Uncertainty, And Underwriting Costs Under Asymmetric Information," **JFR**, 1990, v13(4), 265-278.

Kale, Jayant R., Thomas H. Noe and Gerald D. Gay. "Share Repurchase Through Transferable Put Rights: Theory And Case Study," **JFEC**, 1989, v25(1), 141-160.

Kale, Jivendra. (Hakannsson, Nils H., Avraham Beja and Jivendra Kale. "On The Feasibility Of Automated Market Making By A Programmed Specialist," **JOF**, 1985, v40(1), 1-20.)

Kalish, Lionel, III and R. Alton Gilbert. "The Influence Of Bank Regulation On The Operating Efficiency Of Commercial Banks," **JOF**, 1973, v28(5), 1287-1301.

Kalish, Lionel, III. "A Study Of Money Stock Control," **JOF**, 1970, v25(4), 761-776.

Kalish, Lionel. "A Framework For Evaluating Potential Competition As A Factor In Bank Mergers and Acquisitions," **JMCB**, 1975, v7(4), 527-530.

Kallberg, Jarl G. and Anthony Saunders. "Markov Chain Approaches To The Analysis Of Payment Behavior Of Retail Credit Customers," **FM**, 1983, v12(2), 5-14.

Kallberg, Jarl G. and Duen-Li Kao. "Statistical Models In Credit Management," **AWCM**, 1990, v1(1), 147-176.

Kalle, Hemu. (Davidson, Sidney, George H. Sorter, and Hemu Kalle. "Measuring The Defensive Position Of A Firm," **FAJ**, 1964, v20(1), 23-29.)

Kallio, Markku. (Ohlson, James A. and Markku Kallio. "A Note On The Representation Of Bounded Utility Functions Defined On [a,oo]," **JFQA**, 1975, v10(2), 377-379.)

Kallman, Jonathan. "Panel: Clearance, Payment, And Settlement Systems In The Futures, Options, And Stock Markets," **RFM**, 1988, v7(3), 392-394.

Kalogeras, Gus. "In Defense Of The Lecture Method Of Instruction," **JFED**, 1976, v5, 45-47.

Kalotay, A. J. "Innovations In Corporate Finance: Deep Discount Private Placements," **FM**, 1982, v11(1), 55-57.

Kalotay, A. J. "On The Advanced Refunding Of Discounted Debt," FM, 1978, v7(2), 14-18.

Kalotay, A. J. "On The Structure And Valuation Of Debt Refundings," FM, 1982, v11(1), 41-42.

Kalotay, A. J. "Sinking Funds And The Realized Cost Of Debt," FM, 1982, v11(1), 43-54.

Kalotay, A. J. (Boyce, W. M. and A. J. Kalotay. "Tax Differentials And Callable Bonds," JOF, 1979, v34(4), 825-838.)

Kalotay, Andrew J. "An Analysis Of Original Issue Discount Bonds," FM, 1984, v13(3), 29-38.

Kalotay, Andrew J. "Notes On The Computation Of IRR," JFED, 1982, v11, p. 75.

Kalotay, Andrew J. "Notes On The Definition Of The Cost Of Capital," JFED, 1982, v11, 76-78.

Kalotay, Andrew J. "On The Management Of Sinking Funds," FM, 1981, v10(3), 34-40.

Kalotay, Andrew J. "Refunding Considerations Under Rate-Base Regulation," FM, 1984, v13(3), 11-14.

Kalotay, Andrew J. "The After-Tax Duration Of Original Issue Discount Bonds," JPM, 1984-85, v11(2), 70-72.

Kaluzny, Richard. (Brewster, J. Alan, Irving Crespi, Richard Kaluzny, James Ohls and Cynthia Thomas. "Homeowner Warranties: A Study Of The Need And Demand For Protection Against Unanticipated Repair Expenses," AREUEA, 1980, v8(2), 207-217.)

Kalymon, Basil A. "Estimation Risk In The Portfolio Selection Model," JFQA, 1971, v6(1), 559-582.

Kamara, Avraham and Andrew F. Siegel. "Optimal Hedging In Futures Markets With Multiple Delivery Specifications," JOF, 1987, v42(4), 1007-1021.

Kamara, Avraham. "Delivery Uncertainty And The Efficiency Of Futures Markets," JFQA, 1990, v25(1), 45-64.

Kamara, Avraham. "Forecasting Accuracy And Development Of A Financial Market: The Treasury Bill Futures Market," JFM, 1990, v10(4), 397-406.

Kamara, Avraham. "Issues In Futures Markets: A Survey," JFM, 1982, v2(3), 261-294.

Kamara, Avraham. "Market Trading Structures And Asset Pricing: Evidence From The Treasury-Bill Markets," RFS, 1988-89, v1(4), 357-375.

Kamara, Avraham. "The Behavior Of Futures Prices: A Review Of Theory And Evidence," FAJ, 1984, v40(4), 68-75.

Kamarotou, H. and J. O'Hanlon. "Informational Efficiency In The UK, US, Canadian And Japanese Equity Markets: A Note," JBFA, 1989, v16(2), 183-192.

Kamas, Linda. "The Balance Of Payments Offset To Monetary Policy: Monetarist, Portfolio Balance, And Keynesian Estimates For Mexico And Venezuela," JMCB, 1986, v18(4), 467-481.

Kamath, Ravindra R., Shahriar Khaksari, Heidi Hylton Meier and John Winklepleck. "Management Of Excess Cash: Practices And Developments," FM, 1985, v14(3), 70-77.

Kamath, Ravindra. (Khaksari, Shahriar, Ravindra Kamath and Robin Grieves. "A New Approach To Determining Optimum Portfolio Mix," JPM, 1989, v15(3), 43-49.)

Kamath, Shyam J. (Rugman, Alan M. and Shyam J. Kamath. "International Diversification And Multinational Banking," RDIBF, 1987, v1, 35-60.)

Kamer, Pearl. "The Changing Spatial Relationship Between Residences And Worksites In The New York Metropolitan Region: Implications For Public Policy," AREUEA, 1977, v5(4), 434-454.

Kamer, Pearl. (Rubin, Marilyn, Ilene Wagner and Pearl Kamer. "Industrial Migration: A Case Study Of Destination By City-Suburban Origin Within The New York Metorpolitan Area," AREUEA, 1978, v6(4), 417-437.)

Kamerschen, David R. "A Note On Economies Of Scale In Life Insurance," JRI, 1972, v39(3), 473-474.

Kamerschen, David R. "An Economic Explanation Of The Relative Decline In Household Reserves In Life Insurance," JRI, 1979, v46(3), 531-539.

Kamerschen, David R. "Are Conglomerate Insurance Mergers Sui Generis?," JRI, 1974, v41(3), 463-482.

Kamerschen, David R. "The Determination Of Profit Rates In 'Oligopolistic Industries'," JOB, 1969, v42(3), 293-301.

Kamerschen, David R. "The Return Of Target Pricing?," JOB, 1975, v48(2), 242-252.

Kamerschen, David R. and John J. Pascucci. "The Retail Price Structure In American Life Insurance: Comment," JRI, 1969, v36(3), 493-494.

Kamien, Morton I. and Nancy L. Schwartz. "Payment Plans And The Efficient Delivery Of Health Care Services," JRI, 1973, v40(3), 427-436.

Kamin, Jules H. (Fisher, L. and J. Kamin. "Forecasting Systematic Risk: Estimates Of 'Raw' Beta That Take Account Of The Tendency Of Beta To Change And The Heteroskedasticity Of Residual Returns," JFQA, 1985, v20(2),127-150.)

Kaminow, Ira. "The Household Demand For Money: An Empirical Study," JOF, 1969, v24(4), 679-696.

Kaminow, Ira. (Rao, D. C. and Ira Kaminow. "Selective Credit Controls And The Real Investment Mix: A General Equilibrium Approach," JOF, 1973, v28(5), 1103-1118.)

Kamma, Sreenivas, Joseph Weintrop and Peggy Wier. "Investors' Perceptions Of The Delaware Supreme Court Decision In Unocal V. Mesa," JFEC, 1988, v20(1/2), 419-430.

Kamoike, Osamu. "Portfolio Selection When Future Prices Of Consumption Goods May Change: Comment," JOF, 1973, v28(5), 1357-1360.

Kampmeyer, Joan M. (Alexander, Gordon J., P. George Benson and Joan M. Kampmeyer. "Investigating The Valuation Effects Of Announcements Of Voluntary Corporate Selloffs," JOF, 1984, v39(2), 503-517.)

Kanatas, George. "Commercial Paper, Bank Reserve Requirements, And The Informational Role Of Loan Commitments," JBF, 1987, v11(3), 425-448.

Kanatas, George. "Commercial Paper, Bank Reserve Requirements, And The Informational Role Of Loan Commitments: A Reply," JBF, 1989, v13(2), 276-282.

Kanatas, George. "Deposit Insurance And The Discount Window: Pricing Under Asymmetric Information," JOF, 1986, v41(2), 437-450.

Kanatas, George. (Chan, Yuk-Shee and George Kanatas. "Asymmetric Valuations And The Role Of Collateral In Loan Agreements," JMCB, 1985, v17(1), 84-95.)

Kanatas, George. (Deshmukh, Sudhakar D., Stuart I. Greenbaum and George Kanatas. "Lending Policies Of Financial Intermediaries Facing Credit And Funding Risk," JOF, 1983, v38(3), 873-886.)

Kanatas, George. (Deshmukh, Sudhakar D., Stuart I. Greenbaum and George Kanatas. "Bank Forward Lending In Alternative Funding Environments," JOF, 1982, v37(4), 925-940.)

Kanatas, George. (Deshmukh, Sudhakar D., Stuart I. Greenbaum and George Kanatas. "Interest Rate Uncertainty And The Financial Intermediary's Choice Of Exposure," JOF, 1983, v38(1), 141-147.)

Kanatas, George. (Greenbaum, Stuart I., George Kanatas and Itzhak Venezia. "Equilibrium Loan Pricing Under The Bank-Client Relationship," JBF, 1989, v13(2), 221-236.)

Kanatas, George. (Igawa, Kazuhiro and George Kanatas. "Asymmetric Information, Collateral, And Moral Hazard," JFQA, 1990, v25(4), 469-490.)

Kandel, Shmuel and Robert F. Stambaugh. "On Correlations And Inferences About Mean--Variance Efficiency," JFEC, 1987, v18(1), 61-90.

Kandel, Shmuel and Robert F. Stambaugh. "A Mean-Variance Framework For Tests Of Asset Pricing Models," RFS, 1989, v2(2), 125-156.

Kandel, Shmuel and Robert F. Stambaugh. "Expectations And Volatility Of Consumption And Asset Returns," RFS, 1990, v3(2), 207-232.

Kandel, Shmuel. "On The Exclusion Of Assets From Tests Of The Mean Variance Efficiency Of The Market Portfolio," JOF, 1984, v39(1), 63-75.

Kandel, Shmuel. "The Geometry Of The Maximum Likelihood Estimator Of The Zero-Beta Return," JOF, 1984, v41(2), 339-346.

Kandel, Shmuel. "The Likelihood Ratio Test Statistic Of Mean-Variance Efficiency Without A Riskless Asset," JFEC, 1984, v13(4), 575-592.

Kandel, Shmuel. (Ferson, Wayne E., Shmuel Kandel and Robert F. Stambaugh. "Tests Of Asset Pricing With Time-Varying Expected Risk Premiums And Market Betas," JOF, 1987, v42(2), 201-220.)

Kandel, Shmuel. (Huberman, Gur, Shmuel Kandel and Robert F. Stambaugh. "Mimicking Portfolios And Exact Arbitrage Pricing," JOF, 1987, v42(1), 1-9.)

Kandel, Shmuel. (Huberman, Gur and Shmuel Kandel. "Value Line Rank And Firm Size," JOB, 1987, v60(4), 577-590.)

Kandel, Shmuel. (Huberman, Gur and Shmuel Kandel. "Mean-Variance Spanning," JOF, 1987, v42(4), 873-888.)

Kandel, Shmuel. (Huberman, Gur and Shmuel Kandel. "Market Efficiency And Value Line's Record," JOB, 1990, v63(2), 187-216.)

Kane, Alex and Alan J. Marcus. "Conversion Factor Risk And Hedging In The Treasury-Bond Futures Market," JFM, 1984, v4(1), 55-64.

Kane, Alex and Alan J. Marcus. "The Quality Option In The Treasury Bond Futures Market: An Empirical Assessment," JFM, 1986, v6(2), 231-248.

Kane, Alex and Alan J. Marcus. "Valuation And Optimal Exercise Of The Wild Card Option In The Treasury Bond Futures Market," JOF, 1986, v41(1), 195-208.

Kane, Alex and Leonard Rosenthal. "International Interest Rates And Inflationary Expectations," JIMF, 1982, v1(1), 97-110.

Kane, Alex and Alan J. Marcus. "The Delivery Option On Forward Contracts: A Note," JFQA, 1988, v23(3), 337-342.

Kane, Alex and Stephen G. Marks. "The Delivery Of Market Timing Services: Newsletters Versus Market Timing Funds," JFI, 1990, v1(2), 150-166.

Kane, Alex and Stephen Gary Marks. "The Rocking Horse Analyst," JPM, 1986-87, v13(3), 32-37.

Kane, Alex and Stephen Gary Marks. "Performance Evaluation Of Market Timers: Theory And Evidence," JFQA, 1988, v23(4), 425-436.

Kane, Alex, Alan J. Marcus and Robert L. McDonald. "How Big Is The Tax Advantage To Debt?," JOF, 1984, v39(3), 841-853.

Kane, Alex, Alan J. Marcus and Robert L. McDonald. "Debt Policy And The Rate Of Return Premium To Leverage," JFQA, 1985, v20(4), 479-500.

Kane, Alex, Leonard Rosenthal and Greta Ljung. "Tests Of The Fisher Hypothesis With International Data: Theory And Evidence," JOF, 1983, v38(2), 539-551,

Kane, Alex, Young Ki Lee and Alan Marcus. "Earnings And Dividend Announcements: Is There A Corroboration Effect?," JOF, 1984, v39(4), 1091-1099.

Kane, Alex. "Coins: Anatomy Of A Fad Asset," JPM, 1983-84, v10(2), 44-51.

Kane, Alex. "Skewness Preference And Portfolio Choice," JFQA, 1982, v17(1), 15-25.

Kane, Alex. (Bodie, Zvi, Alex Kane and Robert McDonald. "Why Haven't Nominal Rates Declined?," FAJ, 1984, v40(2), 16-19,22-27.)

Kane, E. "No Room For Weak Links In The Chain Of Deposit Insurance Reform," JFSR, 1987, v1(1),77-111.

Kane, Edward J. and Alvin K. Klevorick. "Absence Of Money Illusion: A 'Sine Qua Non' For Neutral Money?," JOF, 1967, v22(3),419-423.

Kane, Edward J. and Stephen A. Buser. "Portfolio Diversification At Commercial Banks," JOF, 1979, v34(1), 19-34.

Kane, Edward J. "A Comparison Of Stabilization Policies: 1966-67 And 1969-70" Comment," JMCB, 1973, v5(1), 39-42.

Kane, Edward J. "Accelerating Inflation, Technological Innovation, And The Decreasing Effectiveness Of Banking Regulation," JOF, 1981, v36(2), 355-367.

Kane, Edward J. "Changing Incentives Facing Financial-Services Regulators," JFSR, 1989, v2(3), 265-274.

Kane, Edward J. "Costs And Benefits Of The Proposed Tax Credit On Residential Mortgage Income," JBR, 1975-76, v6(2), 88-99.

Kane, Edward J. "Getting Along Without Regulation Q: Testing The Standard View Of Deposit-Rate Competition During The 'Wild-Card Experience'," JPM, 1978, v33(3), 921-932.

Kane, Edward J. "Good Intentions And Unintended Evil: The Case Against Selective Credit Allocation," JMCB, 1977, v9(1), 55-69.

Kane, Edward J. "Market Incompleteness And Divergences Between Forward And Future Interest Rates," JOF, 1980, v35(2), 221-234.

Kane, Edward J. "Panel Discussion On The Teaching Of Money And Banking," JFQA, 1976, v11(4), 613-616.

Kane, Edward J. "Principal-Agent Problems In S&L Salvage," JOF, 1990, v45(3), 755-764.

Kane, Edward J. "Regulatory Structure In Futures Markets: Jurisdictional Competition Between The SEC, The CFTC, And Other Agencies," JFM, 1984, v4(3), 367-384.

Kane, Edward J. "Short-Changing The Small Saver: Federal Government Discrimination Against The Small Saver During The Vietnam War," JMCB, 1970, v2(4), 513-522.

Kane, Edward J. "Technological And Regulatory Forces In The Developing Fusion Of Financial-Services Competition," JOF, 1984, v39(3), 759-772.

Kane, Edward J. "The Central Bank As Big Brother: A Comment," JMCB, 1973, v5(4), 979-981.

Kane, Edward J. "The Re-Politicization Of The Fed," JFQA, 1974, v9(5), 743-752.

Kane, Edward J. "The Term Structure Of Interest Rates: An Attempt To Reconcile Teaching with Practice," JOF, 1970, v25(2), 361-374.

Kane, Edward J. "Wealth-Based Engels Curves For Financial And Real Estate Assets," RIF, 1986, v6, 233-246.

Kane, Edward J. (Buser, Stephen A., Andrew H. Chen And Edward J. Kane. "Federal Deposit Insurance, Regulatory Policy, And Optimal Bank Capital," JOF, 1981, v36(1), 51-60.)

Kane, Edward J. (Goldfeld, Stephen M. and Edward J. Kane. "The Determinants Of Member Bank Borrowing: A Reply," JOF, 1968, v23(5), 838-847.)

Kane, Edward J. (Goldfeld, Stephen M. and Edward J. Kane. "The Determinants Of Member-Bank Borrowing: An Econometric Study," JOF, 1966, v21(3), 499-514.)

Kane, Edward J. (Unal, Haluk and Edward J. Kane. "Two Approaches To Assessing The Interest-Rate Sensitivity Of Deposit-Institutions' Equity Returns," RIF, 1988, v7, 113-138.)

Kane, Edward J. (Walker, David A., Richard C. Aspinwall, Stuart I. Greenbaum, Edward J. Kane and Perry D. Quick. "Panel Discussion On Federal Reserve Membership Issues," FR, 1979, v14(2), 58-74.)

Kane, Edward J. and Haluk Unal. "Change In Market Assessments Of Deposit-Institution Riskiness," JFSR, 1988, v12(2), 207-230.

Kane, Edward J. and Haluk Unal. "Modeling Structural And Temporal Variation In The Market's Valuation Of Banking Firms," JOF, 1990, v45(1), 113-136.

Kang, Han Bin and Alan K. Reichert. "An Evaluation Of Alternative Estimation Techniques And Functional Forms In Developing Statistical Appraisal Models," JRER, 1987, v2(1), 1-29.

Kang, Han Bin and Mona J. Gardner. "Selling Price And Marketing Time In The Residential Real Estae Market," JRER, 1989, v4(1), 21-35.

Kang, Han Bin. (Doherty, Neil A. and Han Bin Kang. "Interest Rates And Insurance Price Cycles," JBF, 1988, v12(2), 199-214.)

Kang, Han Bin. (Gardner, Mona J., Han Bin Kang and Dixie L. Mills. "Consumer Profiles And Acceptance Of ARM Features: An Application Of Logit Regression," JRER, 1987, v2(2), 63-74.)

Kang, Heejoon. (Fratianni, Michele, Hyung-Doh Hur and Heejoon Kang. "Random Walk And Monetary Causality In Five Exchange Markets," JIMF, 1987, v6(4), 505-514.)

Kania, John J. (McKean, John R. and John J. Kania. "An Industry Approach To Owner-Manager Control And Profit Performance," JOB, 1978, v51(2), 327-342.)

Kannan, Srinivasan. (Fraser, Donald R. and Srinivasan Kannan. "Deregulation And Risk: Evidence From Earnings Forecasts And Stock Prices," FM, 1990, v19(4), 68-76.)

Kannan, Srinivasan. (Fraser, Donald R. and Srinivasan Kannan. "The Risk Implications Of Forecast Errors Of Bank Earnings, 1976-1986," JFR, 1989, v12(3), 261-268.)

Kanniainen, Vesa and Vesa Kurikka. "On The Effects Of Inflation In The Stock Market: Empirical Evidence With Finnish Data 1968-1981," JBFA, 1984, v11(2), 139-150.

Kanniainen, Vesa. "Unanticipated Inflation, Taxation, And Common Stocks," JBFA, 1982, v8(4), 459-470.

Kanter, Herschel, Arnold Moore and Neil Singer. "The Allocation Of Computer Time By University Computer Centers," JOB, 1968, v41(3), 375-384.

Kantor, Michael. "Market Sensitivities," FAJ, 1971, v27(1), 64-68.

Kao, Chihwa and Chunchi Wu. "Sinking Funds And The Agency Costs Of Corporate Debt," FR, 1990, v25(1), 95-114.

Kao, Duen-Li. (Frydman, Halina, Edward I. Altman and Duen-Li Kao. "Introducing Recursive Partitioning For Financial Classification: The Case Of Financial Distress," JOF, 1985, v40(1), 269-291.)

Kao, Duen-Li. (Kallberg, Jarl G. and Duen-Li Kao. "Statistical Models In Credit Management," AWCM, 1990, v1(1), 147-176.)

Kao, G. Wenchi. (Ma, Christopher K. and G. Wenchi Kao. "On Exchange Rate Changes And Stock Price Reactions," JBFA, 1990, v17(3), 441-450.)

Kaplan, Donald M. and B. G. Hartzog, Jr. "Residential Mortgage Markets: Current Developments And Future Prospects," AREUEA, 1977, v5(3), 302-312.

Kaplan, Gilbert E. "A Tenth Anniversary," JPM, 1984-85, v11(1), 3.

Kaplan, Howard M. "Farmland As A Portfolio Investment," JPM, 1984-85, v11(2), 73-78.

Kaplan, Mortimer. "Yields On Recently Issued Corporate Bonds: A New Index," JOF, 1962, v17(1), 81-109.

Kaplan, R. and R. W. Roll. "Accounting Changes And Stock Prices," FAJ, 1973, v29(1), 48-53.

Kaplan, Robert S. and Roman L. Weil. "Risk And The Value Line Contest," FAJ, 1973, v29(4), 56-61.

Kaplan, Robert S. and Gabriel Urwitz. "Statistical Models Of Bond Ratings: A Methodological Inquiry," JOB, 1979, v52(2), 231-262.

Kaplan, Robert S. and Richard Roll. "Investor Evaluation Of Accounting Information: Some Empirical Evidence," JOB, 1972, v45(2), 225-257.

Kaplan, Seymour. "Computer Algorithms For Finding Exact Rates Of Return," JOB, 1967, v40(4), 389-392.

Kaplan, Steven N. and David Reishus. "Outside Directorships And Corporate Performance," JFEC, 1990, v27(2), 389-410.

Kaplan, Steven N. "Campeau's Acquisition Of Federated: Value Destroyed Or Value Added," JFEC, 1989, v25(2), 191-212.

Kaplan, Steven N. and Jeremy C. Stein. "How Risky Is The Debt Of Highly Leveraged Transactions?," JFEC, 1990, v27(1), 215-246.

Kaplan, Steven. "Management Buyouts: Evidence On Taxes As A Source Of Value," JOF, 1989, v44(3), 611-632.

Kaplan, Steven. "The Effects Of Management Buyouts On Operating Performance And Value," JFEC, 1989, v24(2), 217-254.

Kaplanis, Costas P. "Options, Taxes, And Ex-Dividend Day Behavior," JOF, 1986, v41(2), 411-424.

Kaplanis, Evi C. "Stability And Forecasting Of The Comovement Measures Of International Stock Market Returns," JIMF, 1988, v7(1), 63-76.

Kapplin, Steven D. (Dale-Johnson, David, M. Chapman Findlay, Arthur L. Schwartz, Jr. and Stephen D. Kapplin. "Valuation And Efficiency In The Market For Creatively Financed Houses," AREUEA, 1985, v13(4), 388-403.)

Kapplin, Steven D. and Arthur L. Schwartz, Jr. "Public Real Estate Limited Partnership Returns: A Preliminary Comparison With Other Investments," AREUEA, 1988, v16(1), 63-68.

Kapplin, Steven D. and Arthur L. Schwartz, Jr. "An Anlaysis Of Recent Rates Of Return And Of The Secondary Market For Public Real Estate Limited Partnerships," JRER, 1986, v1(1), 33-44.

Karady, Gyorgy G. "The Effect Of Temporal Risk Aversion On Liquidity Preference," JFEC, 1982, v10(4), 467-483.

Karafiath, Imre and John Glascock. "Intra-Industry Effects Of A Regulatory Shift: Capital Market Evidence From Penn Square," FR, 1989, v24(1), 123-134.

Karafiath, Imre. "A Stochastic Model Of The Competitive Banking Firm With Lagged And Contemporaneous Reserve Accounting," JMCB, 1985, v17(2), 253-257.

Karafiath, Imre. "Using Dummy Variables In The Event Methodology," FR, 1988, v23(3), 351-358.

Karafiath, Imre. "Will A Risk-Averse Competitive Banking Firm Prefer Contemporaneous Reserve Accounting?," FR, 1985, v20(1), 111-115.

Karafiath, Imre. (Chandy, P. R. and Imre Karafiath. "The Effect Of The WPPSS Crisis On Utility Common Stock Returns," JBFA, 1989, v16(4), 531-542.)

Karamouzis, Nicholas and Raymond E. Lombra. "Forecasts And U.S. Monetary Policy, 1974-78: The Role Of Openness," JMCB, 1988, v20(3), Part 1, 402-408.

Karamouzis, Nicholas. "An Evaluation Of M1 Forecasting Errors By The Federal Reserve Staff In The 1970s," JMCB, 1985, v17(4), Part 1, 512-516.

Karan, Vijay. (Furtado, Eugene P. H. and Vijay Karan. "Causes, Consequences, And Shareholder Wealth Effects Of Management Turnover: A Review Of The Empirical Evidence," FM, 1990, v19(2), 60-75.)

Karber, James W. "Regulatory Philosophy - A Regulator Speaks," FAJ, 1965, v21(1), 49-52.

Kare, D. D. (Herbst, A. F., D. D. Kare and S. C. Caples. "Hedging Effectiveness And Minimum Risk Hedge Ratios In The Presence Of Autocorrelation: Foreign Currency Futures," JFM, 1989, v9(3), 185-198.)

Kareken, John H. and Neil Wallace. "The Monetary Instrument Variable Choice: How Important?: A Comment," JMCB, 1972, v4(3), 723-729.

Kareken, John H. "Federal Bank Regulatory Policy: A Description And Some Observations," JOB, 1986, v59(1), 3-48.

Kareken, John H. "On The Relative Merits Of Reserve-Ratio Changes And Open-Market Operations," JOF, 1961, v16(1), 65-72.

Kareken, John H. "Some Observations On The Radcliffe Report," JOF, 1960, v15(4), 481-503.

Kareken, John H. "The Emergence And Regulation Of Contingent Commitment Banking," JBF, 1987, v11(3), 359-378.

Kareken, John H. "The Mix Of Monetary And Fiscal Policies," JOF, 1967, v22(2), 241-246.

Kareken, John H. "The Optimum Monetary Instrument Variable: A Comment," JMCB, 1970, v2(3), 385-390.

Kareken, John H. and Neil Wallace. "Deposit Insurance And Bank Regulation: A Partial-Equilibrium Exposition," JOB, 1978, v51(3), 413-438.

Karels, Gordon V. (DeFusco, Richard A., Gordon V. Karels and Thomas S. Zorn. "Agency Theory: An Application To Grading Group Projects," JFED, 1989, v18, 43-44.)

Karels, Gordon V. (Prakash, Arun J., Krishnan Dandapani and Gordon V. Karels. "Simple Resource Allocation Rules," JBFA, 1988, v15(3), 447-452.)

Karels, Gordon V. and Arun J. Prakash. "Multivariate Normality And Forecasting Of Business Bankruptcy," JBFA, 1987, v14(4), 573-594.

Karels, Gordon V., Arun J. Prakash and Emmanuel Roussakis. "The Relationship Between Bank Capital Adequacy And Market Measures Of Risk," JBFA, 1989, v16(5), 663-674.

Karfakis, Costas J. and Demetrios M. Moschos. "Interest Rate Linkages Within The European Monetary System: A Time Series Analysis," JMCB, 1990, v22(3), 388-394.

Karim, R. A. A. (Gambling, T. E. and R. A. A. Karim. "Islam And 'Social Accounting'," JBFA, 1986, v13(1), 39-50.)

Karim, Rifaat Ahmed Abdel and Amal El-Tigani Ali. "Determinants Of The Financial Strategy Of Islamic Banks," JBFA, 1989, v16(2), 193-212.

Karna, Adi S. and Duane B. Graddy. "Bank Holding Company Leverage And The Return On Stockholders' Equity," JBR, 1982-83, v13(1), 42-48.

Karna, Adi S. "Bank Holding Company Profitability: Nonbanking Subsidiaries And Financial Leverage," JBR, 1979-80, v10(1), 28-35.

Karna, Adi S. "The Cost Of Private Versus Public Debt Issues," FM, 1972, v1(2), 65-67.

Karna, Adi S. (Graddy, Duane B. and Adi S. Karna. "Net Interest Margin Sensitivity Among Banks Of Different Sizes," JBR, 1983-84, v14(4), 283-290.)

Karna, Adi S. (Graddy, Duane B., Ghassem Homaifar and Adi S. Karna. "Double Leverage As A Source Of Systematic Risk In Bank Holding Company Stocks," JBR, 1984-85, v15(2), 115-122.)

Karni, Edi and Itzhak Zilcha. "Risk Aversion In The Theory Of Life Insurance: The Fisherian Model," JRI, 1986, v53(4), 606-620.

Karni, Edi. "The Value Of Time And The Demand For Money," JMCB, 1974, v6(1), 45-64.

Karo, Margherita. "Cosmetics/Toiletries Industry," FAJ, 1968, v24(5), 34-44.

Karo, Margherita. "The Cosmetics/Toiletries Industry," FAJ, 1967, v23(3), 27-32.

Karo, Margherita. "The Jewelry Business," FAJ, 1968, v24(2), 49-56,88.

Karpoff, Jonathan M. "A Theory Of Trading Volume," JOF, 1986, v41(5), 1060-1088.

Karpoff, Jonathan M. "Costly Short Sales And The Correlation Of Returns With Volume," JFR, 1988, v11(3), 173-188.

Karpoff, Jonathan M. "The Relation Between Price Changes And Trading Volume, A Survey," JFQA, 1987, v22(1), 109-126.

Karpoff, Jonathan M. and Edward M. Rice. "Organizational Form, Share Transferability, And Firm Performance: Evidence From The ANCSA Corporations," JFEC, 1989, v24(1), 69-106.

Karpoff, Jonathan M. and Paul H. Malatesta. "The Wealth Effects Of Second-Generation State Takeover Legislation," JFEC, 1989, v25(2), 291-322.

Karpoff, Jonathan M. and Ralph A. Walkling. "Short-Term Trading Around Ex-Dividend Days: Additional Evidence," JFEC, 1988, v21(2), 291-298.

Karson, Marvin J. and Terrence F. Martell. "On The Interpretation Of Individual Variables In Multiple Discriminant Analysis," JFQA, 1980, v15(1), 211-217.

Karson, Marvin J. (Rudolph, Patricia M., Leonard V. Zumpano and Marvin J. Karson. "Mortgage Markets And Inter-Regional Differences In Convention Mortgage Terms," AREUEA, 1982, v10(1), 94-110.)

Kaserman, David L. "Evidence On The Decline Of FHA," JMCB, 1978, v10(2), 194-205.

Kaserman, David L. (Blair, Roger D., David L. Kaserman and Patricia L. Pacey. "A Note On Purchased Power Adjustment Clauses," JOB, 1985, v58(4), 409-418.)

Kaserman, David L. (Blair, Roger D. and David L. Kaserman. "Tying Arrangements And Uncertainty," RIF, 1983, v4, (Supp), 1-14.)

Kaserman, David L. and John W. Mayo. "Advertising And The Residential Demand For Electricity," JOB, 1985, v58(4), 399-408.

Kaserman, David L. and John W. Mayo. "Regulation, Advertising, And Economic Welfare," JOB, 1991, v64(2), 255-268.

Kashyap, Anil. (Hoshi, Takeo, Anil Kashyap and David Scharfstein. "The Role Of Banks In Reducing The Costs Of Financial Distress In Japan," JFEC, 1990, v27(1), 67-88.)

Kasibhatla, Krishnamoorti. A Monetary Model Of The Brazilian Balance Of Payments," IJOF, 1989, v1(2), 52-59.

Kassam, Rehman P. (Barnhill, Theodore M., William W. Hardgrave and Rehman P. Kassam. "An Empirical Study Of T-Bond Futures Contract Price Change Patterns Around U.S. Treasury Quarterly Refundings," RFM, 1985, v4(1), 106-131.)

Kassaye, W. Wossen. "Some Sources Of Personal Prejudice In Student-Instructor Evaluations," JFED, 1984, v13, 33-39.

Kasserman, David L. (Jackson, Jerry R. and David L. Kasserman. "Default Risk On Home Mortgage Loans: A Test Of Competing Hypotheses," JRI, 1980, v47(4), 678-690.)

Kassouf, Sheen T. "Measuring The Measurers: The Economist As Performer," JPM, 1974-75, v1(4), 20-22.

Kassouf, Sheen T. "Warrant Price Behavior, 1945-1964," FAJ, 1968, v24(1), 123-126.

Kassouf, Sheen T. (Lewis, Alan L., Sheen T. Kassouf, R. Dennis Brehm and Jack Johnston. "The Ibbotson-Sinquefield Simulation Made Easy," JOB, 1980, v53(2), 205-214.)

Kato, Kiyoshi and James S. Schallheim. "Seasonal And Size Anomalies In The Japanese Stock Market," JFQA, 1985, v20(2), 243-260.

Kato, Kiyoshi. "Being A Winner In The Tokyo Stock Market," JPM, 1990, v16(4), 52-56.

Katsimbris, George M. "The Relationship Between The Inflation Rate, Its Variability, And Output Growth Variability: Disaggregated International Evidence," JMCB, 1985, v17(2), 179-188.

Katti, Shriniwas K. (Dickerson, O. D., Shriniwas K. Katti and Alfred E. Hofflander. "Loss Distributions In Non-Life Insurance," JRI, 1961, v28(3), 45-54.)

Katz, Larry. (Rosen, Kenneth T. and Larry Katz. "Money Market Mutual Funds: An Experiment In Ad Hoc Deregulation: A Note," JOF, 1983, v38(3),1011-1017.)

Katz, Lawrence F. "Some Recent Developments In Labor Economics And Their Implications For Macroeconomics," JMCB, 1988, v20(3), Part 2, 507-522.

Katz, Lawrence F. (Rosen, Kenneth T. and Lawrence F. Katz. "Growth Management And Land Use Controls: The San Francisco Bay Area Experience," AREUEA, 1981, v9(4), 321-344.)

Katz, Michael L. "Firm-Specific Differentiation And Competition Among Multiproduct Firms," JOB, 1984, v57(1), Part 2, S149-S166.

Katz, Richard C. "Time Quartile Analysis: A Forecasting Technique," JPM, 1976-77, v3(2), 65-70.

Katz, Steven, Steven Lilien and Bert Nelson. "Stock Market Behavior Around Bankruptcy Model Distress And Recovery Predictions," FAJ, 1985, v41(1), 70-74.

Katz, Steven. "The Price Adjustment Process Of Bonds To Rating Reclassifications: A Test Of Bond Market Efficiency," JOF, 1974, v29(2), 551-559.

Katz, Steven. (Bar-Lev, Dan and Steven Katz. "Fuel Procurement In The Electric Utility Industry," JOF, 1976, v31(3), 933-947.)

Katz, Steven. (Grier, Paul and Steven Katz. "The Differential Effects Of Bond Rating Changes Among Industrial And Public Utility Bonds By Maturity," JOB, 1976, v49(2), 226-239.)

Katzen, M. (Cooke, H. J. and M. Katzen. "The Public Debt Limit," JOF, 1954, v9(3), 298-303.)

Katzman, Martin T. "Pollution Liability Insurance And Catastrophic Environmental Risk," JRI, 1988, v55(1), 75-100.

Kau, James B. and Donald Keenan. "The Theory Of Housing And Interest Rates," JFQA, 1980, v15(4),833-847.

Kau, James B. (Epperson, James F., James B. Kau, Donald C. Keenan and Walter J. Muller, III. "Pricing Default Risk In Mortgages," AREUEA, 1985, v13(3), 261-272.)

Kau, James B. and Donald Keenan. "Taxes, Points And Rationality In The Mortgage Market," AREUEA, 1987, v15(3), 168-184.

Kau, James B., Donald C. Keenan, Walter J. Muller, III and James F. Epperson. "The Valuation And Securitization Of Commercial And Multifamily Mortgages," JBF, 1987, v11(3), 525-546.

Kau, James B., Donald C. Keenan, Walter J. Muller, III and James P. Epperson. "Rational Pricing Of Adjustable Rate Mortgages," AREUEA, 1985, v13(2), 117-128.

Kau, James B., Donald C. Keenan, Walter J. Muller, III and James F. Epperson. "Pricing Commercial Mortgages And Their Mortgage-Backed Securities," JREFEC, 1990, v3(4), 333-356.

Kaufman, Daniel J., Jr. "Factors Affecting The Magnitude Of Premiums Paid To Target-Firm Shareholders In Corporate Acquisitions," FR, 1988, v23(4), 465-482.

Kaufman, Daniel. (Mohan, Nancy, M. Fall Ainina, Daniel Kaufman and Bernard J. Winger. "Acquisition/Divestiture Valuation Practices In Major U.S. Firms," FPE, 1991, v1(1), 73-82.)

Kaufman, G. G. (Bierwag, G. O., G. G. Kaufman, R. Schweitzer and A. Toevs. "The Art Of Risk Management In Bond Portfolios," JPM, 1980-81, v7(3),27-36.)

Kaufman, George C. (Bierwag, Gerald O., Charles J. Corrado and George C. Kaufman. "Computing Durations For Bond Portfolios," JPM, 1990, v17(1), 51-55.)

Kaufman, George G. and Cynthia M. Latta. "The Demand For Money: Preliminary Evidence From Industrial Countries," JFQA, 1966, v1(3), 75-89.

Kaufman, George G. "A Proposed Experiment," FAJ, 1968, v24(6), 90-93.

Kaufman, George G. "A Proposal For Eliminating Interest-Rate Ceilings On Thrift Institutions: A Comment," JMCB, 1972, v4(3), 735-743.

Kaufman, George G. "Bank Employment: A Cross-Section Analysis Of The World's Largest Banks: A Comment," JMCB, 1970, v2(1), 129-131.

Kaufman, George G. "Deposit Variability And Bank Size," JFQA, 1972, v7(5), 2087-2096.

Kaufman, George G. "Duration, Planning Period And Tests Of The Capital Asset Pricing Model," JFR, 1980, v3(1), 1-9.

Kaufman, George G. "Federal Bank Regulatory Policy: Comment On Kareken," JOB, 1986, v59(1), 69-78.

Kaufman, George G. "How Not To Control The Money Supply," FAJ, 1972, v28(5), 20-23,26,57.

Kaufman, George G. "Measuring Risk And Return For Bonds: A New Approach," JBR, 1978-79, v9(2), 82-90.

Kaufman, George G. "Municipal Bond Underwriting: Market Structure," JBR, 1981-82, v12(1), 24-31.

Kaufman, George G. "Rankings Of Finance Departments By Faculty Representation On Editorial Boards Of Professional Journals: A Note," JOF, 1984, v39(4), 1189-1197.

Kaufman, George G. "Search Theory And The Prohibition Against Commercial Bank Underwriting Of Municipal Revenue Bonds," JFR, 1982, v5(3), 201-205.

Kaufman, George G. "Securities Activities Of Commercial Banks: Recent Changes In The Economic And Legal Environments," JFSR, 1988, v1(2), 183-199.

Kaufman, George G. "Teaching Of The Basic Money And Financial Institutions Course," JFQA, 1976, v11(4), 607-612.

Kaufman, George G. "The Academic Preparation Of Economists Employed By Commercial And Investment Banks," JMCB, 1984, v16(3), 351-359.

Kaufman, George G. "The Case For Mortgage Rate Insurance," JMCB, 1975, v7(4), 515-519.

Kaufman, George G. "The Fed's Post-October 1979 Technical Operating Procedures Under Lagged Reserve Requirements," FR, 1982, v17(4), 279-294.

Kaufman, George G. "The Strange Journey Of Monetary Indicators," JFQA, 1972, v7(2), 1625-1639.

Kaufman, George G. "The Tax Treatment Of Municipal Discount Bonds: Rebuttal And Expansion," FM, 1982, v11(4), 48-51.

Kaufman, George G. "The Thrift Institution Problem Further Reconsidered: Reply," JBR, 1974-75, v5(1), 52-54.

Kaufman, George G. "The Thrift Institution Problem Reconsidered," JBR, 1972-73, v3(1), 26-33.

Kaufman, George G. "The Thrift Institution Problem Reconsidered: A Historical Oversight Corrected," JBR, 1976-77, v7(2), 179-180.

Kaufman, George G. "'Is The Federal Reserve System Really Necessary?': Comment," JOF, 1965, v20(3), 485-485.

Kaufman, George G. (Albaum, Gerald and George G. Kaufman. "The Mortgage Acquisition Process: A Comparison Of VRM And FRM Borrowers," AREUEA, 1979, v7(2), 253-264.)

Kaufman, George G. (Bierwag, G. O., George G. Kaufman and Cynthia M. Latta. "Bond Portfolio Immunization: Tests Of Maturity, One-And Two-Factor Duration Matching Strategies," FR, 1987, v22(2), 203-220.)

Kaufman, George G. (Bierwag, G. O. and George G. Kaufman. "Duration Gap For Financial Institutions," FAJ, 1985, v41(2), 68-71.)

Kaufman, George G. (Bierwag, G. O. and George G. Kaufman. "Coping With The Risk Of Interest-Rate Fluctuations: A Note," JOB, 1977, v50(3), 364-370.)

Kaufman, George G. (Bierwag, G. O., George G. Kaufman and Aldan Toevs. "Bond Portfolio Immunization And Stochastic Process Risk," JBR, 1982-83, v13(4),282-291.)

Kaufman, George G. (Bierwag, G. O., George G. Kaufman and Cynthia M. Latta. "Duration Models: A Taxonomy," JPM, 1988-89, v15(1), 50-54.)

Kaufman, George G. (Bierwag, G. O., George G. Kaufman, Cynthia M. Latta and Gordon S. Roberts. "The Usefulness Of Duration: Response To Critics" 1986-87, v13(2), 48-52.)

Kaufman, George G. (Bierwag, G. O., George G. Kaufman and Alden Toevs. "Duration: Its Development And Uses In Bond Portfolio Management," FAJ, 1983, v39(4), 15-35.)

Kaufman, George G. (Bierwag, G. O. and George G. Kaufman. "Durations Of Non-Default-Free Securities," FAJ, 1988, v44(4), 39-46.)

Kaufman, George G. (Bierwag, G. O., George G. Kaufman and Alden

Keen, Howard, Jr. "The Impact Of A Dividend Cut Announcement On Bank Share Prices," JBR, 1982-83, v13(4), 274-281.

Keenan, Donald C. (Epperson, James F., James B. Kau, Donald C. Keenan and Walter J. Muller, III. "Pricing Default Risk In Mortgages," AREUEA, 1985, v13(3), 261-272.)

Keenan, Donald C. (Kau, James B., Donald C. Keenan, Walter J. Muller, III and James F. Epperson. "The Valuation And Securitization Of Commercial And Multifamily Mortgages," JBF, 1987, v11(3), 525-546.)

Keenan, Donald C. (Kau, James B., Donald C. Keenan, Walter J. Muller, III and James P. Epperson. "Rational Pricing Of Adjustable Rate Mortgages," AREUEA, 1985, v13(2), 117-128.)

Keenan, Donald C. (Kau, James B., Donald C. Keenan, Walter J. Muller, III and James F. Epperson. "Pricing Commercial Mortgages And Their Mortgage-Backed Securities," JREFEC, 1990, v3(4), 333-356.)

Keenan, Donald. (Kau, James B. and Donald Keenan. "The Theory Of Housing And Interest Rates," JFQA, 1980, v15(4), 833-847.)

Keenan, Donald. (Kau, James B. and Donald Keenan. "Taxes, Points And Rationality In The Mortgage Market," AREUEA, 1987, v15(3), 168-184.)

Keenan, Michael and Rita M. Maldonado. "The Redundancy Of Earnings Leverage In A Cost Of Capital Decision Framework," JBFA, 1976, v3(2), 43-56.

Keenan, Michael. "Models Of Equity Valuation: The Great Serm Bubble," JOF, 1970, v25(2), 243-273.

Keenan, Michael. (Goldberg, Lawrence G., Gerald A. Hanweck, Michael Keenan and Allan Young. "Economies Of Scale And Scope In The Securities Industry," JBF, 1991, v15(1), 91-107.)

Keeton, Robert E. "Beyond Current Reforms In Automobile Reparations," JRI, 1973, v40(1), 31-37.

Keeton, Robert E. and Jeffrey O'Connell. "Basic Protection - A New Plan Of Automobile Insurance," JRI, 1965, v32(4), 539-548.

Keezer, Dexter Merriam. "The Short-Run Outlook For Business Investment In New Plant And Equipment," JOB, 1955, v28(3), 165-168.

Keim, Donald B. and Robert F. Stambaugh. "A Further Investigation Of The Weekend Effect In Stock Returns," JOF, 1984, v39(3), 819-835.

Keim, Donald B. and Robert F. Stambaugh. "Predicting Returns In The Stock And Bond Markets," JFEC, 1986, v17(2), 357-390.

Keim, Donald B. "A New Look At The Effects Of Firm Size And E/P Ratio On Stock Returns," FAJ, 1990, v46(2), 56-67.

Keim, Donald B. "Dividend Yields, Size And The January Effect," JPM, 1985-86, v12(2), 54-60.

Keim, Donald B. "Dividend Yields And Stock Returns: Implications Of Abnormal January Returns," JFEC, 1985, v14(3), 473-489.

Keim, Donald B. "Size-Related Anomalies And Stock Return Seasonality: Further Empirical Evidence," JFEC, 1983, v12(1), 13-32.

Keim, Donald B. "The CAPM And Equity Return Regularities," FAJ, 1986, v42(3), 19-34.

Keim, Donald B. "The Daily Returns-Size Connection," JPM, 1986-87, v13(2), 41-47.

Keim, Donald B. "Trading Patterns, Bid-Ask Spreads, And Estimated Security Returns: The Case Of Common Stocks At Calendar Turning Points," JFEC, 1989, v25(1), 75-98.

Keim, Donald B. (Blume, Marshall E. and Donald B. Keim. "Lower-Grade Bonds: Their Risks And Returns," FAJ, 1987, v43(4), 26-33.)

Keim, Donald B. (Blume, Marshall E., Donald B. Keim and Sandeep A. Patel. "Returns And Volatility Of Low-Grade Bonds, 1977-1989," JOF, 1991, v46(1), 49-74.)

Keim, Donald B. (Brown, Philip, Donald Keim, Allan Kleidon and Terry Marsh. "Stock Return Seasonalities And The Tax-Loss Selling Hypothesis: Analysis Of The Arguments And Australian Evidence," JFEC, 1983, v12(1), 105-127.)

Keim, Donald B. (Jaffe, Jeffrey, Donald B. Keim and Randolph Westerfield. "Earnings Yields, Market Values, And Stock Returns," JOF, 1989, v44(1), 135-148.)

Keintz, Richard J. and Clyde P. Stickney. "Immunization Of Pension Funds And Sensitivity To Actuarial Assumptions," JRI, 1980, v47(2), 223-239.

Keir, Jack C. "A Second Look At Programmed Learning In The C.L.U. Diploma Program," JRI, 1966, v33(4), 631-638.

Keir, Jack C. "Cash Flow And Solvency Of Life Insurance Companies: Comment," JRI, 1966, v33(1), 139-144.

Keiser, Norman F. "The Development Of The Concept Of 'Automatic Stabilizers'," JOF, 1956, v11(4), 422-441.

Keith, E. Gordon. "The Future Of The Corporation Income Tax," JOF, 1956, v11(2), 195-204.

Kekish, Bohdan J. "Moody's Averages," FAJ, 1967, v23(3), 65-69.

Kekish, Bohdan J. (Gostomski, Adam and Bohdan J. Kekish. "A Criterion Of Business Activity," FAJ, 1965, v21(2), 37-41.)

Kekish, Bohdan J. (Gostomski, Adam and Bohdan J. Kekish. "Composite Indicators: A Rejoinder," FAJ, 1965, v21(6), 60.)

Kelenson, Milton. (Crary David, Gary Fromm and Milton Kelenson. "Financial And Nonfinancial Data For Detailed U.S. Industries," JMCB, 1980, v12(2), Part 2, 308-316.)

Keller, L. Robin. (Daniels, Richard L. and L. Robin Keller. "An Experimental Evaluation Of The Descriptive Validity Of Lottery-Dependent Utility Theory," JRU, 1990, v3(2), 115-134.)

Keller, Philip R. "Utility Stocks Vs. Bonds," FAJ, 1968, v24(3), 127-132.

Keller, Stuart B. "Reporting Timeliness In The Presence Of Subject To Audit Qualifications," JBFA, 1986, v13(1), 117-122.

Keller, Thomas F. and Russell J. Peterson. "Optimal Financial Structure, Cost Of Capital, And The Lease-Or-Buy Decision," JBFA, 1974, v1(3), 405-414.

Keller, Werner E. (Akemann, Charles A. and Werner E. Keller. "Relative Strength Does Persist!," JPM, 1977-78, v4(1), 38-45.)

Kelley, Michael. (Granito, Michael R. and Michael Kelley. "The Performance Of A Class Of Long-Term Currency Hedges," RDIBF, 1987, v1, 117-134.)

Kellison, Stephen G. "A Linear Programming Model Of Profitability, Capacity And Regulation In Insurance Management: Comment," JRI, 1969, v36(4), 637-639.

Kellner, S. and Frank Mathewson. "Entry, Size Distribution, Scale, And Scope Economies In The Life Insurance Industry," JOB, 1983, v56(1), 25-44.

Kellogg, Chester M. "Joint ARIA-IASA Program," JRI, 1962, v29(1), 69-74.

Kellogg, Chester M. "The Capacity Problem," JRI, 1949, v16, 5-13.

Kellow, Ahmed. "Decomposition Of Stock Returns," JBFA, 1990, v17(4), 481-496.

Kelly, Alex K. (Courchene, Thomas J. and Alex K. Kelly. "Money Supply And Money Demand: An Econoteric Analysis For Canada," JMCB, 1971, v3(2), Part 1, 219-244.)

Kelly, Ambrose B. "Confusion Thrice Confounded," JRI, 1963, v30(2), 286-288.

Kelly, Ambrose B. "Current Developments And Problems In Property Insurance," JRI, 1960, v27(1), 23-28.

Kelly, Francis H. M. "Illusions And The Poison Of Defeat," JPM, 1979-80, v6(1), 22-23.

Kelly, Francis H. M. "The Looming Impact Of Technological Drift," JPM, 1975-76, v2(2), 44-49.

Kelly, Gary Wayne. "Some Regulatory Determinants Of Bank Risk Behavior: Comment," JMCB, 1988, v20(2), 265-269.

Kelly, Marvin. (Vaughn, Richard, Frank Hochheimer and Marvin Kelly. "Identifying Seasonality In Futures Prices Using X-11," JFM, v1(1), 93-102.)

Kelly, Thomas M., Jr. "Arbitrage In Government Security Markets," RFM, 1986, v5(1), 44-52.

Kelly, William A., Jr. and James A. Miles. "Darby And Fisher: Resolution Of A Paradox," FR, 1984, v19(1), 103-110.

Kelly, William A., Jr. and Donald R. Chambers. "Inflation, Taxes, And Savings 'Incentives'," FR, 1984, v19(2), 222-231.

Kelly, William A., Jr. (Ezzell, John R. and William A. Kelly, Jr. "An APV Analysis Of Capital Budgeting Under Inflation," FM, 1984, v13(3), 49-54.)

Kelly, William A., Jr. and James A. Miles. "Capital Structure Theory And The Fisher Effect," FR, 1989, v24(1), 53-74.

Keim, Kathryn. (Howe, John S. and Kathryn Kelm. "The Stock Price Impacts Of Overseas Listings," FM, 1987, v16(3), 51-56.)

Kelne, Nicholas. "Commodity Option Exemptions," JFM, 1981, v1(Supp), 543-546.

Kelsey, R. Wilfred. "Visual Aids In Life Insurance Teaching," JRI, 1951, v18, 5-13.

Kelso, Charles M., Jr. (Arnott, Robert D., Charles M. Kelso, Jr., Stephan Kiscadden and Rosemary Macedo. "Forecasting Factor Returns: An Intriguing Possibility," JPM, 1989, v16(1), 28-35.)

Kemirguc-Kunt, Asli. (Dezhbakhsh, Hashem and Asli Demirguc-Kunt. "On The Presence Of Speculative Bubbles In Stock Prices," JFQA, 1990, v25(1), 101-112.)

Kemmerer, Donald L. "Recent Actions Of Federal Reserve Authorities," FAJ, 1950, v6(4), 7-10.

Kemna, A. G. Z. and A. C. F. Vorst. "A Pricing Method For Options Based On Average Asset Values," JBF, 1990, v14(1), 113-130.

Kemna, Angelien G. Z. and Ton C. F. Vorst. "A Futures Contract On An Index Of Existing Bonds: A Reasonable Alternative?," RFM, 1988, v7(Supp), 468-479.

Kemp, Kathleen A. "Party Realignments And The Growth Of Federal Economic Regulation,1861-1986," JFSR, 1989, v2(3), 213-226.

Kemp, Robert S. (Overstreet, George A., Lawrence C. Pettit and Robert S. Kemp. "A Professional Approach To Building An Undergraduate Finance Program: The McIntire Experience," JFED, 1986, v15, 42-52.)

Kemp, Robert S. (Trent, Robert H. and Robert S. Kemp. "The Writings Of Henry A. Latane: A Compilation And Analysis," JFR, 1984, v7(2), 161-174.)

Kemper, James S., Jr. "The Highway Safety Legislation: Its Implications For Insurance," JRI, 1968, v35(1), 67-74.

Kenadjian, N. D. "European Markets In 1961: A Challenge," FAJ, 1961, v17(1), 13-14.

Kenadjian, N. D. "The Dollar Gap," FAJ, 1961, v17(4), 19-20.

Kenadjian, Vahe H. "Constant Safety Versus Sound Profitability," FAJ, 1955, v11(4), 77-82.

Kenagy, H. G. "A Life Insurance Executive Looks At The Academic Program Of Education In Insurance," JRI, 1949, v16, 18-20.

Kendall, Coleman S. (Hertzel, Michael G., Coleman S. Kendall and Peter E. Kretzmer. "The Volatility Of Asset Returns During Trading And Nontrading Hours: Some Evidence From The Foreign Exchange Markets," JIMF, 1990, v9(3), 335-343.)

Kendall, Glen. (Carleton, Willard T., Glen Kendall And Sanjiv Tandon. "Application Of The Decomposition Principle To The Capital Budgeting Problem In A Decentralized Firm," JOF, 1974, v29(3), 815-827.)

Kenen, Peter B. "The Balance Of Payments And Policy Mix: Simulations Based On A U.S. Model," JOF, 1974, v29(2), 631-654.

Kenkel, James. (Williams, Alex O., William Beranek and James Kenkel. "Default Risk In Urban Mortgages: A Pittsburgh Prototype Analysis," AREUEA, 1974, v2(2), 101-116.)

Kennedy, Brian A. "How To Measure Fixed Income Performance Correctly: Comment," JPM, 1985-86, v12(2), 84-86.

Kennedy, Charles. "Fixed Assets And The Hyde Gearing Adjustment," JBFA, 1978, v5(4), 393-406.

Kennedy, Charles. "Holding Gains, Debt-Financing, Working Capital And Current Cost Accounting: Comment," JBFA, 1976, v3(3), 123-128.

Kennedy, Charles. "Inflation Accounting, Profits, Profitability, And Share Valuation," JBFA, 1976, v3(1), 137-146.

Kennedy, Kenneth F. and Robert I. Mehr. "A Case Study In Private V. Public Enterprise: The Manitoba Experience With Automobile Insurance," JRI, 1977, v44(4), 595-622.

Kennedy, Peter E. "Direct Wealth Effects In Macroeconomic Models: The Saving Vs. The Definitional Approach," JMCB, 1978, v10(1), 94-98.

Kennedy, Robert E. and Millie H. Wilson. "Investor Relations And Security Analysts," FAJ, 1980, v36(2), 63-69.

Kennedy, Robert E. Jr. "Profiting By Parkinson's Law (A Satire)," FAJ, 1961, v17(3), 43-47.

Kennedy, Robert E. (Sharma, J. L. and Robert E. Kennedy. "A Comparative Analysis Of Stock Price Behavior On The Bombay,

London, And New York Stock Exchanges," JPQA, 1977, v12(3), 391-413.)

Kennedy, Robert E., Jr. "An Approach To Pricing Growth Stocks," FAJ, 1957, v13(4), 31-34.

Kennedy, Robert E., Jr. "Growth Stocks: Opportunity Or Illusion," FAJ, 1960, v16(2), 27-31.

Kennedy, Robert E., Jr. "Growth Stocks: Chemical Products," FAJ, 1959, v15(1), 51-60.

Kennedy, Roger G. "The Risks Of More Give Than Take," JPM, 1975-76, v2(4), 15-18.

Kennedy, Roger G. "What Happened At The Ford Foundation?," JPM, 1974-75, v1(3), 52-58.

Kennedy, William F. and David F. Scott, Jr. "Some Observations On The Dividend Policies Of Large Commercial Banks," JBR, 1982-83, v13(4), 292-296.

Kennedy, William F. (Krueger, Thomas M. and William F. Kennedy. "An Examination Of The Super Bowl Stock Market Predictor," JOF, 1990, v45(2), 691-698.)

Kennedy, William F. (O'Brien, Thomas J. and William F. Kennedy. "Simultaneous Option And Stock Prices: Another Look at The Black-Scholes Model," FR, 1982, v17(4), 219-227.)

Kennelly, John W. (Brown, Philip and John W. Kennelly. "The Informational Content Of Quarterly Earnings: An Extension And Some Further Evidence," JOB, 1972, v45(3), 403-415.)

Kenney, Roger. "Critique Of American Agency System," JRI, 1958, v25(1), 42-49.

Kensicki, Peter R. "Consumer Valuation Of Life Insurance - A Capital Budgeting Approach," JRI, 1974, v41(4), 655-666.

Kensicki, Peter R. "Replacement Of Life Insurance: A Financial Approach," JRI, 1974, v41(2), 207-219.

Kensicki, Peter R. "Replacement Of Life Insurance: Reply," JRI, 1976, v43(1), 161-163.

Kensicki, Peter R. and David Richmond. "Consumerism And Automobile Insurance," JRI, 1973, v40(2), 209-220.

Kensinger, John W. (Chan, Su Han, John D. Martin and John W. Kensinger. "Corporate Research And Development Expenditures And Share Value," JFEC, 1990, v26(2), 255-276.)

Kensinger, John W. (Chen, Andrew H. and John W. Kensinger. "Innovations In Corporate Financing: Tax-Deductible Equity," FM, 1985, v14(4), 44-51.)

Kensinger, John W. (Chen, Andrew H. and John W. Kensinger. "Puttable Stock: A New Innovation In Equity Financing," FM, 1988, v17(1), 27-37.)

Kensinger, John W. (Chen, Andrew H. and John W. Kensinger. "Beyond The Tax Benefits Of ESOP Financing," JACF, 1988, v1(1), 67-75.)

Kensinger, John W. (Chen, Andrew H. and John W. Kensinger. "An Analysis Of Market-Index Certificates Of Deposit," JFSR, 1990, v4(2), 93-110.)

Kensinger, John W. and John D. Martin. "The Quiet Restructuring," JACF, 1988, v1(1), 16-25.

Kensinger, John W. and John D. Martin. "Project Finance: Raising Money The Old-Fashioned Way," JACF, 1988, v1(3), 69-81.

Kensinger, John W. and John D. Martin. "Project Financing For Research And Development," RIF, 1990, v8, 119-148.

Kent, Richard J. "An Analysis Of Countercyclical Policies Of The FHLBB," JOF, 1981, v36(1), 61-79.

Kent, Richard J. "Credit Rationing And The Home Mortgage Market," JMCB, 1980, v12(3), 488-501.

Kent, Richard J. "Dynamic Credit Rationing In The Home Mortgage Market," AREUEA, 1987, v15(4), 300-320.

Kent, Russell A. "The Outlook For The Bond Market," FAJ, 1960, v16(1), 64-67.

Kent, W. A. and J. Lewison. "Wall Street's Cultural Hangup," FAJ, 1971, v27(2), 33-35.

Kenyon, David E. (Jordan, James V., William E. Seale, Stephen J. Dinehart and David E. Kenyon. "The Intraday Variability Of Soybean Futures Prices: Information And Trading Effects," RFM, 1988, v7(1), 96-109.)

Kenyon, David E. (Jordan, James V., William E. Seale, Nancy C. McCabe and David E. Kenyon. "Transaction Data Tests Of The Black Model For Soybean Futures Options," JFM, 1987, v7(5), 535-554.)

Kenyon, David and John Clay. "Analysis Of Profit Margin Hedging Strategies For Hog Producers," JFM, 1987, v7(2), 183-202.

Kenyon, David, Kenneth Kling, Jim Jordan, William Seale and Nancy McCabe. "Factors Affecting Agricultural Futures Price Variance," JFM, 1987, v7(1), 73-92.

Keown, Arthur J. and John D. Martin. "An Integer Goal Programming Model For Capital Budgeting In Hospitals," FM, 1976, v5(3), 28-35.

Keown, Arthur J. and John D. Martin. "Capital Budgeting In The Public Sector: A Zero-One Goal Programming Approach," FM, 1978, v7(2), 21-27.

Keown, Arthur J. and John M. Pinkerton. "Merger Announcements And Insider Trading Activity: An Empirical Investigation," JOF, 1981, v36(4), 855-869.

Keown, Arthur J. (Benesh, Gary A., Arthur J. Keown and John M. Pinkerton. "An Examination Of Market Reaction To Substantial Shifts In Dividend Policy," JFR, 1984, v7(2), 131-140.)

Keown, Arthur J. (Chen, Son-Nan and Arthur J. Keown. "Risk Composition And Portfolio Diversification When Beta Is Nonstationary: A Note," JOF, 1981, v36(4), 941-947.)

Keown, Arthur J. (Chen, Son-Nan and Arthur J. Keown. "Group Effects And Beta Nonstationarity," JBFA, 1985, v12(4), 595-608.)

Keown, Arthur J. (Chen, Son-Nan and Arthur J. Keown. "An Examination Of The Relationship Between Pure Residual And Market Risk: A Note," JOF, 1981, v36(5), 1202-1209.)

Keown, Arthur J. (Martin, John D. and Arthur J. Keown. "Interest Rate Sensitivity And Portfolio Risk," JPQA, 1977, v12(2), 181-195.)

Keown, Arthur J. (Martin, John and Arthur Keown. "One-Bank Holding Company Formation And The 1970 Bank Holding Company Act Amendment: An Empirical Examination Allowing For Industry Group Effects," JBF, 1987, v11(2),213-222.)

Keown, Arthur J., Jr. (Martin, John D., Arthur J. Keown, Jr. and James L. Farrell, Jr. "Do Fund Objectives Affect Diversification Policies?," JPM, 1981-82, v8(2), 19-28.)

Keown, Arthur J., John M. Pinkerton and Son Nan Chen. "Portfolio Selection Based Upon P/E Ratios: Diversification, Risk Decomposition And Implications," JBFA, 1987, v14(2), 187-198.

Keown, Arthur. (Martin, John D. and Arthur Keown. "A Misleading Feature Of Beta For Risk Measurement," JPM, 1976-77, v3(4), 31-34.)

Keppler, A. Michael. "The Importance Of Dividend Yields In Country Selection," JPM, 1991, v17(2), 24-29.

Keran, Michael W. "Forecasting Stock Prices," JPM, 1974-75, v1(2), 52-60.

Kerby, Joe Kent. "Borrowing From The Behavioral Sciences," JOB, 1969, v42(2), 152-161.

Keren, Michael and David Levhari. "Optimal Span Of Control And The Shape Of Average Costs Of Large Private Or Public Bureaucracies," RIF, 1983, v4, (Supp), 85-112.

Kerley, James J. "Financial Problems Of The Airlines," FAJ, 1967, v23(2), 73-82.

Kerns, Michael W. "The Supply-Side Miracle," JPM, 1989, v15(4), 73-77.

Kerr, Charles Jr. "Locomotives - Today And Tomorrow," FAJ, 1946, v2(4), 44-54.

Kerr, Charles, Jr. "Economic Possibilities Of New Types Of Motive Power," FAJ, 1950, v6(3), 13-18.

Kerr, Charles, Jr. "The Diesel Locomotive," FAJ, 1953, v9(2), 43-46.

Kerr, Charles, Jr. (Brecht, W. A. and Charles Kerr Jr. "Electric Locomotives With Identical Basic Components," FAJ, 1948, v4(3), 33-44.)

Kerr, Dixon. "Teaching Entrepreneurship," JFED, 1973, v2, 35-36.

Kerr, Halbert S. "A Bibliography For FINANCIAL MANAGEMENT," FM, 1981, v10(2), Tenth Anniversary Edition, 123-134.

Kerr, Halbert S. "The Battle Of Insider Trading Vs. Market Efficiency," JPM, 1979-80, v6(4), 47-50.

Kerr, Halbert S. "The Evaluation Of Acquisition Candidates As A Comprehensive Financial Management Project," JFED, 1980, v9, 19-23.

Kerr, Halbert S. (Fuller, Russell J. and Halbert S. Kerr. "Estimating The Divisional Cost Of Capital: An Analysis Of The Pure-Play Technique," JOF, 1981, v36(5), 997-1008.)

Kerr, Halbert S. (Petry, Glenn H. and Halbert S. Kerr. "The Rising Incidence Of Coauthorship As A Function Of Institutional Reward Systems," JFED, 1981, v10, 78-84.)

Kerrigan, Thomas J. "Behavior Of The Short Interest Ratio," FAJ, 1974, v30(6), 45-49.

Kerrigan, Thomas J. "When Forecasting Earnings, It Pays To Watch Forecasts," JPM, 1983-84, v10(4),19-26.

Kessler, Daniel. "Discount Retailing And Leased Departments," FAJ, 1963, v19(3), 99-102.

Kester, George W. "A Group Project Approach To Teaching Finance Cases," JFED, 1989, v18, 38-42.

Kester, George W. "A Note On Solving The Balancing Problem," FM, 1987, v16(1), 52-54.

Kester, George W. "An Integrative Model For Presenting Common Stock Valuation," JFED, 1990, v19, 46-48.

Kester, George W. "An Overview Of Dow Jones News/Retrieval For Teaching Investments," JFED, 1987, v16, 19-25.

Kester, George W. "Market Timing With Small Versus Large-Firm Stocks: Potential Gains And Required Predictive Ability," FAJ, 1990, v46(5), 63-69.

Kester, W. Carl. "Capital And Ownership Structure: A Comparison Of United States And Japanese Manufacturing Corporations," FM, 1986, v15(1), 5-16.

Kester, W. Carl. "The Hidden Costs Of Japanese Success," JACF, 1991, v3(4), 90-97.

Ketcham, Stanley R. "Self-Employed Pension Bill," FAJ, 1953, v9(4), 69-70.

Ketcham, Stanley R. "The Strange Case Of Mrs. Berry," FAJ, 1950, v6(3), 61-63.

Ketcher, David. (Swidler, Steve and David Ketcher. "Economic Forecasts, Rationality, And The Processing Of New Information Over Time," JMCB, 1990, v22(1), 65-76.)

Ketchum, J. C. "Medical Society And Hospital-Sponsored Plans," JRI, 1948, v15, 52-56.

Ketchum, Marshall D. "A Seminar For Financial Analysts," FAJ, 1956, v12(1), 93-95.

Ketchum, Marshall D. "Forecasting Capital Formation In Residential Housing," JOB, 1954, v27(1), 32-40.

Ketchum, Marshall D. "Is Financial Analysis A Profession?," FAJ, 1967, v23(6), 33-37.

Ketz, J. Edward. "Are Constant Dollar Disclosures Informative?," FAJ, 1983, v39(2), 52-54.

Ketz, J. Edward. (Gombola, Michael J., Mark E. Haskins, J. Edward Ketz and David D. Williams. "Cash Flow In Bankruptcy Prediction," FM, 1987, v16(4),55-65.)

Ketz, J. Edward. (Gombola, Michael J. and J. Edward Ketz. "A Caveat On Measuring Cash Flow And Solvency," FAJ, 1983, v39(5), 66-72.)

Ketz, J. Edward. (Gombola, Michael J. and J. Edward Ketz. "Financial Ratio Patterns In Retail And Manufacturing Organizations," FM, 1983, v12(2), 45-56.)

Kewley, T. J. and R. A. Stevenson. "The Odd Lot Theory," FAJ, 1967, v23(5), 103-106.

Kewley, Thomas J. and R. A. Stevenson. "The Odd-Lot Theory: A Reply," FAJ, 1969, v25(1), 99-104.

Key, Dwayne. (Stine, Bert and Dwayne Key. "Reconciling Degrees Of Freedom When Partitioning Risk: A Teaching Note," JFED, 1990, v19, 19-22.)

Keyfitz, Nathan and Andrei Rogers. "Simplified Multiple Contingency Calculations," JRI, 1982, v49(1), 59-72.

Keynes, John Maynard. "The Stock Market And The Beauty Contest," JPM, 1974-75, v1(1), 88-90.

Khajuria, Sajay. (Beenstock, Michael, Gerry Dickinson and Sajay Khajuria. "The Relationship Between Property-Liability Insurance Premiums And Income: An International Analysis," JRI, 1988, v55(2), 259-272.)

Khaksari, Shahriar, Ravindra Kamath and Robin Grieves. "A New Approach To Determining Optimum Portfolio Mix," JPM, 1989, v15(3), 43-49.

Khaksari, Shahriar. (Kamath, Ravindra R., Shahriar Khaksari, Heidi Hylton Meier and John Winklepleck. "Management Of Excess Cash: Practices And Developments," **FM**, 1985, v14(3), 70-77.)

Khan, Mohsin S. and Malcolm D. Knight. "Unanticipated Monetary Growth And Inflationary Finance," **JMCB**, 1982, v14(3), 347-364.

Khan, Mohsin S. (Brillembourg, Arturo and Mohsin S. Khan. "The Relationship Between Money, Income, And Prices: Has Money Mattered Historically?," **JMCB**, 1979, v11(3), 358-365.)

Khang, Chulsoon. "A Dynamic Global Portfolio Immunization Strategy In The World Of Multiple Interest Rate Changes: A Dynamic Immunization And Minimax Strategy," **JFQA**, 1983, v18(3), 355-363.

Khang, Chulsoon. "Bond Immunization When Short-Term Interest Rates Fluctuate More Than Long-Term Rates," **JFQA**, 1979, v14(5), 1085-1090.

Khang, Chulsoon. "Expectations, Prices, Coupons And Yields: Comment," **JOF**, 1975, v30(4), 1137-1140.

Khang, Chulsoon. (Bierwag, G. O., George G. Kaufman and Chulsoon Khang. "Duration And Bond Portfolio Analysis: An Overview," **JFQA**, 1978, v13(4), 671-681.)

Khang, Chulsoon. (Bierway, G. O. and Chulsoon Khang. "An Immunization Strategy Is A Minimax Strategy," **JOF**, 1979, v34(2), 389-399.)

Khanna, Naveen. (Berkovitch, Elazar and Naveen Khanna. "How Target Shareholders Benefit From Value-Reducing Defensive Strategies In Takeovers," **JOF**, 1990, v45(1), 137-156.)

Khouja, Mohamad W. (Konstas, Panos and Mohamad W. Khouja. "The Keynesian Demand-For-Money Function: Another Look And Some Additional Evidence," **JMCB**, 1969, v1(4), 765-777.)

Khoury, Nabil T. and Jean-Marc Martel. "Optimal Futures Hedging In The Presence Of Asymmetric Information," **JFM**, 1985, v5(4), 595-605.

Khoury, Nabil T. (Fortin, Michel and Nabil T. Khoury. "Effectiveness Of Hedging Interest Rate Risks And Stock Market Risks With Financial Futures," **JFM**, 1988, v8(3), 319-334.)

Khoury, Nabil T. and Jean-Marc Martel. "A Supply Of Storage Theory With Asymmetric Information," **JFM**, 1989, v9(6), 573-582.

Khoury, Nabil T. and Pierre Yourougou. "The Informational Content Of The Basis: Evidence From Canadian Barley, Oats, And Canola Futures Markets," **JFM**, 1991, v11(1), 69-80.

Khoury, Nabil T. and Pierre Yourougou. "Price Discovery Performance And Maturity Effects In The Canadian Feed Wheat Market," **RFM**, 1989, v8(3), 402-419.

Khoury, Sarkis J. and Gerald L. Jones. "Daily Price Limits On Futures Contracts: Nature, Impact, And Justification," **RFM**, 1984, v3(1), 22-36.

Khoury, Sarkis J. "Dow Theory Is Alive And Well: Comment," **JPM**, 1983-84, v10(3), 81-83.

Khoury, Sarkis J. (Dambolena, Ismael G. and Sarkis J. Khoury. "Ratio Stability And Corporate Failure," **JOF**, 1980, v35(4), 1017-1026.)

Khoury, Sarkis J., Bajis Dodin and Hirokazu Takada. "Multiple Time Series Analysis Of National Stock Markets And Their Structure: Some Implications," **RDIBF**, 1987, v1, 169-186.

Khoury, Sarkis J., David Nickerson and Venkatraman Sadanand. "Exchange Rate Uncertainty And Precommitment In Symmetric Duopoly: A New Theory Of Multinational Production," **RDIBF**, 1991, v4/5, 439-473.

Khumawala, Saleha B., Neil W. Polhemus and Woody M. Liao. "The Predictability Of Quarterly Cash Flows," **JBFA**, 1981, v8(4),493-510.

Khumuwala, Saleha. (Brandon, Charles, Jeffrey Jarrett and Saleha Khumuwala. "On The Predictability Of Growth In Earnings Per Share," **JBFA**, 1983, v10(3), 373-387.)

Kidd, Phillip E. "Changing Role Of Mortgage Banking In The Secondary Market," **AREUEA**, 1975, v3(2), 43-50.

Kidd, Phillip E. "Housing Statistics: Some Sources And Some Limitations," **AREUEA**, 1977, v5(3), 337-398.

Kidder, R. (Appelbaum, E., J. Burns, R. Evans, J. Gould, T. Hamachek, R. Kidder, M. Jensen, J. Johnstone, M. Murray, R. Sim, J. Stern, B. Stewart and C. Zaner. "Panel: CEO Roundtable On Corporate Structure And Management Incentives," **JACF**, 1990, v3(3), 6-35.)

Kidwell, David S. and Charles A. Trzcinka. "Municipal Bond Pricing And The New York City Fiscal Crisis," **JOF**, 1982, v37(5), 1239-1246.

Kidwell, David S. and Charles A. Trzcinka. "The Impact Of The New York City Fiscal Crisis On The Interest Cost Of New Issue Municipal Bonds," **JFQA**, 1983, v18(3), 381-399.

Kidwell, David S. and Charles A. Trzcinka. "The Risk Structure Of Interest Rates And The Penn-Central Crisis," **JOF**, 1979, v34(3), 751-760.

Kidwell, David S. and Eric H. Sorensen. "Pricing Of Municipal Bond Underwritings: It May Pay To Invest When Underwriters Don't," **FAJ**, 1983, v39(2),58-64.

Kidwell, David S. and Robert J. Rogowski. "State Bond Bank Issues: Method Of Sale And Market Acceptance Over Time," **FM**, 1983, v12(2), 15-20.

Kidwell, David S. and Timothy W. Koch. "The Behavior Of The Interest Rate Differential Between Tax-Exempt Revenue And General Obligation Bonds: A Test Of Risk Preferences And Market Segmentation," **JOF**, 1982, v37(1), 73-85.

Kidwell, David S. and Timothy W. Koch. "Why And When Do Revenue Bonds Yield More Than GOs?," **JPM**, 1981-82, v8(4), 51-56.

Kidwell, David S. and Timothy W. Koch. "Market Segmentation And The Term Structure Of Municipal Yields," **JMCB**, 1983, v15(1), 40-55.

Kidwell, David S. "The Inclusion And Exercise Of Call Provisions By State And Local Governments," **JMCB**, 1976, v8(3), 391-398.

Kidwell, David S. (Benson, Earl D., David S. Kidwell, Timothy W. Koch and Robert J. Rogowski. "Systematic Variation In Yield Spreads For Tax-Exempt General Obligation Bonds," **JFQA**, 1981, v16(5), 685-702.)

Kidwell, David S. (Blackwell, David W. and David S. Kidwell. "An Investigation Of Cost Differences Between Public Sales And Private Placements Of Debt," **JFEC**, 1988, v22(2), 253-278.)

Kidwell, David S. (Hays, Patrick A., David S. Kidwell and M. Wayne Marr. "The Effect Of Market Uncertainty On Negotiated And Competitively Underwritten Public Utility Bonds," **FR**, 1984, v19(4), 339-350.)

Kidwell, David S. (Hendershott, Patric H. and David S. Kidwell. "The Impact Of Relative Security Supplies: A Test With Data From A Regional Tax Exempt Bond Market," **JMCB**, 1978, v10(3), 337-347.)

Kidwell, David S. (Hsueh, L. Paul and David S. Kidwell. "Bond Ratings: Are Two Better Than One?," **FM**, 1988, v17(1), 46-53.)

Kidwell, David S. (Joehnk, Michael D. and David S. Kidwell. "The Impact Of Market Uncertainty On Municipal Bond Underwriting Spread," **FM**, 1984, v13(1), 37-44.)

Kidwell, David S. (Joehnk, Michael D. and David S. Kidwell. "Comparative Costs Of Competitive And Negotiated Underwritings In The State And Local Bond Market," **JOF**, 1979, v34(3), 725-731.)

Kidwell, David S. (Simonson, Donald G. and David S. Kidwell. "The MBA Financial Markets Course -- A Survey On Teaching Approaches," **JFED**, 1982, v11, 25-31.)

Kidwell, David S., M. Wayne Marr and G. Rodney Thompson. "Eurodollar Bonds, Alternative Financing For U.S. Companies: A Correction," **FM**, 1986, v15(1), 78-79.

Kidwell, David S., M. Wayne Marr and G. Rodney Thompson. "SEC Rule 415: The Ultimate Competitive Bid," **JFQA**, 1984, v19(2), 183-195.

Kidwell, David S., M. Wayne Marr and G. Rodney Thompson. "Eurodollar Bonds: Alternative Financing For U.S. Companies," **FM**, 1985, v14(4), 18-27.

Kidwell, David S., Eric H. Sorensen and John M. Wachowicz, Jr. "Estimating The Signaling Benefits Of Debt Insurance: The Case Of Municipal Bonds," **JFQA**, 1987, v22(3), 299-314.

Kidwell, David S., M. Wayne Marr and Joseph P. Ogden. "The Effect Of A Sinking Fund On The Reoffering Yields Of New Public Utility Bonds," **JFI**, 1989, v12(1), 1-14.

Kiefer, Donald W. "The Effects Of Alternative Regulatory Treatments Of The Investment Tax Credit In The Public Utility Industry," **JOB**, 1981, v54(4),549-578.

Kiel, Katherine A. and Richard T. Carson. "An Examination Of Systematic Differences In The Appreciation Of Individual Housing Units," **JRER**, 1990, v5(3), 301-318.

Kienlen, T. W. "The Future Of Coal," **FAJ**, 1954, v10(4), 77-82.

Kiernan, Loyd J. "The Passenger Deficit: A Look At The Facts," **FAJ**, 1955, v11(4), 46-50.

Kiguel, Miguel A. "Budget Deficits, Stability, And The Dynamics Of Hyperinflation," **JMCB**, 1989, v21(2), 148-157.

Kiguel, Miguel A. "The Non-Dynamic Equivalence Of Monetary And Exchange Rate Rules Under Imperfect Capital Mobility And Rational Expectations," **JIMF**, 1987, v6(2), 207-214.

Kihlstrom, Richard E. and Alvin E. Roth. "Risk Aversion And The Negotiation Of Insurance Contracts," **JRI**, 1982, v49(3), 372-387.

Kihlstrom, Richard E. and Steven A. Matthews. "Managerial Incentives In An Entrepreneurial Stock Market Model," **JFI**, 1990, v1(1), 57-79.

Kiker, B. F. (Hunt, Janet C. and B. F. Kiker. "Valuation Of Household Services: Methodology And Estimation," **JRI**, 1979, v46(4), 697-706.)

Kilbride, Bernard J., Bill McDonald and Robert E. Miller. "A Reexamination Of Economies Of Scale In Banking Using A Generalized Functional Form," **JMCB**, 1986, v18(4), 519-526.

Kilbridge, Maurice D. "Reduced Costs Through Job Enlargement: A Case," **JOB**, 1960, v33(4), 357-362.

Kilbridge, Maurice D. "The Effort Bargain In Industrial Society," **JOB**, 1960, v33(1), 10-20.

Kilcollin, Thomas Eric. "Difference Systems In Financial Futures Markets," **JOF**, 1982, v37(5), 1183-1197.

Kilcollin, Thomas Eric. "Tandem T-Bill And CD Spreads," **JFM**, 1982, v2(1), 51-61.

Kilgannon, John J. (Celebuski, Matthew J., Joanne M. Hill and John J. Kilgannon. "Managing Currency Exposures In International Portfolios," **FAJ**, 1990, v46(1), 16-23.)

Killough, Larry N. (Koh, Hian C. and Larry N. Killough. "The Use Of Multiple Discriminant Analysis In The Assessment Of Going-Concern Status Of An Audit Client," **JBFA**, 1990, v17(2), 179-192.)

Kilpatrick, Michael A. (Mabert, Vincent A., Randy Fairhurst and Michael A. Kilpatrick. "Chemical Bank's Encoder Daily Shift Scheduling System," **JBR**, 1979-80, v10(3), 173-180.)

Kilpatrick, Wylie. "Florida City Debt - A Case Study," **JOF**, 1955, v10(3), 350-362.

Kim, Andrew B. "Air Cargo," **FAJ**, 1967, v23(5), 41-48.

Kim, Andrew B. "Is Indexing Really The Answer?," **JPM**, 1977-78, v4(1), 65-69.

Kim, Chan-Wung. (Chang, Eric C. and Chan-Wung Kim. "Day Of The Week Effects And Commodity Price Changes," **JFM**, 1988, v8(2), 229-242.)

Kim, Daesik and Anthony M. Santomero. "Risk In Banking And Capital Regulation," **JOF**, 1988, v43(5), 1219-1233.

Kim, E. Han and John J. McConnell. "Corporate Mergers And The Co-Insurance Of Corporate Debt," **JOF**, 1977, v32(2), 349-365.

Kim, E. Han and John D. Schatzberg. "Voluntary Corporate Liquidations," **JFEC**, 1987, v19(2), 311-328.

Kim, E. Han, John J. McConnell and Paul R. Greenwood. "Capital Structure Rearrangements And Me-First Rules In An Efficient Capital Market," **JOF**, 1977, v32(3), 789-810.

Kim, E. Han, Wilbur G. Lewellen and John J. McConnell. "Sale-And-Leaseback Agreements And Enterprise Valuation," **JFQA**, 1978, v13(5), 871-883.

Kim, E. Han, Wilbur G. Lewellen and John J. McConnell. "Financial Leverage Clienteles: Theory And Evidence," **JFEC**, 1979, v7(1), 83-109.

Kim, E. Han. "A Mean-Variance Theory Of Optimal Capital Structure And Corporate Debt Capacity," **JOF**, 1978, v33(1), 45-63.

Kim, E. Han. "Corporate Takeovers: Winners, Losers, And Some Remaining Issues," **RDIBF**, 1991, v4/5, 92-114.

Kim, E. Han. "Miller's Equilibrium, Shareholder Leverage Clienteles, And Optimal Capital Structure," **JOF**, 1982, v37(2), 301-319.

Kim, E. Han. (Asquith, Paul and E. Han Kim. "The Impact Of Merger Bids On The Participating Firms' Security Holders," **JOF**, 1982, v37(5), 1209-1228.)

Kim, E. Han. (Berkovitch, Elazar and E. Han Kim. "Financial Contracting And Leverage Induced Over- And Under-Investment Incentives," **JOF**, 1990, v45(3), 765-794.)

Kim, E. Han. (Bradley, Michael, Anand Desai and E. Han Kim. "The Rationale Behind Interfirm Tender Offers," *JFEC*, 1983, v11(1), 183-206.)

Kim, E. Han. (Bradley, Michael, Anand Desai and E. Han Kim. "Synergistic Gains From Corporate Acquisitions And Their Division Between The Stockholders Of Target And Acquiring Firms," *JFEC*, 1988, v21(1), 3-40.)

Kim, E. Han. (Bradley, Michael, Gregg A. Jarrell and E. Han Kim. "On The Existence Of An Optimal Capital Structure: Theory And Evidence," *JOF*, 1984, v39(3), 857-878.)

Kim, E. Han. (Chen, A. H., E. Han Kim and S. J. Kon. "Cash Demand, Liquidation Costs And Capital Market Equilibrium Under Uncertainty," *JFEC*, 1975, v2(3), 293-308.)

Kim, E. Han. (Chen, Andrew H., E. Han Kim and Stanley J. Kon. "Cash Demand, Liquidation Costs, And Capital Market Equilibrium Under Uncertainty: Reply," *JFEC*, 1976, v3(3), 297-298.)

Kim, E. Han. (Chen, Andrew H. and E. Han Kim. "Theories Of Corporate Debt Policy: A Synthesis," *JOF*, 1979, v34(2), 371-384.)

Kim, E. Han. (Eades, Kenneth M., Patrick J. Hess and E. Han Kim. "Market Rationality And Dividend Annoucements," *JFEC*, 1985, v14(4), 581-604.)

Kim, E. Han. (Eades, Kenneth M., Patrick J. Hess and E. Han Kim. "On Interpreting Security Returns During The Exdividend Period," *JFEC*, 1984, v13(1),3-34.)

Kim, E. Han. (Hagerman, Robert L. and E. Han Kim. "Capital Asset Pricing With Price Level Changes," *JFQA*, 1976, v11(3), 381-391.)

Kim, Gew-Rae and Harry M. Markowitz. "Investment Rules, Margin, And Market Volatility," *JPM*, 1989, v16(1), 45-52.

Kim, H. Youn. "Economies Of Scale And Economies Of Scope In Multiproduct Financial Institutions: Further Evidence From Credit Unions," *JMCB*, 1986, v18(2), 220-226.

Kim, Hyun. (Lee, Jae K., Robert R. Trippi, Seok C. Chu and Hyun Kim. "K-FOLIO: Integrating The Markowitz Model With A Knowledge-Based System," *JPM*, 1990, v17(1), 89-93.)

Kim, In Joon. "The Analytic Valuation Of American Options," *RFS*, 1990, v3(4), 547-572.

Kim, Inchul. "A Partial Adjustment Theory Of The Balance Of Payments," *JIMF*, 1983, v2(1), 17-26.

Kim, Inchul. "Exchange Market Pressure In Korea: An Application Of The Girton-Roper Monetary Model," *JMCB*, 1985, v17(2), 258-263.

Kim, Jeong-Bon and Roland Lipka. "Effects Of Accounting Choice On The Explanation Of The Market Risk In The Oil And Gas Industry," *JBFA*, 1991, v18(1), 61-84.

Kim, Joo-hyun and Roger D. Stover. "The Role Of Bank Letters Of Credit In Corporate Tax-Exempt Financing," *FM*, 1987, v16(1), 31-37.

Kim, Kee S. "The Theoretical Relationship Between Systematic Risk And Financial (Accounting) Variables: Comment," *JOF*, 1981, v36(3), 747-748.

Kim, Kee S. (Goebel, Paul R. and Kee S. Kim. "Performance Evaluation Of Finite-Life Real Estate Investment Trusts," *JRER*, 1989, v4(2), 57-69.)

Kim, Kee S. (Wurtzebach, Charles H. and Kee S. Kim. "An Investment Analysis And Decision Making Framework For Real Estate Development," *AREUEA*, 1979, v7(3), 410-426.)

Kim, M. and V. Maksimovic. "Technology, Debt And The Exploitation Of Growth Options," *JBF*, 1990, v14(6), 1113-1132.

Kim, Moon and Geoffrey Booth. "Yield Structure Of Taxable Vs. Nontaxable Bonds," *JFR*, 1985, v8(2), 95-105.

Kim, Moon H. (Reilly, Raymond R., Eugene F. Brigham, Charles M. Linke, Moon H. Kim and James S. Ang. "Weighted Average Vs. True Cost Of Capital: Reilly, Brigham, Linke and Kim Versus Ang," *FM*, 1974, v3(1), 80-85.)

Kim, Moon K. and Allan Young. "Rewards And Risks From Warrant Hedging," *JPM*, 1979-80, v6(4),65-68.

Kim, Moon K. "Inflationary Effects In The Capital Investment Process: An Empirical Examination," *JOF*, 1979, v34(4), 941-950.

Kim, Moon K. (Linke, Charles M. and Moon K. Kim. "More On The Weighted Average Cost Of Capital: A Comment And Analysis," *JFQA*, 1974, v9(6), 1069-1080.)

Kim, Moon K. and Chunchi Wu. "Macro-Economic Factors And Stock Returns," *JFR*, 1987, v10(2), 87-98.

Kim, Moon K. and Chunchi Wu. "Effects Of Inflation On Capital Structure," *FR*, 1988, v23(2),183-200.

Kim, Moon K. and J. Kenton Zumwalt. "An Analysis Of Risk In Bull And Bear Markets," *JFQA*, 1979, v14(5), 1015-1025.

Kim, Moshe and Vojislav Maksimovic. "Debt And Input Misallocation," *JOF*, 1990, v45(3), 795-816.

Kim, Moshe. "Scale Economies In Banking: A Methodological Note," *JMCB*, 1985, v17(1), 96-102.

Kim, Sang-Hoon and Hussein H. Elsaid. "Safety Margin Allocation And Risk Assessment Under The NPV Method," *JBFA*, 1985, v12(1), 133-144.

Kim, Sang-Hoon and Hussein H. Elsaid. "Estimation Of Periodic Standard Deviations Under The PERT And Derivation Of Probabilistic Information," *JBFA*, 1988, v15(4), 557-572.

Kim, Sang-Hoon. "The Effect Of Refunding Decisions On The Relationship Between Interest Rates And Stock Prices: An Empirical Test," *JBFA*, 1986, v13(3), 405-424.

Kim, Sang-Hoon. (Fuller, Russell J. and Sang-Hoon Kim. "Inter-Temporal Correlation Of Cash Flows And The Risk Of Multi-Period Investment Projects," *JFQA*, 1980, v15(5), 1149-1162.)

Kim, Sangphill. (DeGennaro, Ramon P. and Sangphill Kim. "The CAPM And Beta In An Imperfect Market: Comment," *JPM*, 1985-86, v12(4), 78-80.)

Kim, Sangphill. (Diallo, Alahassame and Sangphill Kim. "Asymmetric Information, Captive Insurer's Formation, And Manager's Welfare Gain," *JRI*, 1989, v56(2), 233-251.)

Kim, Suk H. and Henry J. Guithues. "A Survey Of Graduate Finance Case Courses," *JFED*, 1982, v11, 83-86.

Kim, Sun-Woong. "Capitalizing On The Week-End Effect," *JPM*, 1987-88, v14(3), 59-63.

Kim, Tae-Hyuk. (Gay, Gerald D. and Tae-Hyuk Kim. "An Investigation Into Seasonality In The Futures Market," *JFM*, 1987, v7(2), 169-182.)

Kim, Taewon. "A Contingent Claims Analysis Of Price Level-Adjusted Mortgages," *AREUEA*, 1987, v15(3), 117-131.

Kim, Taewon. "Bidding In Real Estate: A Game Theoretic Approach," *JREFEC*, 1989, v2(4), 239-252.

Kim, Tye. "An Assessment Of The Performance Of Mutual Fund Management: 1969-1975," *JFQA*, 1978, v13(3), 385-406.

Kim, Wi Saeng and Eric H. Sorensen. "Evidence On The Impact Of The Agency Costs Of Debt On Corporate Debt Policy," *JFQA*, 1986, v21(2), 131-144.

Kim, Wi Saeng, Jae Won Lee and Jack Clark Francis. "Investment Performance Of Common Stocks In Relation To Insider Ownership," *FR*, 1988, v23(1), 53-64.

Kim, Y. H. (Srinivasan, V., Y. H. Kim and P. J. Bolster. "A Framework For Integrating The Leasing Alternative With The Capital Budgeting Decision," *AFPAF*, 1989, v3(1), 75-94.)

Kim, Yong Cheol and Rene M. Stulz. "The Eurobond Market And Corporate Financial Policy: A Test Of The Clientele Hypothesis," *JFEC*, 1988, v22(2), 189-206.

Kim, Yong H. and Joseph C. Atkins. "Evaluating Investments In Accounts Receivable: A Wealth Maximizing Framework," *JOF*, 1978, v33(2), 403-412.

Kim, Yong H. (Atkins, Joseph C. and Yong H. Kim. "Comment And Correction: Opportuny Cost In The Evaluation Of Investment In Accounts Receivable," *FM*, 1977, v6(4), 71-74.)

Kim, Yong H. (McKenna, Fred W. and Yong H. Kim. "Managerial Risk Preferences, Real Pension Costs, And Long-Run Corporate Pension Fund Investment Policy," *JRI*, 1986, v53(1), 29-48.)

Kim, Yong H. (Srinivasan, Venkat and Yong H. Kim. "Credit Granting: A Comparative Analysis Of Classification Procedures," *JOF*, 1987, v42(3), 665-681.)

Kim, Yong H. (Srinivasan, Venkat and Yong H. Kim. "Designing Expert Financial Systems: A Case Study Of Corporate Credit Management," *FM*, 1988, v17(3),32-44.)

Kim, Yong H. (Srinivasan, Venkat, Susan E. Moeller and Yong H. Kim. "International Cash Management: State-Of-The-Art And Research Directions," *AFPAF*, 1990, v5(1), 161-194.)

Kim, Yong H. (Srinivasan, Venkat and Yong H. Kim. "Decision Support For Working Capital Management: A Conceptual Framework," *AWCM*, 1990, v1(1), 187-216.)

Kim, Yong H. (Srinivasan, Venkat and Yong H. Kim. "Integrating Corporate Strategy And Multinational Capital Budgeting: An Analytical Framework," *RDIBF*, 1988, v2, 381-398.)

Kim, Yong H. and Kee H. Chung. "An Integrated Evaluation Of Investment In Inventory And Credit: A Cash Flow Approach," *JBFA*, 1990, v17(3), 381-390.

Kim, Yong O. "Informative Conversion Ratios: A Signalling Approach," *JFQA*, 1990, v25(2), 229-244.

Kim, Yoonbai. "Purchasing Power Parity In The Long Run: A Cointegration Approach," *JMCB*, 1990, v22(4), 491-503.

Kim, Young Y. (Meyer, James E. and Young Y. Kim. "An Autoregressive Forecast Of The World Sugar Future Option Market," *JFQA*, 1975, v10(5), 821-835.)

Kimball, Peter and D. Robert Papera. "Effect Of Stock Splits On Short-Term Market Prices," *FAJ*, 1964, v20(3), 75-80.

Kimball, Miles S. (Basu, Susanto, Miles S. Kimball, N. Gregory Mankiw and David N. Weil. "Optimal Advice For Monetary Policy," *JMCB*, 1990, v22(1), 19-36.)

Kimball, Spencer J. "The Goals Of Insurance Law: Means Versus Ends," *JRI*, 1962, v29(1), 19-30.

Kimball, Spencer L. "Sketches From A Comparative Study Of American And European Insurance Regulation," *JRI*, 1965, v32(2), 195-210.

Kimball, Spencer L. "The Context Of 'No-Fault'," *JRI*, 1985, v52(4), 662-666.

Kimball, Spencer L. (Friedman, Lloyd K., Harold A. Jensen, Jr., Spencer L. Kimball and Jon S. Hanson. "The Regulation Of Specialty Policies In Life Insurance: Comment," *JRI*, 1966, v33(2), 305-316.)

Kimber, Albert W. "Growth Factor Can Reduce Common Share Earnings," *FAJ*, 1947, v3(2), 16-25.

Kimber, John R. "Stock Market Maturity In Canada," *FAJ*, 1968, v24(2), 173-174.

Kimbrough, Kent P. "An Examination Of The Effects Of Government Purchases In An Open Economy," *JIMF*, 1985, v4(1), 113-134.

Kimbrough, Kent P. "Exchange-Rate Policy And Monetary Information," *JIMF*, 1983, v2(3), 333-346.

Kimbrough, Kent P. "Inflation, Employment, And Welfare In The Presence Of Transactions Costs," *JMCB*, 1986, v18(2), 127-140.

Kimbrough, Kent P. "The Derivation And Interpretation Of The Lucas Supply Function: A Comment," *JMCB*, 1984, v16(3), 367-377.

Kimbrough, Kent P. "The Information Content Of The Exchange Rate And The Stability Of Real Output Under Alternative Exchange-Rate Regimes," *JIMF*, 1983, v2(1), 27-38.

Kindleberger, Charles P. "The International Causes And Consequences Of The Great Crash," *JPM*, 1979-80, v6(1), 11-14.

King, A. Thomas. "Mortgage Lending, Social Responsibility, And Public Policy: Some Perspectives On HMDA And CRA," *AREUEA*, 1980, v8(1), 77-90.

King, A. Thomas. "Thrift Institution Deposits: The Influence Of MMCs And MMMFs," *JMCB*, 1984, v16(3), 328-334.

King, Alan L. "The Market Performance Of Diversified And Non-Diversified Organizations Within The PL Insurance Industry," *JRI*, 1975, v42(3), 471-501.

King, B. Frank. "Future Holding Company Lead Banks: Federal Reserve Standards And Record," *JBR*, 1982-83, v13(2), 72-79.

King, Benjamin F. "Market And Industry Factors In Stock Price Behavior," *JOB*, 1966, v39(1), Part II, 139-190.

King, Christopher Q. (Tueting, William F. and Christopher Q. King. "Funds Protections: An Overview Of What Happens When A Commodity Broker Becomes Insolvent," *JFM*, 1987, v7(1), 93-102.)

King, Donald A., Jr. (Roulac, Stephen E. and Donald A. King, Jr. "Institutional Strategies For Real Estate Investment," *JPM*, 1976-77, v3(4), 58-65.)

King, Francis P. "An Increasing Annuity Based On Nominal Interest Rates And Debt Instruments," *JRI*, 1984, v51(4), 624-639.

King, Francis P. "Men, Women, And Life Annuities," *JRI*, 1976, v43(4), 553-568.

King, Mervyn A. and Sushil Wadhwani. "Transmission Of Volatility Between Stock Markets," RFS, 1990, v3(1), 5-33.

King, Paul. "A Short Note On 'Is The Emphasis Of Capital Budgeting Theory Misplaced?'," JBFA, 1977, v4(3), 379-382.

King, Paul. "Is The Emphasis Of Capital Budgeting Theory Misplaced?," JBFA, 1975, v2(1), 69-82.

King, Raymond. "Convertible Bond Valuation: An Empirical Test," JFR, 1986, v9(1), 53-69.

King, Stephen R. "Monetary Transmission: Through Bank Loans Or Bank Liabilities?," JMCB, 1986, v18(3), 290-303.

King, William R. (McGuigan, James and William R. King. "Evaluating Alternative Stock Option Timing Strategies," JFQA, 1974, v9(4), 567-578.)

King, William R. (McGuigan, James R. and William R. King. "Security Option Strategy Under Risk Aversion: An Analysis," JFQA, 1973, v8(1), 1-15.)

Kingery, Dorothy. (Nourse, Hugh O. and Dorothy Kingery. "Survey Of Approaches To Disposing Of Suplus Corporate Real Estate," JRER, 1987, v2(1), 51-59.)

Kingsland, Louis. "Projecting The Financial Condition Of A Pension Plan Using Simulation Analysis," JOF, 1982, v37(2), 577-584.

Kingsman, Brian G. "The Relationship Between European And U.S. Prices For Soyabeans And Corn, 1966-1988," RFM, 1988, v7(Supp), 528-553.

Kingsman, Brian G. (Taylor, Stephen J. and Brian G. Kingsman. "Comment: An Autoregressive Forecast Of The World Sugar Future Option Market," JFQA, 1977, v12(5), 883-890.)

Kingston, Geoffrey H. (Boyer, Russell S. and Geoffrey H. Kingston. "Currency Substitution Under Finance Constraints," JIMF, 1987, v6(3), 235-250.)

Kinnard, William N., Jr. "Junior Mortgages In Real Estate Finance: A Case Study," JOF, 1956, v11(1), 42-57.

Kinnard, William N., Herman G. Berkman, Hugh O. Nourse and John C. Weicher. "The First Twenty Years Of AREUEA," AREUEA, 1988, v16(2), 189-205.

Kinnard, William. (Dasso, Jerome, William Kinnard and Joseph Rabianski. "Corporate Real Estate: A Course Outline And Rationale," JRER, 1989, v4(3), 35-46.)

Kinney, William R., Jr. (Pinches, George E. and William R. Kinney, Jr. "The Measurement Of The Volatility Of Common Stock Prices," JOF, 1971, v26(1), 119-125.)

Kinney, William R., Jr. (Rozeff, Michael S. and William R. Kinney, Jr. "Capital Market Seasonality: The Case Of Stock Returns," JFEC, 1976, v3(4), 379-402.)

Kinsman, Michael. (Robichek, Alexander, Robert C. Higgins and Michael Kinsman. "The Effect Of Leverage On The Cost Of Equity Capital Of Electric Utility Firms," JOF, 1973, v28(2), 353-367.)

Kirby, Robert G. "Lessons Learned And Never Learned," JPM, 1979-80, v6(1), 52-55.

Kirby, Robert G. "The Coffee Can Portfolio," JPM, 1984-85, v11(1), 76-80.

Kirby, Robert G. "Whose Company Is It, Anyway?," JPM, 1989, v16(1), 13-18.

Kirkwood, John B. "The Great Depression: A Structural Analysis," JMCB, 1972, v4(4), 811-837.

Kirshner, Daniel. (Udinsky, Jerald H. and Daniel Kirshner. "A Comparison Of Relative Predictive Power For Financial Models Of Rates Of Return," JFQA, 1979, v14(2), 293-315.)

Kiscadden, Stephen. (Arnott, Robert D., Charles M. Kelso, Jr., Stephan Kiscadden and Rosemary Macedo. "Forecasting Factor Returns: An Intriguing Possibility," JPM, 1989, v16(1), 28-35.)

Kiser, Clyde V. "Population And Security," FAJ, 1952, v8(2), 51-56.

Kishimoto, Naoki. "Pricing Contingent Claims Under Interest Rate And Asset Price Risk," JOF, 1989, v44(3), 571-590.

Kisor, M. Jr. and V. S. Whitbeck. "A New Tool In Investment Decision-Making," FAJ, 1963, v19(3), 55-62.

Kisor, Manown, Jr. and Van A. Messner. "Filter Approach To Earnings," FAJ, 1969, v25(1), 109-115.

Kisor, Manown, Jr. "The Financial Aspects Of Growth," FAJ, 1964, v20(2), 46-51.

Kitchen, John and Mark Denbaly. "Commodity Prices, Money Surprises, And Fed Credibility: Comment," JMCB, 1987, v19(2), 246-251.

Kitchen, John. (Husted, Steven and John Kitchen. "Some Evidence On The International Transmission Of U.S. Money Supply Announcement Effects," JMCB, 1985, v17(4), Part 1, 456-466.)

Klaassen, Eldon J. (Foody, Walter M. and Eldon J. Klaassen. "Financing Medical Care For The Aged," JRI, 1962, v29(2), 221-228.)

Klaffke, Stephen. (Jahnke, Gregg, Stephen Klaffke and Henry R. Oppenheimer. "Price Earnings Ratios And Security Performance," JPM, 1987-88, v14(1), 39-47.)

Klaffky, Thomas E. (Leibowitz, Martin L., Thomas E. Klaffky, Steven Mandel and Alfred Weinberger. "Horizon Matching: A New Approach To Dedicated Portfolios," JPM, 1984-85, v11(1), 93-96.)

Klahr, David. "A Study Of Consumers' Cognitive Structure For Cigarette Brands," JOB, 1970, v43(2), 190-204.

Klaman, Saul B. "Mortgage Companies In The Postwar Mortgage Market," JOF, 1957, v12(2), 148-158.

Klaman, Saul B. "Mortgage Market Prospects," JOF, 1963, v18(2), 404-409.

Klaman, Saul B. "The Mortgage Market," JOF, 1961, v16(2), 255-260.

Klaman, Saul B. "The Plenitude Of Scarcity," FAJ, 1967, v23(4), 59-61.

Klammer, Thomas. "Empirical Evidence Of The Adoption Of Sophisticated Capital Budgeting Techniques," JOB, 1972, v45(3), 387-397.

Klarman, Herbert E. "Economic Aspects Of Hospital Care," JOB, 1951, v24(1), 1-24.

Klarman, Herbert E. "Medical Care Costs And Voluntary Health Insurance," JRI, 1957, v24(1), 23-41.

Klarman, Herbert E. "Reimbursing The Hospital - The Differences The Third Party Makes," JRI, 1969, v36(4), 553-566.

Klarman, Herbert E. "Reimbursing The Hospital - The Differences The Third Party Makes: Reply," JRI, 1971, v38(1), 139-141.

Klass, Michael J. (Garman, Mark B. and Michael J. Klass. "On The Estimation Of Security Price Volatilities From Historical Data," JOB, 1980, v53(1), 67-78.)

Klatzky, S. R. "Automation, Size, And The Locus of Decision Making: The Cascade Effect," JOB, 1970, v43(2), 141-151.

Kleemeier, Robert W. "Age Changes In Psychomotor Capacity And Productivity," JOB, 1954, v27(2),146-155.

Kleidon, Allan W. "Anomalies In Financial Economics: Blueprint For Change?," JOB, 1986, v59(4), Part 2, S469-S500.

Kleidon, Allan W. "Bias In Small Sample Tests Of Stock Price Rationality," JOB, 1986, v59(2), Part 1, 237-262.

Kleidon, Allan W. (Brown, Philip, Donald Keim, Allan Kleidon and Terry Marsh. "Stock Return Seasonalities And The Tax-Loss Selling Hypothesis: Analysis Of The Arguments And Australian Evidence," JFEC, 1983, v12(1), 105-127

Kleidon, Allan W. (Brown, Philip, Allan W. Kleidon and Terry A. Marsh. "New Evidence On The Nature Of Size-Related Anomalies In Stock Prices," JFEC, 1983, v12(1), 33-56.)

Kleiman, Robert T. "The Shareholder Gains From Leveraged Cash-Outs: Some Preliminary Evidence," JACF, 1988, v1(1), 46-53.

Kleiman, Robert T. and Anandi P. Sahu. "Life Insurance Companies As Investment Managers: New Implications For Consumers," FSR, 1991, v1(1), 27-40.

Klein, April and James Rosenfeld. "The Influence Of Market Conditions On Event-Study Residuals," JFQA, 1987,v22(3),345-352.

Klein, April and James Rosenfeld. "The Impact Of Targeted Share Repurchases On The Wealth Of Non-Participating Shareholders," JFR, 1988, v11(2), 89-98.

Klein, April and James Rosenfeld. "Targeted Share Repurchases And Top Management Changes," JFEC, 1988, v20(1), 493-506.

Klein, April. "The Timing And Substance Of Divestiture Announcements: Individual, Simultaneous And Cumulative Effects," JOF, 1986, v41(3), 685-695.

Klein, Benjamin. "Competing Monies: A Comment," JMCB, 1976, v8(4), 513-519.

Klein, Benjamin. "Income Velocity, Interest Rates, And The Money Supply Multiplier: A Reinterpretation Of The Long-Term Evidence," JMCB, 1973, v5(2), 656-668.

Klein, Benjamin. "The Competitive Supply Of Money," JMCB, 1974, v6(4), 423-453.

Klein, Benjamin. (Alchian Armen A. and Benjamin Klein. "On A Correct Measure Of Inflation," JMCB, 1973, v5(1), 173-191.)

Klein, Daniel P. (Whittaker, Gregg, Linda E. Bowyer and Daniel P. Klein. "The Effect Of Futures Trading On The Municipal Bond Market," RFM, 1987, v6(2), 196-204.)

Klein, Hans E. "The Impact Of Planning On Growth And Profit," JBR, 1981-82, v12(2), 105-109.

Klein, Lawrence R. "Money In The Wharton Quarterly Model: A Reply," JMCB, 1984, v16(1), 76-78.

Klein, Lawrence R. (Johnson, Keith and Lawrence R. Klein. "Link Model Simulations Of International Trade: An Evaluation Of The Effects Of Currency Realignment," JOF, 1974, v29(2), 617-630.)

Klein, Lawrence R., Edward Friedman and Stephen Able. "Money In The Wharton Quarterly Model," JMCB, 1983, v15(2), 237-259.

Klein, Linda S. and David R. Peterson. "Investor Expectations Of Volatility Increases Around Large Stock Splits As Implied In Call Option Premia," JFR, 1988, v11(1), 71-80.

Klein, Linda S. and David R. Peterson. "Earnings Forecast Revisions Associated With Stock Split Announcements," JFR, 1989, v12(4), 319-328.

Klein, Manfred. (Bland, Christopher, Manfred Klein, Henri Blanchet and Christian Moretti. "Perspectives On Restructuring In Europe: Interviews With Four European Executives," JACF, 1991, v3(4), 37-45.)

Klein, Michael A. and Neil B. Murphy. "The Pricing Of Bank Deposits: A Theoretical And Empirical Analysis," JFQA, 1971, v6(2), 747-761.

Klein, Michael A. "A Theory Of The Banking Firm," JMCB, 1971, v3(2), Part 1, pp 205-218.

Klein, Michael A. "On The Causes And Consequences Of Savings And Loan Deposit Rate Inflexibility," JOF, 1972, v27(1), 79-87.

Klein, Michael A. "Optimal Life Insurance: Comment," JOF, 1975, v30(3), 904-908.

Klein, Michael A. "The Economics Of Security Divisibility And Financial Intermediation," JOF, 1973, v28(4), 923-931.

Klein, Michael A. "The Membership Problem Of The Federal Reserve: An Alternative Proposal," JMCB, 1980, v12(1), 17-29.

Klein, Michael W. "Macroeconomic Aspects Of Exchange Rate Pass-Through," JIMF, 1990, v9(4), 376-387.

Klein, Michael W. "Sectoral Effects Of Exchange Rate Volatility On United States Exports," JIMF, 1990, v9(3), 299-308.

Klein, Michael. "Credit Standards And Tight Money: A Comment," JMCB, 1973, v5(2), 708-712.

Klein, Richard H. (Harris, John M., Jr. and Richard H. Klein. "Analysis Of Leveraged Buyouts: Application Of A Simple Option Pricing Model," JFED, 1988, v17, 6-14.)

Klein, Richard. "Teaching Computer-Based Financial Modeling," JFED, 1980, v9, 83-88.

Klein, Richard. (Johnson, Rodney and Richard Klein. "Corporate Motives In Repurchases Of Discounted Bonds," FM, 1974, v3(3), 44-49.)

Klein, Roger W. and Vijay S. Bawa. "The Effect Of Limited Information And Estimation Risk On Optimal Portfolio Diversification," JFEC, 1977, v5(1), 89-111.

Klein, Roger W. and Vijay S. Bawa. "The Effect Of Estimation Risk On Optimal Portfolio Choice," JFEC, 1976, v3(3), 215-231.

Kleindorfer, Paul R. (Berger, Lawrence A., Paul R. Kleindorfer and Howard Kunreuther. "A Dynamic Model Of The Transmission Of Price Information In Auto Insurance Markets," JRI, 1989, v56(1), 17-33.)

Kleinman, David C. (Callard, Charles G. and David C. Kleinman. "Inflation-Adjusted Accounting: Does It Matter?," FAJ, 1985, v41(3), 51-59.)

Kleinschmidt, Elko J. (Findlay, M. Chapman, III and Elko J. Kleinschmidt. "Error-Learning In The Eurodollar Market," JFQA, 1975, v10(3), 429-446.)

Klem, Margaret C. "Prepayment Medical Care Organizations," JRI, 1945, v12, 22-31.

Klemkosky, Robert C. and Bruce G. Resnick. "Put-Call Parity And Market Efficiency," JOF, 1979, v34(5), 1141-1155.

Klemkosky, Robert C. and Bruce G. Resnick. "An Ex Ante Analysis Of Put Call Parity," **JFEC**, 1980, v8(4), 363-378.

Klemkosky, Robert C. and Dennis J. Lasser. "An Efficiency Analysis Of The T-Bond Futures Market," **JFM**, 1985, v5(4), 607-620.

Klemkosky, Robert C. and Donald L. Tuttle. "A Ranking Of Doctoral Programs By Financial Research Contributions Of Graduates," **JFQA**, 1977, v12(3), 491-497.

Klemkosky, Robert C. and Donald L. Tuttle. "The Institutional Source And Concentration Of Financial Research," **JOF**, 1977, v32(3), 901-908.

Klemkosky, Robert C. and John D. Martin. "The Effect Of Market Risk On Portfolio Diversification," **JOF**, 1975, v30(1), 147-154.

Klemkosky, Robert C. and John D. Martin. "The Adjustment Of Beta Forecasts," **JOF**, 1975, v30(4), 1123-1128.

Klemkosky, Robert C. and Kwang W. Jun. "The Monetary Impact On Return Variability And Market Risk Premia," **JFQA**, 1982, v17(5), 663-681.

Klemkosky, Robert C. and Terry S. Maness. "The Predictability Of Real Portfolio Risk Levels," **JOF**, 1978, v33(2), 631-639.

Klemkosky, Robert C. and Terry S. Maness. "The Impact Of Options On The Underlying Securities," **JPM**, 1979-80, v6(2), 12-18.

Klemkosky, Robert C. and William P. Miller. "When Forecasting Earnings, It Pays To Be Right!," **JPM**, 1983-84, v10(4), 13-18.

Klemkosky, Robert C. "Additional Evidence On The Risk Level Discriminatory Powers Of The Wiesenberger Classifications," **JOB**, 1976, v49(1), 48-50.

Klemkosky, Robert C. "How Consistently Do Managers Manage?," **JPM**, 1976-77, v3(2), 11-15.

Klemkosky, Robert C. "The Bias In Composite Performance Measures," **JFQA**, 1973, v8(3), 505-514.

Klemkosky, Robert C. "The Impact Of Option Expirations On Stock Prices," **JFQA**, 1978, v13(3), 507-518.

Klemkosky, Robert C. "The Impact And Efficiency Of Institutional Net Trading Imbalances," **JOF**, 1977, v32(1), 79-86.

Klemkosky, Robert C. (Martin, John D. and Robert C. Klemkosky. "The Effect Of Homogeneous Stock Groupings On Portfolio Risk," **JOB**, 1976, v49(3),339-349.)

Klemkosky, Robert C. (Martin, John D. and Robert C. Klemkosky. "Evidence Of Heteroscedasticity In The Market Model," **JOB**, 1975, v48(1), 81-86.)

Klesch, A. Gary. "Interpreting The Prudent Man Rule Of ERISA," **FAJ**, 1977, v33(1), 26-32.

Kleschick, Helen M. (Roenfeldt, Rodney L, Robert J. Sweeney, Steven J. Goldstein and Helen M. Kleschick. "Commentary On 1982 FMA Program," **FM**, 1982, v11(4), 52-54.)

Klevorick, Alvin K. (Alcaly, Roger E. and Alvin K. Klevorick. "Food Prices In Relation To Income Levels In New York City," **JOB**, 1971, v44(4), 380-397.)

Klevorick, Alvin K. (Kane, Edward J. and Alvin K. Klevorick. "Absence Of Money Illusion: A 'Sine Qua Non' For Neutral Money?," **JOF**, 1967, v22(3), 419-423.)

Klevorick, Alvin K. and Richard C. Levin. "A Welfare Analysis Of Constraints On Pricing To Deter Entry," **RIF**, 1983, v4, (Supp), 113-132.

Kliman, M. L. and E. H. Oksanen. "The Keynesian Demand-For-Money Function: A Comment," **JMCB**, 1973, v5(1), 215-220.

Kline, Chester A. "A Visual Aids Program For The College Teacher Of Insurance," **JRI**, 1957, v24(4), 76-88.

Kline, Kristin and Sylvia Lane. "Levels Of Consumer Satisfaction Under Three Subsidized Low Income Housing Programs," **AREUEA**, 1975, v3(2), 83-102.

Kling, Arnold. "How The Stock Market Can Learn To Live With Index Futures And Options," **FAJ**, 1987, v43(5), 33-39.

Kling, Arnold. "The Rise In Bank Failures From A Macroeconomic Perspective," **JFSR**, 1988, v1(4), 353-364.

Kling, John L. "Oil Price Shocks And Stock Market Behavior," **JPM**, 1985-86, v12(1), 34-39.

Kling, John L. "Predicting The Turning Points Of Business And Economic Time Series," **JOB**, 1987, v60(2), 201-238.

Kling, John L. (Fuller, Russell J. and John L. Kling. "Is The Stock Market Predictable?," **JPM**, 1990, v16(4), 28-36.)

Kling, John L. and David A. Bessler. "Calibration-Based Predictive Distributions: An Application Of Prequential Analysis To Interest Rates, Money, Prices, And Output," **JOB**, 1989, v62(4), 477-500.

Kling, John L. and Thomas E. McCue. "Office Building Investment And The Macroeconomy: Empirical Evidence, 1973-1985," **AREUEA**, 1987, v15(3), 234-255.

Kling, Kenneth. (Kenyon, David, Kenneth Kling, Jim Jordan, William Seale and Nancy McCabe. "Factors Affecting Agricultural Futures Price Variance," **JFM**, 1987, v7(1), 73-92.)

Klingman, Darwin D. (Crum, Roy L., Darwin D. Klingman and Lee A. Tavis. "Implementation Of Large-Scale Financial Planning Models: Solution Efficient Transformations," **JFQA**, 1979, v14(1), 137-152.)

Klingstedt, John P. "Full Costing And The Oil Companies," **FAJ**, 1970, v26(5), 79-86.

Klinsky, Steven B. (Little, Wm. Brian and Steven B. Klinsky. "How Leveraged Buy-Outs Can Really Work: A Look At Three Cases," **JACF**, 1989, v2(1), 71-75.)

Klock, David R. "Competitive Rating Laws And Insurer Conduct," **JRI**, 1972, v39(4), 589-601.

Klock, David R. (Babbel, David F. and David R. Klock. "Insurance Pedagogy: Executive Opinions And Priorities," **JRI**, 1988, v55(4), 701-712.)

Klock, David R. (Mehr, Robert I. and David R. Klock. "Student Research And The Insurance Regulator," **JRI**, 1972, v39(1), 119-123.)

Klock, David R. and Sang M. Lee. "A Note On Decision Models For Insurers," **JRI**, 1974, v41(3), 537-543.

Klock, David R. and T. W. Bonham. "Life Insurance Agents And Executives: A Test Of Incongruent Perceptions," **JRI**, 1974, v41(2), 249-258.

Klopstock, Fred H. "The International Money Market: Structure, Scope And Instruments," **JOF**, 1965, v20(2), 182-208.

Klovland, Jan Tore. "The Stability Of The Demand For Money In The Interwar Years: The Case Of Norway, 1925-39," **JMCB**, 1982, v14(2), 252-264.

Kluger, Brian D. and Norman G. Miller. "Measuring Residential Real Estate Liquidity," **AREUEA**, 1990, v18(2), 145-159.

Kluger, Brian. (Hagigi, Moshe and Brian Kluger. "Safety-First: An Alternative Performance Measure," **JPM**, 1986-87, v13(4), 34-40.)

Kluger, Brian. (Hagigi, Moshe and Brian Kluger. "Assessing Risk And Return Of Pension Funds' Portfolios By The Telser Safety-First Approach," **JBFA**, 1987, v14(2), 241-254.)

Klugman, Stuart A. and Michael L. Murray. "Bodily Injury Claim Payments As A Function Of Automobile Liability Insurance Limits," **JRI**, 1984, v51(3), 412-432.

Klugman, Stuart. "Experience Rating In Medical Professional Liability Insurance: Comment," **JRI**, 1989, v56(2), 329-332.

Kneass, George B. "The Money Market," **FAJ**, 1959, v15(4), 9-14.

Knepper, William E. "Law, Insurance And The Automobile Accident Victim," **JRI**, 1962, v29(2), 159-168.

Knetsch, Jack L. (Kahneman, Daniel, Jack L. Knetsch and Richard H. Thaler. "Fairness And The Assumptions Of Economics," **JOB**, 1986, v59(4), Part 2, S285-S300.)

Kniesner, Thomas J. and John D. Leeth. "Compensating Wage Differentials For Fatal Injury Risk In Australia, Japan, And The United States," **JRU**, 1991, v4(1), 75-90.

Knight, Kenneth E. "A Descriptive Model Of The Intra-Firm Innovation Process," **JOB**, 1967, v40(4), 478-496.

Knight, Malcolm D. (Khan, Mohsin S. and Malcolm D. Knight. "Unanticipated Monetary Growth And Inflationary Finance," **JMCB**, 1982, v14(3), 347-364.)

Knight, R. F. and J. F. Affleck-Graves. " The Impact Of Disclosure Requirements On The Systematic Risk Of South African Companies," **JBFA**, 1986, v13(1), 87-94.

Knight, Rory F. (Barr, Graham D. and Rory F. Knight. "Some Geometrical Characteristics Of The Risk-Return Plane," **JBFA**, 1988, v15(3), 437-446.)

Knight, Rory F. and John F. Affleck-Graves. "Further Evidence On The Market Response To LIFO Adoptions," **JBFA**, 1988, v15(2), 169-184.

Knight, W. D. "Working Capital Management - Satisficing Versus Optimization," **FM**, 1972, v1(1),33-40.

Knobel, Abraham. "The Demand For Reserves By Commercial Banks," **JMCB**, 1977, v9(1), 32-47.

Knobel, Roland J. and Beaufort B. Longest, Jr. "Cost-Benefit Assumptions In Analysis For Hospitals," **FM**, 1972, v1(1), 63-65.

Knobler, William M. "Food Stocks," **FAJ**, 1967, v23(3), 35-40.

Knodel, H. William. "Household Durable Goods Trends," **FAJ**, 1956, v12(2), 103-108.

Knodel, H. William. "Method Of Appraising The Stock Market," **FAJ**, 1948, v4(4), 43-53.

Knodel, H. William. "Textile Industry In Transition," **FAJ**, 1959, v15(5), 61-68.

Knodel, H. William. "The Textile Renaissance," **FAJ**, 1955, v11(4), 67-72.

Knoeber, Charles R. (Flath, David and Charles R. Knoeber. "Taxes, Failure Costs, And Optimal Industry Capital Structure: An Empirical Test," **JOF**, 1980, v35(1), 99-117.)

Knopp, Jacky, Jr. "Branding And The Robinson-Patman Act," **JOB**, 1966, v39(1), Part I, 24-34.

Knortz, Herbert C. "The Realities Of Business Combinations," **FAJ**, 1970, v26(4), 28-32.

Knowlton, Winthrop. "The Seven Percent Investment Credit," **FAJ**, 1963, v19(2), 13-15.

Knudsen, Odin. "A Historical-Logical-Ethical Approach To Professional Training," **JFED**, 1974, v3, 25-27.

Knutson, Dennis L. and Henry Wichmann, Jr. "The Accounting Standards Overload Problem For American Small Business," **JBFA**, 1985, v12(3), 387-397.

Ko, Kwang-Soo and Sang-Bin Lee. "A Comparative Analysis Of The Daily Behavior Of Stock Returns: Japan, The US And The Asian NICs," **JBFA**, 1991, v18(2), 219-234.

Kocan, Peter. "Peculiarities Of Railroad Accounting," **FAJ**, 1957, v13(2), 85-92.

Koch, Albert R. "Money Market Developments - From The 'Accord' To Mid-1952," **JOF**, 1955, v10(2), 286-295.

Koch, P. D. (Kawaller, I. G., P. D. Koch and T. W. Koch. "Intraday Relationships Between Volatility In S&P 500 Futures Prices And Volatility In The S&P 500 Index," **JBF**, 1990, v14(2/3), 373-398.)

Koch, Paul D. (Kawaller, Ira G., Paul D. Koch and Timothy W. Koch. "The Temporal Price Relationship Between S&P 500 Futures And The S&P 500 Index," **JOF**, 1987, v42(5), 1309-1329.)

Koch, Paul D., Jeffrey A. Rosenzweig and Joseph A. Whitt, Jr. "The Dynamic Relationship Between The Dollar And US Prices: An Intensive Empirical Investigation," **JIMF**, 1988, v7(2), 181-204.

Koch, T. W. (Kawaller, I. G., P. D. Koch and T. W. Koch. "Intraday Relationships Between Volatility In S&P 500 Futures Prices And Volatility In The S&P 500 Index," **JBF**, 1990, v14(2/3), 373-398.)

Koch, Timothy W. "Commercial Bank Size, Relative Profitability And The Demand For Tax-Exempt Securities," **JBR**, 1981-82, v12(3), 136-144.

Koch, Timothy W. (Benson, Earl D., David S. Kidwell, Timothy W. Koch and Robert J. Rogowski. "Systematic Variation In Yield Spreads For Tax-Exempt General Obligation Bonds," **JFQA**, 1981, v16(5), 685-702.)

Koch, Timothy W. (Hendershott, Patric H. and Timothy W. Koch. "The Demand For Tax-Exempt Securities By Financial Institutions," **JOF**, 1980, v35(3), 717-727.)

Koch, Timothy W. (Kawaller, Ira G., Paul D. Koch and Timothy W. Koch. "The Temporal Price Relationship Between S&P 500 Futures And The S&P 500 Index," **JOF**, 1987, v42(5), 1309-1329.)

Koch, Timothy W. (Kawaller, Ira G. and Timothy W. Koch. "Managing Cash Flow Risk In Stock Index Futures: The Tail Hedge," **JPM**, 1988-89, v15(1), 41-44.)

Koch, Timothy W. (Kawaller, Ira G. and Timothy W. Koch. "Cash-And-Carry Trading And The Pricing Of Treasury Bill Futures," **JFM**, 1984, v4(2), 115-124.)

Koch, Timothy W. (Kawaller, Ira G. and Timothy W. Koch. "Yield Opportunities And Hedge Ratio Considerations With Fixed Income Cash-And-Carry Trades," **JFM**, 1989, v9(6), 539-546.)

Koch, Timothy W. (Kidwell, David S. and Timothy W. Koch. "Market Segmentation And The Term Structure Of Municipal Yields," JMCB, 1983, v15(1), 40-55.)

Koch, Timothy W. (Kidwell, David S. and Timothy W. Koch. "Why And When Do Revenue Bonds Yield More Than GOs?," JPM, 1981-82, v8(4), 51-56.)

Koch, Timothy W. (Kidwell, David S. and Timothy W. Koch. "The Behavior Of The Interest Rate Differential Between Tax-Exempt Revenue And General Obligation Bonds," JOF, 1982, v37(1), 73-85.)

Koch, Timothy W. (MacDonald, S. Scott, Richard L. Peterson and Timothy W. Koch. "Using Futures To Improve Treasury Bill Performance," JFM, 1988, v8(2),167-184.)

Kochanowski, Paul S. and Madelyn V. Young. "Deterrent Aspects Of No-Fault Automobile Insurance: Some Empirical Findings," JRI, 1985, v52(2), 269-288.

Kochenberger, Gary A. (Davis, Samuel G., Gary A. Kochenberger and Edward T. Reutzel. "Expressend: A Check Clearing Decision Support System For Endpoint Selection," JBR, 1983-84, v14(3), 203-211.)

Kocherlakota, Narayana R. "Disentangling The Coefficient Of Relative Risk Aversion From The Elasticity Of Intertemporal Substitution: An Irrelevance Result," JOF, 1990, v45(1), 175-190.

Kochin, Levis A. "Are Future Taxes Anticipated By Consumers?: A Comment," JMCB, 1974, v6(3), 385-394.

Kochin, Levis A. (Choudhri, Ehsan U. and Levis A. Kochin. "The Exchange Rate And The International Transmission Of Business Cycle Disturbances: Some Evidence From The Great Depression," JMCB, 1980, v12(4), Part 1, 565-574.)

Kochin, Levis A. (Gilbert, R. Alton and Levis A. Kochin. "Local Economic Effects Of Bank Failures," JFSR, 1989, v3(4), 333-346.)

Kochin, Levis A. (Hamburger, Michael J. and Levis A. Kochin. "Money And Stock Prices: The Channels Of Influence," JOF, 1972, v27(2), 231-249.)

Kochin, Levis A. (Tanner, J. Ernest and Levis A. Kochin. "The Determinants Of The Difference Between Bid And Ask Prices On Government Bonds," JOB, 1971, v44(4), 375-379.)

Kochin, Levis A. and Richard W. Parks. "Was The Tax-Exempt Bond Market Inefficient Or Were Future Expected Tax Rates Negative?," JOF, 1988, v43(4),913-931.

Kochman, Ladd Michael. "Intrayear Discounting: Uses And Misuses," JFED, 1986, v15, 12-16.

Kodde, David A. and Hein Schreuder. "Forecasting Corporate Revenue And Profit: Time-Series Models Versus Management And Analysts," JBFA, 1984, v11(3), 381-395.

Kodres, Laura E. "Tests Of Unbiasedness In Foreign Exchange Futures Markets: The Effects Of Price Limits," RFM, 1988, v7(1), 138-166.

Koedijk, Kees G. (Bomhoff, Eduard J. and Kees G. Koedijk. "Bilateral Exchange Rates And Risk Premia," JIMF, 1988, v7(2), 205-220.)

Koedijk, Kees and Peter Schotman. "Dominant Real Exchange Rate Movements," JIMF, 1989, v8(4), 517-532.

Koehler, Gary. (Manaster, Steven and Gary Koehler. "The Calculation Of Implied Variances From The Black-Scholes Model: A Note," JOF, 1982, v37(1),227-230.)

Koehn, Michael and Anthony M. Santomero. "Regulation Of Bank Capital And Portfolio Risk," JOF, 1980, v35(5), 1235-1244.

Koehn, Michael F., Paul W. MacAvoy and Harindra De Silva. "Market Responses To Asbestos In Buildings," JREFEC, 1990, v3(3), 213-232.

Koenigsberg, Ernest. "Uncertainty, Capacity, And Market Share In Oligopoly: A Stochastic Theory Of Product Quality," JOB, 1980, v53(2), 151-164.

Kofman, Paul and Casper G. De Vries. "Potato Futures Returns: A Tail Investigation," RFM, 1989, v8(2), 244-258.

Kogelman, Stanley. (Langetieg, Terence C., Martin L. Leibowitz and Stanley Kogelman. "Duration Targeting And The Management Of Multiperiod Returns," FAJ, 1990, v46(5), 35-45.)

Kogelman, Stanley. (Leibowitz, Martin L., Stanley Kogelman and Eric B. Lindenberg. "A Shortfall Approach To The Creditor's Decision: How Much Leverage Can A Firm Support?," FAJ, 1990, v46(3), 43-52.)

Kogelman, Stanley. (Leibowitz, Martin L. and Stanley Kogelman. "Inside The P/E Ratio: The Franchise Factor," FAJ, 1990, v46(6), 17-35.)

Kogelman, Stanley. (Leibowitz, Martin L. and Stanley Kogelman. "Asset Allocation Under Shortfall Constraints," JPM, 1991, v17(2), 18-23.)

Koh, Francis and Terry Walter. "A Direct Test Of Rock's Model Of The Pricing Of Unseasoned Issues," JFEC, 1989, v23(2), 251-272.

Koh, Hian C. and Larry N. Killough. "The Use Of Multiple Discriminant Analysis In The Assessment Of Going-Concern Status Of An Audit Client," JBFA, 1990, v17(2), 179-192.

Koh, Hian-Chye. (Low, Lay-Chin, Pearl Hock-Neo Tan and Hian-Chye Koh. "The Determination Of Audit Fees: An Analysis In The Singapore Context," JBFA, 1990, v17(2), 285-296.)

Kohane, Yehuda. (Krislov, Joseph and Yehuda Kohane. "Worker's Compensation Coverage For The Self-Employed: The Israeli Experience," JRI, 1979, v46(2), 113-122.)

Kohers, Theodor. (Rao, Spuma and Theodor Kohers. "The Effect Of Selected U.S. Market Conditions And Exchange Rate Variability On Merger And Acquisition Activities Of Foreign Companies In The United States," GFJ, 1990, v1(2), 139-152.)

Kohers, Theodor. (Simpson, W. Gary and Theodor Kohers. "The Effect Of Organizational Form On Performance In The Savings And Loan Industry," FR, 1979, v14(3), 1-12.)

Kohlberg Kravis Roberts And Co. "Leveraged Buy-Outs," JACF, 1989, v2(1), 64-70.

Kohlhagen, Steven W. "The Stability Of Exchange Rate Expectations And Canadian Capital Flows," JOF, 1977, v32(5), 1657-1669.

Kohlhagen, Steven W. (Garman, Mark B. and Steven W. Kohlhagen. "Inflation And Foreign Exchange Rates Under Production And Monetary Uncertainty," JFQA, 1980, v15(4), 949-967.)

Kohlhagen, Steven W. (Garman, Mark B. and Steven W. Kohlhagen. "Foreign Currency Option Values," JIMF, 1983, v2(3), 231-237.)

Kohlhepp, Daniel B. (Gau, George W. and Daniel B. Kohlhepp. "The Financial Planning And Management Of Real Estate Developments," FM, 1980, v9(1), 46-52.)

Kohlhepp, Daniel B. (Gau, George W. and Daniel B. Kohlhepp. "Reinvestment Rates And The Sensitivity Of Rates Of Return In Real Estate Investment," AREUEA, 1976, v4(3), 69-84.)

Kohlhepp, Daniel B. (Gau, George W. and Daniel B. Kohlhepp. "Multicollinearity And Reduced-Form Price Equations For Residential Markets," AREUEA, 1978, v6(1), 50-69.)

Kohlhepp, Daniel B. (Gau, George W. and Daniel B. Kohlhepp. "Alternative Estimation Methods For Reduced Form Price Equations Under Conditions Of Multicollinearity: Reply," AREUEA, 1979, v7(3), 437-441.)

Kohlhepp, Daniel B. and Charles A. Ingene. "The Effect Of Municipal Services And Local Taxes On Housing Values," AREUEA, 1979, v7(3), 318-343.

Kohli, Ulrich. "A Note On Banknote Characteristics And The Demand For Currency By Denomination," JBF, 1988, v11(3), 389-400.

Kohn, Donald L. (Burghardt, Galen, Jr. and Donald L. Kohn. "Comments On 'Margins And Futures Contracts'," JFM, v1(2), 255-257.)

Kokus, John, Jr. (Marcin, Thomas C. and John Kokus, Jr. "Economic And Demographic Factors Affecting Housing Demand Into The 1980s And 1990s," AREUEA, 1975, v3(3), 81-94.)

Kolari, James and John DiClemente. "A Case Study Of Geographic Deregulation: The New Illinois Bank Holding Company Act," JBR, 1985-86, v16(3), 150-157.

Kolari, James W. and Vincent P. Apilado. "Bond Risk Premiums, Financial Data, And The Effect Of Market Segmentation," JBFA, 1982, v8(2), 207-218.

Kolari, James W. "An Analytical Model Of Risky Yield Curves," JFR, 1987, v10(4), 295-304.

Kolari, James W. (Fraser, Donald R. and James W. Kolari. "The 1982 Depository Institutions Act And Security Returns In The Savings And Loan Industry," JFR, 1990, v13(4), 339-348.)

Kolari, James W. (French, Dan W., John C. Groth and James W. Kolari. "Current Investor Expectations And Better Betas," JPM, 1983-84, v10(1), 12-17.)

Kolari, James W. (Rose, Peter S., James W. Kolari and Kenneth W. Riener. "A National Survey Study Of Bank Services And Prices Arrayed By Size And Structure," JBR, 1985-86, v16(2), 72-85.)

Kolari, James W. (Uselton, Gene C., James W. Kolari and Donald R. Fraser. "Long-Term Trends In The Riskiness Of Electric Utility Shares," JBFA, 1986, v13(3), 453-459.)

Kolari, James, Arvind Mahajan and Edward M. Saunders. "The Effect Of Changes In Reserve Requirements On Bank Stock Prices," JBF, 1988, v12(2), 183-198.

Kolari, James, Thomas H. McInish and Erwin M. Saniga. "A Note On The Distribution Types Of Financial Ratios In The Commercial Banking Industry," JBF, 1989, v13(3), 463-472.

Kolari, James. (Zardkoohi, Asghar, Nanda Rangan and James Kolari. "Homogeneity Restrictions On The Translog Cost Model: A Note," JOF, 1986, v41(5), 1153-1156.)

Kolb, Burton A. "Capital Budgeting," FAJ, 1968, v24(6), 170-174.

Kolb, Burton A. "Research, Development And Common Stock Values," FAJ, 1962, v18(5), 9-16.

Kolb, Burton A. "Risk, Technological Change, And Long-Term Financing," FAJ, 1965, v21(6), 141-146.

Kolb, Burton A. "The Rise And Fall Of Public Utilities: An Appraisal Of Risk," JOB, 1964, v37(4), 329-345.

Kolb, Robert W. (Chiang, Raymond C., Gerald D. Gay and Robert W. Kolb. "Commodity Exchange Seat Prices," RFM, 1987, v6(1), 1-10.)

Kolb, Robert W. and Gerald D. Gay. "Immunizing Bond Portfolios With Interest Rate Futures," FM, 1982, v11(2), 81-89.

Kolb, Robert W. and Gerald D. Gay. "A Pricing Anomaly In Treasury Bill Futures," JFR, 1985, v8(2), 157-167.

Kolb, Robert W. and Gerald D. Gay. "The Performance Of Live Cattle Futures As Predictors Of Subsequent Spot Prices," JFM, 1983, v3(1), 55-63.

Kolb, Robert W. and Raymond Chiang. "Duration, Immunization, And Hedging With Interest Rate Futures," JFR, 1982, v5(2), 161-170.

Kolb, Robert W. and Raymond Chiang. "Improving Hedging Performance Using Interest Rate Futures," FM, 1981, v10(4), 72-79.

Kolb, Robert W. "Including Costs Of Misclassification In Discriminant Analyses: A Practical Approach," FR, 1981, v16(2), 59-64.

Kolb, Robert W. (Barrett, W. Brian, Andrea J. Heuson and Robert W. Kolb. "The Differential Effects Of Sinking Funds On Bond Risk Premia," JFR, 1986, v9(4), 303-312.)

Kolb, Robert W. (Barrett, W. Brian, Andrea J. Heuson, Robert W. Kolb and Gabriele H. Schropp. "The Adjustment Of Stock Prices To Completely Unanticipated Events," JBF, 1987, v22(4), 345-354.)

Kolb, Robert W. (Barrett, W. Brian, Andrea J. Heuson and Robert W. Kolb. "The Effect Of Three Mile Island On Utility Bond Risk Premia: A Note," JOF, 1986, v41(1), 255-262.)

Kolb, Robert W. (Bidwell, Clinton M., III and Robert W. Kolb. "The Impact And Value Of Broker's Sell Recommendations," FR, 1980, v15(3), 58-68.)

Kolb, Robert W. (Chiang, Raymond and Robert W. Kolb. "An Analytical Model Of The Relationship Between Maturity And Bonds Risk Differentials," FR, 1986, v21(2), 191-209.)

Kolb, Robert W. (Gay, Gerald D. and Robert W. Kolb. "Removing Bias In Duration Based Hedging Models: A Note," JFM, 1984, v4(2), 225-228.)

Kolb, Robert W. (Gay, Gerald D., Robert W. Kolb and Raymond Chiang. "Interest Rate Hedging: An Empirical Test Of Alternative Strategies," JFR, 1983, v6(3), 187-197.)

Kolb, Robert W. (Gay, Gerald D. and Robert W. Kolb. "The Management Of Interest Rate Risk," JPM, 1982-83, v9(2), 65-70.)

Kolb, Robert W. (Gay, Gerald D. and Robert W. Kolb. "Interest Rate Futures As A Tool For Immunization," JPM, 1983-84, v10(1),65-70.)

Kolb, Robert W. (Gay, Gerald D., William C. Hunter and Robert W. Kolb. "A Comparative Analysis Of Futures Contract Margins," JFM, 1986, v6(2), 307-324.)

Kolb, Robert W. (Gay, Gerald D., Robert W. Kolb and Kenneth Yung. "Trader Rationality In The Exercise Of Futures Options," JFEC, 1989, v23(2), 339-362.)

Kolb, Robert W. (Nye, David J. and Robert W. Kolb. "Inflation, Interest Rates And Property-Liability Insurer Risk," JRI, 1986, v53(1), 144-154.)

Kolb, Robert W. and Ricardo J. Rodriguez. "Friday The Thirteenth: 'Part VII'–A Note," JOF, 1987, v42(5), 1385-1387.

Kolb, Robert W. and Ricardo J. Rodriguez. "The Regression Tendencies Of Betas: A Reappraisal," FR, 1989, v24(2), 319-334.

Kolb, Robert W. and Ricardo J. Rodriguez. "Markov Chains And Regression Toward The Mean," FR, 1991, v26(1), 115-125.

Kolb, Robert W. and Ricardo J. Rodriguez. "Is The Distribution Of Betas Stationary?," JFR, 1990, v13(4), 279-284.

Kolb, Robert W., Gerald D. Gay and William C. Hunter. "Liquidity And Capital Requirements For Futures Market Hedges," RFM, 1985, v4(1), 1-25.

Kolb, Robert W., Gerald D. Gay and James V. Jordan. "Managing Foreign Interest Rate Risk," JFM, 1982, v2(2), 151-158.

Kolb, Robert W., Gerald D. Gay and James V. Jordan. "Markets Are There Arbitrage Opportunities In The Treasury-Bond Futures Markets," JFM, 1982, v2(3), 217-230.

Kolb, Robert W., Gerald D. Gay and William C. Hunter. "Liquidity Requirements For Financial Futures Investments," FAJ, 1985, v41(3), 60-68.

Kolb, Robert W., James V. Jordan and Gerald D. Gay. "Futures Prices And Expected Future Spot Prices," RFM, 1983, v2(1), 110-123.

Kolb, Robert W., Roger A. Morin and Gerald D. Gay. "Regulation, Regulatory Lag, And The Use Of Futures Markets," JOF, 1983, v38(2), 405-418.

Kolb, Robert W., Stephen G. Timme and Gerald D. Gay. "Macro Versus Micro Futures Hedges At Commercial Banks," JFM, 1984, v4(1), 47-54.

Kolluri, Bharat R. "Anticipated Price Changes, Inflation Uncertainty, And Capital Stock Returns," JFR, 1982, v5(2), 135-149.

Kolodny, Richard and Diane Rizzuto Suhler. "Changes In Capital Structure, New Equity Issues, And Scale Effects," JFR, 1985, v8(2), 127-136.

Kolodny, Richard, Peter Seeley and Murray E. Polakoff. "The Effect Of Compensating Balance Requirements On The Profitability Of Borrowers And Lenders," JFQA, 1977, v12(5), 801-815.)

Kolodny, Richard, Martin Laurence and Arabinda Ghosh. "In Search Of Excellence ... For Whom?," JPM, 1989, v15(3), 56-60.

Kolodny, Richard. "The Refunding Decision In Near Perfect Markets," JOF, 1974, v29(5), 1467-1477.

Kolodny, Richard. (Arbel, Avner, Richard Kolodny and Josef Lakonishok. "The Relationship Between Risk Of Default And Return On Equity: An Empirical Investigation," JFQA, 1977, v12(4), 615-625.)

Kolodny, Richard. (Eun, Cheol S., Richard Kolodny and Bruce G. Resnick. "U.S.-Based International Mutual Funds: A Performance Evaluation," JPM, 1991, v17(3), 88-94.)

Kolodny, Richard. (Jaggi, Bikki and Richard Kolodny. Selection Of The LIFO Method Of Inventory Valuation: Mangement's Motives And Investor's Reaction," FR, v12(1), 1-19.)

Komar, Robert I. "Developing A Liquidity Management Model," JBR, 1971-72, v2(1), 38-53.

Kon, S. J. (Chen, A. H., E. Han Kim and S. J. Kon. "Cash Demand, Liquidation Costs And Capital Market Equilibrium Under Uncertainty," JFEC, 1975, v2(3), 293-308.)

Kon, Stanley J. and Frank C. Jen. "Estimation Of Time-Varying Systematic Risk And Performance For Mutual Fund Portfolios: An Application Of Switching Regression," JOF, 1978, v33(2), 457-475.

Kon, Stanley J. and W. Patrick Lau. "Specification Tests For Portfolio Regression Parameter Stationarity And The Implications For Empirical Research," JOF, 1979, v34(2), 451-465.

Kon, Stanley J. "Models Of Stock Returns - A Comparison," JOF, 1984, v39(1), 147-165.

Kon, Stanley J. "The Market-Timing Performance Of Mutual Fund Managers," JOB, 1983, v56(3), 323-348.

Kon, Stanley J. (Chen, Andrew H., E. Han Kim and Stanley J. Kon. "Cash Demand, Liquidation Costs, And Capital Market Equilibrium Under Uncertainty: Reply," JFEC, 1976, v3(3), 297-298.)

Kon, Stanley J. (Figlewski, Stephen and Stanley J. Kon. "Portfolio Management With Stock Index Futures," FAJ, 1982, v38(1), 52-60.)

Kon, Stanley J. (Kadapakkam, Palani-Rajan and Stanley J. Kon. "The Value Of Shelf Registration For New Debt Issues," JOB, 1989, v62(2), 271-292.)

Kon, Stanley J. and Frank C. Jen. "The Investment Performance Of Mutual Funds: An Empirical Investigation Of Timing, Selectivity, And Market Efficiency," JOB, 1979, v52(2), 263-290.

Kon, Stanley J. and John G. Thatcher. "The Effect Of Bankruptcy Laws On The Valuation Of Risky Consumer Debt," FR, 1989, v24(3), 371-396.

Kon-Ya, Fumiko. (Yonezawa, Yasuhiro and Fumiko Kon-Ya. "The Japanese Market And The Economic Enviornment," JPM, 1982-83, v9(1), 36-45.)

Konrath, Larry F. "Accounting For Changing Price Levels," FAJ, 1974, v30(6), 50-56.

Konstas, Panos and Mohamad W. Khouja. "The Keynesian Demand-For-Money Function: Another Look And Some Additional Evidence," JMCB, 1969, v1(4), 765-777.

Konstas, Panos and Mohamad W. Kouja. "The Keynesian Money Demand - Another Look At The Evidence," JMCB, 1975, v7(4), 521-526.

Koo, Suk Mo. (Elton, Edwin J., Martin J. Gruber and Suk Mo Koo. "Effect Of Quarterly Earnings Announcements On Analysts' Forecasts," RIF, 1986, v6, 247-260.)

Koontz, Stephen R., Philip Garcia and Michael A. Hudson. "Dominant-Satellite Relationships Between Live Cattle Cash And Futures Markets," JFM, 1990, v10(2), 123-136.

Koop, Dwight. "Pricing Options: Variations On The Black-Scholes Model," RFM, 1986, v5(1), 80-89.

Koot, Ronald S. and David A. Walker. "Rules Versus Discretion: An Analysis Of Income Stability And The Money Supply: A Comment," JMCB, 1974, v6(2),253-261.

Koot, Ronald S. "A Factor Analytic Approach To An Empirical Definition Of Money," JOF, 1975, v30(4), 1081-1089.

Koot, Ronald S. "On Economies Of Scale In Credit Unions," JOF, 1978, v33(4), 1087-1094.

Koot, Ronald S. "On The St. Louis Equation And An Alternative Definition Of The Money Supply," JOF, 1977, v32(3), 917-920.

Koot, Ronald S. "The Demand For Credit Union Shares," JFQA, 1976, v11(1), 133-141.

Kopcke, Richard W. and Peter C. Aldrich. "A Real Estate Crisis: Averted Or Just Postponed?," JPM, 1983-84, v10(3), 21-29.

Kopecky, Kenneth J. "A Mean-Variance Framework For Analyzing Reserve Requirements And Monetary Control," JBF, 1988, v12(1), 151-160.

Kopecky, Kenneth J. "Monetary Control Under Reverse Lag And Contemporaneous Reserve Accounting: A Comparison: A Comment," JMCB, 1984, v16(1), 81-88.

Kopecky, Kenneth J. "Nonmember Banks And Empirical Measures Of The Variability Of Reserves And Money: A Theoretical Appraisal," JOF, 1978, v33(1), 311-318.

Kopecky, Kenneth J. "Nonmember Banks And Monetary Control: Reply," JOF, 1980, v35(3), 807.

Kopp, Bennett S. "Conglomerates In Portfolio," FAJ, 1968, v24(2), 145-148.

Koppenhaver, G. D. "An Empirical Analysis Of Bank Hedging In Futures Markets," JFM, 1990, v10(1), 1-12.

Koppenhaver, G. D. "Bank Funding Risks, Risk Aversion, And The Choice Of Futures Hedging Instrument," JOF, 1985, v40(1), 241-255.

Koppenhaver, G. D. "Selective Hedging Of Bank Assets With Treasury Bill Futures Contracts," JFR, 1984, v7(2), 105-119.

Koppenhaver, G. D. "The Forward Pricing Efficiency Of The Live Cattle Futures Market," JFM, 1983, v3(3), 307-319.

Koppenhaver, G. D. "Variable-Rate Loan Commitments, Deposit Withdrawal Risk, And Anticipatory Hedging," JFM, 1985, v5(3), 317-330.

Koppenhaver, G. D. and Cheng F. Lee. "Alternative Instruments For Hedging Inflation Risk In The Banking Industry," JFM, 1987, v7(6), 619-636.

Koppenhaver, Gary D. "Regulating Financial Intermediary Use Of Futures And Options," RFM, 1987, v6(2), 144-164.

Kopprasch, Robert W. (Pitts, Mark and Robert W. Kopprasch. "Reducing Inter-Temporal Risk In Financial Futures Hedging," JFM, 1984, v4(1), 1-14.)

Kopprasch, Robert W., Jr. (Yates, James W., Jr. and Robert W. Kopprasch, Jr. "Writing Covered Call Options: Profits And Risks," JPM, 1980-81, v7(1), 74-79.)

Kopprasch, Robert. (Hakanoglu, Erol, Robert Kopprasch and Emmanuel Roman. "Constant Proportion Portfolio Insurance For Fixed-Income Investment," JPM, 1989, v15(4), 58-66.)

Korajczyk, Robert A. (Connor, Gregory and Robert A. Korajczyk. "Performance Measurement With The Arbitrage Pricing Theory: A New Framework For Analysis," JFEC, 1986, v15(3), 373-394.)

Korajczyk, Robert A. (Connor, Gregory and Robert A. Korajczyk. "Risk And Return In An Equilibrium APT: Application Of A New Test Methodology," JFEC, 1988, v21(2), 255-290.)

Korajczyk, Robert A. (Connor, Gregory and Robert A. Korajczyk. "An Intertemporal Equilibrium Beta Pricing Model," RFS, 1989, v2(3), 373-392.)

Korajczyk, Robert A. (Connor, Gregory and Robert A. Korajczyk. "The Attributes, Behavior And Performance Of U.S. Mutual Funds," RQFA, 1991, v1(1), 5-26.)

Korajczyk, Robert A. (Jagannathan, Ravi and Robert A. Korajczyk. "Assessing The Market Timing Performance Of Managed Portfolios," JOB, 1986, v59(2), Part 1, 217-236.)

Korajczyk, Robert A. and Claude J. Viallet. "An Empirical Investigation Of International Asset Pricing," RFS, 1989, v2(4), 553-586.

Koray, Faik. "Government Debt, Economic Activity, And Transmission Of Economic Disturbances," JMCB, 1987, v19(3), 361-375.

Koray, Faik. "Money And Functional Distribution Of Income," JMCB, 1989, v21(1), 33-48.

Koray, Faik. (Lastrapes, William D. and Faik Koray. "International Transmission Of Aggregate Shocks Under Fixed And Flexible Exchange Rate Regimes: United Kingdom, France, And Germany, 1959 To 1985," JIMF, 1990, v9(4), 402-423.)

Koreisha, Sergio. (James, Christopher, Sergio Koreisha and Megan Partch. "A Varma Analysis Of The Causal Relations Among Stock Returns, Real Output, And Nominal Interest Rates," JOF, 1985, v40(5), 1375-1384.)

Korkie, Bob M. (Jobson, J. D. and Bob M. Korkie. "Performance Hypothesis Testing With The Sharpe And Treynor Measures," JOF, 1981, v36(4), 889-908.)

Korkie, Bob. "Corrections For Trading Frictions In Multivariate Returns," JOF, 1989, v44(5), 1421-1434.

Korkie, Bob. "External Vs. Internal Performance Evaluation," JPM, 1982-83, v9(3), 36-42.

Korkie, Bob. "Market Line Deviations And Market Anomalies With Reference To Small And Large Firms," JFQA, 1986, v21(2), 161-180.

Korkie, Bob. (Jobson, J. D. and Bob Korkie. "On The Jensen Measure And Marginal Improvements In Portfolio Performance: A Note," JOF, 1984, v39(1),245-251.)

Korkie, Bob. (Jobson, J. D. and Bob Korkie. "Potential Performance And Tests Of Portfolio Efficiency," JFEC, 1982, v10(4), 433-466.)

Korkie, Bob. (Jobson, J. D. and Bob Korkie. "Statistical Inference In Two-Parameter Portfolio Theory With Multiple Regression Software," JFQA, 1983, v18(2), 189-197.)

Korkie, Bob. (Jobson, J. D. and Bob Korkie. "Putting Markowitz Theory To Work," JPM, 1980-81, v7(4), 70-74.)

Korkie, Bob. (Jobson, J. D. and Bob Korkie. "A Performance Interpretation Of Multivariate Tests Of Asset Set Intersection, Spanning, And Mean-Variance Efficiency," JFQA, 1989, v24(2), 185-204.)

Korkie, R. M. (Mumey, G. A. and R. M. Korkie. "Balance Sheet Additivity Of Risk Measures," JFQA, 1971, v6(4), 1123-1133.)

Kormendi, Roger C. and Philip Meguire. "A Multicountry Characterization Of The Nonstationarity Of Aggregate Output," JMCB, 1990, v22(1), 77-93.

Kormendi, Roger C., Victor L. Bernard, S. Craig Pirrong and Edward A. Snyder. "The Origins And Resolution Of The Thrift Crisis," JACF, 1989, v2(3), 85-99.

Kormendi, Roger and Robert Lipe. "Earnings Innovations, Earnings Persistence, And Stock Returns," **JOB**, 1987, v60(3), 323-346.

Kormes, Mark. "Statistical Problems And Methods Of Pre-Paid Blue Cross And Blue Shield Hospital And Medical Plans," **JRI**, 1950, v17, 13-23.

Korn, Donald H. (Bradley, James W. and Donald H. Korn. "Acquisition And Merger Trends," **FAJ**, 1977, v33(6), 65-70.)

Kornbluth, Jonathan S. H. and Joseph D. Vinso. "Capital Structure And The Financing Of The Multinational Corporation: A Fractional Multiobjective Approach," **JFQA**, 1982, v17(2), 147-178.

Korschot, Benjamin C. "Measuring Research Analysts' Performance," **FAJ**, 1978, v34(4), 41-46.

Korschot, Benjamin C. "Prudence Before And After ERISA," **FAJ**, 1977, v33(4), 18-21.

Korschot, Benjamin C. (Patterson, Solon P., Dennis R. Bouwer, Theodore R. Lilley and Benjamin C. Korschot. "Long-Range Planning In The FAF," **FAJ**, 1979, v35(1), 23-26.)

Kortanek, K. (Byrne, R., A. Charnes, W. Cooper and K. Kortanek. "A Chance-Constrained Approach To Capital Budgeting With Portfolio Type Payback And Liquidity Constraints And Horizon Posture Controls," **JFQA**, 1967, Vol(4), 339-364.)

Korth, Christopher M. (Schroath, Frederick W. and Christopher M. Korth. "Managerial Barriers To The Internationalization Of U.S. Property And Liability Insurers: Theory And Perspectives," **JRI**, 1989, v56(4), 630-648.)

Korwar, Ashok N. (Masulis, Ronald W. and Ashok N. Korwar. "Seasoned Equity Offerings: An Empirical Investigation," **JFEC**, 1986, v15(1/2), 91-118.)

Koshal, Manjulika and Rajindar K. Koshal. "Consumer Demand And Supply Of Installment Credit: A Simultaneous Equations Approach," **FR**, 1981, v16(1), 14-26.

Koshal, Rajindar K. (Koshal, Manjulika and Rajindar K. Koshal. "Consumer Demand And Supply Of Installment Credit: A Simultaneous Equations Approach," **FR**, 1981, v16(1), 14-26.)

Kosmicke, Ralph and Scott D. Opsal. "The Effect Of Volatility On Investment Returns," **JPM**, 1987-88, v14(2), 14-19.

Kosmicke, Ralph. "The Contradiction Between Keynes And The EMH," **JPM**, 1984-85, v11(1), 41-43.

Kosmicke, Ralph. "The Limited Relevance Of Volatility To Risk," **JPM**, 1986-87, v13(1), 18-20.

Kosobud, Richard F. "Folklore Into Fact: Appraising Forecasting Methods," **JOB**, 1978, v51(4),569-572.

Kothari, S. P. (Ball, Ray and S. P. Kothari. "Nonstationary Expected Returns: Implications For Tests Of Market Efficiency And Serial Correlations In Returns," **JFEC**, 1989, v25(1), 51-74.)

Kothari, S. P. (Handa, Puneet, S. P. Kothari and Charles Wasley. "The Relation Between The Return Interval And Betas: Implications For The Size Effect," **JFEC**, 1989, v23(1), 79-100.)

Kotler, Philip and Randall L. Schultz. "Marketing Simulations: Review And Prospects," **JOB**, 1970, v43(3), 237-295.

Kotler, Philip. "Elements In A Theory Of Growth Stock Valuation," **FAJ**, 1962, v18(3), 35-44.

Kotlikoff, Laurence J. "What Microeconomics Teaches Us About The Dynamic Macro Effects Of Fiscal Policy," **JMCB**, 1988, v20(3), Part 2, 479-495.

Kott, Phillip S. "Returns To Scale In The U.S. Life Insurance Industry: Comment," **JRI**, 1983, v50(3), 506-507.

Kouja, Mohamad W. (Konstas, Panos and Mohamad W. Kouja. "The Keynesian Money Demand - Another Look At The Evidence," **JMCB**, 1975, v7(4), 521-526.)

Kourday, Michael. "Preparing An Oil Share Analyzer," **FAJ**, 1957, v13(1), 39-44.

Kourday, Michael. "Relative Values - A Method Of Outperforming The Market," **FAJ**, 1963, v19(6), 35-44.

Koveos, Peter and Bruce Seifert. "Purchasing Power Parity And Black Markets," **FM**, 1985, v14(3), 40-46.

Koveos, Peter E. (Booth, G. Geoffrey, Fred R. Kaen and Peter E. Koveos. "Currency Interdependence In Foreign Exchange Markets," **FR**, 1980, v15(3), 36-44.)

Koveos, Peter E. (Booth, G. Geoffrey, Fred R. Kaen and Peter E. Koveos. "Persistent Dependence In Gold Prices," **JFR**, 1982, v5(1), 85-93.)

Koveos, Peter E. (Booth, G. Geoffrey and Peter E. Koveos. "A Programming Model For Bank Hedging Decisions," **JFR**, 1986, v9(3), 271-279.)

Koveos, Peter E. (Booth, G. Geoffrey, James E. Duggan and Peter E. Koveos. "Deviations From Purchasing Power Parity, Relative Inflation, And Exchange Rates: The Recent Experience," **FR**, 1985, v20(2),195-218.)

Koveos, Peter E. (Booth, G. Geoffrey and Peter E. Koveos. "Purchasing Power Parity: A Reexamination Of Prediction Errors," **AFPAF**, 1989, v3(1), 143-162.)

Koveos, Peter E. (Chang, Rosita P., Peter E. Koveos and S. Ghon Rhee. "Financial Planning For International Long-Term Debt Financing," **AFPAF**, 1990, v5(1), 33-58.)

Koveos, Peter E. (Milonas, Nicholaos T., Peter E. Koveos and G. Geoffrey Booth. "Memory In Commodity Futures Contracts: A Comment," **JFM**, 1985, v5(1), 113-114.)

Kowalski, Joseph G. and Peter F. Colwell. "Market Versus Assessed Values Of Industrial Land," **AREUEA**, 1986, v14(2), 361-373.

Kozelka, Richard L. (Arbuckle, Ernest C., Richard L. Kozelka and Arthur M. Weimer. "Dean's Forum: The Place Of Insurance In The Collegiate Curriculum," **JRI**, 1960, v27(3), 67-70.)

Kozub, Robert. (Golen, Steven and Robert Kozub. "Systems Flowchart: A Key To Understanding The Concepts Of Present And Future Value," **JFED**, 1981, v10, 74-77.)

Kracaw, William A. (Blum, Gerald A., William A. Kracaw and Wilbur G. Lewellen. "Determinants Of The Execution Costs Of Common Stock Trades By Individual Investors," **JFR**, 1986, v9(4), 291-301.)

Kracaw, William A. (Campbell, Tim S. and William A. Kracaw. "Optimal Managerial Incentive Contracts And The Value Of Corporate Insurance," **JFQA**, 1987, v22(3), 315-328.)

Kracaw, William A. (Campbell, Tim S. and William A. Dracaw. "Information Production, Market Signalling, And The Theory Of Financial Intermediation: A Reply," **JOF**, 1982, v37(4), 1097-1099.)

Kracaw, William A. (Campbell, Tim S. and William A. Kracaw. "The Market For Managerial Labor Services And Capital Market Equilibrium," **JFQA**, 1985, v20(3), 277-298.)

Kracaw, William A. (Campbell, Tim S. and William A. Kracaw. "Sorting Equilibria In Financial Markets: The Incentive Problem," **JFQA**, 1981, v16(4), 477-492.)

Kracaw, William A. (Campbell, Tim S. and William A. Kracaw. "Information Production, Market Signalling, And The Theory Of Financial Intermediation," **JOF**, 1980, v35(4), 863-882.)

Kracaw, William A. (Campbell, Tim S. and William A. Kracaw. "Corporate Risk Management And The Incentive Effects Of Debt," **JOF**, 1990, v45(5), 1673-1686.)

Kracaw, William A. (Campbell, Tim S. and William A. Kracaw. "Bank Funding Risks, Risk Aversion, And The Choice Of Futures Hedging Instrument: Comment," **JOF**, 1990, v45(5), 1705-1708.)

Kracaw, William A. (Huang, Roger D. and William A. Kracaw. "Stock Market Returns And Real Activity: A Note," **JOF**, 1984, v39(1), 267-273.)

Kracaw, William A. (Johnston, Elizabeth Tashijan, William A. Kracaw and John J. McConnell. "Day-Of-The-Week Effects In Financial Futures: An Analysis Of GNMA, T-Bond, T-Note, And T-Bill Contracts," **JFQA**, 1991, v26(1), 23-44.)

Kracaw, William A. (Lewellen, Wilbur G. and William A. Kracaw. "Inflation, Corporate Growth, And Corporate Leverage," **FM**, 1987, v16(4), 29-36.)

Krackhardt, David M. (Dalton, Dan R., David M. Krackhardt and Lyman W. Porter. "The Impact Of Teller Turnover In Banking: First Appearances Are Deceiving," **JBR**, 1983-84, v14(3), 184-192.)

Kraft, Arthur. (Barth, James, Arthur Kraft and Philip Wiest. "A Utility Maximization Approach To Individual Bank Asset Selection," **JMCB**, 1977, v9(2), 316-327.)

Kraft, Arthur. (Kraft, John and Arthur Kraft. "Income Velocity And Interest Rates: A Time Series Test Of Causality: A Comment," **JMCB**, 1976, v8(1), 123-125.)

Kraft, Arthur. (Kraft, John and Arthur Kraft. "Determinants Of Common Stock Prices: A Time Series Analysis," **JOF**, 1977, v32(2), 417-425.)

Kraft, John and Arthur Kraft. "Income Velocity And Interest Rates: A Time Series Test Of Causality: A Comment," **JMCB**, 1976, v8(1), 123-125.

Kraft, John and Arthur Kraft. "Determinants Of Common Stock Prices: A Time Series Analysis," **JOF**, 1977, v32(2), 417-425.

Krainer, Robert E. "A Neglected Issue In Capital Rationing - The Asset Demand For Money," **JOF**, 1966, v21(4), 731-736.

Krainer, Robert E. "A Pedagogic Note On Dividend Policy," **JFQA**, 1971, v6(4), 1147-1154.

Krainer, Robert E. "A Reexamination Of The Theory Of Monopsonistic Discrimination In The Capital Market," **JOB**, 1974, v47(3), 429-439.

Krainer, Robert E. "Interest Rates, Leverage, And Investor Rationality," **JFQA**, 1977, v12(1), 1-16.

Krainer, Robert E. "Liquidity Preference And Stock Market Speculation," **JFQA**, 1969, v4(1), 89-97.

Krainer, Robert E. "Resource Endowment And The Structure Of Foreign Investment," **JOF**, 1967, v22(1),49-57.

Krainer, Robert E. "The Structure Of Foreign Investment: Reply," **JOF**, 1967, v22(4), 655-656.

Krainer, Robert E. "Wealth Redistribution Risk And The Modern Theory Of Finance: An Analysis Of Inflation And Bankruptcy," **JMCB**, 1977, v9(3), 460-468.

Kraizberg, E. "The Market Making Of Forward Contracts With Premature Delivery Provision," **JBF**, 1990, v14(4), 691-716.

Kraizberg, Elli. "The Option To Deliver Prematurely Associated With Forward Contracts: Analysis Of A Timing Option," **RDIBF**, 1988, v2, 227-258.

Kramer, Donald. "Current Accounting Practices," **FAJ**, 1969, v25(1), 92-97.

Kramer, Donald. "Life Insurance Profit Margins," **FAJ**, 1965, v21(6), 85-90.

Kramer, Robert L. "Arbitrage In U.S. Government Bonds: A Management Science Approach," **JBR**, 1970-71, v1(2), 30-44.

Kramer, Robert L. "Forecasting Branch Bank Growth Patterns," **JBR**, 1970-71, v1(4), 17-24.

Kramer, Robert L. "The Lock Box Problem: Comment," **JBR**, 1971-72, v2(1), 54-55.

Krasker, William S. "Minimax Behavior In Portfolio Selection," **JOF**, 1982, v37(2), 609-614.

Krasker, William S. "Stock Price Movements In Response To Stock Issues Under Asymmetric Information," **JOF**, 1986, v41(1), 93-106.

Krasker, William S. (Bell, David E. and William S. Krasker. "Estimating Hedge Ratios," **FM**, 1986, v15(2), 34-39.)

Krasker, William S. (Leibowitz, Martin L. and William S. Krasker. "The Persistence Of Risk: Stocks Versus Bonds Over The Long Term," **FAJ**, 1988, v44(6), 40-47.)

Krasker, William S. (Leibowitz, Martin L., William S. Krasker and Ardavan Nozari. "Spread Duration: A New Tool For Bond Portfolio Management," **JPM**, 1990, v16(3), 46-53.)

Krasnakevich, John. (Hisrich, Robert D., Michael P. Peters and John Krasnakevich. "Effectively Managing Consumer Credit Through Computer Graphics," **JBR**, 1982-83, v13(4), 304-308.)

Krasniewski, Raymond J. (Hite, Gailen L. and Raymond J. Krasniewski. "The 1981 Tax Act: Cost Recovery Choices For Real Property," **AREUEA**, 1982, v10(2), 200-208.)

Kraus, A. (Brennan, M. J. and A. Kraus. "The Geometry Of Separation And Myopia," **JFQA**, 1976, v11(2), 171-194.)

Kraus, Alan and Gordon A. Sick. "Communication Of Aggregate Preferences Through Market Prices," **JPM**, 1979, v14(4), 695-703.

Kraus, Alan and Gordon A. Sick. "Distinguishing Beliefs And Preferences In Equilibrium Prices," **JOF**, 1980, v35(2), 335-344.

Kraus, Alan and Hans R. Stoll. "Price Impacts Of Block Trading On The New York Stock Exchange," **JOF**, 1972, v27(3), 569-588.

Kraus, Alan and Hans R. Stoll. "Parallel Trading By Institutional Investors," **JFQA**, 1972, v7(5), 2107-2138.

Kraus, Alan and Robert H. Litzenberger. "Market Equilibrium In A Multiperiod State Preference Model With Logarithmic Utility," **JOF**, 1975, v30(5), 1213-1227.

Kraus, Alan and Robert H. Litzenberger. "A State-Preference Model Of Optimal Financial Leverage," JOF, 1973, v28(4), 911-922.

Kraus, Alan and Robert H. Litzenberger. "Skewness Preference And The Valuation Of Risk Assets," JOF, 1976, v31(4), 1085-1100.

Kraus, Alan and Robert Litzenberger. "On The Distributional Conditions For A Consumption-Oriented Three Moment CAPM," JOF, 1983, v38(5), 1381-1391.

Kraus, Alan and Stephen A. Ross. "The Determination Of Fair Profits For The Property-Liability Insurance Firm," JOF, 1982, v37(4), 1015-1028.

Kraus, Alan and Maxwell Smith. "Market Created Risk," JOF, 1989, v44(3), 557-570.

Kraus, Alan, Christian Janssen and Alan McAdams. "The Lock-Box Location Problem," JBR, 1970-71, v1(3), 50-58.

Kraus, Alan. "The Bond Refunding Decision In An Efficient Market," JFQA, 1973, v8(5), 793-806.

Kraus, Alan. (Brennan, M. J. and Alan Kraus. "Necessary Conditions For Aggregation In Securities Markets," JFQA, 1978, v13(3), 407-418.)

Kraus, Alan. (Brennan, Michael and Alan Kraus. "Efficient Financing Under Asymmetric Information," JOF, 1987, v42(5), 1225-1243.)

Kraus, Alan. (Heinkel, Robert and Alan Kraus. "Measuring Event Impacts In Thinly Traded Stocks," JFQA, 1988, v23(1), 71-88.)

Kraus, Alan. (Melnik, Arie and Alan Kraus. "More On The Short Cycles Of Interest Rates," JFQA, 1971, v6(3), 1047-1052.)

Kraus, Alan. (Melnik, Arie and Alan Kraus. "Short-Run Interest Rate Cycles In The U. S.: 1954-1967," JFQA, 1969, v4(3), 291-299.)

Krause, Lawrence B. "Fixed, Flexible, And Gliding Exchange Rates," JMCB, 1971, v3(2), Part 2, 321-338.

Kravitt, Jason H. P. (Rosenberg, Richard M. and Jason H. P. Kravitt. "Legal Issues In Securitization," JACF, 1988, v1(3), 61-68.)

Kreiser, Larry and Charles Nagy. "A Student Model For Product Costing And Pricing In An Inflationary Environment," JFED, 1981, v10, 54-58.

Kreps, Clifton H., Jr. and David T. Lapkin. "Public Regulation And Operating Conventions Affecting Sources Of Funds Of Commercial Banks And Thrift Institutions," JOF, 1962, v17(2), 289-301.

Kreps, Clifton H., Jr. and Richard F. Wacht. "A More Constructive Role For Deposit Insurance," JOF, 1971, v26(2), 605-614.

Kreps, Clifton H., Jr. "Professor Slichter On Budget Deficits And The Future Money Supply," JOF, 1950, v5(4), 400-409.

Kreps, Juanita M., Joseph J. Spengler and Walter Williams. "The Social Security And Pension Fund Systems - Their Place In The American Value Structure: Comment," JRI, 1965, v32(4), 621-638.

Kretlow, William J. "Role-Playing On Acquisition: A Case For Advanced Courses In Managerial Finance," JFED, 1974, v3, 76-78.

Kretlow, William. (Moyer, R. Charles and William Kretlow. "A Note On Investment Opportunities, Dividend Policy And Uncertainty Resolution," FR, 1979, v14(3), 68-73.)

Kretzmer, Peter E. (Hertzel, Michael G., Coleman S. Kendall and Peter E. Kretzmer. "The Volatility Of Asset Returns During Trading And Nontrading Hours: Some Evidence From The Foreign Exchange Markets," JIMF, 1990, v9(3), 335-343.)

Krinsky, I. and W. Rotenberg. "Signalling And The Valuation Of Unseasoned New Issues Revisited," JFQA, 1989, v24(2), 257-265.

Krinsky, Itzhak. "Mean-Variance Utility Functions, Separable Functional Forms, And The Investment Behaviour Of Canadian Life Insurers," JRI, 1985, v52(2), 241-268.

Krinsky, Itzhak. (Aivazian, V.A., J.L. Callen, I. Krinsky and C.C.Y. Kwan. "Mean-Variance Utility Functions And The Demand For Risky Assets: An Empirical Analysis Using Flexible Functional Forms," JFQA, 1983, v18(4),411-424.)

Krinsky, Itzhak. (Aivazian, Varouj A., Jeffrey L. Callen, Itzhak Krinsky and Clarence C. Y. Kwan. "International Exchange Risk And Asset Substitutability," JIMF, 1986, v5(4), 449-466.)

Krinsky, Itzhak. (Chan, M. W. Luke and Itzhak Krinsky. "Expectations Formation And Portfolio Models For Life Insurers," JRI, 1988, v55(4), 682-700.)

Krinsky, Itzhak. (Chan, M. W. Luke, Itzhak Krinsky and Dean C. Mountain. "Analysis Of Productivity At The Firm Level: An Application To Life Insurers: Comment," JRI, 1989, v56(2), 336-340.)

Kripke, Homer. "Can The SEC Make Disclosure Policy Meaningful?," JPM, 1975-76, v2(4), 32-45.

Kripke, Homer. "Inside Information And Efficient Markets," FAJ, 1980, v36(2), 20-24.

Kripotos, Spero L. (Levy, Robert A. and Spero L. Kripotos. "Sources Of Relative Price Strength," FAJ, 1969, v25(6), 60,63-64.)

Krislov, Joseph and Yehuda Kohane. "Worker's Compensation Coverage For The Self-Employed: The Israeli Experience," JRI, 1979, v46(2), 113-122.

Kristof, Frank S. "Housing Policy In A Nongrowth Era: Problems Of The Northeast United States," AREUEA, 1977, v5(2), 171-188.

Kristof, Frank S. "Rent Control Within The Rental Housing Parameters Of 1975," AREUEA, 1975, v3(3), 47-60.

Kristof, Frank S. "The Role Of Housing Finance And Development Agencies In Future Federal Housing Programs," AREUEA, 1973, v1(2), 53-72.

Kritzman, Mark and James C. Ryan. "A Short-Term Approach To Asset Allocation," JPM, 1980-81, v7(1),45-49.

Kritzman, Mark P. "Incentive Fees: Some Problems And Some Solutions," FAJ, 1987, v43(1), 21-26.

Kritzman, Mark. "A Simple Solution For Optimal Currency Hedging," FAJ, 1989, v45(6), 47-50.

Kritzman, Mark. "Can Bond Managers Perform Consistently?," JPM, 1982-83, v9(4), 54-56.

Kritzman, Mark. "How To Build A Normal Portfolio In Three Easy Steps," JPM, 1986-87, v13(4), 21-23.

Kritzman, Mark. "How To Detect Skill In Management Performance," JPM, 1985-86, v12(2), 16-20.

Kritzman, Mark. "Serial Dependence In Currency Returns: Investment Implications," JPM, 1989, v16(1), 96-102.

Kritzman, Mark. "What's Wrong With Portfolio Insurance," JPM, 1986-87, v13(1), 13-17.

Kritzman, Mark. (Estep, Tony and Mark Kritzman. "TIPP: Time Invariant Portfolio Protection," JPM, 1987-88, v14(4), 38-42.)

Kritzman, Mark. (Ryan, James C. and Mark Kritzman. "Catch 500: The Irony Of Indexing," JPM, 1979-80, v6(2), 30-32.)

Kritzman, Mark. (Ryan, James C. and Mark Kritzman. "Catch 500: The Irony Of Indexing: Reply," JPM, 1980-81, v7(1), 82.)

Kriz, Miroslav A. "Gold And International Liquidity," FAJ, 1964, v20(3), 89-96.

Kriz, Miroslav A. "The Gold Picture Today," FAJ, 1965, v21(2), 78-82.

Kroch, Eugene. "Do Futures Markets Help Intertemporal Allocation Of Resources?," JFM, 1982, v2(4), 317-332.

Krogh, Harold C. "Accident Proneness And The Uninsured Motorist," JRI, 1961, v28(2), 99-102.

Krogh, Harold C. "Compassion And Insurance," JRI, 1971, v38(4), 501-503.

Krogh, Harold C. "Faculty Retirement And Insurance Programs In Midwestern Universities," JRI, 1958, v25(4), 55-60.

Krogh, Harold C. "Insurer Post-Insolvency Guaranty Funds," JRI, 1972, v39(3), 431-450.

Krogh, Harold C. and Murray S. Levin. "Recent Trends: State Insurance Guaranty Funds And Insurance Company Insurance Assessment Operations," JRI, 1986, v53(2), 335-342.

Krogh, Harold C., W. O. Bryson, Jr., William M. Howard and Robert M. Stevenson. "The Insurance Curriculum In Collegiate Business Education," JRI, 1959, v26(1), 76-81.

Krol, Robert. "The Interdependence Of The Term Structure Of Eurocurrency Interest Rates," JIMF, 1986, v5(2), 245-253.

Krol, Robert. "The Term Structure Of Eurodollar Interest Rates And Its Relationship To The US Treasury-Bill Market," JIMF, 1987, v6(3), 339-354.

Kroll, Mark J. (Smith, Charles A. and Mark J. Kroll. "Utility Theory And Rent Optimization: Utilizing Cluster Analysis To Segment Rental Markets," JRER, 1989, v4(1), 61-71.)

Kroll, Mark J. and Charles Smith. "Buyer's Response Technique - A Framework For Improving Comparable Selection And Adjustment In Single-Family Appraising," JRER, 1988, v3(1), 27-35.

Kroll, Yoram and Haim Levy. "Stochastic Dominance: A Note," JOF, 1982, v37(3), 871-875.

Kroll, Yoram and Haim Levy. "Stochastic Dominance With A Riskless Asset: An Imperfect Market," JFQA, 1979, v14(2), 179-204.

Kroll, Yoram and Haim Levy. "Sampling Errors And Portfolio Efficient Analysis," JFQA, 1980, v15(3), 655-688.

Kroll, Yoram and Haim Levy. "Stochastic Dominance: A Review And Some New Evidence," RIF, 1980, v2, 163-227.

Kroll, Yoram, Haim Levy and Harry M. Markowitz. "Mean-Variance Versus Direct Utility Maximization," JOF, 1984, v39(1), 47-62.

Kroll, Yoram. "Analytical Examination Of A Business Tax Reform Under Rapid Inflation: The Israeli Case," JBFA, 1988, v15(3), 353-372.

Kroll, Yoram. "On The Differences Between Accrual Accounting Figures And Cash Flows: The Case Of Working Capital," FM, 1985, v14(1), 75-82.

Kroll, Yoram. "Stochastic Choice In Insurance And Risk Sharing: A Comment," JOF, 1983, v38(3), 1033-1035.

Kroll, Yoram. (Briys, Eric, Yehuda Kahane and Yoram Kroll. "Voluntary Insurance Coverage, Compulsory Insurance, And Risky-Riskless Portfolio Opportunities," JRI, 1988, v55(4), 713-722.)

Kroll, Yoram. (Levy, Haim and Yoram Kroll. "Stochastic Dominance With Riskless Assets," JFQA, 1976, v11(5), 743-778.)

Kroll, Yoram. (Levy, Haim and Yoram Kroll. "Ordering Uncertain Options With Borrowing And Lending," JOF, 1978, v33(2), 553-574.)

Kroncke, Charles O. "The Process Of Classifying Drivers: A Suggestion For Insurance Ratemaking," JRI, 1971, v38(4), 543-551.

Kroncke, Charles O. "The Process Of Classifying Drivers: A Suggestion For Insurance Ratemaking: Reply," JRI, 1973, v40(1), 147-148.

Kroncke, Charles O. (Frank, Werner G. and Charles O. Kroncke. "Classifying Conversions Of Convertible Debentures Over Four Years," FM, 1974, v3(2),33-39.)

Kroncke, Charles O. (Haugen, Robert A. and Charles O. Kroncke. "Rate Regulation And The Cost Of Capital In The Insurance Industry," JFQA, 1971, v6(5), 1283-1305.)

Kroncke, Charles O. (Haugen, Robert A. and Charles O. Kroncke. "Optimizing The Structure Of Capital Claims And Assets Of A Stock Insurance Company," JRI, 1970, v37(1), 41-48.)

Kroncke, Charles O. (Haugen, Robert A. and Charles O. Kroncke. "Optimizing The Structure Of Capital Claims And Assets Of A Stock Insurance Company: Reply," JRI, 1972, v39(2), 313-316.)

Kroncke, Charles O. (Ward, David J. and Charles O. Kroncke. "An Analysis Of Voluntary Cash Demands On Life Insurance Companies," JRI, 1975, v42(3), 389-402.)

Kroncke, Charles O. and Patrick T. O'Neill. "The Wisconsin State Insurance Fund And Campus Unrest," JRI, 1970, v37(4), 655-658.

Kroner, Kenneth F. and Stijn Claessens. "Optimal Dynamic Hedging Portfolios And The Currency Composition Of External Debt," JIMF, 1991, v10(1), 131-148.

Kronfeld, Morris and Arthur Rock. "Some Considerations Of The Infinite," FAJ, 1958, v14(5), 87-90.

Krooss, Herman E. "Did The Federal Reserve Study Answer The Question," JOF, 1958, v13(2), 153-162.

Krooss, Herman E. "Monetary History And Monetary Policy: A Review Article," JOF, 1964, v19(4), 662-667.

Kross, William and Douglas A. Schroeder. "Firm Prominence And The Differential Information Content Of Quarterly Earnings Announcements," JBFA, 1989, v16(1), 55-74.

Kross, William and Douglas Schroeder. "An Investigation Of Seasonality In Stock Price Responses To Quarterly Earnings Announcements," JBFA, 1990, v17(5), 649-676.

Kross, William. "Predictive Ability Of Alternative Income Numbers In Nonlife Insurance," JRI, 1978, v45(3), 473-489.

Kross, William. "Profitability, Earnings Announcement Time Lags, And Stock Prices," JBFA, 1982, v8(3), 313-328.

Kross, William. "The Size Effect Is Primarily A Price Effect," JFR, 1985, v8(3), 169-179.

Kroszner, Randall. (Cowen, Tyler and Randall Kroszner. "Scottish Banking Before 1845: A Model For Laissez-Faire?," JMCB, 1989, v21(2), 221-231.)

Krouse, Clement G. and Wayne Y. Lee. "Optimal Equity Financing Of The Corporation," JFQA, 1973, v8(4), 539-563.

Krouse, Clement G. "Portfolio Balancing Corporate Assets And Liabilities With Special Application To Insurance Management," JFQA, 1970, v5(1), 77-104.

Krouse, Clement G. "Measuring Allocative Efficiency With Technological Uncertainty," JOF, 1976, v31(2), 685-700.

Krouse, Clement G. "Optimal Financing And Capital Structure Programs For The Firm: Reply," JOF, 1976, v31(3), 976.

Krouse, Clement G. "Optimal Financing And Capital Structure Programs For The Firm," JOF, 1972, v27(5), 1057-1071.

Krueger, Thomas M. "Seasonal Aspects Of Anomaly Explanatory Power," JBFA, 1990, v17(4), 541-556.

Krueger, Thomas M. and William F. Kennedy. "An Examination Of The Super Bowl Stock Market Predictor," JOF,1990,v45(2),691-698.

Krugman, Paul. "A Model Of Balance-Of-Payments Crises," JMCB, 1979, v11(3), 311-325.

Krugman, Paul. "Vehicle Currencies And The Structure Of International Exchange," JMCB, 1980, v12(3), 513-526.

Kruizenga, Richard J. "Comment On 'Puts And Calls: A Factual Survey'," JOF, 1959, v14(1), 67-70.

Krull, Steven. (Eytan, T. Hanan, Giora Harpaz and Steven Krull. "The Pricing Of Dollar Index Futures Contracts," JFM, 1988, v8(2), 127-140.)

Krull, Steven. (Harpaz, Gioria, Steven Krull and Joseph Yagil. "The Efficiency Of The US Dollar Index Futures Market," JFM, 1990, v10(5), 469-480.)

Kruschwitz, Lutz. "The Role Of The Payback Period In The Theory And Application Of Duration To Capital Budgeting: A Comment," JBFA, 1985, v12(1), 165-168.

Kruskal, William H. and Lester G. Telser. "Rejoinder: Food Prices And The Bureau Of Labor," JOB, 1960, v33(3), 285.

Kruskal, William H. and Lester G. Telser. "Food Prices And The Bureau Of Labor Statistics," JOB, 1960, v33(3), 258-279.

Kryzanowski, Lawrence and Abolhassan Jalilvand. "Statistical Tests Of The Accuracy Of Alternative Forecasts: Some Results For U.S. Utility Betas," FR, 1986, v21(2), 319-336.

Kryzanowski, Lawrence and Minh Chau To. "The Telescopic Effect Of Past Return Realizations On Ex-Post Beta Estimates," FR, 1984, v19(1), 1-25.

Kryzanowski, Lawrence and Minh Chau To. "On Traditional Market Models As Stochastic Return-Generating Models," FR, 1982, v17(3), 165-173.

Kryzanowski, Lawrence and To Minh Chau. "Asset Pricing Models When The Number Of Securities Held Is Constrained: A Comparison And Reconciliation Of The Mao And Levy Models," JFQA, 1982, v17(1), 63-73.

Kryzanowski, Lawrence and Minh Chau To. "The E-V Stationarity Of Security Returns: Some Empirical Evidence," JBF, 1987, v11(1), 117-136.

Kryzanowski, Lawrence. "The Efficacy Of Trading Suspensions: A Regulatory Action Designed To Prevent The Exploitation Of Monopoly Information," JOF, 1979, v34(5), 1187-1200.

Kryzanowski, Lawrence. (Rahman, Abdul, Lawrence Kryzanowski and Ah Boon Sim. "Systematic Risk In A Purely Random Market Model: Some Empirical Evidence For Individual Public Utilities," JFR, 1987, v10(2),143-152.)

Kudla, Ronald J. (McGuire, Dan C. and Ronald J. Kudla. "Option Prices As An Indicator Of Stock Return Expectations," JBFA, 1991, v18(3), 421-430.)

Kudla, Ronald J. and Manjeet S. Dhatt. "An Empirical Test Of Operating Synergism," JBFA, 1988, v15(3), 427-436.

Kuehl, Charles R. "Leader Effectiveness In Committee-Like Groups," JOB, 1977, v50(2), 223-230.

Kuehl, Charles R. (Gustafson, David P. and Charles R. Kuehl. "Citation Age Distributions For Three Areas Of Business," JOB, 1974, v47(3), 440-447.)

Kuehn, A. A. (Cohen, K. J., R. M. Cyert, W. R. Dill, A. A. Kuehn, M. H. Miller, T. A. VanWormer, and P. R. Winters. "The Carnegie Tech Management Game," JOB, 1960, v33(4), 303-321.)

Kuehn, Alfred A. "Demonstration Of A Relationship Between Psychological Factors And Brand Choice," JOB, 1963, v36(2), 237-241.

Kugler, Peter. "The Term Structure Of Euro Interest Rates And Rational Expectations," JIMF, 1990, v9(2), 234-244.

Kuhanza, Michael J. (Epps, T. W. and Michael J. Kukanza. "Predictions Of Returns To Commodities Speculation Based On Current Information: Some Evidence Of Informational Inefficiency In Futures Markets," RFM, 1985, v4(3), 366-382.)

Kuhle, James L. "Portfolio Diversification And Return Benefits - Common Stock Vs. Real Estate Investment Trusts (REITs)," JRER, 1987, v2(2), 1-9.

Kuhle, James L. (Grissom, Terry, James Kuhle and Carl Walther. "Diversification Works In Real Estate, Too," JPM, 1986-87, v13(2), 66-71.

Kuhle, James L. (Johnson, Larry J., James L. Kuhle and Carl H. Walther. "An Elasticity Approach To Equity Risk Evaluation," JRER, 1987, v2(1), 41-49.)

Kuhle, James L. and Josef D. Moorehead. "Applying The Bootstrap Technique To Real Estate Appraisal: An Empirical Analysis," JRER, 1990, v5(1), 33-40.

Kuhle, James L., Carl H. Walther and Charles H. Wurtzebach. "The Financial Performance Of Real Estate Investment Trusts," JRER, 1986, v1(1), 67-75.

Kuhn, Betsy A. "A Note: Do Futures Prices Always Reflect The Cheapest Deliverable Grade Of The Commodity?," JFM, 1988, v8(1), 99-102.

Kulatilaka, Nalin and Alan J. Marcus. "A General Formulation Of Corporate Real Options," RIF, 1988, v7, 183-200.

Kulessa, Matthias. (Mack, Thomas and Matthias Kulessa. "Reinsurance Decision Making And Expected Utility: Comment," JRI, 1985, v52(2), 311.)

Kulp, C. A. "Investment Of Unemployment Insurance Funds," JRI, 1934, v1, 1-12.

Kulp, C. A. "Tomorrow In The Automobile Liability Business," JRI, 1955, v22, 23-27.

Kulp, Clarence A. "Alternate Solutions: Voluntary And Compulsory Medical Care Insurance," JRI, 1951, v18, 88-95.

Kumar, Praveen. "Shareholder-Manager Conflict And The Information Content Of Dividends," RFS, 1988-89, v1(2), 111-136.

Kummer, Donald R., Nasser Arshadi and Edward C. Lawrence. "Incentive Problems In Bank Insider Borrowing," JFSR, 1989, v3(1), 17-32.

Kunreuther, Howard c. (Schoemaker, Paul J. H. and Howard C. Kunreuther. "An Experimental Study Of Insurance Decisions," JRI, 1979, v46(4), 603-618.)

Kunreuther, Howard and Robin M. Hogarth. "Risk, Ambiguity, And Insurance," JRU, 1989, v2(1), 5-36.

Kunreuther, Howard. "Disaster Insurance: A Tool For Hazard Mitigation," JRI, 1974, v41(2), 287-304.

Kunreuther, Howard. (Berger, Lawrence A., Paul R. Kleindorfer and Howard Kunreuther. "A Dynamic Model Of The Transmission Of Price Information In Auto Insurance Markets," JRI, 1989, v56(1), 17-33.)

Kunreuther, Howard. (Camerer, Colin and Howard Kunreuther. "Experimental Markets For Insurance," JRU, 1989, v2(3), 265-300.)

Kuo, Shyanjaw. (Ritchken, Peter H. and Shyanjaw Kuo. "Option Bounds With Finite Revision Opportunities," JOF, 1988, v43(2), 301-308.)

Kupiec, Paul H. "A Survey Of Exchange-Traded Basket Instruments," JFSR, 1990, v4(3), 175-190.

Kupiec, Paul H. "Initial Margin Requirements And Stock Returns Volatility: Another Look," JFSR, 1989, v3(2/3), 287-301.

Kurtz, Robert D. (Elliehausen, Gregory E. and Robert D. Kurtz. "Scale Economies And Compliance Costs For Federal Consumer Credit Regulations," JFSR, 1988, v1(2), 147-160.)

Kuserk, Gregory J. "Limit Moves And Price Resolution: The Case Of The Treasury Bond Futures Market: A Comment," JFM, 1990, v10(6), 673-674.

Kushner, Joseph. (Fortura, Peter and Joseph Kushner. "Canadian Inter-City House Price Differentials," AREUEA, 1986, v14(4), 525-536.)

Kutner, George W. "A Computerized Black-Scholes Option Valuation Model With Applications," JFED, 1988, v17, 94-103.

Kutner, George W. "Black-Scholes Revisited: Some Important Details," FR, 1988, v23(1), 95-104.

Kutner, George W. and James A. Seifert. "The Valuation Of Mortgage Loan Commitments Using Option Pricing Estimates," JRER, 1989, v4(2), 13-20.

Kutner, George W. and James A. Seifert. "A Note On The Valuation Of Mortgage Loan Commitments: Incorporating The Commitment Cost In The Valuation Rate," JRER, 1990, v5(2), 281-284.

Kwan, Clarence C. Y. (Callen, Jeffrey L., M. W. Luke Chan and Clarence C. Y. Kwan. "Spot And Forward Exchange Rates: A Causality Analysis," JBFA, 1989, v16(1), 105-118.)

Kwan, Clarence C. Y. (Chamberlain, Trevor W., C. Sherman Cheung and Clarence C. Y. Kwan. "Expiration-Day Effects Of Index Futures And Options: Some Canadian Evidence," FAJ, 1989, v45(5), 67-71.)

Kwan, Clarence C. Y. (Cheung, C. Sherman and Clarence C. Y. Kwan. "A Note On Simple Criteria For Optimal Portfolio Selection," JOF, 1988, v43(1), 241-245.)

Kwan, Clarence C. Y. (Cheung, C. Sherman, Clarence C. Y. Kwan and Patrick C. Y. Yip. "The Hedging Effectiveness Of Options And Futures: A Mean-Gini Approach," JFM, 1990, v10(1), 61-74.)

Kwan, Clarence C. Y. and Yufei Yuan. "Optimal Sequential Selection In Capital Budgeting: A Shortcut," FM, 1988, v17(1), 54-59.

Kwast, Myron L. "The Impact Of Underwriting And Dealing On Bank Returns And Risks," JBF, 1989, v13(1), 101-126.

Kwok, Chuck C. Y. "The Numeraire Problem, Forward Hedges And International Portfolio Selection," GFJ, 1990, v1(2), 95-120.

Kwok, Chuck C. Y. (Folks, William R., Jr. and Chuck C. Y. Kwok. "A New Way To Cover Foreign Currency Bonds," RDIBF, 1987, v1, 103-116.)

Kyle, Albert S. "Trading Halts And Price Limits," RFM, 1988, v7(3), 426-434.

Kyle, S. C. and R. G. Wirick. "The Impact Of Soverign Risk On The Market Valuation Of U.S. Bank Equities," JBF, 1990, v14(4), 761-780.

LLL

LaChapelle, Chris A. (Neuberger, Brian M. and Chris A. La Chapelle. "Unseasoned New Issue Price Performance On Three Tiers: 1975-1980," FM, 1983, v12(3), 23-28.)

LaCivita, C. J. (LeRoy, Stephen F. and C. J. LaCivita. "Risk Aversion And The Dispersion Of Asset Prices," JOB, 1981, v54(4), 535-548.)

LaCivita, Charles J. "Currency, Trade, And Capital Flows In General Equilibrium," JOB, 1987, v60(1), 113-136.

LaFarge, Francis W. "Methods Of Evaluating Future Price Levels Of The Dow-Jones Industrial Average," FAJ, 1945, v1(4), 49-55.

LaFarge, Francis W. "Timing Common Stock Purchases And Sales," FAJ, 1954, v10(1), 47-50.

LaForge, R. Lawrence and D. Robley Wood, Jr. "The Use Of Operations Research In The Planning Activities Of Large U.S. Banks," JBR, 1980-81, v11(3), 179-183.

LaMotte, Lynn Roy. (Simonds, Richard R., Lynn Roy LaMotte and Archer McWhorter, Jr. "Testing For Nonstationarity Of Market Risk: An Exact Test And Power Considerations," JFQA, 1986, v21(2), 209-220.)

LaTourette, William I. "Television," FAJ, 1951, v7(4), 85-87.

LaValle, Irving H. and Yongsheng Xu. "Information Evaluation Under Nonadditive Expected Utility," JRU, 1990, v3(3), 261-276.

Laatsch, Francis E. and Thomas V. Schwarz. "Price Discovery And Risk Transfer In Stock Index Cash And Futures Markets," RFM, 1988, v7(2), 272-289.

Labarge, Karin Peterson. "Daily Trading Estimates For Treasury Bond Futures Contract Prices," JFM, 1988, v8(5), 533-562.

Laber, Gene. "Bond Covenants And Managerial Flexibility: Two Cases Of Special Redemption Provisions," FM, 1990, v19(1), 82-89.

Laber, Gene. "How Do Call Provisions Influence Bond Yields?: A Comment," JPM, 1978-79, v5(4), 70-71.

Laber, Gene. "Implications Of Discount Rates And Financing Assumptions For Bond Refunding Decisions," FM, 1979, v8(1),7-12.

Laber, Gene. "Repurchases Of Bonds Through Tender Offers: Implications For Shareholder Wealth," **FM**, 1978, v7(2), 7-13.

Laber, Gene. "The Effect Of Bond Refunding On Shareholder Wealth: Comment," **JOF**, 1979, v34(3),795-799.

Laber, Gene. "The Use Of Inflation Factors In Determining Settlements In Personal Injury And Death Suits: Comment," **JRI**, 1977, v44(3), 469-473.

Laborde, P. "A Note On Net And Double Gains, Or Losses, In Spreading Operations," **JFM**, 1982, v2(4), 409-414.

Labuszewski, John W. (Frey, Norman E. and John W. Labuszewski. "Newspaper Articles And Their Impact On Commodity Price Formation - Case Study: Copper," **JFM**, v1(1), 89-91.)

Labuszewski, John W. (Meisner, James F. and John W. Labuszewski. "Treasury Bond Futures Delivery Bias," **JFM**, 1984, v4(4), 569-577.)

Labuszewski, John W. (Meisner, James F. and John W. Labuszewski. "Modifying The Black-Scholes Option Pricing Model For Alternative Underlying Instruments," **FAJ**, 1984, v40(6), 23-27,30.)

Lacey, N. J. (Nawalkha, S. K. and N. J. Lacey. "Generalized Solutions Of Higher-Order Duration Measures," **JBF**, 1990, v14(6), 1143-1150.)

Lacey, Nelson J. and Donald R. Chambers. "The Investigation Of A Systematic Prepayment Option In GNMA Futures," **RFM**, 1985, v4(3), 338-353.

Lacey, Nelson J. "Recent Evidence On The Liability Crisis," **JRI**, 1988, v55(3), 499-508.

Lacey, Nelson J. (Nawalkha, Sanjay K. and Nelson J. Lacey. "Closed-Form Solutions Of Higher-Order Duration Measures," **FAJ**, 1988, v44(6), 82-84.)

Lacey, Nelson J. (Nawalkha, Sanjay K., Nelson J. Lacey and Thomas Schneeweis. "Closed-Form Solutions Of Convexity And M-Square," **FAJ**, 1990, v46(1), 75-77.)

Lacey, Nelson J. and Nikolaos T. Milonas. "The Determinants Of GNMA Prepayments: A Pool-By-Pool Analysis," **JRER**, 1989, v4(2), 21-32.

Lachman, Ran. (Mandell, Lewis, Ran Lachman and Yair Orgler. "Interpreting The Image Of Banking," **JBR**, 1981-82, v12(2), 96-104.)

Lacker, Jeffrey M., Robert J. Levy and John A. Weinberg. "Incentive-Compatible Financial Contracts, Asset Prices, And The Value Of Control," **JFI**, 1990, v1(1), 31-56.

Lackman, C. L. "The Impact Of Capital Adequacy Constraints On Bank Portfolios," **JBFA**, 1986, v13(4), 587-596.

Lackman, Conway L. and Warren N. Minami. "Market Profiles By Lending Institutions," **JBR**, 1978-79, v9(3), 186-190.

Lackman, Conway. "Forecasting Commercial Paper Rates," **JBFA**, 1988, v15(4), 499-524.

Ladd, Edward H. "Thoughts On The Long-Term Implications Of Inflation: A Look At American Inflation From A British Perspective," **FAJ**, 1981, v37(4), 48-56.

Ladenson, Mark L. and Kenneth J. Bombara. "Entry In Commercial Banking: 1962-78," **JMCB**, 1984, v16(2), 165-174.

Ladenson, Mark L. "Money Stock Control: The Effects Of A Reduction In The Number Of Depository Institutions," **JBR**, 1984-85, v15(3), 160-166.

Ladenson, Mark L. and Kenneth J. Bombara. "Entry In Commercial Banking: A Reply," **JMCB**, 1986, v18(3), 390-391.

Laffer, ARthur B. (Fama, Eugene F. and Arthur B. Laffer. "Information And Capital Markets," **JOB**, 1971, v44(3), 289-298.)

Laffer, Arthur B. and R. David Ranson. "Some Practical Applications Of The Efficient-Market Concept," **FM**, 1978, v7(2), 63-75.

Laffer, Arthur B. and R. David Ranson. "1065 And All That," **FAJ**, 1971, v27(3), 8-9,82,94.

Laffer, Arthur B. "Fixed Vs. Flexible Exchange Rates," **FAJ**, 1974, v30(4), 26-28,30,32,76-82.

Laffer, Arthur B. "Monetary Policy And The Balance Of Payments," **JMCB**, 1972, v4(1), 13-22.

Laffer, Arthur B. "Supply-Side Economics," **FAJ**, 1981, v37(5), 29-43.

Laffer, Arthur B. (Canto, Victor A., Arthur B. Laffer and James C. Turney. "Trade Policy And The U.S. Economy," **FAJ**, 1982, v38(5), 27-46.)

Laffer, Arthur B. (Canto, Victor A. and Arthur B. Laffer. "A Not-So-Odd Couple: Small-Cap Stocks And The State Competitive Environment," **FAJ**, 1989, v45(2), 75-78.)

Laffer, Arthur B. and R. David Ranson. "A Formal Model Of The Economy," **JOB**, 1971, v44(3), 247-270.

Lafferty, J. (Amihud, Y., C. Brunie, C. Ferenbach, R. Fredericks, J. Grundfest, J. Lafferty, B. Lev, B. Shorts, J. Stern, B. Stewart and R. Zeckhauser. "Panel: 'Lead Steer' Roundtable," **JACF**, 1989, v2(3), 24-44.)

Laffont, Jean-Jacques. (Cresta, Jean-Paul and Jean-Jacques Laffont. "Incentive Compatibility Of Insurance Contracts And The Value Of Information," **JRI**, 1987, v54(3), 520-540.)

Lafrance, Robert and Daniel Racette. "The Canadian-US Dollar Exchange Rate: A Test Of Alternative Models For The Seventies," **JIMF**, 1985, v4(2), 237-252.

Lahey, Karen E. and Robert L. Conn. "Sensitivity Of Acquiring Firms' Returns To Alternative Model Specifications And Disaggregation," **JBFA**, 1990, v17(3), 421-440.

Lahiri, Kajal and Jungsoo Lee. "On The Constancy Of Real Interest Rates And The Mundell Effect," **JBF**, 1981, v5(4), 557-574.

Lahiri, Kajal and Mark Zaporowski. "A Note On The Variability Of Real Interest Rates, Business Cycles, And The Livingston Data," **JBF**, 1984, v8(3), 483-490.

Lahiri, Kajal, Christie Teigland and Mark Zaporowski. "Interest Rates And The Subjective Probability Distribution Of Inflation Forecasts," **JMCB**, 1988, v20(2), 233-248.

Lai, Ching-chong. (Chen, Chau-nan, Ching-chong Lai and Tien-wang Tsaur. "The Loanable Funds Theory And The Dynamics Of Exchange Rates: The Mundell Model Revisited," **JIMF**, 1988, v7(2), 221-230.)

Lai, Tsong-Yeu. (Ang, James S. and Tsong-Yue Lai. "Functional Forms Of The Capital Asset Pricing Model Under Different Market Risk Regimes," **FR**, 1988, v23(3), 345-350.)

Lai, Tsong-Yue and A. James Boness. "Investment In The Long Run," **FR**, 1984, v19(4), 285-300.

Lai, Tsong-Yue. "An Equilibrium Model Of Asset Pricing With

Lai, Tsong-Yue. (Ang, James S. and Tsong-Yue Lai. "A Simple Rule For Multinational Capital Budgeting," **GFJ**, 1989, v1(1), 71-76.)

Lai, Tsong-Yue. (Ang, James S. and Tsong-Yue Lai. "Insurance Premium Pricing And Ratemaking In Competitive Insurance And Capital Asset Markets," **JRI**, 1987, v54(4), 767-779.)

Lai, Tsong-Yue. (Chiang, Raymond, Tsong-Yue Lai and David C. Ling. "Retail Leasehold Interests: A Contingent Claim Analysis," **AREUEA**, 1986, v14(2), 216-229.)

Lai, Tsong-Yue. (Huang, Roger D. and Tsong-Yue Lai. "Methodological And Empirical Comparisons Of Statistical Classifications Of Bond Ratings," **AFPAF**, 1985, v1(1), 145-166.)

Lai, Tsong-Yue. (Huang, Roger D. and Tsong-Yue Lai. "Financial Asset Substitutability And International Asset Pricing," **AFPAF**, 1989, v4(Supp), 171-196.)

Laibstain, S. and Thomas Huff. "Reporting Of Revised Loss Estimates," **FAJ**, 1971, v27(3), 62-69.

Laiderman, Richard. "The Sinking Fund Bond Game," **FAJ**, 1980, v36(6), 33-36.

Laidler, David. "Expectations, Adjustment, And The Dynamic Response Of Income To Policy Changes," **JMCB**, 1973, v5(1), 157-172.

Laidler, David. "Friedman And Schwartz On Monetary Trends: A Review Article," **JIMF**, 1982, v1(3),293-305.

Laidler, David. "The Definition Of Money: Theoretical And Empirical Problems," **JMCB**, 1969, v1(3), 508-525.

Laird, J. M. "Should Surrender And Loan Values Be Restricted," **JRI**, 1934, v1, 1-7.

Lake, Peter S. (Moylan, James J., Laren A. Ukman and Peter S. Lake. "Exchange Memberships: An Overview Of The Issues Pertaining To The Property Rights Of A Bankrupt Member And His Creditors," **JFM**, 1989, v9(5), 461-468.)

Lake, Robert W. "Introduction: Housing The Nation - Part I," **AREUEA**, 1977, v5(2), 141-146.

Lakonishok, Josef and Alan C. Shapiro. "Systematic Risk, Total Risk And Size As Determinants Of Stock Market Returns," **JBF**, 1986, v10(1), 115-132.

Lakonishok, Josef and Alan C. Shapiro. "Stock Returns, Beta, Variance And Size: An Empirical Analysis," **FAJ**, 1984, v40(4), 36-41.

Lakonishok, Josef and Maurice Levi. "Weekend Effects On Stock Returns: A Reply," **JOF**, 1985, v40(1), 351-352.

Lakonishok, Josef and Maurice Levi. "Weekend Effects On Stock Returns: A Note," **JOF**, 1982, v37(3), 883-889.

Lakonishok, Josef and Seymour Smidt. "Trading Bargains In Small Firms At Year-End," **JPM**, 1985-86, v12(3), 24-29.

Lakonishok, Josef and Seymour Smidt. "Capital Gain Taxation And Volume Of Trading," **JOF**, 1986, v41(4), 951-976.

Lakonishok, Josef and Seymour Smidt. "Volume And Turn-Of-The-Year Behavior," **JFEC**, 1984, v13(3), 435-455.

Lakonishok, Josef and Simcha Sadan. "Information Sets, Macroeconomic Reform, And Stock Prices," **JFQA**, 1981, v16(4), 495-510.

Lakonishok, Josef and Theo Vermaelen. "Tax Reform And Ex-Dividend Day Behavior," **JOF**, 1983, v38(4), 1157-1179.

Lakonishok, Josef and Theo Vermaelen. "Tax-Induced Trading Around Ex-Dividend Days," **JFEC**, 1986, v16(3), 287-319.

Lakonishok, Josef and Baruch Lev. "Stock Splits And Stock Dividends: Why, Who, And When," **JOF**, 1987, v42(4), 913-932.

Lakonishok, Josef and Edwin Maberly. "The Weekend Effect: Trading Patterns Of Individual And Institutional Investors," **JOF**, 1990, v45(1), 231-244.

Lakonishok, Josef and Seymour Smidt. "Are Seasonal Anomalies Real? A Ninety-Year Perspective," **RFS**, 1988-89, v1(4), 403-425.

Lakonishok, Josef and Seymour Smidt. "Past Price Changes And Current Trading Volume," **JPM**, 1989, v15(4), 18-25.

Lakonishok, Josef and Theo Vermaelen. "Anomalous Price Behavior Around Repurchase Tender Offers," **JOF**, 1990, v45(2), 455-478.

Lakonishok, Josef. "Performance Of Mutual Funds Versus Their Expenses," **JBR**, 1981-82, v12(2), 110-113.

Lakonishok, Josef. "Stock Market Return Expectations: Some General Properties," **JOF**, 1980, v35(4), 921-932.

Lakonishok, Josef. (Baran, Arie, Josef Lakonishok and Aharon R. Ofer. "The Value Of General Price Level Adjusted Data To Bond Rating," **JBFA**, 1980, v7(1), 135-149.)

Lakonishok, Josef. (Bjerring, James H., Josef Lakonishok and Theo Vermaelen. "Stock Prices And Financial Analysts' Recommendations," **JOF**, 1983, v38(1), 187-204.)

Lakonishok, Josef. (Carleton, Willard T. and Josef Lakonishok. "Risk And Return On Equity: The Use And Misuse Of Historical Estimates," **FAJ**, 1985, v41(1), 38-47,62.)

Lakonishok, Josef. (Carleton, Willard T., Donald R. Chambers and Josef Lakonishok. "Inflation Risk And Regulatory Lag," **JOF**, 1983, v38(2),419-431.)

Lakonishok, Josef. (Carleton, Willard T. and Josef Lakonishok. "The Size Anomaly: Does Industry Group Matter?," **JPM**, 1985-86, v12(3), 36-40.)

Lakonishok, Josef. (Eisenbeis, Robert A., Robert S. Harris and Josef Lakonishok. "Benefits Of Bank Diversification: The Evidence From Shareholder Returns," **JOF**, 1984, v39(3), 881-892.)

Lakonishok, Josef. (Givoly, Dan and Josef Lakonishok. "Financial Analysts' Forecasts Of Earnings: Their Value To Investors," **JBF**, 1980, v4(3), 221-234.)

Lakonishok, Josef. (Givoly, Dan and Josef Lakonishok. "The Quality Of Analysts' Forecasts Of Earnings," **FAJ**, 1984, v40(5), 40-47.)

Lakonishok. Josef. (Arbel, Avner, Richard Kolodny and Josef Lakonishok. "The Relationship Between Risk Of Default And Return On Equity: An Empirical Investigation," **JFQA**, 1977, v12(4), 615-625.)

Lam, Chun H. and Andrew H. Chen. "A Note On Optimal Credit And Pricing Policy Under Uncertainty: A Contingent-Claims Approach," **JOF**, 1986, v41(5), 1141-1148.

Lam, Chun H. and Andrew H. Chen. "Joint Effects Of Interest Rate Deregulation And Capital Requirements On Optimal Bank Portfolio Adjustments," **JOF**, 1985, v40(2), 563-575.

Lam, Chun H. and Kenneth J. Boudreaux. "Compensating Balances, Deficiency Fees, And Lines Of Credit," **JBF**, 1983, v7(3), 307-322.

Lam, Chun H. and Kenneth J. Boudreaux. "Conglomerate Merger, Wealth Redistribution And Debt: A Note," **JOF**, 1984, v39(1), 275-281.

Lam, Chun H. and Kenneth J. Boudreaux. "Compensating Balance, Rationality, And Optimality," **JBF**, 1981, v5(4), 451-466.

Lam, Chun H. (Cohen Kalman J. and Chun H. Lam. "A Linear Programming Planning Model For Bank Holding Companies," **JBR**, 1979-80, v10(3), 152-164.)

Lam, Swee-Sum. "Venture Capital Financing: A Conceptual Framework," **JBFA**, 1991, v18(2), 137-150.

Lambert, E. W. and A. E. Hofflander. "Liquidity In Investing," **FAJ**, 1967, v23(5), 141-145.

Lambert, Eugene W., Jr. "Bank Debt Securities: The Investor's Viewpoint," **FAJ**, 1966, v22(3), 93-99.

Lambert, Eugene W., Jr. (Duvall, Richard M., Alfred E. Hofflander, Jr. and Eugene W. Lambert, Jr. "Optimum Liquidity Levels For Multiple Line Insurance Companies," **JRI**, 1968, v35(2), 199-205.)

Lambert, Eugene W., Jr. and Alfred E. Hofflander. "Impact Of New Multiple Line Underwriting On Investment Portfolios Of Property-Liability Insurers," **JRI**, 1966, v33(2), 209-223.

Lambert, Richard A., William N. Lanen and David F. Larcker. "Executive Stock Option Plans And Corporate Dividend Policy," **JFQA**, 1989, v24(4), 409-426.

Lamberton, D. McL. "Economic Growth And Stock Prices: The Australian Experience," **JOB**, 1958, v31(3), 200-212.

Lambin, Jean-Jacques. "Is Gasoline Advertising Justified?," **JOB**, 1972, v45(4), 585-619.

Lambin, Jean-Jacques. "Optimal Allocation Of Competitive Marketing Efforts: An Empirical Study," **JOB**, 1970, v43(4), 468-484.

Lambinos, James and Oskar R. Harmon. "An Empirical Evaluation Of Two Methods For Estimating Economic Damages," **JRI**, 1989, v56(4), 733-739.

Lambourne, Richard W. "Institutional Investing," **FAJ**, 1961, v17(6), 61-68.

Lambourne, Richard W. "Is It Another 1929 In The Market?," **FAJ**, 1955, v11(2), 19-24.

Lambourne, Richard W. "The Position Of Common Stocks," **FAJ**, 1956, v12(1), 79-84.

Lambrinos, James. "On The Use Of Historical Data In The Estimation Of Economic Losses," **JRI**, 1985, v52(3), 464-476.

Lamle, Hugh R. "Ginnie Mae: Age Equals Beauty," **JPM**, 1980-81, v7(2), 75-79.

Lamm-Tennant, Joan. "Asset/Liability Management For The Life Insurer: Situation Analysis And Strategy Formulation," **JRI**, 1989, v56(3), 501-517.

Lamon, Russell. "Turnpike Revenue Bonds," **FAJ**, 1954, v10(5), 47-52.

Lamoureux, C. G. (Frankurter, G. M. and C. G. Lamoureux. "The Relevance Of The Distributional Form Of Common Stock Returns To The Construction Of Optimal Portfolios: Reply," **JFQA**, 1989, v24(1), 131.)

Lamoureux, Christopher G. (Frankurter, George M. and Christopher G. Lamoureux. "The Relevance Of The Distributional Form Of Common Stock Returns To The Construction Of Optimal Portfolios," **JFQA**, 1987, v22(4), 505-511.)

Lamoureux, Christopher G. (Frankurter, George M. and Christopher G. Lamoureux. "Stock Selection And Timing--A New Look At Market Efficiency," **JBFA**, 1988, v15(3), 385-400.)

Lamoureux, Christopher G. (Frankurter, George M. and Christopher G. Lamoureux. "Estimation And Selection Bias In Mean-Variance Portfolio Selection," **JFR**, 1989, v12(2), 173-181.)

Lamoureux, Christopher G. and James W. Wansley. "Market Effects Of Changes In The Standard & Poor's 500 Index," **FR**, 1987, v22(1), 53-70.

Lamoureux, Christopher G. and Percy Poon. "The Market Reaction To Stock Splits," **JOF**, 1987, v42(5), 1347-1370.

Lamoureux, Christopher G. and James W. Wansley. "The Pricing Of When-Issued Securities," **FR**, 1989, v24(2), 183-198.

Lamoureux, Christopher G. and Gary C. Sanger. "Firm Size And Turn-Of-The-Year Effects In The OTC/NASDAQ Market," **JOF**, 1989, v44(5), 1219-1246.

Lamoureux, Christopher G. and William D. Lastrapes. "Heteroskedasticity In Stock Return Data: Volume Versus GARCH Effects," **JOF**, 1990, v45(1), 221-230.

Lampman, Robert J. and S. F. Miyamoto. "Effects Of Coverage Of Home And Office Calls In A Physician-Sponsored Health Insurance Plan," **JRI**, 1961, v28(3), 1-16.

Lamport, Anthony M. "The Community Antenna Television Industry," **FAJ**, 1965, v21(1), 53-55.

Lamy, Pascal and Jean-Francois Vincensini. "The Decentralization Of Credit: A Selected Summary Of The Mayoux Report," **JBF**, 1980, v4(1), 57-63.

Lamy, Robert E. and G. Rodney Thompson. "Penn Square, Problem Loans, And Insolvency Risk," **JFR**, 1986, v9(2), 103-111.

Lamy, Robert E. (Allen, David S., Robert E. Lamy and G. Rodney Thompson. "Agency Costs And Alternative Call Provisions: An Empirical Investigation," **FM**, 1987, v16(4), 37-44.)

Lamy, Robert E. (Allen, David S., Robert E. Lamy and G. Rodney Thompson. "The Shelf Registration Of Debt And Self Selection Bias," **JOF**, 1990, v45(1), 275-288.)

Lamy, Robert E. (Billingsley, Randall S., Robert E. Lamy and G. Rodney Thompson. "Valuation Of Primary Issue Con- vertible Bonds," **JFR**, 1986, v9(3), 251-260.)

Lamy, Robert E. (Billingsley, Randall S., Robert E. Lamy, M. Wayne Marr and G. Rodney Thompson. "Split Ratings And Bond Reoffering Yields," **FM**, 1985, v14(2), 59-65.)

Lamy, Robert E. (Billingsley, Randall S. and Robert E. Lamy. "Market Reaction To The Formation Of One-Bank Holding Companies And The 1970 Bank Holding Company Act Amendment," **JBF**, 1984, v8(1), 21-33.)

Lamy, Robert E. (Billingsley, Randall S. and Robert E. Lamy. "The Regulation Of International Lending: IMF Support, The Debt Crisis, And Bank Stockholder Wealth," **JBF**, 1988, v12(2), 255-274.)

Lamy, Robert E. (Billingsley, Randall S., Robert E. Lamy and G. Rodney Thompson. "The Choice Among Debt, Equity, And Convertible Bonds," **JFR**, 1988, v11(1), 43-56.)

Lamy, Robert E. (Billingsley, Randall S., Robert E. Lamy and David M. Smith. "Units Of Debt With Warrants: Evidence Of The 'Penalty-Free' Issuance Of An Equity-Like Security," **JFR**, 1990, v13(3), 187-200.)

Lamy, Robert E. and G. Rodney Thompson. "Risk Premia And The Pricing Of Primary Issue Bonds," **JBF**, 1988, v11(4), 585-601.

Lancaster, Kelvin. "Competition And Product Variety," **JOB**, 1980, v53(3), 2, S79-S104.

Lancaster, Kent M. (Boyer, Kenneth D. and Kent M. Lancaster. "Are There Scale Economies In Advertising?," **JOB**,1986,v59(3),509-526.)

Landa, Diego. (Irwin, Scott H. and Diego Landa. "Real Estate, Futures, And Gold As Portfolio Assets," **JPM**, 1987-88, v14(1), 29-34.)

Landes, William J. (Glasgo, Philip W., William J. Landes and A. Frank Thompson. "Bank Discount, Coupon Equivalent, And Compound Yields," **FM**, 1982, v11(3), 80-84.)

Landes, William J., John D. Stoffels and James A. Seifert. "An Empirical Test Of A Duration-Based Hedge: The Case Of Corporate Bonds," **JPM**, 1985, v5(2),173-182.

Landis, John D. (Dowall, David E. and John D. Landis. "Land-Use Controls And Housing Costs: An Examination Of San Francisco Bay Area Communities," **AREUEA**, 1982, v10(1), 67-93.)

Landon, Charles E. "Freight Traffic On The Ohio River," **FAJ**, 1961, v17(3), 51-57.

Landon, Charles E. "Technological Progress In Transportation On The Mississippi River System," **JOB**, 1960, v33(1), 43-62.

Landry, Robert J. (George, Edwin B. and Robert J. Landry. "The Federal Reserve Board Report On Small-Business Financing," **JOB**, 1959, v32(3), 212-228.)

Landsberger, Michael and Isaac Meilijson. "A Tale Of Two Tails: An Alternative Characterization Of Comparative Risk," **JRU**, 1990, v3(1), 65-82.

Landskroner, Yoram and David Ruthenberg. "Optimal Bank Behavior Under Uncertain Inflation," **JOF**, 1985, v40(4), 1159-1171.

Landskroner, Yoram and Nissan Liviatan. "Risk Premia And The Sources Of Inflation," **JMCB**, 1981, v13(2), 205-214.

Landskroner, Yoram and David Ruthenberg. "How Variable Interest Rates Affect Bank Duration And Immunization," **FAJ**, 1989, v45(4), 77-80.

Landskroner, Yoram. "Effects Of Interest Rate Policy On External Balances," **JBF**, 1978, v2(3),295-301.

Landskroner, Yoram. "Intertemporal Determination Of The Market Price Of Risk," **JOF**, 1977, v32(5), 1671-1681.

Landskroner, Yoram. (Bar-Yosef, Sasson and Yoram Landskroner. "The Impact Of The Government Sector On Financial Equilibrium And Corporate Financial Decisions," **JBFA**, 1984, v11(1), 13-27.)

Landskroner, Yoram. (Friend, Irwin, Yoram Landskroner and Etienne Losq. "The Demand For Risky Assets Under Uncertain Inflation," **JOF**, 1976, v31(5), 1287-1297.)

Landsman, Wayne R. (Beaver, William H., Paul A. Griffin and Wayne R. Landsman. "How Well Does Replacement Cost Income Explain Stock Return?," **FAJ**, 1983, v39(2), 26-30,39.)

Landwehr, Jan L. (Etebari, Ahmad, James O. Horrigan and Jan L. Landwehr. "To Be Or Not To Be--Reaction Of Stock Returns To Sudden Deaths Of Corporate Chief Executive Officers," **JBFA**, 1987, v14(2), 255-278.)

Lane, John T. (McCall, Alan S. and John T. Lane. "Multi-Office Banking And The Safety And Soundness Of Commercial Banks," **JBR**, 1980-81, v11(2), 87-94.)

Lane, Jonathan S. (Vandell, Kerry D. and Jonathan S. Lane. "The Economics Of Architecture And Urban Design: Some Preliminary Findings," **AREUEA**, 1989, v17(2), 235-260.)

Lane, Julia and Dennis Glennon. "The Estimation Of Age/Earnings Profiles In Wrongful Death And Injury Cases," **JRI**, 1985, v52(4), 686-695.

Lane, Julia and Dennis Glennon. "The Estimation Of Age/Earnings Profiles In Wrongful Death And Injury Cases: Reply," **JRI**, 1988, v55(1), 174-179.

Lane, Julia. (Glennon, Dennis and Julia Lane. "Imputing A Housewife's Earnings In A Wrongful Death And Injury Case," **JRI**, 1986, v53(4), 734-743.)

Lane, Morton. "Applying Risk/Return Analysis To Short-Term Fixed-Income Portfolios," **JPM**, 1978-79, v9(1), 26-37.

Lane, Morton. "Asset Allocation: Let The Managers' Market Decide!," **JPM**, 1976-77, v3(4), 5-9.

Lane, Morton. "Fixed-Income Managers Must Time The Market!," **JPM**, 1978-79, v5(4), 36-40.

Lane, Morton. "Short-Term Money Management For Bank Portfolios," **JBR**, 1974-75, v5(2), 102-119.

Lane, Morton. (Burghardt, Galen and Morton Lane. "How To Tell If Options Are Cheap," **JPM**, 1990, v16(2), 72-78.)

Lane, Sylvia. "Submarginal Credit Risk Classification," **JFQA**, 1972, v7(1), 1379-1385.

Lane, Sylvia. (Kline, Kristin and Sylvia Lane. "Levels Of Consumer Satisfaction Under Three Subsidized Low Income Housing Programs," **AREUEA**, 1975, v3(2), 83-102.)

Lane, William R. (Caks, John, William R. Lane, Robert W. Greenleaf and Reginald G. Joules. "A Simple Formula For Duration," **JFR**, 1985, v8(3), 245-249.)

Lane, William R. (Chance Don M. and William R. Lane. "A Re-Examination Of Interest Rate Sensitivity In The Common Stocks Of Financial Institutions," **JFR**, 1980, v3(1), 49-55.)

Lane, William R. (Wansley, James W., William R. Lane and Ho C. Yang. "Gains To Bidder Firms In Cash And Securities Transactions," **FR**, 1987, v22(4), 403-414.)

Lane, William R. (Wansley, James W., William R. Lane and Ho C. Yang. "Abnormal Returns To Acquired Firms By Type Of Acquisition And Method Of Payment," **FM**, 1983, v12(3), 16-22.)

Lane, William R. (Wansley, James W., William R. Lane and Ho C. Yang. "Shareholder Returns To USA Acquired Firms In Foreign And Domestic Acquisitions," **JBFA**, 1983, v10(4), 647-656.)

Lane, William R. (Wansley, James W. and William R. Lane. A Financial Profile Of The Dividend Initiating Firm," **JBFA**, 1987, v14(3), 425-436.)

Lane, William R. (Wansley, James W., William R. Lane and Salil Sarkar. "Managements' View On Share Repurchase And Tender Offer Premiums," **FM**, 1989, v18(3), 97-110.)

Lane, William R. (Yang, Ho C., James W. Wansley and William R. Lane. "Stock Market Recognition Of Multinationality Of A Firm And International Events," JBFA, 1985, v12(2), 263-274.)

Lane, William R. (Yang, Ho C., James W. Wansley and William R. Lane. "A Direct Test Of The Diversification Service Hypothesis Of Foreign Direct Investment," AFPAF, 1989, v4(Supp), 215-238.)

Lane, William R., Stephen W. Looney and James W. Wansley. "An Application Of The Cox Proportional Hazards Model To Bank Failure," JBF, 1986, v10(4), 511-532.

Lanen, William N. (Lambert, Richard A., William N. Lanen and David F. Larcker. "Executive Stock Option Plans And Corporate Dividend Policy," JFQA, 1989, v24(4), 409-426.)

Laney, Leroy O. and Thomas D. Willett. "The International Liquidity Explosion And Worldwide Inflation: The Evidence From Sterilization Coefficient Estimates," JIMF, 1982, v1(2), 141-152.

Lang, Arthur H. "The Investment Aspects Of Water Flooding," FAJ, 1963, v19(5), 71-73.

Lang, Bruno R. (Cosandier, Pierre-Alexis and Bruno R. Lang. "Interest Rate Parity Tests: Switzerland And Some Major Western Countries," JBF, 1981, v5(2), 187-200.)

Lang, Frank. "Insurance Managers And Conglomerates," FAJ, 1970, v26(2), 100-103.

Lang, Frank. "Research In Insurance," JRI, 1954, v21, 27-36.

Lang, James R. and Wesley H. Jones. "Hedonic Property Valuation Models: Are Subjective Measures Of Neighborhood Amenities Needed?," AREUEA, 1979, v7(4), 451-465. 3!?8

Lang, Larry H. P. (Friend, Irwin and Larry H. P. Lang. "An Empirical Test Of The Impact Of Managerial Self-Interest On Coprorate Capital Structure," JOF, 1988, v43(2), 271-281.)

Lang, Larry H. P. (Friend, Irwin and Larry H. P. Lang. "The Size Effect On Stock Returns: Is It Simply A Risk Effect Not Adequately Reflected By The Usual Measures?," JBF, 1988, v12(1), 13-30.)

Lang, Larry H. P. (Gilson, Stuart C., Kose John and Larry H. P. Lang. "Troubled Debt Restructurings: An Empirical Study Of Private Reorganiztion Of Firms In Default," JFEC, 1990, v27(2), 315-354.)

Lang, Larry H. P. and Robert H. Litzenberger. "Dividend Announcements: Cash Flow Signalling Vs. Free Cash Flow Hypothesis?," JFEC, 1989, v24(1), 181-192.

Lang, Larry H. P., Rene M. Stulz and Ralph A. Walkling. "Managerial Performance, Tobin's Q, And The Gains From Successful Tender Offers," JFEC, 1989, v24(1), 137-154.

Lang, Pascal. (Jacque, Laurent L., Pascal Lang and Charles S. Tapiero. "Towards An Expected Utility Paradigm For Foreign Exchange Risk Management: The Long And Short Of It," RDIBF, 1989, v3, 191-228.)

Lang, William W. and Leonard I. Nakamura. "Information Losses In A Dynamic Model Of Credit," JOF, 1989, v44(3), 731-746.

Langdana, Farrokh K. Central Bank Intervention And Domestic Fiscal Policy," IJOF, 1990, v3(1), 170-184.

Lange, Bruce. (Einzig, Robert and Bruce Lange. "Swaps At Transamerica: Applications And Analysis," JACF, 1990, v2(4), 48-58.)

Lange, David R. (Carpenter, Michael D., David R. Lange, Donald S. Shannon and William Thomas Stevens. "Methodologies Of Valuing Lost Earnings: A Review, A Criticism, And A Recommendation," JRI, 1986, v53(1), 104-118.)

Lange, Jeffrey T. "Application Of A Mathematical Concept Of Risk To Property-Liability Insurance Ratemaking," JRI, 1969, v36(3), 383-392.

Langen, Dieter. "An Interactive Multi-Objective Decision Model For Bank Asset Liability Management," RDIBF, 1989, v3, 263-294.

Langer, Leonard C. R. "A Financial Practitioner's View Of Professional Finance Associations," FM, 1981, v10(2), Tenth Anniversary Edition, 116-122.

Langer, Martha J. (Goodman, Laurie S. and Martha J. Langer. "Accounting For Interest Rate Futures In Bank Asset-Liability Management," JFM, 1983, v3(4), 415-428.)

Langetieg, T. C., M. C. Findlay and L. F. J. da Motta. "Multiperiod Pension Plans And ERISA," JFQA, 1982, v17(4), 603-631.

Langetieg, Terence C. "A Multivariate Model Of The Term Structure," JOF, 1980, v35, No. 71-97.

Langetieg, Terence C. "An Application Of A Three-Factor Performance Index To Measure Stockholder Gains From Merger," JFEC, 1978, v6(4), 365-384.

Langetieg, Terence C. "Stochastic Control Of Corporate Investment When Output Affects Future Prices," JFQA, 1986, v21(3), 239-263.

Langetieg, Terence C. (Haugen, Robert A. and Terence C. Langetieg. "An Empirical Test For Synergism In Merger," JOF, 1975, v30(4), 1003-1014.)

Langetieg, Terence C. (Kalaba, Robert E., Terence C. Langetieg, Nima Rasakhoo and Mark I. Weinstein. "Estimation Of Implicit Bankruptcy Costs," JOF, 1984, v39(3), 629-642.)

Langetieg, Terence C. (Leibowitz, Martin L. and Terence C. Langetieg. "Shortfall Risk And The Asset Allocation Decision: A Simulation Analysis Of Stock And Bond Risk Profiles," JPM, 1989, v16(1), 61-68.)

Langetieg, Terence C., Robert A. Haugen and Dean W. Wichern. "Merger And Stockholder Risk," JFQA, 1980, v15(3), 689-717.

Langetieg, Terence C., Martin L. Leibowitz and Stanley Kogelman. "Duration Targeting And The Management Of Multiperiod Returns," FAJ, 1990, v46(5), 35-45.

Langetieg, Terrence C. (Hartzell, David J., David G. Shulman, Terrence C. Langetieg and Martin L. Leibowitz. "A Look At Real Estate Duration," JPM, 1988-89, v15(1), 16-24.)

Langley, William C., Jr. "Strategies In Today's Capital Environment," JBR, 1975-76, v6(3), 177-178.

Langmuir, Dean. "Common Sense And Investment Techniques," FAJ, 1947, v3(1), 3-10.

Langohr, Herwig and Anthony M. Santomero. "Commercial Bank Refinancing And Economic Stability: An Analysis Of European Features," JBF, 1985, v9(4),535-552.

Langohr, Herwig and Anthony M. Santomero. "The Extent Of Equity Investment By European Banks," JMCB, 1985, v17(2), 243-252.

Langohr, Herwig M. and Claude J. Viallet. "Compensation And Wealth Transfers In The French Nationalizations: 1981-1982," JFEC, 1986, v17(2), 273-312.

Langohr, Herwig. "Alternative Approaches To The Theory Of The Banking Firm: A Note," JBF, 1982, v6(2), 297-304.

Langohr, Herwig. "Bank Refinancing With The Central Bank: Reexamination Of Its Interest Rate Elasticities For Belgium 1960-1973," JBF, 1980, v4(2),175-187.

Langohr, Herwig. (Eckbo, B. Espen and Herwig Langohr. "Information Disclosure, Method Of Payment, And Takeover Premiums: Public And Private Tender Offers In France," JFEC, 1989, v24(2), 363-404.)

Langrehr, Frederick W. "Money Market Mutual Fund Investors' Savings Account Holdings And Demographic Profile," JBR, 1982-83, v13(3), 202-206.

Langsam, Joseph A. (Bookstaber, Richard and Joseph A. Langsam. "Portfolio Insurance Trading Rules," JFM, 1988, v8(1), 15-32.)

Lanser, Howard P. and John A. Halloran. "Evaluating Cash Flow Systems Under Growth," FR, 1986, v21(2), 309-318.

Lanser, Howard P. (Bernardo, John J. and Howard P. Lanser. "A Capital Budgeting Decision Model With Subjective Criteria," JFQA, 1977, v12(2), 261-275.)

Lanser, Howard P. (Halloran, John A. and Howard P. Lanser. "The Credit Policy Decision In An Inflationary Environment," FM, 1981, v10(5), 31-38.)

Lanser, Howard P. (Halloran, John A. and Howard P. Lanser. "Inflation-Induced Biases In The Evaluation And Selection Of Capital Investments," FR, 1983, v18(4), 314-325.)

Lanser, Howard P. (Johnson, James M. and Howard P. Lanser. "Dividend Risk Measurement And Tests Of The CAPM," JPM, 1980-81, v7(2), 50-54.)

Lanser, Howard P. (Lewellen, Wilbur G., Howard P. Lanser and John J. McConnell. "Payback Substitutes For Discounted Cash Flow," FM, 1973, v2(2), 17-23.)

Lanstein, Ronald and William F. Sharpe. "Duration And Security Risk," JFQA, 1978, v13(4), 653-668.

Lanstein, Ronald. (Rosenberg, Barr, Kenneth Reid and Ronald Lanstein. "Persuasive Evidence Of Market Inefficiency," JPM, 1984-85, v11(3), 9-17.)

Lanzillotti, R. F. and T. R. Saving. "State Branching Restrictions And The Availablity Of Branching Services: A Comment," JMCB, 1969, v1(4), 778-788.

Lapan, Harvey. (Howe, Keith M. and Harvey Lapan. "Inflation And Asset Life: The Darby Versus The Fisher Effect," JFQA, 1987, v22(2), 249-258.)

Lapkin, David T. (Kreps, Clifton H., Jr. and David T. Lapkin. "Public Regulation And Operating Conventions Affecting Sources Of Funds Of Commercial Banks And Thrift Institutions," JOF, 1962, v17(2), 289-301.)

Lapp, John S. "The Determination Of Savings And Loan Association Deposit Rates In The Absence Of Rate Ceilings: A Cross-Section Approach," JOF, 1978, v33(1), 215-230.

Lapp, John S. (Grennes, Thomas and John S. Lapp. "Neutrality Of Inflation In The Agricultural Sector," JIMF, 1986, v5(2), 231-243.)

Lapsley, Irvine. "Income Measurement At A State Railway Corporation: The 'Social Profit' Illusion?," JBFA, 1981, v8(4), 529-548.

Lapsley, Irvine. "The Use Of Accounting Information In Consensus Management Teams," JBFA, 1979, v6(4), 539-558.

Larcker, David F. "Short-Term Compensation Contracts And Executive Decisions: The Case Of Commercial Banks," JFQA, 1987, v22(1), 33-50.

Larcker, David F. (Fornell, Claes and David F. Larcker. "The Use Of Canonical Correlation Analysis In Accounting Research," JBFA, 1980, v7(3), 455-474.)

Larcker, David F. (Lambert, Richard A., William N. Lanen and David F. Larcker. "Executive Stock Option Plans And Corporate Dividend Policy," JFQA, 1989, v24(4), 409-426.)

Larcker, David F. and Thomas Lys. "An Empirical Analysis Of The Incentives To Engage In Costly Information Acquisition: The Case Of Risk Arbitrage," JFEC, 1987, v18(1), 111-126.

Larcker, David F., Lawrence A. Gordon and George E. Pinches. "Testing For Market Efficiency: A Comparison Of The Cumulative Average Residual Methodology And Intervention Analysis," JFQA, 1980, v15(2), 267-287.

Lareau, Thomas J. (Bloch, Howard R. and Thomas J. Lareau. "Should We Invest In 'Socially Irresponsible' Firms?," JPM, 1984-85, v11(4), 27-31.)

Largay, J. A. (Hausman, W. H., R. R. West and J. A. Largay. "Stock Splits, Price Changes, And Trading Profits: A Synthesis," JOB, 1971, v44(1), 69-77.)

Largay, James A., III and Clyde P. Stickney. "Cash Flows, Ratio Analysis And The W. T. Grant Company Bankruptcy," FAJ, 1980, v36(4), 51-54.

Largay, James A., III and J. Leslie Livingstone. "Current Value Accounting Neglects Liabilities," FAJ, 1978, v34(2), 65-71.

Largay, James A., III. "100% Margins: Combating Speculation In Individual Security Issues," JOF, 1973, v28(4), 973-986.

Largay, James A., III. (Greer, Willis R., Jr. and James A. Largay, III. "Interim Inventory Estimation Error And The Volatility Of Stock Prices," JBFA, 1980, v7(3), 401-414.)

Largay, James A., III. (Greer, Willis R., Jr. and James A. Largay, III. "Decision Model Diagnostics: A Key To Information System Design," FR, 1979, v14(2), 36-44.)

Largay, James A., III. (West, Richard R. and James A. Largay, III. "Premium On Convertible Bonds: Comment," JOF, 1972, v27(5), 1156-1162.)

Larre, Rene. "Facts Of Life About The Integration Of National Capital Markets," JMCB, 1969, v1(3), 319-327.

Larrick, George P. "The Impact Of New Federal Regulations On Research And Development In The Pharmaceutical Industry," FAJ, 1964, v20(4), 31-32.

Larsen, James E. "Money Illusion And Residential Real Estate Transfers," JRER, 1989, v4(1), 13-19.

Larsen, James E. (Zorn, Thomas S. and James E. Larsen. "The Incentive Effects Of Flat-Fee And Percentage Commissions For Real Estate Brokers," AREUEA, 1986, v14(4), 24-47.)

Larsen, James E. and Won J. Park. "Non-Uniform Percentage Brokerage Commissions And Real Estate Market Performance," AREUEA, 1989, v17(4), 422-438.

Larsen, Norma L. "Defining Equity In Surplus Distribution," **JRI**, 1979, v46(4), 672-682.

Larsen, Norma L. "Implications Of Using An Investment Year Interest Factor In Dividend Calculations," **JRI**, 1980, v47(2), 258-278.

Larsen, Norma L. "Policy Loan Utilization Factors In Dividend Distribution Formulas," **JRI**, 1981, v48(1), 80-94.

Larsen, Normal L. and Gerald D. Martin. "Income Growth Factors: Error Introduced Through The Application Of Cohort Data," **JRI**, 1981, v48(1), 143-147.

Larsen, R. A. and J. E. Murphy, Jr. "Why Does Earnings Per Share Change?," **FAJ**, 1975, v31(2), 77-83.

Larson, Arthur. "A Method Of Automatically Adjusting The Maximum Earnings Base Under OASDI: Comment," **JRI**, 1965, v32(3), 472-473.

Larson, John C. and Joel N. Morse. "Intervalling Effects In Hong Kong Stocks," **JFR**, 1987, v10(4), 353-362.

Larson, Richard C. "Capital, Debt And National Growth," **FAJ**, 1964, v20(5), 41-43.

Larson, Richard C. "Self-Administered Pension Funds," **FAJ**, 1969, v25(4), 135-137.

Larson, Robert E. "Note On The Education Of Actuarial Students," **JRI**, 1958, v25(2), 64-66.

Larson, Robert E. "The Actuarial Curriculum: Comment," **JRI**, 1966, v33(3), 475-477.

Lash, Nicholas A. (Batavia, Bala and Nicholas A. Lash. "The Impact Of Bank Portfolio Composition On GNP," **JMCB**, 1982, v14(4), Part 1, 517-524.)

Laskar, Daniel M. "Short-Run Independence Of Monetary Policy Under A Pegged-Exchange-Rates System: An Econometric Approach," **JIMF**, 1982, v1(1), 57-80.

Lasman, Daniel A. and Roman L. Weil. "Adjusting The Debt-Equity Ratio," **FAJ**, 1978, v34(5), 49-58.

Lasser, Dennis J. "A Measure Of Ex Ante Hedging Effectiveness For The Treasury Bill And Treasury Bond Futures Markets," **RFM**, 1987, v6(2), 278-295.

Lasser, Dennis J. "Influence Of Treasury Bill Futures Trading On The Primary Sale Of The Deliverable Treasury Bill," **FR**, 1987, v22(4), 391-402.

Lasser, Dennis J. (Chiang, Raymond and Dennis J. Lasser. "Tax Timing Options On Futures Contracts And The 1981 Economic Recovery Act," **FR**, 1989, v24(1), 75-92.)

Lasser, Dennis J. (Hassell, John M., Robert H. Jennings and Dennis J. Lasser. "Management Earnings Forecasts: Their Usefulness As A Source Of Firm-Specific Information To Security Analysts," **JFR**, 1988, v11(4), 303-320.)

Lasser, Dennis J. (Heuson, Andrea J. and Dennis J. Lasser. "Tax-Timing Options And The Pricing Of Government Bonds," **JFR**, 1990, v13(2), 93-104.)

Lasser, Dennis J. (Klemkosky, Robert C. and Dennis J. Lasser. "An Efficiency Analysis Of The T-Bond Futures Market," **JFM**, 1985, v5(4), 607-620.)

Lasser, Dennis J. and W. Brian Barrett. "New Issue Yield Spreads In The 30-Year Treasury Bond Market," **FR**, 1991, v26(2), 237-248.

Lassiter, Roy L., Jr. "The Wife's Contribution To Family Income," **JRI**, 1961, v28(4), 33-40.

Lastavica, John. "Asset Management And Other Financial Simulation Models," **JBR**, 1971-72, v2(1), 69-70.

Lastrapes, William D. "Exchange Rate Volatility And U.S. Monetary Policy: An ARCH Application," **JMCB**, 1989, v21(1), 66-77.

Lastrapes, William D. (Lamoureux, Christopher G. and William D. Lastrapes. "Heteroskedasticity In Stock Return Data: Volume Versus GARCH Effects," **JOF**, 1990, v45(1), 221-230.)

Lastrapes, William D. and Faik Koray. "International Transmission Of Aggregate Shocks Under Fixed And Flexible Exchange Rate Regimes: United Kingdom, France, And Germany, 1959 To 1985," **JIMF**, 1990, v9(4), 402-423.

Latainer, Gary D. (Platt, Robert B. and Gary D. Latainer. "Risk-Return Tradeoffs Of Contingent Insurance Strategies For Active Bond Portfolios," **FAJ**, 1984, v40(3), 34-39.)

Latainer, Gary D. (Tilley, James A. and Gary D. Latainer. "A Synthetic Option Framework For Asset Allocation," **FAJ**, 1985, v41(3), 32-43.)

Latane, Henry A. (Alhadeff, D., P. Bernstein, C. Campbell, L. Chandler, E. Ettin, V. Farhi, J. Guttentag, H. Latane and K. Poole. "The Commission On Money And Credit's Research Studies," **JOF**, 1964, v19(3), 497-533. Latane, Henry A.

Latane, Henry A. and Charles P. Jones. "Standardized Unexpected Earnings - 1971-77," **JOF**, 1979, v34(3), 717-724.

Latane, Henry A. and Charles P. Jones. "Standardized Unexpected Earnings - A Progress Report," **JOF**, 1977, v32(5), 1457-1465.

Latane, Henry A. and Donald L. Tuttle. "Criteria For Portfolio Building," **JOF**, 1967, v22(3), 359-373.

Latane, Henry A. and Donald L. Tuttle. "Decision Theory And Financial Management," **JOF**, 1966, v21(2), 228-244.

Latane, Henry A. and Donald L. Tuttle. "Probability In Industry Analysis," **FAJ**, 1968, v24(4), 51-61.

Latane, Henry A. and Richard J. Rendleman, Jr. "Standard Deviations Of Stock Price Ratios Implied In Option Prices," **JOF**, 1976, v31(2), 369-381.

Latane, Henry A. and William E. Young. "Test Of Portfolio Building Rules," **JOF**, 1969, v24(4), 595-612.

Latane, Henry A. and William E. Young. "Test Of Portfolio Building Rules: Reply," **JOF**, 1971, v26(4), 976-981.

Latane, Henry A. "Cross-Section Regularities In Returns On Investment In Common Stocks," **JOB**, 1973, v46(4), 512-516.

Latane, Henry A. "Individual Risk Preference In Portfolio Selection," **JOF**, 1960, v15(1), 45-52.

Latane, Henry A. "Price Changes In Equity Securities," **JOF**, 1954, v9(3), 252-264.

Latane, Henry A. "The CAPM And The Investment Horizon," **JPM**, 1981-82, v8(1), 64-65.

Latane, Henry A. "The Geometric-Mean Principle Revisited: A Reply," **JBF**, 1978, v2(4), 395-398.

Latane, Henry A. "The Geometric Mean Criterion Continued," **JBF**, 1979, v3(4), 309-311.

Latane, Henry A. (Jones, Charles P., Richard J. Rendleman, Jr. and Henry A. Latane. "Earnings Announcements: Pre-And-Post Responses," **JPM**, 1984-85, v11(3), 28-33.)

Latane, Henry A. (Rendleman, Richard J., Jr., Charles P. Jones and Henry A. Latane. "Further Insight Into The Standardized Unexpected Earnings Anomaly: Size And Serial Correlation Effects," **FR**, 1987, v22(1), 131-144.)

Latane, Henry A. (Rendleman, Richard J., Jr., Charles P. Jones and Henry A. Latane. "Empirical Anomalies Based On Unexpected Earnings And The Importance Of Risk Adjustment," **JFEC**, 1982, v10(3), 269-287.)

Latane, Henry A., Donald L. Tuttle and C. P. Jones. "E/P Ratios V. Changes In Earnings," **FAJ**, 1969, v25(1), 117-120.

Latane, Henry A., Donald L. Tuttle and William E. Young. "How To Choose A Market Index," **FAJ**, 1971, v27(5), 75-85.

Latane, Henry A., O. Maurice Joy and Charles P. Jones. "Quarterly Data, Sort-Rank Routines, And Security Evaluation," **JOB**, 1970, v43(4), 427-438.

Latane, Henry. (Jones, Charles P., Richard J. Rendleman, Jr. and Henry Latane. "Stock Returns And SUEs During The 1970s," **JPM**, 1983-84, v10(2), 18-22.)

Latham, Mark. "Informational Efficiency And Information Subsets," **JOF**, 1986, v41(1), 39-52.

Latham, Mark. "The Arbitrage Pricing Theory And Supershares," **JOF**, 1989, v44(2), 263-282.

Latta, Cynthia M. (Bierwag, G. O., George G. Kaufman and Cynthia M. Latta. "Duration Models: A Taxonomy," **JPM**, 1988-89, v15(1), 50-54.)

Latta, Cynthia M. (Bierwag, G. O., George G. Kaufman, Cynthia M. Latta and Gordon S. Roberts. "The Usefulness Of Duration: Response To Critics" **JPM**, 1986-87, v13(2), 48-52.)

Latta, Cynthia M. (Bierwag, G. O., George G. Kaufman and Cynthia M. Latta. "Bond Portfolio Immunization: Tests Of Maturity, One- And Two-Factor Duration Matching Strategies," **FR**, 1987, v22(2), 203-220.)

Latta, Cynthia M. (Hamburger, Michael J. and Cynthia M. Latta. "The Term Structure Of Interest Rates: Some Additional Evidence," **JMCB**, 1969, v1(1), 71-83.)

Latta, Cynthia M. (Kaufman, George G. and Cynthia M. Latta. "The Demand For Money: Preliminary Evidence From Industrial Countries," **JFQA**, 1966, v1(3), 75-89.)

Lau, Hon-Shiang and John R. Wingender. "The Analytics Of The Intervaling Effect On Skewness And Kurtosis Of Stock Returns," **FR**, 1989, v24(2), 215-234.

Lau, Hon-Shiang. "An Effective Approach For Estimating The Aggregate Loss Of An Insurance Portfolio," **JRI**, 1984, v51(1), 20-30.

Lau, S. C. (Wagner, W. H. and S. C. Lau. "The Effect Of Diversification On Risk," **FAJ**, 1971, v27(5), 48-53.)

Lau, Sheila C., Stuart R. Quay and Carl M. Ramsey. "The Tokyo Stock Exchange And The Capital Asset Pricing Model," **JOF**, 1974, v29(2), 507-514.

Lau, W. Patrick. (Kon, Stanley J. and W. Patrick Lau. "Specification Tests For Portfolio Regression Parameter Stationarity And The Implications For Empirical Research," **JOF**, 1979, v34(2), 451-465.)

Laub, P. Michael. "On The Informational Content Of Dividends," **JOB**, 1976, v49(1), 73-80.

Lauch, Louis H. and Neil B. Murphy. "A Test Of The Impact Of Branching On Deposit Variability," **JFQA**, 1970, v5(3), 323-327.

Laudadio, Leonard. "Size Of Bank, Size Of Borrower, And The Rate Of Interest," **JOF**, 1963, v18(1), 20-28.

Lauer, J. Alan. "A Model For Determining The Rate Of Return On Investment In Life Insurance Policies: Comment," **JRI**, 1968, v35(3), 476-481.

Lauer, Joseph R. (Singleton, J. Clay and Joseph R. Lauer. "The Implications Of Recursiveness In Capital Markets--Theory And Empirical Tests," **JFQA**, 1979, v14(1), 59-76.)

Laufenberg, Daniel E. "Contemporaneous Versus Lagged Reserve Accounting: A Comment," **JMCB**, 1976, v8(2), 239-245.

Laufenberg, Daniel E. "Optimal Reserve Requirement Ratios Against Bank Deposits For Short-Run Monetary Control," **JMCB**, 1979, v11(1), 99-105.

Laufenberg, Daniel E. "Reserve Measures As Operating Variables Of Monetary Policy," **JOF**, 1976, v31(3), 853-864.

Laufer, Edward B. "Plastics Come Of Age," **FAJ**, 1947, v3(1), 32-42.

Laufer, Edward B. "Retailing," **FAJ**, 1951, v7(4), 88-90.

Laufer, Edward B. "The Antibiotic Field," **FAJ**, 1949, v5(3), 20-23.

Laughhunn, D. J. (Forsyth, J. D. and D. J. Laughhunn. "Rationing Capital In A Telephone Company," **FM**, 1974, v3(3), 36-43.)

Laughhunn, Dan J. and C. Ronald Sprecher. "Probability Of Loss And The Capital Asset Pricing Model," **FM**, 1977, v6(1), 18-25.

Laughhunn, Dan J. (Crum, Roy L., Dan J. Laughhunn and John W. Payne. "Risk-Seeking Behavior And Its Implications For Financial Models," **FM**, 1981, v10(5), 20-27.)

Laughlin, Eugene J. (Richards, Verlyn D. and Eugene J. Laughlin. "A Cash Conversion Cycle Approach To Liquidity Analysis," **FM**, 1980, v9(1), 32-38.)

Laughlin, Richard C. and Anthony G. Puxty. "Accounting Regulation: An Alternative Perspective: A Reply," **JBFA**, 1984, v11(4), 593-596.

Laughlin, Richard C. and Anthony G. Puxty. "Accounting Regulation: An Alternative Perspective," **JBFA**, 1983, v10(3), 451-479.

Laughlin, Richard C. "Accounting Objectives And The Corporate Report," **JBFA**, 1977, v4(1), 115-130.

Laughlin, Richard C. "On The Nature Of Accounting Methodology," **JBFA**, 1981, v8(3), 329-351.

Laughlin, Richard C., E. Anthony Lowe and Anthony G. Puxty. "Towards A Value-Neutral Positive Science Of Accounting: A Comment," **JBFA**, 1982, v8(4), 567-572.

Laughlin, Richard. (Puxty, Anthony G. and Richard Laughlin. "A Rational Reconstruction Of The Decision-Usefulness Criterion," **JBFA**, 1983, v10(4), 543-559.)

Laumas, G. S. and Y. P. Mehra. "The Stability Of The Demand For Money Function, 1900-1974," **JOF**, 1977, v32(3), 911-916.

Laumas, G. S. "Statistical Tests Of The Keynesian Demand Function For Money: Comment," **JOF**, 1968, v23(4), 674-677.

Laumas, Prem S. and Richard Zerbe. "The Relative Stability Of Monetary Policy And Investment Multiplier In Canada: A Comment," **JMCB**, 1971, v3(4), 867-877.

Laumas, Prem S. "The Role Of Savings Deposits As Money: A Comment," JMCB, 1969, v1(4), 789-795.

Laumer, J. Ford, Jr. (McCord, Sammy O., J. Ford Laumer, Jr. and Dolores R. Wright. "Student Internships In Finance," JFED, 1976, v5, 55-57.)

Launie, J. J. "Price Differentials In Life Insurance," JRI, 1968, v35(2), 283-288.

Launie, J. J. "Shifting Of The Life Insurance Company Income Tax," JRI, 1971, v38(1), 81-92.

Launie, J. J. "The Cost Of Capital Of Insurance Companies," JRI, 1971, v38(2), 263-268.

Launie, J. J. "The Cost Of Capital Of Insurance Companies: Reply," JRI, 1972, v39(3), 492-495.

Launie, J. J. "The Supply Function Of Urban Property Insurance," JRI, 1969, v36(2), 269-284.

Launie, J. J. "The Supply Function Of Urban Property Insurance: Reply," JRI, 1970, v37(3), 463-464.

Launstein, Howard C. "Managerial Accounting Tools For Casualty Insurance Companies," JRI, 1957, v24(4), 22-35.

Launstein, Howard C. "The Agent's Responsibility For Developing Sound Insurance Programs," JRI, 1959, v26(3), 61-68.

Laurence, Martin M. "Weak-Form Efficiency In The Kuala Lumpur And Singapore Stock Markets," JBF, 1986, v10, JBF, 1986, v10(3), 431-446.

Laurence, Martin M. (Severn, Alan K. and Martin M. Laurence. "Direct Investment, Research Intensity, And Profitability," JFQA, 1974, v9(2), 181-190.)

Laurence, Martin. (Kolodny, Richard, Martin Laurence and Arabinda Ghosh. "In Search Of Excellence ... For Whom?," JPM, 1989, v15(3), 56-60.)

Laurent, C. R. "Improving The Efficiency And Effectiveness Of Financial Ratio Analysis," JBFA, 1979, v6(3), 401-413.

Laurent, Robert D. "Currency In Circulation And The Real Value Of Notes," JMCB, 1974, v6(2), 213-226.

Laurent, Robert D. "Monetary Control Under Reverse Lag And Contemporaneous Reserve Accounting: A Comparison: A Reply," JMCB, 1984, v16(1), 89-92.

Laurent, Robert D. "Reserve Requirements: Are They Lagged In The Wrong Direction?," JMCB, 1979, v11(3), 301-310.

Laurent, Robert D. "Reserve Requirements, Deposit Insurance, And Monetary Control," JMCB, 1981, v13(3), 314-324.

Lauterbach, Beni and Margaret Monroe. "Evidence On The Effect Of Information And Noise Trading On Intraday Gold Futures Returns," JFM, 1989, v9(4), 297-306.

Lauterbach, Beni and Margaret A. Monroe. "A Transaction Data Examination Of The Weekend Effect In Futures Markets," RFM, 1989, v8(3), 370-383.

Lauterbach, Beni and Paul Schultz. "Pricing Warrants: An Empirical Study Of The Black-Scholes Model And Its Alternatives," JOF, 1990, v45(4), 1181-1209.

Lauterbach, Beni. "Consumption Volatility, Production Volatility, Spot-Rate Volatility, And The Returns On Treasury Bills And Bonds," JFEC, 1989, v24(1), 155-180.

Lauwers, M. (Eeckhoudt, L., J. F. Outreville, M. Lauwers and F. Calcoen. "The Impact Of A Probationary Period On The Demand For Insurance," JRI, 1988, v55(2), 217-228.)

Lavely, Joe, Gordon Wakefield and Bob Barrett. "Toward Enhancing Beta Estimates," JPM, 1979-80, v6(4), 43-46.

Lavely, Joe. "More About Stock Prices And Inflation," JPM, 1976-77, v3(4), 43-47.

Lavely, Joe. "Warrant Beta's," FR No. 1, 1975, 64-69.

Lavely, Joseph A. "Relative Stock Valuation Made Simple," JPM, 1974-75, v1(4), 62-64.

Lavin, David and Robert Libby. "The Effect Of The Perceived Independence Of The Auditor On The Loan Decision," JBR, 1977-78, v8(2), 118-121.

Law, Warren A. "Senior Securities And Bank Stock Prices," FAJ, 1966, v22(3), 101-103.

Lawler, Thomas A. "Default, Risk, And Yield Spreads: A Clarification," JPM, 1981-82, v8(4), 65-66.

Lawler, Thomas A. "Federal Reserve Policy Strategy And Interest Rate Seasonality," JMCB, 1979, v11(4), 494-499.

Lawler, Thomas A. "Reserve Requirements And The Structure Of The CD Market: A Note," JPM, 1981, v36(4), 935-940.

Lawler, Thomas A. "Yield Spreads, Relative Yield Spreads, And Default Risk," FR, 1980, v15(1), 55-60.

Lawrence, Colin and Aloysius Siow. "Interest Rates And Investment Spending: Some Empirical Evidence For Postwar U.S. Producer Equipment, 1947-1980," JOB, 1985, v58(4), 359-376.

Lawrence, Colin. "Banking Costs, Generalized Functional Forms, And Estimation Of Economies Of Scale And Scope," JMCB, 1989, v21(3), 368-379.

Lawrence, Edward C. and Gregory E. Elliehausen. "The Impact Of Federal Interest Rate Regulations On The Small Saver: Further Evidence," JOF, 1981, v36(3),677-684.

Lawrence, Edward C. and Robert M. Bear. "Corporate Bankruptcy Prediction And The Impact Of Leases," JBFA, 1986, v13(4), 571-585.

Lawrence, Edward C. "Learning Portfolio Management By Experience: University Student Investment Funds," FR, 1990, v25(1), 165-173.

Lawrence, Edward C. (Arshadi, Nasser and Edward C. Lawrence. "An Empirical Investigation Of New Bank Performance," JBF, 1987, v11(1), 33-48.)

Lawrence, Edward C. (Kummer, Donald R., Nasser Arshadi and Edward C. Lawrence. "Incentive Problems In Bank Insider Borrowing," JFSR, 1989, v3(1), 17-32.)

Lawrence, Edward C. and Nasser Arshadi. "The Distributional Impact Of Foreign Deposits On Federal Deposit Insurance Premia," JBF, 1988, v12(1), 105-116.

Lawrence, Robert J. and Duane Lougee. "Determinants Of Correspondent Banking Relationships," JMCB, 1970, v2(3), 358-369.

Lawrence, S. R. "The Application Of Analysis Of Variance To Interfirm Comparison Ratios," JBFA, 1982, v8(4), 523-530.

Lawrenz, David W. "The Effects Of Corporate Taxation On The Cost Of Equity Capital," FM, 1976, v5(1), 53-57.

Lawson, Eric W. "A Federal Department Of Finance - A Proposal," JOF, 1952, v7(1), 1-9.

Lawson, G. H. "Holding Gains, Debt-Financing, Working Capital And Current Cost Accounting," JBFA, 1976, v3(1), 105-114.

Lawson, G. H. "Holding Gains, Debt-Financing, Working Capital And Current Cost Accounting: A Reply," JBFA, 1976, v3(3), 129-136.

Lawson, Gerald H. (Aziz, Abdul and Gerald H. Lawson. "Cash Flow Reporting And Financial Distress Models: Testing Of Hypotheses," FM, 1989, v18(1), 55-63.)

Lawson, Raef A. (Brief, Richard P. and Raef A. Lawson. "Estimating Security Returns: A Further Note," FAJ, 1986, v42(6), 75-77.)

Lawson, Raef A. (Brief, Richard P. and Raef A. Lawson. "Approximate Error In Using Accounting Rates Of Return To Estimate Economic Returns," JBFA, 1991, v18(1), 13-20.)

Lay, Paul E. "Common Stock Investments Of Mutual Fire And Casualty Insurance Companies," JRI, 1961, v28(4), 41-48.

Laycock, Mark S. and Dean A. Paxson. "Hedging Noncoetaneous Cash Positions With Eurodollar Futures," RFM, 1988, v7(Supp), 484-500.

Lazarcik, Gregor. "Scientific Research, Earnings And Stock Prices," FAJ, 1962, v18(1), 49-53.

Lazear, Edward P. "Salaries And Piece Rates," JOB, 1986, v59(3), 405-432.

Le Compte, Richard L. B. and Stephen D. Smith. "Changes In The Cost Of Intermediation: The Case Of Savings And Loans," JOF, 1990, v45(4), 1337-1346.

LeBaron, Blake. (Scheinkman, Jose A. and Blake LeBaron. "Nonlinear Dynamics And Stock Returns," JOB, 1989, v62(3), 311-338.)

LeBaron, Dean and Evan Schulman. "Trading: The Fixable Leak," JPM, 1981-82, v8(1), 10-12.

LeBaron, Dean, Gail Farrelly and Susan Gula. "Facilitating A Dialogue On Risk: A Questionnaire Approach," FAJ, 1989, v45(3), 19-24.

LeBaron, Dean. "A Psychological Profile Of The Portfolio Manager," JPM, 1974-75, v1(1), 13-16.

LeBaron, Dean. "Reflections On Market Inefficiency," FAJ, 1983, v39(3), 16-17,23.

LeBon, Gustave. "The Mind Of Crowds," JPM, 1979-80, v6(4), 69-70.

LeRoy, Stephen F. "Efficient Capital Markets: Comment," JOF, 1976, v31(1), 139-141.

LeRoy, Stephen F. "Expectations Models Of Asset Prices: A Survey Of Theory," JOF, 1982, v37(1),185-217.

LeRoy, Stephen F. "Nominal Prices And Interest Rates In General Equilibrium: Money Shocks," JOB, 1984, v57(2), 177-196.

LeRoy, Stephen F. (Gilles, Christian and Stephen F. LeRoy. "A Note On The Local Expectations Hypothesis: A Discrete-Time Exposition--Erratum," JOF, 1987, v42(2), 473-474.)

LeRoy, Stephen F. (Gilles, Christian and Stephen F. LeRoy. "A Note On The Local Expectations Hypothesis: A Discrete-Time Exposition," JOF, 1986, v41(4), 975-980.)

LeRoy, Stephen F. and C. J. LaCivita. "Risk Aversion And The Dispersion Of Asset Prices," JOB, 1981, v54(4), 535-548.

Lea, Michael J. (Zorn, Peter M. and Michael J. Lea. "Mortgage Borrower Repayment Behavior: A Microeconomic Analysis With Canadian Adjustable Rate Mortgage Data," AREUEA, 1989, v17(1), 118-136.)

Lea, Michael J. and Peter M. Zorn. "Adjustable-Rate Mortgages, Economic Fluctuations, And Lender Portfolio Change," AREUEA, 1986, v14(3), 432-447.

Leabo, Dick A. and Richard J. Rogalski. "Warrant Price Movements And The Efficient Market Model," JOF, 1975, v30(1), 163-177.

Leach, H. Derrick. "Canadian Chartered Banks," FAJ, 1969, v25(2), 133-140.

Leach, J. H. Colin. "U. K. Ordinary Share Market," FAJ, 1969, v25(4), 163-166.

Leach, Ralph F. (Cox, Albert H., Jr. and Ralph F. Leach. "Open Market Operations And Reserve Settlement Periods: A Proposed Experiment," JOF, 1964, v19(3), 534-539.)

Leach, Ralph F. (Cox, Albert H., Jr. and Ralph F. Leach. "Defensive Open Market Operations And The Reserve Settlement Periods Of Member Banks," JOF, 1964, v19(1), 76-93.)

Leader, Stefan H. "How Much For Defense?," JPM, 1975-76, v2(1), 62-71.

Leaffer, Frederick H. (Mason, John M. and Frederick H. Leaffer. "The Preferences Of Financial Institutions For Construction And Permanent Mortgage Lending On Multi-Unit Residential And Commercial Income Properties," AREUEA, 1976, v4(1), 41-56.)

Lean, Jane. (Mueller, Eva and Jane Lean. "The Savings Account As A Source For Financing Large Expenditures," JOF, 1967, v22(3), 375-393.)

Lease, Ronald C. (Bhagat, Sanjai, James A. Brickley and Ronald C. Lease. "Incentive Effects Of Stock Purchase Plans," JFEC, 1985, v14(2), 195-216.)

Lease, Ronald C. (Bhagat, Sanjai, James A. Brickley and Ronald C. Lease. "The Authorization Of Additional Common Stock: An Empirical Investigation," FM, 1986, v15(3), 45-53.)

Lease, Ronald C. (Boardman, Calvin M., Frederick H. Dark and Ronald C. Lease. "On The Listing Of Corporate Debt: A Note," JFQA, 1986, v21(1), 107-114.)

Lease, Ronald C. (Brickley, James A., Ronald C. Lease and Clifford W. Smith, Jr. "Ownership Structure And Voting On Antitakeover Amendments," JFEC, 1988, v20(1/2), 267-292.)

Lease, Ronald C. (Cohn, Richard A., Wilbur G. Lewellen, Ronald C. Lease and Gary G. Schlarbaum. "Individual Investor Risk Aversion And Investment Portfolio Composition," JOF, 1975, v30(2), 605-620.)

Lease, Ronald C. (Groth, John C., Wilbur G. Lewellen, Gary G. Schlarbaum and Ronald C. Lease. "Security Analysts: Some Are More Equal," JPM, 1977-78, v4(3), 43-48.)

Lease, Ronald C. (Groth, Stephen C., Wilbur G. Lewellen, Gary G. Schlarbaum and Ronald C. Lease. "How Good Are Broker's Recommendations?," FAJ, 1979, v35(1), 32-40.)

Lease, Ronald C. (Lewellen, Wilbur G., Kenneth L. Stanley, Ronald C. Lease and Gary G. Schlarbaum. "Some Direct Evidence On The Dividend Clientele Phenomenon," JOF, 1978, v33(5), 1385-1399.)

Lease, Ronald C. (Lewellen, Wilbur G., Ronald C. Lease and Gary G. Schlarbaum. "Investment Performance And Investor Behavior," JFQA, 1979, v14(1), 29-57.)

Lease, Ronald C. (Lewellen, Wilbur G., Ronald C. Lease and Gary G. Schlarbaum. "The Personal Investments Of Professional Managers," **FM**, 1979, v8(4), 28-36.)

Lease, Ronald C. (Lewellen, Wilbur G., Ronald C. Lease and Gary C. Schlarbaum. "Patterns Of Investment Strategy And Behavior Among Individual Investors," **JOB**, 1977, v50(3), 296-333.)

Lease, Ronald C. (Pinegar, J. Michael and Ronald C. Lease. "The Impact Of Preferred-For-Common Exchange Offers On Firm Value," **JOF**, 1986, v41(4), 795-814.)

Lease, Ronald C. (Schallheim, James S., Ramon E. Johnson, Ronald C. Lease and John J. McConnell. "The Determinants Of Yields On Financial Leasing Contracts," **JFEC**, 1987, v19(1), 45-68.)

Lease, Ronald C. (Schlarbaum, Gary G., Wilbur G. Lewellen and Ronald C. Lease. "Realized Returns On Common Stock Investments: The Experience Of Individual Investors," **JOB**, 1978, v51(2), 299-326.)

Lease, Ronald C. (Schlarbaum, Gary G., Wilbur G. Lewellen and Ronald C. Lease. "The Common Stock-Portfolio Performance Record Of Individual Investors: 1954-70," **JOF**, 1978, v33(2), 429-441.)

Lease, Ronald C. (Ying, Louis K. W., Wilbur G. Lewellen, Gary G. Schlarbaum and Ronald C. Lease. "Stock Exchange Listings And Securities Returns," **JFQA**, 1977, v12(3), 415-432.)

Lease, Ronald C., John J. McConnell and Wayne H. Mikkelson. "The Market Value Of Control In Publicly-Traded Corporations," **JFEC**, 1983, v11(1), 439-471.

Lease, Ronald C., Wilbur G. Lewellen and Gary G. Schlarbaum. "The Individual Investor: Attributes And Attitudes," **JOF**, 1974, v29(2), 413-433.

Lease, Ronald C., Wilbur G. Lewellen and Gary G. Schlarbaum. "Market Segmentation And The Retail Investor," **FAJ**, 1976, v32(5), 53-60.

Lease, Ronald C., John J. McConnell and Wayne H. Mikkelson. "The Market Value Of Differential Voting Rights In Closely Held Corporations," **JOB**, 1984, v57(4), 443-468.

Lease, Ronald C., John J. McConnell and James S. Schallheim. "Realized Returns And The Default And Prepayment Experience Of Financial Leasing Contracts," **FM**, 1990, v19(2), 11-20.

Leason, J. Walter. "Leading Companies In The Petroleum Industry," **FAJ**, 1951, v7(4), 53-58.

Leason, J. Walter. "Standard Dividend Concept For Electric Utilities," **FAJ**, 1953, v9(4), 41-44.

Leatherwood, Marya L. (Conlon, Edwin J. and Marya L. Leatherwood. "Sunk Costs And Financial Decision Making: Integration And Implications," **AFPAF**, 1989, v3(1), 37-62.)

Leavitt, Gordon and Calvin H. Brainard. "Reviews Of 'Savings Bank Life Insurance': Comment," **JRI**, 1966, v33(2), 329-332.

Leavitt, Gordon. "Relationship Between Benefits And Premiums In Life Insurance: Comment," **JRI**, 1970, v37(2), 312-313.

Leavitt, Harold J. "A Note On Some Experimental Findings About The Meanings Of Price," **JOB**, 1954, v27(3), 205-210.

Leavitt, Harold J. "On The Export Of American Management Education," **JOB**, 1957, v30(3), 153-161.

Leavitt, Harold J. "Selling And The Social Scientist," **JOB**, 1954, v27(1), 41-50.

Leavitt, Harold J. "Small Groups In Large Organizations," **JOB**, 1955, v28(1), 8-17.

Lebow, David. (Feltenstein, Andrew, David Lebow and S. Van Wijnbergen. "Savings, Commodity Market Rationing, And The Real Rate Of Interest In China," **JMCB**, 1990, v22(2), 234-252.)

Lebrenz, Gene. "Desired Academic Characteristics For Bank Loan Officer Trainees," **JFED**, 1975, v4, 37-39.

Lechner, A. B. and D. J. Londoner. "Brokerage Profits After May Day," **FAJ**, 1976, v32(1), 12-17,31.

Ledolter, Johannes and Mark L. Power. "A Study Of ERISA's Impact On Private Retirement Plan Growth," **JRI**, 1984, v51(2), 225-243.

Ledolter, Johannes. (Collins, Daniel W., Johannes Ledolter and Judy Rayburn. "Some Further Evidence On The Stochastic Properties Of Systematic Risk," **JOB**, 1987, v60(3), 425-448.)

Lee, Adrian F. "International Asset And Currency Allocation," **JPM**, 1987-88, v14(1), 68-73.

Lee, Benny M. S. (Bond, Gary E., Stanley R. Thompson and Benny M. S. Lee. "Application Of A Simplified Hedging Rule," **JFM**, 1987, v7(1), 65-72.)

Lee, Bong-Soo. "A Nonlinear Expectations Model Of The Term Structure Of Interest Rates With Time-Varying Risk Premia," **JMCB**, 1989, v21(3), 348-367.

Lee, Boyden E. "The Euro-Dollar Multiplier," **JOF**, 1973, v28(4), 867-874.

Lee, C. Jevons. "Capital Budgeting Under Uncertainty: The Issue Of Optimal Timing," **JBFA**, 1988, v15(2), 155-168.

Lee, C. Jevons. "Fundamental Analysis And The Stock Market," **JBFA**, 1987, v14(1), 131-142.

Lee, C. Jevons. "The Pricing Of Corporate Debt," **JOF**, 1981, v36(5), 1187-1189.

Lee, Chan Keun. "A Study On The Efficiency Of The Eurobond Market," **RDIBF**, 1988, v2, 131-192.

Lee, Charles, Andrei Shleifer and Richard Thaler. "Investor Sentiment And The Closed-End Fund Puzzle," **JOF**, 1991, v46(1), 75-110.

Lee, Cheng F. and Chunchi Wu. "The Impacts Of Kurtosis On Risk Stationarity: Some Empirical Evidence," **FR**, 1985, v20(4), 263-269.

Lee, Cheng F. and Frank C. Jen. "Effects Of Measurement Errors On Systematic Risk And Performance Measure Of A Portfolio," **JFQA**, 1978, v13(1), 299-312.

Lee, Cheng F. and Kirnio Morimune. "Time Aggregation, Coefficient Of Determination And Systematic Risk Of The Market Model," **FR**, 1978, v13(1), 36-47.

Lee, Cheng F. and Manak C. Gupta. "An Inter-Temporal Approach To The Optimization Of Dividend Policy With Predetermined Investment: A Further Comment," **JOF**, 1977, v32(4), 1358-1361.

Lee, Cheng F. and William P. Lloyd. "The Capital Asset Pricing Model Expressed As A Recursive System: An Empirical Investigation," **JFQA**, 1976, v11(2), 237-249.

Lee, Cheng F. (Bubnys, Edward L. and Cheng F. Lee. "The Structure Of International Interest Rates Under Different Exchange Rate Regimes: An Empirical Analysis," **AFPAF**, 1985, v1(1), 187-208.)

Lee, Cheng F. "A Note On The Interdependent Structure Of Security Returns," **JFQA**, 1976, v11(1),73-86.

Lee, Cheng F. "Functional Form And The Dividend Effect In The Electric Utility Industry," **JOF**, 1976, v31(5), 1481-1486.

Lee, Cheng F. "Functional Form, Skewness Effect, And The Risk-Return Relationship," **JFQA**, 1977, v12(1), 55-72.

Lee, Cheng F. "On The Relationship Between The Systematic Risk And The Investment Horizon," **JFQA**, 1976, v11(5), 803-815.

Lee, Cheng F. (Chang, Hui-shyong and Cheng F. Lee. "Using Pooled Time-Series And Cross-Section Data To Test The Firm And Time Effects In Financial Analyses," **JFQA**, 1977, v12(3), 457-471.)

Lee, Cheng F. (Fabozzi, Frank J., Jack C. Francis and Cheng F. Lee. "Generalized Functional Form For Mutual Fund Returns," **JFQA**, 1980, v15(5), 1107-1120.)

Lee, Cheng F. (Gentry, James A. and Cheng F. Lee. "Financial Forecasting And The X-11 Model: Preliminary Evidence," **AFPAF**, 1987, v2(1), 27-50.)

Lee, Cheng F. (Hilliard, Jimmy E., Cheng F. Lee and Robert A. Leitch. "Stochastic Analysis Of Earnings And Leverage Measures," **FR**, 1983, v18(2), 220-233.)

Lee, Cheng F. (Junkus, Joan C. and Cheng F. Lee. "Use Of Three Stock Index Futures In Hedging Decisions," **JFM**, 1985, v5(2), 201-222.)

Lee, Cheng F. (Koppenhaver, G. D. and Cheng F. Lee. "Alternative Instruments For Hedging Inflation Risk In The Banking Industry," **JFM**, 1987, v7(6), 619-636.)

Lee, Cheng F. (Lloyd, William P. and Cheng F. Lee. "Block Recursive Systems In Asset Pricing Models," **JOF**, 1976, v31(4), 1101-1113.)

Lee, Cheng F. (Lynge, Morgan J., Jr. and Cheng F. Lee. "Financial Ratio Comparison Of Savings And Loan Associations And Commercial Banks," **AFPAF**, 1989, v3(1), 195-230.)

Lee, Cheng F. and Chunchi Wu. "Using Zellner's Errors-In-Variables Model To Reexamine MM's Valuation Model For Electric Utility Industry," **AFPAF**, 1989, v3(1), 63-74.

Lee, Cheng F. and Hun Y. Park. "Value Line Investment Survey Rank Changes And Beta Coefficients," **FAJ**, 1987, v43(5), 70-72.

Lee, Cheng F. and Morgan J. Lynge, Jr. "Return, Risk And Cost Of Equity For Stock S&L Firms: Theory And Empirical Results," **AREUEA**, 1985, v13(2), 167-180.

Lee, Cheng F. and Shafiqur Rahman. "New Evidence On Timing And Security Selection Skill Of Mutual Fund Managers," **JPM**, 1991, v17(2), 80-83.

Lee, Cheng F. and Stephen W. Forbes. "Dividend Policy, Equity Value, And Cost Of Capital Estimates For The Property And Liability Insurance Industry," **JRI**, 1980, v47(2), 205-222.

Lee, Cheng F. and Stephen W. Forbes. "Income Measures, Ownership, Capacity Ratios And The Dividend Decision Of The Non-Life Insurance Industry: Some Empirical Evidence," **JRI**, 1982, v49(2), 269-289.

Lee, Cheng F. and Walter J. Primeaux, Jr. "Impacts Of Rate Base Methods On Firm Operating Elasticity And Capital Structure: Theory And Evidence," **AFPAF**, 1985, v1(1), 103-124.

Lee, Cheng F., Paul Newbold, Joseph E. Finnerty and Chen-Chin Chu. "On Accounting-Based, Market-Based And Composite-Based Beta Predictions: Methods And Implications," **FR**, 1986, v21(1), 51-68.

Lee, Cheng F., Raymond M. Leuthold and Jean E. Cordier. "The Stock Market And The Commodity Futures Market: Diversification And Arbitrage Potential," **FAJ**, 1985, v41(4), 53-60.

Lee, Cheng F., Chunchi Wu and K. C. John Wei. "The Heterogeneous Investment Horizon And The Capital Asset Pricing Model: Theory And Implications," **JFQA**, 1990, v25(3), 361-376.

Lee, Cheng F., Donald H. Wort and Doug Han. "The Relationship Between Dividend Yield And Earnings Yield And Its Implication For Forecasting," **AFPAF**, 1987, v2(1), 155-178.

Lee, Cheng F., Frank C. Jen and K. C. John Wei. "The Real And Nominal Parameters In The CAPM: A Responsive Coefficient Approach," **IJOF**, 1988, v1(1), 113-130.

Lee, Cheng Few and J. Kenton Zumwalt. "Associations Between Alternative Accounting Profitability Measures And Security Returns," **JFQA**, 1981, v16(1), 71-93.

Lee, Cheng Few and William P. Lloyd. "Block Recursive Systems In Asset Pricing Models: An Extension," **JOF**, 1978, v33(2), 640-644.

Lee, Cheng Few and Edward L. Bubnys. "The Relationship Between Inflation And Short-Term Interest Rates: An International Comparison," **AFPAF**, 1989, v4(Supp), 123-150.

Lee, Cheng Few. (Francis, Jack Clark and Cheng Few Lee. "Investment Horizon, Risk Proxies, Skewness, And Mutual Fund Performance: A Theoretical Analysis And Empirical Investigation," **RIF**, 1983, v4, 1-20.)

Lee, Cheng-Few and Shafiqur Rahman. "Market Timing, Selectivity, And Mutual Fund Performance: An Empirical Investigation," **JOB**, 1990, v63(2), 261-278.

Lee, Cheng-Few. (Wei, K. C. John, Cheng-few Lee and Andrew H. Chen. "Multivariate Regression Tests Of The Arbitrage Pricing Theory: The Instrumental-Variables Approach," **RQFA**, 1991, v1(2), 191-208.)

Lee, Chi-Wen Jevons. "Market Model Stationarity And Timing Of Structural Change," **FR**, 1985, v20(4), 329-342.

Lee, Chi-Wen Jevons. "The Tax Effect Hypothesis And Inventory Accounting," **JBFA**, 1989, v16(4), 515-530.

Lee, Edward J. Q. (Sweeney, Richard J. and Edward J. Q. Lee. "Trading Strategies In Forward Exchange Markets," **AFPAF**, 1989, v4(Supp), 55-80.)

Lee, Feng-Yao. "Exports And Taiwan's Economic Growth," **AFPAF**, 1985, v1(Supp), 119-138.

Lee, Feng-Yao. "On The Dummy Variable Technique And Covariance Analysis In Testing Equality Among Sets Of Coefficients In Linear Regressions: An Expository Note," **JFQA**, 1974, v9(3), 491-495.

Lee, Haeduck. (Blackley, Dixie M., James R. Follain and Haeduck Lee. "An Evaluation Of Hedonic Price Indexes For 34 Large SMSAs," **AREUEA**, 1986, v14(2), 179-205.)

Lee, Hei Wai. (Gentry, James A., R. Vaidyanathan and Hei Wai Lee. "A Weighted Cash Conversion Cycle," **FM**, 1990, v19(1), 90-99.)

Lee, Hyong J. and George E. Pinches. "On Optimal Insurance Purchasing," **JRI**, 1988, v55(1), 145-149.

Lee, Insup and Steve B. Wyatt. "The Effects Of International Joint Ventures On Shareholder Wealth," **FR**, 1990, v25(4), 641-650.

Lee, Insup and Robert Schweitzer. "Shareholder Wealth Effects In Interstate Banking: The Case Of Delaware's Financial Center Development Act," **JFSR**, 1989, v2(2), 65-72.

Lee, Insup, R. Richardson Pettit and Ronald F. Singer. "Offer Premiums In Stock Exchange Mergers And The Distribution Of Stockholder's Wealth," **IJOF**, 1990, v2(2), 67-87.

Lee, Insup, R. Richardson Pettit and Mark V. Swankoski. "Daily Return Relationships Among Asian Stock Markets," **JBFA**, 1990, v17(2), 265-284.

Lee, Insup. (Fry, Clifford L. and Insup Lee. "OSHA Sanctions And The Value Of The Firm," **FR**, 1989, v24(4), 599-610.)

Lee, Insup. (Horvitz, Paul M., Insup Lee and Kerry L. Robertson. "Valuation Effects Of New Securities Issuance By Bank Holding Companies: New Evidence," **FR**, 1991, v26(1), 91-104.)

Lee, J. Finley. "The Competitive Role Of The Associated Factory Mutuals," **JRI**, 1969, v36(3), 401-418.

Lee, J. Finley. (Headen, Robert S. and J. Finley Lee. "Life Insurance Demand And Household Portfolio Behavior," **JRI**, 1974, v41(4), 685-698.)

Lee, J. Finley. (Headen, Robert S. and J. Finley Lee. "Life Insurance Demand And Household Portfolio Behavior: Reply," **JRI**, 1976, v43(2), 331-334.)

Lee, Jae K., Robert R. Trippi, Seok C. Chu and Hyun Kim. "K-FOLIO: Integrating The Markowitz Model With A Knowledge-Based System," **JPM**, 1990, v17(1), 89-93.

Lee, Jae Won. (Kim, Wi Saeng, Jae Won Lee and Jack Clark Francis. "Investment Performance Of Common Stocks In Relation To Insider Ownership," **FR**, 1988, v23(1), 53-64.)

Lee, Johng Y. (Hartman, Bart P. and Johng Y. Lee. "Influence Of Company Debt Burden On Reported Replacement Cost Values," **JBR**, 1981-82, v12(1), 56-59.)

Lee, Jungsoo. (Lahiri, Kajal and Jungsoo Lee. "On The Constancy Of Real Interest Rates And The Mundell Effect," **JBF**, 1991, v5(4), 557-574.)

Lee, Kam-Hon. (Wehrung, Donald, Kam-Hon Lee, David K. Tse and Ilan B. Vertinsky. "Adjusting Risky Situations: A Theoretical Framework And Empirical Test," **JRU**, 1989, v2(2), 189-212.)

Lee, Keun Chang and Stephen P. D'Arcy. "The Optimal Investment Strategy Through Variable Universal Life Insurance," **JRI**, 1989, v56(2), 201-217.

Lee, Keun, Chang. (D'Arcy, Stephen P. and Keun Chang Lee. "Universal Variable Life Insurance Versus Similar Unbundled Investment Strategies," **JRI**, 1987, v54(3), 452-477.)

Lee, Kyung W. (Rejda, George E. and Kyung W. Lee. "State Unemployment Compensation Programs: Immediate Reforms Needed," **JRI**, 1989, v56(4), 649-669.)

Lee, Li Way. "Co-Insurance And Conglomerate Merger," **JOF**, 1977, v32(5), 1527-1537.

Lee, Luch Chao. (Ferber, Robert and Luch Chao Lee. "Asset Accumulation In Early Married Life," **JOF**, 1980, v35(5), 1173-1188.)

Lee, Lucy Choa. (Ferber, Robert and Lucy Choa Lee. "Acquisition And Accumulation Of Life Insurance In Early Married Life," **JRI**, 1980, v47(4), 713-734.)

Lee, Maurice W. "Hydroelectric Power In The Columbia Basin," **JOB**, 1953, v26(3), 173-189.

Lee, Maurice W. (Gaumnitz, Erwin A., George E. Manners, James R. Surface, Maurice W. Lee and Paul Garner. "Dean's Forum: The Place Of Insurance In The Collegiate Curriculum," **JRI**, 1960, v27(4), 113-120.

Lee, Moon H. and Josef Zechner. "Debt, Taxes, And International Equilibrium," **JIMF**, 1984, v3(3), 343-355.

Lee, Moon H. and Halim Bishara. "Recent Canadian Experience On The Profitability Of Insider Trades," **FR**, 1989, v24(2), 235-250.

Lee, Moon. (Naik, Vasanttilak and Moon Lee. "General Equilibrium Pricing Of Options On The Market Portfolio With Discontinuous Returns," **RFS**, 1990, v3(4), 493-522.)

Lee, S. L. and C. W. R. Ward. "The Association Of Stock Market Volatility And Parallel Trading By UK Institutional Investors," **JBFA**, 1980, v7(3),415-425.

Lee, Sang Bin. (Ho, Thomas S. Y. and Sang Bin Lee. "Interest Rate Futures Options And Interest Rate Options," **FR**, 1990, v25(3), 345-370.)

Lee, Sang Bin. (Ho, Thomas S. Y. and Sang Bin Lee. "Pricing Of The Call And Sinking Fund Provisions On Corporate Bonds Under Interest Rate Risk: Empirical Evidence," **IJOF**, 1989, v2(1), 1-17.)

Lee, Sang Bin. (Ho, Thomas S. Y. and Sang Bin Lee. "The Pricing Of Corporate Bond Provisions Under Interest Rate Risks," **RIF**, 1988, v7, 139-162.)

Lee, Sang M. and A. J. Lerro. "Optimizing The Portfolio Selection For Mutual Funds," **JOF**, 1973, v28(5), 1087-1101.

Lee, Sang M. and A. J. Lerro. "Capital Budgeting For Multiple Objectives," **FM**, 1974, v3(1), 58-66.

Lee, Sang M. and A. Joseph Lerro. "A Cash Management Model For Health Care Clinics," **FR**, 1973, v8(1), 1-10.

Lee, Sang M. and Delton L. Chesser. "Goal Programming For Portfolio Selection," **JPM**, 1979-80, v6(3), 22-26.

Lee, Sang M. (Klock, David R. and Sang M. Lee. "A Note On Decision Models For Insurers," **JRI**, 1974, v41(3), 537-543.)

Lee, Sang M., Anthony J. Lerro and Bruce R. McGinnis. "Optimization Of Tax Switching For Commercial Banks: A Comment," **JMCB**, 1971, v3(2), Part 1, 293-303.

Lee, Sang-Bin. (Ho, Thomas S. Y. and Sang-Bin Lee. "Term Structure Movements And Pricing Interest Rate Contingent Claims," **JOF**, 1986, v41(5), 1011-1030.)

Lee, Sang-Bin. (Ko, Kwang-Soo and Sang-Bin Lee. "A Comparative Analysis Of The Daily Behavior Of Stock Returns: Japan, The US And The Asian NICs," **JBFA**, 1991, v18(2), 219-234.)

Lee, Suk Hun. "Ability And Willingness To Service Debt As Explanation For Commercial And Official Rescheduling Cases," **JBF**, 1991, v15(1), 5-27.

Lee, T. A. and A. W. Stark. "A Cash Flow Disclosure Of Government-Supported Enterprises' Results," **JBFA**, 1984, v11(1), 1-11.

Lee, T. A. "A Note On The Nature And Determination Of Income," **JBFA**, 1974, v1(1), 145-148.

Lee, T. A. "Accounting For And Disclosure Of Business Combinations," **JBFA**, 1974, v1(1), 1-33.

Lee, T. A. "Cash Flow Accounting And The Allocation Problem," **JBFA**, 1982, v8(3), 341-352.

Lee, T. A. "Sandilands And User Comprehension," **JBFA**, 1976, v3(1), 85-95.

Lee, T. A. "The Contribution Of Fisher To Cash Flow Accounting," **JBFA**, 1979, v6(3), 321-330.

Lee, T. A. "The Contribution Of Fisher To Enterprise Income Theory: A Comment," **JBFA**, 1975, v2(3), 373-376.

Lee, Terry N. (Call, Ivan T., Terry N. Lee and Gary F. McKinnon. "Teaching Financial Management As Part Of An Integrated Management Core," **JFED**, 1975, v4, 19-27.)

Lee, Tong Hun. "Substitutability Of Non-Bank Intermediary Liabilities For Money: The Empirical Evidence," **JOF**, 1966, v21(3), 441-457.

Lee, Wayne L., Anjan V. Thakor and Gautam Vora. "Screening, Market Signalling, And Capital Structure Theory," **JOF**, 1983, v38(5), 1507-1518.

Lee, Wayne Y. and Andrew J. Senchack, Jr. "On The Social Optimality Of The Value Maximization Criterion," **JFQA**, 1980,v15(2),379-389.

Lee, Wayne Y. and Kanwal S. Sachdeva. "The Role Of The Multinational Firm In The Integration Of Segmented Capital Markets," **JOF**, 1977, v32(2),479-492.

Lee, Wayne Y. and Michael E. Solt. "Insider Trading: A Poor Guide To Market Timing," **JPM**, 1985-86, v12(4), 65-71.

Lee, Wayne Y. "Diversification And Time: Do Investment Horizons Matter?," **JPM**, 1990, v16(3), 21-26.

Lee, Wayne Y. (Goldberg, Michael A. and Wayne Y. Lee. "The Cost Of Capital And Valuation Of A Two-Country Firm: Comment," **JOF**, 1977, v32(4), 1348-1353.)

Lee, Wayne Y. (Krouse, Clement G. and Wayne Y. Lee. "Optimal Equity Financing Of The Corporation," **JFQA**, 1973, v8(4), 539-563.)

Lee, Wayne Y. (Tuttle, Donald L., Wayne Y. Lee and Terry S. Maness. "Stochastic Cash Flow Constraints And The Term Structure Of Interest," **JBF**, 1978, v2(2), 143-162.)

Lee, Wayne Y. (Weston, J. Fred and Wayne Y. Lee. "Cost Of Capital For A Division Of A Firm: Comment," **JOF**, 1977, v32(5), 1779-1780.)

Lee, Wayne Y., John D. Martin and Andrew J. Senchack. "The Case For Using Options To Value Salvage Values In Financial Leases," **FM**, 1982, v11(3), 33-41.

Lee, Wayne Y., Ramesh K. S. Rao and J. F. G. Auchmuty. "Option Pricing In A Lognormal Securities Market, With Discrete Trading," **JFEC**, 1981, v9(1),75-102.

Lee, Wayne Y., Terry S. Maness and Donald L. Tuttle. "Nonspeculative Behavior And The Term Structure," **JFQA**, 1980, v15(1), 53-83.

Lee, William. (Gilster, John E., Jr. and William Lee. "The Effects Of Transaction Costs And Different Borrowing And Lending Rates On The Option Pricing Model: A Note," **JOF**, 1984, v39(4), 1215-1221.)

Lee, Winson B. (Cooperman, Elizabeth S., Winson B. Lee and James P. Lesage. "Commercial Bank And Thrift Interdependence And Local Market Competition For Retail Certificates Of Deposit," **JFSR**, 1990, v4(1), 37-52.)

Lee, Winson B. and Elizabeth S. Cooperman. "Conglomerates Is The 1980s: A Performance Appraisal," **FM**, 1989, v18(1), 45-54.

Lee, Yoong-Sin. "A Graphical Treatment Of The Coinsurance Clause," **JRI**, 1985, v52(4), 644-661.

Lee, Young Ki. (Kane, Alex, Young Ki Lee and Alan Marcus. "Earnings And Dividend Announcements: Is There A Corroboration Effect?," **JOF**, 1984, v39(4), 1091-1099.)

Leech, Stewart A., Denis J. Pratt and W. G. W. Magill. "Company Asset Revaluations And Inflation In Australia, 1950 To 1975," **JBFA**, 1978, v5(4), 353-362.

Lees, Francis A. "The U.S. Balance Of Payments In The Postwar Period," **FAJ**, 1965, v21(3), 31-38.

Lees, Francis A. (Bruck, Nicholas K. and Francis A. Lees. "Foreign Content Of U.S. Corporate Activities," **FAJ**, 1966, v22(5), 127-132.)

Leeth, John D. (Kniesner, Thomas J. and John D. Leeth. "Compensating Wage Differentials For Fatal Injury Risk In Australia, Japan, And The United States," **JRU**, 1991, v4(1), 75-90.)

Leeth, John D. and Jonathan A. Scott. "The Incidence Of Secured Debt: Evidence From The Small Business Community," **JFQA**, 1989, v24(3), 379-394.

Lefebvre, Olivier. "Risk Sharing In The Bank Deposit Contract," **JBFA**, 1986, v13(4), 547-559.

Leffler, Keith. "Comments: On The Economics Of Product Positioning," **JOB**, 1980, v53(3), 2, S105-S114.

Lefkoe, M. R. "Government Intervention - Freedom's Greatest Threat," **FAJ**, 1962, v18(4), 21-30.

Lefkoe, M. R. "Saving And Loan Holding Companies," **FAJ**, 1961, v17(4), 31-42.

Lefoll, J. (Calvet, A. L. and J. Lefoll. "Performance And Systematic Risk Stability Of Canadian Mutual Funds Under Inflation," **JBFA**, 1981, v8(2), 279-289.)

Lefoll, J. (Calvet, A. L. and J. Lefoll. "Information Asymmetry And Wealth Effect Of Canadian Corporate Acquisitions," **FR**, 1987, v22(4), 415-432.)

Lefoll, Jean. (Caperaa, Philippe and Jean Lefoll. "Changes In The Riskless Rate Of Interest And Financial Markets' Equilibrium," **FR**, 1982, v17(4), 252-258.)

Lefoll, Jean. (Ryan, Peter J. and Jean Lefoll. "A Comment On Mean-Variance Portfolio Selection With Either A Singular Or A Non-Singular Variance-Covariance Matrix," **JFQA**, 1981,v16(3),389-395.)

Leftwich, R. (Agnello, W., W. Brueggeman, G. Decker, R. Griffith, R. Leftwich, R. Moore, J. Neal, B. Sternlicht, B. Wallach, W. Wardrop and C. Zinngrabe. "Panel: Corporate Real Estate Roundtable," **JACF**, 1990, v3(1), 6-38.)

Leftwich, Richard W. (Holthausen, Robert W., Richard W. Leftwich and David Mayers. "The Effect Of Large Block Transactions On Security Prices: A Cross-Sectional Analysis," **JFEC**, 1987, v19(2), 237-268.)

Leftwich, Richard W. (Holthausen, Robert W. and Richard W. Leftwich. "The Effect Of Bond Rating Changes On Common Stock Prices," **JFEC**, 1986, v17(1), 57-90.)

Leftwich, Richard W. (Holthausen, Robert W., Richard W. Leftwich and David Mayers. "Large-Block Transactions, The Speed Of

Response, And Temporary And Permanent Stock-Price Effects," **JFEC**, 1990, v26(1), 71-96.)

Leftwich, Richard. (Bloomfield, T. R., Richard Leftwich and J. B. Long, Jr. "Portfolio Strategies And Performance," **JFEC**, 1977, v5(2), 210-218.)

Leftwich, Richard. (Dodd, Peter and Richard Leftwich. "The Market For Coprorate Charters: 'Unhealthy Competition' Versus Federal Regulation," **JOB**, 1980, v53(3), 259-284.)

Legan, Robert W. "The DJIA @ 2100 In Ten Years," **FAJ**, 1969, v25(1), 129-133.

Leganger, Gunnar. "A Note On The Norwegian School Of Insurance," **JRI**, 1958, v25(4), 79-81.

Legler, John B. (Billings, C. David and John B. Legler. "Financing Equal Educational Opportunity," **FR**, 1972, v2(2), 122-133.)

Lehman, E. R. "Outlook For Liquefied Petroleum Gas Industry," **FAJ**, 1962, v18(6), 63-65.

Lehmann, Bruce and Arthur Warga. "Optimal Distribution-Free Tests And Further Evidence Of Heteroscedasticity In The Market Model: A Comment," **JOF**, 1985, v40(2), 603-605.

Lehmann, Bruce N. "Orthogonal Frontiers And Alternative Mean-Variance Efficiency Tests," **JOF**, 1987, v42(3), 601-619.

Lehmann, Bruce N. and David M. Modest. "The Empirical Foundations Of The Arbitrage Pricing Theory," **JFEC**, 1988, v21(2), 213-254.

Lehmann, Bruce N. and David M. Modest. "Mutual Fund Performance Evaluation: A Comparison Of Benchmarks And Benchmark Comparisons," **JOF**, 1987, v42(2),233-265.

Lehman, Bruce N. "My Experience With The Press The Day Of The Nobel Prizes For Harry M. Markowitz, Merton H. Miller, And william F. Sharpe," **RQFA**, 1991, v1(2), 217-218.

Lehmann, Bruce. (Adler, Michael and Bruce Lehmann. "Deviations From Purchasing Power Parity In The Long Run," **JOF**, 1983, v38(5), 1471-1487.)

Lehmann, Donald R. (Farley, John U., Donald R. Lehmann and Michael J. Ryan. "Generalizing From 'Imperfect' Replication," **JOB**, 1981, v54(4), 597-610.)

Lehmann, Henry W. "The Federal Municipal Bankruptcy Act," **JOF**, 1950, v5(3), 241-256.

Lehn, Kenneth and Annette Poulsen. "Free Cash Flow And Stockholder Gains In Going Private Transactions," **JOF**, 1989, v44(3), 771-788.

Lehn, Kenneth, Jeffry Netter and Annette Poulsen. "Consolidating Corporate Control: Dual-Class Recapitalizations Versus Leveraged Buyouts," **JFEC**, 1990, v27(2) 557-580.

Lehn, Kenneth. (Mitchell, Mark L. and Kenneth Lehn. "Do Bad Bidders Make Good Targets?," **JACF**, 1990, v3(2), 60-69.)

Leibowitt, S. David. "A Corporate Lawyer Looks At Industry," **FAJ**, 1959, v15(5), 45-50.

Leibowitz, Martin L. and Alfred Weinberger. "Contingent Immunization - Part II: Problem Areas," **FAJ**, 1983, v39(1), 35-50.

Leibowitz, Martin L. and Alfred Weinberger. "The Uses Of Contingent Immunization," **JPM**, 1981-82, v8(1), 51-55.

Leibowitz, Martin L. and Alfred Weinberger. "Contingent Immunization - Part I: Risk Control Procedures," **FAJ**, 1982, v38(6), 17-31.

Leibowitz, Martin L. "A Yield Basis For Financial Futures," **FAJ**, 1981, v37(1), 42-51.

Leibowitz, Martin L. "Bond Equivalents Of Stock Returns," **JPM**, 1977-78, v4(3), 25-30.

Leibowitz, Martin L. "Goal-Oriented Bond Portfolio Management," **JPM**, 1978-79, v5(4), 13-18.

Leibowitz, Martin L. "Horizon Analysis For Managed Bond Portfolios," **JPM**, 1974-75, v1(3), 23-34.

Leibowitz, Martin L. "How Financial Theory Evolves Into The Real World-Or Not: The Case Of Duration And Immunization," **FR**, 1983, v18(4), 271-280.

Leibowitz, Martin L. "Liability Returns: A New Look At Asset Allocation," **JPM**, 1986-87, v13(2), 11-18.

Leibowitz, Martin L. "Pension Asset Allocation Through Surplus Management," **FAJ**, 1987, v43(2),29-40.

Leibowitz, Martin L. "The Dedicated Bond Portfolio In Pension Funds - Part II: Immunization, Horizon Matching And Contingent Procedures," **FAJ**, 1986, v42(2), 47-57.

Leibowitz, Martin L. "The Dedicated Bond Portfolio In Pension Funds - Part I: Motivations And Basics," **FAJ**, 1986, v42(1), 68-75.

Leibowitz, Martin L. "The Horizon Annuity," **FAJ**, 1979, v35(3), 68-74.

Leibowitz, Martin L. "Total Portfolio Duration: A New Perspective On Asset Allocation," **FAJ**, 1986, v42(5), 18-29,77.

Leibowitz, Martin L. "Understanding Convertible Securities," **FAJ**, 1974, v30(6), 57-67.

Leibowitz, Martin L. "Volatility In Tax-Exempt Bonds: A Theoretical Model," **FAJ**, 1981, v37(6), 31-33,35-39,41-47,49-52.

Leibowitz, Martin L. (Hartzell, David J., David G. Shulman, Terrence C. Langetieg and Martin L. Leibowitz. "A Look At Real Estate Duration," **JPM**, 1988-89, v15(1), 16-24.)

Leibowitz, Martin L. (Langetieg, Terence C., Martin L. Leibowitz and Stanley Kogelman. "Duration Targeting And The Management Of Multiperiod Returns," **FAJ**, 1990, v46(5), 35-45.)

Leibowitz, Martin L and Roy D. Henriksson. "Portfolio Optimization Within A Surplus Framework," **FAJ**, 1988, v44(2), 43-51.

Leibowitz, Martin L and Roy D. Henriksson. "Portfolio Optimization With Shortfall Constraints: A Confidence-Limit Approach To Managing Downside Risk," **FAJ**, 1989, v45(2), 34-41.

Leibowitz, Martin L. and Stanley Kogelman. "Inside The P/E Ratio: The Franchise Factor," **FAJ**, 1990, v46(6), 17-35.

Leibowitz, Martin L. and Stanley Kogelman. "Asset Allocation Under Shortfall Constraints," **JPM**, 1991, v17(2), 18-23.

Leibowitz, Martin L. and Terence C. Langetieg. "Shortfall Risk And The Asset Allocation Decision: A Simulation Analysis Of Stock And Bond Risk Profiles," **JPM**, 1989, v16(1), 61-68.

Leibowitz, Martin L. and William S. Krasker. "The Persistence Of Risk: Stocks Versus Bonds Over The Long Term," **FAJ**, 1988, v44(6), 40-47.

Leibowitz, Martin L., Thomas E. Klaffky, Steven Mandel and Alfred Weinberger. "Horizon Matching: A New Approach To Dedicated Portfolios," **JPM**, 1984-85, v11(1), 93-96.

Leibowitz, Martin L., Eric H. Sorensen, Robert D. Arnott and H. Nicholas Hanson. "A Total Differential Approach To Equity Duration," **FAJ**, 1989, v45(5), 30-37.

Leibowitz, Martin L., Stanley Kogelman and Eric B. Lindenberg. "A Shortfall Approach To The Creditor's Decision: How Much Leverage Can A Firm Support?," **FAJ**, 1990, v46(3), 43-52.

Leibowitz, Martin L., William S. Krasker and Ardavan Nozari. "Spread Duration: A New Tool For Bond Portfolio Management," **JPM**, 1990, v16(3), 46-53.

Leidenberger, Bruce E. (Lusht, Kenneth M. and Bruce E. Leidenberger. "A Research Note On Factors Associated With Troubled Residential Construction Loans," **AREUEA**, 1979, v7(2), 243-252.)

Leiderman, Leonardo and Assaf Razin. "Foreign Trade Shocks And The Dynamics Of High Inflation: Israel, 1978-85," **JIMF**, 1988, v7(4), 411-424.

Leiderman, Leonardo and Assaf Razin. "Testing Ricardian Neutrality With An Intertemporal Stochastic Model," **JMCB**, 1988,v20(1),1-21.

Leiderman, Leonardo. "Interest Rates As Predictors Of Inflation In A High-Inflation Semi-Industrialized Economy," **JOF**, 1979, v34(4), 1019-1025.

Leiderman, Leonardo. (Cukierman, Alex and Leonardo Leiderman. "Price Controls And The Variability Of Relative Prices," **JMCB**, 1984, v16(3), 271-284.)

Leinbach, Philip A. (Lustig, Ivan L. and Philip A. Leinbach. "The Small Firm Effect," **FAJ**, 1983, v39(3), 46-49.)

Leistikow, Dean. "Announcements And Futures Price Variability," **JFM**, 1989, v9(6), 477-486.

Leistikow, Dean. "The Relative Responsiveness To Information And Variability Of Storable Commodity Spot And Futures Prices," **JFM**, 1990, v10(4), 377-396.

Leisy, Herbert F. and Robert D. Milne. "What Are Bank Earnings?," **FAJ**, 1968, v24(2), 89-94.

Leisy, Herbert F. and Robert D. Milne. "Bank Portfolio Gains And Losses: A Comment," **FAJ**, 1969, v25(1), 91.

Leit, Stephen D. (McConnell, Walter S. and Stephen D. Leit. "Inflation, Stock Prices And Job Creation," **FAJ**, 1977, v33(2), 25-29.)

Leitch, Robert A. (Hilliard, Jimmy E., Cheng F. Lee and Robert A. Leitch. "Stochastic Analysis Of Earnings And Leverage Measures," **FR**, 1983, v18(2), 220-233.)

Leitch, Robert A. (Hilliard, Jimmy E. and Robert A. Leitch. "Analysis Of The Warrant Hedge In A Stable Paretian Market," **JFQA**, 1977, v12(1), 85-103.)

Leite, Sergio Pereira. "International Reserve Flows: A Comment," **JOF**, 1977, v32(4), 1372-1373.

Leiter, Robert D. "Free Speech In Labor Relations," **JOB**, 1950, v23(1), 40-47.

Leland, Hayne E. and David H. Pyle. "Informational Asymmetries, Financial Structure, And Financial Intermediation," **JOF**, 1977, v32(2), 371-387.

Leland, Hayne E. "Option Pricing And Replication With Transactions Costs," **JOF**, 1985, v40(5), 1283-1301.

Leland, Hayne E. "Who Should Buy Portfolio Insurance?," **JOF**, 1980, v35(2), 581-594.

Leland, Hayne E. (Rubinstein, Mark and Hayne E. Leland. "Replicating Options With Positions In Stock And Cash," **FAJ**, 1981, v37(4), 63-72.)

Leland, Simeon E. "The Government, The Banks And The National Debt," **JOF**, 1946, v1(1), 5-26.

Lemaire, Jean. "A Comparative Analysis Of Most European And Japanese Bonus-Malus Systems," **JRI**, 1988, v55(4), 660-681.

Lemmon, Richard C. (Hendershott, Patric H. and Richard C. Lemmon. "The Financial Behavior Of Households: Some Empirical Estimates," **JOF**, 1975, v30(3), 733-759.)

Lempert, Leonard H. "Do The Leading Indicators Lead?," **FAJ**, 1967, v23(6), 19-27.

Lempert, Leonard H. "Forecasting The Leading Indicator Of Stock Prices," **FAJ**, 1961, v17(5), 13-21.

Lempert, Leonard H. "Just Give Me The Necessary Data, Please!," **JPM**, 1977-78, v4(4), 47-52.

Lempert, Leonard H. "The Use Of Composite Indicators," **FAJ**, 1965, v21(6), 57-59.

Lenders, C. T. (Theil, H. and C. T. Leenders. "Tomorrow On The Amsterdam Stock Exchange," **JOB**, 1965, v38(3), 277-284.)

Lent, George E. "A More Permanent Formula For The Taxation Of Life Insurance," **JRI**, 1960, v27(4), 63-74.

Lentz, George H. (Fisher, Jeffrey D. and George H. Lentz. "Tax Reform And The Value Of Real Estate Income Property," **AREUEA**, 1986, v14(2), 287-315.)

Lentz, George H. (Fisher, Jeffrey D. and George H. Lentz. "Business Enterprise Value In Shopping Malls: An Empirical Test," **JRER**, 1990, v5(1), 167-175.)

Lentz, George H. and Jeffrey D. Fisher. "Tax Reform And Organizational Forms For Holding Investment Real Estate: Corporation Vs. Partnership," **AREUEA**, 1989, v17(3), 314-337.

Leonard, David C. and Michael E. Solt. "Recent Evidence On The Accuracy And Rationality Of Popular Inflation Forecasts," **JFR**, 1986, v9(4), 281-290.

Leonard, David C. and Nicholas R. Noble. "Estimation Of Time-Varying Systematic Risk And Investment Performance: Closed-End Investment Companies," **JFR**, 1981, v4(2), 109-120.

Leonard, David C. and Michael E. Solt. "Stock Market Signals Of Changes In Expected Inflation," **JFR**, 1987, v10(1), 57-64.

Leonard, David C. and Michael E. Solt. "On Using The Black-Scholes Model Of Value Warrants," **JFR**, 1990, v13(2), 81-92.

Leonard, James W. "Federal Reserve Membership And Discrimination: A Comment," **JOF**, 1965, v20(3), 483-484.

Leonard, John B. (Anderson, R. N., John A. Haslem and John B. Leonard. "An Empirical Analysis Of The Impact Of Branching On Demand Deposit Variability," **JFQA**, 1976, v11(3), 455-464.)

Leonard, Paul A. (Forbes, Ronald W. and Paul A. Leonard. "The Effects Of Statutory Portfolio Constraints On Tax-Exempt Interest Rates," **JMCB**, 1984, v16(1), 93-99.)

Leonard, Paul H. (Bierwag, G. O., George G. Kaufman and Paul H. Leonard. "Interest Rate Effects Of Commercial Bank Underwriting Of Municipal Revenue Bonds: Additional Evidence," **JBF**, 1984, v8(1), 35-50.)

Leonard, William N. "Network Television Pricing: A Comment," **JOB**, 1969, v42(1), 93-103.

Leonard, William R. and Louis A. Shapiro. "Heavy-Duty Tools For The Market Analyst," **FAJ**, 1952, v8(3), 73-78.

Leong, Kenneth K. and Janis K. Zaima. "Further Evidence Of The Small Firm Effect: A Comparison Of NYSE-AMEX And OTC Stocks," **JBFA**, 1991, v18(1), 117-124.

Leong, Kenneth K., Janis K. Zaima and Thomas Buchman. "The Effect Of Ownership Control Status On Stock Price Reaction To The Adoption Of LIFO Inventory," **JBFA**, 1991, v18(3), 405-420.

Leontiades, Milton. "Conglomerates: Another Look," **FAJ**, 1969, v25(3), 80-86.

Leontiades, Milton. "The Use Of Capital Markets," **FAJ**, 1967, v23(2), 19-23.

Leppel, Karen. "A Trinomial Logit Analysis Of Household Composition," **AREUEA**, 1986, v14(4), 537-556.

Lere, John C. "Deterministic Net Present Value As An Approximation Of Expected Net Present Value," **JBFA**, 1980, v7(2), 245-259.

Lerman, Donald L. and William J. Reeder. "The Affordability Of Adequate Housing," **AREUEA**, 1987, v15(4), 389-404.

Lerman, Zvi. "The Structure Of Interest Rates And Inflation," **RIF**, 1983, v4, 183-215.

Lerman, Zvi. (Levy, Haim and Zvi Lerman. "Testing P/E Ratio Filters With Stochastic Dominance," **JPM**, 1984-85, v11(2), 31-40.)

Lerman, Zvi. (Levy, Haim and Zvi Lerman. "The Benefits Of International Diversification In Bonds," **FAJ**, 1988, v44(5), 56-64.)

Lerman, Zvi. (Levy, Haim and Zvi Lerman. "Testing The Predicitve Power Of Ex-Post Efficient Portfolios," **JFR**, 1988, v11(3), 241-254.)

Lerner, E. M. (Rappaport, A. and E. M. Lerner. "Reporting By Diversified Firms," **FAJ**, 1970, v26(1), 54-64.)

Lerner, Eugene M. and Marvin Schwartz. "Supermarkets: Relationship Between Sales, Rents And Profits," **FAJ**, 1961, v17(3), 7-10.

Lerner, Eugene M. and Pochara Theerathorn. "The Returns Of Different Investment Strategies," **JPM**, 1982-83, v9(4), 26-28.

Lerner, Eugene M. and Rolf Auster. "Market Discounts Potential Dilution?," **FAJ**, 1969, v25(4), 118-121.

Lerner, Eugene M. and Willard T. Carleton. "Financing Decisions Of The Firm," **JOF**, 1966, v21(2), 202-214.

Lerner, Eugene M. and Willard T. Carleton. "A Note On The Lerner-Carleton Analysis: Reply," **JOF**, 1968, v23(5), 862-864.

Lerner, Eugene M. "Rate Of Return On Common Stocks," **FAJ**, 1960, v16(5), 47-49.

Lerner, Eugene M. "Three Financial Problems Facing Bank Holding Companies: A Comment," **JMCB**, 1972, v4(2), 445-455.

Lerner, Eugene M. (Breen, William J. and Eugene M. Lerner. "Corporate Financial Strategies And Market Measures Of Risk And Return," **JOF**, 1973, v28(2),339-351.)

Lerner, Eugene M. (Carleton, Willard T. and Eugene M. Lerner. "Statistical Credit Scoring Of Municipal Bonds," **JMCB**, 1969, v1(4), 750-764.)

Lerner, Eugene M. (Carleton, Willard T. and Eugene M. Lerner. "Measuring Corporate Profit Opportunities," **JFQA**, 1967, v2(3), 225-240.)

Lerner, Eugene M. (Jacobs, Donald P., Eugene M. Lerner and Joseph S. Moag. "Guidelines For Designing Bank Planning Models And Information Systems," **JBR**, 1971-72, v2(1), 14-24.)

Lerner, Eugene M. (Machol, Robert E. and Eugene M. Lerner. "Risk, Ruin And Investment Analysis," **JFQA**, 1969, v4(4), 473-492.)

Lerner, Eugene M. (Moag, Joseph S., Willard T. Carleton and Eugene M. Lerner. "Defining The Finance Function: A Model-Systems Approach," **JOF**, 1967, v22(4), 543-555.)

Lerner, Eugene M. (Moag, Joseph S. and Eugene M. Lerner. "Capital Budgeting Decisions Under Imperfect Market Conditions - A Systems Framework," **JOF**, 1969, v24(4), 613-621.)

Lerro, A. J. (Lee, Sang M. and A. J. Lerro. "Optimizing The Portfolio Selection For Mutual Funds," **JOF**, 1973, v28(5), 1087-1101.)

Lerro, A. J. (Lee, Sang M. and A. J. Lerro. "Capital Budgeting For Multiple Objectives," **FM**, 1974, v3(1), 58-66.)

Lerro, A. Joseph. (Lee, Sang M. and A. Joseph Lerro. "A Cash Management Model For Health Care Clinics," **FR**, 1973, v8(1), 1-10.)

Lerro, Anthony J. (Lee, Sang M., Anthony J. Lerro and Bruce R. McGinnis. "Optimization Of Tax Switching For Commercial Banks: A Comment," **JMCB**, 1971, v3(2), Part 1, 293-303.)

Lesage, James P. (Cooperman, Elizabeth S., Winson B. Lee and James P. Lesage. "Commercial Bank And Thrift Interdependence And Local Market Competition For Retail Certificates Of Deposit," **JFSR**, 1990, v4(1), 37-52.)

Leslie, Neale. "A New Approach To Life Insurance Evaluation," **FAJ**, 1966, v22(5), 75-78.

Leslie, Peter E. "Nature Of Interaction Between Market Structures And Forces And Institutional Systems," **JBF**, 1982, v6(3), 437-442.

Leslie, William, Jr. "Comments Concerning Curricular Concepts," **JRI**, 1962, v29(4), 569-570.

Leslie, William. "Automobile Insurance - A Major Property Insurance Problem," **JRI**, 1953, v20, 24-28.

Leslie, William. "The Condition Of The Workmen's Compensation Business," **JRI**, 1935, v2, 65-71.

Leslie, William. "Training Courses Conducted By Casualty Insurance Companies," **JRI**, 1938, v5, 26-36.

Lessard, Donald R. "Global Competition And Corporate Finance In The 1900s," **JACF**, 1991, v3(4), 59-72.

Lessard, Donald R. "International Diversification," **FAJ**, 1976, v32(1), 32-38.

Lessard, Donald R. "International Portfolio Diversification: A Multivariate Analysis For A Group Of Latin American Countries," **JOF**, 1973, v28(3), 619-633.

Lessard, Donald R. "World, National, And Industry Factors In Equity Returns," **JOF**, 1974, v29(2), 379-391.

Lessard, Donald R. (Agmon, Tamir and Donald R. Lessard. "Investor Recognition Of Corporate International Diversification," **JOF**, 1977, v32(4), 1049-1055.)

Lessard, Donald R. (Bower, Richard S. and Donald R. Lessard. "An Operational Approach To Risk-Screening," **JOF**, 1973, v28(2), 321-337.)

Lessard, Donald R. (Cohn, Richard A. and Donald R. Lessard. "The Effect Of Inflation On Stock Prices: International Evidence," **JOF**, 1981, v36(2), 277-289.)

Lessard, Donald R. (Cohn, Richard A. and Donald R. Lessard. "Recent Research On Indexation And The Housing Market," **JOF**, 1976, v31(2), 403-413.)

Lessard, Donald R. (Colton, Kent W., Donald R. Lessard and Arthur P. Solomon. "Borrower Attitudes Toward Alternative Mortgage Instruments," **AREUEA**, 1979, v7(4), 581-609.)

Lessard, Donald R. (Flood, Eugene, Jr. and Donald R. Lessard. "On The Measurement Of Operating Exposure To Exchange Rates: A Conceptual Approach," **FM**, 1986, v15(1), 25-36.)

Lessard, Donald R. and Adrian E. Tschoegl. "Panama's International Banking Center: The Direct Employment Effects," **JBF**, 1988, v12(1), 43-50.

Lessard, Donald. "North-South: The Implications For Multinational Banking," **JBF**, 1983, v7(4),521-536.

Lessard, Donald. (Agmon, Tamir and Donald Lessard. "Investor Recognition Of Corporate International Diversification: A Note," **JOF**, 1981, v36(1), 191-192.)

Lessiq, V. Parker. (Panton, Don B., V. Parker Lessiq and O. Maurice Joy. "Comovement Of International Equity Markets: A Taxonomic Approach," **JFQA**, 1976, v11(3), 415-432.)

Lesso, William. (Teichroew, Daniel, William Lesso, Kevin Rice and Gordon Wright. "Optimizing Models Of After-Tax Earnings Incorporating Depletion Allowance," **JFQA**, 1967, v2(3), 265-297.)

Lett, Monica R. "Rent Control: The Potential For Equity," **AREUEA**, 1976, v4(1), 57-82.

Leuck, Richard C. and Raymond M. Leuthold. "Agribusiness Firms As Users Of Financial Futures: The Case Of Grain Elevators," **RFM**, 1984, v3(3), 222-234.

Leung Wai K. "Option Theory And Defaultable Mortgage Pricing," **JRER**, 1989, v4(1), 53-59.

Leung, Wai K. and C. F. Sirmans. "A Lattice Approach To Fixed-Rate Mortgage Pricing With Default And Prepayment Options," **AREUEA**, 1990, v18(1), 91-104.

Leuthold, Raymond M. (Leuck, Richard C. and Raymond M. Leuthold. "Agribusiness Firms As Users Of Financial Futures: The Case Of Grain Elevators," **RFM**, 1984, v3(3), 222-234.)

Leuthold, Raymond M. "Commercial Use And Speculative Measures Of The Livestock Commodity Futures Markets," **JFM**, 1983, v3(2), 113-135.

Leuthold, Raymond M. "On The Methodology Of Testing For Independence In Futures Prices: Comment," **JOF**, 1976, v31(3), 984-985.

Leuthold, Raymond M. "Random Walk And Price Trends: The Live Cattle Futures Market," **JOF**, 1972, v27(4), 879-889.

Leuthold, Raymond M. (Garcia, Philip, Raymond M. Leuthold and Hector Zapata. "Lead-Lag Relationships Between Trading Volume And Price Variability: New Evidence," **JFM**, 1986, v6(1), 1-10.)

Leuthold, Raymond M. (Hudson, Michael A., Raymond M. Leuthold and Gboroton F. Sarassoro. "Commodity Futures Price Changes: Recent Evidence For Wheat, Soybeans And Live Cattle," **JFM**, 1987, v7(3), 287-302.)

Leuthold, Raymond M. (Lee, Cheng F., Raymond M. Leuthold and Jean E. Cordier. "The Stock Market And The Commodity Futures Market: Diversification And Arbitrage Potential," **FAJ**, 1985, v41(4), 53-60.)

Leuthold, Raymond M. (Peterson, Paul E. and Raymond M. Leuthold. "A Portfolio Approach To Optimal Hedging For A Commercial Cattle Feedlot," **JFM**, 1987, v7(4), 443-458.)

Leuthold, Raymond M. (Tzang, Dah-Nein and Raymond M. Leuthold. "Hedge Ratios Under Inherent Risk Reduction In A Commodity Complex," **JFM**, 1990, v10(5), 497-504.)

Leuthold, Raymond M. and Paul E. Peterson. "A Portfolio Approach To Optimal Hedging For A Commercial Cattle Feedlot," **JFM**, 1987, v7(2), 119-134.

Leuthold, Steven C. "Interest Rates, Inflation And Deflation," **FAJ**, 1981, v37(1), 28-41.

Leuthold, Steven C. "The Causes (And Cures?) Of Market Volatility," **JPM**, 1975-76, v2(2), 21-25.

Lev, B. (Amihud, Y., C. Brunie, C. Ferenbach, R. Fredericks, J. Grundfest, J. Lafferty, B. Lev, B. Shorts, J. Stern, B. Stewart and R. Zeckhauser. "Panel: 'Lead Steer' Roundtable," **JACF**, 1989, v2(3), 24-44.)

Lev, Baruch and Dov Pekelman. "A Multiperiod Adjustment Model For The Firm's Capital Structure," **JOF**, 1975, v30(1), 75-91.

Lev, Baruch and Yair E. Orgler. "Analysis Of The Lease-Or-Buy Decision: Comment," **JOF**, 1973, v28(4), 1022-1023.

Lev, Baruch and Gershon Mandelker. "Rejoinder To Reid And Honeycutt: The Microeconomic Consequences Of Corporate Mergers," **JOB**, 1975, v48(2), 281-303.

Lev, Baruch and Gershon Mandelker. "The Microeconomic Consequences Of Corporate Mergers," **JOB**, 1972, v45(1), 85-104.

Lev, Baruch. "Decomposition Measures For Financial Analysis," **FM**, 1973, v2(1), 56-63.

Lev, Baruch. "On The Association Between Operating Leverage And Risk," **JFQA**, 1974, v9(4), 627-641.

Lev, Baruch. (Amihud, Yakov, Baruch Lev and Nickolaos G. Travlos. "Corporate Control And The Choice Of Investment Financing: The Case Of Corporate Acquisitions," **JOF**, 1990, v45(2), 603-616.)

Lev, Baruch. (Bar-Yosef, Sasson and Baruch Lev. "Historical Cost Earnings Versus Inflation-Adjusted Earnings In The Dividend Decision," **FAJ**, 1983, v39(2),41-50.)

Lev, Baruch. (Lakonishok, Josef and Baruch Lev. "Stock Splits And Stock Dividends: Why, Who, And When," **JOF**, 1987, v42(4), 913-932.)

Levacic, Rosalind and Alex Rebmann-Huber. "The Tax-Deductibility Of Interest Payments And The Weighted Average Cost Of Capital Once Again," **JBFA**, 1979, v6(1), 101-110.

Levasseur, Michel G. "An Option Model Approach To Firm Liquidity Management," **JBF**, 1977, v1(1), 13-28.

Levasseur, Michel. (Altman, Edward I., Bertrand Jacquillat And Michel Levasseur. "Comparative Analysis Of Risk Measures: France And The United States," **JOF**, 1974, v29(5), 1495-1511.)

Leveen, Serpil S. (Meric, Gulser, Serpil S. Leveen and Ilhan Meric. "The Financial Characteristics Of Commercial Banks Involved In Interstate Acquisitions," **FR**, 1991, v26(1), 75-90.)

Level, Leon J. "Meeting The Needs Of Multinational Corporations,"

JBR, 1985-86, v16(4), 254-257.

Leventakis, John A. (Brissimis, Sophocles N. and John A. Leventakis. "An Empirical Inquiry Into The Short-Run Dynamics Of Output, Prices, And Exchange Market Pressure," JIMF, 1984, v3(1), 75-89.)

Leverett, E. J., Jr. "A Profit Calculation For Agency Management: Comment," JRI, 1967, v34(2), 336-339.

Leverett, E. J., Jr. "Attracting Insurance Majors," JRI, 1970, v37(4), 630-639.

Leverett, E. J., Jr. "Paid-In Surplus And Capital Requirements Of A New Life Insurance Company," JRI, 1971, v38(1), 15-28.

Leverett, E. J., Jr. (Belth, Joseph M. and E. J. Leverett, Jr. "Industrial Life Insurance Prices," JRI, 1965, v32(3), 367-384.)

Leverett, E. J., Jr. (Trieschmann, James S., K. Roscoe Davis and E. J. Leverett, Jr. "A Probabilistic Valuation Model For A Property-Liability Insurance Agency," JRI, 1975, v42(2), 289-302.)

Leverett, E. J., Jr. (Trieschmann, James S. and E. J. Leverett, Jr. "Self-Insurance Of Workers' Compensation Losses," JRI, 1978, v45(4), 635-650.)

Leverett, E. J., Jr. (Trieschmann, James S. and E. J. Leverett, Jr. "A Sensitivity Analysis Of Selected Variables In Agency Valuation," JRI, 1987, v54(2), 357-363.)

Leveson, Sidney M. "Have We Solved The Dilution Problem?," FAJ, 1968, v24(5), 69-70.

Leveson, Sidney M. "The Dividend-Payout Paradox," FR, 1969, v1(4), 253-254.

Levhari, David and Nissan Liviatan. "The Effects Of Increasing Uncertainty Of Inflation On Consumer's Behavior With And Without Indexation," RIF, 1979, v1, 77-94.

Levhari, David. (Keren, Michael and David Levhari. "Optimal Span Of Control And The Shape Of Average Costs Of Large Private Or Public Bureaucracies," RIF, 1983, v4, (Supp), 85-112.)

Levi, Donald R. (Dotzour, Mark G. and Donald R. Levi. "Reducing The Cost Of Corporate Employee Relocation," JRER, 1989, v4(3), 157-168.)

Levi, Donald R. and Curtis D. Terflinger. "A Legal-Economic Analysis Of Changing Liability Rules Affecting Real Estate Brokers And Appraisers," JRER, 1988, v3(2), 133-149.

Levi, Maurice D. and John H. Makin. "Fisher, Phillips, Friedman And The Measured Impact Of Inflation On Interest: A Reply," JOF, 1981, v36(4), 963-969.

Levi, Maurice D. and John H. Makin. "Fisher, Phillips, Friedman And The Measured Impact Of Inflation On Interest," JOF, 1979, v34(1), 35-52.

Levi, Maurice D. "Money And Corporate Earnings," JMCB, 1980, v12(1), 84-94.

Levi, Maurice D. "Underutilization Of Forward Markets Or Rational Behavior?," JOF, 1979, v34(4), 1013-1017.

Levi, Maurice D. (Kupferman, Martin and Maurice D. Levi. "Taxation And Interest Rate Parity," FAJ, 1978, v34(4), 61-64.)

Levi, Maurice. "Spot Versus Forward Speculation And Hedging: A Diagrammatic Exposition," JIMF, 1984, v3(1), 105-109.

Levi, Maurice. (Lakonishok, Josef and Maurice Levi. "Weekend Effects On Stock Returns: A Reply," JOF, 1985, v40(1), 351-352.)

Levi, Maurice. (Lakonishok, Josef and Maurice Levi. "Weekend Effects On Stock Returns: A Note," JOF, 1982, v37(3), 883-889.)

Levin, Bertram F. "Monetary Policy And Economic Stability: Speed And Scale Of Action," JOF, 1959, v14(2), 161-171.

Levin, Fred J. and Ann-Marie Meulendyke. "Monetary Policy: Theory And Practice: A Comment," JMCB, 1982, v14(3), 399-403.

Levin, Fred J. "Examination Of The Money-Stock Control Approach Of Burger, Kalishn, And Babb," JMCB, 1973, v5(4), 924-938.

Levin, Jay H. "A Financial Sector Analysis Of The Eurodollar Market," JOF, 1974, v29(1), 103-117.

Levin, Jay H. "Capital Mobility And Endogenous Stabilization Policy Under Flexible Exchange Rates," JMCB, 1977, v9(4), 572-585.

Levin, Jay H. "Does Leaning Against The Wind Improve Exchange-Rate Performance?," JIMF, 1985, v4(1), 135-150.

Levin, Jay H. "Trade Flow Lags, Monetary And Fiscal Policy, And Exchange-Rate Overshooting," JIMF, 1986, v5(4), 485-495.

Levin, Jesse. "Budget Deficits And Inflation," FAJ, 1974, v30(4), 44-47.

Levin, Jesse. "Prophetic Leaders," FAJ, 1970, v26(4), 87-90.

Levin, Jesse. "The Bigger They Come The Harder They Fall," FAJ, 1972, v28(6), 71-77.

Levin, Murray S. (Krogh, Harold C. and Murray S. Levin. "Recent Trends: State Insurance Guaranty Funds And Insurance Company Insurance Assessment Operations," JRI, 1986, v53(2), 335-342.)

Levin, Richard C. (Klevorick, Alvin K. and Richard C. Levin. "A Welfare Analysis Of Constraints On Pricing To Deter Entry," RIF, 1983, v4, (Supp), 113-132.)

Levine, David A. "The Causes And Dangers Of Interest Rate Volatility," JPM, 1976-77, v3(1), 14-21.

Levine, David A. (Trainer, Francis H., Jr., David A. Levine and Jonathan A. Reiss. "A Systematic Approach To Bond Management In Pension Funds," JPM, 1983-84, v10(3), 30-35.)

Levine, J. M. (Safer, A. E. and J. M. Levine. "Analysis Of Institutional Holdings," FAJ, 1970, v26(4), 74-86.)

Levine, Kenneth C. "Corporate Modeling Of A Life Insurance Company: A Developmental Game Plan," JRI, 1973, v40(4), 555-564.

Levine, Louis. "University Consultation On Employment Security - A Cooperative Venture," JRI, 1962, v29(1), 107-114.

Levine, Ross. "The Pricing Of Forward Exchange Rates," JIMF, 1989, v8(2), 163-180.

Levis, Mario. "Stock Market Anomalies: A Re-Assessment Based On The U.K. Evidence," JBF, 1989, v13(4/5), 675-696.

Levitt, Theodore. "Investment, Depression, And The Assurance Of Prosperity," JOF, 1954, v9(3), 235-251.

Levitt, Theodore. "Professor Levitt On 'Investment, Depression, And The Assurance Of Prosperity': Reply," JOF, 1955, v10(3), 378-380.

Levitz, Gerald D. "Market Risk In Institutional Portfolios," FAJ, 1974, v30(1), 53-60.

Levy, Azriel. "A Note On The Relationship Between Forward And Futures Contracts," JFM, 1989, v9(2), 171-174.

Levy, Azriel. (Levy, Haim and Azriel Levy. "Ordering Uncertain Options Under Inflation: A Note," JOF, 1984, v39(4), 1223-1229.)

Levy, Azriel. (Levy, Haim and Azriel Levy. "Equilibrium Under Uncertain Inflation: A Discrete Time Approach," JFQA, 1987, v22(3), 285-298.)

Levy, Ferdinand K. "The Allocation, Characteristics, And Outcome Of The Firm's Research And Development Portfolio: Comment," JOB, 1968, v41(1), 89-90.

Levy, Haim and Azriel Levy. "Ordering Uncertain Options Under Inflation: A Note," JOF, 1984, v39(4), 1223-1229.

Levy, Haim and Fred D. Arditti. "Valuation, Leverage And The Cost Of Capital In The Case Of Depreciable Assets: A Reply," JOF, 1975, v30(1), 221-223.

Levy, Haim and Fred D. Arditti. "Valuation, Leverage, And The Cost Of Capital In The Case Of Depreciable Assets," JOF, 1973, v28(3), 687-695.

Levy, Haim and Giora Hanoch. "Relative Effectiveness Of Efficiency Criteria For Portfolio Selection," JFQA, 1970, v5(1), 63-76.

Levy, Haim and Jehuda Kahane. "Profitability Of Saving Through Insurance Companies," JRI, 1970, v37(2), 233-240.

Levy, Haim and Marshall Sarnat. "Safety First - An Expected Utility Principle," JFQA, 1972, v7(3), 1829-1834.

Levy, Haim and Marshall Sarnat. "Exchange Rate Risk And The Optimal Diversification Of Foreign Currency Holdings," JMCB, 1978, v10(4), 453-463.

Levy, Haim and Marshall Sarnat. "Alternative Efficiency Criteria: An Empirical Analysis," JOF, 1970, v25(5), 1153-1158.

Levy, Haim and Marshall Sarnat. "Diversification, Portfolio Analysis And The Uneasy Case For Conglomerate Mergers," JOF, 1970, v25(4), 795-802.

Levy, Haim and Marshall Sarnat. "Risk, Dividend Policy, And The Optimal Pricing Of A Rights Offering: A Comment," JMCB, 1971, v3(4), 840-849.

Levy, Haim and Marshall Sarnat. "A Note On Portfolio Selection And Investors' Wealth," JFQA, 1971, v6(1), 639-642.

Levy, Haim and Marshall Sarnat. "Two-Period Portfolio Selection And Investors' Discount Rates," JOF, 1971, v26(3), 757-761.

Levy, Haim and Marshall Sarnat. "Reply: Safety First - An Expected Utility Principle," JFQA, 1974, v9(6), 1063-1064.

Levy, Haim and Marshall Sarnat. "Leasing, Borrowing, And Financial Risk," FM, 1979, v8(4), 47-54.

Levy, Haim and Marshall Sarnat. "The Case For Mutual Funds," FAJ, 1972, v28(2), 77-81.

Levy, Haim and Robert Brooks. "Financial Break-Even Analysis And The Value Of The Firm," FM, 1986, v15(3), 22-26.

Levy, Haim and Yoram Kroll. "Ordering Uncertain Options With Borrowing And Lending," JOF, 1978, v33(2), 553-574.

Levy, Haim and Yoram Kroll. "Stochastic Dominance With Riskless Assets," JFQA, 1976, v11(5), 743-778.

Levy, Haim and Zvi Lerman. "Testing P/E Ratio Filters With Stochastic Dominance," JPM, 1984-85, v11(2), 31-40.

Levy, Haim and Azriel Levy. "Equilibrium Under Uncertain Inflation: A Discrete Time Approach," JFQA, 1987, v22(3), 285-298.

Levy, Haim and James A. Yoder. "Applying The Black-Scholes Model After Large Market Shocks," JPM, 1989, v16(1), 103-106.

Levy, Haim and Marshall Sarnat. "A Pedagogic Note On Alternative Formulations Of The Goal Of The Firm," JOB, 1977, v50(4), 526-528.

Levy, Haim and Robert Brooks. "An Empirical Analysis Of Term Premiums Using Stochastic Dominance," JBF, 1989, v13(2),245-260.

Levy, Haim and Zvi Lerman. "Testing The Predicitve Power Of Ex-Post Efficient Portfolios," JFR, 1988, v11(3), 241-254.

Levy, Haim and Zvi Lerman. "The Benefits Of International Diversification In Bonds," FAJ, 1988, v44(5), 56-64.

Levy, Haim. "A Comment On Payback: A Reply," JFQA, 1971, v6(4), 1161-1161.

Levy, Haim. "A Note On The Payback Method," JFQA, 1968, v3(4), 433-443.

Levy, Haim. "A Test Of The CAPM Via A Confidence Level Approach," JPM, 1982-83, v9(1), 56-61.

Levy, Haim. "A Utility Function Depending On The First Three Moments: Comment," JOF, 1969, v24(4), 715-719.

Levy, Haim. "Economic Evaluation Of Voting Power Of Common Stock," JOF, 1983, v38(1), 79-93.

Levy, Haim. "Futures, Spots, Stocks And Bonds: Multi-Asset Portfolio Analysis," JFM, 1987, v7(4), 383-396.

Levy, Haim. "Measuring Risk And Performance Over Alternative Investment Horizons," FAJ, 1984, v40(2), 61-68.

Levy, Haim. "Optimal Portfolio Of Foreign Currencies With Borrowing And Lending," JMCB, 1981, v13(3), 325-341.

Levy, Haim. "Possible Explanation Of No-Synergy Merger And Small Firm Effect By The Generalized CAPM," RQFA, 1991, v1(1), 101-128.

Levy, Haim. "Stochastic Dominance Rules For Truncated Normal Distributions: A Note," JOF, 1982, v37(5), 1299-1303.

Levy, Haim. "The CAPM And Beta In An Imperfect Market," JPM, 1979-80, v6(2), 5-11.

Levy, Haim. "The CAPM And The Investment Horizon: Reply," JPM, 1982-83, v9(1), 66-68.

Levy, Haim. "The CAPM And The Investment Horizon," JPM, 1980-81, v7(2), 32-40.

Levy, Haim. "The Capital Asset Pricing Model, Inflation, And The Investment Horizon: The Israeli Experience," JFQA, 1980, v15(3), 561-593.

Levy, Haim. "The Connection Between Pre-Tax And Post-Tax Rates Of Return," JOB, 1968, v41(4),477-483.

Levy, Haim. "The Demand For Assets Under Conditions Of Risk," JOF, 1973, v28(1), 79-96.

Levy, Haim. "The Demand For Assets Under Conditions Of Risk: Reply," JOF, 1977, v32(3), 930-932.

Levy, Haim. "The Yield Curve And Expected Inflation," FAJ, 1982, v38(6), 37-42.

Levy, Haim. "Upper And Lower Bonds Of Put And Call Option Value: Stochastic Dominance Approach-Erratum," JOF, 1986, v41(5), 1181-1182.

Levy, Haim. "Upper And Lower Bounds Of Put And Call Option Value: Stochastic Dominance Approach," JOF, 1985, v40(4), 1197-1217.

Levy, Haim. "Voting Power, The CAPM, And Market Efficiency," **RIF,** 1983, v4, (Supp), 133-168.

Levy, Haim. (Arditti, Fred D. and Haim Levy. "The Weighted Average Cost Of Capital As A Cutoff Rate: A Critical Analysis Of The Classical Textbook Weighted Average," **FM,** 1977, v6(3), 24-34.)

Levy, Haim. (Arditti, Fred D. and Haim Levy. "Portfolio Efficiency Analysis In Three Moments: The Multiperiod Case," **JOF,** 1975, v30(3), 797-809.)

Levy, Haim. (Arditti, Fred D. and Haim Levy. "Distribution Moments And Equilibrium: A Comment," **JFQA,** 1972, v7(1), 1429-1433.)

Levy, Haim. (Arditti, Fred D., Haim Levy and Marshall Sarnat. "Taxes, Uncertainty And Optimal Dividend Policy," **FM,** 1976, v5(1), 46-52.)

Levy, Haim. (Bae, Sung C. and Haim Levy. "The Valuation Of Firm Commitment Underwriting Contracts For Seasoned New Equity Issues: Theory And Evidence," **FM,** 1990, v19(2), 48-59.)

Levy, Haim. (Barlev, Benzion and Haim Levy. "Using Accounting Data For Portfolio Management," **JPM,** 1987-88, v14(3), 70-77.)

Levy, Haim. (Barlev, Benzion and Haim Levy. "The Information Content Of Accounting Data And The Management Of Security Portfolios," **JBFA,** 1981, v8(2), 221-248.)

Levy, Haim. (Ben-Horim, Moshe and Haim Levy. "Management Of Accounts Receivable Under Inflation," **FM,** 1983, v12(1), 42-48.)

Levy, Haim. (Ben-Horim, Moshe and Haim Levy. "Total Risk, Diversifiable Risk And Non-Diversifiable Risk: A Pedagogic Note," **JFQA,** 1980, v15(2), 289-298.)

Levy, Haim. (Brooks, Robert, Haim Levy and Jim Yoder. "Using Stochastic Dominance To Evaluate The Performance Of Portfolios With Options," **FAJ,** 1987, v43(2), 79-82.)

Levy, Haim. (Brooks, Robert, Haim Levy and Miles Livingston. "The Coupon Effect On Term Premiums," **JFI,** 1989, v12(1), 15-22.)

Levy, Haim. (Hanoch, Giora and Haim Levy. "Efficient Portfolio Selection With Quadratic And Cubic Utility," **JOB,** 1970, v43(2), 181-189.)

Levy, Haim. (Kahane, Yehuda and Haim Levy. "Regulation In The Insurance Industry: Determination Of Premiums In Automobile Insurance," **JRI,** 1975, v42(1), 117-132.)

Levy, Haim. (Kroll, Yoram and Haim Levy. "Stochastic Dominance: A Note," **JOF,** 1982, v37(3), 871-875.)

Levy, Haim. (Kroll, Yoram and Haim Levy. "Sampling Errors And Portfolio Efficient Analysis," **JFQA,** 1980, v15(3), 655-688.)

Levy, Haim. (Kroll, Yoram and Haim Levy. "Stochastic Dominance With A Riskless Asset: An Imperfect Market," **JFQA,** 1979, v14(2), 179-204.)

Levy, Haim. (Kroll, Yoram and Haim Levy. "Stochastic Dominance: A Review And Some New Evidence," **RIF,** 1980, v2, 163-227.)

Levy, Haim. (Kroll, Yoram, Haim Levy and Harry M. Markowitz. "Mean-Variance Versus Direct Utility Maximization," **JOF,** 1984, v39(1), 47-62.)

Levy, Haim. (Sarnat, Marshall and Haim Levy. "The Relationship Of Rules Of Thumb To The Internal Rate Of Return: A Restatement And Generalization," **JOF,** 1969, v24(3), 479-489.)

Levy, Kenneth N. (Jacobs, Bruce I. and Kenneth N. Levy. "Calendar Anomalies: Abnormal Returns At Calendar Turning Points," **FAJ,** 1988, v44(6), 28-39.)

Levy, Kenneth N. (Jacobs, Bruce I. and Kenneth N. Levy. "On The Value Of 'Value'," **FAJ,** 1988, v44(4), 47-62.)

Levy, Kenneth N. (Jacobs, Bruce I. and Kenneth N. Levy. "Forecasting The Size Effect," **FAJ,** 1989, v45(3), 38-54.)

Levy, Kenneth. (Jacobs, Bruce I. and Kenneth N. Levy. "The Complexity Of The Stock Market," **JPM,** 1989, v16(1), 19-27.)

Levy, Kenneth. (Jacobs, Bruce I. and Kenneth N. Levy. "Disentangling Equity Return Regularities: New Insights And Investment Opportunities," **FAJ,** 1988, v44(3), 18-44.)

Levy, Mickey D. "The Case For Extending Social Security Coverage To Government Employees," **JRI,** 1980, v47(1), 78-90.

Levy, Mickey D. "The Case For Extending Social Security To Government Employees: Reply," **JRI,** 1982, v49(3), 468-471.

Levy, Robert A. and Spero L. Kripotos. "Sources Of Relative Price Strength," **FAJ,** 1969, v25(6), 60,63-64.

Levy, Robert A. "Beta As A Predictor Of Return," **FAJ,** 1974, v30(1), 61-69.

Levy, Robert A. "Conceptual Foundations Of Technical Analysis," **FAJ,** 1966, v22(4), 83-89.

Levy, Robert A. "How To Measure Research Performance," **JPM,** 1974-75, v1(1), 44-49.

Levy, Robert A. "Measurement Of Investment Performance," **JFQA,** 1968, v3(1), 35-57.

Levy, Robert A. "On The Safety Of Low P/E Stocks," **FAJ,** 1973, v29(1), 57-59.

Levy, Robert A. "Random Walks: Reality Or Myth-Reply," **FAJ,** 1968, v24(1), 129-132.

Levy, Robert A. "Random Walks: Reality Or Myth," **FAJ,** 1967, v23(6), 69-77.

Levy, Robert A. "Relative Strength As A Criterion For Investment Selection," **JOF,** 1967, v22(4), 595-610.

Levy, Robert A. "Stationarity Of Beta Coefficients," **FAJ,** 1971, v27(6), 55-62.

Levy, Robert A. "Stocks, Bonds, Bills, And Inflation Over 52 Years," **JPM,** 1977-78, v4(4), 18-19.

Levy, Robert A. "The Predictive Significance Of Five-Point Chart Patterns," **JOB,** 1971, v44(3), 316-323.

Levy, Robert A. and James M. Jondrow. "The Adjustment Of Employment To Technical Change In The Steel And Auto Industries," **JOB,** 1986, v59(3), 475-492.

Levy, Robert J. (Lacker, Jeffrey M., Robert J. Levy and John A. Weinberg. "Incentive-Compatible Financial Contracts, Asset Prices, And The Value Of Control," **JFI,** 1990, v1(1), 31-56.)

Levy, Seymour and Gordon Donhowe. "Exploration Of A Biological Model Of Industrial Organization," **JOB,** 1962, v35(4), 335-342.

Levy, Sidney J. "Consumer Views Of Bank Services," **JBR,** 1973-74, v4(2), 100-104.

Levy-Garboua, V. and G. Maarek. "Bank Behavior And Monetary Policy," **JBF,** 1978, v2(1), 15-46.

Lew, Edward A. "Insurance Mortality Investigations Of Physical Impairments," **JRI,** 1954, v21, 43-55.

Lewellen, Wilbur G. and Douglas R. Emery. "On The Matter Of Parity Among Financial Obligations," **JOF,** 1981, v36(1), 97-111.

Lewellen, Wilbur G. and Douglas R. Emery. "Corporate Debt Management And The Value Of The Firm," **JFQA,** 1986, v21(4), 415-426.

Lewellen, Wilbur G. and George A. Racette. "Convertible Debt Financing," **JFQA,** 1973, v8(5), 777-792.

Lewellen, Wilbur G. and James S. Ang. "Inflation, Security Values, And Risk Premia," **JFR,** 1982, v5(2), 105-123.

Lewellen, Wilbur G. and John J. McConnell. "Tax Reform, Firm Valuation, And Capital Costs," **FM,** 1977, v6(4), 59-66.

Lewellen, Wilbur G. and Michael G. Ferri. "Strategies For The Merger Game: Management And The Market," **FM,** 1983, v12(4), 25-35.

Lewellen, Wilbur G. and Robert O. Edmister. "A General Model For Accounts-Receivable Analysis And Control," **JFQA,** 1973, v8(2), 195-206.

Lewellen, Wilbur G. "A Conceptual Reappraisal Of Cost Of Capital," **FM,** 1974, v3(4), 63-70.

Lewellen, Wilbur G. "A Pure Financial Rationale For The Conglomerate Merger," **JOF,** 1971, v26(2), 521-537.

Lewellen, Wilbur G. "Finance Subsidiaries And Corporate Borrowing Capacity," **FM,** 1972, v1(1), 21-31.

Lewellen, Wilbur G. "Management And Ownership In The Large Firm," **JOF,** 1969, v24(2), 299-323.

Lewellen, Wilbur G. "Some Observations On Risk-Adjusted Discount Rates," **JOF,** 1977, v32(4), 1331-1338.

Lewellen, Wilbur G. "Some Observations On Risk-Adjusted Discount Rates: Reply," **JOF,** 1979, v34(4), 1065-1066.

Lewellen, Wilbur G. (Ang, James S. and Wilbur G. Lewellen. "Risk Adjustment In Capital Investment Project Evaluations," **FM,** 1982, v11(2), 5-14.)

Lewellen, Wilbur G. (Badrinath, S. G. and Wilbur G. Lewellen. "Evidence On Tax-Motivated Securities Trading Behavior," **JOF,** 1991, v46(1), 369-382.)

Lewellen, Wilbur G. (Blum, Gerald A., William A. Kracaw and Wilbur G. Lewellen. "Determinants Of The Execution Costs Of Common Stock Trades By Individual Investors," **JFR,** 1986, v9(4), 291-301.)

Lewellen, Wilbur G. (Blum, Gerald A. and Wilbur G. Lewellen. "Negotiated Brokerage Commissions And The Individual Investor," **JFQA,** 1983, v18(3), 331-343.)

Lewellen, Wilbur G. (Chang, Eric C. and Wilbur G. Lewellen. "An Arbitrage Pricing Approach To Evaluating Mutual Fund Performance," **JFR,** 1985, v8(1), 15-30.)

Lewellen, Wilbur G. (Chang, Eric C. and Wilbur G. Lewellen. "Market Timing And Mutual Fund Investment Performance," **JOB,** 1984, v57(1), Part 1, 57-72.)

Lewellen, Wilbur G. (Cohn, Richard A., Wilbur G. Lewellen, Ronald C. Lease and Gary G. Schlarbaum. "Individual Investor Risk Aversion And Investment Portfolio Composition," **JOF,** 1975, v30(2), 605-620.)

Lewellen, Wilbur G. (Emery, Douglas R. and Wilbur G. Lewellen. "Refunding Noncallable Debt," **JFQA,** 1984, v19(1), 73-82.)

Lewellen, Wilbur G. (Emery, Douglas R., Wilbur G. Lewellen and David C. Mauer. "Tax-Timing Options, Leverage, And The Choice Of Corporate Form," **JFR,** 1988, v11(2), 99-110.)

Lewellen, Wilbur G. (Groth, Stephen C., Wilbur G. Lewellen, Gary G. Schlarbaum and Ronald C. Lease. "How Good Are Broker's Recommendations?," **FAJ,** 1979, v35(1), 32-40.)

Lewellen, Wilbur G. (Groth, John C., Wilbur G. Lewellen, Gary G. Schlarbaum and Ronald C. Lease. "Security Analysts: Some Are More Equal," **JPM,** 1977-78, v4(3), 43-48.)

Lewellen, Wilbur G. (Hughes, John S. and Wilbur G. Lewellen. "Programming Solution To Capital Rationing Problems," **JBFA,** 1974, v1(1), 55-74.)

Lewellen, Wilbur G. (Johnson, Robert W. and Wilbur G. Lewellen. "Analysis Of The Lease-Or-Buy Decision: Reply," **JOF,** 1973, v28(4), 1024-1028.)

Lewellen, Wilbur G. (Johnson, Robert W. and Wilbur G. Lewellen. "Analysis Of The Lease-Or-Buy Decision," **JOF,** 1972, v27(4), 815-823.)

Lewellen, Wilbur G. (Kim, E. Han, Wilbur G. Lewellen and John J. McConnell. "Financial Leverage Clienteles: Theory And Evidence," **JFEC,** 1979, v7(1), 83-109.)

Lewellen, Wilbur G. (Kim, E. Han, Wilbur G. Lewellen and John J. McConnell. "Sale-And-Leaseback Agreements And Enterprise Valuation," **JFQA,** 1978, v13(5), 871-883.)

Lewellen, Wilbur G. (Lease, Ronald C., Wilbur G. Lewellen and Gary G. Schlarbaum. "Market Segmentation And The Retail Investor," **FAJ,** 1976, v32(5), 53-60.)

Lewellen, Wilbur G. (Lease, Ronald C., Wilbur G. Lewellen and Gary G. Schlarbaum. "The Individual Investor: Attributes And Attitudes," **JOF,** 1974, v29(2), 413-433.)

Lewellen, Wilbur G. (Mauer, David C. and Wilbur G. Lewellen. "Debt Management Under Corporate And Personal Taxation," **JOF,** 1987, v42(5), 1275-1291.)

Lewellen, Wilbur G. (Mauer, David C. and Wilbur G. Lewellen. "Securityholder Taxes And Corporate Restructurings," **JFQA,** 1990, v25(3), 341-360.)

Lewellen, Wilbur G. (Schlarbaum, Gary G., Wilbur G. Lewellen and Ronald C. Lease. "The Common Stock-Portfolio Performance Record Of Individual Investors: 1954-70," **JOF,** 1978, v33(2), 429-441.)

Lewellen, Wilbur G. (Schlarbaum, Gary G., Wilbur G. Lewellen and Ronald C. Lease. "Realized Returns On Common Stock Investments: The Experience Of Individual Investors," **JOB,** 1978, v51(2), 299-326.)

Lewellen, Wilbur G. (Stanley, Kenneth L., Wilbur G. Lewellen and Gary G. Schlarbaum. "Further Evidence On The Value Of Professional Investment Research," **JFR,** 1981, v4(1), 1-9.)

Lewellen, Wilbur G. (Stanley, Kenneth L., Wilbur G. Lewellen and Gary G. Schlarbaum. "Investor Response To Investment Research," **JPM,** 1979-80, v6(4), 20-27.)

Lewellen, Wilbur G. (Ying, Louis K. W., Wilbur G. Lewellen, Gary G. Schlarbaum and Ronald C. Lease. "Stock Exchange Listings And Securities Returns," **JFQA,** 1977, v12(3), 415-432.)

Lewellen, Wilbur G. and David C. Mauer. "Tax Options And Corporate Capital Structures," JFQA, 1988, v23(4), 387-400.

Lewellen, Wilbur G. and William A. Kracaw. "Inflation, Corporate Growth, And Corporate Leverage," FM, 1987, v16(4), 29-36.

Lewellen, Wilbur G., Howard P. Lanser and John J. McConnell. "Payback Substitutes For Discounted Cash Flow," FM, 1973, v2(2), 17-23.

Lewellen, Wilbur G., John J. McConnell and Jonathan A. Scott. "Capital Market Influences On Trade Credit Policies," JFR, 1980, v3(2), 105-113.

Lewellen, Wilbur G., Kenneth L. Stanley, Ronald C. Lease and Gary G. Schlarbaum. "Some Direct Evidence On The Dividend Clientele Phenomenon," JOF, 1978, v33(5), 1385-1399.

Lewellen, Wilbur G., Michael S. Long and John J. McConnell. "Asset Leasing In Competitive Capital Markets," JOF, 1976, v31(3), 787-798.

Lewellen, Wilbur G., Ronald C. Lease and Gary G. Schlarbaum. "Investment Performance And Investor Behavior," JFQA, 1979, v14(1), 29-57.

Lewellen, Wilbur G., Ronald C. Lease and Gary G. Schlarbaum. "The Personal Investments Of Professional Managers," FM, 1979, v8(4), 28-36.

Lewellen, Wilbur G., Ronald C. Lease and Gary C. Schlarbaum. "Patterns Of Investment Strategy And Behavior Among Individual Investors," JOB, 1977, v50(3), 296-333.

Lewellen, Wilbur, Claudio Loderer and Ahron Rosenfeld. "Mergers, Executive Risk Reduction, And Stockholder Wealth," JFQA, 1989, v24(4), 459-472.

Lewent, Judy C. and A. John Kearney. "Identifying, Measuring, And Hedging Currency Risk At Merck," JACF, 1990, v2(4), 19-28.

Lewin, Wayne B. "NCEFT Recommendations: An Overview," JBR, 1977-78, v8(4), 200-204.

Lewin, Wayne B. "The Check Collection System: Present And Future Status," JBR, 1978-79, v9(1), 38-42.

Lewis, Alan L. "A Simple Algorithm For The Portfolio Selection Problem," JOF, 1988, v43(1), 71-82.

Lewis, Alan L. "Semivariance And The Performance Of Portfolios With Options," FAJ, 1990, v46(4), 67-76.

Lewis, Alan L., Sheen T. Kassouf, R. Dennis Brehm and Jack Johnston. "The Ibbotson-Sinquefield Simulation Made Easy," JOB, 1980, v53(2), 205-214.

Lewis, Craig M. "A Multiperiod Theory Of Corporate Financial Policy Under Taxation," JFQA, 1990, v25(1), 25-44.

Lewis, Craig M. (Day, Theodore E. and Craig M. Lewis. "The Behavior Of The Volatility Implicit In The Prices Of Stock Index Options," JFEC, 1988, v22(1), 103-122.)

Lewis, David C. (Porter, R. Burr, Roger P. Bey and David C. Lewis. "The Development Of A Mean-Semivariance Approach To Capital Budgeting," JFQA, 1975, v10(4), 639-649.)

Lewis, David L. (Reinmuth, Dennis F. and David L. Lewis. "Review Article - The Case Of The Missing Insurance Entrepreneur," JRI, 1970, v37(2), 291-299.)

Lewis, David L. (Reinmuth, Dennis F. and David L. Lewis. "The Insurance Hall Of Fame," JRI, 1971, v38(1), 61-69.)

Lewis, George M. "Livestock And Meat Supply," FAJ, 1952, v8(3), 85-92.

Lewis, John H. and Dillard B. Tinsley. "Personnnel Administration In Bank Holding Companies," JBR, 1978-79, v9(1), 38-42.

Lewis, John H. and Dillard B. Tinsley. "Curriculum Development For Commercial Bank Management," JFED, 1977, v6, 36-39.

Lewis, John H. "Review And Outlook For The Airlines," FAJ, 1958, v14(2), 35-40.

Lewis, John H. "Review Of Domestic Airline Industry," FAJ, 1955, v11(5), 13-20.

Lewis, John H. "The Air Transport Industry," FAJ, 1952, v8(2), 39-44.

Lewis, John P. "Short-Term General Business Conditions Forecasting: Some Comments On Method," JOB, 1962, v35(4), 343-356.

Lewis, John R. "A Critical Review Of The Federal Riot Reinsurance System," JRI, 1971, v38(1), 29-42.

Lewis, Karen K. "Inflation Risk And Asset Market Disturbances: The Mean-Variance Model Revisited," JIMF, 1988, v7(3), 273-288.

Lewis, Karen K. "The Behavior Of Eurocurrency Returns Across Different Holding Periods And Monetary Regimes," JOF, 1990, v45(4), 1211-1236.

Lewis, Karen K. "The Persistence Of The 'Peso Problem' When Policy Is Noisy," JIMF, 1988, v7(1), 5-22.

Lewis, Kenneth A. and Francis F. Breen. "Empirical Issues In The Demand For Currency: A Multinational Study," JOF, 1975, v30(4), 1065-1079.

Lewis, Kenneth A. "A Note On The Interest Elasticity Of Transaction Demand For Cash," JOF, 1974, v29(4), 1149-1152.

Lewis, Robert E. "Some Factors In The Growth Of Consumer Credit," JOF, 1956, v11(2), 249-256.

Lewis, Tracy. (Giammarino, Ronald and Tracy Lewis. "A Theory Of Negotiated Equity Financing," RFS, 1988-89, v1(3), 265-288.)

Lewis, Virginia L. (Churchill, Neil C. and Virginia L. Lewis. "Profitability Of Small-Business Lending," JBR, 1985-86, v16(2), 63-71.)

Lewis, W. Cris and Paul J. McNutt. "The Incidence Of Property Taxes On Single-Family Housing," AREUEA, 1979, v7(3), 344-361.

Lewis, William F. (Gitman, Lawrence J., William F. Lewis and Rebecca M. J. Yates. "An Approach For Assessing, Selecting And Using Finance Cases," JFED, 1987, v16, 56-64.)

Lewison, J. (Kent, W. A. and J. Lewison. "Wall Street's Cultural Hangup," FAJ, 1971, v27(2), 33-35.)

Leyder, R. (DeBrabander, B., D. Deschoolmeester, R. Leyder and E. Vanlommel. "The Effect Of Task Volume And Complexity Upon Computer Use," JOB, 1972, v45(1), 56-84.)

Li, Jane-Yu. "Do Commercial Banks Speculate On The Foreign Exchange Market?," AFPAF, 1989, v4(Supp), 151-170.

Liang, Ming-Yih. "Bank Flost, Mail Float And The Definition Of Money," JBF, 1986, v10(4), 467-635.

Liano, Kartono and Benton E. Gup. "The Day-Of-The-Week Effect In Stock Returns Over Business Cycles," FAJ, 1989, v45(4), 74-77.

Liao, Shu S. "A Spreadsheet Approach To Receivable Payments Pattern Analysis," JFED, 1987, v16, 78-85.

Liao, Shu S. "Shareholder Oriented Managers," FAJ, 1975, v31(6), 62-71.

Liao, Shu S. "Spreadsheet-Based Simulation Modeling For Risk Analysis," JFED, 1990, v19, 49-58.

Liao, Shu S. (Chang, Davis L. S. and Shu S. Liao. "Forecasting And Control Of Accounts Receivable Characterized By Unstable Payment Patterns: A Field Test," AFPAF, 1985, v1(1), 241-264.)

Liao, Shutsung. "Science And Technology-Related Research Publications From Taiwan And China: An Overall Comparison With Other Asian And European Countries," AFPAF, 1985, v1(Supp), 261-276.

Liao, Woody M. (Khumawala, Saleha B., Neil W. Polhemus and Woody M. Liao. "The Predictability Of Quarterly Cash Flows," JBFA, 1981, v8(4), 493-510.)

Liaw, K. Thomas. "A Microeconomic Approach To Tariff Reform In The Taiwanese Automobile Market," AFPAF, 1985, v1(Supp), 213-242.

Liaw, K. Thomas. Systematic Risk, Monopoly Power, And Factor Prices," IJOF, 1990, v22(2), 46-51.

Liaw, Thomas. (Hsu, Chih-Chang and Thomas Liaw. "Partial Equity Interests And Mangerial Incentives," IJOF, 1989, v1(2), 72-81.)

Libby, Robert. (Lavin, David and Robert Libby. "The Effect Of The Perceived Independence Of The Auditor On The Loan Decision," JBR, 1977-78, v8(2), 118-121.)

Liberman, Joseph. "Human Capital And The Financial Capital Market," JOB, 1980, v53(2), 165-192.

Lichtenberg, Frank R. and Donald Siegel. "The Effect Of Control Changes On The Productivity Of U.S. Manufacturing Plants," JACF, 1989, v2(2), 60-67.

Lichtenberg, Frank R. and Donald Siegel. "The Effects Of Leveraged Buyouts On Productivity And Related Aspects Of Firm Behavior," JFEC, 1990, v27(1), 165-194.

Lichtenstein, Sarah. (Slovic, Paul, Baruch Fischhoff, Sarah Lichtenstein, Bernard Corrigan and Barbara Combs. "Preference For Insuring Against Probable Small Losses: Insurance Implications," JRI, 1977, v44(2), 237-258.)

Liddell, Donald M., Jr. "Wheels Within Wheels," FAJ, 1954, v10(2), 51-54.

Lieber, Harvey and Bruce Rosinoff. "Evaluating The State's Role In Water Pollution Control," AREUEA, 1973, v1(2), 73-87.

Lieber, Zvi and Yair E. Orgler. "Optimal Borrowing And Bank Lending Policies: An Interactive Approach," JBF, 1986, v10(2), 255-266.

Lieber, Zvi. (Elton, Edwin J., Martin J. Gruber and Zvi Lieber. "Valuation, Optimum Investment And Financing For The Firm Subject To Regulation," JOF, 1975, v30(2), 401-425.)

Lieber, Zvi. (Garbade, Kenneth and Zvi Lieber. "On The Independence Of Transactions On The N.Y. Stock Exchange," JBF, 1977, v1(2), 151-172.)

Lieber, Zvi. (Schiff, Michael and Zvi Lieber. "A Model For The Integration Of Credit And Inventory Management," JOF, 1974, v29(1), 133-140.)

Lieberman, Charles. "The Long-Run And Short-Run Demand For Money, Revisited," JMCB, 1980, v12(1), 43-57.

Lieberman, Charles. (Clotfelder, Charles and Charles Lieberman. "On The Distributional Impact Of Federal Interest Rate Restrictions," JOF, 1978, v33(1), 199-213.)

Lieberman, Yehoshua. (Eppen, Gary D. and Yehoshua Liebermann. "Why Do Retailers Deal? An Inventory Explanation," JOB, 1984, v57(4), 519-530.)

Liebert, Albert C. "The Important Place Of Security Analyzation," FAJ, 1958, v14(2), 53-56.

Liebling, Herman I., Peter T. Bidwell and Karen E. Hall. "The Recent Performance Of Anticipation Surveys And Econometric Model Projections Of Investment Spending In The United States," JOB, 1976, v49(4), 451-477.

Lien, Da-Hsiang Donald. "A Note On Hedging Performance And Portfolio Effects," JFM, 1990, v10(2), 201-204.

Lien, Da-Hsiang Donald. "Asymmetric Arbitrage In Futures Markets: An Empirical Study," JFM, 1986, v6(4), 575-592.

Lien, Da-Hsiang Donald. "Cash Settlement Provisions On Futures Contracts," JFM, 1989, v9(3), 263-270.

Lien, Da-Hsiang Donald. "Entry-Deterring Contract Specification On Futures Markets," JFM, 1990, v10(1), 89-96.

Lien, Da-Hsiang Donald. "Hedger Response To Multiple Grades Of Delviery On Futures Markets," JFM, 1988, v8(6), 687-702.

Lien, Da-Hsiang Donald. "Optimal Hedging And Spreading On Wheat Futures Markets," JFM, 1989, v9(2), 163-170.

Lien, Da-Hsiang Donald. "Optical Settlement Specification On Futures Contracts," JFM, 1989, v9(4), 355-358.

Lien, Da-Hsiang Donald. "Sampled Data As A Basis Of Cash Settlement Price," JFM, 1989, v9(6), 583-588.

Lien, Da-Hsiang Donald. "The Inventory Effect In Commodity Futures Markets: An Empirical Study," JFM, 1987, v7(6), 637-652.

Liesz, Thomas J. and Mario G. C. Reyes. "The Use Of Piagetian Concepts To Enhance Student Performance In The Introductory Finance Course," JFED, 1989, v18, 8-14.

Lieu, Derming. "Option Pricing With Futures-Style Margining," JFM, 1990, v10(4), 327-338.

Lifson, K. A. and Brian R. Blackmarr. "Simulation And Optimization Models For Asset Deployment And Funds Sources Balancing Profit, Liquidity And Growth," JBR, 1973-74, v4(3), 239-255.

Lifton, Robert K. "An Understanding Of Public Realty Firms," FAJ, 1962, v18(5), 29-38.

Light, Jay O. (Bodie, Zvi, Jay O. Light, Randall Morck and Robert A. Taggart, Jr. "Corporate Pension Policy: An Empirical Investigation," FAJ, 1985, v41(5), 10-16.)

Lightstone, John B. (Elton, Edwin J., Martin J. Gruber and John B. Lightstone. "The Impact Of Bankruptcy On The Firm's Capital Structure, The Reasonableness Of Mergers, And The Risk Independence Of Projects," RFF, 1981, v3, 143-156.)

Lihara, Yoshio. (Kunimura, Michio and Yoshio Lihara. "Valuation Of Underwriting Agreements For Raising Capital In The Japanese Capital Market," JFQA, 1985, v20(2), 231-242.)

Likert, Rensis and William C. Pyle. "Human Resource Accounting - II," FAJ, 1971, v27(1), 75-84.

Lilien, Steven. (Katz, Steven, Steven Lilien and Bert Nelson. "Stock Market Behavior Around Bankruptcy Model Distress And Recovery Predictions," **FAJ**, 1985, v41(1), 70-74.)

Liljeblom, Eva (Berglund, Tom, Eva Liljeblom and Anders Loflund. "Estimating Betas On Daily Data For A Small Stock Market," **JBF**, 1989, v13(1), 42-64.)

Liljeblom, Eva. "The Informational Impact Of Announcements Of Stock Dividends And Stock Splits," **JBFA**, 1989, v16(5), 681-698.

Liljeblom, Eva. (Berglund, Tom and Eva Liljeblom. "Market Serial Correlation On A Small Security Market: A Note," **JOF**, 1988, v43(5), 1265-1274.)

Lilley, T. R. "European Equities For American Pension Funds," **FAJ**, 1959, v15(3), 37-40.

Lilley, Theodore R. (Patterson, Solon P., Dennis R. Bouwer, Theodore R. Lilley and Benjamin C. Korschot. "Long-Range Planning In The FAF," **FAJ**, 1979, v35(1), 23-26.)

Lilly, Claude C. (Dukes, William P. and Claude C. Lilly. "Short Term Risk-Return Impact Of The Holding Company Movement," **JRI**, 1977, v44(2), 320-328.)

Lilly, Claude C. and John M. Gleason. "A Dynamic Programming Approach To Equipment Loss Analysis," **JRI**, 1977, v44(2), 305-310.

Lim, J. (Saunders, A. and J. Lim. "Underpricing And The New Issue Process In Singapore," **JBF**, 1990, v14(2/3), 291-310.)

Lim, Kian-Guan. "A New Test Of The Three-Moment Capital Asset Pricing Model," **JFQA**, 1989, v24(2), 205-216.

Lim, Suk-Pil. (Narayanan, M. P. and Suk-Pil Lim. "On The Call Provision In Corporate Zero-Coupon Bonds," **JFQA**, 1989, v24(1), 91-104.)

Limmack, R. J. and C. W. R. Ward. "The October 1987 Stock Market Crash: An Exploratory Analysis Of Share Price Models," **JBF**, 1990, v14(2/3), 273-290.

Lin, Cheyeh. "A Price Index For Life Insurance," **JRI**, 1971, v38(4), 563-570.

Lin, Cheyeh. "A Price Index For Life Insurance: Reply," **JRI**, 1973, v40(4), 630.

Lin, Cheyeh. "Investment Experience And The Price Of Life Insurance," **JRI**, 1975, v42(3), 461-470.

Lin, Ji-Chai and John S. Howe. "Insider Trading In The OTC Market," **JOF**, 1990, v45(4), 1273-1284.

Lin, Kuan-Pin and John S. Oh. "Stability Of The U.S. Short-Run Money Demand Function, 1959-81," **JOF**, 1984, v39(5), 1383-1396.

Lin, Steven A. Y. "Effects Of Monetary Policy And Credit Conditions On The Housing Sector," **AREUEA**, 1973, v1(1), 8-30.

Lin, W. Thomas. "Applications Of Goal Programming In Accounting," **JBFA**, 1979, v6(4), 559-578.

Lin, Winston T. and Frank C. Jen. "Consumption, Investment, Market Price Of Risk, And The Risk-Free Rate," **JFQA**, 1980, v15(5), 1025-1040.

Lin, Winston T. "The Valuation Of Risk Assets And Prediction Of Money Changes Under Conditions Of Uncertainty," **FR**, 1979, v14(2), 1-20.

Lincoln, Mervyn. "An Empirical Study Of The Usefulness Of Accounting Ratios To Describe Levels Of Insolvency Risk," **JBF**, 1984, v8(2), 321-340.

Lindahl, Mary. "Measuring Hedging Effectiveness With R-Square: A Note," **JFM**, 1989, v9(5), 469-475.

Lindahl-Stevens, Mary. "Redefining Bull And Bear Markets," **FAJ**, 1980, v36(6), 76-77.

Lindahl-Stevens, Mary. "Some Popular Uses And Abuses Of Beta," **JPM**, 1977-78, v4(2), 13-17.

Lindenberg, E. B. (Bawa, Vijay S. and E. B. Lindenberg. "Capital Market Equilibrium In A Mean-Lower Partial Moment Framework," **JFEC**, 1977, v5(2), 189-200.)

Lindenberg, Eric B. (Leibowitz, Martin L., Stanley Kogelman and Eric B. Lindenberg. "A Shortfall Approach To The Creditor's Decision: How Much Leverage Can A Firm Support?," **FAJ**, 1990, v46(3), 43-52.)

Lindenberg, Eric B. and Stephen A. Ross. "Tobin's q Ratio And Industrial Organization," **JOB**, 1981, v54(1), 1-32.

Lindert, Peter H. "The Payments Impact Of Foreign Investment Controls," **JOF**, 1971, v26(5),1083-1099.

Lindert, Peter H. "The Payments Impact Of Foreign Investment Controls: Reply," **JOF**, 1976, v31(5), 1505-1508.

Lindholm, R. W. "The Federal National Mortgage Association," **JOF**, 1951, v6(1), 54-61.

Lindholm, Richard W. "Adjusting The Posture Of The U. S. Economy To Facilitate Corporate Freedom In International Actions," **JOF**, 1966, v21(2), 253-265.

Lindholm, Richard W. "Comment: Michigan's Employment Problem And The Elasticity Of Substitution," **JOB**, 1965, v38(2), 207-209.

Lindholm, Richard W. "Some Value-Added Tax Impacts On The International Competitiveness Of Producers," **JOF**, 1968, v23(4), 659-665.

Lindley, James T. (Moser, James T. and James T. Lindley. "A Simple Formula For Duration: An Extension," **FR**, 1989, v24(4), 611-615.)

Lindley, James T. (Sealey, C. W. and James T. Lindley. "Inputs, Outputs, And A Theory Of Production And Cost Of Depository Financial Institutions," **JOF**, 1977, v32(4), 1251-1266.)

Lindley, James T., Billy P. Helms and Mahmoud Haddad. "A Measurement Of The Errors In Intra-Period Compounding And Bond Valuation," **FR**, 1987, v22(1),33-52.

Lindow, Wesley. "In Defense Of Bank Liability Management," **JPM**, 1974-75, v1(4), 23-27.

Lindow, Wesley. "The Outlook For The Money Market," **JOF**, 1958, v13(2), 311-317.

Lindsay, Robert. "Housing Finance In The 1980's," **AREUEA**, 1980, v8(1), 118-147.

Lindsey, Lawrence B. (Bolster, Paul J., Lawrence B. Lindsey and Andrew Mitrusi. "Tax-Induced Trading: The Effect Of The 1986 Tax Reform Act On Stock Market Activity," **JOF**, 1989, v44(2), 327-344.)

Lindsley, David A. and Douglas V. Austin. "A Sensational New Investment," **FAJ**, 1977, v33(4), 53-54.

Lindsley, David A. (Austin, Douglas V. and David A. Lindsley. "Ohio Usury Ceiling And Residential Real Estate Development," **AREUEA**, 1976, v4(1), 83-96.)

Lindvall, John R. "New Issue Corporate Bonds, Seasoned Market Efficiency And Yield Spreads," **JOF**, 1977, v32(4), 1057-1068.

Lindvall, John R. (Logue, Dennis E. and John R. Lindvall. "The Behavior Of Investment Bankers: An Econometric Investigation," **JOF**, 1974, v29(1), 203-215.)

Ling, Cyril C. "Management By Objectives - Contemporary University Applications," **JRI**, 1970, v37(2), 269-277.

Ling, David C. (Chiang, Raymond, Tsong-Yue Lai and David C. Ling. "Retail Leasehold Interests: A Contingent Claim Analysis," **AREUEA**, 1986, v14(2), 216-229.)

Ling, David C. (Follain, James R. and David C. Ling. "Another Look At Tenure Choice, Inflation, And Taxes," **AREUEA**, 1988, v16(3), 207-229.)

Ling, David C. (Hendershott, Patric H. and David C. Ling. "Prospective Changes In The Tax Law And The Value Of Depreciable Real Estate," **AREUEA**, 1984, v12(3), 297-317.)

Ling, David C. and Michael J. Whinihan. "Valuing Depreciable Real Estate: A New Methodology," **AREUEA**, 1985, v13(2), 181-194.

Ling, David. (Chen, Andrew and David Ling. "Optimal Mortgage Refinancing With Stochastic Interest Rates," **AREUEA**, 1989, v17(3), 278-299.)

Ling, Robert F. and Harry V. Roberts. "IDA: An Approach To Interactive Data Analysis In Teaching And Research," **JOB**, 1975, v48(3), 411-451.

Link, Charles R. "Graduate Education, School Quality, Experience, Student Ability, And Earnings," **JOB**, 1975, v48(4), 477-491.

Linke, Charles M. and J. Kenton Zumwalt. "Estimation Biases In Discounted Cash Flow Analyses Of Equity Capital Cost In Rate Regulation," **FM**, 1984, v13(3),15-21.

Linke, Charles M. and Moon K. Kim. "More On The Weighted Average Cost Of Capital: A Comment And Analysis," **JFQA**, 1974, v9(6), 1069-1080.

Linke, Charles M. "The Use Of Inflation Factors In Determining Settlements In Personal Injury And Death Suits: Comment," **JRI**, 1977, v44(3), 474-478.

Linke, Charles M. (Bryan, William R. and Charles M. Linke. "The Estimation Of The Age/Earnings Profiles In Wrongful Death And Injury Cases: Comment," **JRI**, 1988, v55(1), 168-173.)

Linke, Charles M. (Bryan, William R. and Charles M. Linke. "Estimating Present Value Of Future Earnings: Experience With Dedicated Portfolios," **JRI**, 1988, v55(2), 273-286.)

Linke, Charles M. (Bryan, William R. and Charles M. Linke. "Estimating The Present Value Of Future Income Losses: An Historical Simulation 1900-1982: Comment," **JRI**, 1989, v56(3), 555-559.)

Linke, Charles M. (Bryan, William R., Thomas Gruca and Charles M. Linke. "The Present Value Of Future Earnings: Contemporaneous Differentials And The Performance Of Dedicated Portfolios," **JRI**, 1990, v57(3), 530-539.)

Linke, Charles M. (Gentry, James A. and Charles M. Linke. "Characteristics Of Life Insurers Entering The Mutual Fund Industry," **JRI**, 1971, v38(2), 237-250.)

Linke, Charles M. (Gilster, John E., Jr. and Charles M. Linke. "More On The Estimation Of Beta For Public Utilities: Biases Resulting From Structural Shifts In True Beta," **FM**, 1978, v7(3), 60-65.)

Linke, Charles M. (Reilly, Raymond R., Eugene F. Brigham, Charles M. Linke, Moon H. Kim and James S. Ang. "Weighted Average Vs. True Cost Of Capital: Reilly, Brigham, Linke and Kim Versus Ang," **FM**, 1974, v3(1), 80-85.)

Linke, Charles M. and J. Kenton Zumwalt. "The Irrelevance Of Compounding Frequency In Determining A Utility's Cost Of Equity," **FM**, 1987, v16(3), 65-69.

Linke, Charles M. and James A. Gentry. "Life Insurers, Variable Annuities And Mutual Funds: A Critical Study: Comment," **JRI**, 1971, v38(3), 477-483.

Linn, Scott C. and John J. McConnell. "An Empirical Investigation Of The Impact Of 'Antitakeover' Amendments On Common Stock Prices," **JFEC**, 1983, v11(1), 361-399.

Linn, Scott C. (Handa, Puneet and Scott C. Linn. "Equilibrium Factor Pricing With Heterogeneous Beliefs," **JFQA**, 1991, v26(1), 11-22.)

Linn, Scott C. (Lockwood, Larry J. and Scott C. Linn. "An Examination Of Stock Market Return Volatility During Overnight And Intraday Periods, 1964-1989," **JOF**, 1990, v45(2), 591-602.)

Linn, Scott C. and J. Michael Pinegar. "The Effect Of Issuing Preferred Stock On Common And Preferred Stockholder Wealth," **JFEC**, 1988, v22(1), 155-184.

Linn, Scott C. and Larry J. Lockwood. "Short-Term Stock Price Patterns: NYSE, AMEX, OTC," **JPM**, 1987-88, v14(2), 30-34.

Linn, Scott C. and Michael S. Rozeff. "The Effect Of Voluntary Spin-Offs On Stock Prices: The Anergy Hypothesis," **AFPAF**, 1985, v1(1), 265-292.

Linneman, Peter and Susan Wachter. "The Impacts Of Borrowing Constraints On Homeownerhip," **AREUEA**, 1989, v17(4), 389-402.

Linneman, Peter. (Gyourko, Joseph and Peter Linneman. "Owner-Occupied Homes, Income-Producing Properties, And REITs As Inflation Hedges: Empirical Findings," **JREFEC**, 1988, v1(4), 347-372.)

Linsmeier, Thomas J., R. D. Nair and Jerry J. Weygandt. "UK Tax Legislation And The Switch To The Liability Method For Income Taxes," **JBFA**, 1988, v15(3), 335-352.

Lintner, John. "Inflation And Security Returns," **JOF**, 1975, v30(2), 259-280.

Lintner, John. "Security Prices, Risk, And Maximal Gains From Diversification," **JOF**, 1965, v20(4), 587-615.

Lintner, John. "The Aggregation Of Investor's Diverse Judgments And Preferences In Purely Competitive Security Markets," **JFQA**, 1969, v4(4), 347-400.

Lintner, John. "The Cost Of Capital And Optimal Financing Of Corporate Growth," **JOF**, 1963, v18(2), 292-310.

Lintner, John. "The Effect Of Short Selling And Margin Requirements In Perfect Capital Markets," **JFQA**, 1971, v6(5), 1173-1195.

Lintner, John. (Butters, J. Keith and John Lintner. "Tax And Non-Tax Motivations For Mergers," **JOF**, 1951, v6(4), 361-382.)

Linton, M. Albert. "Permanent Insurance Vs. Term And Separate Investment," **JRI**, 1939, v6, 5-19.

Linton, M. Albert. "The Effect Of Inflation Upon Life Insurance," **JRI**,

1934, v1, 1-8.

Linton, M. Albert. "The Variable Annuity: Problems And Prospects," *JOF*, 1956, v11(2), 121-141.

Lipe, Robert. (Kormendi, Roger and Robert Lipe. "Earnings Innovations, Earnings Persistence, And Stock Returns," *JOB*, 1987, v60(3), 323-346.)

Lipka, Roland. "Effects Of Taxation Of Social Security Benefits On Portfolio Revisions," *JRI*, 1987, v54(4), 737-751.

Lipka, Roland. (Kim, Jeong-Bon and Roland Lipka. "Effects Of Accounting Choice On The Explanation Of The Market Risk In The Oil And Gas Industry," *JBFA*, 1991, v18(1), 61-84.)

Lipman, Barton L. (Bagnoli, Mark and Barton L. Lipman. "Successful Takeovers With Exclusion," *RFS*, 1988-89, v1(1), 89-110.)

Lipman, Barton. (Bagnoli, Mark, Roger Gordon and Barton L. Lipman. "Stock Repurchase As A Takeover Defense," *RFS*, 1989, v2(3), 423-443.)

Lippincott, Lincoln H. "A General System Of Social Insurance Is Not A Practicable Ideal," *JRI*, 1935, v2, 48-55.

Lippitt, Jeffrey. (Brown, Sudro and Jeffrey Lippitt. "Are Deferred Taxes Discountable?," *JBFA*, 1987, v14(1), 121-130.)

Lippman, Steven A. "Optimal Reinsurance," *JFQA*, 1972, v7(5), 2151-2155.

Lippman, Steven A., John M. McCall and Wayne L. Winston. "Constant Absolute Risk Aversion, Bankruptcy, And Wealth-Dependent Decisions," *JOB*, 1980, v53(3), 285-296.

Lipscomb, Joseph B. and J. Brian Gray. "An Empirical Investigation Of Four Market-Derived Ajustment Methods," *JRER*, 1990, v5(1), 53-66.

Lipton, M. (Boies, D., D. Carroll, A. Fleischer, J. Grundfest, J. Ira Harris, M. Lipton, R. Monks, A. Oliver, L. Sachnoff and J. Wilcox. "Panel: Corporate Governance: The Role Of Boards Of Directors In Takeover Bids And Defenses," *JACF*, 1989, v2(2), 6-35.)

Lipton, Milton. "Productivity Trends," *FAJ*, 1956, v12(2), 87-92.

Liro, Joseph R. (Hill, Joanne M. and Joseph R. Liro. "Incorporating Expected Inflation Into Market Model Estimates," *FR*, 1982, v17(3), 112-127.)

Liro, Joseph. (Hill, Joanne, Joseph Liro and Thomas Schneeweis. "Hedging Performance Of GNMA Futures Under Rising And Falling Interest Rates," *JFM*, 1983, v3(4), 403-413.)

Liss, Herman. "A Backward Glance O'er Travelled Roads," *FAJ*, 1982, v38(2), 55-59.

Lister, Roger J. "Business Finance - An Evolving Field Of Study," *JBFA*, 1978, v5(1), 1-26.

Lister, Roger J. "Interest, Morality, Orthodoxy, Gambling And Karim," *JBFA*, 1988, v15(4), 585-596.

Lister, Roger. "The Cost Of Retained Earnings: A Further Note, An Illustration And A Computer Program," *JBFA*, 1983, v10(3), 389-393.

Lister, Roger. "The Cost Of Retained Earnings: A Comment On Some Recent Work," *JBFA*, 1981, v8(2), 155-160.

Litschert, Robert L. (Nicholson, Edward A. and Robert L. Litschert. "Long-Range Planning In Banking: Ten Cases In The U.S. And Britain," *JBR*, 1973-74, v4(1), 31-40.)

Litterman, Robert and Thomas Iben. "Corporate Bond Valuation And The Term Structure Of Credit Spreads," *JPM*, 1991, v17(3), 52-64.

Little, John D. C. and Jeremy F. Shapiro. "A Theory For Pricing Nonfeatured Products In Supermarkets," *JOB*, 1980, v53(3), S199-S210.

Little, Patricia Knain. "Financial Futures And Immunization," *JFR*, 1986, v9(1), 1-12.

Little, Patricia Knain. "Negative Cash Flows, Duration, And Immunization: A Note," *JOF*, 1984, v39(1), 283-288.

Little, Wm. Brian and Steven B. Klinsky. "How Leveraged Buy-Outs Can Really Work: A Look At Three Cases," *JACF*, 1989, v2(1), 71-75.

Litts, Raymond N. "Another Interesting Tool For Stock Appraisal," *FAJ*, 1954, v10(5), 59-62.

Litzenberger, R. H. and A. P. Budd. "Secular Trends In Risk Premiums," *JOF*, 1972, v27(4), 857-864.

Litzenberger, R. H. and O. M. Joy. "Target Rates Of Return And Corporate Asset And Liability Structure Under Uncertainty," *JFQA*, 1971, v6(2), 675-686.

Litzenberger, R. H. (Budd, A. P. and R. H. Litzenberger. "Changes In The Supply Of Money, The Firm's Market Value And Cost Of Capital," *JOF*, 1973, v28(1), 49-57.)

Litzenberger, Robert H. (Lang, Larry H. P. and Robert H. Litzenberger. "Dividend Announcements: Cash Flow Signalling Vs. Free Cash Flow Hypothesis?," *JFEC*, 1989, v24(1), 181-192.)

Litzenberger, Robert H. and Charles P. Jones. "The Capital Structure And The Cost Of Capital: Comment," *JOF*, 1970, v25(3), 669-673.

Litzenberger, Robert H. and Howard B. Sosin. "The Performance And Potential Of Dual Purpose Funds," *JPM*, 1977-78, v4(3), 56-68.

Litzenberger, Robert H. and Howard B. Sosin. "The Structure And Management Of Dual Purpose Funds," *JFEC*, 1977, v4(2), 203-230.

Litzenberger, Robert H. and Howard B. Sosin. "A Comparison Of Capital Structure Decisions Of Regulated And Non-Regulated Firms," *FM*, 1979, v8(3), 17-21.

Litzenberger, Robert H. and Krishna Ramaswamy. "Dividends, Short Selling Restrictions, Tax-Induced Investor Clienteles And Market Equilibrium," *JOF*, 1980, v35(2), 469-482.

Litzenberger, Robert H. and Ehud I. Ronn. "A Utility-Based Model Of Common Stock Price Movements," *JOF*, 1986, v41(1), 67-92.

Litzenberger, Robert H. and Cherukuri U. Rao. "Portfolio Theory And Industry Cost-Of-Capital Estimates," *JFQA*, 1972, v7(2), 1443-1462.

Litzenberger, Robert H. and Howard Sosin. "Taxation And The Incidence Of Home Ownership Across Income Groups," *JOF*, 1978, v33(3), 947-961.

Litzenberger, Robert H. and James C. Van Horne. "Elimination Of The Double Taxation Of Dividends And Corporate Financial Policy," *JOF*, 1978, v33(3), 737-750.

Litzenberger, Robert H. and Charles P. Jones. "Adjusting For Risk In The Capital Budget Of A Growth-Oriented Company: Comment," *JFQA*, 1969, v4(3), 301-304.

Litzenberger, Robert H. and Jacques Rolfo. "An International Study Of Tax Effects On Government Bonds," *JOF*, 1984, v39(1), 1-22.

Litzenberger, Robert H. and Krishna Ramaswamy. "The Effects Of Dividends On Common Stock Prices: Tax Effects Or Information Effects?," *JOF*, 1982, v37(2), 429-443.

Litzenberger, Robert H. and A. P. Budd. "A Note On Geometric Mean Portfolio Selection And The Market Prices Of Equities," *JFQA*, 1971, v6(5), 1277-1282.

Litzenberger, Robert H. and Jacques Rolfo. "Arbitrage Pricing, Transaction Costs And Taxation Of Capital Gains: A Study Of Government Bonds With The Same Maturity Date," *JFEC*, 1984, v13(3), 337-351.

Litzenberger, Robert H. and Howard B. Sosin. "The Theory Of Recapitalizations And The Evidence Of Dual Purpose Funds," *JOF*, 1977, v32(5), 1433-1455.

Litzenberger, Robert H. and Krishna Ramaswamy. "The Effect Of Personal Taxes And Dividends On Capital Asset Prices: Theory And Empirical Evidence," *JFEC*, 1979, v7(2), 163-196.

Litzenberger, Robert H. and O. Maurice Joy. "Decentralized Capital Budgeting Decisions And Shareholder Wealth Maximization," *JOF*, 1975, v30(4), 993-1002.

Litzenberger, Robert H. and David P. Rutenberg. "Size And Timing Of Corporate Bond Flotations," *JFQA*, 1972, v7(1), 1343-1359.

Litzenberger, Robert H. and Alan P. Rudd. "Corporate Investment Criteria And The Valuation Of Risk Assets," *JFQA*, 1970, v5(4), 395-419.

Litzenberger, Robert H. "Equilibrium In The Equity Market Under Uncertainty," *JOF*, 1969, v24(4), 663-671.

Litzenberger, Robert H. "Some Observations On Capital Structure And The Impact Of Recent Recapitalizations On Share Prices," *JFQA*, 1986, v21(1), 59-71.

Litzenberger, Robert H. "The Effect Of Credit On The Interest Elasticity Of The Transaction Demand For Cash: Comment," *JOF*, 1971, v26(5), 1161-1162.

Litzenberger, Robert H. (Barclay, Michael J. and Robert H. Litzenberger. "Announcement Effects Of New Equity Issues And The Use Of Intraday Price Data," *JFEC*, 1988, v21(1), 71-100.)

Litzenberger, Robert H. (Barclay, Michael J., Robert H. Litzenberger and Jerold B. Warner. "Private Information, Trading Volume, And Stock-Return Variances," *RFS*, 1990, v3(2), 233-254.)

Litzenberger, Robert H. (Breeden, Douglas T. and Robert H. Litzenberger. "Prices Of State-Contingent Claims Implicit In Option Prices," *JOB*, 1978, v51(4), 621-652.)

Litzenberger, Robert H. (Breeden, Douglas T., Michael R. Gibbons and Robert H. Litzenberger. "Empirical Tests Of The Consumption-Oriented CAPM," *JOF*, 1989, v44(2), 231-262.)

Litzenberger, Robert H. (Glenn, David W. and Robert H. Litzenberger. "An Interindustry Approach To Econometric Cost Of Capital Estimation," *RIF*, 1979, v1, 53-76.)

Litzenberger, Robert H. (Grauer, Frederick L. A. and Robert H. Litzenberger. "The Pricing Of Commodity Futures Contracts, Nominal Bonds And Other Risky Assets Under Commodity Price Uncertainty," *JOF*, 1979, v34(1), 69-83.)

Litzenberger, Robert H. (Grauer, Frederick L. A., Robert H. Litzenberger and Richard E. Stehle. "Sharing Rules And Equilibrium In An International Market Under Uncertainty," *JFEC*, 1976, v3(3), 233-256.)

Litzenberger, Robert H. (Jones, Charles P. and Robert H. Litzenberger. "Earnings Seasonality And Stock Prices," *FAJ*, 1969, v25(6), 57-59.)

Litzenberger, Robert H. (Jones, Charles P. and Robert H. Litzenberger. "Quarterly Earnings Reports And Intermediate Stock Price Trends," *JOF*, 1970, v25(1), 143-148.)

Litzenberger, Robert H. (Kraus, Alan and Robert H. Litzenberger. "A State-Preference Model Of Optimal Financial Leverage," *JOF*, 1973, v28(4), 911-922.)

Litzenberger, Robert H. (Kraus, Alan and Robert H. Litzenberger. "Skewness Preference And The Valuation Of Risk Assets," *JOF*, 1976, v31(4), 1085-1100.)

Litzenberger, Robert H. (Kraus, Alan and Robert H. Litzenberger. "Market Equilibrium In A Multiperiod State Preference Model With Logarithmic Utility," *JOF*, 1975, v30(5), 1213-1227.)

Litzenberger, Robert H. (Rao, Cherukuri U. and Robert H. Litzenberger. "Leverage And The Cost Of Capital In A Less Developed Capital Market: Comment," *JOF*, 1971, v26(3), 777-782.)

Litzenberger, Robert H. (Tuttle, Donald L. and Robert H. Litzenberger. "Leverage, Diversification And Capital Market Effects On A Risk-Adjusted Capital Budgeting Framework," *JOF*, 1968, v23(3), 427-443.)

Litzenberger, Robert H., O. Maurice Joy and Charles P. Jones. "Ordinal Predictions And The Selection Of Common Stocks," *JFQA*, 1971, v6(4), 1059-1068.

Litzenberger, Robert, Krishna Ramaswamy and Howard Sosin. "On The CAPM Approach To The Estimation Of A Public Utility's Cost Of Equity Capital," *JOF*, 1980, v35(2), 369-383.

Litzenberger, Robert. (Gatto, Mary Ann, Robert Geske, Robert Litzenberger and Howard Sosin. "Mutual Fund Insurance," *JFEC*, 1980, v8(3), 283-317.)

Litzenberger, Robert. (Gonzales, Nestor, Robert Litzenberger and Jacques Rolfo. "On Mean Variance Models Of Capital Structure And The Absurdity Of Their Predictions," *JFQA*, 1977, v12(2), 165-179.)

Litzenberger, Robert. (Huang, Chi-fu and Robert Litzenberger. "On The Necessary Condition For Linear Sharing And Separation: A Note," *JFQA*, 1985, v20(3), 381-384.)

Litzenberger, Robert. (Kraus, Alan and Robert Litzenberger. "On The Distributional Conditions For A Consumption-Oriented Three Moment CAPM," *JOF*, 1983, v38(5), 1381-1391.)

Liu, Crocker H. (Dotzour, Mark G., Terry V. Grissom, Crocker H. Liu and Thomas Pearson. "Highest And Best Use: The Evolving Paradigm," *JRER*, 1990, v5(1), 17-32.)

Liu, Crocker H. (Grissom, Terry V., David Hartzell and Crocker H. Liu. "An Approach To Industrial Real Estate Market Segmentation And Valuation Using The Arbitrage Pricing Paradigm," *AREUEA*, 1987, v15(3), 199-219.)

Liu, Crocker H., David J. Hartzell, Terry V. Grissom and Wylie Grieg. "The Composition Of The Market Portfolio And Real Estate Investment Performance," *AREUEA*, 1990, v18(1), 49-75.

Liu, Crocker H., David J. Hartzell, Wylie Greig and Terry V. Grissom. "The Integration Of The Real Estate Market And The Stock Market: Some Preliminary Evidence," JREFEC, 1990, v3(3), 261-282.

Liu, Crocker H., Terry V. Grissom and David J. Hartzell. "The Impact Of Market Imperfections On Real Estate Returns And Optimal Investment Portfolios," AREUEA, 1990, v18(4), 453-478.

Liu, Jin Tan and V. Kerry Smith. "Risk Communication And Attitude Change: Taiwan's National Debate Over Nuclear Power," JRU, 1990, v3(4), 331-350.

Liu, Pu and Anjan V. Thakor. "Interest Yields, Credit Ratings, And Economic Characteristics Of State Bonds: An Empirical Analysis," JMCB, 1984, v16(3), 344-351.

Liu, Pu and Anjan V. Thakor. "Interest Yields, Credit Ratings, And Economic Characteristics Of State Bonds: Reply," JMCB, 1988, v20(4), 696-697.

Liu, Pu and William T. Moore. "The Impact Of Split Bond Ratings On Risk Premia," FR, 1987, v22(1), 71-86.

Liu, Pu, Stanley D. Smith and Azmat A. Syed. "Stock Price Reactions To The Wall Street Journal's Securities Recommendations," JFQA, 1990, v25(3), 399-410.

Liu, Pu. (Perry, Larry G., Pu Liu and Dorla A. Evans. "Modified Bond Ratings: Further Evidence On The Effect Of Split Ratings On Corporate Bond Yields," JBFA, 1988, v15(2), 231-242.)

Liu, Pu. (Syed, Azmat A., Pu Liu and Stanley D. Smith. "The Exploitation Of Inside Information At The Wall Street Journal: A Test Of Strong Form Efficiency," FR, 1989, v24(4), 567-580.)

Liu, Y. Angela. (Hsueh, L. Paul and Y. Angela Liu. "An Examination Of The Biases In Estimating The Benefit Of Debt Insurance," FR, 1990, v25(3), 473-486.)

Liu, Y. Angela. (Hsueh, L. Paul and Y. Angela Liu. "The Effectiveness Of Debt Insurance As A Valid Signal Of Bond Quality," JRI, 1990, v57(4), 691-700.)

Liviatan, Nissan. (Landskroner, Yoram and Nissan Liviatan. "Risk Premia And The Sources Of Inflation," JMCB, 1981, v13(2), 205-214.)

Liviatan, Nissan. (Levhari, David and Nissan Liviatan. "The Effects Of Increasing Uncertainty Of Inflation On Consumer's Behavior With And Without Indexation," RIF, 1979, v1, 77-94.)

Livingston, D. T. and James B. Henry. "The Effect Of Employee Stock Ownership Plans On Corporate Profits," JRI, 1980, v47(3), 491-505.

Livingston, D. T. and James B. Henry. "The Effect Of Employee Stock Ownership Plans On Corporate Profits: Reply," JRI, 1983, v50(3), 498-499.

Livingston, M. (Brooks, R. and M. Livingston. "A Note On The Variance Of Spot Interest Rates," JBF, 1990, v14(1), 215-226.)

Livingston, Miles and John Caks. "A 'Duration' Fallacy," JOF, 1977, v32(1), 185-187.

Livingston, Miles and Suresh Jain. "Flattening Of Bond Yield Curves For Long Maturities," JOF, 1982, v37(1), 157-167.

Livingston, Miles. "A Note On The Issue Of Long-Term Pure Discount Bonds," JOF, 1979, v34(1), 241-246.

Livingston, Miles. "A Theory Of Humpbacked Bond Yield Curves," JOF, 1977, v32(5), 1747-1751.

Livingston, Miles. "Bond Refunding Reconsidered: Comment," JOF, 1980, v35(1), 191-195.

Livingston, Miles. "Bond Taxation And The Shape Of The Yield-To-Maturity Curve," JOF, 1979, v34(1), 189-196.

Livingston, Miles. "Comment: Convertible Debt Financing," JFQA, 1977, v12(3), 515-518.

Livingston, Miles. "Duration And Risk Assessment For Bonds And Common Stocks: A Note," JOF, 1978, v33(1), 293-295.

Livingston, Miles. "Flattening Of Bond Yield Curves," JFR, 1987, v10(1), 17-24.

Livingston, Miles. "Industry Movements Of Common Stocks," JOF, 1977, v32(3), 861-874.

Livingston, Miles. "Measuring Bond Price Volatility," JFQA, 1979, v14(2), 343-349.

Livingston, Miles. "Measuring The Benefit Of A Bond Refunding: The Problem Of Nonmarketable Call Options," FM, 1987, v16(1), 38-40.

Livingston, Miles. "Taxation And Bond Market Equilibrium In A World Of Uncertain Future Interest Rates: Reply," JFQA, 1981, v16(5), 779-781.

Livingston, Miles. "Taxation And Bond Market Equilibrium In A World Of Uncertain Future Interest Rates," JFQA, 1979, v14(1), 11-27.

Livingston, Miles. "The Cheapest Deliverable Bond For The CBT Treasury Bond Futures Contract," JFM, 1984, v4(2), 161-172.

Livingston, Miles. "The Delivery Option On Forward Contracts," JFQA, 1987, v22(1), 79-88.

Livingston, Miles. "The Effect Of Bond Refunding On Shareholder Wealth: Comment," JOF, 1979, v34(3), 801-804.

Livingston, Miles. "The Effect Of Coupon Level On Treasury Bond Futures Delivery," JFM, 1987, v7(3), 301-310.

Livingston, Miles. "The Pricing Of Municipal Bonds," JFQA, 1982, v17(2), 179-193.

Livingston, Miles. "The Pricing Of Premium Bonds," JFQA, 1979, v14(3), 517-527.

Livingston, Miles. "The Pricing Of Premium Bonds: Reply," JFQA, 1981, v16(3), 403-406.

Livingston, Miles. (Arditti, Fred D. and Miles Livingston. "The Relative Price Volatility Of Taxable And Non-Taxable Bonds: A Note," JOF, 1982, v37(3), 877-881.)

Livingston, Miles. (Brooks, Robert, Haim Levy and Miles Livingston. "The Coupon Effect On Term Premiums," JFI, 1989, v12(1), 15-22.)

Livingstone, J. Leslie and Anis D. Sherali. "Construction Work In Progress In The Public Utility Rate Base: The Effect Of Multiple Projects And Growth," FM, 1979, v8(1), 42-50.

Livingstone, J. Leslie. (Largay, James A., III and J. Leslie Livingstone. "Current Value Accounting Neglects Liabilities," FAJ, 1978, v34(2), 65-71.)

Livnat, Joshua and Ashwinpaul C. Sondhi. "Finance Subsidiaries: Their Formation And Consolidation," JBFA, 1986, v13(1), 137-148.

Livnat, Joshua. "Disclosure Of Pension Liabilities: The Information Content Of Unfunded Vested Benefits And Unfunded Past Service Cost," JBFA, 1984, v11(1), 73-88.

Livnat, Joshua. (Amit, Raphael and Joshua Livnat. "Grouping Of Conglomerates By Their Segments' Economic Attributes: Towards A More Meaningful Ratio Analysis," JBFA, 1990, v17(1), 85-100.)

Livnat, Joshua. (Bar-Yosef, Sasson, Jeffrey L. Callen and Joshua Livnat. "Autoregressive Modeling Of Earnings--Investment Causality," JOF, 1987, v42(1), 11-28.)

Livnat, Joshua. (Barlev, Benzion and Joshua Livnat. "The Statement Of Changes In Financial Position: It Relationship With Security Prices," JBFA, 1986, v13(2), 223-238.)

Livnat, Joshua. (Barlev, Benzion, Joshua Livnat and Aharon Yoran. "Advance Payments During Inflationary Periods," JBFA, 1982, v8(3), 413-426.)

Lizondo, Jose Saul and Donald J. Mathieson. "The Stability Of The Demand For International Reserves," JIMF, 1987, v6(3), 251-282.

Ljung, Greta. (Kane, Alex, Leonard Rosenthal and Greta Ljung. "Tests Of The Fisher Hypothesis With International Data: Theory And Evidence," JOF, 1983, v38(2), 539-551,)

Lloyd, Richmond M. (Brown, George F., Jr. and Richmond M. Lloyd. "Static Models Of Bank Credit Expansion," JFQA, 1971, v6(3), 995-1014.)

Lloyd, Sam R. "Insurance Education In The Business Schools: Growing Or Going?," JRI, 1969, v36(4), 632-636.

Lloyd, William P. and Cheng F. Lee. "Block Recursive Systems In Asset Pricing Models," JOF, 1976, v31(4), 1101-1113.

Lloyd, William P. and Naval K. Modani. "Stocks, Bonds, Bills, And Time Diversification," JPM, 1982-83, v9(3), 7-11.

Lloyd, William P. and Richard L. Haney, Jr. "Time Diversification: Surest Route To Lower Risk," JPM, 1979-80, v6(3), 5-9.

Lloyd, William P. and Richard A. Shick. "A Test Of Stone's Two-Index Model Of Return," JFQA, 1977, v12(3), 363-376.

Lloyd, William P. and Steven J. Goldstein. "Simulation Of Portfolio Returns: Varying Numbers Of Securities And Holding Periods," JFR, 1982, v5(1), 27-38.

Lloyd, William P. and Steven J. Goldstein. "Called Bonds: How Does The Investor Fare?," JPM, 1981-82, v8(1), 62-63.

Lloyd, William P. "A Note On The Use Of The Two-Stage Least Squares Estimator In Financial Models," JFQA, 1975, v10(1), 143-149.

Lloyd, William P. (Hand, John H., William P. Lloyd and Robert B. Rogow. "Agency Relationships In The Close Corporation," FM, 1982, v11(1), 25-30.)

Lloyd, William P. (Jahera, John S., Jr., William P. Lloyd and Daniel E. Page. "The Relationship Between Financial Performance And Stock Market Based Measures Of Corporate Diversification," FR, 1987, v22(4),379-390.)

Lloyd, William P. (Jahera, John S., Jr. and William P. Lloyd. "Exchange Listing And Size: Effects On Excess Returns," JBFA, 1989, v16(5), 675-680.)

Lloyd, William P. (Lee, Cheng Few and William P. Lloyd. "Block Recursive Systems In Asset Pricing Models: An Extension," JOF, 1978, v33(2), 640-644.)

Lloyd, William P. (Lee, Cheng F. and William P. Lloyd. "The Capital Asset Pricing Model Expressed As A Recursive System: An Empirical Investigation," JFQA, 1976, v11(2), 237-249.)

Lloyd, William P., John H. Hand and Naval K. Modani. "The Effect Of Portfolio Construction Rules On The Relationship Between Portfolio Size And Effective Diversification," JFR, 1981, v4(3), 183-193.

Lloyd, William P., John S. Jahera, Jr. and Steven J. Goldstein. "The Relation Between Returns, Ownership Structure, And Market Value," JFR, 1986, v9(2), 171-177.

Lloyd, William P., Steven J. Goldstein and Robert B. Rogow. "International Portfolio Diversification Of Real Assets: An Update," JBFA, 1981, v8(1), 45-50.

Lloyd-Davies, Peter R. "Optimal Financial Policy In Imperfect Markets," JFQA, 1975, v10(3), 457-482.

Lloyd-Davies, Peter R. (Goldberg, Michael A. and Peter R. Lloyd-Davies. "Standby Letters Of Credit: Are Banks Overextending Themselves?," JBR, 1985-86, v16(1), 28-39.)

Lloyd-Davies, Peter and Michael Canes. "Stock Prices And The Publication Of Second-Hand Information," JOB, 1978, v51(1), 43-56.

Lloyd-Davies, Peter. (Rosen, Richard J., Peter Lloyd-Davies and David B. Humphrey. "New Banking Powers: A Portfolio Analysis Of Bank Investment In Real Estate," JBF, 1989, v13(3), 355-366.)

Lo, Andrew W. "Semi-Parametric Upper Bounds For Option Prices And Expected Payoffs," JFEC, 1987, v19(2), 373-388.

Lo, Andrew W. "Statistical Tests Of Contingent-Claims Asset-Pricing Models: A New Methodology," JFEC, 1986, v17(1), 143-174.

Lo, Andrew W. and A. Craig MacKinlay. "Stock Market Prices Do Not Follow Random Walks: Evidence From A Simple Specification Test," RFS, 1988-89, v1(1), 41-66.

Lo, Andrew W. and A. Craig MacKinlay. "When Are Contrarian Profits Due To Stock Market Overreaction?," RFS, 1990, v3(2), 175-206.

Lo, Andrew W. and A. Craig MacKinlay. "Data-Snooping Biases In Tests Of Financial Asset Pricing Models," RFS, 1990, v3(3), 431-468.

Lobo, Gerald J., R. D. Nair and In Man Song. "Additional Evidence On The Information Content Of Dividends," JBFA, 1986, v13(4), 597-608.

Lobue, Marie. "Categorical Bank Acquisitions," JBR, 1983-84, v14(4), 274-282.

Lochoff, Roland. (Kahn, Ronald N. and Roland Lochoff. "Convexity And Exceptional Return," JPM, 1990, v16(2), 43-47.)

Locke, Stuart M. (Bird, Ronald G. and Stuart M. Locke. "Financial Accounting Reports: A Market Model Of Disclosure," JBFA, 1981, v8(1), 27-44.)

Locke, Stuart. (Bird, Ron and Stuart Locke. "Financial Accounting Reports: A Market Model Of Disclosure: A Reply," JBFA, 1983, v10(3), 495-497.)

Lockett, A. Geoffrey and Anthony E. Gear. "Multistage Capital Budgeting Under Uncertainty," JFQA, 1975, v10(1), 21-36.

Lockett, A. Geoffrey and Cyril Tomkins. "The Discount Rate Problem In Capital Rationing Situations: Comment," JFQA, 1970, v5(2), 245-260.

Lockwood, L. J. and T. H. McInish. "Tests Of Stability For Variances And Means Of Overnight/Intraday Returns During Bull And Bear

Markets," *JBF*, 1990, v14(6), 1243-1254.

Lockwood, Larry J. (Brown, Keith C., Larry J. Lockwood and Scott L. Lummer. "An Examination Of Event Dependency And Structural Change In Security Pricing Models," *JFQA*, 1985, v20(3), 315-334.)

Lockwood, Larry J. (Linn, Scott C. and Larry J. Lockwood. "Short-Term Stock Price Patterns: NYSE, AMEX, OTC," *JPM*, 1987-88, v14(2), 30-34.)

Lockwood, Larry J. and K. Rao Kadiyala. "Measuring Investment Performance With A Stochastic Parameter Regression Model," *JBF*, 1988, v11(3), 457-468.

Lockwood, Larry J. and Scott C. Linn. "An Examination Of Stock Market Return Volatility During Overnight And Intraday Periods, 1964-1989," *JOF*, 1990, v45(2), 591-602.

Lockyer, F. G. "Cash As An Item Of Stock: A Reply," *JBFA*, 1979, v6(1), 120.

Loderer, Claudio P. and Dennis P. Sheehan. "Corporate Bankruptcy And Managers' Self-Serving Behavior," *JOF*, 1989, v44(4), 1059-1076;.

Loderer, Claudio and Heinz Zimmermann. "Stock Offerings In A Different Institutional Setting: The Swiss Case, 1973-1983," *JBF*, 1988, v11(3), 353-378.

Loderer, Claudio and Kenneth Martin. "Corporate Acquisitions By Listed Firms: The Experience Of A Comprehensive Sample," *FM*, 1990, v19(4), 17-33.

Loderer, Claudio. "A Test Of The OPEC Cartel Hypothesis: 1974-1983," *JOF*, 1985, v40(3), 991-1006.

Loderer, Claudio. (Benelli, Giuseppe, Claudio Loderer and Thomas Lys. "Labor Participation In Corporate Policy-Making Decisions: West Germany's Experience With Codetermination," *JOB*, 1987, v60(4),553-576.)

Loderer, Claudio. (Lewellen, Wilbur, Claudio Loderer and Ahron Rosenfeld. "Mergers, Executive Risk Reduction, And Stockholder Wealth," *JFQA*, 1989, v24(4), 459-472.)

Lodge, Howard R. "Variations In The Use Of Futures By Commercial Banks," *RFM*, 1985, v4(2),178-184.

Loeb, Gerald M. "Buy Chesapeake & Ohio - Sell St. Paul," *FAJ*, 1964, v20(5), 48.

Loeb, Gerald M. "Peter And Leonard At Annual Meeting," *FAJ*, 1971, v27(3), 28-31.

Loeb, Martin. (Aharony, Joseph and Martin Loeb. "Mean-Variance Vs. Stochastic Dominance: Some Empirical Findings On Efficient Sets," *JBF*, 1977, v1(1), 95-102.)

Loeb, Thomas F. "Trading Cost: The Critical Link Between Investment Information And Results," *FAJ*, 1983, v39(3), 39-44.

Loeffler, Thomas A. (Fielitz, Bruce D. and Thomas A. Loeffler. "A Linear Programming Model For Commercial Bank Liquidity Management," *FM*, 1979, v8(3), 41-50.)

Loescher, Samuel M. "Geographical Pricing Policies And The Law," *JOB*, 1954, v27(3), 211-224.

Loewenstein, George and Jane Mather. "Dynamic Processes In Risk Perception," *JRU*, 1990, v3(2), 155-176.

Loewenstein, Uri. (Bhagat, Sanjai, James A. Brickley and Uri Loewenstein. "The Pricing Effects Of Interfirm Cash Tender Offers," *JOF*, 1987, v42(4), 965-986.)

Loewenstein, Uri. (Coles, Jeffrey L. and Uri Loewenstein. "Equilibrium Pricing And Portfolio Composition In The Presence Of Uncertain Parameters," *JFEC*, 1988, v22(2), 279-304.)

Loewenstein, Uri. (Kalay, Avner and Uri Loewenstein. "The Informational Content Of The Timing Of Dividend Announcements," *JFEC*, 1986, v16(3),373-388.)

Loewenstein, Uri. (Kalay, Avner and Uri Loewenstein. "Predictable Events And Excess Returns: The Case Of Dividend Announcements," *JFEC*, 1985, v14(3), 423-449.)

Loewy, Harris. "Net Cash Moneyflows Through Life Insurance Companies," *JOF*, 1956, v11(4), 442-462.

Loeys, Jan. (Berlin, Mitchell and Jan Loeys. "Bond Covenants And Delegated Monitoring," *JOF*, 1988, v43(2), 397-412.)

Loflund, Anders. (Berglund, Tom, Eva Liljeblom and Anders Loflund. "Estimating Betas On Daily Data For A Small Stock Market," *JBF*, 1989, v13(1), 42-64.)

Loftis, John D. "Rock Island's Convert-A-Frate," *FAJ*, 1957, v13(2), 15-18.

Logan, John E. (Pritchett, S. Travis and John E. Logan. "Economies Of Size For Worker's Compensation Business," *JRI*, 1976, v43(3), 533-540.)

Logue, D. E. (Barnea, A. and D. E. Logue. "Risk And The Market Maker's Spread," *FAJ*, 1975, v31(6), 45-49.)

Logue, Dennis E. and Donald L. Tuttle. "Brokerage House Investment Advice," *FR*, 1973, v8(1), 38-54.

Logue, Dennis E. and George S. Oldfield. "What's So Special About Foreign Exchange Markets?," *JPM*, 1976-77, v3(3), 19-24.

Logue, Dennis E. and George S. Oldfield. "Managing Foreign Assets When Foreign Exchange Markets Are Efficient," *FM*, 1977, v6(2), 16-22.

Logue, Dennis E. and John R. Lindvall. "The Behavior Of Investment Bankers: An Econometric Investigation," *JOF*, 1974, v29(1), 203-215.

Logue, Dennis E. and Larry J. Merville. "Financial Policy And Market Expectations," *FM*, 1972, v1(2), 37-44.

Logue, Dennis E. and Lemma W. Senbet. "External Currency Market Equilibrium And Its Implications For Regulation Of The Eurocurrency Market," *JOF*, 1983, v38(2), 435-447.

Logue, Dennis E. and Richard James Sweeney. "Inflation And Real Growth: Some Empirical Results," *JMCB*, 1981, v13(4), 497-501.

Logue, Dennis E. and Richard James Sweeney. "'White-Noise' In Imperfect Markets: The Case Of The Franc/Dollar Exchange Rate," *JOF*, 1977, v32(3), 761-768.

Logue, Dennis E. and Richard James Sweeney. "Aspects Of International Monetary Influences," *JFQA*, 1978, v13(1), 143-156.

Logue, Dennis E. and Richard James Sweeney. "The Premia On Euro Rates," *JOF*, 1984, v39(3), 747-755.

Logue, Dennis E. and Richard J. Rogalski. "Offshore Alphas: Should Diversification Begin At Home?: Reply," *JPM*, 1979-80, v6(2), 76-78.

Logue, Dennis E. and T. Craig Tapley. "Performance Monitoring And The Timing Of Cash Flows," *FM*, 1985, v14(3), 34-39.

Logue, Dennis E. and Robert A. Jarrow. "Negotiated Vs. Competitive Bidding In The Sale Of Securities By Public Utilities," *FM*, 1978, v7(3), 31-39.

Logue, Dennis E. "An Experiment In International Diversification," *JPM*, 1982-83, v9(1), 22-27.

Logue, Dennis E. "Are Stock Markets Becoming Riskier?," *JPM*, 1975-76, v2(3), 13-19.

Logue, Dennis E. "Comment: Some Observations On The Significance Of The Research Requirements In Academia," *FPE*, 1991, v1(1), 13-16.

Logue, Dennis E. "Market-Making And The Assessment Of Market Efficiency," *JOF*, 1975, v30(1), 115-123.

Logue, Dennis E. "On The Pricing Of Unseasoned Equity Issues: 1965-1969," *JFQA*, 1973, v8(1),91-103.

Logue, Dennis E. (Barnea, Amir and Dennis E. Logue. "Evaluating The Forecasts Of A Security Analyst," *FM*, 1973, v2(2), 38-45.)

Logue, Dennis E. (Barnea, Amir and Dennis E. Logue. "Stock Trading And Portfolio Performance," *JBR*, 1976-77, v7(2), 150-157.)

Logue, Dennis E. (Berkowitz, Stephen A., Dennis E. Logue and Eugene A. Noser, Jr. "The Total Cost Of Transactions On The NYSE," *JOF*, 1988, v43(1), 97-112.)

Logue, Dennis E. (Berkowitz, Stephen A. and Dennis E. Logue. "The Portfolio Turnover Explosion Explored," *JPM*, 1986-87, v13(3), 38-45.)

Logue, Dennis E. (Bower, Dorothy H., Richard S. Bower and Dennis E. Logue. "Arbitrage Pricing Theory And Utility Stock Returns," *JOF*, 1984, v39(4), 1041-1054.)

Logue, Dennis E. (Bower, Dorothy H., Richard S. Bower and Dennis E. Logue. "Equity Screening Rates Using Arbitrage Pricing Theory," *AFPAF*, 1985, v1(1), 29-48.)

Logue, Dennis E. (Hughes, John S., Dennis E. Logue and Richard James Sweeney. "Corporate International Diversification And Market Assigned Measures Of Risk And Diversification," *JFQA*, 1975, v10(4), 627-637.)

Logue, Dennis E. (Maloney, Kevin J. and Dennis E. Logue. "Neglected Complexities In Structured Bond Portfolios," *JPM*, 1989, v15(2), 59-68.)

Logue, Dennis E. (Simkowitz, Michael A. and Dennis E. Logue. "The Interdependent Structure Of Security Returns," *JFQA*, 1973, v8(2), 259-272.)

Logue, Dennis E. (Yawitz, Jess B., Amir Barnea and Dennis E. Logue. "Evaluating The Forecasts Of A Security Analyst: Yawitz Vs. Barnea And Logue," *FM*, 1973, v2(4), 47-49.)

Lohman, Philipp H. "History An Orderly Process Despite Technology," *FAJ*, 1960, v16(6), 103-111.

Lohmann, Jack R. and R. V. Oakford. "The Effects Of Borrowing On The Rate Of Growth Of Capital And The Risk Of Ruin Of A Firm," *JBFA*, 1982, v8(2), 219-238.

Loman, H. J. "A Course Of Study For Students Specializing In Insurance," *JRI*, 1936, v3, 1-9.

Loman, H. J. "Is A Change In Investment Policy Of Life Insurance Companies Towards Greater Liquidity Desirable?," *JRI*, 1934, v1, 1-4.

Loman, H. J., E. L. Bowers and J. E. Partington. "Report Of The Committee On Standards And Topics For Courses In Insurance," *JRI*, 1937, v4, 5-9.

Loman, Harry J. "College Education For Insurance: A Minimum Program," *JRI*, 1955, v22, 5-18.

Loman, Harry J. "Report Of Committee On Collegiate Preparation For Insurance Careers," *JRI*, 1942, v9, 17-19.

Loman, Harry J. "The Future Of Risk And Insurance As A Collegiate Subject Of Study," *JRI*, 1966, v33(1), 57-62.

Loman, Harry J. "The Insurance Curriculum," *JRI*, 1959, v26(1), 1-7.

Loman, Harry J. (McCahan, David and Harry J. Loman. "College Education For Insurance: A Minimum Program," *JRI*, 1947, v14, 5-24.)

Lombra, Raymond and Frederick Struble. "Monetary Aggregate Targets And The Volatility Of Interest Rates: A Taxonomic Discussion," *JMCB*, 1979, v11(3), 284-300.

Lombra, Raymond E. (Karamouzis, Nicholas and Raymond E. Lombra. "Forecasts And U.S. Monetary Policy, 1974-78: The Role Of Openness," *JMCB*, 1988, v20(3), 402-408.)

Lombra, Raymond. (Gooptu, Sudarshan and Raymond Lombra. "Aggregation Across Heterogeneous Depository Institutions," *FR*, 1987, v22(4), 369-378.)

London, Jack, Bernard Karsh, Joel Seidman and Richard Hammett. "Management Views The Local Union," *JOB*, 1953, v26(2), 91-102.

Londoner, D. J. (Lechner, A. B. and D. J. Londoner. "Brokerage Profits After May Day," *FAJ*, 1976, v32(1), 12-17,31.)

Londoner, David J. "Steel Industry Profit Outlook," *FAJ*, 1968, v24(4), 63-68.

Long, Blair M. "University Insurance Instruction: It Is Time To Teach Problem Solving," *JRI*, 1983, v50(2), 315-322.)

Long, C. Richard and Mark L. Gardner. "Alternative U.S. Monetary And Deficit Reduction Policies For The 1980s," *JMCB*, 1988, v20(3), 336-352.

Long, Hugh W. (Boudreaux, Kenneth J. and Hugh W. Long. "The Weighted Average Cost Of Capital As A Cutoff Rate: A Further Analysis," *FM*, 1979, v8(2), 7-14.)

Long, Hugh W. (Boudreaux, Kenneth J. and Hugh W. Long. "Incorporating The Capital Asset Pricing Model Into The Basic Finance Course," *JFED*, 1976, v5, 15-20.)

Long, Hugh W. (Dyl, Edward A. and Hugh W. Long. "Abandonment Value And Capital Budgeting: Comment," *JOF*, 1969, v24(1), 88-95.)

Long, J. B., Jr. "Efficient Portfolio Choice With Differential Taxation Of Dividends And Capital Gains," *JFEC*, 1977, v5(1), 25-53.

Long, J. B., Jr. (Bloomfield, T. R., Richard Leftwich and J. B. Long, Jr. "Portfolio Strategies And Performance," *JFEC*, 1977, v5(2), 210-218.)

Long, John B., Jr. "Stock Prices, Inflation, And The Term Structure Of Interest Rates," *JFEC*, 1974, v1(2), 131-170.

Long, John B., Jr. "The Market Valuation Of Cash Dividends: A Case To Consider," *JFEC*, 1978, v6(2/3), 235-264.

Long, John B., Jr. "The Numeraire Portfolio," *JFEC*, 1990, v26(1), 29-70.

Long, John D. "Confessions Of A Delphi Panelist," **JRI**, 1970, v37(2), 247-251.

Long, John D. "Curricular Concepts In Risk And Insurance," **JRI**, 1963, v30(2), 289-294.

Long, John D. "Curricular Concepts In Risk And Insurance," **JRI**, 1963, v30(3), 465-472.

Long, John D. "Doctoral Study In Insurance," **JRI**, 1965, v32(3), 401-412.

Long, John D. "Four Points Of Confusion About Reinsurance," **JRI**, 1964, v31(2), 273-278.

Long, John D. "Four Points Of Confusion About Reinsurance: Reply," **JRI**, 1965, v32(1), 136-138.

Long, John D. "Insurance Subsidies And Welfare Economics," **JRI**, 1972, v39(3), 341-349.

Long, John D. "Insurance Subsidies And Welfare Economics: Reply," **JRI**, 1975, v42(3), 542-544.

Long, John D. "Is The U.S. Insurance Poor?," **JRI**, 1972, v39(4), 555-571.

Long, John D. "Proposal For A New Course: Risk In The Enterprise System," **JRI**, 1961, v28(3), 55-64.

Long, John D. "Rates Of Return In The Property And Liability Insurance Industry: A Comparative Analysis: Comment," **JRI**, 1969, v36(2), 201-216.

Long, John D. "Research On Property Agency Continuation," **JRI**, 1956, v23, 152-156.

Long, John D. "Risk, Uncertainty And Moral Hazard: Comment," **JRI**, 1972, v39(1), 130-135.

Long, John D. "Should Punitive Damages Be Insured?," **JRI**, 1977, v44(1), 1-20.

Long, John D. "The Future And Insurance - Presidential Address," **JRI**, 1967, v34(4), 515-523.

Long, John. "Wealth, Welfare, And The Price Of Risk," **JOF**, 1972, v27(2), 419-433.

Long, Michael S. and George A. Racette. "Stochastic Demand, Output And The Cost Of Capital," **JOF**, 1974, v29(2), 499-506.

Long, Michael S. and George Racette. "Stochastic Demand And The Equity Capitalization Rate," **JBFA**, 1979, v6(4), 475-493.

Long, Michael S. "Credit Screening System Selection," **JFQA**, 1976, v11(2), 313-328.

Long, Michael S. "Effect Of Lending Rate Ceilings And Money Costs On Extensions Of Consumer Credit," **JBR**, 1976-77, v7(3), 206-212.

Long, Michael S. "Leasing And The Cost Of Capital," **JFQA**, 1977, v12(4), 579-586.

Long, Michael S. (Lewellen, Wilbur G., Michael S. Long and John J. McConnell. "Asset Leasing In Competitive Capital Markets," **JOF**, 1976, v31(3), 787-798.)

Long, Michael S. and Stephan E. Sefcik. "Participation Financing: A Comparison Of The Characteristics Of Convertible Debt And Straight Bonds Issued In Conjunction With Warrants," **FM**, 1990, v19(3), 23-34.

Long, Robert D. (Hradsky, Gregory T. and Robert D. Long. "High-Yield Default Losses And The Return Performance Of Bankrupt Debt," **FAJ**, 1989, v45(4), 38-49.)

Long, Robert H. "Planning For Tomorrow's Customer," **JBR**, 1973-74, v4(2), 93-99.

Long, Robert H. "The Impact Of Technological Change On Bank Products And Customers," **JBR**, 1974-75, v5(3), 141-144.

Long, Susan W. "Risk-Premium Curve Vs. Capital Market Line: Differences Explained," **FM**, 1978, v7(1), 60-64.

Long, Susan W. (Bolten, Steven E. and Susan W. Long. "A Note On Cyclical And Dynamic Aspects Of Stock Market Price Cycles," **FR**, 1986, v21(1), 149-150.)

Longbottom, D. A. and L. Wiper. "Capital Appraisal And The Case For Average Rate Of Return: A Reply," **JBFA**, 1979, v6(2), 243-244.

Longbottom, D. A. and L. Wiper. "Capital Appraisal And The Case For Average Rate Of Return," **JBFA**, 1977, v4(4), 419-426.

Longbottom, David A. and Linda Wiper. "Necessary Conditions For The Existence Of Multiple Rates In The Use Of Internal Rate Of Return," **JBFA**, 1978, v5(4), 295-304.

Longbottom, J. Andrew. (Beenstock, Michael and J. Andrew Longbottom. "The Term Structure Of Interest Rates In A Small Open Economy," **JMCB**, 1981, v13(1), 44-59.)

Longbrake, William A. and H. Douglas Merrill. "Demand For Commercial Bank Production Workers And Administrators: Demand Deposit Operations," **JMCB**, 1976, v8(3), 275-295.

Longbrake, William A. and John A. Haslem. "Productive Efficiency In Commercial Banking: The Effects Of Size And Legal Form Of Organization On The Cost Of Producing Demand Deposit Services," **JMCB**, 1975, v7(3), 317-330.

Longbrake, William A. and Sandra B. Cohan. "The Now Account Experiment," **JBR**, 1974-75, v5(2), 71-85.

Longbrake, William A. "Commercial Bank Capacity To Pay Interest On Demand Deposits. Part Two: Earnings And Cost Analysis," **JBR**, 1976-77, v7(2), 134-149.

Longbrake, William A. "Commercial Bank Capacity To Pay Interest On Demand Deposits," **JBR**, 1976-77, v7(1), 8-21.

Longbrake, William A. "Computers And The Cost Of Producing Banking Services: Planning And Control Considerations," **JBR**, 1973-74, v4(3), 194-202.

Longbrake, William A. "Computers And The Cost Of Producing Various Types Of Banking Services," **JOB**, 1974, v47(3), 363-381.

Longbrake, William A. "Financial Management Of Banks And Bank Holding Companies," **FM**, 1974, v3(4), 10-24.

Longbrake, William A. "Murphy's Method For Determining The Weights Assigned To Demand Deposit Items: A Clarification And Extension," **JBR**, 1973-74, v4(2), 139-144.

Longbrake, William A. "Statistical Cost Analysis," **FM**, 1973, v2(1), 48-55.

Longbrake, William A. (Daniel, Donnie L., William A. Longbrake and Neil B. Murphy. "The Effect Of Technology On Bank Economies Of Scale For Demand Deposits," **JOF**, 1973, v28(1), 131-146.)

Longbrake, William A. (Gilbert, Gary G. and William A. Longbrake. "The Effects Of Branching By Financial Institutions On Competition, Productive Efficiency And Stability," **JBR**, 1973-74, v4(4), 298-307.)

Longbrake, William A. (Gilbert, Gary and William Longbrake. "The Effects Of Branching By Financial Institutions On Competition, Productive Efficiency, And Stability," **JBR**, 1973-74, v4(3), 154-167.)

Longbrake, William A. (Haslem, John A. and William A. Longbrake. "A Note On Average Interest Charges On Bank Loans, The Loan Mix, And Measures Of Competition," **JOF**, 1971, v26(1), 159-164.)

Longbrake, William. (Haslem, John A. and William Longbrake. "A Credit-Scoring Model For Commercial Loans: A Comment," **JMCB**, 1972, v4(3), 733-734.)

Longest, Beaufort B., Jr. (Knobel, Roland J. and Beaufort B. Longest, Jr. "Cost-Benefit Assumptions In Analysis For Hospitals," **FM**, 1972, v1(1), 63-65.)

Longford, Nicholas. (Fieldsend, Susan, Nicholas Longford and Stuart McLeay. "Industry Effects And The Proportionality Assumption In Ratio Analysis: A Variance Component Analysis," **JBFA**, 1987, v14(4), 497-518.)

Longley, F. A. and G. S. Sarlo. "Current Trends In Integrated Circuits," **FAJ**, 1967, v23(5), 65-69.

Longley-Cook, L. H. "Trends In Property Insurance Rate Making," **JRI**, 1963, v30(1), 23-28.

Longo, Mechthild. (Gregg, Davis W. and Mechthild K. Longo. "Insurance Education Abroad," **JRI**, 1960, v27(4), 121-125.)

Longstaff, Francis A. "A Nonlinear General Equilibrium Model Of The Term Structure Of Interest Rates," **JFEC**, 1989, v23(2), 195-224.

Longstaff, Francis A. "Pricing Options With Extendible Maturities: Analysis And Applications," **JOF**, 1990, v45(3), 935-958.

Longstaff, Francis A. "Temporal Aggregation And The Continuous-Time Capital Asset Pricing Model," **JOF**, 1989, v44(4), 871-888.

Longstaff, Francis A. "The Valuation Of Options On Yields," **JFEC**, 1990, v26(1), 97-122.

Longstaff, Francis A. "Time Varying Term Premia And Traditional Hypotheses About The Term Structure," **JOF**, 1990, v45(4), 1307-1314.

Longstaff, Francis A. (Choi, Jin W. and Francis A. Longstaff. "Pricing Options On Agricultural Futures: An Application Of The Constant Elasticity Of Variance Option Pricing Model," **JFM**, 1985, v5(2), 247-258.)

Longstreet, J. R. and Fred B. Power. "A Capital Budgeting Analysis Of Life Insurance Contracts," **JRI**, 1970, v37(4), 599-608.

Longstreet, James R. (Meyer, Richard L., Scott Besley and James R. Longstreet. "An Examination Of Capital Budgeting Decision Alternatives For Mutually Exclusive Investments With Unequal Lives," **JBFA**, 1988, v15(3), 415-426.)

Longstreth, Bevis. "Takeovers, Corporate Governance, And Stock Ownership: Some Disquieting Trends," **JPM**, 1990, v16(3), 54-59.

Longworth, David. "Exchange Rates And 'News': A Comment," **JIMF**, 1984, v3(1), 119-122.

Longworth, David. "Testing The Efficiency Of The Canadian-U.S. Exchange Market Under The Assumption Of No Risk Premium," **JOF**, 1981, v36(1), 43-49.

Longworth, David. (Boothe, Paul and David Longworth. "Foreign Exchange Market Efficiency Tests: Implications Of Recent Empirical Findings," **JIMF**, 1986, v5(2), 135-152.)

Loo, Jean C. H. "Common Stock Returns, Expected Inflation, And The Rational Expectations Hypothesis," **JFR**, 1988, v11(2), 165-170.

Loo, Jean C. H. (Chang, Jack S. K. and Jean C. H. Loo. "Marking-To-Market, Stochastic Interest Rates And Discounts On Stock Index Futures," **JFM**, 1987, v7(1), 15-20.)

Loo, Jean C. H. (Chang, Jack S. K., Jean C. H. Loo and Carolyn C. Wu Chang. "The Pricing Of Futures Contracts And The Arbitrage Pricing Theory," **JFR**, 1990, v13(4), 297-306.)

Loomes, Graham. "Evidence Of A New Violation Of The Independence Axiom," **JRU**, 1991, v4(1), 91-108.

Loomis, Daniel P. "Behind The Rail Stock Paradox," **FAJ**, 1964, v20(5), 55-57.

Loomis, Daniel P. "Railroads Aim To Win (Union) Battle," **FAJ**, 1959, v15(2), 33-36.

Loomis, Daniel P. "The Transportation Act Of 1958," **FAJ**, 1958, v14(5), 57-62.

Loomis, Daniel P. "Transport Diversification: Today's Answer," **FAJ**, 1960, v16(6), 39-43.

Loomis, Philip A., Jr. "Broker Research After May Day," **FAJ**, 1975, v31(4), 14-16,18.

Loomis, Philip, George S. Bissell, John G. Gillis and Walter P. Stern. "Corporate Disclosure And Inside Information," **FAJ**, 1972, v28(3), 20-21,24-25,82-84,86-88.

Looney, Stephen W. (Lane, William R., Stephen W. Looney and James W. Wansley. "An Application Of The Cox Proportional Hazards Model To Bank Failure," **JBF**, 1986, v10(4), 511-532.)

Loopesko, Bonnie E. "Relationships Among Exchange Rates, Intervention, And Interest Rates: An Empirical Investigation," **JIMF**, 1984, v3(3), 257-277.

Lorant, John H. (Sloan, Frank A. and John H. Lorant. "The Role Of Waiting Time: Evidence From Physicians' Practices," **JOB**, 1977, v50(4), 486-507.)

Lord, Blair M. (Chang, Rosita P., Blair M. Lord and S. Ghon Rhee. "Inflation-Caused Wealth-Transfer: A Case Of The Insurance Industry," **JRI**, 1985, v52(4), 627-643.)

Lord, Blair. (Carlson, Severin and Blair Lord. "Unisex Retirement Benefits And The Market For Annuity 'Lemons'," **JRI**, 1986, v53(3), 409-418.)

Lord, Graham. (Jacob, David P., Graham Lord and James A. Tilley. "A Generalized Framework For Pricing Contingent Cash Flows," **FM**, 1987, v16(3), 5-14.)

Lord, J. Dennis. (Olson, Lola M. and J. Dennis Lord. "Market Area Characteristics And Branch Bank Performance," **JBR**, 1979-80, v10(2), 102-110.)

Lorie, J. H. and M. T. Hamilton. "New Focus For Investment Counselling," **FAJ**, 1973, v29(4), 46-50.

Lorie, J. H. (Fisher, L. and J. H. Lorie. "Rates Of Return On Investments In Common Stocks," **JOB**, 1964, v37(1), 1-21.)

Lorie, James H. and Harry V. Roberts. "Some Comments On Experimentation In Business Research," **JOB**, 1950, v23(2), 94-102.

Lorie, James H. "A Particularly Unhappy Anniversary," **JPM**, 1979-80, v6(1), 42-46.

Lorie, James H. "Diversification: Old And New," **JPM**, 1974-75, v1(2), 25-28.

Lorie, James H. "Forecasting The Demand For Consumer Durable Goods," JOB, 1954, v27(1), 62-70.

Lorie, James H. "NABAC Study On Pension Funds," FAJ, 1968, v24(2), 139-143.

Lorie, James H. "Some Comments On Recent Quantitative And Formal Research On The Stock Market," JOB, 1966, v39(1), Part II, 107-110.

Lorie, James H. "Two Important Problems In Sales Forecasting," JOB, 1957, v30(3), 172-179.

Lorie, James H. (Fisher, Lawrence and James H. Lorie. "Rates Of Return On Investments In Common Stock: The Year-By-Year Record, 1926-65," JOB, 1968, v41(3), 291-316.)

Lorie, James H. (Fisher, Lawrence and James H. Lorie. "Some Studies Of Variability Of Returns On Investments In Common Stocks," JOB, 1970, v43(2), 99-134.)

Lorie, James H. (Fisher, Lawrence and James H. Lorie. "Knowledge Makes A Difference - A Reply To Dr. Leo Barnes," FAJ, 1965, v21(6), 118-120.)

Lorie, James H. and Leonard J. Savage. "Three Problems In Rationing Capital," JOB, 1955, v28(4),229-239.

Losey, Robert L. and John C. Talbott, Jr. "Back On The Track With The Efficient Markets Hypothesis," JOF, 1980, v35(4), 1039-1043.

Losq, Etienne and John Peter D. Chateau. "A Generalization Of The CAPM Based On A Property Of The Covariance Operator," JFQA, 1982, v17(5), 783-797.

Losq, Etienne. (Errunza, Vihang R. and Etienne Losq. "The Behavior Of Stock Prices On LDC Markets," JBF, 1985, v9(4), 561-575.)

Losq, Etienne. (Errunza, Vihang and Etienne Losq. "How Risky Are Emerging Markets," JPM, 1987-88, v14(1), 62-67.)

Losq, Etienne. (Errunza, Vihang and Etienne Losq. "International Asset Pricing Under Mild Segmentation: Theory And Test," JOF, 1985, v40(1), 105-124.)

Losq, Etienne. (Errunza, Vihang and Etienne Losq. "Capital Flow Controls, International Asset Pricing, And Investors' Welfare: A Multi-Country Framework," JOF, 1989, v44(4), 1025-1038.)

Losq, Etienne. (Friend, Irwin, Yoram Landskroner and Etienne Losq. "The Demand For Risky Assets Under Uncertain Inflation," JOF, 1976, v31(5), 1287-1297.)

Lothian, James R. "Political Factors In International Economics: An Overview," JIMF, 1991, v10(Supp), S4-S15.

Lothian, James R. "Real Dollar Exchange Rates Under The Bretton-Woods And Floating Exchange-Rate Regimes," JIMF, 1986, v5(4), 429-448.

Lothian, James R. (Huffman, Wallace E. and James R. Lothian. "Money In The United Kingdom, 1833-80," JMCB, 1980, v12(2), Part 1, 155-174.)

Lotruglio, Anthony F. "How To Measure Fixed Income Performance Correctly: Comment," JPM, 1985-86, v12(2), 87.

Louberge, Henri. "A Portfolio Model Of International Reinsurance Operations," JRI, 1983, v50(1), 44-60.

Louberge, Henri. "The Management Of Research In Risk And Insurance At The Geneva Association," JRI, 1981, v48(2), 309-321.

Louberge, Henri. (Briys, Eric P. and Henri Louberge. "On The Theory Of Rational Insurance Purchasing: A Note," JOF, 1985, v40(2), 577-581.)

Louberge, Henri. (Eeckhoudt, Louis and Henri Louberge. "Export Credit Insurance: Comment," JRI, 1988, v55(4), 742-747.)

Loucks, Christine. (Johnson, Linda L. and Christine Loucks. "The Effect Of State Licensing Regulations On The Real Estate Brokerage Industry," AREUEA, 1986, v14(4), 567-582.)

Loudon, G. F. "American Put Pricing: Australian Evidence," JBFA, 1990, v17(2), 297-322.

Lougee, Duane. (Lawrence, Robert J. and Duane Lougee. "Determinants Of Correspondent Banking Relationships," JMCB, 1970, v2(3), 358-369.)

Lovata, Linda M. and Kirk L. Philipich. "Does Replacement Cost Restatement Affect The Intra-Industry Ranking Of Firms?," FAJ, 1986, v42(3), 72-75.

Lovata, Linda M., William D. Nichols and Kirk L. Philipich. "Defeasing Discounted Debt: An Economic Analysis," FM, 1987, v16(1), 41-45.

Love, Douglas A. "The Use And Abuse Of Leverage," FAJ, 1975, v31(2), 51-57,88.

Love, Kathryn S. (Ibbotson, Roger G., Laurence B. Siegel and Kathryn S. Love. "World Wealth: Market Values And Returns," JPM, 1985-86, v12(1), 4-23.)

Lovell, Robert M., Jr. "Alternative Investments," FAJ, 1980, v36(3), 19-21.

Lovell, Robert M., Jr. "Whose Efficient Market?," JPM, 1976-77, v3(2), 60-64.

Loviscek, Anthony L. and Frederick D. Crowley. "What Is In A Municipal Bond Rating?," FR, 1990, 25(1), 25-54.

Low, Lay-Chin, Pearl Hock-Neo Tan and Hian-Chye Koh. "The Determination Of Audit Fees: An Analysis In The Singapore Context," JBFA, 1990, v17(2), 285-296.

Low, Stuart. (Boyes, W. J., Dennis Hoffman and Stuart Low. "Lender Reactions To Information Restrictions: The Case Of Banks And The ECOA," JMCB, 1986, v18(2), 211-219.)

Lowe, E. A. and A. M. Tinker. "Siting The Accounting Problematic: Towards An Intellectual Emancipation Of Accounting," JBFA, 1977, v4(3), 263-276.

Lowe, E. A. (Tinker, A. M. and E. A. Lowe. "A Rationale For Corporate Social Reporting: Theory And Evidence From Organizational Research," JBFA, 1980, v7(1), 1-17.)

Lowe, E. Anthony. (Laughlin, Richard C., E. Anthony Lowe and Anthony G. Puxty. "Towards A Value-Neutral Positive Science Of Accounting: A Comment," JBFA, 1982, v8(4), 567-572.)

Lowinger, Thomas C., Clas Wihlborg and Elliott S. Willman. "OPEC In World Financial Markets: Oil Prices And Interest Rates," JIMF, 1985, v4(2), 253-266.

Luan, David C. and Norman C. Miller. "A Monetary Approach To International Capital Flows Applied To The United States," JMCB, 1979, v11(1), 87-90.

Lublin, Gerson D. "Market Trends Vs. Security Values," FAJ, 1960, v16(6), 91-94.

Lublin, Gerson D. "Today's Analyst," FAJ, 1955, v11(4), 55-58.

Lucas, Deborah J. and Robert L. McDonald. "Equity Issues And Stock Price Dynamics," JOF, 1990, v45(4), 1020-1043.

Lucas, Deborah and Robert L. McDonald. "Bank Portfolio Choice With Private Information About Loan Quality: Theory And Implications For Regulation," JBF, 1987, v11(3), 473-498.

Lucas, Frank A. W. "Can Taxation Be Constructive?," FAJ, 1956, v12(1), 55-58.

Lucas, Robert E., Jr. "Adaptive Behavior And Economic Theory," JOB, 1986, v59(4), Part 2, S401-S426.

Lucas, Robert E., Jr. "Methods And Problems In Business Cycle Theory," JMCB, 1980, v12(4), Part 2, 696-715.

Lucas, Vane B. "Revision Of The C.L.U. Diploma Program," JRI, 1970, v37(1), 115-124.

Lucas, Vane B. and James M. Daily. "An Adult Learning Research Center At Bryn Mawr," JRI, 1969, v36(1), 125-128.

Lucas, Vane B., Jr. "Private Pension Issues Under Collective Bargaining," JRI, 1965, v32(4), 549-558.

Luce, R. Duncan and Peter C. Fishburn. "Rank- And Sign-Dependent Linear Utility Models For Finite First-Order Gambles," JRU, 1991, v4(1), 29-60.

Luce, R. Duncan. "Rank-Dependent, Subjective Expected-Utility Representations," JRU, 1988, v1(3), 305-332.

Luck, Thomas J. "The Insurance Industry And The Insurance Professor," JRI, 1967, v34(2), 301-304.

Luckett, Dudley G. and Allen R. Soltow. "Determinants Of Interest Rate Expectations," JMCB, 1972, v4(2), 272-282.

Luckett, Dudley G. and Glenn T. Potts. "Monetary Policy And Partisan Politics," JMCB, 1980, v12(3), 540-546.

Luckett, Dudley G. "Compensatory Cyclical Bank Asset Adjustments: Reply," JOF, 1962, v17(4), 655-657.

Luckett, Dudley G. "Compensatory Cyclical Bank Asset Adjustments," JOF, 1962, v17(1), 53-62.

Luckett, Dudley G. "Credit Standards And Tight Money," JMCB, 1970, v2(4), 420-434.

Luckett, Dudley G. "On The Effectiveness Of The Federal Reserve's Margin Requirement," JOF, 1982, v37(3), 783-795.

Luckett, Peter F. "ARR Vs. IRR: A Review And An Analysis," JBFA, 1984, v11(2), 213-232.

Luft, Carl F. and Bruce D. Fielitz. "An Empirical Test Of The Commodity Option Pricing Model Using Ginnie Mae Call Options," JFR, 1986, v9(2), 137-151.

Lui, Y. H. and K. V. Peasnell. "Time Series Behaviour, Predictability And Speculation In The Hong Kong Foreign Exchange Market," JBFA, 1989, v16(2), 145-164.

Lukac, Louis P. (Brorsen, B. Wade and Louis P. Lukac. "Optimal Portfolios For Commodity Futures Funds," JFM, 1990, v10(3), 247-258.)

Lukac, Louis P. and B. Wade Brorsen. "A Comprehensive Test Of Futures Market Disequilibrium," FR, 1990, v25(4), 593-622.

Lukac, Louis P. and B. Wade Brorsen. "The Usefulness Of Historical Data In Selecting Parameters For Technical Trading Systems," JFM, 1989, v9(1), 55-66.

Lukac, Louis P., B. Wade Brorsen and Scott H. Irwin. "Similarity Of Computer Guided Technical Trading Systems," JFM, 1988, v8(1), 1-14.

Lukaczer, Moses. "The Farm Wage Worker In The Social Security Program: His Earnings Profile," JRI, 1969, v36(1), 103-116.

Luke, Dawson B. (Miller, Stephen E. and Dawson B. Luke. "Alternative Techniques For Cross-Hedging Wholesale Beef Prices," JFM, 1982, v2(2), 121-129.)

Luksetich, William A. (Riley, William B. and William A. Luksetich. "The Market Prefers Republicans: Myth Or Reality," JFQA, 1980, v15(3), 541-560.)

Lummer, Scott L. (Alderson, Michael J., Keith C. Brown and Scott L. Lummer. "Dutch Auction Rate Preferred Stock," FM, 1987, v16(2), 68-73.)

Lummer, Scott L. (Brown, Keith C., Larry J. Lockwood and Scott L. Lummer. "An Examination Of Event Dependency And Structural Change In Security Pricing Models," JFQA, 1985, v20(3), 315-334.)

Lummer, Scott L. (Brown, Keith C. and Scott L. Lummer. "A Reexamination Of The Covered Call Option Strategy For Corporate Cash Management," FM, 1985, v15(2), 13-17.)

Lummer, Scott L. (Brown, Keith C. and Scott L. Lummer. "The Cash Management Implications Of A Hedged Dividend Capture Strategy," FM, 1984, v13(4), 7-17.)

Lummer, Scott L. and John J. McConnell. "Further Evidence On The Bank Lending Process And The Capital-Market Response To Bank Loan Agreements," JFEC, 1989, v25(1), 99-122.

Lund, Adrian. (Zador, Paul and Adrian Lund. "Re-Analyses Of The Effects Of No-Fault Auto Insurance On Fatal Crashes," JRI, 1986, v53(2), 226-241.)

Lund, Harry A., Walter J. Casey and Philip K. Chamberlain. "A Financial Analysis Of The ESOT," FAJ, 1976, v32(1), 55-61.

Lundholm, Russell J. (DeJong, Douglas V., Robert Forsythe and Russell J. Lundholm. "Ripoffs, Lemons, And Reputation Formation In Agency Relationships: A Laboratory Market Study," JOF, 1985, v40(3), 809-820.)

Lundsten, Lorman L. (Mandell, Lewis and Lorman L. Lundsten. "Diversion Of Credit Life Insurance Commissions By Bankers," JBR, 1977-78, v8(2), 72-76.)

Lupoletti, William M. and Roy H. Webb. "Defining And Improving The Accuracy Of Macroeconomic Forecasts: Contributions From A VAR Model," JOB, 1986, v59(2), Part 1, 263-286.

Lurie, Arlene J. and Victor S. Pastena. "Prompt Disclosure Of Company Problems," FAJ, 1975, v31(5), 55-61.

Lurie, Sidney B. "Our Changed And Changing Business," FAJ, 1954, v10(1), 19-22.

Lusby, R. Newell. "The Uninsured Motorist - Several Points Of View," JRI, 1957, v24(1), 114-122.

Lusht, Kenneth M. "Inflation And Real Estate Investment Value," AREUEA, 1978, v6(1), 37-49.

Lusht, Kenneth M. "Inflation And Real Estate Investment Value: A Reply," AREUEA, 1980, v8(4), 402-403.

Lusht, Kenneth M. and Bruce M. Leidenberger. "A Research Note On Factors Associated With Troubled Residential Construction Loans," AREUEA, 1979, v7(2), 243-252.

Lusht, Kenneth M. "Real Estate Valuation And Appraisal," AREUEA, 1986, v14(2), 175-178.

Lusht, Kenneth M. "The Real Estate Pricing Puzzle," AREUEA, 1988, v16(2), 95-104.

Lusht, Kenneth M. and Edward M. Saunders. "Direct Tests Of The Divergence Of Opinion Hypothesis In The Market For Racetrack Betting," JFR, 1989, v12(4), 285-292.

Lusht, Kenneth M. and Jeffrey D. Fisher. "Anticipated Growth And The Specification Of Debt In Real Estate Value Models," AREUEA, 1984, v12(1), 1-11.

Luskin, Donald L. "The Marketplace For 'Composite Assets'," JPM, 1987-88, v14(1), 12-19.

Lustgarten, Steven and Allan I. Mendelowitz. "The Covariability Of Industrial Concentration And Employment Fluctuations," JOB, 1979, v52(2), 291-304.

Lustgarten, Steven and Stavros Thomadakis. "Mobility Barriers And Tobin's q," JOB, 1987, v60(4), 519-538.

Lustig, Ivan L. and Philip A. Leinbach. "The Small Firm Effect," FAJ, 1983, v39(3), 46-49.

Lusztig, P. A. (White, R. W. and P. A. Lusztig. "The Price Effects Of Rights Offerings," JFQA, 1980, v15(1), 25-40.)

Lusztig, Peter and Bernhard Schwab. "A Note On The Application Of Linear Programming To Capital Budgeting," JFQA, 1968, v3(4), 427-431.

Lusztig, Peter and Bernhard Schwab. "The Discount Rate Problem In Capital Rationing Situations: Reply," JFQA, 1970, v5(2), 261-261.

Lusztig, Peter A. "Rate Control And Government Competition In Australian Non-Life Insurance: Comment," JRI, 1970, v37(2), 310-311.

Lusztig, Peter and Bernhard Schwab. "A Note On The Application Of Multiple Regression Analysis To Expense Allocation In The Insurance Industry," JRI, 1970, v37(3), 485-488.

Lusztig, Peter. "Analysis Of The Lease-Or-Buy Decision: Comment," JOF, 1973, v28(4), 1017-18.

Lusztig, Peter. (Schwab, Bernhard and Peter Lusztig. "Apportioning Foreign Exchange Risk Through The Use Of Third Currencies: Some Questions On Efficiency," FM, 1978, v7(3), 25-30.)

Lusztig, Peter. (Schwab, Bernhard and Peter Lusztig. "A Comparative Analysis Of The Net Present Value And The Benefit-Cost Ratio As Measures Of The Economic Desirability Of Investments," JOF, 1969, v24(3), 507-516.)

Lusztig, Peter. (Schwab, Bernhard and Peter Lusztig. "A Note On Investment Evaluations In Light Of Uncertain Future Opportunities," JOF, 1972, v27(5), 1093-1100.)

Lusztig, Peter. (Schwab, Bernard and Peter Lusztig. "A Note On Abandonment Value And Capital Budgeting," JFQA, 1970, v5(3), 377-379.)

Lutes, Terry. (Follain, James R., Terry Lutes and David A. Meier. "Why Do Some Real Estate Salespeople Earn More Than Others?," JRER, 1987, v2(1), 73-81.)

Lybeck, Johan A. "On Political Risk - The Turnover Tax On The Swedish Money And Bond Markets Or How To Kill A Market Without Really Trying," RDIBF, 1991, v4/5, 147-169.

Lyles, Henry F. "What Is The Real Value Of Education To The Life Agent?," JRI, 1964, v31(3), 371-380.

Lyn, Esmeralda O. (Gilbert, Erika W. and Esmeralda O. Lyn. "The Impact Of Target Managerial Resistence On The Shareholders Of Bidding Firms," JBFA, 1990, v17(4), 497-510.)

Lynge, Morgan J., Jr. "Money Supply Announcements And Stock Prices," JPM, 1981, 40-43.

Lynge, Morgan J., Jr. (Jahankhani, Ali and Morgan J. Lynge, Jr. "Commercial Bank Financial Policies And Their Impact On Market-Determined Measures Of Risk," JBR, 1980, v11(3), 169-178.)

Lynge, Morgan J., Jr. (Lee, Cheng F. and Morgan J. Lynge, Jr. "Return, Risk And Cost Of Equity For Stock S&L Firms: Theory And Empirical Results," AREUEA, 1985, v13(2), 167-180.)

Lynge, Morgan J., Jr. (Shin, Tai S. and Morgan J. Lynge, Jr. "Rural Banking Markets In Illinois: An Empirical Test," JBR, 1979, v10(2), 124-127.)

Lynge, Morgan J., Jr. and Cheng F. Lee. "Financial Ratio Comparison Of Savings And Loan Associations And Commercial Banks," AFPAF, 1989, v3(1), 195-230.

Lynge, Morgan J., Jr. and J. Kenton Zumwalt. "An Empirical Study Of Interest Rate Sensitivity Of Commercial Bank Returns: A Multi-Index Approach," JFQA, 1980, v15(3), 731-742.

Lynk, William J. "Information, Advertising, And The Structure Of The Market," JOB, 1981, v54(2), 271-304.

Lynk, William J. "Interpreting Rising Concentration: The Case Of Beer," JOB, 1984, v57(1), Part 1, 43-56.

Lynk, William J. "The Price And Output Of Beer Revisited," JOB, 1985, v58(4), 433-437.

Lynn, Arthur D., Jr. "Contributions To Risk And Insurance Theory From The Field Of Law," JRI, 1962, v29(3), 351-354.

Lynn, Laurence E., Jr. "The Behavioral Foundations Of Public Policy-Making," JOB, 1986, v59(4), Part 2, S379-S384.

Lynn, Richard. (Dwyer, Hubert J. and Richard Lynn. "Small Capitalization Companies: What Does Financial Analysis Tell Us About Them?," FR, 1989, v24(3), 397-416.)

Lyon, Robert A. (Grinyer, John R. and Robert A. Lyon. "The Need For Ex Post EEI," JBFA, 1989, v16(3), 303-316.)

Lyons, Daniel J. "The Revision Of Section 213 - A Major Life Insurance Problem," JRI, 1953, v20, 12-17.

Lyons, Richard K. "Tests Of The Foreign Exchange Risk Premium Using The Expected Second Moments Implied By Option Pricing," JIMF, 1989, v8(1), 91-108.

Lypny, Gregory J. "Hedging Foreign Exchange Risk With Currency Futures: Portfolio Effects," JFM, 1988, v8(6), 703-716.

Lys, Thomas. (Benelli, Giuseppe, Claudio Loderer and Thomas Lys. "Labor Participation In Corporate Policy-Making Decisions: West Germany's Experience With Codetermination," JOB, 1987, v60(4), 553-576.)

Lys, Thomas. (Larcker, David F. and Thomas Lys. "An Empirical Analysis Of The Incentives To Engage In Costly Information Acquisition: The Case Of Risk Arbitrage," JFEC, 1987, v18(1), 111-126.)

Ma, Christopher K. and Garry M. Weed. "Fact And Fancy Of Takeover Junk Bonds," JPM, 1986-87, v13(1), 34-37.

Ma, Christopher K. "A Further Investigation Of The Day-Of-The-Week Effect In The Gold Market," JFM, 1986, v6(3), 409-420.

Ma, Christopher K. "Loan Loss Reserves And Income Smoothing: The Experience In The US Banking Industry," JBFA, 1988, v15(4), 487-498.

Ma, Christopher K. "Mean Reversions In GNMA Returns," AREUEA, 1990, v18(2), 207-226.

Ma, Christopher K. "Spreading Between The Gold And Silver Markets: Is There A Parity?," JFM, 1985, v5(4), 579-594.

Ma, Christopher K. (Fabozzi, Frank J. and Christopher K. Ma. "The Over-The-Counter Market And New York Stock Exchange Trading Halts," FR, 1988, v23(4), 427-438.)

Ma, Christopher K. (Fabozzi, Frank J., Eileen Moran and Christopher K. Ma. "Market Uncertainty And The Least-Cost Offering Method Of Public Utility Debt: A Note," JOF, 1988, v43(4), 1025-1034.)

Ma, Christopher K. (Hein, Scott E., Christopher K. Ma and S. Scott MacDonald. "Testing Unbiasedness In Futures Markets: A Clarification," JFM, 1990, v10(5), 555-562.)

Ma, Christopher K. and G. Wenchi Kao. "On Exchange Rate Changes And Stock Price Reactions," JBFA, 1990, v17(3), 441-450.

Ma, Christopher K. and Luc A. Soenen. "Arbitrage Opportunities In Metal Futures Markets," JFM, 1988, v8(2), 199-209.

Ma, Christopher K. and M. E. Ellis. "Selecting Industries As Inflation Hedges," JPM, 1989, v15(4), 45-48.

Ma, Christopher K. and Ramesh P. Rao. "Information Asymmetry And Options Trading," FR, 1988, v23(1), 39-52.

Ma, Christopher K., G. Wenchi Wong and Edwin D. Maberly. "The Daily Effect In The Gold Market: A Reply," JFM, 1989, v9(2), 175-178.

Ma, Christopher K., Ramesh P. Rao and Herbert J. Weinraub. "The Seasonality In Convertible Bond Markets: A Stock Effect Or Bond Effect?," JFR, 1988, v11(4), 335-348.

Ma, Christopher K., Ramesh P. Rao and Richard L. Peterson. "The Resiliency Of The High-Yield Bond Market: The LTV Default," JOF, 1989, v44(4), 1085-1098.

Ma, Christopher K., Ramesh P. Rao and R. Stephen Sears. "Volatility, Price Resolution, And The Effectiveness Of Price Limits," JFSR, 1989, v3(2/3), 165-200.

Ma, Christopher K., Ramesh P. Rao and R. Stephen Sears. "Limit Moves And Price Resolution: The Case Of The Treasury Bond Futures Market," JFM, 1989, v9(4), 321-336.

Ma, Christopher K., William H. Dare and Darla R. Donaldson. "Testing Rationality In Futures Markets," JFM, 1990, v10(2), 137-152.

Ma, Christopher. (Jaffe, Jeffrey F., Randolph Westerfield and Christopher Ma. "A Twist On The Monday Effect In Stock Prices: Evidence From The U.S. And Foreign Stock Markets," JBF, 1989, v13(4/5), 641-650.)

Ma, Cindy W. "Forecasting Efficiency Of Energy Futures Prices," JFM, 1989, v9(5), 393-420.

Ma, Cindy. (Edwards, Franklin R. and Cindy Ma. "Commodity Pool Performance: Is The Information Contained In Pool Prospectuses Useful?," JFM, 1988, v8(5), 589-616.)

Ma, James C. "A Survey Of Finance Department Computer Usage In The California State University And Colleges," JFED, 1989, v18, 71-74.

Ma, Ronald. (Bloomfield, Ted and Ronald Ma. "The Weighted Average Cost Of Capital: Some Questions On Its Definition, Interpretation, And Use: Comment," JOF, 1975, v30(3), 887-888.)

Ma, Tai. (Hansen, Robert S., John M. Pinkerton and Tai Ma. "On The Rightholders' Subscription To The Underwritten Rights Offering," JBF, 1986, v10(4), 595-604.)

Ma, Tai. (Hansen, Robert S., John M. Pinkerton and Tai Ma. "The Allocation Ratio Decision In The Underwritten Rights Offering," RIF, 1988, v7, 201-226.)

Maarek, G. (Levy-Garboua, V. and G. Maarek. "Bank Behavior And Monetary Policy," JBFR, 1978, v2(1), 15-46.)

Maatman, Gerald L. "A Proposal For Change: Affordable Automobile Insurance," JRI, 1989, v56(3), 518-524.

Maberly, Edwin D. "An Analysis Of Trading And Nontrading Period Returns For The Value Line COmposite Index; Spot Versus Futures: A Note," JFM, 1987, v7(5), 497-500.

Maberly, Edwin D. "Testing Futures Market Efficiency - A Restatement," JFM, 1985, v5(3), 425-432.

Maberly, Edwin D. "The Delivery Period And Daily Price Limits: A Comment," JFM, 1982, v2(1), 105-106.

Maberly, Edwin D. "The Informational Content Of The Interday Price Change With Respect to Stock Index Futures," JFM, 1986, v6(3), 385-396.

Maberly, Edwin D. "The Other Friday 'Bull' Effect: A Chance Occurrence Or The Harbinger Of Yet Another Puzzling Anomaly? A Note!," JFM, 1988, v8(6), 723-724.

Maberly, Edwin D. "The Relationship Between Stock Indices And Stock Index Futures From 3:00-3:15: A Note," JFM, 1989, v9(3), 271-273.

Maberly, Edwin D. (Dyl, Edward A. and Edwin D. Maberly. "A Possible Explanation Of The Weekend Effect," FAJ, 1988, v44(3), 83-84.)

Maberly, Edwin D. (Dyl, Edward A. and Edwin D. Maberly. "The Anomaly That Isn't There: A Comment On Friday The Thirteenth," JOF, 1988, v43(5), 1285-1286.)

Maberly, Edwin D. (Dyl, Edward A. and Edwin D. Maberly. "The Weekly Pattern In Stock Index Futures: A Further Note," JOF, 1986, v41(5), 1149-1152.)

Maberly, Edwin D. (Dyl, Edward A. and Edwin D. Maberly. "The Daily Distribution Of Changes In The Price Of Stock Index Futures," JFM, 1986, v6(4), 513-522.)

Maberly, Edwin D. (Herbst, Anthony F. and Edwin D. Maberly. "A Further Investigation Of The Day-Of-The-Week Effect In The Gold Market: A Comment," JFM, 1988, v8(3), 389-390.)

Maberly, Edwin D. (Herbst, Anthony F. and Edwin D. Maberly. "Stock Index Futures, Expiration Day Volatility, And The 'Special' Friday Opening: A Note," JFM, 1990, v10(3), 323-325.)

Maberly, Edwin D. (Ma, Christopher K., G. Wenchi Wong and Edwin

D. Maberly. "The Daily Effect In The Gold Market: A Reply," JFM, 1989, v9(2), 175-178.)

Maberly, Edwin D., David S. Allen and Roy F. Gilbert. "Stock Index Futures And Cash Market Volatility," FAJ, 1989, v45(6), 75-77.

Maberly, Edwin. (Herbst, Anthony F. and Edwin Maberly. "Shoes And Ships And Sealing Wax, Cabbages And Kings: Now Tail-Wagged Dogs And Stock Index Futures," FAJ, 1987, v43(6), 73-75.)

Maberly, Edwin. (Herbst, Anthony F., Edwin Maberly and Hans U. Sieber. "Sovereign Debt: Historical Perspective As Portent For Today," RDIBF, 1989, v3, 45-68.)

Maberly, Edwin. (Lakonishok, Josef and Edwin Maberly. "The Weekend Effect: Trading Patterns Of Individual And Institutional Investors," JOF, 1990, v45(1), 231-244.)

Mabert, Vincent A. and Robert C. Radcliffe. "Forecasting - A Systematic Modeling Methodology," FM, 1974, v3(3), 59-67.

Mabert, Vincent A. and Robert Stocco. "Managing And Monitoring A Forecasting System: The Chemical Bank Experience," JBR, 1982-83, v13(3), 195-201.

Mabert, Vincent A. (Boyd, Kevin and Vincent A. Mabert. "A Two Stage Forecasting Approach At Chemical Bank Of New York For Check Processing," JBR, 1977-78, v8(2), 101-107.)

Mabert, Vincent A., Randy Fairhurst and Michael A. Kilpatrick. "Chemical Bank's Encoder Daily Shift Scheduling System," JBR, 1979-80, v10(3), 173-180.

Mabry, Rodney H. and Arthur D. Sharplin. "The Relative Importance Of Journals Used In Finance Research," JFR, 1985, v8(4), 287-296.

Mabry, Rodney H. (Halperin, Sanford B. and Rodney H. Mabry. "Property And Casualty Insurance Lines Comparison: A Shift-Share Analysis," JRI, 1984, v51(3), 524-535.)

MacArthur, J. B. "The Valuation Of Fixed Assets In The Financial Accounts Of UK Nationalised Industries And The Implications For Monitoring Performance: A Reply" JBFA, 1982, v8(2), 273-276.

MacArthur, John B. "The Valuation Of Fixed Assets In The Financial Accounts Of U.K. Nationalised Industries And The Implications For Monitoring Performance," JBFA, 1980, v7(1), 75-87.

MacAvoy, Paul W. (Hansen, Ronald W., Paul W. MacAvoy and Clifford W. Smith, Jr. "Compensation Alternatives For Occupational Disease And Disability," JRI, 1989, v56(2), 252-274.)

MacAvoy, Paul W. (Koehn, Michael F., Paul W. MacAvoy and Harindra De Silva. "Market Responses To Asbestos In Buildings," JREFEC, 1990, v3(3), 213-232.)

MacBeth, J. D. (Fama, Eugene F. and J. D. MacBeth. "Tests Of The Multi-Period Two-Parameter Model," JFEC, 1974, v1(1), 43-66.)

MacBeth, James D. and Larry J. Merville. "An Empirical Examination Of The Black-Scholes Call Option Pricing Model," JOF, 1979, v34(5), 1173-1186.

MacBeth, James D. and Larry J. Merville. "Tests Of The Black-Scholes And Cox Call Option Valuation Models," JOF, 1980, v35(2), 285-303.

MacBeth, James D. (Emanuel, David C. and James D. MacBeth. "Further Results On The Constant Elasticity Of Variance Call Option Pricing Model," JFQA, 1982, v17(4), 533-554.)

MacBeth, James D. (Fama, Eugene F. and James D. MacBeth. "Long-Term Growth In A Short-Term Market," JOF, 1974, v29(3), 857-885.)

MacCrimmon, Kenneth R. and Donald A. Wehrung. "The Risk In-Basket," JOB, 1984, v57(3), 367-388.

MacDonald, D. L. "Life Insurance: A Study In Location Of Industry," JRI, 1960, v27(2), 93-100.

MacDonald, Don N. (Taube, Paul M. and Don N. MacDonald. "The Job Market For Finance Ph.D's," JFED, 1989, v18, 54-59.)

MacDonald, Don N. (Taube, Paul M. and Don N. MacDonald. "A Note On Residential Mortgage Selection: Borrower Decisions And Inflation Expectations," JRER, 1989, v4(1), 73-79.)

MacDonald, Don N., Harry L. White, Paul M. Taube and William L. Huth. "Flood Hazard Pricing And Insurance Premium Differentials: Evidence From The Housing Market," JRI, 1990, v57(4), 654-663.

MacDonald, Ronald. "The Norman Conquest Of $4.86 And The Asset Approach To The Exchange Rate," JIMF, 1985, v4(3), 373-387.

MacDonald, S. Scott and Scott E. Hein. "Future Rates And Forward Rates As Predictors Of Near-Term Treasury Bill Rates," JFM, 1989, v9(3), 249-262.

MacDonald, S. Scott, Richard L. Peterson and Timothy W. Koch. "Using Futures To Improve Treasury Bill Performance," JFM, 1988, v8(2), 167-184.

MacDonald, S. Scott. (Hein, Scott E., Christopher K. Ma and S. Scott MacDonald. "Testing Unbiasedness In Futures Markets: A Clarification," JFM, 1990, v10(5), 555-562.)

MacDonald, S. Scott. (Hein, Scott E. and S. Scott MacDonald. "On The Difference Between Daily Treasury Bill Futures Contract Rates And Implied Forward Rates," RFM, 1989, v8(3), 446-470.)

MacIntyre, Duncan M. "Rate Philosophy And Health Insurance Competition," JRI, 1965, v32(4), 525-538.

MacKay, Robert J. and Warren E. Weber. "Consumer Behavior And Quantity Constraints: Some Implications For Monetary Theory," JMCB, 1977, v9(1), 21-31.

MacKay, Robert S. (Jordan, James V., Robert S. Mackay and Eugene Moriarty. "The New Regulation Of Hybrid Debt Instruments," JACF, 1990, v2(4), 72-84.)

MacKie-Mason, Jeffrey K. "Do Taxes Affect Corporate Financing Decisions?," JOF, 1990, v45(5), 1471-1494.

MacKinlay, A. Craig and Krishna Ramaswamy. "Index-Futures Arbitrage And The Behavior Of Stock Index Futures Prices," RFS, 1988-89, v1(2), 137-158.

MacKinlay, A. Craig. "On Multivariate Tests Of The CAPM," JFEC, 1987, v18(2), 341-372.

MacKinlay, A. Craig. (Blume, Marshall E., A. Craig MacKinlay and Bruce Terker. "Order Imbalances And Stock Price Movements On October 19 And 20, 1987," JOF, 1989, v44(4), 827-848.)

MacKinlay, A. Craig. (Lo, Andrew W. and A. Craig MacKinlay. "Stock Market Prices Do Not Follow Random Walks: Evidence From A Simple Specification Test," RFS, 1988-89, v1(1), 41-66.)

MacKinlay, A. Craig. (Lo, Andrew W. and A. Craig MacKinlay. "When Are Contrarian Profits Due To Stock Market Overreaction?," RFS, 1990, v3(2), 175-206.)

MacKinlay, A. Craig. (Lo, Andrew W. and A. Craig MacKinlay. "Data-Snooping Biases In Tests Of Financial Asset Pricing Models," RFS, 1990, v3(3), 431-468.)

MacLaury, Bruce K. "OPEC Surpluses And World Financial Stability," JFQA, 1978, v13(4), 737-743.

MacMinn, Richard D. "A General Diversification Theorem: A Note," JOF, 1984, v39(2), 541-550.

MacMinn, Richard D. "Forward Markets, Stock Markets, And The Theory Of The Firm," JOF, 1987, v42(5), 1167-1185.

MacMinn, Richard D. "Insurance And Corporate Risk Management," JRI, 1987, v54(4), 658-677.

MacMinn, Richard D. and John D. Martin. "Uncertainty, The Fisher Model, And Corporate Financial Theory," RIF, 1988, v7, 227-264.

MacMinn, Richard D. and Li-Ming Han. "Limited Liability, Corporate Value, And The Demand For Liability Insurance," JRI, 1990, v57(4), 581-607.

MacPhee, Craig R. "Insurance And Reciprocity: Comment," JRI, 1973, v40(1), 139-141.

MacRae, C. Duncan. "The Relation Between Unemployment And Inflation In The Laffer-Ranson Model," JOB, 1972, v45(4), 513-518.

MacRae, C. Duncan. (Fredland, J. Eric and C. Duncan MacRae. "FHA Multifamily Financial Failure: A Review Of Empirical Studies," AREUEA, 1979, v7(1), 95-122.)

MacRae, C. Duncan. (Fullerton, David J. and C. Duncan MacRae. "FHA, Racial Discrimination And Urban Mortgages," AREUEA, 1978, v6(4), 451-470.)

Macaluso, Donald. (Hawkins, Robert G. and Donald Macaluso. "The Avoidance Of Restrictive Monetary Policies In Host Countries By Multinational Firms," JMCB, 1977, v9(4), 562-571.)

Macaulay, Frederick R. "The Social Sciences And The Unknown Future," JPM, 1974-75, v1(4), 66-72.

Maccini, Louis J. and Robert J. Rossana. "Joint Production, Quasi-Fixed Factors Of Production, And Investment In Finished Goods Inventory," JMCB, 1984, v16(2), 218-236.

Macedo, Rosemary. (Arnott, Robert D., Charles M. Kelso, Jr., Stephan Kiscadden and Rosemary Macedo. "Forecasting Factor Returns: An Intriguing Possibility," JPM, 1989, v16(1), 28-35.)

Machado, Ezequiel L. and Willard T. Carleton. "Financial Planning In A Regulated Environment," JFQA, 1978, v13(4), 759-777.

Macharzina, K. (Coenenberg, A. and K. Macharzina. "Accounting For Price Changes: An Analysis Of Current Developments In Germany," JBFA, 1976, v3(1), 53-68.)

Machlup, Fritz. "Comments On 'The Balance Of Payments,' And A Proposal To Reduce The Price Of Gold," JOF, 1961, v16(2), 186-193.

Machlup, Fritz. "International Monetary Arrangement," FAJ, 1968, v24(4), 25-30.

Machlup, Fritz. "The Teaching Of Money And Banking," JOF, 1949, v4(3), 227-230.

Machol, Robert E. and Eugene M. Lerner. "Risk, Ruin And Investment Analysis," JFQA, 1969, v4(4), 473-492.

Macirowski, T. (Yawitz, J., H. Kaufold, T. Macirowski and M. Smirlock. "The Pricing And Duration Of Floating Rate Bonds," JPM, 1986-87, v13(4), 49-56.)

Mack, Margery J. "Retirement Planning Program," JOB, 1954, v27(2), 169-175.

Mack, Thomas and Matthias Kulessa. "Reinsurance Decision Making And Expected Utility: Comment," JRI, 1985, v52(2), 311.

Mackey, Judith. (Kavesh, Robert A. And Judith Mackey. "A Financial Framework For Economic Growth," JOF, 1961, v16(2), 202-225.)

Mackey, Judith. (Kavesh, Robert A. and Judith Mackey. "Financial Aspects Of The Disarmament Process," JOF, 1963, v18(2), 130-150.)

Mackin, John J. "Machine Tool Industry," FAJ, 1968, v24(5), 53-57.

Mackintosh, George. "Chemical Producers And The Fertilizer Industry," FAJ, 1965, v21(3), 69-72.

Mackintosh, George. "Valuation Of Growth Stocks," FAJ, 1945, v1(1), 6-14.

Macomber, W. Sturgis. "Canadian Investment Opportunities," FAJ, 1957, v13(4), 85-90.

Macomber, W. Sturgis. "Canadian Mineral Exploration Companies," FAJ, 1953, v9(4), 59-61.

Macomber, W. Sturgis. "Improved Outlook For Canadian Oil Equities," FAJ, 1954, v10(2), 47-50.

Macomber, W. Sturgis. "Spotlight On Canadian Oil Industry," FAJ, 1956, v12(2), 21-24.

Macris, Richard G. (Ho, Thomas S. Y. and Richard G. Macris. "Dealer Bid-Ask Quotes And Transaction Prices: An Empirical Study Of Some AMEX Options," JOF, 1984, v39(1), 23-45.)

Macurda, Donald B. "Abandonment Of Basing Point System," FAJ, 1948, v4(4), 28-33.

Macurda, Donald B. "Brewing Industry Achieving Investment Status," FAJ, 1950, v6(1), 31-40.

Macurda, Donald B. "Investment Opportunities In India," FAJ, 1952, v8(5), 29-32.

Macurda, Donald B. "Plant Expansion In Relation To Consumption Capacity," FAJ, 1952, v8(3), 39-44.

Madan, Dilip B. and Eugene Seneta. "The Variance Gamma (V.G.) Model For Share Market Returns," JOB, 1990, v63(4), 511-524.

Madan, Dilip B., Frank Milne and Hersh Shefrin. "The Multinomial Option Pricing Model And Its Brownian And Poisson Limits," RFS, 1989, v2(2), 251-266.

Madansky, A. (Gastineau, G. L. and A. Madansky. "Simulation Is No Guide To Option Strategies," FAJ, 1979, v35(5), 61-76.)

Madansky, Albert. "Introduction To Symposium On Forecasting With Econometric Methods," JOB, 1978, v51(4), 547-548.

Madansky, Albert. "On Conjoint Analysis And Quantal Choice Models," JOB, 1980, v53(3), Part 2, S37-S44.

Madansky, Albert. (Banks, Seymour and Albert Madansky. "Estimation Of Multimagazine Readership," JOB, 1958, v31(3), 235-242.)

Madansky, Albert. (Gastineau, Gary L. and Albert Madansky. "Some Comments On The CBOE Call Option Index," FAJ, 1984, v40(4), 58-67.)

Madansky, Albert. (Gastineau, Gary and Albert Madansky. "S&P 500 Stock Index Futures Evaluation Tables," FAJ, 1983, v39(6), 68-76.)

Maddala, G. S. (Vogel, Robert C. and G. S. Maddala. "Cross-Section Estimates Of Liquid Asset Demand By Manufacturing Corporations," JOF, 1967, v22(4),557-575.)

Madden, Gerald P. "Potential Corporate Takeovers And Market Efficiency: A Note," JOF, 1981, v36(5), 1191-1197.

Madden, Gerald P. "The Performance Of Common Stocks After Intensive Trading By Insiders," FR, 1979, v14(2), 27-35.

Madden, Gerald P. "Using Value/Screen Plus For A Portfolio Management Project," JFED, 1989, v18, 65-70.

Madden, Gerald P. (Fischer, Donald E. and Gerald P. Madden. "Improving The Investments Course With A Securities Trading Game," JFED, 1979, v8, 71-76.)

Madden, Gerald P. (Meador, Joseph W., Gerald P. Madden and David J. Johnston. "On The Probability Of Acquisition Of Non-Life Insurers," JRI, 1986, v53(4), 621-643.)

Madden, Gerald P. (Nunn, Kenneth P., Jr., Gerald P. Madden and Michael J. Gombola. "Are Some Insiders More 'Inside' Than Others?," JPM, 1982-83, v9(3), 18-22.)

Madden, Gerald P., Kenneth P. Nunn, Jr. and Alan Wiemann. "Mutual Fund Performance And Market Capitalization," FAJ, 1986, v42(4), 67-70.

Madden, Gerald P., Lynn W. Marples and Lal C. Chugh. "A Stock Market Evaluation Of Management Buyouts," JBFA, 1990, v17(3), 351-358.

Madison, James. "The Passion Of Faction And Its Control," JPM, 1975-76, v2(3), 67-70.

Madsen, Howard C. (Scherr, Bruce A. and Howard C. Madsen. "Observations On The Relationship Between Agricultural Commodity Prices And Real Interest Rates," JFM, 1983, v3(1), 47-54.)

Madura, J. (Howe, J. S. and J. Madura. "The Impact Of International Listings On Risk: Implications For Capital Market Integration," JBF, 1990, v14(6), 1133-1142.)

Madura, Jeff and E. Joe Nosari. "Optimal Portfolio Of Foreign Currencies With Borrowing And Lending: A Comment," JMCB, 1982, v14(4), Part 1, 531.

Madura, Jeff and Wallace Reiff. "A Hedge Strategy For International Portfolios," JPM, 1985-86, v12(1), 70-74.

Madura, Jeff and Richard H. Fosberg. "The Impact Of Financing Sources On Multinational Projects," JFR, 1990, v13(1), 61-70.

Madura, Jeff and Wm. R. McDaniel. "The Reaction Of Bank Holding Company Share Prices To Citicorp's $1 Billion Stock Issue," IJOF, 1990, v3(1), 101-120.

Madura, Jeff and Wm. R. McDaniel. "Market Reaction To Increased Loan Loss Reserves At Money-Center Banks," JFSR, 1989, v3(4), 359-369.

Madura, Jeff, Ann Marie White and Wm. R. McDaniel. "Reaction Of British Bank Share Prices To Citicorp's Announced $3 Billion Increase In Loan-Loss Reserves," JBF, 1991, v15(1), 151-163.

Madura, Jeff. "Empirical Measurement Of Exchange Rate Betas," JPM, 1982-83, v9(4), 43-46.

Maese, Judy E. "Competitive Versus Negotiated Municipal Revenue Bond Issues: An Investigation Of Underpricing," FM, 1985, v14(1), 26-32.

Maeshiro, Asatoshi. (Cohen, Jacob and Asatoshi Maeshiro. "The Significance Of Money On the State Level," JMCB, 1977, v9(4), 672-678.)

Maffei, Richard B. "Simulation, Sensitivity, And Management Decision Rules," JOB, 1958, v31(3), 177-186.

Magarick, Patrick. "Training Problems Involved In The Handling Of Foreign Claims," JRI, 1961, v28(3), 107-109.

Magat, Wesley A., W. Kip Viscusi and Joel Huber. "Consumer Processing Of Hazard Warning Information," JRU, 1988, v1(2), 201-232.

Magee, H. Robert and Gordon S. Roberts. "On Portfolio Theory, Holding Period Assumptions, And Bond Maturity Diversification," FM, 1979, v8(4), 68-71.

Magee, John F. "Assessing A Company's Technological Program," FAJ, 1982, v38(4), 56-59.

Magee, John H. "The Position Of The Government As An Insurer Of Ocean Marine War Risks," JRI, 1943, v10, 46-58.

Magee, Robert P. "An Evaluation Of Prospective-Payment Plans For Hospitals," JOB, 1977, v50(4), 448-461.

Magen, S. D. "Cost Of Capital And Dividend Policies In Commercial Banks," JFQA, 1971, v6(2),733-746.

Maggi, P. G. (Feuerstein, A. E. and P. G. Maggi. "Computer Investment Research," FAJ, 1968, v24(1), 154-158.)

Magid, James I. "The Mobile Home Industry," FAJ, 1969, v25(5), 29-34.

Magill, W. G. W. (Leech, Stewart A., Denis J. Pratt and W. G. W. Magill. "Company Asset Revaluations And Inflation In Australia, 1950 To 1975," JBFA, 1978, v5(4), 353-362.)

Magrath, Joseph J. "The Proposed Revision Of The New York Insurance Law," JRI, 1938, v5, 40-46.

Maguire, W. G. "Natural Gas: New Era For A Growth Industry," FAJ, 1962, v18(5), 19-21.

Mahajan, Arvind and Dileep Mehta. "Swaps, Expectations, And Exchange Rates," JBF, 1986, v10(1), 7-20.

Mahajan, Arvind and Dileep Mehta. "Strong Form Efficiency Of The Foreign Exchange Market And Bank Positions," JFR, 1984, v7(3), 197-207.

Mahajan, Arvind. "Pricing Expropriation Risk," FM, 1990, v19(4), 77-86.

Mahajan, Arvind. (Abeysekera, Sarath P. and Arvind Mahajan. "A Test Of The APT In Pricing UK Stocks," JBFA, 1987, v14(3), 377-392.)

Mahajan, Arvind. (Kolari, James, Arvind Mahajan and Edward M. Saunders. "The Effect Of Changes In Reserve Requirements On Bank Stock Prices," JBF, 1988, v12(2), 183-198.)

Mahajan, Arvind. (Saunders, Edward M., Jr. and Arvind Mahajan. "An Empirical Examination Of Composite Stock Index Futues Pricing," JFM, 1988, v8(2), 210-228.)

Mahan, Alfred T. "What Price 'Defensive' Stocks?," FAJ, 1965, v21(5), 69-78.

Mahapatra, S., M. Chase and W. Rogers. "Information Interaction Effects Of Inflation Adjusted Accounting Data On Individual Decision-Maker's Sophistication And Risk Preference," JBFA, 1989, v16(5), 635-650.

Mahapatra, Sitikantha. "Investor Reaction To Corporate Social Accounting," JBFA, 1984, v11(1),29-40.

Maher, John E. "The Interpretation Of Wage Data," JOB, 1957, v30(1), 44-49.

Maheshwari, Arun. (Green, Paul E. and Arun Maheshwari. "Common Stock Perception And Preference: An Application Of Multidimensional Scaling," JOB, 1969, v42(4), 439-457.)

Mahlmann, Karsten. (Fleischman, Edward H., William E. Seale, Karsten Mahlmann and Hans R. Stoll. "Panel Discussion On Regulatory Issues Facing The Futures Industry," RFM, 1988, v7(1), 200-216.)

Mahoney, James M. (Dunetz, Mark L. and James M. Mahoney. "Using Duration And Convexity In The Analysis Of Callable Bonds," FAJ, 1988, v44(3), 53-73.)

Mai, Chao-Cheng. (Hwang, Hong and Chao-Cheng Mai. "Sequential Entry And Plant Location In Oligopolistic Competition," JREFEC, 1990, v3(1), 43-54.)

Maier, Steven F. and James H. Vander Weide. "What Lockbox And Disbursement Models Really Do," JOF, 1983, v38(2), 361-371.

Maier, Steven F. and James H. Vander Weide. "A Unified Location Model For Cash Disbursements And Lock-Box Collections," JBR, 1976-77, v7(2), 166-172.

Maier, Steven F. and James H. Vander Weide. "A Practical Approach To Short-Run Financial Planning," FM, 1978, v7(4), 10-16.

Maier, Steven F. and James H. Vander Weide. "The Lock-Box Location Problem: A Practical Reformulation," JBR, 1974-75, v5(2), 92-95.

Maier, Steven F. "Float Management: The Impact Of Regulatory And Technological Changes, Electronic Funds Transfer And National Banking," AWCM, 1990, v1(1), 67-78.

Maier, Steven F. (Cohen, Kalman J., Steven F. Maier, Robert A. Schwartz and David K. Whitcomb. "Limit Orders, Market Structure, And The Returns Generation Process," JOF, 1978, v33(3), 723-736.)

Maier, Steven F. (Cohen, Kalman J., Stephen F. Maier, Robert A. Schwartz and David K. Whitcomb. "Market Makers And The Market Spread: A Review Of Recent Literature," JFQA, 1979, v14(4), 813-835.)

Maier, Steven F. (Cohen, Kalman J., Steven F. Maier, Robert A. Schwartz and David K. Whitcomb. "The Returns Generating Process, Returns Variance, And The Effect Of Thinness In Securities Markets," JOF, 1978, v33(1), 149-167.)

Maier, Steven F. (Cohen, Kalman J., Steven F. Maier, Robert A. Schwartz and David K. Whitcomb. "An Analysis Of The Economic Justification For Consolidation In A Secondary Security Market," JBF, 1982, v6(1),117-136.)

Maier, Steven F. (Cohen, Kalman J., Gabriel A. Hawawini, Steven F. Maier, Robert Schwartz And David K. Whitcomb. "Implications Of Microstructure Theory For Empirical Research On Stock Price Behavior," JOF, 1980, v35(2),249-257.)

Maier, Steven F. (Cohen, Kalman J., Gabriel A. Hawawini, Steven F. Maier, Robert A. Schwartz and David K. Whitcomb. "Friction In The Trading Process And The Estimation Of Systematic Risk," JFEC, 1983, v12(2), 263-278.)

Maier, Steven F. (Cohen, Kalman J., Steven F. Maier, Walter L. Ness, Jr., Hitoshi Okuda, Robert A. Schwartz and David K. Whitcomb. "The Impact Of Designated Market Makers On Security Prices," JBF, 1977, v1(3), 219-247.)

Maier, Steven F., David W. Peterson and James VanderWeide. "Monte Carlo Investigation Of Characteristics Of Optimal Geometric Mean Portfolios," JFQA, 1977, v12(2), 215-233.

Maier, Steven F., David W. Robinson and James H. Vander Weide. "A Short-Term Disbursement Forecasting Model," FM, 1981, v10(1), 9-20.

Main, Brian G. M. "Corporate Insurance Purchases And Taxes," JRI, 1983, v50(2), 197-223.

Main, Brian G. "Risk Management And The Theory Of The Firm: Comment," JRI, 1983, v50(1), 140-144.

Maine, Robert F. "Common Stocks As Life Insurance Investments," JRI, 1947, v14, 48-54.

Mains, Norman E. "Risk, The Pricing Of Capital Assets, And The Evaluation Of Investment Portfolios: Comment," JOB, 1977, v50(3), 371-384.

Mais, Eric L., William T. Moore and Ronald C. Rogers. "A Re-Examination Of Shareholder Wealth Effects Of Calls Of Convertible Preferred Stock," JOF, 1989, v44(5), 1401-1410.

Maisel, Sherman J. and Robert Jacobson. "Interest Rate Changes And Commercial Bank Revenues And Costs," JFQA, 1978, v13(4), 687-700.

Maisel, Sherman J. "Some Relationships Between Assets And Liabilities Of Thrift Institutions," JOF, 1968, v23(2), 367-378.

Maisel, Sherman J. "The Economic And Finance Literature And Decision Making," JOF, 1974, v29(2),313-322.

Majd, Saman and Robert S. Pindyck. "Time To Build, Option Value, And Investment Decisions," JFEC, 1987, v18(1), 7-28.

Majluf, Nicholas S. (Myers, Stewart C. and Nicholas S. Majluf. "Corporate Financing And Investment Decisions When Firms Have Information That Investors Do Not Have," JFEC, 1984, v13(2), 187-221.)

Mak, King-Tim. (Chan, Yuk-Shee and King-Tim Mak. "Depositors' Welfare, Deposit Insurance, And Deregulation," JOF, 1985, v40(3), 959-974.)

Mak, Yuen Teen. "Contingency Fit, Internal Consistency And Financial Performance," JBFA, 1989, v16(2), 273-300.

Makhija, Anil K. and Howard E. Thompson. "Some Aspects Of Equilibrium For A Cross-Section Of Firms Signalling Profitability With Dividends: A Note," JOF, 1986, v41(1), 249-254.

Makhija, Anil K. (Bhandari, Arvind, Theoharry Grammatikos, Anil K. Makhija and George Papaioannou. "Risk And Return On Newly Listed Stocks: The Post-Listing Experience," JFR, 1989, v12(2), 93-102.)

Makhija, Anil K. (Ferris, Stephen, Robert Haugen and Anil K. Makhija. "Predicting Contemporary Volume With Historic Volume At Differential Price Levels: Evidence Supporting The Disposition Effect," JOF, 1988, v43(3), 677-697.)

Makin, John H. "Anticipated Inflation And Interest Rates In An Open Economy," JMCB, 1978, v10(3),275-289.

Makin, John H. "Identifying A Reserve Base For The Euro-Dollar System," JOF, 1973, v28(3), 609-617.

Makin, John H. "Portfolio Theory And The Problem Of Foreign Exchange Risk," **JOF**, 1978, v33(2), 517-534.

Makin, John H. "Portfolio Theory And The Problem Of Foreign Exchange Risk: Reply," **JOF**, 1981, v36(3),743-745.

Makin, John H. "The Problem Of Coexistence Of SDRs And A Reserve Currency," **JMCB**, 1972, v4(3),509-528.

Makin, John H. (Levi, Maurice D. and John H. Makin. "Fisher, Phillips, Friedman And The Measured Impact Of Inflation On Interest," **JOF**, 1979, v34(1), 35-52.)

Makin, John H. (Levi, Maurice D. and John H. Makin. "Fisher, Phillips, Friedman And The Measured Impact Of Inflation On Interest: A Reply," **JOF**, 1981, v36(4), 963-969.)

Makin, John H. (Niho, Yoshio and John H. Makin. "The Solution To The Inverse Problem Of Optimal Control," **JMCB**, 1978, v10(3), 371-377.)

Makinen, G. E. "On Balance-Of-Payments Payback Periods: A Reply," **JOB**, 1972, v45(3), 422-426.

Makinen, G. E. "The 'Payoff' Period Of Direct Foreign Investment By The Untied States Automotive Industry," **JOB**, 1970, v43(4), 395-409.

Makinen, G. E. (Bomberger, W. A. and G. E. Makinen. "The Fischer Effect: Graphical Treatment And Some Econometric Implications," **JOF**, 1977, v32(3), 719-733.)

Makinen, Gail E. (Anderson, Robert, William Bomberger, and Gail Makinen. "The Demand For Money, The 'Reform Effect,' And The Money Supply Process In Hyperinflation: The Evidence From Greece And Hungary," **JMCB**, 1988, v20(4), 653-672.)

Makinen, Gail E. and G. Thomas Woodward. "The Taiwanese Hyperinflation And Stabilization Of 1945-1952," **JMCB**, 1989, v21(1), 90-105.

Makinen, Gail F. (Gray, H. Peter and Gail F. Makinen. "The Balance-Of-Payments Contributions Of Multinational Corporations," **JOB**, 1967, v40(3), 339-343.)

Makowski, Louis and Lynne Pepall. "Easy Proofs Of Unanimity And Optimality Without Spanning: A Pedagogical Note," **JOF**, 1985, v40(4), 1245-1250.

Makridakis, Spyros G. and Steven C. Wheelwright. "An Analysis Of the Interrelationships Among The Major World Stock Exchanges," **JBFA**, 1974, v1(2), 195-215.

Maksimovic, V. (Kim, M. and V. Maksimovic. "Technology, Debt And The Exploitation Of Growth Options," **JBF**, 1990, v14(6), 1113-1132.)

Maksimovic, Vojislav, Gordon Sick and Josef Zechner. "Forward Markets, Stock Markets, And The Theory Of The Firm: Comment," **JOF**, 1989, v44(2), 525-528.

Maksimovic, Vojislav. "Product Market Imperfections And Loan Commitments," **JOF**, 1990, v45(5), 1641-1654.

Maksimovic, Vojislav. (Brennan, Michael J., Vojislav Maksimovic and Josef Zechner. "Vendor Financing," **JOF**, 1988, v43(5), 1127-1141.)

Maksimovic, Vojislav. (Cadsby, Charles Bram, Murray Frank and Vojislav Maksimovic. "Pooling, Separating, And Semiseparating Equilibria In Financial Markets: Some Experimental Evidence," **RFS**, 1990, v3(3), 315-342.)

Maksimovic, Vojislav. (Eckbo, B. Espen, Vojislav Maksimovic and Joseph Williams. "Consistent Estimation Of Cross-Sectional Models In Event Studies," **RFS**, 1990, v3(3), 343-366.)

Maksimovic, Vojislav. (Kim, Moshe and Vojislav Maksimovic. "Debt And Input Misallocation," **JOF**, 1990, v45(3), 795-816.)

Maksy, Mostafa M. (Bernstein, Leopold A. and Mostafa M. Maksy. "Again Now: How Do We Measure Cash Flow From Operations?," **FAJ**, 1985, v41(4), 74-77.)

Malatesta, Paul H. and Rex Thompson. "Partially Anticipated Events: A Model Of Stock Price Reactions With An Application To Corporate Acquisitions," **JFEC**, 1985, v14(2), 237-250.

Malatesta, Paul H. "Measuring Abnormal Performance: The Event Parameter Approach Using Joint Generalized Least Squares," **JFQA**, 1986, v21(1), 27-38.

Malatesta, Paul H. "The Wealth Effect Of Merger Activity And The Objective Functions Of Merging Firms," **JFEC**, 1983, v11(1), 155-181.

Malatesta, Paul H. (Karpoff, Jonathan M. and Paul H. Malatesta. "The Wealth Effects Of Second-Generation State Takeover Legislation," **JFEC**, 1989, v25(2), 291-322.)

Malatesta, Paul H. and Ralph A. Walkling. "Poison Pill Securities: Stockholder Wealth, Profitability, And Ownership Structure," **JFEC**, 1988, v20(1/2), 347-376.

Malatesta, Paul H. and Rex Thompson. "Stock Price Reactions To Partially Anticipated Events: Evidence On The Economic Impact Of Corporate Acquisition Attempts," **RIF**, 1986, v6, 119-148.

Maldonado, Rita and Anthony Saunders. "Foreign Exchange Futures And The Law Of One Price," **FM**, 1983, v12(1), 19-23.

Maldonado, Rita and Anthony Saunders. "International Portfolio Diversification And The Inter-Temporal Stability Of International Stock Market Relationships, 1957-1978," **FM**, 1981, v10(4), 54-63.

Maldonado, Rita M. (Keenan, Michael and Rita M. Maldonado. "The Redundancy Of Earnings Leverage In A Cost Of Capital Decision Framework," **JBFA**, 1976, v3(2), 43-56.)

Malick, William M. and Ronald W. Ward. "Stock Effects And Seasonality In The FCOJ Futures Basis," **JFM**, 1987, v7(2), 157-168.

Malin, Max. "Investing In Uranium," **FAJ**, 1955, v11(2), 117-121.

Malindretos, John. The Keynesian And The Monetary Approaches To International Finance: A Reexamination," **IJOF**, 1988, v1(1), 46-89.

Maling, Charles. "On The Consumers' Surplus Of Money Holders And The Measuring Of Money's Services," **JMCB**, 1987, v19(4), 469-483.

Malisoff, Harry and William O'Donnell. "Is Social Insurance A Profession?," **JRI**, 1969, v36(1), 159-162.

Malisoff, Harry. "Beyond The Limits Of State Workmen's Compensation: Comment," **JRI**, 1973, v40(2), 287-290.

Malisoff, Harry. "Duration Issues In Unemployment Insurance," **JRI**, 1962, v29(2), 199-204.

Malisoff, Harry. "Reimbursing The Hospital - The Differences The Third Party Makes: Comment," **JRI**, 1971, v38(1), 137-139.

Malisoff, Harry. "Review Article - The Scope Of Manpower," **JRI**, 1968, v35(2), 289-291.

Malisoff, Harry. "Social Insurance In The Liberal Arts Curriculum," **JRI**, 1967, v34(2), 311-314.

Malisoff, Harry. "The Informational Problem In Social Insurance Research And Instruction," **JRI**, 1968, v35(1), 133-138.

Malisoff, Harry. "The Insurance Principle And Unemployment Insurance," **JRI**, 1961, v28(2), 103-106.

Malisoff, Harry. "Welfare And Social Insurance In A Great Society," **JRI**, 1966, v33(4), 513-527.

Malitz, Ileen B. "A Re-Examination Of The Wealth Expropriation Hypothesis: The Case Of Captive Finance Subsidiaries," **JOF**, 1989, v44(4), 1039-1048.

Malitz, Ileen and Richard Cohn. "The Nonequivalence Of Subordinated Debt And Equity From The Senior Creditor's Standpoint: A Pedagogical Note," **JFED**, 1987, v16, 1-5.

Malitz, Ileen. "On Financial Contracting: The Determinants Of Bond Covenants," **FM**, 1986, v15(2), 18-25.

Malizia, Emil E. "A Note On Real Estate Marketing Research," **JRER**, 1990, v5(3), 393-401.

Malkiel, Burton G. and Paul B. Firstenberg. "A Winning Strategy For An Efficient Market," **JPM**, 1977-78, v4(4), 20-25.

Malkiel, Burton G. and Richard Quandt. "The Supply Of Money And Common Stock Prices: Comment," **JOF**, 1972, v27(4), 921-926.

Malkiel, Burton G. "The Brady Commission Report: A Critique," **JPM**, 1987-88, v14(4), 9-13.

Malkiel, Burton G. "The Capital Formation Problem In The United States," **JOF**, 1979, v34(2), 291-306.

Malkiel, Burton G. "The Rejection Of The Tiffin Plan And The Alternative Accepted," **JOF**, 1963, v18(3), 511-536.

Malkiel, Burton G. "The Valuation Of Closed-End Investment-Company Shares," **JOF**, 1977, v32(3), 847-859.

Malkiel, Burton G. (Asch, Peter, Burton G. Malkiel and Richard E. Quandt. "Racetrack Betting And Informed Behavior," **JFEC**, 1982, v10(2), 187-194.)

Malkiel, Burton G. (Asch, Peter, Burton G. Malkiel and Richard E. Quandt. "Market Efficiency In Racetrack Betting," **JOB**, 1984, v57(2), 165-176.)

Malkiel, Burton G. (Asch, Peter, Burton G. Malkiel and Richard E. Quandt. "Market Efficiency In Racetrack Betting: Further Evidence And A Correction," **JOB**, 1986, v59(1), 157-160.)

Malkiel, Burton G. (Cragg, John G. and Burton G. Malkiel. "The Consensus And Accuracy Of Some Predictions Of The Growth Of Corporate Earnings," **JOF**, 1968, v23(1), 67-84.)

Malkiel, Burton G. (Von Furstenberg, George M. and Burton G. Malkiel. "Financial Analysis In An Inflationary Environment," **JOF**, 1977, v32(2), 575-588.)

Malkiel, Burton G., George M. Von Furstenberg and Harry S. Watson. "Expectations, Tobin's q, And Industry Investment," **JOF**, 1979, v34(2), 549-561.

Malkiel, Burton. (Fair, Ray and Burton Malkiel. "The Determination Of Yield Differentials Between Debt Instruments Of The Same Maturity," **JMCB**, 1971, v3(4), 733-749.)

Malkiel, Burton. (Miller, Merton H., Burton Malkiel, Myron Scholes and John D. Hawke, Jr. "Stock Index Futures And The Crash Of '87," **JACF**, 1989, v1(4), 6-17.)

Malley, Susan L. and Susan Jayson. "Why Do Financial Executives Manage Pensions Funds The Way They Do?," **FAJ**, 1986, v42(6), 56-62.

Malley, Susan L. "Unfunded Pension Liabilities And The Cost Of Equity Capital," **FR**, 1983, v18(2),133-145.

Malley, Susan. (Perez, Robert and Susan Malley. "Asset Allocation And The Social Security System," **FM**, 1983, v12(1), 29-35.)

Malliaris, A. G. "Approaches To The Cash Management Problem," **AFPAF**, 1989, v3(1), 231-244.

Malliaris, A. G. and Jorge L. Urrutia. "Linkages Of National Stock Markets: Statistical Evidence Before, During And After The October 1987 Crash," **RDIBF**, 1991, v4/5, 336-369.

Malliaris, A. G. and Jorge Urrutia. "Tests Of Random Walk Of Hedge Ratios And Measures Of Hedging Effectiveness For Stock Indexes And Foreign Currencies," **JFM**, 1991, v11(1), 55-68.

Mallman, Thomas L. "Volatility In Municipal Bonds: Estimating And Using Volatility Factors," **FAJ**, 1981, v37(6), 54-59.

Malone, Erwin L. "The Non-Linear Systems Experiment In Participative Management," **JOB**, 1975, v48(1), 52-64.

Malone, John R. "The Capital Expenditure For Owner-Occupied Housing: A Study Of Determinants," **JOB**, 1966, v39(3), 359-365.

Malone, R. Phil. (Atkinson, Stanley M. and R. Phil Malone. "The Use Of Low-Cost Microcomputers In Teaching Investments And Corporate Finance," **JFED**, 1983, v12, 78-81.)

Malone, R. Phil. (Pettway, Richard H. and R. Phil Malone. "Automatic Dividend Reinvestment Plans Of Nonfinancial Corporations," **FM**, 1973, v2(4), 11-18.)

Malone, R. Phil. (Sareewiwatthana, Paiboon and R. Phil Malone. "Market Behavior And The Capital Asset Pricing Model In The Securities Exchange Of Thailand: An Empirical Application," **JBFA**, 1985, v12(3), 439-452.)

Maloney, Kevin J. and Jess B. Yawitz. "Interest Rate Risk, Immunization, And Duration," **JPM**, 1985-86, v12(3), 41-49.

Maloney, Kevin J. and Thomas I. Selling. "Simplifying Tax Simplification: An Analysis Of Its Impact On The Profitability Of Capital Investment," **FM**, 1985, v14(2), 33-42.

Maloney, Kevin J. (Yawitz, Jess B. and Kevin J. Maloney. "Evaluating The Decision To Issue Original Issue Discount Bonds: Term Structue And Tax Effects," **FM**, 1983, v12(4), 36-46.)

Maloney, Kevin J. (Yawitz, Jess B., Kevin J. Maloney and William J. Marshall. "The Term Structure And Callable Bond Yield Spreads," **JPM**, 1982-83, v9(2), 57-63.)

Maloney, Kevin J. (Yawitz, Jess B., Kevin J. Maloney and Louis H. Ederington. "Taxes, Default Risk, And Yield Spreads," **JOF**, 1985, v40(4), 1127-1140.)

Maloney, Kevin J. and Dennis E. Logue. "Neglected Complexities In Structured Bond Portfolios," **JPM**, 1989, v15(2), 59-68.

Maloney, Kevin J. and Mark J. Byrne. "An Equilibrium Debt Option Pricing Model In Discrete Time," **JBF**, 1989, v13(3), 421-442.

Maloney, Kevin J. and Richard J. Rogalski. "Call-Option Pricing And The Turn Of The Year," **JOB**, 1989, v62(4), 539-552.

Maloney, Kevin J., William J. Marshall and Jess B. Yawitz. "The Effect Of Risk On The Firm's Optimal Capital Stock: A Note," **JOF**, 1983, v38(4), 1279-1284.

Maloney, Michael T. and Robert E. McCormick. "A Theory Of Cost And Intermittent Production," *JOB*, 1983, v56(2), 139-154.

Maloney, Peter J. "Managing Currency Exposure: The Case Of Western Mining," *JACF*, 1990, v2(4), 29-34.

Malouin, Jena-Louis. (Outreville, J. Francois and Jean-Louis Malouin. "What Are The Major Journals That Members Of ARIA Read?," *JRI*, 1985, v52(4), 723-733.)

Man, King's. "Is The Committee On General Insurance Terminology Really General?: Comment," *JRI*, 1965, v32(1), 139.

Manage, Neela. (Barth, James R., Padma Gotur, Neela Manage and Anthony M. J. Yezer. "The Effect Of Government Regulations On Personal Loan Markets: A Tobit Estimation Of A Microeconomic Model," *JOF*, 1983, v38(4), 1233-1251.

Manakyan, Herman and Carolyn Carroll. "An Empirical Examination Of The Existence Of A Signaling Value Function For Dividends," *JFR*, 1990, v13(3), 201-210.

Manaster, Steven and Gary Koehler. "The Calculation Of Implied Variances From The Black-Scholes Model: A Note," *JOF*, 1982, v37(1), 227-230.

Manaster, Steven and Richard J. Rendleman, Jr. "Option Prices As Predictors Of Equilibrium Stock Prices," *JOF*, 1982, v37(4), 1043-1057.

Manaster, Steven. "Real And Nominal Efficient Sets," *JOF*, 1979, v34(1), 93-102.

Manaster, Steven. (Carter, Richard and Steven Manaster. "Initial Public Offerings And Underwriter Reputation," *JOF*, 1990, v45(4), 1045-1067.)

Manaster, Steven. (Chiras, Donald P. and Steven Manaster. "The Information Content Of Option Prices And A Test Of Market Efficiency," *JFEC*, 1978, v6(2/3), 213-234.)

Manaster, Steven. (Gay, Gerald D. and Steven Manaster. "Hedging Agains Commodity Price Inflation: Stocks And Bills As Substitutes For Futures Contracts," *JOB*, 1982, v55(2), 317-344.)

Manaster, Steven. (Gay, Gerald D. and Steven Manaster. "The Quality Option Implicit In Futures Contracts," *JFEC*, 1984, v13(3), 353-370.)

Manaster, Steven. (Gay, Gerald D. and Steven Manaster. "Implicit Delivery Options And Optimal Delivery Strategies For Financial Futures Contracts," *JFEC*, 1986, v16(1), 41-72.)

Manchester, Joyce. "How Money Affects Real Output," *JMCB*, 1989, v21(1), 16-32.

Mancke, Richard B. "The Future Of OPEC," *JOB*, 1975, v48(1), 11-19.

Mandel, Steven. (Leibowitz, Martin L., Thomas E. Klaffky, Steven Mandel and Alfred Weinberger. "Horizon Matching: A New Approach To Dedicated Portfolios," *JPM*, 1984-85, v11(1), 93-96.)

Mandelbrot, Benoit B. "Correction Of An Error In 'The Variation Of Certain Speculative Prices' (1963)," *JOB*, 1972, v45(4), 542-543.

Mandelbrot, Benoit. "Forecasts Of Future Prices, Unbiased Markets, And 'Martingale' Models," *JOB*, 1966, v39(1), Part II, 242-255.

Mandelbrot, Benoit. "The Variation Of Some Other Speculative Prices," *JOB*, 1967, v40(4), 393-413.

Mandelbrot, Benoit. "The Variation Of Certain Speculative Prices," *JOB*, 1963, v36(4), 394-419.

Mandelker, Daniel R. "Zoning Reform: Comment," *AREUEA*, 1978, v6(3), 335-336.

Mandelker, Gershon and Artur Raviv. "Investment Banking: An Economic Analysis Of Optimal Underwriting Contracts," *JOF*, 1977, v32(3), 683-694.

Mandelker, Gershon and Kishore Tandon. "Common Stock Returns, Real Activity, Money, And Inflation: Some International Evidence," *JIMF*, 1985, v4(2), 267-286.

Mandelker, Gershon N. (Agrawal, Anup and Gershon N. Mandelker. "Managerial Incentives And Corporate Investment And Financing Decisions," *JOF*, 1987, v42(4), 823-838.)

Mandelker, Gershon N. (Agrawal, Anup and Gershon N. Mandelker. "Large Shareholders And The Monitoring Of Managers: The Case Of Antitakeover Charter Amendments," *JFQA*, 1990, v25(2), 143-162.)

Mandelker, Gershon N. and S. Ghon Rhee. "The Impact Of The Degrees Of Operating And Financial Leverage On Systematic Risk Of Common Stock," *JFQA*, 1984, v19(1), 45-57.

Mandelker, Gershon. "Risk And Return: The Case Of Merging Firms," *JFEC*, 1974, v1(4), 303-335.

Mandelker, Gershon. (Jaffe, Jeffrey F. and Gershon Mandelker. "The Value Of The Firm Under Regulation," *JOF*, 1976, v31(2), 701-713.)

Mandelker, Gershon. (Jaffe, Jeffrey F. and Gershon Mandelker. "The 'Fisher Effect' For Risky Assets: An Empirical Investigation," *JOF*, 1976, v31(2), 447-458.)

Mandelker, Gershon. (Jaffe, Jeffrey F. and Gershon Mandelker. "Inflation And The Holding Period Returns On Bonds," *JFQA*, 1979, v14(5), 959-979.)

Mandelker, Gershon. (Lev, Baruch and Gershon Mandelker. "Rejoinder To Reid And Honeycutt," *JOB*, 1975, v48(2), 281-303.)

Mandelker, Gershon. (Lev, Baruch and Gershon Mandelker. "The Microeconomic Consequences Of Corporate Mergers," *JOB*, 1972, v45(1), 85-104.)

Mandell, Lewis and Lorman L. Lundsten. "Diversion Of Credit Life Insurance Commissions By Bankers," *JBR*, 1977-78, v8(2), 72-76.

Mandell, Lewis, Ran Lachman and Yair Orgler. "Interpreting The Image Of Banking," *JBR*, 1981-82, v12(2), 96-104.

Mandell, Lewis. "Consumer Perception Of Incurred Interest Rates: An Empirical Test Of The Efficacy Of The Truth-In-Lending Law," *JOF*, 1971, v26(5),1143-1153.

Mandell, Lewis. "Diffusion Of EFTS Among National Banks," *JMCB*, 1977, v9(2), 341-348.

Mandell, Lewis. (Murphy, Neil B. and Lewis Mandell. "Reforming The Structure And Regulation Of Financial Institutions: The Evidence From The State Of Maine," *JBR*, 1978-79, v9(4), 200-212.)

Mandell, Lewis. (Murphy, Neil B. and Lewis Mandell. "Consumer Response To Restructured Financial Institutions: The Case Of Maine," *JMCB*, 1979, v11(1), 91-98.)

Mandell, Lewis. (Struck, Peter L. and Lewis Mandell. "The Effect Of Bank Deregulation On Small Business: A Note," *JOF*, 1983, v38(3), 1025-1031.)

Manegold, James. (Beaver, William and James Manegold. "The

Association Between Market-Determined And Accounting-Determined Measures Of Systematic Risk: Some Further Evidence," *JFQA*, 1975, v10(2), 231-284.)

Maness, Terry S. and A. J. Senchack. "Futures Hedging And The Reported Financial Position Of Thrift Institutions," *RFM*, 1986, v5(2), 142-159.

Maness, Terry S. "A Financial Planning Model: A Teaching Tool," *JFED*, 1979, v8, 90-93.

Maness, Terry S. "Optimal Versus Naive Buy-Hedging With T-Bill Futures," *JFM*, v1(3), 393-403.

Maness, Terry S. (Henderson, James W. and Terry S. Maness. "Financial Analysis And Forecasting: A Cash Flow Approach," *JFED*, 1983, v12, 92-99.)

Maness, Terry S. (Klemkosky, Robert C. and Terry S. Maness. "The Predictability Of Real Portfolio Risk Levels," *JOF*, 1978, v33(2), 631-639.)

Maness, Terry S. (Klemkosky, Robert C. and Terry S. Maness. "The Impact Of Options On The Underlying Securities," *JPM*, 1979-80, v6(2), 12-18.)

Maness, Terry S. (Lee, Wayne Y., Terry S. Maness and Donald L. Tuttle. "Nonspeculative Behavior And The Term Structure," *JFQA*, 1980, v15(1), 53-83.)

Maness, Terry S. (Tuttle, Donald L., Wayne Y. Lee and Terry S. Maness. "Stochastic Cash Flow Constraints And The Term Structure Of Interest," *JBF*, 1978, v2(2), 143-162.)

Manfrini, Joseph. "Branch Bank Stocks Cited As 'Better'," *FAJ*, 1959, v15(1), 77-80.

Manfrini, Joseph. "Interstate Banking For Interstate Commerce," *FAJ*, 1953, v9(4), 62-64.

Manfrini, Joseph. "Selecting A Bank Stock," *FAJ*, 1954, v10(2), 69-72.

Mangoletsis, I. D. "The Microeconomics Of Indirect Finance," *JOF*, 1975, v30(4), 1055-1063.

Mankiw, N. Gregory and Lawrence H. Summers. "Money Demand And The Effects Of Fiscal Policies," *JMCB*, 1986, v18(4), 415-429.

Mankiw, N. Gregory and Lawrence H. Summers. "Money Demand And The Effects Of Fiscal Policies: Reply," *JMCB*, 1988, v20(4), 715-717.

Mankiw, N. Gregory, David Romer And Matthew D. Shapiro. "An Unbiased Reexamination Of Stock Market Volatility," *JOF*, 1985, v40(3), 677-687.

Mankiw, N. Gregory. "Recent Developments In Macroeconomics: A Very Quick Refresher Course," *JMCB*, 1988, v20(3), Part 2, 436-449.

Mankiw, N. Gregory. "The Equity Premium And The Concentration Of Aggregate Shocks," *JFEC*, 1986, v17(1), 211-219.

Mankiw, N. Gregory. (Basu, Susanto, Miles S. Kimball, N. Gregory Mankiw and David N. Weil. "Optimal Advice For Monetary Policy," *JMCB*, 1990, v22(1), 19-36.)

Mann, Bruce D. and Michael Veseth. "Moderate Rent Controls: A Microeconomic And Public Choice Analysis," *AREUEA*, 1983, v11(3), 333-343.

Mann, Maurice. "How Does Monetary Policy Affect The Economy?," *JMCB*, 1969, v1(3), 538-548.

Mann, Steven V. and Neil W. Sicherman. "The Agency Costs Of Free Cash Flow: Acquisition Activity And Equity Issues," *JOB*, 1991, v64(2), 213-228.

Mann, Steven. (Zorn, Thomas S. and Steven Mann. "Investors' Reactions To Inflation: A Rational Expectations Test," *FAJ*, 1986, v42(3), 75-80.)

Manners, George E. (Gaumnitz, Erwin A., George E. Manners, James R. Surface, Maurice W. Lee and Paul Garner. "Dean's Forum: The Place Of Insurance In The Collegiate Curriculum," *JRI*, 1960, v27(4), 113-120.)

Manning, Christopher A. "Explaining Intercity Home Price Differences," *JREFEC*, 1989, v2(2), 131-149.

Manning, Christopher A. "Intercity Differences In Home Price Appreciation," *JRER*, 1986, v1(1), 45-66.

Manning, Richard L., Matilde K. Stephenson and Jerry D. Todd. "Information Technology In The Insurance Industry: A Forecast Of Utilization And Impact," *JRI*, 1985, v52(4), 711-722.

Mano, Ronald M. and Ted Burr. "IRAs Versus Nonsheltered Alternatives For Retirement Savings Goals," *FAJ*, 1984, v40(3), 67-75.

Mano, Ronald M. (Jorgensen, Jerry L. and Ronald M. Mano. "FASB Statement No. 5: Throwing Out The Baby (Disclosure) With The Bathwater (Accrual)," *FAJ*, 1982, v38(3), 64-66.)

Mano, Ronald M. (Jorgensen, Jerry L. and Ronald M. Mano. "Financial Statement Disclosure Of Uninsured Risks," *JRI*, 1985, v52(1), 133-143.)

Mansfield, Edwin and Richard Brandenburg. "Reply: The Allocation, Characteristics, And Outcome Of The Firm's Research And Development Portfolio," *JOB*, 1968, v41(1), 91-93.

Mansfield, Edwin and Richard Brandenburg. "The Allocation, Characteristics, And Outcome Of The Firm's Research And Development Portfolio," *JOB*, 1966, v39(4), 447-464.

Mansfield, Edwin and Samuel Wagner. "Organizational And Strategic Factors Associated With Probabilities Of Success In Industrial R & D," *JOB*, 1975, v48(2), 179-198.

Mansfield, Edwin. (Beardsley, George and Edwin Mansfield. "A Note On The Accuracy Of Industrial Forecasts Of The Profitability Of New Products And Processes," *JOB*, 1978, v51(1), 127-136.)

Mansinghka, Surendra K. (Weston, J. Fred and Surendra K. Mansinghka. "Performance Of Conglomerate Firms: Reply," *JOF*, 1973, v28(3), 759.)

Mansinghka, Surendra K. (Weston, J. Fred and Surendra K. Mansinghka. "Conglomerate Performance Measurement: Comment," *JOF*, 1974, v29(3), 1011-1012.)

Mansinghka, Surendra K. (Weston, J. Fred and Surendra K. Mansinghka. "Tests Of The Efficiency Performance Of Conglomerate Firms," *JOF*, 1971, v26(4), 919-936.)

Manski, Charles F. and Kenneth T. Rosen. "The Implications Of Demand Instability For The Behavior Of Firms: The Case Of Residential Construction," *AREUEA*, 1978, v6(2), 204-226.

Manson, William D. (Mumy, Gene E. and William D. Manson. "Payroll Taxes, Social Security, And The Unique Tax Advantage Of Company Pensions," *JRI*, 1983, v50(1), 161-165.)

Mansur, Iqbal, Steven J. Cochran and David K. Seagers. "The

Relationship Between The Argentinean Debt Rescheduling Announcement And Bank Equity Returns," **FR**, 1990, v25(2), 321-334.

Mantell, Edmund H. "Forecasting Aggregate Changes In U.S. Manufacturing And Nonmanufacturing Inventory Investment," **JOB**, 1977, v50(1), 40-49.

Mantell, Edmund H. "How To Measure Expected Returns On Foreign Investments," **JPM**, 1983-84, v10(2), 38-43.

Mantell, Edmund H. "The Relationship Of Rent-Seeking Behavior To Impacted Information In Public Utility Regulation," **JOB**, 1990, v63(4), 525-536.

Mantis, George and Richard N. Farmer. "Demand For Life Insurance," **JRI**, 1968, v35(2), 247-256.

Mantis, George and Richard N. Farmer. "Demand For Life Insurance: Reply," **JRI**, 1970, v37(1), 156-159.

Manton, E. A. G. "Insuring American Risks Abroad," **JRI**, 1965, v32(3), 447-454.

Manton, Kenneth G. (Tolley, H. Dennis, Kenneth G. Manton and James Vertrees. "An Evaluation Of Three Payment Strategies For Capitation For Medicare," **JRI**, 1987, v54(4), 678-690.)

Manuel, Donald E. "Insurance Stocks - Measuring Values And Earnings," **JRI**, 1965, v32(1), 85-90.

Manus, Peter C. "The Inventory Syndrome," **FAJ**, 1967, v23(4), 27-28.

Manzur, Meher. "An International Comparison Of Prices And Exchange Rates: A New Test Of Purchasing Power Parity," **JIMF**, 1990, v9(1), 75-91.

Mao, James C. T. and Carl E. Sarndal. "Cash Management: Theory And Practice," **JBFA**, 1978, v5(3), 329-338.

Mao, James C. T. and Carl Erik Sarndal. "Controlling Risk In Accounts Receivable Management," **JBFA**, 1974, v1(3), 395-404.

Mao, James C. T. and John F. Helliwell. "Investment Decisions Under Uncertainty: Theory And Practice," **JOF**, 1969, v24(2), 323-338.

Mao, James C. T. and Roger L. Wright. "A Chance-Constrained Approach To Urban Renewal Decisions," **JFQA**, 1968, v3(2), 135-150.

Mao, James C. T. "Essentials Of Portfolio Diversification Strategy," **JOF**, 1970, v25(5), 1109-1121.

Mao, James C. T. "Models Of Capital Budgeting, E-V Vs. E-S," **JFQA**, 1970, v5(5), 657-676.

Mao, James C. T. "Quantitative Analysis Of Urban Renewal Investment Decisions," **JOF**, 1967, v22(2), 195-207.

Mao, James C. T. "Security Pricing In An Imperfect Capital Market," **JFQA**, 1971, v6(4), 1105-1116.

Mao, James C. T. "Survey Of Budgeting: Theory And Practice," **JOF**, 1970, v25(2), 349-360.

Mao, James C. T. "The Impact Of Federal Mortgage Insurance Programs On Ann Arbor's Home Mortgage Market, 1956," **JOF**, 1958, v13(3), 412-416.

Mao, James C. T. "The Valuation Of Growth Stocks: The Investment Opportunities Approach," **JOF**, 1966, v21(1), 95-102.

Mao, Jennifer. (Boyle, Phelim P. and Jennifer Mao. "An Exact Solution For The Optimal Stop Loss Limit," **JRI**, 1983, v50(4), 719-726.)

Mar-Molinero, Cecilio. (Ezzamel, Mahmoud, Judith Brodie and Cecilio Mar-Molinero. "Financial Patterns Of UK Manufacturing Companies," **JBFA**, 1987, v14(4), 519-536.)

Mar-Molinero, Cecilio. (Ezzamel, Mahmoud, Cecilio Mar-Molinero and Alistair Beecher. "On The Distributional Properties Of Financial Ratios," **JBFA**, 1987, v14(4), 463-482.)

Mar-Molinero, Cocillo. (Ezzamel, Mahmoud and Cocillo Mar-Molinero. "The Distributional Properties Of Financial Ratios In UK Manufacturing Companies," **JBFA**, 1990, v17(1), 1-30.)

Marais, Laurentius, Katherine Schipper and Abbie Smith. "Wealth Effects Of Going Private For Senior Securities," **JFEC**, 1989, v23(1), 155-191.

Marathe, Vinay. (Rosenberg, Barr and Vinay Marathe. "Test Of Capital Asset Pricing Hypotheses," **RIF**, 1979, v1, 115-224.)

Maravall, Agustin. (Pierce, David A., Darrel W. Parke, William P. Cleveland and Agustin Maravall. "Uncertainty In The Monetary Aggregates: Sources, Measurement And Policy Effects," **JOF**, 1981, v36(2),507-515.)

Marbacher, Josef. "Characteristics And Problems Of Modern Payment Systems," **JBR**, 1980-81, v11(4), 206-213.

Marchand, Patrick H. (Followill, Richard A., Michael Schellenger and Patrick H. Marchand. "Economic Order Quantities, Volume Discounts, And Wealth Maximization," **FR**, 1990, v25(1), 143-152.)

Marchesini, Roberto. (Skantz, Terrance R. and Roberto Marchesini. "The Effect Of Voluntary Corporate Liquidation On Shareholder Wealth," **JFR**, 1987, v10(1), 65-76.)

Marcin, Thomas C. and John Kokus, Jr. "Economic And Demographic Factors Affecting Housing Demand Into The 1980s And 1990s," **AREUEA**, 1975, v3(3), 81-94.

Marcis, Richard G. and V. Kerry Smith. "Efficient Estimation Of Multivariate Financial Relationships," **JOF**, 1974, v29(5), 1415-1423.

Marcis, Richard G. and V. Kerry Smith. "The Demand For Liquid Asset Balances By U. S. Manufacturing Corporations: 1959-1970," **JFQA**, 1973, v8(2),207-218.

Marcis, Richard G. "Implications Of Financial Innovation And Reform For The Savings And Loan Industry," **AREUEA**, 1980, v8(1), 148-155.

Marcis, Richard G. (Kaufman, Herbert M. and Richard G. Marcis. "The Hunt Commission Recommendations And The Determination And Control Of The Money Supply," **JMCB**, 1975, v7(3), 343-358.)

Marcis, Richard G. (Smith, V. Kerry and Richard G. Marcis. "Post Accord Interest Rates: A Reply," **JOF**, 1974, v29(4), 1326-1327.)

Marcis, Richard G. (Smith, V. Kerry and Richard G. Marcis. "A Time Series Analysis Of Post-Accord Interest Rates," **JOF**, 1972, v27(3), 589-605.)

Marcis, Richard G. (Sullivan, James A. and Richard G. Marcis. "Forecasting Consumer Installment Credit: An Application Of Parametric Time Series Modeling," **JOB**, 1975, v48(1), 98-107.)

Marcis, Richard. "Variable Rate Mortgages: Their Uses And Impact In The Mortgage And Capital Markets," **AREUEA**, 1974, v2(1), 21-38.

Marcus, Alan and Israel Shaked. "The Relationship Between Accounting Measures And Prospective Probabilities Of Insolvency: An Application To The Banking Industry," **FR**, 1984, v19(1), 67-83.

Marcus, Alan J. and David M. Modest. "The Valuation Of A Random Number Of Put Options: An Application To Agricultural Price Supports," **JFQA**, 1986, v21(1), 73-86.

Marcus, Alan J. and Israel Shaked. "The Valuation Of FDIC Deposit Insurance Using Option-Pricing Estimates," **JMCB**, 1984, v16(4), Part 1, 446-460.

Marcus, Alan J. "Depreciation Rules And Rate Shock In Rate Of Return Regulation," **FM**, 1986, v15(4),61-68.

Marcus, Alan J. "Deregulation And Bank Financial Policy," **JBF**, 1984, v8(4), 557-565.

Marcus, Alan J. "Spinoff/Terminations And The Value Of Pension Insurance," **JOF**, 1985, v40(3),911-924.

Marcus, Alan J. "The Bank Capital Decision: A Time Series-Cross Section Analysis," **JOF**, 1983, v38(4), 1217-1232.

Marcus, Alan J. "The Magellan Fund And Market Efficiency," **JPM**, 1990, v17(1), 85-88.

Marcus, Alan J. (Kane, Alex and Alan J. Marcus. "The Quality Option In The Treasury Bond Futures Market: An Empirical Assessment," **JFM**, 1986, v6(2), 231-248.)

Marcus, Alan J. (Kane, Alex and Alan J. Marcus. "The Delivery Option On Forward Contracts: A Note," **JFQA**, 1988, v23(3), 337-342.)

Marcus, Alan J. (Kane, Alex and Alan J. Marcus. "Valuation And Optimal Exercise Of The Wild Card Option In The Treasury Bond Futures Market," **JOF**, 1986, v41(1), 195-208.)

Marcus, Alan J. (Kane, Alex and Alan J. Marcus. "Conversion Factor Risk And Hedging In The Treasury-Bond Futures Market," **JFM**, 1984, v4(1), 55-64.)

Marcus, Alan J. (Kane, Alex, Alan J. Marcus and Robert L. McDonald. "How Big Is The Tax Advantage To Debt?," **JOF**, 1984, v39(3), 841-853.)

Marcus, Alan J. (Kane, Alex, Alan J. Marcus and Robert L. McDonald. "Debt Policy And The Rate Of Return Premium To Leverage," **JFQA**, 1985, v20(4), 479-500.)

Marcus, Alan J. (Kulatilaka, Nalin and Alan J. Marcus. "A General Formulation Of Corporate Real Options," **RIF**, 1988, v7, 183-200.)

Marcus, Alan. (Kane, Alex, Young Ki Lee and Alan Marcus. "Earnings And Dividend Announcements: Is There A Corroboration Effect?," **JOF**, 1984, v39(4), 1091-1099.)

Marcus, Edward. "The Effectiveness Of Canadian Fiscal Policy," **JOF**, 1952, v7(4), 559-579.

Marcus, M. (Arzac, E. R. and M. Marcus. "Flotation Cost Allowance For The Regulated Firm: A Reply," **JOF**, 1984, v39(1), 293-294.)

Marcus, Matityahu and Uzi Yaari. "How A Closed-End Fund Can Out-Perform Its Own Stock Portfolio," **IJOF**, 1988, v1(1), 1-14.

Marcus, Matityahu, Dan Palmon and Uzi Yaari. "Growth And The Decision To Incorporate: A Financial Theory Of The U.S. Tax System," **RIF**, 1986, v6, 29-50.

Marcus, Matityahu. (Arzac, Enrique R. and Matityahu Marcus. "Flotation Cost Adjustment In Rate Of Return Regulation: A Reply," **JOF**, 1984, v39(2), 563.)

Marcus, Matityahu. (Arzac, Enrique R. and Matityahu Marcus. "Flotation Cost Allowance In Rate Of Return Regulation: A Note," **JOF**, 1981, v36(5), 1199-1202.)

Marcus, Matityahu. (Arzac, Enrique R. and Matityahu Marcus. "Flotation Cost Allowance In Rate Of Return Regulation: A Reply," **JOF**, 1983, v38(4), 1339-1341.)

Marcus, Matityahu. (Yaari, Uzi, Dan Palmon and Matityahu Marcus. "Stock Prices Under Inflation With Taxation Of Nominal Gains," **FR**, 1980, v15(1), 38-54.)

Marcus, Richard D. (Zivney, Terry L. and Richard D. Marcus. "The Day The United States Defaulted On Treasury Bills," **FR**, 1989, v24(3), 475-490.)

Marcus, Richard D., Donald Solberg and Terry L. Zivney. "A Reexamination Of The Benefits To International Diversification," **RDIBF**, 1991, v4/5, 310-335.

Marcus, Robert P. "Residual Value And The Cost Of Leasing," **FAJ**, 1978, v34(2), 58-60.

Marcus, Warren R. "Financing Tomorrow's Bank Growth," **JBR**, 1974-75, v5(3), 156-160.

Margaine, Michel. (Altman, Edward I., Michel Margaine, Michel Schlosser and Pierre Vernimmen. "Financial And Statistical Analysis For Commercial Loan Evaluation: A French Experience," **JFQA**, 1974, v9(2), 195-211.)

Margolis, Julius. "The Analysis Of The Firm: Rationalism, Conventionalism, And Behaviorism," **JOB**, 1958, v31(3), 187-199.

Margolis, Julius. "Traditional And Revisionist Theories Of The Firm: A Comment," **JOB**, 1959, v32(2), 178-182.

Margolis, Marvin S. (Roberts, Steven M. and Marvin S. Margolis. "Control Of The Money Stock With A Reserve Aggregate," **JMCB**, 1976, v8(4), 457-476.)

Margolis, Stephen E. "Monopolistic Competition And Multiproduct Brand Names," **JOB**, 1989, v62(2), 199-210.

Margoshes, S. L. "Cost Of Capital - Guide To Managerial Decision-Making," **FAJ**, 1963, v19(4), 49-53.

Margoshes, Sanford L. "Debt Financing And Investment Value Of Common Stock," **FAJ**, 1962, v18(4), 67-72.

Margoshes, Sanford L. "Modified Present Value Profile," **FAJ**, 1968, v24(2), 97-104.

Margoshes, Sanford L. "Price Earnings Ratio In Financial Analysis," **FAJ**, 1960, v16(6), 125-132.

Margoshes, Sanford L. "'Present Value' Techniques Of Stock Valuation," **FAJ**, 1961, v17(2), 37-42.

Margrabe, William. "The Value Of An Option To Exchange One Asset For Another," **JOF**, 1978, v33(1),177-186.

Margrabe, William. (Handorf, William C. and William Margrabe. "The Dow-Jones Futures Market: A Role-Playing Case," **JFED**, 1982, v11, 87-93.)

Marien, Edward J. (Niendorf, Robert N., Edward J. Marien and Duane R. Wood. "Integrating Finance, Marketing, And Management Courses Using Behavioral Objectives," **JFED**, 1973, v2, 20-32.)

Marini, Giancarlo. "Flexible Exchange Rates And Stabilizing Speculation," **JIMF**, 1988, v7(2), 251-257.

Marion, Nancy P. (Flood, Robert P. and Nancy P. Marion. "Exchange-Rate Regimes In Transition: Italy 1974," **JIMF**, 1983, v2(3), 279-294.)

Marioni, Robert J. (Copeland, Ronald M. and Robert J. Marioni. "Executives' Forecasts Of Earnings Per Share Versus Forecasts Of Naive Models," JOB, 1972, v45(4), 497-512.)

Maris, Brian A. "Analysis Of Bond Refunding With Overlapping Interest," JBFA, 1989, v16(4), 587-591.

Maris, Brian A. "FHLB Advances And The Cost And Availability Of Funds To S&Ls: A Comment," JOF, 1981, v36(4), 971-974.

Maris, Brian A. "Indirect Evidence On The Efficacy Of Selective Credit Controls: The Case Of Consumer Credit," JMCB, 1981, v13(3), 388-390.

Maris, Brian A. (Wansley, James W., Fayez A. Elayan and Brian A. Maris. "Preferred Stock Returns, CreditWatch, And Preferred Stock Rating Changes," FR, 1990, v25(2), 265-286.)

Maris, Brian A. and Fayez A. Elayan. "Capital Structure And The Cost Of Capital For Untaxed Firms: The Case Of REITS," AREUEA, 1990, v18(1), 22-39.

Maris, Brian A. and Harry L. White. "Valuing And Hedging Fixed-Rate Mortgage Commitments," JREFEC, 1989, v2(3), 223-232.

Mark, Jonathan H. "An Empirical Examination Of The Stability Of Housing Price Equations Over Time," AREUEA, 1983, v11(3), 397-415.

Mark, Jonathan H. and Michael A. Goldberg. "Land Use Controls: The Case Of Zoning In Vancouver," AREUEA, 1981, v9(4), 418-435.

Mark, Jonathan H. and Michael A. Goldberg. "Alternative Housing Price Indices: An Evaluation," AREUEA, 1984, v12(1), 30-49.

Mark, Jonathan. (Boehm, Thomas P. and Jonathan Mark. "A Principal Component Logistic Analysis Of The Mobility Decision In Transitional Neighborhoods," AREUEA, 1980, v8(3), 299-319.)

Mark, Morris, Marvin L. Baris, Ronald K. Lytle and Leonard Marx, Jr. "Pitfalls In Real Estate Accounting," FAJ, 1972, v28(1), 29-36.

Mark, Nelson C. "Some Evidence On The International Inequality Real Interest Rates," JIMF, 1985, v4(2), 189-208.

Mark, Nelson C. "Time-Varying Betas And Risk Premia In The Pricing Of Forward Foreign Exchange Contracts," JFEC, 1988, v22(2), 335-354.

Mark, Nelson C. (Cantor, Richard and Nelson C. Mark. "International Debt And World Business Fluctuations," JIMF, 1987, v6(2), 153-166.)

Markese, John D. and John L. Houston. "Bond Portfolio Management: Emphasis Missing - Treatment Required," JFED, 1981, v10, 3-5.

Markese, John. "Applied Security Analysis And Portfolio Management," JFED, 1984, v13, 65-67.

Market, F. Lynn. (Pohlman, Randolph A., Emmanuel S. Santiago and F. Lynn Markel. "Cash Flow Estimation Practices Of Large Firms," FM, 1988, v17(2), 71-79.)

Markham Edwin. "The Man With The Hoe," JPM, 1978-79, v5(2), 75.

Markland, Robert E. (Furst, Richard W. and Robert E. Markland. "Exploiting Imperfections In Markets: A Preliminary Test Of A Mechanical Trading Rule," FR, 1971, v2(1), 44-78.)

Markland, Robert E. (Nauss, Robert M. and Robert E. Markland. "Solving Lock Box Location Problems," FM, 1979, v8(1), 21-31.)

Markland, Robert E. (Smith, L. Douglas and Robert E. Markland. "Measurement Of Business Risk For Inter-Industry Comparisons," FM, 1981, v10(3), 49-63.)

Markle, John L. "Profitability In The Property And Liability Insurance Industry: Comment," JRI, 1972, v39(3), 479-483.

Markle, John L. and Alfred E. Hofflander. "A Quadratic Programming Model Of The Non-Life Insurer," JRI, 1976, v43(1), 99-120.

Markowitz, Barbara G. (Goldstein, Alice B. and Barbara G. Markowitz. "SOFASIM: A Dynamic Insurance Model With Investment Structure, Policy Benefits And Taxes," JOF, 1982, v37(2), 595-604.)

Markowitz, Harry M. and Andre F. Perold. "Portfolio Analysis With Factors And Scenarios," JOF, 1981, v36(4), 871-877.

Markowitz, Harry M. "Individual Versus Institutional Investing," FSR, 1991, v1(1), 1-9.

Markowitz, Harry M. "Investment For The Long Run: New Evidence For An Old Rule," JOF, 1976, v31(5), 1273-1286.

Markowitz, Harry M. "Markowitz Revisited," FAJ, 1976, v32(5), 47-52.

Markowitz, Harry M. "Nonnegative Or Not Nonnegative: A Question About CAPMs," JOF, 1983, v38(2), 283-295.

Markowitz, Harry M. "The Two Beta' Trap," JPM, 1984-85, v11(1), 12-20.

Markowitz, Harry M. (Kim, Gew-Rae and Harry M. Markowitz. "Investment Rules, Margin, And Market Volatility," JPM, 1989, v16(1), 45-52.)

Markowitz, Harry M. (Kroll, Yoram, Haim Levy and Harry M. Markowitz. "Mean-Variance Versus Direct Utility Maximization," JOF, 1984, v39(1), 47-62.)

Markowitz, Harry. "Portfolio Selection," JOF, 1952, v7(1), 77-91.

Marks, Barry R. "A Reevaluation Of The Arditti And Levy Capital Budgeting Procedure," JFR, 1979, v2(2), 153-159.

Marks, Barry R. "Calculating The Rate Of Return On A Leveraged Lease - A Constant Leverage Approach," JBR, 1982-83, v13(4), 297-299.

Marks, Barry R. (Braswell, Ronald C., Barry R. Marks, Walter J. Reinhart and DeWitt L. Sumners. "The Effect Of Term Structure And Taxes On The Issuance Of Discount Bonds," FM, 1988, v17(4), 92-103.)

Marks, Herbert J. (Hagaman, T. Carter and Herbert J. Marks. "Earnings Stability: Key To The Equity Market," JBR, 1975-76, v6(3), 183-185.)

Marks, John H. D. "Australian Investment Outlook," FAJ, 1967, v23(4), 107-110.

Marks, Lawrence J. "In Defense Of Performance," FAJ, 1967, v23(6), 135-137.

Marks, Peter C. (Simonson, Donald G. and Peter C. Marks. "Breakeven Balances On NOW Accounts: Perils In Pricing," JBR, 1980-81, v11(3), 187-191.)

Marks, Stephen G. (Kane, Alex and Stephen G. Marks. "The Delivery Of Market Timing Services: Newsletters Versus Market Timing Funds," JFI, 1990, v1(2), 150-166.)

Marks, Stephen Gary. (Kane, Alex and Stephen Gary Marks. "The Rocking Horse Analyst," JPM, 1986-87, v13(3), 32-37.)

Marks, Stephen Gary. (Kane, Alex and Stephen Gary Marks. "Performance Evaluation Of Market Timers: Theory And Evidence," JFQA, 1988, v23(4), 425-436.)

Markstein, David L. "Investing In Tomorrow's Bright New World," FAJ, 1959, v15(2), 83-88.

Marlin, John T. "Stock Market Game -- Wall Street Letters," JFED, 1973, v2, 75-77.

Marlin, John Tepper. "Proposal For A Modular Financial Game," JFED, 1972, v1, 79-84.

Marlin, John Tepper. "Rewards And Problems Of The World's Largest B-School," JFED, 1972, v1, 153-155.

Marlin, John Tepper. "Student Tests Of Theories, Social Performance," JFED, 1972, v1, 24-26.

Marlin, John Tepper. "Survey Of Curricular Emphases And Requirements In Major MBA Programs," JFED, 1972, v1, 27-62.

Marlin, John Tepper. (Benston, George J. and John Tepper Marlin. "Bank Examiners' Evaluation Of Credit: An Analysis Of The Usefulness Of Substandard Loan Data," JMCB, 1974, v6(1), 23-44.)

Marlin, Paul. "Fitting The Log-Normal Distribution To Loss Data Subject To Multiple Deductibles," JRI, 1984, v51(4), 687-701.

Marlow, Michael L. "Entry And Performance In Financial Markets," JBR, 1983-84, v14(3), 227-230.

Marmer, Harry S. "Portfolio Model Hedging With Canadian Dollar Futures: A Framework For Analysis," JFM, 1986, v6(1), 83-92.

Marples, Lynn W. (Madden, Gerald P., Lynn W. Marples and Lal C. Chugh. "A Stock Market Evaluation Of Management Buyouts," JBFA, 1990, v17(3), 351-358.)

Marples, William F. "Pensions And The Cost Of Living," JRI, 1960, v27(4), 19-32.

Marquette, R. Penny and Dana Johnson. "Ridge Regression And The Multicollinearity Problem In Financial Research: A Case Study," JFR, 1980, v3(1), 33-47.

Marquez, Jaime. "Money Demand In Open Economies: A Currency Substitution Model For Venezuela," JIMF, 1987, v6(2), 167-178.

Marr, M. Wayne and G. Rodney Thompson. "The Pricing Of New Convertible Bond Issues," FM, 1984, v13(2), 31-37.

Marr, M. Wayne and G. Rodney Thompson. "The Influence Of Offering Yield On Underwriting Spread," JFR, 1984, v7(4), 323-328.

Marr, M. Wayne, Robert W. Rogowski and John L. Trimble. "The Competitive Effects Of U.S. And Japanese Commercial Bank Participation In Eurobond Underwriting," FM, 1989, v18(4), 47-54.

Marr, M. Wayne. (Bhagat, Sanjai, M. Wayne Marr and G. Rodney Thompson. "The Rule 415 Experiment: Equity Markets," JOF, 1985, v40(5), 1385-1401.)

Marr, M. Wayne. (Billingsley, Randall S., Robert E. Lamy, M. Wayne Marr and G. Rodney Thompson. "Split Ratings And Bond Reoffering Yields," FM, 1985, v14(2), 59-65.)

Marr, M. Wayne. (Blackwell, David W., M. Wayne Marr and Michael F. Spivey. "Shelf Registration And The Reduced Due Diligence Argument: Implications Of The Underwriter Certification And The Implicit Insurance Hypotheses," JFQA, 1990, v25(2), 245-260.)

Marr, M. Wayne. (Blackwell, David W., M. Wayne Marr and Michael F. Spivey. "Plant-Closing Decisions And The Market Value Of The Firm," JFEC, 1990, v26(2), 277-288.)

Marr, M. Wayne. (Chance, Don M., M. Wayne Marr and G. Rodney Thompson. "Hedging Shelf Registrations," JPM, 1986, v6(1), 11-28.)

Marr, M. Wayne. (Hays, Patrick A., David S. Kidwell and M. Wayne Marr. "The Effect Of Market Uncertainty On Negotiated And Competitively Underwritten Public Utility Bonds," FR, 1984, v19(4), 339-350.)

Marr, M. Wayne. (Kidwell, David S., M. Wayne Marr and G. Rodney Thompson. "Eurodollar Bonds: Alternative Financing For U.S. Companies," FM, 1985, v14(4), 18-27.)

Marr, M. Wayne. (Kidwell, David S., M. Wayne Marr and G. Rodney Thompson. "SEC Rule 415: The Ultimate Competitive Bid," JFQA, 1984, v19(2), 183-195.)

Marr, M. Wayne. (Kidwell, David S., M. Wayne Marr and Joseph P. Ogden. "The Effect Of A Sinking Fund On The Reoffering Yields Of New Public Utility Bonds," JFI, 1989, v12(1), 1-14.)

Marr, Wayne and John Trimble. "The Persistent Borrowing Advantage In Eurodollar Bonds: A Plausible Explanation," JACF, 1988, v1(2), 65-70.

Marschak, Thomas. "Capital Budgeting And Pricing In The French Nationalized Industries," JOB, 1960, v33(2), 133-156.

Marschner, Donald C. "Theory Versus Practice In Allocating Advertising Money," JOB, 1967, v40(3), 286-302.

Marsh, Gene A. and Leonard V. Zumpano. "Agency Theory And The Changing Role Of The Real Estate Broker: Conflicts And Possible Solutions," JRER, 1988, v3(2), 151-164.

Marsh, P. R. (Dimson, E. and P. R. Marsh. "The Stability Of UK Risk Measures And The Problem Of Thin Trading," JOF, 1983, v38(3), 753-783.)

Marsh, P. (Dimson, E. and P. Marsh. "Volatility Forecasting Without Data-Snooping," JBF, 1990, v14(2/3), 399-422.)

Marsh, Paul. "Equity Rights Issues And The Efficiency Of The UK Stock Market," JOF, 1979, v34(4), 839-862.

Marsh, Paul. "The Choice Between Equity And Debt: An Empirical Study," JOF, 1982, v37(1), 121-144.

Marsh, Paul. "Valuation Of Underwriting Agreements For UK Rights Issues," JOF, 1980, v35(3), 693-716.

Marsh, Paul. (Dimson, Elroy and Paul Marsh. "Event Study Methodologies And The Size Effect: The Case Of UK Press Recommendations," JFEC, 1986, v17(1), 113-142.)

Marsh, Paul. (Dimson, Elroy and Paul Marsh. "An Analysis Of Brokers' And Analysts' Unpublished Forecasts Of UK Stock Returns," JOF, 1984, v39(5), 1257-1292.)

Marsh, Terry A. and Eric R. Rosenfeld. "Non-Trading Market Making, And Estimates Of Stock Price Volatility," JFEC, 1986, v15(3), 359-372.

Marsh, Terry A. and Eric R. Rosenfeld. "Stochastic Processes For Interest Rates And Equilibrium Bond Prices," JOF, 1983, v38(2), 635-646.

Marsh, Terry A. (Brown, Philip, Allan W. Kleidon and Terry A. Marsh. "New Evidence On The Nature Of Size-Related Anomalies In Stock Prices," JFEC, 1983, v12(1), 33-56.)

Marsh, Terry A. (Brown, Philip, Donald B. Keim, Allan W. Kleidon and Terry A. Marsh. "Stock Return Seasonalities And The Tax-Loss Selling Hypothesis: Analysis Of The Arguments And Australian Evidence," JFEC, 1983, v12(1), 105-127.)

Marsh, Terry A. and Robert C. Merton. "Dividend Behavior For The Aggregate Stock Market," **JOB**, 1987, v60(1), 1-40.
Marsh, Terry A. and Robert I. Webb. "Information Dissemination Uncertainty, The Continuity Of Trading, And The Structure Of International Futures Markets, **RFM**, 1983, v2(1), 36-71.
Marsh, Terry. "Equilibrium Term Structure Models: Test Methodology," **JOF**, 1980, v35(2), 421-435.
Marshall, Alf. "Capacity, Employment And Prices," **FAJ**, 1974, v30(3), 46-47.
Marshall, Alf. "Friedman And The Flat Tire," **FAJ**, 1971, v27(2), 8-10.
Marshall, David W. (Colwell, Peter F. and David W. Marshall. "Market Share In The Real Estate Brokerage Industry," **AREUEA**, 1986, v14(4), 583-599.)
Marshall, Earle and James D. Wolfensohn. "Oil And Gas In Australia," **FAJ**, 1964, v20(5), 151-158.
Marshall, Earle. "North Sea Gas Discoveries," **FAJ**, 1966, v22(6), 139-144.
Marshall, John M. "Welfare Analysis Under Uncertainty," **JRU**, 1989, v2(4), 385-404.
Marshall, Peyton J. (Jung, Woo S. and Peyton J. Marshall. "Inflation And Economic Growth: Some International Evidence On Structuralist And Distortionist Positions," **JMCB**, 1986, v18(2), 227-232.)
Marshall, Robert A. and Steven N. Weisbart. "Issues Involved In The Integration Of Traditional And Nontraditional University Curricula," **JRI**, 1976, v43(2), 335-341.
Marshall, Ronald. (Cheng, Peter, Fredric Jacobs and Ronald Marshall. "Cost Variance Investigation In A Linear Programming Framework," **JBFA**, 1984, v11(2), 233-244.)
Marshall, S. Brooks. (Hamilton, Arthur J. and S. Brooks Marshall. "The Chartered Financial Analyst Certification: Implications For The Finance Curriculum," **JFED**, 1987, v16, 32-39.)
Marshall, W. J. (Yawitz, J. B., G. H. Hempel and W. J. Marshall. "Is Average Maturity A Proxy For Risk?," **JPM**, 1975-76, v2(3), 60-63.)
Marshall, Wayne S. and Alan E. Young. "A Mathematical Model For Re-Acquisition Of Small Shareholdings," **JFQA**, 1968, v3(4), 463-469.
Marshall, William and Jess B. Yawitz. "Optimal Terms Of The Call Provision On A Corporate Bond," **JFR**, 1980, v3(2), 203-211.
Marshall, William J. and Jess B. Yawitz. "Lower Bounds On Portfolio Performance: An Extension Of The Immunization Strategy," **JFQA**, 1982, v17(1), 101-113.
Marshall, William J. (Maloney, Kevin J., William J. Marshall and Jess B. Yawitz. "The Effect Of Risk On The Firm's Optimal Capital Stock: A Note," **JOF**, 1983, v38(4), 1279-1284.)
Marshall, William J. (Trainer, Francis H., Jr., Jess B. Yawitz and William J. Marshall. "Holding Period Is The Key To Risk Thresholds," **JPM**, 1978-79, v5(2), 48-54.)
Marshall, William J. (Yawitz, Jess B. and William J. Marshall. "Measuring The Effect Of Callability On Bond Yields," **JMCB**, 1981, v13(1), 60-71.)
Marshall, William J. (Yawitz, Jess B. and William J. Marshall. "Risk And Return In The Government Bond Market," **JPM**, 1976-77, v3(4), 48-52.)
Marshall, William J. (Yawitz, Jess B., Kevin J. Maloney and William J. Marshall. "The Term Structure And Callable Bond Yield Spreads," **JPM**, 1982-83, v9(2), 57-63.)
Marshall, William J. (Yawitz, Jess B., George H. Hempel and William J. Marshall. "A Risk-Return Approach To The Selection Of Optimal Government Bond Portfolios," **FM**, 1976, v5(3), 36-47.)
Marshall, William J. (Yawitz, Jess B., George H. Hempel and William J. Marshall. "The Use Of Average Maturity As A Risk Proxy In Investment Portfolios," **JOF**, 1975, v30(2), 325-333.)
Marshall, William J. (Yawitz, Jess B. and William J. Marshall. "The Shortcomings Of Duration As A Risk Measure For Bonds," **JFR**, 1981, v4(2),91-101.)
Marshall, William J. (Yawitz, Jess B. and William J. Marshall. "The Use Of Futures In Immunized Portfolios," **JPM**, 1984-85, v11(2), 51-58.)
Marshall, William J., Jess B. Yawitz and Edward Greenberg. "Optimal Regulation Under Uncertainty," **JOF**, 1981, v36(4), 909-921.
Marshall, William. (Smirlock, Michael and William Marshall. "An Examination Of The Empirical Relationship Between The Dividend And Investment Decisions: A Note," **JOF**, 1983, v38(5), 1659-1667.)
Marston, R. C. "Systematic Movements In Real Exchange Rates In The G-5: Evidence On The Integration Of Internal And External Markets," **JBF**, 1990, v14(5), 1023-1044.
Marston, Richard C. "Real Wages And The Terms Of Trade: Alternative Indexation Rules For An Open Economy," **JMCB**, 1984, v16(3), 285-301.
Martel, Jean-Marc. (Khoury, Nabil T. and Jean-Marc Martel. "Optimal Futures Hedging In The Presence Of Asymmetric Information," **JFM**, 1985, v5(4), 595-605.)
Martel, Jean-Marc. (Khoury, Nabil T. and Jean-Marc Martel. "A Supply Of Storage Theory With Asymmetric Information," **JFM**, 1989, v9(6), 573-582.)
Martell, Terrence F. and George C. Philippatos. "Adaptation, Information, And Dependence In Commodity Markets," **JOF**, 1974, v29(2), 493-498.
Martell, Terrence F. and Jerrold E. Salzman. "Cash Settlement For Futures Contracts Based On Common Stock Indices: An Economic And Legal Perspective," **JFM**, v1(3), 291-301.
Martell, Terrence F. and Robert L. Pitts. "Determinants Of Bank Trust Department Usage," **JBR**, 1978-79, v9(1), 8-14.
Martell, Terrence F. "The Accuracy Of Deposit Forecasts Generated By The Bank Chartering Process," **JBR**, 1982-83, v13(4), 309-311.
Martell, Terrence F. (Helms, Billy P. and Terrence F. Martell. "An Examination Of The Distribution Of Futures Price Changes," **JFM**, 1985, v5(2), 259-272.)
Martell, Terrence F. (Karson, Marvin J. and Terrence F. Martell. "On The Interpretation Of Individual Variables In Multiple Discriminant Analysis," **JFQA**, 1980, v15(1), 211-217.)
Martell, Terrence F. and Avner S. Wolf. "Determinants Of Trading Volume In Futures Markets," **JFM**, 1987, v7(3), 233-244.
Martell, Terrence F. and Ruben C. Trevino. "The Intraday Behavior Of Commodity Futures Prices," **JFM**, 1990, v10(6), 661-672.
Martin, A. "Notes On Selecting Growth Industries," **FAJ**, 1954, v10(1), 71-72.
Martin, Charles G. (Ferri, Michael G. and Charles G. Martin. "The Cyclical Pattern In Corporate Bond Quality," **JPM**, 1979-80, v6(2), 26-29.)
Martin, Dale R. and William R. Sloane. "Financial Leverage: A More Precise Approach," **JBFA**, 1980, v7(4), 585-590.
Martin, Daniel. "Early Warning Of Bank Failure: A Logit Regression Approach," **JBF**, 1977, v1(3), 249-276.
Martin, Daniel. (Smith, Terrence R. and Daniel Martin. "The Determinants Of Manpower Costs In The Examination Of Banks In The Second Federal Reserve District," **JBR**, 1978-79, v9(3), 161-167.)
Martin, Donald Dewayne. "Justification For Probability Depreciation," **JBFA**, 1977, v4(1), 83-98.
Martin, George. (Melitz, Jacques and George Martin. "Financial Intermediaries, Money Definition, And Monetary Control: A Comment," **JMCB**, 1971, v3(3), 693-701.)
Martin, Gerald D. "Gender Discrimination In Pension Plans," **JRI**, 1976, v43(2), 203-214.
Martin, Gerald D. "Gender Discrimination In Pension Plans: Reply," **JRI**, 1977, v44(1), 145-149.
Martin, Gerald D. "Gender Discrimination In Pension Plans Revisited: The Results Of Court Ordered Implementation," **JRI**, 1979, v46(4), 727-732.
Martin, Gerald D. (Larsen, Normal L. and Gerald D. Martin. "Income Growth Factors: Error Introduced Through The Application Of Cohort Data," **JRI**, 1981, v48(1), 143-147.)
Martin, H. (Rao, M. R. and H. Martin. "A Note On Optimal Municipal Bond Coupon Schedules: Maximum Difference Between The Highest And Lowest Coupon," **JBR**, 1972-73, v3(1), 63-64.)
Martin, John D. and Arthur J. Keown. "Market Reaction To The Formation Of One-Bank Holding Companies," **JBF**, 1981, v5(3), 383-394.
Martin, John D. and Arthur J. Keown. "Interest Rate Sensitivity And Portfolio Risk," **JFQA**, 1977, v12(2), 181-195.
Martin, John D. and Arthur Keown. "A Misleading Feature Of Beta For Risk Measurement," **JPM**, 1976-77, v3(4), 31-34.
Martin, John D. and David F. Scott, Jr. "A Discriminant Analysis Of The Corporate Debt-Equity Decision," **FM**, 1974, v3(4), 71-79.
Martin, John D. and David F. Scott, Jr. "Debt Capacity And The Capital Budgeting Decision," **FM**, 1976, v5(2), 7-14.
Martin, John D. and David F. Scott. "Debt Capacity And The Capital Budgeting Decision: A Revisitation," **FM**, 1980, v9(1), 23-26.
Martin, John D. and J. William Petty. "An Analysis Of The Performance Of Publicly Traded Venture Capital Companies," **JFQA**, 1983, v18(3), 401-410.
Martin, John D. and R. Malcolm Richards. "The Seasoning Process For Corporate Bonds," **FM**, 1981, v10(3), 41-48.
Martin, John D. "Alternative Net Present Value Models," **AFPAF**, 1987, v2(1), 51-66.
Martin, John D. (Anderson, Paul F. and John D. Martin. "Lease Vs. Purchase Decisions: A Survey Of Current Practice," **FM**, 1977, v6(1), 41-47.)
Martin, John D. (Chan, Su Han, John D. Martin and John W. Kensinger. "Corporate Research And Development Expenditures And Share Value," **JFEC**, 1990, v26(2), 255-276.)
Martin, John D. (Chen, Son-Non and John D. Martin. "Beta Nonstationarity And Pure Extra-Market Covariance Effects On Portfolio Risk," **JFR**, 1980, v3(3),269-282.)
Martin, John D. (Granatelli, Andy and John D. Martin. "Management Quality And Investment Performance," **FAJ**, 1984, v40(6), 72-74.)
Martin, John D. (Kensinger, John W. and John D. Martin. "The Quiet Restructuring," **JACF**, 1988, v1(1), 16-25.)
Martin, John D. (Kensinger, John W. and John D. Martin. "Project Finance: Raising Money The Old-Fashioned Way," **JACF**, 1988, v1(3), 69-81.)
Martin, John D. (Kensinger, John W. and John D. Martin. "Project Financing For Research And Development," **RIF**, 1990, v8,119-148.)
Martin, John D. (Keown, Arthur J. and John D. Martin. "Capital Budgeting In The Public Sector: A Zero-One Goal Programming Approach," **FM**, 1978, v7(2), 21-27.)
Martin, John D. (Keown, Arthur J. and John D. Martin. "An Integer Goal Programming Model For Capital Budgeting In Hospitals," **FM**, 1976, v5(3), 28-35.)
Martin, John D. (Klemkosky, Robert C. and John D. Martin. "The Adjustment Of Beta Forecasts," **JOF**, 1975, v30(4), 1123-1128.)
Martin, John D. (Klemkosky, Robert C. and John D. Martin. "The Effect Of Market Risk On Portfolio Diversification," **JOF**, 1975, v30(1), 147-154.)
Martin, John D. (Lee, Wayne Y., John D. Martin and Andrew J. Senchack. "The Case For Using Options To Evaluate Salvage Values In Financial Leases," **FM**, 1982, v11(3), 33-41.)
Martin, John D. (Rao, Ramesh K. S. and John D. Martin. "Another Look At The Use Of Options Pricing Theory To Evaluate Real Asset Investment Opportunities," **JBFA**, 1981, v8(3), 421-429.)
Martin, John D. (Richards, R. Malcolm and John D. Martin. "Revisions In Earnings Forecasts: How Much Response?," **JPM**, 1978-79, v5(4), 47-52.)
Martin, John D. (Scott, David F., Jr. and John D. Martin. "Industry Influence On Financial Structure," **FM**, 1974, v4(1), 67-73.)
Martin, John D. (Senchack, A. J., Jr. and John D. Martin. "The Relative Performance Of The PSR And PER Investment Strategies," **FAJ**, 1987, v43(2), 46-56.)
Martin, John D. (Winger, Bernard J., Carl R. Chen, John D. Martin, J. William Petty and Steven C. Hayden. "Adjustable Rate Preferred Stock," **FM**, 1986, v15(1), 48-57.)
Martin, John D. and A. J. Senchack, Jr. "Program Trading And Systematic Stock Price Behavior," **FAJ**, 1989, v45(3), 61-67.
Martin, John D. and A. J. Senchack, Jr. "Index Futures, Program Trading, And The Covariability Of The Major Market Index Stocks," **JFM**, 1991, v11(1), 95-112.
Martin, John D. and Arthur J. Keown. "One-Bank Holding Company Formation And The 1970 Bank Holding Company Act Amendment: An Empirical Examination Allowing For Industry Group Effects," **JBF**, 1987, v11(2), 213-222.

Martin, John D. and Robert C. Klemkosky. "Evidence Of Heteroscedasticity In The Market Model," **JOB**, 1975, v48(1), 81-86.

Martin, John D. and Robert C. Klemkosky. "The Effect Of Homogeneous Stock Groupings On Portfolio Risk," **JOB**, 1976, v49(3), 339-349.

Martin, John D., Arthur J. Keown, Jr. and James L. Farrell, Jr. "Do Fund Objectives Affect Diversification Policies?," **JPM**, 1981-82, v8(2), 19-28.

Martin, John D., David F. Scott, Jr. and Robert F. Vandell. "Equivalent Risk Classes: A Multidimensional Examination," **JFQA**, 1979, v14(1), 101-118.

Martin, John. (MacMinn, Richard D. and John D. Martin. "Uncertainty, The Fisher Model, And Corporate Financial Theory," **RIF**, 1988, v7, 227-264.)

Martin, Kenneth. (Loderer, Claudio and Kenneth Martin. "Corporate Acquisitions By Listed Firms: The Experience Of A Comprehensive Sample," **FM**, 1990, v19(4), 17-33.)

Martin, Larry J. (Braga, Francesco S. and Larry J. Martin. "Hedging The Corn And Wheat Variable Import Levy Of The European Community," **RFM**, 1987, v6(3),390-408.)

Martin, Larry J. and David Hope. "Risk And Returns From Alternative Marketing Strategies For Corn Producers," **JFM**, 1984, v4(4), 513-530.

Martin, Larry J. (Braga, Francesco S., Larry J. Martin and Karl D. Meilke. "Cross Hedging The Italian Lira/US Dollar Exchange Rate With Deutsch Mark Futures," **JFM**, 1989, v9(2), 87-100.)

Martin, Larry J. (Braga, Francesco S. and Larry J. Martin. "Out Of Sample Effectiveness Of A Joint Commodity And Currency Hedge: The Case Of Soybean Meal In Italy," **JFM**, 1990, v10(3), 229-246.)

Martin, Linda J. and Glenn V. Henderson, Jr. "On Bond Ratings And Pension Obligations: A Note," **JFQA**, 1983, v18(4), 463-470.

Martin, Linda J. and Glenn V. Henderson, Jr. "The Effect Of ERISA On Capital Structure Measures," **FR**, 1980, v15(2), 39-49.

Martin, Linda J. "Uncertain? How Do You Spell Relief?," **JPM**, 1984-85, v11(3), 5-8.

Martin, Linda J. (French, Dan W. and Linda J. Martin. "The Measurement Of Option Mispricing," **JBF**, 1988, v11(4), 537-550.)

Martin, Linda J. (Glascock, John L., Glenn V. Henderson, Jr. and Linda J. Martin. "When E. F. Hutton Talks," **FAJ**, 1986, v42(3), 69-72.)

Martin, Preston. "Affluence And High Household Liquidity: Problems And Opportunities," **JFQA**, 1966, v1(1), 30-52.

Martin, Stanley A. and Ronald W. Spahr. "Futures Market Efficiency As A Function Of Market Speculation," **FR**, 1983, v2(3), 314-328.

Martin, Stanley A. (Dyl, Edward A. and Stanley A. Martin. "Rules Of Thumb For The Analysis Of Tax Swaps," **JPM**, 1983-84, v10(1), 71-74.)

Martin, Stanley A. (Joy, O. Maurice, Don B. Panton, Frank K. Reilly and Stanley A. Martin. "Comovements Of Major International Equity Markets," **FR**, 1976, v11(1), 1-20.)

Martin, Stanley A., Jr. (Dyl, Edward A. and Stanley A. Martin, Jr. "Setting Terms For Leveraged Leases," **FM**, 1977, v6(4), 20-27.)

Martin, Stanley A., Jr. (Dyl, Edward A. and Stanley A. Martin, Jr. "Weekend Effects On Stock Returns: A Comment," **JOF**, 1985, v40(1), 347-350.)

Martin, Stanley A., Jr. (Dyl, Edward A. and Stanley A. Martin, Jr. "Another Look At Barbells Versus Ladders," **JPM**, 1985-86, v12(3), 54-59.)

Martin, William McChesney, Jr. "Monetary Policy And International Payments," **JOF**, 1963, v18(1), 1-10.

Marty, Alvin L. "Inflation, Taxes, And The Public Debt," **JMCB**, 1978, v10(4), 437-452.

Marty, Alvin L. "Inside Money, Outside Money, And The Wealth Effect: A Review Essay," **JMCB**, 1969, v1(1), 101-111.

Marty, Alvin L. "Some Notes On Money And Economic Growth," **JMCB**, 1969, v1(2), 252-265.

Marty, Alvin L. and Frank J. Chaloupka. "Optimal Inflation Rates: A Generalization," **JMCB**, 1988, v20(1), 141-144.

Maru, Junko and Toshiharu Takahashi. "Recent Developments Of Interdealer Brokerage In The Japanese Secondary Bond Markets," **JFQA**, 1985, v20(2), 193-210.

Marx, Leonard, Jr. (Mark, Morris, Marvin L. Baris, Ronald K. Lytle and Leonard Marx, Jr. "Pitfalls In Real Estate Accounting," **FAJ**, 1972, v28(1), 29-36.)

Mascia, Joseph S. "Corporate Earnings Predictions," **FAJ**, 1969, v25(4), 107-110.

Mascia, Joseph S. "Personal Credit In New York State," **FAJ**, 1968, v24(3), 42-51.

Mascia, Joseph S. "Review Of Recent Treasury Refundings," **FAJ**, 1970, v26(6), 98-104.

Masojada, Bronek. (Aczel, Michael, Jack Broyles and Bronek Masojada. "Participation In The Lloyd's Insurance Market As A Portfolio Investment," **JBFA**, 1990, v17(5), 609-634.)

Mason, Arthur, Jr. "The Role Of Insurance And Risk In The Curriculum," **JRI**, 1972, v39(2), 271-274.

Mason, Edward S. "The Apologetics Of 'Managerialism'," **JOB**, 1958, v31(1), 1-11.

Mason, J. M. "Modeling Mutual Funds And Commercial Banks: A Comparative Analysis," **JBF**, 1979, v3(4), 347-353.

Mason, J. M. (Moroney, J. R. and J. M. Mason. "The Dynamic Impacts Of Autonomous Expenditures And The Monetary Base On Aggregate Income," **JMCB**, 1971, v3(4), 793-814.)

Mason, John M. "A Structural Study Of The Income Velocity Of Circulation," **JOF**, 1974, v29(4),1077-1086.

Mason, John M. "The Supply Curve For Housing," **AREUEA**, 1979, v7(3), 362-377.

Mason, John M. and Frederick H. Leaffer. "The Preferences Of Financial Institutions For Construction And Permanent Mortgage Lending On Multi-Unit Residential And Commercial Income Properties," **AREUEA**, 1976, v4(1), 41-56.

Mason, Joseph Barry and Morris L. Mayer. "Consumer Perceptions Of Affiliated Banking," **JBR**, 1972-73, v3(3), 189-191.

Mason, Joseph Barry and J. B. Wilkinson. "Mispricing And Unavailability Of Advertised Food Products In Retail Food Outlets," **JOB**, 1976, v49(2), 219-225.

Mason, R. Hal and Maurice B. Goudzwaard. "Performance Of Conglomerate Firms: A Portfolio Approach," **JOF**, 1976, v31(1), 39-48.

Mason, R. Hal. "The Myth Makers Of The Swinging Sixties," **JPM**, 1976-77, v3(3), 49-51.

Mason, Richard O. and Alfred E. Hofflander. "Management Information Systems In Insurance," **JRI**, 1972, v39(1), 65-77.

Mason, Scott P. and Sudipto Bhattacharya. "Risky Debt, Jump Processes, And Safety Covenants," **JFEC**, 1981, v9(3), 281-307.

Mason, Scott P. (Baldwin, Carliss Y. and Scott P. Mason. "The Resolution Of Claims In Financial Distress: The Case Of Massey Ferguson," **JOF**, 1983, v38(2), 505-516.)

Mason, Scott P. (Jones, E. Philip, Scott P. Mason and Eric Rosenfeld. "Contingent Claims Analysis Of Corporate Capital Structures: An Empirical Investigation," **JOF**, 1984, v39(3), 611-625.)

Mason, Scott P. (Jones, E. Philip and Scott P. Mason. "Valuation Of Loan Guarantees," **JBF**, 1980, v4(1), 89-107.)

Mason, William F. "Air Freight," **FAJ**, 1967, v23(5), 49-56.

Massaro, Vincent G. "An Econometric Study Of Eurodollar Borrowing By New York Banks And The Rate Of Interest On Eurodollars: Comment," **JOF**, 1972, v27(4), 927-930.

Masse, Isidore J. (Bart, John and Isidore J. Masse. "Divergence Of Opinion And Risk," **JFQA**, 1981, v16(1), 23-34.)

Massey, Paul H. "The Mutual Fund Liquidity Ratio: A Trap For The Unwary," **JPM**, 1975-76, v2(2), 18-21.

Masson, Dubos J. "Planning And Forecasting Of Cash Flows For The Multinational Firm: International Cash Management," **AFPAF**, 1990, v5(1), 195-228.

Masson, Paul R. "Portfolio Balance And Exchange Rate Stability: A Comment," **JMCB**, 1980, v12(2), Part 2, 228-230.

Masson, Robert Tempest. "'Concentration And Profits' By Stanley I. Ornstein: A Comment," **JOB**, 1977, v50(4), 529-535.

Massy, William F. (Frank, Ronald E. and William F. Massy. "Market Segmentation And The Effectiveness Of A Brand's Price And Dealing Policies," **JOB**, 1965, v38(2), 186-200.)

Masten, John T. (Hobson, Hugh A., John T. Masten and Jacobus T. Severiens. "Holding Company Acquisitions And Bank Performance: A Comparative Study," **JBR**, 1978-79, v9(2), 105-120.)

Mastrapasqua, Frank and Steven Bolten. "A Note On Financial Analyst Evaluation," **JOF**, 1973, v28(3), 707-712.

Masulis, Ronald W. and Ashok N. Korwar. "Seasoned Equity Offerings: An Empirical Investigation," **JFEC**, 1986, v15(1/2), 91-118.

Masulis, Ronald W. "Changes In Ownership Structure: Conversions Of Mutual Savings And Loans To Stock Charter," **JFEC**, 1987, v18(1), 29-60.

Masulis, Ronald W. "Stock Repurchase By Tender Offer: An Analysis Of The Causes Of Common Stock Price Changes," **JOF**, 1980, v35(2), 305-319.

Masulis, Ronald W. "The Effects Of Capital Structure Change On Security Prices: A Study Of Exchange Offers," **JFEC**, 1980, v8(2), 139-177.

Masulis, Ronald W. "The Impact Of Capital Structure Change On Firm Value: Some Estimates," **JOF**, 1983, v38(1), 107-126.

Masulis, Ronald W. (DeAngelo, Harry and Ronald W. Masulis. "Leverage And Dividend Irrelevancy Under Corprate And Personal Taxation," **JOF**, 1980, v35(2), 453-464.)

Masulis, Ronald W. (DeAngelo, Harry and Ronald W. Masulis. "Optimal Capital Structure Under Corporate And Personal Taxation," **JFEC**, 1980, v8(1), 3-27.)

Masulis, Ronald W. (Galai, Dan and Ronald W. Masulis. "The Option Pricing Model And The Risk Factor Of Stock," **JFEC**, 1976, v3(1/2), 53-81.)

Masulis, Ronald W. (Grinblatt, Mark S., Ronald W. Masulis and Sheridan Titman. "The Valuation Effects Of Stock Splits And Stock Dividends," **JFEC**, 1984, v13(4), 461-490.)

Masulis, Ronald W. (Hamao, Yasushi, Ronald W. Masulis and Victor Ng. "Correlations In Price Changes And Volatility Across International Stock Markets," **RFS**, 1990, v3(2), 281-308.)

Masulis, Ronald W. and Brett Trueman. "Corporate Investment And Dividend Decisions Under Differential Personal Taxation," **JFQA**, 1988, v23(4), 369-386.

Matatko, J. (Woodward, R. S. and J. Matatko. "Factors Affecting The Behaviour Of UK Closed End Fund Discounts 1968 to 1977," **JBFA**, 1982, v8(4), 501-509.)

Mather, Jane. (Loewenstein, George and Jane Mather. "Dynamic Processes In Risk Perception," **JRU**, 1990, v3(2), 155-176.)

Matheson, G. Lloyd. "No Fault Auto Insurance In Canada," **JRI**, 1972, v39(1), 27-30.

Mathews, H. Lee and John W. Slocum, Jr. "Correlates Of Commercial Bank Credit Card Use," **JBR**, 1971-72, v2(4), 20-27.

Mathewson, Frank. (Kellner, S. and Frank Mathewson. "Entry, Size Distribution, Scale, And Scope Economies In The Life Insurance Industry," **JOB**, 1983, v56(1), 25-44.)

Mathewson, G. F. "A Consumer Theory Of Demand For The Media," **JOB**, 1972, v45(2), 212-224.

Mathewson, G. F. and R. A. Winter. "Vertical Integration By Contractual Restraints In Spatial Markets," **JOB**, 1983, v56(4), 497-518.

Mathieson, Donald J. (Lizondo, Jose Saul and Donald J. Mathieson. "The Stability Of The Demand For International Reserves," **JIMF**, 1987, v6(3), 251-282.)

Mathieson, Robert F. "Input-Output: A Tool For Investment Research," **JBR**, 1971-72, v2(3), 31-38.

Matolcsy, Z. P. "The Distributive Nominal And Real Micro Effects Of Inflation On Security Returns: Some Australian Evidence," **JBF**, 1986, v10(3), 361-376.

Matolcsy, Z. P. (Castagna, A. D. and Z. P. Matolcsy. "The Evaluation Of Traded Options Pricing Models In Australia," **JBFA**, 1983, v10(2), 225-233.)

Matolcsy, Z. P. (Castagna, A. D. and Z. P. Matolcsy. "A Two Stage Experimental Design To Test The Efficiency Of The Market For Traded Stock Options And The Australian Evidence," **JBF**, 1982, v6(4), 521-532.)

Matolcsy, Z. P. (Castagna, A. D. and Z. P. Matolcsy. "The Market Characteristics Of Failed Companies: Extensions And Further Evidence," **JBFA**, 1981, v8(4), 467-484.)

Matolcsy, Z. P. (Castagna, A. D. and Z. P. Matolcsy. "The Marginal Information Content Of Selected Items In Financial Statements," **JBFA**, 1989, v16(3), 317-334.) 3Q?8

Matsumoto. (Upson, Roger B., Paul F. Jessup and Matsumoto. "Portfolio Diversification Strategies," FAJ, 1975, v31(3), 86-88.)

Mattar, Edward Paul, III and John Francis Hilson. "Exposure Of Corporate Directors: An Overview Of Indemnification And Liability Insurance," JRI, 1979, v46(3), 411-424.

Matteson, Archibald C. "In Defense Of Municipal Ratings," FAJ, 1968, v24(4), 99-103.

Matteson, David M. "The Insurance Industry And Futures Markets: Regulatory Problems," RFM, 1985, v4(2), 212-217.

Matthews, C. A. "A Note On Monetary Controls And Capital Values," JOF, 1959, v14(3), 415-422.

Matthews, Kent and Patrick Minford. "Private Sector Expenditure And Financial Asset Accumulation In The U.K.," JMCB, 1980, v12(4), Part 1, 644-653.

Matthews, Steven A. (Kihlstrom, Richard E. and Steven A. Matthews. "Managerial Incentives In An Entrepreneurial Stock Market Model," JFI, 1990, v1(1), 57-79.)

Mattingly, Garrett. "Kondratieff 1588," JPM, 1979-80, v6(3), 70-71.

Mattu, Ravi K. (Arditti, Fred D., Sirri Ayaydin, Ravi K. Mattu and Stephen Rigsbee. "A Passive Futures Strategy That Outperforms Active Management," FAJ, 1986, v42(4), 63-67.)

Matulich, Serge. "Borrowing Rates, Alternative Investment Sets, And The Life Insurance Purchase Decision: Comment," JRI, 1977, v44(3), 493-501.

Matulich, Serge. "Portfolio Performance With Lending Or Borrowing," JBFA, 1975, v2(3), 341-347.

Matulich, Serge. (Falk, Haim and Serge Matulich. "The Effect Of Personal Characteristics On Attitudes Toward Risk," JRI, 1976, v43(2), 215-241.)

Matulis, Margaret K. (Greenwald, Douglas and Margaret K. Matulis. "McGraw-Hill Survey Of Profits," FAJ, 1969, v25(2), 44-46.)

Mauer, David C. (Emery, Douglas R., Wilbur G. Lewellen and David C. Mauer. "Tax-Timing Options, Leverage, And The Choice Of Corporate Form," JFR, 1988, v11(2), 99-110.)

Mauer, David C. (Lewellen, Wilbur G. and David C. Mauer. "Tax Options And Corporate Capital Structures," JFQA, 1988, v23(4), 387-400.)

Mauer, David C. and Wilbur G. Lewellen. "Debt Management Under Corporate And Personal Taxation," JOF, 1987, v42(5), 1275-1291.

Mauer, David C. and Wilbur G. Lewellen. "Securityholder Taxes And Corporate Restructurings," JFQA, 1990, v25(3), 341-360.

Mauer, Laurence Jay. "Commercial Bank Maturity Demand For United States Government Securities And The Determinants Of The Term Structure Of Interest Rates," JFQA, 1969, v4(1), 37-52.

Mauldin, Patrick D., Brian F. Olasov and Craig K. Ruff. "The Use Of Mortgage-Derivative Products By Southeastern Thrifts," FAJ, 1990, v46(3), 71-76.

Maunders, K. T. and B. J. Foley. "Accounting Information, Employees And Collective Bargaining," JBFA, 1974, v1(1), 109-127.

Maupin, Rabekah J., C.M. Bidwell and A.K. Ortegren. "An Empirical Investigation Of The Characteristics Of Publicly-Quoted Corporations Which Change To Closely-Held Ownership Through Management Buyouts," JBFA, 1984, v11(4),435-450.

Maxwell, Charles E. (Gitman, Lawrence J. and Charles E. Maxwell. "Financial Activities Of Major U.S. Firms: Survey And Analysis Of Fortune's 1000," FM, 1985, v14(4), 57-65.)

Maxwell, Chris D. "Commercial Banks And Financial Futures: Current Practice," RFM, 1985, v4(2), 170-177.

Maxwell, James A. "Professor Maxwell And Fiscal Equity: Reply," JOF, 1955, v10(1), 71-72.

Maxwell, James A. "The Equalizing Effects Of Federal Grants," JOF, 1954, v9(2), 209-215.

Maxwell, W. David. (Belth, Joseph M. and W. David Maxwell. "Implications Of Viewing Interest Foregone As An Opportunity Cost Of Life Insurance: Comment," JRI, 1970, v37(2), 316-321.)

May, A. Wilfred. "To The Rescue Of The Investor," FAJ, 1948, v4(1), 49-57.

May, Alan M. (Durand, David and Alan M. May. "The Ex-Dividend Behavior Of American Telephone And Telegraph Stock," JOF, 1960, v15(1), 19-31.)

May, Catherine. (Chottiner, Sherman, Catherine May, and Nicholas Molodovsky. "Common Stock Valuation: Theory And Tables," FAJ, 1965, v21(2), 104-123.)

May, Frederick E. "Buying Behavior: Some Research Findings," JOB, 1965, v38(4), 379-396.

Mayer, Morris L. (Mason, Joseph Barry and Morris L. Mayer. "Consumer Perceptions Of Affiliated Banking," JBR, 1972-73, v3(3), 189-191.)

Mayer, Raymond R. "A Case Study Of Effective Communication In Industry," JOB, 1958, v31(4), 344-350.

Mayer, Robert W. "Analysis Of Flow Of Funds Through Capital Market," FAJ, 1961, v17(1), 71-77.

Mayer, Robert W. "Business Risk And The Earnings Multiplier," FAJ, 1965, v21(5), 19-21.

Mayer, Robert W. "Internal Risk In Individual Firms," FAJ, 1959, v15(5), 91-96.

Mayer, Robert W. "Price Earnings Ratios: A Prospect," FAJ, 1967, v23(6), 109.

Mayer, Robert W. "Swiss International Investment Trusts," FAJ, 1964, v20(3), 137-147.

Mayer, Thomas and Harold Nathan. "Mortgage Rates And Regulation Q," JMCB, 1983, v15(1), 107-115.

Mayer, Thomas. "Competitive Equality As A Criterion For Financial Reform," JBF, 1980, v4(1), 7-15.

Mayer, Thomas. "Financial Guidelines And Credit Controls," JMCB, 1972, v4(2), 360-374.

Mayer, Thomas. "Interest Payments On Required Reserve Balance," JOF, 1966, v21(1), 116-118.

Mayer, Thomas. "Is The Portfolio Control Of Financial Institutions Justified?," JOF, 1962, v17(2), 311-317.

Mayer, Thomas. "Our Financial Institutions: What Needs Changing?," JMCB, 1971, v3(1), 13-20.

Mayer, Thomas. "Plant And Equipment Lead Times," JOB, 1960, v33(2), 127-132.

Mayer, Thomas. "Regulating Banks: Comment On Kareken," JOB, 1986, v59(1), 87-96.

Mayer, Thomas. "Should Large Banks Be Allowed To Fail?," JFQA, 1975, v10(4), 603-610.

Mayer, Thomas. "Tests Of The Permanent Income Theory With Continuous Budgets," JMCB, 1972, v4(4), 757-778.

Mayer, Thomas. "The Federal Reserve's Policy Procedures," JMCB, 1972, v4(3), 529-550.

Mayers, David and Clifford W. Smith, Jr. "Ownership Structure And Control: The Mutualization Of Stock Life Insurance Companies," JFEC, 1986, v16(1), 73-98.

Mayers, David and Edward M. Rice. "Measuring Portfolio Performance And The Empirical Content Of Asset Pricing Models," JFEC, 1979, v7(1), 3-28.

Mayers, David and Clifford W. Smith, Jr. "Contractual Provisions, Organizational Structure, And Conflict Control In Insurance Markets," JOB, 1981, v54(3), 407-434.

Mayers, David and Clifford W. Smith, Jr. "Death And Taxes: The Market For Flower Bonds," JOF, 1987, v42(3), 685-698.

Mayers, David and Clifford W. Smith, Jr. "On The Corporate Demand For Insurance," JOB, 1982, v55(2), 281-296.

Mayers, David and Clifford W. Smith, Jr. "On The Corporate Demand For Insurance: Evidence From The Reinsurance Market," JOB, 1990, v63(1), Part 1, 19-40.

Mayers, David and Clifford W. Smith, Jr. "Corporate Insurance And The Underinvestment Problem," JRI, 1987, v54(1), 45-54.

Mayers, David. "Nonmarketable Assets, Market Segmentation, And The Level Of Asset Prices," JFQA, 1976, v11(1), 1-12.

Mayers, David. "Nonmarketable Assets And The Determination Of Capital Asset Prices In The Absence Of A Riskless Asset," JOB, 1973, v46(2), 258-267.

Mayers, David. "Portfolio Theory, Job Choice And The Equilibrium Structure Of Expected Wages," JFEC, 1974, v1(1), 23-42.

Mayers, David. (Chen, Nai-Fu, Thomas E. Copeland and David Mayers. "A Comparison Of Single And Multifactor Portfolio Performance Methodologies," JFQA, 1987, v22(4), 401-418.)

Mayers, David. (Copeland, Thomas E. and David Mayers. "The Value Line Enigma (1965-1978): A Case Study Of Performance Evaluation Issues," JFEC, 1982, v10(3), 289-322.)

Mayers, David. (Dann, Larry Y., David Mayers and Robert J. Raab, Jr. "Trading Rules, Large Blocks And The Speed Of Price Adjustment," JFEC, 1977, v4(1), 3-22.)

Mayers, David. (Holthausen, Robert W., Richard W. Leftwich and David Mayers. "The Effect Of Large Block Transactions On Security Prices: A Cross-Sectional Analysis," JFEC, 1987, v19(2), 237-268.)

Mayers, David. (Holthausen, Robert W., Richard W. Leftwich and David Mayers. "Large-Block Transactions, The Speed Of Response, And Temporary And Permanent Stock-Price Effects," JFEC, 1990, v26(1), 71-96.)

Mayerson, Allen L. "An Inside Look At Insurance Regulation," JRI, 1965, v32(1), 51-76.

Mayerson, Allen L. "Comments On The Curry And Reeder Papers," JRI, 1964, v31(2), 231-236.

Mayerson, Allen L. "How To Rewrite An Insurance Code," JRI, 1967, v34(1), 95-120.

Mayerson, Allen L. "Is A New Mortality Table Needed?," JRI, 1958, v25(2), 22-36.

Mayerson, Robert. (Hill, Joanne, Thomas Schneeweis and Robert Mayerson. "An Analysis Of The Impact Of Marking-To-Market In Hedging With Treasury Bond Futures," RFM, 1983, v2(1), 136-159.)

Maynard, John. "The Most Rapidly Changing Industry," FAJ, 1971, v27(6), 41-47.

Maynard, Walter. "Economic Growth And The Capital Gains Tax," FAJ, 1954, v10(2), 15-20.

Maynard, Walter. "Problems Of Investing In Growth Stocks," FAJ, 1956, v12(4), 27-30.

Maynard, Walter. "Role Of Savings In The American Economy," FAJ, 1952, v8(3), 45-48.

Mayne, L. S. and G. E. Philips. "Investment Assets And Bank Earnings," FAJ, 1972, v28(1), 61-65.

Mayne, Lucile S. (Forbes, Shawn M. and Lucille S. Mayne. "A Friction Model Of The Prime," JBF, 1989, v13(1), 127-136.)

Mayne, Lucile S. "A Comparative Study Of Bank Holding Company Affiliates And Independent Banks, 1969-1972," JOF, 1977, v32(1), 147-158.

Mayne, Lucile S. "Bank Dividend Policy And Holding Company Affiliation," JFQA, 1980, v15(2), 469-480.

Mayne, Lucile S. "Banking Holding Company Characteristics And The Upstreaming Of Bank Funds," JMCB, 1980, v12(2), Part 1, 209-214.

Mayne, Lucile S. "Deposit Reserve Requirements: Time For Change," JBR, 1975-76, v6(4), 268-274.

Mayne, Lucile S. "Funds Transfer Between Bank Holding Companies And Their Affiliates," JBR, 1980-81, v11(1), 20-27.

Mayne, Lucile S. "Management Policies Of Bank Holding Companies And Bank Performance," JBR, 1976-77, v7(1), 37-48.

Mayne, Lucile S. "Supervisory Influence On Bank Capital," JOF, 1972, v27(3), 637-651.

Mayne, Lucile S. "The Deposit Reserve Requirement Recommendations Of The Commission On Financial Structure & Regulation: An Analysis And Critique," JBR, 1973-74, v4(1), 41-51.

Mayo, Cesar. (Viswanathan, P. and Cesar Mayo. "The Feds RCPC Performance: Comment," JBR, 1975-76, v6(1), 70-72.)

Mayo, Herbert. "Advising College Students," JFED, 1978, v7, 42-43.

Mayo, John W. (Kaserman, David L. and John W. Mayo. "Advertising And The Residential Demand For Electricity," JOB, 1985, v58(4), 399-408.)

Mayo, John W. (Kaserman, David L. and John W. Mayo. "Regulation, Advertising, And Economic Welfare," JOB, 1991, v64(2), 255-268.)

Mayo, John W. and Joseph E. Flynn. "The Effects Of Regulation On Research And Development: Theory And Evidence," JOB, 1988, v61(3), 321-336.

Mayo, Robert P. "Government Bond Market And Debt-Management Policy," JOF, 1961, v16(2), 272-279.

Mayor, Thomas H. and Kenneth G. McCoin. "The Rate Of Discount In Bond Refunding," FM, 1974, v3(3), 54-58.

Mayor, Thomas H. and Kenneth G. McCoin. "Bond Refunding: One Or Two Faces?," JOF, 1978, v33(1),349-353.

Mayor, Thomas H. and Lawrence R. Pearl. "Life-Cycle Effects, Structural Change, And Long-Run Movements In The Velocity Of Money," *JMCB*, 1984, v16(2), 175-184.

Mayor, Thomas H. "Short Trading Activities And The Price Of Equities: Some Simulation And Regression Results," *JFQA*, 1968, v3(3), 283-298.

Mays, Elizabeth. "A Profit-Maximizing Model Of Federal Home Loan Bank Behavior," *JREFEC*, 1989, v2(4), 331-348.

Mays, Elizabeth and Edward J. DeMarco. "The Demand For Federal Home Loan Bank Advances By Thrift Institutions: Some Recent Evidence," *AREUEA*, 1989, v17(3), 363-379.

Mays, Milton W. "The Half-Century In Property-Casualty Insurance," *JRI*, 1951, v18, 46-53.

Mays, Milton W. "The Place Of The College Graduate In Fire And Casualty Insurance Company Home Offices," *JRI*, 1956, v23, 42-46.

Mayshar, Joram. "Transaction Costs And The Pricing Of Assets," *JOF*, 1981, v36(3), 583-597.

Mazze, Edward M. (Hamelman, Paul W. and Edward M. Mazze. "Citation Patterns In Finance Journals," *JOF*, 1974, v29(4), 1295-1301.)

Mazzeo, Michael A. (Jennings, Robert H. and Michael A. Mazzeo. "Stock Price Movements Around Acquisition Announcements And Management's Response," *JOB*, 1991, v64(2), 139-164.)

Mazzoleni, P. "The Influence Of Reserve Regulation And Capital On Optimal Bank Asset Management," *JBF*, 1977, v1(3), 297-309.

Mazzolini, Renato. "Creating Europe's Multinationals: The International Merger Route," *JOB*, 1975, v48(1), 39-51.

McAdams, Alan. (Kraus, Alan, Christian Janssen and Alan McAdams. "The Lock-Box Location Problem," *JBR*, 1970-71, v1(3), 50-58.)

McAdams, Lloyd. "How To Anticipate Utility Bond Rating Changes," *JPM*, 1980-81, v7(1), 56-60.

McAlister, M. Khris and George A. Overstreet. "Comparative Job Satisfaction Levels Among Bank Managers," *JBR*, 1978-79, v9(4), 213-217.

McAllister, Harry E. "Comments On 'Administered Prices And Oligopolistic Inflation: A Reply'," *JOB*, 1964, v37(1), 84-86.

McAuliff, Joseph L. "The Impact Of Selected Socio-Economic Factors On Life Insurance: A Case Study Of Arkansas," *JRI*, 1958, v25(3), 39-42.

McBride, Richard D. "Finding The Integer Efficient Frontier For Quadratic Capital Budgeting Problems," *JFQA*, 1981, v16(2), 247-253.

McCabe, George M. and Charles T. Franckle. "The Effectiveness Of Rolling The Hedge Forward In The Treasury Bill Futures Market," *FM*, 1983, v12(2), 21-29.

McCabe, George M. and James M. Blackwell. "The Hedging Strategy: A New Approach To Spread Management Banking And Commercial Lending," *JBR*, 1981-82, v12(2), 114-118.

McCabe, George M. "The Empirical Relationship Between Investment And Financing: A New Look," *JFQA*, 1979, v14(1), 119-135.

McCabe, George M. (Guerard, John B., Jr. and George M. McCabe. "A Further Look At The Interdependencies Of Corporate Expenditures And Implications For Strategic-Planning Models," *RIF*, 1990, v8, 149-178.)

McCabe, George M. (Howe, Keith M. and George M. McCabe. "On Optimal Asset Abandonment And Replacement," *JFQA*, 1983, v18(3), 295-305.)

McCabe, George M. and Donald P. Solberg. "Hedging In The Treasury Bill Futures Market When The Hedged Instrument And The Deliverable Instrument Are Not Matched," *JFM*, 1989, v9(6), 529-538.

McCabe, George M. and Robert C. Witt. "Insurer Optimizing Behavior And Capital Market Equilibrium," *JRI*, 1977, v44(3), 447-468.

McCabe, George M. and Robert C. Witt. "Insurance Pricing And Regulation Under Uncertainty: Pay Chance-Constrained Approach," *JRI*, 1980, v47(4), 607-635.

McCabe, Nancy C. (Jordan, James V., William E. Seale, Nancy C. McCabe and David E. Kenyon. "Transaction Data Tests Of The Black Model For Soybean Futures Options," *JFM*, 1987, v7(5), 535-554.)

McCabe, Nancy. (Kenyon, David, Kenneth Kling, Jim Jordan, William Seale and Nancy McCabe. "Factors Affecting Agricultural Futures Price Variance," *JFM*, 1987, v7(1), 73-92.)

McCafferty, Stephen. (Driskill, Robert and Stephen McCafferty. "Equilibrium Price-Output Dynamics And The (Non) Insulating Properties Of Fixed Exchange Rates," *JIMF*, 1982, v1(3), 325-332.)

McCahan, David and Harry J. Loman. "College Education For Insurance: A Minimum Program," *JRI*, 1947, v14, 5-24.

McCahan, David. "Report On Survey Of College And University Courses In Insurance And Related Subjects," *JRI*, 1949, v16, 21-26.

McCahan, David. "The Half-Century In Insurance Education," *JRI*, 1951, v18, 54-72.

McCahan, David. "University Instruction For Insurance Leadership," *JRI*, 1935, v2, 9-21.

McCall, Alan S. and David A. Walker. "The Effects Of Control Status On Commercial Bank Profitability," *JFQA*, 1973, v8(4), 637-645.

McCall, Alan S. and Donald T. Savage. "Branching Policy: The Options," *JBR*, 1980-81, v11(2), 122-126.

McCall, Alan S. and John T. Lane. "Multi-Office Banking And The Safety And Soundness Of Commercial Banks," *JBR*, 1980-81, v11(2), 87-94.

McCall, Alan S. and Manferd O. Peterson. "The Impact Of DE NOVO Commercial Bank Entry," *JOF*, 1977, v32(5), 1587-1604.

McCall, Alan S. and Manfred O. Peterson. "A Critical Level Of Commercial Bank Concentration: An Application Of Switching Regressions," *JBF*, 1980, v4(4), 353-370.

McCall, Alan S. and Neil B. Murphy. "A Note On Evaluating Liquidity Under Conditions Of Uncertainty In Mutual Savings Banks," *JFQA*, 1971, v6(4), 1165-1169.

McCall, Alan S. "Economies Of Scale, Operating Efficiencies And The Organizational Structure Of Commercial Banks," *JBR*, 1980-81, v11(2), 95-100.

McCall, Alan S. "The Impact Of Bank Structure On Bank Service To Local Communities," *JBR*, 1980-81, v11(2), 101-110.

McCall, Alan S. (Beighley, H. Prescott and Alan S. McCall. "Market Power And Structure And Commercial Bank Installment Lending,"

JMCB, 1975, v7(4), 449-467.)

McCall, Alan S. (Eisenbeis, Robert A. and Alan S. McCall. "Some Effects Of Affiliations Among Mutual Savings And Commercial Banks," *JOF*, 1972, v27(4), 865-877.)

McCall, Alan S. (Eisenbeis, Robert A. and Alan S. McCall. "The Impact Of Legislation Prohibiting Director-Interlocks Among Depository Financial Institutions," *JBF*, 1978, v2(4), 323-337.)

McCall, John J. "An Analysis Of Poverty: Some Preliminary Findings," *JOB*, 1971, v44(2), 125-147.

McCall, John J. "An Analysis Of Poverty: A Suggested Methodology," *JOB*, 1970, v43(1), 31-43.

McCall, John J. "The Economics Of Information And Optimal Stopping Rules," *JOB*, 1965, v38(3), 300-317.

McCall, John M. (Lippman, Steven A., John M. McCall and Wayne L. Winston. "Constant Absolute Risk Aversion, Bankruptcy, And Wealth-Dependent Decisions," *JOB*, 1980, v53(3), Part 1, 285-296.)

McCallum, Bennet T. "Postwar Developments In Business Cycle Theory: A Moderately Classical Perspective," *JMCB*, 1988, v20(3), Part 2, 459-471.

McCallum, Bennett T. and James G. Hoehn. "Instrument Choice For Money Stock Control With Contemporaneous And Lagged Reserve Requirements," *JMCB*, 1983, v15(1), 96-101.

McCallum, Bennett T. "On Consequences And Criticisms Of Monetary Targeting," *JMCB*, 1985, v17(4), Part 2, 570-597.

McCallum, Bennett T. "On 'Real' And 'Sticky-Price' Theories Of The Business Cycle," *JMCB*, 1986, v18(4), 397-414.

McCallum, Bennett T. "Price Level Adjustments And The Rational Expectations Approach To Macroeconomic Stabilization Policy," *JMCB*, 1978, v10(4), 418-436.

McCallum, Bennett T. "Rational Expectations And Macroeconomic Stabilization Policy: An Overview," *JMCB*, 1980, v12(4), Part 2, 716-746.

McCallum, Bennett T. "Sluggish Price Adjustments And The Effectiveness Of Monetary Policy Under Rational Expectations: A Reply," *JMCB*, 1981, v13(1),103-104.

McCallum, J. S. (Carr, J. L., P. J. Halpern and J. S. McCallum. "Correcting The Yield Curve: A Re-Interpretation Of The Duration Problem," *JOF*, 1974, v29(4), 1287-1294.)

McCallum, J. S. (Carr, J. L., P. J. Halpern and J. S. McCallum. "Comments On Single-Valued Duration Measures," *JOF*, 1978, v33(4), 1241-1243.)

McCallum, John S. "A Comment On Implementing Mean-Variance Theory In Selection Of U.S. Government Bond Portfolios," *JBR*, 1983-84, v14(2), 175-176.

McCallum, John S. "An Examination Of The Yields Of Corporate Bonds And Stocks: Comment," *JOF*, 1977, v32(1), 203-205.

McCallum, John S. "On Portfolio Theory, Holding Period Assumptions, And Bond Maturity Diversification: Comment," *FM*, 1980, v9(3), 74-76.

McCallum, John S. "Return And Risk In The Canadian Federal Bond Market," *JBR*, 1982-83, v13(1), 59-61.

McCallum, John S. "The Canadian Conversion Loan: A Remembrance," *JBR*, 1980-81, v11(1), 54-56.

McCallum, John S. "The Canadian Chartered Banks & The Government Of Canada Bond Market: Ex Post Efficient Portfolios And Actual Holding," *JBR*, 1976-77, v7(1), 78-87.

McCallum, John S. "The Empirical Impact Of Changes In Government On Bond Yields: The Canadian Provencial Experience," *JBR*, 1980-81, v11(4), 245-247.

McCallum, John S. "The Expected Holding Period Return, Uncertainty And The Term Structure Of Interest Rates," *JOF*, 1975, v30(2), 307-323.

McCallum, John S. (Gordon, Myron J. and John S. McCallum. "Valuation And The Cost Of Capital For Regulated Utilities: Comment," *JOF*, 1972, v27(5), 1141-1146.)

McCallum, John S. (Hutchings, Murray R. and John S. McCallum. "Bond Price Volatility: A Numerical Analysis," *JRI*, 1975, v42(4), 669-672.)

McCallum, John. "Is Increased Credibility Stabilizing?," *JMCB*, 1988, v20(2), 155-166.

McCandlish, Randolph W., Jr. "Security Analysts I Have Known," *FAJ*, 1971, v27(1), 36-39,85-87.

McCandlish, Randolph W., Jr. "Some Methods For Measuring Performance Of A Pension Fund," *FAJ*, 1965, v21(6), 105-110.

McCandlish, Randolph W., Jr. "Portfolio Evaluation," *FAJ*, 1967, v23(6), 147-150.

McCardle, Kevin F. and Robert L. Winkler. "All Roads Lead To Risk Preference: A Turnpike Theorem For Conditionally Independent Returns," *JFQA*, 1989, v24(1), 13-28.

McCarthy, E. J. "Organization For New Product Development?," *JOB*, 1959, v32(2), 128-132.

McCarthy, E. J. "Wage Guarantees And Annual Earnings: A Case Study Of George A. Hormell And Company," *JOB*, 1956, v29(1), 41-51.

McCarthy, E. J. "Wage Guaranties At Hormel: A Reply," *JOB*, 1956, v29(3), 216-217.

McCarthy, E. Jayne. (Anderson, Richard G., E. Jayne McCarthy and Leslie A. Patten. "Valuing The Core Deposits Of Financial Institutions: A Statistical Analysis," *JBR*, 1986-87, v17(1), 9-17.)

McCarthy, Franklin L. (Rhee, S. Ghon and Franklin L. McCarthy. "Corporate Debt Capacity And Capital Budgeting Analysis," *FM*, 1982, v11(2), 42-50.)

McCarthy, Joseph, Mohammad Najand and Bruce Seifert. "Empirical Tests Of The Proxy Hypothesis," *FR*, 1990, v25(2), 251-264.

McCarthy, Joseph. (Zaima, Janis K. and Joseph McCarthy. "The Impact Of Bond Rating Changes On Common Stocks And Bonds: Tests Of The Wealth Redistribution Hypothesis," *FR*, 1988, v23(4), 483-498.)

McCarthy, Michael D. "Current Prospects For Productivity Growth," *JOF*, 1978, v33(3), 977-988.

McCarthy, Terence. "The Corporate Balance Sheet During The Reconversion Period," *FAJ*, 1945, v1(4),22-29.

McCarty, Daniel E. and Philip M. Scherer. "The Demand For Finance Majors By Financial Institutions In The Southwest," *JFED*, 1977, v6, 40-44.

McCarty, Daniel E. and William R. McDaniel. "A Note On Expensing

Versus Depreciating Under The Accelerated Cost Recovery System: Comment," **FM**, 1983, v12(2), 37-39.

McCarty, Daniel E. (Jessell, Kenneth A. and Daniel E. McCarty. "A Note On Marginal Analysis, NPV Criterion And Wealth Maximization," **JFED**, 1987, v16, 12-14.)

McCarty, Daniel E. (McDaniel, William R., Daniel E. McCarty and Kenneth A. Jessell. "Discounted Cash Flow With Explicit Reinvestment Rates: Tutorial And Extension," **FR**, 1988, v23(3), 369-385.)

McCarty, Daniel E. (Mears, Peter, Daniel E. McCarty and Robert Osborn. "An Empirical Investigation Of Banking Customers' Perception Of Bank Machines," **JBR**, 1978-79, v9(2), 112-115.)

McCarty, Daniel E. (Osteryoung, Jerome S., Daniel E. McCarty and Karen Fortin. "Optimal Tax Lives Of Depreciable Assets: Comment," **FM**, 1980, v9(3), 77-78.)

McCarty, Daniel E. (Osteryoung, Jerome S., Daniel E. McCarty and Gordon S. Roberts. "Riding A Hedged Yield Curve With Treasury Bill Futures," **JBR**, 1983-84, v14(4), 266-273.)

McCarty, Daniel E. (Osteryoung, Jerome S., Daniel E. McCarty and Gordon S. Roberts. "Riding The Yield Curve With Treasury Bills," **FR**, 1981, v16(3), 57-66.)

McCarty, Daniel E. (Osteryoung, Jerome S., Daniel E. McCarty and William R. McDaniel. "The Use Of Visicalc In The Teaching Of Corporate Finance," **JFED**, 1983, v12, 82-91.)

McCarty, Spencer L. "The Revision Of Section 213 - A Major Life Insurance Problem," **JRI**, 1953, v20, 18-23.

McCauley, Peter B. "The Quick Asset Effect: Missing Key To The Relation Between Inflation And The Investment Value Of The Firm," **FAJ**, 1980, v36(5), 57-66.

McClain, David. (Shaked, Israel, Allen Michel and David McClain. "The Foreign Acquirer Bonanza: Myth Or Reality?," **JBFA**, 1991, v18(3), 431-448.)

McClaren, Constance H. (Bauman, W. Scott and Constance H. McClaren. "An Asset Allocation Model For Active Portfolios," **JPM**, 1981-82, v8(2), 76-86.)

McClay, Marvin. "A Rational Approach To Debt/Equity Allocation," **JPM**, 1976-77, v3(1), 50-56.

McClay, Marvin. "Is The Equity Market Becoming More Volatile?," **JPM**, 1980-81, v7(3), 51-54.

McClay, Marvin. "The Penalties Of Incurring Unsystematic Risk," **JPM**, 1977-78, v4(3), 31-35.

McClelland, Harold F. "Do Variable Annuities Have A Tax Advantage?," **JRI**, 1962, v29(2), 245-255.

McClung, Nelson. "The Economics Of Pension Finance," **JRI**, 1969, v36(3), 425-432.

McClure, J. Harold, Jr. "Welfare-Maximizing Inflation Rates Under Fractional Reserve Banking With And Without Deposit Rate Ceilings," **JMCB**, 1986, v18(2), 233-238.

McClure, J. Harold. "PPP, Interest Rate Parities, And The Modified Fisher Effect In The Presence Of Tax Agreements: A Comment," **JIMF**, 1988, v7(3),347-350.

McCoin, Kenneth G. (Mayor, Thomas H. and Kenneth G. McCoin. "The Rate Of Discount In Bond Refunding," **FM**, 1974, v3(3), 54-58.)

McCoin, Kenneth G. (Mayor, Thomas H. and Kenneth G. McCoin. "Bond Refunding: One Or Two Faces?," **JOF**, 1978, v33(1), 349-353.)

McCollough, W. Andrew. (Arditti, Fred D. and W. Andrew McCollough. "Real Versus Randomly Generated Stock Prices," **FAJ**, 1978, v34(6), 70-74.)

McCollum, James F. "Price-Expectations Effects On Interest Rates: Comment," **JOF**, 1973, v28(3), 746-750.

McConkey, C. William. (Warren, William E., Robert E. Stevens and C. William McConkey. "Using Demographic And Lifestyle Analysis To Segment Individual Investors," **FAJ**, 1990, v46(2), 74-77.)

McConnell, Dennis, John A. Haslem and Virginia R. Gibson. "The President's Letter To Stockholders: A New Look," **FAJ**, 1986, v42(5), 66-70.

McConnell, J. Douglas. "An Experimental Examination Of The Price-Quality Relationship," **JOB**, 1968, v41(4), 439-444.

McConnell, J. Douglas. "The Alphabet And Price As Independent Variables: A Note On The Price:Quality Question," **JOB**, 1970, v43(4), 448-451.

McConnell, John J. and Carl M. Sandberg. "The Weighted Average Cost Of Capital: Some Questions On Its Definition, Interpretation, And Use: Comment," **JOF**, 1975, v30(3), 883-886.

McConnell, John J. and Chris J. Muscarella. "Corporate Capital Expenditure Decisions And The Market Value Of The Firm," **JFEC**, 1985, v14(3), 399-422.

McConnell, John J. and Eduardo S. Schwartz. "LYON Taming," **JOF**, 1986, v41(3), 561-575.

McConnell, John J. and Gary G. Schlarbaum. "Another Foray Into The Backwaters Of The Market," **JPM**, 1980-81, v7(1), 61-65.

McConnell, John J. and Gary C. Sanger. "A Trading Strategy For New Listings On The NYSE," **FAJ**, 1984, v40(1), 34-48.

McConnell, John J. and James S. Schallheim. "Valuation Of Asset Leasing Contracts," **JFEC**, 1983, v12(2), 237-261.

McConnell, John J. and Timothy J. Nantell. "Corporate Combinations And Common Stock Returns: The Case Of Joint Ventures," **JOF**, 1985, v40(2), 519-536.

McConnell, John J. "Mortgage Company Bids On the GNMA Auction," **JBR**, 1976-77, v7(4), 294-302.

McConnell, John J. "Price Distortions Induced By The Revenue Structure Of Federally-Sponsored Mortgage Loan Programs," **JOF**, 1977, v32(4), 1201-1206.

McConnell, John J. "Valuation Of A Mortgage Company's Servicing Portfolio," **JFQA**, 1976, v11(3), 433-453.

McConnell, John J. (Ang, James S., Jess H. Chua and John J. McConnell. "The Administrative Costs Of Corporate Bankruptcy: A Note," **JOF**, 1982, v37(1),219-226.)

McConnell, John J. (Berges, Angel, John J. McConnell and Gary G. Schlarbaum. "The Turn-of-the-Year In Canada," **JOF**, 1984, v39(1), 185-192.)

McConnell, John J. (Crawford, Peggy J., Charles P. Harper and John J. McConnell. "Further Evidence On The Terms Of Financial Leases," **FM**, 1981, v10(4), 7-14.)

McConnell, John J. (Dennis, Debra K. and John J. McConnell. "Corporate Mergers And Security Returns," **JFEC**, 1986, v16(2), 143-187.)

McConnell, John J. (Dunn, Kenneth B. and John J. McConnell. "Valuation Of GNMA Mortgage-Backed Securities," **JOF**, 1981, v36(3), 599-616.)

McConnell, John J. (Dunn, Kenneth B. and John J. McConnell. "A Comparison Of Alternative Models For Pricing GNMA Mortgage-Backed Securities," **JOF**, 1981, v36(2), 471-484.)

McConnell, John J. (Dunn, Kenneth B. and John J. McConnell. "Rate Of Return Indexes For GNMA Securities," **JPM**, 1980-81, v7(2), 65-74.)

McConnell, John J. (Dunn, Kenneth B. and John J. McConnell. "Rates Of Return On GNMA Securities: The Cost Of Mortgage Funds," **AREUEA**, 1980, v8(3), 320-336.)

McConnell, John J. (Johnston, Elizabeth Tashijan, William A. Kracaw and John J. McConnell. "Day-Of-The-Week Effects In Financial Futures: An Analysis Of GNMA, T-Bond, T-Note, And T-Bill Contracts," **JFQA**, 1991, v26(1), 23-44.)

McConnell, John J. (Johnston, Elizabeth Tashijan and John J. McConnell. "Requiem For A Market: An Analysis Of The Rise And Fall Of A Financial Futures Contract," **RFS**, 1989, v2(1), 1-24.)

McConnell, John J. (Kim, E. Han, Wilbur G. Lewellen and John J. McConnell. "Financial Leverage Clienteles: Theory And Evidence," **JFEC**, 1979, v7(1), 83-109.)

McConnell, John J. (Kim, E. Han, John J. McConnell and Paul R. Greenwood. "Capital Structure Rearrangements And Me-First Rules In An Efficient Capital Market," **JOF**, 1977, v32(3), 789-810.)

McConnell, John J. (Kim, E. Han and John J. McConnell. "Corporate Mergers And The Co-Insurance Of Corporate Debt," **JOF**, 1977, v32(2), 349-365.)

McConnell, John J. (Kim, E. Han, Wilbur G. Lewellen and John J. McConnell. "Sale-And-Leaseback Agreements And Enterprise Valuation," **JFQA**, 1978, v13(5), 871-883.)

McConnell, John J. (Lease, Ronald C., John J. McConnell and Wayne H. Mikkelson. "The Market Value Of Differential Voting Rights In Closely Held Corporations," **JOB**, 1984, v57(4), 443-468.)

McConnell, John J. (Lease, Ronald C., John J. McConnell and Wayne H. Mikkelson. "The Market Value Of Control In Publicly-Traded Corporations," **JFEC**, 1983, v11(1), 439-471.)

McConnell, John J. (Lease, Ronald C., John J. McConnell and James S. Schallheim. "Realized Returns And The Default And Prepayment Experience Of Financial Leasing Contracts," **FM**, 1990, v19(2), 11-20.)

McConnell, John J. (Lewellen, Wilbur G., John J. McConnell and Jonathan A. Scott. "Capital Market Influences On Trade Credit Policies," **JFR**, 1980, v3(2), 105-113.)

McConnell, John J. (Lewellen, Wilbur G., Howard P. Lanser and John J. McConnell. "Payback Substitutes For Discounted Cash Flow," **FM**, 1973, v2(2), 17-23.)

McConnell, John J. (Lewellen, Wilbur G. and John J. McConnell. "Tax Reform, Firm Valuation, And Capital Costs," **FM**, 1977, v6(4), 59-66.)

McConnell, John J. (Lewellen, Wilbur G., Michael S. Long and John J. McConnell. "Asset Leasing In Competitive Capital Markets," **JOF**, 1976, v31(3),787-798.)

McConnell, John J. (Linn, Scott C. and John J. McConnell. "An Empirical Investigation Of The Impact Of 'Antitakeover' Amendments On Common Stock Prices," **JFEC**, 1983, v11(1), 361-399.)

McConnell, John J. (Lummer, Scott L. and John J. McConnell. "Further Evidence On The Bank Lending Process And The Capital-Market Response To Bank Loan Agreements," **JFEC**, 1989, v25(1), 99-122.)

McConnell, John J. (Sanger, Gary C. and John J. McConnell. "Stock Exchange Listings, Firm Value, And Security Market Efficiency: The Impact Of NASDAQ," **JFEC**, 1986, v21(1), 1-25.)

McConnell, John J. (Schallheim, James S. and John J. McConnell. "A Model For The Determination Of 'Fair' Premiums On Lease Cancellation Insurance Policies," **JOF**, 1985, v40(5), 1439-1457.)

McConnell, John J. (Schallheim, James S., Ramon E. Johnson, Ronald C. Lease and John J. McConnell. "The Determinants Of Yields On Financial Leasing Contracts," **JFEC**, 1987, v19(1), 45-68.)

McConnell, John J. (Van Drunen, Leonard D. and John J. McConnell. "Valuing Mortgage Loan Servicing," **JREFEC**, 1988, v1(1), 5-22.)

McConnell, John J. and Gary C. Sanger. "The Puzzle In Post-Listing Common Stock Returns," **JOF**, 1987, v42(1), 119-140.

McConnell, John J. and Gary G. Schlarbaum. "Returns, Risks, And Pricing Of Income Bonds, 1956-76 (Does Money Have An Odor?)," **JOB**, 1981, v54(1), 33-64.

McConnell, John J. and Henri Servaes. "Additional Evidence On Equity Ownership And Corporate Value," **JFEC**, 1990, v27(2), 595-612.

McConnell, Virginia D. (Harris, Curtis C., Jr. and Virginia D. McConnell. "Surpluses In Disequilibrium Urban Land Markets," **AREUEA**, 1987, v15(4), 359-373.)

McConnell, Walter S. and Stephen D. Leit. "Inflation, Stock Prices And Job Creation," **FAJ**, 1977, v33(2), 25-29.

McConnell, Walter S. "The Investment Standing Of The Steels," **FAJ**, 1958, v14(4), 53-56.

McCord, Sammy O., J. Ford Laumer, Jr. and Dolores R. Wright. "Student Internships In Finance," **JFED**, 1976, v5, 55-57.

McCormack, J. Patrick. (Fraser, Donald R. and J. Patrick McCormack. "Large Bank Failures And Investor Risk Perceptions: Evidence From The Debt Market," **JFQA**, 1978, v13(3), 527-532.)

McCormack, Joseph P. (Herbst, Anthony F. and Joseph P. McCormack. "An Examination Of The Risk/Return Characteristics Of Portfolios Combining Commodity Futures Contracts With Common Stocks," **RFM**, 1987, v6(3), 416-425.)

McCormack, Joseph P. (Herbst, Anthony F., Joseph P. McCormack and Elizabeth N. West. "Investigation Of A Lead-Lag Relationship Between Spot Indices And Their Futures Contracts," **JFM**, 1987, v7(4),373-382.)

McCormick, Robert E. (French, Kenneth R. and Robert E. McCormick. "Sealed Bids, Sunk Costs, And The Process Of Competition," **JOB**, 1984, v57(4), 417-442.)

McCormick, Robert E. (Maloney, Michael T. and Robert E. McCormick. "A Theory Of Cost And Intermittent Production," **JOB**, 1983, v56(2), 139-154.)

McCosker, Joseph S. "Need For Backlog Information," **FAJ**, 1968, v24(6), 37-43.

McCoy, George R. (Hanchett, Paul E. and George R. McCoy. "An Actuarial Appraisal Of Congressional Proposals For Hospital Insurance For The Aged," JRI, 1964, v31(4), 597-602.)

McCracken, Paul W. "Are Variable Annuities The Answer To Inflation," JOF, 1956, v11(2), 142-150.

McCracken, Paul W. "The Present Status Of Monetary And Fiscal Policy," JOF, 1950, v5(1), 24-48.

McCracken, Paul W. "The Public Debt: Hindrance Or Advantage To Credit Control?," JOF, 1953, v8(2), 159-168.

McCrae, William. "Legal Aspects Of Automobile Compensation," JRI, 1962, v29(2), 185-198.

McCrary, Dennis P. (Anstaett, Kurt W., Dennis P. McCrary and Stephen T. Monahan, Jr. "Practical Debt Policy Considerations For Growth Companies: A Case Study Approach," JACF, 1988, v1(2), 71-78.)

McCrary, Dennis and Jo Ousterbout. "The Development And Future Of The Loan Sales Market," JACF, 1989, v2(3), 74-84.

McCue, Thomas E. (Kling, John L. and Thomas E. McCue. "Office Building Investment And The Macroeconomy: Empirical Evidence, 1973-1985," AREUEA, 1987, v15(3), 234-255.)

McCue, Tom. (Miles, Mike and Tom McCue. "Diversification In The Real Estate Portfolio," JFR, 1984, v7(1), 57-68.)

McCue, Tom. (Miles, Mike and Tom McCue. "Historic Returns And Institutional Real Estate Portfolios," AREUEA, 1982, v10(2), 184-199.)

McCulley, Paul A. (Carnes, W. Stansbury, Gerald D. Gay and Paul A. McCulley. "Fed-Watching, Monetary Policy Regimes, And The Response Of Financial Futures To Money Announcements," RFM, 1989, v8(3), 384-401.)

McCulloch, J. Huston. "Bank Regulation And Deposit Insurance," JOB, 1986, v59(1), 79-86.

McCulloch, J. Huston. "Continuous Time Processes With Stable Increments," JOB, 1978, v51(4), 601-620.

McCulloch, J. Huston. "Foreign Exchange Option Pricing With Log-Stable Uncertainty," RDIBF, 1987, v1, 231-246.

McCulloch, J. Huston. "Interest-Risk Sensitive Deposit Insurance Premia: Stable ACH Estimates," JBF, 1985, v9(1), 137-156.

McCulloch, J. Huston. "Measuring The Term Structure Of Interest Rates," JOB, 1971, v44(1), 19-31.

McCulloch, J. Huston. "The Monotonicity Of The Term Premium: A Closer Look," JFEC, 1987, v18(1), 185-192.

McCulloch, J. Huston. "The Tax-Adjusted Yield Curve," JOF, 1975, v30(3), 811-830.

McCullough, Roy C. "Fables Of Reinsurance," JRI, 1964, v31(2), 259-264.

McCullough, Roy C. "Philosophy And Background Of Multiple-Line Underwriting," JRI, 1958, v25(1), 11-14.

McCullough, W. Andrew. (Gapenski, Louis C. and W. Andrew McCullough. "A Televised Replay Approach To Teaching The Basic Finance Course," JFED, 1982, v11, 1-4.)

McCurdy, Thomas H. (Gregory, Allan W. and Thomas H. McCurdy. "Testing The Unbiasedness Hypothesis In The Forward Foreign Exchange Market: A Specification Analysis," JIMF, 1984, v3(3), 357-368.)

McDaniel, William R. "Convertible Bonds In Perfect And Imperfect Markets," JFR, 1983, v6(1), 51-65.

McDaniel, William R. "Sinking Fund Preferred Stock," FM, 1984, v13(1), 45-52.

McDaniel, William R. "The Economic Ordering Quantity Problem And Wealth Maximization," FR, 1986, v21(4), 527-536.

McDaniel, William R. (McCarty, Daniel E. and William R. McDaniel. "A Note On Expensing Versus Depreciating Under The Accelerated Cost Recovery System: Comment," FM, 1983, v12(2), 37-39.)

McDaniel, William R. (Osteryoung, Jerome S., Daniel E. McCarty and William R. McDaniel. "The Use Of Visicalc In The Teaching Of Corporate Finance," JFED, 1983, v12, 82-91.)

McDaniel, William R. (Trivoli, George W. and William R. McDaniel. "Uncertainty, Capital Immobility And Capital Rationing In The Investment Decision," JBFA, 1987, v14(2), 215-228.)

McDaniel, William R., Daniel E. McCarty and Kenneth A. Jessell. "Discounted Cash Flow With Explicit Reinvestment Rates: Tutorial And Extension," FR, 1988, v23(3), 369-385.

McDaniel, Wm. R. "A Pedagogical Approach To The Stock Repurchase Dilemma," JFED, 1986, v15, 8-11.

McDaniel, Wm. R. "Operating Leverage And Operating Risk," JBFA, 1984, v11(1), 113-125.

McDaniel, Wm. R. (Madura, Jeff and Wm. R. McDaniel. "The Reaction Of Bank Holding Company Share Prices To Citicorp's $1 Billion Stock Issue," JOF, 1990, v3(1), 101-120.)

McDaniel, Wm. R. (Madura, Jeff, Ann Marie White and Wm. R. McDaniel. "Reaction Of British Bank Share Prices To Citicorp's Announced $3 Billion Increase In Loan-Loss Reserves," JBF, 1991, v15(1), 151-163.)

McDaniel, Wm. R. (Madura, Jeff and Wm. R. McDaniel. "Market Reaction To Increased Loan Loss Reserves At Money-Center Banks," JFSR, 1989, v3(4), 359-369.)

McDermed, Ann Archibald. (Clark, Robert L. and Ann Archibald McDermed. "Inflation, Pension Benefits, And Retirement," JRI, 1982, v49(1), 19-38.)

McDermott, John. "Exchange-Rate Indexation In A Monetary Model: Theory And Evidence," JIMF, 1983, v2(2), 197-213.

McDiarmid, F. J. "Current Trends In Institutional Investments," JOF, 1949, v4(2), 119-128.

McDiarmid, F. J. "Inflation And Life Insurance," JRI, 1959, v26(2), 59-62.

McDiarmid, F. J. "Some Broader Aspects OF The Insurance Investment Problem," FAJ, 1945, v1(4), 39-48.

McDonald, Bill and Michael H. Morris. "The Statistical Validity Of The Ratio Method In Financial Analysis: An Empirical Examination," JBFA, 1984, v11(1), 89-97.

McDonald, Bill and Michael H. Morris. "The Existence Of Heteroscedasticity And Its Effect On Estimates Of The Market Model Parameters," JFR, 1983, v6(2), 115-126.

McDonald, Bill and Michael H. Morris. "The Statistical Validity Of The Ratio Method In Financial Analysis: An Empirical Examination: A Reply," JBFA, 1986, v13(4), 633-635.

McDonald, Bill and William D. Nichols. "Nonstationarity Of Beta And Tests Of Market Efficiency," JFR, 1984, v7(4), 315-322.

McDonald, Bill. "Beta Non-Stationarity: An Empirical Test Of Stochastic Forms," FR, 1983, v18(2), 175-183.

McDonald, Bill. "Beta Nonstationarity And The Use Of The Chen And Lee Estimator: A Note," JFR, 1983, v38(3), 1005-1009.

McDonald, Bill. "Event Studies And Systems Methods: Some Additional Evidence," JFQA, 1987, v22(4), 495-504.

McDonald, Bill. "Functional Forms And The Capital Asset Pricing Model," JFQA, 1983, v18(3), 319-329.

McDonald, Bill. "Making Sense Out Of Unstable Alphas And Betas," JPM, 1984-85, v11(2), 19-22.

McDonald, Bill. (Affleck-Graves, John and Bill McDonald. "Nonnormalities And Tests Of Asset Pricing Theories," JOF, 1989, v44(4), 889-908.)

McDonald, Bill. (Affleck-Graves, John and Bill McDonald. "Multivariate Tests Of Asset Pricing: The Comparative Power Of Alternative Statistics," JFQA, 1990, v25(2), 163-186.)

McDonald, Bill. (Balvers, Ronald J., Thomas F. Cosimano and Bill McDonald. "Predicting Stock Returns In An Efficient Market," JOF, 1990, v45(4), 1109-1128.)

McDonald, Bill. (Hegde, Shantaram P. and Bill McDonald. "On The Informational Role Of Treasury Bill Futures," JFM, 1986, v6(4), 629-643.)

McDonald, Bill. (Kilbride, Bernard J., Bill McDonald and Robert E. Miller. "A Reexamination Of Economies Of Scale In Banking Using A Generalized Functional Form," JMCB, 1986, v18(4), 519-526.)

McDonald, Bill. (Morris, Michael H. and Bill McDonald. "Asset Pricing And Financial Reporting With Changing Prices," JBFA, 1982, v8(3), 383-395.)

McDonald, Bill. (Nichols, William D. and Bill McDonald. "Stock Splits And Market Anomalies," FR, 1983, v18(4), 237-256.)

McDonald, J. G. and A. K. Fisher. "New-Issue Stock Price Behavior," JOF, 1972, v27(1), 97-102.

McDonald, Jack. "The Mochiai Effect: Japanese Corporate Cross-Holdings," JPM, 1989, v16(1), 90-95.

McDonald, James B. (Bookstaber, Richard M. and James B. McDonald. "A Generalized Option Valuation Model For The Pricing Of Bond Options," RFM, 1985, v4(1), 60-73.)

McDonald, James B. (Bookstaber, Richard M. and James B. McDonald. "A General Distribution For Describing Security Price Returns," JOB, 1987, v60(3), 401-424.)

McDonald, James L. (Davidson, Wallace N., III and James L. McDonald. "Evidence Of The Effect On Shareholder Wealth Of Corporate Spinoffs: The Creation Of Royalty Trusts," JFR, 1987, v10(4), 321-328.)

McDonald, James L. (Walker, Michael C. and James L. McDonald. "A Note On Discounting Risk-Adjusted Cash Flow Streams In The Capital Budgeting Process," JFED, 1986, v15, 1-7.)

McDonald, John G. and Alfred E. Osborne, Jr. "Forecasting The Market Return On Common Stocks," JBFA, 1974, v1(2), 217-237.

McDonald, John G. and Bruno H. Solnik. "Valuation And Strategy For Gold Stocks," JPM, 1976-77, v3(3), 29-33.

McDonald, John G. and Donald C. Baron. "Risk And Return On Short Positions In Common Stocks," JOF, 1973, v28(1), 97-107.

McDonald, John G. and Richard E. Stehle. "How Do Institutional Investors Perceive Risk?," JPM, 1975-76, v2(1), 11-16.

McDonald, John G. "Are Coupons Worth More Than Principal Return?," JPM, 1974-75, v1(3), 35-37.

McDonald, John G. "Diversification And Exposure To Risk," FAJ, 1975, v31(2), 42-50.

McDonald, John G. "French Mutual Fund Performance: Evaluation Of Internationality-Diversified Portfolios," JOF, 1973, v28(5), 1161-1180.

McDonald, John G. "Objectives And Performance Of Mutual Funds, 1960-1969," JFQA, 1974, v9(3), 311-333.

McDonald, John G. (Jacquillat, Bertrand C., John G. McDonald and Jacques Rolfo. "French Auctions Of Common Stock: New Issues, 1966-1974," JBF, 1978, v2(4), 305-322.)

McDonald, John G. (Van Horne, James C. and John G. McDonald. "Dividend Policy And New Equity Financing," JOF, 1971, v26(2), 507-519.)

McDonald, John G. and Bertrand C. Jacquillat. "Pricing Of Initial Equity Issues: The French Sealed-Bid Auction," JOB, 1974, v47(1), 37-47.

McDonald, John G., Bertrand Jacquillat and Maurice Nussenbaum. "Dividend, Investment And Financing Decisions: Empirical Evidence On French Firms," JFQA, 1975, v10(5), 741-755.

McDonald, Robert and Daniel Siegel. "A Note On The Design Of Commodity Options Contracts: A Comment," JFM, 1983, v3(1), 43-46.

McDonald, Robert and Daniel Siegel. "Option Pricing When The Underlying Asset Earns A Below-Equilibrium Rate Of Return: A Note," JOF, 1984, v39(1), 261-265.

McDonald, Robert L. "Taxes And The Hedging Of Forward Commitments," JFM, 1986, v6(2), 207-222.

McDonald, Robert L. (Kane, Alex, Alan J. Marcus and Robert L. McDonald. "Debt Policy And The Rate Of Return Premium To Leverage," JFQA, 1985, v20(4), 479-500.)

McDonald, Robert L. (Kane, Alex, Alan J. Marcus and Robert L. McDonald. "How Big Is The Tax Advantage To Debt?," JOF, 1984, v39(3), 841-853.)

McDonald, Robert L. (Lucas, Deborah and Robert L. McDonald. "Bank Portfolio Choice With Private Information About Loan Quality: Theory And Implications For Regulation," JBF, 1987, v11(3), 473-498.)

McDonald, Robert L. (Lucas, Deborah J. and Robert L. McDonald. "Equity Issues And Stock Price Dynamics," JOF, 1990, v45(4), 1020-1043.)

McDonald, Robert. (Bodie, Zvi, Alex Kane and Robert McDonald. "Why Haven't Nominal Rates Declined?," FAJ, 1984, v40(2), 16-19,22-27.)

McDonald, Stephen L. "Some Factors Affecting The Increased Relative Use Of Currency Since 1939," JOF, 1956, v11(3), 313-327.

McDonald, Stephen L. "The Internal Drain And Bank Credit Expansion," JOF, 1953, v8(4), 407-421.

McDonnell, Jack. (Chaney, John and Jack McDonnell. "An Experiment In A Completely Self-Paced Home Study Finance Course," JFED, 1976, v5, 40-42.)

McDougall, Gerald S. (Cho, Dong W. and Gerald S. McDougall. "The Supply Of Storage In Energy Futures Markets," JFM, 1990, v10(6), 611-622.)

McElhone, Josephine. (Cassidy, Henry J. and Josephine McElhone. "The Pricing Of Variable Rate Mortgages," FM, 1974, v4(4),37-45.)

McElreath, Robert B., Jr. and C. Donald Wiggins. "Using The COMPUSTAT Tapes In Financial Research: Problems And Solutions," FAJ, 1984, v40(1), 71-76.

McElroy, Majorie B. (Burmeister, Edwin and Marjorie B. McElroy. "Joint Estimation Of Factor Sensitivities And Risk Premia For The Arbitrage Pricing Theory," JOF, 1988, v43(3), 721-733.)

McElroy, Majorie B. (Burmeister, Edwin and Marjorie B. McElroy. "The Residual Market Factor, The APT, And Mean-Variance Efficiency," RQFA, 1991, v1(1), 27-50.)

McElroy, Marjorie B. (Berry, Michael A., Edwin Burmeister and Marjorie B. McElroy. "Sorting OUt Risks Using Known APT Factors," FAJ, 1988, v44(2), 29-42.)

McEnally, Richard W. and Calvin M. Boardman. "Aspects Of Corporate Bond Portfolio Diversification," JFR, 1979, v2(1), 27-36.

McEnally, Richard W. and David E. Upton. "A Reexamination Of The Ex Post Risk-Return Tradeoff On Common Stocks," JFQA, 1979, v14(2), 395-419.

McEnally, Richard W. and Edward A. Dyl. "Risk Of Selling Short," FAJ, 1969, v25(6), 73-76.

McEnally, Richard W. and Michael L. Rice. "Hedging Possibilities In The Flotation Of Debt Securities," FM, 1979, v8(4), 12-18.

McEnally, Richard W. "A Note On The Return Behavior Of High Risk Common Stocks," JOF, 1974, v29(1), 199-202.

McEnally, Richard W. "An Investigation Of The Extrapolative Determinants Of Short-Run Earnings Expectations," JFQA, 1971, v6(2), 687-706.

McEnally, Richard W. "Duration As A Practical Tool For Bond Management," JPM, 1976-77, v3(4), 53-57.

McEnally, Richard W. "How To Neutralize Reinvestment Rate Risk," JPM, 1979-80, v6(3), 59-63.

McEnally, Richard W. "Latane's Bequest: The Best Of Portfolio Strategies," JPM, 1985-86, v12(2), 21-30.

McEnally, Richard W. "On The Use Of The CAPM In Public Utility Rate Cases: Comment," FM, 1978, v7(3), 69-70.

McEnally, Richard W. "Rethinking Our Thinking About Interest Rates," FAJ, 1985, v41(2), 62-67.

McEnally, Richard W. "Risk-Premium Curves For Different Classes Of Long-Term Securities, 1950-1966: Comment," JOF, 1972, v27(4), 933-939.

McEnally, Richard W. "Some Portfolio-Relevant Risk Characteristics Of Long-Term Marketable Securities," JFQA, 1973, v8(4), 565-585.

McEnally, Richard W. "Time Diversification: The Surest Route To Lower Risk?," JPM, 1984-85, v11(4), 24-26.

McEnally, Richard W. "What Causes Bond Prices To Change," JPM, 1980-81, v7(3), 5-12.

McEnally, Richard W. (Boardman, Calvin M. and Richard W. McEnally. "Factors Affecting Seasoned Corporate Bond Prices," JFQA, 1981, v16(2), 207-226.)

McEnally, Richard W. (Chambers, Donald R., Willard T. Carleton and Richard W. McEnally. "Immunizing Default-Free Bond Portfolios With A Duration Vector," JFQA, 1988, v23(1), 89-104.)

McEnally, Richard W. (Rendleman, Richard J., Jr. and Richard W. McEnally. "Assessing The Costs Of Portfolio Insurance," FAJ, 1987, v43(3), 27-37.)

McEnally, Richard W. (Todd, Jerry D. and Richard W. McEnally. "Profitability And Risk In The Title Insurance Industry - The Texas Experience," JRI, 1974, v41(3), 415-433.)

McEnally, Richard W. and Lee A. Tavis. "Spatial Risk' And Return Relationships: A Reconsideration," JRI, 1972, v39(3), 351-368.

McEnally, Richard W. and Lee A. Tavis. "Further Studies Of Property-Liability Return Adequacy: Comment," JRI, 1973, v40(3), 443-459.

McEnally, Richard W. and Lee A. Tavis. "Spatial Risk And Return Relationships: A Reconsideration: Reply," JRI, 1975, v42(2), 330-337.

McEnroe, John E. (Benjamin, Wahjudi P. and John E. McEnroe. "The SEC Overruling Of SFAS 19 And The Behavior Of Security Returns," JBFA, 1983, v10(2), 235-249.)

McEnroe, John E. (Benjamin, Wahjudi P. and John E. McEnroe. "The FASB's Policy Intervention And The Behavior Of Security Returns," JBFA, 1981, v8(3),303-327.)

McEvoy, Raymond H. "Variation In Bank Asset Portfolios," JOF, 1956, v11(4), 463-473.

McEwen, Ruth Ann. (Comiskey, Eugene E., Ruth Ann McEwen and Charles W. Mulford. "A Test Of Pro Forma Consolidation Of Finance Subsidiaries," FM, 1987, v16(3), 45-50.)

McFadden, Daniel. "Econometric Models For Probabilistic Choice Among Products," JOB, 1980, v53(3), Part 2, S13-S30.

McFarland, Henry. "Did Railroad Deregulation Lead To Monopoly Pricing? An Application Of q," JOB, 1987, v60(3), 385-400.

McFarland, James W., R. Richardson Pettit and San K. Sung. "The Distribution Of Foreign Exchange Price Changes: Trading Day Effects And Risk Measurement," JOF, 1982, v37(3), 693-715.

McFarland, James W., R. Richardson Pettit and Sam K. Sung. "The Distribution Of Foreign Exchange Price Changes: Trading Day Effects And Risk Measurement—A Reply," JOF, 1987, v42(1), 189-194.

McFarland, M. Carter. "Major Developments In The Financing Of Residential Construction Since World War II," JOF, 1966, v21(2), 382-394.

McGee, John S. "The Decline And Fall Of Quantity Discounts: The Quantity Limit Rule In Rubber Tires And Tubes," JOB, 1954, v27(3), 225-234.

McGee, John S. (Schweiger, Irving and John S. McGee. "Chicago Banking," JOB, 1961, v34(3),203-366.)

McGee, L. Randolph. (Hultman, Charles W. and L. Randolph McGee. "Factors Affecting The Foreign Banking Presence In The U.S.," JBF, 1989, v13(3), 383-396.)

McGee, Robert T. and Richard T. Stasiak. "Does Anticipated Monetary Policy Matter? Another Look," JMCB, 1985, v17(1), 16-27.

McGee, Robert T. (Feige, Edgar L. and Robert T. McGee. "Federal Reserve Policy And Interest Rate Instability," FR, 1982, v17(1), 50-62.)

McGee, Robert. (Feige, Edgar L. and Robert McGee. "Money Supply Control And Lagged Reserve Accounting," JMCB, 1977, v9(4), 536-551.)

McGee, Robert. (Feige, Edgar L. and Robert McGee. "Has The Federal Reserve Shifted From A Policy Of Interest Rate Targets To A Policy Of Monetary Aggregate Targets?," JMCB, 1979, v11(4), 381-404.)

McGibany, James M. and Farrokh Nourzad. "Money Demand And The Effects Of Fiscal Policies: Comment," JMCB, 1988, v20(4), 706-714.

McGill, Dan. "The Basic Life Insurance Course In The Curriculum," JRI, 1954, v21, 5-9.

McGinnis, Bruce R. (Lee, Sang M., Anthony J. Lerro and Bruce R. McGinnis. "Optimization Of Tax Switching For Commercial Banks: A Comment," JMCB, 1971, v3(2), Part 1, 293-303.)

McGrath, Brian. "Implications Of The Government Budget Constraint: A Comparison Of Two Models," JMCB, 1977, v9(2), 304-315.

McGrath, Earl J. "College Schools Of Business: A Further Appraisal," JOF, 1963, v18(2), 438-450.

McGrath, Earl J. "College Schools Of Business: A Further Appraisal," JRI, 1963, v30(1), 1-10.

McGraw, Patricia. (Fooladi, Iraj, Patricia McGraw and Gordon S. Roberts. "Preferred Stock And Taxes," JBFA, 1991, v18(1), 99-108.)

McGugan, Vincent J. and Richard E. Caves. "Integration And Competition In The Equipment Leasing Industry," JOB, 1974, v47(3), 382-396.

McGuigan, James and William R. King. "Evaluating Alternative Stock Option Timing Strategies," JFQA, 1974, v9(4), 567-578.

McGuigan, James R. and William R. King. "Security Option Strategy Under Risk Aversion: An Analysis," JFQA, 1973, v8(1), 1-15.

McGuinnes, Paul. (Keasey, Kevin and Paul McGuinness. "The Failure Of UK Industrial Firms For The Period 1976-1984, Logistic Analysis And Entropy Measures," JBFA, 1990, v17(1), 119-136.)

McGuinness, John S. "The Job Of Insurance Company Top Management," JRI, 1957, v24(4), 9-21.

McGuire, Dan C. and Ronald J. Kudla. "Option Prices As An Indicator Of Stock Return Expectations," JBFA, 1991, v18(3), 421-430.

McGuire, Joseph W. "The Changing Nature Of Business Responsibilities," JRI, 1969, v36(1), 55-62.

McGuire, Thomas G. "Financing Psychotherapy," JRI, 1986, v53(3), 484-491.

McGuire, Thomas G. (Ellis, Randall P., Cynthia L. Gallup and Thomas G. McGuire. "Should Medical Professional Liability Insurance Be Experience Rated?," JRI, 1990, v57(1), 66-78.)

McHugh, A. J. (Bird, R. G. and A. J. McHugh. "Financial Ratios - An Empirical Study," JBFA, 1977, v4(1), 29-46.)

McHugh, Donald P. "Towards A Rational Regulatory System - Discussion," JRI, 1967, v34(4), 575-580.

McIndoe, Robert A. (Johnston, George S., M. Louise Curley and Robert A. McIndoe. "Dual-Purpose Funds Undervalued?," FAJ, 1968, v24(6), 157-163.)

McInish, T. H. (Lockwood, L. J. and T. H. McInish. "Tests Of Stability For Variances And Means Of Overnight/Intraday Returns During Bull And Bear Markets," JBF, 1990, v14(6), 1243-1254.)

McInish, T. H. (Srivastava, R. K., H. R. Isakson, L. Price and T. H. McInish. "Analysis Of The Characteristics Of Individual Investors In Real Estate Securities And Income-Producing Property," AREUEA, 1984, v12(4), 521-541.)

McInish, T. H. and R. A. Wood. "A Transactions Data Analysis Of The Variability Of Common Stock Returns During 1980-1984," JBF, 1990, v14(1), 99-112.

McInish, T. H. and R. A. Wood. "An Analysis Of Transactions Data For The Toronto Stock Exchange: Return Patterns And End-Of-The-Day Effect," JBF, 1990, v14(2/3), 441-458.

McInish, Thomas H. and Donald Puglisi. "The Efficiency Of The International Money Markets: A Reply," JBFA, 1984, v11(4), 583-584.

McInish, Thomas H. and Donald J. Puglisi. "The Efficiency Of The International Money Markets," JBFA, 1982, v8(2), 167-177.

McInish, Thomas H. and Rajendra K. Srivastava. "Ex-Ante Expectations And Portfolio Selection," FR, 1984, v19(1), 84-96.

McInish, Thomas H. and Rajendra K. Srivastava. "Teaching The Art Of Market Making With A Game Simulation," JFED, 1982, v11, 94-96.

McInish, Thomas H. and Robert A. Wood. "Adjusting For Beta Bias: An Assessment Of Alternate Techniques: A Note," JOF, 1986, v41(1), 277-286.

McInish, Thomas H. and Robert A. Wood. "Intertemporal Differences In Movements Of Minute-To-Minute Stock Returns," FR, 1984, v19(4), 359-371.

McInish, Thomas H. and Robert A. Wood. "Intraday And Overnight Returns And Day-Of-The-Week Effects," JFR, 1985, v8(2), 119-126.

McInish, Thomas H. "Teaching The Art Of Market Making With A Game Simulation," JFED, 1980, v9, 74-76.

McInish, Thomas H. (Saniga, Erwin M., Thomas H. McInish and Bruce K. Gouldey. "The Effect Of Differencing Interval Length On Beta," JFR, 1981, v4(2), 129-135.)

McInish, Thomas H. "The Determinants Of Municipal Bond Risk Premiums By Maturity," JFR, 1980, v3(2), 129-138.

McInish, Thomas H. (Srivastava, Rajendra K., Thomas H. McInish and Linda L. Price. "Information Costs And Portfolio Selection," JBF, 1984, v8(3), 417-429.)

McInish, Thomas H. (Gehrlein, William V. and Thomas H. McInish. "Cyclical Variability Of Bond Risk Premia: A Note," JBF, 1985, v9(1), 157-166.)

McInish, Thomas H. (Kolari, James, Thomas H. McInish and Erwin M. Saniga. "A Note On The Distribution Types Of Financial Ratios In The Commercial Banking Industry," JBF, 1989, v13(3), 463-472.)

McInish, Thomas H. and Robert Wood. "Proxies For Nonsynchronous Trading," FR, 1983, v18(2),206-213.

McInish, Thomas H. and Robert A. Wood. "A New Approach To Controlling For Thin Trading," JFR, 1985, v8(1), 69-75.

McInish, Thomas H. (Wood, Robert A., Thomas H. McInish and J. Keith Ord. "An Investigation Of Transactions Data For NYSE Stocks," JOF, 1985, v40(3), 723-739.)

McInish, Thomas H. and Robert A. Wood. "Autocorrelation Of Daily Index Returns: Intraday-to-Intraday Versus Close-To-Close Intervals," JBF, 1991, v15(1), 193-206.

McInnes, W. M. (Davies, J. R. and W. M. McInnes. "The Valuation Of Fixed Assets In The Financial Accounts Of UK Nationalised Industries And The Implications For Monitoring Performance: A Comment," JBFA, 1982, v8(2), 267-272.)

McInstosh, Willard. (Webb, James R. and Willard McIntosh. "Real Estate Investment Acquisition Rules For REITs: A Survey," JRER, 1986, v1(1), 77-98.)

McIntosh, Kenneth L. "Risk: Comment," JRI, 1963, v30(4), 587-589.

McIntosh, Willard and Glenn V. Henderson, Jr. "Efficiency Of The Office Properties Market," JREFEC, 1989, v2(1), 61-70.

McIntosh, Willard, Dennis T. Officer and Jeffrey A. Born. "The Wealth Effects Of Merger Activities: Further Evidence From Real Estate Investment Trusts," JRER, 1989, v4(3), 141-155.

McIntosh, Willard. (Albert, Joseph D. and Willard McIntosh. "Identifying Risk-Adjusted Indifference Rents For Alternative Operating Leases," JRER, 1989, v4(3), 81-93.)

McKean, John R. "A Note On Administered Prices With Fluctuating Demand," JFQA, 1969, v4(1), 15-23.

McKean, John R. and John J. Kania. "An Industry Approach To Owner-Manager Control And Profit Performance," JOB, 1978, v51(2), 327-342.

McKean, Roland N. (Fagg, Donald R., Carl Kaysen, and Roland N. McKean. "What The Factory Worker Knows About His Factory," JOB, 1958, v31(3), 213-234.)

McKenna, Fred W. "Pension Plan Cost Risk," JRI, 1982, v49(2), 193-217.

McKenna, Fred W. and Yong H. Kim. "Managerial Risk Preferences, Real Pension Costs, And Long-Run Corporate Pension Fund Investment Policy," JRI, 1986, v53(1), 29-48.

McKenney, James L. "An Evaluation Of A Business Game In An MBA Curriculum," JOB, 1962, v35(3), 278-286.

McKenzie, George and Stephen Thomas. "Liquidity, Credit Creation And International Banking: An Econometric Investigation," JBF, 1983, v7(4), 467-480.

McKenzie, George W. "Regulating The Euro-Markets," JBF, 1981, v5(1), 109-134.

McKenzie, Joseph A. "Who Holds Alternative Market-Yield Accounts?", JFR, 1984, v7(2), 175-183.

McKenzie, Joseph A. (Boehm, Thomas P. and Joseph A. McKenzie. "Inflation, Taxes, And The Demand For Housing," AREUEA, 1982, v10(1), 25-38.) 3?8

McKeon, James J. "Corporate External Financing," FAJ, 1969, v25(5), 25-28.

McKeown, James C. (Jensen, Daniel L. and James C. McKeown. "Multiple-Step Investigations Of Standard Cost Variances," JBFA, 1977, v4(2), 247-256.)

McKeown, Patrick G. (Miller, Norman G. and Patrick G. McKeown. "Optimizing The Distributions Of Limited Partnership Returns," AREUEA, 1979, v7(3), 378-392.)

McKeown, Patrick G. (Trieschmann, James S. and Patrick G. McKeown. "Sensitivity Analysis Of Workers' Compensation Costs," JRI, 1980, v47(4), 735-752.)

McKersie, R. (Baloff, N. and R. McKersie. "Motivating Startups," JOB, 1966, v39(4), 473-484.)

McKersie, Robert B. and William W. Shropshire, Jr. "Avoiding Written Grievances: A Successful Program," JOB, 1962, v35(2), 135-152.

McKibben, Walt. "Econometric Forecasting Of Common Stock Investment Returns: A New Methodology Using Fundamental Operating Data," JOF, 1972, v27(2), 371-380.

McKibben, Walt. (Rosenberg, Barr and Walt McKibben. "The Prediction Of Systematic And Specific Risk In Common Stocks," JFQA, 1973, v8(2), 317-333.)

McKibbin, Warwick J. and Jeffrey D. Sachs. "Comparing The Global Performance Of Alternative Exchange Arrangements," JIMF, 1988, v7(4), 387-410.

McKinley, Gordon W. "Life Insurance Company Lending To Small Business," JOF, 1961, v16(2), 291-303.

McKinley, Gordon W. "The Federal Home Loan Bank System And The Control Of Credit," JOF, 1957, v12(3), 319-332.

McKinley, Gordon W. "The Federal Home Loan Bank System And The Control Of Credit: Reply," JOF, 1958, v13(4), 545-546.

McKinnell, Cathy S. (Curtis, Charles E., Jr., Kandice H. Kahl and Cathy S. McKinnell. "Risk-Efficient Soybean Marketing: The Contribution Of Commodity Options To The Producing Firm," RFM, 1987, v6(2), 176-190.)

McKinney, George W., Jr. "Residential Mortgage Lenders," JOF, 1952, v7(1), 28-46.

McKinney, George. "A Perspective On The Use Of Models In The Management Of Bank Funds," JBR, 1977-78, v8(2), 122-127.

McKinnon, Gary F. (Call, Ivan T., Terry N. Lee and Gary F. McKinnon. "Teaching Financial Management As Part Of An Integrated Management Core," JFED, 1975, v4, 19-27.)

McKinnon, Ronald I. "Exchange-Rate Flexibility And Monetary Policy," JMCB, 1971, v3(2), Part 2, 339-355.

McKinnon, S. M. "A Cost-Benefit Study Of Disclosure Requirements For Multinational Corporations," JBFA, 1984, v11(4), 451-468.

McKinnon, Sharon M. "How Important Are Those Foreign Operations? A Flow-Chart Approach To Loan Analysis," FAJ, 1985, v41(1), 75-78.

McKinnon, Sharon. (Copeland, Ronald M. and Sharon McKinnon. "Financial Distortion' And Consolidation Of Captive Finance Subsidiaries In The General Merchandising Industry," JBFA, 1987, v14(1), 77-98.)

McKnight, David W. "The Worth Of Food Securities," FAJ, 1949, v5(4), 20-23.

McKnight, John L. ("Smithsonian," Edward J. Mitchell and John L. McKnight. "Nuggets: Hares, Lynx, Energy, And Crooked Teeth," JPM, 1977-78, v4(3), 5-11.)

McLaughlin, Frank C. and John L. Moore, Jr. "Planning To Meet Retirement Costs," FAJ, 1968, v24(5), 13-23.

McLaughlin, Frank C. "International Monetary System," FAJ, 1968, v24(3), 23-27.

McLaughlin, Hugh S. (Peterson, Manferd O. and Hugh S. McLaughlin. "Conflict Of Interest And The Financing Of Commercial Bank Stock Ownership," JBR, 1974-75, v5(1), 7-12.)

McLean, Ephraim R. "An Appraisal Of Computerized Life Insurance Estate Planning," JRI, 1974, v41(3), 497-510.

McLean, James H. "Depreciation: Its Relationship To Funds," FAJ, 1963, v19(3), 73-82.

McLean, W. R. "Statistical Approach To Railway Efficiency," FAJ, 1953, v9(4), 45-47.

McLeavey, Dennis W. (Belkin, Jacob, Donald J. Hempel and Dennis W. McLeavey. "An Empirical Study Of Time On Market Using Multidimensional Segmentation Of Housing Markets," AREUEA, 1976, v4(2), 57-76.)

McLeay, Stuart. "Student's t And The Distribution Of Financial Ratios," JBFA, 1986, v13(2), 209-222.

McLeay, Stuart. (Fieldsend, Susan, Nicholas Longford and Stuart McLeay. "Industry Effects And The Proportionality Assumption In Ratio Analysis: A Variance Component Analysis," JBFA, 1987, v14(4), 497-518.)

McLeod, A. N. "Security-Reserve Requirements In The United States And The United Kingdom: A Comment," JOF, 1959, v14(4), 531-542.

McLeod, Robert W. (Thistle, Paul D., Robert W. McLeod and B. Lynne Conrad. "Interest Rates And Bank Portfolio Adjustments," JBF, 1989, v13(1), 151-162.)

McLure, Charles E., Jr. "Investment Life Insurance Versus Term Insurance And Separate Investment: A Determination Of Expected-Return Equivalents: Comment," JRI, 1973, v40(2), 291-293.

McMahon, Walter W. (Soldofsky, Robert M. and Walter W. McMahon. "A Comment On Variable Annuities," JOF, 1957, v12(3), 372-376.)

McMenamin, J. Stuart. (Cohen, Darrel and J. Stuart McMenamin. "The Role Of Fiscal Policy In A Financially Disaggregated Macroeconomic Model," JMCB, 1978, v10(3), 322-336.)

McMillan, Henry M. "Nonassignable Pensions And The Price Of Risk," JMCB, 1986, v18(1), 60-75.

McMillan, T. E., Jr., Louis E. Buck, Jr. and James Deegan. "The 'Fisher Theorem' - An Illusion, But Whose?," FAJ, 1984, v40(6), 63-69.

McMillan, W. B. "Retailing Frozen Foods," FAJ, 1946, v2(3), 22-31.

McMillin, W. Douglas. "A Dynamic Analysis Of The Impact Of Fiscal Policy On The Money Supply," JMCB, 1981, v13(2), 221-226.

McMillin, W. Douglas. "Money Growth Volatility And The Macroeconomy," JMCB, 1988, v20(3), Part 1, 319-335.

McNamara, Michael J. (Rejda, George E., James R. Schmidt and Michael J. McNamara. "The Impact Of Social Security Tax Contributions On Group Life Insurance Premiums," JRI, 1987, v54(4), 712-720.)

McNamee, Patrick. (Bhaskar, Krish and Patrick McNamee. "Multiple Objectives In Accounting And Finance," JBFA, 1983, v10(4), 595-621.)

McNees, Stephen K. "Are Econometricians Useful? Folklore Versus Fact," JOB, 1978, v51(4), 573-578.

McNeill, Thomas J. (Thompson, Sarahelen, Thomas J. McNeill and James S. Eales. "Expiration And Delivery On The World Sugar Futures Contract," JFM, 1990, v10(2), 153-168.)

McNelis, Paul D. (Browne, Francis X. and Paul D. McNelis. "Exchange Controls And Interest Rate Determination With Traded And Nontraded Assets: The Irish-United Kingdom Experience," JIMF, 1990, v9(1), 41-59.)

McNichols, Maureen and Ajay David. "Stock Dividends, Stock Splits and Signaling," JOF, 1990, v45(3), 857-880.

McNichols, Maureen. (Grundy, Bruce D. and Maureen McNichols. "Trade And Revelation Of Information Through Prices And Direct Disclosure," RFS, 1989, v2(4), 495-526.)

McNown, Robert and Myles S. Wallace. "National Price Levels, Purchasing Power Parity, And Cointegration: A Test Of Four High Inflation Economies," JIMF, 1989, v8(4), 533-546.

McNulty, James E. "The Pricing Of Interest Rate Swaps," JFSR, 1990, v4(1), 53-64.

McNutt, Paul J. (Lewis, W. Cris and Paul J. McNutt. "The Incidence Of Property Taxes On Single-Family Housing," AREUEA, 1979, v7(3), 344-361.)

McPartlin, Kenneth J. (Bower, Richard S. and Kenneth J. McPartlin. "Oh, To Be In Equities, Now That Winter's Here," JPM, 1975-76, v2(1), 39-45.)

McPherrin, John W. (Greene, Mark R., John W. McPherrin and Herbert W. Florer. "Curricular Concepts In Risk And Insurance," JRI, 1963, v30(1), 129-132.)

McPherson, James Roland. "Multiple-Multiple Lines," JRI, 1957, v24(1), 145-150.

McPherson, James Roland. "The Trillion Dollar Question," JRI, 1957, v24(2), 43-55.

McQueen, Grant and Steven Thorley. "Are Stock Returns Predictable? A Test Using Markov Chains," JOF, 1991, v46(1), 239-264.

McQuown, J. A. "Research: Building An Effective Trilogy," JBR, 1970-71, v1(1), 7-12.

McQuown, J. A. "Technical And Fundamental Analysis And Capital Market Theory," JBR, 1973-74, v4(1), 8-17.

McQuown, J. A. (Vasicek, O. A. and J. A. McQuown. "The Efficent Market Model," FAJ, 1972, v28(5), 71-84.)

McRae, James J. and Francis Tapon. "A New Test Of The Administered Pricing Hypothesis With Canadian Data," JOB, 1979, v52(3), 409-428.

McShane, R. W. and I. G. Sharpe. "A Time Service/Cross Section Analysis Of The Determinants Of Australian Trading Bank Loan/Deposit Interest Margins: 1962-1981," JBF, 1985, v9(1), 115-136.

McTague, Peter J. (Gatti, James F., John R. Mills and Peter J. McTague. "The Feasibility Of Small Denomination Consumer Note Issues As A Source Of Funds For Non-Financial Borrowers," FM, 1981, v10(4), 41-53.)

McWhinney, Madeline. "Money Markets Developments June, 1953 To December, 1954," JOF, 1955, v10(2), 296-301.

McWhorter, Archer, Jr. "A Consideration Of The Decision To Self-

Insure A Small Fleet Of Automobiles," JRI, 1979, v46(2), 139-148.

McWhorter, Archer, Jr. "Drawing Inferences From Medical Malpractice Closed Claim Studies," JRI, 1978, v45(1), 79-94.

McWhorter, Archer, Jr. (Simonds, Richard R., Lynn Roy LaMotte and Archer McWhorter, Jr. "Testing For Nonstationarity Of Market Risk: An Exact Test And Power Considerations," JFQA, 1986, v21(2),209-220.)

McWhorter, Archer, Jr. (Steves, Buddy, Archer McWhorter, Jr. and Lee Fisher. "An Empirical Analysis Of The Capacity Crisis In Medical Malpractice Insurance," JRI, 1979, v46(1), 139-146.)

McWhorter, Suzanne S. "Advertising And Public Relations Activities Of Insurance Companies: With Special Emphasis On Health Insurers," JRI, 1958, v25(3), 8-20.

McWilliams, James D. and James Wei. "Some Like To-Matoes And Some Like To-Matoes," JPM, 1980-81, v7(4), 43-47.

McWilliams, James D. "A Closer Look At Incentive Fees For Bank Managed Pension Funds," JBR, 1972-73, v3(4), 238-246.

McWilliams, James D. "Prices, Earnings And P-E Ratios," FAJ, 1966, v22(3), 137-142.

McWilliams, James D. "The Benefits And Costs Of Timing Equity Investments," JBR, 1976-77, v7(1), 22-29.

McWilliams, James D. "'Watchman, Tell Us Of The Night!'," JPM, 1983-84, v10(3), 75-80.

McWilliams, Victoria B. "Managerial Share Ownership And The Stock Price Effects Of Antitakeover Amendment Proposals," JOF, 1990, v45(5), 1627-1640.

Mead, Edgar T., Jr. "Corporate Relations - A New Glimpse," FAJ, 1964, v20(1), 35-36.

Meade, Nigel. "The Random Walk And A Thin Market," JBFA, 1978, v5(3), 321-328.

Meador, Mark. "The Effects On Mortgage Repayment Of Restrictions On The Enforcement Of Due-On-Sale Clauses: The California Experience," AREUEA, 1982, v10(4), 465-474.

Meador, Joseph W. (Chugh, Lal C. and Joseph W. Meador. "The Stock Valuation Process: The Analysts' View," FAJ, 1984, v40(6), 41-43,46-48.)

Meador, Joseph W. (Roden, Peyton Foster and Joseph W. Meador. "An Analysis Of The Audit Guide's Impact On The Sensitivity Of Life Company Stocks," JRI, 1980, v47(4), 660-677.)

Meador, Joseph W., Gerald P. Madden and David J. Johnston. "On The Probability Of Acquisition Of Non-Life Insurers," JRI, 1986, v53(4), 621-643.

Mears, Peter, Daniel E. McCarty and Robert Osborn. "An Empirical Investigation Of Banking Customers' Perception Of Bank Machines," JBR, 1978-79, v9(2), 112-115.

Meckling, W. H. (Jensen, M. C. and W. H. Meckling," "Can The Corporation Survive?," FAJ, 1978, v34(1), 31-37.)

Meckling, William H. "Karl Brunner At The University Of Rochester," JMCB, 1977, v9(1), Part 2, 253-254.

Meckling, William H. (Brunner, Karl and William H. Meckling. "The Perception Of Man And The Conception Of Government," JMCB, 1977, v9(1), 70-85.)

Meckling, William H. (Jensen, Michael C. and William H. Meckling. "Rights And Production Functions: An Application To Labor-Managed Firms And Codetermination," JOB, 1979, v52(4), 469-506.)

Meckling, William H. (Jensen, Michael C. and William H. Meckling. "Theory Of The Firm: Managerial Behavior, Agency Costs And Ownership Structure," JFEC, 1976, v3(4), 305-360)

Meehan, John P. and Ellen M. Hays. "Hidden Dangers In Modern Portfolio Theory," JPM, 1978-79, v5(3), 48-51.

Meeker, Larry G. and Forest E. Myers. "Financing Bank Stock Ownership: A Question Of Control Of Interest," JBF, 1980, v4(2), 111-124.

Meeker, Larry G. and Laura Gray. "A Note On Non-Performing Loans As An Indicator Of Asset Quality," JBF, 1987, v11(1), 161-168.

Meeker, Larry G. and O. Maurice Joy. "Price Premiums For Controlling Shares Of Closely Held Bank Stock," JOB, 1980, v53(3), Part 1, 297-314.

Meeker, Larry G., O. Maurice Joy and Kenneth O. Cogger. "Valuation Of Controlling Shares In Closely Held Banks," JBF, 1983, v7(2), 175-188.

Meeks, Sue E. (Baker, H. Kent and Sue E. Meeks. "Research On Exchange Listings And Delistings: A Review And Synthesis," FPE, 1991, v1(1), 57-72.)

Meese, Richard A. and Kenneth J. Singleton. "On Unit Roots And The Empirical Modeling Of Exchange Rates," JOF, 1982, v37(4), 1029-1035.

Meese, Richard A. "Is The Sticky Price Assumption Reasonable For Exchange Rate Models?," JIMF, 1984, v3(2), 131-139.

Meese, Richard and Kenneth Rogoff. "Was It Real? The Exchange Rate-Interest Differential Relation Over The Modern Floating-Rate Period," JOF, 1988, v43(4), 933-948.

Megginson, William L. "Restricted Voting Stock, Acquisition Premiums, And The Market Value Of Corporate Control," FR, 1990, v25(2), 175-198.

Megginson, William L. (Ang, James S., David W. Blackwell and William L. Megginson. "The Effect Of Taxes On The Relative Valuation Of Dividends And Capital Gains: Evidence From Dual-Class British Investment Trusts," JOF, 1991, v46(1), 383-400.)

Megginson, William L. (Ang, James S. and William L. Megginson. "Restricted Voting Shares, Ownership Structure, And The Market Value Of Dual-Class Firms," JFR, 1989, v12(4), 301-318.)

Megginson, William L. (Ang, James S. and William L. Megginson. "A Test Of The Before-Tax Versus After-Tax Equilibrium Models Of Corporate Debt," RIF, 1990, v8, 97-118.)

Megginson, William L. (Boehmer, Ekkehart and William L. Megginson. "Determinants Of Secondary Market Prices For Developing Country Syndicated Loans," JOF, 1990, v45(5), 1517-1540.)

Meguire, Philip. (Kormendi, Roger C. and Philip Meguire. "A Multicountry Characterization Of The Nonstationarity Of Aggregate Output," JMCB, 1990, v22(1), 77-93.)

Mehdian, Seyed M. (Elyasiani, Elyas and Seyed M. Mehdian. "A Nonparametric Approach To Measurement Of Efficiency And Technological Change: The Case Of Large U.S. Commercial Banks," JFSR, 1990, v4(2), 157-168.)

Mehr, Robert I. "A Blueprint For Long-Range Planning By Insurance Companies," JRI, 1957, v24(3), 70-77.

Mehr, Robert I. "A Philosophy Of Learning - A Summary View," JRI, 1958, v25(1), 23-25.

Mehr, Robert I. "A University Professor's Viewpoint," JRI, 1949, v16, 27-34.

Mehr, Robert I. "Channels Of Distribution In Insurance," JRI, 1969, v36(4), 583-596.

Mehr, Robert I. "Education: Animal, Vegetable, Or Mineral," JRI, 1969, v36(1), 1-10.

Mehr, Robert I. "New Settings For Old Stones," JRI, 1967, v34(3), 477-480.

Mehr, Robert I. "Review Article - A Look At Change For Automobile Claims," JRI, 1968, v35(3), 425-436.

Mehr, Robert I. "Some Thoughts On Product Development In Life Insurance," JRI, 1968, v35(4), 553-567.

Mehr, Robert I. "Tax-Sheltered Annuities: Purchase Decisions," JRI, 1968, v35(2), 207-226.

Mehr, Robert I. "The Concept Of The Level-Premium Whole Life Insurance Policy - Reexamined," JRI, 1975, v42(3), 419-432.

Mehr, Robert I. "The Concept Of Level Premium Whole Life Policy - Re-Examined: Reply," JRI, 1977, v44(3), 505-507.

Mehr, Robert I. "The Effect Of Mass Merchandising On The Agency System," JRI, 1970, v37(1), 142-147.

Mehr, Robert I. "The Variable Annuity: Security Or Insurance," JOF, 1958, v13(3), 386-411.

Mehr, Robert I. (Kennedy, Kenneth F. and Robert I. Mehr. "A Case Study In Private V. Public Enterprise: The Manitoba Experience With Automobile Insurance," JRI, 1977, v44(4), 595-622.)

Mehr, Robert I. (Rose, Terry and Robert I. Mehr. "Flexible Income Programming," JRI, 1980, v47(1), 44-60.)

Mehr, Robert I. (Rose, Terry and Robert I. Mehr. "A Computer Model For Flexible Income Programming," JRI, 1981, v48(2), 308.)

Mehr, Robert I. (Rose, Terry and Robert I. Mehr. "Flexible Income Programming: Reply," JRI, 1982, v49(2), 297-299.)

Mehr, Robert I. and Bob A. Hedges. "New Perspectives On Risk Management: Comment," JRI, 1968, v35(4), 615-623.

Mehr, Robert I. and David R. Klock. "Student Research And The Insurance Regulator," JRI, 1972, v39(1), 119-123.

Mehr, Robert I. and Gary W. Eldred. "Should The 'No-Fault' Concept Be Applied To Automobile Property Damage?," JRI, 1975, v42(1), 17-33.

Mehr, Robert I. and Gary W. Eldred. "Public Desires And Automobile Property Damage Insurance," JRI, 1975, v42(1), 151-155.

Mehr, Robert I. and George R. Jordan. "A Life Adjustment Policy," JRI, 1961, v28(2), 59-70.

Mehr, Robert I. and Mack H. Shumate. "Primacy In Automobile Bodily Injury Coverage," JRI, 1975, v42(2), 201-225.

Mehr, Robert I. and Seev Neumann. "Delphi Forecasting Project," JRI, 1970, v37(2), 241-246.

Mehr, Robert I. and Stephen W. Forbes. "The Risk Management Decision In The Total Business Setting," JRI, 1973, v40(3), 389-402.

Mehr, Robert I., R. W. Osler and Meyer Melnikoff. "Has The Life Insurance Company Product Become Obsolete?," JRI, 1962, v29(1), 31-48.

Mehra, Rajnish. "On The Financing And Investment Decisions Of Multinational Firms In The Presence Of Exchange Risk," JFQA, 1978, v13(2), 227-244.

Mehra, Y. P. (Laumas, G. S. and Y. P. Mehra. "The Stability Of The Demand For Money Function, 1900-1974," JOF, 1977, v32(3), 911-916.)

Mehra, Yash P. "Velocity And The Variability Of Money Growth: Evidence From Granger-Causality Tests: Comment," JMCB, 1989, v21(2), 262-271.

Mehra, Yash P. (Hetzel, Robert L. and Yash P. Mehra. "The Behavior Of Money Demand In The 1980s," JMCB, 1989, v21(4), 455-463.)

Mehrez, Avraham. (Bulmash, Samuel B. and Avraham Mehrez. "Sharing Rule Contracts Between Management And Investors And Their Effect On Management's Attitude Towards Risk," JBFA, 1985, v12(3), 399-413.)

Mehta, Cyrus R. and William Beranek. "Tracking Asset Volatility By Means Of A Bayesian Switching Regression," JFQA, 1982, v17(2), 241-263.

Mehta, Dileep R. and David T. Whitford. "Lease Financing And The M&M Propositions," FR, 1979, v14(1), 47-58.

Mehta, Dileep R. "The Impact Of Outstanding Convertible Bonds On Corporate Dividend Policy," JOF, 1976, v31(2), 489-506.

Mehta, Dileep R. (Deschamps, Benoit and Dileep R. Mehta. "Predictive Ability And Descriptive Validity Of Earnings Forecasting Models," JOF, 1980, v35(4), 933-949.)

Mehta, Dileep R., Edward A. Moses, Benoit Deschamps and Michael C. Walker. "The Influence Of Dividends, Growth, And Leverage On Share Prices In The Electric Utility Industry: An Econometric Study," JFQA, 1980, v15(5), 1163-1196.

Mehta, Dileep R., Michael D. Curley and Hung-Gay Fung. "Inflation, Cost Of Capital, And Capital Budgeting Procedures," FM, 1984, v13(4), 48-54.

Mehta, Dileep R., Peter C. Eisemann, Edward A. Moses and Benoit Deschamps. "Capital Structure And Capital Adequacy Of Bank Holding Companies: A Market Test," JBF, 1979, v3(1), 5-22.

Mehta, Dileep. "Optimal Credit Policy Selection: A Dynamic Approach," JFQA, 1970, v5(4), 421-444.

Mehta, Dileep. (Mahajan, Arvind and Dileep Mehta. "Strong Form Efficiency Of The Foreign Exchange Market And Bank Positions," JFR, 1984, v7(3), 197-207.)

Mehta, Dileep. (Mahajan, Arvind and Dileep Mehta. "Swaps, Expectations, And Exchange Rates," JBF, 1986, v10(1), 7-20.)

Meidan, Arthur. "Marketing Strategies, Organisation And Performance Control In Insurance," JRI, 1982, v49(3), 388-404.

Meier, David A. (Follain, James R., Terry Lutes and David A. Meier. "Why Do Some Real Estate Salespeople Earn More Than Others?," JRER, 1987, v2(1), 73-81.)

Meier, Heidi Hylton. (Kamath, Ravindra R., Shahriar Khaksari, Heidi Hylton Meier and John Winklepleck. "Management Of Excess Cash: Practices And Developments," FM, 1985, v14(3), 70-77.)

Meier, R. L. "Automatism In The American Economy," JOB, 1956, v29(1), 14-27.

Meier, Robert C. "The Application Of Optimum-Seeking Techniques To Simulation Studies: A Preliminary Evaluation," JFQA, 1967, v2(1), 30-51.

Meigs, A. James. "The Changing Role Of Banks In The Market For Equities," JOF, 1965, v20(2), 368-378.

Meigs, A. James. "The Fed And Financial Markets: Is It Killing Them With Kindness?," FAJ, 1981, v37(1), 18-27.

Meilijson, Isaac. (Landsberger, Michael and Isaac Meilijson. "A Tale Of Two Tails: An Alternative Characterization Of Comparative Risk," JRU, 1990, v3(1), 65-82.)

Meilke, Karl D. (Braga, Francesco S., Larry J. Martin and Karl D. Meilke. "Cross Hedging The Italian Lira/US Dollar Exchange Rate With Deutsch Mark Futures," JFM, 1989, v9(2), 87-100.)

Meinster, David R. and Alan K. Severn. "Correspondent Balances, Services, And The Money Supply," JBF, 1982, v6(2), 195-214.

Meinster, David R. and Rajesh K. Mohindru. "Determinants Of The Demand For Correspondent Balances By Small & Medium Sized Banks," JBR, 1975-76, v6(1), 25-34.

Meinster, David R. (Johnson, Rodney D. and David R. Meinster. "The Analysis Of Bank Holding Company Acquisitions: Some Methodological Issues," JBR, 1973-74, v4(1), 58-61.)

Meinster, David R. (Johnson, Rodney D. and David R. Meinster. "The Performance Of Bank Holding Company Acquisitions: A Multivariate Analysis," JOB, 1975, v48(2), 204-212.)

Meinster, David R. (Severn, Alan K. and David R. Meinster. "The Use Of Multicurrency Financing By The Financial Manager," FM, 1978, v7(4), 45-53.)

Meinster, David R. and Elyas Elyasiani. "The Performance Of Foreign Owned, Minority Owned, And Holding COmpany Owned Banks In The U.S.," JBF, 1988, v12(2), 293-314.

Meiselman, David. "A Comparison Of Stabilization Policies: 1966-67 And 1969-70: Comment," JMCB, 1973, v5(1), 43-46.

Meiselman, David. "New Economics And Monetary Policy," FAJ, 1967, v23(6), 95-100.

Meisner, James F. and John W. Labuszewski. "Treasury Bond Futures Delivery Bias," JFM, 1984, v4(4), 569-577.

Meisner, James F. and John W. Labuszewski. "Modifying The Black-Scholes Option Pricing Model For Alternative Underlying Instruments," FAJ, 1984, v40(6), 23-27,30.

Mejia, Edwin J. " Aluminum In World Affairs," FAJ, 1952, v8(5), 39-41.

Melamed, Leo. "The Futures Market: Liquidity And The Technique Of Spreading," JFM, v1(3),405-411.

Melander, E. R. (Hammond, J. D., E. R. Melander and N. Shilling. "Risk, Return, And The Capital Market: The Insurer Case," JFQA, 1976, v11(1), 115-131.)

Melander, E. R. (Hammond, J. D., and E. R. Melander. "The Long Term Crisis In Life Insurance: Comment," JRI, 1968, v35(1), 147-148.)

Melander, E. R. (Hammond, J. D., E. R. Melander and N. Shilling. "Economies of Scale In The Property And Liability Insurance Industry," JRI, 1971, v38(2), 181-191.)

Melander, Eugene R. (Hammond, J. D., David B. Houston and Eugene R. Melander. "Determinants Of Household Life Insurance Premium Expenditures," FAJ, 1967, v34(3), 397-408.)

Melchert, David and Joel L. Naroff. "Central City Revitalization: A Predictive Model," AREUEA, 1987, v15(1), 664-683.

Melicher, Ronald W. and David F. Rush. "Evidence On The Acquisition-Related Performance Of Conglomerate Firms," JOF, 1974, v29(1), 141-149.

Melicher, Ronald W. and David F. Rush. "Systematic Risk, Financial Data, And Bond Rating Relationships In A Regulated Industry Environment," JOF, 1974, v29(2), 537-544.

Melicher, Ronald W. and David F. Rush. "The Performance Of Conglomerate Firms: Recent Risk And Return Experience," JOF, 1973, v28(2), 381-388.

Melicher, Ronald W. "Financing With Convertible Preferred Stock: Comment," JOF, 1971, v26(1),144-147.

Melicher, Ronald W. "Financial Factors Which Influence Beta Variations Within An Homogeneous Industry Environment," JFQA, 1974, v9(2), 231-241.

Melicher, Ronald W. (D'Antonio, Louis J. and Ronald W. Melicher. "Changes In Federal Reserve Membership: A Risk-Return Profitability Analysis," JOF, 1979, v34(4), 987-997.)

Melicher, Ronald W. (Hays, Patrick A., Michael D. Joehnk and Ronald W. Melicher. "Differential Determinants Of Risk Premiums In The Public And Private Corporate Bond Markets," JFR, 1979, v2(2), 143-152.)

Melicher, Ronald W. (Nielsen, James F. and Ronald W. Melicher. "A Financial Analysis Of Acquisition And Merger Premiums," JFQA, 1973, v8(2),139-148.)

Melicher, Ronald W. (Rush, David F. and Ronald W. Melicher. "An Empirical Examination Of Factors Which Influence Warrant Prices," JOF, 1974, v29(5), 1449-1466.)

Melicher, Ronald W. (Tallman, Gary D., David F. Rush and Ronald W. Melicher. "Competitive Versus Negotiated Underwriting Costs For Regulated Industries," FM, 1974, v3(2), 49-55.)

Melicher, Ronald W., David F. Rush and Daryl N. Winn. "Industry Concentration, Financial Structure And Profitability," FM, 1976, v5(3), 48-53.

Melicher, Ronald W., David F. Rush and Daryl N. Winn. "Degree Of Industry Concentration And Market Risk-Return Performance," JFQA, 1976, v11(4), 627-635.

Melitz, Jacques and George Martin. "Financial Intermediaries, Money Definition, And Monetary Control: A Comment," JMCB, 1971, v3(3), 693-701.

Melitz, Jacques and Morris Pardue. "The Demand And Supply Of Commercial Bank Loans," JMCB, 1973, v5(2), 669-692.

Melitz, Jacques. "On The Optimality Of Satiation In Money Balances," JOF, 1972, v27(3), 683-698.

Melitz, Jacques. "The Welfare Case For The European Monetary System," JIMF, 1985, v4(4),485-506.

Mellon, W. G. (Brick, Ivan E., W. G. Mellon, Julius Surkis and Murray Mohl. "Optimal Capital Structure: A Multi-Period Programming Model For Use In Financial Planning," JBF, 1983, v7(1), 45-68.)

Mellon, W. Giles. "On The Use Of Time Series Analysis For Financial Prediction," JOF, 1964, v19(2), Part 1, 170-185.

Mellon, W. Giles. "The Future Of The Electric Utilities," FAJ, 1976, v32(1), 62-74.

Melnik, A. and M. A. Pollatschek. "Debt Capacity, Diversification And Conglomerate Mergers," JOF, 1973, v28(5), 1263-1273.

Melnik, A. (Sofianos, G., P. Wachtel and A. Melnik. "Loan Commitments And Monetary Policy," JBF, 1990, v14(4), 677-690.)

Melnik, Arie and Aharon R. Ofer. "Determinants Of Commission Rates For Bank Trust Stock Transactions," JBF, 1978, v2(4), 355-366.

Melnik, Arie and Aharon R. Ofer. "Competitive Commission Rates, Execution Quality, And Customer's Market Power," JMCB, 1980, v12(2), Part 2, 221-227.

Melnik, Arie and Alan Kraus. "More On The Short Cycles Of Interest Rates," JFQA, 1971, v6(3),1047-1052.

Melnik, Arie and Alan Kraus. "Short-Run Interest Rate Cycles In The U.S.: 1954-1967," JFQA, 1969, v4(3), 291-299.

Melnik, Arie and Steven E. Plaut. "The Economics Of Loan Commitment Contracts: Credit Pricing And Utilization," JBF, 1986, v10(2), 267-280.

Melnik, Arie and Steven Plaut. "Loan Commitment Contracts, Terms Of Lending, And Credit Allocation," JOF, 1986, v41(2), 425-436.

Melnik, Arie and Steven E. Plaut. "Interest Rate Indexation And The Pricing Of Loan Commitment Contracts," JBF, 1987, v11(1), 137-146.

Melnik, Arie and Steven E. Plaut. "International Lending, Private-Sector 'Country Risk,' And Stabilization Policy," RDIBF, 1988, v2, 121-130.

Melnik, Arie. "Demand Deposit Variability In Banks: A Time Series Analysis," JBR, 1979-80, v10(2), 97-101.

Melnik, Arie. "Short Run Determinants Of Commercial Bank Investment Portfolios: An Empirical Analysis," JOF, 1970, v25(3), 639-649.

Melnikoff, Meyer. (Mehr, Robert I., R. W. Osler and Meyer Melnikoff. "Has The Life Insurance Company Product Become Obsolete?," JRI, 1962, v29(1), 31-48.)

Melone, Joseph J. "Actuarial Cost Methods - New Pension Terminology," JRI, 1963, v30(3), 456-464.

Melone, Joseph J. "Are Non-Insured Pension Plans Engaged In The Business Of Insurance?," JRI, 1963, v30(4), 505-516.

Melone, Joseph J. "Implications Of Vested Benefits In Private Pension Plans," JRI, 1965, v32(4), 559-570.

Melrose, Kendrick B. "An Empirical Study On Optimizing Advertising Policy," JOB, 1969, v42(3), 282-292.

Meltzer, Allan H. and Robert H. Rasche. "Is The Federal Reserve's Monetary Control Policy Misdirected?," JMCB, 1982, v14(1), 119-147.

Meltzer, Allan H. "Aggregative Consequences Of Removing Restrictions," JBR, 1972-73, v3(2), 72-83.

Meltzer, Allan H. "Anticipated Inflation And Unanticipated Price Change: A Test Of The Price-Specie Flow Theory And The Phillips Curve," JMCB, 1977, v9(1), Part 2, 182-205.

Meltzer, Allan H. "Credit Availability And Economic Decisions: Some Evidence From The Mortgage And Housing Markets," JOF, 1974, v29(3), 763-777.

Meltzer, Allan H. "Improvement In The Balance Of Payments: A Response To Monetary Policy Or To Ad Hoc Fiscal Policies," JOB, 1965, v38(3), 267-276.

Meltzer, Allan H. "Public Policies As Causes Of Fluctuations," JMCB, 1970, v2(1), 45-55.

Meltzer, Allan H. "The Political And Economic Aspects Of Policymaking: A Symposium: Introduction," JMCB, 1972, v4(1), 1-2.

Meltzer, Allan H. "What The Commission Didn't Recommend," JMCB, 1972, v4(4), 1005-1009.

Meltzer, Allan H. (Arcelus, Francisco and Allan H. Meltzer. "The Markets For Housing And Housing Services," JMCB, 1973, v5(1), 78-99.)

Meltzer, Allan H. (Arcelus, Francisco and Allan H. Meltzer. "A Reply To Craig Swan," JMCB, 1973, v5(4), 973-978.)

Meltzer, Allan H. (Bruner, Karl, Michele Fratianni, Jerry L. Jordan, Allan H. Meltzer and Manfred J. Neumann. "Fiscal And Monetary Policies In Moderate Inflation," JMCB, 1973, v5(1), Part II, 313-354.)

Meltzer, Allan H. (Brunner, Karl and Allan H. Meltzer. "Auerbach's Defense Of Defensive Operations: Comment," JOF, 1965, v20(3), 500-502.)

Meltzer, Allan H. (Brunner, Karl and Allan H. Meltzer. "Some Further Investigations Of Demand And Supply Functions For Money," JOF, 1964, v19(2), Part 1, 240-283.)

Meltzer, Allan H. (Brunner, Karl and Allan H. Meltzer. "Predicting Velocity: Implications For Theory And Policy," JOF, 1963, v18(2), 319-354.)

Meltzer, Allan H. (Clarkson, Geoffrey P. and Allan H. Meltzer. "Portfolio Selection: A Heuristic Approach," JOF, 1960, v15(4), 465-480.)

Melvin, Donald J. "Future Direction Of Bank Regulation And Legislation," JBR, 1974-75, v5(3), 161-164.

Melvin, Michael and David Bernstein. "Trade Concentration, Openness, And Deviations From Purchasing Power Parity," JIMF, 1984, v3(3), 369-376.

Melvin, Michael and Don Schlagenhauf. "Risk In International Lending: A Dynamic Factor Analysis Applied To France And Mexico," JIMF, 1986, v5(Supp), S31-S48.

Melvin, Michael and Jahangir Sultan. "South African Political Unrest, Oil Prices, And The Time Varying Risk Premium In The Gold Futures Market," JFM, 1990, v10(2), 103-112.

Melvin, Michael. "The Choice Of An Exchange Rate System And Macroeconomic Stability," JMCB, 1985, v17(4), Part 1, 467-478.

Melvin, Michael. (Hogan, Ked, Michael Melvin and Dan J. Roberts. "Trade Balance News And Exchange Rates: Is There A Policy Signal?," (Supp), S90-S99.)

Memdelson, Haim. (Amihud, Yakov and Haim Mendelson. "The Effects Of Beta, Bid-Ask Spread, Residual Risk, And Size On Stock Returns," JOF, 1989, v44(2), 479-486.)

Mendelowitz, Allan I. (Lustgarten, Steven and Allan I. Mendelowitz.

"The Covariability Of Industrial Concentration And Employment Fluctuations," JOB, 1979, v52(2), 291-304.)

Mendelson, H. (Amihud, Y., H. Mendelson and M. Murgia. "Stock Market, Microstructure And Return Volatility: Evidence From Italy," JBF, 1990, v14(2/3), 423-440.)

Mendelson, Haim. "Consolidation, Fragmentation, And Market Performance," JFQA, 1987, v22(2), 189-208.

Mendelson, Haim. (Amihud, Yakov and Haim Mendelson. "Liquidity And Stock Returns," FAJ, 1986, v42(3), 43-48.)

Mendelson, Haim. (Amihud, Yakov and Haim Mendelson. "Trading Mechanisms And Stock Returns: An Empirical Investigation," JOF, 1987, v42(3), 533-553.)

Mendelson, Haim. (Amihud, Yakov and Haim Mendelson. "Relative Price Dispersion And Economic Shocks: An Inventory-Adjustment Approach," JMCB, 1982, v14(3), 390-398.)

Mendelson, Haim. (Amihud, Yakov and Haim Mendelson. "Asset Price Behavior In A Dealership Market," FAJ, 1982, v38(3), 50-59.)

Mendelson, Haim. (Amihud, Yakov and Haim Mendelson. "Liquidity And Asset Prices: Financial Management Implications," FM, 1988, v17(1), 5-15.)

Mendelson, Haim. (Amihud, Yakov and Haim Mendelson. "Asset Pricing And The Bid-Asked Spread," JFEC, 1986, v17(2), 223-249.)

Mendelson, Haim. (Amihud, Yakov and Haim Mendelson. "Dealership Market: Market-Making With Inventory," JFEC, 1980, v8(1), 31-53.)

Mendelson, Haim. (Amihud, Yakov and Haim Mendelson. "Are Trading Rule Profits Feasible?," JPM, 1987-88, v14(1), 77-78.)

Mendelson, Haim. (Amihud, Yakov and Haim Mendelson. "Liquidity And Cost Of Capital: Implications For Corporate Management," JACF, 1989, v2(3), 65-73.)

Mendelson, Haim. (Amihud, Yakov and Haim Mendelson. "Explaining Intra-Day And Overnight Price Behavior: Comment," JPM, 1990, v16(2), 85-86.)

Mendelson, Haim. (Amihud, Yakov, Haim Mendelson and Robert A. Wood. "Liquidity And The 1987 Stock Market Crash," JPM, 1990, v16(3), 65-69.)

Mendelson, M. and J. W. Peake. "Which Way To A National Market System?," FAJ, 1979, v35(5), 31-34, 37-42.

Mendelson, Morris. "Closed-End Fund Discounts Revisited," FR, 1978, v13(1), 48-72.

Mendelson, Morris. "Determinants Of Underwriters' Spreads On Tax-Exempt Bond Issues: Comment," JFQA, 1968, v3(2), 215-224.

Mendelson, Morris. "Leverage, Dividend Policy And The Cost Of Capital: A Comment," JOF, 1970, v25(4), 898-903.

Mendelson, Morris. "The Eurobond And Capital Market Integration," JOF, 1972, v27(1), 110-126.

Mendelson, Morris. "The Flow Of Funds Through The Capital Market, 1953-55: A Progress Report," JOF, 1957, v12(2), 159-166.

Mendelson, Robert E. (Elliott, Donald S., Jr., Michael A. Quinn and Robert E. Mendelson. "Maintenance Behavior Of Large-Scale Landlords And Theories Of Neighborhood Succession," AREUEA, 1985, v13(4), 424-445.)

Mendelson, Robert E. (Quinn, Michael A., Donald S. Elliott, Jr., Robert E. Mendelson and Jeffrey A. Thoman. "Maintenance Effort And The Professional Landlord: An Empirical Critique Of Neighborhood Decline," AREUEA, 1980, v8(4), 345-369.)

Mendelson, Morris. "A Comment On Payback," JFQA, 1971, v6(4), 1159-1160.

Menefee, George H. (Pashigian, B. Peter, Lawrence L. Schkade and George H. Menefee. "The Selection Of An Optimal Deductible For A Given Insurance Policy," JOB, 1966, v39(1), Part I, 35-44.)

Menefee, George H. (Schkade, Lawrence L. and George H. Menefee. "A Normative Model For Deductible Collision Insurance Selection," JRI, 1966, v33(3), 427-436.)

Menippus. "Some Self-Criticism Of Institutional Investing," FAJ, 1950, v6(4), 29-31.

Mennis, Daniel L. (Mennis, Edmund A., Jerome L. Valentine and Daniel L. Mennis. "New Perspectives On Pension Fund Management," JPM, 1980-81, v7(3), 46-50.)

Mennis, Edmund A. and John M. Birmingham, Jr. "Diffusion Analysis As An Investment Guide," FAJ, 1957, v13(2), 47-58.

Mennis, Edmund A. "A Fresh Reappraisal Of The Steel Industry," FAJ, 1963, v19(6), 27-32.

Mennis, Edmund A. "A New Method For Evaluating Pension Fund Portfolios," JPM, 1978-79, v5(2), 34-40.

Mennis, Edmund A. "An Integrated Investment System," FAJ, 1974, v30(2), 38-40,42-46,86.

Mennis, Edmund A. "Different Measures Of Corporate Profits," FAJ, 1962, v18(5), 69-78.

Mennis, Edmund A. "Economics And Investment Management," FAJ, 1966, v22(6), 17-23.

Mennis, Edmund A. "Growing Pension Funds," FAJ, 1968, v24(2), 122-131.

Mennis, Edmund A. "Long-Term Trends Of Metal Consumption," FAJ, 1952, v8(5), 75-80.

Mennis, Edmund A. "New Tools For Profits Analysis," FAJ, 1969, v25(1), 25-33.

Mennis, Edmund A. "Profit Trends And Values In Mid-1965," FAJ, 1965, v21(4), 63-66.

Mennis, Edmund A. "Reappraisal Of The Steel Industry," FAJ, 1959, v15(4), 15-24.

Mennis, Edmund A. "Security Prices And Business Cycles," FAJ, 1955, v11(1), 79-86.

Mennis, Edmund A. "Trends In Institutional Investing," FAJ, 1968, v24(4), 133-138.

Mennis, Edmund A., Jerome L. Valentine and Daniel L. Mennis. "New Perspectives On Pension Fund Management," JPM, 1980-81, v7(3), 46-50.

Mennis, Edward A. "The Investment Manager Of The Future," FAJ, 1960, v16(2), 23-24.

Mennis, Sidney and Edmund A. Cottle. "Corporate Earnings - Short Term," FAJ, 1971, v27(4), 24-25,51, 53,55,57,59,61.

Mennis, Sidney. (Cottle, Edmund A., Sidney Mennis and Robert A. Schuelke. "Corporate Earnings - Long Term," FAJ, 1971, v27(4), 22-23,50-52, 54, 56, 58, 60, 62,64.)

Menon, Krishnagopal. (Gilbert, Lisa R., Krishnagopal Menon and Kenneth B. Schwartz. "Predicting Bankruptcy For Firms In Financial Distress," JBFA, 1990, v17(1), 161-171.)

Mensah, Samuel (Gagnon, Louis, Samuel Mensah and Edward Blinder. "Hedging Canadian Corporate Debt: A Comparative Study Of The Hedging Effectiveness Of Canadian And U.S. Bond Futures," JFM, 1989, v9(1), 29-40.)

Menshikov, Stanislav M. "Stagflation And Ways To Tackle It," JPM, 1975-76, v2(1), 58-61.

Mepham, M. J. "The Residual Income Debate," JBFA, 1980, v7(2), 183-199.

Mercer, R. (Gilmour, A., M. Jensen, R. Mercer, N. Minow, J. Morley, R. Siefert, B. Stewart, L. Summers and I. Harris. "Panel: The Economic Consequences Of High Leverage And Stock Market Pressures On Corporate Management: A Roundtable Discussion," JACF, 1990, v3(2), 6-37.)

Mercier, Leo J. "Bridging The Gap With GAAP And The IRC In The Replacement Decision," JFED, 1982, v11, 71-74.

Mercurio, Vincent A. (Gitman, Lawrence J. and Vincent A. Mercurio. "Cost Of Capital Techniques Used By Major U.S. Firms: Survey And Analysis Of Fortune's 1000," FM, 1982, v11(4), 21-29.)

Meredith, L. Douglas. "Liquidity: A Growing Attribute Of Mortgage Loan Portfolios," JOF, 1950, v5(4), 316-323.

Meric, G. (Hutchinson, P., I. Meric and G. Meric. "The Financial Characteristics Of Small Firms Which Achieve Quotation On The UK Unlisted Securities Market," JBFA, 1988, v15(1), 9-20.)

Meric, Gulser and Ilhan Meric. "Industry Effect Of Financial Structure In Multinational Corporations," IJOF, 1989, v1(2), 60-63. 3N?8

Meric, Gulser, Serpil S. Leveen and Ilhan Meric. "The Financial Characteristics Of Commercial Banks Involved In Interstate Acquisitions," FR, 1991, v26(1), 75-90.

Meric, Gulser. (Meric, Ilhan and Gulser Meric. "Potential Gains From International Portfolio Diversification And Intertemporal Stability And Seasonality In International Stock Market Relationships," JBF, 1989, v13(4/5), 627-640.)

Meric, I. (Hutchinson, P., I. Meric and G. Meric. "The Financial Characteristics Of Small Firms Which Achieve Quotation On The UK Unlisted Securities Market," JBFA, 1988, v15(1), 9-20.)

Meric, Ilhan and Gulser Meric. "Potential Gains From International Portfolio Diversification And Intertemporal Stability And Seasonality In International Stock Market Relationships," JBF, 1989, v13(4/5), 627-640.

Meric, Ilhan. (Meric, Gulser, Serpil S. Leveen and Ilhan Meric. "The Financial Characteristics Of Commercial Banks Involved In Interstate Acquisitions," FR, 1991, v26(1), 75-90.)

Meric, Ilhan. (Meric, Gulser and Ilhan Meric. "Industry Effect Of Financial Structure In Multinational Corporations," IJOF, 1989, v1(2), 60-63.)

Merrett, A. J. and Gerald D. Newbold. "Integrating Financial Performance And Stock Valuation," JPM, 1983-84, v10(1), 27-35.

Merrett, A. J. and Gerald D. Newbould. "CEPS: The Illusion Of Corporate Growth," JPM, 1982-83, v9(1), 5-10.

Merrick, John J., Jr. and Anthony Saunders. "Bank Regulation And Monetary Policy," JMCB, 1985, v17(4), Part 2, pp 691-717.

Merrick, John J., Jr. "Early Unwindings And Rollovers Of Stock Index Futures Arbitrage Programs: Analysis And Implications For Predicting Expiration Day Effects," JFM, 1989, v9(2), 101-112.

Merrick, John J., Jr. "Financial Market Efficiency, The Decomposition Of 'Anticipated' Verus 'Unanticipated' Money Growth, And Further Tests Of The Relation Between Money And Real Output," JMCB, 1983, v15(2), 222-232.

Merrick, John J., Jr. "Hedging With Mispriced Futures," JFQA, 1988, v23(4), 451-464.

Merrick, John J., Jr. "Portfolio Insurance With Stock Index Futures," JFM, 1988, v8(4), 441-456.

Merrick, John J., Jr. "Volume Determination In Stock And Stock Index Futures Markets: An Analysis Of Arbitrage And Volatility Effects," JFM, 1987, v7(5), 483-496.

Merrick, John J., Jr. (Ferson, Wayne E. and John J. Merrick, Jr. "Non-Stationarity And Stage-Of-The-Business-Cycle Effects In Consumption-Based Asset Pricing Relations," JFEC, 1987, v18(1), 127-146.)

Merriken, Harry E. (Edmister, Robert O. and Harry E. Merriken. "Pricing Efficiency In The Mortgage Market," AREUEA, 1988, v16(1), 50-62.)

Merriken, Harry E. (Edmister, Robert O. and Harry E. Merriken. "Measuring Interest Rate Sensitivity Of Consumer Depositors," JFSR, 1989, v2(2), 133-145.)

Merriken, Harry. "Mortgage Loan Market Segmentation And Lender Pricing Behavior," JRER, 1988, v3(1), 9-18.

Merrill, H. Douglas. (Longbrake, William A. and H. Douglas Merrill. "Demand For Commercial Bank Production Workers And Administrators: Demand Deposit Operations," JMCB, 1976, v8(3), 275-295.)

Merris, Randall C. "Explicit Interest And Demand Deposit Service Charges," JMCB, 1985, v17(4), Part 1, 528-533.

Merris, Randall C. (Greenbaum, Stuart I., Mukhtar M. Ali and Randall C. Merris. "Monetary Policy And Banking Profits," JOF, 1976, v31(1), 89-101.)

Merris, Randall C. (Reichert, Alan K., William Strauss and Randall C. Merris. "An Economic Analysis Of Short-Run Fluctuations In Federal Reserve Wire Transfer Volume," JBR, 1984-85, v15(4), 222-228.)

Merton, Robert C. and Paul A. Samuelson. "Fallacy Of The Log-Normal Approximation To Optimal Portfolio Decision-Making Over Many Periods," JFEC, 1974, v1(1), 67-94.

Merton, Robert C. "An Analytic Derivation Of The Cost Of Deposit Insurance And Loan Guarantees: An Application Of Modern Option Pricing Theory," JBF, 1977, v1(1), 3-11.

Merton, Robert C. "An Analytic Derivation Of The Efficient Portfolio Frontier," JFQA, 1972, v7(4), 1851-1872.

Merton, Robert C. "On Estimating The Expected Return On The Market: An Exploratory Investigation," JFEC, 1980, v8(4), 323-361.

Merton, Robert C. "On Market Timing And Investment Performance. I. An Equilibrium Theory Of Value For Market Forecasts," JOB, 1981, v54(3), 363-406.

Merton, Robert C. "On The Cost Of Deposit Insurance When There Are Surveillance Costs," **JOB**, 1978, v51(3), 439-452.
Merton, Robert C. "On The Pricing Of Corporate Debt: The Risk Structure Of Interest Rates," **JOF**, 1974, v29(2), 449-470.
Merton, Robert C. "On The Pricing Of Contingent Claims And The Modigliani-Miller Theorem," **JFEC**, 1977, v5(2), 241-249.
Merton, Robert C. "Option Pricing When Underlaying Stock Returns Are Discontinuous," **JFEC**, 1976, v3(1/2), 125-144.
Merton, Robert C. "Presidential Address: A Simple Model Of Capital Market Equilibrium With Incomplete Information," **JOF**, 1987, v42(3), 483-510.
Merton, Robert C. "The Impact On Option Pricing Of Specification Error In The Underlying Stock Price Returns," **JOF**, 1976, v31(2), 333-350.
Merton, Robert C. "The Relationship Between Put And Call Option Prices: Comment," **JOF**, 1973, v28(1), 183-184.
Merton, Robert C. "Theory Of Finance From The Perspective Of Continuous Time," **JFQA**, 1975, v10(4), 659-674.
Merton, Robert C. (Henriksson, Roy D. and Robert C. Merton. "On Market Timing And Investment Performance. II. Statistical Procedures For Evaluating Forecasting Skills," **JOB**, 1981, v54(4), 513-534.)
Merton, Robert C. (Marsh, Terry A. and Robert C. Merton. "Dividend Behavior For The Aggregate Stock Market," **JOB**, 1987, v60(1), 1-40.)
Merton, Robert C. (Samuelson, Paul A. and Robert C. Merton. "Generalized Mean-Variance Tradeoffs For Best Perturbation Correction To Approximate Portfolio Decisions," **JOF**, 1974, v29(1), 27-40.)
Merton, Robert C., Myron S. Scholes and Mathew L. Gladstein. "The Returns And Risk Of Alternative Call Option Portoflio Investment Strategies," **JOB**, 1978, v51(2), 183-242.
Merton, Robert C., Myron S. Scholes and Mathew L. Gladstein. "The Returns And Risks Of Alternative Put-Option Portfolio Investment Strategies," **JOB**, 1982, v55(1), 1-56.
Mertz, Arthur C. "The Uninsured Motorist," **JRI**, 1957, v24(1), 123-132.
Merville, L. J. and L. A. Tavis. "A Total Real Asset Planning System," **JFQA**, 1974, v9(1),107-115.
Merville, L. J. and L. A. Tavis. "A Generalized Model For Capital Investment," **JOF**, 1973, v28(1), 109-118.
Merville, L. J. and L. A. Tavis. "Optimal Working Capital Policies: A Chance-Constrained Programming Approach," **JFQA**, 1973, v8(1), 47-59.
Merville, L. J. and L. A. Tavis. "Financial Planning In A Decentralized Firm Under Conditions Of Competitive Capital Markets," **FM**, 1977, v6(3), 17-23.
Merville, Larry J. and Lee A. Tavis. "Long-Range Financial Planning," **FM**, 1974, v3(2), 56-63.
Merville, Larry J. (Chen, Andrew H. and Larry J. Merville. "An Analysis Of Divestiture Effects Resulting From Deregulation," **JOF**, 1986, v41(5), 997-1010.)
Merville, Larry J. (Jaffe, Jeffrey F. and Larry J. Merville. "Stock Price Dependencies And The Valuation Of Risky Assets with Discountinuous Temporal Returns," **JOF**, 1974, v29(5), 1437-1448.)
Merville, Larry J. (Jaffe, Jeffrey F. and Larry J. Merville. "The Value Of Risk-Reducing Information," **JFQA**, 1974, v9(5), 697-707.)
Merville, Larry J. (Logue, Dennis E. and Larry J. Merville. "Financial Policy And Market Expectations," **FM**, 1972, v1(2), 37-44.)
Merville, Larry J. (MacBeth, James D. and Larry J. Merville. "Tests Of The Black-Scholes And Cox Call Option Valuation Models," **JOF**, 1980, v35(2), 285-303.)
Merville, Larry J. (MacBeth, James D. and Larry J. Merville. "An Empirical Examination Of The Black-Scholes Call Option Pricing Model," **JOF**, 1979, v34(5), 1173-1186.)
Merville, Larry J. and Dan R. Pieptea. "Stock-Price Volatility, Mean-Reverting Diffusion, And Noise," **JFEC**, 1989, v24(1), 193-214.
Messina, Richard J. (Oldfield, George S. and Richard J. Messina. "Forward Exchange Price Determination In Continuous Time," **JFQA**, 1977, v12(3), 473-481.)
Messmore, Thomas E. "The Duration Of Surplus," **JPM**, 1990, v16(2), 19-22.
Messner, Stephen D. (Babcock, Guilford C., M. Chapman Findlay, III and Stephen D. Messner. "FMRR And Duration: Implications For Real Estate Investment Analysis," **AREUEA**, 1976, v4(3), 49-68.)
Messner, Stephen D. (Findlay, M. Chapman, III, Carl W. Hamilton, Stephen D. Messner and Jonathan S. Yormark. "Optimal Real Estate Portfolios," **AREUEA**, 1979, v7(3), 298-317.)
Messner, Van A. (Kisor, Manown, Jr. and Van A. Messner. "Filter Approach To Earnings," **FAJ**, 1969, v25(1), 109-115.)
Mester, Loretta J. "A Multiproduct Cost Study Of Savings And Loans," **JOF**, 1987, v42(2), 423-445.
Mester, Loretta J. "Multiple Market Contact Between Savings And Loans," **JMCB**, 1987, v19(4), 538-549.
Mesznick, Roger. (Bar-Yosef, Sasson and Roger Mesznick. "On Some Definitional Problems With The Method Of Certainty Equivalents," **JOF**, 1977, v32(5), 1729-1737.)
Metcalf, R. W. (Fuller, R. J. and R. W. Metcalf. "How Analysts Use Management Forecasts," **FAJ**, 1978, v34(2), 55-57.)
Metghalchi, Massoud. (Deravi, M. Keivan and Massoud Metghalchi. "The European Monetary System: A Note," **JBF**, 1988, v11(3), 505-512.)
Methe, David T. (Baesel, Jerome B., David T. Methe and David Shulman. "Teaching Managerial Finance To Public Sector Students," **JFED**, 1981, v10, 23-32.)
Metzger, Bert L. "Insurance Industry Begins To Court Profit Sharing Funds With Equity-Based Products," **JRI**, 1969, v36(3), 437-446.
Metzger, C. B. "The Company Executive Looks At Life Insurance Instruction At The University Level," **JRI**, 1950, v17, 79-85.
Meulendyke, Ann-Marie. (Levin, Fred J. and Ann-Marie Meulendyke. "Monetary Policy: Theory And Practice: A Comment," **JMCB**, 1982, v14(3), 399-403.)
Meurer, Emil M., Jr. (Rejda, George E. and Emil M. Meurer, Jr. "An Analysis Of State Crime Compensation Plans," **JRI**, 1975, v42(4), 599-614.)
Meyer, Carl F. and Andre B. Corbeau. "The Application Of Spectral Analysis To Demonstrate The Stochastic Distortion In The Delta Midrange Of Price Series," **JFQA**, 1975, v10(2), 221-230.
Meyer, Hans. "The Role Of The Swiss National Bank In The Payment System," **JBR**, 1985-86, v16(4), 190-193.
Meyer, Harald. (Whisler, Thomas L., Harald Meyer, Bernard H. Baum and Peter F. Sorensen, Jr. "Centralization Of Organizational Control: An Empirical Study Of ITs Meaning And Measurement," **JOB**, 1967, v40(1), 10-26.)
Meyer, Jack R. (Good, Walter R. and Jack R. Meyer. "Adjusting The Price-Earnings Ratio Gap," **FAJ**, 1973, v29(6), 42,44,48-49,81-84.)
Meyer, Jack and Michael B. Ormiston. "Deterministic Transformation Of Random Variables And The Comparative Statics Of Risk," **JRU**, 1989, v2(2), 179-188.
Meyer, Jack. "Further Applications Of Stochastic Dominance To Mutual Fund Performance," **JFQA**, 1977, v12(2), 235-242.
Meyer, Jack. "Mean-Variance Efficient Sets And Expected Utility," **JOF**, 1979, v34(5), 1221-1229.
Meyer, Jack. (Gronberg, Timothy J. and Jack Meyer. "Spatial Pricing And Its Effect On Product Transportability," **JOB**, 1982, v55(2), 269-280.)
Meyer, James E. and Young Y. Kim. "An Autoregressive Forecast Of The World Sugar Future Option Market," **JFQA**, 1975, v10(5), 821-835.
Meyer, John R. (Strong, John S. and John R. Meyer. "Asset Writedowns: Managerial Incentives And Security Returns," **JOF**, 1987, v42(3), 643-661.)
Meyer, Kenneth R. "Sinking Fund Values In A Dynamic Environment," **JPM**, 1976-77, v3(2), 50-52.
Meyer, Kenneth R. "The Dividends From Active Bond Management," **JPM**, 1974-75, v1(3), 18-22.
Meyer, Kenneth R. "Yield Spreads And Interest Rate Levels," **FAJ**, 1978, v34(6), 58-63.
Meyer, Kenneth R. (Johnson, Brian D. and Kenneth R. Meyer. "Managing Yield Curve Risk In An Index Environment," **FAJ**, 1989, v45(6), 51-59.)
Meyer, Laurence H. and Jess B. Yawitz. "The Interest-Induced Wealth Effect And The Behavior Of Real And Nominal Interest Rates: A Comment," **JOF**, 1977, v32(3), 939-948.
Meyer, Laurence H. "Wealth Effects And The Effectiveness Of Monetary And Fiscal Policies," **JMCB**, 1974, v6(4), 481-502.
Meyer, Laurence H. (Yawitz, Jess B. and Laurence H. Meyer. "An Empirical Investigation Of The Extent Of Tax Discounting: A Comment," **JMCB**, 1976, v8(2), 247-254.)
Meyer, Paul A. and Howard W. Pifer. "Prediction Of Bank Failures," **JOF**, 1970, v25(4), 853-868.
Meyer, Paul A. "Interest Rates On Mortgages And Dividend Rates On Savings And Loan Shares: Comment," **JOF**, 1967, v22(3), 467-470.
Meyer, Paul A. "Price Discrimination, Regional Loan Rates, And The Structure Of The Banking Industry," **JOF**, 1967, v22(1), 37-48.
Meyer, Richard F. (Baldwin, Carliss Y. and Richard F. Meyer. "Liquidity Preference Under Uncertainty: A Model Of Dynamic Investment In Illiquid Opportunities," **JFEC**, 1979, v7(4), 347-374.)
Meyer, Richard L. and Murad J. Anitia. "A Note On The Calculation Of Probabilistic Betas," **FR**, 1986, v21(1), 151-156.
Meyer, Richard L. "A Note On Capital Budgeting Techniques And The Reinvestment Rate," **JOF**, 1979, v34(5), 1251-1254.
Meyer, Richard L. (Antia, Murad J. and Richard L. Meyer. "The Growth Optimal Capital Structure: Manager Versus Shareholder Objectives," **JFR**, 1984, v7(3), 259-267.)
Meyer, Richard L. and Fred B. Power. "Total Insurance Costs And The Frequency Of Premium Payments," **JRI**, 1973, v40(4), 599-606.
Meyer, Richard L. and Fred B. Power. "The Investment Value Of Corporate Insurance," **JRI**, 1983, v50(1), 151-156.
Meyer, Richard L., Scott Besley and James R. Longstreet. "An Examination Of Capital Budgeting Decision Alternatives For Mutually Exclusive Investments With Unequal Lives," **JBFA**, 1988, v15(3), 415-426.
Meyer, Robert A. (Cargill, Thomas F. and Robert A. Meyer. "Municipal Interest Rates And The Term Structure Of Inflationary Expectations," **FR**, 1984, v19(2), 135-152.)
Meyer, Robert A. (Cargill, Thomas F. and Robert A. Meyer. "The Term Structure Of Inflationary Expectations And Market Efficiency," **JOF**, 1980, v35(1), 57-70.)
Meyer, Robert A. (Cargill, Thomas F. and Robert A. Meyer. "Estimating Term Structure Phenomena From Data Aggregated Over Time," **JMCB**, 1974, v6(4), 503-515.)
Meyer, Robert A. (Cargill, Thomas F. and Robert A. Meyer. "Intertemporal Stability Of The Relationship Between Interest Rates And Price Changes," **JOF**, 1977, v32(4), 1001-1015.)
Meyer, Robert A. (Cargill, Thomas F. and Robert A. Meyer. "Multiperiod Portfolio Optimization And The Value Of Risk Information," **AFPAF**, 1987, v2(1), 245-268.)
Meyer, Robert A. (Cargill, Thomas F. and Robert A. Meyer. "Estimating The Value Of Risk Information," **RIF**, 1983, v4, 43-62.)
Meyer, Robert A. (Smith, Donald J., Thomas F. Cargill and Robert A. Meyer. "An Economic Theory Of A Credit Union," **JOF**, 1981, v36(2), 519-528.)
Meyer, Stephen A. and Richard Startz. "Real Versus Nominal Forecast Errors In The Prediction Of Foreign Exchange Rates," **JIMF**, 1982, v1(2), 193-200.
Meyerholz, John C. "Competition And Investment Management," **FAJ**, 1966, v22(1), 97-105.
Meyers, Stephen L. "Avoiding Depreciation Influences On Investment Decisions," **FM**, 1972, v1(3),17-24.
Meyers, Steven L. "A Re-Examination Of Market And Industry Factors In Stock Price Behavior," **JOF**, 1973, v28(3), 695-705.
Miceli, Thomas J. "Housing Rental Contracts And Adverse Selection With An Application To The Rent-Own Decision," **AREUEA**, 1989, v17(4), 403-421.
Miceli, Thomas J. "Information Costs And The Organization Of The Real Estate Brokerage Industry In The U.S. And Great Britain," **AREUEA**, 1988, v16(2), 173-188.
Miceli, Thomas J. "The Optimal Duration Of Real Estate Listing Contracts," **AREUEA**, 1989, v17(3), 267-277.
Micha, Bernard. "Analysis Of Business Failures In France," **JBF**, 1984, v8(2), 281-292.
Michael, Robert T. "Variation Across Households In The Rate Of

Inflation," *JMCB*, 1979, v11(1), 32-46.

Michaelsen, Jacob B. and Robert C. Goshay. "Portfolio Selection Financial Intermediaries: A New Approach," *JFQA*, 1967, v2(2), 166-199.

Michaelsen, Jacob B. "The Determinants Of Corporate Dividend Policies," *JFQA*, 1966, v1(1),29-29a.

Michaelsen, Jacob B. "The Term Structure Of Interest Rates And Yields On Government Securities," *JOF*, 1965, v20(3), 444-463.

Michaely, Roni. (Elton, Edwin J., Martin J. Gruber and Roni Michaely. "The Structure Of Spot Rates And Immunization," *JOF*, 1990, v45(2), 629-642.)

Michaely, Roni. (Ho, Thomas S. Y. and Roni Michaely. "Information Quality And Market Efficiency," *JFQA*, 1988, v23(1), 53-70.)

Michas, Nicholas A. "The Performance Measurement And Evaluation Of A Corporate Retirement Plan: A Case Study," *FR*, 1986, v21(4), 537-549.

Michaud, Richard O. and Paul L. Davis. "Valuation Model Bias And The Scale Structure Of Dividend Discount Returns," *JOF*, 1982, v37(1), 562-573.

Michaud, Richard O. "A Scenario-Dependent Dividend Discount Model: Bridging The Gap Between Top-Down Investment Information And Bottom-Up Forecasts," *FAJ*, 1985, v41(6), 49-59.

Michaud, Richard O. "Risk Policy And Long-Term Investment," *JFQA*, 1981, v16(2), 147-167.

Michaud, Richard O. "Should Dividend Discount Models Be Yield-Tilted?: Comment," *JPM*, 1983-84, v10(4), 85.

Michaud, Richard O. "The Markowitz Optimization Enigma: Is 'Optimized' Optimal?," *FAJ*, 1989, v45(1), 31-42.

Michel, Allen and Israel Shaked. "Industry Influence On Pension Funding," *JPM*, 1985-86, v12(3),71-77.

Michel, Allen and Israel Shaked. "Japanese Leverage: Myth Or Reality," *FAJ*, 1985, v41(4), 61-67.

Michel, Allen and Israel Shaked. "Airline Performance Under Deregulation: The Shareholders' Perspective," *FM*, 1984, v13(2), 5-14.

Michel, Allen and Israel Shaked. "Does Business Diversification Affect Performance?," *FM*, 1984, v13(4), 18-25.

Michel, Allen J. and Israel Shaked. "Country And Industry Influence On Dividend Policy: Evidence From Japan And The U.S.A.," *JBFA*, 1986, v13(3), 365-382.

Michel, Allen J. "Municipal Bond Ratings: A Discriminant Analysis Approach," *JFQA*, 1977, v12(4), 587-598.

Michel, Allen and Israel Shaked. "Airline Deregulation And The Probability Of Air Carrier Insolvency," *FR*, 1987, v22(1), 159-174.

Michel, Allen and Israel Shaked. "Corporate Takeovers: Excess Returns And The Multiple Bidding Phenomena," *JBFA*,1988,v15(2),263-274.

Michel, Allen and Israel Shaked. "Trucking Deregulation And Motor-Carrier Performance: The Shareholders' Perspective," *FR*, 1987, v22(2), 295-312.

Michel, Allen and Israel Shaked. "The LBO Nightmare: Fraudulent Conveyance Risk," *FAJ*, 1990, v46(2), 41-50.

Michel, Allen and Israel Shaked. "Are Conglomerates Safer?," *RIF*, 1985, v5, 243-261.

Michel, Allen and James Norris. "On The Determination Of Appropriate Profit Margins In Insurance Industry Regulation," *JRI*, 1982, v49(4), 628-633.

Michel, Allen. "Industry Influence On Dividend Policy," *FM*, 1979, v8(3), 22-26.

Michel, Allen. (Shaked, Israel, Allen Michel and David McClain. "The Foreign Acquirer Bonanza: Myth Or Reality?," *JBFA*, 1991, v18(3), 431-448.)

Michel, Pierre A. (Hawawini, Gabriel A., Pierre A. Michel and Albert Corhay. "New Evidence On Beta Stationarity And Forecast For Belgian Common Stocks," *JBF*, 1985, v9(4), 553-560.)

Michel, Pierre A. (Hawawini, Gabriel A., Pierre A. Michel and Claude J. Viallet. "As Assessment Of Risk And Return Of French Common Stocks," *JBFA*, 1983, v10(3), 333-350.)

Michel, Pierre A. (Hawawini, Gabriel A. and Pierre A. Michel. "The Pricing Of Risky Assets On The Belgian Stock Market," *JBF*, 1982, v6(2), 161-178.)

Michel, Pierre. (Corhay, Albert, Gabriel Hawawini and Pierre Michel. "Seasonality In The Risk-Return Relationship: Some International Evidence," *JOF*, 1987, v42(1), 49-68.)

Michelbacher, G. F. "How Can The Universities And University Teachers Best Serve In Their Fields?," *JRI*, 1936, v3, 68-79.

Micossi, S. and S. Rebecchini. "A Case Study On The Effectiveness Of Foreign Exchange Market Intervention: The Italian Lira (September 1975-March 1977)," *JBF*, 1984, v8(4), 535-555.

Mikesell, Raymond F. "The Eurodollar Market And The Foreign Demand For Liquid Dollar Assets," *JMCB*, 1972, v4(3), 643-683.

Mikkelson, Wayne H. and M. Megan Partch. "Valuation Effects Of Security Offerings And The Issuance Process," *JFEC*, 1986, v15(1/2), 31-60.

Mikkelson, Wayne H. and M. Megan Partch. "Stock Price Effects And Costs Of Secondary Distributions," *JFEC*, 1985, v14(2), 165-194.

Mikkelson, Wayne H. and Richard S. Ruback. "An Empirical Analysis Of The Interfirm Equity Investment Process," *JFEC*, 1985, v14(4), 523-553.

Mikkelson, Wayne H. "Convertible Calls And Stock Price Declines," *FAJ*, 1985, v41(4), 63-69.

Mikkelson, Wayne H. "Convertible Calls And Security Returns," *JFEC*, 1981, v9(3), 237-264.

Mikkelson, Wayne H. (Dann, Larry Y. and Wayne H. Mikkelson. "Convertible Debt Issuance, Capital Structure Change And Financing-Related Information: Some New Evidence," *JFEC*, 1984, v13(2), 157-186.)

Mikkelson, Wayne H. (Lease, Ronald C., John J. McConnell and Wayne H. Mikkelson. "The Market Value Of Control In Publicly-Traded Corporations," *JFEC*, 1983, v11(1), 439-471.)

Mikkelson, Wayne H. (Lease, Ronald C., John J. McConnell and Wayne H. Mikkelson. "The Market Value Of Differential Voting Rights In Closely Held Corporations," *JOB*, 1984, v57(4), 443-468.)

Mikkelson, Wayne H. and M. Megan Partch. "Withdrawn Security Offerings," *JFQA*, 1988, v23(2), 119-134.

Mikkelson, Wayne H. and M. Megan Partch. "Managers' Voting Rights And Corporate Control," *JFEC*, 1989, v25(2), 263-290.

Milano, Duane R., Stephen L. Avard and John Russell Arens. "Microcomputer Applications For Preparing Tests In Entry Level Financial Management Courses," *JFED*, 1986, v15, 68-78.

Milbourne, Ross. "Financial Innovation And The Demand For Liquid Assets," *JMCB*, 1986, v18(4), 506-511.

Milde, Hellmuth. (Baltensperger, Ernst and Hellmuth Milde. "Reserve Demand, Information Costs, And Bank Portfolio Behavior," *JOF*, 1976, v31(3), 835-843.)

Mildenstein, Ekart and Harold Schleef. "The Optimal Pricing Policy Of A Monopolistic Market-Maker In The Equity Market," *JOF*, 1983, v38(1), 218-231.

Miles, James and Dosoung Choi. "Comment: Evaluating Negative Benefits," *JFQA*, 1979, v14(5),1095-1099.

Miles, James A. and James D. Rosenfeld. "The Effect Of Voluntary Spin-off Announcements On Shareholder Wealth," *JOF*, 1983, v38(5), 1597-1606.

Miles, James A. and John R. Ezzell. "The Weighted Average Cost Of Capital, Perfect Capital Markets, And Project Life: A Clarification," *JFQA*, 1980, v15(3), 719-730.

Miles, James A. and John R. Ezzell. "Reformulating Tax Shield Valuation: A Note," *JOF*, 1985, v40(5), 1484-1492.

Miles, James A. "Growth Options And The Real Determinants Of Systematic Risk," *JBFA*, 1986, v13(1), 95-105.

Miles, James A. "Taxes And The Fisher Effect: A Clarifying Analysis," *JOF*, 1983, v38(1), 67-77.

Miles, James A. (Beranek, William and James A. Miles. "The Excess Return Argument And Double Leverage," *FR*, 1988, v23(2), 143-150.)

Miles, James A. (Ezzell, John R. and James A. Miles. "Capital Project Analysis And The Debt Transaction Plan," *JFR*, 1983, v6(1), 25-31.)

Miles, James A. (Kelly, William A., Jr. and James A. Miles. "Darby And Fisher: Resolution Of A Paradox," *FR*, 1984, v19(1), 103-110.)

Miles, James A. (Kelly, William A., Jr. and James A. Miles. "Capital Structure Theory And The Fisher Effect," *FR*, 1989, v24(1), 53-74.)

Miles, James A. (Sinkey, Joseph F., Jr. and James A. Miles. "The Use Of Warrants In The Bail Out Of First Pennsylvania Bank: An Application Of Option Pricing," *FM*, 1982, v11(3), 27-32.)

Miles, James A. and Raj Varma. "Using Financial Market Data To Make Trade Credit Decisions," *JBFA*, 1986, v13(4), 505-518.

Miles, Joseph E. "Formulas For Pricing Bonds," *FAJ*, 1969, v25(4), 156-161.

Miles, Joseph E. "Insurance Portfolio Strategies," *FAJ*, 1967, v23(5), 147-154.

Miles, Marc A. and D. Sykes Wilford. "Foreign Exchange Market Efficiency Under Flexible Exchange Rates: Comment," *JOF*, 1979, v34(3), 787-789.

Miles, Mike and Arthur Esty. "How Well Do Commingled Real Estate Funds Perform?," *JPM*, 1981-82, v8(2), 62-68.

Miles, Mike and R. Stephen Sears. "An Econometric Approach To The FNMA Free Market System Auction," *JFQA*, 1981, v16(2), 177-192.

Miles, Mike and Tom McCue. "Diversification In The Real Estate Portfolio," *JFR*, 1984, v7(1), 57-68.

Miles, Mike E. (Hartzell, David, John S. Hekman and Mike E. Miles. "Real Estate Returns And Inflation," *AREUEA*, 1987, v15(1), 617-637.)

Miles, Mike and Tom McCue. "Historic Returns And Institutional Real Estate Portfolios," *AREUEA*, 1982, v10(2), 184-199.

Miles, Mike, John Pringle and Brian Webb. "Modeling The Corporate Real Estate Decision," *JRER*, 1989, v4(3), 47-66.

Miles, Mike, Rebel Cole and David Guikey. "A Different Look At Commercial Real Estate Returns," *AREUEA*, 1990, v18(4), 403-430.

Miles, Mike. (Conroy, Robert and Mike Miles. "Commercial Forestland In The Pension Portfolio: The Biological Beta," *FAJ*, 1989, v45(5), 46-54.)

Miles, Mike. (Guilkey, David, Mike Miles and Rebel Cole. "The Motivation For Institutional Real Estate Sales And Implications For Asset Class Returns," *AREUEA*, 1989, v17(1), 70-86.)

Miles, Mike. (Hartzell, David, John Hekman and Mike Miles. "Diversification Categories In Investment Real Estate," *AREUEA*, 1986, v14(2), 230-254.)

Miles, R. (Franks, J. R., R. Miles and J. Bagwell. "A Review Of Acquisition Valuation Models," *JBFA*, 1974, v1(1), 35-53.)

Miles, Richard. "Britain Views Common Market-Free Trade Area," *FAJ*, 1959, v15(1), 13-16.

Milgrom, Paul R. (Glosten, Lawrence R. and Paul R. Milgrom. "Bid, Ask And Transaction Prices In A Specialist Market With Heterogeneously Informed Traders," *JFEC*, 1985, v14(1), 71-100.)

Millar, James A. and Bruce D. Fielitz. "Stock-Split And Stock-Dividend Decisions," *FM*, 1973, v2(4), 35-45.

Millar, James A. and Stanley R. Stansell. "Variable Rate Mortgage Experience Of The Farm Credit System," *FM*, 1974, v4(4), 46-57.

Millar, James A. "Primary And Fully Diluted Earnings Per Share: Some Clarifying Comments," *JFED*, 1990, v19, 10-14.

Millar, James A. (Arndt, Terry L. and James A. Millar. "Some Empirical Results On Financial Characteristics And Unusual Stock Prices," *FR*, 1977, v12(2), 18-32.)

Millar, James A. (Cole, Charles W. and James A. Millar. "The Impact Of Municipal Bond Banking On Municipal Interest Costs," *FM*, 1982, v11(1), 70-76.)

Millar, James A. (Nunthirapakorn, Thakol and James A. Millar. "Changing Prices, Accounting Earnings And Systematic Risk," *JBFA*, 1987, v14(1), 1-26.)

Millar, James A. (Stansell, Stanley R. and James A. Millar. "An Empirical Study Of Mortgage Payment To Income Ratios In A Variable Rate Mortgage Program," *JOF*, 1976, v31(2), 415-425.)

Millar, James A. and Ted Nunthirapakorn. "Earnings Per Share Reporting For Canadian Companies With Complex Capital Structures," *JBFA*, 1991, v18(1), 109-116.

Millar, James A., Thakol Nunthirapakorn and Steve Courtenay. "A Note On The Information Content Of Primary And Fully Diluted Earnings Per Share," *FAJ*, 1987, v43(5), 77-79.

Millar, James R. and James A. Gentry. "The Soviet Experiment With Domestic Lottery Bonds," *FM*, 1980, v9(4), 21-29.

Millar, James R. and Stanley R. Stansell. "Variable Rate Mortgage Lending: Some Empirical Results," *AREUEA*, 1975, v3(3), 95-117.

Miller, A. Van Court. "The Buyer's Viewpoint On Insurance," **JRI**, 1940, v7, 53-58.

Miller, Alexander B. "The Standby Purchase Agreement," **FAJ**, 1971, v27(4), 71-73,86-87.

Miller, Arjay. "A Proposal For A National Goals Institute," **JOF**, 1969, v24(2), 173-179.

Miller, Deborah H. (Speidell, Lawrence S., Deborah H. Miller and James R. Ullman. "Portfolio Optimization: A Primer," **FAJ**, 1989, v45(1), 22-30.)

Miller, Donald C. "Financial Markets Under Stress," **FAJ**, 1968, v24(1), 83-81.

Miller, Donald C. "Reconciling Monetary Management And Debt Management Policies," **JOF**, 1950, v5(4), 368-386.

Miller, Edward M. "A Counter Example To The Random Walk," **FAJ**, 1979, v35(4), 55-56,67.

Miller, Edward M. "Atomic Bombs, The Depression, And Equilibrium," **JPM**, 1990, v16(4), 37-41.

Miller, Edward M. "Bank Deposits In The Monetary Theory Of Keynes," **JMCB**, 1984, v16(2), 242-245.

Miller, Edward M. "Bounded Efficient Markets: A New Wrinkle To The EMH," **JPM**, 1986-87, v13(4), 4-13.

Miller, Edward M. "Comment: The Optimal Price To Trade," **JFQA**, 1979, v14(3), 645-647.

Miller, Edward M. "Explaining Intra-Day And Overnight Price Behavior," **JPM**, 1989, v15(4), 10-17.

Miller, Edward M. "Explaining Intra-Day And Overnight Price Behavior: Reply," **JPM**, 1990, v16(2), 87.

Miller, Edward M. "Portfolio Selection In A Fluctuating Economy," **FAJ**, 1978, v34(3), 77-83.

Miller, Edward M. "Risk, Uncertainty, And Divergence Of Opinion," **JOF**, 1977, v32(4), 1151-1168.

Miller, Edward M. "The Competitive Market Assumption And Capital Budgeting Criteria," **FM**, 1987, v16(4), 22-28.

Miller, Edward M. "Time Preference And Interest Rates In An Uncertain Multiperiod World," **JFR**, 1981, v4(2), 161-168.

Miller, Edward M. "Uncertainty Induced Bias In Capital Budgeting," **FM**, 1978, v7(3), 12-18.

Miller, Edward M., Jr. "Why A Weekend Effect?," **JPM**, 1987-88, v14(4), 43-49.

Miller, Edward M., Jr. "How To Win At The Loser's Game," **JPM**, 1978-79, v5(1), 17-24.

Miller, Edward. "Tax-Induced Bias In Markets For Futures Contracts," **FR**, 1980, v15(2), 35-38.

Miller, Elbert G. (Hoffer, George E. and Elbert G. Miller. "The Distribution Of Automobile Liability Insurance: An Alternative," **JRI**, 1979, v46(3), 441-450.)

Miller, Elbert G. and George E. Hoffer. "Pay-At-The-Pump Automobile Liability Insurance: Reply," **JRI**, 1983, v50(3), 487-492.

Miller, Eugene. "Trends In Private Pension Funds," **JOF**, 1961, v16(2), 313-327.

Miller, F. Byers. "Research In The 1970's," **JBR**, 1970-71, v1(2), 59-60.

Miller, G. William. "Toward Monetary Stability With An Understanding Of Social Costs," **FR**, 1979, v14(2), 75-83.

Miller, Glenn R. "Long-Term Small Business Financing From The Underwriter's Point Of View," **JOF**, 1961, v16(2), 280-290.

Miller, Glenn R. "New Industries In The Chicago Area," **FAJ**, 1953, v9(1), 71-74.

Miller, Jack E. (Carpenter, Michael D. and Jack E. Miller. "A Reliable Framework For Monitoring Accounts Receivable," **FM**, 1979, v8(4), 37-40.)

Miller, James M. (Stover, Roger D. and James M. Miller. "Additional Evidence On The Capital Market Effect Of Bank Failures," **FM**, 1983, v12(1), 36-41.)

Miller, Jerry D. "Longevity Of Stock Purchase Warrants," **FAJ**, 1971, v27(6), 78-85.

Miller, John H. "The Impact Of New Disability Coverages On The Life Insurance Companies," **JRI**, 1952, v19, 29-39.

Miller, M. H. (Charnes, A., W. W. Cooper, and M. H. Miller. "Application Of Linear Programming To Financial Budgeting And The Costing Of Funds," **JOB**, 1959, v32(1), 20-46.)

Miller, M. H. (Cohen, K. J., R. M. Cyert, W. R. Dill, A. A. Kuehn, M. H. Miller, T. A. VanWormer, and P. R. Winters. "The Carnegie Tech Management Game," **JOB**, 1960, v33(4), 303-321.)

Miller, Marcus H. (Turnovsky, Stephen J. and Marcus H. Miller. "The Effects Of Government Expenditure On The Term Structure Of Interest Rates," **JMCB**, 1984, v16(1), 16-33.)

Miller, Merton H. and Charles W. Upton. "Leasing, Buying, And The Cost Of Capital Services," **JOF**, 1976, v31(3), 761-786.

Miller, Merton H. and Charles W. Upton. "The Pricing Of Oil And Gas: Some Further Results," **JOF**, 1985, v40(3), 1009-1018.

Miller, Merton H. and Daniel Orr. "The Demand For Money By Firms: Extensions Of Analytic Results," **JOF**, 1968, v23(5), 735-759.

Miller, Merton H. and Kevin Rock. "Dividend Policy Under Asymmetric Information," **JOF**, 1985, v40(4), 1031-1051.

Miller, Merton H. and Myron S. Scholes. "Dividends And Taxes," **JFEC**, 1978, v6(4), 333-364.

Miller, Merton H. "Behavioral Rationality In Finance: The Case Of Dividends," **JOB**, 1986, v59(4), Part 2, S451-S468.

Miller, Merton H. "Debt And Taxes," **JOF**, 1977, v32(2), 261-275.

Miller, Merton H. "Financial Innovation: The Last Twenty Years And The Next," **JFQA**, 1986, v21(4), 459-471.

Miller, Merton H. "The Modigliani-Miller Propositions After Thirty Years," **JACF**, 1989, v2(1), 6-18.

Miller, Merton H. "Who Should Set Futures Margins?," **RFM**, 1988, v7(3), 398-404.

Miller, Merton H. (Banz, Rolf W. and Merton H. Miller. "Prices For State-Contingent Claims: Some Estimates And Applications," **JOB**, 1978, v51(4), 653-672.)

Miller, Merton H. (Black, Fischer, Merton H. Miller and Richard A. Posner. " An Approach To The Regulation Of Bank Holding Companies," **JOB**, 1978, v51(3), 379-412.)

Miller, Merton H. (Grossman, Sanford J. and Merton H. Miller. "Economic Costs And Benefits Of The Proposed One-Minute Time Bracketing Regulation," **JFM**, 1986, v6(1), 141-166.)

Miller, Merton H. (Grossman, Sanford J. and Merton H. Miller. "Liquidity And Market Structure," **JOF**, 1988, v43(3), 617-633.)

Miller, Merton H. (Hsieh, David A. and Merton H. Miller. "Margin Regulation And Stock Market Volatility," **JOF**, 1990, v45(1), 3-30.)

Miller, Merton H. and Franco Modigliani. "Dividend Policy, Growth, And The Valuation Of Shares," **JOB**, 1961, v34(4), 411-433.

Miller, Merton H., Burton Malkiel, Myron Scholes and John D. Hawke, Jr. "Stock Index Futures And The Crash Of '87," **JACF**, 1989, v1(4), 6-17.

Miller, Merton H. "The International Competitiveness Of U.S. Futures Exchanges," **JACF**, 1991, v3(4), 6-20.

Miller, Norman and Stan West. "Why The NYSE Common Stock Indexes?," **FAJ**, 1967, v23(3), 49-54.

Miller, Norman C. and Marina V. N. Whitman. "Alternative Theories And Tests Of U. S. Short-Term Foreign Investment," **JOF**, 1973, v28(5), 1131-1150.

Miller, Norman C. and Sherry S. Askin. "Monetary Policy And The Balance Of Payments In Brazil And Chile," **JMCB**, 1976, v8(2), 227-238.

Miller, Norman C. "Concentration In Institutional Common-Stock Portfolios," **JOF**, 1961, v16(1), 38-51.

Miller, Norman C. "The Structure Of Open Economy Macro-Models," **JIMF**, 1986, v5(1), 75-89.

Miller, Norman C. (Luan, David C. and Norman C. Miller. "A Monetary Approach To International Capital Flows Applied To The United States," **JMCB**, 1979, v11(1), 87-90.)

Miller, Norman G. "Time On The Market And Selling Price," **AREUEA**, 1978, v6(2), 164-174.

Miller, Norman G. (Kluger, Brian D. and Norman G. Miller. "Measuring Residential Real Estate Liquidity," **AREUEA**, 1990, v18(2), 145-159.)

Miller, Norman G. (Sklarz, Michael A., Norman G. Miller and Will Gersch. "Forecasting Using Long-Order Autoregressive Processes: An Example Using Housing Starts," **AREUEA**, 1987, v15(4), 374-388.)

Miller, Norman G. (Solt, Michael E. and Norman G. Miller. "Managerial Incentives: Implications For The Financial Performance Of Real Estate Investment Trusts," **AREUEA**, 1985, v13(4), 404-423.)

Miller, Norman G. and Michael A. Sklarz. "A Note On Leading Indicators Of Housing Market Price Trends," **JRER**, 1986, v1(1), 99-109.

Miller, Norman G. and Michael A. Sklarz. "Pricing Strategies And Residential Property Selling Prices," **JRER**, 1987, v2(1), 31-40.

Miller, Norman G. and Michael A. Sklarz. "Tax Rates And Implicit Rates Of Return On Owner-Occupied Single-Family Housing: A Comment," **JRER**, 1989, v4(1), 81-84.

Miller, Norman G. and Patrick G. McKeown. "Optimizing The Distributions Of Limited Partnership Returns," **AREUEA**, 1979, v7(3), 378-392.

Miller, Norman G., Michael A. Sklarz and Nicholas Ordway. "Japanese Purchases, Exchange Rates And Speculation In Residential Real Estate Markets," **JRER**, 1988, v3(3), 39-49.

Miller, Oscar M. "Retrogression In Stockholders Reports?," **FAJ**, 1945, v1(1), 49-51.

Miller, P. F., Jr. (Beach, T. E. and P. F. Miller, Jr. "Price-Earnings Ratios: A Reply," **FAJ**, 1967, v23(3), 109-110.)

Miller, Paul F., Jr. "Managing Investment Portfolios: A Review Article," **JPM**, 1982-83, v9(4), 57-58.

Miller, Paul F., Jr. "The Dangers Of Retrospective Myopia," **JPM**, 1979-80, v6(1), 67-73.

Miller, Paul F., Jr. "The Financial Analyst's Handbook: A Review Article," **JPM**, 1974-75, v1(4), 5-6.

Miller, Preston J. "Forecasting With Econometric Methods: A Comment," **JOB**, 1978, v51(4), 579-584.

Miller, Randall J. "A Note On The Cost Analysis Of A Commercial Bank Regulatory Agency As A Multiproduct Firm: Implications For Regulatory Reorganization," **JBR**, 1978-79, v9(4), 246-250.

Miller, Randall J. "Examination Man-Hour Cost For Independent, Joint And Divided Examination Programs," **JBR**, 1980-81, v11(1), 28-35.

Miller, Robert B. (Cramer, Robert H. and Robert B. Miller. "Dynamic Modeling Of Multivariate Time Series For Use In Bank Analysis," **JMCB**, 1976, v8(1), 85-96.)

Miller, Robert B. (Cramer, Robert H. and Robert B. Miller. "Multivariate Time Series Analysis Of Bank Financial Behavior," **JFQA**, 1978, v13(5), 1003-1017.)

Miller, Robert B. (Cramer, Robert H. and Robert B. Miller. "Development Of A Deposit Forcasting Procedure For Use In Bank Financial Management," **JBR**, 1973-74, v4(2), 122-138.)

Miller, Robert B. (Hickman, James C. and Robert B. Miller. "Insurance Premiums And Decision Analysis," **JRI**, 1970, v37(4), 567-578.)

Miller, Robert E. and Michael H. Morris. "Multiproduct C-V-P Analysis And Uncertainty: A Linear Programming Approach," **JBFA**, 1985, v12(4), 495-505.

Miller, Robert E. and Adam K. Gehr. "Sample Size Bias And Sharpe's Performance Measure: A Note," **JFQA**, 1978, v13(5), 943-946.

Miller, Robert E. (Affleck-Graves, John and Robert E. Miller. "Regulatory And Procedural Effects On The Underpricing Of Initial Public Offerings," **JFR**, 1989, v12(3), 193-202.)

Miller, Robert E. (Bowers, Helen M. and Robert E. Miller. "Choice Of Investment Banker And Shareholders' Wealth Of Firms Involved In Acquisitions," **FM**, 1990, v19(4), 34-44.)

Miller, Robert E. (Hegde, Shantaram P. and Robert E. Miller. "Market-Making In Initial Public Offerings Of Common Stocks: An Empirical Analysis," **JFQA**, 1989, v24(1), 75-90.)

Miller, Robert E. (Johnson, James M. and Robert E. Miller. "Investment Banker Prestige And The Underpricing Of Initial Public Offerings," **FM**, 1988, v17(2), 19-29.)

Miller, Robert E. (Kilbride, Bernard J., Bill McDonald and Robert E. Miller. "A Reexamination Of Economies Of Scale In Banking Using A Generalized Functional Form," **JMCB**, 1986, v18(4), 519-526.)

Miller, Robert E. and Frank K. Reilly. "An Examination Of Mispricing, Returns, And Uncertainty For Initial Public Offerings," **FM**, 1987, v16(2), 33-38.

Miller, Roger L. (Soldofsky, Robert M. and Roger L. Miller. "Risk-Premium Curve Vs. Capital Line: A Further Work," **FM**, 1978, v7(1), 65-72.)

Miller, Roger L. (Soldofsky, Robert M. and Roger L. Miller. "Risk-Premium Curves For Different Classes Of Long-Term Securities, 1950-1966," **JOF**, 1969, v24(3), 429-445.)

Miller, Roger L. (Soldofsky, Robert M. and Roger L. Miller. "Risk-Premium Curves For Different Classes Of Long-Term Securities, 1950-1966: Reply," **JOF**, 1972, v27(4), 940-943.)

Miller, Ronald K. (Hershbarger, Robert A. and Ronald K. Miller. "A Procedure For Calculating The Annual Change In Value For Investment," **JRI**, 1975, v42(4), 663-668.)

Miller, Ronald K. (Hershbarger, Robert A. and Ronald K. Miller. "The Impact Of Economic Conditions On The Incidence Of Arson," **JRI**, 1978, v45(2), 275-290.)

Miller, Ronald K. (Hershbarger, Robert A. and Ronald K. Miller. "The Investment Performance Of Minority Controlled Life Insurance Companies," **JRI**, 1982, v49(3), 436-442.)

Miller, Ronald K. (Hershbarger, Robert A. and Ronald K. Miller. "The Impact Of Economic Conditions On The Incidence Of Arson: Reply," **JRI**, 1988, v55(4), 755-757.)

Miller, Stanley R. "Recent Trends In Corporate Finance," **FAJ**, 1953, v9(1), 51-54.

Miller, Stephen E. and Dawson B. Luke. "Alternative Techniques For Cross-Hedging Wholesale Beef Prices," **JFM**, 1982, v2(2), 121-129.

Miller, Stephen E. and Kandice H. Kahl. "Forward Pricing When Yields Are Uncertain," **RFM**, 1987, v6(1), 20-39.

Miller, Stephen E. "Forward Pricing Feeder Pigs," **JFM**, 1982, v2(4), 333-340.

Miller, Stephen E. "Forward Cash Contracting Of Cotton," **JFM**, 1986, v6(2), 249-260.

Miller, Stephen E. "Simple And Multiple Cross-Hedging Of Millfeeds," **JFM**, 1985, v5(1), 21-28.

Miller, Stephen E. and Kandice H. Kahl. "Performance Of Estimated Hedging Ratios Under Yield Uncertainty," **JFM**, 1989, v9(4), 307-320.

Miller, Stephen M. "A Simple Model Of Information And Lending Behavior: Comment," **JOF**, 1977, v32(1), 208-210.

Miller, Stephen M. "Measures Of Risk Aversion: Some Clarifying Comments," **JFQA**, 1975, v10(2), 299-309.

Miller, Stephen M. (Katsimbris, George M. and Stephen M. Miller. "Money Illusion, Distribution Effects And The Household And Business Demands For Money," **JBF**, 1982, v6(2), 215-231.)

Miller, Stephen M. (Noulas, Athanasios G., Subhash C. Ray and Stephen M. Miller. "Returns To Scale And Input Substitution For Large U.S. Banks," **JMCB**, 1990, v22(1), 94-108.)

Miller, Stephen M. (Warner, P. D., III and Stephen M. Miller. "The Deficient Treatment Of Money In Basic Undergraduate Texts: An Opposing View: A Reply," **JMCB**, 1974, v6(1), 119-121.)

Miller, Tom W. and Bernell K. Stone. "Daily Cash Forecasting And Seasonal Resolution: Alternative Models And Techniques For Using The Distribution Approach," **JFQA**, 1985, v20(3), 335-352.

Miller, Tom W. and Nicholas Gressis. "Nonstationarity And Evaluation Of Mutual Fund Performance," **JFQA**, 1980, v15(3), 639-654.

Miller, Tom W. "A Systems View Of Short-Term Investment Management," **AWCM**, 1990, v1(1), 39-66.

Miller, Tom W. (Stone, Bernell K. and Tom W. Miller. "Daily Cash Forecasting With Multiplicative Models Of Cash Flow Patterns," **FM**, 1987, v16(4), 45-54.)

Miller, Walter N. "Variable Life Insurance Product Design," **JRI**, 1971, v38(4), 527-542.

Miller, Walter N. "Variable Life Insurance Product Design: Reply," **JRI**, 1972, v39(3), 499.

Miller, William P. (Klemkosky, Robert C. and William P. Miller. "When Forecasting Earnings, It Pays To Be Right!," **JPM**, 1983-84, v10(4), 13-18.)

Millican, Charles N. "The Financial Policies Of Churches," **JOF**, 1951, v6(4), 419-428.

Millman, Gregory J. "Financing The Uncreditworthy: New Financial Structures For LDCs," **JACF**, 1991, v3(4), 83-89.

Millon, Marcia H. (Chen, Andrew H. and Marcia H. Millon. "The Secondary Market And Dynamic Swap Management," **RDIBF**, 1989, v3, 131-148.)

Millon, Marcia H. and Anjan V. Thakor. "Moral Hazard And Information Sharing: A Model Of Financial Information Gathering Agencies," **JOF**, 1985, v40(5), 1403-1422.

Millon-Cornett, Marcia H. "Stock Market Reactions To The Depository Institutions Deregulation And Monetary Control Act Of 1980," **JBF**, 1989, v13(1), 81-100.

Mills, Dixie L. (Gardner, Mona J. and Dixie L. Mills. "Evaluating The Likelihood Of Default On Deliquent Loans," **FM**, 1989, v18(4), 55-63.)

Mills, Dixie L. (Gardner, Mona J. and Dixie L. Mills. "Financial Institutions Management Courses: A Survey Of Current Content And The Outlook For The 1990s," **JFED**, 1990, v19, 1-4.)

Mills, Dixie L. (Gardner, Mona J., Han Bin Kang and Dixie L. Mills. "Consumer Profiles And Acceptance Of ARM Features: An Application Of Logit Regression," **JRER**, 1987, v2(2), 63-74.)

Mills, Dixie L. (Scott, William L., Mona J. Gardner and Dixie L. Mills. "Expense Preference And Minority Banking: A Note," **FR**, 1988, v23(1), 105-116.)

Mills, Edwin S. "Are Real Estate Markets Becoming More Efficient?," **JREFEC**, 1988, v1(1), 75-83.

Mills, Edwin S. "Has The United States Overinvested In Housing?," **AREUEA**, 1987, v15(1), 601-616.

Mills, Edwin S. "Housing Tenure Choice," **JREFEC**, 1990, v3(4), 323-332.

Mills, Edwin S. "Social Returns To Housing And Other Fixed Capital," **AREUEA**, 1989, v17(2), 197-211.

Mills, Harlan D. "On The Measurement Of Fund Performance," **JOF**, 1970, v25(5), 1125-1132.

Mills, James C. (Severn, Alan D., James C. Mills and Basil L. Copeland, Jr. "Capital Gains Taxes After Tax Reform," **JPM**, 1986-87, v13(3), 69-75.)

Mills, John R. (Gatti, James F., John R. Mills and Peter J. McTague. "The Feasibility Of Small Denomination Consumer Note Issues As A Source Of Funds For Non-Financial Borrowers," **FM**, 1981, v10(3), 41-53.)

Mills, Robert H. "Accounting For The Investment Credit," **FAJ**, 1971, v27(6), 71-77.

Mills, Robert H. "Cash Flow And Solvency Of Life Insurance Companies," **JRI**, 1964, v31(4), 621-630.

Mills, Robert H. (Fraine, Harold G. and Robert H. Mills. "Effect Of Defaults And Credit Deterioration On Yields Of Corporate Bonds," **JOF**, 1961, v16(3), 423-434.)

Mills, Terence C. and Geoffrey E. Wood. "Econometric Evaluation Of Alternative Money Stock Series, 1880-1913," **JMCB**, 1982, v14(2), 265-277.

Milne, F. "Choice Over Asset Economies: Default Risk And Corporate Leverage," **JFEC**, 1975, v2(2), 165-185.

Milne, Frank and Clifford Smith, Jr. "Capital Asset Pricing With Proportional Transaction Costs," **JFQA**, 1980, v15(2), 253-266.

Milne, Frank. "Borrowing, Short-Sales, Consumer Default, And The Creation Of New Assets," **JFQA**, 1979, v14(2), 255-273.

Milne, Frank. (Madan, Dilip B., Frank Milne and Hersh Shefrin. "The Multinomial Option Pricing Model And Its Brownian And Poisson Limits," **RFS**, 1989, v2(2), 251-266.)

Milne, Robert D. "Benchmarks For A Diversified Portfolio," **FAJ**, 1958, v14(5), 51-56.

Milne, Robert D. "The Dow-Jones Industrial Average Re-Examined," **FAJ**, 1966, v22(6), 83-88.

Milne, Robert D. (Leisy, Herbert F. and Robert D. Milne. "Bank Portfolio Gains And Losses: A Comment," **FAJ**, 1969, v25(1), 91.)

Milne, Robert D. (Leisy, Herbert F. and Robert D. Milne. "What Are Bank Earnings?," **FAJ**, 1968, v24(2), 89-94.)

Milonas, Nikolaos T. and Ashok Vora. "Sources Of Nonstationarity In Cash And Futures Prices," **RFM**, 1985, v4(3), 314-326.

Milonas, Nikolaos T. "A Note On Agricultural Options And The Variance Of Futures Prices," **JFM**, 1986, v6(4), 671-676.

Milonas, Nikolaos T. "Liquidity And Price Variability In Futures Markets," **FR**, 1986, v21(2), 211-237.

Milonas, Nikolaos T. "Price Variability And The Maturity Effect In Futures Markets," **JFM**, 1986, v6(3), 443-460.

Milonas, Nikolaos T. "The Effects Of USDA Crop Announcements On Commodity Prices," **JFM**, 1987, v7(5), 571-590.

Milonas, Nikolaos T., Peter E. Koveos and G. Geoffrey Booth. "Memory In Commodity Futures Contracts: A Comment," **JFM**, 1985, v5(1), 113-114.

Milonas, Nikolaos. (Lacey, Nelson J. and Nikolaos T. Milonas. "The Determinants Of GNMA Prepayments: A Pool-By-Pool Analysis," **JRER**, 1989, v4(2), 21-32.)

Milutinovich, Jugoslav S. and Stephen C. Stremmel. "Reduction Of Terminal Response Time In An Expanding Real Time Banking System" **JBR**, 1975-76, v6(4), 275-282.

Minami, Warren N. (Lackman, Conway L. and Warren N. Minami. "Market Profiles By Lending Institutions," **JBR**, 1978-79, v9(3), 186-190.)

Minard, Donald C. "New Market Opportunity For Air Conditioning," **FAJ**, 1955, v11(1), 35-38.

Minassian, Donald P. "Information Diversity And Market Behavior: A Comment," **JOF**, 1984, v39(1), 295-297.

Mindell, Joseph. "How News Affects Market Trends," **FAJ**, 1961, v17(1), 31-34.

Mindell, Joseph. "News And The Market Trend," **FAJ**, 1945, v1(4), 30-38.

Miner, Robert B. "Application Of The Theory Of Marketing Tangible Goods To The Marketing Of Insurance," **JRI**, 1961, v28(1), 35-40.

Minet, Lawrence J. (Fischer, Gerald C. and Lawrence J. Minet. "No-Load Mutual Funds," **FAJ**, 1964, v20(1), 64-68.)

Minford, Patrick. "Equilibrium Price-Output Dynamics And The (Non)Insulating Properties Of Fixed Exchange Rates: A Comment," **JIMF**, 1983, v2(3), 355-356.

Minford, Patrick. (Matthews, Kent and Patrick Minford. "Private Sector Expenditure And Financial Asset Accumulation In The U.K.," **JMCB**, 1980, v12(4), Part 1, 644-653.)

Mingo, John and Benjamin Wolkowitz. "The Effects Of Regulation On Bank Balance Sheet Decisions," **JOF**, 1977, v32(5), 1605-1616.

Mingo, John J. "Capital Management And Profitability Of Prospective Holding Company Banks," **JFQA**, 1975, v10(2), 191-203.

Mingo, John J. "Regulatory Influence On Bank Capital Investment," **JOF**, 1975, v30(4), 1111-1121.

Mingo, John J. "The Effect Of Deposit Rate Ceilings On Bank Risk," **JBF**, 1978, v2(4), 367-378.

Mingo, John J. "The Microeconomics Of Deposit Rate Ceilings: Inferences For NOW Accounts And Interest On Checking Accounts," **JBF**, 1980, v4(4), 387-395.

Mingo, John J. (Chase, Samuel B., Jr. and John J. Mingo. "The Regulation Of Bank Holding Companies," **JOF**, 1975, v30(2), 281-292.)

Mingo, John J. (Heggestad, Arnold A. and John J. Mingo. "Capital Management By Holding Company Banks," **JOB**, 1975, v48(4), 500-505.)

Mingo, John J. (Heggestad, Arnold A. and John J. Mingo. "On The Usefulness Of Functional Cost Analysis Data," **JBR**, 1977-78, v8(4), 251-256.)

Mingo, John J. (Heggestad, Arnold A. and John J. Mingo. "Prices, Nonprices, And Concentration In Commercial Banking," **JMCB**, 1976, v8(1), 107-117.)

Mingo, John J. (Heggestad, Arnold A. and John J. Mingo. "The Competitive Condition Of U. S. Banking Markets And The Impact Of Structural Form," **JOF**, 1977, v32(3), 649-661.)

Mingo, Kent A. (Pinches, George E. and Kent A. Mingo. "A Multivariant Analysis Of Industrial Ratings," **JOF**, 1973, v28(1), 1-18.)

Mingo, Kent A. (Pinches, George E. and Kent A. Mingo. "The Role Of Subordination And Industrial Bond Ratings," **JOF**, 1975, v30(1), 201-206.)

Mingo, Kent A. (Pinches, George E., Kent A. Mingo and J. Kent Caruthers. "The Stability Of Financial Patterns In Industrial Organizations," **JOF**, 1973, v28(2), 389-396.)

Minnes, Gordon. "Sketch Of The New President," **FAJ**, 1959, v15(3), 49-52.

Minow, N. (Gilmour, A., M. Jensen, R. Mercer, N. Minow, J. Morley, R. Siefert, B. Stewart, L. Summers and I. Harris. "Panel: The Economic Consequences Of High Leverage And Stock Market Pressures On Corporate Management: A Roundtable Discussion," **JACF**, 1990, v3(2), 6-37.)

Reply," **JMCB**, 1969, v1(1), 112-120.)

Moeller, Charles, Jr. "Economic Implications Of The Life Insurance Industry's Investment Program In The Central Cities," **JRI**, 1969, v36(1), 93-102.

Moeller, Charles. "New Areas For Research - Some Practical Aspects," **JRI**, 1963, v30(1), 53-60.

Moeller, Susan E. (Srinivasan, Venkat, Susan E. Moeller and Yong H. Kim. "International Cash Management: State-Of-The-Art And Research Directions," **AFPAF**, 1990, v5(1), 161-194.)

Moffet, Denis. "An Analysis Of The Demand For Life Insurance: Mathematical Foundations," **JRI**, 1979, v46(2), 87-98.

Moffet, Denis. "An Analysis Of The Demand For Life Insurance: The Consumers' Problem," **JRI**, 1979, v46(2), 99-112.

Moffet, Denis. "Optimal Deductible And Consumption Theory," **JRI**, 1977, v44(4), 669-682.

Moffett, Michael H. "The J-Curve Revisited: An Empirical Examination For The United States," **JIMF**, 1989, v8(3), 425-444.

Moffitt, George Wilber, Jr. "Management Achievement Of Open-End Investment Companies," **JOB**, 1952, v25(2), 71-88.

Mohan, Nancy K. (Ainina, M. Fall and Nancy K. Mohan. "When LBOs Go IPO," **JBFA**, 1991, v18(3), 393-404.)

Mohan, Nancy and Carl R. Chen. "A Review Of The RJR-Nabisco Buyout," **JACF**, 1990, v3(2), 102-108.

Mohan, Nancy, M. Fall Ainina, Daniel Kaufman and Bernard J. Winger. "Acquisition/Divestiture Valuation Practices In Major U.S. Firms," **FPE**, 1991, v1(1), 73-82.

Mohindru, Rajesh K. (Meinster, David R. and Rajesh K. Mohindru. "Determinants Of The Demand For Correspondent Balances By Small & Medium Sized Banks," **JBR**, 1975-76, v6(1), 25-34.)

Mohl, Murray. (Brick, Ivan E., W. G. Mellon, Julius Surkis and Murray Mohl. "Optimal Capital Structure: A Multi-Period Programming Model For Use In Financial Planning," **JBF**, 1983, v7(1), 45-68.)

Mohr, Rosanne M. "The Operating Beta Of A U.S. Multi-Activity Firm: An Empirical Investigation," **JBFA**, 1985, v12(4), 575-593.

Mohr, Rosanne M. (Callahan, Carolyn M. and Rosanne M. Mohr. "The Determinants Of Systematic Risk: A Synthesis," **FR**, 1989, v24(2), 157-182.)

Moizer, Peter and Stuart Turley. "Changes In The UK Market For Audit Services: 1972-1982," **JBFA**, 1989, v16(1), 41-54.

Mokkelbost, Per B. "Unsystematic Risk Over Time," **JFQA**, 1971, v6(2), 785-796.

Mokkelbost, Per B. (Emery, Douglas R., Philip C. Parr, Per B. Mokkelbost, David Gandhi and Anthony Saunders. "An Investigation Of Real Investment Decision Making With The Options Pricing Model," **JBFA**, 1978, v5(4), 363-369.)

Molho, Lazaros E. "Loan Rates As A Selective Credit Control," **JBF**, 1984, v8(1), 79-98.

Molho, Lazaros E. "On Testing The Efficacy Of Selective Credits Controls: A Comment," **JMCB**, 1983, v15(1), 120-122.

Mollenauer, James F. "The Computer In The Laboratory," **FAJ**, 1966, v22(3), 121-124.

Molnar, Daniel E. and T. H. Rockwell. "Analysis Of Policy Movement In A Merit-Rating Program: An Application Of Markov-Processes," **JRI**, 1966, v33(2), 265-276.

Molodovsky, Nicholas. "A Theory Of Price-Earnings Ratios," **FAJ**, 1953, v9(5), 65-80.

Molodovsky, Nicholas. "Building A Stock Market Measure," **FAJ**, 1967, v23(3), 43-46.

Molodovsky, Nicholas. "Dow-Jones Industrials: A Reappraisal," **FAJ**, 1961, v17(2), 13-19.

Molodovsky, Nicholas. "Economic Insight: Historical Vignettes," **FAJ**, 1963, v19(4), 27-31,74-82.

Molodovsky, Nicholas. "For The Record," **FAJ**, 1964, v20(3), 125-128.

Molodovsky, Nicholas. "General Motors: Appraisal Of A Colossus," **FAJ**, 1959, v15(2), 67-74.

Molodovsky, Nicholas. "Growth Stocks: A Note," **FAJ**, 1968, v24(5), 103-106.

Molodovsky, Nicholas. "It's Good To Own Growth Stocks!" **FAJ**, 1963, v19(2), 75-86,93-99.

Molodovsky, Nicholas. "Mergers And Antitrust Policy," **FAJ**, 1968, v24(2), 23-33.

Molodovsky, Nicholas. "Recent Studies Of P/E Ratios," **FAJ**, 1967, v23(3), 101-108.

Molodovsky, Nicholas. "Some Aspects Of Price-Earnings Ratios," **FAJ**, 1953, v9(2), 65-80.

Molodovsky, Nicholas. "Stock Values And Stock Prices. Part II," **FAJ**, 1960, v16(4), 53-64.

Molodovsky, Nicholas. "Stock Values And Stock Prices," **FAJ**, 1960, v16(3), 9-14.

Molodovsky, Nicholas. "Stock Prices And Current Earnings," **FAJ**, 1955, v11(4), 83-95.

Molodovsky, Nicholas. "Stock Values And Stock Prices," **FAJ**, 1968, v24(6), 134-148..

Molodovsky, Nicholas. "The Business Corporation," **FAJ**, 1968, v24(3), 29-39.

Molodovsky, Nicholas. "The Core And The Margin," **FAJ**, 1954, v10(4), 17-32.

Molodovsky, Nicholas. "The Many Aspects Of Yields," **FAJ**, 1962, v18(2), 49-86.

Molodovsky, Nicholas. "The Many Aspects Of Yields," **JPM**, 1978-79, v5(1), 66-71.

Molodovsky, Nicholas. "The Summer Of Our Discontent," **FAJ**, 1961, v17(4), 81-88.

Molodovsky, Nicholas. "Valuation Of Common Stocks," **FAJ**, 1959, v15(1), 23-28.

Molodovsky, Nicholas. (Chottiner, Sherman, Catherine May, and Nicholas Molodovsky. "Common Stock Valuation: Theory And Tables," **FAJ**, 1965, v21(2), 104-123.)

Monahan, James and Kenneth Monahan. "Company Contributions To Discretionary Profit-Sharing Plans: Reply," **JOF**, 1976, v31(3), 991-994.

Monahan, James P. "Some Programming Models For Administering Discretionary Profit Sharing," **FR**, 1976, v11(1), 49-58.

Monahan, James P. and Kenneth B. Monahan. "Company Contributions To Discretionary Profit-Sharing Plans: A Quantitative Approach," **JOF**, 1974, v29(3), 981-994.

Monahan, James P. (Berger, Paul D. and James P. Monahan. "A Planning Model To Cope With Absenteeism," **JOB**, 1974, v47(4), 512-517.)

Monahan, Kenneth B. (Monahan, James P. and Kenneth B. Monahan. "Company Contributions To Discretionary Profit-Sharing Plans: A Quantitative Approach," **JOF**, 1974, v29(3), 981-994.)

Monahan, Kenneth. (Monahan, James and Kenneth Monahan. "Company Contributions To Discretionary Profit-Sharing Plans: Reply," **JOF**, 1976, v31(3), 991-994.)

Monahan, Stephen T. (Anstaett, Kurt W., Dennis P. McCrary and Stephen T. Monahan, Jr. "Practical Debt Policy Considerations For Growth Companies: A Case Study Approach," **JACF**, 1988, v1(2), 71-78.)

Money, Arthur H. (Carter, Kevin J., John F. Affleck-Graves and Arthur H. Money. "Are Gold Shares Better Than Gold For Diversification?," **JPM**, 1982-83, v9(1), 52-55.)

Moniez, Jean-Claude. "The Smart Card In France," **JBR**, 1985-86, v16(4), 221-222.

Monissen, Hans G. "Karl Brunner At The University Of Konstanz, 1969-73," **JMCB**, 1977, v9(2), Part 2, 251-253.

Monke, Eric A. and Alessandro Sorrentino. "Exchange Rate Changes And Commodity Futures Prices," **RFM**, 1987, v6(2), 218-238.

Monks, Joseph G. "Nuclear Fuel Industry Trends," **FAJ**, 1968, v24(6), 45-53.

Monks, R. (Boies, D., D. Carroll, A. Fleischer, J. Grundfest, J. Ira Harris, M. Lipton, R. Monks, A. Oliver, L. Sachnoff and J. Wilcox. "Panel: Corporate Governance: The Role Of Boards Of Directors In Takeover Bids And Defenses," **JACF**, 1989, v2(2), 6-35.)

Monroe, Margaret A. and Richard A. Cohn. "The Relative Efficiency Of The Gold And Treasury Bill Futures Markets," **JFM**, 1986, v6(3), 477-494.

Monroe, Margaret A. "Indeterminacy Of Price And Quantity In Futures Markets," **JFM**, 1988, v8(5), 575-588.

Monroe, Margaret A. "On The Estimation Of Supply And Demand Functions: The Case Of Interest Rate Futures Markets," **RIF**, 1983, v4, 91-122.

Monroe, Margaret A. (Lauterbach, Beni and Margaret A. Monroe. "A Transaction Data Examination Of The Weekend Effect In Futures Markets," **RFM**, 1989, v8(3), 370-383.)

Monroe, Margaret. (Lauterbach, Beni and Margaret Monroe. "Evidence On The Effect Of Information And Noise Trading On Intraday Gold Futures Returns," **JFM**, 1989, v9(4), 297-306.)

Monroe, Robert J. and James Trieschmann. "Portfolio Performance Of Property-Liability Insurance Companies," **JFQA**, 1972, v7(2), 1595-1611.

Monroe, Robert J. (Trieschmann, James S. and Robert J. Monroe. "Investment Performance Of Property-Liability Insurers' Common Stock Portfolios," **JRI**, 1972, v39(4), 545-554.)

Monroe, Robert J. (Trieschmann, James S. and Robert J. Monroe. "Investment Performance Of P.L. Insurers' Common Stock Portfolios: Reply," **JRI**, 1975, v42(1), 173-177.)

Monroe, Wilbur F. "Exchange Controls In Japan: 1971-72," **FAJ**, 1972, v28(6), 43-46,48,91.

Montgomery, Austin H., Jr. (Riley, William B. and Austin H. Montgomery, Jr. "The Use Of Interactive Computer Programs In Security Analysis And Portfolio Management," **JFED**, 1980, v9,89-92.)

Montgomery, David B. and Donald G. Morrison. "A Note On Adjusting R Square," **JOF**, 1973, v28(4), 1009-1013.

Montgomery, Edward. "Aggregate Dynamics And Staggered Contracts: A Test Of The Importance Of Spillover Effects," **JMCB**, 1984, v16(4), Part 1, 505-514.

Montgomery, John O. "Regulatory Tests In The Life And Health Insurance Industry," **JRI**, 1976, v43(3), 411-430.

Montgomery, Royal E., Irwin M. Stelzer, and Rosalind Roth. "Collective Bargaining Over Profit Sharing: The Automobile Union's Effort To Extend Its Frontier Of Control," **JOB**, 1958, v31(4), 318-334.

Monti, Antonio. "Recent Trends In International Banking," **JBF**, 1982, v6(3), 389-399.

Mookerjee, Rajen. (Dadkhah, Kamran M. and Rajen Mookerjee. "Money And Corporate Profits In A Developing Country: Theory And Evidence," **JBF**, 1989, v13(2), 191-206.)

Moon, Philip and Stewart Hodges. "Implications Of The Recent Tax Changes For Corporate Capital Investment," **JBFA**, 1989, v16(1), 25-40.

Moon, Philip. "Paradoxes In The Cost Allocation For Joint Products," **JBFA**, 1989, v16(3), 443-448.

Moondra, Shyam L. "An L.P. Model For Workforce Scheduling For Banks," **JBR**, 1975-76, v6(4), 299-301.

Mooney, Steven P. "Cash Equivalency In Dichotomous Residential Markets," **JRER**, 1990, v5(1), 89-106.

Moor, Roy E. "Economic Disciplines For Economic Disciples," **JPM**, 1974-75, v1(2), 61-69.

Moor, Roy E. "Economics And Investment Analysis," **FAJ**, 1971, v27(6), 63-69.

Moore, Arnold. (Kanter, Herschel, Arnold Moore and Neil Singer. "The Allocation Of Computer Time By University Computer Centers," **JOB**, 1968, v41(3), 375-384.)

Moore, B. J. (Higgins, W. W. and B. J. Moore. "Market Structure Versus Information Costs As Determinants Of Underwriters' Spreads On Municipal Bonds," **JFQA**, 1980, v15(1), 85-97.)

Moore, Basil J. "Monetary Trends In The United States And In The United Kingdom, A Review," **FR**, 1983, v18(2), 146-166.

Moore, Basil J. "The Difficulty Of Controlling The Money Stock," **JPM**, 1980-81, v7(4), 7-14.

Moore, David G. and Richard Renck. "The Professional Employee In Industry," **JOB**, 1955, v28(1), 58-66.

Moore, Geoffrey H. "Changes In Income Distribution," **FAJ**, 1952, v8(5), 33-36.

Moore, Geoffrey H. "Stock Prices And The Business Cycle," **JPM**, 1974-75, v1(3), 59-64.

Moore, Geoffrey H. "The Quality Of Credit In Booms And Depressions," **JOF**, 1956, v11(2), 288-300.

Moore, Geoffrey H. (Zarnowitz, Victor and Geoffrey H. Moore. "Sequential Signals Of Recession And Recovery," **JOB**, 1982, v55(1), 57-86.)

Moore, Geoffrey. "Measuring The 1957-58 Recession," **FAJ**, 1959, v15(1), 17-22.

Moore, Giora. (Berg, Menachem and Giora Moore. "Foreign Exchange Strategies: Spot, Forward And Options," **JBFA**, 1991, v18(3), 449-457.)

Moore, J. S. and A. K. Reichert. "An Analysis Of The Financial Management Techniques Currently Employed By Large U.S. Corporations," **JBFA**, 1983, v10(4), 623-645.

Moore, James S. "An Investigation Of The Major Influences Of Residential Liquidity: A Multivariate Approach," **AREUEA**, 1987, v15(1), 684-703.

Moore, James S. (Reichert, Alan K., James S. Moore and Ezra Byler. "Financial Analysis Among Large US Corporations: Recent Trends And The Impact Of The Personal Computer," **JBFA**, 1988, v15(4), 469-486.)

Moore, James S. (Reichert, Alan K. and James S. Moore. "Using Latent Root Regression To Identify Nonpredictive Collinearity In Statistical Appraisal Models," **AREUEA**, 1986, v14(1), 136-152.)

Moore, James S., Alan K. Riechert and Chien-Ching Cho. "Analyzing The Temporal Stability Of Appraisal Model Coefficients: An Application Of Ridge Regression Techniques," **AREUEA**, 1984, v12(1), 50-71.

Moore, John L., Jr. (McLaughlin, Frank C. and John L. Moore, Jr. "Planning To Meet Retirement Costs," **FAJ**, 1968, v24(5), 13-23.)

Moore, Laurence J. (Scott, David F., Jr., Laurence J. Moore, Andre Saint-Denis, Edouard Archer and Bernard W. Taylor, III. "Implementation Of A Cash Budget Simulator At Air Canada," **FM**, 1979, v8(2), 46-52.)

Moore, Laurence J. (Taylor, Bernard W., III and Laurence J. Moore. "A Simulation Approach To Planning Bank Projects," **JBR**, 1976-77, v7(3), 225-228.)

Moore, Marion Chapman. (Moore, Michael J. and Marion Chapman Moore. "Adaptive Learning, Adaptive Utility, And Rational Behavior In A Repeated Prisoner's Dilemma," **JRU**, 1989, v2(4), 367-384.)

Moore, Michael J. "Dual Exchange Rates, Capital Controls, And Sticky Prices," **JIMF**, 1989, v8(4), 547-558.

Moore, Michael J. and Marion Chapman Moore. "Adaptive Learning, Adaptive Utility, And Rational Behavior In A Repeated Prisoner's Dilemma," **JRU**, 1989, v2(4), 367-384.

Moore, Michael J. and W. Kip Viscusi. "Models For Estimating Discount Rates For Long-Term Health Risks Using Labor Market Data," **JRU**, 1990, v3(4), 381-402.

Moore, Norman H. (Peterson, Pamela P., David R. Peterson and Norman H. Moore. "The Adoption Of New-Issue Dividend Reinvestment Plans And Shareholder Wealth," **FR**, 1987, v22(2), 221-232.)

Moore, Norman H. and Stephen W. Pruitt. "The Market Pricing Of Net Operating Loss Carryforwards: Implications Of The Tax Motivations Of Mergers," **JFR**, 1987, v10(2), 153-160.

Moore, Norman H. and Stephen W. Pruitt. "Excess Asset Reversions And Shareholder Wealth: Comment," **JOF**, 1990, v45(5), 1709-1714.

Moore, Norman H., David R. Peterson and Pamela P. Peterson. "Shelf Registrations And Shareholder Wealth: A Comparison Of Shelf And Traditional Equity Offerings," **JOF**, 1986, v41(2), 451-464.

Moore, R. (Agnello, W., W. Brueggeman, G. Decker, R. Griffith, R. Leftwich, R. Moore, J. Neal, B. Sternlicht, B. Wallach, W. Wardrop and C. Zinngrabe. "Panel: Corporate Real Estate Roundtable," **JACF**, 1990, v3(1), 6-38.)

Moore, Scott B. (Ferri, Michael G., Scott B. Moore and David C. Schirm. "Investor Expectations About Callable Warrants," **JPM**, 1987-88, v14(3), 84-86.)

Moore, Scott B. (Ferri, Michael G., Scott B. Moore and David C. Schirm. "The Listing, Size, And Value Of Equity Warrants," **FR**, 1989, v24(1), 135-146.)

Moore, W. Robert. "Large Value Payment Systems," **JBR**, 1985-86, v16(4), 232-234.

Moore, W. Robert. "The Impact Of Technological Change On Internal Bank Operations," **JBR**, 1974-75, v5(3), 136-140.

Moore, William T. and Son-Nan Chen. "Implementing the IRR Criterion When Cash Flow Parameters Are Unknown," **FR**, 1984, v19(4), 351-358.

Moore, William T. and William L. Satoris. "Dividends And Taxes: Another Look At The Electric Utility Industry," **FR**, 1985, v20(1), 1-20.

Moore, William T. (Boquist, John A. and William T. Moore. "Inter-Industry Leverage Differences And The DeAngelo-Masulis Tax Shield Hypothesis," **FM**, 1984, v13(1), 5-9.)

Moore, William T. (Boquist, John A. and William T. Moore. "Estimating The Systematic Risk Of An Industry Segment: A Mathematical Programming Approach," **FM**, 1983, v12(4), 11-18.)

Moore, William T. (Chen, Son-Nan and William T. Moore. "Investment Decisions Under Uncertainty: Application Of Estimation Risk In The Hillier Approach," **JFQA**, 1982, v17(3), 425-440.)

Moore, William T. (Chen, Son-Nan and William T. Moore. "Project Abandonment Under Uncertainty: A Bayesian Approach," **FR**, 1983, v18(4), 306-313.)

Moore, William T. (Chen, Son-Nan and William T. Moore. "Uncertain Inflation And Optimal Portfolio Approach: A Simplified Approach," **FR**, 1985, v20(4), 343-356.)

Moore, William T. (Chen, Son-Nan and William T. Moore. "Multi-Period Asset Pricing: The Effects Of Uncertain Inflation," **FR**, 1984, v19(2), 208-221.)

Moore, William T. (Chen, Son-Nan and William T. Moore. "The Expected Net Present Value Rule Under Informative And Noninformative Prior Distributions," **AFPAF**, 1985, v1(1), 209-224.)

Moore, William T. (Eberhart, Allan C., William T. Moore and Rodney L. Roenfeldt. "Security Pricing And Deviations From The Absolute Priority Rule In Bankruptcy Proceedings," **JOF**, 1990, v45(5), 1457-1470.)

Moore, William T. (Guffey, Daryl M. and William T. Moore. "Direct Bankruptcy Costs: Evidence From The Trucking Industry," **FR**, 1991, v26(2), 223-236.)

Moore, William T. (Liu, Pu and William T. Moore. "The Impact Of Split Bond Ratings On Risk Premia," **FR**, 1987, v22(1), 71-86.)

Moore, William T. (Mais, Eric L., William T. Moore and Ronald C. Rogers. "A Re-Examination Of Shareholder Wealth Effects Of Calls Of Convertible Preferred Stock," **JOF**, 1989, v44(5), 1401-1410.)

Moore, William T. and Joan T. Schmit. "The Risk Retention Act Of 1986: Effects On Insurance Firm Shareholders' Wealth," **JRI**, 1989, v56(1), 137-145.

Moore, William T., Donald G. Christensen and Rodney L. Roenfeldt. "Equity Valuation Effects Of Forming Master Limited Partnerships," **JFEC**, 1989, v24(1), 107-124.

Moorehead, Josef D. (Kuhle, James L. and Josef D. Moorehead. "Applying The Bootstrap Technique To Real Estate Appraisal: An Empirical Analysis," **JRER**, 1990, v5(1), 33-40.)

Moorhead, E. J. "A Profit Calculation For Agency Management: Comment," **JRI**, 1967, v34(2), 339-341.

Moorhead, E. J. "The Impact Of Lapse Rates On Life Insurance Prices," **JRI**, 1969, v36(1), 163-164.

Moorhead, E. J. and Herbert S. Bright. "Cost Of Life Insurance To The Policyholder: Comment," **JRI**, 1962, v29(3), 424-426.

Moorhead, E. J. and Joseph M. Belth. "A Practical Improvement On The Traditional Method Of Comparing Net Costs Of Participating Life Insurance Policies," **JRI**, 1965, v32(4), 639-644.

Moosa, Suleman A. "Dynamic Portfolio-Balance Behavior Of Time Deposits And 'Money'," **JOF**, 1977, v32(3), 709-717.

Moosa, Suleman A. "Inflation And Common Stock Prices," **JFR**, 1980, v3(2), 115-128.

Moran, Eileen. (Fabozzi, Frank J., Eileen Moran and Christopher K. Ma. "Market Uncertainty And The Least-Cost Offering Method Of Public Utility Debt: A Note," **JOF**, 1988, v43(4), 1025-1034.)

Morande, Felipe G. "Domestic Currency Appreciation And Foreign Capital Inflows: What Comes First? (Chile, 1977-82)," **JIMF**, 1988, v7(4), 447-466.

Morard, Bernard and Ahmed Naciri. "Options And Investment Strategies," **JFM**, 1990, v10(5), 505-518.

Morck, Randall and Bernard Yeung. "Why Investors Value Multinationality," **JOB**, 1991, v64(2), 165-188.

Morck, Randall, Andrei Shleifer and Robert W. Vishny. "Management Ownership And Market Valuation: An Empirical Analysis," **JFEC**, 1988, v20(1/2), 293-316.

Morck, Randall, Andrei Shleifer and Robert W. Vishny. "Do Managerial Objectives Drive Bad Acquisitions?," **JOF**, 1990, v45(1), 31-48.

Morck, Randall, Eduardo Schwartz and David Stangeland. "The Valuation Of Foresty Resources Under Stochastic Prices And Inventories," **JFQA**, 1989, v24(4), 473-488.

Morck, Randall. (Bodie, Zvi, Jay O. Light, Randall Morck and Robert A. Taggart, Jr. "Corporate Pension Policy: An Empirical Investigation," **FAJ**, 1985, v41(5), 10-16.)

Morck, Randall. (Feldstein, Martin and Randall Morck. "Pension Funds And The Value Of Equities," **FAJ**, 1983, v39(5), 29-39.)

Moreau, Arthur F. (Errunza, Vihang R. and Arthur F. Moreau. "Debt-For-Equity Swaps Under A Rational Expectations Equilibrium," **JOF**, 1989, v44(3), 663-680.)

Morehouse, M. Dutton. "Consumer Debt And The Business Cycle," **FAJ**, 1953, v9(4), 11-14.

Morehouse, M. Dutton. "The Financial Analysts Seminar," **FAJ**, 1956, v12(5), 13-18.

Morehouse, M. Dutton. "The Money-Price Relationship," **FAJ**, 1953, v9(2), 47-52.

Morehouse, M. Dutton. "The Search For Facts," **FAJ**, 1956, v12(4), 9-12.

Morelli, D. "Payment Systems In Eleven Developed Countries," **JBR**, 1985-86, v16(4), 173-174.

Moretti, Christian. (Bland, Christopher, Manfred Klein, Henri Blanchet and Christian Moretti. "Perspectives On Restructuring In Europe: Interviews With Four European Executives," **JACF**, 1991, v3(4), 37-45.)

Morgan, Fred W., Jr. "Are Early Triers Heavy Users?," **JOB**, 1979, v52(3), 429-434.

Morgan, George E. (Kaufman, George G. and George E. Morgan. "Standardizing Yields On Mortgages And Other Securities," **AREUEA**, 1980, v8(2), 163-179.)

Morgan, George Emir and Susan M. Becker. "Environmental Factors In Pricing NOW Accounts In 1981," **JBR**, 1982-83, v13(3), 168-178.

Morgan, George Emir and Stephen D. Smith. "Maturity Intermediation And Intertemporal Lending Policies Of Financial Intermediaries," **JOF**, 1987, v42(4), 1023-1034.

Morgan, George Emir and Stephen D. Smith. "The Role Of Capital Adequacy Regulation In The Hedging Decisions Of Financial Intermediaries," **JFR**, 1987, v10(1), 33-46.

Morgan, George Emir, III and Stephen D. Smith. "Basis Risk, Partial Takedown And Hedging By Financial Intermediaries," **JBF**, 1986, v10(4), 467-490.

Morgan, George Emir, III. "On The Adequacy Of Bank Capital Regulation," **JFQA**, 1984, v19(2), 141-162.

Morgan, George Emir, Dilip K. Shome and Stephen D. Smith. "Optimal Futures Positions For Large Banking Firms," **JOF**, 1988, v43(1), 175-195.

Morgan, George Emir. "Floating Rate Securities And Immunization: Some Further Results," **JFQA**, 1986, v21(1), 87-94.

Morgan, George Emir. "Forward And Futures Pricing Of Treasury Bills," **JBF**, 1981, v5(4), 483-496.

Morgan, George Emir. (Jordan, James V. and George Emir Morgan. "Default Risk In Futures Markets: The Customer-Broker Relationship," **JOF**, 1990, v45(3), 909-934.)

Morgan, I. G. "Dividends And Capital Asset Prices," **JOF**, 1982, v37(4), 1071-1086.

Morgan, I. G. "Grouping Procedures For Portfolio Formation," **JOF**, 1977, v32(5), 1759-1765.

Morgan, I. G. "Market Proxies And The Conditional Prediction Of Returns," **JFEC**, 1978, v6(4), 385-398.

Morgan, I. G. "Prediction Of Return With The Minimum Variance Zero-Beta Portfolio," **JFEC**, 1975, v2(4), 361-376.

Morgan, I. G. "Stock Prices And Heteroscedasticity," **JOB**, 1976, v49(4), 496-508.

Morgan, James N. (Cohen, Jacob and James N. Morgan. "The Effect Of Cash Buying And Credit Buying On Consumer Liquid Savings," **JOF**, 1962, v17(1), 110-120.)

Morgan, Karen E. (Baker, H. Kent, Patricia L. Gallagher and Karen E. Morgan. "Management's View Of Stock Repurchase Programs," JFR, 1981, v4(3), 233-247.)

Morgan, N. C. "An Analysis Of Selected Hospice Programs," JRI, 1984, v51(1), 99-114.

Morgan, Norma. "The Case For Extending Social Security To Government Employees: Comment," JRI, 1982, v49(3), 464-467.

Morgan, William K. "The Financial Analyst And A Mature Life Insurance Company," JRI, 1965, v32(3), 423-426.

Morgenegg, C. (Muller, U. A., M. M. Dacorogna, R. B. Olsen, O. V. Pictet, M. Schwarz and C. Morgenegg. "Statistical Study Of Foreign Exchange Rates, Empirical Evidence Of A Price Change Scaling Law, And Intraday Analysis," JBF, 1990, v14(6), 1189-1208.)

Morgenroth, William M. (Stern, Louis W. and William M. Morgenroth. "Concentration, Mutually Recognized Interdependence, And The Allocation Of Marketing Resources," JOB, 1968, v41(1), 56-67.)

Moriarity, Shane. (Walker, Michael C., John D. Stowe and Shane Moriarity. "Decomposition Analysis Of Financial Statements," JBFA, 1979, v6(2), 173-186.)

Moriarty, D. P. and J. Balog. "Use Of Scientific Knowledge," FAJ, 1967, v23(4), 76-79.

Moriarty, Eugene J. and Paula A. Tosini. "Futures Trading And The Price Volatility Of GNMA Certificates - Further Evidence," JFM, 1985, v5(4), 633-641.

Moriarty, Eugene J. (Gordon, J. Douglas, Eugene J. Moriarty and Paula A. Tosini. "Stock Index Futures: Does The Dog Wag The Tail?," FAJ, 1987, v43(6), 72-73.)

Moriarty, Eugene J. (Tosini, Paula A. and Eugene J. Moriarty. "Potential Hedging Use Of A Futures Contract Based On A Composite Stock Index," JFM, 1982, v2(1), 83-104.)

Moriarty, Eugene, Susan Phillips and Paula Tosini. "A Comparison Of Options And Futures In The Management Of Portfolio Risk," FAJ, 1981, v37(1), 61-67.

Moriarty, Eugene. (Jordan, James V., Robert S. Mackay and Eugene Moriarty. "The New Regulation Of Hybrid Debt Instruments," JACF, 1990, v2(4), 72-84.)

Morimune, Kirnio. (Lee, Cheng F. and Kirnio Morimune. "Time Aggregation, Coefficient Of Determination And Systematic Risk Of The Market Model," FR, 1978, v13(1), 36-47.)

Morin, Roger A. and A. Fernandez Suarez. "Risk Aversion Revisited," JOF, 1983, v38(4), 1201-1216.

Morin, Roger A. (Kolb, Robert W., Roger A. Morin and Gerald D. Gay. "Regulation, Regulatory Lag, And The Use Of Futures Markets," JOF, 1983, v38(2),405-418.)

Morley, J. (Gilmour, A., M. Jensen, R. Mercer, N. Minow, J. Morley, R. Siefert, B. Stewart, L. Summers and I. Harris. "Panel: The Economic Consequences Of High Leverage And Stock Market Pressures On Corporate Management: A Roundtable Discussion," JACF, 1990, v3(2), 6-37.)

Morley, Samuel A. "The Relationship Between Money, Income And Prices In The Short And Long Run," JOF, 1973, v28(5), 1119-1130.

Moroney, J. R. and J. M. Mason. "The Dynamic Impacts Of Autonomous Expenditures And The Monetary Base On Aggregate Income," JMCB, 1971, v3(4), 793-814.

Moroney, John R. and Barry J. Wilbratte. "Money And Money Substitutes: A Reply," JMCB, 1978, v10(1), 115-116.

Moroney, John R. and Barry J. Wilbratte. "Money And Money Substitutes: A Time Series Analysis Of Household P ortfolios," JMCB, 1976, v8(2), 181-198.

Morowitz, Jacob J. "Speculation In The Metals Markets," RFM, 1986, v5(1), 1-14.

Morris, Edward L. "Agent-Aided Private Placements," FAJ, 1971, v27(3), 83-88.

Morris, Frank E. "Impact Of Monetary Policy On State And Local Governments: An Empirical Study," JOF, 1960, v15(2), 232-249.

Morris, James R. "A Model For Corporate Debt Maturity Decisions," JFQA, 1976, v11(3), 339-357.

Morris, James R. "An Application Of The Decomposition Principle To Financial Decision Models," JFQA, 1975, v10(1), 37-65.

Morris, James R. "Job Rotation," JOB, 1956, v29(4), 268-273.

Morris, James R. "On Corporate Debt Maturity Strategies," JOF, 1976, v31(1), 29-37.

Morris, James R. "Taxes, Bankruptcy Costs And The Existence Of An Optimal Capital Structure," JFR, 1982, v5(3), 285-299.

Morris, James R. "The Role Of Cash Balances In Firm Valuation," JFQA, 1983, v18(4), 533-545.

Morris, James R. (Bosch, Jean-Claude, James R. Morris and Steve B. Wyatt. "The Investment In Housing As A Forward Market Transaction: Implications For Tenure Choice And Portfolio Selection," AREUEA, 1986, v14(3), 385-405.)

Morris, Joe. (Cudd, Mike and Joe Morris. "Bias In Journal Ratings," FR, 1988, v23(1), 117-125.)

Morris, Michael H. and Bill McDonald. "Asset Pricing And Financial Reporting With Changing Prices," JBFA, 1982, v8(3), 383-395.

Morris, Michael H. (McDonald, Bill and Michael H. Morris. "The Existence Of Heteroscedasticity And Its Effect On Estimates Of The Market Model Parameters," JFR, 1983, v6(2), 115-126.)

Morris, Michael H. (McDonald, Bill and Michael H. Morris. "The Statistical Validity Of The Ratio Method In Financial Analysis: An Empirical Examination," JBFA, 1984, v11(1), 89-97.)

Morris, Michael H. (McDonald, Bill and Michael H. Morris. "The Statistical Validity Of The Ratio Method In Financial Analysis: An Empirical Examination: A Reply" JBFA, 1986, v13(4), 633-635.)

Morris, Michael H. (Miller, Robert E. and Michael H. Morris. "Multiproduct C-V-P Analysis And Uncertainty: A Linear Programming Approach," JBFA, 1985, v12(4), 495-505.)

Morris, Michael H., William D. Nichols and James W. Pattillo. "Capitalization Of Interest, Materiality Judgement Divergence And Users' Information Needs," JBFA, 1984, v11(4), 547-555.

Morris, R. C. and P. F. Pope. "The Jensen Measure Of Portfolio Performance In An Arbitrage Pricing Theory Context," JBFA, 1981, v8(2), 203-220.

Morris, R. C. (El Hennawy, R. H. A. and R. C. Morris. "The Significance Of Base Year In Developing Failure Prediction Models," JBFA, 1983, v10(2), 209-223.)

Morris, R. C. (El Hennawy, R. H. A. and R. C. Morris. "Market Anticipation Of Corporate Failure In The UK," JBFA, 1983, v10(3), 359-372.)

Morris, R. C. (Pope, P. F., R. C. Morris and D. A. Peel. "Insider Trading: Some Evidence On Market Efficiency And Directors' Share Dealings In Great Britain," JBFA, 1990, v17(3), 359-380.)

Morris, Robert B., III. "Fundamental Factors Affecting Electric Utility Bond Ratings: A Quantitative Approach," FAJ, 1982, v38(5), 59-61.

Morris, Russell D. "An Empirical Analysis Of Costs And Revenue Requirements For Point-Of-Sale EFTS," JBR, 1978-79, v9(3), 136-145.

Morris, Russell D. "The FED's RCPC Performance: What Does It Imply For Electronic Funds Transfer?," JBR, 1974-75, v5(2), 86-91.

Morris, Russell D. "The Fed's RCPC Performance: What Does It Imply For EFTS?: Reply," JBR, 1974-75, v5(4), 257-259.

Morris, Russell D. "The Feds RCPC Performance: Reply," JBR, 1975-76, v6(1), 72-73.

Morris, Victor F. "Central Value In Review," JPM, 1985-86, v12(1), 44-49.

Morris, Victor F. "Central Value In Review: Reply," JPM, 1985-86, v12(4), 76-77.

Morris, Victor F. "Revising Graham's 1974 Valuation Formula," FAJ, 1976, v32(6), 21-26.

Morris, Walter S. "Corporate Takeovers And Professional Investors," FAJ, 1983, v39(1), 75-80.

Morrisey, Michael A. (Wedig, Gerard, Frank A. Sloan, Mahmud Hassan and Michael A. Morrisey. "Capital Structure, Ownership, And Capital Payment Policy: The Case Of Hospitals," JOF, 1988, v43(1), 21-40.)

Morrison, Donald G. (Montgomery, David B. and Donald G. Morrison. "A Note On Adjusting R Square," JOF, 1973, v28(4), 1009-1013.)

Morrison, George R. "A Further Note On Time Deposit Interest Rates," JOF, 1959, v14(1), 75-77.

Morrison, James and Paul Morrison. "Accounting And Business Acquisitions," FAJ, 1967, v23(1), 51-56.

Morrison, John C. "Medical Cost Containment For Workers' Compensation," JRI, 1990, v57(4), 646-653.

Morrison, Laurence S. "Selling Method In Life Insurance," JRI, 1939, v6, 40-51.

Morrison, Paul L. "Trends In Investment Policies Of Individuals," JOF, 1949, v4(2), 156-176.

Morrison, Paul. (Morrison, James and Paul Morrison. "Accounting And Business Acquisitions," FAJ, 1967, v23(1), 51-56.)

Morrison, Russell J. "Investment (Savings) Elaborated - With Special Reference To Japan," FAJ, 1982, v38(3), 45-48.

Morrison, Russell J. "Musings Of A Portfolio Manager," FAJ, 1975, v31(3), 37-40.

Morrison, Russell J. "Speculation In Portfolio Management," FAJ, 1976, v32(1), 18-22.

Morrison, Russell J. "The Bullish Bias," FAJ, 1964, v20(2), 77-78.

Morrison, Russell J. "The Warrants Or The Stock?," FAJ, 1957, v13(5), 51-54.

Morrissey, Thomas F. "The Demand For Mortgage Loans And The Concomitant Demand For Home Loan Bank Advances By Savings And Loan Associations," JOF, 1971, v26(3), 687-698.

Morrissey, Thomas F. and Chor Huang. "A Nomogram For Estimating Duration," FAJ, 1987, v43(1), 65-67.

Mors, Wallace P. "Recent Trends In State Regulation Of Instalment Credit," JOF, 1960, v15(2),191-205.

Mors, Wallace P. "State Regulation Of Retail Installment Financing--Progress And Problems, II," JOB, 1951, v24(1), 43-71.

Mors, Wallace P. "State Regulation Of Retail Instalment Financing - Progress And Problems," JOB, 1950, v23(4), 199-218.

Morse, Chandler. "Forecasting Net Foreign Investment," JOB, 1954, v27(1), 51-61.

Morse, Dale and Cathy Deely. "Regional Differences In Municipal Bond Ratings," FAJ, 1983, v39(6), 54-59.

Morse, Dale and Wayne Shaw. "Investing In Bankrupt Firms," JOF, 1988, v43(5), 1193-1206.

Morse, Dale. "Asymmetrical Information In Securities Markets And Trading Volume," JFQA, 1980, v15(5), 1129-1148.

Morse, Dale. "Wall Street Journal Announcements And The Securities Markets," FAJ, 1982, v38(2),69-76.

Morse, Dale. (Beaver, William and Dale Morse. "What Determines Price-Earnings Ratios?," FAJ, 1978, v34(4), 65-76.)

Morse, Dale. (Brent, Averil, Dale Morse and E. Kay Stice. "Short Interest: Explanations And Tests," JFQA, 1990, v25(2), 273-289.)

Morse, Dale. (Divecha, Arjun and Dale Morse. "Market Responses To Dividend Increases and Changes In Payout Ratios," JFQA, 1983, v18(2), 163-173.)

Morse, Joel N. "Index Futures And The Implied Volatility Of Options," RFM, 1988, v7(2), 324-333.

Morse, Joel N. (Larson, John C. and Joel N. Morse. "Intervalling Effects In Hong Kong Stocks," JFR, 1987, v10(4), 353-362.)

Morse, Joseph. "What Price Profits?," FAJ, 1964, v20(5), 118-120.

Morse, Richard S. "New Developments On The Research Front," FAJ, 1953, v9(2), 117-122.

Mortimer, Terry. "Reporting Earnings: A New Approach," FAJ, 1979, v35(6), 67-71.

Morton, Andrew. (Heath, David, Robert Jarrow and Andrew Morton. "Bond Pricing And The Term Structure Of Interest Rates: A Discrete Time Approximation," JFQA, 1990, v25(4), 419-440.)

Morton, Gene A. "Additional Aspects Of Insurance Education: LOMA Profiles," JRI, 1974, v41(4), 711-718.

Morton, Gregory. (Johnson, Keith B., Gregory Morton and M. Chapman Findlay, III. "An Analysis Of The Flotation Cost Of Utility Bonds, 1971-76," JFR, 1979, v2(2), 133-142.)

Morton, John. (Hooper, Peter and John Morton. "Fluctuations In The Dollar: A Model Of Nominal And Real Exchange Rate Determination," JIMF, 1982, v1(1), 39-56.)

Morton, T. Gregory and Jacob M. Duker. "Black Financial Institutions: An Appraisal," FM, 1978, v7(2), 28-36.

Morton, T. Gregory. "A Discriminant Function Analysis Of Residential Mortgage Delinquency And Foreclosure," AREUEA, 1975, v3(1), 73-90.

Morton, T. Gregory. "Narrow Versus Wide Stratification Of Data In The Development Of Regression Appraisal Models," **AREUEA,** 1976, v4(2), 7-18.

Morton, T. Gregory. (Johnson, Keith B., T. Gregory Morton And M. Chapman Findlay, III. "An Empirical Analysis Of The Flotation Cost Of Corporate Securities, 1971-1972," **JOF,** 1975, v30(4), 1129-1133.)

Morton, T. Gregory. (Johnson, Keith B., T. Gregory Morton and M. Chapman Findlay, III. "An Analysis Of The Flotation Cost Of Corporate Quasi-Equity Securities, 1971-72," **FM,** 1974, v4(4), 12-17.)

Moschos, Demetrios M. (Karfakis, Costas J. and Demetrios M. Moschos. "Interest Rate Linkages Within The European Monetary System: A Time Series Analysis," **JMCB,** 1990, v22(3), 388-394.)

Moser, James T. "Public Policy Intervention Through Futures Market Operations," **JFM,** 1990, v10(6), 567-572.

Moser, James T. (Born, Jeffrey A., James T. Moser and Dennis T. Officer. "Changes In Dividend Policy And Subsequent Earnings," **JPM,** 1987-88, v14(4), 56-62.)

Moser, James T. (Born, Jeffrey A. and James T. Moser. "An Investigation Into The Role Of The Market Portfolio In The Arbitrage Pricing Theory," **FR,** 1988, v23(3), 287-300.)

Moser, James T. (Born, Jeffrey A. and James T. Moser. "Bank-Equity Returns And Changes In The Discount Rate," **JFSR,** 1990, v4(3), 223-242.)

Moser, James T. (DeGennaro, Ramon P. and James T. Moser. "Delivery, Failed And Daily Treasury Bill Returns," **JFSR,** 1990, v4(3), 203-222.)

Moser, James T. and Billy Helms. "An Examination Of Basis Risk Due To Estimation," **JFM,** 1990, v10(5), 457-468.

Moser, James T. and James T. Lindley. "A Simple Formula For Duration: An Extension," **FR,** 1989, v24(4), 611-615.

Moses, Edward A. (Bonin, Joseph M. and Edward A. Moses. "Seasonal Variations In Prices Of Individual Dow Jones Industrial Stocks," **JFQA,** 1974, v9(6), 963-991.)

Moses, Edward A. (Eisemann, Peter C. and Edward A. Moses. "Stock Dividends: Management's View," **FAJ,** 1978, v34(4), 77-83.)

Moses, Edward A. (Gitman, Lawrence J., Edward A. Moses and I. Thomas White. "An Assessment Of Corporate Cash Management Practices," **FM,** 1979, v8(1), 32-41.)

Moses, Edward A. (Mehta, Dileep R., Edward A. Moses, Benoit Deschamps and Michael C. Walker. "The Influence Of Dividends, Growth, And Leverage On Share Prices In The Electric Utility Industry," **JFQA,** 1980, v15(5), 1163-1196.)

Moses, Edward A. (Mehta, Dileep R., Peter C. Eisemann, Edward A. Moses and Benoit Deschamps. "Capital Structure And Capital Adequacy Of Bank Holding Companies: A Market Test," **JBF,** 1979, v3(1), 5-22.)

Moses, Edward A., John M. Cheyney and E. Theodore Veit. "A New And More Complete Performance Measure," **JPM,** 1986-87, v13(4), 24-33.

Moses, Jonathan D. "Implied Private Rights Of Action: If The Supreme Court Says 'Yes'," **JFM,** 1981, v1(Supp), 515-517.

Moses, Leon N. and Ian Savage. "The Effect Of Airline Pilot Characteristics On Perception Of Job Safety Risks," **JRU,** 1989, v2(4), 335-352.

Moses, O. Douglas. "On Analysts' Earnings Forecasts For Failing Firms," **JBFA,** 1990, v17(1), 101-118.

Moses, Ronald P. "On Benishay's Evaluation Of Policy: A Comment," **JMCB,** 1975, v7(3), 377-379.

Mosich, A. N. "Retroactive Poolings In Corporate Mergers," **JOB,** 1968, v41(3), 352-362.

Moskowitz, Arnold X. and George A. Harben. "Keep Profits: The True Discount Factor," **JPM,** 1977-78, v4(4), 5-15.

Moskowitz, Arnold X. "Beyond The Monetarist Mind Set: 'Keep' Profits," **JPM,** 1975-76, v2(2), 9-20.

Moskowitz, Arnold X. (Murphy, J. Michael and Arnold X. Moscowitz. "Keep Profits: Comments," **JPM,** 1975-76, v2(4), 69-72.)

Mossavar-Rahmani, Sharmin. "Customized Benchmarks In Structured Management," **JPM,** 1986-87, v13(4), 65-68.

Mossin, Jan. "Merger Agreements: Some Game-Theoretic Considerations," **JOB,** 1968, v41(4), 460-471.

Mossin, Jan. "Optimal Multiperiod Portfolio Policies," **JOB,** 1968, v41(2), 215-229.

Mote, Larry R. (Kaufman, George G., Larry R. Mote and Harvey Rosenblum. "Consequences Of Deregulation For Commercial Banking," **JOF,** 1984, v39(3), 789-803.)

Mote, Larry. (Kaufman, George, Larry Mote and Harvey Rosenblum. "Implications Of Deregulation For Product Lines And Geographical Markets Of Financial Institutions," **JBR,** 1983-84, v14(1), 8-20.)

Motley, Brian. "A Demand-For-Money Function For The Household Sector - Some Preliminary Findings," **JOF,** 1967, v22(3), 405-418.

Motley, Brian. "Inflation And Common Stock Values: Comment," **JOF,** 1969, v24(3), 530-535.

Mountain, Dean C. (Chan, M. W. Luke, Itzhak Krinsky and Dean C. Mountain. "Analysis Of Productivity At The Firm Level: An Application To Life Insurers: Comment," **JRI,** 1989, v56(2), 336-340.)

Mounts, William Stewart. (Boyes, William J., William Stewart Mounts and Clifford Sowell. "The Federal Reserve As A Bureaucracy: An Examination Of Expense-Preference Behavior," **JMCB,** 1988, v20(2), 181-190.)

Mowbray, A. H. "Content, Arrangement And Method Of A General Course For Students Not Specializing In Insurance," **JRI,** 1936, v3, 10-22.

Mowbray, Albert H. "How Far Should Further Increase In Insurance Facilities Be Permitted?," **JRI,** 1934, v1, 1-12.

Moy, Ronald L. "On Father's Day In Finance," **RQFA,** 1991, v1(2), 218.

Moyer, R. Charles and Edward Sussna. "Registered Bank Holding Company Acquisitions: A Cross-Section Analysis," **JFQA,** 1973, v8(4), 647-661.

Moyer, R. Charles and William Kretlow. "A Note On Investment Opportunities, Dividend Policy And Uncertainty Resolution," **FR,** 1979, v14(3), 68-73.

Moyer, R. Charles, Robert E. Chatfield and Phillip M. Sisneros. "Security Analyst Monitoring Activity: Agency Costs And Information Demands," **JFQA,** 1989, v24(4), 503-512.

Moyer, R. Charles. "Finance Courses For The Public Administration Student," **JFED,** 1974, v3, 63-65.

Moyer, R. Charles. "Forecasting Financial Failure: A Re-Examination," **FM,** 1977, v6(1), 11-17.

Moyer, R. Charles. "Growth, Consolidation And Mergers In Banking: Comment," **JOF,** 1976, v31(4), 1231-1232.

Moyer, R. Charles. "Lease Evaluation And The Investment Tax Credit: A Framework For Analysis," **FM,** 1974, v4(2), 39-42.

Moyer, R. Charles. "Reply To 'Examining Moyer's Re-Examination Of Forecasting Financial Failure'," **FM,** 1978, v7(4), 80-81.

Moyer, R. Charles. (Buell, Stephen G., Carl Beidleman and R. Charles Moyer. "On The Linkage Between Corporate Savings And Earnings Growth," **JFR,** 1981, v4(2), 121-128.)

Moyer, R. Charles. (Chatfield, Robert E. and R. Charles Moyer. "'Putting' Away Bond Risk: An Empirical Examination Of The Value Of The Put Option On Bonds," **FM,** 1986, v15(2), 26-33.)

Moyer, R. Charles. (Chatfield, Robert E., Scott E. Hein and R. Charles Moyer. "Long-Term Earnings Forecasts In The Electric Utility Industry: Accuracy And Valuation Implications," **FR,** 1990, v25(3), 421-440.)

Moyer, R. Charles. (Spudeck, Raymond E. and R. Charles Moyer. "Reverse Splits And Shareholder Wealth: The Impact Of Commissions," **FM,** 1985, v14(4), 52-56.)

Moyer, Reed. "Trade And Economic Progress: An International Comparison," **JOB,** 1967, v40(3), 270-279.

Moylan, James J. and Laren Ukman. "Dispute Resolution Systems In The Commodity Futures Industry," **JFM,** 1986, v6(4), 659-670.

Moylan, James J. "Self-Regulation In The Commodity Futures Industry," **JFM,** 1981, v1(Supp), 501-504.

Moylan, James J., Laren A. Ukman and Peter S. Lake. "Exchange Memberships: An Overview Of The Issues Pertaining To The Property Rights Of A Bankrupt Member And His Creditors," **JFM,** 1989, v9(5), 461-468.

Moynihan, Eugene O. "The Financial Analyst And The Computer," **FAJ,** 1964, v20(2), 115-119.

Mudaliar, Vishwa. (Canto, Victor A., J. Kimball Dietrich, Adish Jain and Vishwa Mudaliar. "Protectionism And The Stock Market: The Determinants And Consequences Of Trade Restrictions," **FAJ,** 1986, v42(5), 32-42.)

Mueller, Curt D. "Waiting For Physicians' Services: Model And Evidence," **JOB,** 1985, v58(2), 173-190.

Mueller, Dennis C. "The Effects Of Conglomerate Mergers: A Survey Of The Empirical Evidence," **JBF,** 1977, v1(4), 315-347.

Mueller, Eva and Jane Lean. "The Savings Account As A Source For Financing Large Expenditures," **JOF,** 1967, v22(3), 375-393.

Mueller, Eva. "Consumers' Attitudes Towards Saving And Their Investment Preferences," **FAJ,** 1957, v13(5), 33-40.

Mueller, F. W., Jr. "Corporate Working Capital And Liquidity," **JOB,** 1953, v26(3), 157-172.

Mueller, F. W., Jr. "The Treasury-Federal Reserve Accord," **JOF,** 1952, v7(4), 580-599.

Mueller, Paul A. "Covered Options: An Alternative Investment Strategy," **FM,** 1981, v10(4), 64-71.

Mueller, Thomas. (James, Franklin J. and Thomas Mueller. "Environmental Impact Evaluation, Land Use Planning, And The Housing Consumer," **AREUEA,** 1977, v5(3), 279-301.)

Mueller, Willard F. (Stocking, George W. and Willard F. Mueller. "Business Reciprocity And The Size Of Firms," **JOB,** 1957, v30(2), 73-95.)

Mueller, William J. "Hospital Financial Management," **FM,** 1972, v1(1), 58-62.

Mukherjee, Tarun K. and Larry M. Austin. "An Empirical Investigation Of Small Bank Stock Valuation And Dividend Policy," **FM,** 1980, v9(1), 27-31.

Mulford, Charles W. (Comiskey, Eugene E., Charles W. Mulford and Thomas L. Porter. "Forecast Error, Earnings Variability And Systematic Risk: Additional Evidence," **JBFA,** 1986, v13(2), 257-265.)

Mulford, Charles W. (Comiskey, Eugene E., Ruth Ann McEwen and Charles W. Mulford. "A Test Of Pro Forma Consolidation Of Finance Subsidiaries," **FM,** 1987, v16(3), 45-50.)

Mulherin, J. Harold and Walter J. Muller, III. "Resolution Of Incentive Conflicts In The Mortgage Industry," **JREFEC,** 1988, v1(1), 35-46.

Mulherin, J. Harold and Walter J. Muller, III. "Resolution Of Incentive Conflicts In The Mortgage Industry: A Reply," **JREFEC,** 1989, v2(1), 73-74.

Mulherin, J. Harold. (Mitchell, Mark L. and J. Harold Mulherin. "The Stock Price Response To Pension Terminations And The Relation Of Terminations With Corporate Takeovers," **FM,** 1989, v18(3), 41-56.)

Muller, Frederick L. (Fielitz, Bruce D. and Frederick L. Muller. "A Simplified Approach To Common Stock Valuation," **FAJ,** 1985, v41(6), 35-41.)

Muller, Frederick L. (Fielitz, Bruce D. and Frederick L. Muller. "The Asset Allocation Decision," **FAJ,** 1983, v39(4), 44-50.)

Muller, Frederick L. and Bruce D. Fielitz. "Standard & Poor's Quality Rankings Revisited," **JPM,** 1986-87, v13(3), 64-68.

Muller, Frederick L., Bruce D. Fielitz and Myron T. Greene. "Portfolio Performance In Relation To Quality, Earnings, Dividends, Firm Size, Leverage, And Return On Equity," **JPM,** 1987(1), 17-26.

Muller, Frederick L., Bruce D. Fielitz and Myron T. Greene. "S&P Quality Group Rankings: Risk And Return," **JPM,** 1982-83, v9(4), 39-42.

Muller, U. A., M. M. Dacorogna, R. B. Olsen, O. V. Pictet, M. Schwarz and C. Morgenegg. "Statistical Study Of Foreign Exchange Rates, Empirical Evidence Of A Price Change Scaling Law, And Intraday Analysis," **JBF,** 1990, v14(6), 1189-1208.

Muller, Walter J. (Kau, James B., Donald C. Keenan, Walter J. Muller, III and James P. Epperson. "Rational Pricing Of Adjustable Rate Mortgages," **AREUEA,** 1985, v13(2), 117-128.)

Muller, Walter J., III. (Epperson, James F., James B. Kau, Donald C. Keenan and Walter J. Muller, III. "Pricing Default Risk In Mortgages," **AREUEA,** 1985, v13(3), 261-272.)

Muller, Walter J., III. (Kau, James B., Donald C. Keenan, Walter J. Muller, III and James F. Epperson. "Pricing Commercial Mortgages

And Their Mortgage-Backed Securities," **JREFEC**, 1990, v3(4), 333-356.)

Muller, Walter J., III. (Mulherin, J. Harold and Walter J. Muller, III. "Resolution Of Incentive Conflicts In The Mortgage Industry," **JREFEC**, 1988, v1(1), 35-46.)

Muller, Walter J., III. (Mulherin, J. Harold and Walter J. Muller, III. "Resolution Of Incentive Conflicts In The Mortgage Industry: A Reply," **JREFEC**, 1989, v2(1), 73-74.)

Muller, Walter, J., III. (Kau, James B., Donald C. Keenan, Walter J. Muller, III and James F. Epperson. "The Valuation And Securitization Of Commercial And Multifamily Mortgages," **JBF**, 1987, v11(3), 525-546.)

Muller-Lutz, Heinz L. "Property-Liability Insurance Distribution In Germany," **JRI**, 1958, v25(4), 61-69.

Mullick, Satinder K. "Optimal Design Of A Stochastic System With Dominating Fixed Costs," **JFQA**, 1966, v1(3), 55-74.

Mullineaux, Donald J. "Branching Restrictions And Commercial-Bank Costs," **JOB**, 1976, v49(3), 402-407.

Mullineaux, Donald J. "Deposit-Rate Ceilings And Noncompetitive Bidding For U.S. Treasury Bills," **JMCB**, 1973, v5(1), 201-212.

Mullineaux, Donald J. "Economies Of Scale, And Organizational Efficiency In Banking: A Profit-Function Approach," **JOF**, 1978, v33(1), 259-280.

Mullineaux, Donald J. (Gorton, Gary and Donald J. Mullineaux. "The Joint Production Of Confidence: Endogenous Regulation And Nineteenth Century Commercial-Bank Clearinghouses," **JMCB**, 1987, v19(4), 457-468.)

Mullineaux, Donald J. (Park, Jeong Yun, Donald J. Mullineaux and It-Keong Chew. "Are REITs Inflation Hedges?," **JREFEC**, 1990, v3(1), 91-103.)

Mullins, David W., Jr. (Asquith, Paul and David W. Mullins, Jr. "Equity Issues And Offering Dilution," **JFEC**, 1986, v15(1/2), 61-89.)

Mullins, David W., Jr. (Asquith, Paul, Robert F. Bruner and David W. Mullins, Jr. "The Gains To Bidding Firms From Merger," **JFEC**, 1983, v11(1), 121-139.)

Mullins, David W., Jr. (Asquith, Paul and David W. Mullins, Jr. "Signalling With Dividends, Stock Repurchases, And Equity Issues," **FM**, 1986, v15(3), 27-44.)

Mullins, David W., Jr. (Asquith, Paul and David W. Mullins, Jr. "The Impact Of Initiating Dividend Payments On Shareholders' Wealth," **JOB**, 1983, v56(1), 77-96.)

Mullins, David W., Jr. (Asquith, Paul, David W. Mullins, Jr. and Eric D. Wolff. "Original Issue High Yield Bonds: Aging Analyses Of Defaults, Exchanges, And Calls," **JOF**, 1989, v44(4), 923-952.)

Mullins, David Wiley, Jr. "Restrictions On The Rate Of Interest On Demand Deposits And A Theory Of Compensating Balances," **JOF**, 1976, v31(2), 233-252.

Mumey, G. A. and R. M. Korkie. "Balance Sheet Additivity Of Risk Measures," **JFQA**, 1971, v6(4),1123-1133.

Mumey, G. A. "Premiums On Convertible Bonds: Comment," **JOF**, 1970, v25(4), 928-930.

Mumey, Glen A. "An Amendment To The Note On The Cost Of Debt," **JFQA**, 1967, v2(2), 200-201.

Mumey, Glen A. "Earnings Probabilities And Capital Costs," **JOB**, 1967, v40(4), 450-461.

Mumey, Glen. "Auto Insurance Reform," **JRI**, 1970, v37(2), 185-190.

Mumey, Glen. "Auto Insurance Reform: Reply," **JRI**, 1971, v38(2), 304-306.

Mumford, M. J. "Monetary Assets And Capital Gearing," **JBFA**, 1978, v5(3), 293-308.

Mumy, Gene E. and William D. Manson. "Payroll Taxes, Social Security, And The Unique Tax Advantage Of Company Pensions," **JRI**, 1983, v50(1), 161-165.

Mundell, Robert A. "The Monetary Consequences Of Jacque Rueff: Review Article," **JOB**, 1973, v46(3), 384-395.

Mundell, Robert. "Toward A Better International Monetary System," **JMCB**, 1969, v1(3), 625-648.

Munnell, Alicia H. "The Troubled Future Of Private Pension Plans," **JPM**, 1978-79, v5(3), 35-42.

Muoghalu, Michael I. Valuation Of Toxic Waste Mismanagement Lawsuits: A Capital Market Approach," **IJOF**, 1990, v3(1), 65-85.

Murali, Ramaswami and Jonathan B. Welch. "Agents, Owners, Control And Performance," **JBFA**, 1989, v16(3), 385-398.

Murgia, M. (Amihud, Y., H. Mendelson and M. Murgia. "Stock Market, Microstructure And Return Volatility: Evidence From Italy," **JBF**, 1990, v14(2/3), 423-440.)

Murnighan, J. Keith, Alvin E. Roth and Francoise Schoumaker. "Risk Aversion In Bargaining: An Experimental Study," **JRU**, 1988, v1(1), 101-124.

Murphy, Austin and Doug Gordon. "An Empirical Note On Hedging Mortgages With Puts," **JFM**, 1990, v10(1), 75-78.

Murphy, Austin and Kevin Nathan. "An Analysis Of Merger Financing," **FR**, 1989, v24(4), 551-566.

Murphy, Henry C. "How The Patman 'Textbooks' Were Written," **JOF**, 1953, v8(2), 152-158.

Murphy, Henry C. "The Role Of Interest Rates In A Changing World," **JOF**, 1951, v6(2), 238-251.

Murphy, J. Austin and Jimmy E. Hilliard. "An Investigation Into The Equilibrium Structure Of The Commodity Futures Market Anomaly," **FR**, 1989, v24(1), 1-18.

Murphy, J. Austin. "Analyzing Sub-Classes Of General Motors Common Stock," **FM**, 1989, v18(1), 64-71.

Murphy, J. Austin. "Futures Fund Performance: A Test Of The Effectiveness Of Technical Analysis," **JFM**, 1986, v6(2), 175-186.

Murphy, J. Austin. "Stable Distributions, Futures Prices, And The Measurement Of Trading Performance: A Reply," **JFM**, 1987, v7(1), 103-108.

Murphy, J. Austin. "The Effect Of Portfolio Insurance On The Probability Distribution Of Return," **JFED**, 1987, v16, 6-11.

Murphy, J. Austin. "Using Bayesian Betas To Estimate Risk-Return Parameters: An Empirical Investigation," **JBFA**, 1990, v17(3), 471-477.

Murphy, J. Austin. "Using The CAPM As A General Framework For Asset Pricing Analysis," **JFR**, 1990, v13(3), 233-242.

Murphy, J. Carter. "Illiquidity And The Limits To Interest Arbitrage: Comment," **JOF**, 1968, v23(4), 667-669.

Murphy, J. E. and M. F. M. Osborne. "Predicting The Volatility Of Interest Rates," **JPM**, 1984-85, v11(2), 66-69.

Murphy, J. E., Jr. and H. W. Stevenson. "P/E Ratios And Future Growth," **FAJ**, 1967, v23(6), 111-114.

Murphy, J. E., Jr. and J. R. Nelson. "Five Financial Principles," **FAJ**, 1971, v27(2), 38-52.

Murphy, J. E., Jr. (Larsen, R. A. and J. E. Murphy, Jr. "Why Does Earnings Per Share Change?," **FAJ**, 1975, v31(2), 77-83.)

Murphy, J. Michael and Arnold X. Moscowitz. "'Keep Profits': Comments," **JPM**, 1975-76, v2(4), 69-72.

Murphy, J. Michael. "Efficient Markets, Index Funds, Illusion, And Reality," **JPM**, 1977-78, v4(1), 5-20.

Murphy, J. Michael. "Why No One Can Tell Who's Winning," **FAJ**, 1980, v36(3), 49-57.

Murphy, J. Michael. "Why You Can't Win," **JPM**, 1976-77, v3(1), 45-49.

Murphy, J. Michael. (Griffith, Reynolds and J. Michael Murphy. "'Why You Can't Win'," **JPM**, 1977-78, v4(2), 76-78.)

Murphy, James M. and Allen Rappaport. "A Multiple Discriminant Analysis Of BHC Commercial Paper Ratings: A Comment," **JBF**, 1986, v10(1), 143-144.

Murphy, John H. (Cunningham, William H., W. Thomas Anderson, Jr. and John H. Murphy. "Are Students Real People?," **JOB**, 1974, v47(3), 399-409.)

Murphy, John Michael. "The Value Line Contest: 1969," **FAJ**, 1970, v26(3), 94-100.

Murphy, Joseph E., Jr. and J. Russell Nelson. "Stability Of P/E Ratios," **FAJ**, 1969, v25(2), 77-80.

Murphy, Joseph E., Jr. and J. Russell Nelson. "Random And Nonrandom Relationships Among Financial Variables: A Financial Model," **JFQA**, 1971, v6(2),875-885.

Murphy, Joseph E., Jr. and M. F. M. Osborne. "Games Of Chance And The Probability Of Corporate Profit Or Loss," **FM**, 1979, v8(2), 82-88.

Murphy, Joseph E., Jr. and M. F. M. Osborne. "Brownian Motion In The Bond Market," **RFM**, 1987, v6(3), 306-320.

Murphy, Joseph E., Jr. "Earnings Growth And Price Change," **FAJ**, 1968, v24(1), 97-99.

Murphy, Joseph E., Jr. "Relative Growth Of Earnings Per Share," **FAJ**, 1966, v22(6), 73-75.

Murphy, Joseph E., Jr. "Return, Payout, And Growth," **FAJ**, 1967, v23(3), 91-93.

Murphy, Joseph E., Jr. "Some Effects Of Leverage," **FAJ**, 1968, v24(4), 121-124.

Murphy, Joseph E., Jr. (Osborne, M. F. M. and Joseph E. Murphy, Jr. "Financial Analogs Of Physical Brownian Motion, As Illustrated By Earnings," **FR**, 1984, v19(2), 153-172.)

Murphy, Kevin J. (Baker, George P., Michael C. Jensen and Kevin J. Murphy. "Compensation And Incentives: Practice Vs. Theory," **JOF**, 1988, v43(3), 593-616.)

Murphy, Kevin J. (Jensen, Michael C. and Kevin J. Murphy. "CEO Incentives - It's Not How Much You Pay, But How," **JACF**, 1990, v3(3), 36-49.)

Murphy, Mary E. "Domestic Planning By The British Labor Party," **JOB**, 1951, v24(3), 165-180.

Murphy, Mary E. "Education For Management In Great Britain," **JOB**, 1953, v26(1), 37-47.

Murphy, Neil B. and Harry Weintrob. "Evaluating Liquidity Under Conditions Of Uncertainty In Mutual Savings Banks," **JFQA**, 1970, v5(5), 559-568.

Murphy, Neil B. and Lewis Mandell. "Consumer Response To Restructured Financial Institutions: The Case Of Maine," **JMCB**, 1979, v11(1), 91-98.

Murphy, Neil B. and Lewis Mandell. "Reforming The Structure And Regulation Of Financial Institutions: The Evidence From The State Of Maine," **JBR**, 1978-79, v9(4), 200-212.

Murphy, Neil B. and Ronald C. Rogers. "The Line Of Commerce In Retail Financial Institution Mergers: Some Evidence From Consumer Data In New England," **JBR**, 1984-85, v15(1), 21-25.

Murphy, Neil B. and Ronald C. Rogers. "Life Cycle And The Adoption Of Consumer Financial Innovation: An Empirical Study Of The Adoption Process," **JBR**, 1986-87, v17(1), 3-8.

Murphy, Neil B. and Yair E. Orgler. "Cost Analysis For Branching Systems: Methodology, Test Results, And Implications For Management," **JFR**, 1982, v5(2), 181-188.

Murphy, Neil B. "A Cross-Section Analysis Of Demand Deposit Variability," **JFQA**, 1968, v3(1), 87-95.

Murphy, Neil B. "A Cross-Sectional Analysis Of The Cost Of Operations Of Trust Departments," **JMCB**, 1969, v1(1), 84-100.

Murphy, Neil B. "A Reestimation Of The Benston-Bell-Murphy Cost Functions For A Larger Sample With Greater Size And Geographic Dispersion," **JFQA**, 1972, v7(5), 2097-2105.

Murphy, Neil B. "A Statistical Approach To Determining The Weights To Be Assigned Activity Items In The Demand Deposit Function," **JBR**, 1971-72, v3(2),61-63.

Murphy, Neil B. "A Test Of The Deposit Relationship Hypothesis," **JFQA**, 1967, v2(1), 51-59.

Murphy, Neil B. "Banking Research: Objectives Goals And Priorities," **JBR**, 1970-71, v1(2), 57-59.

Murphy, Neil B. "Determinants Of The Demand For Bank Examiner Manpower In The First National Bank Region," **JMCB**, 1977, v9(3), 500-503.

Murphy, Neil B. "Determinants Of ATM Activity: The Impact Of Card Base, Location, Time In Place And System," **JBR**, 1983-84, v14(3), 231-233.

Murphy, Neil B. "Determinants Of Household Check Writing: The Impacts Of The Use Of Electronic Banking Services And Alternative Pricing Of Services," **FSR**, 1991, v1(1), 41-51.

Murphy, Neil B. "Disclosure Of The Problem Bank Lists: A Test Of The Impact," **JBR**, 1979-80, v10(1), 86-96.

Murphy, Neil B. "Economies Of Scale In The Cost Of Compliance With Consumer Credit Protection Laws: The Case Of The Implementation Of The Equal Credit Opportunity Act Of 1974," **JBR**, 1979-80, v10(4), 248-250.

Murphy, Neil B. "Removing Deposit Interest Ceilings: An Analysis Of Deposit Flows, Portfolio Response And Income Effects In Boston Co-Operative Banks," **JBR**, 1976-77, v7(4), 256-265.

Murphy, Neil B. "The Demand For New York State Mutual Savings Bank Deposits: 1960-1969," **JOF**, 1971, v26(3), 713-718.

Murphy, Neil B. "The Implications Of Econometric Analysis Of Bank Cost Functions For Bank Planning," **JBR**, 1973-74, v4(3), 203-206.

Murphy, Neil B. "The Relationship Between Organizational Size And The Administrative Component Of Banks: A Comment," **JOB**, 1976, v49(1), 62-65.

Murphy, Neil B. (Daniel, Donnie L., William A. Longbrake and Neil B. Murphy. "The Effect Of Technology On Bank Economies Of Scale For Demand Deposits," **JOF**, 1973, v28(1), 131-146.)

Murphy, Neil B. (Fields, Joseph A. and Neil B. Murphy. "An Analysis Of Efficiency In The Delivery Of Financial Services: The Case Of Life Insurance Agencies," **JFSR**, 1989, v2(4), 343-356.)

Murphy, Neil B. (Gilbert, Gary G. and Neil B. Murphy. "Competition Between Thrift Institutions And Commercial Banks: An Examination Of The Evidence," **JBR**, 1971-72, v2(2), 8-18.)

Murphy, Neil B. (Klein, Michael A. and Neil B. Murphy. "The Pricing Of Bank Deposits: A Theoretical And Empirical Analysis," **JFQA**, 1971, v6(2), 747-761.)

Murphy, Neil B. (Lauch, Louis H. and Neil B. Murphy. "A Test Of The Impact Of Branching On Deposit Variability," **JFQA**, 1970, v5(3), 323-327.)

Murphy, Neil B. (McCall, Alan S. and Neil B. Murphy. "A Note On Evaluating Liquidity Under Conditions Of Uncertainty In Mutual Savings Banks," **JFQA**, 1971, v6(4), 1165-1169.)

Murphy, Neil B. (Rogers, Ronald C., Neil B. Murphy and James E. Owers. "Financial Innovation, Balance Sheet Cosmetics And Market Response: The Case Of Equity-For-Debt Exchanges In Banking," **JBR**, 1985-86, v16(3), 145-149.)

Murphy, Paul A. "Opportunities In Closer Valuation Of Stocks," **FAJ**, 1955, v11(1), 55-56.

Murphy, Paul A. "Valuing The Dow Jones Industrial Average," **FAJ**, 1955, v11(4), 73-74.

Murphy, Paul. "Investment Opportunities In Hosiery," **FAJ**, 1952, v8(3), 59-62.

Murphy, Robert G. "Capital Mobility And The Relationship Between Saving And Investment Rates In OECD Countries," **JIMF**, 1984, v3(3), 327-342.

Murphy, Robert G. "Import Pricing And The Trade Balance In A Popular Model Of Exchange Rate Determination," **JIMF**, 1989, v8(3), 345-358.

Murphy, Thomas T. (West, Stan and Thomas T. Murphy. "Caveats For Market Technicians," **FAJ**, 1978, v34(5), 42-48.)

Murray, Dennis. "Further Evidence On The Liquidity Effects Of Stock Splits And Stock Dividends," **JFR**, 1985, v8(1), 59-67.

Murray, Dennis. (Elgers, Pieter T. and Dennis Murray. "LIFO-FIFO, Accounting Ratios And Market Risk: A Re-Assessment," **JBFA**, 1984, v11(3), 313-325.)

Murray, Dennis. (Elgers, Pieter T. and Dennis Murray. "Financial Characteristics Related To Managements' Stock Split And Stock Dividend Decisions," **JBFA**, 1985, v12(4), 543-551.)

Murray, G. L. (Argy, V. E. and G. L. Murray. "Effects Of Sterilising A Balance Of Payments Surplus On Domestic Yields - A Formal Analysis," **JIMF**, 1985, v4(2), 223-236.)

Murray, John D. And Robert W. White. "Economies Of Scale And Economies Of Scope In Multiproduct Financial Institutions: A Study Of British Columbia Credit Unions," **JOF**, 1983, v38(3), 887-902.

Murray, John D. and Robert W. White. "Economies Of Scale And Deposit-Taking Financial Institutions In Canada: A Study Of British Columbia Credit Unions," **JMCB**, 1980, v12(1), 58-70.

Murray, John D. "The Tax Sensitivity Of US Direct Investment In Canadian Manufacturing," **JIMF**, 1982, v1(2), 117-140.

Murray, M. (Appelbaum, E., J. Burns, R. Evans, J. Gould, T. Hamachek, R. Kidder, M. Jensen, J. Johnstone, M. Murray, R. Sim, J. Stern, B. Stewart and C. Zaner. "Panel: CEO Roundtable On Corporate Structure And Management Incentives," **JACF**, 1990, v3(3), 6-35.)

Murray, Merrill G. "Social Insurance Perspectives: Background Philosophy And Early Program Developments," **JRI**, 1963, v30(2), 183-196.

Murray, Michael J. and Frank C. Reid. "Financial Style And Corporate Control," **JACF**, 1988, v1(1), 76-84.

Murray, Michael L. "A Deductible Selection Model - Development And Application," **JRI**, 1971, v38(3), 423-436.

Murray, Michael L. "An Alternative To Workers' Compensation - 24 Hour Benefits," **JRI**, 1986, v53(4), 744-754.

Murray, Michael L. "Analyzing The Investment Value Of Cash Value Life Insurance," **JRI**, 1976, v43(1), 121-128.

Murray, Michael L. "Empirical Utility Functions And Insurance Consumption Decisions," **JRI**, 1972, v39(1), 31-42.

Murray, Michael L. "Review Of Economics And Insurance: Reply," **JRI**, 1975, v42(1), 164.

Murray, Michael L. "Tax-Benefit Ratios And Rates Of Return Under OASI: 1974 Retirees And Entrants: Comment," **JRI**, 1976, v43(1), 142-144.

Murray, Michael L. "The Theory And Practice Of Innovation In The Private Insurance Industry," **JRI**, 1976, v43(4), 653-671.

Murray, Michael L. "The Theory And Practice Of Innovation In The Private Insurance Industry: Reply," **JRI**, 1978, v45(4), 691-692.

Murray, Michael L. (Dymits, Lee and Michael L. Murray. "Another Look At Implied Tax Rates," **JBF**, 1986, v10(1), 133-142.)

Murray, Michael L. (Greene, Mark R. and Michael L. Murray. "Self-Insurance Of State-Owned Property," **JRI**, 1978, v45(1), 109-120.)

Murray, Michael L. (Klugman, Stuart A. and Michael L. Murray. "Bodily Injury Claim Payments As A Function Of Automobile Liability Insurance Limits," **JRI**, 1984, v51(3), 412-432.)

Murray, Roger F. "A New Role For Options," **JFQA**, 1979, v14(4), 895-899.

Murray, Roger F. "An Overview Of The Life Insurance - Mutual Fund Combination," **JRI**, 1969, v36(3), 419-424.

Murray, Roger F. "Graham And Dodd: A Durable Discipline," **FAJ**, 1984, v40(5), 18-19,22-23.

Murray, Roger F. "Impact Of Federal Taxes And Controls On Corporate Profit Margins," **FAJ**, 1951, v7(1), 49-52.

Murray, Roger F. "What Yield Do You Use?," **FAJ**, 1955, v11(4), 15-18.

Murray, Roger F. "Institutional Influences On The Stock Market," **FAJ**, 1958, v14(2), 15-18.

Murray, Roger F. "Investment Aspects Of The Accumulation Of Pension Funds," **JOF**, 1952, v7(2), 252-259.

Murray, Roger F. "Let's Not Blame The Institutions," **FAJ**, 1974, v30(2), 18-20.

Murray, Roger F. "New Life In The Corporate Bond Market," **FAJ**, 1953, v9(5), 13-18.

Murray, Roger F. "Pension Funds In The American Economy," **JOF**, 1968, v23(2), 331-336.

Murray, Roger F. "Pension Funds: Newest Among Major Financial Institutions," **JBR**, 1972-73, v3(4), 247-260.

Murray, Roger F. "The Market For Equities," **JOF**, 1964, v19(2), Part 1, 416-419.

Murray, Roger F. "The Outlook For The Stock Market," **JOF**, 1963, v18(2), 410-412.

Murray, Roger F. "The Penn Central Debacle: Lessons For Financial Analysis," **JOF**, 1971, v26(2), 327-332.

Murray, Rogert F. "The Future Of Private Pensions: Some Economic Aspects," **JRI**, 1967, v34(1), 27-32.

Muscarella, Chris J. "Price Performance Of Initial Public Offerings Of Master Limited Partnership Units," **FR**, 1988, v23(4), 513-521.

Muscarella, Chris J. (Barry, Christopher B., Chris J. Muscarella, John W. Peavy, III and Michael R. Vetsuypens. "The Role Of Venture Capital In The Creation Of Public Companies: Evidence From The Going-Public Process," **JFEC**, 1990, v27(2), 447-472.))

Muscarella, Chris J. (McConnell, John J. and Chris J. Muscarella. "Corporate Capital Expenditure Decisions And The Market Value Of The Firm," **JFEC**, 1985, v14(3), 399-422.)

Muscarella, Chris J. and Michael R. Vetsuypens. "The British Petroleum Stock Offering: An Application Of Option Pricing," **JACF**, 1989, v1(4), 74-80.

Muscarella, Chris J. and Michael R. Vetsuypens. "Efficiency And Organizational Structure: A Study Of Reverse LBOs," **JOF**, 1990, v45(5), 1389-1414.

Muscarella, Chris J. and Michael R. Vetsuypens. "A Simple Test Of Baron's Model Of IPO Underpricing," **JFEC**, 1989, v24(1), 125-136.

Muscarella, Chris J. and Michael R. Vetsuypens. "The Underpricing Of 'Second' Initial Public Offerings," **JFR**, 1989, v12(3), 183-192.

Mussa, Michael. "A Monetary Approach To Balance-Of-Payments Analysis," **JMCB**, 1974, v6(3), 333-351.

Mussa, Michael. "Equities, Interest, And The Stability Of The Inflationary Process," **JMCB**, 1975, v7(4), 433-448.

Mussa, Michael. "Safety And Soundness As An Objective Of Regulation Of Depository Institutions: Comment On Kareken," **JOB**, 1986, v59(1), 97-118.

Mussa, Michael. "The Welfare Cost Of Inflation And The Role Of Money As A Unit Of Account," **JMCB**, 1977, v9(2), 276-286.

Musumeci, James J. and Joseph F. Sinkey, Jr. "The International Debt Crisis, Investor Contagion, And Bank Security Returns In 1987: The Brazilian Experience," **JMCB**, 1990, v22(2), 209-220.

Musumeci, James J. and Joseph F. Sinkey, Jr. "The International Debt Crisis And Bank Loan-Loss-Reserve Decisions: The Signaling Content Of Partially Anticipated Events," **JMCB**, 1990, v22(3), 370-387.

Muth, Richard F. "Interest Rates, Contract Terms, And The Allocation Of Mortgage Funds," **JOF**, 1962, v17(1), 63-80.

Myddelton, D. R. "Why Sandilands Is Unacceptable," **JBFA**, 1976, v3(1), 97-104.

Myers, Barbara C. (Bower, Richard S., Christopher E. Nugent, Barbara C. Myers and J. Peter Williamson. "A Language For Financial Analysts," **FAJ**, 1967, v23(1), 121.)

Myers, Calvin R. "Comment: An Economic Model Of Trade Credit," **JFQA**, 1977, v12(3), 519-524.

Myers, Charles A. "Lessons From Abroad For American Management," **JOB**, 1960, v33(1), 1-9.

Myers, Daniel A., Richard V. Burkhauser and Karen C. Holden. "The Transition From Wife To Widow: The Importance Of Survivor Benefits To Widows," **JRI**, 1987, v54(4), 752-759.

Myers, Forest E. and Joe Van Walleghem. "Management Transferability In Rural Banks," **JBR**, 1984-85, v15(4), 229-233.

Myers, Forest E. and Thomas Hoenig. "Relative Operating Performance Of Withdrawing 10th Federal Reserve District Member Banks," **JBR**, 1979-80, v10(3), 181-183.

Myers, Forest E. (Meeker, Larry G. and Forest E. Myers. "Financing Bank Stock Ownership: A Question Of Conflict Of Interest," **JBF**, 1980, v4(2), 111-124.)

Myers, John H. "Depreciation For Fun And Profits," **FAJ**, 1967, v23(6), 117-123.

Myers, John H. "Federal Taxation Of Fire And Casualty Insurance Companies," **JRI**, 1959, v26(4), 69-71.

Myers, John H. "Irregular Wording In Auditor's Certificates," **FAJ**, 1953, v9(4), 52-54.

Myers, John H. "More On Depreciation Manipulation," **FAJ**, 1969, v25(5), 47-56.

Myers, Margaret G. "The Control Of Consumer Credit In Australia," **JOF**, 1961, v16(3), 409-422.

Myers, Phyllis Schiller and S. Travis Pritchett. "Rate Of Return On Differential Premiums For Selected Participating Life Insurance Contracts," **JRI**, 1983, v50(4), 569-586.

Myers, Phyllis Schiller. (Pritchett, S. Travis and Phyllis Schiller Myers. "Changes In Life Insurer Operating Expenses During Inflation," **JRI**, 1980, v47(2), 346-357.)

Myers, Robert J. "A Consideration Of Several Financing Proposals For Social Security," **JRI**, 1977, v44(3), 487-492.

Myers, Robert J. "A Method Of Automatically Adjusting The Maximum Earnings Base Under The OASDI," **JRI**, 1964, v31(3), 329-340.

Myers, Robert J. "A Method Of Automatically Adjusting The Maximum Earnings Base Under OASDI: Author's Comment," **JRI**, 1966, v33(2), 333-335.

Myers, Robert J. "An Actuarial Appraisal Of Congressional Proposals For Hospital Insurance For The Aged: Comment," **JRI**, 1966, v33(1), 135-138.

Myers, Robert J. "Analysis Of Perpetual Insurance: Comment," **JRI**, 1970, v37(3), 481-482.

Myers, Robert J. "Current Developments And Problems In Social Insurance," JRI, 1960, v27(1), 11-22.

Myers, Robert J. "Employee Social Insurance Contributions And Regressive Taxation," JRI, 1967, v34(4), 611-616.

Myers, Robert J. "Estimating Time-Varying Optimal Hedge Ratios On Futures Markets," JFM, 1991, v11(1), 39-54.

Myers, Robert J. "Factors In Interpreting Mortality After Retirement," JRI, 1954, v21, 56-63.

Myers, Robert J. "Gender Discrimination In Pension Plans: Comment," JRI, 1977, v44(1), 144-145.

Myers, Robert J. "Income Of Social Security Beneficiaries As Affected By Earnings Test And Income Taxes On Benefits," JRI, 1985, v52(2), 289-300.

Myers, Robert J. "Insuring The Senior Citizen - A Case Study: Comment," JRI, 1962, v29(4), 556.

Myers, Robert J. "Note On Funding Procedures And Investments Of Government Employee Retirement Systems," JRI, 1972, v39(1), 136-137.

Myers, Robert J. "Okun's Law And The Carter Social Security Proposals," JRI, 1978, v45(2), 335-339.

Myers, Robert J. "Role Of Social Insurance In Providing Fringe Benefits," JRI, 1965, v32(2), 267-272.

Myers, Robert J. "Social Security And Family Income Requirements: Comment," JRI, 1967, v34(3), 483-484.

Myers, Robert J. "Some Factual Points On Papers Dealing With Social Insurance And Social Security Perspective," JRI, 1963, v30(4), 584-586.

Myers, Robert J. "Tax-Benefit Ratios And Rates Of Return Under OASI: 1974 Retirees And Entrants: Comment," JRI, 1976, v43(1), 139-142.

Myers, Robert J. "The Case For Extending Social Security To Government Employees: Comment," JRI, 1982, v49(3), 463.

Myers, Robert J. "The Family Assistance Plan As A Solution To The Welfare Crisis: Comment," JRI, 1972, v39(3), 471-472.

Myers, Robert J. "The Impact Of Zero Population Growth On The OASDHI Program: Comment," JRI, 1975, v42(4), 659-660.

Myers, Robert J. "The Social Security Principle: Comment," JRI, 1961, v28(2), 120-122.

Myers, Robert J. "Various Proposals To Change The Financing Of Social Security," JRI, 1969, v36(3), 355-364.

Myers, Robert J. "What Would 'Medicare' Cost?: Comment," JRI, 1967, v34(1), 141-147.

Myers, Stewart C. and Gerald A. Pogue. "A Programming Approach To Corporate Financial Management," JOF, 1974, v29(2), 579-596.

Myers, Stewart C. and Nicholas S. Majluf. "Corporate Financing And Investment Decisions When Firms Have Information That Investors Do Not Have," JFEC, 1984, v13(2), 187-221.

Myers, Stewart C. and Stuart M. Turnbull. "Capital Budgeting And The Capital Asset Pricing Model: Good News And Bad News," JOF, 1977, v32(2), 321-333.

Myers, Stewart C. "A Note On Linear Budgeting And Capital Budgeting," JOF, 1972, v27(1), 89-92.

Myers, Stewart C. "A Time-State-Preference Model Of Security Valuation," JFQA, 1968, v3(1), 1-33.

Myers, Stewart C. "Determinants Of Corporate Borrowing," JFEC, 1977, v5(2), 147-175.

Myers, Stewart C. "Interactions Of Corporate Financing And Investment Decisions - Implications For Capital Budgeting: Comment," JOF, 1977, v32(1), 218-220.

Myers, Stewart C. "Interactions Of Corporate Financing And Investment Decisions - Implications For Capital Budgeting," JOF, 1974, v29(1), 1-25.

Myers, Stewart C. "Notes On An Expert System For Capital Budgeting," FM, 1988, v17(3), 23-31.

Myers, Stewart C. "On The Use Of Modern Portfolio Theory In Public Utility Rate Cases: Comment," FM, 1978, v7(3), 66-68.

Myers, Stewart C. "Presidential Address: The Capital Structure Puzzle," JOF, 1984, v39(3),575-592.

Myers, Stewart C. (Robichek, Alexander A. and Stewart C. Myers. "Valuation Of The Firm: Effects Of Uncertainty In A Market Context," JOF, 1966, v21(2), 215-227.)

Myers, Stewart C. (Robichek, Alexander A. and Stewart C. Myers. "Problems In The Theory Of Optimal Capital Structure," JFQA, 1966, v1(2), 1-35.)

Myers, Stewart C. (Robichek, Alexander A. and Stewart C. Myers. "Valuation Under Uncertainty: Comment," JFQA, 1968, v3(4), 479-483.)

Myers, Stewart C. (Robichek, Alexander A. and Stewart C. Myers. "Conceptual Problems In The Use Of Risk-Adjusted Discount Rates," JOF, 1966, v21(4),727-730.)

Myers, Stewart C., David A. Dill and Alberto J. Bautista. "Valuation Of Financial Lease Contracts," JOF, 1976, v31(3), 799-819.

Myrick, Donald. "Value-Added Ratios In Investment Analysis," FAJ, 1954, v10(5), 85-89.

NNN

Nachman, David C. "Spanning And Completeness With Options," RFS, 1988-89, v1(3), 311-328.

Nachman, David C. (John, Kose and David C. Nachman. "Risky Debt, Investment Incentives, And Reputation In A Sequential Equilibrium," JOF, 1985, v40(3), 863-878.)

Nachman, David C. (Neave, Edwin H. and David C. Nachman. "A Framework For Evaluating Securities Performance Forecasts," JBR, 1971-72, v2(2), 19-29.)

Naciri, Ahmed. (Morard, Bernard and Ahmed Naciri. "Options And Investment Strategies," JFM, 1979, v10(5), 505-518.)

Nader, Jahid S. "Duration, Systematic Risk, And Employee Valuation Of Default-Free Pension Claims," JRI, 1990, v57(4), 623-633.

Nadler, Marcus. "Impact Of The International Situation On Security Prices," FAJ, 1951, v7(1), 9-10.

Nadler, Marcus. "The Outlook For Money Rates," JOF, 1956, v11(2), 221-222.

Nadler, Paul S. "Commercial Banking In The Sixties," JOF, 1961, v16(2), 226-240.

Naert, Philippe A. (Hughes, G. David and Philippe A. Naert. "A Computer-Controlled Experiment In Consumer Behavior," JOB, 1970, v43(3), 354-372.)

Naes, Jude L., Jr. (Welch, Patrick J. and Jude L. Naes, Jr. "The Merger Guidelines, Concentration And Excess Capacity In Local Commercial Banking Markets," JBR, 1985-86, v16(3), 158-160.)

Naess, Ragnar D. "Changing Patterns Of Individual Equity Investment," FAJ, 1964, v20(4), 74-83.

Naess, Ragnar D. "Investment Management In 1955," FAJ, 1955, v11(1), 21-24.

Naess, Ragnar D. "Long Term Trend In American Economy," FAJ, 1947, v3(2), 26-37.

Naess, Ragnar D. "Managing Investments In A Changing Economy," FAJ, 1953, v9(2), 59-64.

Naess, Ragnar D. "Postwar Business Prospects," FAJ, 1945, v1(2), 3-10.

Naess, Ragnar D. "The Economy Faces A New Environment," FAJ, 1970, v26(1), 22-24.

Naess, Ragnar D. "The Enigma Of Investment Management," FAJ, 1949, v5(3), 5-10.

Nagarajan, Nandu J. (Agrawal, Anup and Nandu J. Nagarajan. "Corporate Capital Structure, Agency Costs, And Ownership Control: The Case Of All-Equity Firms," JOF, 1990, v45(4), 1325-1331.

Nagarajan, Nandu J. (Balachandran, Bala V., Nandu J. Nagarajan and Alfred Rappaport. "Threshold Margins For Creating Economic Value," FM, 1986, v15(1), 68-77.)

Nagata, Ernest A. "The Cost Structure Of Consumer Finance Small-Loan Operations," JOF, 1973, v28(5), 1327-1337.

Nagatani, Keizo. "A Monetary Growth Model With Variable Employment," JMCB, 1969, v1(2), 188-206.

Nagle, Thomas. "Economic Foundations For Pricing," JOB, 1984, v57(1), Part 2, S3-S34.

Nagorniak, John J. "Risk Adjusted Equity Performance Measurement," JOF, 1982, v37(2), 555-561.

Nagy, Charles. (Kreiser, Larry and Charles Nagy. "A Student Model For Product Costing And Pricing In An Inflationary Environment," JFED, 1981, v10, 54-58.)

Naik, Vasanttilak and Moon Lee. "General Equilibrium Pricing Of Options On The Market Portfolio With Discontinuous Returns," RFS, 1990, v3(4), 493-522.

Nair, R. D. (Linsmeier, Thomas J., R. D. Nair and Jerry J. Weygandt. "UK Tax Legislation And The Switch To The Liability Method For Income Taxes," JBFA, 1988, v15(3), 335-352.)

Nair, R. D. (Lobo, Gerald J., R. D. Nair and In Man Song. "Additional Evidence On The Information Content Of Dividends," JBFA, 1986, v13(4), 597-608.)

Nair, Richard S. "Investment Banking: Judge Medina In Retrospect," FAJ, 1960, v16(4), 35-40.

Najand, Mohammad. (McCarthy, Joseph, Mohammad Najand and Bruce Seifert. "Empirical Tests Of The Proxy Hypothesis," FR, 1990, v25(2), 251-264.)

Nakamura, Leonard I. (Lang, William W. and Leonard I. Nakamura. "Information Losses In A Dynamic Model Of Credit," JOF, 1989, v44(3), 731-746.)

Nally, Robert V. "The Computer And Home Office Management Development In Life Insurance," JRI, 1969, v36(3), 393-400.

Nammacher, Scott A. (Altman, Edward I. and Scott A. Nammacher. "The Default Rate Experience On High-Yield Corporate Debt," FAJ, 1985, v41(4), 25-41.)

Nantell, Timothy J. and Barbara Price. "An Analytical Comparison Of Variance And Semivariance Capital Market Theories," JFQA, 1979, v14(2), 221-242.

Nantell, Timothy J. and C. Robert Carlson. "The Cost Of Capital As A Weighted Average," JOF, 1975, v30(5), 1343-1355.

Nantell, Timothy J. "Equivalence Of Lease Vs. Buy Analyses," FM, 1973, v2(3), 61-65.

Nantell, Timothy J. (Dielman, Terry, Timothy J. Nantell and Roger L. Wright. "Price Effects Of Stock Repurchasing: A Random Coefficient Regression Approach," JFQA, 1980, v15(1), 175-189.)

Nantell, Timothy J. (McConnell, John J. and Timothy J. Nantell. "Corporate Combinations And Common Stock Returns: The Case Of Joint Ventures," JOF, 1985, v40(2), 519-536.)

Nantell, Timothy J. (Price, Kelly, Barbara Price and Timothy J. Nantell. "Variance And Lower Partial Moment Measures Of Systematic Risk: Some Analytical And Empirical Results," JOF, 1982, v37(3), 843-855.)

Nantell, Timothy J., Kelly Price and Barbara Price. "Mean-Lower Partial Moment Asset Pricing Model: Some Empirical Evidence," JFQA, 1982, v17(5), 763-782.

Naqvi, Nadeem. (Batra, Raveendra N. and Nadeem Naqvi. "International Debt, Factor Accumulation, And The Balance Of Payments," RIF, 1986, v6, 261-277.)

Narasimhan, Chakravarthi. "Competitive Promotional Strategies," JOB, 1988, v61(4), 427-450.

Narasimhan, Chakravarthi. (Jeuland, Abel P. and Chakravarthi Narasimhan. "Dealing--Temporary Price Cuts--By Seller As A Buyer Discrimination Mechanism," JOB, 1985, v58(3), 295-308.)

Narayanan, M. P. "Debt Versus Equity Under Asymmetric Information," JFQA, 1988, v23(1), 39-52.

Narayanan, M. P. "Managerial Incentives For Short-Term Results," JOF, 1985, v40(5), 1469-1484.

Narayanan, M. P. "Managerial Incentives For Short-Term Results: A Reply," JOF, 1987, v42(4), 1103-1104.

Narayanan, M. P. "Observability And The Payback Criterion," JOB, 1985, v58(3), 309-324.

Narayanan, M. P. "On The Resolution Of Agency Problems By Complex Financial Instruments: A Comment," JOF, 1987, v42(4), 1083-1090.

Narayanan, M. P. (Berkovitch, Elazar and M. P. Narayanan. "Competition And The Medium Of Exchange In Takeovers," RFS, 1990, v3(2), 153-174.)

Narayanan, M. P. and Suk-Pil Lim. "On The Call Provision In Corporate Zero-Coupon Bonds," JFQA, 1989, v24(1), 91-104.

Narayanan, P. (Altman, Edward I., Robert G. Haldeman and P. Narayanan. "ZETA Analysis: A New Model To Identify Bankruptcy Risk Of Corporations," JBF, 1977, v1(1), 29-54.)

Narayanaswamy, C. R. "A Mean-Variance Synthesis Of Corporate Financial Theory: A Note," JOF, 1988, v43(2), 529-530.

Naroff, Joel L. (Hill, Joanne and Joel L. Naroff. "The Effect Of Location On The Performance Of High Technology Firms," FM, 1984, v13(1), 27-36.)

Naroff, Joel L. (Melchert, David and Joel L. Naroff. "Central City Revitalization: A Predictive Model," AREUEA, 1987, v15(1), 664-683.)

Nash, Lee J. "The New Era Of Finance," FR, 1968, v1(3), 171-180.

Nash, Robert T. (Gramm, William P. and Robert T. Nash. "The Impact Of Changes In The Stock Of Money On Agricultural Income And Investment: A Comment," JMCB, 1971, v3(3), 709-711.)

Naslund, Bertil. "A Model Of Capital Budgeting Under Risk," JOB, 1966, v39(2), 257-271.

Nast, Donald A. (Osteryoung, Jerome S., Rodney L. Roenfeldt and Donald A. Nast. "Capital Asset Pricing Model And Traditional Risk For Capital Budgeting: A Reply," FR, 1978, v13(1), 90-93.)

Nast, Donald A. (Osteryoung, Jerome S., Rodney L. Roenfeldt and Donald A. Nast. Capital Asset Pricing Model And Traditional Risk For Capital Budgeting," FR, v12(1), 48-58.)

Natarajan, Ashok. (Ofer, Aharon R. and Ashok Natarajan. "Convertible Call Policies: An Empirical Analysis Of An Information-Signaling Hypothesis," JFEC, 1987, v19(1), 91-108.)

Nathan, Harold C. "Economic Analysis Of Usury Laws," JBR, 1979-80, v10(4), 200-211.

Nathan, Harold C. "Nonbank Organizations And The McFadden Act," JBR, 1980-81, v11(2), 80-86.

Nathan, Harold. (Mayer, Thomas and Harold Nathan. "Mortgage Rates And Regulation Q," JMCB, 1983, v15(1), 107-115.)

Nathan, Kevin S. and Terrence B. O'Keefe. "The Rise In Takeover Premiums: An Exploratory Study," JFEC, 1989, v23(1), 101-120.

Nathan, Kevin. (Murphy, Austin and Kevin Nathan. "An Analysis Of Merger Financing," FR, 1989, v24(4), 551-566.)

Nathan, Richard P. "The Uses Of Shared Revenue," JOF, 1975, v30(2), 557-565.

National Bureau Exploratory Committee On Research In The Capital Markets. "Research In The Capital Markets," JOF, 1964, v19(2), Part 2, 1-43.

Natrella, Vito. "Tax Returns Vs. Company Books," FAJ, 1969, v25(2), 37-43.

Nattress, Dayle. (Girton, Lance and Dayle Nattress. "Monetary Innovations And Interest Rates," JMCB, 1985, v17(3), 289-297.)

Naumann-Etienne, Ruediger. "A Framework For Financial Decisions In Multinational Corporations--Summary Of Recent Research," JFQA, 1974, v9(5), 859-874.

Nauss, Robert M. and Bradford R. Keeler. "Optimizing Municipal Bond Bids: Reply To A Comment," JBR, 1983-84, v14(3), 239-240.

Nauss, Robert M. and Bradford R. Keeler. "Optimizing Municipal Bond Bids", 1981-82, v12(3), 174-181.

Nauss, Robert M. and Robert E. Markland. "Solving Lock Box Location Problems," FM, 1979, v8(1), 21-31.

Nauss, Robert M. "Generating Optimal True Interest Cost Bids For New Municipal Bond Competitive Issues," JBF, 1987, v11(2), 329-344.

Navarre, Joseph A. "Perfecting The System Of State Regulation Of The Business Of Insurance," JRI, 1958, v25(1), 65-68.

Navarro, Peter. "How Wall Street Ranks The Public Utility Commissions," FAJ, 1983, v39(6), 46-49.

Navarro, Peter. "Why Do Corporations Give To Charity?," JOB, 1988, v61(1), 65-94.

Navratil, Frank J. "An Aggregate Model Of The Credit Union Industry," JOF, 1981, v36(2), 539-549.

Navratil, Frank J. "The Estimation Of Mortgage Prepayment Rates," JFR, 1985, v8(2), 107-117.

Navratil, Frank J. (Clayton, Ronnie J. and Frank J. Navratil. "The Management Of Interest Rate Risk: Comment," JPM, 1984-85, v11(4), 64-66)

Navratil, Frank J. (Wolken, John D. and Frank J. Navratil. "Economies Of Scale In Credit Unions: Further Evidence," JOF, 1980, v35(3), 769-777.)

Navratil, Frank J. (Wolken, John D. and Frank J. Navratil. "The Economic Impact Of The Federal Credit Union Usury Ceiling," JOF, 1981, v36(5), 1157-1168.)

Nawalkha, S. K. and N. J. Lacey. "Generalized Solutions Of Higher-Order Duration Measures," JBF, 1990, v14(6), 1143-1150.

Nawalkha, Sanjay K. and Nelson J. Lacey. "Closed-Form Solutions Of Higher-Order Duration Measures," FAJ, 1988, v44(6), 82-84.

Nawalkha, Sanjay K., Nelson J. Lacey and Thomas Schneeweis. "Closed-Form Solutions Of Convexity And M-Square," FAJ, 1990, v46(1), 75-77.

Nawrocki, David N. "Development Of Computer Programs For Application Of Portfolio Theory In The Classroom," JFED, 1980, v9, 93-97.

Nawrocki, David N. (Philippatos, George C. and David N. Nawrocki. "The Information Inaccuracy Of Stock Market Forecasts: Some New Evidence Of Dependence On The New York Stock Exchange," JFQA, 1973, v8(3), 445-458.)

Nawrocki, David. "A Comparison Of Risk Measures When Used In A Simple Portfolio Selection Heuristic," JBFA, 1983, v10(2), 183-194.

Nawrocki, David. "Entropy, Bifurcation, And Dynamic Market Disequilibrium," FR, 1984, v19(2), 266-284.

Nawrocki, David. "Short Sales And Mechanical Trading Rules," FR, 1981, v16(2), 16-29.

Nayar, Nandkumar. (Cowan, Arnold R., Nandkumar Nayar and Ajai K. Singh. "Stock Returns Before And After Calls Of Convertible Bonds," JFQA, 1990, v25(4), 549-554.)

Ndubizu, Gordian, Augustine C. Arize and P. R. Chandy. "The Market Model Specification And The Structural Stability Of The Beta," IJOF, 1989, v1(2), 1-14.

Ndubizu, Gordian. (Arize, Augustine and Gordian Ndubizu. "Modelling Money Demand Functions With Exchange Rates: Regression Estimates And Diagnostic Tests," IJOF, 1990, v2(2), 88-104.)

Neal, Gregory L. (Shannon, Donald S., Keith H. Johnson and Gregory L. Neal. "How To Beat Those Index Funds," JPM, 1977-78, v4(1), 28-33.)

Neal, J. (Agnello, W., W. Brueggeman, G. Decker, R. Griffith, R.

Leftwich, R. Moore, J. Neal, B. Sternlicht, B. Wallach, W. Wardrop and C. Zinngrabe. "Panel: Corporate Real Estate Roundtable," JACF, 1990, v3(1), 6-38.)

Neal, Kathleen. "Informational Efficiency In The Gold Futures Market: A Semistrong Form Test," RFM, 1988, v7(1), 78-88.

Neal, Kathleen. "Informational Efficiency In The Gold Futures Market: A Semistrong Form Test," RFM, 1988, v7(1), 78-88.

Neal, Robert R. "Current Developments And Problems In Health Insurance," JRI, 1960, v27(1), 1-10.

Neal, Robert. "Potential Competition And Actual Competition In Equity Options," JOF, 1987, v42(3), 511-531.

Neal, Robert. (Bonser-Neal, Catherine, Greggory Brauer, Robert Neal and Simon Wheatley. "International Investment Restrictions And Closed-End Country Fund Prices," JOF, 1990, v45(2), 523-548.)

Neamann, Seev. "Ownership And Performance: Stock And Mutual Life Insurance Companies: Comment," JRI, 1973, v40(4), 631-635.

Neave, Edwin H. and C. Harvey Rorke. "Risk, Ruin, And Investment Analysis: A Comment," JFQA, 1973, v8(3), 517-526.

Neave, Edwin H. and David C. Nachman. "A Framework For Evaluating Securities Performance Forecasts," JBR, 1971-72, v2(2), 19-29.

Neely, Walter P. "Banking Acquisitions: Acquirer And Target Shareholder Returns," FM, 1987, v16(4),66-73.

Neely, Walter P. and David P. Rochester. "Operating Performance And Merger Benefits: The Savings And Loan Experience," FR, 1987, v22(1), 111-130.

Neenan, William B. "Review Of Institutional Activity In The Equity Market, 1951-54," JOF, 1957, v12(4), 468-488.

Neff, David. (Hauser, Robert J. and David Neff. "Pricing Options On Agricultural Futures: Departures From Traditional Theory," JFM, 1985, v5(4), 539-577.)

Neftci, Salih N. and Andrew J. Policano. "Can Chartists Outperform The Market? Market Efficiency Tests For 'Technical Analysis'," JFM, 1984, v4(4), 465-478.

Neftci, Salih N. (Edwards, Franklin R. and Salih N. Neftci. "Extreme Price Movements And Margin Levels In Futures Markets," JFM, 1988, v8(6), 639-656.)

Neggers, Joseph. (Dickerson, O. D. and Joseph Neggers. "A General Risk Theory," JRI, 1964, v31(3), 451-462.)

Negishi, Takashi. "The Supply Of Money, Innovations, And The Business Cycle In Japan: A Review Article," JOF, 1968, v23(5), 875-886.

Neidig, C. P. "World Chemical Companies," FAJ, 1968, v24(1), 51-65.

Neil, Herbert E., Jr. and William C. Norby. "Dynamic Factors In Corporate Profits," FAJ, 1962, v18(4), 33-39.

Neil, Herbert E., Jr. "Implications Of The Proposed Tax Cut," FAJ, 1963, v19(4), 65-72.

Neil, Herbert E., Jr. "Incidence Of Inflation Upon Consumer Spending Units, 1949-58," JOF, 1962, v17(3), 405-431.

Neil, Herbert E., Jr. "International Monetary Situation," FAJ, 1970, v26(1), 70-81.

Neil, Herbert E., Jr. "Moderating Inflation In 1969," FAJ, 1969, v25(3), 21-28.

Neil, Herbert E., Jr. "The Consumer's Tomorrow's Buying," FAJ, 1967, v23(3), 18-24.

Neil, Herbert E., Jr. "The Surtax," FAJ, 1967, v23(6), 105-107.

Neil, Herbert E., Jr. "The U.S. Balance Of Payments Position - Deficit Or Surplus?," FAJ, 1964, v20(4), 135-139.

Neil, Herbert E., Jr. "Unemployment - Structural?," FAJ, 1964, v20(3), 32-37.

Neill, Humphrey B. "I Was There," JPM, 1974-75, v1(2), 81-84.

Nelli, Humbert O. "Insurance Transactions And The U.S. Balance Of Payments," JRI, 1964, v31(1), 1-12.

Nelli, Humbert O. "Insurance And The Bicentennial," JRI, 1976, v43(2), 191-201.

Nelli, Humbert O. "The Earliest Insurance Contract - A New Discovery," JRI, 1972, v39(2), 215-220.

Nelson, Bert. (Katz, Steven, Steven Lilien and Bert Nelson. "Stock Market Behavior Around Bankruptcy Model Distress And Recovery Predictions," FAJ, 1985, v41(1), 70-74.)

Nelson, Charles R. "Adjustment Lags Versus Information Lags: A Test Of Alternative Explanations Of The Phillips Curve Phenomenon," JMCB, 1981, v13(1), 1-11.

Nelson, Charles R. "Adjustment Lags Versus Information Lags: A Test Of Alternative Explanations Of The Phillips Curve Phenomenon: A Comment," JMCB, 1981, v13(4), 494-496.

Nelson, Charles R. "Inflation And Rates Of Return On Common Stock," JOF, 1976, v31(2), 471-483.

Nelson, Charles R. "Inflation And Capital Budgeting," JOF, 1976, v31(3), 923-931.

Nelson, Charles R. "Rational Expectations And The Predictive Efficiency Of Economic Models," JOB, 1975, v48(3), 331-343.

Nelson, Charles R. (Cooper, J. Phillip and Charles R. Nelson. "The Ex Ante Prediction Performance Of The St. Louis And FRB-MIT-PENN Econometric Models And Some Results On Composite Predictors," JMCB, 1975, v7(1), 1-32.)

Nelson, Charles R. (Siegel, Andrew F. and Charles R. Nelson. "Long-Term Behavior Of Yield Curves," JFQA, 1988, v23(1), 105-110.)

Nelson, Charles R. (Turner, Christopher M., Richard Startz and Charles R. Nelson. "A Markov Model Of Heteroskedasticity, Risk, And Learning In The Stock Market," JFEC, 1989, v25(1), 3-20.)

Nelson, Charles R. and Andrew F. Siegel. "Parsimonious Modeling Of Yield Curves," JOB, 1987, v60(4), 473-490.

Nelson, Charles R. and Richard Startz. "The Distribution Of The Instrumental Variables Estimator And Its t-Ratio When The Instrument Is A Poor One," JOB, 1990, v63(1), Part 2, S125-S140.

Nelson, Daniel B. and Krishna Ramaswamy. "Simple Binomial Processes As Diffusion Approximations In Financial Models," RFS, 1990, v3(3), 393-430.

Nelson, Harry L., Jr. "Make Investment Advisers Accountable!," FAJ, 1973, v29(1), 19-22.

Nelson, J. R. (Murphy, J. E., Jr. and J. R. Nelson. "Five Financial Principles," FAJ, 1971, v27(2), 38-52.)

Nelson, J. Russell. "Price Effects In Rights Offerings," JOF, 1965, v20(4), 647-650.

Nelson, J. Russell. (Murphy, Joseph E., Jr. and J. Russell Nelson.

"Stability Of P/E Ratios," FAJ, 1969, v25(2), 77-80.)

Nelson, J. Russell. (Murphy, Joseph E., Jr. and J. Russell Nelson. "Random And Nonrandom Relationships Among Financial Variables: A Financial Model," JFQA, 1971, v6(2), 875-885.)

Nelson, Jack M. (Harrington, Scott E. and Jack M. Nelson. "A Regression-Based Methodology For Solvency Surveillance In The Property-Liability Insurance Industry," JRI, 1986, v53(4), 583-605.)

Nelson, Phillip. "The Economic Consequences Of Advertising," JOB, 1975, v48(2), 213-241.

Nelson, Phillip. "Wages And The Cost Of Search," JOB, 1970, v43(2), 210-216.

Nelson, Ray D. and Robert A. Collins. "A Measure Of Hedging's Performance," JFM, 1985, v5(1), 45-55.

Nelson, Richard R. "The Economics Of Invention: A Survey Of The Literature," JOB, 1959, v32(2), 101-127.

Nelson, Richard W. "Branching, Scale Economies, And Banking Costs," JBF, 1985, v9(2), 177-192.

Nelson, Robert A. "Interest Conflicts In Transportation," JOB, 1964, v37(2), 167-178.

Nelson, Robert E. "Property-Liability Company Exits," JRI, 1971, v38(3), 357-366.

Nelson, Susan Logan. (Nelson, Theron R. and Susan Logan Nelson. "Franchise Affiliation And Brokerage Firm Selection: A Perceptual Investigation," JRER, 1988, v3(2), 87-107.)

Nelson, Theron R. and Joseph Rabianski. "Consumer Preferences In Housing Market Analysis: An Application Of Multidimensional Scaling Techniques," AREUEA, 1988, v16(2), 138-159.

Nelson, Theron R. and Susan Logan Nelson. "Franchise Affiliation And Brokerage Firm Selection: A Perceptual Investigation," JRER, 1988, v3(2), 87-107.

Nelson, William. (Imai, Yutaka and William Nelson. "The Erroneous MEC Function: Comment," JOF, 1972, v27(1), 136-137.)

Nemmers, Erwin Esser and George E. Rejda. "The Impact Of The Business Cycle On New Life Insurance Purchases: Comment," JRI, 1964, v31(4), 631-640.

Nerlove, Marc. "On The Efficiency Of The Coal Industry," JOB, 1959, v32(3), 271-278.

Nerlove, S. H. "Common Stocks As Investments For American Life Insurance Companies. A Non-Academic View II," JOF, 1949, v4(1), 60-77.

Nerlove, S. H. "Common Stocks As Investments For American Life Insurance Companies, A Non-Academic View. I," JOF, 1948, v3(3), 39-51.

Nerlove, S. H. "Professor Machlup On Monopoly," JOB, 1953, v26(3), 200-208.

Nerlove, S. H. "Some Problems Related To Life Insurance Receiverships," JRI, 1934, v1, 3-9.

Nesbitt, Stephen L. (Davanzo, Lawrence E. and Stephen L. Nesbitt. "Performance Fees For Investment Management," FAJ, 1987, v43(1), 14-20.)

Ness, Walter L., Jr. "A Linear Programming Approach To Financing The Multinational Corporation," FM, 1972, v1(3), 88-100.

Ness, Walter L., Jr. (Cohen, Kalman J., Walter L. Ness, Jr., Hitoshi Okuda, Robert A. Schwartz and David K. Whitcomb. "The Determinants Of Common Stock Returns Volatility: An International Comparison," JOF, 1976, v31(2), 733-739.)

Ness, Walter L., Jr. (Cohen, Kalman J., Steven F. Maier, Walter L. Ness, Jr., Hitoshi Okuda, Robert A. Schwartz and David K. Whitcomb. "The Impact Of Designated Market Makers On Security Prices," JBF, 1977, v1(3), 219-247.)

Neter, J., C. A. Williams, Jr. and G. A. Whitmore. "Comparison Of Independent And Joint Decision-Making For Two Insurance Decisions," JRI, 1968, v35(1), 87-105.

Neter, John and C. Arthur Williams, Jr. "Acceptability Of Three Normative Methods In Insurance Decision Making," JRI, 1971, v38(3), 385-408.

Neter, John and C. Arthur Williams, Jr. "Acceptability Of Three Normative Methods In Insurance Decision Making: Reply," JRI, 1972, v39(4), 466-467.

Neter, John and C. Arthur Williams, Jr. "Acceptability Of Three Normative Methods In Insurance Decision Making: An Alternative Hypothesis: Reply," JRI, 1974, v41(2), 366.

Neter, John. (Greene, Mark R., John Neter and Lester I. Tenney. "Annuity Rents And Rates - Guaranteed Vs. Current," JRI, 1977, v44(3), 383-401.)

Netter, Jeffry M. (Mitchell, Mark L. and Jeffry M. Netter. "Triggering The 1987 Stock Market Crash: Antitakeover Provisions In The Proposed House Ways And Means Tax Bill," JFEC, 1989, v24(1), 37-68.)

Netter, Jeffry M. and Mark L. Mitchell. "Stock-Repurchase Announcements And Insider Transactions After The October 1987 Stock Market Crash," FM, 1989, v18(3), 84-96.

Netter, Jeffry and Annette Poulsen. "State Corporation Laws And Shareholders: The Recent Experience," FM, 1989, v18(3), 29-40.

Netter, Jeffry. (Lehn, Kenneth, Jeffry Netter and Annette Poulsen. "Consolidating Corporate Control: Dual-Class Recapitalizations Versus Leveraged Buyouts," JFEC, 1990, v27(2) 557-580.)

Netter, Joseph, II. "Dual-Purpose Funds," FAJ, 1967, v23(4), 85-87.

Nettles, G. Fuhrman. "Investment Opportunities In Electrical Equipment Industry," FAJ, 1958, v14(5), 41-44.

Netzer, Dick and Abner D. Goldstine. "Types Of Money Use In The 1950's," JOF, 1962, v17(4), 606-621.

Netzer, Dick. "State-Local Response To Changing Credit Conditions: The Institutional Obstacles," JOF, 1960, v15(2), 221-231.

Neuberger, Anthony. (Hodges, Stewart D. and Anthony Neuberger. "Optimal Replication Of Contingent Claims Under Transactions Costs," RFM, 1989, v8(2), 222-239.)

Neuberger, Brian M. and Carl T. Hammond. "A Study Of Underwriters' Experience With Unseasoned New Issues," JFQA, 1974, v9(2), 165-177.

Neuberger, Brian M. and Chris A. La Chapelle. "Unseasoned New Issue Price Performance On Three Tiers: 1975-1980," FM, 1983, v12(3), 23-28.

Neuhauser, John. (Viscione, Jerry and John Neuhauser. "Capital Expenditure Decisions In Moderately Sized Firms," FR, 1974, v9(1), 16-23.)

Neumann, Manfred J. M. "Intervention In The Mark/Dollar Market: The Authorities' Reaction Function," JIMF, 1984, v3(2), 223-240.

Neumann, Manfred J. M. "Price Expectations And The Interest Rate In An Open Economy: Germany, 1960-72," JMCB, 1977, v9(1), Part 2, 206-227.

Neumann, Manfred J. M. "The 1972 Report Of The German Council Of Economic Experts: Inflation And Stabilization," JMCB, 1973, v5(4), 950-959.

Neumann, Manfred J. (Bruner, Karl, Michele Fratianni, Jerry L. Jordan, Allan H. Meltzer and Manfred J. Neumann. "Fiscal And Monetary Policies In Moderate Inflation," JMCB, 1973, v5(1), Part II, 313-354.)

Neumann, Seev and Eli Segev. "Human Capital And Risk Management: A Proposal For A New Insurance Product," JRI, 1978, v45(2), 344-352.

Neumann, Seev and Eli Segev. "Human Capital And Risk Management: A Proposal For A New Insurance Product," JRI, 1978, v45(3), 522-530.

Neumann, Seev and Yehuda Shenhav. "Short-Term Impact Of War Economy On The Insurance Industry In Israel," JRI, 1977, v44(1), 87-102.

Neumann, Seev. "Demand For Life Insurance: Comment," JRI, 1970, v37(1), 151-156.

Neumann, Seev. "Inflation And Sales Of Life Insurance: Comments," JRI, 1968, v35(4), 629-635.

Neumann, Seev. "Inflation And Saving Through Life Insurance," JRI, 1969, v36(4), 567-582.

Neumann, Seev. "Inflation And Saving Through Life Insurance: Reply," JRI, 1972, v39(2), 326-330.

Neumann, Seev. "Insurance Subsidies And Welfare Economics: Comment," JRI, 1975, v42(3), 529-536.

Neumann, Seev. "Quantitative Determinants Of Income With Some Implications To Insurance: Comment," JRI, 1971, v38(1), 153-157.

Neumann, Seev. "Spatial Risk And Return Relationships: A Reconsideration: Comment," JRI, 1975, v42(2), 323-329.

Neumann, Seev. (Adar, Zvi and Seev Neumann. "On Optimal Property Insurance Policies," JRI, 1978, v45(1), 95-108.)

Neumann, Seev. (Mehr, Robert I. and Seev Neumann. "Delphi Forecasting Project," JRI, 1970, v37(2), 241-246.)

Neumann, Seev. (Pfeffer, Irving and Seev Neumann. "The Survival Probability Of A New Life Insurance Company," JRI, 1966, v33(4), 597-602.)

Neumann, Seev. (Pfeffer, Irving and Seev Neumann. "The Survival Probability Of A New Life Insurance Company," JRI, 1967, v34(1), 9-13.)

Neumark, David, P. A. Tinsley and Suzanne Tosini. "After-Hours Stock Prices And Post-Crash Hangovers," JOF, 1991, v46(1), 159-178.

Neupert, Peter M. (Dawson, James P., Peter M. Neupert and Clyde P. Stickney. "Restating Financial Statements For Alternative GAAPs: Is It Worth The Effort?," FAJ, 1980, v36(6), 38-46.)

Neveu, Raymond P. "A Note On Environmental Planning For Banks," JBR, 1975-76, v6(3), 222-223.

Neveu, Raymond P. "Teamwork In Student Programming Projects," JFED, 1972, v1, 105.

Nevin, John R. (Anderson, Dan R. and John R. Nevin. "Determinants Of Young Marrieds' Life Insurance Purchasing Behavior: An Empirical Investigation," JRI, 1975, v42(3), 375-387.)

Newberg, Bruce L. (Greenblatt, Joel M., Richard Pzena and Bruce L. Newberg. "How The Small Investor Can Beat The Market," JPM, 1980-81, v7(4), 48-52.)

Newbold, P. (Bos, T. and P. Newbold. "An Empirical Investigation Of The Possibility Of Stochastic Systematic Risk In The Market Model," JOB, 1984, v57(1), Part 1, 35-42.)

Newbold, Paul. (Gentry, James A., Paul Newbold and David T. Whitford. "Funds Flow Components, Financial Ratios, And Bankruptcy," JBFA, 1987, v14(4), 595-606.)

Newbold, Paul. (Gentry, James A., David T. Whitford and Paul Newbold. "Predicting Industrial Bond Ratings With A Probit Model And Funds Flow Components," FR, 1988, v23(3), 269-286.)

Newbold, Paul. (Gentry, James A., Paul Newbold and David T. Whitford. "Predicting Bankruptcy: If Cash Flow's Not The Bottom Line, What Is?," FAJ, 1985, v41(5), 47-56.)

Newbold, Paul. (Gentry, James A., Paul Newbold and David T. Whitford. "Profiles Of Cash Flow Components," FAJ, 1990, v46(5), 41-48.)

Newbold, Paul. (Lee, Cheng F., Paul Newbold, Joseph E. Finnerty and Chen-Chin Chu. "On Accounting-Based, Market-Based And Composite-Based Beta Predictions: Methods And Implications," FR, 1986, v21(1), 51-68.)

Newbould, G. D. and K. W. Wilson. "Alternative Measures Of Company Size - A Note For Researchers," JBFA, 1977, v4(1), 131-132.

Newbould, Gerald D. (Merrett, A. J. and Gerald D. Newbould. "CEPS: The Illusion Of Corporate Growth," JPM, 1982-83, v9(1), 5-10.)

Newbould, Gerald D. (Merrett, A. J. and Gerald D. Newbould. "Integrating Financial Performance And Stock Valuation," JPM, 1983-84, v10(1), 27-35.)

Newcomb, Robinson. "Forecasting 1958," FAJ, 1958, v14(1), 41-44.

Newell, Gale E. "Adequacy Of Quarterly Financial Data," FAJ, 1969, v25(6), 37-43.

Newell, Gale E. "Revisions Of Reported Quarterly Earnings," JOB, 1971, v44(3), 282-285.

Newhouse, Joseph P. and Vincent Taylor. "The Subsidy Problem In Hospital Insurance: A Proposal," JOB, 1970, v43(4), 452-456.

Newhouse, Joseph P. and Vincent Taylor. "A New Type Of Hospital Insurance," JRI, 1971, v38(4), 601-612.

Newlyn, Walter T. "The Definition Of Money: Net Wealth And Neutrality As Criteria: A Reply," JMCB, 1972, v4(1), 118-120.

Newman, D. Paul. "Monitoring Decisions In An Agency Setting," JBFA, 1979, v6(2), 203-222.

Newman, John L. (Boschen, John F. and John L. Newman. "Monetary Effects On The Real Interest Rate In An Open Economy: Evidence From The Argentine Indexed Bond Market," JIMF, 1989, v8(2), 201-218.)

Newman, Joseph A. and John M. Wachowicz, Jr. "Memorandums In The Classroom," JFED, 1989, v18, 25-28.

Newman, Monroe. "Issues In Temporary Disability Insurance," **JRI**, 1957, v24(1), 61-72.

Newman, Monroe. "Joint Administration Of Social Insurance Programs," **JRI**, 1958, v25(4), 43-50.

Newman, R. F. "Which Department Stores?," **FAJ**, 1956, v12(5), 55-60.

Newman, Ruth. (Branch, Ben and Ruth Newman. "Term Papers In Investments: Alternatives And Style," **JFED**, 1985, v14, 47-59.)

Newman, Sandra and James Reschovsky. "An Evaluation Of The One-Time Capital Gains Exclusion For Older Homeowners," **AREUEA**, 1987, v15(1), 704-724.

Newman, William H. "Basic Objectives Which Shape The Character Of A Company," **JOB**, 1953, v26(4), 211-223.

Newton, Robert L. "Investment Evaluation Of Scientific Research," **FAJ**, 1960, v16(2), 81-84.

Newton, Robert (Bohmfalk, John F., Jr. and Robert L. Newton. "A Look Ahead For Chemical Industry," **FAJ**, 1957, v13(2), 33-38.)

Ng, D. S. "Information Accuracy And Social Welfare Under Homogeneous Beliefs," **JFEC**, 1975, v2(1),53-70.

Ng, D. (Winsen, J. and D. Ng. "Investor Behavior And Changes In Accounting Methods," **JFQA**, 1976, v11(5), 873-881.)

Ng, David S. "Pareto-Optimality Of Authentic Information," **JOF**, 1977, v32(5), 1717-1728.

Ng, Francis K. W. (Fisher, Lawrence, Ivan E. Brick and Francis K. W. Ng. "Tax Incentives And Financial Innovation: The Case Of Zero-Coupon And Other Deep-Discount Corporate Bonds," **FR**, 1983, v18(4), 292-305.)

Ng, Nancy. "Detecting Spot Price Forecasts In Futures Prices Using Causality Tests," **RFM**, 1987, v6(2), 250-267.

Ng, Victor. (Hamao, Yasushi, Ronald W. Masulis and Victor Ng. "Correlations In Price Changes And Volatility Across International Stock Markets," **RFS**, 1990, v3(2), 281-308.)

Nga, Nguyen Anh. "Monetary Policy, Inflation, And Devaluation: A Case Study Of The Philippines," **JMCB**, 1979, v11(2), 235-242.

Nguyen, D. T. and R. A. Whittaker. "Inflation, Replacement And Amortisation Funds: A Case Study Of U.K. Industries," **JBFA**, 1976, v3(1), 43-52.

Nguyen, D. T. "Inflation, Inflation Accounting, And The Corporate Viability Condition," **JBFA**, 1976, v3(3), 117-122.

Nguyen, Duc-Tho and Stephen J. Turnovsky. "Monetary And Fiscal Policies In An Inflationary Economy: A Simulation Approach," **JMCB**, 1979, v11(3), 259-283.

Nguyen, Dung. "Advertising, Random Sales Response, And Brand Competition: Some Theoretical And Econometric Implications," **JOB**, 1987, v60(2), 259-280.

Nguyen, Hong V. "Money In The Aggregate Production Function: Reexamination And Further Evidence," **JMCB**, 1986, v18(2), 141-151.

Niarchos, N. A. and C. W. J. Granger. "The Gold Sovereign Market In Greece - An Unusual Speculative Market," **JOF**, 1972, v27(5), 1127-1135.

Nicholas, James C. "Housing Costs And Prices Under Regional Regulation," **AREUEA**, 1981, v9(4), 384-396.

Nicholls, Des. (Hodgson, Allan and Des Nicholls. "The Impact Of Index Futures Markets On Australian Sharemarket Volatility," **JBFA**, 1991, v18(2), 267-280.)

Nichols, Alan. "A Note On The Lerner-Carleton Analysis," **JOF**, 1968, v23(5), 857-861.

Nichols, Alan. "Elasticity Of Capital Supply And Second Order Conditions: Comment," **JOF**, 1967, v22(4), 665-667.

Nichols, Alan. "The Optimal Rate Of Investment In A Firm: Comment," **JOF**, 1970, v25(3), 682-684.

Nichols, Archie. "The Liquidation Of Insurance Carriers In The Commonwealth Of Pennsylvania," **JRI**, 1961, v28(2), 45-50.

Nichols, Donald A. "A Note On Inflation And Common Stock Values," **JOF**, 1968, v23(4), 655-657.

Nichols, Donald R. "A Study Of The Market Valuation Of Extraordinary Items Reported In Financial Statements," **FR**, 1977, v12(2), 1-17.

Nichols, Donald R. "Operating Income And Distributable Income Under Replacement Cost Accounting: The Long-Life Asset Replacement Problem," **FAJ**, 1982, v38(1), 68-73.

Nichols, Donald R. (Brown, Homer A., Jr. and Donald R. Nichols. "A Deterrent To Investment Mobility," **FAJ**, 1969, v25(3), 131-137.

Nichols, Donald R. (Pan, Judy, Donald R. Nichols and O. Maurice Joy. "Sales Forecasting Practices Of Large U.S. Industrial Firms," **FM**, 1977, v6(3), 72-77.)

Nichols, Len M. (Jose, Manuel L., Len M. Nichols and Jerry L. Stevens. "Contributions Of Diversification, Promotion, And R&D To The Value Of Multiproduct Firms: A Tobin's q Approach," **FM**, 1986, v15(4), 33-42.)

Nichols, William D. and Bill McDonald. "Stock Splits And Market Anomalies," **FR**, 1983, v18(4), 237-256.

Nichols, William D. and Stewart L. Brown. "Assimilating Earnings And Split Information: Is The Capital Market Becoming More Efficient?," **JFEC**, 1981, v9(3), 309-315.

Nichols, William D. "Security Price Reaction To Occasional Small Stock Dividends," **FR**, 1981, v16(1), 54-62.

Nichols, William D. (Lovata, Linda M., William D. Nichols and Kirk L. Philipich. "Defeasing Discounted Debt: An Economic Analysis," **FM**, 1987, v16(1),41-45.)

Nichols, William D. (McDonald, Bill and William D. Nichols. "Nonstationarity Of Beta And Tests Of Market Efficiency," **JFR**, 1984, v7(4), 315-322.)

Nichols, William D. (Morris, Michael H., William D. Nichols and James W. Pattillo. "Capitalization Of Interest, Materiality Judgement Divergence And Users' Information Needs," **JBFA**, 1984, v11(4), 547-555.)

Nicholson, Edward A. and Robert L. Litscher. "Long-Range Planning In Banking: Ten Cases In The U.S. And Britain," **JBR**, 1973-74, v4(1), 31-40.

Nicholson, G. A., Jr. and T. E. O'Hara. "Investment Clubs," **FAJ**, 1968, v24(3), 141-146.

Nicholson, S. F., M. Smith and R. B. Willis. "Investment Perspectives - 150 Years," **FAJ**, 1979, v35(6), 23-37.

Nicholson, S. Francis. "Price-Earnings Ratios," **FAJ**, 1960, v16(4), 43-45.

Nicholson, S. Francis. "Price Ratios," **FAJ**, 1968, v24(1), 105-109.

Nickelsburg, Gerald. "Rediscounting Private Dollar Debt And Capital Flight In Ecuador," **JIMF**, 1986, v5(4), 497-503.

Nickerson, David. (Khoury, Sarkis J., David Nickerson and Venkatraman Sadanand. "Exchange Rate Uncertainty And Precommitment In Symmetric Duopoly: A New Theory Of Multinational Production," **RDIBF**, 1991, v4/5, 439-473.)

Nickle, Carl O. "Oil And Gas And Canada's Future," **FAJ**, 1952, v8(5), 61-65.

Nickson, Jack W., Jr. and R. Bryan Grinnan III. "Should Banks Enter The Leasing Field?," **FR**, 1968, v1(3), 181-190.

Nicol, David J. "A Note On Capital Budgeting Techniques And The Reinvestment Rate: Comment," **JOF**, 1981, v36(1), 193-195.

Nicols, Alfred. "Economic Issues In THe DuPont-General Motors Case," **JOB**, 1960, v33(3), 227-251.

Nicosia, F. M. "Marketing And Alderson's Functionalism," **JOB**, 1962, v35(4), 403-413.

Nicosia, Francesco M. "Perceived Risk, Information Processing, And Consumer Behavior: A Review Article," **JOB**, 1969, v42(2), 162-166.

Niebuhr, W. David. (Robichek, Alexander A. and W. David Niebuhr. "Tax-Induced Bias In Reported Treasury Yields," **JOF**, 1970, v25(5), 1081-1090.)

Niederhoffer, Victor and Patrick Regan. "Earnings Changes And Stock Prices," **FAJ**, 1972, v28(3), 65-71.

Niederhoffer, Victor and Richard Zeckhauser. "Market Index Futures Contracts," **FAJ**, 1980, v36(1),49-55.

Niederhoffer, Victor. "A New Look At Clustering Of Stock Prices," **JOB**, 1966, v39(2), 309-313.

Niederhoffer, Victor. "Some Properties Of Stock Prices," **FAJ**, 1968, v24(2), 105-111.

Niederhoffer, Victor. "The Analysis Of World Events And Stock Prices," **JOB**, 1971, v44(2), 193-219.

Niederhoffer, Victor. "The Predictive Content Of First Quarter Earnings Reports," **JOB**, 1970, v43(1), 60-62.

Niederhoffer, Victor. (Brown, Philip and Victor Niederhoffer. "The Predictive Content Of Quarterly Earnings," **JOB**, 1968, v41(4), 488-497.)

Niederhoffer, Victor. (Zeckhauser, Richard and Victor Niederhoffer. "The Performance Of Market Index Futures Contracts," **FAJ**, 1983, v39(1), 59-65.)

Niehans, Jurg and John Hewson. "The Eurodollar Market And Monetary Theory," **JMCB**, 1976, v8(1), 1-27.

Niehans, Jurg. "Classical Monetary Theory, New And Old," **JMCB**, 1987, v19(4), 409-424.

Niehans, Jurg. "Efficient Monetary And Fiscal Policies In Balanced Growth," **JMCB**, 1969, v1(2), 228-251.

Niehans, Jurg. "Financial Innovation, Multinational Banking, And Monetary Policy," **JBF**, 1983, v7(4), 537-551.

Niehans, Jurg. "Further Comment," **JBF**, 1986, v10(4), 615-616.

Niehans, Jurg. "Innovation In Monetary Policy: Challenge And Response," **JBF**, 1982, v6(1), 9-28.

Niehans, Jurg. "Monetary Policy And Investment Dynamics In Interdependent Economics," **JMCB**, 1987, v19(1), 33-45.

Niehans, Jurg. "Money In A Statistic Theory Of Optimal Payment Arrangements," **JMCB**, 1969, v1(4), 706-726.

Niehans, Jurg. "The International Division Of Assets As Determined By Comparative Advantage," **JIMF**, 1986, v5(2), 153-166.

Niehans, Jurg. "Veendorp On Optimal Payment Arrangements: A Reply," **JMCB**, 1973, v5(1), 213-214.

Niehaus, Greg. "Government Pension Policy And The Cost Of Labor And Capital," **JFSR**, 1989, v2(1), 5-20.

Niehaus, Greg. (Chaplinksy, Susan and Greg Niehaus. "The Tax And Distributional Effects Of Leveraged ESOPs," **FM**, 1990, v19(1), 29-38.)

Niehaus, Gregory R. "The PBGCs Flat Fee Schedule, Moral Hazard, And Promised Pension Benefits," **JBF**, 1990, v14(1), 55-68.

Nielsen, James F. and Ronald W. Melicher. "A Financial Analysis Of Acquisition And Merger Premiums," **JFQA**, 1973, v8(2), 139-148.

Nielsen, James F. "Empirical Evidence Of Institutional Timing Ability," **FR**, v12(1), 36-47.

Nielsen, James F. "Trading Small Bank Stocks: An Oregon Case Study," **JBR**, 1982-83, v13(1), 49-52.

Nielsen, James F. (Conn, Robert L. and James F. Nielsen. "An Empirical Test Of The Larson-Gonedes Exchange Ratio Determination Model," **JOF**, 1977, v32(3), 749-759.)

Nielsen, James F. (Joehnk, Michael D. and James F. Nielsen. "The Effects Of Conglomerate Merger Activity On Systematic Risk," **JFQA**, 1974, v9(2), 215-225.)

Nielsen, Lars Tyge. "Portfolio Selection In The Mean-Variance Model: A Note," **JOF**, 1987, v42(5), 1371-1376.

Nielsen, Lars Tyge. "Positively Weighted Frontier Portfolios: A Note," **JOF**, 1987, v42(2), 471.

Nielsen, Lars Tyge. "Uniqueness Of Equilibrium In The Classical Capital Asset Pricing Model," **JFQA**, 1988, v23(3), 329-336.

Nielsen, Niels Christian. "On The Financing And Investment Decisions Of The Firm," **JBF**, 1978, v2(1), 79-102.

Nielsen, Niels Christian. "The Investment Decision Of The Firm Under Uncertainty And The Allocative Efficiency Of Capital Markets," **JOF**, 1976, v31(2), 587-602.

Nielson, Norma. "Capacity Of The Property-Casualty Insurance Industry," **JRI**, 1984, v51(3), 393-411.

Niemi, Albert W., Jr. "Institutional Contributions To The Leading Finance Journals, 1975 Through 1986: A Note," **JOF**, 1987, v42(5), 1389-1397.

Niendorf, Robert N., Edward J. Marien and Duane R. Wood. "Integrating Finance, Marketing, And Management Courses Using Behavioral Objectives," **JFED**, 1973, v2, 20-32.

Nieswiadomy, Michael L. and D. J. Slottje. "Estimating Lost Future Earnings Using The New Worklife Tables: Comment," **JRI**, 1988, v55(3), 539-544.

Nieswiadomy, Michael and Eugene Silberberg. "Calculating Changes In Worklife Expectancies And Lost Earnings In Personal Injury Cases," **JRI**, 1988, v55(3), 492-498.

Niho, Yoshio and H. Makin. "The Solution To The Inverse Problem Of Optimal Control," **JMCB**, 1978, v10(3), 371-377.

Nilsen, James B. "The Use Of Formula Timing Plans For Investment By Property And Casualty Insurance Companies," **JRI**, 1960, v27(3),

19-28.

Nimrod, Vance L. and Richard S. Bower. "Commodities And Computers," **JFQA**, 1967, v2(1), 58-73.

Niskanen, William and Robert Berry. "The 1973 Economic Report Of The President," **JMCB**, 1973, v5(2), 693-703.

Nissan, Edward. (Hamwi, Iskandar S. and Edward Nissan. "Determination Of Net Rate In Property And Liability Insurance: An Alternative Approach," **JRI**, 1984, v51(3), 536-548.)

Nissen, William J. (Hunt, Lawrence H., Jr. and William J. Nissen. "Section 4a(1) Should Be Revised," **FAJ**, 1981, v1(Supp), 461-464.)

Nitzan, Shmuel and Uzi Rosen. "A Note On Reinsurance And The Technology Of Risk," **JRI**, 1977, v44(3), 403-410.

Nixon, Clair J., Casper Wiggins and I. Richard Johnson. "Repeal Of The Investment Tax Credit And Financial Statement Analysis," **FAJ**, 1987, v43(1),52-55.

No Author. "Payment Systems In Norway," **JBR**, 1980-81, v11(4), 242-244.

No Author. "Proposals For The Reform Of Commercial Accounting Law In Germany," **JBFA**, 1979, v6(3), 331-338.

Noan, Eli M. "The Interaction Of Building Codes And Housing Prices," **AREUEA**, 1982, v10(4), 394-404.

Nobbe, Edward Owen. "Dr. Kilowatt And Mr. Hyde," **FAJ**, 1953, v9(5), 42-44.

Nobes, C. W. "A Judgemental International Classification Of Financial Reporting Practices," **JBFA**, 1983, v10(1), 1-19.

Nobes, C. W. and R. H. Parker. "True And Fair': A Survey Of UK Financial Directors," **JBFA**, 1991, v18(3), 359-376.

Noble, Nicholas R. "Granger Causality And Expectational Rationality," **JMCB**, 1982, v14(4), Part 1, 532-537.

Noble, Nicholas R. (Hall, Thomas E. and Nicholas R. Noble. "Velocity And The Variability Of Money Growth: Evidence From Granger-Causality Tests," **JMCB**, 1987, v19(1), 112-116.)

Noble, Nicholas R. (Leonard, David C. and Nicholas R. Noble. "Estimation Of Time-Varying Systematic Risk And Investment Performance: Closed-End Investment Companies," **JFR**, 1981, v4(2), 109-120.)

Noe, Thomas H. "Capital Structure And Signaling Game Equilibria," **RFS**, 1988-89, v1(4), 331-355.

Noe, Thomas H. (Kale, Jayant R., Thomas H. Noe and Gerald D. Gay. "Share Repurchase Through Transferable Put Rights: Theory And Case Study," **JFEC**, 1989, v25(1), 141-160.)

Noe, Thomas H. (Kale, Jayant R. and Thomas H. Noe. "Risky Debt Maturity Choice In A Sequential Game Equilibrium," **JFR**, 1990, v13(2), 155-166.)

Noe, Thomas H. (Kale, Jayant R. and Thomas H. Noe. "Dividends, Uncertainty, And Underwriting Costs Under Asymmetric Information," **JFR**, 1990, v13(4), 265-278.)

Noetzlin, Bernard. (Solnik, Bruno and Bernard Noetzlin. "Optimal International Asset Allocation," **JPM**, 1982-83, v9(1), 11-21.)

Noland, Charles W. "Assessing Hedonic Indexes For Housing," **JFQA**, 1979, v14(4), 783-800.

Noll, Roger G. (Hahn, Robert W. and Roger G. Noll. "Environmental Markets In The Year 2000," **JRU**, 1990, v3(4), 351-368.)

Noon, Theodore W., Jr. "Oil Company Analysis: Estimating Buy And Sell Prices," **FAJ**, 1962, v18(6),96-97.

Norby, William C. and Frances Stone. "Objectives Of Financial Reporting," **FAJ**, 1972, v28(4), 39-45, 76-81.

Norby, William C. and John C. Burton. "Financial Reporting In The 1980s," **FAJ**, 1980, v36(1), 64-68.

Norby, William C. "Applications Of Inflation-Adjusted Accounting Data," **FAJ**, 1983, v39(2), 33-39.

Norby, William C. "Profile Of The Financial Analyst," **FAJ**, 1972, v28(2), 35-37.

Norby, William C. "The Financial Analysts Seminar," **FAJ**, 1958, v14(2), 11-14.

Norby, William C. (Neil, Herbert E., Jr. and William C. Norby. "Dynamic Factors In Corporate Profits," **FAJ**, 1962, v18(4), 33-39.)

Norby, William C. (Stern, Walter P. and William C. Norby. "Research And Market Structure," **FAJ**, 1972, v28(1), 24-28,85-87.)

Nordhaus, William D. "The Effects Of Inflation On The Distribution Of Economic Welfare," **JMCB**, 1973, v5(1), Part II, 465-504.

Nordhauser, Fred. "Using Stock Index Futures To Reduce Market Risk," **JPM**, 1983-84, v10(3), 56-62.

Norgaard, C. T. (Grinnell, D. J. and C. T. Norgaard. "Reporting Rules For Marketable Equity Securities," **FAJ**, 1980, v36(1), 69-74.)

Norgaard, Corine T. "Comprehensive Income Tax Allocation," **FAJ**, 1969, v25(1), 81-85.

Norgaard, Corine. (Dyl, Edward A., Richard E. White, Richard Norgaard and Corine Norgaard "A Critical Examination Of Share Repurchase: Dyl And White Versus Norgaard And Norgaard," **FM**, 1974, v3(3), 68-73.)

Norgaard, Corine. (Norgaard, Richard and Corine Norgaard. "A Critical Examination Of Share Repurchase," **FM**, 1974, v3(1), 44-50.)

Norgaard, R. L. and D. T. Crary. "Insurance Industry Merger Targets," **FAJ**, 1970, v26(1), 91-94.

Norgaard, Richard and Corine Norgaard. "A Critical Examination Of Share Repurchase," **FM**, 1974, v3(1), 44-50.

Norgaard, Richard L. "A Monte Carlo Simulation In Insurance Company Portfolio Management," **JRI**, 1966, v33(3), 459-468.

Norgaard, Richard L. "An Examination Of The Yields Of Corporate Bonds And Stocks: Reply," **JOF**, 1977, v32(1), 206-207.

Norgaard, Richard L. "An Examination Of The Yields Of Corporate Bonds And Stocks," **JOF**, 1974, v29(4), 1275-1286.

Norgaard, Richard L. "Are GNMAs A Good Investment?," **JPM**, 1978-79, v5(1), 49-52.

Norgaard, Richard L. "Evaluating Intercorporate Risk, Returns, And Trends," **JFQA**, 1971, v6(4), 1069-1082.

Norgaard, Richard L. "The Evolution Of Business Finance Textbooks," **FM**, 1981, v10(2), Tenth Anniversary Edition, 34-45.

Norgaard, Richard L. "What Is A Reciprocal?," **JRI**, 1964, v31(1), 51-62.

Norgaard, Richard and George Schick. "Profitability In The Property And Liability Insurance Industry," **JRI**, 1970, v37(4), 579-587.

Norgaard, Richard and George Schick. "Profitability In The Property And Liability Insurance Industry: Reply," **JRI**, 1972, v39(3), 483-485.

Norgaard, Richard. "Bond Indices And Optimal Portfolios," **FR**, 1978, v13(2), 12-21.

Norgaard, Richard. (Dyl, Edward A., Richard E. White, Richard Norgaard and Corine Norgaard. "A Critical Examination Of Share Repurchase: Dyl And White Versus Norgaard And Norgaard," **FM**, 1974, v3(3), 68-73.)

Norman, A. (Tinsley, P., G. Fries, B. Garrett, A. Norman, P.A.V.B. Swamy and P. Von Zur Muehlen. "The Impact Of Uncertainty On The Feasibility Of Humphrey-Hawkins Objectives," **JOF**, 1981, v36(2), 489-496.)

Norr, David. "Accounting And Analysis," **FAJ**, 1964, v20(3), 38-45.

Norr, David. "Currency Translation And The Analyst," **FAJ**, 1976, v32(4), 46-54.

Norr, David. "Investment Theories And Applications," **FAJ**, 1960, v16(4), 121-124.

Norr, David. "Management And The Investor," **FAJ**, 1979, v35(2), 45-48.

Norr, David. "Some Elements Of Oil Profitability," **FAJ**, 1973, v29(6), 58-66.

Norrbin, Stefan. (Guntermann, Karl L. and Stefan Norrbin. "Explaining The Variability Of Apartment Rents," **AREUEA**, 1987, v15(4), 321-340.)

Norris, James. (Michel, Allen and James Norris. "On The Determination Of Appropriate Profit Margins In Insurance Industry Regulation," **JRI**, 1982, v49(4), 628-633.)

Norstrom, Carl J. "A Comment On Two Simple Decision Rules In Capital Rationing," **JBFA**, 1976, v3(2), 63-70.

Norstrom, Carl J. "A Sufficient Condition For A Unique Nonnegative Internal Rate Of Return," **JFQA**, 1972, v7(3), 1835-1839.

Norstrom, Carl J. (Bernhard, Richard H. and Carl J. Norstrom. "A Further Note On Unrecovered Investment, Uniqueness Of The Internal Rate, And The Question Of Project Acceptability," **JFQA**, 1980, v15(2), 421-423.)

North, Joseph E. "The Cosmetics And Toiletries Industry," **FAJ**, 1963, v19(1), 39-50.

Northcutt, David. (Reichert, Alan, William Strauss, David Northcutt and Warren Spector. "The Impact Of Economic Conditions And Electronic Payments Technology On Federal Reserve Check Volume," **JBR**, 1983-84, v14(4), 291-296.)

Northrup, Herbert R. "Engineers, Unions, And Management Organization: A Review Article," **JOB**, 1962, v35(2), 191-195.

Northrup, Herbert R. and Richard L. Rowan. "State Seizure In Public Interest Disputes," **JOB**, 1963, v36(2), 210-227.

Norton, Curtis L. (Everett, John O. and Curtis L. Norton. "Evaluating The Effectiveness Of Code Section 1091 As A Deterrent To Wash Sales," **FR**, 1981, v16(3), 44-56.)

Norton, Edgar. "Determinants Of Capital Structure: A Survey," **APFAF**, 1989, v3(1), 323-350.

Norton, Frank E. "Administrative Organization In Capital Budgeting," **JOB**, 1955, v28(4), 291-295.

Norton, Seth W. "An Empirical Look At Franchising As An Organizational Form," **JOB**, 1988, v61(2), 197-218.

Norwood, Samuel W., III. (Gup, Benton E. and Samuel W. Norwood, III. "Divisional Cost Of Capital: A Practical Approach," **FM**, 1982, v11(1), 20-24.)

Nosal, Ed. (Giammarino, Ronald M. and Ed Nosal. "Debt Overhang And The Efficiency Of International Rescheduling," **RDIBF**, 1991, v4/5, 474-504.)

Nosari, E. Joe. (Braswell, Ronald C., E. Joe Nosari and DeWitt L. Summers. "A Comparison Of The True Interest Costs Of Competitive And Negotiated Underwritings In The Municipal Bond Market," **JMCB**, 1983, v15(1), 102-106.)

Nosari, E. Joe. (Braswell, Ronald C., E. Joe Nosari and Mark A. Browning. "The Effect Of Private Municipal Bond Insurance On The Cost To The Issuer," **FR**, 1982, v17(4), 240-251.)

Nosari, E. Joe. (Madura, Jeff and E. Joe Nosari. "Optimal Portfolio Of Foreign Currencies With Borrowing And Lending: A Comment," **JMCB**, 1982, v14(4), Part 1, 531.)

Noser, Eugene A., Jr. (Berkowitz, Stephen A., Dennis E. Logue and Eugene A. Noser, Jr. "The Total Cost Of Transactions On The NYSE," **JOF**, 1988, v43(1), 97-112.)

Nothaft, Frank E. (Gabriel, Stuart A. and Frank E. Nothaft. "Rental Housing Markets And The Natural Vacancy Rate," **AREUEA**, 1988, v16(4), 419-429.)

Nothaft, Frank E. (Rothberg, James P., Frank E. Nothaft and Stuart A. Gabriel. "On The Determinants Of Yield Spreads Between Mortgage Pass-Through And Treasury Securities," **JREFEC**, 1989, v2(4), 301-316)

Noulas, Athanasios G., Subhash C. Ray and Stephen M. Miller. "Returns To Scale And Input Substitution For Large U.S. Banks," **JMCB**, 1990, v22(1), 94-108.

Nourse, Hugh O. "A Cynic's View Of Zoning Reform," **AREUEA**, 1978, v6(3), 327-334.

Nourse, Hugh O. "A Cynic's View Of Zoning Reform: Response," **AREUEA**, 1978, v6(3), 341-342.

Nourse, Hugh O. "Can We Design The Housing Allowance For Learning?," **AREUEA**, 1976, v4(1), 97-109.

Nourse, Hugh O. "Comment On Rental Price Adjustment And Investment In The Office Market," **AREUEA**, 1986, v14(1), 163-164.

Nourse, Hugh O. (Ball, Jay N. and Hugh O. Nourse. "Testing The Conventional Representation Model For Residential Real Estate Brokerage," **JRER**, 1988, v3(2), 119-131.)

Nourse, Hugh O. (Johnson, Joyce M., Hugh O. Nourse and Ellen Day. "Factors Related To The Selection Of A Real Estate Agency," **JRER**, 1988, v3(2), 109-118.)

Nourse, Hugh O. (Kinnard, William N., Herman G. Berkman, Hugh O. Nourse and John C. Weicher. "The First Twenty Years Of AREUEA," **AREUEA**, 1988, v16(2), 189-205.)

Nourse, Hugh O. (Rutherford, Ronald C. and Hugh O. Nourse. "The Impact Of Corporate Real Estate Unit Formation On The Parent Firm's Value," **JRER**, 1988, v3(3), 73-84.)

Nourse, Hugh O. and Dorothy Kingery. "Survey Of Approaches To Disposing Of Suplus Corporate Real Estate," **JRER**, 1987, v2(1), 51-59.

Nourzad, Farrokh. (McGibany, James M. and Farrokh Nourzad. "Money Demand And The Effects Of Fiscal Policies: Comment," **JMCB**, 1988, v20(4), 706-714.)

Novack, David E. "Liquidity Ratios And Recent British Monetary Experience," **JOF**, 1958, v13(4), 510-526.

Novak, David E. "Security-Reserve Requirements In The United States And The United Kingdom: Reply," **JOF**, 1959, v14(4), 543-545.

Novak, Joseph J. "Plan For User Fees," **JFM**, 1981, v1(Supp), 495-496.

Novomestky, Frederick. (Choie, Kenneth S. and Frederick Novomestky. "Replication Of Long-Term With Short-Term Options," **JPM**, 1989, v15(2), 17-19.)

Noyes, Alexander Dana. "God Help The Surplus!", **JPM**, 1981-82, v8(2), 88-90.

Noyes, Guy E. "Pressures In Credit Markets (Keynote Review)," **FAJ**, 1966, v22(5), 9-11.

Nozari, Ardavan. (Leibowitz, Martin L., William S. Krasker and Ardavan Nozari. "Spread Duration: A New Tool For Bond Portfolio Management," **JPM**, 1990, v16(3), 46-53.)

Nugent, Christopher E. (Bower, Richard S., Christopher E. Nugent, Barbara C. Myers and J. Peter Williamson. "A Language For Financial Analysts," **FAJ**, 1967, v23(1), 121.)

Nunn, Kenneth P., Jr. "The Strategic Determinants Of Working Capital: A Product-Line Perspective," **JFR**, 1981, v4(3), 207-219.

Nunn, Kenneth P., Jr. (Finnerty, Joseph E. and Kenneth P. Nunn, Jr. "Comparative Yield Spreads On U.S. Corporate Bonds And $Eurobonds," **FAJ**, 1985, v41(4), 68-73.)

Nunn, Kenneth P., Jr. (Finnerty, Joseph E. and Kenneth P. Nunn, Jr. "Valuation And The Impact Of Corporate Firm, Taxes, And Leverage On Multinational Net Income Under FASB #8 And FASB #52," **AFPAF**, 1987, v2(1), 87-102.)

Nunn, Kenneth P., Jr. (Gombola, Michael J. and Kenneth P. Nunn, Jr. "Valuation Of The Preferred Stock Sinking Fund Feature: A Time-Series Approach," **JFR**, 1988, v11(1), 33-42.)

Nunn, Kenneth P., Jr. (Hegde, Shantaram P. and Kenneth P. Nunn, Jr. "Non-Infinitesimal Rate Changes And Macaulay Duration," **JPM**, 1987-88, v14(2), 69-78.)

Nunn, Kenneth P., Jr. (Hegde, Shantaram P. and Kenneth P. Nunn, Jr. "Interest Rate Volatility, Trading Volume, And The Hedging Performance Of T-Bond And GNMA Futures - A Note," **JFM**, 1985, v5(2), 273-286.)

Nunn, Kenneth P., Jr. (Hegde, Shantaram P. and Kenneth P. Nunn, Jr. "A Multivariate Analysis Of The Cross-Hedging Performance Of T-Bond And GNMA Futures Markets," **FR**, 1985, v20(2), 143-163.)

Nunn, Kenneth P., Jr. (Madden, Gerald P., Kenneth P. Nunn, Jr. and Alan Wiemann. "Mutual Fund Performance And Market Capitalization," **FAJ**, 1986, v42(4), 67-70.)

Nunn, Kenneth P., Jr. and Gerald P. Madden and Michael J. Gombola. "Are Some Insiders More 'Inside' Than Others?," **JPM**, 1982-83, v9(3), 18-22.

Nunn, Kenneth P., Jr., Joanne Hill and Thomas Schneeweis. "Corporate Bond Price Data Sources And Return/Risk Measurement," **JFQA**, 1986, v21(2), 197-208.

Nunnally, Bennie H., Jr. (O'Brien, Thomas J. and Bennie H. Nunnally, Jr. "A 1982 Survey Of Corporate Leasing Analysis," **FM**, 1983, v12(2), 30-36.)

Nunthirapakorn, Ted. (Millar, James A. and Ted Nunthirapakorn. "Earnings Per Share Reporting For Canadian Companies With Complex Capital Structures," **JBFA**, 1991, v18(1), 109-116.)

Nunthirapakorn, Thakol and James A. Millar. "Changing Prices, Accounting Earnings And Systematic Risk," **JBFA**, 1987, v14(1), 1-26.

Nunthirapakorn, Thakol. (Millar, James A., Thakol Nunthirapakorn and Steve Courtenay. "A Note On The Information Content Of Primary And Fully Diluted Earnings Per Share," **FAJ**, 1987, v43(5), 77-79.)

Nurnberg, Hugo. "An Unrecognized Ambiguity Of The High-Low Method," **JBFA**, 1977, v4(4), 427-442.

Nussenbaum, Maurice. (McDonald, John G., Bertrand Jacquillat and Maurice Nussenbaum. "Dividend, Investment And Financing Decisions: Empirical Evidence On French Firms," **JFQA**, 1975, v10(5), 741-755.)

Nye, Blaine F. (Hofflander, Alfred E. and Blaine F. Nye. "Self-Insurance, Captives And Income Taxation," **JRI**, 1984, v51(4), 702-709.)

Nye, Blaine F. (Hofflander, Alfred E. and Blaine F. Nye. "An Analysis Of Premium Tax Revenue And Rate In California: The Case Of Structured Settlement Annuities," **JRI**, 1987, v54(4), 760-766.)

Nye, Blaine F. (Venezian, Emilio C., Blaine F. Nye and Alfred E. Hofflander. "The Distribution Of Claims For Professional Malpractice: Some Statistical And Public Policy Aspects," **JRI**, 1989, v56(4), 686-701.)

Nye, Blaine F. and Aflred E. Hofflander. "Economics Of Oligopoly: Medical Malpractice Insurance As A Classic Illustration," **JRI**, 1987, v54(3), 502-519.

Nye, Blaine F. and Alfred E. Hofflander. "Experience Rating In Medical Professional Liability Insurance," **JRI**, 1988, v55(1), 150-157.

Nye, Blaine F. and Alfred E. Hofflander. "Experience Rating In Medical Professional Liability Insurance: Reply," **JRI**, 1989, v56(2), 333-335.

Nye, David J. (Archer, Wayne R. and David J. Nye. "An Insurance Approach To Risk Analysis Of Debt Home Equity Conversion Programs," **AREUEA**, 1987, v15(3), 185-198.)

Nye, David J. (Cummins, J. David and David J. Nye. "Optimizing The Structure Of Capital Claims And Assets Of A Stock Insurance Company: Comment," **JRI**, 1972, v39(2), 310-313.)

Nye, David J. (Cummins, J. David and David J. Nye. "The Cost Of Capital Of Insurance Companies: Comment," **JRI**, 1972, v39(3), 487-491.)

Nye, David J. (Cummins, J. David and David J. Nye. "The Stochastic Characteristics Of Property-Liability Insurance Company Underwriting Profits," **JRI**, 1980, v47(1), 61-77.)

Nye, David J. and Robert W. Kolb. "Inflation, Interest Rates And Property-Liability Insurer Risk," **JRI**, 1986, v53(1), 144-154.

Nye, David. (Kahane, Yehuda and David Nye. "A Portfolio Approach To The Property-Liability Insurance Industry," **JRI**, 1975, v42(4), 579-598.)

Nye, William A. "The Case For Social Insurance In The Undergraduate Curriculum," **JRI**, 1966, v33(1), 115-124.

O'Brien, Edward J. "Publication Waiting Line," **JOB**, 1971, v44(3), 286-288.

O'Brien, James J. "A Review Of The Vending Industry," **FAJ**, 1962, v18(6), 81-87.

Oakes, Ralph H. "Resale Price Maintenance In Chicago, 1953-55 (A Study Of Three Products)," **JOB**, 1957, v30(2), 109-130.

Oakford, R. V. and Arturo Salazar. "The Long Term Effectiveness Of 'Exact' And Approximate Capital Rationing Procedures Under Uncertainty And Incomplete Information," **JBFA**, 1981, v8(1), 113-137.

Oakford, R. V. (Lohmann, Jack R. and R. V. Oakford. "The Effects Of Borrowing On The Rate Of Growth Of Capital And The Risk Of Ruin Of A Firm," **JBFA**, 1982, v8(2), 219-238.)

Oates, Wallace E. "Budget Balance And Equilibrium Income: A Comment On The Efficacy Of Fiscal And Monetary Policy In An Open Economy," **JOF**, 1966, v21(3), 489-498.

Oaxaca, Ronald L. (Cox, James C. and Ronald L. Oaxaca. "Laboratory Experiments With A Finite-Horizon Job-Search Model," **JRU**, 1989, v2(3), 301-329.)

Oberhelman, H. Dennis. (D'Souza, Rudolph E., LeRoy D. Brooks and H. Dennis Oberhelman. "A General Stationary Stochastic Regression Model For Estimating And Predicting Beta," **FR**, 1989, v24(2), 299-318.)

Oberhelman, H. Dennis. (Ferri, Michael G., H. Dennis Oberhelman and Rodney L. Roenfeldt. "Market Timing And Mutual Fund Portfolio Composition," **JFR**, 1984, v7(2), 143-150.)

Oberhelman, H. Dennis. (Ferri, Michael G. and H. Dennis Oberhelman. "A Study Of The Management Of Money Market Mutual Funds, 1975-1980," **FM**, 1981, v10(4), 24-29.)

Oberhelman, H. Dennis. (Ferri, Michael G., H. Dennis Oberhelman and Steven J. Goldstein. "Yield Sensitivities Of Short-Term Securities," **JPM**, 1981-82, v8(3), 65-71.)

Oberhelman, H. Dennis. (Ferri, Michael G. and H. Dennis Oberhelman. "How Well Do Money Market Funds Perform?," **JPM**, 1980-81, v7(3), 18-26.)

Oberhelman, H. Dennis. (Ferri, Michael G., Steven J. Goldstein and H. Dennis Oberhelman. "The Performance Of The When-Issued Market For T-Bills," **JPM**, 1984-85, v11(3), 57-61.)

Obersteiner, Erich. "Should The Foreign Affiliate Remit Dividends Or Reinvest?," **FM**, 1973, v2(1), 88-93.

Oblak, David J. and Roy J. Helm, Jr. "Survey And Analysis Of Capital Budgeting Methods Used By Multinationals," **FM**, 1980, v9(4), 37-41.

O'Brien, James M. "Estimating The Information Value Of Immediate Disclosure Of The FOMC Policy Directive," **JOF**, 1981, v36(5), 1047-1061.

O'Brien, James M. "Liquidity Preference And The Flow Of Finance: A Comment," **JMCB**, 1972, v4(3), 730-732.

O'Brien, James M. "On The Incidence Of Selective Credit And Related Policies In A Multi-Asset Framework," **JOF**, 1977, v32(5), 1539-1556.

O'Brien, James M. "The Information Value Of The FOMC Policy Directive Under The New Operating Procedures," **JMCB**, 1984, v16(2), 151-164.

O'Brien, John W. "Applications Of Market Theory," **FAJ**, 1970, v26(4), 91-103.

O'Brien, John W. "Investment Objectives, Policy, And Risk," **JPM**, 1974-75, v1(4), 29-33.

O'Brien, John. (Ferguson, Robert and John O'Brien. "Stabilizing Forwards: For A More Stable Market," **JPM**, 1987-88, v14(4), 4.)

O'Brien, Thomas J. and Bennie H. Nunnally, Jr. "A 1982 Survey Of Corporate Leasing Analysis," **FM**, 1983, v12(2), 30-36.

O'Brien, Thomas J. and Michael J. P. Selby. "Option Pricing Theory And Asset Expectations: A Review And Discussion In Tribute To James Boness," **FR**, 1986, v21(4), 399-418.

O'Brien, Thomas J. and Peter M. Schwarz. "Ex Ante Evidence Of Backwardation/Contango In Commodities Futures Markets," **JPM**, 1982, v2(2), 159-168.

O'Brien, Thomas J. and William F. Kennedy. "Simultaneous Option And Stock Prices: Another Look at The Black-Scholes Model," **FR**, 1982, v17(4), 219-227.

O'Brien, Thomas J. "A Discrete Time Option Model Dependent And Expected Return: A Note," **JOF**, 1986, v41(2), 515-520.

O'Brien, Thomas J. "Portfolio Insurance Mechanics," **JPM**, 1987-88, v14(3), 40-47.

O'Brien, Thomas J. "The Constant Growth Model And Personal Taxes," **JBFA**, 1991, v18(1), 121-132.

O'Brien, Thomas J. (Harris, Robert S., Thomas J. O'Brien and Doug Wakeman. "Divisional Cost-Of-Capital Estimation For Multi-Industry Firms," **FM**, 1989, v18(2), 74-84.)

O'Brien, Thomas J. (Rendleman, Richard J., Jr. and Thomas J. O'Brien. "The Effects Of Volatility Misestimation On Option-Replication Portfolio Insurance," **FAJ**, 1990, v46(3), 61-70.)

O'Brien, Thomas J. and Paul A. Vanderheiden. "Empirical Measurement Of Operating Leverage For Growing Firms," **FM**, 1987, v16(2), 45-53.

O'Brien, Thomas. (Gandar, John, Richard Zuber, Thomas O'Brien and Ben Russo. "Testing Rationality In The Point Spread Betting Market," **JOF**, 1988, v43(4), 995-1008.)

Obst, Norman P. and Robert H. Rasche. "Price Expectations And Interest Rates: Some Clarifying Comments: A Comment," **JMCB**, 1976, v8(1), 119-122.

Obstfeld, Maurice. "Balance-Of-Payments Crises And Devaluation," **JMCB**, 1984, v16(2), 208-217.

Obstfeld, Maurice. "Intertemporal Price Speculation And The Optimal Current-Account Deficit," **JIMF**, 1983, v2(2), 135-145.

Obstfeld, Maurice. (Cumby, Robert E. and Maurice Obstfeld. "A Note On Exchange-Rate Expectations And Nominal Interest Differentials: A Test Of The Fisher Hypothesis," **JOF**, 1981, v36(3), 697-703.)

Ocampo, Juan M. (Rosenthal, James A. and Juan M. Ocampo. "Analyzing The Economic Benefits Of Securitized Credit," **JACF**, 1988, v1(3), 32-44.)

Ocampo, Juan M. and James A. Rosenthal. "The Future Of

Securitization And The Financial Services Industry," *JACF*, 1988, v1(3), 90-100.

Ochs, Jack and Mark Rush. "The Persistence Of Interest-Rate Effects On The Demand For Currency," *JMCB*, 1983, v15(4), 499-505.

O'Connell, James A. "The Policy Level Management Gap In Corporate Pension Administration (And How One Corporation Bridged It)," *FAJ*, 1987, v43(2), 76-79.

O'Connell, Jeffrey. (Keeton, Robert E. and Jeffrey O'Connell. "Basic Protection - A New Plan Of Automobile Insurance," *JRI*, 1965, v32(4), 539-548.)

O'Connell, Joan. "Sterilization And Interest Rates," *JIMF*, 1988, v7(4), 425-428.

O'Connell, John J. and Dwight Anderson. "Risk And Insurance As Part Of Teaching Financial Analysis," *JFED*, 1980, v9, 79-82.

O'Connell, Lehahan. (Goolsby, William C. and Lehahan O'Connell. "Overbuilt Housing: Criteria For Success," *JRER*, 1988, v3(1), 51-59.)

O'Conner, Dennis J. and Alberto T. Bueso. "The New Managerial Finance: The Key Course In The Business Administration Curriculum," *JFED*, 1980, v9, 8-11.

O'Conner, Dennis J. "Personalized System Of Instruction: An Alternative To The Lecture Format," *JFED*, 1974, v3, 5-15.

O'Conner, Melvin C. (Collins, Daniel W., Warren T. Dent and Melvin C. O'Conner. "Has Full Cost Accounting Helped Share Prices?," *FAJ*, 1978, v34(6), 48-57.)

O'Conner, Dennis J. and Alberto T. Bueso. "The Theory Of Finance As A Conceptual Framework For Teaching Basic Finance," *JFED*, 1981, v10, 66-68.

O'Connor, Dennis J. "Personalized Self-Paced Courses In Finance: A New Direction In University Teaching," *JFED*, 1975, v4, 3-8.

O'Connor, Dennis J. (Stickels, James P. and Dennis J. O'Connor. "A Multi-Section Self-Paced Basic Finance Course: A Postmortem," *JFED*, 1981, v10, 10-13.)

O'Connor, James C. "All-Line Insurance," *JRI*, 1959, v26(1), 57-60.

O'Connor, James C. "Fire Insurance In Wartime," *JRI*, 1943, v10, 41-45.

O'Connor, Kevin J. "The Insurance Industry And Futures Markets: Current Practice," *RFM*, 1985, v4(2), 218-223.

O'Connor, William P., Jr. "The Path To Higher Yields And Faster Growth," *JPM*, 1975-76, v2(3), 56-59.

O'Dell, Bruce T. (Burgess, Richard C. and Bruce T. O'Dell. "An Empirical Examination Of Index Efficiency: Implications For Index Funds," *JFQA*, 1978, v13(1), 93-100.)

Odgen, Joseph P., Alan L. Tucker and Timothy W. Vines. "Arbitraging American Gold Spot And Futures Options," *FR*, 1990, v25(4), 577-592.

O'Donnell, John L. "Operating Confusion In Accounting-Two Reports Or One?," *JOB*, 1964, v37(1), 49-50.

O'Donnell, John L. "Some Postwar Trends In Municipal Bond Financing," *JOF*, 1962, v17(2), 259-268.

O'Donnell, William. "Is Social Insurance A Profession?," *JRI*, 1967, v34(3), 417-422.

O'Donnell, William. (Malisoff, Harry and William O'Donnell. "Is Social Insurance A Profession?," *JRI*, 1969, v36(1), 159-162.)

Odum, Eugene P. "Energy, Ecosystem Development And Environmental Risk," *JRI*, 1976, v43(1), 1-16.

Odurtha, James N., Jr. (Bawa, Vijay S., James N. Odurtha, Jr., M. R. Rao and Hira L. Suri. "On Determination Of Stochastic Dominance Optimal Sets," *JOF*, 1985, v40(2), 417-431.)

Oellermann, Charles M. and Paul L. Farris. "Futures Or Cash: Which Market Leads Live Beef Cattle Prices?," *JFM*, 1985, v5(4), 529-538.

Oellermann, Charles M. and Paul L. Farris. "Trader Concentration Effects In Live Cattle Futures," *JFM*, 1986, v6(4), 565-574.

Oellermann, Charles M. (Brorsen, B. Wade, Charles M. Oellermann and Paul L. Farris. "The Live Cattle Futures Market And Daily Cash Price," *JFM*, 1989, v9(4), 273-282.)

Oellermann, Charles M., B. Wade Brorsen and Paul L. Farris. "Price Discovery For Feeder Cattle," *JFM*, 1989, v9(2), 113-122.

Oettinger, Martin P. "Responsible Democracy Or Democratic Irresponsibility," *FAJ*, 1966, v22(2), 27-33.

O'Farrell, David J. (Ellis, John W. and David J. O'Farrell. "Utilizing Mixed Integer Programming In The Construction Of Income-Oriented Portfolios," *JFED*, 1978, v7, 83-85.)

Ofer, A. R. (Agmon, T., A. R. Ofer and A. Tamir. "Variable Rate Debt Instruments And Corporate Debt Policy," *JOF*, 1981, v36(1), 113-125.)

Ofer, Aharon R. and Robert A. Taggart. "'Bond Refunding Reconsidered': Reply," *JOF*, 1980, v35(1), 197-200.

Ofer, Aharon R. and Robert A. Taggart, Jr. "Bond Refunding: A Clarifying Analysis," *JOF*, 1977, v32(1), 21-30.

Ofer, Aharon R. "Investors' Expectation Of Earnings Growth, Their Accuracy And Effects On The Structure Of Realized Rates," *JOF*, 1975, v30(2), 509-523.

Ofer, Aharon R. "The Evaluation Of The Lease Versus Purchase Alternatives," *FM*, 1976, v5(2),67-74.

Ofer, Aharon R. (Breen, William, Ravi Jagannathan and Aharon R. Ofer. "Correcting For Heteroscedasticity In Tests For Market Timing Ability," *JOFA*, 1986, v59(4), Part 1, 585-598.)

Ofer, Aharon R. (Chari, V. V., Ravi Jagannathan and Aharon R. Ofer. "Seasonalities In Security Returns: The Case Of Earnings Announcements," *JFEC*, 1988, v21(1), 101-122.)

Ofer, Aharon R. (Israel, Ronen, Aharon R. Ofer and Daniel R. Siegel. "The Information Content Of Equity-For-Debt Swaps: An Investigation Of Analyst Forecasts Of Firm Cash Flows," *JFEC*, 1989, v25(2), 349-370.)

Ofer, Aharon R. (McNally, Graeme M. "Responsibility Accounting And Organisational Control: Some Perspectives And Prospects," *JBFA*, 1980, v7(2), 165-181.)

Ofer, Aharon R. (Melnik, Arie and Aharon R. Ofer. "Competitive Commission Rates, Execution Quality, And Customer's Market Power," *JMCB*, 1980, v12(2), Part 2, 221-227.)

Ofer, Aharon R. (Melnik, Arie and Aharon R. Ofer. "Determinants Of Commission Rates For Bank Trust Stock Transactions," *JBF*, 1978, v2(4), 355-366.)

Ofer, Aharon R. and Anjan V. Thakor. "A Theory Of Stock Price Responses To Alternative Corporate Cash Disbursement Methods: Stock Repurchases And Dividends," *JOF*, 1987, v42(2), 365-394.

Ofer, Aharon R. and Ashok Natarajan. "Convertible Call Policies: An Empirical Analysis Of An Information-Signaling Hypothesis," *JFEC*, 1987, v19(1), 91-108.

Ofer, Aharon R. and Daniel R. Siegel. "Corporate Financial Policy, Information, And Market Expectations: An Empirical Investigation Of Dividends," *JOF*, 1987, v42(4), 889-911.

Ofer, Aharon. (Dotan, Amihud and Aharon Ofer. "Variable Versus Stationary Beta In The Market Model: A Comparative Analysis," *JBF*, 1984, v8(4), 525-534.)

Offenbacher, Edward. (Barnett, William, Edward Offenbacher and Paul Spindt. "New Concepts Of Aggregated Money," *JOF*, 1981, v36(2), 497-505.)

Officer, Dennis T. and Gary L. Trennepohl. "Price Behavior Of Corporate Equities Near Option Expiration Dates," *FM*, 1981, v10(3), 75-80.

Officer, Dennis T. and Richard L. Smith, II. "Announcement Effects Of Withdrawn Security Offerings: Evidence On The Wealth Redistribution Hypothesis," *JFR*, 1986, v9(3), 229-238.

Officer, Dennis T. and William J. Boyes. "The Behavior Of Brokerage Firm Shares," *FAJ*, 1984, v40(3), 41-46.

Officer, Dennis T. (Booth, James R. and Dennis T. Officer. "Expectations, Interest Rates, And Commercial Bank Stocks," *JFR*, 1985, v8(1), 51-58.)

Officer, Dennis T. (Born, Jeffrey A., James T. Moser and Dennis T. Officer. "Changes In Dividend Policy And Subsequent Earnings," *JPM*, 1987-88, v14(4), 56-62.)

Officer, Dennis T. (Cole, Charles W. and Dennis T. Officer. "The Interest Cost Effect Of Private Municipal Bond Insurance," *JRI*, 1981, v48(3), 435-449.)

Officer, Dennis T. (McIntosh, Willard, Dennis T. Officer and Jeffrey A. Born. "The Wealth Effects Of Merger Activities: Further Evidence From Real Estate Investment Trusts," *JRER*, 1989, v4(3), 141-155.)

Officer, Dennis T. and J. Ronald Hoffmeister. "ADRs: A Substitute For The Real Thing?," *JPM*, 1986-87, v13(2), 61-65.

Officer, Lawrence H. and Thomas D. Willett. "The Covered-Arbitrage Schedule: A Critical Survey Of Recent Developments," *JMCB*, 1970, v2(2), 247-257.

Officer, Lawrence H. "Reserve-Asset Preferences In The Crisis Zone, 1958-67," *JMCB*, 1974, v6(2), 191-212.

Officer, Lawrence H. "The Demand For International Liquidity: A Test Of The Square-Root Law," *JMCB*, 1976, v8(3), 325-337.

Officer, R. R. "Seasonality In Australian Capital Markets: Market Efficiency And Empirical Issues," *JFEC*, 1975, v2(1), 29-52.

Officer, R. R. "The Variability Of The Market Factor Of The New York Stock Exchange," *JOB*, 1973, v46(3), 434-453.

Ogden, Joseph P. "An Analysis Of Yield Curve Notes," *JOF*, 1987, v42(1), 99-110.

Ogden, Joseph P. "Determinants Of The Ratings And Yields On Corporate Bonds: Tests Of The Contingent Claims Model," *JFR*, 1987, v10(4), 329-340.

Ogden, Joseph P. "Determinants Of The Relative Interest Rate Sensitivities Of Corporate Bonds," *FM*, 1987, v16(1), 22-30.

Ogden, Joseph P. "The End Of The Month As A Preferred Habitat: A Test Of Operational Efficiency In The Money Market," *JFQA*, 1987, v22(3), 329-344.

Ogden, Joseph P. "Turn-Of-Month Evaluations Of Liquid Profits And Stock Returns: A Common Explanation For The Monthly And January Effects," *JOF*, 1990, v45(4), 1259-1272.

Ogden, Joseph P. (Kidwell, David S., M. Wayne Marr and Joseph P. Ogden. "The Effect Of A Sinking Fund On The Reoffering Yields Of New Public Utility Bonds," *JFI*, 1989, v12(1), 1-14.)

Ogden, Joseph P. and Alan J. Tucker. "The Relative Valuation Of American Currency Spot And Futures Options: Theory And Empirical Tests," *JFQA*, 1988, v23(4), 351-368.

Ogden, Joseph P. and Alan J. Tucker. "Empirical Tests Of The Efficiency Of The Currency Futures Options Market," *JFM*, 1987, v7(6), 695-704.

Ogden, William, Jr., Nanda Rangan and Thomas Stanley. "Risk Reduction In S&L Mortgage Loan Portfolios Through Geographic Diversification," *JFSR*, 1989, v2(1), 39-48.

Ogilvie, Nigel R. "Foreign Banks In The U.S. And Geographic Restrictions On Banking," *JBR*, 1980-81, v11(2), 72-79.

O'glove, T. L. (Olstein, R. A. and T. L. O'glove. "Devaluation And Multinational Reporting," *FAJ*, 1973, v29(5), 65-69,80-84.)

O'glove, Thornton and Robert Olstein. "How Well Do Accountants Understand Materiality?," *JPM*, 1976-77, v3(2), 19-25.

O'glove, Thornton L. "Finance Company Accounting," *FAJ*, 1968, v24(1), 37-44.

O'Grady, James Patrick, Jr. "Sales Forecasting Techniques Used By Selected Life Insurance Companies," *JRI*, 1965, v32(1), 113-120.

Oh, John S. "Opportunity Cost In The Evaluation Of Investment In Accounts Receivable," *FM*, 1976, v5(2), 32-36.

Oh, John S. (Lin, Kuan-Pin and John S. Oh. "Stability Of The U.S. Short-Run Money Demand Function, 1959-81," *JOF*, 1984, v39(5), 1383-1396.)

O'Hanlon, J. (Choy, A. Y. F. and J. O'Hanlon. "Day Of The Week Effects In The UK Equity Market: A Cross Sectional Analysis," *JBFA*, 1989, v16(1), 89-104.)

O'Hanlon, J. (Condoyanni, L., J. O'Hanlon and C.W.R. Ward. "Day Of The Week Effects On Stock Returns: International Evidence," *JBFA*, 1987, v14(1), 159-174.)

O'Hanlon, J. (Kamarotou, H. and J. O'Hanlon. "Informational Efficiency In The UK, US, Canadian And Japanese Equity Markets: A Note," *JBFA*, 1989, v16(2), 183-192.)

O'Hanlon, John and Charles W. R. Ward. "How To Lose At Winning Strategies," *JPM*, 1985-86, v12(3), 20-23.

O'Hanlon, John. "The Relationship In Time Between Annual Accounting Returns And Annual Stock Market Returns In The UK," *JBFA*, 1991, v18(3), 305-314.

O'Hara, M. "Financial Contracts And International Lending," *JBF*, 1990, v14(1), 11-32.

O'Hara, Maureen and George S. Oldfield. "The Microeconomics Of Market Making," *JFQA*, 1986, v21(4), 361-376.

O'Hara, Maureen and Wayne Shaw. "Deposit Insurance And Wealth Effects: The Value Of Being 'Too Big To Fail'," *JOF*, 1990, v45(5), 1587-1600.

O'Hara, Maureen. "A Dynamic Theory Of The Banking Firm," **JOF,** 1983, v38(1), 127-140.

O'Hara, Maureen. "Commodity Bonds And Consumption Risks," **JOF,** 1984, v39(1), 193-206.

O'Hara, Maureen. "Tax-Exempt Financing: Some Lessons From History," **JMCB,** 1983, v15(4), 425-441.

O'Hara, Maureen. (Burdett, Kenneth and Maureen O'Hara. "Building Blocks: An Introduction To Block Trading," **JBF,** 1987, v11(2), 193-212.)

O'Hara, Maureen. (Easley, David and Maureen O'Hara. "Price, Trade Size, And Information In Securities Markets," **JFEC,** 1987, v19(1), 69-90.)

O'Hara, T. E. (Nicholson, G. A., Jr. and T. E. O'Hara. "Investment Clubs," **FAJ,** 1968, v24(3), 141-146.)

O'Hara, Michael. "Improvement Of Owner-Occupied Rental Housing: A Game-Theoretic Study Of The Decision To Invest," **AREUEA,** 1981, v9(1), 54-66.

O'Haria, Maureen. (Jarrow, Robert A. and Maureen O'Hara. "Primes And Scores: An Essay On Market Imperfections," **JOF,** 1989, v44(5), 1263-1288.)

O'Hay, Charles F. and Charles T. Casazza. "A New Screen For Superior Stock Selection," **JPM,** 1975-76, v2(3), 45-52.

Ohls, James. (Brewster, J. Alan, Irving Crespi, Richard Kaluzny, James Ohls and Cynthia Thomas. "Homeowner Warranties: A Study Of The Need And Demand For Protection Against Unanticipated Repair Expenses," **AREUEA,** 1980, v8(2), 207-217.)

Ohlson, J. A. and W. T. Ziemba. "Portfolio Selection In A Lognormal Market When The Investor Has A Power Utility Function," **JFQA,** 1976, v11(1), 57-71.

Ohlson, James A. and A. Gregory Buckman. "Toward A Theory Of Financial Accounting," **JOF,** 1980, v35(2), 537-547.

Ohlson, James A. and Mark B. Garman. "A Dynamic Equilibrium For The Ross Arbitrage Model," **JOF,** 1980, v35(3), 675-684.

Ohlson, James A. and Markku Kallio. "A Note On The Representation Of Bounded Utility Functions Defined On [a,oo]," **JFQA,** 1975, v10(2), 377-379.

Ohlson, James A. and Stephen H. Penman. "Volatility Increases Subsequent To Stock Splits: An Empirical Abberation," **JFEC,** 1985, v14(2), 251-266.

Ohlson, James A. "Ex Post Stockholder Unanimity," **JBF,** 1985, v9(3), 387-399.

Ohlson, James A. "Portfolio Selection In A Log-Stable Market," **JFQA,** 1975, v10(2), 285-298.

Ohlson, James A. "Risk, Return, Security-Valuation, And The Stochastic Behavior Of Accounting Numbers," **JFQA,** 1979, v14(2), 317-336.

Ohlson, James A. "The Structure Of Asset Prices And Socially Useless/Useful Information," **JOF,** 1984, v39(5), 1417-1435.

Ohlson, James A. (Garman, Mark B. and James A. Ohlson. "Valuation Of Risky Assets In Arbitrage-Free Economies With Transactions Costs," **JFEC,** 1981, v9(3), 271-280.)

Ohlson, James A. (Hakansson, Nils H., J. Gregory Kunkel and James A. Ohlson. "Sufficient And Necessary Conditions For Information To Have Social Value In Pure Exchange(5), 1169-1181.)

Ohlson, James A. (Rosenberg, Barr and James A. Ohlson. "The Stationary Distribution Of Returns And Portfolio Separation In Capital Markets: A Fundamental Contradiction," **JFQA,** 1976, v11(3), 393-402.)

Ohlson, James and Barr Rosenberg. "Systematic Risk Of The CRSP Equal-Weighted Common Stock Index: A History Estimated By Stochastic-Parameter Regression," **JOB,** 1982, v55(1), 121-146.

Ohmae, Kenichi. "Lies, Damned Lies, And Statistics': Why The Trade Deficit Doesn't Matter In A Borderless World," **JACF,** 1991, v3(4), 98-106.

Ohrsuka, Eisaku. (Babbel, David F. and Eisaku Ohrsuka. "Aspects Of Optimal Multiperiod Life Insurance," **JRI,** 1989, v56(3), 460-481.)

O'Keef, Michael and Robert Van Order. "Mortgage Pricing: Some Provisional Empirical Results," **AREUEA,** 1990, v18(3), 313-322.

O'Keefe, Terrence B. (Nathan, Kevin S. and Terrence B. O'Keefe. "The Rise In Takeover Premiums: An Exploratory Study," **JFEC,** 1989, v23(1), 101-120.)

Okner, Benjamin A. "The Social Security Payroll Tax: Some Alternatives For Reform," **JOF,** 1975, v30(2), 567-578.

Oksanen, E. H. (Kliman, M. L. and E. H. Oksanen. "The Keynesian Demand-For-Money Function: A Comment," **JMCB,** 1973, v5(1), 215-220.)

Okuda, Hitoshi. (Cohen, Kalman J., Walter L. Ness, Jr., Hitoshi Okuda, Robert A. Schwartz and David K. Whitcomb. "The Determinants Of Common Stock Returns Volatility: An International Comparison," **JOF,** 1976, v31(2), 733-739.)

Okuda, Hitoshi. (Cohen, Kalman J., Steven F. Maier, Walter L. Ness, Jr., Hitoshi Okuda, Robert A. Schwartz and David K. Whitcomb. "The Impact Of Designated Market Makers On Security Prices," **JBF,** 1977, v1(3), 219-247.)

Okun, Arthur M. "A Review Of Some Economic Forecasts For 1955-57," **JOB,** 1959, v32(3), 199-211.

Okun, Arthur M. "On The Appraisal Of Cyclical Turning-Point Predictors," **JOB,** 1960, v33(2), 101-120.

Okun, Arthur M. "Political Economy: Some Lessons Of Recent Experience," **JMCB,** 1972, v4(1), 23-39.

Okun, Arthur M. "Rational-Expectations-With-Misperceptions As A Theory Of The Business Cycle," **JMCB,** 1980, v12(4), Part 2, 817-825.

Okunev, John. "An Alternative Measure Of Mutual Fund Performance," **JBFA,** 1990, v17(2), 247-264.

Okunev, John. "The Generation Of Mean Gini Efficient Sets," **JBFA,** 1991, v18(2), 209-218.

Olasov, Brian F. (Mauldin, Patrick D., Brian F. Olasov and Craig K. Ruff. "The Use Of Mortgage-Derivative Products By Southeastern Thrifts," **FAJ,** 1990, v46(3), 71-76.)

O'Leary, James J. "Economic Outlook For 1968," **FAJ,** 1968, v24(3), 17-21.

O'Leary, James J. "Outlook For Interest Rates," **FAJ,** 1969, v25(1), 39-44.

O'Leary, James J. "Outlook For The Long-Term Capital Market," **JOF,** 1956, v11(2), 223-228.

O'Leary, James J. "The Economic And Investment Outlook," **FAJ,** 1966, v22(1), 22-24.

O'Leary, James J. "The Effects Of Monetary Policies On The Mortgage Market," **JOF,** 1958, v13(2), 176-187.

O'Leary, James J. "The Effects Of Recent Credit And Debt Management Policies Upon Life Insurance Company Investments," **JOF,** 1952, v7(2), 307-320.

O'Leary, James J. "The Investment Research Program Of The Life Insurance Association Of America," **JRI,** 1964, v31(3), 355-370.

O'Leary, James J. "The Outlook For The Bond Market," **JOF,** 1963, v18(2), 413-416.

O'Leary, James J. "Valuation Of Life Insurance Company Holding Of Corporate Bonds And Stocks - Some Recent Developments," **JOF,** 1954, v9(2), 160-177.

Oldfield, George S. and Carlos E. Rovira. "Futures Contract Options," **JFM,** 1984, v4(4), 479-490.

Oldfield, George S. and Richard J. Messina. "Forward Exchange Price Determination In Continuous Time," **JFQA,** 1977, v12(3), 473-481.

Oldfield, George S. "Financial Aspects Of The Private Pension System," **JMCB,** 1977, v9(1), 48-54.

Oldfield, George S. "The Free Market Regulation Of Bank Capital," **FM,** 1976, v5(4), 56-58.

Oldfield, George S. (Jarrow, Robert A. and George S. Oldfield. "Forward Contracts And Futures Contracts," **JFEC,** 1981, v9(4), 373-382.)

Oldfield, George S. (Juncker, George R. and George S. Oldfield. "Projecting Market Structure By Monte Carlo Simulation: A Study Of Bank Expansion In New Jersey," **JOF,** 1972, v27(5), 1101-1126.)

Oldfield, George S. (Logue, Dennis E. and George S. Oldfield. "Managing Foreign Assets When Foreign Exchange Markets Are Efficient," **FM,** 1977, v6(2), 16-22.)

Oldfield, George S. (Logue, Dennis E. and George S. Oldfield. "What's So Special About Foreign Exchange Markets?," **JPM,** 1976-77, v3(3), 19-24.)

Oldfield, George S. (O'Hara, Maureen and George S. Oldfield. "The Microeconomics Of Market Making," **JFQA,** 1986, v21(4), 361-376.)

Oldfield, George S., Jr. and Richard J. Rogalski. "Treasury Bill Factors And Common Stock Returns," **JOF,** 1981, v36(2), 337-354.

Oldfield, George S., Jr. and Richard J. Rogalski. "A Theory Of Common Stock Returns Over Trading And Non-Trading Periods," **JOF,** 1980, v35(3), 729-751.

Oldfield, George S., Jr. (Bierman, Harold, Jr. and George S. Oldfield, Jr. "Corporate Debt And Corporate Taxes," **JOF,** 1979, v34(4), 951-956.)

Oldfield, George S., Jr., R. J. Rogalski and Robert A. Jarrow. "An Autoregressive Jump Process For Common Stock Returns," **JFEC,** 1977, v5(3), 389-418.

Oliver, A. (Boies, D., D. Carroll, A. Fleischer, J. Grundfest, J. Ira Harris, M. Lipton, R. Monks, A. Oliver, L. Sachnoff and J. Wilcox. "Panel: Corporate Governance: The Role Of Boards Of Directors In Takeover Bids And Defenses," **JACF,** 1989, v2(2), 6-35.)

Oliver, Bruce L. "Selected Insights On Bankers' Loan Decisions," **JBR,** 1973-74, v4(4), 311-313.

Oliver, Jan and Eric Flamholtz. "Human Resource Replacement Cost Numbers, Cognitive Information Processing, And Personnel Decisions: A Laboratory Experiment," **JBFA,** 1978, v5(2), 137-158.

Oliver, Thomas W. (Finnerty, Joseph E. and Thomas W. Oliver. "The Impact Of Qualified Audit Opinions On Systematic Risk," **AFPAF,** 1985, v1(1), 293-306.)

Olivera, J. H. G. "Passive Money, Inflation, And Economic Growth: A Comment," **JMCB,** 1971, v3(1), 137-144.

Olsen, E. Odgers, Jr. "The Role Of Time In The Neoclassical Theory Of The Firm," **JOB,** 1976, v49(4), 541-554.

Olsen, Edgar O. "What Do Economists Know About The Effect Of Rent Control On Housing Maintenance?," **JREFEC,** 1988, v1(3), 295-308.

Olsen, Eric E. (Brzozowski, Leonard J., Lee D. Turner and Eric E. Olsen. "Project Financing Evaluation: A Simulation Approach," **JBR,** 1977-78, v8(1), 40-49.)

Olsen, J. A. and T. A. Blaney. "The Copper Industry Study," **FAJ,** 1968, v24(2), 35-39.

Olsen, John A. "The Evolution Of The Investment Advisers Act," **FR,** 1967, v1(2), 58-65.

Olsen, R. B. (Muller, U. A., M. M. Dacorogna, R. B. Olsen, O. V. Pictet, M. Schwarz and C. Morgenegg. "Statistical Study Of Foreign Exchange Rates, Empirical Evidence Of A Price Change Scaling Law, And Intraday Analysis," **JBF,** 1990, v14(6), 1189-1208.)

Olsen, Robert A. "Lease Vs. Purchase Or Lease Vs. Borrow: Comment," **FM,** 1978, v7(2), 82-83.

Olsen, Robert A. "The Effect Of Interest-Rate Risk On Liquidity Premiums: An Empirical Investigation," **JFQA,** 1979, v9(5), 901-909.

Olsen, Robert M. "Allocating Sales Effort To Branches," **JRI,** 1970, v37(3), 361-368.

Olsen, Robert. "Sample Size And Markowitz Diversification," **JPM,** 1983-84, v10(1), 18-22.

Olson, Douglas G. (Cummins, J. David and Douglas G. Olson. "An Analysis Of The Black Lung Compensation Program," **JRI,** 1974, v41(4), 633-654.)

Olson, Lola M. and J. Dennis Lord. "Market Area Characteristics And Branch Bank Performance," **JBR,** 1979-80, v10(2), 102-110.

Olson, Ronald L. and Donald G. Simonson. "Gap Management And Market Rate Sensitivity In Banks," **JBR,** 1982-83, v13(1), 53-58.

Olstein, R. A. and T. L. O'glove. "Devaluation And Multinational Reporting," **FAJ,** 1973, v29(5), 65-69,80-84.

Olstein, Robert. (O'glove, Thornton and Robert Olstein. "How Well Do Accounts Understand Materiality?," **JPM,** 1976-77, v3(2), 19-25.)

O'Malley, Terence P. (Gooding, Arthur E. and Terence P. O'Malley. "Market Phase And The Stationarity Of Beta," **JFQA,** 1977, v12(5), 833-857.)

Omberg, Edward. "A Note On The Convergence Of Binomial-Pricing And Compound-Option Models," **JOF,** 1987, v42(2), 463-469.

Omberg, Edward. "Efficient Discrete Time Jump Process Models In Option Pricing," **JFQA,** 1988, v23(2), 161-174.

Omberg, Edward. "The Expected Utility Of The Doubling Strategy," **JOF,** 1989, v44(2), 515-524.

O'Neill, Daniel E. (Allvine, Fred C. and Daniel E. O'Neill. "Stock

Osteryoung, Jerome S., Daniel E. McCarty and Gordon S. Roberts. "Riding A Hedged Yield Curve With Treasury Bill Futures," **JBR**, 1983-84, v14(4), 266-273.

Osteryoung, Jerome S., Elton Scott and Gordon S. Roberts. "Selecting Capital Projects With The Coefficient Of Variation," **FM**, 1977, v6(2), 65-70.

Osteryoung, Jerome S., Rodney L. Roenfeldt and Donald A. Nast. "Capital Asset Pricing Model And Traditional Risk For Capital Budgeting: A Reply," **FR**, 1978, v13(1), 90-93.

Osteryoung, Jerome S., Ronald C. Braswell and Dallas R. Blevins. "PIC: An Alternative Approach To Accepting Bids On Local And State Government Bonds," **FM**, 1979, v8(2), 36-41.

Ostry, Jonathan D. (Edwards, Sebastian and Jonathan D. Ostry. "Anticipated Protectionist Policies, Real Exchange Rates, And The Current Account: The Case Of Rigid Wages," **JIMF**, 1990, v9(2), 206-219.)

Otis, George G. "Marketing Research - A New Tool For Security Analysis," **FAJ**, 1958, v14(4), 31-34.

Otjen, Theo P. and Arthur J. Pabst. "Updating Life Insurance Settlement Options," **JRI**, 1960, v27(4), 75-84.

Otley, D. T. (Emmanuel, C. R. and D. T. Otley. "The Usefulness Of Residual Income," **JBFA**, 1976, v3(4), 43-51.)

Otley, David T. "The Accuracy Of Budgetary Estimates: Some Statistical Evidence," **JBFA**, 1985, v12(3), 415-428.

Ott, Attiat F. (Ott, David J. and Attiat F. Ott. "Budget Balance And Equilibrium Income," **JOF**, 1965, v20(1), 71-77.)

Ott, David J. and Attiat F. Ott. "Budget Balance And Equilibrium Income," **JOF**, 1965, v20(1), 71-77.

Ott, Mack. (Batten, Dallas S. and Mack Ott. "The Interrelationship Of Monetary Policies Under Floating Exchange Rates," **JMCB**, 1985, v17(1), 103-110.)

Ott, Mack. (Belongia, Michael T. and Mack Ott. "The US Monetary Policy Regime, Interest Differentials, And Dollar Exchange Rate Risk Premia," **JIMF**, 1989, v8(1), 137-146.)

Ott, Robert A., Jr. "The Duration Of An Adjustable-Rate Mortgage And The Impact Of The Index," **JOF**, 1986, v41(4), 923-934.

Otto, Frederick J. "Status Of Discretionary Commodity Accounts: Security Laws Applicability," **JFM**, 1991, v1(Supp), 453-456.

Otto, Ingolf H. E. "Capacity," **JRI**, 1961, v28(1), 53-70.

Otto, Ingolf H. E. "The British Insurance Scene," **JRI**, 1961, v28(1), 105-111.

Otto, Ingolf H. E. "The Hierarchic Hubris Of Abstractions," **JRI**, 1961, v28(4), 117-123.

Ou, Charles C. F. "Demand For Short-Term Foreign Assets By The German Banks," **JOF**, 1972, v27(3),653-662.

Ouattara, Korotoumou, Ted C. Schroeder and L. Orlo Sorenson. "Potential Use Of Futures Markets For International Marketing Of Cote D'Ivoire Coffee," **JFM**, 1990, v10(2), 113-122.

Oudet, Bruno A. "The Variation Of The Return On Stocks In Periods Of Inflation," **JFQA**, 1973, v8(2), 247-258.

Ousterbout, Jo. (McCrary, Dennis and Jo Ousterbout. "The Development And Future Of The Loan Sales Market," **JACF**, 1989, v2(3), 74-84.)

Outreville, J. F. (Eeckhoudt, L., J. F. Outreville, M. Lauwers and F. Calcoen. "The Impact Of A Probationary Period On The Demand For Insurance," **JRI**, 1988, v55(2), 217-228.)

Outreville, J. Francois and Jean-Louis Malouin. "What Are The Major Journals That Members of ARIA Read?," **JRI**, 1985, v52(4), 723-733.

Outreville, J. Francois and Carole Helie. "More Evidence On The Systematic Underwriting Risk In Automobile Insurance," **JRI**, 1986, v53(4), 755-766.

Outreville, J. Francois and Michel Zins. "Job-Related Responses Of Insurance Agents: More Evidence," **JRI**, 1987, v54(4), 800-803.

Outreville, J. Francois. "Report On Canadian And United States Risk And Insurance Curricula," **JRI**, 1982, v49(3), 472-476.

Outreville, J. Francois. "The Transactions Demand For Cash Balances By Property And Liability Insurance Companies," **JRI**, 1987, v54(3), 557-568.

Outreville, J. Francois. "The Economic Significance Of Insurance Markets In Developing Countries," **JRI**, 1990, v57(3), 487-498.

Outreville, J. Francois. (Cummins, J. David and J. Francois Outreville. "An International Analysis Of Underwriting Cycles In Property-Liability Insurance," **JRI**, 1987, v54(2), 246-262.)

Outreville, Jean-Francois. "The Impact Of The Government No-Fault Plan For Automobile Insurance In The Province Of Quebec," **JRI**, 1984, v51(2), 320-335.

Ouyang, Ling-Nan. "Joint Ventures In China: Problems And Solutions," **FR**, 1988, v23(2), 175-182.

Ovadia, Arie. (Givoly, Dan and Arie Ovadia. "Year-End Tax-Induced Sales And Stock Market Seasonality," **JOF**, 1983, v38(1), 171-185.)

Overdahl, James A. and Dennis R. Starleaf. "The Hedging Performance Of The CD Futures Market," **JFM**, 1986, v6(1), 71-82.

Overdahl, James A. "The Early Exercise Of Options On Treasury Bond Futures," **JFQA**, 1988, v23(4), 437-450.

Overdahl, James A. "The Use Of Crude Oil Futures By The Governments Of Oil-Producing States," **JFM**, 1987, v7(6), 603-618.

Overman, Edwin S. "Evolution Of A Science - An Introduction," **JRI**, 1962, v29(3), 305-320.

Overman, Edwin S. "The Most Appropriate Generic Term To Identify The Property-Casualty Field Of Insurance," **JRI**, 1962, v29(4), 558-566.

Overstreet, George A. (McAlister, M. Khris and George A. Overstreet. "Comparative Job Satisfaction Levels Among Bank Managers," **JBR**, 1978-79, v(4), 213-217.)

Overstreet, George A., Lawrence C. Pettit and Robert S. Kemp. "A Professional Approach To Building An Undergraduate Finance Program: The McIntire Experience," **JFED**, 1986, v15, 42-52.

Overstreet, George A., Jr. (Van Matre, Joseph G. and George A. Overstreet, Jr. "Motor Vehicle Inspection And Accident Mortality: A Reexamination," **JRI**, 1982, v49(3), 423-435.)

Overturf, Stephen Frank. "Interest Rate Expectations And Interest Parity," **JIMF**, 1986, v5(1), 91-98.

Owen, C. F. "Cost Factors In The Integration Of Company Unemployment Benefits And Unemployment Insurance," **JOB**, 1957, v30(1), 50-59.

Owen, Joel and Ramon Rabinovitch. "The Cost Of Information And Equilibrium In The Capital Asset Market," **JFQA**, 1980, v15(3), 497-508.

Owen, Joel and Ramon Rabinovitch. "On The Class Of Elliptical Distributions And Their Application To The Theory Of Portfolio Choice," **JOF**, 1983, v38(3),745-752.

Owen, Joel. "Analysis Of Variance Tests For Local Trends In The Standard And Poor's Index," **JOF**, 1968, v23(3), 509-514.

Owen, Joel. (Brief, R. P. and Joel Owen. "Accounting And Investment Analysis," **FAJ**, 1975, v31(1), 52-56.)

Owen, Joel. (Brief, Richard P. and Joel Owen. "A Note On Earnings Risk And The Coefficient Of Variation," **JOF**, 1969, v24(5), 901-904.)

Owen, Joel. (Brief, Richard P. and Joel Owen. "A Note On The Inclusion Of Earnings Risk In Measures Of Return: A Reply," **JOF**, 1977, v32(4), 1367.)

Owen, Joel. (Rabinovitch, Ramon and Joel Owen. "Nonhomogeneous Expectations And Information In The Capital Asset Market," **JOF**, 1978, v33(2), 575-587.)

Owens, B. D. "Some Legal Aspects Of International Life Insurance," **JRI**, 1964, v31(2), 257-252.

Owens, Hugh F. "Investment Adviser Regulation," **FAJ**, 1973, v29(1), 12-14,18,86-87.

Owens, Robert W. and G. Lee Willinger. "Investment Potential Of An Individual Retirement Account," **JBR**, 1985-86, v16(3), 161-168.

Owers, James E. (Hite, Gailen L. and James E. Owers. "Security Price Reactions Around Corporate Spin-Off Announcements," **JFEC**, 1983, v12(4),409-436.)

Owers, James E. (Hite, Gailen L., James E. Owers and Ronald C. Rogers. "The Market For Interfirm Asset Sales: Partial Sell-Offs And Total Liquidations," **JFEC**, 1987, v18(2), 229-252.)

Owers, James E. (Hite, Gailen L., James E. Owers and Ronald C. Rogers. "The Separation Of Real Estate Operations By Spin-Off," **AREUEA**, 1984, v12(3), 318-331.)

Owers, James E. (Rogers, Ronald C. and James E. Owers. "Equity For Debt Exchanges And Stockholder Wealth," **FM**, 1985, v14(3), 18-26.)

Owers, James E. (Rogers, Ronald C., Neil B. Murphy and James E. Owers. "Financial Innovation, Balance Sheet Cosmetics And Market Response: The Case Of Equity-For-Debt Exchanges In Banking," **JBR**, 1985-86, v16(3), 145-149.)

Owers, James E. (Rogers, Ronald C. and James E. Owers. "The Impact Of Value Line Special Situation Recommendations On Stock Prices," **FR**, 1984, v19(2), 195-207.)

Owers, James E. (Rogers, Ronald C. and James E. Owers. "The Investment Of Performance Of Public Real Estate Limited Partnerships," **AREUEA**, 1985, v13(2), 153-166.)

Oxelheim, Lars and Clas G. Wihlborg. "Hedging And Managing Exchange Rate And Related Macroeconomic Exposure," **RDIBF**, 1988, v2, 321-348.

Oxelheim, Lars and Clas G. Wihlborg. "Using Financial Instruments To Hedge Macroeconomic Exposure," **RFM**, 1988, v7(Supp), 504-522.

Oxelheim, Lars and Clas Wihlborg. "Exchange Rate-Related Exposures In A Macroeconomic Perspective," **RDIBF**, 1987, v1, 87-102.

Oxelheim, Lars. "Proposals For New Accounting Standards For Foreign Monetary Items," **JBFA**, 1983, v10(2), 257-288.

Oxenfeldt, Alfred R. "Valuation Of Closely Held Securities," **FAJ**, 1953, v9(4), 33-38.

Ozanne, Larry. "The Financial Stakes In Due-On-Sale: The Case Of California's State-Chartered Savings And Loans," **AREUEA**, 1984, v12(4), 473-494.

PPP

Paarlberg, Don. "The Economic Challenge Of The Soviet Union," **JOB**, 1960, v33(2), 93-100.

Pabst, Arthur J. (Otjen, Theo P. and Arthur J. Pabst. "Updating Life Insurance Settlement Options," **JRI**, 1960, v27(4), 75-84.)

Pace, R. Kelley and Otis W. Gilley. "Estimation Employing A Priori Information Within Mass Appraisal And Hedonic Pricing Models," **JREFEC**, 1990, v3(1), 55-72.

Pace, R. Kelley. (Gilley, Otis W. and R. Kelley Pace. "A Hybrid Cost And Market-Based Estimator For Appraisal," **JRER**, 1990, v5(1), 75-88.)

Pacey, Patricia L. (Blair, Roger D., David L. Kaserman and Patricia L. Pacey. "A Note On Purchased Power Adjustment Clauses," **JOB**, 1985, v58(4), 409-418.)

Pack, Janet Rothenberg. "Evaluating The Usefulness Of Land Use Models For Policy Analysis," **AREUEA**, 1974, v2(2), 25-46.

Packer, Arnold H. "A Budget Structured To Reflect Economic Objectives," **JOF**, 1973, v28(2), 467-480.

Packer, Stephen B. "A Defense Of Monetary Policy," **FAJ**, 1965, v21(1), 83-89.

Packer, Stephen B. "A Look At The Balance Of Payments," **FAJ**, 1972, v28(6), 20-21,24-25,28-29,86.

Packer, Stephen B. "Economic Significance Of Fiscal Drag," **FAJ**, 1965, v21(6), 127-133.

Packer, Stephen B. "Flow Of Funds Analysis - Its Uses And Limitations," **FAJ**, 1964, v20(4), 117-123.

Packer, Stephen B. "Forecasting Consumer Spending For Durable Goods," **FAJ**, 1962, v18(6), 53-60.

Packer, Stephen B. "Higher Interest Rates Forever?," **FAJ**, 1968, v24(1), 84-90.

Packer, Stephen B. "Monetary Policy - A Current Perspective," **FAJ**, 1966, v22(6), 107-114.

Packer, Stephen B. "Municipal Bond Ratings," **FAJ**, 1968, v24(4), 93-97.

Packer, Stephen B. "New Era For The Capital Markets," **FAJ**, 1970, v26(4), 10-16.

Packer, Stephen B. "New Game Plan In Perspective," **FAJ**, 1972, v28(1), 44-48,91-94.

Packer, Stephen B. "Population Growth And Market Forecasting," **FAJ**, 1966, v22(2), 13-18.

Packer, Stephen B. "The Credit 'Crunch' - '69 Vs. '66," **FAJ**, 1969, v25(5), 18-24.

Packer, Stephen B. "Why Buy Bonds?," **FAJ**, 1961, v17(1), 23-29.

Padberg, Manfred W. (Elton, Edwin J., Martin J. Gruber and Manfred W. Padberg. "Simple Criteria For Optimal Portfolio Selection," **JOF**, 1976, v31(5), 1341-1357.)

Padberg, Manfred W. (Elton, Edwin J., Martin J. Gruber and Manfred W. Padberg. "Simple Rules For Optimal Portfolio Selection: The Multi Group Case," **JFQA**, 1977, v12(3), 329-345.)

Padberg, Manfred W. (Elton, Edwin J., Martin J. Gruber and Manfred W. Padberg. "Optimal Portfolios From Simple Ranking Devices," **JPM**, 1977-78, v4(3), 15-19.)

Padberg, Manfred W. (Elton, Edwin, Martin J. Gruber and Manfred W. Padberg. "Simple Criteria For Optimal Portfolio Selection: Tracing Out The Efficient Frontier," **JOF**, 1978, v33(1), 296-302.)

Padhan, Mahmood. (Blake, David and Mahmood Pradhan. "Debt-Equity Swaps As Bond Conversions: Implications For Pricing," **JBF**, 1991, v15(1), 29-41.)

Padmanabhan, Prasad. (Errunza, Vihang R. and Prasad Padmanabhan. "Further Evidence On The Benefits Of Portfolio Investments In Emerging Markets," **FAJ**, 1988, v44(4), 76-78.)

Padoa-Schioppa, Tommaso. (Caligiuri, Gian Franco, Antonio Fazio and Tommaso Padoa-Schioppa. "Demand And Supply Of Bank Credit In Italy," **JMCB**, 1974, v6(4), 455-479.)

Padoan, P. C. (Gandolfo, G., P. C. Padoan and G. Paladino. "Exchange Rate Determination: Single-Equation Or Economy-Wide Models? A Test Against The Random Walk," **JBF**, 1990, v14(5), 965-992.)

Pagan, Adrian. "A Note On The Magnitude Of Risk Premia," **JIMF**, 1988, v7(1), 109-110.

Page, Albert L. (Cowen, Scott S. and Albert L. Page. "Factors Affecting The Performance Of Loans To Minority Small Businessmen: A Case Study," **JBR**, 1979-80, v10(3), 184-188.)

Page, Alfred N. "Residential Construction: Exploration Of The Statistical Series," **JOB**, 1967, v40(1), 36-43.

Page, Alfred N. "The Variation Of Mortgage Interest Rates," **JOB**, 1964, v37(3), 280-294.

Page, Alfred N. and Richard R. West. "Evaluating Student Performance In Graduate Schools Of Business," **JOB**, 1969, v42(1), 36-41.

Page, Daniel E. (Harris, John M., Jr. and Daniel E. Page. "Rate Level Index Mortgage: An Evaluation," **AREUEA**, 1985, v13(2), 195-207.)

Page, Daniel E. (Jahera, John S., Jr., William P. Lloyd and Daniel E. Page. "The Relationship Between Financial Performance And Stock Market Based Measures Of Corporate Diversification," **FR**, 1987, v22(4), 379-390.)

Page, E. W., Jr. (Gumperz, Julian and E. W. Page, Jr. "Pension Fund Performance," **FAJ**, 1970, v26(3), 30-32,72-77.)

Page, Frank H., Jr. and Anthony B. Sanders. "A General Derivation Of The Jump Process Option Pricing Formula," **JFQA**, 1986, v21(4), 437-446.

Page, John R. and Paul Hooper. "Financial Statements For Security Analysts," **FAJ**, 1979, v35(5),50-55.

Page, John R. (Young, S. David, Michael A. Berry, David W. Harvey and John R. Page. "Systematic Risk And Accounting Information Under The Arbitrage Pricing Theory," **FAJ**, 1987, v43(5), 73-76.)

Paget, Richard M. "What Management Can Do About The Profit Squeeze," **FAJ**, 1964, v20(2), 43-45.

Pak, Simon. (Garcia, Gillian and Simon Pak. "The Rate Of Currency To Demand Deposits In The United States," **JOF**, 1979, v34(3), 703-715.)

Pakkala, A. L. "Accounting Of Multinational Companies," **FAJ**, 1975, v31(2), 32-34,36,38-40,76.

Pakkala, A. L. "Fixed Costs And Earnings Predictions," **FAJ**, 1979, v35(1), 46-48.

Pakkala, A. L. "The Market For Amateur Photography," **FAJ**, 1977, v33(5), 48-52.

Pakkala, A. L. "There Is A Free Lunch," **FAJ**, 1988, v44(5), 83-87.

Pakkala, A. L. "Trust Department Income," **FAJ**, 1968, v24(4), 140-144.

Pakonen, R. Rodney. "'Chicago Banking': Additional Comment," **JOB**, 1970, v43(1), 56-59.

Paladino, G. (Gandolfo, G., P. C. Padoan and G. Paladino. "Exchange Rate Determination: Single-Equation Or Economy-Wide Models? A Test Against The Random Walk," **JBF**, 1990, v14(5), 965-992.)

Palasvirta, A. P. (Fischer, K. P. and A. P. Palasvirta. "High Road To A Global Marketplace: The International Transmission Of Stock Market Fluctuations," **FR**, 1990, v25(3), 371-394.)

Palda, Kristian S. "The Measurement Of Cumulative Advertising Effects," **JOB**, 1965, v38(2), 162-179.

Palepu, Krishna G. "Consequences Of Leveraged Buyouts," **JFEC**, 1990, v27(1), 247-262.

Palepu, Krishna G. (Healy, Paul M. and Krishna G. Palepu. "Earnings Information Conveyed By Dividend Initiations And Omissions," **JFEC**, 1988, v21(2), 149-176.)

Palepu, Krishna G. (Healy, Paul M. and Krishna G. Palepu. "How Investors Interpret Changes In Corporate Financial Policy," **JACF**, 1989, v2(3), 59-64.)

Palfrey, Thomas R. (Forsythe, Robert, Thomas R. Palfrey and Charles R. Plott. "Futures Markets And Information Efficiency: A Laboratory Examination," **JOF**, 1984, v39(4), 955-981.)

Palme, Lennart A., Jr. and James Graham. "The Systematic Downward Bias In Live Cattle Futures: An Evaluation," **JFM**, v1(3), 359-366.

Palmer, Bruce A. "Illustrated And Realized Policyowner Dividends: An Empirical Analysis," **JRI**, 1976, v43(4), 673-692.

Palmer, Bruce A. "Tax Reform And Retirement Income Replacement Ratios," **JRI**, 1989, v56(4), 702-725.

Palmer, Bruce A. (Burnett, John J. and Bruce A. Palmer. "Reliance On Life Insurance Agents: A Demographic And Psychographic Analysis Of Consumers," **JRI**, 1983, v50(3), 510-520.)

Palmer, Bruce A. (Burnett, John J. and Bruce A. Palmer. "Examining Life Insurance Ownership Through Demographic And Psychographic Characteristics," **JRI**, 1984, v51(3), 453-467.)

Palmer, Gilbert H. "An Approach To Stock Valuation," **FAJ**, 1956, v12(2), 17-20.

Palmer, Gilbert H. "Earnings Per Share - Growth And Dilution Factors," **FAJ**, 1954, v10(2), 61-64.

Palmer, Michael. "Money Supply And Stock Prices," **FAJ**, 1970, v26(4), 19-22.

Palmer, Michael. (Gordon, Kenneth R. and Michael Palmer. "A Comparison Of The Financial Institutions' View And The Market's View Of Country Creditworthiness," **JFSR**, 1989, v2(2), 73-88.)

Palmer, W. (Hand, Herbert H. and W. Palmer. "A Bibliography Of Operating Expense Information Sources For Small Businesses," **JFED**, 1979, v8, 97-98.)

Palmon, Dan and Meir I. Schneller. "The Relationship Between Securities' Abnormal Price Movements And Wall Street Journal News," **JBF**, 1980, v4(3), 235-248.

Palmon, Dan and Uzi Yaari. "Retention And Tax Avoidance: A Clarification," **FM**, 1981, v10(1), 29-36.

Palmon, Dan and Uzi Yaari. "Share Values, Inflation, And Escalating Tax Rates," **JBF**, 1981, v5(3), 395-403.

Palmon, Dan and Uzi Yaari. "Personal Taxes And The Fair Rate Of Return Doctrine," **FR**, 1983, v18(2), 167-174.

Palmon, Dan and Uzi Yaari. "Stock Repurchase As A Tax-Saving Distribution," **JFR**, 1981, v4(1),69-79.

Palmon, Dan. (Givoly, Dan and Dan Palmon. "Insider Trading And The Exploitation Of Inside Information: Some Empirical Evidence," **JOB**, 1985, v58(1), 69-88.)

Palmon, Dan. (Givoly, Dan, Dan Palmon and Mier Schneller. "Perception Of Stock Similarity By Financial Analysts," **FR**, 1981, v16(3), 30-43.)

Palmon, Dan. (Marcus, Matityahu, Dan Palmon and Uzi Yaari. "Growth And The Decision To Incorporate: A Financial Theory Of The U.S. Tax System," **RIF**, 1986, v6, 29-50.)

Palmon, Dan. (Yaari, Uzi, Dan Palmon and Matityahu Marcus. "Stock Prices Under Inflation With Taxation Of Nominal Gains," **FR**, 1980, v15(1), 38-54.)

Palmon, Oded. (Ben-Horim, Moshe, Shalom Hochman and Oded Palmon. "The Impact Of The 1986 Tax Reform Act On Corporate Financial Policy," **FM**, 1987, v16(3), 29-35.)

Palmon, Oded. (Hochman, Shalom and Oded Palmon. "Expected Inflation And The Real Rates Of Interest On Taxable And Tax-Exempt Bonds," **JMCB**, 1987, v19(1), 90-103.)

Palmon, Oded. (Hochman, Shalom and Oded Palmon. "A Tax-Induced Clientele For Index-Linked Corporate Bonds," **JOF**, 1988, v43(5), 1257-1263.)

Palmon, Oded. (Hochman, Shalom and Oded Palmon. "The Impact Of Inflation On The Aggregate Debt-Asset Ratio," **JOF**, 1985, v40(4), 1115-1125.)

Palmon, Oded. (Hochman, Shalom and Oded Palmon. "The Irrelevance Of Capital Structure For The Impact Of Inflation On Investment," **JOF**, 1983, v38(3), 785-794.)

Pan, Fung-Shine and James W. Hoag. "The Pricing Of GNMA Futures Using Dealer Quotations And Spot Transactions," **RFM**, 1984, v3(3), 244-255.

Pan, Judy, Donald R. Nichols and O. Maurice Joy. "Sales Forecasting Practices Of Large U.S. Industrial Firms," **FM**, 1977, v6(3), 72-77.

Panimon, Charlotte. (Caldwell, J. E. and Charlotte Panimon. "Projective Testing In An Industrial Research Organization: One Experience," **JOB**, 1955, v28(1), 67-71.)

Panjer, Harry H. "Direct Calculation Of Ruin Probabilities," **JRI**, 1986, v53(3), 521-529.

Panjer, Harry H. (Bellhouse, David R. and Harry H. Panjer. "Stochastic Modelling Of Interest Rates With Applications To Life Contingencies - Part II," **JRI**, 1981, v48(4), 628-637.)

Panjer, Harry H. and David R. Bellhouse. "Stochastic Modelling Of Interest Rates With Applications To Life Contingencies," **JRI**, 1980, v47(1), 91-110.

Pankoff, Lyn D. "Market Efficiency And Football Betting," **JOB**, 1968, v41(2), 203-214.

Pankratz, Alan. "On Modernized Liquidity Preference Theory: A Comment," **JMCB**, 1972, v4(4), 1010-1015.

Pantalone, Coleen C. (Platt, Harlan D. and Coleen C. Pantalone. "Riding The Yield Curve," **JFED**, 1984, v13, 5-9.)

Pantalone, Colleen C. and Marjorie B. Platt. "Predicting Failure Of Savings And Loan Associations," **AREUEA**, 1987, v15(2), 46-64.

Panton, Don B. and William A. Verdini. "A FORTRAN Program For Applying Sturm's Theorem In Counting Internal Rates Of Return," **JFQA**, 1981, v16(3), 381-388.

Panton, Don B. "Approximating The Cumulative Distribution Function In Programming The B-S Call Valuation Model," **JFED**, 1985, v14, 86-91.

Panton, Don B. "The Relevance Of The Distributional Form Of Common Stock Returns To The Construction Of Optimal Portfolios: Comment," **JFQA**, 1989, v24(1), 129-131.

Panton, Don B. (Grube, R. Corwin, O. Maurice Joy and Don B. Panton. "Market Responses To Federal Reserve Changes In The Initial Margin Requirement," **JOF**, 1979, v34(3), 659-674.)

Panton, Don B. (Grube, R. Corwin and Don B. Panton. "How Well Do Filter-Rule Strategies Work For Options?," **JPM**, 1977-78, v4(2), 52-57.)

Panton, Don B. (Grube, R. Corwin, Don B. Panton and J. Michael Terrell. "Risks And Rewards In Covered Call Positions," **JPM**, 1978-79, v5(2), 64-68.)

Panton, Don B. (Joy, O. Maurice, Don B. Panton, Frank K. Reilly and Stanley A. Martin. "Comovements Of Major International Equity Markets," **FR**, 1976, v11(1), 1-20.)

Panton, Don B., V. Parker Lessiq and O. Maurice Joy. "Comovement Of International Equity Markets: A Taxonomic Approach," **JFQA**, 1976, v11(3), 415-432.

Pany, Kurt and Lawrence F. Sherman. "Information Analysis Of Several Large Failed Banks," **JBR**, 1979-80, v10(3), 145-151.

Papadia, F. and S. Rossi. "More On Monetarist Arithmetic," **JBF**, 1990, v14(1), 145-154.

Papadia, Francesco and Salvatore Rossi. "Are Asymmetric Exchange Controls Effective?," **JIMF**, 1991, v10(1), 149-160.

Papadia, Francesco. "Estimates Of Ex Ante Real Rates Of Interest In The EEC Countries And In The United States, 1973-82," **JMCB**, 1984, v16(3), 335-344.

Papadia, Francesco. "Forward Exchange Rates As Predictors Of Future Spot Rates And The Efficiency Of The Foreign Exchange Market," **JBF**, 1981, v5(2), 217-240.

Papaioannou, George J. (Grammatikos, Theoharry and George J. Papaioannou. "The Informational Value Of Listing On The New York Stock Exchange," **FR**, 1986, v21(4), 485-499.)

Papaioannou, George. (Grammatikos, Theoharry and George Papaioannou. "Market Reaction to NYSE Listings: Tests Of The

Marketability Gains Hypothesis," **JFR**, 1986, v9(3), 215-228.)

Papaioannou, George. (Bhandari, Arvind, Theoharry Grammatikos, Anil K. Makhija and George Papaioannou. "Risk And Return On Newly Listed Stocks: The Post-Listing Experience," JFR, 1989, v12(2), 93-102.)

Papell, David H. "Activist Monetary Policy And Exchange-Rate Overshooting: The Deutsche Mark/Dollar Rate," JIMF, 1984, v3(3), 293-310.

Papell, David H. "Anticipated And Unanticipated Disturbances: The Dynamics Of The Exchange Rate And The Current Account," JIMF, 1984, v3(2), 179-193.

Papera, D. Robert. (Kimbali, Peter and D. Robert Papera. "Effect Of Stock Splits On Short-Term Market Prices," FAJ, 1964, v20(3), 75-80.)

Papier, William. "What's Wrong With Unemployment Insurance?," JRI, 1970, v37(1), 63-74.

Pappas, J. L. and E. F. Brigham. "Growth Rate Changes And Common Stock Prices," FAJ, 1966, v22(3), 157-162.

Pappas, James L. and George P. Huber. "Probabilistic Short-Term Financial Planning," FM, 1973, v2(3), 36-44.

Pappas, James L. "A Note On The Inclusion Of Earnings Risk In Measures Of Return: A Comment," JOF, 1977, v32(4), 1363-1366.

Pappas, James L. (Brigham, Eugene F. and James L. Pappas. "Rates Of Return On Common Stock," JOB, 1969, v42(3), 302-316.)

Pappas, James L. (Haugen, Robert A. and James L. Pappas. "Equilibrium In The Pricing Of Capital Assets, Risk-Bearing Debt Instruments, And The Question Of Optimal Capital Structure," JFQA, 1971, v6(3), 943-953.)

Pappas, James L. (Haugen, Robert A. and James L. Pappas. "Equilibrium In Pricing Of Capital Assets, Risk-Bearing Debt Instruments, And The Question Of Optimal Capital Structure: A Reply," JFQA, 1972, v7(4), 2005-2008.)

Pappas, James L. (Haugen, Robert A. and James L. Pappas. "A Comment On The Capital Structure And The Cost Of Capital: A Suggested Exposition," JOF, 1970, v25(3), 674-677.)

Pardue, Morris. (Melitz, Jacques and Morris Pardue. "The Demand And Supply Of Commercial Bank Loans," JMCB, 1973, v5(2), 669-692.)

Pares, Antonio. "The Return On Equity Decomposition (ROED) And Its Importance To Financial Statement Analysis," JBFA, 1980, v7(3), 365-376.

Pares, Antonio. (Stonehill, Arthur, Theo Beekhuisen, Richard Wright, Lee Remmers, Norman Toy, Antonio Pares, Alan Shapiro, Douglas Egan and Thomas Bates. "Financial Goals And Debt Ratio Determinants," FM, 1974, v4(3), 27-41.)

Parhizgari, A. M. (Prakash, Arun J., A. M. Parhizgari and Gerald W. Perritt. "The Effect Of Listing On The Parameters Of Characteristic Lines Models," JBFA, 1989, v16(3), 335-342.)

Pari, Robert A. and Son-Nan Chen. "An Empirical Test Of The Arbitrage Pricing Theory," JFR, 1984, v7(2), 121-130.

Pari, Robert A. and Son-Nan Chen. "Estimation Risk And Optimal Portfolios," JPM, 1985-86, v12(1), 40-43.

Pari, Robert A. "Wall Street Week Recommendations: Yes Or No?," JPM, 1987-88, v14(1), 74-76.

Pari, Robert A. (Benesh, Gary A. and Robert A. Pari. "Performance Of Stocks Recommended On The Basis Of Insider Trading Activity," FR, 1987, v22(1), 145-158.)

Pari, Robert A. (Chatterjee, Sangit and Robert A. Pari. "Bootstrapping The Number Of Factors In The Arbitrage Pricing Theory," JFR, 1990, v13(1), 15-22.)

Pari, Robert A. (Johnson, James M., Robert A. Pari and Leonard Rosenthal. "The Impact Of In-Substance Defeasance On Bondholder And Shareholder Wealth," JOF, 1989, v44(4), 1049-1058.)

Pari, Robert and John Caks. "A Note On Bond Defeasance," FR, 1988, v23(2), 233-236.

Pari, Robert, Steven Carvell and Timothy Sullivan. "Analyst Forecasts And Price/Earnings Ratios," FAJ, 1989, v45(2), 60-62.

Park, Hun Y. and Andrew H. Chen. "Differences Between Futures And Forward Prices: A Further Investigation Of The Marking-to-Market Effect," JFM, 1985, v5(1), 77-88.

Park, Hun Y. and R. Stephen Sears. "Estimating Stock Index Futures Volatility Through The Prices Of Their Options," JFM, 1985, v5(2), 223-238.

Park, Hun Y. and R. Stephen Sears. "Changing Volatility And The Pricing Of Options On Stock Index Futures," JFR, 1985, v8(4), 265-274.

Park, Hun Y. "Reexamination Of Normal Backwardation Hypothesis In Futures Markets," JFM, 1985, v5(4), 505-515.

Park, Hun Y. (Chen, Andrew H., Neil A. Doherty and Hun Y. Park. "The Optimal Capital Structure Decision Of Depository Financial Intermediaries: A Contingent-Claim Analysis," RIF, 1988, v7, 91-112.)

Park, Hun Y. (Colwell, Peter F. and Hun Y. Park. "Seasonality And Size Effects: The Case Of Real-Estate-Related Investment," JREFEC, 1990, v3(3), 251-260.)

Park, Hun Y. (Finnerty, Joseph E. and Hun Y. Park. "Stock Index Futures: Does The Tail Wag The Dog?," FAJ, 1987, v43(2), 57-61.)

Park, Hun Y. (Finnerty, Jospeh E. and Hun Y. Park. "How To Profit From Program Trading," JPM, 1987-88, v14(2), 40-46.)

Park, Hun Y. (Follain, James R. and Hun Y. Park. "Hedging The Interest Rate Risk Of Mortgages With Prepayment Options," RFM, 1989, v8(1), 62-78.)

Park, Hun Y. (Lee, Cheng F. and Hun Y. Park. "Value Line Investment Survey Rank Changes And Beta Coefficients," FAJ, 1987, v43(5), 70-72.)

Park, Hun Y. and Anil K. Bera. "Interest-Rate Volatility, Basis Risk And Heteroscedasticity In Hedging Mortgages," AREUEA, 1987, v15(2), 79-97.

Park, Hun. (Bera, Anil, Edward Bubnys and Hun Park. "Conditional Heteroscedasticity In The Market Model And Efficient Estimates Of Betas," FR, 1988, v23(2), 201-214.)

Park, Jeong Yun, Donald J. Mullineaux and It-Keong Chew. "Are REITs Inflation Hedges?," JREFEC, 1990, v3(1), 91-103.

Park, Keehwan. "Tests Of The Hypothesis Of The Existence Of Risk Premium In The Foreign Exchange Market," JIMF, 1984, v3(2),

169-178.

Park, Keehwan. (Fujihara, Roger and Keehwan Park. "The Probability Distribution Of Futures Prices In The Foreign Exchange Market: A Comparison Of Candidate Processes," JFM, 1990, v10(6), 623-642.)

Park, Sang Yong and Marc R. Reinganum. "The Puzzling Price Behavior Of Treasury Bills That Mature At The Turn Of Calendar Months," JFEC, 1986, v16(2), 267-283.

Park, Sang Yong and Joseph Williams. "Taxes, Capital Structure, And Bondholder Clienteles," JOB, 1985, v58(2), 203-224.

Park, Soo-Bin. "Spot And Forward Rates In The Canadian Treasury Bill Market," JFEC, 1982, v10(1), 107-114.

Park, Timothy and Frances Antonovitz. "Basis Risk And Optimal Decision Making For California Feedlots," JFM, 1990, v10(3), 259-272.

Park, Won J. (Larsen, James E. and Won J. Park. "Non-Uniform Percentage Brokerage Commissions And Real Estate Market Performance," AREUEA, 1989, v17(4), 422-438.)

Park, Yung Chul. "The Transmission Process And The Relative Effectiveness Of Monetary And Fiscal Policy In A Two-Sector Neoclassical Model," JMCB, 1973, v5(2), 595-622.

Parke, Darrel W. (Pierce, David A., Darrel W. Parke, William P. Cleveland and Agustin Maravall. "Uncertainty In The Monetary Aggregates: Sources, Measurement And Policy Effects," JOF, 1981, v36(2), 507-515.)

Parker, Barbara. (White, Charles S., Marilyn M. Helms and Barbara Parker. "Simulations Versus Cases: Impact On The Analysis And Interpretation Of Financial Statements," JFED, 1990, v19, 33-36.)

Parker, C. Reed. "The Trueblood Report," FAJ, 1975, v31(1), 32-41.

Parker, G. G. C. and S. S. Stewart, Jr. "Risk And Investment Performance," FAJ, 1974, v30(3), 49-51.

Parker, G. G. C. (Van Horne, James C. and G. G. C. Parker. "An Empirical Test," FAJ, 1967, v23(6),87-92.)

Parker, G. G. C. (Van Horne, James C. and G. G. C. Parker. "Technical Trading Rules," FAJ, 1968, v24(4), 128-132.)

Parker, George G. C. and Daniel Cooperman. "Competitive Bidding In The Underwriting Of Public Utilities Securities," JFQA, 1978, v13(5), 885-902.

Parker, George G. C. and Robert P. Shay. "Some Factors Affecting Awareness Of Annual Percentage Rates In Consumer Installment Credit Transactions," JOF, 1974, v29(1), 217-225.

Parker, George G. C. (Seelenfreund, Alan, George G. C. Parker and James C. Van Horne. "Stock Price Behavior And Trading," JFQA, 1968, v3(3), 263-281.)

Parker, Jack W. and Robert T. Daigler. "Hedging Money Market CDs With Treasury-Bill Futures," JFM, v1(4), 597-606.

Parker, James E. "New Rules For Determining EPS," FAJ, 1970, v26(1), 49-53.

Parker, Joel. (Pittman, Robert and Joel Parker. "A Survey Of Corporate Real Estate Executives On Factors Influencing Corporate Real Estate Performance," JRER, 1989, v4(3), 107-119.)

Parker, R. H. (Nobes, C. W. and R. H. Parker. "True And Fair': A Survey Of UK Financial Directors," JBFA, 1991, v18(3), 359-376.)

Parker, Stephen. (Pettijohn, James, Gerald Udell and Stephen Parker. "The Quest For AACSB Accreditation: Must Finance Faculty Really Publish Or Perish?," FPE, 1991, v1(1), 53-56.)

Parkes, Robert H. "Use And Abuse Of Financial And Monetary Data," JPM, 1974-75, v1(3), 65-73.

Parkhill, Roberta L. (Ennis, Richard M. and Roberta L. Parkhill. "South African Divestment: Social Responsibility Or Fiduciary Folly?," FAJ, 1986, v42(4), 30-38.)

Parkin, Michael. "The Transition From Fixed Exchange Rates To Money Supply Targets," JMCB, 1977, v9(1), Part 2, 228-242.

Parkinson, Michael. "Empirical Warrant-Stock Relationships," JOB, 1972, v45(4), 563-569.

Parkinson, Michael. "Option Pricing: The American Put," JOB, 1977, v50(1), 21-36.

Parkinson, Michael. "The Valuation Of GNMA Options," FAJ, 1982, v38(5), 66-76.

Parks, Richard W. (Kochin, Levis A. and Richard W. Parks. "Was The Tax-Exempt Bond Market Inefficient Or Were Future Expected Tax Rates Negative?," JOF, 1988, v43(4), 913-931.)

Parks, Robert H. "Monetary Policy And The Creation Of Near-Money," FAJ, 1965, v21(5), 85-93.

Parks, Robert H. "Portfolio Operations Of Commercial Banks And The Level Of Treasury Security Prices," JOF, 1959, v14(1), 52-66.

Parks, William H. (Richards, Larry E. and William H. Parks. "A Note On Model Specification," JFQA, 1972, v7(3), 1847-1850.)

Paroush, Jacob and Yoram C. Peles. "Search For Information And Portfolio Selection," JBF, 1978, v2(2), 163-177.

Paroush, Jacob and Avner Wolf. "Production And Hedging Decisions In The Presence Of Basis Risk," JFM, 1989, v9(6), 547-564.

Paroush, Jacob and Jacques Sibler. "The Stochastic Dominance Criteria, Mortality Risk And Investment In Education: A Cross-Country Comparison," RIF, 1980, v2, 111-120.

Paroush, Jacob and Meir Sokoler. "The Firm's Trade Credit Under Uncertainty And Some Macro Implications," RIF, 1983, v4, 153-164.

Paroush, Jacob. "A Note On Relative Efficiency And Risk Aversion," JBF, 1981, v5(2), 277-280.

Paroush, Jacob. "The Domino Effect And The Supervision Of The Banking System," JOF, 1988, v43(5), 1207-1218.

Paroush, Jacob. (Prager, Jonas and Jacob Paroush. "On The Differential Effects Of Tight Money: Comment," JOF, 1971, v26(4), 951-954.)

Parr, Philip C. (Emery, Douglas R., Philip C. Parr, Per B. Mokkelbost, David Gandhi and Anthony Saunders. "An Investigation Of Real Investment Decision Making With The Options Pricing Model," JBFA, 1978, v5(4), 363-369.)

Parrino, Robert. (Vandell, Robert F. and Robert Parrino. "A Purposeful Stride Down Wall Street," JPM, 1985-86, v12(2), 31-39.)

Parry, C. L., G. L. Amrhein and C. D. Spangler. "Interim Report Of The Committee On Insurance Bibliography," JRI, 1937, v4, 25-27.

Parry, Corliss L. "The Insurance Industry In Defense And War Finance," JRI, 1942, v9, 53-62.

Parry, Robert T. (Thomson, Thomas D., James L. Pierce and Robert T. Parry. "A Monthly Money Market Model," JMCB, 1975, v7(4), 411-431.)

Parry, Robert W., Jr. and Stuart K. Webster. "City Leases: Up Front, Out Back, In The Closet," FAJ, 1980, v36(5), 41-47.

Parsons John E. and Arthur Raviv. "Underpricing Of Seasoned Issues," JFEC, 1985, v14(3), 377-397.

Parsons, John E. "Estimating The Strategic Value Of Long-Term Forward Purchase Contracts Using Auction Models," JOF, 1989, v44(4), 981-1010.

Partch, M. Megan. "The Creation Of A Class Of Limited Voting Common Stock And Shareholder Wealth," JFEC, 1987, v18(2), 313-340.

Partch, M. Megan. (Mikkelson, Wayne H. and M. Megan Partch. "Valuation Effects Of Security Offerings And The Issuance Process," JFEC, 1986, v15(1/2), 31-60.)

Partch, M. Megan. (Mikkelson, Wayne H. and M. Megan Partch. "Stock Price Effects And Costs Of Secondary Distributions," JFEC, 1985, v14(2), 165-194.)

Partch, M. Megan. (Mikkelson, Wayne H. and M. Megan Partch. "Withdrawn Security Offerings," JFQA, 1988, v23(2), 119-134.)

Partch, M. Megan. (Mikkelson, Wayne H. and M. Megan Partch. "Managers' Voting Rights And Corporate Control," JFEC, 1989, v25(2), 263-290.)

Partch, Megan. (James, Christopher, Sergio Koreisha and Megan Partch. "A Varma Analysis Of The Causal Relations Among Stock Returns, Real Output, And Nominal Interest Rates," JOF, 1985, v40(5), 1375-1384.)

Partington, G. H. "The Tax-Deductibility Of Interest Payments And The Weighted Average Cost of Capital: A Comment," JBFA, 1979, v6(1), 95-100.

Partington, Graham H. "Dividend Policy And Its Relationship To Investment And Financing Policies: Empirical Evidence," JBFA, 1985, v12(4), 531-542.

Partington, Graham H. "Financial Decisions, The Cost(s) Of Capital And The Capital Asset Pricing Model," JBFA, 1981, v8(1), 97-112.

Partington, Graham H. "Variables Influencing Dividend Policy In Australia: Survey Results," JBFA, 1989, v16(2), 165-182.

Partington, J. E. (Loman, H. J., E. L. Bowers and J. E. Partington. "Report Of The Committee On Standards And Topics For Courses In Insurance," JRI, 1937, v4, 5-9.)

Pascucci, John J. (Kamerschen, David R. and John J. Pascucci. "The Retail Price Structure In American Life Insurance: Comment," JRI, 1969, v36(3), 493-494.)

Pashigian, B. Peter. Lawrence L. Schkade and George H. Menefee. "The Selection Of An Optimal Deductible For A Given Insurance Policy," JOB, 1966, v39(1), Part I, 35-44.

Pashigian, B. Peter. "The Political Economy Of Futures Market Regulation," JOB, 1986, v59(2), Part 2, S55-S84.

Pashigian, B. Peter. (Frenkel, Jacob A. and B. Peter Pashigian. "Regulation And Economic Demand: A General-Equilibrium Approach," JOB, 1972, v45(3), 379-384.)

Pashley, Mary M. (Shrieves, Ronald E. and Mary M. Pashley. "Evidence On The Association Between Mergers And Capital Structure," FM, 1984, v13(3), 39-48.)

Pastena, Victor S. (Lurie, Arlene J. and Victor S. Pastena. "Prompt Disclosure Of Company Problems," FAJ, 1975, v31(5), 55-61.)

Pastoriza, Hugh. "Growth Of Share Earnings In Regulated Industries," FAJ, 1958, v14(5), 45-50.

Pastre, Olivier. "International Bank-Industry Relations: An Empirical Assessment," JBF, 1981, v5(1), 65-76.

Patel, Jayendu and Richard Zeckhauser. "Treasury Bill Futures As Unbiased Predictors: New Evidence And Relation To Unexpected Inflation," RFM, 1989, v8(3), 352-369.

Patel, Kanaklata and Dean A. Paxson. "Basis Convergence And Rate Volatility In Sterling LIBOR Futures," RFM, 1989, v8(2), 262-284.

Patel, Kiritkumar A. (Ang, James S. and Kiritkumar A. Patel. "Bond Rating Methods: Comparison And Validation," JOF, 1975, v30(2), 631-640.)

Patel, Sandeep A. (Blume, Marshall E., Donald B. Keim and Sandeep A. Patel. "Returns And Volatility Of Low-Grade Bonds, 1977-1989," JOF, 1991, v46(1), 49-74.)

Patell, James M. and Mark A. Wolfson. "The Intraday Speed Of Adjustment Of Stock Prices To Earnings And Dividend Announcements," JFEC, 1984, v13(2), 223-252.

Paternotte, William L. "Supplying The Food Service Industry," FAJ, 1973, v29(6), 50,52,54,56-57,80.

Patinkin, Don. "Inside Money, Monoply Bank Profits, And The Real-Balance Effect: A Comment," JMCB, 1971, v3(2), Part 1, 271-275.

Patinkin, Don. "The Chicago Tradition, The Quantity Theory, And Friedman," JMCB, 1969, v1(1), 46-70.

Patten, Leslie A. (Anderson, Richard G., E. Jayne McCarthy and Leslie A. Patten. "Valuing The Core Deposits Of Financial Institutions: A Statistical Analysis," JBR, 1986-87, v17(1), 9-17.)

Patterson, Cleveland S. "Debt And Taxes: Empirical Evidence," JBFA, 1985, v12(2), 187-206.

Patterson, Cleveland S. "Flotation Cost Allowance In Rate Of Return Regulation: Comment," JOF, 1983, v38(4), 1335-1338.

Patterson, Cleveland S. "Some Notes On The Cost Of New Equity: A Comment," JBFA, 1986, v13(2), 149-152.

Patterson, Cleveland S. "The Effects Of Leverage On Revenue Requirements Of Public Utilities," FM, 1983, v12(3), 29-39.

Patterson, Cleveland S. "The Financing Objectives Of Large U.S. Electric Utilities," FM, 1984, v13(2), 15-23.

Patterson, Douglas M. (Ashley, Richard A. and Douglas M. Patterson. "A Nonparametric, Distribution-Free Test For Serial Independence In Stock Returns," JFQA, 1986, v21(2), 221-227.)

Patterson, Douglas. (Ashley, Richard and Douglas Patterson. "A Nonparametric Distribution-Free Test For Serial Independence In Stock Returns: A Comment," JBFA, 1990, v25(3), 417-418.)

Patterson, Gardner. "Impact Of Deficit Financing In Underdeveloped Countries: Sometimes Neglected Aspects," JOF, 1957, v12(2), 178-189.

Patterson, James H. (Howe, Keith M. and James H. Patterson. "Capital Investment Decisions Under Economies Of Scale In Flotation Costs," FM, 1985, v14(3),61-69.)

Patterson, Robert T. "A Major Error In Refunding," JOF, 1952, v7(3), 421-433.

Patterson, Solon P., Dennis R. Bouwer, Theodore R. Lilley and Benjamin C. Korschot. "Long-Range Planning In The FAF," FAJ, 1979, v35(1), 23-26.

Pattillo, James W. (Morris, Michael H., William D. Nichols and James W. Pattillo. "Capitalization Of Interest, Materiality Judgement Divergence And Users' Information Needs," JBFA, 1984, v11(4), 547-555.)

Pattison, John C. and Patrick S. T. Chan. "Cash Management Of Foreign Note Holdings By Banks," JBF, 1981, v5(4), 511-522.

Pattison, John C. "Bank Deposit Variability: Some Further Evidence" JBR, 1973-74, v4(4), 308-310.

Patton, Henry H. "Investing In Latin America," FAJ, 1967, v23(4), 119-126.

Patton, Macon G. "The Textile Mill Producing Industry," FAJ, 1964, v20(3), 58-61.

Patz, Dennis H. "The State Of The Art In Translation Theory," JBFA, 1977, v4(3), 311-325.

Paul, Chris W. (Forbes, Shawn M. and Chris W. Paul. "Reply: Eduation, Publishing And Academic Markets," FPE, 1991, v1(1), 21-24.)

Paul, Chris W. and Paul H. Rubin. "Teaching And Research: The Human Capital Paradigm," FPE, 1991, v1(1), 7-10.

Paul, Jack W. "Do Timely Interim Reviews Lessen Accounting Error?," FAJ, 1986, v42(4), 70-73.

Paul, Ronda S. "Valuation, Leverage And The Cost Of Capital In The Case Of Depreciable Assets: Comment," JOF, 1975, v30(1), 211-213.

Paul, Ronda S. (Sartoris, William L. and Ronda S. Paul. "Lease Evaluation - Another Capital Budgeting Decision," FM, 1973, v2(2), 46-52.)

Pauling, N. G. "Experience With An Industrial Research Program In The Social Sciences," JOB, 1961, v34(2), 140-152.

Pauling, Norman G. "Some Neglected Areas Of Research On The Effects Of Automation And Other Technological Change On Workers," JOB, 1964, v37(3), 261-273.

Paulson, Albert S. and Peter C. Ho. "Portfolio Selection Via Factor Analysis," JPM, 1979-80, v6(3), 27-30.

Pauly, Mark V. "The Welfare Economics Of Community Rating," JRI, 1970, v37(3), 407-418.

Paxson, Dean A. (Laycock, Mark S. and Dean A. Paxson. "Hedging Noncoetaneous Cash Positions With Eurodollar Futures," RFM, 1988, v7(Supp), 484-500.)

Paxson, Dean A. (Patel, Kanaklata and Dean A. Paxson. "Basis Convergence And Rate Volatility In Sterling LIBOR Futures," RFM, 1989, v8(2), 262-284.)

Payne, John W. (Crum, Roy L., Dan J. Laughhunn and John W. Payne. "Risk-Seeking Behavior And Its Implications For Financial Models," FM, 1981, v10(5), 20-27.)

Pazner, Elisha A. and Assaf Razin. "On Expected Value Vs. Expected Future Value," JOF, 1975, v30(3), 875-877.

Peach, W. N. "Treasury Investment Funds And Open-Market Operations," JOF, 1951, v6(1), 46-53.

Peacock, Leslie C. "Monetary Policy And International Financial Objectives," JOF, 1966, v21(2), 354-359.

Peacock, Peter and Harry L. Davis. "The Alphabet As An Independent Variable: A Reply To J. Douglas McConnell," JOB, 1970, v43(2), 205-209.

Peake, J. W. (Mendelson, M. and J. W. Peake. "Which Way To A National Market System?," FAJ, 1979, v35(5), 31-34,37-42.)

Peake, Junius W. "The National Market System," FAJ, 1978, v34(4), 25-33.

Peale, Mundy J. "Research & Development - The True Capital Of The Space Age," FAJ, 1963, v19(5), 45-47.

Pearce, Douglas K. and V. Vance Roley. "The Reaction Of Stock Prices To Unanticipated Changes In Money: A Note," JOF, 1983, v38(4), 1323-1333.

Pearce, Douglas K. "An Empirical Analysis Of Expected Stock Price Movements," JMCB, 1984, v16(3), 317-327.

Pearce, Douglas K. "Comparing Survey And Rational Measures Of Expected Inflation: Forecast Performance And Interest Rate Effects," JMCB, 1979, v11(4), 447-456.

Pearce, Douglas K. "Short-Term Inflation Expectations: Evidence From A Monthly Survey," JMCB, 1987, v19(3), 388-395.

Pearce, Douglas K. (Jones, Charles P., Douglas K. Pearce and Jack W. Wilson. "Can Tax-Loss Selling Explain The January Effect? A Note," JOF, 1987, v42(2), 453-461.)

Pearce, Douglas K. and V. Vance Roley. "Firm Characteristics, Unanticipated Inflation, And Stock Returns," JOF, 1988, v43(4), 965-981.

Pearce, Douglas K. and V. Vance Roley. "Stock Prices And Economic News," JOB, 1985, v58(1), 49-68.

Pearl, Lawrence R. (Mayor, Thomas H. and Lawrence R. Pearl. "Life-Cycle Effects, Structural Change, And Long-Run Movements In The Velocity Of Money," JMCB, 1984, v16(2), 175-184.)

Pearson, Charles. (Fong, Gifford, Charles Pearson and Oldrich Vasicek. "Bond Performance: Analyzing Sources Of Return," JPM, 1982-83, v9(3), 46-50.)

Pearson, Thomas D. "Assessment Ratios And Property Tax Burdens In Norfolk, Virginia, 1974-1975," AREUEA, 1979, v7(2), 190-203.

Pearson, Thomas. (Dotzour, Mark G., Terry V. Grissom, Crocker H. Liu and Thomas Pearson. "Highest And Best Use: The Evolving Paradigm," JRER, 1990, v5(1), 17-32.)

Pease, Fred. "The Warrant - Its Powers And Its Hazards," FAJ, 1963, v19(1), 25-32.

Peasnell, K. V. and L. C. L. Skerratt. "Long-Term Debt And Shareholder Wealth: A Comment," JBFA, 1976, v3(3), 137-142.

Peasnell, K. V. and L. C. L. Skerratt. "Price Indices For Current Cost Accounting - A Reply And Some Further Evidence," JBFA, 1977, v4(1), 139-144.

Peasnell, K. V. and L. C. L. Skerratt. "Performance Of A Relative Decline Model: An Efficient Markets Interpretation Of Some Results Of Jones, Tweedie And Whittington," JBFA, 1978, v5(2), 261-267.

Peasnell, K. V. "Some Formal Connections Between Economic Values And Yields And Accounting Numbers," JBFA, 1982, v8(3), 361-381.

Peasnell, K. V. "The Present Value Concept In Financial Reporting," JBFA, 1977, v4(2), 153-168.

Peasnell, K. V. "The Present Value Concept In Financial Reporting: A Reply," JBFA, 1978, v5(3), 395.

Peasnell, K. V. (Lui, Y. H. and K. V. Peasnell. "Time Series Behaviour, Predictability And Speculation In The Hong Kong Foreign Exchange Market," JBFA, 1989, v16(2), 145-164.)

Peasnell, K. V., L. C. L. Skerratt and P. A. Taylor. "An Arbitrage Rationale For Tests Of Mutual Fund Performance," JBFA, 1979, v6(3), 373-400.

Peavy, John W. and S. Michael Edgar. "An Expanded Commercial Paper Rating Scale: Classification Of Industrial Issuers," JBFA, 1984, v11(3), 397-407.

Peavy, John W., III and David A. Goodman. "How Inflation, Risk And Corporate Profitability Affect Common Stock Returns," FAJ, 1985, v41(5), 59-65.

Peavy, John W., III and David A. Goodman. "The Significance Of P/Es For Portfolio Returns," JPM, 1982-83, v9(2), 43-47.

Peavy, John W., III and Jonathan A. Scott. "The Effect Of Stock For Debt Swaps On Security Returns," FR, 1985, v20(4), 303-327.

Peavy, John W., III and Jonathan A. Scott. "A Closer Look At Stock-For-Debt Swaps," FAJ, 1985, v41(3), 44-50.

Peavy, John W., III and S. Michael Edgar. "A Multiple Discriminant Analysis Of BHC Commercial Paper Ratings: A Reply," JBF, 1986, v10(1), 145-146.

Peavy, John W., III and S. Michael Edgar. "A Multiple Discriminant Analysis Of BHC Commercial Paper Ratings," JBF, 1983, v7(2), 161-174.

Peavy, John W., III and George H. Hempel. "The Effect Of The WPPSS Crisis On The Tax-Exempt Bond Market," JFR, 1987, v10(3), 239-248.

Peavy, John W., III and George H. Hempel. "The Penn Square Bank Failure: Effect On Commercial Bank Security Returns--A Note," JBF, 1988, v12(1), 141-150.

Peavy, John W., III. "Closed-End Fund IPOs: Caveat Emptor," FAJ, 1989, v45(3), 71-74.

Peavy, John W., III. "Returns On Initial Public Offerings Of Closed-End Funds," RFS, 1990, v3(4), 695-709.

Peavy, John W., III. (Barry, Christopher B., Chris J. Muscarella, John W. Peavy, III and Michael R. Vetsuypens. "The Role Of Venture Capital In The Creation Of Public Companies: Evidence From The Going-Public Process," JFEC, 1990, v27(2), 447-472.)

Peavy, John W., III. (Barry, Christopher B. and John W. Peavy, III. "Risk Characteristics Of Closed-End Stock Fund IPOs," JFSR, 1990, v4(1), 65-76.)

Peavy, John W., III. (Chalk, Andrew J. and John W. Peavy, III. "Initial Public Offerings: Daily Returns, Offering Types And The Price Effect ," FAJ, 1987, v43(5), 65-69.)

Peavy, John W., III. (Chalk, Andrew J. and John W. Peavy, III. "Understanding The Pricing Of Initial Public Offerings," RIF, 1990, v8, 203-240.)

Peavy, John W., III. (Goodman, David A. and John W. Peavy, III. "The Risk Universal Nature Of The P/E Effect," JPM, 1984-85, v11(4), 14-16.)

Peavy, John W., III. (Goodman, David A. and John W. Peavy, III. "The Interaction Of Firm Size And Price-Earnings Ratio On Portfolio Performance," FAJ, 1986, v42(1), 9-12.)

Peavy, John W., III. (Goodman, David A. and John W. Peavy, III. "Industry Relative Price-Earnings Ratios As Indicators Of Investment Returns," FAJ, 1983, v39(4), 60-66.)

Peavy, John W., III. (Scott, Jonathan A., George H. Hempel and John W. Peavy, III. "The Effect Of Stock-For-Debt Swaps On Bank Holding Companies," JBF, 1985, v9(2), 233-251.)

Pechman, Clarice. (Dornbusch, Rudiger and Clarice Pechman. "The Bid-Ask Spread In The Black Market For Dollars In Brazil," JMCB, 1985, v17(4), Part 1, 517-520.)

Pechman, Joseph A. "Distribution Of Federal And State Income Taxes By Income Class," JOF, 1972, v27(2), 179-191.

Pechman, Joseph A. "Individual Income Tax Provisions Of The Revenue Act Of 1964," JOF, 1965, v20(2), 247-272.

Peck, Anne E. "Comments On 'The Economics Of Hedging And Spreading In Futures Markets'," JFM, v1(2), 287-289.

Peck, James. "Liquidity Without Money: A General Equilibrium Model Of Market Microstructure," JFI, 1990, v1(1), 80-103.

Peck, Leslie G. "A Critique Of The Filter Technique," FAJ, 1966, v22(3), 156.

Peckman, Morris. "A Means For Measuring Market Movements," FAJ, 1955, v11(5), 71-78.

Peek, Joe and James A. Wilcox. "The Postwar Stability Of The Fisher Effect," JOF, 1983, v38(4), 1111-1124.

Peek, Joe and James A. Wilcox. "Monetary Policy Regimes And The Reduced Form For Interest Rates," JMCB, 1987, v19(3), 273-291.

Peek, Joe. "Capital Gains And Personal Saving Behavior," JMCB, 1983, v15(1), 1-23.

Peel, D. A. and P. F. Pope. "Corporate Accounting Data, Capital Market Information And Wage Increases Of The Firm," JBFA, 1984, v11(2), 177-188.

Peel, D. A. (Pope, P. F. and D. A. Peel. "Information Disclosure To Employees And Rational Expectations," JBFA, 1981, v8(1), 139-146.)

Peel, D. A. (Pope, P. F., R. C. Morris and D. A. Peel. "Insider Trading: Some Evidence On Market Efficiency And Directors' Share Dealings In Great Britain," JBFA, 1990, v17(3), 359-380.)

Peel, D. A. and P. F. Pope. "Stock Returns And Expected Inflation In The UK: Some New Evidence," JBFA, 1988, v15(4), 459-468.

Peel, David A. and Peter F. Pope. "Testing The Fisherian Hypothesis: Some Methodological Issues And Further Evidence For The UK," JBFA, 1985, v12(2), 297-312.

Peet, William. "Should Consultants In Different Disciplines Merge?," JRI, 1967, v34(2), 333-334.

Pefley, Norman G. (Kuberek, Robert C. and Norman G. Pefley. "Hedging Corporate Debt With U.S. Treasury Bond Futures," JFM, 1983, v3(4), 345-353.)

Peiser, Richard B. "Land Development Regulation: A Case Study Of Dallas And Houston, Texas," AREUEA, 1981, v9(4), 397-417.

Peiser, Richard B. "Risk Analysis In Land Development," AREUEA, 1984, v12(1), 12-29.

Peiser, Richard B. (Brueggeman, William B. and Richard B. Peiser.

"Housing Choice And Relative Tenure Prices," JFQA, 1979, v14(4), 735-751.)

Peiser, Richard B. and Lawrence B. Smith. "Homeownership Returns, Tenure Choice And Inflation," AREUEA, 1985, v13(4), 343-360.

Pekelman, Dov. (Lev, Baruch and Dov Pekelman. "A Multiperiod Adjustment Model For The Firm's Capital Structure," JOF, 1975, v30(1), 75-91.)

Peles, Yoram C. "Goodwill: Financial Statements And Valuation," RIF, 1979, v1, 95-114.

Peles, Yoram C. (Arditti, Fred D. and Yoram C. Peles. "The Regulatory Process And The Firm's Capital Structure," FR, 1980, v15(1), 1-8.)

Peles, Yoram C. (Paroush, Jacob and Yoram C. Peles. "Search For Information And Portfolio Selection," JBF, 1978, v2(2), 163-177.)

Peles, Yoram C. and Marshall Sarnat. "Government Intervention And Financial Policy: The Impact Of Corporate Taxation On Capital Structure," RIF, 1983, v4, (Supp), 169-188.

Peles, Yoram. "A Note On Risk And The Theory Of Asset Value," JFQA, 1971, v6(1), 643-647.

Peles, Yoram. "Economies Of Scale In Advertising Beer And Cigarettes," JOB, 1971, v44(1), 32-37.

Pell, Ricardo. (Saaty, Thomas L., Paul C. Rogers and Ricardo Pell. "Portfolio Selection Through Hierarchies," JPM, 1979-80, v6(3), 16-21.)

Pellatt, Peter G. K. "The Analysis Of Real Estate Investments Under Uncertainty," JOF, 1972, v27(2), 459-471.

Peltason, J. W. "Universities In Jeopardy," JRI, 1969, v36(1), 11-18.

Peltzman, Sam. "Bank Stock Prices And The Effects Of Regulation Of The Banking Structure," JOB, 1968, v41(4), 413-430.

Peltzman, Sam. "The Banking Structure And The Transmission Of Monetary Policy," JOF, 1969, v24(3), 387-411.

Peltzman, Samuel. "The Costs Of Competition: An Appraisal Of The Hunt Commission Report," JMCB, 1972, v4(4), 1001-1004.

Penati, Alessandro. "Budget Deficit, External Official Borrowing, And Sterilized Intervention Policy In Foreign Exchange Markets," JIMF, 1986, v5(1),99-113.

Penati, Alessandro. "The Sources Of The Movements In Interest Rates: An Empirical Investigation," JBF, 1986, v10(3), 343-360.

Penati, Alessandro. (Gultekin, Mustafa N., N. Bulent Gultekin and Alessandro Penati. "Capital Controls And International Capital Market Segmentation: The Evidence From The Japanese And American Stock Markets," JOF, 1989, v44(4), 849-870.)

Pendlebury, M. W. "The Application Of Information Theory To Accounting For Groups Of Companies," JBFA, 1980, v7(1), 105-117.

Pendlebury, Maurice and Rowan Jones. "Budget Auditing In Governmental Organisations Financed By Taxation," JBFA, 1983, v10(4), 585-594.

Penman, Stephen H. "A Comparison Of The Information Content Of Insider Trading And Management Earnings Forecasts," JFQA, 1985, v20(1), 1-18.

Penman, Stephen H. "Insider Trading And The Dissemination Of Firms' Forecast Information," JOB, 1982, v55(4), 479-504.

Penman, Stephen H. "The Distribution Of Earnings News Over Time And Seasonalities In Aggregate Stock Returns," JFEC, 1987, v18(2), 199-228.

Penman, Stephen H. "The Predictive Content Of Earnings Forecasts And Dividends," JOF, 1983, v38(4), 1181-1199.

Penman, Stephen H. (Ohlson, James A. and Stephen H. Penman. "Volatility Increases Subsequent To Stock Splits: An Empirical Abberation," JFEC, 1985, v14(2), 251-266.)

Penn, Robert E. "The Economics Of The Market In Modern Prints," JPM, 1980-81, v7(1), 25-32.

Pennacchi, George G. "A Reexamination Of The Over-(Or Under-) Pricing Of Deposit Insurance," JMCB, 1987, v19(3), 340-360.

Pennacchi, George G. "Alternative Forms Of Deposit Insurance: Pricing And Bank Incentive Issues," JBF, 1987, v11(2), 291-312.

Pennacchi, George G. "Loan Sales And The Cost Of Bank Capital," JOF, 1988, v43(2), 375-396.

Pennacchi, George. (Gorton, Gary and George Pennacchi. "Financial Intermediaries And Liquidity Creation," JOF, 1990, v45(1), 49-72.)

Penno, Mark and Daniel T. Simon. "Accounting Choices: Public Versus Private Firms," JBFA, 1986, v13(4), 561-569.

Pennypacker, James C. (Zakon, Alan J. and James C. Pennypacker. "An Analysis Of The Advance-Decline Line As A Stock Market Indicator," JFQA, 1968, v3(3), 299-314.)

Pentikainen, Teivo. "The Theory Of Risk And Some Applications," JRI, 1980, v47(1), 16-43.

Pepall, Lynne. (Makowski, Louis and Lynne Pepall. "Easy Proofs Of Unanimity And Optimality Without Spanning: A Pedagogical Note," JOF, 1985, v40(4), 1245-1250.)

Percival, John R. (Cummins, J. David, John R. Percival, Randolph Westerfield and J. G. Ramage. "Effects Of ERISA On The Investment Policies Of Private Pension Plans: Survey Evidence," JRI, 1980, v47(3), 447-476.)

Percival, John. A Comment: "Short-Run Interest Rate Cycles In The U. S.: 1954-1967", JFQA, 1971, v6(3), 1043-1045.

Percy, Allan L. "Electric Contacts And Controls," FAJ, 1954, v10(4), 67-68.

Percy, Allan L. "Fansteel And The Refractory Metals," FAJ, 1953, v9(2), 89-96.

Perez, Robert and Susan Malley. "Asset Allocation And The Social Security System," FM, 1983, v12(1), 29-35.

Perg, Wayne F. "Leveraged Leasing: The Problem Of Changing Leverage," FM, 1978, v7(3), 47-51.

Perin, George L. "Modern Underwriting Technique," FAJ, 1945, v1(2), 33-43.

Peristiani, Stavros. (Allen, Linda, Stavros Peristiani and Anthony Saunders. "Bank Size, Collateral, And Net Purchase Behavior In The Federal Funds Market: Empirical Evidence," JOB, 1989, v62(4), 501-516.)

Perlet, Harry F. "Impact Of Multiple Line Underwriting On Coverages, Contracts, And Operating Results," JRI, 1958, v25(1), 15-22.

Perlick, Walter W. "Bank Hiring Practices And Training Programs," JFED, 1978, v7, 30-33.

Perold, Andre F. "The Implementation Shortfall: Paper Versus Reality," JPM, 1987-88, v14(3), 4-9.

Perold, Andre F. (Gammill, James F., Jr. and Andre F. Perold. "The Changing Character Of Stock Market Liquidity," **JPM**, 1989, v15(3), 13-18.)

Perold, Andre F. (Markowitz, Harry M. and Andre F. Perold. "Portfolio Analysis With Factors And Scenarios," **JOF**, 1981, v36(4), 871-877.)

Perold, Andre F. and Evan C. Schulman. "The Free Lunch In Currency Hedging: Implications For Investment Policy And Peformance Standards," **FAJ**, 1988, v44(3), 45-52.

Perold, Andre F. and William F. Sharpe. "Dynamic Strategies For Asset Allocation," **FAJ**, 1988, v44(1), 16-27.

Perrakis, Stylianos and John Zerbinis. "Indentifying The SSD Portion Of The EV Frontier: A Note," **JFQA**, 1978, v13(1), 167-171.

Perrakis, Stylianos and Peter J. Ryan. "Option Pricing Bounds In Discrete Time," **JOF**, 1984, v39(2), 519-525.

Perrakis, Stylianos. "A Note On Optimal Equity Financing Of The Corporation," **JFQA**, 1976, v11(1), 157-164.

Perrakis, Stylianos. "Capital Budgeting And Timing Uncertainty Within The Capital Asset Pricing Model," **FM**, 1979, v8(3), 32-40.

Perrakis, Stylianos. "Certainty Equivalents And Timing Uncertainty," **JFQA**, 1975, v10(1), 109-118.

Perrakis, Stylianos. "Option Bounds In Discrete Time: Extensions And The Pricing Of The American Put," **JOB**, 1986, v59(1), 119-142.

Perreault, William D., Jr. (Spiro, Rosann L. and William D. Perreault, Jr. "Influence Use By Industrial Salesmen: Influence-Strategy Mixes And Situational Determinants," **JOB**, 1979, v52(3), 435-455.)

Perreault, William D., Jr., Warren A. French and Clyde E. Harris, Jr. "Use Of Multiple Discriminant Analysis To Improve The Salesman Selection Process," **JOB**, 1977, v50(1), 50-62.

Perrin, J. R. "Inflation Accounting: Survey Of Academic Opinion," **JBFA**, 1976, v3(1), 183-199.

Perritt, Gerald W. (Prakash, Arun J., A. M. Parhizgari and Gerald W. Perritt. "The Effect Of Listing On The Parameters Of Characteristic Lines Models," **JBFA**, 1989, v16(3), 335-342.)

Perry, Donald. (Van Fenstermaker, J. and Donald Perry. "An Examination Of A Charge Card System Operating In A Smaller Community Through Correspondent Banks," **JBR**, 1971-72, v2(1), 9-13.)

Perry, George L. "The Success Of Anti-Inflation Policies In The United States," **JMCB**, 1973, v5(1), Part II, 569-593.

Perry, Kevin J. and Robert A. Taggart, Jr. "The Growing Role Of Junk Bonds In Corporate Finance," **JACF**, 1988, v1(1), 37-45.

Perry, Larry and Timothy P. Cronan. "A Note On Rank Transformation Discriminant Analysis: An Alternative Procedure For Classifying Bank Holding Company Commercial Paper Ratings," **JBF**, 1986, v10(4), 605-610.

Perry, Larry G. "The Effect Of Bond Rating Agencies On Bond Rating Models," **JFR**, 1985, v8(4), 307-315.

Perry, Larry G. (Cronan, Timothy P., Donald R. Epley and Larry G. Perry. "The Use Of Rank Transformation And Multiple Regression Analysis In Estimating Residential Property Values With A Small Sample," **JRER**, 1986, v1(1), 19-31.)

Perry, Larry G., Glenn V. Henderson, Jr. and Timothy P. Cronan. "Multivariate Analysis Of Corporate Bond Ratings And Industry Classifications," **JFR**, 1984, v7(1), 27-36.

Perry, Larry G., Pu Liu and Dorla A. Evans. "Modified Bond Ratings: Further Evidence On The Effect Of Split Ratings On Corporate Bond Yields," **JBFA**, 1988, v15(2), 231-242.

Perry, Larry G., Timothy P. Cronan and Donald R. Epley. "A Procedure For Unconvering Acceptable And Nonacceptable Mortgage Applications Through Discriminant Analysis Using Ranked Data," **JRER**, 1987, v2(1), 61-72.

Perry, Larry. (Epley, Donald R., Timothy P. Cronan and Larry Perry. "A Research Note On Discrimination In Mortgage Lending," **AREUEA**, 1985, v13(4), 446-451.)

Perry, Philip R. "More Evidence On The Nature Of The Distribution Of Security Returns," **JFQA**, 1983, v18(2), 211-221.

Perry, Philip R. "Portfolio Serial Correlation And Nonsynchronous Trading," **JFQA**, 1985, v20(4), 517-523.

Perry, Philip R. "The Time-Variance Relationship Of Security Returns: Implications For The Return-Generating Stochastic Process," **JOF**, 1982, v37(3), 857-870.

Pertl, Mars A. (Sprecher, C. Ronald and Mars A. Pertl. "Risk Retention And The Market Implied Probability Of Loss," **JRI**, 1980, v47(2), 279-290.)

Pertl, Mars A. (Sprecher, C. Ronald and Mars A. Pertl. "Large Losses, Risk Management And Stock Prices," **JRI**, 1983, v50(1), 107-117.)

Pesando, James E. and Adonis Yatchew. "Real Versus Nominal Interest Rates And The Demand For Consumer Durables In Canada," **JMCB**, 1977, v9(3), 428-436.

Pesando, James E. "Alternative Models Of The Determination Of Nominal Interest Rates: The Canadian Evidence," **JMCB**, 1976, v8(2), 209-218.

Pesando, James E. "Determinants Of Term Premiums In The Market For United States Treasury Bills," **JOF**, 1975, v30(5), 1317-1327.

Pesando, James E. "Investment Risk, Bankruptcy Risk, And Pension Reform In Canada," **JOF**, 1982, v37(3), 741-749.

Pesando, James E. "On Forecasting Long-Term Interest Rates: Is The Success Of The No-Change Prediction Surprising: Comment," **JOF**, 1980, v35(4), 1045-1047.

Pesando, James E. "On The Accuracy And Formation Of Life Insurance Company Cash Flow Forecasts," **JOB**, 1975, v48(1), 20-26.

Pesando, James E. "On The Random Walk Characteristics Of Short- And Long-Term Interest Rates In An Efficient Market," **JMCB**, 1979, v11(4), 457-466.

Pesando, James E. "The Interest Sensitivity Of The Flow Of Funds Through Life Insurance Companies: An Econometric Analysis," **JOF**, 1974, v29(4), 1105-1121.

Pesando, James E. "The Supply Of Money And Common Stock Prices: Further Observations On The Econometric Evidence," **JOF**, 1974, v29(3), 909-921.

Pesando, James E. "The Usefulness Of The Wind-Up Measure Of Pension Liabilities: A Labor Market Perspective," **JOF**, 1985, v40(3), 927-940.

Pesando, James E. and Andre Plourde. "The October 1979 Change In The U.S. Monetary Regime: Its Impact On The Forecastability Of Canadian Interest Rates," **JOF**, 1988, v43(1), 217-239.

Pesaran, M. Hashem. "Consistency Of Short-Term And Long-Term Expectations," **JIMF**, 1989, v8(4), 511-516.

Peseau, Dennis E. and Thomas M. Zepp. "On The Use Of The CAPM In Public Utility Rate Cases: Comment," **FM**, 1978, v7(3), 52-56.

Pesek, B. P. "Equilibrium Level Of Transaction Services Of Money," **JOF**, 1973, v28(3), 647-660.

Pesek, B. P. "Four Ways Of Aggregating Monies," **JFQA**, 1972, v7(2), 1641.

Peskin, Michael W. (Gold, Jeremy and Michael W. Peskin. "Longing For Duration," **FAJ**, 1988, v44(6), 68-71.)

Peslak, Alan R. (Grambo, Ralph W. and Alan R. Peslak. "MAXFINANCE: A Package Of Programs For Comprehensive Capital Budgeting Cases," **JFED**, 1977, v6, 79-80.)

Pessemier, E. A. (Bass, F. M., E. A. Pessemier and D. J. Tigert. "A Taxonomy Of Magazine Readership Applied To Problems In Marketing Starategy And Media Selection," **JOB**, 1969, v42(3), 337-363.)

Pessemier, Edgar A. "An Experimental Method For Estimating Demand," **JOB**, 1960, v33(4), 373-383.

Peterman, John L. "Differences Between The Levels Of Spot And Network Television Advertising Rates," **JOB**, 1979, v52(4), 549-562.

Peterman, John L. and Michael Carney. "A Comment On Television Network Price Discrimination," **JOB**, 1978, v51(2), 343-352.

Peters, Donald H. "Coupon Rate Of Return," **FM**, 1972, v1(3), 25-35.

Peters, Donald H. (Haessler, Robert W. and Donald H. Peters. "More On The Coupon Rate Of Return: Haesser Versus Peters," **FM**, 1973, v2(3), 45-49.)

Peters, Donald J. "Valuing A Growth Stock," **JPM**, 1991, v17(3), 49-51.

Peters, Ed. "The Growing Efficiency Of Index-Futures Markets," **JPM**, 1984-85, v11(4), 52-56.

Peters, Edgar E. "Fractal Structure In The Capital Markets," **FAJ**, 1989, v45(4), 32-37.

Peters, Michael P. (Hisrich, Robert D., Michael P. Peters and John Krasnakevich. "Effectively Managing Consumer Credit Through Computer Graphics," **JBR**, 1982-83, v13(4), 304-308.)

Peters, Robert M. and William Poppei. "An Accelerated Program For Bankers In Accounting/Finance," **JFED**, 1980, v9, 42-45.

Petersen, H. Craig. "The Effect Of 'Fair Value' Rate Base Valuation In Electric Utility Regulation," **JOF**, 1976, v31(5), 1487-1490.

Peterson, David and Michael L. Rice. "A Note On Ambiguity In Portfolio Performance Measures," **JOF**, 1980, v35(5), 1251-1256.

Peterson, David and Pamela Peterson. "The Effect Of Changing Expectations Upon Stock Returns," **JFQA**, 1982, v17(5), 799-813.

Peterson, David R. and Donald M. Waldman. "A Model Of Heterogeneous Expectations As A Determinant Of Short Sales," **JFR**, 1984, v7(1), 1-16.

Peterson, David R. "A Transaction Data Study Of Day-Of-The-Week And Intraday Patterns In Option Returns," **JFR**, 1990, v13(2), 117-132.

Peterson, David R. "An Empirical Test Of An Ex-Ante Model Of The Determination Of Stock Return Volatility," **JFR**, 1986, v9(3), 203-214.

Peterson, David R. "Security Price Reactions To Initial Reviews Of Common Stock By The Value Line Investment Survey," **JFQA**, 1987, v22(4), 483-494.

Peterson, David R. "Stock Return Seasonalities And Earnings Information," **JFQA**, 1990, v25(2), 187-202.

Peterson, David R. (Ang, James S. and David R. Peterson. "Return, Risk, And Yield: Evidence From Ex Ante Data," **JOF**, 1985, v40(2), 537-548.)

Peterson, David R. (Ang, James S. and David R. Peterson. "An Empirical Study Of The Diffusion Process Of Securities And Portfolios," **JFR**, 1984, v7(3), 219-229.)

Peterson, David R. (Ang, James S. and David R. Peterson. "Empirical Properties Of The Elasticity Coefficient In The Constant Elasticity Of Variance Model," **FR**, 1984, v19(4), 372-380.)

Peterson, David R. (Ang, James S. and David R. Peterson. "Optimal Debt Versus Debt Capacity: A Disequilibrium Model Of Corporate Debt Behavior," **RIF**, 1986, v6, 51-72.)

Peterson, David R. (Dickinson, Amy and David R. Peterson. "Seasonality In The Option Market," **FR**, 1989, v24(4), 529-540.)

Peterson, David R. (Fehrs, Donald H., Gary A. Benesh and David R. Peterson. "Evidence Of A Relation Between Stock Price Reactions Around Cash Dividend Changes And Yields," **JFR**, 1988, v11(2), 111-124.)

Peterson, David R. (Klein, Linda S. and David R. Peterson. "Investor Expectations Of Volatility Increases Around Large Stock Splits As Implied In Call Option Premia," **JFR**, 1988, v11(1), 71-80.)

Peterson, David R. (Klein, Linda S. and David R. Peterson. "Earnings Forecast Revisions Associated With Stock Split Announcements," **JFR**, 1989, v12(4), 319-328.)

Peterson, David R. (Moore, Norman H., David R. Peterson and Pamela P. Peterson. "Shelf Registrations And Shareholder Wealth: A Comparison Of Shelf And Traditional Equity Offerings," **JOF**, 1986, v41(2), 451-464.)

Peterson, David R. (Peterson, Pamela P., David R. Peterson and James S. Ang. "Direct Evidence On The Marginal Rate Of Taxation On Dividend Income," **JFEC**, 1985, v14(2), 267-282.)

Peterson, David R. (Peterson, Pamela P., David R. Peterson and Norman H. Moore. "The Adoption Of New-Issue Dividend Reinvestment Plans And Shareholder Wealth," **FR**, 1987, v22(2), 221-232.)

Peterson, David R. (Peterson, Pamela Parrish and David R. Peterson. "Divergence Of Opinion And Return," **JFR**, 1982, v5(2), 125-134.)

Peterson, David R. (Pruitt, Stephen W. and David R. Peterson. "Security Price Reactions Around Product Recall Announcements," **JFR**, 1986, v9(2), 113-122.)

Peterson, David R. (Sullivan, Michael J., Pamela P. Peterson and David R. Peterson. "Two-Stage Acquisitions, Free-Riding, And Corporate Control," **FR**, 1990, v25(3), 405-420.)

Peterson, David R. (Tucker, Alan L., David R. Peterson and Elton Scott. "Tests Of The Black-Scholes And Constant Elasticity Of Variance Currency Call Option Valuation Models," **JFR**, 1988, v11(3), 201-214.)

Peterson, David R. (Wall, Larry D. and David R. Peterson. "Capital Changes At Large Affiliated Banks," **JFSR**, 1988, v1(3), 253-276.)

Peterson, David R. (Wall, Larry D. and David R. Peterson. "The Effect Of Capital Adequacy Guidelines On Large Bank Holding Companies," **JBF**, 1987, v11(4), 581-600.)

Peterson, David R. and Alan L. Tucker. "Implied Spot Rates As Predictors Of Currency Returns: A Note," **JOF**, 1988, v43(1), 247-258.

Peterson, David W. (Maier, Steven F., David W. Peterson and James VanderWeide. "Monte Carlo Investigation Of Characteristics Of Optimal Geometric Mean Portfolios," **JFQA**, 1977, v12(2), 215-233.)

Peterson, David. (Ang, James, David Peterson and Pamela Peterson. "Marginal Tax Rates: Evidence From Nontaxable Corporate Bonds: A Note," **JOF**, 1985, v40(1), 327-332.)

Peterson, David. (Peterson, Pamela, David Peterson and James Ang. "The Extinguishment Of Debt Through InSubstance Defeasance," **FM**, 1985, v14(1), 59-67.)

Peterson, Donald M. "Are Financial Ratios Worth The Effort?," **JPM**, 1975-76, v2(1), 51-54.

Peterson, Donald M. "Know Your Investment Philosophy!," **JPM**, 1978-79, v5(2), 27-33.

Peterson, Harries-Clichy. "Titanium: Progress, Problems, Prospects," **FAJ**, 1954, v10(1), 61-66.

Peterson, James D. (Sanger, Gary C. and James D. Peterson. "An Empirical Analysis Of Common Stock Delistings," **JFQA**, 1990, v25(2), 261-272.)

Peterson, Manferd O. and Hugh S. McLaughlin. "Conflict Of Interest And The Financing Of Commercial Bank Stock Ownership," **JBR**, 1974-75, v5(1), 7-12.

Peterson, Manferd O. (Gilbert, Gary G. and Manferd O. Peterson. "Uniform Reserve Requirements On Demand Deposits: Some Policy Issues: Comment," **JBR**, 1974-75, v5(1), 38-44.)

Peterson, Manferd O. (Gilbert, Gary G. and Manferd O. Peterson. "The Impact Of Changes In Federal Reserve Membership On Commercial Bank Performance," **JOF**, 1975, v30(3), 713-720.)

Peterson, Manferd O. (McCall, Alan S. and Manferd O. Peterson. "The Impact Of DE NOVO Commercial Bank Entry," **JOF**, 1977, v32(5), 1587-1604.)

Peterson, Manferd O. (McCall, Alan S. and Manferd O. Peterson. "A Critical Level Of Commercial Bank Concentration: An Application Of Switching Regressions," **JBF**, 1980, v4(4), 353-370.)

Peterson, Manferd. (Boorman, John T. and Manferd Peterson. "The Hunt Commission & The Mortgage Market: An Appraisal," **JBR**, 1972-73, v3(3), 155-165.)

Peterson, Pamela P. and Gary A. Benesh. "A Reexamination Of The Empirical Relationship Between Investment And Financing Decisions," **JFQA**, 1983, v18(4), 439-453.

Peterson, Pamela P. (Alexander, John, Delbert Goff and Pamela P. Peterson. "Profitability Of A Trading Strategy Based On Unexpected Earnings," **FAJ**, 1989, v45(4), 65-71.)

Peterson, Pamela P. (Ang, James and Pamela P. Peterson. "The Leasing Puzzle," **JOF**, 1984, v39(4), 1055-1065.)

Peterson, Pamela P. (Benesh, Gary A. and Pamela P. Peterson. "On The Relation Between Earnings, Changes, Analysts' Forecasts And Stock Price Fluctuations," **FAJ**, 1986, v42(6), 29-39,55.)

Peterson, Pamela P. (Moore, Norman H., David R. Peterson and Pamela P. Peterson. "Shelf Registrations And Shareholder Wealth: A Comparison Of Shelf And Traditional Equity Offerings," **JOF**, 1986, v41(2), 451-464.)

Peterson, Pamela P. (Sullivan, Michael J., Pamela P. Peterson and David R. Peterson. "Two-Stage Acquisitions, Free-Riding, And Corporate Control," **FR**, 1990, v25(3), 405-420.)

Peterson, Pamela P., David R. Peterson and James S. Ang. "Direct Evidence On The Marginal Rate Of Taxation On Dividend Income," **JFEC**, 1985, v14(2), 267-282.

Peterson, Pamela P., David R. Peterson and Norman H. Moore. "The Adoption Of New-Issue Dividend Reinvestment Plans And Shareholder Wealth," **FR**, 1987, v22(2), 221-232.

Peterson, Pamela Parrish and David R. Peterson. "Divergence Of Opinion And Return," **JFR**, 1982, v5(2), 125-134.

Peterson, Pamela Parrish. "A Re-Examination Of Seemingly Unrelated Regressions Methodology Applied To Estimation Of Financial Relationships," **JFR**, 1980, v3(3), 297-308.

Peterson, Pamela. David Peterson and James Ang. "The Extinguishment Of Debt Through In-Substance Defeasance," **FM**, 1985, v14(1), 59-67.

Peterson, Pamela. "Reincorporation: Motives And Shareholder Wealth," **FR**, 1988, v23(2), 151-160.

Peterson, Pamela. (Ang, James, David Peterson and Pamela Peterson. "Marginal Tax Rates: Evidence From Nontaxable Corporate Bonds: A Note," **JOF**, 1985, v40(1), 327-332.)

Peterson, Pamela. (Peterson, David and Pamela Peterson. "The Effect Of Changing Expectations Upon Stock Returns," **JFQA**, 1982, v17(5), 799-813.)

Peterson, Paul E. (Leuthold, Raymond M. and Paul E. Peterson. "A Portfolio Approach To Optimal Hedging For A Commercial Cattle Feedlot," **JFM**, 1987, v7(2), 119-134.)

Peterson, Paul E. and Raymond M. Leuthold. "A Portfolio Approach To Optimal Hedging For A Commercial Cattle Feedlot," **JFM**, 1987, v7(4), 443-456.

Peterson, Peter G. "Quantity Discounts And The Morton Salt Case," **JOB**, 1952, v25(2), 108-123.

Peterson, Ray M. "A Method Of Automatically Adjusting The Maximum Earnings Base Under OASDI: Comment," **JRI**, 1965, v32(3), 470-472.

Peterson, Ray M. "Actuarial Soundness In Pension Plans With Insurance Companies," **JRI**, 1953, v20, 48-53.

Peterson, Ray M. "The Challenge Of Aging To Insurance: Comment," **JRI**, 1961, v28(3), 93-97.

Peterson, Ray M. "The Future Of Private Pension Plans," **JRI**, 1966, v33(4), 603-620.

Peterson, Ray M. "The Social Security Principle: Comment," **JRI**, 1961, v28(2), 115-119.

Peterson, Richard E. "A Cross Section Study Of The Demand For Money: The United States, 1960-62," **JOF**, 1974, v29(1), 73-88.

Peterson, Richard L. and Dan A. Black. "Consumer Credit Search," **JMCB**, 1984, v16(4), Part 1, 527-536.

Peterson, Richard L. and Michael D. Ginsberg. "Determinants Of Commercial Bank Auto Loan Rates," **JBR**, 1981-82, v12(1), 46-55.

Peterson, Richard L. "Creditors' Use Of Collection Remedies," **JFR**, 1986, v9(1), 71-86.

Peterson, Richard L. "Factors Affecting The Growth Of Bank Credit Card And Check Credit," **JOF**, 1977, v32(2), 553-564.

Peterson, Richard L. "Investor Preferences For Futures Straddles," **JFQA**, 1977, v12(1), 105-120.

Peterson, Richard L. "On The Effects Of Statutory Interest Rate Ceilings: Comment," **JOF**, 1977, v32(5), 1809-1810.

Peterson, Richard L. "The Impact Of General Credit Restraint On The Supply Of Commercial Bank Consumer Installment Credit: A Comment," **JMCB**, 1976, v8(4), 527-535.

Peterson, Richard L. "Usury Laws And Consumer Credit: A Note," **JOF**, 1983, v38(4), 1299-1304.

Peterson, Richard L. (Ma, Christopher K., Ramesh P. Rao and Richard L. Peterson. "The Resiliency Of The High-Yield Bond Market: The LTV Default," **JOF**, 1989, v44(4), 1085-1098.)

Peterson, Richard L. (MacDonald, S. Scott, Richard L. Peterson and Timothy W. Koch. "Using Futures To Improve Treasury Bill Performance," **JFM**, 1988, v8(2), 167-184.)

Peterson, Richard L. (Scott, William L. and Richard L. Peterson. "Interest Rate Risk And Equity Values Of Hedged And Unhedged Financial Intermediaries," **JFR**, 1986, v9(4), 325-329.)

Peterson, Robert A., William Rudelius and Glenn L. Wood. "Spread Of Marketing Innovations In A Service Industry," **JOB**, 1972, v45(4), 485-496.

Peterson, Russell J. (Keller, Thomas F. and Russell J. Peterson. "Optimal Financial Structure, Cost Of Capital, And The Lease-Or-Buy Decision," **JBFA**, 1974, v1(3), 405-414.)

Peterson, T. S. "Management: Corporate Responsibility Abroad," **FAJ**, 1959, v15(2), 9-14.

Peterson, Timothy M. "Loss Reserving - Property/Casualty Insurance: A Summary Of The Book," **JRI**, 1984, v51(1), 115-121.

Peterson, William H. "Risk Capital - Key To Continued Prosperity," **FAJ**, 1956, v12(2), 41-44.

Petrenas, Algimantas M. "The U. S. Balance Of Payments," **FAJ**, 1970, v26(1), 83-89.

Petrucci, Adriana. (Gebotys, Robert J., Alan Auerbach and Adriana Petrucci. "The Insurance Branch Manager: Correlates Of Success," **JRI**, 1987, v54(1), 157-161.)

Petruzzi, Chirstoher, Marguerite Del Valle and Stephen Judlowe. "Patent And Copyright Protection For Innovations In Finance," **FM**, 1988, v17(4), 66-71.

Petry, Glenn H. and Halbert S. Kerr. "The Rising Incidence Of Coauthorship As A Function Of Institutional Reward Systems," **JFED**, 1981, v10, 78-84.

Petry, Glenn H. and Russell J. Fuller. "A Comparison Of Institutions Publishing In Finance Journals With Those Presenting Papers At Finance Association Meetings," **JFED**, 1979, v8, 53-57.

Petry, Glenn H. and Russell J. Fuller. "The Geographic Distribution Of Papers At The Seven Finance Associations In The United States," **JFQA**, 1978, v13(4), 785-794.

Petry, Glenn H. "A History And Analysis Of Scholarly Papers Presented At The Seven Academic Finance Associations From 1939 Through 1980," **FM**, 1981, v10(2), Tenth Anniversary Editon,93-104.

Petry, Glenn H. "Economic Feasibility Studies As Assigned In The Graduate Finance Course," **JFED**, 1977, v6, 62-65.

Petry, Glenn H. "Empirical Evidence On Cost Of Capital Weights," **FM**, 1974, v4(4), 58-65.

Petry, Glenn H. "Lack Of Student Awareness Of Literature In Finance," **JFED**, 1975, v4, 60-61.

Petry, Glenn H. (Fuller, Russell J. and Glenn H. Petry. "Inflation, Return On Equity, And Stock Prices," **JPM**, 1980-81, v7(4), 19-25.)

Petry, Glenn H. (Hickman, Kent and Glenn H. Petry. "A Comparison Of Stock Price Predictions Using Court Accepted Formulas, Dividend Discount, And P/E Models," **FM**, 1990, v19(2), 76-87.)

Petry, Glenn H. (Settle, John W., Glenn H. Petry and Chi-Cheng Hsia. "Synergy, Diversification, And Incentive Effects Of Corporate Merger On Bondholder Wealth: Some Evidence," **JFR**, 1984, v7(4), 329-339.)

Petry, Glenn H. (Sweetser, Albert G. and Glenn H. Petry. "A History Of The Seven Academic Finance Associations And Their Contributions To Development Of The Discipline," **FM**, 1981, v10(2), Tenth Anniversary Edition, 46-70.)

Pettengill, Glenn N. "Holiday Closings And Security Returns," **JFR**, 1989, v12(1), 57-68.

Pettengill, Glenn N. "Persistent Seasonal Return Patterns," **FR**, 1985, v20(4), 271-286.

Pettengill, Glenn N. and Bradford D. Jordan. "A Comprehensive Examination Of Volume Effects And Seasonality In Daily Security Returns," **JFR**, 1988, v11(1), 57-70.

Pettengill, Glenn N. and Bradford D. Jordan. "The Overreaction Hypothesis, Firm Size, And Stock Market Seasonality," **JPM**, 1990, v16(3), 60-64.

Pettijohn, James B. "Hedging: A Forgotten Topic In The Introductory Financial Management Text," **JFED**, 1982, v11, 17-20.

Pettijohn, James, Gerald Udell and Stephen Parker. "The Quest For AACSB Accreditation: Must Finance Faculty Really Publish Or Perish?," **FPE**, 1991, v1(1), 53-56.

Pettit, Laurence C. (DeMong, Richard F., Laurence C. Pettit and B. J. Campsey. "Finance Curriculum For The Future: Perceptions Of Practitioners Versus Academicians," **JFED**, 1979, v8, 45-48.)

Pettit, Laurence C., Jr. "A Course In Small Business Finance," **JFED**, 1979, v8, 77-79.

Pettit, Lawrence C. (Overstreet, George A., Lawrence C. Pettit and Robert S. Kemp. "A Professional Approach To Building An Undergraduate Finance Program: The McIntire Experience," **JFED**, 1986, v15, 42-52.)

Pettit, R. Richardson and Randolph Westerfield. "Using The Capital Asset Pricing Model And The Market Model To Predict Security Returns," **JFQA**, 1974, v9(4), 579-605.

Pettit, R. Richardson and Randolph Westerfield. "A Model Of Capital Asset Risk," **JFQA**, 1972, v7(2), 1649-1668.

Pettit, R. Richardson and Ronald F. Singer. "Small Business Finance: A Research Agenda," **FM**, 1985, v14(3), 47-60.

Pettit, R. Richardson and Ronald F. Singer." Instant Option Betas," FAJ, 1986, v42(5), 51-62.

Pettit, R. Richardson. "Dividend Announcements, Security Performance, And Capital Market Efficiency," JOF, 1972, v27(5), 993-1007.

Pettit, R. Richardson. "Taxes, Transaction Costs And The Clientele Effect Of Dividends," JFEC, 1977, v5(3), 419-436.

Pettit, R. Richardson. "The Impact Of Dividend And Earnings Announcements: A Reconciliation," JOB, 1976, v49(1), 86-96.

Pettit, R. Richardson. "The Weighted Average Cost Of Capital: Some Questions On Its Definition, Interpretation, And Use: Comment," JOF, 1975, v30(3), 881-882.

Pettit, R. Richardson. (Lee, Insup, R. Richardson Pettit and Ronald F. Singer. "Offer Premiums In Stock Exchange Mergers And The Distribution Of Stockholder's Wealth," IJOF, 1990, v2(2), 67-87.)

Pettit, R. Richardson. (Lee, Insup, R. Richardson Pettit and Mark V. Swankoski. "Daily Return Relationships Among Asian Stock Markets," JBFA, 1990, v17(2), 265-284.)

Pettit, R. Richardson. (McFarland, James W., R. Richardson Pettit and Sam K. Sung. "The Distribution Of Foreign Exchange Price Changes: Trading Day Effects And Risk Measurement--A Reply," JOF, 1987, v42(1), 189-194.)

Pettit, R. Richardson. (McFarland, James W., R. Richardson Pettit and San K. Sung. "The Distribution Of Foreign Exchange Price Changes: Trading Day Effects And Risk Measurement," JOF, 1982, v37(3), 693-715.)

Pettit, Rich. (Jacob, Nancy and Rich Pettit. "Research Output And Capital Market Efficiency Under Alternative Commission Rate Structures," JFR, 1978, v1(1), 45-60.)

Pettway, R. H. and H. J. Weinraub. "Some Tax Aspects Of Bond Trading," FAJ, 1969, v25(6), 125-128.

Pettway, Richard H. and Bradford D. Jordan. "Diversification, Double Leverage, And The Cost Of Capital," JFR, 1983, v6(4), 289-300.

Pettway, Richard H. and Jack W. Trifts. "Do Banks Overbid When Acquiring Failed Banks?," FM, 1985, v14(2), 5-15.

Pettway, Richard H. and Joseph F. Sinkey, Jr. "Establishing On-Site Bank Examination Priorities: An Early-Warning System Using Accounting And Market Information," JOF, 1980, v35(1), 137-150.

Pettway, Richard H. and R. Phil Malone. "Automatic Dividend Reinvestment Plans Of Nonfinancial Corporations," FM, 1973, v2(4), 11-18.

Pettway, Richard H. and Robert D. Radcliffe. "Impacts Of New Equity Sales Upon Electric Utility Share Prices," FM, 1985, v14(1), 16-25.

Pettway, Richard H. and Takeshi Yamada. "Mergers In Japan And Their Impacts Upon Stockholders' Wealth," FM, 1986, v15(4), 43-52.

Pettway, Richard H. "Integer Programming In Capital Budgeting: A Note On Computational Experience," JFQA, 1973, v8(4), 665-672.

Pettway, Richard H. "Market Tests Of Capital Adequacy Of Large Commercial Banks," JOF, 1976, v31(3), 865-875.

Pettway, Richard H. "Mathematical Programming For Business Finance," JFED, 1973, v2, 82-90.

Pettway, Richard H. "Potential Insolvency, Market Efficiency And Bank Regulation Of Large Commercial Banks," JFQA, 1980, v15(1), 219-236.

Pettway, Richard H. "The Effects Of Large Bank Failures Upon Investors' Risk Cognizance In The Commercial Banking Industry," JFQA, 1976, v11(3), 465-477.

Pettway, Richard H. (Brigham, Eugene F. and Richard H. Pettway. "Capital Budgeting By Utilities," FM, 1973, v2(3), 11-22.)

Pettway, Richard H. (Celec, Stephen E. and Richard H. Pettway. "Some Observations On Risk-Adjusted Discount Rates: A Comment," JOF, 1979, v34(4), 1061-1063.)

Pettway, Richard H. (Jordan, Bradford D. and Richard H. Pettway. "The Pricing Of Short-Term Debt And The Miller Hypothesis: A Note," JOF, 1985, v40(2), 589-594.)

Pettway, Richard H. (Scanlon, Kevin P., Jack W. Trifts and Richard H. Pettway. "Impacts Of Relative Size And Industrial Relatedness On Returns To Shareholders Of Acquiring Firms," JFR, 1989, v12(2), 103-112.)

Pettway, Richard H. (Sicherman, Neil W. and Richard H. Pettway. "Acquisition Of Divested Assets And Shareholders' Wealth," JOF, 1987, v42(5), 1261-1273.)

Pettway, Richard H. and Bradford D. Jordan. "APT Vs. CAPM Estimates Of The Return-Generating Function Parameters For Regulated Public Utilities," JFR, 1987, v10(3), 227-238.

Pettway, Richard H., T. Craig Tapley and Takeshi Yamada. "The Impacts Of Financial Deregulation Upon Trading Efficiency And The Levels Of Risk And Return Of Japanese Banks," FR, 1988, v23(3), 243-268.

Petty, J. William and Oswald D. Bowlin. "The Financial Manager And Quantitative Decision Models," FM, 1976, v5(4), 32-41.

Petty, J. William, II and Ernest W. Walker. "Optimal Transfer Pricing For The Multinational Firm," JOF, 1972, v1(3), 74-87.

Petty, J. William, II. (Scott, David F., Jr. and J. William Petty, II. "Capital Budgeting Practices In Large American Firms: A Retrospective Analysis And Synthesis," FR, 1984, v19(1), 111-123.)

Petty, J. William, II. (Walker, Ernest W. and J. William Petty, II. "Financial Differences Between Large And Small Firms," FM, 1978, v7(4), 61-68.)

Petty, J. William, III. (Joehnk, Michael D. and J. William Petty, III. "The Interest Sensitivity Of Common Stock Prices," JPM, 1979-80, v6(2), 19-25.)

Petty, J. William. (Joehnk, Michael D., Oswald D. Bowlin and J. William Petty. "Preferred Dividend Rolls: A Viable Strategy For Corporate Money Managers?," FM, 1980, v9(2), 78-87.)

Petty, J. William. (Martin, John D. and J. William Petty. "An Analysis Of The Performance Of Publicly Traded Venture Capital Companies," JFQA, 1983, v18(3), 401-410.)

Petty, J. William. (Scott, David F., Jr. and J. William Petty. "A Note On The Relevance Of Dividend Policy," FR, 1979, v14(1), 59-65.)

Petty, J. William. (Winger, Bernard J., Carl R. Chen, John D. Martin, J. William Petty and Steven C. Hayden. "Adjustable Rate Preferred Stock," FM, 1986, v15(1), 48-57.)

Petzel, Todd E. "Comments On Merton Miller," RQFA, 1991, v1(2), 218-219.

Pfaff, Philip. "Evaluation Of Some Money Stock Forecasting Models," JOF, 1977, v32(5), 1639-1646.

Pfaff, Philip. "Modern Portfolio Theory On A Microcomputer," JFED, 1981, v10, 85-87.

Pfaffenberger, Roger C. (Porter, R. Burr and Roger C. Pfaffenberger. "Efficient Algorithms For Conducting Stochastic Dominance Tests On Large Numbers Of Portfolios: Reply," JFQA, 1975, v10(1), 181-185.)

Pfaffenberger, Roger C. (Stein, William E., Roger C. Pfaffenberger and Dan W. French. "Sampling Error In First Order Stochastic Dominance," JFR, 1987, v10(3), 259-268.)

Pfaffenberger, Roger. (Stein, William, Roger Pfaffenberger and P. C. Kumar. "On The Estimation Risk In First-Order Stochastic Dominance: A Note," JFQA, 1983, v18(4), 471-476.)

Pfeffer, Irving and Seev Neumann. "The Survival Probability Of A New Life Insurance Company," JRI, 1966, v33(4), 597-602.

Pfeffer, Irving and Seev Neumann. "The Survival Probability Of A New Life Insurance Company," JRI, 1967, v34(1), 9-13.

Pfeffer, Irving. "A Survey Of Current Faculty Retirement Programs In American Universities And Colleges," JRI, 1956, v23, 82-93.

Pfeffer, Irving. "Measuring The Profit Potential Of A New Life Insurance Company," JRI, 1965, v32(3), 413-422.

Pfeffer, Irving. "Non-Tariff Barriers To Alien Insurance In The United States," JRI, 1976, v43(2), 275-290.

Pfeffer, Irving. "Residual Risks In Europe," JRI, 1974, v41(1), 41-56.

Pfeffer, Irving. "The Social Responsibility Of Insurance: A Case Study At Watts," JRI, 1967, v34(4), 525-537.

Pfeifer, Phillip E. "Market Timing And Risk Reduction," JFQA, 1985, v20(4), 451-460.

Pfeifer, Phillip E. (Williams, Alex O. and Phillip E. Pfeifer. "Estimating Security Price Risk Using Duration And Price Elasticity," JOF, 1982, v37(2), 399-411.)

Pfenenger, John W., II. (Barrett, W. Brian and John W. Pfenenger, II. "Proper Cash-Flow Discounting For Pension Fund Liabilities," FAJ, 1989, v45(2), 68-70.)

Pflaum, Christopher C. (Roenfeldt, Rodney L., Gary L. Griepentrog and Christopher C. Pflaum. "Further Evidence On The Stationarity Of Beta Coefficients," JFQA, 1978, v13(1), 117-121.)

Pfleiderer, Paul. "Finance Anthropology," JPM, 1985-86, v12(1), 52-53.

Pfleiderer, Paul. (Admati, Anat R., Sudipto Bhattacharya, Paul Pfleiderer and Stephen A. Ross. "On Timing And Selectivity," JOF, 1986, v41(3), 715-729.)

Pfleiderer, Paul. (Admati, Anat R. and Paul Pfleiderer. "A Theory Of Intraday Patterns: Volume And Price Variability," RFS, 1988-89, v1(1), 3-40.)

Pfleiderer, Paul. (Admati, Anat R. and Paul Pfleiderer. "Divide And Conquer: A Theory Of Intraday And Day-Of-The-Week Mean Effects," RFS, 1989, v2(2), 189-224.)

Phaup, E. Dwight and Alan Kusinitz. "Monetary Control Under Fixed Exchange Rates: A Time Series Approach," JMCB, 1977, v9(4), 552-561.

Phaup, E. Dwight. "A Reinterpretation Of The Modern Theory Of Forward Exchange Rates," JMCB, 1981, v13(4), 477-484.

Phelps, Bruce D. (Samorajski, Gregory S. and Bruce D. Phelps. "Using Treasury Bond Futures To Enhance Total Return," FAJ, 1990, v46(1), 58-65.)

Phelps, Edmund S. "Commodity-Supply Shock And Full-Employment Monetary Policy," JMCB, 1978, v10(2), 206-221.

Phelps, Edmund. (Burmesiter, Edwin and Edmund Phelps. "Money, Public Debt, Inflation, And Real Interest," JMCB, 1971, v3(2), Part 1, 153-182.)

Phelps, John R. (Johnson, Larry J. and John R. Phelps. "The Development And Solution Of A Tax-Adjusted Model Of Personal Injury Awards: A Clarification," JRI, 1985, v52(3), 518-519.)

Phelps, Thomas W. "Investing In The "New" World Of The Nineteen Sixties," FAJ, 1966, v22(3), 13-17.

Philipich, Kirk L. (Lovata, Linda M. and Kirk L. Philipich. "Does Replacement Cost Restatement Affect The Intra-Industry Ranking Of Firms?," FAJ, 1986, v42(3), 72-75.)

Philipich, Kirk L. (Lovata, Linda M., William D. Nichols and Kirk L. Philipich. "Defeasing Discounted Debt: An Economic Analysis," FM, 1987, v16(1), 41-45.)

Philipp, Michael G. (Schneeweis, Thomas R., Joanne M. Hill and Michael G. Philipp. "Hedge Ratio Determination Based On Bond Yield Forecasts," RFM, 1983, v2(3), 338-349.)

Philippatos, G. C. (Gressis, N., G. C. Philippatos and J. Hayya. "Multiperiod Portfolio Analysis And The Inefficiency Of The Market Portfolio," JOF, 1976, v31(4), 1115-1126.)

Philippatos, G. C. (Nressis, N., G. Vlahos and G. C. Philippatos. "A CAPM-Based Analysis Of Stock Index Futures," JPM, 1983-84, v10(3), 47-52.)

Philippatos, G. C., A. Christofi and P. Christofi. "The Inter-Temporal Stability Of International Stock Market Relationships: Another View," FM, 1983, v12(4), 63-69.

Philippatos, George C. and David N. Nawrocki. "The Information Inaccuracy Of Stock Market Forecasts: Some New Evidence Of Dependence On The New York Stock Exchange," JFQA, 1973, v8(3), 445-458.

Philippatos, George C. (Choi, Dosoung and George C. Philippatos. "Post-Merger Performance Among Homogeneous Firm Samples," FR, 1984, v19(2), 173-194.)

Philippatos, George C. (Choi, Dosoung and George C. Philippatos. "An Examination Of Merger Synergism," JFR, 1983, v6(3), 239-256.)

Philippatos, George C. (DeFusco, Richard A., George C. Philippatos and Dosoung Choi. "Differences In Factor Structures Between U.S. Multinational And Domestic Corporations: Evidence From Bilinear Paradigm Tests," FR, 1990, v25(3), 395-404.)

Philippatos, George C. (Gressis, Nicholas, George C. Philippatos and George Vlahos. "Net Selectivity As A Component Measure Of Investment Performance," FR, 1986, v21(1), 103-110.)

Philippatos, George C. (Kumar, P. C., George C. Philippatos and John R. Ezzell. "Goal Programming And The Selection Of Portfolios By Dual-Purpose Funds," JOF, 1978, v33(1), 303-310.)

Philippatos, George C. (Martell, Terrence F. and George C. Philippatos. "Adaptation, Information, And Dependence In Commodity Markets," JOF, 1974, v29(2), 493-498.)

Philippatos, George. (Gressis, Nicholas, Jack Hayya and George Philippatos. "Multiperiod Portfolio Efficiency Analysis Via The Geometric Mean," FR, 1974, v9(1), 46-63.)

Philippi, Dieter R. "Maximum Return On University Funds," FR, 1967, v1(2), 55-57.

Philips, G. E. (Mayne, L. S. and G. E. Philips. "Investment Assets And Bank Earnings," FAJ, 1972, v28(1), 61-65.)

Philips, Richard A. (Agarwal, Vinod B. and Richard A. Philips. "The Effects Of Assumption Financing Across Housing Price Categories," AREUEA, 1985, v13(1), 48-57.)

Phillips, Almarin. "CMC, Heller, Hunt, FIA, FRA, And FINE: The Neglected Aspect Of Financial Reform," JMCB, 1977, v9(4), 636-641.

Phillips, Almarin. "Competition, Confusion, And Commercial Banking," JOF, 1964, v19(1), 32-45.

Phillips, Almarin. "Regulatory Reform For The Deposit Financial Institutions--Retrospect And Prospects," JFQA, 1974, v9(5), 795-802.

Phillips, Almarin. (Jacobs, Donald P. and Almarin Phillips. "The Commission On Financial Structure And Regulation: Its Organization And Recommendations," JOF, 1972, v27(2), 319-328.)

Phillips, G. Michael. (Dale-Johnson, David and G. Michael Phillips. "Housing Attributes Associated With Capital Gain," AREUEA, 1984, v12(2), 162-175.)

Phillips, G. Michael. (Jennings, William P. and G. Michael Phillips. "Risk As A Discount Rate Determinant In Wrongful Death And Injury Cases," JRI, 1989, v56(1), 122-127.)

Phillips, Herbert E. and John P. Seagle. "Data: A Mixed Blessing In Portfolio Selection?," FM, 1974, v4(3), 50-53.

Phillips, Herbert E. "Research And Methodology: The Textbook Literature," FR, 1978, v13(1), 88-89.

Phillips, Herbert E. (Frankfurter, George M., Herbert E. Phillips and John P. Seagle. "Performance Of The Sharpe Portfolio Selection Model: A Comparison," JFQA, 1976, v11(2), 195-204.)

Phillips, Herbert E. (Frankfurter, George M. and Herbert E. Phillips. "MPT Plus Security Analysis For Better Performance," JPM, 1981-82, v8(4), 29-36.)

Phillips, Herbert E. (Frankfurter, George M. and Herbert E. Phillips. "Efficient Algorithms For Conducting Stochastic Dominance Tests On Large Numbers Of Portfolios: A Comment," JFQA, 1975, v10(1), 177-179.)

Phillips, Herbert E. (Frankfurter, George M. and Herbert E. Phillips. "Portfolio Selection: An Analytic Approach For Selecting Securities From A Large Universe," JFQA, 1980, v15(2), 357-377.)

Phillips, Herbert E. (Frankfurter, George M., Herbert E. Phillips and John P. Seagle. "Portfolio Selection: The Effects Of Uncertain Means, Variances, And Covariances," JFQA, 1971, v6(5), 1251-1262.)

Phillips, Herbert E. (Frankfurter, George M. and Herbert E. Phillips. "Alpha-Beta Theory: A Word Of Caution," JPM, 1976-77, v3(4), 35-42.)

Phillips, Herbert E. (Frankfurter, George M., Herbert E. Phillips and John P. Seagle. "Estimation Risk In The Portfolio Selection Model: A Comment," JFQA, 1972, v7(1), 1423-1424.)

Phillips, Herbert E. (Frankfurter, George M., Herbert E. Phillips and John P. Seagle. "A Proposed Normative Procedure For Portfolio Selection Under Conditions Of Uncertainty," FM, 1977, v6(4), 43-50.)

Phillips, Herbert E. (Frankfurter, George E. and Herbert M. Phillips. "Catch 500: The Irony Of Indexing: Comment," JPM, 1980-81, v7(1), 80-81.)

Phillips, Lawrence C. "Impact Of New Tax Law," FAJ, 1970, v26(3), 21-26.

Phillips, Llad and John Pippenger. "The Term Structure Of Interest Rates In The MIT-PENN-SSRC Model: Reality Or Illusion?," JMCB, 1979, v11(2), 151-164.

Phillips, Paul D., John C. Groth and R. Malcolm Richards. "Financing The Alaskan Project: The Experience Of Sohio," FM, 1979, v8(3), 7-16.

Phillips, Richard A. (Agarwal, Vinod B. and Richard A. Phillips. "The Effect Of Mortgage Rate Buydowns On Housing Prices: Recent Evidence From FHA-VA Transactions," AREUEA, 1983, v11(4), 491-503.)

Phillips, Susan M. "Regulation Of Futures Markets: Theory And Practice," RFM, 1984, v3(2), 150-158.

Phillips, Susan M. and Clifford W. Smith, Jr. "Trading Costs For Listed Options: The Implications For Market Efficiency," JFEC, 1980, v8(2), 179-201.

Phillips, Susan M. and Paula A. Tosini. "A Comparison Of Margin Requirements For Options And Futures," FAJ, 1982, v38(6), 54-58.

Phillips, Susan M. "The Supreme Court's Decision On The Daniel Case: Implications For Pension Regulations," JRI, 1980, v47(1), 157-164.

Phillips, Susan Meridith and Linda Pickthorne Fletcher. "The Cost Of Funding Benefits Under The ERISA: A Statistical Survey: Reply," JRI, 1978, v45(1), 137-140.

Phillips, Susan and Linda Pickthorne Fletcher. "The Cost Of Funding Benefits Under ERISA: A Statistical Survey," JRI, 1976, v43(4), 569-585.

Phillips, Susan. (Fletcher, Linda Pickthorne and Susan Phillips. "The Cost Of Funding Benefits Under The ERISA: A Statistical Survey: Reply," JRI, 1979, v46(3), 547-549.)

Phillips, Susan. (Moriarty, Eugene, Susan Phillips and Paula Tosini. "A Comparison Of Options And Futures In The Management Of Portfolio Risk," JFQA, 1981, v37(1), 61-67.)

Phillips, W. S. "Teaching Risk Analysis By The Case Study Method," JRI, 1970, v37(1), 125-129.

Phillips, Wallace, Jr. (Fraser, Donald R., Wallace Phillips, Jr. and Peter S. Rose. "A Canonical Analysis Of Bank Performance," JFQA, 1974, v9(2), 287-295.)

Phillips, Willard R., Jr. "Fiduciaries And Futures," JFM, v1(3), 317-328.

Phillips-Patrick, Frederick J. and Thomas Schneeweis. "The 'Weekend Effect' For Stock Indexes And Stock Indexes Future: Dividend And Interest Rate Effects," JFM, 1988, v8(1), 115-122.

Phillips-Patrick, Frederick J. "Ownership, Asset Structure, And Political Risk," AFPAF, 1989, v4(Supp), 239-256.

Phillips-Patrick, Frederick J. "The Effect Of Asset And Ownership Structure On Political Risk: Some Evidence From Mitterand's Election In France," JBF, 1989, v13(4/5), 651-674.

Phylaktis, Kate. "Capital Controls: The Case Of Argentina," JIMF, 1988, v7(3), 303-320.

Piccini, Raymond. "Stock Market Behavior Around Business Cycle Peaks," FAJ, 1980, v36(4), 55-57.

Picconi, Mario J. (Coyne, Thomas J., Waldemar M. Goulet and Mario J. Picconi. "Residential Real Estate Versus Financial Assets," JPM, 1980-81, v7(1), 20-24.)

Pick, R. H. (Emmanuel, C. R. and R. H. Pick. "The Predictive Ability Of UK Segment Reports," JBFA, 1980, v7(2), 201-218.)

Pickersgill, Joyce E. "A Long-Run Demand Function For Money In The Soviet Union: A Comment," JMCB, 1970, v2(1), 123-128.

Pickett, Ralph R. "Textbook Publishing Companies," FAJ, 1969, v25(3), 59-62.

Pickle, Hal B. and Brian S. Rungeling. "Empirical Investigation Of Entrepreneurial Goals And Customer Satisfaction," JOB, 1973, v46(2), 268-273.

Pictet, O. V. (Muller, U. A., M. M. Dacorogna, R. B. Olsen, O. V. Pictet, M. Schwarz and C. Morgenegg. "Statistical Study Of Foreign Exchange Rates, Empirical Evidence Of A Price Change Scaling Law, And Intraday Analysis," JBF, 1990, v14(6), 1189-1208.)

Picur, Ronald D. (Belkaoui, Ahmed and Ronald D. Picur. "The Smoothing Of Income Numbers: Some Empirical Evidence On Systematic Differences Between Core And Periphery Industrial Sectors," JBFA, 1984, v11(4), 527-546.)

Picur, Ronald D. (Belkaoui, Ahmed and Ronald D. Picur. "Sources Of Feedback In A CPA Firm," JBFA, 1987, v14(2), 175-186.)

Pieptea, Dan R. (Geske, Robert L. and Dan R. Pieptea. Controlling Interest Rate Risk And Return With Futures," RFM, 1987, v6(1), 64-86.)

Pieptea, Dan R. "Decision Support Systems For Bond Portfolio Management: A Review Of Underlying Theory And Empirical Work," AFPAF, 1989, v3(1), 95-120.

Pieptea, Dan R. "Leveraged Bond Portfolio Optimization Under Uncertainty," FR, 1987, v22(1),87-110.

Pieptea, Dan R. (Merville, Larry J. and Dan R. Pieptea. "Stock-Price Volatility, Mean-Reverting Diffusion, And Noise," JFEC, 1989, v24(1), 193-214.)

Pieptea, Daniel R. (Briys, Eric, Michel Crouhy and Daniel R. Pieptea. "Hedging Versus Speculating With Interest Rate Futures," RFM, 1988, v7(Supp), 620-635.)

Pieraerts, Pierre. (Cholerton, Kenneth, Pierre Pieraerts and Bruno Solnik. "Why Invest In Foreign Currency Bonds?," JPM, 1985-86, v12(4), 4-8.)

Pierce, David A. "Money Supply Control: Reserves Under Lagged Accounting," JOF, 1976, v31(3), 845-852.

Pierce, David A., Darrel W. Parke, William P. Cleveland and Agustin Maravall. "Uncertainty In The Monetary Aggregates: Sources, Measurement And Policy Effects," JOF, 1981, v36(2), 507-515.

Pierce, Frederic M. "The Responsibility Of The Insurance Industry," JRI, 1961, v28(1), 45-52.

Pierce, James L. and Thomas D. Thomson. "Short-Term Financial Models At The Federal Reserve Board," JOF, 1974, v29(2), 349-357.

Pierce, James L. "How Regulations Affect Monetary Control," JMCB, 1982, v14(4), Part 2, 775-787.

Pierce, James L. "The FINE Study," JMCB, 1977, v9(4), 605-618.

Pierce, James L. "The Political Economy Of Arthur Burns," JOF, 1979, v34(2), 485-496.

Pierce, James L. (Craine, Roger N. and James L. Pierce. "Interest Rate Risk," JFQA, 1978, v13(4), 719-734.)

Pierce, James L. (Thomson, Thomas D., James L. Pierce and Robert T. Parry. "A Monthly Money Market Model," JMCB, 1975, v7(4), 411-431.)

Pierson, Harry M. "Annual Losses For Straight Deductible Coverage: Comment," JRI, 1980, v47(4), 753.

Piesse, Jenifer. (Wood, Douglas and Jenifer Piesse. "The Information Value Of MDA Based Financial Indicators," JBFA, 1987, v14(1), 27-38.)

Pifer, Howard W. (Meyer, Paul A. and Howard W. Pifer. "Prediction Of Bank Failures," JOF, 1970, v25(4), 853-868.)

Pike, Albert. "Commercial Group Medical-Hospitalization Covers," JRI, 1948, v15, 47-51.

Pike, John R. (Gentry, James A. and John R. Pike, "Dual Funds Revisited," FAJ, 1968, v24(2), 149-157.)

Pike, John R. (Gentry, James A. and John R. Pike. "Rates Of Return On Common Stock Portfolios Of Life Insurance Companies," JRI, 1969, v36(4), 545-552.)

Pike, John. (Gentry, James and John Pike. "An Empirical Study Of The Risk-Return Hypothesis Using Common Stock Portfolios Of Life Insurance Companies," JFQA, 1970, v5(2), 179-185.)

Pike, Richard H. "The Capital Budgeting Behaviour And Corporate Characteristics Of Capital Constrained Firms," JBFA, 1983, v10(4), 663-671.

Pillion, Joseph. (Berolzheimer, Howard, Edwin A. Gaumnitz, C. M. Kahler and Joseph Pillion. "Round Table Discussion: The Objectives And Content Of The Survey Course In Insurance," JRI, 1941, v8, 5-38.)

Pilotte, Eugene. "The Economic Recovery Tax Act Of 1981 And Corporate Capital Structure," FM, 1990, v19(4), 98-107.

Pinches, George E. and Gary Simon. "An Analysis Of Portfolio Accumulation Strategies Employing Low-Priced Common Stocks," JFQA, 1972, v7(3), 1773-1796.

Pinches, George E. and J. Clay Singleton. "The Adjustment Of Stock Prices To Bond Rating Changes," JOF, 1978, v33(1), 29-44.

Pinches, George E. and Kent A. Mingo. "The Role Of Subordination And Industrial Bond Ratings," JOF, 1975, v30(1), 201-206.

Pinches, George E. and Kent A. Mingo. "A Multivariant Analysis Of Industrial Ratings," JOF, 1973, v28(1), 1-18.

Pinches, George E. and William R. Kinney, Jr. "The Measurement Of The Volatility Of Common Stock Prices," JOF, 1971, v26(1), 119-125.

Pinches, George E. "Financing With Convertible Preferred Stock, 1960-1967: Reply," JOF, 1971, v26(1), 150-151.

Pinches, George E. "Financing With Convertible Preferred Stock, 1960-

1967," **JOF**, 1970, v25(1), 53-63.

Pinches, George E. "Myopia, Capital Budgeting And Decision Making," **FM**, 1982, v11(3), 6-19.

Pinches, George E. "The Random Walk And Technical Analysis," **FAJ**, 1970, v26(2), 104-109.

Pinches, George E. "A Multivariate Analysis Of Industrial Bond Ratings' And The Role Of Subordination: Reply," **JOF**, 1978, v33(1), 336-344.

Pinches, George E. (Bey, Roger P. and George E. Pinches. "Additional Evidence Of Heteroscedasticity In The Market Model," **JFQA**, 1980, v15(2), 299-322.)

Pinches, George E. (Jahankhani, Ali and George E. Pinches. "Duration And The Nonstationarity Of Systematic Risk For Bonds," **JFR**, 1982, v5(2), 151-160.)

Pinches, George E. (Larcker, David F., Lawrence A. Gordon and George E. Pinches. "Testing For Market Efficiency: A Comparison Of The Cumulative Average Residual Methodology And Intervention Analysis," **JFQA**, 1980, v15(2), 267-287.)

Pinches, George E. (Lee, Hyong J. and George E. Pinches. "On Optimal Insurance Purchasing," **JRI**, 1988, v55(1), 145-149.)

Pinches, George E. (Schwendiman, Carl J. and George E. Pinches. "An Analysis Of Alternative Measures Of Investment Risk," **JOF**, 1975, v30(1), 193-200.)

Pinches, George E. (Trieschmann, James S. and George E. Pinches. "A Multivariate Model For Predicting Financially Distressed P-L Insurers," **JRI**, 1973, v40(3), 327-338.)

Pinches, George E. and James S. Trieschmann. "The Efficiency Of Alternative Models For Solvency Surveillance In The Insurance Industry," **JRI**, 1974, v41(4), 563-577.

Pinches, George E. and James S. Trieschmann. "Discriminant Analysis, Classification Results, And Financially Distressed P-L Insurers," **JRI**, 1977, v44(2), 289-298.

Pinches, George E., J. Clay Singleton and Ali Jahankhani. "Fixed Coverage As A Determinant Of Electric Utility Bond Ratings," **FM**, 1978, v7(2), 45-55.

Pinches, George E., Kent A. Mingo and J. Kent Caruthers. "The Stability Of Financial Patterns In Industrial Organizations," **JOF**, 1973, v28(2), 389-396.

Pinedo, Michael and David Shpilberg. "Stochastic Models With Memory For Seismic Risk Evaluation," **JRI**, 1981, v48(1), 46-58.

Pinegar, J. Michael and Ronald C. Lease. "The Impact Of Preferred-For-Common Exchange Offers On Firm Value," **JOF**, 1986, v41(4), 795-814.

Pinegar, J. Michael (Chang, Eric C. and J. Michael Pinegar. "Risk And Inflation," **JFQA**, 1987, v22(1), 89-100.)

Pinegar, J. Michael and Lisa Wilbricht. "What Managers Think Of Capital Structure Theory: A Survey," **FM**, 1989, v18(4), 82-91.

Pinegar, J. Michael. (Chang, Eric C. and J. Michael Pinegar. "Return Seasonality And Tax-Loss Selling In The Market For Long-Term Government And Corporate Bonds," **JFEC**, 1986, v17(2), 391-416.)

Pinegar, J. Michael. (Chang, Eric C. and J. Michael Pinegar. "A Fundamental Study Of The Seasonal Risk-Return Relationship: A Note," **JOF**, 1988, v43(4), 1035-1039.)

Pinegar, J. Michael. (Chang, Eric C. and J. Michael Pinegar. "Does The Market Reward Risk In Non-January Months?," **JPM**, 1988-89, v15(1), 55-57.)

Pinegar, J. Michael. (Chang, Eric C. and J. Michael Pinegar. "Seasonal Fluctuations In Industrial Production And Stock Market Seasonals," **JFQA**, 1989, v24(1), 59-74.)

Pinegar, J. Michael. (Chang, Eric C. and J. Michael Pinegar. "Stock Market Seasonals And Prespecified Multifactor Pricing Relations," **JFQA**, 1990, v25(4), 517-534.)

Pinegar, J. Michael. (Chang, Eric C. and J. Michael Pinegar. "Another Look At Risk And Reward In January And Non-January Months: Reply," **JPM**, 1990, v16(4), 82-83.)

Pinegar, J. Michael. (Linn, Scott C. and J. Michael Pinegar. "The Effect Of Issuing Preferred STock On Common And Preferred Stockholder Wealth," **JFEC**, 1988, v22(1), 155-184.)

Pines, David. (Eldor, Rafael, David Pines and Abba Schwartz. "Determinants Of An Individual's Demand For Hedging Instruments," **JPM**, 1989, v9(2), 135-142.)

Pines, David. (Eldor, Rafael, David Pines and Aba Schwartz. "The Demand For Domestic Assets And Consumption Risk," **RDIBF**, 1988, v2, 349-362.)

Pink, Louis H. "The Problems Of A Superintendent Of Insurance," **JRI**, 1936, v3, 43-54.

Pinkerton, John M. (Arditti, Fred D. and John M. Pinkerton. "The Valuation And Cost Of Capital Of The Levered Firm With Growth Opportunities," **JOF**, 1978, v33(1), 65-73.)

Pinkerton, John M. (Benesh, Gary A., Arthur J. Keown and John M. Pinkerton. "An Examination Of Market Reaction To Substantial Shifts In Dividend Policy," **JFR**, 1984, v7(2), 131-140.)

Pinkerton, John M. (Hansen, Robert S. and John M. Pinkerton. "Direct Equity Financing: A Resolution Of A Paradox," **JOF**, 1982, v37(3), 651-665.)

Pinkerton, John M. (Hansen, Robert S. and John M. Pinkerton. "Direct Equity Financing: A Resolution Of A Paradox: A Reply," **JOF**, 1984, v39(5), 1619-1624.)

Pinkerton, John M. (Hansen, Robert S., John M. Pinkerton and Ma, Tai. "On The Rightholders' Subscription To The Underwrittin Rights Offering," **JBF**, 1986, v10(4), 595-604.)

Pinkerton, John M. (Hansen, Robert S., John M. Pinkerton and Tai Ma. "The Allocation Ratio Decision In The Underwritten Rights Offering," **RIF**, 1988, v7, 201-226.)

Pinkerton, John M. (Keown, Arthur J., John M. Pinkerton and Son Nan Chen. "Portfolio Selection Based Upon P/E Ratios: Diversification, Risk Decomposition And Implications," **JBFA**, 1987, v14(2), 187-198.)

Pinkerton, John M. (Keown, Arthur J. and John M. Pinkerton. "Merger Announcements And Insider Trading Activity: An Empirical Investigation," **JOF**, 1981, v36(4), 855-869.)

Pinkerton, John M. (Shome, Dilip K., Stephen D. Smith and John M. Pinkerton. "The Purchasing Power Of Money And Nominal Interest Rates: A Re-Examination," **JOF**, 1988, v43(5), 1113-1125.)

Pinkus, Scott M. and Marie A. Chandohl. "The Relative Price Volatility Of Mortgage Securities," **JPM**, 1985-86, v12(4), 9-22.

Pinkyck, Robert S. (Majd, Saman and Robert S. Pindyck. "Time To Build, Option Value, And Investment Decisions," **JFEC**, 1987, v18(1), 7-28.)

Pinnell, W. George. "Residential Real Estate Finance In The 1960's," **JOF**, 1960, v15(2), 250-262.

Pinney, Alexander. "A New Look For Municipals?," **FAJ**, 1956, v12(2), 83-86.

Pinney, Alexander. "A New Responsibility For Management," **FAJ**, 1955, v11(4), 51-54.

Pinney, Alexander. "Gold - A Split Personality," **FAJ**, 1958, v14(2), 29-34.

Pinney, Alexander. "The Plight Of The Stock Exchange," **FAJ**, 1954, v10(4), 99-102.

Piper, Thomas R. and Steven J. Weiss. "The Profitability Of Multibank Holding Company Acquisitions," **JOF**, 1974, v29(1), 163-174.

Pippenger, John E. "A Time Series Analysis Of Post-Accord Interest Rates: Comment," **JOF**, 1974, v29(4), 1320-1325.

Pippenger, John E. "The Determination Of The Stock Of Reserves And The Balance Of Payments In A Neo-Keynesian Model: A Comment," **JMCB**, 1973, v5(2),713-719.

Pippenger, John. "Some Evidence On The Relationship Between Spot And Forward Exchange Rates," **JIMF**, 1982, v1(1), 111-113.

Pippenger, John. "Spot Rates, Forward Rates, And Interest-Rate Differentials," **JMCB**, 1972, v4(2), 375-383.

Pippenger, John. (Bui, Nhuong and John Pippenger. "Commodity Prices, Exchange Rates And Their Relative Volatility," **JIMF**, 1990, v9(1), 3-20.)

Pippenger, John. (Phillips, Llad and John Pippenger. "The Term Structure Of Interest Rates In The MIT-PENN-SSRC Model: Reality Or Illusion?," **JMCB**, 1979, v11(2), 151-164.)

Piros, Christopher D. "Taxable Vs. Tax-Exempt Bonds: A Note On The Effect Of Uncertain Taxable Income," **JOF**, 1987, v42(2), 447-451.

Pirrong, S. Craig. (Kormendi, Roger C., Victor L. Bernard, S. Craig Pirrong and Edward A. Snyder. "The Origins And Resolution Of The Thrift Crisis," **JACF**, 1989, v2(3), 85-99.)

Pitbladdo, Richard. (Harrison, J. Michael, Richard Pitbladdo and Stephen M. Schaefer. "Continuous Price Processes In Frictionless Markets Have Infinite Variation," **JOB**, 1984, v57(3), 353-366.)

Pittman, Robert and Joel Parker. "A Survey Of Corporate Real Estate Executives On Factors Influencing Corporate Real Estate Performance," **JRER**, 1989, v4(3), 107-119.

Pitts, C. G. C. and M. J. P. Selby. "The Pricing Of Corporate Debt: A Further Note," **JOF**, 1983, v38(4), 1311-1313.

Pitts, Mark and Robert W. Kopprasch. "Reducing Inter-Temporal Risk In Financial Futures Hedging," **JPM**, 1984, v4(1), 1-14.

Pitts, Mark. "The Management Of Interest Rate Risk: Reply," **JPM**, 1984-85, v11(4), 67-69.

Pitts, Mark. "The Pricing Of Options On Debt Securities," **JPM**, 1984-85, v11(2), 41-50.

Pitts, Mark. "The Valuation Of Currency Options: Comment," **FM**, 1984, v13(2), 51-52.

Pitts, Robert E. (Reidenbach, R. Eric, Donald L. Moak and Robert E. Pitts. "The Impact Of Marketing Operating On Bank Performance: A Structural Investigation," **JBR**, 1986-87, v17(1), 18-27.)

Planisek, Sandra L. "International Topics In Corporate Finance: What To Teach?," **JFED**, 1989, v18, 45-53.

Planisek, Sandra L. and James P. Sanford. "Video Case Materials For Enhanced Classroom Learning: Observations And Student Reactions," **JFED**, 1988, v17, 44-54.

Platt, Harlan D. and Coleen C. Pantalone. "Riding The Yield Curve," **JFED**, 1984, v13, 5-9.

Platt, Harlan D. and Marjorie B. Platt. "Development Of A Class Of Stable Predictive Variables: The Case Of Bankruptcy Prediction," **JBFA**, 1990, v17(1), 31-52.

Platt, Marjorie B. (Platt, Harlan D. and Marjorie B. Platt. "Development Of A Class Of Stable Predictive Variables: The Case Of Bankruptcy Prediction," **JBFA**, 1990, v17(1), 31-52.)

Platt, Marjorie B. (Pantalone, Colleen C. and Marjorie B. Platt. "Predicting Failure Of Savings And Loan Associations," **AREUEA**, 1987, v15(2), 46-64.)

Platt, Robert B. and Gary D. Latainer. "Risk-Return Tradeoffs Of Contingent Insurance Strategies For Active Bond Portfolios," **FAJ**, 1984, v40(3), 34-39.

Platt, Robert B. "The Interest Rate On Federal Funds: An Empirical Approach," **JOF**, 1970, v25(3), 585-597.

Platt, W. H. "Analysis Of Aspects Of The Treatment Of Monetary Gains And Losses In The Hyde Guidelines And ED24," **JBFA**, 1979, v6(4), 579-601.

Plaut, Steven E. "The Theory Of Collateral," **JBF**, 1985, v9(3), 401-419.

Plaut, Steven E. (Melnik, Arie and Steven E. Plaut. "The Economics Of Loan Commitment Contracts: Credit Pricing And Utilization," **JBF**, 1986, v10(2), 267-280.)

Plaut, Steven E. (Melnik, Arie and Steven E. Plaut. "Interest Rate Indexation And The Pricing Of Loan Commitment Contracts," **JBF**, 1987, v11(1), 137-146.)

Plaut, Steven E. (Melnik, Arie and Steven E. Plaut. "International Lending, Private-Sector 'Country Risk,' And Stabilization Policy," **RDIBF**, 1988, v2, 121-130.)

Plaut, Steven. (Melnik, Arie and Steven Plaut. "Loan Commitment Contracts, Terms Of Lending, And Credit Allocation," **JOF**, 1986, v41(2), 425-436.)

Pliska, Stanley R. (Bassett, Gilbert W., Jr., Virginia G. France and Stanely R. Pliska. "Kalman Filter Estimation For Valuing Nontrading Securities, With Applications To The MMI Cash-Futures Spread On October 19 And 20, 1987," **RQFA**, 1991, v1(2), 135-152.)

Pliska, Stanley R. (France, Virginia G., Gilbert W. Bassett, Jr. and Stanley R. Pliska. "The MMI Cash-Futures Spread On October 19, 1987," **RFM**, 1989, v8(1), 118-138.)

Plotkin, Irving H. "Rate Of Return In The Property And Liability Insurance Industry," **JRI**, 1972, v39(2), 331.

Plotkin, Irving H. "Rates Of Return In The Property And Liability Insurance Industry: A Comparative Analysis," **JRI**, 1969, v36(2), 173-200.

Plott, Charles R. "Rational Choice In Experimental Markets," **JOB**, 1986, v59(4), Part 2, S301-S328.

Plott, Charles R. (Forsythe, Robert, Thomas R. Palfrey and Charles R. Plott. "Futures Markets And Information Efficiency: A Laboratory Examination," JOF, 1984, v39(4), 955-981.)

Plourde, Andre. (Pesando, James E. and Andre Plourde. "The October 1979 Change In The U.S. Monetary Regime: Its Impact On The Forecastability Of Canadian Interest Rates," JOF, 1988, v43(1), 217-239.)

Pluhar, Darwin M., Carl E. Shafer and Thomas L. Sporleder. "The Systematic Downward Bias In Live Cattle Futures: A Further Evaluation," JFM, 1985, v5(1), 11-20.

Plummer, Carlyle J. "A Senior-Security Investment Plan," FAJ, 1961, v17(4), 23-28.

Png, I. P. L. (Hirshleifer, David and I. P. L. Png. "Facilitation Of Competing Bids And The Price Of A Takeover Target," RFS, 1989, v2(4), 587-606.)

Png, I. P. L. and D. Hirshleifer. "Price Discrimination Through Offers To Match Price," JOB, 1987, v60(3), 365-384.

Poapst, J. V. and W. R. Waters. "Rates Of Return On Consumer Durables," JOF, 1964, v19(4), 673-677.

Poapst, J. V. and W. R. Waters. "Individual Investment: Canadian Experience," JOF, 1963, v18(4), 647-665.

Poapst, J. V. "Canada's Federal Mortgage Exchange Corporation," AREUEA, 1975, v3(3), 7-22.

Podrasky, G. J. (Butler, H. L., Jr., G. J. Podrasky and J. D. Allen. "Aerospace Industry Re-Revisited," FAJ, 1977, v33(4), 32-35.)

Podrasky, George J. (Butler, Hartman L., Jr., George J. Podrasky and J. Devon Allen. "Aerospace II - Commercial Aircraft," FAJ, 1977, v33(5), 53-66.)

Pogue, G. A. "An Extension Of The Markowitz Portfolio Selection Model To Include Variable Transactions' Costs, Short Sales, Leverage Policies And Taxes," JOF, 1970, v25(5), 1005-1027.

Pogue, Gerald A. and Bruno H. Solnik. "The Market Model Applied To European Common Stocks: Some Empirical Results," JFQA, 1974, v9(6), 917-944.

Pogue, Gerald A. "An Inter-Temporal Model For Investment Management," JBR, 1970-71, v1(1), 17-34.

Pogue, Gerald A. (Modigliani, Franco and Gerald A. Pogue. "An Introduction To Risk And Return - II," FAJ, 1974, v30(3), 69-86.)

Pogue, Gerald A. (Modigliani, Franco and Gerald A. Pogue. "An Introduction To Risk And Return," FAJ, 1974, v30(2), 68-80.)

Pogue, Gerald A. (Myers, Stewart C. and Gerald A. Pogue. "A Programming Approach To Corporate Financial Management," JOF, 1974, v29(2), 579-596.)

Pogue, Jerry A. (Cohen, Kalman J. and Jerry A. Pogue. "Some Comments Concerning Mutual Fund Versus Random Portfolio Performance," JOB, 1968, v41(2), 180-190.)

Pogue, Jerry A. (Cohen, Kalman J. and Jerry A. Pogue. "An Empirical Evaluation Of Alternative Portfolio Selection Models," JOB, 1967, v40(2), 166-193.)

Pogue, Thomas F. and Robert M. Soldofsky. "What's In A Bond Rating?," JFQA, 1969, v4(2), 201-228.

Pohlman, Lawrence F. (Wolf, Avner S. and Lawrence F. Pohlman. "Tests Of The Black And Whaley Models For Gold And Silver Futures Options," RFM, 1987, v6(3), 328-344.)

Pohlman, Randolph A. and Robert D. Hollinger. "Information Redundancy In Sets Of Financial Ratios," JBFA, 1981, v8(4), 511-528.

Pohlman, Randolph A., James S. Ang and Robert D. Hollinger. "Performance And Timing: A Test Of Hedge Funds," JPM, 1977-78, v4(3), 69-72.

Pohlman, Randolph A., Emmanuel S. Santiago and F. Lynn Markel. "Cash Flow Estimation Practices Of Large Firms," FM, 1988, v17(2), 71-79.

Pointon, John. "Taxation And Mathematical Programming," JBFA, 1982, v8(1), 43-50.

Poitras, Geoff. "Optimal Futures Spread Positions," JFM, 1989, v9(2), 123-134.

Poitras, Geoffrey. "Hedging Canadian Treasury Bill Positions With U.S. Money market Futures Contracts," RFM, 1988, v7(1), 176-191.

Poitras, Geoffrey. "Arbitrage Boundaries, Treasury Bills, And Covered Interest Parity," JIMF, 1988, v7(4), 429-446.

Poitras, Geoffrey. "Hedging Canadian Treasury Bill Positions With U.S. Money Market Futures Contracts," RFM, 1988, v7(1), 176-191.

Poitras, Geoffrey. "The Distribution Of Gold Futures Spreads," JFM, 1990, v10(6), 643-660.

Poitras, Geoffrey. "'Golden Turtle Tracks': In Search Of Unexploited Profits In Gold Spreads," JFM, 1987, v7(4), 397-412.

Pol, Louis and Rebecca F. Guy. "Discrimination In Home Improvement Loans: A Rejoinder," JBR, 1981-82, v12(3), 192.

Polakoff, Michael A. "A Note On The Role Of Futures Indivisibility: Reconciling The Theoretical Literature," JFM, 1991, v11(1), 117-120.

Polakoff, Murray E. and William L. Silber. "Reluctance And Member-Bank Borrowing: Additional Evidence: A Note," JOF, 1967, v22(1), 88-92.

Polakoff, Murray E. "Member-Bank Borrowing: A Rejoinder," JOF, 1961, v16(1), 94-97.

Polakoff, Murray E. "Public Pension Funds," FAJ, 1966, v22(3), 75-81.

Polakoff, Murray E. "Reluctance Elasticity, Least Cost, And Member-Bank Borrowing: A Suggested Integration," JOF, 1960, v15(1), 1-18.

Polakoff, Murray E. (Kolodny, Richard, Peter Seeley and Murray E. Polakoff. "The Effect Of Compensating Balance Requirements On The Profitability Of Borrowers And Lenders," JFQA, 1977, v12(5), 801-815.)

Polakoff, Murray E. (Rangarajan, C. and Murray E. Polakoff. "A Note On A 'Keynesian' Model Of Aggregate Demand: Reply," JOF, 1969, v24(1), 104-105.)

Polakoff, Murray E. (Silber, William L. and Murray E. Polakoff. "On The Differential Effects Of Tight Money: Reply," JOF, 1971, v26(4), 955-958.)

Polakoff, Murray E. (Silber, William L. and Murray E. Polakoff. "The Differential Effects Of Tight Money: An Econometric Study," JOF, 1970, v25(1), 83-97.)

Polhemus, Neil W. (Khumawala, Saleha B., Neil W. Polhemus and Woody M. Liao. "The Predictability Of Quarterly Cash Flows," JBFA, 1981, v8(4), 493-510.)

Policano, Andrew J. (Fethke, Gary C. and Andrew J. Policano. "Long-Term Contracts And The Effectiveness Of Demand And Supply Policies," JMCB, 1981, v13(4), 439-453.)

Policano, Andrew J. (Neftci, Salih N. and Andrew J. Policano. "Can Chartists Outperform The Market? Market Efficiency Tests For 'Technical Analysis'," JFM, 1984, v4(4), 465-478.)

Policano, Michael A. (Rohman, Mark C. and Michael A. Policano. "Financing Chapter 11 Companies In The 1990s," JACF, 1990, v3(2), 96-101.)

Pollard, Stephen K. (Canarella, Giorgio and Stephen K. Pollard. "Efficiency Of Commodity Futures: A Vector Autoregression Analysis," JFM, 1985, v5(1), 57-76.)

Pollard, Stephen K. (Canarella, Giorgio and Stephen K. Pollard. "Efficiency In Foreign Exchange Markets: A Vector Autoregression Approach," JIMF, 1988, v7(3), 331-346.)

Pollard, Stephen K. (Canarella, Giorgio and Stephen K. Pollard. "The Efficiency Of The London Metal Exchange: A Test With Overlapping And Non-Overlapping Data," JBF, 1986, v10(4), 575-594.)

Pollatschek, M. A. (Melnik, A. and M. A. Pollatschek. "Debt Capacity, Diversification And Conglomerate Mergers," JOF, 1973, v28(5), 1263-1273.)

Polli, Rolando E. (Frank, Ronald E., Susan P. Douglas and Rolando E. Polli. "Household Correlates Of 'Brand Loyalty' For Grocery Products," JOB, 1968, v41(2), 237-245.)

Polli, Rolando and Victor Cook. "Validity Of The Product Life Cycle," JOB, 1969, v42(4), 385-400.

Polonchek, John A. (Slovin, Myron B., Marie E. Sushka and John A. Polonchek. "Corporate Sale-And-Leasebacks And Shareholder Wealth," JOF, 1990, v45(1), 289-300.)

Polonchek, John, Myron B. Slovin and Marie E. Sushka. "Valuation Effects Of Commercial Bank Securities Offerings: A Test Of The Information Hypothesis," JBF, 1989, v13(3), 443-462.

Poloz, Stephen S. "Currency Substitution And The Precautionary Demand For Money," JIMF, 1986, v5(1), 115-124.

Pomerantz, Steven. (Bookstaber, Richard M. and Steven Pomerantz. "An Information-Based Model Of Market Volatility," FAJ, 1989, v45(6), 37-46.)

Pomeranz, Robert J. "Thrift Industry Usage Of Financial Futures: A Regulator's Perspective," RFM, 1985, v4(2), 190-195.

PonArul, Richard. "Treatment Of Flotation Cost Of Equity In Capital Budgeting," JFED, 1990, v19, 44-45.

PonArul, Richard. (Chen, Charng Y. and Richard PonArul. "On The Tax Incentive For Corporate Insurance Purchase," JRI, 1989, v56(2), 306-311.)

Poncet, Patrice. "Optimum Consumption And Portfolio Rules With Money As An Asset," JBF, 1983, v7(2), 231-252.

Pontius, Marcia L. (Vandell, Robert F. and Marcia L. Pontius. "The Impact Of Tax Status On Stock Selection," JPM, 1980-81, v7(4), 35-42.)

Pool, A. A. "Attitudes Toward Consumer Banking Packages: An Empirical Analysis," JBR, 1976-77, v7(1), 88-92.

Pool, Albert A. "Application Of Discriminant Analysis In Formulation Of Promotional Strategy For Cash Dispensing Machines," JBR, 1974-75, v5(1), 13-19.

Poole, Alan C. "Canadian Austerity Program And Its Effect On American Economy," FAJ, 1962, v18(5), 23-24.

Poole, Alan C. "Gold, Money And The Economy - 1962," FAJ, 1962, v18(2), 17-19.

Poole, Alan C. "Senior Financial Analysts Look Into Future (Beloit Seminar)," FAJ, 1962, v18(6), 89-92.

Poole, Alan C. "Socio-Political Effects On Western European Economies," FAJ, 1961, v17(3), 67-74.

Poole, Alan C. "Stocks And The Berlin Crisis," FAJ, 1961, v17(5), 9-11.

Poole, Alan C. "United States And The Free World Economy," FAJ, 1963, v19(2), 9-11.

Poole, Kenyon E. (Alhadeff, D., P. Bernstein, C. Campbell, L. Chandler, E. Ettin, V. Farhi, J. Guttentag, H. Latane and K. Poole. "The Commission On Money And Credit's Research Studies," JOF, 1964, v19(3), 497-533.)

Poole, William. "A Proposal For Reforming Bank Reserve Requirements In The United States," JMCB, 1976, v8(2), 137-147.

Poole, William. "Burnsian Monetary Policy: Eight Years Of Progress?," JOF, 1979, v34(2), 473-484.

Poole, William. "Commercial Bank Reserve Management In A Stochastic Model: Implications For Monetary Policy," JOF, 1968, v23(5), 769-791.

Poole, William. "Federal Reserve Operating Procedures: A Survey And Evaluation Of The Historical Record Since October 1979," JMCB, 1982, v14(4), Part 2, 575-596.

Poole, William. "The Relationship Of Monetary Decelerations To Business Cycle Peaks: Another Look At The Evidence," JOF, 1975, v30(3), 697-719.

Poon, Percy. (Lamoureux, Christopher G. and Percy Poon. "The Market Reaction To Stock Splits," JOF, 1987, v42(5), 1347-1370.)

Poor, Riva. "4-Days, 40-Hours: Reporting A Revolution In Work And Leisure," JBR, 1970-71, v1(3), 21-28.

Pope, P. F. and D. A. Peel. "Information Disclosure To Employees And Rational Expectations," JBFA, 1981, v8(1), 139-146.

Pope, P. F. (Morris, R. C. and P. F. Pope. "The Jensen Measure Of Portfolio Performance In An Arbitrage Pricing Theory Context," JBFA, 1981, v8(2), 203-220.)

Pope, P. F. (Peel, D. A. and P. F. Pope. "Corporate Accounting Data, Capital Market Information And Wage Increases Of The Firm," JBFA, 1984, v11(2), 177-188.)

Pope, P. F. (Peel, D. A. and P. F. Pope. "Stock Returns And Expected Inflation In The UK: Some New Evidence," JBFA, 1988, v15(4), 459-468.)

Pope, P. F., R. C. Morris and D. A. Peel. "Insider Trading: Some Evidence On Market Efficiency And Directors' Share Dealings In Great Britain," JBFA, 1990, v17(3), 359-380.

Pope, Peter F. "Information Asymmetries In Participative Budgeting: A Bargaining Approach," JBFA, 1984, v11(1), 41-59.

Pope, Peter F. (Peel, David A. and Peter F. Pope. "Testing The Fisherian Hypothesis: Some Methodological Issues And Further Evidence For The UK," JBFA, 1985, v12(2), 297-312.)

Pope, Peter F. (Yadav, Pradeep K. and Peter F. Pope. "Stock Index Futures Arbitrage: International Evidence," JFM, 1990, v10(6), 573-604.)

Pope, Ralph A. "An Analysis Of The Need To Develop A Tax Course," JFED, 1987, v16, 46-55.

Popkin, Philip. (Ferguson, Robert and Philip Popkin. "Pulling Rabbits Out Of Hats In The Oil Business - And Elsewhere," FAJ, 1982, v38(2), 24-27.)

Poppei, William M. (Berry, Thomas D. and William M. Poppei. "An Alternative Methodology For Developing Certainty Equivalents," JFED, 1983, v12, 51-53.)

Poppei, William. (Peters, Robert M. and William Poppei. "An Accelerated Program For Bankers In Accounting/ Finance," JFED, 1980, v9, 42-45.)

Porat, M. Moshe. (Kahane, Yehuda and M. Moshe Porat. "Financial Analysis Of Underwriting Results - A Corrected Approach To Loss Ratio Analysis, With Special Reference To Inflation," JRI, 1984, v51(4), 710-719.)

Porter, Albert. "Intelligence-Test Score As A Predictor Of Executive Success," JOB, 1963, v36(1), 65-68.

Porter, David M. (Brueggeman, William B., Jeffrey D. Fisher and David M. Porter. "Rethinking Corporate Real Estate," JACF, 1990, v3(1), 39-50.)

Porter, Lyman W. (Dalton, Dan R., David M. Krackhardt and Lyman W. Porter. "The Impact Of Teller Turnover In Banking: First Appearances Are Deceiving," JBR, 1983-84, v14(3), 184-192.)

Porter, Michael E. "Industry Structure And Competitive Strategy: Keys To Profitability," FAJ, 1980, v36(4), 30-41.

Porter, R. Burr and Roger C. Pfaffenberger. "Efficient Algorithms For Conducting Stochastic Dominance Tests On Large Numbers Of Portfolios: Reply," JFQA, 1975, v10(1), 181-185.

Porter, R. Burr and Roger P. Bey. "An Evaluation Of The Empirical Significance Of Optimal Seeking Algorithms In Portfolio Selection," JOF, 1974, v29(5), 1479-1490.

Porter, R. Burr, James R. Wart and Donald L. Ferguson. "Efficient Algorithms For Conducting Stochastic Dominance Tests On Large Numbers Of Portfolios," JFQA, 1973, v8(1), 71-81.

Porter, R. Burr, Roger P. Bey and David C. Lewis. "The Development Of A Mean-Semivariance Approach To Capital Budgeting," JFQA, 1975, v10(4), 639-649.

Porter, R. Burr. "An Empirical Comparison Of Stochastic Dominance And Mean-Variance Portfolio Choice Criteria," JFQA, 1973, v8(4), 587-608.

Porter, R. Burr. (Ezzell, John R. and R. Burr Porter. "Flotation Costs And The Weighted Average Cost Of Capital," JFQA, 1976, v11(3), 403-413.)

Porter, R. Burr. (Ezzell, John R. and R. Burr Porter. "Correct Specification Of The Cost Of Capital And Net Present Value," FM, 1979, v8(2), 15-17.)

Porter, R. Burr. (Joy, O. Maurice and R. Burr Porter. "Stochastic Dominance And Mutual Fund Performance," JFQA, 1974, v9(1), 25-31.)

Porter, Thomas L. (Comiskey, Eugene E., Charles W. Mulford and Thomas L. Porter. "Forecast Error, Earnings Variability And Systematic Risk: Additional Evidence," JBFA, 1986, v13(2), 257-265.)

Portis, Bernard. "Negroes And Fashion Interest," JOB, 1966, v39(2), 314-323.

Portney, Paul R. (Cropper, Maureen L. and Paul R. Portney. "Discounting And The Evaluation Of Lifesaving Programs," JRU, 1990, v3(4), 369-380.)

Porzecanski, Arturo C. "Patterns Of Monetary Policy In Latin America," JMCB, 1979, v11(4), 427-437.

Porzecanski, Arturo C. "The International Financial Role Of U. S. Commercial Banks: Past And Future," JBF, 1981, v5(1), 5-16.

Poskitt, D. S. (Jones-Lee, M. W. and D. S. Poskitt. "An Existence Proof For Equilibrium In A Capital Asset Market," JBFA, 1975, v2(3), 349-360.)

Poșnak, Robert L. "Perspectives On Life Insurance Financial Reporting," JRI, 1973, v40(1), 7-30.

Posner, Richard A. (Black, Fischer, Merton H. Miller and Richard A. Posner. " An Approach To The Regulation Of Bank Holding Companies," JOB, 1978, v51(3), 379-412.)

Possen, Uri M. (Ebrill, Liam P. and Uri M. Possen. "Inflation And The Taxation Of Equity In Corporations And Owner-Occupied Housing," JMCB, 1982, v14(1), 33-47.)

Post, Lawrence E. "Yield To Early Maturity In Usable Bonds," FAJ, 1973, v29(6), 70-73,84.

Postelwaite, Andrew. (Allen, Franklin and Andrew Postelwaite. "Rational Expectations And The Measurement Of A Stock's Elasticity Of Demand," JOF, 1984, v39(4), 1119-1125.)

Potepan, Michael J. (Harmon, Oskar R. and Michael J. Potepan. "Housing Adjustment Costs: Their Impact On Mobility And Housing Demand Elasticities," AREUEA, 1988, v16(4), 459-478.)

Poterba, James M. and Lawrence H. Summers. "New Evidence That Taxes Affect The Valuation Of Dividends," JOF, 1984, v39(5), 1397-1415.

Poterba, James M. "The Market Valuation Of Cash Dividends: The Citizens Utilities Cash Reconsidered," JFEC, 1986, v15(3), 395-406.

Poterba, James M. (Cutler, David M., James M. Poterba and Lawrence H. Summers. "What Moves Stock Prices?," JPM, 1989, v15(3), 4-12.)

Poterba, James M. and Julio J. Rotemberg. "Inflation And Taxation With Optimizing Governments," JMCB, 1990, v22(1), 1-18.

Poterba, James M. and Lawrence H. Summers. "Mean Reversion In Stock Prices: Evidence And Implications," JFEC, 1988, v22(1), 27-60.

Potter, Roger E. (Hoeke, Robert S. and Roger E. Potter. "Stock Investor Objectives Of Demographic Segments," FR, 1975, v10(1), 1-11.)

Potts, Glenn T. (Luckett, Dudley G. and Glenn T. Potts. "Monetary Policy And Partisan Politics," JMCB, 1980, v12(3), 540-546.)

Potts, Tom L. and William Reichenstein. "The Optimal Allocation Of Pension Fund Assets: An Individual's Perspective," FSR, 1991, v1(1), 11-26.

Poudyal, Sri Ram. (Thornton, John and Sri Ram Poudyal. "Money And Capital In Economic Development: A Test Of The McKinnon Hypothesis For Nepal," JMCB, 1990, v22(3), 395-399.)

Poulsen, Annette B. "Japanese Bank Regulation And The Activities Of The U.S. Officies Of Japanese Banks," JMCB, 1986, v18(3), 366-373.

Poulsen, Annette B. (Jarrell, Gregg A. and Annette B. Poulsen. "Dual-Class Recapitalizations As Antitakeover Mechanisms: The Recent Evidence," JFEC, 1988, v20(1/2), 129-152.)

Poulsen, Annette B. (Jarrell, Gregg A. and Annette B. Poulsen. "Shark Repellents And Stock Prices: The Effects Of Antitakeover Amendments Since 1980," JFEC, 1987, v19(1), 127-168.)

Poulsen, Annette B. (Jarrell, Gregg A. and Annette B. Poulsen. "The Returns To Acquiring Firms In Tender Orders: Evidence From Three Decades," FM, 1989, v18(3), 12-19.)

Poulsen, Annette. (Lehn, Kenneth and Annette Poulsen. "Free Cash Flow And Stockholder Gains In Going Private Transactions," JOF, 1989, v44(3), 771-788.)

Poulsen, Annette. (Lehn, Kenneth, Jeffry Netter and Annette Poulsen. "Consolidating Corporate Control: Dual-Class Recapitalizations Versus Leveraged Buyouts," JFEC, 1990, v27(2) 557-580.)

Poulsen, Annette. (Netter, Jeffry and Annette Poulsen. "State Corporation Laws And Shareholders: The Recent Experience," FM, 1989, v18(3), 29-40.)

Pound, G. D. and J. R. Francis. "The Accounting Services Market: Theory And Evidence," JBFA, 1981, v8(3), 353-371.

Pound, G. (Francis, J. R. and G. Pound. "The Accounting Services Market: Theory And Evidence: A Reply," JBFA, 1983, v10(2), 323-324)

Pound, John and Richard Zeckhauser. "Clearly Heard On The Street: The Effect Of Takeover Rumors On Stock Prices," JOB, 1990, v63(3), 291-308.

Pound, John and Robert J. Shiller. "Are Institutional Investors Speculators?," JPM, 1986-87, v13(3), 46-52.

Pound, John. "Proxy Contests And The Efficiency Of Shareholder Oversight," JFEC, 1988, v20(1/2), 237-266.

Pound, John. (Gordon, Lilli A. and John Pound. "ESOPs And Corporate Control," JFEC, 1990, v27(2), 525-556.)

Pound, John. The Information Effects Of Takeover Bids And Resistance," JFEC, 1988, v22(2), 207-228.

Pounds, Henry M. "Covered Call Option Writing: Strategies And Results," JPM, 1977-78, v4(2), 31-42.

Pourian, Heydar. "International Securities Markets: Integration, Regulation, And Methods For Extraterritorial Conflict Resolution," RDIBF, 1988, v2, 105-120.

Powell, James. (Barnhill, Theodore M. and James Powell. "Silver Price Volatility: A Perspective On the July 1979-April 1980 Period," JFM, v1(4), 619-647.)

Powell, John R. P. and Roger C. Vergin. "A Heuristic Model For Planning Corporate Financing," FM, 1974, v4(2), 13-20.

Power, Donald C. "Communications In A Changing World," FAJ, 1960, v16(6), 9-14.

Power, Fred B. (Longstreet, J. R. and Fred B. Power. "A Capital Budgeting Analysis Of Life Insurance Contracts," JRI, 1970, v37(4), 599-608.)

Power, Fred B. (Meyer, Richard L. and Fred B. Power. "Total Insurance Costs And The Frequency Of Premium Payments," JRI, 1973, v40(4), 599-606.)

Power, Fred B. (Meyer, Richard L. and Fred B. Power. "The Investment Value Of Corporate Insurance," JRI, 1983, v50(1), 151-156.)

Power, Fred B. (Shows, E. Warren, Fred B. Power and Dale A. Johnson. "Lump-Sum Awards In Workers' Compensation: Comment," JRI, 1988, v55(4), 734-739.)

Power, Fred B. and E. Warren Shows. "A Status Report On The National Flood Insurance Program - Mid 1978," JRI, 1979, v46(2), 61-76.

Power, Mark L. (Ledolter, Johannes and Mark L. Power. "A Study Of ERISA's Impact On Private Retirement Plan Growth," JRI, 1984, v51(2), 225-243.)

Powers, James T. "APB Opinion No. 15," FAJ, 1970, v26(3), 69-77.

Powers, Mark J. "Trading Tactics," JFM, 1986, v6(4), 681-682.

Powers, R. William. "A Survey Of Bank Check Volume," JBR, 1975-76, v6(4), 245-256.

Pozen, Robert C. "The Prudent Man Rule And ERISA," FAJ, 1977, v33(2), 30-35.

Pozen, Robert C. "When To Purchase A Protective Put," FAJ, 1978, v34(4), 47-60.

Pozo, Susan. "The ECU As International Money," JIMF, 1987, v6(2), 195-206.

Praetz, P. D. "A General Test Of A Filter Effect," JFQA, 1979, v14(2), 385-394.

Praetz, Peter D. "A Comparison Of The Stable And Student Distributions As Statistical Models For Stock Prices: Comment," JOB, 1977, v50(1), 76-77.

Praetz, Peter D. "On The Methodology Of Testing For Independence In Futures Prices: Comment," JOF, 1976, v31(3), 977-979.

Praetz, Peter D. "Rates Of Return On Filter Tests," JOF, 1976, v31(1), 71-75.

Praetz, Peter D. "Testing For A Flat Spectrum On Efficient Market Price Data," JOF, 1979, v34(3), 645-658.

Praetz, Peter D. "The Distribution Of Share Price Changes," JOB, 1972, v45(1), 49-55.

Praetz, Peter. "A Note On Economies Of Scale In The United Kingdom Property-Liability Insurance Industry," JRI, 1985, v52(2), 315-320.

Praetz, Peter. "Returns To Scale In The U.S. Life Insurance Industry," JRI, 1980, v47(3), 525-533.

Praetz, Peter. "Returns To Scale In The U.S. Life Insurance Industry: Reply," JRI, 1983, v50(3), 508-509.

Prager, Jonas and Jacob Paroush. "On The Differential Effects Of Tight Money: Comment," JOF, 1971, v26(4), 951-954.

Prager, Robin A. "The Effects Of Regulatory Policies On The Cost Of Debt For Electric Utilities: An Empirical Investigation," JOB, 1989, v62(1), 33-54.

Prais, Zmira. "Real Money Balances As A Variable In The Production Function," JMCB, 1975, v7(4), 535-544.

Prakash, Arun J. and Robert M. Bear. "A Simplifying Performance Measure Recognizing Skewness," FR, 1986, v21(1), 135-144.

Prakash, Arun J., Krishnan Dandapani and Gordon V. Karels. "Simple Resource Allocation Rules," JBFA, 1988, v15(3), 447-452.

Prakash, Arun J. (Anderson, Gary A. and Arun J. Prakash. "A Note On Simple Resource Allocation Rules: The Case Of Arithmetic Growth," JBFA, 1990, v17(5), 759-762.)

Prakash, Arun J. (Karels, Gordon V. and Arun J. Prakash. "Multivariate Normality And Forecasting Of Business Bankruptcy," JBFA, 1987, v14(4), 573-594.)

Prakash, Arun J. (Karels, Gordon V., Arun J. Prakash and Emmanuel Roussakis. "The Relationship Between Bank Capital Adequacy And Market Measures Of Risk," JBFA, 1989, v16(5), 663-674.)

Prakash, Arun J., A. M. Parhizgari and Gerald W. Perritt. "The Effect Of Listing On The Parameters Of Characteristic Lines Models," JBFA, 1989, v16(3), 335-342.

Pratt, Denis J. (Leech, Stewart A., Denis J. Pratt and W. G. W. Magill. "Company Asset Revaluations And Inflation In Australia, 1950 To 1975," JBFA, 1978, v5(4), 353-362.)

Pratt, Eugene J. "Myths Associated With Closed-End Investment Company Discounts," FAJ, 1966, v22(4), 79-82.

Pratt, Frank T. (Goodfriend, Herbert E. and Frank T. Pratt. "Community Antenna Television," FAJ, 1970, v26(2), 48-57.)

Pratt, John W. and John S. Hammond, III. "Evaluating And Comparing Projects: Simple Detection Of False Alarms," JOF, 1979, v34(5), 1231-1242.

Pratt, John W. "Aversion To One Risk In The Presence Of Others," JRU, 1988, v1(4), 395-414.

Pratt, John W. "The Logic Of Partial-Risk Aversion: Paradox Lost," JRU, 1990, v3(2), 105-114.

Pratt, John W. and Richard Zeckhauser. "The Impact Of Risk Sharing On Efficient Decision," JRU, 1989, v2(3), 219-234.

Pratt, Leila J. (Mixon, J. Wilson, Jr., Leila J. Pratt and Myles S. Wallace. "Cross-National Money To Income Causality: U.S. Money To U.K. Income," JMCB, 1979, v11(4), 419-426.)

Pratt, Richard T. (Johnson, Ramon E., Richard T. Pratt and Samuel S. Stewart, Jr. "The Economic Consequences Of ESOPs," JFR, 1982, v5(1), 75-82.)

Preddy, R. Keith. (Wofford, Larry E. and R. Keith Preddy. "Real Estate Investment Perception: A Multidimensional Analysis," AREUEA, 1978, v6(1), 22-36.)

Preddy, R. Keith. (Wofford, Larry E. and R. Keith Preddy. "Assessing Student Perception Of Real Estate Careers," AREUEA, 1980, v8(4), 417-427.)

Preiss, Beth. (Bloom David E., Beth Preiss and James Trussell. "Mortgage Lending Discrimination And The Decision To Apply: A Methodological Note," AREUEA, 1983, v11(1), 97-103.)

Prelec, Drazen. "A 'Pseudo-Endowment' Effect, And Its Implications For Some Recent Nonexpected Utility Models," JRU, 1990, v3(3), 247-260.

Press, S. James. "A Compound Events Model For Security Prices," JOB, 1967, v40(3), 317-335.

Prestopino, Chris Joseph. "Do Higher Reserve Requirements Discourage Federal Reserve Membership?," JOF, 1976, v31(5), 1471-1480.

Prezas, Alexandros P. "Effects Of Debt On The Degrees Of Operating And Financial Leverage," FM, 1987, v16(2), 39-44.

Price, Barbara. (Nantell, Timothy J., Kelly Price and Barbara Price. "Mean-Lower Partial Moment Asset Pricing Model: Some Empirical Evidence," JFQA, 1982, v17(5), 763-782.)

Price, Barbara. (Nantell, Timothy J. and Barbara Price. "An Analytical Comparison Of Variance And Semivariance Capital Market Theories," JFQA, 1979, v14(2), 221-242.)

Price, Barbara. (Price, Kelly, Barbara Price and Timothy J. Nantell. "Variance And Lower Partial Moment Measures Of Systematic Risk: Some Analytical And Empirical Results," JOF, 1982, v37(3), 843-855.)

Price, Kelly and John R. Brick. "Daily Interest Rate Relationships," JMCB, 1980, v12(2), Part 1, 215-220.

Price, Kelly, Barbara Price and Timothy J. Nantell. "Variance And Lower Partial Moment Measures Of Systematic Risk: Some Analytical And Empirical Results," JOF, 1982, v37(3), 843-855.

Price, Kelly. (Nantell, Timothy J., Kelly Price and Barbara Price. "Mean-Lower Partial Moment Asset Pricing Model: Some Empirical Evidence," JFQA, 1982, v17(5), 763-782.)

Price, L. (Srivastava, R. K., H. R. Isakson, L. Price and T. H. McInish. "Analysis Of The Characteristics Of Individual Investors In Real Estate Securities And Income-Producing Property," AREUEA, 1984, v12(4), 521-541.)

Price, Lee N. "Choosing Between Growth And Yield," FAJ, 1979, v35(4), 57-67.

Price, Lee N. (Barrett, M. Edgar, Lee N. Price and Judith Ann Gehrke. "What Investors Need To Know About Japan," FAJ, 1974, v30(2), 60-67,59.)

Price, Lee N. (Barrett, M. Edgar, Lee N. Price and Judith Ann Gehrke. "What Investors Need To Know About Japan," FAJ, 1974, v30(1), 33-44.)

Price, Linda L. (Srivastava, Rajendra K., Thomas H. McInish and Linda L. Price. "Information Costs And Portfolio Selection," JBF, 1984, v8(3), 417-429.)

Price, Robert. (Freeman, Orville L., Patrick J. James, and Robert Price. "World Food Needs: A Discussion," FAJ, 1967, v23(5), 19-25.)

Price, Vera. (Theobald, Michael and Vera Price. "Seasonality Estimation In Thin Markets," JOF, 1984, v39(2), 377-392.)

Priest, Donald E. "The Uncharted Trend: Toward Increasing Public-Private Cooperation For Housing Development," AREUEA, 1977, v5(2), 242-253.

Priest, W. W. (Treynor, Jack L., P. J. Regan and W. W. Priest. "Pension Claims And Corporate Assets," FAJ, 1978, v34(3), 84-88.)

Priest, William W., Jr. "Evaluating Research And Development Expenditures," FAJ, 1966, v22(4), 43-47.

Priest, William W., Jr. "Rate Of Return As A Criterion For Investment Decisions," FAJ, 1965, v21(4), 109-113.

Priest, William W., Jr. (Beebower, Gilbert L. and William W. Priest, Jr. "The Tricks Of The Trade," JPM, 1979-80, v6(2), 36-42.)

Priest, William W., Jr. (Treynor, Jack L., William W. Priest, Jr., Lawrence Fisher and Catherine A. Higgins. "Risk Estimates," FAJ, 1968, v24(5),93-100.)

Priewasser, Erich. "Implementation Of OR/MS Models In German Banks," JBR, 1981-82, v12(2), 124-127.

Primeaux, Walter J. (Bomball, Mark R., Walter J. Primeaux and Donald E. Pursell. "Forecasting Stage 2 Of The Family Life Cycle," JOB, 1975, v48(1), 65-73.)

Primeaux, Walter J., Jr. "The Effect Of Consumer Knowledge And Bargaining Strength On Final Selling Price: A Case Study," JOB, 1970, v43(4), 419-426.

Primeaux, Walter J., Jr. "The Newspaper Rate Differential: Another Element In The Explanation-Reply," JOB, 1977, v50(1), 86-87.

Primeaux, Walter J., Jr. "The Newspaper Rate Differential: Another Element In The Explanation," JOB, 1975, v48(4), 492-499.

Primeaux, Walter J., Jr. "The Interdependence Of The Life Cycle And Strategic Group Concepts: Theory And Evidence," AFPAF, 1987, v2(1), 67-86.

Primeaux, Walter J., Jr. (Fiegenbaum, Avi and Walter J. Primeaux, Jr. "An Empirical Examination Of Strategic Groups In Three Manufacturing Industries," AFPAF, 1989, v3(1), 281-310.)

Primeaux, Walter J., Jr. (Lee, Cheng F. and Walter J. Primeaux, Jr. "Impacts Of Rate Base Methods On Firm Operating Elasticity And Capital Structure: Theory And Evidence," AFPAF, 1985, v1(1), 103-124.)

Pringle, J. J. (Franks, J. R. and J. J. Pringle. "Debt Financing, Corporate Financial Intermediaries And Firm Valuation," JOF, 1982, v37(3), 751-761.)

Pringle, J. Maxwell. "The Mortgage Market," FAJ, 1966, v22(3), 105-106.

Pringle, John J. "A Theory Of The Banking Firm," JMCB, 1973, v5(4), 990-996.

Pringle, John J. "Bank Capital And The Performance Of Banks As Financial Intermediaries," JMCB, 1975, v7(4), 545-559.

Pringle, John J. "Managing Foreign Exchange Exposure," JACF, 1991, v3(4), 73-82.

Pringle, John J. "Price/Earnings Ratios, Earnings Per Share, And Financial Management," FM, 1973, v2(1), 34-40.

Pringle, John J. "The Capital Decision In Commercial Banks," JOF, 1974, v29(3), 779-795.

Pringle, John J. "The Imperfect-Markets Model Of Commercial Bank Financial Management," JFQA, 1974, v9(1), 69-87.

Pringle, John J. (Chambers, Donald R., Robert S. Harris and John J. Pringle. "Treatment Of Financing Mix In Analyzing Investment Opportunities," FM, 1982, v11(2), 24-41.)

Pringle, John J. (Cohn, Richard A. and John J. Pringle. "Imperfections In International Financial Markets: Implications For Risk Premia And The Cost Of Capital To Firms," JOF, 1973, v28(1), 59-66.)

Pringle, John J. (Harris, Robert S. and John J. Pringle. "Implications Of Miller's Argument For Capital Budgeting," JFR, 1983, v6(1), 13-23.)

Pringle, John J. (Harris, Robert S. and John J. Pringle. "Risk-Adjusted Discount Rates - Extensions From The Average-Risk Case," JFR, 1985, v8(3), 237-244.)

Pringle, John J. (Robichek, Alexander A., Richard A. Cohn and John J. Pringle. "Returns On Alternative Investment Media And Implications For Portfolio Construction," JOB, 1972, v45(3), 427-443.)

Pringle, John J. (Wall, Larry D. and John J. Pringle. "Alternative Explanations Of Interest Rate Swaps: A Theoretical And Empirical Analysis," FM, 1989, v18(2), 59-73.)

Pringle, John. (Miles, Mike, John Pringle and Brian Webb. "Modeling The Corporate Real Estate Decision," JRER, 1989, v4(3), 47-66.)

Prisman, E. Z. "Bond Pricing In Markets With Taxes: The Tax-Clientele Model Vs. The Non-Clientele Model," JBF, 1990, v14(1), 33-40.

Prisman, Eliezer Z. "A Unified Approach To Term Structure Estimation: A Methodology For Estimating The Term Structure In A Market With Frictions," JFQA, 1990, v25(1), 127-141.

Prisman, Eliezer Z. "Immunization As A Maxmim Strategy: A New Look," JBF, 1986, v10(4), 491-510.

Prisman, Eliezer Z. "Valuation Of Risky Assets In Arbitrage Free Economies With Frictions," JOF, 1986, v41(3), 545-556.

Prisman, Eliezer Z. and Marilyn R. Shores. "Duration Measures For Specific Term Structure Estimations And Applications To Bond Portfolio Immunization," JBF, 1988, v11(3), 493-504.

Prisman, Eliezer Zeev. (Dermody, Jaime Cuevas and Eliezer Zeev Prisman. "Term Structure Multiplicity And Clientele In Markets With Transactions Costs And Taxes," JOF, 1988, v43(4), 893-911.)

Pritchard, Leland J. "Toward A More Meaningful Statistical Concept of The Money Supply: Reply," JOF, 1955, v10(1), 66-68.

Pritchard, Leland J. "Toward A More Meaningful Statistical Concept Of The Money Supply," JOF, 1954, v9(1), 41-48.

Pritchett, Clayton P. "The Effect Of Regional Growth Characteristics On Regional Housing Prices," AREUEA, 1977, v5(2), 189-208.

Pritchett, S. Travis and Benjamin Y. Brewster, Jr. "Comparison Of Ordinary Life Operating Expense Ratios For Agency And Nonagency Insurers," JRI, 1979, v46(1), 61-74.

Pritchett, S. Travis and Harvey W. Rubin. "A Case Study Of Flood Losses: Implications For Flood Insurance Produce Development," JRI, 1975, v42(1), 105-116.

Pritchett, S. Travis and James S. Trieschmann. "Faculty Benefits At Fifty Major Universities," JRI, 1974, v41(1), 93-108.

Pritchett, S. Travis and John E. Logan. "Economies Of Size For Worker's Compensation Business," JRI, 1976, v43(3), 533-540.

Pritchett, S. Travis and Phyllis Schiller Myers. "Changes In Life Insurer Operating Expenses During Inflation," JRI, 1980, v47(2), 346-357.

Pritchett, S. Travis and Ronald P. Wilder. "Company Characteristics And Policyowner Cost Structures For Cash Value Life Insurance," JRI, 1977, v44(3), 355-372.

Pritchett, S. Travis. "1980 Presidential Address - The Underdeveloped Concepts Of Profitability And Dividend Payout Ratios For Mutual Life Insurers," JRI, 1980, v47(4), 592-606.

Pritchett, S. Travis. "An Intercompany Expense Comparison For Thirty Life Insurers," JRI, 1971, v38(4), 553-562.

Pritchett, S. Travis. "Operating Expenses Of Life Insurers, 1961-70: Implication For Economies Of Size," JRI, 1973, v40(2), 157-165.

Pritchett, S. Travis. "The Problem Drinker And Group Weekly Indemnity Insurance Claims," JRI, 1970, v37(4), 589-597.

Pritchett, S. Travis. (Myers, Phyllis Schiller and S. Travis Pritchett. "Rate Of Return On Differential Premiums For Selected Participating Life Insurance Contracts," JRI, 1983, v50(4), 569-586.)

Pritchett, S. Travis. (Schmit, Joan T., S. Travis Pritchett and Paige Fields. "Punitive Damages: Punishment Or Further Compensation?," JRI, 1988, v55(3), 453-466.)

Prochazka, Jaroslav. "Insurance In Czechoslovakia," JRI, 1959, v26(3), 57-60.

Prochnow, Herbert V. "Bank Liquidity And The New Doctrine Of Anticipated Income," JOF, 1949, v4(4), 298-314.

Proctor, Jim. (Yandle, Bruce and Jim Proctor. "Effect Of State Usury Laws On Housing Starts: Comments," JFQA, 1978, v13(3), 549-557.)

Prodhan, Bimal K. "Geographical Segment Disclosure And Multinational Risk Profile," JBFA, 1986, v13(1), 15-38.

Prodhan, Bimal K. and Malcolm C. Harris. "Systematic Risk And The Discretionary Disclosure Of Geographical Segments: An Empirical Investigation Of US Multinationals," JBFA, 1989, v16(4), 467-492.

Proffitt, Dennis and Keith Taylor. "Evaluating Negative Composite Performance Scores," JPED, 1985, v14, 17-21.

Prohaska, Charles R. and Walton Taylor. "Minimizing Losses In A Hostile Environment: The Costs Of Defending One's Castle," JRI, 1973, v40(3), 375-388.

Projector, Murray. "A Profit Calculation For Agency Management: Comment," JRI, 1967, v34(2), 335-336.

Projector, Murray. "Relationship Between Benefits And Premiums In Life Insurance: Comment," JRI, 1970, v37(2), 313-315.

Proschansky, Harris. "Anti-Insurance Activities," JRI, 1967, v34(3), 481-482.

Protopapadakis, Aris and Hans R. Stoll. "Spot And Futures Prices And The Law Of One Price," JOF, 1983, v38(5), 1431-1455.

Protopapadakis, Aris A. and Hans R. Stoll. "The Law Of One Price In International Commodity Markets: A Reformulation And Some Formal Tests," JIMF, 1986, v5(3), 335-360.

Protopapadakis, Aris A. (Flannery, Mark J. and Aris A. Protopapadakis. "From T-Bills To Common Stocks: Investigating The Generality Of Intra-Week Return Seasonality," JOF, 1988, v43(2), 431-450.)

Protopapadakis, Aris A. and Jeremy J. Siegel. "Are Money Growth And Inflation Related To Government Deficits? Evidence From Ten Industrialized Economies," JIMF, 1987, v6(1), 31-48.

Protopapadakis, Aris. "Expectations, Exchange Rates, And Monetary Theory: The Case Of The German Hyperinflation," JIMF, 1983, v2(1), 47-65.

Protopapadakis, Aris. "Some Indirect Evidence On Effective Capital Gains Tax Rates," JOB, 1983, v56(2), 127-138.

Protopapadakis, Aris. (Benninga, Simon and Aris Protopapadakis. "The Equilibrium Pricing Of Exchange Rates And Assets When Trade Takes Time," JIMF, 1988, v7(2), 129-150.)

Protopapadakis, Aris. (Benninga, Simon and Aris Protopapadakis. "General Equilibrium Properties Of The Term Structure Of Interest Rates," JFEC, 1986, v16(3), 389-410.)

Provenzano, George and Chunchi Wu. "Combining Financial And Production Constraints In Investment Planning For Electrical Power Supply," AFPAF, 1985, v1(1), 167-186.

Provost, Theodore E. "Payment Of Claims Under The Uniform Simultaneous Death Acts," JRI, 1960, v27(3), 7-18.

Prowse, Stephen D. "Institutional Investment Patterns And Corporate Financial Behavior In The United States And Japan," JFEC, 1990, v27(1), 43-66.

Pruitt, Stephen W. and David R. Peterson. "Security Price Reactions Around Product Recall Announcements," JFR, 1986, v9(2), 113-122.

Pruitt, Stephen W. (Bansal, Vipul K., Stephen W. Pruitt and K. C. John Wei. "An Empirical Reexamination Of The Impact Of CBOE Option Initiation On Volatility And Trading Volume Of The Underlying Equities: 1973-1986," FR, 1989, v24(1), 19-30.)

Pruitt, Stephen W. (Hoffer, George E., Stephen W. Pruitt and Robert J. Reilly. "Automotive Recalls And Informational Efficiency," FR, 1987, v22(4), 433-442.)

Pruitt, Stephen W. (Moore, Norman H. and Stephen W. Pruitt. "The Market Pricing Of Net Operating Loss Carryforwards: Implications Of The Tax Motivations Of Mergers," JFR, 1987, v10(2), 153-160.)

Pruitt, Stephen W. (Moore, Norman H. and Stephen W. Pruitt. "Excess Asset Reversions And Shareholder Wealth: Comment," JOF, 1990, v45(5), 1709-1714.)

Pruitt, Stephen W. and K. C. John Wei. "Institutional Ownership And Changes In The S&P 500," JOF, 1989, v44(2), 509-514.

Pruitt, Stephen W. and Lawrence J. Gitman. "Capital Budgeting Forecast Biases: Evidence From The Fortune 500," FM, 1987, v16(1), 46-51.

Pruitt, Stephen W. and Richard E. White. "Who Says Technical Analysis Can't Beat The Market?," JPM, 1987-88, v14(3), 55-58.

Pruitt, Stephen W. and Richard E. White. "Exchange-Traded Options And CRISMA Trading," JPM, 1989, v15(4), 55-57.

Pruitt, Stephen W., Wittipan Tawarangkoon and K. C. John Wei. "Chernobyl, Commodities And Chaos: An Examination Of The Reaction Of Commodity Futures Prices To Evolving Information," JFM, 1987, v7(5), 555-570.

Pryor, Frederic L. "The Origins Of Money," JMCB, 1977, v9(3), 391-409.

Puckett, Richard H. and Susan B. Vroman. "Rules Versus Discretion: A Simulation Study," JOF, 1973, v28(4), 853-865.

Puckett, Richard H. "Monetary Policy Effectiveness: The Case Of A Positively Sloped I-S Curve: Comment," JOF, 1973, v28(5), 1362-1364.

Puder, Virginia B. "The Revolution In Life Insurance," FAJ, 1970, v26(4), 50-62.

Pugh, William N. and John S. Jahera, Jr. "State Antitakeover Legislation And Shareholder Wealth," JFR, 1990, v13(3), 221-232.

Pugh, William and John S. Jahera, Jr. "Stock Repurchases And Excess Returns: An Empirical Examination," FR, 1990, v25(1), 127-142.

Puglisi, D. J. (Hettenhouse, G. W. and D. J. Puglisi. "Investor Experience With Options," FAJ, 1975, v31(4), 53-58.)

Puglisi, Donald J. and Anthony J. Vignola, Jr. "An Examination Of Federal Agency Debt Pricing Practices," JFR, 1983, v6(2), 83-92.

Puglisi, Donald J. "Is The Futures Market For Treasury Bills Efficient?," JPM, 1977-78, v4(2), 64-67.

Puglisi, Donald J. (McInish, Thomas H. and Donald J. Puglisi. "The Efficiency Of The International Money Markets," JBFA, 1982, v8(2), 167-177.)

Puglisi, Donald J. and Rudolph E. D'Souza. "A Note On Fiscal Agent Pricing Of Federal Agency Debt," JBF, 1989, v13(2), 311-320.

Puglisi, Donald. (McInish, Thomas H. and Donald Puglisi. "The Efficiency Of The International Money Markets: A Reply," JBFA, 1984, v11(4), 583-584.)

Pullara, S. J. and L. R. Walker. "The Evaluation Of Capital Expenditure Proposals: A Survey Of Firms In The Chemical Industry," JOB, 1965, v38(4), 403-408.

Pulley, Lawrence B. "A General Mean-Variance Approximation To Expected Utility For Short Holding Periods," JFQA, 1981, v16(2), 361-373.

Pulley, Lawrence B. "Comment On 'Mean-Variance Versus Direct Utility Maximization'," JOF, 1985, v40(2), 601-602.

Pulliam, Ken P. "How To Beat These Index Funds: Comment," JPM, 1979-80, v6(3), 72-74.

Pulliam, Kenneth P. "A Liquidity Portfolio Management Strategy Approach," JBR, 1977-78, v8(1), 50-58.

Pulliam, Kenneth P. "How To Produce Value From Portfolio Measurement," JPM, 1981-82, v8(1), 13-16.

Punter, Alan. "Optimal Cash Management Under Conditions Of Uncertainty," JBFA, 1982, v8(3), 329-340.

Pupp, Roger L. "Community Rating And Cross Subsidies In Health Insurance," JRI, 1981, v48(4), 610-627.

Pupp, Roger. (Bloch, Howard and Roger Pupp. "The January Barometer Revisited And Rejected," JPM, 1982-83, v9(2), 48-50.)

Purcell, Wayne D. and Michael A. Hudson. "The Certificate System For Delivery In Live Cattle: Conceptual Issues And Measures Of Performance," JFM, 1986, v6(3), 461-476.

Purdy, Derek E. "Accounting For Convertible Debt," JBFA, 1977, v4(1), 99-114.

Purdy, Derek E. "The Enterprise Theory: An Extension," JBFA, 1983, v10(4), 531-541.

Pursell, Donald E. (Bomball, Mark R., Walter J. Primeaux and Donald E. Pursell. "Forecasting Stage 2 Of The Family Life Cycle," JOB, 1975, v48(1), 65-73.)

Pursell, Garry L. "Rate Control And Government Competition In Australian Non-Life Insurance," JRI, 1967, v34(2), 237-254.

Purvis, Douglas D. (Harris, Richard G. and Douglas D. Purvis. "Incomplete Information And Equilibrium Determination Of The Forward Exchange Rate," JIMF, 1982, v1(3), 241-254.)

Purvis, Douglas. (Backus, David and Douglas Purvis. "An Integrated Model Of Household Flow-Of-Funds Allocations," JMCB, 1980, v12(2), Part 2, 400-421.)

Putnam, Bluford H. (Akhtar, M. A. and Bluford H. Putnam. "Money Demand And Foreign Exchange Risk: The German Case, 1972-1976," JOF, 1980, v35(3), 787-794.)

Putnam, Bluford H. and John J. Van Belle. "A Monetary Approach To Afghanistan's Flexible Exchange Rate: A Comment," JMCB, 1978, v10(1), 117-118.

Putnam, Bluford H. (Akhtar, M. A., Bluford H. Putnam and D. Sykes Wilford. "Fiscal Constraints, Domestic Credit, And International Reserves Flows In The United Kingdom, 1952-71," JMCB, 1979, v11(2), 202-208.)

Putnam, Harrington. "A Review Of Some Problems In Foreign Insurance," JRI, 1967, v34(4), 593-601.

Putnam, Samuel. "Harvard College Versus Amory," JPM, 1976-77, v3(1), 67-71.

Puxty, Anthony G. and Richard Laughlin. "A Rational Reconstruction Of The Decision-Usefulness Criterion," JBFA, 1983, v10(4), 543-559.

Puxty, Anthony G. (Laughlin, Richard C. and Anthony G. Puxty. "Accounting Regulation: An Alternative Perspective," JBFA, 1983, v10(3), 451-479.)

Puxty, Anthony G. (Laughlin, Richard C. and Anthony G. Puxty. "Accounting Regulation: An Alternative Perspective: A Reply," JBFA, 1984, v11(4), 593-596.)

Puxty, Anthony G. (Laughlin, Richard C., E. Anthony Lowe and Anthony G. Puxty. "Towards A Value-Neutral Positive Science Of Accounting: A Comment," JBFA, 1982, v8(4), 567-572.)

Pye, Gordon and Ian Young. "The Effect Of Deposit Rate Ceilings On Aggregate Income," JOF, 1972, v27(5), 1023-1034.

Pye, Gordon. "A Note On Diversification," JFQA, 1974, v9(1), 131-136.

Pye, Gordon. "A Stock Valuation Paradox," FAJ, 1970, v26(3), 103-106.

Pye, Gordon. "Gauging The Default Premium," FAJ, 1974, v30(1), 49-52.

Pye, Gordon. "Minimax Portfolio Policies," FAJ, 1972, v28(2), 56-60.

Pye, Gordon. "Present Values For Imperfect Capital Markets," JOB, 1966, v39(1), Part I, 45-51.

Pye, Gordon. "State Of The Finance Field: Reply," JOF, 1968, v23(5), 853-856.

Pye, Gordon. "The Value Of Call Deferment On A Bond: Some Empirical Results," JOF, 1967, v22(4), 623-636.

Pyhrr, Stephen A. "A Computer Simulation Model To Measure The Risk In Real Estate Investment," AREUEA, 1973, v1(1), 48-78.

Pyhrr, Stephen A. (Gentry, James A. and Stephen A. Pyhrr. "Simulating An EPS Growth Model," FM, 1973, v2(2), 68-75.)

Pyhrr, Stephen A., Waldo L. Born and James R. Webb. "Development Of A Dynamic Investment Strategy Under Alternative Inflation Cycle Scenarios," JRER, 1990, v5(2), 177-193.

Pyle, David H. and Stephen J. Turnovsky. "The Dynamics Of Government Policy In An Inflationary Economy: An 'Intermediate-Run' Analysis," JMCB, 1976, v8(4), 411-437.

Pyle, David H. "Capital Regulation And Deposit Insurance," JBF, 1986, v10(2), 189-201.

Pyle, David H. "Descriptive Theories Of Financial Institutions Under Uncertainty," JFQA, 1972, v7(5), 2009-2029.

Pyle, David H. "On The Theory Of Financial Intermediation," JOF, 1971, v26(3), 737-747.

Pyle, David H. (Cootner, Paul H. and David H. Pyle, Ed. "Capital Asset Pricing In A General Equilibrium Framework," JFQA, 1978, v13(4), 613-624.)

Pyle, David H. (Leland, Hayne E. and David H. Pyle. "Informational Asymmetries, Financial Structure, And Financial Intermediation," JOF, 1977, v32(2), 371-387.)

Pyle, David. (Gurel, Eitan and David Pyle. "Bank Income Taxes And Interest Rate Risk Management: A Note," JOF, 1984, v39(4), 1199-1206.)

Pyle, William C. "Human Resource Accounting," **FAJ**, 1970, v26(5), 69-77.

Pyle, William C. (Likert, Rensis and William C. Pyle. "Human Resource Accounting - II," **FAJ**, 1971, v27(1), 75-84.)

Pyun, C. S. "A Note On Capital Asset Pricing Model Under Uncertain Inflation," **JFQA**, 1980, v15(2), 425-434.

Pyun, C. S. "DJIA AT 2100 In Ten Years' Examined," **FAJ**, 1969, v25(3), 118-121.

Pzena, Richard. (Greenblatt, Joel M., Richard Pzena and Bruce L. Newberg. "How The Small Investor Can Beat The Market," **JPM**, 1980-81, v7(4), 48-52.)

QQQ

Qualls, P. David. "Market Structure And The Cyclical Flexibility Of Price-Cost Margins," **JOB**, 1979, v52(2), 305-325.

Quan, Daniel C. and John M. Quigley. "Inferring An Investment Return Series For Real Estate From Observations On Sales," **AREUEA**, 1989, v17(2), 218-230.

Quandt, Richard E. (Asch, Peter, Burton G. Malkiel and Richard E. Quandt. "Market Efficiency In Racetrack Betting: Further Evidence And A Correction," **JOB**, 1986, v59(1), 157-160.)

Quandt, Richard E. (Asch, Peter, Burton G. Malkiel and Richard E. Quandt. "Racetrack Betting And Informed Behavior," **JFEC**, 1982, v10(2), 187-194.)

Quandt, Richard E. (Asch, Peter, Burton G. Malkiel and Richard E. Quandt. "Market Efficiency In Racetrack Betting," **JOB**, 1984, v57(2), 165-176.)

Quandt, Richard E. (Baumol, William J., Richard E. Quandt and Harold T. Shapiro. "Oligopoly Theory And Retail Food Pricing," **JOB**, 1964, v37(4), 346-363.)

Quandt, Richard. (Malkiel, Burton G. and Richard Quandt. "The Supply Of Money And Common Stock Prices: Comment," **JOF**, 1972, v27(4), 921-926.)

Quantius, Frances. "Duplication Of Government Insurance In Commercial Banks," **JRI**, 1959, v26(3), 75-78.

Quantius, Frances. "Federal Loan Insurance: Its Relation To Federal Reserve Policy," **JRI**, 1958, v25(4), 51-54.

Quay, S. R. (Wagner, W. H. and S. R. Quay. "New Concepts In Portfolio Management," **JPM**, 1972-73, v3(2), 102-110.)

Quay, Stuart R. (Lau, Sheila C., Stuart R. Quay and Carl M. Ramsey. "The Tokyo Stock Exchange And The Capital Asset Pricing Model," **JOF**, 1974, v29(2), 507-514.)

Quay, Stuart. (Wahner, Wayne and Stuart Quay. "Ten Myths About Beta," **JPM**, 1974-75, v1(1), 37-40.)

Que, Agustin V. (Walter, James E. and Agustin V. Que. "The Valuation Of Convertible Bonds," **JOF**, 1973, v28(3), 713-732.)

Queen, Maggie and Richard Roll. "Firm Mortality: Using Market Indicators To Predict Survival," **FAJ**, 1987, v43(3), 9-26.

Quek, J. P. (Dodds, J. C. and J. P. Quek. "Effect Of Mergers On Share Price Movement Of The Acquiring Firms: A UK Study," **JBFA**, 1985, v12(2), 285-296.)

Quenneville, Charles E. (Hutchins, Robert C. and Charles E. Quenneville. "Rate Of Return Versus Interest-Adjusted Cost," **JRI**, 1975, v42(1), 69-80.)

Querin, Scott F. (Tomek, William G. and Scott F. Querin. "Random Processes In Prices And Technical Analysis," **JPM**, 1984, v4(1), 15-23.)

Quick, Perry D. (Walker, David A., Richard C. Aspinwall, Stuart I. Greenbaum, Edward J. Kane and Perry D. Quick. "Panel Discussion On Federal Reserve Membership Issues," **FR**, 1979, v14(2), 58-74.)

Quigley, John M. (Quan, Daniel C. and John M. Quigley. "Inferring An Investment Return Series For Real Estate From Observations On Sales," **AREUEA**, 1989, v17(2), 218-230.)

Quigley, John M. and Robert Van Order. "Efficiency In The Mortgage Market: The Borrower's Perspective," **AREUEA**, 1990, v18(3), 237-252.

Quinn, J. J. (Haas, G. M. and J. J. Quinn. "American Corporation Earnings," **FAJ**, 1950, v6(4), 25-28.)

Quinn, James J. "Aerospace 'Envelope' (A New Conception)," **FAJ**, 1962, v18(6), 41-44.

Quinn, James J. "Airlines Earnings Perspective," **FAJ**, 1965, v21(5), 40-48.

Quinn, James J. "Kinetonics - A New Tool In Aircraft Analysis," **FAJ**, 1958, v14(4), 41-46.

Quinn, James J. "The Nucleonic Imperative And Investment Dollar," **FAJ**, 1964, v20(1), 83-92.

Quinn, James. "Renegotiation And Reneging," **FAJ**, 1956, v12(1), 61-66.

Quinn, Judith L. (Duvall, Richard M. and Judith L. Quinn. "Skewness Preference In Stable Markets," **JFR**, 1981, v4(3), 249-263.)

Quinn, Michael A. (Elliott, Donald S., Jr. and Michael A. Quinn. "Concentrated Housing Code Enforcement In St. Louis," **AREUEA**, 1983, v11(3), 344-370.)

Quinn, Michael A. (Elliott, Donald S., Jr., Michael A. Quinn and Robert E. Mendelson. "Maintenance Behavior Of Large-Scale Landlords And Theories Of Neighborhood Succession," **AREUEA**, 1985, v13(4), 424-445.)

Quinn, Michael A., Donald S. Elliott, Jr., Robert E. Mendelson and Jeffrey A. Thoman. "Maintenance Effort And The Professional Landlord: An Empirical Critique Of Neighborhood Decline," **AREUEA**, 1980, v8(4), 345-369.

Quinn, Thomas E. (Bodurtha, Stephen G. and Thomas E. Quinn. "Does Patient Program Trading Really Pay?," **FAJ**, 1990, v46(6), 35-42.)

Quirin, G. David and William R. Waters. "Market Efficiency And The Cost Of Capital: The Strange Case Of Fire And Casualty Insurance Companies," **JOF**, 1975, v30(2), 427-445.

RRR

Raab, Robert J., Jr. (Dann, Larry Y., David Mayers and Robert J. Raab, Jr. "Trading Rules, Large Blocks And The Speed Of Price Adjustment," **JFEC**, 1977, v4(1), 3-22.)

Rabb, J. Mac. (Davis, Samuel G., Nicholas Ceto, Jr. and J. Mac. Rabb. "A Comprehensive Check Processing Simulation Model," **JBR**, 1982-83, v13(3), 185-194.)

Rabel, W. H. "Increasing Knowledge As A Technique For Treating Risk: A Reconsideration Of Principles," **JRI**, 1969, v36(2), 296-298.

Rabel, W. H. "New Perspectives On Risk Management: Comment," **JRI**, 1968, v35(4), 610-615.

Rabianski, Joseph and Jackson Harris. "A Descriptive Analysis Of The AREUEA Members: 1978," **AREUEA**, 1979, v7(4), 610-620.

Rabianski, Joseph. (Dasso, Jerome, William Kinnard and Joseph Rabianski. "Corporate Real Estate: A Course Outline And Rationale," **JRER**, 1989, v4(3), 35-46.)

Rabianski, Joseph. (Nelson, Theron R. and Joseph Rabianski. "Consumer Preferences In Housing Market Analysis: An Application Of Multidimensional Scaling Techniques," **AREUEA**, 1988, v16(2), 138-159.)

Rabin, Michael. (Apsel, David, Jack Cogen and Michael Rabin. "Hedging Long Term Commodity Swaps With Futures," **GFJ**, 1989, v1(1), 77-93.)

Rabinovitch, Ramon and Joel Owen. "Nonhomogeneous Expectations And Information In The Capital Asset Market," **JOF**, 1978, v33(2), 575-587.

Rabinovitch, Ramon. "Pricing Stock And Bond Options When The Default-Free Rate Is Stochastic," **JFQA**, 1989, v24(4), 447-458.

Rabinovitch, Ramon. (Hochman, Shalom and Ramon Rabinovitch. "Financial Leasing Under Inflation," **FM**, 1984, v13(1), 17-26.)

Rabinovitch, Ramon. (Kalay, Avner and Ramon Rabinovitch. "On Individual Loans Pricing Credit Rationing And Interest Rate Regulation," **JOF**, 1978, v33(4), 1071-1085.)

Rabinovitch, Ramon. (Owen, Joel and Ramon Rabinovitch. "The Cost Of Information And Equilibrium In The Capital Asset Market," **JFQA**, 1980, v15(3), 497-508.)

Rabinovitch, Ramon. (Owen, Joel and Ramon Rabinovitch. "On The Class Of Elliptical Distributions And Their Application To The Theory Of Portfolio Choice," **JOF**, 1983, v38(3), 745-752.)

Rabinovitch, Ramon. The Valuation Of Options Embedded In Government Agricultural Loans," **IJOF**, 1989, v2(1), 30-49.

Racette, Daniel. (Lafrance, Robert and Daniel Racette. "The Canadian-US Dollar Exchange Rate: A Test Of Alternative Models For The Seventies," **JIMF**, 1985, v4(2), 237-252.)

Racette, George A. "The Role Of Financial Theory In Educating The Financial Manager," **JFED**, 1979, v8, 33-39.

Racette, George A. (Boquist, John A., George A. Racette and Gary G. Schlarbaum. "Duration And Risk Assessment For Bonds And Common Stocks: A Note," **JOF**, 1975, v30(5), 1360-1365.)

Racette, George A. (Lewellen, Wilbur G. and George A. Racette. "Convertible Debt Financing," **JFQA**, 1973, v8(5), 777-792.)

Racette, George A. (Long, Michael S. and George A. Racette. "Stochastic Demand, Output And The Cost Of Capital," **JOF**, 1974, v29(2), 499-506.)

Racette, George. (Long, Michael S. and George Racette. "Stochastic Demand And The Equity Capitalization Rate," **JBFA**, 1979, v6(4), 475-493.)

Racster, Ronald L. and Robert Howard. "Evaluation Of Multiple Subsidy Programs In A Local Market," **AREUEA**, 1973, v1(2), 104-118.

Racz-Ecker, L. L. "Whiter State And Local Finance?," **JOF**, 1964, v19(2), Part 1, 370-381.

Radcliffe, Robert C. and William G. Gillespie. "The Price Impact Of Reverse Splits," **FAJ**, 1979, v35(1), 63-67.

Radcliffe, Robert C. "Liquidity Costs And Block Trading," **FAJ**, 1973, v29(4), 73-80.

Radcliffe, Robert C. (Fogler, H. Russell and Robert C. Radcliffe. "A Note On Measurement Of Skewness," **JFQA**, 1974, v9(3), 485-489.)

Radcliffe, Robert C. (Mabert, Vincent A. and Robert C. Radcliffe. "Forecasting - A Systematic Modeling Methodology," **FM**, 1974, v3(3), 59-67.)

Radcliffe, Robert C. (Pettway, Richard H. and Robert C. Radcliffe. "Impacts Of New Equity Sales Upon Electric Utility Share Prices," **FM**, 1985, v14(1), 16-25.)

Rader, Lawrence A. "A Stock Is A Company Is People," **FAJ**, 1969, v25(5), 105-108.

Rader, Louis T. "Automation - Some Economic Implications," **FAJ**, 1965, v21(5), 113-118.

Rafael, Fred J. "Demand For Wool And The Inventory Cycle," **FAJ**, 1950, v6(1), 27-30

Raftopoulos, Dimitri. "Pinning Down The Small-Stock Universe," **FAJ**, 1990, v46(5), 77-79.

Ragazzi, Giorgio. "Index-Linking And General Welfare: A Comment," **JMCB**, 1976, v8(2), 261-263.

Ragazzi, Giorgio. "On The Relation Between Ownership Dispersion And The Firm's Market Value," **JBF**, 1981, v5(2), 261-276.

Raghid, Muhammad and Devinder K. Gandhi. "Tax And Savings Implications Of The Canadian Registered Retirement Savings Plans," **FR**, 1986, v21(4), 463-471.

Rahman, Abdul, Lawrence Kryzanowski and Ah Boon Sim. "Systematic Risk In A Purely Random Market Model: Some Empirical Evidence For Individual Public Utilities," **JFR**, 1987, v10(2), 143-152.

Rahman, Abdul. (Doukas, John and Abdul Rahman. "Foreign Currency Futures And Monetary Policy Announcements: An Intervention Analysis," **JFM**, 1986, v6(3), 343-374.)

Rahman, Abdul. (Doukas, John and Abdul Rahman. "Unit Roots Tests: Evidence From The Foreign Exchange Futures Market," **JFQA**, 1987, v22(1), 101-108.)

Rahman, Abdul. (Doukas, John and Abdul Rahman. "Stable Distributions, Futures Prices, And The Measurement Of Trading Performance: A Comment," **JFM**, 1986, v6(3), 505-506.)

Rahman, M. Zubaidur and Robert W. Scapens. "Transfer Pricing By Multinationals: Some Evidence From Bangladesh," **JBFA**, 1986, v13(3), 383-391.

Rahman, Shafiqur. (Lee, Cheng-Few and Shafiqur Rahman. "Market Timing, Selectivity, And Mutual Fund Performance: An Empirical Investigation," **JOB**, 1990, v63(2), 261-278.)

Rahman, Shafiqur. (Lee, Cheng F. and Shafiqur Rahman. "New Evidence On Timing And Security Selection Skill Of Mutual Fund Managers," JPM, 1991, v17(2), 80-83.)

Raia, Anthony P. "A Study Of The Educational Value Of Management Games," JOB, 1966, v39(3), 339-352.

Raina, Dijjotam. (Hawley, Delvin D., John D. Johnson and Dijjotam Raina. "Artificial Neural Systems: A New Tool For Financial Decision-Making," FAJ, 1990, v46(6), 63-72.)

Raine, P. S., R. B. Flavell and G. R. Salkin. "A Likelihood Control System For Use With Formal Planning Models," JBFA, 1981, v8(2), 249-266.

Rajaraman, Indira. "Testing The Rationality Of Futures Prices For Selected LDC Agricultural Exports," JFM, 1986, v6(4), 523-540.

Rakich, Jonathan S. (Williams, John Daniel and Jonathan S. Rakich. "Investment Evaluation In Hospitals," FM, 1973, v2(2), 30-35.)

Ralston, August. "Insurance Subsidies And Welfare Economics: Comment," JRI, 1975, v42(3), 538-541.

Ralston, August. "Pollution Liability And Insurance: An Application Of Economic Theory," JRI, 1979, v46(3), 497-513.

Ramage, J. G. (Cummins, J. David, John R. Percival, Randolph Westerfield and J. G. Ramage. "Effects Of ERISA On The Investment Policies Of Private Pension Plans: Survey Evidence," JRI, 1980, v47(3), 447-476.)

Ramakrishnan, Ram T. S. and Anjan V. Thakor. "Moral Hazard, Agency Costs, And Asset Prices In A Competitive Equilibrium," JFQA, 1982, v17(4), 503-532.

Ramakrishnan, Ram T. S. and Anjan V. Thakor. "The Valuation Of Assets Under Moral Hazard," JOF, 1984, v39(1), 229-238.

Ramaswami, Murali. "Multiple Versus Multivariate Valuation Models," FAJ, 1990, v46(5), 73-77.

Ramaswami, Murali. "Stock Market Perception Of Industrial Firm Bankruptcy," FR, 1987, v22(2), 267-280.

Ramaswamy, Krishna and Suresh M. Sundaresan. "The Valuation Of Floating-Rate Instruments: Theory And Evidence," JFEC, 1986, v17(2), 251-272.

Ramaswamy, Krishna and Suresh M. Sundaresan. "The Valuation Of Options On Futures Contracts," JOF, 1985, v40(5), 1319-1340.

Ramaswamy, Krishna and Suresh M. Sundaresan. "The Pricing Of Derivative Assets In Foreign Exchange Markets," RDIBF, 1987, v1, 187-202.

Ramaswamy, Krishna. (Litzenberger, Robert H. and Krishna Ramaswamy. "The Effects Of Dividends On Common Stock Prices: Tax Effects Or Information Effects?," JOF, 1982, v37(2), 429-443.)

Ramaswamy, Krishna. (Litzenberger, Robert, Krishna Ramaswamy and Howard Sosin. "On The CAPM Approach To The Estimation Of A Public Utility's Cost Of Equity Capital," JOF, 1980, v35(2), 369-383.)

Ramaswamy, Krishna. (Litzenberger, Robert H. and Krishna Ramaswamy. "The Effect Of Personal Taxes And Dividends On Capital Asset Prices: Theory And Empirical Evidence," JFEC, 1979, v7(2), 163-196.)

Ramaswamy, Krishna. (Litzenberger, Robert H. and Krishna Ramaswamy. "Dividends, Short Selling Restrictions, Tax-Induced Investor Clienteles And Market Equilibrium," JOF, 1980, v35(2), 469-482.)

Ramaswamy, Krishna. (MacKinlay, A. Craig and Krishna Ramaswamy. "Index-Futures Arbitrage And The Behavior Of Stock Index Futures Prices," RFS, 1988-89, v1(2), 137-158.)

Ramaswamy, Krishna. (Nelson, Daniel B. and Krishna Ramaswamy. "Simple Binomial Processes As Diffusion Approximations In Financial Models," RFS, 1990, v3(3), 393-430.)

Ramey, W. J. "Anti-Selection Of Agents Through Selection Of Field Management," JRI, 1962, v29(4), 517-522.

Ramjee, Anju. (Bhattacharya, Anand K., Anju Ramjee and Balasubramani Ramjee. "The Causal Relationship Between Futures Price Volatility And The Cash Price Volatility Of GNMA Securities," JFM, 1986, v6(1), 29-40.)

Ramsay, Colin M. "An Optimum And Equitable Net Risk Premium Payment Plan," JRI, 1986, v53(2), 294-300.

Ramsey, Carl M. (Lau, Sheila C., Stuart P. Quay and Carl M. Ramsey. "The Tokyo Stock Exchange And The Capital Asset Pricing Model," JOF, 1974, v29(2), 507-514.)

Ramsey, David D. and Paul E. Smith. "Relative Lags In The Effect Of Monetary And Fiscal Policy," JBR, 1971-72, v2(2), 45-55.

Randall, Jesse W. "Insurance - The American Way," JRI, 1950, v17, 90-96.

Randall, Maury R. "Investment Strategy And Inflation," FR, 1981, v16(1), 63-68.

Randall, Maury R. "Investment Planning In An Inflationary Environment," FAJ, 1981, v37(1), 68-70.

Randall, Maury R. (Greenfield, Robert L., Maury R. Randall and John C. Woods. "Financial Leverage And Use Of The Net Present Value Investment Criterion," FM, 1983, v12(3), 40-44.)

Randall, Maury R. (Woods, John C. and Maury R. Randall. "The Net Present Value Of Future Investment Opportunities: Its Impact On Shareholder Wealth And Implications For Capital Budgeting Theory," FM, 1989, v18(2), 85-92.)

Randell, Donald H. "A Reappraisal Of The World's Economy," FAJ, 1959, v15(4), 55-58.

Randell, Donald H. "A Report: Financial Analysts Seminar (Beloit) 1963," FAJ, 1963, v19(5), 75-76.

Randell, Donald H. "Evolution Of The Financial Analyst," FAJ, 1961, v17(2), 67-75.

Randell, Donald H. "Shareholder Interest In Europe Growing," FAJ, 1961, v17(3), 87-90.

Randell, Donald H. "The Future Of Analysts' Societies," FAJ, 1951, v7(4), 65-66.

Randolph, William Lewis and John E. Gilster, Jr. "Modeling Futures Options: The State-Variable Issue," RFM, 1988, v7(2), 334-344.

Randolph, William Lewis. "The Relative Pricing Of Options On Futures And Options On The Spot," RFM, 1986, v5(3), 198-215.

Randolph, William Lewis. "Use Of The Mean Reversion Model In Predicting Stock Market Volatility," JPM, 1991, v17(3), 22-26.

Rangan, Nanda K. (Thomas H., Donald R. Fraser and Nanda K. Rangan. "Debt-Equity Swaps, Regulation K, And Bank Stock Returns," JBF, 1989, v13(6), 853-868.)

Rangan, Nanda. (Ogden, William, Jr., Nanda Rangan and Thomas Stanley. "Risk Reduction In S&L Mortgage Loan Portfolios Through Geographic Diversification," JFSR, 1989, v2(1), 39-48.)

Rangan, Nanda. (Zardkoohi, Asghar, Nanda Rangan and James Kolari. "Homogeneity Restrictions On The Translog Cost Model: A Note," JOF, 1986, v41(5), 1153-1156.)

Rangarajan, C. and Alan K. Severn. "Bank Responses To Reserve Changes: Reply," JOF, 1966, v21(3), 542-543

Rangarajan, C. and Alan K. Severn. "The Response Of Banks To Changes In Aggregate Reserves," JOF, 1965, v20(4), 651-664.

Rangarajan, C. and Murray E. Polakoff. "A Note On A 'Keynesian' Model Of Aggregate Demand: Reply," JOF, 1969, v24(1), 104-105.

Rangarajan, C. (Hawkins, Robert G. and C. Rangarajan. "On The Distribution Of New International Reserves," JOF, 1970, v25(4), 881-891.)

Ranson, R. David and Charles E. Babin. "What's Holding Up Capital Investment?," FAJ, 1978, v34(5), 30-41.

Ranson, R. David and William G. Shipman. "Institutional Buying Power And The Stock Market," FAJ, 1981, v37(5), 62-68.

Ranson, R. David. (Laffer, Arthur B. and R. David Ranson. "1065 And All That," FAJ, 1971, v27(3), 8-9,82,94.)

Ranson, R. David. (Laffer, Arthur B. and R. David Ranson. "Some Practical Applications Of The Efficient-Market Concept," FM, 1978, v7(2), 63-75.)

Ranson, R. David. (Laffer, Arthur B. and R. David Ranson. "A Formal Model Of The Economy," JOB, 1971, v44(3), 247-270.)

Rao, Cherukuri U. and Robert H. Litzenberger. "Leverage And The Cost Of Capital In A Less Developed Capital Market: Comment," JOF, 1971, v26(3), 777-782.

Rao, Cherukuri U. (Litzenberger, Robert H. and Cherukuri U. Rao. "Portfolio Theory And Industry Cost-Of-Capital Estimates," JFQA, 1972, v7(2), 1443-1462.)

Rao, D. C. and Ira Kaminow. "Selective Credit Controls And The Real Investment Mix: A General Equilibrium Approach," JOF, 1973, v28(5), 1103-1118.

Rao, D. C. "Selective Credit Policy: Is It Justified And Can It Work?," JOF, 1972, v27(2), 473-479.

Rao, K. S. Hanumanta. (Sarma, L. V. L. N. and K. S. Hanumanta Rao. "Leverage And The Value Of The Firm," JOF, 1969, v24(4), 673-677.)

Rao, K. S. Hanumanta. (Sarma, L. V. L. N. and K. S. Hanumanta Rao. "Leverage And The Cost Of Capital In A Less Developed Capital Market: Reply," JOF, 1971, v26(3), 783-785.)

Rao, M. R. and H. Martin. "A Note On Optimal Municipal Bond Coupon Schedules: Maximum Difference Between The Highest And Lowest Coupon," JBR, 1972-73, v3(1), 63-64.

Rao, M. R. (Bawa, Vijay S., James N. Odurtha, Jr., M. R. Rao and Hira L. Suri. "On Determination Of Stochastic Dominance Optimal Sets," JOF, 1985, v40(2), 417-431.)

Rao, N. Krishna. "Equivalent-Risk Class Hypothesis: An Empirical Study," JFQA, 1972, v7(3), 1763-1771.

Rao, Ramesh K. S. and John D. Martin. "Another Look At The Use Of Options Pricing Theory To Evaluate Real Asset Investment Opportunities," JBFA, 1981, v8(3), 421-429.

Rao, Ramesh K. S. "Modern Option Pricing Models: A Dichotomous Classification," JFR, 1981, v4(1), 33-44.

Rao, Ramesh K. S. "The Impact Of Yield Changes On The Systematic Risk Of Bonds," JFQA, 1982, v17(1), 115-127.

Rao, Ramesh K. S. (Ancel, Esther Weinstock and Ramesh K. S. Rao. "Stock Returns And Option Prices: An Exploratory Study," JFR, 1990, v13(3), 173-186.)

Rao, Ramesh K. S. (Barry, Christopher B., Dan W. French and Ramesh K. S. Rao. "Estimation Risk And Adaptive Behavior In The Pricing Of Options," FR, 1991, v26(1), 15-30.) 3¦?8

Rao, Ramesh K. S. (Harlow, W. V. and Ramesh K. S. Rao. "Asset Pricing In A Generalized Mean-Lower Partial Moment Framework: Theory And Evidence," JFQA, 1989, v24(3), 285-312.)

Rao, Ramesh K. S. (Lee, Wayne Y., Ramesh K. S. Rao and J. F. G. Auchmuty. "Option Pricing In A Lognormal Securities Market, With Discrete Trading," JFEC, 1981, v9(1), 75-102.)

Rao, Ramesh P. (Aggarwal, Raj and Ramesh P. Rao. "Institutional Ownership And Distribution Of Equity Returns," FR, 1990, v25(2), 211-230.)

Rao, Ramesh P. (Aggarwal, Raj, Ramesh P. Rao and Takato Hiraki. "Skewness And Kurtosis In Japanese Equity Returns: Empirical Evidence," JFR, 1989, v12(3), 253-260.)

Rao, Ramesh P. (Aggarwal, Raj, Ramesh P. Rao and Takato Hiraki. "Regularities In Tokyo Stock Exchange Security Returns: P/E, Size, And Seasonal Influences," JFR, 1990, v13(3), 249-263.)

Rao, Ramesh P. (Gupta, Yash P., Ramesh P. Rao and Prabir K. Bagchi. "Linear Goal Programming As An Alternative To Multivariate Discriminant Analysis: A Note," JBFA, 1990, v17(4), 593-598.)

Rao, Ramesh P. (Ma, Christopher K., Ramesh P. Rao and Herbert J. Weinraub. "The Seasonality In Convertible Bond Markets: A Stock Effect Or Bond Effect?," JFR, 1988, v11(4), 335-348.)

Rao, Ramesh P. (Ma, Christopher K. and Ramesh P. Rao. "Information Asymmetry And Options Trading," FR, 1988, v23(1), 39-52.)

Rao, Ramesh P. (Ma, Christopher K., Ramesh P. Rao and Richard L. Peterson. "The Resiliency Of The High-Yield Bond Market: The LTV Default," JOF, 1989, v44(4), 1085-1098.)

Rao, Ramesh P. (Ma, Christopher K., Ramesh P. Rao and R. Stephen Sears. "Volatility, Price Resolution, And The Effectiveness Of Price Limits," JFSR, 1989, v3(2/3), 165-200.)

Rao, Ramesh P. (Ma, Christopher K., Ramesh P. Rao and R. Stephen Sears. "Limit Moves And Price Resolution: The Case Of The Treasury Bond Futures Market," JFM, 1989, v9(4), 321-336.)

Rao, Spuma and Theodor Kohers. "The Effect Of Selected U.S. Market Conditions And Exchange Rate Variability On Merger And Acquisition Activities Of Foreign Companies In The United States," GFJ, 1990, v2(1), 139-152.

Rao, Vithala R. "Pricing Research In Marketing: The State Of The Art," JOB, 1984, v57(1), Part 2, S39-S60.

Rao, Vithala R. (Bierman, Harold, Jr. and Vithala R. Rao. "Investment Decisions With Sampling," FM, 1978, v7(3), 19-24.)

Raphaelson, Arnold H. (Hall, Charles P., Jr., Stanley M. Henemier and Arnold H. Raphaelson. "Some Issues In Limiting Hospital Cost

Reimbursement: A Maryland Experience," **JRI**, 1977, v44(2), 267-288.)

Rapkin, Chester. "Growth And Prospects Of Private Mortgage Insurance Activity," **AREUEA**, 1974, v2(1), 89-106.

Rapkin, Chester. "New Towns For America: From Picture To Process," **JOF**, 1967, v22(2), 208-219.

Rapoport, Alice. (Cameron, Stephen, Kevin Holme and Alice Rapoport. "Managing Interest Rate Risk," **JACF**, 1990, v3(1), 56-64.)

Rapp, Walter E. "The Case For Increasing The Savings Bank Life Insurance Policy Limit In Connecticut," **JRI**, 1967, v34(4), 621-627.

Rapp, Wilbur A. "Treasury-Stock Purchases: Their Effects Upon The Price-Earnings Ratio," **FR**, 1969, v1(4), 255-263.

Rapp, Wilbur A. (Cole, David W. and Wilbur A. Rapp. "University Courses In Commercial Banking And Other Financial Institutions," **FR**, 1970, v1(5), 348-358.)

Rappaport, A. and E. M. Lerner. "Reporting By Diversified Firms," **FAJ**, 1970, v26(1), 54-64.

Rappaport, Alfred and Robert A. Taggart, Jr. "Evaluation Of Capital Expenditure Proposals Under Inflation," **FM**, 1982, v11(1), 5-13.

Rappaport, Alfred. "The Affordable Dividend Approach To Equity Valuation," **FAJ**, 1986, v42(4), 52-58.

Rappaport, Alfred. (Balachandran, Bala V., Nandu J. Nagarajan and Alfred Rappaport. "Threshold Margins For Creating Economic Value," **FM**, 1986, v15(1), 68-77.)

Rappaport, Alfred. (Hong, Hai and Alfred Rappaport. "Debt Capacity, Optimal Capital Structure, And Capital Budgeting Analysis," **FM**, 1978, v7(3), 7-11.)

Rappaport, Allen and Anne Johnstone. "Toward Better Case Writing In Financial Management," **JFED**, 1984, v13, 55-64.

Rappaport, Allen. "Integrating The Behavioral Aspects Of Budgeting Into The Basic Finance Course," **JFED**, 1981, v10, 20-22.

Rappaport, Allen. (Murphy, James M. and Allen Rappaport. "A Multiple Discriminant Analysis Of BHC Commercial Paper Ratings: A Comment," **JBF**, 1986, v10(1), 143-144.)

Rappaport, Anna Maria. "Life Insurance Product Innovations: Comment," **JRI**, 1972, v39(1), 138-139.

Rasakhoo, Nima. (Kalaba, Robert E., Terence C. Langetieg, Nima Rasakhoo and Mark I. Weinstein. "Estimation Of Implicit Bankruptcy Costs," **JOF**, 1984, v39(3), 629-642.)

Rasche, Robert H. "Simulations Of Stabilization Policies For 1966-1970," **JMCB**, 1973, v5(1), 1-25.

Rasche, Robert H. (Anderson, Richard G. and Robert H. Rasche. "What Do Money Market Models Tell Us About How To Implement Monetary Policy?," **JMCB**, 1982, v14(4), Part 2, 796-828.)

Rasche, Robert H. (Gilbert, R. Alton and Robert H. Rasche. "Federal Reserve Bank Membership: Effects On Bank Profits," **JMCB**, 1980, v12(3), 448-461.)

Rasche, Robert H. (Johannes, James M. and Robert H. Rasche. "Can The Reserves Approach To Monetary Control Really Work?," **JMCB**, 1981, v13(3), 298-313.)

Rasche, Robert H. (Meltzer, Allan H. and Robert H. Rasche. "Is The Federal Reserve's Monetary Control Policy Misdirected?," **JMCB**, 1982, v14(1), 119-147.)

Rasche, Robert H. (Obst, Norman P. and Robert H. Rasche. "Price Expectations And Interest Rates: Some Clarifying Comments: A Comment," **JMCB**, 1976, v8(1), 119-122.)

Rasche, Robert. (Modigliani, Franco, Robert Rasche and J. Philip Cooper. "Central Bank Policy, The Money Supply, And The Short-Term Rate Of Interest," **JMCB**, 1970, v2(2), 166-218.)

Rashid, Muhammad and Ben Amoako-Adu. "Personal Taxes, Inflation, And Market Valuation," **JFR**, 1987, v10(4), 341-352.

Rashid, Muhammad. (Gandhi, Devinder K., Muhammad Rashid and Kenneth D. Riener. "Intertemporal Resolution Of Uncertainty And Portfolio Behavior," **FR**, 1989, v24(3), 491-498.)

Rasmussen, Bo Sandemann. "Stabilization Policies In Open Economies With Imperfect Current Information," **JIMF**, 1988, v7(2), 151-166.

Rassekh, Farhad and Barry Wilbratte. "The Effect Of Import Price Changes On Domestic Inflation: An Empirical Test Of The Ratchet Effect," **JMCB**, 1990, v22(2), 263-267.

Ratchford, B. U. "Practical Limitations To The Net Income Tax - General," **JOF**, 1952, v7(2), 203-213.

Ratchford, B. U. "Some Constitutional Aspects Of Federal Expenditures," **JOF**, 1955, v10(4), 459-482.

Ratchford, B. U. "State And Local Financing," **JOF**, 1961, v16(2), 261-264.

Ratchford, Brian T. and Gary T. Ford. "A Study Of Prices And Market Shares In The Computer Mainfraime Industry," **JOB**, 1976, v49(2), 194-218.

Ratchford, Brian T. and Gary T. Ford. "A Study Of Prices And Market Shares In The Computer Mainframe Industry: Reply," **JOB**, 1979, v52(1), 125-129.

Ratcliffe, David T. "The Case Method Of Instruction In Insurance," **JRI**, 1958, v25(1), 26-31.

Ratcliffe, Davis T. "Risk," **JRI**, 1963, v30(2), 269-272.

Ratcliffe, Davis T. "Teaching The Meaning Of Risk," **JRI**, 1971, v38(3), 455-461.

Ratcliffe, Davis T. "The Omnibus Clause," **JRI**, 1972, v39(3), 457-458

Rathbun, Daniel B. "Liquid Assets: A Neglected Factor In The Formulation Of Housing Finance Policies," **JOF**, 1952, v7(4), 546-558.

Rathbun, Daniel B. (Wendt, Paul F. and Daniel B. Rathbun. "The Role Of Government In The San Francisco Bay Area Mortgage Market," **JOF**, 1951, v6(4), 383-397.)

Rausser Gordon C. (Gordon, Kathryn M. and Gordon C. Rausser. "Country Hedging For Real Income Stabilization: A Case Study Of South Korea And Egypt," **JFM**, 1984, v4(4), 449-464.)

Rausser, Gordon C. (Cargill, Thomas F. and Gordon C. Rausser. "Temporal Price Behavior In Commodity Futures Markets," **JOF**, 1975, v30(4), 1043-1053.)

Raveh, Adi. "A Note On Factor Analysis And Arbitrage Pricing Theory," **JBF**, 1985, v9(2), 317-322.

Raveh, Adi. (BarNiv, Ran and Adi Raveh. "Identifying Financial Distress: A New Nonparametric Approach," **JBFA**, 1989, v16(3), 361-384.)

Ravichandran, R. (Brauer, Greggory A. and R. Ravichandran. "How Sweet Is Silver?," **JPM**, 1985-86, v12(4), 33-42.)

Ravichandran, R. and J. Sa-Aadu. "Resource Combination And Security Price Reactions: The Case Of Real Estate Joint Ventures," **AREUEA**, 1988, v16(2), 105-122.

Ravid, S. Abraham and Eli Talmor. "Government Financing, Taxation, And Capital Markets," **RIF**, 1988, v7, 21-52.

Ravid, S. Abraham. "On Interactions Of Production And Financial Decisions," **FM**, 1988, v17(3),87-99.

Ravid, S. Abraham. (Brick, Ivan E. and S. Abraham Ravid. "On The Relevance Of Debt Maturity Structure," **JOF**, 1985, v40(5), 1423-1437.)

Ravid, S. Abraham. (Brick, Ivan E. and S. Abraham Ravid. "Interest Rate Uncertainty And The Optimal Debt Maturity Structure," **JFQA**, 1991, v26(1), 63-82.)

Ravid, S. Abraham. (Dotan, Amihud and S. Abraham Ravid. "On The Interaction Of Real And Financial Decisions Of The Firm Under Uncertainty," **JOF**, 1985, v40(2), 501-517.)

Raviv, Arthur. (Parsons John E. and Arthur Raviv. "Underpricing Of Seasoned Issues," **JFEC**, 1985, v14(3), 377-397.)

Raviv, Arthur. (Harris, Milton and Artur Raviv. "Corporate Control Contests And Capital Structure," **JFEC**, 1988, v20(1/2), 55-86.)

Raviv, Arthur. (Harris, Milton and Artur Raviv. "Corporate Governance: Voting Rights And Majority Rules," **JFEC**, 1988, v20(1/2), 203-236.)

Raviv, Arthur. (Harris, Milton and Artur Raviv. "A Sequential Signalling Model Of Convertible Debt Call Policy," **JOF**, 1985, v40(5), 1263-1281.)

Raviv, Arthur. (Harris, Milton and Artur Raviv. "Capital Structure And The Informational Role Of Debt," **JOF**, 1990, v45(2), 321-350.)

Raviv, Arthur. (Harris, Milton and Artur Raviv. "The Theory Of Capital Structure," **JOF**, 1991, v46(1), 297-356.)

Raviv, Arthur. (Harris, Milton and Artur Raviv. "The Design Of Securities," **JFEC**, 1989, v24(2), 255-288.)

Raviv, Arthur. (Mandelker, Gershon and Artur Raviv. "Investment Banking: An Economic Analysis Of Optimal Underwriting Contracts," **JOF**, 1977, v32(3), 683-694.)

Rawls, S. Waite, III and Charles W. Smithson. "The Evolution Of Risk Management Products," **JACF**, 1989, v1(4), 18-26.

Rawls, S. Waite, III and Charles W. Smithson. "Strategic Risk Management," **JACF**, 1990, v2(4), 6-18.

Ray, Subhash C. (Noulas, Athanasios G., Subhash C. Ray and Stephen M. Miller. "Returns To Scale And Input Substitution For Large U.S. Banks," **JMCB**, 1990, v22(1), 94-108.)

Rayburn, Judy. (Collins, Daniel W., Johannes Ledolter and Judy Rayburn. "Some Further Evidence On The Stochastic Properties Of Systematic Risk," **JOB**, 1987, v60(3), 425-448.)

Rayburn, William, Michael Devaney and Richard Evans. "A Test Of Weak-Form Efficiency In Residential Real Estate Returns," **AREUEA**, 1987, v15(3), 220-233.

Rayburn, William. (Devaney, Michael and William Rayburn. "When A House Is More Than A Home: Performance Of The Household Portfolio," **JRER**, 1988, v3(1), 75-85.)

Raymond, Arthur J. and Gordon Weil. "Diversification Benefits And Exchange-Rate Changes," **JBFA**, 1989, v16(4), 455-466.

Raymond, Michael V. (Brown, Keith C. and Michael V. Raymond. "Risk Arbitrage And The Prediction Of Successful Corporate Takeovers," **FM**, 1986, v15(3), 54-63.)

Raynauld, Jacques and Jacques Tessier. "Risk Premiums In Futures Markets: An Empirical Investigation," **JFM**, 1984, v4(2), 189-211.

Raynauld, Jacques. (Gregory, Allan W. and Jacques Raynauld. "An Econometric Model Of Canadian Monetary Policy Over The 1970s," **JMCB**, 1985, v17(1), 43-58.)

Raynolds, David R. "The United States Balance Of Payments," **FAJ**, 1963, v19(6), 11-16.

Razin, Assaf and Lars E. O. Svensson. "The Current Account And The Optimal Government Debt," **JIMF**, 1983, v2(2), 215-224.

Razin, Assaf. "Rational Insurance Purchasing," **JOF**, 1976, v31(1), 133-137.

Razin, Assaf. (Leiderman, Leonardo and Assaf Razin. "Testing Ricardian Neutrality With An Intertemporal Stochastic Model," **JMCB**, 1988, v20(1), 1-21.)

Razin, Assaf. (Leiderman, Leonardo and Assaf Razin. "Foreign Trade Shocks And The Dynamics Of High Inflation: Israel, 1978-85," **JIMF**, 1988, v7(4), 411-424.)

Razin, Assaf. (Pazner, Elisha A. and Assaf Razin. "On Expected Value Vs. Expected Future Value," **JOF**, 1975, v30(3), 875-877.

Rea, James B. "Remembering Benjamin Graham - Teacher And Friend," **JPM**, 1976-77, v3(4), 66-72.

Rea, John D. "Monetary Policy And The Cyclical Behavior Of The Money Supply," **JMCB**, 1976, v8(3), 347-358.

Rea, Samuel A., Jr. "Consumption Stabilizing Annuities With Uncertain Inflation," **JRI**, 1981, v48(4), 596-609.

Read, Colin. "Advertising And Natural Vacancies In Rental Housing Markets," **AREUEA**, 1988, v16(4), 354-363.

Read, Colin. "Price Strategies For Idiosyncratic Goods - The Case Of Housing," **AREUEA**, 1988, v16(4), 379-395.

Reader, A. Constant. "Diary Of A Portfolio Manager's Business Trip," **FAJ**, 1983, v39(3), 70-72.

Reader, A. Constant. "The Care And Feeding Of Buy-Side Analysts," **FAJ**, 1981, v37(2), 42-43,51.

Reagan, Patricia B. and Rene M. Stulz. "Contracts, Delivery Lags, And Currency Risk," **JIMF**, 1989, v8(1), 89-104.

Reagan, Patricia B. and Rene M. Stulz. "Risk-Bearing, Labor Contracts, And Capital Markets," **RIF**, 1986, v6, 217-232.

Reavis, Marshall W. "The Corporate Risk Manager's Contribution To Profit," **JRI**, 1969, v36(3), 473-480.

Reback, Robert. "Nonrandom Price Changes In Association With Trading In Large Blocks: A Comment," **JOB**, 1974, v47(4), 564-565.

Reback, Robert. "Risk And Return In Option Trading," **FAJ**, 1975, v31(4), 42-52.

Reback, Robert. "Risks And Returns In Continuous Option Writing: Comment," **JPM**, 1979-80, v6(2),71-73.

Reback, Robert. "The Single Index Model For Portfolio Selection With Unstable Parameters," **JBR**, 1974-75, v5(1), 35-37.

Reback, Robert. (Stone, Bernell K. and Robert Reback. "Constructing

A Model For Managing Portfolio Revisions," **JBR**, 1975-76, v6(1), 48-60.)

Rebecchini, S. (Micossi, S. and S. Rebecchini. "A Case Study On The Effectiveness Of Foreign Exchange Market Intervention: The Italian Lira (September 1975-March 1977)," **JBF**, 1984, v8(4), 535-555.)

Rebmann-Huber, Alex. (Levacic, Rosalind and Alex Rebmann-Huber. "The Tax-Deductibility Of Interest Payments And The Weighted Average Cost Of Capital Once Again," **JBFA**, 1979, v6(1), 101-110.)

Recker, Charles E. "Real Property Development," **FAJ**, 1969, v25(4), 138-142.

Reckers, Philip M. J. (Bedingfield, James P., Philip M. J. Reckers and A. J. Stagliano. "Distributions Of Financial Ratios In The Commercial Banking Industry," **JFR**, 1985, v8(1), 77-81.)

Record, Eugene E., Jr. and Mary Ann Tynan. "Incentive Fees: The Basic Issues," **FAJ**, 1987, v43(1), 39-43.

Reder, M. W. "An Analysis Of A Small, Closely Observed Labor Market: Starting Salaries For University Of Chicago M.B.A.'s," **JOB**, 1978, v51(2), 263-298.

Reder, M. W. "Introduction To The Symposium On Bank Regulation," **JOB**, 1986, v59(1), 1-2.

Redfield, Corey B. "A Theoretical Analysis Of The Volatility Premium In The Dollar Index Contract," **JFM**, 1986, v6(4), 619-628.

Redhead, Keith J. "Stock Appreciation And The Definition Of Profit - A Macroeconomic Perspective," **JBFA**, 1976, v3(4), 169-178.

Redman, Arnold L. and John R. Tanner. "The Acquisition And Disposition Of Real Estate By Corporate Executives: A Survey," **JRER**, 1989, v4(3), 67-80.

Redman, Milton. "The Computer In The Classroom: The Case Of Money Creation," **JFED**, 1974, v3, 90-95.

Reece, B. F. "The Price-Adjustment Process For Rental Housing: Some Further Evidence," **AREUEA**, 1988, v16(4), 411-418.

Reece, Franklin A. "Where Is The Country's Manufacturing Plant Headed?," **FAJ**, 1954, v10(5), 55-58.

Reed, Henry H. "War Problems In Marine Insurance," **JRI**, 1940, v7, 5-10.

Reed, J. David. (Hutchinson, Peter M., James R. Ostas and J. David Reed. "A Survey And Comparison Of Redlining Influences In Urban Mortgage Lending Markets," **AREUEA**, 1977, v5(4), 463-472.)

Reed, Joel L. "Evaluating Oil And Gas Reserves," **FAJ**, 1978, v34(6), 42-47.

Reed, Vergil D. "Export Crazy And Import Blind," **FAJ**, 1952, v8(3), 49-54.

Reede, Arthur H. "The Impact Of The War Upon Workmen's Compensation Underwriting And Loss Prevention," **JRI**, 1943, v10, 26-40.

Reeder, C. L. "Health Insurance For Impaired Risks," **JRI**, 1964, v31(2), 225-230.

Reeder, William J. (Lerman, Donald L. and William J. Reeder. "The Affordability Of Adequate Housing," **AREUEA**, 1987, v15(4), 389-404.)

Rees, Albert. "An Incomes Policy For The United States?," **JOB**, 1965, v38(4), 374-378.

Rees, Albert. "The Waste-Makers And The String-Savers," **JOB**, 1961, v34(3), 367-373.

Reese, Richard M. and Wilbur W. Stanton. "Further Segmenting A Minority Bank's Customer Set," **JBR**, 1983-84, v14(4), 297-301.

Reeve, James M. "Loan Evaluations Under Accounting Disclosure Alternatives," **JBR**, 1983-84, v14(3), 234-236.

Reeve, James M. (Zavgren, Christine V., Michael T. Dugan and James M. Reeve. "The Association Between Probabilities Of Bankruptcy And Market Responses--A Test Of Market Anticipation," **JBFA**, 1988, v15(1), 27-46.)

Regan, P. J. (Treynor, Jack L., P. J. Regan and W. W. Priest. "Pension Claims And Corporate Assets," **FAJ**, 1978, v34(3), 84-88.)

Regan, Patrick J. "The 1976 BEA Pension Survey," **FM**, 1977, v6(1), 48-65.

Regan, Patrick J. "The Pension Burden Under ERISA," **FAJ**, 1976, v32(2), 26-32.

Regan, Patrick. (Niederhoffer, Victor and Patrick Regan. "Earnings Changes And Stock Prices," **FAJ**, 1972, v28(3), 65-71.)

Regan, William J. "Economic Growth And Services," **JOB**, 1963, v36(2), 200-209.

Rege, Udayan P. "Accounting Ratios To Locate Take-Over Targets," **JBFA**, 1984, v11(3), 301-311.

Regier, Philip R. (Mittelstaedt, H. Fred and Philip R. Regier. "Further Evidence On Excess Asset Reversions And Shareholder Wealth," **JRI**, 1990, v57(3), 471-486.)

Reich, Kenneth E., Kenneth B. Gray, Jr. and Wolfgang P. Hoehenwarter. "Balance Sheet Management: A Simulation Approach," **JBR**, 1970-71, v1(3), 59-62.

Reichenstein, William R. (Farrelly, Gail E. and William R. Reichenstein. "Risk Perceptions Of Institutional Investors," **JPM**, 1983-84, v10(4), 5-12.)

Reichenstein, William. "Martingles And Efficient Forecasts Of Effective Mortgage Rates," **JREFEC**, 1989, v2(4), 317-330.

Reichenstein, William. "On Standard Deviation And Risk," **JPM**, 1986-87, v13(2), 39-40.

Reichenstein, William. "When Stock Is Less Risky Than Treasury Bills," **FAJ**, 1986, v42(6), 71-75.

Reichenstein, William. (Potts, Tom L. and William Reichenstein. "The Optimal Allocation Of Pension Fund Assets: An Individual's Perspective," **FSR**, 1991, v1(1), 11-26.)

Reichert, A. K. (Moore, J. S. and A. K. Reichert. "An Analysis Of The Financial Management Techniques Currently Employed By Large U.S. Corporations," **JBFA**, 1983, v10(4), 623-645.)

Reichert, Alan K. "The Impact Of Interest Rates, Income, And Employment Upon Regional Housing Prices," **JREFEC**, 1990, v3(4), 373-391.

Reichert, Alan K. (Brewer, Elijah, III, Gillian G. Garcia and Alan K. Reichert. "A Statistical Analysis Of S&L Accounting Profits," **AFPAF**, 1989, v3(1), 163-194.)

Reichert, Alan K. (Kang, Han Bin and Alan K. Reichert. "An Evaluation Of Alternative Estimation Techniques And Functional Forms In Developing Statistical Appraisal Models," **JRER**, 1987, v2(1), 1-29.)

Reichert, Alan K. and James S. Moore. "Using Latent Root Regression To Identify Nonpredictive Collinearity In Statistical Appraisal Models," **AREUEA**, 1986, v14(1), 136-152.

Reichert, Alan K., William Strauss and Randall C. Merris. "An Economic Analysis Of Short-Run Fluctuations In Federal Reserve Wire Transfer Volume," **JBR**, 1984-85, v15(4), 222-228.

Reichert, Alan K., James S. Moore and Ezra Byler. "Financial Analysis Among Large US Corporations: Recent Trends And The Impact Of The Personal Computer," **JBFA**, 1988, v15(4), 469-486.

Reichert, Alan, William Strauss, David Northcutt and Warren Spector. "The Impact Of Economic Conditions And Electronic Payments Technology On Federal Reserve Check Volume," **JBR**, 1983-84, v14(4), 291-296.

Reid, Clifford E. "The Reliability Of Fair Housing Audits To Detect Racial Discrimination In Rental Housing Markets," **AREUEA**, 1984, v12(1), 86-96.

Reid, Donald V. (Tew, Bernard V., Donald W. Reid and Craig A. Witt. "The Opportunity Cost Of A Mean-Variance Efficient Choice," **FR**, 1991, v26(1), 31-44.)

Reid, Donald W. (Tew, Bernard V. and Donald W. Reid. "More Evidence On Expected Value-Variance Analysis Versus Direct Utility Maximization," **JFR**, 1987, v10(3), 249-258.)

Reid, Donald W. (Tew, Bernard V. and Donald W. Reid. "Mean-Variance Versus Direct Utility Maximization: A Comment," **JOF**, 1986, v41(5), 1177-1180.)

Reid, Frank C. (Murray, Michael J. and Frank C. Reid. "Financial Style And Corporate Control," **JACF**, 1988, v1(1), 76-84.)

Reid, Gary and Robert Schafer. "Multifamily Housing Demand: Comment," **AREUEA**, 1979, v7(1), 123-129.

Reid, Kenneth. (Rosenberg, Barr, Kenneth Reid and Ronald Lanstein. "Persuasive Evidence Of Market Inefficiency," **JPM**, 1984-85, v11(3), 9-17.)

Reid, Samuel R. "A Reply To The Weston/Mansinghka Criticisms Dealing With Conglomerate Mergers," **JOF**, 1971, v26(4), 937-946.

Reid, Samuel R. "Conglomerate Performance Measurement: Reply," **JOF**, 1974, v29(3), 1013-1015.

Reid, Samuel R. "Petroleum Mergers, Multinational Investments, Refining Capacity And Performance In The Energy Crisis," **FM**, 1973, v2(4), 50-56.

Reid, Samuel Richardson. "The Microeconomic Consequences Of Corporate Mergers: Comment," **JOF**, 1975, v48(2), 275-280.

Reid, Samuel Richardson. (Cohen, Kalman J. and Samuel Richardson Reid. "The Benefits And Costs Of Bank Mergers," **JFQA**, 1966, v1(4), 15-57.)

Reidenbach, R. Eric, Donald L. Moak and Robert E. Pitts. "The Impact Of Marketing Operating On Bank Performance: A Structural Investigation," **JBR**, 1986-87, v17(1), 18-27.

Reierson, Roy L. "Factors And Prospects In The Money Market," **JOF**, 1955, v10(2), 302-314.

Reierson, Roy L. "Monetary Policy And The Money Market," **JOF**, 1961, v16(2), 247-254.

Reierson, Roy L. "New Forces In The Money Market," **JOF**, 1962, v17(2), 220-229.

Reierson, Roy L. "Prospects For The Credit Markets," **JOF**, 1963, v18(2), 423-437.

Reierson, Roy L. "The Changing Capital Markets," **JOF**, 1960, v15(2), 289-298.

Reierson, Roy L. "The Credit Outlook," **JOF**, 1959, v14(2), 279-287.

Reierson, Roy L. "The Outlook For Federal Reserve And Treasury Policy," **JOF**, 1958, v13(2), 318-322.

Reierson, Roy L. "Working Of The Credit Mechanism," **JOF**, 1953, v8(2), 177-189.

Reierson, Roy L. (Riddle, J. H. and Roy L. Reierson. "An Analysis Of The Certificate Reserve Plan," **JOF**, 1946, v1(1), 27-51.)

Reif, William E. (Euske, Kenneth J., Donald W. Jackson, Jr. and William E. Reif. "Performance And Satisfaction Of Bank Managers," **JBR**, 1980-81, v11(1), 36-42.)

Reiff, Wallace W. (Veit, E. Theodore and Wallace W. Reiff. "Commercial Banks And Interest Rate Futures: A Hedging Survey," **JFM**, 1983, v3(3), 283-293.)

Reiff, Wallace. (Madura, Jeff and Wallace W. Reiff. "A Hedge Strategy For International Portfolios," **JPM**, 1985-86, v12(1), 70-74.)

Reilly, F. K., G. L. Johnson and R. E. Smith. "Inflation Hedges And Common Stocks," **FAJ**, 1970, v26(1), 104-110.

Reilly, Frank G. and Thomas J. Zeller. "An Analysis Of Relative Industry Price-Earnings Ratios," **FR**, 1974, v8(1), 17-33.

Reilly, Frank K. and David J. Wright. "Block Trading And Aggregate Stock Price Volatility," **FAJ**, 1984, v40(2), 54-60.

Reilly, Frank K. and Eugene F. Drzycimski. "Exchange Specialists And World Events," **FAJ**, 1975, v31(4), 27-32.

Reilly, Frank K. and Eugene F. Drzycimski. "Short-Run Profits From Stock Splits," **FM**, 1981, v10(3), 64-74.

Reilly, Frank K. and Kenneth Hatfield. "Experience With New Stock Issues," **FAJ**, 1969, v25(5), 73-78.

Reilly, Frank K. and Michael D. Joehnk. "The Association Between Market-Determined Risk Measures For Bonds And Bond Ratings," **JOF**, 1976, v31(5), 1387-1403.

Reilly, Frank K. and Rupinder S. Sidhu. "The Many Uses Of Bond Duration," **FAJ**, 1980, v36(4), 58-72.

Reilly, Frank K. and Sandra G. Gustavson. "Investing In Options On Stocks Announcing Splits," **FR**, 1985, v20(2), 121-142.

Reilly, Frank K. and William C. Slaughter. "The Effect Of Dual Markets On Common Stock Market Making," **JFQA**, 1973, v8(2), 167-182.

Reilly, Frank K. "A Three Tier Stock Market In Corporate Financing," **FM**, 1974, v4(3), 7-16.

Reilly, Frank K. "Evidence Regarding A Segmented Stock Market," **JOF**, 1972, v27(3), 607-625.

Reilly, Frank K. "First Look At O-T-C Volume," **FAJ**, 1969, v25(1), 124-128.

Reilly, Frank K. "Further Evidence On Short-Run Results For New Issues Investors," **JFQA**, 1973, v8(1), 83-90.

Reilly, Frank K. "How To Use Common Stocks As An Inflation Hedge," **JPM**, 1974-75, v1(4), 38-43.

Reilly, Frank K. "Institutions On Trial: Not Guilty!," **JPM**, 1976-77, v3(2), 5-10.

Reilly, Frank K. "Misdirected Emphasis In Stock Valuation," **FAJ**, 1973, v29(1), 54-56,59-60.

Reilly, Frank K. "New Issues Revisited," **FM**, 1977, v6(4), 28-42.

Reilly, Frank K. "Stock Price Changes By Market Segment," **FAJ**, 1971, v27(2), 54-59.

Reilly, Frank K. "What Determines Ratio Of Exchange In Corporate Mergers?," **FAJ**, 1962, v18(6), 47-50.

Reilly, Frank K. (Johnson, Glenn L., Frank K. Reilly and Ralph E. Smith. "Individual Common Stocks As Inflation Hedges," **JFQA**, 1971, v6(3), 1015-1024.)

Reilly, Frank K. (Joy, O. Maurice, Don B. Panton, Frank K. Reilly and Stanley A. Martin. "Comovements Of Major International Equity Markets," **FR**, 1976, v11(1), 1-20.)

Reilly, Frank K. (Miller, Robert E. and Frank K. Reilly. "An Examination Of Mispricing, Returns, And Uncertainty For Initial Public Offerings," **FM**, 1987, v16(2), 33-38.)

Reilly, Frank K. (Schultz, Joseph J., Jr., Sandra G. Gustavson and Frank K. Reilly. "Factors Influencing The New York Stock Exchange Specialists' Price-Setting Behavior: An Experiment," **JFR**, 1985, v8(2), 137-144.)

Reilly, Frank K. (Smith, Ralph E. and Frank K. Reilly. "Price-Level Accounting And Financial Analysis," **FM**, 1974, v4(2), 21-26.)

Reilly, Frank K. (Whitford, David T. and Frank K. Reilly. "What Makes Stock Prices Move?," **JPM**, 1984-85, v11(2), 23-30.)

Reilly, Frank K. and David J. Wright. "A Comparison Of Published Betas," **JPM**, 1987-88, v14(3),64-69.

Reilly, Frank K. and David T. Whitford. "A Test Of The Specialists' Short Sale Ratio," **JPM**, 1981-82, v8(2), 12-18.

Reilly, Frank K. and Edward A. Dyl. "Inflation And Portfolio Management: Be Nimble!," **JPM**, 1975-76, v2(3), 20-26.

Reilly, Frank K. and Eugene F. Drzycimski. "An Analysis Of The Effects Of A Multi-Tiered Stock Market," **JFQA**, 1981, v16(4), 559-575.

Reilly, Frank K. and Eugene F. Drzycimski. "Alternative Industry Performance And Risk," **JFQA**, 1974, v9(3), 423-446.

Reilly, Frank K. and John M. Wachowicz, Jr. "How Institutional Trading Reduces Market Volatility," **JPM**, 1978-79, v5(2), 11-17.

Reilly, Frank K., Frank T. Griggs and Wenchi Wong. "Determinants Of The Aggregate Stock Market Earnings Multiple," **JPM**, 1983-84, v10(1), 36-45.

Reilly, Frank K. Ralph E. Smith and Glenn L. Johnson. "A Correction And Update Regarding Individual Common Stocks As Inflation Hedges," **JFQA**, 1975, v10(5), 871-880.

Reilly, James F. "Comments On Testimony," **FAJ**, 1968, v24(3), 65-66.

Reilly, James F. "The Outlook For Municipal Bonds," **FAJ**, 1967, v23(5), 93-95.

Reilly, Raymond R. and William E. Wecker. "On The Weighted Average Cost Of Capital," **JFQA**, 1973, v8(1), 123-126.

Reilly, Raymond R. and William E. Wecker. "On The Weighted Average Cost Of Capital: Reply," **JFQA**, 1975, v10(2), 367.

Reilly, Raymond R., Eugene F. Brigham, Charles M. Linke, Moon H. Kim and James S. Ang. "Weighted Average Vs. True Cost Of Capital: Reilly, Brigham, Linke and Kim Versus Ang," **FM**, 1974, v3(1), 80-85.

Reilly, Robert J. "Some Evidence On The Reliability Of Variance As A Proxy For Risk," **JRI**, 1983, v50(4), 697-702.

Reilly, Robert J. (Hoffer, George E., Stephen W. Pruitt and Robert J. Reilly. "Automotive Recalls And Informational Efficiency," **FR**, 1987, v22(4), 433-442.)

Reim, John F. (Beatty, Randolph P., John F. Reim and Robert F. Schapperle. "The Effect Of Barriers To Entry On Bank Shareholder Wealth: Implications For Interstate Banking," **JBR**, 1985-86, v16(1), 8-15.)

Reimer, Richard D. "A Comment On Oligopoly Pricing Practices And Economic Theory," **JOB**, 1965, v38(2), 210-211.

Reimer, Richard. (Starleaf, Dennis R. and Richard Reimer. "Statistical Tests Of The Keynesian Demand Function For Money: Reply," **JOF**, 1968, v23(4), 676-678.)

Reimer, Richard. (Starleaf, Dennis R. and Richard Reimer. "The Keynesian Demand Function For Money: Some Statistical Tests," **JOF**, 1967, v22(1), 71-76.)

Reinemann, Roger T. (Johnson, Alton C. and Roger T. Reinemann. "Recruiting Practices And Attitudes In Selected Insurance Companies," **JRI**, 1961, v28(4), 73-78.)

Reinemann, Roger T. (Johnson, Alton C. and Roger T. Reinemann. "Reactions Of Students And Agents To Recruiting Practices," **JRI**, 1962, v29(2), 239-244.)

Reinganum, Marc R. "A Direct Test Of Roll's Conjecture On The Firm Size Effect," **JOF**, 1982, v37(1), 27-35.

Reinganum, Marc R. "A New Empirical Perspective On The CAPM," **JFQA**, 1981, v16(4), 439-462.

Reinganum, Marc R. "Abnormal Returns In Small Firm Portfolios," **FAJ**, 1981, v37(2), 52-56,71.

Reinganum, Marc R. "Is Time Travel Impossible? A Financial Proof," **JPM**, 1986-87, v13(1), 10-12.

Reinganum, Marc R. "Misspecification Of Capital Asset Pricing: Empirical Anomalies Based On Earnings' Yields And Market Values," **JFEC**, 1981, v9(1), 19-46.

Reinganum, Marc R. "Portfolio Strategies For Small Caps Versus Large," **JPM**, 1982-83, v9(2), 29-36.

Reinganum, Marc R. "The Anatomy Of A Stock Market Winner," **FAJ**, 1988, v44(2), 16-28.

Reinganum, Marc R. "The Anomalous Stock Market Behavior Of Small Firms In January: Empirical Tests For Tax-Loss Selling Effects," **JFEC**, 1983, v12(1),89-104.

Reinganum, Marc R. "The Arbitrage Pricing Theory: Some Empirical Results," **JOF**, 1981, v36(2), 313-321.

Reinganum, Marc R. (Canto, Victor A., M. C. Findlay and Marc R. Reinganum. "Inflation, Money, And Stock Prices: An Alternative Interpretation," **FR**, 1985, v20(1), 95-101.)

Reinganum, Marc R. (Cornell, Bradford and Marc R. Reinganum. "Forward And Futures Prices: Evidence From The Foreign Exchange Markets," **JOF**, 1981, v36(5), 1035-1045.)

Reinganum, Marc R. (Park, Sang Yong and Marc R. Reinganum. "The Puzzling Price Behavior Of Treasury Bills That Mature At The Turn Of Calendar Months," **JFEC**, 1986, v16(2), 267-283.)

Reinganum, Marc R. and Alan C. Shapiro. "Taxes And Stock Return Seasonality: Evidence From The London Stock Exchange," **JOB**, 1987, v60(2), 281-296.

Reinganum, Marc R. and Partha Gangopadhyay. "On Information Release And The January Effect: Accounting-Information Hypothesis," **RQFA**, 1991, v1(2), 169-176.

Reinhardt, U. E. "Break-Even Analysis For Lockheed's Tri Star: An Application Of Financial Theory," **JOF**, 1973, v28(4), 821-838.

Reinhart, Vincent. "Targeting Nominal Income In A Dynamic Model," **JMCB**, 1990, v22(4), 427-443.

Reinhart, Walter J. (Ang, James A., Jess H. Chua and Walter J. Reinhart. "Monetary Appreciation And Inflation-Hedging Characteristics Of Comic Books," **FR**, 1983, v18(2), 196-205.)

Reinhart, Walter J. (Boardman, Calvin M., Walter J. Reinhart and Stephen E. Celec. "The Role Of The Payback Period In The Theory And Application Of Duration To Capital Budgeting," **JBFA**, 1982, v8(4), 511-522.)

Reinhart, Walter J. (Braswell, Ronald C., Barry R. Marks, Walter J. Reinhart and DeWitt L. Sumners. "The Effect Of Term Structure And Taxes On The Issuance Of Discount Bonds," **FM**, 1988, v17(4), 92-103.)

Reinhart, Walter J. (Braswell, Ronald C., Walter J. Reinhart and James R. Hasselback. "The Tax Treatment Of Municipal Discount Bonds: Correction Of A Fallacy," **FM**, 1982, v11(1), 77-81.)

Reinmuth, Dennis F. "Managerial Control Of The Reciprocal: A Regulatory Void," **JRI**, 1967, v34(1), 69-80.

Reinmuth, Dennis F. "What Is A Reciprocal?: Comment," **JRI**, 1964, v31(4), 641-646.

Reinmuth, Dennis F. and David L. Lewis. "Review Article - The Case Of The Missing Insurance Entrepreneur," **JRI**, 1970, v37(2), 291-299.

Reinmuth, Dennis F. and David L. Lewis. "The Insurance Hall Of Fame," **JRI**, 1971, v38(1), 61-69.

Reinmuth, Dennis. "Insurer Views On Property And Liability Insurance Rate Regulation: Comment," **JRI**, 1970, v37(2), 305-308.

Reinmuth, James E. and Dick R. Wittink. "Recursive Models For Forecasting Seasonal Processes," **JFQA**, 1974, v9(4), 659-684.

Reints, William and Pieter Vandenberg. "Investment Performance Of Levered Bank Stocks," **FAJ**, 1977, v33(1), 66-70.

Reints, William W. and Pieter A. Vandenberg. "The Impact Of Changes In Trading Location On A Security's Systematic Risk," **JFQA**, 1975, v10(5), 881-890.

Reints, William W. and Pieter A. Vandenberg. "A Comment On The Risk Level Discriminatory Powers Of The Wiesenberger Classifications," **JOB**, 1973, v46(2), 278-283.

Reischer, Otto R. "Adjustment To Imports And The National Interest," **JOB**, 1953, v26(4), 254-262.

Reischer, Otto R. "Assistance In Adjusting To A Tariff Reduction," **JOB**, 1953, v26(2), 103-109.

Reishus, David. (Kaplan, Steven N. and David Reishus. "Outside Directorships And Corporate Performance," **JFEC**, 1990, v27(2), 389-410.)

Reisman, Arnold. (Sloane, William R. and Arnold Reisman. "Stock Evaluation Theory: Classification, Reconciliation, And General Model," **JFQA**, 1968, v3(2), 171-204.)

Reisman, Haim. (John, Kose and Haim Reisman. "Fundamentals, Factor Structure, And Multibeta Models In Large Asset Markets," **JFQA**, 1991, v26(1), 1-10.)

Reiss, Jonathan A. (Trainer, Francis H., Jr., David A. Levine and Jonathan A. Reiss. "A Systematic Approach To Bond Management In Pension Funds," **JPM**, 1983-84, v10(3), 30-35.)

Reitano, Robert R. "Non-Parallel Yield Curve Shifts And Durational Leverage," **JPM**, 1990, v16(4), 62-67.

Reitano, Robert R. "Non-Parallel Yield Curve Shifts And Spread Leverage," **JPM**, 1991, v17(3), 82-87.

Reiter, Sara A. and David A. Ziebart. "Bond Yields, Ratings, And Financial Information: Evidence From Public Utility Issues," **FR**, 1991, v26(1), 44-74.

Reiter, Stanley. "A System For Managing Job-Shop Production," **JOB**, 1966, v39(3), 371-393.

Rejda, George E. "1977 Presidential Address - New Directions For The American Risk And Insurance Association," **JRI**, 1978, v45(1), 1-5.

Rejda, George E. "Family Allowances As A Program For Reducing Poverty," **JRI**, 1970, v37(4), 539-554.

Rejda, George E. "Social Security And The Paradox Of The Welfare State," **JRI**, 1970, v37(1), 1-9.

Rejda, George E. "The Family Assistance Plan As A Solution To The Welfare Crisis," **JRI**, 1971, v38(2), 169-179.

Rejda, George E. "The Impact Of The Business Cycle On New Life Insurance Purchases," **JRI**, 1963, v30(4), 525-534.

Rejda, George E. "The Role Of Dollar Averaging In The Common Stock Investment Operations Of Life Insurance Companies," **JRI**, 1962, v29(4), 533-546.

Rejda, George E. "Unemployment Insurance As An Automatic Stabilizer," **JRI**, 1966, v33(2), 195-208.

Rejda, George E. (Nemmers, Erwin Esser and George E. Rejda. "The Impact Of The Business Cycle On New Life Insurance Purchases: Comment," **JRI**, 1964, v31(4), 631-640.)

Rejda, George E. and David I. Rosenbaum. "Unemployment Insurance And Full-Cost Experience Rating: The Impact On Seasonal Hiring," **JRI**, 1990, v57(3), 519-529.

Rejda, George E. and Emil M. Meurer, Jr. "An Analysis Of State Crime Compensation Plans," **JRI**, 1975, v42(4), 599-614.

Rejda, George E. and James R. Schmidt. "The Impact Of The Social Security Program On Private Pension Contributions," **JRI**, 1979, v46(4), 636-651.

Rejda, George E. and James R. Schmidt. "The Impact Of Social Security And ERISA On Insured Private Pension Contributions," **JRI**, 1984, v51(4), 640-651.

Rejda, George E. and Kyung W. Lee. "State Unemployment Compensation Programs: Immediate Reforms Needed," **JRI**, 1989, v56(4), 649-669.

Rejda, George E. and Richard J. Shepler. "The Impact Of Zero Population Growth On The OASDHI Program," **JRI**, 1973, v40(3), 313-325.

Rejda, George E., James R. Schmidt and Michael J. McNamara. "The

Impact Of Social Security Tax Contributions On Group Life Insurance Premiums," JRI, 1987, v54(4), 712-720.

Rejda, George E., Joseph M. Belth and Glenn L. Wood. "Life Insurance Policy Loans: The Emergency Fund Concept: Comment," JRI, 1966, v33(2), 317-328.

Remaley, William A. "Suboptimization In Mean-Variance Efficient Set Analysis," JOF, 1973, v28(2), 397-403.

Remaley, William A. (Gressis, Nicholas and William A. Remaley. "Comment: Safety First - An Expected Utility Principle," JFQA, 1974, v9(6), 1057-1061.)

Remmers, Lee, Arthur Stonehill, Richard Wright and Theo Beekhuisen. "Industry And Size As Debt Ratio Determinants In Manufacturing Internationally," FM, 1974, v3(2), 24-32.

Remmers, Lee. (Stonehill, Arthur, Theo Beekhuisen, Richard Wright, Lee Remmers, Norman Toy, Antonio Pares, Alan Shapiro, Douglas Egan and Thomas Bates. "Financial Goals And Debt Ratio Determinants," FM, 1974, v4(3), 27-41.)

Remmers, Lee. (Toy, N., A. Stonehill, L. Remmers, R. Wright and T. Beekhuisen. "A Comparative International Study Of Growth, Profitability, And Risk As Determinants Of Corporate Debt Ratios," JFQA, 1974, v9(5), 875-886.)

Renck, Richard. (Moore, David G. and Richard Renck. "The Professional Employee In Industry," JOB, 1955, v28(1), 58-66.)

Render, Barry, William Wagoner, James R. Bobo and Stephen Corliss. "Finance Doctorates In The South: A 1977-1981 Supply And Demand Analysis," JFED, 1978, v7, 37-41.

Rendleman, Richard J., Jr. "Commentary On The Effects Of Stock Index Futures Trading On The Market For Underlying Stocks," RFM, 1986, v5(3), 174-187.

Rendleman, Richard J., Jr. and Brit J. Bartter. "The Pricing Of Options On Debt Securities," JFQA, 1980, v15(1), 11-24.

Rendleman, Richard J., Jr. and Brit J. Bartter. "Two-State Option Pricing," JOF, 1979, v34(5), 1093-1110.

Rendleman, Richard J., Jr. and Christopher E. Carabini. "The Efficiency Of The Treasury Bill Futures Market," JOF, 1979, v34(4), 895-914.

Rendleman, Richard J., Jr. "The Effects Of Default Risk On The Firm's Investment And Financing Decisions," FM, 1978, v7(1), 45-53.

Rendleman, Richard J., Jr. "Optimal Long-Run Option Investment Strategies," FM, 1981, v10(1), 61-76.

Rendleman, Richard J., Jr. "Ranking Errors In CAPM Capital Budgeting Applications," FM, 1978, v7(4), 40-44.

Rendleman, Richard J., Jr. (Jones, Charles P., Richard J. Rendleman, Jr. and Henry Latane. "Stock Returns And SUEs During The 1970s," JPM, 1983-84, v10(2), 18-22.)

Rendleman, Richard J., Jr. (Jones, Charles P., Richard J. Rendleman, Jr. and Henry A. Latane. "Earnings Announcements: Pre-And-Post Responses," JPM, 1984-85, v11(3), 28-33.)

Rendleman, Richard J., Jr. (Conroy, Robert M. and Richard J. Rendleman, Jr. "A Test Of Market Efficiency In Government Bonds," JPM, 1986-87, v13(4), 57-64.)

Rendleman, Richard J., Jr. (Manaster, Steven and Richard J. Rendleman, Jr. "Option Prices As Predictors Of Equilibrium Stock Prices," JOF, 1982, v37(4), 1043-1057.)

Rendleman, Richard J., Jr. (Latane, Henry A. and Richard J. Rendleman, Jr. "Standard Deviations Of Stock Price Ratios Implied In Option Prices," JOF, 1976, v31(2), 369-381.)

Rendleman, Richard J., Jr. (Conroy, Robert M. and Richard J. Rendleman, Jr. "Pricing Commodities When Both Price And Output Are Uncertain," JFM, 1983, v3(4), 439-450.)

Rendleman, Richard J., Jr. (Bartter, Brit J. and Richard J. Rendleman, Jr. "Fee-Based Pricing Of Fixed Rate Bank Loan Commitments," FM, 1979, v8(1), 13-20.)

Rendleman, Richard J., Jr. and Richard W. McEnally. "Assessing The Costs Of Portfolio Insurance," FAJ, 1987, v43(3), 27-37.

Rendleman, Richard J., Jr. and Thomas J. O'Brien. "The Effects Of Volatility Misestimation On Option-Replication Portfolio Insurance," FAJ, 1990, v46(3), 61-70.

Rendleman, Richard J., Jr., Charles P. Jones and Henry A. Latane. "Empirical Anomalies Based On Unexpected Earnings And The Importance Of Risk Adjustment," JFEC, 1982, v10(3), 269-287.

Rendleman, Richard J., Jr., Charles P. Jones and Henry A. Latane. "Further Insight Into The Standardized Unexpected Earnings Anomaly: Size And Serial Correlation Effects," FR, 1987, v22(1), 131-144.

Rennie, Edward P. and Thomas J. Cowhey. "The Successful Use Of Benchmark Portfolios: A Case Study," FAJ, 1990, v46(5), 18-26.

Rennie, Robert A. "An Experiment In Limited Absolute Liability," JRI, 1962, v29(2), 177-184.

Rennie, Robert A. "Management's Approach To Alternative Methods Of Insurance Distribution," JRI, 1957, v24(3), 32-41.

Rennie, Robert A. "The Measurement Of Risk," JRI, 1961,v28(1),83-92.

Renshaw, Anthony and Edward Renshaw. "Does Gold Have A Role In Investment Portfolios?," JPM, 1981-82, v8(3), 28-31.

Renshaw, Ed. "A Note On The Arithmetic Of Capital Budgeting Decisions," JOB, 1957, v30(3), 193-201.

Renshaw, Ed. "Utility Regulation: A Re-Examination," JOB, 1958, v31(4), 335-343.

Renshaw, Edward F. and Paul J. Feldstein. "The Case For An Unmanaged Investment Co.," FAJ, 1960, v16(1), 43-46.

Renshaw, Edward F. and Vernon D. Renshaw. "Test Of The Random Walk Hypothesis," FAJ, 1970, v26(5), 51-59.

Renshaw, Edward F. "A Note On Behavior In The Stock Market," FAJ, 1958, v14(4), 19-24.

Renshaw, Edward F. "A Note On Economic Activity And Alternative Definitions Of The Money Supply," JMCB, 1975, v7(4), 507-513.

Renshaw, Edward F. "A Risk Premium Model For Market Timing," JPM, 1984-85, v11(4), 33-35.

Renshaw, Edward F. "Foundations Of Security Analysis," FAJ, 1958, v14(1), 57-62.

Renshaw, Edward F. "Money, Prices And Output," JOF, 1976, v31(3), 956-959.

Renshaw, Edward F. "Portfolio Theory," FAJ, 1968, v24(2), 114-119.

Renshaw, Edward F. "Portfolio Balance Models In Perspective: Some Generalizations That Can Be Derived From The Two-Asset Case," JFQA, 1967, v2(2), 123-149.

Renshaw, Edward F. "Return On S&P Industrials," FAJ, 1969, v25(1), 121-123.

Renshaw, Edward F. "Short Selling And Financial Arbitrage," FAJ, 1977, v33(1), 58-65.

Renshaw, Edward F. "Stock Market Instability," FAJ, 1967, v23(4), 80-83.

Renshaw, Edward F. "Stock Market Panics: A Test Of The Efficient Market Hypothesis," FAJ, 1984, v40(3), 48-51.

Renshaw, Edward F. "The Anatomy Of Stock Market Cycles," JPM, 1983-84, v10(1), 53-57.

Renshaw, Edward F. "The Rationality Model Revisited," JFM, 1988, v8(2), 157-166.

Renshaw, Edward F. "The Stock Market And Prosperity," FAJ, 1967, v23(1), 88-89.

Renshaw, Edward. "A Consensus Approach To The Determination Of Not-So-Good Years To Own Common Stock," FAJ, 1989, v45(1), 71-72.

Renshaw, Edward. "Some Evidence In Support Of Stock Market Bubbles," FAJ, 1990, v46(2), 71-73.

Renshaw, Edward. (Hofflander, Alfred E., Edward Renshaw and Vernon Renshaw. "Optimal Insurance," JRI, 1971, v38(2), 207-214.)

Renshaw, Edward. (Kaimakliotis, Michael and Edward Renshaw. "Some Self-Perpetuating Patterns In The Stock Market?," JPM, 1991, v17(2), 41-43.)

Renshaw, Edward. (Renshaw, Anthony and Edward Renshaw. "Does Gold Have A Role In Investment Portfolios?," JPM, 1981-82, v8(3), 28-31.)

Renshaw, Vernon D. (Renshaw, Edward F. and Vernon D. Renshaw. "Test Of The Random Walk Hypothesis," FAJ, 1970, v26(5), 51-59.)

Renshaw, Vernon. (Hofflander, Alfred E., Edward Renshaw and Vernon Renshaw. "Optimal Insurance," JRI, 1971, v38(2), 207-214.)

Rentz, William F. (Henin, Claude and William F. Rentz. "Call Purchases, Stock Purchases, And Subjective Stochastic Dominance," JBFA, 1984, v11(1), 127-138.)

Rentz, William F. (Spellman, Lewis J., Robert C. Witt and William F. Rentz. "Investment Income And Non-Life Insurance Pricing," JRI, 1975, v42(4), 567-577.)

Rentzler, Joel C. "Trading Treasury Bond Spreads Against Treasury Bill Futures - A Model And Empirical Test Of The Turtle Trade," JFM, 1986, v6(1), 41-62.

Rentzler, Joel C. (Elton, Edwin J., Martin J. Gruber and Joel C. Rentzler. "Professionally Managed, Publicly Traded Commodity Funds," JOB, 1987, v60(2), 175-200.)

Rentzler, Joel. (Elton, Edwin, Martin Gruber and Joel Rentzler. "The Arbitrage Pricing Model And Returns On Assets Under Uncertain Inflation," JOF, 1983, v38(2), 525-537.)

Rentzler, Joel. (Elton, Edwin, Martin Gruber and Joel Rentzler. "A Simple Examination Of The Empirical Relationship Between Dividend Yields And Deviations From The CAPM," JBF, 1983, v7(1), 135-146.)

Rentzler, Joel. (Elton, Edwin J., Martin J. Gruber and Joel Rentzler. "The Ex-Dividend Day Behavior Of Stock Prices; A Reexamination Of The Clientele Effect: A Comment," JOF, 1984, v39(2), 551-556.)

Rentzler, Joel. (Elton, Edwin J., Martin J. Gruber and Joel Rentzler. "The Performance Of Publicly Offered Commodity Funds," FAJ, 1990, v46(4), 23-30.)

Rentzler, Joel. (Elton, Edwin J., Martin J. Gruber and Joel Rentzler. "New Public Offerings, Information, And Investor Rationality: The Case Of Publicly Offered Commodity Funds," JOB, 1989, v62(1), 1-16.)

Renwick, Fred B. "Asset Management And Investor Portfolio Behavior: Theory And Practice," JOF, 1969, v24(2), 181-206.

Reschovsky, James D. "Residential Immobility Of The Elderly: An Empirical Investigation," AREUEA, 1990, v18(2), 160-183.

Reschovsky, James. (Newman, Sandra and James Reschovsky. "An Evaluation Of The One-Time Capital Gains Exclusion For Older Homeowners," AREUEA, 1987, v15(1), 704-724.)

Resek, Robert W. "Multidimensional Risk And The Modigliani-Miller Hypothesis: Reply," JOF, 1971, v26(4), 963-964.

Resek, Robert W. "Multidimensional Risk And The Modigliani-Miller Hypothesis," JOF, 1970, v25(1), 47-51.

Resek, Robert W. "Uncertainty And The Precautionary Demand For Money: Comment," JOF, 1967, v22(4), 657-662.

Resnick, Bruce G. "The Relationship Between Futures Prices For U.S. Treasury Bonds," RFM, 1984, v3(1), 88-104.

Resnick, Bruce G. and Elizabeth Hennigar. "The Relationship Between Futures And Cash Prices For U.S. Treasury Bonds," RFM, 1983, v2(3), 282-299.

Resnick, Bruce G. (Alexander, Gordon J. and Bruce G. Resnick. "More On Estimation Risk And Simple Rules For Optimal Portfolio Selection," JOF, 1985, v40(1), 125-133.)

Resnick, Bruce G. (Alexander, Gordon J. and Bruce G. Resnick. "Using Linear And Goal Programming To Immunize Bond Portfolios," JBF, 1985, v9(1), 35-54.)

Resnick, Bruce G. (Eun, Cheol S. and Bruce G. Resnick. "Estimating The Correlation Structure Of International Share Prices," JOF, 1984, v39(5), 1311-1324.)

Resnick, Bruce G. (Eun, Cheol S. and Bruce G. Resnick. "Exchange Rate Uncertainty, Forward Contracts, And International Portfolio Selection," JOF, 1988, v43(1), 197-215.)

Resnick, Bruce G. (Eun, Cheol S. and Bruce G. Resnick. "Estimating The Dependence Structure Of Share Prices: A Comparative Study Of The United States And Japan," FR, 1988, v23(4), 387-402.)

Resnick, Bruce G. (Eun, Cheol S., Richard Kolodny and Bruce G. Resnick. "U.S.-Based International Mutual Funds: A Performance Evaluation," JPM, 1991, v17(3), 88-94.)

Resnick, Bruce G. (Eun, Cheol S. and Bruce G. Resnick. "International Diversification Under Estimation Risk: Actual Versus Potential Gains," RDIBF, 1987, v1, 135-148.)

Resnick, Bruce G. (Klemkosky, Robert C. and Bruce G. Resnick. "Put-Call Parity And Market Efficiency," JOF, 1979, v34(5), 1141-1155.)

Resnick, Bruce G. (Klemkosky, Robert C. and Bruce G. Resnick. "An Ex Ante Analysis Of Put Call Parity," JFEC, 1980, v8(4), 363-378.)

Resnick, Bruce. (Alexander, Gordon, Thomas R. Hoffman and Bruce Resnick. "Immunization: A Computer Program Involving The Implementation Of A Bond Portfolio Immunization Strategy," JFED, 1985, v14, 60-69.)

Reuss, W. Wendell. "Elements Of Strength In Railroad Industry," FAJ, 1948, v4(1), 3-9.

Reutzel, Edward T. (Davis, Samuel G., Gary A. Kochenberger and Edward T. Reutzel. "Expressend: A Check Clearing Decision Support System For Endpoint Selection," JBR, 1983-84, v14(3), 203-211.)

Revell, Jack. "Payment Systems Over The Next Decade," JBR, 1984-85, v15(4), 200-210.

Revsine, Lawrence. "General Reports Vs. User's Needs," FAJ, 1969, v25(5), 37-46.

Revsine, Lawrence. "Improving Comparability Of Accounting," FAJ, 1975, v31(1), 45-51.

Revsine, Lawrence. "Inflation Accounting For Debt," FAJ, 1981, v37(3), 20-29.

Revsine, Lawrence. "Understanding Financial Accounting Standard 87," FAJ, 1989, v45(1), 61-68.

Revzan, David A. "Distribution In A High-Level Economy: A Review Article," JOB, 1966, v39(3), 413-417.

Reyes, Mario G. C. (Liesz, Thomas J. and Mario G. C. Reyes. "The Use Of Piagetian Concepts To Enhance Student Performance In The Introductory Finance Course," JFED, 1989, v18, 8-14.)

Reynolds, Fred D. and William D. Wells. "Life Style Analysis: A Dimension For Future-Oriented Bank Research," JBR, 1978-79, v9(3), 181-185.

Rezaee, Zabihollah. "Capital Market Reactions To Accounting Policy Deliberations: An Empirical Study Of Accounting For Foreign Currency Translation 1974-1982," JBFA, 1990, v17(5), 635-648.

Reznik, Neil D. "Risk And Insurance Curricula In The Two-Year Colleges," JRI, 1967, v34(4), 602-605.

Rhee, S. Ghon and Franklin L. McCarthy. "Corporate Debt Capacity And Capital Budgeting Analysis," FM, 1982, v11(2), 42-50.

Rhee, S. Ghon. "Stochastic Demand And A Decomposition Of Systematic Risk," RIF, 1986, v6, 197-216.

Rhee, S. Ghon. (Chang, Rosita P. and S. Ghon Rhee. "Does The Stock Market React To Announcements Of The Producer Price Index?," FR, 1986, v21(1), 125-134.)

Rhee, S. Ghon. (Chang, Rosita P., Peter E. Koveos and S. Ghon Rhee. "Financial Planning For International Long-Term Debt Financing," AFPAF, 1990, v5(1), 33-58.)

Rhee, S. Ghon. (Chang, Rosita P. and S. Ghon Rhee. "The Impact Of Personal Taxes On Corporate Dividend Policy And Capital Structure Decisions," FM, 1990, v19(2), 21-31.)

Rhee, S. Ghon. (Chang, Rosita P., Blair M. Lord and S. Ghon Rhee. "Inflation-Caused Wealth-Transfer: A Case Of The Insurance Industry," JRI, 1985, v52(4), 627-643.)

Rhee, S. Ghon. (Mandelker, Gershon N. and S. Ghon Rhee. "The Impact Of The Degrees Of Operating And Financial Leverage On Systematic Risk Of Common Stock," JFQA, 1984, v19(1), 45-57.)

Rhee, Thomas A. and Fuad A. Abdullah. "The Intermarket Pricing Relations In The Foreign Currency Option Market," IJOF, 1989, v2(1), 50-57.

Rhine, Sherrie L. W. "The Determinants Of Fringe Benefits: Additional Evidence," JRI, 1987, v54(4), 790-799.

Rhoades, S. A. and A. J. Yeats. "Growth, Consolidation And Mergers In Banking," JOF, 1974, v29(5), 1397-1405.

Rhoades, Stephen A. and Alice P. White. "Output In Relation To Labor Input In The Banking And Savings And Loan Industries: 1927-1979," JBF, 1984, v8(1), 119-130.

Rhoades, Stephen A. "A Clarification Of The Potential Competition Doctrine In Bank Merger Analysis," JBR, 1975-76, v6(1), 35-42.

Rhoades, Stephen A. "Bank Expansion And Merger Activity By State, 1960-1975," JBR, 1981-82, v12(4), 254-256.

Rhoades, Stephen A. "Concentration Of World Banking And The Role Of U. S. Banks Among The 100 Largest, 1956-1980," JBF, 1983, v7(3), 427-437.

Rhoades, Stephen A. "Entry And Competition In Banking," JBF, 1980, v4(2), 143-150.

Rhoades, Stephen A. "Sharing Arrangements In An Electronic Funds Transfer System" JBR, 1977-78, v8(1), 8-15.

Rhoades, Stephen A. "The Effect Of Bank-Holding-Company Acquisitions Of Mortgage Bankers On Mortgage Lending Activity," JOB, 1975, v48(3), 344-348.

Rhoades, Stephen A. "The Relative Size Of Banks And Industrial Firms In The U. S. And Other Countries: A Note," JBF, 1982, v6(4), 579-585.

Rhoades, Stephen A. (Greer, Douglas F. and Stephen A. Rhoades. "Evaluation Of A Study On Competition In Financial Services: Comment," JBR, 1975-76, v6(1), 61-66)

Rhoades, Stephen A. (Yeats, Alexander J., Edward D. Irons and Stephen A. Rhoades. "An Analysis Of New Bank Growth," JOB, 1975, v48(2), 199-203.)

Rhodes, James E. (Arbit, Harold L. and James E. Rhodes. "Performance Goals In A Generally Efficient Market," JPM, 1976-77, v3(1), 57-61.)

Rhomberg, Rudolf R. "Comments On Papers By Gramlich And By Sargent And Wallace," JMCB, 1971, v3(2), Part 2, 546-549.

Rice, Edward M. (DeAngelo, Harry and Edward M. Rice. "Antitakeover Charter Amendments And Stockholder Wealth," JFEC, 1983, v11(1), 329-360.)

Rice, Edward M. (Karpoff, Jonathan M. and Edward M. Rice. "Organizational Form, Share Transferability, And Firm Performance: Evidence From The ANCSA Corporations," JFEC, 1989, v24(1), 69-106.)

Rice, Edward M. (Mayers, David and Edward M. Rice. "Measuring Portfolio Performance And The Empirical Content Of Asset Pricing Models," JFEC, 1979, v7(1), 3-28.)

Rice, John G. and John A. Haslem. "Use Of Computer-Based Simulation Cases For Educational Programs In Financial Institutions," JFED, 1981, v10, 91-108.

Rice, Kevin. (Teichroew, Daniel, William Lesso, Kevin Rice and Gordon Wright. "Optimizing Models Of After-Tax Earnings Incorporating Depletion Allowance," JFQA, 1967, v2(3), 265-297.)

Rice, Michael L. (McEnally, Richard W. and Michael L. Rice. "Hedging Possibilities In The Flotation Of Debt Securities," FM, 1979, v8(4), 12-18.)

Rice, Michael L. (Peterson, David and Michael L. Rice. "A Note On Ambiguity In Portfolio Performance Measures," JOF, 1980, v35(5), 1251-1256.)

Rich, G. "Exchange-Rate Management Under Floating Exchange Rates: A Skeptical Swiss View," JBF, 1990, v14(5), 993-1022.

Rich, Georg. "A Theoretical And Empirical Analysis Of The Eurodollar Market," JMCB, 1972, v4(3),616-635.

Richard, Denis and Dan Villaneuva. "Relative Economic Efficiency Of Banking Systems In A Developing Country," JBF, 1980, v4(4), 315-334.

Richard, Donald L. "Fiscal Use And Financial Reporting," FAJ, 1968, v24(5), 113-115.

Richard, Scott F. and M. Sundaresan. "A Continuous Time Equilibrium Model Of Forward Prices And Future Prices In A Multigood Economy," JFEC, 1981, v9(4), 347-371.

Richard, Scott F. "An Arbitrage Model Of The Term Structure Of Interest Rates," JFEC, 1978, v6(1), 33-57.

Richard, Scott F. "Optimal Consumption, Portfolio And Life Insurance Rules For An Uncertain Lived Individual In A Continuous Time Model," JFEC, 1975, v2(2), 187-204.

Richard, Scott F. and Richard Roll. "Prepayments On Fixed-Rate Mortgage-Backed Securities," JPM, 1989, v15(3), 74-82.

Richards, Daniel J. "Unanticipated Money And The Political Business Cycle," JMCB, 1986, v18(4), 447-457.

Richards, Daniel J. (Garman, David M. and Daniel J. Richards. "Policy Rules, Inflationary Bias, And Cyclical Stability," JMCB, 1989, v21(4), 409-421.)

Richards, Kenneth E. "A New Concept Of Performance Appraisal," JOB, 1959, v32(3), 229-243.

Richards, Larry E. and William H. Parks. "A Note On Model Specification," JFQA, 1972, v7(3), 1847-1850.

Richards, R. Malcolm and John D. Martin. "Revisions In Earnings Forecasts: How Much Response?," JPM, 1978-79, v5(4), 47-52.

Richards, R. Malcolm, Don R. Fraser and John C. Groth. "Winning Strategies For Closed-End Funds," JPM, 1980-81, v7(1), 50-55.

Richards, R. Malcolm, Donald R. Fraser and John C. Groth. "The Attractions Of Closed-End Bond Funds," JPM, 1981-82, v8(2), 56-61.

Richards, R. Malcolm, James J. Benjamin and Robert H. Strawser. "An Examination Of The Accuracy Of Earnings Forecasts," FM, 1977, v6(3), 78-86.

Richards, R. Malcolm, Donald R. Fraser and John C. Groth. "Premiums, Discounts, And The Volatility Of Closed-End Mutual Funds," FR, 1979, v14(3), 25-33.

Richards, R. Malcolm. "Analysts' Performance And The Accuracy Of Corporate Earnings Forecasts," JOB, 1976, v49(3), 350-357.

Richards, R. Malcolm. (Cooper, Kerry and R. Malcolm Richards. "Investing The Alaskan Project Cash Flows: The Sohio Experience," FM, 1988, v17(2), 58-70.)

Richards, R. Malcolm. (Fraser, Donald R., R. Malcolm Richards and Richard H. Fosberg. "A Note On Deposit Rate Deregulation, Super Nows, And Bank Security Returns," JBF, 1985, v9(4), 585-596.)

Richards, R. Malcolm. (Fraser, Donald R. and R. Malcolm Richards. "The Penn Square Failure And The Inefficient Market," JPM, 1984-85, v11(3), 34-36.)

Richards, R. Malcolm. (Martin, John D. and R. Malcolm Richards. "The Seasoning Process For Corporate Bonds," FM, 1981, v10(3), 41-48.)

Richards, R. Malcolm. (Phillips, Paul D., John C. Groth and R. Malcolm Richards. "Financing The Alaskan Project: The Experience Of Sohio," FM, 1979, v8(3),7-16.)

Richards, T. M. (Smith, R. F. and T. M. Richards. "Asset Mix And Investment Strategy," FAJ, 1976, v32(2), 67-71.)

Richards, Thomas M., Jr. "The Role Of The Active Manager For The Pension Fund," JPM, 1978-79, v5(3), 43-47.

Richards, Verlyn D. and Eugene J. Laughlin. "A Cash Conversion Cycle Approach To Liquidity Analysis," FM, 1980, v9(1), 32-38.

Richardson, David H. and Mickey T. C. Wu. "Tests Of The Goods Market Integration Hypothesis," JMCB, 1982, v14(1), 92-97.

Richardson, David H. and Richard Thalheimer. "Alternative Methods Of Variable Selection: An Application To Real Estate Assessment," AREUEA, 1979, v7(3), 393-409.

Richardson, Dennis W. "The Emerging Era Of Electronic Money: Some Implications For Monetary Policy," JBR, 1972-73, v3(4), 261-264.

Richardson, Frederick M. and Lewis F. Davidson. "On Linear Discrimination With Accounting Ratios," JBFA, 1984, v11(4), 511-525.

Richardson, Frederick M. and Lewis F. Davidson. "An Exploration Into Bankruptcy Discriminant Model Sensitivity," JBFA, 1983, v10(2), 195-207.

Richardson, Frederick M. (Albrecht, W. David and Frederick M. Richardson. "Income Smoothing By Economy Sector," JBFA, 1990, v17(5), 713-730.)

Richardson, Gary. (Evans, Bruce D. and Gary Richardson. "Stop Loss Reinsurance - A New Look," JRI, 1971, v38(2), 251-262.)

Richardson, Gordon, Stephen E. Sefcik and Rex Thompson. "A Test Of Dividend Irrelevance Using Volume Reactions To A Change In Dividend Policy," JFEC, 1986, v17(2), 313-333.

Richardson, James G. (Fogler, H. Russell, William A. Groves and James G. Richardson. "Bond Management: Are 'Dumbbells,' Smart?," JPM, 1975-76, v2(2), 54-60.)

Richardson, James G. (Fogler, H. Russell, William A. Groves and James G. Richardson. "Bond Portfolio Strategies, Returns, And Skewness: A Note," JFQA, 1977, v12(1), 127-140.)

Richardson, Lemont K. "Airline Traffic Forecasting," FAJ, 1970, v26(5), 119-125.

Richardson, Lemont K. "Commercial Airplane Programs," FAJ, 1969, v25(3), 37-48.

Richardson, Lemont K. "Do High Risks Lead To High Returns?," FAJ, 1970, v26(2), 88-99.

Richardson, Lemont K. "Misconceptions About Earnings Dilution In Electric Utility Analysis," FAJ, 1964, v20(5), 58-62.

Richardson, Matthew and James H. Stock. "Drawing Inferences From Statistics Based On Multiyear Asset Returns," JFEC, 1989, v25(2), 323-348.

Richardson, William C. (Williams, Stephen J., Paula Diehr, William L. Drucker and William C. Richardson. "Limitations And Exclusions In Two Provider Systems With Comprehensive Care," JRI, 1982, v49(3), 448-462.)

Richebacher, Kurt. "The Problems And Prospects Of Integrating European Capital Markets," JMCB, 1969, v1(3), 336-346.

Richins, Marsha L., William C. Black and C. F. Sirmans. "Strategic Orientation And Marketing Strategy: An Analysis Of Residential Real Estate Brokerage Firms," JRER, 1987, v2(2), 41-54.

Richken, Peter H. (Salkin, Harvey M. and Peter H. Richken. "Option Spreading: Comment," JPM, 1980-81, v7(2), 89-93.)

Richmond, David. (Kensicki, Peter R. and David Richmond. "Consumerism And Automobile Insurance," JRI, 1973, v40(2), 209-220.)

Richmond, Richard D. (Hagerman, Robert L. and Richard D. Richmond. "Random Walks, Martingales And The OTC," JOF, 1973, v28(4), 897-909.)

Rickard, John A. (Russell, Allen M. and John A. Rickard. "An Algorithm For Determining Unique Nonnegative Internal Rates Of Return," JBFA, 1984, v11(3), 355-366.)

Rickard, John A. (Stanton, Harry G. and John A. Rickard. "The 'Rule Of 78' Cost Penalty: An Alternative Perspective," JBFA, 1989, v16(2), 255-266.)

Rickard, John. (Collins, Brett, John Rickard and Michael Selby. "Discounting Of Deferred Tax Liabilities," JBFA, 1990, v17(5), 757-758.)

Ricketts, Donald and Roger Stover. "An Examination Of Commercial Bank Financial Ratios," JBR, 1978-79, v9(2), 121-124.

Ricketts, Donald E. and Michael J. Barrett. "Corporate Operating Income Forecasting Ability," FM, 1973, v2(2), 53-62.

Ricks, David A. and Leroy Carpenter. "An Annotated Bibliography For International Finance," JFED, 1973, v2, 92-108.

Ricks, David A. (Bavishi, Vinod B., Michael R. Czinkota, Harry A. Shawky and David A. Ricks. "International Financial Management -- A Survey Of Research Trends And An Annotated Bibliography, 1977-1976," JFED, 1977, v6, 93-95.)

Ricks, Michael. (Wilson, William W., Hung-Gay Fung and Michael Ricks. "Option Price Behavior In Grain Futures Markets," JFM, 1988, v8(1), 47-66.)

Ricks, R. Bruce and J. Fred Weston. "Land As A Growth Investment," FAJ, 1966, v22(4), 69-78.

Ricks, R. Bruce. "Imputed Equity Returns On Real Estate Finances with Life Insurance Company Loans," JOF, 1969, v24(5), 921-937.

Ricks, R. Bruce. "Tight Money And Investment Management," FAJ, 1967, v23(1), 104-105.

Rickwood, C. P. and R. E. V. Groves. "Tax And The Integration Of Finance And Investment," JBFA, 1979, v6(2), 157-172.

Riding, A. L. (Jog, V. M. and A. L. Riding. "Some Canadian Findings Regarding Infrequent Trading And Instability In The Single Factor Market Model," JBFA, 1986, v13(1), 125-135.)

Riding, Allan J. (Jog, Vijay M. and Allan L. Riding. "Lunar Cycles In Stock Prices," FAJ, 1989, v45(2), 63-68.)

Riding, Allan L. "The Information Content Of Dividends: An Other Test," JBFA, 1984, v11(2), 163-176.

Riding, Allan L. (Jog, Vijay M. and Allan L. Riding. "Price Effects Of Dual-Class Shares," FAJ, 1986, v42(1), 58-67.)

Riding, Allan L. (Jog, Vijay M. and Allan L. Riding. "Underpricing In Canadian IPOs," FAJ, 1987, v43(6), 48-55.)

Riding, Allan L. (Jog, Vijay M. and Allan L. Riding. "A Note On Insider Trading And Issuances Of Restricted-Voting Common Shares," JBFA, 1990, v17(3), 461-470.)

Rie, Daniel. "How Trustworthy Is Your Valuation Model?," FAJ, 1985, v41(6), 42-48.

Rieber, Michael. "Some Characteristics Of Treasury Bill Dealers In The Auction Market," JOF, 1965, v20(1), 49-58.

Riechenstein, William. "Another Look At Risk And Reward In January And Non-January Months: Comment," JPM, 1990, v16(4), 79-81.

Riechert, Alan K. (Moore, James S., Alan K. Riechert and Chien-Ching Cho. "Analyzing The Temporal Stability Of Appraisal Model Coefficients: An Application Of Ridge Regression Techniques," AREUEA, 1984, v12(1), 50-71.)

Riefler, Winfield W. "Monetary Policy," JOB, 1954, v27(3), 235-242.

Riegel, Robert. "Content, Arrangement And Method Of A General Course For Students Not Specializing In Insurance," JRI, 1936, v3, 23-30.

Riegel, Robert. "Life Insurance And The Moratorium," JRI, 1934,v1,1-7.

Riegle, D. W. (Blake, C. W. and D. W. Riegle. "Data Processing," FAJ, 1968, v24(1), 134-146.)

Riehle, Robert C. "Moody's Municipal Ratings," FAJ, 1968,v24(3),71-73.

Riener, Kenneth D. "A Pedagogic Note On The Cost Of Capital With Personal Taxes And Risky Debt," FR, 1985, v20(2), 229-235.

Riener, Kenneth D. "Financial Structure Effects Of Bond Refunding," FM, 1980, v9(2), 18-23.

Riener, Kenneth D. (Gandhi, Devinder K., Muhammad Rashid and Kenneth D. Riener. "Intertemporal Resolution Of Uncertainty And Portfolio Behavior," FR, 1989, v24(3), 491-498.)

Riener, Kenneth D. (Hill, Ned C. and Kenneth D. Riener. "Determining The Cash Discount In The Firm's Credit Policy," FM, 1979, v8(1), 68-73.)

Riener, Kenneth D. (Rose, Peter S., James W. Kolari and Kenneth D. Riener. "A National Survey Study Of Bank Services And Prices Arrayed By Size And Structure," JBR, 1985-86, v16(2), 72-85.)

Riesman, David and Mark Benney. "Asking And Answering," JOB, 1956, v29(4), 225-236.

Riesz, Peter C. "Size Versus Price, Or Another Vote For Tonypandy," JOB, 1973, v46(3), 396-403.

Riesz, Peter C. "The Great Tonypandy Debate Continued," JOB, 1976, v49(1), 70-72.

Riggs, Henry E. "The Economics Of 'Tax Switching'," FAJ, 1963, v19(5), 25-31.

Rigsbee, Stephen. (Arditti, Fred D., Sirri Ayaydin, Ravi K. Mattu and Stephen Rigsbee. "A Passive Futures Strategy That Outperforms Active Management," FAJ, 1986, v42(4), 63-67.)

Riley, William B. and Austin H. Montgomery, Jr. "The Use Of Interactive Computer Programs In Security Analysis And Portfolio Management," JFED, 1980, v9, 89-92.

Riley, William B. and William A. Luksetich. "The Market Prefers Republicans: Myth Or Reality," JPQA, 1980, v15(3), 541-560.

Riley, William B. (Hobbs, Gerald R. and William B. Riley. "Profiting From A Presidential Election," FAJ, 1984, v40(2), 46-52.)

Rimlinger, Frank. (Fisk, Charles and Frank Rimlinger. "Nonparametric Estimates Of LDC Repayment Prospects," JOF, 1979, v34(2), 429-436.)

Rinfret, Pierre A. "Changing Population And Changing Demand," FAJ, 1961, v17(5), 75-78.

Rinfret, Pierre A. "Investment Managers Are Needed," FAJ, 1968, v24(2), 163-170.

Ringer, L. Ray. "My Reaction To Property And Casualty Insurance Education On The University Level," JRI, 1950, v17, 74-78.

Ripley, Duncan M. "Capital Control Policies And Foreign Share Prices," JOF, 1975, v30(3), 865-868.

Rippe, Richard D. and Richard L. Feldman. "The Impact Of Residential Consturction On The Demand For Automobiles: An Omitted Variable," JOB, 1976, v49(3), 389-401.

Rippy, J. Fred. "A Bond-Selling Extravaganza Of The 1920's," JOB, 1950, v23(4), 238-247.

Rippy, J. Fred. "Background For Point Four: Samples Of Profitable British Investments In The Underdeveloped Countries," JOB, 1953, v26(2), 110-124.

Rippy, J. Fred. "British Economic Activities In Uruguay: An Example Of Profitable Foreign Investment," JOB, 1952, v25(2), 124-129.

Rippy, J. Fred. "British Income From Latin-American Investments, 1939 And 1948," JOB, 1950, v23(2), 110-116.

Rippy, J. Fred. "English Investments In Mexico: A Story Of Bonanzas And Heartbreaks," JOB, 1952, v25(4), 242-248.

Rippy, J. Fred. "Point Four Background: A Decade Of Income From Briitish Overseas Investment," JOB, 1953, v26(4), 231-237.

Rippy, J. Fred. "The Boom In British Africa," JOB, 1953,v26(3),190-199.

Rischer, Gunter. "Computers And The Stock Market (A Brief Comment)," FAJ, 1961, v17(4),91-93.

Rist, Marcel. "Letters From France," FAJ, 1968, v24(2), 175-181.

Rist, Marcel. "The Investment Outlook In France," FAJ, 1966, v22(1), 130-135.

Ritchey, Robert J. "Call Option Valuation For Discrete Normal Mixtures," JFR, 1990, v13(4), 285-296. 3E?8

Ritchken, Peter H. and Harvey M. Salkin. "Safety First Selection Techniques For Option Spreads," JPM, 1982-83, v9(3), 61-67.

Ritchken, Peter H. "Enhancing Mean-Variance Analysis With Options," JPM, 1984-85, v11(3), 67-71.

Ritchken, Peter H. "On Option Pricing Bounds," JOF, 1985, v40(4), 1219-1233.

Ritchken, Peter H. (Salkin, Harvey M. and Peter H. Ritchken. "Option Spreading: Rejoinder," JPM, 1980-81, v7(2), 89-93.)

Ritchken, Peter H. and Michael G. Ferri. "Recursion Models For Warrant Pricing," RDIBF, 1987, v1, 257-272.

Ritchken, Peter H. and Shyanjaw Kuo. "Option Bounds With Finite Revision Opportunities," JOF, 1988, v43(2), 301-308.

Ritchken, Peter H. and Wen-Kuei Chen. "Downside Risk Option Pricing Models," RDIBF, 1988, v2, 205-226.

Ritchken, Peter and Kiekie Boenawan. "On Arbitrage-Free Pricing Of Interest Rate Contingent Claims," JOF, 1990, v45(1), 259-264.

Ritchken, Peter and L. Sankarasubramanian. "On Valuing Complex Interest Rate Claims," JFM, 1990, v10(5), 443-456.

Ritchken, Peter, L. Sandarasubramanian and Anand M. Vijh. "Averaging Options For Capping Total Costs," FM, 1990, v19(3), 35-41.

Ritter, Jay R. "Signaling And The Valuation Of Unseasoned New Issues: A Comment," JOF, 1984, v39(4), 1231-1237.

Ritter, Jay R. "The Buying And Selling Behavior Of Individual Investors At The Turn Of The Year," JOF, 1988, v43(3), 701-717.

Ritter, Jay R. "The Costs Of Going Public," JFEC, 1987, v19(2), 269-282.

Ritter, Jay R. "The Long Run Performance Of Initial Public Offerings," JOF, 1991, v46(1), 3-28.

Ritter, Jay R. "The 'Hot Issue' Market Of 1980," JOB, 1984, v57(2), 215-240.

Ritter, Jay R. (Beatty, Randolph P. and Jay R. Ritter. "Investment Banking, Reputation, And The Underpricing Of Initial Public Offerings," JFEC, 1986, v15(1/2), 213-232.)

Ritter, Jay R. (Ibbotson, Roger G., Jody L. Sindelar and Jay R. Ritter. "Initial Public Offerings," JACF, 1988, v1(2), 37-45.)

Ritter, Jay R. and Navin Chopra. "Portfolio Rebalancing And The Turn-Of-The-Year Effect," JOF, 1989, v44(1), 149-166.

Ritter, Lawrence S. and Thomas R. Atkinson. "Monetary Theory And Policy In the Payments System Of The Future," JMCB, 1970, v2(4), 493-503.

Ritter, Lawrence S. "A Note On The Retirement Of Public Debt During Inflation," JOF, 1951, v6(1), 66-70.

Ritter, Lawrence S. "An Exposition Of The Structure Of The Flow-Of-Funds Accounts," JOF, 1963, v18(2), 219-230.

Ritter, Lawrence S. "On The Fundamental Role Of Transactions Costs In Monetary Theory: Two Illustrations From Casino Gambling," JMCB, 1978, v10(4), 522-528.

Ritter, Lucy E. "A Sense Of Values," FAJ, 1967, v23(1), 98-99.

Ritter, Lucy E. "Common Stocks For Life Insurance Portfolios," FAJ, 1966, v22(1), 109-112.

Ritter, Lucy E. "Reflections On The Corporate Exercise Of Proxies," FAJ, 1966, v22(5), 89-91.

Ritter, Lucy E. "Variable Annuity Suggestions," FAJ, 1970, v26(1), 111-113.

Rivel, Robert B. "Bank Reserve Requirements In Australia," JOF, 1951, v6(3), 291-299.

Rivel, Robert B. "The Use Of Average Maturity In The Analysis Of Commercial Bank Investments," JOF, 1949, v4(4), 342-347.

Rivers, Anthony U. (Dietz, Peter O., H. Russell Fogler and Anthony U. Rivers. "Duration, Nonlinearity, And Bond Portfolio Performance," JPM, 1980-81, v7(3), 37-41.)

Rivers, Richard and D. Larry Crumbley. "The Timing Problem For The Unified Estate And Gift Tax," JRI, 1979, v46(1), 125-138.

Rivoli, Pietra. (Aggarwal, Reena and Pietra Rivoli. "Fads In The Initial Public Offering Market?," **FM**, 1990, v19(4), 45-57.)

Rivoli, Pietra. (Aggarwal, Reena and Pietra Rivoli. "Seasonal And Day-Of-The-Week Effects In Four Emerging Stock Markets," **FR**, 1989, v24(4), 541-550.)

Rivoli, Pietra. (Brewer, Thomas L. and Pietra Rivoli. "Politics And Perceived Country Creditworthiness In International Banking," **JMCB**, 1990, v22(3), 357-369.)

Rizzo, John A. "The Impact Of Medical Malpractice Insurance Rate Regulation," **JRI**, 1989, v56(3), 482-500.

Rizzuto, Ronald and Hugh Grove. "How To Lie With Accounting: A Unique Extension Of Security Analysis," **JFED**, 1981, v10, 33-37.

Ro, Byung T. (Haw, In-Mu and Byung T. Ro. "Firm Size, Reporting Lags And Market Reactions To Earnings Releases," **JBFA**, 1990, v17(4), 557-574.)

Ro, Byung T. "An Analytical Approach To Accounting Materiality," **JBFA**, 1982, v8(3), 397-412.

Roach, Stephen S. "Living With Corporate Debt," **JACF**, 1989, v2(1), 19-29.

Roach, William L. "Pay-At-The-Pump Automobile Liability Insurance," **JRI**, 1983, v50(1), 131-139.

Robb, A. Leslie. (Serletis, Apostolos and A. Leslie Robb. "Divisia Aggregation And Substitutability Among Monetary Assets," **JMCB**, 1986, v18(4), 430-446.)

Robbie, Ken. (Thompson, Steve, Mike Wright and Ken Robbie. "Management Buy-Outs, Debt, And Efficiency: Some Evidence From The U.K.," **JACF**, 1989, v2(1), 76-86.)

Robbie, Ken. (Wright, Mike, Ken Robbie and Steve Thompson. "Corporate Restructuring, Buy-Outs, And Managerial Equity: The European Dimension," **JACF**, 1991, v3(4), 46-58.)

Robbins, Edward Henry and John D. Schatzberg. "Callable Bonds: A Risk-Reducing Signalling Mechanism," **JOF**, 1986, v41(4), 935-950.

Robbins, Edward Henry and John D. Schatzberg. "Callable Bonds: A Risk-Reducing Signalling Mechanism--A Reply," **JOF**, 1988, v43(4), 1067-1073.

Robbins, Edward Henry. "Pricing Municipal Debt," **JFQA**, 1984, v19(4), 467-483.

Robbins, Edward Henry. (Jacklin, Charles J. and Edward Henry Robbins. "Costly Information Production And Optimal Capital Structuring: Theory And Implications For Finance And Accounting," **RQFA**, 1991, v1(2), 153-168.)

Robbins, Rainard B. "The Effect Of Social Security Legislation On Private Pension Plans," **JRI**, 1938, v5, 47-55.

Robbins, Sidney and Edward Foster, Jr. "Profit-Planning And The Finance Function," **JOF**, 1957, v12(4), 451-467.

Robbins, Sidney M. and Robert B. Stobaugh. "Financing Foreign Affiliates," **FM**, 1972, v1(3), 56-65.

Robbins, Sidney M. "Investor Guideposts In Comparing Income Statements," **JOF**, 1952, v7(1), 47-65.

Robbins, Sidney M. "The Fixed-Charge Coverage Test Under Changing Economic Conditions," **JOB**, 1951, v24(3), 203-219.

Robbins, Sidney M. "The Need For More Complete Cost Data In Annual Reports," **FAJ**, 1957, v13(1), 9-12.

Robbins, Sidney M., Robert B. Stobaugh, Francis L. Sterling and Thomas H. Howe. "The Impact Of Exchange-Traded Options On The Market For New Issues Of Common Stock Of Small Companies," **FR**, 1979, v14(1), 1-22.

Robbins, Sidney and Walter Werner. "Professor Stigler Revisited," **JOB**, 1964, v37(4), 406-413.

Robbins, Stuart M. "Market Penetration And Profits," **FAJ**, 1976, v32(5), 41-46.

Robbins, Stuart M. "The Fabric Retailing Industry," **FAJ**, 1973, v29(3), 70-74,92-101.

Robert, David L. (Anderson, Gary A. and David L. Robert. "Stability In The Present Value Assessment Of Lost Earnings," **JRI**, 1989, v56(1), 50-66.)

Roberts, Dan J. (Hogan, Ked, Michael Melvin and Dan J. Roberts. "Trade Balance News And Exchange Rates: Is There A Policy Signal?," (Supp), S90-S99.)

Roberts, Brian E. (Ederington, Louis H., Jess B. Yawitz and Brian E. Roberts. "The Informational Content Of Bond Ratings," **JFR**, 1987, v10(3), 211-226.)

Roberts, Charles Dewitt and Edna N. Roberts. "Exact Determination Of Earnings Risk By The Coefficient Of Variation," **JOF**, 1970, v25(5), 1161-1165.

Roberts, David L. (Anderson, Gary A. and David L. Roberts. "A Historical Perspective On The Present Value Assessment Of Medical Care," **JRI**, 1989, v56(2), 218-232.)

Roberts, E. A. "The Rubber Industry," **FAJ**, 1952, v8(2), 77-82.

Roberts, Edna N. (Roberts, Charles Dewitt and Edna N. Roberts. "Exact Determination Of Earnings Risk By The Coefficient Of Variation," **JOF**, 1970, v25(5), 1161-1165.)

Roberts, Edward B. (Davis, William A., Jr. and Edward B. Roberts. "The Management Of Department Of Defense Laser Research Contracts," **JOB**, 1970, v43(1), 44-55.)

Roberts, Gordon S. and Arthur C. Gudikunst. "Equipment Financial Leasing Practices And Costs: Comment," **FM**, 1978, v7(2), 79-81.

Roberts, Gordon S. and Jerry A. Viscione. "Captive Finance Subsidiaries: The Manager's View," **FM**, 1981, v10(1), 36-42.

Roberts, Gordon S. and Jerry A. Viscione. "Note On Who Pays The Agency Costs Of Debt," **FR**, 1984, v19(2), 232-239.

Roberts, Gordon S. and Jerry A. Viscione. "The Impact Of Seniority And Security Covenants On Bond Yields: A Note," **JOF**, 1984, v39(5), 1597-1602.

Roberts, Gordon S. "Endogenous Endowments And Capital Asset Prices," **JOF**, 1975, v30(1), 155-162.

Roberts, Gordon S. "Term Premiums In The Term Structure Of Interest Rates," **JMCB**, 1980, v12(2), Part 1, 184-197.

Roberts, Gordon S. (Bierwag, G. O., George G. Kaufman, Cynthia M. Latta and Gordon S. Roberts. "The Usefulness Of Duration: Response To Critics" **JPM**, 1986-87, v12(2), 48-52.)

Roberts, Gordon S. (Bierwag, G. O. and Gordon S. Roberts. "Single-Factor Duration Models: Canadian Tests," **JFR**, 1990, v13(1), 23-38.)

Roberts, Gordon S. (Bildersee, John S. and Gordon S. Roberts. "Beta Instability When Interest Rate Levels Change," **JFQA**, 1981, v16(3), 375-380.)

Roberts, Gordon S. (Dipchand, Cecil R., Gordon S. Roberts and Jerry A. Viscione. "Agency Costs And Captive Finance Subsidiaries In Canada," **JFR**, 1982, v5(2), 189-199.)

Roberts, Gordon S. (Dipchand, Cecil R., Arthur C. Gudikunst and Gordon S. Roberts. "An Empirical Analysis Of Canadian Railroad Leases," **JFR**, 1980, v3(1), 57-68.)

Roberts, Gordon S. (Fooladi, Iraj and Gordon S. Roberts. "On Preferred Stock," **JFR**, 1986, v9(4), 319-324.)

Roberts, Gordon S. (Fooladi, Iraj and Gordon S. Roberts. "Dividend Changes And Preferred Stock Returns," **IJOF**, 1988, v1(1), 96-112.)

Roberts, Gordon S. (Fooladi, Iraj, Patricia McGraw and Gordon S. Roberts. "Preferred Stock And Taxes," **JBFA**, 1991, v18(1), 99-108.)

Roberts, Gordon S. (Magee, H. Robert and Gordon S. Roberts. "On Portfolio Theory, Holding Period Assumptions, And Bond Maturity Diversification," **FM**, 1979, v8(4), 68-71.)

Roberts, Gordon S. (Osteryoung, Jerome S., Daniel E. McCarty and Gordon S. Roberts. "Riding A Hedged Yield Curve With Treasury Bill Futures," **JBR**, 1983-84, v14(4), 266-273.)

Roberts, Gordon S. (Osteryoung, Jerome S., Elton Scott and Gordon S. Roberts. "Selecting Capital Projects With The Coefficient Of Variation," **FM**, 1977, v6(2), 65-70.)

Roberts, Gordon S. (Osteryoung, Jerome S., Daniel E. McCarty and Gordon S. Roberts. "Riding The Yield Curve With Treasury Bills," **FR**, 1981, v16(3), 57-66.)

Roberts, Gordon S. and Jerry A. Viscione. "Agency Costs, Bond Covenants, And Bond Yields," **RIF**, 1986, v6, 73-100.

Roberts, Gordon. (Fooladi, Iraj, Gordon Roberts and Jerry Viscione. "Captive Finance Subsidiaries: Overview And Synthesis," **FR**, 1986, v21(2), 259-275.)

Roberts, Harry V. "Current Problems In The Economics Of Capital Budgeting," **JOB**, 1957, v30(1), 12-16.

Roberts, Harry V. "Stock-Market 'Patterns' And Financial Analysis: Methodological Suggestions," **JOF**, 1959, v14(1), 1-10.

Roberts, Harry V. "The New Business Statistics," **JOB**, 1960, v33(1), 21-30.

Roberts, Harry V. (Evans, Franklin B. and Harry V. Roberts. "Fords, Chevrolets, And The Problem Of Discrimination," **JOB**, 1963, v36(2), 242-249.)

Roberts, Harry V. (Ling, Robert F. and Harry V. Roberts. "IDA: An Approach To Interactive Data Analysis In Teaching And Research," **JOB**, 1975, v48(3), 411-451.)

Roberts, Harry V. (Lorie, James H. and Harry V. Roberts. "Some Comments On Experimentation In Business Research," **JOB**, 1950, v23(2), 94-102.)

Roberts, Mark O. "Mandatory Pretrial Disclosure Of Automobile Liability Insurance Limits," **JRI**, 1960, v27(3), 1-6.

Roberts, Steven M. and Marvin S. Margolis. "Control Of The Money Stock With A Reserve Aggregate," **JMCB**, 1976, v8(4), 457-476.

Roberts, William W. (Friedman, Richard M. and William W. Roberts. "The Carry-Forward Provision And Management Of Bank Reserves," **JOF**, 1983, v38(3), 845-855.)

Robertson, Dan H. and Danny N. Bellenger. "Identifying Bank Market Segments," **JBR**, 1976-77, v7(4), 276-283.

Robertson, Dan H. (Bellenger, Danny N., Dan H. Robertson and Barnett A. Greenberg. "Female Attitudes Toward The Use Of Credit Vs. Cash," **JBR**, 1979-80, v10(1), 54-57.)

Robertson, Kerry L. (Horvitz, Paul M., Insup Lee and Kerry L. Robertson. "Valuation Effects Of New Securities Issuance By Bank Holding Companies: New Evidence," **FR**, 1991, v26(1), 91-104.)

Robertson, Matthew. "A Note On The Flow Of Capital In Outstanding Common And Preferred Shares Between Canada And The United States," **JFQA**, 1972, v7(1), 1425-1427.

Robertson, Terry D. (Stowe, John D., Collin J. Watson and Terry D. Robertson. "Relationships Between The Two Sides Of The Balance Sheet: A Canonical Correlation Analysis," **JOF**, 1980, v35(4), 973-980.)

Robertson, Terry. (Stock, Duane and Terry Robertson. "Improved Techniques For Predicting Municipal Bond Ratings," **JBR**, 1981-82, v12(3), 153-160.)

Robichek, Alexander A. and James C. Van Horne. "Abandonment Value And Capital Budgeting," **JOF**, 1967, v22(4), 577-589.

Robichek, Alexander A. and James C. Van Horne. "Abandonment Value And Capital Budgeting: Reply," **JOF**, 1969, v24(1), 96-97.

Robichek, Alexander A. and Marcus C. Bogue. "A Note On The Behavior Of Expected Price/Earnings Ratios Over Time," **JOF**, 1971, v26(3), 731-735.

Robichek, Alexander A. and Mark R. Eaker. "Foreign Exchange Hedging And The Capital Asset Pricing Model," **JOF**, 1978, v33(3), 1011-1018.

Robichek, Alexander A. and Mark R. Eaker. "Debt Denomination And Exchange Risk In International Capital Markets," **FM**, 1976, v5(3), 11-18.

Robichek, Alexander A. and Richard A. Cohn. "The Economic Determinants Of Systematic Risk," **JOF**, 1974, v29(2), 439-447.

Robichek, Alexander A. and Stewart C. Myers. "Valuation Under Uncertainty: Comment," **JFQA**, 1968, v3(4), 479-483.

Robichek, Alexander A. and Stewart C. Myers. "Valuation Of The Firm: Effects Of Uncertainty In A Market Context," **JOF**, 1966, v21(2), 215-227.

Robichek, Alexander A. and Stewart C. Myers. "Problems In The Theory Of Optimal Capital Structure," **JFQA**, 1966, v1(2), 1-35.

Robichek, Alexander A. and Stewart C. Myers. "Conceptual Problems In The Use Of Risk-Adjusted Discount Rates," **JOF**, 1966, v21(4), 727-730.

Robichek, Alexander A. and W. David Niebuhr. "Tax-Induced Bias In Reported Treasury Yields," **JOF**, 1970, v25(5), 1081-1090.

Robichek, Alexander A. "Interpreting The Results Of Risk Analysis: A Note," **JOF**, 1975, v30(5), 1384-1388.

Robichek, Alexander A. "Regulation And Modern Finance Theory," **JOF**, 1978, v33(3), 693-705.

Robichek, Alexander A. "Risk And The Value Of Securities," **JFQA**, 1969, v4(4), 513-538.

Robichek, Alexander A., Richard A. Cohn and John J. Pringle. "Returns On Alternative Investment Media And Implications For Portfolio Construction," **JOB**, 1972, v45(3), 427-443.

Robichek, Alexander, Robert C. Higgins and Michael Kinsman. "The Effect Of Leverage On The Cost Of Equity Capital Of Electric Utility Firms," **JOF,** 1973, v28(2), 353-367.

Robins, Philip K. "The Effects Of State Usury Ceilings On Single Family Homebuilding," **JOF,** 1974, v29(1), 227-235.

Robinson, Anthony W. (Ibbotson, Roger G., Richard C. Carr and Anthony W. Robinson. "International Equity And Bond Returns," **FAJ,** 1982, v38(4), 61-83.)

Robinson, David W. (Maier, Steven F., David W. Robinson and James H. Vander Weide. "A Short-Term Disbursement Forecasting Model," **FM,** 1981, v10(1), 9-20.)

Robinson, Joan. "Quantity Theories Old And New," **JMCB,** 1970, v2(4), 504-512.

Robinson, Joan. "Unwinding The Stagflation Puzzle," **JPM,** 1978-79, v5(4), 5-10.

Robinson, Randall S. "Bank Mod: An Interactive Simulation Aid For Bank Financial Planning," **JBR,** 1973-74, v4(3), 212-224.

Robinson, Randall S. "Measuring The Risk Dimension Of Investment Performance," **JOF,** 1970, v25(2), 455-467.

Robinson, Roland I. "A New Supervisory View Of Bank Capital," **JOF,** 1950, v5(1), 95-109.

Robinson, Roland I. "Factors Accounting For The Sharply Increased Cost Of State And Local Government Borrowing," **JOF,** 1957, v12(2), 126-135.

Robinson, Roland I. "Forecasting Interest Rates," **JOB,** 1954, v27(1), 87-100.

Robinson, Roland I. "The Hunt Commission Report: A Search For Politically Feasible Solutions To The Problems Of Financial Structure," **JOF,** 1972, v27(4), 765-777.

Robinson, Roland I. "The Teaching Of Money And Banking," **JOF,** 1949, v4(3), 237-242.

Robinson, Roland I. "What Should We Teach In A Money And Banking Course?," **JOF,** 1966, v21(2), 403-410.

Robinson, Romney. "Cost In The Minimum Pricing Of Railroad Services: A Comment," **JOB,** 1963, v36(3), 341-347.

Robinson, Thomas R. "Life Insurance Companies And The Commercial Mortgage Market, 1960-73," **AREUEA,** 1975, v3(1), 49-72.

Robison, Jesse. "Labor Unions - A Challenge To Wall Street," **FAJ,** 1955, v11(1), 97-99.

Robison, Lindon and Peter J. Barry. "Risk Efficiency Using Stochastic Dominance And Expected Gain-Confidence Limits," **JOF,** 1978, v33(4), 1244-1249.

Robock, Stefan H. "Overseas Financing For U. S. International Business," **JOF,** 1966, v21(2), 297-307.

Rochester, David P. and Samuel C. Hadaway, Jr. "Further Evidence Of Seasonal Adjustment Of Time Series Data," **JFQA,** 1978, v13(1), 133-141.

Rochester, David P. (Neely, Walter P. and David P. Rochester. "Operating Performance And Merger Benefits: The Savings And Loan Experience," **FR,** 1987, v22(1), 111-130.)

Rock, Arthur. (Kronfeld, Morris and Arthur Rock. "Some Considerations Of The Infinite," **FAJ,** 1958, v14(5), 87-90.)

Rock, Kevin. "Why New Issues Are Underpriced," **JFEC,** 1986, v15(1/2), 187-212.

Rock, Kevin. (Miller, Merton H. and Kevin Rock. "Dividend Policy Under Asymmetric Information," **JOF,** 1985, v40(4), 1031-1051.)

Rockness, Joanne W. "An Assessment Of The Relationship Between US Corporate Environmental Performance And Disclosure," **JBFA,** 1985, v12(3), 339-354.

Rockoff, Hugh. "The Free Banking Era: A Reexamination," **JMCB,** 1974, v6(2), 141-167.

Rockwell, T. H. (Molnar, Daniel E. and T. H. Rockwell. "Analysis Of Policy Movement In A Merit-Rating Program: An Application Of Markov-Processes," **JRI,** 1966, v33(2), 265-276.)

Rodda, William H. "Multiple Line Underwriting: Rating Methods," **JRI,** 1957, v24(1), 133-144.

Roddewig, Clair M. "A Breakthrough To Higher Rail Earnings," **FAJ,** 1959, v15(1), 69-71.

Roddewig, Clair M. "Competition Or Price Rigging By Government?," **FAJ,** 1961, v17(3), 37-40.

Roddewig, Clair M. "Diversification: Key To Transportation Progress," **FAJ,** 1961, v17(2), 53-56.

Roddewig, Clair M. "Showdown Looms In Rail Transportation," **FAJ,** 1962, v18(5), 85-88.

Roden, Peyton Foster and Robert L. Bland. "Issuer Sophistication And Underpricing In The Negotiated Municipal Bond Market," **JFR,** 1986, v9(2), 163-170.

Roden, Peyton Foster and Joseph W. Meador. "An Analysis Of The Audit Guide's Impact On The Sensitivity Of Life Company Stocks," **JRI,** 1980, v47(4), 660-677.

Rodermund, Matthew. "Four Points Of Confusion About Reinsurance: Comment," **JRI,** 1965, v32(1), 133-136.

Rodha, Rodney R. "Variable Life Insurance Product Design: Comment," **JRI,** 1972, v39(3), 497-499.

Rodowskas, Christopher A., Jr. (Gagnon, Jean P. and Christopher A. Rodowskas, Jr. "Two Controversial Problems In Third-Party Outpatient Prescription Plans," **JRI,** 1972, v39(4), 603-611.)

Rodowskas, Christopher A., Jr. (Gagnon, Jean P. and Christopher A. Rodowskas, Jr. "Two Controversial Problems In Third-Party Outpatient Prescription Plans: Reply," **JRI,** 1974, v41(4), 742-747.)

Rodriguez, Carlos. (Frenkel, Jacob A. and Carlos Rodriguez. "Wealth Effects And The Dynamics Of Inflation: A Comment," **JMCB,** 1975, v7(2), 259-268.)

Rodriguez, Ricardo J. "A Generalization Of The Tree Harvesting Paradigm," **FR,** 1990, v25(3), 501-515.

Rodriguez, Ricardo J. "Default Risk, Yield Spreads, And Time To Maturity," **JFQA,** 1988, v23(1), 111-117.

Rodriguez, Ricardo J. "Investment Horizon, Taxes And Maturity Choice For Discount Coupon Bonds," **FAJ,** 1988, v44(5), 67-69.

Rodriguez, Ricardo J. "The Quadratic Approximation To The Yield To Maturity," **JFED,** 1988, v17, 19-25.

Rodriguez, Ricardo J. "The Wealth Maximizing Ordering Quantity: An Extension," **FR,** 1988, v23(2), 227-232.

Rodriguez, Ricardo J. (Kolb, Robert W. and Ricardo J. Rodriguez. "The Regression Tendencies Of Betas: A Reappraisal," **FR,** 1989, v24(2), 319-334.)

Rodriguez, Ricardo J. (Kolb, Robert W. and Ricardo J. Rodriguez. "Markov Chains And Regression Toward The Mean," **FR,** 1991, v26(1), 115-125.)

Rodriguez, Ricardo J. (Kolb, Robert W. and Ricardo J. Rodriguez. "Is The Distribution Of Betas Stationary?," **JFR,** 1990, v13(4), 279-284.)

Rodriguez, Rita M. "Corporate Exchange Risk Management: Theme And Aberrations," **JOF,** 1981, v36(2), 427-438.

Rodriguez, Rita M. "FASB No. 8: What Has It Done To Us?," **FAJ,** 1977, v33(2), 40-47.

Rodriguez, Rita M. "Management Of Foreign Exchange Risk In The U. S. Multinationals," **JFQA,** 1974, v9(5), 849-857.

Rodriguez, Rita M. "Measuring Multinationals' Exchange Risk," **FAJ,** 1979, v35(6), 49-55.

Rodriquez, Ricardo J. (Kolb, Robert W. and Ricardo J. Rodriguez. "Friday The Thirteenth: 'Part VII'--A Note," **JOF,** 1987, v42(5), 1385-1387.)

Rodriquez, Rita M. (Carter, E. Eugene and Rita M. Rodriquez. "Internationalizing The Corporate Finance Course According To AACSB Guidelines," **JFED,** 1980, v9, 3-7.)

Roe, Mark J. "Political And Legal Restraints On Ownership And Control Of Public Companies," **JFEC,** 1990, v27(1), 7-42.

Roe, Terry. (Antonovitz, Frances and Terry Roe. "Effects Of Expected Cash And Futures Prices On Hedging And Production," **JFM,** 1986, v6(2), 187-206.)

Roehl, Tom. "Data Sources For Research In Japanese Finance," **JFQA,** 1985, v20(2), 273-276.

Roell, Ailsa. "Dual-Capacity Trading And The Quality Of The Market," **JFI,** 1990, v1(2), 105-124.

Roenfeldt, Rodney I., Robert J. Sweeney, Steven J. Goldstein and Helen M. Kleschick. "Commentary On 1982 FMA Program," **FM,** 1982, v11(4), 52-54.

Roenfeldt, Rodney L. and James B. Henry. "Lease-Cost Measurement Of Hospital Equipment Under Cost-Based Reimbursement," **FM,** 1979, v8(2), 24-35.

Roenfeldt, Rodney L. and Jerome S. Osteryoung. "Analysis Of Financial Leases," **FM,** 1973, v2(1), 74-87.

Roenfeldt, Rodney L. and Philip L. Cooley. "Predicting Corporate Profitability For Investment Selection," **JBFA,** 1978, v5(1), 57-65.

Roenfeldt, Rodney L. (Cooley, Philip L., Rodney L. Roenfeldt and Naval K. Modani. "Interdependence Of Market Risk Measures," **JOB,** 1977, v50(3), 356-363.)

Roenfeldt, Rodney L. (Cooley, Philip L. and Rodney L. Roenfeldt. "A Comparative Multivariate Analysis Of Factors Affecting Stock Returns," **FR,** 1975, v10(1), 31-41.)

Roenfeldt, Rodney L. (Cooley, Philip L., Rodney L. Roenfeldt and It-Keong Chew. "Clarification Of Three Capital Budgeting Criteria," **FR,** v12(1), 20-27.)

Roenfeldt, Rodney L. (Cooley, Philip L., Rodney L. Roenfeldt and It-Keong Chew. "Capital Budgeting Procedures Under Inflation," **FM,** 1974, v4(4), 18-27.)

Roenfeldt, Rodney L. (Copley, Ronald E., Philip L. Cooley and Rodney L. Roenfeldt. "Autocorrelation In Market Model Residuals," **JBFA,** 1984, v11(3), 409-417.)

Roenfeldt, Rodney L. (Eberhart, Allan C., William T. Moore and Rodney L. Roenfeldt. "Security Pricing And Deviations From The Absolute Priority Rule In Bankruptcy Proceedings," **JOF,** 1990, v45(5), 1457-1470.)

Roenfeldt, Rodney L. (Ferri, Michael G., H. Dennis Oberhelman and Rodney L. Roenfeldt. "Market Timing And Mutual Fund Portfolio Composition," **JFM,** 1984, v7(2), 143-150.)

Roenfeldt, Rodney L. (Findlay, M.C., III, A.W. Frankle, P.L. Cooley, R.L. Roenfeldt and It-Keong Chew. "Capital Budgeting Procedures Under Inflation: Cooley, Roenfeldt, And Chew Vs. Findlay And Frankle," **FM,** 1976, v5(3),83-95.)

Roenfeldt, Rodney L. (Gombola, Michael J., Rodney L. Roenfeldt and Philip L. Cooley. "Some Additional Evidence On Pricing Efficiency Of CBOE Options," **FR,** 1980, v15(1), 9-19.)

Roenfeldt, Rodney L. (Gombola, Michael J., Rodney L. Roenfeldt and Philip L. Cooley. "Spreading Strategies In CBOE Options: Evidence On Market Performance," **JFR,** 1978, v1(1), 35-44.)

Roenfeldt, Rodney L. (Harris, John M., Jr., Rodney L. Roenfeldt and Philip L. Cooley. "Evidence Of Financial Leverage Clienteles," **JOF,** 1983, v38(4), 1125-1132.)

Roenfeldt, Rodney L. (Modani, Naval K., Philip L. Cooley and Rodney L. Roenfeldt. "Stability Of Market Risk Surrogates," **JFR,** 1983, v6(1), 33-40.)

Roenfeldt, Rodney L. (Modani, Naval K., Philip L. Cooley and Rodney L. Roenfeldt. "Covariation Of Risk Measures Under Inflation," **JBFA,** 1980, v7(3), 393-400.)

Roenfeldt, Rodney L. (Moore, William T., Donald G. Christensen and Rodney L. Roenfeldt. "Equity Valuation Effects Of Forming Master Limited Partnerships," **JFEC,** 1989, v24(1), 107-124.)

Roenfeldt, Rodney L. (Osteryoung, Jerome S., Rodney L. Roenfeldt and Donald A. Nast. Capital Asset Pricing Model And Traditional Risk For Capital Budgeting," **FR,** v12(1), 48-58.)

Roenfeldt, Rodney L. (Osteryoung, Jerome S., Rodney L. Roenfeldt and Donald A. Nast. "Capital Asset Pricing Model And Traditional Risk For Capital Budgeting: A Reply," **FR,** 1978, v13(1), 90-93.)

Roenfeldt, Rodney L. (Trifts, Jack W., Neil W. Sicherman, Rodney L. Roenfeldt and Francisco De Cossio. "Divestiture To Unit Managers And Shareholder Wealth," **FR,** 1990, v13(2), 167-172.)

Roenfeldt, Rodney L. (Wansley, James W., Rodney L. Roenfeldt and Philip L. Cooley. "Abnormal Returns From Merger Profiles," **JFQA,** 1983, v18(2), 149-162.)

Roenfeldt, Rodney L., Gary L. Griepentrog and Christopher C. Pflaum. "Further Evidence On The Stationarity Of Beta Coefficients," **JFQA,** 1978, v13(1), 117-121.

Roering, Kenneth J. and Paul E. Smith. "A Distributed Lag Forecasting Model For Bank Loans And The Money Supply," **JBR,** 1978-79, v9(2), 104-111.

Rogalski, R. J. (Oldfield, George S., Jr., R. J. Rogalski and Robert A. Jarrow. "An Autoregressive Jump Process For Common Stock Returns," **JFEC,** 1977, v5(3), 389-418.)

Rogalski, Richard and Seha M. Tinic. "The January Size Effect: Anomaly Or Risk Mismeasurement?," **FAJ,** 1986, v42(6), 63-70.

Rogalski, Richard J. and Joseph D. Vinso. "Heteroscedastic Security Returns," **FR**, 1978, v13(2), 1-11.

Rogalski, Richard J. and Joseph D. Vinso. "Stock Returns, Money Supply And The Direction Of Causality," **JOF**, 1977, v32(4), 1017-1030.

Rogalski, Richard J. and Joseph D. Vinso. "An Analysis Of Monetary Aggregates," **JMCB**, 1978, v10(2), 252-266.

Rogalski, Richard J. "New Findings Regarding Day-Of-The-Week Returns Over Trading And Non-Trading Periods: A Note," **JOF**, 1984, v39(5), 1603-1614.

Rogalski, Richard J. "Trading In Warrants By Mechanical Systems," **JOF**, 1977, v32(1), 87-101.

Rogalski, Richard J. "Variances And Options Prices In Theory And Practice," **JPM**, 1977-78, v4(2), 43-51.

Rogalski, Richard J. (Gultekin, N. Bulent and Richard J. Rogalski. "Alternative Duration Specifications And The Measurement Of Basis Risk: Empirical Tests," **JOB**, 1984, v57(2), 241-264.)

Rogalski, Richard J. (Gultekin, N. Bulent and Richard J. Rogalski. "Comment: A Test Of Stone's Two-Index Model Of Returns," **JFQA**, 1979, v14(3), 629-639.)

Rogalski, Richard J. (Gultekin, N. Bulent and Richard J. Rogalski. "Government Bond Returns, Measurement Of Interest Rate Risk, And The Arbitrage Pricing Theory," **JOF**, 1985, v40(1), 43-61.)

Rogalski, Richard J. (Leabo, Dick A. and Richard J. Rogalski. "Warrant Price Movements And The Efficient Market Model," **JOF**, 1975, v30(1), 163-177.)

Rogalski, Richard J. (Logue, Dennis E. and Richard J. Rogalski. "Offshore Alphas: Should Diversification Begin At Home?: Reply," **JPM**, 1979-80, v6(2), 76-78.)

Rogalski, Richard J. (Maloney, Kevin J. and Richard J. Rogalski. "Call-Option Pricing And The Turn Of The Year," **JOB**, 1989, v62(4), 539-552.)

Rogalski, Richard J. (Oldfield, George S., Jr. and Richard J. Rogalski. "A Theory Of Common Stock Returns Over Trading And Non-Trading Periods," **JOF**, 1980, v35(3), 729-751.)

Rogalski, Richard J. (Oldfield, George S., Jr. and Richard J. Rogalski. "Treasury Bill Factors And Common Stock Returns," **JOF**, 1981, v36(2), 337-354.)

Rogalski, Richard J. and Seha M. Tinic. "Risk-Premium Curve Vs. Capital Line: A Re-Examination," **FM**, 1978, v7(1), 73-84.

Rogalski, Richard. (Gultekin, N. Bulent, Richard Rogalski and Seha M. Tinic. "Option Pricing Model Estimates: Some Empirical Results," **FM**, 1982, v11(1), 58-69.)

Rogers, Andrei. (Keyfitz, Nathan and Andrei Rogers. "Simplified Multiple Contingency Calculations," **JRI**, 1982, v49(1), 59-72.)

Rogers, George E. "The Risk Manager And Insurance Legislation," **JRI**, 1963, v30(3), 447-450.

Rogers, John H. "Foreign Inflation Transmission Under Flexible Exchange Rates And Currency Substitution," **JMCB**, 1990, v22(2), 195-208.

Rogers, Karen. (Goldberg, Craig J. and Karen Rogers. "An Introduction To Asset Backed Securities," **JACF**, 1988, v1(3), 20-31.)

Rogers, Paul C. (Saaty, Thomas L., Paul C. Rogers and Ricardo Pell. "Portfolio Selection Through Hierarchies," **JPM**, 1979-80, v6(3), 16-21.)

Rogers, Paul P. "A Survey Of Insurance In The USSR," **JRI**, 1963, v30(2), 273-280.

Rogers, Paul P. "Gosstrakh: Ten Years Later," **JRI**, 1980, v47(3), 534-547.

Rogers, Paul P. "The 1967 Insurance Law Of Yugoslavia," **JRI**, 1970, v37(2), 326-329.

Rogers, Paul P. "The Structure Of Soviet Insurance," **JRI**, 1965, v32(2), 237-254.

Rogers, Robert P. (Bernard, Jules E., Gary G. Gilbert and Robert P. Rogers. "Final Report Of The National Commission On Electronic Fund Transfers," **JBR**, 1977-78, v8(4), 209-217.)

Rogers, Ronald C. and James E. Owers. "Equity For Debt Exchanges And Stockholder Wealth," **FM**, 1985, v14(3), 18-26.

Rogers, Ronald C. and James E. Owers. "The Impact Of Value Line Special Situation Recommendations On Stock Prices," **FR**, 1984, v19(2), 195-207.

Rogers, Ronald C. "The Relationship Between Earnings Yield And Market Value: Evidence From The American Stock Exchange," **FR**, 1988, v23(1), 65-80.

Rogers, Ronald C. (Clauretie, Terrence M., Mel Jameson and Ronald C. Rogers. "A Note On Refinancing Costs, Prepayment Assumptions, And The Value Of Mortgage-Backed Securities," **JREFEC**, 1990, v3(3), 295-300.)

Rogers, Ronald C. (Hite, Gailen L., James E. Owers and Ronald C. Rogers. "The Market For Interfirm Asset Sales: Partial Sell-Offs And Total Liquidations," **JFEC**, 1987, v18(2), 229-252.)

Rogers, Ronald C. (Hite, Gailen L., James E. Owers and Ronald C. Rogers. "The Separation Of Real Estate Operations By Spin-Off," **AREUEA**, 1984, v12(3), 318-331.)

Rogers, Ronald C. (Mais, Eric L., William T. Moore and Ronald C. Rogers. "A Re-Examination Of Shareholder Wealth Effects Of Calls Of Convertible Preferred Stock," **JOF**, 1989, v44(5), 1401-1410.)

Rogers, Ronald C. (Murphy, Neil B. and Ronald C. Rogers. "The Line Of Commerce In Retail Financial Institution Mergers: Some Evidence From Consumer Data In New England," **JBR**, 1984-85, v15(1), 21-25.)

Rogers, Ronald C. (Murphy, Neil B. and Ronald C. Rogers. "Life Cycle And The Adoption Of Consumer Financial Innovation: An Empirical Study Of The Adoption Process," **JBR**, 1986-87, v17(1), 3-8.)

Rogers, Ronald C. and James E. Owers. "The Investment Of Performance Of Public Real Estate Limited Partnerships," **AREUEA**, 1985, v13(2), 153-166.

Rogers, Ronald C., Neil B. Murphy and James E. Owers. "Financial Innovation, Balance Sheet Cosmetics And Market Response: The Case Of Equity-For-Debt Exchanges In Banking," **JBR**, 1985-86, v16(3), 145-149.

Rogers, Stephen. "Accounting Practices: A Critique," **FAJ**, 1967, v23(1), 31-32.

Rogers, Stephen. "Valuation Methods And Portfolio Performance," **JPM**, 1974-75, v1(1), 80-83.

Rogers, W. (Mahapatra, S., M. Chase and W. Rogers. "Information Interaction Effects Of Inflation Adjusted Accounting Data On Individual Decision-Maker's Sophistication And Risk Preference," **JBFA**, 1989, v16(5), 635-650.)

Rogoff, Donald L. "Problems Of Teaching Case Courses: A Survey," **JFED**, 1972, v1, 72.

Rogoff, Donald L. (Eckarkt, Walter L., Jr. and Donald L. Rogoff. "100% Margins Revisited," **JOF**, 1976, v31(3), 995-1001.)

Rogoff, Kenneth. (Meese, Richard and Kenneth Rogoff. "Was It Real? The Exchange Rate-Interest Differential Relation Over The Modern Floating-Rate Period," **JOF**, 1988, v43(4), 933-948.)

Rogow, Robert B. (Hand, John H., William P. Lloyd and Robert B. Rogow. "Agency Relationships In The Close Corporation," **FM**, 1982, v11(1), 25-30.)

Rogow, Robert B. (Lloyd, William P., Steven J. Goldstein and Robert B. Rogow. "International Portfolio Diversification Of Real Assets: An Update," **JBFA**, 1981, v8(1), 45-50.)

Rogowsky, Robert J. and Eric H. Sorensen. "Deregulation In Investment Banking: Shelf Registrations, Structure, And Performance," **FM**, 1985, v14(1), 5-15.

Rogowsky, Robert J. "Pricing The Money Market Deposit And Super-NOW Accounts In 1983," **JBR**, 1984-85, v15(2), 72-81.

Rogowsky, Robert J. "Underwriting Competition And Issuer Borrowing Costs In The Municipal Revenue Bond Market," **JBR**, 1979-80, v10(4), 212-220.

Rogowski, Robert J. (Benson, Earl D. and Robert J. Rogowski. "The Cyclical Behavior Of Risk Spreads On New Municipal Issues," **JMCB**, 1978, v10(3), 348-362.)

Rogowski, Robert J. (Benson, Earl D., David S. Kidwell, Timothy W. Koch and Robert J. Rogowski. "Systematic Variation In Yield Spreads For Tax-Exempt General Obligation Bonds," **JFQA**, 1981, v16(5), 685-702.)

Rogowski, Robert J. (Kidwell, David S. and Robert J. Rogowski. "State Bond Bank Issues: Method Of Sale And Market Acceptance Over Time," **FM**, 1983, v12(2), 15-20.)

Rogowski, Robert W. (Marr, M. Wayne, Robert W. Rogowski and John L. Trimble. "The Competitive Effects Of U.S. And Japanese Commercial Bank Participation In Eurobond Underwriting," **FM**, 1989, v18(4), 47-54.)

Rogowski, Robert. "The Cyclical Pattern Of Corporate Bond Supply: Comment," **JPM**, 1980-81, v7(2), 94.

Rohman, Mark C. and Michael A. Policano. "Financing Chapter 11 Companies In The 1990s," **JACF**, 1990, v3(2), 96-101.

Rohrlich, George F. "The Place Of Social Insurance In The Pursuit Of The General Welfare," **JRI**, 1969, v36(3), 333-354.

Rohrlich, Goerge F. "Problems Of Social Insurance Coordination - The Case Of Puerto Rico," **JRI**, 1978, v45(2), 239-259.

Rokes, Willis P. "Consumerism And Insurance," **JRI**, 1971, v38(1), 119-122.

Rokes, Willis P. "The Role Of The Sales Finance Company Insurance Affiliate In Writing Automobile Insurance," **JRI**, 1962, v29(1), 115-122.

Rokes, Willis P. "The Saskatchewan Plan," **JRI**, 1962, v29(3), 373-384.

Rokes, Willis Park. "Remedies Afforded Private Parties Against Insurers For Unfair Claims Practices," **JRI**, 1987, v54(3), 478-501.

Roley, V. Vance. "Forecasting Interest Rates With A Structural Model," **JPM**, 1981-82, v8(3), 53-63.

Roley, V. Vance. "Money Demand Predictability," **JMCB**, 1985, v17(4), Part 2, 611-641.

Roley, V. Vance. "The Determinants Of The Treasury Security Yield Curve," **JOF**, 1981, v36(5), 1103-1126.

Roley, V. Vance. "The Effects Of Money Announcements Under Alternative Monetary Control Procedures," **JMCB**, 1987, v19(3), 292-307.

Roley, V. Vance. "The Response Of Short-Term Interest Rates To Weekly Money Announcements," **JMCB**, 1983, v15(3), 344-354.

Roley, V. Vance. "The Response Of Short-Term Interest Rates To Weekly Money Announcements: A Reply," **JMCB**, 1985, v17(2), 271-273.

Roley, V. Vance. "The Role Of Commercial Banks' Portfolio Behavior In The Determination Of Treasury Security Yields," **JMCB**, 1980, v12(2), Part 2, 353-369.

Roley, V. Vance. "US Money Announcements And Covered Interest Parity: The Case Of Japan," **JIMF**, 1987, v6(1), 57-70.

Roley, V. Vance. (Friedman, Benjamin M. and V. Vance Roley. "Models Of Long-Term Interest Rate Determination," **JPM**, 1979-80, v6(3), 35-45.)

Roley, V. Vance. (Pearce, Douglas K. and V. Vance Roley. "Firm Characteristics, Unanticipated Inflation, And Stock Returns," **JOF**, 1988, v43(4), 965-981.)

Roley, V. Vance. (Pearce, Douglas K. and V. Vance Roley. "Stock Prices And Economic News," **JOB**, 1985, v58(1), 49-68.)

Roley, V. Vance. (Pearce, Douglas K. and V. Vance Roley. "The Reaction Of Stock Prices To Unanticipated Changes In Money: A Note," **JOF**, 1983, v38(4), 1323-1333.)

Rolfo, Jacques. (Gonzales, Nestor, Robert Litzenberger and Jacques Rolfo. "On Mean Variance Models Of Capital Structure And The Absurdity Of Their Predictions," **JFQA**, 1977, v12(2), 165-179.)

Rolfo, Jacques. (Jacquillat, Bertrand C., John G. McDonald and Jacques Rolfo. "French Auctions Of Common Stock: New Issues, 1966-1974," **JBF**, 1978, v2(4), 305-322.)

Rolfo, Jacques. (Litzenberger, Robert H. and Jacques Rolfo. "Arbitrage Pricing, Transaction Costs And Taxation Of Capital Gains: A Study Of Government Bonds With The Same Maturity Date," **JFEC**, 1984, v13(3), 337-351.)

Rolfo, Jacques. (Litzenberger, Robert H. and Jacques Rolfo. "An International Study Of Tax Effects On Government Bonds," **JOF**, 1984, v39(1), 1-22.)

Roll, R. W. (Kaplan, R. and R. W. Roll. "Accounting Changes And Stock Prices," **FAJ**, 1973, v29(1), 48-53.)

Roll, Richard and Stephen A. Ross. "A Note On Qualitative Results For Investment Proportions: Comment," **JFEC**, 1977, v5(2), 265-268.

Roll, Richard and Stephen A. Ross. "The Arbitrage Pricing Theory

Approach To Strategic Portfolio Planning," **FAJ**, 1984, v40(3), 14-26.

Roll, Richard and Stephen A. Ross. "A Critical Reexamination Of The Empirical Evidence On The Arbitrage Pricing Theory: A Reply," **JOF**, 1984, v39(2), 347-350.

Roll, Richard and Stephen A. Ross. "An Empirical Investigation Of The Arbitrage Pricing Theory," **JOF**, 1980, v35(5), 1073-1103.

Roll, Richard. "A Critique Of The Asset Pricing Theory's Tests; Part I: On Past And Potential Testability Of Theory," **JFEC**, 1977, v4(2), 129-176.

Roll, Richard. "A Note On The Geometry Of Shanken's CSR T-Squared Test For Mean/Variance Efficiency," **JFEC**, 1985, v14(3), 349-358.

Roll, Richard. "A Possible Explanation Of The Small Firm Effect," **JOF**, 1981, v36(4), 879-888.

Roll, Richard. "A Simple Implicit Measure Of The Effective Bid-Ask Spread In An Efficient Market," **JOF**, 1984, v39(4), 1127-1139.

Roll, Richard. "After-Tax Investment Results From Long-Term Vs. Short-Term Discount Coupon Bonds," **FAJ**, 1984, v40(1), 43-54.

Roll, Richard. "Ambiguity When Performance Is Measured By The Securities Line," **JOF**, 1978, v33(4), 1051-1069.

Roll, Richard. "An Analytic Valuation Formula For Unprotected American Call Options On Stocks With Known Dividends," **JFEC**, 1977, v5(2), 251-258.

Roll, Richard. "Assets, Money, And Commodity Price Inflation Under Uncertainty: Demand Theory," **JMCB**, 1973, v5(4), 903-923.

Roll, Richard. "Bias In Fitting The Sharpe Model To Time Series Data," **JFQA**, 1969, v4(3), 271-289.

Roll, Richard. "Evidence On The 'Growth-Optimum' Model," **JOF**, 1973, v28(3), 551-566.

Roll, Richard. "Interest Rates On Monetary Assets And Commodity Price Index Changes," **JOF**, 1972, v27(2), 251-277.

Roll, Richard. "Investment Diversification And Bond Maturity," **JOF**, 1971, v26(1), 51-66.

Roll, Richard. "Measuring Portfolio Performance And The Empirical Content Of Asset Pricing Models: A Reply," **JFEC**, 1979, v7(3), 391-400.

Roll, Richard. "On Computing Mean Returns And The Small Firm Premium," **JFEC**, 1983, v12(3), 371-386.

Roll, Richard. "Orthogonal Portfolios," **JFQA**, 1980, v15(5), 1005-1023.

Roll, Richard. "Performance Evaluation And Benchmark Errors," **JPM**, 1979-80, v6(4), 5-12.

Roll, Richard. "Performance Evaluation And Benchmark Errors (II)," **JPM**, 1980-81, v7(2), 17-22.

Roll, Richard. "Presidential Address: R-Square," **JOF**, 1988, v43(3), 541-566.

Roll, Richard. "Price Volatility, International Market Links, And Their Implications For Regulatory Policies," **JFSR**, 1989, v3(2/3), 211-246.

Roll, Richard. "The Hubris Hypothesis Of Corporate Takeovers," **JOB**, 1986, v59(2), Part 1, 197-216.

Roll, Richard. "The International Crash Of October 1987," **FAJ**, 1988, v44(5), 19-35.

Roll, Richard. "Vas Ist Das?," **JPM**, 1982-83, v9(2), 18-28.

Roll, Richard. (Berk, Jonathan and Richard Roll. "Adjustable Rate Mortgages: Valuation," **JREFEC**, 1988, v1(2), 163-184.)

Roll, Richard. (Bogue, Marcus C. and Richard Roll. "Capital Budgeting Of Risky Projects With 'Imperfect' Markets For Physical Capital," **JOF**, 1974, v29(2), 601-613.)

Roll, Richard. (Chen, Nai-Fu, Richard Roll and Stephen A. Ross. "Economic Forces And The Stock Market," **JOB**, 1986, v59(3), 383-404.)

Roll, Richard. (French, Kenneth R. and Richard Roll. "Stock Return Variances: The Arrival Of Information And The Reaction Of Traders," **JFEC**, 1986, v17(1), 5-26.)

Roll, Richard. (Geske, Robert and Richard Roll. "On Valuing American Call Options With The Black-Scholes European Formula," **JOF**, 1984, v20(5), 443-455.)

Roll, Richard. (Geske, Robert and Richard Roll. "The Fiscal And Monetary Linkage Between Stock Returns And Inflation," **JOF**, 1983, v38(1), 1-33.)

Roll, Richard. (Geske, Robert, Richard Roll and Kuldeep Shastri. "Over-the-Counter Option Market Dividend Protection And 'Biases' In The Black-Scholes Model: A Note," **JOF**, 1983, v38(4), 1271-1277.)

Roll, Richard. (Hinich, Melvin J. and Richard Roll. "Measuring Nonstationarity In The Parameters Of The Market Model," **RIF**, 1981, v3, 1-52.)

Roll, Richard. (Jacquillat, Bertrand and Richard Roll. "French Index-Linked Bonds For U.S. Investors," **JPM**, 1978-79, v5(3), 24-30.)

Roll, Richard. (Kaplan, Robert S. and Richard Roll. "Investor Evaluation Of Accounting Information: Some Empirical Evidence," **JOB**, 1972, v45(2), 225-257.)

Roll, Richard. (Queen, Maggie and Richard Roll. "Firm Mortality: Using Market Indicators To Predict Survival," **FAJ**, 1987, v43(3), 9-26.)

Roll, Richard. (Richard, Scott F. and Richard Roll. "Prepayments On Fixed-Rate Mortgage-Backed Securities," **JPM**, 1989, v15(3), 74-82.)

Rolland, Louis J. "Ethical Drug Industry Has Unlimited Frontiers," **FAJ**, 1953, v9(2), 127-129.

Rollins, Garry M. "Minimum Deposit Plans - Miracles Or Mirages," **JRI**, 1979, v46(2), 23-44.

Rollins, J. R. (Bishop, E. L., III and J. R. Rollins. "Lowry's Reports: A Denial Of Market Efficiency," **JPM**, 1977-78, v4(1), 21-27.)

Rolph, Earl R. "Review Article: The Taxation Of Income From Capital," **JOF**, 1971, v44(2), 175-179.

Rolph, John E. "Some Statistical Evidence On Merit Rating In Medical Malpractice Insurance," **JRI**, 1981, v48(2), 247-260.

Rolph, John E., James K. Hammitt and Robert L. Houchens. "Automobile Accident Compensation: Who Pays How Much How Soon?," **JRI**, 1985, v52(4), 667-685.

Roman, Emmanuel. (Hakanoglu, Erol, Robert Kopprasch and Emmanuel Roman. "Constant Proportion Portfolio Insurance For Fixed-Income Investment," **JPM**, 1989, v15(4), 58-66.)

Romer David. (Mankiw, N. Gregory, David Romer and Matthew D. Shapiro. "An Unbiased Reexamination Of Stock Market Volatility," **JOF**, 1985, v40(3), 677-687.)

Ronen, Joshua and Simcha Sadan. "Income Smoothing Via Classification," **FAJ**, 1975, v31(5), 62-68.

Ronen, Joshua and George H. Sorter. "Relevant Accounting," **JOB**, 1972, v45(2), 258-282.

Ronen, Joshua. (Amihud, Yakov, Jacob Y. Kamin and Joshua Ronen. "'Management', 'Ownerism', And Risk," **JBF**, 1983, v7(2), 189-196.)

Ronen, Joshua. (Ingberman, Monroe, Joshua Ronen and George H. Sorter. "Lease Capitalization And Financial Ratios," **FAJ**, 1979, v35(1), 28-31.)

Rones, Arthur. (Goodman, Laurie S., Raj Daryanani and Arthur Rones. "The Credit Exposure Of Cross-Currency And Nondollar Interest Rate Swaps," **RDIBF**, 1988, v2, 193-204.)

Ronk, Sally S. "The Acceleration Of Corporate Income Tax Payments," **JOF**, 1956, v11(4), 474-481.

Ronn, Aimee Gerbarg and Ehud I. Ronn. "The Box Spread Arbitrage Conditions: Theory, Tests, And Investment Strategies," **RFS**, 1989, v2(1), 91-108.

Ronn, Ehud I. (Flesaker, Bjorn and Ehud I. Ronn. "Inflation Futures And A Riskless Real Interest Rate," **RFM**, 1988, v7(1), 36-67.)

Ronn, Ehud I. and Avinash K. Verma. "Pricing Risk-Adjusted Deposit Insurance: An Option-Based Model," **JOF**, 1986, v41(4), 871-896.

Ronn, Ehud I. "A New Linear Programming Approach To Bond Portfolio Management," **JFQA**, 1987, v22(4), 439-466.

Ronn, Ehud I. "On The Rationality Of Common Stock Return Volatility," **FR**, 1986, v21(4), 355-381.

Ronn, Ehud I. (Bliss, Robert R., Jr. and Ehud I. Ronn. "Arbitrage-Based Estimation Of Nonstationary Shifts In The Term Structure Of Interest Rates," **JOF**, 1989, v44(3), 591-610.)

Ronn, Ehud I. (Flesaker, Bjorn and Ehud I. Ronn. "Inflation Futures And A Riskless Real Interest Rate," **RFM**, 1988, v7(1), 36-67.)

Ronn, Ehud I. (Litzenberger, Robert H. and Ehud I. Ronn. "A Utility-Based Model Of Common Stock Price Movements," **JOF**, 1986, v41(1), 67-92.)

Ronn, Ehud I. (Ronn, Aimee Gerbarg and Ehud I. Ronn. "The Box Spread Arbitrage Conditions: Theory, Tests, And Investment Strategies," **RFS**, 1989, v2(1), 91-108.)

Ronn, Ehud I. and Avinash K. Verma. "A Multi-Attribute Comparative Evaluation Of Relative Risk For A Sample Of Banks," **JBF**, 1987, v11(3), 499-524.

Ronn, Ehud I. and Avinash K. Verma. "Risk-Based Capital Adequacy Standards For A Sample Of 43 Major Banks," **JBF**, 1989, v13(1), 21-30.

Ronning, Gerd. (Davies, Laurie and Gerd Ronning. "A Note On The Uniqueness Of Portfolio Choice," **JFQA**, 1976, v11(3), 481-484.)

Rood, Henry F. "An Evaluation Of The Life Insurance Company Income Tax Act Of 1959: Comment," **JRI**, 1964, v31(2), 285-293.

Roos, Leslie L., Jr. "Managing The Public Sector - Automobile Insurance In Western Canada," **JRI**, 1977, v44(4), 555-570.

Roos, Nestor R. "Life Insurance In Mexico," **JRI**, 1959, v26(3), 41-56.

Roos, Nestor R. "Recent Federal Activity In Insurance Regulation," **JRI**, 1957, v24(1), 174-180.

Roos, Nestor R. "The Fundamental Nature Of Blue Cross And Blue Shield: Comment," **JRI**, 1963, v30(1), 109-111.

Roosa, Robert V. "Balance Of Payments Adjustment And International Liquidity," **JOF**, 1964, v19(1), 1-15.

Roosa, Robert V. "Controlling Inflation And The Inflationary Mentality," **JOF**, 1970, v25(2), 233-241.

Roosa, Robert V. "Reconciling Internal And External Financial Policies," **JOF**, 1962, v17(1), 1-16.

Roosa, Robert V. (Friedman, Milton and Robert V. Roosa. "Free Versus Fixed Exchange Rates: A Debate," **JPM**, 1976-77, v3(3), 68-83.)

Roose, Kenneth D. "The Role Of Net Government Contribution To Income In The Recession And Revival Of 1937-38," **JOF**, 1951, v6(1), 1-18.

Roper, Burns W. "Solving The Problems Of Marketing Research," **FAJ**, 1964, v20(5), 44-47.

Roper, Don. (Girton, Lance and Don Roper. "Theory And Implications Of Currency Substitution," **JMCB**, 1981, v13(1), 12-30.)

Rorke, C. Harvey. "On The Portfolio Effects Of Nonmarketable Assets: Government Transfers And Human Capital Payments," **JFQA**, 1979, v14(2), 167-177.

Rorke, C. Harvey. (Fowler, David J., C. Harvey Rorke and Vijay M. Jog. "A Note On Beta Stability And Thin Trading On The Toronto Stock Exchange," **JBFA**, 1981, v8(2), 267-278.)

Rorke, C. Harvey. (Fowler, David J., C. Harvey Rorke and Vijay M. Jog. "Heteroscedasticity, R-Squared And Thin Trading On The Toronto Stock Exchange," **JOF**, 1979, v34(5), 1201-1210.)

Rorke, C. Harvey. (Fowler, David J., and C. Harvey Rorke. "Risk Measurement When Shares Are Subject To Infrequent Trading: Comment," **JFEC**, 1983, v12(2), 279-283.)

Rorke, C. Harvey. (Fowler, David J., C. Harvey Rorke and Vijay M. Jog. "A Bias-Correcting Procedure For Beta Estimation In The Presence Of Thin Trading," **JFI**, 1989, v12(1), 23-32.)

Rorke, C. Harvey. (Fowler, J. and C. Harvey Rorke. "Capital Budgeting, Capital Asset Pricing And Externalities," **JBFA**, 1979, v6(2), 145-156.)

Rorke, C. Harvey. (Neave, Edwin H. and C. Harvey Rorke. "Risk, Ruin, And Investment Analysis: A Comment," **JFQA**, 1973, v8(3), 517-526.)

Rosa, Robert V. "Some Small Business Problems Indicated By The Industrial Loan Experience Of The Federal Reserve Bank Of New York," **JOF**, 1947, v2(1), 91-100.

Rosansky, Victor I. (Bodie, Zvi and Victor I. Rosansky. "Risk And Return In Commodity Futures," **FAJ**, 1980, v36(3), 27-31,33-39.)

Rose, Andrew K. "An Alternative Approach To The American Demand For Money," **JMCB**, 1985, v17(4), Part 1, 439-455.

Rose, Andrew K. "Is The Real Interest Rate Stable?," **JOF**, 1988, v43(5), 1095-1112.

Rose, Harold B. "The Competition For Deposits And The Impact Of Monetary Policy," **JBF**, 1980, v4(1), 17-32.

Rose, Hugh. "Real And Monetary Factors In The Business Cycle," **JMCB**, 1969, v1(2), 138-152.

Rose, John T. and Donald T. Savage. "Bank Holding Company De Novo Entry And Banking Market Performance," **JBR**, 1986-87, v17(1), 45-50.

Rose, John T. and Donald T. Savage. "Bank Holding Company De Novo Entry And Banking Market Deconcentration," JBR, 1982-83, v13(2), 96-100.

Rose, John T. and Donald T. Savage. "De Novo Entry And Performance: Bank Holding Companies Versus Independent Banks," JBR, 1984-85, v15(2), 95-107.

Rose, John T. and Peter S. Rose. "The Burden Of Federal Reserve System Membership: A Review Of The Evidence," JBF, 1979, v3(4), 331-346.

Rose, John T. and Roger D. Rutz. "Organization Form And Risk In Bank-Affiliated Mortgage Companies," JMCB, 1981, v13(3), 375-380.

Rose, John T. and Samuel H. Talley. "Financial Transactions Within Bank Holding Companies," JFR, 1984, v7(3), 209-217.

Rose, John T. "Branch Banking And The State/National Charter Decision," JBR, 1983-84, v14(2), 170-172.

Rose, John T. "Entry In Commercial Banking, 1962-78," JMCB, 1986, v18(2), 247-249.

Rose, John T. "Federal Reserve System Attrition Since 1960," JBR, 1979-80, v10(1), 8-27.

Rose, John T. "Growth, Consolidation And Mergers In Banking: Comment," JOF, 1976, v31(4), 1233-1237.

Rose, John T. "The Attractiveness Of Banking Markets For De Novo Entry," JBR, 1976-77, v7(4), 284-293.

Rose, John T. "The Effect Of Federal Home Loan Bank System Membership On Mutual Savings Bank Financial Performance," FR, 1978, v13(2), 22-35.

Rose, John T. "The Weighted Average Cost Of Capital And The Marginal Cost Of Capital: A Pedagogical Note," JFED, 1987, v16, 16-18.

Rose, John T. (Curry, Timothy J. and John T. Rose. "Multibank Holding Companies: Recent Evidence On Competition And Performance In Banking Markets," JBR, 1983-84, v14(3), 212-220.)

Rose, John T. (Curry, Timothy J. and John T. Rose. "Bank Holding Company Presence And Banking Market Performance," JBR, 1983-84, v14(4), 259-265.)

Rose, John T. (Goldberg, Lawrence G. and John T. Rose. "The Effect On Nonmember Banks Of The Imposition Of Member Bank Reserve Requirements - With And Without Federal Reserve Services," JOF, 1976, v31(5), 1457-1469.)

Rose, John T. (Goldberg, Lawrence G. and John T. Rose. "Mutual Savings Bank Membership In The FHLBS: Motivations Behind Recent Membership Growth," JBF, 1981, v5(2), 241-260.)

Rose, John T. (Goldberg, Lawrence G. and John T. Rose. "Do State Reserve Requirements Matter?," JBR, 1977-78, v8(1), 31-39.)

Rose, John T. (Kwast, Myron L. and John T. Rose. "Pricing, Operating Efficiency, And Profitability Among Large Commercial Banks," JBF, 1982, v6(2), 233-254.)

Rose, John T. and John D. Wolken. "Geographic Diversification In Banking, Market Share Changes, And The Viability Of Small Independent Banks," JFSR, 1990, v4(1), 5-20.

Rose, Joseph R. "The Role Of Cost In The Minimum Pricing Of Railroad Services: A Comment," JOB, 1963, v36(3), 336-337.

Rose, Lawrence C. (Smith, Dean G. and Lawrence C. Rose. "The Effects Of Insurance Policy Limits On Product Choice," JRI, 1986, v53(3), 514-520.)

Rose, Michael. (Finnerty, John D. and Michael Rose. "Arbitrage-Free Spread: A Consistent Measure Of Relative Value," JPM, 1991, v17(3), 65-81.)

Rose, Peter S. and Lacy H. Hunt, II. "The Relative Importance Of Monetary And Fiscal Variables In Determining Price Level Movements: Reply," JOF, 1973, v28(1), 191-193.

Rose, Peter S. and Lacy H. Hunt, II. "The Relative Importance Of Monetary And Fiscal Variables In Determining Price Level Movements: A Note," JOF, 1971, v26(1), 31-37.

Rose, Peter S. "Banker Attitudes Toward The Federal Reserve System: Survey Results," JBR, 1977-78, v8(2), 77-84.

Rose, Peter S. "Diversification Of The Banking Firm," FR, 1989, v24(2), 251-280.

Rose, Peter S. "The Pattern Of Bank Holding Company Acquisitions," JBR, 1976-77, v7(3), 236-240.

Rose, Peter S. (Fraser, Donald R., Wallace Phillips, Jr. and Peter S. Rose. "A Canonical Analysis Of Bank Performance," JFQA, 1974, v9(2), 287-295.)

Rose, Peter S. (Fraser, Donald R. and Peter S. Rose. "Bank Entry And Bank Performance," JOF, 1972, v27(1), 65-78.)

Rose, Peter S. (Fraser, Donald R. and Peter S. Rose. "Commercial Bank Adjustments To Monetary Policy: The Peed Of Response," JBR, 1977-78, v8(4), 233-241.)

Rose, Peter S. (Fraser, Donald R. and Peter S. Rose. "More On Banking Structure And Performance: The Evidence From Texas," JFQA, 1971, v6(1), 601-611.)

Rose, Peter S. (Fraser, Donald R. and Peter S. Rose. "Short-Run Bank Portfolio Behavior: An Examination Of Selected Liquid Assets," JOF, 1973, v28(2), 531-537.)

Rose, Peter S. (Fraser, Donald R., Peter S. Rose and Gary L. Schugart. "Federal Reserve Membership And Bank Performance: The Evidence From Texas," JOF, 1975, v30(2), 641-658.)

Rose, Peter S. (Giroux, Gary A. and Peter S. Rose. "An Update Of Bank Planning Systems: Results Of A Nationwide Survey Of Large U.S. Banks," JBR, 1984-85, v15(3), 136-147.)

Rose, Peter S. (Rose, John T. and Peter S. Rose. "The Burden Of Federal Reserve System Membership: A Review Of The Evidence," JBF, 1979, v3(4), 331-346.)

Rose, Peter S., James W. Kolari and Kenneth W. Riener. "A National Survey Study Of Bank Services And Prices Arrayed By Size And Structure," JBR, 1985-86, v16(2), 72-85.

Rose, Terry L. and John H. Hand. "The Effects Of Risk Reduction Inherent In Universal Life Insurance: Comment," JRI, 1981, v48(4), 682-689.

Rose, Terry and Robert I. Mehr. "Flexible Income Programming," JRI, 1980, v47(1), 44-60.

Rose, Terry and Robert I. Mehr. "A Computer Model For Flexible Income Programming," JRI, 1981, v48(2), 308.

Rose, Terry and Robert I. Mehr. "Flexible Income Programming: Reply," JRI, 1982, v49(2), 297-299.

Rosen, Charles S. (Schneller, Meir I. and Charles S. Rosen. "Time-Variance Relationship: Evidence On Correlation In Common Stock Returns: Comment," JOF, 1979, v34(5), 1271-1272.)

Rosen, Corey M. "The Effect Of Employee Stock Ownership Plans On Corporate Profits: Comment," JRI, 1983, v50(3), 493-494.

Rosen, Corey. "The Record Of Employee Ownership," FM, 1990, v19(1), 39-47.

Rosen, Harvey S. (Eaton, Jonathan and Harvey S. Rosen. "Agency, Delayed Compensation, And The Structure Of Executive Remuneration," JOF, 1983, v38(5), 1489-1505.)

Rosen, Jeffrey S. "The Impact Of The Futures Trading Act of 1982 Upon Commodity Regulation," JFM, 1983, v3(3), 235-258.

Rosen, Kenneth T. and David E. Bloom. "A Microeconomic Model Of Federal Home Loan Mortgage Corporate Activity," JOF, 1980, v35(4), 959-971.

Rosen, Kenneth T. and Larry Katz. "Money Market Mutual Funds: An Experiment In Ad Hoc Deregulation: A Note," JOF, 1983, v38(3), 1011-1017.

Rosen, Kenneth T. "A Regional Model Of Multifamily Housing Starts," AREUEA, 1979, v7(1), 63-76.

Rosen, Kenneth T. "Toward A Model Of The Office Building Sector," AREUEA, 1984, v12(3), 261-269.

Rosen, Kenneth T. (Jaffee, Dwight M. and Kenneth T. Rosen. "Estimates Of The Effectiveness Of Stabilization Policies For The Mortgage And Housing Markets," JOF, 1978, v33(3), 933-946.)

Rosen, Kenneth T. (Manski, Charles F. and Kenneth T. Rosen. "The Implications Of Demand Instability For The Behavior Of Firms: The Case Of Residential Construction," AREUEA, 1978, v6(2), 204-226.)

Rosen, Kenneth T. and Lawrence F. Katz. "Growth Management And Land Use Controls: The San Francisco Bay Area Experience," AREUEA, 1981, v9(4), 321-344.

Rosen, Kenneth T. and Lawrence B. Smith. "The Resale Housing Market," AREUEA, 1986, v14(4), 510-524.

Rosen, Kenneth. (Jaffee, Dwight and Kenneth Rosen. "The Changing Liability Structure Of Savings And Loan Associations," AREUEA, 1980, v8(1), 33-49.)

Rosen, Richard J., Peter Lloyd-Davies and David B. Humphrey. "New Banking Powers: A Portfolio Analysis Of Bank Investment In Real Estate," JBF, 1989, v13(3), 355-366.

Rosen, Sherwin. "The Value Of Changes In Life-Expectancy," JRU, 1988, v1(3), 285-304.

Rosen, Uzi. (Nitzan, Shmuel and Uzi Rosen. "A Note On Reinsurance And The Technology Of Risk," JRI, 1977, v44(3), 403-410.)

Rosenbaum, David I. (Rejda, George E. and David I. Rosenbaum. "Unemployment Insurance And Full-Cost Experience Rating: The Impact On Seasonal Hiring," JRI, 1990, v57(3), 519-529.)

Rosenberg, Barr and Andrew Rudd. "Factor Related And Specific Returns Of Common Stocks: Serial Correlation And Market Efficiency," JOF, 1982, v37(2), 543-554.

Rosenberg, Barr and James A. Ohlson. "The Stationary Distribution Of Returns And Portfolio Separation In Capital Markets: A Fundamental Contradiction," JFQA, 1976, v11(3), 393-402.

Rosenberg, Barr and James Guy. "Beta And Investment Fundamentals," FAJ, 1976, v32(3), 60-72.

Rosenberg, Barr and James Guy. "Beta And Investment Fundamentals - II," FAJ, 1976, v32(4),62-70.

Rosenberg, Barr and Michel Houglet. "Error Rates In CRSP And COMPUSTAT Data Bases And Their Implications," JOF, 1974, v29(4), 1303-1310.

Rosenberg, Barr and Walt McKibben. "The Prediction Of Systematic And Specific Risk In Common Stocks," JFQA, 1973, v8(2), 317-333.

Rosenberg, Barr and Vinay Marathe. "Test Of Capital Asset Pricing Hypotheses," RIF, 1979, v1, 115-224.

Rosenberg, Barr, Kenneth Reid and Ronald Lanstein. "Persuasive Evidence Of Market Inefficiency," JPM, 1984-85, v11(3), 9-17.

Rosenberg, Barr. "Extra-Market Components Of Covariance In Security Returns," JFQA, 1974, v9(2), 263-273.

Rosenberg, Barr. "How Active Should Your Portfolio Be?," FAJ, 1979, v35(1), 49-62.

Rosenberg, Barr. "Prediction Of Common Stock Betas," JPM, 1984-85, v11(2), 5-14.

Rosenberg, Barr. "Prediction Of Common Stock Investment Risk," JPM, 1984-85, v11(1), 44-53.

Rosenberg, Barr. "Statistical Analysis Of Price Series Obscured By Averaging Measures," JFQA, 1971, v6(4), 1083-1094.

Rosenberg, Barr. "The Capital Asset Pricing Model And The Market Model," JPM, 1980-81, v7(2), 5-16.

Rosenberg, Barr. "The Current State And Future Of Investment Research," FAJ, 1982, v38(1), 43-50.

Rosenberg, Barr. (Errunza, Vihang R. and Barr Rosenberg. "Investment In Developed And Less Developed Countries," JFQA, 1982, v17(5), 741-762.)

Rosenberg, Barr. (Fouse, William L., William W. Jahnke and Barr Rosenberg. "Is Beta Phlogiston?," FAJ, 1974, v30(1), 70-80.)

Rosenberg, Barr. (Ohlson, James and Barr Rosenberg. "Systematic Risk Of The CRSP Equal-Weighted Common Stock Index: A History Estimated By Stochastic-Parameter Regression," JOB, 1982, v55(1), 121-146.)

Rosenberg, Barr. (Rudd, Andrew and Barr Rosenberg. "Market Model In Investment Management," JPM, 1980-81, v7(2), 597-607.)

Rosenberg, Claude, Jr. and Paul Sack. "The High Risks Of Open-End Real Estate Funds," JPM, 1975-76, v2(1), 55-57.

Rosenberg, Marvin. "Institutions And Market Liquidity," FAJ, 1974, v30(2), 53-59.

Rosenberg, Michael R. "A Framework For Formulating International Fixed-Income Strategy," JPM, 1990, v16(4), 70-76.

Rosenberg, Moses K. "Historical Perspective Of The Development Of Rate Regulation Of Title Insurance," JRI, 1977, v44(2), 193-210.

Rosenberg, Moses K. (Roussel, H. Lee and Moses K. Rosenberg. "The High Price Of 'Reform': Title Insurance Rates And The Benefits Of Rating Bureaus," JRI, 1981, v48(4), 638-648.)

Rosenberg, Richard M. and Jason H. P. Kravitt. "Legal Issues In Securitization," JACF, 1988, v1(3), 61-68.

Rosenberg, Samuel D. "Credit Unions In North Carolina," JOB, 1950, v23(3), 182-190.

Rosenberg, Sidney B. and John B. Corgel. "Agency Costs In Property Management Contracts," AREUEA, 1990, v18(2), 184-201.

Rosenbloom, Jerry S. "1981 Presidential Address - Is ARIA Facing A Mid-Life Crisis?," JRI, 1982, v49(1), 8-18.

Rosenbloom, Jerry S. "Fixed Dollar Tax Deferred Annuities - An Evaluation," JRI, 1978, v45(4), 611-634.

Rosenbloom, Jerry S. "Programmed Learning And The C.L.U. Curriculum," JRI, 1970, v37(3), 451-457.

Rosenbloom, Jerry S. and Gary K. Stone. "Social Aspects Of The Rate Structure Of Medical Malpractice Insurance," JRI, 1978, v45(1), 53-64.

Rosenblum, Harvey. (Kaufman, George G., Larry R. Mote and Harvey Rosenblum. "Consequences Of Deregulation For Commercial Banking," JOF, 1984, v39(3), 789-803.)

Rosenblum, Harvey. (Kaufman, George, Larry Mote and Harvey Rosenblum. "Implications Of Deregulation For Product Lines And Geographical Markets Of Financial Institutions," JBR, 1983-84, v14(1), 8-20.)

Rosenfeld, Ahron. (Lewellen, Wilbur, Claudio Loderer and Ahron Rosenfeld. "Mergers, Executive Risk Reduction, And Stockholder Wealth," JFQA, 1989, v24(4), 459-472.)

Rosenfeld, Eric R. (Jarrow, Robert A. and Eric R. Rosenfeld. "Jump Risks And The Intertemporal Capital Asset Pricing Model," JOB, 1984, v57(3), 337-352.)

Rosenfeld, Eric R. (Marsh, Terry A. and Eric R. Rosenfeld. "Non-Trading Market Making, And Estimates Of Stock Price Volatility," JFEC, 1986, v15(3), 359-372.)

Rosenfeld, Eric R. (Marsh, Terry A. and Eric R. Rosenfeld. "Stochastic Processes For Interest Rates And Equilibrium Bond Prices," JOF, 1983, v38(2), 635-646.)

Rosenfeld, Eric. (Jones, E. Philip, Scott P. Mason and Eric Rosenfeld. "Contingent Claims Analysis Of Corporate Capital Structures: An Empirical Investigation," JOF, 1984, v39(3), 611-625.)

Rosenfeld, James D. "Additional Evidence On The Relation Between Divestiture Announcements And Shareholder Wealth," JOF, 1984, v39(5), 1437-1448.

Rosenfeld, James D. "Returns On High-Quality And Low-Quality Preferred Stocks In Periods Of Common-Stock Dividend Reductions," JFR, 1984, v7(3), 255-258.

Rosenfeld, James D. (Miles, James A. and James D. Rosenfeld. "The Effect Of Voluntary Spin-off Announcements On Shareholder Wealth," JOF, 1983, v38(5), 1597-1606.)

Rosenfeld, James. "The Effect Of Common-Stock Dividend Reductions On The Returns Of Nonconvertible Preferred Stocks: A Note," JOF, 1983, v38(3), 1019-1024.

Rosenfeld, James. (Klein, April and James Rosenfeld. "Targeted Share Repurchases And Top Management Changes," JFEC, 1988, v20(1), 493-506.)

Rosenfeld, James. (Klein, April and James Rosenfeld. "The Impact Of Targeted Share Repurchases On The Wealth Of Non-Participating Shareholders," JFR, 1988, v11(2), 89-98.)

Rosenfeld, James. (Klein, April and James Rosenfeld. "The Influence Of Market Conditions On Event-Study Residuals," JFQA, 1987, v22(3), 345-352.)

Rosenfeld, Lawrence. "Electronic Computers And Their Place In Securities Analyses," FAJ, 1957, v13(1), 51-54.

Rosenman, Robert E. (Helms, Billy P., Fred R. Kaen and Robert E. Rosenman. "Memory In Commodity Futures Contracts," JFM, 1984, v4(4), 559-567.)

Rosenstein, Stuart and David F. Rush. "The Stock Return Performance Of Corporations That Are Partially Owned By Other Corporations," JFR, 1990, v13(1), 39-52.

Rosenstein, Stuart and Jeffrey G. Wyatt. "Outside Directors, Board Independence, And Shareholder Wealth," JFEC, 1990, v26(2), 175-192.

Rosenthal, James A. (Ocampo, Juan M. and James A. Rosenthal. "The Future Of Securitization And The Financial Services Industry," JACF, 1988, v1(3), 90-100.)

Rosenthal, James A. and Juan M. Ocampo. "Analyzing The Economic Benefits Of Securitized Credit," JACF, 1988, v1(3), 32-44.

Rosenthal, Leonard and Timothy G. Sullivan. "Some Estimates Of The Impact Of Corporate Diversification On The Valuation And Leverage Of USA Firms: Estimates From 1972 Data," JBFA, 1985, v12(2), 275-284.

Rosenthal, Leonard and Colin Young. "The Seemingly Anomalous Price Behavior Of Royal Dutch/Shell And Unilever N.V./PLC," JFEC, 1990, v26(1), 123-142.

Rosenthal, Leonard. "An Empirical Test Of The Efficiency Of The ADR Market," JBF, 1983, v7(1), 17-30.

Rosenthal, Leonard. (Johnson, James M., Robert A. Pari and Leonard Rosenthal. "The Impact Of In-Substance Defeasance On Bondholder And Shareholder Wealth," JOF, 1989, v44(4), 1049-1058.)

Rosenthal, Leonard. (Kane, Alex and Leonard Rosenthal. "International Interest Rates And Inflationary Expectations," JIMF, 1982, v1(1), 97-110.)

Rosenthal, Leonard. (Kane, Alex, Leonard Rosenthal and Greta Ljung. "Tests Of The Fisher Hypothesis With International Data: Theory And Evidence," JOF, 1983, v38(2), 539-551.)

Rosenthal, Leonard. (Samuelson, William and Leonard Rosenthal. "Price Movements As Indicators Of Tender Offer Success," JOF, 1986, v41(2), 481-500.)

Rosenzweig, Jeffrey A. (Koch, Paul D., Jeffrey A. Rosenzweig and Joseph A. Whitt, Jr. "The Dynamic Relationship Between The Dollar And US Prices: An Intensive Empirical Investigation," JIMF, 1988, v7(2), 181-204.)

Rosenzweig, Adelle R. "The Random Walk Hypothesis, Domestic Borrowing, And Others: A Glossary Of Contemporary Financial Terms," JOF, 1973, v28(5), 1371-1372.

Rosett, Joshua G. "Do Union Wealth Concessions Explain Takeover Premiums? The Evidence On Contract Wages," JFEC, 1990, v27(1), 263-282.

Rosinoff, Bruce. (Lieber, Harvey and Bruce Rosinoff. "Evaluating The State's Role In Water Pollution Control," AREUEA, 1973, v1(2), 73-87.)

Ross, Carl D. "Is It Safe To Invest In Mexico?," FAJ, 1959, v15(4),67-70.

Ross, Carl D. "The Changing Mexican Market," FAJ, 1964, v20(3), 149-153.

Ross, Carl D. "The Mexican Stock Market," FAJ, 1962, v18(3), 57-64.

Ross, Caroline. (Friedman, Bernard, Caroline Ross and Glen Misek. "On The Surprisingly Low Cost Of State Catastrophic Health Insurance Programs," JRI, 1984, v51(1), 31-48.)

Ross, H. Laurence. "Auto Insurance Reform: Comment," JRI, 1971, v38(2), 303-304.

Ross, H. Laurence. "Basic Protection For The Traffic Victim," JRI, 1967, v34(4), 647-652.

Ross, Ivan. "Self-Concept And Brand Preference," JOB, 1971, v44(1), 38-50.

Ross, Knud. (Feder, Gershon and Knud Ross. "Risk Assessments And Risk Premiums In The Eurodollar Market," JOF, 1982, v37(3), 679-691.)

Ross, Knud. (Feder, Gershon, Richard Just and Knud Ross. "Projecting Debt Servicing Capacity Of Developing Countries," JFQA, 1981, v16(5), 651-669.)

Ross, Lawrence. "Paper Industry - Wood Costs," FAJ, 1967, v23(5), 71-72.

Ross, Leonard. (Tobin, James and Leonard Ross. "A Reply To Gordon Tullock," JMCB, 1972, v4(2), 431-436.)

Ross, Marc. "Capital Budgeting Practices Of Twelve Large Manufacturers," FM, 1986, v15(4), 15-22.

Ross, Stephen A. "A Reply to Dhrymes: APT Is Empirically Relevant," JPM, 1984-85, v11(1), 54-56.

Ross, Stephen A. "A Simple Approach To The Valuation OF Risky Streams," JOB, 1978, v51(3), 453-476.

Ross, Stephen A. "Debt And Taxes And Uncertainty," JOF, 1985, v40(3), 637-657.

Ross, Stephen A. "Information And Volatility: The No-Arbitrage Martingale Approach To Timing And Resolution Irrelevancy," JOF, 1989, v44(1), 1-18.

Ross, Stephen A. "Innovation In The Financial Markets," RDIBF, 1991, v4/5, 81-91.

Ross, Stephen A. "On The Empirical Relevance Of APT: Reply," JPM, 1984-85, v11(4), 72-73.

Ross, Stephen A. "Portfolio Turnpike Theorems For Constant Policies," JFEC, 1974, v1(2), 171-198.

Ross, Stephen A. "Presidential Address: Institutional Markets, Financial Marketing, And Financial Innovation," JOF, 1989, v44(3), 541-556.

Ross, Stephen A. "The Capital Asset Pricing Model (CAPM), Short-Sale Restrictions And Related Issues," JOF, 1977, v32(1), 177-183.

Ross, Stephen A. (Admati, Anat R. and Stephen A. Ross. "Corrigendum," JOB, 1986, v59(2), Part 1, 367.)

Ross, Stephen A. (Admati, Anat R. and Stephen A. Ross. "Measuring Investment Performance In A Rational Expectations Equilibrium Model," JOB, 1985, v58(1), 1-26.)

Ross, Stephen A. (Admati, Anat R., Sudipto Bhattacharya, Paul Pfleiderer and Stephen A. Ross. "On Timing And Selectivity," JOF, 1986, v41(3), 715-729.)

Ross, Stephen A. (Chen, Nai-Fu, Richard Roll and Stephen A. Ross. "Economic Forces And The Stock Market," JOB, 1986, v59(3), 383-404.)

Ross, Stephen A. (Cox, John C., Jonathan E. Ingersoll, Jr., and Stephen A. Ross. "Duration And The Measurement Of Basis Risk," JOB, 1979, v52(1), 51-62.)

Ross, Stephen A. (Cox, John C., Stephen A. Ross and Mark Rubinstein. "Option Pricing: A Simplified Approach," JFEC, 1979, v7(3), 229-264.)

Ross, Stephen A. (Cox, John C. and Stephen A. Ross. "The Valuation Of Options For Alternative Stochastic Processes," JFEC, 1976, v3(1/2), 145-166.)

Ross, Stephen A. (Cox, John C., Jonathan E. Ingersoll, Jr. and Stephen A. Ross. "The Relation Between Forward Prices And Futures Prices," JFEC, 1981, v9(4), 321-346.)

Ross, Stephen A. (Cox, John C., Jonathan E. Ingersoll, Jr. and Stephen A. Ross. "A Re-examination Of Traditional Hyptheses About The Term Structure Of Interest Rates," JOF, 1981, v36(4), 769-799.)

Ross, Stephen A. (Cox, John C. and Stephen A. Ross. "A Survey Of Some New Results In Financial Option Pricing Theory," JOF, 1976, v31(2), 383-402.)

Ross, Stephen A. (Cox, John C., Jonathan E. Ingersoll, Jr. and Stephen A. Ross. "An Analysis Of Variable Rate Loan Contracts," JOF, 1980, v35(2), 389-403.)

Ross, Stephen A. (Dybvig, Philip H. and Stephen A. Ross. "Performance Measurement Using Differential Information And A Security Market Line," JOF, 1985, v40(2), 383-399.)

Ross, Stephen A. (Dybvig, Philip H. and Stephen A. Ross. "Tax Clienteles And Asset Pricing," JOF, 1986, v41(3), 751-771.)

Ross, Stephen A. (Dybvig, Philip H. and Stephen A. Ross. "Yes, The APT Is Testable," JOF, 1985, v40(4), 1173-1188.)

Ross, Stephen A. (Dybvig, Philip H. and Stephen A. Ross. "The Analytics Of Performance Measurement Using A Security Market Line," JOF, 1985, v40(2), 401-416.)

Ross, Stephen A. (Firstenberg, Paul M., Stephen A. Ross and Randall C. Zisler. "Real Estate: The Whole Story," JPM, 1987-88, v14(3), 22-34.)

Ross, Stephen A. (Kraus, Alan and Stephen A. Ross. "The Determination Of Fair Profits For The Property-Liability Insurance Firm," JOF, 1982, v37(4), 1015-1028.)

Ross, Stephen A. (Lindenberg, Eric B. and Stephen A. Ross. "Tobin's q Ratio And Industrial Organization," JOB, 1981, v54(1), 1-32.)

Ross, Stephen A. (Roll, Richard and Stephen A. Ross. "An Empirical Investigation Of The Arbitrage Pricing Theory," JOF, 1980, v35(5), 1073-1103.)

Ross, Stephen A. (Roll, Richard and Stephen A. Ross. "A Critical Reexamination Of The Empirical Evidence On The Arbitrage Pricing Theory: A Reply," JPM, 1984, v39(2), 347-350.)

Ross, Stephen A. (Roll, Richard and Stephen A. Ross. "A Note On Qualitative Results For Investment Proportions: Comment," JFEC, 1977, v5(2), 265-268.)

Ross, Stephen. "The Current Status Of The Capital Asset Pricing Model," JOF, 1978, v33(3), 885-901.

Ross, Stephen. "Some Notes On Financial Incentive-Signalling Models, Activity Choice And Risk Preferences," JOF, 1978, v33(3), 777-794.

Ross

Ross, Stephen A. (Roll, Richard and Stephen A. Ross. "The Arbitrage Pricing Theory Approach To Strategic Portfolio Planning," FAJ, 1984, v40(3), 14-26.)

Ross, Susan. (Goodman, Laurie S., Susan Ross and Frederick Schmidt. "Are Foreign Currency Options Overvalued? The Early Experience Of The Philadelphia Stock Exchange," JFM, 1985, v5(3), 349-359.)

Ross, Thomas W. "The Costs Of Regulating Price Differences," JOB, 1986, v59(1), 143-156.

Rossana, Robert J. (Maccini, Louis J. and Robert J. Rossana. "Joint Production, Quasi-Fixed Factors Of Production, And Investment In Finished Goods Inventory," JMCB, 1984, v16(2), 218-236.)

Rossi, S. (Papadia, F. and S. Rossi. "More On Monetarist Arithmetic," JBF, 1990, v14(1), 145-154.)

Rossi, Salvatore. (Papadia, Francesco and Salvatore Rossi. "Are Asymmetric Exchange Controls Effective?," JIMF, 1991, v10(1), 149-160.)

Rossiter, Lewis F., Killard W. Adamche and Tamara Faulknier. "A Blended Sector Rate Adjustment For The Medicare AAPCC When Risk-Based Market Penetration Is High," JRI, 1990, v57(2), 220-239.

Rotch, William. "Venture Capital Financing," FAJ, 1968, v24(5), 141-147.

Rotemberg, Julio J. "Supply Shocks, Sticky Prices, And Monetary Policy," JMCB, 1983, v15(4), 489-498.

Rotemberg, Julio J. (Poterba, James M. and Julio J. Rotemberg. "Inflation And Taxation With Optimizing Governments," JMCB, 1990, v22(1), 1-18.)

Rotemberg, Julio J. and David S. Scharfstein. "Shareholder-Value Maximization And Product-Market Competition," RFS, 1990, v3(3), 367-392.

Rotenberg, W. (Krinsky, I. and W. Rotenberg. "Signalling And The Valuation Of Unseasoned New Issues Revisited," JFQA, 1989, v24(2), 257-265.)

Roth, Alvin E. "Risk Aversion And The Relationship Between Nash's Solution And Subgame Perfect Equilibrium Of Sequential Bargaining," JRU, 1989, v2(4), 353-366.

Roth, Alvin E. (Kihlstrom, Richard E. and Alvin E. Roth. "Risk Aversion And The Negotiation Of Insurance Contracts," JRI, 1982, v49(3), 372-387.)

Roth, Alvin E. (Murnighan, J. Keith, Alvin E. Roth and Francoise Schoumaker. "Risk Aversion In Bargaining: An Experimental Study," JRU, 1988, v1(1), 101-124.)

Roth, Kendall. (Schmit, Joan T. and Kendall Roth. "Cost Effectiveness Of Risk Management Practices," JRI, 1990, v57(3), 455-470.)

Roth, Rosalind. (Montgomery, Royal E., Irwin M. Stelzer, and Rosalind Roth. "Collective Bargaining Over Profit Sharing: The Automobile Union's Effort To Extend Its Frontier Of Control," JOB, 1958, v31(4), 318-334.)

Rothberg, James P., Frank E. Nothaft and Stuart A. Gabriel. "On The Determinants Of Yield Spreads Between Mortgage Pass-Through And Treasury Securities," JREFEC, 1989, v2(4), 301-316

Rothenberg, Jerome. "Welfare Implications Of Alternative Methods Of Financing," JRI, 1951, v18, 96-106.

Rothmeier, Steven G. "The Effect Of Financial Leverage On Air Carrier Earnings: Comment," FM, 1980, v9(1), 88-89.

Rothstein, Marvin. "On Geometric And Arithmetic Portfolio Performance Indexes," JFQA, 1972, v7(4), 1983-1992.

Rothstein, Marvin. "The Geometric Index Revisited: A Rejoinder," JFQA, 1974, v9(3), 505-506.

Rothstein, Morton. "The Rejection And Acceptance Of A Marketing Innovation: Hedging In The Late 19th Century," RFM, 1983, v2(2), 200-214.

Rotnem, Ralph A. "The European Field Trip," FAJ, 1959, v15(3), 9-12.

Rotnem, Ralph. "Methods For Determining Stock Market Trends," FAJ, 1946, v2(3), 12-21.

Rottenberg, Simon. "The Distribution Of 'Chit Fund' Gains And Losses," JOB, 1968, v41(2), 246-250.

Rottenberg, Simon. "The Irrelevance Of Union Apprentice/ Journeyman Ratios," JOB, 1961, v34(3), 384-386.

Rottman, Dick L. "Analysis Of Perpetual Insurance," JRI, 1969, v36(3), 365-382.

Rottman, Dick L. "Analysis Of Perpetual Insurance: Reply," JRI, 1970, v37(3), 482-484.

Rottman, Dick L. "Corporate Risk Manager's Contribution To Profit: Comment," JRI, 1971, v38(2), 299-302.

Rottman, Dick L. "The Long Term Crisis In Life Insurance: Comment," JRI, 1968, v35(1), 148-152.

Rottman, Dick L. (Hustedt, W. J. and Dick L. Rottman. "Insurance Professors' Relationships With Risk Managers," JRI, 1969, v36(4), 643-647.)

Rottman, Dick L. (Wood, Glenn L. and Dick L. Rottman. "Policy Loan Interest Rates: A Critical Evaluation: Reply," JRI, 1972, v39(1), 160-162.)

Rottman, Rich L. (Wood, Glenn L. and Rich L. Rottman. "Policy Loan Interest Rates: An Critical Evaluation," JRI, 1970, v37(4), 555-566.)

Roubini, Nouriel. "Economic And Political Determinants Of Budget Deficits In Developing Countries," JIMF, 1991, v10(Supp), S49-S72.

Roulac, Stephen E. and Donald A. King, Jr. "Institutional Strategies For Real Estate Investment," JPM, 1976-77, v3(4), 58-65.

Roulac, Stephen E. "Can Real Estate Returns Outperform Common Stock?," JPM, 1975-76, v2(2), 26-43.

Roulac, Stephen E. "How To Structure Real Estate Investment Management," JPM, 1981-82, v8(1), 32-35.

Roulac, Stephen E. "Real Estate Securities Valuation," JPM, 1987-88, v14(3), 35-39.

Roulac, Stephen E. "Real Estate Appraisals: Critique And Analysis," JPM, 1978-79, v5(2), 69-74.

Roulac, Stephen E. "Using Live Cases In Teaching Finance," JFED, 1976, v5, 61-64.

Roulac, Stephen. "The Use Of The Case Method In Financial Education," JFED, 1975, v4, 63-71.

Roumi, Ebrahim. (Schnabel, Jacques A. and Ebrahim Roumi. "Corporate Insurance And The Underinvestment Problem: An Extension," JRI, 1989, v56(1), 155-159.)

Roussakis, Emmanuel. (Karels, Gordon V., Arun J. Prakash and Emmanuel Roussakis. "The Relationship Between Bank Capital Adequacy And Market Measures Of Risk," JBFA, 1989, v16(5), 663-674.)

Roussel, H. Lee and Moses K. Rosenberg. "The High Price Of 'Reform': Title Insurance Rates And The Benefits Of Rating Bureaus," JRI, 1981, v48(4), 638-648.

Rousslang, Donald J. (Feinberg, Robert M. and Donald J. Rousslang. "The Economic Effects Of Intellectual Property Right Infringements," JOB, 1990, v63(1), Part 1, 79-90.)

Roux, F. J. P. and B. P. Gilbertson. "The Behaviour Of Share Prices On The Johannesburg Stock Exchange," JBFA, 1978, v5(2), 223-232.

Rovelli, R. (Corradi, V., M. Galeotti and R. Rovelli. "A Cointegration Analysis Of The Relationship Between Bank Reserves, Deposits And Loans: The Case Of Italy, 1965-1987," JBF, 1990, v14(1), 199-214.)

Rovira, Carlos E. (Oldfield, George S. and Carlos E. Rovira. "Futures Contract Options," JFM, 1984, v4(4), 479-490.)

Rowan, Richard L. "Discrimination And Apprentice Regulation In The Building Trades," JOB, 1967, v40(4), 435-447.

Rowan, Richard L. (Northrup, Herbert R. and Richard L. Rowan. "State Seizure In Public Interest Disputes," JOB, 1963, v36(2), 210-227.)

Rowell, Dexter R. (Francis, Jack Clark and Dexter R. Rowell. "A Simultaneous Equation Model Of The Firm For Financial Analysis And Planning," FM, 1978, v7(1), 29-44.)

Rowell, Dexter R. (Grablowsky, Bernie J. and Dexter R. Rowell. "The Market For Finance Majors: The Myths And Realities Reconsidered," JFED, 1980, v9, 33-41.)

Rowen, Henry S. "Problems Of American Society," FAJ, 1967, v23(5), 13-16.

Roy, Asim. "Optimal Acquisition Fraction And A Theory For Partial Acquisitions," JBFA, 1988, v15(4), 543-556.

Roy, Asim. "Partial Acquisition Strategies For Business Combinations," FM, 1985, v14(2), 16-23.

Roy, J. (Barrett, M. E. and J. Roy. "Financial Reporting In France," FAJ, 1976, v32(1), 39-49.)

Roy, Tapan S. and Robert Charles Witt. "Leverage, Exposure Ratios And The Optimal Rate Of Return On Capital For The Insurer," JRI, 1976, v43(1), 53-72.

Royer, Marc H. "Simulation At Banque De Bruxelles," JBR, 1974-75, v5(4), 237-245.

Rozeff, Michael S. and William R. Kinney, Jr. "Capital Market Seasonality: The Case Of Stock Returns," JFEC, 1976, v3(4), 379-402.

Rozeff, Michael S. "Dividend Yields Are Equity Risk Premiums," JPM, 1984-85, v11(1), 68-75.

Rozeff, Michael S. "Growth, Beta And Agency Costs As Determinants Of Dividend Payout Ratios," JFR, 1982, v5(3), 249-259.

Rozeff, Michael S. "Money And Stock Prices: Market Efficiency And The Lag In Effect Of Monetary Policy," JFEC, 1974, v1(3), 245-302.

Rozeff, Michael S. "The Association Between Firm Risk And Wealth Transfers Due To Inflation," JFQA, 1977, v12(2), 151-163.

Rozeff, Michael S. "The Money Supply And The Stock Market," FAJ, 1975, v31(5), 18-20,22-24,26,76.

Rozeff, Michael S. "The Three-Phase Dividend Discount Model And The ROPE Model," JPM, 1990, v16(2), 36-42.

Rozeff, Michael S. (Bowlin, Lyle and Michael S. Rozeff. "Do Specialists' Short Sales Predict Returns?," JPM, 1986-87, v13(3), 59-63.)

Rozeff, Michael S. (Brown, Lawrence D. and Michael S. Rozeff. "The Superiority Of Analyst Forecasts As Measures Of Expectations: Evidence From Earnings," JOF, 1978, v33(1), 1-16.)

Rozeff, Michael S. (Brown, Lawrence D. and Michael S. Rozeff. "Analysts Can Forecast Accurately!," JPM, 1979-80, v6(3), 31-34.)

Rozeff, Michael S. (Cook, Thomas J. and Michael S. Rozeff. "Coskewness, Dividend Yield And Capital Asset Pricing," JFR, 1984, v7(3), 231-241.)

Rozeff, Michael S. (Cook, Thomas J. and Michael S. Rozeff. "Size And Earnings/Price Ratio Anomalies: One Effect Or Two?," JFQA, 1984, v19(4), 449-466.)

Rozeff, Michael S. (Furtado, Eugene P. H. and Michael S. Rozeff. "The Wealth Effects Of Company Initiated Management Changes," JFEC, 1987, v18(1), 147-160.)

Rozeff, Michael S. (Linn, Scott C. and Michael S. Rozeff. "The Effect Of Voluntary Spin-Offs On Stock Prices: The Anergy Hypothesis," AFPAF, 1985, v1(1), 265-292.)

Rozeff, Michael S. and Mir A. Zaman. "Market Efficiency And Insider Trading: New Evidence," JOB, 1988, v61(1), 25-44.

Rozeff, Michael. (Stevenson, Richard A. and Michael Rozeff. "Are The Backwaters Of The Market Efficient?," JPM, 1978-79, v5(3), 31-34.)

Rozelle, James P. and Bruce D. Fielitz. "Skewness In Common Stock Returns," FR, 1980, v15(3), 1-23.

Rozelle, James P. and Bruce D. Fielitz. "Stationarity Of Common Stock Returns," JFR, 1980, v3(3), 229-242.

Rozental, Alek A. "Variable-Return Bonds - The French Experience," JOF, 1959, v14(4), 520-530.

Rua, Ernest J., Jr. "Analyzing A Motor Carrier's Balance Sheet," FAJ, 1966, v22(3), 57-61.

Ruback, Richard S. "Assessing Competition In The Market For Corporate Acquisitions," JFEC, 1983, v11(1), 141-153.

Ruback, Richard S. "Calculating The Market Value Of Riskless Cash Flows," JFEC, 1986, v15(3), 323-340.

Ruback, Richard S. "Coercive Dual-Class Exchange Offers," JFEC, 1988, v20(1/2), 153-174.

Ruback, Richard S. "The Cities Service Takeover: A Case Study," JOF, 1983, v38(2), 319-330.

Ruback, Richard S. "The Effect Of Discretionary Price Control Decisions On Equity Values," JFEC, 1982, v10(1), 83-105.

Ruback, Richard S. (Baldwin, Carliss Y. and Richard S. Ruback. "Inflation, Uncertainty And Investment," JOF, 1986, v41(3), 657-667.)

Ruback, Richard S. (Jensen, Michael C. and Richard S. Ruback. "The Market For Corporate Control," JFEC, 1983, v11(1), 5-50.)

Ruback, Richard S. (Mikkelson, Wayne H. and Richard S. Ruback. "An Empirical Analysis Of The Interfirm Equity Investment Process," JFEC, 1985, v14(4), 523-553.)

Ruback, Richard. (Dodd, Peter and Richard Ruback. "Tender Offers And Stockholder Returns: An Empirical Analysis," *JFEC*, 1977, v5(3), 351-373.)

Rubens, Jack A. (Webb, James R. and Jack A. Rubens. "How Much In Real Estate? A Surprising Answer," *JPM*, 1986-87, v13(3), 10-14.)

Rubens, Jack H. (Webb, James R. and Jack H. Rubens. "Portfolio Considerations In The Valuation Of Real Estate," *AREUEA*, 1986, v14(3), 465-495.)

Rubens, Jack H. (Webb, James R. and Jack H. Rubens. "The Effect Of Alternative Return Measures On Restricted Mixed-Asset Portfolios," *AREUEA*, 1988, v16(2), 123-137.)

Rubens, Jack H. (Webb, James R. and Jack H. Rubens. "Tax Rates And Implicit Rates Of Return On Owner-Occupied Single-Family Housing," *JRER*, 1987, v2(2), 11-28.)

Rubens, Jack H. (Webb, James R. and Jack H. Rubens. "Tax Rates And Implicit Rates Of Return On Owner-Occupied Single-Family Housing: A Reply," *JRER*, 1989, v4(1), 85-86.)

Rubens, Jack H., Michael T. Bond and James R. Webb. "The Inflation-Hedging Effectiveness Of Real Estate," *JRER*, 1989, v4(2), 45-55.

Rubiales, Carlos. (Ezzell, John R. and Carlos Rubiales. "An Empirical Analysis Of The Determinants Of Stock Splits," *FR*, 1975, v10(1), 21-30.)

Rubin, Harvey W. (Davis, Herbert J. and Harvey W. Rubin. "Perceived Benefits Of Professional Certification," *JRI*, 1976, v43(1), 152-155.)

Rubin, Harvey W. (Pritchett, S. Travis and Harvey W. Rubin. "A Case Study Of Flood Losses: Implications For Flood Insurance Produce Development," *JRI*, 1975, v42(1), 105-116.)

Rubin, Harvey W. and Peter A. Zuger. "Prospects For Selling Life Insurance Through Retail Banking Outlets," *JRI*, 1975, v42(2), 303-312.

Rubin, Marilyn, Ilene Wagner and Pearl Kamer. "Industrial Migration: A Case Study Of Destination By City-Suburban Origin Within The New York Metorpolitan Area," *AREUEA*, 1978, v6(4), 417-437.

Rubin, Marilyn. "The Suburbanization Of Industry And Its Effects Upon Labor Force Participation Rates Of Suburban Women," *AREUEA*, 1977, v5(1), 111-127.

Rubin, Paul H. (Paul, Chris W. and Paul H. Rubin. "Teaching And Research: The Human Capital Paradigm," *FPE*, 1991, v1(1), 7-10.)

Rubin, harvey W. (Blalack, Richard O., Herbert J. Davis and Harvey W. Rubin. "Sources Of Job Stress For The FLMI: A Comparative Analysis," *JRI*, 1979, v46(2), 123-138.)

Rubinstein, Mark and Hayne E. Leland. "Replicating Options With Positions In Stock And Cash," *JPM*, 1981, v37(4), 63-72.

Rubinstein, Mark E. "A Comparative Statics Analysis Of Risk Premiums," *JOB*, 1973, v46(4), 605-615.

Rubinstein, Mark E. "A Mean-Variance Synthesis Of Corporate Financial Theory," *JOF*, 1973, v28(1), 167-181.

Rubinstein, Mark E. "Corporate Financial Policy In Segmented Securities Markets," *JFQA*, 1973, v8(5), 749-761.

Rubinstein, Mark E. "The Fundamental Theorem Of Parameter-Preference Security Valuation," *JFQA*, 1973, v8(1), 61-69.

Rubinstein, Mark. "A Discrete-Time Synthesis Of Financial Theory," *RIF*, 1981, v3, 53-102.

Rubinstein, Mark. "A Simple Formula For The Expected Rate Of Return Of An Option Over A Finite Holding Period," *JOF*, 1984, v39(5), 1503-1509.

Rubinstein, Mark. "Alternative Paths To Portfolio Insurance," *FAJ*, 1985, v41(4), 42-52.

Rubinstein, Mark. "An Aggregation Theorem For Securities Market," *JFEC*, 1974, v1(3), 225-244.

Rubinstein, Mark. "Displaced Diffusion Option Pricing," *JOF*, 1983, v38(1), 213-217.

Rubinstein, Mark. "Market Basket Alternatives," *FAJ*, 1989, v45(5), 20-29.

Rubinstein, Mark. "Nonparametric Tests Of Alternative Option Pricing Models Using All Reported Trades And Quotes On The 30 Most Active CBOE Option Classes From August 23, 1976 Through August 31, 1978," *JOF*, 1985, v40(2), 455-480.

Rubinstein, Mark. "Portfolio Insurance And The Market Crash," *FAJ*, 1988, v44(1), 38-47.

Rubinstein, Mark. "The Irrelevancy Of Dividend Policy In An Arrow-Debreu Economy," *JOF*, 1976, v31(4), 1229-1230.

Rubinstein, Mark. "The Strong Case For The Generalized Logarithmic Utility Model As The Premier Model Of Financial Markets," *JOF*, 1976, v31(2), 551-571.

Rubinstein, Mark. (Cox, John C., Stephen A. Ross and Mark Rubinstein. "Option Pricing: A Simplified Approach," *JFEC*, 1979, v7(3), 229-264.)

Rubinstein, Mark. (Imai, Yutaka and Mark Rubinstein. "Equilibrium In The Pricing Of Capital Assets, Risk-Bearing Debt Instruments, And The Question Of Optimal Capital Structure: A Comment," *JFQA*, 1972, v7(4), 2001-2003.)

Rubio, G. (Alonso, A. and G. Rubio. "Overreaction In The Spanish Equity Market," *JBF*, 1990, v14(2/3), 469-482.)

Rubio, G. (Alonso, A., G. Rubio and F. Tusell. "Asset Pricing And Risk Aversion In The Spanish Stock Market," *JBF*, 1990, v14(2/3), 351-370.)

Rubio, Gonzalo. "An Empirical Evaluation Of The Intertemporal Capital Asset Pricing Model: The Stock Market In Spain," *JBFA*, 1989, v16(5), 729-744.

Rubio, Gonzalo. "Further International Evidence On Asset Pricing: The Case Of The Spanish Capital Market," *JBF*, 1988, v12(2), 221-242.

Rudd, Andrew and Barr Rosenberg. "Market Model" In Investment Management," *JOF*, 1980, v35(2), 597-607.

Rudd, Andrew T. "The Revised Dow Jones Industrial Average," *FAJ*, 1979, v35(6), 57-61,63.

Rudd, Andrew. "A Note On Qualitative Results For Investment Proportions," *JFEC*, 1977, v5(2), 259-263.

Rudd, Andrew. "Divestment Of South African Equities: How Risky?," *JPM*, 1978-79, v5(3), 5-10.

Rudd, Andrew. "Optimal Selection Of Passive Portfolios," *FM*, 1980, v9(1), 57-66.

Rudd, Andrew. "Using Options To Increase Reward And Decrease Risk," *JBR*, 1981-82, v12(3), 182-191.

Rudd, Andrew. (Evnine, Jeremy and Andrew Rudd. "Option Portfolio Risk Analysis," *JPM*, 1983-84, v10(2), 23-27.)

Rudd, Andrew. (Evnine, Jeremy and Andrew Rudd. "Index Options: The Early Evidence," *JOF*, 1985, v40(3), 743-758.)

Rudd, Andrew. (Fung, W. K. H. and Andrew Rudd. "Pricing New Corporate Bond Issues: An Analysis Of Issue Cost And Seasoning Effects," *JOF*, 1986, v41(3), 633-642.)

Rudd, Andrew. (Grinold, Richard and Andrew Rudd. "Incentive Fees: Who Wins? Who Loses?," *FAJ*, 1987, v43(1), 27-38.)

Rudd, Andrew. (Grinold, Richard, Andrew Rudd and Dan Stefek. "Global Factors: Fact Or Fiction?," *JPM*, 1989, v16(1), 79-89.)

Rudd, Andrew. (Jarrow, Robert and Andrew Rudd. "A Comparison Of The APT And CAPM: A Note," *JBF*, 1983, v7(2), 295-303.)

Rudd, Andrew. (Jarrow, Robert and Andrew Rudd. "Approximate Option Valuation For Arbitrary Stochastic Processes," *JFEC*, 1982, v10(3), 347-369.)

Rudd, Andrew. (Rosenberg, Barr and Andrew Rudd. "Factor Related And Specific Returns Of Common Stocks: Serial Correlation And Market Efficiency," *JOF*, 1982, v37(2), 543-554.)

Rudebusch, Glenn D. (Diebold, Francis X. and Glenn D. Rudebusch. "Scoring The Leading Indicators," *JOB*, 1989, v62(3), 369-392.)

Rudelius, William and Glenn L. Wood. "Life Insurance Product Innovations," *JRI*, 1970, v37(2), 169-184.

Rudelius, William and Glenn L. Wood. "Life Insurance Product Innovations: Reply," *JRI*, 1972, v39(1), 142-149.

Rudelius, William. (Peterson, Robert A., William Rudelius and Glenn L. Wood. "Spread Of Marketing Innovations In A Service Industry," *JOB*, 1972, v45(4), 485-496.)

Rudelius, William. (Wood, Glenn L. and William Rudelius. "The Product Performance Of The Life Insurance Industry: Revisited: Comment," *JRI*, 1972, v39(4), 651-652.)

Rudolph, J. Allan. "Stock Prices And The Money Supply," *FAJ*, 1972, v28(2), 19-25.

Rudolph, Patricia M. "The Insolvent Thrifts Of 1982: Where Are They Now?," *AREUEA*, 1989, v17(4), 450-462.

Rudolph, Patricia M. (Zumpano, Leonard V. and Patricia M. Rudolph. "Another Look At Residential Mortgage Lending By Savings And Loans," *JFR*, 1981, v4(1), 59-67.)

Rudolph, Patricia M. (Zumpano, Leonard V., Patricia M. Rudolph and David C. Cheng. "The Demand And Supply Of Mortgage Funds And Mortgage Loan Terms," *AREUEA*, 1986, v14(1), 91-109.)

Rudolph, Patricia M. and Bassum Hamden. "An Analysis Of Post-Deregulation Savings-And-Loan Failures," *AREUEA*, 1988, v16(1), 17-33.

Rudolph, Patricia M., Leonard V. Zumpano and Marvin J. Karson. "Mortgage Markets And Inter-Regional Differences In Convention Mortgage Terms," *AREUEA*, 1982, v10(1), 94-110.

Ruff, Craig K. (Mauldin, Patrick D., Brian F. Olasov and Craig K. Ruff. "The Use Of Mortgage-Derivative Products By Southeastern Thrifts," *FAJ*, 1990, v46(3), 71-76.)

Ruff, Raymond T. "Effect Of A 'Stock Of The Month' Recommendation," *FAJ*, 1963, v19(2), 41-43.

Ruffin, Roy J. "An Econometric Model Of The Impact Of Open Market Operations On Various Bank Classes," *JOF*, 1968, v23(4), 625-637.

Rugman, Alan M. and Shyam J. Kamath. "International Diversification And Multinational Banking," *RDIBF*, 1987, v1, 35-60.

Rukeyser, Merryle Stanley. "Auditing Reuther's Economic Ideas," *FAJ*, 1958, v14(5), 9-14.

Rukeyser, Merryle Stanley. "Intangible Phases Of Security Analysis," *FAJ*, 1954, v10(5), 17-20.

Rukeyser, Merryle Stanley. "A Larger Sphere For Analysts," *FAJ*, 1950, v6(4), 11-14.

Ruland, William. "On The Choice Of Simple Extrapolative Model Forecasts Of Annual Earnings," *FM*, 1980, v9(2), 30-37.

Ruland, William. "Stock Prices And Management Forecasts Of Future Earnings," *FR*, 1978, v13(1), 22-35.

Ruland, William. "The Behavior Of Changes In Accounting Risk Measures," *JBFA*, 1981, v8(3), 373-387.

Ruland, William. "The Time Series Of Earnings For Forecast Reporting And Nonreporting Firms," *JBFA*, 1979, v6(2), 187-201.

Ruland, William. (Beedles, William L., O. Maurice Joy and William Ruland. "Conglomeration And Diversification," *FR*, 1981, v16(1), 1-13.)

Ruland, William. (Haw, In-Mu, William Ruland and Ahmed Hamdallah. "Investor Evaluation Of Overfunded Pension Plan Terminations," *JFR*, 1988, v11(1),81-88.)

Ruml, Beardsley. "Tax Policies For Prosperity," *JOF*, 1946, v1(1), 81-90.

Rumsey, John. "Pricing Cross-Currency Options," *JFM*, 1991, v11(1), 89-94.

Rungeling, Brian S. (Pickle, Hal B. and Brian S. Rungeling. "Empirical Investigation Of Entrepreneurial Goals And Customer Satisfaction," *JOB*, 1973, v46(2), 268-273.)

Rungeling, Brian. (Scott, David F., Jr. and Brian Rungeling. "Business Doctoral Programs: What Are The Incremental Costs Of Starting New Ones?," *JFED*, 1988, v17, 80-88.)

Runyon, L. Richard. "The Use Of A Computer Simulation Game In The Investments Course," *JFED*, 1978, v7, 76-79.

Ruser, John W. and Robert S. Smith. "The Effect Of OSHA Records-Check Inspections On Reported Occupational Injuries In Manufacturing Establishments," *JRU*, 1988, v1(4), 415-435.

Rush, David F. and Ronald W. Melicher. "An Empirical Examination Of Factors Which Influence Warrant Prices," *JOF*, 1974, v29(5), 1449-1466.

Rush, David F. (Melicher, Ronald W., David F. Rush and Daryl N. Winn. "Degree Of Industry Concentration And Market Risk-Return Performance," *JFQA*, 1976, v11(4), 627-635.)

Rush, David F. (Melicher, Ronald W., David F. Rush and Daryl N. Winn. "Industry Concentration, Financial Structure And Profitability," *FM*, 1976, v5(3), 48-53.)

Rush, David F. (Melicher, Ronald W. and David F. Rush. "Evidence On The Acquisition-Related Performance Of Conglomerate Firms," *JOF*, 1974, v29(1), 141-149.)

Rush, David F. (Melicher, Ronald W. and David F. Rush. "The Performance Of Conglomerate Firms: Recent Risk And Return Experience," *JOF*, 1973, v28(2), 381-388.)

Rush, David F. (Melicher, Ronald W. and David F. Rush. "Systematic Risk, Financial Data, And Bond Rating Relationships In A Regulated Industry Environment," *JOF*, 1974, v29(2), 537-544.)

Rush, David F. (Rosenstein, Stuart and David F. Rush. "The Stock Return Performance Of Corporations That Are Partially Owned By Other Corporations," JFR, 1990, v13(1), 39-52.)

Rush, David F. (Tallman, Gary D., David F. Rush and Ronald W. Melicher. "Competitive Versus Negotiated Underwriting Costs For Regulated Industries," FM, 1974, v3(2), 49-55.)

Rush, Mark. "A Classical Model Of A Small Fixed Exchange Rate Economy," JIMF, 1984, v3(1), 31-49.

Rush, Mark. "Unexpected Money And Unemployment: 1920 to 1983," JMCB, 1986, v18(3), 259-274.

Rush, Mark. (Hakkio, Craig S. and Mark Rush. "Market Efficiency And Cointegration: An Application To The Sterling And Deutschemark Exchange Markets," JIMF, 1989, v8(1), 75-88.)

Rush, Mark. (Ochs, Jack and Mark Rush. "The Persistence Of Interest-Rate Effects On The Demand For Currency," JMCB, 1983, v15(4), 499-505.)

Rushinek, Avi and Sara Rushinek. "A Note To Barlev-Levy Theory Of The Information Content Of Accounting Data And The Management Of Security Portfolios Which Include The Least Correlated Stocks," JBFA, 1985, v12(1), 117-131.

Rushinek, Sara. (Rushinek, Avi and Sara Rushinek. "A Note To Barlev-Levy Theory Of The Information Content Of Accounting Data And The Management Of Security Portfolios," JBFA, 1985, v12(1), 117-131.)

Russek, Frank S. (Barth, James R., Frank S. Russek and George H. K. Wang. "The Measurement And Significance Of The Cyclically Adjusted Federal Budget And Debt: A Comment," JMCB, 1986, v18(4), 527-538.)

Russell, Allen M. and John A. Rickard. "An Algorithm For Determining Unique Nonnegative Internal Rates Of Return," JBFA, 1984, v11(3), 355-366.

Russell, Hugh. "Ethical Obligations In The Student-Professor Relationship," JRI, 1964, v31(3), 393-404.

Russell, Thomas. (Sheffrin, Steven M. and Thomas Russell. "Sterling And Oil Discoveries: The Mystery Of Nonappreciation," JIMF, 1984, v3(3), 311-326.)

Russell, William R. and Tae Kun Seo. "An Application Of Stochastic Dominance To A Portfolio Problem," RIF, 1980, v2, 121-138.

Russo, Ben. (Gandar, John, Richard Zuber, Thomas O'Brien and Ben Russo. "Testing Rationality In The Point Spread Betting Market," JOF, 1988, v43(4), 995-1008.)

Rutemiller, Herbert C. (Tull, Donald S. and Herbert C. Rutemiller. "A Note On The Relationship Of Actual And Predicted Sales And Profits In New-Product Introductions," JOB, 1968, v41(3), 385-387.)

Rutenberg, David P. (Cohen, Kalman J. and David P. Rutenberg. "Toward A Comprehensive Framework For Bank Financial Planning," JBR, 1970-71, v1(4), 41-57.)

Rutenberg, David P. (Litzenberger, Robert H. and David P. Rutenberg. "Size And Timing Of Corporate Bond Flotations," JFQA, 1972, v7(1), 1343-1359.)

Rutenberg, David P. (Shapiro, Alan C. and David P. Rutenberg. "Managing Exchange Risks In A Floating World," FM, 1976, v5(2), 48-58.)

Ruth, Stephen R. (Guy, Donald C., John L. Hysom and Stephen R. Ruth. "The Effect Of Subsidized Housing On Values Of Adjacent Housing," AREUEA, 1985, v13(4), 378-387.)

Ruthenberg, David. (Landskroner, Yoram and David Ruthenberg. "Optimal Bank Behavior Under Uncertain Inflation," JOF, 1985, v40(4), 1159-1171.)

Ruthenberg, David. (Landskroner, Yoram and David Ruthenberg. "How Variable Interest Rates Affect Bank Duration And Immunization," FAJ, 1989, v45(4), 77-80.)

Rutherford, B. A. "Cash Flow Reporting And Distributional Allocations: A Note," JBFA, 1983, v10(2), 313-316.

Rutherford, B. A. "The Explication Of The True And Fair View Doctrine: A Reply," JBFA, 1988, v15(1), 125-127.

Rutherford, B. A. "The True And Fair View Doctrine: A Search For Explication," JBFA, 1985, v12(4), 483-494.

Rutherford, Ronald C. "Empirical Evidence On Shareholder Value And The Sale-Leaseback Of Corporate Real Estate," AREUEA, 1990, v18(4), 522-529.

Rutherford, Ronald C. and Hugh O. Nourse. "The Impact Of Corporate Real Estate Unit Formation On The Parent Firm's Value," JRER, 1988, v3(3), 73-84.

Rutherford, Ronald and Robert Stone. "Corporate Real Estate Unit Formation: Rationale, Industry And Type Of Unit," JRER, 1989, v4(3), 121-129.

Rutner, Jack L. (Auerbach, Robert D. and Jack L. Rutner. "A Negative View Of The Negative Money Multiplier: Comment," JOF, 1977, v32(5), 1814-1817.)

Rutz, Roger D. "Key Features Of The Municipal Bond Futures Contract," RFM, 1985, v4(2), 252-259.

Rutz, Roger D. "Clearance, Payment, And Settlement Systems In The Futures, Options, And Stock Markets," RFM, 1988, v7(3), 346-370.

Rutz, Roger D. (Coleman, Thomas C. and Roger D. Rutz. "Self-Regulation And Government Regulation Of Futures And Options Markets: Introduction," JOB, 1986, v59(2), Part 2, S1-S4.)

Rutz, Roger D. (Kahl, Kandace H., Roger D. Rutz and Jeanne C. Sinquefield. "The Economics Of Performance Margins In Futures Markets," JFM, 1985, v5(1), 103-112.)

Rutz, Roger D. (Rose, John T. and Roger D. Rutz. "Organization Form And Risk In Bank-Affiliated Mortgage Companies," JMCB, 1981, v13(3), 375-380.)

Ruuhela, Reijo. (Salmi, Timo and Reijo Ruuhela. "Estimating The Internal Rate Of Return From Published Financial Statements: A Reply," JBFA, 1985, v12(4), 611-612.)

Ryan, Cornelius. (Branch, Ben and Cornelius Ryan. "Tax Loss Trading: An Inefficiency Too Large To Ignore," FR, 1980, v15(1), 20-29.)

Ryan, James C. and Mark Kritzman. "Catch 500: The Irony Of Indexing: Reply," JPM, 1980-81, v7(1), 82.

Ryan, James C. and Mark Kritzman. "Catch 500: The Irony Of Indexing," JPM, 1979-80, v6(2), 30-32.

Ryan, James C. (Kritzman, Mark and James C. Ryan. "A Short-Term Approach To Asset Allocation," JPM, 1980-81, v7(1), 45-49.)

Ryan, John. "Bank Capital And Size And Location Of Banks," JOB, 1952, v25(4), 225-241.

Ryan, Michael J. (Farley, John U., Donald R. Lehmann and Michael J. Ryan. "Generalizing From 'Imperfect' Replication," JOB, 1981, v54(4), 597-610.)

Ryan, Peter J. and Jean Lefoll. "A Comment On Mean-Variance Portfolio Selection With Either A Singular Or A Non-Singular Variance-Covariance Matrix," JFQA, 1981, v16(3), 389-395.

Ryan, Peter J. (Perrakis, Stylianos and Peter J. Ryan. "Option Pricing Bounds In Discrete Time," JOF, 1984, v39(2), 519-525.)

Ryan, Robert J. "Capital Market Theory - A Case Study In Methodological Conflict," JBFA, 1982, v8(4), 443-458.

Ryan, Robert J. "Towards A Value-Neutral Positive Science Of Accounting: A Comment," JBFA, 1982, v8(4), 565-566.

Ryan, Robert J. (Scapens, Robert W., Robert J. Ryan and Leslie Fletcher. "Explaining Corporate Failure: A Catastrophe Theory Approach," JBFA, 1981, v8(1), 1-26.)

Ryan, Scott W. "The Search For An Integrated Options Strategy," JPM, 1976-77, v3(1), 41-44.

Ryan, Stephen G. (Beaver, William H. and Stephen G. Ryan. "How Well Do Statement No. 33 Earnings Explain Stock Returns?," FAJ, 1985, v41(5), 66-71.)

Ryan, Terence M. "Dividend Policy And Market Valuation In British Industry," JBFA, 1974, v1(3), 415-428.

Ryan, Terence M. "Security Prices As Markov Processes," JFQA, 1973, v8(1), 17-36.

Rychel, Dwight F. "Capital Budgeting With Mixed Integer Linear Programming: An Application," FM, 1977, v6(4), 11-19.

Rydqvist, K. (Bergstrom, C. and K. Rydqvist. "The Determinants Of Corporate Ownership: An Empirical Study Of Swedish Data," JBF, 1990, v14(2/3), 237-254.)

Rydqvist, K. (Bergstrom, C. and K. Rydqvist. "Ownership Of Equity In Dual-Class Firms," JBF, 1990, v14(2/3), 255-270.)

Ryngaert, Michael D. "Firm Valuation, Takeover Defenses, And The Delaware Supreme Court," FM, 1989, v18(3), 20-28.

Ryngaert, Michael. "The Effect Of Poison Pill Securities On Shareholder Wealth," JFEC, 1988, v20(1/2), 377-418.

Rystrom, David S. "Costs Of Regulation Of Futures Markets: The 1958 Onion Futures Act," RFM, 1989, v8(1), 44-55.

Rystrom, David S. and Earl D. Benson. "Investor Psychology And The Day-Of-The-Week Effect," FAJ, 1989, v45(5), 75-78.

Rystrom, David. "Inflation And Real Estate Investment Value: A Comment," AREUEA, 1980, v8(4), 395-401.

Rzepczynski, Mark S. "The Behavior Of Primary Government Security Dealers And Their Use Of Financial Futures," RFM, 1984, v3(3), 282-317.

Rzepczynski, Mark S. "Risk Premiums In Financial Futures Markets: The Case Of Treasury Bond Futures," JFM, 1987, v7(6), 653-662.

Rzepczynski, Mark. (Stein, Jerome L., Mark Rzepczynski and Robert Selvaggio. "A Theoretical Explanation Of The Empirical Studies Of Futures Markets In Foreign Exchange And Financial Instruments," FR, 1983, v18(1), 1-32.)

SSS

Sa-Aadu, J. "Another Look At The Economics Of Demand-Side Versus Supply-Side Strategies In Low-Income Housing," AREUEA, 1984, v12(4), 427-460.

Sa-Aadu, J. "Consumer Welfare Under The Adjustable Rate Mortgage: Some Empirical Evidence," AREUEA, 1987, v15(3), 132-151.

Sa-Aadu, J. (Ravichandran, R. and J. Sa-Aadu. "Resource Combination And Security Price Reactions: The Case Of Real Estate Joint Ventures," AREUEA, 1988, v16(2), 105-122.)

Sa-Aadu, J. and C. F. Sirmans. "The Pricing Of Adjustable Rate Mortgage Contracts," JREFEC, 1989, v2(4), 253-266.

Sa-Aadu, J. and James D. Shilling. "Ranking Of Contributing Authors To The AREUEA Journal By Doctoral Origin And Employer," AREUEA, 1988, v16(3), 257-270.

Sa-Aadu, J., C. F. Sirmans and John D. Benjamin. "Financing And House Prices," JFR, 1989, v12(1), 83-91.

Saaty, Thomas L., Paul C. Rogers and Ricardo Pell. "Portfolio Selection Through Hierarchies," JPM, 1979-80, v6(3), 16-21.

Saba, Richard P. (Bellante, Don and Richard P. Saba. "Human Capital And Life-Cycle Effects On Risk Aversion," JFR, 1986, v9(1), 41-51.)

Saba, Richard. (Ault, Richard and Richard Saba. "The Economic Effects Of Long-Term Rent Control: The Case Of New York City," JREFEC, 1990, v3(1), 25-42.)

Sachdeva, Kanwal S. and Lawrence J. Gitman. "Accounts Receivable Decisions In A Capital Budgeting Framework," FM, 1981, v10(5), 45-49.

Sachdeva, Kanwal S. and William E. Sterk. "Projecting Finance Student Final Course Scores Based On Initial Exam Scores," JFED, 1982, v11, 55-60.

Sachdeva, Kanwal S. (Lee, Wayne Y. and Kanwal S. Sachdeva. "The Role Of The Multinational Firm In The Integration Of Segmented Capital Markets," JOF, 1977, v32(2), 479-492.)

Sachdeva, Kanwal. "On The Equality Of Two Lower Bounds On The Call Price: A Note," JFQA, 1986, v21(2), 235-237.

Sachlis, J. Minor. "A Business Finance Simulation," JFED, 1979, v8, 80-85.

Sachlis, J. Minor. (Handorf, William C. and J. Minor Sachlis. "A Note On The Accounting Model For Problem Real Estate Loans," JRER, 1990, v5(3), 381-391.)

Sachnoff, L. (Boies, D., D. Carroll, A. Fleischer, J. Grundfest, J. Ira Harris, M. Lipton, R. Monks, A. Oliver, L. Sachnoff and J. Wilcox. "Panel: Corporate Governance: The Role Of Boards Of Directors In Takeover Bids And Defenses," JACF, 1989, v2(2), 6-35.)

Sachs, Alexander. "The A.T.&T. Case In A Changed Economy," FAJ, 1966, v22(5), 13-19.

Sachs, Jeffrey D. (McKibbin, Warwick J. and Jeffrey D. Sachs. "Comparing The Global Performance Of Alternative Exchange Arrangements," JIMF, 1988, v7(4), 387-410.)

Sachs, Jeffrey. (Alesina, Alberto and Jeffrey Sachs. "Political Parties And The Business Cycle In The United States, 1948-1984," JMCB, 1988, v20(1), 63-82.)

Sack, Paul. (Rosenberg, Claude, Jr. and Paul Sack. "The High Risks Of Open-End Real Estate Funds," JPM, 1975-76, v2(1), 55-57.)

Sacks, Seymour. "Metropolitan Fiscal Disparities: Their Nature And Determinants," JOF, 1968, v23(2), 229-250.

Sadan, Simcha. (Lakonishok, Josef and Simcha Sadan. "Information Sets, Macroeconomic Reform, And Stock Prices," JFQA, 1981, v16(4), 495-510.)

Sadan, Simcha. (Ronen, Joshua and Simcha Sadan. "Income Smoothing Via Classification," FAJ, 1975, v31(5), 62-68.)

Sadanand, Venkatraman. (Khoury, Sarkis J., David Nickerson and Venkatraman Sadanand. "Exchange Rate Uncertainty And Precommitment In Symmetric Duopoly: A New Theory Of Multinational Production," RDIBF, 1991, v4/5, 439-473.)

Safanda, C. F. (Herman, E. S. and C. F. Safanda. "Allocating Investment Information," FAJ, 1973, v29(1), 23-28,88-91.)

Safarian, A. E. "Perspectives On Foreign Direct Investment From The Viewpoint Of A Capital Receiving Country," JOF, 1973, v28(2), 419-438.

Safavi, Farrokh. "'Case Feeding': A Student Oriented Approach To Case-Writing," JFED, 1973, v2, 49-56.

Safer, A. E. and J. M. Levine. "Analysis Of Institutional Holdings," FAJ, 1970, v26(4), 74-86.

Safian, Kenneth and Kenneth B. Smilen. "Relative Earnings: A Fresh Perspective," FAJ, 1964, v20(5), 104-107.

Safra, Zvi, Uzi Segal and Avia Spivak. "The Becker-DeGroot-Marschak Mechanism And Non-Expected Utility," JRU, 1990, v3(2), 177-190.

Sagalyn, Lynne B. "Real Estate Risk And The Business Cycle: Evidence From Security Markets," JRER, 1990, v5(2), 203-219.

Sagan, John. "Toward A Theory Of Working Capital Management," JOF, 1955, v10(2), 121-129.

Sahasakul, Chaipat. (Barro, Robert J. and Chaipat Sahasakul. "Average Marginal Tax Rates From Social Security And The Individual Income Tax," JOB, 1986, v59(4), Part 1, 555-566.)

Sahasakul, Chaipat. (Barro, Robert J. and Chaipat Sahasakul. "Measuring The Average Marginal Tax Rate From The Individual Income Tax," JOB, 1983, v56(4), 419-452.)

Sahin, Izzet and Yves Balcer. "Qualifying Service Under ERISA Vesting Standards: A Comparative Analysis," JRI, 1979, v46(3), 483-496.

Sahin, Izzet. "Bruce's Spider And The Employee's Risk Under A Pension System," JRI, 1984, v51(1), 143-149.

Sahin, Izzet. (Balcer, Yves and Izzet Sahin. "Probabilistic Models For Pension Benefits," JRI, 1979, v46(1), 99-124.)

Sahin, Izzet. (Balcer, Yves and Izzet Sahin. "Modeling The Impact Of Pension Reform - A Case Study," JRI, 1982, v49(2), 158-192.)

Sahin, Izzet. (Balcer, Yves and Izzet Sahin. "Dynamics Of Pension Reform: The Case Of Ontario," JRI, 1984, v51(4), 652-686.)

Sahlman, William A. "Aspects Of Financial Contracting In Venture Capital," JACF, 1988, v1(2), 23-36.

Sahlman, William A. "The Structure And Governance Of Venture-Capital Organizations," JFEC, 1990, v27(2), 473-522.

Sahu, Anandi P. (Kleiman, Robert T. and Anandi P. Sahu. "Life Insurance Companies As Investment Managers: New Implications For Consumers," FSR, 1991, v1(1), 27-40.)

Saidi, Nasser H. "Expectations, International Business Cycles, And The Balance Of Payments," JMCB, 1982, v14(3), 327-346.

Saidi, Nasser H. "Fluctuating Exchange Rates And The International Transmissions Of Economic Disturbances," JMCB, 1980, v12(4), Part 1, 575-591.

Sailor, Vance L. "Bank Supervision And The Business Cycle," JOF, 1948, v3(3), 65-77.

Saini, Krishan G. and Philip S. Bates. "A Survey Of The Quantitative Approaches To Country Risk Analysis," JBF, 1984, v8(2), 341-356.

Saint-Denis, Andre. (Scott, David F., Jr., Laurence J. Moore, Andre Saint-Denis, Edouard Archer and Bernard W. Taylor, III. "Implementation Of A Cash Budget Simulator At Air Canada," FM, 1979, v8(2), 46-52.)

Saito, Mitsuo. "Household Flow-Of-Funds Equations: Specification And Estimation," JMCB, 1977, v9(1), 1-20.

Sakakibara, Eisuke. (Hewson, John and Eisuke Sakakibara. "A General Equilibrium Approach To The Eurodollar Market," JMCB, 1976, v8(3), 297-323.)

Sakakibara, Eisuke. (Hewson, John and Eisuke Sakakibara. "A Qualitative Analysis Of Euro-Currency Controls," JOF, 1975, v30(2), 377-400.)

Sakakibara, Eisuke. (Hewson, John and Eisuke Sakakibara. "The Effect Of U. S. Controls On The U. S. Commercial Bank Borrowing In The Euro-Dollar Market," JOF, 1975, v30(4), 1101-1110.)

Sakata, Shintaro. "Japan's Economy And Securities Market," FAJ, 1969, v25(5), 111-122.

Salamon, Gerald L. and Dan S. Dhaliwal. "Company Size And Financial Disclosure Requirements With Evidence From The Segmental Reporting Issue," JBFA, 1980, v7(4), 555-568.

Salamon, Gerald L. and E. Dan Smith. "Additional Evidence On The Time Series Properties Of Reported Earnings Per Share: Comment," JOF, 1977, v32(5), 1795-1801.

Salandro, Dan. (Choi, J. Y., Dan Salandro and Kuldeep Shastri. "On The Estimation Of Bid-Ask Spreads: Theory And Evidence," JFQA, 1988, v23(2), 219-230.)

Salant, Walter S. "Projecting, Forecasting, And Hindcasting: A Reply," JMCB, 1971, v3(2), Part 1, 281-287.

Salazar, Arturo. (Oakford, R. V. and Arturo Salazar. "The Long Term Effectiveness Of 'Exact' And Approximate Capital Rationing Procedures Under Uncertainty And Incomplete Information," JBFA, 1991, v8(1), 113-137.)

Sale, J. Timothy. (Scapens, Robert W. and J. Timothy Sale. "Performance Measurement And Formal Capital Expenditure Controls In Divisionalised Companies," JBFA, 1981, v8(3), 389-419.)

Salemi, Michael K. "Expected Exchange Depreciation And The Demand For Money In Hyperinflation Germany," JMCB, 1980, v12(4), Part 1, 592-602.

Salinger, Michael A. "Stock Market Margin Requirements And Volatility: Implications For Regulation Of Stock Index Futures," JFSR, 1989, v3(2/3), 121-138.

Salkin, G. R. (Christofides, N., R. D. Hewins and G. R. Salkin. "Graph Theoretic Approaches To Foreign Exchange Operations," JFQA, 1979, v14(3), 481-500.)

Salkin, G. R. (Flavell, R. B. and G. R. Salkin. "A Sequential Analysis Of Large-Scale Investment Projects," JBFA, 1974, v1(1), 75-91.)

Salkin, G. R. (Raine, P. S., R. B. Flavell and G. R. Salkin. "A Likelihood Control System For Use With Formal Planning Models," JBFA, 1981, v8(2), 249-266.)

Salkin, Harvey M. and Peter H. Ritchken. "Option Spreading: Rejoinder," JPM, 1980-81, v7(2), 89-93.

Salkin, Harvey M. and Peter H. Richken. "Option Spreading: Comment," JPM, 1980-81, v7(2), 89-93.

Salkin, Harvey M. (Ritchken, Peter H. and Harvey M. Salkin. "Safety First Selection Techniques For Option Spreads," JPM, 1982-83, v9(3), 61-67.)

Salmi, Timo and Reijo Ruuhela. "Estimating The Internal Rate Of Return From Published Financial Statements: A Reply," JBFA, 1985, v12(4), 611-612.

Salmi, Timo. "Estimating The Internal Rate Of Return From Published Financial Statements," JBFA, 1982, v8(1), 63-74.

Salton, A. "Sales Prospects Of Department Stores And Mail Order Houses," FAJ, 1945, v1(4), 13-21.

Salvino, S. M. "Rate Of Return Dilemma Of Utilities," FAJ, 1967, v23(6), 45-49.

Salyer, Kevin D. "The Term Structure And Time Series Properties Of Nominal Interest Rates: Implications From Theory," JMCB, 1990, v22(4), 478-490.

Salz, Frank. "Gross National Product And The Investor's Focus," FAJ, 1966, v22(4), 28-32.

Salz, Frank. "Is The Long-Term Investor Facing Bleak Years Ahead? - Part II," FAJ, 1964, v20(6), 31-40.

Salz, Frank. "Is The Long-Term Investor Facing Bleak Years Ahead?," FAJ, 1964, v20(5), 33-40.

Salzman, Gary. "Murder, Wagering, And Insurable Interest In Life Insurance," JRI, 1963, v30(4), 555-562.

Salzman, Jerrold E. and Daniel A. Clune. "Judicial Review Of CFTC's Invocation Of Emergency Powers," JFM, 1981, v1(Supp), 465-467.

Salzman, Jerrold E. (Martell, Terrence F. and Jerrold E. Salzman. "Cash Settlement For Futures Contracts Based On Common Stock Indices: An Economic And Legal Perspective," JFM, v1(3), 291-301.)

Sametz, Arnold W. "Patterns Of Business Financing: Reply," JOF, 1965, v20(4), 708-718.

Sametz, Arnold W. "Trends In The Volume And Composition Of Equity Finance," JOF, 1964, v19(3), 450-469.

Sametz, Arnold. (Wachtel, Paul, Arnold Sametz and Harry Shuford. "Capital Shortages: Myth Or Reality?," JOF, 1976, v31(2), 269-286.)

Samorajski, Gregory S. and Bruce D. Phelps. "Using Treasury Bond Futures To Enhance Total Return," FAJ, 1990, v46(1), 58-65.

Samprone, Joseph C., Jr. "Rate Regulation And Nonprice Competition In The Property And Liability Insurance Industry," JRI, 1979, v46(4), 683-696.

Sampson, A. A. "Liquidity Constraints On Investment And Dividends," JBFA, 1976, v3(2), 131-142.

Sampson, Anthony A. "Measuring The Rate Of Return On Capital," JOF, 1969, v24(1), 61-74.

Sampson, Richard. (Froland, Charles, Robert Gorlow and Richard Sampson. "The Market Risk Of Real Estate," JPM, 1985-86, v12(3), 12-19.)

Samson, Danny and Howard Thomas. "Reinsurance Decision Making And Expected Utility," JRI, 1983, v50(2), 249-264.

Samson, Danny and Howard Thomas. "Reinsurance Decision Making And Expected Utility: Reply," JRI, 1985, v52(2), 312-314.

Samson, William D. (Curatola, Anthony P., Kent T. Fields and William D. Samson. "The Benefits Of The Salary Reduction Plan," FAJ, 1984, v40(3), 53-58.)

Samuels, J. M. (Briscoe, G., J. M. Samuels and D. J. Smyth. "The Treatment Of Risk In The Stock Market," JOF, 1969, v24(4), 707-713.)

Samuels, J. M. (Groves, R. E. V. and J. M. Samuels. "A Note On The Cost Of Retained Earnings And Deferred Taxes In The U.K.," JBFA, 1976, v3(4), 143-149.)

Samuelson, Paul A. and Robert C. Merton. "Generalized Mean-Variance Tradeoffs For Best Perturbation Correction To Approximate Portfolio Decisions," JOF, 1974, v29(1), 27-40.

Samuelson, Paul A. "Asset Allocation Could Be Dangerous To Your Health," JPM, 1990, v16(3), 5-8.

Samuelson, Paul A. "Challenge To Judgment," JPM, 1974-75, v1(1), 17-19.

Samuelson, Paul A. "Efficient Portfolio Selection For Pareto-Levy Investments," JFQA, 1967, v2(2), 107-122.

Samuelson, Paul A. "General Proof That Diversification Pays," JFQA, 1967, v2(1), 1-13.

Samuelson, Paul A. "How A Certain Internal Consistency Entails The Expected Utility Dogma," JRU, 1988, v1(4), 389-394.

Samuelson, Paul A. "Limited Liability, Short Selling, Bounded Utility, And Infinite-Variance Stable Distributions," JFQA, 1976, v11(3), 485-503.

Samuelson, Paul A. "Myths And Realities About The Crash And Depression," JPM, 1979-80, v6(1), 7-10.

Samuelson, Paul A. "Paradise Lost & Refound: The Harvard ABC Barometers," JPM, 1986-87, v13(3), 4-9.

Samuelson, Paul A. "The Judgment Of Economic Science On Rational Portfolio Management: Indexing, Timing, And Long-Horizon Effects," JPM, 1989, v16(1), 4-12.

Samuelson, Paul A. "Why We Should Not Make Mean Log Of Wealth Big Though Years To Act Are Long," JBF, 1979, v3(4), 305-308.

Samuelson, Paul A. (Merton, Robert C. and Paul A. Samuelson. "Fallacy Of The Log-Normal Approximation To Optimal Portfolio Decision-Making Over Many Periods," JFEC, 1974, v1(1), 67-94.)

Samuelson, Paul. "Reflections On Recent Federal Reserve Policy," JMCB, 1970, v2(1), 33-44.

Samuelson, Victor E. (Boyle, Alexander R. M. and Victor E. Samuelson. "Disclosure Of Long-Term Leases," FAJ, 1962, v18(2), 35-40.)

Samuelson, William and Leonard Rosenthal. "Price Movements As Indicators Of Tender Offer Success," JOF, 1986, v41(2), 481-500.

Samuelson, William and Richard Zeckhauser. "Status Quo Bias In Decision Making," JRU, 1988, v1(1), 7-60.

Sand, Ole Christian. (Cornell, Bradford and Ole Christian Sand. "The Value Of Base Rate Options In The Eurocredit Market," JBR, 1985-86, v16(1), 22-27.)

Sand, Ole Christian. (Schollhammer, Hans and Ole Christian Sand. "Lead-Lag Relationships Among National Equity Markets: An Empirical Investigation," RDIBF, 1987, v1, 149-168.)

Sandarasubramanian, L. (Ritchken, Peter, L. Sandarasubramanian and Anand M. Vijh. "Averaging Options For Capping Total Costs," FM, 1990, v19(3), 35-41.)

Sandberg, Carl M. (McConnell, John J. and Carl M. Sandberg. "The Weighted Average Cost Of Capital: Some Questions On Its Definition, Interpretation, And Use: Comment," JOF, 1975, v30(3), 883-886.)

Sandelin, Bo. "Price Behavior And Capital Gains On Residential Real Estate: The Case Of Sweden," AREUEA, 1981, v9(3), 241-264.

Sanders, Anthony B. (Buser, Stephen A. and Anthony B. Sanders. "Tenure Decisions Under A Progressive Tax Structure," AREUEA, 1983, v11(3), 371-381.)

Sanders, Anthony B. (Buser, Stephen A., Patric H. Hendershott and Anthony B. Sanders. "Pricing Life Of Loan Rate Caps On Default-Free Adjustable-Rate Mortgages," AREUEA, 1985, v13(3), 248-260.)

Sanders, Anthony B. (Chan, K. C., Patric H. Hendershott and Anthony B. Sanders. "Risk And Return On Real Estate: Evidence From Equity REITs," AREUEA, 1990, v18(4), 431-452.)

Sanders, Anthony B. (Hite, Gailen L. and Anthony B. Sanders. "Excess Depreciation And The Maximum Tax," AREUEA, 1981, v9(2), 134-147.)

Sanders, Anthony B. (Page, Frank H., Jr. and Anthony B. Sanders. "A General Derivation Of The Jump Process Option Pricing Formula," JFQA, 1986, v21(4), 437-446.)

Sanders, Anthony B. and Haluk Unal. "On The Intertemporal Behavior Of The Short-Term Rate Of Interest," JFQA, 1988, v23(4), 417-424.

Sanders, Barkev S. "What Would 'Medicare' Cost?," JRI, 1965, v32(4), 579-594.

Sanders, Barkev S. "What Would 'Medicare' Cost?: Reply," JRI, 1967, v34(1), 148-166.

Sanders, Douglas O., Jr. "Methods Of Simulating The Random Components Of Life Insurance Company Financial Results," JRI, 1968, v35(3), 393-410.

Sanderson, G. Robert. "Intuitive Versus Analytical Thinking In Investment Decision-Making," JFED, 1980, v9, 12-16.

Sanderson, George R. "Active Participation As An Integral Part Of Financial Education," JFED, 1975, v4, 41-45.

Sanderson, George R. "Five Levels Of Decision Making In Finance," JFED, 1973, v2, 9-12.

Sanderson, George R. "The Teaching Of Critical Inquiry Through Financial Analysis," JFED, 1974, v3, 39-42.

Sanderson, George Robert. "A Bank Management Simulation Game As A Learning Device," JFED, 1978, v7, 21-24.

Sanderson, George Robert. "The Classroom Professor As A Manager," JFED, 1977, v6, 51-53.

Sanderson, George Robert. "Teaching Financial Management Through Small Business Consulting," JFED, 1976, v5, 51-54.

Sandor, Richard L. "Some Empirical Findings On The Legal Costs Of Patenting," JOB, 1972, v45(3), 375-378.

Sandor, Richard L. and Howard B. Sosin. "The Determinants Of Mortgage Risk Premiums: A Case Study Of The Portfolio Of A Savings And Loan Association," JOB, 1975, v48(1), 27-38.

Sands, Gary. "A Vacancy Transfer Model Of The Structure Of The Local Housing Market," AREUEA, 1977, v5(1), 128-138.

Sanford, James P. (Planisek, Sandra L. and James P. Sanford. "Video Case Materials For Enhanced Classroom Learning: Observations And Student Reactions," JFED, 1988, v17, 44-54.)

Sanger, Gary C. and John J. McConnell. "Stock Exchange Listings, Firm Value, And Security Market Efficiency: The Impact Of NASDAQ," JFQA, 1986, v21(1), 1-25.

Sanger, Gary C. (Chen, Andrew H. and Gary C. Sanger. "An Analysis Of The Impact Of Regulatory Change: The Case Of Natural Gas Deregulation," FR, 1985, v20(1), 36-54.)

Sanger, Gary C. (Lamoureux, Christopher G. and Gary C. Sanger. "Firm Size And Turn-Of-The-Year Effects In The OTC/NASDAQ Market," JOF, 1989, v44(5), 1219-1246.)

Sanger, Gary C. (McConnell, John J. and Gary C. Sanger. "A Trading Strategy For New Listings On The NYSE," FAJ, 1984, v40(1), 34-48.)

Sanger, Gary C. (McConnell, John J. and Gary C. Sanger. "The Puzzle In Post-Listing Common Stock Returns," JOF, 1987, v42(1), 119-140.)

Sanger, Gary C. and James D. Peterson. "An Empirical Analysis Of Common Stock Delistings," JFQA, 1990, v25(2), 261-272.

Sanghvi, Arun P. and Gordon H. Dash, Jr. "Core Securities: Widening The Decision Dimensions," JPM, 1977-78, v4(3), 20-24.

Saniga, Erwin M. and Jack C. Hayya. "Simple Goodness-Of-Fit Tests For Symmetric Stable Distributions," JFQA, 1977, v12(2), 276-289.

Saniga, Erwin M. (Kolari, James, Thomas H. McInish and Erwin M. Saniga. "A Note On The Distribution Types Of Financial Ratios In The Commercial Banking Industry," JBF, 1989, v13(3), 463-472.)

Saniga, Erwin M., Thomas H. McInish and Bruce K. Gouldey. "The Effect Of Differencing Interval Length On Beta," JFR, 1981, v4(2), 129-135.

Saniga, Erwin, Nicholas Gressis and Jack Hayya. "The Effects Of Sample Size And Correlation On The Accuracy Of The EV Efficient Criterion," JFQA, 1979, v14(3), 615-628.

Sankarasubramanian, L. (Ritchken, Peter and L. Sankarasubramanian. "On Valuing Complex Interest Rate Claims," JFM, 1990, v10(5), 443-456.)

Sant, Donald T. "Estimating Expected Losses In Auto Insurance," JRI, 1980, v47(1), 133-151.

Santesmases, Miguel. "An Investigation Of The Spanish Stock Market Seasonalities," JBFA, 1986, v13(2), 267-276.

Santiago, Emmanuel S. (Pohlman, Randolph A., Emmanuel S. Santiago and F. Lynn Markel. "Cash Flow Estimation Practices Of Large Firms," FM, 1988, v17(2), 71-79.)

Santomero, Anthony J. (Barro, Robert J. and Anthony J. Santomero. "Household Money Holdings And The Demand Deposit Rate," JMCB, 1972, v4(2), 397-413.)

Santomero, Anthony M. and Jeremy J. Siegel. "A General Equilibrium Money And Banking Paradigm," JOF, 1982, v37(2), 357-369.

Santomero, Anthony M. and Joseph D. Vinso. "Estimating The Probability Of Failure For Commercial Banks And The Banking System," JBF, 1977, v1(2), 185-205.

Santomero, Anthony M. and Ronald D. Watson. "Determining Optimal Capital Standard For The Banking Industry," JOF, 1977, v32(4), 1267-1282.

Santomero, Anthony M. "A Model Of The Demand For Money By Households," JOF, 1974, v29(1), 89-102.

Santomero, Anthony M. "A Note On Interest Rates And Prices In General Equilibrium," JOF, 1973, v28(4), 997-1000.

Santomero, Anthony M. "Bank Capital: A Regulation Perspective," FM, 1976, v5(4), 59-64.

Santomero, Anthony M. "Controlling Monetary Aggregates: The Discount Window," JOF, 1983, v38(3), 827-843.

Santomero, Anthony M. "Fixed Versus Varible Rate Loans," JOF, 1983, v38(5), 1363-1380.

Santomero, Anthony M. "Modeling The Banking Firm: A Survey," JMCB, 1984, v16(4), Part 2, 576-602.

Santomero, Anthony M. "The Error-Learning Hypothesis And The Term Structure Of Interest Rates In Eurodollars," JOF, 1975, v30(3), 773-783.

Santomero, Anthony M. "The Economic Effects Of NASDAQ: Some Preliminary Results," JFQA, 1974, v9(1), 13-24.

Santomero, Anthony M. (Goodman, Laurie S. and Anthony M. Santomero. "Variable-Rate Deposit Insurance: A Re-Examination," JBF, 1986, v10(2), 203-218.)

Santomero, Anthony M. (Gorton, Gary and Anthony M. Santomero. "Market Discipline And Bank Subordinated Debt," JMCB, 1990, v22(1), 119-128.)

Santomero, Anthony M. (Gultekin, Bulent and Anthony M. Santomero. "Indexation, Expectations, And Stability," JMCB, 1979, v1(1), 1-21.)

Santomero, Anthony M. (Kim, Daesik and Anthony M. Santomero. "Risk In Banking And Capital Regulation," JOF, 1988, v43(5), 1219-1233.)

Santomero, Anthony M. (Koehn, Michael and Anthony M. Santomero. "Regulation Of Bank Capital And Portfolio Risk," JOF, 1980, v35(5), 1235-1244.)

Santomero, Anthony M. (Langohr, Herwig and Anthony M. Santomero. "Commercial Bank Refinancing And Economic Stability: An Analysis Of European Features," JBF, 1985, v9(4), 535-552.)

Santomero, Anthony M. (Langohr, Herwig and Anthony M. Santomero. "The Extent Of Equity Investment By European Banks," JMCB, 1985, v17(2), 243-252.)

Santoni, G. J. (Belongia, Michael T. and G. J. Santoni. "Interest Rate Risk, Market Value, And Hedging Financial Portfolios," JFR, 1987, v10(1), 47-57.)

Santow, Leonard Jay. "Cost Of Long-Term Capital From A Corporate Point Of View," FAJ, 1963, v19(3), 43-50.

Santow, Leonard Jay. "Ultimate Demise Of Preferred Stock As A Source Of Corporate Capital," FAJ, 1962, v18(3), 47-54.

Sanvicente, Antonio Z. (Griffin, Paul A. and Antonio Z. Sanvicente. "Common Stock Returns And Rating Changes: A Methodological Comparison," JOF, 1982, v37(1), 103-119.)

Sapolsky, Harvey M. "Organizational Structure And Innovation," JOB, 1967, v40(4), 497-510.

Sappington, David E. M. and Birger Wernerfelt. "To Brand Or Not To Brand? A Theoretical And Empirical Question," JOB, 1985, v58(3), 279-294.

Sarason, Harry M. "Association Insurance," JRI, 1961, v28(4), 79-84.

Sarassoro, Gboroton F. (Hudson, Michael A., Raymond M. Leuthold and Gboroton F. Sarassoro. "Commodity Futures Price Changes: Recent Evidence For Wheat, Soybeans And Live Cattle," JFM, 1987, v7(3), 287-302.)

Sareewiwatthana, Paiboon and R. Phil Malone. "Market Behavior And The Capital Asset Pricing Model In The Securities Exchange Of Thailand: An Empirical Application," JBFA, 1985, v12(3), 439-452.

Sargeant, Ann H. "Investor Optimism And Security Pricing," FAJ, 1964, v20(5), 130-132.

Sargen, Nicholas P. "Exchange Rate Flexibility And Demand For Money," JOF, 1977, v32(2), 531-544.

Sargent, Thomas J. and Neil Wallace. "Market Transaction Costs, Asset Demand Functions, And The Relative Potency Of Monetary And Fiscal Policy," JMCB, 1971, v3(2), Part 2, 469-506.

Sargent, Thomas J. "A Note On The 'Accelerationist' Controversy," JMCB, 1971, v3(3), 721-725.

Sargent, Thomas J. "Interest Rates And Prices In The Long Run," JMCB, 1973, v5(1), Part II, 385-449.

Sargent, Thomas J. "Rational Expectation And The Term Structure Of Interest Rates," JMCB, 1972, v4(1), 74-97.

Sargent, Thomas J. (Frost, Peter A. and Thomas J. Sargent. "Money-Market Rates, The Discount Rate, And Borrowing From The Federal Reserve," JMCB, 1970, v2(1), 56-82.)

Sarig, Oded and James Scott. "The Puzzle Of Financial Leverage Clienteles," JOF, 1985, v40(5), 1459-1467.

Sarig, Oded H. "On Mergers, Divestments, And Options: A Note," JFQA, 1985, v20(3), 385-390.

Sarig, Oded and Arthur Warga. "Some Empirical Estimates Of The Risk Structure Of Interest Rates," JOF, 1989, v44(5), 1351-1360.

Sarig, Oded and Arthur Warga. "Bond Price Data And Bond Market Liquidity," JFQA, 1989, v24(3), 367-378.

Sarin, Rakesh I. (Becker, Joao L. and Rakesh K. Sarin. "Decision Analysis Using Lottery-Dependent Utility," JRU, 1989, v2(1), 105-118.)

Sarkar, Salil. (Wansley, James W., William R. Lane and Salil Sarkar. "Managements' View On Share Repurchase And Tender Offer Premiums," FM, 1989, v18(3), 97-110.)

Sarlo, G. S. (Longlev, F. A. and G. S. Sarlo. "Current Trends In Integrated Circuits," FAJ, 1967, v23(5), 65-69.)

Sarma, L. V. L. N. and K. S. Hanumanta Rao. "Leverage And The Cost Of Capital In A Less Developed Capital Market: Reply," JOF, 1971, v26(3), 783-785.

Sarma, L. V. L. N. and K. S. Hanumanta Rao. "Leverage And The Value Of The Firm," JOF, 1969, v24(4), 673-677.

Sarnat, Marshall and Haim Levy. "The Relationship Of Rules Of Thumb To The Internal Rate Of Return: A Restatement And Generalization," JOF, 1969, v24(3), 479-489.

Sarnat, Marshall. "A Note On The Prediction Of Portfolio Performance From Ex Post Data," JOF, 1972, v27(4), 903-906.

Sarnat, Marshall. "A Note On The Implications Of Quadratic Utility For Portfolio Theory," JFQA, 1974, v9(4), 687-689.

Sarnat, Marshall. "Capital Market Imperfections And The Composition Of Optimal Portfolios," JOF, 1974, v29(4), 1241-1253.

Sarnat, Marshall. "Purchasing Power Risk, Portfolio Analysis, And The Case For Index-Linked Bonds: A Comment," JMCB, 1973, v5(3), 836-845.

Sarnat, Marshall. (Arditti, Fred D., Haim Levy and Marshall Sarnat. "Taxes, Uncertainty And Optimal Dividend Policy," FM, 1976, v5(1), 46-52.)

Sarnat, Marshall. (Ben-Shahar, Haim and Marshall Sarnat. "Reinvestment And The Rate Of Return On Common Stock," JOF, 1966, v21(4), 737-742.)

Sarnat, Marshall. (Levy, Haim and Marshall Sarnat. "A Pedagogic Note On Alternative Formulations Of The Goal Of The Firm," JOB, 1977, v50(4), 526-528.)

Sarnat, Marshall. (Levy, Haim and Marshall Sarnat. "Leasing, Borrowing, And Financial Risk," FM, 1979, v8(4), 47-54.)

Sarnat, Marshall. (Levy, Haim and Marshall Sarnat. "Reply: Safety First - An Expected Utility Principle," JFQA, 1974, v9(6), 1063-1064.)

Sarnat, Marshall. (Levy, Haim and Marshall Sarnat. "Safety First - An Expected Utility Principle," JFQA, 1972, v7(3), 1829-1834.)

Sarnat, Marshall. (Levy, Haim and Marshall Sarnat. "Risk, Dividend Policy, And The Optimal Pricing Of A Rights Offering: A Comment," JMCB, 1971, v3(4), 840-849.)

Sarnat, Marshall. (Levy, Haim and Marshall Sarnat. "Two-Period Portfolio Selection And Investors' Discount Rates," JOF, 1971, v26(3), 757-761.)

Sarnat, Marshall. (Levy, Haim and Marshall Sarnat. "A Note On Portfolio Selection And Investors' Wealth," JFQA, 1971, v6(1), 639-642.)

Sarnat, Marshall. (Levy, Haim and Marshall Sarnat. "Exchange Rate Risk And The Optimal Diversification Of Foreign Currency Holdings," JMCB, 1978, v10(4), 453-463.)

Sarnat, Marshall. (Levy, Haim and Marshall Sarnat. "Diversification, Portfolio Analysis And The Uneasy Case For Conglomerate Mergers," JOF, 1970, v25(4), 795-802.)

Sarnat, Marshall. (Levy, Haim and Marshall Sarnat. "The Case For Mutual Funds," FAJ, 1972, v28(2), 77-81.)

Sarnat, Marshall. (Levy, Haim and Marshall Sarnat. "Alternative Efficiency Criteria: An Empirical Analysis," JOF, 1970, v25(5), 1153-1158.)

Sarnat, Marshall. (Peles, Yoram C. and Marshall Sarnat. "Government Intervention And Financial Policy: The Impact Of Corporate Taxation On Capital Structure," RIF, 1983, v4, (Supp), 169-188.)

Sarndal, Carl E. (Mao, James C. T. and Carl E. Sarndal. "Cash Management: Theory And Practice," JBFA, 1978, v5(3), 329-338.)

Sarndal, Carl Erik. (Mao, James C. T. and Carl Erik Sarndal. "Controlling Risk In Accounts Receivable Management," JBFA, 1974, v1(3), 395-404.)

Sartoris, William L. and M. Lynn Spruill. "Goal Programming And Working Capital Management," FM, 1974, v3(1), 67-74.

Sartoris, William L. and Ned C. Hill. "A Generalized Cash Flow Approach To Short-Term Financial Decisions," JOF, 1983, v38(2), 349-360.

Sartoris, William L. and Ned C. Hill. "Evaluating Credit Policy Alternatives: A Present Value Framework," JFR, 1981, v4(1), 81-89.

Sartoris, William L. and Ronda S. Paul. "Lease Evaluation - Another Capital Budgeting Decision," FM, 1973, v2(2), 46-52.

Sartoris, William L. "The Effect Of Regulation, Population Characteristics, And Competition On The Market For Personal Cash Loans," JFQA, 1972, v7(4), 1931-1956.

Sartoris, William L. (Moore, William T. and William L. Satoris. "Dividends And Taxes: Another Look At The Electric Utility Industry," FR, 1985, v20(1), 1-20.)

Sartoris, William L. and Ned C. Hill. "The Relationship Between Credit Policies And Firm Financial Characteristics," AWCM, 1990, v1(1), 99-114.

Sastry, A. S. Rama. "The Effect Of Credit On The Interest Elasticity Of The Transaction Demand For Cash: Reply," JOF, 1971, v26(5), 1163-1165.

Sastry, A. S. Rama. "The Effect Of Credit On Transactions Demand For Cash," JOF, 1970, v25(4), 777-781.

Sau, Ranjit K. "The Optimal Rate Of Investment In A Firm: Reply," JOF, 1970, v25(3), 685-686.

Sau, Ranjit K. "The Optimal Rate Of Investment In A Firm," JOF, 1969, v24(1), 1-12.

Saubert, Lynn K. (Wolk, Harry I., Lynn K. Saubert and Frank M. Tiernan. "A Further Note On Discounting Deferred Taxes," JBFA, 1984, v11(2), 253-255.)

Saudagaran, Shahrokh M. "An Investigation Of Selected Factors Influencing Multiple Listing And The Choice Of Foreign Stock Exchanges," AFPAP, 1990, v5(1), 75-122.

Sauerhaft, Daniel. (Wang, George H. K. and Daniel Sauerhaft. "Examination Ratings And The Identification Of Problem/Non-Problem Thrift Institutions," JFSR, 1989, v2(4), 319-342.)

Sauerlender, Owen H. (Gamble, Hays B., Roger H. Downing and Owen H. Sauerlender. "Community Growth Around Nuclear Power Plants," AREUEA, 1980, v8(3), 268-280.)

Saulnier, R. J. "Insurance Company Urban Mortgage Lending And The Business Cycle," JOF, 1950, v5(4), 295-306.

Saulnier, Raymond J. "The Financial Research Program Of The National Bureau Of Economic Research," JOF, 1947, v2(1), 5-14.

Saulnier, Raymond J. "The President's Economic Report: A Critique," JPM, 1974-75, v1(4), 15-16.

Saulnier, Raymond J. "The President's Economic Report: A Critique," JPM, 1975-76, v2(4), 57-58.

Saulnier, Raymond J. "The President's Economic Report: A Critique," JPM, 1976-77, v3(4), 23-24.

Saulnier, Raymond J. "The President's Economic Report: A Critique," JPM, 1977-78, v4(4), 45-46.

Saulnier, Raymond J. "The President's Economic Report: A Critique," JPM, 1978-79, v5(4), 11-12.

Saulnier, Raymond J. "The President's Economic Report: A Critique," JPM, 1979-80, v6(4), 37-39.

Saulnier, Raymond J. "The President's Economic Report: A Critique," JPM, 1980-81, v7(4), 17-18.

Saulnier, Raymond J. "The President's Economic Report: A Critique," JPM, 1981-82, v8(4), 50.

Saulnier, Raymond J. "The President's Economic Report: A Critique," JPM, 1982-83, v9(4), 58-59.

Saulnier, Raymond J. "The President's Economic Report: A Critique," JPM, 1983-84, v10(4), 81-83.

Saulnier, Raymond J. "The President's Economic Report: A Critique," JPM, 1984-85, v11(4), 61-62.

Saulnier, Raymond J. "The President's Economic Report: A Critique," JPM, 1985-86, v12(4), 72-73.

Saulnier, Raymond J. "The President's Economic Report: A Critique," JPM, 1986-87, v13(4), 83-86.

Saulnier, Raymond J. "The President's Economic Report: A Critique," JPM, 1987-88, v14(4), 66-67.

Saulnier, Raymond J. "The President's Economic Report: A Critique," JPM, 1989, v15(4), 78-80.

Saulnier, Raymond J. "The President's Economic Report: A Critique," JPM, 1990, v16(4), 77-78.

Saulnier, Raymond J. "Three Federal Budget Concepts," FAJ, 1967, v23(4), 19-24.

Saunders, A. (Ward, C. W. R. and A. Saunders. "U.K. Unit Trust Performance 1964-74," JBFA, 1976, v3(4), 83-100.)

Saunders, A. and J. Lim. "Underpricing And The New Issue Process In Singapore," JBF, 1990, v14(2/3), 291-310.

Saunders, Anthony and Richard S. Woodward. "Gains From International Portfolio Diversification: A Reply," JBFA, 1979, v6(1), 51-52.

Saunders, Anthony and Richard S. Woodward. "Gains From International Portfolio Diversification: UK Evidence 1971-75," JBFA, 1977, v4(3), 299-309.

Saunders, Anthony B. (Buser, Stephen A., Patric H. Hendershott and Anthony B. Saunders. "Determinants Of The Value Of Call Options On Default-Free Bonds," JOB, 1990, v63(1), Part 2, S33-S50.)

Saunders, Anthony and Michael Smirlock. "Intra- And Interindustry Effects Of Bank Securities Market Activities: The Case Of Discount Brokerage," JFQA, 1987, v22(4), 467-482.

Saunders, Anthony and Stanley Sienkiewicz. "The Hedging Performance Of ECU Futures Contracts," JFM, 1988, v8(3), 335-352.

Saunders, Anthony and Thomas Urich. "The Effects Of Shifts In Monetary Policy And Reserve Accounting Regimes On Bank Reserve Management Behavior In The Federal Funds Markets," JBF, 1988, v11(4), 523-536.

Saunders, Anthony, Charles Ward and Richard Woodward. "Stochastic Dominance And The Performance Of U.K. Unit Trusts," JFQA, 1980, v15(2), 323-330.

Saunders, Anthony, Elizabeth Strock and Nickolaos G. Travlos. "Ownership Structure, Deregulation, And Bank Risk Taking," JOF, 1990, v45(2), 643-654.

Saunders, Anthony. "Expected Inflation, Unexpected Inflation And The Return On U.K. Shares, 1961-1973," JBFA, 1978, v5(3), 309-320.

Saunders, Anthony. (Aharony, Joseph, Anthony Saunders and Itzhak Swary. "The Effects Of The International Banking Act On Domestic Bank Profitability And Risk," JMCB, 1985, v17(4), Part 1, 493-506.)

Saunders, Anthony. (Allen, Linda and Anthony Saunders. "The Large-Small Bank Dichotomy In The Federal Funds Market," JBF, 1986, v10(2), 219-230.)

Saunders, Anthony. (Allen, Linda, Stavros Peristiani and Anthony Saunders. "Bank Size, Collateral, And Net Purchase Behavior In The Federal Funds Market: Empirical Evidence," JOB, 1989, v62(4), 501-516.)

Saunders, Anthony. (Emery, Douglas R., Philip C. Parr, Per B. Mokkelbost, David Gandhi and Anthony Saunders. "An Investigation Of Real Investment Decision Making With The Options Pricing Model," JBFA, 1978, v5(4), 363-369.)

Saunders, Anthony. (Gandhi, Devinder K., Robert Hausmann, Jr. and Anthony Saunders. "On Syndicate Sharing Rules For Unanimous Project Rankings," JBF, 1985, v9(4), 517-534.)

Saunders, Anthony. (Gandhi, Devinder K. and Anthony Saunders. "The Superiority Of Stochastic Dominance Over Mean-Variance Efficiency Criteria: Some Clarifications," JBFA, 1981, v8(1), 51-59.)

Saunders, Anthony. (Gandhi, Devinder K., Anthony Saunders, Richard Woodward and Charles Ward. "The British Investor's Gains From International Portfolio Investment," JBF, 1981, v5(2), 155-165.)

Saunders, Anthony. (Goldberg, Lawrence G. and Anthony Saunders. "The Causes Of U.S. Bank Expansion Overseas: The Case Of Great Britain," JMCB, 1980, v12(4), Part 1, 630-634.)

Saunders, Anthony. (Goldberg, Lawrence G. and Anthony Saunders. "The Determinants Of Foreign Banking Activity In The United States," JBF, 1981, v5(1), 17-32.)

Saunders, Anthony. (Goldberg, Lawrence G. and Anthony Saunders. "The Growth Of Organizational Forms Of Foreign Banks In The U.S.," JMCB, 1981, v13(3), 365-374.)

Saunders, Anthony. (Grammatikos, Theoharry, Anthony Saunders and Itzhak Swary. "Returns And Risks Of U. S. Bank Foreign Currency Activities," JOF, 1986, v41(3), 670-681.)

Saunders, Anthony. (Grammatikos, Theoharry and Anthony Saunders. "Futures Price Variability: A Test Of Maturity And Volume Effects," JOB, 1986, v59(2), Part 1, 319-330.)

Saunders, Anthony. (Grammatikos, Theoharry and Anthony Saunders. "Stability And The Hedging Performance Of Foreign Currency Futures," JFM, 1983, v3(3), 295-305.)

Saunders, Anthony. (Ho, Thomas and Anthony Saunders. "A Catastrophe Model Of Bank Failure," JOF, 1980, v35(5), 1189-1207.)

Saunders, Anthony. (Ho, Thomas S. Y. and Anthony Saunders. "A Micro Model Of The Federal Funds Market," JOF, 1985, v40(3), 977-988.)

Saunders, Anthony. (Ho, Thomas S. Y. and Anthony Saunders. "The Determinants Of Bank Interest Margins: Theory And Empirical Evidence," JFQA, 1981, v16(4), 581-600.)

Saunders, Anthony. (Ho, Thomas S. Y. and Anthony Saunders. "Fixed Rate Loan Commitments, Take-Down Risk, And The Dynamics Of Hedging With Futures," **JFQA**, 1983, v18(4), 499-516.)

Saunders, Anthony. (John, Kose and Anthony Saunders. "Asymmetry Of Information, Regulatory Lags And Optimal Incentive Contracts: Theory And Evidence," **JOF**, 1983, v38(2), 391-404.)

Saunders, Anthony. (Kallberg, Jarl G. and Anthony Saunders. "Markov Chain Approaches To The Analysis Of Payment Behavior Of Retail Credit Customers," **FM**, 1983, v12(2), 5-14.)

Saunders, Anthony. (Maldonado, Rita and Anthony Saunders. "Foreign Exchange Futures And The Law Of One Price," **FM**, 1983, v12(1), 19-23.)

Saunders, Anthony. (Maldonado, Rita and Anthony Saunders. "International Portfolio Diversification And The Inter-Temporal Stability Of International Stock Market Relationships, 1957-1978," **FM**, 1981, v10(4), 54-63.)

Saunders, Anthony. (Merrick, John J., Jr. and Anthony Saunders. "Bank Regulation And Monetary Policy," **JMCB**, 1985, v17(4), Part 2, 691-717.)

Saunders, Anthony. Aharony, Joseph, Anthony Saunders and Itzhak Swary. "The Effects Of DIDMCA On Bank Stockholders' Returns And Risk," **JBF**, 1988, v11(3), 317-332.)

Saunders, Edward M. (Kolari, James, Arvind Mahajan and Edward M. Saunders. "The Effect Of Changes In Reserve Requirements On Bank Stock Prices," **JBF**, 1988, v12(2), 183-198.)

Saunders, Edward M. (Lusht, Kenneth M. and Edward M. Saunders. "Direct Tests Of The Divergence Of Opinion Hypothesis In The Market For Racetrack Betting," **JFR**, 1989, v12(4), 285-292.)

Saunders, Edward M., Jr. "Developing A Real-Time Microcomputerized Investment Arbitrage Course," **JFED**, 1990, v19, 15-18.

Saunders, Edward M., Jr. and Arvind Mahajan. "An Empirical Examination Of Composite Stock Index Futures Pricing," **JFM**, 1988, v8(2), 210-228.

Saunders, R. Duane. "The Development Of The Flow Of Institutional Savings In The Analysis Of Treasury Borrowing Problems," **JOF**, 1956, v11(2), 277-287.

Saunders, Robert J. "Further Comment: Cross-Sectional Differences Among Commercial Banks," **JFQA**, 1974, v9(6), 1053-1055.

Saunders, Robert J. "On The Interpretation Of Models Explaining Cross Section Differences Among Commercial Banks," **JFQA**, 1969, v4(1), 25-35.

Saunders, Robert J. (Bahl, Roy W. and Robert J. Saunders. "Factors Associated With Variation In State And Local Government Spending," **JOF**, 1966, v21(3), 523-534.)

Saurman, David S. "Currency Substitution, The Exchange Rate, And The Real Interest Rate (Non)Differential: Shipping The Bad Money In," **JMCB**, 1986, v18(4), 512-518.

Saurman, David S. "Transactions Costs, Foreign Exchange Demands, And The Expected Rates Of Change Of Exchange Rates," **JMCB**, 1982, v14(1), 20-32.

Sauvain, Harry C. "Changing Interest Rates And The Investment Portfolio," **JOF**, 1959, v14(2), 230-244.

Sauvain, Harry C. "Investment Management (A Review)," **FAJ**, 1966, v22(4), 91-92.

Sauvain, Harry. "The State Of The Finance Field: Comment," **JOF**, 1967, v22(4), 541-542.

Savage, Donald T. and David Burras Humphrey. "Branching Laws And Banking Offices," **JMCB**, 1979, v11(2), 227-230.

Savage, Donald T. and Elinor H. Solomon. "Branch Banking: The Competitive Issues," **JBR**, 1980-81, v11(2), 110-121.

Savage, Donald T. "Bank Home Office Protection Laws And Intercity Branching In Statewide Branch Banking States," **JMCB**, 1979, v11(4), 500-505.

Savage, Donald T. "Branch Banking Laws, Deposits, Market Share And Profitability Of New Banks," **JBR**, 1981-82, v12(4), 200-206.

Savage, Donald T. (McCall, Alan S. and Donald T. Savage. "Branching Policy: The Options," **JBR**, 1980-81, v11(2), 122-126.)

Savage, Donald T. (Rose, John T. and Donald T. Savage. "Bank Holding Company De Novo Entry And Banking Market Performance," **JBR**, 1986-87, v17(1), 45-50.)

Savage, Donald T. (Rose, John T. and Donald T. Savage. "Bank Holding Company De Novo Entry And Banking Market Deconcentration," **JBR**, 1982-83, v13(2), 96-100.)

Savage, Donald T. (Rose, John T. and Donald T. Savage. "De Novo Entry And Performance: Bank Holding Companies Versus Independent Banks," **JBR**, 1984-85, v15(2), 95-107.)

Savage, E. Linwood, Jr. "Conclusions Regarding Annual Reports," **FAJ**, 1954, v10(1), 51-54.

Savage, G. P. (Doyle, P., I. Fenwick and G. P. Savage. "A Model For Evaluating Branch Location And Performance," **JBR**, 1981-82, v12(2), 90-95.)

Savage, Ian. (Moses, Leon N. and Ian Savage. "The Effect Of Airline Pilot Characteristics On Perception Of Job Safety Risks," **JRU**, 1989, v2(4), 335-352.)

Savage, James. (Breen, William and James Savage. "Portfolio Distribution And Tests Of Security Selection Models," **JOF**, 1968, v23(5), 805-819.)

Savage, Leonard J. (Lorie, James H. and Leonard J. Savage. "Three Problems In Rationing Capital," **JOB**, 1955, v28(4), 229-239.)

Savarino, James E. (Frost, Peter A. and James E. Savarino. "For Better Performance: Constrain Portfolio Weights," **JPM**, 1988-89, v15(1), 29-34.)

Savarino, James E. (Frost, Peter A. and James E. Savarino. "An Empirical Bayes Approach To Efficient Portfolio Selection," **JFQA**, 1986, v21(3), 293-305.)

Savarino, James E. (Frost, Peter A. and James E. Savarino. "Portfolio Size And Estimation Risk," **JPM**, 1985-86, v12(4), 60-64.)

Saving, T. R. "Inside Money, Short-Run Rents, And The Real-Balance Effect: A Reply," **JMCB**, 1971, v3(2), Part 1, 276-280.

Saving, T. R. "The Value Of Time And Economies Of Scale In The Demand For Cash Balances: A Comment," **JMCB**, 1974, v6(1), 122-124.

Saving, T. R. (Lanzillotti, R. F. and T. R. Saving. "State Branching Restrictions And The Availablity Of Branching Services: A Comment," **JMCB**, 1969, v1(4), 778-788.)

Saving, Thomas R. "Money Supply Theory With Competitively Determined Deposit Rates And Activity Charges," **JMCB**, 979, v11(1), 22-31.

Saving, Thomas R. "Outside Money, Inside Money, And The Real Balance Effect," **JMCB**, 1970, v2(1), 83-111.

Saving, Thomas R. "Portfolio Choice And Monetary Theory: A Review Essay," **JMCB**, 1970, v2(2), 258-267.

Saving, Thomas R. "Toward A Competitive Financial Sector," **JMCB**, 1972, v4(4), 897-914.

Saving, Thomas R. "Transactions Cost Function And The Inventory-Theoretic Approach To Money Demand," **JMCB**, 1976, v8(3), 339-345.

Saving, Thomas R. (Parkinson, Michael. "The Extreme Value Method For Estimating The Variance Of The Rate Of Return," **JOB**, 1980, v53(1), 61-66.)

Saving, Thomas. "Transaction Costs And The Demand For Money," **JMCB**, 1972, v4(2), 245-259.

Savit, Robert. "Nonlinearities And Chaotic Effects In Options Prices," **JFM**, 1989, v9(6), 507-518.

Savit, Robert. "When Random Is Not Random: An Introduction To Chaos In Market Prices," **JFM**, 1988, v8(3), 271-290.

Savoie, Leonard M. "Financial Reports," **FAJ**, 1968, v24(2), 67-79.

Savoie, Leonard M. "Meeting Financial Consumer Needs," **FAJ**, 1969, v25(2), 47-51.

Savoie, Leonard M. "The Accounting Principles Board," **FAJ**, 1965, v21(3), 53-57.

Savvides, Andreas. "Bank Loan Rate Indexation In The Eurocurrency Market," **JIMF**, 1987, v6(3), 355-372.

Savvides, Andreas. "Real Exchange Rate Variability And The Choice Of Exchange Rate Regime By Developing Countries," **JIMF**, 1990, v9(4), 440-454.

Sawaya, William J. (Dyl, Edward A. and William J. Sawaya. "The Bond Issue Size Decision Revisited," **FM**, 1979, v8(4), 60-67.)

Sawyer, E. W. "Liability At Law And Insurance Against It," **JRI**, 1937, v4, 72-78.

Sawyer, Elmer Warren. "Meeting The Problems Of Insurance As Interstate Commerce," **JRI**, 1947, v14, 57-67.

Saxe, Jo W. "Concessionary Lending To Developing Countries," **JBF**, 1981, v5(1), 135-148.

Saxon, O. Glenn, Jr. "Gold Mining In South Africa," **FAJ**, 1953, v9(5), 61-64.

Saxon, O. Glenn. "Commodity And Paper Dollars: 1619-1792," **FAJ**, 1953, v9(2), 35-42.

Saxon, O. Glenn. "The Federal Debt And Its Implications," **FAJ**, 1951, v7(1), 25-30.

Scadding, John L. "The Fiscal Element In Monetary Policy: 1965-68," **JMCB**, 1971, v3(2), Part 2, 391-411.

Scanlan, F. V. and C. S. Goodwin. "The Advertising Industry," **FAJ**, 1968, v24(1), 71-76.

Scanlon, J. J. "Long-Range Outlook For Financing," **JOF**, 1957, v12(2), 272-278.

Scanlon, John J. "Bell System Financial Policies," **FM**, 1972, v1(2), 16-26.

Scanlon, Kevin P. (Trifts, Jack W. and Kevin P. Scanlon. "Interstate Bank Mergers: The Early Evidence," **JFR**, 1987, v10(4), 305-312.)

Scanlon, Kevin P., Jack W. Trifts and Richard H. Pettway. "Impacts Of Relative Size And Industrial Relatedness On Returns To Shareholders Of Acquiring Firms," **JFR**, 1989, v12(2), 103-112.

Scapens, Robert W. and J. Timothy Sale. "Performance Measurement And Formal Capital Expenditure Controls In Divisionalised Companies," **JBFA**, 1981, v8(3), 389-419.

Scapens, Robert W. "A Neoclassical Measure Of Profit: An Extension For Uncertainty," **JBFA**, 1983, v10(3), 409-418.

Scapens, Robert W. "Profit Measurement In Divisionalised Companies," **JBFA**, 1979, v6(3), 281-306.

Scapens, Robert W. "The Gearing Adjustment: An Economic Profit Perspective," **JBFA**, 1983, v10(4), 503-520.

Scapens, Robert W. (Rahman, M. Zubaidur and Robert W. Scapens. "Transfer Pricing By Multinationals: Some Evidence From Bangladesh," **JBFA**, 1986, v13(3), 383-391.)

Scapens, Robert W., Robert J. Ryan and Leslie Fletcher. "Explaining Corporate Failure: A Catastrophe Theory Approach," **JBFA**, 1981, v8(1), 1-26.

Scarth, William. "Deficits And Debt In An Open Economy," **JIMF**, 1988, v7(3), 351-358.

Schaack, Christian. (Hiller, Randall S. and Christian Schaack. "A Classification Of Structured Bond Portfolio Modeling Techniques," **JPM**, 1990, v17(1), 37-50.)

Schaaf, A. H. "Regional Differences In Mortgage Financing Costs," **JOF**, 1966, v21(1), 85-94.

Schachter, Barry. "A Note On The Welfare Consequences Of New Option Markets," **JOF**, 1986, v41(1), 263-268.

Schachter, Barry. (Butler, J. S. and Barry Schachter. "Unbiased Estimation Of The Black/Scholes Formula," **JFEC**, 1986, v15(3), 341-357.)

Schachter, Barry. (Butler, J. S. and Barry Schachter. "The Investment Decision: Estimation Risk And Risk Adjusted Discount Rates," **FM**, 1989, v18(4), 13-22.)

Schachter, Barry. (Golbe, Devra L. and Barry Schachter. "The Net Present Value Rule And An Algorithm For Maintaining A Constant Debt-Equity Ratio," **FM**, 1985, v14(2), 53-58.)

Schadrack, Frederick C., Jr. "Demand And Supply In The Commercial Paper Market," **JOF**, 1970, v25(4), 837-852.

Schaede, Ulrike. "Forwards And Futures In Tokugawa-Period Japan: A New Perspective On The Dojima Rice Market," **JBF**, 1989, v13(4/5), 487-514.

Schaefer, Jeffrey M. and Adolphe J. Warner. "Concentration In The Securities Industry," **FAJ**, 1977, v33(6), 29-34.

Schaefer, Jeffrey M. and Adolphe J. Warner. "Rejoinder To West And Tinic," **FAJ**, 1978, v34(3), 47-49.

Schaefer, S. M. (Hodges, S. D. and S. M. Schaefer. "A Model For Bond Portfolio Improvement," **JFQA**, 1977, v12(2), 243-260.)

Schaefer, Stephen M. and Eduardo S. Schwartz. "A Two-Factor Model Of The Term Structure: An Approximate Analytical Solution," **JFQA**, 1984, v19(4), 413-424.

Schaefer, Stephen M. "Tax-Induced Clientele Effects In The Market For British Government Securities: Placing Bounds On Security

Values In An Incomplete Market," *JFEC*, 1982, v10(2), 121-159.

Schaefer, Stephen M. "Taxation And Bond Market Equilibrium In A World Of Uncertain Future Interest Rates: Comment," *JFQA*, 1981, v16(5), 773-777.

Schaefer, Stephen M. "The Problem With Redemption Yields," *FAJ*, 1977, v33(4), 59-67.

Schaefer, Stephen M. (Harrison, J. Michael, Richard Pitbladdo and Stephen M. Schaefer. "Continuous Price Processes In Frictionless Markets Have Infinite Variation," *JOB*, 1984, v57(3), 353-366.)

Schaefer, Stephen M. and Eduardo S. Schwartz. "Time-Dependent Variance And The Pricing Of Bond Options," *JOF*, 1987, v42(5), 1113-1128.

Schaefer, Stephen. (Brealey, Richard and Stephen Schaefer. "Term Structure And Uncertain Inflation," *JOF*, 1977, v32(2), 277-289.)

Schaefer, Stephen. (Hodges, Stewart and Stephen Schaefer. "The Interpretation Of The Geometric Mean: A Note," *JFQA*, 1974, v9(3), 497-504.)

Schafer, Robert. (Reid, Gary and Robert Schafer. "Multifamily Housing Demand: Comment," *AREUEA*, 1979, v7(1), 123-129.)

Schaffer, Burton F. and D. Ordell Calkins. "An Appraisal Of Prerequisites To Business Finance," *JFED*, 1980, v9, 51-55.

Schaffer, Burton F. and D. Ordell Calkins. "Compustat: Bringing The Real World Into The Classroom," *JFED*, 1977, v6, 75-78.

Schall, Lawrence D. and Gary L. Sundem. "Capital Budgeting Methods And Risk: A Further Analysis," *FM*, 1980, v9(1), 7-11.

Schall, Lawrence D. "Analytic Issues In Lease Vs. Purchase Decisions," *FM*, 1987, v16(2), 17-20.

Schall, Lawrence D. "Asset Valuation, Firm Investment, And Firm Diversification," *JOB*, 1972, v45(1), 11-28.

Schall, Lawrence D. "Firm Financial Structure And Investment," *JFQA*, 1971, v6(3), 925-942.

Schall, Lawrence D. "Taxes, Inflation And Corporate Financial Policy," *JOF*, 1984, v39(1), 105-126.

Schall, Lawrence D. "The Lease-Or-Buy And Asset Acquisition Decisions," *JOF*, 1974, v29(4), 1203-1214.

Schall, Lawrence D. (Haley, Charles W. and Lawrence D. Schall. "A Note On Investment Policy With Imperfect Capital Martkets," *JOF*, 1972, v27(1), 93-96.)

Schall, Lawrence D. (Haley, Charles W. and Lawrence D. Schall. "Problems With The Concept Of The Cost Of Capital," *JFQA*, 1978, v13(5), 847-870.)

Schall, Lawrence D. (Higgins, Robert C. and Lawrence D. Schall. "Corporate Bankruptcy And Conglomerate Merger," *JOF*, 1975, v30(1), 93-113.)

Schall, Lawrence D., Gary L. Sundem and William R. Geijsbeek, Jr. "Survey And Analysis Of Capital Budgeting Methods," *JOF*, 1978, v33(1), 281-287.

Schallheim, James and Robin DeMagistris. "New Estimates Of The Market Parameters," *FM*, 1980, v9(3), 60-68.

Schallheim, James S. and John J. McConnell. "A Model For The Determination Of "Fair" Premiums On Lease Cancellation Insurance Policies," *JOF*, 1985, v40(5), 1439-1457.

Schallheim, James S. (Brickley, James A. and James S. Schallheim. "Lifting The Lid On Closed-End Investment Companies: A Case Of Abnormal Returns," *JFQA*, 1985, v20(1), 107-118.)

Schallheim, James S. (Kato, Kiyoshi and James S. Schallheim. "Seasonal And Size Anomalies In The Japanese Stock Market," *JFQA*, 1985, v20(2), 243-260.)

Schallheim, James S. (Lease, Ronald C., John J. McConnell and James S. Schallheim. "Realized Returns And The Default And Prepayment Experience Of Financial Leasing Contracts," *FM*, 1990, v19(2), 11-20.)

Schallheim, James S. (McConnell, John J. and James S. Schallheim. "Valuation Of Asset Leasing Contracts," *JFEC*, 1983, v12(2), 237-261.)

Schallheim, James S., Ramon E. Johnson, Ronald C. Lease and John J. McConnell. "The Determinants Of Yields On Financial Leasing Contracts," *JFEC*, 1987, v19(1), 45-68.

Schapira, Steffen. "An Insurance Plan To Guarantee Reverse Mortgage: Comment," *JRI*, 1990, v57(4), 712-714.

Schapiro, Morris A. "Factors In Bank Stock Appraisal," *FAJ*, 1949, v5(2), 36-39.

Schapperle, Robert F. (Beatty, Randolph P., John F. Reim and Robert F. Schapperle. "The Effect Of Barriers To Entry On Bank Shareholder Wealth: Implications For Interstate Banking," *JBR*, 1985-86, v16(1), 8-15.)

Scharfstein, David S. (Froot, Kenneth A., David S. Scharfstein and Jeremy C. Stein. "LDC Debt: Forgiveness, Indexation, And Investment Incentives," *JOF*, 1989, v44(5), 1335-1350.)

Scharfstein, David S. (Rotemberg, Julio J. and David S. Scharfstein. "Shareholder-Value Maximization And Product-Market Competition," *RFS*, 1990, v3(3), 367-392.)

Scharfstein, David. (Hoshi, Takeo, Anil Kashyap and David Scharfstein. "The Role Of Banks In Reducing The Costs Of Financial Distress In Japan," *JFEC*, 1990, v27(1), 67-88.)

Schatzberg, John D. (Kim, E. Han and John D. Schatzberg. "Voluntary Corporate Liquidations," *JFEC*, 1987, v19(2), 311-328.)

Schatzberg, John D. (Robbins, Edward Henry and John D. Schatzberg. "Callable Bonds: A Risk-Reducing Signalling Mechanism--A Reply," *JOF*, 1988, v43(4), 1067-1073.)

Schatzberg, John D. (Robbins, Edward Henry and John D. Schatzberg. "Callable Bonds: A Risk-Reducing Signalling Mechanism," *JOF*, 1986, v41(4), 935-950.)

Schatzberg, John. (Corrado, Charles J. and John Schatzberg. "A Nonparametric Distribution-Free Test For Serial Independence In Stock Returns: A Correction," *JFQA*, 1990, v25(3), 411-416.)

Schechtman, Edna. (Bigman, David, David Goldfarb and Edna Schechtman. "Futures Market Efficiency And The Time Content Of The Information Sets," *JFM*, 1983, v3(3), 321-334.)

Scheel, William C. "A Critique Of The Interest-Adjusted Net Cost Index," *JRI*, 1973, v40(2), 245-262.

Scheel, William C. "A Critique Of The Interest-Adjusted Net Cost Index: Reply," *JRI*, 1975, v42(3), 553-559.

Scheel, William C. "Company Retention - An Unreliable Indicator Of The Cost Of Life Insurance To The Policyowner," *JRI*, 1975, v42(1), 81-104.

Scheel, William C. "Comparisons Of Riskiness As Measured By The Coefficient Of Variation," *JRI*, 1978, v45(1), 148-152.

Scheel, William C. "Efficient Simulation Of Mortality Experience For A Closed Cohort Of Lives," *JRI*, 1977, v44(4), 571-584.

Scheel, William C. "Optimizing The Structure Of Capital Claims And Assets Of A Stock Insurance Company: Comment," *JRI*, 1972, v39(2), 305-310.

Scheel, William C. "The Concept Of Level Premium Whole Life Policy - Re-Examined: Comment," *JRI*, 1977, v44(3), 502-505.

Scheel, William C. "The Cost Of Funding Benefits Under The ERISA: A Statistical Survey: Comment," *JRI*, 1978, v45(1), 133-136.

Scheel, William C. "The Effects Of Risk Reduction Inherent In Universal Life Insurance," *JRI*, 1979, v46(2), 45-60.

Scheel, William C. "The Effects Of Risk Reduction In Universal Life Insurance: Part II," *JRI*, 1979, v46(3), 451-482.

Scheel, William C. "The Effects Of Risk Reduction Inherent In Universal Life Insurance: Reply," *JRI*, 1981, v48(4), 690-693.

Scheel, William C. "The Impropriety Of Benefits-Premiums Ratios In Life Insurance Price Disclosure," *JRI*, 1974, v41(2), 356-359.

Scheel, William C. "The Rate Of Return On The Savings Element In Cash-Value Life Insurance: Comment," *JRI*, 1977, v38(4), 633-637.

Scheel, William C. "Yearly Prices Of Protection And Rates Of Return In A System Of Life Insurance Cost Disclosure," *JRI*, 1977, v44(1), 37-54.

Scheel, William C. (Cummins, J. David, Herbert S. Denenberg and William C. Scheel. "Concentration In The U.S. Life Insurance Industry," *JRI*, 1972, v39(2), 177-200.)

Scheel, William C. and Jack L. VanDerhei. "Replacement Of Life Insurance: Its Regulation And Current Activity," *JRI*, 1978, v45(2), 189-216.

Scheidell, John M. (Bower, Richard S. and John M. Scheidell. "Operationalism In Finance And Economics," *JFQA*, 1970, v5(4), 469-495.)

Scheiner, James H. "Income Smoothing: An Analysis In The Banking Industry," *JBR*, 1981-82, v12(2), 119-123.

Scheinfeld, Aaron. "A Proposal To Accelerate The Flow Of Private Capital Into Under-Developed Nations," *JOB*, 1965, v38(1), 12-17.

Scheinkman, Jose A. and Blake LeBaron. "Nonlinear Dynamics And Stock Returns," *JOB*, 1989, v62(3), 311-338.

Schellbach, Lewis L. "When Did The DJIA Top 1200?," *FAJ*, 1967, v23(3), 71-73.

Schellbach, Lewis L. "Yardsticks For The Market," *FAJ*, 1955, v11(5), 33-36.

Schellenger, Michael. (Followill, Richard A., Michael Schellenger and Patrick H. Marchand. "Economic Order Quantities, Volume Discounts, And Wealth Maximization," *FR*, 1990, v25(1), 143-152.)

Schenk, Robert E. "A Theory Of Vacant Urban Land," *AREUEA*, 1978, v6(2), 153-163.

Schenk, Robert E. "On Finding Determinants Of Money-Stock Cycles," *JMCB*, 1980, v12(3), 502-512.

Scherer, Joseph. "Labor Force: Concepts, Measurement, And Use Of Data," *JOB*, 1958, v31(1), 38-62.

Scherer, Joseph. "On Measuring Fiscal Policy," *JOF*, 1965, v20(4), 683-690.

Scherer, Philip M. (McCarty, Daniel E. and Philip M. Scherer. "The Demand For Finance Majors By Financial Institutions In The Southwest," *JFED*, 1977, v6, 40-44.)

Scherr, Bruce A. and Howard C. Madsen. "Observations On The Relationship Between Agricultural Commodity Prices And Real Interest Rates," *JFM*, 1983, v3(1), 47-54.

Scherr, Frederick C. "A Multiperiod Mean-Variance Model Of Optimal Capital Structure," *FR*, 1987, v22(1), 1-32.

Scherr, Frederick C. (Sugrue, Timothy F. and Frederick C. Scherr. "An Empirical Test Of Ross's Cash Flow Beta Theory Of Capital Structure," *FR*, 1989, v24(3), 355-370.)

Schick, George. (Norgaard, Richard and George Schick. "Profitability In The Property And Liability Insurance Industry," *JRI*, 1970, v37(4), 579-587.)

Schick, George. (Norgaard, Richard and George Schick. "Profitability In The Property And Liability Insurance Industry: Reply," *JRI*, 1972, v39(3), 483-485.)

Schiff, Allen. (Fried, Dov and Allen Schiff. "Audit Committies And Their Objectives," *FAJ*, 1976, v32(6), 46-48.)

Schiff, Michael and Zvi Lieber. "A Model For The Integration Of Credit And Inventory Management," *JOF*, 1974, v29(1), 133-140.

Schilling, Don. "Estimating The Present Value Of Future Income Losses: An Historical Simulation 1900-1982," *JRI*, 1985, v52(1), 100-116.

Schilling, Don. "Estimating The Present Value Of Future Income Losses: An Historical Simulation 1900-1982: Reply," *JRI*, 1989, v56(3), 560-563.

Schilling, Don. "Forward Exchange And Currency Position," *JOF*, 1969, v24(5), 875-885.

Schilling, Don. "Implicit Inflation And Interest Rates In Discounting Personal Injury Economic Losses: Reply," *JRI*, 1986, v53(3), 496-497.

Schilling, Judith M. (Cohen, Ayala, Judith M. Schilling and Irma Terpenning. "Dealer-Issued Commercial Paper: Analysis Of Data," *RIF*, 1985, v5, 77-106.)

Schinasi, Garry J. and P. A. V. B. Swamy. "The Out-Of-Sample Forecasting Performance Of Exchange Rate Models When Coefficients Are Allowed To Change," *JIMF*, 1989, v8(3), 375-390.

Schink, William A. and John S. Y. Chiu. "A Simulation Study Of Effects Of Multicollinearity And Autocorrelation On Estimates Of Parameters," *JFQA*, 1966, v1(2), 36-67.

Schipper, Katherine and Abbie Smith. "A Comparison Of Equity Carve-Outs And Seasoned Equity Offerings: Share Price Effects And Corporate Restructuring," *JFEC*, 1986, v15(1/2), 153-186.

Schipper, Katherine and Abbie Smith. "Effects Of Recontracting On Shareholder Wealth: The Case Of Voluntary Spin-Offs," *JFEC*, 1983, v12(4), 437-468.

Schipper, Katherine and Rex Thompson. "Evidence On The Capitalized Value Of Merger Activity For Acquiring Firms," *JFEC*, 1983, v11(1), 85-119.

Schipper, Katherine and Rex Thompson. "Common Stocks As Hedges Against Shifts In The Consumption Or Investment Opportunity Set," *JOB*, 1981, v54(2), 305-328.

Schipper, Katherine. (Marais, Laurentius, Katherine Schipper and Abbie Smith. "Wealth Effects Of Going Private For Senior Securities," JFEC, 1989, v23(1), 155-191.)

Schirm, David C. (Ferri, Michael G., Scott B. Moore and David C. Schirm. "Investor Expectations About Callable Warrants," JPM, 1987-88, v14(3), 84-86.)

Schirm, David C. (Ferri, Michael G., Scott B. Moore and David C. Schirm. "The Listing, Size, And Value Of Equity Warrants," FR, 1989, v24(1), 135-146.)

Schirm, David C., Richard G. Sheehan and Michael G. Ferri. "Financial Market Responses To Treasury Debt Announcements," JMCB, 1989, v21(3), 394-400.

Schkade, Lawrence L. (Pashigian, B. Peter, Lawrence L. Schkade and George H. Menefee. "The Selection Of An Optimal Deductible For A Given Insurance Policy," JOB, 1966, v39(1), Part I, 35-44.)

Schkade, Lawrence L. and George H. Menefee. "A Normative Model For Deductible Collision Insurance Selection," JRI, 1966, v33(3), 427-436.

Schlagenhauf, Don E. (Hoffman, Dennis L. and Don E. Schlagenhauf. "The Impact Of News And Alternative Theories Of Exchange Rate Determination," JMCB, 1985, v17(3), 328-346.)

Schlagenhauf, Don E. (Kaufman, Herbert M. and Don E. Schlagenhauf. "FNMA Auction Results As A Forecaster Of Residential Mortgage Yields," JMCB, 1981, v13(3), 352-364.)

Schlagenhauf, Don. (Melvin, Michael and Don Schlagenhauf. "Risk In International Lending: A Dynamic Factor Analysis Applied To France And Mexico," JIMF, 1986, v5(Supp), S31-S48.)

Schlais, Dennis. "A Class-Owned And Operated Corporation As A Learning Vehicle," JFED, 1976, v5, 58-60.

Schlarbaum, Gary C. "Investment Performance Of P.L. Insurers' Common Stock Portfolios: Comment," JRI, 1975, v42(1), 167-173.

Schlarbaum, Gary C. (Lewellen, Wilbur G., Ronald C. Lease and Gary C. Schlarbaum. "Patterns Of Investment Strategy And Behavior Among Individual Investors," JOB, 1977, v50(3), 296-333.)

Schlarbaum, Gary G. "The Investment Performance Of The Common Stock Portfolios Of Property-Liability Insurance Companies," JFQA, 1974, v9(1), 89-106.

Schlarbaum, Gary G. (Berges, Angel, John J. McConnell and Gary G. Schlarbaum. "The Turn-of-the-Year In Canada," JOF, 1984, v39(1), 185-192.)

Schlarbaum, Gary G. (Boquist, John A., George A. Racette and Gary G. Schlarbaum. "Duration And Risk Assessment For Bonds And Common Stocks: A Note," JOF, 1975, v30(5), 1360-1365.)

Schlarbaum, Gary G. (Brinson, Gary P., Jeffrey J. Diermeier and Gary G. Schlarbaum. "A Composite Portfolio Benchmark For Pension Plans," FAJ, 1986, v42(2), 15-24.)

Schlarbaum, Gary G. (Cohn, Richard A., Wilbur G. Lewellen, Ronald C. Lease and Gary G. Schlarbaum. "Individual Investor Risk Aversion And Investment Portfolio Composition," JOF, 1975, v30(2), 605-620.)

Schlarbaum, Gary G. (Edmister, Robert O. and Gary G. Schlarbaum. "Credit Policy In Lending Institutions," JFQA, 1974, v9(3), 335-356.)

Schlarbaum, Gary G. (Groth, Stephen C., Wilbur G. Lewellen, Gary G. Schlarbaum and Ronald C. Lease. "How Good Are Broker's Recommendations?," FAJ, 1979, v35(1), 32-40.)

Schlarbaum, Gary G. (Groth, John C., Wilbur G. Lewellen, Gary G. Schlarbaum and Ronald C. Lease. "Security Analysts: Some Are More Equal," JPM, 1977-78, v4(3), 43-48.)

Schlarbaum, Gary G. (Howe, John S. and Gary G. Schlarbaum. "SEC Trading Suspensions: Empirical Evidence," JFQA, 1986, v21(3), 323-333.)

Schlarbaum, Gary G. (Lease, Ronald C., Wilbur G. Lewellen and Gary G. Schlarbaum. "The Individual Investor: Attributes And Attitudes," JOF, 1974, v29(2), 413-433.)

Schlarbaum, Gary G. (Lease, Ronald C., Wilbur G. Lewellen and Gary G. Schlarbaum. "Market Segmentation And The Retail Investor," FAJ, 1976, v32(5), 53-60.)

Schlarbaum, Gary G. (Lewellen, Wilbur G., Kenneth L. Stanley, Ronald C. Lease and Gary G. Schlarbaum. "Some Direct Evidence On The Dividend Clientele Phenomenon," JOF, 1978, v33(5), 1385-1399.)

Schlarbaum, Gary G. (Lewellen, Wilbur G., Ronald C. Lease and Gary G. Schlarbaum. "Investment Performance And Investor Behavior," JFQA, 1979, v14(1), 29-57.)

Schlarbaum, Gary G. (Lewellen, Wilbur G., Ronald C. Lease and Gary G. Schlarbaum. "The Personal Investments Of Professional Managers," FM, 1979, v8(4), 28-36.)

Schlarbaum, Gary G. (McConnell, John J. and Gary G. Schlarbaum. "Returns, Risks, And Pricing Of Income Bonds, 1956-76 (Does Money Have An Odor?)," JOB, 1981, v54(1), 33-64.)

Schlarbaum, Gary G. (McConnell, John J. and Gary G. Schlarbaum. "Another Foray Into The Backwaters Of The Market," JPM, 1980-81, v7(1), 61-65.)

Schlarbaum, Gary G. (Oppenheimer, Henry R. and Gary G. Schlarbaum. "Investing With Ben Graham: An Ex Ante Test Of The Efficient Markets Hypothesis," JFQA, 1981, v16(3), 341-360.)

Schlarbaum, Gary G. (Stanley, Kenneth L., Wilbur G. Lewellen and Gary G. Schlarbaum. "Investor Response To Investment Research," JPM, 1979-80, v6(4), 20-27.)

Schlarbaum, Gary G. (Stanley, Kenneth L., Wilbur G. Lewellen and Gary G. Schlarbaum. "Further Evidence On The Value Of Professional Investment Research," JFR, 1981, v4(1), 1-9.)

Schlarbaum, Gary G. (Ying, Louis K. W., Wilbur G. Lewellen, Gary G. Schlarbaum and Ronald C. Lease. "Stock Exchange Listings And Securities Returns," JFQA, 1977, v12(3), 415-432.)

Schlarbaum, Gary G., Wilbur G. Lewellen and Ronald C. Lease. "The Common Stock-Portfolio Performance Record Of Individual Investors: 1954-70," JOF, 1978, v33(2), 429-441.

Schlarbaum, Gary G., Wilbur G. Lewellen and Ronald C. Lease. "Realized Returns On Common Stock Investments: The Experience Of Individual Investors," JOB, 1978, v51(2), 299-326.

Schlater, John E., Robert A. Haugen and Dean W. Wichern. "Trading Based On Forecasts Of Earnings Per Share: A Test Of The Efficient Market Hypothesis," JBF, 1980, v4(2), 197-211.

Schlee, Edward. "The Value Of Information In Anticipated Utility Theory," JRU, 1990, v3(1), 83-92.

Schleef, Harold J. "Whole Life Cost Comparisons Based Upon The Year Of Required Protection," JRI, 1989, v56(1), 83-103.

Schleef, Harold. (Mildenstein, Ekart and Harold Schleef. "The Optimal Pricing Policy Of A Monopolistic Market-Maker In The Equity Market," JOF, 1983, v38(1), 218-231.)

Schlender, W. F. (Craig, Paul G. and W. F. Schlender. "Some Relationships Between GAW And Seniority," JOB, 1957, v30(1), 1-11.)

Schlesinger, Harris and Neil A. Doherty. "Incomplete Markets For Insurance: An Overview," JRI, 1985, v52(3), 402-423.

Schlesinger, Harris. "Choosing A Deductible For Insurance Contracts: Best Or Worst Insurance Policy?," JRI, 1985, v52(3), 522-527.

Schlesinger, Harris. "Ex Ante Loss Control By Insurers: Public Interest For Higher Profit," JFSR, 1990, v4(2), 83-92.

Schlesinger, Harris. "Monopoly Profits For Contingent-Claims Contracts When Preferences Are State Dependent," JRI, 1987, v54(1), 179-184.

Schlesinger, Harris. "Nonlinear Pricing Strategies For Competitive And Monopolistic Insurance Markets," JRI, 1983, v50(1), 61-83.

Schlesinger, Harris. "Optimal Insurance For Irreplaceable Commodities," JRI, 1984, v51(1), 131-137.

Schlesinger, Harris. "Optimal Insurance Coverage: Comment," JRI, 1987, v54(4), 810-812.

Schlesinger, Harris. "The Optimal Level Of Deductibility In Insurance Contracts," JRI, 1981, v48(3), 465-481.

Schlesinger, Harris. (Briys, Eric, Michel Crouhy and Harris Schlesinger. "Optimal Hedging Under Intertemporally Dependent Preferences," JOF, 1990, v45(4), 1315-1324.)

Schlesinger, Harris. (Briys, Eric, Michel Crouhy and Harris Schlesinger. "An Intertemporal Model Of Consumption And Hedging," RFM, 1988, v7(Supp), 456-466.)

Schlesinger, Harris. (Doherty, Neil A. and Harris Schlesinger. "The Optimal Deductible For An Insurance Policy When Initial Wealth Is Random," JOB, 1983, v56(4), 555-565.)

Schlosser, Michel. (Altman, Edward I., Michel Margaine, Michel Schlosser and Pierre Vernimmen. "Financial And Statistical Analysis For Commercial Loan Evaluation: A French Experience," JFQA, 1974, v9(2), 195-211.)

Schmalensee, Richard and Robert R. Trippi. "Common Stock Volatility Expectations Implied By Option Premia," JOF, 1978, v33(1), 129-147.

Schmalensee, Richard, Alvin J. Silk and Robert Bojanek. "The Impact Of Scale And Media Mix On Advertising Agency Costs," JOB, 1983, v56(4), 453-476.

Schmalensee, Richard. "Gaussian Demand And Commodity Bundling," JOB, 1984, v57(1), Part 2, S211-S230.

Schmalensee, Richard. "Risk And Return On Long-Lived Tangible Assets," JFEC, 1981, v9(2), 185-205.

Schmidt, Charles H. "Meeting The Long-Term Capital Requirements Of Small Business," JOF, 1951, v6(2), 143-149.

Schmidt, Frederick. (Goodman, Laurie S., Susan Ross and Frederick Schmidt. "Are Foreign Currency Options Overvalued? The Early Experience Of The Philadelphia Stock Exchange," JPM, 1985, v5(3), 349-359.)

Schmidt, James R. (Rejda, George E. and James R. Schmidt. "The Impact Of The Social Security Program On Private Pension Contributions," JRI, 1979, v46(4), 636-651.)

Schmidt, James R. (Rejda, George E. and James R. Schmidt. "The Impact Of Social Security And ERISA On Insured Private Pension Contributions," JRI, 1984, v51(4), 640-651.)

Schmidt, James R. (Rejda, George E., James R. Schmidt and Michael J. McNamara. "The Impact Of Social Security Tax Contributions On Group Life Insurance Premiums," JRI, 1987, v54(4), 712-720.)

Schmidt, Peter. (Amsler, Christine E. and Peter Schmidt. "A Monte Carlo Investigation Of The Accuracy Of Multivariate CAPM Tests," JFEC, 1985, v14(3), 359-376.)

Schmidt, Reinhart. "Early Warning Of Debt Rescheduling," JBF, 1984, v8(2), 357-370.

Schmidt, Richard F. "Does A Deductible Curb Moral Hazard?," JRI, 1961, v28(3), 89-92.

Schmit, Joan T. "A New View Of The Requisites Of Insurability," JRI, 1986, v53(2), 320-329.

Schmit, Joan T. "Lump-Sum Awards In Workers' Compensation," JRI, 1987, v54(2), 332-340.

Schmit, Joan T. "Lump-Sum Awards In Workers' Compensation: Reply," JRI, 1988, v55(4), 740-741.

Schmit, Joan T. (Moore, William T. and Joan T. Schmit. "The Risk Retention Act Of 1986: Effects On Insurance Firm Shareholders' Wealth," JRI, 1989, v56(1), 137-145.)

Schmit, Joan T. and Kendall Roth. "Cost Effectiveness Of Risk Management Practices," JRI, 1990, v57(3), 455-470.

Schmit, Joan T., S. Travis Pritchett and Paige Fields. "Punitive Damages: Punishment Or Further Compensation?," JRI, 1988, v55(3), 453-466.

Schmitt, Thomas G. (Johnson, Timothy E. and Thomas G. Schmitt. "Effectiveness Of Earnings Per Share Forecasts," FM, 1974, v3(2), 64-72.)

Schnabel, Constance. (Sobotka, Stephen P. and Constance Schnabel. "Linear Programming As A Device For Depicting Market Value: Prices Of Used Commercial Aircraft, 1959-65," JOB, 1961, v34(1), 10-30.)

Schnabel, J. A. "A Note On Inflation, The Capital Asset Pricing Model, And Beta Estimation With Nominal Data," JFR, 1980, v3(3), 261-267.

Schnabel, Jacques A. "Is Benter Better: A Cautionary Note On Maximizing Convexity," FAJ, 1990, v46(1), 78-79.

Schnabel, Jacques A. "Optimal Output In An Option Pricing Framework: An Agency-Theoretic Perspective," JBFA, 1990, v17(5), 745-750.

Schnabel, Jacques A. "Variable Transactions Costs, The Capital Asset Pricing Model And The Corporate Dividend Decision: A Comment," JBFA, 1982, v4(4), 559-562.

Schnabel, Jacques A. (Chua, Jess H. and Jacques A. Schnabel. "Nonpecuniary Benefits And Asset Market Equilibrium," FR, 1986, v21(2), 185-190.)

Schnabel, Jacques A. and Ebrahim Roumi. "Corporate Insurance And

The Underinvestment Problem: An Extension," JRI, 1989, v56(1), 155-159.

Schnabel, Morton. "A Challenge To A Vote For Tonypandy," JOB, 1976, v49(1), 68-69.

Schnabel, Morton. "Defining A Product," JOB, 1976, v49(4), 517-529.

Schnabel, Morton. "The Subsidy Problem In Hospital Insurance: A Comment," JOB, 1972, v45(2), 302-304.

Schnader, M. H. and H. O. Stekler. "Evaluating Predictions Of Change," JOB, 1990, v63(1), Part 1, 99-108.

Schnee, Jerome E. "Development Cost: Determinants And Overruns," JOB, 1972, v45(3), 347-374.

Schneeweis, Thomas and J. Randall Woolridge. "Capital Market Seasonality: The Case Of Bond Returns," JFQA, 1979, v14(5), 939-958.

Schneeweis, Thomas and Joanne Hill. "A Note On The Comovement Of International Equity And Bond Markets," FR, 1980, v15(1), 30-37.

Schneeweis, Thomas R., Joanne M. Hill and Michael G. Philipp. "Hedge Ratio Determination Based On Bond Yield Forecasts," RFM, 1983, v2(3), 338-349.

Schneeweis, Thomas. (Elgers, Pieter, Joanne Hill and Thomas Schneeweis. "Research Design For Systematic Risk Prediction," JPM, 1981-82, v8(3), 43-52.)

Schneeweis, Thomas. (Finnerty, Joseph E., Thomas Schneeweis and Shantaram P. Hegde. "Interest Rates In The $Eurobond Market," JFQA, 1980, v15(5), 743-755.)

Schneeweis, Thomas. (Hill, Joanne, Thomas Schneeweis and Robert Mayerson. "An Analysis Of The Impact Of Marking-To-Market In Hedging With Treasury Bond Futures," RFM, 1983, v2(1), 136-159.)

Schneeweis, Thomas. (Hill, Joanne M. and Thomas Schneeweis. "Reducing Volatility With Financial Futures," FAJ, 1984, v40(6), 34-40.)

Schneeweis, Thomas. (Hill, Joanne, Joseph Liro and Thomas Schneeweis. "Hedging Performance Of GNMA Futures Under Rising And Falling Interest Rates," JFM, 1983, v3(4), 403-413.)

Schneeweis, Thomas. (Hill, Joanne and Thomas Schneeweis. "A Note On The Hedging Effectiveness Of Foreign Currency Futures," JFM, 1981, v1(4), 659-664.)

Schneeweis, Thomas. (Hill, Joanne and Thomas Schneeweis. "The Hedging Effectiveness Of Foreign Currency Futures," JFR, 1982, v5(1), 95-104.)

Schneeweis, Thomas. (Hill, Joanne and Thomas Schneeweis. "The Effect Of Interval Selection On The Parameters Of The Market Model As Applied To Bond Returns," FR, 1979, v14(3), 34-51.)

Schneeweis, Thomas. (Hill, Joanne and Thomas Schneeweis. "International Diversification Of Equities And Fixed-Income Securities," JFR, 1983, v6(4), 333-343.)

Schneeweis, Thomas. (Hill, Joanne and Thomas Schneeweis. "The Effect Of Three Mile Island On Electric Utility Stock Prices: A Note," JOF, 1983, v38(4), 1285-1292.)

Schneeweis, Thomas. (Hill, Joanne and Thomas Schneeweis. "On The Estimation Of Hedge Ratios For Corporate Bond Positions," AFPAF, 1985, v1(1), 307-323.)

Schneeweis, Thomas. (Hill, Joanne, Thomas Schneeweis and Jot Yau. "International Trading/Non Trading Time Effects On Risk Estimation In Futures Markets," JFM, 1990, v10(4), 407-424.)

Schneeweis, Thomas. (Nawalkha, Sanjay K., Nelson J. Lacey and Thomas Schneeweis. "Closed-Form Solutions Of Convexity And M-Square," FAJ, 1990, v46(1), 75-77.)

Schneeweis, Thomas. (Nunn, Kenneth P., Jr., Joanne Hill and Thomas Schneeweis. "Corporate Bond Price Data Sources And Return/Risk Measurement," JFQA, 1986, v21(2), 197-208.)

Schneeweis, Thomas. (Phillips-Patrick, Frederick J. and Thomas Schneeweis. "The 'Weekend Effect' For Stock Indexes And Stock Indexes Future: Dividend And Interest Rate Effects," JFM, 1988, v8(1), 115-122.)

Schneeweis, Thomas. (Schweser, Carl and Thomas Schneeweis. "Risk Return And The Multi-Dimensional Security Pricing Market," JFR, 1980, v3(1), 23-31.)

Schneeweis, Tom. (Schweser, Carl, Robert M. Soldofsky and Tom Schneeweis. "The Meaning Of The Mean," JPM, 1978-79, v5(4), 23-27.)

Schneider, Arnold. "Simultaneous Determination Of Cost Allocations And Cost-Plus Prices For Joint Products," JBFA, 1986, v13(2), 187-195.

Schneider, Carl W. "SEC Filings - Their Use To The Professional," FAJ, 1965, v21(1), 33-38.

Schneider, Carl W. "SEC Filings - Their Content And Use," FAJ, 1965, v21(2), 42-48.

Schneider, Henry S. "Two Formula Methods For Choosing Common Stocks," FAJ, 1951, v6(2), 229-237.

Schneider, Richard B. "New Aspects Of The Chemical Industry," FAJ, 1947, v3(1), 11-17.

Schneider, Richard B. "Recent Developments In Petroleum Chemistry," FAJ, 1949, v5(2), 17-19.

Schneider, Theodore H. "Measuring Performance," FAJ, 1969, v25(3), 105-111.

Schneiderman, Gerald. "Maximizing Creativity: The Individual And The System," FAJ, 1984, v40(4), 76-78.

Schneller, Meir I. and Charles S. Rosen. "Time-Variance Relationship: Evidence On Correlation In Common Stock Returns: Comment," JOF, 1979, v34(5), 1271-1272.

Schneller, Meir L "Are Betas Worth The Trouble?," FAJ, 1983, v39(4), 74-77.

Schneller, Meir I. "Efficient Frontiers In Factor Economies," JPM, 1990, v16(2), 23-25.

Schneller, Meir I. "Mean-Variance Portfolio Composition When Investors' Revision Horizon Is Very Long," JOF, 1975, v30(5), 1293-1300.

Schneller, Meir I. "Taxes And The Optimal Capital Structure Of The Firm," JOF, 1980, v35(1), 119-127.

Schneller, Meir I. "The Arbitrage Pricing Theories: A Synthesis And Critical Review," RIF, 1990, v8, 1-22.

Schneller, Meir I. (Galai, Dan and Meir I. Schneller. "Pricing Of Warrants And The Value Of The Firm," JOF, 1978, v33(5), 1333-1342.)

Schneller, Meir I. (Palmon, Dan and Meir I. Schneller. "The Relationship Between Securities' Abnormal Price Movements And Wall Street Journal News," JBF, 1980, v4(3), 235-248.)

Schneller, Meir. (Givoly, Dan, Dan Palmon and Meir Schneller. "Perception Of Stock Similarity By Financial Analysts," FR, 1981, v16(3), 30-43.)

Schnepper, Jeff A. "'Going Private' And Minority Shareholders," FAJ, 1978, v34(2), 45-57.

Schneweis, Thomas. (Hill, Joanne, Thomas Schneeweis and Jot Yau. "International Multi-Asset Diversification: A Further Analysis," AFPAF, 1989, v4(Supp), 197-214.)

Schniederjans, Marc J. (Hoffman, James J., Marc J. Schniederjans and G. Stacy Sirmans. "A Multi-Criteria Model For Corporate Property Evaluation," JRER, 1990, v5(3), 285-300.)

Schnitzel, Paul. "Do Deposit Rates Cause Mortgage Loan Rates?: The Evidence From Causality Tests," AREUEA, 1986, v14(3), 448-464.

Schoemaker, Paul J. H. (Hershey, John C. and Paul J. H. Schoemaker. "Risk Taking And Problem Context In The Domain Of Losses: An Expected Utility Analysis," JRI, 1980, v47(1), 111-132.)

Schoemaker, Paul J. H. and Howard C. Kunreuther. "An Experimental Study Of Insurance Decisions," JRI, 1979, v46(4), 603-618.

Schoemaker, Paul. "Preferences For Information On Probabilities Vs. Prizes: The Role Of Risk Taking Attitudes," JRU, 1989, v1(1), 37-60.

Schoeplein, Robert N. "The Effect Of Pension Plans On Other Retirement Saving," JOF, 1970, v25(3), 633-637.

Schoetz, Robert F. "Profit Margins In The U.S. And Europe," FAJ, 1967, v23(2), 25-33.

Scholes, Myron and Joseph T. Williams. "Estimating Betas From Nonsynchronous Data," JFEC, 1977, v5(3), 309-327.

Scholes, Myron S. "The Economics Of Hedging And Spreading In Futures Markets," JPM, v1(2), 265-286.

Scholes, Myron S. "The Market For Securities: Substitution Versus Price Pressure And The Effects Of Information On Share Prices," JOB, 1972, v45(2), 179-211.

Scholes, Myron S. (Constantinides, George M. and Myron S. Scholes. "Optimal Liquidation Of Assets In The Presence Of Personal Taxes: Implications For Asset Pricing," JOF, 1980, v35(2), 439-449.)

Scholes, Myron S. (Merton, Robert C., Myron S. Scholes and Mathew L. Gladstein. "The Returns And Risks Of Alternative Put-Option Portfolio Investment Strategies," JOB, 1982, v55(1), 1-56.)

Scholes, Myron S. (Merton, Robert C., Myron S. Scholes and Mathew L. Gladstein. "The Returns And Risk Of Alternative Call Option Portoflio Investment Strategies," JOB, 1978, v51(2), 183-242.)

Scholes, Myron S. (Miller, Merton H. and Myron S. Scholes. "Dividends And Taxes," JFEC, 1978, v6(4), 333-364.)

Scholes, Myron S. and Mark A. Wolfson. "Employee Stock Ownership Plans And Corporate Restructuring: Myths And Realities," FM, 1990, v19(1), 12-28.

Scholes, Myron S. and Mark A. Wolfson. "The Effects Of Changes In Tax Laws On Corporate Reorganization Activity," JOB, 1990, v63(1), Part 2, S141-S164.

Scholes, Myron S. and Mark A. Wolfson. "Decentralized Investment Banking: The Case Of Discount Dividend-Reinvestment And Stock-Purchase Plans," JFEC, 1989, v24(1), 7-36.

Scholes, Myron S., G. Peter Wilson and Mark A. Wolfson. "Tax Planning, Regulatory Capital Planning, And Financial Reporting Strategy For Commercial Banks," RFS, 1990, v3(4), 625-650.

Scholes, Myron. "Taxes And The Pricing Of Options," JOF, 1976, v31(2), 319-332.

Scholes, Myron. (Black, Fischer and Myron Scholes. "The Valuation Of Option Contracts And A Test Of Market Efficiency," JOF, 1972, v27(2), 399-417.)

Scholes, Myron. (Black, Fischer and Myron Scholes. "The Effects Of Dividend Yield And Dividend Policy On Common Stock Prices And Returns," JFEC, 1974, v1(1), 1-22.)

Scholes, Myron. (Black, Fischer and Myron Scholes. "From Theory To A New Financial Product," JOF, 1974, v29(2), 399-412.)

Scholes, Myron. (Miller, Merton H., Burton Malkiel, Myron Scholes and John D. Hawke, Jr. "Stock Index Futures And The Crash Of '87," JACF, 1989, v1(4), 6-17.) 3(?8

Schollhammer, Hans and Chang Young Chung. "The Effect Of Exchange Rate Changes On The Interdependence Among National Equity Markets: An Empirical Investigation Of The United States, Japan, Britain And Germany," RDIBF, 1989, v3, 229-246.

Schollhammer, Hans and Ole Christian Sand. "Lead-Lag Relationships Among National Equity Markets: An Empirical Investigation," RDIBF, 1987, v1, 149-168.

Schollmeyer, H. Edward. "Packaging Materials For Consumer Goods," FAJ, 1965, v21(4), 78-83.

Scholz, John T. and Wayne B. Gray. "OSHA Enforcement And Workplace Injuries: A Behavioral Approach To Risk Assessment," JRU, 1990, v3(3), 283-305.

Schonberger, Richard J. "Management Information Systems In Insurance: Comment," JRI, 1973, v40(2), 294-296.

Schonfeld, Eugene P. (Boyd, John H. and Eugene P. Schonfeld. "The Effect Of Financial Press Advertising On Stock Prices," FM, 1977, v6(2), 42-51.)

Schoomer, B. Alva, Jr. "American Stock Exchange Index System," FAJ, 1967, v23(3), 57-61.

Schotland, Roy A. "Divergent Investing For Pension Funds," FAJ, 1980, v36(5), 29-39.

Schotman, Peter. (Koedijk, Kees and Peter Schotman. "Dominant Real Exchange Rate Movements," JIMF, 1989, v8(4), 517-532.)

Schott, Brian. "Annual Losses For Straight Deductible Coverage," JRI, 1979, v46(4), 619-635.

Schott, Brian. "Annual Losses For Straight Deductible Coverage: Reply," JRI, 1980, v47(4), 754.

Schott, Brian. "Using A Business Simulation Game To Teach Risk Management," JRI, 1976, v43(3), 526-532.

Schott, Francis H. "Disintermediation Through Policy Loans At Life Insurance Companies," JOF, 1971, v26(3), 719-729.

Schott, Francis H. "Investment Implications Of The Actuarial Design Of Life Insurance Products: Comment," JRI, 1972, v39(4), 655-658.

Schott, Francis H. "Life Insurers, Variable Annuities And Mutual Funds: A Critical Study: Comment," JRI, 1971, v38(3), 463-476.

Schott, Werner S. "The Valuation Of British Equities," **FAJ**, 1960, v16(3), 15-19.

Schotta, Charles, Jr. "The Real Balance Effect In The United States, 1947-1963," **JOF**, 1964, v19(4), 619-630.

Schotta, Charles. (Bonomo, Vittorio and Charles Schotta. "Federal Open Market Operations And Variations In The Reserve Base: Reply," **JOF**, 1972, v27(3), 730-732.)

Schotta, Charles. (Bonomo, Vittorio and Charles Schotta. "Federal Open Market Operations And Variations In The Reserve Base," **JOF**, 1970, v25(3), 659-667.)

Schoumaker, Francoise. (Murnighan, J. Keith, Alvin E. Roth and Francoise Schoumaker. "Risk Aversion In Bargaining: An Experimental Study," **JRU**, 1988, v1(1), 101-124.)

Schrader, William J. (Cramer, Joe J., Jr. and William J. Schrader. "Elements Of 'Pension Costs'," **JRI**, 1968, v35(2), 237-245.)

Schram, Emil. "A Message From The President Of The New York Stock Exchange," **FAJ**, 1945, v1(2), 11-14.

Schreder, Harold X. "Impact Of Business Conditions On Investment Policies," **JOF**, 1952, v7(2), 138-173.

Schreder, Harold X. "The Stock Market," **JOF**, 1962, v17(2), 245-258.

Schreiber, Paul S. and Robert A. Schwartz. "Price Discovery In Securities Markets," **JPM**, 1985-86, v12(4), 43-48.

Schreiber, S. Van Zandt, Jr. "Outlook For The Farm Equipment Industry," **FAJ**, 1966, v22(6), 49-52.

Schreiner, John C. (Smith, Keith V. and John C. Schreiner. "Direct Vs. Indirect Diversification," **FAJ**, 1970, v26(5), 33-38.)

Schreiner, John C. (Smith, Keith V. and John C. Schreiner. "A Portfolio Analysis Of Conglomerate Diversification: Reply," **JOF**, 1970, v25(4), 915-916.)

Schreiner, John C. (Smith, Keith V. and John C. Schreiner. "A Portfolio Analysis Of Conglomerate Diversification," **JOF**, 1969, v24(3), 413-427.)

Schreiner, John. "Comparing Commission Proposals," **FAJ**, 1971, v27(4), 75-84.

Schreiner, John. "Portfolio Revision: A Turnover-Constrained Approach," **JPM**, 1980, v9(1), 67-75.

Schremer, John C. and Keith V. Smith. "The Impact Of Mayday On Diversification Costs," **JPM**, 1979-80, v6(4), 28-36.

Schrems, Edward L. "The Tax Treatment Of Workers Compensation Costs And Safety And Health Incentives," **JRI**, 1981, v48(2), 272-285.

Schrems, Edward L. (Stock, Duane and Edward L. Schrems. "Municipal Bond Demand Premiums And Bond Price Volatility: A Note," **JOF**, 1984, v39(2), 535-539.)

Schreuder, Hein. (Kodde, David A. and Hein Schreuder. "Forecasting Corporate Revenue And Profit: Time-Series Models Versus Management And Analysts," **JBFA**, 1984, v11(3), 381-395.)

Schreyer, William A. "The Future Of The Financial Services Industry," **FAJ**, 1982, v38(4), 51-54.

Schroath, Frederick W. and Christopher M. Korth. "Managerial Barriers To The Internationalization Of U.S. Property And Liability Insurers: Theory And Perspectives," **JRI**, 1989, v56(4), 630-648.

Schroder, Mark. "Adapting The Binomial Model To Value Options On Assets With Fixed-Cash Payouts," **FAJ**, 1988, v44(6), 54-62.

Schroder, Mark. "Computing The Constant Elasticity Of Variance Option Pricing Formula," **JOF**, 1989, v44(1), 211-220.

Schroeder, Douglas A. (Kross, William and Douglas A. Schroeder. "Firm Prominence And The Differential Information Content Of Quarterly Earnings Announcements," **JBFA**, 1989, v16(1), 55-74.)

Schroeder, Douglas. (Kross, William and Douglas Schroeder. "An Investigation Of Seasonality In Stock Price Responses To Quarterly Earnings Announcements," **JBFA**, 1990, v17(5), 649-676.)

Schroeder, Edmund R. "CFTC Reauthorization: Some Possible Implications For Futures Trading On Foreign Markets And For Foreign Trading On U.S. Markets," **JPM**, 1981, v1(Supp), 555-564.

Schroeder, George W. "A Simple System For Managing And Monitoring," **JPM**, 1975-76, v2(4), 52-56.

Schroeder, Juergen. "International Risk And Exchange Rate Overshooting," **JIMF**, 1990, v9(2), 193-205.

Schroeder, Ted C. (Hayenga, M. L., D. D. Dipietre, J. M. Skadberg and T. C. Schroeder. "Profitable Hedging Opportunities And Risk Premiums For Producers In Live Cattle And Live Hog Futures Markets," **JFM**, 1984, v4(2), 141-154.)

Schroeder, Ted C. (Ouattara, Korotoumou, Ted C. Schroeder and L. Orlo Sorenson. "Potential Use Of Futures Markets For International Marketing Of Cote D'Ivoire Coffee," **JFM**, 1990, v10(2), 113-122.)

Schroeder, Ted C. (Witt, Harvey J., Ted C. Schroeder and Marvin L. Hayenga. "Comparison Of Analytical Approaches For Estimating Hedge Ratios For Agricultural Commodities," **JFM**, 1987, v7(2), 135-146.)

Schroeder, Ted C. and Marvin L. Hayenga. "Comparison Of Selective Hedging And Options Strategies In Cattle Feedlot Risk Management," **JFM**, 1988, v8(2), 141-156.

Schroeter, John R. and Scott L. Smith. "A Reexamination Of The Rationality Of The Livingston Price Expectations," **JMCB**, 1986, v18(2), 239-246.

Schropp, Gabriele H. (Barrett, W. Brian, Andrea J. Heuson, Robert W. Kolb and Gabriele H. Schropp. "The Adjustment Of Stock Prices To Completely Unanticipated Events," **FR**, 1987, v22(4), 345-354.)

Schuelke, Robert A. (Cottle, Edmund A., Sidney Mennis and Robert A. Schuelke. "Corporate Earnings - Long Term," **FAJ**, 1971, v27(4), 22-23,50-52,54,56,58,60, 62,64.)

Schugart, Gary L. (Fraser, Donald R., Peter S. Rose and Gary L. Schugart. "Federal Reserve Membership And Bank Performance: The Evidence From Texas," **JOF**, 1975, v30(2), 641-658.)

Schugart, Gary L. (Grossman, Steven D., Gary L. Schugart and Robert H. Strawser. "An Intra And Inter-Industry Comparison Of Performance Measures Based On Alternative Income Concepts," **FR**, 1979, v14(3), 13-24.)

Schulkin, Peter A. "Conflicts Of Interest In REITs," **FAJ**, 1971, v27(3), 33-40,74-78.

Schulman, Evan C. (Perold, Andre F. and Evan C. Schulman. "The Free Lunch In Currency Hedging: Implications For Investment Policy And Peformance Standards," **FAJ**, 1988, v44(3), 45-52.)

Schulman, Evan. "A Parable Of Tulips," **JPM**, 1985-86, v12(3), 10-11.

Schulman, Evan. "Can The Market Forecast Itself?," **JPM**, 1977-78, v4(1), 57-58.

Schulman, Evan. "Central Value In Review: Comment," **JPM**, 1985-86, v12(1), 50-51.

Schulman, Evan. "Let The Facts Speak For Themselves," **JPM**, 1990, v16(3), 86.

Schulman, Evan. (Lebaron, Dean and Evan Schulman. "Trading: The Fixable Leak," **JPM**, 1981-82, v8(1), 10-12.)

Schultz, Joseph J., Jr. (Gustavson, Sandra G. and Joseph J. Schultz, Jr. "Property-Liability Loss Reserve Certification: Independent Or In-House?," **JRI**, 1983, v50(2), 307-314.)

Schultz, Joseph J., Jr., Sandra G. Gustavson and Frank K. Reilly. "Factors Influencing The New York Stock Exchange Specialists' Price-Setting Behavior: An Experiment," **JFR**, 1985, v8(2), 137-144.

Schultz, Paul. "Personal Income Taxes And The January Effect: Small Firm Stock Returns Before The War Revenue Act Of 1917: A Note," **JOF**, 1985, v40(1), 333-343.

Schultz, Paul. "Transaction Costs And The Small Firm Effect: A Comment," **JFEC**, 1983, v12(1), 81-88.

Schultz, Paul. (Lauterbach, Beni and Paul Schultz. "Pricing Warrants: An Empirical Study Of The Black-Scholes Model And Its Alternatives," **JOF**, 1990, v45(4), 1181-1209.)

Schultz, Randall L. (Kotler, Philip and Randall L. Schultz. "Marketing Simulations: Review And Prospects," **JOB**, 1970, v43(3), 237-295.)

Schultz, Raymond G. "Administrative Issues In Workmen's Compensation," **JRI**, 1967, v34(3), 423-434.

Schultz, Raymond G. "Investment Income And Casualty Insurance Profits," **JRI**, 1959, v26(3), 33-40.

Schultz, Raymond G. "Trends In Life Insurance Company Competition For Pension Funds," **JRI**, 1964, v31(2), 193-206.

Schultz, Raymond G. (Schultz, Robert E. and Raymond G. Schultz. "The Regulation Of Life Insurance Company Investments," **JRI**, 1960, v27(4), 57-62.)

Schultz, Raymond G. and Robert E. Schultz. "The Regulation Of Multiple-Line Insurance Company Investments," **JRI**, 1961, v28(4), 49-56.

Schultz, Robert E. (Schultz, Raymond G. and Robert E. Schultz. "The Regulation Of Multiple-Line Insurance Company Investments," **JRI**, 1961, v28(4), 49-56.)

Schultz, Robert E. and Raymond G. Schultz. "The Regulation Of Life Insurance Company Investments," **JRI**, 1960, v27(4), 57-62.

Schulze, William. (Gerking, Shelby, Menno De Haan and William Schulze. "The Marginal Value Of Job Safety: A Contingent Valuation Study," **JRU**, 1988, v1(2), 185-200.)

Schumacher, Arnold C. "Changes In The Money Forces During 1955 And Their Implications," **FAJ**, 1956, v12(2), 45-50.

Schumacher, Arnold C. "Is Outstanding Debt At A Danger Point?," **FAJ**, 1965, v21(4), 33-39.

Schumacher, Arnold C. "Monetary Forces And The Stock Market," **FAJ**, 1959, v15(2), 95-100.

Schumacher, Arnold C. "Relationship Of Money Forces To Equity Prices," **FAJ**, 1955, v11(1), 15-20.

Schurman, James H. "Canada - A Reappraisal," **FAJ**, 1960, v16(1), 11-12.

Schuster, Leo. "Concentration And Competition In Banking," **JBR**, 1986-87, v17(1), 51-53.

Schuster, Leo. "Profitability And Market Share Of Banks," **JBR**, 1984-85, v15(1), 56-61.

Schutt, Leonard D. "Implementing Investment Policy," **FAJ**, 1966, v22(2), 105-112.

Schwab, Bernard and Peter Lusztig. "A Note On Abandonment Value And Capital Budgeting," **JFQA**, 1970, v5(3), 377-379.

Schwab, Bernhard and Peter Lusztig. "A Note On Investment Evaluations In Light Of Uncertain Future Opportunities," **JOF**, 1972, v27(5), 1093-1100.

Schwab, Bernhard and Peter Lusztig. "A Comparative Analysis Of The Net Present Value And The Benefit-Cost Ratio As Measures Of The Economic Desirability Of Investments," **JOF**, 1969, v24(3), 507-516.

Schwab, Bernhard and Peter Lusztig. "Apportioning Foreign Exchange Risk Through The Use Of Third Currencies: Some Questions On Efficiency," **FM**, 1978, v7(3), 25-30.

Schwab, Bernhard. "Conceptual Problems In The Use Of Risk-Adjusted Discount Rates With Disaggregated Cash Flows," **JBFA**, 1978, v5(4), 281-293.

Schwab, Bernhard. (Brumelle, Shelby L. and Bernhard Schwab. "Capital Budgeting With Uncertain Future Opportunities: A Markovian Approach," **JFQA**, 1973, v8(1), 111-122.)

Schwab, Bernhard. (Everett, James E. and Bernhard Schwab. "On The Proper Adjustment For Risk Through Discount Rates In A Mean-Variance Framework," **FM**, 1979, v8(2), 61-65.)

Schwab, Bernhard. (Lusztig, Peter and Bernhard Schwab. "The Discount Rate Problem In Capital Rationing Situations: Reply," **JFQA**, 1970, v5(2), 261-261.)

Schwab, Bernhard. (Lusztig, Peter and Bernhard Schwab. "A Note On The Application Of Linear Programming To Capital Budgeting," **JFQA**, 1968, v3(4), 427-431.)

Schwab, Bernhard. (Lusztig, Peter and Bernhard Schwab. "A Note On The Application Of Multiple Regression Analysis To Expense Allocation In The Insurance Industry," **JRI**, 1970, v37(3), 485-488.)

Schwann, Gregory M. (Capozza, Dennis R. and Gregory M. Schwann. "The Asset Approach To Pricing Urban Land: Empirical Evidence," **AREUEA**, 1989, v17(2), 161-174.)

Schwann, Gregory M. (Capozza, Dennis R. and Gregory M. Schwann. "The Value Of Risk In Real Estate Markets," **JREFEC**, 1990, v3(2), 117-140.)

Schwartz, A. "The Lender Of Last Resort And The Federal Safety Net," **JFSR**, 1987, v1(1), 1-18.

Schwartz, Aba. (Eldor, Rafael, David Pines and Aba Schwartz. "The Demand For Domestic Assets And Consumption Risk," **RDIBF**, 1988, v2, 349-362.)

Schwartz, Abba. (Eldor, Rafael, David Pines and Abba Schwartz. "Determinants Of An Individual's Demand For Hedging Instruments," **JFM**, 1989, v9(2), 135-142.)

Schwartz, Anna J. "Reflections On The Gold Commission Report,"

JMCB, 1982, v14(4), Part 1, 538-551.

Schwartz, Anna J. "Secular Price Change In Historical Perspective," **JMCB**, 1973, v5(1), Part II, 243-269.

Schwartz, Anna J. "The Aliber, Dewald, And Gordon Papers," **JMCB**, 1972, v4(4), 978-984.

Schwartz, Anna J. (Bordo, Michael D., Ehsan U. Choudhri and Anna J. Schwartz. "The Behavior Of Money Stock Under Interest Rate Control: Some Evidence For Canada," **JMCB**, 1987, v19(2), 181-198.)

Schwartz, Anna J. (Cagan, Phillip and Anna J. Schwartz. "Has The Growth Of Money Substitutes Hindered Monetary Policy?," **JMCB**, 1975, v7(2), 137-159.)

Schwartz, Anna J. (Friedman, Milton and Anna J. Schwartz. "The Definition Of Money: Net Wealth And Neutrality As Criteria," **JMCB**, 1969, v1(1), 1-14.)

Schwartz, Anna J. (Friedman, Milton and Anna J. Schwartz. "Interrelations Between The United States And The United Kingdom, 1873-1975," **JIMF**, 1982, v1(1), 3-19.)

Schwartz, Arthur L. (Hopewell, Michael H. and Arthur L. Schwartz. "Temporary Trading Suspensions In Individual NYSE Securities," **JOF**, 1978, v33(5), 1355-1373.)

Schwartz, Arthur L., Jr. "The Adjustment Of Individual Stock Prices During Periods Of Unusual Disequilibria," **FR**, 1982, v17(4), 228-239.

Schwartz, Arthur L., Jr. (Dale-Johnson, David, M. Chapman Findlay, Arthur L. Schwartz, Jr. and Stephen D. Kapplin. "Valuation And Efficiency In The Market For Creatively Financed Houses," **AREUEA**, 1985, v13(4), 388-403.)

Schwartz, Arthur L., Jr. (Hopewell, Michael H. and Arthur L. Schwartz, Jr. "Stock Price Movement Associated With Temporary Trading Suspensions: Bear Market Versus Bull Market," **JFQA**, 1976, v11(4), 577-590.)

Schwartz, Arthur L., Jr. (Kapplin, Steven D. and Arthur L. Schwartz, Jr. "Public Real Estate Limited Partnership Returns: A Preliminary Comparison With Other Investments," **AREUEA**, 1988, v16(1), 63-68.)

Schwartz, Arthur L., Jr. (Kapplin, Steven D. and Arthur L. Schwartz, Jr. "An Anlaysis Of Recent Rates Of Return And Of The Secondary Market For Public Real Estate Limited Partnerships," **JRER**, 1986, v1(1), 33-44.)

Schwartz, E. S. (Brennan, M. J. and E. S. Schwartz. "Convertible Bonds: Valuation And Optimal Strategies For Call And Conversion," **JOF**, 1977, v32(5), 1699-1715.)

Schwartz, E. S. (Brennan, M. J. and E. S. Schwartz. "Corporate Income Taxes, Valuation, And The Problem Of Optimal Capital Structure," **JOB**, 1978, v51(1), 103-114.)

Schwartz, E. S. (Brennan, M. J. and E. S. Schwartz. "Evaluating Natural Resource Investments," **JOB**, 1985, v58(2), 135-158.)

Schwartz, Eduardo S. "The Valuation Of Warrants: Implementing A New Approach," **JFEC**, 1977, v4(1), 79-93.

Schwartz, Eduardo S. (Ananthanarayanan, A. L. and Eduardo S. Schwartz. "Retractable And Extendible Bonds: The Canadian Experience," **JOF**, 1980, v35(1), 31-47.)

Schwartz, Eduardo S. (Boyle, Phelim P. and Eduardo S. Schwartz. "Equilibrium Prices Of Guarantees Under Equity-Linked Contracts," **JRI**, 1977, v44(4), 639-660.)

Schwartz, Eduardo S. (Brennan, Michael J. and Eduardo S. Schwartz. "Alternative Investment Strategies For The Issuers Of Equity Linked Life Insurance Policies With An Asset Value Guarantee," **JOB**, 1979, v52(1), 63-94.)

Schwartz, Eduardo S. (Brennan, Michael J. and Eduardo S. Schwartz. "A Continuous Time Approach To The Pricing Of Bonds," **JBF**, 1979, v3(2), 133-156.)

Schwartz, Eduardo S. (Brennan, Michael J. and Eduardo S. Schwartz. "An Equilibrium Model Of Bond Pricing And A Test Of Market Efficiency," **JFQA**, 1982, v17(3), 301-329.)

Schwartz, Eduardo S. (Brennan, Michael J. and Eduardo S. Schwartz. "The Valuation Of American Put Options," **JOF**, 1977, v32(2), 449-462.)

Schwartz, Eduardo S. (Brennan, Michael J. and Eduardo S. Schwartz. "Time-Invariant Portfolio Insurance Strategies," **JOF**, 1988, v43(2), 283-299.)

Schwartz, Eduardo S. (Brennan, Michael J. and Eduardo S. Schwartz. "Optimal Financial Policy And Firm Valuation," **JOF**, 1984, v39(3), 593-607.)

Schwartz, Eduardo S. (Brennan, Michael J. and Eduardo S. Schwartz. "Savings Bonds, Retractable Bonds And Callable Bonds," **JFEC**, 1977, v5(1), 67-88.)

Schwartz, Eduardo S. (Brennan, Michael J. and Eduardo S. Schwartz. "On The Geometric Mean Index: A Note," **JFQA**, 1985, v20(1), 119-122.)

Schwartz, Eduardo S. (Brennan, Michael J. and Eduardo S. Schwartz. "Conditional Predictions Of Bond Prices And Returns," **JOF**, 1980, v35(2), 405-417.)

Schwartz, Eduardo S. (Brennan, Michael J. and Eduardo S. Schwartz. "Analyzing Convertible Bonds," **JFQA**, 1980, v15(4), 907-929.)

Schwartz, Eduardo S. (Brennan, Michael J. and Eduardo S. Schwartz. "Finite Difference Methods And Jump Processes Arising In The Pricing Of Contingent Claims: A Synthesis," **JFQA**, 1978, v13(3), 461-474.)

Schwartz, Eduardo S. (Brennan, Michael J. and Eduardo S. Schwartz. "Bond Pricing And Market Efficiency," **FAJ**, 1982, v38(5), 49-56.)

Schwartz, Eduardo S. (Brennan, Michael J. and Eduardo S. Schwartz. "Regulation And Corporate Investment Policy," **JOF**, 1982, v37(2), 289-300.)

Schwartz, Eduardo S. (Brennan, Michael J. and Eduardo S. Schwartz. "The Pricing Of Equity-Linked Life Insurance Policies With An Asset Value Guarantee," **JFEC**, 1976, v3(3), 195-213.)

Schwartz, Eduardo S. (Brennan, Michael J. and Eduardo S. Schwartz. "The Case For Convertibles," **JACF**, 1988, v1(2), 55-64.)

Schwartz, Eduardo S. (Brennan, Michael J. and Eduardo S. Schwartz. "Determinants Of GNMA Mortgage Prices," **AREUEA**, 1985, v13(3), 209-228.)

Schwartz, Eduardo S. (Brennan, Michael J. and Eduardo S. Schwartz. "Portfolio Insurance And Financial Market Equilibrium," **JOB**, 1989, v62(4), 455-472.)

Schwartz, Eduardo S. (Brennan, Michael J. and Eduardo S. Schwartz. "Arbitrage In Stock Index Futures," **JOB**, 1990, v63(1), Part 2, S7-S32.)

Schwartz, Eduardo S. (Gibson, Rajna and Eduardo S. Schwartz. "Stochastic Convenience Yield And The Pricing Of Oil Contingent Claims," **JOF**, 1990, v45(3), 959-976.)

Schwartz, Eduardo S. (Heinkel, Robert and Eduardo S. Schwartz. "Rights Versus Underwritten Offerings: An Asymmetric Information Approach," **JOF**, 1986, v41(1), 1-18.)

Schwartz, Eduardo S. (McConnell, John J. and Eduardo S. Schwartz. "LYON Taming," **JOF**, 1986, v41(3), 561-575.)

Schwartz, Eduardo S. (Schaefer, Stephen M. and Eduardo S. Schwartz. "A Two-Factor Model Of The Term Structure: An Approximate Analytical Solution," **JFQA**, 1984, v19(4), 413-424.)

Schwartz, Eduardo S. (Schaefer, Stephen M. and Eduardo S. Schwartz. "Time-Dependent Variance And The Pricing Of Bond Options," **JOF**, 1987, v42(5), 1113-1128.)

Schwartz, Eduardo S. and Walter N. Torous. "Prepayment And The Valuation Of Mortgage-Backed Securities," **JOF**, 1989, v44(2), 375-392.

Schwartz, Eduardo and Robert Van Order. "Valuing The Implicit Guarantee Of The Federal National Mortgage Association," **JREFEC**, 1988, v1(1), 23-34.

Schwartz, Eduardo. (Dietrich-Campbell, Bruce and Eduardo Schwartz. "Valuing Debt Options: Empirical Evidence," **JFEC**, 1986, v16(3), 321-343.)

Schwartz, Eduardo. (Jorion, Philippe and Eduardo Schwartz. "Integration Vs. Segmentation In The Canadian Stock Market," **JOF**, 1986, v41(3), 603-613.)

Schwartz, Eduardo. (Morck, Randall, Eduardo Schwartz and David Stangeland. "The Valuation Of Foresty Resources Under Stochastic Prices And Inventories," **JFQA**, 1989, v24(4), 473-488.)

Schwartz, Eduargo S. "The Pricing Of Commodity-Linked Bonds," **JOF**, 1982, v37(2), 525-539.

Schwartz, Eli and J. Richard Aronson. "How To Integrate Corporate And Personal Income Taxation," **JOF**, 1972, v27(5), 1073-1080.

Schwartz, Eli and J. Richard Aronson. "Some Surrogate Evidence In Support Of The Concept Of Optimal Financial Structure," **JOF**, 1967, v22(1), 10-18.

Schwartz, Eli and James A. Greenleaf. "A Comment On Investment Decisions, Repetitive Games And The Unequal Distribution Of Wealth," **JOF**, 1978, v33(4), 1222-1227.

Schwartz, Eli and Roger C. Van Tassel. "Some Suggested Changes In The Corporate Tax Structure," **JOF**, 1950, v5(4), 410-420.

Schwartz, Eli. "A Contribution To The Theory Of Capital Budgeting - The Multi-Investment Case: A Comment," **JOF**, 1964, v19(4), 668-670.

Schwartz, Eli. "Note On A Theory Of Firm Growth," **JOB**, 1965, v38(1), 29-33.

Schwartz, Eli. "The Cost Of Capital And Investment Criteria In The Public Sector," **JOF**, 1970, v25(1), 135-142.

Schwartz, Eli. "The Refunding Decision," **JOB**, 1967, v40(4), 448-449.

Schwartz, Eli. "Theory Of The Capital Structure Of The Firm," **JOF**, 1959, v14(1), 18-39.

Schwartz, Irwin. "Water Pollution: Market Potential," **FAJ**, 1966, v22(1), 123-126.

Schwartz, Kenneth B. (Gilbert, Lisa R., Krishnagopal Menon and Kenneth B. Schwartz. "Predicting Bankruptcy For Firms In Financial Distress," **JBFA**, 1990, v17(1), 161-171.)

Schwartz, Marvin. (Lerner, Eugene M. and Marvin Schwartz. "Supermarkets: Relationship Between Sales, Rents And Profits," **FAJ**, 1961, v17(3), 7-10.)

Schwartz, Nancy L. (Kamien, Morton I. and Nancy L. Schwartz. "Payment Plans And The Efficient Delivery Of Health Care Services," **JRI**, 1973, v40(3), 427-436.)

Schwartz, R. A. "Corporate Philanthropic Contributions," **JOF**, 1968, v23(3), 479-497.

Schwartz, R. A. "The Income Elasticity Of Corporate Philanthropy: Reply," **JOF**, 1970, v25(1), 153-157

Schwartz, Robert A. and David K. Whitcomb. "Comment: Assessing The Impact Of Stock Exchange Specialists On Stock Volatility," **JFQA**, 1976, v11(5), 901-908.

Schwartz, Robert A. and David K. Whitcomb. "On Time-Variance Analysis: Reply," **JOF**, 1979, v34(5), 1273-1275.

Schwartz, Robert A. and David K. Whitcomb. "Evidence On The Presence And Causes Of Serial Correlation In Market Model Residuals," **JFQA**, 1977, v12(2), 291-313.

Schwartz, Robert A. and David K. Whitcomb. "The Time-Variance Relationship: Evidence On Autocorrelation In Common Stock Returns," **JOF**, 1977, v32(1), 41-55.

Schwartz, Robert A. and Edward I. Altman. "Volatility Behavior Of Industrial Stock Price Indices," **JOF**, 1973, v28(4), 957-971.

Schwartz, Robert A. "A Proposal To Stabilize Stock Prices," **JPM**, 1988-89, v15(1), 4-11.

Schwartz, Robert A. "A Proposal To Stabilize Stock Prices: Reply," **JPM**, 1990, v16(2), 82-84.

Schwartz, Robert A. "An Economic Model Of Trade Credit," **JFQA**, 1974, v9(4), 643-657.

Schwartz, Robert A. "Institutionalization Of The Equity Markets," **JPM**, 1991, v17(2), 44-49.

Schwartz, Robert A. (Altman, Edward I. and Robert A. Schwartz. "Common Stock Price Volatility Measures And Patterns," **JFQA**, 1970, v5(5), 603-626.)

Schwartz, Robert A. (Arzac, Enrique R., Robert A. Schwartz and David K. Whitcomb. "The Leverage Structure Of Interest Rates," **JMCB**, 1981, v13(1), 72-88.)

Schwartz, Robert A. (Bloch, Ernest and Robert A. Schwartz. "The Great Debate Over NYSE Rule 390," **JPM**, 1978-79, v5(1), 5-10.)

Schwartz, Robert A. (Cohen, Kalman J., Steven F. Maier, Robert A. Schwartz and David K. Whitcomb. "The Returns Generating Process, Returns Variance, And The Effect Of Thinness In Securities Markets," **JOF**, 1978, v33(1), 149-167.)

Schwartz, Robert A. (Cohen, Kalman J., Steven F. Maier, Walter L. Ness, Jr., Hitoshi Okuda, Robert A. Schwartz and David K. Whitcomb. "The Impact Of Designated Market Makers On Security Prices," **JBF**, 1977, v1(3), 219-247.)

Schwartz, Robert A. (Cohen, Kalman J., Walter L. Ness, Jr., Hitoshi Okuda, Robert A. Schwartz and David K. Whitcomb. "The Determinants Of Common Stock Returns Volatility: An International Comparison," **JOF**, 1976, v31(2), 733-739.)
Schwartz, Robert A. (Cohen, Kalman J., Gabriel A. Hawawini, Steven F. Maier, Robert A. Schwartz and David K. Whitcomb. "Friction In The Trading Process And The Estimation Of Systematic Risk," **JFEC**, 1983, v12(2), 263-278.)
Schwartz, Robert A. (Cohen, Kalman J., Steven F. Maier, Robert A. Schwartz and David K. Whitcomb. "Limit Orders, Market Structure, And The Returns Generation Process," **JOF**, 1978, v33(3), 723-736.)
Schwartz, Robert A. (Cohen, Kalman J., Steven F. Maier, Robert A. Schwartz and David K. Whitcomb. "An Analysis Of The Economic Justification For Consolidation In A Secondary Security Market," **JBF**, 1982, v6(1), 117-136.)
Schwartz, Robert A. (Cohen, Kalman J., Stephen F. Maier, Robert A. Schwartz and David K. Whitcomb. "Market Makers And The Market Spread: A Review Of Recent Literature," **JFQA**, 1979, v14(4), 813-835.)
Schwartz, Robert A. (Fung, William K. H., Robert A. Schwartz and David K. Whitcomb. "Adjusting For The Intervalling Effect Bias In Beta," **JBF**, 1985, v9(3), 443-460.)
Schwartz, Robert A. (Goodman, Laurie S. and Robert A. Schwartz. "Coffee Pots And Limit Orders," **JPM**, 1982-83, v9(3), 5-6.)
Schwartz, Robert A. (Hasbrouck, Joel and Robert A. Schwartz. "Liquidity And Execution Costs In Equity Markets," **JPM**, 1987-88, v14(3), 10-17.)
Schwartz, Robert A. (Ho, Thomas S. Y., Robert A. Schwartz and David K. Whitcomb. "The Trading Decision And Market Clearing Under Transaction Price Uncertainty," **JOF**, 1985, v40(1), 21-42.)
Schwartz, Robert A. (Schreiber, Paul S. and Robert A. Schwartz. "Price Discovery In Securities Markets," **JPM**, 1985-86, v12(4), 43-48.)
Schwartz, Robert. (Cohen, Kalman J., Gabriel A. Hawawini, Steven F. Maier, Robert Schwartz And David K. Whitcomb. "Implications Of Microstructure Theory For Empirical Research On Stock Price Behavior," **JOF**, 1980, v35(2), 249-257.)
Schwartz, William D. "The Domestic Toy Industry," **FAJ**, 1968, v24(5), 45-48.
Schwartz, William. "Convertibles Get Realistic Image," **FAJ**, 1967, v23(4), 55-57.
Schwartz, William. "Warrants: A Form Of Equity Capital," **FAJ**, 1970, v26(5), 87-101.
Schwarz, Peter M. (O'Brien, Thomas J. and Peter M. Schwarz. "Ex Ante Evidence Of Backwardation/Contango In Commodities Futures Markets," **JFM**, 1982, v2(2), 159-168.)
Schwarz, Thomas V. (Laatsch, Francis E. and Thomas V. Schwarz. "Price Discovery And Risk Transfer In Stock Index Cash And Futures Markets," **RFM**, 1988, v7(2), 272-289.)
Schwarz, Thomas. (Ang, James S. and Thomas Schwarz. "Risk Aversion And Information Structure: An Experimental Study Of Price Variability In The Securities Markets," **JOF**, 1985, v40(3), 825-844.)
Schwarzbach, Henry. "The Role Of Independent Audit Reports In Commercial Bank Business Loan Decision Making: A Study Of Rhode Island Banks," **JBR**, 1977-78, v8(4), 249-250.
Schwarzchild, Stuart. "Rights Of Creditors In Life Insurance Policies," **JRI**, 1961, v28(2), 51-58.
Schwarzschild, Stuart. "A Model For Determining The Rate Of Return On Investment In Life Insurance Policies," **JRI**, 1967, v34(3), 435-444.
Schwarzschild, Stuart. "A Note On The Accounting Treatment Of The Acquisition Expenses Of Life Insurance Companies," **JRI**, 1965, v32(2), 273-276.
Schwarzschild, Stuart. "Alexander Hoover - A Life Insurance Case Study," **JRI**, 1968, v35(2), 301-306.
Schwarzschild, Stuart. "Rates Of Return On The Investment Differentials Between Life Insurance Policies," **JRI**, 1968, v35(4), 583-596.
Schwatz, M. (Muller, U. A., M. M. Dacorogna, R. B. Olsen, O. V. Pictet, M. Schwarz and C. Morgenegg. "Statistical Study Of Foreign Exchange Rates, Empirical Evidence Of A Price Change Scaling Law, And Intraday Analysis," **JBF**, 1990, v14(6), 1189-1208.)
Schweiger, Irving and John S. McGee. "Chicago Banking," **JOB**, 1961, v34(3), 203-366.
Schweiger, Irving. "1965 Forecast Of Gross National Product, Consumer Spending, Saving, And Housing," **JOB**, 1965, v38(1), 9-11.
Schweiger, Irving. "1967 Forecast Of Gross National Product, Consumer Spending, Saving, And Housing," **JOB**, 1967, v40(1), 5-9.
Schweiger, Irving. "1968 Forecast Of Gross National Product, Consumer Spending, Saving, And Housing," **JOB**, 1968, v41(1), 5-9.
Schweiger, Irving. "1969 Forecast Of Gross National Product, Consumer Spending, Saving, And Housing," **JOB**, 1969, v42(1), 7-11.
Schweiger, Irving. "1970 Forecast Of Gross National Product, Consumer Spending, Saving, And Housing," **JOB**, 1970, v43(1), 6-9.
Schweiger, Irving. "1971 Forecast Of Gross National Product, Consumer Spending, Saving, And Housing," **JOB**, 1971, v44(1), 6-9.
Schweiger, Irving. "1972 Forecast Of Gross National Product, Consumer Spending, Saving And Housing," **JOB**, 1972, v45(1), 6-10.
Schweiger, Irving. "1973 Forecast Of Gross National Product, Consumer Spending, Saving, And Housing," **JOB**, 1973, v46(1), 6-10.
Schweiger, Irving. "1974 Forecast Of Gross National Product, Consumer Spending, Saving, And Housing," **JOB**, 1974, v47(1), 5-10.
Schweiger, Irving. "1975 Forecast Of Gross National Product, Consumer Spending, Saving, And Housing," **JOB**, 1975, v48(1), 5-10.
Schweiger, Irving. "1976 Forecast Of Gross National Product, Consumer Spending, Saving, And Housing," **JOB**, 1976, v49(1), 5-10.
Schweiger, Irving. "Adequacy Of Financing For Small Business Since World War II," **JOF**, 1958, v13(3), 323-347.
Schweiger, Irving. "Forecasting Short-Term Consumer Demand From Consumer Anticipations," **JOB**, 1956, v29(2), 90-100.
Schweiger, Irving. "Gross National Product, Consumer Spending, Saving, And Housing," **JOB**, 1966, v39(1), Part I, 9-11.
Schweiger, Irving. "Gross National Product, Consumer Spending, Saving, And Housing," **JOB**, 1964, v37(1), 28-31.
Schweiger, Irving. "Gross National Product, Consumer Spending, Saving, And Housing," **JOB**, 1963, v36(1), 10-13.
Schweitzer, Arthur. "Fixing Of Cost Prices: An Experiment Of World War II," **JOB**, 1950, v23(4), 219-237.
Schweitzer, Arthur. "Schacht's Regulation Of Money And The Capital Markets," **JOF**, 1948, v3(2), 1-18.
Schweitzer, Paul and Joshua Greene. "Determinants And Consequences Of Market Entry: A Case Study Of Two Wisconsin Banking Markets," **JBR**, 1978-79, v9(4), 218-226.
Schweitzer, Paul R. and Joshua E. Greene. "The Johnson Wax Effect: Reply," **JBR**, 1980-81, v11(3), 192.
Schweitzer, R. (Bierwag, G. O., G. G. Kaufman, R. Schweitzer and A. Toevs. "The Art Of Risk Management In Bond Portfolios," **JPM**, 1980-81, v7(3), 27-36.)
Schweitzer, Robert L. (Black, Harold and Robert L. Schweitzer. "Discrimination In The Lending Decision: Home Improvement Loans," **JBR**, 1980-81, v11(3), 184-186.)
Schweitzer, Robert L. (Black, Harold A. and Robert L. Schweitzer. "Black-Controlled Credit Unions: A Comparative Analysis," **JFR**, 1985, v8(3), 193-202.)
Schweitzer, Robert L. (Black, Harold A. and Robert L. Schweitzer. "An Analysis Of Market Segmentation In Mortgage Lending Between A Commercial Bank And A Mutual Savings Bank," **AREUEA**, 1981, v9(3), 234-240.)
Schweitzer, Robert L. (Black, Harold A., M. Andrew Fields and Robert L. Schweitzer. "Changes In Interstate Banking Laws: The Impact On Shareholder Wealth," **JOF**, 1990, v45(5), 1663-1672.)
Schweitzer, Robert. (Bundt, Thomas P. and Robert Schweitzer. "Deregulation, Deposit Markets, And Banks' Cost Of Funds," **FR**, 1989, v24(3), 417-430.)
Schweitzer, Robert. (Havrilesky, Thomas and Robert Schweitzer. "Non-Price Competition Among Banking Firms," **JBR**, 1975-76, v6(2), 113-121.)
Schweitzer, Robert. (Lee, Insup and Robert Schweitzer. "Shareholder Wealth Effects In Interstate Banking: The Case Of Delaware's Financial Center Development Act," **JFSR**, 1989, v2(2), 65-72.)
Schwendiman, Carl J. and George E. Pinches. "An Analysis Of Alternative Measures Of Investment Risk," **JOF**, 1975, v30(1), 193-200.
Schwentker, Frank J. "The Life Insurance Agency System," **JRI**, 1958, v25(1), 50-60.
Schwentker, Frank J. "The Structure Of Life Insurance Agents' Compensation," **JRI**, 1960, v27(2), 69-72.
Schwert, G. William and Paul J. Seguin. "Heteroskedasticity In Stock Returns," **JOF**, 1990, v45(4), 1129-1155.
Schwert, G. William. "Indexes Of U.S. Stock Prices From 1802 To 1987," **JOB**, 1990, v63(3), 399-426.
Schwert, G. William. "Margin Requirements And Stock Volatility," **JFSR**, 1989, v3(2/3), 153-164.
Schwert, G. William. "Size And Stock Returns, And Other Empirical Regularities," **JFEC**, 1983, v12(1), 3-12.
Schwert, G. William. "Stock Exchange Seats As Capital Assets," **JFEC**, 1977, v4(1), 51-78.
Schwert, G. William. "Stock Market Volatility," **FAJ**, 1990, v46(3), 23-34.
Schwert, G. William. "Stock Returns And Real Activity: A Century Of Evidence," **JOF**, 1990, v45(4), 1237-1257.
Schwert, G. William. "Stock Volatility And The Crash Of '87," RFS, 1990, v3(1), 77-102.
Schwert, G. William. "The Adjustment Of Stock Prices To Information About Inflation," **JOF**, 1981, v36(1), 15-29.
Schwert, G. William. "Why Does Stock Market Volatility Change Over Time?," **JOF**, 1989, v44(5), 1115-1154.
Schwert, G. William. (Fama, Eugene F. and G. William Schwert. "Human Capital And Capital Market Equilibrium," **JFEC**, 1977, v4(1), 95-125.)
Schwert, G. William. (Fama, Eugene F. and G. William Schwert. "Inflation, Interest, And Relative Prices," **JOB**, 1979, v52(2), 183-210.)
Schwert, G. William. (Fama, Eugene F. and G. William Schwert. "Asset Returns And Inflation," **JFEC**, 1977, v5(2), 115-146.)
Schwert, G. William. (French, Kenneth R., G. William Schwert and Robert F. Stambaugh. "Expected Stock Returns And Volatility," **JFEC**, 1987, v19(1), 3-30.)
Schweser, C. "Multidimensional Security Pricing: A Correction," **JFQA**, 1978, v13(1), 177-183.
Schweser, Carl and Thomas Schneeweis. "Risk Return And The Multi-Dimensional Security Pricing Market," **JFR**, 1980, v3(1), 23-31.
Schweser, Carl, Robert M. Soldofsky and Tom Schneeweis. "The Meaning Of The Mean," **JPM**, 1978-79, v5(4), 23-27.
Schweser, Carl. "The Doctoral Origins Of Contributors To The **JOF** From 1964 Through 1975," **JOF**, 1977, v32(3), 908-910.
Schwinn, Leslie B. "Growth Of Credit Unions," **FAJ**, 1963, v19(4), 55-58.
Scigliano, Robert G. "Trade-Unionism And The Industrial Foreman," **JOB**, 1954, v27(4), 293-300.
Scott, Charlotte H. "Higher Interest Rates On Time Deposits: Comment," **JOF**, 1965, v20(1), 78-85.
Scott, Cuthbert L., III. "Effects Of Differing Unemployment Insurance Taxable Wage Bases On System Capacity," **JRI**, 1986, v53(3), 454-470.
Scott, David F. (Martin, John D. and David F. Scott. "Debt Capacity And The Capital Budgeting Decision: A Revisitation," **FM**, 1980, v9(1), 23-26.)
Scott, David F., Jr. and Dana J. Johnson. "Financing Policies And Practices In Large Corporations," **FM**, 1982, v11(2), 51-59.
Scott, David F., Jr. and J. William Petty. "A Note On The Relevance Of Dividend Policy," **FR**, 1979, v14(1), 59-65.
Scott, David F., Jr. and J. William Petty, II. "Capital Budgeting Practices In Large American Firms: A Retrospective Analysis And Synthesis," **FR**, 1984, v19(1), 111-123.
Scott, David F., Jr. and John D. Martin. "Industry Influence On Financial Structure," **FM**, 1974, v4(1), 67-73.
Scott, David F., Jr. "Evidence On The Importance Of Financial Structure," **FM**, 1972, v1(2), 45-50.
Scott, David F., Jr. (Kennedy, William F. and David F. Scott, Jr. "Some Observations On The Dividend Policies Of Large Commercial Banks," **JBR**, 1982-83, v13(4), 292-296.)
Scott, David F., Jr. (Martin, John D., David F. Scott, Jr. and Robert F.

Vandell. "Equivalent Risk Classes: A Multidimensional Examination," JFQA, 1979, v14(1), 101-118.)

Scott, David F., Jr. (Martin, John D. and David F. Scott, Jr. "A Discriminant Analysis Of The Corporate Debt-Equity Decision," FM, 1974, v3(4), 71-79.)

Scott, David F., Jr. (Martin, John D. and David F. Scott, Jr. "Debt Capacity And The Capital Budgeting Decision," FM, 1976, v5(2), 7-14.)

Scott, David F., Jr. and Brian Rungeling. "Business Doctoral Programs: What Are The Incremental Costs Of Starting New Ones?," JFED, 1988, v17, 80-88.

Scott, David F., Jr., Laurence J. Moore, Andre Saint-Denis, Edouard Archer and Bernard W. Taylor, III. "Implementation Of A Cash Budget Simulator At Air Canada," FM, 1979, v8(2), 46-52.

Scott, David G. "Life Insurance And Accounting Statements," JRI, 1970, v37(3), 447-450.

Scott, David M. (Ausman, Evan L., David M. Scott and Raymond T. Smith. "Life Insurance Stocks," FAJ, 1956, v12(4), 87-93.)

Scott, Eldred H. "Probable Impact Of Atomic Energy On Electric Public Utility Securities," JOF, 1954, v9(2), 136-147.

Scott, Elton and Stewart Brown. "Biased Estimators And Unstable Betas," JOF, 1980, v35(1), 49-55.

Scott, Elton and Alan L. Tucker. "Predicting Currency Return Volatility," JBF, 1989, v13(6), 839-852.

Scott, Elton. "On The Financial Application Of Discriminant Analysis: Comment," JFQA, 1978, v13(1), 201-205.

Scott, Elton. (Osteryoung, Jerome S., Elton Scott and Gordon S. Roberts. "Selecting Capital Projects With The Coefficient Of Variation," FM, 1977, v6(2), 65-70.)

Scott, Elton. (Tucker, Alan L. and Elton Scott. "A Study Of Diffusion Processes For Foreign Exchange Rates," JIMF, 1987, v6(4), 465-478.)

Scott, Elton. (Tucker, Alan L., David R. Peterson and Elton Scott. "Tests Of The Black-Scholes And Constant Elasticity Of Variance Currency Call Option Valuation Models," JFR, 1988, v11(3), 201-214.)

Scott, Ira O., Jr. (Fand, David I. and Ira O. Scott, Jr. "The Federal Reserve System's 'Bills Only' Policy: A Suggested Interpretation," JOB, 1958, v31(1), 12-18.)

Scott, Ira. "The Changing Significance Of Treasury Obligations In Commercial Bank Portfolios," JOF, 1957, v12(2), 213-222.

Scott, James and Charles R. Wolf. "Bidding On Treasury Bills," JPM, 1979-80, v6(3), 46-52.

Scott, James H., Jr. "Ambiguities In The Cross-Section Analysis Of Per Share Financial Data: Comment," JOF, 1977, v32(3), 933-936.

Scott, James H., Jr. "Bankruptcy, Secured Debt, And Optimal Capital Structure: Reply," JOF, 1979, v34(1), 253-260.

Scott, James H., Jr. "Bankruptcy, Secured Debt, And Optimal Capital Structure," JOF, 1977, v32(1), 1-19.

Scott, James H., Jr. "On The Theory Of Conglomerate Mergers," JOF, 1977, v32(4), 1235-1250.

Scott, James H., Jr. "The Tax Effects Of Investment In Marketable Securities On Firm Valuation," JOF, 1979, v34(2), 307-324.

Scott, James H., Jr. (Chatterjee, Sris and James H. Scott, Jr. "Explaining Differences In Corporate Capital Structure: Theory And New Evidence," JBF, 1989, v13(2), 283-310.)

Scott, James. "The Probability Of Bankruptcy: A Comparison Of Empirical Predictions And Theoretical Models," JBF, 1981, v5(3), 317-344.

Scott, James. (Sarig, Oded and James Scott. "The Puzzle Of Financial Leverage Clienteles," JOF, 1985, v40(5), 1459-1467.)

Scott, James. (Stumpp, Mark and James Scott. "Does Liquidity Predict Stock Returns?," JPM, 1991, v17(2), 35-40.)

Scott, Jonathan A. and Terrence C. Smith. "The Effect Of The Bankruptcy Reform Act Of 1978 On Small Business Loan Pricing," JFEC, 1986, v16(1), 119-140.

Scott, Jonathan A. and William C. Dunkelberg. "Rural Versus Urban Bank Performance: An Analysis Of Market Competition For Small Business Loans," JBR, 1984-85, v15(3), 167-178.

Scott, Jonathan A. (Dunkelberg, William C., Jonathan A. Scott and Edwin L. Cox. "Small Business And The Value Of Bank-Customer Relationships," JBR, 1983-84, v14(4), 248-258.)

Scott, Jonathan A. (Leeth, John D. and Jonathan A. Scott. "The Incidence Of Secured Debt: Evidence From The Small Business Community," JFQA, 1989, v24(3), 379-394.)

Scott, Jonathan A. (Lewellen, Wilbur G., John J. McConnell and Jonathan A. Scott. "Capital Market Influences On Trade Credit Policies," JFR, 1980, v3(2), 105-113.)

Scott, Jonathan A. (Peavy, John W., III and Jonathan A. Scott. "A Closer Look At Stock-For-Debt Swaps," FAJ, 1985, v41(3), 44-50.)

Scott, Jonathan A. (Peavy, John W., III and Jonathan A. Scott. "The Effect Of Stock For Debt Swaps On Security Returns," FR, 1985, v20(4), 303-327.)

Scott, Jonathan A., George H. Hempel and John W. Peavy, III. "The Effect Of Stock-For-Debt Swaps On Bank Holding Companies," JBF, 1985, v9(2), 233-251.

Scott, Louis "Do Prices Reflect Market Fundamentals In Real Estate Markets?," JREFEC, 1990, v3(1), 5-24.

Scott, Louis O. "Option Pricing When The Variance Changes Randomly: Theory, Estimation, And An Application," JFQA, 1987, v22(4), 419-438.

Scott, Louis O. "The Stationarity Of The Conditional Mean Of Real Rates Of Return On Common Stocks: An Empirical Investigation," JFQA, 1984, v19(2), 217-230.

Scott, Louis. (Chesney, Marc and Louis Scott. "Pricing European Currency Options: A Comparison Of The Modified Black-Scholes Model And A Random Variance Model," JFQA, 1989, v24(3), 267-284.)

Scott, Robert C. and Philip A. Horvath. "On The Direction Of Preference For Moments Of Higher Order Than The Variance," JOF, 1980, v35(4), 915-919.

Scott, Robert C. (Horvath, Philip A. and Robert C. Scott. "An Expected Utility Explanation Of Plunging And Dumping Behavior," FR, 1985, v20(2), 219-228.)

Scott, Robert Haney. "A Conditional Theory Of Banking Enterprise," JFQA, 1966, v1(2), 84-98.

Scott, Robert Haney. "Estimates Of Hicksian IS And LM Curves For The United States," JOF, 1966, v21(3), 479-487.

Scott, Robert Haney. "Some Additional Estimates Of The Liquidity Preference Function For The United States," JFQA, 1967, v2(3), 299-312.

Scott, Robert Haney. "Teaching The Financial Markets Course," JFQA, 1976, v11(4), 591-594.

Scott, William L. and Richard L. Peterson. "Interest Rate Risk And Equity Values Of Hedged And Unhedged Financial Intermediaries," JFR, 1986, v9(4), 325-329.

Scott, William L., Mona J. Gardner and Dixie L. Mills. "Expense Preference And Minority Banking: A Note," FR, 1988, v23(1), 105-116.

Scott, William R. (Atkinson, Anthony A. and William R. Scott. "Current Cost Depreciation: A Programming Perspective," JBFA, 1982, v8(1), 19-42.)

Scruggs, L. S. "A Note On Scale Economies In Investment Advising: Reexamination Of The SEC Findings," JOB, 1976, v49(3), 408-411.

Scully, Gerald W. "Business Cycles And Industrial Strike Activity," JOB, 1971, v44(4), 359-374.

Scully, Gerald W. and Lowell E. Gallaway. "A Spectral Analysis Of The Demographic Structure Of American Unemployment," JOB, 1973, v46(1), 87-102.

Seagers, David K. (Mansur, Iqbal, Steven J. Cochran and David K. Seagers. "The Relationship Between The Argentinean Debt Rescheduling Announcement And Bank Equity Returns," FR, 1990, v25(2), 321-334.)

Seagle, John P. (Duchessi, Peter, Hany Shawky and John P. Seagle. "A Knowledge-Engineered System For Commercial Loan Decisions," FM, 1988, v17(3), 57-65.)

Seagle, John P. (Frankfurter, George M., Herbert E. Phillips and John P. Seagle. "A Proposed Normative Procedure For Portfolio Selection Under Conditions Of Uncertainty," FM, 1977, v6(4), 43-50.)

Seagle, John P. (Frankfurter, George M., Herbert E. Phillips and John P. Seagle. "Performance Of The Sharpe Portfolio Selection Model: A Comparison," JFQA, 1976, v11(2), 195-204.)

Seagle, John P. (Frankfurter, George M., Herbert E. Phillips and John P. Seagle. "Portfolio Selection: The Effects Of Uncertain Means, Variances, And Covariances," JFQA, 1971, v6(5), 1251-1262.)

Seagle, John P. (Frankfurter, George M., Herbert E. Phillips and John P. Seagle. "Estimation Risk In The Portfolio Selection Model: A Comment," JFQA, 1972, v7(1), 1423-1424.)

Seagle, John P. (Phillips, Herbert E. and John P. Seagle. "Data: A Mixed Blessing In Portfolio Selection?," FM, 1974, v4(3), 50-53.)

Seale, William E. (Jordan, James V., William E. Seale, Stephen J. Dinehart and David E. Kenyon. "The Intraday Variability Of Soybean Futures Prices: Information And Trading Effects," RFM, 1988, v7(1), 96-109.)

Seale, William E. (Barnhill, Theodore M., James V. Jordan and William E. Seale. "Maturity And Refunding Effects On Treasury-Bond Futures Price Variance," JFR, 1987, v10(2), 121-132.)

Seale, William E. (Barnhill, Theodore M. and William E. Seale. "Optimal Exercise Of The Switching Option In Treasury Bond Arbitrages," JFM, 1988, v8(5), 517-532.)

Seale, William E. (Fleischman, Edward H., William E. Seale, Karsten Mahlmann and Hans R. Stoll. "Panel Discussion On Regulatory Issues Facing The Futures Industry," RFM, 1988, v7(1), 200-216.)

Seale, William E. (Jordan, James V., William E. Seale, Nancy C. McCabe and David E. Kenyon. "Transaction Data Tests Of The Black Model For Soybean Futures Options," JFM, 1987, v7(5), 535-554.)

Seale, William E. (Jordan, James V., William E. Seale, Stephen J. Dinehart and David E. Kenyon. "The Intraday Variability Of Soybean Futures Prices: Information And Trading Effects," RFM, 1988, v7(1), 96-109.)

Seale, William E. (Kenyon, David, Kenneth Kling, Jim Jordan, William Seale and Nancy McCabe. "Factors Affecting Agricultural Futures Price Variance," JFM, 1987, v7(1), 73-92.)

Sealey, C. W. and James T. Lindley. "Inputs, Outputs, And A Theory Of Production And Cost Of Depository Financial Institutions," JOF, 1977, v32(4), 1251-1266.

Sealey, C. W., Jr. and Robert Heinkel. "Asymmetric Information And A Theory Of Compensating Balances," JBF, 1985, v9(2), 193-205.

Sealey, C. W., Jr. "Credit Rationing In The Commercial Loan Market: Estimates Of A Structural Model Under Conditions Of Disequilibrium," JOF, 1979, v34(3), 689-702.

Sealey, C. W., Jr. "Deposit Rate-Setting, Risk Aversion And The Theory Of Depository Financial Intermediaries," JOF, 1980, v35(5), 1139-1154.

Sealey, C. W., Jr. "Financial Planning With Multiple Objectives," FM, 1978, v7(4), 17-23.

Sealey, C. W., Jr. "Portfolio Separation For Stockholder Owned Depository Financial Intermediaries," JBF, 1985, v9(4), 477-490.

Sealey, C. W., Jr. "Utility Maximization And Programming Models For Capital Budgeting," JBFA, 1978, v5(3), 355-366.

Sealey, C. W., Jr. "Valuation, Capital Structure, And Shareholder Unanimity For Depository Financial Intermediaries," JOF, 1983, v38(3), 857-875.

Sealey, C. W., Jr. (Eatman, John L. and C. W. Sealey, Jr. "A Multiobjective Linear Programming Model For Commercial Bank Balance Sheet Management," JBR, 1978-79, v9(4), 227-236.)

Sealey, Calvin W., Jr. (Eatman, John L. and Calvin W. Sealey, Jr. "A Spectral Analysis Of Aggregate Commercial Bank Liability Management And Its Relationship To Short-Run Earning Asset Behavior," JFQA, 1977, v12(5), 767-778.)

Sears, R. Stephen and Gary L. Trennepohl. "Diversification And Skewness In Option Portfolios," JFR, 1983, v6(3), 199-212.

Sears, R. Stephen and Gary L. Trennepohl. "Measuring Portfolio Risk In Options," JFR, 1983, v17(3), 391-409.

Sears, R. Stephen and K. C. John Wei. "The Structure Of Skewness Preferences In Asset Pricing Models With Higher Moments: An Empirical Test," FR, 1988, v23(1), 25-38.

Sears, R. Stephen. (Chen, Andrew H., K. C. Chen and R. Stephen Sears. "The Value Of Loan Guarantees: The Case Of Chrysler Corporation," RIF, 1986, v6, 101-118.)

Sears, R. Stephen. (Chen, K. C., R. Stephen Sears and Dah-Nein Tzang. "Oil Prices And Energy Futures," JFM, 1987, v7(5), 501-518.)

Sears, R. Stephen. (Chen, K. C. and R. Stephen Sears. "How Many Small Firms Are Enough?," JFR, 1984, v7(4), 341-349.)

Sears, R. Stephen. (Chen, K. C. and R. Stephen Sears. "Pricing The SPIN," FM, 1990, v19(2), 36-47.)

Sears, R. Stephen. (Ma, Christopher K., Ramesh P. Rao and R. Stephen Sears. "Volatility, Price Resolution, And The Effectiveness Of Price Limits," JFSR, 1989, v3(2/3), 165-200.)

Sears, R. Stephen. (Ma, Christopher K., Ramesh P. Rao and R. Stephen Sears. "Limit Moves And Price Resolution: The Case Of The Treasury Bond Futures Market," JFM, 1989, v9(4), 321-336.)

Sears, R. Stephen. (Miles, Mike and R. Stephen Sears. "An Econometric Approach To The FNMA Free Market System Auction," JFQA, 1981, v16(2), 177-192.)

Sears, R. Stephen. (Park, Hun Y. and R. Stephen Sears. "Estimating Stock Index Futures Volatility Through The Prices Of Their Options," JFM, 1985, v5(2), 223-238.)

Sears, R. Stephen. (Park, Hun Y. and R. Stephen Sears. "Changing Volatility And The Pricing Of Options On Stock Index Futures," JFR, 1985, v8(4), 265-274.)

Sears, Stephen and K. C. John Wei. "Asset Pricing, Higher Moments, And The Market Risk Premium: A Note," JOF, 1985, v40(4), 1251-1253.

Seater, John J. "Are Future Taxes Discounted?," JMCB, 1982, v14(3), 376-389.

Seater, John J. "On The Estimation Of Permanent Income," JMCB, 1982, v14(1), 76-83.

Seaver, William L. and Donald R. Fraser. "Branch Banking And The Availability Of Banking Services In Metropolitan Areas," JFQA, 1979, v14(1), 153-160.

Seaver, William L. (Skomp, Stephen E., Timothy P. Cronan and William L. Seaver. "On Application Of The Rank Transformation Discrimination Method To Financial Problems," FR, 1986, v21(4), 473-483.)

Sedgwick, R. Minturn. "Alternative To Conventional Investing?," FAJ, 1973, v29(4), 41-44.

Seelenfreund, Alan, George G. C. Parker and James C. Van Horne. "Stock Price Behavior And Trading," JFQA, 1968, v3(3), 263-281.

Seeley, Peter. (Kolodny, Richard, Peter Seeley and Murray E. Polakoff. "The Effect Of Compensating Balance Requirements On The Profitability Of Borrowers And Lenders," JFQA, 1977, v12(5), 801-815.)

Seelig, Steven A. "Rising Interest Rates And Cost Push Inflation," JOF, 1974, v29(4), 1049-1061.

Seevers, Gary L. "Comments On 'Innovation, Competition, And New Contract Design In Futures Contracts'," JFM, v1(2), 157-159.

Sefcik, Stephan E. (Long, Michael S. and Stephan E. Sefcik. "Participation Financing: A Comparison Of The Characteristics Of Convertible Debt And Straight Bonds Issued In Conjunction With Warrants," FM, 1990, v19(3), 23-34.)

Sefcik, Stephen E. (Richardson, Gordon, Stephen E. Sefcik and Rex Thompson. "A Test Of Dividend Irrelevance Using Volume Reactions To A Change In Dividend Policy," JFEC, 1986, v17(2), 313-333.)

Seff, Eric J. (Choie, Kenneth S. and Eric J. Seff. "TIPP: Insurance Without Complexity: Comment," JPM, 1989, v16(1), 107-108.)

Segal, Uzi and Avia Spivak. "Non-Expected Utility Risk Premiums: The Cases Of Probability Ambiguity And Outcome Uncertainty," JRU, 1988, v1(3), 333-347.)

Segal, Uzi. "Probabilistic Insurance And Anticipated Utility," JRI, 1988, v55(2), 287-297.

Segal, Uzi. (Safra, Zvi, Uzi Segal and Avia Spivak. "The Becker-DeGroot-Marschak Mechanism And Non-Expected Utility," JRU, 1990, v3(2), 177-190.)

Segall, Joel E. (Weil, Roman L., Joel E. Segall and David Green, Jr. "Premiums On Convertible Bonds: Reply," JOF, 1970, v25(4), 931-933.)

Segall, Joel E. (Weil, Roman L., Jr., Joel E. Segall and David Green, Jr. "Premiums On Convertible Bonds," JOF, 1968, v23(3), 445-463.)

Segall, Joel E. (Weil, Roman L, Joel E. Segall and David O. Green. "Premium On Convertible Bonds: Reply," JOF, 1972, v27(5), 1163-1170.)

Segall, Joel. "The Effect Of Maturity On Price Fluctuations," JOB, 1956, v29(3), 202-206.

Segall, Joel. "The Propagation Of Bulldozers: A Review Article," JOB, 1965, v38(4), 397-402.

Segall, Joel. (Green, David, Jr. and Joel Segall. "Return Of Strawman," JOB, 1970, v43(1), 63-65.)

Segall, Joel. (Green, David, Jr. and Joel Segall. "The Predictive Power Of First-Quarter Earnings Reports," JOB, 1967, v40(1), 44-55.)

Segall, Joel. (Green, David, Jr. and Joel Segall. "Brickbats And Straw Men: A Reply To Brown And Niederhoffer," JOB, 1968, v41(4), 498-502.)

Segev, Eli. (Neumann, Seev and Eli Segev. "Human Capital And Risk Management: A Proposal For A New Insurance Product," JRI, 1978, v45(2), 344-352.)

Segev, Eli. (Neumann, Seev and Eli Segev. "Human Capital And Risk Management: A Proposal For A New Insurance Product," JRI, 1978, v45(3), 522-530.)

Seguin, Paul J. (Jarrell, Gregg A. and Paul J. Seguin. "A Proposal To Stabilize Stock Prices: Comment," JPM, 1990, v16(2), 79-81.)

Seguin, Paul J. (Schwert, G. William and Paul J. Seguin. "Heteroskedasticity In Stock Returns," JOF, 1990, v45(4), 1129-1155.)

Seiber, Hans U. (Herbst, Anthony F., Edwin Maberly and Hans U. Sieber. "Sovereign Debt: Historical Perspective As Portent For Today," RDIBF, 1989, v3, 45-68.)

Seiden, Martin H. "Pricing A Banking Service - The Special Checking Account," JOF, 1960, v15(3), 371-386.

Seidenverg, Edward. "A Case Of Confused Identity," FAJ, 1988, v44(4), 63-67.

Seiders, David F. "Major Developments In Residential Mortgage And Housing Markets Since The Hunt Commission," AREUEA, 1980, v8(1), 4-32.

Seiders, David S. "Managing Mortgage Interest-Rate Risks In Forward,

Futures, And Options Markets," AREUEA, 1983, v11(2), 237-263.

Seiders, David S. "Mortgage Pass-Through Securities: Progress And Prospects," AREUEA, 1983, v11(2), 264-287.

Seidler, L. J. (Benjes, W. D. and L. J. Seidler. "Interim Financial Statements," FAJ, 1967, v23(5), 109-115.)

Seidman, Joel and Glen G. Cain. "Unionized Engineers And Chemists: A Case Study Of A Professional Union," JOB, 1964, v37(3), 238-257.

Seidman, Joel. (London, Jack, Bernard Karsh, Joel Seidman and Richard Hammet. "Management Views The Local Union," JOB, 1953, v26(2), 91-102.)

Seidman, Laurence S. "Supplementary Health Insurance And Cost-Consciousness Strategy," JRI, 1978, v45(2), 291-310.

Seifert, Bruce. (Akgiray, Vedat, G. Geoffrey Booth and Bruce Seifert. "Distribution Properties Of Latin American Black Market Exchange Rates," JIMF, 1988, v7(1), 37-48.)

Seifert, Bruce. (Eddy, Albert and Bruce Seifert. "Dividend Changes Of Financially Weak Firms," FR, 1986, v21(4), 419-431.)

Seifert, Bruce. (Eddy, Albert and Bruce Seifert. "Inflation, The Fisher Hypothesis, And Long-Term Bonds," FR, 1985, v20(1), 21-35.)

Seifert, Bruce. (Eddy, Albert and Bruce Seifert. "Firm Size And Dividend Announcements," JFR, 1988, v11(4), 295-302.)

Seifert, Bruce. (Koveos, Peter and Bruce Seifert. "Purchasing Power Parity And Black Markets," FM, 1985, v14(3), 40-46.)

Seifert, Bruce. (McCarthy, Joseph, Mohammad Najand and Bruce Seifert. "Empirical Tests Of The Proxy Hypothesis," FR, 1990, v25(2), 251-264.)

Seifert, James A. (Cramer, Robert H. and James A. Seifert. "Measuring The Impact Of Maturity On Expected Return And Risk," JBR, 1976-77, v7(3), 229-235.)

Seifert, James A. (Kutner, George W. and James A. Seifert. "The Valuation Of Mortgage Loan Commitments Using Option Pricing Estimates," JRER, 1989, v4(2), 13-20.)

Seifert, James A. (Kutner, George W. and James A. Seifert. "A Note On The Valuation Of Mortgage Loan Commitments: Incorporating The Commitment Cost In The Mortgage Rate," JRER, 1990, v5(2), 281-284.)

Seifert, James A. (Landes, William J., John D. Stoffels and James A. Seifert. "An Empirical Test Of A Duration-Based Hedge: The Case Of Corporate Bonds," JFM, 1985, v5(2), 173-182.)

Seiler, Robert E. (Jenkins, Elizabeth and Robert E. Seiler. "The Impact Of Executive Compensation Schemes Upon The Level Of Discretionary Expenditures And Growth In Stockholder Wealth," JBFA, 1990, v17(4), 585-592.)

Seitz, Neil E. (Abbott, Jarold G. and Neil E. Seitz. "An Evaluation Of An Innovative Approach To Graduate Business Education," JFED, 1974, v3, 28-38.)

Seitz, Neil E. (Cotner, John S. and Neil E. Seitz. "A Simplified Approach To Short-Term International Diversification," FR, 1987, v22(2), 249-266.)

Seitz, Neil. "Shareholder Goals, Firm Goals And Firm Financing Decisions," FM, 1982, v11(3), 20-26.

Seix, Christina and Ravi Akhoury. "Bond Indexation: The Optimal Quantitative Approach," JPM, 1985-86, v12(3), 50-53.

Sekaran, Chandra P. (Garbade, Kennth D. and Chandra P. Sekaran. "Opening Prices On The New York Stock Exchange," JBF, 1981, v5(3), 345-355.)

Sekely, William S. (Collins, J. Markham and William S. Sekely. "The Relationship Of Headquarters Country And Industry Classification To Financial Structure," FM, 1983, v12(3), 45-51.)

Selby, Edward B., Jr. "The Recognition Lag Of The Federal Advisory Council," JOF, 1979, v34(1), 237-240.

Selby, Edward B., Jr. "The Role Of Director Deposits In New Bank Growth," JBR, 1981-82, v12(1), 60-61.

Selby, Edward B., Jr. (Beranek, William and Edward B. Selby, Jr. "Accelerated Depreciation And Income Growth," AREUEA, 1981, v9(1), 67-73.)

Selby, M. J. P. (Pitts, C. G. C. and M. J. P. Selby. "The Pricing Of Corporate Debt: A Further Note," JOF, 1983, v38(4), 1311-1313.)

Selby, Michael J. P. (O'Brien, Thomas J. and Michael J. P. Selby. "Option Pricing Theory And Asset Expectations: A Review And Discussion In Tribute To James Boness," FR, 1986, v21(4), 399-418.)

Selby, Michael. (Collins, Brett, John Rickard and Michael Selby. "Discounting Of Deferred Tax Liabilities," JBFA, 1990, v17(5), 757-758.)

Selden, Larry. "A New Approach To The Joint Consumption-Portfolio Problem," JMCB, 1980, v12(3), 429-447.

Selden, Richard T. "The Postwar Rise In The Velocity Of Money: A Sectoral Analysis," JOF, 1961, v16(4), 483-545.

Seligman, Barnard. "A Note On Cost Of Living Adjustment In Annuities," JRI, 1964, v31(1), 111-112.

Seligman, Barnard. "Financial Indexing - The 'Variable Payments' Approach To Fixed Income Investment," FAJ, 1963, v19(2), 59-64.

Seligman, Barnard. "Tax Effects Of State Investment Policy," FAJ, 1967, v23(2), 113-115.

Seligman, Barnard. "The Use Of Public Credit For Private Business Through Bond Issues," FAJ, 1966, v22(2), 141-143.

Seligman, Stephanie. (Feldstein, Martin and Stephanie Seligman. "Pension Funding, Share Prices, And National Savings," JOF, 1981, v36(4), 801-824.)

Sellers, Richard M. "Life Insurance In Its New Competitive Frame," JRI, 1956, v23, 61-68.

Sellers, Ronald. (Ang, James S., Jess H. Chua and Ronald Sellers. "Generating Cash Flow Estimates: An Actual Study Using The Delphi Technique," FM, 1979, v8(1), 64-67.)

Selling, Thomas I. and George H. Sorter. "FASB Statement No. 52 And Its Implications For Financial Statement Analysis," FAJ, 1983, v39(3), 64-69.

Selling, Thomas I. (Maloney, Kevin J. and Thomas I. Selling. "Simplifying Tax Simplification: An Analysis Of Its Impact On The Profitability Of Capital Investment," FM, 1985, v14(2), 33-42.)

Selling, Thomas I. and Clyde P. Stickney. "The Effects Of Business Environment And Strategy On A Firm's Rate Of Return On Assets," FAJ, 1989, v45(1), 43-52.

Selling, Thomas I, Ashwinpaul C. Sondhi and George H. Sorter.

"Consolidating Captive Finance Subsidiaries: The Impact Of SFAS 94 On Financial Statements," **FAJ**, 1989, v45(6), 72-75.

Selmer, Brian. "Stock Index Futures Trading," **RFM**, 1986, v5(1), 60-69.

Selmer, David R. "Customer 'Suitability'," **JFM**, 1981, v(Supp), 527-530.

Seltzer, John. "Pension-Fund Investing," **FR**, 1967, v1(2), 15-25.

Selvaggio, Robert. (Stein, Jerome L., Mark Rzepczynski and Robert Selvaggio. "A Theoretical Explanation Of The Empirical Studies Of Futures Markets In Foreign Exchange And Financial Instruments," **FR**, 1983, v18(1), 1-32.)

Sen, Subrata K. (Horsky, Dan and Subrata K. Sen. "Interfaces Between Marketing And Economics: An Overview," **JOB**, 1980, v53(3), Part 2, S5-S12.)

Senbet, Lemma W. and Howard E. Thompson. "The Equivalence Of Alternative Mean-Variance Capital Budgeting Models," **JOF**, 1978, v33(2), 395-401.

Senbet, Lemma W. and Howard E. Thompson. "Growth And Risk," **JFQA**, 1982, v17(3), 331-340.

Senbet, Lemma W. and Robert A. Taggart, Jr. "Capital Structure Equilibrium Under Market Imperfections And Incompleteness," **JOF**, 1984, v39(1), 93-103.

Senbet, Lemma W. "Generalized Separation Of The Portfolio Decision Process Under Uncertain Inflation And Asset Pricing Implications," **JBF**, 1982, v6(2), 263-275.

Senbet, Lemma W. "International Capital Market Equilibrium And The Multinational Firm Financing And Investment Policies," **JFQA**, 1979, v14(3), 455-480.

Senbet, Lemma W. (Barnea, Amir, Robert A. Haugen and Lemma W. Senbet. "A Rationale For Debt Maturity Structure And Call Provisions In The Agency Theoretic Framework," **JOF**, 1980, v35(5), 1223-1234.)

Senbet, Lemma W. (Barnea, Amir, Robert A. Haugen and Lemma W. Senbet. "Market Imperfections, Agency Problems, And Capital Structure: A Review," **FM**, 1981, v10(3), 7-22.)

Senbet, Lemma W. (Barnea, Amir, Robert A. Haugen and Lemma W. Senbet. "An Equilibrium Analysis Of Debt Financing Under Costly Tax Arbitrage And Agency Problems," **JOF**, 1981, v36(3), 569-581.)

Senbet, Lemma W. (Barnea, Amir, Robert A. Haugen and Lemma W. Senbet. "Management Of Corporate Risk," **AFPAF**, 1985, v1(1), 1-28.)

Senbet, Lemma W. (Bodurtha, James N., Jr., D. Chinhyung Cho and Lemma W. Senbet. "Economic Forces In The Stock Market: An International Perspective," **GFJ**, 1989, v1(1), 21-46.)

Senbet, Lemma W. (Cho, D. Chinhyung, Cheol S. Eun and Lemma W. Senbet. "International Arbitrage Pricing Theory: An Empirical Investigation," **JOF**, 1986, v41(2), 313-330.)

Senbet, Lemma W. (Dammon, Robert M. and Lemma W. Senbet. "The Effect Of Taxes And Depreciation On Corporate Investment And Financial Leverage," **JOF**, 1988, v43(2), 357-373.)

Senbet, Lemma W. (Errunza, Vihang R. and Lemma W. Senbet. "International Corporate Diversification, Market Valuation, And Size-Adjusted Evidence," **JOF**, 1984, v39(3), 727-743.)

Senbet, Lemma W. (Errunza, Vihang R. and Lemma W. Senbet. "The Effects Of International Operations On The Market Value Of The Firm: Theory And Evidence," **JOF**, 1981, v36(2), 401-417.)

Senbet, Lemma W. (Hagerman, Robert L. and Lemma W. Senbet. "A Test Of Accounting Bias And Market Structure," **JOB**, 1976, v49(4), 509-514.)

Senbet, Lemma W. (Haugen, Robert A. and Lemma W. Senbet. "Resolving The Agency Problems Of External Capital Through Options," **JOF**, 1981, v36(3), 629-647.)

Senbet, Lemma W. (Haugen, Robert A. and Lemma W. Senbet. "The Insignificance Of Bankruptcy Costs To The Theory Of Optimal Capital Structure," **JOF**, 1978, v33(2), 383-393.)

Senbet, Lemma W. (Haugen, Robert A. and Lemma W. Senbet. "The Role Of Options In The Resolution Of Agency Problems: A Reply," **JOF**, 1986, v41(5), 1171-1174.)

Senbet, Lemma W. (Haugen, Robert A. and Lemma W. Senbet. "On The Resolution Of Agency Problems By Complex Financial Instruments: A Reply," **JOF**, 1987, v42(4), 1091-1095.)

Senbet, Lemma W. (Haugen, Robert A. and Lemma W. Senbet. "New Perspectives On Informational Asymmetry And Agency Relationships," **JFQA**, 1979, v14(4), 671-694.)

Senbet, Lemma W. (Haugen, Robert A. and Lemma W. Senbet. "Bankruptcy And Agency Costs: Their Significance To The Theory Of Optimal Capital Structure," **JFQA**, 1988, v23(1), 27-38.)

Senbet, Lemma W. (Haugen, Robert A. and Lemma W. Senbet. "Corporate Finance And Taxes: A Review," **FM**, 1986, v15(3), 5-21.)

Senbet, Lemma W. (Haugen, Robert A., Lemma W. Senbet and Eli Talmor. "Debt, Dividends, And Taxes: Equilibrium Conditions For Simultaneous Tax Neutrality Of Debt And Dividend Policies," **RIF**, 1986, v6, 1-28.)

Senbet, Lemma W. (Hodder, James E. and Lemma W. Senbet. "International Capital Structure Equilibrium," **JOF**, 1990, v45(5), 1495-1516.)

Senbet, Lemma W. (Logue, Dennis E. and Lemma W. Senbet. "External Currency Market Equilibrium And Its Implications For Regulation Of The Eurocurrency Market," **JOF**, 1983, v38(2), 435-447.)

Senchack, A. J. (Maness, Terry S. and A. J. Senchack. "Futures Hedging And The Reported Financial Position Of Thrift Institutions," **RFM**, 1986, v5(2), 142-159.)

Senchack, A. J., Jr. (Easterwood, John C. and A. J. Senchack, Jr. "Arbitrage Opportunities With T-Bill/T-Bond Futures Combinations," **JFM**, 1986, v6(3), 433-442.)

Senchack, A. J., Jr. (Martin, John D. and A. J. Senchack, Jr. "Program Trading And Systematic Stock Price Behavior," **FAJ**, 1989, v45(3), 61-67.)

Senchack, A. J., Jr. (Martin, John D. and A. J. Senchack, Jr. "Index Futures, Program Trading, And The Covariability Of The Major Market Index Stocks," **JFM**, 1991, v11(1), 95-112.)

Senchack, A. J., Jr. (Woodruff, Catherine S. and A. J. Senchack, Jr. "Intradaily Price-Volume Adjustments Of NYSE Stocks To Unexpected Earnings," **JOF**, 1988, v43(2), 467-491.)

Senchack, A. J., Jr. and John D. Martin. "The Relative Performance Of The PSR And PER Investment Strategies," **FAJ**, 1987, v43(2), 46-56.

Senchack, Andrew J. (Lee, Wayne Y., John D. Martin and Andrew J. Senchack. "The Case For Using Options To Evaluate Salvage Values In Financial Leases," **FM**, 1982, v11(3), 33-41.)

Senchack, Andrew J., Jr. and William L. Beedles. "Is Indirect International Diversification Desirable?," **JPM**, 1979-80, v6(2), 49-57.

Senchack, Andrew J., Jr. and Don M. Heep. "Auction Profits In The Treasury Bill Market," **FM**, 1974, v4(2), 45-52.

Senchack, Andrew J., Jr. and John C. Easterwood. "Cross Hedging CDs With Treasury Bill Futures," **JFM**, 1983, v3(4), 429-438.

Senchack, Andrew J., Jr. and William L. Beedles. "Price Behavior In A Regional Over-The-Counter Securities Market," **JFR**, 1979, v2(2), 119-131.

Senchack, Andrew J., Jr. "A Bibliography Of Corporate Financial Theory And Empirics," **JFED**, 1978, v7, 95-96.

Senchack, Andrew J., Jr. "Modern Capital Market Theory: A Bibliography Of Its Influence In The Finance, Economics, And Accounting Literature," **JFED**, 1977, v6, 97-98.

Senchack, Andrew J., Jr. "The Firm's Optimal Financing Policies: Solution, Equilibrium And Stability," **JFQA**, 1975, v10(4), 543-555.

Senchack, Andrew J., Jr. (Franckle, Charles T. and Andrew J. Senchack, Jr. "Economic Considerations In The Use Of Interest Rate Futures," **JFM**, 1982, v2(1), 107-116.)

Senchack, Andrew J., Jr. (Lee, Wayne Y. and Andrew J. Senchack, Jr. "On The Social Optimality Of The Value Maximization Criterion," **JFQA**, 1980, v15(2), 379-389.)

Seneca, Joseph J. "Short Interest: Bullish Or Bearish?: Reply," **JOF**, 1968, v23(3), 524-527.

Seneca, Joseph J. "Short Interest: Bearish Or Bullish?," **JOF**, 1967, v22(1), 67-70.

Seneca, Joseph J. (Smith, V. Kerry and Joseph J. Seneca. "A Further Note On The Cost Implications Of Fluctuating Demand," **JFQA**, 1970, v5(3), 369-376.)

Seneta, Eugene. (Madan, Dilip B. and Eugene Seneta. "The Variance Gamma (V.G.) Model For Share Market Returns," **JOB**, 1990, v63(4), 511-524.)

Sennetti, John T. "Bernoulli, Sharpe, Financial Risk And St. Petersburg Paradox," **JOF**, 1976, v31(3), 960-962.

Senshack, Andrew J., Jr. "FINANAL: A Computerized Financial Statement Analysis Program," **JFED**, 1975, v4, 103-105.

Senteney, David L. "Dealers' Adverse Selection Costs And The Evaluation Of Alternative Measures Of The Earnings Release Signal," **FR**, 1990, v25(2), 199-210.

Seo, Tae Kun. (Hadar, Josef and Tae Kun Seo. "Ross' Measure Of Risk Aversion And Portfolio Selection," **JRU**, 1990, v3(1), 93-99.)

Seo, Tae Kun. (Hadar, Josef and Tae Kun Seo. "Stochastic Dominance And The Case For Specialization," **RIF**, 1980, v2, 99-110.)

Seo, Tae Kun. (Russell, William R. and Tae Kun Seo. "An Application Of Stochastic Dominance To A Portfolio Problem," **RIF**, 1980, v2, 121-138.)

Sepe, James F. (Statman, Meir and James F. Sepe. "Managerial Incentive Plans And The Use Of The Payback Method," **JBFA**, 1984, v11(1), 61-65.)

Sepe, James R. (Statman, Meir and James F. Sepe. "Project Termination Announcements And The Market Value Of The Firm," **FM**, 1989, v18(4), 74-81.)

Sephton, Peter S. "On Exchange Intervention, Sterlization, And Bank Reserve Accounting," **JIMF**, 1989, v8(3), 445-450.

Seppi, Duane J. "Equilibrium Block Trading And Asymmetric Information," **JOF**, 1990, v45(1), 73-94.

Serbein, Oscar N. "Paying For Medical Care In The United States," **JRI**, 1956, v23, 120-122.

Sercu, Piet. "A Note On Real And Nominal Efficient Sets," **JOF**, 1981, v36(3), 721-737.

Sercu, Piet. (Beckers, Stan and Piet Sercu. "Foreign Exchange Pricing Under Free Floating Versus Admissible Band Regimes," **JIMF**, 1985, v4(3), 317-329.)

Serfaty, Abraham. "The Kinked Supply Function For Savings Banks Deposits," **JBR**, 1976-77, v7(1), 93-96.

Serletis, Apostolos and A. Leslie Robb. "Divisia Aggregation And Sub-stitutability Among Monetary Assets," **JMCB**, 1986, v18(4), 430-446.

Servaes, Henri. "Tobin's Q And The Gains From Takeovers," **JOF**, 1991, v46(1), 409-420.

Servaes, Henri. (McConnell, John J. and Henri Servaes. "Additional Evidence On Equity Ownership And Corporate Value," **JFEC**, 1990, v27(2), 595-612.)

Seth, S. B. (Woo, J. C. H. and S. B. Seth. "Replacement Costs And Historical Performance," **FAJ**, 1978, v34(2), 48-54.)

Sethi, Suresh P. and Gerald L. Thompson. "Applications Of Mathematical Control Theory To Finance: Modeling Simple Dynamic Cash Balance Problems," **JFQA**, 1970, v5(4), 381-394.

Sethi, Suresh P. "A Note On A Planning Horizon Model Of Cash Management," **JFQA**, 1971, v6(1), 659-664.

Sethi, Suresh P. "A Note On Modeling Simple Dynamic Cash Balance Problem: Errata," **JFQA**, 1978, v13(3), 585-586.

Sethi, Suresh P. "A Note On Modeling Simple Dynamic Cash Balance Problems," **JFQA**, 1973, v8(4), 685-687.

Sethi, Suresh P. "Optimal Equity And Financing Model Of Krouse And Lee: Corrections And Extensions," **JFQA**, 1978, v13(3), 487-505.

Settle, John W. (Fuller, Russell J. and John W. Settle. "Determinants Of Duration And Bond Volatility," **JPM**, 1983-84, v10(4), 66-72.)

Settle, John W., Glenn H. Petry and Chi-Cheng Hsia. "Synergy, Diversification, And Incentive Effects Of Corporate Merger On Bondholder Wealth: Some Evidence," **JFR**, 1984, v7(4), 329-339.

Severiens, Jacobus T. (Fitzpatrick, John D. and Jacobus T. Severiens. "Hickman Revisited: The Case For Junk Bonds," **JPM**, 1977-78, v4(4), 53-57.)

Severiens, Jacobus T. (Hobson, Hugh A., John T. Masten and Jacobus T. Severiens. "Holding Company Acquisitions And Bank Performance: A Comparative Study," **JBR**, 1978-79, v9(2), 116-120.)

Severiens, Jacobus T. and Mark R. Greene. "Variable Life Insurance In The Netherlands - A Case Study," **JRI**, 1974, v41(3), 511-522.

Severn, Alan D., James C. Mills and Basil L. Copeland, Jr. "Capital Gains Taxes After Tax Reform," **JPM**, 1986-87, v13(3), 69-75.

Severn, Alan K. and David R. Meinster. "The Use Of Multicurrency Financing By The Financial Manager," **FM**, 1978, v7(4), 45-53.

Severn, Alan K. and Martin M. Laurence. "Direct Investment, Research Intensity, And Profitability," **JFQA**, 1974, v9(2), 181-190.

Severn, Alan K. "Investor Evaluation Of Foreign And Domestic Risk," **JOF**, 1974, v29(2), 545-550.

Severn, Alan K. "The Structure Of Foreign Investment: Comment," **JOF**, 1967, v22(4), 653-654.

Severn, Alan K. (Clayman, Charles F. and Alan K. Severn. "The Effect Of Random Disturbances In Float On The Federal Funds Rate," **JBR**, 1979-80, v10(1), 58-60.)

Severn, Alan K. (Meinster, David R. and Alan K. Severn. "Correspondent Balances, Services, And The Money Supply," **JBF**, 1982, v6(2), 195-214.)

Severn, Alan K. (Rangarajan, C. and Alan K. Severn. "The Response Of Banks To Changes In Aggregate Reserves," **JOF**, 1965, v20(4), 651-664.)

Severn, Alan K. (Rangarajan, C. and Alan K. Severn. "Bank Responses To Reserve Changes: Reply," **JOF**, 1966, v21(3), 542-543.)

Severns, Roger E. (Berekson, Leonard L. and Roger E. Severns. "Insurance Executives' Perceptions Of Insurance Instruction At The College And University Level," **JRI**, 1981, v48(2), 322-333.)

Sevier, John C. "Life Insurance Reserves And Aggregate Savings," **JRI**, 1959, v26(4), 65-68.

Seward, J. Allen. (Ambrose, Jan Mills and J. Allen Seward. "Best's Ratings, Financial Ratios And Prior Probabilities In Insolvency Prediction," **JRI**, 1988, v55(2), 229-244.)

Seward, James K. "Corporate Financial Policy And The Theory Of Financial Intermediation," **JOF**, 1990, v45(2), 351-378.

Sexton, Donald E., Jr. "Determining Good And Bad Credit Risks Among High- And Low-Income Families," **JOB**, 1977, v50(2), 236-239.

Sexton, Donald E., Jr. "Food Sales Mix And Profitability: Ghetto Supermarkets Revisited," **JOB**, 1974, v47(4), 538-542.

Sexton, Jr. Donald E. "A Microeconomic Model Of The Effects Of Advertising," **JOB**, 1972, v45(1), 29-41.

Seyhun, H. Nejat. "Do Bidder Managers Knowingly Pay Too Much For Target Firms?," **JOB**, 1990, v63(4), 439-464.

Seyhun, H. Nejat. "Insiders' Profits, Cost Of Trading, And Market Efficiency," **JFEC**, 1986, v16(2), 189-212.

Seyhun, H. Nejat. "Overreaction Or Fundamentals: Some Lessons From Insiders' Response To The Market Crash Of 1987," **JOF**, 1990, v45(5), 1363-1388.

Seyhun, H. Nejat. "The Information Content Of Aggregate Insider Trading," **JOB**, 1988, v61(1), 1-24.

Seyhun, H. Nejat. "The January Effect And Aggregate Insider Trading," **JOF**, 1988, v43(1), 129-141.

Seyhun, H. Nejat. (Chaplinsky, Susan and H. Nejat Seyhun. "Dividends And Taxes: Evidence On Tax-Reduction Strategies," **JOB**, 1990, v63(2), 239-260.)

Seyhun, H. Nejat. (Kaul, Gautam and H. Nejat Seyhun. "Relative Price Variability, Real Shocks, And The Stock Market," **JOF**, 1990, v45(2), 479-496.)

Shafer, Carl E. (Pluhar, Darwin M., Carl E. Shafer and Thomas L. Sporleder. "The Systematic Downward Bias In Live Cattle Futures: A Further Evaluation," **JFM**, 1985, v5(1), 11-20.)

Shafer, Carl E. (Wood, Wendell C., Carl E. Shafer and Carl G. Anderson. "Frequency And Duration Of Profitable Hedging Margins For Texas Cotton Producers, 1980-1986," **JFM**, 1989, v9(6), 519-528.)

Shaffer, Sherrill. "Cross-Subsidization In Checking Accounts," **JMCB**, 1984, v16(1), 100-109.

Shaftel, Timothy L. (Barr, James L. and Timothy L. Shaftel. "Solution Properties Of Deterministic Auctions," **JFQA**, 1976, v11(2), 287-311.)

Shah, Anup. "Crowding Out, Capital Accumulation, The Stock Market, And Money-Financed Fiscal Policy," **JMCB**, 1984, v16(4), Part 1, 461-473.

Shah, Salman and Anjan V. Thakor. "Private Versus Public Ownership: Investment, Ownership Distribution, And Optimality," **JOF**, 1988, v43(1), 41-59.

Shaked, Israel, Allen Michel and David McClain. "The Foreign Acquirer Bonanza: Myth Or Reality?," **JBFA**, 1991, v18(3), 431-448.

Shaked, Israel. "International Equity Markets And The Investment Horizon," **JPM**, 1984-85, v11(2), 80-84.

Shaked, Israel. "Measuring Prospective Probabilities Of Insolvency: An Application To The Life Insurance Industry," **JRI**, 1985, v52(1), 59-80.

Shaked, Israel. (Freiman, Howard A. "Understanding The Economics Of Leveraged ESOPs," **FAJ**, 1990, v46(2), 51-55.)

Shaked, Israel. (Marcus, Alan J. and Israel Shaked. "The Valuation Of FDIC Deposit Insurance Using Option-Pricing Estimates," **JMCB**, 1984, v16(4), Part 1, 446-460.)

Shaked, Israel. (Marcus, Alan and Israel Shaked. "The Relationship Between Accounting Measures And Prospective Probabilities Of Insolvency: An Application To The Banking Industry," **FR**, 1984, v19(1), 67-83.)

Shaked, Israel. (Michel, Allen and Israel Shaked. "Airline Performance Under Deregulation: The Shareholders' Perspective," **FM**, 1984, v13(2), 5-14.)

Shaked, Israel. (Michel, Allen and Israel Shaked. "Japanese Leverage: Myth Or Reality," **FAJ**, 1985, v41(4), 61-67.)

Shaked, Israel. (Michel, Allen and Israel Shaked. "Airline Deregulation And The Probability Of Air Carrier Insolvency," **FR**, 1987, v22(1), 159-174.)

Shaked, Israel. (Michel, Allen J. and Israel Shaked. "Country And Industry Influence On Dividend Policy: Evidence From Japan And The U.S.A.," **JBFA**, 1986, v13(3), 365-382.)

Shaked, Israel. (Michel, Allen and Israel Shaked. "Does Business Diversification Affect Performance?," **FM**, 1984, v13(4), 18-25.)

Shaked, Israel. (Michel, Allen and Israel Shaked. "Corporate Takeovers: Excess Returns And The Multiple Bidding Phenomena," **JBFA**, 1988, v15(2), 263-274.)

Shaked, Israel. (Michel, Allen and Israel Shaked. "Industry Influence On Pension Funding," **JPM**, 1985-86, v12(3), 71-77.)

Shaked, Israel. (Michel, Allen and Israel Shaked. "Trucking Deregulation And Motor-Carrier Performance: The Shareholders' Perspective," **FR**, 1987, v22(2), 295-312.)

Shaked, Israel. (Michel, Allen and Israel Shaked. "Are Conglomerates Safer?," **RIF**, 1985, v5, 243-261.)

Shalen, C. T. "The Optimal Maturity Of Hedges And Participation Of Hedgers In Futures And Forward Markets," **JFM**, 1989, v9(3), 215-224.

Shalit, Haim and Shlomo Yitzhaki. "Mean-Gini, Portfolio Theory, And The Pricing Of Risky Assets," **JOF**, 1984, v39(5), 1449-1468.

Shalit, Haim and Shlomo Yitzhaki. "Evaluating The Mean-Gini Approach To Portfolio Selection," **IJOF**, 1989, v1(2), 15-31.

Shalit, Sol S. "A Doctor-Hospital Cartel Theory," **JOB**, 1977, v50(1), 1-20.

Shalit, Sol S. "On The Mathematics Of Financial Leverage," **FM**, 1974, v4(1), 57-66.

Shalit, Sol S. (Ben-Zion, Uri and Sol S. Shalit. "Size, Leverage, And Dividend Record As Determinants Of Equity Risk," **JOF**, 1975, v30(4), 1015-1026.)

Shangquan, Patricia. (Einhorn, Steven G. and Patricia Shangquan. "Using The Dividend Discount Model For Asset Allocation," **FAJ**, 1984, v40(3), 30-32.)

Shank, John K. "How Good Is FASB Statement No. 8?," **FAJ**, 1976, v32(4), 55-61.

Shank, John K. "Long Range Planning Systems: Achieving Both 'Realism' And 'Reach'," **JBR**, 1973-74, v4(3), 185-193.

Shank, John K., Jessie F. Dillard and Joseph F. Bylinski. "What 'Subject To' Opinions Tell Investors," **FAJ**, 1979, v35(1), 41-45.

Shanken, Jay. "A Bayesian Approach To Testing Portfolio Efficiency," **JFEC**, 1987, v19(2), 195-216.

Shanken, Jay. "Multi-Beta CAPM Or Equilibrium APT?: A Reply," **JOF**, 1985, v40(4), 1189-1196.

Shanken, Jay. "Multivariate Proxies And Asset Pricing Relations: Living With The Roll Critique," **JFEC**, 1987, v18(1), 91-110.

Shanken, Jay. "Multivariate Tests Of The Zero-Beta CAPM," **JFEC**, 1985, v14(3), 327-348.

Shanken, Jay. "Nonsynchronous Data And The Covariance-Factor Structure Of Returns," **JOF**, 1987, v42(2), 221-231.

Shanken, Jay. "On The Exclusion Of Assets From Tests Of The Mean Variance Efficiency Of The Market Portfolio: An Extension," **JOF**, 1986, v41(2), 331-338.

Shanken, Jay. "Testing Portfolio Efficiency When The Zero-Beta Rate Is Unknown: A Note," **JOF**, 1986, v41(1), 269-276.

Shanken, Jay. "The Arbitrage Pricing Theory: Is It Testable?," **JOF**, 1982, v37(5), 1129-1140.

Shanken, Jay. (Gibbons, Michael R. and Jay Shanken. "Subperiod Aggression And The Power Of Multivariate Tests Of Portfolio Efficiency," **JFEC**, 1987, v19(2), 389-394.)

Shanker, Latha. "The Effect Of Differential Inflation On Conglomerates And Single-Industry Firms," **RIF**, 1985, v5, 163-206.

Shanker, Latha. (Chang, Jack S. K. and Latha Shanker. "Option Pricing And The Arbitrage Pricing Theory," **JFR**, 1987, v10(1), 1-16.)

Shanker, Latha. (Chang, Jack S. K. and Latha Shanker. "Hedging Effectiveness Of Currency Options And Currency Futures," **JFM**, 1986, v6(2), 289-306.)

Shanker, Latha. (Chang, Jack S. K. and Latha Shanker. "A Risk-Return Measure Of Hedging Effectiveness: A Comment," **JFQA**, 1987, v22(3), 373-376.)

Shanker, Roy J. and Andris A. Zoltners. "An Extension Of The Lock-Box Location Problem: Comment," **JBR**, 1971-72, v2(4), 62.

Shanker, Roy J. and Andris A. Zoltners. "The Corporate Payment Problem," **JBR**, 1972-73, v3(1), 47-53.

Shanno, David. (Johnson, Herb and David Shanno. "Option Pricing When The Variance Is Changing," **JFQA**, 1987, v22(2), 143-152.)

Shannon, D. S. (Johnson, Keith H. and D. S. Shannon. "A Note Of Diversification And The Reduction Of Dispersion," **JFEC**, 1974, v1(4), 365-372.)

Shannon, Don. (Barnes, Tom, Keith Johnson and Don Shannon. "A Test Of Fixed-Income Markets," **JPM**, 1983-84, v10(2), 60-65.)

Shannon, Donald S. and Keith H. Johnson. "Error Terms And Asset Allocation Schemes," **FR**, 1975, v10(1), 55-63.

Shannon, Donald S. "Some Evidence Of Imperfections In The Market For Municipal Bonds," **FR**, 1974, v9(1), 64-78.

Shannon, Donald S. (Carpenter, Michael D., David R. Lange, Donald S. Shannon and William Thomas Stevens. "Methodologies Of Valuing Lost Earnings: A Review, A Criticism, And A Recommendation," **JRI**, 1986, v53(1), 104-118.)

Shannon, Donald S. (Upton, David E. and Donald S. Shannon. "The Stable Paretian Distribution, Subordinated Stochastic Processes, And Asymptotic Lognormality: An Empirical Investigation," **JOF**, 1979, v34(4), 1031-1039.)

Shannon, Donald S., Keith H. Johnson and Gregory L. Neal. "How To Beat Those Index Funds," **JPM**, 1977-78, v4(1), 28-33.

Shapiro, Alan C. and David P. Rutenberg. "Managing Exchange Risks In A Floating World," **FM**, 1976, v5(2), 48-58.

Shapiro, Alan C. "Capital Budgeting For The Multinational Corporation," **FM**, 1978, v7(1), 7-16.

Shapiro, Alan C. "Currency Risk And Relative Price Risk," **JFQA**, 1984, v19(4), 365-373.

Shapiro, Alan C. "Currency Risk And Country Risk In International Banking," **JOF**, 1985, v40(3), 881-891.

Shapiro, Alan C. "Defining Exchange Risk," **JOB**, 1977, v50(1), 37-39.

Shapiro, Alan C. "Exchange Rate Changes, Inflation, And The Value Of The Multinational Corporation," **JOF**, 1975, v30(2), 485-502.

Shapiro, Alan C. "Financial Structure And Cost Of Capital In The Multinational Corporation," **JFQA**, 1978, v13(2), 211-226.

Shapiro, Alan C. "In Defense Of The Traditional Weighted Average Cost Of Capital As A Cutoff Rate," **FM**, 1979, v8(2), 22-23.

Shapiro, Alan C. "International Cash Management--The Determination Of Multicurrency Cash Balances," **JFQA**, 1976, v11(5), 893-900.

Shapiro, Alan C. "Nominal Contracting In A World Of Uncertainty," **JBF**, 1983, v7(1), 69-82.

Shapiro, Alan C. "Risk In International Banking," **JFQA**, 1982, v17(5), 727-740.

Shapiro, Alan C. "The Economic Import Of Europe 1992," **JACF**, 1991, v3(4), 25-36.

Shapiro, Alan C. "What Does Purchasing Power Parity Mean?," **JIMF**, 1983, v2(3), 295-318.

Shapiro, Alan C. "Why The Budget Deficit Doesn't Matter," **JACF,**

Shapiro, Alan C. "Why The Trade Deficit Does Not Matter," **JACF**, 1989, v2(1), 87-96.

Shapiro, Alan C. (Cornell, Bradford and Alan C. Shapiro. "The Reaction Of Bank Stock Prices To The International Debt Crisis," **JBF**, 1986, v10(1), 55-73.)

Shapiro, Alan C. (Cornell, Bradford and Alan C. Shapiro. "Interest Rates And Exchange Rates: Some New Empirical Results," **JIMF**, 1985, v4(4), 431-442.)

Shapiro, Alan C. (Cornell, Bradford and Alan C. Shapiro. "Corporate Stakeholders And Corporate Finance," **FM**, 1987, v16(1), 5-14.)

Shapiro, Alan C. (Cornell, Bradford and Alan C. Shapiro. "Financing Corporate Growth," **JACF**, 1988, v1(2), 6-22.)

Shapiro, Alan C. (Cornell, Bradford and Alan C. Shapiro. "The Mispricing Of U.S. Treasury Bonds: A Case Study," **RFS**, 1989, v2(3), 297-310.)

Shapiro, Alan C. (Lakonishok, Josef and Alan C. Shapiro. "Stock Returns, Beta, Variance And Size: An Empirical Analysis," **FAJ**, 1984, v40(4), 36-41.)

Shapiro, Alan C. (Lakonishok, Josef and Alan C. Shapiro. "Systematic Risk, Total Risk And Size As Determinants Of Stock Market Returns," **JBF**, 1986, v10(1), 115-132.)

Shapiro, Alan C. (Reinganum, Marc R. and Alan C. Shapiro. "Taxes And Stock Return Seasonality: Evidence From The London Stock Exchange," **JOB**, 1987, v60(2), 281-296.)

Shapiro, Alan. "Optimal Inventory And Credit-Granting Strategies Under Inflation And Devaluation," **JFQA**, 1973, v8(1), 37-46.

Shapiro, Alan. (Stonehill, Arthur, Theo Beekhuisen, Richard Wright, Lee Remmers, Norman Toy, Antonio Pares, Alan Shapiro, Douglas Egan and Thomas Bates. "Financial Goals And Debt Ratio Determinants: A Survey Of Practice

Shapiro, Alan. (Stonehill, In Five Countries)," **FM**, 1974, v4(3), 27-41.)

Shapiro, Arnold F. "A Stochastic Model For Determining The Contingency Charge In Group Life Insurance," **JRI**, 1976, v43(3), 463-486.

Shapiro, Arnold F. "Contributions To The Evolution Of Pension Cost Analysis," **JRI**, 1985, v52(1), 81-99.

Shapiro, Arnold F. "The Interest-Only Method As An Interim Funding Option For Public Pension Plans," **JRI**, 1978, v45(4), 693-698.

Shapiro, Arnold F. "The Interest-Only Method As An Interim Funding Option For Public Pension Plans: Reply," **JRI**, 1979, v46(4), 735.

Shapiro, Arnold F. "The Relevance Of Expected Persistency Rates When Projecting Pension Costs," **JRI**, 1977, v44(4), 623-638.

Shapiro, David L. "Conglomerate Mergers And Optimal Investment Policy," **JFQA**, 1970, v5(5), 643-656.

Shapiro, David. "Recent Trends In The Independent Telephone Industry," **FAJ**, 1962, v18(6), 29-31.

Shapiro, Eli and William L. White. "Patterns Of Business Financing: Some Comments," **JOF**, 1965, v20(4), 693-707.

Shapiro, Eli and Joseph N. Froomkin. "Devaluation Procedures And The Role Of The International Monetary Fund," **JOB**, 1950, v23(2), 103-109.

Shapiro, Eli. "The Market For Corporate Securities: A Progress Report," **JOF**, 1957, v12(2), 136-147.

Shapiro, Eli. "The Postwar Market For Corporate Securities: 1946-55," **JOF**, 1959, v14(2), 196-217.

Shapiro, Eli. (Goldsmith, Raymond W. and Eli Shapiro. "An Estimate Of Bank-Administered Personal Trust Funds," **JOF**, 1959, v14(1), 11-17.)

Shapiro, H. T. "The Efficacy Of Monetary And Fiscal Policy: A Comment," **JMCB**, 1971, v3(2), Part 2, 550-554.

Shapiro, Harold T. (Baumol, William J., Richard E. Quandt and Harold T. Shapiro. "Oligopoly Theory And Retail Food Pricing," **JOB**, 1964, v37(4), 346-363.)

Shapiro, Harold T. (Baxter, Nevins D. and Harold T. Shapiro. "Compensating-Balance Requirements: The Results Of A Survey," **JOF**, 1964, v19(3), 483-496.)

Shapiro, Jeremy F. (Little, John D. C. and Jeremy F. Shapiro. "A Theory For Pricing Nonfeatured Products In Supermarkets," **JOB**, 1980, v53(3), Part 2, S199-S210.)

Shapiro, Matthew D. (Mankiw, N. Gregory, David Romer and Matthew D. Shapiro. "An Unbiased Reexamination Of Stock Market Volatility," **JOF**, 1985, v40(3), 677-687.)

Shapiro, Robert. "Financial Intermediaries, Credit Availability, And Aggregate Demand," **JOF**, 1966, v21(3), 459-478.

Sharir, Shmuel. "Brand Loyalty' And The Household's Cost Of Time," **JOB**, 1974, v47(1), 53-55.

Sharkawy, M. Atef. "Evaluating Spatiotemporal Consistency Of Secondary Office Market Data," **JRER**, 1990, v5(3), 341-354.

Sharma, J. L. and Robert E. Kennedy. "A Comparative Analysis Of Stock Price Behavior On The Bombay, London, And New York Stock Exchanges," **JFQA**, 1977, v12(3), 391-413.

Sharp, Karen Chant. (Berndt, Ernst R., Karen Chant Sharp and G. Campbell Watkins. "Utility Bond Rates And Tax Normalization," **JOF**, 1979, v34(5), 1211-1220.)

Sharp, Keith P. "Mortgage Rate Insurance Pricing Under An Interest Rate Diffusion With Drift," **JRI**, 1989, v56(1), 34-49.)

Sharp, Mitchell W. "Deferred Depreciation - A Canadian Anti-Inflationary Measure," **JOF**, 1952, v7(2), 331-346.

Sharp, Robert F. (Greenberg, Ralph H., Robert F. Sharp and Eric E. Spires. "A Practical Method Of Measuring Current Costs Of Technologically Inferior Assets," **JBFA**, 1989, v16(3), 433-442.)

Sharp, Roger R. "The Growth Of The Man-Made Fiber Industry," **FAJ**, 1964, v20(1), 43-48.

Sharpe, Eddie J. "A Review Of The Food Industry," **FAJ**, 1966, v22(1), 63-68.

Sharpe, I. G. (McShane, R. W. and I. G. Sharpe. "A Time Service/Cross Section Analysis Of The Determinants Of Australian Trading Bank Loan/Deposit Interest Margins: 1962-1981," **JBF**, 1985, v9(1), 115-136.)

Sharpe, Ian G. "Australian Money Supply Analysis: The Relationship Between The Monetary Base, Secondary Reserves And The Money Supply," **JBF**, 1980, v4(3), 283-300.

Sharpe, Steven A. "Asymmetric Information, Bank Lending, And Implicit Contracts: A Stylized Model Of Customer Relationships," **JOF**, 1990, v45(4), 1069-1087.

Sharpe, W. F. and G. M. Cooper. "NYSE Stocks Classified By Risk, 1931-1967," **FAJ**, 1972, v28(2), 46-54,81.

Sharpe, W. F. and H. B. Sosin. "Risk, Return And Yield On Common Stock," **FAJ**, 1976, v32(2), 33-42.

Sharpe, W. F. "Decentralized Investment Management," **JOF**, 1981, v36(2), 217-234.

Sharpe, W. F. "Mutual Fund Performance And The Theory Of Capital Asset Pricing: Reply," **JOB**, 1968, v41(2), 235-236.

Sharpe, William F. and Allen Silver. "'Sideways Betas': Further Comments," **JPM**, 1975-76, v2(4), 67-68.

Sharpe, William F. "A Linear Programming Approximation For The General Portfolio Analysis Problem," **JFQA**, 1971, v6(5), 1263-1275.

Sharpe, William F. "Adjusting For Risk In Performance Measurement," **JPM**, 1974-75, v1(2), 29-34.

Sharpe, William F. "Are Gains Likely From Market Timing," **FAJ**, 1975, v31(2), 60-69.

Sharpe, William F. "Bank Capital Adequacy, Deposit Insurance, And Security Values," **JFQA**, 1978, v13(4), 701-718.

Sharpe, William F. "Bonds Vs. Stocks: Capital Market Theory," **FAJ**, 1973, v29(6), 74-80.

Sharpe, William F. "Capital Asset Prices: A Theory Of Market Equilibrium Under Conditions Of Risk," **JOF**, 1964, v19(3), 425-442.

Sharpe, William F. "Computer-Assisted Economics," **JFQA**, 1970, v5(3), 353-366.

Sharpe, William F. "Corporate Pension Funding Policy," **JFEC**, 1976, v3(3), 183-193.

Sharpe, William F. "Diversification And Portfolio Risk," **FAJ**, 1972, v28(1), 74-79.

Sharpe, William F. "Factor Models, CAPMs, And The ABT," **JPM**, 1984-85, v11(1), 21-25.

Sharpe, William F. "Factors In NYSE Security Returns, 1931-1979," **JPM**, 1981-82, v8(4), 5-19.

Sharpe, William F. "Imputing Expected Security Returns From Portfolio Composition," **JFQA**, 1974, v9(3), 462-472.

Sharpe, William F. "Integrated Asset Allocation," **FAJ**, 1987, v43(5), 25-32.

Sharpe, William F. "Library Catalog, 20 Programs And Files Usable In Finance Courses," **JFED**, 1972, v1, 97-99.

Sharpe, William F. "Major Investment Styles," **JPM**, 1977-78, v4(2), 68-74.

Sharpe, William F. "Mutual Fund Performance," **JOB**, 1966, v39(1), Part II, 119-138.

Sharpe, William F. "On Capital Asset Prices: Reply," **JOF**, 1965, v20(1), 94-95.

Sharpe, William F. "On The Use Of The CAPM In Public Utility Rate Cases: Comment," **FM**, 1978, v7(3), 71.

Sharpe, William F. "Portfolio Analysis," **JFQA**, 1967, v2(2), 76-84.

Sharpe, William F. "Risk-Aversion In The Stock Market: Some Empirical Evidence," **JOF**, 1965, v20(3), 416-422.

Sharpe, William F. "Security Prices, Risk, And Maximal Gains From Diversification: Reply," **JOF**, 1966, v21(4), 743-744.

Sharpe, William F. "Simple Strategies For Portfolio Diversification: Comment," **JOF**, 1972, v27(1), 127-129.

Sharpe, William F. "Simple Strategies For Portfolio Diversification: Comment: A Correction," **JOF**, 1972, v27(3), 733.

Sharpe, William F. (Grossman, Blake R. and William F. Sharpe. "Financial Implications Of South African Divestment," **FAJ**, 1986, v42(4), 15-29.)

Sharpe, William F. (Lanstein, Ronald and William F. Sharpe. "Duration And Security Risk," **JFQA**, 1978, v13(4), 653-668.)

Sharpe, William F. (Perold, Andre F. and William F. Sharpe. "Dynamic Strategies For Asset Allocation," **FAJ**, 1988, v44(1), 16-27.)

Sharpe, William F. and Lawrence G. Tint. "Liabilities - A New Approach," **JPM**, 1990, v16(2), 5-10.

Sharplin, Arthur D. (Mabry, Rodney H. and Arthur D. Sharplin. "The Relative Importance Of Journals Used In Finance Research," **JFR**, 1985, v8(4), 287-296.)

Shashua, L. and Y. Goldschmidt. "An Index For Evaluating Financial Performance," **JOF**, 1974, v29(3), 797-814.

Shastri, Kuldeep and Kishore Tandon. "Options On Futures Contracts: A Comparison Of European And American Pricing Models," **JFM**, 1986, v6(4), 593-618.

Shastri, Kuldeep and Kishore Tandon. "An Empirical Test Of A Valuation Model For American Options On Futures Contracts," **JFQA**, 1986, v21(4), 377-392.

Shastri, Kuldeep and Kishore Tandon. "Arbitrage Tests Of The Efficiency Of The Foreign Currency Options Market," **JIMF**, 1985, v4(4), 455-468.

Shastri, Kuldeep and Kishore Tandon. "On The Use Of European Models To Price American Options On Foreign Currency," **JFM**, 1986, v6(1), 93-108.

Shastri, Kuldeep and Kishore Tandon. "Valuation Of Foreign Currency Options: Some Empirical Tests," **JFQA**, 1986, v21(2), 145-160.

Shastri, Kuldeep and Kishore Tandon. "Valuation Of American Options On Foreign Currency," **JBF**, 1987, v11(2), 245-270.

Shastri, Kuldeep and Kulpatra Wethyavivorn. "The Valuation Of Currency Options For Alternate Stochastic Processes," **JFR**, 1987, v10(4), 283-294.

Shastri, Kuldeep and Kulpatra Wethyavivorn. "Pricing Of Foreign Currency Options For Arbitrary Stochastic Processes," **JBFA**, 1990, v17(2), 323-334.

Shastri, Kuldeep. "The Differential Effects Of Mergers On Corporate Security Values," **RIF**, 1990, v8, 179-202.

Shastri, Kuldeep. (Choi, J. Y., Dan Salandro and Kuldeep Shastri. "On The Estimation Of Bid-Ask Spreads: Theory And Evidence," **JFQA**, 1988, v23(2), 219-230.)

Shastri, Kuldeep. (Choi, J. Y. and Kuldeep Shastri. "Bid-Ask Spreads And Volatility Estimates: The Implications For Option Pricing," **JBF**, 1989, v13(2), 207-220.)

Shastri, Kuldeep. (Denning, Karen Craft and Kuldeep Shastri. "Single Sale Divestments: The Impact On Stockholders And Bondholders," **JBFA**, 1990, v17(5), 731-744.)

Shastri, Kuldeep. (Geske, Robert, Richard Roll and Kuldeep Shastri. "Over-the-Counter Option Market Dividend Protection And 'Biases' In The Black-Scholes Model: A Note," **JOF**, 1983, v38(4), 1271-1277.)

Shastri, Kuldeep. (Geske, Robert and Kuldeep Shastri. "Valuation By Approximation: A Comparison Of Alternative Option Valuation Techniques," JFQA, 1985, v20(1), 45-72.)

Shastri, Kuldeep. (Geske, Robert and Kuldeep Shastri. "The Early Exercise Of American Puts," JBF, 1985, v9(2), 207-219.)

Shastri, Kuldeep. (Jayaraman, Narayanan and Kuldeep Shastri. "The Valuation Impacts Of Specially Designated Dividends," JFQA, 1988, v23(3), 301-312.)

Shatto, Gloria. "Government Securities And The Cyclical Investment Behavior Of Corporations And Commercial Banks: A Note," JOB, 1972, v45(3), 385-386.

Shatto, Gloria. "Money Substitutes For The Corporate Business Sector: A Note," JOF, 1967, v22(1), 83-85.

Shattuck, Leroy A., Jr. "The Recapture Of Insiders' Profits," JOF, 1953, v8(3), 319-332.

Shaviro, Frieda W. "An Analysis Of Cash And Futures Prices In The Delivery Period Of Maturing Contracts In The Coffee 'C' Market, 1972-1981," JFM, 1987, v7(4), 413-442.

Shaw, David C. "The Performance Of Primary Common Stock Offerings: A Canadian Comparison," JOF, 1971, v26(5), 1101-1113.

Shaw, David C. (Fry, Joseph N., David C. Shaw, C. Haehling Von Lanzenauer and Cecil R. Dipchand. "Customer Loyalty To Banks: A Longitudinal Study," JOB, 1973, v46(4), 517-525.)

Shaw, Edward S. (Gurley, John G. and Edward S. Shaw. "Financial Intermediaries And The Saving-Investment Process," JOF, 1956, v11(2), 257-276.)

Shaw, Michael J. and James A. Gentry. "Using An Expert System With Inductive Learning To Evaluate Business Loans," FM, 1988, v17(3), 45-56.

Shaw, Robert B. "Dow Jones Industrials Vs. Dow Jones Industrial Average," FAJ, 1955, v11(5), 37-42.

Shaw, Robert B. "Justifiable Invasion Of Principal," FAJ, 1956, v12(5), 65-68.

Shaw, Robert. "History Of The Dollar," FAJ, 1958, v14(2), 77-82.

Shaw, Wayne. (Morse, Dale and Wayne Shaw. "Investing In Bankrupt Firms," JOF, 1988, v43(5), 1193-1206.)

Shaw, Wayne. (O'Hara, Maureen and Wayne Shaw. "Deposit Insurance And Wealth Effects: The Value Of Being Too Big To Fail," JOF, 1990, v45(5), 1587-1600.)

Shawky, Hany A. and Philip J. Fischer. "Imperfect Contracts, Me-First Rules, And Firm Value," FR, 1983, v18(1), 79-93.

Shawky, Hany A. "An Update On Mutual Funds: Better Grades," JPM, 1981-82, v8(2), 29-34.

Shawky, Hany, Ronald Forbes and Alan Frankle. "Liquidity Services And Capital Market Equilibrium: The Case For Money Market Mutual Funds," JFR, 1983, v6(2), 141-152.

Shawky, Hany. (Duchessi, Peter, Hany Shawky and John P. Seagle. "A Knowledge-Engineered System For Commercial Loan Decisions," FM, 1988, v17(3), 57-65.)

Shawky, Harry A. (Bavishi, Vinod B., Michael R. Czinkota, Harry A. Shawky and David A. Ricks. "International Financial Management – A Survey Of Research Trends And An Annotated Bibliography, 1977-1976," JFED, 1977, v6, 93-95.)

Shay, Brian. (Fernholz, Robert and Brian Shay. "Stochastic Portfolio Theory And Stock Market Equilibrium," JOF, 1982, v37(2), 615-624.)

Shay, Robert P. "Factors Affecting Price, Volume And Credit Risk In The Consumer Finance Industry," JOF, 1970, v25(2), 503-515.

Shay, Robert P. "Major Developments In The Market For Consumer Credit Since The End Of World War II," JOF, 1966, v21(2), 369-381.

Shay, Robert P. "New-Automobile Finance Rates, 1924-1962," JOF, 1963, v18(3), 461-493.

Shay, Robert P. "The Price Of New Automobile Financing," JOF, 1964, v19(2), Part 1, 205-221.

Shay, Robert P. (Parker, George G. C. and Robert P. Shay. "Some Factors Affecting Awareness Of Annual Percentage Rates In Consumer Installment Credit Transactions," JOF, 1974, v29(1), 217-225.)

Shay, Robert. "Postwar Developments In The Market For Consumer Instalment Credit," JOF, 1956, v11(2), 229-248.

Shea, Gary S. "Interest Rate Term Structure Estimation With Exponential Splines: A Note," JOF, 1985, v40(1), 319-325.

Shea, Gary S. "Pitfalls In Smoothing Interest Rate Term Structure Data: Equilibrium Models And Spline Approximations," JFQA, 1984, v19(3), 253-269.

Sheales, Terence C. and William G. Tomek. "Hedging Australian Wheat Exports Using Futures Markets," JFM, 1987, v7(5), 519-534.

Shear, William B. "A Note On Occupancy Turnover In Rental Housing Units," AREUEA, 1983, v11(4), 525-538.

Shear, William B. and Anthony M. J. Yezer. "An Indirect Test For Differential Treatment Of Borrowers In Mortgage Markets," AREUEA, 1982, v10(4), 405-420.

Shearon, Winston. (Giroux, Gary, Winston Shearon and Steven Grossman. "How Does Inflation Affect A BHCs Rate Of Return?," JBR, 1983-84, v14(2), 164-169.)

Shedd, Peter. "Land Use Controls: Can Landowners Force Government Bodies To Pay?," AREUEA, 1981, v9(4), 457-473.

Sheehan, Dennis P. (Holderness, Clifford G. and Dennis P. Sheehan. "Raiders Or Saviors? The Evidence On Six Controversial Investors," JFEC, 1985, v14(4), 555-579.)

Sheehan, Dennis P. (Holderness, Clifford G. and Dennis P. Sheehan. "The Role Of Majority Shareholders In Publicly Held Corporations: An Exploratory Analysis," JFEC, 1988, v20(1/2), 317-346.)

Sheehan, Dennis P. (Loderer, Claudio P. and Dennis P. Sheehan. "Corporate Bankruptcy And Managers' Self-Serving Behavior," JOF, 1989, v44(4), 1059-1076;.)

Sheehan, Richard G. (Schirm, David C., Richard G. Sheehan and Michael G. Ferri. "Financial Market Responses To Treasury Debt Announcements," JMCB, 1989, v21(3), 394-400.)

Sheehey, Edmund J. "Monetary Policy And The Balance Of Payments In Brazil And Chile: A Comment," JMCB, 1980, v12(3), 547-549.

Sheehey, Edmund J. "The Neutrality Of Money In The Short Run: Some Tests," JMCB, 1984, v16(2), 237-241.

Sheen, Jeffrey. "Modelling The Floating Australian Dollar," JIMF, 1989, v8(2), 253-276.

Sheffrin, Steven M. and Thomas Russell. "Sterling And Oil Discoveries: The Mystery Of Nonappreciation," JIMF, 1984, v3(3), 311-326.

Sheffrin, Steven M. (Cordes, Joseph J. and Steven M. Sheffrin. "Estimating The Tax Advantage Of Corporate Debt," JOF, 1983, v38(1), 95-105.)

Sheffrin, Steven M. and Wing Thye Woo. "Testing An Optimizing Model Of The Current Account Via The Consumption Function," JIMF, 1990, v9(2), 220-233.

Shefrin, Hersh and Meir Statman. "The Disposition To Sell Winners Too Early And Ride Losers Too Long: Theory And Evidence," JOF, 1985, v40(3), 777-782.

Shefrin, Hersh M. and Meir Statman. "Explaining Investor Preference For Cash Dividends," JFEC, 1984, v13(2), 253-282.

Shefrin, Hersh. (Madan, Dilip B., Frank Milne and Hersh Shefrin. "The Multinomial Option Pricing Model And Its Brownian And Poisson Limits," RFS, 1989, v2(2), 251-266.)

Sheikh, Aamir M. "Stock Splits, Volatility Increases, And Implied Volatilities," JOF, 1989, v44(5), 1361-1372.

Shelby, Donald. "Some Implications Of The Growth Of Financial Intermediaries," JOF, 1958, v13(4), 527-541.

Sheldon, Randall E. "Options Contracts," RFM, 1984, v3(2), 166-170.

Shelor, Roger M. and Mark L. Cross. "Insurance Firm Market Response To California Proposition 103 And The Effects Of Firm Size," JRI, 1990, v57(4), 682-690.

Shelor, Roger M., Dwight C. Anderson and Mark L. Cross. "The Impact Of The California Earthquake On Real Estate Firms' Stock Value," JRER, 1990, v5(3), 335-340.

Shelton, David H. "Private Insurance In Latin America: Prospects And Problems," JRI, 1958, v25(3), 43-56.

Shelton, John P. "An Evaluation Of Merger-Hedges," FAJ, 1965, v21(2), 49-52.

Shelton, John P. "Influence Of Six-Month Capital Gains Rule On Short-Term Transactions," FAJ, 1962, v18(5), 99-101.

Shelton, John P. "New Research And The Investment Profession (Keynote Review)," FAJ, 1966, v22(6), 65-67.

Shelton, John P. "The Value Line Contest: A Test Of The Predictability Of Stock-Price Changes," JOB, 1967, v40(3), 254-269.

Shelton, John P. "Warrant, Stock-Price Relations - Part II," FAJ, 1967, v23(4), 88-99.

Shelton, John P. "Warrant, Stock-Price Relations - Part I," FAJ, 1967, v23(3), 143-151.

Shelton, John P. (Cheng, Pao L. and John P. Shelton. "A Contribution To The Theory Of Capital Budgeting - The Multi-Investment Case," JOF, 1963, v18(4), 622-636.)

Shelton, John P. (Cheng, Pao L. and John P. Shelton. "A Contribution To The Theory Of Capital Budgeting - The Multi-Investment Case: Reply," JOF, 1964, v19(4), 671-672.)

Shelton, John P. (Holt, Charles C. and John P. Shelton. "The Implications Of The Capital Gains Tax For Investment Decisions," JOF, 1961, v16(4), 559-580.)

Shelton, John P. (Warren, James M. and John P. Shelton. "A Simultaneous Equation Approach To Financial Planning," JOF, 1971, v26(5), 1123-1142.)

Shelton, John P. (Warren, James M. and John P. Shelton. "A Simultaneous Equation Approach To Financial Planning: Reply," JOF, 1973, v28(4), 1039-1042.)

Shelton, John P., Eugene F. Brigham and Alfred E. Hofflander, Jr. "Dual Funds: An Appraisal," FAJ, 1967, v23(3), 131-139.

Shelton, Judy. "Equal Access And Miller's Equilibrium," JFQA, 1981, v16(4), 603-623.

Shen, Chung-Hua and Lee-Rong Wang. "Examining The Validity Of A Test Of Futures Market Efficiency: A Comment," JFM, 1990, v10(2), 195-196.

Shen, F. C. (Grauer, R. R., N. H. Hakansson and F. C. Shen. "Industry Rotation In The U.S. Stock Market: 1934-1986 Returns On Passive, Semi-Passive, And Active Strategies," JBF, 1990, v14(2/3), 513-538.)

Shenhav, Yehuda. (Neumann, Seev and Yehuda Shenhav. "Short-Term Impact Of War Economy On The Insurance Industry In Israel," JRI, 1977, v44(1), 87-102.)

Shepard, Herbert A. "Innovation-Resisting And Innovation-Producing Organizations," JOB, 1967, v40(4), 470-477.

Shepard, Herbert A. "Patterns Of Organization For Applied Research And Development," JOB, 1956, v29(1), 52-58.

Shepard, Herbert A. "Superiors And Subordinates In Research," JOB, 1956, v29(4), 261-267.

Shepard, Lawrence. "How Good Is Investment Advice For Individuals?," JPM, 1976-77, v3(2), 32-36.

Shepherd, Pearce. "War Clauses In Life Insurance," JRI, 1940, v7, 75-82.

Shepler, Richard J. (Rejda, George E. and Richard J. Shepler. "The Impact Of Zero Population Growth On The OASDHI Program," JRI, 1973, v40(3), 313-325.)

Shepp, Lawrence A. (Goldman, M. Barry, Howard B. Sosin and Lawrence A. Shepp. "On Contingent Claims That Insure Ex-post Optimal Stock Market Timing," JOF, 1979, v34(2), 401-414.)

Sheppard, C. Stewart. "Professionalization Of The Analyst," FAJ, 1967, v23(6), 39-41.

Sherali, Anis D. (Livingstone, J. Leslie and Anis D. Sherali. "Construction Work In Progress In The Public Utility Rate Base: The Effect Of Multiple Projects And Growth," FM, 1979, v8(1), 42-50.)

Sherden, William A. "An Analysis Of The Determinants Of The Demand For Automobile Insurance," JRI, 1984, v51(1), 49-62.

Sherman, Eugene J. "A Gold Pricing Model," JPM, 1982-83, v9(3), 68-70.

Sherman, Eugene J. "Gold: A Conservative, Prudent Diversifier," JPM, 1981-82, v8(3), 21-27.

Sherman, H. David and Franklin Gold. "Bank Branch Operating Efficiency: Evaluation With Data Envelopment Analysis," JBF, 1985, v9(2), 297-316.

Sherman, Jerome F. (Johnson, Robert R. and Jerome F. Sherman. "The Financial World: A Campus And Travel Course," JFED, 1987, v16, 26-31.)

Sherman, John C. "A Device To Measure Portfolio Performance," FAJ, 1966, v22(1), 106-108.

Sherman, Larry. (Stanhouse, Bryan and Larry Sherman. "A Note On Information In The Loan Evaluation Process," *JOF*, 1979, v34(5), 1263-1269.)

Sherman, Lawrence F. "A Proposed Method For Financial Case Analysis," *JFED*, 1980, v9, 57-65.

Sherman, Lawrence F. (Pany, Kurt and Lawrence F. Sherman. "Information Analysis Of Several Large Failed Banks," *JBR*, 1979-80, v10(3), 145-151.)

Sherman, Lawrence F. (Shick, Richard A. and Lawrence F. Sherman. "Bank Stock Prices As An Early Warning System For Changes In Condition," *JBR*, 1980-81, v11(3), 136-146.)

Sherman, Lawrence F., Case M. Sprenkle and Bryan E. Stanhouse. "Reserve Requirements And Control Of The Money Supply," *JMCB*, 1979, v11(4), 486-493.

Sherwood, Charles S. (Dudley, D. A. and Charles S. Sherwood. "Which Computer Skills For Finance Graduates?," *JFED*, 1984, v13, 80-86.)

Sheshinski, Eytan and Yoram Weiss. "Optimum Pricing Policy Under Stochastic Inflation," *RIF*, 1983, v4, (Supp), 189-208.

Shetler, Douglas. "Monetary Aggregates Prior To The Civil War: A Closer Look: A Comment," *JMCB*, 1973, v5(4), 1000-1006.

Shick, Richard A. and Frank C. Jen. "Merger Benefits To Shareholders Of Acquiring Firms," *FM*, 1974, v3(4), 45-53.

Shick, Richard A. and James S. Trieschmann. "Some Future Evidence On The Performance Of Property-Liability Insurance Companies' Stock Portfolios," *JFQA*, 1978, v13(1), 157-166.

Shick, Richard A. and James A. Verbrugge. "An Analysis Of Bank Price-Earnings Ratios," *JBR*, 1975-76, v6(2), 140-149.

Shick, Richard A. and Lawrence F. Sherman. "Bank Stock Prices As An Early Warning System For Changes In Condition," *JBR*, 1980-81, v11(3), 136-146.

Shick, Richard A. "The Analysis Of Mergers And Acquisitions," *JOF*, 1972, v27(2), 495-502.

Shick, Richard A. (Lloyd, William P. and Richard A. Shick. "A Test Of Stone's Two-Index Model Of Return," *JFQA*, 1977, v12(3), 363-376.)

Shick, Richard A. (Verbrugge, James A., Richard A. Shick And Kenneth J. Thygerson. "An Analysis Of Savings And Loan Profit Performance," *JOF*, 1976, v31(5), 1427-1442.)

Shiller, Robert J. and Franco Modigliani. "Coupon And Tax Effects On New And Seasoned Bond Yields And The Measurement Of The Cost Of Debt Capital," *JFEC*, 1979, v7(3), 297-318.

Shiller, Robert J. "Comovements In Stock Prices And Comovements In Dividends," *JOF*, 1989, v44(3), 719-730.

Shiller, Robert J. "Rational Expectations And The Term Structure Of Interest Rates: A Comment," *JMCB*, 1973, v5(3), 856-860.

Shiller, Robert J. "The Use Of Volatility Measures In Assessing Market Efficiency," *JOF*, 1981, v36(2), 291-304.

Shiller, Robert J. "Theories Of Aggregate Stock Price Movements," *JPM*, 1983-84, v10(2), 28-37.

Shiller, Robert J. (Campbell, John Y. and Robert J. Shiller. "The Dividend-Price Ratio And Expectations Of Future Dividends And Discount Factors," *RFS*, 1988-89, v1(3), 195-228.)

Shiller, Robert J. (Case, Karl E. and Robert J. Shiller. "Forecasting Prices And Excess Returns In The Housing Market," *AREUEA*, 1990, v18(3), 253-273.)

Shiller, Robert J. (Grossman, Sanford J. and Robert J. Shiller. "Consumption Correlatedness And Risk Measurement In Economies With Non-Traded Assets And Heterogeneous Information," *JFEC*, 1982, v10(2), 195-210.)

Shiller, Robert J. (Pound, John and Robert J. Shiller. "Are Institutional Investors Speculators?," *JPM*, 1986-87, v13(3), 46-52.)

Shilling, James D. "On The Gains To Acquiring Capital-Stock Savings And Loan Associations In Merger Conversions: A Re-Examination Of The Regulatory-Approval Hypothesis," *JBF*, 1991, v15(1), 165-172.

Shilling, James D. (Benjamin, John D., James D. Shilling and C. F. Sirmans. "Contracts As Options: Some Evidence From Condominium Developments," *AREUEA*, 1985, v13(2), 143-152.)

Shilling, James D. (Dhillon, Upinder S., James D. Shilling and C. F. Sirmans. "Choosing Between Fixed And Adjustable Rate Mortgages," *JMCB*, 1987, v19(2), 260-267.)

Shilling, James D. (Hendershott, Patric H., James D. Shilling and Kevin E. Villani. "Measurement Of The Spreads Between Yields On Various Mortgage Contracts And Treasury Securities," *AREUEA*, 1983, v11(4), 476-490.)

Shilling, James D. (Hendershott, Patric H. and James D. Shilling. "Valuing ARM Rate Caps: Implications Of 1970-84 Interest Rate Behavior," *AREUEA*, 1985, v13(3), 317-332.)

Shilling, James D. (Hendershott, Patric H. and James D. Shilling. "Reforming Conforming Loan Limits: The Impact On Thrift Earnings And Taxpayer Outlays," *JFSR*, 1989, v3(4), 311-332.)

Shilling, James D. (Hendershott, Patric H. and James D. Shilling. "The Impact Of The Agencies On Conventional Fixed-Rate Mortgage Yields," *JREFEC*, 1989, v2(2), 101-116.)

Shilling, James D. (Howe, James S. and James D. Shilling. "REIT Advisor Performance," *AREUEA*, 1990, v18(4), 479-500.)

Shilling, James D. (Howe, John S. and James D. Shilling. "Capital Structure Theory And REIT Security Offerings," *JOF*, 1988, v43(4), 983-993.)

Shilling, James D. (Jameson, Mel, James D. Shilling and C. F. Sirmans. "Regional Variation Of Mortgage Yields And Simultaneity Bias," *JFR*, 1990, v13(3), 211-220.)

Shilling, James D. (Sa-Aadu, J. and James D. Shilling. "Ranking Of Contributing Authors To The AREUEA Journal By Doctoral Origin And Employer," *AREUEA*, 1988, v16(3), 257-270.)

Shilling, James D. and C. F. Sirmans. "Pricing Fast-Pay Mortgages: Some Simulation Results," *JFR*, 1987, v10(1), 25-32.

Shilling, James D. and C. F. Sirmans. "The Effects Of Occupational Licensing On Complaints Against Real Estate Agents," *JRER*, 1988, v3(2), 1-9.

Shilling, James D., C. F. Sirmans and John D. Benjamin. "On Option-Pricing Models In Real Estate: A Critique," *AREUEA*, 1987, v15(1), 742-752.

Shilling, James D., John D. Benjamin and C. F. Sirmans. "Estimating Net Realizable Value For Distressed Real Estate," *JRER*, 1990, v5(1), 129-140.

Shilling, N. (Hammond, J. D., E. R. Melander and N. Shilling. "Risk, Return, And The Capital Market: The Insurer Case," *JFQA*, 1976, v11(1), 115-131.)

Shilling, N. (Hammond, J. D. and N. Shilling. "Review Article - The Little Report On Prices And Profits In The Property And Liability Insurance Industry," *JRI*, 1969, v36(1), 129-144.)

Shilling, N. (Hammond, J. D., E. R. Melander and N. Shilling. "Economies Of Scale In The Property And Liability Insurance Industry," *JRI*, 1971, v38(2), 181-191.)

Shilling, N. (Hammond, J. D. and N. Shilling. "Some Relationships Of Portfolio Theory To The Regulation Of Insurer Solidity," *JRI*, 1978, v45(3), 377-400.)

Shilling, Ned. (Hammond, J. D. and Ned Shilling. "Review Article: Some Empirical Implications Of The Return On Investible Funds Measure Of Profitability," *JRI*, 1970, v37(4), 659-663.)

Shillinglaw, Gordon. "Profit Analysis For Abandonment Decisions," *JOB*, 1957, v30(1), 17-29.

Shillinglaw, Gordon. "Residual Values In Investment Analysis," *JOB*, 1955, v28(4), 275-284.

Shilton, Leon G. and James R. Webb. "Commercial Loan Underwriting And Option Valuation," *JRER*, 1989, v4(1), 1-12.

Shim, Jae K. "Estimating Cash Collection Rates From Credit Sales: A Lagged Regression Approach," *FM*, 1981, v10(5), 28-30.

Shim, Sangdal. (Eun, Cheol S. and Sangdal Shim. "International Transmission Of Stock Market Movements," *JFQA*, 1989, v24(2), 241-256.)

Shimerda, Thomas A. (Chen, Kung H. and Thomas A. Shimerda. "An Empirical Analysis Of Useful Financial Ratios," *FM*, 1981, v10(1), 51-60.)

Shimko, David C. "The Equilibrium Valuation Of Risky Discrete Cash Flows In Continuous Time," *JOF*, 1989, v44(5), 1373-1384.

Shimrat, Adam. (Kalay, Avner and Adam Shimrat. "Firm Value And Seasoned Equity Issues: Price Pressure, Wealth Redistribution, Or Negative Information," *JFEC*, 1987, v19(1), 109-126.)

Shimrat, Adam. (Kalay, Avner and Adam Shimrat. "The Maintained Flexibility Of Divided Constraints: A Cross-Sectional And Time Series Analysis," *RIF*, 1990, v8, 77-96.)

Shin, Tai S. and Morgan J. Lynge, Jr. "Rural Banking Markets In Illinois: An Empirical Test," *JBR*, 1979-80, v10(2), 124-127.

Shin, Tai S. and Elbert T. Hubbard. "Current Status Of Doctoral Programs In Finance," *JFED*, 1988, v17, 64-79.

Shinjo, Koji. "Predictive Ability And Dynamic Multiplier Properties Of Alternative Treatments Of The Monetary Mechanism," *JOF*, 1972, v27(2), 481-493.

Shinnar, Reuel, Ofer Dressler, C. A. Feng and Alan I. Avidan. "Estimation Of The Economic Rate Of Return For Industrial Companies," *JOB*, 1989, v62(3), 417-446.

Shinoda, Phillip. (Brooker, George and Phillip Shinoda. "Peer Ratings Of Graduate Programs For Business," *JOB*, 1976, v49(2), 240-251.)

Shipman, William G. (Ranson, R. David and William G. Shipman. "Institutional Buying Power And The Stock Market," *FAJ*, 1981, v37(5), 62-68.)

Shishko, Irwin. "Why Gold?," *JPM*, 1976-77, v3(3), 34-40.

Shiskin, Julius. "Application Of Electronic Computers To Economic Time-Series Analysis," *FAJ*, 1955, v11(2), 35-38.

Shiskin, Julius. "Electronic Computers And Business Indicators," *JOB*, 1957, v30(4), 219-267.

Shleifer, Andrei and Robert W. Vishny. "Management Entrenchment: The Case Of Manager-Specific Investments," *JFEC*, 1989, v25(1), 123-140.

Shleifer, Andrei. "Do Demand Curves For Stocks Slope Down?," *JOF*, 1986, v41(3), 579-590.

Shleifer, Andrei. (De Long, J. Bradford, Andrei Shleifer, Lawrence H. Summers and Robert J. Waldmann. "The Survival Of Noise Traders In Financial Markets," *JOB*, 1991, v64(1), 1-20.)

Shleifer, Andrei. (De Long, J. Bradford, Andrei Shleifer, Lawrence H. Summers and Robert J. Waldmann. "Positive Feedback Investment Strategies And Destabilizing Rational Speculation," *JOF*, 1990, v45(2), 379-396.)

Shleifer, Andrei. (DeLong, J. Bradford, Andrei Shleifer, Lawrence H. Summers and Robert J. Waldmann. "The Size And Incidence Of The Losses From Noise Trading," *JOF*, 1989, v44(3), 681-696.)

Shleifer, Andrei. (Jaffee, Dwight and Andrei Shleifer. "Costs Of Financial Distress, Delayed Calls Of Convertible Bonds, And The Role Of Investment Banks," *JOB*, 1990, v63(1), Part 2, S107-S124.)

Shleifer, Andrei. (Lee, Charles, Andrei Shleifer and Richard Thaler. "Investor Sentiment And The Closed-End Fund Puzzle," *JOF*, 1991, v46(1), 75-110.)

Shleifer, Andrei. (Morck, Randall, Andrei Shleifer and Robert W. Vishny. "Management Ownership And Market Valuation: An Empirical Analysis," *JFEC*, 1988, v20(1/2), 293-316.)

Shleifer, Andrei. (Morck, Randall, Andrei Shleifer and Robert W. Vishny. "Do Managerial Objectives Drive Bad Acquisitions?," *JOF*, 1990, v45(1), 31-48.)

Shoenthal, Edward R. "Classification Of Accounting Systems Using Competencies As A Discriminating Variable: A Great Britain - United States Study," *JBFA*, 1989, v16(4), 549-564.

Shogren, Jason F. "The Impact Of Self-Perception And Self-Insurance On Individual Response To Risk," *JRU*, 1990, v3(2), 191-204.

Shohet, Ruben. "Investing In Foreign Securities," *FAJ*, 1974, v30(5), 55-72.

Shohet, Ruben. "New Investment Environment For The U. S.," *FAJ*, 1973, v29(5), 26-32.

Sholund, J. Douglas. "The Impact Of Financial Futures On The Firm's Cost Of Capital And Investment Decisions," *RFM*, 1985, v4(1), 36-49.

Shome, Dilip K. (Brigham, Eugene F., Dilip K. Shome and Steve R. Vinson. "The Risk Premium Approach To Measuring A Utility's Cost Of Equity," *FM*, 1985, v14(1), 33-45.)

Shome, Dilip K. (Ferris, Stephen P., Dana J. Johnson and Dilip K. Shome. "Regulatory Environment And Market Response To Public Utility Rate Decisions," *JFR*, 1986, v9(4), 313-318.)

Shome, Dilip K. (Morgan, George Emir, Dilip K. Shome and Stephen D. Smith. "Optimal Futures Positions For Large Banking Firms," *JOF*, 1988, v43(1), 175-195.)

Shome, Dilip K. and Stephen D. Smith. "An Econometric Analysis Of Equity Costs And Risk Premiums In The Electric Utility Industry: 1971-1985," **FR**, 1988, v23(4), 439-452.

Shome, Dilip K., Stephen D. Smith and Arnold A. Heggestad. "Capital Adequacy And The Valuation Of Large Commercial Banking Organizations," **JFR**, 1986, v9(4), 331-341.

Shome, Dilip K., Stephen D. Smith and John M. Pinkerton. "The Purchasing Power Of Money And Nominal Interest Rates: A Re-Examination," **JOF**, 1988, v43(5), 1113-1125.

Shores, Marilyn R. (Prisman, Eliezer Z. and Marilyn R. Shores. "Duration Measures For Specific Term Structure Estimations And Applications To Bond Portfolio Immunization," **JBF**, 1988, v11(3), 493-504.)

Short, Brock K. and Delano P. Villanueva. "Further Evidence On The Role Of Savings Deposits As Money In Canada," **JMCB**, 1977, v9(3), 437-446.

Short, Brock K. "Bank Employment In The World's Largest Banks: A Comment," **JMCB**, 1971, v3(3), 712-720.

Short, Brock K. "The Relation Between Commercial Bank Profit Rates And Banking Concentration In Canada, Western Europe, And Japan," **JBF**, 1979, v3(3), 209-219.

Short, Daniel G. "The Impact Of Price-Level Adjustment On The Meaning Of Accounting Ratios," **JBFA**, 1980, v7(3), 377-391.

Short, Eugenie Dudding. "A New Look At Real Money Balances As A Variable In The Production Function," **JMCB**, 1979, v11(3),326-339.

Shorts, B. (Amihud, Y., C. Brunie, C. Ferenbach, R. Fredericks, J. Grundfest, J. Lafferty, B. Lev, B. Shorts, J. Stern, B. Stewart and R. Zeckhauser. "Panel: 'Lead Steer' Roundtable," **JACF**, 1989, v2(3), 24-44.)

Shoup, Carl S. "Some Considerations On The Incidence Of The Corporation Income Tax," **JOF**, 1951, v6(2), 187-199.

Shoup, Carl S. Surrey's Pathways To Tax REform - A Review Article," **JOF**, 1975, v30(5), 1329-1341.

Shoup, Donald C. "Effects Of Suboptimization On Urban Government Decision Making," **JOF**, 1971, v26(2), 547-564.

Shoven, John B. (Green, Jerry and John B. Shoven. "The Effects Of Interest Rates On Mortgage Prepayments," **JMCB**, 1986, v18(1), 41-59.)

Shows, E. Warren, Fred B. Power and Dale A. Johnson. "Lump-Sum Awards In Workers' Compensation: Comment," **JRI**, 1988, v55(4), 734-739.

Shows, E. Warren. (Power, Fred B. and E. Warren Shows. "A Status Report On The National Flood Insurance Program - Mid 1978," **JRI**, 1979, v46(2), 61-76.)

Shows, George. (Baesel, Jerome, George Shows and Edward Thorp. "Can Joe Granville Time The Market?," **JPM**, 1981-82, v8(3), 5-9.)

Shows, George. (Baesel, Jerome B., George Shows and Edward Thorp. "The Cost Of Liquidity Services In Listed Options: A Note," **JOF**, 1983, v38(3), 989-995.)

Shpilberg, David and Richard De Neufville. "Use Of Decision Analysis For Optimizing Choice Of Fire Protection And Insurance: An Airport Study," **JRI**, 1975, v42(1), 133-150.

Shpilberg, David. "The Probability Distribution Of Fire Loss Amount," **JRI**, 1977, v44(1), 103-116.

Shpilberg, David. (Pinedo, Michael and David Shpilberg. "Stochastic Models With Memory For Seismic Risk Evaluation," **JRI**, 1981, v48(1), 46-58.)

Shreiber, Chanoch. (Williams, David J. and Chanoch Shreiber. "Cost-Volume-Profit Complications Using A Simplified Form," **JBFA**, 1983, v10(3), 481-488.)

Shrieves, R. E. (Dahl, D. and R. E. Shrieves. "The Impact Of Regulation On Bank Equity Infusions," **JBF**, 1990, v14(6), 1209-1228.)

Shrieves, Ronald E. and Donald L. Stevens. "Bankruptcy Avoidance As A Motive For Merger," **JFQA**, 1979, v14(3), 501-515.

Shrieves, Ronald E. and John M. Wachowicz, Jr. "A Utility Theoretic Basis For 'Generalized' Mean-Coefficient Of Variation (MCV) Analysis," **JFQA**, 1981, v16(5), 671-683.

Shrieves, Ronald E. and Mary M. Pashley. "Evidence On The Association Between Mergers And Capital Structure," **FM**, 1984, v13(3), 39-48.

Shrieves, Ronald E. (Dahl, Drew and Ronald E. Shrieves. "Evidence On The Role Of Holding Company Acquisitions In The Management Of Bank Capital," **JFSR**, 1989, v2(1), 21-38.)

Shrieves, Ronald E. (Wachowicz, John M., Jr. and Ronald E. Shrieves. "An Argument For 'Generalized' Mean-Coefficient Of Variation Analysis," **FM**, 1980, v9(4), 51-58.)

Shriver, Keith A. (Dugan, Michael T. and Keith A. Shriver. "The Effects Of Estimation Period, Industry, And Proxy On The Calculation Of The Degree Of Operating Leverage," **FR**, 1989, v24(1), 109-122.)

Shropshire, William O. "Can The FED Control The Money Supply?," **FAJ**, 1976, v32(3), 20-24.

Shropshire, William W., Jr. (McKersie, Robert B. and William W. Shropshire, Jr. "Avoiding Written Grievances: A Successful Program," **JOB**, 1962, v35(2), 135-152.)

Shubik, Martin. "Approaches To The Study Of Decision-Making Relevant To The Firm," **JOB**, 1961, v34(2), 101-118.

Shubik, Martin. "Competitive Equilibrium Contingent Commodities And Information," **JOF**, 1977, v32(1), 189-193.

Shuford, Harry. (Wachtel, Paul, Arnold Sametz and Harry Shuford. "Capital Shortages: Myth Or Reality?," **JOF**, 1976, v31(2), 269-286.)

Shukla, Ravi and Charles Trzcinka. "Sequential Tests Of The Arbitrage Pricing Theory: A Comparison Of Principal Components And Maximum Likelihood Factors," **JOF**, 1990, v45(5), 1541-1564.

Shukla, Ravi and Charles Trzcinka. "Research On Risk And Return: Can Measures Of Risk Explain Anything?," **JPM**, 1991,v17(3),15-21.

Shulansky, Ralph M. "The Case Against Increasing The Savings Bank Life Insurance Policy Limit In Connecticut," **JRI**, 1967, v34(4), 628-634.

Shulman, David G. (Hartzell, David J., David G. Shulman, Terrence C. Langetieg and Martin L. Leibowitz. "A Look At Real Estate Duration," **JPM**, 1988-89, v15(1), 16-24.)

Shulman, David G. (Hartzell, David J., David G. Shulman and Charles H. Wurtzebach. "Refining The Analysis Of Regional Diversification For Income-Producing Real Estate," **JRER**, 1987, v2(2), 85-95.)

Shulman, David. "Real Estate Valuation Under Rent Control: The Case Of Santa Monica," **AREUEA**, 1981, v9(1), 38-53.

Shulman, David. (Baesel, Jerome B., David T. Methe and David Shulman. "Teaching Managerial Finance To Public Sector Students," **JFED**, 1981, v10, 23-32.)

Shulman, David. (Hofflander, Alfred E. and David Shulman. "The Distribution Of Title Insurance: The Unregulated Intermediary," **JRI**, 1977, v44(3), 435-446.)

Shulman, David. (Smith, Keith V. and David Shulman. "The Performance Record Of The Equity REIT's," **FAJ**, 1976, v32(5), 61-66.)

Shulman, Joel M. (Dambolena, Ismael G. and Joel M. Shulman. "A Primary Rule For Detecting Bankruptcy: Watch The Cash," **FAJ**, 1988, v44(5), 74-78.)

Shultz, George P. "A Note On Forecasting," **JOB**, 1963, v36(1), 1.

Shultz, Hon. George P. "Joint Session AFA-AEA Address Reflections On Political Economy," **JOF**, 1974, v29(2), 323-330.

Shumate, Mack H. (Mehr, Robert I. and Mack H. Shumate. "Primacy In Automobile Bodily Injury Coverage," **JRI**, 1975, v42(2), 201-225.)

Shuptrine, F. Kelly. "On The Validity Of Using Students As Subjects In Consumer Behavior Investigations," **JOB**, 1975, v48(3), 383-390.

Shurtleff, Lynn. "Where Is The Market Headed?," FAJ, v7(3), 59-62.

Shute, Clyde. "Construction Today," **FAJ**, 1952, v8(2), 73-76.

Shute, Clyde. "Construction Possibilities - 1953," **FAJ**, 1953, v9(2), 29-34.

Shyy, Gang. "Gambler's Ruin And Optimal Stop Loss Strategy," **JFM**, 1989, v9(6), 565-572.

Sibert, Anne C. (Canzoneri, Matthew B. and Anne C. Sibert. "The Macroeconomic Implications Of Contract Models With Asymmetric Information," **JMCB**, 1990, v22(3), 273-287.)

Sibert, Anne. "The Risk Premium In The Foreign Exchange Market," **JMCB**, 1989, v21(1), 49-65.

Sibler, Jacques. (Paroush, Jacob and Jacques Sibler. "The Stochastic Dominance Criteria, Mortality Risk And Investment In Education: A Cross-Country Comparison," **RIF**, 1980, v2, 111-120.)

Sibley, A. M. "Some Evidence On The Cash Flow Effects Of Bond Refunding," **FM**, 1974, v3(3), 50-53.

Sichel, Werner. "Fire Insurance: Imperfectly Regulated Collusion," **JRI**, 1966, v33(1), 95-114.

Sicherman, Neil W. (Mann, Steven V. and Neil W. Sicherman. "The Agency Costs Of Free Cash Flow: Acquisition Activity And Equity Issues," **JOB**, 1991, v64(2), 213-228.)

Sicherman, Neil W. (Trifts, Jack W., Neil W. Sicherman, Rodney L. Roenfeldt and Francisco De Cossio. "Divestiture To Unit Managers And Shareholder Wealth," **JFR**, 1990, v13(2), 167-172.)

Sicherman, Neil W. and Richard H. Pettway. "Acquisition Of Divested Assets And Shareholders' Wealth," **JOF**, 1987, v42(5), 1261-1273.

Sick, Gordon A. "A Certainty-Equivalent Approach To Capital Budgeting," **FM**, 1986, v15(4), 23-32.

Sick, Gordon A. "Multiperiod Risky Project Valuation: A Mean-Covariance Certainty-Equivalent Approach," **AFPAF**, 1989, v3(1), 1-36.

Sick, Gordon A. (Kraus, Alan and Gordon A. Sick. "Distinguishing Beliefs And Preferences In Equilibrium Prices," **JOF**, 1980, v35(2), 335-344.)

Sick, Gordon A. (Kraus, Alan and Gordon A. Sick. "Communication Of Aggregate Preferences Through Market Prices," **JFQA**, 1979, v14(4), 695-703.)

Sick, Gordon. (Chua, Jess H., Gordon Sick and Richard S. Woodward. "Diversifying With Gold Stocks," **FAJ**, 1990, v46(4), 76-79.)

Sick, Gordon. (Maksimovic, Vojislav, Gordon Sick and Josef Zechner. "Forward Markets, Stock Markets, And The Theory Of The Firm: Comment," **JOF**, 1989, v44(2), 525-528.)

Sidhu, Rupinder S. (Reilly, Frank K. and Rupinder S. Sidhu. "The Many Uses Of Bond Duration," **FAJ**, 1980, v36(4), 58-72.)

Siefert, R. (Gilmour, A., M. Jensen, R. Mercer, N. Minow, J. Morley, R. Siefert, B. Stewart, L. Summers and I. Harris. "Panel: The Economic Consequences Of High Leverage And Stock Market Pressures On Corporate Management: A Roundtable Discussion," **JACF**, 1990, v3(2), 6-37.)

Sieff, John A. "Measuring Investment Performance: The Unit Approach," **FAJ**, 1966, v22(4), 93-99.

Sieff, John A. "Retirement Fund Portfolios," **FAJ**, 1965, v21(4), 89-94.

Siegel, Andrew F. (Kamara, Avraham and Andrew F. Siegel. "Optimal Hedging In Futures Markets With Multiple Delivery Specifications," **JOF**, 1987, v42(4), 1007-1021.)

Siegel, Andrew F. (Nelson, Charles R. and Andrew F. Siegel. "Parsimonious Modeling Of Yield Curves," **JOB**, 1987, v60(4), 473-490.)

Siegel, Andrew F. and Charles R. Nelson. "Long-Term Behavior Of Yield Curves," **JFQA**, 1988, v23(1), 105-110.

Siegel, Daniel R. (Israel, Ronen, Aharon R. Ofer and Daniel R. Siegel. "The Information Content Of Equity-For-Debt Swaps: An Investigation Of Analyst Forecasts Of Firm Cash Flows," **JFEC**, 1989, v25(2), 349-370.)

Siegel, Daniel R. (Ofer, Aharon R. and Daniel R. Siegel. "Corporate Financial Policy, Information, And Market Expectations: An Empirical Investigation Of Dividends," **JOF**, 1987, v42(4), 889-911.)

Siegel, Daniel. (Hayes, Beth and Daniel Siegel. "Rate Of Return Regulation With Price Flexibility," **JOB**, 1986, v59(4), Part 1, 537-554.)

Siegel, Daniel. (McDonald, Robert and Daniel Siegel. "A Note On The Design Of Commodity Options Contracts: A Comment," **JFM**, 1983, v3(1), 43-46.)

Siegel, Daniel. (McDonald, Robert and Daniel Siegel. "Option Pricing When The Underlying Asset Earns A Below-Equilibrium Rate Of Return: A Note," **JOF**, 1984, v39(1), 261-265.)

Siegel, Donald. (Lichtenberg, Frank R. and Donald Siegel. "The Effect Of Control Changes On The Productivity Of U.S. Manufacturing Plants," **JACF**, 1989, v2(2), 60-67.)

Siegel, Donald. (Lichtenberg, Frank R. and Donald Siegel. "The Effects Of Leveraged Buyouts On Productivity And Related Aspects Of Firm Behavior," **JFEC**, 1990, v27(1), 165-194.)

Siegel, Irving H. "Technological Change And Long-Run Forecasting," **JOB**, 1953, v26(3), 141-156.

Siegel, Jeremy J. and Jerold B. Warner. "Indexation, The Risk-Free Asset, And Capital Market Equilibrium," **JOF**, 1977, v32(4), 1101-1107.

Siegel, Jeremy J. "Bank Reserves And Financial Stability," **JOF**, 1981, v36(5), 1073-1084.

Siegel, Jeremy J. "Technological Change And The Superneutrality Of Money," JMCB, 1983, v15(3), 363-367.

Siegel, Jeremy J. "The Application Of The DCF Methodology For Determining The Cost Of Equity Capital," FM, 1985, v14(1), 46-53.

Siegel, Jeremy J. (Protopapadakis, Aris A. and Jeremy J. Siegel. "Are Money Growth And Inflation Related To Government Deficits? Evidence From Ten Industrialized Economies," JIMF, 1987, v6(1), 31-48.)

Siegel, Jeremy J. (Santomero, Anthony M. and Jeremy J. Siegel. "A General Equilibrium Money And Banking Paradigm," JOF, 1982, v37(2), 357-369.)

Siegel, Joel G. "The 'Quality Of Earnings' Concept - A Survey," FAJ, 1982, v38(2), 60-68.

Siegel, Joel G. (Bernstein, Leopold A. and Joel G. Siegel. "The Concept Of Earnings Quality," FAJ, 1979, v35(4), 72-75.)

Siegel, Laurence B. (Diermeier, Jeffrey J., Roger G. Ibbotson and Laurence B. Siegel. "The Supply Of Capital Market Returns," FAJ, 1984, v40(2), 74-80.)

Siegel, Laurence B. (Ibbotson, Roger G. and Laurence B. Siegel. "The World Market Wealth Portfolio," JPM, 1982-83, v9(2), 5-17.)

Siegel, Laurence B. (Ibbotson, Roger G., Laurence B. Siegel and Kathryn S. Love. "World Wealth: Market Values And Returns," JPM, 1985-86, v12(1), 4-23.)

Siegel, Laurence B. (Ibbotson, Roger G., Jeffrey J. Diermeier and Laurence B. Siegel. "The Demand For Capital Market Returns: A New Equilibrium Theory," FAJ, 1984, v40(1), 22-33.)

Siegel, Laurence B. (Ibbotson, Roger G. and Laurence B. Siegel. "Real Estate Returns: A Comparison With Other Investments," AREUEA, 1984, v12(3), 219-242.)

Siegel, Mayer. "The Impact Of Pension Reform On Portfolio Management," JPM, 1974-75, v1(2), 21-24.

Siegelman, Louis. "Inflation Control Through A National Wage Policy," JOF, 1952, v7(1), 66-76.

Siegfried, John J. (Evans, Kaye D., John J. Siegfried and George H. Sweeney. "The Economic Cost Of Suboptimal Manufacturing Capacity," JOB, 1983, v56(1), 55-76.)

Siegfried, John J. (Zak, Thomas A., Cliff J. Huang and John J. Siegfried. "Production Efficiency: The Case Of Professional Basketball," JOB, 1979, v52(3), 379-392.)

Siegman, Charles J. (Fisher, Robert Moore and Charles J. Siegman. "Patterns Of Housing Experience During Periods Of Credit Restraint In Industrialized Countries," JOF, 1972, v27(2), 193-205.)

Sienkiewicz, Stanley. (Saunders, Anthony and Stanley Sienkiewicz. "The Hedging Performance Of ECU Futures Contracts," JFM, 1988, v8(3), 335-352.)

Siklos, Pierre L. "The End Of The Hungarian Hyperinflation Of 1945-1946," JMCB, 1989, v21(2), 135-147.

Silber, William L. and Murray E. Polakoff. "On The Differential Effects Of Tight Money: Reply," JOF, 1971, v26(4), 955-958.

Silber, William L. and Murray E. Polakoff. "The Differential Effects Of Tight Money: An Econometric Study," JOF, 1970, v25(1), 83-97.

Silber, William L. "Fiscal Policy In IS-LM Analysis: A Correction," JMCB, 1970, v2(4), 461-472.

Silber, William L. "Innovation, Competition, And New Contract Design In Futures Markets," JFM, v1(2), 123-156.

Silber, William L. "Monetary Policy Effectiveness: The Case Of A Positively Sloped I-S Curve: Reply," JOF, 1973, v28(5), 1365.

Silber, William L. "Monetary Policy Effectiveness: The Case Of A Positively Sloped IS Curve," JOF, 1971, v26(5), 1077-1082.

Silber, William L. "Monetary Channels And The Relative Importance Of Money Supply And Bank Portfolios," JOF, 1969, v24(1), 81-87.

Silber, William L. "The Excess Burden Of Monetary Policy: A Discussion Of The Hodgman And Mayer Papers," JMCB, 1972, v4(2), 414-418.

Silber, William L. "Thinness In Capital Markets: The Case Of The Tel Aviv Stock Exchange," JFQA, 1975, v10(1), 129-142.

Silber, William L. (Ben-Horim, Moshe and William L. Silber. "Financial Innovation: A Linear Programming Approach," JBF, 1977, v1(3), 277-296.)

Silber, William L. (Black, Deborah G., Kenneth D. Garbade and William L. Silber. "The Impact Of The GNMA Pass-through Program On FHA Mortgage Costs," JOF, 1981, v36(2), 457-469.)

Silber, William L. (Garbade, Kenneth D. and William L. Silber. "Cash Settlement Of Futures Contracts: An Economic Analysis," JFM, 1983, v3(4), 451-472.)

Silber, William L. (Garbade, Kenneth D. and William L. Silber. "Technology, Communication And The Performance Of Financial Markets: 1840-1975," JOF, 1978, v33(3), 819-832.)

Silber, William L. (Garbade, Kenneth D. and William L. Silber. "Futures Contracts On COmmodities With Multiple Varieties: An Analysis Of Premiums And Discounts," JOB, 1983, v56(3), 249-272.)

Silber, William L. (Garbade, Kenneth D. and William L. Silber. "Structural Organization Of Secondary Markets: Clearing Frequency, Dealer Activity And Liquidity Risk," JOF, 1979, v34(3), 577-593.)

Silber, William L. (Garbade, Kenneth D. and William L. Silber. "Best Execution In Securities Markets: An Application Of Signaling And Agency Theory," JOF, 1982, v37(2), 493-504.)

Silber, William L. (Polakoff, Murray E. and William L. Silber. "Reluctance And Member-Bank Borrowing: Additional Evidence: A Note," JOF, 1967, v22(1), 88-92.)

Silber, William. "Marketmaker Behavior In An Auction Market: An Analysis Of Scalpers In Futures Markets," JOF, 1984, v39(4), 937-953.

Silberberg, Eugene. (Nieswiadomy, Michael and Eugene Silberberg. "Calculating Changes In Worklife Expectancies And Lost Earnings In Personal Injury Cases," JRI, 1988, v55(3), 492-498.)

Silberman, Irwin H. "A Note On Merger Valuation," JOF, 1968, v23(3), 528-534.

Silberman, Irwin H. (Carleton, Willard T. and Irwin H. Silberman. "Joint Determination Of Rate Of Return And Capital Structure: An Econometric Analysis," JOF, 1977, v32(3), 811-821.)

Silbermann, Joachim. "What Financial Community And Stockholder Relations Mean To Management," FAJ, 1956, v12(4), 61-64.

Silhan, Peter A. and Thomas J. Frecka. "On The Sales Forecasting Benefits Of Form 10-K Backlog Information," JBFA, 1986, v13(3), 425-431.

Silhan, Peter A. "Using Quarterly Sales And Margins To Predict Corporate Earnings: A Time-Series Perspective," JBFA, 1989, v16(1), 131-141.

Silk, Alvin J. (Schmalensee, Richard, Alvin J. Silk and Robert Bojanek. "The Impact Of Scale And Media Mix On Advertising Agency Costs," JOB, 1983, v56(4), 453-476.)

Silk, Leonard S. "The Goals Of Business Education," JRI, 1964, v31(3), 421-428.

Sillcox, L. K. "Cars To Come," FAJ, 1957, v13(5), 83-90.

Sillcox, L. K. "Transportation Equipment Equity," FAJ, 1959, v15(2), 37-42.

Silveira, Antonio M. "Interest Rate And Rapid Inflation: The Evidence From The Brazilian Economy," JMCB, 1973, v5(3), 794-805.

Silveira, Antonio M. "The Demand For Money: The Evidence From The Brazilian Economy," JMCB, 1973, v5(1), 113-140.

Silver, Allen. "Betas: Up, Down, And Sideways," JPM, 1974-75, v1(4), 54-60.

Silver, Allen. (Sharpe, William F. and Allen Silver. "'Sideways Betas': Further Comments," JPM, 1975-76, v2(4), 67-68.)

Silver, Allen. (Williamson, J. Peter and Allen Silver. "Sideways Betas: Criticism And Response," JPM, 1975-76, v2(2), 68-70.)

Silver, Andrew. (Arak, Marcelle, Arturo Estrella, Laurie Goodman and Andrew Silver. "Interest Rate Swaps: An Alternative Explanation," FM, 1988, v17(2), 12-18.)

Silver, Andrew. (Arak, Marcelle and Andrew Silver. "The Value Of The Tax Treatment Of Original-Issue Deep-Discount Bonds: A Note," JOF, 1984, v39(1), 253-259.)

Silver, Morris and Richard Auster. "Entrepreneurship, Profit, And Limits On Firm Size," JOB, 1969, v42(3), 277-281.

Silver, Murray. "An Approximate Solution For The Unknown Rate Of Interest For An Annuity Certain," JRI, 1981, v48(1), 136-142.

Silverberg, Stanley C. "Bank Holding Companies And Capital Adequacy," JBR, 1975-76, v6(3), 202-207.

Silverberg, Stanley C. "Compensatory Cyclical Bank Asset Adjustments: Comment," JOF, 1962, v17(4), 651-654.

Silverberg, Stanley C. "Deposit Costs And Bank Portfolio Policy," JOF, 1973, v28(4), 881-895.

Silverman, Herbert R. "Newer Forms Of Secured Commercial Loans," FAJ, 1955, v11(1), 93-96.

Silverman, Lester P. "Credit Standards And Tight Money: A Comment," JMCB, 1973, v5(1), 221-223.

Silvers, J. B. "An Alternative To The Yield Spread As A Measure Of Risk," JOF, 1973, v28(4), 933-955.

Silvers, J. B. "Liquidity, Risk And Duration Patterns In Corporate Financing," FM, 1976, v5(3), 54-64.

Sim, Ah Boon. (Rahman, Abdul, Lawrence Kryzanowski and Ah Boon Sim. "Systematic Risk In A Purely Random Market Model: Some Empirical Evidence For Individual Public Utilities," JFR, 1987, v10(2), 143-152.)

Sim, R. (Appelbaum, E., J. Burns, R. Evans, J. Gould, T. Hamachek, R. Kidder, M. Jensen, J. Johnstone, M. Murray, R. Sim, J. Stern, B. Stewart and C. Zaner. "Panel: CEO Roundtable On Corporate Structure And Management Incentives," JACF, 1990, v3(3), 6-35.)

Simaan, Yusif. (Tandon, Kishore and Yusif Simaan. "The Reaction Of Effective Exchange Rates To Information About Inflation," FR, 1985, v20(2), 164-179.)

Simkin, Mark G. and Ralph H. Sprague, Jr. "Staffing For Bank Telephone Inquiry Systems: A Decision Analysis," JBR, 1976-77, v7(1), 49-55.

Simkowitz, Michael A. and Charles P. Jones. "A Note On The Simultaneous Nature Of Finance Methodology," JOF, 1972, v27(1), 103-108.

Simkowitz, Michael A. and Dennis E. Logue. "The Interdependent Structure Of Security Returns," JFQA, 1973, v8(2), 259-272.

Simkowitz, Michael A. and William L. Beedles. "Diversification In A Three-Moment World," JFQA, 1978, v13(5), 927-941.

Simkowitz, Michael A. (Beedles, William L. and Michael A. Simkowitz. "A Note On Skewness And Data Errors," JOF, 1978, v33(1), 288-292.)

Simmons, David R. "Visual Aids In Insurance Teaching," JRI, 1967, v34(4), 606-610.

Simmons, Edward C. "A Note On The Causes Of Instability In The Money Supply," JOF, 1951, v6(3), 333-337.

Simmons, Edward C. "A Note On The Revival Of Federal Reserve Discount Policy," JOF, 1956, v11(4), 413-421.

Simmons, Edward C. "Federal Reserve Discount-Rate Policy And Member-Bank Borrowing: 1944-50," JOB, 1952, v25(1), 18-29.

Simmons, Edward C. "Sales Of Government Securities To Federal Reserve Banks Under Repurchase Agreements," JOF, 1954, v9(1), 23-40.

Simmons, LeRoy F. (Cross, Mark L. and LeRoy F. Simmons. "The Underwriting Cycle And The Risk Manager: Reply," JRI, 1988, v55(3), 561-562.)

Simmons, LeRoy F. and Mark L. Cross. "The Underwriting Cycle And The Risk Manager," JRI, 1986, v53(1), 155-163.

Simms, John M., Jr. (Bruner, Robert F. and John M. Simms, Jr. "The International Debt Crisis And Bank Security Returns In 1982," JMCB, 1987, v19(1), 46-55.)

Simon, Daniel T. (Penno, Mark and Daniel T. Simon. "Accounting Choices: Public Versus Private Firms," JBFA, 1986, v13(4), 561-569.)

Simon, David P. "Expectations And The Treasury Bill-Federal Funds Rate Spread Over Recent Monetary Policy Regimes," JOF, 1990, v45(2), 567-578.

Simon, David P. "Expectations And Risk In The Treasury Bill Market: An Instrumental Variables Approach," JFQA, 1989, v24(3), 357-366.

Simon, David P. "Segmentation In The Treasury Bill Market: Evidence From Cash Management Bills," JFQA, 1991, v26(1), 97-108.

Simon, David P. "The Rationality Of Federal Funds Rate Expectations: Evidence From A Survey," JMCB, 1989, v21(3), 388-393.

Simon, David. (Adler, Michael and David Simon. "Exchange Risk Surprises In International Portfolios," JPM, 1985-86, v12(2), 44-53.)

Simon, Gary. (Pinches, George E. and Gary Simon. "An Analysis Of Portfolio Accumulation Strategies Employing Low-Priced Common Stocks," JFQA, 1972, v7(3), 1773-1796.)

Simon, Herbert A. "Rationality In Psychology And Economics," JOB, 1986, v59(4), Part 2, S209-S224.

Simon, Herbert A. (Cyert, Richard M., Herbert A. Simon, and Donald B. Trow. "Observation Of A Business Decision," JOB, 1956, v29(4), 237-248.)

Simon, Julian L. "Regulation Improves Efficiency? In Airline Overbooking - Yes And Maybe," RIF, 1983, v4, (Supp) 209-226.

Simon, Julian L. and Leslie Golembo. "The Spread Of A Cost-Free Business Innovation," JOB, 1967, v40(4), 385-388.

Simon, LeRoy J. "A Theory Of Capacity And The Insurance Of Catastrophe Risks: Comment," JRI, 1975, v42(2), 338-339.

Simon, Simon M. "The Case Method Approach To Teaching Decision Making And Analysis," JFED, 1979, v8, 63-70.

Simon, William E. "Is U.S. Capital Investment Too Low?," JPM, 1975-76, v2(1), 5-10.

Simonds, Richard R. "Case Management Simulation," JFED, 1978, v7, 80-82.

Simonds, Richard R. "Evaluation Of Seller-Financing Offers On Residential Real Estate," JPM, 1985, v11(1), 77-102.

Simonds, Richard R. "Mutual Fund Strategies For IRA Investors," JPM, 1985-86, v12(2), 40-43.

Simonds, Richard R. (Atchison, Michael D., Kirt C. Butler and Richard R. Simonds. "Nonsynchronous Security Trading And Market Index Autocorrelation," JOF, 1987, v42(1), 111-118.)

Simonds, Richard R., Lynn Roy LaMotte and Archer McWhorter, Jr. "Testing For Nonstationarity Of Market Risk: An Exact Test And Power Considerations," JFQA, 1986, v21(2), 209-220.

Simonoff, Jeffrey S. "Application Of Statistical Methodology To The Evaluation Of Timing Devices In Commodities Trading," JFM, v1(4), 649-656.

Simons, Gustave. "Providing Security For The Security Analyst," FAJ, 1955, v11(2), 39-36.

Simonson, Donald G. and David S. Kidwell. "The MBA Financial Markets Course -- A Survey On Teaching Approaches," JFED, 1982, v11, 25-31.

Simonson, Donald G. and George H. Hempel. "Improving Gap Management for Controlling Interest Rate Risk," JBR, 1982-83, v13(2), 109-115.

Simonson, Donald G. and Peter C. Marks. "Breakeven Balances On NOW Accounts: Perils In Pricing," JBR, 1980-81, v11(3), 187-191.

Simonson, Donald G. "Funds Management By State Treasurers: Direct Vs. Socio-Economic Returns," FM, 1977, v6(4), 51-58.

Simonson, Donald G. "The Speculative Behavior Of Mutual Funds," JOF, 1972, v27(2), 381-391.

Simonson, Donald G. (Olson, Ronald L. and Donald G. Simonson. "Gap Management And Market Rate Sensitivity In Banks," JBR, 1982-83, v13(1), 53-58.)

Simonson, Donald G. (Stock, Duane and Donald G. Simonson. "Tax-Adjusted Duration For Amortizing Debt Instruments," JFQA, 1988, v23(3), 313-328.)

Simonson, Donald G., John D. Stowe and Collin J. Watson. "A Canonical Correlation Analysis Of Commercial Bank Asset/Liability Structures," JFQA, 1983, v18(1), 125-140.

Simonson, Henry J., Jr. "Scientific Formula In Operation," FAJ, 1952, v8(2), 35-38.

Simonson, John C. (Clemmer, Richard B. and John C. Simonson. "Trends In Substandard Housing 1940-1980," AREUEA, 1982, v10(4), 442-464.)

Simonson, John. (Buckley, Robert M. and John Simonson. "Effective Property Tax Rates And Capital Formation Issues: Manvel, Acton And Darby," AREUEA, 1987, v15(1), 725-738.)

Simonson, John. (Villani, Kevin E. and John Simonson. "Real Estate Settlement Pricing: A Theoretical Framework," AREUEA, 1982, v10(3), 249-275.)

Simonton, Gail. (Walsh, Cornelius F. and Gail Simonton. "The Confidence Index As A Stock Market Indicator," JBR, 1971-72, v2(2), 40-44.)

Simos, Evangelos O. (Kaen, Fred R., Evangelos O. Simos and George A. Hachey. "The Response Of Forward Exchange Rates To Interest Rate Forecasting Errors," JFR, 1984, v7(4), 281-290.)

Simpson, Gary. "The Cost Of Capital And Break-Even Analysis," JFED, 1984, v13, 28-32.

Simpson, Thomas D. (Farley, Dennis E. and Thomas D. Simpson. "Graduated Reserve Requirements And Monetary Control," JOF, 1979, v34(4), 999-1012.)

Simpson, W. Gary and Brenda P. Sumrall. "The Determinants Of Objective Test Scores By Finance Students," JFED, 1979, v8, 58-62.

Simpson, W. Gary and Theodor Kohers. "The Effect Of Organizational Form On Performance In The Savings And Loan Industry," FR, 1979, v14(3), 1-12.

Simpson, W. Gary and Timothy C. Ireland. "The Impact Of Financial Futures On The Cash Market For Treasury Bills," JFQA, 1985, v20(3), 371-380.

Simpson, W. Gary and Timothy C. Ireland. "The Effect Of Futures Trading On The Price Volatility Of GNMA Securities," JFM, 1982, v2(4), 357-366.

Simpson, W. Gary. "Capital Market Prediction Of Large Commercial Bank Failures: An Alternative Analysis," FR, 1983, v18(1), 33-55.

Sinai, Allen and Houston Stokes. "Real Money Balances As A Variable In The Production Function: A Comment," JMCB, 1977, v9(2), 372-373.

Sinai, Allen. (Brimmer, Andrew and Allen Sinai. "The Effects Of Tax Policy On Capital Formation, Corporate Liquidity And The Availability Of Investible Funds: A Simulation Study," JOF, 1976, v31(2), 287-308.)

Sindelar, Jody L. (Ibbotson, Roger G., Jody L. Sindelar and Jay R. Ritter. "Initial Public Offerings," JACF, 1988, v1(2), 37-45.)

Singer, Daniel and Walter Holman. "The Effective Use Of Writing In Financial Case Analysis," JFED, 1990, v19, 23-26.

Singer, Donald F. (Ho, Thomas and Donald F. Singer. "The Value Of Corporate Debt With A Sinking-Fund Provision," JOB, 1984, v57(3), 315-336.)

Singer, Neil. (Kanter, Herschel, Arnold Moore and Neil Singer. "The Allocation Of Computer Time By University Computer Centers," JOB, 1968, v41(3), 375-384.)

Singer, Ronald F. "Endogenous Marginal Income Tax Rates, Investor Behavior And The Capital Asset Pricing Model," JOF, 1979, v34(3), 609-616.

Singer, Ronald F. (Ho, Thomas S. Y. and Ronald F. Singer. "Bond Indenture Provisions And The Risk Of Corporate Debt," JFEC, 1982, v10(4), 375-406.)

Singer, Ronald F. (Lee, Insup, R. Richardson Pettit and Ronald F. Singer. "Offer Premiums In Stock Exchange Mergers And The Distribution Of Stockholder's Wealth," IJOF, 1990, v2(2), 67-87.)

Singer, Ronald F. (Pettit, R. Richardson and Ronald F. Singer. "Instant Option Betas," FAJ, 1986, v42(5), 51-62.)

Singer, Ronald F. (Pettit, R. Richardson and Ronald F. Singer. "Small Business Finance: A Research Agenda," FM, 1985, v14(3), 47-60.)

Singh, Ajai K. (Cowan, Arnold R., Nandkumar Nayar and Ajai K. Singh. "Stock Returns Before And After Calls Of Convertible Bonds," JFQA, 1990, v25(4), 549-554.)

Singh, S. P. (Jollineau, R. W. and S. P. Singh. "Inflation And The Profitability Of Firms In Canada," JBFA, 1975, v2(1), 105-120.)

Singh, Saraswati P. and Prem P. Talwar. "Monetary And Fiscal Policies And Stock Prices," JBFA, 1982, v8(1), 75-91.

Singhvi, Surendra S. and Harsha B. Desai. "An Overview Of The Case Method Of Instruction," JFED, 1977, v6, 70-74.

Singhvi, Surendra S. "Disclsoure To Whom? Annual Financial Reports To Stockholders And To The Securities And Exchange Commission," JOB, 1968, v41(3), 347-351.

Singhvi, Surendra S. "How Willing Is Management To Disclose," FAJ, 1972, v28(4), 66-73.

Singhvi, Surendra S. "One Financial Executive's Response To Surveys," FM, 1981, v10(5), 82-83.

Singhvi, Surendra. "Teaching Trends: Management Fundamentals - Finance Modules," JFED, 1983, v12, 27-30.

Singleton, J. Clay and John Wingender. "Skewness Persistence In Common Stock Returns," JFQA, 1986, v21(3), 335-341.

Singleton, J. Clay and Joseph R. Lauer. "The Implications Of Recursiveness In Capital Markets—Theory And Empirical Tests," JFQA, 1979, v14(1), 59-76.

Singleton, J. Clay and Robin Grieves. "Synthetic Puts And Portfolio Insurance Strategies," JPM, 1983-84, v10(3), 63-69.

Singleton, J. Clay. "A Stock Options Game," JFED, 1986, v15, 79-88.

Singleton, J. Clay. (Grieves, Robin and J. Clay Singleton. "Analytical Methods Of The All-America Research Team," JPM, 1987-88, v14(1), 4-8.)

Singleton, J. Clay. (Pinches, George E. and J. Clay Singleton. "The Adjustment Of Stock Prices To Bond Rating Changes," JOF, 1978, v33(1), 29-44.)

Singleton, J. Clay. (Pinches, George E., J. Clay Singleton and Ali Jahankhani. "Fixed Coverage As A Determinant Of Electric Utility Bond Ratings," FM, 1978, v7(2), 45-55.)

Singleton, Kenneth J. "Maturity-Specific Disturbances And The Term Structure Of Interest Rates," JMCB, 1980, v12(4), Part 1, 603-614.

Singleton, Kenneth J. (Dunn, Kenneth B. and Kenneth J. Singleton. "An Empirical Analysis Of The Pricing Of Mortgage-Backed Securities," JOF, 1983, v38(2), 613-623.)

Singleton, Kenneth J. (Dunn, Kenneth B. and Kenneth J. Singleton. "Modeling The Term Structure Of Interest Rates Under Non-Separable Utility And Durability Of Goods," JFEC, 1986, v17(1), 27-56.)

Singleton, Kenneth J. (Meese, Richard A. and Kenneth J. Singleton. "On Unit Roots And The Empirical Modeling Of Exchange Rates," JOF, 1982, v37(4), 1029-1035.)

Sinha, Sujata. (Fishe, Raymond P. H., Lawrence G. Goldberg, Thomas F. Gosnell and Sujata Sinha. "Margin Requirements In Futures Markets: Their Relationship To Price Volatility," JFM, 1990, v10(5), 541-554.)

Sinha, Tapen. "The Effects Of Survival Probabilities, Transactions Costs And The Attitude Towards Risk On The Demand For Annuities," JRI, 1986, v53(2), 301-307.

Sinkey, Joseph F., Jr. and David A. Walker. "Problem Banks: Indentification & Characteristics," JBR, 1974-75, v5(4), 208-217.

Sinkey, Joseph F., Jr. and James A. Miles. "The Use Of Warrants In The Bail Out Of First Pennsylvania Bank: An Application Of Option Pricing," FM, 1982, v11(3), 27-32.

Sinkey, Joseph F., Jr. "A Multivariate Statistical Analysis Of The Characteristics Of Problem Banks," JOF, 1975, v30(1), 21-36.

Sinkey, Joseph F., Jr. "A Pedagogical Note On The EOQ Model," FR, 1983, v18(1), 111-113.

Sinkey, Joseph F., Jr. "Adverse Publicity And Bank Deposit Flows: The Cases Of Franklin National Bank Of New York And United States National Bank Of San Diego," JBR, 1975-76, v6(2), 109-112.

Sinkey, Joseph F., Jr. "Identifying Large Problem/Failed Banks: The Case Of Franklin National Bank Of New York," JFQA, 1977, v12(5), 779-800.

Sinkey, Joseph F., Jr. "Identifying 'Problem' Banks: How Do The Banking Authorities Measure A Bank's Risk Exposure," JMCB, 1978, v10(2), 184-193.

Sinkey, Joseph F., Jr. "The Term Structure Of Interest Rates: A Time-Series Test Of The Kane Expected-Change Model Of Interest-Rate Forecasting," JMCB, 1973, v5(1), 192-200.

Sinkey, Joseph F., Jr. "The Performance Of First Pennsylvania Bank Prior To Its Bail Out," JBR, 1983-84, v14(2), 119-133.

Sinkey, Joseph F., Jr. "The Failure Of United States National Bank Of San Diego: A Portfolio & Performance Analysis," JBR, 1975-76, v6(1), 8-24.

Sinkey, Joseph F., Jr. "The Collapse Of Franklin National Bank Of New York," JBR, 1976-77, v7(2), 113-122.

Sinkey, Joseph F., Jr. (Greenawalt, Mary Brady and Joseph F. Sinkey, Jr. "Bank Loan-Loss Provisions And The Income-Smoothing Hypothesis: An Empirical Analysis, 1976-1984," JFSR, 1988, v1(4), 301-318.)

Sinkey, Joseph F., Jr. (Hilliard, Jimmy and Joseph F. Sinkey, Jr. "Duration Analysis As A Tool For Predicting Interest-Sensitive Cash Flows," JFED, 1989, v18, 1-7.)

Sinkey, Joseph F., Jr. (Jahera, John S., Jr. and Joseph F. Sinkey, Jr. "A Note On The Intracyclical Balance-Sheet Behavior Of Large

Commercial Banks: 1972-1978," **JBF**, 1984, v8(1), 109-118.)

Sinkey, Joseph F., Jr. (Kurtz, Robert D. and Joseph F. Sinkey, Jr. "Bank Disclosure Policy And Procedures, Adverse Publicity And Bank Deposit Flows," **JBR**, 1973-74, v4(3), 177-184.)

Sinkey, Joseph F., Jr. (Musumeci, James J. and Joseph F. Sinkey, Jr. "The International Debt Crisis, Investor Contagion, And Bank Security Returns In 1987: The Brazilian Experience," **JMCB**, 1990, v22(2), 209-220.)

Sinkey, Joseph F., Jr. (Musumeci, James J. and Joseph F. Sinkey, Jr. "The International Debt Crisis And Bank Loan-Loss-Reserve Decisions: The Signaling Content Of Partially Anticipated Events," **JMCB**, 1990, v22(3), 370-387.)

Sinkey, Joseph F., Jr. (Pettway, Richard H. and Joseph F. Sinkey, Jr. "Establishing On-Site Bank Examination Priorities: An Early-Warning System Using Accounting And Market Information," **JOF**, 1980, v35(1), 137-150.)

Sinn, Hans-Werner. "Expected Utility, Mu-Sigma Preferences, And Linear Distribution Classes: A Further Result," **JRU**, 1990, v3(3), 277-282.

Sinquefield, Jeanne C. (Kahl, Kandace H., Roger D. Rutz and Jeanne C. Sinquefield. "The Economics Of Performance Margins In Futures Markets," **JFM**, 1985, v5(1), 103-112.)

Sinquefield, R. A. (Ibbotson, R. G. and R. A. Sinquefield. "Stocks, Bonds, Bills And Inflation: Updates," **FAJ**, 1979, v35(4), 40-44.)

Sinquefield, Rex A. (Ibbotson, Roger G. and Rex A. Sinquefield. "Stocks, Bonds, Bills, And Inflation: Year-By-Year Historical Returns (1926-1974)," **JOB**, 1976, v49(1), 11-47.)

Sinquefield, Rex A. (Ibbotson, Roger G. and Rex A. Sinquefield. "Stocks, Bonds, Bills, And Inflation: Simulations Of The Future (1976-2000)," **JOB**, 1976, v49(3), 313-338.)

Siong, Lye Meng. (Ann, Wong Kie and Lye Meng Siong. "Market Values, Earnings' Yields And Stock Returns: Evidence From Singapore," **JBF**, 1990, v14(2/3), 311-326.)

Sioshansi, F. Perry. "Insurance For Irreplaceable Commodities," **JRI**, 1982, v49(2), 309-320.

Siow, Aloysius. (Lawrence, Colin and Aloysius Siow. "Interest Rates And Investment Spending: Some Empirical Evidence For Postwar U.S. Producer Equipment, 1947-1980," **JOB**, 1985, v58(4), 359-376.)

Sirmans, C. F. "An Econometric Analysis Of Urban Travel Behavior Between Residence And Work Site," **AREUEA**, 1976, v4(2), 19-32.

Sirmans, C. F. "Minimum Tax, Recapture And Choice Of Depreciation Methods," **AREUEA**, 1980, v8(3), 255-267.

Sirmans, C. F. (Allen, Paul R. and C. F. Sirmans. "An Analysis Of Gains To Acquiring Firm's Shareholders: The Special Case Of REITs," **JFEC**, 1987, v18(1), 175-184.)

Sirmans, C. F. (Beaton, William and C. F. Sirmans. "Do Syndications Pay More For Real Estate?," **AREUEA**, 1986, v14(2), 206-215.)

Sirmans, C. F. (Benjamin, John D., James D. Shilling and C. F. Sirmans. "Contracts As Options: Some Evidence From Condominium Developments," **AREUEA**, 1985, v13(2), 143-152.)

Sirmans, C. F. (Benjamin, John D., Glenn W. Boyle and C. F. Sirmans. "Retail Leasing: The Determinants Of Shopping Center Rents," **AREUEA**, 1990, v18(3), 302-312.)

Sirmans, C. F. (Colwell, Peter F., Karl L. Guntermann and C. F. Sirmans. "Discount Points And Housing Prices: Comment," **JOF**, 1979, v34(4), 1049-1054.)

Sirmans, C. F. (Dhillon, Upinder S., James D. Shilling and C. F. Sirmans. "Choosing Between Fixed And Adjustable Rate Mortgages," **JMCB**, 1987, v19(2), 260-267.)

Sirmans, C. F. (Glascock, John L., Shirin Jahanian and C. F. Sirmans. "An Analysis Of Office Market Rents: Some Empirical Evidence," **AREUEA**, 1990, v18(1), 105-120.)

Sirmans, C. F. (Glascock, John L., Wallace N. Davidson and C. F. Sirmans. "An Analysis Of The Acquisition And Dispositon Of Real Estate Assets," **JRER**, 1989, v4(3), 131-140.)

Sirmans, C. F. (Jameson, Mel, James D. Shilling and C. F. Sirmans. "Regional Variation Of Mortgage Yields And Simultaneity Bias," **JFR**, 1990, v13(3), 211-220.)

Sirmans, C. F. (Leung, Wai K. and C. F. Sirmans. "A Lattice Approach To Fixed-Rate Mortgage Pricing With Default And Prepayment Options," **AREUEA**, 1990, v18(1), 91-104.)

Sirmans, C. F. (Richins, Marsha L., William C. Black and C. F. Sirmans. "Strategic Orientation And Marketing Strategy: An Analysis Of Residential Real Estate Brokerage Firms," **JRER**, 1987, v2(2), 41-54.)

Sirmans, C. F. (Sa-Aadu, J. and C. F. Sirmans. "The Pricing Of Adjustable Rate Mortgage Contracts," **JREFEC**, 1989, v2(4), 253-266.)

Sirmans, C. F. (Sa-Aadu, J., C. F. Sirmans and John D. Benjamin. "Financing And House Prices," **JFR**, 1989, v12(1), 83-91.) 3e?8

Sirmans, C. F. (Shilling, James D. and C. F. Sirmans. "Pricing Fast-Pay Mortgages: Some Simulation Results," **JFR**, 1987, v10(1), 25-32.)

Sirmans, C. F. (Shilling, James D., C. F. Sirmans and John D. Benjamin. "On Option-Pricing Models In Real Estate: A Critique," **AREUEA**, 1987, v15(1), 742-752.)

Sirmans, C. F. (Shilling, James D. and C. F. Sirmans. "The Effects Of Occupational Licensing On Complaints Against Real Estate Agents," **JRER**, 1988, v3(2), 1-9.)

Sirmans, C. F. (Shilling, James D., John D. Benjamin and C. F. Sirmans. "Estimating Net Realizable Value For Distressed Real Estate," **JRER**, 1990, v5(1), 129-140.)

Sirmans, C. F. (Sirmans, G. Stacy and C. F. Sirmans. "The Historical Perspective Of Real Estate Returns," **JPM**, 1986-87, v13(3), 22-31.)

Sirmans, C. F. (Sirmans, G. Stacy, Stanley D. Smith and C. F. Sirmans. "Assumption Financing And Selling Price Of Single-Family Homes," **JFQA**, 1983, v18(3), 307-317.)

Sirmans, C. F. (Sirmans, G. Stacy, C. F. Sirmans and John D. Benjamin. "Determining Apartment Rent: The Value Of Amenities, Services And External Factors," **JRER**, 1989, v4(2), 33-43.)

Sirmans, C. F. (Sirmans, G. Stacy, C. F. Sirmans and John D. Benjamin. "Rental Concessions And Property Values," **JRER**, 1990, v5(1), 141-151.)

Sirmans, C. F. (Webb, James R. and C. F. Sirmans. "Yields And Risk Measures For Real Estate, 1966-77," **JPM**, 1980-81, v7(1), 14-19.)

Sirmans, C. F. and James R. Webb. "Expected Equity Returns On Real Estate Financed With Life Insurance Company Loans: 1967-1977," **AREUEA**, 1980, v8(2), 218-228.

Sirmans, C. F. and John D. Benjamin. "Pricing Fixed Rate Mortgages: Some Empirical Evidence," **JFSR**, 1990, v4(3), 191-202. 3-?8

Sirmans, G. Stacy and C. F. Sirmans. "The Historical Perspective Of Real Estate Returns," **JPM**, 1986-87, v13(3), 22-31.

Sirmans, G. Stacy, Stanley D. Smith and C. F. Sirmans. "Assumption Financing And Selling Price Of Single-Family Homes," **JFQA**, 1983, v18(3), 307-317.

Sirmans, G. Stacy, C. F. Sirmans and John D. Benjamin. "Determining Apartment Rent: The Value Of Amenities, Services And External Factors," **JRER**, 1989, v4(2), 33-43.

Sirmans, G. Stacy, C. F. Sirmans and John D. Benjamin. "Rental Concessions And Property Values," **JRER**, 1990, v5(1), 141-151.

Sirmans, G. Stacy. (Ferreira, Eurico J. and G. Stacy Sirmans. "Selling Price, Financing Premiums, And Days On The Market," **JREFEC**, 1989, v2(3), 209-222.)

Sirmans, G. Stacy. (Ferreira, Eurico J. and G. Stacy Sirmans. "Interest-Rate Changes, Transaction Costs, And Assumable Loan Value," **JRER**, 1987, v2(2), 29-40.)

Sirmans, G. Stacy. (Harris, John M., Jr. and G. Stacy Sirmans. "Discount Points, Effective Yields And Mortgage Prepayments," **JRER**, 1987, v2(2), 97-104.)

Sirmans, G. Stacy. (Hoffman, James J., Marc J. Schniederjans and G. Stacy Sirmans. "A Multi-Criteria Model For Corporate Property Evaluation," **JRER**, 1990, v5(3), 285-300.)

Sirmans, G. Stacy. (Smith, Stanley D. and G. Stacy Sirmans. "The Shifting Of FHA Discount Points: Actual Vs. Expectations," **AREUEA**, 1984, v12(2), 153-161.)

Sirmon, William A. (Daniel, Donnie L. and William A. Sirmon. "Computerized Bank Financial Statements: Classroom Applications," **JFED**, 1979, v8, 86-89.)

Sisneros, Phillip M. (Moyer, R. Charles, Robert E. Chatfield and Phillip M. Sisneros. "Security Analyst Monitoring Activity: Agency Costs And Information Demands," **JFQA**, 1989, v24(4), 503-512.)

Sitt, Irving. "Mechanical Investment Plans Versus Judgment," **FAJ**, 1946, v2(2), 30-38.

Sitzer, Scott. (Bopp, Anthony E. and Scott Sitzer. "Are Petroleum Prices Good Predictors Of Cash Value?," **JFM**, 1987, v7(6), 705-720.)

Sivesind, Charles M. (Fix, Robert F. and Charles M. Sivesind. "An Assessment Of The Income Stabilization Impact Of Monetary Policy In Twelve Industrialized Countries," **JMCB**, 1978, v10(4), 476-490.)

Sjostrom, Robert A. "What Are Life Insurance Stocks Worth?," **FAJ**, 1962, v18(5), 59-62.

Sjostrom, Robert A. "Which Fire And Casualty Stocks?," **FAJ**, 1957, v13(2), 79-84.

Skaburskis, A. "Determinants Of Canadian Housing Stock Losses," **AREUEA**, 1981, v9(2), 181-184.

Skadberg, J. Marvin. (Hayenga, M.L., D.D. Dipietre, J.M. Skadberg and T.C. Schroeder. "Profitable Hedging Opportunities And Risk Premiums For Producers In Live Cattle And Live Hog Futures Markets," **JFM**, 1984, v4(2), 141-154.)

Skantz, Terrance R. and Roberto Marchesini. "The Effect Of Voluntary Corporate Liquidation On Shareholder Wealth," **JFR**, 1987, v10(1), 65-76.

Skantz, Terrance R. and Thomas H. Strickland. "House Prices And A Flood Event: An Empirical Investigation Of Market Efficiency," **JRER**, 1987, v2(2), 75-83.

Skantz, Terrance R., Dale O. Cloninger and Thomas H. Strickland. "Price-Fixing And Shareholder Returns: An Empirical Study," **FR**, 1990, v25(1), 153-164.

Skelton, Jeffrey L. "Banks, Firms And The Relative Pricing Of Tax-Exempt And Taxable Bonds," **JFEC**, 1983, v12(3), 343-355.

Skelton, Jeffrey L. "Relative Risk In Municipal And Corporate Debt," **JOF**, 1983, v38(2), 625-634.

Skelton, Jeffrey. (Ingersoll, Jonathan E., Jr., Jeffrey Skelton and Roman L. Weil. "Duration Forty Years Later," **JFQA**, 1978, v13(4), 627-650.)

Skelton, Lisa B. (Davidson, Sidney, Lisa B. Skelton and Roman L. Weil. "The FASB's Inflation Accounting Proposal," **FAJ**, 1979, v35(3), 41-54.)

Skerratt, L. C. L. "The Price Determination Of Convertible Loan Stock: A UK Model," **JBFA**, 1974, v1(3), 429-443.

Skerratt, L. C. L. "The Valuation Of Stock Warrants: A Rejoinder," **JBFA**, 1976, v3(2), 151-152.

Skerratt, L. C. L. "The Valuation Of Stock Warrants: A Comment On The Bird Model," **JBFA**, 1975, v2(3), 389-394.

Skerratt, L. C. L. (Peasnell, K. V. and L. C. L. Skerratt. "Performance Of A Relative Decline Model: An Efficient Markets Interpretation Of Some Results Of Jones, Tweedie And Whittington," **JBFA**, 1978, v5(2), 261-267.)

Skerratt, L. C. L. (Peasnell, K. V. and Skerratt, L. C. L. "Long-Term Debt And Shareholder Wealth: A Comment," **JBFA**, 1976, v3(3), 137-142.)

Skerratt, L. C. L. (Peasnell, K. V. and L. C. L. Skerratt. "Price Indices For Current Cost Accounting - A Reply And Some Further Evidence," **JBFA**, 1977, v4(1), 139-144.)

Skerratt, L. C. L. (Peasnell, K. V., L. C. L. Skerratt and P. A. Taylor. "An Arbitrage Rationale For Tests Of Mutual Fund Performance," **JBFA**, 1979, v6(3), 373-400.)

Skinner, David L. and John E. Gilster, Jr. "Dividend Clienteles, The Tax-Clientele Hypothesis, And Utilities," **FR**, 1990, v25(2), 287-296.

Skinner, Douglas J. "Options Markets And Stock Return Volatility," **JFEC**, 1989, v23(1), 61-78.

Skinner, Steven J. (Dubinsky, Alan J., Terry L. Childers, Steven J. Skinner and Esra Gencturk. "Impact Of Sales Supervisor Leadership Behavior On Insurance Agent Attitudes And Performance," **JRI**, 1988, v55(1), 132-144.)

Skinner, Steven J. and Alan J. Dubinsky. "Purchasing Insurance: Predictors Of Family Decision-Making Responsibility," **JRI**, 1984, v51(3), 513-523.

Skipper, Harold D., Jr. "Protectionism In The Provision Of International Insurance Services," **JRI**, 1987, v54(1), 55-85.

Skipper, Harold D., Jr. (Chung, Yosup and Harold D. Skipper, Jr. "The Effect Of Interest Rates On Surrender Values Of Universal Life Policies," **JRI**, 1987, v54(2), 341-347.)

Skipper, Harold, Jr. "Replacement Vulnerability Of Older Non-Participating Ordinary Life Policies," JRI, 1980, v47(4), 691-712.)

Skipper, Harold, Jr. "The Effect Of Premium Payment Frequency On Life Insurance Cost Rankings," JRI, 1980, v47(2), 291-304.

Skipper, Harold, Jr. "The Privacy Implications Of Insurers' Information Practices," JRI, 1979, v46(1), 9-32.

Skipper, Harold, Jr. "The Privacy Implications Of Insurers' Information Practices: Reply," JRI, 1980, v47(2), 341-345.

Sklarz, Michael A. (Miller, Norman G. and Michael A. Sklarz. "A Note On Leading Indicators Of Housing Market Price Trends," JRER, 1986, v1(1), 99-109.)

Sklarz, Michael A. (Miller, Norman G. and Michael A. Sklarz. "Pricing Strategies And Residential Property Selling Prices," JRER, 1987, v2(1), 31-40.)

Sklarz, Michael A. (Miller, Norman G., Michael A. Sklarz and Nicholas Ordway. "Japanese Purchases, Exchange Rates And Speculation In Residential Real Estate Markets," JRER, 1988, v3(3), 39-49.)

Sklarz, Michael A. (Miller, Norman G. and Michael A. Sklarz. "Tax Rates And Implicit Rates Of Return On Owner-Occupied Single-Family Housing: A Comment," JRER, 1989, v4(1), 81-84.)

Sklarz, Michael A., Norman G. Miller and Will Gersch. "Forecasting Using Long-Order Autoregressive Processes: An Example Using Housing Starts," AREUEA, 1987, v15(4), 374-388.

Skogh, Goran. "Returns To Scale In The Swedish Property-Liability Insurance Industry," JRI, 1982, v49(2), 218-228.

Skogh, Goran. "The Transactions Costs Theory Of Insurance: Contracting Impediments And Costs," JRI, 1989, v56(4), 726-732.

Skogstad, Samuel L. (Ederington, Louis H. and Samuel L. Skogstad. "Measurement Of Banking Competition And Geographic Markets: The Market For Checking Account Services," JMCB, 1977, v9(3), 469-482.)

Skogsvik, Kenth. "Current Cost Accounting Ratios As Predictors Of Business Failures: The Swedish Case," JBFA, 1990, v17(1), 137-160.

Skomp, Stephen E. (Henderson, Glenn and Stephen E. Skomp. "Geometric Expositon Of CAPM-Based Capital Budgeting," JFED, 1983, v12, 1-16.)

Skomp, Stephen E. (Henderson, Glenn V., Jr. and Stephen E. Skomp. "A Pedagogical Note On CAPM-Based Capital Budgeting," FR, 1981, v16(2), 51-58.)

Skomp, Stephen E., Timothy P. Cronan and William L. Seaver. "On Application Of The Rank Transformation Discrimination Method To Financial Problems," FR, 1986, v21(4), 473-483.

Slade, Helen. "Edicts Of Kings," FAJ, 1951, v7(1), 59-61.

Slade, Helen. "The Road Of Progress," FAJ, 1949, v5(4), 5-8.

Slatin, Benjamin. "Current Trends In The Paper Industry," FAJ, 1964, v20(1), 35-40.

Slaughter, William C. (Reilly, Frank K. and William C. Slaughter. "The Effect Of Dual Markets On Common Stock Market Making," JPQA, 1973, v8(2), 167-182.)

Slemrod, Joel. (Gordon, Roger H. and Joel Slemrod. "A General Equilibrium Simulation Study Of Subsidies To Municipal Expenditures," JOF, 1983, v38(2), 585-594.)

Slemrod, Joel. (Hendershott, Patric H. and Joel Slemrod. "Taxes And The User Cost Of Capital For Owner-Occupied Housing," AREUEA, 1982, v10(4), 375-393.)

Slesinger, Reuben E. "Broad Economics Of Iron And Steel Industry," FAJ, 1960, v16(1), 15-18.

Slesinger, Reuben E. "Economic Forces Contributing To Inflation," FAJ, 1958, v14(4), 69-72.

Slesinger, Reuben E. "The Federal Reserve System," FAJ, 1959, v15(1), 37-40.

Slinkman, Craig W. (Herbst, Anthony F. and Craig W. Slinkman. "Political-Economic Cycles In The U.S. Stock Market," FAJ, 1984, v40(2), 38-44.)

Slivka, Ronald T. "Call Option Spreading," JPM, 1980-81, v7(3), 71-76.

Slivka, Ronald T. "Risk And Return For Option Investment Strategies," FAJ, 1980, vl. 36(5), 67-73.

Sloan, Frank A. (Hoerger, Thomas J., Frank A. Sloan and Mahmud Hassan. "Loss Volatility, Bankruptcy, And The Demand For Reinsurance," JRU, 1990, v3(3), 221-246.)

Sloan, Frank A. (Steinwald, Bruce and Frank A. Sloan. "Determinants Of Physicians' Fees," JOB, 1974, v47(4), 493-511.)

Sloan, Frank A. (Wedig, Gerard, Frank A. Sloan, Mahmud Hassan and Michael A. Morrisey. "Capital Structure, Ownership, And Capital Payment Policy: The Case Of Hospitals," JOF, 1988, v43(1), 21-40.)

Sloan, Frank A. (Wedig, Gerard J., Mahmud Hassan and Frank A. Sloan. "Hospital Investment Decisions And The Cost Of Capital," JOB, 1989, v62(4), 517-538.)

Sloan, Frank A. and John H. Lorant. "The Role Of Waiting Time: Evidence From Physicians' Practices," JOB, 1977, v50(4), 486-507.

Sloane, William R. and Arnold Reisman. "Stock Evaluation Theory: Classification, Reconciliation, And General Model," JPQA, 1968, v3(2), 171-204.

Sloane, William R. "A Scholarly Approach To The Teaching Of Finance," FR, 1970, v1(5), 358-359.

Sloane, William R. "Life Insurers, Variable Annuities And Mutual Funds: A Critical Study," JRI, 1970, v37(1), 87-104.

Sloane, William R. "Life Insurers, Variable Annuities And Mutual Funds: A Critical Study: Reply," JRI, 1971, v38(3), 483-486.

Sloane, William R. (Martin, Dale R. and William R. Sloane. "Financial Leverage: A More Precise Approach," JBFA, 1980, v7(4), 585-590.)

Slocum, John W., Jr. and Robert H. Strawser. "The Impact Of Job Level, Geographical Location And Organizational Size On The Managerial Satisfaction Of Bankers," JBR, 1970-71, v1(3), 41-49.

Slocum, John W., Jr. (Mathews, H. Lee and John W. Slocum, Jr. "Correlatives Of Commercial Bank Credit Card Use," JBR, 1971-72, v2(4), 20-27.)

Sloss, James. "The Demand For Intercity Motor Freight Transport: A Macroeconomic Analysis," JOB, 1971, v44(1), 62-68.

Slottje, D. J. (Nieswiadomy, Michael L. and D. J. Slottje. "Estimating Lost Future Earnings Using The New Worklife Tables: Comment," JRI, 1988, v55(3), 539-544.)

Slovic, Paul, Baruch Fischhoff, Sarah Lichtenstein, Bernard Corrigan and Barbara Combs. "Preference For Insuring Against Probable Small Losses: Insurance Implications," JRI, 1977, v44(2), 237-258.

Slovic, Paul, Dan Fleissner and W. Scott Bauman. "Analyzing The Use Of Information In Investment Decision Making: A Methodological Proposal," JOB, 1972, v45(2), 283-301.

Slovic, Paul. "Psychological Study Of Human Judgment: Implications For Investment Decision Making," JOF, 1972, v27(4), 779-799.

Slovin, M. B. (Hirschey, M., M. B. Slovin and J. K. Zaima. "Bank Debt, Insider Trading, And The Return To Corporate Selloffs," JBF, 1990, v14(1), 85-98.)

Slovin, M. B. and J. E. Young. "Bank Lending And Initial Public Offering," JBF, 1990, v14(4), 729-740.

Slovin, Myron B. and Marie Elizabeth Sushka. "A Model Of The Commercial Loan Rate," JOF, 1983, v38(5), 583-1596.

Slovin, Myron B. and Marie Elizabeth Sushka. "A Note On The Evidence On Alternative Models Of The Banking Firm: A Cross Section Study Of Commercial Loan Rates," JBF, 1984, v8(1), 99-108.

Slovin, Myron B. and Marie Elizabeth Sushka. "The Structural Shift In The Demand For Money," JOF, 1975, v30(3), 721-731.

Slovin, Myron B. "Financial Disintermediation In A Macroeconomic Framework: Comment," JOF, 1974, v29(3), 1016-1019.

Slovin, Myron B. "On The Relationships Among Monetary Aggregates," JMCB, 1974, v6(3), 353-366.

Slovin, Myron B. (Barrett, W. Brian, Myron B. Slovin and Marie E. Sushka. "Reserve Regulation And Recourse As A Source Of Risk Premia In The Federal Funds Market," JBF, 1988, v11(4), 575-584.)

Slovin, Myron B. (Polonchek, John, Myron B. Slovin and Marie E. Sushka. "Valuation Effects Of Commercial Bank Securities Offerings: A Test Of The Information Hypothesis," JBF, 1989, v13(3), 443-462.)

Slovin, Myron B. (Sushka, Marie Elizabeth and Myron B. Slovin. "The Macroeconomic Impact Of Changes In The Ceilings On Deposit Rates," JOF, 1977, v32(1), 117-130.)

Slovin, Myron B., Marie E. Sushka and Carl D. Hudson. "Corporate Commercial Paper, Note Issuance Facilities, And Shareholder Wealth," JIMF, 1988, v7(3), 289-302.

Slovin, Myron B., Marie E. Sushka and John A. Polonchek. "Corporate Sale-And-Leasebacks And Shareholder Wealth," JOF, 1990, v45(1), 289-300.

Smaistrla, Charles J. and Adrian W. Throop. "A New Inflation In The 1970s?," FAJ, 1980, v36(2), 47-52,54-57.

Smerling, Saul A. "Found: A Realistic Market Measure," FAJ, 1957, v13(2), 59-64.

Smidt, Seymour. "A Bayesian Analysis Of Project Selection And Of Post Audit Evaluations," JOF, 1979, v34(3), 675-688.

Smidt, Seymour. "A New Look At The Random Walk Hypothesis," JPQA, 1968, v3(3), 235-261.

Smidt, Seymour. "Continuous Versus Intermittent Trading On Auction Markets," JPQA, 1979, v14(4), 837-867.

Smidt, Seymour. "Evaluating The Risk Of Investment Projects," FR, 1968, v1(3), 155-165.

Smidt, Seymour. "Investment Horizons And Performance Measurement," JPM, 1977-78, v4(2), 18-22.

Smidt, Seymour. "Long-Run Trends In Equity Turnover," JPM, 1990, v17(1), 66-73.

Smidt, Seymour. "The Road To An Efficient Stock Market," FAJ, 1971, v27(5), 18-20,64-69.

Smidt, Seymour. (Bierman, Harold, Jr. and Seymour Smidt. "Application Of The Capital Asset Pricing Model To Multi-Period Investments," JBFA, 1975, v2(3), 327-340.)

Smidt, Seymour. (Bierman, Harold and Seymour Smidt. "Capital Budgeting And The Problem Of Reinvesting Cash Proceeds," JOB, 1957, v30(4), 276-279.)

Smidt, Seymour. (Brenner, Menachem and Seymour Smidt. "Asset Characteristics And Systematic Risk," FM, 1978, v7(4), 33-39.)

Smidt, Seymour. (Brenner, Menachem and Seymour Smidt. "A Simple Model Of Non-Stationarity Of Systematic Risk," JOF, 1977, v32(4), 1081-1092.)

Smidt, Seymour. (Lakonishok, Josef and Seymour Smidt. "Are Seasonal Anomalies Real? A Ninety-Year Perspective," RFS, 1988-89, v1(4), 403-425.)

Smidt, Seymour. (Lakonishok, Josef and Seymour Smidt. "Trading Bargains In Small Firms At Year-End," JPM, 1985-86, v12(3), 24-29.)

Smidt, Seymour. (Lakonishok, Josef and Seymour Smidt. "Volume And Turn-Of-The-Year Behavior," JFEC, 1984, v13(3), 435-455.)

Smidt, Seymour. (Lakonishok, Josef and Seymour Smidt. "Capital Gain Taxation And Volume Of Trading," JOF, 1986, v41(4), 951-976.)

Smidt, Seymour. (Lakonishok, Josef and Seymour Smidt. "Past Price Changes And Current Trading Volume," JPM, 1989, v15(4), 18-25.)

Smilen, Kenneth B. (Safian, Kenneth and Kenneth B. Smilen. "Relative Earnings: A Fresh Perspective," FAJ, 1964, v20(5), 104-107.)

Smiley, Robert H. and Scott D. Stewart. "White Knights And Takeover Bids," FAJ, 1985, v41(1), 19-26.

Smiley, Robert H. (Dunkelberg, William C. and Robert H. Smiley. "Subsidies In The Use Of Revolving Credit," JMCB, 1975, v7(4), 469-490.)

Smirlock Michael. "Seasonality And Bond Market Returns," JPM, 1984-85, v11(3), 42-44.

Smirlock, M. (Yawitz, J., H. Kaufold, T. Macirowski and M. Smirlock. "The Pricing And Duration Of Floating Rate Bonds," JPM, 1986-87, v13(4), 49-56.)

Smirlock, Michael and Jess Yawitz. "Asset Returns, Discount Rate Changes, And Market Efficiency," JOF, 1985, v40(4), 1141-1158.

Smirlock, Michael and Laura Starks. "A Further Examination Of Stock Price Changes And Transaction Volume," JFR, 1985, v8(3), 227-236.

Smirlock, Michael and Laura Starks. "Day-Of-The-Week And Intraday Effects In Stock Returns," JFEC, 1986, v17(1), 197-210.

Smirlock, Michael and William Marshall. "An Examination Of The Empirical Relationship Between The Dividend And Investment Decisions: A Note," JOF, 1983, v38(5), 1659-1667.

Smirlock, Michael L. (Gilligan, Thomas W. and Michael L. Smirlock. "An Empirical Study Of Joint Production And Scale Economies In Commercial Banking," JBF, 1984, v8(1), 67-78.)

Smirlock, Michael and Howard Kaufold. "Bank Foreign Lending, Mandatory Disclosure Rules, And The Reaction Of Bank Stock Prices To The Mexican Debt Crisis," JOB, 1987, v60(3), 347-364.

Smirlock, Michael and Laura Starks. "An Empirical Analysis Of The Stock Price-Volume Relationship," *JBF*, 1988, v12(1), 31-42.

Smirlock, Michael. "Evidence On The (Non) Relationship Between Concentration And Profitability In Banking," *JMCB*, 1985, v17(1), 69-83.

Smirlock, Michael. "Private Pension Fund Assets: Projected Growth To 1990," *JRI*, 1980, v47(2), 321-330.

Smirlock, Michael. (Benninga, Simon and Michael Smirlock. "An Empirical Analysis Of The Delivery Option, Marking To Market, And The Pricing Of Treasury Bond Futures," *JFM*, 1985, v5(3), 361-374.)

Smirlock, Michael. (Kaufold, Howard and Michael Smirlock. "Managing Corporate Exchange And Interest Rate Exposure," *FM*, 1986, v15(3), 64-72.)

Smirlock, Michael. (Kaufold, Howard and Michael Smirlock. "The Impact Of Credit Risk On The Pricing And Duration Of Floating-Rate Notes," *JBF*, 1991, v15(1), 43-52.)

Smirlock, Michael. (Saunders, Anthony and Michael Smirlock. "Intra-And Interindustry Effects Of Bank Securities Market Activities: The Case Of Discount Brokerage," *JFQA*, 1987, v22(4), 467-482.)

Smith, Abbie J. "Corporate Ownership Structure And Performance: The Case Of Management Buyouts," *JFEC*, 1990, v27(1), 143-164.

Smith, Abbie. (Marais, Laurentius, Katherine Schipper and Abbie Smith. "Wealth Effects Of Going Private For Senior Securities," *JFEC*, 1989, v23(1), 155-191.)

Smith, Abbie. (Schipper, Katherine and Abbie Smith. "A Comparison Of Equity Carve-Outs And Seasoned Equity Offerings: Share Price Effects And Corporate Restructuring," *JFEC*, 1986, v15(1/2), 153-186.)

Smith, Abbie. (Schipper, Katherine and Abbie Smith. "Effects Of Recontracting On Shareholder Wealth: The Case Of Voluntary Spin-Offs," *JFEC*, 1983, v12(4), 437-468.)

Smith, Barry D. "A Model For Workers' Compensation Group Self Insurance: The Delaware Valley School Districts Plan," *JRI*, 1983, v50(3), 521-532.

Smith, Barry D. "A Note On The Application Of The Normal Power Method When Estimating Maximum Probable Yearly Aggregate Loss," *JRI*, 1983, v50(1), 157-160.

Smith, Barry D. "An Analysis Of Auto Liability Loss Reserves And Underwriting Results," *JRI*, 1980, v47(2), 305-320.

Smith, Barry D. "Analyzing The Tax Deductibility Of Premiums Paid To Captive Insurers," *JRI*, 1986, v53(1), 85-103.

Smith, Barry D. "The Effect Of Life Insurance Underwriting Practices On Mortality Results," *JRI*, 1985, v52(3), 441-463.

Smith, Bruce D. "Accelerated Debt Repayment In Leveraged Leases," *FM*, 1982, v11(2), 73-80.

Smith, Bruce D. and Michael J. Stutzer. "Credit Rationing And Government Loan Programs: A Welfare Analysis," *AREUEA*, 1989, v17(2), 177-193.

Smith, Bruce D. and Michael J. Stutzer. "Adverse Selection, Aggregate Uncertainty, And The Role For Mutual Insurance Contracts," *JOB*, 1990, v63(4), 493-510.

Smith, Bruce D. and Michael J. Stutzer. "Adverse Selection And Mutuality: The Case Of The Farm Credit System," *JFI*, 1990, v1(2), 125-149.

Smith, C. R. "How Not To Operate An Airline," *FAJ*, 1956,v12(1),51-54.

Smith, Charles A. and George D. Greenwade. "The Rankings Of Real Estate Publications And Tenure Requirements At AACSB Versus Non-AACSB Schools," *JRER*, 1987, v2(2), 105-112.

Smith, Charles A. and Mark J. Kroll. "Utility Theory And Rent Optimization: Utilizing Cluster Analysis To Segment Rental Markets," *JRER*, 1989, v4(1), 61-71.

Smith, Charles. (Kroll, Mark J. and Charles Smith. "Buyer's Response Technique - A Framework For Improving Comparable Selection And Adjustment In Single-Family Appraising," *JRER*, 1988, v3(1), 27-35.)

Smith, Chas. B. "Rule 144 And Technological Innovation," *FAJ*, 1973, v29(6), 38-41,85.

Smith, Clifford W. and Rene M. Stulz. "The Determinants Of Firms' Hedging Policies," *JFQA*, 1985, v20(4), 391-406.

Smith, Clifford W. "Option Pricing: A Review," *JFEC*, 1976, v3(1/2), 3-51.

Smith, Clifford W., Jr. and Jerold B. Warner. "On Financial Contracting: An Analysis Of Bond Covenants," *JFEC*, 1979, v7(2), 117-162.

Smith, Clifford W., Jr. and L. MacDonald Wakeman. "Determinants Of Corporate Leasing Policy," *JOF*, 1985, v40(4), 895-908.

Smith, Clifford W., Jr. and Jerold B. Warner. "Bankruptcy, Secured Debt, And Optimal Capital Structure: Comment," *JOF*, 1979, v34(1), 247-251.

Smith, Clifford W., Jr. "Alternative Methods For Raising Capital: Rights Versus Underwritten Offerings," *JFEC*, 1977, v5(3), 273-307.

Smith, Clifford W., Jr. "Investment Banking And The Capital Acquisition Process," *JFEC*, 1986, v15(1/2), 3-29.

Smith, Clifford W., Jr. "On The Convergence Of Insurance And Finance Research," *JRI*, 1986, v53(4), 693-717.

Smith, Clifford W., Jr. "Pricing Mortgage Originations," *AREUEA*, 1982, v10(3), 313-330.

Smith, Clifford W., Jr. (Barclay, Michael J. and Clifford W. Smith, Jr., "Corporate Payout Policy: Cash Dividends Versus Open-Market Repurchases," *JFEC*, 1988, v22(1), 61-82.)

Smith, Clifford W., Jr. (Benston, George J. and Clifford W. Smith, Jr. "A Transactions Cost Approach To The Theory Of Financial Intermediation," *JOF*, 1976, v31(2), 215-231.)

Smith, Clifford W., Jr. (Brickley, James A., Ronald C. Lease and Clifford W. Smith, Jr. "Ownership Structure And Voting On Antitakeover Amendments," *JFEC*, 1988, v20(1/2), 267-292.)

Smith, Clifford W., Jr. (Hansen, Ronald W., Paul W. MacAvoy and Clifford W. Smith, Jr. "Compensation Alternatives For Occupational Disease And Disability," *JRI*, 1989, v56(2), 252-274.)

Smith, Clifford W., Jr. (Hess, Alan C. and Clifford W. Smith, Jr. "Elements Of Mortgage Securitization," *JREFEC*, 1988, v1(4), 331-346.)

Smith, Clifford W., Jr. (Mayers, David and Clifford W. Smith, Jr. "Death And Taxes: The Market For Flower Bonds," *JOF*, 1987, v42(3), 685-698.)

Smith, Clifford W., Jr. (Mayers, David and Clifford W. Smith, Jr. "On The Corporate Demand For Insurance," *JOB*, 1982, v55(2), 281-296.)

Smith, Clifford W., Jr. (Mayers, David and Clifford W. Smith, Jr. "Ownership Structure And Control: The Mutualization Of Stock Life Insurance Companies," *JFEC*, 1986, v16(1), 73-98.)

Smith, Clifford W., Jr. (Mayers, David and Clifford W. Smith, Jr. "Contractual Provisions, Organizational Structure, And Conflict Control In Insurance Markets," *JOB*, 1981, v54(3), 407-434.)

Smith, Clifford W., Jr. (Mayers, David and Clifford W. Smith, Jr. "On The Corporate Demand For Insurance: Evidence From The Reinsurance Market," *JOB*, 1990, v63(1), Part 1, 19-40.)

Smith, Clifford W., Jr. (Mayers, David and Clifford W. Smith, Jr. "Corporate Insurance And The Underinvestment Problem," *JRI*, 1987, v54(1), 45-54.)

Smith, Clifford W., Jr. (Phillips, Susan M. and Clifford W. Smith, Jr. "Trading Costs For Listed Options: The Implications For Market Efficiency," *JFEC*, 1980, v8(2), 179-201.)

Smith, Clifford W., Jr., Charles W. Smithson and Lee Macdonald Wakeman. "The Market For Interest Rate Swaps," *FM*, 1988, v17(4), 34-44.

Smith, Clifford W., Jr., Charles W. Smithson and D. Sykes Wilford. "Managing Financial Risk," *JACF*, 1989, v1(4), 27-48.

Smith, Clifford, Jr. (Milne, Frank and Clifford Smith, Jr. "Capital Asset Pricing With Proportional Transaction Costs," *JFQA*, 1980, v15(2), 253-266.)

Smith, Dan Throop. "Government Financial Aid To Small Business: Fiscal Policy," *JOF*, 1951, v6(2), 150-160.

Smith, David B. "A Framework For Analyzing Nonconvertible Preferred Stock Risk," *JFR*, 1983, v6(2), 127-139.

Smith, David B. "Systems Engineering - Implications For Management," *FAJ*, 1965, v21(3), 119-127.

Smith, David B. (Strachan, James L., David B. Smith and William L. Beedles. "The Price Reaction To (Alleged) Corporate Crime," *FR*, 1983, v18(2), 121-132.)

Smith, David L. "Characteristics Of Merging Banks," *FR*, 1970, v1(5), 303-319.

Smith, David L. "The Performance Of Merging Banks," *JOB*, 1971, v44(2), 184-192.

Smith, David M. (Billingsley, Randall S., Robert E. Lamy and David M. Smith. "Units Of Debt With Warrants: Evidence Of The 'Penalty-Free' Issuance Of An Equity-Like Security," *JFR*, 1990, v13(3), 187-200.)

Smith, Dean G. and Lawrence C. Rose. "The Effects Of Insurance Policy Limits On Product Choice," *JRI*, 1986, v53(3), 514-520.

Smith, Donald J. "A Theoretic Framework For The Analysis Of Credit Union Decision Making," *JOF*, 1984, v39(4), 1155-1168.

Smith, Donald J. "Credit Union Rate And Earnings Retention Decisions Under Uncertainty And Taxation," *JMCB*, 1988, v20(1), 119-131.

Smith, Donald J. "Individual Retirement Accounts And Intermediate Term Holding Periods," *FR*, 1984, v19(4), 381-387.

Smith, Donald J. "Risk-Efficient Lottery Bets?!," *JPM*, 1987-88, v14(1), 25-28.

Smith, Donald J. "The Arithmetic Of Financial Engineering," *JACF*, 1989, v1(4), 49-58.

Smith, Donald J. "The Borrower's Choice Between Fixed And Adjustable Rate Loan Contracts," *AREUEA*, 1987, v15(2), 110-115.

Smith, Donald J. "The Demand For And Supply Of Deposits By Credit Unions: The Caisses Populaires' Case-Correction And Comment," *JBF*, 1983, v7(2), 285-287.

Smith, Donald J. "The Duration Of A Bond As A Price Elasticity And A Fulcrum," *JFED*, 1988, v17, 26-38.

Smith, Donald J. "The Pricing Of Bull And Bear Floating Rate Notes: An Application Of Financial Engineering," *FM*, 1988, v17(4), 72-81.

Smith, Donald J. (Brown, Keith C. and Donald J. Smith. "Recent Innovations In Interest Rate Risk Management And The Reintermediation Of Commercial Banking," *FM*, 1988, v17(4), 45-58.)

Smith, Donald J. (Brown, Keith and Donald J. Smith. "Forward Swaps, Swap Options, And The Management Of Callable Debt," *JACF*, 1990, v2(4), 59-71.)

Smith, Donald J., Thomas F. Cargill and Robert A. Meyer. "An Economic Theory Of A Credit Union," *JOF*, 1981, v36(2), 519-528.

Smith, E. Dan. (Salamon, Gerald L. and E. Dan Smith. "Additional Evidence On The Time Series Properties Of Reported Earnings Per Share: Comment," *JOF*, 1977, v32(5), 1795-1801.)

Smith, Edgar Lawrence. "Low Tide In Sunspots - 1964," *FAJ*, 1963, v19(4), 91-92.

Smith, Ephraim P. "Requirements For Stock Option Plans," *FAJ*, 1969, v25(5), 64-70.

Smith, Eric H. "Economic And Competitive Factors In The Nuclear Power Industry," *FAJ*, 1966, v22(1), 116-122.

Smith, Eric H. "Economic And Competitive Factors In The Nuclear Power Industry - Part Two," *FAJ*, 1966, v22(2), 149-155.

Smith, Ethan A., Jr. "The Big Breakthrough In Beryllium," *FAJ*, 1960, v16(6), 51-54.

Smith, Felix C. "An Investment Trust Views The Rails," *FAJ*, 1958, v14(1), 45-48.

Smith, Franklin C. "The Interest-Only Method As An Interim Funding Option For Public Pension Plans: Comment," *JRI*, 1979, v46(4), 733-734.

Smith, Franklin C. "The Use Of Inflation Factors In Determining Settlements In Personal Injury And Death Suits," *JRI*, 1976, v43(3), 369-376.

Smith, Franklin C. "The Use Of Inflation Factors In Determining Settlements In Personal Injury And Death Suits: Reply," *JRI*, 1977, v44(3), 479-480.

Smith, Gary and William Brainard. "The Value Of A Priori Information In Estimating A Financial Model," *JOF*, 1976, v31(5), 1299-1322.

Smith, Gary and William Brainard. "A Disequilibrium Model Of Savings And Loan Associations," *JOF*, 1982, v37(5), 1277-1294.

Smith, Gary and William Starnes. "A Short-Run Two-Sector Model With Immobile Capital," *JMCB*, 1979, v11(1), 47-67.

Smith, Gary. "A Simple Model For Estimating Intrinsic Value," *JPM*, 1981-82, v8(4), 46-49.

Market Research: Evidence On The Small Firm Effect," **JFQA,** 1985, v20(4), 501-516.)

Smith, Richard L., II. (Booth, James R. and Richard L. Smith, II. "The Impact Of The Community Reinvestment Act On Branching Activity Of Financial Institutions," **JBR,** 1984-85, v15(2), 123-128.)

Smith, Richard L., II. (Booth, James R. and Richard L. Smith, II. "Capital Raising, Underwriting And The Certification Hypothesis," **JFEC,** 1986, v15(1/2), 261-281.)

Smith, Richard L., II. (Brown, Stephen W., Richard L. Smith, II and George J. Zurowski. "The Appropriateness And Applicability Of Image Research To Banking," **JBR,** 1977-78, v8(2), 94-100.)

Smith, Richard L., II. (Officer, Dennis T. and Richard L. Smith, II. "Announcement Effects Of Withdrawn Security Offerings: Evidence On The Wealth Redistribution Hypothesis," **JFR,** 1986, v9(3), 229-238.)

Smith, Robert S. (Ruser, John W. and Robert S. Smith. "The Effect Of OSHA Records-Check Inspections On Reported Occupational Injuries In Manufacturing Establishments," **JRU,** 1988, v1(4), 415-435.)

Smith, Rodney T. "An Economic Analysis Of Income Growth By U.S. Oil Firms: The Roles Of U.S. Oil Regulation And OPEC," **JOB,** 1982, v55(4), 427-478.

Smith, Rodney T. "In Search Of The 'Just' U.S. Oil Policy: A Review Of Arrow And Kalt And More," **JOB,** 1981, v54(1), 87-116.

Smith, Scott L. (Schroeter, John R. and Scott L. Smith. "A Reexamination Of The Rationality Of The Livingston Price Expectations," **JMCB,** 1986, v18(2), 239-246.)

Smith, Stanley D. (Liu, Pu, Stanley D. Smith and Azmat A. Syed. "Stock Price Reactions To The Wall Street Journal's Securities Recommendations," **JFQA,** 1990, v25(3), 399-410.)

Smith, Stanley D. (Sirmans, G. Stacy, Stanley D. Smith and C. F. Sirmans. "Assumption Financing And Selling Price Of Single-Family Homes," **JFQA,** 1983, v18(3), 307-317.)

Smith, Stanley D. (Syed, Azmat A., Pu Liu and Stanley D. Smith. "The Exploitation Of Inside Information At The Wall Street Journal: A Test Of Strong Form Efficiency," **FR,** 1989, v24(4), 567-580.)

Smith, Stanley D. and G. Stacy Sirmans. "The Shifting Of FHA Discount Points: Actual Vs. Expectations," **AREUEA,** 1984, v12(2), 153-161.

Smith, Stanley D. and Kenneth L. Stanley. "Social Security Retirement Age: Alternatives And Cost Comparisons," **JRI,** 1981, v48(4), 694-699.

Smith, Stephen D. (Le Compte, Richard L. B. and Stephen D. Smith. "Changes In The Cost Of Intermediation: The Case Of Savings And Loans," **JOF,** 1990, v45(4), 1337-1346.)

Smith, Stephen D. (Morgan, George Emir, III and Stephen D. Smith. "Basis Risk, Partial Takedown And Hedging By Financial Intermediaries," **JBF,** 1986, v10(4), 467-490.)

Smith, Stephen D. (Morgan, George Emir and Stephen D. Smith. "The Role Of Capital Adequacy Regulation In The Hedging Decisions Of Financial Intermediaries," **JFR,** 1987, v10(1), 33-46.)

Smith, Stephen D. (Morgan, George Emir and Stephen D. Smith. "Maturity Intermediation And Intertemporal Lending Policies Of Financial Intermediaries," **JOF,** 1987, v42(4), 1023-1034.)

Smith, Stephen D. (Morgan, George Emir, Dilip K. Shome and Stephen D. Smith. "Optimal Futures Positions For Large Banking Firms," **JOF,** 1988, v43(1), 175-195.)

Smith, Stephen D. (Shome, Dilip K. and Stephen D. Smith. "An Econometric Analysis Of Equity Costs And Risk Premiums In The Electric Utility Industry: 1971-1985," **FR,** 1988, v23(4), 439-452.)

Smith, Stephen D. (Shome, Dilip K., Stephen D. Smith and Arnold A. Heggestad. "Capital Adequacy And The Valuation Of Large Commercial Banking Organizations," **JFR,** 1986, v9(4), 331-341.)

Smith, Stephen D. (Shome, Dilip K., Stephen D. Smith and John M. Pinkerton. "The Purchasing Power Of Money And Nominal Interest Rates: A Re-Examination," **JOF,** 1988, v43(5), 1113-1125.)

Smith, Stephen D., Deborah Wright Gregory and Kathleen A. Weiss. "A Note On Quantity Versus Price Risk And The Theory Of Financial Intermediation," **JOF,** 1987, v42(5), 1377-1383.

Smith, Stephen. (Oren, Shmuel, Stephen Smith and Robert Wilson. "Producing A Product Line," **JOB,** 1984, v57(1), Part 2, S73-S100.

Smith, Terrence C. (Scott, Jonathan A. and Terrence C. Smith. "The Effect Of The Bankruptcy Reform Act Of 1978 On Small Business Loan Pricing," **JFEC,** 1986, v16(1), 119-140.)

Smith, Terrence R. and Daniel Martin. "The Determinants Of Manpower Costs In The Examination Of Banks In The Second Federal Reserve District," **JBR,** 1978-79, v9(3), 161-167.

Smith, V. Kerry and Joseph J. Seneca. "A Further Note On The Cost Implications Of Fluctuating Demand," **JFQA,** 1970, v5(3), 369-376.

Smith, V. Kerry and Richard G. Marcis. "Post Accord Interest Rates: A Reply," **JOF,** 1974, v29(4), 1326-1327.

Smith, V. Kerry and Richard G. Marcis. "A Time Series Analysis Of Post-Accord Interest Rates," **JOF,** 1972, v27(3), 589-605.

Smith, V. Kerry, William H. Desvousges, Ann Fisher and F. Reed Johnson. "Learning About Radon's Risk," **JRU,** 1988, v1(2), 233-258.

Smith, V. Kerry. "A Note On Student's t Test In Multiple Regression," **JFQA,** 1971, v6(3), 1053-1056.

Smith, V. Kerry. "On The Use Of Two-Stage Least Squares In Financial Models: A Comment," **JFQA,** 1976, v11(3), 505-509.

Smith, V. Kerry. (Liu, Jin Tan and V. Kerry Smith. "Risk Communication And Attitude Change: Taiwan's National Debate Over Nuclear Power," **JRU,** 1990, v3(4), 331-350.)

Smith, V. Kerry. (Marcis, Richard G. and V. Kerry Smith. "The Demand For Liquid Asset Balances By U. S. Manufacturing Corporations: 1959-1970," **JFQA,** 1973, v8(2), 207-218.)

Smith, V. Kerry. (Marcis, Richard G. and V. Kerry Smith. "Efficient Estimation Of Multivariate Financial Relationships," **JOF,** 1974, v29(5), 1411-1423.)

Smith, Vernon L. "Experimental Studies Of Discrimination Versus Competition In Sealed-Bid Auction Markets," **JOB,** 1967, v40(1), 56-84.

Smith, Vernon L. (Cox, James C., Vernon L. Smith and James M. Walker. "Theory And Behavior Of Multiple Unit Discriminative Auctions," **JOF,** 1984, v39(4), 983-1010.)

Smith, Vernon L. (Cox, James C., Vernon L. Smith and James M. Walker. "Theory And Individual Behavior Of First-Price Auctions," **JRU,** 1988, v1(1), 61-100.)

Smith, Vernon L. (Walker, James M., Vernon L. Smith and James C. Cox. "Inducing Risk-Neutral Preferences: An Examination In A Controlled Market Environment," **JRU,** 1990, v3(1), 5-24.)

Smith, Vernon L. (Williams, Arlington W. and Vernon L. Smith. "Cyclical Double-Auction Markets With And Without Speculators," **JOB,** 1984, v57(1), Part 1, 1-34.)

Smith, W. B. "The Effect Of The Corporate Financial Plan On The Corporate Risk Management Program," **JOF,** 1964, v19(2), Part 1, 334-339.

Smith, W. James. "Sensitivity Analysis Of Rates Of Return: Comment," **JOF,** 1978, v33(5), 1457-1460.

Smith, Warren L. "The Outlook For Federal Reserve And Treasury Policy," **JOF,** 1959, v14(2), 288-301.

Smith, William. (Findlay, M. Chapman, III and William Smith. "Some Canadian Implications Of International Portfolio Diversification," **FR,** 1976, v11(1), 36-48.)

Smith, Winfield. (Dean, Joel and Winfield Smith. "Has MAPI A Place In A Comprehensive System Of Capital Controls?," **JOB,** 1955, v28(4), 261-274.)

Smithson, Charles W. (Rawls, S. Waite, III and Charles W. Smithson. "The Evolution Of Risk Management Products," **JACF,** 1989, v1(4), 18-26.)

Smithson, Charles W. (Rawls, S. Waite, III and Charles W. Smithson. "Strategic Risk Management," **JACF,** 1990, v2(4), 6-18.)

Smithson, Charles W. (Smith, Clifford W., Jr., Charles W. Smithson and Lee Macdonald Wakeman. "The Market For Interest Rate Swaps," **FM,** 1988, v17(4), 34-44.)

Smithson, Charles W. (Smith, Clifford W., Jr., Charles W. Smithson and D. Sykes Wilford. "Managing Financial Risk," **JACF,** 1989, v1(4), 27-48.)

Smithsonian, Edward J. Mitchell and John L. McKnight. "Nuggets: Hares, Lynx, Energy, And Crooked Teeth," **JPM,** 1977-78, v4(3), 5-11.

Smucker, David E. "The American Railroads In A Changing World," **FAJ,** 1958, v14(1), 37-40.

Smyth, D. J. (Briscoe, G., J. M. Samuels and D. J. Smyth. "The Treatment Of Risk In The Stock Market," **JOF,** 1969, v24(4), 707-713.)

Smyth, Henry D. "Industrial Application Of Atomic Energy," **JOB,** 1954, v27(4), 312-320.

Smyth, T. Lynn. "The Distribution And Movements Of The Aged Population," **JOB,** 1954, v27(2), 109-118.

Snailer, Joseph. (Arak, Marcelle, Laurie S. Goodman and Joseph Snailer. "Duration Equivalent Bond Swaps: A New Tool," **JPM,** 1985-86, v12(4), 26-32.)

Snavely, Howard J. "Pooling Is Good Accounting," **FAJ,** 1968, v24(6), 85-89.

Snider, H. Wayne. "Beneficial Risks," **JRI,** 1968, v35(1), 139-140.

Snider, H. Wayne. "Educational Requirements For Agents' Licensing," **JRI,** 1963, v30(2), 281-285.

Snider, H. Wayne. "Inland Marine Rating And Rate Regulation," **JRI,** 1963, v30(1), 61-80.

Snider, H. Wayne. "Population, Prejudice And Pensions," **JRI,** 1960, v27(3), 37-42.

Snider, H. Wayne. "Problems Of Professionalism," **JRI,** 1963, v30(4), 563-572.

Snider, H. Wayne. "Teaching Risk Management," **JRI,** 1961, v28(2), 41-44.

Snider, H. Wayne. "Toward Building An Insurance Department," **JRI,** 1971, v38(1), 113-116.

Snider, Thomas E. "The Effect Of Merger On The Lending Behavior Of Rural Unit Banks In Virginia," **JBR,** 1973-74, v4(1), 52-57.

Snider, William D. "Building An On-Line Financial Planning Model," **JBR,** 1973-74, v4(3), 232-238.

Snyder, Edward A. (Kormendi, Roger C., Victor L. Bernard, S. Craig Pirrong and Edward A. Snyder. "The Origins And Resolution Of The Thrift Crisis," **JACF,** 1989, v2(3), 85-99.)

Snyder, Gerard L. "A Look At Options," **FAJ,** 1967, v23(1), 100-103.

Snyder, Gerard L. "Alternative Forms Of Options," **FAJ,** 1969, v25(5), 93-99.

Snyder, Gerard L. "Tender Offering For Stock Options," **FAJ,** 1973, v29(4), 30-32.

Snyder, Gerard L. "The Coming Impact Of Mass Transit," **FAJ,** 1966, v22(4), 55-58.

Snyder, W. Howard T. "How To Take A Loss And Like It," **FAJ,** 1957, v13(2), 115-116.

Snyder, Wayne W. "Horse Racing: Testing The Efficient Markets Model," **JOF,** 1978, v33(4), 1109-1118.

Snyderman, Mark P. "A Commercial Mortgage Performance Index," **JPM,** 1990, v16(3), 70-73.

So, Jacky C. "Commodity Future Risk Premium And Unstable Systematic Risk," **JPM,** 1987, v7(3), 311-326.

So, Jacky C. "Some Empirical Evidence On The Outliers And The Non-Normal Distribution Of Financial Ratios," **JBFA,** 1987, v14(4), 483-496.

So, Jacky C. "The Distribtuion Of Foreign Exchange Price Changes: Trading Day Effects And Risk Measurement--A Comment," **JOF,** 1987, v42(1), 181-188.

Sobotka, Stephen P. "Michigan's Employment Problem: The Substitution Against Labor," **JOB,** 1961, v34(2), 119-128.

Sobotka, Stephen P. and Constance Schnabel. "Linear Programming As A Device For Depicting Market Value: Prices Of Used Commercial Aircraft, 1959-65," **JOB,** 1961, v34(1), 10-30.

Sobti, Rajiv. "Increasing Social Variability And Insurance Equilibrium," **JRI,** 1988, v55(3), 509-517.

Soday, Frank J. "Ammonia As A Petrochemical Raw Material," **FAJ,** 1951, v7(4), 41-52.

Soday, Frank J. "Resources And Research Affecting Development Of The South," **FAJ,** 1956, v12(2), 67-74.

Soday, Frank J. "The Chemical Industry Looks South," **FAJ,** 1952, v8(5), 51-60

Soenen, Luc A. (Aggarwal, Raj and Luc A. Soenen. "The Nature And Efficiency Of The Gold Market," **JPM,** 1987-88, v14(3), 18-21.)

Soenen, Luc A. (Ma, Christopher K. and Luc A. Soenen. "Arbitrage Opportunities In Metal Futures Markets," *JFM*, 1988, v8(2), 199-209.)

Soenen, Luc A. and Raj Aggarwal. "Cash And Foreign Exchange Management: Theory And Corporate Practice In Three Countries," *JBFA*, 1989, v16(5), 599-620.

Soenen, Luc. (Beckers, Stan and Luc Soenen. "Gold: More Attractive To Non-U.S. Than To U.S. Investors?," *JBFA*, 1984, v11(1), 107-112.)

Soffer, Benson. (Herrnstadt, Irwin L. and Benson Soffer. "Recent Labor Disputes Over 'Restrictive' Practices And 'Inflationary' Wage Increases," *JOB*, 1961, v34(4), 453-470.)

Sofianos, G., P. Wachtel and A. Melnik. "Loan Commitments And Monetary Policy," *JBF*, 1990, v14(4), 677-690.

Sokoler, Meir. (Gheva, David and Meir Sokoler. "An Alternative Approach To The Problem Of Classification - The Case Of Bank Failures In Israel," *JBR*, 1981-82, v12(4), 228-238.)

Sokoler, Meir. (Paroush, Jacob and Meir Sokoler. "The Firm's Trade Credit Under Uncertainty And Some Macro Implications," *RIF*, 1983, v4, 153-164.)

Solanki, R. (Brennan, M. J. and R. Solanki. "Optimal Portfolio Insurance," *JFQA*, 1981, v16(3), 279-300.)

Solberg, Donald P. (McCabe, George M. and Donald P. Solberg. "Hedging In The Treasury Bill Futures Market When The Hedged Instrument And The Deliverable Instrument Are Not Matched," *JFM*, 1989, v9(6), 529-538.)

Solberg, Donald. (Marcus, Richard D., Donald Solberg and Terry L. Zivney. "A Reexamination Of The Benefits To International Diversification," *RDIBF*, 1991, v4/5, 310-335.)

Solberg, Harry J. "A Method For Consumer Valuation Of Life Insurance Policies By Type: Reply," *JOF*, 1963, v18(4), 688-690.

Solberg, Harry J. "A Method For Consumer Valuation Of Life Insurance Policies By Type," *JOF*, 1962, v17(4), 634-645.

Solberg, Harry J. "An Analysis Of The Aging Of A Life Insurance Program," *JRI*, 1965, v32(3), 395-400.

Solberg, Harry J. "The Profit Factor In Fire Insurance Rates," *JRI*, 1957, v24(2), 24-33.

Solberg, Harry J. (Howard, William M. and Harry J. Solberg. "Perpetual Fire Insurance," *JOF*, 1958, v13(1), 70-79.)

Soldofsky, R. M. "Institutional Ownership Of Common Stock To The Year 2000," *FR*, 1971, v2(1), 15-26.

Soldofsky, R. M. (Johnson, C. R. and R. M. Soldofsky. "Rights Timing," *FAJ*, 1967, v23(4), 101-104.)

Soldofsky, Robert M. and Roger L. Miller. "Risk-Premium Curves For Different Classes Of Long-Term Securities, 1950-1966," *JOF*, 1969, v24(3), 429-445.

Soldofsky, Robert M. and Roger Biderman. "Yield-Risk Measurements Of The Performance Of Common Stocks," *JFQA*, 1968, v3(1), 59-74.

Soldofsky, Robert M. and Roger L. Miller. "Risk-Premium Curves For Different Classes Of Long-Term Securities, 1950-1966: Reply," *JOF*, 1972, v27(4), 940-943.

Soldofsky, Robert M. and Roger L. Miller. "Risk-Premium Curve Vs. Capital Line: A Further Work," *FM*, 1978, v7(1), 65-72.

Soldofsky, Robert M. and Walter W. McMahon. "A Comment On Variable Annuities," *JOF*, 1957, v12(3), 372-376.

Soldofsky, Robert M. "A Note On The History Of Bond Tables And Stock Valuation Models," *JOF*, 1966, v21(1), 103-111.

Soldofsky, Robert M. "College Retirement Benefit Planning: A Snare Of Uncertainty For All Concerned," *JRI*, 1967, v34(2), 269-288.

Soldofsky, Robert M. "Growth Yields," *FAJ*, 1961, v17(5), 43-47.

Soldofsky, Robert M. "Performance Of Convertibles," *FAJ*, 1971, v27(2), 61-65,79.

Soldofsky, Robert M. "Private Placement Loans For Small Business," *JRI*, 1959, v26(4), 51-58.

Soldofsky, Robert M. "Programming The Three-Phase Dividend Model: Comment," *JPM*, 1979-80, v6(2), 74.

Soldofsky, Robert M. "Risk And Return For Long-Term Securities: 1971-1982," *JPM*, 1984-85, v11(1), 57-67.

Soldofsky, Robert M. "Risk-Return Characteristics Of Convertible Preferred Stock: Reply," *JPM*, 1983-84, v10(2), 79.

Soldofsky, Robert M. "Risk-Return Performance Of Convertibles," *JPM*, 1980-81, v7(2), 80-84.

Soldofsky, Robert M. "The Size And Maturity Of Direct-Placement Loans," *JOF*, 1960, v15(1), 32-44.

Soldofsky, Robert M. "Yield-Risk Performance Measurements," *FAJ*, 1968, v24(5), 130-139.

Soldofsky, Robert M. (Bhandari, Shyam B., Robert M. Soldofsky and Warren J. Boe. "Bond Quality Rating Changes For Electric Utilities: A Multivariate Analysis," *FM*, 1979, v8(1), 74-81.)

Soldofsky, Robert M. (Pogue, Thomas F. and Robert M. Soldofsky. "What's In A Bond Rating?," *JFQA*, 1969, v4(2), 201-228.)

Soldofsky, Robert M. (Schweser, Carl, Robert M. Soldofsky and Tom Schneeweis. "The Meaning Of The Mean," *JPM*, 1978-79, v5(4), 23-27.)

Soleil, M. "A New Payment Technique: The Memory Card," *JBR*, 1980-81, v11(4), 214-218.

Solnik, B. H. "The International Pricing Of Risk: An Empirical Investigation Of The World Capital Market Structure," *JOF*, 1974, v29(2), 365-378.

Solnik, B. "International Parity Conditions And Exchange Risk: A Review," *JBF*, 1978, v2(3), 281-293.

Solnik, B. (Brennan, M. J. and B. Solnik. "International Risk Sharing And Capital Mobility," *JIMF*, 1989, v8(3), 359-374.)

Solnik, B. and L. Bousquet. "Day-Of-The-Week Effect On The Paris Bourse," *JBF*, 1990, v14(2/3), 461-468.

Solnik, Bruno and Bernard Noetzlin. "Optimal International Asset Allocation," *JPM*, 1982-83, v9(1), 11-21.

Solnik, Bruno H. and Jean Grall. "Eurobonds: Determining The Demand For Capital And The International Interest Rate Structure," *JBR*, 1974-75, v5(4), 218-230.

Solnik, Bruno H. "An Empirical Investigation Of The Determinants Of National Interest Rate Differences," *JIMF*, 1982, v1(3), 333-339.

Solnik, Bruno H. "An International Market Model Of Security Price Behavior," *JFQA*, 1974, v9(4), 537-554.

Solnik, Bruno H. "Inflation And Optimal Portfolio Choices," *JFQA*,

1978, v13(5), 903-925.

Solnik, Bruno H. "Note On The Validity Of The Random Walk For European Stock Prices," *JOF*, 1973, v28(5), 1151-1159.

Solnik, Bruno H. "Testing International Asset Pricing: Some Pessimistic Views," *JOF*, 1977, v32(2), 503-512.

Solnik, Bruno H. "Why Not Diversify Internationally?," *FAJ*, 1974, v30(4), 48-54.

Solnik, Bruno H. (McDonald, John G. and Bruno H. Solnik. "Valuation And Strategy For Gold Stocks," *JPM*, 1976-77, v3(3), 29-33.)

Solnik, Bruno H. (Pogue, Gerald A. and Bruno H. Solnik. "The Market Model Applied To European Common Stocks: Some Empirical Results," *JFQA*, 1974, v9(6), 917-944.)

Solnik, Bruno and Arlei De Freitas. "International Factors Of Stock Price Behavior," *RDIBF*, 1988, v2, 259-276.

Solnik, Bruno. "International Arbitrage Pricing Theory," *JOF*, 1983, v38(2), 449-457.

Solnik, Bruno. "Stock Prices And Monetary Variables: The International Evidence," *FAJ*, 1984, v40(2), 69-73.

Solnik, Bruno. "The Distribution Of Daily Stock Returns And Settlement Procedures: The Paris Bourse," *JOF*, 1990, v45(5), 1601-1610.

Solnik, Bruno. "The Relation Between Stock Prices And Inflationary Expectations: The International Evidence," *JOF*, 1983, v38(1), 35-48.

Solnik, Bruno. "Using Financial Prices To Test Exchange Rate Models: A Note," *JOF*, 1987, v42(1), 141-149.

Solnik, Bruno. (Cholerton, Kenneth, Pierre Pieraerts and Bruno Solnik. "Why Invest In Foreign Currency Bonds?," *JPM*, 1985-86, v12(4), 4-8.)

Solnik, Bruno. (Garrone, Francois and Bruno Solnik. "A Global Approach To Money Management," *JPM*, 1975-76, v2(4), 5-14.)

Solnik, Bruno. (Jacquillat, Bertrand and Bruno Solnik. "Multinationals Are Poor Tools For Diversification," *JPM*, 1977-78, v4(2), 8-12.)

Solo, Robert A. "Automation: Technique, Mystique, Critique," *JOB*, 1963, v36(2), 166-178.

Solo, Robert A. "Intra-Enterprise Conspiracy And The Theory Of The Firm," *JOB*, 1961, v34(2), 153-166.

Solomon, Arthur P. "A National Policy And Budgetary Framework For Housing And Community Development," *AREUEA*, 1977, v5(2), 147-170.

Solomon, Arthur P. (Colton, Kent W., Donald R. Lessard and Arthur P. Solomon. "Borrower Attitudes Toward Alternative Mortgage Instruments," *AREUEA*, 1979, v7(4), 581-609.)

Solomon, Benjamin and Robert K. Burns. "Unionization Of White-Collar Employees: Extent, Potential, And Implications," *JOB*, 1963, v36(2), 141-165.

Solomon, Benjamin. "The Growth Of The White-Collar Work Force," *JOB*, 1954, v27(4), 268-275.

Solomon, E. Ray. "Inheritance Taxation Of Life Insurance," *JRI*, 1963, v30(3), 393-402.

Solomon, Elinor H. "Bank Merger Policy And Problems: A Linkage Theory Of Oligopoly," *JMCB*, 1970, v2(3), 323-336.

Solomon, Elinor H. (Savage, Donald T. and Elinor H. Solomon. "Branch Banking: The Competitive Issues," *JBR*, 1980-81, v11(2), 110-121.)

Solomon, Ezra. "Economic Growth And Common Stock Values," *JOB*, 1955, v28(3), 213-221.

Solomon, Ezra. "Leverage And The Cost Of Capital," *JOF*, 1963, v18(2), 273-279.

Solomon, Ezra. "Measuring A Company's Cost Of Capital," *JOB*, 1955, v28(4), 240-252.

Solomon, Ezra. "The Arithmetic Of Capital Budgeting-Decisions," *JOB*, 1956, v29(2), 124-129.

Solomon, Ezra. "The Current Recovery: An Analysis," *JOB*, 1955, v28(2), 95-99.

Solomon, Ezra. "The Economic Outlook-1959," *JOB*, 1959, v32(1), 74-78.

Solomon, Ezra. "What Should We Teach In A Course In Business Finance?," *JOF*, 1966, v21(2), 411-415.

Solomon, Ira and Don Vickrey. "Restatement Of The Numerosity Paradox And Criticism Of Its Purported Resolution," *JBFA*, 1980, v7(3), 481-488.

Solomon, Paul J. (Hair, Joseph F., Jr., Paul J. Solomon and Ronald F. Bush. "A Factor Analytic Study Of Black Models In Television Commercials," *JOB*, 1977, v50(2), 208-215.)

Solomon, Robert J. "Testing Techniques In Insurance," *JRI*, 1960, v27(1), 53-64.

Solomons, David. "The Determination Of Asset Values," *JOB*, 1962, v35(1), 28-42.

Soloway, Arnold M. "Economic Aspects Of The British Purchase Tax," *JOF*, 1954, v9(2), 188-208.

Solt, Michael E. (Lee, Wayne Y. and Michael E. Solt. "Insider Trading: A Poor Guide To Market Timing," *JPM*, 1985-86, v12(4), 65-71.)

Solt, Michael E. (Leonard, David C. and Michael E. Solt. "Recent Evidence On The Accuracy And Rationality Of Popular Inflation Forecasts," *JFR*, 1986, v9(4), 281-290.)

Solt, Michael E. (Leonard, David C. and Michael E. Solt. "Stock Market Signals Of Changes In Expected Inflation," *JFR*, 1987, v10(1), 57-64.)

Solt, Michael E. (Leonard, David C. and Michael E. Solt. "On Using The Black-Scholes Model Of Value Warrants," *JFR*, 1990, v13(2), 81-92.)

Solt, Michael E. and Meir Statman. "How Useful Is The Sentiment Index?," *FAJ*, 1988, v44(5), 45-55.

Solt, Michael E. and Meir Statman. "Good Companies, Bad Stocks," *JPM*, 1989, v15(4), 39-44.

Solt, Michael E. and Norman G. Miller. "Managerial Incentives: Implications For The Financial Performance Of Real Estate Investment Trusts," *AREUEA*, 1985, v13(4), 404-423.

Solt, Michael E. and Paul J. Swanson. "On The Efficiency Of The Markets For Gold And Silver," *JOB*, 1981, v54(3), 453-478.

Soltow, Allen R. (Luckett, Dudley G. and Allen R. Soltow. "Determinants Of Interest Rate Expectations," *JMCB*, 1972, v4(2), 272-282.)

Somanath, V. S. "Efficient Exchange Rate Forecasts: Lagged Models Better Than The Random Walk," *JIMF*, 1986, v5(2), 195-220.

Somers, Harold M. "Estate Taxes And Business Mergers: The Effects Of Estate Taxes On Business Structure And Practices In The United States," JOF, 1958, v13(2), 201-210.

Somers, Harold M. "On The Demise Of The Social Discount Rate," JOF, 1971, v26(2), 565-578.

Sommariva, Andrea and Giuseppe Tullio. "International Gold Flows In Gold Standard Germany: A Test Of The Monetary Approach To The Balance Of Payments, 1880-1911," JMCB, 1988, v20(1), 132-140.

Sommariva, Andrea and Giuseppe Tullio. "The German Depression And The Stock Market Crash Of The Thirties: The Role Of Macropolicies And Of The International Business Cycle," JBF, 1989, v13(4/5), 515-536.

Sommer, Armand. "The War And Accident And Health Insurance," JRI, 1943, v10, 59-68.

Sommers, Albert T. "Forecasting And The Diffusion Indexes," FAJ, 1958, v14(1), 23-29.

Sommers, Albert T. "Inflation And Domestic Economic Policy," FAJ, 1975, v31(1), 18-26.

Sondhi, Ashwinpaul C. (Livnat, Joshua and Ashwinpaul C. Sondhi. "Finance Subsidiaries: Their Formation And Consolidation," JBFA, 1986, v13(1), 137-148.)

Sondhi, Ashwinpaul C. (Selling, Thomas I., Ashwinpaul C. Sondhi and George H. Sorter. "Consolidating Captive Finance Subsidiaries: The Impact Of SFAS 94 On Financial Statements," FAJ, 1989, v45(6), 72-75.)

Sondhi, Ashwinpaul C., George H. Sorter and Gerald I. White. "Transactional Analysis," FAJ, 1987, v43(5), 57-64.

Song, In Man. (Lobo, Gerald J., R. D. Nair and In Man Song. "Additional Evidence On The Information Content Of Dividends," JBFA, 1986, v13(4), 597-608.)

Song, Moon H. (Stulz, Rene M., Ralph A. Walkling and Moon H. Song. "The Distribution Of Target Ownership And The Division Of Gains In Successful Takeovers," JOF, 1990, v45(3), 817-834.)

Sono, Kenji. "A Note On Insurance Education In Japan," JRI, 1964, v31(4), 647.

Sontheimer, Kevin. " On The Determination Of Money Prices," JMCB, 1972, v4(3), 489-508.

Sorensen, Eric H. and Clark A. Hawkins. "On The Pricing Of Preferred Stock," JFQA, 1981, v16(4), 515-528.

Sorensen, Eric H. and Clark A. Hawkins. "The Demand For Preferred Stock With Sinking Funds And Without: A Note," JOF, 1982, v37(1), 237-241.

Sorensen, Eric H. and David A. Williamson. "Some Evidence On The Value Of Dividend Discount Models," FAJ, 1985, v41(6), 60-69.

Sorensen, Eric H. and James E. Wert. "A New Tool For Estimating New Issue Bond Yields," JPM, 1980-81, v7(3), 42-45.

Sorensen, Eric H. and Terry Burke. "Portfolio Returns From Active Industry Group Rotation," FAJ, 1986, v42(5), 43-50.

Sorensen, Eric H. "An Analysis Of The Relationship Between Underwriter Spread And The Pricing Of Municipal Bonds," JFQA, 1980, v15(2), 435-447.

Sorensen, Eric H. "Bond Ratings Versus Market Risk Premiums," JPM, 1979-80, v6(3), 64-69.

Sorensen, Eric H. "Negotiated Municipal Bond Underwritings: Implications For Efficiency," JMCB, 1979, v11(3), 366-370.

Sorensen, Eric H. "On The Seasoning Process Of New Bonds: Some Are More Seasoned Than Others," JFQA, 1982, v17(2), 195-208.

Sorensen, Eric H. "Rational Expectations And The Impact Of Money Upon Stock Prices," JFQA, 1982, v17(5), 649-662.

Sorensen, Eric H. "The Impact Of Underwriting Method And Bidder Competition Upon Corporate Bond Interest Cost," JOF, 1979, v34(4), 863-870.

Sorensen, Eric H. (Gould, J. B. and Eric H. Sorensen. "Duration: A Factor In Equity Pricing," JPM, 1986-87, v13(1), 38-43.)

Sorensen, Eric H. (Kidwell, David S., Eric H. Sorensen and John M. Wachowicz, Jr. "Estimating The Signaling Benefits Of Debt Insurance: The Case Of Municipal Bonds," JFQA, 1987, v22(3), 299-314.)

Sorensen, Eric H. (Kidwell, David S. and Eric H. Sorensen. "Pricing Of Municipal Bond Underwritings: It May Pay To Invest When Underwriters Don't," FAJ, 1983, v39(2), 58-64.)

Sorensen, Eric H. (Kim, Wi Saeng and Eric H. Sorensen. "Evidence On The Impact Of The Agency Costs Of Debt On Corporate Debt Policy," JFQA, 1986, v21(2), 131-144.)

Sorensen, Eric H. (Leibowitz, Martin L., Eric H. Sorensen, Robert D. Arnott and H. Nicholas Hanson. "A Total Differential Approach To Equity Duration," FAJ, 1989, v45(5), 30-37.)

Sorensen, Eric H. (Rogowski, Robert J. and Eric H. Sorensen. "Deregulation In Investment Banking: Shelf Registrations, Structure, And Performance," FM, 1985, v14(1), 5-15.)

Sorensen, Eric H. and Robert D. Arnott. "The Risk Premium And Stock Market Performance," JPM, 1987-88, v14(4), 50-55.

Sorensen, Eric. "Who Puts The Slope In The Municipal Yield Curve?," JPM, 1982-83, v9(4), 61-65.

Sorensen, Ivar W. and Ramon E. Johnson. "Equipment Financial Leasing Practices And Costs: An Empirical Study," FM, 1977, v6(1), 33-40.

Sorensen, Peter F., Jr. (Baum, Bernard H. and Peter F. Sorensen, Jr. "Influence Relationships As Administrative Organizational Data," JRI, 1966, v33(1), 63-71.)

Sorensen, Peter F., Jr. (Whisler, Thomas L., Harald Meyer, Bernard H. Baum and Peter F. Sorensen, Jr. "Centralization Of Organizational Control: An Empirical Study Of ITs Meaning And Measurement," JOB, 1967, v40(1), 10-26.)

Sorensen, Roy A. "An 'Essential Reservation' About The EMH," JPM, 1982-83, v9(4), 29-30.

Sorenson, L. Orlo. (Ouattara, Korotoumou, Ted C. Schroeder and L. Orlo Sorenson. "Potential Use Of Futures Markets For International Marketing Of Cote D'Ivoire Coffee," JFM, 1990, v10(2), 113-122.)

Soros, George. "European Financial Analysts' Congress," FAJ, 1966, v22(6), 147-148.

Sorrentino, Alessandro. (Monke, Eric A. and Alessandro Sorrentino. "Exchange Rate Changes And Commodity Futures Prices," RFM, 1987, v6(2), 218-238.)

Sorter, George H. "Reported Income And Inventory Change," JOB, 1959, v32(1), 47-51.

Sorter, George H. (Davidson, Sidney, George H. Sorter, and Hemu Kalle. "Measuring The Defensive Position Of A Firm," FAJ, 1964, v20(1), 23-29.)

Sorter, George H. (Ingberman, Monroe, Joshua Ronen and George H. Sorter. "Lease Capitalization And Financial Ratios," FAJ, 1979, v35(1), 28-31.)

Sorter, George H. (Ronen, Joshua and George H. Sorter. "Relevant Accounting," JOB, 1972, v45(2), 258-282.)

Sorter, George H. (Selling, Thomas I. and George H. Sorter. "FASB Statement No. 52 And Its Implications For Financial Statement Analysis," FAJ, 1983, v39(3), 64-69.)

Sorter, George H. (Selling, Thomas I., Ashwinpaul C. Sondhi and George H. Sorter. "Consolidating Captive Finance Subsidiaries: The Impact Of SFAS 94 On Financial Statements," FAJ, 1989, v45(6), 72-75.)

Sorter, George H. (Sondhi, Ashwinpaul C., George H. Sorter and Gerald I. White. "Transactional Analysis," FAJ, 1987, v43(5), 57-64.)

Sosin, H. B. (Sharpe, W. F. and H. B. Sosin. "Risk, Return And Yield On Common Stock," FAJ, 1976, v32(2), 33-42.)

Sosin, Howard B. "Neutral Recapitalizations: Predictions And Tests Concerning Valuation And Welfare," JOF, 1978, v33(4), 1228-1234.

Sosin, Howard B. "On The Valuation Of Federal Loan Guarantees To Corporations," JOF, 1980, v35(5), 1209-1221.

Sosin, Howard B. (Goldman, M. Barry, Howard B. Sosin and Lawrence A. Shepp. "On Contingent Claims That Insure Ex-post Optimal Stock Market Timing," JOF, 1979, v34(2), 401-414.)

Sosin, Howard B. (Goldman, M. Barry, Howard B. Sosin and Mary Ann Gatto. "Path Dependent Options: 'Buy At The Low, Sell At The High'," JOF, 1979, v34(5), 1111-1127.)

Sosin, Howard B. (Goldman, M. Barry and Howard B. Sosin. "Information Dissemination, Market Efficiency And The Frequency Of Transactions," JFEC, 1979, v7(1), 29-61.)

Sosin, Howard B. (Litzenberger, Robert H. and Howard B. Sosin. "The Structure And Management Of Dual Purpose Funds," JFEC, 1977, v4(2), 203-230.)

Sosin, Howard B. (Litzenberger, Robert H. and Howard B. Sosin. "The Performance And Potential Of Dual Purpose Funds," JPM, 1977-78, v4(3), 56-68.)

Sosin, Howard B. (Litzenberger, Robert H. and Howard B. Sosin. "A Comparison Of Capital Structure Decisions Of Regulated And Non-Regulated Firms," FM, 1979, v8(3), 17-21.)

Sosin, Howard B. (Litzenberger, Robert H. and Howard B. Sosin. "The Theory Of Recapitalizations And The Evidence Of Dual Purpose Funds," JOF, 1977, v32(5), 1433-1455.)

Sosin, Howard B. (Sandor, Richard L. and Howard B. Sosin. "The Determinants Of Mortgage Risk Premiums: A Case Study Of The Portfolio Of A Savings And Loan Association," JOB, 1975, v48(1), 27-38.)

Sosin, Howard. (Gatto, Mary Ann, Robert Geske, Robert Litzenberger and Howard Sosin. "Mutual Fund Insurance," JFEC, 1980, v8(3), 283-317.)

Sosin, Howard. (Litzenberger, Robert H. and Howard Sosin. "Taxation And The Incidence Of Home Ownership Across Income Groups," JOF, 1978, v33(3), 947-961.)

Sosin, Howard. (Litzenberger, Robert, Krishna Ramaswamy and Howard Sosin. "On The CAPM Approach To The Estimation Of A Public Utility's Cost Of Equity Capital," JOF, 1980, v35(2), 369-383.)

Sosnoff, Martin T. "Hedge Fund Management - A New Respectability For Short Selling," FAJ, 1966, v22(4), 105-108.

Soule, Don M. "Shifting Of The Corporate Income Tax: A Dynamic Analysis," JOF, 1959, v14(3), 390-402.

Sowell, Clifford. (Boyes, William J., William Stewart Mounts and Clifford Sowell. "The Federal Reserve As A Bureaucracy: An Examination Of Expense-Preference Behavior," JMCB, 1988, v20(2), 181-190.)

Spahr, Ronald W. (Martin, Stanley A. and Ronald W. Spahr. "Futures Market Efficiency As A Function Of Market Speculation," RFM, 1983, v2(3), 314-328.)

Spahr, Ronald W. (Dyl, Edward A. and Ronald A. Spahr. "Taxes And The Refunding Of Discount Bonds," JFR, 1983, v6(4), 265-273.)

Spahr, Ronald W. (Emery, Douglas R., J. Ronald Hoffmeister and Ronald W. Spahr. "The Case For Indexing A Bond's Call Price," FM, 1987, v16(3), 57-64.)

Spahr, Ronald W. and Edmond L. Escolas. "1979 Automobile Accident Reports: Do Driver Characteristics Support Rate Discrimination?," JRI, 1982, v49(1), 91-103.

Spahr, Ronald W. and Edmond L. Escolas. "Mortgage Guaranty Insurance: A Unique Style Of Insurance," JRI, 1986, v53(2), 308-319.

Spaid, Orieon M. "The Calculated Risk In Business," JRI, 1963, v30(2), 245-256.

Spangler, C. D. (Manes, Alfred. "Relationship Between Insurance Practice And Theory," JRI, 1937, v4, 32-36.)

Spare, Anthony. (Brush, John S. and Anthony Spare. "Change In Dividend Yield And Portfolio Volatility," JPM, 1990, v16(3), 27-32.)

Spatt, Chester S. "Imperfect Price Discrimination And Variety," JOB, 1983, v56(2), 203-216.

Spatt, Chester S. (Dammon, Robert M., Kenneth B. Dunn and Chester S. Spatt. "A Reexamination Of The Value Of Tax Options," RFS, 1989, v2(3), 341-372.)

Spatt, Chester S. (Dunn, Kenneth B. and Chester S. Spatt. "An Analysis Of Mortgage Contracting: Prepayment Penalties And The Due-on-Sale Clause," JOF, 1985, v40(1), 293-308.)

Spatt, Chester S. (Dunn, Kenneth B. and Chester S. Spatt. "A Strategic Analysis Of Sinking Fund Bonds," JFEC, 1984, v13(3), 399-424.)

Spatt, Chester S. (Dunn, Kenneth B. and Chester S. Spatt. "Private Information And Incentives: Implications For Mortgage Contract Terms And Pricing," JREFEC, 1988, v1(1), 47-60.)

Spatt, Chester S. and Frederic P. Sterbenz. "Warrant Exercise, Dividends, And Reinvestment Policy," JOF, 1988, v43(2), 493-506.

Speaker, Paul J. (Clark, Jeffrey A. and Paul J. Speaker. "Compensating Balance Requirements And The Firm's Demand For Transactions Balances," JBF, 1986, v10(3), 411-429.)

Speakes, Jeffrey K. "Risk Measurement And Risk Management," **JPM**, 1983-84, v10(2), 66-70.

Speakes, Jeffrey K. "The Phased-In Money Market Certificate Hedge," **JFM**, 1983, v3(2), 185-190.

Spector, Warren. (Reichert, Alan, William Strauss, David Northcutt and Warren Spector. "The Impact Of Economic Conditions And Electronic Payments Technology On Federal Reserve Check Volume," **JBR**, 1983-84, v14(4), 291-296.)

Speidell, Lawrence S. "Embarrassment And Riches: The Discomfort Of Alternative Investment Strategies," **JPM**, 1990, v17(1), 6-11.

Speidell, Lawrence S., Deborah H. Miller and James R. Ullman. "Portfolio Optimization: A Primer," **FAJ**, 1989, v45(1), 22-30.

Spellman, L. J. "Competition For Savings Deposits In The U.S.: 1936-1966," **JFQA**, 1975, v10(4), 575-576.

Spellman, Lewis J. "Commercial Banks And The Profits Of Savings And Loan Markets," **JBR**, 1981-82, v12(1), 32-36.

Spellman, Lewis J. "Deposit Ceilings And The Efficiency Of Financial Intermediation," **JOF**, 1980, v35(1), 129-136.

Spellman, Lewis J. "Inflation And Housing Prices," **AREUEA**, 1981, v9(3), 205-222.

Spellman, Lewis J. "Nonrate Competition For Savings Deposits," **JBR**, 1977-78, v8(3), 171-178.

Spellman, Lewis J. (Bradford, William D., Alfred E. Osborne, Jr. and Lewis J. Spellman. "The Efficiency And Profitability Of Minority Controlled Savings And Loan Associations," **JMCB**, 1978, v10(1), 65-74.)

Spellman, Lewis J., Alfred E. Osborne, Jr. and William D. Bradford. "The Comparative Operating Efficiency Of Black Savings And Loan Associations," **JOF**, 1977, v32(2), 565-574.

Spellman, Lewis J., Robert C. Witt and William F. Rentz. "Investment Income And Non-Life Insurance Pricing," **JRI**, 1975, v42(4), 567-577.

Spence, James G. "CML To SML: A Graphical Approach," **FR**, 1984, v19(4), 388-393.

Spencer, David E. "Does Money Matter? The Robustness Of Evidence From Vector Autoregressions," **JMCB**, 1989, v21(4), 442-454.

Spencer, P. C. "A Great Future Needs Great Transportation," **FAJ**, 1960, v16(3), 119-121.

Spencer, P. D. "Speculative And Precautionary Balances As Complements In The Portfolio: The Case Of The U.K. Banking Sector 1972-1980," **JBF**, 1989, v13(6), 811-830.

Spencer, Roger W. and Michael J. Heppen. "Economic Conditions And Life Insurance," **FAJ**, 1969, v25(4), 73-79.

Spencer, Roger W. "LIFO Inventory In Meatpacking Industry," **FAJ**, 1967, v23(1), 59-63.

Spencer, Roger W. (Walz, Daniel T. and Roger W. Spencer. "The Informational Content Of Forward Rates: Further Evidence," **JFR**, 1989, v12(1), 69-82.)

Spengler, Joseph J. "Population Movements And Investment. Part II," **JOF**, 1952, v7(1), 10-27.

Spengler, Joseph J. "Population Movements And Investment. Part I," **JOF**, 1951, v6(4), 343-360.

Spengler, Joseph J. (Kreps, Juanita M., Joseph J. Spengler and Walter Williams. "The Social Security And Pension Fund Systems - Their Place In The American Value Structure: Comment," **JRI**, 1965, v32(4), 621-638.)

Spero, L. L. (Barrett, M. E. and L. L. Spero. "Foreign Exchange Gains And Losses," **FAJ**, 1975, v31(2), 26-30.)

Speyrer, Janet Furman. "The Effect Of Land-Use Restrictions On Market Values Of Single-Family Homes In Houston," **JREFEC**, 1989, v2(2), 117-130.

Spiceland, J. David and Jerry E. Trapnell. "The Effect Of Market Conditions And Risk Classifications On Market Model Parameters," **JFR**, 1983, v6(3), 217-222.

Spicer, Barry H. and Don Vickrey. "The Quality Of Disclosure And The Cost Of Capital," **JBFA**, 1979, v6(2), 245-266.

Spicer, Barry H. "Market Risk, Accounting Data And Companies' Pollution Control Records," **JBFA**, 1978, v5(1), 67-83.

Spiegelglas, Stephen. "Margin Requirements And Stock Market Prices," **FAJ**, 1960, v16(6), 35-37.

Spiegelman, Mortimer. "Our Increasing Longevity And What It Means," **FAJ**, 1952, v8(3), 63-68.

Spies, Richard R. "The Dynamics Of Corporate Capital Budgeting," **JOF**, 1974, v29(3), 829-845.

Spigelman, J. H. "Implications Of Recent Advances In Electronic Data Processing - Part II," **FAJ**, 1964, v20(6), 87-93.

Spigelman, J. H. "Implications Of Recent Advances In Electronic Data Processing," **FAJ**, 1964, v20(5), 137-143.

Spigelman, J. H. (Gumperz, Julian and J. H. Spigelman. "Prospects For Nuclear Energy," **FAJ**, 1964, v20(1), 95-101.)

Spigelman, Joseph H. "Technological Transformation Of The Drug Industry - Part II," **FAJ**, 1966, v22(6), 121-133.

Spigelman, Joseph H. "Technological Transformation Of The Drug Industry," **FAJ**, 1966, v22(5), 113-121.

Spigelman, Joseph H. "The Data Service Industry," **FAJ**, 1969, v25(2), 92-102.

Spigelman, Joseph H. "The Data Service Industry - Part II," **FAJ**, 1969, v25(3), 88-99.

Spigelman, Joseph H. "The Data Service Industry - Part III," **FAJ**, 1969, v25(4), 52-70.

Spigelman, Joseph H. "The Knowledge Revolution - I," **FAJ**, 1972, v28(4), 22-24,26-27,30-32.

Spigelman, Joseph H. "The Knowledge Revolution - II," **FAJ**, 1972, v28(5), 33-40.

Spigelman, Joseph H. "What Basis For Superior Performance?," **FAJ**, 1974, v30(3), 32-34,38-39,42, 44,86.

Spilka, Walter, Jr. "An Overview Of The USDA Crop And Livestock Information System," **JFM**, 1983, v3(2), 167-176.

Spiller, Richard. "Life Insurance Product Innovations: Comment," **JRI**, 1972, v39(1), 139-140.

Spiller, Richard. "Ownership And Performance: Stock And Mutual Life Insurance Companies," **JRI**, 1972, v39(1), 17-26.

Spiller, Richard. "Ownership And Performance: Stock And Mutual Life Insurance Companies: Reply," **JRI**, 1973, v40(4), 635-638.

Spindt, Paul A. and Vefa Tarhan. "Bank Reserve Adjustment Process And The Use Of Reserve Carryover As A Reserve Management Tool: A Microeconometric Approach," **JBF**, 1984, v8(1), 5-20.

Spindt, Paul A. and Vefa Tarhan. "Liquidity Structure Adjustment Behavior Of Large Money Center Banks," **JMCB**, 1980, v12(2), Part 1, 198-208.

Spindt, Paul A. (Benveniste, Lawrence M. and Paul A. Spindt. "How Investment Bankers Determine The Offer Price And Allocation Of New Issues," **JFEC**, 1989, v24(2), 343-362.)

Spindt, Paul A. and J. Ronald Hoffmeister. "The Micromechanics Of The Federal Funds Market: Implications For Day-Of-The-Week Effects In Funds Rate Variability," **JFQA**, 1988, v23(4), 401-416.

Spindt, Paul A. and Vefa Tarhan. "Bank Reserve Adjustment Process And The Use Of Reserve Carryover As A Reserve Management Tool: A Reply," **JBF**, 1989, v13(1), 37-40.

Spindt, Paul. (Barnett, William, Edward Offenbacher and Paul Spindt. "New Concepts Of Aggregated Money," **JOF**, 1981, v36(2),497-505.)

Spires, Eric E. (Greenberg, Ralph H., Robert F. Sharp and Eric E. Spires. "A Practical Method Of Measuring Current Costs Of Technologically Inferior Assets," **JBFA**, 1989, v16(3), 433-442.)

Spiro, Harvey M. "The Use Of Economics In Portfolio Decisions," **JPM**, 1975-76, v2(3), 34-38.

Spiro, Peter S. "The Impact Of Interest Rate Changes On Stock Price Volatility," **JPM**, 1990, v16(2), 63-68.

Spiro, Rosann L. and William D. Perreault, Jr. "Influence Use By Industrial Salesmen: Influence-Strategy Mixes And Situational Determinants," **JOB**, 1979, v52(3), 435-455.

Spitz, A. Edward and Andre DeKorvin. "A New Theoretical Model For Depicting Profit Optimality," **JFQA**, 1971, v6(4), 1117-1121.

Spitzfaden, James. (Baker, H. Kent and James Spitzfaden. "The Impact Of Exchange Listing On The Cost Of Equity Capital," **FR**, 1982, v17(3), 128-141.)

Spivack, Joseph. (Altman, Edward I. and Joseph Spivack. "Predicting Bankruptcy: The Value Line Relative Financial Strength System Vs. The Zeta Bankruptcy Classification Approach," **FAJ**, 1983, v39(6), 60-67.)

Spivak, Avia. (Safra, Zvi, Uzi Segal and Avia Spivak. "The Becker-DeGroot-Marschak Mechanism And Non-Expected Utility," **JRU**, 1990, v3(2), 177-190.)

Spivak, Avia. (Segal, Uzi and Avia Spivak. "Non-Expected Utility Risk Premiums: The Cases Of Probability Ambiguity And Outcome Uncertainty," **JRU**, 1988, v1(3), 333-347.)

Spivey, Michael F. "The Cost Of Including A Call Provision In Municipal Debt Contracts," **JFR**, 1989, v12(3), 203-216.

Spivey, Michael F. (Blackwell, David W., M. Wayne Marr and Michael F. Spivey. "Shelf Registration And The Reduced Due Diligence Argument: Implications Of The Underwriter Certification And The Implicit Insurance Hypotheses," **JFQA**, 1990, v25(2), 245-260.)

Spivey, Michael F. (Blackwell, David W., M. Wayne Marr and Michael F. Spivey. "Plant-Closing Decisions And The Market Value Of The Firm," **JFEC**, 1990, v26(2), 277-288.)

Spong, Kenneth and Thomas Hoenig. "An Examination Of Individual Bank Growth," **JBR**, 1976-77, v7(4), 303-310.

Spooner, Malvin C. "Origin Of Fundamental Analysis," **FAJ**, 1984, v40(4), 79-80.

Sporleder, Thomas L. (Pluhar, Darwin M., Carl E. Shafer and Thomas L. Sporleder. "The Systematic Downward Bias In Live Cattle Futures: A Further Evaluation," **JFM**, 1985, v5(1), 11-20.)

Spraakman, Gary P. "The Sensitivity Of Earnings Per Share Growth To Some Of Its Financial Components," **FM**, 1979, v8(4), 41-46.

Sprague, Ralph H., Jr. (Simkin, Mark G. and Ralph H. Sprague, Jr. "Staffing For Bank Telephone Inquiry Systems: A Decision Analysis," **JBR**, 1976-77, v7(1), 49-55.)

Sprague, Ralph. (Cotlar, Morton and Ralph Sprague. "Multi-Media Cases In Finance," **JFED**, 1974, v3, 69-72.)

Sprecher, C. Ronald and Mars A. Pertl. "Risk Retention And The Market Implied Probability Of Loss," **JRI**, 1980, v47(2), 279-290.

Sprecher, C. Ronald and Mars A. Pertl. "Large Losses, Risk Management And Stock Prices," **JRI**, 1983, v50(1), 107-117.

Sprecher, C. Ronald. "A Note On Financing Mergers With Convertible Preferred Stock," **JOF**, 1971, v26(3), 683-685.

Sprecher, C. Ronald. (Durand, Richard M., Donald W. Eckrich and C. Ronald Sprecher. "Bank Image: An Adequacy-Importance Approach," **JBR**, 1978-79, v9(3), 168-172.)

Sprecher, C. Ronald. (Laughhunn, Dan J. and C. Ronald Sprecher. "Probability Of Loss And The Capital Asset Pricing Model," **FM**, 1977, v6(1), 18-25.)

Sprenkle, C. M. (Aigner, D. J. and C. M. Sprenkle. "On Optimal Financing Of Cyclical Cash Needs," **JOF**, 1973, v28(5), 1249-1254.)

Sprenkle, C. M. (Aigner, D. J. and C. M. Sprenkle. "A Simple Model Of Information And Lending Behavior," **JOF**, 1968, v23(1), 151-166.)

Sprenkle, C. M., S. J. Turnovsky and R. A. Fujihara. "Assets, Aggregates And Optimal Monetary Control," **JBF**, 1990, v14(1), 155-178.

Sprenkle, Case M. and Bryan E. Stanhouse. "A Theoretical Framework For Evaluating The Impact Of Universal Reserve Requirements," **JOF**, 1981, v36(4), 825-840.

Sprenkle, Case M. "An Overdue Note On Some 'Ancient But Popular' Literature," **JOF**, 1974, v29(5), 1577-1580.

Sprenkle, Case M. "Comments On The Papers Of Bloch And Of Greenbaum And Haywood," **JMCB**, 1971, v3(2), Part 2, 599-603.

Sprenkle, Case M. "Is The Precautionary Demand For Money Negative?," **JOF**, 1967, v22(1), 77-82.

Sprenkle, Case M. "Liability And Asset Uncertainty For Banks," **JBF**, 1987, v11(1), 147-160.

Sprenkle, Case M. "On The Precautionary Demand For Assets," **JBF**, 1985, v9(4), 499-515.

Sprenkle, Case M. "The Uselessness Of Transaction Demand Models: Comment," **JOF**, 1977, v32(1), 227-230.

Sprenkle, Case M. "The Uselessness Of Transactions Demand Models," **JOF**, 1969, v24(5), 835-847.

Sprenkle, Case M. "Uncertainty And The Precautionary Demand For Money: Reply," **JOF**, 1967, v22(4), 663-664.

Sprenkle, Case M. (Sherman, Lawrence F., Case M. Sprenkle and Bryan E. Stanhouse. "Reserve Requirements And Control Of The Money Supply," **JMCB**, 1979, v11(4), 486-493.)

Spriggs, Dillard. "Forecasting Oil Industry Profits," **FAJ**, 1966, v22(5), 49-52.

Springate, David J. "Designing A Course In Non-Profit Financial Management," JFED, 1977, v6, 24-26.

Springate, David. "The Advantages Of Early Student Exposure To Cases In Finance," JFED, 1974, v3, 73-75.

Springate, David. "Three Alternative Approaches To The Basic Finance Course," JFED, 1976, v5, 43-44.

Springer, Robert F. and H. E. Frech, III. "Deterring Fraud: The Role Of Resale Price Maintenance," JOB, 1986, v59(3), 433-450.

Sprinkel, Beryl W. "1965 Economic And Financial Prospects," JOB, 1965, v38(1), 5-8.

Sprinkel, Beryl W. "1975: A Year Of Recession, Recovery, And Decelerating Inflation," JOB, 1975, v48(1), 1-4.

Sprinkel, Beryl W. "1976: A Year Of Moderate Expansion And Contained Inflation," JOB, 1976, v49(1), 1-4.

Sprinkel, Beryl W. "An End To Economic Euphoria," JOB, 1967, v40(1), 1-4.

Sprinkel, Beryl W. "Continued Expansion In 1973 Amid Growing Prosperity," JOB, 1973, v46(1), 1-5.

Sprinkel, Beryl W. "Economic Achievements, Problems And Prospects," JOB, 1966, v39(1), Part I, 5-8.

Sprinkel, Beryl W. "Environment For Capital Goods Spending (Keynote Review)," FAJ, 1966, v22(6), 13-15.

Sprinkel, Beryl W. "Further Expansion And Less Inflation In 1972," JOB, 1972, v45(1), 1-5.

Sprinkel, Beryl W. "Highly Expansionary Economic Policies In The Midst Of Inflation," JOB, 1968, v41(1), 1-4.

Sprinkel, Beryl W. "Inflation - Its Cause And Cure," FAJ, 1971, v27(3), 11-16.

Sprinkel, Beryl W. "Measuring Impact Of Monetary Policy," FAJ, 1967, v23(5), 85-87.

Sprinkel, Beryl W. "Monetary Policy, Balance Of Payments, And Financial Markets," JOB, 1963, v36(1), 6-9.

Sprinkel, Beryl W. "Monetary Policy, Balance Of Payments, And Financial Markets," JOB, 1964, v37(1), 25-27.

Sprinkel, Beryl W. "Monetary Growth As A Cyclical Predictor," JOF, 1959, v14(3), 333-346.

Sprinkel, Beryl W. "Moving Toward Economic Stability," JOB, 1969, v42(1), 1-5.

Sprinkel, Beryl W. "Outlook For The Government Bond Market," JOF, 1960, v15(2), 299-304.

Sprinkel, Beryl W. "Recent Federal Reserve Policy," FAJ, 1965, v21(4), 45-51.

Sprinkel, Beryl W. "Recovery: Vigorous Or Lethargic?," FAJ, 1971, v27(4), 9-15.

Sprinkel, Beryl W. "Slow Growth And High Inflation For 1974," JOB, 1974, v47(1), 1-4.

Sprinkel, Beryl W. "The Cost Of Restoring Stability," JOB, 1970, v43(1), 1-5.

Sprinkel, Beryl W. "The Management Of Prosperity: A Review Article," JOB, 1967, v40(2), 149-154.

Sprinkel, Beryl W. "Vigorous Growth And Reduced Inflation In 1971," JOB, 1971, v44(1), 1-5.

Sprinkel, Beryl W. and B. Kenneth West. "Effects Of Capital Gains Taxes On Investment Decisions," JOB, 1962, v35(2), 122-134.

Sprinkel, Beryl Wayne. "Economic Consequences Of The Operations Of The Reconstruction Finance Corporation," JOB, 1952, v25(4), 211-224.

Sprinkle, Beryl W. "The Investment Climate - General Prospects," FAJ, 1960, v16(1), 62-64.

Sproul, Allan. "Coordination Of Economic Policy," JOF, 1967, v22(2), 137-146.

Sproul, Allan. "Reflections Of A Central Banker," JOF, 1956, v11(1), 1-14.

Sprouse, Robert T. "Prospects For Progress In Financial Reporting," FAJ, 1979, v35(5), 56-60.

Sprowls, R. Clay. "Computer Education In The Business Curriculum," JOB, 1963, v36(1), 91-96.

Spruill, M. Lynn. (Sartoris, William L. and M. Lynn Spruill. "Goal Programming And Working Capital Management," FM, 1974, v3(1), 67-74.)

Spudeck, Raymond E. and R. Charles Moyer. "Reverse Splits And Shareholder Wealth: The Impact Of Commissions," FM, 1985, v14(4), 52-56.

Spurdle, John W. "The Oil Industry," FAJ, 1949, v5(4), 31-33.

Squier, Albert P. "Training Prospective Security Analysts," FAJ, 1954, v10(2), 39-40.

Srinidhi, B. N. (Balachandran, K. R. and B. N. Srinidhi. "A Stable Cost Application Scheme For Service Center Usage," JBFA, 1988, v15(1), 87-100.)

Srinidhi, B. N. (Balachandran, Kashi R. and B. N. Srinidhi. "A Note On Cost Allocation, Opportunity Costs And Optimal Utilization," JBFA, 1990, v17(4), 579-584.)

Srinivasan, V., Y. H. Kim and P. J. Bolster. "A Framework For Integrating The Leasing Alternative With The Capital Budgeting Decision," AFPAF, 1989, v3(1), 75-94.

Srinivasan, Venkat and Yong H. Kim. "Designing Expert Financial Systems: A Case Study Of Corporate Credit Management," FM, 1988, v17(3), 32-44.

Srinivasan, Venkat and Yong H. Kim. "Credit Granting: A Comparative Analysis Of Classification Procedures," JOF, 1987, v42(3), 665-681.

Srinivasan, Venkat and Yong H. Kim. "Decision Support For Working Capital Management: A Conceptual Framework," AWCM, 1990, v1(1), 187-216.

Srinivasan, Venkat and Yong H. Kim. "Integrating Corporate Strategy And Multinational Capital Budgeting: An Analytical Framework," RDIBF, 1988, v2, 381-398.

Srinivasan, Venkat, Susan E. Moeller and Yong H. Kim. "International Cash Management: State-Of-The-Art And Research Directions," AFPAF, 1990, v5(1), 161-194.

Srinivasulu, S. L. (Dufey, Gunter and S. L. Srinivasulu. "The Case For Corporate Management Of Foreign Exchange Risk," FM, 1983, v12(4), 54-62.)

Srivastava, R. K., H. R. Isakson, L. Price and T. H. McInish. "Analysis Of The Characteristics Of Individual Investors In Real Estate Securities And Income-Producing Property," AREUEA, 1984, v12(4), 521-541.

Srivastava, Rajendra K. (McInish, Thomas H. and Rajendra K. Srivastava. "Ex-Ante Expectations And Portfolio Selection," FR, 1984, v19(1), 84-96.)

Srivastava, Rajendra K. (McInish, Thomas H. and Rajendra K. Srivastava. "Teaching The Art Of Market Making With A Game Simulation," JFED, 1982, v11, 94-96.)

Srivastava, Rajendra K. and Robert T. Green. "Determinants Of Bilateral Trade Flows," JOB, 1986, v59(4), Part I, 623-640.

Srivastava, Rajendra K., Thomas H. McInish and Linda L. Price. "Information Costs And Portfolio Selection," JBF, 1984, v8(3), 417-429.

Srivastava, Sanjay. (Green, Richard C. and Sanjay Srivastava. "Risk Aversion And Arbitrage," JOF, 1985, v40(1), 257-268.)

Srivastava, Sanjay. (Hodrick, Robert J. and Sanjay Srivastava. "The Covariation Of Risk Premiums And Expected Future Spot Exchange Rates," JIMF, 1986, v5(Supp), S5-S21.)

Srivastava, Sanjay. (Hodrick, Robert J. and Sanjay Srivastava. "An Investigation Of Risk And Return In Forward Foreign Exchange," JIMF, 1984, v3(1), 5-29.)

St. Germain, Fernand J. "Consumer Banking Issues," JBR, 1985-86, v16(4), 244-247.

Stafford, Frank. (Becker, Selwyn W. and Frank Stafford. "Some Determinants Of Organizational Success," JOB, 1967, v40(4), 511-518.)

Stagliano, A. J. (Bedingfield, James P., Philip M. J. Reckers and A. J. Stagliano. "Distributions Of Financial Ratios In The Commercial Banking Industry," JFR, 1985, v8(1), 77-81.)

Stagner, Ross. (Derber, Milton, W. Ellison Chalmers, and Ross Stagner. "Collective Bargaining And Management Functions: An Empirical Study," JOB, 1958, v31(2), 107-120.)

Staking, Kim B. (Babbel, David F. and Kim B. Staking. "A Capital Budgeting Analysis Of Life Insurance Costs In The United States: 1950-1979," JOF, 1983, v38(1), 149-170.)

Staking, Kim B. (Babbel, David F. and Kim B. Staking. "An Engel Curve Analysis Of Gambling And Insurance In Brazil," JRI, 1983, v50(4), 688-696.)

Stalnaker, Armand C. "A Look At The Future Life Agency Force," JRI, 1961, v28(4), 65-72.

Stalnaker, Armand C. "What Is The Real Value Of Education To The Life Agent?: Comment," JRI, 1965, v32(2), 289.

Stambaugh, Robert F. "Arbitrage Pricing With Information," JFEC, 1983, v12(3), 357-370.

Stambaugh, Robert F. "On The Exclusion Of Assets From Tests Of The Two-Parameter Model: A Sensitivity Analysis," JFEC, 1982, v10(3), 237-268.

Stambaugh, Robert F. "Testing The CAPM With Broader Market Indexes: A Problem Of Mean-Deficiency," JBF, 1983, v7(1), 5-16.

Stambaugh, Robert F. "The Information In Forward Rates: Implications For Models Of The Term Structure," JFEC, 1988, v21(1), 41-70.

Stambaugh, Robert F. (Blume, Marshall E. and Robert F. Stambaugh. "Biases In Computed Returns: An Application To The Size Effect," JFEC, 1983, v12(3), 387-404.)

Stambaugh, Robert F. (Chen, Nai-Fu, Bruce Grundy and Robert F. Stambaugh. "Changing Risk, Changing Risk Premiums, And Dividend Yield Effects," JOB, 1990, v63(1), Part 2, SS1-S70.)

Stambaugh, Robert F. (Ferson, Wayne E., Shmuel Kandel and Robert F. Stambaugh. "Tests Of Asset Pricing With Time-Varying Expected Risk Premiums And Market Betas," JOF, 1987, v42(2), 201-220.)

Stambaugh, Robert F. (French, Kenneth R., G. William Schwert and Robert F. Stambaugh. "Expected Stock Returns And Volatility," JFEC, 1987, v19(1), 3-30.)

Stambaugh, Robert F. (Huberman, Gur, Shmuel Kandel and Robert F. Stambaugh. "Mimicking Portfolios And Exact Arbitrage Pricing," JOF, 1987, v42(1), 1-9.)

Stambaugh, Robert F. (Kandel, Shmuel and Robert F. Stambaugh. "On Correlations And Inferences About Mean--Variance Efficiency," JFEC, 1987, v18(1), 61-90.)

Stambaugh, Robert F. (Kandel, Shmuel and Robert F. Stambaugh. "A Mean-Variance Framework For Tests Of Asset Pricing Models," RFS, 1989, v2(2), 125-156.)

Stambaugh, Robert F. (Kandel, Shmuel and Robert F. Stambaugh. "Expectations And Volatility Of Consumption And Asset Returns," RFS, 1990, v3(2), 207-232.)

Stambaugh, Robert F. (Keim, Donald B. and Robert F. Stambaugh. "A Further Investigation Of The Weekend Effect In Stock Returns," JOF, 1984, v39(3), 819-835.)

Stambaugh, Robert F. (Keim, Donald B. and Robert F. Stambaugh. "Predicting Returns In The Stock And Bond Markets," JFEC, 1986, v17(2), 357-390.)

Standish, P. E. M. "Implementing Sandilands: Issues For The Steering Group," JBFA, 1976, v3(1), 147-160.

Stanga, Keith G. "Disclosure In Published Annual Reports," FM, 1976, v5(4), 42-53.

Stangeland, David. (Morck, Randall, Eduardo Schwartz and David Stangeland. "The Valuation Of Foresty Resources Under Stochastic Prices And Inventories," JFQA, 1989, v24(4), 473-488.)

Stangle, Bruce E. (Koehn, Michael F. and Bruce E. Stangle. "The Effect Of Deposit-Rate Ceilings On Bank Risk: A Comment," JBF, 1980, v4(4), 381-386.)

Stanhouse, Bryan and Larry Sherman. "A Note On Information In The Loan Evaluation Process," JOF, 1979, v34(5), 1263-1269.

Stanhouse, Bryan E. (Sherman, Lawrence F., Case M. Sprenkle and Bryan E. Stanhouse. "Reserve Requirements And Control Of The Money Supply," JMCB, 1979, v11(4), 486-493.)

Stanhouse, Bryan E. (Sprenkle, Case M. and Bryan E. Stanhouse. "A Theoretical Framework For Evaluating The Impact Of Universal Reserve Requirements," JOF, 1981, v36(4), 825-840.)

Stanhouse, Bryan. "Commercial Bank Portfolio Behavior And Endogenous Uncertainty," JOF, 1986, v41(5), 1103-1114.

Stanhouse, Bryan. (Fackler, James and Bryan Stanhouse. "Rationality Of The Michigan Price Expectations Data," JMCB, 1977, v9(4), 662-666.)

Stanley, Kenneth L. "Measuring The Operational Costs Of Dual Trading: An Analytical Framework," JFM, v1(3), 329-336.

Stanley, Kenneth L. (Lewellen, Wilbur G., Kenneth L. Stanley, Ronald C. Lease and Gary G. Schlarbaum. "Some Direct Evidence On The Dividend Clientele Phenomenon," JOF, 1978, v33(5), 1385-1399.)

Stanley, Kenneth L. (Smith, Stanley D. and Kenneth L. Stanley. "Social Security Retirement Age: Alternatives And Cost Comparisons," JRI, 1981, v48(4), 694-699.)

Stanley, Kenneth L., Wilbur G. Lewellen and Gary G. Schlarbaum. "Further Evidence On The Value Of Professional Investment Research," JFR, 1981, v4(1), 1-9.

Stanley, Kenneth L., Wilbur G. Lewellen and Gary G. Schlarbaum. "Investor Response To Investment Research," JPM, 1979-80, v6(4), 20-27.

Stanley, Majorie T. and Stanley B. Block. "A Survey Of Multinational Capital Budgeting," FR, 1984, v19(1), 36-54.

Stanley, Majorie. (Becker, Charles M. and Marjorie Stanley. "Equations As A Conceptual Basis For The Money And Banking Course," JFED, 1982, v11, 13-16.)

Stanley, Majorie. (Block, Stanley and Majorie Stanley. "The Financial Characteristics And Price Movement Patterns Of Companies Approaching The Unseasoned Securities Market In The Late 1970s," FM, 1980, v9(4), 30-36.)

Stanley, Thomas. (Ogden, William, Jr., Nanda Rangan and Thomas Stanley. "Risk Reduction In S&L Mortgage Loan Portfolios Through Geographic Diversification," JFSR, 1989, v2(1), 39-48.)

Stanley, W. F. "A New Look At Public Utility Depreciation Reserves," FAJ, 1949, v5(3), 15-19.

Stansell, Stanley R. and James A. Millar. "An Empirical Study Of Mortgage Payment To Income Ratios In A Variable Rate Mortgage Program," JOF, 1976, v31(2), 415-425.

Stansell, Stanley R. "Some Further Comments On The Confidence Index," JBR, 1971-72, v2(3), 55-57.

Stansell, Stanley R. (Bhoocha-Oom, Areepong and Stanley R. Stansell. "A Study Of International Financial Market Integration: An Examination Of The US, Hong Kong And Singapore Markets," JBFA, 1990, v17(2), 193-212.)

Stansell, Stanley R. (Edwards, Charles E. and Stanley R. Stansell. " An Inter-Temporal Approach To The Optimization Of Dividend Policy With Predetermined Investments: Comment," JOF, 1974, v29(1), 251-253.)

Stansell, Stanley R. (Fry, Clifford L., Charles P. Harper and Stanley R. Stansell. "An Analysis Of Credit Union Costs: A New Approach To Analyzing Cost Of Financial Institutions," JBR, 1981-82, v12(4), 239-249.)

Stansell, Stanley R. (Millar, James A. and Stanley R. Stansell. "Variable Rate Mortgage Experience Of The Farm Credit System," FM, 1974, v4(4), 46-57.)

Stansell, Stanley R. and Daniel R. Hollas. "An Examination Of The Relative Economic Efficiency Of Mutual Vs. Stock Savings Institutions," JREFEC, 1990, v3(1), 73-90.

Stansell, Stanley. (Millar, James R. and Stanley R. Stansell. "Variable Rate Mortgage Lending: Some Empirical Results," AREUEA, 1975, v3(3), 95-117.)

Stanton, Harry G. and John A. Rickard. "The 'Rule Of 78' Cost Penalty: An Alternative Perspective," JBFA, 1989, v16(2), 255-266.

Stanton, Wilbur W. (Reese, Richard M. and Wilbur W. Stanton. "Further Segmenting A Minority Bank's Customer Set," JBR, 1983-84, v14(4), 297-301.)

Stapleton, R. C. and M. G. Subrahmanyam. "Notes On Multiperiod Valuation And The Pricing Of Options: A Comment," JOF, 1984, v39(1), 303-306.

Stapleton, R. C. and M. G. Subrahmanyam. "The Market Model And Capital Asset Pricing Theory: A Note," JOF, 1983, v38(5), 1637-1642.

Stapleton, R. C. and M. G. Subrahmanyam. "Market Imperfections, Capital Market Equilibrium And Corporation Finance," JOF, 1977, v32(2), 307-319.

Stapleton, R. C. and M. G. Subrahmanyam. "The Valuation Of Multivariate Contingent Claims In Discrete Time Models," JOF, 1984, v39(1), 207-228.

Stapleton, R. C. and M. G. Subrahmanyam. "The Valuation Of Options When Asset Returns Are Generated By A Binomial Process," JOF, 1984, v39(5), 1525-1539.

Stapleton, R. C. and M. G. Subrahmanyam. "Marketability Of Assets And The Price Of Risk," JFQA, 1979, v14(1), 1-10.

Stapleton, R. C. "The Acquisition Decision As A Capital Budgeting Problem," JBFA, 1975, v2(2), 187-202.

Stapleton, R. C. and M. G. Subrahmanyam. "Risk Aversion And The Intertemporal Behavior Of Asset Prices," RFS, 1990, v3(4), 677-694.

Stapleton, Richard C. and Christopher M. Burke. "European Tax Systems And The Neutrality Of Corporate Financing Policy," JBF, 1977, v1(1), 55-70.

Stapleton, Richard C. and Marti G. Subrahmanyam. "Uncertain Inflation, Exchange Rates, And Bond Yields," JBF, 1981, v5(1), 93-108.

Stapleton, Richard C. "Capital Budgeting Under Uncertainty: A Reformation: Comment," JOF, 1974, v29(5), 1583-1584.

Stapleton, Richard C. "Portfolio Analysis, Stock Valuation And Capital Budgeting Decision Rules For Risky Projects," JOF, 1971, v26(1), 95-117.

Stapleton, Robert C. "A Note On Default Risk, Leverage And The MM Theorem," JFEC, 1975, v2(4), 377-381.

Starbuck, W. H. and F. M. Bass. "An Experimental Study Of Risk-Taking And The Value Of Information In A New Product Context," JOB, 1967, v40(2), 155-165.

Stark, A. W. (Gordon, L. A. and A. W. Stark. "Accounting And Economic Rates Of Return: A Note On Depreciation And Other Accruals," JBFA, 1989, v16(3), 425-432.)

Stark, A. W. (Lee, T. A. and A. W. Stark. "A Cash Flow Disclosure Of Government-Supported Enterprises' Results," JBFA, 1984, v11(1), 1-11.)

Stark, Andrew W. "On The Observability Of The Cash Recovery Rate," JBFA, 1987, v14(1), 99-108.

Stark, John R. "Economic Status Of Older People," JOB, 1954, v27(2), 119-130.

Stark, Stanley. "Executive Foresight: Definitions, Illustrations, Importance," JOB, 1961, v34(1), 31-44.

Stark, Stanley. "Research Criteria Of Executive Success," JOB, 1959, v32(1), 1-14.

Starke, Wolfgang. "Efficiencies In Credit-Based Transfer Systems," JBR, 1985-86, v16(4), 223-226.

Starke, Wolfgang. "Payment Methods Of The Future," JBR, 1980-81, v11(4), 223-226.

Starks, Laura T. "Performance Incentive Fees: An Agency Theoretic Approach," JFQA, 1987, v22(1), 17-32.

Starks, Laura T. (Barry, Christopher B. and Laura T. Starks. "Investment Management And Risk Sharing With Multiple Managers," JOF, 1984, v39(2), 477-491.)

Starks, Laura T. (Jennings, Robert H., Laura T. Starks and John C. Fellingham. "An Equilibrium Model Of Asset Trading With Sequential Information Arrival," JOF, 1981, v36(1), 143-161.)

Starks, Laura. (Jennings, Robert and Laura Starks. "Earnings Announcements, Stock Price Adjustment, And The Existence Of Option Markets," JOF, 1986, v41(1), 107-126.)

Starks, Laura. (Smirlock, Michael and Laura Starks. "An Empirical Analysis Of The Stock Price-Volume Relationship," JBF, 1988, v12(1), 31-42.)

Starks, Laura. (Smirlock, Michael and Laura Starks. "Day-Of-The-Week And Intraday Effects In Stock Returns," JFEC, 1986, v17(1), 197-210.)

Starks, Laura. (Smirlock, Michael and Laura Starks. "A Further Examination Of Stock Price Changes And Transaction Volume," JFR, 1985, v8(3), 227-236.)

Starleaf, Dennis R. and James A. Stephenson. "A Suggested Solution To The Monetary-Policy Indicator Problem: The Monetary Full Employment Interest Rate," 1969, v24(4), 623-641.

Starleaf, Dennis R. and James A. Stephenson. "The Full-Employment Interest Rate And The Neutralized Money Stock: Reply," JOF, 1971, v26(1), 137-143.

Starleaf, Dennis R. and Richard Floyd. "Some Evidence With Respect To The Efficacy Of Friedman's Monetary Policy Proposals: A Comment," JMCB, 1972, v4(3), 713-722.

Starleaf, Dennis R. and Richard Reimer. "The Keynesian Demand Function For Money: Some Statistical Tests," JOF, 1967, v22(1), 71-76.

Starleaf, Dennis R. and Richard Reimer. "Statistical Tests Of The Keynesian Demand Function For Money: Reply," JOF, 1968, v23(4), 676-678.

Starleaf, Dennis R. "A Comment On 'Nonmember Banks And Empirical Measures Of The Variability Of Reserves And Money: A Theoretical Appraisal'," JOF, 1980, v35(3), 801-805.

Starleaf, Dennis R. "A Suggestion For Changing The Definition Of The U.S. Money Stock," JMCB, 1976, v8(2), 149-166.

Starleaf, Dennis R. "Nonmember Banks And Monetary Control," JOF, 1975, v30(4), 955-975.

Starleaf, Dennis R. "The Specification Of Money Demand-Supply Models Which Involve The Use Of Distributed Lags," JOF, 1970, v25(4), 743-760.

Starleaf, Dennis R. (Dickson, Harold D. and Dennis R. Starleaf. "Polynomial Distributed Lag Structures In The Demand Function For Money," JOF, 1972, v27(5), 1035-1043.)

Starleaf, Dennis R. (Overdahl, James A. and Dennis R. Starleaf. "The Hedging Performance Of The CD Futures Market," JFM, 1986, v6(1), 71-82.)

Starler, Norman. (Fisher, Warren, Norman Starler and Ann Fisher. "A Method For Building A Property Values' Index For Use In Local Public Policy Decisions," AREUEA, 1976, v4(2), 77-90.)

Starmer, Chris and Robert Sugden. "Probability And Juxtaposition Effects: An Experimental Investigation Of The Common Ratio Effect," JRU, 1989, v2(2), 159-178.

Starnes, William. (Smith, Gary and William Starnes. "A Short-Run Two-Sector Model With Immobile Capital," JMCB, 1979, v11(1), 47-67.)

Starr, J. Philip. "Plan Design In Group Long Term Disability Insurance," JRI, 1965, v32(4), 509-524.

Startz, Richard. "Do Forecast Errors Or Term Premia Really Make The Difference Between Long And Short Rates?," JFEC, 1982, v10(3), 323-329.

Startz, Richard. (Frodin, Joanna H. and Richard Startz. "The NOW Account Experiment And The Demand For Money," JBF, 1982, v6(2), 179-193.)

Startz, Richard. (Meyer, Stephen A. and Richard Startz. "Real Versus Nominal Forecast Errors In The Prediction Of Foreign Exchange Rates," JIMF, 1982, v1(2), 193-200.)

Startz, Richard. (Nelson, Charles R. and Richard Startz. "The Distribution Of The Instrumental Variables Estimator And Its t-Ratio When The Instrument Is A Poor One," JOB, 1990, v63(1), Part 2, S125-S140.)

Startz, Richard. (Turner, Christopher M., Richard Startz and Charles R. Nelson. "A Markov Model Of Heteroskedasticity, Risk, And Learning In The Stock Market," JFEC, 1989, v25(1), 3-20.)

Stasiak, Richard T. (McGee, Robert T. and Richard T. Stasiak. "Does Anticipated Monetary Policy Matter? Another Look," JMCB, 1985, v17(1), 16-27.)

Stassen, John H. "Facts Are Stubborn Things: Section 3 Should Be Revised," JFM, 1981, v1(Supp), 457-459.

Stathas, P. P. "Earnings Outlook: Electric And Gas Utilities," FAJ, 1966, v22(3), 23-27.

Stathas, P. P. "Investment Appraisal Of The Natural Gas Industry," FAJ, 1947, v3(3), 20-26.

Stathas, P. P. "The Outlook For The Electric Utility Industry," FAJ, 1958, v14(1), 73-78.

Statman, Meir and James F. Sepe. "Managerial Incentive Plans And The Use Of The Payback Method," JBFA, 1984, v11(1), 61-65.

Statman, Meir and Tyzoon T. Tyebjee. "Optimistic Capital Budgeting Forecasts: An Experiment," FM, 1985, v14(3), 27-33.

Statman, Meir and David Caldwell. "Applying Behavioral Finance To Capital Budgeting: Project Terminations," FM, 1987, v16(4), 7-15.

Statman, Meir and James F. Sepe. "Project Termination Announcements And The Market Value Of The Firm," FM, 1989, v18(4), 74-81.

Statman, Meir and Neal Ushman. "Another Look At Bonds Versus Stocks," JPM, 1986-87, v13(2), 33-38.

Statman, Meir. "Betas Compared: Merrill Lynch Vs. Value Line," **JPM,** 1980-81, v7(2), 41-44.

Statman, Meir. "Fixed Rate Or Index-Linked Mortgages From The Borrower's Point Of View: A Note," **JFQA,** 1982, v17(3), 451-457.

Statman, Meir. "Growth Opportunities Vs. Growth Stocks," **JPM,** 1983-84, v10(3), 70-74.

Statman, Meir. "How Many Stocks Make A Diversified Portfolio?," **JFQA,** 1987, v22(3), 353-364.

Statman, Meir. (Brick, Ivan E. and Meir Statman. "A Note On Beta And The Probability Of Default," **JFR,** 1981, v4(3), 265-269.)

Statman, Meir. (Brick, Ivan E., Meir Statman and Daniel G. Weaver. "Event Studies And Model Misspecification: Another Look At The Benefits Of Outsiders From Public Information About Insider Trading," **JBFA,** 1989, v16(3), 399-424.)

Statman, Meir. (Clarke, Roger G., Michael T. FitzGerald, Phillip Berent and Meir Statman. "Market Timing With Imperfect Information," **FAJ,** 1989, v45(6), 27-36.)

Statman, Meir. (Clarke, Roger G., Michael T. Fitzgerald, Philip Berent and Meir Statman. "Diversifying Among Asset Allocators," **JPM,** 1990, v16(3), 9-14.)

Statman, Meir. (Clarke, Roger G., Michael T. Fitzgerald, Philip Berent and Meir Statman. "Required Accuracy For Successful Asset Allocation," **JPM,** 1990, v17(1), 12-19.)

Statman, Meir. (Shefrin Hersh and Meir Statman. "The Disposition To Sell Winners Too Early And Ride Losers Too Long: Theory And Evidence," **JOF,** 1985, v40(3), 777-782.)

Statman, Meir. (Shefrin, Hersh M. and Meir Statman. "Explaining Investor Preference For Cash Dividends," **JFEC,** 1984, v13(2), 253-282.)

Statman, Meir. (Solt, Michael E. and Meir Statman. "How Useful Is The Sentiment Index?," **FAJ,** 1988, v44(5), 45-55.)

Statman, Meir. (Solt, Michael E. and Meir Statman. "Good Companies, Bad Stocks," **JPM,** 1989, v15(4), 39-44.)

Staubus, George J. "Earnings Periods For Common Share Analysis," **JOB,** 1968, v41(4), 472-476.

Stauffer, Robert F. "A Reinterpretation Of Velocity Trends In The United States, 1900-1920: A Comment," **JMCB,** 1978, v10(1), 105-111.

Stauffer, Robert F. "The Bank Failures Of 1930-31: A Comment," **JMCB,** 1981, v13(1), 109-113.

Stearns, Linhart. "A Modest Proposal," **JPM,** 1977-78, v4(1), 70-72.

Stedry, Andrew C. "Budgeting And Employee Behavior: A Reply," **JOB,** 1964, v37(2), 195-202.

Steele, A. and N. Tessaromatis. "A Note On Dividend Policy And Beta: A Comment," **JBFA,** 1989, v16(4), 543-548.

Steele, Anthony. "A Note On Estimating The Internal Rate Of Return From Published Financial Statements," **JBFA,** 1986, v13(1), 1-13.

Steele, Anthony. "Difference Equation Solutions To The Valuation Of Lease Contracts," **JFQA,** 1984, v19(3), 311-328.

Steele, Donald C. (Burkhead, Jesse and Donald C. Steele. "The Effect Of State Taxation On The Migration Of Industry," **JOB,** 1950, v23(3), 167-172.)

Steers, Newton I., Jr. "Uranium Demand And Supply," **FAJ,** 1956, v12(2), 75-82.

Stefek, Dan. (Grinold, Richard, Andrew Rudd and Dan Stefek. "Global Factors: Fact Or Fiction?," **JPM,** 1989, v16(1), 79-89.)

Steffen, Walter W. "Recent Developments In Life Reinsurance," **JRI,** 1964, v31(2), 265-272.

Steger, Wilbur A. "Averaging Corporation Income For Tax Purposes: A Statistical Study," **JOF,** 1957, v12(3), 364-371.

Stegman, Michael A. "Multifamily Distress: A Case For National Action," **AREUEA,** 1979, v7(1), 77-94.

Stegman, Michael A. "The Neighborhood Effects Of Filtering," **AREUEA,** 1977, v5(2), 227-241.

Stegman, Michael A. and Howard Sumka. "Nonmetropolitan And Inner-City Housing Investment Markets," **AREUEA,** 1974, v2(2), 81-100.

Stegman, Michael A. and Howard J. Sumka. "Market Implications Of A Direct Cash Assistance Program In Southern Nonmetropolitan Cities," **AREUEA,** 1975, v3(3), 23-46.

Stehle, Richard E. (Grauer, Frederick L. A., Robert H. Litzenberger and Richard E. Stehle. "Sharing Rules And Equilibrium In An International Market Under Uncertainty," **JFEC,** 1976, v3, **JFEC,** 1976, v3(3), 233-256.)

Stehle, Richard E. (McDonald, John G. and Richard E. Stehle. "How Do Institutional Investors Perceive Risk?," **JPM,** 1975-76, v2(1), 11-16.)

Stehle, Richard. "An Empirical Test Of The Alternative Hypotheses Of National And International Pricing Of Risky Assets," **JOF,** 1977, v32(2), 493-502.

Steib, Steve B. "The Demand For Euro-Dollar Borrowings By U. S. Banks," **JOF,** 1973, v28(4), 875-879.

Stein, Avy. (Willis, John R. and Avy Stein. "Financing A Generational Change Of Ownership," **JACF,** 1990, v3(3), 71-76.)

Stein, Garry R. (Baesel, Jerome B. and Garry R. Stein. "The Value Of Information: Inferences From The Profitability Of Insider Trading," **JFQA,** 1979, v14(3), 553-571.)

Stein, Herbert. "Where Stands The New Fiscal Policy?," **JMCB,** 1969, v1(3), 463-473.

Stein, J. L. "Introduction To Special Issue On 'Real And Nominal Exchange Rates'," **JBF,** 1990, v14(5), 839-844.

Stein, J. L. "The Real Exchange Rate," **JBF,** 1990, v14(5), 1045-1078.

Stein, J. L. (Allen, P. R. and J. L. Stein. "Capital Market Integration," **JBF,** 1990, v14(5), 909-928.)

Stein, Jeremy C. (Froot, Kenneth A., David S. Scharfstein and Jeremy C. Stein. "LDC Debt: Forgiveness, Indexation, And Investment Incentives," **JOF,** 1989, v44(5), 1335-1350.)

Stein, Jeremy C. (Kaplan, Steven N. and Jeremy C. Stein. "How Risky Is The Debt Of Highly Leveraged Transactions?," **JFEC,** 1990, v27(1), 215-246.)

Stein, Jeremy. "Overreactions In The Options Market," **JOF,** 1989, v44(4), 1011-1024.

Stein, Jerome L. and Ettore F. Infante. "Optimal Stabilization Paths," **JMCB,** 1973, v5(1), Part II, 525-562.

Stein, Jerome L. "Illiquidity And The Limits To Interest Arbitrage: Reply," **JOF,** 1968, v23(4), 670-671.

Stein, Jerome L. "Inflation And Stagflation," **JBF,** 1978, v2(2), 109-131.

Stein, Jerome L. "Rational, Irrational, And Overregulated Speculative Markets," **RIF,** 1983, v4, (Supp), 227-258.

Stein, Jerome L. "Spot, Forward, And Futures," **RIF,** 1979, v1, 225-310.

Stein, Jerome L. "The Optimum Quantity Of Money," **JMCB,** 1970, v2(4), 397-419.

Stein, Jerome L. "'Neoclassical' And 'Keynes-Wicksell' Monetary Growth Models," **JMCB,** 1969, v1(2), 153-171.

Stein, Jerome L., Mark Rzepczynski and Robert Selvaggio. "A Theoretical Explanation Of The Empirical Studies Of Futures Markets In Foreign Exchange And Financial Instruments," **FR,** 1983, v18(1), 1-32.

Stein, William E., Roger C. Pfaffenberger and Dan W. French. "Sampling Error In First Order Stochastic Dominance," **JFR,** 1987, v10(3), 259-268.

Stein, William L., Esq. (White, Frederick L., Esq. and William L. Stein, Esq. "Broker-Customer Arbitration: An Attractive Alternative," **JFM,** 1987, v7(4), 459-460.)

Stein, William, Roger Pfaffenberger and P. C. Kumar. "On The Estimation Risk In First-Order Stochastic Dominance: A Note," **JFQA,** 1983, v18(4), 471-476.

Stein, William. (White, Frederick L. and William Stein. "Legal And Regulatory Developments," **JFM,** 1986, v6(3), 503-504.)

Steinberg, Joan S. and Larry R. Arnold. "An Interactive Approach For Optimizing Debt Repayment Schedules," **JFR,** 1981, v4(2), 137-146.

Steindl, Frank G. and Maurice D. Weinrobe. "Natural Hazards And Deposit Behavior At Financial Institutions: A Note," **JBF,** 1983, v7(1), 111-118.

Steindl, Frank G. "Money And Income: The View From The Government Budget Restraint," **JOF,** 1974, v29(4), 1143-1148.

Steindl, Frank G. "Price Expectations And Interest Rates," **JMCB,** 1973, v5(4), 939-949.

Steindl, Frank G. "The Negative View Of The Negative Money Multiplier: Reply," **JOF,** 1977, v32(5), 1818-1821.

Steiner, Gary A. "Notes On Franklin B. Evans' 'Psychological And Objective Factors In The Prediction Of Brand Choice'," **JOB,** 1961, v34(1), 57-60.

Steiner, Gary A. "The People Look At Commercials: A Study Of Audience Behavior," **JOB,** 1966, v39(2), 272-304.

Steiner, J. E. "Aircraft Evolution And Airline Growth," **FAJ,** 1967, v23(2), 85-92.

Steinhardt, Michael H. "Investing, Hedge-Fund Style," **FAJ,** 1982, v38(6), 33-35.

Steinhaus, H. W. "1953 Savings In The United States," **FAJ,** 1954, v10(2), 21-24.

Steinhaus, Henry W. "Evaluation Of Life Insurance Companies," **FAJ,** 1958, v14(4), 61-64.

Steinhaus, Henry W. "The Effect Of Pension Fund Investments On Common Stock Prices," **FAJ,** 1958, v14(1), 63-66.

Steinmuller, Heinz. (Forster, Edgar and Heinz Steinmuller. "An Alternative View On Moral Hazard," **JRI,** 1978, v45(3), 531-534.)

Steinwald, Bruce and Frank A. Sloan. "Determinants Of Physicians' Fees," **JOB,** 1974, v47(4), 493-511.

Stekler, H. O. "A Simulation Of The Forecasting Performance Of The Diffusion Index," **JOB,** 1962, v35(2), 196-200.

Stekler, H. O. "An Evaluation Of Quarterly Judgmental Economic Forecasts," **JOB,** 1968, v41(3), 329-339.

Stekler, H. O. "Forecasting The GNP Price Deflator," **JOB,** 1968, v41(4), 431-438.

Stekler, H. O. "The Federal Budget As A Short-Term Forecasting Tool," **JOB,** 1967, v40(3), 280-285.

Stekler, H. O. "The Savings Rate As A Tool Of Economic Analysis," **JOB,** 1976, v49(2), 189-193.

Stekler, H. O. (Enzler, Jared J. and H. O. Stekler. "An Analysis Of The 1968-69 Economic Forecasts," **JOB,** 1971, v44(3), 271-281.)

Stekler, H. O. (Schnader, M. H. and H. O. Stekler. "Evaluating Predictions Of Change," **JOB,** 1990, v63(1), Part 1, 99-108.)

Stelpflug, W. J. "Modern Refrigeration And The Modern Supermarket," **FAJ,** 1954, v10(5), 63-66.

Stelpflug, W. J. "The Food Industry And Refrigeration," **FAJ,** 1950, v6(4), 37-39.

Stelzer, Irwin M. (Montgomery, Royal E., Irwin M. Stelzer, and Rosaland Roth. "Collective Bargaining Over Profit Sharing: The Automobile Union's Effort To Extend Its Frontier Of Control," **JOB,** 1958, v31(4), 318-334.)

Stensland, Gunnar and Dag Tjostheim. "Optimal Investments Using Empirical Dynamic Programming With Application To Natural Resources," **JOB,** 1989, v62(1), 99-120.

Stephan, Jens A. and Robert E. Whaley. "Intraday Price Changes And Trading Volume Relations In The Stock And Stock Option Markets," **JOF,** 1990, v45(1), 191-220.

Stephen, Frank H. "On Deriving The Internal Rate Of Return From The Accountant's Rate Of Return," **JBFA,** 1976, v3(2), 147-149.

Stephens, Mark. (Hsieh, Chang-Tseh and Mark Stephens. "A Simultaneous Equations Model For Examining Taiwan-U.S. Trade Relations," **AFPAF,** 1985, v1(Supp), 139-156.)

Stephenson, James A. (Starleaf, Dennis R. and James A. Stephenson. "A Suggested Solution To The Monetary-Policy Indicator Problem: The Monetary Full Employment Interest Rate," **JOF,** 1969, v24(4), 623-641.)

Stephenson, James A. (Starleaf, Dennis R. and James A. Stephenson. "The Full-Employment Interest Rate And The Neutralized Money Stock: Reply," **JOF,** 1971, v26(1), 137-143.)

Stephenson, James B. "The High-Protection Annuity," **JRI,** 1978, v45(4), 593-610.

Stephenson, Matilde K. (Manning, Richard L., Matilde K. Stephenson and Jerry D. Todd. "Information Technology In The Insurance Industry: A Forecast Of Utilization And Impact," **JRI,** 1985, v52(4), 711-722.)

Sterbenz, Frederic P. (Spatt, Chester S. and Frederic P. Sterbenz. "Warrant Exercise, Dividends, And Reinvestment Policy," **JOF,** 1988, v43(2), 493-506.)

Sterge, Andrew J. "On The Distribution Of Financial Futures Price Changes," **FAJ,** 1989, v45(3), 74-78.

Sterk, William E. "Comparative Performance Of The Black-Scholes And Roll-Geske-Whaley Option Pricing Models," JFQA, 1983, v18(3), 345-354.

Sterk, William E. (Cramer, Robert H. and William E. Sterk. "The Present Value Approach To Commercial Loan Pricing," JBR, 1981-82, v12(4), 207-217.)

Sterk, William E. (Sachdeva, Kanwal S. and William E. Sterk. "Projecting Finance Student Final Course Scores Based On Initial Exam Scores," JFED, 1982, v11, 55-60.)

Sterk, William E. and Pieter A. Vandenberg. "The Market Valuation Of Cash Dividends And The Tax Differential Theory Of Dividend Policy: A Case Revisited," FR, 1990, v25(3), 441-456.

Sterk, William Edward. "Option Pricing: Dividends And The In- And Out-Of-The-Money Bias," FM, 1983, v12(4), 47-53.

Sterk, William. "Tests Of Two Models For Valuing Call Options On Stocks With Dividends," JOF, 1982, v37(5), 1229-1237.

Sterling, C. Ralph. "The Varying Impact Of State Regulation On Public Utility Earning Power," FAJ, 1946, v2(4), 3-19.

Sterling, E. Ralph. "Methods Of Recapitalizing Utility Holding Companies," FAJ, 1945, v1(1), 15-23.

Sterling, Francis L. (Robbins, S. M., R. B. Stobaugh, F. L. Sterling and T. H. Howe. "The Impact Of Exchange-Traded Options On The Market For New Issues Of Common Stock Of Small Companies," FR, 1979, v14(1), 1-22.)

Sterling, Robert R. "Toward A Science Of Accounting," FAJ, 1975, v31(5), 28-36.

Stern, Bruce L., Ronald F. Bush and Joseph F. Hair, Jr. "The Self-Image/Store Image Matching Process: An Empirical Test," JOB, 1977, v50(1), 63-69.

Stern, J. (Amihud, Y., C. Brunie, C. Ferenbach, R. Fredericks, J. Grundfest, J. Lafferty, B. Lev, B. Shorts, J. Stern, B. Stewart and R. Zeckhauser. "Panel: 'Lead Steer' Roundtable," JACF, 1989, v2(3), 24-44.)

Stern, J. (Appelbaum, E., J. Burns, R. Evans, J. Gould, T. Hamachek, R. Kidder, M. Jensen, J. Johnstone, M. Murray, R. Sim, J. Stern, B. Stewart and C. Zaner. "Panel: CEO Roundtable On Corporate Structure And Management Incentives," JACF, 1990, v3(3), 6-35.)

Stern, Jerrold J. (Brueggeman, William B., Jeffrey D. Fisher and Jerrold J. Stern. "Federal Income Taxes, Inflation And Holding Periods For Income-Producing Property," AREUEA, 1981, v9(2), 148-164.)

Stern, Joel M. "Earnings Per Share Doesn't Count," FAJ, 1974, v30(4), 39-43,67-75.

Stern, Joel M. "Maximizing Earnings Per Share," FAJ, 1970, v26(5), 107-112.

Stern, Louis W. and William M. Morgenroth. "Concentration, Mutually Recognized Interdependence, And The Allocation Of Marketing Resources," JOB, 1968, v41(1), 56-67.

Stern, Robert N. (Becker, Theodore M. and Robert N. Stern. "Professionalism, Professionalization, And Bias In The Commercial Human Relations COnsulting Operation: A Survey Analysis," JOB, 1973, v46(2), 230-257.)

Stern, Walter P. and William C. Norby. "Research And Market Structure," FAJ, 1972, v28(1), 24-28,85-87.

Stern, Walter P. "Investing In Japan," FAJ, 1964, v20(1), 105-109.

Stern, Walter P. "Performance-Transitory Or Real?," FAJ, 1968, v24(1), 110-113.

Stern, Walter P. "Planning On Wall Street," FAJ, 1970, v26(3), 27-29.

Stern, Walter P. "The Investment Scene," FAJ, 1969, v25(2), 109-112.

Stern, Walter P. "United States Direct Investments Abroad," FAJ, 1965, v21(1), 92-99.

Stern, Walter P. (Loomis, Philip, George S. Bissell, John G. Gillis and Walter P. Stern. "Corporate Disclosure And Inside Information," FAJ, 1972, v28(3), 20-21,24-25,82-84,86-88.)

Sternberg, Walter. "Future Of The Air Transport Industry," FAJ, 1953, v9(5), 100-102.

Sternlicht, B. (Agnello, W., W. Brueggeman, G. Decker, R. Griffith, R. Leftwich, R. Moore, J. Neal, B. Sternlicht, B. Wallach, W. Wardrop and C. Zinngrabe. "Panel: Corporate Real Estate Roundtable," JACF, 1990, v3(1), 6-38.)

Sternlieb, George and James W. Hughes. "Neighborhood Dynamics And Government Policy," AREUEA, 1974, v2(2), 7-24.

Sternlieb, George and James W. Hughes. "Condominium Conversion Profiles: Governmental Policy," AREUEA, 1975, v3(3), 61-80.

Sternlieb, George and James W. Hughes. "Regional Market Variations: The Northeast Versus The South," AREUEA, 1977, v5(1), 44-67.

Sternlieb, George and Robert W. Burchell. "Multifamily Housing Demand: 1980-2000," AREUEA, 1979, v7(1), 1-38.

Sternlight, Peter D. "Member Bank Reserve Settlement Periods: A Further Comment," JOF, 1964, v19(3), 540-543.

Sternlight, Peter D. "Reserve Settlement Periods Of Member Banks: Comment," JOF, 1964, v19(1), 94-98.

Sternlight, Peter D. (Axilrod, Stephen H. and Peter D. Sternlight. "Is The Federal Reserve's Monetary Control Policy Misdirected?," JMCB, 1982, v14(1), 119-147.)

Stetson, Warren B. "Price-Yield Relationships," FAJ, 1954, v10(5), 67-68.

Stevens, Donald L. "Financial Characteristics Of Merged Firms: A Multivariate Analysis," JFQA, 1973, v8(2), 149-158.

Stevens, Donald L. (Shrieves, Ronald E. and Donald L. Stevens. "Bankruptcy Avoidance As A Motive For Merger," JFQA, 1979, v14(3), 501-515.)

Stevens, Edward J. "Composition Of The Money Stock Prior To The Civil War," JMCB, 1971, v3(1), 84-101.

Stevens, Guy G. V. "Two Problems In Portfolio Analysis: Conditional And Multiplicative Random Variables," JFQA, 1971, v6(5), 1235-1250.

Stevens, Guy V. G. "The Payments Impact Of Foreign Investment Controls: Comment," JOF, 1976, v31(5), 1495-1504.

Stevens, Guy V. G. (Adler, Michael and Guy V. G. Stevens. "The Trade Effects Of Direct Investment," JOF, 1974, v29(2), 655-676.)

Stevens, Jerry L. (Jose, Manuel L. and Jerry L. Stevens. "Product Market Structure, Capital Intensity, And Systematic Risk: Empirical Results From The Theory Of The Firm," JFR, 1987, v10(2), 161-175.)

Stevens, Jerry L. (Jose, Manuel L., Len M. Nichols and Jerry L. Stevens. "Contributions Of Diversification, Promotion, And R&D To The Value Of Multiproduct Firms: A Tobin's q Approach," FM, 1986, v15(4), 33-42.)

Stevens, Jerry L. (Jose, Manuel L. and Jerry L. Stevens. "Capital Market Valuation Of Dividend Policy," JBFA, 1989, v16(5), 651-662.)

Stevens, Jerry L. (Vandell, Robert F. and Jerry L. Stevens. "Personal Taxes And Equity Security Pricing," FM, 1982, v11(1), 31-40.)

Stevens, Jerry L. (Vandell, Robert F. and Jerry L. Stevens. "Evidence Of Superior Performance From Timing," JPM, 1989, v15(3), 38-42.)

Stevens, Robert E. (Warren, William E., Robert E. Stevens and C. William McConkey. "Using Demographic And Lifestyle Analysis To Segment Individual Investors," FAJ, 1990, v46(2), 74-77.)

Stevens, Stanley C. "Evidence For A Weather Persistence Effect On The Corn, Wheat, And Soybean Growing Season Price Dynamics," JFM, 1991, v11(1), 81-88.

Stevens, Stanley C. "The Negative Precautionary Demand For Money Reconsidered," JOF, 1971, v26(3), 749-755.

Stevens, William Thomas. (Carpenter, Michael D., David R. Lange, Donald S. Shannon and William Thomas Stevens. "Methodologies Of Valuing Lost Earnings: A Review, A Criticism, And A Recommendation," JRI, 1986, v53(1), 104-118.)

Stevenson, H. W. (Murphy, J. E., Jr. and H. W. Stevenson. "P/E Ratios And Future Growth," FAJ, 1967, v23(6), 111-114.)

Stevenson, John. "Financing Of Railroad Equipment," FAJ, 1953, v9(5), 27-32.

Stevenson, R. A. (Crepas, K. J. and R. A. Stevenson. "Industrial Aid Bonds," FAJ, 1968, v24(6), 105-109.)

Stevenson, R. A. (Kewley, T. J. and R. A. Stevenson. "The Odd Lot Theory," FAJ, 1967, v23(5), 103-106.)

Stevenson, R. A. (Kewley, Thomas J. and R. A. Stevenson. "The Odd-Lot Theory: A Reply," FAJ, 1969, v25(1), 99-104.)

Stevenson, Richard A. and Michael Rozeff. "Are The Backwaters Of The Market Efficient?," JPM, 1978-79, v5(3), 31-34.

Stevenson, Richard A. and Robert M. Bear. "Commodity Futures: Trends Or Random Walks," JOF, 1970, v25(1), 65-81.

Stevenson, Richard A. "Deep-Discount Convertible Bonds: An Analysis," JPM, 1981-82, v8(4), 57-64.

Stevenson, Richard A. "Odd-Lot Trading In The Stock Market And Its Market Impact: Comment," JFQA, 1973, v8(3), 527-533.

Stevenson, Richard A. "Retirement Of Non-Callable Preferred Stock," JOF, 1970, v25(5), 1143-1152.

Stevenson, Richard A. "The Variability Of Common Stock Quality Ratings," FAJ, 1966, v22(6), 97-101.

Stevenson, Richard A. (Bear, Robert M. and Richard A. Stevenson. "On The Methodology Of Testing For Independence In Futures Prices: Reply," JOF, 1976, v31(3), 980-983.)

Stevenson, Richard A. (Chang, Eric C. and Richard A. Stevenson. "The Timing Performance Of Small Traders," JFM, 1985, v5(4), 517-527.)

Stevenson, Richard. (Frankfurter, George M., Richard Stevenson and Allan Young. "Option Spreading: Theory And An Illustration," JPM, 1978-79, v5(4), 59-63.)

Stevenson, Robert M. (Krogh, Harold C., W. O. Bryson, Jr., William M. Howard and Robert M. Stevenson. "The Insurance Curriculum In Collegiate Business Education," JRI, 1959, v26(1), 76-81.)

Steves, Buddy, Archer McWhorter, Jr. and Lee Fisher. "An Empirical Analysis Of The Capacity Crisis In Medical Malpractice Insurance," JRI, 1979, v46(1), 139-146.

Stewart, B. (Amihud, Y., C. Brunie, C. Ferenbach, R. Fredericks, J. Grundfest, J. Lafferty, B. Lev, B. Shorts, J. Stern, B. Stewart and R. Zeckhauser. "Panel: 'Lead Steer' Roundtable," JACF, 1989, v2(3), 24-44.)

Stewart, B. (Appelbaum, E., J. Burns, R. Evans, J. Gould, T. Hamachek, R. Kidder, M. Jensen, J. Johnstone, M. Murray, R. Sim, J. Stern, B. Stewart and C. Zaner. "Panel: CEO Roundtable On Corporate Structure And Management Incentives," JACF, 1990, v3(3), 6-35.)

Stewart, B. (Gilmour, A., M. Jensen, R. Mercer, N. Minow, J. Morley, R. Siefert, B. Stewart, L. Summers and I. Harris. "Panel: The Economic Consequences Of High Leverage And Stock Market Pressures On Corporate Management: A Roundtable Discussion," JACF, 1990, v3(2), 6-37.)

Stewart, G. Bennett and David Glassman. "The Motives And Methods Of Corporate Restructuring," JACF, 1988, v1(1), 85-99.

Stewart, G. Bennett and David Glassman. "The Motives And Methods Of Corporate Restructuring: Part II," JACF, 1988, v1(2), 79-88.

Stewart, G. Bennett, III. "Announcing The Stern Stewart Performance 1,000: A New Way Of Viewing Corporate America," JACF, 1990, v3(2), 38-59.

Stewart, G. Bennett, III. "Market Myths," JACF, 1989, v2(3), 6-23.

Stewart, G. Bennett, III. "Simulating Ownership For Line Managers," JACF, 1990, v3(3), 62-70.

Stewart, I. C. "The Explication Of The True And Fair View Doctrine: A Comment," JBFA, 1988, v15(1), 115-124.

Stewart, J. C. "Multinational Companies And Transfer Pricing," JBFA, 1977, v4(3), 353-372.

Stewart, John F. (Carleton, Willard T., David K. Guilkey, Robert S. Harris and John F. Stewart. "An Empirical Analysis Of The Role Of The Medium Of Exchange In Mergers," JOF, 1983, v38(3), 813-826.)

Stewart, Richard E. "The End Of Isolationism In Insurance Regulation," JRI, 1969, v36(3), 489-492.

Stewart, S. S., Jr. (Parker, G. G. C. and S. S. Stewart, Jr. "Risk And Investment Performance," FAJ, 1974, v30(3), 49-51.)

Stewart, Samuel S., Jr. "Corporate Forecasts: Research Report," FAJ, 1973, v29(1), 77-85.

Stewart, Samuel S., Jr. "Should A Corporation Repurchase Its Own Stock?," JOF, 1976, v31(3), 911-921.

Stewart, Samuel S., Jr. (Johnson, Ramon E., Richard T. Pratt and Samuel S. Stewart, Jr. "The Economic Consequences Of ESOPs," JFR, 1982, v5(1), 75-82.)

Stewart, Scott D. "Biases In Performance Measurement During Contributions: A Note," FR, 1987, v22(2), 339-343.

Stewart, Scott D. (Smiley, Robert H. and Scott D. Stewart. "White Knights And Takeover Bids," FAJ, 1985, v41(1), 19-26.)

Stice, E. Kay. (Brent, Averil, Dale Morse and E. Kay Stice. "Short Interest: Explanations And Tests," JFQA, 1990, v25(2), 273-289.)

Stich, Robert S. "The Electric Utilities: A Second Look," FAJ, 1970, v26(6), 47-51.

Stickel, Scott E. "The Effect Of Value Line Investment Survey Rank Changes On Common Stock Prices," *JFEC*, 1985, v14(1), 121-143.

Stickel, Scott E. "The Ex-Dividend Behavior Of Nonconvertible Preferred Stock Returns And Trading Volume," *JFQA*, 1991, v26(1), 45-62.

Stickels, James P. and Dennis J. O'Connor. "A Multi-Section Self-Paced Basic Finance Course: A Postmortem," *JFED*, 1981, v10, 10-13.

Stickels, James P. "A Present Value Approach To Teaching The CAPM," *JFED*, 1981, v10, 38-41.

Stickney, Clyde P. "Analyzing Effective Corporate Tax Rates," *FAJ*, 1979, v35(4), 45-54.

Stickney, Clyde P. "Window Dressing The Interim-Earnings Report: An Empirical Assessment For Firms Initially Going Public," *JOB*, 1975, v48(1), 87-97.

Stickney, Clyde P. (Dawson, James P., Peter M. Neupert and Clyde P. Stickney. "Restating Financial Statements For Alternative GAAPs: Is It Worth The Effort?," *FAJ*, 1980, v36(6), 38-46.)

Stickney, Clyde P. (Jargay, James A., III and Clyde P. Stickney. "Cash Flows, Ratio Analysis And The W. T. Grant Company Bankruptcy," *FAJ*, 1980, v36(4), 51-54.)

Stickney, Clyde P. (Keintz, Richard J. and Clyde P. Stickney. "Immunization Of Pension Funds And Sensitivity To Actuarial Assumptions," *JRI*, 1980, v47(2), 223-239.)

Stickney, Clyde P. (Selling, Thomas I. and Clyde P. Stickney. "The Effects Of Business Environment And Strategy On A Firm's Rate Of Return On Assets," *FAJ*, 1989, v45(1), 43-52.)

Stigler, George J. "Administered Prices And Oligopolistic Inflation," *JOB*, 1962, v35(1), 1-13.

Stigler, George J. "Comment: Administered Prices And Oligopolistic Inflation," *JOB*, 1964, v37(1), 82-83.

Stigler, George J. "Comment: Professor Stigler Revisited," *JOB*, 1964, v37(4), 414-422.

Stigler, George J. "Public Regulation Of The Securities Markets," *JOB*, 1964, v37(2), 117-142.

Stigler, George. "The Goals Of Economic Policy," *JOB*, 1958, v31(3), 169-176.

Stiglitz, J. E. (Grossman, S. J. and J. E. Stiglitz. "On Value Maximization And Alternative Objectives Of The Firm," *JOF*, 1977, v32(2), 389-402.)

Stiglitz, Joseph E. "Credit Markets And The Control Of Capital," *JMCB*, 1985, v17(2), 133-152.

Stiglitz, Joseph E. "Pareto Optimality And Competition," *JOF*, 1981, v36(2), 235-251.

Stiglitz, Joseph E. "Using Tax Policy To Curb Speculative Short-Term Trading," *JFSR*, 1989, v3(2/3), 101-116.

Stiglitz, Joseph E. (Gale, Ian and Joseph E. Stiglitz. "The Information Content Of Initial Public Offerings," *JOF*, 1989, v44(2), 469-478.)

Stigum, Marcia L. "Some Further Implications Of Profit Maximization By Savings And Loan Association," *JOF*, 1976, v31(5), 1405-1426.

Stiles, Albert I. "Corporate Management," *FAJ*, 1947, v3(3), 10-13.

Stillman, Robert. "Examining Antitrust Policy Towards Horizontal Mergers," *JFEC*, 1983, v11(1), 225-240.

Stillson, Richard T. "An Analysis Of Information And Transaction Services In Financial Institutions," *JMCB*, 1974, v6(4), 517-535.

Stine, Bert and Dwayne Key. "Reconciling Degrees Of Freedom When Partitioning Risk: A Teaching Note," *JFED*, 1990, v19, 19-22.

Stinton, John E. (Felton, Robert S., William K. Ghee and John E. Stinton. "A Mid-1970 Report On The National Flood Insurance Program," *JRI*, 1971, v38(1), 1-14.)

Stirling, S. Logan. "Outlook For Entertainment Industry," *FAJ*, 1949, v5(4), 17-19.

Stirling, S. Logan. "Outlook For Air-Conditioning Industry," *FAJ*, 1953, v9(1), 75-80.

Stitzel, Thomas E. "Investing In Intrastate Issues Of Common Stock," *JFQA*, 1970, v5(5), 697-706.

Stobaugh, Robert B. (Robbins, Sidney M. and Robert B. Stobaugh. "Financing Foreign Affiliates," *FM*, 1972, v1(3), 56-65.)

Stobaugh, Robert B. (Robbins, Sidney M., Robert B. Stobaugh, Francis L. Sterling and Thomas H. Howe. "The Impact Of Exchange-Traded Options On The Market For New Issues Of Common Stock Of Small Companies," *FR*, v14(1), 1-22.)

Stocco, Robert. (Mabert, Vincent A. and Robert Stocco. "Managing And Monitoring A Forecasting System: The Chemical Bank Experience," *JBR*, 1982-83, v13(3), 195-201.)

Stock, Duane and Edward L. Schrems. "Municipal Bond Demand Premiums And Bond Price Volatility: A Note," *JOF*, 1984, v39(2), 535-539.

Stock, Duane and Terry Robertson. "Improved Techniques For Predicting Municipal Bond Ratings," *JBR*, 1981-82, v12(3), 153-160.

Stock, Duane R. (Gilmer, R. H., Jr. and Duane R. Stock. "Yield Volatility Of Discount Coupon Bonds," *JFR*, 1988, v11(3), 189-200.)

Stock, Duane and Donald G. Simonson. "Tax-Adjusted Duration For Amortizing Debt Instruments," *JFQA*, 1988, v23(3), 313-328.

Stock, Duane. "Does Active Management Of Municipal Bond Portfolios Pay?," *JPM*, 1981-82, v8(2), 51-55.

Stock, Duane. "Empirical Analysis Of Municipal Bond Portfolio Structure And Performance," *JFR*, 1982, v5(2), 171-180.

Stock, Duane. "Price Volatility Of Municipal Discount Bonds," *JFR*, 1985, v8(1), 1-13.

Stock, Duane. "The Analytics Of Tax Effects In Discount Bond Valuation," *FR*, 1986, v21(4), 451-462.

Stock, James H. (Frankel, Jeffrey A. and James H. Stock. "Regression Vs. Volatility Tests Of Efficiency Of Foreign Exchange Markets," *JIMF*, 1987, v6(1), 49-56.)

Stock, James H. (Richardson, Matthew and James H. Stock. "Drawing Inferences From Statistics Based On Multiyear Asset Returns," *JFEC*, 1989, v25(2), 323-348.)

Stockman, Alan C. "On The Roles Of International Financial Markets And Their Relevance For Economic Policy," *JMCB*, 1988, v20(3), Part 2, 531-549.

Stockman, Alan C. "Real Exchange Rates Under Alternative Nominal Exchange-Rate Systems," *JIMF*, 1983, v2(2), 147-166.

Stockum, Steve. (Chen, Carl R. and Steve Stockum. "Selectivity, Market Timing, And Random Beta Behavior Of Mutual Funds: A Generalized Model," *JFR*, 1986, v9(1), 87-96.)

Stoffels, John D. "Stock Recommendations By Investment Advisory Services: Immediate Effects On Market Price," *FAJ*, 1966, v22(2), 77-86.

Stoffels, John D. (Landes, William J., John D. Stoffels and James A. Seifert. "An Empirical Test Of A Duration-Based Hedge: The Case Of Corporate Bonds," *JFM*, 1985, v5(2), 173-182.)

Stokes, Charles J. "How The General Accounting Office Evaluates Urban Housing Policies: An Analysis Of Criteria And Procedures," *AREUEA*, 1973, v1(2), 88-103.

Stokes, Houston. (Sinai, Allen and Houston Stokes. "Real Money Balances As A Variable In The Production Function: A Comment," *JMCB*, 1977, v9(2), 372-373.)

Stoll, Hans R. "Expiration-Day Effects Of Index Futures And Options--Alternative Proposals," *RFM*, 1986, v5(3), 309-312.

Stoll, Hans R. and Anthony J. Curley. "Small Business And The New Issues Market For Equities," *JFQA*, 1970, v5(3), 309-322.

Stoll, Hans R. and Robert E. Whaley. "Transaction Costs And The Small Firm Effect," *JFEC*, 1983, v12(1), 57-80.

Stoll, Hans R. "Causes Of Deviation From Interest-Rate Parity: A Comment," *JMCB*, 1972, v4(1), 113-117.

Stoll, Hans R. "Commodity Futures And Spot Price Determination And Hedging In Capital Market Equilibrium," *JFQA*, 1979, v14(4), 873-894.

Stoll, Hans R. "Dealer Inventory Behavior: An Empirical Investigation Of NASDAQ Stocks," *JFQA*, 1976, v11(3), 359-380.

Stoll, Hans R. "Index Futures, Program Trading, And Stock Market Procedures," *JFM*, 1988, v8(4), 391-412.

Stoll, Hans R. "Inferring The Components Of The Bid-Ask Spread: Theory And Empirical Tests," *JOF*, 1989, v44(1), 115-134.

Stoll, Hans R. "Portfolio Trading," *JPM*, 1987-88, v14(4), 20-24.

Stoll, Hans R. "The Pricing Of Security Dealer Services: An Empirical Study Of NASDAQ Stocks," *JOF*, 1978, v33(4), 1153-1172.

Stoll, Hans R. "The Relationship Between Put And Call Option Prices," *JOF*, 1969, v24(5), 801-824.

Stoll, Hans R. "The Relationship Between Put And Call Option Prices: Reply," *JOF*, 1973, v28(1), 185-187.

Stoll, Hans R. "The Supply Of Dealer Services In Securities Markets," *JOF*, 1978, v33(4), 1133-1151.

Stoll, Hans R. (Fleischman, Edward H., William E. Seale, Karsten Mahlmann and Hans R. Stoll. "Panel Discussion On Regulatory Issues Facing The Futures Industry," *RFM*, 1988, v7(1), 200-216.)

Stoll, Hans R. (Haller, Andreas and Hans R. Stoll. "Market Structure And Transaction Costs: Implied Spreads In The German Stock Market," *JBF*, 1989, v13(4/5), 697-708.)

Stoll, Hans R. (Ho, Thomas S. Y. and Hans R. Stoll. "The Dynamics Of Dealer Markets Under Competition," *JOF*, 1983, v38(4), 1053-1074.)

Stoll, Hans R. (Ho, Thomas and Hans R. Stoll. "On Dealer Markets Under Competition," *JOF*, 1980, v35(2), 259-267.)

Stoll, Hans R. (Ho, Thomas and Hans R. Stoll. "Optimal Dealer Pricing Under Transactions And Return Uncertainty," *JFEC*, 1981, v9(1), 47-73.)

Stoll, Hans R. (Kraus, Alan and Hans R. Stoll. "Price Impacts Of Block Trading On The New York Stock Exchange," *JOF*, 1972, v27(3), 569-588.)

Stoll, Hans R. (Kraus, Alan and Hans R. Stoll. "Parallel Trading By Institutional Investors," *JFQA*, 1972, v7(5), 2107-2138.)

Stoll, Hans R. (Protopapadakis, Aris and Hans R. Stoll. "Spot And Futures Prices And The Law Of One Price," *JOF*, 1983, v38(5), 1431-1455.)

Stoll, Hans R. (Protopapadakis, Aris A. and Hans R. Stoll. "The Law Of One Price In International Commodity Markets: A Reformulation And Some Formal Tests," *JIMF*, 1986, v5(3), 335-360.)

Stoll, Hans R. and Robert E. Whaley. "Volatility And Futures: Message Versus Messenger," *JPM*, 1987-88, v14(2), 20-22.

Stoll, Hans R. and Robert E. Whaley. "Program Trading And Expiration-Day Effects," *FAJ*, 1987, v43(2), 16-28.

Stoll, Hans R. and Robert E. Whaley. "Program Trading And Individual Stock Returns: Ingredients Of The Triple-Witching Brew," *JOB*, 1990, v63(1), Part 2, S165-S192.

Stoll, Hans R. and Robert E. Whaley. "The Dynamics Of Stock Index And Stock Index Futures Returns," *JFQA*, 1990, v25(4), 441-468.

Stoll, Hans R. and Robert E. Whaley. "Stock Market Structure And Volatility," *RFS*, 1990, v3(1), 37-71.

Stoll, Hans R. and Robert E. Whaley. "Futures And Options On Stock Indexes: Economic Purpose, Arbitrage, And Market Structure," *RFM*, 1988, v7(2), 224-249.

Stolz, Richard W. (Booth, James R., Richard L. Smith and Richard W. Stolz. "Use Of Interest Rate Futures By Financial Institutions," *JBR*, 1984-85, v15(1), 15-20.)

Stolz, Richard W. (Jessup, Paul F. and Richard W. Stolz. "Customer Alternatives Among Rural Banks," *JBR*, 1975-76, v6(2), 135-139.)

Stolz, Robert K. "Is Executive Development Coming Of Age?," *JOB*, 1955, v28(1), 48-57.

Stone, Bernell K. and Ned C. Hill. "The Design Of A Cash Concentration System," *JFQA*, 1981, v16(3), 301-322.

Stone, Bernell K. and Ned C. Hill. "Cash Transfer Scheduling For Efficient Cash Concentration," *FM*, 1980, v9(3), 35-43.

Stone, Bernell K. and Ned C. Hill. "Alternative Cash Transfer Mechanisms And Methods: Evaluation Frameworks," *JBR*, 1982-83, v13(1), 7-16.

Stone, Bernell K. and Ned C. Hill. "Portfolio Management And The Shrinking Knapsack Algorithm," *JFQA*, 1979, v14(5), 1071-1083.

Stone, Bernell K. and Robert A. Wood. "Daily Cash Forecasting: A Simple Method For Implementing The Distribution Approach," *FM*, 1977, v6(3), 40-50.

Stone, Bernell K. and Robert Reback. "Constructing A Model For Managing Portfolio Revisions," *JBR*, 1975-76, v6(1), 48-60.

Stone, Bernell K. (Hill, Ned C. and Bernell K. Stone. "Accounting Betas, Systematic Operating Risk, And Financial Leverage: A Risk-Composition Approach To The Determinants Of Systematic Risk," *JFQA*, 1980, v15(3), 595-637.)

Stone, Bernell K. "A General Class Of Three-Parameter Risk Measures," *JOF*, 1973, v28(3), 675-685.

Stone, Bernell K. "A Linear Programming Formulation Of The General Portfolio Selection Problem," *JFQA*, 1973, v8(4), 621-636.

Stone, Bernell K. "Allocating Credit Lines, Planned Borrowing, And Tangible Services Over A Company's Banking System," FM, 1974, v4(2), 65-78.

Stone, Bernell K. "Cash Planning And Credit-Line Determination With A Financial Statement Simulator: A Cash Report On Short-Term Financial Planning," JFQA, 1973, v8(5), 711-729.

Stone, Bernell K. "Lock-Box Selection And Collection-System Design: Objective Function Validity," JBR, 1979-80, v10(4), 251-254.

Stone, Bernell K. "Systematic Interest-Rate Risk In A Two-Index Model Of Returns," JFQA, 1974, v9(5), 709-721.

Stone, Bernell K. "The Cost Of Bank Loans," JFQA, 1972, v7(5), 2077-2086.

Stone, Bernell K. "The Design Of A Company's Banking System," JOF, 1983, v38(2), 373-385.

Stone, Bernell K. "The Payments-Pattern Approach To The Forecasting And Control Of Accounts Receivable," FM, 1976, v5(3), 65-82.

Stone, Bernell K. "The Use Of Forecasts And Smoothing In Control-Limit Models For Cash Management," FM, 1972, v1(1), 72-84.

Stone, Bernell K. "Warrant Financing," JFQA, 1976, v11(1), 143-153.

Stone, Bernell K. (Miller, Tom W. and Bernell K. Stone. "Daily Cash Forecasting And Seasonal Resolution: Alternative Models And Techniques For Using The Distribution Approach," JFQA, 1985, v20(3), 335-352.)

Stone, Bernell K. and Tom W. Miller. "Daily Cash Forecasting With Multiplicative Models Of Cash Flow Patterns," FM, 1987, v16(4), 45-54.

Stone, Charles A. and Anne-Marie Zissu. "Does The Quality Of Investment Banks Foretell The Outcome Of Hostile Tender Offers?," JOF, 1990, v2(2), 1-11.

Stone, Charles A. and Anne-Marie Zissu. "Choosing A Discount Point/Contract Rate Combination," JREFEC, 1990, v3(3), 283-294.

Stone, David B. "Corporate Financing - The Investment Banker's Role," FAJ, 1958, v14(4), 15-18.

Stone, David. "Input-Output And The Multi-Product Firm," FAJ, 1969, v25(4), 96-102.

Stone, Donald E. "Computer-Aided Financial Analysis," FAJ, 1968, v24(1), 149-153.

Stone, Edward C. "Developments In Property-Casualty Insurance Legislation Resulting From Public Law 15," JRI, 1946, v13, 63-70.

Stone, Frances. "Investments: Research And Development," FAJ, 1963, v19(1), 19-23.

Stone, Frances. "Water And Securities," FAJ, 1957, v13(4), 59-64.

Stone, Frances. (Norby, William C. and Frances Stone. "Objectives Of Financial Reporting," FAJ, 1972, v28(4), 39-45,76-81.)

Stone, Gary K. "A Trend In Complaints Processed By State Insurance Departments," JRI, 1967, v34(2), 231-236.

Stone, Gary K. "Insurance In The Undergraduate Curriculum," JRI, 1972, v39(3), 451-456.

Stone, Gary K. "Life Insurance Sales Practices On The College Campus," JRI, 1973, v40(2), 167-179.

Stone, Gary K. (Rosenbloom, Jerry S. and Gary K. Stone. "Social Aspects Of The Rate Structure Of Medical Malpractice Insurance," JRI, 1978, v45(1), 53-64.)

Stone, James M. "A Theory Of Capacity And The Insurance Of Catastrophe Risks (Part I)," JRI, 1973, v40(2), 231-243.

Stone, James M. "A Theory Of Capacity And The Insurance Of Catastrophe Risks (Part II)," JRI, 1973, v40(3), 339-355.

Stone, James M. "A Theory Of Capacity And The Insurance Of Catastrophe Risks: Reply," JRI, 1975, v42(2), 340-341.

Stone, James M. "Principles Of The Regulation Of Futures Markets," JFM, v1(2), 117-122.

Stone, James M. (Gammill, James F., Jr. and James M. Stone. "Options, Futures, And Business Risk," JFM, 1982, v2(2), 141-149.)

Stone, John D. and Michael C. Walker. "The Effect Of Executive Stock Options On Corporate Financial Decisions," JFR, 1980, v3(1), 69-83.

Stone, John R. "A Winning Strategy For An Efficient Market," JPM, 1978-79, v5(2), 82.

Stone, Mark R. "Are Sovereign Debt Secondary Market Returns Sensitive To Macroeconomic Fundamentals?," JIMF, 1991, v10(Supp), S100-S122.

Stone, Robert W. "The Changing Structure Of The Money Market," JOF, 1965, v20(2), 229-238.

Stone, Robert. (Rutherford, Ronald and Robert Stone. "Corporate Real Estate Unit Formation: Rationale, Industry And Type Of Unit," JRER, 1989, v4(3), 121-129.)

Stonehill, Arthur, Theo Beekhuisen, Richard Wright, Lee Remmers, Norman Toy, Antonio Pares, Alan Shapiro, Douglas Egan and Thomas Bates. "Financial Goals And Debt Ratio Determinants," FM, 1974, v4(3), 27-41.

Stonehill, Arthur. "Internationalizing The Business Core: The Finance Component," JFED, 1978, v7, 7-12.

Stonehill, Arthur. (Remmers, Lee, Arthur Stonehill, Richard Wright and Theo Beekhuisen. "Industry And Size As Debt Ratio Determinants In Manufacturing Internationally," FM, 1974, v3(2), 24-32.)

Stonehill, Arthur. (Toy, N., A. Stonehill, L. Remmers, R. Wright and T. Beekhuisen. "A Comparative International Study Of Growth, Profitability, And Risk As Determinants Of Corporate Debt Ratios," JFQA, 1974, v9(5), 875-886.)

Stoney, P. J. M. (Bourn, Michael, P. J. M. Stoney and R. F. Wynn. "Price Indices For Current Cost Accounting," JBFA, 1976, v3(3), 149-172.)

Stoney, P. J. M. (Bourn, Michael, P. J. M. Stoney and R. F. Wynn. "Price Indices For Current Cost Accounting: A Rejoinder," JBFA, 1977, v4(1), 145-150.)

Storer, Robert W. "A Law Of Market Indeterminacy," FAJ, 1959, v15(5), 13-18.

Storer, Robert W. "Comparative Net Yields On Stocks And Municipal Bonds," FAJ, 1957, v13(4), 55-58.

Storer, Robert W. "An Evaluation Of The Stock Market," FAJ, 1960, v16(3), 57-62.

Storer, Robert W. "Bank Portfolio Management," FAJ, 1950, v6(1), 23-26.

Storer, Robert W. "Business Earnings, High Employment And Economic Growth," FAJ, 1962, v18(2), 29-32.

Storer, Robert W. "A Stock-Price Yardstick," FAJ, 1954, v10(4), 51-56.

Storer, Robert W. "Capital Goods - A Puzzling Paradox," FAJ, 1952, v8(3), 69-72.

Storer, Robert W. "Effects Of Yield-Maturity Curve On True Yields," FAJ, 1949, v5(2), 29-33.

Storer, Robert W. "Money Velocity And The Business Cycle," FAJ, 1956, v12(5), 89-98.

Storer, Robert W. "Present - Normal - Future A Study Of Production And Earnings," FAJ, 1956, v12(2), 25-32.

Storer, Robert W. "Problems Of Near-Money Versus Real Money," FAJ, 1965, v21(2), 73-77.

Storer, Robert W. "Psychological Aspects Of Business And The Stock Market," FAJ, 1953, v9(5), 95-96.

Storer, Robert W. "Stock Price Selectivity And Breadth," FAJ, 1960, v16(6), 97-101.

Storer, Robert W. "Stock Signal Criteria For Maximum Gains," FAJ, 1959, v15(1), 35-36.

Storer, Robert W. (Conn, Mabel V. and Robert W. Storer. "Stock Market Leading Indicators," FAJ, 1961, v17(5), 61-64.)

Storey, Reed K. "Conditions Necessary For Developing A Conceptual Framework," FAJ, 1981, v37(3), 51-54,56-58.

Storey, Ronald G. and Cecil R. Dipchand. "Factors Related To The Conversion Record Of Convertible Securities: The Canadian Experience 1946-1975," JFR, 1978, v1(1), 71-83.

Storoy, Sverre, Sten Thore and Marcel Boyer. "Equilibrium In Linear Capital Market Networks," JOF, 1975, v30(5), 1197-1211.

Storrs, Thomas I. "Freedom For Banks," JOF, 1975, v30(2), 293-302.

Stoughton, Neal M. "The Information Content Of Corporate Merger And Acquisition Offers," JFQA, 1988, v23(2), 175-198.

Stoughton, Neal M. (Darrough, Masako N. and Neal M. Stoughton. "Moral Hazard And Adverse Selection: The Question Of Financial Structure," JOF, 1986, v41(2), 501-514.)

Stoughton, Neal M. (Darrough, Masako N. and Neal M. Stoughton. "A Bargaining Approach To Profit Sharing In Joint Ventures," JOB, 1989, v62(2), 237-270.)

Stoughton, Neal M. (Jorion, Philippe and Neal M. Stoughton. "An Empirical Investigation Of The Early Exercise Premium Of Foreign Currency Options," JFM, 1989, v9(5), 365-376.)

Stoughton, Neal M. (Jorion, Philippe and Neal M. Stoughton. "The Valuation Of The Early Exercise Premium In The Foreign Currency Options Market," RDIBF, 1989, v3, 159-190.)

Stout, David E. (Heck, Jean Louis and David E. Stout. "Initial Empirical Evidence On The Relationship Between Finance Test-Question Sequencing And Student Performance Scores," FPE, 1991, v1(1), 41-48.)

Stout, Thomas T. (Asplund, Nathan M., D. Lynn Forster and Thomas T. Stout. "Farmers' Use Of Forward Contracting And Hedging," RFM, 1989, v8(1), 24-37.)

Stover, Roger D. and Gordon J. Alexander. "Bank Managed Equity Common Trust Funds: A Performance Analysis," JBR, 1977-78, v8(4), 218-223.

Stover, Roger D. and James M. Miller. "Additional Evidence On The Capital Market Effect Of Bank Failures," FM, 1983, v12(1), 36-41.

Stover, Roger D. "A Re-Examination Of Bank Holding Company Acquisitions," JBR, 1982-83, v13(2), 101-108.

Stover, Roger D. "The Interaction Between Pricing And Underwriting Spread In The New Issue Convertible Debt Market," JFR, 1983, v6(4), 323-332.

Stover, Roger D. "The Single-Subsidiary Bank Holding Company," JBR, 1980-81, v11(1), 43-50.

Stover, Roger D. (Alexander, Gordon J. and Roger D. Stover. "Pricing In The New Issue Convertible Debt Market," FM, 1977, v6(3), 35-39.)

Stover, Roger D. (Alexander, Gordon J. and Roger D. Stover. "The Effect Of Forced Conversions On Common Stock Prices," FM, 1980, v9(1), 39-45.)

Stover, Roger D. (Alexander, Gordon J., Roger D. Stover and David B. Kuhnau. "Market Timing Strategies In Convertible Debt Financing," JOF, 1979, v34(1), 143-155.)

Stover, Roger D. (Carter, Richard B. and Roger D. Stover. "The Effects Of Mutual To Stock Conversion Of Thrift Institutions On Managerial Behavior," JFSR, 1990, v4(2), 127-144.)

Stover, Roger D. (Christner, Ronald C. and Roger D. Stover. "Institutional Research And Regulation Are On The Wrong Track," JPM, 1974-75, v1(2), 12-20.)

Stover, Roger D. (Cranford, Brian K. and Roger D. Stover. "Interest Yields, Credit Ratings, And Economic Characteristics Of State Bonds: Comment," JMCB, 1988, v20(4), 691-695.)

Stover, Roger D. (Desai, Anand S. and Roger D. Stover. "Bank Holding Company Acquisitions, Stockholder Returns, And Regulatory Uncertainty," JFR, 1985, v8(2), 145-156.)

Stover, Roger D. (Gahlon, James M. and Roger D. Stover. "Diversification, Financial Leverage, And Conglomerate Systematic Risk," JFQA, 1979, v14(5), 999-1013.)

Stover, Roger D. (Gahlon, James M. and Roger D. Stover. "Debt Capacity And The Capital Budgeting Decisions: A Caveat," FM, 1979, v8(4), 55-59.)

Stover, Roger D. (Kim, Joo-hyun and Roger D. Stover. "The Role Of Bank Letters Of Credit In Corporate Tax-Exempt Financing," FM, 1987, v16(1), 31-37.)

Stover, Roger. (Ricketts, Donald and Roger Stover. "An Examination Of Commercial Bank Financial Ratios," JBR, 1978-79, v9(2), 121-124.)

Stowe, John D. "An Integer Programming Solution For The Optimal Credit Investigation/Credit Granting Sequence," FM, 1985, v14(2), 66-76.

Stowe, John D. (Simonson, Donald G., John D. Stowe and Collin J. Watson. "A Canonical Correlation Analysis Of Commercial Bank Asset/Liability Structures," JFQA, 1983, v18(1), 125-140.)

Stowe, John C. (Walker, Michael C., John D. Stowe and Shane Moriarity. "Decomposition Analysis Of Financial Statements," JBFA, 1979, v6(2), 173-186.)

Stowe, John D. and Collin J. Watson. "A Multivariate Analysis Of The Composition Of Life Insurer Balance Sheets," JRI, 1985, v52(2), 222-240.

Stowe, John D. "Life Insurance Company Portfolio Behavior," JRI, 1978, v45(3), 431-447.

Stowe, John D., Collin J. Watson and Terry D. Robertson. "Relationships Between The Two Sides Of The Balance Sheet: A Canonical Correlation Analysis," JOF, 1980, v35(4), 973-980.

Strachan, James L., David B. Smith and William L. Beedles. "The Price Reaction To (Alleged) Corporate Crime," FR, 1983, v18(2), 121-132.

Strahm, Norman D. "Preference Space Evaluation Of Trading System Performance," JFM, 1983, v3(3), 259-281.

Strain, Robert W. "Insurance Pricing And Its Role In Relation To Economic Theory And Marketing Management," JRI, 1966, v33(3), 447-458.

Strain, Robert W. "The Impact Of Increased Life Insurance Purchases On The Consumption Function," JRI, 1958, v25(4), 28-31.

Strain, Robert W. "The Insurance Society As An Integral Part Of An Insurance Program," JRI, 1958, v25(4), 58-63.

Strangways, Raymond and Bruce Yandle, Jr. "Effect Of State Usury Laws On Housing Starts In 1966," JFQA, 1971, v6(1), 665-669.

Strangways, Raymond. (Donaldson, Loraine and Raymond S. Strangways. "Can Ghetto Groceries Price Competitively And Make A Profit?," JOB, 1973, v46(1), 61-65.)

Straszheim, Donald H. "Profits Vs. Phase 2 Margin Guidelines," FAJ, 1972, v28(2), 27-32,83-85.

Straus, Robert. "Recognizing The Problem Drinker In Business And Industry," JOB, 1952, v25(2), 95-100.

Strauss, Anselm L. (Martin, Norman H. and Anselm L. Strauss. "Patterns Of Mobility Within Industrial Organizations," JOB, 1956, v29(2), 101-110.)

Strauss, George. "The Changing Role Of The Working Supervisor," JOB, 1957, v30(3), 202-211.

Strauss, William. (Reichert, Alan, William Strauss, David Northcutt and Warren Spector. "The Impact Of Economic Conditions And Electronic Payments Technology On Federal Reserve Check Volume," JBR, 1983-84, v14(4), 291-296.)

Strauss, William. (Reichert, Alan K., William Strauss and Randall C. Merris. "An Economic Analysis Of Short-Run Fluctuations In Federal Reserve Wire Transfer Volume," JBR, 1984-85, v15(4), 222-228.)

Strawser, Robert H. "A Comparative Study Of Perceived Adequacy Of Financial Reporting Practices Of Commercial Banks," JBR, 1971-72, v2(4), 48-58.

Strawser, Robert H. "Trends In The Financial Reporting Practices Of Commercial Banks," JBR, 1970-71, v1(2), 20-29.

Strawser, Robert H. (Cooper, Kerry and Robert H. Strawser. "Evaluation Of Capital Investment Projects Involving Asset Leases," FM, 1974, v4(1), 44-49.)

Strawser, Robert H. (Grossman, Steven D., Gary L. Schugart and Robert H. Strawser. "An Intra And Inter-Industry Comparison Of Performance Measures Based On Alternative Income Concepts," FR, 1979, v14(3), 13-24.)

Strawser, Robert H. (Richards, R. Malcolm, James J. Benjamin and Robert H. Strawser. "An Examination Of The Accuracy Of Earnings Forecasts," FM, 1977, v6(3), 78-86.)

Strawser, Robert H. (Slocum, John W., Jr. and Robert H. Strawser. "The Impact Of Job Level, Geographical Location And Organizational Size On The Managerial Satisfaction Of Bankers," JBR, 1970-71, v1(3), 41-49.)

Strebel, Paul J. and Avner Arbel. "Pay Attention To Neglected Firms!," JPM, 1982-83, v9(2), 37-42.

Strebel, Paul J. (Carvell, Steven A. and Paul J. Strebel. "Is There A Neglected Firm Effect?," JBFA, 1987, v14(2), 279-290.)

Strebel, Paul. (Arbel, Avner, Steven Carvell and Paul Strebel. "Giraffes, Institutions And Neglected Firms," FAJ, 1983, v39(3), 57-63.)

Strebel, Paul. (Arbel, Avner and Paul Strebel. "The Neglected And Small Firm Effects," FR, 1982, v17(4), 201-218.)

Strebel, Paul. (Carvell, Steven and Paul Strebel. "A New Beta Incorporating Anaysts' Forecasts," JPM, 1984-85, v11(1), 81-85.)

Strebel, Paul. (Grier, Paul and Paul Strebel. "An Implicit Clientele Test Of The Relationship Between Taxation And Capital Structure," JFR, 1983, v6(2), 163-174.)

Strebel, Paul. (Grier, Paul and Paul Strebel. "The Empirical Relationship Between Taxation And Capital Structure," FR, 1980, v15(3), 45-57.)

Street, Donald M. "The Role Of Equipment Obligations In Postwar Railroad Financing," JOF, 1960, v15(3), 333-340.

Street, Robert L. (Beightler, Charles S. and Robert L. Street. "Profit Planning In Non-Life Insurance Companies Through The Use Of A Probability Model," JRI, 1967, v34(2), 255-268.)

Stremmel, Stephen C. (Milutinovich, Jugoslav S. and Stephen C. Stremmel. "Reduction Of Terminal Response Time In An Expanding Real Time Banking System" JBR, 1975-76, v6(4), 275-282.)

Strickland, Thomas H. (Skantz, Terrance R., Dale O. Cloninger and Thomas H. Strickland. "Price-Fixing And Shareholder Returns: An Empirical Study," FR, 1990, v25(1), 153-164.)

Strickland, Thomas H. (Skantz, Terrance R. and Thomas H. Strickland. "House Prices And A Flood Event: An Empirical Investigation Of Market Efficiency," JRER, 1987, v2(2), 75-83.)

Strickland, Thomas H. and Ghassem Homaifar. "Foreign Direct Investment: Evidence From Capital Market Data," GFJ, 1990, v1(2), 153-162.

Strickler, Les. "Undergraduate Finance Education Patterns," JFED, 1985, v14, 22-35.

Strock, Elizabeth. (Saunders, Anthony, Elizabeth Strock and Nickolaos G. Travlos. "Ownership Structure, Deregulation, And Bank Risk Taking," JOF, 1990, v45(2), 643-654.)

Strong, George H. "Management's Fourth Dimension," FAJ, 1967, v23(2), 97-102.

Strong, John S. "The Market Valuation Of Credit Market Debt," JMCB, 1989, v21(3), 307-320.

Strong, John S. and John R. Meyer. "Asset Writedowns: Managerial Incentives And Security Returns," JOF, 1987, v42(3), 643-661.

Strong, N. C. (Appleyard, A. R. and N. C. Strong. "Textbook Inconsistencies In Graphing Valuation Equations: A Note," FR, 1985, v20(4), 361-367.)

Strong, N. (Appleyard, A. R., N. Strong and M. Walker. "Mutual Fund Performance In The Context Of Models Of Equilibrium Capital Asset Pricing," JBFA, 1982, v8(3), 289-296.)

Strong, Robert A. "Do Share Price And Stock Splits Matter?," JPM, 1983-84, v10(1), 58-64.

Strong, Robert A. "The Impact Of Mayday On Diversification Costs: Comment," JPM, 1980-81, v7(3), 77-78.

Strong, Robert A. "Using Gunning's Fog Index With Term Papers And Outside Reading Lists," JFED, 1986, v15, 63-67.

Strong, Robert A. (Choi, Dosoung and Robert A. Strong. "The Pricing Of When-Issued Common Stock: A Note," JOF, 1983, v38(4), 1293-1298.)

Strongin, Steven and Vefa Tarhan. "Money Supply Announcements And The Market's Perception Of Federal Reserve Policy," JMCB, 1990, v22(2), 135-153.

Strotz, Robert H. "On Being Fooled By Figures: The Case Of Trading Stamps," JOB, 1958, v31(4), 304-310.

Strotz, Robert H. "Trading Comments On Trading Stamps: A Rejoinder," JOB, 1959, v32(3), 283-286.

Stroud, Hubert B. "The Land Development Corporation: A System Of Selling Rural Real Estate," AREUEA, 1978, v6(3), 271-286.

Stroyny, Alvin L. (Haugen, Robert A., Alvin L. Stroyny and Dean W. Wichern. "Rate Regulation, Capital Structure, And The Sharing Of Interest Rate Risk In The Electric Utility Industry," JOF, 1978, v33(3), 707-721.)

Struble, Frederick M. "Comments On 'Financial Futures Markets: Is More Regulation Needed?'," JFM, v1(2), 193-199.

Struble, Frederick. (Lombra, Raymond and Frederick Struble. "Monetary Aggregate Targets And The Volatility Of Interest Rates: A Taxonomic Discussion," JMCB, 1979, v11(3), 284-300.)

Struck, Peter L. and Lewis Mandell. "The Effect Of Bank Deregulation On Small Business: A Note," JOF, 1983, v38(3), 1025-1031.

Strunk, Norman. "The Improved Investment Position Of Savings And Loan Associations," JOF, 1947, v2(2), 1-21.

Struyk, Raymond. (Follain, James and Raymond Struyk. "Homeownership Effects Of Alternative Mortgage Instruments," AREUEA, 1977, v5(1), 1-43.)

Stuck, B. W. "Explicit Solutions To Some Single-Period Investment Problems For Risky Log-Stable Stocks," JFEC, 1976, v3(3), 277-294.

Studness, Charles M. "New York Stock Exchange Trading," FAJ, 1968, v24(6), 26-36.

Stuhr, David. (Korobow, Leon and David Stuhr. "Performance Measurement Of Early Warning Models: Comments On West And Other Weakness/Failure Prediction Models," JBF, 1985, v9(2), 267-273.)

Stulz, Rene M. and Herb Johnson. "An Analysis Of Secured Debt," JFEC, 1985, v14(4), 501-522.

Stulz, Rene M. "A Model Of International Asset Pricing," JFEC, 1981, v9(4), 383-406.

Stulz, Rene M. "Asset Pricing And Expected Inflation," JOF, 1986, v41(1), 209-224.

Stulz, Rene M. "Capital Mobility And The Current Account," JIMF, 1988, v7(2), 167-180.

Stulz, Rene M. "Currency Preferences, Purchasing Power Risks, And The Determination Of Exchange Rates," JMCB, 1984, v16(3), 302-316.

Stulz, Rene M. "Managerial Control Of Voting Rights: Financing Policies And The Market For Corporate Control," JFEC, 1988, v20(1/2), 25-54.

Stulz, Rene M. "Managerial Discretion And Optimal Financing Policies," JFEC, 1990, v26(1), 3-28.

Stulz, Rene M. "On The Determinants Of Net Foreign Investment," JOF, 1983, v38(2), 459-468.

Stulz, Rene M. "On The Effects Of Barriers To International Investment," JOF, 1981, v36(4), 923-934.

Stulz, Rene M. "Optimal Hedging Policies," JFQA, 1984, v19(2), 127-140.

Stulz, Rene M. "Options On The Minimum Or The Maximum Of Two Risky Assets: Analysis And Applications," JFEC, 1982, v10(2), 161-185.

Stulz, Rene M. "Real Exchange Rate Dynamics And The Financial Theory Of The Trading Firm," RDIBF, 1989, v3, 247-262.

Stulz, Rene M. (Bailey, Warren and Rene M. Stulz. "The Pricing Of Stock Index Options In A General Equilibrium Model," JFQA, 1989, v24(1), 1-12)

Stulz, Rene M. (Bailey, Warren and Rene M. Stulz. "Benefits Of International Diversification: The Case Of Pacific Basin Stock Markets," JPM, 1990, v16(4), 57-61.)

Stulz, Rene M. (Kim, Yong Cheol and Rene M. Stulz. "The Eurobond Market And Corporate Financial Policy: A Test Of The Clientele Hypothesis," JFEC, 1988, v22(2), 189-206.)

Stulz, Rene M. (Lang, Larry H. P., Rene M. Stulz and Ralph A. Walkling. "Managerial Performance, Tobin's Q, And The Gains From Successful Tender Offers," JFEC, 1989, v24(1), 137-154.)

Stulz, Rene M. (Reagan, Patricia B. and Rene M. Stulz. "Contracts, Delivery Lags, And Currency Risk," JIMF, 1989, v8(1), 89-104.)

Stulz, Rene M. (Reagan, Patricia B. and Rene M. Stulz. "Risk-Bearing, Labor Contracts, And Capital Markets," RIF, 1986, v6, 217-232.)

Stulz, Rene M. (Smith, Clifford W. and Rene M. Stulz. "The Determinants Of Firms' Hedging Policies," JFQA, 1985, v20(4), 391-406.)

Stulz, Rene M., Ralph A. Walkling and Moon H. Song. "The Distribution Of Target Ownership And The Division Of Gains In Successful Takeovers," JOF, 1990, v45(3), 817-834.

Stulz, Rene. (Johnson, Herb and Rene Stulz. "The Pricing Of Options With Default Risk," JOF, 1987, v42(2), 267-280.)

Stumpp, Mark and James Scott. "Does Liquidity Predict Stock Returns?," JPM, 1991, v17(2), 35-40.

Sturrock, Thomas. (Thies, Clifford F. and Thomas Sturrock. "The Pension-Augmented Balance Sheet," JRI, 1988, v55(3), 467-480.)

Stutzer, Michael J. (Smith, Bruce D. and Michael J. Stutzer. "Credit Rationing And Government Loan Programs: A Welfare Analysis," AREUEA, 1989, v17(2), 177-193.)

Stutzer, Michael J. (Smith, Bruce D. and Michael J. Stutzer. "Adverse Selection, Aggregate Uncertainty, And The Role For Mutual Insurance Contracts," JOB, 1990, v63(4), 493-510.)

Stutzer, Michael J. (Smith, Bruce D. and Michael J. Stutzer. "Adverse Selection And Mutuality: The Case Of The Farm Credit System," JFI, 1990, v1(2), 125-149.)

Suarez, A. Fernandez. (Morin, Roger A. and A. Fernandez Suarez. "Risk Aversion Revisited," JOF, 1983, v38(4), 1201-1216.)

Subrahmanyam, M. G. (Stapleton, R. C. and M. G. Subrahmanyam. "The Valuation Of Options When Asset Returns Are Generated By A Binomial Process," JOF, 1984, v39(5), 1525-1539.)

Subrahmanyam, M. G. (Stapleton, R. C. and M. G. Subrahmanyam. "The Market Model And Capital Asset Pricing Theory: A Note," JOF, 1983, v38(5), 1637-1642.)

Subrahmanyam, M. G. (Stapleton, R. C. and M. G. Subrahmanyam. "Market Imperfections, Capital Market Equilibrium And Corporation Finance," JOF, 1977, v32(2), 307-319.)

Subrahmanyam, M. G. (Stapleton, R. C. and M. G. Subrahmanyam. "Notes On Multiperiod Valuation And The Pricing Of Options: A Comment," JOF, 1984, v39(1), 303-306.)

Subrahmanyam, M. G. (Stapleton, R. C. and M. G. Subrahmanyam. "The Valuation Of Multivariate Contingent Claims In Discrete Time Models," JOF, 1984, v39(1), 207-228.)

Subrahmanyam, M. G. (Stapleton, R. C. and M. G. Subrahmanyam. "Marketability Of Assets And The Price Of Risk," JFQA, 1979, v14(1), 1-10.)

Subrahmanyam, M. G. (Stapleton, R. C. and M. G. Subrahmanyam. "Risk Aversion And The Intertemporal Behavior Of Asset Prices," RFS, 1990, v3(4), 677-694.)

Subrahmanyam, Marti G. "On The Optimality Of International Capital Market Integration," JFEC, 1975, v2(1), 3-28.

Subrahmanyam, Marti G. (Brenner, Menachem and Marti G. Subrahmanyam. "Intra-Equilibrium And Inter-Equilibrium Analysis In Capital Market Theory: A Clarification," JOF, 1977, v32(4), 1313-1319.)

Subrahmanyam, Marti G. (Brenner, Menachem and Marti G. Subrahmanyan. "A Simple Formula To Compute The Implied Standard Deviation," FAJ, 1988, v44(5), 80-83.)

Subrahmanyam, Marti G. (Brenner, Menachem, Marti G. Subrahmanyam and Jun Uno. "Arbitrage Opportunities In The Japanese Stock And Futures Markets," FAJ, 1990, v46(2), 14-24.)

Subrahmanyam, Marti G. (Brenner, Menachem, Marti G. Subrahmanyam and Jun Uno. "The Behavior Of Prices In The Nikkei Spot And Futures Market," JFEC, 1989, v23(2), 363-384.)

Subrahmanyam, Marti G. (Kalay, Avner and Marti G. Subrahmanyam. "The Ex-Dividend Day Behavior Of Option Prices," JOB, 1984, v57(1), Part 1, 113-128.)

Subrahmanyam, Marti G. (Stapleton, Richard C. and Marti G. Subrahmanyam. "Uncertain Inflation, Exchange Rates, And Bond Yields," JBF, 1981, v5(1), 93-108.)

Subrahmanyam, Marti. (Brenner, Menachem, Georges Courtadon And Marti Subrahmanyam. "Options On The Spot And Options On Futures," JOF, 1985, v40(5), 1303-1317.)

Subrahmanyam, Marti. (Brenner, Menachem, Georges Courtadon and Marti Subrahmanyam. "Options On Stock Indices And Options On Futures," JBF, 1989, v13(4/5), 773-782.)

Subrahmanyam, Marti. (Brick, Ivan E., William Fung and Marti Subrahmanyam. "Leasing And Financial Intermediation: Comparative Tax Advantages," FM, 1987, v16(1), 55-59.)

Subramanian, N. (Edmister, Robert O. and N. Subramanian. "Determinants Of Brokerage Commission Rates For Institutional Investors: A Note," JOF, 1982, v37(4), 1087-1093.)

Suchanek, Gerry L. (Forsythe, Robert and Gerry L. Suchanek. "The Impossibility Of Efficient Decision Rules For Firms In Competitive Stock Market Economies," JFQA, 1982, v17(4), 555-574.)

Sudit, Ephrain F. (Kinberg, Yoram and Ephrain F. Sudit. "Successive Retention Of Funds, Loan Profitability And Marketing Implications In Banking," JBF, 1978, v2(3), 243-255.)

Sudit, Ephraim F. (Jagpal, Harsharanjeet S., Ephraim F. Sudit and Hrishikesh D. Vinod. "Measuring Dynamic Marketing Mix Interactions Using Translog Functions," JOB, 1982, v55(3), 401-415.)

Sudman, Seymour, Norman M. Bradburn and Galen Gockel. "The Extent And Characteristics Of Racially Integrated Housing In The United States," JOB, 1969, v42(1), 50-92.

Sugars, Edmund G. "A Managerial Theory For The Non-Life Stock Company," JRI, 1972, v39(2), 245-256.

Sugars, Edmund G. "A Risk Theoretic Prescription For Regulated Ratemaking," JRI, 1972, v39(3), 475-478.

Sugars, Edmund G. "Selected Results From A Risk-Theoretic Simulation Of An Insurance Company," JRI, 1974, v41(2), 221-228.

Sugden, Robert. (Starmer, Chris and Robert Sugden. "Probability And Juxtaposition Effects: An Experimental Investigation Of The Common Ratio Effect," JRU, 1989, v2(2), 159-178.)

Sugrue, Timothy F. and Frederick C. Scherr. "An Empirical Test Of Ross's Cash Flow Beta Theory Of Capital Structure," FR, 1989, v24(3), 355-370.

Suhler, Diane Rizzuto. (Kolodny, Richard and Diane Rizzuto Suhler. "Changes In Capital Structure, New Equity Issues, And Scale Effects," JFR, 1985, v8(2), 127-136.)

Sullivan, A. Charlene and Debra Drecnik Worden. "Deregulation, Tax Reform, And The Use Of Consumer Credit," JFSR, 1989, v3(1), 77-91.

Sullivan, Barry F. "Meeting The Challenge Of Controlling Banking Costs And Developing Pricing Strategies," JBR, 1985-86, v16(4), 178-181.

Sullivan, James A. and Richard G. Marcis. "Forecasting Consumer Installment Credit: An Application Of Parametric Time Series Modeling," JOB, 1975, v48(1), 98-107.

Sullivan, James R. "What Price Featherbedding? (Railroads)," FAJ, 1959, v15(1), 29-34.

Sullivan, John L., Jr. "Current Trends In The Reduction Of Stock Certificates," JBR, 1972-73, v3(2), 118-122.

Sullivan, John P. "Why Research?," FAJ, 1955, v11(1), 61-64.

Sullivan, Mary. "Measuring Image Spillovers In Umbrella-Branded Products," JOB, 1990, v63(3), 309-330.

Sullivan, Michael J., Pamela P. Peterson and David R. Peterson. "Two-Stage Acquisitions, Free-Riding, And Corporate Control," FR, 1990, v25(3), 405-420.

Sullivan, Timothy G. "Market Power, Profitability And Financial Leverage," JOF, 1974, v29(5), 1407-1414.

Sullivan, Timothy G. (Rosenthal, Leonard and Timothy G. Sullivan. "Some Estimates Of The Impact Of Corporate Diversification On The Valuation And Leverage Of USA Firms: Estimates From 1972 Data," JBFA, 1985, v12(2), 275-284.)

Sullivan, Timothy J. "Significance Of Population Changes On Investment Trends," FAJ, 1966, v22(6), 25-33.

Sullivan, Timothy P. (Joehnk, Michael D. and Timothy P. Sullivan. "An Annotated Bibliography Of Bond Literature," JFED, 1974, v3, 106-113.)

Sullivan, Timothy. (Pari, Robert, Steven Carvell and Timothy Sullivan. "Analyst Forecasts And Price/Earnings Ratios," FAJ, 1989, v45(2), 60-62.)

Sultan, Jahangir. (Melvin, Michael and Jahangir Sultan. "South African Political Unrest, Oil Prices, And The Time Varying Risk Premium In The Gold Futures Market," JFM, 1990, v10(2), 103-112.)

Sumka, Howard J. (Stegman, Michael A. and Howard J. Sumka. "Market Implications Of A Direct Cash Assistance Program In Southern Nonmetropolitan Cities," AREUEA, 1975, v3(3), 23-46.)

Sumka, Howard. (Stegman, Michael A. and Howard Sumka. "Nonmetropolitan And Inner-City Housing Investment Markets," AREUEA, 1974, v2(2), 81-100.)

Summer, Charles E., Jr. "Five 'Most Useful' Books For Management," JOB, 1965, v38(4), 416-418.

Summers, L. (Gilmour, A., M. Jensen, R. Mercer, N. Minow, J. Morley, R. Siefert, B. Stewart, L. Summers and I. Harris. "Panel: The Economic Consequences Of High Leverage And Stock Market Pressures On Corporate Management: A Roundtable Discussion," JACF, 1990, v3(2), 6-37.)

Summers, Lawrence H. "Does The Stock Market Rationally Reflect Fundamental Values?," JOF, 1986, v41(3), 591-600.

Summers, Lawrence H. "On Economics And Finance," JOF, 1985, v40(3), 633-636.

Summers, Lawrence H. "Selections From The Senate And House Hearings On LBOs And Corporate Debt," JACF, 1989, v2(1), 45-51.

Summers, Lawrence H. (Cutler, David M., James M. Poterba and Lawrence H. Summers. "What Moves Stock Prices?," JPM, 1989, v15(3), 4-12.)

Summers, Lawrence H. (De Long, J. Bradford, Andrei Shleifer, Lawrence H. Summers and Robert J. Waldmann. "The Survival Of Noise Traders In Financial Markets," JOB, 1991, v64(1), 1-20.)

Summers, Lawrence H. (De Long, J. Bradford, Andrei Shleifer, Lawrence H. Summers and Robert J. Waldmann. "Positive Feedback Investment Strategies And Destabilizing Rational Speculation," JOF, 1990, v45(2), 379-396.)

Summers, Lawrence H. (DeLong, J. Bradford, Andrei Shleifer, Lawrence H. Summers and Robert J. Waldmann. "The Size And Incidence Of The Losses From Noise Trading," JOF, 1989, v44(3), 681-696.)

Summers, Lawrence H. (Mankiw, N. Gregory and Lawrence H. Summers. "Money Demand And The Effects Of Fiscal Policies: Reply," JMCB, 1988, v20(4), 715-717.)

Summers, Lawrence H. (Mankiw, N. Gregory and Lawrence H. Summers. "Money Demand And The Effects Of Fiscal Policies," JMCB, 1986, v18(4), 415-429.)

Summers, Lawrence H. (Poterba, James M. and Lawrence H. Summers. "New Evidence That Taxes Affect The Valuation Of Dividends," JOF, 1984, v39(5), 1397-1415.)

Summers, Lawrence H. (Poterba, James M. and Lawrence H. Summers. "Mean Reversion In Stock Prices: Evidence And Implications," JFEC, 1988, v22(1), 27-60.)

Summers, Lawrence H. and Victoria P. Summers. "When Financial Markets Work Too Well: A Cautious Case For A Securities Transactions Tax," JFSR, 1989, v3(2/3), 261-286.

Summers, Timothy. (Veit, E. Theodore, Mary Lee Avey, Jerry L. Corley and Timothy Summers. "The Role Of Stock Options In Bank Trust Departments: Fifth Federal Reserve District Banks," JBR, 1979-80, v10(4), 255-256.)

Summers, Victoria P. (Summers, Lawrence H. and Victoria P. Summers. "When Financial Markets Work Too Well: A Cautious Case For A Securities Transactions Tax," JFSR, 1989, v3(2/3), 261-286.)

Sumner, Howard A. "An Advance In Medicinal Chemistry," FAJ, 1952, v8(5), 81-84.

Sumner, Scott. "The Forerunners Of 'New Monetary Economics' Proposals To Stabilize The Unit Of Account," JMCB, 1990, v22(1), 109-118.

Sumner, Scott. (Grubaugh, Stephen and Scott Sumner. "Commodity Prices, Money Surprises, And Fed Credibility: Comment," JMCB, 1989, v21(3), 407-408.)

Sumners, DeWitt L. (Braswell, Ronald C., Barry R. Marks, Walter J. Reinhart and DeWitt L. Sumners. "The Effect Of Term Structure And Taxes On The Issuance Of Discount Bonds," FM, 1988, v17(4), 92-103.)

Sumners, DeWitt L. (Braswell, Ronald C., E. Joe Nosari and DeWitt L. Sumners. "A Comparison Of The True Interest Costs Of Competitive And Negotiated Underwritings In The Municipal Bond Market," JMCB, 1983, v15(1), 102-106.)

Sumrall, Brenda P. (Simpson, W. Gary and Brenda P. Sumrall. "The Determinants Of Objective Test Scores By Finance Students," JFED, 1979, v8, 58-62.)

Sundaram, Anant K. "Syndications In Sovereign Lending," JIMF, 1989, v8(3), 451-464.

Sundaram, Anant K. and Veena Mishra. "Currency Movements And Corporate Pricing Strategy," RDIBF, 1991, v4/5, 196-235.

Sundaram, Srinivasan. (Barton, Sidney L., Ned C. Hill and Srinivasan Sundaram. "An Empirical Test Of Stakeholder Theory Predictions Of Capital Structure," FM, 1989, v18(1), 36-44.)

Sundararaghavan, P. S. (Aggarwal, Raj and P. S. Sundararaghavan. "Efficiency Of The Silver Futures Market: An Empirical Study Using Daily Data," JBF, 1987, v11(1), 49-64.)

Sundaresan, M. "Constant Absolute Risk Aversion Preferences And Constant Equilibrium Interest Rates," JOF, 1983, v38(1), 205-212.

Sundaresan, M. "Consumption And Equilibrium Interest Rates In Stochastic Production Economies," JOF, 1984, v39(1), 77-92.

Sundaresan, M. (Richard, Scott F. and M. Sundaresan. "A Continuous Time Equilibrium Model Of Forward Prices And Future Prices In A Multigood Economy," JFEC, 1981, v9(4), 347-371.)

Sundaresan, Mahadevan. (Modest, David M. and Mahadevan Sundaresan. "The Relationship Between Spot And Futures Prices In Stock Index Futures Markets: Some Preliminary Evidence," JFM, 1983, v3(1), 15-41.)

Sundaresan, Suresh M. "Equilibrium Valuation Of Natural Resources," JOB, 1984, v57(4), 493-518.

Sundaresan, Suresh M. "Intertemporally Dependent Preferences And The Volatility Of Consumption And Wealth," RFS, 1989, v2(1), 73-90.

Sundaresan, Suresh M. (Ramaswamy, Krishna and Suresh M. Sundaresan. "The Valuation Of Floating-Rate Instruments: Theory And Evidence," JFEC, 1986, v17(2), 251-272.)

Sundaresan, Suresh M. (Ramaswamy, Krishna and Suresh M. Sundaresan. "The Valuation Of Options On Futures Contracts," JOF, 1985, v40(5), 1319-1340.)

Sundaresan, Suresh M. (Ramaswamy, Krishna and Suresh M. Sundaresan. "The Pricing Of Derivative Assets In Foreign Exchange Markets, RDIBF, 1987, v1, 187-202.)

Sundaresan, Suresh. "Valuation Swaps," RDIBF, 1991, v4/5, 390-418.

Sundem, Gary L. "Evaluating Capital Budgeting Models In Simulated Environments," JOF, 1975, v30(4), 977-991.

Sundem, Gary L. (Schall, Lawrence D., Gary L. Sundem and William R. Geijsbeek, Jr. "Survey And Analysis Of Capital Budgeting Methods," JOF, 1978, v33(1), 281-287.)

Sundem, Gary L. (Schall, Lawrence D. and Gary L. Sundem. "Capital Budgeting Methods And Risk: A Further Analysis," FM, 1980, v9(1), 7-11.)

Sunder, Shyam. "Corporate Capital Investment, Accounting Methods And Earnings: A Test Of The Control Hypothesis," JOF, 1980, v35(2), 553-565.

Sunder, Shyam. "Stationarity Of Market Risk: Random Coefficient Tests For Individual Stocks," JOF, 1980, v35(4), 883-896.

Sunderland, Thomas E. "Changing Legal Concepts," JOB, 1951, v24(4), 235-252.

Sunderman, Mark A. (Cannaday, Roger E. and Mark A. Sunderman. "Estimation Of Depreciation For Single-Family Appraisals," AREUEA, 1986, v14(2), 255-273.)

Sunderman, Mark A., John W. Birch, Roger E. Cannaday and Thomas W. Hamilton. "Testing For Vertical Inequity In Property Tax Systems," JRER, 1990, v5(3), 319-334.

Sunderman, Mark A., Roger E. Cannaday and Peter F. Colwell. "The Value Of Mortgage Assumptions: An Empirical Test," JRER, 1990, v5(2), 247-257.

Sung, Sam K. (McFarland, James W., R. Richardson Pettit and Sam K. Sung. "The Distribution Of Foreign Exchange Price Changes: Trading Day Effects And Risk Measurement--A Reply," JOF, 1987, v42(1), 189-194.)

Sung, Sam K. (McFarland, James W., R. Richardson Pettit and San K. Sung. "The Distribution Of Foreign Exchange Price Changes: Trading Day Effects And Risk Measurement," JOF, 1982, v37(3), 693-715.)

Surface, James R. (Gaumnitz, Erwin A., George E. Manners, James R. Surface, Maurice W. Lee and Paul Garner. "Dean's Forum: The Place Of Insurance In The Collegiate Curriculum," JRI, 1960, v27(4), 113-120.)

Suri, Hira L. (Bawa, Vijay S., James N. Odurtha, Jr., M. R. Rao and Hira L. Suri. "On Determination Of Stochastic Dominance Optimal Sets," JOF, 1985, v40(2), 417-431.)

Surkis, Julius. (Brick, Ivan E., W. G. Mellon, Julius Surkis and Murray Mohl. "Optimal Capital Structure: A Multi-Period Programming Model For Use In Financial Planning," JBF, 1983, v7(1), 45-68.)

Surz, Ronald J. "Elaborations On The Tax Consequences Of Long-Run Pension Policy," FAJ, 1981, v37(1), 52-54,60.

Sushka, Marie E. (Barrett, W. Brian, Myron B. Slovin and Marie E. Sushka. "Reserve Regulation And Recourse As A Source Of Risk Premia In The Federal Funds Market," JBF, 1988, v11(4), 575-584.)

Sushka, Marie E. (Polonchek, John, Myron B. Slovin and Marie E. Sushka. "Valuation Effects Of Commercial Bank Securities Offerings: A Test Of The Information Hypothesis," JBF, 1989, v13(3), 443-462.)

Sushka, Marie E. (Slovin, Myron B., Marie E. Sushka and Carl D. Hudson. "Corporate Commercial Paper, Note Issuance Facilities, And Shareholder Wealth," JIMF, 1988, v7(3), 289-302.)

Sushka, Marie E. (Slovin, Myron B., Marie E. Sushka and John A. Polonchek. "Corporate Sale-And-Leasebacks And Shareholder Wealth," JOF, 1990, v45(1), 289-300.)

Sushka, Marie E. and Yvette Bendeck. "Bank Acquisitions And Stockholders' Wealth," JBF, 1988, v11(4), 551-562.

Sushka, Marie Elizabeth and Myron B. Slovin. "The Macroeconomic Impact Of Changes In The Ceilings On Deposit Rates," JOF, 1977, v32(1), 117-130.

Sushka, Marie Elizabeth. (Slovin, Myron B. and Marie Elizabeth Sushka. "The Structural Shift In The Demand For Money," JOF, 1975, v30(3), 721-731.)

Sushka, Marie Elizabeth. (Slovin, Myron B. and Marie Elizabeth Sushka. "A Note On The Evidence On Alternative Models Of The Banking Firm: A Cross Section Study Of Commercial Loan Rates," JBF, 1984, v8(1), 99-108.)

Sushka, Marie Elizabeth. (Slovin, Myron B. and Marie Elizabeth Sushka. "A Model Of The Commercial Loan Rate," JOF, 1983, v38(5), 583-1596.)

Sussman, Jeffrey. "Individualized Student Learning Contracts In Finance," JFED, 1977, v6, 54-56.

Sussman, M. Richard. "A Note On The Implications Of Periodic 'Cash Flow'," JOF, 1962, v17(4), 658-662.

Sussna, Edward. (Moyer, R. Charles and Edward Sussna. "Registered Bank Holding Company Acquisitions: A Cross-Section Analysis," JFQA, 1973, v8(4), 647-661.)

Sutch, Richard and Franco Modigliani. "The Term Structure Of Interest Rates: A Re-examination Of The Evidence: A Reply," JMCB, 1969, v1(1), 112-120.

Sutch, Richard C. (Dobson, Steven W., Richard C. Sutch and David E. Vanderford. "An Evaluation Of Alternative Empirical Models Of

The Firm Structure Of Interest Rates," JOF, 1976, v31(4), 1035-1065.)

Sutcliffe, C. M. S. (Board, J. L. G. and C. M. S. Sutcliffe. "Optimal Portfolio Diversification And The Effects Of Differing Intra Sample Measures Of Return," JBFA, 1985, v12(4), 561-574.)

Sutcliffe, C. M. S. (Board, J. L. G. and C. M. S. Sutcliffe. "The Weekend Effect In UK Stock Market Returns," JBFA, 1988, v15(2), 199-214.)

Sutherland, Ronald J. "Income Velocity And Commercial Bank Portfolios," JOF, 1977, v32(5), 1752-1758.

Sutliff, David G. "Outlook For The Electrical Equipment Industry," FAJ, 1966, v22(3), 28-32.

Sutton, Ben B. "Recent Developments In Pension Planning - A Challenge To The Insurance Industry," JOF, 1954, v9(2), 148-159.

Sutton, Nancy A. (Holland, Rodger G. and Nancy A. Sutton. "The Liability Nature Of Unfunded Pension Obligations Since ERISA," JRI, 1988, v55(1), 32-58.)

Svensson, Lars E. O. (Razin, Assaf and Lars E. O. Svensson. "The Current Account And The Optimal Government Debt," JIMF, 1983, v2(2), 215-224.)

Swadener, Paul. "Gambling And Insurance Distinguished," JRI, 1964, v31(3), 463-468.

Swadener, Paul. "The Loss Ratio Method Of Rating And The Feedback Control Loop Concept," JRI, 1969, v36(4), 615-627.

Swales, George S., Jr. "Another Look At The President's Letter To Stockholders," FAJ, 1988, v44(2), 71-73.

Swamy, P. A. V. B. (Feige, Edgar L. and P. A. V. B. Swamy. "A Random Coefficient Model Of The Demand For Liquid Assets," JMCB, 1974, v6(2), 241-252.)

Swamy, P. A. V. B. (Schinasi, Garry J. and P. A. V. B. Swamy. "The Out-Of-Sample Forecasting Performance Of Exchange Rate Models When Coefficients Are Allowed To Change," JIMF, 1989, v8(3), 375-390.)

Swamy, P.A.V.B. (Tinsley, P., G. Fries, B. Garrett, A. Norman, P.A.V.B. Swamy and P. Von Zur Muehlen. "The Impact Of Uncertainty On The Feasibility Of Humphrey-Hawkins Objectives," JOF, 1981, v36(2), 489-496.)

Swan, Craig. "Housing Subsidies And Housing Starts," AREUEA, 1973, v1(2), 119-140.

Swan, Craig. "Pricing Private Mortgage Insurance," AREUEA, 1982, v10(3), 276-296.

Swan, Craig. "The Markets For Housing And Housing Services: A Comment," JMCB, 1973, v5(4), 960-972.

Swanick, Robert V. (Johnson, Rodney D. and Robert V. Swanick. "New Insights Into Forecasting And Long Range Planning," JBR, 1975-76, v6(1), 77-79.)

Swankoski, Mark V. (Lee, Insup, R. Richardson Pettit and Mark V. Swankoski. "Daily Return Relationships Among Asian Stock Markets," JBFA, 1990, v17(2), 265-284.)

Swanson, Ernst W. "Forecasting Consumer Expenditures On Nondurable Goods And Services," JOB, 1954, v27(1), 71-76.

Swanson, Paul J. (Solt, Michael E. and Paul J. Swanson. "On The Efficiency Of The Markets For Gold And Silver," JOB, 1981, v54(3), 453-478.)

Swanson, Peggy E. "Capital Market Integration Over The Past Decade: The Case Of The US Dollar," JIMF, 1987, v6(2), 215-226.

Swanson, Peggy E. "Compensating Balances And Foreigners' Dollar Deposits In United States Banks," JFR, 1983, v6(3), 257-263.

Swanson, Peggy E. "External Currency Market Data: An Application From BIS Series," JIMF, 1984, v3(1), 111-117.

Swanson, Peggy E. "Interrelationships Among Domestic And Eurocurrency Deposit Yields: A Focus On The U.S. Dollar," FR, 1988, v23(1), 81-94.

Swanson, Peggy E. "The International Transmission Of Interest Rates: A Note On Causal Relationships Between Short-Term External And Domestic U.S. Dollar Returns," JBF, 1988, v11(4), 563-574.

Swars, William B., III. "The Privacy Implications Of Insurers' Information Practices: Comment," JRI, 1980, v47(2), 338-340.

Swary, Itzhak. "Bank Acquisition Of Mortgage Firms And Stockholders' Wealth: An Empirical Analysis," JBF, 1981, v5(2), 201-215.

Swary, Itzhak. "Bank Acquisition Of Non-Bank Firms: An Empirical Analysis Of Administrative Decisions," JBF, 1983, v7(2), 213-230.

Swary, Itzhak. "Stock Market Reaction To Regulatory Action In The Continental Illinois Crisis," JOB, 1986, v59(3), 451-474.

Swary, Itzhak. (Aharony, Joseph and Itzhak Swary. "A Note On Corporate Bankruptcy And The Market Model Risk Measures," JBFA, 1988, v15(2), 275-282.)

Swary, Itzhak. (Aharony, Joseph and Itzhak Swary. "Quarterly Dividend And Earnings Announcements And Stockholders' Returns: An Empirical Analysis," JOF, 1980, v35(1), 1-12.)

Swary, Itzhak. (Aharony, Joseph and Itzhak Swary. "Contagion Effects Of Bank Failures: Evidence From Capital Markets," JOB, 1983, v56(3), 305-322.)

Swary, Itzhak. (Aharony, Joseph, Haim Falk and Itzhak Swary. "Information Content Of Dividend Increases: The Case Of Regulated Utilities," JBFA, 1988, v15(3), 401-414.)

Swary, Itzhak. (Aharony, Joseph, Anthony Saunders and Itzhak Swary. "The Effects Of DIDMCA On Bank Stockholders' Returns And Risk," JBF, 1988, v11(3), 317-332.)

Swary, Itzhak. (Aharony, Joseph, Charles P. Jones and Itzhak Swary. "An Analysis Of Risk And Return Characteristics Of Corporate Bankruptcy Using Capital Market Data," JOF, 1980, v35(4), 1001-1016.)

Swary, Itzhak. (Aharony, Joseph, Anthony Saunders and Itzhak Swary. "The Effects Of The International Banking Act On Domestic Bank Profitability And Risk," JMCB, 1985, v17(4), Part 1, 493-506.)

Swary, Itzhak. (Aharony, Joseph and Itzhak Swary. "Effects Of The 1970 Bank Holding Company Act: Evidence From Capital Markets," JOF, 1981, v36(4), 841-853.)

Swary, Itzhak. (Grammatikos, Theoharry, Anthony Saunders and Itzhak Swary. "Returns And Risks Of U. S. Bank Foreign Currency Activities," JOF, 1986, v41(3), 670-681.)

Sweeney, George H. (Evans, Kaye D., John J. Siegfried and George H. Sweeney. "The Economic Cost Of Suboptimal Manufacturing Capacity," JOB, 1983, v56(1), 55-76.)

Sweeney, Joan and Richard James Sweeney. "Monetary Theory And The Great Capitol Hill Baby Sitting Co-Op Crisis," JMCB, 1977, v9(1), 86-89.

Sweeney, Kevin B. "Radio And Its Booming Next 10 Years," FAJ, 1960, v16(2), 39-40.

Sweeney, R. J. "The Transactions Velocity Of Money And Its Efficiency," JPQA, 1984, v19(3), 339-350.

Sweeney, Richard J. and Arthur D. Warga. "Interest-Sensitive Stocks: An APT Application," FR, 1983, v18(4), 257-270.

Sweeney, Richard J. and Arthur D. Warga. "The Pricing Of Interest-Rate Risk: Evidence From The Stock Market," JOF, 1986, v41(2), 393-410.

Sweeney, Richard J. and Arthur D. Warga. "The Possibility Of Estimating Risk Premia In Asset Pricing Models," FR, 1986, v21(2), 299-308.

Sweeney, Richard J. "Beating The Foreign Exchange Market," JOF, 1986, v41(1), 163-182.

Sweeney, Richard J. "Evidence On Short-Term Trading Strategies," JPM, 1990, v17(1), 20-26.

Sweeney, Richard J. "Some Macro Implications Of Risk," JMCB, 1987, v19(2), 222-234.

Sweeney, Richard J. "Some New Filter Rule Tests: Methods And Results," JPQA, 1988, v23(3), 285-300.

Sweeney, Richard J. "Technical Strategies In Foreign Exchange Markets: An Interim Report," RDIBF, 1991, v4/5, 236-270.

Sweeney, Richard J. "Uncertainty, Capital Formation, And Exchange Rates," RDIBF, 1988, v2, 299-320.

Sweeney, Richard J. and Edward J. Q. Lee. "Trading Strategies In Forward Exchange Markets," AFPAF, 1989, v4(Supp), 55-80.

Sweeney, Richard James. (Hughes, John S., Dennis E. Logue and Richard James Sweeney. "Corporate International Diversification And Market Assigned Measures Of Risk And Diversification," JPQA, 1975, v10(4), 627-637.)

Sweeney, Richard James. (Logue, Dennis E. and Richard James Sweeney. "Inflation And Real Growth: Some Empirical Results," JMCB, 1981, v13(4), 497-501.)

Sweeney, Richard James. (Logue, Dennis E. and Richard James Sweeney. "Aspects Of International Monetary Influences," JPQA, 1978, v13(1), 143-156.)

Sweeney, Richard James. (Logue, Dennis E. and Richard James Sweeney. "'White-Noise' In Imperfect Markets: The Case Of The Franc/Dollar Exchange Rate," JOF, 1977, v32(3), 761-768.)

Sweeney, Richard James. (Logue, Dennis E. and Richard James Sweeney. "The Premia On Euro Rates," JOF, 1984, v39(3), 747-755.)

Sweeney, Richard James. (Sweeney, Joan and Richard James Sweeney. "Monetary Theory And The Great Capitol Hill Baby Sitting Co-Op Crisis," JMCB, 1977, v9(1), 86-89.)

Sweeney, Robert J. (Roenfeldt, Rodney L., Robert J. Sweeney, Steven J. Goldstein and Helen M. Kleschick. "Commentary On 1982 FMA Program," FM, 1982, v11(4), 52-54.)

Sweetser, Albert G. and Glenn H. Petry. "A History Of The Seven Academic Finance Associations And Their Contributions To Development Of The Discipline," FM, 1981, v10(2), Tenth Anniversary Edition, 46-70.

Sweetser, Albert G. "The Financing Of The Seven Academic Finance Associations And Their Journals," FM, 1981, v10(2), Tenth Anniversary Edition, 71-92.

Swidler, Steve and Paul Vanderheiden. "Another Opinion Regarding Divergence Of Opinion And Return," JFR, 1983, v6(1), 47-50.

Swidler, Steve and David Ketcher. "Economic Forecasts, Rationality, And The Processing Of New Information Over Time," JMCB, 1990, v22(1), 65-76.

Swim, Dudley. "Investors: It's On Us," FAJ, 1957, v13(2), 11-14.

Swinnerton, Eugene A., Richard J. Curcio and Richard E. Bennett. "Index Arbitrage Program Trading And The Prediction Of Intraday Stock Price Changes," RFM, 1988, v7(2), 300-323.

Swinyard, William R. "Strategy Development With Importance Analysis," JBR, 1979-80, v10(4), 228-234.

Swoboda, Alexander K. "International Banking: Current Issues In Perspective," JBF, 1982, v6(3), 323-348.

Swoboda, Peter. (Zechner, Josef and Peter Swoboda. "The Critical Implicit Tax Rate And Capital Structure," JBF, 1986, v10(3), 327-341.)

Swofford, James L. and Gerald A. Whitney. "Flexible Functional Forms And The Utility Approach To The Demand For Money: A Nonparametric Analysis," JMCB, 1986, v18(3), 383-389.

Sy, Wilson. "Market Timing: Is It A Folly?," JPM, 1990, v16(4), 11-16.

Syed, Azmat A. (Liu, Pu, Stanley D. Smith and Azmat A. Syed. "Stock Price Reactions To The Wall Street Journal's Securities Recommendations," JPQA, 1990, v25(3), 399-410.)

Syed, Azmat A., Pu Liu and Stanley D. Smith. "The Exploitation Of Inside Information At The Wall Street Journal: A Test Of Strong Form Efficiency," FR, 1989, v24(4), 567-580.

Syron, Richard F. "Administered Prices And The Market Reaction: The Case Of Urban Core Property Insurance," JOF, 1973, v28(1), 147-156.

Szatrowski, Z. Ted. "A Conceptual Overview Of The Electronic Funds Transfer System," JBR, 1974-75, v5(3), 197-199.

Szatrowski, Zenon. "A Statistical Approach To Formula Planning," FAJ, 1955, v11(2), 65-70.

Szego, G. P. "A Note On Co-Variance Properties Of Efficient Portfolios," JBF, 1978, v2(4), 399-401.

Szego, Giorgio P. "Bank Asset Management And Financial Insurance," JBF, 1986, v10(2), 295-308.

Szego, Giorgio P. "The Role Of International Banking In The 'Oil Surplus' Adjustment Process," JBF, 1983, v7(4), 497-518.

Szeplaki, Leslie and Ryland A. Taylor. "Banking, Credit, And Monetary Indicators In Reformed Socialist Planning," JMCB, 1972, v4(3), 572-581.

Szewczyk, Samuel H. and Raj Varma. "The Effect Of Proposition 103 On Insurers: Evidence From The Capital Market," JRI, 1990, v57(4), 671-681.

Szpiro, George G. "Optimal Insurance Coverage," JRI, 1985, v52(4), 704-710.

Szpiro, George G. "Optimal Insurance Coverage: Reply," JRI, 1987, v54(4), 813-815.

Tabell, Anthony W. and Edmund W. Tabell. "The Case For Technical Analysis," FAJ, 1964, v20(2), 67-76.

Tabell, Edmund W. "Stock Market Outlook - The Technical Viewpoint," FAJ, 1960, v16(3), 65-66.

Tabell, Edmund W. "The Importance Of Basic Economic Forces," FAJ, 1957, v13(1), 19-30.

Tabell, Edmund W. (Tabell, Anthony W. and Edmund W. Tabell. "The Case For Technical Analysis," FAJ, 1964, v20(2), 67-76.)

Tabellini, Guido. "Centralized Wage Setting And Monetary Policy In A Reputational Equilibrium," JMCB, 1988, v20(1), 102-118.

Tabellini, Guido. "Learning And The Volatility Of Exchange Rates," JIMF, 1988, v7(2), 425-436.

Tabellini, Guido. "Secrecy Of Monetary Policy And The Variability Of Interest Rates," JMCB, 1987, v19(4), 425-436.

Tabellini, Guido. (Edwards, Sebastian and Guido Tabellini. "Explaining Fiscal Policies And Inflation In Developing Countries," JIMF, 1991, v10(Supp), S16-S48.)

Taff, Conrad. "Dividend Omission As A Buying Signal," FAJ, 1954, v10(1), 67-70.

Taffler, Richard J. "Empirical Models For The Monitoring Of UK Corporations," JBF, 1984, v8(2), 199-228.

Taggart, Robert A. (Bodie, Zvi, Jay O. Light, Randall Morck and Robert A. Taggart, Jr. "Corporate Pension Policy: An Empirical Investigation," FAJ, 1985, v41(5), 10-16.)

Taggart, Robert A. (Bodie, Zvi and Robert A. Taggart. "Future Investment Opportunities And The Value Of The Call Provision On A Bond," JOF, 1978, v33(4), 1187-1200.)

Taggart, Robert A. (Ofer, Ahron R. and Robert A. Taggart. "'Bond Refunding Reconsidered': Reply," JOF, 1980, v35(1), 197-200.)

Taggart, Robert A., Jr. and Stuart I. Greenbaum. "Bank Capital And Public Regulation," JMCB, 1978, v10(2), 158-169.

Taggart, Robert A., Jr. "A Model Of Corporate Financing Decisions," JOF, 1977, v32(5), 1467-1484.

Taggart, Robert A., Jr. "Allocating Capital Among A Firm's Divisions: Hurdle Rates Vs. Budgets," JFR, 1987, v10(3), 177-190.

Taggart, Robert A., Jr. "Capital Budgeting And The Financing Decision: An Exposition," FM, 1977, v6(2), 59-64.

Taggart, Robert A., Jr. "Corporate Financing: Too Much Debt?," FAJ, 1986, v42(3), 35-42.

Taggart, Robert A., Jr. "Effects Of Deposit Rate Ceilings: The Evidence From Massachusetts Savings Banks," JMCB, 1978, v10(2), 139-157.

Taggart, Robert A., Jr. "Rate-of-Return Regulation And Utility Capital Structure Decisions," JOF, 1981, v36(2), 383-393.

Taggart, Robert A., Jr. "Taxes And Corporate Capital Structure In An Incomplete Market," JOF, 1980, v35(3), 645-659.

Taggart, Robert A., Jr. (Bodie, Zvi and Robert A. Taggart, Jr. "Future Investment Opportunities And The Value Of The Call Provision On A Bond: Reply," JOF, 1980, v35(1), 1055-1056.)

Taggart, Robert A., Jr. (Ofer, Aharon R. and Robert A. Taggart, Jr. "Bond Refunding: A Clarifying Analysis," JOF, 1977, v32(1), 21-30.)

Taggart, Robert A., Jr. (Orgler, Yair E. and Robert A. Taggart, Jr. "Implications Of Corporate Capital Structure Theory For Banking Institutions," JMCB, 1983, v15(2), 212-221.)

Taggart, Robert A., Jr. (Perry, Kevin J. and Robert A. Taggart, Jr. "The Growing Role Of Junk Bonds In Corporate Finance," JACF, 1988, v1(1), 37-45.)

Taggart, Robert A., Jr. (Rappaport, Alfred and Robert A. Taggart, Jr. "Evaluation Of Capital Expenditure Proposals Under Inflation," FM, 1982, v11(1), 5-13.)

Taggart, Robert A., Jr. (Senbet, Lemma W. and Robert A. Taggart, Jr. "Capital Structure Equilibrium Under Market Imperfections And Incompleteness," JOF, 1984, v39(1), 93-103.)

Tahai, Alireza. (Epley, Donald R. and Alireza Tahai. "Consumer-Revealed Preferences For A Margin And Other Associated Adjustable-Rate Mortgage Features," JRER, 1989, v4(1), 37-51.)

Takada, Hirokazu. (Khoury, Sarkis J., Bajis Dodin and Hirokazu Takada. "Multiple Time Series Analysis Of National Stock Markets And Their Structure: Some Implications," RDIBF, 1987, v1, 169-186.)

Takagi, Shinji. "Rediscount Policy And Official Capital Flows: A Study Of Monetary Control In Central America In The 1950s," JMCB, 1986, v18(2), 200-210.

Takagi, Shinji. "The Japanese Equity Market: Past And Present," JBF, 1989, v13(4/5), 537-570.

Takagi, Shinji. "Transactions Costs And The Term Structure Of Interest Rates In The OTC Bond Market In Japan," JMCB, 1987, v19(4), 515-527.

Takahashi, Kichinosuke, Yukiharu Kurokawa and Kazunori Watase. "Corporate Bankruptcy Prediction In Japan," JBF, 1984, v8(2), 229-247.

Takahashi, Toshiharu. (Maru, Junko and Toshiharu Takahashi. "Recent Developments Of Interdealer Brokerage In The Japanese Secondary Bond Markets," JPQA, 1985, v20(2), 193-210.)

Talbott, John C., Jr. (Losey, Robert L. and John C. Talbott, Jr. "Back On The Track With The Efficient Markets Hypothesis," JOF, 1980, v35(4), 1039-1043.)

Talley, Samuel H. "Regulating Bank Holding Company Capital," FM, 1976, v5(4), 68-70.

Talley, Samuel H. (Rose, John T. and Samuel H. Talley. "Financial Transactions Within Bank Holding Companies," JFR, 1984, v7(3), 209-217.)

Talley, Walter J., Jr. "New Tools For Evaluating Companies," FAJ, 1959, v15(1), 101-108.

Tallman, Gary D. "Computers In The Financial Management Classroom," JFED, 1983, v12, 69-72.

Tallman, Gary D., David F. Rush and Ronald W. Melicher. "Competitive Versus Negotiated Underwriting Costs For Regulated Industries," FM, 1974, v3(2), 49-55.

Talmor, Eli and Sheridan Titman. "Taxes And Dividend Policy," FM, 1990, v19(2), 32-35.

Talmor, Eli, Robert Haugen and Amir Barnea. "The Value Of The Tax Subsidy On Risky Debt," JOB, 1985, v58(2), 191-202.

Talmor, Eli. "A Normative Approach To Bank Capital Adequacy," JFQA, 1980, v15(4), 785-811.

Talmor, Eli. "Asymmetric Information, Signaling, And Optimal Corporate Financial Decisions," JFQA, 1981, v16(4), 413-435.

Talmor, Eli. "Tax Arbitrage Restrictions And Financial Leverage Clienteles," JBF, 1989, v13(6), 831-838.

Talmor, Eli. (Barnea, Amir, Eli Talmor and Robert A. Haugen. "Debt And Taxes: A Multiperiod Investigation," JBF, 1987, v11(1), 79-98.)

Talmor, Eli. (Benninga, Simon and Eli Talmor. "The Interaction Of Corporate And Government Financing In General Equilibrium," JOB, 1988, v61(2), 233-258.)

Talmor, Eli. (Green, Richard C. and Eli Talmor. "Asset Substitution And The Agency Costs Of Debt Financing," JBF, 1986, v10(3), 391-400.)

Talmor, Eli. (Green, Richard C. and Eli Talmor. "The Structure And Incentive Effects Of Corporate Tax Liabilities," JOF, 1985, v40(4), 1095-1114.)

Talmor, Eli. (Haugen, Robert A., Lemma W. Senbet and Eli Talmor. "Debt, Dividends, And Taxes: Equilibrium Conditions For Simultaneous Tax Neutrality Of Debt And Dividend Policies," RIF, 1986, v6, 1-28.)

Talmor, Eli. (Ravid, S. Abraham and Eli Talmor. "Government Financing, Taxation, And Capital Markets," RIF, 1988, v7, 21-52.)

Talwar, Prem P. (Singh, Saraswati P. and Prem P. Talwar. "Monetary And Fiscal Policies And Stock Prices," JBFA, 1982, v8(1), 75-91.)

Tam, Kar Yan. (Holsapple, Clyde W., Kar Yan Tam and Andrew B. Whinston. "Adapting Expert System Technology To Financial Management," FM, 1988, v17(3), 12-22.)

Tamari, Meir. "The Use Of A Bankruptcy Forecasting Model To Analyze Corporate Behavior In Israel," JBF, 1984, v8(2), 293-302.

Tamarkin, Maurry J. (Burgess, Richard C. and Maurry J. Tamarkin. "Regulatory Influences On Portfolio Performance: Short Selling And Regulation T," JFR, 1982, v5(1), 39-54.)

Tamarkin, Maurry J. (Conine, Thomas E. and Maurry J. Tamarkin. "On Diversification Given Asymmetry In Returns," JOF, 1981, v36(5), 1143-1155.)

Tamarkin, Maurry. (Baxter, Jennefer, Thomas E. Conine, Jr. and Maurry Tamarkin. "On Commodity Market Risk Premiums: Additional Evidence," JFM, 1985, v5(1), 121-125.)

Tamarkin, Maurry. (Conine, Thomas E., Jr. and Maurry Tamarkin. "A Pedagogic Note On The Derivation Of The Comparative Statics Of The Option Pricing Model," FR, 1984, v19(4), 397-400.)

Tamarkin, Maurry. (Conine, Thomas E., Jr. and Maurry Tamarkin. "Implications Of Skewness In Returns For Utilities' Cost Of Equity Capital," FM, 1985, v14(4), 66-71.)

Tamarkin, Maurry. (Conine, Thomas E., Jr. and Maurry Tamarkin. "Divisional Cost Of Capital Estimation: Adjusting For Leverage," FM, 1985, v14(1), 54-58.)

Tamarkin, Maurry. (Conine, Thomas E., Jr. and Maurry Tamarkin. "On Diversification Given Asymmetry In Returns: Erratum," JOF, 1982, v37(4), 1101-1101.)

Tamarkin, Maurry. (Conine, Thomas E., Jr. and Maurry Tamarkin. "Textbook Inconsistencies In Graphing Valuation Equations: A Further Note," FR, 1988, v23(2), 237-241.)

Tamarkin, Maurry. (Conine, Thomas E., Jr., Oscar W. Jensen and Maurry Tamarkin. "On Optimal Output In An Option Pricing Framework," JBFA, 1988, v15(1), 21-26.)

Tamir, A. (Agmon, T., A. R. Ofer and A. Tamir. "Variable Rate Debt Instruments And Corporate Debt Policy," JOF, 1981, v36(1), 113-125.)

Tan, Pearl Hock-Neo. (Low, Lay-Chin, Pearl Hock-Neo Tan and Hian-Chye Koh. "The Determination Of Audit Fees: An Analysis In The Singapore Context," JBFA, 1990, v17(2), 285-296.)

Tan, S. J. and Ilan Vertinsky. "Strategic Management Of International Financial Centers: A Tale Of Two Cities," RDIBF, 1988, v2, 87-104.

Tandon, Kishore and Yusif Simaan. "The Reaction Of Effective Exchange Rates To Information About Inflation," FR, 1985, v20(2), 164-179.

Tandon, Kishore and Thomas Urich. "International Market Response To Announcements Of US Macroeconomic Data," JIMF, 1987, v6(1), 71-84.

Tandon, Kishore. (Mandelker, Gershon and Kishore Tandon. "Common Stock Returns, Real Activity, Money, And Inflation: Some International Evidence," JIMF, 1985, v4(2), 267-286.)

Tandon, Kishore. (Shastri, Kuldeep and Kishore Tandon. "On The Use Of European Models To Price American Options On Foreign Currency," JFM, 1986, v6(1), 93-108.)

Tandon, Kishore. (Shastri, Kuldeep and Kishore Tandon. "Arbitrage Tests Of The Efficiency Of The Foreign Currency Options Market," JIMF, 1985, v4(4), 455-468.)

Tandon, Kishore. (Shastri, Kuldeep and Kishore Tandon. "Valuation Of American Options On Foreign Currency," JBF, 1987, v11(2), 245-270.)

Tandon, Kishore. (Shastri, Kuldeep and Kishore Tandon. "An Empirical Test Of A Valuation Model For American Options On Futures Contracts," JFQA, 1986, v21(4), 377-392.)

Tandon, Kishore. (Shastri, Kuldeep and Kishore Tandon. "Valuation Of Foreign Currency Options: Some Empirical Tests," JFQA, 1986, v21(2), 145-160.)

Tandon, Kishore. (Shastri, Kuldeep and Kishore Tandon. "Options On Futures Contracts: A Comparison Of European And American Pricing Models," JFM, 1986, v6(4), 593-618.)

Tandon, Sanjiv. (Carleton, Willard T., Glen Kendall And Sanjiv Tandon. "Application Of The Decomposition Principle To The Capital Budgeting Problem In A Decentralized Firm," JOF, 1974, v29(3), 815-827.)

Tang, Eric M. P. (Fong, H. Gifford and Eric M. P. Tang. "Immunized Bond Portfolios In Portfolio Protection," JPM, 1987-88, v14(2), 63-68.)

Tang, Roger Y. W. "Environmental Variables Of Multinational Transfer Pricing: A UK Perspective," JBFA, 1982, v8(2), 179-189.

Tannenbaum, Robert. "Managerial Decision-Making," JOB, 1950, v23(1), 22-39.

Tanner, J. Ernest and Levis A. Kochin. "The Determinants Of The Difference Between Bid And Ask Prices On Government Bonds," JOB, 1971, v44(4), 375-379.

Tanner, J. Ernest. "An Empirical Investigation Of Tax Discounting: A Comment," JMCB, 1979, v11(2), 214-218.

Tanner, J. Ernest. "Empirical Evidence On The Short-Run Real Balance Effect In Canada," JMCB, 1970, v2(4), 473-485.

Tanner, J. Ernest. "The Determinants Of Interest Cost On New Municipal Bonds: A Reevaluation," JOB, 1975, v48(1), 74-80.

Tanner, John R. (Cudd, Mike, John R. Tanner and Michael C. Budden. "The Issue Of Student Preparedness: Perceptions Of Finance Professors," JFED, 1989, v18, 60-64.)

Tanner, John R. (Redman, Arnold L. and John R. Tanner. "The Acquisition And Disposition Of Real Estate By Corporate Executives: A Survey," JRER, 1989, v4(3), 67-80.)

Tansey, Michael M. and Patricia Hoon Tansey. "An Analysis Of The Impact Of Usury Ceilings On Conventional Mortgage Loans," AREUEA, 1981, v9(3), 265-282.

Tansey, Patricia Hoon. (Tansey, Michael M. and Patricia Hoon Tansey. "An Analysis Of The Impact Of Usury Ceilings On Conventional Mortgage Loans," AREUEA, 1981, v9(3), 265-282.)

Tanzer, Ellen P. "Housing Quality And The Structure Tax: Evidence From Microdata," AREUEA, 1987, v15(2), 32-45.

Tapiero, Charles S. and Dror Zuckerman. "A Note On The Optimal Control Of A Cash Balance Problem," JBF, 1980, v4(4), 345-352.

Tapiero, Charles S. (Jacque, Laurent L., Pascal Lang and Charles S. Tapiero. "Towards An Expected Utility Paradigm For Foreign Exchange Risk Management: The Long And Short Of It'," RDIBF, 1989, v3, 191-228.)

Tapiero, Charles S. and Laurent Jacque. "The Expected Cost Of Ruin And Insurance Premiums In Mutual Insurance," JRI, 1987, v54(3), 594-602.

Tapley, Mark. "Offshore Alphas: Should Diversification Begin At Home?: Comment," JPM, 1979-80, v6(2), 76-78.

Tapley, T. Craig. (Chiang, Raymond C. and T. Craig Tapley. "Day-Of-The-Week Effects And The Futures Market," RFM, 1983, v2(3), 356-410.

Tapley, T. Craig. (Brigham, Eugene F. and T. Craig Tapley. "Financial Leverage And Use Of The Net Present Value Investment Criterion: A Reexamination," FM, 1985, v14(2), 48-52.)

Tapley, T. Craig. (Logue, Dennis E. and T. Craig Tapley. "Performance Monitoring And The Timing Of Cash Flows," FM, 1985, v14(3), 34-39.)

Tapley, T. Craig. (Pettway, Richard H., T. Craig Tapley and Takeshi Yamada. "The Impacts Of Financial Deregulation Upon Trading Efficiency And The Levels Of Risk And Return Of Japanese Banks," FR, 1988, v23(3), 243-268.)

Tapon, Francis. (McRae, James J. and Francis Tapon. "A New Test Of The Administered Pricing Hypothesis With Canadian Data," JOB, 1979, v52(3), 409-428.)

Tarantello, R. A. (Findlay, M. Chapman, III and R. A. Tarantello. "An M.B.A. Program In Real Estate With A Financial Emphasis," JFED, 1977, v6, 17-18.)

Tarhan, Vefa. "Unanticipated Interest Rates, Bank Stock Returns And The Nominal Contracting Hypothesis," JBF, 1987, v11(1), 99-116.

Tarhan, Vefa. (Spindt, Paul A. and Vefa Tarhan. "Bank Reserve Adjustment Process And The Use Of Reserve Carryover As A Reserve Management Tool: A Microeconometric Approach," JBF, 1984, v8(1), 5-20.)

Tarhan, Vefa. (Spindt, Paul A. and Vefa Tarhan. "Liquidity Structure Adjustment Behavior Of Large Money Center Banks," JMCB, 1980, v12(2), Part 1, 198-208.)

Tarhan, Vefa. (Spindt, Paul A. and Vefa Tarhan. "Bank Reserve Adjustment Process And The Use Of Reserve Carryover As A Reserve Management Tool: A Reply," JBF, 1989, v13(1), 37-40.)

Tarhan, Vefa. (Strongin, Steven and Vefa Tarhan. "Money Supply Announcements And The Market's Perception Of Federal Reserve Policy," JMCB, 1990, v22(2), 135-153.)

Tarleton, Jesse S. "Recommended Courses In International Business For Graduate Business Students," JOB, 1977, v50(4), 438-447.

Tashchian, Armen. (Diskin, Barry A. and Armen Tashchian. "Application Of Logit Analysis To The Determination Of Tenant Absorption In Condominium Conversion," AREUEA, 1984, v12(2), 191-205.) 3a?8

Tatar, Daniel D. "Teaching Securities Analysis With Real Funds," JFED, 1987, v16, 40-45.

Tatham, Charles, Jr. "A Brief History Of The Society," FAJ, 1945, v1(1), 3-5.

Tatham, Charles, Jr. "Book Value And Market Prices Of Electric Utility Common Stocks," FAJ, 1953, v9(5), 33-38.

Tatham, Charles, Jr. "Growth Factor In Electric Utility Earnings," FAJ, 1952, v8(2), 31-34.

Tatham, Charles, Jr. "Investment Value Of Electrical Utility Common Stocks," FAJ, 1954, v10(5), 11-16.

Tatham, Charles, Jr. "Outlook For Electrical Utility Earnings," FAJ, 1951, v7(1), 53-54.

Tatham, Charles, Jr. "Two Useful Ratios In Public Utility Bond Analysis," FAJ, 1945, v1(2), 29-32.

Tatham, Charles. "Are Two Million Investors Wrong?," FAJ, 1960, v16(6), 31-33.

Tatom, John A. "Will A Weaker Dollar Mean A Stronger Economy?," JIMF, 1987, v6(4), 433-448.

Tattersall, Robert. "In Defense Of The Consesus Decision," FAJ, 1984, v40(1), 55-57.

Taub, Allan J. (Bell, Edward B. and Allan J. Taub. "Selecting Income Growth And Discount Rates In Wrongful Death And Injury Cases: Comment," JRI, 1977, v44(1), 122-129.)

Taub, Bart. "Equilibrium Traits Of Durable Commodity Money," JBF, 1985, v9(1), 5-34.

Taube, Paul M. (MacDonald, Don N., Harry L. White, Paul M. Taube and William L. Huth. "Flood Hazard Pricing And Insurance Premium Differentials: Evidence From The Housing Market," JRI, 1990, v57(4), 654-663.)

Taube, Paul M. and Don N. MacDonald. "The Job Market For Finance Ph.D's," JFED, 1989, v18, 54-59.

Taube, Paul M. and Don N. MacDonald. "A Note On Residential Mortgage Selection: Borrower Decisions And Inflation Expectations," JRER, 1989, v4(1), 73-79.

Tauber, Ronald S. "Is Gold A Prudent Investment Under ERISA?," JPM, 1981-82, v8(1), 28-31.

Taubman, Paul. "The Economics Of The Asset Depreciation Range System: The Case Against ADR," JOF, 1972, v27(2), 511-524.

Taussig, R. A. (Hayes, S. L. and R. A. Taussig. "Are Cash Take-Over Bids Unethical?," FAJ, 1967, v23(1), 107-111.)

Tavis, L. A. (Merville, L. J. and L. A. Tavis. "A Total Real Asset Planning System," JFQA, 1974, v9(1), 107-115.)

Tavis, L. A. (Merville, L. J. and L. A. Tavis. "Financial Planning In A Decentralized Firm Under Conditions Of Competitive Capital Markets," FM, 1977, v6(3), 17-23.)

Tavis, L. A. (Merville, L. J. and L. A Tavis. "Optimal Working Capital Policies: A Chance-Constrained Programming Approach," JFQA, 1973, v8(1), 47-59.)

Tavis, L. A. (Merville, L. J. and L. A. Tavis. "A Generalized Model For Capital Investment," JOF, 1973, v28(1), 109-118.)

Tavis, Lee A. (Crum, Roy L. and Lee A. Tavis. "Allocating Multinational Resources When Objectives Conflict: A Problem Of Overlapping Systems," AFPAF, 1990, v5(1), 271-294.)

Tavis, Lee A. (Crum, Roy L., Darwin D. Klingman and Lee A. Tavis. "Implementation Of Large-Scale Financial Planning Models: Solution Efficient Transformations," JFQA, 1979, v14(1), 137-152.)

Tavis, Lee A. (McEnally, Richard W. and Lee A. Tavis. "Spatial Risk' And Return Relationships: A Reconsideration," JRI, 1972, v39(3), 351-368.)

Tavis, Lee A. (McEnally, Richard W. and Lee A. Tavis. "Further Studies Of Property-Liability Return Adequacy: Comment," JRI, 1973, v40(3), 443-459.)

Tavis, Lee A. (McEnally, Richard W. and Lee A. Tavis. "Spatial Risk And Return Relationships: A Reconsideration: Reply," JRI, 1975, v42(2), 330-337.)

Tavis, Lee A. (Merville, Larry J. and Lee A. Tavis. "Long-Range Financial Planning," FM, 1974, v3(2), 56-63.)

Tavlas, George S. "The Chicago Tradition Revisited: Some Neglected Monetary Contributions: Senator Paul Douglas (1892-1976)," JMCB, 1977, v9(4), 529-535.

Tawarangkoon, Wittipan. (Pruitt, Stephen, Wittipan Tawarangkoon and K. John Wei. "Chernobyl, Commodities And Chaos: An Examination Of The Reaction Of Commodity Futures Prices To Evolving Information," JFM, 1987, v7(5), 555-570.)

Taylor, Bernard W., III and Laurence J. Moore. "A Simulation Approach To Planning Bank Projects," JBR, 1976-77, v7(3), 225-228.

Taylor, Bernard W., III. (Scott, David F., Jr., Laurence J. Moore, Andre Saint-Denis, Edouard Archer and Bernard W. Taylor, III. "Implementation Of A Cash Budget Simulator At Air Canada," FM, 1979, v8(2), 46-52.)

Taylor, C. G. "How Can The Universities And University Teachers Best Serve In Their Fields?," JRI, 1936, v3, 55-60.

Taylor, Charles T. "Average Interest Charges, The Loan Mix, And Measures Of Competition: Sixth Federal Reserve District Experience," JOF, 1968, v23(5), 793-804.

Taylor, David P. (Weber, Arnold R. and David P. Taylor. "Procedures For Employee Displacement: Advance Notice Of Plant Shutdown," JOB, 1963, v36(3), 302-315.)

Taylor, Dean G. "A Simple Model Of Monetary Dynamics," JMCB, 1977, v9(1), 107-111.

Taylor, Dean. (Connolly, Michael B. and Dean Taylor. "The Exact Timing Of The Collapse Of An Exchange Rate Regime And Its Impact On The Relative Price Of Traded Goods," JMCB, 1984, v16(2), 194-207.)

Taylor, Dean. (Corrado, Charles J. and Dean Taylor. "The Cost Of A Central Bank Leaning Against A Random Walk," JIMF, 1986, v5(3), 303-314.)

Taylor, Frank W. "An Economic Indemnity Model As The Basis For Life Insurance Programs," JRI, 1975, v42(2), 227-242.

Taylor, Herbert. "Fisher, Phillips, Friedman And The Measured Impact Of Inflation On Interest: A Comment," JOF, 1981, v36(4), 955-962.

Taylor, J. G. "College Revenue Bonds To Finance Self-Supporting Projects," JOF, 1949, v4(4), 328-341.

Taylor, Julian H. "Debt Management And The Term Structure Of Interest Rates: A Comment," JMCB, 1971, v3(3), 702-708.

Taylor, Keith. (Proffitt, Dennis and Keith Taylor. "Evaluating Negative Composite Performance Scores," JFED, 1985, v14, 17-21.)

Taylor, Mark P. (Allen, Helen and Mark P. Taylor. "Chart Analysis And The Foreign Exchange Market," RFM, 1989, v8(2), 288-319.)

Taylor, Mark P. (Hall, Stephen G. and Mark P. Taylor. "Modeling Risk Premia In Commodity Forward Prices: Some Evidence Form The London Metal Exchange," RFM, 1989, v8(2), 200-217.)

Taylor, P. A. (Peasnell, K. V., L. C. L. Skerratt and P. A. Taylor. "An Arbitrage Rationale For Tests Of Mutual Fund Performance," JBFA, 1979, v6(3), 373-400.)

Taylor, P. J. "The Nature And Determinants Of Income: Some Further Comments," JBFA, 1975, v2(2), 233-241.

Taylor, P. J. (Glautier, M. W. E. and P. J. Taylor. "A Comment On The Application Of Group Dynamics In Task Performance Relevant To Accounting," JBFA, 1977, v4(4), 477-480.)

Taylor, Paul A. "The Information Content Of Dividends Hypothesis: Back To The Drawing Board?," JBFA, 1979, v6(4), 495-526.

Taylor, Paul. "Savings Bank Life Insurance," JRI, 1940, v7, 61-69.

Taylor, Peter and Stuart Turley. "Applying Economic Consequences Analysis In Accounting Standard Setting: A Tax Incidence Approach," JBFA, 1986, v13(4), 467-488.

Taylor, R. F. "Channel Or Rut?," FAJ, 1956, v12(2), 97-102.

Taylor, Reese H. "Efficiency' Watchword Of The Oil Industry," FAJ, 1962, v18(3), 81-84.

Taylor, Richard W. "A Three-Phase Quarterly Dividend Discount Model," FAJ, 1988, v44(5), 79-80.

Taylor, Richard W. "A Three-Phase Quarterly Earnings Model," FAJ, 1989, v45(5), 79.

Taylor, Richard W. "Bond Duration Analysis: A Pedagogical Note," FAJ, 1987, v43(4), 72-74.

Taylor, Richard W. "Bond Duration With Geometric Mean Returns," FAJ, 1989, v45(1), 77-80.

Taylor, Richard W. "Future Value Of A Growing Annuity: A Note," JFED, 1986, v15, 17-21.

Taylor, Richard W. "Make Life Easy: Bond Analysis And DDM On The PC," JPM, 1985-86, v12(1), 54-57.

Taylor, Richard W. "Option Valuation For Alternative Instruments With The Black-Scholes Model: A Pedagogical Note," JFED, 1987, v16, 73-77.

Taylor, Richard W. "Portfolio Management With A Hand-Held Calculator," JPM, 1983-84, v10(4), 27-31.

Taylor, Richard W. "The Valuation Of Semiannual Bonds Between Interest Payment Dates," FR, 1988, v23(3), 365-368.

Taylor, Robert F. "It Has Happened Before," FAJ, 1954, v10(4), 97-98.

Taylor, Roger K. (Ziese, Charles H. and Roger K. Taylor. "Advance Refunding: A Practitioner's Perspective," FM, 1977, v6(2), 73-76.)

Taylor, Ryland A. "The Demand For Credit Union Shares: A Cross-Sectional Analysis," JFQA, 1972, v7(3), 1749-1756.

Taylor, Ryland A. (Szeplaki, Leslie and Ryland A. Taylor. "Banking, Credit, And Monetary Indicators In Reformed Socialist Planning," JMCB, 1972, v4(3), 572-581.)

Taylor, Stephen J. and Brian G. Kingsman. "Comment: An Autoregressive Forecast Of The World Sugar Future Option Market," JFQA, 1975(2), 883-890.

Taylor, Stephen J. "How Efficient Are The Most Liquid Futures Contracts? A Study Of Treasury Bond Futures," RFM, 1988, v7(Supp), 574-592.

Taylor, Stephen J. "Tests Of The Random Walk Hypothesis Against A Price-Trend Hypothesis," JFQA, 1982, v17(1), 37-61.

Taylor, Stephen J. "The Efficiency Of The International Money Markets: A Comment," JBFA, 1984, v11(4), 579-581.

Taylor, Stephen. "Uses Of Flow-Of-Funds Accounts In The Federal Reserve System," JOF, 1963, v18(2), 249-258.

Taylor, Vincent. (Newhouse, Joseph P. and Vincent Taylor. "The Subsidy Problem In Hospital Insurance: A Proposal," JOB, 1970, v43(4), 452-456.)

Taylor, Vincent. (Newhouse, Joseph P. and Vincent Taylor. "A New Type Of Hospital Insurance," JRI, 1971, v38(4), 601-612.)

Taylor, Walton. "A Note On Mao's Growth Stock-Investment Opportunities Approach," JOF, 1974, v29(5), 1573-1576.

Taylor, Walton. (Prohaska, Charles R. and Walton Taylor. "Minimizing Losses In A Hostile Environment: The Costs Of Defending One's Castle," JRI, 1973, v40(3), 375-388.)

Taylor, William M. "The Estimation Of Quality-Adjusted Rates Of Return In Stamp Auctions," JOF, 1983, v38(4), 1095-1109.

Taylor, William M. (Cho, D. Chinhyung and William M. Taylor. "The Seasonal Stability Of The Factor Structure Of Stock Returns," JOF, 1987, v42(5), 1195-1211.)

Tearney, Michael G. (Wolk, Harry I. and Michael G. Tearney. "Discounting Deferred Tax Liabilities: Review And Analysis," JBFA, 1980, v7(1), 119-133.)

Teas, R. Kenneth and W. L. Dellva. "Conjoint Measurement Of Consumers' Preferences For Multiattribute Financial Services," JBR, 1985-86, v16(2), 99-112.

Teck, Alan. "Population Study And Age Group Evaluation For Industry Growth," FAJ, 1962, v18(5), 25-27.

Teeters, Nancy. "The Role Of Banks In The International Financial System," JBF, 1983, v7(4), 447-451.

Tehranian, Hassan and Billy P. Helms. "An Empirical Comparison Of Stochastic Dominance Among Lognormal Prospects," JFQA, 1982, v17(2), 217-226.

Tehranian, Hassan and James F. Waegelein. "Short-Term Bonus Plan Adoption And Stock Market Performance - Proxy And Industry Effects: A Note," FR, 1986, v21(2), 345-353.

Tehranian, Hassan, Nickolaos G. Travlos and James F. Waegelein. "The Effect Of Long-Term Performance Plans On Corporate Sell-Off-Induced Abnormal Returns," JOF, 1987, v42(4), 933-942.

Tehranian, Hassan. "Empirical Studies In Portfolio Performance Using Higher Degrees Of Stochastic Dominance," JOF, 1980, v35(1), 159-171.

Tehranian, Hassan. (Booth, James R., Hassan Tehranian and Gary L. Trennepohl. "Efficiency Analysis And Option Portfolio Selection," JFQA, 1985, v20(4), 435-450.)

Tehranian, Hassan. (Cornett, Marcia Millon and Hassan Tehranian. "An Examination Of The Impact Of The Garn-St. Germain Depository Institutions Act Of 1982 On Commercial Banks And Savings And Loans," JOF, 1990, v45(1), 95-112.)

Tehranian, Hassan. (Kaen, Fred R. and Hassan Tehranian. "Information Effects In Financial Distress: The Case Of Seabrook Station," JFEC, 1990, v26(1), 143-171.)

Tehranian, Hassan. (Trennepohl, Gary L., James R. Booth and Hassan Tehranian. "An Empirical Analysis Of Insured Portfolio Strategies Using Listed Options," JFR, 1988, v11(1), 1-12.)

Teichroew, Daniel, William Lesso, Kevin Rice and Gordon Wright. "Optimizing Models Of After-Tax Earnings Incorporating Depletion Allowance," JFQA, 1967, v2(3), 265-297.

Teigen, Ronald L. "A Structural Approach To The Impact Of Monetary Policy," JOF, 1964, v19(2), Part 1, 284-308.

Teigen, Ronald L. (Branson, William H. and Ronald L. Teigen. "Flow And Stock Equilibrium In A Dynamic Metzler Model," JOF, 1976, v31(5), 1323-1339.)

Teigland, Christie. (Lahiri, Kajal, Christie Teigland and Mark Zaporowski. "Interest Rates And The Subjective Probability Distribution Of Inflation Forecasts," JMCB, 1988, v20(2), 233-248.)

Telser, L. G. "A Theory Of Monopoly Of Complementary Goods," JOB, 1979, v52(2), 211-230.

Telser, L. G. "A Theory Of Self-Enforcing Agreements," JOB, 1980, v53(1), 27-44.

Telser, L. G. "Some Aspects Of The Economics Of Advertising," JOB, 1968, v41(2), 166-173.

Telser, Lester G. "Futures And Actual Markets: How They Are Related," JOB, 1986, v59(2), Part 2, S5-S20.

Telser, Lester G. "Genesis Of The Sherman Act," RIF, 1983, v4, (Supp), 259-278.

Telser, Lester G. "Margins And Futures Contracts," JFM, v1(2), 225-253.

Telser, Lester G. (Kruskal, William H. and Lester G. Telser. "Rejoinder: Food Prices And The Bureau Of Labor," JOB, 1960, v33(3), 285.)

Telser, Lester G. (Kruskal, William H. and Lester G. Telser. "Food

Prices And The Bureau Of Labor Statistics," **JOB**, 1960, v33(3), 258-279.)

Temple, Alan H. "Outlook For Second Half," **FAJ**, 1950, v6(3), 31-32.

Templeton, John M. "Airlines, A Growth Industry," **FAJ**, 1959, v15(1), 41-45.

Tennenbaum, Michael E. (Hayes, Samuel L,, III and Michael E. Tennenbaum. "The Impact Of Listed Options On The Underlying Shares," **FM**, 1979, v8(4), 72-76.)

Tenney, Lester I. (Greene, Mark R., John Neter and Lester I. Tenney. "Annuity Rents And Rates - Guaranteed Vs. Current," **JRI**, 1977, v44(3), 383-401.)

Tennyson, B. Mack, Robert W. Ingram and Michael T. Dugan. "Assessing The Information Content Of Narrative Disclosures In Explaining Bankruptcy," **JBFA**, 1990, v17(3), 391-410.

Teplin, Albert M. "Uses And Abuses Of Residential Building Permits In Forecasting Private Housing Starts," **AREUEA**, 1978, v6(1), 86-104.

Tepper, Irwin and A. R. P. Affleck. "Pension Plan Liabilities And Corporate Financial Strategies," **JOF**, 1974, v29(5), 1549-1564.

Tepper, Irwin. "Optimal Financial Strategies For Trusteed Pension Plans," **JFQA**, 1974, v9(3), 357-376.

Tepper, Irwin. "Revealed Preference Methods And The Pure Theory Of The Cost Of Capital," **JOF**, 1973, v28(1), 35-48.

Tepper, Irwin. "Taxation And Corporate Pension Policy," **JOF**, 1981, v36(1), 1-13.

Tepper, Irwin. "The Future Of Private Pension Funding," **FAJ**, 1982, v38(1), 25-31.

Ter Kuile, Curtis V. "Africa: An 'Open End Investment'," **FAJ**, 1959, v15(1), 72-76.

Terborgh, George. "Inflation And Profits," **FAJ**, 1974, v30(3), 19-23.

Terborgh, George. "Some Comments On The Dean-Smith Article On The MAPI Formula," **JOB**, 1958, v31(2), 138-140.

Terborgh, George. "The Decline Of Fiscal Discipline," **FAJ**, 1981, v37(4), 58-62.

Terborgh, George. "The Indexation Issue In Inflation Accounting," **FAJ**, 1980, v36(6), 26-31.

Terflinger, Curtis D. (Levi, Donald R. and Curtis D. Terflinger. "A Legal-Economic Analysis Of Changing Liability Rules Affecting Real Estate Brokers And Appraisers," **JRER**, 1988, v3(2), 133-149.)

Terker, Bruce. (Blume, Marshall E., A. Craig MacKinlay and Bruce Terker. "Order Imbalances And Stock Price Movements On October 19 And 20, 1987," **JOF**, 1989, v44(4), 827-848.)

Terninko, John. (Wrightsman, Dwayne and John Terninko. "On The Measurement Of Opportunity Cost In Transactions Demand Models," **JOF**, 1971, v26(4), 947-950.)

Terpenning, Irma. (Cohen, Ayala, Judith M. Schilling and Irma Terpenning. "Dealer-Issued Commercial Paper: Analysis Of Data," **RIF**, 1985, v5, 77-106.)

Terracciano, Anthony P. (Frieder, Larry A. and Anthony P. Terracciano. "Chase Manhattan/SBI Innovation In Commercial Bank Administration: A Pilot Course," **JFED**, 1984, v13, 10-18.)

Terrell, Henry S. "Wealth Accumulation Of Black And White Families: The Empirical Evidence," **JOF**, 1971, v26(2), 363-377.

Terrell, J. Michael. (Grube, R. Corwin, Don B. Panton and J. Michael Terrell. "Risks And Rewards In Covered Call Positions," **JPM**, 1978-79, v5(2), 64-68.)

Terrell, William T. and William J. Frazer, Jr. "Interest Rates, Portfolio Behavior And Marketable Government Securities," **JOF**, 1972, v27(1), 1-35.

Terry, Brian. (Fawthrop, R. A. and Brian Terry. "The Evaluation Of An Integrated Investment And Lease-Financing Decision," **JBFA**, 1976, v3(3), 79-112.)

Terry, Brian. (Fawthrop, R. A. and Brian Terry. "Debt Management And The Use Of Leasing Finance In UK Corporate Financing Strategies," **JBFA**, 1975, v2(3), 295-314.)

Terry, Brian. (Fawthrop, R. A. and Brian Terry. "The Evaluation Of An Integrated Investment And Lease-Financing Decision: A Reply," **JBFA**, 1979, v6(1), 89-93.)

Tesar, Robert. "Agricultural Options: Practical Usage By A Commercial Firm," **RFM**, 1986, v5(1), 24-34.

Tesoriere, S. A. "Problematical Profits," **FAJ**, 1954, v10(5), 73-78.

Tesoriere, S. A. "Taxation And National Security," **FAJ**, 1958, v14(2), 83-86.

Tessaromatis, N. "Money Supply Announcements And Real Interest Rates: Evidence From The U.K. Index-Linked Bond Market, " (2/3), 637-648.

Tessaromatis, N. (Steele, A. and N. Tessaromatis. "A Note On Dividend Policy And Beta: A Comment," **JBFA**, 1989, v16(4), 543-548.)

Tessema, Asrat. "A Stock Market Game In Teaching Investments," **JFED**, 1989, v18, 33-37.

Tessier, Jacques. (Raynauld, Jacques and Jacques Tessier. "Risk Premiums In Futures Markets: An Empirical Investigation," **JFM**, 1984, v4(2), 189-211.)

Tew, Bernard V. and Donald W. Reid. "Mean-Variance Versus Direct Utility Maximization: A Comment," **JOF**, 1986, v41(5), 1177-1180.

Tew, Bernard V. and Donald W. Reid. "More Evidence On Expected Value-Variance Analysis Versus Direct Utility Maximization," **JFR**, 1987, v10(3), 249-258.

Tew, Bernard V., Donald W. Reid and Craig A. Witt. "The Opportunity Cost Of A Mean-Variance Efficient Choice," **FR**, 1991, v26(1), 31-44.

Teweles, R. J. (Harlow, C. V. and R. J. Teweles. "Commodities And Securities Compared," **FAJ**, 1972, v28(5), 64-70.)

Teweles, Richard J. "Commodity Futures Courses," **JFED**, 1981, v10, 51-53.

Tezel, Ahmet. "A Note On Bond Risk Differential," **JFQA**, 1978, v13(3), 573-576.

Tezel, Ahmet. "Default Risk On Fixed-Income Securities And Some Empirical Results On Installment Loans," **FR**, 1979, v14(1), 40-46.

Tezel, Ahmet. "The Effect Of Inflation On Common Stock Values," **JFR**, 1982, v5(1), 17-25.

Tezel, Ahmet. "The Value Line Stock Rankings And The Option Model Implied Standard Deviations," **JFR**, 1988, v11(3), 215-226.

Thakkar, Rashmi B. "Comment: The Dynamics Of Corporate Debt Management, Decision Rules, And Some Empirical Evidence," **JFQA**, 1974, v9(6), 1065-1066.

Thakor, Anjan V. and Richard Callaway. "Costly Information Production Equilibria In The Bank Credit Market With Applications To Credit Rationing," **JFQA**, 1983, v18(2), 229-256.

Thakor, Anjan V. "An Exploration Of Competitive Signalling Equilibria With 'Third Party' Information Production: The Case Of Debt Insurance," **JOF**, 1982, v37(3), 717-739.

Thakor, Anjan V. "Competitive Equilibrium With Type Convergence In An Asymmetrically Informed Market," **RFS**, 1989, v2(1), 49-72.

Thakor, Anjan V. "Strategic Issues In Financial Contracting: An Overview," **FM**, 1989, v18(2), 39-58.

Thakor, Anjan V. "Towards A Theory Of Bank Loan Commitments," **JBF**, 1982, v6(1), 55-84.

Thakor, Anjan V. (Boot, Arnoud, Anjan V. Thakor and Gregory F. Udell. "Competition, Risk Neutrality And Loan Commitments," **JBF**, 1987, v11(3), 449-472.)

Thakor, Anjan V. (Brennan, Michael J. and Anjan V. Thakor. "Shareholder Preferences And Dividend Policy," **JOF**, 1990, v45(4), 993-1019.)

Thakor, Anjan V. (Chan, Yuk-Shee, Stuart I. Greenbaum and Anjan V. Thakor. "Information Reusability, Competition And Bank Asset Quality," **JBF**, 1986, v10(2), 243-253.)

Thakor, Anjan V. (Chan, Yuk-Shee and Anjan V. Thakor. "Collateral And Competitive Equilibria With Moral Hazard And Private Information," **JOF**, 1987, v42(2), 345-363.)

Thakor, Anjan V. (Deshmukh, Sudhakar D., Stuart I. Greenbaum and Anjan V. Thakor. "Capital Accumulation And Deposit Pricing In Mutual Financial Institutions," **JFQA**, 1982, v17(5), 705-725.)

Thakor, Anjan V. (Greenbaum, Stuart I. and Anjan V. Thakor. "Bank Funding Modes: Securitization Versus Deposits," **JBF**, 1987, v11(3), 379-402.)

Thakor, Anjan V. (Lee, Wayne L., Anjan V. Thakor and Gautam Vora. "Screening, Market Signalling, And Capital Structure Theory," **JOF**, 1983, v38(5), 1507-1518.)

Thakor, Anjan V. (Liu, Pu and Anjan V. Thakor. "Interest Yields, Credit Ratings, And Economic Characteristics Of State Bonds: An Empirical Analysis," **JMCB**, 1984, v16(3), 344-351.)

Thakor, Anjan V. (Liu, Pu and Anjan V. Thakor. "Interest Yields, Credit Ratings, And Economic Characteristics Of State Bonds: Reply," **JMCB**, 1988, v20(4), 696-697.)

Thakor, Anjan V. (Millon, Marcia H. and Anjan V. Thakor. "Moral Hazard And Information Sharing: A Model Of Financial Information Gathering Agencies," **JOF**, 1985, v40(5), 1403-1422.)

Thakor, Anjan V. (Ofer, Aharon R. and Anjan V. Thakor. "A Theory Of Stock Price Responses To Alternative Corporate Cash Disbursement Methods: Stock Repurchases And Dividends," **JOF**, 1987, v42(2), 365-394.)

Thakor, Anjan V. (Ramakrishnan, Ram T. S. and Anjan V. Thakor. "The Valuation Of Assets Under Moral Hazard," **JOF**, 1984, v39(1), 229-238.)

Thakor, Anjan V. (Ramakrishnan, Ram T. S. and Anjan V. Thakor. "Moral Hazard, Agency Costs, And Asset Prices In A Competitive Equilibrium," **JFQA**, 1982, v17(4), 503-532.)

Thakor, Anjan V. (Shah, Salman and Anjan V. Thakor. "Private Versus Public Ownership: Investment, Ownership Distribution, And Optimality," **JOF**, 1988, v43(1), 41-59.)

Thakor, Anjan V. and Gregory F. Udell. "An Economic Rationale For The Pricing Structure Of Bank Loan Commitments," **JBF**, 1987, v11(2), 271-290.

Thakor, Anjan, Hai Hong and Stuart I. Greenbaum. "Bank Loan Commitments And Interest Rate Volatility," **JBF**, 1981, v5(4), 497-510.

Thaler, Richard H. "The Psychology And Economics Conference Handbook: Comments On Simon, On Einhorn And Hogarth, And On Tversky And Kahneman," **JOB**, 1986, v59(4), Part 2, S279-S284.

Thaler, Richard H. (DeBondt, Werner F. M. and Richard H. Thaler. "Further Evidence On Investor Overreaction And Stock Market Seasonality," **JOF**, 1987, v42(3), 557-581.)

Thaler, Richard H. (Kahneman, Daniel, Jack L. Knetsch and Richard H. Thaler. "Fairness And The Assumptions Of Economics," **JOB**, 1986, v59(4), Part 2, S285-S300.)

Thaler, Richard. (DeBondt, Werner F. M. and Richard Thaler. "Does The Stock Market Overreact?," **JOF**, 1985, v40(3), 793-805.)

Thaler, Richard. (Lee, Charles, Andrei Shleifer and Richard Thaler. "Investor Sentiment And The Closed-End Fund Puzzle," **JOF**, 1991, v46(1), 75-110.)

Thalheimer, Richard. (Richardson, David H. and Richard Thalheimer. "Alternative Methods Of Variable Selection: An Application To Real Estate Assessment," **AREUEA**, 1979, v7(3), 393-409.)

Thanassoulis, E. "Selecting A Suitable Solution Method For A Multi Objective Programming Capital Budgeting Problem," **JBFA**, 1985, v12(3), 453-472.

Thatcher, Janet S. "The Choice Of Call Provision Terms: Evidence Of The Existence Of Agency Costs Of Debt," **JOF**, 1985, v40(2), 549-561.

Thatcher, Janet S. and John G. Thatcher. "Timing Performance And The Flotation Of Shelf-Registered Bonds," **FM**, 1988, v17(1), 16-26.

Thatcher, John G. (Hansen, Robert S. and John G. Thatcher. "On The Nature Of Credit Demand And Credit Rationing In Competitive Credit Markets," **JBF**, 1983, v7(2), 273-284.)

Thatcher, John G. (Kon, Stanley J. and John G. Thatcher. "The Effect Of Bankruptcy Laws On The Valuation Of Risky Consumer Debt," **FR**, 1989, v24(3), 371-396.)

Thatcher, John G. (Thatcher, Janet S. and John G. Thatcher. "Timing Performance And The Flotation Of Shelf-Registered Bonds," **FM**, 1988, v17(1), 16-26.)

Thauburn, Bruce E. "Adjusting Railroad Earnings," **FAJ**, 1946, v2(2), 19-29.

Theerathorn, Pochara. (Lerner, Eugene M. and Pochara Theerathorn. "The Returns Of Different Investment Strategies," **JPM**, 1982-83, v9(4), 26-28.)

Theil, H. and C. T. Leenders. "Tomorrow On The Amsterdam Stock Exchange," **JOB**, 1965, v38(3), 277-284.

Theilman, Ward. "Commercial Bank Liability Management And Monetary Control," **JFQA**, 1970, v5(3), 329-339.

Theisen, Rolf D. (Dunn, Patricia C. and Rolf D. Theisen. "How Consistently Do Active Managers Win?," **JPM**, 1982-83, v9(4), 47-50.)

Theobald, M. F. (Fung, W. K. H. and M. F. Theobald. "Taxes, Unequal Access, Public Debt And Corporate Financial Policy In The United Kingdom," JBF, 1987, v11(1), 65-78.)

Theobald, Michael and Richard Thomas. "Time Series Properties Of Liquidating Company Equity Returns," JBF, 1982, v6(4), 495-505.

Theobald, Michael and Vera Price. "Seasonality Estimation In Thin Markets," JOF, 1984, v39(2), 377-392.

Theobald, Michael F. (Fung, William K. H. and Michael F. Theobald. "Dividends And Debt Under Alternative Tax Systems," JFQA, 1984, v19(1), 59-72.)

Theobald, Michael. "A Note On Variable Transactions Costs, The Capital Asset Pricing Model And The Corporate Dividend Decision," JBFA, 1979, v6(1), 9-16.

Theobald, Michael. "An Analysis Of The Market Model And Beta Factors Using U.K. Equity Share Data," JBFA, 1980, v7(1), 49-64.

Theobald, Michael. "Beta Stationarity And Estimation Period: Some Analytical Results," JFQA, 1981, v16(5), 747-757.

Theobald, Michael. "Intertemporal Dividend Models - An Empirical Analysis Using Recent UK Data," JBFA, 1978, v5(1), 123-136.

Theobald, Michael. "On Estimating Betas That Change," JPM, 1982-83, v9(1), 62-65.

Theobald, Michael. "Testing The Relationship Between Forward And Spot Rates In Foreign Exchange Markets," JBFA, 1991, v18(1), 1-12.

Theobald, Michael. "The Analytic Relationship Between Intervaling And Nontrading Effects In Continuous Time," JFQA, 1983, v18(2), 199-209.

Theobald, Michael. "Variable Transactions Costs, The Capital Asset Pricing Model And The Corporate Dividend Decision: A Reply," JBFA, 1982, v8(4), 563-564

Theobald, Thomas C. "Restructuring The U.S. Banking System For Global Competition," JACF, 1991, v3(4), 21-24.

Thibodeau, Thomas G. "Housng Price Indexes From The 1974-83 SMSA Annual Housing Surveys," AREUEA, 1989, v17(1), 100-117.

Thibodeau, Thomas G. (Hendershott, Patric H. and Thomas G. Thidodeau. "The Relationship Between Median And Constant Quality House Prices: Implications For Setting FHA Loan Limits," AREUEA, 1990, v18(3), 323-334.)

Thibodeau, Thomas. (Vandell, Kerry D. and Thomas Thibodeau. "Estimation Of Mortgage Defaults Using Disaggregate Loan History Data," AREUEA, 1985, v13(3), 292-316.)

Thibodeaux, Thomas G. (Giliberto, S. Michael and Thomas G. Thibodeaux. "Modeling Conventional Residential Mortgage Refinancings," JREFEC, 1989, v2(4), 285-300.)

Thies, Clifford F. "Business Price Expectations: 1947-83," JMCB, 1986, v18(3), 336-354.

Thies, Clifford F. "New Estimates Of The Term Structure Of Interest Rates: 1920-1939," JFR, 1985, v8(4), 297-306.

Thies, Clifford F. and Thomas Sturrock. "The Pension-Augmented Balance Sheet," JRI, 1988, v55(3), 467-480.

Thiessen, G. Willard. "Spread Trading In The Grains," RFM, 1982, v1(3), 188-194.

Thistle, Paul D., Robert W. McLeod and B. Lynne Conrad. "Interest Rates And Bank Portfolio Adjustments," JBF, 1989, v13(1), 151-162.

Thistlethwaite, Robert L. (Fox, Harold W. and Robert L. Thistlethwaite. "Variable Annuities At State Universities: The Illinois Case," JRI, 1970, v37(3), 465-473.)

Thomadakis, Stavros B. (Harpaz, Giora and Stavros B. Thomadakis. "Systematic Risk And The Firm's Experimental Strategy," JFQA, 1982, v17(3), 363-389.)

Thomadakis, Stavros B. (Harpaz, Giora and Stavros B. Thomadakis. "Capital Budgeting With Imperfect Information And Bayesian Learning," RIF, 1985, v5, 207-228.)

Thomadakis, Stavros. (Lustgarten, Steven and Stavros Thomadakis. "Mobility Barriers And Tobin's q," JOB, 1987, v60(4), 519-538.)

Thoman, Jeffrey A. (Quinn, Michael A., Donald S. Elliott, Jr., Robert E. Mendelson and Jeffrey A. Thoman. "Maintenance Effort And The Professional Landlord: An Empirical Critique Of Neighborhood Decline," AREUEA, 1980, v8(4), 345-369.)

Thomas, Andrew P. "Towards A Value-Neutral Positive Science Of Accounting," JBFA, 1981, v8(4), 549-572.

Thomas, Andrew P. "Towards A Value-Neutral Positive Science Of Accounting: A Reply," JBFA, 1982, v8(4), 573-578.

Thomas, Arthur. "Accounting And The Allocation Fallacy," FAJ, 1975, v31(5), 37-41,68.

Thomas, Conrad W. "How To Sell Short And Perform Wondrous Feats: Comment," JPM, 1977-78, v4(3), 73-74.

Thomas, Cynthia. (Brewster, J. Alan, Irving Crespi, Richard Kaluzny, James Ohls and Cynthia Thomas. "Homeowner Warranties: A Study Of The Need And Demand For Protection Against Unanticipated Repair Expenses," AREUEA, 1980, v8(2), 207-217.)

Thomas, Douglas P. "Canada-U.S. Auto Trade Agreement," JFM, 1967, v23(4), 113-117.

Thomas, Edward. "Charting Prospective Fundamental Growth Numerically," FAJ, 1951, v7(4), 67-68.

Thomas, Howard. (Samson, Danny and Howard Thomas. "Reinsurance Decision Making And Expected Utility," JRI, 1983, v50(2), 249-264.)

Thomas, Howard. (Samson, Danny and Howard Thomas. "Reinsurance Decision Making And Expected Utility: Reply," JRI, 1985, v52(2), 312-314.)

Thomas, J. (Bierman, H., K. Chopra and J. Thomas. "Ruin Considerations: Optimal Working Capital And Capital Structure," JFQA, 1975, v10(1), 119-128.)

Thomas, Joseph, III and R. V. Evanson. "An Empirical Investigation Of Association Between Financial Ratio Use And Small Business Success," JBFA, 1987, v14(4), 555-572.

Thomas, Kenneth H. (Guttentag, Jack M. and Kenneth H. Thomas. "Branch Banking And Bank Structure: Some Evidence From Alabama," JBR, 1979-80, v10(1), 45-53.)

Thomas, L. Joseph. (Bierman, Harold, Jr. and L. Joseph Thomas. "Ruin Considerations And Debt Issuance," JFQA, 1972, v7(1), 1361-1378.)

Thomas, Lee R. "A Winning Strategy For Currency-Futures Speculation," JPM, 1985-86, v12(1), 65-69.

Thomas, Lee R. "Portfolio Theory And Currency Substitution," JMCB,

1985, v17(3), 347-357.

Thomas, Lee R. "The Performance Of Currency-Hedged Foreign Bonds," FAJ, 1989, v45(3), 25-31.

Thomas, Lee R., III. "Currency Risks In International Equity Portfolios," FAJ, 1988, v44(2), 68-71.

Thomas, Lee R., III. "Random Walk Profits In Currency Futures Trading," JFM, 1986, v6(1), 109-126.

Thomas, Richard. (Theobald, Michael and Richard Thomas. "Time Series Properties Of Liquidating Company Equity Returns," JBF, 1982, v6(4), 495-505.)

Thomas, Robert E. "Profit From Railroad Revenue Dollars," FAJ, 1952, v8(5), 66-69.

Thomas, Roy E. "The Mexican Automobile Insurance Problem For Tourists," JRI, 1963, v30(4), 577-581.

Thomas, Stephen. (McKenzie, George and Stephen Thomas. "Liquidity, Credit Creation And International Banking: An Econometric Investigation," JBF, 1983, v7(4), 467-480.)

Thomas, Woodlief. "Money Trends," FAJ, 1952, v8(3), 15-24.

Thompson, A. Frank, Jr. "Immunization Of Pension Funds And Sensitivity To Actuarial Assumptions: Comment," JRI, 1981, v48(1), 148-153.

Thompson, A. Frank. (Glasgo, Philip W., William J. Landes and A. Frank Thompson. "Bank Discount, Coupon Equivalent, And Compound Yields," FM, 1982, v11(3), 80-84.)

Thompson, A. Peter. "Current Cost Profitability Of British And American Industry," FAJ, 1983, v39(2), 73-78.

Thompson, Arthur A. "Tax-Exempt Development Bonds," FAJ, 1968, v24(6), 99-103.

Thompson, Donald J., II. "Sources Of Systematic Risk In Common Stocks," JOB, 1976, v49(2), 173-188.

Thompson, Donald J., II. (Fielitz, Bruce D. and Donald J. Thompson, II. "Performance Indexes Derived From The Sharpe-Lintner And Two-Factor Asset Pricing Models: Some Comparative Tests," FR, 1977, v12(2), 47-75.)

Thompson, Donald J., II. (Zivney, Terry L. and Donald J. Thompson, II. "Relative Stock Prices And The Firm Size Effect," JFR, 1987, v10(2), 99-110.)

Thompson, Donald J., II. (Zivney, Terry L. and Donald J. Thompson, II. "The Specification And Power Of The Sign Test In Measuring Security Price Performance: Comments And Analysis," FR, 1989, v24(4), 581-588.)

Thompson, Donald J., II. (Zivney, Terry L. and Donald J. Thompson, II. "The Effect Of Market Proxy Rebalancing Policies On Detecting Abnormal Performance," JFR, 1989, v12(4), 293-300.)

Thompson, Donald S. "Changes In Quality Of Bank Credit," JOF, 1956, v11(2), 301-311.

Thompson, Donald S. "Nonfarm Real Estate Finance," JOF, 1947, v2(1), 34-50.

Thompson, Edna M. "Paper Company Stocks," FAJ, 1956, v12(5), 43-44.

Thompson, G. L. (Cyert, R. M. and G. L. Thompson. "Selecting A Portfolio Of Credit Risks By Markov Chains," JOB, 1968, v41(1), 39-46.)

Thompson, G. Rodney and Peter Vaz. "Dual Bond Ratings: A Test Of The Certification Function Of Rating Agencies," FR, 1990, v25(3), 457-472.

Thompson, G. Rodney. (Allen, David S., Robert E. Lamy and G. Rodney Thompson. "Agency Costs And Alternative Call Provisions: An Empirical Investigation," FM, 1987, v16(4), 37-44.)

Thompson, G. Rodney. (Allen, David S., Robert E. Lamy and G. Rodney Thompson. "The Shelf Registration Of Debt And Self Selection Bias," JOF, 1990, v45(1), 275-288.)

Thompson, G. Rodney. (Bhagat, Sanjai, M. Wayne Marr and G. Rodney Thompson. "The Rule 415 Experiment: Equity Markets," JOF, 1985, v40(5), 1385-1401.)

Thompson, G. Rodney. (Billingsley, Randall S., Robert E. Lamy, M. Wayne Marr and G. Rodney Thompson. "Split Ratings And Bond Reoffering Yields," FM, 1985, v14(2), 59-65.)

Thompson, G. Rodney. (Billingsley, Randall S., Robert E. Lamy and G. Rodney Thompson. "The Choice Among Debt, Equity, And Convertible Bonds," JFR, 1988, v11(1), 43-56.)

Thompson, G. Rodney. (Billingsley, Randall S. and G. Rodney Thompson. "Determinants Of Stock Repurchases By Bank Holding Companies," JBR, 1985-86, v16(3), 128-135.)

Thompson, G. Rodney. (Billingsley, Randall S., Robert E. Lamy and G. Rodney Thompson. "Valuation Of Primary Issue Convertible Bonds," JFR, 1986, v9(3), 251-260.)

Thompson, G. Rodney. (Chance, Don M., M. Wayne Marr and G. Rodney Thompson. "Hedging Shelf Registrations," JFM, 1986, v6(1), 11-28.)

Thompson, G. Rodney. (Kidwell, David S., M. Wayne Marr and G. Rodney Thompson. "Eurodollar Bonds: Alternative Financing For U.S. Companies," FM, 1985, v14(4), 18-27.)

Thompson, G. Rodney. (Kidwell, David S., M. Wayne Marr and G. Rodney Thompson. "SEC Rule 415: The Ultimate Competitive Bid," JFQA, 1984, v19(2), 183-195.)

Thompson, G. Rodney. (Kidwell, David S., M. Wayne Marr and G. Rodney Thompson. "Eurodollar Bonds, Alternative Financing For U.S. Companies: A Correction," FM, 1986, v15(1), 78-79.)

Thompson, G. Rodney. (Lamy, Robert E. and G. Rodney Thompson. "Penn Square, Problem Loans, And Insolvency Risk," JFR, 1986, v9(2), 103-111.)

Thompson, G. Rodney. (Lamy, Robert E. and G. Rodney Thompson. "Risk Premia And The Pricing Of Primary Issue Bonds," JBF, 1988, v11(4), 585-601.)

Thompson, G. Rodney. (Marr, M. Wayne and G. Rodney Thompson. "The Pricing Of New Convertible Bond Issues," FM, 1984, v13(2), 31-37.)

Thompson, G. Rodney. (Marr, M. Wayne and G. Rodney Thompson. "The Influence Of Offering Yield On Underwriting Spread," JFR, 1984, v7(4), 323-328.)

Thompson, Gerald L. (Sethi, Suresh P. and Gerald L. Thompson. "Applications Of Mathematical Control Theory To Finance: Modeling Simple Dynamic Cash Balance Problems," JFQA, 1970, v5(4), 381-394.)

Thompson, H. E. (Whitman, A. F. and H. E. Thompson. "Impact Of Alternative Forms Of Life Insurance Company Income Tax

Legislation," **JRI**, 1968, v35(1), 107-117.)

Thompson, Howard E. "A Note On The Value Of Rights In Estimating The Investor Capitalization Rate," **JOF**, 1973, v28(1), 157-160.

Thompson, Howard E. "Coverage Ratios In Public Utilities," **FAJ**, 1972, v28(1), 69-73.

Thompson, Howard E. "Mathematical Programming, The Capital Asset Pricing Model And Capital Budgeting Of Interrelated Projects," **JOF**, 1976, v31(1), 125-131.

Thompson, Howard E. (Aghili, Parvis, Robert H. Cramer and Howard E. Thompson. "Small Bank Balance Sheet Management: Applying Two-Stage Programming Models," **JBR**, 1974-75, v5(4), 246-256.)

Thompson, Howard E. (Ahn, Chang Mo and Howard E. Thompson. "Jump-Diffusion Processes And Term Structure Of Interest Rates," **JOF**, 1988, v43(1), 155-174.)

Thompson, Howard E. (Anderson, John J. and Howard E. Thompson. "Financial Implications Of Over-Reserving In Nonlife Insurance," **JRI**, 1971, v38(3), 333-342.)

Thompson, Howard E. (Brick, John R. and Howard E. Thompson. "The Economic Life Of An Investment And The Appropriate Discount Rate," **JFQA**, 1978, v13(5), 831-846.)

Thompson, Howard E. (Brick, John R. and Howard E. Thompson. "Time Series Analysis Of Interest Rates: Some Additional Evidence," **JOF**, 1978, v33(1), 93-103.)

Thompson, Howard E. (Brick, John R. and Howard E. Thompson. "Portfolio Policies Of Private Mortgage Insurers," **FAJ**, 1981, v37(2), 58-66.)

Thompson, Howard E. (Brick, John R. and Howard E. Thompson. "Investment Portfolios And Regulation Of Private Mortgage Insurance," **JRI**, 1978, v45(2), 261-273.)

Thompson, Howard E. (Hoffmann, Thomas R. and Howard E. Thompson. "Salary Scales And Trends," **JRI**, 1964, v31(3), 437-444.)

Thompson, Howard E. (Makhija, Anil K. and Howard E. Thompson. "Some Aspects Of Equilibrium For A Cross-Section Of Firms Signalling Profitability With Dividends: A Note," **JOF**, 1986, v41(1), 249-254.)

Thompson, Howard E. (Senbet, Lemma W. and Howard E. Thompson. "Growth And Risk," **JFQA**, 1982, v17(3), 331-340.)

Thompson, Howard E. (Senbet, Lemma W. and Howard E. Thompson. "The Equivalence Of Alternative Mean-Variance Capital Budgeting Models," **JOF**, 1978, v33(2), 395-401.)

Thompson, Howard E. (Whitman, Andrew F. and Howard E. Thompson. "The Impact Of The 1959 Income Tax Act On Stock And Mutual Companies: A Simulation Study," **JRI**, 1967, v34(2), 215-230.)

Thompson, Howard E. and Jerry J. Weygandt. "The Rate-Making Treatment Of The Investment Tax Credit For Public Utilities," **JOB**, 1977, v50(4), 508-519.

Thompson, Joel E. "An Alternative Control Model For Event Studies," **JBFA**, 1989, v16(4), 507-514.

Thompson, Joel E. "More Methods That Make Little Difference In Event Studies," **JBFA**, 1988, v15(1), 77-86.

Thompson, Lawrence E. and J. Keith Butters. "Effects Of Taxation On The Investment Policies And Capacity Of Individuals," **JOF**, 1953, v8(2), 137-151.

Thompson, Rex. "Conditioning The Return-Generating Process On Firm-Specific Events: A Discussion Of Event Study Methods," **JFQA**, 1985, v20(2), 151-168.

Thompson, Rex. "The Information Content Of Discounts And Premiums On Closed-End Fund Shares," **JFEC**, 1978, v6(2/3), 151-186.

Thompson, Rex. (Clarkson, Peter M. and Rex Thompson. "Empirical Estimates Of Beta When Investors Face Estimation Risk," **JOF**, 1990, v45(2), 431-454.)

Thompson, Rex. (De Jong, Piet and Rex Thompson. "Testing Linear Hypothesis In The Sur Framework With Identical Explanatory Variables," **RIF**, 1990, v8, 59-76.)

Thompson, Rex. (Malatesta, Paul H. and Rex Thompson. "Partially Anticipated Events: A Model Of Stock Price Reactions With An Application To Corporate Acquisitions," **JFEC**, 1985, v14(2), 237-250.)

Thompson, Rex. (Malatesta, Paul H. and Rex Thompson. "Stock Price Reactions To Partially Anticipated Events: Evidence On The Economic Impact Of Corporate Acquisition Attempts," **RIF**, 1986, v6, 119-148.)

Thompson, Rex. (Richardson, Gordon, Stephen E. Sefcik and Rex Thompson. "A Test Of Dividend Irrelevance Using Volume Reactions To A Change In Dividend Policy," **JFEC**, 1986, v17(2), 313-333.)

Thompson, Rex. (Schipper, Katherine and Rex Thompson. "Common Stocks As Hedges Against Shifts In The Consumption Or Investment Opportunity Set," **JOB**, 1981, v54(2), 305-328.)

Thompson, Rex. (Schipper, Katherine and Rex Thompson. "Evidence On The Capitalized Value Of Merger Activity For Acquiring Firms," **JFEC**, 1983, v11(1), 85-119.)

Thompson, Sarahelen R. and Mark L. Waller. The Intraday Variability Of Soybean Futures Prices: Information And Trading Effects," **RFM**, 1988, v7(1), 110-126.

Thompson, Sarahelen, Thomas J. McNeill and James S. Eales. "Expiration And Delivery On The World Sugar Futures Contract," **JFM**, 1990, v10(2), 153-168.

Thompson, Sarahelen. "Returns To Storage In Coffee And Cocoa Futures Markets," **JFM**, 1986, v6(4), 541-564.

Thompson, Stanley R. (Bond, Gary E. and Stanley R. Thompson. "Optimal Commodity Hedging Within The Capital Asset Pricing Model," **JFM**, 1986, v6(3), 421-432.)

Thompson, Stanley R. (Bond, Gary E., Stanley R. Thompson and Benny M. S. Lee. "Application Of A Simplified Hedging Rule," **JFM**, 1987, v7(1), 65-72.)

Thompson, Steve, Mike Wright and Ken Robbie. "Management Buy-Outs, Debt, And Efficiency: Some Evidence From The U.K.," **JACF**, 1989, v2(1), 76-86.

Thompson, Steve. (Wright, Mike, Ken Robbie and Steve Thompson. "Corporate Restructuring, Buy-Outs, And Managerial Equity: The European Dimension," **JACF**, 1991, v3(4), 46-58.)

Thomsen, T. C. "Improving The Flow Of Corporate Information," **FAJ**, 1958, v14(2), 73-76.

Thomson, James B. "Errors In Recorded Security Prices And The Turn-Of-The-Year Effect," **JFQA**, 1989, v24(4), 513-526.

Thomson, James B. "The Use Of Market Information In Pricing Deposit Insurance," **JMCB**, 1987, v19(4), 528-537.

Thomson, James B. (Osterberg, William P. and James B. Thomson. "Deposit Insurance And The Cost Of Capital," **RIF**, 1990, v8, 255-270.)

Thomson, Lydia and Robert Watson. "Historic Cost Earnings, Current Cost Earnings And The Dividend Decision," **JBFA**, 1989, v16(1), 1-24.

Thomson, Michael R. "Forecasting For Financial Planning," **JBR**, 1973-74, v4(3), 225-231.

Thomson, Thomas D. (Pierce, James L. and Thomas D. Thomson. "Short-Term Financial Models At The Federal Reserve Board," **JOF**, 1974, v29(2), 349-357.)

Thomson, Thomas D., James L. Pierce and Robert T. Parry. "A Monthly Money Market Model," **JMCB**, 1975, v7(4), 411-431.

Thomspon, Sarahelen R. and Mark L. Waller. "Determinants Of Liquidity Costs In Commodity Futures Markets," **RFM**, 1988, v7(1), 110-126.

Thore, Eugene M. "Current Developments And Problems In Life Insurance," **JRI**, 1960, v27(1), 29-36.

Thore, Eugene M. "The Ingratiating Intervention," **JRI**, 1955, v22, 40-51.

Thore, Eugene M. "The Washington Scene," **JRI**, 1963, v30(1), 11-16.

Thore, Sten. "Programming A Credit Network Under Uncertainty," **JMCB**, 1970, v2(2), 219-246.

Thore, Sten. "Spatial Models Of The Eurodollar Market," **JBF**, 1984, v8(1), 51-65.

Thore, Sten. (Charnes, A. and Sten Thore. "Planning For Liquidity In Financial Institutions: The Chance-Constrained Method," **JOF**, 1966, v21(4), 649-674.)

Thore, Sten. (Cohen, Kalman J. and Sten Thore. "Programming Bank Portfolios Under Uncertainty," **JBR**, 1970-71, v1(1), 43-61.)

Thore, Sten. (Storoy, Sverre, Sten Thore and Marcel Boyer. "Equilibrium In Linear Capital Market Networks," **JOF**, 1975, v30(5), 1197-1211.)

Thorelli, Hans B., Robert L. Graves and Lloyd T. Howells. "The International Operations Simulation At The University Of Chicago," **JOB**, 1962, v35(3), 287-297.

Thorley, Steven. (McQueen, Grant and Steven Thorley. "Are Stock Returns Predictable? A Test Using Markov Chains," **JOF**, 1991, v46(1), 239-264.)

Thorne, Daniel. "The Information Content Of The Trend Between Historical Cost Earnings And Current Cost Earnings (United States Of America), (3), 289-304.

Thornton, Daniel B. "The Rule Of 69 In Perspective: A Note On The Force Of Interest," **JOB**, 1976, v49(4), 515-516.

Thornton, Daniel L. and Dallas S. Batten. "Lag-Length Selection And Tests Of Granger Causality Between Money And Income," **JMCB**, 1985, v17(2), 164-178.

Thornton, Daniel L. "The Effect Of Unanticipated Money On The Money And Foreign Exchange Markets," **JIMF**, 1989, v8(4), 573-588.

Thornton, Daniel L. (Batten, Dallas S. and Daniel L. Thornton. "Discount Rate Changes And The Foreign Exchange Market," **JIMF**, 1984, v3(3), 279-292.)

Thornton, Daniel L. (Chrystal, K. Alec and Daniel L. Thornton. "On The Informational Content Of Spot And Forward Exchange Rates," **JIMF**, 1988, v7(3), 321-330.)

Thornton, J. E. (Abdelsamad, M. H. and J. E. Thornton. "An Evaluation Of Business Masters Programs By Graduates," **JFED**, 1979, v8, 49-52.)

Thornton, Jack E. and Henry Tobler, III. "Effective Compustat Tape Utilization By Students And Faculty," **JFED**, 1975, v4, 111-113.

Thornton, Jack E. "The Finance Course: An Industry View," **JFED**, 1974, v3, 56-60.

Thornton, John H. (Cross, Mark L. and John H. Thornton. "The Probable Effect Of An Extreme Hurrican On Texas Catastrophe Plan Insurers," **JRI**, 1983, v50(3), 417-444.)

Thornton, John H. (Cross, Mark L., Wallace N. Davidson, III and John H. Thornton. "The Impact Of Captive Insurer Formation On The Parent Firm's Value," **JRI**, 1986, v53(3), 471-483.)

Thornton, John H. (Cross, Mark L., Wallace N. Davidson, III and John H. Thornton. "Taxes, Stock Returns And Captive Insurance Subsidiaries," **JRI**, 1988, v55(2), 331-338.)

Thornton, John H. (Cross, Mark L., Wallace N. Davidson and John H. Thornton. "The Impact Of Directors And Officers' Liability Suits On Firm Value," **JRI**, 1989, v56(1), 128-136.)

Thornton, John and Sri Ram Poudyal. "Money And Capital In Economic Development: A Test Of The McKinnon Hypothesis For Nepal," **JMCB**, 1990, v22(3), 395-399.

Thornton, John. "The Role Of Rediscount Quotas," **JMCB**, 1985, v17(3), 387-390.

Thornton, Richard M. (Kwon, Jene K. and Richard M. Thornton. "The Effect Of FHLB Bond Operations On Savings Inflows At Savings And Loan Associations: Reply," **JOF**, 1973, v28(1), 203-206.)

Thornton, Richard M. (Kwon, Jene K. and Richard M. Thornton. "An Evaluation Of The Competitive Effect Of FHLB Open Market Operations On Savings Inflows At Savings And Loan Associations," **JOF**, 1971, v26(3), 699-712.)

Thorp, Edward O. (Bicksler, James L. and Edward O. Thorp. "The Capital Growth Model: An Empirical Investigation," **JFQA**, 1973, v8(2), 273-287.)

Thorp, Edward. (Baesel, Jerome, George Shows and Edward Thorp. "Can Joe Granville Time The Market?," **JPM**, 1981-82, v8(3), 5-9.)

Thorp, Edward. (Baesel, Jerome B., George Shows and Edward Thorp. "The Cost Of Liquidity Services In Listed Options: A Note," **JOF**, 1983, v38(3), 989-995.)

Thorsen, Robert. "Multiplicity Of Proceedings And Investigations," **JFM**, 1981, v1(Supp), 525-526.

Thosar, Satish and Lenos Trigeorgis. "Stock Volatility And Program Trading," **JACF**, 1990, v2(4), 91-96.

Thottathil, Pelis. "A Note On Eurodollar Borrowing By U.S. Banks: Derivation Of Reg D Equation," **JBR**, 1985-86, v16(1), 40-44.

Throop, Adrian W. "Capital Investment And Entry In Commercial Banking: A Competitive Model," **JMCB**, 1975, v7(2), 193-214.

Throop, Adrian W. (Smaistrla, Charles J. and Adrian W. Throop. "A New Inflation In The 1970s?," FAJ, 1980, v36(2), 47-52,54-57.)

Thurman, Oliver. "The Future Of Disability Income Insurance," JRI, 1938, v5, 59-65.

Thurston, Thom B. "Regional Interaction And The Reserve Adjustment Lag Within The Commercial Banking Sector," JOF, 1976, v31(5), 1443-1456.

Thurston, Thom B. "The Permanent Income Hypothesis And Monetary Influences On Consumption," JMCB, 1977, v9(4), 586-596.

Thurston, Thom B. (Fabozzi, Frank J. and Thom B. Thurston. "State Taxes And Reserve Requirements As Major Determinants Of Yield Spreads Among Money Market Instruments," JFQA, 1986, v21(4), 427-436.)

Thurston, Thom. (Allen, Linda and Thom Thurston. "Cash-Futures Arbitrage And Forward-Futures Spreads In The Treasury Bill Market," JFM, 1988, v8(5), 563-574.)

Thygerson, Kenneth J. "Hedging Forward Mortgage Loan Commitments: The Option Of Futures And A Future For Options," AREUEA, 1978, v6(4), 357-369.

Thygerson, Kenneth J. (Verbrugge, James A., Richard A. Shick And Kenneth J. Thygerson. "An Analysis Of Savings And Loan Profit Performance," JOF, 1976, v31(5), 1427-1442.)

Tiemann, Jonathan. "Exact Arbitrage Pricing And The Minimum-Variance Frontier," JOF, 1988, v43(2), 327-338.

Tiernan, Frank M. (Wolk, Harry I., Lynn K. Saubert and Frank M. Tiernan. "A Further Note On Discounting Deferred Taxes," JBFA, 1984, v11(2), 253-255.)

Tierney, David E. and Kenneth Winston. "Defining And Using Dynamic Completeness Funds To Enhance Total Fund Efficiency," FAJ, 1990, v46(4), 49-54.

Tieschmann, James S. (Shick, Richard A. and James S. Trieschmann. "Some Future Evidence On The Performance Of Property-Liability Insurance Companies' Stock Portfolios," JFQA, 1978, v13(1), 157-166.)

Tigert, D. J. (Bass, F. M., E. A. Pessemier and D. J. Tigert. "A Taxonomy Of Magazine Readership Applied To Problems In Marketing Starategy And Media Selection," JOB, 1969, v42(3), 337-363.)

Tilley, James A. and Gary D. Latainer. "A Synthetic Option Framework For Asset Allocation," FAJ, 1985, v41(3), 32-43.

Tilley, James A. (Jacob, David P., Graham Lord and James A. Tilley. "A Generalized Framework For Pricing Contingent Cash Flows," FM, 1987, v16(3), 5-14.)

Timberlake, Richard H. "Private Production Of Scrip-Money In The Isolated Community," JMCB, 1987, v19(4), 437-447.

Timberlake, Richard H., Jr. "A Note On The Pigou Effect And The Upward Turning Point," JOF, 1958, v13(3), 417-422.

Timberlake, Richard H., Jr. (Beranek, William, Thomas M. Humphrey and Richard H. Timberlake, Jr. "Fisher, Thornton, And The Analysis Of The Inflation Premium," JMCB, 1985, v17(3), 371-377.)

Timberlake, Richard H., Jr. "The Central Banking Role Of Clearinghouse Associations," JMCB, 1984, v16(1), 1-15.

Timberlake, Richard H., Jr. "Repeal Of Silver Monetization In The Late Nineteenth Century," JMCB, 1978, v10(1), 27-45.

Timbers, Stephen B. "Equity Research After Modern Portfolio Theory," JPM, 1978-79, v5(3), 52-56.

Timbers, Stephen B. "The Non-Efficient Market Is Not For Institutions," JPM, 1977-78, v4(1), 59-64.

Timme, Stephen G. (Eisemann, Peter C. and Stephen G. Timme. "Intraweek Seasonality In The Federal Funds Market," JFR, 1984, v7(1), 47-56.)

Timme, Stephen G. (Hunter, William C. and Stephen G. Timme. "Technical Change, Organizational Form, And The Structure Of Bank Production," JMCB, 1986, v18(2), 152-166.)

Timme, Stephen G. (Hunter, William C., Stephen G. Timme and Won Keun Yang. "An Examination Of Cost Subadditivity And Multiproduct Production In Large U.S. Banks," JMCB, 1990, v22(4), 504-525.)

Timme, Stephen G. (Kolb, Robert W., Stephen G. Timme and Gerald D. Gay. "Macro Versus Micro Futures Hedges At Commercial Banks," JFM, 1984, v4(1), 47-54.)

Timme, Stephen G. and Peter C. Eisemann. "On The Use Of Consensus Forecasts Of Growth In The Constant Growth Model: The Case Of Electric Utilities," FM, 1989, v18(4), 23-35.

Tinbergen, Jan. "International Price Stabilization," FAJ, 1954, v10(4), 103-105.

Tinic, S. M. (Doherty, N. A. and S. M. Tinic. "Reinsurance Under Conditions Of Capital Market Equilibriuim: A Note," JOF, 1981, v36(4), 949-953.)

Tinic, Seha M. and Richard R. West. "Risk And Return: January Vs. The Rest Of The Year," JFEC, 1984, v13(4), 561-574.

Tinic, Seha M. and Richard R. West. "Marketability Of Common Stocks In Canada And The U.S.A.: A Comparison Of Agent Versus Dealer Dominated Markets," JOF, 1974, v29(3), 729-746.

Tinic, Seha M. and Richard R. West. "Competition And The Pricing Of Dealer Service In The Over-The-Counter Stock Market," JFQA, 1972, v7(3), 1707-1727.

Tinic, Seha M. "Anatomy Of Initial Public Offerings Of Common Stock," JOF, 1988, v43(4), 789-822.

Tinic, Seha M. (Brown, Keith C., W. V. Harlow and Seha M. Tinic. "Risk Aversion, Uncertain Information, And Market Efficiency," JFEC, 1988, v22(2), 355-386.)

Tinic, Seha M. (Brown, Keith C., W. V. Harlow and Seha M. Tinic. "How Rational Investors Deal With Uncertainty (Or, Reports Of The Death Of Efficient Market Theory Are Greatly Exaggerated)," JACF, 1989, v2(3), 45-58.)

Tinic, Seha M. (Gultekin, N. Bulent, Richard Rogalski and Seha M. Tinic. "Option Pricing Model Estimates: Some Empirical Results," FM, 1982, v11(1), 58-69.)

Tinic, Seha M. (Rogalski, Richard and Seha M. Tinic. "The January Size Effect: Anomaly Or Risk Mismeasurement?," FAJ, 1986, v42(6), 63-70.)

Tinic, Seha M. (Rogalski, Richard J. and Seha M. Tinic. "Risk-Premium Curve Vs. Capital Line: A Re-Examination," FM, 1978, v7(1), 73-84.)

Tinic, Seha M. (West, Richard R. and Seha M. Tinic. "Corporate Finance And The Changing Stock Market," FM, 1974, v3(3), 14-23.)

Tinic, Seha M. (West, Richard R. and Seha M. Tinic. "Portfolio Returns And The Random Walk Theory: Comment," JOF, 1973, v28(3), 733-741.)

Tinic, Seha M., Giovanni Barone-Adesi and Richard R. West. "Seasonality In Canadian Stock Prices: A Test Of The 'Tax-Loss-Selling' Hypothesis," JFQA, 1987, v22(1), 51-64.

Tinic, Seha. (West, Richard R. and Seha Tinic. "Critique Of Schaefer And Warner," FAJ, 1978, v34(3), 46,50-56.)

Tinker, A. M. and E. A. Lowe. "A Rationale For Corporate Social Reporting: Theory And Evidence From Organizational Research," JBFA, 1980, v7(1), 1-17.

Tinker, A. M. "A Short Note On 'Is The Emphasis Of Capital Budgeting Theory Misplaced?," JBFA, 1976, v3(2), 23-26.

Tinker, A. M. (Lowe, E. A. and A. M. Tinker. "Siting The Accounting Problematic: Towards An Intellectual Emancipation Of Accounting," JBFA, 1977, v4(3), 263-276.)

Tinsley, Dillard B. (Lewis, John H. and Dillard B. Tinsley. "Personnnel Administration In Bank Holding Companies," JBR, 1978-79, v9(1), 38-42.)

Tinsley, Dillard B. (Lewis, John H. and Dillard B. Tinsley. "Curriculum Development For Commercial Bank Management," JFED, 1977, v6, 36-39.)

Tinsley, P. A. "Capital Structure, Precautionary Balances, And Valuation Of The Firm: The Problem Of Financial Risk," JFQA, 1970, v5(1), 33-62.

Tinsley, P. A. (Neumark, David, P. A. Tinsley and Suzanne Tosini. "After-Hours Stock Prices And Post-Crash Hangovers," JOF, 1991, v46(1), 159-178.)

Tinsley, P., G. Fries, B. Garrett, A. Norman, P.A.V.B. Swamy and P. Von Zur Muehlen. "The Impact Of Uncertainty On The Feasibility Of Humphrey-Hawkins Objectives," JOF, 1981, v36(2), 489-496.

Tinsley, Peter A., Helen T. Farr, Gerhard Fries, Bonnie Garrett and Peter von zur Muehlen. "Policy Robustness: Specification And Simulation Of A Monthly Money Market Model," JMCB, 1982, v14(4), Part 2, 829-856.

Tint, Lawrence G. (Sharpe, William F. and Lawrence G. Tint. "Liabilities - A New Approach," JPM, 1990, v16(2), 5-10.)

Tippett, Mark. (Bird, Ron, David Dennis and Mark Tippett. "A Stop Loss Approach To Portfolio Insurance," JPM, 1988-89, v15(1), 35-40.)

Tipton, James. (Fogler, H. Russell, Kose John and James Tipton. "Three Factors, Interest Rate Differentials And Stock Groups," JOF, 1981, v36(2), 323-335.)

Titman, Sheridan and Arthur Warga. "Risk And The Performance Of Real Estate Investment Trusts: A Multiple Index Approach," AREUEA, 1986, v14(3), 414-431.

Titman, Sheridan and Arthur Warga. "Stock Returns As Predictors Of Interest Rates And Inflation," JFQA, 1989, v24(1), 47-58.

Titman, Sheridan and Roberto Wessels. "The Determinants Of Capital Structure Choice," JOF, 1988, v43(1), 1-19.

Titman, Sheridan and Walter Torous. "Valuing Commercial Mortgages: An Empirical Investigation Of The Contingent-Claims Approach To Pricing Risky Debt," JOF, 1989, v44(2), 345-374.

Titman, Sheridan. "The Effect Of Capital Structure On A Firm's Liquidation Decision," JFEC, 1984, v13(1), 137-151.

Titman, Sheridan. "The Effect Of Forward Markets On The Debt-Equity Mix Of Investor Portfolios And The Optimal Capital Structure Of Firms," JFQA, 1985, v20(1), 19-28.

Titman, Sheridan. "The Effects Of Anticipated Inflation On Housing Market Equilibrium," JOF, 1982, v37(3), 827-842.

Titman, Sheridan. (Grinblatt, Mark and Sheridan Titman. "Approximate Factor Structures: Interpretations And Implications For Empirical Tests," JOF, 1985, v40(5), 1367-1373.)

Titman, Sheridan. (Grinblatt, Mark and Sheridan Titman. "How Clients Can Win The Gaming Game," JPM, 1986-87, v13(4), 14-20.)

Titman, Sheridan. (Grinblatt, Mark and Sheridan Titman. "The Relation Between Mean-Variance Efficiency And Arbitrage Pricing," JOB, 1987, v60(1), 97-112.)

Titman, Sheridan. (Grinblatt, Mark S., Ronald W. Masulis and Sheridan Titman. "The Valuation Effects Of Stock Splits And Stock Dividends," JFEC, 1984, v13(4), 461-490.)

Titman, Sheridan. (Grinblatt, Mark and Sheridan Titman. "Factor Pricing In A Finite Economy," JFEC, 1983, v12(4), 497-508.)

Titman, Sheridan. (Grinblatt, Mark and Sheridan Titman. "Mutual Fund Performance: An Analysis Of Quarterly Portfolio Holdings," JOB, 1989, v62(3), 393-416.)

Titman, Sheridan. (Grinblatt, Mark and Sheridan Titman. "Portfolio Performance Evaluation: Old Issues And New Insights," RFS, 1989, v2(3), 393-422.)

Titman, Sheridan. (Talmor, Eli and Sheridan Titman. "Taxes And Dividend Policy," FM, 1990, v19(2), 32-35.)

Tito, Dennis A. (Smith, Keith V. and Dennis A. Tito. "Risk-Return Measures Of Ex Post Portfolio Performance," JFQA, 1969, v4(4), 449-471.)

Tiwari, Kashi Nath. "The Circular Flow Of Dollars In The World Financial Markets," GFJ, 1990, v1(2), 121-138.

Tiwari, Kashi Nath. "The Money Supply Process Under Deregulation," FR, 1986, v21(1), 111-123.

Tjostheim, Dag. (Stensland, Gunnar and Dag Tjostheim. "Optimal Investments Using Empirical Dynamic Programming With Application To Natural Resources," JOB, 1989, v62(1), 99-120.)

To, Eric C. (Chua, Jess H., Richard S. Woodward and Eric C. To. "Potential Gains From Stock Market Timing In Canada," FAJ, 1987, v43(5), 50-56.)

To, Minh Chau. (Kryzanowski, Lawrence and Minh Chau To. "General Factor Models And The Structure Of Security Returns," JFQA, 1983, v18(1), 31-52.)

To, Minh Chau. (Kryzanowski, Lawrence and Minh Chau To. "The E-V Stationarity Of Security Returns: Some Empirical Evidence," JBF, 1987, v11(1), 117-136.)

To, Minh Chau. (Kryzanowski, Lawrence and Minh Chau To. "The Telescopic Effect Of Past Return Realizations On Ex-Post Beta Estimates," FR, 1984, v19(1), 1-25.)

To, Minh Chau. (Kryzanowski, Lawrence and Minh Chau To. "On Traditional Market Models As Stochastic Return-Generating Models," FR, 1982, v17(3), 165-173.)

Tobey, John. "Seven Hundred Years Of Investment Experience," JPM, 1978-79, v5(3), 11-12.

Tobey, Julian E. "Expanding Use Of Coal By Electric Utility Industry," FAJ, 1963, v19(5), 19-23.

Tobier, Emanuel. (Drennan, Matthew and Emanuel Tobier. "Taxation Of Residential Property In New York City: The Sources Of Differential Treatment," AREUEA, 1977, v5(1), 85-110.)

Tobin, James and Leonard Ross. "A Reply To Gordon Tullock," JMCB, 1972, v4(2), 431-436.

Tobin, James. "A General Equilibrium Approach To Monetary Theory," JMCB, 1969, v1(1), 15-29.

Tobin, James. "A Mean-Variance Approach To Fundamental Valuations," JPM, 1984-85, v11(1), 26-32.

Tobin, James. "Are New Classical Models Plausible Enough To Guide Policy?," JMCB, 1980, v12(4), Part 2, 788-799.

Tobin, James. "Deposit Interest Ceilings As A Monetary Control," JMCB, 1970, v2(1), 4-14.

Tobin, James. "Monetary Policy: Rules, Targets, And Shocks," JMCB, 1983, v15(4), 506-518.

Tobin, James. "Money And Finance In The Macroeconomic Process," JMCB, 1982, v14(2), 171-204.

Tobin, James. "More On Inflation: A Reply," JMCB, 1973, v5(4), 982-984.

Tobin, James. "The Burden Of The Public Debt: A Review Article," JOF, 1965, v20(4), 679-682.

Tobin, James. "The Icons Of Public Debt: Reply(3), 547-547.

Tobin, James. (Backus, David, William C. Brainard, Gary Smith and James Tobin. "A Model Of U.S. Financial And Nonfinancial Economic Behavior," JMCB, 1980, v12(2), Part 1, 259-293.)

Tobler, Henry, III. (Thornton, Jack E. and Henry Tobler, III. "Effective Compustat Tape Utilization By Students And Faculty," JFED, 1975, v4, 111-113.)

Todd, Jerry D. "A Reevaluation Of Tax Sheltered Annuity Cost And Performance Measurement Techniques," JRI, 1978, v45(4), 575-592.

Todd, Jerry D. "A Retirement Plan Decision Model For Small Business," JRI, 1984, v51(2), 265-285.

Todd, Jerry D. "The Costing Of Non-Fault Automobile Insurance," JRI, 1976, v43(3), 431-443.

Todd, Jerry D. "The Risk Management Function In Municipal Government," JRI, 1969, v36(2), 285-295.

Todd, Jerry D. (Manning, Richard L., Matilde K. Stephenson and Jerry D. Todd. "Information Technology In The Insurance Industry: A Forecast Of Utilization And Impact," JRI, 1985, v52(4), 711-722.)

Todd, Jerry D. and David N. Goldstein. "A Computerized Simulation Model For Analyzing Profit Sharing Plans," JRI, 1981, v48(4), 662-673.

Todd, Jerry D. and Richard W. McEnally. "Profitability And Risk In The Title Insurance Industry - The Texas Experience," JRI, 1974, v41(3), 415-433.

Toelle, R. Maynard. "A Commentary On Foreign Insurance Practices," JRI, 1958, v25(4), 70-75.

Toevs, A. (Bierwag, G. O., G. G. Kaufman, R. Schweitzer and A. Toevs. "The Art Of Risk Management In Bond Portfolios," JPM, 1980-81, v7(3), 27-36.)

Toevs, Alden L. and David P. Jacob. "Futures And Alternative Hedge Ratio Methodologies," JPM, 1985-86, v12(3), 60-70.

Toevs, Alden L. (Bierwag, G. O., George G. Kaufman and Alden L. Toevs. "Single Factor Duration Models In A Discrete General Equilibrium Framework," JOF, 1982, v37(2), 325-338.)

Toevs, Alden. "Interest Rate Risk And Uncertain Lives," JPM, 1984-85, v11(3), 45-56.

Toevs, Alden. (Bierwag, G. O., George G. Kaufman and Alden Toevs. "Immunization Strategies For Funding Multiple Liabilities," JFQA, 1983, v18(1), 113-123.)

Toevs, Alden. (Bierwag, G. O., George G. Kaufman and Alden Toevs. "Duration: Its Development And Uses In Bond Portfolio Management," FAJ, 1983, v39(4), 15-35.)

Toevs, Alden. (Bierwag, G. O., George G. Kaufman and Alden Toevs. "Bond Portfolio Immunization And Stochastic Process Risk," JBR, 1982-83, v13(4), 282-291.)

Tokutsu, Ichiro. (Friend, Irwin and Ichiro Tokutsu. "The Cost Of Capital To Corporations In Japan And The U.S.A.," JBF, 1987, v11(2), 313-328.)

Tole, Thomas M. and Robert Ford. "Performance Evaluation Of Sources Of Investment Research," FR, 1977, v12(2), 33-46.

Tole, Thomas M. "How To Maximize Stationarity Of Beta: Reply," JPM, 1982-83, v9(4), 67-68.

Tole, Thomas M. "How To Maximize Stationarity Of Beta," JPM, 1980-81, v7(2), 45-49.

Tole, Thomas M. "You Can't Diversify Without Diversifying," JPM, 1981-82, v8(2), 5-11.

Tollefson, John D. (Joy, O. Maurice and John D. Tollefson. "Some Clarifying Comments On Discriminant Analysis," JFQA, 1978, v13(1), 197-200.)

Tollefson, John O. (Joy, O. Maurice and John O. Tollefson. "On The Financial Applications Of Discriminant Analysis," JFQA, 1975, v10(5), 723-739.)

Tolley, H. Dennis, Kenneth G. Manton and James Vertrees. "An Evaluation Of Three Payment Strategies For Capitation For Medicare," JRI, 1987, v54(4), 678-690.

Tolley, H. Dennis, Michael D. Bahr and Peter K. Dotson. "A Statistical Method For Monitoring Social Insurance Claims," JRI, 1989, v56(4), 670-685.

Tollison, Robert D. and Thomas Willett. "A Defense Of The CEA As An Instrument For Giving Economic Policy Advice: A Comment," JMCB, 1975, v7(1), 113-116.

Toman, Michael A. (Bohi, Douglas R. and Michael A. Toman. "Futures Trading And Oil Market Conditions," JFM, 1987, v7(2), 203-222.)

Tomberlin, Thomas J. (Fairley, William B., Thomas J. Tomberlin and Herbert I. Weisberg. "Pricing Automobile Insurance Under A Cross-Classification Of Risks: Evidence From New Jersey," JRI, 1981, v48(3), 505-514.)

Tomberlin, Thomas J. (Weisberg, Herbert I. and Thomas J. Tomberlin. "A Statistical Perspective On Actuarial Methods For Estimating Pure Premiums From Cross-Classified Data," JRI, 1982, v49(4), 539-563.)

Tomczyk, Stephen and Sangit Chatterjee. "Estimating The Market Model Robustly," JBFA, 1984, v11(4), 563-573.

Tomek, William G. and Scott F. Querin. "Random Processes In Prices And Technical Analysis," JFM, 1984, v4(1), 15-23.

Tomek, William G. (Kahl, Kandice H. and William G. Tomek. "Effectiveness Of Hedging In Potato Futures," JFM, 1982, v2(1), 9-18.)

Tomek, William G. (Sheales, Terence C. and William G. Tomek. "Hedging Australian Wheat Exports Using Futures Markets," JFM, 1987, v7(5), 519-534.)

Tomkins, Cyril. "Another Look At 'Residual Income'," JBFA, 1975, v2(1), 39-53.

Tomkins, Cyril. "Residual Income - A Rebuttal Of Professor Amey's Arguments," JBFA, 1975, v2(2), 161-168.

Tomkins, Cyril. (Lockett, A. Geoffrey and Cyril Tomkins. "The Discount Rate Problem In Capital Rationing Situations: Comment," JFQA, 1970, v5(2), 245-260.)

Tomlinson, C. E. "Business Contracts: Developments And Trends In Multiple Line Underwriting," JRI, 1957, v24(1), 151-157.

Tomlinson, Lucile. "Leverage In Investment Company Stocks," FAJ, 1945, v1(1), 52-62.

Tomlinson, Peter. (Smith, Lawrence B. and Peter Tomlinson. "Rent Controls In Ontario: Roofs Or Ceilings?," AREUEA, 1981, v9(2), 93-114.)

Tong, Tom. (Fabozzi, T. Dessa, Tom Tong and Yu Zhu. "Symmetric Cash Matching," FAJ, 1990, v46(5), 46-52.)

Toole, Howard R. (Capettini, Robert, Richard A. Grimlund and Howard R. Toole. "Comment: The Unique, Real Internal Rate Of Return," JFQA, 1979, v14(5), 1091-1094.)

Toole, Howard. (Capettini, Robert and Howard Toole. "Designing Leveraged Leases: A Mixed Integer Linear Programming Approach," FM, 1981, v10(4), 15-23.)

Tootle, Columbus E. "Doctoral Dissertations In Insurance And Closely Related Fields, 1940-1962," JRI, 1963, v30(2), 237-244.

Tootle, Columbus E. "Second Supplement To: Doctoral Dissertations In Insurance And Closely Related Fields, 1940-1962," JRI, 1966, v33(3), 469-470.

Tootle, Columbus E. "Supplement To Doctoral Dissertations In Insurance And Closely Related Fields, 1940-1962," JRI, 1963, v30(4), 593-594.

Torabzadeh, Khalil M. (Bertin, William J., Farrokh Ghazanfari and Khalil M. Torabzadeh. "Failed Bank Acquisitions And Successful Bidders' Returns," FM, 1989, v18(2), 93-100.)

Torabzadeh, Khalil M. and William J. Bertin. "Leveraged Buyouts And Shareholder Returns," JFR, 1987, v10(4), 313-320.

Torell, John R., III. "U. S. Financial Deregulation: Upheaval And Promise," JBF, 1983, v7(4), 561-566.

Torgerson, David A. (White, Hubert D. and David A. Torgerson. "The Fed's Performance: What Does It Imply For EFTS?: Comment," JBR, 1974-75, v5(3), 193-196.)

Torgerson, Harold W. "Developments In Savings And Loan Associations, 1945-53," JOF, 1954, v9(3), 283-297.

Torgerson, Malcolm S. "Some Ideas And More Problems With FINANSIM," JFED, 1972, v1, 85-88.

Torous, Walter N. "Differential Taxation And The Equilibrium Structure Of Interest Rates," JBF, 1985, v9(3), 363-385.

Torous, Walter N. (Ball, Clifford A. and Walter N. Torous. "Bond Price Dynamics And Options," JFQA, 1983, v18(4), 517-531.)

Torous, Walter N. (Ball, Clifford A., Walter N. Torous and Adrian E. Tschoegl. "An Empirical Investigation Of The EOE Gold Options Market," JBF, 1985, v9(1), 101-113.)

Torous, Walter N. (Ball, Clifford A. and Walter N. Torous. "On Jumps In Common Stock Prices And Their Impact On Call Pricing," JOF, 1985, v40(1), 155-173.)

Torous, Walter N. (Ball, Clifford A. and Walter N. Torous. "Investigating Security-Price Performance In The Presence Of Event-Date Uncertainty," JFEC, 1988, v22(1), 123-154.)

Torous, Walter N. (Ball, Clifford A. and Walter N. Torous. "The Maximum Likelihood Estimation Of Security Price Volatility: Theory, Evidence, And Application To Option Pricing," JOB, 1984, v57(1), Part I, 97-112.)

Torous, Walter N. (Ball, Clifford A. and Walter N. Torous. "Futures Options And The Volatility Of Futures Prices," JOF, 1986, v41(4), 857-870.)

Torous, Walter N. (Ball, Clifford A., Walter N. Torous and Adrian E. Tschoegl. "The Degree Of Price Resolution: The Case Of The Gold Market," JFM, 1985, v5(1), 29-43.)

Torous, Walter N. (Ball, Clifford A. and Walter N. Torous. "A Simplified Jump Process For Common Stock Returns," JFQA, 1983, v18(1), 53-65.)

Torous, Walter N. (Ball, Clifford A. and Walter N. Torous and Adrian E. Tschoegl. "Gold And The 'Weekend Effect'," JFM, 1982, v2(2), 175-182.)

Torous, Walter N. (Franks, Julian R. and Walter N. Torous. "An Empirical Investigation Of U.S. Firms In Reorganization," JOF, 1989, v44(3), 747-770.)

Torous, Walter N. (Schwartz, Eduardo S. and Walter N. Torous. "Prepayment And The Valuation Of Mortgage-Backed Securities," JOF, 1989, v44(2), 375-392.)

Torous, Walter. (Titman, Sheridan and Walter Torous. "Valuing Commercial Mortgages: An Empirical Investigation Of The Contingent-Claims Approach To Pricing Risky Debt," JOF, 1989, v44(2), 345-374.)

Torrance, Charles M. "Gross Flows Of Funds Through Savings And Loan Associations," JOF, 1960, v15(2), 157-169.

Torrance, Grant. "Investing Life Insurance Funds," FAJ, 1955, v11(1), 45-50.

Torto, Raymond G. (Wheaton, William C. and Raymond G. Torto. "Vacancy Rates And The Future Of Office Rents," AREUEA, 1988, v16(4), 430-436.)

Torto, Raymond G. (Wheaton, William C. and Raymond G. Torto. "Income And Appraised Values: A Reexamination Of The FRC Returns Data," AREUEA, 1989, v17(4), 439-449.)

Torto, Raymond G. (Wheaton, William C. and Raymond G. Torto. "An Investment Model Of The Demand And Supply For Industrial Real Estate," AREUEA, 1990, v18(4), 530-547.)

Tosi, Henry L. "The Effects Of Expectation Levels And Role Consensus On The Buyer-Seller Dyad," JOB, 1966, v39(4), 516-528.

Tosi, Henry L. (Carroll, Stephen J., Jr. and Henry L. Tosi. "The Relationship Of Characteristics Of The Review Process To The Success Of The 'Management By Objectives' Approach," JOB, 1971, v44(3), 299-305.)

Tosini, Paula A. and Eugene J. Moriarty. "Potential Hedging Use Of A Futures Contract Based On A Composite Stock Index," JFM, 1982, v2(1), 83-104.

Tosini, Paula A. "Stock Index Futures And Stock Market Activity In October 1987," FAJ, 1988, v44(1), 28-37.

Tosini, Paula A. (Gordon, J. Douglas, Eugene J. Moriarty and Paula A. Tosini. "Stock Index Futures: Does The Dog Wag The Tail?," FAJ, 1987, v43(6), 72-73.)

Tosini, Paula A. (Moriarty, Eugene J. and Paula A. Tosini. "Futures Trading And The Price Volatility Of GNMA Certificates - Further Evidence," JFM, 1985, v5(4), 633-641.)

Tosini, Paula A. (Phillips, Susan M. and Paula A. Tosini. "A Comparison Of Margin Requirements For Options And Futures," FAJ, 1982, v38(6), 54-58.)

Tosini, Paula. (Moriarty, Eugene, Susan Phillips and Paula Tosini. "A Comparison Of Options And Futures In The Management Of Portfolio Risk," FAJ, 1981, v37(1), 61-67.)

Tosini, Suzanne. (Neumark, David, P. A. Tinsley and Suzanne Tosini. "After-Hours Stock Prices And Post-Crash Hangovers," JOF, 1991, v46(1), 159-178.)

Tostlebe, Alvin S. "Trends In Capital Formation And Financing In Agriculture," JOF, 1955, v10(2), 234-249.

Toth, J. R. (Burton, J. S. and J. R. Toth. "Forecasting Long-Term Interest Rates," FAJ, 1974, v30(5), 73-87.)

Tower, Edward. "Monetary And Fiscal Policy Under Fixed And Flexible Exchange Rates In The Inter-Run," JMCB, 1972, v4(4), 877-896.

Tower, Edward. "More On The Welfare Cost Of Inflationary Finance: Comment," JMCB, 1971, v3(4), 850-860.

Tower, Edward. (Willett, Thomas O. and Edward Tower. "The Welfare Economics Of International Adjustment," JOF, 1971, v26(2), 287-302.)

Towey, Richard E. "Money Creation And The Theory Of The Banking Firm," JOF, 1974, v29(1), 57-72.

Towey, Richard E. "The Prohibition Of Interest On Demand Deposits," JBR, 1970-71, v1(4), 8-16.

Towl, Andrew R. "Intercollegiate Case Clearing House," JFED, 1973, v2, 57-61.

Town, Donald E. (Cornew, Ronald W., Donald E. Town and Lawrence D. Crowson. "Stable Distributions, Futures Prices, And The Measurement Of Trading Performance," JFM, 1984, v4(4), 531-558.)

Townsend, Frederick S. "Insurance Stocks - Measuring Values And Earnings: Comment," JRI, 1966, v33(3), 485-488.

Townsend, Henry. "Another Look At The Modigliani And Cohn Equation," FAJ, 1986, v42(5), 63-66.

Townsend, Henry. "Stockholder Earnings," FAJ, 1990, v46(1), 47-57.

Toy, Norman, A. Stonehill, L. Remmers, R. Wright and T. Beekhuisen. "A Comparative International Study Of Growth, Profitability, And Risk As Determinants Of Corporate Debt Ratios," JFQA, 1974, v9(5), 875-886.

Toy, Norman. (Stonehill, Arthur, Theo Beekhuisen, Richard Wright, Lee Remmers, Norman Toy, Antonio Pares, Alan Shapiro, Douglas Egan and Thomas Bates. "Financial Goals And Debt Ratio Determinants," FM, 1974, v4(3), 27-41.)

Toy, William W. and Mark A. Zurack. "Tracking The Euro-Pac Index," JPM, 1989, v15(2), 55-58.

Toy, William. (Black, Fischer, Emanuel Derman and William Toy. "A One-Factor Model Of Interest Rates And Its Application To Treasury Bond Options," FAJ, 1990, v46(1), 33-39.)

Tracy, Myles A. "Insurance And Theology: The Background And The Issues," JRI, 1966, v33(1), 85-94.

Trader, William A. "Dealer Uses Of The Municipal Bond Futures Contract," RFM, 1985, v4(2), 268-272.

Trainer, Francis H., Jr. "The Uses Of Treasury Bond Futures In Fixed-Income Portfolio Management," FAJ, 1983, v39(1), 27-34.

Trainer, Francis H., Jr., David A. Levine and Jonathan A. Reiss. "A Systematic Approach To Bond Management In Pension Funds," JPM, 1983-84, v10(3), 30-35.

Trainer, Francis H., Jr., Jess B. Yawitz and William J. Marshall. "Holding Period Is The Key To Risk Thresholds," JPM, 1978-79, v5(2), 48-54.

Trapnell, Jerry E. (Spiceland, J. David and Jerry E. Trapnell. "The Effect Of Market Conditions And Risk Classifications On Market Model Parameters," JFR, 1983, v6(3), 217-222.)

Trauring, Mitchell. "A Capital Asset Pricing Model With Investors' Taxes And Three Categories Of Investment Income," JFQA, 1979, v14(3), 537-545.

Travers, Frank J. "Some Life Insurance Investment Problems," JRI, 1939, v6, 56-61.

Travlos, Nickolaos G. "Corporate Takeover Bids, Methods Of Payment, And Bidding Firms' Stock Returns," JOF, 1987, v42(4), 943-963.

Travlos, Nickolaos G. (Amihud, Yakov, Baruch Lev and Nickolaos G. Travlos. "Corporate Control And The Choice Of Investment Financing: The Case Of Corporate Acquisitions," JOF, 1990, v45(2), 603-616.)

Travlos, Nickolaos G. (Cornett, Marcia Millon and Nickolaos G. Travlos. "Information Effects Associated With Debt-For-Equity And Equity-For-Debt Exchange Offers," JOF, 1989, v44(2), 451-468.)

Travlos, Nickolaos G. (Doukas, John and Nickolaos G. Travlos. "The Effect Of Corporate Multinationalism On Shareholders' Wealth: Evidence From International Acquisitions," JOF, 1988, v43(5), 1161-1175.)

Travlos, Nickolaos G. (Tehranian, Hassan, Nickolaos G. Travlos and James F. Waegelein. "The Effect Of Long-Term Performance Plans On Corporate Sell-Off-Induced Abnormal Returns," JOF, 1987, v42(4), 933-942.)

Travlos, Nickolaos G. (Saunders, Anthony, Elizabeth Strock and Nickolaos G. Travlos. "Ownership Structure, Deregulation, And Bank Risk Taking," JOF, 1990, v45(2), 643-654.)

Trefftzs, Kenneth L. "Let's Avoid The Next Panic," FAJ, 1967, v23(2), 121-122.

Treimer, Ray. "Don't Overlook Corporate Assets," FAJ, 1954, v10(1), 59-60.

Treischmann, James S. (Pinches, George E. and James S. Trieschmann. "Discriminant Analysis, Classification Results, And Financially Distressed P-L Insurers," JRI, 1977, v44(2), 289-298.)

Tremblay, Victor J. "A Reappraisal Of Interpreting Rising Concentration: The Case Of Beer," JOB, 1985, v58(4), 419-432.

Trenchard, G. Ogden. "Outlook For The Rubber Industry," FAJ, 1953, v9(5), 39-41.

Trennepohl, Gary L. and William P. Dukes. "An Empirical Test Of Option Writing And Buying Strategies Utilizing In-The-Money And Out-Of-The-Money Contracts," JBFA, 1981, v8(2), 185-202.

Trennepohl, Gary L. and William P. Dukes. "Return And Risk From Listed Option Investments," JFR, 1979, v2(1), 37-49.

Trennepohl, Gary L. (Booth, James R., Hassan Tehranian and Gary L. Trennepohl. "Efficiency Analysis And Option Portfolio Selection," JFQA, 1985, v20(4), 435-450.)

Trennepohl, Gary L. (Officer, Dennis T. and Gary L. Trennepohl. "Price Behavior Of Corporate Equities Near Option Expiration Dates," FM, 1981, v10(3), 75-80.)

Trennepohl, Gary L. (Sears, R. Stephen and Gary L. Trennepohl. "Diversification And Skewness In Option Portfolios," JFR, 1983, v6(3), 199-212.)

Trennepohl, Gary L. (Sears, R. Stephen and Gary L. Trennepohl. "Measuring Portfolio Risk In Options," JFQA, 1982, v17(3), 391-409.)

Trennepohl, Gary L., James R. Booth and Hassan Tehranian. "An Empirical Analysis Of Insured Portfolio Strategies Using Listed Options," JFR, 1988, v11(1), 1-12.

Trennepohl, Gary. "A Comparison Of Listed Option Premiums And Black And Scholes Model Prices: 1973-1979," JFR, 1981, v4(1), 11-20.

Trent, Robert H. and Robert S. Kemp. "The Writings Of Henry A. Latane: A Compilation And Analysis," JFR, 1984, v7(2), 161-174.

Trent, Robert H. (Young, William E. and Robert H. Trent. "Geometric Mean Approximations Of Individual Security And Portfolio Performance," JFQA, 1969, v4(2), 179-199.)

Trescott, Paul B. "The Behavior Of The Currency-Deposit Ratio During The Great Depression: A Comment," JMCB, 1984, v16(3), 362-365.

Trestrail, Richard W. "Eurodollars And The Money Supply," FAJ, 1972, v28(3), 55-63.

Trevino, Ruben C. (Cornett, Marcia Millon and Ruben C. Trevino. "Monthly Return Patterns On Commodity Futures Contracts," RFM, 1989, v8(1), 86-104.)

Trevino, Ruben C. (Martell, Terrence F. and Ruben C. Trevino. "The Intraday Behavior Of Commodity Futures Prices," JFM, 1990, v10(6), 661-672.)

Treynor, Jack L. and Robert Ferguson. "In Defense Of Technical Analysis," JOF, 1985, v40(3), 757-773.

Treynor, Jack L. "Long-Term Investing," FAJ, 1976, v32(3), 56-59.

Treynor, Jack L. "Market Efficiency And The Bean Jar Experiment," FAJ, 1987, v43(3), 50-53.

Treynor, Jack L. "On The Quality Of Municipal Bonds," FAJ, 1982, v38(3), 25-30.

Treynor, Jack L. "Portfolio Insurance And Market Volatility," FAJ, 1988, v44(6), 71-73.

Treynor, Jack L. "The Economics Of The Dealer Function," FAJ, 1987, v43(6), 27-34.

Treynor, Jack L. "The Financial Objective In The Widely Held Corporation," FAJ, 1981, v37(2), 68-71.

Treynor, Jack L. "The Fiscal Burden," FAJ, 1982, v38(5), 17-24.

Treynor, Jack L. "The Principles Of Corporate Pension Finance," JOF, 1977, v32(2), 627-638.

Treynor, Jack L. "The Trouble With Earnings," FAJ, 1972, v28(5), 41-43.

Treynor, Jack L. "Unemployment And Inflation," FAJ, 1975, v31(3), 21-23,26-28.

Treynor, Jack L. "What Does It Take To Win The Trading Game?," FAJ, 1981, v37(1), 55-60.

Treynor, Jack L. "What Prof. Galbraith Failed To Say On TV," FAJ, 1978, v34(2), 43-44.

Treynor, Jack L. and Fischer Black. "How To Use Security Analysis To Improve Portfolio Selection," JOB, 1973, v46(1), 66-86.

Treynor, Jack L., P. J. Regan and W. W. Priest. "Pension Claims And Corporate Assets," FAJ, 1978, v34(3), 84-88.

Treynor, Jack L., William W. Priest, Jr., Lawrence Fisher and Catherine A. Higgins. "Risk Estimates," FAJ, 1968, v24(5), 93-100.

Treynor, Jack. (Good, Walter R., Robert Ferguson and Jack Treynor. "A Guide To The Index Fund Controversy," FAJ, 1976, v32(6), 27-38.)

Triantis, Alexander J. and James E. Hodder. "Valuing Flexibility As A Complex Option," JOF, 1990, v45(2), 549-566.

Trieschmann, James S. "1982 Presidential Address - The American Risk And Insurance Association Today And Tomorrow," JRI, 1983, v50(1), 8-18.

Trieschmann, James S. "Further Studies Of Property-Liability Return Adequacy: Further Reply," JRI, 1973, v40(3), 463-464.

Trieschmann, James S. "Property-Liability Profits: A Comparative Study," JRI, 1971, v38(3), 437-453.

Trieschmann, James S. "Replacement Of Life Insurance: Comment," JRI, 1976, v43(1), 156-161.

Trieschmann, James S. "Teaching Insurance With An Insurance Management Computer Game," JRI, 1976, v43(1), 43-51.

Trieschmann, James S. (Aiuppa, Thomas A. and James S. Trieschmann. "An Empirical Analysis Of The Magnitude And Accuracy Of Incurred-But-Not-Reported Reserves," JRI, 1987, v54(1), 100-118.)

Trieschmann, James S. (Cather, David A., Sandra G. Gustavson and James S. Trieschmann. "A Profitability Analysis Of Property-Liability Insurers Using Alternative Distribution Systems," JRI, 1985, v52(2), 321-332.)

Trieschmann, James S. (Dotterweich, William and James S. Trieschmann. "Use Of Computers In Teaching Insurance, Revisited," JRI, 1974, v41(3), 553-560.)

Trieschmann, James S. (Gustavson, Sandra G. and James S.

Trieschmann. "Universal Life Insurance As An Alternative To The Joint And Survivor Annuity," **JRI**, 1988, v55(3), 529-538.)

Trieschmann, James S. (Pinches, George E. and James S. Trieschmann. "The Efficiency Of Alternative Models For Solvency Surveillance In The Insurance Industry," **JRI**, 1974, v41(4), 563-577.)

Trieschmann, James S. (Pritchett, S. Travis and James S. Trieschmann. "Faculty Benefits At Fifty Major Universities," **JRI**, 1974, v41(1), 93-108.)

Trieschmann, James S. and E. J. Leverett, Jr. "Self-Insurance Of Workers' Compensation Losses," **JRI**, 1978, v45(4), 635-650.

Trieschmann, James S. and E. J. Leverett, Jr. "A Sensitivity Analysis Of Selected Variables In Agency Valuation," **JRI**, 1987, v54(2), 357-363.

Trieschmann, James S. and George E. Pinches. "A Multivariate Model For Predicting Financially Distressed P-L Insurers," **JRI**, 1973, v40(3), 327-338.

Trieschmann, James S. and Patrick G. McKeown. "Sensitivity Analysis Of Workers' Compensation Costs," **JRI**, 1980, v47(4), 735-752.

Trieschmann, James S. and Robert J. Monroe. "Investment Performance Of Property-Liability Insurers' Common Stock Portfolios," **JRI**, 1972, v39(4), 545-554.

Trieschmann, James S. and Robert J. Monroe. "Investment Performance Of P.L. Insurers' Common Stock Portfolios: Reply," **JRI**, 1975, v42(1), 173-177.

Trieschmann, James S., K. Roscoe Davis and E. J. Leverett, Jr. "A Probabilistic Valuation Model For A Property-Liability Insurance Agency," **JRI**, 1975, v42(2), 289-302.

Trieschmann, James. (Monroe, Robert J. and James Trieschmann. "Portfolio Performance Of Property-Liability Insurance Companies," **JFQA**, 1972, v7(2), 1595-1611.)

Trifts, Jack W. (Pettway, Richard H. and Jack W. Trifts. "Do Banks Overbid When Acquiring Failed Banks?," **FM**, 1985, v14(2), 5-15.)

Trifts, Jack W. (Scanlon, Kevin P., Jack W. Trifts and Richard H. Pettway. "Impacts Of Relative Size And Industrial Relatedness On Returns To Shareholders Of Acquiring Firms," **JFR**, 1989, v12(2), 103-112.)

Trifts, Jack W. and Kevin P. Scanlon. "Interstate Bank Mergers: The Early Evidence," **JFR**, 1987, v10(4), 305-312.

Trifts, Jack W., Neil W. Sicherman, Rodney L. Roenfeldt and Francisco De Cossio. "Divestiture To Unit Managers And Shareholder Wealth," **JFR**, 1990, v13(2), 167-172.

Trigeorgis, Lenos. (Thosar, Satish and Lenos Trigeorgis. "Stock Volatility And Program Trading," **JACF**, 1990, v2(4), 91-96.)

Trigger, Raymond. "Sing Something Simple," **FAJ**, 1956, v12(4), 37-40.

Trimble, John L. (Marr, M. Wayne, Robert W. Rogowski and John L. Trimble. "The Competitive Effects Of U.S. And Japanese Commercial Bank Participation In Eurobond Underwriting," **FM**, 1989, v18(4), 47-54.)

Trimble, John. (Marr, Wayne and John Trimble. "The Persistent Borrowing Advantage In Eurodollar Bonds: A Plausible Explanation," **JACF**, 1988, v1(2), 65-70.)

Trippi, Robert R. "Conventional And Unconventional Methods For Evaluating Investments," **FM**, 1974, v3(3), 31-35.

Trippi, Robert R. (Lee, Jae K., Robert R. Trippi, Seok C. Chu and Hyun Kim. "K-FOLIO: Integrating The Markowitz Model With A Knowledge-Based System," **JPM**, 1990, v17(1), 89-93.)

Trippi, Robert R. (Schmalensee, Richard and Robert R. Trippi. "Common Stock Volatility Expectations Implied By Option Premia," **JOF**, 1978, v33(1), 129-147.)

Trippi, Robert R. and Rebecca Jacob Abraham. "Interest Rates Implied In The Prices Of S&P 100 Options: Evidence And Implications Of An Inverted Ultra-Short Term Structure," **IJOF**, 1990, v2(2), 52-66.

Trivoli, G. William. "The Effects Of Price Concessions On New Automobiles To Dealers During The MOdel Year 1969," **JOB**, 1971, v44(4), 398-407.

Trivoli, George W. "Evaluation Of Pollution Control Expenditures By Lending Corporations," **FM**, 1973, v2(4), 19-24.

Trivoli, George W. "Project Investment Analysis And Anticipated Government Mandated Expenditures," **FM**, 1976, v5(4), 18-25.

Trivoli, George W. and William R. McDaniel. "Uncertainty, Capital Immobility And Capital Rationing In The Investment Decision," **JBFA**, 1987, v14(2), 215-228.

Trivoli, George William. "How To Profit From Insider Trading Information," **JPM**, 1979-80, v6(4), 51-56.

Trolle-Schultz, Erik. "International Money Transfer Developments," **JBR**, 1978-79, v9(2), 72-77.

Trosper, Joseph F. "A Challenge To AAUTI Members," **JRI**, 1959, v26(1), 12-15.

Trosper, Joseph F. "Appraising The Life Value For Key Man Life Insurance," **JRI**, 1960, v27(2), 81-92.

Trosper, Joseph F. "Overinsurance - Its Meaning," **JRI**, 1964, v31(4), 603-612.

Trosper, Joseph F. "The Basic Life Insurance Course In The Curriculum," **JRI**, 1954, v21, 10-12.

Troutt, Marvin D. "A Purchase Timing Model For Life Insurance Decision Support Systems," **JRI**, 1988, v55(4), 628-643.

Trovato, Sal. (Fabozzi, Frank J. and Sal Trovato. "The Use Of Quantitative Techniques In Commercial Banks," **JBR**, 1976-77, v7(2), 173-178.)

Trow, Donald B. (Cyert, Richard M., Herbert A. Simon, and Donald B. Trow. "Observation Of A Business Decision," **JOB**, 1956, v29(4), 237-248.)

Trowbridge, C. L. "Insurance Is A Transfer Mechanism," **JRI**, 1975, v42(1), 1-15.

Trowell, John. "The Addition Of Current Exit Values And The Numerosity Paradox," **JBFA**, 1980, v7(3), 475-479.

Troxel, Emery. "Valuation Of Public Utility Property - A Problem In Efficient Resource Use And Efficient Regulation," **JOB**, 1950, v23(1), 1-21.

Troxel, Terrie E. (Cargill, Thomas F. and Terrie E. Troxel. "Modeling Life Insurance Savings: Some Methodological Issues," **JRI**, 1979, v46(3), 391-410.)

Trued, Merlyn N. "The Great Escape From Gold," **FAJ**, 1970, v26(1), 67-68.

Trueman, Brett. "A Theory Of Noise Trading In Securities Markets," **JOF**, 1988, v43(1), 83-95.

Trueman, Brett. "Motivating Mangement To Reveal Inside Information," **JOF**, 1983, v38(4), 1253-1269.

Trueman, Brett. "Optimality Of The Disclosure Of Private Information In A Production-Exchange Economy," **JOF**, 1983, v38(3), 913-924.

Trueman, Brett. "The Relationship Between The Level Of Capital Expenditures And Firm Value," **JFQA**, 1986, v21(2), 115-129.

Trueman, Brett. (Masulis, Ronald W. and Brett Trueman. "Corporate Investment And Dividend Decisions Under Differential Personal Taxation," **JFQA**, 1988, v23(4), 369-386.)

Truett, Dale B. and Lila J. Truett. "The Demand For Life Insurance In Mexico And The United States: A Comparative Study," **JRI**, 1990, v57(2), 321-328.

Truett, Lila J. (Truett, Dale B. and Lila J. Truett. "The Demand For Life Insurance In Mexico And The United States: A Comparative Study," **JRI**, 1990, v57(2), 321-328.)

Trussell, James. (Bloom David E., Beth Preiss and James Trussell. "Mortgage Lending Discrimination And The Decision To Apply: A Methodological Note," **AREUEA**, 1983, v11(1), 97-103.)

Tryfos, Peter. "On Classification In Automobile Insurance," **JRI**, 1980, v47(2), 331-337.

Tryfos, Peter. "The Equity Of Classification Systems In Automobile Insurance," **JRI**, 1987, v54(3), 569-581.

Trykowski, Ben L. "Integrating A Computerized Examination Generating System Into The Basic Business Finance Course," **JFED**, 1977, v6, 67-89.

Trykowski, Ben L. "Socrates: A Computer System To Design And Evaluate Examinations In Finance," **JFED**, 1975, v4, 114-117.

Trzcinka, Charles A. (Kidwell, David S. and Charles A. Trzcinka. "The Impact Of The New York City Fiscal Crisis On The Interest Cost Of New Issue Municipal Bonds," **JFQA**, 1983, v18(3), 381-399.)

Trzcinka, Charles A. (Kidwell, David S. and Charles A. Trzcinka. "The Risk Structure Of Interest Rates And The Penn-Central Crisis," **JOF**, 1979, v34(3), 751-760.)

Trzcinka, Charles A. (Kidwell, David S. and Charles A. Trzcinka. "Municipal Bond Pricing And The New York City Fiscal Crisis," **JOF**, 1982, v37(5), 1239-1246.)

Trzcinka, Charles. "On The Number Of Factors In The Arbitrage Pricing Model," **JOF**, 1986, v41(2), 347-368.

Trzcinka, Charles. "Risk, Segmentation, And The Municipal Term Structure," **FR**, 1986, v21(4), 501-526.

Trzcinka, Charles. "The Pricing Of Tax-Exempt Bonds And The Miller Hypothesis," **JOF**, 1982, v37(4), 907-923.

Trzcinka, Charles. (Shukla, Ravi and Charles Trzcinka. "Research On Risk And Return: Can Measures Of Risk Explain Anything?," **JPM**, 1991, v17(3), 15-21.)

Trzcinka, Charles. (Shukla, Ravi and Charles Trzcinka. "Sequential Tests Of The Arbitrage Pricing Theory: A Comparison Of Principal Components And Maximum Likelihood Factors," **JOF**, 1990, v45(5), 1541-1564.)

Tsaur, Tien-wang. (Chen, Chau-nan, Ching-chong Lai and Tien-wang Tsaur. "The Loanable Funds Theory And The Dynamics Of Exchange Rates: The Mundell Model Revisited," **JIMF**, 1988, v7(2), 221-230.)

Tsay, Jeffrey J. (Hall, Thomas W. and Jeffrey J. Tsay. "An Evaluation Of The Performance Of Portfolios Selected From Value Line Rank One Stocks: 1976-1982," **JFR**, 1988, v11(3), 227-240.)

Tschirgi, Harvey. (Lentz, Arthur and Harvey Tschirgi. "The Ethical Content Of Annual Reports," **JOB**, 1963, v36(4), 387-393.)

Tschoegl, Adrain E. (Lessard, Donald R. and Adrian E. Tschoegl. "Panama's International Banking Center: The Direct Employment Effects," **JBF**, 1988, v12(1), 43-50.)

Tschoegl, Adrian E. "Concentration Among International Banks: A Note," **JBF**, 1982, v6(4), 567-578.

Tschoegl, Adrian E. "Efficiency In The Gold Market: A Note," **JBF**, 1980, v4(4), 371-379.

Tschoegl, Adrian E. "Size, Growth, And Transnationality Among The World's Largest Banks," **JOB**, 1983, v56(2), 187-202.

Tschoegl, Adrian E. (Ball, Clifford A., Walter N. Torous and Adrian E. Tschoegl. "Gold And The 'Weekend Effect'," **JFM**, 1982, v2(2), 175-182.)

Tschoegl, Adrian E. (Ball, Clifford A., Walter N. Torous and Adrian E. Tschoegl. "An Empirical Investigation Of The EOE Gold Options Market," **JBF**, 1985, v9(1), 101-113.)

Tschoegl, Adrian E. (Ball, Clifford A., Walter N. Torous and Adrian E. Tschoegl. "The Degree Of Price Resolution: The Case Of The Gold Market," **JFM**, 1985, v5(1), 29-43.)

Tschoegl, Adrian E. (Ball, Clifford A. and Adrian E. Tschoegl. "The Decision To Establish A Foreign Bank Branch Or Subsidiary: An Application Of Binary Classification Procedures," **JFQA**, 1982, v17(3), 411-424.)

Tschoegl, Adrian E. (Choi, Sang-Rim and Adrian E. Tschoegl. "Bank Employment In The World's Largest Banks: An Update," **JMCB**, 1984, v16(3), 359-362.)

Tschoegl, Adrian E. (Hodder, James E. and Adrian E. Tschoegl. "Some Aspects Of Japanese Corporate Finance," **JFQA**, 1985, v20(2), 173-192.)

Tse, David K. (Wehrung, Donald, Kam-Hon Lee, David K. Tse and Ilan B. Vertinsky. "Adjusting Risky Situations: A Theoretical Framework And Empirical Test," **JRU**, 1989, v2(2), 189-212.)

Tse, K. S. Maurice and Mark A. White. "The Valuation Of Semiannual Bonds Between Interest Payment Dates: A Correction," **FR**, 1990, v25(4), 659-662.

Tse, Y. K. (Boyle, Phelim P. and Y. K. Tse. "An Algorithm For Computing Values Of Options On The Maximum Or Minimum Of Several Assets," **JFQA**, 1990, v25(2), 215-228.)

Tseng, Kuo C. "Low Price, Price-Earnings Ratio, Market Value, And Abnormal Stock Returns," **FR**, 1988, v23(3), 333-344.

Tsetsekos, George P. and Richard Defusco. "Portfolio Performance, Managerial Ownership, And The Size Effect," **JPM**, 1990, v16(3), 33-39.

Tsiang, S. C. "A Critical Note On The Optimum Supply Of Money," **JMCB**, 1969, v1(2), 266-280.

Tsuji, Masao. (Ansari, Shahid L. and Masao Tsuji. "A Behavioral Extension To The Cost Variances Investigation Decision," **JBFA**, 1981, v8(4), 573-591.)

497

Tsutsui, Yoshiro. (Osano, Hiroshi and Yoshiro Tsutsui. "Implicit Contracts In The Japanese Bank Loan Market," JFQA, 1985, v20(2), 211-230.)

Tuan, Kailin. "A Preliminary Note On The Study Of Hazards," JRI, 1973, v40(2), 279-286.

Tuan, Kailin. "Aviation Insurance In America," JRI, 1965, v32(1), 1-22.

Tuan, Kailin. "Insurance And Society: A Liberal Study," JRI, 1970, v37(2), 281-290.

Tuan, Pham D. (Weston, J. Fred and Pham D. Tuan. "Comment On Analysis Of Credit Policy Changes," FM, 1980, v9(4), 59-63.)

Tubiana, Paul S. (Altman, Edward I. and Paul S. Tubiana. "The Multi-Firm Bond Issue: A Fund-Raising Financial Instrument," FM, 1981, v10(3), 23-33.)

Tuccillo, John A. "The Tax Treatment Of Mortgage Investment," AREUEA, 1983, v11(2), 288-299.

Tuccillo, John A. (Biederman, Kenneth R., John A. Tuccillo and George J. Viksnins. "An Analysis Of The Mortgage Tax Credit Provision Of The Financial Institutions Act," JBR, 1975-76, v6(2), 100-108.)

Tuchi, Ben J. (Dalrymple, Brent B. and Ben J. Tuchi. "Hospital Pricing Under Economic Controls," FR, 1972, v2(2), 156-162.)

Tucker, Alan J. (Ogden, Joseph P. and Alan J. Tucker. "The Relative Valuation Of American Currency Spot And Futures Options: Theory And Empirical Tests," JFQA, 1988, v23(4), 351-368.)

Tucker, Alan L. "Empirical Tests Of The Efficiency Of The Currency Option Market," JFR, 1985, v8(4), 275-285.

Tucker, Alan L. "Exchange Rate Jumps And Currency Options Pricing," RDIBF, 1991, v4/5, 419-438.

Tucker, Alan L. "Foreign Exchange Option Prices As Predictors Of Equilibrium Forward Exchange Rates," JIMF, 1987, v6(3), 283-294.

Tucker, Alan L. (Ang, James S. and Alan L. Tucker. "The Shareholder Wealth Effects Of Corporate Greenmail," JFR, 1988, v11(4), 265-280.)

Tucker, Alan L. (Ehrhardt, Michael C. and Alan L. Tucker. "Pricing CRB Futures Contracts," JFR, 1990, v13(1), 7-14.)

Tucker, Alan L. (Ogden, Joseph P., Alan L. Tucker and Timothy W. Vines. "Arbitraging American Gold Spot And Futures Options," FR, 1990, v25(4), 577-592.)

Tucker, Alan L. (Ogden, Joseph P. and Alan L. Tucker. "Empirical Tests Of The Efficiency Of The Currency Futures Options Market," JFM, 1987, v7(6), 695-704.)

Tucker, Alan L. (Peterson, David R. and Alan L. Tucker. "Implied Spot Rates As Predictors Of Currency Returns: A Note," JOF, 1988, v43(1), 247-258.)

Tucker, Alan L. (Scott, Elton and Alan L. Tucker. "Predicting Currency Return Volatility," JBF, 1989, v13(6), 839-852.)

Tucker, Alan L. and Elton Scott. "A Study Of Diffusion Processes For Foreign Exchange Rates," JIMF, 1987, v6(4), 465-478.

Tucker, Alan L., David R. Peterson and Elton Scott. "Tests Of The Black-Scholes And Constant Elasticity Of Variance Currency Call Option Valuation Models," JFR, 1988, v11(3), 201-214.

Tucker, Donald P. "Financial Innovation And The Mortgage Market: The Possibilities For Liability Management By Thrifts," JOF, 1976, v31(2), 427-437.

Tucker, Donald P. "Macroeconomic Models And The Demand For Money Under Market Disequilibrium," JMCB, 1971, v3(1), 57-83.

Tucker, John M. (Berg, Gordon H. and John M. Tucker. "Techniques For Arranging Hospital Financing," FM, 1972, v1(1), 48-57.)

Tucker, Julia. (Fabozzi, Frank J., Michael G. Ferri, T. Dessa Fabozzi and Julia Tucker. "A Note On Unsuccessful Tender Offers And Stockholder Returns," JOF, 1988, v43(5), 1275-1283.)

Tucker, Michael. "Adjustable-Rate And Fixed-Rate Mortgage Choice: A Logit Analysis," JRER, 1989, v4(2), 81-91.

Tucker, Robert D. "A Discussion Of Benjamin Graham's Central Value Concept," FAJ, 1957, v13(2), 93-96.

Tucker, Rufus S. "Outlook For The Automobile Industry," FAJ, 1949, v5(4), 9.

Tucker, Rufus S. "Principles For Post-War Taxation," FAJ, 1945, v1(1), 24-29.

Tucker, Rufus S. "Some Thoughts On Market Controls," FAJ, 1951, v7(1), 11-12.

Tueting, William F. "Jurisdiction Over Clearinghouse Offset Options," JFM, 1981, v1(Supp), 445-448.

Tueting, William F. "Section 5a(12) Rule Approval: A Ponderous Partner In Exchange Management," JFM, 1981, v1(Supp), 469-473.

Tueting, William F. and Christopher Q. King. "Funds Protections: An Overview Of What Happens When A Commodity Broker Becomes Insolvent," JFM, 1987, v7(1), 93-102.

Tufano, Peter. "Financial Innovation And First-Mover Advantages," JFEC, 1989, v25(2), 213-240.

Tull, D. S., R. A. Boring and M. H. Gonsior. "A Note On The Relationship Of Price And Imputed Quality," JOB, 1964, v37(2), 186-191.

Tull, Donald S. "A Re-Examination Of The Causes Of The Decline In Sales Of Sapolio," JOB, 1955, v28(2), 128-137.

Tull, Donald S. "The Relationship Of Actual And Predicted Sales And Profits In New-Product Introductions," JOB, 1967, v40(3), 233-253.

Tull, Donald S. and Herbert C. Rutemiller. "A Note On The Relationship Of Actual And Predicted Sales And Profits In New-Product Introductions," JOB, 1968, v41(3), 385-387.

Tullio, Giuseppe. "Monetary Equilibrium And Balance-Of-Payments Adjustment: An Empirical Test Of The U.S. Balance Of Payments, 1951-73," JMCB, 1979, v11(1), 68-79.

Tullio, Giuseppe. (Sommariva, Andrea and Giuseppe Tullio. "International Gold Flows In Gold Standard Germany: A Test Of The Monetary Approach To The Balance Of Payments, 1880-1911," JMCB, 1988, v20(1), 132-140.)

Tullio, Giuseppe. (Sommariva, Andrea and Giuseppe Tullio. "The German Depression And The Stock Market Crash Of The Thirties: The Role Of Macropolicies And Of The International Business Cycle," JBF, 1989, v13(4/5), 515-536.)

Tullock, Gordon. "A Modest Proposal: A Comment," JMCB, 1971, v3(2), Part 1, 263-270.

Tullock, Gordon. "Can You Fool All Of The People All Of The Time?," JMCB, 1972, v4(2), 426-430.

Tullock, Gordon. "Competing Monies: A Reply," JMCB, 1976, v8(4),

521-525.

Tullock, Gordon. "Competing Monies," JMCB, 1975, v7(4), 491-497.

Tullock, Gordon. "Inflation And Unemployment: The Discussion Continued: A Comment," JMCB, 1973, v5(3), 826-835.

Tullock, Gordon. "When Is Inflation Not Inflation?," JMCB, 1979, v11(2), 219-221.

Ture, Norman B. "Growth Aspects Of Federal Tax Policy," JOF, 1962, v17(2), 269-279.

Turgeon, Frank L. "The Agricultural Equipment Industry," FAJ, 1957, v13(5), 29-32.

Turkish, Norman A. "Commodities: High Finance In Soybeans," FAJ, 1961, v17(2), 91-101.

Turley, Stuart. (Moizer, Peter and Stuart Turley. "Changes In The UK Market For Audit Services: 1972-1982," JBFA, 1989, v16(1), 41-54.)

Turley, Stuart. (Taylor, Peter and Stuart Turley. "Applying Economic Consequences Analysis In Accounting Standard Setting: A Tax Incidence Approach," JBFA, 1986, v13(4), 467-488.)

Turnbull, Geoffrey K. "The Impact Of Loss Offset Limitations On Project Selection And Development Timing," JREFEC, 1990, v3(2), 141-154.

Turnbull, Geoffrey Keith. "Property Taxes And The Transition Of Land To Urban Use," JREFEC, 1988, v1(4), 393-403.

Turnbull, S. M. "Additional Aspects Of Rational Insurance Purchasing," JOB, 1983, v56(2), 217-229.

Turnbull, S. M. "Market Imperfections And The Capital Asset Pricing Model," JBFA, 1977, v4(3), 327-337.

Turnbull, Stuart M. "Debt Capacity: Erratum," JOF, 1981, v36(1), 197.

Turnbull, Stuart M. "Debt Capacity," JOF, 1979, v34(4), 931-940.

Turnbull, Stuart M. "Discounting The Components Of An Income Stream: Comment," JOF, 1977, v32(1), 221-223.

Turnbull, Stuart M. "Market Value And Systematic Risk," JOF, 1977, v32(4), 1125-1142.

Turnbull, Stuart M. "Measurement Of The Real Rate Of Interest And Related Problems In A World Of Uncertainty," JMCB, 1981, v13(2), 177-191.

Turnbull, Stuart M. "Swaps: A Zero Sum Game?," FM, 1987, v16(1), 15-21.

Turnbull, Stuart M. (Boyle, Phelim P. and Stuart M. Turnbull. "Pricing And Hedging Capped Options," JBM, 1989, v9(1), 41-54.)

Turnbull, Stuart M. (Epstein, Larry G. and Stuart M. Turnbull. "Capital Asset Prices And The Temporal Resolution Of Uncertainty," JOF, 1980, v35(3), 627-643.)

Turnbull, Stuart M. (Halpern, Paul J. and Stuart M. Turnbull. "Empirical Tests Of Boundary Conditions For Toronto Stock Exchange Options," JOF, 1985, v40(2), 481-500.)

Turnbull, Stuart M. (Myers, Stewart C. and Stuart M. Turnbull. "Capital Budgeting And The Capital Asset Pricing Model: Good News And Bad News," JOF, 1977, v32(2), 321-333.)

Turner, Bengt. "Economic And Political Aspects Of Negotiated Rents In The Swedish Housing Market," JREFEC, 1988, v1(3), 257-276.

Turner, Christopher M., Richard Startz and Charles R. Nelson. "A Markov Model Of Heteroskedasticity, Risk, And Learning In The Stock Market," JFEC, 1989, v25(1), 3-20.

Turner, John A. (Ippolito, Richard A. and John A. Turner. "Turnover, Fees And Pension Plan Performance," FAJ, 1987, v43(6), 6-26.)

Turner, Lee D. (Brzozowski, Leonard J., Lee D. Turner and Eric E. Olsen. "Project Financing Evaluation: A Simulation Approach," JBR, 1977-78, v8(1), 40-49.)

Turner, Robert C. "Recent Development And Evaluation Of Direct Controls," JOF, 1950, v5(1), 3-23.

Turner, Robert C. "The Apologetics Of 'Managerialism'": Comment," JOB, 1958, v31(3), 243-248.

Turner, Terry L. "A Multivariate Spectral Analysis Of The Supply Of Money And Credit," JMCB, 1972, v4(4), 848-876.

Turney, James C. (Canto, Victor A., Arthur B. Laffer and James C. Turney. "Trade Policy And The U.S. Economy," FAJ, 1982, v38(5), 27-46.)

Turnovsky, S. J. (Sprenkle, C. M., S. J. Turnovsky and R. A. Fujihara. "Assets, Aggregates And Optimal Monetary Control," JBF, 1990, v14(1), 157-178.)

Turnovsky, Stephen J. and Jagdeep S. Bhandari. "The Degree Of Capital Mobility And The Stability Of An Open Economy Under Rational Expectations," JMCB, 1982, v14(3), 303-326.

Turnovsky, Stephen J. and Marcus H. Miller. "The Effects Of Government Expenditure On The Term Structure Of Interest Rates," JMCB, 1984, v16(1), 16-33.

Turnovsky, Stephen J. "Domestic And Foreign Disturbances In An Optimizing Model Of Exchange-Rate Determination," JIMF, 1985, v4(1), 151-171.

Turnovsky, Stephen J. "Financial Structure And The Theory Of Production," JOF, 1970, v25(5), 1061-1080.

Turnovsky, Stephen J. "Macroeconomic Dynamics And Growth In A Monetary Economy: A Synthesis," JMCB, 1978, v10(1), 1-26.

Turnovsky, Stephen J. "Monetary Policy And Foreign Disturbances Under Flexible Exchange Rates: Stochastic Approach," JMCB, 1981, v13(2), 156-176.

Turnovsky, Stephen J. "Optimal Choice Of Monetary Instrument In A Linear Economic Model With Stochastic Coefficients," JMCB, 1975, v7(1), 51-80.

Turnovsky, Stephen J. "Optimal Monetary Growth With Accommodating Fiscal Policy In A Small Open Economy," JIMF, 1987, v6(2), 179-194.

Turnovsky, Stephen J. "Optimal Monetary Policy And Wage Indexation Under Alternative Disturbances And Information Structures," JMCB, 1987, v19(2), 157-180.

Turnovsky, Stephen J. "The Demand For Money And The Determination Of The Rate Of Interest Under Uncertainty," JMCB, 1971, v3(2), Part 1, 183-204.

Turnovsky, Stephen J. "The Relative Stability Of Alternative Exchange Rate Systems In The Presence Of Random Disturbances," JMCB, 1976, v8(1), 29-50.

Turnovsky, Stephen J. "The Term Structure Of Interest Rates And The Effects Of Macroeconomic Policy," JMCB, 1989, v21(3), 321-347.

Turnovsky, Stephen J. (Eaton, Jonathan and Stephen J. Turnovsky. "Effects Of Monetary Disturbances On Exchange Rates With Risk Averse Speculation," JIMF, 1982, v1(1), 21-37.)

Turnovsky, Stephen J. (Nguyen, Duc-Tho and Stephen J. Turnovsky. "Monetary And Fiscal Policies In An Inflationary Economy: A Simulation Approach," JMCB, 1979, v11(3), 259-283.)

Turnovsky, Stephen J. (Pyle, David H. and Stephen J. Turnovsky. "The Dynamics Of Government Policy In An Inflationary Economy: An 'Intermediate-Run' Analysis," JMCB, 1976, v8(4), 411-437.)

Turov, Daniel. "Warrants Of Dividend-Paying Stocks," FAJ, 1973, v29(2), 76-78.

Turpie, Keith D. (Williams, David J. and Keith D. Turpie. "The Accounting Services Market: Theory And Evidence: A Comment," JBFA, 1983, v10(2), 317-321.)

Turrentine, Gordon H. "Newsmakers In The Texas Gulf Coast Chemical Empire - 1955," FAJ, 1956, v12(2), 109-118.

Turrentine, Gordon H. "Petrochemicals Come Of Age," FAJ, 1953, v9(5), 45-50.

Turvey, Calum G. "Alternative Estimates Of Weighted Implied Volatilities From Soybean And Live Cattle Options," JFM, 1990, v10(4), 353-366.

Tusell, F. (Alonso, A., G. Rubio and F. Tusell. "Asset Pricing And Risk Aversion In The Spanish Stock Market," JBF, 1990, v14(2/3), 351-370.)

Tussing, A. Dale. "Can Monetary Policy Influence The Availability Of Credit?," JOF, 1966, v21(1),1-13.

Tussing, A. Dale. "Stimulating Bank Competition: Comment," JOF, 1965, v20(4), 691-692.

Tuttle, Donald L. and Robert H. Litzenberger. "Leverage, Diversification And Capital Market Effects On A Risk-Adjusted Capital Budgeting Framework," JOF, 1968, v23(3), 427-443.

Tuttle, Donald L. and William L. Wilbur. "Holding-Period Yields On Highest-Grade Corporate Bonds," FR, 1969, v1(4), 227-241.

Tuttle, Donald L. and William L. Wilbur. "A Multivariate Time-Series Investigation Of Annual Returns On Highest Grade Corporate Bonds," JFQA, 1971, v6(2), 707-721.

Tuttle, Donald L. (Beedles, William L. and Donald L. Tuttle. "Portfolio Construction And Clientele Objective," JPM, 1978-79, v5(1), 25-28.)

Tuttle, Donald L. (Finkel, Sidney R. and Donald L. Tuttle. "Determinants Of The Aggregate Profits Margin," JOF, 1971, v26(5), 1067-1075.)

Tuttle, Donald L. (Finkel, Sidney R. and Donald L. Tuttle. "Determinants Of The Aggregate Profit Margin: Reply," JOF, 1976, v31(1), 167-168.)

Tuttle, Donald L. (Klemkosky, Robert C. and Donald L. Tuttle. "The Institutional Source And Concentration Of Financial Research," JOF, 1977, v32(3), 901-908.)

Tuttle, Donald L. (Klemkosky, Robert C. and Donald L. Tuttle. "A Ranking Of Doctoral Programs By Financial Research Contributions Of Graduates," JFQA, 1977, v12(3), 491-497.)

Tuttle, Donald L. (Latane, Henry A., Donald L. Tuttle and William E. Young. "How To Choose A Market Index," FAJ, 1971, v27(5), 75-85.)

Tuttle, Donald L. (Latane, Henry A. and Donald L. Tuttle. "Criteria For Portfolio Building," JOF, 1967, v22(3), 359-373.)

Tuttle, Donald L. (Latane, Henry A. and Donald L. Tuttle. "Probability In Industry Analysis," FAJ, 1968, v24(4), 51-61.)

Tuttle, Donald L. (Latane, Henry A., Donald L. Tuttle and C. P. Jones. "E/P Ratios V. Changes In Earnings," FAJ, 1969, v25(1), 117-120.)

Tuttle, Donald L. (Latane, Henry A. and Donald L. Tuttle. "Decision Theory And Financial Management," JOF, 1966, v21(2), 228-244.)

Tuttle, Donald L. (Lee, Wayne Y., Terry S. Maness and Donald L. Tuttle. "Nonspeculative Behavior And The Term Structure," JFQA, 1980, v15(1), 53-83.)

Tuttle, Donald L. (Logue, Dennis E. and Donald L. Tuttle. "Brokerage House Investment Advice," FR, 1973, v8(1), 38-54.)

Tuttle, Donald L., Wayne Y. Lee and Terry S. Maness. "Stochastic Cash Flow Constraints And The Term Structure Of Interest," JBF, 1978, v2(2), 143-162.

Tversky, Amos and Daniel Kahneman. "Rational Choice And The Framing Of Decisions," JOB, 1986, v59(4), Part 2, S251-S278.

Tversky, Amos. (Heath, Chip and Amos Tversky. "Preference And Belief: Ambiguity And Competence In Choice Under Uncertainty," JRU, 1991, v4(1), 5-28.)

Twardowski, Jan M. (Bogle, John C. and Jan M. Twardowski. "Institutional Investment Performance Compared," FAJ, 1980, v36(1), 33-41.)

Tweedie, D. P. "ED18 And User Comprehension - The Need For An Explanatory Statement," JBFA, 1977, v4(3), 285-298.

Tweedie, D. P. (Jones, C. J., D. P. Tweedie and G. Whittington. "The Regression Portfolio: A Statistical Investigation Of A Relative Decline Model," JBFA, 1976, v3(2), 71-92.)

Tybout, James R. "Interest Controls And Credit Allocation In Developing Countries," JMCB, 1984, v16(4), Part 1, 474-487.

Tyebjee, Tyzoon T. (Statman, Meir and Tyzoon T. Tyebjee. "Optimistic Capital Budgeting Forecasts: An Experiment," FM, 1985, v14(3), 27-33.)

Tyler, George R. and George E. Hoffer. "Reform Of The Non-Commercial Vehicle Liability Insurance Market," JRI, 1973, v40(4), 565-574.

Tynan, Mary Ann. (Record, Eugene E., Jr. and Mary Ann Tynan. "Incentive Fees: The Basic Issues," FAJ, 1987, v43(1), 39-43.)

Tyndall, D. G. "The Value Of Participation In A Loan Contract," FAJ, 1979, v35(1), 68-77.

Tyndall, David Gordon. "A Suggestion For The Control Of Peacetime Inflation," JOF, 1949, v4(4), 315-327.

Tysseland, Milford S. "Further Tests Of The Validity Of The Industry Approach To Investment Analysis," JFQA, 1971, v6(2), 835-847.

Tysseland, Milford S. (Arditti, Fred D. and Milford S. Tysseland. "Three Ways To Present The Marginal Cost Of Capital," FM, 1973, v2(2), 63-67.)

Tzang, Dah-Nein and Raymond M. Leuthold. "Hedge Ratios Under Inherent Risk Reduction In A Commodity Complex," JFM, 1990, v10(5), 497-504.

Tzang, Dah-Nein. (Chen, K. C., R. Stephen Sears and Dah-Nein Tzang. "Oil Prices And Energy Futures," JFM, 1987, v7(5), 501-518.)

Tzang, Daniel T. (Chen, K. C. and Daniel T. Tzang. "Interest-Rate Sensitivity Of Real Estate Investment Trusts," JRER, 1988, v3(3), 13-22.)

UUU

Udell, Gerald. (Pettijohn, James, Gerald Udell and Stephen Parker. "The Quest For AACSB Accreditation: Must Finance Faculty Really Publish Or Perish?," FPE, 1991, v1(1), 53-56.)

Udell, Gregory F. "Loan Quality, Commercial Loan Review And Loan Officer Contracting," JBF, 1989, v13(3), 367-382.

Udell, Gregory F. "Pricing Returned Check Charges Under Asymmetric Information," JMCB, 1986, v18(4), 495-505.

Udell, Gregory F. (Boot, Arnoud, Anjan V. Thakor and Gregory F. Udell. "Competition, Risk Neutrality And Loan Commitments," JBF, 1987, v11(3), 449-472.)

Udell, Gregory F. (Thakor, Anjan V. and Gregory F. Udell. "An Economic Rationale For The Pricing Structure Of Bank Loan Commitments," JBF, 1987, v11(2),271-290.)

Udell, Jon G. (Haugen, Robert A. and Jon G. Udell. "Rates Of Return To Stockholders Of Acquired Companies," JFQA, 1972, v7(1), 1387-1398.)

Udinsky, Jerald H. and Daniel Kirshner. " A Comparison Of Relative Predictive Power For Financial Models Of Rates Of Return," JFQA, 1979, v14(2), 293-315.

Ueda, K. "Japanese Capital Outflows," JBF, 1990, v14(5), 1079-1102.

Uhlenhop, Paul B. "Section 5a(12): Exchange Rule Approval," JFM, 1981, v1(Supp), 483-486.

Uhrig, J. William (Irwin, Scott H. and J. William Uhrig. "Do Technical Analysts Have Holes In Their Shoes?," RFM, 1984, v3(3), 264-277.)

Ukman, Laren A. (Moylan, James J., Laren A. Ukman and Peter S. Lake. "Exchange Memberships: An Overview Of The Issues Pertaining To The Property Rights Of A Bankrupt Member And His Creditors," JFM, 1989, v9(5), 461-468.)

Ukman, Laren. (Moylan, James J. and Laren Ukman. "Dispute Resolution Systems In The Commodity Futures Industry," JFM, 1986, v6(4), 659-670.)

Ulfers, D. D. "Insuring The Senior Citizen - A Case Study," JRI, 1961, v28(4), 1-12.

Ulin, Robert P. "Financing Business Expansion Since Korea," JOF, 1952, v7(2), 347-358.

Ulin, Robert P. "Financing Business Expansion-The Next Five Years," JOB, 1956, v29(3), 185-190.

Ulivi, Richard M. "Teaching Financial Planning To Business Students," JFED, 1982, v11, 5-8.

Ullman, James R. (Speidell, Lawrence S., Deborah H. Miller and James R. Ullman. "Portfolio Optimization: A Primer," FAJ, 1989, v45(1), 22-30.)

Ullman, Joseph. "Reply To Phillip Nelson's Comment: Wages And The Cost Of Search," JOB, 1970, v43(2), 217.

Ullman, Jospeh C. "Interfirm Differences In The Cost Of Search For Clerical Workers," JOB, 1968, v41(2), 153-165.

Ulmer, Melville J. "Long-Term Trends In The Financing Of Regulated Industries, 1870-1950," JOF, 1955, v10(2), 266-276.

Ulrich, Thomas A. "The Management By Objectives Approach Applied To Teaching Financial Management," JFED, 1975, v4, 16-18.

Umbeck, John and Robert E. Chatfield. "The Structure Of Contracts And Transaction Costs," JMCB, 1982, v14(4), Part 1, 511-516.

Umble, M. Michael, Paul F. York and E. J. Everett, Jr. "Agent Retention Rates In The Independent Agency System," JRI, 1977, v44(3), 481-486.

Umble, M. Michael. (Carlson, Rodney L. and M. Michael Umble. "Statistical Demand Functions For Automobiles And Their Use For Forecasting In An Energy Crisis," JOB, 1980, v53(2), 193-204.)

Umstead, David A. and Gary L. Bergstrom. "Dynamic Estimation Of Portfolio Betas," JFQA, 1979, v14(3), 595-614.

Umstead, David A. "Forecasting Stock Market Prices," JOF, 1977, v32(2), 427-441.

Umstead, David A. "Volatility, Growth, And Investment Policy," JPM, 1980-81, v7(2), 55-59.

Unal, Haluk and Edward J. Kane. "Two Approaches To Assessing The Interest-Rate Sensitivity Of Deposit-Institutions' Equity Returns," RIF, 1988, v7, 113-138.

Unal, Haluk. "Impact Of Deposit-Rate Ceiling Changes On Bank Stock Returns," JMCB, 1989, v21(2), 206-220.

Unal, Haluk. (Kane, Edward J. and Haluk Unal. "Change In Market Assessments Of Deposit-Institution Riskiness," JFSR, 1988, v1(3), 207-230.)

Unal, Haluk. (Kane, Edward J. and Haluk Unal. "Modeling Structural And Temporal Variation In The Market's Valuation Of Banking Firms," JOF, 1990, v45(1), 113-136.)

Unal, Haluk. (Sanders, Anthony B. and Haluk Unal. "On The Intertemporal Behavior Of The Short-Term Rate Of Interest," JFQA, 1988, v23(4), 417-424.)

Underwood, Edward F. and Myron C. Nelkin. "Brokerage House Opinion At Turning Points In The Stock Market," FAJ, 1946, v2(4), 39-43.

Ungar, Meyer and Benzion Zilberfarb. "The Demand For Money By Firms: The Stability And Other Issues Reexamined," JOF, 1980, v35(3), 779-785.

Unger, Raymond F. "Using Outside Research," JPM, 1982-83, v9(3), 43-45.

Unland, E. Scott. (Dokko, Yoon, Robert H. Edelstein and E. Scott Unlang. "Does Credit Rationing Affect Residential Investment? Deja Vu All Over Again," JREFEC, 1990, v3(4), 357-372.)

Uno, Jun. (Brenner, Menachem, Marti G. Subrahmanyam and Jun Uno. "Arbitrage Opportunities In The Japanese Stock And Futures Markets," FAJ, 1990, v46(2), 14-24.)

Uno, Jun. (Brenner, Menachem, Marti G. Subrahmanyam and Jun Uno. "The Behavior Of Prices In The Nikkei Spot And Futures Market," JFEC, 1989, v23(2), 363-384.)

Unterman, Israel. "Strategic Planning Of Central American Insurers," JRI, 1977, v44(3), 425-434.

Updegraff, David E. (Coates, Robert and David E. Updegraff. "The Relationship Between Organizational Size And The Administrative Component Of Banks: A Reply," JOB, 1976, v49(1), 66-67.)

Updegraff, David E. (Coates, Robert and David E. Updegraff. "The Relationship Between Organizational Size And The Administrative COmponent Of Banks," JOB, 1973, v46(4), 576-588.)

VVV

VanDerhei, Jack L. "An Empirical Analysis Of Risk-Related Insurance Premiums For The PBGC," *JRI*, 1990, v57(2), 240-259.

VanDerhei, Jack L. (Scheel, William C. and Jack L. VanDerhei. "Replacement Of Life Insurance: Its Regulation And Current Activity," *JRI*, 1978, v45(2), 189-216.)

VanDerhei, Jack L. and Francois P. Joanette. "Economic Determinants For The Choice Of Actuarial Cost Methods," *JRI*, 1988, v55(1), 59-74.

Vanderheiden, Paul A. (O'Brien, Thomas J. and Paul A. Vanderheiden. "Empirical Measurement Of Operating Leverage For Growing Firms," *FM*, 1987, v16(2), 45-53.)

Vanderheiden, Paul. (Swidler, Steve and Paul Vanderheiden. "Another Opinion Regarding Divergence Of Opinion And Return," *JFR*, 1983, v6(1), 47-50.)

Vander Kraats, R. H. and L. D. Booth. "Empirical Tests Of The Monetary Approach To Exchange-Rate Determination," *JIMF*, 1983, v2(3), 255-278.

Vandermeulen, Alice John. "Criteria Of 'Adequate' Governmental Expenditure And Their Implication," *JOF*, 1951, v6(1), 19-31.

Van der Ploeg, Frederick. "Benefits Of Contingent Rules For Optimal Taxation Of A Monetary Economy," *JMCB*, 1987, v19(2), 252-259.

Vander Weide, James H. (Maier, Steven F., David W. Robinson and James H. Vander Weide. "A Short-Term Disbursement Forecasting Model," *FM*, 1981, v10(1), 9-20.)

Vander Weide, James H. (Maier, Steven F. and James H. Vander Weide. "What Lockbox And Disbursement Models Really Do," *JOF*, 1983, v38(2), 361-371.)

Vander Weide, James H. (Maier, Steven F. and James H. Vander Weide. "The Lock-Box Location Problem: A Practical Reformulation," *JBR*, 1974-75, v5(2), 92-95.)

Vander Weide, James H. (Maier, Steven F. and James H. Vander Weide. "A Practical Approach To Short-Run Financial Planning," *FM*, 1978, v7(4), 10-16.)

Vander Weide, James H. (Maier, Steven F. and James H. Vander Weide. "A Unified Location Model For Cash Disbursements And Lock-Box Collections," *JBR*, 1976-77, v7(2), 166-172.)

Vander Weide, James H. and Willard T. Carleton. "Investor Growth Expectations: Analysts Vs. History," *JPM*, 1987-88, v14(3), 78-83.

Vander Weide, James. (Hughes, John S. and James Vander Weide. "Incentive Considerations In The Reporting Of Leveraged Leases," *JBR*, 1982-83, v13(1), 36-41.)

Vander Weide, James. (Maier, Steven F., David W. Peterson and James VanderWeide. "Monte Carlo Investigation Of Characteristics Of Optimal Geometric Mean Portfolios," *JFQA*, 1977, v12(2),215-233.)

Vandeven, William J. "Bank Communication Standards Research," *JBR*, 1970-71, v1(1), 63-64.

Van Drunen, Leonard D. (Davidson, Andrew S., Michael D. Herskovitz and Leonard D. Van Drunen. "The Refinancing Threshold Pricing Model: An Economic Approach To Valuing MBS," *JREFEC*, 1988, v1(2), 117-130.)

Van Drunen, Leonard D. and John J. McConnell. "Valuing Mortgage Loan Servicing," *JREFEC*, 1988, v1(1), 5-22.

van Eck, John C. "The German Stock Market," *FAJ*, 1967, v23(6), 155-158.

van Eck, John C., Jr. "Outlook For The German Stock Market," *FAJ*, 1965, v21(3), 140-147.

van Eck, John C., Jr. "South African Gold Stocks," *FAJ*, 1964, v20(5), 159-163.

Van Fenstermaker, J. and Donald Perry. "An Examination Of A Charge Card System Operating In A Smaller Community Through Correspondent Banks," *JBR*, 1971-72, v2(1), 9-13.

Van Fenstermaker, J. and John E. Filer. "Impact Of The First And Second Banks Of The United States And The Suffolk System On New England Bank Money: 1791-1837," *JMCB*, 1986, v18(1), 28-40.

Van Handel, Robert J. (Budin, Morris and Robert J. Van Handel. "A Rule-Of-Thumb Theory Of Cash Holdings By Firm," *JFQA*, 1975, v10(1), 85-108.)

Van Hoose, David D. "A Note On Discount Rate Policy And The Variability Of Discount Window Borrowing," *JBF*, 1987, v11(4), 563-570.

Van Hoose, David D. "A Note On Interest On Required Reserves As An Instrument Of Monetary Control," *JBF*, 1986, v10(1), 147-156.

Van Hoose, David D. "Bank Market Structure And Monetary Control," *JMCB*, 1985, v17(3), 298-311.

Van Hoose, David D. "Deregulation And Oligopolistic Rivalry In Bank Deposit Markets," *JBF*, 1988, v11(3), 379-388.

Van Hoose, David D. "Monetary Policy Under Alternative Bank Market Structures," *JBF*, 1983, v7(3),383-404.

VanHoose, David D. "Monetary Targeting And Price Level Non-Trend-Stationarity," *JMCB*, 1989, v21(2), 232-239.

VanHoose, David. (Duca, John V. and David VanHoose. "Loan Commitments And Optimal Monetary Policy," *JMCB*, 1990, v22(2), 178-194.)

Van Horne, James C. and G. G. C. Parker. "An Empirical Test," *FAJ*, 1967, v23(6), 87-92.

Van Horne, James C. and G. G. C. Parker. "Technical Trading Rules," *FAJ*, 1968, v24(4), 128-132.

Van Horne, James C. and Hal B. Heaton. "Securities Inventories And Excess Returns," *JFR*, 1983, v6(2), 93-102.

Van Horne, James C. and Hal B. Heaton. "Government Security Dealers' Positions, Information And Interest-Rate Expectations: A Note," *JOF*, 1983, v38(5), 1643-1649.

Van Horne, James C. and John G. McDonald. "Dividend Policy And New Equity Financing," *JOF*, 1971, v26(2), 507-519.

Van Horne, James C. and William F. Glassmire, Jr. "The Impact Of Unanticipated Changes In Inflation On The Value Of Common Stock," *JOF*, 1972, v27(5), 1081-1092.

Van Horne, James C. "A Note On Biases In Capital Budgeting Introduced By Inflation," *JFQA*, 1971, v6(1), 653-658.

Van Horne, James C. "An Application Of The CAPM To Divisional Required Returns," *FM*, 1980, v9(1), 14-19.

Van Horne, James C. "Call Risk And Municipal Bonds," *JPM*, 1986-87, v13(2), 53-57.

Van Horne, James C. "Called Bonds: How Does The Investor Fare?," *JPM*, 1979-80, v6(4), 58-61.

Van Horne, James C. "Implied Tax Rates And The Valuation Of Discount Bonds," *JBF*, 1982, v6(2), 145-160.

Van Horne, James C. "Implied Fixed Costs Of Long-Term Debt Issues," *JFQA*, 1973, v8(5), 821-833.

Van Horne, James C. "New Listings And Their Price Behavior," *JOF*, 1970, v25(4), 783-794.

Van Horne, James C. "Optimal Initiation Of Bankruptcy Proceedings," *JOF*, 1976, v31(3), 897-910.

Van Horne, James C. "Teaching Business Finance With Cases," *JFED*, 1972, v1, 69-71.

Van Horne, James C. "The Effect Of FHLB Bond Operations On Savings Inflows At Savings And Loan Associations: Comment," *JOF*, 1973, v28(1), 194-197.

Van Horne, James C. "The Presidential Address: Of Financial Innovations And Excesses," *JOF*, 1985, v40(3), 621-631.

Van Horne, James C. "The Two-Tier Setting To International Planning Research," *AFPAF*, 1990, v5(1), 145-160.

Van Horne, James C. (Hendershott, Patric H. and James C. Van Horne. "Expected Inflation Implied By Capital Market Rates," *JOF*, 1973, v28(2), 301-314.)

Van Horne, James C. (Litzenberger, Robert H. and James C. Van Horne. "Elimination Of The Double Taxation Of Dividends And Corporate Financial Policy," *JOF*, 1978, v33(3), 737-750.)

Van Horne, James C. (Robichek, Alexander A. and James C. Van Horne. "Abandonment Value And Capital Budgeting: Reply," *JOF*, 1969, v24(1), 96-97.)

Van Horne, James C. (Robichek, Alexander A. and James C. Van Horne. "Abandonment Value And Capital Budgeting," *JOF*, 1967, v22(4), 577-589.)

Van Horne, James C. (Seelenfreund, Alan, George G. C. Parker and James C. Van Horne. "Stock Price Behavior And Trading," *JFQA*, 1968, v3(3), 263-281.)

Van Horne, James. "A Linear-Programming Approach To Evaluating Restrictions Under A Bond Indenture Or Loan Agreement," *JFQA*, 1966, v1(2), 68-83.

Van Horne, James. "Liquidity Premiums And The Government Bond Market," *FAJ*, 1964, v20(5), 127-129.

Vankudre, Prashant. (Herring, Richard J. and Prashant Vankudre. "Growth Opportunities And Risk-Taking By Financial Intermediaries," *JOF*, 1987, v42(3), 583-600.)

Van Landingham, M. H. "The Day Trader: Some Additional Evidence," *JFQA*, 1980, v15(2), 341-355.

van Leeuwen, Peter H. "The Prediction Of Busines Failure At Rabobank," *JBR*, 1985-86, v16(2), 91-98.

Van Lierde, Paul A. "Price-Level Changes And Capital Consumption Allowances," *JOB*, 1959, v32(4), 370-382.

Vanlommel, E. (DeBrabander, B., D. Deschoolmeester, R. Leyder and E. Vanlommel. "The Effect Of Task Volume And Complexity Upon Computer Use," *JOB*, 1972, v45(1), 56-84.)

Vanlommel, E. and B. De Brabander. "The Organization Of Electronic Data Processing (EDP) Activities And Computer Use," *JOB*, 1975, v48(3), 391-410.

Van Marrewijk, C. and C. G. De Vries. "The Customs Union Argument For A Monetary Union," *JBF*, 1990, v14(5), 877-888.

Van Matre, Joseph G. and George A. Overstreet, Jr. "Motor Vehicle Inspection And Accident Mortality: A Reexamination," *JRI*, 1982, v49(3), 423-435.

Van Nieuwkerk, Marius. "Domestic And Foreign Trade Credit In The Netherlands: An Econometric Analysis," *JBF*, 1979, v3(1), 83-105.

Vannebo, Olav. "Horse Racing: Testing The Efficient Markets Model: Comment," *JOF*, 1980, v35(1), 201-202.

Van Order, R. (Hendershott, P. and R. Van Order. "Pricing Mortgages: An Interpretation Of The Model And Results," *JFSR*, 1987, v1(1), 19-56.)

Van Order, Robert A. (Buckley, Robert M. and Robert A. Van Order. "Housing And The Economy: Popular Myths," *AREUEA*, 1982, v10(4), 421-441.)

Van Order, Robert. (Foster, Chester and Robert Van Order. "FHA Terminations: A Prelude To Rational Mortgage Pricing," *AREUEA*, 1985, v13(3), 273-291.)

Van Order, Robert. (O'Keef, Michael and Robert Van Order. "Mortgage Pricing: Some Provisional Empirical Results," *AREUEA*, 1990, v18(3), 313-322.)

Van Order, Robert. (Quigley, John M. and Robert Van Order. "Efficiency In The Mortgage Market: The Borrower's Perspective," *AREUEA*, 1990, v18(3), 237-252.)

Van Order, Robert. (Schwartz, Eduardo and Robert Van Order. "Valuing The Implicit Guar-antee Of The Federal National Mortgage Association," *JREFEC*, 1988, v1(1), 23-34.)

Van Slyke, M. D. (Babb, E. M., M. A. Leslie and M. D. Van Slyke. "The Potential Of Business-Gaming Methods In Research," *JOB*, 1966, v39(4), 465-472.)

Van Steenwyk, E. A. "Non-Profit Health Service Plans," *JRI*, 1945, v12, 32-38.

Van Tassell, Roger C. (Schwartz, Eli And Roger C. Van Tassel. "Some Suggested Changes In The Corporate Tax Structure," *JOF*, 1950, v5(4), 410-420.)

Vanthienen, Lambert and Theo Vermaelen. "The Effect Of Personal Taxes On Common Stock Prices: The Case Of A Belgian Tax Reform," *JBF*, 1987, v11(2), 223-244.

Van Walleghem. Joe. (Myers, Forest E. and Joe Van Walleghem. "Management Transferability In Rural Banks," *JBR*, 1984-85, v15(4), 229-233.)

Van Wijnbergen, S. (Feltenstein, Andrew, David Lebow and S. Van Wijnbergen. "Savings, Commodity Market Rationing, And The Real Rate Of Interest In China," *JMCB*, 1990, v22(2), 234-252.)

VanWormer, T. A. (Cohen, K. J., R. M. Cyert, W. R. Dill, A. A. Kuehn, M. H. Miller, T. A. VanWormer, and P. R. Winters. "The Carnegie Tech Management Game," *JOB*, 1960, v33(4), 303-321.)

Van Zijl, Tony. "Beta Quotient, Beta Loss: Comment," *JPM*, 1984-85, v11(4), 75-78.

Van Zijl, Tony. "Risk Decomposition: Variance Or Standard Deviation--A Reexamination And Extension," *JFQA*, 1987, v22(2), 237-248.

Varaiya, Nikhil P. "An Empirical Investigation Of The Bidding Firms' Gains From Corporate Takeovers," *RIF*, 1986, v6, 149-178.

Varaiya, Nikhil P. (Giliberto, S. Michael and Nikhil P. Varaiya. "The Winner's Curse And Bidder Competition In Acquisitions: Evidence From Failed Bank Auctions," **JOF**, 1989, v44(1), 59-76.)

Varaiya, Nikhil P. and Kenneth R. Ferris. "Overpaying In Corporate Takeovers: The Winner's Curse," **FAJ**, 1987, v43(3), 64-71.

Varela, Oscar and P. R. Chandy. "Market Reaction To Listings And Delistings In The Dow Jones Portfolios," **IJOF**, 1989, v2(1), 67-78.

Varela, Oscar. "Using The COMPUSTAT Tapes In Studying The Dow Jones Portfolios," **FAJ**, 1986, v42(5), 70-75.

Varghese, Matthew. (Ariff, Mohamed and Matthew Varghese. "Risk Reduction From Currency Portfolio Diversification And Revision Gains," **IJOF**, 1990, v3(1), 86-100.)

Varian, Hal R. "Divergence Of Opinion In Complete Markets: A Note," **JOF**, 1985, v40(1), 309-317.

Varian, Hal R. "Nonparametric Tests Of Models Of Investor Behavior," **JFQA**, 1983, v18(3), 269-278.

Varma, Raj and Donald R. Chambers. "The Role Of Financial Innovation In Raising Capital: Evidence From Deep Discount Debt Offers," **JFEC**, 1990, v26(2), 289-298.

Varma, Raj. (Miles, James A. and Raj Varma. "Using Financial Market Data To Make Trade Credit Decisions," **JBFA**, 1986, v13(4), 505-518.)

Varma, Raj. (Szewczyk, Samuel H. and Raj Varma. "The Effect Of Proposition 103 On Insurers: Evidence From The Capital Market," **JRI**, 1990, v57(4), 671-681.)

Vasicek, O. A. and J. A. McQuown. "The Efficent Market Model," **FAJ**, 1972, v28(5), 71-84.

Vasicek, O. "An Equilibrium Characterization Of The Term Structure," **JFEC**, 1977, v5(2), 177-188.

Vasicek, Oldrich A. and H. Gifford Fong. "Term Structure Modeling Using Exponential Splines," **JOF**, 1982, v37(2), 339-348.

Vasicek, Oldrich A. "A Note On Using Cross-Sectional Information In Bayesian Estimation Of Security Betas," **JOF**, 1973, v28(5), 1233-1239.

Vasicek, Oldrich A. (Fong, H. Gifford and Oldrich A. Vasicek. "A Risk Minimizing Strategy For Portfolio Immunization," **JOF**, 1984, v39(5),1541-1546.)

Vasicek, Oldrich A. (Fong, H. Gifford and Oldrich A. Vasicek. "Forecast-Free International Asset Allocation," **FAJ**, 1989, v45(2), 29-33.)

Vasicek, Oldrich. (Fong, Gifford, Charles Pearson and Oldrich Vasicek. "Bond Performance: Analyzing Sources Of Return," **JPM**, 1982-83, v9(3), 46-50.)

Vasicek, Oldrich. (Fong, H. Gifford and Oldrich Vasicek. "The Tradeoff Between Return And Risk In Immunized Portfolios," **FAJ**, 1983, v39(5), 73-78.)

Vatter, William J. "Fund Flows And Fund Statements," **JOB**, 1953, v26(1), 15-25.

Vatter, William J. "Operating Confusion In Accounting-Two Reports Or One?," **JOB**, 1963, v36(3),290-301.

Vaughan, Emmett J. "A Case Study In Municipal Risk Management," **JRI**, 1971, v38(2), 281-284.

Vaughan, Emmett J. "Social Insurance In Yugoslavia," **JRI**, 1965, v32(3), 385-394.

Vaughn, Donald E. and Hite Bennett. "Adjusting For Risk In The Capital Budget Of A Growth-Oriented Company," **JFQA**, 1968, v3(4), 445-461.

Vaughn, Richard, Frank Hochheimer and Marvin Kelly. "Identifying Seasonality In Futures Prices Using X-11," **JFM**, v1(1), 93-102.

Vaughn, Therese M. "The Financial Feasibility Of Tax-Sheltered Individual Retirement Plans: Comment," **JRI**, 1988, v55(1), 158-163.

Vaught, Daniel. (Elam, Emmet W. and Daniel Vaught. "Risk And Return In Cattle And Hog Futures," **JFM**, 1988, v8(1), 79-88.)

Vawter, Jan. "Formula Timing Plans In Investment Analysis," **FAJ**, 1959, v15(1), 67-68.

Vawter, Jay. "End Of The Post-War Bull Market?," **FAJ**, 1961, v17(1), 17-21.

Vaz, Peter. (Thompson, G. Rodney and Peter Vaz. "Dual Bond Ratings: A Test Of The Certification Function Of Rating Agencies," **FR**, 1990, v25(3), 457-472.)

Veale, Peter R. "Managing Corporate Real Estate Assets: Current Executive Attitudes And Prospects For An Emergent Discipline," **JRER**, 1989, v4(3), 1-22.

Veendorp, E. C. H. "Money In A Static Theory Of Optimal Payment Arrangement: A Comment," **JMCB**, 1972, v4(2), 437-440.

Veit, E. Theodore and John M. Cheney. "Are Mutual Funds Market Timers?," **JPM**, 1981-82, v8(2), 35-42.

Veit, E. Theodore and John M. Cheney. "Managing Investment Portfolios: A Survey Of Mutual Funds," **FR**, 1984, v19(4), 321-338.

Veit, E. Theodore and Wallace W. Reiff. "Commercial Banks And Interest Rate Futures: A Hedging Survey," **JFM**, 1983, v3(3), 283-293.

Veit, E. Theodore, Mary Lee Avey, Jerry L. Corley and Timothy Summers. "The Role Of Stock Options In Bank Trust Departments: Fifth Federal Reserve District Banks," **JBR**, 1979-80, v10(4), 255-256.

Veit, E. Theodore. (Cheney, John M. and E. Theodore Veit. "Evidence Of Shifts In Portfolio Asset Composition As A Market Timing Tool," **FR**, 1983, v18(1),56-78.)

Veit, E. Theodore. (Moses, Edward A., John M. Cheyney and E. Theodore Veit. "A New And More Complete Performance Measure," **JPM**, 1986-87, v13(4), 24-33.)

Vellermann, Charles M. and Paul L. Farris. "Note On Trader Concentration Effects In Feeder Cattle Futures And Comparison With Live Cattle," **JFM**, 1988, v8(1), 103-114.

Venezia, Itzhak and Menachem Brenner. "The Optimal Duration Of Growth Investments And Search," **JOB**, 1979, v52(3), 393-408.

Venezia, Itzhak. "A Bayesian Approach To The Optimal Growth Period Problem: A Note," **JOF**, 1983, v38(1), 237-246.

Venezia, Itzhak. "Adaptive Credit Granting Policies," **JBF**, 1980, v4(3), 269-281.

Venezia, Itzhak. "Aspects Of Optimal Automobile Insurance," **JRI**, 1984, v51(1), 63-79.

Venezia, Itzhak. "On The Economic Advantages Of The Coinsurance Clause," **JRI**, 1988, v55(2), 307-314.

Venezia, Itzhak. (Brenner, Menachem and Itzhak Venezia. "The Effects

Of Inflation And Taxes On Growth Investments And Replacement Policies," **JOF**, 1983, v38(5), 1519-1528.)

Venezia, Itzhak. (Greenbaum, Stuart I. and Itzhak Venezia. "Partial Exercise Of Loan Commitments Under Adaptive Pricing," **JFR**, 1985, v8(4), 251-263.)

Venezia, Itzhak. (Greenbaum, Stuart I., George Kanatas and Itzhak Venezia. "Equilibrium Loan Pricing Under The Bank-Client Relationship," **JBF**, 1989, v13(2), 221-236.)

Venezian, Emilio C. "Are Insurers Under-Earning?," **JRI**, 1984, v51(1), 150-156.

Venezian, Emilio C. "Coding Errors And Classification Refinement," **JRI**, 1985, v52(4), 734-742.

Venezian, Emilio C. "Comments On The Exchange Between Hedges And Witt," **JRI**, 1982, v49(4), 618-620.

Venezian, Emilio C. "Cost-Based Pricing And Price-Based Costing In Private Passenger Automobile Insurance," **JRI**, 1984, v51(3), 433-452.

Venezian, Emilio C. "Efficiency And Equity In Insurance," **JRI**, 1984, v51(2), 190-204.

Venezian, Emilio C. "Insurer Capital Needs Under Parameter Uncertainty," **JRI**, 1983, v50(1), 19-32.

Venezian, Emilio C. "Interactions In Insurance Classifications," **JRI**, 1985, v52(4), 571-584.

Venezian, Emilio C. "Ratemaking Methods And Profit Cycles In Property And Liability Insurance," **JRI**, 1985, v52(3), 477-500.

Venezian, Emilio C. "Risk Management And Financial Regret," **JRI**, 1986, v53(3), 395-408.

Venezian, Emilio C. "Use Of Risk Loads And Distributional Fitting In Ratemaking: Comment," **JRI**, 1986, v53(2), 330-333.

Venezian, Emilio C. (Fields, Joseph A. and Emilio C. Venezian. "Investment Income - Is There A Company Effect?," **JRI**, 1987, v54(1), 173-178.)

Venezian, Emilio C. (Fields, Joseph A. and Emilio C. Venezian. "Informational Asymmetries In Retroactive Insurance: Reply," **JRI**, 1988, v55(3), 555-558.)

Venezian, Emilio C. (Fields, Joseph A. and Emilio C. Venezian. "Interest Rates And Profit Cycles: A Disaggregated Approach," **JRI**, 1989, v56(2), 312-319.)

Venezian, Emilio C. and Joseph A. Fields. "Informational Asymmetries In Retroactive Insurance," **JRI**, 1987, v54(4), 780-789.

Venezian, Emilio C., Blaine F. Nye and Alfred E. Hofflander. "The Distribution Of Claims For Professional Malpractice: Some Statistical And Public Policy Aspects," **JRI**, 1989, v56(4), 686-701.

Venkatesh, P. C. and R. Chiang. "Information Asymmetry And The Dealer's Bid-Ask Spread: A Case Study Of Earnings And Dividend Announcements," **JOF**, 1986, v41(5), 1089-1102.

Venkatesh, P. C. "The Impact Of Dividend Initiation On The Information Content Of Earnings Announcements And Returns Volatility," **JOB**, 1989, v62(2), 175-198.

Venkatesh, P. C. (Chiang, Raymond and P. C. Venkatesh. "Insider Holdings And Perceptions Of Information Asymmetry: A Note," **JOF**, 1988, v43(4),1041-1048.)

Venkatesh, P. C. (Jang, Hasung and P. C. Venkateshi. "Consistency Between Predicted And Actual Bid-Ask Quote Revisions," **JOF**, 1991, v46(1), 433-446.)

Verbrugge, James A. and John S. Jahera, Jr. "Expense-Preference Behavior In The Savings And Loan Industry," **JMCB**, 1981, v13(4), 465-476.

Verbrugge, James A. and Steven J. Goldstein. "Risk Return And Managerial Objectives: Some Evidence From The Savings And Loan Industry," **JFR**, 1981, v4(1), 45-58.

Verbrugge, James A. "The Effects Of Pledging Regulations On Bank Asset Composition," **JBR**, 1973-74, v4(3), 168-176.

Verbrugge, James A. (Jordan, Bradford D., James A. Verbrugge and Richard M. Burns. "Returns To Initial Shareholders In Savings Institution Conversions: Evidence And Regulatory Implications," **JFR**, 1988, v11(2), 125-136.)

Verbrugge, James A. (Shick, Richard A. and James A. Verbrugge. "An Analysis Of Bank Price-Earnings Ratios," **JBR**, 1975-76, v6(2), 140-149.)

Verbrugge, James A., Richard A. Shick And Kenneth J. Thygerson. "An Analysis Of Savings And Loan Profit Performance," **JOF**, 1976, v31(5), 1427-1442.

Verdini, William A. (Panton, Don B. and William A. Verdini. "A FORTRAN Program For Applying Sturm's Theorem In Counting Internal Rates Of Return," **JFQA**, 1981, v16(3), 381-388.)

Vergin, Roger C. (Powell, John R. P. and Roger C. Vergin. "A Heuristic Model For Planning Corporate Financing," **FM**, 1974, v4(2), 13-20.)

Verma, Avinash K. (Ronn, Ehud I. and Avinash K. Verma. "A Multi-Attribute Comparative Evaluation Of Relative Risk For A Sample Of Banks," **JBF**, 1987, v11(3), 499-524.)

Verma, Avinash K. (Ronn, Ehud I. and Avinash K. Verma. "Pricing Risk-Adjusted Deposit Insurance: An Option-Based Model," **JOF**, 1986, v41(4), 871-896.)

Verma, Avinash K. (Ronn, Ehud I. and Avinash K. Verma. "Risk-Based Capital Adequacy Standards For A Sample Of 43 Major Banks," **JBF**, 1989, v13(1), 21-30.)

Verma, Vinod K. "A Price Theoretic Approach To The Specification And Estimation Of The Sales-Advertising Function," **JOB**, 1980, v53(3), Part 2, S115-S138.

Vermaelen, Theo. "Common Stock Repurchases And Market Signalling: An Empirical Study," **JFEC**, 1981, v9(2), 138-183.

Vermaelen, Theo. "Repurchase Tender Offers, Signaling, And Managerial Incentives," **JFQA**, 1984, v19(2), 163-181.

Vermaelen, Theo. (Bjerring, James H., Josef Lakonishok and Theo Vermaelen. "Stock Prices And Financial Analysts' Recommendations," **JOF**, 1983, v38(1), 187-204.)

Vermaelen, Theo. (Lakonishok, Josef and Theo Vermaelen. "Tax Reform And Ex-Dividend Day Behavior," **JOF**, 1983, v38(4), 1157-1179.)

Vermaelen, Theo. (Lakonishok, Josef and Theo Vermaelen. "Tax-Induced Trading Around Ex-Dividend Days," **JFEC**, 1986, v16(3), 287-319.)

Vermaelen, Theo. (Lakonishok, Josef and Theo Vermaelen. "Anomalous Price Behavior Around Repurchase Tender Offers," **JOF**, 1990, v45(2), 455-478.)

Vinso, Joseph D. (Rogalski, Richard J. and Joseph D. Vinso. "An Analysis Of Monetary Aggregates," JMCB, 1978, v10(2), 252-266.)

Vinso, Joseph D. (Rogalski, Richard J. and Joseph D. Vinso. "Stock Returns, Money Supply And The Direction Of Causality," JOF, 1977, v32(4), 1017-1030.)

Vinso, Joseph D. (Rogalski, Richard J. and Joseph D. Vinso. "Heteroscedastic Security Returns," FR, 1978, v13(2), 1-11.)

Vinso, Joseph D. (Santomero, Anthony M. and Joseph D. Vinso. "Estimating The Probability Of Failure For Commercial Banks And The Banking System," JBF, 1977, v1(2), 185-205.)

Vinson, Charles E. "Rates Of Return On Convertibles," FAJ, 1970, v26(4), 110-114.

Vinson, Steve R. (Brigham, Eugene F., Dilip K. Shome and Steve R. Vinson. "The Risk Premium Approach To Measuring A Utility's Cost Of Equity," FM, 1985, v14(1), 33-45.)

Viren, Matti. "The Long-Run Relationship Between Interest Rates And Inflation: Some Cross-Country Evidence," JBF, 1989, v13(4/5), 571-588.

Virts, John R. (Cocks, Douglas L. and John R. Virts. "Pricing Behavior Of The Ethical Pharmaceutical Industry," JOB, 1974, v47(3), 349-362.)

Viscione, Jerry and John Neuhauser. "Capital Expenditure Decisions In Moderately Sized Firms," FR, 1974, v9(1), 16-23.

Viscione, Jerry A. and George Aragon. "The Case Method In Undergraduate Finance," JFED, 1978, v7, 49-52.

Viscione, Jerry A. (Dipchand, Cecil R., Gordon S. Roberts and Jerry A. Viscione. "Agency Costs And Captive Finance Subsidiaries In Canada," JFR, 1982, v5(2), 189-199.)

Viscione, Jerry A. (Roberts, Gordon S. and Jerry A. Viscione. "The Impact Of Seniority And Security Covenants On Bond Yields: A Note," JOF, 1984, v39(5), 1597-1602.)

Viscione, Jerry A. (Roberts, Gordon S. and Jerry A. Viscione. "Captive Finance Subsidiaries: The Manager's View," FM, 1981, v10(1), 36-42.)

Viscione, Jerry A. (Roberts, Gordon S. and Jerry A. Viscione. "Note On Who Pays The Agency Costs Of Debt," FR, 1984, v19, 232-239.)

Viscione, Jerry A. (Roberts, Gordon S. and Jerry A. Viscione. "Agency Costs, Bond Covenants, And Bond Yields," RIF, 1986, v6, 73-100.)

Viscione, Jerry. (Fooladi, Iraj, Gordon Roberts and Jerry Viscione. "Captive Finance Subsidiaries: Overview And Synthesis," FR, 1986, v21(2), 259-275.)

Viscusi, W. Kip. "Long-Term Environmental Risks," JRU, 1990, v3(4), 311-314.

Viscusi, W. Kip. "Prospective Reference Theory: Toward An Explanation Of The Paradoxes," JRU, 1989, v2(3), 235-264.

Viscusi, W. Kip. (Grabowski, Henry, W. Kip Viscusi and William N. Evans. "Price And Availability Tradeoffs Of Automobile Insurance Regulation," JRI, 1989, v56(2), 275-299.)

Viscusi, W. Kip. (Magat, Wesley A., W. Kip Viscusi and Joel Huber. "Consumer Processing Of Hazard Warning Information," JRU, 1988, v1(2), 201-232.)

Viscusi, W. Kip. (Moore, Michael J. and W. Kip Viscusi. "Models For Estimating Discount Rates For Long-Term Health Risks Using Labor Market Data," JRU, 1990, v3(4), 381-402.)

Vishny, Robert W. (Morck, Randall, Andrei Shleifer and Robert W. Vishny. "Management Ownership And Market Valuation: An Empirical Analysis," JFEC, 1988, v20(1/2), 293-316.)

Vishny, Robert W. (Morck, Randall, Andrei Shleifer and Robert W. Vishny. "Do Managerial Objectives Drive Bad Acquisitions?," JOF, 1990, v45(1), 31-48.)

Vishny, Robert W. (Shleifer, Andrei and Robert W. Vishny. "Management Entrenchment: The Case Of Manager-Specific Investments," JFEC, 1989, v25(1), 123-140.)

Visser, John R. and Hsiu-Kwang Wu. "The Effects Of Deregulation On Bank Stock Price-Earnings Ratios," FAJ, 1989, v45(5), 62-67.

Viswanath, P. V. "Taxes And The Futures-Forward Price Difference In The 91-Day T-Bill Market," JMCB, 1989, v21(2), 190-205.

Viswanath, P. V. (Hegde, Krishna and P. V. Viswanath. "Structure Stability With Ex-Ante Factor Specification In APT," IJOF, 1990, v3(1), 121-157.)

Viswanathan, P. and Cesar Mayo. "The Feds RCPC Performance: Comment," JBR, 1975-76, v6(1), 70-72.

Viswanathan, S. (Foster, F. Douglas and S. Viswanathan. "A Theory Of The Interday Variations In Volume, Variance, And Trading Costs In Securities Markets," RFS, 1990, v3(4), 593-624.)

Vitaliano, Donald F. "Measuring The Efficiency Cost Of Rent Control," AREUEA, 1986, v14(1), 61-72.

Vlahos, G. (Gresis, N., G. C. Phillipatos and G. Vlahos. "A CAPM-Based Analysis Of Stock Index Futures," JPM, 1983-84, v10(3), 47-52.

Vlahos, George. (Gressis, Nicholas, George Vlahos and George C. Philippatos. "Net Selectivity As A Component Measure Of Investment Performance," FR, 1986, v21(1), 103-110.)

Vogel, Robert C. and G. S. Maddala. "Cross-Section Estimates Of Liquid Asset Demand By Manufacturing Corporations," JOF, 1967, v22(4), 557-575.

Vogel, Robert C. (Joyce, Jon M. and Robert C. Vogel. "The Uncertainty In Risk: Is Variance Unambiguous?," JOF, 1970, v25(1), 127-134.)

Vogel, Ronald J. (Blair, Roger D. and Ronald J. Vogel. "A Survivor Analysis Of Commerical Health Insurers," JOB, 1978, v51(3), 521-530.)

Vogel, Ronald J. (Greenspan, Nancy T. and Ronald J. Vogel. "An Econometric Analysis Of The Effects Of Regulation In The Private Health Insurance Market," JRI, 1982, v49(1), 39-58.)

Vogt, Michael G. and R. S. Hanna. "Variations Of The Federal Funds Rate And Bank Reserve Management," JBR, 1984-85, v15(3), 188-192.

Vogt, Michael G. "Bank Reserve Adjustment Process And The Use Of Reserve Carryover As A Reserve Management Tool: A Comment," JBF, 1989, v13(1), 31-36.

Voith, Richard and Theodore Crone. "National Vacancy Rates And The Persistence Of Shocks In U.S. Office Markets," AREUEA, 1988, v16(4), 437-458.

Volcker, Paul A. "Domestic Expansion And External Responsibilities," JOF, 1971, v26(2), 243-250.

Volk, Harry J. "Bankers Meet Population Boom," FAJ, 1959, v15(4), 73-76.

Volkan, Ara G. (Ismail, Badr E. and Ara G. Volkan. "The Impact Of Current Replacement Costing On Corporate Taxation," FR, 1981, v16(1), 43-53.)

Von Furstenberg, George M. "The Investment Quality Of Home Mortgages," JRI, 1970, v37(3), 437-445.

Von Furstenberg, George M. and R. Jeffrey Green. "Estimation Of Delinquency Risk For Home Mortgage Portfolios," AREUEA, 1974, v2(1), 5-20.

von Furstenberg, George M. and R. Jeffery Green. "Home Mortgage Delinquencies: A Cohort Analysis," JOF, 1974, v29(5), 1545-1548.

von Furstenberg, George M. and Burton G. Malkiel. "Financial Analysis In An Inflationary Environment," JOF, 1977, v32(2), 575-588.

von Furstenberg, George M. "The Long-Term Effects Of Government Deficits On The U. S. Output Potential," JOF, 1978, v33(3), 989-1007.

von Furstenberg, George M. "Risk Structures And The Distribution Of Benefits Within The FHA Home Mortgage Insurance Program," JMCB, 1970, v2(3), 303-322.

von Furstenberg, George M. "Comment On 'Future Markets And The Supply Of Storage With Rational Expectations'," JFM, 1982, v2(4), 415-417.

von Furstenberg, George M. "The Equilibrium Spread Between Variable Rates And Fixed Rates On Long-Term Financing Instruments," JFQA, 1973, v8(5), 807-819.

von Furstenberg, George M. "Interstate Differences In Mortgage Lending Risks: An Analysis Of The Causes," JFQA, 1970, v5(2), 229-242.

von Furstenberg, George M. "Default Risk On FHA-Insured Home Mortgages As A Function Of The Terms Of Financing: A Quantitative Analysis," JOF, 1969, v24(3), 459-477.

von Furstenberg, George M. "Adjustment With IMF Lending," JIMF, 1985, v4(2), 209-222.

von Furstenberg, George M. "The Impact Of GNMA Tandem Plans: A Reply," JMCB, 1978, v10(3),385-387.

von Furstenberg, George M. "Distribution Effects Of GNMA Home Mortgage Purchases And Commitments Under The Tandem Plans," JMCB, 1976, v8(3), 373-389.

von Furstenberg, George M. "New Estimates Of The Demand For Non-Gold Reserves Under Floating Exchange Rates," JIMF, 1982, v1(1), 81-96.

von Furstenberg, George M. (Malkiel, Burton G., George M. von Furstenberg and Harry S. Watson. "Expectations, Tobin's q, And Industry Investment," JOF, 1979, v34(2), 549-561.)

von Germeten, James N. (Arnott, Robert D. and James N. von Germeten. "Systematic Asset Allocation," FAJ, 1983, v39(6), 31-38.)

Von Hagen, Juergen. "Policy Effectiveness In An Open Multi-Market Economy With Risk Neutral Exchange Rate Speculation," JIMF, 1990, v9(2), 110-122.

Von Hagen, Jurgen and Michele Fratianni. "German Dominance In The EMS: Evidence From Interest Rates," JIMF, 1990, v9(4), 358-375.

Von Lanzenauer, C. Haehling. (Fry, Joseph N., David C. Shaw, C. Haehling Von Lanzenauer and Cecil R. Dipchand. "Customer Loyalty To Banks: A Longitudinal Study," JOB, 1973, v46(4), 517-525.)

Von Lanzenauer, Christoph Haehling. "The Expected Cost Hypothesis And The Selection Of An Optimal Deductible For A Given Insurance Policy," JOB, 1971, v44(3), 306-315.

Von Lanzenauer, Christoph Haehling. "Decision Problems In The Canadian Automobile Insurance System," JRI, 1972, v39(1), 79-92.

Von Lanzenauer, Christoph Haehling. "A Model For Determining Optimal Profit Sharing Plans," JFQA, 1969, v4(1), 53-63.

Von Stein, Johann Heinrich and Werner Ziegler. "The Prognosis And Surveillance Of Risks From Commercial Credit Borrowers," JBF, 1984, v8(2),249-268.

Von Zur Muehlen, P. (Tinsley, P., G. Fries, B. Garrett, A. Norman, P.A.V.B. Swamy and P. von zur Muehlen. "The Impact Of Uncertainty On The Feasibility Of Humphrey-Hawkins Objectives," JOF, 1981, v36(2), 489-496.)

Von Zur Muehlen, Peter. (Tinsley, P. A., H. T. Farr, G. Fries, B. Garrett and Peter von zur Muehlen. "Policy Robustness: Specification And Simulation Of A Monthly Money Market Model," JMCB, 1982, v14(4), Part 2, 829-856.)

Von Szeliski, Victor. "Predicting Stock Market Trends By Structure Analysis," FAJ, 1956, v12(2), 51-62.

Voorheis, Frank L. "Bank Trustee And Pension Performance," FAJ, 1972, v28(4), 60-64.

Voorheis, Frank L. "Do Banks Manage Pension Funds Well?," FAJ, 1976, v32(5), 35-40.

Vora, Ashok. (Milonas, Nikolaos T. and Ashok Vora. "Sources Of Nonstationarity In Cash And Futures Prices," RFM, 1985, v4(3), 314-326.)

Vora, Ashok. (Casabona, Patrick A. and Ashok Vora. "The Bias Of Conventional Risk Premiums In Empirical Tests Of The Capital Asset Pricing Model," FM, 1982, v11(2), 90-96.)

Vora, Ashok. (Castelino, Mark G. and Ashok Vora. "Spread Volatility In Commodity Futures: The Length Effect," JFM, 1984, v4(1), 39-46.)

Vora, Ashok. (Goldberg, Michael A. and Ashok Vora. "Bivariate Spectral Analysis Of The Capital Asset Pricing Model," JFQA, 1978, v13(3),435-459.)

Vora, Ashok. (Goldberg, Michael A. and Ashok Vora. "Dividend Yield, Regulation, And The Return On U.S. Public Utility Stocks," JBFA, 1985, v12(1), 47-70.)

Vora, Ashok. (Hawawini, Gabriel A. and Ashok Vora. "The CAPM And The Investment Horizon: Comment," JPM, 1982-83, v9(1), 66-68.)

Vora, Ashok. (Hawawini, Gabriel A. and Ashok Vora. "Investment Horizon, Diversification, And The Efficiency Of Alternative Beta Forecasts," JPM, 1982, v5(1), 1-15.)

Vora, Ashok. (Hawawini, Gabriel A. and Ashok Vora. "Yield Approximations: A Historical Perspective," JOF, 1982, v37(1), 145-156.)

Vora, Ashok. (Hawawini, Gabriel A. and Ashok Vora. "Is Adjusting Beta Estimates An Illusion?," JPM, 1983-84, v10(1), 23-26.)

Vora, Ashok. (Hawawini, Gabriel A. and Ashok Vora. "Evidence Of Intertemporal Systematic Risks In The Daily Price Movements Of NYSE And AMEX Common Stocks," *JFQA*, 1980, v15(2),331-339.)

Vora, Ashok. (Hawawini, Garbriel and Ashok Vora. "Proportional Vs. Logarithmic Models Of Asset Pricing," *RIF*, 1985, v5, 1-24.)

Vora, Gautam. (Lee, Wayne L., Anjan V. Thakor and Gautam Vora. "Screening, Market Signalling, And Capital Structure Theory," *JOF*, 1983, v38(5), 1507-1518.)

Vorst, A. C. F. (Kemna, A. G. Z. and A. C. F. Vorst. "A Pricing Method For Options Based On Average Asset Values," *JBF*, 1990, v14(1), 113-130.)

Vorst, Ton C. F. (Kemna, Angelien G. Z. and Ton C. F. Vorst. "A Futures Contract On An Index Of Existing Bonds: A Reasonable Alternative?," *RFM*, 1988, v7(Supp), 468-479.)

Vroman, Susan B. (Puckett, Richard H. and Susan B. Vroman. "Rules Versus Discretion: A Simulation Study," *JOF*, 1973, v28(4), 853-865.)

Vronen, H. William. (Watson, Hugh J. and H. William Vronen. "A Heuristic Model For Processing Overdrafts," *JBR*, 1972-73, v3(3), 186-188.)

Vrooman, John. "Does The St. Louis Equation Even Believe In Itself?: A Comment," *JMCB*, 1979, v11(1), 111-117.

Vu, Joseph D. "An Anomalous Evidence Regarding Market Efficiency: The Net Current Asset Value Rule," *RIF*, 1990, v8, 241-254.

Vu, Joseph D. "An Empirical Investigation Of Calls Of Non-Convertible Bonds," *JFEC*, 1986, v16(2), 235-265.

Vu, Joseph D. "An Empirical Analysis Of Ben Graham's Net Current Asset Value Rule," *FR*, 1988, v23(2), 215-226.

Vu, Joseph D. and Paul Caster. "Why All The Interest In Short Interest?," *FAJ*, 1987, v43(4), 77-79.

Vu, Joseph. (Cinar, E. Mine and Joseph Vu. "Evidence On The Effect Of Option Expirations On Stock Prices," *FAJ*, 1987, v43(1), 55-57.)

Vuchelen, J. "A Study Of A Monetary System With A Pegged Discount Rate Under Different Market Structures: Comments On The Article By F. Aftalion And L. White," *JBF*, 1978, v2(4), 339-350.

Vultee, Howard F. "No United States Of Europe," *FAJ*, 1956, v12(5), 51-54.

WWW

Waburton, Clark. "Rules And Implements For Monetary Policy," *JOF*, 1953, v8(1), 1-21.

Wachowicz, John M., Jr. and Ronald E. Shrieves. "An Argument For 'Generalized' Mean-Coefficient Of Variation Analysis," *FM*, 1980, v9(4), 51-58.

Wachowicz, John M., Jr. (Kidwell, David S., Eric H. Sorensen and John M. Wachowicz, Jr. "Estimating The Signaling Benefits Of Debt Insurance: The Case Of Municipal Bonds," *JFQA*, 1987, v22(3), 299-314.)

Wachowicz, John M., Jr. (Newman, Joseph A. and John M. Wachowicz, Jr. "Memorandums In The Classroom," *JFED*, 1989, v18, 25-28.)

Wachowicz, John M., Jr. (Reilly, Frank K. and John M. Wachowicz, Jr. "How Institutional Trading Reduces Market Volatility," *JPM*, 1978-79, v5(2), 11-17.)

Wachowicz, John M., Jr. (Shrieves, Ronald E. and John M. Wachowicz, Jr. "A Utility Theoretic Basis For 'Generalized' Mean-Coefficient Of Variation (MCV) Analysis," *JFQA*, 1981, v16(5), 671-683.)

Wacht, Richard F. and David T. Whitford. "A Goal Programming Model For Capital Investment Analysis In Nonprofit Hospitals," *FM*, 1976, v5(2), 37-47.

Wacht, Richard F. "A Financial Management Theory Of The Nonprofit Organization," *JFR*, 1984, v7(1), 37-45.

Wacht, Richard F. "Branch Banking And Risk," *JFQA*, 1968, v3(1), 97-108.

Wacht, Richard F. "Diversification And Capital Budgeting For Commercial Banks," *FR*, 1969, v1(4), 204-209.

Wacht, Richard F. "The Southern Finance Association: The First Twenty Years," *JFR*, 1980, v3(3), 221-228.

Wacht, Richard F. "Toward Rationality In The Allocation Of Hospital Resources," *FM*, 1972, v1(1), 66-71.

Wacht, Richard F. (Kreps, Clifton H., Jr. and Richard F. Wacht. "A More Constructive Role For Deposit Insurance," *JOF*, 1971, v26(2), 605-614.)

Wachtel, P. (Sofianos, G., P. Wachtel and A. Melnik. "Loan Commitments And Monetary Policy," *JBF*, 1990, v14(4), 677-690.)

Wachtel, Paul. (Arnold Sametz and Harry Shuford. "Capital Shortages: Myth Or Reality?," *JOF*, 1976, v31(2), 269-286.)

Wachtel, Paul. "Interrelated Models Of Household Behavior: A Summary And An Extension," *JOF*, 1972, v27(2), 503-506.

Wachtel, Paul. (Urich, Thomas and Paul Wachtel. "The Effects Of Inflation And Money Supply Announcements On Interest Rates," *JOF*, 1984, v39(4), 1177-1188.)

Wachtel, Paul. (Urich, Thomas and Paul Wachtel. "Market Response To The Weekly Money Supply Announcements In The 1970s," *JOF*, 1981, v36(5), 1063-1072.)

Wachter, Susan. (Linneman, Peter and Susan Wachter. "The Impacts Of Borrowing Constraints On Homeownerhip," *AREUEA*, 1989, v17(4), 389-402.)

Wadhwani, Sushil. (King, Mervyn A. and Sushil Wadhwani. "Transmission Of Volatility Between Stock Markets," *RFS*, 1990, v3(1), 5-33.)

Wadsworth, J. S., Jr. (Ellis, C. A. and J. S. Wadsworth, Jr. "U.S. Corporations And The International Capital Market Abroad," *FAJ*, 1966, v22(3), 169-175.)

Waegelein, James F. (Tehranian, Hassan and James F. Waegelein. "Short-Term Bonus Plan Adoption And Stock Market Performance - Proxy And Industry Effects: A Note," *FR*, 1986, v21(2), 345-353.)

Waegelein, James F. (Tehranian, Hassan, Nickolaos G. Travlos and James F. Waegelein. "The Effect Of Long-Term Performance Plans On Corporate Sell-Off-Induced Abnormal Returns," *JOF*, 1987, v42(4), 933-942.)

Wagner, Ilene. (Rubin, Marilyn, Ilene Wagner and Pearl Kamer. "Industrial Migration: A Case Study Of Destination By City-Suburban Origin Within The New York Metropolitan Area," *AREUEA*, 1978, v6(4), 417-437.)

Wagner, John R. "The Pesek-Saving Effect And The Effectiveness Of Open-Market Operations: A Comment," *JMCB*, 1976, v8(3), 399.

Wagner, Ludwig A. and Theodore Bakerman. "Wage Earner's Opinions Of Insurance Fringe Benefits," *JRI*, 1960, v27(2), 17-28.

Wagner, Richard E. "Politics, Bureaucracy, And Budgetary Choice: The Brookings Budget For 1974," *JMCB*, 1974, v6(3), 367-383.

Wagner, Samuel. (Mansfield, Edwin and Samuel Wagner. "Organizational And Strategic Factors Associated With Probabilities Of Success In Industrial R & D," *JOB*, 1975, v48(2), 179-198.)

Wagner, W. H. and C. A. Zipkin. "Better Performance Via Inventory Funds," *FAJ*, 1978, v34(3), 34-36,68.

Wagner, W. H. and S. C. Lau. "The Effect Of Diversification On Risk," *FAJ*, 1971, v27(5), 48-53.

Wagner, W. H. and S. R. Quay. "New Concepts In Portfolio Management," *JBR*, 1972-73, v3(2), 102-110.

Wagner, W. H. (Cuneo, L. J. and W. H. Wagner. "Reducing The Cost Of Stock Trading," *FAJ*, 1975, v31(6), 35-44.)

Wagner, Wayne H. "The Many Dimensions Of Risk," *JPM*, 1987-88, v14(2), 35-39.

Wagner, Wayne H. (Arnott, Robert D. and Wayne H. Wagner. "The Measurement And Control Of Trading Costs," *FAJ*, 1990, v46(6), 73-80.)

Wagner, Wayne H., Allen Emkin and Richard L. Dixon. "South African Divestment: The Investment Issues," *FAJ*, 1984, v40(6), 14-19,22.

Wagoner, William. (Render, Barry, William Wagoner, James R. Bobo and Stephen Corliss. "Finance Doctorates In The South: A 1977-1981 Supply And Demand Analysis," *JFED*, 1978, v7, 37-41.)

Wahlroos, Bjorn and Tom Berglund. "Stock Returns, Inflationary Expectations And Real Activity: New Evidence," *JBF*, 1986, v10(3), 377-389.

Wahlroos, Bjorn. (Berglund, Tom and Bjorn Wahlroos. "The Efficiency Of The Finnish Market For Rights Issues: An Application Of The Black-Scholes Model," *JBFA*, 1985, v12(1), 151-164.)

Wahner, Wayne and Stuart Quay. "Ten Myths About Beta," *JPM*, 1974-75, v1(1), 37-40.

Waill, Robert S. "Old Thoughts On New Growth Rates," *FAJ*, 1962, v18(6), 67-70.

Wainscott, Craig B. "The Stock-Bond Correlation And Its Implications For Asset Allocation," *FAJ*, 1990, v46(4), 55-60.

Wakefield, B. Richard. "APB Is On Wrong Track: Banker's View," *FAJ*, 1970, v26(4), 33-36.

Wakefield, Gordon. (Lavely, Joe, Gordon Wakefield and Bob Barrett. "Toward Enhancing Beta Estimates," *JPM*, 1979-80, v6(4), 43-46.)

Wakeman, Doug. (Harris, Robert S., Thomas J. O'Brien and Doug Wakeman. "Divisional Cost-Of-Capital Estimation For Multi-Industry Firms," *FM*, 1989, v18(2), 74-84.)

Wakeman, L. MacDonald. (Bradley, Michael and L. MacDonald Wakeman. "The Wealth Effects Of Targeted Share Repurchases," *JFEC*, 1983, v11(1), 301-328.)

Wakeman, L. MacDonald. (Smith, Clifford W., Jr. and L. MacDonald Wakeman. "Determinants Of Corporate Leasing Policy," *JOF*, 1985, v40(3), 895-908.)

Wakeman, Lee MacDonald. (Fratianni, Michele and Lee MacDonald Wakeman. "The Law Of One Price In The Eurocurrency Market," *JIMF*, 1982, v1(3), 307-324.)

Wakeman, Lee Macdonald. (Smith, Clifford W., Jr., Charles W. Smithson and Lee Macdonald Wakeman. "The Market For Interest Rate Swaps," *FM*, 1988, v17(4), 34-44.)

Wakoff, Gary I. "On Shareholders' Indifference To The Proceeds Price In Preemptive Rights Offerings," *JFQA*, 1973, v8(5), 835-836.

Walden, Michael L. "Effects Of Housing Codes On Local Housing Markets," *AREUEA*, 1987, v15(2), 13-31.

Walden, Michael L. "Magnet Schools And The Differential Impact Of School Quality On Residential Property Values," *JRER*, 1990, v5(2), 221-230.

Walden, Michael L. "The Whole Life Insurance Policy As An Options Package: An Empirical Investigation," *JRI*, 1985, v52(1), 44-58.

Waldman, Donald M. (Peterson, David R. and Donald M. Waldman. "A Model Of Heterogeneous Expectations As A Determinant Of Short Sales," *JFR*, 1984, v7(1), 1-16.)

Waldman, Donald W. (Chambers, Donald R., Willard T. Carleton and Donald W. Waldman. "A New Approach To Estimation Of The Term Structure Of Interest Rates," *JFQA*, 1984, v19(3), 233-252.)

Waldmann, Robert J. (De Long, J. Bradford, Andrei Shleifer, Lawrence H. Summers and Robert J. Waldmann. "The Survival Of Noise Traders In Financial Markets," *JOB*, 1991, v64(1), 1-20.)

Waldmann, Robert J. (DeLong, J. Bradford, Andrei Shleifer, Lawrence H. Summers and Robert J. Waldmann. "The Size And Incidence Of The Losses From Noise Trading," *JOF*, 1989, v44(3), 681-696.)

Waldmann, Robert J. (De Long, J. Bradford, Andrei Shleifer, Lawrence H. Summers and Robert J. Waldmann. "Positive Feedback Investment Strategies And Destabilizing Rational Speculation," *JOF*, 1990, v45(2), 379-396.)

Walia, Tirlochan S. "Explicit And Implicit Cost Of Changes In The Level Of Accounts Receivable And The Credit Policy Decision Of The Firm," *FM*, 1977, v6(4), 75-78.

Walker, C. James, III. "The United States Wine Industry," *FAJ*, 1973, v29(5), 70-79,32.

Walker, Charles E. "Discount Policy In The Light Of Recent Experience," *JOF*, 1957, v12(2), 223-237.

Walker, David A. "A Recursive Programming Approach To Bank Asset Management," *JFQA*, 1972, v7(5), 2055-2075.

Walker, David A. "An Analysis Of Cash Dispenser And Automated Teller Activity Levels And Costs," *JBR*, 1976-77, v7(4), 266-275.

Walker, David A. "Contrasts Among Banks With Retail Electronic Banking Machines And All Insured Banks: 1974 Versus 1976," *JBR*, 1977-78, v8(3), 159-170.

Walker, David A. "Economies Of Scale In Electronic Funds Transfer Systems," *JBF*, 1978, v2(1), 65-78.

Walker, David A. "Effects Of Deregulation On The Savings And Loan Industry," *FR*, 1983, v18(1), 94-110.

Walker, David A. "U. S. Banking Regulations And Foreign Banks' Entry Into The United States," *JBF*, 1983, v7(4), 569-580.

Walker, David A. (Gupta, Manak C. and David A. Walker. "Dividend Disbursal Practices In Commercial Banking," *JFQA*, 1975, v10(3), 515-529.)

Walker, David A. (Koot, Ronald S. and David A. Walker. "Rules Versus Discretion: An Analysis Of Income Stability And The Money Supply: A Comment," JMCB, 1974, v6(2), 253-261.)

Walker, David A. (Koot, Ronald S. and David A. Walker. "A Statistical Analysis Of The Impact Of Monetary Policy On Credit Union Lending," JBF, 1980, v4(3), 301-312.)

Walker, David A. (McCall, Alan S. and David A. Walker. "The Effects Of Control Status On Commercial Bank Profitability," JFQA, 1973, v8(4), 637-645.)

Walker, David A. (Sinkey, Joseph F., Jr. and David A. Walker. "Problem Banks: Indentification & Characteristics," JBR, 1974-75, v5(4), 208-217.)

Walker, David A., Richard C. Aspinwall, Stuart I. Greenbaum, Edward J. Kane and Perry D. Quick. "Panel Discussion On Federal Reserve Membership Issues," FR, 1979, v14(2), 58-74.

Walker, Ernest W. and J. William Petty, II. "Financial Differences Between Large And Small Firms," FM, 1978, v7(4), 61-68.

Walker, Ernest W. (Petty, J. William, II and Ernest W. Walker. "Optimal Transfer Pricing For The Multinational Firm," FM, 1972, v1(3), 74-87.)

Walker, James M. (Cox, James C., Vernon L. Smith and James M. Walker. "Theory And Behavior Of Multiple Unit Discriminative Auctions," JOF, 1984, v39(4), 983-1010.)

Walker, James M. (Cox, James C., Vernon L. Smith and James M. Walker. "Theory And Individual Behavior Of First-Price Auctions," JRU, 1988, v1(1), 61-100.)

Walker, James M., Vernon L. Smith and James C. Cox. "Inducing Risk-Neutral Preferences: An Examination In A Controlled Market Environment," JRU, 1990, v3(1), 5-24.

Walker, Joe. "Life Among The Finan," JPM, 1989, v15(4), 5-9.

Walker, L. R. (Pullara, S. J. and L. R. Walker. "The Evaluation Of Capital Expenditure Proposals: A Survey Of Firms In The Chemical Industry," JOB, 1965, v38(4), 403-408.)

Walker, M. "Financial Accounting Reports: A Market Model Of Disclosure: A Comment," JBFA, 1983, v10(3), 489-493.

Walker, M. (Appleyard, A. R., N. Strong and M. Walker. "Mutual Fund Performance In The Context Of Models Of Equilibrium Capital Asset Pricing," JBFA, 1982, v8(3), 289-296.)

Walker, M. (Clubb, C. D. B. and M. Walker. "On The Association Between General And Relative Price Movements In The CCA Price Indices," JBFA, 1986, v13(2), 197-208.)

Walker, Martin. "Forecast Disclosure: An Information Economics Perspective," JBFA, 1985, v12(3), 355-371.

Walker, Michael C. and James L. McDonald. "A Note On Discounting Risk-Adjusted Cash Flow Streams In The Capital Budgeting Process," JFED, 1986, v15, 1-7.

Walker, Michael C. "A Course In The Financial Management Of Not-For-Profit Organizations," JFED, 1977, v6, 20-23.

Walker, Michael C. "The Thrift Institution Problem Further Reconsidered: Comment," JBR, 1974-75, v5(1), 45-51.

Walker, Michael C. (Mehta, D.R., E.A. Moses, B. Deschamps and M.C. Walker. "The Influence Of Dividends, Growth, And Leverage On Share Prices In The Electric Utility Industry: An Econometric Study," JFQA, 1980, v15(5), 1163-1196.)

Walker, Michael C. (Stone, John D. and Michael C. Walker. "The Effect Of Executive Stock Options On Corporate Financial Decisions," JFR, 1990, v3(1), 69-83.)

Walker, Michael C., John D. Stowe and Shane Moriarity. "Decomposition Analysis Of Financial Statements," JBFA, 1979, v6(2), 173-186.

Walker, O. Forrest. "Price Freedom For Distributors," FAJ, 1952, v8(5), 14-19.

Walker, O. Forrest. "The Worth Of Retail Securities," FAJ, 1949, v5(4), 40-42.

Walker, R. G. (Birkett, W. P. and R. G. Walker. "Accounting: A Source Of Market Imperfection," JBFA, 1974, v1(2), 171-193.)

Walker, R. W. "Writing A Life Insurance Policy," JRI, 1964, v31(1), 39-50.

Walkling, Ralph A. and Robert O. Edmister. "Are There Commission Cost Side-Effects From Portfolio Management Decisions?," FAJ, 1983, v39(4), 52-59.

Walkling, Ralph A. and Robert O. Edmister. "Determinants Of Tender Offer Premiums," FAJ, 1985, v41(1), 27,30-37.

Walkling, Ralph A. "Predicting Tender Offer Success: A Logistic Analysis," JFQA, 1985, v20(4), 461-478.

Walkling, Ralph A. (Comiskey, Eugene E., Ralph A. Walkling and Michael A. Weeks. "Dispersion Of Expectations And Trading Volume," JBFA, 1987, v14(2), 229-240.)

Walkling, Ralph A. (Edmister, Robert O. and Ralph A. Walkling. "Trends In Institutional Commission Costs Following Deregulation: Evidence From The U.S.A.," JBFA, 1985, v12(4), 553-559.)

Walkling, Ralph A. (Ehrhardt, Michael C., James V. Jordan and Ralph A. Walkling. "An Application Of Arbitrage Pricing Theory To Futures Markets: Tests Of Normal Backwardation," JFM, 1987, v7(1), 21-34.)

Walkling, Ralph A. (Huang, Yen-Sheng and Ralph A. Walkling. "Target Abnormal Returns Associated With Acquisition Announcements: Payment, Acquisition Form, And Managerial Resistance," JFEC, 1987, v19(2), 329-350.)

Walkling, Ralph A. (Karpoff, Jonathan M. and Ralph A. Walkling. "Short-Term Trading Around Ex-Dividend Days: Additional Evidence," JFEC, 1988, v21(2), 291-298.)

Walkling, Ralph A. (Lang, Larry H. P., Rene M. Stulz and Ralph A. Walkling. "Managerial Performance, Tobin's Q, And The Gains From Successful Tender Offers," JFEC, 1989, v24(1), 137-154.)

Walkling, Ralph A. (Malatesta, Paul H. and Ralph A. Walkling. "Poison Pill Securities: Stockholder Wealth, Profitability, And Ownership Structure," JFEC, 1988, v20(1/2), 347-376.)

Walkling, Ralph A. (Stulz, Rene M., Ralph A. Walkling and Moon H. Song. "The Distribution Of Target Ownership And The Division Of Gains In Successful Takeovers," JOF, 1990, v45(3), 817-834.)

Wall, Kent D. (Burmeister, Edwin and Kent D. Wall. "The Arbitrage Pricing Theory And Macroeconomic Factor Measures," FR, 1986, v21(1), 1-20.)

Wall, Larry D. "Callable Bonds: A Risk-Reducing Signalling Mechanism—A Comment," JOF, 1988, v43(4), 1057-1065.

Wall, Larry D. "Interest Rate Swaps In An Agency Theoretic Model With Uncertain Interest Rates," JBF, 1989, v13(2), 261-270.

Wall, Larry D. (Cheng, David C., Benton E. Gup and Larry D. Wall. "Financial Determinants Of Bank Takeovers," JMCB, 1989, v21(4), 524-536.)

Wall, Larry D. and David R. Peterson. "Capital Changes At Large Affiliated Banks," JFSR, 1988, v1(3), 253-276.

Wall, Larry D. and David R. Peterson. "The Effect Of Capital Adequacy Guidelines On Large Bank Holding Companies," JBF, 1987, v11(4), 581-600.

Wall, Larry D. and John J. Pringle. "Alternative Explanations Of Interest Rate Swaps: A Theoretical And Empirical Analysis," FM, 1989, v18(2), 59-73.

Wall, Larry. "Why Are Some Banks More Profitable Than Others?," JBR, 1984-85, v15(4), 240-256.

Wallace, Hugh D. "A Proposed Solution To The Problem Of Compensating Automobile Accident Victims," JRI, 1968, v35(1), 141-146.

Wallace, James E. "Direct Household Assistance And Block Grants," AREUEA, 1983, v11(2), 192-202.

Wallace, Myles S. "World Money Or Domestic Money: Which Predicts US Inflation Best?," JIMF, 1984, v3(2), 241-244.

Wallace, Myles S. (McNown, Robert and Myles S. Wallace. "National Price Levels, Purchasing Power Parity, And Cointegration: A Test Of Four High Inflation Economies," JIMF, 1989, v8(4), 533-546.)

Wallace, Myles S. (Mixon, J. Wilson, Jr., Leila J. Pratt and Myles S. Wallace. "Cross-National Money To Income Causality: U.S. Money To U.K. Income," JMCB, 1979, v11(4), 419-426.)

Wallace, Neil. "An Approach To The Study Of Money And Nonmoney Exchange Structures," JMCB, 1972, v4(4), 838-847.

Wallace, Neil. "The Determination Of The Stock Of Reserves And The Balance Of Payments In A Neo-Keynesian Model," JMCB, 1970, v2(3), 269-290.

Wallace, Neil. "The Term Structure Of Interest Rates And The Maturity Composition Of The Federal Debt," JOF, 1967, v22(2), 301-312.

Wallace, Neil. (Kareken, John H. and Neil Wallace. "The Monetary Instrument Variable Choice: How Important?: A Comment," JMCB, 1972, v4(3), 723-729.)

Wallace, Neil. (Kareken, John H. and Neil Wallace. "Deposit Insurance And Bank Regulation: A Partial-Equilibrium Exposition," JOB, 1978, v51(3), 413-438.)

Wallace, Neil. (Sargent, Thomas J. and Neil Wallace. "Market Transaction Costs, Asset Demand Functions, And The Relative Potency Of Monetary And Fiscal Policy," JMCB, 1971, v3(2), Part 2, 469-506.)

Wallace, Robert F. "Some Reflections On Current War Financing," JOF, 1951, v6(3), 300-310.

Wallace, S. Rains, Jr. "Research In Insurance," JRI, 1954, v21, 22-26.

Wallace, Thomas H. "Pre-Employment Tests And Post-Employment Performance," JOB, 1955, v28(1), 72-75.

Wallach, B. (Agnello, W., W. Brueggeman, G. Decker, R. Griffith, R. Leftwich, R. Moore, J. Neal, B. Sternlicht, B. Wallach, W. Wardrop and C. Zinngrabe. "Panel: Corporate Real Estate Roundtable," JACF, 1990, v3(1), 6-38.)

Waller, Christopher J. "Monetary Policy Games And Central Bank Politics," JMCB, 1989, v21(4), 422-431.

Waller, Mark L. (Thompson, Sarahelen R. and Mark L. Waller. The Intraday Variability Of Soybean Futures Prices: Information And Trading Effects," RFM, 1988, v7(1), 110-126.

Waller, Mark L. (Thomspon, Sarahelen R. and Mark L. Waller. "Determinants Of Liquidity Costs In Commodity Futures Markets," RFM, 1988, v7(1), 110-126.)

Wallich, Henry C. "A Near-Term Look At The Capital Shortage," JFQA, 1976, v11(4), 541-547.

Wallich, Henry C. "Fiscalists Vs. Monetarists," FAJ, 1970, v26(5), 12-20.

Wallich, Henry C. "Investment Income During Inflation," FAJ, 1978, v34(2), 34-37.

Wallich, Henry C. "Money And Growth: A Country Cross-Section Analysis," JMCB, 1969, v1(2), 281-302.

Wallich, Henry C. "One Chance In A Generation: Guideposts For The Commission On Financial Structure And Regulation," JMCB, 1971, v3(1), 21-30.

Wallich, Henry C. "Radical Revisions Of The Distant Future: Then And Now," JPM, 1979-80, v6(1), 36-38.

Wallich, Henry C. "Random Walk And Security Analysts," FAJ, 1968, v24(2), 159-162.

Wallich, Henry C. "Reconstructing Humpty Dumpty," FAJ, 1972, v28(1), 18-22,66-67.

Wallich, Henry C. "Security Operations Of The International Bank," FAJ, 1946, v2(4), 20-25.

Wallich, Henry C. "Techniques Of Monetary Policy," FAJ, 1981, v37(4), 41-46,56.

Wallich, Henry C. "The Bond Market In Inflation: Innovation And Vitality," JPM, 1974-75, v1(2), 70-73.

Wallich, Henry C. "The Philosophy Of Public Debt Management: Some Implications Of The Patman Inquiry," JOF, 1953, v8(2), 196-205.

Wallich, Henry C. "The Spotty Economy," FAJ, 1969, v25(4), 21-24.

Wallingford, Buckner A. "A Survey And Comparison Of Portfolio Selection Models," JFQA, 1967, v2(2), 85-106.

Wallingford, Buckner A. (Brick, Ivan E. and Buckner A. Wallingford. "The Relative Tax Benefits Of Alternative Call Features In Corporate Debt," JFQA, 1985, v20(1), 95-106.)

Wallingford, Buckner A., II. "A Correction To 'An Inter-Temporal Approach To The Optimization Of Dividend Policy With Predetermined Investments'," JOF, 1972, v27(4), 944-945.

Wallingford, Buckner A., II. "An Inter-Temporal Approach To The Optimization Of Dividend Policy With Predetermined Investments: Reply," JOF, 1974, v29(1), 264-266.

Wallingford, Buckner A., II. "An Inter-Temporal Approach To The Optimization Of Dividend Policy With Predetermined Investments," JOF, 1972, v27(3), 627-635.

Walls, Edward L., Jr. "Hospital Dependency On Long-Term Debt," FM, 1972, v1(1), 42-47.

Walsh, Carl E. "Interest Rate Volatility And Monetary Policy," JMCB,

Warfield, Guy T. "The Place Of The College Graduate In Property And Casualty Sales," JRI, 1956, v23, 34-41.

Warga, Arthur D. (Sweeney, Richard J. and Arthur D. Warga. "The Possibility Of Estimating Risk Premia In Asset Pricing Models," FR, 1986, v21(2), 299-308.)

Warga, Arthur D. (Sweeney, Richard J. and Arthur D. Warga. "The Pricing Of Interest-Rate Risk: Evidence From The Stock Market," JOF, 1986, v41(2), 393-410.)

Warga, Arthur D. (Sweeney, Richard J. and Arthur D. Warga. "Interest-Sensitive Stocks: An APT Application," FR, 1983, v18(4), 257-270.)

Warga, Arthur. (Lehmann, Bruce and Arthur Warga. "Optimal Distribution-Free Tests And Further Evidence Of Heteroscedasticity In The Market Model: A Comment," JOF, 1985, v40(2), 603-605.)

Warga, Arthur. (Sarig, Oded and Arthur Warga. "Some Empirical Estimates Of The Risk Structure Of Interest Rates," JOF, 1989, v44(5), 1351-1360.)

Warga, Arthur. (Sarig, Oded and Arthur Warga. "Bond Price Data And Bond Market Liquidity," JFQA, 1989, v24(3), 367-378.)

Warga, Arthur. (Titman, Sheridan and Arthur Warga. "Risk And The Performance Of Real Estate Investment Trusts: A Multiple Index Approach," AREUEA, 1986, v14(3), 414-431.)

Warga, Arthur. (Titman, Sheridan and Arthur Warga. "Stock Returns As Predictors Of Interest Rates And Inflation," JFQA, 1989, v24(1), 47-58.)

Wark, David L. (Blazek, Lubomir J. and David L. Wark. "Profits Hidden In The Balance Sheet," JBR, 1978-79, v9(4), 251-255.)

Warner, Adolphe J. "Inside Europe's Future Capital Market," FAJ, 1967, v23(2), 141-143.

Warner, Adolphe J. "Report On European Trip," FAJ, 1969, v25(2), 125-127.

Warner, Adolphe J. (Schaefer, Jeffrey M. and Adolphe J. Warner. "Concentration In The Securities Industry," FAJ, 1977, v33(6), 29-34.)

Warner, Adolphe J. (Schaefer, Jeffrey M. and Adolphe J. Warner. "Rejoinder To West And Tinic," FAJ, 1978, v34(3), 47-49.)

Warner, Arthur E. and F. Jerry Ingram. "A Test For Discrimination In A Mortgage Market," JBR, 1982-83, v13(2), 116-124.

Warner, Arthur E. (Huffman, Forrest E. and Arthur E. Warner. "Toward The Development Of An Urban Growth Model That Recognizes The Importance Of The Basic Nature Of Services," AREUEA, 1987, v15(4), 341-358.)

Warner, Don C. (Apilado, Vincent P., Don C. Warner and Joel J. Dauten. "Evaluative Techniques In Consumer Finance -- Experimental Results And Policy Implications For Financial Institutions," JFQA, 1974, v9(2), 275-283.)

Warner, Jerold B. "Bankruptcy Costs: Some Evidence," JOF, 1977, v32(2), 337-347.

Warner, Jerold B. "Bankruptcy, Absolute Priority, And The Pricing Of Risky Debt Claims," JFEC, 1977, v4(3), 239-276.

Warner, Jerold B. (Barclay, Michael J., Robert H. Litzenberger and Jerold B. Warner. "Private Information, Trading Volume, And Stock-Return Variances," RFS, 1990, v3(2), 233-254.)

Warner, Jerold B. (Brown, Stephen J. and Jerold B. Warner. "Measuring Security Price Information," JFEC, 1980, v8(3), 205-258.)

Warner, Jerold B. (Brown, Stephen J. and Jerold B. Warner. "Using Daily Stock Returns: The Case Of Event Studies," JFEC, 1985, v14(1), 3-31.)

Warner, Jerold B. (Dodd, Peter and Jerold B. Warner. "On Corporate Governance," JFEC, 1983, v11(1), 401-438.)

Warner, Jerold B. (Jensen, Michael C. and Jerold B. Warner. "The Distribution Of Power Among Corporate Managers, Shareholders, And Directors," JFEC, 1988, v20(1/2), 3-24.)

Warner, Jerold B. (Siegel, Jeremy J. and Jerold B. Warner. "Indexation, The Risk-Free Asset, And Capital Market Equilibrium," JOF, 1977, v32(4), 1101-1107.)

Warner, Jerold B. (Smith, Clifford W., Jr. and Jerold B. Warner. "On Financial Contracting: An Analysis Of Bond Covenants," JFEC, 1979, v7(2), 117-162.)

Warner, Jerold B. (Smith, Clifford W., Jr. and Jerold B. Warner. "Bankruptcy, Secured Debt, And Optimal Capital Structure: Comment," JOF, 1979, v34(1), 247-251.)

Warner, Jerold B. (Watts, Ross L. and Karen H. Wruck. "Stock Prices And Top Management Changes," JFEC, 1988, v20(1), 461-492.

Warner, P. D., III and Stephen M. Miller. "The Deficient Treatment Of Money In Basic Undergraduate Texts: An Opposing View: A Reply," JMCB, 1974, v6(1), 119-121.

Warren, James M. and John P. Shelton. "A Simultaneous Equation Approach To Financial Planning," JOF, 1971, v26(5), 1123-1142.

Warren, James M. and John P. Shelton. "A Simultaneous Equation Approach To Financial Planning: Reply," JOF, 1973, v28(4), 1039-1042.

Warren, James M. "A Note On The Algebraic Equivalence Of The Holt And Malkiel Models Of Share Valuation," JOF, 1974, v29(3), 1007-1010.

Warren, James M. "An Operational Model For Security Analysis And Valuation," JFQA, 1974, v9(3), 395-422.

Warren, James M. (Hogan, William W. and James M. Warren. "Computation Of The Efficient Boundary In The E-S Portfolio Selection Model," JFQA, 1972, v7(4), 1881-1896.)

Warren, James M. (Hogan, William W. and James M. Warren. "Toward The Development Of An Equilibrium Capital-Market Model Based On Semivariance," JFQA, 1974, v9(1), 1-11.)

Warren, Stanton A. (Butler, Arthur D. and Stanton A. Warren. "An Optimal Temporary Loan Model For State Borrowers," JOF, 1977, v32(4), 1305-1312.)

Warren, William E., Robert E. Stevens and C. William McConkey. "Using Demographic And Lifestyle Analysis To Segment Individual Investors," FAJ, 1990, v46(2), 74-77.

Warschauer, Thomas and Antony Cherin. "Optimal Liquidity In Personal Financial Planning," FR, 1987, v22(4), 355-368.

Warschauer, Thomas. "The Use Of Project/Contract Method In The Investments Course," JFED, 1979, v8, 30-32.

Warshawsky, Mark. "Life Insurance Savings And The After-Tax Life Insurance Rate Of Return," JRI, 1985, v52(4), 585-606.

Warshawsky, Mark. "Private Annuity Markets In The United States: 1919-1984," JRI, 1988, v55(3), 518-528.

Warshawsky, Mark. "The Adequacy And Consistency Of Margin Requirements: The Cash, Futures, And Options Segments Of The Equity Market," RFM, 1989, v8(3), 420-437.

Wart, James R. (Porter, R. Burr, James R. Wart and Donald L. Ferguson. "Efficient Algorithms For Conducting Stochastic Dominance Tests On Large Numbers Of Portfolios," JFQA, 1973, v8, 71-81.)

Wasley, Charles. (Handa, Puneet, S. P. Kothari and Charles Wasley. "The Relation Between The Return Interval And Betas: Implications For The Size Effect," JFEC, 1989, v23(1), 79-100.)

Wasserfallen, Walter and Heinz Zimmermann. "The Behavior Of Intra-Daily Exchange Rates," JBF, 1985, v9(1), 55-72.

Wasserfallen, Walter and Daniel Wydler. "Underpricing Of Newly Issued Bonds: Evidence From The Swiss Capital Market," JOF, 1988, v43(5), 1177-1191.

Wasserfallen, Walter. "Expected And Unexpected Changes In Nominal And Real Variables - Evidence From The Capital Markets," JIMF, 1990, v9(1), 92-107.

Wasserfallen, Walter. "Macroeconomics News And The Stock Market: Evidence From Europe," JBF, 1989, v13(4/5), 613-626.

Wasserfallen, Walter. "The Behavior Of Flexible Exchange Rates: Evidence And Implications," FAJ, 1988, v44(5), 36-44.

Wasserfallen, Walter. "Trends, Random Walks, And The Expectations-Augmented Phillips Curve - Evidence From Six Countries," JMCB, 1988, v20(3), Part 1, 306-318.

Wasson, Hilda C. "Some Investment Policies For Commercial Banks," FAJ, 1966, v22(3), 83-91.

Waterman, Merwin H. "Financial Management Of Gas And Electric Utilities By The Securities And Exchange Commission," JOF, 1948, v3(1), 41-58.

Waterman, Robert H., Jr. and William D. Clendenin. "Problem Solving For Commercial Banks," JBR, 1970-71, v1(2), 60-62.

Waters, D. (Awh, R. Y. and D. Waters. "A Discriminant Analysis Of Economic, Demographic, And Attitudinal Characteristics Of Bank Charge-Card Holders: A Case Study," JOF, 1974, v29(3), 973-980.)

Waters, Elinor. "Unionization Of Office Employees," JOB, 1954, v27(4), 285-292.

Waters, W. R. (Poapst, J. V. and W. R. Waters. "Individual Investment: Canadian Experience," JOF, 1963, v18(4), 647-665.)

Waters, W. R. (Poapst, J. V. and W. R. Waters. "Rates Of Return On Consumer Durables," JOF, 1964, v19(4), 673-677.)

Waters, William R. (Quirin, G. David and William R. Waters. "Market Efficiency And The Cost Of Capital: The Strange Case Of Fire And Casualty Insurance Companies," JOF, 1975, v30(2), 427-445.)

Watkins, G. Campbell. (Berndt, Ernst R., Karen Chant Sharp and G. Campbell Watkins. "Utility Bond Rates And Tax Normalization," JOF, 1979, v34(5), 1211-1220.)

Watkins, Marvin G. (Chuppe, Terry M., Hugh R. Haworth and Marvin G. Watkins. "Public Policy Toward The International Bond Markets In The 1980s," AFPAF, 1990, v5(1), 3-30.)

Watkins, Marvin G. (Chuppe, Terry M., Hugh R. Haworth and Marvin G. Watkins. "Global Finance: Causes, Consequences And Prospects For The Future," GFJ, 1989, v1(1), 1-20.)

Watne, Donald A. "Cross-Selling The Bank Customer," JBR, 1979-80, v10(3), 165-172.

Watse, Kazunori. (Takahashi, Kichinosuke, Yukiharu Kurokawa and Kazunori Watase. "Corporate Bankruptcy Prediction In Japan," JBF, 1984, v8(2), 229-247.)

Watson, Collin J. (Simonson, Donald G., John D. Stowe and Collin J. Watson. "A Canonical Correlation Analysis Of Commercial Bank Asset/Liability Structures," JFQA, 1983, v18(1), 125-140.)

Watson, Collin J. (Stowe, John D., Collin J. Watson and Terry D. Robertson. "Relationships Between The Two Sides Of The Balance Sheet: A Canonical Correlation Analysis," JOF, 1980, v35(4), 973-980.)

Watson, Collin J. (Stowe, John D. and Collin J. Watson. "A Multivariate Analysis Of The Composition Of Life Insurer Balance Sheets," JRI, 1985, v52(2), 222-240.)

Watson, Edward T. P. "Distribution Of New Securities In SEC. 77 Reorganizations," JOF, 1950, v5(4), 337-367.

Watson, Harry S. (Malkiel, Burton C., George M. Von Furstenberg and Harry S. Watson. "Expectations, Tobin's q, And Industry Investment," JOF, 1979, v34(2), 549-561.)

Watson, Harry. "The Effects Of Compensation For Uninsured But Insurable Losses," JRI, 1984, v51(3), 498-512.

Watson, Hugh J. and H. William Vronen. "A Heuristic Model For Processing Overdrafts," JBR, 1972-73, v3(3), 186-188.

Watson, J. "A Study Of Possible Gains From International Investment And The Stationarity Of Inter-Country Correlation Coefficients: A Reply," JBFA, 1982, v8(1), 117-118

Watson, J. "A Study Of Possible Gains From International Investment," JBFA, 1978, v5(2), 195-206.

Watson, J. "The Stationarity Of Inter-Country Correlation Coefficients: A Note," JBFA, 1980, v7(2), 297-304.

Watson, Justin T. "A Regulatory View Of Capital Adequacy," JBR, 1975-76, v6(3), 170-172.

Watson, R. (Keasey, K. and R. Watson. "Non-Financial Symptoms And The Prediction Of Small Comapny A Test Of Argenti's Hypotheses," JBFA, 1987, v14(3), 335-354.)

Watson, Robert. "Modelling Directors' Remuneration Decisions In Small And Closely-Held UK Companies," JBFA, 1991, v18(1), 85-98.

Watson, Robert. (Keasey, Kevin and Robert Watson. "Current Cost Accounting And The Prediction Of Small Company Performance," JBFA, 1986, v13(1), 51-70.)

Watson, Robert. (Thomson, Lydia and Robert Watson. "Historic Cost Earnings, Current Cost Earnings And The Dividend Decision," JBFA, 1989, v16(1), 1-24.)

Watson, Ronald D. "Capital Evaluation Tools," FM, 1976, v5(4), 54-55.

Watson, Ronald D. "Tests Of Maturity Structures Of Commercial Bank Government Securities Portfolios: A Simulation Approach," JBR, 1972-73, v3(1), 34-46.

Watson, Ronald D. "The Marginal Cost Of Funds Concept In Banking," JBR, 1977-78, v8(3), 136-147.

Watson, Ronald D. (Santomero, Anthony M. and Ronald D. Watson. "Determining Optimal Capital Standard For The Banking Industry," JOF, 1977, v32(4), 1267-1282.)

Watts, James M. (Wingler, Tony R. and James M. Watts. "Electric Utility Bond Rating Changes: Methodological Issues And Evidence," JFR, 1982, v5(3), 221-235.)

Watts, Ross L. "Systematic 'Abnormal' Returns After Quarterly Earnings Announcements," JFEC, 1978, v6(2/3), 127-150.

Watts, Ross L. (Warner, Jerold B., Ross L. Watts and Karen H. Wruck. "Stock Prices And Top Management Changes," JFEC, 1988, v20(1), 461-492.)

Watts, Ross. "Comments On 'On The Informational Content Of Dividends'," JOB, 1976, v49(1), 81-85.

Watts, Ross. "Comments On The Impact Of Dividend And Earnings Announcements: A Reconciliation," JOB, 1976, v49(1), 97-106.

Watts, Ross. "The Information Content Of Dividends," JOB, 1973, v46(2), 191-211.

Watts, Ross. (Ball, Ray and Ross Watts. "Some Additional Evidence On Survival Biases," JOF, 1979, v34(1), 197-206.)

Watts, Ross. (Ball, Ray and Ross Watts. "Additional Evidence On The Time Series Properties Of Reported Earnings Per Share: Reply," JOF, 1977, v32(5), 1802-1808.)

Watts, Ross. (Ball, Ray and Ross Watts. "Some Time Series Properties Of Accounting Income," JOF, 1972, v27(3), 663-681.)

Waud, Roger N. "CD Behavior And The Use Of Broader Monetary Aggregates," JMCB, 1977, v9(3), 483-490.

Waud, Roger N. "Net Outlay Uncertainty And Liquidity Preference As Behavior Toward Risk," JMCB, 1975, v7(4), 499-506.

Waud, Roger N. (Abrams, Richard K., Richard Froyen and Roger N. Waud. "Monetary Policy Reaction Functions, Consistent Expectations, And The Burns Era," JMCB, 1980, v12(1), 30-42.)

Wearing, R. T. (Arnold, A. J. and R. T. Wearing. "Cash Flows, Exit Prices And British Airways," JBFA, 1988, v15(3), 311-334.)

Weaver, Daniel G. (Brick, Ivan E. and Daniel G. Weaver. "A Comparison Of Capital Budgeting Techniques In Identifying Profitable Investments," FM, 1984, v13(4), 29-39.)

Weaver, Daniel G. (Brick, Ivan E., Meir Statman and Daniel G. Weaver. "Event Studies And Model Misspecification: Another Look At The Benefits Of Outsiders From Public Information About Insider Trading," JBFA, 1989, v16(3), 399-424.)

Weaver, Robert A. "Corporate Officer Analyzes The Analysts," FAJ, 1959, v15(1), 46-50.

Weaver, Robert D. and Aniruddha Banerjee. "Cash Price Variation In The Live Beef Cattle Market: The Causal Role Of Futures Trade," JFM, 1982, v2(4), 367-389.

Weaver, Robert D. and Aniruddha Banerjee. "Does Futures Trading Destabilize Cash Prices? Evidence For U.S. Live Beef Cattle," JFM, 1990, v10(1), 41-60.

Weaver, Wallace Q., Jr. (Findlay, M. Chapman, III, Arthur E. Gooding and Wallace Q. Weaver, Jr. "On The Relevant Risk For Determining Capital Expenditure Hurdle Rates," FM, 1976, v5(4), 9-17.)

Weaver, William C. "Eathquake Events And Real Estate Portfolios: A Survey Result," JRER, 1990, v5(2), 277-280.

Weaver, William M., Jr. "Investment Casting - A Big Growth Industry," FAJ, 1961, v17(6), 29-32.

Webb, Bernard L. "Collective Merchandising Of Automobile Insurance," JRI, 1969, v36(3), 465-472.

Webb, Bernard L. "The Framework For Insurance Marketing Changes," JRI, 1974, v41(2), 239-248.

Webb, Brian. (Miles, Mike, John Pringle and Brian Webb. "Modeling The Corporate Real Estate Decision," JRER, 1989, v4(3), 47-66.)

Webb, Bruce G. "Borrower Risk Under Alternative Mortgage Instruments," JOF, 1982, v37(1), 169-183.

Webb, James R. and C. F. Sirmans. "Yields And Risk Measures For Real Estate, 1966-77," JPM, 1980-81, v7(1), 14-19.

Webb, James R. and Richard J. Curcio. "Interest Rate Illusions And Real Property Purchases," JPM, 1981-82, v8(4), 67-73.

Webb, James R. "On The Exclusion Of Real Estate From The Market Portfolio," JPM, 1990, v17(1), 78-84.

Webb, James R. "Real Estate Investment Acquisition Rules For Life Insurance Companies And Pension Funds: A Survey," AREUEA, 1984, v12(4), 495-520.

Webb, James R. "The Assimilation Of New Services Into The Real Estate Brokerage Firm," JRER, 1988, v3(2), 165-175.

Webb, James R. (Hartzell, David J. and James R. Webb. "Real Estate Risk And Return Expectations: Recent Survey Results," JRER, 1988, v3(3), 31-37.)

Webb, James R. (Pyhrr, Stephen A., Waldo L. Born and James R. Webb. "Development Of A Dynamic Investment Strategy Under Alternative Inflation Cycle Scenarios," JRER, 1990, v5(2), 177-193.)

Webb, James R. (Rubens, Jack H., Michael T. Bond and James R. Webb. "The Inflation-Hedging Effectiveness Of Real Estate," JRER, 1989, v4(2), 45-55.)

Webb, James R. (Shilton, Leon G. and James R. Webb. "Commercial Loan Underwriting And Option Valuation," JRER, 1989, v4(1), 1-12.)

Webb, James R. (Sirmans, C. F. and James R. Webb. "Expected Equity Returns On Real Estate Financed With Life Insurance Company Loans: 1967-1977," AREUEA, 1980, v8(2), 218-228.)

Webb, James R. (Wang, Ko, James R. Webb and Susanne Cannon. "Estimating Project-Specific Absorption," JRER, 1990, v5(1), 107-116.)

Webb, James R. and Jack A. Rubens. "How Much In Real Estate? A Surprising Answer," JPM, 1986-87, v13(3), 10-14.

Webb, James R. and Jack H. Rubens. "Portfolio Considerations In The Valuation Of Real Estate," AREUEA, 1986, v14(3), 465-495.

Webb, James R. and Jack H. Rubens. "The Effect Of Alternative Return Measures On Restricted Mixed-Asset Portfolios," AREUEA, 1988, v16(2), 123-137.

Webb, James R. and Jack H. Rubens. "Tax Rates And Implicit Rates Of Return On Owner-Occupied Single-Family Housing," JRER, 1987, v2(2), 11-28.

Webb, James R. and Jack H. Rubens. "Tax Rates And Implicit Rates Of Return On Owner-Occupied Single-Family Housing: A Reply," JRER, 1989, v4(1), 85-86.

Webb, James R. and Willard McIntosh. "Real Estate Investment Acquisition Rules For REITs: A Survey," JRER, 1986, v1(1), 77-98.

Webb, Robert L. (Marsh, Terry A. and Robert I. Webb. "Information Dissemination Uncertainty, The Continuity Of Trading, And The Structure Of International Futures Markets," RFM, 1983, v2(1), 36-71.)

Webb, Robert L. "A Note On Volatility And Pricing Of Futures Options During Choppy Markets," JFM, 1987, v7(3), 333-338.

Webb, Roy H. (Lupoletti, William M. and Roy H. Webb. "Defining And Improving The Accuracy Of Macroeconomic Forecasts: Contributions From A VAR Model," JOB, 1986, v59(2), Part 1, 263-286.)

Webb, Samuel G. "The Deficient Treatment Of Money In Basic Undergraduate Texts: A Comment," JMCB, 1972, v4(1), 109-112.

Webb, Steven B. "Government Debt And Inflationary Expectations As Determinants Of The Money Supply In Germany: 1919-23," JMCB, 1985, v17(4), Part 1, 479-492.

Webber, Alan. (Capie, Forrest and Alan Webber. "Total Coin And Coin In Circulation In The United Kingdom, 1868-1914," JMCB, 1983, v15(1), 24-39.)

Weber, Arnold R. and David P. Taylor. "Procedures For Employee Displacement: Advance Notice Of Plant Shutdown," JOB, 1963, v36(3), 302-315.

Weber, C. Edward. "Change In Managerial Manpower With Mechanization Of Data-Processing," JOB, 1959, v32(2), 151-163.

Weber, Edward A. "Instalment Credit For Autos: A Literature Survey Of Sources, Terms And Demand Effects," JBR, 1984-85, v15(1), 35-43.

Weber, Gerald I. "Interest Rates On Mortgages And Dividend Rates On Savings And Loan Shares," JOF, 1966, v21(3), 515-521.

Weber, Gerald I. "Interest Rates On Mortgages And Dividend Rates On Savings And Loan Shares: Reply," JOF, 1967, v22(3), 471-473.

Weber, Harry. "God As Portfolio Manager," JPM, 1979-80, v6(2), 67-68.

Weber, Harry. "God As Portfolio Manager," JOF, 1973, v28(5), 1353-1355.

Weber, John A. "A Note On Keeping Abreast Of Developments In The Field Of Finance," JOF, 1973, v28(1), 161-165.

Weber, Paul G. (Johnson, James M. and Paul G. Weber. "The Impact Of The Problem Bank Disclosure On Bank Share Prices," JBR, 1977-78, v8(3), 179-182.)

Weber, Warren E. "Monetary Assets, Net Wealth, And Banking Structures," JMCB, 1975, v7(3), 331-342.

Weber, Warren E. (MacKay, Robert J. and Warren E. Weber. "Consumer Behavior And Quantity Constraints: Some Implications For Monetary Theory," JMCB, 1977, v9(1), 21-31.)

Webster, Paul K. "Method Of Accounting For Emergency Facilities," FAJ, 1953, v9(2), 97-102.

Webster, Stuart K. (Parry, Robert W., Jr. and Stuart K. Webster. "City Leases: Up Front, Out Back, In The Closet," FAJ, 1980, v36(5), 41-47.)

Wecker, William E. "Comments On 'Forecasting With Econometric Methods: Folklore Versus Fact'," JOB, 1978, v51(4), 585-586.

Wecker, William E. "Predicting The Turning Points Of A Time Series," JOB, 1979, v52(1), 35-50.

Wecker, William E. (Reilly, Raymond R. and William E. Wecker. "On The Weighted Average Cost Of Capital," JFQA, 1973, v8(1), 123-126.)

Wecker, William E. (Reilly, Raymond R. and William E. Wecker. "On The Weighted Average Cost Of Capital: Reply," JFQA, 1975, v10(2), 367.)

Wedding, Nugent. "Advertising And Public Relations," JOB, 1950, v23(3), 173-181.

Wedig, Gerard J., Mahmud Hassan and Frank A. Sloan. "Hospital Investment Decisions And The Cost Of Capital," JOB, 1989, v62(4), 517-538.

Wedig, Gerard, Frank A. Sloan, Mahmud Hassan and Michael A. Morrisey. "Capital Structure, Ownership, And Capital Payment Policy: The Case Of Hospitals," JOF, 1988, v43(1), 21-40.

Weed, Garry M. (Ma, Christopher K. and Garry M. Weed. "Fact And Fancy Of Takeover Junk Bonds," JPM, 1986-87, v13(1), 34-37.)

Weeden, Donald E. "Competition: Key To Market Structure," JFQA, 1972, v7(2), Supp, 1696-1701.

Weeks, Michael A. (Comiskey, Eugene E., Ralph A. Walkling and Michael A. Weeks. "Dispersion Of Expectations And Trading Volume," JBFA, 1987, v14(2), 229-240.)

Weeks, Richard E. (Dunn, Marshall and Richard E. Weeks. "Railroad Pro Forma Tabulations," FAJ, 1947, v3(1), 43-51.)

Weese, Samuel H. "A Critical Analysis Of State Surplus Lines Laws," JRI, 1970, v37(2), 191-202.

Weese, Samuel H. "Another Look At Nuclear Liability After Three Mile Island," JRI, 1983, v50(2), 323-327.

Wehrun, Donald A. (MacCrimmon, Kenneth R. and Donald A. Wehrung. "The Risk In-Basket," JOB, 1984, v57(3), 367-388.

Wehrung, Donald, Kam-Hon Lee, David K. Tse and Ilan B. Vertinsky. "Adjusting Risky Situations: A Theoretical Framework And Empirical Test," JRU, 1989, v2(2), 189-212.

Wei, James. (McWilliams, James D. and James Wei. "Some Like To-Matoes And Some Like To-Matoes," JPM, 1980-81, v7(4), 43-47.)

Wei, K. C. John, Cheng-few Lee and Andrew H. Chen. "Multivariate Regression Tests Of The Arbitrage Pricing Theory: The

Wei, K. C. John. "An Asset-Pricing Theory Unifying The CAPM And APT," JOF, 1988, v43(4), 881-892.

Wei, K. C. John. (Bansal, Vipul K., Stephen W. Pruitt and K. C. John Wei. "An Empirical Reexamination Of The Impact Of CBOE Option Initiation On Volatility And Trading Volume Of The Underlying Equities: 1973-1986," FR, 1989, v24(1), 19-30.)

Wei, K. C. John. (Carroll, Carolyn and K. C. John Wei. "Risk, Return, And Equilibrium: An Extension," JOB, 1988, v61(4), 485-500.)

Wei, K. C. John. (Chen, T. J. and K. C. John Wei. "Risk Premiums In Foreign Exchange Markets: Theory And Evidence," AFPAF, 1989, v4(Supp), 23-42.)

Wei, K. C. John. (Lee, Cheng F., Frank C. Jen and K. C. John Wei. "The Real And Nominal Parameters In The CAPM: A Responsive Coefficient Approach," IJOF, 1988, v1(1), 113-130.)

Wei, K. C. John. (Lee, Cheng F., Chunchi Wu and K. C. John Wei. "The Heterogeneous Investment Horizon And The Capital Asset Pricing Model: Theory And Implications," JFQA, 1990, v25(3), 361-376.)

Wei, K. C. John. (Pruitt, Stephen W., Wittipan Tawarangkoon and K. C. John Wei. "Chernobyl, Commodities And Chaos: An Examination Of The Reaction Of Commodity Futures Prices To Evolving Information," JFM, 1987, v7(5), 555-570.)

Wei, K. C. John. (Pruitt, Stephen W. and K. C. John Wei. "Institutional Ownership And Changes In The S&P 500," JOF, 1989, v44(2), 509-514.)

Wei, K. C. John. (Sears, R. Stephen and K. C. John Wei. "The Structure Of Skewness Preferences In Asset Pricing Models With Higher Moments: An Empirical Test," FR, 1988, v23(1), 25-38.)

Wei, K. C. John. (Sears, Stephen and K. C. John Wei. "Asset Pricing, Higher Moments, And The Market Risk Premium: A Note," JOF, 1985, v40(4), 1251-1253.)

Weicher, John C. "New Home Affordability, Equity, And Housing Market Behavior," AREUEA, 1978, v6(4), 395-416.

Weicher, John C. "Re-Evaluating Housing Policy Alternatives: What Do We Really Know?," AREUEA, 1983, v11(1), 1-10.

Weicher, John C. "The Affordability Of New Homes," AREUEA, 1977, v5(2), 209-226.

Weicher, John C. "The Report Of The President's Commission On Housing: Policy Proposals For Subsidized Housing," AREUEA, 1983, v11(2), 117-132.

Weicher, John C. (Clemmer, Richard B. and John C. Weicher. "The Individual Housing Account," AREUEA, 1983, v11(2), 221-236.)

Weicher, John C. (Kinnard, William N., Herman G. Berkman, Hugh O. Nourse and John C. Weicher. "The First Twenty Years Of AREUEA," AREUEA, 1988, v16(2), 189-205.)

Weidenbaum, Murray L. "A Hard Look At The Federal Budget," FAJ, 1973, v29(4), 18-20,88-92.

Weidenbaum, Murray L. "Aircraft: Diversification In The Industry," FAJ, 1959, v15(2), 51-58.

Weidenbaum, Murray L. "Federal Credit Programs," FAJ, 1971, v27(1), 17-21.

Weidenbaum, Murray L. "Government Spending," FAJ, 1968, v24(1), 77-80.

Weidenbaum, Murray L. "Is Fiscal Policy Dead?," FAJ, 1970, v26(2), 31-32.

Weidenbaum, Murray L. "Matching National Goals And Resources," FAJ, 1972, v28(4), 17-19,74-75.

Weidenbaum, Murray L. "The Case Against Government Guarantees Of Electric Utility Bonds," FM, 1974, v3(3), 24-30.

Weidenbaum, Murray L. "The Federal Budget For Fiscal 1975," FAJ, 1974, v30(4), 20-24,61-63.

Weidenbaum, Murray L. "The Inflationary Impact Of The Federal Budget," FAJ, 1966, v22(4), 35-37.

Weidenbaum, Murray L. "The United States Aircraft Industry," FAJ, 1963, v19(2), 49-53.

Weidenbaum, Murray L. "Trend Of The Military Market," FAJ, 1960, v16(1), 21-25.

Weigand, Robert E. "The Marketing Organization, Channels, And Firm Size," JOB, 1963, v36(2), 228-236.

Weil, David N. (Basu, Susanto, Miles S. Kimball, N. Gregory Mankiw and David N. Weil. "Optimal Advice For Monetary Policy," JMCB, 1990, v22(1), 19-36.)

Weil, Gordon. (Raymond, Arthur J. and Gordon Weil. "Diversification Benefits And Exchange-Rate Changes," JBFA, 1989, v16(4), 455-466.)

Weil, R. L. (Davidson, S. and R. L. Weil. "Predicting Inflation - Adjusted Results," FAJ, 1975, v31(1), 27-31.)

Weil, R. L. (Vancil, R. F. and R. L. Weil. "Accounting For Distributable Income," FAJ, 1976, v32(4), 38-45.)

Weil, Roman L. "Annuitants Can Afford CREF's Projecting Earnings At A Rate Larger Than 4 Percent," JRI, 1973, v40(3), 465-472.

Weil, Roman L. "Macaulay's Duration: An Appreciation," JOB, 1973, v46(4), 589-592.

Weil, Roman L. (Davidson, Sidney and Roman L. Weil. "Inflation Accounting And Leases," FAJ, 1975, v31(6), 22-29,57.)

Weil, Roman L. (Davidson, Sidney and Roman L. Weil. "Inflation Accounting And 1974 Earnings," FAJ, 1975, v31(5), 42-54.)

Weil, Roman L. (Davidson, Sidney and Roman L. Weil. "Inflation Accounting For Utilities," FAJ, 1975, v31(3), 30-34,62.)

Weil, Roman L. (Davidson, Sidney and Roman L. Weil. "Replacement Cost Disclosure," FAJ, 1976, v32(2), 57-66.)

Weil, Roman L. (Davidson, Sidney, Lisa B. Skelton and Roman L. Weil. "The FASB's Inflation Accounting Proposal," FAJ, 1979, v35(3), 41-54.)

Weil, Roman L. (Easman, W. S., Jr., A. Falkenstein, Roman L. Weil and D. J. Guy. "Sustainable Income And Stock Returns," FAJ, 1979, v35(5), 44-48.)

Weil, Roman L. (Falkenstein, Angela and Roman L. Weil. "Using Replacement Costs To Measure Income - Part I," FAJ, 1977, v33(1), 46-57.)

Weil, Roman L. (Falkenstein, Angela and Roman L. Weil. "Using Replacement Costs To Measure Income - Part II," FAJ, 1977, v33(2), 48-57.)

Weil, Roman L. (Fisher, Lawrence and Roman L. Weil. "Coping With The Risk Of Interest-Rate Fluctuations: Returns To Bondholders From Naive And Optimal Strategies," JOB, 1971, v44(4), 408-431.)

Weil, Roman L. (Gould, John P. and Roman L. Weil. "The Rule Of 69," JOB, 1974, v47(3), 397-398.)

Weil, Roman L. (Ingersoll, Jonathan E., Jr., Jeffrey Skelton and Roman L. Weil. "Duration Forty Years Later," JFQA, 1978, v13(4), 627-650.)

Weil, Roman L. (Kaplan, Robert S. and Roman L. Weil. "Risk And The Value Line Contest," FAJ, 1973, v29(4), 56-61.)

Weil, Roman L. (Lasman, Daniel A. and Roman L. Weil. "Adjusting The Debt-Equity Ratio," FAJ, 1978, v34(5), 49-58.)

Weil, Roman L. and Lawrence Fisher. "TIAA/CREF: Who Gets What? An Analysis Of Wealth Transfers In A Variable Annuity," JOB, 1974, v47(1), 67-87.

Weil, Roman L., Joel E. Segall and David O. Green. "Premium On Convertible Bonds: Reply," JOF, 1972, v27(5), 1163-1170.

Weil, Roman L., Joel E. Segall and David Green, Jr. "Premiums On Convertible Bonds: Reply," JOF, 1970, v25(4), 931-933.

Weil, Roman L., Jr., Joel E. Segall and David Green, Jr. "Premiums On Convertible Bonds," JOF, 1968, v23(3), 445-463.

Weimer, Arthur M. "Suggestions Regarding Education For Business," JRI, 1959, v26(2), 7-12.

Weimer, Arthur M. (Arbuckle, Ernest C., Richard L. Kozelka and Arthur M. Weimer. "Dean's Forum: The Place Of Insurance In The Collegiate Curriculum," JRI, 1960, v27(3), 67-70.)

Weinberg, Eli. "Solving The Paper Crisis In The Security Industry," JBR, 1970-71, v1(4), 25-40.

Weinberg, John A. (Lacker, Jeffrey M., Robert J. Levy and John A. Weinberg. "Incentive-Compatible Financial Contracts, Asset Prices, And The Value Of Control," JFI, 1990, v1(1), 31-56.)

Weinberg, Michael A. (Kadish, LLoyd and Michael A. Weinberg. "If The Supreme Court Does Not Imply A Private Judicial Cause Of Action Under The Commodity Exchange Act," JFM, 1981, v1(Supp), 519-521.)

Weinberger, Alfred. (Leibowitz, Martin L., Thomas E. Klaffky, Steven Mandel and Alfred Weinberger. "Horizon Matching: A New Approach To Dedicated Portfolios," JPM, 1984-85, v11(1), 93-96.)

Weinberger, Alfred. (Leibowitz, Martin L. and Alfred Weinberger. "The Uses Of Contingent Immunization," JPM, 1981-82, v8(1), 51-55.)

Weinberger, Alfred. (Leibowitz, Martin L. and Alfred Weinberger. "Contingent Immunization - Part II: Problem Areas," FAJ, 1983, v39(1), 35-50.)

Weinberger, Alfred. (Leibowitz, Martin L. and Alfred Weinberger. "Contingent Immunization - Part I: Risk Control Procedures," FAJ, 1982, v38(6), 17-31.)

Weinblatt, J. (Ben-Zion, Uri and J. Weinblatt. "Purchasing Power, Interest Rate Parities And The Modified Fisher Effect In Presence Of Tax Agreements," JIMF, 1984, v3(1), 67-73.)

Weiner, John M. "Business And Investment Outlook In Britain," FAJ, 1965, v21(3), 137-139.

Weiner, John M. "Investment Outlook In Britain (Keynote Review)," FAJ, 1966, v22(5), 123-126.

Weiner, Michael D. and Peter Berman. "Section 17: Registered Futures Associations," JFM, 1981, v1(Supp), 497-500.

Weiner, Michael D. "Dual Investigation/Dual Punishment," JFM, 1981, v1(Supp), 523-524.

Weiner, Neil S. "The Hedging Rationale For A Stock Index Futures Contract," JFM, 1981, v1(1), 59-76.

Weinflash, David H. "Econogenesis," JPM, 1980-81, v7(4), 5-6.

Weinflash, David. "Investor Behavior: Work Or Play?," JPM, 1979-80, v6(2), 69-70.

Weingartner, H. Martin. "Capital Rationing: n Authors In Search Of A Plot," JOF, 1977, v32(5), 1403-1431.

Weingartner, H. Martin. "Leasing, Asset Lives And Uncertainty: Guides To Decision Making," FM, 1987, v16(2), 5-12.

Weingartner, H. Martin. "Rejoinder: Leasing, Asset Lives And Uncertainty," FM, 1987, v16(2), 21-23.

Weingartner, H. Martin. "The Generalized Rate Of Return," JFQA, 1966, v1(3), 1-29.

Weinraub, H. J. (Pettway, R. H. and H. J. Weinraub. "Some Tax Aspects Of Bond Trading," FAJ, 1969, v25(6), 125-128.)

Weinraub, Herbert J. (Ma, Christopher K., Ramesh P. Rao and Herbert J. Weinraub. "The Seasonality In Convertible Bond Markets: A Stock Effect Or Bond Effect?," JFR, 1988, v11(4), 335-348.)

Weinrebe, Earl J. "Appraising Life Insurance Stocks," FAJ, 1958, v14(5), 63-66.

Weinrobe, Maurice D. "Home Equity Conversion Instruments With Fixed Term To Maturity: Alternatives To End Of Term Pay-Off," AREUEA, 1983, v11(1), 83-96.

Weinrobe, Maurice D. (Steindl, Frank G. and Maurice D. Weinrobe. "Natural Hazards And Deposit Behavior At Financial Institutions: A Note," JBF, 1983, v7(1), 111-118.)

Weinrobe, Maurice. "An Analysis Of The Effectiveness Of FHLBB Liquidity Policy, 1971-1975," JOF, 1977, v32(5), 1617-1637.

Weinrobe, Maurice. "An Analysis Of Home Equity Conversion In The RAM Program," AREUEA, 1987, v15(2), 65-78.

Weinrobe, Maurice. "An Insurance Plan To Guarantee Reverse Mortgages," JRI, 1988, v55(4), 644-659.

Weinrobe, Maurice. "Savings And Loan Demand For Liquid Assets: Theory, Evidence And Implications For Policy," AREUEA, 1981, v9(1), 18-37.

Weinrobe, Maurice. (Anderson, Dan and Maurice Weinrobe. "Mortgage Default Risks And The 1971 San Fernando Earthquake," AREUEA, 1986, v14(1), 110-135.)

Weinrobe, Maurice. (Anderson, Dan R. and Maurice Weinrobe. "Insurance Issues Related To Mortgage Default Risks Associated With Natural Disasters," JRI, 1986, v53(3), 501-513.)

Weinstein, David and John U. Farley. "Market Segmentation And Parameter Inequalities In A Buyer Behavior Model," JOB, 1975, v48(4), 526-540.

Weinstein, Mark I. "A Curmudgeon's View Of Junk Bonds," JPM, 1986-87, v13(3), 76-80.

Weinstein, Mark I. "Bond Systematic Risk And The Option Pricing Model," JOF, 1983, v38(5), 1415-1429.

Weinstein, Mark I. "The Effect Of A Rating Change Announcement On Bond Price," JFEC, 1977, v5(3), 329-350.

Weinstein, Mark I. "The Seasoning Process Of New Corporate Bond Issues," JOF, 1978, v33(5), 1343-1354.

Weinstein, Mark I. (Brown, Stephen J. and Mark I. Weinstein. "Derived Factors In Event Studies," JFEC, 1985, v14(3), 491-495.)

Weinstein, Mark I. (Brown, Stephen J. and Mark I. Weinstein. "A New Approach To Testing Asset Pricing Models: The Bilinear Paradigm," JOF, 1983, v38(3), 711-743.)

Weinstein, Mark I. (Clark, Truman A. and Mark I. Weinstein. "The Behavior Of The Common Stock Of Bankrupt Firms," JOF, 1983, v38(2), 489-504.)

Weinstein, Mark I. (Kalaba, Robert E., Terence C. Langetieg, Nima Rasakhoo and Mark I. Weinstein. "Estimation Of Implicit Bankruptcy Costs," JOF, 1984, v39(3), 629-642.)

Weinstein, Mark. "The Equity Component Of Corporate Bonds," JPM, 1984-85, v11(3), 37-41.

Weinstein, Mark. "The Systematic Risk Of Corporate Bonds," JFQA, 1981, v16(3), 257-278.

Weinstein, Mark. (Amihud, Yakov, Peter Dodd and Mark Weinstein. "Conglomerate Mergers, Managerial Motives And Stockholder Wealth," JBF, 1986, v10(3), 401-410.)

Weinstock, Irwin. (Coe, Robert K. and Irwin Weinstock. "Evaluating The Finance Journals: The Department Chairman's Perspective," JFR, 1983, v6(4), 345-349.)

Weintraub, Robert and William R. Hosek. "Further Reflections On And Investigations Of Money Demand," JOF, 1970, v25(1), 109-125.

Weintraub, Robert E. "Money In The Wharton Quarterly Model: A Rejoinder," JMCB, 1984, v16(1), 79-80.

Weintraub, Robert E. "Money In The Wharton Quarterly Model: A Comment," JMCB, 1984, v16(1), 69-75.

Weintraub, Robert E. "On Speculative Prices And Random Walks: A Denial," JOF, 1963, v18(1), 59-68.

Weintraub, Robert E. "Some Neglected Monetary Contributions: Congressman Wright Patman (1893-1976)," JMCB, 1977, v9(4), 517-528.

Weintraub, Robert E. (Hambor, John C. and Robert E. Weintraub. "The Term Structure: Another Look: A Comment," JMCB, 1974, v6(4), 551-557.)

Weintraub, Robert. "Monetary Policy And Karl Brunner," JMCB, 1977, v9(1), Part 2, 255-256.

Weintrob, Harry. (Murphy, Neil B. and Harry Weintrob. "Evaluating Liquidity Under Conditions Of Uncertainty In Mutual Savings Banks," JFQA, 1970, v5(5), 559-568.)

Weintrop, Joseph. (Kamma, Sreenivas, Joseph Weintrop and Peggy Wier. "Investors' Perceptions Of The Delaware Supreme Court Decision In Unocal V. Mesa," JFEC, 1988, v20(1/2), 419-430.)

Weisbach, Michael S. "Outside Directors And CEO Turnover," JFEC, 1988, v20(1/2), 431-460.

Weisbart, Steven N. "Contested Claims In Life Insurance: An Exploratory Study," JRI, 1976, v43(4), 611-628.

Weisbart, Steven N. "Life Insurance Company Expense Limitation Laws, 1905-1907," JRI, 1970, v37(3), 369-380.

Weisbart, Steven N. (Johnson, Joseph E., George B. Flanigan and Steven N. Weisbart. "Returns To Scale In The Property And Liability Insurance Industry," JRI, 1981, v48(1), 18-45.)

Weisbart, Steven N. (Marshall, Robert A. and Steven N. Weisbart. "Issues Involved In The Integration Of Traditional And Nontraditional University Curricula," JRI, 1976, v43(2), 335-341.)

Weisberg, Herbert I. (Fairley, William B., Thomas J. Tomberlin and Herbert I. Weisberg. "Pricing Automobile Insurance Under A Cross-Classification Of Risks: Evidence From New Jersey," JRI, 1981, v48(3), 505-514.)

Weisberg, Herbert I. and Thomas J. Tomberlin. "A Statistical Perspective On Actuarial Methods For Estimating Pure Premiums From Cross-Classified Data," JRI, 1982, v49(4), 539-563.

Weisbrod, Burton A. "Some Problems Of Pricing And Resource Allocation In A Non-Profit Industry-The Hospitals," JOB, 1965, v38(1), 18-28.

Weisbrod, Burton A. "The Per Diem Freight-Car Rate And Railroad Efficiency-The Short-Run Problem," JOB, 1959, v32(4), 383-385.

Weisler, Mark. "Analysis Of Questionnaire Responses," JFED, 1973, v1, 7-8.

Weiss, Donald S. "Leverage Transactions: Survival Or Extinction?," JFM, 1981, v1(Supp), 547-554.

Weiss, Doyle L. (Windal, Pierre M. and Doyle L. Weiss. "An Iterative GLS Procedure For Estimating The Parameters Of Models With Autocorrelated Errors Using Data Aggregted Over Time," JOB, 1980, v53(4), 415-424.)

Weiss, Doyle L., Franklin S. Houston and Pierre Windal. "The Periodic Pain Of Lydia E. Pinkham," JOB, 1978, v51(1), 91-102.

Weiss, Kathleen. "The Post-Offering Price Performance Of Closed-End Funds," FM, 1989, v18(3), 57-67.

Weiss, Lawrence A. "Bankruptcy Resolution: Direct Costs And Violaton Of Priority Of Claims," JFEC, 1990, v27(2), 285-314.

Weiss, Leonard W. "A Note On Time Deposit Interest Rates: Reply," JOF, 1959, v14(1), 77-77.

Weiss, Leonard W. "A Note On Time Deposit Interest Rates," JOF, 1958, v13(1), 96-102.

Weiss, Mary A. "Analysis Of Productivity At The Firm Level: An Application To Life Insurers," JRI, 1986, v53(1), 49-84.

Weiss, Mary A. "Analysis Of Productivity At The Firm Level: An Application To Life Insurers: Reply," JRI, 1989, v56(2), 341-346.

Weiss, Mary A. "Macroeconomic Insurance Output Estimation," JRI, 1987, v54(3), 582-593.

Weiss, Mary. "A Multivariate Analysis Of Loss Reserving Estimates In Property-Liability Insurers," JRI, 1985, v52(2), 199-221.

Weiss, Steven J. (Gonyer, George H. and Steven J. Weiss. "The Competitive Effects Of Demand Deposit Powers For Thrift Institutions In Connecticut," JBR, 1976-77, v7(2), 104-112.)

Weiss, Steven J. (Piper, Thomas R. and Steven J. Weiss. "The Profitability Of Multibank Holding Company Acquisitions," JOF, 1974, v29(1), 163-174.)

Weiss, Yoram. (Sheshinski, Eytan and Yoram Weiss. "Optimum Pricing Policy Under Stochastic Inflation," RIF, 1983, v4, (Supp), 189-208.)

Weissbrod, Doron. "Index-Linked Life Insurance In Israel And The Sharir Committee," JRI, 1984, v51(2), 336-341.

Weissman, Jacob. "The Role Of Law In Education For Business," JOB, 1960, v33(4), 348-356.

Weissman, Rudolph L. "Valuation And Nationalization Of Industry In Britain," FAJ, 1949, v5(3), 24-25.

Welam, Ulf Peter. "Company Contributions To Discretionary Profit-Sharing Plans: Comment," JOF, 1976, v31(3), 986-990.

Welch, Ivo. "Seasoned Offerings, Imitation Costs, And The Underpricing Of Initial Public Offerings," JOF, 1989, v44(2), 421-450.

Welch, Jonathan B. "Explaining Disintermediation At Mutual Savings Banks," FAJ, 1980, v36(3), 71-76.

Welch, Jonathan B. (Murali, Ramaswami and Jonathan B. Welch. "Agents, Owners, Control And Performance," JBFA, 1989, v16(3), 385-398.)

Welch, Patrick J. and Jude L. Naes, Jr. "The Merger Guidelines, Concentration And Excess Capacity In Local Commercial Banking Markets," JBR, 1985-86, v16(3), 158-160.

Welland, Deborah A. "Workers' Compensation Liability Changes And The Distribution Of Injury Claims," JRI, 1986, v53(4), 662-678.

Wellisz, Stanislaw. "The European Common Market And American Foreign Trade And Investment," JOB, 1959, v32(3), 244-257.

Wells, Alfred T., Jr. "Coal Industry Review," FAJ, 1964, v20(5), 63-74.

Wells, Paul. "Liquidity Preference And The Flow Of Finance," JMCB, 1971, v3(1), 123-136.

Wells, Warren. "Titanium - A Metal With A Future," FAJ, 1950, v6(1), 17-18.

Wells, William D. (Reynolds, Fred D. and William D. Wells. "Life Style Analysis: A Dimension For Future-Oriented Bank Research," JBR, 1978-79, v9(3), 181-185.)

Welshans, Merle T. (Dauten, Carl A. and Merle T. Welshans. "Investment Development Companies," JOF, 1951, v6(3), 276-290.)

Welty, Dan M. "A Need For Federal Insurance Regulation," JRI, 1967, v34(2), 329-332.

Wenck, Thomas L. "Eliminating A Traditional Dichotomy," JRI, 1968, v35(3), 461-466.

Wenck, Thomas L. "Financing Senior Citizen Health Care: An Alternative Approach," JRI, 1965, v32(2), 165-176.

Wenck, Thomas L. "Some Observations About Business Schools," JRI, 1969, v36(4), 629-631.

Wenck, Thomas L. "Standard Hospitalization Insurance Contracts," JRI, 1964, v31(1), 73-82.

Wenck, Thomas L. "The Historical Development Of Standard Policies," JRI, 1968, v35(4), 537-550.

Wendel, Jeanne. (Osborne, D. K. and Jeanne Wendel. "A Note On Concentration And Checking Account Prices," JOF, 1981, v36(1), 181-186.)

Wendt, Paul F. and Daniel B. Rathbun. "The Role Of Government In The San Francisco Bay Area Mortgage Market," JOF, 1951, v6(4), 383-397.

Wendt, Paul F. and Sui N. Wong. "Investment Performance: Common Stocks Versus Apartment Houses," JOF, 1965, v20(4), 633-646.

Wendt, Paul F. "Current Growth Stock Valuation Methods," FAJ, 1965, v21(2), 91-103.

Wendt, Paul F. "Determination Of Investment Policy," FAJ, 1968, v24(1), 91-96.

Wendt, Paul F. "Individual Investment Policy And The New Economics," JOF, 1950, v5(2), 201-214.

Wendt, Paul F. "Large-Scale Community Development," JOF, 1967, v22(2), 220-239.

Wendt, Paul F. "New Techniques Of Financing Real Estate," AREUEA, 1973, v1(1), 140-157.

Wendt, Paul F. "Term Loans To Small Business In California, 1945-46," JOF, 1948, v3(2), 45-58.

Wendt, Paul F. "The Availability Of Capital To Small Business In California In 1945-46," JOF, 1947, v2(2), 43-54.

Wendt, Paul F. "The Outlook For California Commercial Banks," FAJ, 1964, v20(4), 59-65.

Wendt, Paul F. "What Should We Teach In An Investment Course?," JOF, 1966, v21(2), 416-422.

Wendt, Paul F. and Richard L. Haney, Jr. "Secondary Mortgage Market Performance Under Pressure," AREUEA, 1975, v3(2), 31-42.

Werboff, Lawrence L. "The Effects Of Instalment Credit Term Variation," JOF, 1959, v14(3), 379-389.

Werczberger, Elia. "The Experience With Rent Control In Israel: From Rental Housing To Condominiums," JREFEC, 1988, v1(3), 277-294.

Wermel, Michael T. "The Role Of Management In Retirement Preparation Programs," JRI, 1960, v27(2), 37-44.

Werner, Frank M. (Ben-Shahar, Haim and Frank M. Werner. "Multiperiod Capital Budgeting Under Uncertainty: A Suggested Application," JFQA, 1977, v12(5), 859-877.)

Werner, Robert F. "The Federal Government And Portfolio Policy," FAJ, 1966, v22(1), 81-82.

Werner, Walter. (Robbins, Sidney and Walter Werner. "Professor Stigler Revisited," JOB, 1964, v37(4), 406-413.)

Wernerfelt, Birger. "Advertising Content When Brand Choice Is A Signal," JOB, 1990, v63(1), Part 1, 91-98.

Wernerfelt, Birger. (Sappington, David E. M. and Birger Wernerfelt. "To Brand Or Not To Brand? A Theoretical And Empirical Question," JOB, 1985, v58(3), 279-294.)

Wert, James E. "Content Orientation In The Introductory Finance Course," JFQA, 1975, v10(4), 695-698.

Wert, James E. (Fredman, Albert J. and James E. Wert. "Secondary Distributions," FAJ, 1968, v24(6), 165-168.)

Wert, James E. (Jen, Frank C. and James E. Wert. "The Effect Of Call Risk On Corporate Bond Yields," JOF, 1967, v22(4), 637-651.)

Wert, James E. (Jen, Frank C. and James E. Wert. "Imputed Yields Of A Sinking Fund Bond And The Term Structure Of Interest Rates," JOF, 1966, v21(4), 697-713.)

Wert, James E. (Jen, Frank C. and James E. Wert. "The Deferred Call Provision And Corporate Bond Yields," JFQA, 1968, v3(2), 157-170.)

Wert, James E. (Jen, Frank C. and James E. Wert. "Sinking Funds And Bond Yields," FAJ, 1967, v23(2), 125-131.)

Wert, James E. (Sorensen, Eric H. and James E. Wert. "A New Tool For Estimating New Issue Bond Yields," JPM, 1980-81, v7(3), 42-45.)

Wessels, R. E. (Van Den Bergh, W. M. and R. E. Wessels. "Stock Market Seasonality And Taxes: An Examination Of The Tax-Loss Selling Hypothesis," JBFA, 1985, v12(4), 515-530.)

Wessels, Roberto. (Titman, Sheridan and Roberto Wessels. "The Determinants Of Capital Structure Choice," JOF, 1988, v43(1), 1-19.)

West, B. Kenneth. (Sprinkel, Beryl W. and B. Kenneth West. "Effects Of Capital Gains Taxes On Investment Decisions," JOB, 1962, v35(2), 122-134.)

West, David A. and Arthur A. Eubank, Jr. "An Automatic Cost Of Capital Adjustment Model For Regulating Public Utilities," FM, 1976, v5(1), 23-31.

West, David A. "Risk Analysis In The 1960's," FAJ, 1967, v23(6), 124-126.

West, David A. and Glenn L. Wood. "Risk Attitudes Of Annuity-Prone Investors," JRI, 1970, v37(1), 9-16.

West, Elizabeth N. (Herbst, Anthony F., Joseph P. McCormack and Elizabeth N. West. "Investigation Of A Lead-Lag Relationship Between Spot Indices And Their Futures Contracts," JFM, 1987, v7(4), 373-382.)

West, Kenneth D. "Bubbles, Fads, And Stock Price Volatility Tests: A Partial Evaluation," JOF, 1988, v43(3), 639-656.

West, Phillip L. "Progress In The Public Interest," FAJ, 1956, v12(1), 29-32.

West, R. R. (Hausman, W. H., R. R. West and J. A. Largay. "Stock Splits, Price Changes, And Trading Profits: A Synthesis," JOB, 1971, v44(1), 69-77.)

West, Richard R. and James A. Largay, III. "Premium On Convertible Bonds: Comment," JOF, 1972, v27(5), 1156-1162.

West, Richard R. and Seha M. Tinic. "Portfolio Returns And The Random Walk Theory: Comment," JOF, 1973, v28(3), 733-741.

West, Richard R. and Seha M. Tinic. "Corporate Finance And The Changing Stock Market," FM, 1974, v3(3), 14-23.

West, Richard R. and Seha Tinic. "Critique Of Schaefer And Warner," FAJ, 1978, v34(3), 46,50-56.

West, Richard R. "Conflicts Of Interest," FAJ, 1971, v27(6), 31-39.

West, Richard R. "Determinants Of Underwriters' Spreads On Tax Exempt Bond Issues," JFQA, 1967, v2(3), 241-263.

West, Richard R. "Mutual Fund Performance And The Theory Of Capital Asset Pricing: Some Comments," JOB, 1968, v41(2), 230-234.

West, Richard R. "Quiet Revolution In The Stock Market," FAJ, 1971, v27(3), 17-24,71-72,78.

West, Richard R. "Simulating Securities Markets Operations: Some Examples, Observations, And Comments," JFQA, 1970, v5(1), 115-137.

West, Richard R. "The Teaching Of Investments - Is 'Witchcraft' Still Appropriate?," JFQA, 1974, v9(5), 789-793.

West, Richard R. "The William Morris Episode," FAJ, 1965, v21(4), 119-122.

West, Richard R. "Two Kinds Of Market Efficiency," FAJ, 1975, v31(6), 30-34.

West, Richard R. "When Is A GIC Not A GIC?," FAJ, 1983, v39(1), 24-26.

West, Richard R. "'Homemade' Diversification Vs. Corporate Diversification," JFQA, 1967, v2(4), 417-420.

West, Richard R. (Fabozzi, Frank J. and Richard R. West. "Negotiated Versus Competitive Underwritings Of Public Utility Bonds: Just One More Time," JFQA, 1981, v16(3), 323-339.)

West, Richard R. (Page, Alfred N. and Richard R. West. "Evaluating Student Performance In Graduate Schools Of Business," JOB, 1969, v42(1), 36-41.)

West, Richard R. (Tinic, Seha M. and Richard R. West. "Marketability Of Common Stocks In Canada And The U.S.A.: A Comparison Of Agent Versus Dealer Dominated Markets," JOF, 1974, v29(3), 729-746.)

West, Richard R. (Tinic, Seha M., Giovanni Barone-Adesi and Richard R. West. "Seasonality In Canadian Stock Prices: A Test Of The 'Tax-Loss-Selling' Hypothesis," JFQA, 1987, v22(1), 51-64.)

West, Richard R. (Tinic, Seha M. and Richard R. West. "Competition And The Pricing Of Dealer Service In The Over-The-Counter Stock Market," JFQA, 1972, v7(3), 1707-1727.)

West, Richard R. (Tinic, Seha M. and Richard R. West. "Risk And Return: January Vs. The Rest Of The Year," JFEC, 1984, v13(4), 561-574.)

West, Richard R. and Harold Bierman, Jr. "Corporate Dividend Policy And Preemptive Security Issues," JOB, 1968, v41(1), 71-75.

West, Richard W. "Comment: Teaching, Research And The Human Capital Paradigm," FPE, 1991, v1(1), 17-20.

West, Richard. "More On The Effects Of Municipal Bond Monopsony," JOB, 1966, v39(2), 305-308.

West, Richard. "New Issue Concessions On Municipal Bonds: A Case Of Monopsony Pricing," JOB, 1965, v38(2), 135-148.

West, Richard. (Bierman, Harold, Jr. and Richard West. "The Acquisition Of Common Stock By The Corporate Issuer," JOF, 1966, v21(4), 687-696.)

West, Richard. (Bierman, Harold, Jr. and Richard West. "The Effect Of Share Repurchase On The Value Of The Firm: Some Further Comments," JOF, 1968, v23(5), 865-869.)

West, Robert Craig. "A Factor-Analytic Approach To Bank Condition," JBF, 1985, v9(2), 253-266.

West, Stan and Thomas T. Murphy. "Caveats For Market Technicians," FAJ, 1978, v34(5), 42-48.

West, Stan. (Miller, Norman and Stan West. "Why The NYSE Common Stock Indexes?," FAJ, 1967, v23(3), 49-54.)

Westerfield, Randolph. "A Note On The Measurement Of Conglomerate Diversification," JOF, 1970, v25(4), 909-914.

Westerfield, Randolph. "The Distribution Of Common Stock Price Changes: An Application Of Transactions Time And Subordinated Stochastic Models," JFQA, 1977, v12(5), 743-765.

Westerfield, Randolph. (Cummins, J. David, John R. Percival, Randolph Westerfield and J. G. Ramage. "Effects Of ERISA On The Investment Policies Of Private Pension Plans: Survey Evidence," JRI, 1980, v47(3), 447-476.)

Westerfield, Randolph. (Cummins, J. David and Randolph Westerfield. "Patterns Of Concentration In Private Pension Plan Common Stock Portfolios Since ERISA," JRI, 1981, v48(2), 201-219.)

Westerfield, Randolph. (Friend, Irwin, Randolph Westerfield and Michael Granito. "New Evidence On The Capital Asset Pricing Model," JOF, 1978, v33(3), 903-917.)

Westerfield, Randolph. (Friend, Irwin and Randolph Westerfield. "Risk And Capital Asset Prices," JBF, 1981, v5(3), 291-315.)

Westerfield, Randolph. (Friend, Irwin and Randolph Westerfield. "Co-Skewness And Capital Assets Pricing," JOF, 1980, v35(4), 897-913.)

Westerfield, Randolph. (Jaffe, Jeffrey F. and Randolph Westerfield. "Leverage And The Value Of A Firm Under A Progressive Income Tax: A Correction And Extension," JBF, 1984, v8(3), 491-494.)

Westerfield, Randolph. (Jaffe, Jeffrey and Randolph Westerfield. "Patterns In Japanese Common Stock Returns: Day Of The Week And Turn Of The Year Effects," JFQA, 1985, v20(2), 261-272.)

Westerfield, Randolph. (Jaffe, Jeffrey and Randolph Westerfield. "The Week-End Effect In Common Stock Returns: The International Evidence," JOF, 1985, v40(2), 433-454.)

Westerfield, Randolph. (Jaffe, Jeffrey and Randolph Westerfield. "Is There A Monthly Effect In Stock Market Returns?: Evidence From Foreign Countries," JBF, 1989, v13(2), 237-244.)

Westerfield, Randolph. (Jaffe, Jeffrey F., Randolph Westerfield and Christopher Ma. "A Twist On The Monday Effect In Stock Prices: Evidence From The U.S. And Foreign Stock Markets," JBF, 1989, v13(4/5), 641-650.)

Westerfield, Randolph. (Jaffe, Jeffrey, Donald B. Keim and Randolph Westerfield. "Earnings Yields, Market Values, And Stock Returns," JOF, 1989, v44(1), 135-148.)

Westerfield, Randolph. (Keeley, Robert H. and Randolph Westerfield. "A Problem In Probability Distribution Techniques For Capital Budgeting," JOF, 1972, v27(3), 703-709.)

Westerfield, Randolph. (Pettit, R. Richardson and Randolph Westerfield. "Using The Capital Asset Pricing Model And The Market Model To Predict Security Returns," JFQA, 1974, v9(4), 579-605.)

Westerfield, Randolph. (Pettit, R. Richardson and Randolph Westerfield. "A Model Of Capital Asset Risk," JFQA, 1972, v7(2), 1649-1668.)

Westergaard, John. (Black, Fischer, Yale Hirsch and John Westergaard. "Nuggets," JPM, 1976-77, v3(2), 71-77.)

Westfield, Fred M. "Practicing Marginal Cost Pricing-A Review," JOB, 1966, v39(1), Part I, 67-73.

Weston, C. R. "Adjustment To Future Dividend Rates In The Prediction Of Ex-Rights Prices," JBFA, 1974, v1(3), 335-342.

Weston, C. R. "The Information Content Of Rights Trading: A Reply," JBFA, 1981, v8(3), 441-443.

Weston, C. R. "The Information Content Of Rights Trading," JBFA, 1978, v5(1), 85-92.

Weston, Frank T. and Sidney Davidson. "Accounting Changes And Earnings," FAJ, 1968, v24(5), 59-66.

Weston, Frank T. "Reporting Earnings Per Share," FAJ, 1967, v23(4), 45-53.

Weston, J. Fred and Nai-Fu Chen. "A Note On Capital Budgeting And The Three Rs," FM, 1980, v9(1), 12-13.

Weston, J. Fred and Pham D. Tuan. "Comment On Analysis Of Credit Policy Changes," FM, 1980, v9(4), 59-63.

Weston, J. Fred and Surendra K. Mansinghka. "Tests Of The Efficiency Performance Of Conglomerate Firms," JOF, 1971, v26(4), 919-936.

Weston, J. Fred and Surendra K. Mansinghka. "Conglomerate Performance Measurement: Comment," JOF, 1974, v29(3), 1011-1012.

Weston, J. Fred and Surendra K. Mansinghka. "Performance Of Conglomerate Firms: Reply," JOF, 1973, v28(3), 759.

Weston, J. Fred and Wayne Y. Lee. "Cost Of Capital For A Division Of A Firm: Comment," JOF, 1977, v32(5), 1779-1780.

Weston, J. Fred. "A Managerial Orientation In The First Finance Course," JF\QA, 1975, v10(4), 699-704.

Weston, J. Fred. "A Not-So-New Era In The Stock Market," FAJ, 1960, v16(6), 57-66.

Weston, J. Fred. "A Note On Merger Valuation: Reply," JOF, 1968, v23(3), 535-536.

Weston, J. Fred. "A Proposed Outline For A Course In The Theory Of Managerial Finance," JFED, 1976, v5, 3-7.

Weston, J. Fred. "Developments In Finance Theory," FM, v10(2), Tenth Anniversary Edition, 5-22.

Weston, J. Fred. "Divestitures: Mistakes Or Learning," JACF, 1989, v2(2), 68-76.

Weston, J. Fred. "From Practice To Theory," FM, 1981, v10, FM, 1981, v10(1), 7-8.

Weston, J. Fred. "Investment Decisions Using The Capital Asset Pricing Model," FM, 1973, v2(1), 25-33.

Weston, J. Fred. "New Themes In Finance," JOF, 1974, v29(1), 237-243.

Weston, J. Fred. "Norms For Debt Levels," JOF, 1954, v9(2), 124-135.

Weston, J. Fred. "The Finance Function," JOF, 1954, v9(3), 265-282.

Weston, J. Fred. "The Industrial Economics Background Of The Penn Central Bankruptcy," JOF, 1971, v26(2), 311-326.

Weston, J. Fred. "The Management Of Corporate Capital: A Review Article," JOB, 1961, v34(2), 129-139.

Weston, J. Fred. "The Recent Merger Movement," JOB, 1952, v25(1), 30-38.

Weston, J. Fred. "The State Of The Finance Field," JOF, 1967, v22(4), 539-540.

Weston, J. Fred. "The State Of The Finance Field," JRI, 1967, v34(4), 617-620.

Weston, J. Fred. "Toward Theories Of Financial Policy," JOF, 1955, v10(2), 130-143.

Weston, J. Fred. "What MM Have Wrought," FM, 1989, v18(2), 29-38.

Weston, J. Fred. (Beranek, William and J. Fred Weston. "Programming Investment Portfolio Construction," FAJ, 1955, v11(2), 51-56.)

Weston, J. Fred. (Copeland, Thomas E. and J. Fred Weston. "A Note On The Evaluation Of Cancellable Operating Leases," FM, 1982, v11(2), 60-67.)

Weston, J. Fred. (Eiteman, David K. and J. Fred Weston. "Economic Trends And Security Values - A Bleak Or Bountiful Future For Investors?," FAJ, 1965, v21(1), 21-32.)

Weston, J. Fred. (Hsia, Chi-Cheng and J. Fred Weston. "Price Behavior Of Deep Discount Bonds," JBF, 1981, v5(3), 357-361.)

Weston, J. Fred. (Ricks, R. Bruce and J. Fred Weston. "Land As A Growth Investment," FAJ, 1966, v22(4), 69-78.)

Wethyavivorn, Kulpatra. (Shastri, Kuldeep and Kulpatra Wethyavivorn. "The Valuation Of Currency Options For Alternate Stochastic Processes," JFR, 1987, v10(4), 283-294.)

Wethyavivorn, Kulpatra. (Shastri, Kuldeep and Kulpatra Wethyavivorn. "Pricing Of Foreign Currency Options For Arbitrary Stochastic Processes," JBFA, 1990, v17(2), 323-334.)

Wetmore, Jill L. T. and John R. Brick. "Interest Rate Risk And The Optimal Gap For Commercial Banks: An Empirical Study," FR, 1990, v25(4), 539-558.

Weygandt, Jerry J. "A Comment On Financing With Convertible Preferred Stock," JOF, 1971, v26(1), 148-149.

Weygandt, Jerry J. (Linsmeier, Thomas J., R. D. Nair and Jerry J. Weygandt. "UK Tax Legislation And The Switch To The Liability Method For Income Taxes," JBFA, 1988, v15(3), 335-352.)

Weygandt, Jerry J. (Thompson, Howard E. and Jerry J. Weygandt. "The Rate-Making Treatment Of The Investment Tax Credit For Public Utilities," JOB, 1977, v50(4), 508-519.)

Whalen, Edward L. "A Cross-Section Study Of Business Demand For Cash," JOF, 1965, v20(3), 423-443.

Whalen, Edward L. "An Extension Of The Baumol-Tobin Approach To The Transactions Demand For Cash," JOF, 1968, v23(1), 113-134.

White, Harry L. (MacDonald, Don N., Harry L. White, Paul M. Taube and William L. Huth. "Flood Hazard Pricing And Insurance Premium Differentials: Evidence From The Housing Market," JRI, 1990, v57(4), 654-663.)

White, Harry L. (Maris, Brian A. and Harry L. White. "Valuing And Hedging Fixed-Rate Mortgage Commitments," JREFEC, 1989, v2(3), 223-232.)

White, Harry. (Barney, L. Dwayne and Harry White. "The Optimal Mortgage Payment Path Under Price Uncertainty," AREUEA, 1986, v14(3), 406-413.)

White, Harry. (Barney, L. Dwayne, Jr., Alan Frankle and Harry White. "Reserve Requirements And The Inflation Tax," JMCB, 1990, v22(3), 400-401.)

White, Hubert D. and David A. Torgerson. "The Fed's Performance: What Does It Imply For EFTS?: Comment," JBR, 1974-75, v5(3), 193-196.

White, I. Thomas. (Gitman, Lawrence J., Edward A. Moses and I. Thomas White. "An Assessment Of Corporate Cash Management Practices," FM, 1979, v8(1), 32-41.)

White, J. R. "Unit Trusts, Homogenous Beliefs And The Separation Property," JBFA, 1981, v8(1), 61-78.

White, Jane H. (Avard, Stephen L. and Jane H. White. "Readability Study Of Principles Of Financial Management Textbooks," JFED, 1986, v15, 53-62.)

White, Joseph. (Guenther, Harry and Joseph White. "EFT System Privacy Safeguards: A Preliminary Inquiry Into The Privacy-Leisure Time Trade-Off," JBR, 1979-80, v10(3), 136-144.)

White, Kenneth J. "The Effect Of Bank Credit On The Household Transactions Demand For Money," JMCB, 1976, v8(1), 51-61.

White, Lawrence H. "Accounting For Non-Interest-Bearing Currency: A Critique Of The Legal Restrictions Theory Of Money," JMCB, 1987, v19(4), 448-456.

White, Lawrence H. "Scottish Banking And The Legal Restrictions Theory: A Closer Look," JMCB, 1990, v22(4), 526-536.

White, Lawrence J. "Price Regulation And Quality Rivalry In A Profit-Maximizing Model: The Case Of Bank Branching," JMCB, 1976, v8(1), 97-106.

White, Lawrence J. "The Title Insurance Industry, Reverse Competition, And Controlled Business - A Different View," JRI, 1984, v51(2), 308-319.

White, Lawrence J. (Aftalion, Florin and Lawrence J. White. "On The Choice Of Immediate Monetary Targets," JBF, 1978, v2(1), 1-13.)

White, Lawrence J. (Aftalion, Florin and Lawrence J. White. "A Study Of A Monetary System With Pegged Discount Rate Under Different Market Structures: A Reply To J. Vuchelen," JBF, 1978, v2(4), 351-354.)

White, Lawrence J. (Aftalion, Florin and Lawrence J. White. "A Study Of A Monetary System With A Pegged Discount Rate Under Different Market Structures," JBF, 1977, v1(4), 349-371.)

White, Mark A. (Tse, K. S. Maurice and Mark A. White. "The Valuation Of Semiannual Bonds Between Interest Payment Dates: A Correction," FR, 1990, v25(4), 659-662.)

White, Michelle J. "Bankruptcy Costs And The New Bankruptcy Code," JOF, 1983, v38(2), 477-488.

White, Michelle J. "Commuting And Congestion: A Simulation Model Of A Decentralized Metropolitan Area," AREUEA, 1990, v18(3), 335-368.

White, R. W. and P. A. Lusztig. "The Price Effects Of Rights Offerings," JFQA, 1980, v15(1), 25-40.

White, Reba. "Coping With The Financial Reporter," FAJ, 1978, v34(2), 38-40.

White, Richard E. (Dyl, Edward A., Richard E. White, Richard Norgaard and Corine Norgaard. "A Critical Examination Of Share Repurchase: Dyl And White Versus Norgaard And Norgaard," FM, 1974, v3(3), 68-73.)

White, Richard E. (Pruitt, Stephen W. and Richard E. White. "Who Says Technical Analysis Can't Beat The Market?," JPM, 1987-88, v14(3), 55-58.)

White, Richard E. (Pruitt, Stephen W. and Richard E. White. "Exchange-Traded Options And CRISMA Trading," JPM, 1989, v15(4), 55-57.)

White, Robert W. (Hatch, James E. and Robert W. White. "A Canadian Perspective On Canadian And United States Capital Market Returns: 1950-1983," FAJ, 1986, v42(3), 60-68.)

White, Robert W. (Murray, John D. and Robert W. White. "Economies Of Scale And Economies Of Scope In Multiproduct Financial Institutions: A Study Of British Columbia Credit Unions," JOF, 1983, v38(3), 887-902.)

White, Robert W. (Murray, John D. and Robert W. White. "Economies Of Scale And Deposit-Taking Financial Institutions In Canada: A Study Of British Columbia Credit Unions," JMCB, 1980, v12(1), 58-70.)

White, Sammis B. "Translating Housing Analysis Into Housing Policy," AREUEA, 1974, v2(2), 59-80.

White, W. L. (Hausman, W. H. and W. L. White. "Theory Of Option Strategy Under Risk Aversion," JFQA, 1968, v3(3), 343-358.)

White, Walter E. "Secular & Cyclical Trends In U. S. Economy," FAJ, 1959, v15(4), 77-80.

White, William G. "What's Ahead For The Motor Freight Carriers?," FAJ, 1965, v21(4), 67-71.

White, William H. "Effects Of Tight Money On 1966 Business Investment: The True Findings Of The Commerce Department-Wharton Survey," JMCB, 1970, v2(4), 446-460.

White, William L. "Debt Management And The Form Of Business Financing," JOF, 1974, v29(2), 565-577.

White, William L. (Shapiro, Eli and William L. White. "Patterns Of Business Financing: Some Comments," JOF, 1965, v20(4), 693-707.)

Whitehead, Louis H. "Electronics Industry In Europe," FAJ, 1959, v15(3), 41-48.

Whitesell, William C. "The Demand For Currency Versus Debitable Accounts," JMCB, 1989, v21(2), 246-251.

Whiteside, Mary M. William P. Dukes and Patrick M. Dunne. "Short Term Impact Of Option Trading On Underlying Securities," JFR, 1983, v6(4), 313-321.

Whitestone, Bruce. "United States And Canadian Stock Markets," FAJ, 1960, v16(4), 49-50.

Whitford, David T. and Frank K. Reilly. "What Makes Stock Prices Move?," JPM, 1984-85, v11(2), 23-30.

Whitford, David T. (Chu, Chen-Chin and David T. Whitford. "Stock Market Returns And Inflationary Expectations: Additional Evidence For 1975-1979," JFR, 1982, v5(3), 261-271.)

Whitford, David T. (Davis, Wayne J. and David T. Whitford. "Tests Of Competition Models For Resource Allocation: Good News And Bad News," AFPAF, 1989, v3(1), 375-393.)

Whitford, David T. (Gentry, James A., David T. Whitford and Paul Newbold. "Predicting Industrial Bond Ratings With A Probit Model And Funds Flow Components," FR, 1988, v23(3), 269-286.)

Whitford, David T. (Gentry, James A., Paul Newbold and David T. Whitford. "Predicting Bankruptcy: If Cash Flow's Not The Bottom Line, What Is?," FAJ, 1985, v41(5), 47-56.)

Whitford, David T. (Gentry, James A., Paul Newbold and David T. Whitford. "Funds Flow Components, Financial Ratios, And Bankruptcy," JBFA, 1987, v14(4), 595-606.)

Whitford, David T. (Gentry, James A., Paul Newbold and David T. Whitford. "Profiles Of Cash Flow Components," FAJ, 1990, v46(4), 41-48.)

Whitford, David T. (Mehta, Dileep R. and David T. Whitford. "Lease Financing And The M&M Propositions," FR, 1979, v14(1), 47-58.)

Whitford, David T. (Reilly, Frank K. and David T. Whitford. "A Test Of The Specialists' Short Sale Ratio," JPM, 1981-82, v8(2), 12-18.)

Whitford, David T. (Wacht, Richard F. and David T. Whitford. "A Goal Programming Model For Capital Investment Analysis In Nonprofit Hospitals," FM, 1976, v5(2), 37-47.)

Whitin, T. M. "Output Dimensions And Their Implications For Cost And Price Analysis," JOB, 1972, v45(2), 305-315.

Whitman, A. F. and H. E. Thompson. "Impact Of Alternative Forms Of Life Insurance Company Income Tax Legislation," JRI, 1968, v35(1), 107-117.

Whitman, Andrew F. (Williams, C. Arthur, Jr. and Andrew F. Whitman. "Open Competition Rating Laws And Price Competition," JRI, 1973, v40(4), 483-496.)

Whitman, Andrew F. and C. Arthur Williams, Jr. "Environmental Hazards And Rating Urban Core Properties," JRI, 1970, v37(3), 419-436.

Whitman, Andrew F. and C. Arthur Williams, Jr. "FAIR Plan And Excess Rate Plan Rates In Minnesota," JRI, 1971, v38(1), 43-59.

Whitman, Andrew F. and Howard E. Thompson. "The Impact Of The 1959 Income Tax Act On Stock And Mutual Companies: A Simulation Study," JRI, 1967, v34(2), 215-230.

Whitman, Marina V. N. "Economic Openness And International Financial Flows," JMCB, 1969, v1(4), 727-749.

Whitman, Marina V. N. "Global Monetarism: Theory, Policy, And Critique," JPM, 1976-77, v3(3), 7-18.

Whitman, Marina V. N. (Miller, Norman C. and Marina V. N. Whitman. "Alternative Theories And Tests Of U. S. Short-Term Foreign Investment," JOF, 1973, v28(5), 1131-1150.)

Whitman, Martin J. "Let's Reform Exchange Prospectuses," FAJ, 1973, v29(5), 44-46,85-89.

Whitman, W. Tate. (Cottle, C. Sidney and W. Tate Whitman. "Testing Formula Plans," JOF, 1951, v6(2), 220-228.)

Whitmarsh, Theodore F. "When To Sell Short Against The Box," FAJ, 1972, v28(3), 80-81,78.

Whitmore, G. A. and Lloyd R. Amey. "Capital Budgeting Under Rationing: Comments On The Lusztig And Schwab Procedure," JFQA, 1973, v8(1), 127-135.

Whitmore, G. A. "A Note On The Exact Calculation Of Accrued Interest And Bond Pricing," FAJ, 1985, v41(2), 76-77.

Whitmore, G. A. "Diversification And The Reduction Of Dispersion: A Note," JFQA, 1970, v5(2), 263-264.

Whitmore, G. A. "Market Demand Curve For Common Stock And The Maximization Of Market Value," JFQA, 1970, v5(1), 105-114.

Whitmore, G. A. "Probability Analysis Of The Cash Outflow For Mortality," JRI, 1970, v37(1), 75-86.

Whitmore, G. A. "Stochastic Dominance Contributions To The Economic Theory Of Search Behavior," RIF, 1980, v2, 139-162.

Whitmore, G. A. (Findlay, M. Chapman, III and G. A. Whitmore. "Beyond Shareholder Wealth Maximization," FM, 1974, v3(4), 25-35.)

Whitmore, G. A. (Neter, J., C. A. Williams, Jr. and G. A. Whitmore. "Comparison Of Independent And Joint Decision-Making For Two Insurance Decisions," JRI, 1968, v35(1), 87-105.)

Whitney, Alan D. "Odd Lot Trading As A Market Barometer," FAJ, 1948, v4(1), 58-66.

Whitney, Alan D. "The Middle Road," FAJ, 1955, v11(1), 91-92.

Whitney, Gerald A. (Swofford, James L. and Gerald A. Whitney. "Flexible Functional Forms And The Utility Approach To The Demand For Money: A Nonparametric Analysis," JMCB, 1986, v18(3), 383-389.)

Whitney, Jack M., II. "The S.E.C. And The Financial Analyst," FAJ, 1963, v19(4), 11-14.

Whitney, Simon N. "Errors In The Concept Of Countervailing Power," JOB, 1953, v26(4), 238-253.

Whitney, Simon N. (Dewhurst, J. Frederic and Simon N. Whitney. "Alternatives," FAJ, 1951, v7(1), 17-20.)

Whitt, Joseph A., Jr. (Koch, Paul D., Jeffrey A. Rosenweig and Joseph A. Whitt, Jr. "The Dynamic Relationship Between The Dollar And US Prices: An Intensive Empirical Investigation," JIMF, 1988, v7(2), 181-204.)

Whittaker, Gregg, Linda E. Bowyer and Daniel P. Klein. "The Effect Of Futures Trading On The Municipal Bond Market," RFM, 1987, v6(2), 196-204.

Whittaker, R. A. (Nguyen, D. T. and R. A. Whittaker. "Inflation, Replacement And Amortisation Funds: A Case Study Of U.K. Industries," JBFA, 1976, v3(1), 43-52.)

Whittall, David. "A Simulation Model," FAJ, 1968, v24(6), 115-118.

Whittington, G. (Jones, C. J., D. P. Tweedie and G. Whittington. "The Regression Portfolio: A Statistical Investigation Of A Relative Decline Model," JBFA, 1976, v3(2), 71-92.)

Whittington, Geoffrey. "A Comment On The Efficient Markets Interpretation Of A Relative Decline Model," JBFA, 1978, v5(2), 269-273.

Whittington, Geoffrey. "Some Basic Properties Of Accounting Ratios," JBFA, 1980, v7(2), 219-232.

Willett, Thomas D. and Edward Tower. "The Welfare Economics Of International Adjustment," JOF, 1971, v26(2), 287-302.

Willett, Thomas D. "Exchange-Rate Volatility, International Trade, And Resource Allocation: A Perspective On Recent Research," JIMF, 1986(Supp), S101-S112.

Willett, Thomas D. (Laney, Leroy O. and Thomas D. Willett. "The International Liquidity Explosion And Worldwide Inflation: The Evidence From Sterilization Coefficient Estimates," JIMF, 1982, v1(2), 141-152.)

Willett, Thomas. (Tollison, Robert D. and Thomas Willett. "A Defense Of The CEA As An Instrument For Giving Economic Policy Advice: A Comment," JMCB, 1975, v7(1), 113-116.)

Willhour, Richard. (Ang, James and Richard Willhour. "The Consumer Loan Supply Function Of A Minority Bank: An Empirical Note: A Comment," JMCB, 1976, v8(2), 255-259.)

William J. Baumol and Associates. "The Role Of Cost In The Minimum Pricing Of Railroad Services," JOB, 1962, v35(4), 357-366.

Williams, Alan C. "Educator Seminar On Insurance," JRI, 1971, v38(1), 117-118.

Williams, Alex O. and Phillip E. Pfeifer. "Estimating Security Price Risk Using Duration And Price Elasticity," JOF, 1982, v37(2), 399-411.

Williams, Alex O., William Beranek and James Kenkel. "Default Risk In Urban Mortgages: A Pittsburgh Prototype Analysis," AREUEA, 1974, v2(2), 101-116.

Williams, Arlington W. "Computerized Double-Auction Markets: Some Initial Experimental Results," JOB, 1980, v53(3), Part 1, 235-258.

Williams, Arlington W. "The Formation Of Price Forecasts In Experimental Markets," JMCB, 1987, v19(1), 1-18.

Williams, Arlington W. and Vernon L. Smith. "Cyclical Double-Auction Markets With And Without Speculators," JOB, 1984, v57(1), Part 1, 1-34.

Williams, Arthur L. "Some Empirical Observations On Term Life Insurance," JRI, 1964, v31(3), 445-450.

Williams, Arthur, III. "The Bond Market Line: Measuring Risk And Reward," JPM, 1979-80, v6(4), 62-64.

Williams, B. Earl. (Born, Waldo and B. Earl Williams. "Electronic Data Transmission Pathways: Implications For Site Selection," JRER, 1989, v4(3), 95-105.)

Williams, C. A., Jr. (Neter, J., C. A. Williams, Jr. and G. A. Whitmore. "Comparison Of Independent And Joint Decision-Making For Two Insurance Decisions," JRI, 1968, v35(1), 87-105.)

Williams, C. Arthur, Jr. "A Method Of Automatically Adjusting The Maximum Earnings Base Under OASDI: Comment," JRI, 1965, v32(3), 465-468.

Williams, C. Arthur, Jr. "Achieving Our Potential," JRI, 1965, v32(4), 501-508.

Williams, C. Arthur, Jr. "An Analysis Of Current Experience And Retrospective Rating Plans," JRI, 1954, v9(4), 377-411.

Williams, C. Arthur, Jr. "Analyzing The Expenses Incurred By Private Workmen's Compensation Insurers," JRI, 1961, v28(1), 71-82.

Williams, C. Arthur, Jr. "Attitudes Toward Speculative Risks As An Indicator Of Attitudes Toward Pure Risks," JRI, 1966, v33(4), 577-586.

Williams, C. Arthur, Jr. "Competitive Bidding And Municipal Property And Liability Insurance," JRI, 1963, v30(3), 345-362.

Williams, C. Arthur, Jr. "Game-Theory And Insurance Consumption," JRI, 1960, v27(4), 47-56.

Williams, C. Arthur, Jr. "Higher Interest Rates, Longer Lifetimes, And The Demand For Life Annuities," JRI, 1986, v53(1), 164-171.

Williams, C. Arthur, Jr. "Insurer Views On Property And Liability Insurance Rate Regulation," JRI, 1969, v36(2), 217-236.

Williams, C. Arthur, Jr. "Insurer Views On Property And Liability Insurance Rate Regulation: Reply," JRI, 1970, v37(2), 308-309.

Williams, C. Arthur, Jr. "Regulatory Property And Liability Insurance Rates Through Excess Profits Statutes," JRI, 1983, v50(3), 445-472.

Williams, C. Arthur, Jr. "Some Economic And Legal Aspects Of Insurance Rate Discrimination," JRI, 1957, v24(2), 9-23.

Williams, C. Arthur, Jr. "Social Insurance - Proper Terminology?," JRI, 1963, v30(1), 112-128.

Williams, C. Arthur, Jr. "The Deductible In Medical Expense Insurance," JRI, 1953, v20, 107-116.

Williams, C. Arthur, Jr. "Trends In Property And Liability Insurance Rate Making: An Academic Viewpoint," JRI, 1963, v30(1), 29-34.

Williams, C. Arthur, Jr. "Workmen's Compensation And The Handicapped," JRI, 1959, v26(2), 13-28.

Williams, C. Arthur, Jr. (Josephson, Halsey D., Glenn L. Wood and C. Arthur Williams, Jr. "High Cash Value Life Insurance Policies And Unfair Discrimination: Comment," JRI, 1966, v33(1), 125-134.)

Williams, C. Arthur, Jr. (Neter, John and C. Arthur Williams, Jr. "Acceptability Of Three Normative Methods In Insurance Decision Making," JRI, 1971, v38(3), 385-408.)

Williams, C. Arthur, Jr. (Neter, John and C. Arthur Williams, Jr. "Acceptability Of Three Normative Methods In Insurance Decision Making: Reply," JRI, 1972, v39(4), 466-467.)

Williams, C. Arthur, Jr. (Neter, John and C. Arthur Williams, Jr. "Acceptability Of Three Normative Methods In Insurance Decision Making: An Alternative Hypothesis: Reply," JRI, 1974, v41(2), 366.)

Williams, C. Arthur, Jr. (Whitman, Andrew F. and C. Arthur Williams, Jr. "Environmental Hazards And Rating Urban Core Properties," JRI, 1970, v37(3), 419-436.)

Williams, C. Arthur, Jr. (Whitman, Andrew F. and C. Arthur Williams, Jr. "FAIR Plan And Excess Rate Plan Rates In Minnesota," JRI, 1971, v38(1), 43-59.)

Williams, C. Arthur, Jr. (Wood, Glenn L. and C. Arthur Williams, Jr. "High Cash Value Life Insurance Policies And Unfair Discrimination," JRI, 1964, v31(4), 557-572.)

Williams, C. Arthur, Jr. and O. D. Dickerson. "Game-Theory And Insurance Consumption: The Worry Factor Revisited," JRI, 1966, v33(3), 411-426.

Williams, C. Arthur, Jr. and Andrew F. Whitman. "Open Competition Rating Laws And Price Competition," JRI, 1973, v40(4), 483-496.

Williams, C. Arthur, Jr. and Michael L. Smith. "FAIR Plan Insureds: Occupancy And Location Characteristics And Experience," JRI, 1975, v42(1), 156-162.

Williams, Dave H. "Changing Shape Of Investment Research," FAJ, 1978, v34(1), 18-21.

Williams, Dave H. "Organizing For Superior Investment Returns," FAJ, 1980, v36(5), 21-23,27.

Williams, David D. "The Potential Determinants Of Auditor Change," JBFA, 1988, v15(2), 243-262.

Williams, David D. (Gombola, Michael J., Mark E. Haskins, J. Edward Ketz and David D. Williams. "Cash Flow In Bankruptcy Prediction," FM, 1987, v16(4), 55-65.)

Williams, David J. and Chanoch Shreiber. "Cost-Volume-Profit Complications Using A Simplified Form," JBFA, 1983, v10(3), 481-488.

Williams, David J. and Keith D. Turpie. "The Accounting Services Market: Theory And Evidence: A Comment," JBFA, 1983, v10(2), 317-321.

Williams, E. E. (Findlay, M. C., III and E. E. Williams. "Better Debt Service Coverage Ratios," FAJ, 1975, v31(6), 58-61.)

Williams, E. E. (Findlay, M. C. and E. E. Williams. "A Positivist Evaluation Of The New Finance," FM, 1980, v9(2), 7-17.)

Williams, Edward E. and M. Chapman Findlay, III. "Discounting Deferred Tax Liabilities: Some Clarifying Comments," JBFA, 1975, v2(1), 121-133.

Williams, Edward E. and M. Chapman Findlay, III. "Capital Budgeting, Cost Of Capital And Ex Ante Static Equilibrium," JBFA, 1979, v6(4), 455-474.

Williams, Edward E. "Accounting And Capital Allocation," FAJ, 1969, v25(4), 37-40.

Williams, Edward E. (Findlay, M. Chapman, III and Edward E. Williams. "A Post Keynesian View Of Modern Financial Economics: In Search Of Alternative Paradigms," JBFA, 1985, v12(1), 1-18.)

Williams, Edward E. (Findlay, M. Chapman, III and Edward E. Williams. "Discounting Deferred Tax Liabilities: A Reply," JBFA, 1981, v8(4), 593-597.)

Williams, Edward E. (Findlay, M. Chapman, III and Edward E. Williams. "The Problem Of 'Unequal Lives' Reconsidered," JBFA, 1981, v8(2), 161-164.)

Williams, Edward E. (Findlay, M. Chapman, III and Edward E. Williams. "Opportunity Cost, Discounting, And Deferred Tax Liabilities: A Final Note," JBFA, 1985, v12(2), 183-185.)

Williams, Edward E. (Findlay, M. Chapman, III and Edward E. Williams. "Owners' Surplus, The Marginal Efficiency Of Capital And Market Equilibrium," JBFA, 1979, v6(1), 17-36.)

Williams, Edward E. (Findlay, M. Chapman, III and Edward E. Williams. "Capital Allocation And The Nature Of Ownership Equities," FM, 1972, v1(2), 68-76.)

Williams, Edward E. (Findlay, M. Chapman, III, Edward E. Williams and Lawrence A. Gordon. "Toward More Adequate Measures Of Lender Protection," FM, 1974, v4(3), 54-61.)

Williams, Edward E. (Findlay, M. Chapman, III and Edward E. Williams. "Better Betas Didn't Help The Boat People," JPM, 1986-87, v13(1), 4-9.)

Williams, George P., Jr. "An Incentive Plan For Bank Managed Pension Funds," JBR, 1971-72, v2(1), 25-30.

Williams, Harold M. "The Future Of ARIA," JRI, 1973, v40(1), 103-114.

Williams, James R. (Daniels, Arthur C., Albert I. Hermalin, Alfred Cranwill and James R. Williams. "The Research Facilities Of The Institute Of Life Insurance," JRI, 1958, v25(1), 32-41.)

Williams, Jeffrey C. "Fractional Reserve Banking In Grain," JMCB, 1984, v16(4), Part 1, 488-496.

Williams, Jeffrey C. (Wright, Brian D. and Jeffrey C. Williams. "A Theory Of Negative Prices For Storage," JPM, 1989, v9(1), 1-14.)

Williams, John Daniel and Jonathan S. Rakich. "Investment Evaluation In Hospitals," FM, 1973, v2(2), 30-35.

Williams, Joseph T. "A Note On Indifference Curves In The Mean-Variance Model," JFQA, 1977, v12(1), 121-126.

Williams, Joseph T. "Capital Asset Prices With Heterogeneous Beliefs," JFEC, 1977, v5(2), 219-239.

Williams, Joseph T. "Risk, Human Capital, And The Investor's Portfolio," JOB, 1978, v51(1), 65-90.

Williams, Joseph T. "Trading And Valuing Depreciable Assets," JFEC, 1985, v14(2), 283-308.

Williams, Joseph T. "Uncertainty And The Accumulation Of Human Capital Over The Life Cycle," JOB, 1979, v52(4), 521-548.

Williams, Joseph T. (Scholes, Myron and Joseph T. Williams. "Estimating Betas From Nonsynchronous Data," JFEC, 1977, v5(3), 309-327.)

Williams, Joseph. "A Message From The President Of The Society For Financial Studies," RFS, 1988-89, v1(1), 1-2.

Williams, Joseph. "Efficient Signalling With Dividends, Investment, And Stock Repurchases," JOF, 1988, v43(3), 737-747.

Williams, Joseph. "Perquisites, Risk, And Capital Structure," JOF, 1987, v42(1), 29-48.

Williams, Joseph. (Ambarish, Ramasastry, Kose John and Joseph Williams. "Efficient Signalling With Dividends And Investments," JOF, 1987, v42(2), 321-343.)

Williams, Joseph. (Dothan, Uri and Joseph Williams. "Banks, Bankruptcy, And Regulation," JBF, 1980, v4(1), 65-87.)

Williams, Joseph. (Dothan, Uri and Joseph Williams. "Education As An Option," JOB, 1981, v54(1), 117-140.)

Williams, Joseph. (Dothan, Uri and Joseph Williams. "Term-Risk Structures And The Valuation Of Projects," JFQA, 1980, v15(4), 875-905.)

Williams, Joseph. (Dothan, Uri and Joseph Williams. "Financial Game: Capital Market Equilibrium," JFED, 1980, v9, 77-78.)

Williams, Joseph. (Eckbo, B. Espen, Vojislav Maksimovic and Joseph Williams. "Consistent Estimation Of Cross-Sectional Models In Event Studies," RFS, 1990, v3(3), 343-366.)

Williams, Joseph. (John, Kose and Joseph Williams. "Dividends, Dilution, And Taxes: A Signalling Equilibrium," JOF, 1985, v40(4), 1053-1070.)

Williams, Joseph. (Park, Sang Yong and Joseph Williams. "Taxes, Capital Structure, And Bondholder Clienteles," JOB, 1985, v58(2), 203-224.)

Williams, Raburn M. (Ibrahim, I. B. and Raburn M. Williams. "The Fisher Relationship Under Different Monetary Standards," JMCB, 1978, v10(3), 363-370.)

Williams, Richard E. and Peter W. Bacon. "Efficient Portfolios Vs. Index Funds: Comment," JPM, 1978-79, v5(1), 72-74.

Williams, Richard. (Bacon, Peter and Richard Williams. "Interest Rate Futures Trading: New Tool For The Financial Manager," **FM**, 1976, v5(1), 32-38.)

Williams, Stephen J., Paula Diehr, William L. Drucker and William C. Richardson. "Limitations And Exclusions In Two Provider Systems With Comprehensive Care," **JRI**, 1982, v49(3), 448-462.

Williams, Stephen L. (Eckardt, Walter L., Jr. and Stephen L. Williams. "The Complete Options Indexes," **FAJ**, 1984, v40(4), 48-57.)

Williams, W. H. and M. L. Goodman. "A Statistical Grouping Of Corporations By Their Financial Characteristics," **JFQA**, 1971, v6(4), 1095-1104.

Williams, W. H. (Davis, E. G., D. M. Dunn and W. H. Williams. "Ambiguities In The Cross-Section Analysis Of Per Share Financial Data," **JOF**, 1973, v28(5), 1241-1248.)

Williams, W. H. (Davis, E. G., D. M. Dunn and W. H. Williams. "Invariance And Scaling In The Per Share Analysis Of Financial Data: Reply," **JOF**, 1977, v32(3), 937-938.)

Williams, Walter. "A Comment On Insurance And The Consumption Function," **JRI**, 1960, v27(2), 109-112.

Williams, Walter. "Insurance As A Segment Of The Liberal Business Education," **JRI**, 1960, v27(3), 43-48.

Williams, Walter. "Measuring The Macroeconomic Effects Of Life And Health Insurance," **JRI**, 1961, v28(2), 77-82.

Williams, Walter. "The Implications Of Retirement Security Systems For Consumer Behavior," **JRI**, 1965, v32(3), 349-366.

Williams, Walter. "The Life Insurance-Consumer Saving Relationship," **JRI**, 1962, v29(3), 355-372.

Williams, Walter. "The Social Security And Pension Fund System - Their Place In The American Value Structures," **JRI**, 1964, v31(3), 341-354.

Williams, Walter. "The Value Of Pension Promises And Consumer Wealth," **JOF**, 1965, v20(1), 36-48.

Williams, Walter. (Hedges, Bob A., Walter Williams and Henry K. Duke. "What Is Wrong With Insurance Theory?," **JRI**, 1964, v31(2), 279-284.)

Williams, Walter. (Kreps, Juanita M., Joseph J. Spengler and Walter Williams. "The Social Security And Pension Fund Systems - Their Place In The American Value Structure: Comment," **JRI**, 1965, v32(4), 621-638.)

Williams, William D. "A Look Behind Reported Earnings," **FAJ**, 1966, v22(1), 38-39.

Williams, William D. "CIC 1976 Awards For Excellence," **FAJ**, 1978, v34(1), 42-45.

Williams, William D. "Industrial Gases," **FAJ**, 1968, v24(1), 66-69.

Williamson, David A. (Sorensen, Eric H. and David A. Williamson. "Some Evidence On The Value Of Dividend Discount Models," **FAJ**, 1985, v41(6), 60-69.)

Williamson, J. M. "Pricing Money Transfer Services," **JBR**, 1980-81, v11(4), 227-232.

Williamson, J. P. and R. S. Bower. "Measuring Pension Fund Performance: Another Comment," **FAJ**, 1966, v22(3), 143-149.

Williamson, J. Peter and Allen Silver. "Sideways Betas: Criticism And Response," **JPM**, 1975-76, v2(2), 68-70.

Williamson, J. Peter. "Bond Switching And The Computer," **FAJ**, 1970, v26(4), 65-72.

Williamson, J. Peter. "Endowment Funds: Income, Growth, And Total Return," **JPM**, 1974-75, v1(1), 74-79.

Williamson, J. Peter. "How Well Are College Endowment Funds Managed?," **JPM**, 1978-79, v5(4), 19-22.

Williamson, J. Peter. "Measuring Mutual Fund Performance," **FAJ**, 1972, v28(6), 78-80,82-84.

Williamson, J. Peter. "Mortgage Loan Extensions After An Interest Rate Change: A Problem In Blended Interest Rates," **JBR**, 1972-73, v3(2), 111-117.

Williamson, J. Peter. "Mutual Funds And Portfolio Selection," **FR**, 1971, v2(1), 1-14.

Williamson, J. Peter. "Should Endowment Funds Invest For Yield?," **JPM**, 1976-77, v3(2), 46-49.

Williamson, J. Peter. (Bower, Richard S., Christopher E. Nugent, Barbara C. Myers and J. Peter Williamson. "A Language For Financial Analysts," **FAJ**, 1967, v23(1), 121.)

Williamson, J. Peter. (Walter, James E. and J. Peter Williamson. "Organized Securities Exchanges In Canada," **JOF**, 1960, v15(3), 307-324.)

Williamson, Oliver E. "Corporate Finance And Corporate Governance," **JOF**, 1988, v43(3), 567-591.

Williamson, Stephen. "Transactions Costs, Inflation, And The Variety Of Intermediation Services," **JMCB**, 1987, v19(4), 484-498.

Williamson, W. R. "Non-Governmental Medical Care Programs," **JRI**, 1948, v15, 57-62.

Williamson, W. Rulon. "The Social Security Principle: Comment," **JRI**, 1961, v28(2), 111-114.

Willinger, G. Lee. (Owens, Robert W. and G. Lee Willinger. "Investment Potential Of An Individual Retirement Account," **JBR**, 1985-86, v16(3), 161-168.)

Willinger, Marc. "Risk Aversion And The Value Of Information," **JRI**, 1989, v56(1), 104-112.

Willinger, Marc. "Risk Aversion And The Value Of Information," **JRI**, 1989, v56(2), 320-328.

Willis, George H. "Convertibility - The Current Approach," **JOF**, 1955, v10(2), 152-169.

Willis, J. Brooke. "Gross Flows Of Funds Through Mutual Savings Banks," **JOF**, 1960, v15(2), 170-190.

Willis, J. Brooke. "Postwar Changes In Commercial Bank Investments In U. S. Government Securities," **JOF**, 1949, v4(2), 140-155.

Willis, J. Brooke. "Secondary Reserve Requirements," **JOF**, 1948, v3(2), 29-44.

Willis, John R. and Avy Stein. "Financing A Generational Change Of Ownership," **JACF**, 1990, v3(3), 71-76.

Willis, John R. and David A. Clark. "An Introduction To Mezzanine Finance And Private Equity," **JACF**, 1989, v2(2), 77-86.

Willis, R. B. (Nicholson, S. F., M. Smith and R. B. Willis. "Investment Perspectives - 150 Years," **FAJ**, 1979, v35(6), 23-37.)

Willman, Elliott S. (Lowinger, Thomas C., Clas Wihlborg and Elliott S. Willman. "OPEC In World Financial Markets: Oil Prices And Interest Rates," **JIMF**, 1985, v4(2), 253-266.)

Willmott, Hugh. "Accounting Regulation: An Alternative Perspective: A Comment," **JBFA**, 1984, v11(4), 583-591.

Wilsey, H. Lawrence. "The Investment Advisers Act Of 1940," **JOF**, 1949, v4(4), 286-297.

Wilsey, H. Lawrence. "The Use Of Sinking Funds In Preferred Stock Issues," **JOF**, 1947, v2(2), 31-42.

Wilson, Brent D. "Improving Finance Education Through Curriculum Planning," **JFED**, 1981, v10, 71-73.

Wilson, Brent D. "Improving Finance Education Through Curriculum Planning," **JFED**, 1982, v11, 47-49.

Wilson, Charles Z. "The Future Of Business Education-Some Further Comments," **JOB**, 1966, v39(1), Part I, 74-75.

Wilson, David T. "Acceptability Of Three Normative Methods In Insurance Decision Making: An Alternative Hypothesis: Comment," **JRI**, 1974, v41(2), 363-365.

Wilson, Edward S. "Financial Analysts' Second Overseas Field Trip," **FAJ**, 1961, v17(3), 63-66.

Wilson, Edward S. "Is Railroad Working Capital Overstated?," **FAJ**, 1956, v12(1), 33-40.

Wilson, G. Peter. (Scholes, Myron S., G. Peter Wilson and Mark A. Wolfson. "Tax Planning, Regulatory Capital Planning, And Financial Reporting Strategy For Commercial Banks," **RFS**, 1990, v3(4), 625-650.)

Wilson, Jack W. and Charles P. Jones. "The Relationship Between Performance And Risk: Whence The Bias?," **JFR**, 1981, v4(2), 103-108.

Wilson, Jack W. (Jones, Charles P. and Jack W. Wilson. "Stocks, Bonds, Paper, And Inflation: 1870-1985," **JPM**, 1987-88, v14(1), 20-24.)

Wilson, Jack W. (Jones, Charles P., Douglas K. Pearce and Jack W. Wilson. "Can Tax-Loss Selling Explain The January Effect? A Note," **JOF**, 1987, v42(2), 453-461.)

Wilson, Jack W. (Jones, Charles P. and Jack W. Wilson. "Is Stock Price Volatility Increasing?," **FAJ**, 1989, v45(6), 20-26.)

Wilson, Jack W. (Jones, Charles P. and Jack W. Wilson. "An Analysis Of The January Effect In Stocks And Interest Rates Under Varying Monetary Regimes," **JFR**, 1989, v12(4), 341-354.)

Wilson, Jack W. and Charles P. Jones. "A Comparison Of Annual Common Stock Returns: 1871-1925 With 1926-85," **JOB**, 1987, v60(2), 239-258.

Wilson, Jack W. and Charles P. Jones. "Common Stock Prices And Inflation: 1857-1985," **FAJ**, 1987, v43(4), 67-72.

Wilson, Jack W. and Charles P. Jones. "Is There A January Effect In Corporate Bond And Paper Returns?," **FR**, 1990, v25(1), 55-80.

Wilson, John F. "Comment On 'Ex Ante Evidence Of Backwardation/Contango In Commodities Futures Markets'," **JFM**, 1982, v2(2), 169-174.

Wilson, Joseph W. and Timothy P. Cronan. "Computer System Use In The Finance Major," **JFED**, 1982, v11, 97-100.

Wilson, K. W. (Newbould, G. D. and K. W. Wilson. "Alternative Measures Of Company Size - A Note For Researchers," **JBFA**, 1977, v4(1), 131-132.)

Wilson, Millie H. (Kennedy, Robert E. and Millie H. Wilson. "Investor Relations And Security Analysts," **FAJ**, 1980, v36(2), 63-69.)

Wilson, Paul N. and Robert I. Cummin. "Saving Management And Transaction Costs," **FAJ**, 1977, v33(2), 58-62.

Wilson, Robert. (Oren, Shmuel, Stephen Smith and Robert Wilson. "Producing A Product Line," **JOB**, 1984, v57(1), Part 2, S73-S100.

Wilson, Stephen D. "Hedging A Mortgage Pipeline," **RFM**, 1984, v3(2), 116-121.

Wilson, William W. "Hedging Effectiveness Of U.S. Wheat Futures Markets," **RFM**, 1984, v3(1), 64-79.

Wilson, William W. "Price Discovery And Hedging In The Sunflower Market," **JFM**, 1989, v9(5), 377-392.

Wilson, William W. and Hung-Gay Fung. "Information Content Of Volatilities Implied By Option Premiums In Grain Futures Markets," **JFM**, 1990, v10(1), 13-28.

Wilson, William W., Hung-Gay Fung and Michael Ricks. "Option Price Behavior In Grain Futures Markets," **JFM**, 1988, v8(1), 47-66.

Wilt, Glenn A., Jr. (Fischer, Donald E. and Glenn A. Wilt, Jr. "Non-Convertible Preferred Stock As A Financing Instrument, 1950-1965," **JOF**, 1968, v23(4), 611-624.)

Wiltbank, Laurel J. (Cummins, J. David and Laurel J. Wiltbank. "Estimating The Total Claims Distribution Using Multivariate Frequency And Severity Distributions," **JRI**, 1983, v50(3), 377-403.)

Wiltman, William J. "Administration Of Union Pension Plans In Multi-Employer Industries," **FR**, 1967, v1(2), 33-40.

Win, Willis F. and Arleigh Hess, Jr. "The Value Of The Call Privilege," **JOF**, 1959, v14(2), 182-195.

Wind, Yoram. (Goldberg, Stephen M., Paul E. Green and Yoram Wind. "Conjoint Analysis Of Price Premiums For Hotel Amenities," **JOB**, 1984, v57(1), Part 2, S111-S132.

Windal, Pierre M. and Doyle L. Weiss. "An Iterative GLS Procedure For Estimating The Parameters Of Models With Autocorrelated Errors Using Data Aggregted Over Time," **JOB**, 1980, v53(4), 415-424.

Windal, Pierre. (Weiss, Doyle L., Franklin S. Houston and Pierre Windal. "The Periodic Pain Of Lydia E. Pinkham," **JOB**, 1978, v51(1), 91-102.)

Winder, James P. (Hendershott, Patric H. and James P. Winder. "Commercial Bank Asset Portfolio Behavior In The United States: Evidence Of A Change In Structure," **JBF**, 1979, v3(2), 113-131.)

Winder, John W. L. (Smith, Lawrence B. and John W. L. Winder. "Interest Rate Expectations And The Demand For Money In Canada: Reply," **JOF**, 1973, v28(1), 213-214.)

Winder, John W. L. (Smith, Lawrence B. and John W. L. Winder. "Price And Interest Rate Expectations And The Demand For Money In Canada," **JOF**, 1971, v26(3), 671-682.)

Windisch, Richard P. "The European Chemical Industry," **FAJ**, 1959, v15(4), 25-34.

Winer, Leon. "Question-Asking Skills: Effective Use Of The First Meeting Of A Case Course," **JFED**, 1972, v1, 74.

Winer, Leon. "Using The Nomograph," **FAJ**, 1969, v25(1), 105-108.

Winer, Russell S. "An Analysis Of The Time-Varying Effects Of Advertising: The Case Of Lydia Pinkham," **JOB**, 1979, v52(4), 563-576.

Winer, Russell S. (Wildt, Albert R. and Russell S. Winer. "Modeling And Estimation In Changing Market Environments," JOB, 1983, v56(3), 365-388.)

Wing, George A. "Capital Budgeting, Circa 1915," JOF, 1965, v20(3), 472-479.

Wingender, John R. (Lau, Hon-Shiang and John R. Wingender. "The Analytics Of The Intervaling Effect On Skewness And Kurtosis Of Stock Returns," FR, 1989, v24(2), 215-234.)

Wingender, John and James E. Groff. "On Stochastic Dominance Analysis Of Day-Of-The-Week Return Patterns," JFR, 1989, v12(1), 51-56.

Wingender, John. (Singleton, J. Clay and John Wingender. "Skewness Persistence In Common Stock Returns," JFQA, 1986, v21(3), 335-341.)

Winger, Alan R. "Local Construction Response To National Credit-Market," JOB, 1966, v39(4), 505-511.

Winger, Alan R. "Mortgage Demands And Supplies," FAJ, 1968, v24(5), 77-84.

Winger, Alan R. "Regional Growth Disparities And The Mortgage Market," JOF, 1969, v24(4), 659-662.

Winger, Bernard J. (Mohan, Nancy, M. Fall Ainina, Daniel Kaufman and Bernard J. Winger. "Acquisition/Divestiture Valuation Practices In Major U.S. Firms," FPE, 1991, v1(1), 73-82.)

Winger, Bernard J., Carl R. Chen, John D. Martin, J. William Petty and Steven C. Hayden. "Adjustable Rate Preferred Stock," FM, 1986, v15(1), 48-57.

Wingler, Tony R. and James M. Watts. "Electric Utility Bond Rating Changes: Methodological Issues And Evidence," JFR, 1982, v5(3), 221-235.

Wingler, Tony R. (Angell, Robert J. and Tony R. Wingler. "A Note On Expensing Versus Depreciating Under The Accelerated Cost Recovery System," FM, 1982, v11(4), 34-35.)

Wingler, Tony R. (Frew, James R., G. Donald Jud and Tony R. Wingler. "The Effects Of Zoning On Population And Employment Density," JREFEC, 1990, v3(2), 155-172.)

Wingler, Tony R. and G. Donald Jud. "Premium Debt Tenders: Analysis And Evidence," FM, 1990, v19(4), 58-67.

Winick, Charles. "The Relationship Among Personality Needs, Objective Factors, And Brand Choice: A Re-Examination," JOB, 1961, v34(1), 61-66.

Winkelmann, Kurt. "Uses And Abuses Of Duration And Convexity," FAJ, 1989, v45(5), 72-75.

Winklepleck, John. (Kamath, Ravindra R., Shahriar Khaksari, Heidi Hylton Meier and John Winklepleck. "Management Of Excess Cash: Practices And Developments," FM, 1985, v14(3), 70-77.)

Winkler, Daniel T. (Flanigan, George B., Joseph E. Johnson, Daniel T. Winkler and William Ferguson. "Experience From Early Tort Reforms: Comparative Negligence Since 1974," JRI, 1989, v56(3), 525-534.)

Winkler, Daniel T. (Frew, James R., G. Donald Jud and Daniel T. Winkler. "Atypicalities And Apartment Rent Concessions," JRER, 1990, v5(2), 195-201.)

Winkler, Daniel T., George B. Flanigan and Joseph E. Johnson. "Solving For The Number Of Cash Flows And Periods In Financial Problems," JFED, 1990, v19, 62-65.

Winkler, Robert L. and Christopher B. Barry. "A Bayesian Model For Portfolio Selection And Revision," JOF, 1975, v30(1), 179-192.

Winkler, Robert L. "Bayesian Models For Forecasting Future Security Prices," JFQA, 1973, v8(3), 387-405.

Winkler, Robert L. (Barry, Christopher B. and Robert L. Winkler. "Nonstationarity And Portfolio Choice," JFQA, 1976, v11(2), 217-235.)

Winkler, Robert L. (Conroy, Robert M. and Robert L. Winkler. "Informational Difference Between Limit And Market Orders For A Market Maker," JFQA, 1981, v16(5), 703-724.)

Winkler, Robert L. (Conroy, Robert M. and Robert L. Winkler. "Market Structure: The Specialist As Dealer And Broker," JBF, 1986, v10(1), 21-36.)

Winkler, Robert L. (Jaffe, Jeffrey F. and Robert L. Winkler. "Optimal Speculation Against An Efficient Market," JOF, 1976, v31(1), 49-61.)

Winkler, Robert L. (McCardle, Kevin F. and Robert L. Winkler. "All Roads Lead To Risk Preference: A Turnpike Theorem For Conditionally Independent Returns," JFQA, 1989, v24(1), 13-28.)

Winklevoss, Howard E. "An Explantory Analysis Of The Insurable Value Concept," JRI, 1973, v40(3), 437-442.

Winklevoss, Howard E. "Cost Sensitivity Analysis Of Mandatory Funding And Vesting Standards In Pension Plans," JRI, 1974, v41(1), 57-73.

Winklevoss, Howard E. "Inflation Based Variable Life Insurance Models," JRI, 1974, v41(4), 601-620.

Winklevoss, Howard E. "Plasm: Pension Liability And Asset Simulation Model," JOF, 1982, v37(2), 585-594.

Winklevoss, Howard E. and Robert A. Zelten. "An Empirical Analysis Of Mutual Life Insurance Company Surplus," JRI, 1973, v40(3), 403-426.

Winn, Daryl N. (Melicher, Ronald W., David F. Rush and Daryl N. Winn. "Industry Concentration, Financial Structure And Profitability," FM, 1976, v5(3), 48-53.)

Winn, Daryl N. (Melicher, Ronald W., David F. Rush and Daryl N. Winn. "Degree Of Industry Concentration And Market Risk-Return Performance," JFQA, 1976, v11(4), 627-635.)

Winn, Edward L., Jr. (Bacon, Peter W. and Edward L. Winn, Jr. "The Impact Of Forced Conversion On Stock Prices," JOF, 1969, v24(5), 871-874.)

Winnick, Louis. "Financing The Rebuilding Of Our Cities," JOF, 1962, v17(2), 371-378.

Winnick, Louis. "The Burden Of The Residential Mortgage Debt," JOF, 1956, v11(2), 166-179.

Winningham, Scott. "More On The Alleged Profitability Of Borrowing At 8% To Lend At 6%: Comment," JBR, 1978-79, v9(2), 125-127.

Winsen, J. and D. Ng. "Investor Behavior And Changes In Accounting Methods," JFQA, 1976, v11(5), 873-881.

Winsen, Joseph K. "A Reformulation Of The API Approach To Evaluating Accounting Income Numbers," JFQA, 1977, v12(3), 499-504.

Winsen, Joseph K. "Investor Behavior And Information," JFQA, 1976, v11(1), 13-37.

Winston, Kenneth. (Tierney, David E. and Kenneth Winston. "Defining And Using Dynamic Completeness Funds To Enhance Total Fund Efficiency," FAJ, 1990, v46(4), 49-54.)

Winston, Wayne L. (Lippman, Steven A., John M. McCall and Wayne L. Winston. "Constant Absolute Risk Aversion, Bankrupty, And Wealth-Dependent Decisions," JOB, 1980, v53(3), Part 1, 285-296.)

Winter, P. R. (Cohen, K. J., R. M. Cyert, W. R. Dill, A. A. Kuehn, M. H. Miller, T. A. VanWormer, and P. R. Winters. "The Carnegie Tech Management Game," JOB, 1960, v33(4), 303-321.)

Winter, R. A. (Mathewson, G. F. and R. A. Winter. "Vertical Integration By Contractual Restraints In Spatial Markets," JOB, 1983, v56(4), 497-518.)

Winter, Ralph A. "On The Choice Of An Index For Disclosure In The Life Insurance Market: An Axiomatic Approach," JRI, 1982, v49(4), 513-538.

Winter, Ralph A. "On The Rate Structure Of The American Life Insurance Market," JOF, 1981, v36(1), 81-96.

Winter, Ralph A. (Farmer, Roger E. A. and Ralph A. Winter. "The Role Of Options In The Resolution Of Agency Problems: A Comment," JOF, 1986, v41(5), 1157-1170.)

Winter, William D. "Marine Insurance In A World At War," JRI, 1942, v9, 39-44.

Winthrop, John. "Layman's View Of Computer Power," FAJ, 1969, v25(5), 101-103.

Wiper, L. (Longbottom, D. A. and L. Wiper. "Capital Appraisal And The Case For Average Rate Of Return," JBFA, 1977, v4(4), 419-426.)

Wiper, L. (Longbottom, D. A. and L. Wiper. "Capital Appraisal And The Case For Average Rate Of Return: A Reply," JBFA, 1979, v6(2), 243-244.)

Wiper, Linda. (Longbottom, David A. and Linda Wiper. "Necessary Conditions For The Existence Of Multiple Rates In The Use Of Internal Rate Of Return," JBFA, 1978, v5(4), 295-304.)

Wippern, Ronald F. "Financial Structure And The Value Of The Firm," JOF, 1966, v21(4), 615-633.

Wippern, Ronald F. "Significance Of Dummy Variables: Reply," JOF, 1968, v23(3), 518-519.

Wippern, Ronald F. "Utility Implications Of Portfolio Selection And Performance Appraisal Models," JFQA, 1971, v6(3), 913-924.

Wippern, Ronald F. (Bower, Richard S. and Ronald F. Wippern. "Risk-Return Measurement In Portfolio Selection And Performance Appraisal Models: Progress Report," JFQA, 1969, v4(4), 417-447.)

Wirick, R. G. (Kyle, S. C. and R. G. Wirick. "The Impact Of Soverign Risk On The Market Valuation Of U.S. Bank Equities," JBF, 1990, v14(4), 761-780.)

Wirth, A. and F. K. Wright. "New-Issue Costs And Project Evaluation: Ezzell And Porter Revisited," JBFA, 1987, v14(3), 393-408.

Wirth, Andrew. "A Note On A Cash Management Model Allowing For Overdrafts," JBFA, 1984, v11(4), 557-561.

Wise, Gordon L. "Differential Pricing And Treatment By New-Car Salesmen: The Effect Of The Propsect's Race, Sex, And Dress," JOB, 1974, v47(2), 218-230.

Wise, Paul S. "The Problem Of The Financially Irresponsible Motorist And The Uncompensated Accident Victim," JRI, 1957, v24(1), 101-113.

Wise, Trevor D. "A Note On Additional Evidence On The Behaviour Of Deferred Tax Credits," JBFA, 1986, v13(3), 433-444.

Witherspoon, William. "Gold - Credit - Money - Spending," FAJ, 1951, v7(4), 61-64.

Witt, Craig A. (Tew, Bernard V., Donald W. Reid and Craig A. Witt. "The Opportunity Cost Of A Mean-Variance Efficient Choice," FR, 1991, v26(1), 31-44.)

Witt, Harvey J., Ted C. Schroeder and Marvin L. Hayenga. "Comparison Of Analytical Approaches For Estimating Hedge Ratios For Agricultural Commodities," JFM, 1987, v7(2), 135-146.

Witt, Horst J. "The Cost Of Developing And Implementing Electronic Payment Systems," JBR, 1985-86, v16(4), 186-189.

Witt, Robert C. "An Economic Appraisal Of Territorial Pricing Issues In Automobile Insurance," JRI, 1979, v46(1), 33-60.

Witt, Robert C. "Underwriting Risk And Return: Some Additional Comments: Reply," JRI, 1981, v48(4), 653-661.

Witt, Robert C. (Brockett, Patrick L. and Robert C. Witt. "The Underwriting Risk And Return Paradox Revisited," JRI, 1982, v49(4), 621-627.)

Witt, Robert C. (Brockett, Patrick L., Samuel H. Cox, Jr. and Robert C. Witt. "Self-Insurance And The Probability Of Financial Regret," JRI, 1984, v51(4), 720-729.)

Witt, Robert C. (Brockett, Patrick L., Samuel H. Cox, Jr. and Robert C. Witt. "Insurance Versus Self-Insurance: A Risk Management Perspective," JRI, 1986, v53(2), 242-257.)

Witt, Robert C. (McCabe, George M. and Robert C. Witt. "Insurer Optimizing Behavior And Capital Market Equilibrium," JRI, 1977, v44(3), 447-468.)

Witt, Robert C. (McCabe, George M. and Robert C. Witt. "Insurance Pricing And Regulation Under Uncertainty: Pay Chance-Constrained Approach," JRI, 1980, v47(4), 607-635.)

Witt, Robert C. (Smith, Michael L. and Robert C. Witt. "An Economic Analysis Of Retroactive Liability Insurance," JRI, 1985, v52(3), 379-401.)

Witt, Robert C. (Smith, Michael L. and Robert C. Witt. "Informational Asymmetries In Retroactive Insurance: A Response," JRI, 1988, v55(3), 548-554.)

Witt, Robert C. (Spellman, Lewis J., Robert C. Witt and William F. Rentz. "Investment Income And Non-Life Insurance Pricing," JRI, 1975, v42(4), 567-577.)

Witt, Robert C. and Jorge Urrutia. "A Comparative Economic Analysis Of Tort Liability And No-Fault Compensation Systems In Automobile Insurance," JRI, 1983, v50(4), 631-669.

Witt, Robert Charles. "Credibility Standards And Pricing In Automobile Insurance," JRI, 1974, v41(3), 375-396.

Witt, Robert Charles. "Pricing Problems In Automobile Insurance: An Economic Analysis," JRI, 1973, v40(1), 75-93.

Witt, Robert Charles. "Pricing And Underwriting Risk In Automobile Insurance: A Probabilistic View," JRI, 1973, v40(4), 509-531.

Witt, Robert Charles. "Pricing, Investment Income, And Underwriting Risk In Auto Insurance: A Stochastic View," **JRI**, 1974, v41(1), 109-134.

Witt, Robert Charles. "Pricing And Underwriting Risk In Automobile Insurance: A Probabilistic View: Reply," **JRI**, 1975, v42(4), 651-658.

Witt, Robert Charles. (Roy, Tapan S. and Robert Charles Witt. "Leverage, Exposure Ratios And The Optimal Rate Of Return On Capital For The Insurer," **JRI**, 1976, v43(1), 53-72.)

Witt, Stephen F. and Richard Dobbins. "A Note On The Effect Of Institutional Trading Activities On The Real Value Of The Financial Times All-Share Index," **JBFA**, 1983, v10(3), 351-358.

Witt, Stephen F. "Cash Flow Forecasting In The International Tourism Industry," **AFPAF**, 1990, v5(1), 229-244.

Witt, Stephen F. (Dobbins, Richard and Stephen F. Witt. "Stock Market Prices And Sector Activity," **JBFA**, 1980, v7(2), 261-276.)

Wittink, Dick R. (Reinmuth, James E. and Dick R. Wittink. "Recursive Models For Forecasting Seasonal Processes," **JFQA**, 1974, v9(4), 659-684.)

Wizman, Thierry A. (Asquith, Paul and Thierry A. Wizman. "Event Risk, Covenants, And Bondholder Returns In Leveraged Buyouts," **JFEC**, 1990, v27(1), 195-214.)

Woerheide, Walt. "Investor Response To Suggested Criteria For The Selection Of Mutual Funds," **JFQA**, 1982, v17(1), 129-137.

Wofford, Larry E. "A Simulation Approach To The Appraisal Of Income Producing Real Estate," **AREUEA**, 1978, v6(4), 370-394.

Wofford, Larry E. (Johnson, Larry J. and Larry E. Wofford. "On Contracts As Options: Some Evidence From Condonimium Developments," **AREUEA**, 1987, v15(1), 739-741.)

Wofford, Larry E. and R. Keith Preddy. "Real Estate Investment Perception: A Multidimensional Analysis," **AREUEA**, 1978, v6(1), 22-36.

Wofford, Larry E. and R. Keith Preddy. "Assessing Student Perception Of Real Estate Careers," **AREUEA**, 1980, v8(4), 417-427.

Woglom, Geoffrey. "A Reexamination Of The Role Of Stocks In The Consumption Function And The Transmission Mechanism," **JMCB**, 1981, v13(2), 215-220.

Woglom, Geoffrey. "Systematic Risk And The Theory Of Wage Indexation," **JOB**, 1990, v63(2), 217-238.

Woglom, Geoffrey. (Kaufman, Roger T. and Geoffrey Woglom. "Estimating Models With Rational Expectations," **JMCB**, 1983, v15(3), 275-285.)

Wohlgenant, Michael K. (Goodwin, Barry K., Thomas Grennes and Michael K. Wohlgenant. "Testing The Law Of One Price When Trade Takes Time," **JIMF**, 1990, v9(1), 21-40.)

Wojdak, Joseph F. (Copeland, Ronald M. and Joseph F. Wojdak. "Goodwill In Merger-Minded Firms," **FAJ**, 1969, v25(5), 57-62.)

Wojdak, Joseph F. (Ferrara, William L. and Joseph F. Wojdak. "Valuation Of Long-Term Leases," **FAJ**, 1969, v25(6), 29-32.)

Wojnilower, Albert M. "Financial Crises And Social Values," **JPM**, 1976-77, v3(1), 11-13.

Wojtyla, Henry L. "Cashing In On Our Investment In People," **FAJ**, 1979, v35(2), 49-52.

Woldow, Robert J. "Panel: Clearance, Payment, And Settlement Systems In The Futures, Options, And Stock Markets," **RFM**, 1988, v7(3), 371-386.

Wolf, Anver. "Options Of Futures: Pricing And The Effect Of An Anticipated Price Change," **JFM**, 1984, v4(4), 491-512.

Wolf, Avner S. and Lawrence F. Pohlman. "Tests Of The Black And Whaley Models For Gold And Silver Futures Options," **RFM**, 1987, v6(3), 328-344.

Wolf, Avner S. (Martell, Trence F. and Avner S. Wolf. "Determinants Of Trading Volume In Futures Markets," **JFM**, 1987, v7(3), 233-244.)

Wolf, Avner, Mark Castelino and Jack Francis. "Hedging Mispriced Options," **JFM**, 1987, v7(2), 147-156.

Wolf, Avner. "Fundamentals Of Commodity Options On Futures," **JFM**, 1982, v2(4), 391-408.

Wolf, Avner. (Castelino, Mark G., Jack C. Francis and Avner Wolf. "Cross-Hedging: Basis Risk And Choice Of The Optimal Hedging Vehicle," **FR**, 1991, v26(2), 179-210.)

Wolf, Avner. (Paroush, Jacob and Avner Wolf. "Production And Hedging Decisions In The Presence Of Basis Risk," **JFM**, 1989, v9(6), 547-564.) 3x?8

Wolf, Chalres R. (Scott, James and Charles R. Wolf. "Bidding On Treasury Bills," **JPM**, 1979-80, v6(3), 46-52.)

Wolf, Charles R. "Bank Portfolio Gains And Losses," **FAJ**, 1969, v25(1), 86-90.

Wolf, Charles R. "Regulation F And The Yield Structure Of The U.S. Government Securities Market: A Comment," **JMCB**, 1970, v2(1), 112-122.

Wolf, Charles. (Johnsen, Thore and Charles Wolf. "The Strategic Profitability Of Borrowing At 8% To Lend At 6%: A Comment," **JBR**, 1977-78, v8(3), 186-187.)

Wolf, Jesse. "Calendar Spreads For Enhanced Index Fund Returns," **FAJ**, 1990, v46(1), 66-74.

Wolfe, Harry D. "Forecasting For Business," **FAJ**, 1956, v12(1), 17-20.

Wolfe, Harry Deane and Gerald Albaum. "Inequality In Products, Orders, Customers, Salesmen, And Sales Territories," **JOB**, 1962, v35(3), 298-301.

Wolfe, Harry Deane. "Science As A Trustworthy Tool," **FAJ**, 1952, v8(2), 45-50.

Wolfe, Joseph and Gary R. Guth. "The Case Approach Versus Gaming In The Teaching Of Business Policy: An Experimental Evaluation," **JOB**, 1975, v48(3), 349-364.

Wolfe, Joseph. "An Evaluation Of A Simulation-Based Business School Curriculum Integration Effort," **JOB**, 1977, v50(3), 343-355.

Wolfe, Wendell W. "Human Relations Laboratory Training: Three Questions," **JOB**, 1966, v39(4), 512-515.

Wolfensohn, James D. (Marshall, Earle and James D. Wolfensohn. "Oil And Gas In Australia," **FAJ**, 1964, v20(5), 151-158.)

Wolff, Christian C. P. "Exchange Rates, Innovations And Forecasting," **JIMF**, 1988, v7(1), 49-62.

Wolff, Christian C. P. "Forward Foreign Exchange Rates, Expected Spot Rates, And Premia: A Signal-Extraction Approach," **JOF**, 1987, v42(2), 395-406.

Wolff, Eric D. (Asquith, Paul, David W. Mullins, Jr. and Eric D. Wolff. "Original Issue High Yield Bonds: Aging Analyses Of Defaults, Exchanges, And Calls," **JOF**, 1989, v44(4), 923-952.)

Wolfson, Mark A. (Barth, Mary E., William H. Beaver and Mark A. Wolfson. "Components Of Earnings And The Structure Of Bank Share Prices," **FAJ**, 1990, v46(3), 53-60.)

Wolfson, Mark A. (Patell, James M. And Mark A. Wolfson. "The Intraday Speed Of Adjustment Of Stock Prices To Earnings And Dividend Announcements," **JFEC**, 1984, v13(2), 223-252.)

Wolfson, Mark A. (Scholes, Myron S. and Mark A. Wolfson. "Employee Stock Ownership Plans And Corporate Restructuring: Myths And Realities," **FM**, 1990, v19(1), 12-28.)

Wolfson, Mark A. (Scholes, Myron S. and Mark A. Wolfson. "The Effects Of Changes In Tax Laws On Corporate Reorganization Activity," **JOB**, 1990, v63(1), Part 2, S141-S164.)

Wolfson, Mark A. (Scholes, Myron S. and Mark A. Wolfson. "Decentralized Investment Banking: The Case Of Discount Dividend-Reinvestment And Stock-Purchase Plans," **JFEC**, 1989, v24(1), 7-36.)

Wolfson, Mark A. (Scholes, Myron S., G. Peter Wilson and Mark A. Wolfson. "Tax Planning, Regulatory Capital Planning, And Financial Reporting Strategy For Commercial Banks," **RFS**, 1990, v3(4), 625-650.)

Wolfson, Mark. "Tax, Incentive, And Risk-Sharing Issues In The Allocation Of Property Rights: The Generalized Lease-Or-Buy Problem," **JOB**, 1985, v58(2), 159-172.

Wolfson, Mark. (Beaver, William and Mark Wolfson. "Foreign Currency Translation Gains And Losses: What Effect Do They Have And What Do They Mean?," **FAJ**, 1984, v40(2), 28-29,32-36.)

Wolk, Harry I. and Michael G. Tearney. "Discounting Deferred Tax Liabilities: Review And Analysis," **JBFA**, 1980, v7(1), 119-133.

Wolk, Harry I., Lynn K. Saubert and Frank M. Tiernan. "A Further Note On Discounting Deferred Taxes," **JBFA**, 1984, v11(2),253-255.

Wolken, John D. and Frank J. Navratil. "The Economic Impact Of The Federal Credit Union Usury Ceiling," **JOF**, 1981, v36(5), 1157-1168.

Wolken, John D. and Frank J. Navratil. "Economies Of Scale In Credit Unions: Further Evidence," **JOF**, 1980, v35(3), 769-777.

Wolken, John D. (Elliehausen, Gregory E. and John D. Wolken. "Market Definition And Product Segmentation For Household Credit," **JFSR**, 1990, v4(1), 21-36.)

Wolken, John D. (Hannan, Timothy H. and John D. Wolken. "Returns To Bidders And Targets In The Acquisition Process: Evidence From The Banking Industry," **JFSR**, 1989, v3(1), 5-16.)

Wolken, John D. (Rose, John T. and John D. Wolken. "Geographic Diversification In Banking, Market Share Changes, And The Viability Of Small Independent Banks," **JFSR**, 1990, v4(1), 5-20.)

Wolkowitz, Benjamin. "The Case For The Federal Reserve Actively Participating In Electronic Funds Transfer," **JBR**, 1978-79, v9(1), 15-25.

Wolkowitz, Benjamin. (Asay, Michael R., Gisela A. Gonzalez and Benjamin Wolkowitz. "Financial Futures, Bank Portfolio Risk, And Accounting," **JFM**, v1(4), 607-618.)

Wolkowitz, Benjamin. (Mingo, John and Benjamin Wolkowitz. "The Effects Of Regulation On Bank Balance Sheet Decisions," **JOF**, 1977, v32(5), 1605-1616.)

Wong, David Y. "What Do Saving-Investment Relationships Tell Us About Capital Mobility?," **JIMF**, 1990, v9(1), 60-74.

Wong, G. Wenchi. (Fuller, Russell J. and G. Wenchi Wong. "Traditional Versus Theoretical Risk Measures," **FAJ**, 1988, v44(2), 52-57.)

Wong, G. Wenchi. (Ma, Christopher K., G. Wenchi Wong and Edwin D. Maberly. "The Daily Effect In The Gold Market: A Reply," **JFM**, 1989, v9(2), 175-178.)

Wong, Shee Q. "The Contribution Of Inflation Uncertainty To The Variable Impacts Of Money On Stock Prices," **JFR**, 1986, v9(1), 97-101.

Wong, Sui N. (Wendt, Paul F. and Sui N. Wong. "Investment Performance: Common Stocks Versus Apartment Houses," **JOF**, 1965, v20(4), 633-646.)

Wong, Wenchi. (Reilly, Frank K., Frank T. Griggs and Wenchi Wong. "Determinants Of The Aggregate Stock Market Earnings Multiple," **JPM**, 1983-84, v10(1), 36-45.)

Wonnacott, Paul. "A Suggestion For The Revaluation Of Gold," **JOF**, 1963, v18(1), 49-55.

Woo, J. C. H. and S. B. Seth. "Replacement Costs And Historical Performance," **FAJ**, 1978, v34(2), 48-54.

Woo, Wing Thye. "Some Evidence Of Specualtive Bubbles In The Foreign Exchange Market," **JMCB**, 1987, v19(4), 499-514.

Woo, Wing Thye. (Sheffrin, Steven M. and Wing Thye Woo. "Testing An Optimizing Model Of The Current Account Via The Consumption Function," **JIMF**, 1990, v9(2), 220-233.)

Wood, Arnold S. "Manager Vs. Client: What's The Difference," **JPM**, 1987-88, v14(4), 63-65.

Wood, D. Robley, Jr. (LaForge, R. Lawrence and D. Robley Wood, Jr. "The Use Of Operations Research In The Planning Activities Of Large U.S. Banks," **JBR**, 1980-81, v11(3), 179-183.)

Wood, David M. "Legal Aspects Of Revenue Bond Financing," **JOF**, 1955, v10(2), 201-208.

Wood, Douglas and Jenifer Piesse. "The Information Value Of MDA Based Financial Indicators," **JBFA**, 1987, v14(1), 27-38.

Wood, Douglas. "The Information Value Of Failure Predictions In Credit Assessment," **JBF**, 1988, v12(2), 275-292.

Wood, Duane R. (Niendorf, Robert N., Edward J. Marien and Duane R. Wood. "Integrating Finance, Marketing, And Management Courses Using Behavioral Objectives," **JFED**, 1973, v2, 20-32.)

Wood, Elmer. "Recent Monetary Policies," **JOF**, 1955, v10(3), 315-325.

Wood, Geoffrey E. (Mills, Terence C. and Geoffrey E. Wood. "Econometric Evaluation Of Alternative Money Stock Series, 1880-1913," **JMCB**, 1982, v14(2), 265-277.)

Wood, Glenn L. "Life Insurance Policy Loans: The Emergency Fund Concept," **JRI**, 1964, v31(3), 411-420.

Wood, Glenn L. (Josephson, Halsey D., Glenn L. Wood and C. Arthur Williams, Jr. "High Cash Value Life Insurance Policies And Unfair Discrimination: Comment," **JRI**, 1966, v33(1), 125-134.)

Wood, Glenn L. (Peterson, Robert A., William Rudelius and Glenn L. Wood. "Spread Of Marketing Innovations In A Service Industry," **JOB**, 1972, v45(4), 485-496.)

Wood, Glenn L. (Rejda, George E., Joseph M. Belth and Glenn L. Wood. "Life Insurance Policy Loans: The Emergency Fund Concept: Comment," JRI, 1966, v33(2), 317-328.)

Wood, Glenn L. (Rudelius, William and Glenn L. Wood. "Life Insurance Product Innovations," JRI, 1970, v37(2), 169-184.)

Wood, Glenn L. (Rudelius, William and Glenn L. Wood. "Life Insurance Product Innovations: Reply," JRI, 1972, v39(1), 142-149.)

Wood, Glenn L. (West, David A. and Glenn L. Wood. "Risk Attitudes Of Annuity-Prone Investors," JRI, 1970, v37(1), 9-16.)

Wood, Glenn L. and C. Arthur Williams, Jr. "High Cash Value Life Insurance Policies And Unfair Discrimination," JRI, 1964, v31(4), 557-572.

Wood, Glenn L. and Dick L. Rottman. "Policy Loan Interest Rates: A Critical Evaluation: Reply," JRI, 1972, v39(1), 160-162.

Wood, Glenn L. and Rich L. Rottman. "Policy Loan Interest Rates: An Critical Evaluation," JRI, 1970, v37(4), 555-566.

Wood, Glenn L. and William Rudelius. "The Product Performance Of The Life Insurance Industry: Revisited: Comment," JRI, 1972, v39(4), 651-652.

Wood, J. Harry. "Training Courses Conducted By Life Insurance Companies," JRI, 1938, v5, 5-12.

Wood, John H. "Two Notes On The Uniqueness Of Commercial Banks," JOF, 1970, v25(1), 99-108.

Wood, Marshall H. "Public Revenue Construction Bond Analysis," FAJ, 1950, v6(3), 33-36.

Wood, Oliver G. "Evolution Of The Concept Of Risk," JRI, 1964, v31(1), 83-92.

Wood, R. A. (McInish, T. H. and R. A. Wood. "A Transactions Data Analysis Of The Variability Of Common Stock Returns During 1980-1984," JBF, 1990, v14(1), 99-112.)

Wood, R. A. (McInish, T. H. and R. A. Wood. "An Analysis Of Transactions Data For The Toronto Stock Exchange: Return Patterns And End-Of-The-Day Effect," JBF, 1990, v14(2/3), 441-458.)

Wood, Ralph C. "The Discipline Of The Balance Of Payments: Postwar Experience In Europe," JOF, 1961, v16(2), 157-166.

Wood, Ramsey. "Government Mortgage Credit Commitments And Economic Stability," JOF, 1956, v11(2), 151-165.

Wood, Robert A. (Amihud, Yakov, Haim Mendelson and Robert A. Wood. "Liquidity And The 1987 Stock Market Crash," JPM, 1990, v16(3), 65-69.)

Wood, Robert A. (McInish, Thomas H. and Robert A. Wood. "A New Approach To Controlling For Thin Trading," JFR, 1985, v8(1), 69-75.)

Wood, Robert A. (McInish, Thomas H. and Robert A. Wood. "Intraday And Overnight Returns And Day-Of-The-Week Effects," JFR, 1985, v8(2), 119-126.)

Wood, Robert A. (McInish, Thomas H. and Robert A. Wood. "Adjusting For Beta Bias: An Assessment Of Alternate Techniques: A Note," JOF, 1986, v41(1), 277-286.)

Wood, Robert A. (McInish, Thomas H. and Robert A. Wood. "Intertemporal Differences In Movements Of Minute-To-Minute Stock Returns," FR, 1984, v19(4), 359-371.)

Wood, Robert A. (McInish, Thomas H. and Robert A. Wood. "Autocorrelation Of Daily Index Returns: Intraday-to-Intraday Versus Close-To-Close Intervals," JBF, 1991, v15(1), 193-206.)

Wood, Robert A. (Stone, Bernell K. and Robert A. Wood. "Daily Cash Forecasting: A Simple Method For Implementing The Distribution Approach," FM, 1977, v6(3), 40-50.)

Wood, Robert A., Thomas H. McInish and J. Keith Ord. "An Investigation Of Transactions Data For NYSE Stocks," JOF, 1985, v40(3), 723-739.

Wood, Robert A., Jr. (Hill, Joanne M., Anshuman Jain and Robert A. Wood, Jr. "Insurance: Volatility Risk And Futures Mispricing," JPM, 1987-88, v14(2), 23-29.)

Wood, Robert. (McInish, Thomas H. and Robert Wood. "Proxies For Nonsynchronous Trading," FR, 1983, v18(2), 206-213.)

Wood, Wendell C., Carl E. Shafer and Carl G. Anderson. "Frequency And Duration Of Profitable Hedging Margins For Texas Cotton Producers, 1980-1986," JFM, 1989, v9(6), 519-528.

Wood, William C. "Nuclear Liability After Three Mile Island," JRI, 1981, v48(3), 450-464.

Wood, William C. "Nuclear Liability After Three Mile Island: Reply," JRI, 1983, v50(2), 328-329.

Woodard, George D. and James E. Goldsberry. "Economic Research As An Aid To Regional Bank Holding Company Expansion," JBR, 1983-84, v14(4), 302-304.

Woodbridge, Richard G., III. "Chemical Process Enterprises," FAJ, 1953, v9(4), 65-68.

Woodbury, John R., III. (White, Betsy Buttrill and John R. Woodbury, III. "Exchange Rate Systems And International Capital Market Integration," JMCB, 1980, v12(2), Part 1, 175-183.)

Woodliff, David R. (Houghton, Keith A. and David R. Woodliff. "Financial Ratios: The Prediction Of Corporte 'Success' And Failure," JBFA, 1987, v14(4), 537-554.)

Woodman, Herbert B. (Cassel, Norman S. and Herbert B. Woodman. "Looking Behind Research Costs," FAJ, 1957, v13(4), 11-14.)

Woodroof, Clarence E. "An Analyst Looks At A Port," FAJ, 1953, v9(4), 31-32.

Woodruff, Catherine S. and A. J. Senchack, Jr. "Intradaily Price-Volume Adjustments Of NYSE Stocks To Unexpected Earnings," JOF, 1988, v43(2), 467-491.

Woods, A. (Bayldon, R., A. Woods and N. Zafiris. "A Note On The 'Pyramid' Technique Of Financial Ratio Analysis Of Firms' Performance," JBFA, 1984, v11(1), 99-106.)

Woods, Donald H. and Eugene F. Brigham. "Stockholder Distribution Decisions: Share Repurchases Or Dividends," JFQA, 1966, v1(1), 15-25.

Woods, Donald H. and Thomas A. Caverly. "Development Of A Linear Programming Model For The Analysis Of Merger/ Acquisition Situations," JFQA, 1970, v5(5), 627-642.

Woods, Donald H. "A New Perspective," FAJ, 1967, v23(4), 73-75.

Woods, John C. and Maury R. Randall. "The Net Present Value Of Future Investment Opportunities: Its Impact On Shareholder Wealth And Implications For Capital Budgeting Theory," FM, 1989, v18(2), 85-92. 3j 3

Woods, John C. (Greenfield, Robert L., Maury R. Randall and John C. Woods. "Financial Leverage And Use Of The Net Present Value Investment Criterion," FM, 1983, v12(3), 40-44.)

Woodside, Arch G. (White, Douglas and Arch G. Woodside. "Marketing In Banking: Philosophies And Actions," JBR, 1972-73, v3(4), 265-268.)

Woodside, Arch G. and J. William Davenport, Jr. "Effects Of Price And Salesman Expertise On Customer Purchasing Behavior," JOB, 1976, v49(1), 51-59.

Woodward, Donald B. "Investment," FAJ, 1951, v7(3), 40.

Woodward, G. Thomas. "The Real Thing: A Dynamic Profile Of The Term Structure Of Real Interest Rates And Inflation Expectations In The United Kingdom, 1982-89," JOB, 1990, v63(3), 373-398.

Woodward, G. Thomas. (Makinen, Gail E. and G. Thomas Woodward. "The Taiwanese Hyperinflation And Stabilization Of 1945-1952," JMCB, 1989, v21(1), 90-105.)

Woodward, Lynn. (Dasso, Jerome and Lynn Woodward. "Real Estate Education: Past, Present And Future - The Search For A Discipline," AREUEA, 1980, v8(4), 404-416.)

Woodward, R. S. and J. Matatko. "Factors Affecting The Behaviour Of UK Closed End Fund Discounts 1968 to 1977," JBFA, 1982, v8(4), 501-509.

Woodward, R. S. "Some New Evidence On The Profitability Of One-Way Versus Round-Trip Arbitrage," JMCB, 1988, v20(4), 645-652.

Woodward, R. S. "The Effect Of Monetary Surprises On Financial Futures Prices," JFM, 1986, v6(3), 375-384.

Woodward, R. S. "The Performance Of U. K. Investment Trusts As Internationally Diversified Portfolios Over The Period 1968 To 1977," JBF, 1983, v7(3), 417-426.

Woodward, R. S. "The Performance Of UK Closed-End Funds: A Comparison Of The Various Ranking Criteria," JBFA, 1983, v10(3), 419-428.

Woodward, R. S. (Chua, J. H. and R. S. Woodward. "The Investment Wizardry Of J. M. Keynes," FAJ, 1983, v39(3), 35-37.)

Woodward, R. S. (Chua, J. and R. S. Woodward. "Gold As An Inflation Hedge: A Comparative Study Of Six Major Industrial Countries," JBFA, 1982, v8(2), 191-197.)

Woodward, Richard S. (Ang, James S., Jess H. Chua and Richard S. Woodward. "A Note On Investment Decision Rules Based On Utility Functions," JBFA, 1983, v10(4), 657-661.)

Woodward, Richard S. (Chua, Jess H., Richard S. Woodward and Eric C. To. "Potential Gains From Stock Market Timing In Canada," FAJ, 1987, v43(5), 50-56.)

Woodward, Richard S. (Chua, Jess H. and Richard S. Woodward. "J. M. Keynes's Investment Performance: A Note," JOF, 1983, v38(1), 232-235.)

Woodward, Richard S. (Chua, Jess H., Gordon Sick and Richard S. Woodward. "Diversifying With Gold Stocks," FAJ, 1990, v46(4), 76-79.)

Woodward, Richard S. (Saunders, Anthony and Richard S. Woodward. "Gains From International Portfolio Diversification: A Reply," JBFA, 1979, v6(1), 51-52.)

Woodward, Richard S. (Saunders, Anthony and Richard S. Woodward. "Gains From International Portfolio Diversification: UK Evidence 1971-75," JBFA, 1977, v4(3), 299-309.)

Woodward, Richard. (Gandhi, Devinder K., Anthony Saunders, Richard Woodward and Charles Ward. "The British Investor's Gains From International Portfolio Investment," JBF, 1981, v5(2), 155-165.)

Woodward, Richard. (Saunders, Anthony, Charles Ward and Richard Woodward. "Stochastic Dominance And The Performance Of U.K. Unit Trusts," JFQA, 1980, v15(2), 323-330.)

Woodworth, A. V., Jr. "Natural Resource Stocks As Inflation Hedge," FAJ, 1959, v15(4), 45-50.

Woodworth, Jay N. "What Kind Of Research Do We Really Need?," FAJ, 1978, v34(1), 38-40.

Woodworth, Kenneth. "National Federation Of Financial Analyst's Societies," FAJ, 1947, v3(4), 51-53.

Woolley, P. K. (Coates, J. H. and P. K. Woolley. "Corporate Gearing In The EEC," JBFA, 1975, v2(1), 1-18.)

Woolley, Paul. (Bostock, Paul, Paul Woolley and Martin Duffy. "Duration-Based Asset Allocation," FAJ, 1989, v45(1), 53-60.)

Woolridge, J. Randall and Chinmoy Ghosh. "Institutional Trading And Security Prices: The Case Of Changes In The Composition Of The S&P 500 Index," JFR, 1986, v9(1), 13-24.

Woolridge, J. Randall and Donald R. Chambers. "Reverse Splits And Shareholder Wealth," FM, 1983, v12(3), 5-15.

Woolridge, J. Randall. "Competitive Decline And Corporate Restructuring: Is A Myopic Stock Market To Blame?," JACF, 1988, v1(1), 26-36.

Woolridge, J. Randall. "Dividend Changes And Security Prices," JOF, 1983, v38(5), 1607-1615.

Woolridge, J. Randall. "Ex-Date Stock Price Adjustment To Stock Dividends: A Note," JOF, 1983, v38(1), 247-255.

Woolridge, J. Randall. "Stock Dividends As Signals," JFR, 1983, v6(1), 1-12.

Woolridge, J. Randall. "The Information Content Of Dividend Changes," JFR, 1982, v5(3), 237-247.

Woolridge, J. Randall. (Calley, Nicholas O., Donald R. Chambers and J. Randall Woolridge. "A Note On Standardized Unexpected Earnings: The Case Of The Electric Utility Industry," FR, 1985, v20(1), 102-110.)

Woolridge, J. Randall. (Ghosh, Chinmoy and J. Randall Woolridge. "An Analysis Of Shareholder Reaction To Dividend Cuts And Omissions," JFR, 1988, v11(4), 281-294.)

Woolridge, J. Randall. (Ghosh, Chinmoy and J. Randall Woolridge. "Dividend Omissions And Stock Market Rationality," JBFA, 1991, v18(3), 315-330.)

Woolridge, J. Randall. (Schneeweis, Thomas and J. Randall Woolridge. "Capital Market Seasonality: The Case Of Bond Returns," JFQA, 1979, v14(5), 939-958.)

Worcester, Dean A., Jr. "Monetary Versus Fiscal Policy At Full Employment," JOF, 1957, v12(1), 1-15.

Worden, Debra Drecnik. (Sullivan, A. Charlene and Debra Drecnik Worden. "Deregulation, Tax Reform, And The Use Of Consumer Credit," JFSR, 1989, v3(1), 77-91.)

Workman, Rosemarie. (Dale, Charles and Rosemarie Workman. "The Arc Sine Law And The Treasury Bill Futures Market," **FAJ**, 1980, v36(6), 71-74.)

Works, John W. "Clustering Of Stock Prices: A New Model," **FR**, 1970, v1(5), 340-347.

Worley, Richard B. and Stanley Diller. "Interpreting The Yield Curve," **FAJ**, 1976, v32(6), 37-45.

Worrall, John D. (Appel, David, John D. Worrall and Richard J. Butler. "Survivorship And The Size Distribution Of The Property-Liability Insurance Industry," **JRI**, 1985, v52(3), 424-440.)

Worrall, John D. and David Appel. "The Wage Replacement Rate And Benefit Utilization In Workers' Compensation Insurance," **JRI**, 1982, v49(3), 361-371.

Worrall, John D., David Appel and Richard J. Butler. "Sex, Marital Status, And Medical Utilization By Injured Workers," **JRI**, 1987, v54(1), 27-44.

Worswick, G. D. N. "Fiscal Policy And Stabilization In Britain," **JMCB**, 1969, v1(3), 474-495.

Wort, Donald H. (Lee, Cheng F., Donald H. Wort and Doug Han. "The Relationship Between Dividend Yield And Earnings Yield And Its Implication For Forecasting," **AFPAF**, 1987, v2(1), 155-178.)

Worthley, Reginald G. (Jonish, James E. and Reginald G. Worthley. "Unemployment Insurance Fund Adequacy: An Alternative Measure," **JRI**, 1972, v39(4), 535-544.)

Worthy, James C. "Education For Business Leadership," **JOB**, 1955, v28(1), 76-82.

Worthy, James C. "Religion And Its Role In The World Of Business," **JOB**, 1958, v31(4), 293-303.

Wrage, Peter. (Bartel, Henry, Michael Daly and Peter Wrage. "Reverse Mortgages: Supplementary Retirement Income From Home-ownership," **JRI**, 1980, v47(3), 477-490.)

Wrapp, H. Edward. "Standards Deterioration Under Wage Incentives," **JOB**, 1953, v26(1), 9-14.

Wright, Arthur L. "The Impact Of Residential Rent Controls On Lender Policies And Activities," **JRER**, 1988, v3(3), 85-90.

Wright, B. V., Jr. "Interest Rates: A Contrary View," **FAJ**, 1974, v30(4), 34-36.

Wright, Brian D. and Jeffrey C. Williams. "A Theory Of Negative Prices For Storage," **JFM**, 1989, v9(1), 1-14.

Wright, David J. (Reilly, Frank K. and David J. Wright. "Block Trading And Aggregate Stock Price Volatility," **FAJ**, 1984, v40(2), 54-60.)

Wright, David J. (Reilly, Frank K. and David J. Wright. "A Comparison Of Published Betas," **JPM**, 1987-88, v14(3), 64-69.)

Wright, David McCord. "Inflation And The Rate Of Interest," **FAJ**, 1960, v16(3), 45-47.

Wright, David McCord. "Community', Mobility, Security: A Footnote On Economic Growth," **JOB**, 1959, v32(1), 15-19.

Wright, Dolores R. (McCord, Sammy O., J. Ford Laumer, Jr. and Dolores R. Wright. "Student Internships In Finance," **JFED**, 1976, v5, 55-57.)

Wright, F. K. "An Economic Analysis Of Value To The Owner: A Comment," **JBFA**, 1984, v11(3), 419-423.

Wright, F. K. "Cash As An Item Of Stock: A Comment," **JBFA**, 1979, v6(1), 115-119.

Wright, F. K. "Project Evaluation And The Managerial Limit," **JOB**, 1964, v37(2), 179-185.

Wright, F. K. (Wirth, A. and F. K. Wright. "New-Issue Costs And Project Evaluation: Ezzell And Porter Revisited," **JBFA**, 1987, v14(3), 393-408.)

Wright, Forrest J. "The Link Between Money And Stock Prices," **FAJ**, 1976, v32(3), 27-32.

Wright, Gordon. (Teichroew, Daniel, William Lesso, Kevin Rice and Gordon Wright. "Optimizing Models Of After-Tax Earnings Incorporating Depletion Allowance," **JFQA**, 1967, v2(3), 265-297.)

Wright, Kenneth M. "Gross Flows Of Funds Through Life Insurance Companies," **JOF**, 1960, v15(2), 140-156.

Wright, Mike, Ken Robbie and Steve Thompson. "Corporate Restructuring, Buy-Outs, And Managerial Equity: The European Dimension," **JACF**, 1991, v3(4), 46-58.

Wright, Mike. "Real Rates Of Return On Capital: Some Estimates For British Gas," **JBFA**, 1980, v7(1), 89-103.

Wright, Mike. (Chiplin, Brian and Mike Wright. "Inter-Industry Differences In The Response Of Trade Credit To Changes In Monetary Policy," **JBFA**, 1985, v12(2), 221-248.)

Wright, Mike. (Thompson, Steve, Mike Wright and Ken Robbie. "Management Buy-Outs, Debt, And Efficiency: Some Evidence From The U.K.," **JACF**, 1989, v2(1), 76-86.)

Wright, Richard. (Remmers, Lee, Arthur Stonehill, Richard Wright and Theo Beekhuisen. "Industry And Size As Debt Ratio Determinants In Manufacturing Internationally," **FM**, 1974, v3(2), 24-32.)

Wright, Richard. (Stonehill, Arthur, Theo Beekhuisen, Richard Wright, Lee Remmers, Norman Toy, Antonio Pares, Alan Shapiro, Douglas Egan and Thomas Bates. "Financial Goals And Debt Ratio Determinants," **FM**, 1974, v4(3), 27-41.)

Wright, Richard. (Toy, N., A. Stonehill, L. Remmers, R. Wright and T. Beekhuisen. "A Comparative International Study Of Growth, Profitability, And Risk As Determinants Of Corporate Debt Ratios," **JFQA**, 1974, v9(5), 875-886.)

Wright, Roger L. (Dielman, Terry, Timothy J. Nantell and Roger L. Wright. "Price Effects Of Stock Repurchasing: A Random Coefficient Regression Approach," **JFQA**, 1980, v15(1), 175-189.)

Wright, Roger L. (Mao, James C. T. and Roger L. Wright. "A Chance-Constrained Approach To Urban Renewal Decisions," **JFQA**, 1968, v3(2), 135-150.)

Wright, William F. (Eskew, Robert K. and William F. Wright. "An Empirical Analysis Of Differential Capital Market Reactions To Extraordinary Accounting Items," **JOF**, 1976, v31(2), 651-674.)

Wrightsman, Dwayne and James O. Horrigan. "Retention, Risk Of Success, And The Price Of Stock: A Note," **JOF**, 1975, v30(5), 1357-1359.

Wrightsman, Dwayne and John Terninko. "On The Measurement Of Opportunity Cost In Transactions Demand Models," **JOF**, 1971, v26(4), 947-950.

Wrightsman, Dwayne. "Tax Shield Valuation And The Capital Structure Decision," **JOF**, 1978, v33(2), 650-656.

Wruck, Karen H. (Baker, George P. and Karen H. Wruck. "Organizational Changes And Value Creation In Leveraged Buyouts: The Case Of The O.M. Scott & Sons Company," **JFEC**, 1989, v25(2), 163-190.)

Wruck, Karen H. (Warner, Jerold B., Ross L. Watts and Karen H. Wruck. "Stock Prices And Top Management Changes," **JFEC**, 1988, v20(1), 461-492.)

Wruck, Karen Hopper. "Equity Ownership Concentration And Firm Value: Evidence From Private Equity Financings," **JFEC**, 1989, v23(1), 3-28.

Wruck, Karen Hopper. "Financial Distress, Reorganiztion, And Organizational Efficiency," **JFEC**, 1990, v27(2), 419-444.

Wu, Chunchi and Peter F. Colwell. "Equilibrium Of Housing And Real Estate Brokerage Markets Under Uncertainty," **AREUEA**, 1986, v14(1), 1-23.

Wu, Chunchi and Peter F. Colwell. "Moral Hazard And Moral Imperative," **JRI**, 1988, v55(1), 101-117.

Wu, Chunchi and Peter F. Colwell. "Moral Hazard And Moral Imperative: Reply," **JRI**, 1990, v57(2), 332-335.

Wu, Chunchi. (Colwell, Peter F., Roger E. Cannaday and Chunchi Wu. "The Analytical Foundations Of Adjustment Grid Methods," **AREUEA**, 1983, v11(1), 11-29.)

Wu, Chunchi. (Kao, Chihwa and Chunchi Wu. "Sinking Funds And The Agency Costs Of Corporate Debt," **FR**, 1990, v25(1), 95-114.)

Wu, Chunchi. (Kim, Moon K. and Chunchi Wu. "Macro-Economic Factors And Stock Returns," **JFR**, 1987, v10(2), 87-98.)

Wu, Chunchi. (Kim, Moon K. and Chunchi Wu. "Effects Of Inflation On Capital Structure," **FR**, 1988, v23(2), 183-200.)

Wu, Chunchi. (Lee, Cheng F. and Chunchi Wu. "The Impacts Of Kurtosis On Risk Stationarity: Some Empirical Evidence," **FR**, 1985, v20(4), 263-269.)

Wu, Chunchi. (Lee, Cheng F. and Chunchi Wu. "Using Zellner's Errors-In-Variables Model To Reexamine MM's Valuation Model For Electric Utility Industry," **AFPAF**, 1989, v3(1), 63-74.)

Wu, Chunchi. (Lee, Cheng F., Chunchi Wu and K. C. John Wei. "The Heterogeneous Investment Horizon And The Capital Asset Pricing Model: Theory And Implications," **JFQA**, 1990, v25(3), 361-376.)

Wu, Chunchi. (Provenzano, George and Chunchi Wu. "Combining Financial And Production Constraints In Investment Planning For Electrical Power Supply," **AFPAF**, 1985, v1(1), 167-186.)

Wu, De-Min. "An Empirical Analysis Of Japanese Direct Investment In Taiwan," **AFPAF**, 1985, v1(Supp), 9-64.

Wu, Hsiu-Kwang and Billy P. Helms. "Confidential Bank Examination Data And The Efficiency Of Bank Share Prices," **FAJ**, 1984, v40(6), 31-33.

Wu, Hsiu-Kwang. "Bank Examiner Criticisms, Bank Loan Defaults, And Bank Loan Quality," **JOF**, 1969, v24(4), 697-705.

Wu, Hsiu-Kwang. "Odd-Lot Trading In The Stock Market And Its Market Impact," **JFQA**, 1972, v7(1), 1321-1341.

Wu, Hsiu-Kwang. "Odd-Lot Trading In The Stock Market And Its Market Impact: A Reply," **JFQA**, 1973, v8(3), 515.

Wu, Hsiu-Kwang. (Visser, John R. and Hsiu-Kwang Wu. "The Effects Of Deregulation On Bank Stock Price-Earnings Ratios," **FAJ**, 1989, v45(5), 62-67.)

Wu, Mickey T. C. (Richardson, David H. and Mickey T. C. Wu. "Tests Of The Goods Market Integration Hypothesis," **JMCB**, 1982, v14(1), 92-97.)

Wu, Rong I. "Economic Development Strategy And The Role Of Direct Foreign Investment In Taiwan," **AFPAF**, 1985, v1(Supp), 65-90.

Wubbels, Rolf E. "Market Letters," **FAJ**, 1952, v8(3), 103-107.

Wubbels, Rolf E. "The French Economic Miracle," **FAJ**, 1979, v35(4), 23-27.

Wubbels, Rolf E. (Glickstein, David A. and Rolf E. Wubbels. "Dow Theory Is Alive And Well!," **JPM**, 1982-83, v9(3), 28-32.)

Wunsch, R. Steven. "Panel: Trading Halts And Price Limits," **RFM**, 1988, v7(3), 440-441.

Wurtzebach, Charles H. "Integrating A Real Estate Sequence Into The Finance Curriculum," **JFED**, 1980, v9, 46-50.

Wurtzebach, Charles H. (Hartzell, David J., David G. Shulman and Charles H. Wurtzebach. "Refining The Analysis Of Regional Diversification For Income-Producing Real Estate," **JRER**, 1987, v2(2), 85-95.)

Wurtzebach, Charles H. (Kuhle, James L., Carl H. Walther and Charles H. Wurtzebach. "The Financial Performance Of Real Estate Investment Trusts," **JRER**, 1986, v1(1), 67-75.)

Wurtzebach, Charles H. and Kee S. Kim. "An Investment Analysis And Decision Making Framework For Real Estate Development," **AREUEA**, 1979, v7(3), 410-426.

Wyatt, Jeffrey G. (Rosenstein, Stuart and Jeffrey G. Wyatt. "Outside Directors, Board Independence, And Shareholder Wealth," **JFEC**, 1990, v26(2), 175-192.)

Wyatt, Steve B. "On The Valuation Of Puts And Calls On Spot, Forward, And Future Foreign Exchange: Theory And Evidence," **AFPAF**, 1989, v4(Supp), 81-104.

Wyatt, Steve B. (Adams, Paul D. and Steve B. Wyatt. "Biases In Option Prices: Evidence From The Foreign Currency Option Market," **JBF**, 1987, v11(4), 549-562.)

Wyatt, Steve B. (Adams, Paul D. and Steve B. Wyatt. "On The Pricing Of European And American Foreign Currency Call Options," **JIMF**, 1987, v6(3), 315-338.)

Wyatt, Steve B. (Adams, Paul D. and Steve B. Wyatt. "On The Pricing Of European And American Foreign Currency Options: A Clarification," **JIMF**, 1989, v8(2), 305-311.)

Wyatt, Steve B. (Bosch, Jean-Claude, James J. Morris and Steve B. Wyatt. "The Investment In Housing As A Forward Market Transaction: Implications For Tenure Choice And Portfolio Selection," **AREUEA**, 1986, v14(3), 385-405.)

Wyatt, Steve B. (Lee, Insup and Steve B. Wyatt. "The Effects Of International Joint Ventures On Shareholder Wealth," **FR**, 1990, v25(4), 641-650.)

Wyckoff, Peter G. "Methods And Motives For Selling Short," **FAJ**, 1959, v15(2), 101-116.

Wyckoff, Peter. "How Safe Is Your Security?," **FAJ**, 1956, v12(4), 65-68.

Wyckoff, Peter. "The Trader's Trilogy," **FAJ**, 1954, v10(5), 69-72.

Wydler, Daniel. "Swiss Stocks, Bonds, And Inflation, 1926-1987," **JPM**, 1989, v15(3), 27-32.

Yawitz, Jess. (Smirlock, Michael and Jess Yawitz. "Asset Returns, Discount Rate Changes, And Market Efficiency," JOF, 1985, v40(4), 1141-1158.)

Yeager, Francis S. "A New Course In Urban Finance," JFED, 1974, v3, 61-62.

Yeager, James H., Jr. "Wealth Effects And The Effectiveness Of Monetary And Fiscal Policies," JMCB, 1975, v7(4), 531-532.

Yeager, Leland B. "The Misconceived Problem Of International Liquidity," JOF, 1959, v14(3), 347-360.

Yeager, Leland B. (Greenfield, Robert L. and Leland B. Yeager. "A Laissez-Faire Approach To Monetary Stability," JMCB, 1983, v15(3), 302-315.)

Yeager, Leland. "Bootstrap Inflation," JOF, 1976, v31(1), 103-112.

Yeakel, John A. (Clancy, Donald K. and John A. Yeakel. "On Reporting Dilutionary Exchanges," FAJ, 1981, v37(5), 70-73.)

Yeasting, Kenneth L. "CD Warrants," FAJ, 1970, v26(2), 44-47.

Yeats, A. J. "A Framework For Evaluating Potential Competition As A Factor In Bank Mergers And Acquisitions: A Comment," JMCB, 1974, v6(3), 395-402.

Yeats, A. J. (Rhoades, S. A. and A. J. Yeats. "Growth, Consolidation And Mergers In Banking," JOF, 1974, v29(5), 1397-1405.)

Yeats, Alexander J. (Erzan, Refik and Alexander J. Yeats. "Implications Of Current Factor Proportions Indices For The Competitive Position Of The U.S. Manufacturing And Service Industries In The Year 2000," JOB, 1991, v64(2), 229-254.)

Yeats, Alexander J., Edward D. Irons and Stephen A. Rhoades. "An Analysis Of New Bank Growth," JOB, 1975, v48(2), 199-203.

Yeats, Alexander. "An Analysis Of The Effect Of Mergers On The Banking Market Structure," JMCB, 1973, v5(2), 623-636.

Yellott, John I. "Coal-Burning Gas Turbine Locomotive," FAJ, 1947, v3(1), 18-31.

Yellott, John I. "Solar Energy - Its Domestic And Foreign Implications," FAJ, 1958, v14(1), 15-22.

Yen, Eva C. (Yen, Gili, T. L. Chang and Eva C. Yen. "On The Measurement Of State-Owned Enterprises In Taiwan: An Application Of Financial Ratio Analysis," AFPAF, 1985, v1(Supp), 243-260.)

Yen, Gili, T. L. Chang and Eva C. Yen. "On The Measurement Of State-Owned Enterprises In Taiwan: An Application Of Financial Ratio Analysis," AFPAF, 1985, v1(Supp), 243-260.

Yen, Gili. "Is Managerial Resistance 'Strategic' Or 'Self-Serving'? A Case Study Of Merger Proposals," AFPAF, 1989, v3(1), 351-374.

Yeo, Edwin H., III. "A Management View Of Financial Planning, Or The Best Laid Schemes," JBR, 1973-74, v4(3), 207-211.

Yeomans, K. A. (Buckland, R., P. J. Herbert and K. A. Yeomans. "Price Discount On New Equity Issues In The UK And Their Relationship To Investor Subscription In The Period 1965-75," JBFA, 1981, v8(1), 79-95.)

Yeomans, K. A. (Davis, E. W. and K. A. Yeomans. "Market Discount On New Issues Of Equity: The Influence Of Firm Size, Method Of Issue And Market Volatility," JBFA, 1976, v3(4), 27-42.)

Yett, Donald E. (Mann, Judith K. and Donald E. Yett. "The Analysis Of Hospital Costs: A Review Article," JOB, 1968, v41(2), 191-202.)

Yeung, Bernard. (Barone-Adesi, Giovanni and Bernard Yeung. "Price Flexibility And Output Volatility: The Case For Flexible Exchange Rates," JIMF, 1990, v9(3), 276-298.)

Yeung, Bernard. (Mirus, Rolf and Bernard Yeung. "The Relevance Of The Invoicing Currency In Intra-Firm Trade Transactions," JIMF, 1987, v6(4), 449-464.)

Yeung, Bernard. (Morck, Randall and Bernard Yeung. "Why Investors Value Multinationality," JOB, 1991, v64(2), 165-188.)

Yew, Madata. "Is The Committee On General Insurance Terminology Really General?: Comment," JRI, 1965, v32(1), 139-140.

Yezer, Anthony M. J. (Barth, James, Padma Gotur, Neela Manage and Anthony Yezer. "The Effect Of Government Regulations On Personal Loan Markets: A Tobit Estimation Of A Microeconomic Model," JOF, 1983, v38(4), 1233-1251.)

Yezer, Anthony M. J. (Barth, James R. and Anthony M. J. Yezer. "Default Risk On Home Mortgages: A Further Test Of Competing Hypotheses," JRI, 1983, v50(3), 500-505.)

Yezer, Anthony M. J. (Shear, William B. and Anthony M. J. Yezer. "An Indirect Test For Differential Treatment Of Borrowers In Mortgage Markets," AREUEA, 1982, v10(4), 405-420.)

Yilmaz, Mustafa R. "The Use Of Risk And Return Models For Multiattribute Decisions With Decomposable Utilities," JFQA, 1983, v18(3), 279-285.

Yim, Hyang K. (Dale-Johnson, David and Hyang K. Yim. "Coastal Development Moratoria And Housing Prices," JREFEC, 1990, v3(2), 173-184.)

Yin, Robert K. "What A National Commission On Neighborhoods Could Do," AREUEA, 1977, v5(3), 255-278.

Ying, Charles. (Gordon, Myron J. and Charles Ying. "The Assignment Of Costs To Joint Products In A Decentralized Firm," JOB, 1968, v41(3), 363-374.)

Ying, Louis K. W., Wilbur G. Lewellen, Gary G. Schlarbaum and Ronald C. Lease. "Stock Exchange Listings And Securities Returns," JFQA, 1977, v12(3), 415-432.

Yip, Patrick C. Y. (Cheung, C. Sherman, Clarence C. Y. Kwan and Patrick C. Y. Yip. "The Hedging Effectiveness Of Options And Futures: A Mean-Gini Approach," JFM, 1990, v10(1), 61-74.)

Yitzhaki, Shlomo. (Shalit, Haim and Shlomo Yitzhaki. "Evaluating The Mean-Gini Approach To Portfolio Selection," IJOF, 1989, v1(2), 15-31.)

Yitzhaki, Shlomo. (Shalit, Haim and Shlomo Yitzhaki. "Mean-Gini, Portfolio Theory, And The Pricing Of Risky Assets," JOF, 1984, v39(5), 1449-1468.)

Yntema, Theodore O. "Economic Adjustments Among Nations," JOF, 1961, v16(1), 1-7.

Yntema, Theodore. "Transferable Skills And Abilities," JOB, 1958, v31(2), 91-94.

Yoder, James A. (Levy, Haim and James A. Yoder. "Applying The Black-Scholes Model After Large Market Shocks," JPM, 1989, v16(1), 103-106.)

Yoder, Jim. (Brooks, Robert, Haim Levy and Jim Yoder. "Using Stochastic Dominance To Evaluate The Performance Of Portfolios With Options," FAJ, 1987, v43(2), 79-82.)

Yohe, W. P. and L. C. Gasper. "Even Keel' Decisions Of The FOMC," FAJ, 1970, v26(6), 105-115.

Yonezawa, Yasuhiro and Fumiko Kon-Ya. "The Japanese Market And The Economic Enviornment," JPM, 1982-83, v9(1), 36-45.

Yoran, Aharon. (Barlev, Benzion, Joshua Livnat and Aharon Yoran. "Advance Payments During Inflationary Periods," JBFA, 1982, v8(3), 413-426.)

York, Paul F. (Umble, M. Michael, Paul F. York and E. J. Everett, Jr. "Agent Retention Rates In The Independent Agency System," JRI, 1977, v44(3), 481-486.)

Yormark, Jonathan S. (Findlay, M. Chapman, III, Carl W. Hamilton, Stephen D. Messner and Jonathan S. Yormark. "Optimal Real Estate Portfolios," AREUEA, 1979, v7(3), 298-317.)

Yoshida, Hiroshi. "Some Comments On CPP Accounting," JBFA, 1976, v3(3), 113-116.

Yoshino, Gakuzo. "Japanese Economy - New Market For Investors," FAJ, 1962, v18(1), 17-28.

Young, Allan E. "The Effects Of Share Distribution On Price Action," FR, 1973, v8(1), 11-16.

Young, Allan E. (Marshall, Wayne S. and Alan E. Young. "A Mathematical Model For Re-Acquisition Of Small Shareholdings," JFQA, 1968, v3(4), 463-469.)

Young, Allan. "Common Stocks After Repurchase," FAJ, 1967, v23(5), 117-121.

Young, Allan. "Parameters For Stock Repurchase," FAJ, 1969, v25(4), 123-128.

Young, Allan. (Franck, Peter and Allan Young. "Stock Price Reaction Of Multinational Firms To Exchange Realignments," FM, 1972, v1(3), 66-73.)

Young, Allan. (Frankfurter, George M., Richard Stevenson and Allan Young. "Option Spreading: Theory And An Illustration," JPM, 1978-79, v5(4), 59-63.)

Young, Allan. (Frankfurter, George and Allan Young. "Option Spreading: Reply," JPM, 1980-81, v7(2), 89-93.)

Young, Allan. (Goldberg, Lawrence G., Gerald A. Hanweck, Michael Keenan and Allan Young. "Economies Of Scale And Scope In The Securities Industry," JBF, 1991, v15(1), 91-107.)

Young, Allan. (Kim, Moon K. and Allan Young. "Rewards And Risks From Warrant Hedging," JPM, 1979-80, v6(4), 65-68.)

Young, C. M. (Brealey, R. A. and C. M. Young. "Debt, Taxes And Leasing - A Note," JOF, 1980, v35(5), 1245-1250.)

Young, Charles W. "Computer-Assisted Analysis As The Focus For A Course In Financial Management," JFED, 1978, v7, 59-62.

Young, Colin M. "The Competitiveness Of Lease Markets: An Empirical Investigation Of The UK Local Authority Lease Market," JBFA, 1984, v11(2), 189-198.

Young, Colin. (Rosenthal, Leonard and Colin Young. "The Seemingly Anomalous Price Behavior Of Royal Dutch/Shell And Unilever N.V./PLC," JFEC, 1990, v26(1), 123-142.)

Young, Harold H. "Factors Influencing Utility Price-Earnings Ratios," FAJ, 1945, v1(1), 45-48.

Young, Harold H. "Near Term Outlook For Public Utilities: 1948 - A Promising Year," FAJ, 1948, v4(1), 23-26.

Young, Harold H. "The Human Side Of Utility Investments," FAJ, 1953, v9(5), 9-12.

Young, Harold. "Desirability Of Public Utility Equities," FAJ, 1950, v6(1), 7-12.

Young, Howard. "A Method Of Automatically Adjusting The Maximum Earnings Base Under OASDI: Comment," JRI, 1965, v32(3), 468-470.

Young, Howard. "Discussion Of Papers On The Future Of Private Pensions," JRI, 1967, v34(1), 33-37.

Young, Ian. (Pye, Gordon and Ian Young. "The Effect Of Deposit Rate Ceilings On Aggregate Income," JOF, 1972, v27(5), 1023-1034.)

Young, J. E. (Slovin, M. B. and J. E. Young. "Bank Lending And Initial Public Offering," JBF, 1990, v14(4), 729-740.)

Young, James R. "Automobile Insurance Reform," JRI, 1972, v39(2), 263-270.

Young, Leslie and Glenn W. Boyle. "Forward And Futures Prices In A General Equilibrium Monetary Model," JFEC, 1989, v24(2), 319-342.

Young, Madelyn V. (Kochanowski, Paul S. and Madelyn V. Young. "Deterrent Aspects Of No-Fault Automobile Insurance: Some Empirical Findings," JRI, 1985, v52(2), 269-288.)

Young, Ralph A. (Fauver, Clarke L. and Ralph A. Young. "Measuring The Impact Of Consumer Credit Controls On Spending," JOF, 1952, v7(2), 388-402.)

Young, S. David, Michael A. Berry, David W. Harvey and John R. Page. "Systematic Risk And Accounting Information Under The Arbitrage Pricing Theory," FAJ, 1987, v43(5), 73-76.

Young, William E. and Robert H. Trent. "Geometric Mean Approximations Of Individual Security And Portfolio Performance," JFQA, 1969, v4(2), 179-199.

Young, William E. (Latane, Henry A., Donald L. Tuttle and William E. Young. "How To Choose A Market Index," FAJ, 1971, v27(5), 75-85.)

Young, William E. (Latane, Henry A. and William E. Young. "Test Of Portfolio Building Rules," JOF, 1969, v24(4), 595-612.)

Young, William E. (Latane, Henry A. and William E. Young. "Test Of Portfolio Building Rules: Reply," JOF, 1971, v26(4), 976-981.)

Youngdahl, C. Richard. "Outlook For U.S. Treasury Securities," JOF, 1962, v17(2), 230-233.

Yourougou, P. "Interest-Rate Risk And The Pricing Of Depository Financial Intermediary Common Stock: Empirical Evidence," JBF, 1990, v14(4), 803-820.

Yourougou, P. (Grammatikos, T. and P. Yourougou. "Market Expectations Of The Effects Of The Tax Reform Act Of 1986 On Banking Organizations," JBF, 1990, v14(6), 1171-1188.)

Yourougou, Pierre. (Khoury, Nabil T. and Pierre Yourougou. "The Informational Content Of The Basis: Evidence From Canadian Barley, Oats, And Canola Futures Markets," JFM, 1991, v11(1), 69-80.)

Yourougou, Pierre. (Khoury, Nabil T. and Pierre Yourougou. "Price Discovery Performance And Maturity Effects In The Canadian Feed Wheat Market," RFM, 1989, v8(3), 402-419.)

Yu, P. L. (Hillmer, S. C. and P. L. Yu. "The Market Speed Of Adjustment To New Information," JFEC, 1979, v7(4), 321-346.)

Yuan, Tsungwei. "Review Article - A Brief On Chinese Insurance Literature," JRI, 1968, v35(4), 639.

Yuan, Yufei. (Kwan, Clarence C. Y. and Yufei Yuan. "Optimal Sequential Selection In Capital Budgeting: A Shortcut," FM, 1988, v17(1), 54-59.)

Yun, Young-Sup. "The Effects Of Inflation And Income Taxes On Interest Rates: Some New Evidence," JPQA, 1984, v19(4), 425-438.

Yung, Kenneth. (Gay, Gerald D., Robert W. Kolb and Kenneth Yung. "Trader Rationality In The Exercise Of Futures Options," JFEC, 1989, v23(2), 339-362.)

Yuravlivker, David E. "Political Shocks, International Reserves And The Real Exchange Rate--The Argentine Case," JIMF, 1987, v6(4), 401-418.

ZZZ

Zacks, Leonard. "EPS Forecasts - Accuracy Is Not Enough," FAJ, 1979, v35(2), 53-55.

Zador, Paul and Adrian Lund. "Re-Analyses Of The Effects Of No-Fault Auto Insurance On Fatal Crashes," JRI, 1986, v53(2), 226-241.

Zaentz, Neil. "Price Performance In Corporate Bonds," FAJ, 1969, v25(4), 146-155.

Zafiris, N. (Bayldon, R., A. Woods and N. Zafiris. "A Note On The 'Pyramid' Technique Of Financial Ratio Analysis Of Firms' Performance," JBFA, 1984, v11(1), 99-106.)

Zafiris, Nicos. "Interest On Equity Capital As An Ex Post Cost: A Comment," JBFA, 1982, v8(1), 119-125.

Zafiris, Nicos. "Interest On Equity Capital As An Ex Post Cost: A Rejoinder," JBFA, 1982, v8(1), 133-134.

Zahn, Douglas A. (Hickman, James C. and Douglas A. Zahn. "Some Mathematical Views Of Risk," JRI, 1966, v33(3), 437-446.)

Zaima, J. K. (Hirschey, M., M. B. Slovin and J. K. Zaima. "Bank Debt, Insider Trading, And The Return To Corporate Selloffs," JBF, 1990, v14(1), 85-98.)

Zaima, Janis K. and Douglas Hearth. "The Wealth Effects Of Voluntary Selloffs: Implications For Divesting And Acquiring Firms," JFR, 1985, v8(3), 217-226.

Zaima, Janis K. (Hearth, Douglas and Janis K. Zaima. "Voluntary Corporate Divestitures And Value," FM, 1984, v13(1), 10-16.)

Zaima, Janis K. (Hearth, Douglas and Janis K. Zaima. "Divestiture Uncertainty And Shareholder Wealth: Evidence From The U.S.A. (1975-1982)," JBFA, 1986, v13(1), 71-85.)

Zaima, Janis K. (Hirschey, Mark and Janis K. Zaima. "Insider Trading, Ownership Structure, And The Market Assessment Of Corporate Sell-Offs," JOF, 1989, v44(4), 971-980.)

Zaima, Janis K. (Leong, Kenneth K. and Janis K. Zaima. "Further Evidence Of The Small Firm Effect: A Comparison Of NYSE-AMEX And OTC Stocks," JBFA, 1991, v18(1), 117-124.)

Zaima, Janis K. (Leong, Kenneth K., Janis K. Zaima and Thomas Buchman. "The Effect Of Ownership Control Status On Stock Price Reaction To The Adoption Of LIFO Inventory," JBFA, 1991, v18(3), 405-420.) 3 ?8

Zaima, Janis K. and Joseph McCarthy. "The Impact Of Bond Rating Changes On Common Stocks And Bonds: Tests Of The Wealth Redistribution Hypothesis," FR, 1988, v23(4), 483-498.

Zak, Thomas A., Cliff J. Huang and John J. Siegfried. "Production Efficiency: The Case Of Professional Basketball," JOB, 1979, v52(3), 379-392.

Zakon, Alan J. and James C. Pennypacker. "An Analysis Of The Advance-Decline Line As A Stock Market Indicator," JPQA, 1968, v3(3), 299-314.

Zaltman, Gerald. "Comments On 'Institutional Contributions To Scholarly Journals Of Business," JOB, 1974, v47(4), 568-570.

Zaman, Mir A. (Rozeff, Michael S. and Mir A. Zaman. "Market Efficiency And Insider Trading: New Evidence," JOB, 1988, v61(1), 25-44.)

Zaner, C. (Appelbaum, E., J. Burns, R. Evans, J. Gould, T. Hamachek, R. Kidder, M. Jensen, J. Johnstone, M. Murray, R. Sim, J. Stern, B. Stewart and C. Zaner. "Panel: CEO Roundtable On Corporate Structure And Management Incentives," JACF, 1989, v3(4), 6-35.)

Zanker, F. W. A. "The Cost Of Capital For Debt-Financed Investments," JBFA, 1977, v4(3), 277-284.

Zapata, Hector. (Garcia, Philip, Raymond M. Leuthold and Hector Zapata. "Lead-Lag Relationships Between Trading Volume And Price Variability: New Evidence," JFM, 1986, v6(1), 1-10.)

Zaporowski, Mark. (Lahiri, Kajal and Mark Zaporowski. "A Note On The Variability Of Real Interest Rates, Business Cycles, And The Livingston Data," JBF, 1984, v8(3), 483-490.)

Zaporowski, Mark. (Lahiri, Kajal, Christie Teigland and Mark Zaporowski. "Interest Rates And The Subjective Probability Distribution Of Inflation Forecasts," JMCB, 1988, v20(2), 233-248.)

Zardkoohi, Asghar, Nanda Rangan and James Kolari. "Homogeneity Restrictions On The Translog Cost Model: A Note," JOF, 1986, v41(5), 1153-1156.

Zarnowitz, Victor and Geoffrey H. Moore. "Sequential Signals Of Recession And Recovery," JOB, 1982, v55(1), 57-86.

Zarnowitz, Victor. "An Analysis Of Annual And Multiperiod Quarterly Forecasts Of Aggregate Income, Output, And The Price Level," JOB, 1979, v52(1), 1-34.

Zarnowitz, Victor. "Cloos On Reference Dates And Leading Indicators: A Comment," JOB, 1963, v36(4), 461-463.

Zarnowitz, Victor. "On Functions, Quality, And Timeliness Of Economic Information," JOB, 1982, v55(1), 87-120.

Zarnowitz, Victor. "On The Dating Of Business Cycles," JOB, 1963, v36(2), 179-199.

Zarowin, Paul. "Does The Stock Market Overreact To Corporate Earnings Information?," JOF, 1989, v44(5), 1385-1400.

Zarowin, Paul. "Short-Run Overreaction: Size And Seasonality Effects," JPM, 1989, v15(3), 26-29.

Zarowin, Paul. "Size, Seasonality, And Stock Market Overreaction," JPQA, 1990, v25(1), 113-126.

Zarruk, Emilio R. "Bank Spread With Uncertain Deposit Level And Risk Aversion," JBF, 1989, v13(6), 797-810.

Zavgren, Christine V. "Assessing The Vulnerability To Failure Of American Industrial Firms: A Logistic Analysis," JBFA, 1985,

v12(1), 19-46.

Zavgren, Christine V., Michael T. Dugan and James M. Reeve. "The Association Between Probabilities Of Bankruptcy And Market Responses--A Test Of Market Anticipation," JBFA, 1988, v15(1), 27-46.

Zbesko, John. "Determinants Of Performance In The Bull Market," JPM, 1989, v15(2), 38-44.

Zecher, J. Richard. "The Effects Of The Current Turbulent Times On American Multinational Banking: An Overview," JBF, 1983, v7(4), 625-637.

Zecher, J. Richard. (Wilford, D. Sykes and J. Richard Zecher. "Monetary Policy And The Balance Of Payments In Mexico, 1955-75," JMCB, 1979, v11(3), 340-348.)

Zecher, Richard. "Monetary Equilibrium And International Reserve Flows In Australia," JOF, 1974, v29(5), 1523-1530.

Zecher, Richard. "Money And Congress: A Review Of Congressional Activity Relating To Monetary Policy," JMCB, 1971, v3(3), 680-692.

Zechner, Josef and Peter Swoboda. "The Critical Implicit Tax Rate And Capital Structure," JBF, 1986, v10(3), 327-341.

Zechner, Josef. "Tax Clienteles And Optimal Capital Structure Under Uncertainty," JOB, 1990, v63(4), 465-492.

Zechner, Josef. (Brennan, Michael J., Vojislav Maksimovic and Josef Zechner. "Vendor Financing," JOF, 1988, v43(5), 1127-1141.)

Zechner, Josef. (Fischer, Edwin O., Robert Heinkel and Josef Zechner. "Dynamic Recapitalization Policies And The Role Of Call Premia And Issue Discounts," JPQA, 1989, v24(4), 427-446.)

Zechner, Josef. (Heinkel, Robert and Josef Zechner. "The Role Of Debt And Preferred Stock As A Solution To Adverse Investment Incentives," JPQA, 1990, v25(1), 1-24.)

Zechner, Josef. (Lee, Moon H. and Josef Zechner. "Debt, Taxes, And International Equilibrium," JIMF, 1984, v3(3), 343-355.)

Zechner, Josef. (Maksimovic, Vojislav, Gordon Sick and Josef Zechner. "Forward Markets, Stock Markets, And The Theory Of The Firm: Comment," JOF, 1989, v44(2), 525-528.)

Zechner, Joserf. (Fischer, Edwin O., Robert Heinkel and Josef Zechner. "Dynamic Capital Structure Choice: Theory And Tests," JOF, 1989, v44(1), 19-40.)

Zeckhauser, R. (Amihud, Y., C. Brunie, C. Ferenbach, R. Fredericks, J. Grundfest, J. Lafferty, B. Lev, B. Shorts, J. Stern, B. Stewart and R. Zeckhauser. "Panel: 'Lead Steer' Roundtable," JACF, 1989, v2(3), 24-44.)

Zeckhauser, Richard and Victor Niederhoffer. "The Performance Of Market Index Futures Contracts," FAJ, 1983, v39(1), 59-65.

Zeckhauser, Richard. (Niederhoffer, Victor and Richard Zeckhauser. "Market Index Futures Contracts," FAJ, 1980, v36(1), 49-55.)

Zeckhauser, Richard. (Patel, Jayendu and Richard Zeckhauser. "Treasury Bill Futures As Unbiased Predictors: New Evidence And Relation To Unexpected Inflation," RFM, 1989, v8(3), 352-369.)

Zeckhauser, Richard. (Pound, John and Richard Zeckhauser. "Clearly Heard On The Street: The Effect Of Takeover Rumors On Stock Prices," JOB, 1990, v63(3), 291-308.)

Zeckhauser, Richard. (Pratt, John W. and Richard Zeckhauser. "The Impact Of Risk Sharing On Efficient Decision," JRU, 1989, v2(3), 219-234.)

Zeckhauser, Richard. (Samuelson, William and Richard Zeckhauser. "Status Quo Bias In Decision Making," JRU, 1988, v1(1), 7-60.)

Zeghal, Daniel. "Firm Size And The Informational Content Of Financial Statements," JPQA, 1984, v19(3), 299-310.

Zeghal, Daniel. "Timeliness Of Accounting Reports And Their Informational Content On The Capital Market," JBFA, 1984, v11(3), 367-380.

Zeikel, Arthur. "After 50 Years, Nothing New, Nor Likely," JPM, 1979-80, v6(1), 26-35.

Zeikel, Arthur. "Coordinating Research Information," FAJ, 1969, v25(2), 119-123.

Zeikel, Arthur. "Future Research In Finance," FR, 1978, v13(1), 79-85.

Zeikel, Arthur. "Group Dynamics," FAJ, 1971, v27(1), 30-34.

Zeikel, Arthur. "On The Threat Of Change," FAJ, 1975, v31(6), 17-20.

Zeikel, Arthur. "Organizing For Creativity," FAJ, 1983, v39(6), 25-29.

Zeikel, Arthur. "Stock Market Outlook: No Metamorphosis," FAJ, 1977, v33(5), 25-28.

Zeikel, Arthur. "The Random Walk And Murphy's Law," JPM, 1974-75, v1(1), 20-30.

Zelhorst, Dick. (De Haan, Jakob and Dick Zelhorst. "The Impact Of Government Deficits On Money Growth In Developing Countries," JIMF, 1990, v9(4), 455-469.)

Zell, Samuel. "From Cassandra, With Love," JACF, 1990, v3(1), 51-55.

Zeller, Thomas J. (Reilly, Frank G. and Thomas J. Zeller. "An Analysis Of Relative Industry Price-Earnings Ratios," FR, 1973, v8(1), 17-33.)

Zellner, Arnold. "Folklore Versus Fact In Forecasting With Econometric Methods," JOB, 1978, v51(4), 587-594.

Zelten, Robert A. "Solvency Surveillance: The Problem And A Solution," JRI, 1972, v39(4), 573-588.

Zelten, Robert A. (Winklevoss, Howard E. and Robert A. Zelten. "An Empirical Analysis Of Mutual Life Insurance Company Surplus," JRI, 1973, v40(3), 403-422.)

Zenoff, D. B. and R. L. Cuneo. "Trading With Eastern Europe," FAJ, 1971, v27(4), 66-70,91-95.

Zepp, Thomas M. (Peseau, Dennis E. and Thomas M. Zepp. "On The Use Of The CAPM In Public Utility Rate Cases: Comment," FM, 1978, v7(3), 52-56.)

Zerbe, Richard. (Laumas, Prem S. and Richard Zerbe. "The Relative Stability Of Monetary Policy And Investment Multiplier In Canada: A Comment," JMCB, 1971, v3(4), 867-877.)

Zerbinis, John. (Perrakis, Stylianos and John Zerbinis. "Indentifying The SSD Portion Of The EV Frontier: A Note," JPQA, 1978, v13(1), 167-171.)

Zerbst, Robert H. and Barbara R. Cambon. "Real Estate: Historical Returns And Risks," JPM, 1983-84, v10(3), 5-20.

Zerbst, Robert H. and William B. Brueggeman. "FHA And VA Mortgage Discount Points And Housing Prices," JOF, 1977, v32(5), 1766-1773.

Zerbst, Robert H. (Brueggeman, William B. and Robert H. Zerbst. "Discount Points And Housing Prices: Reply," JOF, 1979, v34(4), 1055-1060.)

Zerbst, Robert H. (Vandell, Kerry D. and Robert H. Zerbst. "Estimates Of The Effect Of School Desegregation Plans On Housing Values Over Time," AREUEA, 1984, v12(2), 109-135.)

Zervos, David. (Hirschhorn, Eric and David Zervos. "Policies To Change The Priority Of Claimants: The Case Of Depositor Preference Laws," JFSR, 1990, v4(2), 111-126.)

Zhou, Guofu. (Harvey, Campbell R. and Guofu Zhou. "Bayesian Inference In Asset Pricing Tests," JFEC, 1990, v26(2), 221-254.)

Zhu, Yu and Irwin Friend. "The Effects Of Different Taxes On Risky And Risk-Free Investment And On The Cost Of Capital," JOF, 1986, v41(1), 53-66.

Zhu, Yu and Robert C. Kavee. "Performances Of Portfolio Insurance Strategies," JPM, 1987-88, v14(3), 48-54.

Zhu, Yu. (Fabozzi, T. Dessa, Tom Tong and Yu Zhu. "Symmetric Cash Matching," FAJ, 1990, v46(5), 46-52.)

Ziebart, David A. (Reiter, Sara A. and David A. Ziebart. "Bond Yields, Ratings, And Financial Information: Evidence From Public Utility Issues," FR, 1991, v26(1), 44-74.)

Ziebarth, Karl. "On The Estimation Of Railroad Earnings," FAJ, 1966, v22(6), 54-55.

Ziebarth, Karl. "Railroad Review," FAJ, 1966, v22(3), 39-42.

Ziebert, David A. "The Information Content Of Annual Accounting Data: An Empirical Modeling Approach Using Structural Equation Techniques," AFPAF, 1989, v3(1), 121-142.

Ziegert, A. L. "The Demand For Housing Additions: An Empirical Analysis," AREUEA, 1988, v16(4), 479-492.

Ziemba, W. T. (Huang, C. C., I. Vertinsky and W. T. Ziemba. "On Multiperiod Stochastic Dominance," JFQA, 1978, v13(1), 1-13.)

Ziemba, W. T. (Ohlson, J. A. and W. T. Ziemba. "Portfolio Selection In A Lognormal Market When The Investor Has A Power Utility Function," JFQA, 1976, v11(1), 57-71.)

Ziemba, William T. "A Myopic Capital Budgeting Model," JFQA, 1969, v4(3), 305-327.

Ziemba, William T. "Note On 'Optimal Growth Portfolios When Yields Are Serially Correlated'," JFQA, 1972, v7(4), 1995-2000.

Ziemba, William T. "Solving Nonlinear Programming Problems With Stochastic Objective Functions," JFQA, 1972, v7(3), 1809-1827.

Ziemba, William T. (Hausch, Donald B. and William T. Ziemba. "Arbitrage Strategies For Cross-Track Betting On Major Horse Races," JOB, 1990, v63(1), Part 1, 61-78.)

Ziese, Charles H. and Roger K. Taylor. "Advance Refunding: A Practitioner's Perspective," FM, 1977, v6(2), 73-76.

Zilberfarb, Ben Zion. "Overdraft Banking: An Empirical Analysis," JBF, 1989, v13(6), 869-882.

Zilberfarb, Ben-Zion. "The Effect Of Automated Teller Machines On Demand Deposits: An Empirical Analysis," JFSR, 1989, v2(1), 49-57.

Zilberfarb, Benzion. (Ungar, Meyer and Benzion Zilberfarb. "The Demand For Money By Firms: The Stability And Other Issues Reexamined," JOF, 1980, v35(3), 779-785.)

Zilcha, Itzhak and Rafael Eldor. "Exporting Firm And Forward Markets: The Multiperiod Case," JIMF, 1991, v10(1), 108-117.

Zilcha, Itzhak. (Benninga, Simon, Rafael Eldor and Itzhak Zilcha. "Optimal International Hedging In Commodity And Currency Forward Markets," JIMF, 1985, v4(4), 537-552.)

Zilcha, Itzhak. (Benninga, Simon, Rafael Eldor and Itzhak Zilcha. "The Optimal Hedge Ratio In Unbiased Futures Markets," JFM, 1984, v4(2), 155-159.)

Zilcha, Itzhak. (Karni, Edi and Itzhak Zilcha. "Risk Aversion In The Theory Of Life Insurance: The Fisherian Model," JRI, 1986, v53(4), 606-620.)

Zimmer, Ian. (Wilkins, Trevor and Ian Zimmer. "The Reporting Of Investments In Associated Companies And Credit Evaluations: An Experimental Study," JBFA, 1985, v12(2), 207-220.)

Zimmerman, Charles J. "Future Patterns Of Life Insurance Distribution - A Company View," JRI, 1957, v24(3), 21-31.

Zimmerman, Charles J. "The Place Of The College Graduate In Life Insurance Sales," JRI, 1956, v23, 20-26.

Zimmerman, Jerold L. (Gaver, Kenneth M. and Jerold L. Zimmerman. "An Analysis Of Competitive Bidding On BART Contracts," JOB, 1977, v50(3), 279-295.)

Zimmerman, Martin B. (Alt, Christopher B., Michael G. Baumann and Martin B. Zimmerman. "The Economics Of Western Coal Severance Taxes," JOB, 1983, v56(4), 519-536.)

Zimmerman, R. E. "Research In Steel," FAJ, 1952, v8(2), 19-22.

Zimmermann, Heinz. (Loderer, Claudio and Heinz Zimmermann. "Stock Offerings In A Different Institutional Setting: The Swiss Case, 1973-1983," JBF, 1988, v11(3), 353-378.)

Zimmermann, Heinz. (Wasserfallen, Walter and Heinz Zimmermann. "The Behavior Of Intra-Daily Exchange Rates," JBF, 1985, v9(1), 55-72.)

Zinbarg, Edward D. "A Study Of Industrial Common Stock," FAJ, 1959, v15(4), 35-44.

Zinbarg, Edward D. "Supply And Demand Factors In The Stock Market," FAJ, 1964, v20(4), 84-88.

Zinbarg, Edward D. "The Private Placement Loan Agreement," FAJ, 1975, v31(4), 33-35,52.

Zinbarg, Edward D. (Freund, William C. and Edward D. Zinbarg. "Application Of Flow Of Funds To Interest-Rate Forecasting," JOF, 1963, v18(2), 231-248.)

Zinbarg, Edward D. (Harrington, John J., Jr. and Edward D. Zinbarg. "The Stock Market's 'Seasonal Pattern'," FAJ, 1964, v20(1), 53-55.)

Zinner, Shandor M. "The Contribution Of Commercial Receivable Companies And Factors To Financing Small- And Medium-Sized Business," JOF, 1947, v2(1), 76-90.

Zinngrabe, C. (Agnello, W., W. Brueggeman, G. Decker, R. Griffith, R. Leftwich, R. Moore, J. Neal, B. Sternlicht, B. Wallach, W. Wardrop and C. Zinngrabe. "Panel: Corporate Real Estate Roundtable," JACF, 1990, v3(1), 6-38.)

Zins, Michel. (Outreville, J. Francois and Michel Zins. "Job-Related Responses Of Insurance Agents: More Evidence," JRI, 1987, v54(4), 800-803.)

Ziock, Richard W. "A Realistic Profit Model For Individual Non-Participating Life Insurance," JRI, 1973, v40(3), 357-374.

Ziock, Richard W. "A Realistic Profit Model For Individual Non-Participating Life Insurance: Addendum," JRI, 1974, v41(1), 179-182.

Zionts, Stanley. (Chen, Andrew H. Y., Frank C. Jen and Stanley Zionts," JOB, 1971, v44(1), 51-61.)

Zionts, Stanley. (Chen, Andrew H. Y., Frank C. Jen and Stanley Zionts. "The Joint Determination Of Portfolio And Transaction Demands For Money," JOF, 1974, v29(1), 175-186.)

Ziorklui, Sam Q. Devaluation And Inflationary Pressures In The Less Developed Countries: A Test Of The Granger Causality," IJOF, 1990, v2(2), 31-45.

Zipkin, C. A. (Wagner, W. H. and C. A. Zipkin. "Better Performance Via Inventory Funds," FAJ, 1978, v34(3), 34-36,68.)

Zises, Alvin. "Long Term Leases: Case Against Capitalization; For Full Disclosures," FAJ, 1962, v18(3), 13-64.

Ziskind, Ross and Robert Boldin. "A Computer Simulation Model For Investment Portfolio Management," FM, 1973, v2(3), 23-33.

Zisler, Randall C. (Firstenberg, Paul M., Stephen A. Ross and Randall C. Zisler. "Real Estate: The Whole Story," JPM, 1987-88, v14(3), 22-34.)

Zissu, Anne-Marie. (Stone, Charles A. and Anne-Marie Zissu. "Does The Quality Of Investment Banks Foretell The Outcome Of Hostile Tender Offers?," IJOF, 1990, v2(2), 1-11.)

Zissu, Anne-Marie. (Stone, Charles A. and Anne-Marie Zissu. "Choosing A Discount Point/Contract Rate Combination," JREFEC, 1990, v3(3), 283-294.)

Zitnik, Louis J. "Are California Utilities Growth Companies?," FAJ, 1960, v16(2), 59-61.

Zitnik, Louis J. "Changing Pattern Of West Coast Petroleum Industry," FAJ, 1954, v10(2), 77-82.

Zitnik, Louis J. "Research Report Ethics," FAJ, 1966, v22(1), 73-75.

Zivney, Terry L. (Swidler, Steven and Terry L. Zivney. "An Empirical Analysis Of The Early Exercise Premium," RFM, 1987,v6(1),46-56.)

Zivney, Terry L. and Michael J. Alderson. "Hedged Dividend Capture With Stock Index Options," FM, 1986, v15(2), 5-12.

Zivney, Terry L. "The Value Of Early Exercise In Option Prices: An Empirical Investigation," JFQA, 1991, v26(1), 129-138.

Zivney, Terry L. (Alderson, Michael J. and Terry L. Zivney. "Optimal Cross-Hedge Portfolios For Hedging Stock Index Options," JFM, 1989, v9(1), 67-76.)

Zivney, Terry L. (Bertin, William J. and Terry L. Zivney. "The New Hire Market For Finance: Productivity, Salaries And Other Market Factors," FPE, 1991, v1(1), 25-34.)

Zivney, Terry L. (Marcus, Richard D., Donald Solberg and Terry L. Zivney. "A Reexamination Of The Benefits To International Diversification," RDIBF, 1991, v4/5, 310-335.)

Zivney, Terry L. and Donald J. Thompson, II. "Relative Stock Prices And The Firm Size Effect," JFR, 1987, v10(2), 99-110.

Zivney, Terry L. and Donald J. Thompson, II. "The Specification And Power Of The Sign Test In Measuring Security Price Performance: Comments And Analysis," FR, 1989, v24(4), 581-588.

Zivney, Terry L. and Donald J. Thompson, II. "The Effect Of Market Proxy Rebalancing Policies On Detecting Abnormal Performance," JFR, 1989, v12(4), 293-300.

Zivney, Terry L. and Richard D. Marcus. "The Day The United States Defaulted On Treasury Bills," FR, 1989, v24(3), 475-490.

Zobian, Stewart P. "Investment Decision Modelling," FAJ, 1966, v22(3), 151-155.

Zock, Richard. "Injecting Realism Into Computer Games: A Negotiation With The Investment Banker," JFED, 1978, v7, 69-71.

Zock, Richard. "The Cost Of Funding Benefits Under ERISA: A Statistical Survey: Comment," JRI, 1979, v46(3), 540-546.

Zoltners, Andris A. "A Manpower Sizing And Resource Allocation Model For Commercial Lending," JBR, 1983-84, v14(2), 134-143.

Zoltners, Andris A. (Haas, Gary and Andris A. Zoltners. "A Computerized Bank Check Collection Vehicle Routing System," JBR, 1977-78, v8(3), 148-158.)

Zoltners, Andris A. (Shanker, Roy J. and Andris A. Zoltners. "An Extension Of The Lock-Box Location Problem: Comment," JBR, 1971-72, v2(4), 62.)

Zoltners, Andris A. (Shanker, Roy J. and Andris A. Zoltners. "The Corporate Payment Problem," JBR, 1972-73, v3(1), 47-53.)

Zorn, Peter M. "Mobility-Tenure Decisions And Financial Credit: Do Mortgage Qualification Requirements Constrain Home Ownership?," AREUEA, 1989, v17(1), 1-16.

Zorn, Peter M. and Michael J. Lea. "Mortgage Borrower Repayment Behavior: A Microeconomic Analysis With Canadian Adjustable Rate Mortgage Data," AREUEA, 1989, v17(1), 118-136.

Zorn, Peter. (Lea, Michael J. and Peter M. Zorn. "Adjustable-Rate Mortgages, Economic Fluctuations, And Lender Portfolio Change," AREUEA, 1986, v14(3), 432-447.)

Zorn, Thomas S. and Steven Mann. "Investors' Reactions To Inflation: A Rational Expectations Test," FAJ, 1986, v42(3), 75-80.

Zorn, Thomas S. (Beck, Paul J. and Thomas S. Zorn. "Managerial Incentives In A Stock Market Economy," JOF,1982,v37(5),1151-1168.)

Zorn, Thomas S. (DeFusco, Richard A., Gordon V. Karels and Thomas S. Zorn. "Agency Theory: An Application To Grading Group Projects," JFED, 1989, v18, 43-44.)

Zorn, Thomas S. and James E. Larsen. "The Incentive Effects Of Flat-Fee And Percentage Commissions For Real Estate Brokers," AREUEA, 1986, v14(1), 24-47.

Zu Selhausen, Hermann Meyer. "Commercial Bank Balance Sheet Optimization," JBF, 1977, v1(2), 119-142.

Zubay, Eli A. "Feasibility Study Of Operations Research In Insurance," JRI, 1965, v32(3), 325-336.

Zubay, Eli A. (Black, Kenneth, Jr. and Eli A. Zubay. "The Actuarial Curriculum: Reply," JRI, 1966, v33(3), 482-483.)

Zubay, Eli. (Black, Kenneth, Jr. and Eli Zubay. "The Actuarial Curriculum," JRI, 1965, v32(2), 308-311.)

Zuber, Richard. (Gandar, John, Richard Zuber, Thomas O'Brien and Ben Russo. "Testing Rationality In The Point Spread Betting Market," JOF, 1988, v43(4), 995-1008.)

Zuber, Richard. (Johnson, R. Stafford, Lyle C. Fiore and Richard Zuber. "The Investment Performance Of Common Stocks In Relation To Their Price-Earnings Ratios: An Update Of The Basu Study," FR, 1989, v24(3), 499-506.)

Zuckerman, Dror. (Tapiero, Charles S. and Dror Zuckerman. "A Note On The Optimal Control Of A Cash Balance Problem," JBF, 1980, v4(4), 345-352.)

Zuehlke, Thomas W. "Transformations To Normality And Selectivity Bias In Hedonic Price Functions," **JREFEC**, 1989, v2(3), 173-180.

Zufryden, Fred S. "On The Dual Optimization Of Media Reach And Frequency," **JOB**, 1975, v48(4), 558-570.

Zuger, Peter A. (Rubin, Harvey W. and Peter A. Zuger. "Prospects For Selling Life Insurance Through Retail Banking Outlets," **JRI**, 1975, v42(2), 303-312.)

Zulauf, Carl R. (Johnson, Robert L., Carl R. Zulauf, Scott H. Irwin and Mary E. Gerlow. "The Soybean Complex Spread: An Examination Of Market Efficiency From The Viewpoint Of A Production Process," **JFM**, 1991, v11(1), 25-38.)

Zultowski, Walter H. "The Extent Of Buyer-Initiated Life Insurance Sales," **JRI**, 1979, v46(4), 707-714.

Zumpano, Leonard V. and Patricia M. Rudolph. "Another Look At Residential Mortgage Lending By Savings And Loans," **JFR**, 1981, v4(1), 59-67.

Zumpano, Leonard V. (Marsh, Gene A. and Leonard V. Zumpano. "Agency Theory And The Changing Role Of The Real Estate Broker: Conflicts And Possible Solutions," **JRER**, 1988, v3(2), 151-164.)

Zumpano, Leonard V. (Rudolph, Patricia M., Leonard V. Zumpano and Marvin J. Karson. "Mortgage Markets And Inter-Regional Differences In Convention Mortgage Terms," **AREUEA**, 1982, v10(1), 94-110.)

Zumpano, Leonard V. and Donald L. Hooks. "The Real Estate Brokerage Market: A Critical Reevaluation," **AREUEA**, 1988, v16(1), 1-16.

Zumpano, Leonard V., Patricia M. Rudolph and David C. Cheng. "The Demand And Supply Of Mortgage Funds And Mortgage Loan Terms," **AREUEA**, 1986, v14(1), 91-109.

Zumwalt, J. Kenton. (Eubank, Arthur A., Jr. and J. Kenton Zumwalt. "An Analysis Of The Forecast Error Impact Of Alternative Beta Adjustment Techniques And Risk Classes," **JOF**, 1979, v34(3), 761-776.)

Zumwalt, J. Kenton. (Eubank, Arthur A., Jr. and J. Kenton Zumwalt. "How To Determine The Stability Of Beta Values," **JPM**, 1978-79, v5(2), 22-26.)

Zumwalt, J. Kenton. (Gallagher, Timothy J. and J. Kenton Zumwalt. "Risk-Adjusted Discount Rates Revisited," **FR**, 1991, v26(1), 105-114.)

Zumwalt, J. Kenton. (Kim, Moon K. and J. Kenton Zumwalt. "An Analysis Of Risk In Bull And Bear Markets," **JFQA**, 1979, v14(5), 1015-1025.)

Zumwalt, J. Kenton. (Lynge, Morgan J., Jr. and J. Kenton Zumwalt. "An Empirical Study Of The Interest Rate Sensitivity Of Commercial Bank Returns: A Multi-Index Approach," **JFQA**, 1980, v15(3), 731-742.)

Zumwalt, J. Kenton. (Lee, Cheng Few and J. Kenton Zumwalt. "Associations Between Alternative Accounting Profitability Measures And Security Returns," **JFQA**, 1981, v16(1), 71-93.)

Zumwalt, J. Kenton. (Linke, Charles M. and J. Kenton Zumwalt. "The Irrelevance Of Compounding Frequency In Determining A Utility's Cost Of Equity," **FM**, 1987, v16(3), 65-69.)

Zumwalt, J. Kenton. (Linke, Charles M. and J. Kenton Zumwalt. "Estimation Biases In Discounted Cash Flow Analyses Of Equity Capital Cost In Rate Regulation," **FM**, 1984, v13(3), 15-21.)

Zundel, Raulston G. "Conflict And Co-Operation Among Retail Unions," **JOB**, 1954, v27(4), 301-311.

Zupnick, Elliot. "Consumer Credit And Monetary Policy In The United States And The United Kingdom," **JOF**, 1962, v17(2), 342-354.

Zurack, Mark A. (Toy, William W. and Mark A. Zurack. "Tracking The Euro-Pac Index," **JPM**, 1989, v15(2), 55-58.)

Zurowski, George J. (Brown, Stephen W., Richard L. Smith, II and George J. Zurowski. "The Appropriateness And Applicability Of Image Research To Banking," **JBR**, 1977-78, v8(2), 94-100.)

Zusman, Pinhas. (Etgar, Michael and Pinhas Zusman. "The Marketing Intermediary As An Information Seller: A New Approach," **JOB**, 1982, v55(4), 505-516.)

Zuwaylif, Fadil. (Ferber, Robert, Nai-Ruenn Chen and Fadil Zuwaylif. "Employers' Forecasts Of Manpower: An Interview Study," **JOB**, 1961, v34(3), 387-395.)

Zweig, Martin E. "An Investor Expectations Stock Price Predictive Model Using Closed-End Fund Premiums," **JOF**, 1973, v28(1), 67-78.

Zweig, Martin. "A Stock Market Game Using FINANSIM Companies," **JFED**, 1973, v2, 67-74.

Zwick, Burton. "The Interest-Induced Wealth Effect And The Behavior Of Real And Nominal Interest Rates," **JOF**, 1974, v29(5),1425-1435.

Zwick, Burton. "The Interest-Induced Wealth Effect And The Behavior Of Real And Nominal Interest Rates: A Reply," **JOF**, 1977, v32(3), 949-950.

Zwick, Burton. "Yields On Privately Placed Corporate Bonds," **JOF**, 1980, v35(1), 23-29.

Zwick, Burton. "'Snapback' And 'Crowding-Out' Effects In Monetary And Fiscal Policy: Explanation And Interrelation: A Comment," **JMCB**, 1974, v6(4), 559-566.

Zwick, Burton. (Hamburger, Michael J. and Burton Zwick. "The Efficacy Of Selective Credit Policies: An Alternative Test," **JMCB**, 1979, v11(1), 106-110.)

Zwick, Burton. (Hamburger, Michael J. and Burton Zwick. "Installment Credit Controls, Consumer Expenditures And The Allocation Of Real Resources," **JOF**, 1977, v32(5), 1557-1569.)

Zwick, Charles J. "Strategic Planning And Its Role In The Banking Environment Of The Seventies," **JBR**, 1973-74, v4(2), 74-78.

APPENDIX A
MONTHLY AND SEASONAL DESIGNATIONS
USED FOR EACH JOURNAL ISSUE

Advances in Financial Planning and Forecasting

1985,87,89,90 (1) No Designation

Advances in Working Capital Management

1988-89 (1) No Designation

Financial Analysts Journal

1945 (4) Jan, Apr, Jul, Oct
1946-51 (4) First, Second, Third, Fourth Quarter
1952 (4) Feb,Mar,May,Aug,Nov; 1953-58 (4) Feb,May,Jun,Aug,Nov
1959 (4) Feb, May, Jul, Aug, Nov
1960-90 (6) Jan/Feb,Mar/Apr,May/Jun,Jul/Aug,Sep/Oct,Nov/Dec

Financial Management

1972 (3) Spring, Summer, Winter
1973-76 (4) Spring, Summer, Autumn, Winter
1977 (4) Spring, Summer, Fall, Winter
1978-80 (4) Spring, Summer, Autumn, Winter
1981 (5) Spring, Tenth Annv., Summer, Autumn, Winter
1982-90 (4) Spring, Summer, Autumn, Winter

Financial Practice and Education

1991 (2) Spring, Fall

Financial Review

1966-70 (1) Spring; 1971 (1) No. 1; 1972 (1) No. 2
1973-76 (1) No. 10; 1977-78 (2) Spring, Fall
1979-81 (3) Winter, Spring, Fall
1982 (4) May, Proceedings, Sep, Nov
1983 (3) Feb, May, Proceedings, Nov
1984 (3) Mar, May, Proceedings, Nov
1985-87 (4) Feb, May, Proceedings, Nov
1988-90 (4) Feb, May, Aug, Nov

Financial Services Review

1991 (2) Spring, Fall

Global Finance Journal

1989/90 (2) Fall, /Spring

International Journal of Finance

1988/89-90/91 (2) Autumn, /Spring

Journal of the American Real Estate and Urban Econ. Assoc.

1973 (1) Fall; 1974 (1) June; 1975 (3) Spring, Summer, Winter
1976 (3) Spring,Fall,Winter; 1977-90 (4) Spring,Summer,Fall,Winter

Journal of Applied Corporate Finance

1988/89-90/91 (4) Spring, Summer, Fall, /Winter

Journal of Bank Research

1970/71-1985/86 (4) Spring, Summer, Autumn, /Winter

Journal of Banking and Finance

1977 (4) Jun, Aug, Nov, Dec; 1978 (4) Jun, Aug, Oct, Dec
1979 (4) Apr, Jul, Sep, Dec; 1980-85 (4) Mar, Jun, Sep, Dec
1986 (4) Mar, Jun, Oct, Dec; 1987-88 (4) Mar, Jun, Sep, Dec
1989 (5) Mar, May, Jul, Sep, Dec; 1990 (5) Mar, Aug, Oct, Nov, Dec

Journal of Business

1950-90 (4) Jan, Apr, Jul, Oct

Journal of Business Finance and Accounting

1974-75 (3) Spring, Summer, Autumn
1976-90 (4) Spring, Summer, Autumn, Winter

Journal of Finance

1946 (1) Aug; 1947 (2) Apr, Oct; 1948 (3) Feb, Jun, Oct
1949-60 (4) Mar, Jun, Sep, Dec
1961-67 (4) Mar, May, Sep, Dec
1968-83 (5) Mar, May, Jun, Sep, Dec
1984-90 (5) Mar, Jun, Jul, Sep, Dec

Journal of Financial and Quantitative Analysis

1966-69 (4) Mar, Jun, Sep, Dec
1970 (5) Mar, Jun, Sep, Dec, Jan
1971-73 (5) Jan, Mar, Jun, Sep, Dec
1974 (6) Jan, Mar, Jun, Sep, Nov, Dec
1975-82 (5) Mar, Jun, Sep, Nov, Dec
1983-90 (4) Mar, Jun, Sep, Dec

Journal of Financial Economics

1974 (3) May, Jul, Sep, Dec; 1975 (4) Mar, Jun, Sep, Dec
1976 (4) Jan/Mar, Jun, Oct
1977 v(3) Jan, Mar, May; v(3) Aug, Nov, Dec
1978 (4) Mar, Jun/Sep, Dec; 1979-81 (4) Mar, Jun, Sep, Dec
1982 (4) Mar, Jul, Nov, Dec
1983, v11 (1) Apr; v12 (4) Jun, Aug, Nov, Dec
1984-85 (4) Mar, Jun, Sep, Dec
1986 v15 (1) Jan/Feb; v16 (3) May, Jun, Jul; v17 (2) Sep, Dec
1987 v18 (2) Mar, Jun; v19 Sep, Dec
1988 v20 (1) Jan/Mar; v21(2) May, Sep; v22 (2) Oct, Dec
1989 v23 (2) Jun,Aug; v24 (2) Sep,Oct; v25 (2) Nov,Dec
1990 v26 (2) Jul,Aug; v27 (2) Sep,Oct

Journal of Financial Education

1972-90 (1) No designation

Journal of Financial Intermediation

1991 (4) Mar, Jun

Journal of Financial Research

1978 (1) Winter; 1979 (2) Spring, Fall
1980-82 (3) Spring, Summer, Fall
1983-90 (4) Spring, Summer, Fall, Winter

Journal of Financial Services Research

1987/88 (4) Sep, /Jan, Jun, Dec
1989 v2 (4) Feb,Jun,Sep,Oct; v3 (3) Oct,Dec,Dec
1990 (4) Mar, Jul, Oct, Dec

Journal of Futures Markets

1981-90 (4) Spring, Summer, Fall, Winter

Journal of International Money and Finance

1982-84 (3) Apr, Aug, Dec; 1985-90 (4) Mar, Jun, Sep, Dec

Journal of Money, Credit and Banking

1969-90 (4) Feb, May, Aug, Nov

Journal of Portfolio Management

1974/75-90/91 (4) Fall, /Winter, Spring, Summer

Journal of Real Estate Finance and Economics

1988 (4) Apr, Jun, Nov, Dec; 1989-90 (4) Apr, Jun, Sep, Dec

Journal of Real Estate Research

1986 (1) Fall; 1987 (2) Fall, Winter; 1988-90 (3) Spring, Summer, Fall

Journal of Risk and Insurance

1934-56 (1) Mar; 1957/58 (4) Sep, Nov, Dec, /May
1958/59 (4) Jul, Oct, Nov, /Feb; 1959 (4) Spring, Summer, Fall, Winter
1960-90 (4) Mar, Jun, Sep, Dec

Journal of Risk and Uncertainty

1988-90 (4) No Designation

Recent Developments in International Banking and Finance

1988-91 (1) No Designation

Research in Finance

1979,80,81,83,84,85,86,88,90 (1) No Designation

Review of Financial Studies

1988/89-90/91 (4) Spring, Summer, Fall, /Winter

Review of Futures Markets

1982 (3) May 81, Oct 81, Nov 81; 1983 (3) May 82, Sep 82, Oct 82
1984 (3) May 83, Oct 83, Dec 83'; 1985 (3) May 84, Dec 84, May 85
1986 (3) Dec 85, Mar 86, May 86; 1987 (3) Dec 86, May 87, Dec 87
1988 (4) May 88, None, Nov 88, Supp; 1989 (3) None, Sep, None

Issue dates represent when CBOT held seminars that
yielded the articles contained in each issue.

Published under title of "Review of Research
in Futures Markets" through 1986

Review of Quantitative Finance and Accounting

1991 (4) Spring, Summer

The number in ( ) indicates number of issues in that volume. Years separated by a dash (1984-85) designate the years 1984 through 1985. Years separated by a slash (1984/85) designate the volume spans one calendar year into another. Thus, 1984-87 includes 1984, 1985, 1986, and 1987, while 1981/82-1983/84 includes the three journal years of 1981/82, 1982/83 and 1983/84. A single seasonal designation preceded by a slash (/Winter) denotes point in the journal year where volume spans the calendar year. Two seasonal designations joined by a slash (Jan/Feb) denotes that single issue is designated by both months.

FINANCE/ACCOUNTING
LITERATURE DATABASE

FOR THE PERSONAL COMPUTER

This revolutionary database will eliminate most of those time consuming and expensive literature searches at the library. With a few simple commands on your personal computer, nearly all the relevant finance and accounting journal references can be retrieved by keyword.

*Includes nearly 35,000 bibliographic references from the 66 leading finance and accounting journals
*Also includes the leading real estate and insurance journals
*Version 2.0 is updated through 1990 (all citations from journals' inaugural issues)
*Search command compiles listing by author, journal or keyword
*Narrow command reduces selected list by keyword, giving "and/or"capabilities
*Selected references can also be deleted from search list by keyword or "del" key
*Browse command permits scrolling of index when keyword or its spelling is unknown
*Print/Save commands output references to printer or ASCII file
*Typical search time of entire database by keyword is less than one second
*Runs on IBM and compatibles having 640K.RAM and 5 MBytes of disk storage space
*Site license one-time fee is $395, which allows for use on all PCs, or networking, within licensee's building. Purchase orders accepted by phone, mail or FAX
* Bi-annual updates/expansions available
*Reviewed in the Journal of Finance, September 1990

To Order Or For More Information Contact:

Jean Louis Heck
JLH Enterprises
1512 County Line Rd
Bryn Mawr, PA 19010
215-525-8271
FAX: 215-527-0397